ENCYCLOPAEDIA
JUDAICA

ENCYCLOPAEDIA JUDAICA

SECOND EDITION

VOLUME 10
INZ–IZ

FRED SKOLNIK, *Editor in Chief*
MICHAEL BERENBAUM, *Executive Editor*

MACMILLAN REFERENCE USA
An imprint of Thomson Gale, a part of The Thomson Corporation

IN ASSOCIATION WITH
KETER PUBLISHING HOUSE LTD., JERUSALEM

THOMSON
GALE

Detroit • New York • San Francisco • New Haven, Conn. • Waterville, Maine • London

THOMSON
GALE

ENCYCLOPAEDIA JUDAICA, Second Edition

Fred Skolnik, *Editor in Chief*
Michael Berenbaum, *Executive Editor*
Shlomo S. (Yosh) Gafni, *Editorial Project Manager*
Rachel Gilon, *Editorial Project Planning and Control*

Thomson Gale
Gordon Macomber, *President*
Frank Menchaca, *Senior Vice President and Publisher*
Jay Flynn, *Publisher*
Hélène Potter, *Publishing Director*

Keter Publishing House
Yiphtach Dekel, *Chief Executive Officer*
Peter Tomkins, *Executive Project Director*

Complete staff listings appear in Volume 1

For more information, contact
Macmillan Reference USA
An imprint of Thomson Gale
27500 Drake Rd.
Farmington Hills, MI 48331-3535
Or you can visit our internet site at
http://www.gale.com

LIBRARY OF CONGRESS CATALOGING-IN-PUBLICATION DATA

Encyclopaedia Judaica / Fred Skolnik, editor-in-chief ; Michael Berenbaum, executive editor. -- 2nd ed.
v. cm.
Includes bibliographical references and index.
Contents: v.1. Aa-Alp.
ISBN 0-02-865928-7 (set hardcover : alk. paper) -- ISBN 0-02-865929-5 (vol. 1 hardcover : alk. paper) -- ISBN 0-02-865930-9 (vol. 2 hardcover : alk. paper) -- ISBN 0-02-865931-7 (vol. 3 hardcover : alk. paper) -- ISBN 0-02-865932-5 (vol. 4 hardcover : alk. paper) -- ISBN 0-02-865933-3 (vol. 5 hardcover : alk. paper) -- ISBN 0-02-865934-1 (vol. 6 hardcover : alk. paper) -- ISBN 0-02-865935-X (vol. 7 hardcover : alk. paper) -- ISBN 0-02-865936-8 (vol. 8 hardcover : alk. paper) -- ISBN 0-02-865937-6 (vol. 9 hardcover : alk. paper) -- ISBN 0-02-865938-4 (vol. 10 hardcover : alk. paper) -- ISBN 0-02-865939-2 (vol. 11 hardcover : alk. paper) -- ISBN 0-02-865940-6 (vol. 12 hardcover : alk. paper) -- ISBN 0-02-865941-4 (vol. 13 hardcover : alk. paper) -- ISBN 0-02-865942-2 (vol. 14 hardcover : alk. paper) -- ISBN 0-02-865943-0 (vol. 15: alk. paper) -- ISBN 0-02-865944-9 (vol. 16: alk. paper) -- ISBN 0-02-865945-7 (vol. 17: alk. paper) -- ISBN 0-02-865946-5 (vol. 18: alk. paper) -- ISBN 0-02-865947-3 (vol. 19: alk. paper) -- ISBN 0-02-865948-1 (vol. 20: alk. paper) -- ISBN 0-02-865949-X (vol. 21: alk. paper) -- ISBN 0-02-865950-3 (vol. 22: alk. paper)
1. Jews -- Encyclopedias. I. Skolnik, Fred. II. Berenbaum, Michael, 1945-
DS102.8.E496 2007
909'.04924 -- dc22
2006020426

ISBN-13:

978-0-02-865928-2 (set)
978-0-02-865929-9 (vol. 1)
978-0-02-865930-5 (vol. 2)
978-0-02-865931-2 (vol. 3)
978-0-02-865932-9 (vol. 4)
978-0-02-865933-6 (vol. 5)
978-0-02-865934-3 (vol. 6)
978-0-02-865935-0 (vol. 7)
978-0-02-865936-7 (vol. 8)
978-0-02-865937-4 (vol. 9)
978-0-02-865938-1 (vol. 10)
978-0-02-865939-8 (vol. 11)
978-0-02-865940-4 (vol. 12)
978-0-02-865941-1 (vol. 13)
978-0-02-865942-8 (vol. 14)
978-0-02-865943-5 (vol. 15)
978-0-02-865944-2 (vol. 16)
978-0-02-865945-9 (vol. 17)
978-0-02-865946-6 (vol. 18)
978-0-02-865947-3 (vol. 19)
978-0-02-865948-0 (vol. 20)
978-0-02-865949-7 (vol. 21)
978-0-02-865950-3 (vol. 22)

This title is also available as an e-book
ISBN-10: 0-02-866097-8
ISBN-13: 978-0-02-866097-4
Contact your Thomson Gale representative for ordering information.
Printed in the United States of America

10 9 8 7 6 5 4 3 2 1

TABLE OF CONTENTS

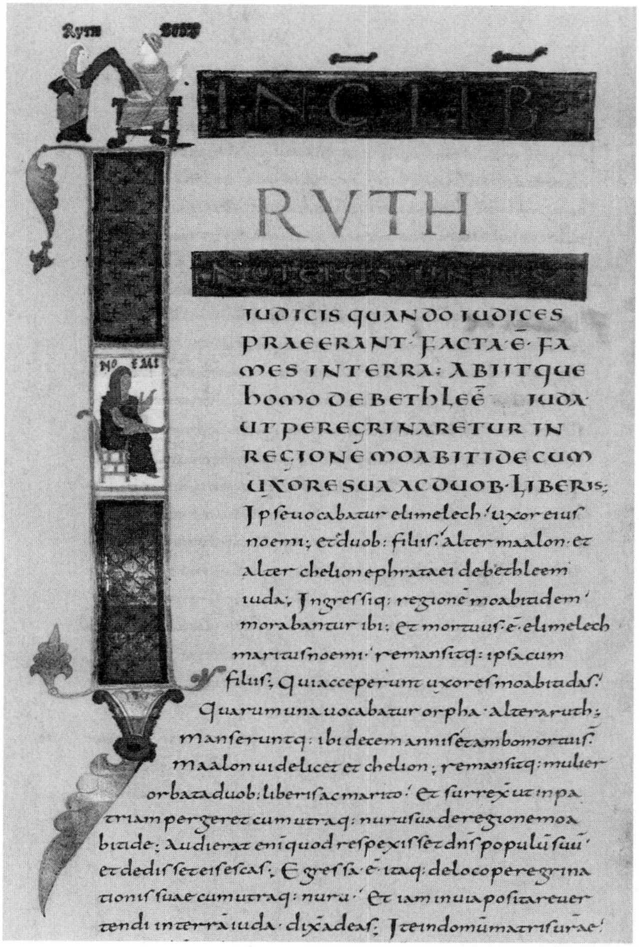

Initial letter "I" of the phrase In diebus unius iudicis *at the beginning of the Book of Ruth from the Latin* Bible *of Charles the Bald, Rheims, ninth century. The illumination shows Ruth and Boaz above the letter and Naomi seated in the middle of it. Paris, Bibliothèque Nationale, Ms. Lat. 1-88v.*

INZ–IZ

IN-ZIKH, the Introspectivist movement in American Yiddish poetry, arose in 1919 and centered on the literary organ *In Zikh* ("In the Self," 1920–40). The founders of the movement included A. *Glanz-Leyeles, Jacob *Glatstein, and N.B. *Minkoff, who in their first volume declared: "The world exists and we are part of it. But for us, the world exists only as it is mirrored in us, as it touches *us*. The world is a nonexistent category, a lie, if it is not related to us. It becomes an actuality only *in* and *through* us." In contrast to *Di Yunge, the Inzikhists espoused all themes, rhythms, and vocabulary, so long as the poetry reflected the poet's individuality. They declared that free verse and social realities must be combined, that poetry required the poet to look into the self (*in zikh*) and thus present a truer image of the psyche and the world. Urbane modernists, the Inzikhists considered associations and allusions as the two most important elements of poetic expression. Dedicating themselves to the Yiddish language and poetry, they published some of the most important poets and prose writers of the 20th century.

BIBLIOGRAPHY: B. Rivkin, *Grunt-Tendentsn fun der Yidisher Literatur in Amerike* (1948); N.B. Minkoff, *Literarishe Vegn* (1955); A. Glanz-Leyeles, *Velt un Vort* (1958); *N.B. Minkof-Bukh* (1959); C. Madison, *Yiddish Literature* (1968), 306–11; S. Liptzin, *Maturing of Yiddish Literature* (1970), 40–65. **ADD. BIBLIOGRAPHY:** B. Harshav, *American-Yiddish Poetry* (1986).

[Sol Liptzin / Anita Norich (2nd ed.)]

IOANNINA (Janina), name of town and region in Greece, N.W. of Athens. According to an old tradition, there was a Jewish community in Ioannina as early as the ninth century; the archaic Greek spoken by the Jewish inhabitants suggests that this may be true. During the first half of the 13th century the town was part of the despotate of *Epirus and the Jewish community suffered from persecutions. Jewish serfs are mentioned in two bulls, dated 1319 and 1321 respectively, issued by Emperor Andronicus II Palaeologus (1282–1328). During his reign the emperor placed the Jews under his direct protection. In 1431 when the town was taken by the Turks, there was a sizable Jewish community, which continued to grow in succeeding generations. When Jewish refugees from Spain settled there, they assimilated into the local Romaniot population and adopted their Greek dialect. There were two synagogues, one known as the "old community," the other as the "new." Apulian and Sicilian Jews also settled in Ioannina and retained special circumcision and Purim customs. In 1612 the Jews were falsely accused of having handed Bishop Dionysios, the leader of a revolt, over to the Turkish authorities, who executed him. Ali Pasha, who was governor of the area from 1788 to 1822, imposed a heavy tax burden on the wealthy Jews. In 1821 when the Greek rebellion broke out, some Jews found refuge in Ioannina. In 1851, the community suffered a major blood libel. The 1869 fire ruined half the Jewish shops in the market. In 1872 there were anti-Jewish riots in the town. The local wealthy banker Effendi Davitchon Levy was one of four Jews in the Ottoman Empire elected to the first national assembly in 1876. The Hebron emissary Rabbi Ḥayyim Shemuel Halevy (*Ha-Ḥasm'al*) remained in Ioannina for more than three decades (1848–81) and prophesied that the redemption of Israel would take place in the year 5708 (1948). Ioannina Jews maintained trade relations with Europe and the East, and also engaged in silk weaving and the manufacture of scarves, veils, and silver belts for sale to the Albanians; there were also goldsmiths, dyers, glaziers, tinsmiths, fishermen, and coachmen among them. The wealthy merchant Meir Gani moved to Jerusalem in 1880 and initiated Jewish settlement in the Christian Quarter of the Old City of Jerusalem owing to his close connections to the Greek Orthodox Church, and he also purchased much land from the latter for the Jewish National Fund in Jerusalem in the Rehavia neighborhood as well the site of the present-day Israel Museum and land in the Dead Sea region (where Kibbutz Bet ha-Aravah was located). At the beginning of the 20th century, there were 7,000 Jews in Ioannina, but due to fear of political instability, compulsory military service, and economic decline, several thousand Jews began emigrating, heading to New York City. In 1910 the Jewish population was 3,000 and on the eve of the Holocaust it was 1,950. In the Depression of the early 1930s, many Ioanniote Jews migrated to Athens for economic betterment. The local Jewish poet, philologist, and teacher Joseph *Eliyia (1901–1931) is remembered and highly revered in contemporary Greece for his prose and poetry. On March 24, 1944, 1,860 Jews were seized by the Nazis and deported to Auschwitz. In 1948 there were 170 Jews living in the town, and by 1967 their number had dwindled to 92. The Ioannina community has continued to maintain the Romaniot prayer rite. A Ioannina synagogue, Bet Avraham ve-Ohel Sarah, exists in Jerusalem in the Maḥaneh Yehudah quarter.

BIBLIOGRAPHY: J.M. Toledano, *Sarid u-Falit* (1945), 32–35; Bees, in: *Byzantinisch-neugriechische Jahrbuecher*, 2 (1921), 159–77. **ADD. BIBLIOGRAPHY:** R. Dalven, *The Jews of Ioannina* (1990); B. Rivlin, "Ioannina," in: *Pinkas Kehillot Yavan* (1999), 131–43.

[Simon Marcus / Yitzchak Kerem (2nd ed.)]

IONESCO, EUGÈNE (1912–1994), Romanian-born French playwright. Ionesco's mother, Thérèse Icard, was a French Jewess who, while teaching in Romania, married a non-Jewish lawyer, Eugène Ionesco. In 1913 the family moved to Paris, returning to Romania in 1925, and a few years later the father abandoned his wife and two children. The young Eugène specialized in French studies. He became a teacher and literary critic, studying in Paris (1938–40). When he returned to Romania he encountered the Fascism which he was later to attack in the bitterest terms, and in 1942 he fled back to France with his wife.

Ionesco's first two books, written in Romanian and published in 1934, were a volume of lyrical poems, *Elegii pentru ființele mici* ("Elegies for Little Souls"), and *Nu* ("No"), a collection of essays criticizing established Romanian authors. Ionesco's plays, which reveal the influence of *Kafka and of the important Romanian dramatist Ion Luca Caragiale, are mostly one-act caricatures of middle-class smugness and philistinism. A mixture of comedy and tragedy, surrealistic and grotesque, they attack what Ionesco terms "the universal petty bourgeoisie … the personification of accepted ideas and slogans, the ubiquitous conformist." This "Theater of the Absurd" (Ionesco himself preferred the designation "Theater of Derision") had its birth in the highly successful play *La Cantatrice chauve* (1949; *The Bald Soprano*, 1958). The best known of the many plays that helped to consolidate Ionesco's reputation were *La Lyçon* (1950; *The Lesson*, 1958), *Les Chaises* (1951; *The Chairs*, 1958), *Victimes du devoir* (1952; *Victims of Duty*, 1958), *Le Nouveau Locataire* (1953; *The New Tenant*, 1958), *Tueur sans gages* (1957; *The Killer*, 1960), *Rhinoceros* (1959), which appeared in an English translation in 1960, and *Le Roi se meurt* (1962; *Exit the King*, 1963). Ionesco's plays were collected in four volumes (1954–66) and have been translated into nearly 30 languages. A series of essays appeared in book form as *Notes et Contrenotes* (1962; *Notes and Counternotes*, 1964), and he also wrote the scripts for several distinguished films. Later plays included *Macbeth* (1973), *Man with Bags* (1975), and *Journey Among the Dead* (1980).

He visited Israel and made declarations in favor of the state on the eve of the Six-Day War. After it was over he wrote about his family history for the first time in the second volume of his memoirs, *Présent Passé, Passé Présent* (1968), a sequel to *Le Journal en Miettes* (1957, *Fragments of a Journal*, 1968), expressing a new awareness of his Jewish origin. Ionesco, whose qualities of wit and mordant satire had led to his being referred to as "the Molière of the Twentieth Century," was elected to the French Academy in 1970.

BIBLIOGRAPHY: R.N. Coe, *Ionesco* (Eng., 1961); P. Sénart, *Ionesco* (Fr., 1964); F. Bradesco, *Le monde étrange de Ionesco* (1967); C. Bonnefoy, *Entretiens avec Eugène Ionesco* (1966); Ben-Jacob, in: *American Zionist*, 59:3 (1968), 19–21; *Le Figaro Littéraire* (July 29, Aug. 5, 12, 1968); Davidowitz, in: *Ariel*, 4 (1963), 18–21. **ADD. BIBLIOGRAPHY:** R.J. North, *Eugene Ionesco: an inaugural lecture delivered at the University of Birmingham* (1970); R. Hayman, *Eugene Ionesco* (1972); R.N. Coe, *Ionesco: A Study of His Plays* (1971); A. Lewis, *Ionesco* (1972); R. Lamont (ed.), *Ionesco: A Collection of Critical Essays* (1973); E. Kern, *The Works of Ionesco* (1974); S. Cavarra, *Ionesco: de l'absurde à la quête*

(1976); A. Kamyabi Mask, *Ionesco et son théâtre* (1987); M.C. Hubert, *Eugene Ionesco* (Fr., 1990); A. Hayman, *Ionesco avant Ionesco: portrait de l' artiste en jeune homme* (1993); G. Plazy, *Eugene Ionesco: le rire et l'espèrance: une biographie* (1994); N. Lane, *Understanding Eugene Ionesco* (1994); D.B. Gaensbauer, *Eugene Ionesco Revisited* (1996); H. Bloom (ed.), *Eugene Ionesco* (2003).

[Claude Gandelman / Rohan Saxena and Dror Franck Sullaper (2nd ed.)]

IOSIFESCU, SILVIAN (1917–), Romanian literary historian and critic. A former illegal Communist, he decided in favor of an academic career and was, from 1948, professor of Literary Theory at the Bucharest University. He wrote on the Romanian classics and problems of aesthetics, and, after a short period of dogmatic Marxist esthetic, Iosifescu became an eminent literary analyst of modern prose. His works include *Drumuri literare* ("Literary Paths," 1957), *In jurul romanului* ("On the Novel," 1959), *Literatura de frontieră* ("The Frontier Literature," 1969), *Mobilitatea privirii* ("The Mobility of Sight," 1976), *Trepte* ("Steps," 1988). Iosifescu translated (partially in collaboration with Vera Călin) from Romain Rolland, H. Taine, John Steinbeck, Robert Graves, and published anthologies of French and English humor.

ADD. BIBLIOGRAPHY: *Dicționarul scriitorilor români*, D-L (1998), 629–31; M. Martin and N. Rata-Dumitriu, in: *Observator cultural*, 157 (2003).

IOWA, state in midwestern U.S. In 2005 Iowa had a Jewish population of 6,100 out of a total of 2,944,000. The largest Jewish community was in Des Moines (3,500), the state capital, where there were four synagogues – Orthodox, Conservative, Reform and Chabad – a Jewish Federation which is situated on the community campus and includes Iowa Jewish Senior Life Center, a synagogue, and the Community Hebrew School. There were also organized Jewish communities with one or more synagogues in Ames, Cedar Rapids, Waterloo, Council Bluffs; Davenport (450); Dubuque (105); Iowa City (200), Sioux City (300), and Postville, now home to 450 Jews, most associated with the kosher meat processing plant, AgriProcessors.

The first mention of Jews in connection with Iowa appeared in a memoir published in London in 1819 by William Robinson, a non-Jewish adventurer and land speculator, who proposed mass colonization of European Jews in Iowa and Missouri. The first known Jewish settler was Alexander Levi, a native of France who arrived from New Orleans in 1833 and established himself in Dubuque in the year the town was laid out. Credited with being the first foreigner naturalized in Iowa (1837), Levi helped develop the lead mines first worked by Julien Dubuque, for whom the town was named. One of Dubuque's leading citizens for 60 years, Levi was elected justice of the peace in 1846. In the late 1830s and early 1840s Jewish peddlers from Germany and Poland reached Dubuque and McGregor, key points for traffic across the Mississippi, in eastern Iowa, as the immigrant tide began pushing westward. Solomon Fine and Nathan Louis were doing business at Fort Madison in 1842. In that year Joseph Newmark opened a store at Dubuque. Among the early settlers in McGregor were the parents of Leo S. Rowe (1871–1946), director-general of the Pan-American Union (1920–46), who was born there. Samuel Jacobs was surveyor of Jefferson County in 1845. In the 1850s Jews were also settled at Davenport, Burlington, and Keokuk. William Krause, the first Jew in Des Moines, arrived with his wife in 1846, when it was still known as Raccoon Forks. His brother Robert came to Davenport about the same time. Krause opened Des Moines' first store in 1848, a year before Joseph and Isaac Kuhn arrived there. Krause was one of the incorporators of Des Moines, helped found the town's first public school, contributed toward the building of Christian churches, and was a leading figure in having the state capital moved from Iowa City to Des Moines. Other pioneer Jews were Michael Raphael, paymaster of the Northwestern Railroad while it was building west from Davenport; Abraham Kuhn, who went to Council Bluffs in 1853; Leopold Sheuerman, who had a store at Muscatine in 1858; and Solomon Hess, who represented Johnson City at the 1856 convention at which the Iowa Republican Party was organized.

The first organized Jewish community was formed at Keokuk in 1855 in the home of S. Gerstle under the name of the Benevolent Children of Israel. This society maintained a cemetery from 1859 on and four years later was incorporated as Congregation B'nai Israel. In 1877 it erected Iowa's first synagogue. Other communities grew up in Dubuque and Burlington in 1857 and in Davenport in 1861. There was a handful of Jews in Sioux City on the banks of the Missouri River in the 1860s, but no congregation was formed until 1884. The Council Bluffs community dates from the late 1870s and that in Ottumwa from 1876. Davenport's Temple Emanuel is the oldest existing congregation (the one in Keokuk went out of existence in the 1920s). Des Moines' pioneer congregation, B'nai Jeshurun, was founded in 1870 and erected the state's second synagogue in 1878.

The best-known Jews in Iowa in the 1880s were Abraham Slimmer, of Waverly, and Moses Bloom, of Iowa City. Slimmer, a recluse, endowed hospitals, schools, and orphanages throughout Iowa and other states and was a generous contributor to synagogues. Bloom was elected mayor of Iowa City in 1869 and 1874 and served in both houses of the state legislature in the 1880s. Benjamin Salinger served on the Iowa State Supreme Court from 1915 to 1921. Joe Katelman was elected mayor of Council Bluffs in 1966. David Henstein was mayor of Glenwood (1892) and Sam Polonetzky was mayor of Valley Junction (1934).

[Bernard Postal]

Des Moines remains the largest center of Jewish life in Iowa. Its Federation, located on a community campus which includes the Jewish Community Relations Commission, the Greater Des Moines Jewish Press, Jewish Family Services, the Iowa Jewish Senior Life Center, and Tifereth Israel, the Conservative synagogue which houses the Federation-run com-

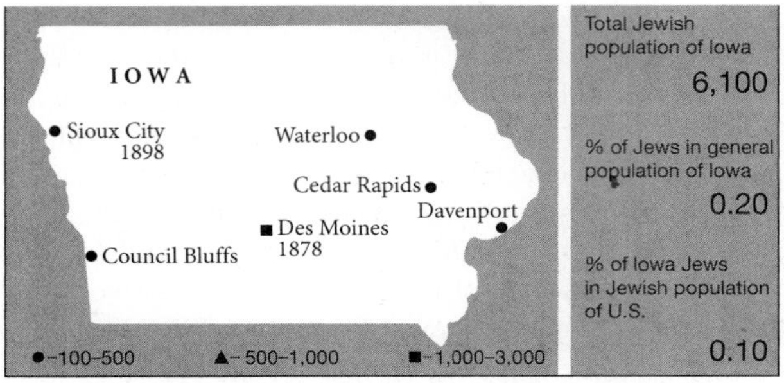

Jewish communities in Iowa, with dates of establishment of first synagogue. Population figures for 2001.

munity Hebrew School, is very active and influential. The Des Moines Jewish Academy, a day school started in 1977 by three families, merged in 2004 with a secular private school to become The Academy, Des Moines' only secular private school. The Academy offers an after-school Jewish curriculum. An additional Federation facility for social, cultural, and recreational activities, the Caspe Terrace, located in nearby Waukee, Iowa, is the site of the children's camp, Camp Shalom, as well as the museum of the Iowa Jewish Historical Society, a committee of the Federation founded in 1989.

Des Moines boasts four synagogues, and ritual practice in most has become more traditional over time. The Reform Temple, B'nai Jeshurun, has the largest membership with Shabbat services now held on both Friday night and Saturday morning. Ritual at the Conservative synagogue, Tifereth Israel, has remained largely unchanged. Beth El Jacob, the Orthodox synagogue which allowed mixed seating beginning in the 1950s, now has a *meḥizah* in both its small chapel and its main sanctuary. Lubavitch of Iowa/Jewish Resource Center, operating with its current rabbi since 1992, holds Shabbat services and publishes a monthly magazine, *The Jewish Spark*, and contains a *mikveh*, as does Beth El Jacob synagogue, less than half a mile away. Beth El Jacob synagogue and Lubavitch of Iowa clashed over a bequest, which resulted in a civil law suit. The resulting settlement led to the establishment of a Chabad-run kosher deli, Maccabee. The Jewish population in Des Moines has moved westward. With the purchase of land west of Des Moines, plans are under discussion for moving the campus that contains both the Federation and Tifereth Israel synagogue.

Perhaps the most interesting development in Iowa has been the growth of an ultra-Orthodox community in rural Postville, where once there were only Christians. Heshy Rubashkin moved to this town of 2300 in 1989 to set up AgriProcessors, a kosher meat processing plant. Five years later, when they opened a Jewish school, more hasidic families followed. Today 75 ḥasidic families live in Postville, which offers K-8 Jewish education for girls and K-11 Jewish education for boys. The Postville Jewish community boasts a Jewish doctor, a family-run kosher cheese manufacturing business, Mitzvah Farms, and a kosher grocery store and adjacent restaurant. Tensions developed between the ḥasidic newcomers and their Christian neighbors. The cross cultural conflict became the subject of much national press coverage, a best-selling book, and a PBS movie. Though tensions still persist, Jews and non-Jews are learning to live with each other. One member of the hasidic community was elected to a term on the Postville City Council. Recently the Lubavitch community, which houses Postville's only synagogue where all types of Ḥasidim pray together, including those of Ger and Bobov, opened a Jewish Resource Center. The JRC, open to all comers including non-Jews, contains a Jewish library, meeting room, gift shop and offers Jewish tutorials for the few non-observant Jews in Postville.

One Postville resident, observing the harmony among diverse Ḥasidim described life in Jewish Postville as "moschiah time."

Sioux City, which was at one time Iowa's second largest Jewish community, now numbers only 300. To address the crisis of a Jewish population decreasing through death and not replenishing with new families, the Conservative and Reform synagogues merged in 1994, maintaining in congregation Beth Shalom affiliation with both the Conservative and Reform movements. Ritual observance at Beth Shalom generally follows the Reform tradition, though Conservative traditions apply to both Shabbat morning and second day holiday prayer. Beth Shalom maintains a K-12 religious school and employs a full-time rabbi, ordained at a trans-denominational seminary.

In Iowa City, home to the University of Iowa, the Reform and Conservative synagogues also merged, and congregation Agudas Achim, with a membership of 200 families, is affiliated with both the Reform and Conservative movements. Services, led by a Conservative-ordained Rabbi, generally follow the Conservative ritual, though once each month Reform services are held. The University of Iowa with a Jewish population of roughly 600 undergraduates and 200 graduate students runs a Hillel in which about 10% of the students are active.

Nearby, Temple Judah of Cedar Rapids, a Reform Congregation, has maintained a stable Jewish community with 125 families and a school enrollment of 53 students.

Davenport, one of the Quad Cities, has a Jewish population of about 450 people, most affiliated with either the Reform Congregation, Temple Emanuel, or a Conservative synagogue across the river in Rock Island, Illinois. An Israeli *shali'aḥ* sent to Davenport's Federation for one year, has helped revitalize Jewish life and promote outreach to the non-Jewish community.

Ames, the home of Iowa State University, maintains the Ames Jewish Congregation, a community of 62 families, affiliated with the Reform Movement since 1962.

BIBLIOGRAPHY: J.S. Wolfe, *A Century with Iowa Jewry* (1941); S. Glazer, *Jews of Iowa* (1904); B. Postal and L. Koppman, *A Jewish Tourist's Guide to the U.S.* (1954), 171–77. Steven Bloom, *Postville: A Clash of Cultures in Heartland America* (2001); *Yiddl in Middle: Growing Up Jewish in Iowa*, a film by Marlene Booth.

[Marlene Booth (2nd ed.)]

IPSWICH, town in southeastern England. A medieval community existed there until 1290 with its own *archa. However, relatively little is known about it. Jews began to resettle in the mid-18th century. A synagogue was built in 1792 and a cemetery acquired in 1796. During the French Revolution, the Jews were suspected of Jacobin sympathies and the magistrates had to intervene to save them from attack. The community ceased to exist during the 19th century. At the outset of the 21st century, no Jewish institutions existed in Ipswich.

BIBLIOGRAPHY: Abrahams, in: JHSET, 2 (1894–95), index; Davis, in: *East Anglian*, 3 (1889–90), 89–93, 105f., 123–7; C. Roth, *Rise of Provincial Jewry* (1950), 71–4; Roth, England, index. **ADD BIBLIOGRAPHY:** M. Brown, "The Jews of Norfolk and Sufflok Before 1840," in: JHSET, 32 (1990–92), 219–36; idem, "An Ipswich Worthy Portrayed by John Constable," in: JHSET, 33 (1992–4), 137–40.

[Cecil Roth]

IQUITOS, city in Peru. Surrounded by the Amazon River and two of its tributaries, and separated from other cities by the vast tropical rain forest and the high Andean summits, Iquitos, located 1,200 miles from Lima, was the most isolated city in South America until the coming of the airplane. Nevertheless, like Manaus and Belén do Pará, it was the hub from which representatives of foreign industries administered their businesses during the rubber boom of the 19th century. Hence, starting in 1870, around 150 Sephardi Jews, mainly from Morocco but also from places such as Gibraltar, Malta, Alsace, and the city of Manchester, made their way to Iquitos in search of quick fortunes working as traders and owners of commercial houses that provided services to the people who exploited rubber in the jungle. In a few years the little town founded by Jesuits became a cosmopolitan city that boasted the only organized Jewish community in Peru besides the one in the capital city of Lima.

In 1905 the Jewish immigrants, who initially had no intention of staying long in the city, built a cemetery to accommodate the inevitable loss of life in a frontier area while refraining from building such permanent structures as a synagogue or a school. By 1909, they had founded and formally registered with the local authorities of the city the Israelite Society of Beneficence of Iquitos in order to provide assistance to fellow Jews, although, they only met for the Jewish high holidays and scarcely developed a Jewish life. Most of the Jews, like all the immigrants, married or had children with local Amazonian women. During the 1910s, with the decline of rubber prices, most of the Jews left the city. The few who stayed, together with the first generation of their descendants, met occasionally for Sabbath services in private homes. Though they continued to intermarry with local Christian natives, the descendants of Jews preserved a strong sense of Jewishness, kept up some Jewish traditions, and made several attempts to sustain a fragile community, which made its first contacts with Lima's Jews during the 1950s, especially after the visit of the Jewish Peruvian geologist Alfredo Rosenzweig, who in 1948 got to know the first generation of Jewish descendants during a trip to the Amazon region. In an article published in 1967 Rosenzweig provided the first detailed account of the presence of Jews in Iquitos, telling about the economic contribution of the big and famous Kahn, Israel, and Cohen commercial houses, among others, and obtaining a copy of the statutes of the Israelite Society and a list with 29 documents concerning community members buried at the Israelite cemetery, where "Israelite," "Hebrew," or "Jewish" is explicitly written as the faith of the deceased.

In 1995 Dr. Ariel Segal visited Iquitos in order to research the syncretic identity of the Jewish descendants of the city after learning that there was still an organized community of self-proclaimed Jews who celebrated the main Jewish holidays. These had been visited twice by Rabbi Guillermo Bronstein of the Conservative Jewish congregation of Lima and by officials of the Jewish Agency who helped those members who expressed an interest in learning about Judaism and immigrating to the State of Israel and whose cases fell under the Law of Return, to make *aliyah*. Their Judaism has been also debated in Orthodox circles after they were visited by a member of Israel's Rabbinate.

Iquitos descendants of Jews still bury members of their congregation in the Israelite cemetery, they celebrate *Kabbalat Shabbat* services – although some of them also attend churches – and speak proudly of their Jewish heritage while a few of them practice some local Amazonian and Christian rituals. They define themselves as members of the "chosen people" with Jewish blood. This sense of lineage and identity is part of the fascinating historical consciousness that Dr. Segal, in the book *Jews of the Amazon*, categorized as *Marranic*, claiming that the identity of the "Jewish *Mestizos*" – *Mestizaje* is understood as biological and cultural miscegenation – resembles the identity of many descendants of Jews forced to convert to Christianity in the Iberian Peninsula, and of other communities that combined Judaism and another religion, such the *Bene Israel of Bombay.

Defining *Marranism* also as an identity, a product of isolation rather than exclusively a result of compulsory conversion to another religion, is, however controversial, useful in understanding the sense of peoplehood of the Iquitos community after living almost 100 years without a rabbi, a synagogue, or a Jewish school.

BIBLIOGRAPHY: A. Rosenzweig, "Judíos en la Amazonía Peruana, 1870–1949," in: *MajShavot* 12 (June 1967); A. Segal, *Jews of the Amazon: Self-Exile in Earthly Paradise* (1999); M. Freund, "Exodus from the Amazon," in *The Jerusalem Post* (Sept. 12, 2003).

[Ariel Segal (2nd ed.)]

IRAN (official name: Islamic Republic of Iran), country in S.W. Asia, before 1935 known as Persia. Iran covers an area of 1,648,195 square km and includes 28 provinces, 714 districts, 718 towns, and 2,258 villages. Up to 1948 Jews were scattered in about 100 towns and villages, their number was then estimated at between 100,000 and 120,000.

The name Iran for the entire Iranian plateau has been in

usage since the Sasanian period (224–650 C.E.) and also in classical literature, e.g., in the *Shāhnāmeh* of Ferdawsi (about 10th century). Persia as a name for the country was used by foreigners; geographically it referred to the Province of Fārs in the south from which the Achaemenian kingdom of Cyrus the Great emerged. It was officially changed to Iran in 1935, most probably under the influence of strong German-Iranian relations during the 1930s. The many German agents in Iran emphasized the so-called Aryan origin of the Iranians, which appealed to the nationalist mood of the time. This type of nationalism in Iran did not allow any social and political activities with ties to foreign countries, and thus Communist and Zionist activities were forbidden in Iran during Reza Shah's reign (1925–41). There were also difficulties faced by Jews who wanted to immigrate to the Land of Israel. However, it must be said that Reza Shah's reign proved to be the beginning of an era of relative freedom and socioeconomic opportunities for Jews and other non-Muslim communities. In this period, Jews were active in trade, industry, and tourism. Several Jews reached the highest levels of fame and prosperity in the modern history of Iran. Among them were Haim Moreh, Morteza Mo'allem, and Soleiman Haim in education and scholarship; Iraj Lālehzāri and Shemooil Rahbar in science; Morteza Ney-Dāvoud and Yonah Dardashti in music; Morād Ariyeh, Habib Elghanaian, Ebrāhim Rād, and many others in economics.

With the occupation of Iran by Russia and Britain in August 1941 and the abdication of Reza Shah in September, Iran experienced a new era of relative democracy and freedom such as it had never had before. Jews began to take advantage of the situation and from 1942 on they started to renew their Zionist and social activities. During the 1940s, a dozen Jewish organizations emerged in *Teheran and in other major cities, such as *Shiraz, *Isfahan, *Hamadan, *Kermanshah, and Sanandaj. Among these organizations were the following: several youth organizations named Kānun-e Javānān; Ha-Histadrut ha-Ẓiyyonit; the Ḥalutz Movement; the Jewish Hospital; the Oẓar ha-Torah Educational Schools; the Women's Organization; ORT Schools; newspapers, such as *'Ālam-e Yahud, Yisrāel, Sinā*, and so on. State universities, colleges, elementary and high schools became more accessible to Jewish students and teachers. Jews were able to find employment in governmental offices with less difficulty than before. This relative freedom also gave rise to fascist parties such as the Pan-Iranism Party that regarded the Jews as an undesirable Semitic foreign element in Iran. The Tudeh Party favored the Jews, whose intellectuals, in general, were sympathetic to it, and a few hundred of them became active members of the party.

Jewish settlements in Iran, 1967 and 2001. 1967 data based on E. Spicehandler, Yahadut Iran, *Jerusalem, 1970.*

Population

The earliest report of a Jewish population in Iran goes back to the 12th century. It was *Benjamin of Tudela who claimed that there was a population of about 600,000 Jews. This number was later reduced to 100,000 in the Safavid period (1501–1736), and it further diminished to 50,000 at the beginning of the 20th century, as reported by the *Alliance Israélite Universelle (AIU) emissaries in Iran. The drastic decrease in number was the result of persecution, forced conversions, Muslim laws of inheritance (which encouraged conversion and allowed the convert to inherit the properties of his Jewish family), and massacres. These problems continued at least up to the Constitutional Revolution in Iran (1905–09). According to unofficial statistics released by the Jewish Agency in Teheran, there were between 100,000 to 120,000 Jews living in Iran in 1948. The following numbers, with some variation, were reported for the Jews of major cities: Teheran, about 50,000 Jews; all Iranian Kurdistan, between 15,000 to 20,000; Shiraz, 17,000; Isfahan, 10,000; Hamadan, 3,000; Kashan, 1,200; *Meshed, 2,500; Kermanshah, 2,864; Yazd/Yezd, 2,000 (uncertain). There are no reliable statistics for other communities scattered in many small towns and villages, such as Borujerd, Dārāb, Fasā, Golpāygān, Gorgān, Kāzrun, Khunsār, Lahijān, Malāyer, Nowbandegān, Rasht, and many more. There were also censuses carried out once every 10 years by the government, beginning in 1956. These censuses usually were not reliable as far as the Jewish communities were concerned, since Jews were not enthusiastic about being identified as such. For example, the official census of 1966 cites 60,683 Jews in Iran, but the Jewish sources put the number much higher than 70,000. The data provided by different sources, especially by those involved or interested in Iran's Jewish community affairs, differ greatly from one another.

Occupation

We do not possess a reliable source regarding the occupations of the Jews in different towns and settlements in Iran. The data varies in time and place, but one may nevertheless find similarities in the reports. We have more reliable statistics concerning the second largest community in Iran, the Jews of Shiraz which may, to some degree, represent the Jewish occupations in other major cities – with the exception of the goldsmiths and musicians who made Shirazi Jews famous. The following was reported by Dr. Laurence Loeb, who resided in Shiraz from August 1967 through December 1968, as investigated and reported on the distribution of occupations. (See table: Occupations in Shiraz.)

Table 1. Occupations in Shiraz, 1967–1968

Occupation	Number	Percentage
Peddler	49	12.10
Cloth store	42	10.37
Goldsmith	27	6.67
Haberdasher	25	6.17
Doctor	19	4.69
Nurse, hospital worker	17	4.17
Teacher, principal	16	3.95
Engineer	12	3.46
Musician	12	2.96
Liquor seller	12	2.96
Moneylender	12	2.96
Spinner	12	2.96
Merchant of gum tragacanth	11	2.72
Druggist	9	2.22
Grocer	9	2.22
Fruit and vegetables	9	2.22
Smith	8	1.98
Mason	7	1.73
Carter	6	1.48
Office worker	6	1.48
Real estate	6	1.48
Butcher	4	0.99
Technician	4	0.99
Tailor	4	0.99
JDC worker	4	0.99
Industrial worker	4	0.99
Household goods shop	4	0.99
School janitor	4	0.99

In addition to what was reported above, Loeb found in Shiraz 41 persons who were dentists, cooks, carpenters, barbers, seed merchants, laborers, librarians, mullas, restaurant workers, bath attendants, leather tanners, photographers, beauty parlor attendants, appliance store clerks, lambswool merchants or dairy store attendants. They constituted 10.12 percent of the work force of the community. There were also 8 unemployed persons (1.98%).

Education

Modern Jewish education in Iran was in general in the hands of the Alliance Israélite Universelle (AIU) from 1898. The AIU was active only in major cities such as Teheran (from 1898), Hamadan (1900), Isfahan (1901), Shiraz (1903), Sanandaj (1903), and Kermanshah (1904). In the second decade of the 20th century it opened schools in Kashan and Yazd, and also in some small towns close to Hamadan, such as Tuyserkān, Borujerd, and Nehāvand. Parallel to the AIU schools, community schools were established in a few towns, such as Koresh in Teheran and Koresh in Rasht. During the Pahlavi regime, some Jews also studied in non-Jewish schools.

In 1946/47, the Oẓar ha-Torah schools were opened in Teheran and other cities. Rabbi Isaac Meir Levi, a Polish Jew who had come to Iran in 1941 to organize the dispatch of parcels to rabbis and synagogues in Russia, was appointed by the Oẓar ha-Torah center in New York to establish a network of schools in Iran.

Given the great wave of immigration to Israel which swept the Jews of Iran in the 1950s, most immigrants being poor and unskilled, the economic prosperity which Iran enjoyed in the 1960s and 1970s, and the rise to wealth of a large segment of the remaining Jewish community, more attention was devoted to education. In 1977/78 there were in Teheran 11 Oẓar ha-Torah schools, 7 AIU schools, and 6 community schools, including one ORT vocational school and the Ettefāq school belonging to Iraqi Jews resident in Teheran. This picture changed drastically with the mass exodus of Jews resulting from the Islamic revolution. Prior to the Islamic Republic of Iran (= IRI) there were three Jewish schools in Shiraz and one Jewish school in each major city. By the end of the 20th century there were generally three Jewish schools in Teheran, one in Shiraz, and one in Isfahan. Most of these schools were funded and sponsored by Oẓar ha-Torah (Netzer, 1996).

Aliyah

Immigration to Israel was facilitated and accelerated through the Zionist Association in Teheran (founded in 1918) and its branches in 18 major cities. The following official statistics published by the Government of Israel show the rate of Iranian Jewish immigration to Israel (the number 3,536 below for the years 1919–1948 does not accurately reflect reality, since thousands of Iranian Jews immigrated to Israel illegally and were consequently not registered by the British Mandate or the Jewish Agency). It is believed that on the eve of independence there were about 20,000 Iranian Jews living in Israel.

Table 2. Immigration of Iranian Jews to Israel, 1919–2001

Period	Number of Immigrants
1919–1948	3,536
1948–1951	21,910
1952–1960	15,699
1961–1964	8,857
1965–1971	10,645
1972–1979	9,550
1980–1989	8,487
1990–2001	257
Total	78,941

In the past, the majority of Iranian Jews lived in Jerusalem, while at the beginning of the 21st century they were to be found primarily in Tel Aviv, Holon, Bat-Yam, Rishon le-Zion, Kefar Saba, Nes Ẓiyyonah, and Reḥovot. A smaller number chose to reside in Jerusalem, Netanyah, Haifa, Ashkelon, Ashdod, and Beersheba. Since 1948, the Jews of Iran have founded several moshavim: Agur, Amishav (now a quarter in Petaḥ Tikvah),

Avdon, Dovev, Eshbol, Givati, Givolim, Hodayah, Margaliyyot, Maslul, Melilot, Nes-Harim, Netiv ha-Shayarah, Neveh Yamin, Nogah, Pa'mei TaShaZ, Patish, Kadimah, Talmei Bilu, Ẓerufah, and others.

With the change of the regime and *Khomeini's rise to power, about three-quarters of Iran's 80,000 Jews left. Many immigrated to Israel and the United States, but a part preferred to settle in European countries. The official statistics of Israel show that in 2001 there were 135,200 Jews who were considered Iranian either as *olim* or as individuals one of whose parents was Iranian-Jewish. The above figure includes 51,300 who were born in Iran and 83,900 who were born in Israel. Iranian Jews in Israel became active and reached high ranks in academic life, in the socioeconomic realm, politics, and the military. Since 1955, they have had about a score of university teachers; Rabbi Ezra Zion *Melamed, professor of Talmud at the Hebrew University of Jerusalem was granted the Israel Prize. There have been several Knesset members, two chief commanders of the Air Force (General Eitan Ben-Eliyahu and General Dan Ḥaluẓ), two army chiefs of staff (Major-General Shaul *Mofaz and Major-General Dan Ḥaluẓ); one defense minister, Shaul Mofaz; one Sephardi chief rabbi (Rabbi *Bakshi Doron); and the president of the State of Israel, Moshe *Katzav.

Jewish Representation in the Majles

The Jewish representatives in the Iranian Parliament (Majles) since its inception (1907) were the following: Azizollah Simāni, a merchant (replaced by Ayatollah Behbāhni after only a few months); Dr. Loqmān Nehoray, a physician (1909–23); Shemuel Haim, a journalist (1923–26); Dr. Loqmān Nehoray (1926–43), Morād Ariyeh, a merchant (1945–56); Dr. Mussa Berāl, a pharmacologist (1956–1960), Morād Ariyeh, (1960–64), Jamshid Kashfi, a merchant (1964–68), Lotfollah Hay, a merchant (1968–75), and Yosef Cohen, a lawyer (1975–79).

Iran-Israel Relations

Relations between the Yishuv and Iran began in 1942, when the Jewish Agency opened a Palestine Office in Teheran, with the aim of assisting the Jewish-Polish refugees from Russia and arranging for their immigration to the Land of Israel. This office continued to function until 1979. Iran voted, together with the Muslim and Arab states in the UN against the partition of Palestine (November 29, 1947). In the Israel-Arab conflict, Iran sided with the Arabs. However, Iran's need for socioeconomic reforms drove it to establish closer relations with the West, especially with the U.S. Consequently, after the Shah's trip to the U.S. in 1949, Iran recognized Israel de-facto in March 1950. The relations between the two countries remained "discreetly unofficial," even though diplomatic missions were operating in Teheran and Tel Aviv. These continued to function until early 1979. Practical relations between the two states existed in a variety of fields such as trade, export-import, regular El-Al flights to Teheran, supply of Iranian oil to Israel, and student exchanges. They developed especially strong relations in three major fields: agriculture, medicine, and the military. Israeli experts assisted Iran in various development projects such as the Qazvin project in the 1960s. The Six-Day War is regarded as the high point of friendly Israel-Iran relations, particularly in the area of the Intelligence Service. The Shah and his military were surprised by the swift Israeli victory over *Syria, *Jordan, and *Egypt. Likewise, the Israeli setback in the Yom Kippur War (1973) induced the Shah's pragmatic diplomacy to develop amicable relations with Anwar *Sadat of Egypt. It has been said that it was this policy of the Shah that encouraged Sadat to make peace with Israel. With the coming to power of Khomeini in February 1979, the friendly relations between the two states changed into strong enmity. In 2006 the growing Iranian nuclear threat and President Ahmadinejad's declaration that Israel should be wiped off the face of the earth led to increasing talk of a preemptive military strike against Iran.

Jews in the Last Year of the Pahlavi Regime

The economic boom of the 1960s and the 1970s in Iran benefited the Jews too. Many Jews became rich, which enabled them to provide higher education for their children. In 1978 there were about 80,000 Jews in the country, constituting one-quarter of one percent of the general population. Of these Jews, 10 percent were very rich, the same percentage were poor (aided by the Joint Distribution Committee) and the rest were classified as from middle class to rich. Approximately, 70 out of 4,000 academicians teaching at Iran's universities were Jews; 600 Jewish physicians constituted six percent of the country's medical doctors. There were 4,000 Jewish students studying in all the universities, representing four percent of the total number of students. Never in their history were the Jews of Iran elevated to such a degree of affluence, education, and professionally as they were in the last decade of the Shah's regime. All this changed with the emergence of the Islamic Republic of Iran (IRI).

Iranian Jews in the IRI

On January 16, 1979, the Shah was forced to leave Iran. Two weeks later Ayatollah Khomeini entered Teheran to assume power, after having lived in exile for almost 15 years. On February 11, 1979, for the first time in the history of Iran, the government of the Ayatollahs came into being, and the kingdom of Iran turned into the Islamic Republic of Iran (IRI). This political phenomenon has significantly changed the demographic map of the Jewish community of Iran. By the end of 20th century – that is to say, at the end of 20 years of the Islamic regime in Iran – taking into consideration the birthrate, there were about 30,000 Jews in Iran, of which 25,000 lived in Teheran, 3,000 in Shiraz, 1,500 in Isfahan, while the rest were scattered in other cities and settlements. In the IRI, Jews as well as other religious minorities were regarded as the supporters of the royal regime, because it was under the Pahlavi dynasty that they had enjoyed prosperity and some measure of relative freedom. When the revolution broke out, Israel-Iran relations and the diplomatic, economic, and military cooperation between the countries were markedly strong. Consequently the situation of the Jews became precarious, because of the anti-Zionist attitude and character of the revolution. The Jews of Iran were accused of being the supporters of the Shah, Israel, the Mossad, the CIA and the U.S. All were defined as "Satan." A few wealthy Jews, among them the former head of the Jewish Community of Teheran, Habib Elghanian, were tried by the revolutionary courts and sentenced to death (May 9, 1979). Jewish-owned property worth at least one billion dollars was confiscated by the regime. This alarming situation caused many Jews to leave Iran.

Under the Islamic Republic of Iran, the following persons represented the Jewish community in the Majles: Eshāq Farahmandpour, a teacher (a few months in 1979 and then Jews had no representative until 1982); Khosrow Nāqi, a lawyer (1982–84); Dr. Manouchehr Nikruz (1984–92); Dr. Kuros Keyvāni (1992–96); Dr. Manouchehr Elyāsi (1996–2000); Moris Mo'tamed, an engineer (2000–).

Iranian Jews Abroad

It is estimated that during the first 10 years of the Islamic regime about 60,000 Jews left Iran; the rest, some 20,000, remained in Teheran, Shiraz, Isfahan, and other provincial cities. Of the 60,000 Jews who emigrated, about 35,000 preferred to immigrate to the U.S.; some 20,000 left for Israel, and the remaining 5,000 chose to live in Europe, mainly in England, France, Germany, Italy, or Switzerland. The spread of the Iranian Jews in the U.S. provides us with the following demographic map: of the total 35,000, some 25,000 live in California, of whom about 20,000 prefer to dwell in Los Angeles; 8,000 Iranian Jews live in the city of New York and on Long Island; the remaining 2,000 live in other cities, mainly in Boston, Baltimore, Washington, Detroit, or Chicago.

In every city abroad, the Jews of Iran tried to establish themselves in their own newly founded organizations and synagogues. In Los Angeles alone, they set up more than 40 organizations, 10 synagogues, about 6 magazines, and one television station. The Iranian Jewish community in the U.S. is, for the most part, well-educated and financially stable. Education is one of the strongest values stressed by the Iranian Jewish community, which considers itself the cream of all immigrant groups in the U.S. The Iranian Jews brought with them money, doctors, engineers, upper-class educated businessmen, and professionals in almost all fields. Many of them became wealthy in their new homes in the U.S., Europe, and Israel.

[Amnon Netzer (2nd ed.)]

Musical Tradition

The musical patrimony of the Iranian Jews contains several different styles. The nature of their non-synagogal music, and the general approach to music and the way it is performed, are identical with those of their non-Jewish neighbors. The attachment to poetry and music which has been characteristic of Iranian culture from its earliest days is also found among the Jews, with similar attention devoted to the cultivation of these arts, the special connection of music with the expressions of sorrow, meditation, and mystical exaltation, and the same ideal of voice color and voice production. Some of these characteristics have of course been transposed in order to suit the specific conditions of a Jewish culture. The tendency toward mysticism finds its fullest expression in a predilection for the *Zohar, which is recited with a special musical intonation. The great importance attached to lamentations for the dead, which constitute a rich and interesting repertoire, may be analogous with the *ta'ziya-t* of the Persian Shi'ites, which are a kind of vernacular religious drama commemorating the tragedies which marked the birth of the Shi'a sect.

Notwithstanding some analogies in style and form, the Iranian influence is, however, hardly traceable in the Iranian synagogal tradition. In the structure of the melodies of free rhythmical or recitative character, A.Z. *Idelsohn found a strong resemblance to the synagogal tradition of the Yemenite Jews. Their tradition of Pentateuch cantillation is among the more archaic ones, being centered almost exclusively on the major divisive accents (see *Masoretic Accents, Musical Rendition). On the other hand, most of the metrical **piyyutim*, mainly those of the High Holidays, are sung to melodies common to all Near Eastern, i.e. "Eastern Sephardi," communities.

In the paraliturgical and secular domain, the poetry and music of the Iranian Jews are simply a part of the general culture, with a few exceptions. Among these are the works of non-Persian Jewish poets, such as Israel *Najara, of which a Judeo-Persian translation is in wide use, and which are sung on such occasions as *se'udah shlishit* and **bakkashot* (among Persians Jews, contrary to other communities, these are performed at home and not in the synagogue).

The most impressive production was in the domain of epic songs. Here, the Persian Jews closely followed the Persian model in language, meter, and musical rendition, though the Jewish poets and musicians naturally sang of the achievements and history of their own people. The chief representative of epic poetry is *Shahin, a Persian Jewish poet of the 14th century. His poetic paraphrase of the narrative parts of the Pentateuch, called in brief *Shāhīn*, is sung in public on Sabbath afternoons and at festive gatherings by specialized "epic singers." The public, although knowing every word by memory, expresses its enthusiasm anew each time. The *Shahīn* also became a favorite in Bukhara, which was considered a cultural province of Persian Jewry. Shahin himself and after him other poets, especially 'Amrani, wrote other epic songs on Jewish topics which also attained great popularity.

Another branch of poetry, but one of a more folkloristic nature, consists of the songs which are improvised in an impromptu competition of poets. These are performed at family celebrations, after wine-drinking bouts, and the competition between the two singer-poets adds to the atmosphere of good cheer. (For the music of the Kurdistan region of Iran see *Kurdistan.)

[Amnon Shiloah]

BIBLIOGRAPHY: E. Abrahamian, *Iran Between the Two Revolutions* (1982); P. Avery, *Modern Iran* (1965); *Bulletin de l'Alliance Israélite Universelle*, Paris; I. Ben-Zvi (1935), *Nidhei Yisrael* (1935, 1965); Sh. Bakhash, *The Reign of the Ayatollas: Iran and the Islamic Revolution* (1984); A. Banani, *The Modernization of Iran: 1921–1941* (1961); U. Bialer, "The Iranian Connection in Israel's Foreign Policy," in: *The Middle East Journal*, 39 (Spring 1985), 292–315; G.N. Curzon,

Persia and the Persian Question, 1–2 (1892), index; R. Graham, *Iran: The Illusion of Power* (1979); F. Halliday, *Iran: Dictatorship and Development* (1979); Sh. Hillel, *Ruah Qadim* (1985); S. Landshut, *Jewish Communities in the Muslim Countries of the Middle East* (1950), 61–6; G. Lenczowski, *Russia and the West in Iran, 1918–1948* (1949); idem, *Iran under the Pahlavis* (1978); H. Levy, *History of the Jews of Iran*, vol.3, (1960); A. Netzer, "*Be'ayot ha-Integrazya ha-Tarbutit, ha-Ḥevratit ve-ha-Politit shel Yehudei Iran*," in: *Gesher*, 25:1–2 (1979), 69–83; idem, "*Yehudei Iran, Israel, ve-ha-Republikah ha-Islamit shel Iran*; in: *ibid.*, 26:1–2 (1980), 45–57; idem, "*Iran ve-Yehudeha be-Parashat Derakhim Historit*," in: *ibid.*, 1/106 (1982), 96–111; idem, "*Tekufot u-Shelavim be-Maẓav ha-Yehudim ve-ha-Pe'ilut ha-Ẓiyyonit be-Iran*," in: *Yahdut Zemanenu*, 1 (1983), 139–62; idem, "*Yehudei Iran be-Arẓot ha-Berit*," in: *Gesher*, 1/110 (1984), 79–90; idem, "Anti-Semitism be-Iran, 1925–1950," in: *Pe'amim*, 29 (1986), 5–31; idem, "Jewish Education in Iran," in: H.S. Himmelfarb and S. DellaPergola (eds.), *Jewish Education Worldwide*, (1989), 447–61; idem, "Immigration, Iranian," in: J. Fischel and S. Pinsker (eds.), *Jewish-American History and Culture* (1992), 265–67; idem, "Persian Jewry and Literature: A Sociocultural View," in: H.E. Goldberg (ed.), *Sephardi and Middle Eastern Jewries* (1996), 240–55; J. Nimrodi, *Massa' Hayyay*, 1–2 (2003); *The Palestine Year Book*, 3 (1947–1948), 77; R.K. Ramazani, *Revolutionary Iran* (1986), 282–5; idem, *The Foreign Policy of Iran: 1500–1941* (1966); Sh. Segev, *Ha-Meshullash ha-Irani* (1981); *Ha-Shenaton ha-Statisti le-Israel* (2002); *Shofar* (Jewish monthly in Persian published on Long Island), 243 (May 2001), 22ff.; B. Souresrafil, *Khomeini and Israel* (1988); J. Upton, *The History of Modern Iran: An Interpretation* (1968); D.N. Wilbur, *Iran, Past and Present* (1948); M. Yazdani, *Records on Iranian Jews Immigration to Palestine (1921–1951)* (1996), 61, 67, 110; Idelson, Melodien, 3 (1922).

IRAQ, country in S.W. Asia (for period prior to 634 C.E. see *Mesopotamia and *Babylonia).

The Diaspora of Iraq was one of the most ancient of the Jewish people. The Jews came to Babylon after the destruction of the First Temple (586 B.C.E.), or even 10 years earlier, with the exile of Jehoiachin. They integrated into their land of captivity and took part in its economic and cultural development.

The contribution of Babylonian Jewry to molding the spirit and character of the Jewish people in the Diaspora was channeled through its famous academies (yeshivot) of *Sura and *Pumpedita. There, the Babylonian Talmud was composed and sealed. The heads of those academies functioned as the leaders of Babylonian Jewry and of other Jews. They continued to do so until the conquest of the country by the *Mongols in 1258 C.E. The decline of the Jewish communities of *Baghdad and *Basra continued for many generations. Only at the end of the 18th and the beginning of the 19th centuries did Baghdad begin to recover economically and culturally and start to function again as a religious center for the Jewish communities of *Kurdistan, *Persia, *India, and *Aden.

Under Islamic Rule

The Jews of Babylonia, who had suffered from persecutions at the end of the rule of the Persian Sasanid dynasty, welcomed the Arab conquest of the land, which became known as Iraq.

The legal status of the Jews, as **dhimmīs*, was defined by the *Shari'a* (the Islamic Law), under which they had certain rights including the right to worship and to administer their own religious law. On the other hand they were required to pay the *jizya* (poll tax) in exchange for protection by the Islamic rulers. They were also exempted from serving in the Muslim armies.

UNDER THE UMAYYAD CALIPHATE (661–750). The extant information on the attitude of the caliphs of the *Umayyad dynasty (661–750) toward the Jews is very limited. During this period the Jews suffered from the political disputes and controversies which took place in Iraq. In the times of the caliph Omar II ibn 'Abd al-Azīz (717–720) the Jews suffered, with other *dhimmīs*, intolerance toward their religion. He forbade the governors to appoint members of non-Muslims as tax collectors and scribes; he also prohibited the *dhimmīs* from dressing like Muslims and sought to degrade them socially (The Covenant of *Omar).

UNDER THE ABBASID CALIPHATE (750–1258). The situation of the Jews during the *Abbasid period was not stable. Some of the rulers were tolerant to them while others oppressed them variously. The caliph Hārūn al-Rashīd (786–809) persecuted the Jews and sought to humiliate them. He imposed heavy taxes and discriminated against them in regard to their dress, commerce, and other matters. The attitude changed under his son, the caliph al-Ma'mūn (813–833), who was a devotee of the sciences. At the beginning of his rule he revealed a tolerant attitude toward the Jews, but at its end he changed this policy for the worse as a result of his advisers' influence. During the reign of the caliph al-Mutawakkil (847–861) the Jewish situation was severely aggravated. This caliph issued, in 850, decrees which degraded the Jews and other non-Muslims. He instituted a yellow head covering and, for the servants and the poor, a yellow patch to be prominently worn on their clothes, on the chest or on the back. Four years later he added some new decrees on the color of clothes and on women's clothing. Various restrictions concerned with living quarters, taxes, and other matters are also attributed to him (see Covenant of *Omar). It may be assumed that not all these decrees were applied. In spite of all the restrictions, many Jews adapted themselves to the values of the Muslim culture. They distinguished themselves as physicians and writers, played important roles in the economic life and held government positions. The fact that it was necessary from time to time to renew the decrees on clothing proves that they were not generally enforced.

During the terms of office of the *gaon* *Aharon b. Joseph ha-Cohen Sargado, Baghdad was conquered by the Buwayhid emirs who ruled Iraq for more than a century (945–1055). This Persian Shi'ite dynasty was extremely fanatic and cruelly persecuted the Sunni Muslims, the Jews, and the Christians. They abolished the former rights of the exilarch to collect the poll tax, and the Jews were compelled to pay it to Muslim collectors who oppressed them severely. The situation of the Jews improved during the rule of the *Seljuks (1055–1150). After the

Seljuks the Abbasid caliphs restored their power, and a change for the worse occurred during the reign of caliph al-Muqtadī (1075–1094), who adopted a harsh attitude toward both the Jews and the Christians. He imposed heavy taxes upon them and compelled them to live according the discriminatory decrees issued by the caliph al-Mutwwakil. After him the situation of the Jews improved and their former autonomy was restored.

*Baghdad was founded by the caliph al-Manṣūr (754–775) and became the capital of the Abbasids. The Jewish community begin to expand until it became the largest one in Iraq and the seat of the *exilarch.

Under Muslim rule the academies of *Sura and *Pumbedita began to prosper. The heads of these academies were known, from then on, as **geonim*. The golden age of the *geonim* parallels the days of splendor of the Abbasid caliphate.

According to the traveler *Benjamin of Tudela, who visited Iraq in about 1170, the caliph was most favorable to the Jews; there were many Jewish officials in his service. The traveler R. *Pethahiah of Regensburg, who visited Iraq at the beginning of the reign of the caliph al-Nāṣir (1180–1225) greatly admired the erudition of the Jews of Babylonia: "... Babylonia is an entirely different world, their occupation consisting of Torah study and the fear of heaven, even the Ishmaelites are trustworthy ... in Babylon there are 30 synagogues in addition to that of Daniel ..." (*Sibbuv Rabbi Petahyah* (1905), 8, 24).

After the death of R. Hai the offices of the head of the academy (*rosh yeshivah*) and the exilarch (*resh galuta*) were both held by *Hezekiah b. David (1038–1058).

The academies of Sura and Pumbedita had been transferred to Baghdad during the 9th and the 10th century. In the middle of the 11th century they ceased to exist and were replaced by the Academy of Baghdad.

Under Mongol Rule (1258–1335)

Following *Mongols' occupation of Iraq in 1258, which caused total destruction and disaster all over the south and the center of the land, the Jewish communities of Baghdad and Basra did not recover for many generations. The attitude of the new rulers toward the Jews at the beginning of their reign changed for the better. Some of them advanced to high positions of state. The first of these was *Saʿd al-Dawla who was appointed a physician of the sultan Arghun Khan (1284–91) and then as a finance minister of the Il-khan kingdom. However, in 1291, when the sultan was in his sickbed, Saʿd al-Dawla was executed. The same fate was met 27 years later by another Jewish personality, *Rashid al-Dawla (1247–1318), who was a physician, capable financier, historian, and philosopher. He attained high rank and was appointed as physician of the khan and the chief minister (vizir); his enemies accused him of having poisoned the khan and had him executed. The situation of the Jews began to worsen when Ghazan Khan (1295–1304) converted to Islam. At that time a number of Jews were compelled to follow suit. In 1333 and 1334 the synagogues of Baghdad were destroyed, Jewish property was looted and, again, a number of Jews converted to Islam.

The occupation of the country by Tamerlane in 1393 caused destruction of a large part of Baghdad and other towns. The Baghdad community did not recover until the end of the 18th and the beginning of the 19th century.

Under Ottoman Rule

The Ottomans occupied Baghdad in 1534; their rule continued until 1917, except for 15 years (1623–38) when the Persians ruled the country and dealt very harshly with the Jews.

The *shariʿa* (the Islamic Code) was the law of the *Ottoman Empire, so the *dhimmīs* were treated according to this religious code. Jews suffered from minor discrimination under the Ottomans, and the Iraqi Jews, in general, lived under a tolerant regime. They paid a moderate poll tax and enjoyed relative freedom. Nevertheless, anti-Jewish crime or agitation on a petty scale was ready to appear. At times the Turkish governors oppressed the Jews and the poll tax was collected with many abuses by the highest bidder.

From 1830 to 1917, 42 Turkish valis governed Iraq. Mustafa Nuri Pasha (1860–61) tried to confiscate the shrine of the prophet *Ezekiel (traditionally considered buried in the village of Kifil) from the Jews; and Mustafa ʿAsim Pasha (1887–89) made false accusations against the Jews. In the time of the last vali, Khalil Pasha, 17 Jewish notables of Baghdad were accused of having engaged in illegal commerce. They were cruelly tortured and then executed. Conversely, there were some enlightened officials who restored order and brought peace to the country. The most prominent of these were Midhat Pasha (1869–72) and Hüseyin Nazim Pasha (1910–11). During their rule the Jews enjoyed security and tranquility.

DEMOGRAPHIC CHANGES. The Jewish population of Baghdad in 1824 was estimated at about 1,500 Jewish families. In 1831 it was reported that about 7,000 Jews were dwelling in a special quarter of the city and that they were employed in various governmental jobs. In 1845 the population of Baghdad was estimated at about 16,000 Jews, 40,000 Muslims, and 4,000 Christians. The traveler R. *Benjamin II (1848) put the number of the Jewish families in Baghdad at 3,000 with nine synagogues.

Scores of small Jewish communities were scattered throughout northern Iraq. The largest was in Mosul, which in 1848 had about 450 Jewish families. The figure of 3,000 Jews in this city remained stable until approximately the beginning the 20th century. The decline of the economic standing of Mosul seems to have contributed to the departure of Jews for Baghdad. According to official figures, there were in 1919 in all the northern districts (Mosul, Arbil, Suleimania, and Kirkuk) 13,835 Jews. According to the census of 1947 there were in the northern districts 19,767 Jews.

The main demographic changes occurred from the mid-19th century on. A considerable internal emigration from north to south followed the opening of the Suez-Canal (1869), which shifted the commercial pathway from the overland route (from Europe to India via *Aleppo in *Syria and Mosul in northern Iraq) to the naval route, thus favoring the Iraqi port of Basra. Economic conditions in the north begin to deteriorate. The

Jews, like others, started to move southward. North to south emigration was also encouraged by changes introduced during the reign of the Vali Midhat Pasha (1869–72), who succeeded in pacifying the tribes of central and southern Iraq and protecting the cities from their attacks. The two small Jewish communities in southern Iraq (Basra and Hilla) had grown larger, and additional communities settled in 'Amara, Qal'at Salih. 'Ali al-Gharbi, and Musyab. The Jewish movement to the south, however, declined after World War I, except for Basra.

The Jewish community of Baghdad continued to increase. In the year 1860 there lived in Baghdad about 20,000 Jews among 70,000 non-Jews. In 1889, they were estimated at about 25,000 among a population of 100,000 Muslims and 5,000 Christians. An account by the British Consul in Baghdad, in February 1910 stated, "The Jewish community at Baghdad is, after that of Salonica, the most numerous, important, and prosperous in Turkey." At the beginning of the 20th century the Jewish community of Baghdad numbered about 45,000, In 1919 the British put the figures of Iraqi Jews at 87,488 among a total population of 2,849,283; that is to say 3.1%. In the Baghdad district there were about 50,000 Jews in a total of 250,000 inhabitants. Official Iraqi statistics, based on the 1947 census, put the total number of Iraqi Jews at 118,000 or 2.6% of the total population of 4.5 million. In spite of this official census, some studies suggest that the real number of Jews in the late 1940s was higher. During the years 1948–51, 123,500 Jews immigrated to Israel, with several thousand others leaving during this period for other countries. About 6,000 Jews remained in Iraq after the mass immigration. This led to the conclusion that the total number of Jews in Iraq in the late 1940s was about 135,000.

Major Jewish Settlements in Iraq, based on the official census of 1947

Provinces	1920	1932	1947
Amara	3,000	2,540	2,145
Baghdad	50,300	42,799	76,825
Basra	6,928	7,260	9,388
Diyala	1,689	2,252	2,850
Diwaniya	6,530	531	809
Dulaym	2,600	897	1,661
Hilla	1,065	1,000	1,893
Irbil	4,800	3,090	c. 4,226
Karbala	—	—	—
Kirkuk	1,400	2,633	c. 4,025
Kut	381	346	359
Mosul	7,635	7,537	c. 8,696
Muntafiq	160	555	644
Sulaimaniya	1,000	1,343	c. 2,256
Total	87,488	72,783	115,777

SOCIAL CHANGE. The reforms in the Ottoman Empire that took place in the second half of the 19th century (*Tanzimat*) improved the legal status of the Jews. Theoretically they became equal in rights and obligations. The traditional poll tax (*jizya*), which symbolized the inferiority of the *dhimmis* and their subject status, was rescinded. The fiscal change was, however, cosmetic in a sense, since the *jizya* was replaced in 1855 by a new levy, *Bedel-i 'Askari* or military substitution tax, which exempted the non-Muslims from military service, for which they had become technically liable with the granting of civil equality. In 1909, shortly after the Young Turks' coup, this tax was canceled, and about 100 young Baghdadi Jews applied for admission to officers training school.

When World War I broke out, several thousands of Iraqi Jews were drafted into the Ottoman Army and sent to distant fronts, from which many of them did not return.

The most far-reaching of the reforms came in the reorganization of the millet all over the Empire. In Baghdad the post of the *Nasi* (the leader of the Jewish community) was suppressed in 1849, and the community was recognized as a millet. Its leadership was vested in a religious personality (the *ḥakham bashi*), "the chief rabbi." Later on, in 1931, under the British Mandate a new law was enacted to replace the Ottoman one. This law permitted the vesting of the leadership of Baghdad's Jewish community in a secular personality. Relying upon this law, it was possible in 1949 to replace Chief Rabbi *Sassoon Kadoorie with Heskel Shemtov.

As a result of the improvement in their civil status deriving from the reforms, the Jews were appointed to positions of judges, lecturers in the universities, officials in governmental service, and police officers. They also were appointed as members of city councils.

In 1869, when Midhat Pasha carried out the vilayet system, he appointed a leading Jewish notable, Menahem *Daniel, as council member of the Baghdad vilayet (*Majlis al-Idāra*). Daniel was also elected to parliament, which was opened in 1877 in Istanbul. This was a precedent which was followed in 1908 by the election of Heskel *Sassoon (1860–1932) to parliament.

The changes in the status of the *dhimmis* did not sit well with the traditionally minded Muslims. Anti-Christian violence erupted in many places in the Middle East, but not in Iraq. However, when the Young Turks tried to bring into force their notions of liberty, equality, and justice in Iraq, the Muslims greeted them with shock and dismay. They reacted on October 15, 1908, with violence against the Jews of Baghdad, which resulted in 40 wounded Jews. This event disabused the Jews of Baghdad of any illusions of equality.

Education and Literature

RELIGIOUS EDUCATION. In 1832 Midrash Talmud Torah was founded in Baghdad, which continued its activity until the mass immigration in the mid-20th century. In 1840 a religious academy, "Yeshivat Bet Zilkha," was founded after 100 years during which there was no such institution. This yeshivah educated rabbis for the Iraqi communities and those of its neighboring countries.

The founding of modern schools accelerated the secular trend in education among Iraqi Jews. The role of the *bet midrash* and the yeshivah was steadily undermined and became insignificant by the 1940s.

SECULAR EDUCATION. The first school of the *Alliance

Israélite Universelle for boys was founded in Baghdad in 1865 and for girls in 1883. More elementary schools were later opened in the provincial towns of Iraq. Those schools introduced modern methods of teaching and included foreign languages in the curriculum alongside Arabic, French, English, and Turkish. It created a real gap between the educational level of the Jews and that of the non-Jews. It qualified the Jews to be businessmen, clerks, and employees in the governmental offices and banks. This gap prevailed until the mass emigration and aroused the jealousy of the non-Jews in the country, causing friction between the Jews and their neighbors.

By the 1920s numerous schools had been established, mostly by Jewish philanthropists, and maintained by both Jewish community funds and regular contributions by the Iraqi government.

The number of the schools supervised by the Jewish community in Baghdad continued to rise, reaching 20 at the time of the mass exodus of 1950–51. In addition to the regular schools, a number of other institutes were established, including a school for the blind, orphanages, a music school, vocational centers, and charitable organizations.

Jewish students began attending universities in Iraq and abroad after World War I, and government schools were open to Jews as well as to other religious and ethnic minorities. In the 1930s there was no restriction on the number of Jewish students in governmental schools and colleges. Later, in the 1940s, a preferential quota introduced for scientific and medical colleges affected Jews' chances of entering these colleges.

The liberal and secular trend brought about a stronger association of Iraqi Jews and Arab culture and led Jews to take a more active role in public and cultural life. A considerable number of prominent Jewish writers and poets emerged, whose works in Arabic were both well known and well regarded; among them were the poet and historian Meir *Basri (1911–) and the poet Anwar *Sha'ul (1904–1984). Jewish journalists founded a number of newspapers and magazines in Arabic, such as *al-Misbah* (1924–1929) and *al-Hasid* (1929–1937). Jewish journalists contributed to the Iraqi press and occasionally wrote for the Arabic press outside Iraq.

From the 1920s a number of Jews were also prominent in the Iraqi theater and performed in Arabic. Many Jews in Iraq distinguished themselves in music as singers, composers, and players of traditional instruments.

Some works by the Jewish intelligentsia were Arabic in essence and expressed the cultural life of the country.

[Abraham Ben-Yaacob and Hayyim J. Cohen / Nissim Kazzaz (2nd ed.)]

British Occupation and Mandate (1917–1932)

The Jews under the British occupation (1917–21) enjoyed full rights of equality and freedom as well as a feeling of security. The majority of the Jews considered themselves as British citizens. Some grew rich, others were employed in the British administration, especially in Baghdad and Basra. They were interested in the continuation of British rule, and they expressed this in 1918, only a week after the armistice went into effect, when the Jewish community of Baghdad presented a petition to the civil commissioner of Baghdad, asking him to make them British subjects. Twice again, in 1919 and 1920, the Jews of Iraq appealed to the British high commissioner and asked him not to allow an Arab government to come to power or at least to grant British citizenship to the Jewish community en masse. The British authorities rejected this request, and the Jews were eventually appeased by personal assurances that ample guaranties would be afforded. However, when in April 1930 the League of Nations decided to adopt the mandate, the Jewish leaders decided to support the establishment of an Iraqi state under the British Mandate.

The Jews were given further assurances by Amir Faysal (1883–1933), who was the leading British candidate for the Iraqi throne. The new monarch-to-be made numerous speeches, including one before the Jewish community of Baghdad on July 18, 1921, one month before his coronation, in which he emphasized the equality of all Iraqis, irrespective of religion.

King Faysal continued to maintain cordial personal relations with individual members of the Jewish elite through his 12-year reign. As his first finance minister, he appointed Sir Sasson *Heskel, the only Jew who ever held cabinet rank in Iraq. Four members represented the Jews in the Iraqi parliament. In 1946 their number increased to six. In the Senate Menahem Salih *Daniel represented them and after him his son, Ezra *Daniel.

Because of their generally superior educational qualifications, Jews and Christians could be found in the civil service during the first decade of the kingdom while it was still under the British Mandate. However, as early as 1921, a strong Arab nationalist element rejected the employment of foreigners and non-Muslims. This opposition intensified after Iraq had gained full independence in 1932 and became even stronger after the death of Faysal the following year.

ZIONIST ACTIVITY DURING THE BRITISH MANDATE. Zionist activity resumed in Iraq about a year after World War I ended; though still unorganized, serious fundraising was undertaken through the initiatives of a few individuals. Despite the substantial sums donated by a few wealthy philanthropists for development projects in the Holy Land, most of the Jewish mercantile elite of Iraq remained unattracted by Zionism. The first organized Zionist group in the postwar period included a schoolteacher, a law student, and a police officer. In 1920 they founded an association in Baghdad with the innocuous name of "Jamʿiyya Adabiyya Isrāʾiliyya" ("Jewish Literary Society"), which published a short-lived journal in Hebrew and Judeo-Arabic, *Yeshurun*. In early 1921, a group within the Jewish Literary Society founded a separate Zionist society, "Al-Jamʿiyya al-Sahyuniyya li-Bilād al-Rāfidayn" ("The Mesopotamian Zionist Society) under the presidency of Aaron Sassoon b. Eliahu *Nahum, who was also known as "ha-Moreh" (the teacher). The society received a permit from the government. Ha-Moreh was very active together with his deputy, the lawyer Joseph Elias

Gabbai, and others. The organization's headquarters were in Baghdad and branches existed in Basra, Khanaqin, Amara and Arbil. Fundraising was the principal object of the Zionists in Iraq during the 1920s. Emissaries from the Holy Land were well received and helped by the authorities of the British Mandate and senior Iraqi officials. The Zionists enjoyed considerable sympathy from the poorer Jewish masses, who demonstrated their support in vocal public gatherings, which offended Arab public opinion, but failed to attract any influential community figures. The unrestrained behavior of the Zionists caused anxiety among members of the upper class such as Menahem Salih Daniel, a leading Baghdadi Jewish notable and later, as noted above, a senator in the Iraqi Senate. In reacting to the request for help in promoting Zionist activities in Iraq, he foresaw the danger to the community because of the political style the Zionists endorsed. Zionist ideology was attacked by another prominent figure, Joseph al-*Kabir, a Baghdadi Jewish lawyer, in a letter published in the *Iraq Times* in November 1938.

British officials and the native Arab authorities also warned both the Zionists and the visiting representative of the movement against public activities and indiscreet statements. The nationalist press was more emphatic in this regard. Therefore, even though no actual ban was imposed upon their activities in Iraq until 1929, the need to maintain a low profile increased when the Zionist committee found it could not renew its permit in 1922, although it was allowed to continue operating unofficially until 1929.

In 1923 a "Keren Hayesod" committee was founded in Baghdad; contributions to the national funds passed through this committee. The size of contributions increased during the early years of British rule (1920–1924), but declined steadily afterwards, and Iraqi Jews were not represented at any international Zionist Congress after 1927. Evidence also shows that Congress representatives of the community before that date were actually foreigners who had succeeded in selling in Iraq the number of shekels required for representation by Zionist Congress rulers.

Short-lived Zionist societies were established at the end of the British Mandate, such as "Agudat Ahi'ever" (1929), whose aim was to spread the Hebrew book; the "Maccabi" sport society (1929–1930); "Histadrut ha-Noʿar ha-Ivri" (1929) and others. Hebrew teachers from the Holy Land were invited to teach Hebrew and Jewish history.

The visit of Sir Alfred Mond (a well-known Zionist) to Baghdad, in February 1928, marked the first anti-Zionist demonstration in the city. Some Jews who passed by were beaten.

The Palestine disturbances, which erupted in August 1929, aroused a widespread and highly vocal reaction in Iraq. The press published exaggerated reports placing the Arab casualties in the thousands. A leading national paper claimed that the Jews had thrown a bomb into a mosque, killing 70 worshipers at Friday prayers. On August 30 some 10,000 Arabs gathered in a Baghdad mosque, where prayers were recited for the victims of British and Zionist aggression. After the speeches, the crowd poured out into the streets for a demonstration march, which turned into violent clashes with the police. Some of the speakers did not differentiate between Zionists and other Iraqi Jews.

From that time the Iraqi government began to persecute Zionism, Palestinian Jewish teachers were expelled. In 1935 ha-Moreh was arrested and forced to leave Iraq for Palestine. After that there was no legal Zionist activity in Iraq.

Fascism and Antisemitism (1933–1941)

Iraqi Jews did not know the kind of *antisemitism that prevailed in some Christian states of Europe. The first attempt to copy modern European antisemitic libels was made in 1924 by Sādiq Rasūl al-Qādirī, a former officer in the White Russian Army. He published his views, particularly that of worldwide conspiracy, in a Baghdadi newspaper. The Jewish response in its own weekly newspaper, *al-Misbah*, compelled al-Qādirī to apologize, although he later published his antisemitic memoirs.

At that time the press drew a clear dividing line between Judaism and Zionism. This line became blurred in the 1930s, along with the demand to remove Jews from the genealogical tree of the Semitic peoples. This anti-Jewish trend coincided with Faysal's death in 1933, which brought about a noticeable change for the Jewish community. His death also came at the same time as the Assyrian massacre, which created a climate of insecurity among the minorities. Iraqi Jewry at that time had been subject to threats and invectives emanating not only from extremist elements, but also from official state institutions as well. Dr. Sāmī Shawkat, a high official in the Ministry of Education in the pre-war years and for a while its director general, was the head of "al-Futuwwa," an imitation of Hitler's Youth. In one of his addresses, "The Profession of Death," he called on Iraqi youth to adopt the way of life of Nazi Fascists. In another speech he branded the Jews as the enemy from within, who should be treated accordingly. In another, he praised Hitler and Mussolini for eradicating their internal enemies (the Jews). Syrian and Palestinian teachers often supported Shawkat in his preaching.

The German ambassador, Dr. F. Grobba, distributed funds and Nazi films, books, and pamphlets in the capital of Iraq, mostly sponsoring the anti-British and the nationalists. Grobba also serialized Hitler's book *Mein Kampf* in a daily newspaper. He and his German cadre maintained a great influence upon the leadership of the state and upon many classes of the Iraqi people, especially through the directors of the Ministry of Education.

The first anti-Jewish act occurred in September 1934, when 10 Jews were dismissed from their posts in the Ministry of Economics and Communications. From then on an unofficial quota was fixed for the number of Jews to be appointed to the civil service.

Pro-Palestinian, anti-British, anti-Jewish, and anti-Zionist sentiments rose to new heights in Iraq in 1936. The Arab general strike and the revolt, which erupted in Palestine that year, gave the conflict a new centrality in Arab politics. The atmosphere in Baghdad became highly charged. The Committee for the Defense of Palestine circulated anti-

Jewish pamphlets. Over a four-week period, extending from mid-September to mid-October, three Jews were murdered in Baghdad and in Basra. A bomb, which however failed to explode, was thrown into a Baghdadi synagogue on Yom Kippur (September 27). Several other bombs were thrown at Jewish clubs, and street gangs roughed up a number of Jews.

The president of the Baghdadi Jewish community, Rabbi Sassoon *Kadoorie, who was himself a staunch anti-Zionist, issued a public statement, in response to a demand from the national press, affirming loyalty to the Arab cause in Palestine and dissociating Iraqi Jewry from Zionism. This did not bring about any real improvement in the situation and, in August 1937, incidents against the Jews were renewed, fostered then and later by Syrians and Palestinians who had settled in Iraq.

THE ANTI-JEWISH POGROM ON JUNE 1–2, 1941 – "AL-FARHUD." On June 1, the first day of Shavuʿot, which in Iraq was traditionally marked by joyous pilgrimages to the tomb of holy men and visits of friends and relatives, the Hashemite regent, ʿAbd al-Ilāh, returned to the capital from his exile in Transjordan. A festive crowd of Jews crossed over the west bank of the Tigris River to welcome the returning prince. On the way back, a group of soldiers, who were soon joined by civilians, turned on the Jews and attacked them, killing one and injuring others. Anti-Jewish riots soon spread throughout the city, especially on the east bank of the Tigris, where most of the Jews lived. By nightfall, a major pogrom was under way, led by soldiers and paramilitary youth gangs, followed by a mob. The rampage of murder and plunder in the Jewish neighborhoods and business districts continued until the afternoon of the following day, when the regent finally gave orders for the police to fire upon the rioters and Kurdish troops were brought in to maintain order.

In the "*Farhud*," 179 Jews of both sexes and all ages were killed, 242 children were left orphans, and 586 businesses were looted, 911 buildings housing more than 12,000 people were pillaged. The total property loss was estimated by the Jewish community's own investigating committee to be approximately 680,000 pounds.

The "*Farhud*" dramatically undermined the confidence of all Iraqi Jewry and, like the Assyrian massacres of 1933, had a highly unsettling effect upon all the Iraqi minorities. Nevertheless, many Jews tried to convince themselves that the worst was over. A factor in this was the commercial boom during the war, of which the Jewish business community was the prime beneficiary. Another factor was the tranquility which prevailed during the next years of the war. But the shadow of the "*Farhud*" continued to hover for years.

The pogrom caused a split between the youth of the Jewish community and its traditional leadership. The new generation turned to two separate directions: the Communist and the Zionist movements, the activity of both being underground.

The Jewish Youth Between Zionism and Communism

IN THE COMMUNIST PARTY. The Communist underground was joined by some young Jewish intellectuals who believed that by changing the regime of the state salvation would come to them as a minority. During the 1940s they played an important part in organizing demonstrations and anti-government activities. Two of them reached the top ranks of the party and were hanged in 1949. In 1946 'Uṣbat Mukāfahat al-Ṣahyūniyya' (the Anti-Zionist League) was authorized by the Iraqi government. This League succeeded in attracting many intellectuals. Its meetings were well attended and its daily newspaper, '*al-'Usba*', was widely read. The League soon established itself as an outspoken representative of the Iraqi Jewish community on the issue of Palestine. It distinguished between Judaism and Zionism, terming the latter a "colonialist phenomenon." In June 1946 the League organized a large demonstration in Baghdad against "the injustice in Palestine." Three months after granting permission, the authorities banned '*al-'Usba*' and closed it. Its leaders were arrested and sentenced to various terms of imprisonment.

The role of Jewish communists was visible in the daily demonstrations of February 1948, which erupted against the Portsmouth Agreement, endangered the regime, and brought down the government. The Jewish communists succeeded in convincing many Jews, including the leadership of the Jewish community, to participate in the demonstrations. By their behavior they stirred the anger of the government, which removed its protection from its Jewish subjects and began to display an official antisemitic policy.

THE ZIONIST UNDERGROUND. The Zionist Movement renewed its activity in March 1942 by forming the youth organization called Tenu'at he-Ḥalutz (the Pioneer Movement) and paramilitary youth, Haganah, among Iraqi Jews. Contrary to the Communist underground, the Zionists did not work against the regime. They concentrated on teaching Hebrew and educating the young generation to Zionism and pioneering. A main purpose was to convince the Jews, mainly the youth, to immigrate to Ereẓ Israel.

The ranks of the Zionist movement in Iraq increased when World War II was over, and the Iraqi press began to address the Palestine question. The Zionist underground organizations in Iraq, despite some crises, were flooded, from 1945 until 1951, with requests for joining. The most dangerous crisis was that of October 1949, which nearly wiped out the Zionist movement in Iraq. The Iraqi authorities arrested about 50 Jews who were accused of Zionism and court-martialed. The second crisis was that of May–June 1951. When the evacuation of the Jews was nearing its end, the Iraqi government uncovered a spy ring in Baghdad, run by two foreigners, Yehuda Tajir and Rodny, who were arrested. The authorities also discovered explosives, guns, files, typewriters, presses, and membership lists hidden in synagogues or buried in private homes. As a result, the police arrested about 80 Jews, 13 of them were sentenced to long terms of imprisonment, two others (Yosef Basri and Shalom Saleh) were sentenced to death and hanged on January 19, 1952. By June 15, 1951, the order was given to the Zionist underground to cease its activity in Iraq.

Official Antisemitism

When World War II was over the former pro-Nazi followers were released and began anew their activities and incitement against the Jews. The General Assembly vote in favor of the partition of Palestine on November 29, 1947, increased tensions between Arabs and Jews in Iraq and the authorities started to oppress the Jews.

The declaration of martial law, before sending Iraqi troops to Palestine, marked the beginning of official antisemitism. At first it was directed mainly against Communists but soon was used against Jews, when it became clear that the Arab offensive in Palestine was encountering serious difficulties. Now the Iraqi authorities seemed increasingly willing to accommodate anti-Jewish demands as a mean of diverting the attention of the Iraqi population from the failure in Palestine and from concern with social and political reforms. From now on, abuses and restrictions characterized the life of the Jews in Iraq. Restrictions were imposed on travel abroad and disposal of property. Hundreds of Jews were dismissed from public service; efforts were made to eliminate Jews from the army and the police; they were prohibited from buying and selling property; they were also discriminated against in obtaining the necessary licenses granting access to some professions.

At the same time the nationalist press opened with aggressive attacks against the Jews, practically daily. The longstanding distinction between Judaism and Zionism was fast becoming blurred, The Jews were held responsible for the economic hardship faced by Iraq in 1948–49, and their leaders were threatened by the national press. The most important effect, which shook the Jewish community to the core, was the hanging of Shafiq Adas, one of the wealthiest Jews in the country, in front of his house in Basra on September 23, 1948. Adas was condemned on the unlikely charge of having supplied scrap metal to the Zionist state.

When Adas was executed about 450 Jews were in the jails; added to these were those arrested the following year, in early October 1949. The detainees were sentenced to terms of imprisonment ranging from 2 to 10 years. In carrying out the arrests the police also arrested another 700 Jews and released them after investigation, most of them were relatives of those who were brought before martial courts.

The Exodus – Operation Ezra and Nehemiah

Throughout 1949, the general disaffection of Iraqi Jewry was exacerbated. With this atmosphere Jewish youths were fleeing the country. The clandestine crossing of the Iranian border began to assume major proportions. Within a few months in 1950, about 10,000 Jews fled Iraq in this way. Once in Iran, most Iraqi Jews were directed to the large refugee camp administered by the Joint Distribution Committee near Teheran, and from there they were airlifted to Israel.

In an attempt to stabilize the situation and to solve the Jewish problem, the government introduced a bill in the Iraqi Parliament at the beginning of March 1950 that would in effect permit Jews who desired to leave the country for good to do so after renouncing their Iraqi citizenship. The bill also provided for the denaturalization of those Jews who had already left the country. The bill was duly passed in the Chamber of Deputies and the Senate as Law No. 1 of 1950.

Iraqi government officials thought that only about 6,000–7,000 and at most 10,000 Jews would take advantage of the new law. The British diplomats in Baghdad and the Israelis shared this view as well. They were all mistaken. The Jews were tired of life in Iraq. And when the Zionist organization in Iraq issued a call at the end of Passover (April 8, 1950) for Jews to come forward and register for emigration in the centers which had been set up at the major synagogues, the call was highly effective. The overwhelming majority of the Jewish community preferred to leave their birthplace. By July 5, 1951, about 105,000 had arrived in Israel.

On March 10, 1951, only one day after the registration deadline had passed, while nearly 65,000 Jews were waiting for departure, the authorities enacted a law which froze the assets of all departing Jews and placed them under the control of a government bureau. Parliament passed a second law, which declared that those Iraqi Jews who were abroad and did not return home within a specific period would forfeit both their nationality and their property. Although some individuals succeeded in smuggling out some money after March 10, 1951, many more were reduced to paupers, being allowed to take out only 50 dinars ($140) per adult and 20 to 30 dinars ($56 to $84) per minor, depending upon the age.

After the Mass Emigration

About 6,000 Jews preferred to remain in Iraq after the mass emigration. Over the years this number fell to about 4,700 in 1957 and about 3,000 in 1968 when the Baʿth Party came to power in Iraq. Their number continued to decline and in the early 21st century there were only a handful of Jews still living in Iraq. Most of those remaining were from the elite and the rich families, who believed that the violent storm which had marked the life of the Jews in Iraq before and during the mass emigration would pass.

The Jewish community, which consisted before the mass emigration of about one quarter of the population of Baghdad, now became a small and unimportant one. These Jews no longer dominated the economic and the financial life of the country, and Jewish youth posed no danger to the regime through activities in the communist underground. So the regime removed some of the restrictions, and the pressure upon them was lightened to some degree. But in principle, the antagonistic attitude to them remained. Still in force were the restrictions on Jews registering in the universities and the sanction of taking away Iraqi nationality from those who did not return to the country within a limited time, which was marked in their passports. In 1954 the authorities nationalized the Jewish Meir Elias Hospital, which was the most modern and largest in Iraq. The Iraqi government also expropriated from the Jewish community the Rima Kheduri Hospital, which treated eye diseases.

Relief came under Brigadier ʿAbd al-Karīm Qāsim (1958–1963), who toppled the monarchy by a military revolution on July 14, 1958. Qāsim canceled all the restrictions against the Jews. He also released Yehuda Tajir and let him go back to Israel. The Jewish golden age under Qāsim was affected however by the confiscation and destruction of the Jewish cemetery, located in the middle of the capital, in order to build a tower to immortalize his name.

Qāsim was assassinated by Colonel ʿAbd al-Salām ʿĀrif, who carried out a successful coup on February 13, 1963. The new rulers reinstated all the restrictions which had been in force before Qāsim, and added others: Passports were not to be issued to Jews; the Jews were prevented from discounting their promissory notes and it was prohibited to grant them credit in the then-nationalized banks; again, Jewish students were not to be admitted to government colleges; a warning was issued to all Jews abroad to return to Iraq within three months, otherwise they would be denationalized and their movable and immovable property in Iraq would be sequestrated; Jews were not allowed to sell their landed property.

After the Six-Day War, the situation of the Iraqi Jews worsened more. They were terrorized and cruelly persecuted. The government opened with a series of detentions, enacted laws, and issued instructions which brought the Jewish community to the threshold of starvation. The measures taken against the small isolated Jewish community of Baghdad after the Six-Day War included: warning the public not to cooperate with them; expelling them from all social clubs; depriving Jewish importers and pharmacists of their licenses; forbidding all transactions with Jews (including access to the banks); prohibiting them from selling their cars and furniture; and cutting off all telephone communications from their homes, offices, or stores.

Under the Baʿth regime (1968–2003), persecution increased and many Jews reached starvation level. Some were jailed, accused of spying or held without any formal charge. Within one year (January 1969–January 1970), 13 were hanged; up to April 1973 the total number of Jews hanged, murdered, kidnapped, or who simply disappeared reached 46; dozens more were jailed.

The shock following the executions of the innocent Jews caused repercussions throughout the world and the world conscience was aroused. The Iraqi government responded to the world reaction by relaxing, for a while, some of its anti-Jewish discriminatory measures, including those limiting travel in Baghdad and throughout Iraq, too. At the same time a peace treaty was signed (March 1970) between the Iraqi government and the Kurdish rebels. Some Jews seized the opportunity and escaped across the Kurdish Mountains, in the summer of 1970, to the Iranian frontier. Up to 300 Jews fled the country in this way. In September 1971 the authorities began to issue passports to the Jews, and about 1,300 Jews left Iraq legally. They sought refuge mainly in England, Canada, the United States, and Israel. In 1975 the Jews in Iraq numbered about 350; over time this figure declined further, reaching c. 120 in 1996. At the beginning of the 21st century, as stated, there were only a handful of Jews there. Thus came to its end the most ancient Diaspora of the Jewish people.

[Nissim Kazzaz (2nd ed.)]

Iraq and Israel

*Jordan and *Syria, including 440 mi. (700 km.) of desert and steppe, come between Iraq and Israel, making Iraq's interests and fears vis-à-vis Israel less realistic than those of the Arab states that border directly upon the latter. Iraq has no territorial questions to settle with Israel, and its own internal and foreign problems (the Kurds, the Persian Gulf, conflicts with *Iran, social and economic unrest, the absence of a stable and representative government) are more pressing and important than the conflict with Israel. The position taken by Iraq toward Israel has been a function of its inter-Arab aspirations and relations; the importance of the Pan-Arab factor among active Iraqi circles, especially the Sunnis, who, under Ṣaddām, were the basic support of the Iraqi authorities; and its interest in an outlet on the Mediterranean Sea. Under both Hashemite and republican rule, Iraq nonetheless displayed active and extreme hostility toward Israel.

There were, however, certain differences in Iraqi policy toward Israel between the Hashemite period and the revolutionary republic established in 1958. During the Hashemite monarchy and Nūrī al-Saʿīd's rule, the latter proposed (in his "Blue Book" of 1943) a certain degree of autonomy for the Jewish community in Palestine in the framework of his plan for a federation of the Fertile Crescent. This period was also characterized by the special ties between Hashemite Iraq and Jordan and the need to justify the alliance between Iraq and Britain by displays of anti-Israel extremism and anti-Israel influence on Britain. On the other hand, in his contacts with the British, Nūrī al-Saʿīd was willing to discuss a compromise solution in Palestine on the basis of the UN partition plan. At the time leftist circles in Iraq did not show any special hostility toward Israel. ʿAbd al-Karīm Qāsim (July 1958–February 1963) exploited anti-Israel positions and support for the Palestinians in his inter-Arab struggles, but he did not actually turn his attention to a struggle against Israel and personally was not particularly extreme in relation to this subject. After Qāsim's fall the combination of a military government and the Pan-Arab ideology of the ruling Baʿth Party exacerbated hostility toward Israel.

Iraq became increasingly one of the most extreme forces in Arab deliberations and often called for the destruction of Israel. This extremism was motivated by Iraq's competition with *Egypt for supremacy in the Arab world and the desire to place Egypt in an untenable position by proposing initiatives that Egypt could not accept and thus making the latter seem to be weak and hesitant. Anti-Israel extremism also served the Iraqi regimes as (a) a pretext for initiatives and intervention in the countries of the Fertile Crescent and competition with Syria, one of the most outspoken of Israel's enemies; (b) in the struggle with the opposition nationalist factors within Iraq, which tend toward Pan-Arabism and hostility toward Israel; (c) as a justification of government policy among the Iraqi public and to deflect attention from more pressing internal problems. It was also motivated by feelings of injured prestige and the longing for revenge, especially among the army following the defeats in the wars against Israel.

Despite the logistical difficulties, Iraq participated in two wars against Israel (1948, 1967), and during the Sinai Campaign (1956) sent troops into Jordan. As early as December 1947, it demanded that regular Arab troops invade that country, following the UN decision to partition Palestine. When irregular Arab forces were waging war in Palestine (end of 1947–May 14, 1948), Iraqis stood out among the officers and soldiers of the Arab "rescue force." The Iraqi deputy chief of staff, General Ismāʿil Ṣafwat, was appointed head of the Palestinian forces and volunteers, and Ṭāhā al-Hāshimī was appointed inspector general of the "rescue force." With the invasion of Palestine by regular Arab forces (May 15, 1948), the Iraqi general Nūr-Din Maḥmūd was appointed acting commander. The Iraqi force that invaded Palestine waged hard-fought battles against the Israel Defense Forces in the Jenin area at the beginning of June 1948. Just before the Six-Day War a token force came from Iraq to Egypt (May 31) and after hostilities broke out an Iraqi brigade entered Jordan (June 5) and an Iraqi plane bombed Netanyah (June 6). The Iraqi brigade that entered Jordan at the beginning of the war was not withdrawn with the cease-fire and was added to later on until the Iraqi expedition force reached 12,000 soldiers. In March 1969 an Iraqi force of 6,000 men entered southern Syria in the framework of the Eastern Arab Command against Israel. The Iraqi contingent in Jordan participated in bombardments of Israel territory a number of times after the Six-Day War.

Iraq objected to the cease-fires of June and July 1948, and refused to conduct negotiations on an armistice with Israel (as Egypt, Jordan, Syria and Lebanon did). In June 1949 Iraq withdrew its forces from the "triangle" sector (Shechem-Jenin-Ṭūl-Karm). It also avoided expressly agreeing to the 1967 cease-fire, replying on June 15, 1967, that its forces were under joint command with Jordan, which agreed to the cease-fire. Iraq strongly opposed the Security Council resolution of Nov. 22, 1967 and any political settlement in Palestine.

Except for times of war there has been a large gap between the ostensible extremism of Iraq and its actual contributions to Arab belligerence against Israel. Among the factors that precluded more active Iraqi participation were internal struggles and difficulties, the extended battles against the Kurds, and tension regarding Iran and the Persian Gulf. Iraqi propaganda also accused Israel of lending support to the Kurds. Iraqi hostility to Israel continued unabated; a symptom was its firing 39 scud missiles into Israel in the 1991 first Gulf War (although Israel was not a participant in that war). The downfall of Saddam Hussein in 2003 did not produce any normalization of Israel–Iraq relations.

Iraq was one of the leading forces in the Arab economic boycott of Israel. On the eve of the UN resolution to partition Palestine, it demanded that the Arab states cancel all Western oil rights. In April 1948, it closed off the IPC oil pipeline to Haifa, and its consequent losses in the period 1948 to 1958 were estimated at more than $400,000,000. In 1967 Iraq was again among the more extreme forces in its desire to use oil as a weapon in order to prevent Western support for Israel (see also *Arab Boycott).

[Asher Goren]

Musical Traditions

In view of the antiquity of the community, one could assume that ancient elements have been preserved in their traditional music. A long period of cultural decline, however, and contact with the powerful and flourishing music of the Muslim world, of which Iraq was for a long time an influential center, deeply marked their music and somehow altered their pre-Islamic heritage. Although it is difficult to trace a borderline between the older and the more recent elements, it would appear that older elements have been preserved only in the biblical cantillations and some of the synagogal melodies.

The second volume of A.Z. *Idelsohn's *Thesaurus of Hebrew-Oriental Melodies* (1923) contains the Babylonian traditions. Idelsohn classified the synagogal melodies according to 13 basic "modes," but these are fairly common to many of the Near Eastern communities. However, the Babylonians also had a number of melodic patterns peculiarly their own. One of these is the "lamentations mode," for which Idelsohn could find an analogy only in the chants of the Syrian Jacobites and the Copts (cf. *Thesaurus* II, no. 17). It has become possible to identify still another Babylonian "lamentations mode," which shows similar archaic features (see A. Herzog and A. Hajdu in: *Yuval 1*, 1968, pp. 194–203). In this context it is surely significant that *Al-Ḥarizi in his *Taḥkemoni* (ch. 18) emphasized the mournful character of their songs, while denigrating the Babylonian poets.

From the early Middle Ages the Babylonian rabbinic authorities were known for their strict adherence to traditional liturgical chant. One of the oldest masters of post-talmudic synagogal chant was *Yehudai b. Naḥman Gaon of Sura (eighth century), whose tradition was supposed to go back to the talmudic period. Two of the earliest documents concerning Jewish music come to us from Babylonian Gaonic circles. The first is a paragraph in *Saadiah Gaon's Sefer *ha-Emunot ve-ha-De'ot* ("Book of Beliefs and Opinions") where he speaks of the influence of the rhythmic modes on the soul; the second is by R. Hai Gaon and it proposes an answer to a question put by the Jews of Gabes (Tunisia) concerning the use of singing and playing during the marriage ceremony. A vivid description of responsorial and even choral singing in tenth-century Baghdad is given in *Nathan b. Isaac ha-Bavli's description of the installation of the Exilarch Oukba, who was himself a poet-musician having composed and performed songs in honor of the caliph. Benjamin of Tudela reports from his travels (c. 1160–80) that Eleazar b. Ẓemaḥ, the head of one of the ten rabbinical academies of Baghdad, and his brothers "know how to sing the hymns according to the manner of the singers of the Temple." Another traveler of the same period, *Pethahiah of Regensburg, gives a most picturesque description of the simultaneous talmudic chanting of the 2,000 pupils of Samuel b. Ali's Yeshivah at Baghdad. He also reports that the Jews there "know a certain number of traditional melodies for each psalm," and on intermediate days (*ḥol ha-mo'ed*) "the psalms are performed with instrumental accompaniment." The instrumental skill went side by side with the creation of a rich repertoire of folk and para-liturgical song in Judeo-Arabic by Babylonian poets. A great number of talented instrumentalists and singers rose to prominent positions in the musical life of the surrounding culture. The best known of these, in the 19th and 20th centuries, were the *kamān* player Biddūn, the singers Reuben Michael Rajwān and Salmān Moshi, the santour player Ṣaliḥ Raḥmūn Fataw and his son, and the composer and *'ud* player Ezra *Aharon. All of them were highly proficient in the performance of the prestigious classical genre known as the *Iraki maqam*. Ezra Aharon led the official group of such distinguished specialist performers who represented Iraq in the first International Congress on Arab music held in Cairo in 1932. This group comprised six Jewish instrumentalists and an Arab vocalist. Not long after this congress, in 1936, composer and violinist Saleh *Kuwaiti and his brother (*'ud* player) founded the first official musical ensemble, that of the Iraq Broadcasting service. Among the finest executants of S. Kuwaiti's works was the famous Umm Kulthum who sang his compositions.

FOLK MUSIC. Folk music was an inseparable part of all events including two main categories: (1) Events connected with the annual cycle (especially those concerning the general religious life affairs of the community); (2) Those connected with life cycle (events chiefly concerning the life of the individual). The rich repertory of folk music comprises men's songs and women's songs whose texts are in Hebrew and in Judeo-Arabic dialect and they are performed either by amateurs or by professionals accompanied by various musical instruments. A special genre held in great favor among Jews is the group of Station's songs in Judeo-Arabic called Kunag sung at the pilgrimage to the Ezekiel and Ezra graves. Jews from many parts of the country were accustomed to spend several days there, during which time music and dance played a prominent role. Since the Kunags are religious in content they were accepted into the category of *piyyutim* and were accorded the status of sacred songs.

Another two popular Hebrew pilgrimage songs to the mentioned graves and another one for Lag ba'Omer were composed by the venerable religious authority R. Yoseph Hayyim (1839–1909). His Lag ba'Omer song (*we-amartem ko leḥay*) and two songs for Simḥat Torah were introduced into the repertory of Israeli songs and published by Idelsohn.

Until 1950 there existed in Baghdad a famous group of four or five woman singers and players on various drums called *Daqaqāt* (Drummers), who performed at Jewish and non-Jewish family rejoicings and festivities. There were also the woman wailers, both professional and private. Their most notable appearances were at the mourning ceremonies for young people not yet married: two groups of women chanted antiphonally, first wedding songs and then lamentations, beating their breasts and scratching their faces.

Many folk songs were written down and are to be found in manuscripts with musical indications, such as the **maqāma* or the name of the song to the melody of which the poem has to be sung (see especially Ms. Sassoon 485). Sometimes the poets composed according to the rhythm, rhyme, and even used the first verse of a given song with slight changes. A number of the songs in Judeo-Arabic have an introduction in Hebrew in the form of a prayer or of a laudatory nature. The public as a refrain usually sings this introduction after each verse sung by a soloist. Almost all the folk songs are performed in this sort of responsorial style.

For the musical traditions of Iraqi Kurdistan, see *Kurdistan, musical tradition.

[Amnon Shiloah (2nd ed)]]

BIBLIOGRAPHY: S.A. Poznański, *Babylonische Geonim im nachgaonaeischen Zeitalter* (1914); B.M. Levin (ed.), *Iggeret Rav Sherira Ga'on* (1921); J. Obermeyer, *Die Landschaft Babylonien* (1929); C. Roth, *Sassoon Dynasty* (1941); A. Ben-Jacob, *Toledot ha-Rav Abdallah Somekh* (1949); idem, *Kehillot Yehudei Kurdistan* (1961); idem, *Yehudei Bavel* (1965), with extensive bibliography; idem, *Shirah u-Fiyyut shel Yehudei Bavel ba-Dorot ha-Aḥaronim* (1970); idem, *Kiẓẓur Toledot Yehudei Bavel* (1970); D. Sassoon, *History of the Jews in Baghdad* (1949); idem, *Massa Bavel* (1955); S. Landshut, *Jewish Communities in the Muslim Countries of the Middle East* (1950); S. Shinah, *Mi-Bavel le-Ẓiyyon* (1955); M. Sicron, *Immigration to Israel, 1948–1953* (1957); A. Agasi, *20 Shanah la-Pera'ot bi-Yhudei Baghdad* (1961); S. Jackson, *The Sassoons* (1968); H.J. Cohen, *Ha-Pe'ilut ha-Ẓiyyonit be-Iraq* (1969); idem, in: JJSO, 11 (1969), 59–66, Y. Atlas, *Ad Ammud ha-Teliyyah* (1969). CONTEMPORARY PERIOD: *Yalkut ha-Mizraḥ ha-Tikhon*, 1–3 (1949–51); R. Alan, in: *Commentary*, 28 (1959), 185–92; J. Caspar, *ibid.*, 193–201; The Baghdad daily newspapers *Al-Zamān* and *Al-Bitād*; N. Rokarion, in: J. Freid (ed.), *Jews in Modern World* (1962), 50–90. **ADD. BIBLIOGRAPHY:** N. Rejwan, *The Jews of Iraq: 300 Years…* (1985); Y. Bar-Moshe, *al-Khurūj min al-'Irāq* (1975); F. al-Barāk, *al-Madāris al-Yahūdiyya fī al-'Irāq* (1985); M. Basri, *'Alam al-Yahūd fī al-'Irāq al-Ḥadīth* (1993); M. Ben-Porat, *Le-Bagdad ve-Ḥazarah* (1996); G. Bekhor, *Fascinating Life and Sensational Death* (1990); A. Ben-Ya'akov, *Yehudei Bavel ba-Tekufot ha-Aḥaronot* (1980); special issue of *Pe'amim*, 8 (1981) on Iraq's Jews; H. Cohen, "The Anti-Jewish Farhud in: Baghdad," in: MES, 3 (1966), 2–17; idem, *Ha-Yehudim be-Arẓot ha-Mizraḥ ha-Tikhon be-Yameinu* (1973); M. Gat, *Kehillah Yehudit be-Mashber* (1989); Y. Ghanima, *Nuzhat al-Mushtāq fī Ta'rīkh Yahūd al-'Irāq* (1924); K. Grünwald, "*Ha-Banka'im ha-Yehudim be-Irak*," in: *Ha-Mizraḥ he-Ḥadash*, 9 (1961), 159–169; *Iraqi Jews Speak for Themselves* (1969); N. Kattan, *Farewell Babylon* (1976); N. Kazzaz, "*Hashpa'at ha-Naẓizm be-Irak ve-ha-Pe'ilut ha-Anti-Yehudit 1933–1941*," in: *Pe'amim*, 29 (1986), 48–71; idem, "*Ha-Pe'ilut ha-Politit shel Yehudei Irak be-Shilhei ha-Tekufah ha-Otomanit*," in: *Pe'amim*, 36 (1988), 35–51; idem, "*Hamarot Dat be-Kerev ha-Yehudim be-Irak ba-Et ha-Ḥadashah*," in: *Pe'amim*, 42 (1990), 157–166; idem, *Yehudei Irak ba-Me'ah ha-Esrim* (1991); idem, "*Ha-Yehudim be-Irak bi-Tekufat ha-General 'Abd al-Karīm Qāsim*," in: *Pe'amim*, 71 (1997), 55–82; idem, *Sofah shel Golah* (2002); E. Kedourie, "The Jews of Baghdad in 1910," in: MES, 3 (1970), 355–61; idem, "The Sack of Basra and the Farhud in Baghdad," in: E. Kedourie, *Arabic Political Memoirs and other Studies* (1974), 283–314; K. N. Ma'ruf, *al-Aqalliyya al-Yahūdiyya fī al-'Irāq bayna Sanat 1921 wa-1952* (1975, 1976); E. Meir, *Ha-Tenu'ah ha-*

Ziyyonit ve-Yehudei Irak (1994); idem, "*Ha-Sikhsukh al Erez Yisrael ve-Yaḥasei Yehudim-Muslemim be-Irak*," in: *Pe'amim*, 62 (1995), 111–131; Y. Meir, *Me'ever la-Midbar* (1973); idem, *Hitpatteḥut Ḥevratit-Tarbutit shel Yehudei Irak* (1989); idem, *Be-Ikar ba-Maḥteret* (1993); A. Sha'ul, *Qiṣṣat Ḥayātii fī Wādī al-Rāfidain* (1980); M. Sawdayee, *All Waiting To Be Hanged* (1974); A. Shiblak, *The Lure of Zion* (1986); M. Shohet, *Benei Adat Moshe* (1979); G. Strasman, *Ba-Ḥazarah min ha-Gardom* (1992); R. Shnir, "*Yaḥasei Yehudim-Muslemim ba-Sifrut u-va-Ittonut shel Yehudei Irak*," in: *Pe'amim* 63 (1995), 5–40; S. G. Haim, "Aspects of Jewish Life in Baghdad under the Monarchy," in: MES, 12 (1976), 188–208; Z. Yehuda (ed.), *Mi-Bavel le-Yerushalayim* (1980). IRAQ AND ISRAEL: E. Berger, *The Covenant and the Sword, 1948–56* (1965). MUSICAL TRADITION: A. Idelsohn, *Thesaurus of Oriental Hebrew Melodies*, 2 (1923); J. al-Ḥanafi, *al-Mughanūn al-Baghdadiyūn* (1964), a directory of Baghdad – including Jewish – musicians. **ADD. BIBLIOGRAPHY:** A. Shiloah, *The Musical Tradition of Iraqi Jews* (1983); Avishur, *Shirat ha-Nashim shel Yehudei Iraq* (1987); S. Manasseh, "Daqqaqat: Jewish Women Musicians from Iraq," in: *International Council for Traditional Music* (UK Chapter), 25 (1990), 7–15; idem, "A Song To Heal Your Wounds. Traditional Lullabies in the Repertoire of the Jews of Iraq," in: *Musica Judaica*, 10 (1991/2), 1–29.

°IRĀQĪ, ELEAZAR BEN AARON HA-KOHEN (d. 1864), Yemenite-*Indian scholar and printer. Though born in Cochin, India, before 1816, ʿIrāqī was of Yemenite parentage. He spent most of his life in Calcutta where he served as teacher, *ḥazzan*, and *shoḥet* in the new Jewish community. He opened a printing press in Calcutta in 1841, becoming the first Jewish printer in India; during the next 16 years he printed 25 ritual books for the use of the Jewish communities of India and the East. He made special efforts to print the works of Yemenite scholars and poets. In the *Sefer ha-Pizmonim* ("Book of Hymns," 1842) which he printed, some of his own poems are also included.

BIBLIOGRAPHY: A. Yaari, *Ha-Defus ha-Ivri be-Arzot ha-Mizraḥ* (1940), 9–13.

[Yehuda Ratzaby]

IRĀQĪ, SHALOM HA-KOHEN (al-Usta; 18th century), community leader in *Yemen. His family originated in *Egypt. He was appointed governor of the mint and he also supervised the collection of taxes and the royal properties at the courts of the Imam al-Mahdī and his successor Imam al-Mansūr (1731–61). During his period of office, the Jewish community enjoyed a brief period of peace and tranquility; this was due partly to his personality and status, and partly to his silencing slanderers by means of bribes. He built synagogues in several towns. The best known was the beautiful Kanīsat al-Usta synagogue in *San'a, the capital of Yemen, which was in use until the dissolution of the Yemenite community. He also made use of his political status to influence decisions in religious and communal affairs. The spread of the Sephardi version of prayer (*Shāmī*) in the communities of Yemen was caused by his generous distribution of printed prayer books to replace the handwritten *maḥzorim* which were in use until then. ʿIrāqī lost his influence in 1761 when the new imam removed him from office, imprisoned him, and levied a heavy fine on him, while at the same time the Jewish community was attacked by the Muslims.

BIBLIOGRAPHY: Ḥ. Ḥabashush, in: *Sefunot*, 2 (1958), 267–71; S. Geridi, *Mi-Teiman le-Ẓiyyon* (1938), 129–31; A. Kare'aḥ, *Sa'arat Teiman* (1954), 16; M. Zadoc, *Yehudei Teiman* (1967), 75–6.

[Yehuda Ratzaby]

ʿIRĀQĪ, SHALOM JOSEPH (1843–1917), leader of the Yemenite community in Jerusalem. Born in San'a (Yemen), in 1882 ʿIrāqī immigrated to Palestine, together with all his family. In Jerusalem he earned his living as a goldsmith, at the same time devoting himself to study in the Sephardi yeshivah of the Old City, and acting as rabbi and leader of the Yemenite community. Because of his relationship with the ʿIrāqī family in India, he was sent to India, together with R. Meyuḥas, as an emissary of the Sephardi *kolel* (congregation). With the separation of the Yemenites from the Sephardi *kolel* in 1908, he was appointed as one of the three leaders of the independent congregation.

[Yehuda Ratzaby]

IRBIL (or **Erbil;** formerly **Arbil**), one of the four important towns of Assyria and now situated in Iraq to the E. of *Mosul, in the fertile plain between the Great Zab and the Small Zab. A Jewish community existed in Irbil continuously from the end of the Second Temple period when it was the capital of the *Adiabene kingdom until the 1950s. At the end of the 12th century and during the first half of the 13th century, Irbil was the capital of an independent principality. During that period there was a large community there; it was considered as one of the most important in northern *Babylonia. In the dispute between the exilarch Samuel and the famous *rosh yeshivah* *Samuel b. Ali at the end of the 12th century the community of Irbil supported the exilarch. At that time there was no lack of intellectuals in the community. Judah *al-Ḥarizi, who visited Iraq at the beginning of the 13th century, mentions poets among the Jews of the town, as well as the "noblemen of Irbil." During the middle of the century the *Gaon* Eli b. Zechariah, the Irbilite, lived in the town. In 1275 *Maimonides' *Guide of the Perplexed* was copied from its Arabic original by Joseph ha-Kohen b. Eli b. Aaron in Irbil (Neubauer, 1237).

There was also an important community in Irbil under the Turkish rule. During the second half of the 16th century Irbil was mentioned by the author-traveler Zakariyyā al-Ẓāhirī, in his *Sefer ha-Musar* ("Book of Ethics"); information on the community during subsequent generations has been preserved in the letters of the Erez Israel emissaries who frequently visited the town. In 1767 the emissary of Tiberias, R. Solomon Aznati, stayed in Irbil. In 1848 the Jerusalemite emissary, R. Pethahiah, died in Irbil, and the Kurds who resented the respect shown to him by the Jews exhumed his body and abused it. However, the Jews also suffered numerous times at the hands of Turkish soldiers. After one such case in 1895 the matter was taken up by R. Isaac Abraham Solomon, the *ḥakham bashi*, with the commander of the army in *Baghdad, where due justice was executed in favor of the Jews of Irbil. The Jews of the town were engaged in commerce and crafts: dyeing, shoemaking, building, and porterage. According to an official estimate made in 1919 some 4,800 Jews lived in the district of Irbil of whom about 250 spoke *Aramaic. This number dwindled to 3,109 in the first census of population taken in 1947. Out of this last number 1,300 lived in the city of Irbil and in 1951 all the Jews of the town emigrated to Israel, in the great exodus of Iraqi Jewry.

BIBLIOGRAPHY: S. Schechter, *Saadyana* (1903), 134; Mann, in: REJ, 73 (1921), 106f.; Yaari, Sheluḥei, index; A. Ben-Jacob, *Yehudei Bavel* (1965), index; Z. Al-Ẓāhirī, *Sefer ha-Musar*, ed. by Y. Ratzaby (1965), 29, 77.

[Eliyahu Ashtor]

Modern Jewish communities in Ireland.

IRELAND, island W. of Britain comprising the Republic of Ireland (Eire, 26 counties) and Northern Ireland or Ulster (part of the United Kingdom, six counties). The *Annals of Inisfallen* record that in 1079 five Jews (apparently a delegation to secure the admission of Jews) went to Ireland bringing gifts for King Toirdelbach of Munster, but were sent back. The beginning of a Jewish settlement dates from the 12th and 13th centuries. The few Jews who established themselves there as merchants and financiers probably had to leave on the expulsion from England (1290). Some refugees from Spain and Portugal settled in Ireland at the close of the 15th century. In the 16th and 17th centuries, persons of Jewish origin held office in Ireland under the English crown. The founding of Trinity College, in its capital *Dublin, in 1591 witnessed the birth of Hebrew studies in the city.

Five or six years after the resettlement in England (1656), a handful of ex-Marranos from Holland, who were engaged in the export trade, went to Dublin as "foreign Protestants." A synagogue is said to have been established in 1661. England's Glorious Revolution (1688) gave a considerable impetus to the tiny community of Dublin. In 1690 Isaac Pereira, a London Sephardi, was appointed commissary general to William III's expeditionary force and employed in his commissariat other Jews who later established themselves in Dublin. At the turn of the 18th century, some Ashkenazi families from Poland and Germany settled in Dublin. During the second half of the 18th century, further Jewish immigrants arrived from Germany, Poland, Holland, Bohemia, France, and England, and the Dublin community increased to approximately 40 families, engaged largely in the jewelry trade, with a few pencil-makers. Some richer Jews were accepted into Christian society, while Freemasonry provided an important sphere for contacts between Jews and the Protestant minority. A number of Jews also established themselves outside Dublin. As early as 1702 a Sephardi Jew was granted the freedom of the city of Waterford. A congregation was established in Cork, as an offshoot of the Dublin community, in about 1725, with its burial ground in Kemp Street. In the 18th century, Cork Jews imported wines and merchandise from Spain and Portugal in their own ships, while others exported preserved meat, certified by the local *shoḥet*, to England and the West Indies. By 1796 the Cork community was defunct, to be revived only some 60 years later. In the latter half of the 18th century, an organized community may have existed in *Belfast where the presence of individual Jews is attested already in the second half of the 17th century. Throughout the 18th century, missionaries were active among the Dublin Jews, some of whom became converted to Christianity. By 1791 the Jewish population had decreased to such an extent that the synagogue had to be closed. Abraham Jacobs (1656–1725?), "priest" of the Dublin Jews, who was baptized in 1706, translated the Anglican Book of Common Prayer into Hebrew in 1717.

From 1743 to 1748 four bills were introduced in the Irish parliament to facilitate the naturalization of foreign Jews, but all were rejected because of the hostility of the peers. Acts of parliament passed in 1780 and 1783, granting aliens the right of naturalization, expressly excluded the Jews. It was not until 1816, when there were only three Jewish families in Dublin and a few others in the rest of the country, that the Irish Naturalization Act of 1783 was repealed.

In 1822, with the arrival of Jews from Germany, Poland, and England, the Jewish community in Dublin was reestablished. By 1881, the number of Jews in the country had grown from a mere handful to about 450, rising by 1901 to 3,769, the majority living in Dublin. This increase was the result of the immigration of Russian Jews after 1881, reinforcing the Dublin, Belfast, and Cork communities and leading to the establishment of new ones such as *Limerick, Waterford, and Londonderry. In 1901 the Jews of Dublin were mainly occupied as petty traders and moneylenders, but they have since played a leading role in the manufacture of clothing, furniture, and jewelry. Apart from some anti-Jewish rioting in Limerick in 1884 and in Cork in 1894 (JC, April 11, 1894), the most serious anti-Jewish agitation took place in Limerick in 1904, when a Catholic priest attacked the local Jews from the pulpit. This resulted in an economic boycott, which remained in force until 1906, and led to the decline of the Jewish community there from 200 to less than 40 people. The antisemitic campaign ceased only with the removal of the priest. During World War I, Limerick had again a congregation of about 40 families.

Modern Period

When in 1921 Southern Ireland became independent of Britain, first as the Irish Free State and later as the Republic of Ireland, the majority of its Jews became, at least *de jure*, independent of the Anglo-Jewish community, under their own chief rabbi and with their own representative council (1938). The 1937 Constitution of the Republic recognized Judaism as a minority faith and guaranteed Jews complete freedom from discrimination. In 1968 the Jewish population numbered 4,000 out of a total population of 2,800,000, of whom 95% were Roman Catholics. There were three main Dublin congregations and four smaller synagogues at the time, and all other Jewish institutions were unified under the Orthodox auspices of the chief rabbi. The Jewish Progressive Congregation of Dublin, comprising about 60 families, functioned independently. The chief rabbinate has been held by Isaac *Herzog (c. 1926–37), Immanuel *Jakobovits (1949–58), Isaac Cohen (1959–79), David Rosen (1979–84), Ephraim Yitzhak Mirvis (1984–92), Gavin Broder (1996–2000), and Yaakov Parlman (from 2002). Community affairs were coordinated by the Jewish Representative Council of Ireland, which was established in 1938 and is responsible for the appointment of the chief rabbi and the *bet din*. The council represents the views of the Jewish community in government departments and in the general public. Autonomous bodies in Dublin administer *sheḥitah*, Hebrew education, welfare, burial, Zionist affairs, youth activities, and student societies. In 1968, 400 pupils, constituting 90% of all Jewish schoolchildren, received Hebrew education in Jewish day schools (primary and secondary) and afternoon classes. In Cork, a rapidly dwindling community of about 50 Jews existed in 1970, dropping to just 21 in the late 1980s. Although friendly relations existed between the Jewish communities of Northern Ireland (see below) and Eire, there was no common activity between them, the former regarding themselves as part of English Jewry, under the authority of the chief rabbi of Great Britain, while the latter operate as an independent body.

The salient feature of Irish Jewish life in the modern period has been the decline of the Jewish population, due both to a fall in the birth rate and to emigration, from 3,255 in 1961 to 2,633 in 1971, 2,127 in 1981, and around 1,300 in the mid-1990s, though in 2004, about 1,790 Jews were recorded, with 1,500 in Dublin. At the turn of the 20th century there were five Orthodox synagogues and one Liberal in Ireland, with four in Dublin and one each in Belfast and Cork. The two major Orthodox synagogues in Dublin were Adelaide Road (which celebrated its centenary in 1992) and Terenure; the two smaller congregations were Machzikei Hadass (formerly St. Kevin's Parade, which celebrated its centenary in 1983) and the Abraham Gittleson synagogue in the Jewish Home for the Aged, opened in 1991. The Dublin Jewish Progressive congregation marked its 40th anniversary in 1986. The Greenville Hall synagogue was sold in 1986 but the developers have retained the original perimeter walls, windows and cupola, and welcome visitors. The *mikveh* was restored in 1984.

The main educational facility, Stratford College, was rebuilt after an arson attack in 1983, and its three-tier educational complex remained in full operation. It was awarded the Jerusalem Prize for Jewish education in 1989. The Edmonstown Golf Club built a new 6,000-square-foot clubhouse, opened in 1990. The old Jewish cemetery at Ballybough, which was in use from 1718 to 1890, was reopened to the public in 1990. An extension to the Jewish Home for the Aged was opened by the Irish president, Mary Robinson, in 1992. The old headquarters of the Board of Guardians and former Talmud Torah premises in Bloomfield Avenue were sold in 1983.

A number of new organizations were founded in the 1980s and 1990s: the Irish Council of Christians and Jews in 1983; the Ireland-Israel Economic and Business Association in 1992; while the Irish-Israel Friendship Association was revived in 1989.

A number of international conferences of Jewish interest were held in Dublin. These included the International Council of Jewish Women (1985); the International Council of Christians and Jews (1985); the International James Joyce Symposium in 1991, which held a session at the Irish Jewish Museum; while the first Irish Genealogical Congress in 1991 held a workshop on Irish Jewry.

Relationships with the authorities continued to be cordial. The president of Ireland, the lord mayor of Dublin, and many dignitaries were guests of honor at Jewish occasions and delegations from the Jewish Representative Council of Ireland have reciprocated with courtesy visits. The chief rabbis continued to make TV appearances on major Jewish festivals.

There has also been a rise in Jewish participation in the top sectors of public life. Throughout various general elections, three Jewish TDs (members of the Dail, the Irish parliament) retained their seats – one for each of the main parties. Ben Briscoe, who represented Fianna Fail, was also lord mayor of Dublin in the city's millennium year (1988), following in the footsteps of his father, Robert *Briscoe. Gerald Goldberg was lord mayor of Cork in 1977. Alan Shatter of Fine Gael was also appointed his party's environment spokesman. Mervyn Taylor of the Labour Party in 1993 became Ireland's first Jewish cabinet minister.

Antisemitism was very low-key, although occasionally exacerbated by casualties suffered by Irish troops serving in

UN units in Lebanon. The tiny Nationalist Socialist Irish Workers' party, which exported anti-Jewish pamphlets to the United Kingdom in 1984, has not surfaced for years. Nevertheless, Ireland has taken high-profile positions at international bodies like the UN which have seen it come into conflict with Israel. A survey by St. Patrick's College, Maynooth, found only 40% of the respondents would marry or welcome Jews into their family (which should be seen partly against religious backgrounds) while 13% did not welcome them as Irish citizens.

Apart from Dublin, the only other community that still exists in the Republic of Ireland is in Cork, which has a burial ground and synagogue. However, services take place only during the High Holy Days when the *minyan* is brought up to strength by volunteers from Dublin. Park Shalom was dedicated by Cork Corporation and the Irish Gas Board, 1989, in fond memory of the city's Jewish community, and is appropriately situated in the area where they lived.

The disused Limerick Jewish cemetery (early 20th century) was restored in 1990 by the Limerick Civic Trust. The ceremony was attended by many church and civic leaders.

[Asher Benson]

In recent years there has been a good deal of interest in the history of the Jews of Ireland, with such works as Dermot Keogh's *Jews in Twentieth-Century Ireland* (1998) and Ray Rivlin's *Shalom Ireland: A Social History of the Jews of Modern Ireland* (2003).

Relations with Israel

Ireland accorded de facto recognition to Israel on Feb. 12, 1949, but only established full diplomatic relations with Israel in 1975 and a residential embassy in 1996. Relations between the two states have been friendly, and Ireland has frequently supported Israel at the United Nations. Trade relations developed satisfactorily; in 1969 Israel exported $800,000 worth of goods to Ireland and imported $700,000 worth.

Israel's president Chaim *Herzog, who was born in Belfast and educated in Dublin, paid a state visit to Ireland in 1985. On this occasion he opened the Irish Jewish Museum in the former Walworth Road Synagogue. A pro-PLO Palestine Information Office was established in Dublin in 1986.

Northern Ireland

By the Anglo-Irish treaty of 1921 the six northwestern counties of Ireland (Ulster) became a self-governing province of the British Crown under the name of Northern Ireland, with the Jewish community recognizing the authority of the British chief rabbi.

The Jewish population was mainly concentrated in its capital, Belfast; a smaller community existed in Londonderry from the 1880s to World War II. The 1964 census recorded about 1,200 Jews living in Northern Ireland. The decrease to 968 recorded in 1971 can be linked to the outbreak of disturbances between the Catholics and Protestants and has continued, with quiet but steady emigration to Australia, Britain, the United States, and Israel. The community is now estimated at about 200 families, maintaining an active communal life.

[Louis Hyman and Isaac Cohen]

BIBLIOGRAPHY: B. Shillman, *Short History of the Jews in Ireland* (1945); idem (with L. Wolf), in: HSET, 11 (1924–27), 143–67; I. Cohen (ed.), *Irish-Jewish Year Book* (1951–); C. Roth, *The Rise of Provincial Jewry* (1950), 56–57; L. Hyman, *History of the Jews in Ireland (until 1910)*, (1972).

IRGUN ẒEVA'I LE'UMMI (Heb. "National Military Organization" – **I.Ẓ.L., Eẓel**, or the **Irgun**], a Jewish underground armed organization founded in Jerusalem in the spring of 1931 by a group of *Haganah commanders, headed by Avraham Tehomi, who had left the Haganah in protest against its defensive character. Joining forces with a clandestine armed group of *Betar members from Tel Aviv, they formed a parallel, more activist defense organization.

In April 1937, during the Arab riots, the organization split over the question of how to react against Arab terrorism, and about half its three thousand members returned to the Haganah, which was controlled by the *Jewish Agency. The rest formed a new Irgun Ẓeva'i Le'ummi, which was ideologically linked with the Revisionist movement and accepted the authority of its leader, Vladimir *Jabotinsky. Rejecting the "restraint" (Heb. *havlagah*) policy of the Jewish Agency and the Haganah, the organization carried out armed reprisals against Arabs, which were condemned by the Jewish Agency as "blemishing the moral achievements of the Jews of Ereẓ Israel, hindering the political struggle, and undermining security." Many members and sympathizers were arrested and one of them, Shelomo *Ben-Yosef, was hanged for shooting at an Arab bus, but IẒL intensified its activities. It also cooperated with the Revisionist movement in *"illegal" immigration, succeeding in smuggling many thousands of Jews into Palestine.

After the publication of the *White Paper in May 1939, IẒL directed its activities against the British Mandatory authorities, sabotaging government property and attacking security officers. The British retaliated with widespread arrests, and at the outbreak of World War II, when hundreds of Revisionists and members of IẒL (including its commander David *Raziel and his staff commanders) were in prison, IẒL declared a truce, which led to a second split (June 1940) and the formation of a new underground group (*Loḥamei Ḥerut Israel, or Leḥi) led by Avraham *Stern. IẒL members contributed to the war effort against the Nazis by joining the British Army's Palestinian units and later the Jewish Brigade. During a clandestine operation by an IẒL unit, in cooperation with British Intelligence, against the pro-Nazi regime of Rashid Ali in Iraq, David Raziel fell at Habbaniya, near Baghdad, on May 20, 1941. Ya'akov Meridor took command, and was succeeded in December 1943 by Menahem *Begin. By this time, the full extent of the Holocaust in the Nazi-occupied territories had become known, and in February 1944 IẒL declared war against the British administration, which continued to implement the White Paper. It attacked and blew up government offices, several CID headquarters, and four police stations, also capturing weapons and ammunition.

The British authorities made many arrests, and 251 prisoners (including Leḥi members) were deported to Eritrea on Oct. 20, 1944. No organized reaction to the deportation was possible because of the repercussions following the assassination of Lord Moyne by Leḥi in Cairo (Nov. 6, 1944). The Jewish Agency and the Haganah moved against the IẒL in a campaign nicknamed by the underground the "saison" ("hunting season"), during which some of IẒL's members (including several leaders) were kidnapped and handed over to the British authorities. The "saison" limited the scope of IẒL's activities, but did not halt them; after the war it began attacking military installations, bridges, and the vital Kirkuk-Haifa oil pipeline (May 25, 1945).

When the British Labour government's anti-Zionist policy disappointed post-war hopes, Haganah, IẒL, and Leḥi formed a united front, sabotaging bridges, railways, and patrol boats. IẒL again attacked CID and police stations, as well as seven army camps, gaining control of their ammunition stores, and damaged planes at two military airfields. The IẒL attacks culminated in blowing up a wing of the King David Hotel in Jerusalem, headquarters of the Palestine government and the military command, on July 22, 1946.

The united fighting front disintegrated in August 1946, after the arrest of the Jewish Agency leaders, but IẒL and Leḥi continued their attacks on military and governmental objectives. The British increased their military strength to a hundred thousand men and reacted with increased ferocity: curfews, arrests, deportations, floggings, and hangings. IẒL reacted by flogging British officers and kidnapping hostages. It also extended its activities abroad, the most striking act being the bombing of the British embassy in Rome on Oct. 31, 1946. Four members of IẒL – Dov Gruner, Yeḥiel Drezner, Mordekhai Alkaḥi, and Eliezer Kashani – were hanged in Acre prison on April 16, 1947, and another two – Meir Feinstein and the Leḥi member Moshe Barazani – who were due to be hanged in Jerusalem, blew themselves up in the condemned cell on April 27. IẒL broke into the fortress at Acre on May 4, and freed 41 IẒL and Leḥi prisoners. Under the pressure of the continual attacks, the British retreated to security zones where they lived in a state of siege. When three other IẒL members, Meir Nakar, Ya'akov Weiss, and Avshalom Ḥaviv, were condemned to death by the British, IẒL kidnapped two British sergeants and hanged them in July, when the three were executed. The IẒL revolt was given wide publicity in the United States, where the Hebrew Committee for National Liberation, led by Peter Bergson (Hillel Kook), was established. In Palestine publicity was conducted through a clandestine radio station, newspapers, and leaflets bearing the IẒL emblem, a hand holding a rifle on the background of a map of Ereẓ Israel including Transjordan.

After the United Nations resolution of November 29, 1947, on the partition of Palestine, IẒL gradually came out of hiding, helped to repulse the Arab attacks, and continued to attack British army camps in order to capture weapons. On April 25, 1948, it began a large-scale attack on Arab Jaffa; the capture of the town was completed by the Haganah. After the Declaration of Independence, the high command of IẒL offered to disband the organization and integrate its members into the army of the new Jewish state, but, until integration was achieved, it acted independently in various sectors, particularly in Jerusalem, where its activities were loosely coordinated with the Haganah. Its attack on the Arab village of Deir Yasin near Jerusalem, which caused many civilian casualties and led to panic among the Arabs, was denounced by the Jewish Agency. On June 20, during the first Arab-Israel cease fire, an IẒL ship, *Altalena*, clandestinely reached the shores of Israel, carrying a huge quantity of weapons and ammunition and about eight hundred young people, some of whom had received military training. During negotiations with the newly established provisional government of Israel, IẒL demanded 20% of the arms for the use of its units in Jerusalem. IẒLrejected a government ultimatum to hand over the ship, and when it appeared off the shore of Tel Aviv it was blown up by Israel artillery. The Jerusalem units of IẒL fought in most sectors of the city and joined the national army on Sept. 21, 1948, on the orders of the provisional government.

BIBLIOGRAPHY: M. Begin, *The Revolt* (1964); Irgun Ẓeva'i Le'ummi, *Hebrew Struggle for National Liberation* (1947); J.B. Schechtman, *Vladimir Jabotinsky Story…*, 2 vols. (1956–61); D. Niv, *Ma'arkhot ha-Irgun ha-Ẓeva'i ha-Le'ummi*, 3 vols. (1965–67); S. Katz, *Days of Fire* (1968); E. Lankin, *Sippuro shel Mefakked Altalena* (1967); Dinur, Haganah, 2 pt. 3 (1963), index; D. Ben-Gurion, *Bi-Medinat Yisrael ha-Meḥuddeshet*, 1 (1969), 175–91, 281–5.

[David Niv]

IR HA-NIDDAḤAT (Heb. עִיר הַנִּדַּחַת, the "subverted" or "apostate" city). Deuteronomy 13:13ff. enjoins the utter destruction of a city, including its inhabitants, its animals, and its inanimate contents, the citizens of which have been "subverted" (*va-yadiḥu*) by "scoundrels" (sons of Belial). In essence it is an extreme example of the *Ḥerem but in the Talmud it is regarded as belonging to a special category. The punishment meted out to an *Ir ha-Niddaḥat* was never applied in practice in talmudic times, and in fact the Tosefta (Sanh. 14:1) enumerates it as one of those things that "never was and never will be," but which was enjoined only so that one should receive the reward for its study. The discussion on it (Sanh. 10:4–6 and the *Gemara* on these passages) is therefore purely theoretical. A city could be declared an *Ir ha-Niddaḥat* only if the majority of its male inhabitants were found guilty of collective apostasy and only the Great Sanhedrin could make the declaration (Sanh. 16a). Jerusalem, however, could never be declared an *Ir ha-Niddaḥat*. The destruction of Jericho and the ban against its rebuilding (Josh. 6:26) were taken as the model. There is a difference of opinion as to whether the verse "it shall not be built again" (Deut. 13:17) meant that it was to be left completely waste, or whether the prohibition of rebuilding referred only to a city, but the site could be turned into gardens and orchards. The wholesale destruction applied to all the property of the transgressors, whether it was in the city or beyond its borders, and to the property of the innocent residents within the city only. With regard to consecrated objects a distinction was made. Animals dedicated to the altar and **terumah* and second tithe were left to rot. Dedications for the repair of the Temple, first fruits, and the first tithe could be redeemed. R. Simeon explains the destruction of the property of the innocent ("righteous") inhabitants of the city by pointing out that since it was the desire for wealth which brought them to reside there, that wealth is destroyed (Sanh. 112a).

BIBLIOGRAPHY: J.N. Epstein, in: *Abhandlungen… H.P. Chajes* (1933), 72–5; C. Tchernowitz, *Toledot ha-Halakhah*, 1 pt. 1 (1934), 37.

[Louis Isaac Rabinowitz]

IRKUTSK, city in Russia. Several Jews settled in Irkutsk at the beginning of the 19th century, of whom the majority were sent there as prisoners or exiles. Subsequently, Jewish soldiers discharged from the army of Nicholas I (see *Cantonists) settled in the city. The Jewish population grew from 1,000 in 1875, to 3,610 in 1897 (7.1% of the total), and 6,100 in 1909 (5.6%). Jews played a considerable role in the city's commerce and industry and in the development of the gold mines in the vicinity. After the 1917 Revolution, a Jewish political exile, P.M. Rubinstein, was appointed president of the newly founded Irkutsk University. There were 7,159 Jews in Irkutsk in 1926 (7.2% of the total population), 7,100 (2.8%) in 1939, and 10,313 in Irkutsk oblast in 1959. In 1970 the city's Jewish population was estimated at about 15,000. There was one synagogue, but no rabbi or cantor. In the early 21st century there were an estimated 5,000 Jews still in the city, with community life revolving around the synagogue and Chabad rabbi Aaron Wagner.

BIBLIOGRAPHY: V. Voitinsky, *Yevrei v Irkutske* (1915).

[Yehuda Slutsky]

IR-NAHASH (Heb. עִיר נָחָשׁ), biblical locality in Judah established by Tehinnah, son of Eshton (I Chron. 4:12). Ir-Nahash ("Serpent City") was probably originally called Ir Neḥoshet ("Copper City") after Tehinnah's craft – brass artisan. It has been tentatively identified with the village of Deir (Dayr) Naḥḥās, 2 mi. (3 km.) northeast of Bet Guvrin, but only remains from the Roman period and later have been discovered there. These include cisterns, remains of a pool, and a tomb with *loculi*. Leases drawn up in the name of Bar Kokhba and dated to 133, which were found in the Murabbaʿāt caves in the Judean Desert, mention that Eleazar the Shilonite, Ḥalifa, son of Joseph, and Judah, son of Rabba, leased land in Ir-Nahash from Hillel, son of Garis, the representative of Bar Kokhba at Herodium. These leases indicate that Ir-Nahash was situated in a crown domain; rent for the land was to be paid in grain.

BIBLIOGRAPHY: Abel, Géog, 2 (1938), 351; Barthélemy-Milik, 2 (1961), 127ff.

[Michael Avi-Yonah]

IRON (Heb. יִרְאוֹן), city in the territory of Naphtali mentioned in the Bible only in Joshua 19:38. It may possibly occur in the inscriptions of Tiglath-Pileser III, among the cities conquered in his campaign of 733 B.C.E., in the fragmentary form Ir-ru-[na], but the reading is uncertain. The Arab village of Yarun on the Israel-Lebanon border is situated near an ancient mound containing Iron Age and later pottery. Iron was apparently one of the cities founded by the Israelites in the mountainous and wooded area of Galilee.

BIBLIOGRAPHY: Maisler (Mazar), in: BJPES, 1 (1933/34), 3; J. Garstang, *Joshua-Judges* (1931), 102, n. 1; Y. Aharoni, *Hitnaḥalut Shivtei Yisrael ba-Galil ha-Elyon* (1957), 130–2; Tadmor, in: H. Hirshberg (ed.), *Kol Ereẓ Naftali* (1967), 63ff.

[Michael Avi-Yonah]

IRON GUARD, right-wing, antisemitic movement and party in Romania. In 1927 nationalist students, headed by Corneliu Zelea Codreanu, founded the Legion of Archangel Michael, which fostered the Iron Guard mass movement in 1930 and merged with it. The Iron Guard became a political party with a Christian-nationalist and totalitarian platform combining elements of fascism, Nazism, and Christian-Orthodox mysticism and symbolism. The Iron Guard press, *Buna Vestire* ("The Annunciation"), and the press under its influence, *Porunca Vremii* ("The Command of Our Times"), instigated antisemitism in the vein of *Der Stuermer*. The Iron Guard held conferences and student rallies that were often accompanied by anti-Jewish riots in which synagogues and Jewish newspapers and shops were destroyed, as in Oradea-Mare and Cluj (1927), and in Timişoara (1938). In the mid-1930s, the Iron Guard, known as *Totul pentru Ţară* ("All for the Fatherland"), became the third largest party in Romania; but it was temporarily dissolved in 1938 by King Carol. On the eve of the dissolution of Greater Romania, the Iron Guard, reconciled for the time being with King Carol, carried out mass slaughters of Jews, especially in Moldavia (June–September 1940). On September 6, the Iron Guard proclaimed a National-Legionary State under joint rule with Ion *Antonescu. Anti-Jewish legislation was enacted to eliminate the Jews of Romania from economic, political, and cultural life. The final goal of Iron Guard policy was the deportation of the Jews (see *Romania, Holocaust).

A struggle for hegemony led to the Legionnaire rebellion in Jan. 19–20, 1941, in which 120 Jews were killed in Bucharest and some 30 in the countryside (notably in *Ploieşti and *Constanţa). The rebellion was quashed by Antonescu; Horia *Sima and other leaders of the rebellion fled the country. Following the outbreak of war against the Soviet Union (June 1941) the German forces and Antonescu's police, joined by Iron Guard elements, committed anti-Jewish outrages, including the *Jassy pogrom (June 29, 1941) and "death train," and other such attacks in Moldavia with thousands of victims. The Romanian anti-Nazi coup of August 1944 put an end to the Iron Guard in Romania, and the Germans set up in December 1944 a Legionnaire government-in-exile in Vienna led by Sima. For more than 25 years after the liquidation of the Iron Guard, Legionnaire emigrant groups were still in existence in some western countries, and post-Communist Romania.

BIBLIOGRAPHY: E. Weber, "The Man of the Archangel," in: G.L. Mosse (ed.), *International Fascism* (1979); Z. Barbu, in: S.J. Woolf (ed.), *Fascism in Europe* (1981); A.Heinen, *Die Legion "Erzengel Michael" in Rumänien* (1986); F. Veiga, *La mistica del ultranacionalismo. Historia de la Guardia de Hierro* (1989); R. Ioanid, *The Sword of the Archangel: Fascist Ideology in Romania* (1990); L.Volovici, *Nationalist Ideology and Antisemitism* (1991).

[Bela Adalbert Vago]

IRVING, AMY (1953–), U.S. actress. Irving was born in Palo Alto, California, the daughter of influential stage director/ producer Jules Irving and actress Priscilla Pointer. Although her father was Jewish, Amy was raised a Christian Scientist like her mother. As a young woman she trained at the American Conservatory Theater in San Francisco before moving to England to study at the prestigious London Academy of Music and Dramatic Art. When Irving was only 17, she made her off-Broadway debut. She appeared in guest roles on several TV shows before landing the role of Sue Snell, the sympathetic supporting character in Brian De Palma's supernatural thriller *Carrie* (1976), launching her career. Romantic leads in such films as *Voices* (1979), *Honeysuckle Rose* (1979), and *The Competition* (1980), not to mention her deep blue eyes and long curly locks, made Irving the idol of young men around the globe. Irving went on to star in mostly mature and independent productions such as *Crossing Delancey* (1988), *Deconstructing Harry* (1997), and *Yentl* (1983), for which she won the Academy Award nomination for Best Supporting Actress. All are popular films that addressed Jewish identity in their own way. Irving remained loyal to the stage, appearing in many acclaimed Broadway productions, most notably *The Heidi Chronicles, Amadeus,* and *The Road to Mecca,* for which she won an Obie Award in 1988. After several years of courtship, Irving married film director Steven *Spielberg in 1985 and had one child with him before their marriage ended in 1989.

[Max Joseph (2nd ed.)]

°**IRVING, JULES** (**Jules Israel**; 1925–1979), U.S. theatrical director. Born in New York, Irving was professor of drama at San Francisco State College. In the early 1950s he co-founded – with his wife, actress Priscilla Pointer, Beatrice Manley, and Herbert *Blau – the Actors' Workshop, which represented the United States at the Brussels Exposition of 1958. In 1965 he and Blau were named directors of the Lincoln Center Repertory Theater, New York. When Blau resigned in 1967, Irving continued as sole director until 1973.

On Broadway, Irving directed such plays as *The Country Wife* (1966); *The Caucasian Chalk Circle* (1966); *Galileo* (1967); *The Little Foxes* (1967); *Tiger at the Gates* (1968); *A Cry of Players* (1968); *Camino Real* (1970); *An Enemy of the People* (1971); *Man of La Mancha* (1972); and *A Streetcar Named Desire* (1973).He was the father of actress Amy *Irving, director David Irving, and singer Katie Irving, and the brother of producer/director Richard Irving.

[Ruth Beloff (2nd ed.)]

IRVING V. LIPSTADT, legal case initiated by Holocaust denier David Irving against defendants Deborah Lipstadt and Penguin Books, tried in a London court from January to March 2001, and resulting in the defeat of Irving. At stake was not the truth of the Holocaust but the quality and nature of Irving's historiography.

David Irving was a Holocaust denier who had written many books on the Third Reich. Deborah Lipstadt was a history professor who had written, among other works, a book about Holocaust denial, *Denying the Holocaust*. It described Irving as a Holocaust denier. He did not care for the description, because he understood it to mean that he was something less than a reputable historian. Therefore he sued Lipstadt and her publishers, Penguin Books, for defamation. He might have sued in the United States, where the book was first published, but then Irving would have had to prove a reckless disregard of truth by Lipstadt. Instead he chose to sue in England because English law gives certain advantages to libel claimants. The defendant must prove the truth of their statements. The case came to trial on January 11, 2000, and lasted five weeks. The evidence of expert witnesses dominated the proceedings. In accordance with defense decisions: no Holocaust survivors were called, for the Holocaust was not on trial; Lipstadt herself did not testify. The case was heard without a jury by Mr. Justice Charles Gray. A 335-page judgment was delivered on April 11, 2000.

The judge decided the case in favor of the defendants, Lipstadt and Penguin. Irving's falsifications and distortions were so egregious, and his animus towards Jews so plain that he won the case for them. They had proved the truth of their allegations against Irving by demonstrating Irving's manipulation of the historical record (which became *the* issue in the case). The multiple concessions made by Irving during the course of the trial did not save him from the judgment that he was indeed a Holocaust denier. The judge also decided that he was an antisemite, a racist, and a falsifier of the historical record. Penguin Books published the judgment, and donated the sale proceeds to a hospital specializing in the treatment of cancer patients. An interim costs order was made against Irving in the sum of £150,000.

Irving, who had represented himself at the trial, instructed lawyers to represent him on his appeal. The appeal was heard in June 2001 and dismissed. Penguin then enforced the costs order and when Irving did not pay, bankrupted him. After the trial, he was asked, "Will you stop denying the Holocaust on the basis of this judgment?" Irving replied, "Good Lord, no." The case attracted a great deal of attention, and large claims continue to be made for its significance. Deniers dismissed it. "Gray's verdict," said a denier, "was predictable, given the display of naked Jewish power during the trial."

David Irving

David Irving (b. 1938) had been writing history books for over 40 years. His first book, published in 1963, was about the bombing of Dresden in February 1945. It wildly overstated the numbers killed, relying in later and foreign editions on a document known by Irving to be a forgery. The intended effect of the book was to narrow the moral distance between the Allied and Axis powers. It introduced into the historiography of World War II the novel concept of the German nation as victim. His principal work, *Hitler's War* (1977; 1991), told the story of World War II from what Irving supposed to be Hitler's perspective, and it thereby made a case for him as an intelligent and even estimable leader. Irving has always been protective of Hitler, and in the earlier part of his career as a writer tended to put the responsibility for the regime's crimes on Hitler's subordinates. He proposed that the Holocaust was executed behind Hitler's back. Irving thus ignored, or explained away, Hitler's own statements about the Jews, the reports on the killings destined for him, and the statements of subordinates that the policy of genocide was determined at the highest level. This special pleading has its own momentum and in due course Irving came to embrace Holocaust denial (among other places, evident in the 1991 edition of *Hitler's War*). Irving came to denial, and then persisted in it, out of tenderness for Hitler and hostility to Jews, and out of a misplaced bravado and a deficient moral sense.

Holocaust Denial

Irving had at various times asserted that the number of Jews killed by the Nazis was far lower than commonly asserted, that gas chambers were not used or used on only an experimental and limited basis, that the killing of the Jews was not systematic, that the Holocaust was an invention of the Allies and that it was then exploited by the Jews to swindle the Germans, to procure a state, and to distract attention from their own crimes. In advancing these theses, he joined a small, ignominious group of published deniers – charlatans, cranks, dedicated haters of Jews. The object of these deniers, or "negationists," is to unwrite the history of the Holocaust.

Deborah Lipstadt

Deborah Lipstadt (b. 1947), a professor at Emory University, Atlanta, was not the first to write about Holocaust denial. She was not even the first to write about Irving's career as a denier, but was the first defendant in a denial libel trial. *Denying the Holocaust* described Irving as a writer of popular historical works. He believed that Britain made a mistake, Lipstadt said, in going to war against Germany, and he regarded the Allies and the Nazis as equally at fault. It was a "disturbing new development," she proposed, that he had "joined the ranks of the deniers." Lipstadt summarized criticisms of his use of evidence and assessed him as being "one of the most dangerous spokespersons for Holocaust denial." She did not allege that Irving was an antisemite, though the charge was implied in the libel proceedings and the defense expressly pleaded his antisemitism.

The Legal Proceedings

In September 1996 David Irving issued a writ against the author and her U.K. publishers, Penguin. He complained that the book represented him to be a Nazi apologist, a manipulator of the historical record, a Holocaust denier, a racist, and an antisemite, and a consorter with racists and antisemites. The defendants broadly agreed that that was indeed what the book maintained, and they insisted that this was the truth about him. The bad history was a consequence of his bad politics, his alliance with the Far Right and his assumed role as apologist for Hitler and the Nazi project. Irving also claimed that he was the victim of an international Jewish conspiracy to silence and discredit him. Here the defendants did not agree, nor did the judge.

In the 3½ years between the start of the legal action and the trial, Irving lost control of his claim. Required to disclose his library of speeches, diaries, and other written materials, he thereby secured the defendants' case against his politics. Confronted by expert reports by scholars such as Richard Evans, Christopher *Browning, Peter Longerich, and Robert Jan Van Pelt that he was unable to counter, he thereby conceded their case against his historiography. The disclosure hanged him; the expert evidence hanged him a second time over. The contribution made by the experts to the defendants' case was considerable, though not in itself determinative of the outcome.

While the disclosure was plainly objectionable, proving the sin of his books required experts. This was hard work, but not difficult work. It needed much checking of sources. The experts demonstrated that Irving mistranslated documents, disputed, overstated or ignored or dismissed adverse, impeccable witnesses and relied upon unreliable witnesses, all to one end. The pattern of deceit was clear: the only witnesses to the Holocaust Irving accepted were those who saw nothing. Euphemistic or otherwise evasive documents were taken at face value; documents that were candid about the extermination process were dismissed as forgeries or otherwise explained away or ignored. An unattainable standard of proof was demanded to "prove" the Holocaust; yet anything, however flimsy and unreliable, was accepted to "disprove" it. There was no consistency to his methodology, only to his politics. It was by the systematic application of "double standards" that Irving honored Hitler's memory.

The Nature of Irving's Antisemitism

The trial exposed the nature of Irving's antisemitism. It was evident both in his performance at the trial itself and in the materials obtained from him in consequence of pre-trial hearings. There was, of course, the desire to rehabilitate Hitler and the Third Reich, and there was the fantasy of a Jewish conspiracy. Irving made wild allegations – Churchill was in the pay of the Jews, the Jews dragged Britain into the war, Jews dominated many of the postwar Communist regimes, the world is in great measure controlled by Jews. There were also lies, including lies told to the judge.

However, so short is the memory, so limited is the understanding, of English newspapers that within a short while of the trial Irving was being referred to by them once again as a historian, his opinions solicited on matters of current controversy. Still, the judgment diminished, though it did not eliminate, Holocaust denial. For the duration of the trial and especially upon the decisive and stinging judgment, the morale of some survivors was lifted. There was the sense that battle had been joined with an antisemite in which the oppressor, for once, did not have the upper hand. Jews and non-Jews of good will came together in defense of the historical truth of the Holocaust, and thereby repelled the attack of an antisemite. It was an act of resistance. And though it was merely one among countless others, it had its own, distinctive merit.

In 2006 an Austrian court sentenced Irving to three years' imprisonment for Holocaust denial.

See also *Holocaust Denial.

[Anthony Julius (2nd ed.)]

ISAAC (Heb. יִצְחָק, יִשְׂחָק), son of *Abraham and *Sarah, second of the *patriarchs of the people of Israel. Isaac was born when Abraham was 100 years old (Gen. 21:5) and Sarah 90 (17:17), exactly a quarter of a century after the family had migrated from Haran, its ancestral homeland, in response to divine prompting and promise of offspring (12:4). By his birth, which took place long after his mother had passed the normal childbearing age (18:11), and in his very person, Isaac represented the fulfillment of the oft-repeated divine assurances of posterity. He alone was the true heir of the Abrahamic tradition and covenant (17:19, 21; 21:12). His name had been preordained by God (17:19), and at the age of eight days he became the first to be circumcised (21:4) in accordance with the divine command (17:12). Further emphasis is given to Isaac's role as Abraham's sole heir by the expulsion of his half-brother *Ishmael in resolution of the domestic crisis which Isaac's birth precipitated (21:9–14).

Nothing is related of Isaac's childhood except the celebration held on the day of his weaning (21:8). Not mentioned as having participated in the burial of Sarah (chapter 23), the only other recorded incident of Isaac's life prior to his marriage is the episode known as "the binding of Isaac" (**Akedah, Aqedah*; chapter 22), where he is the potential victim of child sacrifice. His age at this time is not given, but since he was able to recognize a sacrifice and to ask an intelligent question, he must have been a lad (cf. 22:5).

God ordered Abraham, in a test of his constancy, to sacrifice Isaac, his favored son, the object of his love (22:2; cf. 22:12, 16), as a burnt offering on one of the heights in the land of Moriah. Observing the firestone and the knife in his father's hand, while he himself carried the wood, Isaac asked, "Where is the sheep for the burnt offering?" (22:7–8). From Abraham's evasive reply, "God will see to the sheep for His burnt offering, my son," Isaac must surely have sensed the truth. Although the *Aqedah* was the climactic event in the tales of Abraham, who demonstrated his willingness to obey God even when God contradicted himself (see Rashi to Gen. 22:12), the fact that "the two of them walked on together" (22:8; cf. 22:6), and that Isaac fell completely silent, must be taken as an implication of the lad's surrender to God's purposes. As it is, the narrative closes with a reaffirmation of the divine blessings. Isaac is thus inextricably bound up with God's promises and their fulfillment.

At the age of 40 (25:20), Isaac married *Rebekah, daughter of Bethuel, nephew of Abraham. The story of the marriage, arranged by Abraham who had sent his servant to Haran to bring back a suitable wife, is told in extraordinary detail (chapter 24) and in a manner calculated to show the intervention of Divine Providence in the sequence of events.

Unique among the patriarchs, Isaac remained monogamous, and he was also exceptional in that he did not have concubines (see *Patriarchs) even though Rebekah was barren during the first 20 years of their marriage (25:20, 21, 26). After "Isaac pleaded with the Lord on behalf of his wife" (25:21), Rebekah gave birth to twins, *Esau and *Jacob, who early became rivals (verses 25–34). During her pregnancy, which was very difficult, Rebekah received an oracle from God concerning the destiny of her progeny (verses 21–23).

Isaac's wanderings were restricted to the area around Gerar (26:1, 17), Beer-Sheba (21:32; 22:19; 26:23, 33; 28:10), and Beer-Lahai-Roi (24:62; 25:11). He had wanted to go down to Egypt in time of famine, but was forbidden to do so by God (26:1–2) and, in fact, he never left the land of Canaan (cf. 24:5, 8). At both Gerar and Beer-Sheba he received divine affirmation of the Lord's promise of protection, numerous progeny, and the land (26:3–5, 23–24), and in Beer-Sheba he built an altar and invoked the Lord by name (verse 25) just as his father had done before him (cf. 21:25–33). Unlike the other patriarchs Isaac engaged in agriculture with great success (26:12), becoming a wealthy man, possessed of flocks and herds and a large retinue. On the whole, his relationships with his neighbors were peaceful, but he did arouse their envy (26:13–16). On one occasion he felt compelled to pass off his beautiful wife as his sister, fearing the men of Gerar would murder him in order to possess Rebekah (verses 6–11). On another occasion he clashed with them over watering rights (verses 15, 18–22; cf. verses 25, 32–33). His status and power were such that Abimelech, king of the Philistines in Gerar, came to Beer-Sheba to conclude a pact of mutual nonaggression (verses 28–31).

The final episode in Isaac's life was the oral testament (chapter 27). Old and blind and not knowing how soon he would die, he decided to communicate his blessing to Esau for whom he had quite early shown partiality (25:28), even though Esau had married Canaanite women, of which Isaac and Rebekah, like Abraham before them (24:3–4), had disapproved (26:34–35; cf. 27:46; 28:8). At Rebekah's direction, however, Jacob deceived his father by assuming the guise of Esau and succeeded in gaining the birthright for himself (27:1–29), a situation in which Isaac finally acquiesced (verse 33; cf. 28:3–4). To insure that Jacob would not marry a Canaanite woman Isaac sent him to the home of his wife's family in Paddan-Aram to find a wife (28:1–2).

Isaac lived on for another 20 years. Like the other patriarchs, Isaac lived a fantastically long time, dying in Hebron at 180, "a ripe old age" (35:27–29). His two sons buried him in the cave of Machpelah beside his wife (49:31).

The biblical data concerning Isaac are relatively sparse, and followers of the documentary theory regard them as an amalgam of J and E with an admixture of P (see *Pentateuch). In any event, it appears likely that numerous traditions have been lost. Thus, in treaty negotiations with Laban, the fact that Jacob employed a divine name, *Paḥad Yiẓḥak* ("Fear [or "Kinsman"?] of Isaac"; 31:42), not otherwise attested, implies that there once existed some historic framework in which this epithet had special meaning. Although the narratives of Isaac are set in a time that would in our chronology correspond to the early or mid-second millennium, individual markers such as the encounters with the Philistines, marriage ties with Arameans, and the founding of the city of Beersheba indicate that the oldest Isaac traditions cannot be earlier than the late second millennium, and are probably later. No independent traditions about Isaac have been preserved outside of the Pentateuch. In some respects, Isaac, like Abraham and Jacob, is an allegorical figure whose actions reflect historical personalities and situations of the monarchic period (Sperling).

The triad of Abraham, Isaac, and Jacob appears with great frequency throughout the Pentateuch, and became enshrined in the cultic traditions of Israel. Amos actually employs "Isaac" as a synonym for Israel (7:9, 16), though it is uncertain whether this is the sole biblical remnant of a once more extensive usage, or an oratorical device invented by the prophet for purposes of wordplay.

Although no explanation for Isaac's name is given in Genesis (cf. Gen. 17:19; 21:3), the recurrent association of the laughter of the aged Abraham and Sarah when foretold of the birth of a son (17:17; 18:12–15; 21:6) has suggested the popular etymology that the name comes from *saḥak* (*saḥaq*, "laugh"). In actuality, the name is a verbal form, probably originally accompanied by a divine subject and meaning, "may (God) laugh," i.e., look benevolently upon.

[Nahum M. Sarna / S. David Sperling (2nd ed.)]

In the Aggadah

Isaac was born on the first day of Passover (RH 11a). At his birth, many other barren women were also blessed with children. The sun shone with unparalleled splendor, the like of which will only be seen again in the messianic age (Tanḥ. B, Gen. 107; PR 42:177a–177b). To silence the accusations of slanderers who questioned Abraham's paternity, which they ascribed to Abimelech, Isaac was given the exact appearance of his father (BM 87a). As his name was given by God before his birth (Gen. 17:19), he was the only one of the patriarchs whose name was not later changed (TJ, Ber. 1:9, 4a).

The *Akedah* of Isaac was the result of Satan's complaint after Abraham's celebration of the weaning of Isaac. Satan said to the Almighty: "Sovereign of the Universe! To this old man Thou didst graciously vouchsafe the fruit of the womb at the age of a hundred, yet of all that banquet which he prepared, he did not sacrifice one dove or pigeon to thee!" God therefore decided to show Satan that Abraham would offer up even Isaac to Him. According to another tradition, it was Isaac, then 37 years old, who himself suggested the *Akedah* in response to Ishmael's claim that he was more virtuous since Isaac was circumcised at eight days, whereas he was 13 years of age at the time and could have refused (Sanh. 89b; Gen. R. 55:4). On the way to the *Akedah*, Satan unsuccessfully attempted to dissuade Isaac from obeying his father and, when he failed, tried to impede their journey (*Sefer ha-Yashar*, Va-Yera, 77–78; Gen. R. 56:4). Isaac cooperated fully with his father in the proposed sacrifice, even begging him to bind him tightly lest he might involuntarily struggle and render the sacrifice invalid (Gen. R. 56:8). When Abraham lifted up his knife, the angels cried for Isaac. Their tears fell into Isaac's eyes and they caused his subsequent blindness, which was also attributed to his having looked directly at the *Shekhinah* while on the altar (Gen. R. 65:10). Others attribute it to his constantly looking at his wicked son, Esau. His lack of vision later kept him at home and spared him from hearing people say, "there goes the father of the wicked Esau" (Gen. R. 65:10. According to one tradition, during the *Akedah* Abraham drew one fourth of a log of blood from Isaac which symbolized the essence of life (Mekh. SbY, p. 4). According to another version, Isaac actually lost his life as a result of the terror he experienced when Abraham lifted his knife. He was revived by the heavenly voice admonishing Abraham not to slaughter his son, and he then pronounced the benediction, "Blessed are Thou, O Lord, who quickenest the dead" (PdRE 31). God therefore accounted Isaac's deed as an actual sacrifice, and his harsh judgments against Israel are constantly mitigated when he recalls "Isaac's ashes heaped up upon the altar" (Lev. R. 36:5; Ta'an. 16a). Abraham also prayed that God should mercifully recall his binding Isaac whenever the children of Isaac give way to transgressions and evil deeds (Lev. R. 29:9). The *Akedah* therefore became a central theme in all penitential and **seliḥot* prayers. Isaac is also depicted as the patriarch possessing the deepest feelings and compassion for his descendants. He pleads for them even when they are sinful, and the verse "For thou art our father, for Abraham knoweth us not, and Israel doth not acknowledge us" (Isa. 63:16) is applied to him (Shab. 89b). The institution of the **Minḥah* prayer is attributed to Isaac (Ber. 26b). Like Abraham, he observed the Commandments (PR 25, p. 127b) and made God known in the world (Men. 53a). He was one of three who had a foretaste of the future world while in this world; one of six over whom the angel of death had no power; one of seven whose bodies were not devoured by worms; and one of three upon whom the "evil inclination" had no influence (BB 17a).

[Aaron Rothkoff]

In Christian Tradition

Isaac appears in the New Testament as a type and prefiguration of Christ: "Now to Abraham were the promises spoken, and to his seed. He saith not, And to seeds, as of many; but as of one, And to thy seed, which is Christ" (Gal. 3:16). In the same epistle, Paul also explains that Isaac and Ishmael symbolize the old and the new covenants and thus represent Christians and Jews respectively. Isaac is the heir of the spiritual inheritance and messianic blessing implied in God's promise while Ishmael, the son of the slave, is turned out of his father's house. In the same way, the Christians are delivered from the fetters of the Old Testament commandments and enjoy the freedom granted to God's children (*ibid.* 4:22–31). Isaac's sacrifice, which is interpreted typologically in the Epistle to the Hebrews, prefigures both the Passion by offering, and the resurrection of Jesus.

The Church Fathers developed this typology further: Isaac's miraculous birth by a sterile woman is a prefiguration of the virginal maternity. They also drew more detailed parallels between the sacrifice of Isaac and Jesus on the Cross: in the same way as Isaac was offered by his father Abraham and carried the sacrificial wood, so Jesus was offered by his Father and bore the Cross. Both obey the divine order of death and, because of that, triumph over death. The vicarious death of Jesus is compared to the substitution of the ram for Isaac. The ram represents the visible sacrifice of the flesh and Isaac prefigures the Eternal Word (Christ). Like Philo before them, the Church Fathers also interpreted the marriage of Isaac and Rebekah symbolically, though they did so in a specifically Christian manner. Rebekah symbolizes the Church waiting for a long time; she sees Isaac (i.e., the Messiah) coming toward her as announced by the prophets, and their union is consecrated.

In Islam

Isḥāq (Isaac) and Yaʿqūb (Jacob) were the descendants of Ibrāhīm (Abraham) and both were prophets and righteous men (Koran, Sura 19:50–51; 21:72–73; and in other places such as 6:84). The tale of the binding (37:99–110) does not mention the name of the one destined to be the sacrifice. According to the Ḥadīth which is quoted by al-Ṭabarī (*Taʾrīkh*, 1 (1357 A.H.), 184–5), Muhammad himself declared that the intended one was Isaac. This is also the opinion of Muhammad's colleagues: the caliphs Omar ibn al-Khaṭṭāb and Ali ibn Abī Ṭālib and the members of the second generation (*tābiʿūn*), e.g., *Kaʿb al-Aḥbār (Thaʿlabī, 76). In his *Taʾrīkh* (history) and his *Tafsīr* (commentary) Ṭabarī quotes the Ḥadiths of all the Arab masoretes and exegetes, who were divided as to whether the object of the binding was Isaac or Ishmael. Umayya ibn Abī al-Ṣalt, a contemporary of Muhammad, gives a description of the binding (29:9–21) as it is told in the Bible and in the Midrashim (Hirschberg, in bibl., pp. 58–61, 124–9). In spite of its similarity to the Koran, it is definitely an original poem. In a fragment of the **genizah* of al-Samawʾal al-Kuraẓī there is the mention of the *dhabīḥ* ("the bound one") as he is also referred to in Arab legend; he was redeemed for a lamb, specially created for this purpose.

[Haïm Z'ew Hirschberg]

In the Arts

In most literary treatments of the patriarch Isaac the theme of the binding of Isaac predominates (see *Akedah). This is the case with the medieval English miracle plays (Chester, York, Towneley, Dublin, Brome cycles; the many religious *autos* of the Spanish Renaissance; Metastasio's *Isacco figura del Redentore* (1740); and Laurence Housman's *Abraham and Isaac*, one of the English writer's fiercely anti-biblical *Old Testament Plays* (1950)). The *Akedah* theme inspired a drama in the Aztec language of Mexico (1678), which was later translated into Spanish; and two Italian plays of the 18th century, Pietro van Ghelen's *Isacco, figura del Redentore* (Vienna, 1740) and *Isacco al monte* (Padoya, 1766), a *sacra rappresentazione* in verse by Ferdinando degli Obizzi.

In other works dating from the Middle Ages onward the Sacrifice of Isaac is incidental or omitted. The 12th-century *Ordo de Ysaac et Rebecca et Filiis Eorum* makes Esau the representative of "pharisaical Judaism" and Jacob the spokesman of Christianity. Dramatic works of the 16th–18th centuries include a *Farsa de Isaac* by Diego Sanchez (c. 1530); Francesco Contarini's tragedy *Isaccio* (Venice, 1615); *Izsák házassága* ("The Marriage of Isaac," 1703), a Hungarian play by Ferenc Pápai Páriz; a drama by the Spanish Marrano writer Felipe *Godínez; and *Isaac* (1779?; Eng. 1807), a comedy for young people by the French author Félicité Ducrest de Saint-Aubin, countess de Genlis. The subject declined in importance during the 19th century, an exception being Julius *Zeyer's Czech drama *Z dob ružového jitra* ("From the Times of the Rosy Dawn," 1888), based on Gen. 26, the first of several fresh treatments by Jewish writers. Thus, Edmond *Fleg's poem "La Vision d'Isaac" (in *Ecoute Israël*, 1913–21) dealt with Isaac's traditional plea to God for Israel's preservation. A 20th-century treatment is in Soviet writer Yosif *Brodski's "*Isaak i Avraam*," which only appeared in the West in the verse collection *Stikhotvoreniya i poemy* (1965).

In art, the chief episodes represented are the *Akedah*, the meeting of Eliezer and Rebekah, the marriage of Isaac and Rebekah, and the blessing of Jacob and Esau. The meeting of Eliezer and Rebekah (Gen. 24:15–28) has generally been more popular with artists than the marriage of Isaac and Rebekah. In medieval Christian iconography Isaac was equated with Jesus, and Rebekah with the Virgin Mary, who symbolized the Church. There is a charming early representation of the meeting of Eliezer and Rebekah in the sixth-century Vienna Genesis. It is later found in 12th-century mosaics in the Capella Palatina at Palermo and the cathedral of Monreale, in Sicily; in the St. Louis Psalter (c. 1256); and in the 14th-century English *Queen Mary Psalter*. There are Renaissance and later paintings of the subject by Paolo Veronese at Versailles, by Nicolas Poussin in the Louvre, and by Bartolomé Murillo in the Prado, Madrid. The marriage of Isaac and Rebekah (Gen. 24:63ff.) occurs in an illumination in the *St. Louis Psalter*. A noteworthy representation is the spacious landscape ("The Mill") by Claude Lorrain (1648 National Gallery, London). In the Raphael Loggia in the Vatican there is a representation of Isaac and Rebekah intercepted in their lovemaking by Abimelech (Gen. 26:8–11).

The lyrical subject of Isaac's marriage with Rebekah, preceded by Eliezer's mission, has been treated in several musical works, mainly oratorios. Some examples are G.C. Arresti's *Lo sposalizio di Rebecca* (1675); A. Sacchini's *Lo sposalizio d'Isaaco con Rebecca* (1739); Michael Haydn's *Rebecca als Braut* (also called *Eliezer*), a "Singspiel," i.e., a kind of operetta (1766); Ferdinand *Hiller's *Rebekka*, an "idyll" for solo choir, opus 182 (date unknown); César Franck's *Rebecca*, produced as an oratorio in 1881 and as a one-act "sacred opera" in 1918; and Maurice Jacobson's *Rebecca's Hymn* for choir and orchestra (1930). The meeting of Eliezer and Rebekah at the well was set as a simple children's dialogue song by the Israel composer Yedidya *Admon-Gorochov in the early 1930s (*Na'arah tovah, yefat einayim*), and has remained popular with Israel children.

BIBLIOGRAPHY: For Isaac in the Bible see bibliography to *Abraham and *Patriarchs, and N.M. Sarna, *Understanding Genesis* (1966), 154–165, 170–180. IN THE AGGADAH: Ginzberg, Legends, 1 (1942[2]), 261–6, 271–86, 291–9, 321–36; A.A. Halevy, *Sha'arei ha-Aggadah* (1963), 20–23, 35, 37, 103–5; G. Vermes, *Scripture and Tradition in Judaism* (1961), 193–227. IN THE CHRISTIAN TRADITION: J. Daniélou, *Sacramentum Futuri* (1950), 97–128; idem, in: *Biblica*, 28 (1947), 363–93 (Fr.); Schoeps, in: JBL, 65 (1946), 385–92. IN ISLAM: Tabarī, *Ta'rīkh*, 1 (1357 A.H.), 184–9; idem, *Tafsīr*, 23 (1329 A.H.), 51–54; Tha'labi, *Qiṣaṣ* (1356 A.H. 76–81; Kisā'ī, *Qiṣaṣ*, ed. by I. Eisenberg (1922), 150–3; H.Z. (J.W.) Hirschberg, *Der Dīwān des As-Samu'al ibn ʿAdijā'...* (1931), 33, 631.; idem, *Juedische und christliche Lehren* (1939), 58–61, 124–9. ADD. BIBLIOGRAPHY: R. Martin-Achard, in: ABD, 3:462–70 (incl. bibl.); J. Levenson, *The Death and Resurrection of the Beloved Son* (1993); S.D. Sperling, *The Original Torah* (1998). IN ISLAM: W.M. Watt, "Isḥaḳ," in: EIS[2], 4 (1978), 109–110 (incl. bibl.).

ISAAC (middle of the second century), *tanna*. He is not mentioned in the Mishnah but is often cited in *beraitot*, especially those dealing with halakhic exegesis in the Talmuds, and in the halakhic Midrashim of the school of R. Ishmael: *Mekhilta, Sifrei Numbers*, and *Sifrei Deuteronomy*. It appears that he was a Babylonian, and if so he was one of the earliest known *tannaim* hailing from Babylonia. During the period of persecution following the Bar Kokhba War, when Hananiah, the nephew of R. Joshua b. Hananiah, attempted to proclaim leap years and to sanctify new moons in Babylonia, and thereby make Babylonia independent of Ereẓ Israel, Rabbi (the *nasi* at the time, perhaps *Simeon b. Gamaliel) sent him "three communications through R. Isaac and R. Nathan" so as to restrain the Diaspora from taking this step (TJ, Sanh. 1:2). Isaac moved to Ereẓ Israel, where he debated halakhic matters, particularly with the disciples of R. Ishmael. He also associated with R. *Simeon b. Yoḥai (Gen. R. 35:16), and engaged in dispute with Judah ha-Nasi and others (Ber. 48b, Git. 27b, etc.). Among his expositions of biblical verses some are of an aggadic character: "Remember the Sabbath day, i.e., count not [the days of the week] as others count them, but count them with reference to the Sabbath" (Mekh., Jethro, 7). He also engaged in mystical studies (Ḥag. 13a).

BIBLIOGRAPHY: Bacher, Tann; Hyman, Toledot, 78ff.; Epstein, Tanna'im, 570.

[Zvi Kaplan and Shmuel Safrai]

ISAAC (seventh century), *gaon*, head of the academy in Firuz-Shapur in Babylonia. In 658 the city was captured by Caliph Ali. Isaac, together with other Jewish notables, at the head of 90,000 Jews, welcomed the caliph upon his entry; the conqueror in turn gave the Jewish delegation a cordial reception. No responsa or decisions written by this *gaon* are extant. The commentaries and decisions mentioned in the responsa of the *geonim* and other early authorities and attributed to a R. Isaac (*Sha'arei Teshuvah*, no. 217; Zedekiah *Anav, *Shibbolei ha-Leket*, no. 225; *Abraham b. Isaac of Narbonne, *Sefer ha-Eshkol*, 2 (1868), 158; Aaron ha-Kohen of Lunel, *Orḥot Ḥayyim*, ed. by M. Schlesinger, 2 (1902), 414, et al.) originated with another R. Isaac, a *gaon* of Sura, who was also known as Isaac Zadok.

BIBLIOGRAPHY: A. Harkavy, *Zikkaron la-Rishonim ve-gam la-Aḥaronim*, 1, *Teshuvot ha-Ge'onim* (1887), 355–6; B.M. Lewin (ed.), *Iggeret Rav Sherira Ga'on* (1921), 101; Weiss, Dor, 4 (1904), 7–8; J. Mueller, *Mafte'aḥ li-Teshuvot ha-Ge'onim* (1891), 62; Mann, in: JQR, 8 (1917/18), 340–1.

[Simha Assaf]

ISAAC, Jewish merchant of Aachen, the first Jew in Germany to be mentioned by name. In 797 he was appointed by Charlemagne as guide and interpreter to an official delegation to Harun al-Rashid, entrusted with a delicate and important mission. Charlemagne's ambassadors died on the way and Isaac completed the journey and was received in audience when he returned four years later. He brought with him precious gifts from the caliph, including an elephant. According to one account *Machir, the Babylonian scholar credited with founding a Jewish academy in Narbonne, traveled from the East to Europe with Isaac.

BIBLIOGRAPHY: Germ Jud, 1 (1963), xxviii; Graetz, Hist, 3 (1949), 143; M. Steinschneider, *Jewish Literature* (1965), 81; S. Katz, *Jews in Visigothic Spain and France* (1937), 133; Baron, Social[2], 4 (1957), 45, 257.

ISAAC (**Ishak**; late 12th or early 13th century), Spanish-Hebrew poet. Isaac is only known from his *Mishlei Arav* or *Mishlei Musar*, a translation of an Arabic text which is no longer extant, comprising proverbs, ethical poems, and prose passages. The material is divided into 50 sections called "gates." The last gate includes admonitions and proverbs in poetic form. The most interesting of them is *Ḥidat ha-Nazir ve-ha-Soḥer* ("The Riddle of the Nazirite and the Merchant"), an allegorical tale which in character and presentation is reminiscent of **Ben ha-Melekh ve-ha-Nazir* ("The Prince and the Hermit") of Abraham *Ibn Ḥasdai. These proverbs are of great importance for research into the motifs of Hebrew proverbs and poetry, and they also shed light upon the literary taste of Isaac's time. Several of them are already cited by Menahem b. Solomon *Meiri (1249–1316) in his *Kiryat Sefer* (Smyrna, 1863–1881). The proverbs and poems in the supplement to *Mivḥar ha-Peninim* of *Jedaiah ha-Penini Bedersi (Venice, 1546) are taken in their entirety from the *Mishlei Arav*. In those poems written in the form of an acrostic the name Isḥak appears. According to Steinschneider, the author of the *Mishlei Arav* was in fact

Isaac b. Krispin, author of the *Sefer ha-Musar* mentioned in the *Taḥkemoni* of *al-Ḥarizi, in which case he lived at a much earlier date. His book has been published once only in serial form by S. Sachs in *Ha-Levanon* (vols. 2–6, 1865–69).

BIBLIOGRAPHY: Steinschneider, Uebersetzungen, 884–7; Schirmann, Sefarad, 2 (1960²), 60–66; A.M. Habermann, in: *Sinai*, 25 (1945), 288–99; Davidson, Oẓar, 4 (1933), 423f.

[Abraham David]

ISAAC (Isak), AARON (Aron; 1730–1816), founder of the Jewish community in Sweden. Born in Treuenbrietzen, a small city in the Duchy of Mecklenburg, Isaac started his career as a peddler at the age of 18. Yielding to an artistic impulse, he taught himself seal-engraving, achieving some success in this craft, and settled in Buetzow. During the Seven Years' War (1756–63) he did business with the Prussian and later the Swedish armies. Learning from the Swedish soldiers that there were no seal-engravers in Sweden, Isaac decided to settle in that country, although no Jew had lived there previously. When he arrived in Stockholm in June 1774 after a difficult journey, he was informed that permission to settle would be granted only if he accepted baptism. This he refused to do and petitioned the king, whom he impressed by his sobriety and persistence. His request was granted and Isaac, his brother, and his partner in Germany, with their families, received permission to settle in Stockholm. After these early struggles the fledgling settlement began to flourish, Isaac remaining head of the Stockholm community for many years. His memoirs in Yiddish, completed in 1804 with an introduction in Hebrew, *Sjelfbiografi* (1897), are important not only historically but also for Yiddish philology and have been frequently republished.

BIBLIOGRAPHY: N. Stif and Z. Rejzen (eds.), *Aaron Isaacs Autobiografia* (Yid., 1922); Z. Holm (ed.), *Denkwuerdigkeiten des Aron Isak* (1930); A. Brody and H. Valentin (eds.), *Aaron Isaacs Minnen* (Swedish, 1932), annotated critical edition; L. Schwarz, *Memoirs of my People* (1963²), 166–81; 299; H. Valentin, *Judarnas historia i Sverige* (1924), index; idem, *Judarna i Sverige* (1964), index.

[Hugo Mauritz Valentin]

ISAAC, JULES MARX (1877–1963), French historian. Born in Rennes, he became chief inspector of history teaching at the Ministry of Education. Isaac wrote history textbooks for French secondary schools; his research works concerned the origins of World War I and the problem of the origins of superstitions and popular prejudices. From 1943, traumatically influenced by the Nazi persecutions and the deportation and death of his close relatives, including his wife and daughter, Isaac began to study Christian antisemitism, to which he dedicated the remainder of his life. He did not content himself with the publication of the result of his studies and vigorous polemics against his critics, but also assumed a militant role as founder and member of the executive committee of the Amitié Judéo-Chrétienne. He took an active part in the Judeo-Christian meeting of Seelisberg (1947), whose resolutions called for a revision of the attitude of the churches toward Judaism. After the accession of Pope *John XXIII, the Vatican sought Isaac's advice; upon the request of Cardinal *Bea and after an audience with Pope John in 1960, he drew up a record of the history of the relations between the Catholic Church and Judaism. Isaac's writings had a great influence on the decision to introduce a statement on relations with the Jews at the Vatican Council that ended in 1965.

In his historical works, Isaac points out the falsehood and the tendentious intentions of the claim that the dispersion of Israel was the result of its rejection of the messianism of Jesus. At the same time, he reached the conclusion that there was no reason whatsoever to maintain that antisemitism was as old as Judaism itself. On the contrary, he showed that the Church promoted a system of degradation by gradually burdening the Jews with a lengthy series of restrictions, exclusions, and humiliations which were decreed by the secular governments subjected to ecclesiastic influence. This system was based on the "teaching of contempt," which was essentially the work of the Church Fathers of the fourth century C.E. and whose most harmful thesis was that of describing the Jews as a "deicidal people." Isaac developed his arguments in *Jésus et Israël* (1948; Eng. tr., 1971), *Genèse de l'antisémitisme* (1956), and *L'Enseignement du mépris* (1962; *The Teaching of Contempt*, 1964).

BIBLIOGRAPHY: C.H. Bishop, in: J. Isaac, *The Teaching of Contempt* (1964), introduction. **ADD. BIBLIOGRAPHY:** A. Kaspi, *Jules Isaac ou la passion de la vérité* (2002).

ISAAC, TESTAMENT OF, pseudepigraphical work. There is no reference to an apocryphal book of Isaac in the ancient lists of *apocrypha, such as that of Nicephorus. The Apostolicae Constitutiones 6, 16 may, however, refer to it by its mention of the "apocryphal books of the three Patriarchs." A text entitled *The Testament of Isaac* was published in an English translation from the Arabic by M.R. James. Ethiopic and Coptic texts of the work also exist (see S. Gaselee in bibliography). The book opens with a homiletic preface which is followed by the story of how an angel, resembling Abraham, announces to Isaac his imminent death and commands him to instruct his sons. The instruction that follows is similar in tone to that encountered in some parts of the Testaments of the Twelve Patriarchs, such as those relating Isaac's instructions to Jacob (Test. Patr., Levi, ch. 9). Jubilees 21 also contains similar materials, as do the Greek fragments of the Testament of *Levi and other associated texts. This section of moral instruction is followed by an apocalyptic vision which features the punishments of hell, and in particular the river of fire which can distinguish between the righteous and the wicked. The text concludes with an exhortation for the commemoration of Isaac. It seems that older material may be embedded in the moral instruction, but in its present form the work is probably a late imitation of the Testament of Abraham.

BIBLIOGRAPHY: M.R. James, *Testament of Abraham* (1892), 140–51, 155–61; S. Gaselee, in: G.H. Box, *Testament of Abraham* (1927); J.-B. Frey, in: DBI, Suppl. 1 (1928), 38.

[Michael E. Stone]

ISAAC BAR DORBELO (12th century), one of the best-known pupils of Jacob *Tam. Isaac transmitted details of the various personal practices of Jacob Tam and other scholars, incorporating them in the **Maḥzor Vitry*, which he apparently edited. The book describes the conduct and the teachings of *Rashi and his school (*"de-Vei Rashi"*) and there is no doubt that Isaac's share in it amounted to much more than the passages quoted in his name. Many of his "additions" do not bear his name at all but are simply signed with the letter *tav* (*tosefet*, "addition"). Isaac traveled extensively in France, Germany (*Maḥzor Vitry*, ed. S. Hurwitz (1923), 388), Russia, and Bohemia, where he met *Isaac b. Jacob ha-Lavan (*ibid.*, 243). He also visited Worms where he saw the text of the two queries sent by the Rhenish scholars to Ereẓ Israel – one on the subject of the Messiah, and the other concerning the question of the ritual implications of a cardiac adhesion of the lung in an animal – as well as the replies received. This is the oldest extant German-Jewish document of its kind.

The origin of the name Dorbelo is not certain. It may indicate that his father came from the town Ourville in northern France, but Isaac is not to be identified with the scholar Isaac of Ourville – author of the *Sefer ha-Menahel*, an abridgment of which is included in the ritual compendium **Kol Bo*. It is quite possible that Dorbelo is a personal name, a person of this name appearing in the list of the martyrs of Mainz of 1096 (cf. also responsa of Meir b. Baruch, ed. Prague (1608), no. 501). It may be that both of these are identical with the scholar of this name to whom Rashi addressed a responsum in deferential terms, or that Isaac is his son.

BIBLIOGRAPHY: S.H. Kook, *Iyyunim u-Meḥkarim*, 1 (1959), 292–7; Perles, in: *Jubelschrift… Graetz* (1887), 31–2.

[Israel Moses Ta-Shma]

ISAAC BAR ISRAEL IBN AL-SHUWAYK (c. 1167–1247; known in Arabic as **Fakhr al-Dawla Abu al-Fatḥ Is ḥaq**), head of the *Baghdad academy from 1221 to 1247. Isaac was born in Baghdad. In addition to his erudition, Isaac was a prominent *paytan*. He wrote six *vidduyim* and *tokhaḥot* (penitential *piyyutim*) for the Day of Atonement, which were published in the *maḥzorim* of Sephardi rites. According to the testimony of the historian Ibn al-Fuwaṭī, he also possessed a wide knowledge of astronomy and mathematics. Judah Al-Ḥarizi mentions him in his work *Taḥkemoni* (ed. by A. Kaminka (1899), 190) and praises his noble character. In a letter to him R. Abraham b. Moses b. Maimon refers to him as "the sage of our generation, unequaled in our time, the crown of our heads, the head of our academy…." In a eulogy written for him by the contemporary poet R. Eleazar ha-Bavli, it is said of him that "he was like Koheleth in wisdom." His remains were interred on the Mount of Olives.

BIBLIOGRAPHY: S. Poznański, *Babylonische Geonim im nachgaonaeischen Zeitalter* (1914), index; Mann, Texts, 1 (1931), 225–7; A. Ben-Jacob, *Yehudei Bavel* (1965), 31–3.

[Abraham Ben-Yaacob]

ISAAC BAR JOSEPH (first half of fourth century C.E.), Palestinian *amora*. Isaac was a pupil of *Abbahu and of *Jeremiah who transmitted to him the teachings of *Johanan (Pes. 72a; Git. 11b). He may have studied under Johanan himself in his youth (cf. Yev. 64b). He was among the **neḥutei*, the rabbis who brought to Babylonia the doctrines, traditions, and customs of the Palestinian *amoraim* (Ber. 9a; RH 30a; Av. Zar. 73a; et al.). Statements by him are quoted in the Babylonian Talmud but he is not mentioned in the Jerusalem Talmud. Although on one occasion Abbaye relied upon him in an important matter (Yev. 64b), he was considered less reliable than Rabin, also one of the *neḥutei*. They said: "Rabin is reliable, Isaac *sumka* ['the red'] is not *sumkha* ['reliable']; Rabin *yeshno ba-ḥazarah* ['revises his learning,' so Rashi, *ibid.*], Isaac *sumka* does not revise his learning." According to another interpretation given by Rashi, "Rabin is well acquainted with any change [in the view of R. Johanan] but Isaac 'the red' is not so acquainted."

BIBLIOGRAPHY: Hyman, Toledot, 793–5.

[Zvi Kaplan]

ISAAC BAR RAV JUDAH (end of the third and beginning of the fourth century), Babylonian *amora*. Isaac was the son of *Judah b. Ezekiel, head of the academy of Pumbedita. He studied under his father (Shab. 35b; Pes. 104b; et al.) and was already a distinguished scholar during his father's lifetime, being appointed by him to preach in the *bet ha-midrash* (Ta'an. 13b). He also studied under *Huna (Nid. 17b), *Rabbah b. Naḥamani, who succeeded his father as head of the yeshivah of Pumbedita (Shevu. 36b), *Rami bar Ḥama, and *Sheshet (Zev. 96b). Both halakhic and aggadic statements by him are given in the Talmud (Shab. 21a; Er. 84a; et al.). One of his sayings was: "A man should always pray not to fall sick; for if he falls sick, he is told, 'Show thy merits and be quit'" (Shab. 32a). Isaac refrained from marriage in his youth because he sought a woman of good family and unsullied descent, for which he was rebuked by Ulla (Kid. 71b). His granddaughter, a daughter of his son Isi, was the beautiful Ḥomah, wife of Abbaye (Yev. 64b).

BIBLIOGRAPHY: Hyman, Toledot, 792f.

[Zvi Kaplan]

ISAAC BEN ABBA MARI OF MARSEILLES (1120?–1190?), rabbinical scholar in Provence and Spain. Isaac studied under his father, *Abba Mari b. Isaac, and when only 17 years of age composed a work on the laws of **sheḥitah* and forbidden foods, at his father's behest. Later he went to Barcelona, where he was received with great honor and, at the request of Sheshet *Benveniste, wrote a commentary on chapter 4 of the tractate *Menahot* which deals with the laws concerning **ẓiẓit*, **mezuzah*, and **tefillin*. He corresponded with the most illustrious figures of his generation, such as *Abraham b. David of Posquieres and Jacob *Tam, whom he frequently mentions and quotes. His place in the first rank of rabbinic authorities is due to his encyclopedic work, *Sefer ha-Ittur*, a compilation of the main halakhic laws which are of practical application. Part one deals with the various laws of bills, both financial and of divorce. It is arranged according to subject matter but following a mnemonic acrostic *Tashkef be-Geza Ḥokhmah.* תשקף בגזע חכמה ("Consider the Root of Wisdom"), each letter representing a certain concept. Thus ת stands for *tenai* ("condition"), ש for *shover* ("receipt"), ק for *kiyyum* ("authentication"), etc. Part two includes the laws for the preparation of meat, *sheḥitah*, circumcision, *tefillin*, marriage benedictions, *ẓiẓit*, and a separate section entitled "Ten Commandments" containing ten positive commands which must be performed at specific times. This arrangement is unique in halakhic literature. Isaac b. Abba Mari made use of his vast knowledge of geonic literature and his work is still an important source for that literature. He also made extensive use of Spanish authorities and those of Germany and northern France. He used the Jerusalem Talmud to a considerable extent and also engaged in establishing the correct text of the Talmud on the basis of ancient sources, some of which are no longer extant.

The *Sefer ha-Ittur* was accepted as an authoritative halakhic treatise by the great rabbinical authorities of Spain and Germany and even such renowned talmudic scholars as Naḥmanides made frequent use of it without specifically mentioning it. Both the manuscript and the printed editions (Pt. 1: Venice, 1608; Warsaw, 1801; Pt. 2: Lemberg, 1860) of the text of the *Sefer ha-Ittur* are faulty to the extent of the deletion of entire lines, rendering its study difficult. A new edition of the entire work, together with a commentary, was prepared and published by Meir Jonah (1874–85). Additional fragments, entitled *Tashlum ha-Ittur* were published (from manuscripts) in the Festschrift in honor of Dr. Jakob Freimann (1937) by Alfred Freimann. Besides this work Isaac b. Abba Mari wrote a short treatise on Isaac Alfasi called *Me'ah She'arim* (printed at the end of some of the talmudic tractates in the Romm-Vilna edition).

BIBLIOGRAPHY: Michael, Or, no. 1072; Benedikt, in KS, 25 (1949), 164–6; Assaf, in: HHY, 6 (1922), 289–309.

ISAAC BEN ABRAHAM (Riẓba; 12th century), French tosafist. Isaac is variously referred to as Riẓba, Riba, and Isaac ha-Baḥur of Dampierre. He was the pupil of Isaac b. Samuel ha-Zaken and also studied for a time under Jacob *Tam. He was not a pupil of *Judah b. Isaac-Judah, Sir Leon, as a number of scholars have thought (see Urbach, Tosafot, 269 n. 29). His brother was *Samson of Sens and his maternal grandfather, *Samson of Falaise. He succeeded his teacher as head of the yeshivah of Dampierre.

No complete work by him has survived, but his statements are cited in the *tosafot* to various tractates, chiefly *Eruvin, Yoma, Mo'ed Katan, Yevamot, Ketubbot, Kiddushin, Nedarim, Bava Kamma*, and *Zevaḥim*. He wrote numerous responsa, some of which are quoted in the *Haggahot Maimuniyyot*, the *Or Zaru'a* and in other works. During the Maimonidean controversy, Meir b. Todros Abulafia, an opponent of the books of Maimonides, approached him in 1202 to express his opinion. Among those who addressed problems to him was Jonathan b. David, the leading scholar of Lunel. There is mention of a work by him on the Passover *seder*, entitled *Yesod Rabbenu Yiẓḥak b. Avraham be-Leilei Pesaḥ*. His pupils included Nathan b. Meir and *Judah b. Yakar, the teachers of Naḥmanides, and Samuel b. Elhanan.

BIBLIOGRAPHY: Gross, Gal Jud, 495; Michael, Or, no. 1073; Urbach, Tosafot, 219–26, 269 n. 29, 287 n. 14, 484 n. 106.

[Shlomoh Zalman Havlin]

ISAAC BEN ABRAHAM DI MOLINA (d. before 1580), Egyptian rabbi. Isaac's surname probably derives from the town of Molina in southeast Spain, and it may be assumed that he came to Egypt with the Spanish exiles. His father was a wealthy person and was on friendly terms with the *nagid*, Isaac *Sholal. Isaac appears to have headed the yeshivah of Solomon *Alashkar. R. Isaac himself was wealthy and for a time was the head of the Egyptian mint, a position which was held by other Jews as well in Egypt in the 16th century. He is mentioned in the responsa of Moses di *Trani (Resp. Maharit, vol. 2, no. 16) and of Joseph *Caro (Resp. *Beit Yosef*, EH *Dinei Ketubbot*, 14) as being exceptionally strict with regard to (*Gershom b. Judah's) ban on bigamy, in contrast to Joseph Caro, Moses di Trani, Israel di *Curiel and others, who took a more lenient view. Caro complains that Isaac slighted him and his work *Beit Yosef* in stating that it was a mere digest of the rulings of his predecessors. Isaac is the author of a commentary on the Mishnah. One of his responsa was published in the *Avkat Rokhel* (130) of Caro. A number of his responsa have remained in manuscript and three of them have been published (see bibliography). Isaac's name came to the fore during the scandal surrounding the *Besamin Rosh* (Berlin, 1793), by Saul *Berlin, who falsely claimed the book to contain responsa by *Asher b. Jehiel and his contemporaries which had been collected, annotated, and prepared for publication by Isaac di Molina.

BIBLIOGRAPHY: A. David, in: KS, 44 (1968/69), 553–9. **ADD. BIBLIOGRAPHY:** A. David, in: KS, 46 (1971), 580–2; idem, in: KS, 61 (1986), 368–70;. Z. Havlin, *Shenaton ha-Mishpat ha-Ivri*, 2 (1975), 240–50.

[Abraham David]

ISAAC BEN ABRAHAM HA-GORNI (13th century), Hebrew poet. Born in the city of Aire (i.e., "threshing floor," Heb. *goren*, hence the name Gorni) in southwestern France, Gorni seems to have spent part of his life in Luz (Hautes Pyrénées) and Lucq (Basses Pyrénées). From his verses, it seems that he led a wandering life and he was constantly dependent on patrons. He was, among other places, at Arles, Aix-en-Provence, Manosque, Carpentras, Draguignan, and Perpignan, complaining almost constantly about the shallow culture and the parsimony of their inhabitants. Because of various love affairs he was bitterly persecuted by his compatriots. Several features of his poetry could have been taken from troubadour poetry, and although he uses the meters and rhymes of classical Andalusian poetry, he is far removed from most of its poetical conventions. According to Neubauer, Gorni was on intimate terms in Perpignan in about 1280–90 with Abraham *Bedersi, to whom he addressed many complimentary poems, but received an answer only after a long delay. Their friendship does not seem to have lasted long: Bedersi composed a series of blunt, poetical lampoons ridiculing Gorni and did not consider him worthy of inclusion in his poem, *Ḥerev ha-Mithappekhet* (publ. in *Ḥotem Tokhnit*, 1865), in which he lists the names of the famous contemporary poets. Their way of understanding poetry was too different, and apparently for not a few intellectuals of the time Gorni's poetry, far removed from Andalusian traditions, was not highly esteemed. Gorni was involved in another literary quarrel with Isaiah Debash of Aix, whose friend Shiloni he had violently attacked.

Although in some places his style is uneven and at times awkward, Gorni was undoubtedly a poet of unusual talent and originality. The poem on his fate after death, a kind of "last will and testament," replete with both sarcasm and anxiety, is unique in the literature of the Middle Ages. Two centuries later, his fame was still firmly established: Jacob ben David *Provençal names him together with Al-Ḥarizi and Sulami as the best Hebrew poets of Provence (Letter of the year 1490, ed. by E. Ashkenazi in *Divrei Ḥakhamim* (1849), 70). Gorni's poems were published by M. Steinschneider, H. Gross, A.M. Habermann, and J.H. Schirmann, but they deserve a new critical edition. We know today 18 of his probably much more numerous poems: praising the generosity or fustigating the heartlessness of several Provençal communities, invectives against other poets, etc. He represents himself as one of the wandering jongleurs of his time, going from place to place with his musical instrument, as shown by J.H. Schirmann and A. Brenner.

BIBLIOGRAPHY: Steinschneider, in: A. Bedersi, *Ḥotem Tokhnit*, pt. 3 (1865), 4–6; Renan, Rabbins, 719–25, 747; Gross, in: MGWJ, 31 (1882), 510–23; Schirmann, Sefarad, 2 (1956), 472–84; idem, in: *Sefer Yovel Y. Baer* (1960) 168–72; idem, in: *Lettres Romanes*, 3 (1949), 175–200; J. Zinberg, *Geschihte fun der Literatur bay Yiden*, 2 (1943), 130–4; Davidson, Oẓar, 4 (1933), 420. **ADD. BIBLIOGRAPHY:** A.M. Habermann, *Shirei Avraham ha-Bedersi ve-Yiẓḥak ha-Gorni ve-Ḥugam* (1968), 29–44; Carmi, *The Penguin Book of Hebrew Verse* (1981), 397–400; A. Brenner, in: *Zutot*, 1 (2002), 84–90. Schirmann-Fleischer, *The History of Hebrew Poetry in Christian Spain and Southern France* (1997), 484–98 (Heb.).

[Jefim (Hayyim) Schirmann / Angel Sáenz-Badillos (2nd ed.)]

ISAAC BEN ABRAHAM OF NARBONNE (13th century), halakhist of Provence. Almost no biographical details on him are known. He was a pupil (according to some, a colleague-disciple) of *Naḥmanides and Jonah *Gerondi and one of the teachers of Solomon b. Abraham *Adret. Some identify him with Isaac of Carcassone, who is mentioned in a work on *Pesaḥim* ascribed to Yom Tov *Ishbili (Ritba), in novellae to *Avodah Zarah* by the pupils of Jonah Gerondi, in *Nimmukei Yosef* to *Ketubbot*, and in responsa by Simeon b. Ẓemaḥ *Duran. There is, however, insufficient evidence to establish this identification. Meir (Introduction to *Beit ha-Beḥirah* to *Avot*, ed. by B.Z. Prag (1964), 57) states that Isaac compiled commentaries on *halakhot* by Isaac *Alfasi. Some scholars have attempted to ascribe various commentaries preserved in manuscript to Isaac, but their evidence is doubtful. Benedikt claims that the commentaries ascribed to a pupil of Naḥmanides on the tractates *Beẓah, Megillah, Ta'anit, Pesaḥim*, and *Makkot* are by Isaac; his opinion is shared by Blau and Chavel, but rejected by B. Naeh. A manuscript comprising a commentary by Alfasi to *Ḥullin* has been ascribed to Isaac by Marx, as well as another manuscript comprising a commentary by the same author to *Pesaḥim* (by Sassoon). Naeh has raised serious doubts about these ascriptions, and they cannot be accepted with certainty. Isaac of Carcassone is said to have written commentaries on *halakhot* by Isaac Alfasi to *Pesaḥim, Avodah Zarah, Bava Meẓia*, and *Bava Batra*.

BIBLIOGRAPHY: Marx, in: REJ, 58 (1909), 301–3; D.S. Sassoon, *Ohel David*, 2 (1932), 1075 no. 1050; S. Assaf, *Sifran shel Rishonim* (1935), 53; Benedikt, in: KS, 29 (1953/54), 413–7; M.Y. Blau (ed.), *Perush ha-Ra'ah... Massekhet Berakhot* (1957), 10f. (introd.); idem (ed.), *Shitat ha-Kadmonim... Bava Meẓia* (1967), introd., 15, 30f.; B. Naeh (ed.), in: *Gemara Shelemah*, 1 (1960). 26 (introd.); Chavel, in: *Ha-Darom*, 12 (1960), 32; Hurwitz, *ibid.*, 24 (1967), 43–7.

[Shlomoh Zalman Havlin]

ISAAC BEN ABRAHAM OF POSEN (d. 1685), rabbi and author. Isaac was a pupil of Jonah Teomim and Abraham Meir of Bar. He was on friendly terms with the kabbalist Moses *Zacuto. His first position was as rabbi in Lutsk. In 1664 he was appointed rabbi of Vilna and from there he went to Posen in 1667. His extensive knowledge of the Talmud and Kabbalah earned him the title of R. Isaac the Great, his opinion on halakhic questions being frequently sought by contemporary scholars (see *Magen Avraham* to Sh. Ar., OḤ, 1:7; 32:35; *Gaon Ẓevi* of Ẓevi Hirsch Horowitz (Prague, 1737), 2a–3a). His novellae are mentioned in *Sha'arei Shamayim* of Jehiel Michael ha-Levi (Prague, 1675), 94b; in *Lev Aryeh* of Judah Aryeh Hotchke (Wilhelmdorf, 1674 – on the weekly portion *Toledot*), 16a; *Leket Shemu'el* of Samuel Feivush Katz (Venice, 1694); and in *Even ha-Shoham u-Me'irat Einayim* of Eliezer Goetz b. Meir (Dyhernfuerth, 1733), nos. 11 and 48. Part of his responsa collection was published under the title *Be'er Yiẓḥak* (Vienna, 1894), and part of the remainder was published at the end of Asher b. Jehiel's commentary to *Sukkah* (1903). The whole collection of responsa was in the possession of R. Spira of Munkacs. Isaac died in Posen.

BIBLIOGRAPHY: S.J. Fuenn, *Kiryah Ne'emanah* (1915²), 97; H.N. Maggid-Steinschneider, *Ir Vilna* (1900), 5–7; Kaufmann, in: MGWJ, 39 (1895), 38–46, 91–96.

[Samuel Abba Horodezky]

ISAAC BEN ASHER HA-LEVI (known as **Riba,** initials of **R**abbi **I**saac **B**en **A**sher; second half of 11th and beginning of 12th century), talmudist of Speyer, the first of the German tosafists. He was a pupil of *Rashi and the son-in-law of Rashi's colleague Eliakim b. Meshullam ha-Levi. Contemporary scholars addressed their problems to him and treated him with great respect. His pupils referred to him as "*ha-Kadosh*" ("the Saint," cf. Eliezer b. Nathan, *Sefer Rabban* (Prague, 1610), 149a; Simleul-Silvaniei edition, 1926, 298b). This appellation may be connected with the manner of his death, it being related that he became very ill on the Day of Atonement and on being told by the physicians that if he fasted he would certainly die, but if he ate he might live, he decided to fast and succumbed to his illness (Menaḥem of Recanati, *Sefer Recanati* (*Piskei Halakhot*), Bologna, 1538, no. 166). He compiled *tosafot* to most tractates of the Talmud, but only extracts included in the later collections of *tosafot* are extant. Some of his statements are likewise quoted in subsequent halakhic literature (*Sefer ha-Yashar* of Jacob Tam, *Or Zaru'a* of Isaac b. Moses of Vienna, Meir of Rothenburg, and others). He compiled halakhic collections on loans, on usury, on the tractates *Ḥullin, Bava Batra* chapter 4, *Avodah Zarah, Gittin*, and *Ketubbot*. It is stated that before teaching he went over the *halakhah* by himself four times (Aaron Ha-Kohen, *Orḥot Ḥayyim*, pt. 1, Law of Mondays and Thursdays, no. 20, Jerusalem, 1956 ed., 49). It is also stated that he and his pupils endeavored to create a *Golem by the aid of practical Kabbalah (Commentary to *Sefer Yeẓirah* attributed to Saadiah Gaon, 2:4, Grodno, 1806 ed., 42b). Among his pupils were Isaac b. Mordecai (the Riẓbam), Moses b. Joel Saltman, and Shemariah b. Mordecai.

Isaac b. Asher had a grandson of the same name (first quarter of the 12th century–1195) who is known as Riba II, to distinguish him from his grandfather. He was also known as Riba ha-Baḥur ("The Younger"). He was born in Speyer on the day his grandfather died and they applied to him the verse (Eccles. 1:5), "The sun also ariseth and the sun goeth down" (see Eccles. R. to 1:5; *Da'at Zekenim* to Ex. 7:25). He studied under Shemariah b. Mordecai and Abraham b. Moses of Regensburg. He was a member of the *bet din* among whose other members were Meir b. Kalonymus and alternately Meir's brother Judah. His signature appears with theirs on a responsum to R. Joel. Among his pupils were *Eliezer b. Joel ha-Levi (the Ravyah) and Simḥah b. Samuel of Speyer. He met a martyr's death in 1195 after rioters abused the dead body of his daughter (Narrative of Ephraim of Bonn in *Quellen zur Geschichte der Juden in Deutschland*, 2 (1892), 74f.).

BIBLIOGRAPHY: RIBA I: Michael, Or, no. 1074; V. Aptowitzer, *Mavo le-Sefer Ravyah* (1938), 259, 369f.; Urbach, Tosafot, 141–8, 304–5, and index s.v.; J. Lipschuetz, *Sanhedrei Gedolah* (1968), introd.; I. Ta-Shema, in: KS, 43 (1968), 573, n. 17. RIBA II: Urbach, Tosafot, 304f.

[Shlomoh Zalman Havlin]

ISAAC BEN AVDIMI (late third–early fourth century C.E.), Babylonian *amora*. Almost all Isaac's sayings in the Babylonian Talmud are in the sphere of biblical exegesis and aggadic or halakhic Midrash. His interpretations were regarded as so authoritative that in the following generation *Rava stated that "any biblical verse not explained by Isaac b. Avdimi remains unelucidated" (Zev. 43b). Most of his statements and his discussions on biblical exegesis are given together with the differing view of *Ḥisda (Sanh. 56b) on the verse under discussion. The main figures of the following generation, such as *Abbaye and Rava, transmit his sayings (Zev. 28a, 43b). It would therefore appear that Isaac went from Sura, where Ḥisda lived, to Pumbedita, to the academy of Rabbah, and there Abbaye and Rava heard him. Abbaye introduces the statements of Isaac with the words: "When Isaac b. Avdimi came, he said" etc. (Zev. 28a). The usual meaning of this wording is that he came from Ereẓ Israel to Babylonia, but it cannot have this meaning in this instance since his name is found neither in the Palestinian sources nor in connection with Palestinian scholars. The reference must be to his arrival in Pumbedita from Sura.

BIBLIOGRAPHY: Hyman, Toledot, 786; Ḥ. Albeck, *Mavo la-Talmudim*, 1 (1969), 294f.

[Shmuel Safrai]

ISAAC BEN BEZALEL OF VLADIMIR (d. 1576), Polish rabbi. To Isaac, as to his contemporaries *Shalom Shachna and Kalman of Worms, belongs the credit for the expansion of talmudic studies in Poland. He was considered a front-ranking authority in the halakhic field (cf. resp. Solomon *Luria, nos. 1, 15, 35ff.; resp. She'erit Yosef (Joseph Kohen), 17; resp. Moses *Isserles, 91). An opinion of Isaac on an **agunah* matter is included in the "new" responsa of Joel *Sirkes (no. 4). He also wrote annotations to the Talmud, to *Asher b. Jehiel, and *Mordecai b. Hillel. Numerous decisions of Isaac are quoted by his grandson, *David b. Samuel ha-Levi (*Turei Zahav*, OḤ no. 153; YD no. 113; EH no. 129; ḤM no. 3).

BIBLIOGRAPHY: Ḥ.N. Dembitzer, *Kelilat Yofi*, 1 (1888) 48a–49b; Zunz, *Ir ha-Ẓedek*, n. 28; Fuenn, Kenesset, 601; Kahana, *Anaf Eẓ Avot*, 34; Lewinstein, *Dor Dor ve-Doreshav* (1900), no. 795.

[Samuel Abba Horodezky]

ISAAC BEN ELEAZAR, name of two Palestinian *amoraim*. The first lived during the second half of the second century C.E. He was a relative of R. Johanan and an associate of R. Isaac and of Ḥiyya b. Abba. Although referred to in the Babylonian Talmud as Isaac b. Eleazar, he is also identical with the Isaac Ḥakola or Ben Ḥakola mentioned in both the Talmuds (cf. Ket. 109a; TJ, *ibid.* 13: 1, 35b); the correct reading in *Pesaḥim* 113b (see Dik. Sof., p. 354, no. 100) is "Isaac b. Ḥakola is identical with Isaac b. Eleazar."

The second *amora* of this name lived in the second half of the fourth century. He was a native of Caesarea, and several of the halakhic and aggadic teachings transmitted by him are connected with the town. When R. Mana went to Caesarea he turned to him with a halakhic question (TJ, Dem. 2:1, 22c). Jacob of Kefar Nibburaya, in his sharp criticism of the *nasi* for appointing *dayyanim* because of their wealth, contrasted them with Isaac: "But 'The Lord is in His holy Temple' (Hab. 2:20), is to be applied to Isaac b. Eleazar in the Maradata [turbulent] Synagogue of Caesarea" (TJ, Bik. 3:3, 65d). The leading halakhists and aggadists of the following generation, such as Mana and Tanḥuma, quote sayings in his name (*ibid.*, TJ, Bik. 1:3, 63d). His most distinguished pupil was Oshaya b. Shammai, also a native of Caesarea, who transmitted several *halakhot* in his name. When Oshaya was about to undertake a sea voyage, Isaac instructed him in the *halakhah* of travel by sea during the intermediate days of the festival (TJ, MK 2:3, 81b). Among his aggadic dicta are "That which wisdom has placed as a crown upon its head [i.e., the fear of God] humility has made the heel of its shoe" (TJ, Shab. 1:5, 3c; cf. Tanh. B. Num. 52); and "The prophets know that their God is true. Hence they do not flatter Him" (TJ, Ber. 7:4, 11c).

BIBLIOGRAPHY: Hyman, Toledot, s.v.; Epstein, Mishnah, 167–8; I.W. Rabinowitz, *Sha'arei Torat Bavel* (1961), 457–9; Ḥ. Albeck, *Mavo la-Talmudim* (1969), 186–7, 339–40.

[Shmuel Safrai]

ISAAC BEN ELIAKIM OF POSEN (17th century), Yiddish moralist and author. Isaac wrote *Lev Tov* (Prague, 1620), an ethical-religious work in 20 chapters, providing rules for prayer and correct observance of *mitzvot*, and proper behavior for home and synagogue. It was reprinted with additions by Ḥayyim b. Jacob Orbach (Cracow, 1641). Unlike other Yiddish ethical works, *Lev Tov* was addressed to both men and women. It counseled the men to honor their wives – since they educate the children to keep a Jewish home – and, despite a traditional view of gender relations, stressed that men and women have equal rights. This work became very popular but was criticized in the anonymous Yiddish book, *Hasoges* (*Hassagot*; Amsterdam, c. 1710). Isaac was apparently attracted to Kabbalah. From Venice, Moses *Zacuto sent him his treatise on the laws of writing Torah scrolls, *Tikkun Soferim*, for approval (Oxford, Bodleian Library, Ms. Opp. 554, which also contains Isaac's reply).

BIBLIOGRAPHY: Fuerst, Bibliotheca, 2 (1863), 140f; Zinberg, Sifrut, 4 (1958), 82f.; M. Erik, *Geshikhte fun der Yidisher Literatur* (1923), 294–301. **ADD. BIBLIOGRAPHY:** J. Winter and S. Wünsche, *Juedische Literatur*, 3 (1896), 541–2; J.C. Frakes, *Early Yiddish Texts: 1100–1750* (2004), 536–40.

ISAAC BEN ELIEZER (known as *segan Leviyyah* – meaning a levite; d. 1070), one of the great "scholars of Worms" and a teacher of *Rashi. Isaac b. Eliezer apparently originated from *Vitry (see Asher b. Jehiel, to Ḥul 4:7). He studied at the yeshivah of Mainz under *Eliezer b. Isaac of Worms and thereafter went to Worms, where he headed the yeshivah and where he introduced several regulations into the local liturgy. Of his many disciples there, the most noteworthy were Rashi, Eliakim b. Meshullam, and *Meir b. Samuel. Rashi states that "he was leader and guide of the generation, nothing being done without his approval." Some of his responsa and rulings, written in an unusually terse manner, appear in the books of the "School of Rashi" and in the responsa of Rashi and the scholars of France and Lorraine, along with some of his scriptural interpretations. In his commentary on the Talmud, Rashi refers to him as *Leviyyah* and elsewhere (*Likkutei ha-Pardes*, Munkaes ed. (1897), 36b) "our holy teacher," apparently in allusion to his saintliness and asceticism (cf. *Sefer Ravyah*, ed. by V. Aptowitzer (1964^2), part 2, 659: no. 886). *Piyyutim* by him are also extant. Of his three sons, whom the *rishonim* called "our levite teachers," the best known is Jacob, called *Ya'vez*, whose halakhic rulings are included among those of the *rishonim* and whose elegy on the massacres of 1096, beginning "*Oi li al shivri*" has been preserved.

BIBLIOGRAPHY: Davidson, Oẓar, 4 (1933), 421; Epstein, in: *Tarbiz*, 4 (1932/33), 167–70; V. Aptowitzer, *Mavo le-Sefer Ravyah* (1938), 367–9; Urbach, Tosafot, index; Roth, Dark Ages, 2 (1966), index.

[Israel Moses Ta-Shma]

ISAAC BEN ḤAYYIM BEN ABRAHAM (c. 1500), Spanish-Hebrew poet. Isaac left Spain, according to his own testimony, in the summer of 1492, together with the exiles from the city of Jativa. Later he came to Naples and Apulia. In Adar 1501 he was in Constantinople, where in 1503, he composed a parody on a marriage contract. Isaac's works *Ma'yan Gannim* and *Eẓ Ḥayyim* (manuscript in the Bodleian Library) contain, among others, a detailed work on prosody, *Melekhet ha-Shir*, poems by himself and by his grandfather, Isaac b. Joseph.

BIBLIOGRAPHY: Neubauer, Cat, 2 (1906), 186, no. 2770; M. Drechsler, *Mekonen Evlenu* (1932); Davidson, Oẓar, 4 (1933), 420.

[Jefim (Hayyim) Schirmann]

ISAAC BEN JACOB HA-KOHEN (second half of 13th century), Spanish kabbalist. He was born in Soria and was related to *Shem Tov b. Abraham ibn Gaon. He traveled through Spain and Provence together with his brother *Jacob and also on his own and collected the traditions of the elder kabbalists there. Isaac was among the leading spokesmen of the Gnostic circle in Spanish Kabbalah; his books are full of important material having no counterpart in his colleagues' works; but some of it was incorporated as well as freely edited by his pupil *Moses b. Solomon of Burgos.

Isaac's writings include (1) a treatise on *aẓilut* ("*emanation"; *Madda'ei ha-Yahadut*, 2 (1927), 244–64; other excerpts in *Ha-Ẓofeh*, 13 (1929), 261 and in *Kitvei Yad be-Kabbalah* (1930), 69–70). Another edition of this treatise was edited with additions and elaborations of several passages by Moses of Burgos (*Tarbiz*, 5 (1934), 190–6); (2) *Perush al Merkevet Yeḥezkel* ("Commentary on Ezekiel's Chariot," *Tarbiz*, 2 (1932), 188–218, and additions from the elaborations of Moses of Burgos; *Tarbiz*, 5 (182–90)). This commentary was mistakenly inserted in the commentary of *Moses de Leon on the *Merkabah in his *Mishkan ha-Edut* in some manuscripts; (3) *Ta'amei ha-Nekuddot ve-Ta'amei ha-Te'amim* ("On vowels and accents") on which no author's name appears but whose content and language prove the identity of the author (*Madda'ei ha-Yahadut*, 2 (1927), 265–75); (4) *Inyan Gadol Meva'er Keẓat Ma'aseh Merkavah* ("An important theme, which explains part of the mystery of the chariot"; *ibid.*, 279–84); (5) a commentary on the Torah seen by Isaac b. Samuel of Acre; (6) a speculative work which belonged to Shem Tov *Ibn Shem Tov explaining the doctrine of the *Sefirot* and connecting it with neoplatonic ideas; some quotations from it are quoted by Shem Tov ibn Shem Tov (*ibid.*, 276–9).

Isaac *Albalag mentions Isaac among the three most famous and most authoritative kabbalists of his generation and indeed in several manuscripts of his major treatise he is called "Paragon of the Generation." His treatise on emanation contains the first formulation of the doctrine of left emanation (see *Kabbalah) according to pseudepigraphic sources. This article is composed of different parts, apparently letters which he wrote to his colleagues at different times, and they contain parallel and different versions of this doctrine. As can be seen from his commentary on Ezekiel 1 and remnants of his theoretical book, he had a complete system on the hierarchy of the worlds which came to him from neoplatonic sources in different channels: *olam ha-mitboded* ("the transcendent world of divine unity"), *olam ha-yeẓirah* ("the world of formation") which is also called *olam ha-madda* ("the world of cognition"), *olam ha-nivdal* ("the world of separation," i.e., separate intelligences) or *olam ha-nevu'ah* ("the world of prophecy"), *olam ha-tekhunah* ("the world of astronomy") and *olam ha-beḥinah* ("the world of trial") which is *olam ha-shafel* ("the terrestrial world," *Tarbiz*, 2 (1939), 436–42).

BIBLIOGRAPHY: G. Scholem, in: *Madda'ei ha-Yahadut*, 2 (1927), 163–293; idem, in: *Tarbiz*, 2–5 (1931–34); Toledano, in: *Ha-Ẓofeh* 13 (1931), 261–7; G. Scholem, *Les Origines de la Kabbale* (1966), 310–4, 376–82.

[Gershom Scholem]

ISAAC BEN JACOB HA-LAVAN OF PRAGUE (12th century), tosafist of Bohemia. It has been maintained by some that he was called "ha-Lavan" ("white") because of his white hair and by others that the name is derived from the river Elbe. He was also known as Isaac of Bohemia and Isaac of Regensburg. He was a brother of the well-known traveler *Pethahiah of Regensburg. Isaac lived in Germany and in France, where he studied under *Isaac b. Asher ha-Levi, and under Jacob b. Meir *Tam. He was the author of *tosafot* to *Ketubbot* and *Yoma* which have been published on the basis of various manuscripts – *Ketubbot* (1954) by P.J. Kohn; *Yoma* by D. Genachowski (1956) and by P.J. Kohn (1960) in a different reading of the manuscript. *Eliezer b. Joel ha-Levi possessed a collection of Isaac's responsa. He is known also to have compiled various *piyyutim*. The *Sefer ha-Yashar* of Jacob Tam, containing sayings of Tam preserved by his pupils, also contains traditions transmitted by Isaac (Urbach, *Tosafot*, p. 82 n. 27). Isaac is mentioned in the *tosafot* in the printed editions of the Talmud to *Yevamot, Ketubbot* and *Zevaḥim*, as well as in the following works of the *posekim: Yiḥusei Tanna'im ve-Amora'im, Arugat ha-Bosem, Roke'aḥ* (which includes a responsum by Isaac to *Judah b. Kalonymus b. Moses), the responsa of Isaac Or Zarua, and *Meir b. Baruch of Rothenburg (which quotes a complete responsum by him), *Orḥot Ḥayyim, Kol Bo*, and others. According to Aptowitzer, Isaac died before 1188 but according to Zunz and Tykocinski, after 1193.

BIBLIOGRAPHY: Zunz, Lit Poesie, 313, 489; Zunz, Gesch, index; Gross, Gal Jud, 168, no. 4; S.D. Luzzatto, in: *Kerem Ḥemed*, 7 (1843), 69; V. Aptowitzer, *Mavo le-Sefer Ravyah* (1938), 174, 260, 296, 375f.; G. Scholem, in: *Tarbiz*, 3 (1931/32), 276f.; Tykocinski, in: Germ Jud, 1 (1934), 275f.; and index s.v.; Urbach, Tosafot, index s.v.; D. Ganchowsky, in: *Sinai*, 38 (1956), 288–311; idem (ed.), *Tosefot R. Yizḥak ben Ya'akov ha-Lavan le-Massekhet Yoma* (1956), introduction.

[Shlomoh Zalman Havlin]

ISAAC BEN JACOB MIN HA-LEVIYYIM ("of the levites"; b. 1621), Italian rabbi. He was orphaned at an early age and was brought up in the house of his grandfather, Leone *Modena. He was a printer, proofreader, cantor, and preacher in his native Venice. He was the author of *Ma'asei Ḥakhamim* (Venice, 1647), talmudic *aggadot* based on Jacob ibn *Ḥabib's *Ein Ya'akov*, Leone da Modena's *Beit Yehudah*, with commentaries; *Medabber Tahpukhot*, memoirs (published by L. Blau); *Yizḥak Meẓaḥek*, an anthology of poems, apparently no longer extant (several of Isaac's poems have been printed in other works, e.g., Yom Tov Valvason's *Hed Urim*, Venice, 1662); extracts from Moses *Cordovero's *Pardes Rimmonim* (Salonika n.d., Venice, 1586); and *Pesikta Rabbati*, a collection of decisions (neither of the latter works is extant). Isaac also wrote introductions to numerous works by others, including his grandfather's *Magen va-Ḥerev*. He was one of those who took part in the inquiry against *Nathan of Gaza (see Samuel *Aboab, *Devar Shemu'el*, no. 375).

BIBLIOGRAPHY: L. Blau (ed.), *Leo Modenas Briefe und Schriftstuecke* (1905), 74 (Ger. section), 165 (Heb. section); idem, in: HHY, 2 (1912), 168–71; 3 (1914), 45–54, 69–96; Scholem, Shabbetai Ẓevi, 2 (1957), 417–9; Leone (Judah Aryeh of) Modena, *Ziknei Yehudah*, ed. by S. Simonson (1956), 44 (introd.).

[Umberto (Moses David) Cassuto]

ISAAC BENJAMIN WOLF BEN ELIEZER LIPMAN (d. before 1698), German rabbi. Isaac's father, ELIEZER, was called Goettingen, a name taken from the city of that name in Germany. Isaac studied under Isaac b. Abraham, *av bet din* of Vilna and Posen. He served as rabbi of Landsberg an der Warthe. From 1687 he was rabbi of Slutsk and then of Olyka. While still young, he wrote *Naḥalat Binyamin*, a work in four parts; only the first part was published (Amsterdam, 1682). The book is a pilpulistic commentary on 147 precepts, positive and negative. In the introduction he praises his brother JUDAH, known as Judah Kaẓin ("leader"), one of the heads of the Berlin community. Judah assisted him in covering the cost of the publication of the first part of the work. Isaac's approach is explained in the introduction. He based all his works "on what was possible, without coming to any halakhic decision. That is why I have reviewed all aspects in the hope of arriving at the truth at least in one matter." His novellae to *Bava Meẓia* were also published (1686). Of his sons, ELIEZER, LIPMAN GOETTINGEN, the rabbi of Coblenz, and Aaron, known as ARND BENJAMIN WOLF (1670–1721), who was born in Landsberg, are known. The latter's uncle and father-in-law, Judah Berlin, founded a *bet ha-midrash* in Berlin and appointed Aaron as its head. In 1697 Aaron was appointed deputy to the aged rabbi of Berlin, Shemaiah b.

Abraham Issachar Ber, and when the latter died in 1709 he was appointed the official rabbi of Alt-Mittel-Neumark. From 1713 he served as rabbi of Frankfurt on the Oder and his brother-in-law, Michael (Mikhol) Ḥasid, succeeded him in Berlin.

BIBLIOGRAPHY: E.L. Landshuth, *Toledot Anshei ha-Shem u-Fe'ulatam ba-Adat Berlin* (1884), 1–10; Lassally, in: MGWJ, 80 (1936), 408f.; *Pinkas Slutsk u-Venoteha* (1962), 33f.; J. Meisl, in: *Arim ve-Immahot be-Yisrael*, 1 (1946), 100.

[Yehoshua Horowitz]

ISAAC BEN JOSEPH OF CORBEIL (known as **Semak** after his main work; d. 1280), one of the great French codifiers of the 13th century; son-in-law of *Jehiel of Paris. Isaac was renowned for his piety which is reflected in his *Sefer Mitzvot Katan* (*Se-Ma-K*), "Small" Book of Commandments, for which he is mainly known. In this work, he provided the masses with a compendium of contemporary *halakhah*, interspersed with ethical homilies, parables, and *aggadot*. He divided the precepts into seven "Pillars," corresponding to the seven days of the week, apparently intending that the work be read through every week. In his enumeration of the precepts and their details, though not in his division of the work, Isaac was guided by the *Sefer Mitzvot Gadol* of *Moses of Coucy, but he omitted the extensive halakhic discussions of that work. The *Semak* achieved wide popularity, receiving recognition from outstanding scholars of France and Germany and even being included by some early authorities in the prayer book "so that the precepts could be recited daily… in place of supplications (see **Teḥinnah*) and the reading of psalms." *Meir b. Baruch of Rothenburg's encomium gained wide circulation for the book in Germany, and it soon became an accepted source for the *posekim* ("codifiers"), particularly *Aaron ha-Kohen of Lunel and Joseph *Colon. In the course of time many annotations (the best known being those of *Perez b. Elijah of Corbeil) were added; in later editions, these were sometimes merged with the original text and printed as one. The glosses of Moses of Zurich were known (but never published) as "The *Semak* of Zurich;" this consists of a selection from the works of German and French scholars which were added to the *Sefer Mitzvot Katan*. *Sefer Mitzvot Katan* was first published in Constantinople (1510) and many times later. Many manuscripts still exist, evidence of its wide popularity. Isaac's other writings include his "decisions," collated by one of his disciples from his responsa. His *tosafot* to several tractates are also referred to in rabbinic literature.

BIBLIOGRAPHY: Urbach, Tosafot, 447–57; Waxman, Literature, 2 (1960²) 128f.

[Israel Moses Ta-Shma]

ISAAC BEN JUDAH (c. 1080), liturgical poet. While it is not known where Isaac flourished, his *piyyutim* have been included for the most part in the *Maḥzor Romania*; for that reason Zunz assumed that Isaac must have originally come from the Byzantine Empire. Isaac composed *yoẓerot* with the corresponding *zulatot* (hymns) for the four special *Sabbaths, for Shabbat *ha-Gadol, and for Shabbat *Bereshit. He may also have composed an *ofan*, as well as a *seliḥah*, for the Fast of *Esther. Content, structure, and stylistic peculiarities of Isaac's poetry indicate that he belonged to the old paytanic school.

BIBLIOGRAPHY: Zunz, Lit Poesie, 91, 142–4, 248; Davidson, Oẓar, 4 (1933), 419. **ADD. BIBLIOGRAPHY:** E. Fleischer, *Ha-Yoẓerot be-Hithavutam ve-Hitpatteḥutam* (1984), 616, 624, 690.

[Jefim (Hayyim) Schirmann]

ISAAC BEN JUDAH HA-SENIRI (i.e., of Mount Senir; end of 12th century-beginning of 13th), Provençal *paytan*. He was one of five sons of the scholar *Judah b. Nethanel of Beaucaire whom Judah *Al-Ḥarizi met on his travels. Isaac's brother, Samuel b. Judah, was also a liturgical poet. The dates 1208 and 1220 appear in three of his poems and the poet's productive period can be determined according to them (Zunz, Lit Poesie, 472 nos. 1, 8, 9). In the acrostic of one poem he speaks of himself as "living on [or "at"] Mount Senir." There has been much discussion as to the meaning of Mount Senir, but it almost certainly refers to Mount Ventoux in the region of Carpentras.

Isaac is one of the few non-Spanish poets whom Al-Ḥarizi praises without reservation ("Isaac makes the stars turn pale," *Taḥkemoni, sha'ar* 46). Similarly, Isaac's poems are praised lavishly by his friend *Meshullam de Piera, by Abraham *Bedersi in *Ḥerev ha-Mithappekhet* (verse 139), Menahem de *Lonzano (16th century) in *Shetei Yadot* (Venice 1618). He wrote only liturgical poetry. About 59 of his religious poems have been preserved; most of them formed part of and were printed in the rite of Carpentras and the Comtat Venaissin. Individual poems were also used in the rite of Tripoli (*Siftei Renanot*), Algiers, and others. B. Bar-Tikva (1996) published a complete edition of Ha-Seniri's *piyyutim*. Isaac cultivated almost all styles of the *piyyut*: Bar-Tikva's edition includes nine *yoẓerot* (*me'orah*, *ofan*, *zulat*, *geulah*, *mi-khamokha*), three *kedushta'ot* and *silluk* for the *amidah*, eight *reshuyyot*, some Spanish preferences, such as four *nishmat, kaddish, barekhu* and three *shillum* of Provençal style; 20 of his poems are *seliḥot* of different genres, including four *tokhaḥot*, three *mustagāb*, three *rehuṭot*, one *bakashah*, one *teḥinnah*; two *kinot* for Tishah be-Av, eight *hoshanot* for *Sukkot* (he devoted a large composition, preserved in the *Carpentras Maḥzor*, to Hoshana Rabba which embodies one of the most lengthy and elaborate acrostics on record), and one *petirat Moshe* for *Simḥat Torah*. In some cases, different forms of the same poem have been preserved, reflecting the changes of the time (Einbinder). Sometimes he drew on halakhic material and converted it to poetic form. He is also a witness of the historical conditions of his time and shows in some poems his perceptions of ritual violence. About half of his poems use the Spanish meter, in particular the syllabic one; not a few take strophic patterns. Other poems are written using the language and the technique of the old Palestinian *piyyut*, with stress or word meter. E. Fleischer considers Ha-

Seniri the best and the most representative of the Provençal *paytanim*.

BIBLIOGRAPHY: Zunz, Poesie, 12, 110, 290f.; Zunz, Lit Poesie, 472–75; Landshuth, Ammudei, 118–20; Renan, Rabbins, 715 n. 1; Gross, Gal Jud, 120, 360f.; Kahn, in: REJ, 65 (1913), 182f.; Davidson, Oẓar, 4 (1933), 424f.; Schirmann, Sefarad, 2 (1956), 275–84. **ADD. BIBLIOGRAPHY:** B. Bar-Tikva, *Piyyutei R. Yiẓḥak ha-Sheniri* (1996); Schirmann-Fleischer, *The History of Hebrew Poetry in Christian Spain and Southern France* (1997), 452–64 (Heb.); S. Einbinder, in: REJ, 163 (2004), 111–35.

[Angel Sáenz-Badillos 2nd ed.)]

ISAAC BEN JUDAH OF MAINZ (11th century), German scholar; teacher of *Rashi. Practically no biographical details are known of him or his family. The description given by J.N. Epstein (see bibliography) of the characteristics of the yeshivah of Mainz during the period that Isaac was its head, and the manner in which it differed from the contemporary yeshivah of Worms, has been rejected by Aptowitzer (see bibliography). Isaac was head of the famous yeshivah in Mainz founded by his teacher *Gershom b. Judah, to whom he was apparently related, as he was to Rashi. He seems to have come from France (Zedekiah b. Abraham ha-Rofe, *Shibbolei ha-Leket* ed. by Buber (1886). 66 no. 93). He was also a pupil of *Eliezer ha-Gadol of Metz who was also one of the heads of the Mainz yeshivah. In addition to Rashi, he numbered Eliakim b. Meshullam among his distinguished pupils. Eliakim refers to him as *Moreh Ẓedek* ("the righteous teacher") whenever he mentions him in his commentary to *Yoma* and Rashi uses the same title on *Yoma* 16b and in his responsa. According to Abraham Epstein, the commentary attributed to Rabbenu Gershom in the Romm (Vilna) editions of the Talmud to the tractates *Menaḥot, Bekhorot, Arakhin, Temurah, Keritot, Me'ilah, Tamid, Ḥullin, Ta'anit*, and *Bava Batra* was compiled in Isaac's *bet midrash*. Eight of his responsa are included in the *Teshuvot Ḥakhmei Ẓarefat ve-Loter* (1881), and in the introduction to this work J. Mueller gives a list of 17 of his responsa and novellae which are scattered throughout the literature. I. Elfenbein's edition of Rashi's responsa (1943) contains 38 of Isaac's, mainly directed to Rashi.

BIBLIOGRAPHY: E.M. Lipschuetz, *R. Shelomo Yiẓḥaki* (1912), 18f., 56f.; Epstein, in: *Festschrift… M. Steinschneider* (1896), 115–43; S. Buber (ed.), *Sefer ha-Orah*, 1 (1905), introd. 15–6; idem. (ed.) Zedekiah b. Abraham ha-Rofe, *Shibbolei ha-Leket* (1886), introd. 713; J. Mueller (ed.), *Teshuvot Ḥakhmei Ẓarefat ve-Loter* (1881), introd. 23–5; N. Epstein, in: *Tarbiz*, 4 (1932/33), 167–78; V. Aptowitzer, *Mavo le-Sefer Ravyah* (1938), 260, 296f., 311, 371f., 406f.; S. Hurwitz (ed.), *Maḥzor Vitry* (1923²), introd. 33–6; D. Genachowski (ed.), *Perush R. Elyakim le-Massekhet Yoma* (1964), 12f.; I. Elfenbein (ed.), *Teshuvot Rashi* (1943), introd. and index 403; S. Eidelberg (ed.), *Teshuvot R. Gershom Me'or ha-Golah* (1956), introd. 26–33.

[Shlomoh Zalman Havlin]

ISAAC BEN MEIR (**Ribam**; mid-12th century), one of the first tosafists. Isaac was the brother of *Samuel b. Meir (the Rashbam) and of Jacob *Tam, all of them grandsons of Rashi. No biographical details are known of him. He died during his father's lifetime and left seven orphans. In a responsum to Eliezer b. Nathan, his brother Jacob lamented him: "I cry in the bitterness of my spirit… because the holy ark has been taken" (*Sefer ha-Yashar* (responsa) by F. Rosenthal (1898), 71). His widow later married Judah b. Yom Tov, a grandson of Judah b. Nathan, Rashi's son-in-law (see Urbach from a Ms.). The well-known tosafist *Isaac of Dampierre was his pupil; he subsequently married the daughter of Isaac b. Meir's wife by her second marriage, and asked his mother-in-law for details of various decisions given by her first husband. *Tosafot* written by him on the tractates *Yevamot* and *Nedarim* are referred to. His opinions are frequently quoted in the *tosafot* to many tractates. His appellation Ribam is the same as that of Isaac b. Mordecai, and consequently the two have sometimes been confused.

BIBLIOGRAPHY: V. Aptowitzer, *Mavo le-Sefer Ravyah* (1938), 376f.; Urbach, Tosafot, 52f.

[Shlomoh Zalman Havlin]

ISAAC BEN MELCHIZEDEK OF SIPONTO (c. 1090–1160), the first Italian commentator on the Mishnah. It is unknown whether his commentary covered the whole of the Mishnah, since only the commentaries on *Zera'im* and *Tohorot* are known. The former is printed in the Romm Vilna Talmud, while the latter is quoted by the *tosafot* in the *Sefer ha-Makhri'a* (Leghorn, 1779) of Isaiah di Trani (nos 62, 86, et al.) and by other rabbis. Abraham b. David of Posquières refers to him as "*ha-rav ha-Yevani*," "the Greek rabbi," part of southern Italy being at that time Byzantine. Isaac's commentary is based on the Babylonian and Jerusalem Talmuds, and he quotes from the *Tosefta*, the *Sifra*, the **Sifrei Zuta*, and mentions R. Nissim, R. Daniel of Rome (brother of Nathan, the author of the *Arukh*), the *Arukh*, and Hai Gaon. He often translates Hebrew words into the vernacular, making use of Greek, Italian, and Arabic. His commentary is brief and clear, like that of Rashi, and he does not give halakhic decisions.

BIBLIOGRAPHY: Frankel, Mishnah, index; Ch. Albeck, *Mavo la-Mishnah* (1959), 245; V. Aptowitzer, *Mavo le-Sefer Ravyah* (1938), 261, 283, 377–8; E.E. Urbach, Tosafot, index.

[Hirsch Jacob Zimmels]

ISAAC BEN MENAHEM THE GREAT (11th century), French scholar of the generation of *Rashi's teachers. In his youth Isaac studied in Mainz at the yeshivah of *Eliezer b. Isaac of Worms. Later he settled in France and the correspondence thereafter between Isaac and his teacher shows that the two were very closely attached and contains great praise by Eliezer for Isaac. Rashi made extensive use of Isaac's teachings, both written and oral, particularly in determining the correct text of the Talmud. Isaac had apparently copied out in his own hand several orders of the Mishnah and the Talmud while still in the yeshivah, and Rashi, in at least one case, preferred Isaac's text to that of his own teachers and "of all the manuscripts" (Suk. 40a). Rashi also made use of Isaac's work to explain difficult words (Shab. 67a; BM 7b; et al.). At the same time, Rashi did not hesitate to disagree with one of his rulings and to set it aside completely (J. Mueller (ed.), *Teshuvot Ḥakhmei Ẓarefat ve-Loter* (1881), 10a–b, no. 17), and some of Isaac's other rulings met with opposition from authorities of the time (Tos. to Git. 21b; S. Hurwitz (ed.), *Maḥzor Vitry* (1923²), et al.). His text and explanation of words were generally relied on by scholars, in that they were based on the traditions of the main yeshivah in Mainz (*Maḥzor Vitry*, 610, 635). Many scholars accepted as authoritative the example of the religious practices of his sister, Bella, who apparently grew up in his house and thus learned them from him (*ibid.*).

[Israel Moses Ta-Shma]

ISAAC BEN MERWAN HA-LEVI (11th–12th centuries), Provençal communal leader and halakhist. He headed the *bet din* and the yeshivah in Narbonne. His father, Merwan, was described as a "man of great piety and rich in material things and good deeds, who applied his wealth for the benefit of his brethren and thus obtained the repeal of several oppressive edicts" (addition to the *Sefer ha-Kabbalah* of Abraham ibn Daud, Neubauer, Chronicles, 1 (1887), 83). Isaac studied under Judah b. Moses (ha-Darshan of Toulouse?), a pupil of *Gershom b. Judah of Mainz. In a ruling cited by Menahem b. Solomon Meiri (Pes. 42a, *Beit ha-Beḥirah al Massekhet Pesaḥim* ed. by J. Klein (1964), 142) which bears the signatures of "five scholars of world standing," Isaac's is the first. The five scholars apparently constituted the *bet din* of Narbonne (B.Z. Benedikt, in *Tarbiẓ*, 22 (1951), 107). It is not certain whether Isaac left anything in writing; his words are usually quoted as "having been heard," but sometimes it is stated that "he wrote." Some of his statements were cited by his pupil Abraham b. Isaac, the author of the *Eshkol*; Zerahiah b. Isaac ha-Levi Gerondi in *Ha-Ma'or*; Joseph b. Migash in *Temim De'im*, and Moses ha-Kohen in his **hassagot* to Maimonides' *Mishneh Torah* (Shabbat 6:5; S. Atlas, in: HUCA, 27 (1956), 60), in the *Shibbolei ha-Leket* (Pt. 1, no. 48 and 51, ed. by S.K. Mirsky (1966), 256, 260), etc. Among his pupils were some of the greatest scholars of Provence in the following generation, Moses the son of his brother Joseph, Moses b. Todros ha-Nasi, and Abraham b. Isaac "Av Bet Din." Joseph studied under him. Isaac left no descendants, and he must have died before 1134, since in that year his brother Joseph lodged a claim in connection with his estate (Isaac ha-Sardi, *Sefer ha-Terumot*, 14:5, Prague 1605, 26a).

BIBLIOGRAPHY: Gross, Gal Jud, 412f.; Z.B. Auerbach (ed.), Abraham b. Isaac of Narbonne, *Ha-Eshkol* (1968), introd. 9; S. Albeck (ed.), Abraham b. Isaac of Narbonne, *Ha-Eshkol*, 1 (1935), introd. 3; B.Z. Benedict, in: *Tarbiz*, 19 (1948), 19, n.7, 22 (1951), 96, n. 109, 107; I. Twersky, *Rabad of Posquières* (1962), 236, 239.

[Shlomoh Zalman Havlin]

ISAAC BEN MORDECAI (known as **Ribam,** initials of **R**abbi **I**saac **B**en **M**ordecai; 12th century), German tosafist. Isaac was also known as Isaac b. Mordecai of Bohemia and Isaac b. Mordecai of Prague. The abbreviated form of his name, Ribam, led to his being confused at times with *Isaac b. Meir (see Urbach, Tosafot, 170 no. 37). Active in the community of Regensburg, he served as head of its *bet din* and was regarded as the greatest scholar of the town and its leader (as described by Jacob b. Meir *Tam in *Sefer ha-Yashar*, part of responsa ed. by F. Rosenthal (1898), 178 no. 80). He was a pupil of *Isaac b. Asher ha-Levi (Riba I) of Speyer and of Jacob Tam. He compiled *tosafot* to most tractates of the Talmud, a large part of them while with his teachers. A considerable part of his *tosafot* to *Bava Batra* are included in the printed edition of the Talmud and in the *tosafot* of *Isaiah di Trani. He is known to have written *tosafot* to the tractates *Pesaḥim, Mo'ed Katan*, and *Bava Kamma* compiled before his teacher, Isaac, and to *Shabbat, Ketubbot, Gittin, Sotah, Nazir*, and *Bava Meẓia*. He is quoted in the printed *tosafot* to *Yoma, Ḥagigah, Sanhedrin, Zevaḥim*, and *Ḥullin*, and in *Sefer ha-Ravyah* and *Or Zaru'a*. *Eliezer b. Nathan of Mainz sent his book to him and his colleagues *Ephraim b. Isaac and Moses b. Joel on the *bet din* of Regensburg. They criticized many of his statements and in his reply Eliezer treated them with great respect. He also sent them the well-known responsum on *ḥallonot* ("windows," i.e., the prohibition against disturbing the privacy of a neighbor by opening a window facing his premises).

BIBLIOGRAPHY: Eliezer b. Nathan, *Sefer Rabban*, ed. by S. Albeck (1904), introd. p. XI; V. Aptowitzer, *Mavo le-Sefer Ravyah* (1938), 29, 42f., 288, 378f.; Epstein, in: *Tarbiz*, 12 (1940/41), 200–2; Urbach, Tosafot, 167–70.

[Shlomoh Zalman Havlin]

ISAAC BEN MOSES OF VIENNA (c. 1180-c. 1250), halakhic authority of Germany and France. He is usually referred to as Isaac Or Zaru'a, i.e., by the title of his important halakhic work. Isaac was born in Bohemia which he usually refers to as "the land of Canaan." In his youth he suffered from "poverty and wanderings" (*Or Zaru'a* pt. I, 6d), but as a result of his peregrinations he came in contact with contemporary German and French scholars, by whose teaching he was influenced. Among the scholars of Bohemia under whom he studied were Jacob b. Isaac ha-Lavan of Prague and *Abraham b. Azriel, author of *Arugat ha-Bosem*. In Regensburg he studied under Judah ben Samuel he-Ḥasid and Abraham b. Moses. His chief teachers, "on whom he waited," were, according to him, *Simḥah b. Samuel of Speyer, Eliezer b. Joel ha-Levi (the Ravyah), and *Judah b. Isaac Sir Leon of Paris. He noted their decisions and learned from their conduct and customs. In Wuerzburg he studied under Jonathan b. Isaac, and in France was a pupil of Samson of Coucy. He transmitted a ruling in the name of Samson of Coucy in connection with the decree in 1215 of Pope Innocent III compelling Jews to wear the yellow *badge (*ibid.*, pt. II *Hilkhot Shabbat* 84:3).

Isaac's monumental work *Or Zaru'a* shared the fate of similar halakhic works which were apparently not sufficiently copied because of their extensive nature, and as a result did not achieve large circulation. Only 600 years after his death were the first two parts of the work published (1862) from a manuscript in the possession of Akiva *Lehren of Amsterdam (the adventures related in connection with the manuscript are pure legend). The first part deals with blessings, laws connected with the land of Israel, *niddah* and *mikva'ot*, laws of marriage, and a collection of responsa, mostly by the author, but some by other scholars. Part II contains topics which are now included in the *Oraḥ Ḥayyim* section of the Shulḥan Arukh. Two further parts were published at a later date (1887–90) from a manuscript in the British Museum. These contain halakhic rulings derived from the tractates *Bava Kamma, Bava Meẓia, Bava Batra, Sanhedrin*, and *Avodah Zarah*. A supplement to this section, comprising decisions based on the tractate *Shevu'ot*, which had not been published in the previous collections because they were thought to pertain to tractate *Shevi'it*, was published by A. Freimann (in *Festschrift zu I. Lewy…* (1911), Heb. pt. 10–32). A number of abridgments have been made of the work, the best known of which is that by Isaac's son *Ḥayyim b. Isaac Or Zaru'a, entitled *Simanei Or Zaru'a* which achieved a wide circulation although this work too was not at the disposal of all scholars. The quotations from Isaac Or Zaru'a in the *Haggahot Asheri* of *Israel of Krems are from this abridgment. Although the work did not have a wide circulation, later authorities quote his views to a considerable extent from secondary sources, such as the *Mordecai*, the *Haggahot Maimuniyyot*, etc. The complete work constitutes a valuable collection of the halakhic rulings of German and French scholars as well as being of great value for the history of Jewish communities in Europe during the Middle Ages (for instance, he discusses whether "our brothers in Bohemia" are permitted to carry arms on the Sabbath when they have to guard the city). A great part of the work (according to Aptowitzer, a third) is derived from his teacher *Eliezer b. Joel ha-Levi, whose *Ravyah* was already available to Isaac. There is no definite information as to how the work was composed and edited, or the order in which the various parts were written. One reason pointed out by Urbach (Tosafot, 367 n. 61) is that an examination of the manuscripts indicate that the existing text is not the original. Urbach came to the conclusion that copyists made copies of the work in sections, which were subsequently combined into a unified book. The book itself was compiled over a long period, the author adding various supplements. As a result there are mutual cross references between passages and it is impossible to determine which was written first. Before compiling the book, the author made notes and assembled data which were later written up, as he himself states (*Or Zaru'a*, pt. II, no. 38). He was still engaged in its compilation in 1246 (idem, Av. Zar. no. 107).

BIBLIOGRAPHY: Gross, in: MGWJ, 20 (1871), 248–64; Wellesz, *ibid.*, 48 (1904), 129–44, 209–13, 361–71, 440–56, 710–2; idem, in: JJLG, 4 (1906), 75–124; Vogelstein, in: MGWJ, 49 (1905), 701–6; V. Aptowitzer, *Mavo le-Sefer Ravyah* (1938), 25–32; Tykocinski, in: MGWJ, 55 (1911), 478–500; idem, in: Germ Jud, 1 (1934), 400–10; Urbach, Tosafot, 359–70; Samet, in: KS, 43 (1968), 435.

[Shlomoh Zalman Havlin]

ISAAC BEN NOAH KOHEN SHAPIRA (late 16th–early 17th century), Polish rabbi and author. Isaac received his talmudic education at the yeshivah of his uncle, Ḥayyim b. Samuel, rabbi in Kremenets. At an early age he was appointed rabbi in Gorodnitsa, later serving in Mezhirech. He was the author of an alphabetically arranged compendium in rhymed verse of the four parts of the Shulḥan Arukh under the title *Sefer Zikkaron* (also called *Zikhron Dinim* or *Kiẓẓur Pirkei Dinim*, Cracow?, 1559?). He further published *Petiḥat ha-Lev* (Cracow, 1645?), kabbalistic homilies on the Pentateuch, consisting of extracts from his larger unpublished work "*Harḥavat ha-Lev*."

BIBLIOGRAPHY: Zunz, Gesch, 299; Carmoly, in: *Ha-Karmel*, 6 (1866/67), 301–2; Fuenn, Keneset, 666.

[Jacob Freimann]

ISAAC BEN SAMSON HA-KOHEN (d. 1624), talmudist of Bohemia. Isaac was born in Prague and married the daughter of *Judah Loew b. Bezalel of Prague. He served as a rabbi in Vienna and Nikolsburg, later becoming *dayyan* and leader of the Prague community. He was renowned both for his extensive talmudic knowledge and philanthropic activities. His opinions on halakhic questions, as well as his approbation of contemporary works, were widely sought. He is believed to be the author of a Yiddish translation of the Pentateuch that first appeared in Basle in 1583, or to have supplemented this work with midrashic explanations appearing for the first time in the Prague edition (1610), which contains a poem with his name in acrostics. He wrote a supplement to the *Ḥatan Damim* of Solomon *Runkel on the Pentateuch (Prague, 1606); published Isaac b. Judah ha-Levi's *Pa'ne'aḥ Raza*, with his own introduction (*ibid.*, 1607) and commentary on *Midrash Psalms, Midrash Proverbs*, and *Midrash Samuel* (*ibid.*, 1613). He edited the sermon delivered by his father-in-law on the festival of Shavuot, in Posen in 1592, entitled *Derush al ha-Torah*, adding to it notes, an index of sources, and three introductory poems (*ibid.*, 1953). He also wrote introductions to *Ḥayyim b. Bezalel's *Sefer ha-Ḥayyim* (Cracow, 1593) and to Meir of Rothenburg's responsa (Prague, 1608). A work called *Sidrei Bereshit* remained uncompleted. He accompanied his father-in-law when he was received in audience by the emperor Rudolph in 1592 and reported on the interview. His sons Ḥayyim and *Naphtali also served as rabbis; his daughter Eva married Samuel Bachrach of Worms.

BIBLIOGRAPHY: K. Lieben, *Gal Ed* (1856), no. 84 (Hebrew section); S. Buber (ed.), *Midrash Tehillim (Shoḥer Tov)* (1891), introd., 114 n.4; N. Gruen, *Der Hohe Rabbi Loew* (1895), 24, 29; E. Schulmann, *Sefat Yehudit-Ashkenazit ve-Sifrutah* (1903), 10f; I.Z. Kahana, in: *Arim ve-Immahot be-Yisrael*, 4 (1950), 262f.

[Samuel Abba Horodezky]

ISAAC BEN SAMUEL HA-LEVI (1580–1646?), Polish talmudist and grammarian. Isaac was the elder brother and teacher of *David b. Samuel ha-Levi. He was born in Ludomir, and studied under Joshua *Falk at Lemberg. He served as rabbi of Chelm and in 1627 was appointed *rosh yeshivah* in Posen. He was one of the leading talmudic scholars and sages of his generation and was recognized as a halakhic authority, linguist, and grammarian. He had a sound knowledge of geometry and of German. He was kind and never adopted a didactic attitude toward his questioners, not even to his own students. Isaac is the author of *She'elot u-Teshuvot ve-Ḥiddushei Mahari ha-Levi* (Neuwied, 1736). These show him to have been considerate, balanced in judgment, and inclining toward leniency whenever possible. In his novellae he does not hesitate to attack the views of such outstanding authorities as Solomon *Luria, Samuel *Edels, *Judah Leib b. Bezalel and Levi *Ibn Ḥabib. He possessed a concise style and penetrated to the very heart of the problems under discussion. In his halakhic decisions he takes into consideration the rules of grammar, attaching great value to a knowledge of Hebrew and its grammar. He published *Si'aḥ Yiẓḥak* (Basle, 1627) on the rules of grammar and the conjugation of the verb. To it he appended *Beit ha-Levi*, discussing all compound and doubtful words in the Bible. In its introduction, Isaac complained of "the lack of attention paid to the knowledge of Hebrew. Its study is neglected and its origins are not investigated." He pointed out that the meanings of some words were not known because even scholars had no knowledge of the conjugation being used. Instead of devoting themselves to a thorough study of grammar, they disparaged it as being a mere routine task, requiring no intelligence. Even were this so, he writes, it is still a highly skilled accomplishment, essential for all scholarship, and a prerequisite for all sacred study, since, without it, no one can write or speak Hebrew correctly. The book carried an approbation by Yom Tov Lipman Heller, and was highly praised by Samuel David *Luzzatto. An abbreviated edition, *Derekh Si'aḥ* (Frankfurt, 1693), was published by J.L. Oppenheim. A poem of Isaac's, *Shir Ge'ulim*, commemorating the freeing of Lemberg Synagogue from the hands of the Jesuits, was published in 1609. He left an unpublished manuscript, *Elleh Toledot Yiẓḥak*, a supercommentary on Rashi. Many of his ideas and opinions are incorporated in his brother's *Turei Zahav* and one of his responsa in *Bayit Ḥadash he-Ḥadash* (Korzec, 1785), no. 78. In the 1646 edition of *Turei Zahav* he is referred to as being no longer alive.

BIBLIOGRAPHY: Fuenn, Keneset, 628–9; H.N. Dembitzer, *Kelilat Yofi*, 1 (1888), 50; S. Buber, *Anshei Shem* (1895), 114–5; S.M. Chones, *Toledot ha-Posekim* (1910), 561; S.D. Luzzatto, *Prolegomeni ad una grammatica ragionata della lingua ebraica* (1836), 60; M. Steinschneider, *Jewish Literature* (1857), 240.

[Abram Juda Goldrat]

ISAAC BEN SAMUEL OF ACRE (late 13th–mid-14th century), kabbalist. In his youth Isaac of Acre studied in the yeshivah of Solomon Petit in Acre and he quotes Petit's story in which Aristotle is ridiculed by the wife of Alexander the Great. In 1291 Isaac left Acre for Italy, traveling from there to Spain (where he apparently arrived in 1305). There he met numerous kabbalists and he quotes many of their writings. Of great importance was his meeting with *Moses b. Shem Tov de Leon, whom he questioned concerning the *Zohar – asking whether it had been written by *Simeon b. Yoḥai or whether it was Moses de Leon's own work. Even after the death of Moses de Leon, Isaac continued his investigations, which he described in *Divrei ha-Yamim* (see below). Isaac was close to the circle of Solomon b. Abraham *Adret, but his knowledge of Adret's kabbalistic writings was vague and his testimony should be treated with great reservation. At least three statements which he attributes to Adret were made by *Ezra and *Azriel of Gerona.

Four of Isaac's works have been preserved:

(1) *Me'irat Einayim*, a major commentary on Naḥmanides' mysticism, incorporating a large collection of writings from the Gerona circle and other groups which are not part of his explications of Naḥmanides. Isaac criticizes commentators who discovered ideas in Naḥmanides' writings which were far from the intention of the author – yet he himself deliberately does the same. *Me'irat Einayim* contains references to books and personalities otherwise unknown. Many copies of the work are in existence. Considerable use was made of it by the kabbalists of the 15th and 16th centuries and it has also been an important source for scholars of the 19th and 20th centuries.

(2) *Oẓar Ḥayyim*, a kind of mystical diary of visions and revelations; not an intimate diary, but one written with the object of describing revelations to the reader. Dealing with the *ẓerufim* ("combinations") which he considers essential for prophecy, he sets store on visions, thoughts, and automatic utterances. Most of his revelations came while he was in a state of trance, and many things were revealed through his dreams. Isaac was especially interested in outlining the way to attain prophecy, a subject he had already treated at length in *Me'irat Einayim*. He notes three states in the ladder of ascent leading to the Holy Spirit:

(a) devotion, which means the performance of two actions, one visual. In his mind's eye man sees the letters of YHWH "as if they were written before him in a book," while at the same time he concentrates his thoughts on the aspect of the Divinity, called by the kabbalists **Ein-Sof* ("the infinite"); (b) indifference, i.e., acquiesence in any occurrence in earthly life, except that which is concerned with the Divinity. Only a man who has reached this level of indifference, who is insensitive to the honor or scorn with which men regard him, is able to reach the state in which his soul becomes one with the Divinity; (c) solitude – a complete emptying of the mind of any matter which is not divine. The central focus of Isaac's prophetic ideal is individual spirituality. He applies sayings from the realm of national redemption to the realm of the redemption of the soul, and considers that the public mission of the prophet hampers his intimate contact with the Divinity. The work remains almost in entirety in Ms. 775 of the Guenzburg Collection, Moscow. Selections from it are in *Leket Shoshannim* (Neubauer, Cat, no. 1911). Many extracts are found in various manuscripts (Sassoon Ms. 919, Adler Ms. 1589, et al.).

(3) A commentary on the *Sefer* **Yeẓirah* (ch. 1 only), published by G. *Scholem (KS, vol. 31, 1955/56).

(4) A shortened free translation of the Arabic commentary of Judah b. Nissim ibn Malka on **Pirkei deRabbi Eliezer.* Isaac's comments occupy the main place in the work, which is to be found in Sassoon manuscript 919b.

There is evidence that other works by Isaac also existed, the most important being *Sefer ha-Yamim*, as it is called in *Sefer ha-Yuḥasin* which quotes the large section concerning the composition of the Zohar. No other author who quotes from *Sefer ha-Yamim* is known, but there is no doubt that such a book did exist, since Isaac himself refers to it in his *Oẓar Ḥayyim*, where he calls it *Sefer Divrei ha-Yamim*. Sachs' description of manuscript 775 in the Guenzburg collection led to the belief that this was *Sefer ha-Yamim*, but apparently this is not so. There are no means of knowing from which works the author of *Reshit Ḥokhmah* took the four quotations which he cites in the name of Isaac of Acre. Similarly the nature of the mystical book mentioned in *Novelot Ḥokhmah* by Joseph Solomon *Delmedigo of Candia is not known. David Azulai writes that he saw treatises of Isaac of Acre, according to which he was visited by angels who revealed to him secrets and acts of practical Kabbalah. It is possible that the reference was to the treatises of *Oẓar Ḥayyim*, but this is not certain.

BIBLIOGRAPHY: Graetz-Rabbinowitz, index; A. Jellinek, *Beitraege zur Geschichte der Kabbala* (1852), 72 (Ger. pt.); vi (Heb. pt.); G. Scholem, in: KS, 2 (1926), 102–3; 31 (1955/56), 379–96; idem, in: *Tarbiz*, 3 (1931/32), 59–61; idem, *Ursprung und Anfaenge der Kabbala* (1962), index; idem, in: *Madda'ei ha-Yahadut*, 1 (1920), 17ff.; E. Gottlieb, *Fourth World Congress of Jewish Studies*, 2 (1969), 327–34; idem, *Ha-Kabbalah be-Khitvei R. Baḥya b. Asher* (1970), index; G. Vajda, in: REJ, 115 (1956), 27–71.

[Efraim Gottlieb]

ISAAC BEN SAMUEL OF DAMPIERRE (usually referred to by the initial letters of his name as **Ri** (initials of **R**abbi **I**saac) or **Ri the Elder**, or **Ri of Dampierre**, d. c. 1185), one of the most important of the *tosafists and leading authority of Franco-German Jewry in the second half of the 12th century. Isaac was the nephew and pupil of Jacob *Tam. His father was the son of Simḥah b. Samuel of Vitry, and his wife the daughter of Judah b. Yom Tov, great-grandson of *Rashi. He was thus related to the distinguished Jewish families of scholars and communal leaders of his time. He lived in Ramerupt for many years, accompanying his teacher, Jacob Tam, and helping him with his ramified correspondence. After R. Tam left Ramerupt, Isaac went to live in Dampierre. For some time he also lived in Joinville. Even after leaving his teacher, Isaac regarded himself as completely subordinate to R. Tam until his death, and rarely deviated from his rulings. Together with R. Tam, he is the central pillar of the entire *tosafot* activity, there being hardly a page of the printed *tosafot* where he is not mentioned. His *tosafot* have not survived in their original form except for fragments in some manuscripts and quotations in the works of the *rishonim*. His teachings were interwoven in the published *tosafot*, being handed down by a line of his pupils. Ḥ.J.D. *Azulai still had Isaac's *tosafot* to *Kiddushin* and quotes them in his *Petaḥ Einayim*. However the commentary published in the editions of the Talmud on *Kiddushin* with the title *Perush Ri ha-Zaken* is not by Isaac but by *Abraham b. Isaac of Montpellier. Especially abundant use of Isaac's *tosafot* was made by his pupil, *Samson b. Abraham of Sens, who based his own *tosafot* on them. Another important source for his teachings is the *Haggahot Asheri* of *Israel of Krems. There are historical testimonies (see introduction to the *Ẓeidah la-Derekh* of *Menahem b. Aaron ibn Zeraḥ, as well as a tradition cited by Solomon *Luria in the introduction to his *Yam shel Shelomo* on tractate *Ḥullin*) to the effect that the school of Isaac was the main creative center in which the *tosafot* were developed as a system of study and as a literary genre, and it was there that the system of study whose foundations had been laid by Rashi's sons-in-law reached its peak.

Many of Isaac's responsa are preserved in the works of the *rishonim*. These contain historical and cultural material of great value for a knowledge of the internal lives of the Jews and their relations with their neighbors. Despite his central position in the Jewish world of his time, his responsa lack the note of polemic, controversy, and vehemence that characterizes the responsa of the great tosafists, particularly of R. Tam. Great humility and an exceptionally gentle approach are especially conspicuous. His piety and uprightness were renowned and already in the 14th century there was a legend that he had ascended on high and received information from the angels. A tendency toward mysticism is discernible in his writings, and it is possible that he was in contact with *Samuel, the father of *Judah ben Samuel he-Ḥasid. *Elhanan b. Yakar of London, who wrote a commentary on the *Sefer Yeẓirah* (published by Vajda in *Koveẓ al Yad*, 6 pt. 1 (1966), 147–97) in the succeeding generation, quotes statements he heard in his name. Among his important pupils were *Abraham b. Nathan ha-Yarḥi, who acted as the intermediary between him and *Asher b. Meshullam of Lunel, and his own son *Elhanan who died during his father's lifetime. Noteworthy among his other pupils, all of whom were important tosafists, are *Baruch b. Isaac of Worms, *Isaac b. Abraham, and the above-mentioned Samson of Sens. Isaac's rulings were also known to the early scholars and manuscripts of them are still extant. His *Hilkhot ha-Get*, which he apparently composed toward the end of his life, has recently been published (Kupfer, in *Koveẓ al-Yad*, 6 pt. 1 (1966), 123–44). It is very doubtful whether he wrote a commentary on the *Hilkhot ha-Rif* of Isaac *Alfasi, its ascription to him being due to a printer's error (Responsa of the Rosh (Asher b. Jehiel), Kelal 85, no. 10 (ed. Zolkiew, 1803), 84b).

BIBLIOGRAPHY: A. Aptowitzer, *Mavo le-Sefer Ravyah* (1938), 379–81; Assaf, in: *A. Marx Jubilee Volume* (1950), 9–22 (Heb. section); Benedikt, in: KS, 28 (1952–53), 227–9; Urbach, Tosafot, 195–211, 460ff.; idem, in: *Sefer Assaf* (1953), 18–32; Kupfer, in: *Koveẓ al-Yad*, 6 pt. 1 (1966), 123–44.

[Israel Moses Ta-Shma]

ISAAC BEN SHESHET PERFET (known as **Ribash** from the initials of **R**abbi **I**saac **B**en **Sh**eshet; 1326–1408), Spanish rabbi and halakhic authority. Perfet was born in Barcelona, where he studied under such eminent scholars as *Perez ha-Kohen, Ḥasdai b. Judah Crescas (the grandfather of the philosopher), and *Nissim b. Reuben Gerondi, and where he later acted unofficially as rabbi. In 1370, Isaac, together with Nissim and five other Jewish notables, was arrested on a false charge and imprisoned for several months. After acquittal, he moved to Saragossa, where he accepted the position of rabbi, only to be involved in the first of the many controversies and family tragedies that were to embitter his career. In Saragossa he made strenuous efforts to secure the abolition of certain objectionable customs. He did not succeed, but brought upon himself the opposition of the local scholars. Finally he decided to leave for Calatayud but was persuaded to change his mind. Faced with continued disharmony in the community, he moved to Valencia, where from 1385 he acted as rabbi.

The anti-Jewish riots of 1391 drove him to North Africa. A close reading of the Valencia court records reveals that the authorities asked Perfet to convert as a way to stop the riots. After he refused, they trumped up a charge against him that would have resulted in his death unless he converted. This time Perfet relented and he converted, thereby becoming a Marrano. He was baptized on July 4, 1391, which was the Ninth of Av. A year and a half later, he managed to leave Valencia for North Africa and resume his life as a Jew. A number of his responsa deal with the issue of those compelled to convert to Christianity. After a short stay at Miliana, he finally settled in Algiers, where he was enthusiastically welcomed. Fresh vexations awaited him; however, as another refugee, jealous of Isaac's prestige, launched a violent campaign against the newcomer in the hope that he would leave Algiers. Thanks to the intervention of *Saul Astruc ha-Kohen, the civil authorities put an end to the conflict by appointing Isaac *dayyan* or communal rabbi. Their action, however, antagonized a celebrated refugee from Majorca, Simeon b. Ẓemaḥ *Duran, who declared the appointment invalid, no government having the power of jurisdiction in Jewish communal affairs. Duran relented when he was convinced that Isaac harbored no thoughts of personal aggrandizement, and the latter was left free to enjoy general affection and respect in his last years. On the anniversary of his death pilgrimages were made to his tomb until recent years.

Perfet's most important work is his responsa (Constantinople, 1546). They exercised considerable influence on subsequent *halakhah*, and were one of the pillars upon which the Shulḥan Arukh rested. They contain a vast amount of halakhic material – part derived from sources which are no longer extant – together with much valuable information about popular customs in Spain and North Africa. The collection is of very great importance for knowledge of the history of the Jews in those countries in the 14th century. Perfet was involved as a halakhist and decisor in the great controversy connected with the French chief rabbinate (see *Trèves (Trier)); he was one of the first to discuss the status of *Marranos from the halakhic point of view, which had become one of the crucial problems of Spanish and North African Judaism. He was one of those who established the *minhag* of Algiers regarding the financial rights connected with matrimonial law. Perfet recognized five categories of *minhag*: (a) Those acts that are halakhically acceptable but deemed prohibited by custom, thus creating a defensive "fence" around the Torah; (b) those acts that are halakhically acceptable but which certain communities deemed prohibited by custom; (c) a prohibitive custom based on one opinion in a rabbinic dispute; (d) those behaviors that are not customs but for which the sages avowed that whoever acts in such a way will be blessed; and (e) when a person errs thinking that what he does is correct. Perfet argued that one cannot change the custom in categories (a) through (c). However, the last two categories do not constitute *minhag* and can therefore be changed. On three occasions, Perfet accepted customs based on Islamic customs (see responsa nos. 94, 158, 102, and 148). In each case, the practice was not in violation of *halakhah* and thus acceptable.

Perfet also wrote an extensive commentary on several talmudic tractates, and a commentary on the Pentateuch. Poems and *kinot* composed by him were published in *Ẓafenat Pa'ne'aḥ* (1895). His work shows some knowledge of philosophy, even though he opposed its study and regarded the philosophical preoccupations of *Maimonides and *Levi b. Gershom with misgiving. He also dissociated himself from the Kabbalah. The responsa *She'elot u-Teshuvot ha-Ribash ha-Ḥadashot* (Munkacs, 1901) are not all his.

BIBLIOGRAPHY: A.M. Hershman, *Rabbi Isaac bar Sheshet Perfet and his Times* (1943), Hebrew edition (1956); H.J. Zimmels, *Marranen in der rabbinischen Literatur* (1932), 24, 91ff.; Baer, Spain, index; I. Epstein, Responsa of R. Simon b. Zemach Duran (1930), index. **ADD. BIBLIOGRAPHY:** J. Slotnik, "Rabbi Yizhak bar Sheshet – ha-Rivash" (diss., Touro, 2001); D. Yarden, in: *Sefer Zikaron le-Yizhak Ben-Zvi* 1 (1964); M. Slay, in: *Shanah be-Shanah* (1971), 226–36; idem, in: *Maḥanayim*, 1 (1991), 158–61; Z. Rayrah, in: *Sefunot*, 17 (1983), 11–20; M. Kellner, in: *Tradition*, 15 (1975), 110–18; E. Seroussi, at: http://research.umbc.edu.

[Hirsch Jacob Zimmels / David Derovan (2nd ed.)]

ISAAC BEN SOLOMON (1755–1826), prominent *Karaite scholar and spiritual leader from Chufut-Qaleh, a reformer of the Karaite calendar system, and authority on religious law. He was a disciple of Isaac ben Joseph *Kalfa. At the age of 17 he worked for Benjamin *Aga and went with him to St. Petersburg. After returning to Chufut-Qaleh he engaged in commerce but went bankrupt. In 1776 he was appointed by Benjamin Aga to teach at the school in Chufut-Qaleh and soon was appointed as a *hakham* of the community at the age of 21. In 1795 he traveled with Benjamin Aga and some other community leaders to St. Petersburg with a special mission to the government, which achieved exemption for Crimean

Karaites from the double taxation imposed on all the Jews of the Russian Empire, and the attainment of other rights. Isaac was a physician, who cured Jews and non-Jews of Chufut-Qaleh and the surrounding area. He had a wide knowledge of astronomy, which he studied for six months during his stay in St. Petersburg. In 1806 he was one of the founders of a publishing house in Chufut-Qaleh. He read proofs of Karaite books and prayer books that were printed there and sometimes added introductions to them. Isaac was a prominent religious authority in his generation, establishing several new regulations of Karaite *halakhah*: He forbade the ritual purification of golden and silver vessels without passing them through fire; forbade moving things in the public domain on Shabbat; permitted weddings during the Ten Days of Penitence and so on. His most important innovation was calendar reform (1779). It was an attempt to establish a uniform permanent system of calendation among the Karaites, which was not based on observation. It was supported by most scholars in Crimea and some other communities. His initiative led to a fierce dispute among the communities of Constantinople and the Crimea that lasted 18 years. The opposition to this reform was headed by *Benjamin ben Elijah Duwan, a Karaite leader from Evpatoria. In 1781 Benjamin Duwan came to Chufut-Qaleh at the head of a group of Karaite worthies of his town in order to conduct a debate with Isaac ben Solomon. According to Isaac's report, Benjamin was defeated, and Isaac's calendar calculation was supported by the majority. His book *Or ha-Levana* (Zhitomir 1872) is a detailed exposition of his calendar reform. Isaac also wrote the following works: *Iggeret Pinnat Yiqrat* (Evpatoria 1834), a theological treatise based on the ten principles of faith formulated by Elijah *Bashyazi in *Adderet Eliyahu* (with a Tatar translation of the principles; Nemoy published an English abridged translation of the work, with a detailed appraisal [see bibl.]); it includes many refutations ("replies") of philosophical positions, in which he actually criticized Bashyazi for his theological innovations; *Moladot* – lunar calculations for 34 years for the years 1806–40 (Chufut-Qaleh, 1806) and a commentary on the Song of Songs (Ms B 316 at the St. Petersburg Institute of Oriental Studies of the Russian Academy). He also wrote many liturgical poems, which were included in the Karaite *Siddur*. Many letters, responsa, and short treatises by him are preserved in manuscripts the St. Petersburg Institute of Oriental Studies of the Russian Academy and the Russian National Library.

BIBLIOGRAPHY: G. Akhiezer, in: M. Polliack (ed.), *Karaite Judaism* (2003), 740–2, and index; E. Deinard, *Massa Krim* (1878), 70; R. Fahn, *Sefer ha-Kara'im* (1929), 79–81; J. Mann, Texts, 2, (1935), index; L. Nemoy, in: JQR, 80:1–2 (1989), 49–85.

[Golda Akhiezer (2nd ed.)]

ISAAC BEN TODROS (mid-fourteenth century), known as **Isaac Tauroci (ben Todros)** in Latin; French physician. Isaac ben Todros practiced in Carpentras and audited the accounts of the Jewish community in 1367. He was the pupil of the astronomer, Emmanuel b. Jacob *Bonfils, with whom he calculated the constellations in Avignon during the month of Nisan (April) 1373. Isaac possessed a profound knowledge of theology and philosophy. He wrote a work dealing with the plague in Avignon entitled *Be'er la-Ḥai* ("Source of Life"). This work included a study of the dietetics and the therapeutics of the sick, as well as of the healthy. He declared that there were many Jewish victims of the epidemic. This treatise was published by Baron David *Guenzburg from the only existing Hebrew manuscript on the occasion of the 90th birthday of Leopold *Zunz. Isaac also wrote another medical work on facial convulsion (*Avit ha-Panim*; Oxford, Bodleian Library, Heb. Ms. 2141, 31).

BIBLIOGRAPHY: E. Wickersheimer, *Dictionnaire Biographique des Médecins en France au Moyen Age* (1936), 311f.; Kaufmann, Schriften, 3 (1915), 482–6.

[Isidore Simon]

ISAAC BEN TODROS OF BARCELONA (c. end of the 13th, beginning of the 14th century), Spanish talmudist, a pupil of Naḥmanides. Isaac occupied himself with the *Kabbalah to a considerable extent. No biographical details of him are known. His signature appears on the well-known ban on the study of philosophy promulgated in Barcelona in 1305 (Responsa Rashba 1, nos. 415–6). He was the author of a commentary to the *maḥzor*, remnants of which were discovered by G. Scholem in manuscript (H. Zotenberg, *Catalogues des manuscrits* (1866), 839:11); a commentary to the **seliḥot* (M. Steinschneider, *Die hebraeischen Handschriften... in Muenchen* (1895²), 237); a commentary to the **azharot* of Solomon ibn Gabirol (see bibl. Freimann, introd. 10 (99), n. 45). The work *Be'er la-Ḥai* edited by D. Guenzburg (in: Jubelschrift... L. Zunz; 1884) is not by him (see Freimann p. 11). E. Gottlieb too has shown that the ascription of the commentary on the *Ginnat ha-Bitan* attributed to Isaac is a forgery. Among his pupils were *Shem Tov Gaon b. Abraham who describes his relation with his teacher in the introduction to his *Keter Shem Tov* (not in the printed edition but in the Ms., see bibl., Loewinger, p. 30 and Gottlieb, p. 65). His kabbalistic teachings are included in the works of Naḥmanides' disciples, e.g., *Ibn Shuaib's commentary to the *Sodot ha-Ramban*, Meir b. Solomon Abi *Sahula, *Keter Shem Tov, Me'irat Einayim*, and *Ma'arekhet ha-Elohut*.

BIBLIOGRAPHY: Nathan b. Judah, *Sefer ha-Maḥkim*, ed. by J. Freimann (1909), introd. 9–11 (= *Ha-Eshkol*, 6 (1909), 98–100); Loewinger, in: *Sefunot*, 7 (1963), 11, 27, 38; Gottlieb, in: *Studies in Mysticism and Religion Presented to Gershom G. Scholem* (1967), Heb. pt. 63–86.

[Shlomoh Zalman Havlin]

ISAAC BEN YAKAR (12th century), *paytan*. In two acrostics of his *seliḥot* Isaac adds to his signature *yeled meshu'sha* and in two other acrostics, *millul*. The first designation is probably an allusion to his family name (according to Jer. 31:33), while the second seems to indicate his place of residence. *Gross reads מלוך (*milokh*) for מלול (*millul*) having in mind a French village, probably Luc in the Pyrenees; Lille could hardly have been meant. Six of Isaac's *seliḥot*, with the complete acrostic of his name, are extant; three have appeared in print, among them a very ingeniously constructed *seliḥah*, *Ḥatanu*, consisting only of "ring" words. One of the remaining three *seliḥot* was rendered into German by *Zunz.

BIBLIOGRAPHY: Zunz, Poesie, 90, 110, 251, 271; Zunz, Lit Poesie, 268f., 618; Steinschneider, Kat. Hamburg, 51:134; Ziemlich, in: MWJ, 12 (1885), 137; Fuenn, Keneset, 1 (1886), 615; Davidson, Oẓar, 4 (1933), 419; Gross, Gal Jud, 275f.; D. Goldschmidt, *Seliḥot... Lita* (1965), 228–31, 247–50.

ISAAC THE BLIND (**"Sagi Nahor"**; c. 1160–1235), a central figure among early kabbalists, the son of *Abraham b. David of Posquières. He was usually referred to as "He-Ḥasid" and *Baḥya b. Asher called him "the father of Kabbalah." No biographical facts or details of his life are available, but apparently he lived in Posquières for a time. His name meant hardly anything to 19th century Kabbalah scholars; so little was known of his personality or his work that several incorrect conclusions were drawn about him; for example, that he was the author of Sefer ha-*Bahir (Landauer). In fact, a considerable amount of information concerning Isaac can be gleaned from traditions preserved among his disciples and their disciples, as well as from his pamphlets and those fragments of his other writings that have been preserved.

The question of whether he was born blind remains undecided. His direct disciples do not mention his blindness, but a kabbalistic tradition from the 13th century testifies that "his eyes never saw anything during his lifetime" (*Me'irat Einayim*, Munich Ms. 17, 140b). Several fragments of his writings contain long discussions on the mysticism of lights and colors, which might seem to refute the assumption that he was born blind, but most of his mysticism is not essentially visual. However, as it appears that he was well-versed in books and even states, "this I found in an ancient manuscript," it is possible that he became blind only after reaching maturity.

Shem Tov b. Abraham ibn Gaon (1287–1330) mentions that Isaac could sense "in the feeling of the air" whether a person would live or die (Recanati, *Perush la-Torah, Ki-Teẓe*), and "whether his soul was among the new [meaning that it had not undergone transmigration] or among the old" (*ibid., Va-Yeshev*). To his mystical powers should be added testimonies that he had received "the revelation of Elijah," and magical power in prayer (*ibid., Ki-Teẓe*).

The fragments of his writings about *kavvanah* ("intention") and the various forms of meditation which should be employed in different prayers are constructed on a complete system of the *Sefirot*, the attributes of God, which emanated from Ancient Divine Thought (*Maḥashavah*) as found in *Sefer ha-Bahir*. Isaac speaks of three levels within the Divine: **Ein-Sof*, *Maḥashavah* ("Thought"), and *Dibbur* ("Speech"). His views on *Ein-Sof* or "the Cause of Thought" avoid any positive attributes or personal characteristics and are intentionally couched in unclear, vague language. *Ein-Sof* is "that which cannot be conceived of through thought" or the "annihilation of thought," a realm which is mysterious and transcendent even in relation to Divine Thought itself (which is a certain kind of revelation). In contrast with his brief discussion of the *Ein-Sof*, Isaac deals at length with the first *Sefirah, Maḥashavah*. It appears that he based his system on the theory that *Maḥashavah* should not be included among the ten *Sefirot*, and he adds, in order to complete the number of *Sefirot*, *Haskel* (the "Intellect") – the hypostasis of the intellectual act – placed between the levels of *Maḥashavah* and *Ḥokhmah* ("Wisdom"). The Divine Will, as a force which activates thought and is superior to it, is absent from his system. Thought is the sphere with which every mystic aspires to unite and thence derive sustenance, the object of *kavvanah* around which the religious aspiration is centered. Thought is the revelation of the hidden God; it is called the *Ayin* ("Nothingness," a paradoxical appellation which is used as a symbol of the first emanation). Nothingness symbolizes the higher existence of the Divine in its most hidden manifestation, as well as the annihilation of human thought which desires to contemplate it.

The world of *Dibbur* begins with the *Sefirah Ḥokhmah*. Isaac often uses the concept *devarim* ("words") or *dibburim* ("speeches" or *logoi*; in the language of *Sefer ha-Bahir, ma'amarot*, "sayings") as a synonym for *Sefirot*. This outlook, which underlies Isaac's system, views the development of the world as a linguistic development, the Creator's expression in His language. He sees the materialization of the Divine Speech in all areas of creation. The apparent letters are nothing but a manifestation of the inner letters by which the Divine Words came into being, and they are the bases of the world.

The *Sefirot* are not only attributes of God but are the principles of the world outside the world of the *Sefirot*, which is called the *olam ha-nifradim* ("world of the separables," in the sense of the world of multiple being). There is a continuous stream of emanation from the Divine Transcendence to the "world of the separables"; Isaac's main aim was to show the way (by contemplation, intention, and devotion) to communication with the world of the Divine Attributes. This is the secret of the whole Torah and of prayer. The internal connection between all essences and stages of creation is *ẓepiyyah* ("contemplation"). All things contemplate one another and are connected with one another, and there thus exists a universal dialectical process of emanation and spreading out to the limit of lower existence on the one hand, and contemplating upward (*teshuvah*, "repentance") on the other. The return of things to their origins is an ontological process from unity to plurality and vice versa which exists in every moment of creation and it contains within itself an eschatological significance, for creation is seen as an act of contemplation by God within Himself, and finally a return to the source.

Isaac's writings include commentary to *Sefer Yeẓirah* (many Mss.; first published by G. Scholem at the end of *Ha-Kabbalah be-Provence*, 1963); a mystic treatise on sacrifice (several Mss.); commentary on the beginning of *Midrash*

Konen (Ms.; New York, Jewish Theological Seminary); letter to Naḥmanides and Jonah Gerondi (in *Sefer Bialik* (1934), 143–4); detailed instructions on meditation in prayer (*Reshit ha-Kabbalah* (1948), 245–8).

BIBLIOGRAPHY: G. Scholem, *Reshit ha-Kabbalah* (1948), 99–126; idem, in: *Sefer Bialik* (1934), 141–55; idem in: KS, 6 (1929/30), 389, 398–400; idem in: MGWJ, 78 (1934), 496–503; idem, *Ursprung und Anfaenge der Kabbala* (1962), index; Scholem, Mysticism, index; I. Tishby, in: *Zion*, 9 (1944), 180–2; idem, *Perush ha-Aggadot le-Rabbi Azriel* (1945), 136; Ch. Wirszubski, in: *Tarbiz*, 27 (1957/58), 257–64; A. Jellinek, *Ginzei Ḥokhmat ha-Kabbalah* (1853), 4–5; A.B. Gottlober, *Toledot ha-Kabbalah ve-ha-Ḥasidut* (1869), 64–65.

[Esther (Zweig) Liebes]

ISAAC FROM OURVILLE (second half of the 13th century), rabbinic author. No biographical details are known of him. According to Gross, he originated from Ourville in Normandy, but Schwarzfuchs is of the opinion that the town of Orville on the border of the Champagne district north of Dijon is more probable. Isaac studied under Ḥayyim of Blois. He wrote a halakhic work called *Sefer ha-Menahel* which is no longer extant; however, extracts from it appear in the *Kol Bo* and the *Orḥot Ḥayyim*. The *Kol Bo* has a section (no. 143) headed: "The Laws of Isaac, of blessed memory, author of the *Menahel*." There have also been published: "Ancient **ḥaramot* of Rabbenu *Gershom, copied from the *Sefer ha-Menahel* of Isaac of Ourville" (Schwarzfuchs, see bibl.). Some (including Rapoport and Hurwitz) have tried to identify him with the Isaac b. Durbal mentioned in the *Maḥzor Vitry* who was a pupil of Jacob *Tam. However, there is no basis for such identification, which would be impossible.

BIBLIOGRAPHY: Rapoport, in: *Kerem Ḥemed*, 3 (1838), 200 n.; Jacob Kopel Levy, in: *Shomer Ẓiyyon ha-Ne'eman*, no. 11 (5 Kislev, 1847), 22; J. Hurwitz (ed.), *Maḥzor Vitry* (1923²), 36 (introd.); Berliner, *ibid.*, 177; Gross, Gal Jud, 27f.; Schwarzfuchs, in: REJ, 115 (1956), 109–16; idem, in: *Bar Ilan, Sefer ha-Shanah*, 4–5 (1967), 214.

[Shlomoh Zalman Havlin]

ISAAC NAPPAḤA (third century), Palestinian *amora*. A R. Isaac, without epithet, is frequently mentioned in the Babylonian and Palestinian Talmuds and in the Midrashim. There was another contemporary scholar called Isaac Nappaḥa (i.e., "the smith") who is mentioned in the Babylonian Talmud and in the late Midrashim. Many of the sayings quoted in one source in the name of Isaac are attributed in the parallel passages to Isaac Nappaḥa, and most scholars regard the Isaac without qualification to be Isaac Nappaḥa (for the name of his father, see the vague tradition at the bottom of Pes. 113b, Dik. Sof., *ibid.*, and Rabbenu Hananel and the commentators). Isaac studied under R. Johanan in Tiberias and transmitted many statements in his name in *halakhah* and in *aggadah*. He was highly regarded by his colleagues and Resh Lakish once remarked with reference to the explanation of a verse on which R. Johanan and R. Isaac differed: "The interpretation of the smith [Isaac] is better than that of the son of the smith" (i.e., Johanan; Sanh. 96a). He also transmitted sayings in the names of Resh Lakish and R. Eleazar (Av. Zar. 14a, 70b), and was an older colleague of *Ammi and *Assi (BK 60b). He also served as *dayyan* and halakhic authority in Tiberias and Caesarea together with Ammi, *Abbahu and *Ḥanina b. Pappa (BK 117b; Ned. 57b). He was one of the **neḥutei* who brought teachings of Ereẓ Israel to Babylonia (Er. 27a; et al.), and similarly transmitted some of the teachings of the Babylonian scholars, Rav and R. Judah (Ber. 43a; TJ, Shevu. 4:1, 35c). There is mention of his preaching in the house of the exilarch (MK 24b) and disputing with Naḥman b. Jacob (Ber. 7b), R. Ḥisda, and R. Sheshet (Ber. 27a; Shab. 43b).

Many Babylonian *amoraim* transmit *halakhah* and *aggadah* in his name. On one of his visits to Babylon Isaac was the guest of R. Naḥman. When he was about to take his departure Naḥman requested Isaac to bless him. He replied with a parable: "A man was once journeying in the desert. He was hungry, weary, and thirsty, and chanced across a tree whose fruits were sweet, its shade pleasant, and a stream of water flowed beneath it… When he was about to resume his journey he said: 'Tree, with what shall I bless thee?… That thy fruits be sweet? They are sweet already; that thy shade be pleasant? It is already pleasant; that a stream of water should flow beneath thee? It already flows beneath thee; I pray that all the shoots planted from you be like you'" (Ta'an. 5b). Isaac was renowned both as a halakhist and an aggadist, and the following story is told. Once Ammi and Assi were sitting before him. One of them asked him to expound a *halakhah* and the other an *aggadah*. "He commenced an *aggadah* but was prevented by the one, and when he commenced a *halakhah* he was prevented by the other. He said to them: This may be compared to a man who has two wives, one young and one old. The young one used to pluck out the white hairs to make him appear young and the old one his black ones, to make him appear old. He thus became completely bald" (BK 60b). He devoted himself, however, particularly to the *aggadah* and is numbered among the most important aggadists. He saw in it a means of encouraging the people during the difficult period through which they were passing, as is evident from his saying (PdRK 101): "In the past when money was plentiful people used to crave to hear the words of the Mishnah and the Talmud. Now that money is in short supply and moreover we suffer from the government, people crave to hear the words of Scripture and of the *aggadah*." It was his custom to give an introduction to the homilies he delivered in public and the expression, "Isaac opened (i.e., "his discourse")" is frequently found (see Gen. R. 1:7; et al.). He interlaced his homilies with parables and proverbs and engaged much in biblical exposition. His *aggadah* reflects contemporary events (e.g., Meg. 6a).

The following are some of Isaac's sayings: "If you see fortune favoring the wicked, do not contend with him" (Ber. 7b); "a man should always divide his wealth in three parts, [investing] one in land, one in merchandise, and [keeping] one ready to hand" (BM 42a); "if a man says to you: 'I have labored and not found,' believe him not; 'I have not labored, yet found,' believe him not; 'I have labored and found,' believe him" (Meg. 6b); "a leader should not be appointed over the community without the approval of the community" (Ber. 55a). He was opposed to those who took vows to abstain from permitted worldly pleasures, saying of them: "Are not those things forbidden by the Torah enough, without you wanting to add to them?" (TJ, Ned. 9:1, 41b).

BIBLIOGRAPHY: Hyman, Toledot, 782–4, 800–2; Bacher, Pal Amor, 2 (1896), 205–95; Z.W. Rabinowitz, *Sha'arei Torat Bavel* (1961), 457–8.

[Yitzhak Dov Gilat]

ISAAC OF CHERNIGOV (12th century), one of the first rabbinical scholars in Eastern Europe. Originating from Chernigov, Ukraine, Isaac toured the Jewish communities in Western Europe, and probably also reached England. In rabbinical literature he is also mentioned as Isaac (b. Ezekiel) of Russia, a disciple of R. *Judah he-Ḥasid.

BIBLIOGRAPHY: HḤY, 13 (1929), 224; S.D. Luzzatto, in: *Kerem Ḥemed*, 7 (1843), 69; A.A. Harkavy, *Ha-Yehudim u-Sefat ha-Slavim* (1867), 14, 62; J. Jacobs (ed.), *Jews of Angevin England* (1893), 66, 73.

[Yehuda Slutsky]

ISAAC OF EVREUX (first half of 13th century), brother of *Moses and Samuel of *Evreux, the three of whom were referred to as "the scholars of Evreux." Their well-known school in Evreux, Normandy, was attended by students from various countries, including Spain; among them were some, such as Jonah *Gerondi, who were to become the leading scholars of the next generation. Greater freedom in teaching than was customary at the time was one of the characteristics of the school, the pupils being permitted to study independently and even to disagree with their teachers, provided they produced proof for their statements. Isaac was apparently the youngest of the brothers. His teachings are interwoven with those of his brothers in the collections of *tosafot* that emanated from their school, known among early scholars as *Shitot me-Evreux* ("Opinions of Evreux"). His commentaries on several tractates are also quoted in the printed *tosafot*. According to Urbach, the printed *tosafot* to tractate *Nazir* were edited by Isaac, and those to *Kiddushin* by one of his pupils; while those to *Nedarim* are based upon the *tosafot* of Evreux.

BIBLIOGRAPHY: Urbach, Tosafot, 397–8, 493–5, 519–20; Y. Lipschitz (ed.), Tosafot Evreux (1969), 32–4.

[Israel Moses Ta-Shma]

ISAAC OF SOUTHWARK (d. 1289/90), English lawyer and financier. Isaac appears as a possibly professional lawyer, speaking on behalf of clients, in the Exchequer of the Jews in 1268 and 1270, but later only as a financier lending money. In 1285 he was accused of the murder of Maud of Worcester, but was subsequently cleared of this charge. Not long before his death in 1289/90 he sold his house in Southwark, just south of the river Thames opposite London, to Richard Clerk and his wife, Alice, but his widow, Zipporah, was able to continue living in a house in St Lawrence Jewry in the City of London.

BIBLIOGRAPHY: P. Brand, *Plea Roles of the Exchequer of the Jews*, *VI* (2005); idem, PROME, Parliaments of Edward I, appendix of material related to Roll 2, no. 178; J. Hillaby, "London: The 13th Century Jewry Revisited," in: JHSET, 32 (1990/92).

[Paul Brand (2nd ed.)]

ISAACS, U.S. family prominent in New York City. Founder of the family was SAMUEL MYER ISAACS, born in Leeuwarden, Holland, who immigrated to the United States in 1839 from London, where he had been the principal of an orphan asylum. He was the first *ḥazzan* and preacher of Congregation B'nai Jeshurun in New York. After the congregation split in 1847 Isaacs became rabbi of Congregation Shaarei Tefila, remaining there until his death. In *Jewish Messenger*, a weekly newspaper which he founded (1857), Isaacs took a stand against Reform Judaism, but called for certain minor ritual changes. A supporter of the abolition movement, Isaacs lost southern subscribers as a result. He was associated with the founding of Mount Sinai Hospital in 1852 and became its first vice president. Isaacs also helped found the Hebrew Free School Association of New York City in 1864 and Maimonides College in Philadelphia, the first, though short-lived, American rabbinical school, in 1867. In 1859 he was one of the organizers of the Board of Delegates of American Israelites, an organization that worked for Jewish civil and religious rights in the U.S. and abroad. He helped organize the United Hebrew Charities in 1873 with his eldest son, MYER SAMUEL ISAACS (1841–1904), New York lawyer and community leader. Myer Samuel was born in New York, graduated from NYU (1859) and NYU Law School (1861), and was admitted to the bar in 1862. He then started his own office, founding the family firm M.S. and I.S. Isaacs. In 1880 Isaacs was appointed judge on the City (then Marine) Court to fill an unexpired term. Later he received nominations to the Superior Court (1891) and the Supreme Court (1895). He lectured on real estate law at New York University Law School from 1887 to 1897. Active in community affairs, Isaacs helped his father found the Board of Delegates of American Israelites and the Hebrew Free School Association, serving in leadership positions in both organizations. In civic affairs Isaacs was one of the organizers of the Citizens' Union in 1897 and was instrumental in creating Seward Park for the crowded East Side of New York City. He was a leader in many other Jewish charitable and educational efforts, particularly to aid East European Jewish immigrants, and was editor of the *Jewish Messenger*, which he helped his father found.

ABRAM SAMUEL ISAACS (1852–1920), another son of Samuel Myer Isaacs, who was a rabbi, writer, and educator. Educated at New York University, the University of Breslau (1874–77), and the Breslau rabbinical seminary, Isaacs taught Hebrew, German, and postgraduate German literature at NYU between 1885 and 1906. He was named professor of Semitic languages in 1906, a post which he held until his death. Isaacs was also a preacher at the East 86th Street Synagogue in New

York City and rabbi of the B'nai Jeshurun Congregation in Paterson, N.J. (1896–1906). Following his father's death in 1878 he became an editor of the *Jewish Messenger* until its merger in 1903 with the *American Hebrew.* Isaacs wrote several books for adults and children, including *A Modern Hebrew Poet: The Life and Writings of Moses Chaim Luzzatto* (1878) and *What is Judaism* (1912).

LEWIS MONTEFIORE ISAACS (1877–1944), son of Myer Samuel Isaacs, lawyer and musician. Born in New York City, Isaacs joined the family law firm in 1903. Isaacs was secretary and treasurer of the Beethoven Association, and director of the Musicians Foundation and the Edward Macdowell Association. He wrote songs and compositions for piano and orchestra as well as books about music, notably (with Kurt J. Rahlson), *Koenigskinder, a Guide to Engelbert Humperdinck's and Ernst Rosmer's Opera* (1912) and *Haensel und Gretel, A Guide to Humperdinck's Opera* (1913). He was also a trustee of the family's West End Synagogue (Congregation Shaarei Tefila) and a member and officer of several bar associations. His wife, EDITH JULIET RICH ISAACS (1878–1956), was active in the theatrical world. Born in Milwaukee, she became a literary editor of the *Milwaukee Sentinel* in 1903 and wrote drama criticism for periodicals. Later she was the editor and business manager of the quarterly *Theatre Arts Magazine*, which became the *Theatre Arts Monthly* in 1924. Edith Isaacs edited *Theatre* (1927), a collection of essays; *Plays of American Life and Fantasy* (1929); and *Architecture for the New Theatre* (1935), another collection of essays. She wrote *American Theatre in Social and Educational Life; a Survey of its Needs and Opportunities* (1932) and *Negro in the American Theatre* (1947).

Another son was STANLEY MYER ISAACS (1882–1962), lawyer and New York City official, who practiced law from 1905 until 1919, when he went into the real estate business. A longtime member of the Republican Party, Isaacs was a leading supporter of municipal reform and was elected president of the Borough of Manhattan on the La Guardia fusion ticket in 1937. Failing to be renominated by his party in 1941 as a result of a controversy started when he appointed a Communist to the post of confidential examiner, Isaacs ran and was elected to the New York City Council, where he served until his death, for many years as its only Republican member. An exemplar of civic leadership, Isaacs' many progressive causes included slum housing improvements, laws prohibiting racial discrimination in housing, and the Committee for a Sane Nuclear Policy. He was also active in the settlement houses, notably the Educational Alliance, and in 1934 was president of the United Neighborhood Houses. A trustee of the Federation for the Support of Jewish Philanthropic Societies, Isaacs worked also for many other charitable, civic, and political organizations.

ISAACS, EDITH JULIET (1878–1956), editor of *Theater Arts* magazine from 1919 to 1945. Isaacs tried to make American theatergoers aware of people and movements in the European theater and to make them familiar with the London Old Vic and the Moscow Art Theater. She printed early plays by Eugene O'Neill, Thornton Wilder, and others, and work by American designers. Her magazine also encouraged the growth of pioneer progressive groups. Isaacs was active in the Federal Theater Project and supported black culture. She was married to LEWIS MONTEFIORE ISAACS (1877–1944), a real estate lawyer and accomplished musician who was one of the founders of the Musicians Foundation of New York and the MacDowell Artists Colony in Peterborough, New Hampshire.

Books she edited include *Theater: Essays on the Arts of the Theater* (1927); *Plays of American Life and Fantasy* (1929); and *Architecture for the New Theater* (1935). She wrote *The Negro in the American Theater* (1947).

[Ruth Beloff (2nd ed.)]

ISAACS, SIR ISAAC ALFRED (1855–1948), Australian lawyer and politician who became governor-general and chief justice of Australia. Isaacs' father emigrated from Poland to England and then to Australia at the time of the gold rush (c. 1851). Isaac Isaacs was born in Melbourne. He entered the Government Law Department and studied law at Melbourne University, graduating in 1880. His legal acumen and astute mind soon earned him recognition, and he advanced rapidly. In 1892, Isaacs entered politics and was elected as a member to the state parliament. In the following year he became solicitor general and in 1894 attorney general. He was acting premier of Victoria for a short time in 1899. Active in the debates of the inter-state conventions which led to the formation of the federal government of Australia, Isaacs was elected for the constituency of Indi, in Victoria, when the first federal parliament was formed in 1900. In the federal parliament, he served with distinction as attorney general and in 1906 was appointed a justice of the federal High Court in which he served for 24 years. In 1930, Isaacs became chief justice of Australia. He held strong views on the need for strengthening the power of the federal government as against that of the states and although he did not secure this in the framing of the constitution, his subsequent judgments did much to influence events in that direction. In 1931, after a lengthy public controversy, the Australian Labor government decided on the appointment of an Australian-born governor-general and Isaacs was chosen as the first Australian for this post, which he occupied with dignity, decision, and leadership. He became a privy councillor in 1921 and was knighted in 1928.

Isaacs remained a conscious and practicing Jew but he saw his Jewishness as a religion, rejecting completely its national and political side. Strongly opposed to political Zionism, he engaged in a vigorous public controversy at the age of 90 in which he took a strong anti-Zionist line. He supported the official British government policy on Palestine in 1945–47 as laid down by Ernest *Bevin. Isaacs died a few months before Israeli independence, so that it is impossible to know whether, like many of his non-Zionist associates, he would have fundamentally altered his views on the Jewish state; those who knew him are divided on this point. Even in the last years of his long life, Isaacs preserved his brilliant qualities as a political speaker. The man who, many years later, became Australia's second Jewish governor-general, Zelman Cowen, wrote the authoritative biography, *Isaac Isaacs* (1967).

BIBLIOGRAPHY: M. Gordon, *Sir Isaac Isaacs* (1963). **ADD. BIBLIOGRAPHY:** Australian Dictionary of Biography; H.L. Rubinstein, Australia I, index; W.D. Rubinstein, Australia II, index.

[Isidor Solomon]

ISAACS, ISAIAH (1747–1806), U.S. merchant, communal leader, and public official. Isaacs, who was born in Germany, went to Richmond, Virginia, by 1769, and was Richmond's first permanent Jewish resident. A silversmith by trade, he entered into a prosperous partnership later with Jacob I. Cohen, as merchants and owners of land, houses, and slaves. A founder of Beth Shalome Congregation, he gave part of his land to the congregation for cemetery purposes in 1791. Active in political affairs, Isaacs was appointed clerk of the market (1785), later became a tax assessor, and served as a member of the original Common Council of Richmond along with John Marshall.

[Saul Viener.]

ISAACS, JACOB (c. 1730–1798), U.S. inventor. He lived in Newport, Rhode Island, and was listed as a member of the Jewish community. In 1758 he became involved in a law case against John Merritt of Providence and the king's council decided in his favor. In 1759 he was one of the ten signatories to a letter of thanks sent to the congregation of the Shearith Israel synagogue in New York for their help in the building of the synagogue in Newport. Here the name appears as Jacob Isaacks. In 1760 his name (in the form of Isaacs) appeared in a list of Newport Jews made by Ezra Stiles. His family was listed as five souls and in 1762 he was registered as the owner of a brig. In 1783 he made an offer to build ships and in 1791 he invented a method of water desalination and petitioned the House of Representatives to take over the discovery for payment. He interested George Washington and though Thomas Jefferson recommended it, Congress set the matter aside.

BIBLIOGRAPHY: Friedenwald, in: A.J. Karp (ed.), *The Jewish Experience in America*, 1 (1969), 222–8.

[Samuel Aaron Miller]

ISAACS, JACOB (1896–1973), literary scholar. Born in the East End of London, Isaacs was educated at Oxford and specialized in Shakespearean studies. He was interested in the Hebrew Bible as a literary source, which was reflected in his contribution to H. Wheeler Robinson's *The Bible in Its Ancient and English Versions* (1940). He was the first professor of English at the Hebrew University of Jerusalem (1942–45) and from 1952–64 was professor of English at London University. Isaacs became a well-known broadcaster on English literature on BBC radio and wrote *The Background of Modern Poetry* (1951).

ADD. BIBLIOGRAPHY: ODNB online.

ISAACS, SIR JEREMY (1932–), English producer and arts executive. Isaacs was educated at Oxford, where he was president of the Union in 1955. In television, his main interests were in documentaries and current affairs, and he was responsible for celebrated series and programs both for BBC (Panorama) and Independent Television as producer, controller, editor, and sometimes journalist. The 26-part series *The World at War* about World War II, which received worldwide praise, was initiated and produced by Isaacs in 1974. As an independent, he produced "A Sense of Freedom" for Scottish TV and a series for BBC, *Ireland – a Television History.*

He became founding chief executive of Channel 4 in 1981, serving until 1987. Isaacs created a much envied model for cultural television. He was a major influence in the arts by attaching a high priority to opera and ballet as well as literature and the visual arts.

In 1988–96 Isaacs was general director of the Royal Opera House, Convent Garden, where he had served as a member of the board since 1985. Despite great financial difficulties in the arts and much media criticism of the Royal Opera House, Isaacs brought Covent Garden back to internationally acclaimed artistic levels.

A private and somewhat reserved personality, he is also a distinguished TV interviewer of singular discretion, allowing recognition for the personality being addressed (he rarely appears on the screen himself). He suffered a personal tragedy when his brother was killed by a terrorist bomb in Jerusalem in 1975.

Isaacs has been the recipient of many honors and awards and was a governor of the British Film Institute from 1979. France made him a Commandeur de l'Ordre des Arts et de Lettres in 1988. He also became chairman of *Artsworld,* a non-commercial cable television station. Isaacs was kighted in 1996 and is the author of *Storm Over 4: A Personal Account* (1989).

[Sally Whyte]

ISAACS, JORGE (1837–1895). Colombian novelist and poet. The son of a converted English Jew and a Colombian mother, Isaacs was born in Cali and educated as a Catholic; in 1868 he became a Freemason; he nevertheless assumed what he defined as his "racial" Jewish identity. After publishing a collection of poems (1864), he won instant fame with his novel *María* (1867), a tragic love story in which the partial Jewishness of the main characters plays an important role. The novel became a classic of Latin American literature; it was translated into many languages and an English version by Rollo Ogden appeared in 1890. Some of his poems, such as "La tierra de Córdoba" ("The land of Cordoba"), "A Cali" ("To Cali") and "Río Moro" ("Moro River"), contain allusions to his Jewish origins. Isaacs subsequently entered politics and became a Colombian diplomat, but achieved no further distinction as a writer.

BIBLIOGRAPHY: M. Carvajal, *Vida y pasión de Jorge Isaacs*

(1937). **ADD. BIBLIOGRAPHY:** F. Alegría, *Breve historia de la novela hispano-americana* (1959). G. Arciniegas, *Genio y figura de Jorge Isaacs* (1967); J.S. Brushwood, *Genteel Barbarism: Experiments in Analysis of 19th Century Spanish American Novels* (1981); F.F. Goldberg, *Judaica Latinoamericana 3* (1997); I. Goldberg, "Jewish Writers in South America," in: *The Menorah Journal*, 11:5, 1925; P. Gómez Valderrama, *Jorge Isaacs* (1989); D.B. Lockhart, *Jewish Writers of Latin America. A Dictionary* (1997); D. Sommer, *Foundational Fictions. The National Romances of Latin America* (1991).

[Kenneth R. Scholberg / Florinda F. Goldberg (2nd ed.)]

ISAACS, JOSEPH (1659–1737), New York pioneer. Colonial records afford only glimpses of Isaacs' career. It is known that he enlisted in the provincial militia in 1691 during King William's War; that as a resident of the North and East Wards of New York City he was made a freeman of the city in 1698; that he was a merchant and a butcher, and that he unsuccessfully petitioned the municipal authorities in 1702 for permission to manufacture rum. In addition Isaacs was a party to numerous lawsuits, including one in which he was charged with possessing illegal weights. The assessment rolls of the city indicate that he was one of its less affluent businessmen, yet he contributed to the building of the Shearith Israel synagogue in 1729–30.

[Leo Hershkowitz]

ISAACS, NATHAN (1886–1941), U.S. lawyer, educator, and author. Isaacs taught law at the university of his native Cincinnati (1912–18; interrupted by service in the U.S. Army during World War I), at Harvard (1919–20 and from 1924) and at the University of Pittsburgh (1920–23). He also lectured at Yale Law School (1937–39). Isaacs was active in Jewish affairs and was an American delegate to the first World Jewish Congress in Geneva (1936). His books include *The Law of Business Problems* (1921, revised 1934), and *Course in Business Law* (1922). He co-edited the National Law Library with Roscoe Pound (1939).

ISAACS, NATHANIEL (1808–1872), South African trader and explorer, regarded as one of the founders of Natal. He left a record of his visits to the kraal of the Zulu kings, Chaka and Dingaan, *Travels and Adventures in Eastern Africa*, 1–2 (1836), which is an important contemporary account of Zulu life and customs. Isaacs was a nephew of Saul Solomon, merchant of St. Helena, and was sent from England at the age of 14 to join his uncle's countinghouse. In 1825, befriended by J.S. King, commander of the brig *Mary*, he accompanied him to Port Natal, and decided to explore the interior. His party reached the royal kraal of Chaka 130 miles inland, and was received by the monarch, who already knew King. Isaacs observed tribal life at close quarters and was later able to describe the tyrannical rule of Chaka with much horrifying detail. He traded in ivory and accompanied the Zulus in an expedition against a Swazi tribe (in which he was wounded) and was given the name "Tamboosa" (Brave Warrior). He was granted a concession of land at what is now Durban, which he surrendered to H.F. Fynn, another Natal pioneer. Much of our knowledge of Chaka Zulu derives from him.

After Chaka's assassination by Dingaan, Isaacs vainly urged upon the Cape Government the advisability of colonizing Natal. He was then only 20, and he spent two more years in Natal where he trained the Zulus in cultivation and cattle raising. In 1831 he returned to England, still hoping Natal would be declared a colony, but received no encouragement. Natal was annexed by the British in 1843, but by then Isaacs was in West Africa, trading in Sierra Leone.

BIBLIOGRAPHY: H.G. Mackeurton, *The Cradle Days of Natal* (1930), 125ff.; L. Hermann, *A History of the Jews in South Africa* (1935), 79–82. **ADD. BIBLIOGRAPHY:** M. Jolles, *Samuel Isaac, Saul Isaac and Nathaniel Isaacs* (1998).

ISAACS, SUSAN (1943–), U.S. author. Brooklyn-born Isaacs, a novelist, essayist, and screenwriter, was educated at Queens College. She left before she earned her degree to work as an editorial assistant at *Seventeen* magazine. She rose to senior editor but resigned to stay home with her children. At the same time, she freelanced, writing political speeches and magazine articles. She used her work background in her novels. While living on Long Island, a suburb of New York City, she published her first book, *Compromising Positions*, a comic novel, in 1978. It was a main selection of the Book-of-the-Month Club and was the first of 10 novels, all of which made the bestseller list. The whodunit told the tale of a suburban housewife who investigates, and solves, the murder of a philandering periodontist. In 1985, Isaacs adapted the book into a successful film, with Susan Sarandon playing the investigator-housewife. She also wrote and co-produced a comedy, *Hello Again*, in 1987, with Shelley Long and Judith Ivey.

Isaacs's second novel, *Close Relations*, was a love story set against a background of ethnic, sexual, and New York Democratic Party politics. It was published in 1980 and was a selection of the Literary Guild. Her third, *Almost Paradise*, in 1984, was also a Literary Guild main selection. In this work Isaacs used the saga form to show how the people are molded not only by their histories but also by family fictions that supplant truth. Her fourth novel, *Shining Through*, published in 1988, was set during World War II and a film adaptation starred Michael *Douglas and Melanie Griffith. Her other books include *After All These Years, Lily White, Red White and Blue, Long Time No See,* and *Any Place I Hang My Hat*. Her fiction has been translated into 30 languages.

Isaacs served as chairman of the board of Poets & Writers and was a president of the Mystery Writers of America. She was also a member of the National Book Critics Circle, PEN (Poets, Essayists and Novelists) and served on various educational and family guidance organizations.

[Stewart Kampel (2nd ed.)]

ISAACSOHN, SIEGFRIED (1845–1882), German historian. Isaacsohn wrote a three-volume work on Prussian history, *Geschichte des preussischen Beamtenthums vom Anfang des fuenf-*

zehnten Jahrhunderts bis auf die Gegenwart (1874–84, reprint 1962), and together with Harry Bresslau, *Der Fall zweier preussischer Minister, des Oberpraesidenten Eberhard v. Danckelmann 1697 u. des Grosskanzlers C.J.M. v. Fuerst 1779. Studien zur brandenburgisch-preussischen Geschichte* (1878). He was editor of the tenth volume of the series devoted to the documents of the Elector Frederick William of Brandenburg (1620–1688), *Urkunden und Actenstuecke zur Geschichte des Kurfuersten Friedrich Wilhelm von Brandenburg. Auf Veranlassung Sr. koeniglichen Hoheit des Kronprinzen v. Preussen* (1880).

ADD. BIBLIOGRAPHY: H. Bresslau, Preface to *Geschichte des preussischen Beamtentums*, 3:v-viii (biogr. and bibliogr. notes).

ISAACSON, JOSE (1922–). Argentinian writer, essayist, and lyric poet of Sephardic origin. Many of his works have received awards, including *Amor y Amar* ("Love and To love," 1960), *Elogio de la poesía* ("Praise of Poetry," 1963), *Oda a la alegría* ("Ode to Joy," 1966), and his essay *El poeta en la sociedad de masas* ("The Poet in Mass Society," 1969). Other noteworthy works were *Kafka: la imposibilidad como proyecto* ("Kafka: Impossible as a Project," 1974) and *Cuaderno Spinoza* ("The Spinoza Notebook," 1977) a philosophical poem on the apogee of 18th-century reason before the advent of the crisis of contemporary thought and the alienation of 20th century man. In 1980 he received the Latin American Prize for Intellectual Jewish Merit, conferred by the Latin American Jewish Congress. From the Jewish perspective Isaacson writes about the post-emancipation period and from the perspective of Argentine history; his literary production belongs to the most pluralistic and humanist tradition generated by Liberalism. Thus he appealed both to Jewish intellectuals and to the non-Jewish cultural world which appreciated his human, universal, and abstract values. He was president of the Argentine branch of the International Pen Club. From 1953 to 1970 he was board secretary of the Jewish-Argentine quarterly *Comentario.*

BIBLIOGRAPHY: N. Lindstrom, *Jewish Issues in Argentine Literature* (1989). D.B. Lockhart, *Jewish Writers of Latin America. A Dictionary* (1997). L. Senkman, *La identidad judía en la literatura argentina* (1983). A.E. Weinstein & M.G. Nasatsky (eds.), *Escritores judeo-argentinos. Bibliografía 1900–1987* (1994).

[Jose Luis Nachenson and Noemi Hervits de Najenson]

ISAIAH (Heb. יְשַׁעְיָה, יְשַׁעְיָהוּ "Salvation of YHWH"), one of the eight books (as the Rabbis and the Masorah count them) of the *Nevi'im*, or Prophets, the second division of the Hebrew canon (see *Bible, Canon).

INTRODUCTION

Outside the Book of Isaiah itself, the prophet is mentioned in II Kings 19–20 and II Chronicles 26:22; 32:20, 32. He is called the son of Amoz, who is otherwise unknown. According to a tradition in the Babylonian Talmud (Meg. 10b), Amoz was the brother of *Amaziah, king of Judah. A contemporary of *Micah, Isaiah was preceded slightly by Hosea and Amos, both of whom preached in the Northern Kingdom.

The pseudepigraphical Ascension of *Isaiah relates that Isaiah was "sawn asunder" by the wicked *Manasseh (5:1ff., cf. also Heb. 11:37). A variation of this theme is found in the Babylonian Talmud (Yev. 49b), which relates that a genealogical record in Jerusalem reports the death of Isaiah by the hand of Manasseh: Isaiah was "swallowed by a cedar tree, and the tree was sawn asunder." Also in the Jerusalem Talmud (TJ, Sanh. 10:2, 28c), Isaiah is said to have hidden in a cedar tree which was then "sawn asunder." The tradition is therefore consistent that the prophet was martyred in the days of Manasseh.

For other biblical figures with the name Isaiah see Ezra 8:7; 8:19; Neh. 11:7; I Chron. 3:21; 25:3, 15; 26:25.

SURVEY OF VIEWS OF THE AUTHORSHIP OF ISAIAH. Ben Sira attests that by 180 B.C.E. Isaiah had already reached its present form (Ecclus. 48:17–25). This is corroborated by the Isaiah scroll discovered in the area of the Dead Sea which contains all 66 chapters of Isaiah (but see W.H. Brownlee, *The Meaning of the Qumran Scrolls for the Bible* (1964), who believes, on the basis of a gap following chapter 33 in the Isaiah scroll, that a literary division should be made at that point). On the basis of this evidence, it is highly unlikely that some portions of Isaiah date from the Maccabean period (see R.H. Kennett, *The Composition of the Book of Isaiah in the Light of History and Archaeology* (1910)). The New Testament speaks of the entire book as Isaianic: John 12:38 refers to Isaiah 53:7 by the formula "spoken by the prophet Isaiah" while the next verse, 12:39, refers to Isaiah 6:9, 10 with the statement "For Isaiah again said…" (see further E.J. Young, *Who Wrote Isaiah?* (1958), 11ff.). According to *Bava Batra* 15a, Hezekiah and his colleagues "wrote" Isaiah. However, it was generally axiomatic among the rabbis that the Book of Isaiah was the work of one prophet, and they answered the apparent time discrepancy by attributing the latter chapters to the outcome of prophetic powers. Abraham ibn Ezra, anticipating modern criticism, hints that because chapters 40–66 of Isaiah contain historical material subsequent to the time of Isaiah, it is likely that these chapters were not written by Isaiah ben Amoz (see M. Friedlaender, *Commentary of Ibn Ezra on Isaiah* (1873), 170). Modern criticism began with J.B. Koppe's observation, in the German edition of Lowth's *Commentary* (1780), that chapter 50 may not have come from the prophet. In 1789, J.C. Doederlein denied the Isaianic authorship of chapters 40–66. Taking up the issue, J.G. Eichhorn and E.F.K. Rosenmueller defined the criteria for distinguishing between genuine Isaianic and non-Isaianic portions. By the middle of the 19th century, these views had a very wide following, although they were challenged by C.P. Caspari, J.A. Alexander, and, in his early years, F. Delitzsch. More and more scholars began to write on the subject, refining and correcting previous positions. Among these were G.A. Smith (1889) and B. Duhm, who, in 1892, labeled chapters 40–55 and 56–66 of the book Deutero-Isaiah and Trito-Isaiah, respectively. In 1914, H. Gressmann applied the method of *Formgeschichte* to the study of Isaiah (in: ZAWB, 34 (1914), 254–97). This method, introduced by H. Gunkel and

H. Gressmann, is concerned with identifying the *Gattungen* (literary types) of a given book and placing them in their *Sitz im Leben* (life situation, historical context). C.C. Torrey maintained that chapters 34–66, excluding 36–39, were the work of one author, writing that "the paring process, begun with a penknife, is continued with a hatchet, until the book has been chopped into hopeless chunks" (*The Second Isaiah: A New Interpretation* (1928), 13). There has been a trend toward synthesizing the methods of literary criticism and the methods of *Formgeschichte* in the manner of Childs' *Isaiah and the Assyrian Crisis*, 1967. Y.T. Radday has attempted to utilize computers in determining the authorship of the work (Y.T. Radday, in: *Tarbiz*, 39 (1969/70), 323–41; idem, in: JBL, 89 (1970), 319–24; idem. in: *Computers and the Humanities*, 5 no. 2 (1970), 65ff.). Radday's work concludes that there was at least one other author for the second part of Isaiah. J.H. Hertz put the traditional Jewish viewpoint on this subject thus: "This question can be considered dispassionately. It touches no dogma, or any religious principle in Judaism; and, moreover, does not materially affect the understanding of the prophecies, or of the human conditions of the Jewish people that they have in view" (*The Pentateuch and Haftorahs* (1956), 942). For a more recent survey of Isaiah scholarship see J. Sawyer, DBI I, 549–54.

The virtually unanimous opinion in modern times is that Isaiah is to be considered the work of two distinct authors: First Isaiah (chs. 1–39) whose prophetic career in Jerusalem covers the years c. 740–700 B.C.E., and that of an unknown prophet (Deutero-Isaiah, chs. 40–66; see below) whose prophecies reflect the experience and events of the Babylonian Exile (c. 540 B.C.E.).

The beginning of (First) Isaiah's prophetic career (6:1; "the year of the death of King Uzziah," c. 740 B.C.E.) coincided with the onset of a highly critical period in the fortunes of both the kingdoms of Israel and Judah, and the events of this period furnish the immediate background of Isaiah's prophecies. The march of conquest of both Babylonia and Syria, launched by Tiglath-Pileser III upon his accession to the Assyrian throne (745 B.C.E.), raised a looming threat to the future independence and, indeed, to the very existence of both kingdoms. The coming to power of the usurper Pekah (736 B.C.E.) in Israel marked a concerted effort, in which he was joined by Rezin, king of Damascus, and a few other neighboring principalities, to throw off the yoke of Assyrian domination. Upon King Ahaz of Judah's refusal to join the alliance, his kingdom was invaded by the leaders of the anti-Assyrian alliance who proposed to depose him and replace him with a pro-Aramean puppet, the "son of Tabeel" (II Kings 15:37; 16:5; Isa. 7:1ff.). In that critical hour, in a meeting with the panic-stricken monarch, Isaiah urged the king to be confident and calm. Ahaz spurned the prophet's quietistic counsel and, instead, sent an urgent appeal for help, accompanied by tribute, to Tiglath-Pileser (II Kings 16:7). Thus, the independence of Judah was surrendered. For Isaiah, the fateful act, while buying temporary security for Judah, ultimately invited disaster at the hands of its rescuer. King *Hezekiah (c. 715–687 B.C.E.), Ahaz's son and successor to the throne, cautiously stayed aloof, for a time, from abortive attempts initiated by Egypt to throw off the Assyrian yoke. Perhaps it was the insistence of the prophet on the futility of an alliance with Egypt that prompted this attitude; Isaiah dramatized his insistence by going about barefoot and naked for three years as a symbol of the fate that would overtake Egypt and its ally Nubia at the hands of the Assyrians (ch. 20). Some years later, internal troubles in Assyria apparently persuaded Hezekiah that, despite the prophet's warnings and dire predictions (39:5–7), the hour was ripe to break the yoke of vassalage. Isaiah's warning that dependence upon Egyptian aid could only lead to disaster went unheeded (31:3). In 701 B.C.E. Sennacherib invaded Palestine, after defeating an opposing Egyptian and Nubian force at Eltekeh. The countryside was quickly overrun (22:7), and much of its population deported. Soon afterward Jerusalem was besieged. Isaiah, prompted by his faith in the inviolability of Jerusalem, encouraged Hezekiah to refuse to surrender the city to the invader despite the threats and demands of Sennacherib's high officer (36:4ff.; II Kings 18:17ff.). The prophet predicted that Jerusalem would not be taken and that God would "turn back the invader the way by which he came" (37:22–29). The siege of Jerusalem was lifted, an event credited to a divine visitation (37:36; II Kings 19:36) that devastated the camp of Sennacherib. (For Sennacherib's account see Pritchard, Texts, 287–8; COS II: 302–3; L.L. Honor, *Sennacherib's Invasion of Palestine*, 1926.) Though the political and military events of the prophet's time, briefly described above, help to illuminate a number of passages in Isaiah (essentially, those already cited), the major portion of the book is devoted not to Judah's foreign policy but to the inner state of the nation, its social order, and its religious situation. Isaiah's career began at a time of growing prosperity that brought comfort and luxury. Material growth was accompanied by the territorial expansion of the Kingdom of Judah, achieved by military power cultivated by King Uzziah (II Chron. 26:6–15). The economic and political situation never seemed brighter. A national sense of complacent self-satisfaction and pride could hardly be avoided. Isaiah, however, saw that wealth had been purchased at the price of oppression. Corruption was rife in high places (1:23); the guilty were acquitted for bribes and the innocent were denied justice (5:23); the fatherless went undefended (1:23); the mansions of the rich contained the spoils of the poor (3:14); the poor farmer was evicted from his land to make room for the estate of the plutocrat (5:8). The aristocratic women of Jerusalem, in their elaborate attire and jewelry, especially served the prophet as target for his denunciations and predictions of doom (3:16–24). Foreign trade and imports apparently brought with them idolatrous religious practices and superstitions; at least, the prophet links the two (2:6–8) and he charges that "Everyone worshippeth the work of his own hands" (10:10f.). The prophet does not repudiate the sacrificial cult carried out in the Temple; indeed, he seems to have been a frequent Temple visitor, for it is here that he receives the divine call to prophecy in a vision. However, sacrifice and oblations brought by hands "full of blood" are "vain" and an "abomination" (1:11–15). If the divine demand "to seek justice, relieve the oppressed, judge the fatherless, plead for the widow" (1:17) is heeded, "ye shall eat the good of the land"; if not, "ye shall be devoured by the sword" (1:19, 20). The coming of God in His fierce anger to punish Israel and the nations is a recurrent theme (5:15, 16, 24, 25; 9:14–19; 13:11–13; 30:27, 28; cf. 9:20; 10:4). Yet, the divine anger is but an instrument wherewith to humble the arrogant and punish the evildoers. Once it has accomplished its purpose, God will show His graciousness and mercy (10:25; 26:30; 30:18). The latter are presumably meant for the "holy seed" that will remain when the work of destructive purification has been fulfilled (6:13). Only a remnant of Israel shall return (8:18; 10:21, 22; Heb. *She'ar Yashuv*, the symbolic name of the prophet's son, 7:3). In addition to the concrete historical hope of the survival of a remnant, the prophet holds out an eschatological hope, one to be consummated at the end of days when the whole world will be transformed. Isaiah's eschatology is grounded in his faith in God's permanent attachment to Israel and to Zion (28:16). God's design for the history of the nations is to reach its fulfillment in Zion, to which the nations will repair to learn the ways of God and to walk in His paths (2:2–4, 5; 33:20; 28:16; cf. Micah 4:14). The denouement of history will see the abolition of war and the turning of the nations to peace. Closely linked to Isaiah's eschatology are his visions of the messianic figure. Sprung from the root of Jesse (father of David), he will be endowed with the spirit of God in its fullness. With unblurred vision, he will intervene on behalf of the poor and deliver them from their persecutors, establishing thereby a reign of righteousness and truth. Under his reign, even the ferocity of the wild beasts will be transformed into gentleness (11:1–10). In a similar passage, the prophet invests the messianic king with extraordinary traits, calling him "Wonderful in counsel… the everlasting father, the prince of peace" (9:5 ff.). In summary fashion, the essential doctrines of Isaiah may be described as

(1) an emphasis on the holiness of God;

(2) a rejection of human schemes and wisdom as the means of working out the destiny of Israel and, in their stead, a total reliance on God;

(3) an ardent faith in Jerusalem as the inviolable city of God and its proclamation as the future site of universal acceptance of the God of Israel by the nations;

(4) the delineation of the messianic king under whose reign final justice and peace will be inaugurated;

(5) the doctrine that only a remnant of Israel shall emerge out of the doom to be visited upon it;

(6) the primacy of the moral dimension of the religious life without which ritual observance becomes an abomination in the sight of God.

Chapters 40–66 of the Book of Isaiah constitute the prophecies of an unknown prophet of the Babylonian Exile, commonly referred to as Deutero-(Second) Isaiah. Fairly widely accepted critical opinion (but with exceptions) attributes chapters 56–66 to a different prophet conveniently called Trito-Isaiah. (Since the essential ideas of these latter chapters form a consistent whole with chapters 40–55, for purposes of this article they will be considered in conjunction with them.) The dramatic turn of events of his time, the impending conquest of Babylonia by Cyrus, the Persian king of Anshan (539 B.C.E.), to which the prophet alludes (45:1 ff.; 47:1), enables the prophet's utterances to be dated with approximate accuracy to 540 B.C.E. In the light of the predicted downfall of Babylonia, and hence presumably an end to exile, the prophet's message to his people who are in despair over the ruin of Judah is, in the first instance, one of hope and consolation. He speaks in vivid terms of "the waste and desolate places, the land that has been destroyed" (49:19). Zion is a widow bereaved of her children (49:19 ff.) or a barren mother without offspring (54:1; cf. 51:18–20). It was not only the thought of Zion in ruins that weighed heavily on the mind and heart of the prophet; hardly less oppressive was the fact that thousands of his fellow countrymen, owing to a variety of circumstances, had been widely scattered and were to be found at all points of the compass (43:5; 49:12, 22). To judge from repeated references, the exiles in Babylonia were subject to contempt and hostility (41:11; 51:7, 13, 23; 54:15). A pervasive despair and fear, coupled with a sense of abandonment by God, had overcome the exiles (40:27; 49:14; 50:1). Here and there, some, despairing of the God of Israel's power to deliver them (40:28; 45:24; 46:12; 50:2), had readily succumbed to the lure of Babylonian idolatry (44:17; 48:5). In the midst of the depressing situation, the anonymous prophet reaffirms with striking emphasis and clarity the ancient faith that the God of Israel is not only the creator of heaven and earth (40:26; 44:24; 45:7), but the ultimate arbiter of the destinies of the proud empires, to do with them as he would (40:15 ff.). It was the God of Israel who directed history (43:12) and who, even now, was guiding the course of events in bringing overwhelming victory to Cyrus (41:2 ff., 25). Incisively, he predicts the collapse of the idols of Babylon (46:1 ff.) and sets forth again and again the exclusive divinity of the God of Israel besides whom there is no redeemer (43:10; cf. 44:24; 45:6, 18, 21; 46:9; 48:11 f.). True, Israel had sinned (43:27 f.; cf. 48:1 ff.), but divine wrath and punishment were things of the past, and God had freely pardoned Israel's sins (40:2; 44:22; cf. 48:9; 51:22; 54:6 ff.). As expressions of God's love and His assurance that they had not been abandoned, the prophet employs a whole series of endearing epithets for Israel (43:7; 44:1, 5, 21; 51:4, 16; 54:17). In precise terms, the exiles would be released from Babylonia when that empire had vengeance wreaked upon it for its oppression of Israel (45:1 ff.; 47:1 ff.). It is Cyrus, heir to Babylonia's throne, who would let the exiles go free (45:13; 52:11 ff.). The return to Zion would be led by God Himself (40:9 ff.). The Temple would then rise upon a new foundation, and Zion would gain a new, incomparable splendor (54:11 f.). There would also be a vast ingathering of Israelites out of the lands to which they had been scattered (43:5 f.; cf. 49:12; 51:11; 53:12). Non-Israelites would join the House of Israel in allegiance to its God (44:5). The prophet speaks warmly of the aliens who associate themselves with the faith of Israel and assures them that they will receive an "everlasting memorial" (56:4–8). In a burst of exaltation at the thought of Israel's forthcoming restoration, he sees Israel as supreme over the nations and the latter as subservient to it (43:3; 45:14; 49:22f.; 54:3). A group of passages in Second Isaiah (42:1–4; 49:1–6; 50:4–9; 52:13–53:12) are known as songs of the Servant of the Lord. Around the question of the identity of the figure described in these passages, a vast literature has grown up. The preponderance of scholarly opinion inclines to the conclusion that the Suffering Servant is to be identified with the people of Israel and, at the same time, perhaps with an "individual who both represents the whole community and carries to its supreme point the mission of the nation" (H.H. Rowley, *The Faith of Israel* (1953), 122). The mission of the servant is not only "to raise up the tribes of Jacob" but to be a "light to the nations" (49:6). His task is to set justice in the earth, bringing it forth in truth (42:3, 4), and to serve as liberator (42:7; see *Servant of the Lord).

[Theodore Friedman]

FIRST ISAIAH

Within this can be distinguished (1) the core, chapters 1–33, and (2) the historical appendix, chapters 36–39. The latter, a variant of II Kings 18:13, 17–20:19, does not purport to be by Isaiah, and was only copied from (a variant recension of) the Book of Kings and appended to Isaiah 1–33 because it tells about Isaiah. Even within chapters 1–33 there are some pericopes which are about, rather than by, Isaiah (e.g., ch. 20) and some which are neither by Isaiah nor about him. For the authentic utterances of Isaiah, the dating by the (not Isaian, but editorial) superscription 1:1 "in the reigns of Kings Uzziah, Jotham, Ahaz, and Hezekiah of Judah" is reliable, and the modern student of Isaiah does well to add: "and of Kings Tiglath-Pileser (III, 745–727), Shalmaneser (V, 726–722), Sargon (II, 722–705), and Sennacherib (705–681) of Assyria."

Divisions and Content of Chapters 1–33

The block Isaiah 1–33 falls into two main divisions of unequal length: A. The Diary, chapters 1–12; B. The Archive, chapters 13–33. The Diary has been so named by Ginsberg (1964) because despite deviations (which can be accounted for) its arrangement is chronological (c. 740–715 B.C.E.) in principle, with the result that when read in light of the most up-to-date knowledge of the relevant history it resembles a diary. The Archive, on the other hand, is a repository of prophecies of which only a minority at the end seem to be arranged chronologically.

THE DIARY, CHAPTERS 1–12. The Diary, Chapters 1–12, may be likened to a triptych with a narrow inner panel, chapter 6, and two broad outer panels, chapters 1–5 and 7–12, each of which is divided (horizontally or vertically, according to the reader's preference) into two fields. Panel 1 dates basically from before the death of King Uzziah; Panel 2 – as 6:1 states – from "the year that King Uzziah died"; Panel 3 – as stated by 7:1 – begins in the reign of Ahaz, whether it continues into the reign of Hezekiah depends on whether Ahaz's reign was short (some date his death as early as 727, see below) or long (some have him live till 715). The somewhat detailed discussion which follows will serve as an introduction to the person, background, style, and outlook of Isaiah and will make possible considerable economies of space in the treatment of the Archive.

Panel 1, Field A, Chapter 1. *Ewald titled this chapter "The Great Arraignment." More apt would be "The Great Exhortation" for it appeals for reform (vv. 16–18), and offers total remission of even grave past sins on condition of reform (18–20). S.D. Luzzatto pointed out that *Lekhu na* (note the precative particle *na!*) *ve-nivvakheḥah* (*we-niwwakheḥah*) can only mean "Come, let us reach an understanding," since that is the only meaning that fits both here and in the only other undamaged passage in which the *nifal* of *ykḥ* occurs, Job. 23:7 (Gen. 20:6b is obscure). And escape is offered to everyone in Zion who reforms: verse 27: "In the judgment, Zion shall be saved (as in Job 5:20); in the retribution (so *ẓedakah* (*ẓedaqah*) is also to be rendered in 5:16; 10:22; 28:17), those in her who turn back." Only the rebels and sinners will perish, verse 28. The implication is that they will be a minority. When it is noticed that nowhere else does Isaiah summon to repentance, but only expects it after an ever greater depopulation (even in 31:6, the continuation in the third person in the same verse and in the following one show that *shuvu* [imperative, "turn back!"] is to be emended to *we-shavu*, "The children of Israel will then turn back to him to whom they were so false"), it is clear that chapter 1 belongs exactly where it is, at the beginning of the book; only verses 5–9 (10?) have been added – by Isaiah – either after the extinction of the Kingdom of Ephraim in 722 or after Sennacherib's invasion of Judah, his transfer of some of its territory to the Philistines, and his imposition of a heavy tribute on Hezekiah in 701. The fact that 1:2–20 (apart from the verses just mentioned) is Isaiah's maiden composition may explain its heavy dependence on earlier models. The models in question are the Song of Moses and the message of Amos. Isaiah 1:2 may be said to summarize the whole of Deuteronomy 32:1–18. Isaiah 1:2a = Deuteronomy 32:1–4 minus the elaborate adornment: Let heaven and earth give respectful attention, for these are the words of no other than the Lord. Isaiah 1:2b = Deuteronomy 32:5–18 in a nutshell: children nurtured and reared (Deut. 32, less restrained, also uses five verbs of engendering, Deut. 32:6b, 18) by the Lord have defected from him. Isaiah 1:3 merely repeats the preceding thought: ox and ass acknowledge their master and feeder, Israel does not. In turning from heaven and earth to address Israel reproachfully, Isaiah 1:4 takes its cue from Deuteronomy 32:6, but two of its epithets are inspired by Deuteronomy 32:5: "corrupt children" (Heb. *banim mashḥitim*) goes back to Deuteronomy 32:5a, which even in its mutilated condition has preserved the elements *banaw* and *shiḥet* and which originally may have read very much like *banim mashḥitim yalad*, "He gave birth to corrupt children," while *zera*ʿ *mere*ʿ*im*, "brood of evildoers," is synonymous with Deuteronomy 32:5b, "a crooked and twisted generation." Here the echoes of Deuteronomy 32 in content and diction cease, but its form persists through Isaiah 1:20. For just as in Deuteronomy 32 the speaker alternately utters his own "discourse" (*lekaḥ, leqaḥ*, verse 2), verses 1–18, 36a, 43, and introduces and quotes YHWH, verses 19–35, 36a–42, so Isaiah 1:2–20 gives the following alternation: Isaiah introduces and quotes YHWH, 2–3; Isaiah adds his own comment, 4–9 (but 5–9 were added by him later); Isaiah introduces and quotes YHWH, 10–18; Isaiah adds his own interpretation, 19–20. The idea of disloyal children is repeated in 30:1, 9. The last cited verse is preceded (30:8) by an introduction remarkably reminiscent of the introduction to the Song of Moses, Deuteronomy 31:19, for as the Targum, among other versions, realized, *lʿd* in the former is to be vocalized *le-ʿed*, "for a witness"; but in this case it is hard to decide which passage is dependent on which. As for the message of Isaiah 1:10–17 – the protest against the topsy-turvy scale of values applied to cult and justice – its dependence on Amos 5:21–25 is obvious, and the identical or equivalent elements can be picked out. The themes of the oppression of the poor and the subversion of justice occur again both in Isaiah and in Amos, and it is not difficult to recognize in Amos 2:6b–7a; 3:15; 5:11–12 the elements of Isaiah 5:8–10 (cf. 1:29–30, which speak not of cult gardens but of luxury gardens in view of verse 31 *he-ḥason… u-foʿalo* ("treasure… and he who amassed it"); 5:23, 10:1–2). Not dependent on either the Song of Moses or the words of Amos is the glorification of Jerusalem, Isaiah 1:21–27. Disappointed as he is in her present state, Isaiah firmly believes that she was a faithful city where justice dwelt in the past, and will be such again in the future. He may well have idealized the past unduly. Jerusalem's judges had probably been officials appointed by the king ever since David's conquest, and it seems that in the Ancient Near East it was understood that an official derived much of his income from the gifts of the private persons who needed his services. From the start, therefore, a judge was exposed to a powerful temptation (1) to be too busy to hear an action brought by a widow or an orphan, who could not afford to bring an adequate gift (Isa. 1:23), (2) not only to hear but also to favor a litigant who did bring such a gift. However, Isaiah is to be judged as a prophet, not as a historian. The initial impression of nobility of thought and language is confirmed by the following chapters.

Panel 1, Field B, chapters 2–5. Furnished with a superscription of its own, 2:1, this collection dates from a slightly later period than Field A, as explained above, but the last pronouncement in it, 5:25ff., dates still from the reign of Uzziah, since the latest misfortune it speaks of as having already occurred (though it is not destined to remain the last) is the famous earthquake of Uzziah's reign (Amos 1:1; Zech. 14:5). The pericope 9:7[8]ff., which begins its survey further back in history, also knows of later calamities as having already been endured: it comes to the earthquake in 9:18[19]a, and goes on in 9:18b–20a [19b–21a] to speak of Ephraim's savage civil wars – see II Kings 15:9–16, 23–25 – and of its ensuing attack on Judah, for which see II Kings 16:5–6; Isaiah 7:1ff. The date of this last event is 733, and if there were any merit to the argument that Isaiah 5:25 (with or without 5:26ff.) belongs in the context of 9:7[8]ff. "because it has the same refrain" it would follow that Isaiah 5:25(ff.) likewise dates from 733. However, the said argument begs the question; for a stich that occurs only once is not a refrain, and in chapter 5 the stich "Yet his anger has not turned back, and his arm is outstretched still" (5:25b) occurs only once. No time need be wasted on R. Kittel's egregious suggestion (*Biblia Hebraica*, 1929³, which is not peculiar to him) that the statement at the beginning of 5:25 to the effect that God's anger has been roused against his people and that he has extended his arm to strike it, presupposes four previous occurrences of "Yet his anger has not turned back and his arm is outstretched still." But it is also the opposite of probable that Isaiah contemplated repeating "Yet his anger has not turned back, etc," and going on to depict still further slaughter either in Israel or in Judah at the time when he announced (5:26–29) the coming with uncanny speed "from the end of the earth" of a legendary nation of barbarians equipped with the fangs (for *wšg* [so the consonantal text] read *wšnym, we-shinnayim*), the voracity, and the irresistibleness of lions. (The description no more contemplates a specific, real, nation – like the Assyrians – here than in Deut. 28:49–51; Jer. 5:15–17.) What more was necessary for making the land desolate (Isa. 6:11–12)? See also Panel 3, Field A.

Excursus: The Zion Vision, 2:2–4. This is one of the most remarkable pericopes in the entire Book of Isaiah. It reads as follows (verse 2): "In the days to come, the Mount of the Lord's House shall stand firm above the mountains and tower above the hills; and all the nations shall gaze on it with joy. (3) And the many peoples shall go and shall say: 'Come, // Let us go to the mount of The Lord,/to the House of the God of Jacob;// That he may direct us according to his ways,/And that we may walk in his paths'//For direction shall be forthcoming from Zion,/And words of the Lord from Jerusalem.// (4) Thus he will judge among the nations/And arbitrate for the many peoples,//And they shall beat their swords into plowtips/and their spears into pruning hooks://Nation shall not take up/Sword against nation;//They shall never again know war."//The use of the verb "to direct" (*horah*) of the issuing of messages by the Lord and of the delivering of such messages by prophets is characteristic of Isaiah (9:14; 28:9, 26; 30:20 [bis]), and the use of the noun "direction" (*torah*) of messages from superhuman sources is even more characteristic of him (1:10; 5:24; 8:16, 20; 30:9). This is true of ad hoc prophecy that is characteristic of Isaiah, though occasionally emulated by Habakkuk (2:19). Not merely characteristically Isaian but specifically Isaian is the parallelism "direction//word of the Lord" (or, once, "utterance of the Holy One of Israel"): 1:10; 5:24. In this as in other matters (see below), Isaiah's weaknesses lie in the field of practicality. Isaiah 2:2–4 is unmistakably Isaian not only in its diction but also in its ideology. For both its Zion-centeredness and its concern that other nations beside Israel may be spared the horrors of war (contrast Lev. 25:18; 26:5; Jer. 30:10; 46:27; Hos. 2:20) are in line with much else. Although the prophecy occurs again in Micah 4:1–4, its uniquely Isaian "*Torah*//word of the Lord," which has already been commented upon, makes it unlikely that it is the work of some anonymous genius who preceded both Isaiah and Micah; and both this feature and the ideological congruence with Isaiah and clash with Micah – who cancels the universalism of the passage in the very next verse (Micah 4:5) as well as in 5:7–8, and its Zionism (he was a provincial from Morashah, 1:1) in 3:12 – preclude the priority of Micah (see Kaufmann on Micah).

Panel 2, chapter 6. Both the rabbis and modern research regard this as Isaiah's earliest prophecy (his "inaugural vision"); but Kaplan and Kaufmann have dissented, as have Milgrom, Knierim, and Schmidt. There is a new harshness here. God tells Isaiah to go and harden the hearts of "that people" (*ha-ʿam ha-zeh*, verses 9, 10) – the first occurrence of this deprecating designation; contrast "my people," 1:3 (though God is here reproaching Israel); 3:15 – in order that it may not (*pen*) "turn back and be healed" (cf. 19:22). To Isaiah's shocked question, "How long, O Lord?" – with which is to be compared Ezekiel's horrified exclamation (Ezek. 11:13b), "Oh, Lord YHWH, You are completely destroying the remnant of Israel!" – YHWH replies, just as He does to Ezekiel (Ezek. 11:14–21), that a small remnant shall turn back to the Lord and be spared. Unless *we-hayetah levaʿer* is moved, for purely stylistic reasons, to the end of verse 11, Isaiah 6:13 is to be rendered thus: "But while a tenth part still remains in it, it shall turn back (cf. *She'ar-yashuv* (Shear-Jashub), "a remnant shall turn back," the name of the son with whom Isaiah appears, a year or two later, in 7:3; see also 10:21). For it shall be ravaged (*we-hayetah levaʿer*) like the terebinth and the oak, of which stumps remain even when they are felled; its stump shall be a holy kindred." The only interpolation in Isaiah 6 is verse 12a, "The Lord will remove the population," which – referring to the Lord in the third person in the midst of a speech by the Lord – stems from a post-Exilic glossator who thought the prediction of devastation was a prediction of the exiling of the population to Babylonia (a century and a half later). In the inaugural visions Exodus 3:2–4:17; Jeremiah 1:4–9 (verse 9 makes this a vision); and Ezekiel 1:1–3:13, there are no participants but God and prophet (in the last cited vision the Lord does not address the creatures that bear His throne), and there is no call for a volunteer: the prophet is assigned his mission willy-nilly. The true analogue to Isaiah 6 is I Kings 22:17 ff.; in the former, however, the prophet is purged by a peculiar visionary rite (Isa. 6:6–7) so that he, as well as the celestial creatures of the Lord's council, may participate (imitated in Zech. 3:4–7). No wonder he believes that not only he but also his unnamed wife (she is simply "the Prophetess," perhaps herself a prophet, 8:3) and his children (8:11 ff., 18) – the last word in 8:16 is probably also to be emended to *ba-yeladim*, "in the children" – are something set apart from "the masses" (*rabbim*, 8:15)!

Panel 3, Field A, chapters 7–9. The Arameo-Ephraimite Attempt to Depose the House of David, 734–732. The Arameo-Ephraimite attack is the occasion for 9:7 [8]ff., whereas it is only the starting point of 7:1 – 9:6 [7], which in 8:23 [9:1] alludes to the Assyrian annexation of Sharon (in 734) and of Gilead and Galilee (732) as having already taken place (cf. II Kings 15:29). But 7:1–9:6 [7] was attracted to the vicinity of chapter 6 by the similarity of the openings 6:1 and 7:1. To the attempt to dethrone the Davidic dynasty, Isaiah reacted with the fury of a devout "legitimist." For to him the divine election of the House of David was as axiomatic as the divine election of Zion (see above). Recalling Amos 4:6–12, in which his predecessor had traced a series of disasters which had failed to induce repentance in the Northern Kingdom, because of which he had threatened it with ominous vagueness (Amos 4:12), with something much worse than anything that had preceded, Isaiah first repeated the last two of the disasters to which Amos had already looked back and then paraphrased Amos' threat for the future with appalling explicitness. For in Isaiah 9:7 [8] the Septuagint is unquestionably right in interpreting the consonants of the first two Hebrew words as *dever shillaḥ* ("let[past tense] loose pestilence"), and Ehrlich in changing *we-nafal* to *we-negef* ("plague"). Isaiah 9:7[8] alludes to the same pestilence, and Isaiah 9:10–11[11–12] to the same military disaster(s), as Amos 4:10. For the military disasters, this identity is confirmed by Haran's observation that Amos 1:6 speaks of Gaza (i.e., Philistia generally) handing over Israelite captives to Aram (so read for "Edom"). Then in 9:12[13], Isaiah paraphrases the final clause of Amos 4:10. Accordingly, Isaiah 9:13, 16a[14,17a] spells out the vague threat of Amos 4:12, and the beginning of it must be translated, "The Lord will exterminate from Israel head and tail, palm branch and reed, in one day." After that, Isaiah 9:17–20[18–21] traces the stages in the fulfillment of this threat that have been realized between the time that Amos uttered it (see Amos 1:1) and Israel's attack on Judah. Unlike Isaiah 5:25 ff., therefore, Isaiah 9:7[8] ff. resembles Amos 4:6 ff. in looking back on not one but a whole series of past blows, and so this passage (emphatically not Isa. 5:25 ff.) does, like Amos, employ a refrain. The roughly parallel block 7:1–9:6[7] has preserved the reason for this implacable attitude of Isaiah toward the sister kingdom: the purpose of the attack on Judah was to put an end to the reign of the Davidic dynasty in Judah, 7:6. Isaiah is convinced that Aram and Ephraim have thereby dug their own graves. That Judah will be ravaged by a cruel foe is the gist of 5:26 ff., which has already been dealt with, and presently Isaiah will substitute for this legendary people the Assyrians (8:7–8a); but the Davidic dynasty is inviolable. That its subjects are greatly outnumbered by those of either one of the two attacking kings makes no difference. The entire world outside the Davidic polity is a world without God, whereas YHWH is an integral part of the Davidic polity; and what could even all the nations in the world do against God? (8:8b–10 belongs between 7:9a and 7:9b; see *Immanuel.) But Judah – through its king Ahaz – must exhibit the same faith as Isaiah. If it solicits the aid of heathen Assyria, it thereby implies that it does not credit the Lord with the ability to dispose of Aram and Ephraim unaided. ("You treat my God as helpless," 7:13.) One obvious advantage of taking Isaiah's own word for it, instead of imputing to him the astute diplomatic motive so dear to rationalists who like to believe that the prophets were rationalists like them, is that the same irrational reason explains why Isaiah later opposed enlisting the aid of Egypt in disposing of Assyria, whereas for this the rationalizers have to discover still another secret rational motive. The fact is that only in the latter case can the course advocated by Isaiah also be justified by practical considerations (though they were foreign to Isaiah's thinking). Of the three premises of those who justify on practical grounds the policy advocated by Isaiah in the face of the Arameo-Ephraimite attack, two are at least doubtful: the premise that Tiglath-Pileser had not already imposed his suzerainty on Judah either when he defeated the *Uzziah-led coalition in 738 or when he swept into Philistia in 734; and the premise that although he had not moved betimes against the same *Pekah – who had perhaps been aided by the same *Rezin – when he rebelled against *Pekahiah, the presumably loyal son and successor of Assyrophile *Menahem, he would certainly, and without being solicited, attack Pekah and Rezin in time to save the House of David. The third premise is nonsense: that stronger powers do not subjugate weaker ones which do not either attack them first or solicit their protection! By procuring the aid of Assyria, Ahaz probably saved his dynasty and possibly his nation. Isaiah, however, bitterly confirmed his prediction of chapter 6, of an appalling devastation and added that the very power – Assyria – that Judah had hired to save her would be the instrument of her devastation (7:20). The best farmland (7:23, corresponding to the most hairy parts of the body, verse 20) would be reduced to thornbrakes infested by dangerous beasts. Just the marginal farmland, which could only be tilled with the hoe because too rocky for the plow (corresponding to areas of the body with scant hair), would escape infestation by dangerous beasts and would serve as pasture, the shrunken population being dependent on cows, sheep, and goats for its subsistence. (See also *Immanuel.) Chapter 8 begins, like chapter 7, with a piece of narrative; but unlike chapter 7 and like chapter 6, it is first person narrative. Isaiah's wife bears him a son whom the Lord instructs him to name Maher-(to be vocalized rather *Mihar*?) Shalal-Hash-Baz, "Pillage hastens, looting speeds," in token of the early plundering of two cities: "(4) For before the boy has learned to call 'Father!' and 'Mother!' the wealth of Damascus and the spoils of Samaria (6b) and the delights of Rezin and the son of Remaliah (the respective kings) (4b) shall be carried off before the king of Assyria." Isaiah is also instructed to symbolize this fact by writing an "undertaking (*ʾnwš*, which in 33:8 is parallel to *ʿedim* [so manuscript 1Qisa[a]] and *berit*; perhaps in both passages read *ʾmwn* [i.e., *emun*], since confusion of *sh* and *m*, which resemble each other in the Paleohebraic script [see *Alphabet] is frequent in First Isaiah) to Maher Shalal Hash Baz," and having it formally witnessed. But as in chapter 7, Judah's want of faith must also be punished and through the same agent, Assyria. Unlike Aram and Israel, however, Judah would only be imperiled, not destroyed (8:5–8a). In this connection the opprobrious epithet "that people" is again applied to Judah (8:6), and twice more in 8:11, where Isaiah tells how, when the Lord singled him out (*be-ḥezqat* (*be-ḥezkat*) *ha-yad*, "when He grasped me by the hand"; cf. Isa. 45:1; Jer. 31:31[32]; Job 8:20), He warned him and his household not to walk in the path of "that people" (and here, as verse 14 makes clear, he means "both Houses of Israel," both Ephraim and Judah) so as not to stumble like the masses (verse 15; *rabbim*, as e.g., in Mal. 2:8, means "the many, *hoi polloi*"). On 8:16ff., see Ginsberg 1956, except that verses 20b–22 are to be arranged as follows: "(20b) For him who speaks thus there shall be no dawn. (21bc) Whether he turns upward, (22b) or looks downward (*el ereẓ* = Aram. *laʾaraʿ*<*leraʿ*), behold, distress and darkness with no day-break (reading *meʿif* with 1Q1saa), straitness and gloom with no dawning (read *mi-negoah*). (21a–b*b*) He shall walk in it wretched and hungry, and when he is hungry he shall rage and revolt against his king (better "kings"; vocalize *bi-mlakhaw*) and his divine beings." The sense of 8:23[9:1] is "For if (read *lu* with 1Q1sa[a]) there were to be drawn for her that is in straits, only the former [king, i.e., Pekah] would have brought disgrace on the land of the Zebulunites and the land of the Naphtalites (read *ereẓ ha-zevuloni we-ereẓ ha-naftali*) but the latter [king, i.e., Hoshea] would have brought honor to the other side of the Jordan and Galilee of the nations." In other words, the failure of Hoshea to regain the provinces lost by Pekah shows that the decree of the sack of Samaria (8:4) has not been revoked; its execution has merely been postponed, which dates at least 8:19–23 in the reign of Hoshea (732–725). Verse 5:30 (But on that day there will resound over him (i.e., over the subject of 8:20b–22, once he has learned to spurn his kings and his divine spirits) a roaring like that of the sea; and when he then looks down, behold, distressing darkness with light, darkness with dawn [*beʿefah*]) belongs here and (in a manner analogous to 29:5b*b*–6) it creates a transition from 8:20bff. to 9:1ff. The latter's message is: Following the final liquidation of the Northern Kingdom, its people shall enjoy freedom and happiness again – in a Davidic kingdom which shall again embrace them and be headed by a model king whose reign shall be blessed. Improved restoration and rendering of verses 5–6[6–7] are: "For a child has been born to us, a son has been given to us, and prosperity (?) has become the import of his name (read *shemo*). He has been named 'The Mighty God is planning grace, the Puissant One of Jacob intends well being' (*avir yaʿaqov ʿoseh shalom*), (6) in token of abundant prosperity and measureless well being, etc." (Explanations: Meaning of *hmṣrh* unknown. 1Q1saa reads המשורה, perhaps cf. מְשׂוּרָה "liquid measure." *Avir Yaʿaqov* is synonymous with and commoner than *Avir Yisraʾel* [Isa. 1:24], which, however, is to be restored in 43:15. For the synonymous parallelism of *yʿẓ* and *ʿsy*, cf. 5:19; 29:10. The root *ʿsy* also has this meaning in 5:12; 22:11; 32:6; 37:26. For *peleʾ* ("grace" see 25:1, and Psalms 88:11, 13; 89:6 and Qumran Hebrew.)

Panel 3, Field B, chapters 10–12. Isaiah 10:1–4a is a social protest in the style of 5:3–10. 4b is not a conclusion of what precedes – since 1–4a is not a recollection of a past blow but a threat of a future one. It is rather a repetition of the last clause of chapter 9 intended to serve as a link between the latter and the former (since its key words *af*, "anger," and *yad*, "arm, hand," occur again in 10:5). Since 10:16–19 is a threat against Israel (note, among other things, the resemblance of 10:16 to 17:4) and it originally followed directly on 9:16a [17a] (note, among other things, "in one day," 9:13 [14] and 10:17), what originally stood in its present position may very well have been 14:24–27; note among other things the antithesis between the Lord's purpose (*dimmiti*, 14:24) and Assyria's purpose (*yedammeh*, 10:7). Isaiah 10:5–15; 14:24–27 is a remarkable display of concern for the right of nations – not just Israel – to exist that is worthy of the man who authored 2:2–4; see above, panel 1, field B. The *terminus post quem* is given by the reference in 10:9 to the Assyrian annexation of Carchemish, which took place in 717 B.C.E. At the same time, verses 27b ff. can best be understood against the background of Sargon's Arabian campaign of 715. The date of 10:5–15; 14:24–27 is therefore probably 716. Since the time when Isaiah assigned to Assyria the missions of liquidating the states of Aram and Ephraim and severely chastising Judah (see above), between ten and 15 years have elapsed, and he has been sickened by the ruthlessness (born, like every vice, of pride) of the Assyrian, who is not content to attack the nation he is commissioned to attack but conquers insatiably, and is not content to plunder (in accordance with 8:4; 10:6) but needs must annihilate (10:7), namely by expatriation (10:13bc; the Karatepe inscriptions confirm that *horid* means "to exile [populations]"). Assyria has still to carry out its mission of chastising Judah (8:5–8a), but after that the "Lord… will punish the majestic pride, and overbearing arrogance of the king of Assyria" (10:12). And 14:24–27 tells us in what manner: (24) The Lord of Hosts has sworn this oath: "As I have designed, so shall it happen;/What I have planned, that shall come to pass://(25a) To smash Assyria in my land,/ To trample him on my mountain (i.e., in my country; vocalize *hari* in view of Isa. 11:9; 25:6, 7, 10; 65:25; Ex. 15:17; Ps. 78:54)."/ /(26) That is the plan that is planned/For all the earth;//That is what an arm is poised for/Over all the nation.//(25b) And off them his yoke shall drop,/And his burden shall drop from their backs.//(27) For the Lord of Hosts has planned,/ And who can foil it?//It is His arm that is poised,/And who can stay it?//In 10:27b ff. the prophet anticipates that the predicted imperilment of Judah by Assyria will take place by Sargon marching up the road from the Jordan Valley to Ai but turning southwestward before reaching Ai in order to advance on Jerusalem by way of Michmas and Geba. The only time when Sargon could be expected to march on Jerusalem by way of the Jordan Valley was when he was campaigning in, or returning from, North Arabia, in 716 or 715. The ravaged forest of verses 33–34 is, of course, no less than that in verses 17–18*aa*, 19 and in 9:17[18], the local population, not the invading army. In this passage, however, the ravaging is done with the ax, not with fire, and stumps – including notably the stump of Jesse, 11:1 ff. – can produce new crowns of foliage, and so they shall, 11:1 ff. The stump of the tallest tree of all, "the stump of Jesse shall, in regenerating, produce a marvelous shoot; a prince with a charismatic gift of justice. For he shall be endowed with the charismas of wisdom, resourcefulness and valor, and piety (*daʿat* being, as in Hos. 4:6; Prov 1:29, short for *daʿat elohim*/YHWH, "devotion to, or mindfulness of, God/YHWH"). He shall know the rights and wrongs of a case by instinct, and destroy the wicked by his mere utterance. (For *ruaḥ* (lit. "spirit"), "charisma," cf. e.g., II Kings 2:8–9, 14–15; Hos. 9:7; Micah 3:8). Down to this point, the doctrine of the election of the House of David had merely asserted that his family would reign forever; here the attention is transferred from the perpetuity of the dynasty to the marvelous qualities of the individual ruler. One might therefore say that Isaiah's concern, which has already been noted, about the social ills of his time, particularly the judicial oppression of the poor, has led him (most strikingly here but also in 9:5–6 (1–6) and 16:4b–5) to combine the peculiarly Judahite – really peculiarly Jerusalemite – doctrine of the perpetuity of the Davidic line with the common West Asiatic ideal of kingship as expressed in Israel's wisdom literature (Prov. 16:21b; 20:28; 25:5b; 29:14). By taking this step Isaiah made possible the evolution of the post-biblical idea of "the *Messiah." There followed visions of peace in the animal kingdom (at least within the borders of the Land of Israel, 11:9), the reconciliation of Judah and Ephraim under the Davidic dynasty (11:10, 13), and the reconquest of the dependencies of David (14); finally, the redemption of the Israelites exiled by the kings of Assyria.

THE ARCHIVE, CHAPTERS 13–33. This falls into three parts: I. The Book of Pronouncements *(Massaʾot)*, 13–23, minus the two misplaced "*ah*'s" 17:12–14; 18:1–7 (place these after chapter 33); II. "The Isaiah Apocalypse," chapters 24–27; III. The Book of *Ah*'s: 17:12–18:7, chapters 28–33. (30:6–7 is not a misplaced "pronouncement"; the first three words are corrupt for *bmšwʾt* (Job. 30:3; 38:27) *hngb*, "in the wasteland of the Negev").

The Book of Pronouncements. That there is no chronological arrangement here is easily demonstrated: 14:28 ff. is dated "in the year that King Ahaz died," for which the earliest possible identification is 727 B.C.E.; yet 17:1 ff., which predicts a total and definitive destruction of Damascus, which was taken but not destroyed in 732, cannot date from later than 732 B.C.E. (note that the depopulation of Israel is also still in the future, 17:4–6). The arrangement is actually geographical, namely, in two arcs beginning at Babylon and ending in the West: (a) chapters 13–21 (Babylon, 13:1, 19; 14:4; Assyria, 14:24–27; Philistia, 14:28 ff.; Moab, chapters 15–16; Damascus and Israel, 17:1 ff. [on the two "*ah*'s," 17:12 ff.; 18:1–7, see above]; Egypt, chapter 19; Egypt and Nubia, chapter 20); (b) chapters 21–23 (Babylon, 21:1–10; Dumah, 21:11–12; Northwest Arabia, 21:13–17; Jerusalem, chapter 22; Tyre-Sidon, chapter 23). The material may be classified in four categories:

1. Definitely or probably Isaian. (i) 14:4b–21, a magnificent ode composed in the summer of 705, when the Assyrian defeat and the ignominious death of King Sargon seemed, even though they took place hundreds of miles northeast of "my land//my mountain" (14:24–25, see above) to be the fulfillment of Isaiah's prediction of the crushing of Assyria and the liberation of "all the nations" (14:26, see above). (ii) 14:24–27 (dealt with above, under The Diary, Panel 3, Field B). (iii) 14:28–29, 30b–31 (32, 30a [read *be-kharo*, "in His – YHWH's, referring to 32b – pasture"] belong after 16:5). It would seem that Ahaz died in the same year as Tiglath-Pileser; in any case, not Ahaz but the latter, who invaded Philistia both in 734 and in 733, is the rod of him [i.e., Assyria] that beat Philistia. (iv) 17:1–11 clearly 733–732. (v) 19:1–15. In Isaiah's time the nomes (districts) of Lower Egypt were governed by hereditary princes, which is why his contemporary Sennacherib speaks of defeating "the kings (plural) of Egypt." In line with this is Isaiah's reference to the nomes of Egypt as kingdoms (19:2). In addition, the rhythm and diction of 19:1–15 are typically Isaian; for the presumable occasion see on chapter 22. On verses 16 ff., see below. (vi) chapter 22. The background of this chapter is the situation after the fall of Azekah to the Assyrians in 712 B.C.E., and the feverish preparations in Jerusalem for the eventuality of a siege (whose non-materialization is probably to be ascribed to timely submission). The main target of the Assyrians was Ashdod which headed a revolt of vassal states against Assyria in the years 713 and 712 until it was besieged and captured. As can be seen from Isaiah 20:4ff., the rebels hoped for help from Nubia and Egypt. Isaiah opposed Judah's involvement for the same reason as he had 20 years earlier opposed soliciting the aid of Assyria against Aram and Israel: it signified that Judah relied on the might of heathen Egypt and Ashdod because it had no faith in the Lord's ability to dispose of Assyria – as he surely would, in his own good time. (vii) 23:1–14. The diction is Isaiah's, and the period is the Assyrian one. (The corrupt verse 13 is to be restored something like this: The land of Kittim itself, which [this is one of the instances of the use of *zeh* as a relative pronoun] Sidonians founded – whose turrets they raised, whose ramparts they erected – is a people no more; Assyria has turned it into a ruin.) On verses 14 ff., see below.

2. Not by but about Isaiah, chapter 20. The year of the Assyrian capture of Ashdod is 712 (see above on chapter 22). The account is in the third person, but it obviously contains a historical core. As already mentioned, Isaiah disapproved of his own people's attempting to throw off the Assyrian domination with the help of Egypt and Nubia, and he was convinced that both Egypt and those who relied on her would come to grief. That he took off his clothes and sandals to dramatize – and thus quasi-magically effectuated – the ignominious end of Egypt that he predicted is entirely conceivable (cf. the Maher-Shalal-Hash-Baz sign, 8:3–4). That Isaiah's regular attire was a loincloth, and that he went entirely naked and barefoot for three years are not impossible data; but they may be a distorted recollection that so long as the rebellion lasted he went about in sack-cloth and sandals, and when Ashdod fell he took these off and went naked and barefoot for a while.

3. Definitely neither by nor about Isaiah. (i) 13:1–14:4a, 22–23. Both Isaiah 13 and Zephaniah 1:7, 14ff. announce a day of divine wrath and stress that it is close at hand, but only the latter likens it explicitly to a day of a private sacrificial slaughter, and feast of which one notifies one's guests in advance and "has them cleanse themselves (ritually)" (*hikdish*, *hiqdish*, Zeph. 1:7; cf. *kiddesh*, *qiddesh*, Job 1:5, of having persons on whose behalf burnt offerings are made cleanse themselves ritually). Consequently it is only Zephaniah 1 that enables us to understand why the armies summoned by the Lord to execute the carnage of the day of His wrath are styled by him in Isaiah 13:3 "My ritually cleansed ones." Moreover, the age of prophecies that Media would overthrow Babylon was the Babylonian age; Jeremiah 51 is an indication for Isaiah 13 and Isaiah 21:1–9; naturally, for it was the Median empire whose power balanced that of the neo-Babylonian until the year 550, when King Astyages of Media was defeated and captured by his vassal Cyrus of Anshan, the founder of the Persian empire. For 14:1–2, a comparison with Zechariah 1:12–16 is suggestive, and 14:3–4a, 22–23 are clearly an editorial framework from the Babylonian period to verses 14b–21, representing it as an Isaian prediction of what the Jews will say on the death of the Babylonian tyrant rather than as the expression of Isaiah's own satisfaction – on the ignominious death of the Assyrian king, Sargon II, and the apparent collapse of Assyria, in 705 B.C.E – that it is (see above). (ii) chapter 21.21:1–10 is to be judged in light of what has just been said about predictions about the fall of Babylon to the Medes, and a presumption is thereby created against the enigmatic "pronouncements" 21:11–12 and 21:13 ff. as well.

4. Tantalizing in-betweens. (i) The Moab Pronouncement, chapters 15–16 (with 14:32, 30a restored to its original position after 16:5, as indicated under 1). It seems equally clear that on the one hand the bulk of this composition must be old, and on the other, that it cannot be an Isaian composition pure and simple. As regards the basic text, its dating must take account of the fact that the Moabites are represented as fleeing southward from as far north as Heshbon and Elealeh. However, it is known (from the Mesha inscription) that Moab recovered (from the Israelites, who had dispossessed the Amorites) much of the anciently Moabite territory north of the Arnon; and when Israel was forced out of Transjordan, Moab may very well have emulated Ammon (Amos 1:13), so that the old suggestion, most recently defended by Rudolph, that the basic lament was composed on the occasion of Jeroboam son of Joash's reconquest of Transjordan "from Lebo of Hamath to the Sea of the Arabah (i.e., the Dead Sea)" (II Kings 14:25) still has to be considered. For one has the impression that the old lament already had at 16:1 counsel to the Moabite refugees who have reached the southernmost point in Moab, Zoar (15:5), to cross over to Edom (Moab's southern neighbor) and send messengers from Sela in Edom to Jerusalem requesting asylum; only 16:4b–5; 14:32, 30a; 16:6 seem to have been added

by Isaiah. In 4b–5 the speaker explains to Moab why asylum in Judah would be particularly desirable; "For violence (read *ḥamaẓ*, equivalent to *ḥamas*) has vanished, rapine is ended, /and marauders have perished from this land: //and a throne shall be established in goodness/in the tent of David//and on it shall sit in faithfulness/a ruler devoted to justice/and zealous (read *we-shoḥer*, Ginsberg 1950; *mahir* would require a different construction, see Prov. 22:29; 7:6) for equity." But then in 14:32, 30a; 16:6 he reveals how this ruler will react to the Moabite's petitions (14:32). "And what will he reply to a nation's messenger?// That Zion has been established by YHWH; in it the needy of His people shall find shelter (14:30). In His pasture (read *be-kharo*, see 30:23b) such as are poor may graze/and such as are destitute may lie down secure."// The immediately preceding sentence seems to imply that non-Israelites who seek asylum will be welcomed, but only if they are poor and humble. Verse 5 then explains – and it makes no difference whether the speaker is still the Davidic king or the poet who reports the former's answer – why Moab is not welcome: "We have heard of Moab's pride-/most haughty is he-//of his pride and haughtiness and fury,/and of the iniquity in him" (16:6). There is no such word as bad "falsehood," or "prating." *Baddaw* is the suffixed form of the preposition *bede* (Jer. 51:58; Nah. 2:13; Hab. 2:13; Job 11:3, and what *bdnm* is in the Eshmunazor inscription (Phoenician), line 6). Now if one takes the above translations bit by bit, it is not difficult to find striking parallels to every bit. 16:4b–5 is insistently reminiscent, in content and partly in diction, of 9:3–6 [4–7] and 14:32, 30a, reminiscent of 3:15, of 5:17 (especially if we emend וְרָעוּ כְבָשִׂים כַּר בְּרִיִּים, "and the lambs shall graze the pasture of the fat (rams), etc." – but even also as it stands), and of 11:4a, 9a; while to 16:6 the closest single parallel is 10:7a, 12–15 (cf. 37:23–25), but see also 2:10–17; 3:16–17; 5:15–16; 28:1ff. Indeed, anyone who has not been struck by the importance in Isaiah's thought of the doctrine that pride is the root and essence of wickedness has never done more than skim his book; cf. further 16:5b (reading *we-shoḥer* as above) with 1:17a (reading *shaḥaru ẓedeq* for the insipid "guide the robbed").

(ii) and (iii) the prose, or mainly prose, appendices to the Egypt and Tyre Pronouncements, i.e., 19:16–25 and 23:15ff. The latter does not sound like Isaiah either in diction or in sentiments, but the former is occasionally reminiscent of Isaiah in its diction and is tantalizingly suggestive of events in Isaiah's time by which they could have been suggested to Isaiah: 19:19–20 of the stele Tiglath-Pileser erected on the border of Egypt in token of his sovereignty over it, and verse 23 of Sargon's forcible opening of Egypt to trade with Assyria. And certainly the universalism of 19:24–25 ("my [YHWH's] people Egypt," "Israel… third to Egypt and Assyria") is worthy of Isaiah.

"The Isaiah Apocalypse." (Isa. 24–27). It may be admitted that though the language and the ideas are often Isaian, frequent divergences from Isaiah's style, spirit, and outlook argue that the resemblances are due to imitation of Isaiah rather than Isaian authorship. On the other hand it is unwise to descend below the Babylonian exile, and at least the key passage 25:6–12 sounds like nothing so much as an assurance by an early seventh-century writer that Isaiah's prediction 14:24–27 (translated above in connection with The Diary, Panel 3, Field B) of the liberation of the nations as a result of the Lord's destroying Assyria by trampling it on "his mountains," i.e., in the Holy Land, will yet come true. For consider what 25:1–6 says: It says that the Lord's trampling of a certain entity "on this mountain" is going to result in a feast for "all the peoples" (verse 6) because of the destruction of "the shroud that is drawn over the faces of all the peoples and the covering that is spread over all the nations" (verse 7) and the "destruction of 'death' [i.e., the Assyrian killing of whole peoples, 10:7 (and 14:20, where "countries" and "peoples" should be read for 'your country' and 'your people' of MT)] forever and the wiping away of tears from all faces and the end of the reproach of peoples [so for MT's "his people"] over all the earth" (25:8). – Let who will try to escape the conclusion that first, "this mountain" here is identical with "my mountain" in 14:25 (which stands in parallel with "my country," – and means the Holy Land), and that, secondly, the entity that is to be trampled to death by the Lord on the said mountain must be, here as in 14:25, Assyria. Moab was never of such international importance. The received reading "Moab" might be taken as a cryptogram for "Assyria," though *atbash*, the system by which *ššk* represents *bbl* in Jeremiah 25:26; 51:41 and *lbqmy* represents *kšdym* in Jeremiah 51:1, is of no use here. However, the better explanation of מואב is simply that it was a misreading for אשור (confusion of ב and ר was possible and occurred in all periods, and confusion of ש and מ was possible in the Paleohebraic script in which it has occurred a number of times throughout chapters 1–33. A well-known instance is אִמְרוּ for אַשְׁרֵי ("Happy is"; 3:10), Kaufmann has very plausibly emended עַמְּךָ to עֹשֶׂךָ ("your Maker"; in 2:6); Another possibility is to read אֱמוּן (with the surmised meaning "undertaking" [cf. *amanah*]) for אֱנוֹשׁ in 8:1; 33:8. Further תָּשָׂא is to be emended to אִתָּם (read וֶאֱלִילֵיהֶם אִתָּם ("and their idols along with them")) in 2:9, מַיִם to שִׂמְלָה ("clothing,) in 3:1, and the inapposite שִׂיד of 33:12 to שָׁמִיר ("brambles"; the מ omitted by haplography after the ש which it resembled in the Paleohebraic script) so as to parallel קוֹצִים, cf. 32:13. (The resemblance between *m* and *š* in the Protohebraic script also played a part in the loss of a *m* in *mšlwḥ*), 11:14, and in the double writing of the *m* in *wmmšltk*, 22:21, for *wmšʿntk*.) As has been shown, we must now add *mwʾb*, 25:10, for *ʾšwr*; but we must also add, in the same verse, *khdwš tbn* for *khdwš mtbn* (the *m* is a dittogram of the preceding *š* and *md*(*w*)*šh* for *mdmnh*). For the sense required is not the remarkable "as a *pile* of straw chips [the meaning of *matben* in the Mishnah] is threshed to bits in a dunghill" (?; as a common noun *madmenah* is not otherwise attested) but "as straw chips are threshed to bits in threshing (21:10)." This confusing of *m* and *š* does not extend to Deutero-Isaiah. Consequently the incorporation of "the Isaiah Apocalypse" in the Book of Isaiah antedates that of Deutero-Isaiah. Consequently, though "Assyria" in our verse may conceivably

refer, as e.g., in 52:4, to the neo-Babylonian empire and date from after 605, it cannot refer to the Persian Empire and date from after 539. Finally, the meaning of 25:11 is, "Then he will spread out his hands in their (i.e., the Assyrians') homeland as a swimmer spreads out his hands to swim, and he will humble their pride along with their citadels (read *armenotaw*). Yea, the secure fortification of their walls (read *ḥomotaw*) he will lay low and humble, will raze to the ground, to the very dust." Of course the same – Assyrian or Babylonian – cities are meant in 26:5–6; 27:10.

The Book of "Ah's," chapters 28–33, 17:12–18:7. The background of 30:1ff. and 31:1ff. is obviously Judah's negotiations with Egypt for aid in a contemplated or ongoing revolt against Assyria's suzerainty, and the only doubt is whether the revolt in question is that of 713–712 against Sargon or that of 705–701 against Sennacherib. Skinner still favored the former because of 30:4 (which could be read immediately after verse 2) "For his [Pharaoh's] officers are present [read *yihyu*?] in Tanis [in the eastern Delta], and his monarchs [read *melakhaw*] reach as far as Heracleopolis magna [in Middle Egypt]." That would be a fair description of the eastern and southern limits of the realm of Tefnakhte and Bocchoris, the Pharaohs of the 24th Dynasty, whose residence was Sais in the western Delta and whose rule was terminated in the year 710. If correct, this would mean (so Skinner) that there is no evidence that Isaiah again condemned the policy of attempting to win independence from Assyria with the help of heathen allies during the revolt of 705–701, at the end of which he definitely encouraged Hezekiah, 37:5, 38:6. If chapters 30–31 are nevertheless dated, as with the majority of critics, to the revolt of 705–701, 30:4 must be regarded as formulaic. The Masoretic Text's *mal'akhaw*, "his messengers," cannot be made to refer, along with "his officers," to Hezekiah's delegation (where is Hezekiah mentioned?). That the displaced block of "*Ah*'s" 17:12–18:7 belongs after chapter 33 is suggested by the similarity between 33:21–23 (we shall be as inaccessible to enemies as if surrounded by an impassable sea) and 17:12–14 (the multitudes of our enemies may create a tumult like that of the seas, but they shall be terrified into flight by the roar of YHWH (like the primeval waters, Ps. 104:5–9)). Chapter 33, for its part, seems to date from after the final subjugation of Judah in 701 (Judah's past and future situations (3–6 and 10ff. respectively) are enviable, but the present (7–9) deplorable). There is thus no obstacle in the way of regarding the arrangement of the entire Book of "*Ah*'s" as basically chronological.

THE HISTORICAL APPENDIX, CHAPTERS 36–39. It is of course nothing but a parallel version of II Kings 18:13–20:19, mostly shorter (the most important omission is Hezekiah's abject surrender, II Kings 18:14–16) but with Hezekiah's Psalm, Isaiah 38:9–20, added. It relates three incidents in which Isaiah played a part: (1) the deliverance of Jerusalem, chapters 36–37; (2) Hezekiah's illness and recovery, chapter 38; and (3) the visit of the ambassadors from Babylon, chapter 39.

(1) Within the first, two versions of the manner of Jerusalem's deliverance have been combined: (a) 36:2–37:9a (plus *wa-yishma*c2), 37–38; (b) 37:9b (minus *wa-yishma*c2)–36. The former is full of circumstantial details and virtually dispenses with miracles: Sennacherib, at Lachish, sends the *Rabshakeh (it is a title, not a proper name) with a force to Jerusalem to demand that its people surrender so that they can at least eat decent food and drink decent drink while awaiting Sennacherib's inevitable return to carry them off into an exile which is also tolerable, instead of continuing to put up with the terrible conditions of siege that they are enduring. The Rabshakeh deliberately shouts this, in the Judean language, to the men on the walls of Jerusalem and over the heads of the Judahite officials – their names and offices are given – who were sent out to parley with him in Aramaic. Hezekiah then sends a delegation to Isaiah, who sends back an assurance that a disquieting report will compel Sennacherib to withdraw to his own country, where he will fall by the sword. Returning to Sennacherib, the Rabshakeh finds that he has already moved northward to Libnah, which is to the north of Lachish, because of a report that King Tirhakah of Nubia is advancing upon him. Sennacherib, as a matter of fact, withdraws all the way to his capital Nineveh, and there (some 20 years later but telescoped in the narrative; see *Adrammelech) two of his sons assassinate him; another son, Esarhaddon, succeeds him on the throne. The other version (37:9b–36), on the other hand, is short on details and long on the miraculous: Sennacherib sends anonymous messengers with a written demand of surrender, addressed not to the people but to Hezekiah and supported by the argument not that YHWH Himself has sent the Assyrians because Hezekiah has offended Him but that the Lord is helpless to save him. Isaiah spontaneously sends Hezekiah a reassurance that Sennacherib will never even lay siege to the city but will return to his homeland, and that night an angel of the Lord kills 185,000 men in the Assyrian camp. Although this second account is manifestly farther removed from actual history than the first, it contains in 37:22b–29 what sounds, in thought and in diction, like a genuine Isaian composition. As for the first account, either it refers to an (unlikely) second invasion of Judah by Sennacherib which, occurring after the year 697, the last one that is covered by his annals, is unattested by any Assyrian source, or else its divergences from the course of events in 701 (Tirhakah was then not yet king of Nubia but only a boy who had never left Nubia; Sennacherib did not retreat from Lachish to avoid the advancing Nubian army but met and defeated the Nubian and Egyptian forces at Eltekeh-which is north of Lachish and even of Libnah-apparently before advancing further south and dispatching a force to Jerusalem. See *Hezekiah, *Sennacherib.

(2) Hezekiah's illness and recovery. The legendary sun miracle had an antecedent in the reign of Ahaz, as the rabbis guessed from 38:8; see *Immanuel.

(3) The visit of the ambassadors from Babylon, chapter 39. Since Merodach-Baladan, who had been driven out of Babylon by Sargon in 710, returned on the latter's death in

705 from the Chaldean country by the Persian Gulf to reign in Babylon again until expelled in 703 by Sennacherib, and then successfully eluded him in the southern marshes, the visit by a delegation from the leading anti-Assyrian of the east to the leading anti-Assyrian of the west is presumably historical, but hardly the conversation between Isaiah and Hezekiah reported in 39:3–8.

[Harold Louis Ginsberg]

CHAPTERS 34–35

Chapters 34–35 of Isaiah constitute an independent unit. Chapter 34 contains a prophecy of wrath and destruction of the nations in general and Edom in particular, and chapter 35 deals with the Redemption of Israel and the Return to Zion. Since the beginning of modern biblical criticism scholars have held that chapters 34–35 do not relate to Isaiah son of Amoz, either in terms of content or style, and even certain conservative critics do not attribute them to Isaiah son of Amoz. There is no consensus, however, regarding their inclusion within prophetic units, or their exact time. Some scholars suggested joining these chapters to Isaiah 13–14 and regarding them as the product of a single author (Gesenius); some suggested joining them to Jeremiah 50–51 and regarding them as the product of a single author (Ewald); but the majority tend to relate them to Isaiah 40–66 (but esp. Torrey, who not only related them to Isaiah 40–66 but maintained that originally 34–35 were joined to, and served as, an introduction for 40–66; Steck regards 34–35 as a redactional bridge between First and Second Isaiah when the book was almost complete; the later account of Sennacherib's campaign against Judah, chapters 36–39, was added to them). Most critics tended to attribute them to the time of Deutero-Isaiah, i.e., the second half of the sixth century B.C.E., but some date them later, to after the time of Malachi, i.e., the middle of the fifth century B.C.E. (M.H. Segal), while still others dated them even later, to the fourth century (Pfeiffer). The injunction to "search in the book of Yahweh, read! Not one of these failed" (Isa. 34:16) points to the existence of a collection of written prophecies of destruction that have now materialized (Cf. Blenkinsopp a.l. 454).

Together with the question of the placing and dating of these chapters, scholars also began to doubt that these two chapters are a single unit, and some of them distinguished between them. Graetz was the first (1891) who separated them, attributing chapter 35 to Deutero-Isaiah. He regarded it as an integral part of Deutero-Isaiah and even inserted it into chapter 51 between verses 3 and 4. As for chapter 34, he attributed it to Jeremiah. When a distinction began to be made between Deutero- and Trito-Isaiah (see below), some scholars joined chapter 35 to 40–55, which are seen as part of Deutero-Isaiah (see Olmstead), while some joined it to 56–66, which are seen as part of Trito-Isaiah (Scott). Actually only the dating of these chapters, but not their relation to any particular prophet, can be determined. These two chapters are only part of a multifaceted literature which grew and flourished after the destruction of the First Temple and before the Return of the Exiles, of which Isaiah 40–66 are but the most important part. It was concerned, on the one hand, with announcing the downfall of Babylon the destroyer of Judah and the downfall of Edom the ally of Babylon, and, on the other, with announcing the Redemption of Israel and the Return to Zion. The contents of Isaiah 34–35 bears witness to their time of origin, i.e., after the destruction of Judah and on the eve of the Return to Zion (between c. 580 and 540 B.C.E.). The acts perpetrated by Edom against Judah during the period of the destruction, which were denounced by the prophets (Ezek. 35; Obad.) and poets (Ps. 137; Lam. 4:21–22), are still very much in the mind of the prophet and his audience and are expressed here with extreme wrath (cf. Isa. 63:1–6). Edom is the people whom God has doomed (34:5). The time is a "day of vengeance for the Lord, a year of recompense for the cause of Zion" (34:8), and perhaps there is also an allusion to the destruction of Edom (which also took place in the sixth century). The anticipated and desired destruction of Edom is total, in accordance with the literary tradition of maledictions against breakers of alliances (see esp. Hillers' work, but his attribution of the chapter to the time of Isaiah son of Amoz has been criticized in terms of historical background). Chapter 35 completes the picture and expresses the yearning for the Redemption of Israel and the Return to Zion which will follow the downfall of Israel's enemies. In light of its subject and content it is related in terms of content and style to Isaiah 40–66.

DEUTERO-ISAIAH

DIFFERENTIATION BETWEEN CHAPTERS 1–39 AND 40–66. Hints of a dichotomy between chapters 1–39 and chapters 40–66 of Isaiah are to be found even in medieval Jewish Bible exegesis (see e.g., *Ibn Ezra, Ibn *Gikatilla, and others). The question of the dichotomy between these chapters was revived at the beginning of modern biblical research, in 1775, by the German scholar J.Ch. Doederlin, and since then the dichotomy has been generally maintained as an incontrovertible fact. This differentiation between the two groups is based on a conclusive combination of historical, conceptual, stylistic, and linguistic evidence. One of the characteristics of chapters 40–66 is the scarcity of historical data and the vagueness of the historical background. However, some distinctly historical information (such as the two explicit references to Cyrus, 44:28; 45:1), and the mention of Babylon and the Chaldeans (43:14; 47:1; 48:20), and reflections of the historical background (the Exile and Redemption, the return to Zion and Jerusalem, the exiles and their "joiners"), attest another background which is more than 150 years later than the time of Isaiah son of Amoz. Similarly, there are conceptual differences between the two groups. For example, in the first part the idea of rebuke is predominant, while in the second consolation is the major idea; in the first part there are central motifs such as the idea of the remnant, of the end of days, and of the future king, while in the second these are not mentioned; and, in contrast, the central idea which dominates the second part, the "Servant of God," is neither mentioned nor hinted at in the first. Furthermore, despite important similarities of diction, there are clear and distinct differences between the two parts, which prove that not only were these two parts not written by the same person, but they are not even products of the same period. It appears that there were a number of reasons for joining chapters 40ff. to the group attributed to Isaiah son of Amoz. The first and decisive reason was apparently the intention of the editors of the Prophets to conclude them with chapters of comfort. An additional reason is that despite the differences between the two parts in language and style, there is some relationship between them. Another contributive factor was the paucity of historical data in chapters 40–66. Although they did sense that the two groups were from different periods, the editors' faith in the prophet's ability to envision the distant future allowed them to overcome this difficulty. This view is still held in certain circles, especially fundamentalists. Although the distinction between the two parts has been accepted in biblical research as a fact, several writers in the 20th century have maintained the unity of the book and have attempted to disprove most of the arguments of those who distinguish between the two parts (Zlotnick, Kaminka, et al.).

Structure of 40–66 and its Composition. Critics of the Book of Isaiah have raised the question of whether chapters 40–66 all stem from a single prophet or are the products of two, three, or more prophets. B. Duhm was the first to divide these chapters into two blocs (40–55 and 56–66). According to him, the two blocs are distinct in historical background, conceptual content (attitude to ritual, polemic against the Samaritans), language and style, and place and time of authorship. The first bloc belongs to "the Second (Deutero-) Isaiah," who lived during the time of Cyrus, while the second bloc, 56–66, belongs to another prophet whom he called "the Third (Trito-) Isaiah," who lived in Jerusalem close to the time of Ezra and Nehemiah. This differentiation into two blocs and two prophets was accepted, with various modifications, by many scholars – E.S. Sellin and Elliger held that the "Third Isaiah" was a disciple of the "Second" and edited his prophecies, that he lived at the end of the sixth century, the time of Haggai and Zechariah, and that the prophecies were written in Jerusalem. Some scholars follow Duhm in maintaining that the group is divided into two blocs, but they hold that it is impossible that chapters 56–66 were the work of one author and were produced during the lifetime of one prophet. Rather, they maintain that there are in this bloc prophecies from different periods, differing, however, in the times they assign to the prophecies. Some limit the period of time reflected in these prophecies to that between Ezekiel and Ezra-Nehemiah (Cheyne, Smith, Kittel). Some expand it to the period from the seventh to the third centuries B.C.E. (Budde, Volz, Eissfeldt). Other scholars, such as Glahn, Klausner, Segal, Kaufmann, and Haran, defend the unity of chapters 40–66. Kaufmann made the greatest attempts to disprove the arguments of those who maintained division into blocs and into separate prophets or prophecies, by determining that the historical background of chapters 40–66 is explicitly before the building of the Second Temple. He also emphasized that these prophecies contain no reflection of what befell those who returned from the Babylonian Exile to Palestine. Kaufmann concluded that these prophecies date from before the building of the Second Temple and their location is in Babylon. Segal also supported the unity of the book and its author, but unlike Kaufmann he held that the background reflected is that of Palestine. M. Haran has argued for the unity of the book and the author, but not of the place, as did Segal and Kaufmann. It is Haran's opinion that chapters 40–48 originated in Babylon. In the return to Palestine, which the prophet had foretold, he too returned to Jerusalem with the exiles, and chapter 49 on reflects the Palestinian background. This is expressed especially in these chapters in which there is a direct address to Jerusalem (49:14–26; 51:17–23; 54:1ff.; 60:1ff.; 62:1–9). More recent study has moved in the direction that chapters 56–66 do not come from one hand or one time period (Blenkinsopp (2003), 59).

SONGS OF THE SERVANT OF THE LORD. In dividing chapters 40–66 into two blocs and two authors, Duhm also maintained that there are additions and editing of other authors in both blocs. The word *'eved*, "slave," "servant," occurs 20 times in chapters 40–55 (once in the plural in 54:17). In 13 of these instances the servant is Israel the people. From the first bloc, 40–55, Duhm first separated four poems which he called "Songs of the Servant of the Lord," maintaining that they are by a different prophetic personality, not by Deutero-Isaiah. The four songs according to Duhm, are (1) 42:1–4; (2) 49:1–6; (3) 50:4–9; and (4) 52:13–53:12. According to Duhm and his followers, the servant is not Israel, but an idealized figure who is predestined by God for a function on account of which he suffers greatly. (Although "Israel" is found in most versions of Isa. 49:3, it is inconsistent with the mission to Israel in 5–6, and is probably a gloss; see Blenkinsopp, a.l. 297–98.) Some scholars who agree with the isolation of the "Songs of the Servant of the Lord" and their unity of content did not accept Duhm's method of dividing them and rightly added to what is called the first song, 42:1–4, verses 5–7 of the chapter, whose subject matter is similar to that of the preceding verses. Some scholars consider verses 1–9 as a unit, despite the differences in person and approach. Similarly, verse 7 is added to what is called the second song, 49:1–6, and there are some scholars who attribute to it even some of the following verses. There is also doubt about the inclusion of what is called the third song, 50:4–9, among the other songs. It seems that there are verses outside these four songs which may be identified with verses of the four songs, both in terms of content and in terms of style (e.g., 41:8; 42:1–25; 44:1–2, 21–22, 26; 50:10; 51:16; 61:1–3). Furthermore, a detailed analysis of the language and style of what are called the "Songs of the Servant of the Lord" within the other chapters shows no differences among them (see Ch. North, *The Suffering Servant in Deutero-Isaiah*, 1956[2]). In consequence, it has been argued that any distinction between these units and their contexts is somewhat arbitrary (cf. also Haran). The "servant" of Duhm's fourth song (52:13–53:12) received special attention because of the New Testament's identification of him with Jesus (directly in Acts 8 8:26–40 and implied elsewhere, e.g., Mark 10:45).

LITERARY UNITS IN 40–66. The analysis of the boundaries and scope of the literary and prophetic units that comprise chapters 40–66 has gone through several stages. The stage that preceded Gunkel and Gressmann recognized a prophetic unit of the length of a chapter or more. Skinner, for example, divided the first section, chapters 40–48, into six units, each of which was delivered at a different time, and whose order reflects the prophet's reactions to the events of his time. Budde regarded chapters 40–66 as a planned book which included four prophecies with a prologue and epilogue. This was followed by the approach associated with Gunkel, who originated the method of "form criticism." Gunkel maintained that the prophetic books are composed of small units of separate "oracles," which were joined together by editors. He determined the limits of the units by the formal criteria of opening and conclusion. Gressmann applied this method of Gunkel to Deutero-Isaiah, and in his literary analysis (1914) attempted to prove that chapters 40–55 are composed of 49 small independent units. Gressmann also classified the prophecies into about 12 "types," comprising nine prophetic *Gattungen* and three non-prophetic ones. This method played a major role in German biblical criticism. Koehler distinguished 70 units in chapters 40–55, while Volz distinguished 50 units (apart from the "Songs of the Servant of the Lord"). Mowinckel divided these chapters into 41 units (excluding the "Songs of the Servant of the Lord"), while Begrich pointed to the existence of more than 70 units. The protagonists of the small unit attempted to discover the system according to which these units were arranged. Mowinckel stated that these small prophecies, which were at first separate, were later organized according to the principle of "key words" (*Stichwörter*). Similar words or expressions appeared at the beginnings and ends of prophecies and served the editors as guides. Sometimes this principle of verbal associations was combined with, or varied by, conceptual associations. In the third stage there appeared a reaction to the method of *Gattungen* and small units, and several scholars attempted to show that the prophetic units are longer. Kaufmann strongly rejected the "form critical" method and maintained that "the error of this approach is the confusion of the formal or typological unit with the unit of composition." An author can fashion his creation out of many separate units formally joined together, which nevertheless combine into one composition. Kaufmann holds that Mowinckel's theory of "key words" is a mechanical approach which is unacceptable. The verbal linkings are not a matter of technical arrangement, but rather a phenomenon of composition: it is the author, not an editor, who is fond of such associations and more than once strains the meaning of a word in order to be able to repeat it. Kaufmann maintains that the prophecies in Isaiah 40–66 – both the units of the books and the separate prophecies within each unit – are arranged chronologically. According to him there are 14 prophecies in the first unit, 40–48; in the second unit, 49–57, he counts about 20 prophecies; while in the third unit, 58–66, he finds nine prophecies. According to him the traditional division into three sections is primary and reflects the stages in which these prophecies came into being. Similarly Muilenburg maintains that the literary units are large. According to him section 40–48 contains 14 prophecies (the same number as that of Kaufmann but with minor divergences). He maintains, however, that the prophecies of Deutero-Isaiah are made up of strophes which are joined in various ways by means of openings and conclusions, and, in this way, Muilenburg sought a formal structure in each and every prophecy. Haran affirmed the system of the long prophetic units, but according to him the criterion for the division of the prophecies has to be based not on formal mechanics but rather on the context of the individual cycles: formal linguistic considerations can be added subsequently by way of confirmation. The construction of the complete prophecies is accomplished by linking a concatenation of short sections, each of which contains a new idea or a new poetic image. The combination of the separate parts results in a kind of sum total of ideas and images, subjects and motifs, which is repeated several times throughout the first division 40–48. Each consecutive set of strophes which approaches a sum total makes up a whole literary unit. Each image or motif serves as a typical component of a prophecy, while the total prophecy is made up of a set which includes most of the components. It is not necessary, according to Haran, that the internal order of the components be uniform. The prophet can combine the typical components in a different order every time. There is a certain consistency in the total content of the set but not within the arrangement of components within it. The number of prophetic units in division 40–48, according to Haran, is 10, including the satirical lamentation for Babylon in chapter 47. More recent work (see Sweeney 1993, Sawyer) has focused on redactional analysis that studies the connections between the prophetic speeches and the extant prophetic book at the literary level, with the goal of explicating independent literary layers, the original foundation, and added-on layers not only in Deutero-Isaiah but in the entire canonical book (Kratz, Steck, Vermeylen). Other approaches are those of Baltzer, who views chapters 40–55 as liturgical drama, and Lau, who understands chapter 56–66 as a composite collection of texts brought together as "scribal prophecy" by scholars working within circles of transmitters of prophetic tradition.

CONCEPTUAL ASPECTS. *Exile and Redemption.* The Book of Ezekiel attests the frame of mind of the exiles of Judah and Jerusalem. The depression and despair of the exiles are expressed in the words of the people in the vision of the dry bones: "Our bones are dried up and our hope is lost" (Ezek. 37:11). This same pessimistic view of the relationship between the people and its God and of the future of the people persisted among the exiles. Some time (about 20 years) later, when the prophet who is called Deutero-Isaiah appeared, he found that the people believed that God was "hiding His face" from them and that their case was hopeless: "Why do you say, O Jacob, and speak O Israel, My way is hid from the Lord, and my right is disregarded by my God" (40:27). Against the background of this depression and despair, the prophet of comfort and encouragement arose and, like Ezekiel in his later years, he began at the outset of his career to comfort and encourage the exiles of Judah and Jerusalem and breathe new life into them. He brought the people tidings of the end of the time of wrath and the beginning of God's goodwill. The sin of Jerusalem was expiated, since she had atoned doubly for all her transgressions. The prophet tirelessly wove into all his early prophecies (40–48) words of comfort and tidings of redemption, describing God as the creator and director of history who has erased the guilt of His people and is about to redeem them from the captivity and exile, by both natural and supernatural means, according to His will and power. Despite the miraculous and eschatological nature of the described redemption, it is no mere consolation for the end of days but is rather based on, and connected with, current events. In the same way that God, the guide of history, created Babylon "to punish His obedient people, to destroy Jerusalem, and burn its Temple, so He has set up Cyrus" to promote the redemption of the Israelite people, to rebuild Jerusalem, and reestablish its Temple (44:28; 45:13). The prophet proclaims that the time has come for Babylon and Chaldea to be punished (43:14; 46:1; 47:1ff.), and actual events serve as proof of the truth of his words. The defeat of Babylon by Cyrus is seen as evidence that just as God fulfilled the "first promises" (probably the fall of Babylon; see Haran, *Bein Rishonot le-Ḥadashot*, 1963), so he will fulfill the "new promises" – the tidings of redemption, of the revival of the people, and of their return to Zion. The description of the redemption is not limited to the redemption of the people but includes also the redemption of Judah and Jerusalem. The redemption of the forsaken Jerusalem, the forgotten and widowed, the "bereaved and barren" (49:14, 21), is described in poetic and hyperbolic terms. She will shake herself out of the dust of her mourning, she will put on her power and her glory, her justice and her salvation will be seen by the nations and the kings, she will draw exiles to her from all corners of the land until there will not be room to contain them, and all the nations will stream to her to render her honor and glory (see 49:14–26; 51:17–23; 52:11ff.; 54:1ff.; 60:1ff.; 62:1ff.). Actually, the dreams of redemption foretold by the prophet were not fulfilled and realized, and there is, in fact, a discrepancy between the redemption as envisioned by the prophet and the actual Return. Apparently the prophet was among the first returnees, fulfilling what he had foretold. From Jerusalem he called on the people still in exile to forsake their exile (52:11). Although Jerusalem, the holy city, did not become the mother city of all the lands and nations, the returnees did rebuild its ruins.

Comfort and Rebuke. Prophecies of comfort and salvation predominate among the prophet's first prophecies, especially in the first section, chapters 40–48. The sin of the people was forgiven and the transgressions erased and pardoned, but even these first prophecies contain a tone of rebuke. Together with the notion that the sin was forgiven because they had paid "double for all their sins," there is the view that God pardoned the transgressions of Israel and would not bear their sins in mind not because of Israel's merit but for the sake of God's name (43:25). The words of comfort and tidings of redemption apparently did not arouse within Israel the anticipated reaction, and for this they are rebuked by the prophet (see 42:18–20; 43:8; 46:9–13). The wrathful rebuke, which is not merely implied but elaborated, is contained in the last chapter (48:1–11) of the first group, which is replete with prophecies of comfort, and which is also intended for those of little faith. Beginning with chapter 50, the prophet appears as an instrument of rebuke, and the rebuke overshadows the element of comfort. The subjects of rebuke are many and varied: he repeats his rebuke against those of little faith (chapter 50), against the forsaking of God (51:12–13). Whether or not chapters 56–66 are the words of this prophet, rebukes continue against the wicked among the people (chapter 56), against giving priority to ritual over social morality (chapter 58), against social transgressions (chapter 59), and against idolatry (chapter 65).

The Servant of the Lord. The biblical descriptions of the Servant are not unequivocal – he is sometimes portrayed as an individual, either biographically or autobiographically, while at other times he appears as a collective figure, identified with the People of Israel. This lack of clarity gave rise to varied and ramified interpretations among both Jews and Christians in all generations. The methods of interpreting the image of the Servant of the Lord have varied. The Servant has been seen as an individual personality, as a collective, and as a figure of myth with associated ritual. The individual approach is based on the assumption that what is written about the Servant is a description of an individual figure. Those who adopt this method disagree about the identity of this figure. In attempting to identify him, they identify him variously, as a figure from the past (the historical approach); as a contemporary of the prophet, including possibly the prophet himself; as one whom the prophet envisions as destined to appear in the future (the eschatological approach). These methods are intimated in early interpretations, and explicitly stated and argued in modern studies and commentaries. Numerous varied and strange proposals have been advanced concerning the identification of the Servant of God with historical figures from the Bible. The Servant was identified with various kings of the House of David and their descendants, whose biographies include some feature or features suggestive of the Servant, such as – among the Kings – Uzziah's leprosy, Hezekiah's dangerous illness, Josiah's untimely death despite his righteousness, or Jehoiachin's captivity. Among the post-Exilic members of the House of David with whom he is identified are Zerubbabel, the object of unfulfilled messianic hopes, Elioenai (a scion of the House of David, I Chron. 3:23), and Anani (last in the list of the Davidic line, 3:24). Other individuals with whom the Servant of the Lord has been identified were selected from among the prophets: e.g., Isaiah son of Amoz, who, according to the *aggadah*, was killed by Manasseh; the much-suffering Jeremiah; or Ezekiel, who bore the burden of the sin of the House of Israel (Ezek. 4:4–8). Still others are historical figures such as Moses or Job. According to the biographical approach, the prophet was describing a contemporary figure, known to himself and his listeners. The figures proposed for identification were Cyrus, Zerubbabel, or an anonymous person. Some maintained that the prophet was describing himself, or that he was being described by a disciple. According to the eschatological approach, the Servant of God is the destined redeemer, the Messiah. The approach is found at first in Targum Jonathan ("my servant the Messiah," at 52:13), but it has left few traces in Jewish exegesis, in contrast to its important role in Christianity, which identified the Servant of God with Jesus (beginning with the New Testament; see above). According to the collective method of interpretation, the Servant is Israel. If there are any personal elements in the description they are merely allegorical. It is explicitly stated in a number of places that the Servant is Israel (see e.g., 41:8; 44:1, 2, 21; 45:4; 59:1). While there are some who maintain that this refers to all of Israel, the real Israel, this is difficult since the real Israel is sinful and the Servant, free of sin. Therefore the Servant is identified with an ideal Israel, not the Israel of the present but the Israel of the future. Some adherents of the collective method hold that it is not all of Israel which is being referred to, but rather an elite within Israel, and there are varied opinions regarding the nature of this elite. Some maintain that it refers to the prophets, while others maintain that it refers to the priests. Still others speak of an undefined minority, "the righteous of Israel," and there are some who see the Servant as a visionary figure, the symbol of the righteous Israel. According to the mythological method, in portraying the figure of the Servant of God the prophet utilized a mythological figure, ignoring certain mythological traits and adopting several other characteristic traits. The image is that of a god who died and is resurrected, like the god Tammuz or Adonis (Baal). The central part of the Songs of the Servant of the Lord, 52:13–53:12, basically corresponds to the hymns sung during the Mesopotamian ritual of mourning the death of the god. According to this view there existed in Israel the ceremony of mourning for Tammuz and there was also the "bewailing of Hadadrimmon in the plain of Megiddo" (Zech. 12:11) which is assumed to have originated in the tragic death of Josiah at Megiddo (II Kings 23:29). These two wailing rites were combined into one ceremony and served as the basis for the description of the figure of the Servant of the Lord. Thus, the description of the Servant was influenced by a historical figure (Josiah) and a mythological figure (Tammuz). This method was associated with the Scandinavian school of myth and ritual. The "individual approach" and the "collective approach" are both plausible. It is, however, possible to interpret what is written about the Servant of the Lord in other ways. Some point to a lack of firm distinction in Hebraic thought between the particular or the individual – the prophet – and the general or the many – the people. Such fluidity could give rise to prophecies having both an "individual" and a "collective" style, i.e., the prophet Deutero-Isaiah, like his predecessors Hosea, Isaiah, Jeremiah, and Ezekiel, saw himself as a symbol of, and an "examplar" and model for, the people. His personal life was interwoven with the life of the people, the private domain became commingled with the public, and events from his personal life were interpreted by him as allegories of the people. There was also an opposite process, i.e., the image of the Servant of the Lord refers both to the prophet and to the people. At times, the individual type of description predominates, while at others, the collective style is prominent, referring also to Jacob and Israel. In the same way that the preceding prophets had interpreted their private and family lives as a sign and model for the people, so biographical details of the prophet were interwoven with the description of the Servant. The above hypotheses are based on the assumption of a unified conception of the Servant on the part of a writer or editor, which is far from certain.

Israel and the Nations. The relationship between Israel and the nations had political significance as well as religio-social significance. With the political victory of Babylon, Judah lost its political and territorial framework, and there was a danger that, as in the case of other nations, Israel's loss of a state would lead to its loss of religious identity, and that the people would assimilate among the nations. In the face of this danger, the prophet called Deutero-Isaiah played a decisive role in the crystallization of a well-informed national-religious group and the later crystallization of Judaism. Earlier biblical writings stressed monolatry, the principle that Israelites must serve Yahweh alone, but left open the possibility that other gods existed and might be worshipped by gentiles (Ex. 20:3; Deut. 4:19). It is in Deutero-Isaiah, followed by Trito-Isaiah, that we find for the first time a militant full-blown monotheism that denies the existence of all other gods but Yahweh, and calls gentiles to his service (Isa. 42:8; 43:10–11; 44:6–8; 45:5–7, 18–22; 46:9; 49:6; 56:1–8; 66:21–3). The victorious, conquering gods, the advanced material culture, and the impressive idolatrous ceremonies of Babylon constituted a danger that the exiles in Babylon would be attracted to assimilation. This prophet described in harsh polemic and with mockery and loathing the practices of idolatry and its followers (e.g., 40:17, 26; 44:6–20). He placed Israel vis-à-vis the gods of the nations, emphasizing the opposition between them. Israel and its God are lined up against the nations and their gods for "battle" and judgment. Opponents who strive and contend against Him rise up against Israel (41:11–12; 45:24). Some of the nations taunt and revile Israel (49:7; 51:7) and some of them blaspheme the name of the God of Israel (52:5). This religious-national battle recurs a number of times. But this is only for the present.

Chapters 40–66 are replete with the faith that the law of God will be disseminated by His Servant, Israel, among the nations which will be led from darkness to light. Israel will be "a light (or rather, 'a salvation') unto the nations" and Jerusalem will be the place of God's shining glory to which all the nations will stream with song and praise. They will emerge from spiritual darkness to the light which will shine for them in Zion. In Israel's redemption the world will also be redeemed and in the end of days all men will come to bow down before God (66:23). Traces of the envisioned end of days were already seen at this time. Israel's presence among the nations gave rise to the phenomenon of the "joiners" (chapter 66) who forsook idolatry and joined the religion of Israel. Questions were raised with regard to their status within the people of Israel and its future. The prophecies found in Isaiah 40–66 confront these problems and provide a positive response.

[Isaac Avishur]

IN THE AGGADAH

Amoz, the father of Isaiah, was also a prophet, for "when the name of the prophet's father is given, the father was likewise a prophet" (PdRE 118; Lev. R. 6:6). Isaiah came from Jerusalem, for "whenever the city of a prophet is not specified, he hailed from Jerusalem" (Lam. R., proem 24, beginning). An ancient *aggadah* reports that Amoz and Amaziah, king of Judah, were brothers (Meg. 10b.). "Because Isaiah was the king's nephew, he used to chastise Israel" (PdRK, 117). Isaiah uttered words of censure at the very outset of his prophecy. When the call came to him (Isa. 6:8), God said to him, "Isaiah! My children are obstinate and troublesome, are you ready to be beaten and degraded by them?" (PdRK, 125). As he stood bewildered he uttered words saying, "I am a man of unclean lips, and I dwell in the midst of a people of unclean lips" (Isa. 6:5), whereupon the Holy One blessed be He said to him, "You are permitted to say 'I am a man of unclean lips,' since you are your own master, but are you the master of My children that you refer to them as a people of unclean lips?" He was punished on the spot; Isaiah 6:6–7 are interpreted to mean that his mouth was scorched (PR 33:150), for having transgressed "Slander not a servant to his master" (Prov. 30:10). When Sennacherib besieged Jerusalem, Shebna and his companions wished to submit and conclude peace with him: "King Hezekiah, afraid lest the Holy One blessed be He be with the majority, was told by Isaiah, 'It is a conspiracy of wicked men, and a conspiracy of wicked men is to be disregarded'" (Sanh. 26a; cf. Isa. 8:12). When Hezekiah fell ill and was told by Isaiah that he would die (II Kings 20:1) because of his refusal to beget children, he attempted to justify himself by explaining that it had been foretold to him that he would beget a wicked son; whereupon Isaiah proposed to him that he marry his daughter in the hope that a worthy son would result from the union. In spite of this, however, only a wicked son was born to him (TJ, Sanh. 10:2, 28b–c). Of that wicked son, Manasseh, it is written that he "filled Jerusalem (with blood) from one end to the other" (II Kings 21:16). Scripture is silent as to the victims of Manasseh and the reason for his killing. According to Josephus (Ant., 10:38) "Manasseh killed all the righteous men among the Hebrews, nor did he spare even the prophets, everyday putting some to death." Many aggadists, however, see Manasseh's blood spilling as confined to Isaiah alone (TJ, Sanh. 10:2, 28c). According to the *aggadah* Manasseh accused Isaiah of being a false prophet. Isaiah, knowing that whatever he said in his defense would not be accepted, said nothing, both to absolve Manasseh and his people from the responsibility for deliberately murdering a prophet, and to prevent his blood from bubbling like that of the prophet Zechariah. Isaiah's silence was regarded as a confession and he was sentenced to death. When the sentence was about to be carried out, however, he uttered the ineffable name and was swallowed by a cedar tree. The tree was sawn, but the saw was powerless against Isaiah's body, which had become like a pillar of marble. One organ, alone, his mouth, was vulnerable, because of its having uttered the words, "And I dwell in the midst of a people of unclean lips." As a result, when the saw reached Isaiah's lips, he died (Yev. 49b).

[Elimelech Epstein Halevy]

Christian View

For discussion of the Christian use of Isaiah see *Immanuel, and Servant of the Lord (above).

IN ISLAM

Slightly altering the version in II Kings 18:13–21 the authors Tabarī and Thaʿlabī, related that Shaʿyā (Isaiah) ibn Amaṣya (Amaziah) (!) the prophet was sent during the reign of Zedikah (Zedekiah) to lead the king along the righteous path and to warn the people of Israel to repent. Allah sent the Assyrian king Sennacherib with a force of 600,000 soldiers against them. At the command of God, Shaʿyā informed the king that his death was imminent and that he should make his will and appoint a successor. Zedikah prayed to Allah, who lengthened his life by 15 years and also delivered him from Sennacherib. Sennacherib's army was annihilated and only he and five dignitaries and scribes escaped to a cave, where they were found by the king of Judah. Sennacherib confessed that he had heard of God, even before he left his country, but weakness of his mind had prevented him from reaching the right conclusion. The king of Judah let Sennacherib and his scribes circle the Temple for 70 days, giving them two loaves of bread made of barley daily. He sent Sennacherib home, according to God's command, in order that he might serve as a sign of warning. However, Tabarī (p. 381) also knew the correct name of the king, which was Hezekiah. In their tales on Isaiah, Umāra and Thaʿlabī quote paraphrases of his prophecies (ch. 1, etc.). After Hezekiah, his son Manasseh ruled for 55 years (II Kings 20:21–21:1). Tabarī also knew of Amon and Josiah, who reigned after Manasseh. Concerning Isaiah's end, Tabarī and Thaʿlabī relate that the people of Israel persecuted him for his prophecies and rebukes and that he escaped into a tree. Satan however held the fringes of his garment, which thus could be seen from without. They then brought a saw and cut through Isaiah. This tale was handed down by Wahb ibn Munabbih; its Jewish source is evident.

[Haïm Z'ew Hirschberg]

IN THE ARTS

The prophecies of Isaiah have found stronger echoes in art and music than in literature. In the 12th-century Anglo-Norman *Jeu d'Adam* Isaiah is one of the Old Testament prophets consigned to Hell after submitting reluctant evidence to the truths of Christianity; and he also figures in the medieval *Ordo Prophetarum*. Thereafter, Isaiah played only a minor part in literature until the 19th century, when the French writer Victor Hugo produced an appreciative sketch in his apocalyptic study *William Shakespeare* (1864; Eng. tr. 1864). The first Jewish writer to deal with the theme was Abraham *Mapu, the creator of the modern Hebrew novel; his *Ahavat Ẓiyyon* (1853, *In the Days of Isaiah*, 1902) was remarkable less for its characterization than for its Haskalah ideas and local color. *Ahavat Ẓiyyon* enjoyed amazing success and was translated into several languages, including no less than three English versions. Mapu later wrote another historical novel set in the times of Isaiah, *Ashmat Shomeron* (1865–66). In the 20th century, various plays were devoted to the subject. A modern Jewish treatment of the theme was *Der Novi* (1955; *The Prophet*, 1955), a novel about Deutero-Isaiah by Sholem *Asch.

Isaiah was represented by artists from early Christian times onward and owed his great popularity in the Middle Ages to three biblical passages thought to foretell the Incarnation and Nativity. More than any other prophet, Isaiah benefited from the cult of the Virgin. The passage, "the young woman shall conceive and bear a son" (Isa. 7:14), was seen as a prediction of the birth of Jesus. Even in the oldest surviving representation of the prophet, a second-century mural from the catacomb of Priscilla, Rome, Isaiah is shown seated opposite the Virgin and Child. Another prophecy, that of the "twig" that "shall grow from the roots of Jesse" (Isa. 11:1), gave rise to genealogical trees purporting to trace the ancestry of Jesus to the house of David. The distinguishing symbols of Isaiah in art are these "Jesse Trees" or one of his prophecies inscribed on his phylactery. Scenes from the life of Isaiah are found in Byzantine and premedieval art. Figures of the prophet often appear among the sculptures of 12th-century French Romanesque churches such as Vézelay and Moissac. The most striking example is the tempestuous swirling image from the abbey church at Souillac. There are also 13th-century sculptures of Isaiah in the great Gothic cathedrals of Chartres, Amiens, Burgos, and Bramberg. At the same period, his image adorned the wing of a painted "life of Christ" by the Sienese artist Duccio (1282–1319). In the 15th century, Isaiah appeared chiefly in painting and sculpture. Naturalistic sculpture by Claus Sluter adorns the fountain of the Chartreuse at Dijon. Renaissance treatments of the subject include a round painting by Perugino (Nantes Museum); and figures of Isaiah from the fresco by Raphael in Sant' Agostino, Rome, and from the Sistine Chapel ceiling by Michelangelo. A painting of the subject by Fra Bartolommeo is in the Uffizi Galleries, Florence. The German Renaissance artist Matthias Gruenewald included a figure of Isaiah in his painting of the Annunciation, which forms part of his Isenheim altarpiece in the Colmar Museum. Although the subject later lost favor, the 18th-century artist Tiepolo painted a figure of Isaiah for the ceiling of the Archbishop's Palace in Udine. Artists have also illustrated a number of episodes from the Book of Isaiah. There is an amusing painting called *Isaiah Rebuking the Women of Jerusalem* (on Isa. 3:16ff.) by the 19th-century English artist *Salaman. Isaiah's vision of God enthroned amid the Seraphim (Isa. 6:1–4) was quite a common theme in Byzantine and medieval art (see *Cherubim and *Seraphim). The purification of the prophet's lips with a burning coal (Isa. 6:5–7) is illustrated in premedieval and medieval manuscripts, including the 15th-century breviary of the Duke of Bedford (Bibliothèque Nationale); in murals; and in the 13th-century stained glass of La Sainte Chapelle, Paris. The visits of the prophet to the dying Hezekiah and the miraculous prolongation of the monarch's life (Isa. 38:1–8) are treated in an eighth-century fresco at Santa Maria Antiqua, Rome, where Isaiah is shown standing by the bedside of the sick king. The rabbinic tradition that Isaiah met his death by being sawn asunder in the hollow of a cedar is illustrated in various murals, including a sixth-century Coptic fresco, and in medieval sculpture and manuscripts.

In music, composers have dealt either with the "Triple Sanctus" or with the inspiring figure of the prophet himself. The "Thrice Holy" acclamation of the angels in the vision of Isaiah (Isa. 6:3) is the main text of the *Sanctus* section of the Roman Catholic mass; it is followed by the jubilant *Hosanna in excelsis*, the mystically interpreted *Benedictus*, and by a repetition of the *Hosanna*, the combination having been adapted from Matthew 21:9, Mark 11:9–10, and John 12:13. It has 21 traditional ("Gregorian") chant melodies dating from the tenth to the 13th centuries. In some of these, the initial "*Sanctus*" is rather florid and its reiterations are expressed in progressively rising phrases. This restrained attempt at word painting was carried much further in the *Sanctus* of the mass compositions, which date from the 14th century onward. Although these works naturally reflect the varieties of individual expression and the style of their era, certain conventions in the setting of the *Sanctus* can, nevertheless, be identified. The angelic acclamation is interpreted either as an outpouring of sweet sounds, often by two or three high solo voices (as in most of the 16th-century works), or as a mighty thundering of massed praise (as in Bach's *Mass in B Minor*). The *Sanctus* in Beethoven's *Missa Solemnis* (1823) is an exception, since it begins with a whispered stammering of awe. All composers take advantage of the differences in mood suggested throughout the sequence of *Sanctus, Hosanna, Benedictus*, and *Hosanna*. For the Protestant liturgy Martin *Luther created the rhymed "German Sanctus" (*Jesaia dem Propheten das geschah*, 1526), the melody of which is also attributed to the reformer. There are two settings by Bach of simple chorale tunes, based on the "Gregorian" melodies, with the Latin or German (*Heilig, Heilig, Heilig*) text. The many works for concert performance based on extended passages from the Book of Isaiah include Antonio Caldara's oratorio *Le profezie evangeliche d'Isaia* (1729; text by A. Zeno); Granville Bantock's *Seven Burdens of Isaiah* for men's choir *a cappella* (1927); Willy Burkhard's oratoria *Das GesichtJesaias* (1933–36; première 1936); Alexandre *Tansman's oratorio *Isaïe le prophète* (1951); Bernard Rogers' cantata *The Prophet Isaiah* (1954; published 1961); Robert *Starer's *Ariel, Visions of Isaiah* (1959); Bohuslav Martinu's cantata *The Prophecy of Isaiah* (première in Jerusalem, 1963); and Ben Zion *Orgad's *Isaiah's Vision*. Another modern work was Jacob *Weinberg's *Isaiah* (1947), an oratorio for solo voices and chorus with organ accompaniment and trumpet obbligato. The first part of Handel's oratorio *The Messiah* (première in Dublin, 1742), for which the text was compiled by Charles Jennens, contains so many passages from Isaiah (beginning with "Comfort ye, comfort ye my people") that it may almost be considered an Isaiah oratorio. Some of the most striking parts of Brahms' *Deutsches Requiem* (1857–68), for which the composer himself compiled the text from the Old and New Testaments, also originate in this biblical book. Settings of single verses or brief passages for liturgical or concert use are numerous. There are also traditional tunes from the various Jewish communities, ḥasidic melodies, and modern Israel folksongs.

[Bathja Bayer]

BIBLIOGRAPHY: O. Eissfeldt, *The Old Testament, an Introduction* (1965), 301–30, 754–56, contains copious bibliography on all aspects of Isaiah; (a) Medieval Jewish: Rashi; David Kimḥi, ed. by L. Finkelstein (1926); Ibn Ezra, ed. by M. Friedlaender, 2 vols. (1873–77, reprint 1964); (b) Modern: S.D. Luzzatto (Italian translation and Hebrew Commentary; 1855–67, reprint 1966); J. Skinner (*The Cambridge Bible*, rev. ed. 1915, reprint 1958–60); O. Procksch (Ger., 1930); E.J. Kissane (Eng., 1941). Other Works: M. Dyman (Haran), in: BJPES, 13 (1947), 7–13; H.L. Ginsburg, in: *Tarbiz*, 20 (1949), 29–32 (also publ. in *J.N. Epstein Jubilee Volume*, 1950); idem, in: JBL, 69 (1950), 51–60; idem, in: *Mordecai M. Kaplan Jubilee Volume* (1953), 245–59 (Eng. sect.); idem, in: *Eretz Israel*, 5 (1956), 61–65 (Eng. sect.); idem, in: *Oz le-David* (Ben Gurion, 1964), 335–50; idem, in: *Fourth World Congress of Jewish Studies, Papers 1* (1967), 91–93; idem, in: *Conservative Judaism*, 22, no. 1 (1967), 1–18; idem, in: JAOS, 88 (1968), 47–53, also publ. in *Essays in Memory of E.A. Speiser* (1968); idem, in: VTS, 17 (1968), 103 n. 2; R. Knierim, in: VT, 18 (1968),47–68; E.G. Kraeling, in: JBL, 50 (1931), 277–97; J. Milgrom, in: VT, 14 (1964), 164–82; H.M. Orlinsky, in: *Essays in Honor of Herbert Gordon May* (1970), 206–36; W. Rudolph, in: *Hebrew and Semitic Studies Presented to Godfrey Rolles Driver* (1963), 130–143; H.M. Schmidt, in: VT, 21 (1971), 68–90; H. Tadmor, in: *Journal of Cuneiform Studies*, 12 (1958), 22–40, 77–100; M.M. Kaplan, in: JBL. 45 (1926), 251–59; Kaufmann Y., Toledot, 3 (1947), 147–256, 293–318; W. Rudolph, in: D.W. Thomas and W.D. McHardy (eds.), *Hebrew and Semitic Studies Presented to G.R. Driver*... (1963), 130–43; M. Haran, in: VT, 17 (1967), 266–97; idem, in: iej, 18 (1968), 201–12; B.S. Childs, *Isaiah and the Assyrian Crisis* (1967); See also bibliography, *Immanuel. CHAPTERS 34–35: H. Graetz, in: JQR, 4 (1891/92), 1–8; A.T. Olmstead, in: AJSLL, 53 (1936/37), 251–3; C.C. Torrey, *The Second Isaiah* (1928), 103–4, 279–304; idem, in: JBL, 57 (1938), 109–34; M. Pope, *ibid.*, 71 (1952), 235–43; W. Caspari, in: ZAW, 49 (1931), 67–86; P. Wernberg-Moeller, *ibid.*, 69 (1957), 71–73; D.R. Hillers, *Treaty-Curses and the Old Testament Prophets* (1964); DEUTERO-ISAIAH: A.B. Ehrlich, *Mikra ki-Feshuto* (1901); S. Krauss, in: A. Kahana (ed). *Sefer Yeshayahu* (1904); B. Duhm, *Das Buch Jesaya* (19224); J. Skinner, *The Book of the Prophet Isaiah*, chs. XL–LXVI (1917); C. Torrey, *The Second Isaiah* (1922); K. Budde, *Das Buch Jesaya* (1922); E. Koenig, *Das Buch Jesaya* (1926); H. Odeberg, *Trito-Isaiah* (1931); P. Volz, *Jesaya II Kapital 40–66* (1932); D. Yellin, *Ḥikrei Mikra* (1939); E.J. Kissane, *The Book of Isaiah* (1943); J. Muilenburg, *The Book of Isaiah*, chs. 40–66 (1956), 381–773; C.R. North, *The Second Isaiah* (1964); N.H. Tur-Sinai, *Peshuto shel Mikra*, 3 (1967); J.L. McKenzie, *Second Isaiah* (1968); C. Westermann, *Isaiah*, 40–66 (1969). SELECTED STUDIES: Y. Zlotnick, *Aḥdut Yeshayahu* (1928); A. Kaminka, *Meḥkarim*, (1938), 1–89; N. Raban, in: *Tarbiz*, 14 (1943), 19–26; Ch. R. North *The Suffering Servant in Deutero-Isaiah* (1956^2), incl. bibl.; A. Neubauer and S.R. Driver, *The Fifty-Third Chapter of Isaiah According to the Jewish Interpretations* (2 vols, 1970); P.A.H. De Boer, *Second Isaiah's Message* (1956); S. Mowinckel, *He That Cometh* (1956), 187–257; Kaufmann Y., Toledot, 4 (1960), 51–156; M. Haran, *Beyn Rishonot le-Ḥadashot* (1963); idem, in: VTS, 9 (1963), 127–55; H.H. Rowley, *The Servant of the Lord* (1965^2); W. Zimmerly and J. Jeremias, *The Servant of God* (1965 rev. ed); H.M. Orlinsky and N.H. Snaith, *Studies on the Second Part of the Book of Isaiah* (1967). IN THE AGGADAH: Ginzberg, Legends, index. IN ISLAM: Ṭabarī, *Ta'rikh*, 1 (01357H), 378–82; Tha'labī, *Qiṣaṣ* (1356^4), 271–81; 'Umāra ibn Wathīma, *Qiṣaṣ*, Vatican, Ms. Borgia 165, fols. 106v–110f. **ADD. BIBLIOGRAPHY:** P. Machinist, in: JAOS, 103 (1983), 719–37; O. Steck, *Bereitete Heimkehr*... (1985; additional publications on Isaiah apud Blenkinsopp 2003, 117–18); J. Vermeylen (ed.), *The Book of Isaiah* (1989); C. Seitz, in: ABD, 3:472–88 (with bibliography); idem, in: JBL 115 (1996), 219–40; M. Sweeney, in: A. Hauser and P. Selow (eds.), *Currents in Research: Biblical Studies I* (1993), 141–62; idem, in: *Isaiah 1–39* (1996); R. Kratz, *Kyros im Deuterojesaja-Buch*...(1993); W. Lau, *Schriftgelehrte Prophetie in Jes 56–66*...(1994); M. Goshen-Gottstein (ed.), *The Book of Isaiah* (critical edition; 1995); J. Blenkinsopp, *Isaiah 1–39* (AB; 2000; bibliography 115–67); *Isaiah 40–55* (AB; 2000; bibliography, 127–74); *Isaiah 56–66* (AB; 2003; bibliography, 93–126); K. Baltzer, *Deutero-Isaiah: A Commentary on Isaiah 40–55* (Hermeneia; 2001); R.G. Kratz, in: *Review of Biblical Literature* (bookreviews.org; 03/2003), 1–8. IN ISLAM: B. Levine, in: *Iraq* 67 (2005), 411–27.

ISAIAH, ASCENSION OF, early Christian apocalypse, containing the Jewish apocryphon t*he Martyrdom of *Isaiah*. The *aggadah* about Isaiah's violent death was already known at the beginnings of Christianity (see Acts 8: 34). Thus the Jewish apocryphon was expounded by Christians as early as in the first century of Christianity. Of the Greek original only a papyrus fragment is extant and parts of Latin, Slavonic, and Coptic translations have been preserved. The whole work exists only in an Ethiopic translation. The apocryphal description of Jesus' birth, life, and resurrection (11:1–21) is a later interpolation lacking in the Latin version and in the three Slavonic versions. In the Christian part of the book Isaiah is described as a seer according to the spirit of apocalyptic literature. His violent death is regarded as revealing the coming of Jesus and the early history of the Church (3:13–31). This passage and the following chapter (4) containing a description of the *Antichrist are very important witnesses for the oldest Christian history and beliefs. The author sees inter alia the degeneration of contemporary Christianity in the small number of Christian prophets, an institution which disappeared in the second century. He is the oldest witness to Peter's martyrdom by Nero (4: 3). At the end of days Beliar (Belial), "the great prince, the king of this world," will descend from heaven in the shape of Nero; he will do many wonders and lead humanity astray, but he will finally be destroyed. This description reflects an Antichrist tradition more or less independent of the New Testament, whose main motifs are taken from Jewish sources.

It is very probable that the description of Isaiah's ascent to the seven heavens was also written by the same Christian author (chapters 6–11). The similarities between this vision and similar visions in Jewish apocalyptic literature and old Jewish mysticism are noteworthy. According to the book, Isaiah also saw the miraculous descent of Jesus from the seventh heaven and his future ascent after his resurrection. This description resembles the similar motifs of the *Epistola Apostolorum* ("Letter of the Apostles"), a Christian work of the beginning of the second century. The mystical theology of the Christian parts of the *Ascension of Isaiah* is imbued by Jewish mystical and apocalyptical material, and its opinion about the heavenly nature of Jesus is close to gnostic speculations, although the book is, compared with contemporary Christian products, not heterodox. Later, when orthodox Christian tenets were firmly established, the book was used by Christian sects with gnostic elements and even by Arians.

BIBLIOGRAPHY: R.H. Charles, *Ascension of Isaiah* (1900; repr. with intr. by G.H. Box, 1917); B.P. Grenfell and A.S. Hunt, *Amherst Papyri* (1902); E. Tisserant, *Ascension d'Isaïe* (1909); J. Flemming and H. Duensing, in: E. Hennecke and W. Schneemelcher (eds.), *Neutestamentliche Apocryphen*, 2 (1964³), 454–68; M. Meslin, *Les Ariens d'Occident* (1967), 242–3.

[David Flusser]

ISAIAH, MARTYRDOM OF, one of the source documents discerned by scholars in the *Ascension of Isaiah* (see *Isaiah, Ascension of), relating Isaiah's persecution and eventual martyr's death at the hands of *Manasseh, king of Judah. From the first publication in 1819 of the Ethiopic version with Latin translation (the most important text) by R. Laurence, the martyrdom legend was recognized as of Jewish origin. Gesenius in 1821 first distinguished two parts (1–5, 6–11) and the two most important divisions of the material were those of A. Dillmann (*Ascensio Isaiae, aethiopice et latine*, 1877) and R.H. Charles (*Ascension of Isaiah*, 1900). Dillmann considers that the material falls into (1) a Jewish martyrdom of Isaiah (2:1–3:12 + 5:2–14); (2) a Christian ascension of Isaiah (6:1–11:1 + 23–40); (3) Christian editorial reworkings of these two (ch. 1, except 1, 3, 4 and 11:42–43); (4) a final Christian editing which added the apocalypse (3:13–5:1) and certain other passages. Charles concluded that the work is composed of three documents: (1) martyrdom of Isaiah (1:1, 2, 6–13; 2:1–8, 10–3:12; 5:1–14 – substantially identical with Dillmann's first document); (2) testament of Hezekiah (3:13–4:18); and (3) vision of Isaiah (6:1–11:14). Both the latter are Christian. Charles' hypothesis has been widely accepted, although C.C. Torrey, for example (*The Apocryphal Literature* (1945), 133–5) queries the existence of the martyrdom as a separate work.

In view of the obviously composite nature of the *Ascension* and the wide circulation of the story of the martyrdom in Jewish sources (e.g., Yev. 49b; Sanh. 103b; TJ, Sanh. 10:2, 28c; PR 84:14, cf. Ginzberg, Legends (1928), 373ff.), it seems likely that the work is of Jewish origin. It is probably to be connected with the traditions about the deaths of prophets (Mart. Isa. 5:12 and parallels; Jub. 1:12; cf. II Chron. 24:19, I En. 89:51–53, 4Qp-Hosb 2:4–6; et al.) and with a type of hagiographic literature of which the *Vitae Prophetarum* is an example. Eissfeldt relates it to the martyrdom legends of the period of Antiochus Epiphanes, such as those of Eleazar and of the mother and her seven sons (II Macc. 6:18–7:42). Flusser (IEJ, 3 (1953), 30–47) interprets the work as a typological representation of the story of the Qumran Teacher of Righteousness. This interpretation is carried to great extremes by M. Philonenko (*Pseudépigraphes de l'Ancien Testament et manuscrits de la Mer Morte* (1967), 1–10). Certainly notable is the use of the name Beliar (2:4 et al.) along with Satan (e.g., 2:2) and Sammael (1:8). The name Belchira (with variants) for the false prophet, Isaiah's opponent, remains without conclusive explanation. The book may supply important information about the life and mores of apocalyptic seers, and is an example of little-known Jewish hagiographic writing. The transmission of the work is complex and is dealt with by Charles, E. Tisserant (*Ascension d'Isaïs*, 1909), and others. As well as the Ethiopic text, there are fragments or versions in Greek, Slavonic (Vaillant, in *Revue des Etudes Slaves*, 42 (1963), 109–21), Latin, and Coptic (Lacau, in *Le Muséon*, 59 (1946), 453–67).

BIBLIOGRAPHY: Beer, in: *Apokryphen und Pseudepigraphen...*, ed. by E. Kautzsch, 2 (1900), 119–27; Charles, Apocrypha, 2 (1913), 155–62; Rist, in: IDB, 2 (1962), 744ff., s.v. *Isaiah, Ascension of* (contains bibliography); E. Hennecke and W. Schneemelcher, *Neutestamentliche Apocryphen*, 2 (1964³), 454–65; O. Eissfeldt, *The Old Testament, an Introduction* (1965), 609f. (contains bibliography).

[Michael E. Stone]

ISAIAH BEN ABRAHAM (d. 1723), rabbi and kabbalist, grandson of *David b. Samuel ha-Levi. He wrote *Ba'er Heitev*, a commentary on the Shulḥan Arukh, *Oraḥ Ḥayyim*, which the title page describes as "a digest of the legal decisions of all the early and later halakhic authorities, and of all extant responsa." The book, which contains many kabbalistic quotations, particularly from Isaac Luria, achieved immediate acclaim, many editions appearing within a few years (first ed. in Shulḥan Arukh, *Oraḥ Ḥayyim*, Amsterdam, 1708). In 1742, however, Judah *Ashkenazi, *dayyan* of Tiktin, published a book serving the same purpose, with the same form and content and even the same name. Because the later book treated the material in greater detail, the earlier one lost its popularity, and whereas Ashkenazi's edition was published with the Shulḥan Arukh, Isaiah's was forgotten. His work on the other sections of the Shulḥan Arukh was never published. Isaiah, his wife, and his daughter met their death in an inn fire in Mogilev, on their way to Ereẓ Israel.

BIBLIOGRAPHY: Azulai, 2 (1852), 12, no. 17; H.N. Maggid-Steinschneider, *Ir-Vilna* (1900), 139 n.2; Ch. Tchernowitz, *Toledot ha-Posekim*, 3 (1947), 306–8.

[Abram Juda Goldrat]

ISAIAH BEN ELIJAH DI TRANI (the Younger, "Riaz"; d. c. 1280), rabbinical scholar; grandson of Isaiah b. Mali di *Trani (the Elder). Little is known of his life, and even his works have remained mostly in manuscript. His novellae are known mainly from quotations in Joshua Boaz' *Shiltei ha-Gibborim* on the *Halakhot* of *Alfasi. Isaiah's halakhic works on a few tractates (*Berakhot* and *Shabbat* (Jerusalem, 1964) and on *Eruvin, Pesaḥim, Yoma*, and *Sukkah* (*ibid.*, 1966)) have been published and several fragments appear in the *Me'at Devash* of D. Sassoon (1928). He frequently quotes his grandfather, and his own *Kunteres ha-Re'ayot*, apparently an extensive work in which he enlarged on his brief decisions. In his halakhic works Isaiah disputes philosophical interpretations while he deals with the *aggadah*. Isaiah adopted a less tolerant attitude toward philosophy and the general sciences than did his grandfather. The *Perush Rabbenu Yeshayah*, printed in *Mikra'ot Gedolot*, as well as the commentaries on the Prophets and Hagiographa recently published as the work of his grandfather, should apparently be ascribed to him.

BIBLIOGRAPHY: Guedemann, Gesch Erz, 2 (1884), 189ff. (= A.S. Friedberg, *Ha-Torah ve-ha-Ḥayyim* (1898), 165–8); Joel, in: KS, 10 (1933/34), 545–52; A.I. Wertheimer, *Perush Nevi'im u-Khetuvim le-Rabbenu Yeshayah ha-Rishon mi-Trani* (1959), 11–56.

[Israel Moses Ta-Shma]

ISAIAH BEN MALL DI TRANI (the Elder; c. 1200–before 1260), early Italian halakhist, scion of a well-known rabbinic and scholarly family. Born in Trani, he is mainly known as the author of extensive commentaries and *pesakim* ("decisions") on the Talmud. Isaiah was a pupil of Simḥah of Speier and kept in contact with German scholars. His responsa are to be found in the *Or Zaru'a* of *Isaac b. Moses of Vienna, who greatly esteemed him. He traveled in the Mediterranean countries, spending some time in Greece and in Ereẓ Israel. Among the scholars whom he quotes mention should be made of Baruch "of Greece" (see *Baruch b. Isaac of Aleppo) while Zedekiah b. Abraham *Anav, author of *Shibbolei ha-Leket*, quotes him extensively.

Isaiah's works cover a wide range. They include (1) *Pesakim* on the Talmud, containing a summary of the subject under discussion, along the lines of *Alfasi, with additional comments on unresolved difficulties and a final decision on the conflicting views in the manner of *Hananel b. Ḥushi'el. The following *pesakim* have been published: on *Berakhot* and *Shabbat* (1964); on *Eruvin, Pesaḥim, Yoma*, and *Sukkah* (1966); on *Sukkah* alone in *Sam Ḥayyim* (Leghorn, 1801); on *Beẓah* (in *Maḥaneh David*, 1889, wrongly described as *Tosafot Rid*); on *Rosh Ha-Shanah, Ta'anit* and *Ḥagigah* (in *Oholei Yiẓḥak*, Leghorn, 1821); on *Yevamot* (called *Tosafot Rid*, 1931); on *Ketubbot* and *Gittin* (in margin of TB, Vilna edition, wrongly described as *Tosafot Rid*); on *Kiddushin* (1965); on *Makkot* (in: *Talpioth*, 8, 1963); on *Horayot* (*ibid.*, 9, 1965); on *Ḥullin* (first chapter, in *Ha-Segullah*, 1940), and on *Niddah* (1963). His *pesakim* on the *Halakhot Ketannot* have also been published (Leghorn, 1801). The remainder are still in manuscript. (2) *Sefer ha-Makhri'a* (Leghorn, 1779) deals principally with important *halakhot* in regard to which the codifiers were in dispute, and which Isaiah attempts to resolve. (3) *Sefer ha-Leket* (not extant) is similar in nature to *ha-Makhri'a*. (4) *Tosafot Rid*, novellae to the Talmud. Extant are his novellae to the tractates: *Shabbat, Eruvin, Pesaḥim, Yoma, Sukkah, Beẓah, Rosh Ha-Shanah, Megillah, Ḥagigah, Mo'ed Katan, Nedarim, Nazir, Bava Kamma, Bava Meẓi'a, Bava Batra, Avodah Zarah*, and *Niddah* (Lemberg, 1862–68; new edition in preparation partly printed); *Kiddushin* (Sabionetta, 1553, and subsequent editions, such as, New York, 1965); *Ta'anit* (at end of *Sefer ha-Makhri'a*). *Tosafot Rid* was compiled in several "editions" in the form of pamphlets in which Isaiah retracted or supplemented his previous statements. The exact relationship between this book and his *pesakim* has not been established, as much of the material is common to both and in addition the printers added to the confusion. (5) Responsa (1967). (6) Commentary on the Pentateuch. Extracts from this commentary were published by Ḥ.J.D. *Azulai in his *Penei David* (Leghorn, 1792). The commentaries on the other books of the Bible, published under his name in Jerusalem in 1959, are apparently to be ascribed to his grandson. (7) *Piyyutim*.

Isaiah was an independent thinker with considerable originality of approach and with a critical attitude to the opinions of his predecessors. Occasionally he sharply rejects the teachings of *geonim*, such as *Hai Gaon and *Samuel b. Hophni, and of other distinguished predecessors. He even criticizes his own works, commenting, "All that I have written is valueless (*hevel*)." He is not awed by authority and is concerned only with examination of the source material. His books are distinguished by clarity of explanation, careful choice of correct readings, and methodological approach to talmudic principles and lines of reasoning.

BIBLIOGRAPHY: Guedemann, Gesch Erz, 2 (1884), 184–9, 320–6; Gross, in: ZHB, 13 (1909), 46–58, 87–92, 118–23; Marx, *ibid.*, 188f.; M. Higger, *Halakhot ve-Aggadot* (1933), 11–27; H. Tchernowitz, *Toledot ha-Posekim*, 2 (1947), 62–68; A.I. Wertheimer (ed.), *Perush Nevi'im u-Khetuvim le-Rabbi Yeshayah ha-Rishon mi-Trani* (1959), 11–56 (introd.); idem (ed.), *Teshuvot ha-Rid* (1967), 17–66 (introd.); Rosenfeld, in: *Sinai*, 54 (1963/64), 290–301; S.K. Mirsky (ed.), *Shibbolei ha-Leket* (1966), 29–34 (introd.); idem, in: *Talpioth*, 9 (1964), 49–109; S. Abramson, in: *Sinai*, 65 (1969), 103–8.

[Israel Moses Ta-Shma]

ISAIAH BEN UZZIAH HA-KOHEN, medieval Karaite scholar of uncertain date (12th–15th centuries). He was the author of a work in Arabic known under the Hebrew title *Siddur* or *Sefer ha-Mitzvot*, of which two different versions are known. The first part deals with prayer and ritual matters (fasts and feasts, Sabbath, circumcision, marriage, diet, etc.). The second part deals with dogmatic theology, Hebrew grammar, etc., as well as with some subjects already covered in the first part; this second part refers to Isaiah in the third person, and may therefore be by another hand. Isaiah is generally referred to in Karaite sources by the title *al-Muʿallim al-Fāḍil* ("the excellent preceptor").

BIBLIOGRAPHY: Steinschneider, Arab Lit, 242–3; L. Nemoy (ed.), *Karaite Anthology* (1952), 235.

[Leon Nemoy]

ISAIAH ḤASID FROM ZBARAZH (17th–18th centuries), Shabbatean scholar, the son-in-law of *Judah he-Ḥasid. In 1700 Isaiah Ḥasid immigrated to Jerusalem with his father-in-law and his companions. When the kabbalist Abraham *Rovigo arrived in *Jerusalem in 1702 and founded there a *bet midrash* for ten select members, he took Isaiah Ḥasid's advice as to who should be admitted to it. Isaiah's name occurs among the signatories of a letter sent from Jerusalem to Breslau seeking help for the Ashkenazi community in Jerusalem. As a result of falling under the influence of Shabbatean beliefs and performing "strange deeds," he was compelled, apparently before 1706, to leave Jerusalem. Settling in Mannheim, Germany, he installed himself in the Shabbatean *bet midrash* of the philanthropist Asher Lemmle Regenheim. From there, together with others of the sect, he spread Shabbatean propaganda in the communities of Germany and Poland. He became a follower of the Shabbatean leader Loebele *Prossnitz, who he believed to be the Messiah. In 1725, when Moses Meir Kamenker, the emissary of the Polish Shabbateans, came to Mannheim, he entered into a conspiracy with Isaiah. The two disseminated writings condemning the Talmud and hinting that adherents of the Talmud did not believe in the God of Israel. They even wanted to proclaim Jonathan *Eybeschuetz as the Messiah. When their activity became publicly known the rabbis of Frankfurt excommunicated them, a ban which was also proclaimed in Altona, Amsterdam, Mannheim, and other communities.

BIBLIOGRAPHY: I. Rivkind, in: *Reshumot*, 4 (1926), 318–20; J. Mann, in: *Me'assef Ẓiyyon*, 6 (1934), 67–68; G. Scholem, in: *Zion*, 9 (1944), 32; M.A. Perlmutter, *Rabbi Yehonatan Eybeschuetz ve-Yaḥaso el ha-Shabbeta'ut* (1947), 29, 41–4; M. Benayahu, in: *Sefunot*, 3–4 (1960), 141, 153, 158, 163–4, 166–7.

[David Tamar]

ISAIAH MENAHEM BEN ISAAC (d. 1599), rabbi in Poland. In accordance with the custom prevalent in his time, his father-in-law's name was added to his and he was referred to as "Mendel [Menahem] Avigdors." Isaiah Menahem was one of the chief spokesmen of the *Council of Four Lands. He served as rabbi of Praga (a suburb of Warsaw), head of the yeshivah of Szczebrzeszyn, rabbi of Lodomeria, and in 1591 succeeded *Meir of Lublin as rabbi of Cracow. While rabbi of Lodomeria, he drew up a new formula for the *hetter iska* (permitting the lending of money on interest), which was opposed by Mordecai *Jaffe and Joshua *Falk. As a result, when he became rabbi of Cracow, he amended the formula. This amended formula, known as *Shetar Hetter Iska ke-Tikkun Muram* (Morenu Rav Mendel), was wrongly attributed to Moses *Isserles. In his *Naḥalat Shivah*, *Samuel b. David ha-Levi defends the formula and highly praises Isaiah Menahem. Isaiah Menahem was among the signatories of the *takkanah* adopted by the Council of Four Lands at Lublin in 1587, prohibiting anyone from acquiring rabbinic office by payment or other unjust means. He is referred to in the responsa Baḥ of Joel *Sirkes (no. 77) and in the *Matenat Kehunnah* on the *Midrash Rabbah* (Lev. R. 2) of Issacher Ashkenazi who acknowledges his indebtedness to him for the explanation of a certain passage. Together with his son Moses he wrote notes to the *Ammudei ha-Golah* of *Isaac of Corbeil which were published with the text (Cracow, 1596). He wrote a supercommentary on Rashi's commentary on the Pentateuch (*Be'urim Kabbedu ha-Shem*, Cracow, 1604). One of his *piyyutim* was published in the *Ḥag ha-Pesaḥ* of J. Kitzingen (Cracow, c. 1597).

BIBLIOGRAPHY: A. Walden, *Shem ha-Gedolim he-Ḥadash*, 1 (1864), 486 no. 52; J.M. Zunz, *Ir ha-Ẓedek* (1874), 45–49; Azulai, 1 (1905), 214 no. 118 *(Pelelat Soferim)*; H.D. (B.) Friedberg, *Luḥot Zikkaron*; Halpern, Pinkas, 6, 8, 63, 74.

[Abram Juda Goldrat]

ISBAKH, ALEXANDER ABRAMOVICH (**Itzhak Bakhrakh**; 1904–1977), Russian writer and literary scholar. Isbakh was born in Daugavpils, Latvia, and graduated from the Literary Department of Moscow University in 1924. He published poems and novels about the Red Army, including descriptions of Jewish soldiers. During World War II he was an army correspondent. He was also a member of the editorial staff of the journals *Oktober* and *Znamia*, and taught in the university. In 1949 he was arrested as a "cosmopolitan" and sentenced to 10 years in forced labor camps. He was released in 1959, rehabilitated, and returned to writing. He published a number of autobiographical novels and a book about the French Resistance (1960), always using Jewish imagery and themes. He also published a personal account of the Nazi offensive, *Front* (1941). His literary studies include one on Louis Aragon (1957) and *Na literatunykh barrikadakh* ("On the Barricades of Literature," 1964). He later wrote the fictional family chronicle *Masterovoy* ("The Artisan," 1966).

[Shmuel Spector (2nd ed.)]

ISCANDARI (originally **Al-Iscandari,** from al-Iscandria = *Alexandria, also written as **Ascandarani, Scandarani,** and **Scandari**), family of talmudists and authors, heads of the *Mustaʿrab (Arabic-speaking Jews) community who were in close touch with government circles in Ereẓ Israel and Egypt in the 17th and 18th centuries. According to Joseph *Sambari, the family originated in *Spain, the first of the family to immigrate to *Egypt being a certain Joseph who settled in Alexandria and, on moving to *Cairo, was called Scandari. This is, however, doubtful; it is almost certain that the Iscandaris were an ancient Mustaʿrab family.

(1) JOSEPH BEN ABRAHAM ASCANDARANI (1430?–after 1507) lived in *Jerusalem. He studied together with Obadiah of *Bertinoro and according to Jacob *Berab was a most erudite scholar. He moved to *Safed, c. 1491, where he became the head of a Mustaʿrab yeshivah; he spent the rest of his life there. He wrote commentaries on the *Yad* of Maimonides and on the *Tur* of *Jacob b. Asher. The letter he sent in about 1507 to the *nagid*, Isaac ha-Kohen *Sholal, in Egypt, is one of the most important documents about the Jewish community in Ereẓ Israel after the expulsion from Spain. He described the yeshivah, and asked for Sholal's intervention in a dispute he had with Moses ha-Dayyan who was responsible for its administration.

(2) JOSEPH SCANDARI (after 1527), rabbi and physician. He is said to have lived first in Alexandria before moving to Cairo, where he became one of five appointed leaders of the Mustaʿrabim community.

(3) ABRAHAM THE ELDER, son of Joseph (2), was also a rabbi and physician, and succeeded to his father's post in the community. Ḥayyim Joseph David Azulai possessed a manuscript of his halakhic rulings.

(4) ELEAZAR B. ABRAHAM SCANDARI (d. 1620; called Aba, after the initials of his name), son of Abraham, court physician of Sinan Pasha, the Turkish governor of Egypt. He healed Sinan of a severe illness, whereupon the latter appointed him finance minister of his dominion. Eleazar was the head of the Mustaʿrabs. In 1591 when Sinan was appointed chief vizier, Scandari moved to Constantinople where he became the leader of the Jewish community. As a result of his participation in the formulation of Turkish policy in Moldavia and Transylvania, he became involved in a dispute with the Moldavian governor, Aron-Wodah, who did not fulfill the promises he had made to Scandari. On one occasion when Scandari accompanied Sinan Pasha to Jassy, he was arrested by the governor and held captive in Transylvania until 1596. On his release he returned to Cairo and in 1618 was awarded the Turkish title, *chelebi*. He was put to death on the orders of the Turkish governor of Egypt after he had been falsely accused by the Muslims. According to Joseph *Sambari, he was the author of glosses on the *Yad* of Maimonides.

(5) ABRAHAM B. ELEAZAR ISCANDARI (1565?–1650), one of the four sons of Eleazar, was one of the greatest Egyptian rabbis and halakhists. He was a pupil of Abraham *Monzon I. He maintained a yeshivah in his own home and possessed a large and valuable library, containing many manuscripts. Through him an impressive collection of the responsa of Maimonides was copied. From his responsa, copies and digests were made, some of which were published in the books of the scholars in Egypt, Palestine, and Turkey. The historians Joseph Sambari and David *Conforte resided with him and assisted with his library. He also engaged in the study of Kabbalah and copied the *Sifra de-Ẓeni'uta* with the commentary of Isaac *Luria, adding his own glosses (Benayahu collection). Collections of his sermons are extant in manuscript (Ms. Guenzburg, Moscow, no. 1055).

(6) JOSEPH HA-LEVI ISCANDARI (d. 1768) was head both of the Mustaʿrabim and the general Egyptian community where he also served as a tax collector. Ḥayyim Joseph David Azulai was one of his friends. He was executed by Ali-Bey.

BIBLIOGRAPHY: Conforte, Kore, 30b, 41, 49b, 51a; Neubauer, Chronicles, 1 (1887), 155–6, 158, 162; Ḥ.Y.D. Azulai, *Ma'gal Tov ha-Shalem*, ed. by A. Freimann, 1 (1921), 51, 53; R.A. Ben-Shimon, *Tuv Miẓrayim* (1908), 5a–7a, 9a, 13b–14b; Rosanes, Togarmah, 3 (1938), 316–8, 358–60; Ashtor, Toledot, 2 (1951), 487–9; Benayahu, in: *Sefer Assaf* (1953), 111–3; idem, *Rabbi D. Azulai* (Heb., 1959), 22, 549, 572–3; Ben-Ze'ev, in: *Sefunot*, 9 (1965), 272–6, 278, 292–3; Baer, Spain, index, s.v. *Ascandrani*; Tamar, in: *Rabbi Yoseph Caro*, ed. by I. Raphael (Heb., 1969), 12ff.

ISENSTEIN, KURT HARALD (1898–1980), Danish sculptor, born in Hanover. Isenstein directed an art school in Germany, which he reestablished when he moved to Denmark. His works include portraits of Einstein, Hindenburg, and Pirandello. He carved a monument in memory of the Danish refugees in Sweden (1943–45) and two memorials to the Norwegian Jews who perished at Auschwitz. The latter are found in the Jewish cemeteries in Oslo and Trondheim, Norway.

ISER, JOSIF (1881–1958), Romanian artist and draftsman. Iser, who studied in Munich and then in Paris under Derain, began his career as a draftsman. However, after World War I, he devoted himself entirely to painting, working until 1928 at Neuilly-sur-Seine. Iser's work is characterized by the almost linear manner in which he emphasizes the contours of people and objects. His style is a mixture of neoclassicism and impressionism, influenced by Cézanne. Some of his recurring themes are the Oriental landscapes of Romania (Doboudja), old Turks in cafés, and interiors with odalisques.

BIBLIOGRAPHY: Jancou, in: *Menorah Journal*, 15 (1928). 340; *Iser* (1962).

[Isac Bercovici]

ISFAHAN, city in Iran on the route from Teheran to the Persian Gulf. The origin of the Jewish settlement in Isfahan, one of the oldest in Persia, has been ascribed by Pehlevi, Armenian, and Muslim sources to various early historical periods. Though not mentioned in the Talmud, the city's Jewish community is first recorded in the time of the Sassanid ruler Fīrūz (472 C.E.) who, according to Ḥamza al-Iṣfahānī, put to death half the Jewish population in Isfahan on a charge of killing two Magian priests. When the Arabs conquered Persia (641), they found a strong Jewish community in Isfahan. The Arab chronicler Abu Nuʿaym reported that at that time the Jews were celebrating, dancing, and playing music in expectation of a "Jewish king." Under the caliphate, the Jewish quarter in Isfahan, known as *Jayy*, had grown to such a degree in number and size that Arab and Persian geographers called it *al-Yahūdiyya*, "the city of the Jews." Isfahan was the birthplace of the first Jewish sectarian movement, led by *Abu ʿIsā of Isfahan, in the time of the Umayyad caliph ʿAbd al-Malik (685–705). Abu ʿIsā, claiming to be a messiah and a religious reformer, gained a considerable following among the Jews of Isfahan and other places and it is reported that his followers, known as "Isavis" or "Isfahanis," still existed in Isfahan in the tenth century.

*Maimonides mentioned the Jews in Isfahan in his *Iggeret Teiman* (Epistle to Yemen); the city was regarded as a center of Hebrew grammar and exegesis. About 1166 *Benjamin of Tudela estimates their number at 15,000 and also mentions the chief rabbi Sar Shalom, who had been appointed by the exilarch of Baghdad, with authority over all the communities of Persia. When the Safavid dynasty made Isfahan its capital (1598), the Jews prospered economically and were engaged as craftsmen, artisans, and merchants in drugs, spices, antiquities, jewelry, and textiles. They suffered greatly when the persecution and forced conversion, initiated under Shah *Abbas I and renewed under Shah *Abbas II, swept throughout the Jewish communities of Persia in the 17th century. Their sufferings were described in the Judeo-Persian chronicles of *Babai ibn Luṭf and *Babai ibn Farḥad, and by Carmelite, Jesuit, and other eyewitnesses.

Religious life in Isfahan had a rigid traditional rabbinical basis, with the Sabbath and dietary laws strictly enforced. There existed several synagogues, schools, and other communal institutions, and the community was well organized. A *Karaite group also existed there. On the instructions of *Nādir Shah (d. 1747), the Isfahani Jew Bābā ibn Nuriel translated the Psalms and the Pentateuch into Persian in 1740. Bible manuscripts in Judeo-Persian were found in Isfahan at the beginning of the 17th century by the Italian scholar and traveler G. Vechietti, who cooperated with Jewish scholars there in the transliteration of Judeo-Persian manuscripts.

With the advent of the Qājār dynasty (1794–1925) and the transfer of the capital to *Teheran, Isfahan and its Jewish population lost much of its cultural and political prominence. European travelers of the 19th century, such as *David d'Beth Hillel (1828), *Benjamin II (1850), and E. *Neumark (1884), estimated the number of Jews in Isfahan at between 300 and 400 families. Jewish cultural life in Isfahan was threatened by the activities of the *Bahai movement and the Christian missionary societies, who, exploiting the plight of the Jews, began to work in the Jewish ghettos and established a missionary school in Isfahan in 1889. These inroads were counteracted in 1901 by the establishment of a Jewish school in Isfahan by the *Alliance Israélite Universelle. Isfahan is the seat of some revered "holy places," especially the alleged burial place of Serah bat Asher b. Jacob (granddaughter of the patriarch mentioned in Num. 26:46), situated in the vicinity of Pir Bakran, 20 miles (30 km.) south of Isfahan and a popular place of pilgrimage for all Isfahan Jews, who bury their dead there, with an inscription dated 1133 C.E.

[Walter Joseph Fischel / Amnon Netzer (2nd ed.)]

Contemporary Period

Of the 10,000–12,000 Jews who lived in Isfahan in 1948, about 2,500 remained in 1968. Many had settled in Israel, while others moved to Teheran. According to the census of 1956, Isfahan was the third-largest Jewish community in Iran, after Teheran and Shiraz. The number of synagogues had dropped from 18 to 13 by 1961. Most Jews were poor peddlers; in 1952 it was estimated that only 1% lived in reasonable circumstances, while 80% were poverty-stricken, and the rest lived on the verge of poverty. Most of the poorest left for Israel. In 1968 the town had an Alliance Israélite Universelle school with high school classes, and schools run by *ORT and *Oẓar ha-Torah. In 1961, 150 pupils attended Jewish high school; 897 attended elementary school; other children attended government schools, while there were about 50 Jews at Isfahan University. However, even in 1967 many Jewish children did not attend any educational institution. In 1968 Isfahan had a branch of the Iranian Jewish Women's Organization and of the Zionist youth organization He-Ḥalutz, founded before 1948. At the beginning of the Islamic regime in Iran (1979) there were an estimated 3,000 Jews in Isfahan, reduced to 1,500 by the end of the 20th century.

BIBLIOGRAPHY: W. Bacher, "Un épisode de l'histoire des Juifs de Perse," in: REJ, 47 (1903), 262–82; idem, "Les Juifs de Perse aux XVIIe et XVIIIe siècles daprès les chroniques poétiques de Babai b. Loutf et de Babai b. Farhad," in: REJ, 51 (1906), 121–36, 265–79; 52 (1906), 77–97, 234–71; 53 (1907), 85–110; F. Baer, "Eine juedische Messiasprophetie auf das Jahr 1186 und der 3. Kreuzzug," in: MGWJ, 50 (1926), 155ff; W.J. Fischel, "Isfahan: The Story of a Jewish Community in Persia," in: *Joshua Starr Memorial Volume* (1953), 111–28; V.B. Moreen, *Iranian Jewry's Hour of Peril and Heroism* (1987), index; A. Netzer, "*Redifot u-Shemadot be-Toledot Yehudei Iran be-Me'ah ha-17*," in: *Pe'amim*, 6 (1980), 32–56; P. Schwarz, *Iran im Mittelalter nach den arabischen Geographer* (1969), 582ff, esp. p. 586; M. Seligsohn, "Quatre poésies judéo-persanes sur les persécutions des juifs d'Ispahan," in: *Revue des études juives*, 44 (1902), 87–103, 244–259; E. Spicehandler, "The Persecution of the Jews of Isfahan under Shāh ʿAbbās II (1642–1666)," in: *Hebrew Union College Annual*, 46 (1975), 331–356; G. Widengren, "The Status of the Jews in the Sassanian Empire," in: *Iranica Antiqua*, 1 (1961), 117–162.

[Hayyim J. Cohen / Amnon Netzer (2nd ed.)]

ISH-BOSHETH (Heb. אִישׁ־בֹּשֶׁת), son of *Saul; reigned over Israel for two years (II Sam. 2:10), at the same time that David reigned over Judah in Hebron. The name Ish-Bosheth is a dysphemism (*Baal* = *Boshet*; see *Euphemism and Dysphemism) for his true name, Eshbaal (Heb. אֶשְׁבַּעַל, I Chron. 8:33; 9:39). The meaning of the syllable *'esh* is unclear. It is possibly derived from the root איש, whose meaning (as in Ugaritic) is "to give [a present]"; the name would then mean "given by Baal" (cf. the Phoenician name Matanbaal and the Hebrew names Mattaniah, Nethanel, et al.). Others explain the name as meaning "man of Baal" or see in the radical אש a form corresponding to יש.

After Saul and his three sons (including his firstborn) died in the battle against the Philistines at Mount Gilboa

(I Sam. 31), *Abner son of Ner, the uncle and general of Saul, took Eshbaal (Ish-Bosheth), the son of Saul, and proclaimed him king "over Gilead, and over the Ashurites [= Asherites], and over Jezreel, and over Ephraim, and over Benjamin, and over all Israel" (II Sam. 2:8–9). The capital was fixed in Mahanaim on the eastern bank of the Jordan, at a distance from the Philistine garrisons, who controlled western Israel (I Sam. 31:7), and from the borders of Judah, where David reigned. By enthroning Ish-Bosheth, Abner intended, on the one hand, to prevent David from reigning over the whole of Israel and, on the other, to govern, in fact, the northern tribes; Ish-Bosheth, the legal successor of Saul, would be king in title but dependent on the will and mercy of Abner, the general of the army. Indeed, Abner concentrated the full authority of the government in his hands and led the war against David (II Sam. 2:12–17; 3:6). It is a measure of Abner's power and Ish-Bosheth's impotence that Abner dared to cohabit with *Rizpah daughter of Aiah, the concubine of Saul. It is not surprising that Ish-Bosheth reproached him for it; for he might well regard it as not only an affront to the memory of Saul, but also reason for suspecting Abner of ambitions to the throne (cf. 16:21–22; I Kings 2:17–22). Abner for his part regarded Ish-Bosheth's rebuke as an act of ingratitude for his efforts in preventing David from reigning over all Israel (II Sam. 3:8). It is also possible that Abner, realizing that the military situation was in favor of David (3:1), welcomed Ish-Bosheth's rebuke as a pretext for coming to terms with David and thus assured his continuing in the position of army commander in Israel (3:12–21). The dispute sealed Ish-Bosheth's fate. He had lost his main supporter (4:1) and the hope of remaining in power. According to II Samuel 4, Ish-Bosheth was murdered by two officers, Rechab and Baanah. It can be assumed that the conspirators, who came from the town of Beeroth, one of the four Hivite towns (Josh. 9:17), murdered Ish-Bosheth in order to avenge the execution of the Gibeonites by Saul (II Sam. 21:1).

BIBLIOGRAPHY: Bright, Hist, 175–7; Tsevat, in: JSS, 3 (1958), 237ff.; de Vaux, Anc Isr, 45, 94–95, 116, 220; EM, 1 (1965), 749–50, includes bibliography. **ADD. BIBLIOGRAPHY:** D. Edelman, in: ABD, 3, 509–10; S. Bar-Efrat, *II Samuel* (1996), 17.

[Bustanay Oded]

ISH-KISHOR, EPHRAIM (1863–1945), one of the first followers of *Ḥibbat Zion and of political Zionism in England. Born in Ponjemon, Lithuania, he lived from the beginning of the 1880s in England, where he taught Hebrew. He was one of the first to promote Ḥibbat Zion in England through essays, stories, and poems in Yiddish newspapers that he published and edited at the end of the 1880s and the beginning of the 1890s. Ish-Kishor adhered to Herzl upon his first appearance in England, and in his diary, on July 15, 1896, Herzl mentions that Ish-Kishor came to see him and proposed the establishment of an organization to be headed by Herzl: "A hundred persons will gather in the East End; they will enlist members in all the countries and they will create propaganda for a Jewish state." Ish-Kishor later participated in the First Zionist Congress and was active in the Zionist Federation of Great Britain. In 1907 he went to the United States, where he continued his Zionist work. He was also among the founders of the Judea Insurance Company and worked for it when he settled in Palestine in 1933. His daughter, SHULAMITH ISH-KISHOR (1896–1977), who lived in New York, was a noted children's writer whose work included *Our Eddie* (1970).

BIBLIOGRAPHY: *Sefer ha-Congress*, 2 (1950), 85–86, 361; *T. Herzl Complete Diaries*, ed. by R. Patai, 5 vols. (1960), index; *Haolam* (Oct. 4, 1945).

[Getzel Kressel]

ISHMAEL (Heb. יִשְׁמָעֵאל; "God hears," wordplays on the name occur in Gen. 16:11–12; 17:20; 21:13, 17), the first son of Abraham, born to him when he was 86 years old. Ishmael's mother was the Egyptian *Hagar, the maidservant of Sarah (Gen. 16). After Hagar had conceived, she became insolent toward her barren mistress, and Sarah treated her harshly. She fled to the wilderness but eventually returned and submitted to Sarah's torments, as commanded by an angel of the Lord. However, after the birth of Isaac many years later, Abraham, with divine consent, acceded to Sarah's demand and expelled Hagar and Ishmael (Gen. 21). The relationships among Abraham, Sarah, and Hagar have analogs in ancient Near Eastern family law and practice. Ishmael is the eponymous ancestor of the *Ishmaelites. His circumcision at age 13 (Gen. 17:25) reflects a practice among Arabs of circumcision as a rite of puberty. The reference to him as a bowman (Gen. 21:21) reflects the tradition that Arabs were marksmen (Isa. 21:17). According to Gen. 25:9, Isaac and Ishmael together buried their father Abraham.

In the New Testament (Gal. 4:21–31) Paul treats the banishment of Hagar and Ishmael as an allegory for the replacement of God's old covenant with the Jews through law by God's new covenant with the Christians through promise.

[Yehuda Elitzur / S. David Sperling (2nd ed.)]

In the Aggadah

Abraham tried to train Ishmael in the right way (Gen. R. 148:13), but failed, his excessive love for him causing him to "spare the rod and spoil the child" (Ex. R. 1:1). Abraham closed his eyes to Ishmael's evil ways and was reluctant to send him away (Gen. R. 53:12). Sarah, on the other hand, fully recognized the true character of Ishmael, for he dishonored women, worshiped idols, and attempted to kill Isaac (Gen. R. 53:11; Tosef. Sot. 6:6). He also mocked those who rejoiced at the birth of Isaac (Gen. R. 53:11). Ishmael is identified with one of the two lads who accompanied Abraham to the *Akedah*. He was left behind with *Eliezer and the ass at the foot of Mount Moriah because he could not see the divine cloud which enveloped the mountain (Lev. R. 26:7). When abandoned by Hagar, Ishmael prayed for a quick end rather than a slow torturous death from thirst (PdRE 30). The angels hastened to indict Ishmael, exclaiming to God, "Wilt Thou bring up a well for one whose descendants will one day slay Thy children with thirst?" Nevertheless, God provided the well that was created during the twilight of the Sabbath of Creation for Ishmael since he was at that time righteous, and God judges man "only as he is at the moment" (Gen. R. 53:14; PdRE 30).

Ishmael's skill in archery was so great (Gen. 21:20) that he became the master of all the bowmen (Gen. R. 53:15). He married a Moabitess named Ayesha. When Abraham later visited them, Ishmael was away and his wife was inhospitable. Abraham thereupon left a message with her that Ishmael should "change the peg of his tent." Ishmael understood the message, divorced his wife, and married a Canaanite woman, Fatima. Three years later, when Abraham next visited, Fatima received him kindly and Abraham declared that the peg was good. Ishmael was so pleased with his father's approval that he moved his entire family to the land of the Philistines so that they could be near Abraham (PdRE 30; *Sefer Yashar, Va-Yera*, 41a–b. Ayesha (ʿAi'sha) and Fatima are the names of Muhammad's wife and daughter respectively, and the Midrash is obviously a late one). Ishmael became a genuine penitent at the end of his father's lifetime and he later stood aside out of deference for Isaac at his father's funeral (BB 16b). A man who sees Ishmael in a dream will have his prayers answered by God (Ber. 56b; cf. Gen. 21:17). Gradually Ishmael became identified not only as the ancestor of the Ishmaelites but also of the Arabs, who were often named Ishmael in the Middle Ages (see Ginzberg, Legends, 5, 223, 234).

In Islam

Ismāʿīl was a prophet (Sura 19:55; 21:85; 38:48), but it was only in *Medina that it became known to *Muhammad that he was the son of Abraham, one of the founders of the cult at the Kaaba in Mecca, one of the forefathers of the Arabs, and, like Abraham, Isaac, and Jacob, one of the worshipers of Allah, even though he was neither Jew nor Christian (Sura 2:119, 127, 130; 3:78; 14:44; 19:55). In the tale of the binding (Sura 37:99–110) Muhammad identified the son who was to be sacrificed as Ishmael and, indeed, the opinions of the traditionalists were also divided on this subject (cf. *Isaac). It is related that a renowned traditionalist of Jewish origin, from the *Qurayẓa tribe, and another Jewish scholar, who converted to Islam, told the caliph Omar ibn Abd al-Azīz (717–20) that the Jews were well informed that Ismāʿil was the one who was bound, but that they concealed this out of jealousy (Tabarī, *Ta'rīkh*, 1:189; idem, *Tafsīr*, 23:54; Thaʿlabī, *Qiṣaṣ*, 77). Muslim legend also adds details on Hājar (Hagar), the mother of Ismāʿīl. After Abraham drove her and her son out, she wandered between the hills of al-Ṣafā and al-Marwa (in the vicinity of Mecca) in her search for water. At that time the waters of the spring Zemzem began to flow. Her acts became the basis for the hallowed customs of Muslims during the Ḥajj. According to Arab genealogists, Ismāʿīl was the progenitor of the northern Arabs, the *Mustaʿriba, i.e., Aramite tribes which were assimilated among the Arabs.

[Haïm Z'ew Hirschberg]

BIBLIOGRAPHY: A. Musil, *Arabia Deserta* (1927), 477ff.; T.A. Montgomery, *Arabia and the Bible* (1934), 45ff.; H.Z. Hirschberg, *Yisrael be-Arav* (1946), 2ff. IN THE AGGADAH: Ginzberg, Legends, 1 (1942), 237–40, 263–9; 5 (1947), 230–3, 246–7. IN ISLAM: Heller, in: MGWJ, 69 (1925), 47–50; J. Horovitz, *Koranische Untersuchungen* (1926), 91–92; H. Speyer, *Biblische Erzählungen...* (1961), 171–4; R. Paret, "Ismāʿīl," in: EIS², 4 (1978), 184–5 (incl. bibl.). **ADD. BIBLIOGRAPHY:** N. Sarna, *JPS Torah Commentary Genesis* (1989), 148. See also bibliography to *Isaac.

ISHMAEL, son of Nethaniah son of Elishama, one of the military commanders in the period after the destruction of the First Temple (II Kings 25:25; Jer. 41:1). Ishmael, a descendant of the Judahite royal family, assassinated *Gedaliah son of Ahikam (Jer. 40:13–14), who presided over the Judean puppet government set up by Nebuchadnezzar. It would appear that Ishmael's assassination of Gedaliah at Mizpah was both personally and politically motivated. Ishmael may have been jealous of Gedaliah, who had been appointed by the Babylonians as head of the remnant of the population in Judah, and therefore may have wished to kill him for that reason alone; but he could hardly have hoped that the Babylonians would reward him for the murder by appointing him in Gedaliah's stead. His only hope to gain a positive advantage lay in continued resistance to Babylon, which would, if successful, result in his succession to the throne of David. *Baalis, the king of Ammon, with whom Ishmael found refuge, apparently encouraged Ishmael, because Gedaliah was a collaborator whereas the Ammonites were in open revolt against Babylon (cf. Ezek. 21:24–27, and Zedekiah's attempt to flee across the Jordan, II Kings 25:4–5), and not, as some scholars maintain, because they hoped that after the murder of Gedaliah, the Babylonians would punish the Judahite remnant and attach what was left of the territory of Judah to Ammon. After killing Gedaliah (and 70 other Israelites who had later come to Mizpah to worship), Ishmael attempted the forcible transfer to Ammon of the remnants of the Judean population left at Mizpah (Jer. 41:2–10). However, this plan was frustrated by *Johanan son of Kareah and the military commanders with him. They met Ishmael and his captives at Gibeon and took them back to Mizpah; only Ishmael and eight of his men escaped to the Ammonite king (Jer. 41: 11–15).

BIBLIOGRAPHY: Bright, Hist, 310; Klausner, Bayit Sheni, 1 (1963⁵), 55ff.; Ginsberg, in: *A. Marx Jubilee Volume* (1950), 366ff.; Yeivin, in: *Tarbiz*, 12 (1940/41), 261–2, 265–6; W. Rudolph, *Jeremia* (Ger., 1947), 685ff. **ADD. BIBLIOGRAPHY:** M. Cogan and H. Tadmor, *II Kings* (AB; 1988), 326–27.

[Josef Segal]

ISHMAEL BEN ABRAHAM ISAAC HA-KOHEN (1723–1811), Italian rabbi. Ishmael ha-Kohen, rabbi of Modena, enjoyed a high standing in the Jewish world generally and was the last Italian rabbi who was accepted throughout the rabbinic world as a halakhic authority. He was among those to whom Naphtali Hirsch *Wessely appealed in his *Divrei Shalom ve-Emet* (Berlin, 1782) to defend the introduction of secular studies in Jewish schools. Though formally disassociating himself from the ideology of the *maskilim*, in practice he concurred with it. It is of note that he occasionally wrote secular poems. Ishmael was among those invited by Napoleon to answer questions put to the *Assembly of Jewish Notables which took place in Paris in 1806. From his replies on this occasion as well as from his other halakhic rulings, both published and in manuscript, he emerges as a rabbi alive to the needs of the times and inclined to narrow the gap between them and traditions. His realistic and moderate approach is clearly revealed in his responsa published under the name *Zera Emet* (pt. 1, Leghorn, 1785; pt. 2, *ibid.*, 1796; pt. 3, Reggio, n.d.), see especially pt. 1, nos. 69, 74, and 89; pt. 2, no. 107; and pt. 3, nos. 32, 33, and 42. Many responsa remain unpublished.

BIBLIOGRAPHY: J. Rosenthal, *Meḥkarim*, 2 (1966), 513–32; Shirmann, in: *Zion*, 29 (1964), 88; M. Benayahu (ed.), *Sefer ha-Ḥida* (1959), 36–38; idem, *R. Ḥayyim Yosef David Azulai* (1959), index.

[Moshe Shraga Samet]

ISHMAEL BEN ELISHA (first half of the second century C.E.), *tanna*, the Ishmael generally mentioned without patronymic. Ishmael was one of the sages the stamp of whose personality and teachings had a permanent effect on tannaitic literature and on Judaism as a whole. He was a kohen (Ket. 105b), and in a *baraita* (Tosef., Ḥal. 1:10) it is stated that he once took an oath "by the [priestly] garments worn by my father and by the miter which he set between his eyes"; this suggests that his father was a high priest, but since no high priest called Elisha is known during the relevant period, he may have had an ancestor in mind. Still a child at the time of the destruction of the Second Temple, he was taken captive to Rome and ransomed by R. Joshua (Git. 58a), whose pupil he became (Tosef., Par. 10:3). He also studied under Neḥunyah b. ha-Kanah, who was his teacher in halakhic Midrash (Shev. 26a). Ishmael lived at Kefar Aziz, south of Hebron near Idumea (Kil. 6:4; Ket. 5:8), and appears to have taken local tradition into account in his decisions (Ket. 5:8). One of the chief spokesmen among the sages of *Jabneh, he took part in and expressed his view at all its meetings and assemblies and was present, too, on the day when Eleazar b. Azariah was appointed in the yeshiva (Yad. 4:3). In the debate concerning the commandments for which one should suffer martyrdom rather than transgress, he was of the opinion that it was permissible to transgress the prohibition against idolatry in order to save one's life, as long as it was not done in public (Sifra, Aḥarei Mot. 13:14).

His most intimate colleague was *Akiva, and he disputed with him on *halakhah*, *aggadah*, and in halakhic expositions of the Bible. Both of them laid down and evolved different systems of exposition and the derivation of the *halakhah*, and different schools were named after them: De-Vei ("the house (or school) of") R. Ishmael and De-Vei R. Akiva. Most of the extant halakhic Midrashim belong to one of those schools, the *Mekhilta de-R. Ishmael* on Exodus, and the *Sifrei* on Numbers coming from Ishmael's school, the *Sifra* on Leviticus and the *Sifrei* on Deuteronomy coming from Akiva's school. For the fundamental differences between these two schools see **Midreshei Halakhah*, section II.

Many of the actions and ethical sayings ascribed to Ishmael testify to his love of mankind, and especially of every Jew. On one occasion, when mentioning "the children of Israel," he added: "May I be an atonement for them" (Neg. 2:1); on another he said: "All Israel are to be regarded as princes" (i.e., there can be no distinctions between Jews; BM 113b). He declared that mourning over the destruction of the Second Temple would demand abstinence from meat and wine, were it not for the principle that no restriction is imposed on the public unless the majority can endure it; similarly the prohibition instituted by the Roman authorities against the study of the Torah and the observance of the *mitzvot* would require that one should not marry or beget children, so "that the seed of Abraham might cease of itself. But let Israel go their way. Better that they err unwittingly than presumptuously" (BB 60b, and parallels). The following story is told in the Mishnah (Ned. 9:10): "It once happened that a man vowed to have no benefit from his sister's daughter (i.e., not to marry her); and they brought her to the house of R. Ishmael and beautified her. R. Ishmael said to him, 'My son, didst thou vow to abstain from this one?' And he said, 'No!' And R. Ishmael released him from his vow. In that same hour R. Ishmael wept and said, 'The daughters of Israel are comely but poverty destroys their comeliness.' When R. Ishmael died the daughters of Israel raised a lament saying, 'Ye daughters of Israel, weep over R. Ishmael!'" His very human approach is evidenced in his aphorism: "Receive all men joyfully" (Avot 3:12). From his school came the dictum, "One should always use decorous language" (Pes. 3a), as well as an ethical explanation of why the whole ear is hard and only the lobe is soft – "so that if one hears anything improper, one may stop up the ear with the lobe" (Ket. 5b).

According to the Talmud he opposed the extreme view of Simeon b. Yoḥai, who encouraged men to refrain from mundane pursuits, such as plowing, sowing, reaping, threshing, and winnowing, in order to fulfill the literal interpretation of the verse, "This book of the law shall not depart out of thy mouth" (Josh. 1:8). For his part, Ishmael recalled that the Bible states, "Thou shalt gather in thy corn" (Deut. 9:14), thus teaching that the study of the Torah is to be combined with a worldly occupation (Ber. 35b). Yet the Talmud states that he prohibited Eleazar b. Dama, his sister's son, from learning Greek wisdom because this would be at the expense of studying the Torah (Men. 99b). He adopted an uncompromising attitude toward the Christian sectarians, then still within the Jewish fold, and several of his statements against them and their writings are couched in harsh terms (Shab. 116a, and see Av. Zar. 27b).

It is doubtful whether Ishmael survived until the Bar Kokhba revolt. His name is apparently included among the first martyred sages killed in the persecutions which followed that revolt (Mekh. Nezikin 18; and parallels, but cf. Tosef., Sot. 13:4). Later *aggadot* combined various traditions on the martyrs into a single literary work, making their martyrdom take place simultaneously (see *Ten Martyrs) and dwelling in legendary terms on the personality of Ishmael. This legendary figure of the high priest's son (see Tosef., Ḥal. 1:10 above), who is said to have himself been a high priest, knew the Tetragrammaton, by means of which he was able, at the request of his companions, to ascend to heaven to learn whether the decree of death had indeed been issued from on high. While Akiva, the leading figure among the "four who entered the *pardes*," served as the protagonist of the early *heikhalot* text, *Heikhalot Zutarti*, it was R. Ishmael who took over this role in later works like *Heikhalot Rabbati*, and similar works relating to *Ma'aseh Bereshit*, and *Ma'aseh Merkavah* (see *Kabbalah and *Merkabah Mysticism). Among his pupils were Illai, the father of R. Judah (Git. 6b), Meir (Er. 13a), Jonathan, and Josiah (Men. 57b), who are most mentioned in the halakhic Midrashim of the school of Ishmael.

BIBLIOGRAPHY: Hyman, Toledot, 3–29; I. Konowitz, *Ma'arekhot Tanna'im*, 2 (1968), 261–367; Frankel, Mishnah (1923²), 112–8; J. Bruell, *Mevo ha-Mishnah 1* (1876), 103–16; Graetz-Rabbinowitz, 2 (1893), 191–4, 231f.; D. Hoffmann, in: *Jahresbericht des Rabbiner-Seminars zu Berlin 5647 (1886/87)*, 5ff.; Bacher, Tann; M. Petuchowski, *Der Tanna R. Ismael* (1894); M. Auerbach, in: *Jeschurum*, 10 (1923), 60–66, 81–88 (Heb. pt.); Allon, Toledot, 1 (1959³) index; 2 (1961²), 11f.; Zeitlin, in: JQR, 36 (1945/46), 1–11.

[Shmuel Safrai]

ISHMAEL BEN JOHANAN BEN BEROKA (middle of the second century), *tanna*. He was a contemporary of *Simeon b. Gamaliel II, and he is often quoted as being in agreement or disagreement with him (Tosef., Er. 5 (4):2; Tosef., Yev. 13:5). He is mentioned three times in the Mishnah (BK 10:2, San 11:1, Avot 4:5), about 30 times in the Tosefta, in all areas of *halakhah*, and about the same number of times in Babylonian Talmud and the Jerusalem Talmud. He is mentioned several times in connection with the scholars of Jabneh (Tosef., Yev. 6:6, 10:3). His only aggadic teaching is included in *Avot* (4:5): "He who learns in order to teach, Heaven will grant him the opportunity both to learn and to teach; but he who learns in order to practice, Heaven will grant him the opportunity to learn and to teach, to observe and to practice."

BIBLIOGRAPHY: Bacher, Tann; Frankel, Mishnah, 195f.; Weiss, Dor, 2, 149f.

[Harry Freedman]

ISHMAEL BEN PHIABI (Phabi) II, high priest, appointed by Agrippa II in 59 C.E. He is not to be confused with a high priest of the same name appointed by the procurator Valerius Gratus in 15 C.E. The Phiabi family was one of the few from whose ranks the high priests were chosen. The name suggests an Egyptian origin and the immigration of the family to Ereẓ Israel seems to have taken place in the time of Herod, when Joshua b. Phiabi held office as high priest (Jos., Ant. 15:322). According to Josephus, Ishmael was a member of the delegation sent to Rome in connection with Agrippa II's opposition to the wall erected at the Temple by the priests (see Sabina *Poppaea). Though Nero upheld the appeal (Jos., Ant. 20:194–6), Ishmael was detained in Rome as one of the hostages and Joseph b. Simeon was appointed to succeed him. He apparently held office for a period of two years only. An Ishmael b. Phiabi is mentioned on various occasions in the Talmud as a righteous man, but it is not clear which of them is referred to. A well-known *baraita* (Pes. 57a; Ker. 28b; Tosef., Men. 13:21) states: "Woe is me because of the house of Ishmael b. Phiabi, woe is me because of their fists," etc., but it continues that "the Temple court cried out, 'Lift up your heads, O ye gates, and let Ishmael the son of Phiabi, Phinehas' disciple, enter and serve as high priest.'" The Mishnah also states that with his death the glory of the high priesthood departed (Sot. 9:15). He was one of those who prepared the ashes of the *red heifer, of which only seven (or nine) were prepared in the whole history of the Second Temple (3:5). A slightly different version is given in the Tosefta (Par. 3:6; cf. Num. R. 19:10), which suggests that he prepared two, the first not in accordance with the Pharisaic requirements, whereupon he prepared the second. According to Buechler, this accounts for the favorable mention of a Sadducean priest by the Talmud. Derenbourg is of the opinion that this act is to be ascribed to the first Ishmael.

BIBLIOGRAPHY: Derenbourg, Hist, 237ff., 250; Hyman, Toledot, 838–9, s.v.; A. Buechler, *Das Synedrion in Jerusalem* (1902), 96; Schuerer, Gesch, 2 (1907⁴), 269, 272; A. Zacut(o), *Sefer Yuḥasin ha-Shalem*, ed. by H. Filipowski (1925²), 24; Graetz, Hist, 2 (1949), 246; Klausner, Bayit Sheni, 5 (1951²), 21–22, 24–26.

[Lea Roth]

ISHMAEL BEN YOSE BEN ḤALAFTA (end of the second century C.E.), *tanna*. He is not mentioned by name in the Mishnah (apart from *Avot*, see below), and most of the halakhic sayings transmitted by him in the Tosefta are in his father's name (Tosef. Ter. 4:2, Maas. 1:2, Kel. BK 5:16; Oho.18:14; Nid. 4:12. Ṭoh. 10:12). He was mentioned as a member of a *bet din* (along with R. Eleazar Hakappar and R. Pinhas ben Yair) who discussed the establishment of *halakhot* and *takkanot* (Tosef., Oho. 18:18). According to the Talmud Ishmael was the eldest son of *Yose b. Ḥalafta (Shab. 118b) and succeeded him in the leadership of the town of Sepphoris (Er. 86b). The sources note Ishmael's extensive knowledge of the whole of the Bible (TJ, *ibid.*). He was greatly occupied with civil law and much is related of his exceptional care to maintain his impartiality and not to allow any suspicion or hint of bribery to attach to him, so that to him was applied the verse (Isa. 33:15): "That shaketh his hands from holding of bribes" (Mak. 24a). His great experience as a judge made him say: "He who shuns the judicial office rids himself of hatred, robbery, and vain swearing; but he who presumptuously lays down decisions is foolish, wicked, and of an arrogant spirit." He used to say: "Judge not alone. For none may judge alone save God" (Avot 4:8). Ishmael was appointed by the government, against his will, to head the local police. He is criticized for not fleeing abroad in order to avoid having to deliver Jews to the government (BM 83b). According to the Talmud he died prior to the death of Judah ha-Nasi (Pes. 118b). The great pupils of Judah, such as *Ḥanina b. Ḥama in Ereẓ Israel and *Rav in Babylon, transmitted some of his teachings and customs (Kid. 71a; Ber. 27b). One of his aggadic sayings is: "The older scholars grow, the more wisdom they acquire ... but as for the ignorant, the older they become the more foolish they become" (Shab. 152a).

BIBLIOGRAPHY: Hyman, Toledot, s.v.; Epstein, Tanna'im, 181.

[Shmuel Safrai]

ISHMAELITES (Heb. יִשְׁמְעֵאלִים), a group of nomadic tribes related according to the Bible to *Ishmael, son of Abraham and Hagar. In Genesis 25:13–15 and I Chronicles 1:29–31 there is a list of "the sons of Ishmael," which requires special consideration (see below). Apart from this list, the designation "Ishmaelite(s)" is found in Genesis 37:25–28; Judges 8:24; Psalms 83:3; I Chronicles 2:17 and 27:30. To date no mention of Ishmaelites as a designation of nomads has been found in other sources of the biblical period. The assumptions concerning the identification of the name Sumu(')ilu in the inscriptions of Sennacherib and Ashurbanipal, kings of Assyria, with Ishmael (J. Lewy, R. Campbell Thompson) are based on incorrect interpretations of these texts.

Knowledge of the area and the characteristics of the nomads called Ishmaelites can be derived, therefore, only from the biblical references to the Ishmaelites (apart from the list of the "sons of Ishmael"), as well as from what is related in Genesis about Ishmael. The "father" of these nomads is definitely connected with the desert regions between Ereẓ Israel and Egypt, and he is the son of Hagar, the Egyptian maidservant (Gen. 16:1, 3). Hagar's meeting with the angel of God who brought her tidings of Ishmael's forthcoming birth and his destined greatness is connected with the "spring of water in the wilderness, the spring on the road to Shur," which is later called Beer-lahai-roi, and "is between Kadesh and Bered" (*ibid.*, 16:7, 14). After having been expelled by Abraham, Hagar and Ishmael are saved by an angel of God in the wilderness of Beer-Sheba (21:14–19). When he grew up and became a bowman, Ishmael lived in the wilderness of Paran, and his mother got a wife for him from Egypt (21:21). The Ishmaelites' area of habitation is defined in Genesis 25:18: "from Havilah, by Shur, which is close to Egypt ..." This area includes the region in which Saul defeated Amalek: "from Havilah as far as Shur, which is east of Egypt" (I Sam. 15:7). The exact location of the Havilah mentioned in these passages is unknown, but according to the description of Saul's battle with the Amalekites it can be established with certainty that this place is in southern Palestine.

The Ishmaelites are described as Bedouin who live in the desert, raise camels (see especially the inclusion of Obil the Ishmaelite, who was "over the camels," among David's officers, I Chron. 27:30), are desert robbers (cf. Gen. 16:12), and periodically overrun the permanent settlement and plunder it (Ps. 83:7; Judg. 8:24). In addition, the Ishmaelites engaged in caravan trade (Gen. 37:25). (For relations of kinship and intermarriage between the Ishmaelite groups, who were close to the borders of settled areas, and the permanent inhabitants cf. Gen. 28:9, 36:3; I Chron 2:17.)

At the time when the Midianites, Amalekites, and Bene Kedem had become a rare sight in the land of Israel a biblical writer explained to his contemporaries that these were a species of Ishmaelites (cf. Judg. 6:3, 33; 7:12; 8:10, 22, 26 with 8:24). The account of the sale of Joseph mentions an Ishmaelite caravan on its way from Gilead to Egypt (Gen. 37:25, 27; 39:1). The same account also calls these traders Midianites (37:28) or Medanites (37:36). The identification of the Midianites, Medanites, and Amalekites with the Ishmaelites, as well as the inclusion of the latter's areas of habitation with that of the Amalekites, support the assumption that during a specific period the Ishmaelites were the principal group of nomads on the borders of Palestine (cf. Gen. 16:12: "He shall dwell alongside of all his kinsmen"; 25:18: "they camped alongside of all his kinsmen"; and 21:18: "... for I will make a great nation of him"). It is also possible that groups that were not directly related to the Ishmaelites were sometimes called by their name (Midian and Medan are listed among the sons of Abraham and Keturah, Gen. 25:2; I Chron. 1:32; Amalek is listed among the descendants of Esau, i.e., Edom, Gen. 36: 12, 16; I Chron. 1:36). It appears that this period ended no later than around the middle of the tenth century B.C.E., from which time on there is no mention of the Ishmaelites in the historiographic and literary sources in the Bible.

Genesis 25:13–15 and I Chronicles 1:29–31 contain the list of "the sons of Ishmael," in which 12 groups are listed by name: Nebaioth, Kedar, Adbeel, Mibsam, Mishma, Dumah, Massa, Hadad, Tema, Jetur, Naphish, Kedmah (for the number of the 12 sons of Ishmael cf. also Gen. 17:20). Of these, Kedar, Mibsam, Mishma, Dumah, Massa, Jetur, and Naphish are mentioned in other passages of the Bible. Assyrian and North-Arabian inscriptions mention Nebaioth, Kedar, Adbeel, Dumah, Massa, and Tema; while Greek sources from the second century B.C.E. on mention also the sons of Jetur. It should be noted that apart from the genealogical list, not one of these groups is mentioned in any source from the period preceding the tenth century B.C.E. In light of what is known about the peoples just mentioned, especially from Assyrian sources, it can be seen that they are not connected with the unified framework of the Ishmaelite tribes mentioned above: the scope of their wanderings is much greater than that of the Ishmaelites and covers an area from northern Sinai (Adbeel) to the edge of Wadi Sizhan (Duma) and the western border of Babylonia (Kedar, Nebaioth, and Massa). The collective name for these groups in all the sources is "Arabs" (Aribi, Arabu, Arbaia, etc.), and there is no doubt that this is the name by which they called themselves. On the other hand, the Assyrian sources make no mention of an ethnic framework called Ishmael; and there is no evidence that the nomads were called by this name.

According to this view the list of "the sons of Ishmael"

is composed of nomadic peoples who dwelt on the borders of Palestine and in the wide desert area in North Arabia and the Syrian-Arabian desert from the eighth century B.C.E. on, and who were called the "Sons of Ishmael" although the ancient Ishmaelites by this time – as a result of the battles of Saul and David with the nomads on the borders of their kingdom and the appearance of new nomadic groups who forcefully pushed them away from the areas adjacent to Palestine – no longer inhabited this area.

BIBLIOGRAPHY: Ed. Meyer, *Die Israeliten und ihre Nachbarstaemme* (1906), 322–8; F. Hommel, *Ethnologie und Geographie des alten Orients* (1926), 591–7; A. Musil, *Arabia Deserta* (1927), 477–93; J.A. Montgomery, *Arabia and the Bible* (1934), 45–46; Y. Liver, in: EM, 3 (1958), 902–6; F.V. Winnett and W.L. Reed, *Ancient Records from North Arabia* (1970), 29–31, 90–91, 95, 99–102.

[Israel Eph'al]

ISHMAEL OF ʿUKBARA (Ar. **Ismāʿīl al-ʿUkbarī**; ninth century), sectarian teacher from ʿUkbarā, near *Baghdad. *Al-Qirqisānī asserts that Ishmael dubbed *Anan b. David, the titular founder of *Karaism, an ass, yet some of his own teachings were so absurd as to cause ridicule. Nevertheless, when he felt his end approaching, he instructed his followers to inscribe upon his tombstone "The chariots of Israel and the horsemen thereof" (II Kings, 2:12). Ishmael did not recognize the Masoretic emendations (*keri*) in the biblical text, and ruled that it should be read as written (*ketiv*), yet at the same time he asserted that some passages reflect a corrupt reading. He permitted the consumption on the Sabbath of food cooked or gathered on that day by persons of other faiths. He permitted a person to use the income of a business operating seven days a week, such as a bathhouse or a shop, provided he devoted the proceeds of each seventh and forty-ninth or fiftieth day for charity (on the analogy of the Sabbatical and Jubilee years for agricultural produce). He also prohibited the consumption of meat.

His followers appear to have been comparatively few, and Al-Qirqisānī states that in his day (tenth century) none was left. They were presumably absorbed in the slowly consolidating Karaite sect. In ʿUkbarā, Ishmael was succeeded by Mīshawayh al-ʿUkbarī, who organized a separate group of his own disciples.

BIBLIOGRAPHY: L. Nemoy, in: HUCA, 7 (1930), 329, 388; idem (ed.), *Karaite Anthology* (1952), 52, 335.

[Leon Nemoy]

ISIDOR, LAZARE (1814–1888), French rabbi. Born in Lixheim, Lorraine, he became rabbi of Pfalzburg in 1838, of Paris in 1847, and chief rabbi of France in 1867. While rabbi of Pfalzburg, he refused to permit a member of the congregation of Saverne to pronounce the humiliating *oath *more Judaico*, in the synagogue of Saverne when requested by the tribunal of Sarrebourg. As rabbi in charge, Isidor closed the synagogue, and was consequently prosecuted (1839). A brilliant defense by Adolphe *Crémieux brought about Isidor's acquittal. This and similar cases contributed to the final abolition of the oath *more Judaico* in France (1846).

BIBLIOGRAPHY: AI, 49 (1888), 310; Consistoire Central des Israélites de France, *La mort de M. Lazare Isidor* (funeral orations, 1888); L. Berman, *Histoire des juifs de France* (1937), 412.

°ISIDORE OF SEVILLE (**Isidorus Hispalensis**; c. 560–636), archbishop of Seville, theologian, and encyclopedist; one of the last Church *Fathers. Isidore was probably born in Cartagena, but when he was still a child his family moved to Seville. He was educated by his elder brother Leander, archbishop of Seville, and after his brother's death in 600, Isidore succeeded him in the episcopate, which he held until his death. In his numerous writings Isidore encompassed all the sciences of his time; his great erudition was mainly expressed in his book *Originum, sive etymologiarum*. His most important historical work is *Historia de Regibus Gothorum Vandalorum et Suevorum*.

During his episcopate, Isidore presided over several regional and national church councils in Visigothic Spain, most important of which was the fourth national council of Toledo in 633, which determined the authority of the Visigothic kingdom and the status of the Church. Though the council agreed with Isidore's fundamental views against forced conversion of Jews, it may be assumed that he prompted the numerous laws decreed by this council against converts of Jewish origin who had remained faithful to Judaism. While Isidore was strictly opposed to forced conversion, he believed that the political status of the Jews should be exploited to bring about their voluntary conversion, an attitude he expressed in his polemical writings against Judaism. In the first of these, *Isaiae testimonia de Christo Domino*, he tries to prove that Isaiah's prophecies herald Jesus as Messiah. In his main apologetic book *De fide catholica ex Veteri et Novo Testamento contra Iudaeos*, he tries to find evidence for the truth of Christianity in all the biblical books. Despite its title, the book does not contain any dogmatic evidence against the Jews from the New Testament. In both these works Isidore does not refer to the original Hebrew text of the Bible nor does he appear to have any knowledge of talmudic literature. His information in this field is based mainly on the writings of the Church Fathers, *Jerome in particular. Despite his missionary fervor, his writings are characterized by their moderate and restrained language, contrary to the prevailing anti-Jewish polemics.

In his exegetical works Isidore generally preferred mystical and allegorical interpretations, especially in *Mysticorum expositiones sacramentorum seu quaestiones in Vetus Testamentum*, where he tries to reconcile divergencies between the Old and New Testaments. This work was designed to support Christian arguments in anti-Jewish disputations. His book *Liber de variis quaestionibus adversus Iudaeos*, attributed by some scholars to a later period, was aimed at bringing back into the fold of the Church those converts who had returned to Judaism.

Isidore's works were widely read in the Middle Ages, as attested by the great number of manuscripts remaining as well as the translation into German of *De fide catholica…*, made at a relatively early date. Up to the 12th century all anti-Jewish apologetic writers in Western Europe were inspired by Isidore's writings and his influence on the anti-Jewish disputations in Spain lasted even longer. Isidore's writings are collected in Migne's *Patrologia Latina* (vols. 81–84, 1850–62).

BIBLIOGRAPHY: Baron, Social², index; A. Lukyn Williams, *Adversus Judaeos* (1935), index; J. Fontaine, *Isidore de Séville et la culture classique dans l'Espagne wisigothique*, 2 vols. (1959); M.C. Diaz y Diaz (ed.), *Isidoriana* (Sp., 1961), includes bibliography.

ISIS, Egptian deity, at whose instigation, it was said, the Jews were forced to leave Egypt. Cheremon, the enemy of the Jews, asserted that the goddess Isis had appeared to the Egyptian king Amenophis, and had censured him because her sanctuary had been destroyed; whereupon the priest Phritibantes told the king that the terrible vision would not recur if he would purge Egypt of the "foul people." Then the departure of the Jews from Egypt took place (Jos., Apion I, 32). Tacitus has a different version, according to which the Jews were natives of Egypt, and had emigrated during the reign of Isis (Hist. V, 2–5). In the Epistle of Jeremiah (30–40) either the cult of Isis or that of Cybele is described. The violation of the chaste Paulina in the Temple of Isis at Rome was one of the reasons for the expulsion of the Jews from that city by Tiberius (Jos., Ant. XVIII, 3:4). After the destruction of Jerusalem, Vespasian and Titus celebrated their triumph in the Temple of Isis at Rome (Jos., Wars VII, 5:4).

ISKENDERUN (formerly **Alexandretta**), harbor town on the Mediterranean coast of Turkey on the gulf of the same name; population (2004), 173,900. The town (along with its district), first attached to Syria under the French mandate, was annexed to Turkey in 1939. Jews settled in Iskenderun in the Middle Ages. They were expelled by the Crusaders in 1098, but returned during the 16th century. During the 17th century the Jews of Iskenderun were among the supporters of Shabbetai *Ẓevi. The community was small and numbered some tens of families. After World War I about 20 families remained in Iskenderun. Most of the Jews emigrated from Iskenderun to Israel with the establishment of the State.

BIBLIOGRAPHY: A. Galanté, *Histoire des Juifs d' Istanbul* (1941). **ADD. BIBLIOGRAPHY:** EIS², 4 (1960), 138.

[David Kushner (2nd ed.)]

ISKOWITZ, GERSHON (1921–1988), Canadian painter. Iskowitz was born in Kielce, Poland. He registered at the Warsaw Academy of Art in 1939. With the German invasion of Poland, he was put to forced labor. In 1942, his parents and sister were taken to Treblinka. A year later, he and his brother were transported to Auschwitz. In the fall of 1944, he was transferred to Buchenwald. Liberated on April 11, 1945, he was the only member of his family to survive the Holocaust. In 1947 he studied at the Munich Academy of Art and privately, for a short time, with Oskar Kokoschka. In September 1949 he emigrated to Canada and settled in Toronto. He held his first solo exhibition in Toronto in 1957.

Only a few of Iskowitz's early sketches recording life in the ghetto and the camps survived. His memories and the horrors of the war, however, remained a principal focus of his drawings into the 1950s. In 1952 Iskowitz began taking sketching trips into the countryside around Toronto. This work became the basis for the development of the dramatic, painterly abstract canvases for which he is best known, a direction that was confirmed on the first of several trips into the Canadian north; the first, by helicopter, was funded by a Canada Council grant. These large-scale abstractions, which begin with the perception of landscape, have been described as radiant and joyful expressions that transform the immediacy of vision into colored light.

Iskowitz exhibited regularly in Toronto; after 1964, with the Gallery Moos. He was one of two artists selected to represent Canada at the 1972 Venice Biennale. In 1982, the Art Gallery of Ontario held a major retrospective of his work. In 1985, he established the Gershon Iskowitz Foundation that continues to award an annual prize to experienced, professional Canadian artists.

BIBLIOGRAPHY: A. Freeman,*Gershon Iskowitz: Painter of Light* (1982); D. Burnett, *Iskowitz* (1982).

[Joyce Zemans (2nd ed.)]

ISLAM. The word conveys the sense of total and exclusive submission to Allah and is the name of the religion enunciated by the Prophet *Muhammad in the city of Mecca at the beginning of the seventh century C.E. An adherent of it is called a Muslim, a person who submits to Allah totally and exclusively. While the word is normally used in this sense, in traditional Muslim usage the word also denotes the ancient monotheistic faith associated with *Abraham. It is in this sense that Abraham is explicitly designated as Muslim in *Koran 3:67; the same designation is implicit for the Old Testament prophets and for Jesus as well. Liberal-minded modern Muslims tend to interpret this as a reflection of Muslim tolerance and recognition of the prophets of Judaism and Christianity; viewed from a different perspective, the idea may also be construed as an appropriation of Jewish and Christian religious history by Muslims.

In contradistinction to other religions whose names were frequently given to them by outsiders (cf. W.C. Smith, *The Meaning and End of Religion*, (1963), 80–82), the name Islam is indigenous and appears in the Koran eight times; moreover, the Koran maintains that Allah himself approved of Islam (Koran 5:5) and it is "*the* religion in the eyes of Allah" (Koran 3:19). Conversely, "whoever desires a religion other than Islam, it will not be accepted from him, and he will be in the hereafter one of the losers" (Koran 3:85). Muslims use Islam as the only name for their religion; other names by which Islam has been known until recently in European languages – such as "Mohammedanism" or "Mahométanisme" – are totally unacceptable to them. Nevertheless, in medieval Muslim texts one occasionally encounters expressions such as "Muhammadan way" (*ṭarīqa muḥammadiyya*) in a sense identical with Islam. In the literature of tradition, the terms Islam and Muslim are sometimes also given a more sublime significance; playing on the various meanings of the Arabic root *s-l-m*, a tradition says that "a Muslim is someone by whose hands and tongue the Muslims are not harmed" (al-Bukhārī, *Ṣaḥīḥ, Kitāb al-īmān,* 4; ed. Krehl, vol. 1, 11). Recent interpretations according to which Islam is related to *salām* ("peace") seem to have no basis in traditional literature, though the linguistic root of the two words is identical.

In the pre-Islamic period (called the era of barbarism and ignorance, *al-Jāhiliyya*), Arab inhabitants of the Peninsula believed in a multiplicity of gods but were not unaware of Allah whom they believed to be the strongest among these. In the Muslim tradition, this is called "associationism" (*shirk*), the belief that Allah has associates (*shurakāʾ*) in His divinity. These associates were believed to have an essential mediatory role between human beings and Allah. Muslim tradition maintains, nevertheless, that pre-Islamic Arabs understood that Allah was more powerful than all other gods and in times of extreme danger they placed their trust in Him alone, becoming, in a manner of speaking, "temporary monotheists" (cf. Koran 29:65–66, 31:22; Izutsu, *God and Man*, 102–103). In the Peninsula there were also Jewish and Christian communities. The Jews lived in the northern city of *Khaybar and in *Medina where the Prophet Muhammad was active from 622 C.E. until his death ten years later. The Christians inhabited the town of Najrān and also lived elsewhere: the Christian tribe of Taghlib lived first in the Najd region of the Peninsula and later on the lower Euphrates (M. Lecker, "Taghlib" EIS², s.v.). Small Zoroastrian communities probably existed in the eastern part of the Peninsula. Islam developed out of polemics with these religious communities and a substantial part of Muslim belief and ritual can only be understood against this background.

"The Pillars of Islam" (arkān al-islām)

In contradistinction to Judaism which speaks of 613 (*taryag*) commandments, the Muslim tradition does not keep count of the commandments incumbent on a Muslim. However, five of these have acquired a special standing in Islamic tradition. One of them is related to the manner in which an unbeliever embraces Islam, while the other four belong to the ritual aspect of the religion. Each of these commandments is mentioned several times in the Koran, but there they do not appear as a separate group. However, in the literature of prophetic tradition (**ḥadīth*), the five commandments are grouped and designed as the pillars on which Islam stands. In the collection compiled by al-Bukhārī (d. 870 C.E.), we read: "Islam is built on five (pillars): Witnessing that there is no god but Allah and that Muhammad is the messenger of Allah, and the performance of prayer, and giving of alms, and pilgrimage, and the fast of Ramaḍān" (al-Bukhārī, *Ṣaḥīḥ, Kitāb al-īmān,* 2; ed. Krehl, 1, 10).

1. The double formula saying that "there is no god but Allah and Muhammad is the messenger of Allah" (called in Arabic *shahāda* ("witnessing"), *kalima* ("word"), or *kalimat al-ikhlāṣ* ("the word of exclusive devotion") does not appear in the Koran as one unit. Its first part appears with slight modifications several times. Koran 3:18 reads: "Allah witnessed that there is no god except Him." (Cf. Koran 2:255, 37:35 and elsewhere.) The second part appears only once, in Koran 48:29: "Muhammad is the messenger of Allah. And those who are with him are hard against the unbelievers, merciful one to another..." This formula is the most distinctive expression of Muslim monotheism and of the central position accorded in Islam to the Prophet Muhammad. It is an important part of worship, appearing in the call to prayer and in the prayer itself. It is also the formal requirement for joining the Muslim community. Like other Muslim rituals, this formula seems also to have undergone certain developments before reaching its final form. The tradition maintains that the first part of the *shahāda*, affirming the oneness of Allah, was sufficient to indicate the conversion of Arab polytheists to Islam because it is unambiguous in the rejection of their former belief in multiple gods. When the call to Islam was directed at Christians and Jews, this part of the *shahāda* was no longer sufficient: an affirmation of Allah's oneness by monotheist Jews or Christians does not indicate their conversion to Islam because Christians and Jews may identify with the first part of the *shahāda* without changing their religious affiliation. For a Jew or a Christian, therefore, the acknowledgment of Muhammad's prophethood was considered essential. And since some Jewish groups were willing to acknowledge Muhammad's prophethood but restricted its validity to Arabs alone (see Y. Erder, "The Doctrine of Abū Īsā al-Isfahānī and Its Sources," in: *Jerusalem Studies in Arabic and Islam*, 20 (1996), 162–99), Jews and Christians were obliged – according to some traditions – not only to pronounce the double *shahāda*, but also unequivocally to renounce their former faiths.

2. Prayer (*ṣalāt*): Pre-Islamic Arabs did not observe an obligatory daily routine which could be seen as an inspiration for the Islamic prayer. It is therefore significant to observe that *ṣalāt* ("prayer") is an Aramaic loan word which means bowing or prostration. Nevertheless, prayer is mentioned as an obligation of the believer already in the Meccan period of the Koran (Koran 108:1–2; 107:4–5). It seems that in the first stage of the development, the Prophet spoke of two daily prayers: in the evening and at dawn. Koran 17:80 enjoins the Muslims to "perform the prayer at the sinking of the sun to the darkening of the night and the recital of dawn (*Koran al-fajr*)...." Later developments in this field are not very clear, but it appears that after the *hijra* to *Medina an additional prayer, called the "middle" one, was added when the Koran says: "Be watchful over the prayers and the middle prayer..." (Koran 2:239). The "middle prayer" is variously explained as the noon or the afternoon prayer.

If we assume that the prayers mentioned in the first part of the verse are the two prayers which had been referred to in the Meccan period, we reach the conclusion that after the *hijra* the number of prayers reached three. Though there is no hard evidence to substantiate this notion, some scholars tend to speculate that this happened under the influence of the Jews with whom the Prophet came into contact in Medina. The number of the Muslim prayers eventually reached five, but we do not know exactly when this development took place. There is some evidence to suggest that during the *Umayyad period in *Syria the number of the obligatory prayers was not generally known, and at the time of the Umayyad caliph ʿOmar b. ʿAbd al-ʿAzīz (r. 717–720 C.E.) the proper time for prayer was not known either (Goldziher, *Muslim Studies*, 2, 39–40). As for the reasons why the Muslims eventually decided on the number of five daily prayers, these are not clear. Goldziher maintains that the number was influenced by the Zoroastrian tradition which had five daily prayers. Islamic tradition connects the establishment of the five prayers with Muhammad's miraculous nocturnal journey to heaven (*isrāʾ, miʿrāj*). According to this tradition, Allah intended to impose on the Muslim community 50 daily prayers, but after some negotiations (which Muhammad conducted with Allah in compliance with the advice of Moses), the number was reduced to five. The tradition maintains, however, that these five prayers have the value of fifty.

In any case, post-Koranic Muslim tradition established five daily prayers: morning (*fajr*), noon (*ẓuhr*), afternoon (*ʿaṣr*), evening (*maghrib*), and night (*isha*). Before each prayer it is necessary to perform an ablution (*wuḍu*), which involves washing the hands up to the elbows, rinsing the mouth and nose, and washing the feet including the ankles. If water is not available, sand may be used; in this case the procedure is called *tayammum* (Koran 5:8–9). In preparation for the Friday prayer washing the entire body (*ghusl*) is required. The prayer itself consists of a prescribed sequence of bodily movements (*rakʿa*), including bending, standing, prostration, and half-kneeling, half sitting. The only texts which are essential for the prayer being valid are the formula *Allāhu Akbar* and the *Fātiḥa*, the opening chapter of the Koran.

Three elements associated with Muslim prayer will serve as an illustration of the idea that Islam developed out of polemics with, and attempts to differentiate itself from, Judaism and Christianity. As is well known, Muslims now pray barefoot. However, there is evidence to suggest that in the early days of Islam, Muslims prayed with their shoes on. This was recommended, even enjoined, in order to distinguish between Muslims and Jews who are said to have prayed barefoot. The second element is the *adhān*, the call preceding each prayer. The tradition maintains that in the beginning the Prophet used a horn "like the horn of the Jews" for this purpose. Later he disliked this and ordered the clapper (*nāqūs*) to be used to summon the believers, in emulation of Eastern Christians. Eventually, ʿOmar b. al-Khaṭṭāb, the second caliph, had a vision in which he was told: "Do not use the clapper, rather call to prayer (with human voice)." In this way the characteristic Muslim call to prayer is said to have emerged. This call now consists of pronouncing the formula "Allahu Akbar" four times, the *shahāda* twice, the formula "come to prayer, come to success" twice, "Allahu Akbar" twice again, and, finally, the *shahāda*.

The development of the Muslim direction of prayer (*qibla*) is the most famous reflection of the progressive dissociation of Islam from Judaism. The Muslim direction of prayer underwent several changes. The relevant traditions are reasonably clear, but there is no way to verify their historicity. Koran 2:216, considered by some commentators to be abrogated, seems to belittle the importance of the direction of prayer, saying that "To God belong the East and the West; wherever you turn, there is the face of God." On the other hand, we have three traditions concerning the direction of prayer in Mecca before Muhammad's migration to Medina in 622. According to one of them, in Mecca the Prophet faced the Kaʿba while praying; according to another, he faced Jerusalem; according to a third, which constitutes an attempt to harmonize between the first two ones, he faced Jerusalem, but took care to have the Kaʿba on the straight line between himself and Jerusalem. In this way, the tradition maintains, he faced both sanctuaries.

Regarding the period of the Prophet's sojourn in Medina (622–632 C.E.), the tradition is unanimous and maintains that for the first 16 or 18 months of his stay in Medina, the Prophet and the Muslims with him prayed toward Jerusalem; this is why Jerusalem came to be known in Islam as "the first *qibla* and the third sanctuary" (after Mecca and Medina) (*ūlā al-qiblatayn wa thālith al-ḥaramayn*). There is no record of a divine command to do this; nevertheless, some commentators think that such a command was issued, while others maintain that praying in the direction of Jerusalem was the Prophet's own decision. Some suggest that the Prophet was commanded to pray toward Jerusalem "in order to conciliate the Jews." Frequently we read that at some point in time the Prophet became averse to this direction of prayer, and Koran 2:150, which commands the Muslims to pray in the direction of Mecca, was revealed in response to the Prophet's desire. The change of the *qibla* to Mecca introduced a crucial Arabian element into Islam and was a major step in its disengagement from Judaism.

The five daily prayers may be performed in public or in private, though according to the tradition public prayer is always preferable. The only prayer which must always be performed in public is the noon prayer on Friday (*jumʿa*).

Naturally, no congregational prayer was held before the *hijra* in Mecca because of the precarious position of the few Meccan Muslims in that period. Though there are some references to the *jumʿa* prayer in Medina before the *hijra*, it is clear that the *jumʿa* prayer acquired its central standing in Muslim ritual in the Medinan period of the Prophet's career. The choice of Friday as the Muslim day of congregational prayer was explained in various ways. Some thought that it was just to differentiate Islam from Judaism and Christianity; but this argument is good for any day except Saturday and Sunday. A classical tradition observes that although the Jews and the

Christians were given their holy books before the Muslims, the Muslims precede them in their day of prayer, in order to do them justice. The most widely accepted scholarly explanation was given by S.D. Goitein ("The Origin and Nature of the Muslim Friday Worship," *Studies in Islamic history and institutions* (1968), 111–25). Goitein suggests that Friday was chosen because on that day the Jews of Medina used to prepare provisions for the Sabbath; because of this Friday became a market day on which not only the inhabitants of Medina, but also the inhabitants of the adjacent areas assembled in the city and engaged in commerce. Since Koran 62:9–11 clearly says that commercial activity must cease when the call to prayer is sounded, this explanation sounds convincing.

The Friday prayer is the only prayer during which a sermon (*khuṭba*) is delivered. The sermon normally includes praise of Allah, a prayer for the Prophet, exhortation to good deeds, and a chapter from the Koran. It is also customary to mention the ruler. This custom has great political importance: it is a symbol of the worshipers' allegiance to the government in power. Mentioning the ruler's name in the sermon is considered indicative of the preacher's (and the congregation's) political loyalty, while its omission is considered a symbol of rebellion. *Mutatis mutandis*, sermons are at times used for political statements in the modern period as well. Religiously speaking, Friday is not a day of rest like the Jewish Sabbath. As is clear from Koran 62:9–11, work is prohibited only during the prayer itself; after the prayer is concluded, all activities may be resumed. Nevertheless, Friday has acquired in Islam the characteristics of a holiday and is the official day of rest in many Muslim states.

3. Pilgrimage (*ḥajj*): In contradistinction to prayer, the Muslim pilgrimage has clear antecedents in the pre-Islamic period. Muslim tradition maintains that pre-Islamic Arabs performed pilgrimage to the Kaʿba in Mecca, which was then a pagan place of worship, with images of idols. The transformation of the Kaʿba into a Muslim sanctuary and of the pilgrimage into a Muslim ritual necessitated an infusion of monotheistic elements into the history of both. This was achieved by describing the pilgrimage as a ritual which had begun long before Arabian idolatry came into being and was a part of the ancient monotheistic religion associated with Abraham "who was neither a Jew nor a Christian but a *ḥanīf* Muslim and was not of the idolaters" (Koran 3:67). According to the Koranic account, Abraham was the man who built the Kaʿba together with his son Ishmael and made it into a pure place of worship (Koran 2:125, 3:95–97).

Hence the Kaʿba, an idolatrous sanctuary in the pre-Islamic period, became the holiest place in Islam. The way was now open for the next step, transformimg the pilgrimage to Mecca into an Islamic commandment: "It is the duty of all people to come to the House as pilgrim, if he is able to make his way there" (Koran 3:97). Thus the pilgrimage is a case in which Islam did not abolish a pre-Islamic ritual, but rather filled it with new content and significance. The identity of the Muslim rituals with the pre-Islamic ones caused misgivings among some early believers and at least in one case a special revelation was needed to give legitimacy to such a ritual.

The pilgrimage is held annually in the month of Dhū al-Ḥijja, the last month of the Islamic year. It is obligatory for every Muslim once in a lifetime, if he has the means to perform it. At the outskirts of Mecca, the pilgrims enter into the state of sacredness (*iḥrām*), symbolized by the white, seamless garment worn during the pilgrimage. The uniform clothing is understood as symbolizing the equality of all believers. When the pilgrim reaches Mecca, he starts the ritual by circumambulating the Kaʿba seven times (*ṭawāf*). Then he covers seven times the distance between the hills of al-Safā and al-Marwa (*saʿy*). This is understood as commemorating Hagar's search of water for her son Ishmael. The collective rituals, so characteristic of the annual Muslim pilgrimage, begin on the 8th of Dhū al-Ḥijja, when the pilgrims set out for the plain of ʿArafāt, east of Mecca. On the 9th of the month the pilgrims stand there and listen to a sermon at the time of the noon-prayer. This is the central ritual of the pilgrimage (*wuqūf*). On the way back to Mecca, the pilgrims throw stones at Minā; this is meant to symbolize the stoning of the devil. On the 10th, 11th, and 12th of the month the Feast of Sacrifice (*ʿīd al-aḍḥā*) is celebrated. The sacrifice of an animal is obligatory on every free Muslim who can afford it. After this, the pilgrims return to Mecca and can come out of their state of sacredness.

The pilgrimage has acquired tremendous importance in Islam. It allows millions of Muslims from all parts of the world to meet, exchange ideas, and get acquainted with each other. The pilgrimage is therefore an extraordinary event: in recent years, about two million Muslims participate in it. It gives the Muslims a sense of belonging to a large, universal community and strengthens the feeling of unity in the Muslim world.

4. Fasting (*ṣawm*): The development of the Muslim commandment of fasting began with the migration of the Prophet to Medina in 622, when the Prophet instructed the Muslims to fast the *ʿāshūrāʾ* (cf. *ʿasor*, Lev. 16:29) on the 10th of Muḥarram, the first month in the Muslim calendar. One version of this tradition maintains that this was in emulation of, or in competition with, the Day of Atonement. Other traditions deny any Jewish connection and hold that the *ʿāshūrāʾ* commemorates the saving of Noah during the flood, or a fast observed by the tribe of Quraysh in the pre-Islamic period. In 2 A.H./624 C.E., Koran 2:185 was revealed, instituting the month of Ramaḍān as the month of fasting, from sunrise to sunset. This is another example of the progressive dissociation of Islam from the Jewish tradition. Henceforth, *ʿāshūrāʾ* was downgraded to a voluntary fast, but there are indications for its persistence into the Muslim period. Later the fast of *ʿāshūrāʾ* merged with the Shīʿī commemoration of the death of al-Hūsayn, the Prophet's grandson, in Karbalāʾ in 680 C.E.

Throughout Ramaḍān, the believer must refrain from food, drink, and sexual relations during the daytime. *Imsāk* is the beginning of the fast at dawn, while *ifṭār* signifies the breaking of the fast after sunset. Unrelated to Ramaḍān is fasting of various durations as expiation for failing to fulfill an oath (Koran 5:92), for repudiating a wife in a forbidden way (*ẓihār*, Koran 58:4), for failing to perform the pilgrimage rituals properly (Koran 2:196), or for an accidental killing of a believer (Koran 4:91).

5. Alms-giving (*zakā*). The pre-Islamic secular value of generosity was transformed into mandatory almsgiving in Islam. In the early Sūras of the Koran, the commandment is phrased in very general terms (Koran 13:24–26). In the late Medinan period, the tone is much more specific and the purposes for which the collected money may be used are specified: "The alms are for the poor and the needy, and those who collect them, and those whose hearts are to be reconciled, and to free the captives, and the debtors, and for the sake of Allah and for the wayfarers; a duty imposed by Allah" (Koran 9:60). Those "whose hearts are to be reconciled" are understood to be people who needed economic incentive to join Islam, while "for the sake of Allah" is interpreted as the *jihād* (q.v.). This suggests that the Prophet used the alms money not only as help for the needy, but also for political purposes. According to some prophetic traditions, the payment of the alms "purifies" the property retained by the payer. The Qur'an does not specify the amount to be paid as alms. Koran 2:219 seems to indicate that one should give as alms whatever is his surplus (for details on this in Islamic law, see A. Zysow, "Zakāt," EIS², 11, 406–22).

The Expansion of Islam

The first wave of conquests by Muslim Arabs, completed at the beginning of the eighth century C.E., included the Fertile Crescent, *Iran, *Egypt, North Africa, *Spain, the western fringes of *India, and some parts of Central Asia. From the 10th century Turkish people originating on the steppes between the Caspian Sea and the Altai mountains became increasingly important as political and military champions of Islam. The conquest of South Asia (comprising today India, *Pakistan, and Bangladesh) began with the Indian campaigns of Maḥmūd Ghaznawī in the early 11th century, and was almost completed by the Delhi Sultanate in the 13th. The conversion of the *Mongols to Islam which began in the 13th century significantly extended the boundaries of Islam. The manner in which Islam came to South East Asia has not been satisfactorily described so far, but it is clear that it was not by way of conquest. The presence of Muslims in the Indonesian archipelago has been attested since the late 13th century. Muslim merchants and mystics are normally credited with bringing Islam to these areas. It is clear that Muslim conquests and the establishment of Muslim dynasties are not coterminous with the spread of Islam among the population and that the former aspects of Muslim history are known much better than the processes by which Islam became the religion of a substantial part of Asian and African populations.

The number of Muslims was estimated in 2000 at 1,262 million, 77% of these living in countries where the majority of the population is Muslim. The largest concentration of Muslim population is found in the three countries of South Asia (India, Pakistan, and Bangladesh) which are home to 384.3 million Muslims. Indonesia is the largest single Muslim political unit, with 212.1 million Muslims. The Arabic-speaking countries of North Africa (including the Sudan) and the Middle East comprise 257 million Muslims. Turkey follows with 66.5 million, Iran with 62.2 million, the five Muslim states of Central Asia (Uzbekistan, Turkmenistan, Tajikistan, Kirgyzstan, and Kazakhstan) with 41.5 million, and Afghanistan with 22.5 million. In Africa 58.9 million Muslims live in West Africa (south of the Sahara) and 47.1 in East Africa. The Muslim minority of China is estimated at 19.2 million, of Russia at 14.7 million, and of Europe (including the Balkans, France, and the U.K.) at 8.1 million. The number of Muslims in the U.S. and Canada is put at 2 million, although some Muslim organizations in the U.S. speak of 6 million Muslims in the U.S. alone. Reference to religion in demographic statistics is not universal, and these figures must therefore be viewed with caution. It is estimated that the number of Muslims will reach 1.8 billion by 2025; the Muslims are then expected to form almost a quarter of the global population.

General Characteristics

The general character of Islam is determined by two main factors: its foundational literature and its global expansion. The foundational literature – including the Koran, the prophetic tradition (*ḥadīth*), the jurisprudence (**fiqh*) and mysticism (*taṣawwuf*) – should be seen as unifying factors. The global expansion of Islam, the diverse conditions in the various areas, the different degrees to which the classical sources of Islam were internalized, the different degrees of modernization – all these explain the distinct characteristics of Islam in various areas of the world.

In addition to its fierce monotheism, the universal, global appeal of Islam seems to be its most conspicuous general feature. It is based on the firm belief that in contradistinction to all other prophets who had been sent to specific communities, Muhammad was sent to all humanity. Furthermore, Muḥammad is considered the last prophet to be sent to earth. Consequently, Islam and the Koran – the consummate embodiment of the divine will – will remain valid until the end of days: no prophet will ever be sent in order to bring another revelation or another sacred law. Therefore, Islam does not countenance the establishment of any new religion after the coming of Muhammad. Also, the Koran is considered to be the only scripture which was transmitted reliably and suffered no interpolation, while the Torah and the New Testament had allegedly been tampered willfully by the Jews and the Christians (*taḥrīf*). As a result of these and similar considerations, Muslims are "the best community ever brought forth to mankind" (Koran 3:110), and "Islam is exalted and nothing is exalted above it" (*al-Islām yaʿlū wa lā yuʿlā* (al-Bukhārī, *Ṣaḥīḥ*, *Kitāb al-janāʾiz 80*; ed. Krehl, 1, 337–38). The idea of Islamic exaltedness has numerous ramifications for the relationship between Islam and other faiths (Friedmann, *Tolerance and Coercion*, 34–39).

The Muslim ideas relevant to this relationship have been subject to significant changes since the earliest period of Islam. Even the Koran includes divergent ideas about the relationship between Islam and other religions. On the one hand, it includes verses which seem to promise divine reward for the Jews and the Christians without mentioning their conversion to Islam as a precondition (Koran 2:62; cf. 5:69). On the other hand, it speaks about the humiliation inflicted upon them (Koran 2:61, 3:112), instructs the Muslims not to forge alliances with them (Koran 5:51), and calls upon the Muslims to fight them "until they pay the poll-tax (**jizya*) out of hand while being humiliated (Koran 9:29). These and verses of similar import have been extensively commented upon in Muslim tradition and jurisprudence. The Muslim attitude to the Jews and Christians gradually moved from an initial conciliatory approach in the direction of increased rigor. (See Friedmann, *Tolerance and Coercion*, 194–99.)

The Koran and the prophetic tradition (*ḥadīth*) (q.v.) constitute the major unifying factors in Islam. The Koran is considered to be the literal word of Allah. Muslim theologians debated whether it has existed since all eternity and is uncreated (*ghayr makhlūq*), or was created (*makhlūq*) at a certain point in time. Perceived as divine in origin, its style is considered inimitable (*muʿjiz*) in the sense that no human being is capable of producing a book of so sublime a stylistic standard. This is the dogma known as *iʿjāz al- Koran*, the idea that the Koran renders human beings unable to imitate it. The distinctive character of Koranic style is unmistakable; from the secular vantage point it may derive from the fact that the Koran is the only extant literary work from seventh-century Arabia. In any case, the Koran has always been the subject of boundless veneration by Muslims. Although the Koran considers itself as "a book in which there is no doubt" (Koran 2:2) and as a revelation in "clear Arabic language" (Koran 26:195), many verses are difficult to understand and the book has inspired a vast literary corpus of exegesis (*tafsīr*). Once the meaning of a verse was agreed upon by mainstream exegetes, the accepted meaning acquired an uncontested normative value in Muslim law and piety.

The prophetic tradition (*hadīth*) has developed out of the conviction that a pious Muslim should emulate the Prophet in whatever he did, recall whatever he said, and even keep a record of things which gained his tacit approval. This attitude is based on the firm conviction that Muhammad possessed a perfect personality and should be treated with utmost respect. Any action which is judged incompatible with this basic idea is rejected with great severity. Therefore, one of the most meritorious actions which a Muslim can do is to revive a custom of the Prophet (*sunna*) which for some reason fell into disuse. The customs of the Prophet were recorded in the *ḥadīth* which has become a major part of Muslim religious literature, a major source of Muslim law and an important vehicle through which later generations could influence the development of Islam. The desire to emulate the Prophet brought about a tremendous proliferation of the *ḥadīth*, which soon became an extensive branch of Muslim religious literature.

According to the traditional Muslim view, a considerable part of the *hadīth*, which has a reliable chain of transmitters and thus can pass the traditional test of authenticity, was actually pronounced by the Prophet and has therefore a normative value second only to the Koran itself. Modern scholarship, on the other hand, maintains that the authenticity of this material is unverifiable: since we have no extant books of *hadīth* from the lifetime of the Prophet, there is no reliable method which can establish whether a certain saying was pronounced by the Prophet, or originated in a later period and was attributed to the Prophet in order to prove a point of law or an idea in the religious thought of a Muslim group. In some cases it is possible to discern the religious tendency or political interest embedded in a tradition; but in the countless traditions of general ethical content lacking a point of historical reference this is frequently impossible. In the brilliant formulation of *Goldziher, whose study of the *hadīth,* written in the late 19th century, is still an indispensable masterpiece, "the *hadīth* will not serve as a document for the history of the infancy of Islam, but rather as a reflection of the tendencies which appeared in the community during the maturer stages of its development. It contains invaluable evidence for the evolution of Islam during the years when it was forming itself into an organized whole from powerful mutually opposed forces. This makes the proper appreciation and study of the *hadīth* so important for the understanding of Islam in the evolution of which the most notable phases are accompanied by successive stages in the creation of the *hadīth*" (Goldziher, *Muslim Studies*, vol. 2, 19).

The third unifying factor is Islamic jurisprudence (**sharīʿa*, **fiqh*). From the very beginning, Islam strove to control the life of the community in all fields. Like Judaism, Islam is not satisfied with regulating man's obligation toward God, but also aspires to regulate his daily behavior and legislates in matters which in other cultures belong to the field of civil or secular law. Legal matters do not constitute a major part of the Koran, though topics such as the law of marriage, divorce, inheritance, and penalties for a restricted number of transgressions (theft, highway robbery, wine drinking, unlawful sexual intercourse and false accusation thereof) are discussed in some detail. Beginning in the last decades of the 8th century C.E., major compendia of Muslim jurisprudence began to emerge. Numerous schools of legal thinking (*madhhab*, pl. *madhāhib*) came into being in the formative period of Islam. Four of them (Ḥanafīs, Ḥanbalīs, Mālikīs, and Shāfiʿīs) survived and are regarded as valid versions of the religious law of Islam. The Ḥanafī school, which originated in the Iraqi city of Kūfa, is the most widespread. It was the dominant school in the *Abbāsid empire, in the *Ottoman empire, in the *Moghul empire in India and in Central Asia. The Mālikīs school was predominant in Muslim Spain, and still is in North Africa. The Shāfiʿīs school is deeply rooted in Egypt and has many adherents in the Fertile Crescent. The Ḥanbalīs have official status in *Saudi Arabia and numerous adherents elsewhere.

While the division into schools of law may indicate some measure of diversity, the common denominator between the schools is more than sufficient to consider the law as a unifying factor in Islam. The law is administered by a judge (*qāḍī*), sometimes assisted by a legal specialist authorized to issue legal opinions (*fatwā* pl. *fatāwā*).

The formative period of Islam was characterized by immense worldly success. The great conquests of the first century of Muslim history, in which Muslims took control of vast areas in the Middle East, in the western fringes of India, in Central Asia, in North Africa and in the Iberian peninsula, transformed the history of these regions and brought them under the aegis of Islam. Later expansion and conquests did the same for other areas of the world. The chronicles of the early conquests abound in descriptions of the wealth accumulated in the course of these events, and the conquerors do not seem to have had any qualms about the riches which they amassed. Mainstream Islam legitimized this and regulated the ways in which booty may be taken and used. This reflects a positive approach of Islam to worldly success (cf. Smith, *Islam in Modern History*, 22–23). Yet at the same time, one can discern in early Islam a completely different trend of thought: a trend which is contemplative, stresses the uselessness of this world and sees it only as a corridor through which one must pass, but which has no real value when compared with the everlasting bliss promised to the believers in the hereafter. This was the attitude of early Muslim ascetics (*zuhhād*, sg. *zāhid*) who spared no effort to revile this world, to describe it as "a corpse pursued by dogs," as a place of unbearable stench, a place which is a prison for the believer and Paradise for the infidel. These were the precursors of the Ṣūfī movement (see *Sufism) which developed into a major trend in Muslim religiosity. Since the 10th century C.E., Ṣūfī thinkers produced numerous manuals in which they described the path (*ṭarīqa*) to God and which served as guides on the seeker's (*murīd*) way to spiritual perfection. These manuals, of which "The book of (mystical) flashes in Ṣūfism" (*Kitāb al-luma' fī al-taṣawwuf*) by Abū Naṣr al-Sarrāj (d. 988 C.E.) is a prime example, surveys the practices and modes of thinking of the Ṣūfīs. The book speaks about the standing of the Ṣūfīs among the believers and reaches the conclusion that they are more assiduous than others in observance and do not try to avoid the inconvenient commandments by seeking allegorical explanations and legal evasions. Thus, they not only obey the letter of the law, but go beyond it and reach degrees of religiosity which can not be attained by jurists and others. They leave aside all irrelevant matters and cut every connection which may interfere with attaining their objective, which is God alone. The book also describes in great detail the spiritual stages on the Ṣūfī's way to God.

In a later stage, from the 12th century onward, the Ṣūfīs were not only individuals exploring divine mysteries, but also organized themselves into Ṣūfī orders (*ṭuruq*, sg. *ṭarīqa*) which spread all over the Muslim world from the Maghrib in the West to Indonesia in the East. These orders developed around Ṣūfī masters (*shuyūkh*, sg. *shaykh*, or *pīr* in the eastern part of the Muslim world). These orders were of considerable importance in the life of the Muslim communities everywhere. It stands to reason that participation in the Ṣūfī ritual, such as the communal *dhikr* (the constant repetition of God's name), gave the common man a spiritual satisfaction unachievable by other means. Trimmingham (*The Ṣūfī Orders*, 229) sees a similarity between the spiritual role of a Ṣūfī order and that of a local church in Europe; another possible comparison is with the Ḥasidic movement in Judaism.

While the orders developed numerous disparate characteristics in the various parts of the Muslim world, the similarities between them are sufficient to include Ṣūfism among the unifying factors of Islam. The more unified picture of Islam can be found in Islamic literature, while its diversity can be most profitably studied in anthropological research. Anthropological fieldwork in various areas of the Muslim world has revealed numerous characteristics which show the extent to which Islam was influenced by local cultures, especially in rural areas. In almost every Muslim house in the Indian district of Purnea a little shrine existed in which prayers were offered both to Allah and to the Indian goddess Kālī. In the same place, a part of the Muslim marriage ceremony was conducted in a shrine of the goddess Bhagvatī (Mujeeb, *The Indian Muslims*, 13–14). There is substantial literature about the existence of caste system among Indian Muslims, despite the classical Islamic principle of equality of all believers (Ahmad, *Caste and Social Stratification…*). Geertz (*Islam observed*, 66) maintains that in Indonesia, "the mass of the peasantry remained devoted to local spirits, domestic rituals and familiar charms. … Christians and pagans apart, all these people, gentry and peasantry alike, conceived themselves to be Muslims." Muslims for whom the classical literature of Islam is the only guide as to what constitutes Islam will probably consider such phenomena as cases of incomplete Islamization; but, of course, there is no guarantee that the Muslims in question will ever be transformed into believers conforming to the ideal of Islam as embodied in the classical tradition.

Modern Islam

Barring a few exceptions, classical and medieval Muslim thought developed against the background of a dominant Muslim civilization. Both in the formative period of Islam and in the later pre-modern centuries, Muslim thinkers were active in areas which were part of secure and relatively stable political systems, headed by Muslim rulers. This situation began to change with the first Western incursions into the Muslim world and with the gradually developing sense that Islam had lost its erstwhile primacy in its relationship with other civilizations. The reaction of Muslim thinkers to this evolving situation was manifold. During the second half of the 19th century, the Muslim modernist movement came into being. In Egypt, the prominent intellectual figure was that of Muhammad 'Abduh (1849–1905). At various times, he was teacher, journalist, and judge; his career culminated between 1899 and

1905, when he served as the *muftī* of Egypt. His leading ideas included the insistence on the compatibility of Islam with reason and modern science, since the Koran encouraged the study of the physical universe; the preference of reason when it conflicts with traditional knowledge; rejection of the blind following of the tradition (*taqlīd*); and the revitalization of independent reasoning (*ijtihād*). He also maintained that the restrictions placed in Islam on polygamy (the obligation to treat the wives with equality and justice; cf. Koran 4:3) are such that they amount to prohibition, and advocated the education of girls. Among his numerous followers, mention should be made of Qāsim Amīn (1865–1908), who became famous because of his advocacy of women's rights, and ʿAlī ʿAbd al-Rāziq (1888–1966), who maintained that Islam "is a religion, not a state" (*dīn lā dawla*). In other words, and in contradistinction to the prevalent view, he advocated the separation of religion and state in Islam. This idea aroused serious opposition and caused him to be expelled from the ranks of the *ʿulamāʾ* and from his position as a religious judge.

In the Indian subcontinent, the modernist movement was launched by Sir Sayyid Aḥmad Khān (1817–1898). Having been knighted for his loyal behavior during the Indian uprising of 1857, he devoted his life to the improvement of the Indian Muslims' relationship with the British rulers and to the advancement of modern education among Indian Muslims. In 1875 he established (with British support) the Anglo-Muhammadan Oriental College, which came to be known since 1920 as Aligarh Muslim University, and served as an important Muslim institution of higher learning in which modern science was taught alongside the humanities. He promoted the idea that there can be no contradiction between the word of God and laws of nature which are God's doing. Therefore, there can be no contradiction between the Koran, Islam, and the laws of nature, and there can be no objection in Islam to the study of modern Western sciences. Aḥmad Khān also devoted considerable effort to the demythologizing of Islam and interpreting its leading ideas as conforming to human intellect. In his attempt to improve the relationship between Islam and Christianity, he disagreed with the classical Muslim accusation that Christians and Jews had falsified the Scriptures, maintained that the books of the Bible are to be considered genuine and denounced the Indian Muslim custom of refusal to dine with Christians. Like Muhammad ʿAbduh, he maintained that Islam actually prohibited polygamy by insisting on the equal treatment of all wives, an attitude of which men are emotionally incapable.

Sayyid Aḥmad Khān's views found support among numerous Indian Muslim thinkers. Chirāgh ʿAlī (1844–1895) devoted much attention to the interpretation of *jihād* and argued that "all wars of Mohammad were defensive." He argued that "there are certain points in which the Mohammadan Common Law is irreconcilable with the modern needs of Islam, whether in India or Turkey, and requires modification. The several chapters of the Common Law, as those on political institutes, slavery, concubinage, marriage, divorce, and disabilities of non-Moslem fellow-subjects are to be remodeled and rewritten in accordance with the strict interpretations of the Koran...." He also opposed the blind following (*taqlīd*) of the Islamic schools of jurisprudence which were "never intended to be either divine or finite." It may be said that Chirāgh ʿAlī was one of the most radical reformers in Indian Islam. His definition of the *sharīʿa* as "common law" which may be changed by human intervention is a major departure from traditional norms.

The most famous among Indian Muslim modernists was Muhammad Iqbal (1875–1938). A poet, a philosopher and a political thinker – he is a towering figure among the Indian Muslims in the 20th century. He enjoyed immense popularity among the Indian Muslims, mainly because of his powerful and compelling poetry in Urdu and Persian, although his philosophical and political ideas also played a role in the development of his popularity. His *Reconstruction of Religious Thought in Islam*, which reflects his Islamic upbringing as well as his knowledge of European philosophy, is the most systematic formulation of his thought, though some of the arguments proffered in it are not clear. A substantial part of this work is dedicated to the description of Islam as a dynamic force in human history and to the analysis of the reasons which caused its stagnation in modern times. In Iqbal's view, the stagnation of Islam was caused by several reasons. One is the failure of the Muʿtazila which he considers a rationalist school of thought. Like other modernists, Iqbal is severely critical of Ṣūfism which preferred other-worldliness and caused the Muslims to neglect the concrete world which had been, in his view, at the center of the Koran's attention. He maintains, however, that Islam is capable of renewal and maintains that the belief in the finality of Muhammad's prophethood is a powerful intellectual tool that can be used for this purpose. In contradistinction to the classical interpretation, which used this belief as a proof of the eternal validity of the Koran and of Islamic law, Iqbal maintains that "in Islam prophecy reached its perfection in discovering the need for its own abolition." Finality of prophethood means that after the completion of Muhammad's mission nobody can ever claim personal authority of supernatural origin. Man has reached a stage in which he can open new horizons without being hampered by any constraints. The ideal believer is, therefore characterized by creativity, vitality, abhorrence of stagnation, and love of perpetual movement. Together with the use of the reinterpretation of Islamic law (*ijtihād*), these are the qualities which can revitalize Islam and restore its original dynamic character.

The modernist movement, which aimed at bringing Islam into conformity with the modern world and was characteristic of Islamic thought in the second half of the 19th century and the first half of the 20th, gradually lost its primacy and was replaced by radical trends of thought. Driven by the acute sense that modernity failed to deliver on its promise and stands in sharp contrast with the traditional Islamic ideal, radical Muslim thinkers, such as Abū al-Aʿlā Mawdūdī (1903–1979) in India and Sayyid Quṭb (1906–1966) in Egypt, initiated scathing attacks on the modernist approach. A central component of these attacks has been a categorical rejection of modern Western civilization which is seen as corrupt, licentious, irreligious and dangerous for Islam. The *leitmotif* of Mawdūdī's thought is that all sovereignty in the world belongs to God alone; no other source of authority, such as the will of the people, or laws promulgated by elected legislative assemblies is legitimate. In 1941, Mawdūdī juxtaposed obedience to divine law – which is Islam – with obedience to manmade laws and customs; the latter he called Jāhiliyya, a term traditionally used for the pre-Islamic, pagan period in Arab history. When Pakistan was established in 1947, Mawdūdī (and the "Islamic Group," Jamāt-i Islāmī organization which he founded) immersed himself in a struggle to enhance as much as possible the Islamic characteristics of the newly established state. While he saw himself as the vanguard of opposition to things modern and desirous of implementing the classical ideal of Islam, in many details modern ideas and modern conditions influenced his understanding of the ideal. Sayyid Quṭb, the leader of the Muslim Brethren in Egypt (executed in 1966), gave much currency to the dichotomy between Islam and the Jāhiliyya which is, in his as well as in Mawdūdī's view, not only a specific historical period but also a state of affairs and a mentality which allows people to choose a way of life different from the one prescribed by God and by the Prophet Muhammad. Jāhilī society is not only that which denies the existence of God, but also that which does not deny it, but relegates God to the kingdom of heaven and does not apply His law on earth. Such societies, including those which are nominally Muslim, have to be replaced by societies living under the divine Muslim law. The radical Muslim trends which we exemplified by reference to Abū al-Aʿlā Mawdūdī and Sayyid Quṭb have gained much currency since the middle of the 20th century.

As a religion and a civilization, Islam has been in existence since the seventh century. At the beginning of the 21st century, Muslims live in dozens of countries in most areas of the world. These plain facts go a long way to explain the diversity of the Islamic experience. Islam has always been many things. Muslims have been warriors, rulers, mystics, writers, poets, artisans, and scholars in various fields; they have been, and still are, engaged in the whole range of human activity in widely differing circumstances. Within one century of Muslim history, they conquered a substantial part of the then known world. During the first three centuries of that history, Muslim writers produced a rich historiography, extensive literature in linguistics and lexicography, literary criticism, poetry, and jurisprudence. They stood for a long period at the cutting edge of scientific development. In its formative period, Muslim religious thought was characterized by a wide variety of views on numerous subjects. The variety of views and the nature of the arguments marshaled by their protagonists testify to the vibrant intellectual life of Islam in the early period of its history. Muslims have differed on questions such as determinism versus free will; the existence of the Koran since all eternity versus its being created at a certain point in time, with the rest of creation; the equality of all prophets versus the unquestioned superiority of Muhammad; the validity of personal reasoning versus the irrefutable authority of the prophetic tradition in jurisprudential matters; the identity of unbelievers who may be offered the status of protected communities (**dhimmīs*) rather than being forced to embrace Islam; the extent of tolerance to non-Muslims living under Muslim rule and the measure of humiliation to be imposed on them. The list of these much debated issues could easily be augmented. This diversity of Muslim thought and experience has crucial significance. It means that all Muslims, in any place and historical period, must choose the type of Islamic thought and belief most appropriate to the circumstances of their lives and to their world view. It also means that the Muslim tradition includes material capable of substantiating almost any interpretation of Islam which a Muslim may want to develop. He may choose to be a fundamentalist or a modernist. He may choose to view Judaism and Christianity as basically illegitimate and corrupt versions of the divine will, or adopt a more pluralistic view of religious diversity. Professional men of religion tend to promote the view that their interpretation is the only legitimate one, and they are frequently supported by the autocratic regimes in many Muslim states. Such attitudes are belied by the long history of intellectual controversy in Islam and by the various forms which Islam took on in various times and places. Since the middle of the 20th century, radical interpretations of Islam have held sway in some of the most important areas of the Muslim world, but there is no doubt that the building bricks for a different version of Islam are readily available in the Muslim tradition.

[Yohanan Friedmann (2nd ed.)]

Polemics against Judaism

Islamic polemics directed against Judaism and Jews are substantial neither in quantity nor in quality. The great masses of Christian subjects within the Islamic domain and the Christian powers outside caused Islamic polemics to focus on Christianity. On the whole, Arabic lore and literature reflect a negative attitude toward the Jews, one of distrust and suspicion, contempt and animosity. It is argued that from the days of the Prophet the Jews were enemies of Islam, either in direct military confrontation with the Prophet, or in plots to undermine Islam through heresy, subversion, and cunning ill will. An 11th-century admirer of *Samuel b. Joseph ha-Nagid or the 14th-century mystic al-Jīlī (I. Goldziher in JZWL, 11 (1875), 68 ff.) are exceptions in their positive attitude toward the Jews. The prevailing attitude may have come from Christian polemics which in turn were rooted to some extent in classical anti-Jewish lore. This holds true even concerning the Koran (T. Andrae, *Ursprung des Islams…* (1923–25), 198 f.; cf. Waardenburg in *Liber Amicorum, Studies… C.J. Bleeker*, 1969). It is not surprising that the ever-growing mass of Christian converts to Islam should have contributed to the anti-Jewish mood. As early as the ninth century, al-Jāḥiz stated that although Judaism may seem closer to Islam than Christianity, Muslims are more negative in their attitude toward Jews than toward Christians (ed. and tr. by J. Finkel, in JAOS, 47 (1927), 311–34).

Polemic remarks appear in the Koran and the *Ḥadith* (G. Vajda in JA, 229 (1937), 57–127) and in numerous theological works. Systematic treatment appears in courses and manuals on theology, heresies, and comparative religion. Muslim scholars displayed a very limited knowledge of Judaism and were not acquainted with original Jewish sources, and only rarely with translations. For example, the historian Ibn Khaldūn (14th century) even quoted the Bible from the 10th century historian al-Masʿūdī. The judgments and references of the polemists were usually based on sets of passages, presumably supplied by Jews converted to Islam, and, in the critique of post-biblical Judaism, possibly going back to some *Karaite material. Sometimes polemics may have been geared to social-political public agitation and mob riots. For example, the enemies of the family of Samuel ha-Nagid accused Jewish dignitaries and officials of selling *terefah* meat to the believers. The Moroccan al-Maghribī (G. Vajda in *Étude à la mémoire de Lévi-Provençal*, 2 (1962), 805–13) voiced a similar argument.

CONTENT. The subject matter of polemics can be reduced to a few points. Islam claims to be the final dispensation, following the abrogation (Ar. *naskh*) of Judaism and Christianity, and regards the development of Judaism, after its abrogation, as abnormal and as a human invention (*bidʿa*) contrary to divine dispensation (*sharʿ*). This is demonstrated by a critique of the Bible. Jews are charged with tampering (*tabdīl*) and distorting (*taḥrīf*) the texts, either in reading or in interpretation. Indeed, the Scriptures contain accounts unworthy of and senseless in a divine book (e.g., the stories of Lot, Judah and Tamar, kings of Edom, stations in the wilderness). Many of the numerical computations seem faulty; contradictions and anthropomorphisms (*tajsīm*) abound. Conversely, the Scriptures fail to elaborate on reward and punishment in the hereafter. Disrupted by the Babylonian captivity, the transmission of events (*tawātur*) is defective. Finally, if the Scriptures are authentic, they must contain annunciations (*aʿlām*) of the advent of Muhammad. The latter are gleaned from **gematria*, the interpretation of the numerical value of significant words (Muhammad = 92 = *bi-me'od me'od* in Gen. 17:2; Paran wilderness = Mecca) etc. (cf. Strauss-Ashtor, in *Sefer ha-Zikkaron le-Veit ha-Midrash le-Rabbanim be-Vinah* (1946), 182–97).

HISTORICAL SURVEY. A tenth-century compendium by the theologian Bāqillānī presents a discussion of Judaism (Brunschvig, in *Homenaje a Millás Vallicrosa*). Partly provoked by the high position attained by Samuel ha-Nagid, the philosopher and historian Ibn Ḥazm (11th century) composed a substantial attack on Judaism in vitriolic language (M. Perlmann, in PAAJR, 18 (1948/49), 269–90). In the 12th century, a Jewish convert to Islam, *Samuel ibn Abbas al-Maghribī produced the most important polemic work (idem, in PAAJR, 32, 1964), which was often used and plagiarized by later polemists such as Qarāfī (13th century) and Ibn Qayyim ibn al-Jawziya (14th century). The Egyptian Jew Saʿīd b. Hasan of Alexandria who converted to Islam in 1298 (I. Goldziher, in REJ, 30 (1895), 1–23; S.A. Weston, in JAOS, 24 (1903), 312–83) and the Moroccan convert ʿAbd al-Ḥaqq al Islāmī (14th century) wrote popular tracts. In about 1360, Abu Zakariyyā Yaḥyā al-Rāqilī, a Morisco in Christian Spain, wrote a manual of disputation against the Jews who "loosen their tongues… against our prophet" (as in Palacios, in *Mélanges Hartwig Derenbourg* (1909), 343–66). As late as the 19th century, the account of Tabātabaʾī's disputation and the pamphlet *Risāla Sabʿiyya* appeared in Egyptian editions of Samuel's aforesaid tract (1939, 1962^2).

Jewish replies to the Islamic contentions began to appear in the tenth century and their authors include the philosophers *Saadiah Gaon, *Judah Halevi, Abraham ibn Daud, and *Maimonides. The former three were also outstanding polemists against the Karaites. Separate tracts against Islam were rare. *Ma'amar ʿal Yishma'el* (13th century), ascribed to Solomon b. Abraham Adret (J. Perles, 1863; M. Zikier, in *Festschrift A. Kaminka*, 1937), and *Keshet u-Magen* (M. Steinschneider, in MWJ, 7 (1880), 1–48) of R. Simeon b. Ẓemaḥ Duran (d. 1444) came from the Jewish milieu peculiar to Christian Spain. While Jewish polemists were bitter about oppression and humiliation under Islam, they were aware that Islam showed greater affinity to Judaism than did Christianity, despite the biblical background shared with the latter.

[Moshe Perlmann]

Judaism and Islam

Centuries before the rise of Islam many Jewish communities were scattered over *Arabia, so that Judaism, in its normative and also sectarian versions, was known to the sedentary population and even to the Bedouin tribes. It was especially widespread in South Arabia, where Judaized groups and proselytes were very common. The deciphering of the South Arabian inscriptions, some of which were discovered only in the 1950s, confirm the many accounts and reports of early, pre-Islamic Christian writers about Jewish missionary activities and the persecutions of the Christians, especially in *Najrān by *Yūsuf Dhū Nuwās, the Jewish (proselyte) king of *Himyar. Raḥmān, the Merciful, as a name of God, without any other attribute, has been found many times in those inscriptions and indicates their Jewish origin. Arab historians and biographers of Muhammad's life describe the Jewish communities and tribes living in Hejaz generations before his rise. The years spent by Muhammad the Prophet and Messenger of God in the Jewish Yathrib-Medina gave him many opportunities (positive and negative) to come into close contact with the Jewish tribes living in that group of oases. This historical background explains the fact of the strict uncompromising monotheism preached by Muhammad (who objected to the Christian belief that Jesus was the son of God). Most of the *Bible tales to be found in the Koran and the normative form of Islam based on precepts are to be traced to the Bible and to the Oral Law. At the same time, some descriptions of the Last Judgment and of eschatological events which preoccupied Muhammad in his early period in Mecca, and also some historical tales, stem from Christian sources and inspirations. But the main eschatological beliefs belong to the common Jewish-Christian heritage, even though they were transmitted by Christian monks. In a *Ḥadith* ʿAisha, Muhammad's wife, is said to have heard the tradition about the punishment in the grave (*ḥibbuṭ ha-kever*) from two old Jewish women in Medina. More Jewish elements can be found in those beliefs after Jerusalem was accepted as the location of the Last Judgment.

Nonetheless, the Arabian character of the Koran must always be stressed as it was Muhammad's genius which founded and established Islam. The fact that some of his contemporaries, prophets, and *ḥanifs* tried unsuccessfully to spread monotheism in Arabia cannot lower Muhammad's stature. A large number of Jewish teachings, sayings, and normative and ethical precepts have been included in the **Ḥadith* literature, sometimes in the name of Jews or Jewish converts to Islam although most were inserted anonymously. Much of the narrative material gathered in the *Qiṣaṣ al-Anbiyāʾ* ("Legends of the Prophets") goes back to *Kaʿb al-Aḥbār, the Jewish convert to Islam who accompanied the caliph *Omar during his visit to Jerusalem, or to *Wahb b. Munabbih, also a convert or son of a Jewish convert. All of this *Ḥadith* literature (and the legends are also systematically arranged like the oral tradition) shows an astonishing knowledge of the **halakhah* and **aggadah* as laid down in talmudic and midrashic literature. As in Judaism, at first there was opposition in Islam to writing down the sayings and teachings which were transmitted, by *isnād* (lit., leaning, ascription of an oral religious tradition), a chain of traditioners (see below). The caliph Omar disapproved of the literary fixing of the *sunna* (the sayings and exemplary actions of Muhammad): "Would you like to have a [written] *mathnat* like the *mathnat* [Aramaic: *mathnitha* – Heb. Mishnah] of the Jews?" (Ibn Saʿd v, p. 140).

It is not always possible to postulate a clear-cut dependence of Islamic teachings and methods on Judaism. The fundamental similarity of Judaism and Islam, both based on religious laws in principles, methods, and legislation, caused parallel developments in later centuries. It is a well-known fact that the **geonim*, the heads of the two famous talmudic academies in *Sura and in *Pumbedita, received questions concerning legal and social matters; there are many tens of thousands of their responsa extant. This was also the practice of the Muslim muftis, a category of jurists from whom every Muslim could ask a *fatwā*, a legal opinion based on the religious law. The *fatwā* and the responsum both possessed legal power. It is difficult to decide if the development of this branch of literature in both religions was independent or whether this was an example of mutual influence. For example, at the end of the typical question one finds in the *fatwā* and in the responsum the formula: "May our rabbi (or mufti) give his instruction [= decision] and his reward will be doubled by Heaven [= God]." Goldziher (ZDMG 52, p. 645) sees an Islamic influence in this formula of the responsum.

In the first centuries of Islam the jurists were allowed to use their independent judgment (*ijtihād*) in their decisions, but had to base it on primary sources. Later they were restricted in their freedom of independent decision and were obliged to follow the *taqlīd* (precedent) and to rely on former judgments. One finds a parallel development in rabbinic Judaism, in which even the *geonim* were obliged to follow the authority of their predecessors. Nonetheless, social and economic transformations sometimes demanded departure from accepted laws and rules. Thus the *geonim* and the later generations of rabbis were obliged to establish ordinances adjusted to the new situation. A similar principle was current in the *madhhab* (legal school) of Mālik b. Anas, i.e., the *istiṣlāḥ*, the adaptation (or correction) of laws, for the benefit of the community.

The influence of **fiqh* (Islamic jurisprudence) is clear in the systematic dealings of the *geonim* with halakhic materials according to their contents, e.g., the laws of inheritance, gifts, deposits, oaths, usury, witness and writs, loans, and obligations, as they were arranged by Saadiah, Hai, Samuel b. Ḥophni, who wrote their works in Arabic. This is especially clear in Maimonides' code, *Mishneh Torah*, written in Hebrew and preceded by *Sefer ha-Miẓvot* (Book of Precepts), the first exposition of the 613 precepts. Maimonides' arrangement of these works indicates knowledge of the methods and principles of the *fiqh* literature and of the *Ḥadith* collections of al-Bukhārī, Muslims, and others. Maimonides applied the *ijmāʿ* (consensus), one of the four *uṣūl al-fiqh* (roots of *fiqh*), in his code. In his introduction to this code he gives the chain of the teachers and rabbis who during 40 generations transmitted the Oral Law from Moses to R. Ashi. This is a classic illustration of how the *isnād* – the method of verification of the sayings of Muhammad and his companions – was taken over by early Islam from Judaism, which traced the chain of tradition from Moses to the Men of the Great Synagogue (Avot 1); and in turn was used by Maimonides as a principle to verify the *halakhah*.

But Islamic influence was not restricted to methodology. Some Muslim customs concerning ablutions, prostrations, and general behavior during prayer were accepted by Maimonides and his son Abraham, and aroused disagreement among the majority of the Jewish society. Jewish apocalypses ascribed to R. Simeon b. *Yoḥai, and pseudepigraphic works such as *Pirkei de Rabbi Eliezer* and *Targum Jonathan* show traces of Islamic influence. Note should be made of the book of R. Nissim b. Jacob (Kairouan, first half of the 11th century) called *Ḥibbur Yafe me-ha-Yeshuʿah* ("A Fine Treatise on Salvation"), which in its Hebrew translation was known for centuries and was often reprinted because of its popular religious contents. Its Arabic original (the exact title of which is unknown) was found in the last decade of the 19th century (ed. by J. Obermann, 1933). In Jewish literature it is the only representative of a type known in Islamic literature as *Kutub al-Faraj baʿda al-Shidda* ("Books of Comfort after Disaster"). A detailed comparison between the *Ḥibbur* and the Muslim books shows that Nissim, who was head of the talmudic academy in *Kairouan, knew the stories then current in his non-Jewish environment, whether in literary form or as folktales.

Islamic culture, which had absorbed the legacy of Greece and the Hellenistic world, made a tremendous impact on some aspects of Jewish thought and science. After centuries of complete disruption between that world and Judaism, the works of the Greek philosophers and scientists came back to the orbit of Jewish thinkers and scholars through Arabic translations (from earlier translations in the Syriac language). From the tenth century on, Aristotle, Plato, and Neoplatonism influenced Jewish philosophers of religion, theologians, poets, and scientists. The most famous include: Saadiah, Isaac Israeli (from Kairouan), *Ibn Gabirol, Baḥya ibn *Paquda, Judah *Halevi, *Abraham ibn Daud, Maimonides, and his younger contemporary Joseph ibn Aknin (not to be mistaken for Maimonides' pupil of the same name). As S.D. *Goitein has shown, early *Sufism was also supplemented by Jewish sources. In its higher and later states, Sufism was inspired by Greek philosophy. Sufi influence is to be found in the poems of Ibn Gabirol, but the classic work which wholeheartedly advocates asceticism is Baḥya ibn *Paquda's *Ḥovot ha-Levavot*, which was written in Arabic. Although there is a great deal of eclecticism in this work, it is modeled mainly on Muslim sources. The most prominent representative of Sufism in Judaism is Abraham b. Moses b. *Maimon. In his book *Kifāyat al-ʿĀbidīn* Sufi traces are discernible, even more than in the work of Baḥya. Abraham recommends study and contemplation in order to perfect the soul engaged in the service of God. He used the term "highways" as a means that lead to perfection. In its highest degree, perfection culminates in ecstasy through the praise of God in love. Pure, humble, and sincere souls have access to the esoteric, inner mystical sense of the Torah. Baḥya's *Ḥovot ha-Levavot* and Abraham's *Kifāyat al-ʿĀbidīn* especially influenced the Jewish communities in the East, and played an important role in some later mystic movements; sometimes these mystics found common ways with Muslim Sufis (cf. also *Isrāʾīliyat, *Naḍīr, *Qurayẓa, *Qaynuqāʿa).

[Haïm Z'ew Hirschberg]

BIBLIOGRAPHY: I. Goldziher, *Muhammedanische Studien*, 2 vols. (1889–90); N. Wieder, *Islamic Influences on the Jewish Worship* (1947); S.D. Goitein, *Jews and Arabs* (1955); E.I.J. Rosenthal, *Judaism and Islam* (1961). POLEMICS: Baron, Social², 3 (1957), 76–85, 87, 156f.; 5 (1957), 82–105, 117–21, 136, 326–37; M. Steinschneider, *Polemische und apologetische Literatur*...(1887); I. Goldziher, in: JZWL, 1–11 (1862–75); idem, in: REJ, 30 (1895), 1–23; 43 (1901), 1–14; 60 (1910), 32–8; idem, in: M. Brann and F. Rosenthal (eds.), *Gedenkbuch...David Kaufmann* (1900), 86–102; M. Schreiner, *Beitraege zur Geschichte der theologischen Bewegungen im Islam* (1899, offprint from ZDMG, vols. 52–53, 1898–99); I. Friedlaender, in: ZA, 26 (1912), 93–110; A.S. Tritton, in: *Islamic Studies*, 1, no. 2 (1962), 60–4. **ADD. BIBLIOGRAPHY:** POLEMICS: I.Y. al-Shāhabī, *Istrātījiyyat al-Qurʾān al-Karīm fī muwājahat al-Yahūdiyya al-ʿālamiyya* (1997); M.I. Khalaf, *Qiyam al-Yahūd fī al-qiṣaṣ al-Qurʾāniyya*...(2001). JUDAISM AND ISLAM: M. Maas, *Bibel und Koran* (1893); A.I. Katsh, *Judaism in Islam* (1954); Abraham Geiger, *Judaism and Islam* (1969); R. Roberts, *The Social Laws of the Qoran* (1925, 1971²); H. Schwarzbaum, *Mi-Mekor Israel we Ishmaʿel: Yahadūt we-Islām be-aspaklariyyat ha-folklor* (1975).

ISLE-SUR-LA-SORGUE, L' (Heb. לישלאה), town in the Vaucluse department, S.E. France. The L'Isle community, smallest of the four communities of *Comtat Venaissin, was formed at the latest at the close of the 13th century. During the French Revolution, the *carrière* (Jewish quarter) of L'Isle was all but abandoned. At the time of the Reign of Terror, when there was a controversy over the sale of the silver belonging to the synagogue, no Jew intervened; it can therefore be assumed that the community had ceased to exist. Known scholars of L'Isle were the brothers Isaac and Jacob Gard (mid-16th century) and Ḥayyim Judah b. Jacob Segre, who died in L'Isle in 1633.

BIBLIOGRAPHY: Gross, Gal Jud, 310f.; J. de Joannis, *Le Fédéralisme ... à L'Isle* (1884), 240; I. Loeb, in: REJ, 12 (1886), 170, and index volume; Z. Szajkowski, *Franco-Judaica* (1962), index.

[Bernhard Blumenkranz]

ISOU (Goldstein), ISIDORE (1925–), poet. Isou immigrated to France from Romania. He wrote verse and created *Lettrisme*, an ephemeral literary theory which advocated the dislocation of the word and a return to the original letter; in this some critics have seen an unconscious echo of the Kabbalah. In his essay, *L'agrégation d'un Nom et d'un Messie* (1947), Isou pessimistically foretold a second Auschwitz that would engulf surviving Jewry.

ISRAEL (Heb. יִשְׂרָאֵל).

(1) The name of honor given to *Jacob after his mysterious struggle with the angel, "Thy name shall be called no more Jacob but Israel, for thou hast striven [*sarita* from the root *sarah*, שרה] with God [*El*, אֵל] and with men and hast prevailed" (Gen. 32:28, 29). The explanation of the name is not etymological, and was probably not meant to be. More likely, the name literally means "El-is-Just/ Straight/ Upright." It may be noted that the name occurs in Ugaritic as a proper name, and is spelled with *shin*. Despite the apparent prohibition contained in this verse against the subsequent use of the name Jacob, in the following scriptural narrative the names Jacob and Israel are both used indiscriminately with regard to the father and his sons (cf. Gen. 49:2 and 46:5): "and the sons of Israel carried Jacob their father." The discrepancy between Genesis 32:28–29 and the subsequent use of the name is due to different sources. The Talmud specifically states that both names may be employed; Israel, however, shall be of greater importance (Ber. 13a).

(2) When the immediate descendants of Jacob, "the children [*benei*, "sons"] of Israel" (Ex. 1:1), grew into a people, they were called "the people of the children of Israel" (idem, 1:9), and henceforth, until the division of the kingdom under *Rehoboam, "Israel" or "the children of Israel" were the only designations for what is now known as the Jewish people. If the "Israel" mentioned in the inscription of Merne-ptah (king

of Egypt, c. 1225 B.C.E.) is to be identified with Israel and not, as some have suggested, with Jezreel, it is the earliest known use of the name outside the Bible.

(3) With the division of the kingdom during the reign of Rehoboam, the Southern Kingdom, consisting of the two tribes which remained loyal to the House of David, Judah, and Benjamin, took the name Judah; the Northern Kingdom, consisting of the 10 defecting tribes, was called the Kingdom of Israel (cf. I and II Kings with regard to the respective kings, and Amos 2:4, 2:6).

(4) After the Kingdom of Israel fell in 721 B.C.E., only the southern Kingdom of Judah remained, the inhabitants of which were referred to as "Judahites" (*Yehudim*), from which derives the alternative name "Jew." Thus Esther 2:5 reads "There was a certain *Yehudi* in Shushan, whose name was Mordecai … a Benjamite," *Yehudi* being his people and Benjamin his tribe. The designation becomes reinforced by the fact that under Roman rule the land was designated as the province of Judea. Nevertheless, the name Israel continues to be used in the Bible in the books written after the end of the Northern Kingdom as well as in rabbinic literature, especially in the *aggadah*, to denote the Jewish people as a whole, and continues in the post-talmudic period.

(5) The term "Ereẓ Israel" ("Land of Israel") to denote the country of the people of Israel is first used in the Mishnah.

(6) Although the name Israelites was revived in some Western countries in the 19th century to designate the Jews, it is of little historical or theological significance, and is primarily due to the pejorative association which the word Jew had acquired in literature.

(7) The word Israel is also used to designate a Jew who is neither a *kohen nor a *levite.

(8) When the Jewish state was established, the decision was taken to call it the State of Israel. Since 1948, therefore, Israel has become a national connotation and Jew a religious one. The term Israeli applies to all citizens of the state, irrespective of religion.

(9) Mention should also be made of the native Indian Jews, who call themselves *Bene Israel, and of the Ethiopian Jews who call themselves *Beta Israel.

BIBLIOGRAPHY: E. Sachsse, in: ZAW, 34 (1914), 1–16; idem, in: *Zeitschrift für Semitistik*, 4 (1925), 63–9; W. Casperi, *ibid.*, 3 (1924), 194–211; W.F. Albright, in: JBL, 46 (1927), 156–68; S. Feist, in: MGWJ, 73 (1929), 317–20; M. Naor, in: ZAW, 49 (1931), 317–21; R. Marcus, in: JBL, 60 (1941) 141–50; G.A. Dannel, *Studies in the Name Israel in the Old Testament* (1946); EM, 3 (1958), 938–43.

[Louis Isaac Rabinowitz]

ISRAEL. This entry is arranged according to the outline below. Bibliography for a section is indicated by (†).

LAND OF ISRAEL

GEOGRAPHICAL SURVEY

Names

The name Ereẓ Israel (the Land of Israel) designates the land which, according to the Bible was promised as an inheritance to the Israelite tribes. In the course of time it came to be regarded first by the Jews and then also by the Christian world as the national homeland of the Jews and the Holy Land. The concept of *ha-Areẓ* ("the land") had apparently become permanently rooted in the consciousness of the Jewish people by the end of the Second Temple period, at which time the term Ereẓ Israel also became fixed and its usage widespread. Prior to this there was no name in existence, or at any rate in general use, to denote the land in its entirety. At different periods there were names that designated parts of the country, either alone or together with an adjacent territory; in some periods it was regarded as part of a wider geographical unit.

During the Egyptian Middle Empire and the beginning of the New Empire (up to the 19th Dynasty), Ereẓ Israel together with part of Syria (and the Lebanon) was called Retune (Rtnw). In the New Empire period, especially from the 19th Dynasty (14th–13th centuries B.C.E.) onward, Ereẓ Israel and (central-southern) Syria were referred to as Ḫurru (Ḫù-rú) chiefly as an ethnic term, after the Horites who inhabited the country, especially Syria. The term *pa-Ḫurru* ("[Land of] the Hori[tes]") is still found as late as 238 B.C.E. (Ptolemaic period) in the Greek text of the Canopus inscription as the synonym for "Syria." An additional name employed from the late 14th to the 12th century B.C.E. is P3-Knʿn. For two important designations of pre-Israelite Ereẓ Israel, *Ereẓ ha-Emori* (Land of the Amorites) and *Ereẓ Kenaʿan*, see *Amorites, *Canaan, and *Phoenicia.

With the Israelite conquest began an entirely new period in the history of Ereẓ Israel, as is expressed in its names. An early term with a widespread usage is *Ereẓ ha-Ivrim* ("land of the Hebrews" – Gen. 40:15). Even later writers, especially Josephus and Pausanias (second century C.E.) sometimes employ this term. After the Israelite conquest, the name Canaan became merely an historical concept but many generations passed before the term Ereẓ Israel became standard usage. The expressions "*ereẓ bene Israel*" ("land of the children of Israel") in Joshua 11:22 and Ereẓ Israel in I Samuel 13:19 refer only to the area inhabited by the Israelites and not to the country as a single geographical entity within its natural boundaries.

Saul, David, and Solomon reigned over the kingdom of Israel, but it is doubtful whether their dominions had an official designation. The biblical references to Ereẓ Israel in the days of David (I Chron. 22:2; II Chron. 2:16) apparently reflect the later period of their composition. After the first split of the united monarchy early in David's reign, "Judah and Israel" sometimes appear side by side to indicate the territory of all the Israelite tribes, but this expression is also considered an anticipation (Josh. 11:21; II Sam. 3:10; 5:5; I Kings 4:20; 5:5). With the final division of the kingdom the name Israel was restricted to the area of the kingdom of Ephraim while the kingdom of the Davidic dynasty was known as the land of Judah. The land of Israel mentioned in II Kings 5:2 refers to the kingdom of all the tribes. In Ezekiel, Gilead and Judah in one reference are explicitly excluded from the territory of Ereẓ Israel; in another Jerusalem, though in Judah, is included in Ereẓ Israel (27:17; 40:2; 47:18).

The shortened form *ha-Areẓ* is already found in Leviticus 19:23; Joshua 11:23; 12:1; Ezekiel 45:1; Ruth 1:1; but the Mishnah, which also uses it, is the first to employ the term Ereẓ Israel to denote the "land of the children of Israel." After the Assyrian Exile, when the remnants of the people in the country centered in Judah, the name Jew (*Yehudi*) became a synonym for Israelite and Hebrew (Jer. 34:9). In the post-Exilic period, Judah (*Yehud* in Aramaic) was the official name of the autonomous area of Jewish settlement and later of the Hasmonean and Herodian kingdoms, even though these extended over a much larger area than that of Judah in the First Temple period. The Persian authorities in their Aramaic documents used the name Yehud and it also appears on coins struck by the province; the Greeks (Iouda, Ioudaia) and the Romans (Judaea) continued it. After the Bar Kokhba War (132–135), the Romans changed its name to Palaestina so as to emphasize that the rebellious Jewish nation had lost its right in its homeland. Coins from the Hasmonean period do not mention Israel but only *Ḥever ha-Yehudim ("Council of the Jews"), which perhaps designates the governing body of the nation and not the territory. On the other hand, coins issued during the Jewish and Bar Kokhba Wars bore the inscription Israel (e.g., *"Shekel Yisrael," "Le-Ḥer[ut] Yisrael"*) but whether this referred to the people or the country is unknown. The name Judah in its broader meaning disappeared almost entirely from Hebrew literature and the Aramaic language and in the end it was replaced by the terms Ereẓ Israel and the Aramaic Ar'a de-Yisra'el and the name Ereẓ Israel entered all the languages spoken by Jews throughout the Diaspora.

The name "*Palestine" was originally an adjective derived from Philistia (*Peleshet*). It is first mentioned by Herodotus 1.105 in the form Συρία ἡ Παλαιστίνη, i.e., "the Philistine Syria"; it was subsequently shortened, the adjective "Palaistinei" becoming a proper noun. The emperor Hadrian, who applied it to the whole country in order to eradicate the name Judea, revived it and from Byzantine times became the accepted name of Ereẓ Israel in non-Jewish languages. (For fuller details, see *Palestine.) On May 14, 1948, the Jewish-held part of Western Palestine was given the name the "State of Israel" in the declaration of independence promulgated by the People's Council. Transjordan, together with Arab-inhabited parts of Western Palestine, the so-called "West Bank," later became the Hashemite Kingdom of *Jordan, and a strip on the southwestern coast, occupied by Egypt, became known as the *Gaza Strip. The *Six-Day War brought the whole area, including the *Golan Heights, which were captured from Syria, under Israeli control, though only the formerly Jordanian-occupied part of Jerusalem and the Golan Heights were formally annexed by Israel. Internationally, all these areas were commonly referred to as the "occupied territories." On part of them the Palestinians established the *Palestinian Authority, which embraced most of the Gaza Strip and certain areas, including the Arab towns, of the West Bank. The common Israeli terms for these areas are "Judea and Samaria" (Yehudah ve-Shomron) for the West Bank and Ḥevel Aza (the Gaza District) for the Gaza Strip.

[Abraham J. Brawer]

Boundaries

ACCORDING TO BIBLE AND TALMUD. Eretz Israel is an abstract geographical name. Its boundaries were never agreed upon and up today, there are lots of definitions concerning the dispersion of the area. Jewish sources distinguish between three borders of Ereẓ Israel:

(1) "the boundary of the Patriarchs," based on Genesis 15:18–21: "from the river of Egypt (the Nile) unto the great river, the river Euphrates…"; (2) "the boundary of those coming out of Egypt," based on Deuteronomy 1:7–8; 11:24; Joshua 1:4; 13:2–5, which was interpreted as extending from the coastal Galilee (not including Acre-Akko) to the Brook of Egypt (Wadi el-Arish; Tosef., Ter. 2:12; Tosef., Ḥal. 2:11; Git. 8a, et al.); and (3) "the boundary of those returning from Babylonia," within which the halakhic rules for Ereẓ Israel applied, i.e., this is the actual area of Jewish settlement in talmudic times (Tosef., Shev. 4:11; Sif. Deut. 51; TJ, Shev. 6:1, 36c). According to this definition, the border extended from the coast of the Mediterranean Sea in the western Galilee (south of Acre) to the Golan, continued to the Hauran in the east, followed the desert road down to Amman and Petra, returned to the coast along the Roman *limes,* excluding the southern coastal cities up to, and excluding, Ashkelon.

The biblical expression "from Dan even to Beer-Sheba" is used in II Samuel 24:2 and I Kings 5:5 to designate Ereẓ Israel in its limited sense corresponding to the area "from the valley of Arnon unto mount Hermon" in the lands beyond the Jordan (Josh. 12:1). The term Holy Land (Terra Sancta) which is used in Christian sources also never defines the exact limits of this area.

NATURAL FEATURES IN HISTORICAL SOURCES. The ancient texts do not mention all of the country's natural geographical features. Those found include the principal rivers of the Coastal Plain, Litas (Egyptian *Ntn*, cf. Theophanes, *Chronography*, 6235), Belus (Jos., Wars, 2:189), Kishon (Judg. 5:21; I Kings 18:40), Chorseus (Ptolemy, *Geography*, 5:14, 3), Shihor-Libnath

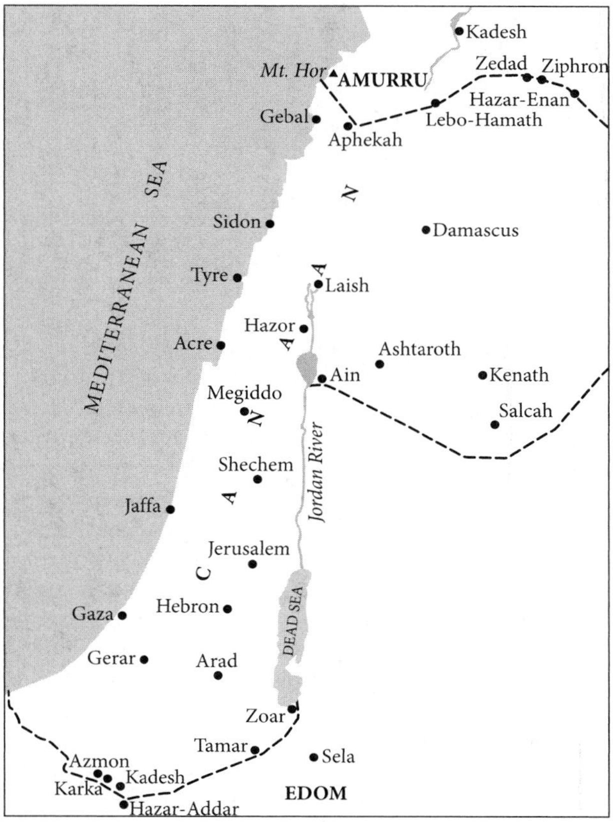

Map 1. The borders of the Egyptian province of Canaan (early 13th century B.C.E.*). After Y. Aharoni,* Carta's Atlas of the Bible, *Jerusalem 1964.*

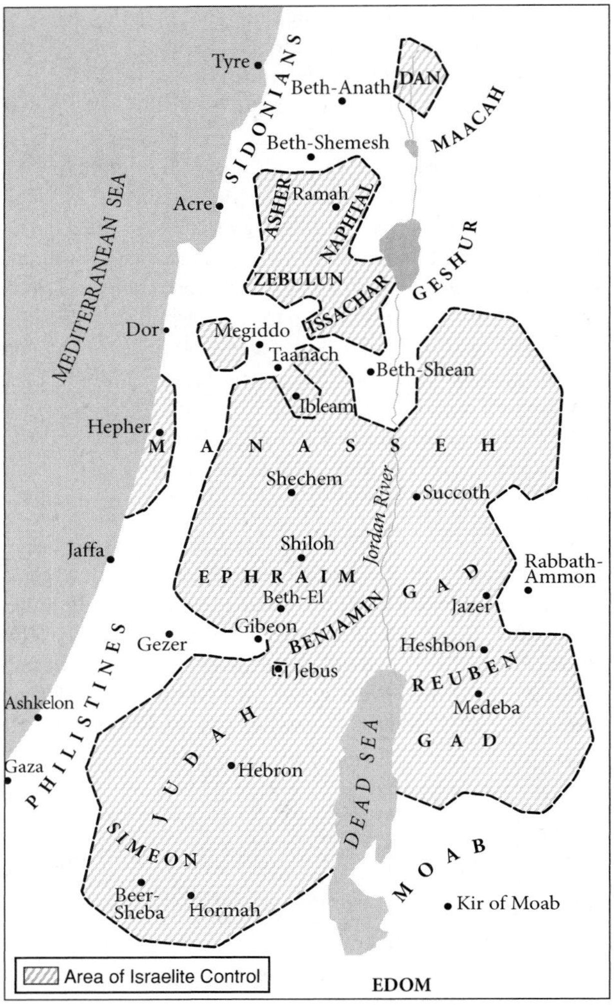

Map 2. The limits of Israelite control in the time of the Judges (12th century B.C.E.*). After Y. Aharoni,* Carta's Atlas of the Bible.

(Josh. 19:26), and Yarkon (Josh. 19:46). In the central mountain range, termed the "hill country of Naphtali" (Josh. 20:7), Mts. Tabor and Moreh are prominent landmarks (Josh. 19:22; Judg. 7:1). South of the Jezreel Valley (Judg. 6:33), also known as the "Great Plain" (I Macc. 12:49), are Mt. Carmel, the *rosh kadosh* ("sacred promontory," as it is already called in inscriptions of Thutmosis III, c. 1469 B.C.E.) in the west, and Mt. Gilboa in the east (I Sam. 28:4). These mountains are outcrops of Mt. Ephraim (Josh. 17:15) whose most outstanding peaks are Mts. Gerizim and Ebal (Deut. 11:29). Baal-Hazor (II Sam. 13:23) marks the beginning of the Judean mountains, where the famous Mount of Olives stands (Zech. 14:4). The Sharon and the Shephelah extend to the west of the central mountain range which ends in the Negev (Isa. 65:10; Josh. 9:1; Deut. 1:7). The four main rivers of Ereẓ Israel east of the Jordan are the Hieromices (Yarmuk; Pliny, *Natural History*, 5:16, 74), Yabbok (Josh. 212:2), Arnon (Deut. 2:24), and the Zered (Num. 21:12), of which the latter two empty into the Dead Sea. The Jordan itself flows through Lake Semechonitis (Lake Ḥuleh, Jos., Wars, 4:3) and Lake Gennesareth or Chinnereth (Num. 34:11 – modern Lake Kinneret) and completes its course in the Salt Sea (Num. 34:3, now known as the Dead Sea) which is also called Lake Asphaltitis (Pliny, *Natural History*, 5:12, 72; Jos., Wars, 4:476). The term Aravah is applied to the whole of the Jordan Valley and the area south of the Dead Sea (Deut. 1:7; 34:1–3). The latter area is also called the Valley of Salt (II Sam. 8:13). To the east beyond the Jordan are the mountains of Bashan (Ps. 68:16), Gilead (Gen. 31:25), Seir (Gen. 14:6), and the most prominent – Mt. Nebo (or Pisgah, Deut. 32:48–50; 34:1) from which Moses beheld the Promised Land.

HISTORICAL BOUNDARIES AND SUBDIVISIONS. The earliest complete description of the boundaries of Ereẓ Israel is contained in Numbers 34. Scholars regard this description as

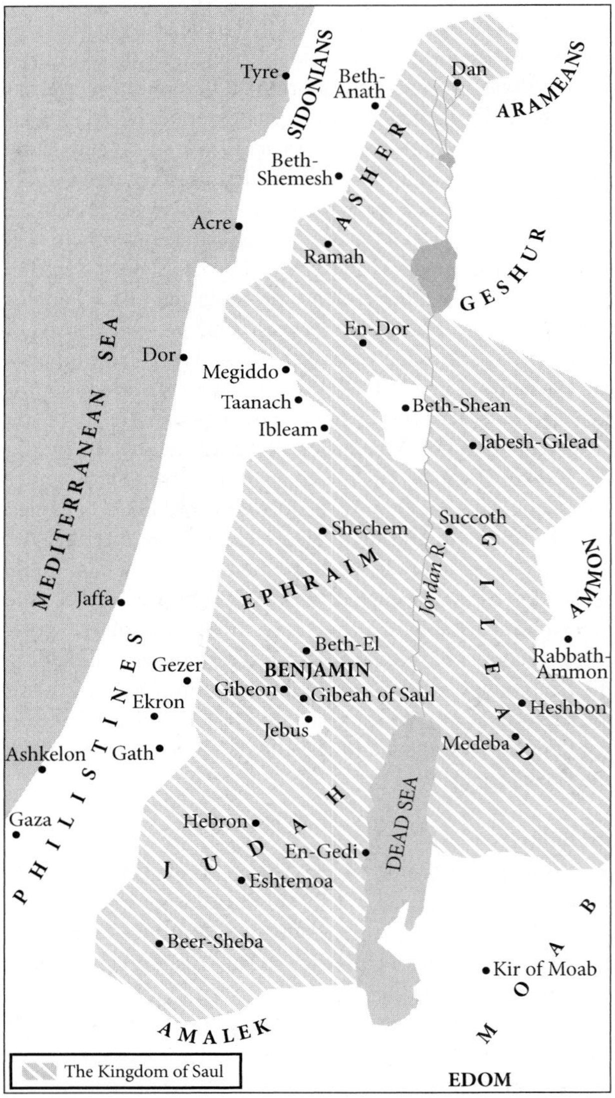

Map 3. The limits of Saul's kingdom (end of 11th century B.C.E.*). After Y. Aharoni,* Carta's Atlas of the Bible.

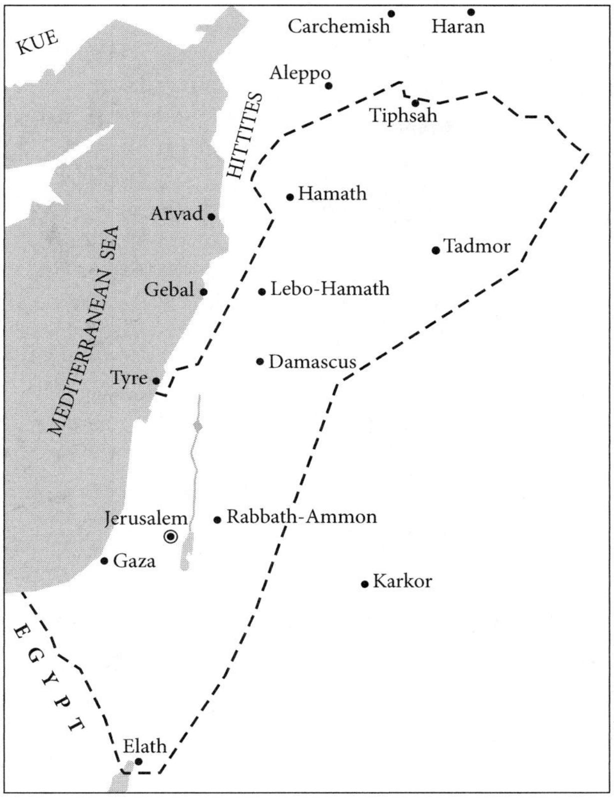

Map 4. The limits of the kingdom of David and Solomon (10th century B.C.E.). After Y. Aharoni, Carta's Atlas of the Bible.

a definition of the limits of the Egyptian province of Canaan as established in the peace treaty between Ramses II and the Hittites (c. 1270 B.C.E.). The province of Canaan included the entire area west of the Jordan, Phoenicia up to Mt. Hor north of Byblos, and the Bashan, Hauran, and Hermon areas. No subdivisions of this area are known – the system of Canaanite city-states did not lend itself to any clear administrative organization. The next detailed account of the borders appears in Joshua 13–19. Scholars dispute the date of this source and of the various fragments of lists from which it was compiled. It is nevertheless evident from the list of unconquered Canaanite cities in Judges 1:21–35 that the ideal and actual limits of Israelite power did not coincide. The theoretical boundaries extended from Sidon in the north and Lebo-Hamath in the northeast to the Brook of Egypt and the Negev in the south and included east of the Jordan the Bashan and Hauran, and Gilead and Moab down to the Arnon. In actual fact, however, the area occupied by the Israelite tribes before the time of David was limited to the mountains of Galilee and Ephraim, Judah to the southern end of the Dead Sea, and most of the area between the Yarmuk and the Arnon, excluding Ammon. In the Coastal Plain Israelite control was tenuous and Canaanite enclaves in the Jezreel Valley and around Jerusalem virtually cut Israelite territory into three separate parts. South of Jaffa the entire Coastal Plain remained the domain of the Philistines who threatened to encroach on the territory held by the Israelites.

The lands of the tribes were divided as follows: the Bilhah tribes, Dan and Naphtali, held eastern Galilee (Dan being a latecomer to the area after an unsuccessful attempt to take possession of part of the Shephelah west of Jerusalem); three tribes of the Leah-Zilpah group, Issachar, Asher, and Zebulun, settled western and southern Galilee; the central group of tribes, the House of Joseph (Ephraim and Manasseh) together with the allied Benjamite tribe – all three of the Rachel group – occupied the hill country from Jerusalem to the Jezreel Valley, with Manasseh overspilling into Issachar and east of the Jordan (Josh. 17:11; Judg. 1:27; Num. 32:33); the

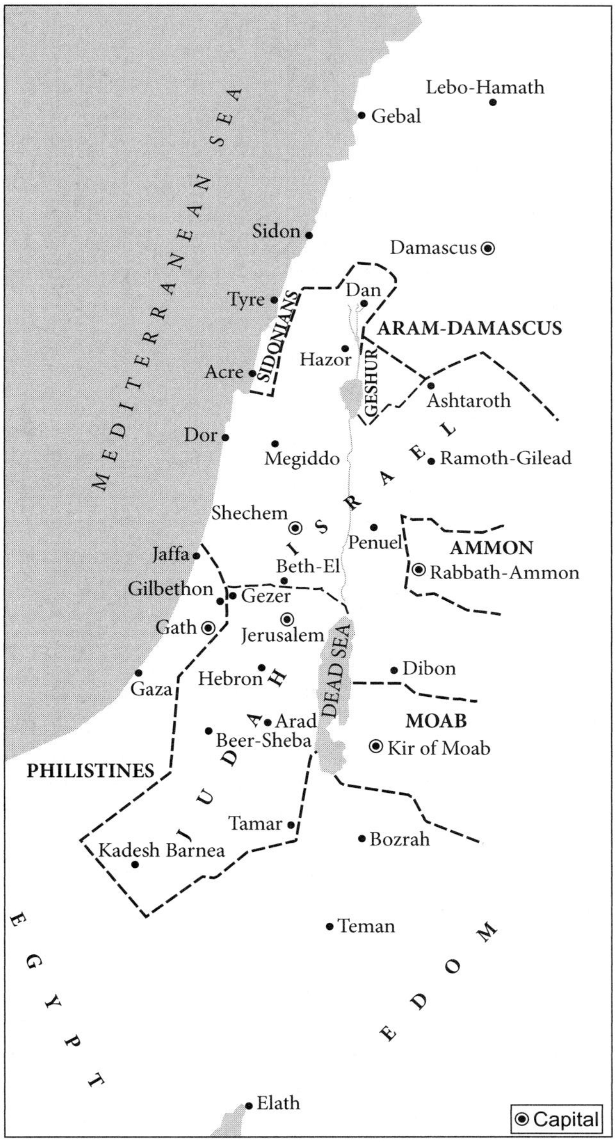

Map 5. The divided kingdom of Israel and Judah in the time of Jeroboam and Rehoboam (end of 10th century B.C.E.). After Y. Aharoni, Carta's Atlas of the Bible.

southern group included the Leah tribes of Judah, centered upon Hebron, and the weak tribe of Simeon on the borders of the Negev; Reuben, Gad, and half of Manasseh occupied the lands east of the Jordan with Reuben subject to Gad as was Simeon to Judah.

From the time of King David onward, the ideal borders of Ereẓ Israel came much closer to realization. According to the Bible, David closed the gaps dividing the tribes by conquering Jerusalem, the Jezreel Valley, and the coastal area between Jaffa and Acre. Jerusalem, originally within Benjamin, was made a royal domain outside the tribal system. David, moreover, subdued all the lands up to Lebo-Hamath, annexed Ammon, Moab, and Edom (thereby reaching the Arabah and the Red Sea) and dominated the kings of Hamath and the Philistines by means of vassal treaties. David's kingdom thus extended from the Brook of Egypt to Tiphsah on the Euphrates, although not all his entire domain was regarded as Ereẓ Israel proper. He established a network of levitical cities to serve as administrative centers uniting the kingdom. Solomon reorganized the kingdom into 12 districts (excluding Judah), unequal in size, but equal in economic importance. Each district was to supply his court with its needs during one month of the year. Some of these districts were identical with the old tribal areas while others were new units. According to I Kings 4:7–19, the districts included:

(1) Mount Ephraim;
(2) Makaz (from Beth-Shemesh to the coast);
(3) Hepher (the Sharon coast);
(4) Dor and its region;
(5) Jezreel Valley;
(6) northern Gilead;
(7) southern Gilead (Mahanaim);
(8) Naphtali;
(9) Asher;
(10) Issachar;
(11) Benjamin;
(12) Gad.

Judah's exclusion from this tax-paying area was one of the causes of the subsequent split of the monarchy. As to the external boundaries of the kingdom, Solomon gained Gezer, but gave Cabul to Hiram of Tyre as well as *Aram-Damascus, which deprived him of access to the Euphrates.

With the division of the monarchy under Rehoboam, the northern kingdom of Israel consisted of Ephraim, Galilee, Gilead, and the rest of Israelite territory east of the Jordan. The southern kingdom of Judah retained Benjamin. The subject areas of Ammon, Moab, and Edom soon liberated themselves from the overlordship of weakened Israel and Judah. Apart from some futile attempts by Abijah of Judah to advance into Israel (c. 911 B.C.E.) and of Baasha of Israel to push the frontier closer to Jerusalem, the boundaries of the two kingdoms remained fairly stable. Their external borders, however, changed according to the vicissitudes of their power. On the northern front the house of Omri, and of Ahab in particular, waged several wars with Aram-Damascus and in the end lost Ramoth-Gilead (c. 850 B.C.E.). With the weakening of Aram under Assyrian pressure, *Jehoash and Jeroboam II (c. 790–770) advanced to Damascus and Lebo-Hamath, almost restoring the boundaries of David. Moab was definitely lost to Mesha in approximately 855 B.C.E. In Judah, Asa or Jehoshaphat (c. 860 B.C.E.) advanced to Elath, which, together with Edom, was later lost but reconquered in the days of Uzziah (c. 750 B.C.E.) who also extended the frontier of the Judahite monarchy in the direction of Philistia (II Chron. 26:6). As to the internal administration of the two kingdoms, the capital of Israel was first at Shechem, then – perhaps already under Jeroboam in the tenth century B.C.E. – at Tirzah, and from

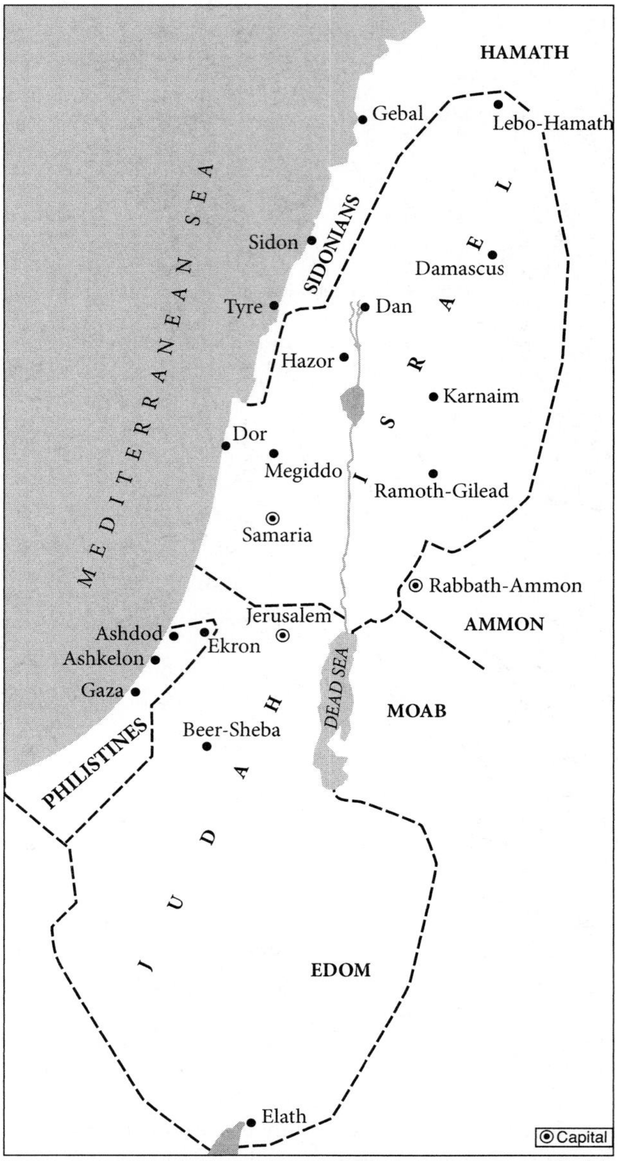

Map 6. The borders of the kingdoms of Israel and Judah in the time of Jeroboam II and Uzziah (mid-eighth century B.C.E.). After Y. Aharoni, Carta's Atlas of the Bible.

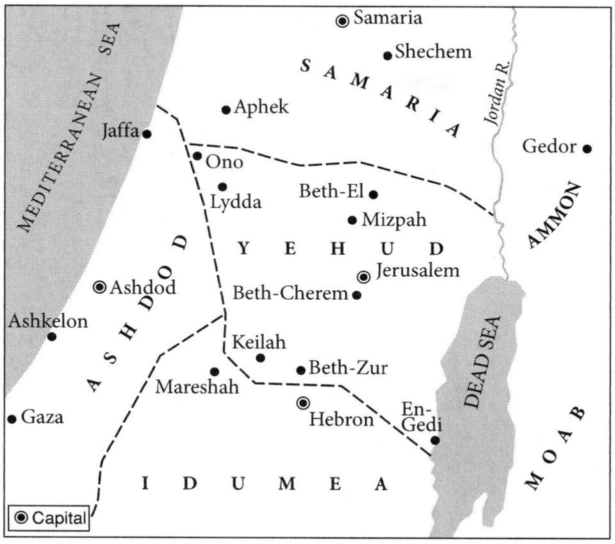

Map 7. The borders of the Persian province of Yehud in the days of the Return (mid-fifth century B.C.E.*). After M. Avi-Yonah* Carta's Atlas of the Period of the Second Temple, the Mishnah and the Talmud.

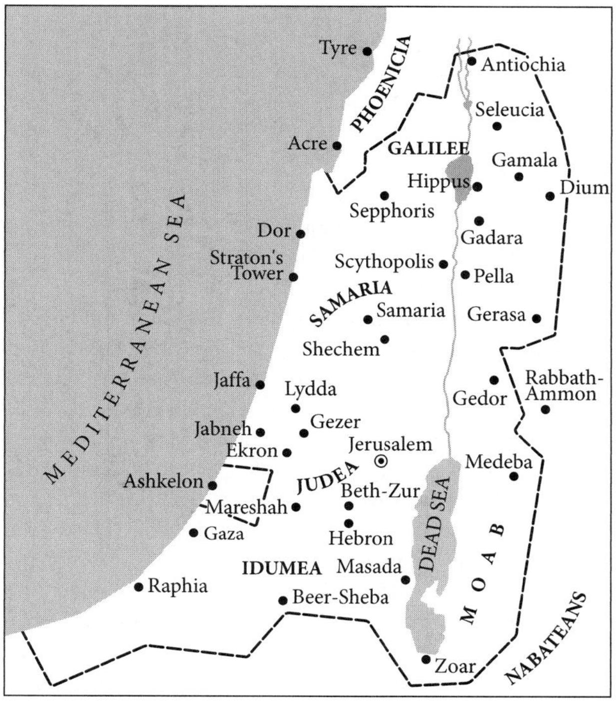

Map 8. The borders of the kingdom of Alexander Yannai (103–76 B.C.E.*). After M. Avi-Yonah* Carta's Atlas of the Period of the Second Temple, the Mishnah and the Talmud.

the time of Omri (882–871 B.C.E.) at Samaria. Ostraca found at Samaria provide information on the division of the kingdom into districts in the eighth century B.C.E. The division of the Judahite monarchy into 12 districts is preserved in Joshua 15:21–62; 18:25–28. From the eighth century onward, the Assyrians began reducing the boundaries of Israel. In 732 B.C.E.

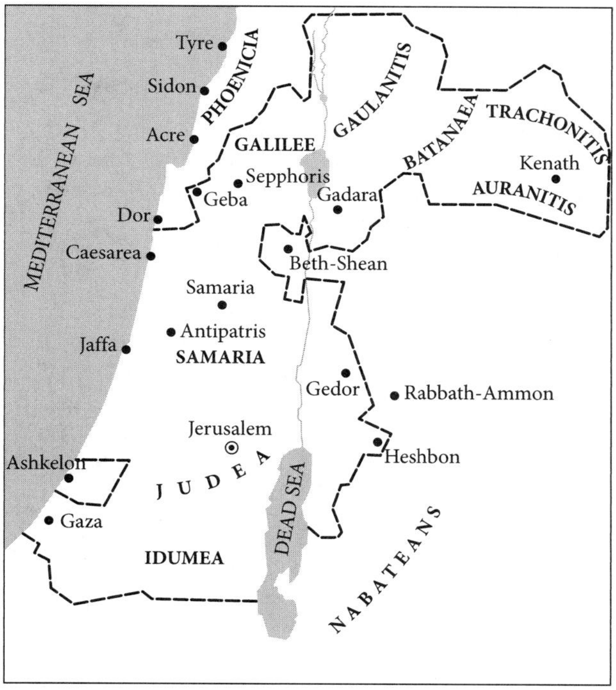

Map 9. The borders of the kingdom of Herod (37–4 B.C.E.*). After M. Avi-Yonah* Carta's Atlas of the Period of the Second Temple, the Mishnah and the Talmud.

Tiglath-Pileser III captured Galilee and Gilead, leaving only Samaria to Israel. In the conquered territory he established the Assyrian provinces of Megiddo, Dor, Karnaim, Hauran, and Gilead. Sargon II (722–705 B.C.E.) conquered the rest of the Northern Kingdom (721 B.C.E.) and Philistia and organized them into two additional provinces: Samaria and Ashdod. Assyria's decline in the seventh century enabled Josiah of Judah (639–609 B.C.E.) once again to extend the rule of the Davidic dynasty over most of Samaria and Galilee, but the Babylonian conquest in 587 B.C.E. brought about the final downfall of Judah. The Babylonians diminished its borders and established an additional province in Edom south of Judah.

After the establishment of Persian rule (539 B.C.E.) all of Ereẓ Israel was included in its fifth satrapy called ʿAbarnaharah ("beyond the river," i.e., the Euphrates). Its satrap residing at Damascus had under his control the various provinces as inherited from the Assyrians and Babylonians. The province of Judah (officially called Yehud) extended from Beth-El in the north to Beth-Zur in the south and from Emmaus and Keilah in the west to the Jordan in the east. The province was subdivided into six districts (called *pelekh* in Hebrew), each with a capital and subcapital. These included Jerusalem with Netophah as its subcapital in the center of Judah; Beth-Cherem (Ein Kerem) in the west Zanoah as its subcapital, Keilah with Adullam in the southwest; Beth-Zur with Tekoa in the south; Jericho with Hassenaah in the east; Mizpah (Tell en-Nasbeh) with Gibeon in the north. The Persians continued the Babylonian provinces but added the province of Ammon which was administered by the Jewish Tobiad family (see *Tobias). The coastal area was divided between the Phoenician cities Tyre and Sidon.

The Hellenistic conquest (332 B.C.E.) did not alter the country's internal subdivision for the time being. The Ptolemies, kings of Egypt, who ruled the whole of Ereẓ Israel from 301 to 198 B.C.E., granted autonomy to the coastal cities and gave Greek names to various cities (e.g., Acre became Ptolemais, Rabbath-Ammon became Philadelphia, etc.). The Tobiads were restricted to the Western part of their district. All of Ereẓ Israel was administered from Alexandria. When the Seleucid monarchy under Antiochus III conquered Ereẓ Israel, larger units, eparchies, were established, each of which included several smaller districts or hyparchies. Thus Samaria now ruled over Judea and Galilee and Perea of the Tobiads. Idumea remained a separate district, the coastal cities were joined into one district, and Paralia and all the lands east of the Jordan were combined into Galaaditis, except for Perea. The Seleucids, who were energetic Hellenizers, particularly Antiochus IV (175–164 B.C.E.), founded many Greek poleis, such as Scythopolis (Beth-Shean), Pella, Gerasa, Gadara, and Hippus. Samaria had been a Macedonian colony since the time of Alexander.

The main events in the period between the outbreak of the Hasmonean revolt (167 B.C.E.) and the death of Alexander Yannai (76 B.C.E.) were the expansion of the Jewish state, paralleled by the disintegration of Seleucid rule. In 147 B.C.E. Jonathan, the first ruler of the Hasmonean dynasty, received Ekron and the three districts of Lydda, Arimathea, and Aphaerema. Some time before 144 B.C.E. he was also ceded Perea. His brother Simeon (142–135 B. C.E.) annexed Jaffa and Gezer, thus open the sea for his state. Simeon's son John Hyrcanus I (135–104 B.C.E.) extended his sway over Idumea, Samaria, Scythopolis, and the inner Carmel, as well as Heshbon and Medeba east of the Jordan. Judah Aristobulus I, the son of Hyrcanus, who barely reigned one year, added Galilee. The last of the conquering Hasmoneans, Alexander Yannai (103–76 B.C.E.), captured the whole coast from Rhinocorura (El-Arish) on the Brook of Egypt to the Carmel promontory, all of Western Gilead from Paneas (Banias) to Gerasa, and all the lands around the Dead Sea. Only Acre-Ptolemais, Philadelphia, and Ascalon remained outside his rule, the last with Yannai's consent. In their internal organization of the state, the Hasmoneans preserved the basic subdivision – toparchy – of which there were 24, corresponding to the 24 *ma'amadot* (literally, "place of standing") of the Temple service. They also followed Ptolemaic practice by establishing a larger administrative unit called *meris*, and divided the country into five of them: Galilee, Samaria, Judea, Idumea, and Perea.

Roman intervention under Pompey put an end to the expansion of the Hasmonean State. Under Pompey's settlement of 63 B.C.E. the Jewish State was reduced to Judea, including Idumea and Perea, and to Galilee. The Greek cities conquered by the Hasmoneans were "freed." Those cities along the coast were placed under the supervision of the Roman governor of Syria and those east of the Jordan were united into a league of ten cities, known as the Decapolis. The Samaritans regained their independence, the Itureans obtained the Golan and Paneas, and the Nabateans, the Negev and the lands around the Dead Sea. Pompey's harsh arrangements were somewhat alleviated by Julius Caesar, who in 47 B.C.E. restored Jaffa and the Plain of Jezreel to Judea. When Herod replaced the Hasmonean dynasty in 40 B.C.E., he was given, in addition to the lands held by Mattathias Antigonus, the last Hasmonean ruler, the region of Marisa and the lands of the Samaritans. In 30 B.C.E. Augustus granted him the coastal area from Gaza to Caesarea (originally called Straton's Tower) as well as Samaria (renamed Sebaste), Gadara, and Hippus in the interior. In 23 B.C.E. Herod received Batanea (Bashan), Trachonitis, and the Hauran, and in 20 B.C.E. Augustus finally added Paneas and the Gaulan. Herod's kingdom was administered on a dual basis: the Greek cities were more or less autonomous, while the remainder, the "King's country," was ruled directly by royal officials. Herod retained the division into *merides* and toparchies. Two lists of his toparchies have been preserved: one by Pliny (*Natural History*, 5:15, 70) who enumerates them as follows:

(1) Jericho;
(2) Emmaus;
(3) Lydda;
(4) Joppa (Jaffa);
(5) Acrabitene;
(6) Gophna;
(7) Thamna;
(8) Betholeptephene (Beit Nattif);
(9) Orine (Jerusalem);
(10) Herodium.

To this list Josephus adds Idumea, En-Gedi, and Jamnia (Wars, 3: 54–55). After Herod's death (4 B.C.E.) his kingdom was divided among his three sons. Archelaus received Judea, Idumea, Samaria, and Caesarea; Herod Antipas received Galilee and Perea; Philip received Caesarea Philippi and the lands east of the Jordan. The Greek cities were placed under the governor of Syria. When Archelaus was deposed in 6 C.E., his lands were administered by a Roman procurator. This was the situation in Jesus' time. After the death of Philip, his nephew Agrippa I received his inheritance, to which were added the lands of Antipas in 39 C.E., and in 41 C.E. also those of Archelaus. When Agrippa I died in 44 C.E., part of his kingdom was reserved for his son Agrippa II (Philip's share and eastern Galilee) but most of it was administered by Roman procurators up to the Jewish War (66–73).

After the siege and destruction of Jerusalem, the Provincia Judaea was under the rule of Roman governors. Urbanization progressed rapidly in the following centuries. Vespasian turned the lands of the Samaritans into the city of Neapolis; Hadrian set up Aelia Capitolina on the ruins of Jerusalem; Septimius Severus turned Lydda into Diospolis and Bet Guvrin into Eleutheropolis until finally only Upper Galilee, the Gaulan and, and the Jordan Valley remained non-urban areas. Under Diocletian (284) the southern part of the Roman province of Arabia was attached to the province of Palaestina, which was partitioned in Byzantine times. In 358 the Negev and southern Transjordan were detached and formed into Palaestina Salutaris. In approximately 400 the remainder was subdivided into Palaestina Prima (with its capital at Caesarea) and Palaestina Secunda (with its capital at Scythopolis) and the third province, Palaestina Salutaris, was now called Palaestina Tertia; its governor resided in Petra.

This threefold division continued under the Arabs who conquered the area in the 7th century: Palaestina Prima became Jund Filastīn, Palaestina Secunda, Jund al-Urdunn, and Palaestina Tertia was abandoned to the Bedouins. The province of Filastīn was administered from the new city of Ramleh and Urdunn from Tiberias. The Crusaders who came in 1099 first established themselves on the coast and to the west of the Jordan; at the zenith of their power their kingdom (the Kingdom of Jerusalem) included all of Ereẓ Israel west of the Jordan to Deir el-Balah, the Jordan Valley, and the Seir Mountains down to Elath. Their feudal administration was centered on a royal domain around Jerusalem with royal vassals in the rest of the country: the principality of Galilee, the seigniories of Jaffa and Ashkelon, Caesarea, St. Jean d'Acre (Acre), Naples (Nablus), St. Abraham (Hebron), Toron (northern Galilee), and Outre Jourdain. After the debacle at the hands of Saladin in 1187, Richard the Lion-Hearted in 1192 reconstituted the Crusader kingdom along the coast from Jaffa to Tyre and included western Galilee. In 1228 Frederick II added a corridor to Jerusalem and Bethlehem, and Richard of Cornwall (1240/41) added the area southward to Ashkelon and Beit Guvrin and eastward to the Jordan near Jericho and in Galilee. From 1250 the kingdom gradually shrank under Mamluk attacks which finally led to the capture of Acre, the Crusader capital, in 1291. The Mamluks (1250–1516) divided Ereẓ Israel into a number of "mamlakas": Ghazza (coast); Safed (Galilee); Dimashq (Damascus; Samaria, Judea, northern Transjordan); and el-Kerak (southern Transjordan). Under the Turks, who took over the country in 1517, a Wali (governor) at Acre ruled from the Carmel to Galilee, while his colleagues at Esh-Sham (Damascus) held the rest of Ereẓ Israel, which was subdivided into the sanjaks of Nablus (including Al-Salt), Al-Quds (Jerusalem), Gaza, Hauran, and Kerak. From 1874 Jerusalem with southern Judea was administered directly from Constantinople as a separate sanjak or *mutessarifliq*. The Turks reestablished their rule over the Negev, but in 1906 the British, who ruled Egypt from 1882, forced them to cede the Sinai Peninsula to Egypt. The British, who took over Palestine in 1917, were the first to establish it as a modern political entity with clear boundaries. The Zionist Organization requested a more extensive area, including the lower Litani River and Mt. Hermon in the north, a line just west of the Hejaz Railway in the east, and a line running from Aqaba to El Arish in the southwest. The British, in agreement with the French, established a boundary which ran from Ras el Naqura between Acre and Tyre on the Mediterranean shore to Metullah and then to El Hama, east of the Sea of Galilee. In the east the Jordan River, the Dead Sea, and the Arava Valley marked the boundary line, while in the south the British adopted the 1906 line between Egypt and the Ottoman Empire. Thus the Mandatory area of Palestine (from which Transjordan was detached in 1922) extended from Dan (Metullah) to Umm Rashrash (today Eilat), and from the Mediterranean coast at Ras en-Naqura to the sources of the Jordan River. This area is seen today by most people dealing with the area as Palestine or Ereẓ Israel. During the 30 years of the British Mandate, the subdivision of the country varied from six districts to two (with a separate Jerusalem division). In 1946, at the end of the Mandate, there were six: Galilee, Haifa, Samaria, Jerusalem, Gaza, and "Lydda," so called because, although it contained the largest city in Ereẓ Israel – Tel Aviv – the Mandatory officials refused to honor it with the name of a district.

From 1949 to 1967 the State of Israel was bounded by the lines of the Armistice Agreements (the "Green Line"). The Six-Day War established ceasefire lines on the Suez Canal, along the Jordan River, and east of the Golan. These lines were partially changed after the *Yom Kippur War of 1973. As stipulated by the peace treaty between Israel and Egypt (1979), both countries accepted the Mandatory line (Rafah – Taba) as the international boundary between them. The peace treaty between Israel and the Hashemite Kingdom of Jordan (1994) also adopted the Mandatory line, with some modifications, as the international boundary. (See also Israel, State of: Historical Survey below.)

ETHNOGRAPHY. The earliest inhabitants of Ereẓ Israel of whom there is historical documentation are the West Semitic tribes known as Amurru (Amorites). In the Bible they are subdivided into a large number of groups, known collectively as Canaanites, a name properly belonging to the Phoenicians. In the Bronze Age, peoples of Indo-Aryan origin (Hittites and Mitanni) became the rulers of various cities in Ereẓ Israel. The Israelite conquest and the Philistine entrenchment on the southern coast (c. 1200 B.C.E.) produced a change in the population balance. The Canaanites were gradually absorbed by the Semitic Israelites, while the Philistines retained their separate character. The Assyrian deportations created a new mixed element, the Samaritans, in Mt. Ephraim. Under Babylonian rule, the Edomites settled in southern Judea, the Nabateans occupied the Negev and southern Transjordan, and a remnant of Jews clung to Jerusalem. In Persian times Jews returned from captivity in Babylonia and the Phoenicians and some Greek settlers inhabited the coast. Hellenistic rule brought an influx of Greeks as officials, soldiers, merchants, and estate owners and the coastal areas and part of the inland cities became Hellenized. At that time there was an overspill of Jews northward into Samaria and eastward into Perea. The Hasmoneans made the Idumeans (Edomites) and the Galileans assimilate with the Jews. During Herod's rule Jewish settlements in northern Transjordan expanded, while a sprinkling of Romans and Greeks settled in Judea and Galilee. After the Bar Kokhba War, the Jews were expelled from Judea and replaced by Syrian and Arab colonists; Galilee, however, remained Jewish up to the end of Byzantine times.

Arabs gradually began to infiltrate into Ereẓ Israel in the late Byzantine period, even before the Arab conquest. After their conquest the Christians in the country slowly became Islamized. The Crusader period brought an incursion of West Europeans, mainly French, Normans, and Italians, but they were unable to root themselves in the country and withdrew after the Crusader collapse. From the ninth century onward, Seljuk, Kurdish, and Turkish mercenaries settled in the country, remaining its rulers until the World War I. The German Templars resumed European colonization on a small scale in the late 19th century, and many other Europeans and Americans settled in the cities in that period for religious or commercial reasons. The Jews, who had clung to the "Four Holy Cities" (Jerusalem, Safed, Tiberias, and Hebron) and were reinforced from time to time by newcomers from Europe and the Ottoman Empire, began to expand their settlement from 1878 onward, assisted first by the Rothschilds and later by the Zionist Organization. From a population of 55,000 in 1918 they increased to 5.5 million in 2003, mostly by immigration from Eastern and Central Europe, Asia, and North Africa.

For natural boundaries, see Israel, Land of: *Physiography.

BIBLIOGRAPHY: Abel, Geog; Aharoni, Land; idem, *Carta Atlas of the Bible* (2004[4]); Y. Aharoni and M. Avi-Yonah, *Macmillan Bible Atlas* (1992[3]); Avi-Yonah, Land; Avi-Yonah, Geog; G. Le Strange, *Palestine under the Moslems* (1890); Neubauer, Geog; Press, Ereẓ; G.A. Smith, *Historical Geography of the Holy Land* (1896[4]); P. Thomsen, *Loca Sancta* (1907).

[Michael Avi-Yonah / Gideon Biger (2nd ed.)]

Physiography

INTRODUCTION. (Official transliteration of place-names can be found in *The New Israel Atlas*; 1969.) Despite its historical origin and usage, the name Ereẓ Israel (Land of Israel) may very appropriately be applied to designate a major regional entity within the Fertile Crescent, wedged between the Mediterranean on the west and the Syrian and Arabian Deserts on the east and southeast. Throughout historical and very likely also prehistorical times, this area served as a bridge between adjacent African and Asian regions. It is adequately defined by "natural boundaries," i.e., major physiographical features beyond which relief configuration or climatic conditions and associated surface phenomena change markedly, as postulated by regional geography for the concept of a major unit of the earth's surface. The region is distinctively delimited on the west by the vast expanse of the Levantine Basin of the Mediterranean. Moreover, along this particular section of the coastline there are no islands, which could complicate proper delineation. Similarly, the coast of Eilat, by which Ereẓ Israel has access to the Indian Ocean, clearly demarcates the maximum extension toward the south. On the east, northeast, southeast, and southwest, Ereẓ Israel is bounded by extensive tracts of the great global, subtropical desert belt (Syrian Desert, Arabian Desert, and Sinai Desert). The marginal areas of this desert belt, in which the climatic conditions undergo a change from semiarid to fully arid, form the historical border zone of Ereẓ Israel as well. In the Sinai Peninsula, the Negev plains continue without interruption up to the Wadi el-Arish, the Brook of Egypt according to the tradition. To the east, an adequate, though not continuous, delineation is afforded by a watershed zone between rivers west and east of it. Although it is not a prominent relief feature, this zone also denotes a sort of a border between the semiarid and Mediterranean areas to the west and the arid ones to the east. The northern boundaries of Ereẓ Israel are fairly well defined. There the valley of Qasimiye – the lower course of the Leontes (Litani) River – and, further east, the towering Hermon Massif form a marked natural boundary between Ereẓ Israel and the Lebano-Syrian region.

Ereẓ Israel, however, is not considered a regional entity merely because of its natural confines. These are mainly concomitant consequences of the fact that the area is morphogenetically a very consistent surface unit in almost all its physiographical aspects. The area is decidedly influenced by a singular major phenomenon: the Jordan-Dead Sea-Arabah Rift Valley, which also forms the meridional axis of Ereẓ Israel along its entire length. The morphogenetic impact of the Rift Valley is outwardly expressed by the main drainage pattern of the region. About 70% of Ereẓ Israel's rivers (and far more of its overall runoff, if the quantities of the inflow are considered) discharge into the Rift Valley, in relation to which the areas with river outlets into the Mediterranean form a sort of foreland. From the hydrographical point of view alone, Ereẓ Israel thus represents primarily the catchment area of the Rift Valley, which, within this region, is characterized by some unique topographical features. It is the deepest continental depression on the earth and contains an inland sea (the Dead Sea) whose level is about 1,300 ft. (400 m.) lower than that of the Mediterranean with one of the highest mineral contents of any body of water in the world. Its second large body of water is Lake Kinneret, which is the lowest freshwater body on the earth's surface, about 660 ft. (200 m.) below sea level. The two bodies of water are connected by a river (Jordan River) whose bed, accordingly, is the lowest in the world. This hydrographical condition, namely the predominance of the endoreic area (i.e., an area without outlet into an ocean or a major body of water connected with it), is only one of the many influences exerted by the formation of the Rift Valley upon almost all of the surface configuration of Ereẓ Israel.

From the anthropogeographical point of view, however, the Rift Valley has proven a rather disuniting element. Due to its relative depth, and still more to the height and steepness of the mountain slopes ascending from it to highlands more than 3,300 ft. (1,000 m.) above its floor, enclosing it wall-like with a single wider breach giving access to it only from the west, the Rift Valley was throughout history one of the main factors for the division of the region into two parts, very infrequently – and then only partially – united into a single state.

The Rift Valley is thus the prime cause of Ereẓ Israel's subdivision into two main parts: a western one – Mediterranean-oriented Cisjordan (referred to as western Palestine in political and historical geography) – and an eastern one – Transjordan (eastern Palestine). The first may be regarded from the geographic point of view as the mainland, the second as the backland of the entire region.

Situated between the Mediterranean on the west and an almost continuous desert belt on the south and east, and being long and relatively narrow – about 280 mi. (450 km.) in length and about 110 mi. (180 km.) at maximum width – Ereẓ Israel also morphogenetically represents a transition zone. It contains almost all the major relief elements characteristic of the adjacent countries, although generally on a much smaller scale and in somewhat subdued form; coastal plains; mountain ranges, partly continuing the systems of folds fully developed and culminating in Lebanon-Syria and Asia Minor; plateaus, much smaller and more discontinuous here than in the neighboring countries; and basins of all kinds, most of which are greatly affected by and subordinated to the dominant relief feature – the Rift Valley. The same is true of lithological conditions. Outcrops of most kinds of rocks, from basement (magmatic, metamorphic) to sedimentary ones of most recent ages, form its bedrock. Volcanic rocks (basalts, tuffs) are also widely distributed there, as are evaporites (i.e., sediments mainly generated by deposition in outletless inland seas given to intensive evaporation and thus to concentration and consequent consolidation of their solutional contents).

Located between the Mediterranean and the deserts, Ereẓ Israel exhibits complex climatic gradations and transitions ranging from conditions mainly influenced by the sea and manifested primarily by the amount of precipitation to those which already show all the characteristics of a fully desert region – manifested, inter alia, by the relatively extensive surfaces composed of evaporites. A most important characteristic of the region, and particularly of Cisjordan, is therefore the proximity of greatly differing landscapes within relatively small areas resulting mainly from the structural, lithological, and climatic conditions changing over very small distances. The region's very mosaic-like quality is also crucially important as physiographical background to its history, illuminating, e.g., the tendency to regional particularism throughout the area. Notwithstanding the great number of small, highly different regions, it is customary to subdivide Ereẓ Israel into only four major units: (1) the Coastal Plains, (2) the Western Mountain Zone, (3) the Rift Valley, and (4) the Transjordan Plateau.

THE COASTAL PLAINS. *The Coastal Zone.* Ereẓ Israel is bordered on the west by the Mediterranean Sea. The length of its coastline is about 170 mi. (270 km.) from the mouth of Wadi el-Arish to that of the Qasimiye River. From the morphogenetic and typological points of view, the coast of Ereẓ Israel represents a transition between the coasts of Egypt and Sinai, which are mainly deltaic, and the Lebano-Syrian coast, whose configuration is primarily determined by faulting. The coast of Ereẓ Israel is fairly smooth, without any islands representing detached parts of the mainland. A shelf zone, relatively wide at the southern portion and progressively narrower toward the north, extends along the coast up to about 500 ft. (150 m.) in depth. The coastal zone (i.e., the areas adjacent to the coastline that are directly influenced by the sea) consists of two main parts: a rather uniform southern part, extending from the mouth of the Wadi el-Arish to Tel Aviv-Jaffa, and a northern one that extends up to the mouth of the Qasimiye River. The northern part is far more complex in its origin and consequently in its outline. The southern part of the coastline is almost straight, and its course accords with that of the series of anticlines that form the mountainous backbone of Cisjordan. Sandy beaches, attaining several hundreds of meters in width, extend along the coastline, broken only at the alluvia-filled valley-exits of the rivers discharging into the Mediterranean. Breaks also occur at four other spots: Deir al-Balah, a portion of the coast south of Gaza, Ashkelon, and Mīnat Rūbīn (south of the mouth of the valley of the River Sorek), where coastal cliffs border almost immediately on the sea. The beaches are covered almost exclusively by quartz sands brought from the Nile delta and from the coast of Sinai by currents running close to the shore. Inland, the beach zone is delimited mainly by low ridges composed of sand grains cemented by calcareous material – a rock type called *kurkar* in the vernacular – and passes into areas covered by shifting dunes. The sands of these dunes are mainly of marine origin, i.e., they were brought to the coast by shore currents and waves and then transported inland by winds. The width of the sand-dune belt varies considerably; it attains its maximum – about 4.5 mi. (7 km.) – in the vicinity of Rishon le-Zion.

The northern coastal zone is rather different, in some aspects even opposite, in configuration. It is no longer straight throughout, but indented at some sections by small embayments, several of which form coves (e.g., at Dor and Athlit). Off-branchings of the inland mountains, the Carmel and the Ḥanitah Range (Rosh ha-Nikrah), border immediately upon the sea, forming high and steep headlands, north of which the coastline recesses to form wide embayments. Only the first of these, at Haifa, represents a true bay, extending southeast for about 4 mi. (6 km.) and even forming a small secondary bay at its northern extremity at Acre. The rest of the northern coastline is bordered along its entire length by cliffs of *kurkar.* These cliffs are high as far north as Athlit – attaining a maximum height of about 130 ft. (40 m.) in the vicinity of Netanyah – and then becoming progressively lower. A very discontinuous small abrasion platform, i.e., a rocky, narrow shore-plane generated by progressive down-and-back erosion of the cliff faces, extends along the greater part of the coast. Waves undercut the cliffs at their bases, and as the cliffs are worn back, their bases form a progressively widening plane. The seaward parts of the platform, subject to the continuous and generally very intensive impact of the waves, in turn gradually become destroyed, with only small isolated remains –

reefs – evidencing the earlier extension of the coast 1.2–1.8 mi. (2–3 km.) west of its present course. Beaches are very poorly developed along this northern portion of the coast zone. They exist mostly around coastal indentations or along the bases of cliffs, where they are somewhat protected against the onslaught of waves by an outlying strip of reefs close to the shore or tiers of beachrock (i.e., coarse sands, pebbles, and shells cemented into rocks). Areas of sand dunes are small and can be found only where the valleys of rivers discharging into the Mediterranean breach the cliffs, creating sufficiently wide gaps for the landward intrusion of wind-borne sands accumulating on the shore. Thus only at the bay of Haifa are beach and dune areas fully developed.

The Coastal Plains. In the narrow sense, the Coastal Plains are lowlands covered mainly by alluvial soils that extend from the coastal dune areas and the coastal cliff zone, respectively, to the bases of the inland mountains. The plains exhibit a large number of minor relief features, particularly isolated hillocks or those forming small ridges composed of *kurkar* and a fairly well-developed drainage net, which is more dense toward the north and sometimes exhibits minute gorge-like valleys where traversing the *kurkar* ridges. The ridges extend without a major break from the mouth of Wadi el-Arish to the headland of the Carmel, and from there to the Rosh ha-Nikrah promontory, recurring on a very small scale as far as the valley of the Qasimiye River. From the earliest times the Coastal Plains were one of the most densely populated and intensively cultivated parts of the country, although secondary in historical importance to the mountainous interior regions. They may be rather arbitrarily subdivided into seven units: the Southern Plains (frequently referred to as the Negev Plains); the Judean Plain (including the Philistine Plain as its southern part); the Sharon; the Carmel Coast Plain (usually referred to only as Carmel Coast); the Haifa (Zebulun) Plain; the Galilean Plain (Acre Plain); the Tyre Plain, north of the cape of Rosh ha-Nikrah. Each of the last three units is usually referred to in Hebrew as *emek*, i.e., valley or narrow lowland, because of their limited width.

The Southern Coastal Plains. These plains are separated from the Mediterranean by a relatively narrow belt of sand dunes, 2 mi. (3 km.) wide on the average. Their most important characteristics are determined by climatic conditions. They receive the smallest amount of precipitation in comparison with the other units of the Coastal Plains – El-Arish, approximately 8 in. (200 mm.); Gaza, somewhat less than 16 in. (400 mm.). Due to its proximity to the desert areas, the soils of this plain are composed predominantly of wind-borne loess, probably redistributed by surface flow, and exhibit many intermixing gradations with sands in the southern parts of the plains and with the red-sand soils (called *ḥamra* in the vernacular) at its northern limits. Only two main ephemeral streams (Naḥal Besor and Naḥal Shikmah), about 12 mi. (20 km.) apart at their debouchures into the Mediterranean, traverse the region. Naḥal Besor and its tributaries have turned part of the loess zone into spectacular "badlands," i.e., intensively dissected surfaces that form a microrelief landscape of miniature hillocks and gullies of the most variegated shapes.

Three major topographical zones may be distinguished more or less parallel to the coast. East of the coastal sands, where some dunes attain heights of several tens of meters, a relatively low zone extends, delimited to some extent by discontinuous *kurkar* ridges. This zone forms a gradual ascent to a hillock region in the east and to relatively large areas covered by inland sands of eolian origin in the southeast. Because of its narrowness, elongated shape, and low topography (in comparison with the bordering zones), this area is frequently referred to in the regional geography of Ereẓ Israel as the *marzevah* ("corridor"). This is also a major topographical feature on the plains farther north and had a decisive influence in the past on the sites of settlements and communication lines (Via Maris).

Judean Plain. Rather wide in its southern part – about 15 mi. (25 km.) – the Judean Plain narrows progressively toward the north – about 10 mi. (17 km.), a characteristic common to all the plain regions described below. The plain is separated from the sea by a dune belt, which attains its maximum width – about 4 mi. (7 km.) – here. The "corridor" between the sand zone and the base of the hill country to the east of the plain (the "Shephelah") is more distinct and forms a fairly uniform surface with far fewer and smaller remains of *kurkar* ridges than are found in the Negev Plain. Climatic conditions are fully Mediterranean – 16–20 in. (400–500 mm.) annual average precipitation – and are reflected in the soil cover – loess in the southernmost part and *ḥamra* covering almost the whole remaining area with rather large enclaves of heavy soils of alluvial and swamp origin. The genesis of the latter types of soil is connected with the greater number of rivers draining the plain. Although only four of these rivers reach the sea, their courses are frequently deflected to run meridionally by the extension, width, and continuity of the dune belts.

Sharon Plain. Lengthwise, the Sharon Plain extends from the Yarkon, the largest river in Cisjordan discharging into the Mediterranean, up to the Zikhron Ya'akov spur of Mount Carmel. Its width varies considerably, generally narrowing northward to a minimum of about 2½ mi. (4 km.). It also exhibits a distinct meridional zonation, far more pronounced than that of the Judean Plain. Dune areas between the sea and the plain proper, as mentioned before, are rather sporadic there, narrow and short, and restricted to the cliffless parts of the coast, i.e., to the vicinity of the river exits into the sea. Elsewhere, the plain begins immediately behind the zone of the cliffs, which attain considerable height and are continuous, thus preventing the ingress and accumulation of sand further inland. More or less parallel to the sea cliffs appear two major, though discontinuous, closely spaced *kurkar* ridges which indicate the former coastline. Between them are situated elongated and narrow lowlands, of which only the eastern one attains a width of about 2 mi. (3 km.), whereas the western one is much narrower. East from the *kurkar* ridge zone the "corridor" extends up to the outliers of the Samarian Highland. In contrast to the two above-mentioned intermediate areas between the *kurkar* ridges, with their prevailing *ḥamra* cover, the soil of the "corridor" is mainly alluvial. The amount of precipitation is approximately 4 in. (100 mm.) greater than in the Judean Plain, exceeding an annual average of 24 in. (600 mm.) in some places. This was one of the main preconditions for the large forested areas characteristic of the Sharon in the past. The river network is relatively dense, with far more rivers discharging into the sea than on the Judean Plain. The exits of the rivers here have also been largely blocked both by the dune areas and the *kurkar* ridges. Consequently, large tracts of the Sharon became swampy, particularly in the environs of Ḥaderah and the Ḥefer Plain (the latter was drained by Jewish settlers only in the 1930s).

Carmel Coast Plain. About 22 mi. (35 km.) long, 2–2.5 mi. (3–4 km.) wide at its southern end and a few hundred meters wide at its northern limit, the Carmel Coast Plain ends prominently at the Carmel Headland. The shape of this land unit would fully justify the omission of the term "plain" or even "valley" in its usual meaning. Like the Sharon, a considerable part of this plain consists of *kurkar* ridges, the westernmost of which is almost entirely transformed by marine erosion and ingression into reefs and abrasion platforms and is mainly characterized by several kinds of indentations, including some coves and minute headlands. The other two ranges of *kurkar* ridges are still preserved, particularly in the southern portion, and greatly impede the passage of the numerous streamlets descending from the Carmel, so that in the past artificial outlets had to be cut into the ridges. Another characteristic of this plain is the relative scarcity of *ḥamra* in comparison with the alluvial soils that are derived mainly from Mount Carmel by erosion and river deposition.

Haifa Bay Plain. Tectonically, this plain represents the westernmost component of the Beth-Shean–Harod–Jezreel Valley system that traverses the entire width of Cisjordan from the Jordan Rift Valley to the Mediterranean. Flanked on the southeast by the high and steep slopes of the Carmel, it exhibits several features absent from the adjacent parts of the coastal plain north and south of it. Along the coast a relatively wide and continuous beach reappears, followed by a belt of sand dunes about a mile wide; no cliff formations are interposed between the plain and the sea. Farther inland it borders the relatively low and gently sloping Yodefat Hills – outliers of the Lower Galilee Mountains. The eastern part of the plain is covered by heavy alluvial soils, partly in consequence of the extensive swamps that existed here in the past. The southern portion of the plain is drained by the sluggishly meandering Kishon River; the northern part is drained by the Na'aman River, fed by springs and extensive swamps behind the sand area. For several kilometers the Na'aman flows parallel to the coastline and along the inland margin of the dune belt.

Acre-Tyre Plain (Galilean Coastal Plain). The coastal plain north of Acre terminates abruptly in the promontory of Rosh ha-Nikrah. It bears some resemblance to the Sharon and still more to the coastal plain of the Carmel. Here the coast is bordered by cliffs (albeit inconsiderable in height) accompanied by an extensive abrasion platform, disjointed parts of which can be discerned in the form of reefs at a distance of 1.2–1.8 mi. (2–3 km.) from the coastline. There are several very small indentations in the coast, which is subject to strong marine erosion. The paucity and smallness of beaches and their predominant cover of coarse sands are also the result of wave erosion. No larger dune-sand accumulations intervene between the coast and the plain, and there are only few and small remnants of *kurkar* ridges. The narrow plain – 4 mi. (7 km.) maximum width – is bordered on the east by interfluves, i.e., mountain spurs created by the numerous rivers from the Upper Galilee Mountains discharging into the Mediterranean. These rivers also supply the bulk of the heavy soil material that forms the cover of the plain almost exclusively. The promontory of Rosh ha-Nikrah (the biblical "Tyrian Ladder"), the seaward scarp of an Upper Galilean mountain range along which the present-day border between the State of Israel and Lebanon runs, sharply delimits the Acre Plain. The headland, of a type frequently encountered along the Lebano-Syrian coast and bordering immediately on the sea for a length of about 7 mi. (12 km.), consists of calcareous rock, and its base contains deep sea caves cut in by wave erosion. Beyond the promontory the coastline curves gently in and out, and along it extend beaches and even a continuous, although very small, dune belt. Of specific interest here is Tyre, formerly situated on a reef island but now connected to the mainland as if by a tombolo. This transformation was caused by the accumulations of sand at the dam constructed during the siege of this harbor town by Alexander the Great, and it is one of the countless instances of major landscape transformations effected by man in the Middle East. The coastal plain east of the sand zone is narrower than the Acre Plain and irregularly confined by the east-west-oriented spurs of the Lebanese-Galilee Mountains. It is traversed by a relatively great number of ephemeral rivers which are the main suppliers of the predominantly alluvial soil cover of the plain.

THE WESTERN MOUNTAIN ZONE. Often referred to metaphorically as the backbone of Cisjordan, the Western Mountain Zone extends from Eilat to the Valley of Qasimiye along the entire length of the region. Within the Levant, it tectonically represents the southernmost outliers of the great Alpine orogenic system and accordingly consists mainly of rather simple and short fold structures generally of medium height. The latter characteristic is also reflected in the term "Hills" (Judean Hills, Samarian Hills, etc.), which is frequently used in this region. In addition to folding, the formation of these mountains was strongly affected by faulting, particularly in the vicinity of the Rift Valley and in Galilee. Despite its moderate elevation above sea level and in relation to the lower surroundings (valleys and basin floors), the relief of this mountainous region, which occupies more than two-thirds of the Cisjordan area, is very pronounced. Steep slopes often appear as major and minor scarp and cliff faces, and surface roughness even on moderate slopes is frequently accentuated, particularly in the southern part of the Mountain Zone, by the almost complete absence of soil and vegetation cover. In the central and northern parts, large tracts were once covered by forests (now largely reduced to sporadic maquis and garigue – brush-and-thorn vegetation), and the slopes were terraced, creating a main area of cultivation. These terraces, now largely disused and in disrepair, form one of the most conspicuous external features of the slopes. The slopes that were not terraced and the mostly flat or gently domed summit surfaces are covered by coarse detritus of different sizes or are pitted by mostly small and shallow depressions, as a result of strong weathering (especially solutional) of the bare surfaces (which are composed mainly of limestone).

The bold relief of the Cisjordan Mountains is mainly a result of deep incisions by the watercourses, which created valleys that frequently take the form of gorges or even canyons. In the other types of valleys as well, most of the slopes are very steep, and often no valley floors developed along the river beds. The relatively high frequency of intramontane basins of all sizes is another very important characteristic of the overall relief that contributes greatly to the multiformity and mosaic-like composition of the mountainous region. The extremely variegated pattern of the mountainous zone, resulting in a large number of small regions – and thus contributing to the particularist tendencies of its inhabitants throughout history – was brought about by the complexity of its tectonic, lithological, and climatic conditions. Tectonically, the most characteristic aspect of Cisjordan – in sharp contrast to Transjordan – is the most intensive intermixing of major features originating through up- and downfolding, mostly with subsequent forms produced by faulting. In the southern and central parts of the Mountain Zone the first group of processes determined – mainly in the form of anti- and synclines – the build-up, extension, and course of the principal ranges, whereas the latter played a decisive role in their disruption. Particularly in the northern part, faulting and associated features virtually obliterate the former structures, creating a relief mainly characterized by intramontane tectonic valleys and ranges, the extent and orientation of which is determined by these valleys. The role of some major subsidence regions (Rift Valley, Beth-Shean-Harod-Jezreel Valley and Haifa Bay) in relation to general exterior configuration has already been pointed out. Fault zones and lines also exert decisive influence upon the drainage system of a greater part of Cisjordan.

The lithology of the Cisjordan Mountain Zone is rather diversified, considering the small size of the area. Most of the mountains consist of calcareous rocks, with only small areas of outcropping sandstones, magmatic, metamorphic, and volcanic rocks. Due to the great differences in their composition (limestone, dolomites, chalk, calcareous marls, etc.) and frequent intercalations – each responding rather dissimilarly to denudational processes – these calcareous formations greatly contribute to the diversification of the landscape, determining major and minor morphological features specific to the predominant bedrock. The influence of climatic factors, mainly the amount and type of precipitation, is even greater. The southern part of the Cisjordan Mountain Zone, although consisting predominantly of the same types of rock as the central and northern parts, differs greatly from the latter in its morphological physiognomy. Weathering processes are dissimilar here in degree and even to some extent in kind. For example, farther north solutional processes exert the greatest influence upon the surface configuration by creating karstic features that dominate the landscape, particularly in Galilee. These processes are almost entirely lacking in the southern highlands. Runoff is much greater and consequently erosion is much more intensive here than in regions receiving much larger amounts of precipitation. The eastern flank of the central area is semiarid and arid (the Judean Desert), due to its location leeward of the Judean Mountains, with the precipitation caused by the moisture-bearing winds from the Mediterranean consequently decreased. This area also exhibits a specific set of morphological features, in many respects similar to those of the Negev, which is also mainly affected by climatic conditions.

Mainly in accordance with the three criteria mentioned above (tectonic, lithological, and climatic conditions), the mountain region of Cisjordan can be subdivided into the following major physiographical units: the Negev Highlands, the Central Mountain Massif, and the Galilean Mountains. Each of these units comprises several subregions determined by geological, tectonic, lithological, climatic, and consequently morphological conditions. Each is very different from the others in the overall character of its landscape. The width of the Mountain Zone varies proportionately with that of Cisjordan as a whole (i.e., the distance from the Mediterranean coast to the Rift Valley), decreasing from about 50 mi. (80 km.) in the Negev Highlands to about 22 mi. (35 km.) in Galilee.

Negev Highlands. In many respects, the Negev Highlands represent a direct continuation of the plateau and mountainous regions of the Sinai Peninsula, exhibiting great similarity of tectonic, lithological, and climatic conditions and, consequently, relief. The similarities are most evident in the southern part of the Highlands, the Eilat Mountains, which extend from the Gulf of Eilat to Bikat Sayyarim and Bikat Uvdah in the north. Here, though confined to a comparatively small area, are found ranges and blocks composed of magmatic and metamorphic rocks that build up the larger part of the southern apex of the Sinai Peninsula and are not found in any other region of Cisjordan, with the exception of Makhtesh Ramon. Similarly, outcrops of Nubian Sandstone, exposed only on the floors and the foot of the slopes of the *makhteshim* (see below), are relatively widely distributed here as surface rocks. These types of rock are in very close contact with calcareous ones, creating relief forms of singular diversity and even contrast. The extremely variegated composition of the crystalline rocks makes them particularly susceptible to granular weathering, exfoliation, and sheeting. These processes result in steep, serrated, and crenulated ridges (Jehoshafat, Shelomo, Roded, Sheḥoret), separated from one another by steep fault-conditioned valleys. Even more spectacular are the relief features that developed from Nubian Sandstone. Columnar jointing – of which the Solomon Pillars in the Timna region, about 15 mi. (25 km.) north of Eilat, are but one outstanding example. Column relicts in the form of mushroom rocks, castellated rocks, rocking stones, and intensive alveolation, producing cave-like tafoni and canyons – deeply incised in the multicolored sandstone by the extremely strong erosive action of the many river courses (the Red Canyon, Naḥal Amran, etc.) carrying only flash floods once or twice within a year – give rise to landscapes even far more diversified in ever-changing micro-features than those which developed in the crystalline bedrock. In sharp contrast to these landforms are those which developed on other bedrock, limestone in particular. The relief in limestone is generally far more uniform and massive and is mainly characterized by flat-topped ranges and small plateau-like elevations covered by angular gravels. The latter are produced by weathering, which imparts to the surfaces covered by them the appearance of typical *ḥamada* (block-strewn desert surfaces).

The Paran Plateau. This area comprises mainly the Cisjordan catchment area of the Paran River, a major tributary of the Arabah, which is the collecting stream of the Rift Valley south of the Dead Sea. The headrivers of the Paran drain the parts of the Sinai adjacent to the Eilat Mountains in a relatively dense network of wide channels filled with sand and pebbles. The highest elevations of the Paran Plateau – some of which form mountain blocks or ridges – are on its northeastern side – Har Nes, 3,329 ft. (1,015 m.); Har Saggi, 3,229 ft. (1,006 m.). In the eastward direction, elevations become lower and surfaces generally more uniform. In strong contrast to the variegated lithology of the Eilat Mountains, the tableland here is built up almost exclusively of calcareous strata: limestones interbedded with chalk, marls, and thin layers of chert. The surface of the plateau features the widest areas of "desert pavement" found in Cisjordan, i.e., areas covered by angular gravels (*ḥamada*) or rounder pebble-like debris (a desert surface type morphologically known as "serir"). At the southern periphery of the plateau, Bikat Sayyarim and the far larger Bikat Uvdah represent typical intramontane desert basins covered and filled by sands. They are subject to occasional flooding and drain – albeit through very indistinct channel beds – into the Ḥiyyon River, a major tributary of the Arabah River, running about 12 mi. (20 km.) south of the Paran. To the northeast the tableland is delimited by the gravel-covered Ha-Meshar Basin, which, from the hydrographical point of view, belongs to the Central Negev region.

The Central Negev Highlands. The anticline of Ramon is essentially the only major structure of the Central Negev Highlands. This upfold extends approximately 43 mi. (70 km.) in length from the biblical Kadesh-Barnea in the Sinai almost to the very escarpments bordering the western side of the Arabah Rift. It is not only the highest portion of the Negev Highlands – Har Ramon, 3,395 ft. (1,035 m.) – but also structurally and morphologically the most complex. This is very evident in one of the most pronounced occurrences of relief inversion, i.e., the conversion of a major structural element into a morphologically "negative," i.e., reverse form. Here the anticline was transformed, chiefly by erosion, into a wide, elongated, valley-like basin, about 28 mi. (45 km.) in length, enclosed by almost perpendicular slopes, some of them about 1,000 ft. (300 m.) high. This specific form, which also occurs in some anticlines of northern Sinai and in the northern part of the Negev Highlands, is referred to in Hebrew as *makhtesh* ("mortar" or "mixing bowl"), which in the geomorphology of arid regions is now becoming a general term to denote affinite landforms. The greatest influence upon the formation, lithology, and configuration of Makhtesh Ramon was exerted by faulting along its southern flank. Accordingly, magmatic-volcanic rocks are exposed here. Wherever the enclosure is composed of these rocks, it assumes the form of a serrated range, resembling those in the crystalline Eilat Mountains and strongly contrasting with the other enclosured portions of the *makhtesh*, which consist of Nubian Sandstones in the lower and hard limestone in the upper parts of their slopes. The floor of Makhtesh Ramon, covered mainly by detritus of Nubian Sandstone, reveals many small elevations, preponderantly in the form of flat-topped basalt-covered remains of former surface levels. The *makhtesh* is drained by the multichanneled Ramon River, which breaches the eastern enclosure in a narrow steep gorge to join the Arabah River system. To the northwest of the *makhtesh*, its foreland forms a rather level, or gently undulating, tableland up to its very rim; only at the periphery of the plateau does the relief become mountainous (Har Loẓ, Har Ḥorshah, Rekhes-Nafḥa).

The Northern Negev Highlands. On the northeast, the Central Negev Highlands are separated from the Northern Highlands by the wide, deeply incised Valley of the Zin River. This tectonically conditioned valley begins as a wide erosive cirque, the southwestern side of which forms precipitous, almost perpendicular, scarps. At a small distance from the northern side of the valley two *makhteshim* are situated: Ha-Makhtesh ha-Gadol (the "Big Makhtesh") and Ha-Makhtesh ha-Katan (the "Little Makhtesh"). They differ from Makhtesh Ramon not only by their smaller size and almost regular oval shape, but also in structure, lithology, and consequently morphology. Not affected by faulting, they represent upfolds turned into deep valley-basins, on the floors of which older sedimentary strata became exposed through erosion by the watercourses draining them. Their almost perpendicularly sloping walls of Nubian Sandstone are overlaid by much more resistant limestones and dolomites. The Ḥatirah and Ḥaẓevah Rivers, running parallel to the long axes of Ha-Makhtesh ha-Gadol and Ha-Makhtesh ha-Katan, respectively, breach their eastern walls in impressive gorges to join the Zin River. Toward the west and northwest elevations become progressively lower, although there are several upfolds rising above their surroundings as short ridges with moderate slopes, frequently worn down to isolated table-hills. In the west the plateau margins are partly covered by relatively large areas of sand dunes (Ḥaluẓah, Agur), which form a transition zone to the Plain of the Negev. On the northern side, the highlands terminate in the wide Beersheba Basin and its much narrower eastern continuation, the Valley of Arad. Structurally, and in particular climatically, these two intramontane depressions form a marked border zone between the arid Negev Highlands and the mountains north of it, where Mediterranean conditions prevail. In the Beersheba Basin, the mean annual precipitation is 10 in. (250 mm.), a quantity indicating the transition from semiarid to subhumid conditions. The thick loess cover and the amount of precipitation together give rise to the most convenient conditions for agriculture within the Negev. The main drainage artery of this part of the Negev is the Beersheba River (a tributary of the Besor River), and several of its confluents originate in the Hebron Mountains, although its almost annually recurring floodings are mainly caused by the tributaries crossing the relatively impervious loess areas.

The Central Mountain Massif. This range extends from the Beersheba Basin up to the Beth-Shean–Harod–Jezreel Valley sequence in the north. It represents the most compact and continuous mountain region of Cisjordan. Its basic structures are relatively large, meridionally trending anticlinoria, i.e., systems usually composed of one major upfold flanked by downfolds and smaller anticlines. Faulting does not exert a great influence upon the configuration of the southern part of the area; its effect is far stronger in the northern portion, though not yet as decisive in determining the landscape as in Galilee. According to climatic, lithological, and hypsographical conditions, this area can be subdivided into several major units. The most important difference exists between the western part, which is fully exposed to the climatic influences of the Mediterranean, and the eastern flank descending into the Dead Sea and Jordan Valley. The landscape of the eastern portion, which is leeward of the precipitation-bearing winds, is consequently semi-desertic and desertic in character (Judean Desert). The difference is accentuated by lithological variance. The western flank is built predominantly of limestone and dolomite strata, whereas in the eastern one chalks and marls prevail. To the west a subregion or different lithology and elevation is interposed between the southern part of the Central Mountain Massif and the Coastal Plains. Considerably lower and built mainly of chalky rock, it is a hill region gradually rising toward the massif but separated from it in a very pronounced manner by a series of valleys running parallel to the foot of the massif. Toward the north, two major protrusions of the massif can be regarded as distinct mountain regions: a smaller one – the Gilboa – separating the valleys of Harod and Jezreel, and another, much larger and more complex in structure – the Carmel, in the broad sense – which, as already mentioned, delimits the southern Coastal Plains. According to the criteria enumerated above, the Central Mountain Massif can be subdivided into the following regions: Judean Mountains, comprising the Mediterranean southern portion of the massif; Judean Desert; Shephelah (the hill region to the west of the Judean Mountains); Samarian Highlands (the northern part of the massif) and its two subunits, Gilboa and Carmel.

The Judean Mountains. The core region of Cisjordan, the Judean Mountains consist structurally of two consecutive large anticlinoria, whose axes – in contrast to the upfolds in the Negev, which trend mainly southwest-northeast – run almost meridionally. Built up of limestone and dolomite strata with chalky and marly intercalations (the latter very important as groundwater horizons), the mountains' main topographical features are an almost continuous watershed zone (rather uniform in height and delimiting them toward the Judean Desert) and the many interfluves (i.e., ridge-like mountainous spurs separated by deeply incised valleys) extending mainly westward. The watershed zone is generally flat and widens considerably in many places. Its topography thus provided suitable conditions for defense and the development of communications by means of a highway between the cities that were built in this area from earliest times.

Not far from this divide, watercourses begin to incise progressively deeper valleys, the steep slopes of which almost fully converge at the narrow rocky river beds; generally there are no accompanying floodplains. The slopes rising from the valley floors are, for the most part, intensively terraced and end in almost flat or only slightly domed tops separated by wide gentle saddles. Both the mountain tops and the slopes (where not terraced) are densely covered by block detritus, deeply corroded by solutional processes, which also produced the many rounded depressions, holes, and cavities in the slope surfaces as well as many caverns and caves. The prevalent terra rossa is mainly another product of this weathering process, here strongly effective due to the considerable amounts of precipitation – about 20 in. (500 mm.) on the annual average. From the orographic point of view, three parts of the Judean Mountains, very unequal in size, are distinguished: Hebron Mountains, Jerusalem Mountains, Beth-El (Ramallah) Mountains.

The Hebron Mountains extend from the Beersheba Basin up to the Wadi Arṭās in the north (a valley belonging to the drainage area of the Dead Sea), the site of the Solomon Pools. They rise steeply from the Beersheba Basin (one of the southward protrusions of these mountains separates the latter from the Arad Basin) to heights of about 2,600 ft. (800 m.), culminating in summits near Ḥalḥul (north of Hebron) that rise to 3,300 ft. (1,000 m.). The Hebron Mountains are also the largest constituent of the Judean Mountains, with an area greatly exceeding the total of the two other subunits. From the morphological point of view, the southern portion of the Hebron Mountains can be subdivided into two main parts, separated by the relatively wide, mostly flat-floored, and not very deeply incised valley of the Hebron River, a tributary of the Beersheba River, which runs for about 18 mi. (30 km.) almost parallel to the meridional axis of the mountains. The mountains here thus consist of two main ridges. An eastern, higher one is called the Eshtemoa (Samūʿ) Range after one of the villages, the name and site of which have remained virtually unchanged since biblical times. Along this ridge extends the divide between the dry valleys (except at times of flood) descending into the Dead Sea Rift and the southern and western ones that drain into the Mediterranean. The western ridge is named after the village of Adoraim (Dūrā), also mentioned in the Bible. The highway connecting Beersheba with the townships and villages of the watershed zone runs along this ridge. Also characteristic of the Hebron Mountains are several topographic depressions, the largest of which, the valley of Berachah, is distinguished by an abundant spring. The waters of this spring, together with those of others issuing in the vicinity, feed the Solomon Pools, which were the most important source of water for Jerusalem in the past. Near Hebron the two ridges merge to form a single watershed zone that continues along the entire length of the Judean Mountains. Climatically, the Hebron Mountains represent a transition zone from semiarid to Mediterranean conditions. Whereas at al-Ẓāhiriyya, the southernmost village along the main highway, the annual precipitation is only about 12 in. (300 mm.), it increases to 20 in. (500 mm.) in Hebron, and 28 in. (700 mm.) in the region of the highest elevations, where snowfall is frequent. Accordingly, the larger part of the soil cover (where preserved) in the Hebron Mountains is terra rossa.

The Jerusalem Mountains are about 500 ft. (150 m.) lower on the average than the Hebron and Beth-El Mountains – highest elevation, al-Nabī Samwīl, 2,870 ft. (875 m.) – and form a wide saddle-like region between these sections. This topographical feature somewhat facilitates the ascent from the Coastal Plains to the watershed region, with its settlements and highway, and the descent into the Rift Valley, in particular to Jericho, the most important township of the Valley region throughout history. The Jerusalem Mountains are also intensively dissected into interfluvial ridges. One of these, Mount of Olives – Mount Scopus, immediately east of Jerusalem, forms a conspicuous border with the Judean Desert. The Judean Mountains are drained mainly by the Sorek River, one of the major watercourses of the Central Mountain Massif. The Sorek River discharges into the Mediterranean, and its markedly meandering valley proved sufficiently wide for the construction of the railway connecting Jerusalem with the Coastal Plains.

The Beth-El Mountains, covering an area similar in size to that of the Jerusalem Mountains – about 9 mi. (15 km.) in length – rise to summit heights exceeding 3,300 ft. (1,000 m.) – Baal-Hazor, 3,332 ft. (1,016 m.). One of their most important characteristics is that the watershed attains considerable width there. A road along one of the interfluves extending to the west (Beth-Horon Ridge) was formerly the main approach to Jerusalem from the Coastal Plains and consequently of particular strategic importance.

The Judean Desert. According to its appearance, the Judean Desert could be regarded as a northward extension of the arid Negev lands that border on it at the valley of the Ḥemar River. Genetically, however, it belongs to the orographic types of deserts, whose aridity – much less pronounced than in "true" deserts – is due mainly to the fact that the area is situated on the leeward side of the massive and high Judean Mountains, which intercept the rain-bearing winds. This effect is made more pronounced by the steepness of the eastern flank of the Judean anticlinoria toward the Dead Sea–Jordan Rift Valley, about 1,000–1,300 ft. (300–400 m.) below sea level. Actually, only the lower portions of this flank are arid. Even there, the larger part of the area receives more than 4 in. (100 mm.) of rain per annum – Jericho receives about 6 in. (150 mm.) – whereas on the upper portions the precipitation decreases gradually from about 16 in. (400 mm.) near the watershed region to the amounts mentioned above. The Judean Desert also comprises the eastern flank of the Samarian Mountains up to the wide valley of Wadi Fāriʿa and the spur of Qeren Sartaba protruding from the Samarian Mountains into the Jordan Rift Valley. It differs markedly from the Judean Mountains in lithology as well as in structure and is composed predominantly of chalky formations younger in origin than those forming the bulk of the Judean Mountains. In contrast to the latter, faulting – syngenetical with that which created the Dead Sea-Jordan Rift Valley – exerted a great influence upon the configuration of this desert, particularly by creating the step-like descent toward the Rift Valley. The relative imperviousness of the bedrock, the much lower resistance to erosion, and the steep overall declivity caused by a difference in elevation of about 4,000 ft. (1,200 m.) from the watershed zone to the Dead Sea, over a distance of only 19 mi. (30 km.) result in most of the precipitation turning into highly erosive runoff. Consequently, the Judean Desert represents a "mountain wilderness," an apparently chaotic landscape of innumerable valleys of all kinds. Many of them are canyons cut in harder rock exposed along the flexures and fault lines (Ẓe'elim, Agurot, Mishmar), whereas the higher-lying portions form a maze of mostly flat-topped hills (some of which are famous as sites of ancient fortresses such as Herodium and Masada). In the Ḥatrurim area these hills impart to the landscape the appearance of badlands. It was mainly this type of relief, the absence of productive soils of the terra rossa type, and the very short duration and scantiness of the vegetation cover – almost excluding trees and actually confined to a few weeks during the rainy season – that throughout historical times rendered it a region of "desolation" and a refuge for fugitives from the law and prevented any permanent settlement or the establishment of communication networks.

Shephelah. Topographically, the Shephelah represents a transition zone between the Coastal Plains and the Hebron and Jerusalem Mountains. It is relatively narrow – about 8 mi. (13 km.) – in proportion to its south-north extension – about 35 mi. (60 km.). Though they form the foothills of the Judean Mountains, the Shephelah hills differ from the former in almost all respects. Structurally, they form a major synclinal part of the south Judean anticlinorium, composed mainly of chalky formations of Senonian-Eocene origin. Hypsographically, the Shephelah consists of two parts: a western one (the "Low Shephelah"), rising to a height of about 600 ft. (200 m.) above the Coastal Plains, and an eastern one (the "High Shephelah") about 600 ft. (200 m.) higher than the former. On the north the Shephelah borders on the tectonically conditioned Aijalon Valley, one of the main natural approaches to the Judean Mountains. The Shephelah is a region of gently sloped hills separated by the confluents of the major rivers descending into the area from the Judean Mountains. At their entrance into the Shephelah, these rivers, and several of their tributaries, form relatively wide-floored valleys that run for a considerable stretch along the border between the hill and the mountain region. Passage between these longitudinal valleys is relatively convenient, and this natural communication channel has been very important throughout history.

The Samarian Mountains. Morphotectonically, the Samarian Mountains (less frequently referred to as the Ephraim Mountains) form a transitional link between the massive Judean Mountains, which are influenced little by faulting, and those of the Galilees, where faulting has all but obliterated the other tectonic elements. No topographic features form any pronounced boundary between the two parts of the Central Mountain Massif, and it is only by convention that the upper reaches of the Shiloh River – a tributary of the Yarkon – are used for this demarcation. Structurally, the Samarian Mountains consist of two main parts: an eastern anticlinal one, built up of Cretaceous formations, and a synclinal western one, consisting mainly of rocks of Eocene origin. Characteristically, the highest elevations are found in the latter part. Here the twin mountains of Ebal and Gerizim attain heights of 3,083 ft. (940 m.) and 2,890 ft. (881 m.), respectively. Northward, approaching the valleys of Beth-Shean and Jezreel, respectively, elevations become progressively smaller – about 1,300 ft. (400 m.) above sea level. The structure and its morphological expression are mainly influenced by faulting, which produced tectonic valleys and almost enclosed basins (the latter additionally affected and shaped by solution processes). Sequences of short ranges and mountain blocks thus rise steeply above their flat surroundings, which sometimes form relatively extensive intramontane plains. Thus, the wide tectonic valley of Shechem (Nablus) separates Ebal from Gerizim and continues eastward as Wadi Fāriʿa, which separates the southern, higher part of the Samarian Mountains from the spurs of a much lower northern part. The broad, tectonic valley of Dothan delimits the Samarian Mountains, in the narrow sense, in the direction of the Carmel, whereas in the interior parts, several wide alluvia-filled basins (Emek Shiloh, the Lubban Valley, Emek Hamikhmetat, and the largest of them, Marj Sānūr) endow the region with some features characteristic of Lower Galilee. The shorter distance between the Samarian Mountains and the sea, with no intervening foothill region, the many and wide valley openings, and the smaller amount of depression in the Rift Valley bordering it to the east resulted in a Mediterranean climate for almost all of Samaria, except for a narrow belt adjacent to the Jordan Rift, where semiarid conditions still prevail. Samaria receives larger amounts of precipitation than the Judean Mountains – 28–36 in. (700–800 mm.) annual average rainfall – and the soil cover (terra rossa and rendzina) is also much more continuous. There is a great deal of evidence that considerable parts of Samaria were once covered by woods.

Mount Gilboa. According to its situation and structure, Mount Gilboa represents a direct continuation of the Samarian Mountains, although almost separated from the main body of these mountains by the Jenin Plain – an extension of the Jezreel Plain. It is bordered on the east and southeast by steep fault-scarps, which, together with some outcrops of volcanic rocks, indicate the complex tectonic processes that caused the separation of the Samarian from the Galilee Mountains, also resulting in the formation of the Harod-Jezreel Valley. Composed of Eocene strata, with outcrops of Senonian ones on the northeast side, the surface here is mostly barren, block-strewn, and covered by soil in patches only – probably as the result of intensive slopewash and consequent soil erosion, mainly caused by the difference in elevations of about 1,600 ft. (500 m.) over a distance of only about a mile between the mountain crest and the floor of the surrounding valleys. Precipitation amounts to about 18 in. (450 mm.) on the annual average. The barrenness of the Gilboa, in such strong contrast to the once forested landscapes of Samaria, may serve as the factual background to the explanation of the well-known biblical curse laid upon this mountain. Nowhere in Cisjordan is there such a concentration of springs, some very abundant in discharge, as is found at the bases of the fault escarpments of the Gilboa (Ein Moda, Ein Ḥumah, Ein Amal, En-Harod). These are now one of the most important sources of irrigation for the Harod and Beth-Shean Valleys.

Carmel Mountain. To the northwest a highland body branches off from the Samarian Mountains, differing from the latter in many respects, particularly in structure. In the regional literature of Cisjordan, this branch is usually referred to as the Carmel, although it consists of three very distinct parts of very different structure, lithology, topography, and consequent relief features. The Carmel, therefore, represents a triplet mountain body about 35 mi. (60 km.) long along its median axis and stretching southeast-northwest – a single major occurrence within Cisjordan, although recurring in some lesser ranges. Its general shape is that of an elongated triangle, the relatively short base of which is formed by the Dothan Valley, separating it from Samaria, with the two long sides facing the northern Sharon Plain on the west and the Plain of Haifa and the Jezreel Valley on the northeast. The apex of this triangle – the Carmel headland – abuts almost immediately on the Mediterranean; this is a feature that recurs only at Rosh ha-Nikrah. All the flanks of the mountain, as well as those of its parts, exhibit high and steep slopes, mainly created by faulting, rising abruptly above the adjacent plains. The three subunits of the Carmel (from southeast to northwest) are the Umm al-Faḥm Block, separated from Samaria by the wide Dothan Valley; the Manasseh region, disjointed from the former by the tectonically conditioned Iron Valley; and the Carmel, in the narrow sense, its largest component, separated from the Manasseh region by the Jokneam–Tut Valley sequence, also of tectonic origin.

The Umm al-Faḥm Block (lately also called the Amir Range) forms a quadrangle-shaped plateau, whose undulating surface provides a gradual descent toward the southwest. Toward its northeast confines, the plateau becomes higher, with bolder relief, and ends in a scarp descent facing the Jezreel Valley. Structurally, it represents an upwarped and uplifted part of the Carmel and accordingly consists of resistant Cenomanian limestone and dolomite formations framed at the periphery of the block by formations of Turonian age. Relatively large areas are covered by basalts and volcanic tuff, a lithological feature recurring in the two other subunits of the Carmel. It receives a mean annual precipitation of about 20 in. (500 mm.) and the prevailing soils are of terra rossa type. There are very scanty remains of forests, and still larger areas covered by maquis, their degraded forms, indicate that in the past extensive areas here were wooded. With the exception of its southernmost part, the area is drained almost exclusively by tributaries of the Kishon River.

The region of Manasseh, similar in its quadrangular outline to that of Umm al-Faḥm, contrasts with it in almost all other respects. Composed predominantly of soft Eocene chalks, which also accounts for the scantiness of terra rossa and the wide distribution of rendzina soils in this area, its originally tabular surface became intensively dissected. The dominant relief features of the region are thus hills with moderate slopes rising to relatively small heights above the valley floors. The overall height of the region above sea level is about 600 ft. (200 m.) less than than Umm al-Faḥm Block and still less than that of the Carmel. Its slopes to the Jezreel Valley are also far lower and less steep and continuous than those of the two adjacent units. Due to the relative impermeability of the surface rock, and consequently the considerable percentage of runoff and particularly the erodibility of the bedrock, the drainage net is rather dense, flowing to the Kishon River in the north and to Ha-Tanninim ("Crocodile") and Daliyyah Rivers in the south, both of which discharge directly into the Mediterranean.

The singularity of the Carmel within Cisjordan – used in the Scriptures, together with Mount Tabor, as a paradigm of beautiful mountainous scenery – is based on the following factors: it appears as a very regularly shaped mountain block, well defined on all its sides, and conspicuously elevated above the surrounding plain; it is the only major mountain – about 22 mi. (35 km.) long along its central axis – in Cisjordan with an extended slope rising only a small distance from the Mediterranean; its apex forms a most conspicuous headland, and beyond its northern flank the coastline recedes, forming the only true bay of the country; fully exposed on both its flanks to the Mediterranean, it receives large amounts of rain – about 32 in. (800 mm.) per annum – and dew; arboreal vegetation persisted here, due to its great regenerative power, mainly as a result of favorable climatic conditions. Structurally the Carmel represents a sort of counterpart to the Umm al-Faḥm Block. It, too, was upwarped and uplifted and is mainly composed of Cenomanian-Turonian limestones and dolomites. Volcanic outcrops, in particular tuff, are relatively widespread, and the latter greatly influence the form of valleys. Whereas the valleys incised into the hard, intensively jointed calcareous rocks are deep, narrow, and have steep slopes – frequently actually minor canyons (Naḥal Me'arot, Daliyyah, Oren), those which developed in the tuffs are conspicuously wide and flat-floored, and exhibit relatively gentle valley slopes (Kerem Maharal, Shefeyah Valley). The calcareous parts are strongly affected by solutional weathering. Thoroughly corroded blocks cover large portions of the surfaces, and many of the almost perpendicular valley slopes contain caves, some of which are of considerable prehistoric importance. The Carmel is strongly affected by faulting, which not only gave rise to the almost uninterrupted slopes descending steeply to the Haifa Plain and to the Jezreel Valley and less pronounced ones along the Jokneam trough, which separates it from the Manasseh region, but also strongly influenced the relief of its interior parts. Faulting here gave rise to several depressions and had a major influence upon the course of some of the valleys. The Carmel, like its adjacent mountain units, consists of two topographically differentiated parts: a higher one, its summit region, along its northeast flank – from Rosh ha-Carmel, 1,790 ft. (546 m.), to the somewhat lower Keren ha-Carmel – referred to in regional literature as the "High Carmel," and a far larger part sloping down to the Carmel Coast, the "Low Carmel." The latter consists mainly of broad interfluves, created by the many valleys descending to the Coastal Plain. The drainage net is characteristically varied in catchment area and pattern, in close accordance with the relief differentiation described above. The divide between the watercourses descending on the northeastern slopes and tributary to the Kishon runs a very small distance from the scarp rim. The valleys of these watercourses are short and relatively straight and are joined by very few tributaries. The watercourses running west and draining more than three-quarters of the total area of the Carmel are more numerous and intensely ramified, particularly the Oren and Daliyyah Rivers. Toward the south the Carmel juts out into the Plain of Sharon and up to the valley of the Ha-Tanninim River in a large spur separated from the main body by the valley of the Daliyyah River. Called the Zikhron Ya'akov

Mountains, after the principal settlement, the spur encloses the Carmel Coastal Plain to the west and separates it from the Plain of Binyaminah, a northward extension of the Sharon.

THE VALLEY SEQUENCE. From the Jordan Rift Valley to the coast of the Mediterranean, Cisjordan is traversed by an east-west sequence of large, interconnected, elongated basins that are of preeminent physio- and anthropogeographical importance. These are the Harod Valley, named after its main water artery, the Harod River; the Jezreel Plain, the largest component of the sequence; and the Plain of Haifa, which, genetically, forms the continental terminal part of this tectonic trough and continues westward as the Bay of Haifa. The three basins form relatively wide plains, enclosed on their southern and northern sides by abruptly rising, steep mountains, and constitute a marked discontinuity within the Cisjordan highlands north of the Beersheba Basin. The vale sequence subdivides the highlands very conspicuously into two main mountain complexes: a larger, southern one (Judean Mountains, Samarian Mountains, and Carmel) and a northern one, approximately one-third the size of the former, the Galilees.

The Harod Valley. The Harod Valley – the easternmost component of the sequence – represents, hypsographically, topographically, climatically, and lithologically, a westward salient of the Beth-Shean Valley. There is no major relief feature that could serve as demarcation between these two units; therefore the travertine terraces, more correctly their remnants near Beth-Shean, are used by convention for this purpose. Their correlative characteristics are as follows: the surface of the eastern part of the funnel-shaped vale gradually descends to below sea level and merges imperceptibly with the depression of the Beth-Shean and Jordan Valleys; temperatures and precipitation (in both amount and distribution) are very similar to those of the Beth-Shean Valley; a close likeness of the soil cover in two valleys, particularly in the types resulting from decomposition of basalts and travertine; the already mentioned abundance of springs, particularly at the foot of the Gilboa scarps. In the past the Harod Valley was partly covered by swamps due to the relative impermeability of some of its soil cover, heavy flooding by the many watercourses reaching it from the nearby high, steep mountain enclosure, and the incapacity of the bed of the Harod to contain the floodwaters. The many springs were an additional cause of swamp formation.

The Jezreel Valley. The largest of all intramontane basins in Cisjordan is the Valley of Jezreel, formerly also known as the Plain of Armageddon (after the fortress of Megiddo, which was renowned in the annals of the Fertile Crescent). Roughly triangular in shape, it is bordered on the southwest by the Carmel, Manasseh Plateau, and the Umm al-Faḥm Block; on the north by the Lower Galilee Mountains; and on the east, discontinuously, by Mount Tabor, Givat ha-Moreh, and the Gilboa Mountains. The shape of this valley is straight only along the Carmel; at the other borders there are several embayment-like extensions of the plain into the surrounding mountains. The largest of these extensions is the Plain of Jenin, enclosed on the east by the Gilboa and joined on the southwest by the Dothan Valley. Eastward, the Jezreel Valley downgrades imperceptibly in the vicinity of Afulah into the Harod Valley and intrudes deeply into the Lower Galilee Mountains, separating their outliers, Mount Tabor and Givat ha-Moreh, by the wide Chesulloth Plain. The Jezreel Valley is connected at its apex with the Haifa Plain by a narrow passage 1,600 ft. (500 m.) wide created by the valley of the Kishon (at Kiryat Ḥaroshet) near the site of Bet She'arim, between the Carmel and the Lower Galilee Mountains. The winding course of the Kishon River begins near Afulah, less than 230 ft. (70 m.) above sea level and at a distance of about 25 mi. (40 km.) from the Mediterranean, into which it discharges. In the past it was inadequate to drain the valley, particularly in the rainy season. Its many affluents from the enclosing mountains, which receive about 8 in. (200 mm.) more precipitation than the Jezreel Valley, together with the many local topographic depressions and poorly permeable alluvial heavy soil cover, turned a large part of the valley into swamps. Consequently, it was sparsely populated and little utilized agriculturally. Only after the marshes were drained and malaria, once endemic in this area, eradicated, did the valley become the area of the most intensive and continuous cultivation within the mountain zone of Cisjordan. The physiognomy of the Jezreel Valley, and to some extent also of the Harod Valley, is largely determined by the two massive, high mountain blocks rising abruptly above the plain; Mount Tabor and Givat ha-Moreh. Pronouncedly isolated from each other and from the highlands to the north and south, their summits attain heights of over 1,600 ft. (500 m.) above sea level and only slightly less above the surrounding plain. Because of the almost perfect dome shape of Mount Tabor, it was, together with the Carmel, often used to exemplify the beauty of mountainous scenery. Differing as they do in lithological structure (limestones and dolomites in Mount Tabor, outcrops of volcanic rocks in Givat ha-Moreh), these two mountains probably represent remnants of a highland zone connecting the Samarian Mountains with those of the Galilees that was shattered by the tectonic movements, which also formed the entire basin sequence.

Haifa Plain. Despite its being a part of the Coastal Plains, according to its situation and surface configuration, the Haifa Plain (formerly referred to also as the Zebulun Plain) morphotectonically represents the westernmost unit of the vale sequence. The plain continues in its submerged part as the Bay of Haifa. Accordingly, the interior part of the plain, east of the dune belt, is covered by heavy alluvial soils with very little *ḥamra*. Drainage here was also greatly impeded, mainly by the dune belt (as evidenced by the deferred debouchures of its two main streams, Kishon and Na'aman), and marsh areas persisted up to the time of Jewish colonization.

THE GALILEE MOUNTAINS. Occupying a smaller area than the Judean or the Samarian Highlands, the Galilee Mountains are nevertheless far more complex in lithology, structure, and consequently morphology. Basalts (there is even a remnant of a true volcano – Karnei Ḥittin, the "Horns" of Ḥittin) cover large tracts in the eastern parts, a feature recurring only in Transjordan. This cover imparts to several of its landscapes a peculiar plateau-like relief of great uniformity, in vivid contrast to areas of much more variegated configuration in the west, where the surfaces consist of calcareous rocks. Faulting, however, has exerted a far more decisive influence. In the Negev and in the Central Highlands, fold structures are found almost everywhere and are visually recognizable as the most important tectonic element that determines the relief of the region even in its minor features. In the Galilees, however, the influence of fold structures upon the relief is largely upset, permuted, and even inverted by faulting. Tectonic activity seems to be continuing at present, as evidenced by the relatively frequent, and sometimes strong, earthquakes affecting the region. Generally characteristic of the landscape of the Galilees as a whole are closely spaced sequences of basins or valleys and mountain ranges that are uplifted unequally and thus tilted, so that one slope is much steeper than the opposite. Here mountain blocks, separated from their surroundings by faults and upthrusting, constitute some of the highest summit regions of Cisjordan. Since the prevailing direction of the major fault lines is west–east, the general trend of Galilean ranges follows this direction, in strong contrast to the Central Mountain Zone's prevailing meridional trend and particularly to the Judean Mountains, where a continuous watershed zone running south–north emphasizes the compactness of this body. Tectonic conditions, resulting in an increase of rock exposures, and the relatively large amounts of precipitation produced relatively abundant karst features in the Galilees. Among these there are simple and complex dolines (small solution basins), sinkholes, even a large polje, and caves several of which contain speleothems (stalactites, stalagmites, etc.) or, they are caves which are of prime importance as prehistoric sites. Thus, lithologically, and still more so morphologically, the Galilees form the most contrasted and variegated mountain province (excluding the Eilat Mountains) of Cisjordan. Although strongly disjointed by the numerous basins, tectonic valleys, and uplifted blocks, the Galilee may be clearly subdivided into two main regions: a southern one of comparatively moderate height, Lower Galilee, and a northern one, separated from the first by an extended tectonic valley (Valley of Beth-Cherem), and rising immediately behind it to maximum summit heights in Cisjordan, Upper Galilee.

Lower Galilee. The Lower Galilee Highlands, which rise abruptly and steeply from the vale sequence in an in- and outcurving front, are markedly subdivided into an eastern part and a western one. The first is characterized by a widespread basalt cover of considerable thickness that buried a former, probably intensively sculptured relief, turning the area into groups of plateau-topped mountain bodies. This landscape, which is geologically recent, is now subject to vigorous dissection by rivers (many of them perennial) that discharge into Lake Kinneret or into the Jordan (Ammud, Ẓalmon, Ha-Yonim and Tabor Rivers). They flow through deeply incised gorges created by their great erosive power, resulting from very considerable height differences between their respective source regions and their places of debouchure, which are respectively about 700 ft. (200 m.) above and 800 ft. (250 m.) below sea level and are only 12 mi. (20 km.) apart. The rivers also subdivide eastern Lower Galilee into many units, several of which form small plateaus, rising steplike, one above the other (Kokhav – the site of the Crusader fortress of Belvoir – and the Jabneel-Kefar Tabor plateau are the largest of them). In the other two-thirds of Lower Galilee, the surface rock consists of limestone (subject to strong solutional processes and to the formation of karstic features, such as dolines, sinkholes, caverns), chalk and marl, generally intensively interbedded. In this part of Lower Galilee almost all of the landforms bear visible evidence of the decisive role played by faulting in determining the relief of the present landscape.

Central Galilee consists of a series of basins, separated by generally narrower ranges, usually representing remnants, partially uplifted portions, of the former highland surface. The series begins with the Plain of Jezreel, which, from the general morphotectonic point of view, represents the foreland of Lower Galilee. It is separated from the Tiran Basin by the abruptly rising, steeply sloping Nazareth Mountains. Beyond the Tiran Basin lies that of Beit Netofah (the largest one), separated from the Tiran Basin by the Tiran Range. The Tiran Basin now contains a large storage lake, part of the National Water Carrier System. It is bordered on the north by the Yodefat Range, which, in turn, separates it from the Sakhnīn Basin. The Shezor (Sājūr) Ridge extends north of the Sakhnīn Basin, near the boundary valley of Beth-Cherem, beyond which the first group of the Upper Galilee Mountains rises, wall-like to heights exceeding 3,280 ft. (1,000 m.). The interbasin ranges are not compact, but rather form series of rounded hills separated by wide saddles, being the short fluviatile valleys of tributaries of the major rivers that drain the basins (Ẓippori and Ḥillazon Rivers). The rivers draining the basins, however, were inadequate to collect and carry off the waters flowing down to them from the enclosing ridges. Large areas of them were flooded during the rainy season and the thick cover of heavy soils, mainly a product of slope erosion, greatly impeded infiltration. In addition to the flatness of the basin floors, the sluggishness of the flow of waters in their main channels, due to the very small gradient, strongly enhanced marshy conditions.

Upper Galilee. Most of the essential differences between the Lower and the Upper Galilee are conspicuous at their boundary, Valley of Beth-Cherem, one of the most distinct morphotectonic border zones of Cisjordan. Here, without any transition, the slopes of several mountain blocks rise abruptly to the highest summit heights in Cisjordan – Mount ha-Ari, 3,434 ft. (1,047 m.), Mount Kefir, 3,221 ft. (982 m.) – culminating slightly to the north in the three summits of the Meron Block with heights of 3,621, 3,745, and 3,962 ft. (1,104, 1,151, and 1,208 m.). Structurally these mountains, as well as the majority of the mountains throughout Upper Galilee, are horsts, i.e., blocks separated from their surroundings by faults and partially uplifted to very considerable heights. The relative abundance of the horsts, which predominate over other tectonic structures, seems to be a result of the variety of fault directions. Whereas in the Lower Galilee the major fault lines generally trend east–west, conditioning the pattern of basins and intervening ranges that follow the same directions in Upper Galilee, faults running in these directions are intersected obliquely or even at right angles by other faults. This is one of the prime causes of the isolation of the individual blocks and their apparently random pattern. The difference in height between the blocks is primarily the result of the amount of uplift rather than of different rates of denudation. The Upper Galilee Highlands, as a whole, slope down to the northwest, and their lowest parts, already within the boundaries of Lebanon (Lebanese Galilee), are adjacent to the Qasimiye Valley. Faults also strongly influence the pattern and the individual courses of the valleys, which form almost parallel gorges only several kilometers apart (Ga'aton, Chezib, Beẓet Rivers within Israel; Shamaʿ and ʿArriya in the Lebanese Galilee). In contrast to Lower Galilee, Upper Galilee is predominantly built up of Cenomanian and Turonian limestone formations, framed in the west by a belt of less resistant Senonian ones, which also form the surface rock of the region's intramontane basins. Eocene formations, generally consisting of hard rock sequences, are more extensive in the eastern part of the region. Another important difference between the Lower and Upper Galilee is the much smaller surface covered by basalts in the latter, where they are virtually restricted to some small plateaus (Dalton, Ram Plateaus).

Upper Galilee, being northernmost of all the mountain regions of Cisjordan, with only a narrow coastal plain interposed between it and the Mediterranean to "intercept" the early rains, in particular, and affect their amounts, as in the case of the Judean Mountains, is the region with comparatively the highest precipitation within Cisjordan. Very few parts of the region receive less than 24 in. (600 mm.), while the amount of precipitation on its summit areas exceeds 40 in. (1,000 mm.) annually. Snowfall occurs almost yearly. The large amounts of precipitation combined with the hard, intensively jointed limestone bedrock and the abundance of exposed surfaces (the result of tectonic shattering and fracturing and of the erosive activity of the watercourses) have made Upper Galilee the region most strongly affected by solution processes. Accordingly, it contains almost a full inventory of subaerial and subsurface karstic features. This is the only area where a sort of "holokarst" has developed, i.e., landscapes whose surfaces are primarily affected by solution and that display almost the whole gamut of specific features. Large surfaces are rilled and corroded into a maze of small, sharp-crested ridgelets separated by even narrower minute channels (lapies). Dolines are widespread (particularly in the vicinity of Sa'sa and Alma) as are sinkholes, many of which are tens of meters deep. This is also the site of the only large "true" polje within Cisjordan, i.e., a basin of considerable size (Kadesh Naphtali), mainly a product of solution. Upper Galilee is, in addition, the site of the most abundant and intricate caves in Ereẓ Israel (some of which include a full inventory of speleothems – stalactites, stalagmites, stalagnates, dripstone-draperies, etc.).

The same basic conditions – the large amounts of precipitation and the prevalence of limestone-dolomite surface rock – produced a relatively continuous cover of terra rossa on most moderately sloping areas. These conditions also apply to the relatively large areas of forest, which have great regenerative ability, so that even in the past, when forests were utterly depleted through man's agency, considerable parts of Upper Galilee remained covered by high-grade maquis.

Upper Galilee is an analogue of Lower Galilee in its physiographic subdivision, on the basis of lithological and morphotectonic conditions. The eastern part of Upper Galilee was apparently affected by faulting to a smaller extent, imparting to the landscape a more uniform aspect than in the adjacent parts. Several areas form small plateaus, mainly due to their basalt cover. Basins of considerable size, as well as relatively long mountain ranges, running almost unbroken and not partitioned into isolated blocks, are found here. One of these, the Naphtali Range, with summits over 2,900 ft. (900 m.) high, extends almost due north up to the Qasimiye River. Its eastward slope is precipitous – 1,600 ft. (500 m.) difference in height over a distance of only about a mile – a marked fault-scarp facing the upper Jordan Valley, the Ḥuleh Basin and the Marj ʿAyyūn Basin farther north. Plateau-like on its top surfaces, and strongly affected by karstification, the Naphtali Range forms a wall-like enclosure around the Ḥuleh Basin, uninterrupted by major valleys, and a pronounced watershed zone between this basin and the rivers draining to the Mediterranean. South of this range lies the Safed region, flanked on its east by Mount Canaan and on the west by the dominant Meron Block. Here the surface is divided into individual mountain groups, due largely to the numerous steeply incised valleys of the tributaries of the Ammud River. The central Upper Galilee Highlands are separated from the eastern Highlands by the gorge of the Ammud River, running almost due north-south. Here, as in the portion extending southward to the Beth-Cherem Valley, typical Mediterranean mountain scenery reaches its climax within Cisjordan. Slopes, mostly terraced, rise from deep valley gorges to heights surpassing 3,000 ft. (1,000 m.) above sea level. Covered by patches of trees or scrub growth, they culminate in the gently domed summits of large mountain bodies such as Mount ha-Ari, Mount Hillel, and Mount Addir, which are overshadowed by the summit region of the massive Mount Meron. The western part of Upper Galilee, much lower in absolute and relative heights, is characterized primarily by a large number of valleys (originating in the Central Highlands). As noted earlier, the valleys are very closely spaced, and form deep gorges in their upper and middle reaches (Chezib and Beẓet in the Israeli part of the area and Samara, Shamaʿ, and ʿAzziyya in the Lebanese). These intensively dissected highlands mainly form extended interfluve ranges, the widest of which, the Ḥanitah-Rosh ha-Nikrah Range, ends with a headland into the Mediterranean (Rosh ha-Nikrah).

RIFT VALLEY. The Rift Valley, within Ereẓ Israel, is part of the approximately 3,700 mi. (6,000 km.) Rift Valley system that begins in Africa near the Zambezi Valley and peters out north of the Amanus Mountains. The Red Sea and its two gulfs, Eilat and Suez, are submerged parts of the system, whereas in Ereẓ Israel, as mentioned earlier, the Rift Valley is the prime determining factor of a complex of morphotectonic features unique in the world. Some of the tectonic movements that generated the Rift Valley seem to be still active here, as proved by the frequent earthquakes affecting the valley and the adjacent regions. Other evidence is provided by the many hot springs along the boundaries of the Rift Valley, indicating the presence of near-surface magmatic bodies. Geologically recent volcanic activity also played a major role in forming the basic surface configuration of the valley and its adjacent regions. Streams of lava, extruding mainly in the Bashan (particularly in the Hauran and Golan), formed an almost continuous basalt cover extending as far as to the south of the Yarmuk Valley. The lava moved down into the northern part of the present Jordan Valley, consolidated, and dammed up the valley, thus differentiating it into the Ḥuleh Valley – the head part of the Jordan River system – and a section lying about 800 ft. (250 m.) lower, at present occupied by Lake Kinneret. A vast inland sea covered the Rift Valley floor in the Middle Pleistocene, extending from the present Lake Kinneret to far beyond the southern shores of the Dead Sea. It is termed the Lashon (Lisān) Lake after the wide peninsula, or "tongue" (Heb. *lashon*; Ar. *lisān*), that protrudes into the present Dead Sea and divides it into two basins connected by a narrow strait. The level of the Lashon Lake was once about 700 ft. (200 m.) higher than that of the Dead Sea. Sediments deposited on the floor of the Lashon Lake (accordingly called the Lashon formation) – overlying very thick sediment accumulations of former lake formations, which appeared and disappeared in accordance with climatic variations during the Pliocene and Lower Pleistocene eras, and other fill-in material – are of very specific character. They consist of thinly layered clastic material, particularly clays, and evaporites, i.e., sediments produced by chemical precipitation caused mainly by evaporation. With the gradual regression of the Lashon Lake (evidenced by the many terraces along the Dead Sea slope enclosures marking the former coastlines), the Lashon formation sediments were bared. These sediments, covering the floor and the slope bases of the Rift Valley from Lake Kinneret in the north to Ein Ḥaẓevah about 20 mi. (30 km.) south of the Dead Sea, are easily eroded and thus condition microreliefing processes of the highest intensity. These processes create mazes of badlands containing almost the entire gamut of configuration features in miniature, due mainly to the innumerable gullies that dissect this former floor of the Lashon Lake. Another extremely important lithological characteristic of the Rift Valley is the abundance of rock salt and gypsum forming the bedrock of prominent features (e.g., Mount Sodom).

The Rift Valley, sunk in, troughlike, in some places to considerable depths below the sea level, forms a unique climatic region with very distinct characteristics and exerting great influence upon its adjacent zones. Climatic conditions in the Rift Valley have a decisive influence on the surface relief of its southern and central parts, i.e., from the Gulf of Eilat to Lake Kinneret. The Rift Valley receives very small amounts of precipitation, as it is leeward of the moisture-bearing winds coming from the Mediterranean, due to the interposition of the highlands of Cisjordan. Precipitation averages 1 in. (25 mm.) annually at Eilat, 2 in. (50 mm.) at the southern end, and less than 4 in. (100 mm.) at the northern end of the Dead Sea and gradually increases to approximately 12 in. (300 mm.) annually at Lake Kinneret, the terminal area of the depression below sea level. North of Lake Kinneret, where the Rift Valley floor is well above the level of the Mediterranean, precipitation is 16 in. (400 mm.) annually, imparting to this section subhumid characteristics. The topographical conditions that influence the amounts of precipitation are also the major reason for the generally extreme temperatures and their variations in the Rift Valley. Geomorphologically more important than the temperatures themselves, which frequently reach the highest values within Ereẓ Israel, is the extreme evaporation potential they cause, which greatly influences the bedrock and the processes affecting it, particularly weathering. The above-mentioned climatic conditions, together with particular lithological conditions (the high proportion of evaporites), have resulted in large parts of the Rift Valley being devoid of proper soil and vegetational cover, and these develop here only under specific hydrographic or hydrological conditions. The Jordan, for instance, from its exit from Lake Kinneret almost up to its debouchure, is accompanied by a dense gallery forest covering its floodplain. In the vicinity of springs and in areas where topographical conditions cause the formation of salt marshes a type of tree oasis is common.

Hydrographically, the Rift Valley is a vast endoreic basin (i.e., without a discharge outlet to the sea), presently in a state of equilibrium between the amount of inflow from its catchment area – about 15,500 sq. mi. (40,000 sq. km.) in area – and the amount of loss caused by evaporation and infiltration. The level of the Dead Sea, its discharge terminal, does not change in height appreciably from year to year. From the physiographical, and particularly morphotectonic, points of view, the portion of the Rift Valley within Ereẓ Israel may be subdivided into the following major units (dealt with here according to their south-north sequence, which to some degree also follows their genetical order of succession): Arabah, Dead Sea Region, Ḥuleh Basin, and the Jordan Sources Region.

Arabah. North of the Red Sea and the Gulf of Eilat, the Great Rift Valley again becomes a continental feature. Its first portion here extends for about 100 mi. (160 km.) up to the Dead Sea, constituting the longest and largest Rift unit within Ereẓ Israel. It is relatively narrow, as its maximum width is only about 12 mi. (20 km.), and, according to its topography (especially its hydrographic conditions), it consists of two parts. The southern part, about 43 mi. (70 km.) long, ascends gradually from the Eilat coast to a divide between the latter and the Dead Sea about 600 ft. (200 m.) above sea level. From here the valley floor slopes down to below sea level in its last third and merges with the large salt marsh at the southern shore of the Dead Sea. This northern area is drained by the Arabah River and its many tributaries, whereas the southern area lacks any organized drainage, particularly any distinct river channel discharging into the Gulf of Eilat. Another significant characteristic of the southern portion of the Arabah is several major topographical depressions that function as discharge terminals for various very short, sporadic watercourses flowing in shallow, indistinct, rill-like beds and for the sheet floods occurring after each heavy rain.

Southern Arabah. The southern section of the Arabah is bordered by the coast of Eilat-Akaba, which is less than 6 mi. (10 km.) long and runs southwest-northeast. This coast differs in several respects from that bordering the Mediterranean. It is covered by coarse sands and shingle, created by the disintegration of magmatic rocks and Nubian Sandstone, which compose the mountains framing the Gulf of Eilat and the Arabah and by fragments of corals and associated organisms that populate the Gulf. The widely distributed beachrock consists mainly of pebbly material deposited on the coast by the rivers descending from the crystalline Eilat Mountains and their Transjordanian counterpart, the Edom Mountains, in addition to the above-mentioned organogenic material. After somewhat protracted or concentrated rainfall, the coastal part of the Arabah is frequently flooded. In the absence of discharge channels it becomes a kind of playa (i.e., salty marsh) that, after its ensuing desiccation, exhibits wide areas of polygonal clay shards encrusted by salt crystals. Farther north the floor of the Arabah is covered by detritus of various sizes reaching a depth of more than 3,300 ft. (1,000 m.). This layer has been deposited by numerous streambeds that carry only floodwaters (from Roded, Shekhoret, Amram, Reḥam, and Timna on the western enclosure and Yitm, Mulghān, and Muhtadī on the eastern one). Another very important depositional factor is slope wash and gravitational movements (rockfall, sliding, slumping, particle creep) that continuously take place on the mountain slopes flanking the Arabah, which lack stabilization by soil and vegetational cover. These slopes, as mentioned earlier, are lithologically heterogeneous. In the southern part of the Cisjordan Arabah, they are composed mainly of magmatic-metamorphic rocks and Nubian Sandstone (Eilat and Timna Massifs); farther north limestones and dolomites prevail. The Transjordanian side of the mountainous enclosure consists predominantly of crystalline rocks and Nubian Sandstone.

The floor of the southern part of the Arabah is not flat. It is differentiated by many rises and wide shallow depressions. The former originate in alluvial fans spreading out widely into the Arabah at the exits of all the valleys. The fans on the east side are generally more numerous, larger, and longer as a result of the larger supply of detritus. The abundance of this supply is conditioned by several factors. The mountains bordering the Arabah to the east are much higher than the Negev Highlands and receive far larger amounts of precipitation because of their westerly exposure. These two factors endow the watercourses descending from the eastern side with considerably greater erosive power. In addition, the bedrock there, which consists of crystalline rock and sandstones almost along the entire extension of this flank, is subject to intensive disintegration under the prevailing arid conditions and supplies the watercourses with the bulk of the coarse material that is borne down and deposited at their exit into the Arabah. Thus, on the east side an almost continuous detritus apron of coalesced fans envelops the bases and the lower slopes. Where the fans extend farther into the Arabah or meet fans formed by watercourses from the west side (generally smaller in size), rises or topographical swells originate. The floor between the rises is basin-like; runoff is deflected into these basins with consequent flooding and salt marshes of short duration are formed. In several of these basins (Avronah, Yotvatah, and Sa'idiyin are the largest), halophytic vegetation has developed and even trees are able to subsist on brackish subsurface water. Another characteristic of both the southern and northern Arabah is the relatively wide areas of dunes, particularly between the basins of Yotvatah and Saʿīdiyīn.

Northern Arabah. The northern, larger part of the Arabah, which begins with a wide protrusion of the Paran Plateau into the trough valley, differs in several respects from the southern part. The latter is relatively narrow, limited on the east by the relatively straight and continuous fault scarps of the Edom Highlands and on the west by the irregular outline of the southern Negev Highlands with their many mountain outliers and riverhead cirques. The influence of faulting is less pronounced there. Conversely, the northern Arabah often widens into the mountains bordering it, which are in turn frequently interrupted by wide valleys intruding deeply into the confining mountain flanks. The most significant difference between the southern and the northern parts of the Arabah, however, is the presence of a river course almost throughout the length of the latter. It is very indistinct and erratic, functioning mainly as a collecting artery of the many tributaries joining it from the east and west. The existence of this relatively dense drainage net, although it carries flash-flood waters almost exclusively, precludes the existence of any major basins turning into a salt marsh or extensive dune areas. The bed of the Arabah River, several hundred meters wide, is not contained by any permanent or continuous banks and is defined mainly by the accumulation of pebbles and associated fluviatile material. It does not run along the median axis of this part of the Rift Valley, but consistently deviates westward due to the fans growing and spreading out from the eastern side of the valley. These fans receive more alluvial material than those spreading out from the Negev, due to the greater height, larger amounts of precipitation, and consequently greater erosive and tractive capacities of the Transjordanian affluents.

The northernmost part of the Arabah was covered in the Middle Pleistocene by the Lashon Lake. Its surface accordingly consists mostly of laminated, highly erodible marls. The Arabah River and several others (in particular the Amaẓyahu River, almost parallel in course to the former) have cut spectacular canyons into these sediments, accompanied by labyrinthal badlands. The Arabah River does not reach the Dead Sea through a clearly defined bed channel, but disappears in the Sodom playa – the salt marshes south of the Dead Sea – which is flooded periodically by any considerable rise of the Dead Sea and/or by the rivers that discharge into the Dead Sea. Only one river in this area, however, the Zered (Ḥasā') – delimiting Edom from Moab – has a direct debouchure into the Dead Sea. It drains an area in Transjordan that reaches heights of over 3,280 ft. (1,000 m.), receives over 10 in. (250 mm.) precipitation on the annual average, and is fed by numerous springs. Due to these factors, the Zered exhibits perennial flow up to its entrance into the Rift Valley, and after rains it discharges very large quantities of floodwater. A large spring is also located in that section of the valley through which the Zered flows, and this northeast corner of the Arabah (the region of Zoar) forms a sort of an enclave, characterized by plentiful, almost tropical vegetation.

Dead Sea. The deepest part of the Rift Valley is covered by an inland sea about 50 mi. (80 km.) long, 10 mi. (17 km.) wide, and generally similar in shape to the rift lakes in East Africa. With no outlet to the sea and an inflow of river water balanced by evaporation from its surface area of over 380 sq. mi. (1,000 sq. km.), the salt contents of the sea (mainly magnesium, sodium, and calcium chlorides), carried as solutions by the rivers and the other sources of discharge into it (such as springs with a high mineral content), became progressively concentrated. This salt content now amounts to about 28–33%, depending on the depth of the water layer. The Dead Sea consists of two widely differing parts: a southern, small, and very shallow basin – 20 ft. (6 m.) deep – with a higher percentage of salinity; and a northern basin, over three times the size of the southern one, and considerably deeper than it – about 1,300 ft. (400 m.). The two basins are connected by a strait about 2 mi. (3 km.) wide, formed by the westward protrusion of the Lashon Peninsula into the sea. According to topographical and historical indications, the strait was formerly shallower and probably narrower, and it is assumed that in the geologically recent past the two basins were virtually separated. The Lashon Peninsula rises about 200 ft. (60 m.) above the Dead Sea and was probably formed by diapiric movements of underlying deep-seated salt masses (i.e., an upward thrust of salt deposits rendered plastic and mobile by the pressure exerted on them). Its tabloid surface consists of Lashon Marls, as do the steep sides of the peninsula, which are subject to strong wave abrasion. Except for its northern and southern coast and small stretches along its sides, the Dead Sea does not have any shore flats. It is almost immediately bordered along its entire length by steep slopes that sometimes protrude into the sea and form bold capes (Rās Fashkha, south of the site of Qumran, is the most pronounced). Conversely, many rivers, particularly those coming from the Judean Desert, create rather extensive deltas quite close to the exits of their canyons (Kidron, Daraja, the combined deltas of Mishmar, Ẓe'elim and Masada). These deltas impart to the western coast its sinuous outline, in contrast to the relatively straight coastline on the eastern side, where the deltas built out into the sea are fewer in number and generally far smaller in size. Thus, e.g., the delta of the Arnon River, second only to the Jordan in the amount of water it supplies to the Dead Sea, is small; when the sea is at its high-water stage, its waters even extend up to the river's canyon exit. Even less pronounced is the subaerial delta of the Zarqā Mā'īn River, the third most important contributor to the Dead Sea. This variance in delta size seems primarily to be the result of the greater depth of the sea floor near its eastern coast, probably a consequence of the major fault line running close to it.

A singular relief feature found on the southeastern side of the sea is Mount Sodom. It rises over 600 ft. (200 m.) above the sea, with jagged, almost perpendicular slopes, close to the water line, and gradually slopes down on its western flank. About 6 mi. (10 km.) long, it is composed mainly of salt and gypsum layers capped by Lashon Marls. The mountain is of diapiric origin, i.e., salt and other evaporites have been squeezed upward along an elongated fault, thus uplifting the overlying sediments and then spreading them out sideways. The great solubility and erodibility of the evaporites, augmented by their strong tendency to form cracks as a result of the enormous stresses exerted on the rock masses when they are thrust up and intensively contorted, resulted in the formation of this almost unique mountain ridge. Closely spaced fissures (continually widened and deepened by solution), washout, and corrasion by gully waters created a multitude of pillar-like features ("Lot's Wife"). Their surfaces are pitted by innumerable hollows, crisscrossed by rills ("salt-lapies"); in their flank facing the Dead Sea caverns developed, one of them an actual cave, connected with the upper mountain surface by a chimney-like conduit. The interior of this cave exhibits a rich inventory of speleothems (stalactites, etc.), somewhat more elaborate than those found in limestone caves.

The Lower Jordan Valley. The Lower Jordan Valley morphogenetically represents the floor of the Lashon Lake laid bare after its recession. The valley of the Jordan progressively developed on this floor, as did the lowermost courses of its tributaries, which formerly discharged into the Lashon Lake.

Hypsographical, lithological, and climatic conditions resulted in the formation of a unique riverscape, connected with and focused on the course of the Jordan River from its exit from Lake Kinneret to its debouchure into the Dead Sea. The Jordan and its tributaries are deeply entrenched in the layers of the Lashon formations, which thicken progressively southward. They did not succeed, although greatly aided by the innumerable gullies that developed on the former Lashon Lake floor, in dissecting and reducing it considerably, so that two distinct surface levels exist along the Lower Jordan Valley. The higher one, generally flat, featureless, and only moderately affected by river dissection, is the remnant of the Lashon Lake floor and is referred to as the Ghor (Kikkar ha-Yarden in Hebrew). On both sides it borders high and steep mountainous slopes, formed mainly by scarps and composed predominantly of hard limestones and dolomites. Near the Jordan course, however, the Ghor becomes intensively dissected by innumerable gullies that turn it into intensive and characteristic badlands. Tens of meters below the Ghor extends the alluvial valley of the Jordan formed by its vertical and lateral erosion and much narrower than the Ghor. The Jordan valley, in the narrow sense, consists of the riverbed, about 80–100 ft. (25–30 m.) wide when not in bankful or overflooding stage, and a discontinuous floodplain covered by a dense gallery forest. Walled in by the steep, intensively gullied badland slopes, it contacts the bases of the mountain slopes enclosing the Rift Valley in only a few places.

The length of the Rift Valley between Lake Kinneret and the Dead Sea is about 65 mi. (105 km.); the course of the Jordan along this part of the Rift Valley, however, is approximately 125 mi. (205 km.). The near doubling in length is the result of the river's intricate meandering, despite the great drop in height between its exit from Lake Kinneret and its entrance into the Dead Sea. Despite its tortuous course, the river's gradient and the velocity of its current are still quite considerable, endowing it with great erosive power – factors which are generally adverse to the full development of a meandering course. The intensive meandering of the Jordan – often cited as an example of the phenomenon – seems causally to be connected with the tributaries joining it, which built out progressively, growing fans into its valley, and thus deviate from its course. The rivers contributing the greatest amounts of discharge to the Lower Jordan are its affluents from the Transjordanian side: the Yarmuk contributes about 17 billion cu. ft. (480 million cu. m.) annual discharge, compared with about almost 18 billion cu. ft. (500 million cu. m.) of the Jordan flowing at their confluence; the Jabbok provides approximately 2 billion cu. ft. (about 60 million cu. m.); the Arabah River, over 1 billion cu. ft. (30 million cu. m.); and the other major tributaries contribute only 210–350 million cu. ft. (6–10 million cu. m.) Because the tributaries coming in from the western side of the valley discharge far less, the Jordan is permanently deflected westward. Another factor in determining the river's course is the larger amounts of river-borne material supplied by the eastern affluents (particularly at the flood stages), due to the greater height at which these rivers originate, the larger amounts of precipitation their catchment areas receive, and consequently their far greater erosive and tractive capacities. In addition, exceedingly large amounts of material are delivered to the river from the Rift floor, particularly from the badland zone. Since this material is deposited within the riverbed, where the current is extremely unequal, irregular, and frequently deviated in its course by the outbuilt fans, the large discharge injections are an additional major factor behind the meandering tendency. Finally, waste movements, activated by undermining the river erosion banks, or even – although far more rarely – by earthquakes, bring vast amounts of debris down into the riverbed. According to both historical and contemporary eyewitnesses, this activity has even caused temporary cessation of the river's flow for some time.

The Lower Jordan Valley is fringed on its eastern side by the high scarp-slopes of the Transjordanian plateaus, which are only insignificantly punctuated by the canyon exits of the rivers descending into the Rift Valley. Less linear in outline is the western enclosure, in which the Jordan tributaries created wide valleys, extending far into the eastern flank of the Judean and particularly the Samarian Mountains (ʿAwjā and Fāriʿa Rivers). Some 18 mi. (30 km.) south of Lake Kinneret, the western mountain enclosure is broken by the tectonic valley of Beth-Shean, which begins the valley sequence traversing the width of Cisjordan. Hypsographically and climatically it represents a transition zone. The valley's level rises progressively from about 800 ft. (250 m.) below sea level at its eastern limit – the Jordan River – to about 300 ft. (100 m.) above sea level at its conjunction with the Harod Valley. Two surface levels exist within this embayment of the Rift Valley: a higher one adjacent to Mount Gilboa and predominantly composed of travertine, precipitated mainly from the many fault-conditioned springs at the base of this mountain; and an eastern, lower one, separated from the former by a step slope (now indistinct because of cultivation), merging imperceptibly with the Ghor. The Beth-Shean and Jordan valleys exhibit semiarid characteristics, mainly as a result of the amounts of precipitation (exceeding 12 in. (300 mm.) on the annual average). Conversely, the prevailing temperatures are still very similar to those in the southern part of the Lower Jordan Valley.

Kinneret Region. The Kinneret Region comprises Lake Kinneret (also called the Sea of Galilee or Lake Tiberias) and the narrow plains situated between it and the high, steep mountain slopes enclosing it to the west and east. To the south the plain into which the Jordan exits from the lake and in which the embouchure of the Yarmuk into the Kinneret is situated merges imperceptibly with the Beth-Shean Valley. The lake, however, covers a larger area – about 70 sq. mi. (170 sq. km.) – than all its surrounding plains combined. Lake Kinneret itself, whose maximum depth is only about 200 ft. (60 m.), was created by complex and protracted tectonic movements involving faulting and volcanic activities (the mountains enclosing the lake are to a large extent covered by basalts). These movements, which seem to continue to this day, as may be inferred from the earthquakes of considerable strength that affect the region from time to time (the town of Tiberias was heavily damaged and about 700 people were killed in the earthquake of 1837) and from the presence of hot springs (Tiberias, al-Ḥamma, the ancient Hammath-Gader, in the Yarmuk Valley). Another indirect source of evidence is the many mineral springs issuing from the lake bottom and contributing considerably to the relatively high salinity of the waters – 300 mg./liter. Fault lines are the main factor behind the pronounced asymmetry of the shoreline. Whereas the eastern shore, conditioned by a fairly meridional fault sequence, runs relatively straight, the western one curves out sharply due to crescent-shaped fault lines. Asymmetry is also characteristic of most of the other features of the lakescape. Steep, high slopes rising almost immediately from the eastern and western sides of the lake face littoral plains on the opposite shores. The northern and southern shores of the lake are also very different in configuration. At its northern tip the Jordan River enters the lake in a complex braided course; several branches of it split up and join alternatively, uniting into a single bed only a small distance from the embouchure. The small river plain thus formed is the head of the al-Buṭayḥa (Bet Ẓayyada) Plain, which extends farther southeast and is composed mainly of the alluvial deposits of six small streams descending from the Golan Heights into the lake. South of this plain, and separated from it by a steep mountain spur, extends the shore plain of Ein Gev, dominated by Mount Susita and progressively widening and finally merging with the Yarmuk Plain.

In bold contrast to the northern and eastern sides of the lake, where alluvial plains are prograded into the lake, the southern shore is subject to incessant, strong abrasion and thus to regrading by the wave activity caused by the prevailing north winds. The recession of the shore is strongly aided by the high erodibility of the Lashon formation materials framing the lake. Into this bedrock, which also contains many basalt outcrops, the Jordan has cut its bed in a course that meanders almost from its exit from the lake. The west side of Lake Kinneret is fringed from the exit of the Jordan up to the debouchure of the Arbel River by a steep slope rising in several steps to about 600–800 ft. (200–250 m.) above the level of the lake – 700 ft. (212 m.) below sea level. A large littoral plain – the plain of Ginnosar – developed only at its northwest corner. This plain was created by the coalescence of deposits brought down from Eastern Galilee by several rivers (Arbel, Zalmon, Ammud).

Huleh Basin and Jordan Source Region. At least two subsequent lava flows, descending from the Golan Heights into the Rift Valley north of the present Kinneret Lake and consolidating there, formed a basalt sill that dammed up the flow of the Jordan southward. A result of this stoppage was the formation of a lake whose waters quickly reached a level higher than the sill and finally began to overflow it. This process resulted in the formation of a riverbed incised progressively deeper into the basalt block, and the lake eventually became greatly reduced in surface area and depth. This reduction was probably accomplished in a relatively short time because of the considerable difference in height between the floor of the basin and the surface of Lake Kinneret that must have existed before the up-damming. At present the difference in height amounts to about 900 ft. (270 m.) over a distance of only 10 mi. (17 km.) – the steepest gradient in the Jordan's course, giving it great erosive power, despite the hardness of the basaltic bedrock (as evidenced also by the steepness of the banks along the bed cut into it). The Ḥuleh Lake, which was small – about 5 sq. mi. (14 sq. km.) – and only about 20 ft. (6 m.) deep, and the adjacent Ḥulatah swamps, which occupied an area of about 12 sq. mi. (30 sq. km.) covered by papyrus and kindred hydrophilic plants and populated by waterfowl, buffalo, etc., represented the natural remnants of the former lakescape. Drained off by the lowering, widening, and straightening of the Jordan bed and by artificial channels dug through the marshy areas in the 1930s – uncovering soils extremely rich in organic matter and thick layers of peat – the region underwent one of the most pronounced anthropogenous landscape transformations within Ereẓ Israel. At present it is one of the most intensively cultivated areas in the country (with the exception of a small reservation where the former conditions are preserved); however, it faces the problem of surface subsidence due to the progressive shrinkage of its underground, caused by the draining off of its interstitial water contents into the channels.

North of the former swamp area and lake, which occupied the lowest part of the basin, the land surface gradually rises to the Hills of Metullah, interposed between the Naphtali Range in the west and the Golan Heights in the east. This region is characterized mainly by its many watercourses – the headrivers of the Jordan: namely, from west to east: the Senir (al-Ḥaṣbānī), Dan, and Hermon (Banias) Rivers. All these rivers, as well as several brooks that discharged independently into the Ḥulatah swamps – like the Ijon (ʿAyyūn), which drains the basin bearing the same name farther north – are fed mainly by spring waters. The springs are partly supplied by rainfall and snow melting on the Hermon and fed by subterranean conduits, created by solution. The three above-mentioned headrivers, of which the Senir has the longest course, beginning at the northwest base of the Hermon, flow in deeply incised, precipitously sloped valleys in beds with very irregular gradients, which at times become highly steep and form waterfalls. There are several waterfalls along the course of the Hermon River and some smaller ones along that of the Dan. The most impressive waterfall within Cisjordan, however, is the *Tannur* ("Chimney") of the Ijon River near Metullah.

The Hermon River first joins the Dan, and only some distance from their confluence with the Senir does the Jordan River begin its course in a single bed. Before the swamps were drained, this united flow continued for only a small distance, after which the flatness of the basin bottom and the marshes covering it caused a division of the Jordan's course into several indistinct branches that discharged into the swamps and contributed to their existence. Thus the Jordan proper, in terms of the continuity of the river, and the singleness of its bed, began only at its exit from the Ḥuleh Basin. All these conditions were essentially changed by the draining of the Ḥulatah swamps and the regulation of the river courses discharging into it. The numerous watercourses perennially flowing down from the Hermon foothills, the Golan Heights, and the Naphtali Range – totaling an average annual inflow of over 26 billion cu. ft. (about 740 million cu. m.) – and the abundant springs (among them the largest in Ereẓ Israel) impart to the source region of the Jordan hydrographic characteristics infrequently encountered in the Levant.

Ijon Region The 8.5 sq. mi. (22 sq. km.) basin of Ijon (Marj ʿAyyūn) which is situated within Lebanon, is separated from the Ḥuleh Basin by the Metullah Hills. It represents the northernmost portion of the Rift Valley drained by the Jordan, and also of the endoreic part of the Great Rift Valley System. The basin is over 1,600 ft. (500 m.) above sea level and it also is a tectonically conditioned depression. It is much smaller than the Ḥuleh Basin, with which it shares some properties, particularly its considerable marsh areas and associated vegetation. On its north the Rift Valley continues in the Beqa, which divides the Lebano-Syrian region into two main physiographical parts: a western one (Lebanon, Ansariye, Amanus Mountains) and an eastern one (Antilebanon, Syrian Plateau). In this area as well, both structure and hydrography are largely conditioned by the Rift, but drainage is essentially different from that of the Rift Valley within Ereẓ Israel: the two collecting trunk rivers (Leontes and Orontes) flow in opposite directions and discharge into the Mediterranean.

TRANSJORDAN. The other main part of Ereẓ Israel, Transjordan, comprises the regions east of the Rift Valley from the Gulf of Eilat in the south up to the Hermon and the Damascus Basin in the north. The eastern confines of Transjordan are not marked by any distinct relief features, and most of it gradually merges with the Syrian Desert. Thus only the zone adjacent to the Rift Valley, where the climate is still Mediterranean to semiarid and the water-courses discharge into the Rift Valley, may actually be regarded as the eastern part of Ereẓ Israel, according to its definition as a major natural unit. The zone averages only about 25 mi. (40 km.) in width and has always been politically, culturally, and economically connected with and dependent upon Cisjordan. The Rift Valley is more than just an external disconnection between Cisjordan and Transjordan. In spite of their spatial juxtaposition and the relatively narrow Rift Valley separating them, several differences, although not fundamental, do exist between these two areas. These differences pertain to lithology, tectonics, and consequently to surface features. Lithologically, almost all rock formations (except for the *kurkar* outcropping in Cisjordan) are present in Transjordan, although their areal distribution varies greatly. Formations that form the bedrock of relatively small surfaces in Cisjordan cover large areas in Transjordan, and vice versa. For example, basement rock of magmatic-metamorphic origin, found almost exclusively in the southernmost tip of Cisjordan (the Eilat Mountains), constitutes the surface of a large section of southern Transjordan, extending about 60 mi. (100 km.) north of the Gulf of Eilat. The same is true of Nubian Sandstone and various massive sediments of Paleozoic origin. Similarly, volcanic formations, which are of major importance as surface rock in Cisjordan only in Eastern Galilee, cover much larger areas of Transjordan. North of the Yarmuk they form the almost exclusive surface rock and create in the Bashan a volcanic region, also in all the morphological aspects. Volcanic formations are also widely distributed farther south in Transjordan, i.e., in regions whose counterparts in Cisjordan are almost entirely composed of calcareous rocks. Although the latter is also the most widely distributed type of rock in Transjordan, its predominance in Cisjordan is far more outstanding. These facts, together with studies of tectonic features (mainly the prominence and continuity of the fault lines bordering the Rift Valley to the east), have recently led to the following hypothesis: the formation of the Rift Valley, which continued through several geological ages, involved horizontal displacement and a northward movement of about 60 mi. (100 km.) of the eastern flank of the Rift Valley, whereas the western flank was apparently not affected by a similar movement.

The lithological conditions described above are indicative, albeit indirectly, of tectonic variances between Cisjordan and Transjordan. In Cisjordan, beginning with the Central Negev, folding played a decisive role in determining structure and relief; in Transjordan it appears to have been of subordinate importance, although large-scale up- and downwarping participated in the formation of the region. In the interior of Transjordan, faulting did not produce the basins and tectonic valleys so characteristic of Cisjordan, where it formed the most pronounced features, culminating in the valley sequence of Beth-Shean-Haifa Plain and a large number of small individual regions. In no part of Transjordan did faulting, subsidence, and uplifting influence small-scale relief as strongly as it did in the Galilees. In a general morphological sense, Transjordan can be defined as a plateau, very uniform in surface configuration and elevations. As no large intramontane basins exist there, lowlands covered by alluvial soils can be found only in Ghor, east of the Jordan. The ascent from the valley to the plateau is extremely steep, almost wall-like, interrupted only by the gorges of rivers exiting into the Rift Valley. These gorges are so narrow and steep that nowhere do they provide convenient access to the surfaces of the plateaus.

It is probable that together with the subsidence of the Rift Valley, its eastern flank was subject to strong uplifting, which particularly affected the immediately adjacent zone. This theory would explain why the eastern zone reaches great heights and gradually slopes down eastward at a small distance from Rift Valley. Only the western zone was transformed into a mountainous relief by numerous deeply incised rivers; eastward, as the elevation gradually becomes smaller and the relief flatter, or only gently undulating, the plateau character of the terrain becomes more marked. Further east, the surfaces generally rise again, forming a sort of a broad rise where the major rivers that cut into the plateau and discharge into the Rift Valley originate. Only at Edom does the rise become a mountainous range, from which the plateau gradually slopes down eastward to the large desert basins at the border between Transjordan and Arabian Desert and the riverine lowlands of the Euphrates. This configuration, which represents the general watershed zone between the Rift Valley and the Syro-Arabian Desert, extends only up to the Yarmuk River, beyond which the landforms are primarily volcanic in origin.

The most significant topographical feature of almost all regions of Transjordan is thus the tablelands, which attain greater heights than those facing them on the west. This feature is accentuated by summits several hundred meters higher than the highest ones in Cisjordan. As the highest parts of the plateau almost abut on the Rift Valley, only a relatively narrow zone is effectively exposed to the rain-bearing, mainly westerly winds. This zone is only 20–30 mi. (30–50 km.) wide (broadening considerably only in the Bashan) and its climate is Mediterranean, although the amounts of precipitation it receives exceed those of the opposite regions in Cisjordan only in the highest areas of Edom – 16 in. (400 mm.) as against 2–4 in. (50–100 mm.) in the Negev Highlands. Another significant difference between this part of Transjordan and the highlands of Cisjordan is that most of the main rivers of Transjordan carry flow throughout the year, mainly as a result of the deep valleys reaching aquiferous strata and a large number of springs that feed the rivers.

Climatic and topographic conditions strongly influence the prevalence and distribution of soil types. Due to the relatively smaller areas of limestones and the narrowness of the zone receiving at least 16 in. (400 mm.) mean annual precipitation, the cover of terra rossa is less extensive and continuous here than in Cisjordan. Rendzina soils, *ḥamra* soils, and loess are not found frequently here. In contrast, however, large areas, particularly north of the Yarmuk, are covered by heavy soils produced by the decomposition of volcanic rocks. Alluvial soils form a rather continuous belt on the Rift Valley floor along the course of the Lower Jordan, whereas on the plateau, due to the narrowness of the fluviatile valleys and the absence of intramontane basins, the distribution of alluvial soils is rather patchy. Farther east and south, yellow and gray soils, peculiar to desert-like conditions, become more extensive. Topographic and more extreme climatic conditions produced the natural vegetational cover in Transjordan, which is considerably different both in character and in spatial distribution from that in Cisjordan. Whereas in the latter, whole regions were covered in early historical times by forests, which persisted for many centuries, relatively small areas south of the Yarmuk, characteristically including the highest parts of Edom (Seir), seem to have been forested.

Transjordan may be subdivided physiographically into four main regions and a transitional one. These are, from south to north: Edom, Moab-Ammon, Gilead, and Bashan. The Hermon Massif (which, because of its position, orography, and particularly hydrography, morphotectonically constitutes a part of the Antilebanon system) forms the terminal and transitional arch between the two flanks of the endoreic Rift Valley.

Edom. Like its western counterpart, the Negev, Edom is the longest unit of Transjordan. No major natural feature distinguishes Edom from the northern part of the Arabian Peninsula (the biblical Midian), whereas, on the north the Zered (Ḥasaʾ) River – one of the major watercourses traversing the entire width of Transjordan and draining into the Dead Sea – forms a marked border between Edom and Moab. Nowhere else in Ereẓ Israel are basement rocks Paleozoic sediments, and particularly Paleo-Mesozoic Nubian Sandstone so widespread or exert such influence upon the landscape as in this region. Even the name Edom (red) is thought by some to be derived from the prevalent color of the granite and the predominant reddish-brown hues of the Nubian Sandstone. Farther east the formations are younger (up to Eocene) and the topography is progressively lower, so that structurally the area bears resemblance to a pan. This description applies particularly to the Maon (Maʿon, Maʿān) Basin in the central-eastern part of Edom, where this structure is strongly accentuated by a drainage pattern that converges centripetally toward its lowest part.

As in southern Sinai and the Eilat Mountains, the areas of crystalline rocks in Edom have serrated crenulated ridges and bold dome-shaped summits. The slopes of these ridges are very steep and their bases are buried in debris, mainly produced by weathering under arid conditions. The rock waste progressively fills up the valleys between the ridges and individual mountain blocks. Conversely, the parts composed mostly of horizontally bedded Nubian Sandstones form broad flat-topped ridges, frequently dissected into isolated blocks, mesas, and buttes (i.e., larger and smaller table-mountains, the uppermost beds of which consist of resistant rock that preserves the flatness of the surface). Their steep slopes are pitted by alveoli of various sizes and are strongly subject to disjointing, giving rise to pillar-like columns, mushroom rocks, etc. In contrast, the forms developed by the calcareous formations, which are far less subject to disintegration, usually appear massive, and generally exhibit characteristics of plateaus, mountain-like only where dissection by rivers was more intensive. The climate of Edom is like that of the Negev – as a whole arid. Nevertheless, several regions within it are still exposed to Mediterranean influence, due to their considerable height above sea level and still more – over 1,000 ft. (300 m.) on the average – above the Negev Highlands, which interpose between Edom and the sea. The mean annual precipitation on these summits therefore amounts to more than 12 in. (300 mm.), and even snow is frequent. The precipitation also accounts for the relatively dense drainage net, the rivers of which (with the exception of Zered) carry water only immediately following rain and in the form of flash floods. The great difference of elevation between the head areas of these rivers and the Arabah on the west and the topographical depressions (described later) into which the rivers discharge on the east endows them with very great erosive power, manifested in the deep, almost perpendicularly walled gorges and the very large debris fans at their mouths; these fans coalesce to form an almost continuous waste apron at the foot of slopes along the Arabah. Edom can be subdivided physiographically into the following three parts: Southern Edom, including the al-Ḥismā depression; Central Edom, generally referred to as the Seir (al-Sharaʾ), and including the Maon (Maʿān) Basin on the east; and Northern Edom, also called the Jebel (al-Jibāl) region.

Southern Edom The scarp slopes of the highland of Southern Edom rise abruptly above the Arabah. There are no major breaks in their continuity except for the valley exit of the al-Yitm River discharging into the Gulf of Eilat, which facilitated the construction of the only road (Akaba-Maʾon) traversing the entire width of the Edom Mountains. The plateau reaches heights of more than 5,000 ft. (1,500 m.) at a distance of no more than 6 mi. (10 km.) from the Rift Valley: Jebel Bāqir, 4,020 ft. (1,592 m.); Jebel al-Aḥmar, 5,220 ft. (1,588 m.). In Southern Edom the belt of basement rocks is the widest in all of Ereẓ Israel – about 12 mi. (20 km.) – as are the areas covered by sandstones. Within the latter zone lies the Ḥismā depression, an elongated, triangularly shaped, tectonically conditioned basin running northwest-southeast. It also contains the head-valley of the Yitm and merges gradually with the plateau of Midian. Considerably lower than the adjacent tableland, the floor of the basin contains a sequence of local depressions (sing. qāʿ) that become saline marshes in the rainy season. Many plateaus bordered by steep slopes – the remains of a former continuous table-mountain surface – still stand high above the basin floor but are subject to incessant reduction by weathering and fluviatile erosion. Notwithstanding its much higher elevation, climatic conditions in Southern Edom are generally similar to those of the southern Negev, as evidenced by the scarcity of soil and vegetational cover and the complete lack of permanent settlement throughout historical times.

Central Edom. The central part of Edom, also referred to as the Seir Mountains (al-Sharaʾ), represents the area's largest region in both meridional and east-west extension. It is, except for the Hermon, the highest land unit within Ereẓ Israel, with large surface areas exceeding 3,500–5,000 ft. (1,200–1,500 m.) in height and several summits above 5,500 ft. (1,700 m.). In contrast to Southern Edom the Seir Mountains proper appear as a continuous range towering high above the Rift Valley, only 12 mi. (20 km.) from their summit region, and sloping down far more gradually towards the east to the Basin of Maon. Relevant lithological differences also exist between Southern and Central Edom. Basement rocks in Central Edom are less widespread than Nubian Sandstones or Mesozoic calcareous rocks, and most significantly the belt of highest elevations extends along the zone of sedimentary formations. Structurally the area differs from Southern Edom by its greater frequency of fault lines, which greatly contributed to the prevailing pattern in the magmatic zone of isolated mountains and to the frequent interspersing of areas composed of magmatic-metamorphic rocks with those consisting of Nubian Sandstones and even of Mesozoic calcareous formations. The Seir Mountains form a very distinct watershed between the relatively short watercourses descending to the Arabah and those – far greater in number – discharging into the Maon Basin in a very pronounced concentric pattern. Due to the extremely steep gradient of the westward-flowing rivers and the prevalently hard bedrock into which they are incised, their valleys usually form very deep and narrow canyons, at times widening into small, intramontane, cirque-like basins (e.g., the Wadi Mūsā at Petra, accessible only through the spectacular al-Siq gorge).

Central Edom rises about 1,900 ft. (600 m.) higher than the Negev Highlands and thus receives relatively large amounts of precipitation, rather frequently in the form of snow. Consequently areas covered, albeit patchwise, by productive soils and vegetation are abundant in comparison with Southern Edom, particularly in the vicinity of the relatively numerous springs. These conditions allowed for the existence of some permanent settlements in the area throughout most historical times, the most important of which was Petra (near the Mūsā spring), the famous Nabatean center. A great deal of natural and historical evidence also leads to the conclusion that up to the first decade of the present century some parts of the Seir Mountains were forested. Toward the east the slopes of the Seir Mountains descend into the Maʾon Basin, which is enclosed on the north by large outcrops of volcanic rock. As most of the precipitation that falls on the Seir Mountains runs off into this basin, whose floor is wide and flat, the valleys descending into it become progressively wider and indistinct after forming vast fans at their entrance into the basin. The widespread deposits of large amounts of alluvia brought by the rivers created considerable tracts of cultivable soils, particularly in the vicinity of Maʾon (Maʿān) the capital of Edom, throughout history.

Northern Edom. Northern Edom, the Jebel (al-Jibāl) region, differs in many regards from Central Edom. Its mean elevation is considerably lower, although some summits still exceed 3,300 ft. (1,000 m.). There is no range-like alignment such as the Seir Mountains, but individual, small mountain bodies are separated by valleys, many of which have wide floors. The significant difference in lithology between the two areas is a major cause of this configuration. Crystalline rocks, widely distributed in the other parts of Edom and constituting the backbone of its structure, and the bulk of the ramparts sloping down to the Arabah occupy far smaller areas in Northern Edom than do sedimentary rocks. The scarp-slopes facing the Arabah consist mainly of Nubian Sandstone and are thus less steep than those composed of crystalline rocks. The greater erodibility of the Nubian Sandstone and certain other sedimentary rocks is also an important explanation for the relative prevalence of wide valleys in this area. The orientation of the valleys is largely determined by intensively developed and complex fault lines. Northern Edom also receives relatively considerable amounts of precipitation. Because of this factor, as well as the many springs, the wide valley floors, and the location, i.e., the relative proximity of the area to the core region of Transjordan (Gilead), Northern Edom became the most densely populated part of Edom.

Moab-Ammon. The Edom Highlands descend gradually to the valley of the Zered River (Wadi al-Ḥasa'), the first major river, deeply incised into aquiferous strata and draining a large catchment area – 675 sq. mi. (1,750 sq. km.) – far larger than any catchment area in Cisjordan. The Zered flows throughout the year, discharging into the Sodom Sabkhah (salt marsh), and its course traverses the whole width of the Transjordanian plateau south of the Dead Sea, with head rivers beginning as far as 45 mi. (70 km.) from the Rift Valley. The Moab-Ammon region is delimited on the north by the Jabbok (Nahr al-Zarqa') Valley – one of the most pronounced canyons in Transjordan. Morphologically, this area represents the most compact and homogeneous part of Transjordan. This effect seems mainly to be the result of lithological conditions, namely the prevalence of almost horizontally bedded sedimentary rock formations (sandstones and calcareous rocks) and larger areas of volcanic extrusions (even a major extinct volcano). The elevation of the plateau is relatively high, averaging 3,300 ft. (1,000 m.) with some summits exceeding 4,000 ft. (1,200 m.). Moab is separated from Ammon by the Heshbon (Ḥisbān) River and borders on the Dead Sea along its entire length. With the exception of the low, tabular Lashon Peninsula – morphogenetically a part of the Rift Valley floor – the plateau rises abruptly from the sea, with almost no intervening shore flats, so that it attains a height of 3,300 ft. (1,000 m.) at a distance of only 6–9 mi. (10–15 km.) from the Dead Sea in the southern portion of Moab and of 2,300 ft. (700 m.) at a distance of 6 mi. (10 km.) in the northern one. The ascent to the Ammon Plateau from the Jordan Valley bordering it on the west is much more gradual, although the mean elevation of Ammon is about 600 ft. (200 m.) greater than Moab.

The western parts of Moab and Edom – which are about 18 mi. (30 km.) wide – exhibit the main, albeit marginal, characteristics of the Mediterranean zone. Not only do relatively large amounts of precipitation – more than 24 in. (600 mm.) – fall on their higher parts, but the variations in the amounts of precipitation from year to year, so characteristic of the Edom, are far smaller. Due to the topography and the prevalence of calcareous surface rock, terra rossa and rendzina soils are relatively widely distributed and utilized. Also quite a large number of springs contribute to the perennial flow of the Arnon River, which drains most of Moab – 1,650 sq. mi. (4,460 sq. km.) – and subdivides the region into southern and northern Moab (almost equal in size). Similar hydrographical conditions are responsible for the perennial flow of the Zarqā', Mā'īn, and Heshbon rivers. Topographic and climatic conditions and the considerable areas of cultivable soils, which in the past even produced grain surpluses, were reasons for the area being densely populated in comparison with the southern regions, a large percentage of the population being concentrated in several townships. One of these Rabbath-Ammon (Amman), the capital of the present Hashemite Kingdom of Jordan, is connected to Jerusalem by a highway via Jericho. Kerak (Kir Moab), the principal town of Moab, Madeba, and most of the nearby villages lie along the highway running almost straight and parallel to the Dead Sea coast at a small distance from the prevalently wide watershed between the rivers draining into the Rift Valley and those discharging to the east.

Gilead. The Jabbok (Zarqā') River – after the Yarmuk the most important tributary of the Jordan – whose catchment area is about 1,100 sq. mi. (3,000 sq. km.), with about 2 million cu. ft. (70 million cu. m.) mean annual discharge, divides Gilead from Ammon. Gilead represents one of the largest regions of Transjordan south of the Yarmuk, not so much because of its length – which, between the Jabbok and Yarmuk rivers, is 46 mi. (75 km.) – as by its width, which averages 35 mi. (60 km.). It exhibits some morphotectonic similarities to the central mountains of Cisjordan due to the influence exerted upon its morphogenesis by fold structures and by its mountainous appearance, resulting from relatively intensive dissection by rivers. The larger and higher southern part of the region is traversed by four major, perennially flowing tributaries of the Jordan: Rājib, Kafranjī, Yābis (Jabesh), and Siqlāb. In the northern part, which is only about 1,600 ft. (600 m.) high and is drained only by the Arab River, the relief is far less pronounced. The east-west oriented valleys of the rivers and of their many confluents – which are increasingly numerous farther east – give rise to a landscape of mainly short, interfluvial ranges composed of rounded hills whose slopes are terraced to a considerable extent. These ranges do not attain great heights; the highest summit in Gilead, Umm al-Daraj, is somewhat less than 4,100 ft. (1,250 m.). This configuration also reflects the prevalent lithological and climatic conditions. The southern part of Gilead is composed of mainly Cenomanian-Turonian calcareous formations, whereas in the northern one, younger (Senonian-Eocene), generally less resistant strata form the bedrock. Immediately south of the Yarmuk there are several outcrops of volcanic rocks – outliers of the Bashan basalt cover.

Despite its considerably lower elevation (than more southerly regions of Transjordan), Gilead receives the relatively largest amounts of precipitation – more than 20 in. (500 mm.) annual mean on most of the area, whereas in the highest regions in the south precipitation amounts to about 28 in. (700 mm.). Moreover, the 16 in. (400 mm.) isohyet, still the most useful means of delineating regions of Mediterranean-type from those of semiarid climate, runs here at a distance of about 30 mi. (50 km.) from the Rift Valley. Consequently, soils (mainly of terra rossa type) are rather common and extensively cultivated here, which again accounts for the population throughout history being much more dense than in other parts of Transjordan. There is strong evidence that considerable parts of Gilead were forested in the past. The area is relatively easily accessible from the Rift Valley, particularly along the Siqlāb Valley, where the gentle relief near the watershed greatly facilitates communication along the entire length of the region. The divide conditioned the site of a relatively large number of townships (ʿAjlūn in the south and Irbid in the north are the most important) and villages situated along or near the meridional highway and at the springs, particularly abundant in the plateau parts adjacent to the Rift Valley. In the past, Gilead was the region most closely connected with Cisjordan historically, particularly during the Roman era, when Geresh (Gerasha; Ar. Jarash), Arbel (Irbid), and Gadera (Umm Qays) formed part of the Dekapolis.

Bashan. The deeply incised valley of the Yarmuk, the second largest river of Ereẓ Israel – with a catchment area about 2,670 sq. mi. (7,250 sq. km.) – forms a prominent natural border between central Transjordan and its northern region, Bashan. The latter covers about 4,600 sq. mi. (12,000 sq. km.) and differs in almost all physiographical aspects, primarily in morphotectonics and lithology, from the regions south of the Yarmuk. The landscapes of Bashan were formed mainly by volcanic activities that probably persisted from the Pliocene up to prehistoric times. Consequently, almost the whole of the Bashan is covered by extrusive rocks, in many places attaining a thickness of several hundreds of meters. The relief is also determined by these activities, which resulted primarily in vast plains built of consolidated lava sheets that are overtopped by elevations of eruptive origin. Large parts of the terrain still exhibit the characteristics of block fields. Others are covered by heavy soils formed through the decomposition of the basaltic bedrock or from the disintegration of the volcanic tuff. Since the Bashan is the northernmost region of Transjordan, and because its eastern most part is considerably high, the Mediterranean type of climate prevails over an area two to three times wider and extending far further east than the regions having a similar climate south of the Yarmuk. Topographically, Bashan can be subdivided into three major regions: Golan, Bashan Plain, and Hauran.

Golan. The plateau of Golan, situated between the Hermon Massif and the Upper Jordan Valley on the west and the Ruqqād River (a tributary of the Yarmuk) on the east, is only about 15 mi. (25 km.) wide. Its continuous steep slopes rise abruptly above the Ḥuleh Basin and are even steeper in the region of the sources of the Jordan, attaining heights of 3,300 ft. (1,000 m.) at a distance of only about 9 mi. (15 km.) from the latter. Morphotectonically the Golan represents a plateau of lava sheets whose prevalent flatness is accentuated by a number of isolated cones rising without any transitional forms above the vast surrounding plain. These cones are composed mainly of volcanic cinder and extend in a more or less straight line from north to south. This orientation indicates their causal connection with a meridionally running fissure system, along which they originated at spots where lava extrusions and cinder ejections were more intensive, persistent, or recent. The most pronounced of these cones are Tell al-Sheikha, about 4,000 ft. (1,300 m.) high, in the northern part of Golan and Tell Abu Nidāʾ, which contains a crater with a circumference of about 2½ mi. (4 km.), followed by lesser ones (Tell Abu Khanzīr, Tell Yūsuf, and Tell Faras) in the south. In the northern part of Golan a small shallow lake of almost perfect oval shape, Birkat Rām, was in ancient times thought to be one of the sources of the Jordan connected with the Banias Spring by subterranean conduits. It is not, however, a crater lake – as was also formerly assumed, as a part of its enclosure consists of sedimentary rock – but is probably a depression produced by subsidence of pyroclastic material.

According to topographic and surface-rock conditions, two main subregions can be distinguished in the Golan Plateau: a higher, northern one, adjacent to the Hermon, and a considerably lower, south part, consistently sloping down to the Yarmuk Valley. Volcanic cones and extensive block fields with intermittent soil and plant cover characterize the former, whereas most of the surface of the latter is covered by extensively utilized heavy basaltic and tuff soils. Golan receives comparatively large amounts of precipitation, exceeding 32 in. (800 mm.) annual mean in some areas; consequently, large tracts were once covered by forests. Because of the amount of precipitation and the relative impermeability of the bedrock, it has a rather dense net of watercourses, although few of them flow perennially. The northern part of this net drains into the Jordan through a series of almost equidistant and parallel valleys. These are not yet incised deeply in the plateau proper and form gorges only at their entrance into the Rift Valley, where they can erode the far less resistant calcareous formations underlying the plateau basalts. A large part of the southern Golan belongs to the catchment area of the Yarmuk and is drained mainly by the deeply incised Ruqqād and its affluents. The western portion drains into Lake Kinneret in a series of short watercourses, the most important of which is the Samak River.

Bashan Plain. The largest and lowest regional unit of the Bashan – as indicated by its current Arabic name, al-Nuqra ("The Hollow"), the Bashan Plain is situated between the Golan Highlands on the west and the still higher Hauran Massif on the east. The plain is about 40 mi. (60 km.) wide and it is not uniform in elevation. Its slopes descend gradually both from north to south and from east to west where they abut on the Hauran. Unlike in the Golan, no volcanic cones were formed here, but the same difference exists between its northern and southern parts. The former contains large expanses of lava-block fields, whereas the latter exhibits an almost continuous cover of volcanic soils, which rendered the region one of the granaries of the Mediterranean lands in ancient times. Although it is on the leeward side of the Golan Heights, the

Bashan Plain still receives an annual mean precipitation exceeding 16 in. (400 mm.) and its main rivers, Wadi ʿAllān and Wadi al-Iḥrayr, affluents of the Yarmuk, flow perennially.

Hauran. In the eastern part of Bashan, Hauran (the ancient Auranitis, now usually referred to as Jebel al-Druze), relief forms originating in volcanic activities are the most pronounced within Ereẓ Israel. This oval-shaped massif, about 60 mi. (100 km.) long from south to north and 25–30 mi. (40–50 km.) wide, is mainly composed of extinct volcanoes, many of which contain craters and rise to heights above 5,500 ft. (1,700 m.) – the highest summit is Tell al-Janynā, 5,900 ft. (1,800 m.). The massif exhibits two main levels: a lower – up to 4,500 ft. (1500 m.) – comprising most of its southern portion; and a northern portion – 650 ft. (200 m.) higher, in which the relief forms are also much bolder. Due to its height, the Hauran still receives considerable quantities of precipitation, and snowfall is frequent in winter. On the north and east the Hauran Massif is surrounded by lava deserts called *al-ḥarra* in the vernacular. They consist of consolidated "ropy" lava, which forms labyrinth-like serrated ridges of blocks separated by oblong depressions. Only the northwestern lava field, al-Lijaʾ (the ancient Trachonitis), is at least historically connected with Ereẓ Israel.

Hermon. Morphotectonically, the Hermon Massif, the main source area of the Jordan and the northernmost element of the endoreic Rift Valley within Ereẓ Israel, is the southernmost part of the Antilebanon upfold system, strongly affected by faulting, uplifted along their lines, and thus turned into a pronounced horst structure. It is separated from the Antilebanon proper by the Valley of Zabadānī, where the source springs of the Barada River issue. This river irrigates the Ghūṭa (oasis) of Damascus. Composed predominantly of calcareous Jurassic strata, it forms an oblong dome-like mountain block whose three main summits rise to heights of 6,760 ft. (2,465 m.), 7,720 ft. (2,810 m.), and 7,350 ft. (2,680 m.) respectively. It exhibits a rather subdued topography of rounded summits separated by wide and flat saddles. Although the area receives a mean annual precipitation of more than 60 in. (1,500 mm.) and snow cover persists on its higher parts until August, its surfaces have not yet been affected by river erosion, with the consequent formation of deeply incised valleys and associated slopes, nor does it seem to have been glaciated in the Pleistocene as has been assumed.

BIBLIOGRAPHY: *Atlas of Israel* (1970); E. Orni and E. Efrat, *Geography of Israel* (1980[4]); D. Ashbel, *Bio-Climatic Atlas of Israel* (1948); C.R. Conder and H.H. Kitchener, *Survey of Western Palestine* (1881–83): K.O. Emery and D. Neev, in: *Bulletin Geological Survey of Israel*, 26 (1960), 1–13; M.G. Ionides, *Report on the Water Resources of Transjordan and their Development* (1940); Y. Karmon, *The Northern Huleh Valley* (1956); L. Picard, in: *Bulletin Geological Department Hebrew University Jerusalem*, 4 (1943), 1–134; A.M. Quennel in: *Proceedings of the Geological Society London* (1954), 14–20; I. Schattner, in: *Scripta Hierosolymitana*, 11 (1962), 1–123; G.A. Smith, *Historical Geography of the Holy Land* (1931[25]).

[Isaac Schattner]

Climate

INTRODUCTION. Ereẓ Israel is situated between subtropical arid (Egypt) and subtropical wet (Lebanon) zones. This location helps to explain the great climatic contrast between the light rainfall in the south and the heavy rainfall in the north in all three orographic belts: Coastal Plain, Western Mountain Ridge and Jordan Valley. In the rainy season the centers of the barometric depressions crossing the eastern Mediterranean from the west normally pass over Cyprus. Most of Egypt and southern Ereẓ Israel lie in and partly outside this area of cloudiness and precipitation, whereas northern Ereẓ Israel is nearer to the center of the vortex. The cyclonic depressions of the eastern Mediterranean are usually smaller, both in area and in axis length, than the Atlantic depressions. The difference in pressure between the center and the periphery does not exceed 10–13 millibars, with differences between highs and lows not exceeding 17–20 mb. Pressure gradients in winter storms in Ereẓ Israel, however, are just as steep as those in Europe or America.

In the winter, depressions arrive in Ereẓ Israel from the west along two trajectories. The first, of decisive influence on the climate of the country, comes from northern Italy along the Adriatic Sea to Greece and the Aegean Sea. There it divides into two sections, one leading to the Black Sea and the other to Syria. The second leads from southern Italy and Sicily to the central Mediterranean and thence to the southeastern corner of the Mediterranean and Ereẓ Israel. A rare path extends along the North African coast through Egypt to Ereẓ Israel. Depressions sometimes pass along a narrow belt from the Red Sea northward and cause sudden cloudbursts accompanied by torrential floods in the normally dry Sinai Desert, Negev, Jordan Valley, and Syrian Desert. Mediterranean depressions are prevalent in the eight months from October until early June, when cold air penetrates from Eastern Europe through the Balkans to the Mediterranean, influencing the activity of the depressions. Rainfall in the eastern Mediterranean, including Ereẓ Israel, is directly related to the intensity of cold airstreams over Eastern Europe in the winter. The lower the temperatures fall in Eastern Europe, the stronger the influence of the cold airstreams on the depressions moving into the eastern Mediterranean. A narrow belt of high pressure descends from the Balkans and pushes depressions lying to the east. If, simultaneously, a second area of high pressure zones, connected to the great Siberian winter high-pressure system, extends over northern Iraq and Turkey, the activity of the eastern Mediterranean depression increases. Depressions are followed by high pressures, normally centered over northern Syria and Turkey, which are usually connected to the winter anticyclones of central Asia. In such cases, cold air descends from the high mountains of Armenia, which, though warming in descent – sometimes through tens of degrees – is often cold enough upon reaching Israel to cause freezing and frost. Visibility is exceptional. Snowcapped Mt. Hermon and the mountains of Lebanon are then visible from Mt. Carmel – a distance of 60 mi. (100 km.) – and even from Tel Aviv and high points west of Jerusalem – over 100 mi. (nearly 180 km.) away. Barometric pressures are higher in winter than in summer, being low only on stormy days. The difference between winter and summer pressures is smaller in Ereẓ Israel than in Turkey or Iraq.

Lower summer pressures result from Ereẓ Israel's location on the western periphery of the extensive low-pressure system of southern Asia, which causes the Indian monsoon. There is a summer monsoon in Ereẓ Israel too, though it is not accompanied by the heavy precipitation typical of Indian monsoons. The latter, however, affect summer conditions in Ereẓ Israel. Normal monsoons in India result in normal summers in Ereẓ Israel; insufficient pressure gradients and abnormal Indian monsoons cause "abnormal summers" in Ereẓ Israel and the entire eastern Mediterranean. In a normal summer, strong, humid, westerly and northwesterly sea breezes prevail continuously for weeks or months, resulting in extensive dew formation. These are the "etesian winds" known to the ancient Greeks. Other airstreams arise only in the transition months of spring and fall, arriving chiefly from the hot and dry deserts in the east. These are the *ḥamsin* (or *sharav*) winds (see below). *Sharav* winds from July to October are abnormal in summer, indicating undeveloped Indian monsoons.

CLOUDINESS. The frequency of depressions between October and May and their scarcity or total absence between June and September result in marked differences in cloud forms. Between October and May, or sometimes even June, all forms of high, medium, and low clouds occur. In summer only low clouds form through condensation of marine air currents ascending the mountain slopes. Toward the end of September, high ice clouds, then medium, and finally water-laden low cumulus clouds form. Summer clouds are also of the cumulus type, but they are higher than winter clouds. In summer low clouds also approach from the west, carrying more humidity than in winter, but they do not cause rain, lacking ice crystals and the necessary conditions for rainfall. Over high mountains, such as Mt. Hermon and the Lebanon range to the north, these summer clouds reduce penetration of the sun's rays. An afternoon mist that rises from the sea mostly covers the western, seaward slopes and valleys. Clouds over the mountains of Ereẓ Israel at night are very low, while during the day they occur at altitudes of 6,500–10,000 ft. (2–3 km.). Mist clouds are found in mountain valleys on summer mornings and disappear after sunrise. In Upper Galilee summer cloudiness exceeds that in the south, and morning mists are more prevalent. In the winter, cloudiness in the mountains exceeds that in the coastal region; the opposite is true in summer. The Jordan Valley differs from the rest of the country in this respect as few clouds occur even in winter.

There are no completely overcast days in summer: a quarter of the summer days are partly cloudy; the rest are completely clear. Mist occurs in the Coastal Plain in winter and the transition months. In the inland valleys, such as the Jezreel Valley, mists occur mostly in summer. Heavy morning fogs cover the coast on *sharav* days, while morning mists in inland valleys are the result of temperature inversion. Low places in the Jezreel Valley have mist on clear winter mornings and on summer mornings with no easterly wind. Unique fogs rise in the winter from the Ḥuleh Basin and the Dead Sea. The former is covered by heavy mists on cold nights; over the latter, fogs form after sunrise in the wake of depressions, when cold air flows in pushing the local air up the slopes of the Judean Mountains in the west and the Moab Mountains in the east. After sunrise, these fogs ascend to the mountains tops, over altitude differences of 4,000–5,000 ft. (1,200–1,500 m.). They reach Jerusalem late in the morning, thicken toward noon, and scatter in the late afternoon, though they sometimes remain until evening or even throughout the night. Fogs do not cross the mountain crests to the west, but remain stationary in the strong westerly wind as a westward-pointed wedge hundreds of meters thick.

RADIATION. Ereẓ Israel is a sunny country because of its location in the subtropical zone, its low degree of cloudiness, and its extensive desert areas. In the long summer days the sun ascends to over 80° above the horizon, and radiation reaches the ground in 98% of all potential hours of sunshine; in the winter the sky is cloudy, on the average, through half the day. The annual mean daily radiation is 5 million calories on each square meter. On a summer day it is about 7.5 million, on a clear winter day 3 million, and on a cloudy winter day 1 million. Few countries can compete with Ereẓ Israel in abundance of sunshine. Horizontal surfaces receive illumination of some 90 kilo-lux-hours at noon in summer, and an area perpendicular to the sun's rays receives over 130 k.l.h., nearly the absolute maximum the sun can provide. These quantities are reduced by one-third in the winter. Southern slopes as well as southern-oriented walls and rooms receive the greatest amount of sunshine in the winter. In other directions, no marked differences exist between the various seasons.

RAIN. Rainfall normally begins in Ereẓ Israel in November, increases in intensity to about January-February, and decreases again to May, which is sometimes completely dry. First rains sometimes fall earlier and sometimes later. Likewise, the rainy season may end before Purim (March), though small quantities of rain may fall until Shavuot (around the end of May). Most of the rainfall, some 72% of the seasonal total, occurs in December, January, and February. Five types of yearly rainfall can be discerned: (1) normal, with even distribution; (2) rainy in early winter and dry in its second half; (3) dry in early winter and rainy later; (4) heavy rains in the middle of winter with relatively dry early and late seasons; (5) twin – (or even multiple) – peaked season, with dry intervals between peaks. The first type occurs in Jerusalem in about 33% and in Haifa in some 42% of the winters. The second type is found in Jerusalem and the Judean Mountains in about 20% of the winters and only in 6% in northern Israel.

The third type is more frequent in the north (31% in Haifa) than in the south (13% in Jerusalem). The fourth type is rare, occurring in 2–3% of all years. The fifth type is most frequent in the Judean Mountains (35%), with some 24% in Haifa. Regional differences in rainfall are much larger in Ereẓ Israel than in other countries of comparable size. In Israel there is an absolute desert with under 1.2 in. (30 mm.) rain per annum – the Arava: semi-desert areas with 2–3 in. (50–75 mm.) to 6–8 in. (150–200 mm.) – the Negev and Dead Sea Valley; agricultural regions with 12–18 in. (300–600 mm.): and mountain areas with 20–32 in. (500–800 mm.) in Judea and Samaria and up to 44 in. (1,100 mm.) in Upper Galilee. Mountains receive more rain than the Coastal Plain or the Jezreel Valley. Amounts of rainfall increase from south to north in all regions: the Coastal Plain, the western and eastern mountain ridges, and the Jordan Valley. Similarly, the number of rainy days in northern Ereẓ Israel exceeds that in the south. In dry years both the amount of rain and the number of rainy days are reduced; in very wet years both may be doubled. Most cultivated areas are those with over 12 in. (300 mm.) rainfall per annum. Contrary to common belief, the amount of rainfall in agricultural areas in Ereẓ Israel is no less than that in agricultural countries in the temperate zones. The difference lies not in the annual amount of rain, but in the number of rainy days and in the intensity of rain per hour or per day. In Ereẓ Israel the entire annual amount falls in 40 to 60 days in a season of seven to eight months. In temperate climates precipitation occurs on 180 days spread over 12 months.

DEW. The formation and amount of dew are dependent both on meteorological conditions – relative humidity and nocturnal cooling – and on the properties of the cooling surfaces – soil and vegetation. The regional distribution of the number of dew nights and the amount of dew is greatly diverse. Richest in dew are the northwestern Negev and the western and central Jezreel Valley, followed by the Coastal Plain from Gaza to Binyaminah. The central Ḥuleh Basin and parts of the lower Beth-Shean Valley also have large amounts of dew. The Golan and the Naphtali Mountain slopes, which are dry on most nights of the year, surround them. Hilly coast regions (Mt. Carmel), regions near the mountains (Western Galilee), and the Jezreel Valley have smaller amounts of dew and fewer dew nights per month and per year. Still smaller is the amount of dew in the mountains of Jerusalem and Galilee. The eastern slopes of the mountain ridge descending into the Jordan Valley, as well as the western foothills, receive smaller and sometimes negligible amounts of dew. The Carmel foothills and those of western Galilee, Ephraim, and Judea have almost no dew at all. The mean annual number of dew nights exceeds 200 in the entire Coastal Plain and the Jezreel Valley and 250 in the northwestern Negev. The mountains have only 150–180 dew (and fog) nights per year; the western foothills have 100, and the Jordan Valley (excluding lower Beth-Shean Valley and central Ḥuleh Basin) has fewer than 50. An abundance of dew is important for agriculture and settlement. For example, as a result of the dew formation on most summer nights, the vicinity of Khan Yunis in the western Negev, which receives only scanty winter rainfall, is a center for growing watermelons, a typical summer crop. Unirrigated summer field crops (sorghum, corn, and sesame) can be grown only in areas with sufficient dew.

SNOW. In certain mountain areas snow is a normal occurrence. Mountains of 2,500–4,000 ft. (800–1,000 m.), such as those of Hebron and the Upper Galilee – elevation 4,000–5,500 ft. (1,300–1,700 m.) – have snow nearly every year. Mt. Hermon, rising to some 10,000 ft. (3,000 m.) above sea level, receives most of its precipitation as snow, which feeds a relatively large number of perennial streams. Most snow falls in Ereẓ Israel in January or February, but it has been known to occur in November and December and even in March and April. The heaviest snowfall recorded in Jerusalem in the last century was 38 in. (97 cm.) in February 1920.

TEMPERATURE. Air temperature depends on elevation and distance from the sea. Valleys have higher, mountains lower mean temperatures; the higher the location, the lower the air temperature. The highest temperatures are recorded in the Rift Valley, a few hundred meters below sea level, with peak temperatures in the Arava, south of the Dead Sea. The lowest mean temperature is found in Upper Galilee. The mean annual temperature in the coastal regions is 68°–70° F (20°–21° C) with differences between coastal plains that are near mountains and coastal plains that are not. Haifa has lower temperatures than Acre, Netanyah or Tel Aviv. Coastal temperatures vary only slightly in summer, and even in winter their fluctuations are smaller than elsewhere. The Maximum temperatures in summer are not high and winter minima not very low. Fluctuations increase with the distance from the sea; the maximum rises and the minimum decreases markedly. The annual mean temperature is 3° C lower in Jerusalem than in Tel Aviv – difference in elevation 2,624 ft. (800 m.) – but in the winter the difference is larger.

The annual means in the Jezreel Valley and the Coastal Plain are similar, but monthly fluctuations inland, as well as differences between maximums and minimums, are larger than on the coast. Temperatures are lower in the Ḥuleh Basin than around Lake Kinneret or the Dead Sea. The mean annual temperature at the southern end of the Dead Sea is 78.3° F (25.7° C); at the northern end, 74.3° F (23.4° C); at Tirat Ẓevi 71.6° F (22.0° C); and at Kinneret, 72.1° F (22.3° C). The annual mean in the Ḥuleh Basin is similar to that on the coast – 67.8° F (19.9° C) – though the extremes differ widely. Great climatic differences are hidden by a similarity of mean annual temperatures; evaluation of climatic conditions must also take into account the extremes of diurnal cycles and of hourly differences.

DIURNAL CYCLE. Regional differences are most outstanding in the daily temperature cycle. On the coast temperatures reach their maximum values long before noon. The sea breeze prevents any further increase and the temperature remains almost constant until late afternoon. A flat ridge thus replaces the temperature peak. The same is true of the minimum at night, which lasts for several hours after midnight. But, with increasing distance from the sea, both maximal and minimal temperatures decrease in duration. In the Jordan Valley the diurnal cycle is different. Near the northern Dead Sea in the summer there are two peaks. There is an early morning and a late afternoon maximum near the Dead Sea. At Ein Gev on Lake Kinneret the two daily peaks are less developed but still quite prominent. Along the entire Jordan Valley the afternoon peak in temperature results from the adiabatic warming of the westerly wind that descends from the western mountain ridge into the deep Jordan depression. On the southern shore of the Dead Sea the cycle is similar to that near the Mediterranean coast, but the basis temperature values are entirely different. The mountains to the west of this area are not as high and adiabatic heating of the descending air does not increase the temperature above that prevailing locally. The shallow water at the southern end of the Dead Sea has an equalizing effect on daytime temperatures and also maintains high values at night.

HEAT WAVES. A *ḥamsin*, or heat wave, occurs when depression approaches Israel from the west, with easterly winds backing first to south and later to west. It is broken when cool and humid maritime air replaces the hot air; when this occurs temperatures may fall by 45° F (20° C) or more. During a *ḥamsin* the temperature always rises and the humidity decreases. In midwinter, clear days with temperatures rising by 10° C or more in a day are a pleasant phenomenon. Such a temperature rise in spring or fall, however, is far from pleasant, since air temperature may reach body temperature. Mountains are hit first by a heat wave and, although temperature rises are relatively small, it is felt strongly because it lasts longer than in the valleys near sea level. When a *ḥamsin* reaches the valleys temperatures are always higher than in the mountains and reach the absolute maxima recorded in Ereẓ Israel. In May and June and in October and November there are often such severe days with high temperatures. But they may occur in the rainy season, with its centers of low and high pressure arriving from the west.

Another type of *ḥamsin* develops with rising barometric pressure under anticyclonic conditions. A northeasterly wind, turning easterly, blows toward the area from a center of high pressure over Iraq, Syria, and sometimes also Turkey. Such a strong east wind in winter is referred to in the Bible as *kadim* (e.g., Ex. 10:13; Ps. 48:8; Jonah 4:8). Owing to the very low humidity, the air is very clear. At first the temperature is low, but it rises daily while the air becomes both dry and hazy. When pressure begins to fall, the conditions are similar to those occurring in a depression *ḥamsin*, but an anticyclonic *ḥamsin* is not only as hard to bear, but it is often stationary and of longer duration. The action of the sun's rays is weakened during such days, and there is only a slight wind. Humans and other warm-blooded creatures feel unwell because the normal functioning of the body's cooling processes are impaired. Delicate winter plants wither in a spring *ḥamsin* because high evaporation causes excessive loss of moisture and the winter green vanishes as if by magic. The *ḥamsin* is harder to bear near the coast than in the mountains, chiefly because of the high relative humidity of the hot air, which prevents the evaporation of perspiration.

COLD WAVES Every barometric depression is followed by a high-pressure system generally centered over Syria or Turkey. Air flowing in from the northeast usually comes from Siberia in winter, reaching Ereẓ Israel after some warming over the mountains of Armenia, Iran, and Turkey, or, if coming from the north, northwest, or west, over the Black and Mediterranean seas. Such cold waves bring air at a temperature of 14°–19° F (-7° to -10° C) to the Euphrates Valley and 23° F (-5° C) in the Transjordanian Mountains. Each cold wave from the east penetrates first into the Jordan Valley before reaching the Western mountain ridge. In such cases, temperatures near the Dead Sea start to fall some 12 hours earlier than in Jerusalem. The danger of frost in winter is thus greater in the northern Jordan Valley than in the western valleys or the Coastal Plain.

TEMPERATURE EXTREMES. The highest temperature ever recorded in Israel was 131° F (54° C, Tirat Ẓevi, Beth-Shean Valley, June 1942). On the same day the temperature was 122° F (51.5° C) at the Dead Sea, 113° F (45° C) on the Coastal Plain, and 118° F (48° C) in the Jezreel Valley. In the mountains, temperatures exceeding 111° F (44° C) have not been recorded for the past 100 years. In most heat waves, temperatures rise to 110°–113° F (43°–45° C) in the Jordan Valley and 97°–100° F (36°–38° C) on the Coastal Plain; 100° F (38° C) is considered very hot for the mountains. The lowest temperature recorded in Jerusalem in the past 100 years was 19.4° F (−7° C). Even in the Jordan Valley 28°–32° F (-2° to 0° C) was repeatedly recorded. The Coastal Plain, however, seems to be immune to frosts; only twice on record did temperatures fall below freezing. In early 1950, all of northern and central Ereẓ Israel down to the Mediterranean was covered by snow.

HUMIDITY. The relative humidity of the air is highest near the coast and higher at night in summer than in winter. Humidity reaches its daily minimum around noon. Mountain areas are drier, and the humidity there in winter exceeds that in summer, in spite of the dry easterly winds. Conditions in the Jezreel Valley are similar to those near the coast, with high nocturnal humidity in summer. Humidity is lowest in the Rift Valley, especially in the Arava, and around the Dead Sea. The Dead Sea has higher humidity at the northern end than at the southern end; but the diurnal cycle is different at each end. In all areas the daily cycle is simple, with a minimum at noon and a maximum late at night or throughout the night. At the northern end, however, the relative humidity rises to its maximum at noon in summer when the Dead Sea breeze lowers the temperature. In the afternoon and near sunset, when temperatures reach a maximum, the humidity is minimal due to the western breeze that warms up while descending into the valley.

Absolute humidity in the valleys is higher than in the mountains. The Coastal Plain not only has a high relative but also a high absolute humidity, which causes physical discomfort in summer. Absolute humidity near the Mediterranean is similar to that near the Dead Sea, or even exceeding the latter in summer, although temperatures near the coast are lower. In the Beth-Shean Basin the absolute humidity is also high because of the very high summer temperatures. Since a low humidity facilitates evaporation of perspiration, conditions in the mountains are more pleasant.

WINDS. Simple wind conditions prevail on the Coastal Plain. In summer, a sea breeze blows all day and a land breeze blows at night. Wind conditions on clear winter days are similar to those in the summer, but when a barometric depression covers the sea, easterly winds blow at first, slowly backing to the south and southwest. These winds bring clouds and sometimes rain from the sea, until northerly winds disperse the clouds and the sky clears. In summer northwesterly winds blow over the mountains for weeks and even months on end. The strength of the wind rises from near calm in the morning to a maximum in the late afternoon. Local winds are rare in the mountains, where mainly regional winds blow. These winds are dependent upon pressure distribution around centers of high or low pressure. Local winds occur in summer around the lakes of the Jordan Valley as well as near the Mediterranean. The latter receives the sea breeze throughout the day, while the inland lakes generate land breezes only at certain hours. This is a result of the Mediterranean breeze neutralizing all local activity on reaching the Jordan Valley, so that even the lakes become involved in the general climatic conditions. The landward breeze from the lakes is of biological importance in the hot season. The Mediterranean's sea breeze generally has a cooling effect; but upon descending into the valleys lying hundreds of meters below the surrounding mountains and even below sea level, the breeze undergoes such a rise in temperature that, instead of cooling, it heats the area. In summer the westerly winds in the entire Jordan Valley are thus hot and dry. The biological cooling effect of the westerly winds in the Jordan Valley seems to vary. A moist and perspiring body is cooled by it; but upon drying, only the effect of moving air remains, imparting a false sensation of cooling.

Weak winds prevail in the Coastal Plain, the Jezreel Valley, and the Negev. The mountains and the Rift Valley, especially the southern Arava, experience strong winds. Average wind force is higher in summer than in winter throughout the country; but in a winter storm, velocities in January and February equal or surpass those in the summer. Isolated cases of high winds in winter often lead to a general impression of high winter averages. Wind speeds may reach 50 mph. (80 kph.) and even more in winter, but between storms near calm may prevail. In summer, on the other hand, strong winds blow regularly at certain hours. While these are not as strong as the winter storms, summer averages are generally higher than winter ones. In the Manarah ridge in Upper Galilee, e.g., winds of "winter force" blow on summer days, especially at dusk. The diurnal cycle of wind strength in the mountains reaches its maximum in the afternoon, and on the coast and in the Jezreel Valley at noon. Mornings are usually calm in most areas of the country, as are nights, except in the mountains and the southern Arava.

HISTORY OF CLIMATE RESEARCH IN ISRAEL. Scientific climate research in Palestine started in the mid-19th century. The first instruments for weather observation were used at the English Hospital in Jerusalem in 1845, where regular observations were taken until World War I. The records of the first 14 years have been lost, but those for 1860–1913 have been preserved intact. The Scottish Mission also took observations at various places, which were supervised from 1860 by the Palestine Exploration Fund and its meteorologist, G. Glaisher (until 1903). M. Blanckenhorn took meteorological observations for the Deutscher Palaestina-Verein from the mid-1890s.

The first results of these observations are assembled in F.M. Exner's work *Zum Klima von Palaestina* (1910), including the first rainfall map of Ereẓ Israel and the adjacent areas. French and American convents, schools, and scientific institutions also set up meteorological stations in Palestine, Syria, and Lebanon. Jews entered the field of climatic research in Ereẓ Israel only in the 20th century. In 1910 the Palestine Office of the World Zionist Organization set up rainfall stations in several towns and villages. Soon after World War I Dov Ashbel set up a network of meteorological stations in Jewish villages from Metullah to the Negev, and a number of stations were installed by the British Mandatory administration. Meteorological research after 1937 was conducted at two centers. One was at the meteorological station maintained by the government Department of Civil Aviation at Lydda Airport, where upper-air conditions were studied with advanced technical equipment. The other was run by the department of meteorology of the Hebrew University of Jerusalem, which controlled the network of meteorological stations in Jewish settlements. The government set up stations in parts of the country populated by Arabs, formerly inaccessible to Jewish research. During World War I, the opposing air forces studied upper winds and upper-air meteorology in Palestine. In World War II, the Allied air forces in the whole Middle East theater systematically collected a mass of meteorological data resulting in a revision of concepts of the conditions in the area. The network of Jewish stations was extended in the latter years of the Mandate.

After the establishment of the State of Israel, both the civil authorities and the Israeli Air Force developed meteorological operations on a national scale for both civilian and military needs. These operations include extensive upper-air observations with radio-sondes as well as meteorological satellite research in collaboration with other countries. The universities in Israel, especially departments of geography, earth science, and geophysics undertook extensive research on climatic conditions for human needs. Their research placed Israel in the front ranks of meteorological and climatic research in the academic world.

BIBLIOGRAPHY: D. Ashbel, *Aklim Ereẓ Yisrael le-Ezoreha* (1952); E. Orni and E. Efrat, *Geography of Israel* (1980[4]), 105–25; F.M. Exner, *Zum Klima von Palaestina* (1910); H. Klein, *Das Klima Palaestinas auf Grund alter hebraeischer Quellen* (1914); *Atlas of Israel* (1970).

[Dov Ashbel]

Geology

STRATIGRAPHIC EVOLUTION. *The Precambrian Basement.* Upper Tertiary to Recent faulting and uplift led to many exposures of the basement rocks along the flanks of the Arabah graben, the southeastern corner of the Dead Sea, the Eilat area, and eastern Sinai. The morphology of the Precambrian basement rocks is characterized in Sinai and in the Ḥejaz, situated opposite Sinai, by a conspicuously barren and rugged relief (e.g., Mount Sinai, Wadi Yitm), contrasting remarkably with the tabular landscape of the Paleozoic-Mesozoic sedimentary cover. Varieties of granite and granite-porphyry, syenite, diorite, and gabbro, interchanging with gneiss and mica schists, constitute the principal plutonic and metamorphic basement rocks. Volcanic tuffs and lava sheets also occur, as well as abundant acid and basic dikes. Swarms of dikes invade the whole of the crystalline complex, as well as the unmetamorphosed sediments of the Saramūj series.

The Saramūj series consists principally of multicolored conglomerates analogous in rock character and deposition to the Molasse and Verucano of the Alps. Like these Alpine formations the Saramūj series are of simple fold structure, giving reason to assume strong mountain building during the late Precambrian. The Precambrian "Alps" were then leveled on a regional scale, only a few monadnocks remaining on the enormous erosion and abrasion surface of the Lipalian peneplain. Ore deposits of economic importance have not yet been discovered in the basement complex. The feldspar-, barite-, and mica-bearing pegmatites are of very limited economic value.

Paleozoics. Above the Lipalian peneplain (principal unconformity) there is an extensive cover of continental and marine sediments of Paleozoic to Recent age. The sedimentary material is derived either from a landmass in the east, the "Arabo-Nubian" shield, or from the transgressive "Tethys" sea in the west. The few marine Lower Paleozoic outcrops known from Timna, Eilat, and Petra or from Wadi al-Ḥasaʾ and Zarqā Māʿīn at the Dead Sea all appear as thin beds of shallow epicontinental limestone-dolomite, shales, and littoral sands; these are intercalated between sandstones hundreds of meters thick. This continental, as well as littoral, sandy complex is included in the Nubian Sandstone. Reminiscent of the "Old Red" of Europe or the "continental intercalaire" of Africa, the Nubian Sandstone has built the impressive colorful rock escarpments of Petra and the eastern cliffs of the Dead Sea. Erosion and corrosion have sculptured these sandstones to fantastic rock forms, especially well developed in the Ḥismā plains and in the Wadi al-Rūm of the Ḥejaz province. It is also in this region that the complete atmospheric disintegration of the Nubian Sandstone has supplied the sandy fillings of the present extensive valleys of the Ḥismā; in the region outside our map it has provided the material for the large belts of dunes of the Ḍahna and Nafūd of inner Arabia. Copper of an average 1.5% is found as a cementing carbonate in the Paleozoic Nubian Sandstone and is mined at Timna. In the same area, manganese deposits have been mapped (mostly psilomelane) but their economic value is still under discussion.

Mesozoics. Dating the Nubian Sandstone is a persistent difficulty, particularly where there are no marine intercalations. This is the case in the Arabah and Dead Sea graben. Thus in the north-south canyons and steep western slopes of Moab, Sodom, and Midian and in the area opposite, between Eilat and Timna, Triassic and Jurassic marine interbeds are remarkably absent. There the massive sandstone rests directly on the Precambrian or the marine Lower Paleozoic Cambro-Silurian beds and is overlaid by marine Cenomanian strata. In this part of the country the Nubian Sandstone may therefore be of any age from Paleozoic to Mesozoic. Fossil plants found in the uppermost layers of sandstone (here somewhat clayey and shaly) are of continental Lower Cretaceous or Wealden character. Genuine marine Triassic in the Transjordanian part of our map is known from the surroundings of the northeastern corner of the Dead Sea and from the deeper wadi-cuts of the Jabbok River. In the high Negev of Sinai and Israel, Triassic is exposed in the erosion windows of Mt. Arif and Ramon. The predominantly calcareous, occasionally marly beds display lithological affinities with the "Germanic" epicontinental Trias – the Muschelkalk – though their fauna also contain many "Mediterranean" elements. Quasi-continental conditions during the Upper Triassic led to the deposition of gypsum evaporites and to faunistically sterile dolomite varves and Keuper-like variegated marls. The lowermost outcropping strata of the marine Triassic again appear in the "Nubian" facies.

Marine Jurassic is recorded from the neighborhood of the Triassic outcrops of Transjordan and on the Cisjordanian side from the anticlinal cores in Makhtesh Ramon, Ha-Makhtesh ha-Gadol and Ha-Makhtesh ha-Katan; yet none of the calcareous and marly epicontinental formations of the Jurassic or Triassic in Transjordan and in the Negev are completely devoid of sandy intercalations, demonstrating shallow sea conditions in the vicinity of a dune-framed continent. At Ramon, terrestrial influence is also marked by residual deposits of bog-iron and flint clays (up to 55% Al_2O_3) at the Jurassic-Triassic boundary, as well as by a few hundred meters of continental Nubian Sandstone containing some thin intercalations of marine Jurassic. Striking gravel formations recorded from the Jurassic-Cretaceous transition beds of the Ramon in the Negev, as well as of the Lebanon, indicate uplift and widespread erosion at the end of the Jurassic.

The Ramon outcrops are finally distinguished by numerous trachytic dikes and sills of possibly Upper Jurassic age, since they penetrate both Jurassic and Triassic sediments. The syenite-essexite plutonics of the anticlinal core have also been assigned to the Jurassic. The "intermediary" magmatics differ somewhat in rock type from the more basic volcanics, which are extensively represented in the Hermon-Lebanon mountains. In contrast to the continental and epicontinental Jurassic of the Negev and Transjordan, the Middle and Upper Jurassic of Lebanon and Hermon are developed as a 1,000–1,500-meter-thick marine complex prevalently of dolomite and limestone, suggesting deposition in an oceanic basin fairly remote from shore and land.

The recent material obtained from oil-exploration drilling in Israel leads to the conclusion that the Mid-Upper-Jurassic marine sedimentary troughs of Lebanon-Hermon extended south and southwest to Galilee, Carmel, Judea, the Coastal Plain, and the western Negev lowlands. The continental sphere of influence during this period is restricted to the Negev proper and to Transjordan. This paleogeographic zoning of sedimentary conditions persists to a greater extent in the following epoch, during the Lower Cretaceous. Thus in Transjordan and in the Negev-Arabah, the principal representative of the Lower Cretaceous is a uniform sandstone of continental habitus assigned in the map to the "Nubian" complex. Mostly regarded as the time-equivalent of the Wealden, this Lower Cretaceous Nubian Sandstone (kaolinic at the base) is again well exposed in the erosion windows of Ramon, the Makhtesh ha-Gadol, and the Makhtesh ha-Katan. There are, howevever, a few thin marine intercalations.

In the western regions, in the Coastal Plain as well as on Mount Carmel and in Galilee, evidence of the hegemony of the Tethys sea during the Lower Cretaceous is found in the cuttings and core samples from the recent wells at Ḥeleẓ, Tel Ẓafit, Moẓa, Zikhron Ya'akov, Caesarea, Haifa, Ein Na'aman (Kurdāna), Mount Tabor, and Tiberias, as well as in the outcrops of central and northern Galilee (Sartaba-Tabor, Bet Netophah, Har Ḥazon, Har ha-Ari, Manarah) and of eastern Samaria (Wadi Māliḥ-Fāriʿa). The lithology of the Lower Cretaceous is predominantly marly and occasionally sandy. Limestones are less frequent and like the other formations are of shelf and littoral character. The presence of lignite in the sandy beds also indicates the proximity of the continent. The abundance of hydroxides and oxides of iron gives the Lower Cretaceous rocks of Galilee their dominant and characteristic brown colors. Enrichment in a shallow sea led to the deposition of oolitic iron ores. The best ore (28% Fe) was found in the "minette" of the Aptian of Manarah in northernmost Israel (30,000,000 tons of minable ore have been evaluated).

Cenomanian-Turonian. Whereas the Triassic, Jurassic, and Lower Cretaceous appear in restricted outcrops in the anticlinal erosion cirques, Makhtesh Ramon, Ha-Makhtesh ha-Gadol, and Ha-Makhtesh ha-Katan, in the wadi-cuts at Ramallah and Wadi Māliḥ-Fārīʿa, and in the uplifted fault blocks of Galilee, more than half of the exposed mountain formations of Israel belong to the marine Cenomanian-Turonian. Thus the prominent mountain bodies of the northern Negev, Judea-Samaria, Carmel, and Galilee are built of Cenomanian-Turonian rocks up to 2,500 ft. (800 m.) thick. The principal strata, hard limestone and dolomite, weather to a rough and rocky karstic landscape characteristic of Mediterranean calcareous terrains. Subdivided by very thin marly (e.g., Moẓa Marl) or by thicker flint-bearing chalk beds (e.g., the Carmel promontory of Haifa), these dolomites and limestones have become the main groundwater aquifer exploited during the last few decades in Israel.

In the central Transjordan section, in the Arabah-Dead Sea Rift Valley, and in the southernmost Negev (Timna), the Cenomanian limestone protrudes as a hard, vertical cliff overlying the rim of Nubian Sandstone escarpments. In southern Transjordan, the lower stage of the Cenomanian is still in the Nubian Sandstone facies. The main Cretaceous transgression starts there only with the Upper Cenomanian, or even, in places, with the Turonian. In northern Transjordan, however, in the upwarped region of the Jabbok-ʿAjlūn, the marine development of the Cenomanian is again complete, of considerable thickness and surface distribution. The landscape here is very reminiscent of the Judean-Samarian uplands. In the Carmel and Umm al-Faḥm mountains, submarine lavas and tuffs are interspersed in the Cenomanian-Turonian.

Senonian (Including Paleocene). The Cenomanian upwarps and anticlines of the Israeli mountain bodies are everywhere framed on their flanks by narrow strips of Senonian, which continue in larger extension in the synclinal areas. Flint-bearing hogbacks and flat-irons are characteristic morphologic features of the asymmetrical slopes of the Negev and Judean anticlines. The greatest surface extension, however, is that of the synclinorial downwarps of the Judean Desert, the Desert of Zin, and the Paran (Jirāfi) and Ẓenifim deserts in the southern Negev. The dominating Senonian of these regions is also distinguished in the landscape by a white to light gray color and badland dissection of its principal rock type, the chalk. Where unexposed to the atmosphere, the Senonian chalk is usually bituminous. Intercalated flints and the now exploited phosphatic limestones are other representative rock-types of the Senonian. In the Negev section of Sinai and of Edom, opposite, the harder flints are the principal components of the pebble pavement of the large Ḥamada plains and plateaus.

Eocene. The surface occurrence of the Eocene is similarly associated with the downwarped regions. The anticlinal ridges of the Cenomanian-Turonian, including their asymmetrical flanks, are practically devoid of Eocene. Eocene is of great extension west of the Ramon and Dimonah ranges in the structural depressions which start from the Avedat plateau down to Niẓẓanah, Revivim, and Beersheba. From Beersheba to the north it extends along the western foothills as far as Ḥuldah. Eocene is likewise extensively represented in the downwarped fold region of Paran and ʿAqof (ʿIqfi) in the southern Negev.

The folds of these synclinorial regions (and this applies also to those of the north) are usually smaller, shallower, more symmetric, and frequently of the brachy-anticline type. Undulations of this kind are developed in the uplifted high plateaus of Transjordan. In Samaria the exposed Eocene is distributed between Ebal-Gerizim and the Umm al-Faḥm range and in Ephraim proper between Umm al-Faḥm and Mount Carmel. A large area of Eocene is analogously situated (though disturbed by faults of the Kishon Valley) between Carmel and southwestern Galilee (Shepharam to Nazareth). In spite of the strong block-faulting which dissected the Galilee in the Pleistocene and the extensive basalt and Neogene cover, it is nevertheless possible to trace the Eocene on the southeastern flanks of the Galilean upwarp. On the western flank of this upwarp, parallel to the Senonian-Paleocene sedimentary girdle, Eocene appears in sporadic outcrops, intimating that its major portion lies hidden below the Coastal Plain and the sea. The Eocene in the foothill region of the Negev and Judea, western Galilee, and Ephraim consists primarily of chalk interspersed with flint and chalky marl. Lithologically it frequently resembles the Senonian and is accordingly marked by a common egg-shaped smooth hill-morphology. Harder limestones in the higher Negev (Avedat plateau) and in Sinai produce an esplanade landscape with enormous regional plateaus and cuestas. In the Lower Eocene table landscape of Edom-Moab, there is much interstratification of phosphatic limestone. Harder limestone and marble limestone of uppermost Lower to Middle Eocene age are widely distributed in central and eastern Galilee, evolving a pronounced karstic rough-hewn landscape which differs sharply from the smoother relief forms found in the foothill regions of Israel. There, rare occurrences of Upper Eocene are still developed in the chalky marly facies of the Middle to Lower Eocene foothills. Some of Galilee's largest springs derive from the Eocene karst, e.g., Gilboa, Migdal, Naḥal Ammud, Kinnerot (al-Ṭabigha), Kefar Giladi.

Oligocene. The Oligocene Tethys sea never reached far inland. The few limited outcrops in the foothills of Bet Guvrin, Ramleh, and Ephraim, as well as the drilling samples of the Coastal Plain, all point to shore deposits of chalky and detritic character. Marine Oligocene, therefore, plays no significant role in Israel's surface formations; continental Oligocene has not, so far, been discovered. Israel's emergence from the sea may have commenced in the Late Eocene from submarine ridges which already existed here and there in the Senonian; but the major elevation and hence the final anticlinal-synclinal fold pattern came about at the end of the Oligocene or earliest Miocene.

Marine Neogene. The beginning of the Neogene coincides with the most widespread rising of the region above the sea since the end of the Precambrian, i.e., since before the first appearance of the Paleozoic Tethys (Lipalian interval). Emergences had taken place before, such as at the end of the Triassic and Jurassic and the end of the Lower Cenomanian, but the whole of the country was not affected then, as shown by the results of recent deep borings in the Coastal Plain.

With the approach of the Miocene, the Tethys ceased to exist, its waters merging with and filling the Atlantic and Indian Oceans. At a later time, this region became connected with these two oceans only by means of small sea branches. Europe and Africa-Arabia were then united by isthmuses or divided by inland seas and the Mediterranean originated. In place of the widespread Mesozoic and Eocene transgressions of the Tethys, marine ingressions are henceforth limited to local embayments of the Mediterranean. These occurred primarily during the two Neogene stages, the Miocene Vindobonian and the Pliocene Astian-Plaisancian. Surface outcrops of the marine Neogene are very small in Israel and restricted to the foothill area or to the Beersheba and Kishon plains. Marine Neogene thus plays a very minor role in the morphology of the country.

The littoral Miocene is found today from Haifa Bay and the Ephraim Hills (Ein ha-Shofet) in the north to Beersheba and Dimonah in the Negev, up to a height of 1,600 ft. (500 m.) above sea level. In all the known exposures, it appears with sharp erosional unconformity on folded Eocene and Cretaceous rocks. The marine Miocene strata consist of lagoonal, sandy marls, beach sands, coarse-grained sands, and coral limestone. Both the facies and the fauna point to a connection with the Red Sea and the Indian Ocean. After the retreat of the Miocene sea, due to uplift in the Pontian of some 700–1,000 ft. (200–300 m.), there followed a new subsidence, accompanied by the Pliocene ingression.

The Pliocene sea in the north again occupied the Kishon Valley, the Jezreel Valley, and eastern Galilee as far as Tiberias. In the south it reached Nevatim, east of Beersheba, and again washed the foothills bounding the present Coastal Plain. The character of the Pliocene (Astian) littoral sediments is similar to the Miocene, except for the absence of coral reef limestone, indicating disconnection from the Red Sea and Indian Ocean. Uplift movements at the end of the Pliocene and during the Pleistocene brought the Pliocene littoral beds to their present height of 700–1,000 ft. (200–300 m.) and the Miocene to 1,600 ft. (500 m.). Where subaerial erosion has removed the Neogene sediments, the ancient abrasion planes often appear as tilted "peneplains."

The marine Miocene-Pliocene lying below the Quaternary of the Coastal Plain has been studied in hundreds of water wells and in many petroleum-exploration drillings. As so-called Sāqiyya beds, it consists of several hundred meters of plastic clays, silty marls, and marly sands; there are some local lumachelle layers and even basalt flows. In the deeper horizons it becomes markedly lagoonal, with several gypsum horizons, but this part of the section may be assigned to the Miocene-Oligocene.

Continental Neogene. The varying relief of Israel and neighboring Levant countries demonstrated by the Neogene irregular gulf and headland coastal configuration is also expressed by the development of large intermontane depressions, with their fill of predominantly continental deposits. Limnic freshwater and brackish sediments, evaporites (Menaḥemiyyah gypsum, Sodom salt), fluviatile gravel, red beds, and desert sands attaining hundreds of meters of thickness have been described under various formation names: Herod, Sodom, Ḥaẓevah (Ḥoṣeb), etc. They occur in the Jezreel Valley, the Jordan Valley, the Negev, and near the Dead Sea. Although of lesser thickness and geographical extension, these inland sediments may be compared in facies and age with the Bakhtiyārī and Fars series of Iran, Iraq, and Syria.

The continental Neogene, like its contemporaneous marine Mio-Pliocene, rests discordantly upon all pre-Miocene formations, frequently starting with a basal conglomerate, e.g., Kefar Giladi, Har Hordos, al-Dhrāʿ, Dimonah, etc. In the folded mountains of the Negev it is associated with synclinal basins (as in the Palmyra chains of Syria), e.g., Naḥal Malḥata (Wadi Milḥ) east of Beersheba, synclinal valleys between Yeroḥam and the Ha-Makhtesh ha-Gadol (Ḥatirah) anticlines, the Ḥaẓevah-Sodom-al-Dhrāʿ basin, and the Upper Paran downwarp. In the Jezreel Valley and eastern Galilee the continental Neogene occurs as filling masses within the huge fault depressions that extend from the Kishon to the Tiberias area. This is the same region of tectonic tension in which Upper Miocene and, more visibly, Upper Pliocene continental basalt eruptions took place and even continued during the Pleistocene. Pleistocene and Pliocene sheet lavas have built up the extensive volcanic plateaus of Hauran and eastern Galilee. They cover Neogene and pre-Neogene sediments, which, due to Pleistocene block and rift faulting, are exposed along the slopes of the Jordan graben and in the transversal fault valleys of Naḥal Tabor (Wadi Bīra), Harod, and eastern Dayshūn.

Quaternary. Uplift and desiccation of the inland lakes not only brought the marine and continental Pliocene into a higher topographic position, but was also accompanied by the complete retreat of the sea far to the west of the present Levant shores. Contemporary with this uplift, fault-dissection on a regional scale produced the graben-trough of Eilat-Arabah, the Dead Sea, and the Jordan Valley and accompanying step-fault blocks. The branching off of diagonal faults both in Cis- and Transjordan gave origin to transversal fault valleys and fault-block mountains, which are especially well developed in Samaria and the Galilee. The Negev, south Judea, Shephelah, and Sharon were far less affected by fault tectonics, and thus the mid-Tertiary fold pattern of anticlinal ridges and synclinal valleys, upwarps and downwarps, remained well preserved. In the synclinal valleys and on the ḥamada-plateaus of the Paran hinterland, continental deposition may have continued from Upper Tertiary to Recent.

Along the western border of the Judean Mountains, gravel fans and terraces plunge below the Coastal Plain (as far west as the Mediterranean) and are found in groundwater exploration wells at depths of 330 ft. (100 m.) overlying the Neogene strata. These clastics are assigned to the Lower Pleistocene or Villafranchian, indicating the extremely high precipitation of this Pluvial stage, synchronized with the Guenz-Mindel glacial time of Europe. Younger gravels of Mid-Upper Pleistocene age interfinger the fossil indurated dunes of the Coastal Plain, known as *kurkar* sandstone. The *kurkar*, which constitutes another important aquifer, is frequently subdivided by a terra-rossa-like, sandy, loamy soil, the *ḥamra* (Ar. *ḥamrāʾ*) or "red sands" of our citrus belt. The unconsolidated dunes are of Recent age. They run along the Coastal Plain and extend into the northern Negev, as far inland as the neighborhood of Beersheba. The undifferentiated Quaternary signifies the loamy, loess, and swampy soils, as well as recent gravels and silts blanketing the coastal and interior alluvial plains. Pleistocene marine sediments are found as foraminiferal limestone in the Haifa-Acre plain (e.g., Kurdaneh) and as marine *kurkar* around the western Carmel border. The water boreholes in the Coastal Plain encountered marine Pleistocene only as far inland as Rishon le-Zion, but this is missing in the Jezreel Valley and the Shephelah foothills. The lower Pleistocene is thus the most insignificant of the ingressions of the Cenozoic Mediterranean Sea. During the Upper Pleistocene, Mousterian man already lived near the present shores.

In the newly formed Quaternary Dead Sea-Jordan graben, the Lower to Middle Pleistocene is distinguished by gravel and freshwater lake and swamp deposits. At the southern end of Lake Tiberias (ʿUbaydiyya), many extinct mammals, skeleton remains of primitive man, and implements both of pebble culture and of Abbevillian were discovered. Slightly younger, but not older than Middle Pleistocene, were the proto-Acheulean tools and extinct fauna found at the Jordan, south of Lake Ḥuleh. During this period volcanic activity was renewed and many basalt layers accumulated, derived in part from the Hauran district. They were partly responsible for separating the Ḥuleh graben section from the Tiberias and southern Jordan graben and for the accumulation of thick peat deposits in the Ḥuleh Valley. The Tiberias region, the middle and southern Jordan valley, the Dead Sea, and the northernmost Arabah valley were occupied during the Upper Pleistocene (some 60,000 years ago) by a large brackish inland lake in which were deposited fine-bedded clays, gypsum, and chalk, called the Lashon (lisān) formation. This formation is interfingered with large fluviatile deposits of gravel and silt. At the end of the Pleistocene (some 20,000 to 15,000 years ago), the ancient Lisān lake receded from its highest stand at the -720 ft. (-220 m.) level to about -1,300 ft. (-400 m.), the present level of the Dead Sea. Young rivers spread their gravels upon the dried-up Lisān lake and cut out the present floodplain of the Jordan River. The raising of the Sodom salt mountain also started in the Lower Pleistocene.

STRUCTURAL PATTERN. The tectonic structures formed by the folding movements that modeled their final features during the Mid-Tertiary are best preserved in the dry climate of the Negev. However, south of the Yotvatah area, the influence of the Plio-Pleistocene graben faulting with its step faults, parallel and transversal to the Arabah graben depression, markedly disturbs the fold pattern that is still well observable at Ẓenifim. From Naḥal Paran as far as Makhtesh Ramon the direction of the folds is close to east-west and this trend persists into Sinai. The folds then turn in a northeast-southwest direction and dominate the central and northern Negev. Their anticlines are mostly asymmetrical on the eastern flanks and frequently limited by reverse strike-faults. These folds are grouped into one unit forming the main anticlinorial uplift, with culminations in the Makhtesh Ramon and Ha-Makhtesh ha-Gadol. In the structurally low areas, such as the central Arabah Valley and the synclinorium of Ḥaluẓah, the folds are smaller and more symmetrical, representing small domes and brachy-anticlines.

The mountainous region of Judea and Samaria is a broad arch, rising to a considerable height, that is subdivided into folds by the anticlines of Maon, Yatta, Ẓāhiriyya, Modi'im, etc. and the synclines of Netiv ha-Lamed-He and Ẓorah. The arch and its folds, again with a northeast–southwest trend, are distinctly asymmetrical, descending unequally to the Coastal Plain in the west and to the Jordan-Dead Sea graben in the east. Thus the pronounced northwest asymmetry observed on the western slopes of the Judean arch contrasts with the southeast asymmetry of the dominant folds of the Judean Desert and the northern Negev. These asymmetrical anticlinal folds are difficult to relate to pressure exerted by the Arabo-Nubian massif, but are apparently connected with the mechanism of epeirogenic and taphrogenic uplifts.

As in most rift valleys of regional extent, it is not always possible to define the exact location of the main border faults. In the case of the Pleistocene Jordan–Dead Sea graben, a throw of a thousand meters or more has been determined at a number of places. The western cliffs of the Dead Sea graben and the graben slopes between Beth-Shean and Lake Kinneret are, moreover, divided by numerous step faults that run parallel to the main border fault. They are also hidden to some extent by *en échelon* faults that have their origin in the main graben. A number of transversal faults, such as those between Wadi Fāriʿa and Jericho, as well as in the foothill region near Tulkarm, cut the anticlinorium of the Judean Mountains.

On the Coastal Plain, just as in the northern Negev and the southern part of the Judean Mountains, the structural lines are directed northeast-southwest. It is not yet clear whether this direction applies only to the folds or, as in the Ḥeleẓ area, to deep-seated faults as well. Petroleum wells of the Ḥeleẓ-Beror Ḥayil ridge indicate the presence of a wide and deep depression filled with Tertiary sediments, constituting the regional (Ashkelon) fault-conditioned trough.

In the Sharon a number of small transversal faults have been observed. It is possible that these constitute the continuation of faults exposed in the foothill area. There are no surface indications of a main, larger border fault, as found along the Jordan graben. Nevertheless one may assume that the great thickness of Tertiary sediments in the Sharon Plain is the outcome of a downfaulted coastal depression that began during or at the end of the Mid-Tertiary, as presumed also for the Ashkelon trough. If the existence of main faults below the young fill on the Coastal Plain and the continental slope area of the Mediterranean should be proved, then a general tectonic picture would evolve presenting Judea as a major horst limited on both sides by major grabens or by downfaulted depressions.

Mount Carmel forms a structural unit by itself. It is an extensive faulted uplift. The direction of some of the smaller anticlines (ʿUsifiyyā, Oren) is northwest-southeast. That is to say, they are not in harmony with the strike of other fold structures in the country. The view has been expressed that the major faults that limit Mount Carmel to the north have been responsible for producing the small anticlinal bends of this exceptional direction. Although the folds in Upper Galilee are more or less obliterated by the predominance of faulting, a certain east-southeast asymmetry of the rudimentary folds, and especially of the central upwarp, is still noticeable. Whereas in eastern Galilee faults are primarily directed northwest-southeast and their fault escarpments face north, in western Galilee, i.e., west of the main watershed, the faults run principally east-west, and their tilted block escarpments usually face south. The region of the watershed thus serves as a structural backbone where both the western and eastern fault systems meet. It is here, at Mount Tabor, Ḥazon, Ha-Ari, Meron, and Addir, that the faults frame the horst blocks on all sides.

In geological maps of Transjordan, many faults are indicated. Among the principal ones, there is the northeast-southwest Wadi Shu'eib fault, which turns into a north-south fault in the Dead Sea, thus becoming the eastern boundary fault of the graben. Between Wadi Ḥasaʾ and Petra, sets of faults in various directions build an extensive series of blocks in which the influence of the graben tectonics is heavily felt. The most outstanding of these faults extend southward from Petra, forming the eastern boundary fault of the southern Arabah graben and the western boundary of the Midian horst.

BIBLIOGRAPHY: M.A. Avnimelech (comp.), *Bibliography of Levant Geology*, 2 vols. (1965–9); idem, *Etudes géologiques dans la région de la Shephélah* (1936), includes illustrations; L. Lartet, *Essai sur la géologie de la Palestine* (1869); M. Blanckenhorn, in: *Handbuch der regionalen Geologie*, 5 no. 4 (1914), 1–159, includes illustrations; G.S. Blake, *The Stratigraphy of Palestine and its Building Stones* (1936); L. Picard, in: *Bulletin of the Geological Department, Hebrew University, Jerusalem*, 4 no. 2–4 (1943), 1–134; idem, in: *Israel Economic Forum*, 6 no. 3 (1954), 8–38, 146–50: idem, in: BRCI, 8G (1959), 1–30: idem, in: *American Geological Society, Special Paper*, no. 84 (1965), 337–66, includes illustrations; Y. Bentor, in: BRCI, 10G (1961), 17–64; S.H. Shaw, *Southern Palestine Geological Map* (1947), with explanatory notes; M.W. and D. Ball, in: *American Association of Petroleum Geology*, 37 no. 1 (1953), 1–113. See also Geological Survey of Israel Reports.

[Leo Picard]

Flora and Fauna

FLORA. The flora of Ereẓ Israel is among the richest and most varied of any country in the world. On both sides of the Jordan River there are close to 2,300 species belonging to about 700 genera, which in turn belong to 115 families of flora. To these should be added scores of species found in Golan. No other place in the world has such floral wealth concentrated within such a comparatively small area. This density of species is due to several factors. Among them are the varied history of the region's landscape, the diversity of its topography and climate, the lengthy period of its agriculture, and especially the fact that it is the meeting place of three phytogeographic areas: the Mediterranean, the Irano-Turanic, and the Saharo-Sindic, with enclaves here and there of the Sudano-Deccanic.

The Flora of the Mediterranean Area. Of the three phytogeographic areas, the most important is the Mediterranean, which includes agricultural land in the mountains and valleys. In it the amount of water precipitation varies from 14–40 in. (350–1,000 mm.). This precipitation, the result of winter rains (with a small additional amount of melted snow from the high mountains), makes the nonirrigated cultivation of plantations and of winter and summer crops possible. The area is subdivided into mountain and coastal subareas.

The Mountain Subarea. This was once agriculturally the most developed area (having since been superseded in importance by farming lands in the valleys and the Coastal Plain). The intensive agricultural cultivation of mountain lands has curtailed or prevented the development of forests in this, their natural habitat, so that only remnants of forests and groves are left. In this subarea several types of forests are to be found containing the common *oak, the Palestine *terebinth, the mastic terebinth, the *carob, the arbutus, and the rhamnus, as well as many shrubs and wild grasses. The **Aleppo pine* (*Pinus halepensis*), thought to be native to the country, is mainly a newcomer, brought by human activities in the last 500 years. Most of the woods in Israel consist of the group of the common oak (*Quercus calliprinos*), and the Palestine terebinth (*Pistacia palaestina*), which can reach a considerable height but are usually shrubby as a result of having been cut or gnawed by sheep and particularly goats. This bush grows extensively on mountains of an altitude between 1,000–4,000 ft. (300–1,200 m.) above sea level. There is also the gall oak (*Quercus infectoria* (*boissieri*)), a deciduous tree with a tall trunk, alongside which grows the hawthorn (*Crataegus azarolus*). Under favorable humid conditions there also grow in this subarea the sweet *bay (*Laurus nobilis*) and the Judas tree (*Cercis siliquastrum*), which in spring adorns the mountains with its lilac flowers. On the western ridges of the Carmel and Western Galilee and on the western slopes of the Judean mountains, there is maquis, where grow the group of the carob (*ceratonia siliqua*) and the mastic terebinth (*Pistacia tentiscus*), along with many species of shrubs, climbers, annuals, and perennials. A third genus of oak – the Tabor oak (*Quercus ithaburensis*) – predominates on the western ranges of the Lower Galilean mountains, accompanied by the *storax tree (*Styrax officinalis*). In the northern Ḥuleh Valley it grows alongside the Atlantic terebinth (*Pistacia atlantica*). These two species of trees are the largest in Israel, some in the neighborhood of Dan having trunks 20 ft. (6 m.) in circumference and reaching a height of c. 65 ft. (20 m.).

All these are types of forest trees. Another genus of Mediterranean plant comprises flora groups called garrigue, which in Israel consist predominantly of shrubs and dwarf shrubs no taller than a man. The characteristic plants of the garrigue are the calycotome thorn bush (*Calycotome villosa*), the rock rose (*Cistus villosus*), and the salvia (*Salvia tribola*). At times the garrigue flora groups are the developing stage of a forest, at others an indication of the former presence there of a forest since destroyed. Characteristic of the unforested Mediterranean landscape are dwarf shrubs, of which the most widespread is the poterium thorn (*Poterium spinosum*). Reaching a height of less than half a meter, it grows densely and is one of the principal factors in preventing the erosion of mountain soil. Where being used either for firewood or for burning lime has destroyed these plants, the eroding effects of wind and rain have denuded the ground.

The Coastal Subarea. The soil here is sandy or a mixture of sandy chalk and sandy clay, which, being poor in organic substances and in its capacity to retain rainwater, is unsuitable for the growth of plants (unless irrigated). In this subarea grows flora that strikes deep roots, and desert and Aravah plants that can exist on small amounts of water, as well as annuals which sprout and ripen during the rainy winter months. Here can be found flora of Israel's three phytogeographic areas, as well as that of the Sudanoz-Deccanic, such as the *sycamore (*Ficus sycomorus*) and the wild *jujube (*Zizyphus spina-Christi*). Sand flora is in constant danger of being covered by moving sands and of having the sand under its roots blown away by the wind. Yet many sand plants are able to survive under such conditions, either by striking deep roots or by developing new shoots above the branches covered by sand. Near the sea, where the winds carry sea spray onto the flora, plants grow which are insensitive to sea water, such as the Russian thistle (*Salsola kali*) and species of fig marigold (*Mesembryanthemum*). Most of the sandy-clay soil is planted with citrus groves. The flora group of the love grass (*Eragrostis bipinnata*) and of the thistle (*Centaurea procurrens*) grow extensively here, as do the group of the cistus and of the calycotome on the brittle sandy-chalk hills in the Coastal Plain area, and the group of the carob and of the mastic in the hard sandy-chalk soil.

The Flora of the Irano-Turanic Area. This is concentrated in the loess or arid soil of the northern Negev and the Judean Desert. Here the climate is dry, with a rainfall varying from 8–14 in. (200–300 mm.), these being the limits for nonirrigated plants which thrive in rainy years (cf. Gen. 26:12). In this area there are almost no forests, but only sparse trees, such as the plant association of the Atlantic terebinth and the lotus jujube (*Zizyphus lotus*). Characteristic of the slopes bordering on the Jordan and Beth-Shean Valleys is the *Retama duriaei* association. Here the most important plant association is of a species of *wormwood (*Artemisia herba-alba*) which grows extensively in the Negev and in the Judean Desert.

The Flora of the Saharo-Sindic Area. This area, which extends over most of Israel but has the poorest flora, includes the southern Negev and the Aravah. Its rainfall, which is limited to a shorter period in winter, does not exceed c. 8 in. (200 mm.) and is usually much less, and there are even parts which in some years are almost completely rainless. The soil here is infertile and includes hammada, desert, gravel, and rocks. Trees grow only in wadi fissures. There are saline tracts bare of all flora, which is in any event very sparse here. The most typical plant in the hammada is the small shrub *Zygophyllum dumosum*, which is capable of surviving in areas with a rainfall of less than 2 in. (50 mm.). Since desert plants have to contend with a severe shortage of water, only those with special properties are able to survive here. Most of them spring up and flower quickly after a shower of rain; some of them, only a few weeks after germinating, scatter their seeds, which are capable of preserving their power of germination for many years. Other species here are bulbous plants that hibernate in dry periods. Generally, desert flora has long roots so as to utilize the sparse amount of water over a wide area, and hence the infrequency of these plants. Many species of desert flora have a great ability to absorb groundwater; one species, the *Reaumaria palaestina*, developing an osmotic capacity of more than 200 atmospheres. Other desert plants shed their leaves in a dry season, thereby curtailing the area of evaporation. Still other species are succulents, which are equipped with cells that in the rainy season store water for the dry period.

In sandy desert regions the flora is usually more abundant, the predominant species here being the haloxylon and the broom (*Retama roetam*). In the Aravah and in the lower Jordan Valley, where there is widespread salinity, saline flora, including species of atriplex and salicornia, grows densely.

In desert regions near sources of water there are oases, where tropical Sudano-Deccanic flora grows, the characteristic plants here being species of acacia, wild jujube, etc. These also grow in wadi fissures in desert regions. In places where the ground becomes sodden from winter floods, crops can be grown and plantations established.

Hydrophylic flora grows near expanses of water in all the areas of Israel. Large numbers of the poplar (*Populus euphratica*), as well as species of the *willow (*Salix*) and of the *tamarisk (*Tamarix*), grow on river banks, as do the *plane (*Platanus orientalis*) and the Syrian ash (*Fraxinus syriaca*) on the banks of streams in the north. Alongside these trees there usually grows the *oleander (*Nerium oleander*), together with numerous species of annuals and perennials. The reed and the cattail are found near almost every expanse of water. The papyrus once flourished extensively in the Ḥuleh swamps, but since they were drained it grows in extremely limited areas. Due to the draining of swamps in Israel and the piping of river water, hydrophytic flora has progressively decreased. On the other hand, some species of riparian plants flourish near fishponds, the area of which has greatly increased.

Cultivated Plants. Ereẓ Israel has a long and varied history of *agriculture. In addition to the older plants cultivated in the country for centuries, many have been introduced from various parts of the world, especially from Australia (mainly many species of the eucalyptus and the acacia) and from America, among these being numerous ornamental plants. Together with these plants, their companion wild grasses have also come into Israel and have flourished alongside the older wild grasses, in particular the prickly species which are a characteristic feature of Israel's landscape, especially in the burning hot days of summer.

FAUNA. *History.* The history of the fauna of Ereẓ Israel is a long one, going back to the earliest geological periods. Of these the Pleistocene epoch was the most dynamic and decisive in this respect by reason of the considerable changes which took place in its zoological character, mainly as a result of the influx of animals from various regions. In this period, fauna at present characteristic of East African savannas predominated in the country. To this period belong the bones, uncovered in the country, of animals no longer extant in Israel, such as warthog, hippopotamus, rhinoceros, and striped hyena, as well as various species of gazelle. The bones of elephants and of mastodons, brought to light in the Jordan Valley, belong to the Lower Pleistocene Age. In later periods animals penetrated to the country from Western and Central Asia, among them the wild horse, the wild ass, gazelles, wolves, and badgers. From the north there was a limited influx of animals as a result of the Ice Age in Europe.

During the Upper Pleistocene Age a tropical climate, warm and humid, predominated in Ereẓ Israel. This was followed by a dry period, which led to the destruction of the tropical fauna. And indeed an examination of the bones of animals found in the caves of prehistoric man in the Carmel shows that the principal game hunted by him consisted of mammals still extant in Israel. This is true also of the bones of birds brought to light in Early Stone Age caves, although several mammals and birds are of species extinct in the country in historical times. As early as the end of the Stone Age (4,000 B.C.E.) there was to be found in the country the fauna characteristic of it since biblical days.

With the enlargement of the settled area in the biblical and later in the Byzantine period, changes took place in the distribution of animals, now forced into the uninhabited areas (see *Animals of the Bible). The invention of rifles led to the extinction of the large carnivores as well as of the large ruminant game.

The present-day Jewish agricultural settlements have altered the distribution of the various animals. Some of them have disappeared, while others, finding favorable conditions in developed farming areas, have begun to multiply. Thus the increase in waterfowl is due directly to the increase of fishponds, in which aquatic mammals (such as the marsh lynx) have also begun to establish themselves. New species of birds have started to nest in plantations and citrus groves. The State of Israel's fauna preservation laws have saved several mammals from threatened extinction and some have begun to multiply greatly, such as the *gazelle, at present to be found in various parts of the country. The *ibex, too, has increased in number and herds of it may be seen in the mountains of En-Gedi and Eilat. On the other hand, toxic substances used to exterminate agricultural pests and jackals have led to the extinction of birds, particularly carrion-feeding ones. In this way the griffon *vultures, found in large numbers in the country up to the 1930s, have become almost extinct, only a few surviving at present.

The Zoogeography of Ereẓ Israel. The fauna in the country is extremely varied, the reason for this being, as in the case of the flora, that Israel is the meeting place of three climatic and floral regions. The regional distribution of the fauna corresponds almost exactly to that of the flora. To the Mediterranean fauna belong the *hare, chukar *partridge, swallow, agama, and others; to the Saharo-Sindic, the desert mouse, desert lark, sandgrouse, *gecko, cobra, and many other species; to the Irano-Turanic, animals that inhabit the northern Negev and the Judean Desert, such as the tiger weasel (*Vormela*), bustard, isolepis, and agama.

The Sudano-Deccanic animals inhabit the Jordan Valley as far as the Aravah. Here are to be found representatives also of tropical fauna, such as the cheetah, honey badger, tropical cuckoo, and carpet viper. In contrast to these animals that love the warmth, there are also representatives of the Holarctic fauna, such as the shrew and meadow pipit.

The catalogue of the names of animals thus far studied testifies to a wealth of fauna. At present approximately 100 species of mammals are known, nearly 400 of birds, more than 70 of reptiles, more then 400 of sweet and salt water fish, and seven of Amphibia. Much larger is the number of invertebrates. These are extensively represented among the insects, of which some 8,000 species are known in the country, their aggregate number being 22,000 according to Bodenheimer, who maintains that there are about 900 species of other *Arthropoda*. Of the invertebrates, other than the *Arthropoda*, some 300 species are known, their total number being estimated at about 2,750.

BIBLIOGRAPHY: FLORA. A. Eig, et al., *Magdir le-Ẓimḥei Ereẓ Yisrael* (1948); M. Zohari, *Olam ha-Ẓemaḥim* (1954); idem, *Geobotanikah* (1955); idem, *Plant Life of Palestine* (1962); J. Feliks, *Olam ha-Ẓome'aḥ ha-Mikra'i* (1957); N. Feinbrun-Dothan, *Wild Plants in the Land of Israel* (1960). FAUNA. Lewysohn, Zool; F.S. Bodenheimer, *Animal and Man in Bible Lands* (1960); J. Feliks, *The Animal World of the Bible* (1962). **ADD. BIBLIOGRAPHY:** J. Feliks, *Ḥai ve-Ẓomaḥ ba-Torah* (1984).

[Jehuda Feliks]

HISTORY

For Prehistory see *Archaeology; for Biblical and Second Temple periods, see *History.

Destruction of the Second Temple until the Arab Conquest (70–640 C.E.)

THE EFFECTS OF THE WAR OF 66–70 C.E. The Jewish war against the Romans, which lasted more than four years and encompassed the entire country, the continuing siege of the fortresses of *Machaerus, *Herodium, and *Masada, the last falling only in 73, the capture of *Jerusalem and the destruction of the *Temple – all these gravely affected the Jewish people and the cities and villages of Ereẓ Israel. Josephus (Wars, 6:420) states that during the siege of Jerusalem alone more than a million Jews fell, while his contemporary Tacitus places the number at 600,000 (*Historiae*, 5:13). To these figures are to be added those killed at various stages of the war in Judea, Galilee, and Transjordan. Many fell in the battles fought and the massacres perpetrated by the inhabitants of the Greek cities against the local Jews, such as in *Caesarea, *Beth-Shean, *Acre, and *Ashkelon. In addition to the slain, many were taken captive before the siege of Jerusalem; tens of thousands were sold into slavery, sent to toil in ships and mines, or presented to the non-Jewish cities adjacent to Ereẓ Israel to fight against wild animals in the theaters. While the figures given by the early historians are undoubtedly exaggerated, it is certain that tens upon tens of thousands of Jews were killed or taken prisoner. Cities and villages were burnt and destroyed either in the course of the war or as an act of revenge and intimidation. Agriculture in particular suffered. Fruit trees on the mountains and in the valleys were cut down by the army for use in the siege or by military detachments in order to cow the population. That they might not be utilized by the enemy, many fruit trees were uprooted by the Jewish fighters, as were also the groves of balsam trees in the vicinity of Jericho which, of a quality unequaled in the world, were deliberately destroyed by the Jews, according to Pliny. Several cities and villages, which were demolished and of which Josephus tells that they were razed to the ground and burnt, were not actually destroyed but were damaged in one form or another. Some, like Jaffa, were already rebuilt during the war, others were completely destroyed or never restored.

With the destruction of the Temple, Jerusalem, although continuing to be inhabited by impoverished Jews, completely lost not only its spiritual significance but also its importance as a populated and economic center. Contemporary sages give distressing accounts of the plight of the surviving members of wealthy Jerusalem families (Mekh., Ba-Ḥodesh, 1; TJ, Ket. 5:13, 30b; TB *ibid.*, 67a). A considerable proportion of the inhabitants of Jerusalem and its immediate vicinity had derived their livelihood from the service and the supplies as also from other public duties associated with the Temple, as well as from the pilgrimages. With the destruction of the Temple and of Jerusalem they lost their sole means of support. The protracted war greatly increased the hostility of the soldiers and the authorities toward the Jews, undermining their position and bringing religious persecutions in its wake. The sources attest to the destruction of synagogues and the building of theaters on their sites or with their plunder, "so as to wound the feelings of the Jews." More grievous were the tortures inflicted on the Jews to compel them to transgress the commandments of their religion (Jos., Wars, 2:150 ff.; Apion, 1:43). For a time after the destruction of the Temple the Jews had the legal status of *dediticii*, that is, of a people that had unconditionally surrendered itself, its property, territory, and towns to the Roman state; they were deprived of their communal and religious rights by imperial edict; and were the arbitrary victims both in theory and in practice of unrestrained acts of lawlessness, as were also the Jewish communities in the immediate neighborhood of Ereẓ Israel. The authorities searched out the Jewish families descended from the house of David in order to destroy them and thus eradicate the last remnant of the nation's hope of the restoration of the Davidic kingdom. There was also *Vespasian's decree that, instead of the half shekel which each Jew contributed to the Temple in Jerusalem, a tax of two drachmas was to be imposed on every Jew in Ereẓ Israel and the Diaspora, and given annually to the imperial treasury for Jupiter Capitolinus, the Roman god, whose temple was on the Capitol. More than being a serious financial burden, this tax, which was paid also by women and children, was humiliating and oppressive, in addition to indirectly enforcing idolatry on the Jews. Although levied until the days of Julian the Apostate in the middle of the fourth century, its connection with Jupiter was discontinued some years after the destruction of the Temple. The memory of the war against the Romans and of the subjugation of Judea, with all that these implied, was kept alive by the Flavian emperors who throughout that dynasty's reign struck coins commemorating the victory and emphasizing the fact that Judea had been conquered.

THE ORGANIZATIONAL AND SPIRITUAL CRISIS. No less grave were the consequences in the spiritual and organizational spheres. The destruction of the country, the capture of Jerusalem, the burning of the Temple, and in their wake the abolition of the leading institutions – the high priesthood and the Sanhedrin – brought stupefaction and confusion in spiritual and communal life. Associated with the Temple and its divine service were communal and judicial institutions that had their seat in the Temple. There was the Sanhedrin, which administered justice, proclaimed the new months, and intercalated the year. There was the high priesthood, which had lost none of its commanding spiritual splendor despite its diminished prestige during the generations preceding the destruction of the Second Temple, its curtailed power, and the widespread criticism leveled at it. The destruction of the Temple brought an end to the sacrifices that atoned for Israel's sins and to the pilgrimages, and many categories of *mitzvot* connected with the Temple and its service fell into disuse, and so to some extent did numerous other *mitzvot* associated with festivals, such as the blowing of the *shofar* on the New Year and the waving of the *lulav* on Tabernacles, which were mainly observed in the Temple and only partially outside it. The Temple was also the political, juridical basis of the Jewish communal structure. Centering round it in the Persian and Hellenistic periods, Judea derived its constitutional power from the Temple, the nation's glory as far as the outside world was concerned and the focal point of the Jewish people both in Ereẓ Israel and in the Diaspora. In the Second Temple period Jerusalem was not only the capital of the state but also the theater of every spiritual creativity and political occasion. Coalescing as it were with the Temple, the city was intertwined in the practical life of the people and in the complex of the basic values of the nation's thought. The destruction of the city and of the Temple left a vacuum in the spiritual and practical life of the Jews. The crises that followed the revival and the fervent hopes aroused during the war against the Romans were calculated to undermine the nation's faith both in its teachings and in its future. One senses in the tannaitic literature and in the apocryphal works, composed in the generation after the destruction of the Temple and Jerusalem, the somber sorrow and pain that afflicted many contemporary circles. Some abstained from flesh and wine, for the altar had been destroyed on which flesh had been offered and wine poured out in libations. Many lived in caves and in fasting and self-mortification awaited the messianic era, which would soon dawn. There was no speedy transition to the spiritual, religious reality necessary to rebuild the sole basis of a hope of redemption – the life of the nation, now deprived of its Temple and its political framework.

THE ADMINISTRATIVE CHANGES AND THE REGIME AFTER DESTRUCTION. With the destruction of Jerusalem and the Temple, Judea, except for those settlements (like Caesarea) which, within the confines of Jewish Ereẓ Israel, enjoyed city status, passed under the direct control of the Roman administration. At Motza a colony was set up consisting of 800 Roman veterans, who received confiscated Jewish land. Jaffa and Flavia Neapolis, founded near Shechem, were granted city rights. No new cities were established within the limits of Jewish settlement, except *Tiberias and *Sepphoris which, having previously had city status, in the course of time regained their rights. The province of Judea, *provincia Judaea*, which was now founded, included all the coastal cities from Caesarea to Rafa, the whole of Idumea, Judea, Samaria, Perea in Transjordan, Galilee, and all the cities of the Decapolis, except Damascus and Canatha. After the death of *Agrippa II (92), the last ruler of the Herodian dynasty, a considerable part of his kingdom, comprising territories in Perea, Tiberias, Magdala, and Gaulanitis, was added to Judea. In contrast to the period preceding the destruction, the province was now subject to the authority of a Roman senator who had formerly served as a *praetor* and whose title was *legatus Augusti pro praetore provincia Judaea*.

Contrary to the prevailing Roman imperial practice of stationing legions only in the provinces bordering on the empire, *Vespasian stationed in Judea, an "internal" country, a permanent garrison, the tenth legion, *legio decima Fretensis*, that had taken part in the war against the Jews. During the entire period of the Roman imperial rule of Ereẓ Israel this legion was permanently stationed in the country, and inscriptions and seals of it have been uncovered at its various encampments. Its main camp, located on the city's ruins, was in Jerusalem; its commander was the governor, who resided in Caesarea. To facilitate contact between the military headquarters in the center of the country and the administrative seat of government at Caesarea, a branch of the coastal road was built from Antipatris to Jerusalem. Encamped near the legion were other military units, auxiliary troops, etc., that had been brought from distant lands. The auxiliary forces which had been stationed in Ereẓ Israel before the destruction and which, consisting of soldiers from Caesarea and from Sebaste, were distinguished for their hatred of the Jews whom they had provoked to acts of war, were transferred by Vespasian to other provinces. Assisting the governor was a procurator who was in charge of financial affairs. It is doubtful whether the province of Judea became independent after the destruction and was not annexed to Syria, as it had been before the war, since civil, legal, and military issues of decisive importance still required the decision of the Syrian governor who resided in Antioch. Josephus tells that Vespasian ordered that all Jewish territory was to be hired out, for he founded no city in it (Wars, 7:216). Since in point of fact many Jewish farmers remained on their land as owners, Josephus' statement refers to that land which was confiscated and which indeed constituted a considerable proportion of Jewish territory. Contemporary literature echoes a poignant cry against the Roman tax-collectors (*conductores*) who held land throughout Ereẓ Israel. Some was actually transferred to non-Jews, such as to the 800 veterans, and its former owners were dispossessed. Other land was given to favorites and loyal friends of the Jewish and non-Jewish authorities or to large tenants, the *conductores*. The former owners were not ejected from most of the confiscated land but cultivated their own as tenant farmers, for which they had to pay a high rental in kind, expecting nevertheless to be evicted at any time on the pretext of not paying the rent or some other excuse.

Taxes. On unconfiscated land a tax was levied which was increased after the destruction and from which only a few imperial court favorites, such as Josephus in the days of Domitian, were exempted. But whereas some in the territories of the Roman Empire were liable to a land but not to a poll tax, the Jews in Ereẓ Israel had to pay both. A Roman writer of a generation or two after the destruction states that, because of their rebelliousness, the tax imposed on the Jews of Ereẓ Israel was more severe than that demanded of the inhabitants of the neighboring countries. After the destruction the tax for the provision and maintenance of the army and of the enlarged Roman officialdom in the country, levied in kind (*annona*) from dough, animals, and all locally produced or imported agricultural and industrial products, was increased. There were bitter complaints against the excessive demands and the harshness employed in collecting them, as also against the various forms of forced labor, whereby the authorities and especially the army compelled the population, both urban and rural, to perform work, such as haulage, or repairing and making roads, with their own persons and with the help of their temporary or permanently requisitioned draught animals. A short time after the destruction small watchtower stations were erected along the borders and along the main roads in many places in Ereẓ Israel. In the years following the destruction, under the Flavian dynasty (until 96), a system of defense, known by its latter name of *limes Palaestinae* was established in southern Ereẓ Israel. Extending from Menois, north of Rafa, to the Dead Sea, the *limes* consisted of a series of fortresses connected by a road, along which, on allotments of land, military colonists enjoying a special status were settled. In the rear of the *limes* were two military bases: *Carmel and *Hebron. While its establishment brought security to the country's southern settlements, it further increased the already large non-Jewish population in the country.

THE INCEPTION OF A CENTRAL LEADERSHIP. The renewal in post-destruction Ereẓ Israel of Jewish communal life – which also reconstructed Judaism in the Diaspora – without the framework of a state and without a Temple which was the foundation of Jewish religious and spiritual existence, is associated with the name of Rabban *Johanan b. Zakkai and with his activities in the semi-Greek city of *Jabneh. One of the greatest Pharisaic sages in Jerusalem before the destruction, he vehemently opposed the Sadducees and the Sadducean high priesthood. He was deputy to the president of the Sanhedrin, Rabban *Simeon b. Gamaliel, who was the leader of the government set up after Cestius Gallus had been forced to retreat and with whom he signed the letters sent throughout Ereẓ Israel and the Diaspora in connection with tithes and the intercalation of the year (Mid. Tan. 26:13). To him is ascribed the abolition of the ceremony of the bitter water in the examination of a wife suspected of infidelity (Sot. 9:9). Although a priest, he is depicted as a scholar and teacher who in his statements and teachings protested and strove against the priests' haughtiness and aloofness. It is possible that he gave no support to the revolt against Rome. At any rate, warning the rebels against fanaticism and impetuous acts, he called on them to display moderation in their relations with gentiles and toward their sacred objects: "Be not precipitate in tearing down the altars of gentiles that you do not have to rebuild them with your own hands, that you do not tear down those made of brick and be ordered: Make them of stone…." (ARN[2] 31, 66). He was in besieged Jerusalem, but left the city during the siege, apparently in the spring of 68 when Vespasian was closing in on the city. His departure then left a deep impression on talmudic tradition, and there are different versions of his appearance before Vespasian when he prophesied that the latter would become the emperor (which Josephus ascribes to himself, and various sources to different persons in the east). According to later traditions in the Babylonian Talmud, he obtained from the emperor "Jabneh with its sages" and "the dynasty of Rabban Gamaliel" (Git. 56b). But this tradition, which contains much taken from somewhat later circumstances, reflects the time when "Jabneh with its sages" was already established under the leadership of Rabban *Gamaliel, the son of Rabban Simeon b. Gamaliel, and the foundations had been laid for the succeeding dynasty of *nesi'im* who presided over the Sanhedrin and led the nation for more than 300 years. The earlier traditions embodied in the Ereẓ Israel literature (Lam. R. 1:5, no. 31; ARN[1] 40, 22–23; ARN[2] 60, 19–20) indicate that Johanan b. Zakkai was first held in custody at Gophna and later transferred, apparently under duress, to Jabneh, which was used together with other cities such as Ashdod, on account of their large non-Jewish population, as a place for concentrating and imprisoning the Jews, and especially the prominent ones, who had surrendered to the Romans. According to one source, he only requested of the emperor, who granted his request, that certain persons be saved; according to others he succeeded in obtaining Jabneh "to teach his pupils" or "to observe the *mitzvot* and study the Torah" there.

The general circumstances prevailing during the war against the Romans, as also the usual procedures adopted by Vespasian and his son *Titus, support these earlier versions of the origin of Jabneh. When requesting "Jabneh with its sages," Johanan b. Zakkai did not presumably ask of and receive from Rome permission to establish a national or even merely a spiritual center. Although the official permission he received was extremely restricted, he in effect began, with or without the authorities' knowledge, to rehabilitate Jewish life theoretically and to fill in practice the vacuum created by the destruction. He reestablished the *Sanhedrin, and in Jabneh commenced to proclaim the new months and intercalate the years, on which the entire calendar of Jewish festivals depended. The proclamation of the new month, based on the testimony of witnesses, and the intercalation of the year, dependent on the decision of the *bet din*, which were previously done in the Temple in Jerusalem, were now transferred to Jabneh, and the information was transmitted to all the cities of Ereẓ Israel and the Diaspora. By this action alone Jabneh became the leading center and place of assembly for all Israel. To it was transferred some of the authority and activities that pertained to the Temple courtyards in Jerusalem. Several of Johanan b. Zakkai's regulations deal with the proclamation of the new month at Jabneh. He decreed that the *shofar* was to be blown at Jabneh also on a New Year that fell on a Sabbath, which had previously only been done in the Temple and in Jerusalem. Another regulation lays down "that even if the head of the *bet din* is in some other place, the witnesses (who testify when the new moon appeared) should still go only to the place of the assembly" (RH 4:4). His other regulations were likewise intended to fill the void created by the destruction and to rebuild Jewish life while retaining a remembrance of the Temple, so as to rehabilitate the former without the latter. He instituted that the *lulav* be waved all the seven days of Tabernacles, contrary to the situation that obtained during the existence of the Temple when it was waved seven days in the Temple and only one day in other parts of the country (*ibid.* 4:3). He ordained that the priests bless the people during prayers in the synagogue without their shoes on, as had been done at the end of the service in the Temple. According to the *halakhah*, a proselyte, on his conversion, had to bring a sacrifice to the Temple, but with its destruction he set aside a quarter shekel for a sacrifice to be offered when the Temple would be rebuilt, a regulation abolished by Johanan b. Zakkai (*ibid.* 31b). To the people, shaken by the destruction of the Temple, "where the sins of Israel were expiated," he taught: "My son, be not grieved. We have another means of expiation like it. What is it? It is deeds of loving-kindness" (ARN[1] 4, 21). He laid the foundations for the structure of organized life by instituting or renewing the ordination of sages and the title of "rabbi" for ordained sages, a fact of great significance not only for the religious life, law, and leadership in Ereẓ Israel, but also for the country's hegemony over the Diaspora, since the right of granting ordination was restricted to the leading institutions in Ereẓ Israel. The title of rabbi also indicated that its bearer was a member of the Sanhedrin and acted in its name. Furthermore, Johanan b. Zakkai began to work for the consolidation and unity of the nation amid the various trends and movements which appeared in all their destructive virulence during the last days of the Temple's existence. Nevertheless Johanan b. Zakkai's activities are limited in comparison with those that marked the days of Rabban Gamaliel. This is not to be ascribed only to the difficult external conditions then prevailing and the Roman Empire's nonrecognition of the leadership at Jabneh. It is also due to the fact that many sages dissociated themselves from Johanan b. Zakkai and his actions at Jabneh. Conspicuous by their absence were not only the priestly sages who ministered in the Temple and ranked among the influential members of Pharisaic circles, but also many others, some of whom went to Jabneh after the days of Johanan b. Zakkai. Of his five pupils, only two, *Eliezer b. Hyrcanus and *Joshua b. Hananiah, accompanied him to Jabneh. Apparently a considerable number of the sages were unable to reconcile themselves with him, with his leaving besieged Jerusalem, his surrender to the Romans, and his throwing himself on the emperor's mercy. These circles, however, cooperated with Rabban Gamaliel, his successor and a member of the dynasty of the *nasi*.

IN THE DAYS OF THE NASI RABBAN GAMALIEL. A change in the status of Judaism in Ereẓ Israel took place when the Flavian dynasty came to an end with the murder of Domitian (96). The policy of encouraging informers in Rome against those suspected of Judaism was abolished, as was that of persecuting proselytes. To this period is to be assigned the accession of Rabban Gamaliel to the position of *nasi* after having previously been compelled to go into hiding from the Romans. In contrast to Johanan b. Zakkai who according to the evidence had no contact with the authorities during his tenure of the office of *nasi*, Rabban Gamaliel traveled to Antioch where he obtained authorization from "the governor in Syria" (Eduy. 7:7). Roman imperial emissaries were sent to ascertain the nature of Hebrew civil law, then reintroduced and extensively in vogue. There were the journeys to Rome undertaken by Rabban Gamaliel together with the leading members of the Sanhedrin, Eliezer b. Hyrcanus, *Eleazar b. Azariah, Joshua, and *Akiva, their meeting with the authorities, and their visit to the Jews in the city. Under Rabban Gamaliel the center in Jabneh assumed most of the functions fulfilled by the Sanhedrin in Second Temple times. To it questions were addressed from all the cities of Ereẓ Israel and the Diaspora. During this period missions were reintroduced on behalf of the *nasi* and the Sanhedrin to the communities of Ereẓ Israel and the Diaspora, some of the most eminent sages, such as Eliezer b. Hyrcanus, Joshua b. Hananiah, Akiva, and *Ishmael, acting as emissaries and being sometimes accompanied by the *nasi* himself. These missions also had great economic importance, since the emissaries brought back with them the money collected in the Diaspora for the maintenance of the central authority in Ereẓ Israel. The ties that the emissaries formed with the cities of Ereẓ Israel and with the Diaspora had not only an organizational significance but also established a personal link between these places and the great teachers of the Torah acting in the name of the *nasi*. Wherever they went, they gave practical decisions on the questions submitted to them, brought with them the innovations decided upon in the *battei midrashot* in Ereẓ Israel, supervised the communal arrangements and institutions, and established those essential for the life of a Jewish community, such as charitable, educational and other similar ones. The emissaries decisively influenced the appointment of leaders in the cities and villages of Ereẓ Israel and the communities of the Diaspora, and even had the power to depose them if their leadership was found to be defective. During this period the character of the Sanhedrin assumed definite form as a *bet midrash*, a legislature and a dominant executive body.

Many discussions and actions that marked those years until the Bar Kokhba revolt (132) had not only then a decisive effect on the life of the Jews in Ereẓ Israel and in the Diaspora but shaped and directed the existence of the nation throughout all subsequent generations. Amid much argument and conflict the *halakhah* was decided according to Bet Hillel, a fact of great influence on the entire history of the *halakhah*. A final decision was taken on numerous problems concerned with proselytization, priestly dues, tithes, and other subjects. In this period the concept crystallized that study is greater than action, since "study leads to action" (Kid. 40b). At one assembly which took place at Lydda in keeping with the custom of meeting on occasion elsewhere than at the permanent center at Jabneh, it was decided that a Jew, if forced to transgress the *mitzvot* of the Torah, may do so to save his life except in the three instances of idolatry, murder, and incest. But at a time of open religious persecution intended to compel Jews to sin against their religion, a Jew should suffer death and not transgress even a minor custom (TJ, Sanh. 3:6, 21a). At Jabneh the form of the festivals was laid down under the circumstances prevailing after the destruction, when there were now no pilgrimages, sacrifices, or Temple. The order was also fixed of the four fasts instituted after the destruction of the First Temple but either observed partially or totally disregarded in the Second Temple period. Under the direction of the sages of Jabneh, *Aquila the proselyte of Pontus translated the Bible anew into Greek. The earlier Septuagint did not mirror the later halakhic and aggadic interpretation of the Pentateuch and the Prophets, thereby creating a barrier between the Jews who used it and the halakhic and aggadic expositions they heard from the sages. That the Septuagint had been adopted and canonized by the Church and several of its passages were used as a basis for the Church Fathers' interpretations may have influenced the sages to produce a new translation. The Jews did not entirely discard the Septuagint but Aquila's version was adopted in synagogues and in Jewish life. On Rabban Gamaliel's explicit instructions the order was fixed of the prayer of Eighteen Benedictions, known already in Second Temple times (see *Amidah). While it is not certain what precisely was done in the days of Gamaliel, at all events from this period the prayer was permanently instituted for private and public worship two or three times daily.

In the days of Jabneh, too, the breach and separation between Judaism and *Christianity took place. Pharisaic Judaism had in the Second Temple period shown tolerance alike to Gentile and Judeo-Christians. But after the destruction came the separation. The Judeo-Christians dissociated themselves from the war against the Romans and from the tragedy that had come upon the nation. Nor did some share the hope of deliverance, which had, in their view, been fulfilled with the advent of their Messiah. Many of them saw in the destruction of the Temple and of Jerusalem a proof of the truth of Christianity, in that Israel had been punished for killing their Messiah, and Jesus' prophecy regarding the destruction of the Temple had been fulfilled. Some even held that with its destruction and the discontinuance of many commandments, all the *mitzvot* had been annulled and Judaism's hour had passed. Thus they used the destruction of the Temple for propagating Christianity. To this the sages of Jabneh answered with actions calculated to bring about a breach and a separation between the Jews and Judeo-Christianity and especially those trends in Judeo-Christianity that approximated to Gentile Christianity. A notable factor that had a decisive influence in the Jewish community's rejection of Judeo-Christianity was the introduction in the Eighteen Benedictions of an additional blessing directed against its adherents: "To apostates let there be no hope if they return not to Thy Torah, and may the Nazarenes and the sectarians perish as in a moment" (such or something similar was the ancient Ereẓ Israel version). This prayer in effect excluded Judeo-Christianity from the Jewish people.

THE EDUCATIONAL ACTIVITIES OF THE SAGES OF JABNEH INSIDE THE CONFINES OF THE HOUSE OF ASSEMBLY.

The sages of Jabneh succeeded not only in reconstructing the life of the nation but also in achieving the efflorescence of its spiritual and social existence. This was largely due to the activities of the leaders of the *bet midrash* and the Sanhedrin as also to the great personalities with whom that period was favored. Most of them were ordained rabbis and functioned officially as members of the Sanhedrin. But there were also those – and some of them represented the most outstandingly creative and constructive forces – who, unordained, continued as "disciples" and worked as itinerant teachers of the Torah in Ereẓ Israel unhampered by any official obligations. Almost none of the personalities who established and consolidated the institutions of the communal national leadership at Jabneh emanated from the circles that, during Second Temple times, had constituted the social elite, whether of the priestly or the social-economic aristocracy. Some of the sages were indeed priests and even well-to-do or rich, but many, and they included some of the most eminent figures, were poor and of undistinguished birth, their standing being determined only by their learning and their rich personalities. In addition to the *bet midrash* at Jabneh, others flourished in the towns and villages, being found in all parts of the country from the south to the north, at Kefar Aziz in the south, where Ishmael was active; at *Bene Berak, where Akiva lived; at Lydda, the seat of Eliezer b. Hyrcanus and of *Tarfon; at Peki'in, which was under the leadership of Joshua b. Hananiah; and in Galilean cities, such as at Sepphoris, where *Ḥalafta was active, at *Sikhnin, the seat of *Ḥananiah b. Teradyon, and at Tiberias, where *Yose b. Kisma taught. The heads of the local *battei midrashot* came regularly to Jabneh which some made their main place of residence, paying only short visits to their own *battei midrashot*.

RESETTLEMENT AND ECONOMIC RECOVERY. Despite the considerable suffering endured as a consequence of the war, Jewish Ereẓ Israel made a rapid recovery. Many captives, freed with the help of the local Jewish population or by other means, returned to their homes. As a result of the teachings of the contemporary sages, the significance of Ereẓ Israel, its settlement, and the redemption of its land now assumed the character of a basic principle in Jewish thought and action. Large tracts of land were redeemed from the non-Jews, plantations were restored, and new ones planted. Agricultural knowledge increased, and industry in Ereẓ Israel, consisting of processed agricultural products, quickly recovered. Craftsmen's associations plied their trades; farmers reaped bounteous harvests; agricultural and industrial products were exported. Already toward the end of the first century C.E. the economic position had improved considerably. In general, Jewish cities destroyed during the war were rebuilt and rehabilitated. All the Greek cities, whose Jewish settlement had been destroyed during the war, were repopulated by Jews. By the end of the first century C.E. there were flourishing Jewish communities in places like Caesarea, Ashkelon, Acre, Beth-Shean, and elsewhere. Great assistance in the speedy rehabilitation of the Jewish nation in Ereẓ Israel was rendered by those cities which had not revolted against Rome or had at an early stage in the war stopped fighting, while the basis for the restoration of a normal economic life was provided by those cities and circles which had not participated in the war. By reason both of postwar military requirements and of the economic and commercial prosperity of the Roman Empire under the Antonines (96–180), the network of roads in Ereẓ Israel was extended and many bridges were built. In 106 the *Nabatean kingdom was annexed to the Roman Empire, and in 111 a start was made with constructing a road linking Damascus and Akaba. A large part of the foreign trade with the Arabian Peninsula and with India passed along this route, to the benefit of the cities, including the Jewish settlements, adjoining this road and of the Jews in the Greek cities in Transjordan. The Jewish population increased, too, in Akaba, that is, Ezion-Geber.

THE WAR OF QUIETUS. In 115–117 the Jews in the Diaspora rose in a widespread revolt which, embracing Libya, Cyrenaica, Egypt, Cyprus, and Mesopotamia, was marked both by battles between the Jews and the Greeks and uprisings against Roman rule in the east. The focal point of the revolt was in the Diaspora and the early historical sources speak explicitly only of the revolt and the destruction of Diaspora Jewry and especially of North African countries. But epigraphic evidence about military missions sent at that time to Ereẓ Israel and fragmentary literary information indicate that there were uprisings on a considerable scale in Ereẓ Israel too. In Jewish tradition these uprisings are known as "the war of Quietus" (Sot. 9:14), after the Moorish commander Lusius Quietus, who, having ruthlessly suppressed the revolt of the Jews in Mesopotamia, was sent to stamp out the revolt in Judea and was then appointed its governor until recalled to Rome, where he was executed at the beginning of Hadrian's rule (118).

Talmudic traditions tell of meetings on the Temple Mount in Jerusalem, of the revolt spreading to *Galilee, the destruction of various cities in Ereẓ Israel, and the execution of its leaders, *Pappus and Lulianus, whose activities extended also to the Diaspora (Sifra 8:9). With the suppression of the revolt religious persecutions were reinstituted. In an act of deliberate provocation, an idol was set up on the Temple Mount (Ta'an. 4:6).

THE BAR KOKHBA REVOLT. The accession of *Hadrian (117) brought with it a trend to restore peace in the east and to rehabilitate and reconstruct the region on an extensive scale. Apparent in Hadrian's actions was a regard for the national character, predilections, and needs of the provinces. Ereẓ Israel and the Jews, too, benefited from this trend. In his efforts to restore devastated areas, the emperor promised the Jews that he would rebuild and return Jerusalem to them, and permit the rebuilding of the Temple. Jews began to flock to Jerusalem, and organizational and financial preparations were made for rebuilding the Temple (Or. Sibyll. 5:252–4; Epistle of Barnabas, 16: 1–5; Epiphanius, *Liber de Mensuris et Ponderibus*, 170; Gen. R. 64:10). A few years after his accession Hadrian, changing his mind, abandoned the plan of rebuilding Jerusalem as a Jewish city and instead decided to continue its construction as a pagan Roman city. Even the coins struck in Ereẓ Israel in those days show a tendency to ignore the prevailing facts of Jewish existence. It is difficult to determine Hadrian's motives for this change of mind. He may have been prompted to adopt this new course by the profound echo which his promise produced among the Jews and by the political fears he entertained at restoring Jerusalem to the Jewish people. His attitude to Judaism may also have changed, for during his reign and already at the beginning of the twenties he displayed indubitable pan-Hellenistic tendencies, his policy being aimed at introducing in the empire and particularly in its eastern regions the later universal Hellenistic outlook and mode of life. This found expression alike in the erection of buildings and monuments, the passing of laws against Oriental usages, and, inclusion in the ban against castration which was punishable with death, the prohibition of circumcision.

This last was not specifically directed against Judaism, since its practice was also forbidden to others in the east who circumcised their sons. But for no other people did circumcision occupy so significant a place in its thought. Nor did any other people so scrupulously insist on circumcising every single boy. Hadrian, who before becoming emperor had been the governor of Syria and had come into contact with the Jews and their sages, was undoubtedly aware of what these arrangements of his meant for the Jews. But in his resolve to reshape and reconstitute life in Ereẓ Israel, he deliberately ignored the Jewish nation and its past in the country. No wonder that one historian, *Dio Cassius, mentions this resolve of Hadrian as the cause of the revolt: "For it was terrible in the eyes of the Jews that non-Jews should dwell in their city and that gentile temples should be erected in it" (*Historia Romana*, 69:12–14), while another source gives the prohibition of circumcision as the reason for the revolt (*Historia Augusta*: Hadrian, 14). These actions, coming as they did after the spiritual elation engendered by the permission to rebuild Jerusalem and the Temple, led to a profound agitation among the Jews and to military preparations against Rome, to the surreptitious construction of various fortifications, and to the accumulation of arms. Dio Cassius tells that the Jews purposely damaged the weapons they made for the Romans, so that these should be rejected and remain in the possession of the Jews without their stockpiling arousing suspicion. While Hadrian was in Ereẓ Israel and its neighborhood (128–132) the Jews did not openly rebel, but the grave terrorist acts then committed in the country found the permanent Roman forces there insufficient to cope with the situation. An additional legion, the *Sexta Ferrata*, was brought to Ereẓ Israel, and remained in the country after the revolt, being stationed in Kefar Otnai at the entrance to the Valley of Jezreel. The authorities were also compelled to reinforce the tenth legion by recruiting soldiers from nearby countries. When Hadrian left the east, the revolt broke out and assumed large proportions, since "the Jews throughout the entire world were in an uproar too, and joined them, inflicting openly or by stealth great losses on the Romans. They were moreover helped by non-Jews" (Dio Cassius loc. cit.). The *Samaritans, or at least some of them, also joined.

In contrast to the rebellion against the Romans in 66–70, the revolt was distinguished by national unity and centralized leadership. There are references to local heroes and to various messiahs and pretenders to the royal title who flourished in the first stages of the revolt, but conspicuous during its course and until its end were the leadership and the central figure of *Simeon bar Kokhba. It is he who is mentioned in the historical sources, round whose personality are centered talmudic traditions and legends, and in whose name – Simeon, Nasi of Israel – coins were struck. Documents and letters, dating from the time of the war and found in the caves of the Judean Desert, were taken there by fugitives from En-Gedi and its vicinity. In them it is "Simeon bar Kosiba, Nasi of Israel," who issues instructions and commands; in his name public lands are leased out. Christian sources state that he was called Bar Kokhba by reason of the messianic traits ascribed to him. Akiva, too, acknowledged his messiahship and declared: "This is the King Messiah" (TJ, Ta'an. 4:8, 68d). With Simeon the Nasi there also appears on some coins "Eleazar the priest," apparently *Eleazar of Modi'in, a sage of Jabneh, whom talmudic tradition associates with Bar Kokhba. The headquarters of Bar Kokhba and of the commanders of the Jewish fighters was at *Bethar situated at the extremity of a mountain ridge to the southwest of Jerusalem. In the intervening period between the war against the Romans and the Bar Kokhba revolt, the town, having been rebuilt after its destruction, flourished as a commercial and inhabited center for the region in place of Jerusalem. Shortly before the revolt, the Sanhedrin and the household of the *nasi* moved to Bethar, in which not only schools for study of Torah were established but also one for Greek learning. It is not known what connection the household of the *nasi* had with the revolt or with Bar Kokhba, or to what extent the Sanhedrin was associated with the revolt, but it is clear that the sages supported it.

The revolt began with a great offensive. Bar Kokhba succeeded in gaining control of the whole of Judea, including Jerusalem, as well as of a considerable part of the rest of Ereẓ Israel, and in introducing in the territory under his rule an independent Jewish order. The rebels defeated Tinnius Rufus, the Roman governor, and Publius Marcellius, the governor of Syria, who arrived with the legions stationed in Syria and to whose assistance the legions stationed in Egypt and Arabia had been dispatched. The 22nd Legion, which had come from Egypt, was annihilated. At this juncture the Jewish fighters invaded the coastal region and the Romans engaged in sea battles against the Jews. In those days Rome enjoyed complete security, peace prevailed on its borders, and hence it was able to mobilize large numbers of men and forces even from distant places. Hadrian summoned Julius Severus, the governor of Britain, who arrived with his forces and with legions from Danubian countries. There were about 12 legions in all, composed of their full complement or of detachments of them.

Julius Severus, "refraining from engaging in open warfare," forced the Jewish fighters back step by step amid heavy losses to the Roman army, compelled them to retreat to fortresses which were taken one by one. "Fifty strongholds … and 985 of the most important settlements were destroyed"; hundreds of thousands were killed. In the first stage, Galilee, which was not seriously affected, was captured, and the main burden of war fell on Judea. Eventually, the Jewish fighters were thrust back to their last stronghold, Bethar, which fell after a protracted siege. Tradition records that Bethar was captured on Av 9 (the summer of 135), on the anniversary of the destruction of the First and Second Temples (Ta'an. 4:6). With its fall and the death of Simeon bar Kosiba there came an end to the struggle which had lasted three and a half years, although there were sieges and skirmishes in the region of the Judean Desert caves to which the fighters had escaped in the final stages of the revolt, even as had been the case with the fortress at Masada after the war against the Romans. In conformity with Roman custom, Jerusalem was now plowed up with a yoke of oxen, and thus the limits were fixed of the Roman colony, henceforth called *Colonia *Aelia Capitolina* in Roman sources.

Consequences of the Revolt. In addition to the destruction of populated areas and the large-scale massacre, there were great numbers of Jewish captives who filled the slave markets in Ereẓ Israel and in distant lands. Especially notorious was the market under the terebinth near Hebron where a Jewish slave was sold for the price of a horse's feed. Many settlements, especially in Judea, were not rebuilt. The central Judean Mountains were largely depopulated of their Jewish inhabitants. In Galilee, which suffered less from the aftermath of the revolt, the olive plantations were destroyed (TJ, Pe'ah 7:1, 20a). Hadrian now resolved to launch a war of annihilation against the Torah and to expunge the name of Israel from the land. To this end decrees were issued against the observance of the *mitzvot*, gatherings in synagogues for the purposes of prayer or study were prohibited, *battei din* were forbidden to meet. In a description of those times a contemporary Babylonian sage commented: "'Of them that love Me and keep My commandments' (Ex. 19:6) – 'These are the Jews who live in Ereẓ Israel and jeopardize their lives for the sake of the *mitzvot*.' 'Why are you being led out to be decapitated?' 'Because I circumcised my son.' 'Why are you being led out to be burnt?' 'Because I read the Torah.' 'Why are you being led out to be crucified?' 'Because I ate unleavened bread.' 'Why are you being whipped with the scourge?' 'Because I performed the *mitzvah* of the *lulav*'" (Mekh., ba-Ḥodesh, 6). Jews were forbidden to stay in Jerusalem and only once a year, on Tishah be-Av (Av 9), were they permitted to enter the city to weep over the remains of their holy places. Desirous of blotting out, too, all reference to the Jews' association with Ereẓ Israel, Hadrian changed the name of Judea to Syria Palaestina, by which it henceforth came to be known in non-Jewish literature. The authorities confiscated land on an extensive scale on the strength of martial law or of offenses against the new decrees, such as the prohibition of circumcision. Large tracts of land lay waste, their owners having been taken captive or compelled to flee. The Jews in the country underwent a harsh period of persecution. Many, and they included the nation's most eminent men and sages such as Akiva, Ishmael, Hananiah b. Teradyon, Tarfon, and others, were killed in the persecutions, many went into hiding in Ereẓ Israel, large numbers fled abroad and never returned or did so only after several years. There were numerous martyrs, this being the generation that bequeathed to the Jewish people the tradition of martyrdom (see *Kiddush ha-Shem*). From the end of the revolt until the close of Hadrian's reign (i.e., from 135 to 138) the Jews of Ereẓ Israel bore the full brunt of the anti-religious decrees.

The repressive measures were somewhat relaxed only on the accession of *Antoninus Pius. He neither annulled them nor immediately restored to the Jews the status they had enjoyed before the revolt. Gradually, however, their situation improved. Apparently at the beginning of Antoninus Pius' reign, circumcision was permitted, a law enacted by him having allowed the Jews to circumcise their sons but not slaves or proselytes. For the Samaritans the prohibition remained in force, and for a long time they circumcised their sons at great risk. But alike in the days of the Antonines as in those of Hadrian, a harsh military regime prevailed in Ereẓ Israel.

Recovery After the Revolt: Usha. The first signs of the recovery of communal life appeared in Galilee, to which the center of Jewish life henceforth passed and where the main population as also the seat of the Sanhedrin and of the *nasi* remained until the end of the period. The Sanhedrin had first gone to *Usha, whence it moved for a short time to *Shepharam and from there to *Bet She'arim and Sepphoris. In the third century it finally settled at Tiberias, the capital of Galilee. But Judea still had its Jewish population, its *battei midrashot*, and sages – at Lydda there was a large *bet midrash*, which enjoyed independence in many spheres of Jewish life. But the central authority and the focal point of spiritual creativity were in Galilee, where the main work of collecting and of finally redacting the tannaitic and amoraic literature was done.

The leaders who restored the religious and communal life comprised several of Akiva's younger pupils who survived the massacre and who had not yet gained renown in the generation of Jabneh: *Meir, *Judah b. Ilai, *Jose b. Ḥalafta, *Simeon b. Yoḥai, and *Nehemiah. The early meetings of the Sanhedrin were still held in temporary quarters and under semi-underground conditions in the Valley of Bet Rimmon, and only after many years, at "the end of the religious persecutions," did it meet at Usha (Song R. 2:5 no. 3). Among its first decisions was to declare the levitical cleanness of Tiberias. From its foundation at the beginning of the first century C.E. many Jews and especially priests refrained from living there for fear that it had been built on a cemetery. Hadrian had wanted to give the city a pagan character but the temple which he had begun to build was not completed. After the revolt Tiberias was almost entirely Jewish. Simeon b. Yoḥai sought to declare it levitically clean and following protracted discussions it was recognized as such (TJ, Shev. 9:1, 38d). This facilitated the city's growth and enabled it to serve during the years as the spiritual center. Simeon b. Gamaliel, the son of Rabban Gamaliel of Jabneh, did not take part in the Sanhedrin in the early stages of its reestablishment, for he, too, had been compelled to go into hiding for several years. After some time he is mentioned as the head of the Sanhedrin at Usha.

The period not only of his tenure of the office of *nasi* (c. 140–170) but of the entire reign of the Antonines (until 193) was a difficult one both politically and economically. The authorities showed a growing contempt and suspicion of the Jews, and when Marcus Aurelius passed through Ereẓ Israel in 175 he expressed himself in opprobrious terms about them. They, for their part, displayed considerable rebelliousness, hoping as they did for the downfall of Rome, a hope that grew with the latter's clashes and preparations for war with the Parthians. Simeon b. Yoḥai asserted: "If you see a Persian horse tied in the burial places of Ereẓ Israel, expect the Messiah" (Song R. 8:9). This rebelliousness was responsible for the fact that the Jews of Ereẓ Israel, like the other peoples of the east, supported Avidius Cassius who had proclaimed himself emperor and was assassinated shortly before Marcus Aurelius' arrival in the country. Brigandage, too, increased greatly at this time, and although this was due to economic difficulties, it also had overtones of political insurrection. In Ereẓ Israel as a whole the economic situation was quite good during this period, although the country suffered in 166 from a plague which spread in the east. Like other provinces, Ereẓ Israel profited from the expanded international trade. Roads were built and bridges constructed, public institutions were established, markets and grain exchanges were set up and wells dug, creating a sense of security and promoting commerce, so that many cities flourished at this time. There were Jews, too, who benefited from this prosperity.

In Rome two inscriptions of Jews from Tiberias have been found that testify to commercial stations in the city, and some Jews, who were imperial court favorites, rose to positions of eminence. But the Jewish community as a whole lived in dire poverty. Thus reference is made to "the generation of R. Judah b. Illai ... six of whose pupils covered themselves with one garment and studied the Torah" (Sanh. 20a). The nonrecognition of the Jews' religious rights brought in its train economic difficulties. Up to the Bar Kokhba revolt the authorities had exempted the Jews from land taxes during the sabbatical year, when they had no income from agricultural produce. After the revolt they had to pay these taxes, and were hard put to find a way of meeting the burden of taxation while observing, at least to some extent, the sabbatical year (Sanh. 3:3 et al.). This circumstance is the background to the *halakhah* which lays down that "if at the present time a man wishes to become a proselyte, he is to be addressed as follows: 'What reason have you for wanting to become a proselyte? Do you not know that at present Jews are persecuted and oppressed, despised, harassed, and burdened with afflictions ... and do not conduct themselves in public like other peoples?'" (Yev. 47a; Tractate *Gerim*, beginning). As a result of the harsh conditions, there was an increasing emigration, either temporary or permanent, from Ereẓ Israel. Seeking to stem it, the sages enacted *halakhot* to curtail this tendency.

Despite the difficult political conditions and the imperial nonrecognition, the sages of the generation of Usha and Rabban Simeon b. Gamaliel succeeded in consolidating the leadership of the central authority and in restoring to Ereẓ Israel its hegemony over the Diaspora. During the persecutions, when the house of assembly ceased to function, one of the Ereẓ Israel sages, *Hananiah, the nephew of Joshua, who had been sent to Babylonia, began to proclaim the new months and intercalate years there, and would not desist even when the central authority was reestablished in Ereẓ Israel. Only by resolute persuasion, by appeasement, and with the support of the Babylonian sages was the *nasi* able to make the separatist circles in Babylonia cease their activities, whereupon the Jews there once again submitted to the authority of Ereẓ Israel. In the days of Rabban Simeon b. Gamaliel, the office of *nasi* assumed the form of a triumvirate, consisting of the *nasi* himself, the *av bet din*, and a sage, who was the authorized halakhist. For some time, *Nathan, the son of the exilarch in Babylonia, was the *av bet din*, thereby enabling the *nasi* to associate with his office also a representative of that large Diaspora community. This set an example for future generations, the great majority of those occupying the position of *av bet din* in the tannaitic and amoraic period having been sages who immigrated to Ereẓ Israel from Babylonia.

In the generation following the Bar Kokhba revolt the Samaritans began a large-scale expansion beyond the confines of "the land of the Cutheans." Their expansion to the north having been halted by the Beth-Shean and Jezreel Valleys, they spread northwest along the coast and especially southwest along the southern coastal plain. The reasons for this may have been the Jews' diminished power as well as the plight in which the Samaritans found themselves on account of religious persecution. They therefore sought refuge among the Jewish population, perhaps because of the close contacts established between them during the Bar Kokhba revolt. The Samaritans' expansion into the Jewish areas led to considerable friction, and there were assertions by sages that, since leaving their villages, they had become lax in the observance of *mitzvot*. In contrast to the earlier *halakhah*, they were now more and more adjudged as non-Jews.

THE SEVERAN DYNASTY. R. JUDAH HA-NASI. A period of political and economic efflorescence came to the Jews of Ereẓ Israel under the Severan emperors (193–235), coinciding largely with the tenure of the office of *nasi* by Judah I, the eldest son of Rabban Simeon b. Gamaliel and known as Rabbi. After the murder of Commodus (192) an armed struggle broke out between Pescennius Niger and Septimius *Severus which divided the east, including Ereẓ Israel and the legions stationed there. Pescennius Niger had, as governor of Syria, been ruthless in his attitude to the Jews. When they had asked him to lighten the burden of taxation, he had answered that were it possible he would tax the very air they breathed. He severely punished the cities which supported his rival. While the tenth legion sided with him, the house of the *nasi* and the Jews of Ereẓ Israel supported Severus, whose victory was regarded as a deliverance. The good relations that existed between the Jews of Ereẓ Israel and the Severans, which continued throughout that dynasty's reign, influenced several Severan emperors in their predilection and love for Judaism and for a syncretism in which it, too, was included. Alexander *Severus was derisively called *archisynagogus* (head of the synagogue). The political position of the Jews in Ereẓ Israel improved and they were able to occupy notable positions in the Greek and Roman cities. Their more influential status found expression mainly in an increased autonomy, both public and judicial. The *nasi* was permitted to levy taxes for the maintenance of the central authority, civil and criminal cases were tried, and judgment could be enforced against the guilty party. When necessary, the *nasi* could also try capital cases. While this right was not officially recognized by Roman law, it was not exercised surreptitiously (Origen, *Epistola ad Africanum*, 28:14).

The relations between the Roman Empire and *Judah ha-Nasi were particularly good. Extensive areas of state land in the Valley of Jezreel, Golan, and elsewhere were given to him as a gift or on lease. The *aggadah* frequently mentions the close ties between him and the Roman emperor *Antoninus, but since several Severans bore this name, it is difficult to determine which of them is meant. From what is known of the stay of the emperors in the neighborhood of Ereẓ Israel and their association with Judaism, this reference is probably to *Caracalla (198–217 C.E.) or Alexander Severus (222–235 C.E.). The Jews were grateful to the Severan dynasty and both in Ereẓ Israel (at Kaisan in Upper Galilee) and in the Diaspora synagogues dedicated to the emperors of that dynasty have been found. In their days there was a great expansion of settlement. Thus at this time there were included within the halakhic limits of Ereẓ Israel areas in the north and south, which halakhically had not belonged to Ereẓ Israel since the majority of their inhabitants had been non-Jews and to which the commandments applicable to Ereẓ Israel, such as those relating to priestly dues and tithes, had not previously applied. At this time, too, there was established in Jerusalem a permanent Jewish settlement, known in talmudic tradition as the "the holy community in Jerusalem" (*kehilla kadisha de-bi-Yrushalayim*). While presumably the prohibition against Jews' settling in Jerusalem was not officially rescinded, the authorities chose to ignore it. At this time, too, the economic position of the Jews of Ereẓ Israel improved. The extensive urbanization initiated by the Severan emperors had favorable economic repercussions. Septimius Severus bestowed city rights on *Bet Guvrin, now called Eleutheropolis, and granted it large areas which included the whole of Idumea. Land was even detached from Aelia Capitolina and the *limes* and given to it. Lydda, too, obtained city status, was named Diospolis, and granted considerable areas of land. In 220–221 C.E. the district of *Emmaus was made a city and named Nicopolis. This completed the urbanization of western Ereẓ Israel. Except for the part of Upper Galilee known as Tetracomia (the four villages) and the imperial estates in the *limes* and in the Valley of Jericho, the whole of western Ereẓ Israel became a city area enjoying special privileges.

Emigration from Ereẓ Israel was now replaced by immigration from the Diaspora, among the immigrants being people with expert knowledge, initiative, and money, who developed new branches of the economy, such as flax-growing, and of agricultural industry, such as the manufacture of clothes and dyeing.

The improved economic and political position found expression in splendid *synagogues which were built throughout the country and remains of which have been uncovered, chiefly in Galilee, such as at Kefar Naḥum (*Capernaum), Korazim (*Chorazin), Baram, and elsewhere.

The Jewish people in Ereẓ Israel saw in the enlargement of their power and in the aggrandizement of the *nasi* the beginnings of the redemption. A messianic aura surrounded him. From the days of Judah ha-Nasi and onward the *nasi*'s court was distinguished by an outer splendor, great opulence, and regal pomp. He succeeded in attracting to his court and to a participation in public leadership the heads of the large cities and the financial aristocracy, whom he prevailed on to accept the responsibilities of public office and national discipline. This led to a protest on the part of the popular *Ḥasidean sages, the extremists among whom became estranged from Judah ha-Nasi. In internal affairs, too, Judah ha-Nasi's authority was extensive. The right to grant ordination and the control of the Sanhedrin were concentrated in his hands. Under him the central authority exercised increased supervision over the cities and communities in the Diaspora. Under him, too, there was considerable legislation in the spheres of communal religion, of apportioning the burden of taxes, and the manner of levying them. While not charged with collecting the taxes, he, by virtue of the authority of his office and of being a rabbi, gave decisions on various financial problems, among them being some which impressed their stamp on Jewish communal arrangements for generations, such as exempting scholars, who devote themselves wholly to the study of the Torah, from taxes and civic obligations. He also exempted areas in southern and northern Ereẓ Israel from priestly dues, tithes, and from the laws of the sabbatical year, from which last-named he sought to grant a total exemption, but due to the opposition of *Phinehas b. Jair, a Ḥasidean sage, the question was not brought up for discussion and a final decision.

His activities included the final redaction of the *Mishnah, which constitutes the summary and crystallization of most of the halakhic material of the Oral Law. Judah ha-Nasi was not the first to undertake the task of committing the *Oral Law to writing and of summarizing it in an halakhic compilation. Already in Second Temple times, and especially in the generation of Jabneh, this was done by *tannaim*, but their Mishnah collections were incorporated, either wholly or in part, in that of Judah ha-Nasi, whose compilation is the more comprehensive and extensive. Assembling the teachings and collections of preceding generations, he arranged them in *sedarim* and tractates according to subject matter, *Shabbat, Pesaḥim, Gittin, Kiddushin*, etc., and subdivided these into chapters, generally set out in a logical development of the subject. The final redaction of the Mishnah constitutes a compilation of the Oral Law without deciding between the various views but including also the decisions arrived at and the laws enacted in Judah ha-Nasi's *bet midrash*. His humility in teaching the Torah and in halakhic judgments, his readiness to pay heed to and examine different opinions, his spiritual independence, his exalted status, and his lengthy tenure of the office of *nasi* – all these contributed to the compilation of the Mishnah and its acceptance as the basic work for the study of the Oral Law and as the principal foundation of Jewish jurisprudence. Within a short time his Mishnah, having superseded and consigned to oblivion earlier or contemporaneous collections, became the basis and the prototype of the continued creation of the Oral Law. The close of the Mishnah represents a turning point and a landmark in the history of the Oral Law, which was further elucidated and defined throughout the generations. The literature created up to the close of the Mishnah, even if redacted shortly afterward, is the tannaitic, that which followed it the amoraic, literature. All *halakhot* mentioned in the Mishnah and in the other tannaitic productions are more authoritative than those in the amoraic works. Except for a number of Aramaic and Greek words and expressions, the language of the Mishnah is mishnaic Hebrew, reflecting the prevailing circumstances in Ereẓ Israel from Second Temple times onward. The death of Judah ha-Nasi (c. 225) initiated a process that led to a separation between the office of *nasi* and the Sanhedrin. The last testament ascribed to him states that Rabban *Gamaliel, his eldest son, was to be the *nasi* and the sage *Ḥanina b. Ḥama the president of the Sanhedrin (TJ, Ta'an. 4:2, 68a).

In the following generation the separation was almost complete. Then the Sanhedrin, presided over by Johanan (from c. 240), had its seat at Tiberias, while the office of *nasi* occupied by *Judah ha-Nasi II, had its seat for a considerable time at Sepphoris. Under normal circumstances a sage was the president of the Sanhedrin or the Great Bet Din, which was independent, but not entirely so, of the *nasi*, since the latter was theoretically its president, and in certain areas, as also in particular instances, its dependence on the *nasi* was maintained. Thus the ordination of sages was contingent on the sanction of the *nasi*, who continued to exercise the sole right to enact regulations. There was also cooperation between them in political matters. Alongside the central *bet midrash* or the Sanhedrin at Tiberias there were in amoraic times other *battei midrashot* which, as the centers of instruction and leadership for their immediate vicinity, taught the Torah and appointed *dayyanim* for the neighborhood. At Lydda there was the center, founded by *Joshua b. Levi, for the southern settlements; at Caesarea one established by *Hoshaiah; and a smaller one in Upper Galilee at Akbara, under the leadership of *Yannai, where a considerable nucleus of his companions lived a communal life for several generations. Each of these *battei midrashot* was distinct in its teachings and method of instruction, but in special instances their heads were invited to assemblies, the sages of the south (Lydda) in particular often meeting with the members of the Sanhedrin at Tiberias.

THE PERIOD OF ANARCHY (235–289 C.E.) In this period of the frequent change of emperors, of chaos and collapse throughout the Roman Empire, Jewish Ereẓ Israel in particular suffered. There was indeed no religious persecution of the Jews, and even when the Christians and Samaritans were compelled to participate in emperor worship, the rights of the Jews were recognized and respected. The contemporary diatribes against the evil "Esau" who oppressed "Jacob" were mainly directed against Esau, the robber and plunderer, a circumstance conspicuous, too, in the non-Hebrew sources of the nations neighboring on Israel. The rural population suffered greatly from economic hardship, from taxation, and from oppression at the hands of soldiers, and since the economy of Jewish Ereẓ Israel was largely agricultural, the Jews were affected more than the non-Jewish population. During the period of anarchy there was a decline in agriculture, not because of the diminished fertility of the soil but because of the corrupt administrative arrangements that led to a neglect of the land and lack of interest in fostering the cultivation of the soil. During this period, too, the country suffered from privation and an extremely severe famine. Emigration increased, and although there was also a considerable immigration to Ereẓ Israel, it was not large enough to balance the number of those leaving the country. Despite the upheavals and wars which occurred in the east with the accession and onslaught of the Sassanid kings, there were increasing contacts between Ereẓ Israel and the Diaspora, especially that in Babylonia. In the days of the principal generations of the **amoraim* the contacts between these two Jewish communities were considerable, numerous, and frequent. As a result of the situation created by the fact that the Roman Empire was in the process of disintegration and by the Persian attacks, the kingdom of Palmyra (Tadmor) enlarged its power. This buffer state, situated between Persia and Rome, and subordinate to the latter, first forged ahead from 260 C.E. under Odaenathus within the ambit of the Roman Empire. Later, under Queen Zenobia (267–272), having proclaimed its independence and freed itself from Roman suzerainty, it initiated a policy of conquest and expansion directed against the countries of the east, including Ereẓ Israel. The Palmyrene regime was not only a continuation of Roman rule but also contained elements conducive to creating an independent eastern state. Although wide circles in the east supported it, at the decisive moment, when Rome reconquered the east from Zenobia, the great majority of them refrained from coming to its assistance and instead helped the Romans. When Odaenathus was a client king under Roman patronage, Jewish tradition charged him with being "a brother" (because of the eastern elements in his regime) who had come to the aid of "Esau" (Rome) in the latter's hour of weakness. "Happy is he," declared R. Johanan, the leader of that generation of Jews, "who witnesses the downfall of Tadmor [Palmyra]" (TJ, Ta'an. 4:8, 69b). But with Zenobia, whose attitude toward them was one of protectiveness and esteem, the relations of the Jews were friendlier, the clash between her and Rome even raising messianic hopes in some circles.

STABILITY RETURNS TO THE ROMAN EMPIRE. At the end of the third century (284) Diocletian became emperor and succeeded in transforming the regime and the system of the Roman Empire into a despotic monarchy on the Byzantine pattern with its exaggerated hierarchy and extensive bureaucracy. By dividing each of the provinces into two or three, their number was increased. Ereẓ Israel, one of the smallest among them, was likewise subdivided into several parts, so that from 358 to the beginning of the fifth century (429) it comprised Palaestina Prima, which consisted of Judea, Samaria, the Coastal Plain, Idumea, and Perea (Jewish Transjordan), and whose capital remained Caesarea; Palaestina Secunda, which embraced Galilee, the *Decapolis, and *Golan, and whose capital was Scythopolis (Beth-Shean); and Palaestina Tertia, which comprised the Negev and whose capital was *Petra. As in other provinces, the civil ruler, the *praeses*, was distinct from the military head, the *dux*. Instead of reforming the corrupt government system, the new regime perpetuated it, increasing its sway over the population. Participation in all the associations became compulsory and was enforced, ranging from performing municipal duties to the organization of craftsmen's unions from which all workmen were excluded, and to the obligation of children to continue in their parents' occupation. All the associations were at the disposal of the empire for levying taxes and providing services. During this period land tenancy assumed such proportions that the petty independent farmer, typical of Jewish Ereẓ Israel, all but disappeared. The land passed into the possession of the proprietors of large estates and its former owners became tenant farmers. The imperial law of the *colonatus* was introduced, binding the farmer in perpetuity to the soil. This perpetual tenancy was hereditary and was marked by several expressions of the tenant farmer's servitude to the landlord. The imperial tenant farmers were similarly bound in perpetuity to their tenancy and their holdings. Because land in Ereẓ Israel was retained in the possession of petty farmers for a longer time, the *lex colonatus* was introduced in the country at a comparatively late period, 383–388, about 50 years later than in the other provinces. At the beginning of the fourth century, the Jews were progressively becoming a minority in their ownership of land.

With the stabilization of the imperial regime, a new force emerged in the world: Christianity was gaining a commanding position, commencing with Constantine's recognition of the Christian religion (313). This was destined to have a decisive effect on the status of Ereẓ Israel and of its Jews, henceforth called upon to undertake a joint political self-defense. Hitherto the Jews had struggled culturally against a pagan world, which by its very nature acknowledged the existence of national religions. Even the Roman regime recognized in theory, and for most of the time in practice too, the Jewish religious reality in Ereẓ Israel. Christianity, which within a short period became the imperial religion, did not, as is the way of a monotheistic religion, recognize or tolerate other religions, and in this displayed a greater bigotry and inflexibility than Judaism. Although the Christian Church had a special interest in converting Jews, and particular those in Ereẓ Israel, Judaism was not declared illegal either in that country or in the Roman Empire, which nevertheless fostered an enmity toward and a contempt for Judaism. In addition to the hostility originating in the separation between them the Roman Christians were the object of much of the contempt for Jews prevalent in circles of the pagan Roman aristocracy. The hostile attitude to Judaism was expressed in the emperors' anti-Jewish legislation with its insulting language, and in the attacks of fanatics on Jews and their institutions, such as the campaign of the bigoted monk Bar Sauma of Nisibis who, with his band, passed through Ereẓ Israel in 419–422 C.E. destroying synagogues. Not only did Christianity have an interest in the *holy places, such as the site of the Crucifixion, the sepulcher of Jesus, and others, it also based its gospel on the destruction of Jerusalem and God's rejection of the people of Israel, so that the whole of the patriarchal blessing, including Ereẓ Israel, now belonged to it. Henceforward it was not the Jews alone who sought to have possession of Ereẓ Israel. Many Christian congregations were established in the country. The inhabitants of villages and of the large cities, most of which remained faithful to *Hellenism, had to fight for their continued pagan existence. Constantine and his mother Helena, who was devoted to Christianity and even immigrated to Ereẓ Israel in her old age, set about building magnificent churches, one – the Church of the Nativity – at *Bethlehem, and two – those of the Holy Sepulcher and of the Ascension – in Jerusalem, as also at Abraham's Oak. The Church Father Epiphanius has preserved a detailed account of the manner in which the emperor helped the apostate Joseph to build churches in the Jewish centers, at Tiberias, Sepphoris, and other localities holy to Christianity, such as Kefar Naḥum (Capernaum) and Nazareth, places inhabited exclusively by Jews. The Jews fought Joseph who consequently succeeded only in building a small church at Tiberias (Epiphanius, *Panarion adversus Haereses*, 1:2, XXX, 4). The Christian population increased by reason of the conversion of non-Jews in Ereẓ Israel and of the arrival of Christians or pilgrims who settled in the country. The many monasteries which were first built in the fourth century and multiplied in the fifth and sixth also attracted devout Christians from abroad. There were instances of Jews who were converted to Christianity, as in the case of Joseph, but the number was not large either among them or among the Samaritans.

THE REVOLT AGAINST GALLUS. In June 351 a revolt of the Jews broke out at Sepphoris against Gallus, the Roman ruler in the east. The rebels had heard of various uprisings in the west and of Constantius' reverses in his campaign to suppress them. They also relied on obtaining assistance from the *Persians whose attacks, some of them successful, had increased at that time. Having appointed a leader named Patricius, of whom little is known, the Jews defeated the Roman army in the city. From there the revolt spread through Galilee and reached Lydda in the south. It bore no anti-Christian character, nor were Christians or their institutions attacked, the revolt being directed solely against Gallus' corrupt rule. Ursicinus, an experienced commander, was dispatched against the rebels. The decisive battle took place near Acre. From there the enemy advanced against centers in Galilee inhabited by Jews, and several Jewish settlements and cities were destroyed. Some of them, such as Tiberias, Sepphoris, and Lydda, were rebuilt shortly after the revolt, but there were places like Bet She'arim which were now left with only a meager population. It is not known where the seat of the Sanhedrin and of the *nasi* was during the revolt, but not long after it they were once again engaged in their usual activities. During the years immediately following the revolt the authorities interfered with assemblies for the intercalation of the year and especially with emissaries sent to inform the Diaspora of it (Sanh. 12a). It was therefore apparently decided to draw up a permanent calendar (TJ, Er. 3:11, 21c) which, according to a later tradition, was done by *Hillel II in 359 (*Sefer ha-Ibbur*, 97). Even after the calendar had been laid down and until it received its definitive form, questions were addressed to the sages of Ereẓ Israel to elucidate various problems. In Ereẓ Israel they continued even afterward to proclaim the new month and to celebrate the occasion as had formerly been done when its proclamation was made by the Great Bet Din.

JULIAN THE APOSTATE. Excitement mounted in Ereẓ Israel and the Diaspora during the brief reign of *Julian (360–363) who endeavored to resuscitate Hellenism, to which he was devoted, by diminishing the image of Christianity in the empire. Wishing to reinstitute the sacrificial service of the Jews, which he regarded as more important than anything else in their Bible, he announced and promised in his letters to the "Community of the Jews" and to the *nasi* that he would rebuild "with great diligence the Temple of the supreme God" and "the holy Jerusalem which you have for many years longed to see rebuilt and which I shall restore." When he set out to fight the Persians, a special emissary, Alypius of Antioch, was appointed who filled important duties in connection with the rebuilding and to whom large sums of money were allocated. By this act the emperor may have sought, as he departed for war, to win over the Babylonian Jews, and assure their support, but all his letters are marked by friendship and sympathy toward the Jews. Moreover, he revoked the decrees relating to the special Jewish taxes, such as that of the two drachmas, and even asked the *nasi* to reduce the tax levied for the needs of his high office from the Jews. Julian's proclamations and actions created a ferment among the Jews, who flocked to Jerusalem and began to collect money from Italy and as far afield as Babylonia and Persia. Jews settled in the city, started to expel Christians from certain parts of it, and set up a synagogue in one of the colonnades on the Temple Mount. The Christians were furious, and their writers tell of a fire that broke out when the pagan shrines, abandoned with the rise of Christianity, were removed from the Temple site. It is possible that the Christians, desirous of interrupting the work of building, started the fire. When Julian was killed, apparently by a Christian Arab soldier, on the Persian front, the matter was ended.

After Julian's death, the Christians began to attack the Jewish settlements in the south where the Jews were greatly in the minority. Christian sources report the destruction "in the south of 21 cities of pagans, Jews, and Samaritans, who had had a share in Julian the Apostate's sin." Even after this the Jewish settlements in the south did not cease entirely but were reduced in number and impoverished. In the period between the death of Julian and the accession of *Theodosius I (379) there was no anti-Jewish legislation, and several laws were even enacted which enhanced their status and that of the *nasi*, one law exempting officials of the communities subject to "the illustrious *nasi*" from sitting on municipal councils, another of 368 prohibiting the billeting of soldiers in synagogues. This period was a congenial one for the Jews either because Julian's personality and activities had fostered a tolerant attitude toward other religions and arrested the Church's domination or because the emperor Valens (364–378) acted with moderation due to his not wishing to add to his enemies, since the adherents of Arianism, of which he was one, were already then in the minority. Under Theodosius I and his sons Honorius and Arcadius as also under Theodosius II until the abolition of the office of the *nasi* (i.e., from 379 to 428) there was intensified anti-Jewish legislation which assigned an inferior status to Judaism and the Jews.

THE CLOSE OF THE JERUSALEM TALMUD AND THE ABOLITION OF THE OFFICE OF THE NASI. In the second half of the fourth century C.E. the Jerusalem *Talmud was finalized and redacted in Ereẓ Israel, for the most part at Tiberias. In it was summarized all that was said, initiated, and thought in the world of Ereẓ Israel's sages in the century and a half that elapsed since the close of the Mishnah. No tradition is extant of the time taken to redact it or who its redactors were. The date of its redaction is fixed on the basis of the last sages and of the latest historical events – the revolt against Gallus and the emperor Julian's activities – mentioned in it (TJ, Meg. 3:1, 74a; TJ, Ned. 3:2, 37d). Dating from the end of the fourth century are evidences which combine to portray the firm status of the office of *nasi*, his right to collect money and to appoint and depose the leaders of communities in the Diaspora. At the beginning of the fifth century the position of the last *nasi*, Rabban *Gamaliel VI, was undermined. Accused of contravening the imperial laws by building synagogues, circumcising Christian slaves, and acting as a judge in cases involving Christians, he was deposed from the rank of "Honorary *praefectus*." The existence of the office of *nasi*, who claimed descent from the house of David, was not to the liking of the Church, which tried to diminish his image and spiritual stature. An order in the *Codex Theodosianus* of the year 429 mentions the death of the *nasi* and instructs the Sanhedrins in the two Palestines to transfer to the imperial treasury the money previously collected on behalf of the *nasi*. Taking advantage of the death of Rabban Gamaliel VI and of the "babes who died" (according to Jewish tradition), the authorities refrained from approving the appointment of another *nasi*. With the abolition of this office, the nation lost its leading institution which had persisted for three and a half centuries after the destruction of Jerusalem and the Temple. The Sanhedrin continued to exist, money was sent to it even without official permission, and Jewry was obedient to it and its leaders who were called "the heads of the school" (*rashei ha-perek*), but it progressively lost its hegemony over the Diaspora. With the accession in 520 of Mar *Zutra, the son of the exilarch Mar Zutra, the title of Head of the Sanhedrin was bestowed on him, and until the Arab conquest his descendants continued to occupy that position.

BYZANTINE RULE IN EREẒ ISRAEL. During this period the economic position of the country improved. Many Christians, among them men of wealth and influence, immigrated to Ereẓ Israel. The visits, too, of Christians, as also the existence and export of the bones of patriarchs, prophets, and saints, whose graves were purported to have been discovered, brought much wealth to the land. In this period agricultural settlement, particularly in the Negev, was extended to areas never previously nor subsequently tilled, as evidenced by the remains not only of agricultural cultivation but also of cities in the Negev which flourished at this time. The period from the second half of the fifth century until the revival under *Justinian (527–565) of the aggressive Christian policy was a tranquil one for the Jews in Ereẓ Israel. The Christians were absorbed in a theological controversy between the orthodox and the monophysites on the relation between the human and the divine nature of Jesus, a controversy which was associated with political, military, and communal clashes, so that they had no time to concern themselves with the Jews. The latter benefited from the economic prosperity that had come to the country, as attested by the building, extension, and renovation of synagogues whose remains have been found in the north (Bet Alfa, Hammath-Gader, and elsewhere) and in the south (Jericho, Naaran, Ashkelon, Gaza, and in other places). Although the erection and renovation of synagogues were prohibited, the Jews were able to circumvent various repressive laws. The difficult position of the Samaritans and their hopes of receiving help from the Persians emboldened them to organize in 485 and in 529 two large revolts. At first successful, they set up their own brief government in a small area around Samaria, but the revolts were speedily suppressed with such ruthlessness that the Samaritans were considerably reduced in number. There followed a relentless religious persecution. Justinian's reign was the last glorious period of Roman-Byzantine rule in Ereẓ Israel. He fortified the borders, provided the cities with a water supply, and built magnificent churches in various places in the country. But his reign was marked by the beginning of a harsh legislative attack on Judaism and by the Church's growing obduracy in its policy toward the Jews. When the old laws were selected from the *Codex Theodosianus* for inclusion in Justinian's new legal compilation, several which confirmed the rights of the Jews were omitted, while others depriving them of rights were added.

THE PERSIAN INVASION. In 603 the Persians renewed their attempt to assail the Roman Empire. In 611 they arrived at Antioch, in 613 they entered Damascus, in 614 they reached Ereẓ Israel. The approach of the Persians inspired messianic hopes. Contact was made with the conquerors and the Jews gave them effective help in capturing Galilee. From there the Persians marched on Caesarea; proceeding along the coast, advanced against Lydda, and wound their way up to Jerusalem (May 614), in whose capture Jewish forces also took part. The Persians handed the city over to the Jews who, settling in it, began to remove from it the Christians and their churches. The leader in Jerusalem was one known only by the name of Nehemiah b. Ḥushi'el b. Ephraim b. Joseph, his messianic designation, and a beginning may even have been made to reintroduce sacrifices. His rule in Jerusalem lasted for three years. In 617 the Persians retracted, perhaps in order to gain the support of the Christians for their rule. The Jews did not acquiesce in this and the Persian regime was compelled to fight against them. Nehemiah and some of his closest adherents were killed by the Persians (*Sefer Zerubbabel*). In the meantime *Heraclius, the *Byzantine emperor, having begun to grow powerful, set out in the spring of 622 on a campaign of conquest against Persia. In 627 the Persians, accepting their defeat, agreed to withdraw to their own country and the Byzantine army regained control of Ereẓ Israel. In 629 Heraclius appeared at the gateways of the country. The Jewish leaders made a vain attempt to enter into a compact with him. They presented him with many gifts, he promised to overlook their past actions, and even made an agreement with them, binding himself by oath to observe it. One of the Jewish leaders, *Benjamin of Tiberias, who was extremely wealthy, lodged the emperor in his home there, maintained him and the army accompanying him, and even joined him on his journey to Jerusalem. On March 21, 629, the emperor entered Jerusalem in a typically magnificent Byzantine procession and restored to their site the remnants of the cross given to him by the Persians. The emperor, who was not an antisemite, wished to keep his promises but under pressure from the Church revoked them. A decree was issued expelling the Jews from Jerusalem and its vicinity, and Jews were put on trial. Many were killed and many fled. In the period between Heraclius' return and the Arab conquest there were forced conversions and persecutions by the Byzantine Empire. The Arab conquest brought relief to the Jewish population, but in the Arab period the Jews of Ereẓ Israel lost their central position in the leadership of Jewry.

[Shmuel Safrai]

Arab Period (634–1099)

THE ARAB CONQUEST. The raids against Syria and Ereẓ Israel carried out by Arab tribes from the Hejaz toward the end of *Muhammad's lifetime differed little from the attacks mounted by the inhabitants of the Arabian desert against the agricultural and trading settlements of the border lands from the ancient period on. The Byzantines, heirs of Roman power in the Near East, founded an Arab "state" embracing the territory that had formerly belonged to the Nabateans and Palmyra. In reality, though, it was a drifting camp of nominally Christian (Monophysite) Bedouin of the Ghasn tribe that constituted a buffer between the settled lands and the desert. These semi-barbarians were hired to stand guard against the barbarians of the hinterland, but after defeating the Persians and expelling them from Ereẓ Israel (628) and other lands they had conquered, Heraclius did not think it necessary to spend any more on his Bedouin mercenaries. The Byzantines did not grasp the impact of the rise of Islam in Arabia and did not regard the events seriously. The advance of Arabian bands probing their frontier and raids and incursions into Transjordan, and even into Ereẓ Israel, seemed no more than the usual Bedouin border attacks.

In 629 the Arabs suffered a defeat near Mu'ta (east of the southern extremity of the Dead Sea). According to Arab historians, after the death of Muhammad (632) three commanders were assigned the mission of occupying Syria and Ereẓ Israel. ʿAmr ibn-al ʿAṣ was given the task of conquering "Filasṭīn," i.e., Judea and the southern Coastal Plain; Shuraḥbīl ibn-Ḥasana was to take Galilee and the valleys of the upper Jordan and Jezreel, an area later called Jund Urdunn (the military district of the Jordan); and Yazīd ibn Abī-Sufyān marched on Damascus. ʿAmr invaded Palestine by way of Elath, while the other two advanced along the caravan route from Tabk to the Balqāʾ between the Jabbok and Arnon winter streams. The Byzantines suffered three serious defeats in 633–634, as the Arabs relentlessly pushed them back toward the sea from the east and south, and retreated to Beisan (Beth-Shean). For six months the Arabs raided towns and villages without capturing a single fortified city. When they marched on Beisan, the Byzantines withdrew to Fiḥl (or Faḥl-Pella) in Transjordan after destroying the Jordan River dams to impede the enemy's progress. Defeated near Fiḥl, the Byzantine troops fled to Damascus, with the Arabs in pursuit. The Arabs then briefly occupied Damascus, which they abandoned – along with other cities taken in Syria – when they received news of a large Byzantine force gathering at Aleppo and Antioch. This army, however, composed of about 50,000 Armenian and Arab mercenaries, was crushed in a decisive engagement at the confluence of the Ruqqād and Yarmuk rivers (in Golan) on August 20, 636. By the end of the year, all of Syria as far north as Aleppo was in Arab hands.

In Ereẓ Israel, Jerusalem, Caesarea, and Ashkelon were still garrisoned by Byzantine troops. Jerusalem surrendered in 637 or 638, after the Byzantine commander deserted, ending a two-year siege. Patriarch Sophronius conducted the

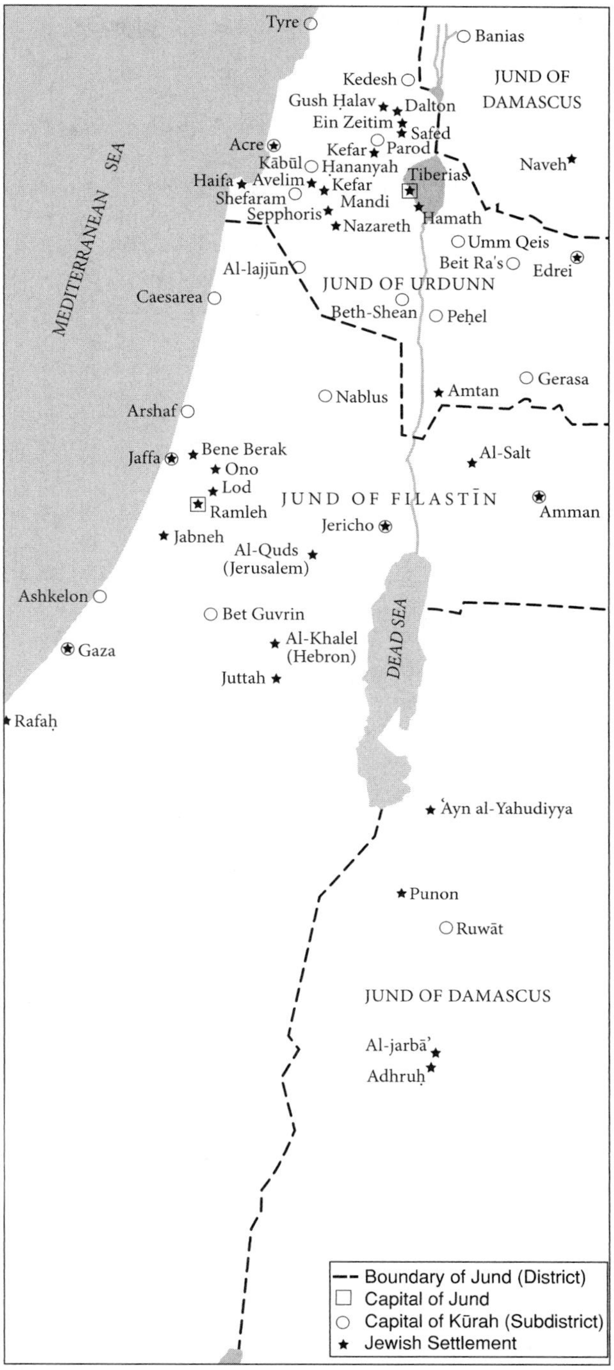

Map 1. The Land of Israel under Arab rule (8th century C.E.). After Atlas of Israel, *Survey of Israel, 1970.*

negotiations with the Arabs, who promised not to harm the Christian churches there. Caesarea was apparently taken by Muʿāwiya in 640, ending a seven-year siege, after a Jew showed the Arabs a secret passage into the city. (According to an Arab historian, there were 700,000 "Roman" soldiers, 200,000 Jews, and 300,000 Samaritans inside the city.) The fall of Ashkelon followed soon after (641). The Arab conquest of Ereẓ Israel was a major event in the history of the Western world. It opened a gateway to the West for the inhabitants of the desert and brought them into direct contact with a 2,000-year-old culture. Had they been satisfied with their conquest of the Persian Empire, it is doubtful whether their influence on civilization would have been any greater than that of the Sassanids or Zoroastrians.

The conquerors did not change the administrative system in Ereẓ Israel. Northern Ereẓ Israel (the Byzantine Palaestina Secunda) became the military province (*jund*) of Urdunn (Jordan), with Tiberias as its capital, and southern Ereẓ Israel (the Byzantine Palaestine Prima) became *Jund Filastīn*, with Lydda as its capital. The latter province comprised Judea and Samaria and, according to the Arab geographers of the tenth century, the Negev, as well as the southern districts of Transjordan, were annexed to it. The conquest was followed by the migration of Arabs into the area. When taking a town, the Arabs sometimes stipulated that half of its area be handed over to them. Arabic historians record that this was the case in Tiberias and Beisan. At first, most of the Arabs lived in great camps, e.g., al-Jābiya in Golan and Emmaus in the Judean plain, where they soon began to acquire estates and settle down. The number who became landlords and engaged in agriculture increased when Muʿāwiya became governor of Syria and Ereẓ Israel. Arabs bought estates, settled down and became peasants throughout the country. Muʿāwiya also founded colonies of Arabs and other Muslims in the coastal towns as a military safeguard against Byzantine attacks on this vulnerable area.

The Ummayyads also granted lands to Bedouin tribes. Whereas most of the Arabs living in Transjordan and regions to the north before the Muslim conquest belonged to south Arabian Kalb tribes, under Ummayyad rule the North Arabian Qays tribes became predominant. Many Qaysites moved into Galilee, Golan, Hauran, and al-Balqā'. On the other hand, the Arabs who settled in Tiberias and Bet Guvrin were Kalbites. The majority of the Arabs of southern Palestine belonged to the Lakhm and Judhām tribes (South Arabians). In the course of the ninth century, the number of Qaysites continued to increase in northern Ereẓ Israel and Transjordan. After the dissolution of the military camps, their inhabitants dispersed and settled in the established towns, and both Islam and the Arabic language proliferated. Nevertheless, these towns did not change completely: a great portion of the town dwellers remained Christians, as borne out by Al-Maqdis (985) in his account of Jerusalem. Ramleh was probably the one exception. Founded by the caliph Suleiman (715–17), who resided there, it became the flourishing capital of the south.

The decline of the Abbasid caliphate began in the ninth century, when Turkish princes established semiautonomous principalities. Ahmad ibn-Ṭūlūn founded an independent kingdom in Egypt (868) and ten years later conquered Ereẓ Israel and Syria; his son defeated the caliph's brother in battle at the Yarkon River (*nahr* abī Fuṭrus – Antipatris) in 885. After Ahmad's death, the Qarmatians – one of the Shiʿite sects from the Syrian desert – began to carry out fierce raids against Syria and Ereẓ Israel in 906. A bit later, Ikhshidi princes became masters over Egypt (935) and Palestine (942) and set out to engage forces with the Turkish rulers of Aleppo. In the second half of the tenth century, the Fatimid Shiʿite dynasty assumed power in Egypt. The Ikhshidis attempted to prevent the Fatimids from taking control of Palestine, but were defeated in a battle near Ramleh in 969.

FATIMIDS AND SELJUKS. During the early period of Fatimid rule in Palestine, the enemies of the dynasty carried out a number of incursions into the country. The first to invade Palestine were the Qarmatians, who captured the entire country except the coastal fortresses in 971. Although their attempt to penetrate into Egypt failed, they remained in control of Palestine for three years. In 974 the Qarmatians were driven out by Fatimid troops, but after a short time they managed to reestablish their authority for a few months. The confusion in Palestine was exploited by the Byzantines, who attacked the Abbasid caliph and, under the emperor Tsimiskes, undertook what modern scholars have called the Byzantine Crusade, penetrating as far as Beisan in 975. They were compelled to retreat from the areas conquered in Syria, but meanwhile the Qarmatians renewed their attacks. After joining forces with the Turkish leader Alptekin, the ruler of Damascus, the Qarmatians defeated the Fatimid troops near Ramleh and laid siege to Ashkelon; however, they were vanquished in 977 by the Egyptian caliph al-Aziz in a battle near Ramleh.

Even after defeating the Qarmatians, the Fatimids could not establish a stable government in the country because of the rising power of Ṭayyi' Bedouin, who had been supported by the Egyptian caliphs in the hope that they would be useful against their governors in Damascus. In effect, the Bedouin chiefs of banū Jarrāḥ, who lived in Ramleh, were the real masters of the country, and the governors of the Fatimid regime were content to maintain their authority only in the coastal towns. In 998 the Bedouin chief Al-Mufarrij ibn Danfal ibn al-Jarrāḥ revolted against the caliph Al-Ḥākim and installed the sharif of Mecca as caliph at Ramleh. Later, the Bedouin were reconciled with the government, but Al-Mufarrij's power continued until his death in 1013, when the Egyptian Fatimid authorities sent a large army to Palestine to put an end to Bedouin rule. At first the caliph Al-Ẓāhir maintained peaceful relations with Al-Mufarrij's son and successor, Hasan; however, when relations again deteriorated, Hasan concluded an alliance with a league of Bedouin tribes ruling Syria, intending to make himself master of the entire region from the Taurus to the Egyptian border. Initially, the Bedouin scored a number of victories, taking Ramleh in 1024 and ruling the country for five years. In 1029, however, they were defeated by a Fatimid army near Lake Kinneret. In 1042 the banū Jarrāḥ again attempted to conquer the country. Fatimid power was already unstable at this period and the first Seljuk forays into Ereẓ Israel had begun.

The Seljuks were a Turkish people that had established an empire in Western Asia in the middle of the 11th century. In 1071 the Seljuk general Atsiz captured Jerusalem and most of the rest of Ereẓ Israel. Although his invasion of Egypt ended in failure, the rebellion that broke out in Jerusalem while he was occupied there was later suppressed. The Seljuk conquest brought an end to Arab rule in Ereẓ Israel, although the struggle between the Fatimids and the Seljuks lasted until the end of the 11th century; the Fatimids held the Coastal Plain and in 1098, a year before the arrival of the Crusaders, even recaptured Jerusalem.

The detailed description of the political events in the 10th–11th centuries indicates a gloomy picture of the living conditions in that period, which is also confirmed by contemporary letters found in the Cairo *Genizah*. Agriculture was predominant in the economic life of the country. The dams near Beisan were quickly repaired and the region soon became famous for its dates, rice, and indigo. Other sectors lost importance, compared to previous periods and neighboring countries. Ereẓ Israel was self-sufficient in the growing of cereals and exported olive oil, dried figs, and raisins. In the Jordan Valley and the Coastal Plain sugar plantations developed considerably, and the Arabs introduced the lemon and orange to Ereẓ Israel. In spite of the flourishing agriculture in the first centuries of Arab rule, heavy fiscal pressure exacerbated the peasants and provoked revolts, e.g., the uprising of Abu-Ḥarb, who in 842, caused turmoil in Ereẓ Israel. The volume of industry decreased, however, when the coastal towns shrank in size as a result of the loss of overseas markets. The interruption of international trade in the Mediterranean area was a foremost phenomenon in the economic history of Syria and Ereẓ Israel under the caliphs. Industry, therefore, produced mostly for local markets, although soap (made from olive oil) and glass vessels were sold in Egypt and Transjordan. On the whole, the decay of maritime trade in the Mediterranean world was outweighed by the intensification of commercial relations with countries that had belonged to other economic regions before the Arab conquest. Ereẓ Israel's economy thus remained intact under the caliphs. Its decline and the subsequent general impoverishment of the population began in the tenth century, due to changes in the political structure, as described above.

In the south (the Negev), however, the deterioration of the economy began even earlier. With the consolidation of the Muslim empire from Spain to India, it became safe for travelers to journey by land, a permanent postal system was established, and new overland trade routes between Europe and the East came into being. These developments eliminated the Negev trade routes, which had functioned as a factor in international commerce, during the Roman and Byzantine periods, and the Negev's key position disappeared for centuries to come. Its cities declined as their inhabitants lost the transit trade and their livelihoods from dyeing and weaving, and the population dwindled. As the markets for agricultural products disappeared, the farmers also moved away, and villages ceased to exist. Ramleh, the headquarters of the administration, was then an important commercial center, and other larger cities were Ashkelon, Caesarea, and Jerusalem. These cities, however, declined like the rest of the country during the period of Fatimid rule. The constant Bedouin raids made life quite difficult for the inhabitants, and, in addition to man-made disasters, earthquakes, which occurred in 1016 and 1033, contributed still further to the country's impoverishment.

The Muslim population of Palestine was for the most part Sunni, and the Shiʿite propaganda of the Fatimid government met with little success. There were large groups of Shiʿites in Tiberias and a number of other places. Most of the inhabitants of Nablus and its environs were Samaritans. In Jerusalem, Bethlehem, Nazareth, and Tiberias, the majority of the population was Christian and enjoyed the protection of the Byzantines who cared for the Christian shrines. The spoken language of all the inhabitants, regardless of religion, was Arabic, although Arabic culture had not struck roots in the country. The intellectual level of the population was lower than that of the neighboring countries. In 985 the Jerusalem geographer al-Maqdisī wrote that it was difficult to find a Muslim intellectual in Ereẓ Israel in his time. The cultural level of the Christians was higher than that of the Muslims, which explains the fact that Christians held most of the government positions. Talented and ambitious members of the population immigrated to the adjacent countries, where the chances of advancement in a number of fields were much greater.

THE JEWISH POPULATION. In the period preceding the Arab invasion, there were Jewish agricultural and trade settlements in the Negev, south of the Dead Sea, along the shores of the Gulf of Elath, and in Transjordan. Delegations sent to conclude protective treaties with Muhammad, once his fame had begun to spread, included Jews from Transjordan and the Gulf of Elath, Maqnā, a small port along the southern portion of the Gulf, was a Jewish community inhabited by the banū Janbā, warriors who earned their livelihood from agriculture, fishing, trade, and home crafts. From the clothing they pledged to deliver to Muhammad, it is apparent that they were wealthy. The delegation from Elath was accompanied by groups of Jews from the neighboring communities of Adhruḥ and Jarbā, between Petra and Maʿān in Transjordan. The region between Edreʿi and Jericho was inhabited by Jews as late as the 10th and 11th centuries, but they disappeared completely during the Crusades. *Estori ha-Parhi, however, mentions a Jewish community in Edreʿi in his time (13th century).

The southern coastal towns continued to flourish after the Arab conquest. In the 11th century there were still Jewish communities in Gaza, Rafa, and El-Arish, but they disintegrated with the Crusades, when the population as a whole declined. Many villages and small towns were destroyed in the Crusader wars against the Fatimids and the Ayyubids, but the disappearance of much of the population in the borderland was also due to the complete cessation of transit trade in the Negev during this period. Controversial reports exist about the resettlement of the Jews in Jerusalem after the Arab conquest. According to Arab sources, the treaty between the caliph *Omar and Patriarch Sophronius about the surrender of Jerusalem to the Arabs contained the condition that the Jews should not be allowed to settle in the city. On the other hand, a document in the Cairo *Genizah* testifies that Omar gave 70 Jewish families from Tiberias permission to settle in Jerusalem. A later Arabic source reports that Jewish families attended the Mosque of Omar in the Temple area. The sources about Jerusalem as seat of the academy do not indicate the date of this event (see section on Religious and Spiritual Life below).

In general, Jewish and Christian communities in Ereẓ Israel prospered during the first 50 years of Arab rule. The founder of the Ummayyad dynasty, Caliph Muʿāwiya (661–680), devoted himself to organizing and expanding his realm. His regime displayed tolerance toward the people under Muslim protection and afforded numerous opportunities to both Jews and Christians. Muʿāwya settled Jews in Tripoli because he regarded them as loyal to the Arabs and wanted to strengthen reliable elements there. The situation changed for the worse when Omar II (717–720) became caliph and introduced numerous restrictions against non-Muslims (see *Omar Covenant). These laws severely affected the public conduct, religious observances, and legal status of the people under Muslim protection. During the Abbasid rule, Jews were sometimes forced to wear yellow turbans, Christians, blue ones, and Samaritans, red ones. These regulations, however, were not strictly observed and had to be stressed from time to time in public proclamations. In 1009–13 the Fatimid caliph *Al-Ḥākim issued severe restrictions against the dhimmi (protected non-Muslim population) that affected the Christians more than the Jews. He also revived the regulations about prescribed garb and ordered the destruction of churches and synagogues. Finally, Jews and Christians were presented with the ultimatum of either adopting Islam or leaving the country. During this period, the Church of the Holy Sepulcher in Jerusalem was demolished. Soon afterward, however, while Al-Ḥākim was still alive, the orders were rescinded and permission was granted to rebuild the houses of worship and allow persons who pretended to adopt Islam to profess their own religions openly.

Economic Conditions. Because of the heavy land taxes imposed on non-Muslim farmers, Jews ceased to cultivate the soil. They settled in the towns, where economic conditions were better and they were safer, and engaged in crafts such as dyeing and tanning, which became exclusively Jewish occupations for centuries to come. With the exception of Al-Ḥākim's decrees, the attitude of the authorities toward the Jews in the Fatimid period was generally favorable and better than the treatment accorded to the Christians, who sometimes provoked the Muslims with their arrogance. Whereas it was strictly forbidden to employ members of the protected faiths in government posts during the Abbasid period, under Fatimid rule, Jews and Christians were in the service of the caliphs, who had come to learn that the protected peoples were more loyal to them than the Sunni Muslims.

The Jews of Ramleh derived benefits from the trade caravans passing through the city. They traded with Egypt and Syria, as well as with North Africa. However, Bedouin depredations and severe earthquakes, which caused unusual damage to Ramleh, undermined the city's position. The economic status of Jerusalem was less satisfactory because of the city's distance from trade routes and its proximity to the desert. Whenever disorders and highway robberies increased, the number of Jewish and Christian pilgrims to the Holy City fell off. In addition, the tax burden in Jerusalem was heavier than in other Palestinian cities. Most of the Jewish population lived off contributions from foreign Jewish communities or visitors. Whatever Jewish merchants there were in Jerusalem were dependent on those in Ramleh. A number of copyists supported themselves from copying manuscripts to be sold abroad.

Religious and Spiritual Life. In the last century of Byzantine rule, Tiberias was again the center of Jewish spiritual and religious leadership. Mar *Zutra, a scion of the exilarchs, settled there in 520 and was appointed head of the academy. Even the persecutions of the emperor Justinian (527–565) could not destroy the community that had fostered the development of Jewish scholarship. Tiberias was the center of the masoretes (see *Masorah) and the inventors of the Tiberian system of vocalizing Hebrew, the most important cultural achievement of the period. This system superseded two others, the Babylonian and the Palestinian, and came into current use in all Jewish communities. The Tiberian pronunciation became famous for its precision and clarity, and many scholars went to Tiberias to study the proper tradition of reading the Torah. The city also attained renown for its liturgical poets. One of the most famous of them was *Yannai b. Yannai, several hundred of whose *piyyutim* have remained. Fragments from a halakhic work *Sefer ha-Ma'asim li-Venei Ereẓ Yisrael* ("Book of the Deeds of the Ereẓ Israel Jews"), in which important decisions on religious, social, and economic matters have been collected, provide a glimpse into the life of the period. Although the exact date of the collection is still controversial – the end of the Byzantine or beginning of the Muslim period – there is no doubt about its importance as one of the few halakhic works of that period from Ereẓ Israel to have survived. It is not known exactly when the academy passed from Tiberias to Jerusalem and Ramleh. From some hints in the letters of the Ereẓ Israel *Gaon* *Aaron b. Meir (a contemporary and an opponent of *Saadiah Gaon), it can be assumed that the move occurred in the ninth century. It may also be ventured that the transfer of the academy to Jerusalem was caused at least partially by the settlement of the *Karaites (see below) in the city. Among the outstanding heads of the academy during the period, in addition to Aaron b. Meir, were R. *Solomon b. Judah (1025–1051) and *Daniel b. Azariah (1051–1062), a scion of the Babylonian exilarchs who signed with the title "*gaon* of Tiberias," although his seat was in Jerusalem. The last *gaon* whose seat was in Jerusalem was *Elijah b. Solomon. After the Seljuk conquest of Jerusalem (1071) he had to move the academy to Tyre, where it remained until the Crusades. It then moved to Ḥadrak near Damascus and subsequently to Damascus itself. The academy existed in Syria for about a century and was still known as the Academy of the Holy Land.

The Karaites in Jerusalem. In the ninth century a number of Karaites left Iraq and Persia and settled in Jerusalem, which became an important center of Karaism. A letter written by Aaron b. Meir testifies that among them were *nesi'im* (princes), so styled because they belonged to the exilarchic family. The Karaites occupied a special quarter and called themselves "mourners of Zion"; the foremost among them were styled "*shoshannim*" (lilies). A genealogical list of Karaite Davidides published by Mann (Texts, 2 (1935), 131) tells that Ẓemaḥ the prince (third generation after Anan) was also head of the academy, whereas his brother Jehoshaphat was called "head of the academy, the pride (*Gaon*) of Jacob." Abramson (Merkazim, 27) is inclined to assume that Ẓemaḥ was head of the academy in Jerusalem. In any case it seems that the rivalry between the Rabbanites and Karaites in Jerusalem was one of the reasons for the reestablishment of the seat of the Rabbanite academy in Jerusalem (for later developments, see *Karaites: in Palestine).

Leadership. After the extinction of the patriarchate (c. 429), the leadership of the Jewish population passed to the scholars and heads of the academy, rather than to descendants of the Davidic dynasty, although the Karaites attempted to revive the office of the *nasi (patriarch) from the family of Anan, of the family of the exilarchs who were of Davidic stock. In the 11th century a Rabbanite descendant of the exilarchs, R. *Daniel b. Azariah who styled himself "patriarch (*nasi*) and *Gaon*," ascended to the leadership of the community. In an epistle to Egypt, he wrote: "Since we came to this holy place, we guide Israel, with God's help, in the whole of Palestine and Syria, and administer justice even to those in distant places. In all towns and settlements prayers are recited for us. The *Ḥaverim* and judges in every place are authorized by us. Nobody else has any influence even over a small town...." (Mann, Egypt, 1 (1920), 179; 2 (1922), 216). Daniel concentrated the powers of the exilarch and the *gaon* in Iraq in his hands. From the many letters of Solomon b. Judah, Daniel's predecessor in the office as head of the Palestinian academy, it is assumed that he was the acknowledged representative of the Jewish population vis-à-vis the Muslim authorities. The *geonim* *Elijah b. Solomon and his son *Abiathar also assumed leadership beyond the boundaries of Ereẓ Israel.

The *ḥaverim* mentioned in Daniel b. Azariah's epistle were authorized to head the local communities and sometimes also served as *dayyanim*. The judges were paid by their communities, but it is learned from many letters that they did not always receive their fixed emoluments or collections made to pay their salaries. In one of his letters, Solomon b. Judah mentions how the Jerusalemites induced him to become their *ḥazzan* before he became the head of the academy, because he was satisfied with a small livelihood; but two years passed and his services went entirely unrewarded, due to the great distress prevailing in the Holy City (Mann, Texts, 2 (1935), 318). One of Solomon b. Judah's main tasks was to request support for his communities and their functionaries from the Ereẓ Israel congregations in Egypt. The *Gaon* Josiah remarks in a letter (Mann, Egypt, 2 (1922), 69–70) that the academy used to be maintained by the Fatimid government, but this support ceased (during the Al-Ḥākim persecutions?), and the academy was in great distress. These financial problems increased with deteriorating political and economic conditions. At the end of the 11th century the Jewish population in Ereẓ Israel diminished and lost its firm organizational and spiritual features.

[Haïm Z'ew Hirschberg]

Crusader Period (1099–1291)

In 1095 Pope Urban II appealed to the French at Clermont to rescue the Holy Land and recover it for Christendom. The response was instantaneous: Peter the Hermit, a Fleming from Amiens, harangued crowds; fanatical bands of peasants streamed eastward, passing through southern Germany, Hungary, and the Balkans, destroying the Jewish communities on the way; but this first mob "army" did not reach the Holy Land and was destroyed by the Turks (July–October 1096). Two years elapsed before the mailed Christian chivalry could be organized, and it took another year before that military expedition reached the coastal road leading from Lebanon into Ereẓ Israel (May 1099). The coastal cities agreed, out of fear, to furnish the advancing expedition with provisions and funds. The army made its way from Caesarea to Ramleh (whose population fled) on the way to conquer Jerusalem, the proclaimed aim of the *Crusade movement. The Crusaders besieged Jerusalem from June 7 to July 15, 1099, and the city capitulated after Godfrey de Bouillon's troops had broken through the northern wall and Raymond of Toulouse's men had broken through at "Mt. Zion." The conquerors carried out a mass massacre of the population, which numbered between 20,000 and 30,000. The Jews, who had heroically defended their quarter, were in part killed and burned in their synagogue and in part taken captive and sold into slavery in Italy. Only few managed to flee to Ashkelon and Egypt.

Having conquered the capital, the Crusaders proceeded to occupy the rest of the country. Bethlehem had surrendered even before the conquest of Jerusalem; the city was in fact handed over to the Crusaders by its Eastern Christian inhabitants, who constituted the majority of its population. Jericho and Nablus had also surrendered when Tancred took both Tiberias and Beisan without a battle, turning the former into the capital of a new principality. The last serious Fatimid attempt to combat the Crusaders ended in the defeat of the Fatimids at the battle of Ashkelon (August 1099), and the Crusaders were thus free to proceed with the occupation of the coastal cities. Like Ramleh, Jaffa was abandoned by its Muslim population and for a while served the Crusaders as their main port; during this first stage in the existence of their state, they were totally dependent on the supply of men, horses, arms, and provisions from overseas. It took the Crusaders ten years (1100–10) to conquer most of the coastal cities. *Haifa, then a small fortress (1100), was important because of its shipyards; the Jewish community, which resided there by special arrangement with the Fatimids, played an important role in its defense. Arsūf (April 1101), Caesarea (1101), Acre (May 1104), Beirut (1101), and Sidon (December 1110) followed suit. The conquest of the port cities facilitated the renewal of military and commercial ties with Europe and also provided the main residential centers of the Crusader community, which never struck roots in agricultural areas. Ashkelon constituted a serious danger to the Crusaders and was finally captured from the Egyptians in 1153.

Crusader expansion into the southern part of Transjordan had begun by 1100. In spite of the deterring efforts of the rulers of Damascus, the Crusaders succeeded first in establishing control over the local nomad population. In 1107 they captured Wadi Mūsā; in 1112 they fortified Shawbak, calling it Montreal; in 1113 they conquered Elath; and, finally, the fortification of Le Crac (Kerak), captured in 1142, secured their control over the area, the land connection between Syria and Egypt, and the "Pilgrims' Road" from the north to Mecca and Medina. Omitting further details it should be pointed out that from the standpoint of territorial expanse, the Kingdom of Jerusalem (or the Kingdom of David and even Israel, as it was called during the period of *Saladin's rise to power in Egypt (1174)) was at its height. Its border in the north went along the Muʿāmalatayn River (or Nahr Ibrahim) between Giblet (which belonged to the principality of Tripoli) and Beirut and continued in the west along the coast southward to Dayr-al-Balaḥ (Daron of the Crusaders). It extended eastward from Beirut to encompass the sources of the Jordan and reached the foot of Mount Hermon. From there the border turned southward and encompassed parts of Horan and Bashan, Gilead, and all the territory of Moab up to Elath. The desert region of the Negev (Grande Barrie, from the Arabic *bariyya* (desert)) completed the borderline between Elath and Daron.

Saladin, Ayyub's son, directed his policy toward the unification of Syria and Iraq with Egypt, a goal that was fulfilled with his conquest of Aleppo (1183). His halting attempts to attack the Crusaders' borders during the lifetime of Nur al-Din (Gaza, 1170; Montreal and Elath, 1171; Crac, 1173) took on the appearance of a planned mission in 1177, when he attacked southern Gaza, captured Ramleh, besieged Lydda, and reached Arsūf. But at the battle of Gezer (Montgisard, as it was called by the Crusaders), he was routed by Baldwin IV, and his attempts to impose a sea blockade on the Crusaders (1179–82), accompanied by attacks on Montreal, Galilee, Beisan, and Beirut, ended in yet another Crusader victory in the battle of Forbelet (1182). In 1183 Saladin captured Beisan and Zarʿīn, besieged Crac, and destroyed Nablus, Samaria, and Jezreel. His victories terminated in the battle of Hattin (July 1187) with the crushing defeat of the Crusader camp, which had left Sepphoris to come to the aid of besieged Tiberias. As a result of this battle, all the Crusader cities and fortresses, including Jerusalem (November 1187), surrendered to Saladin almost without a fight. Tyre, which was not conquered due to Conrad Montferrat, now became the center of the remaining Crusaders, under the leadership of their king, Guy de Lusignan. The prolonged siege imposed on Acre by the Crusaders (August 1189–July 1191) and their conquest of the city constituted the beginning of a renewed conquest under the leadership of Richard the Lion-Hearted; but, as a result of the conflict between the kings of France and England, this endeavor produced poor results. According to the peace treaty of September 1192, the Crusader state was established in the area between Tyre and Jaffa (the Lydda-Ramleh area was divided between the two sides); in addition, the Christians obtained the right of pilgrimage to Jerusalem, which remained in Muslim hands.

Upon Saladin's death (1193), the Muslim empire was once again broken up. The Crusaders, however, were no longer able to exploit this situation, despite the fact that their state continued to expand by virtue of the various Crusades (such as the German Crusade that succeeded in capturing Beirut in 1197). The treaty of 1204 returned Jaffa (which fell to the Egyptians in 1197), as well as part of the territories of Sidon and Nazareth, to the Crusaders. The Fourth Crusade, which might have brought aid to the Crusaders in Ereẓ Israel, turned to the capture of Constantinople and resulted in the diversion of the European forces to Cyprus (captured by Richard in 1189). The military Crusade of the kings of Hungary and Cyprus in 1217 spent itself in undirected missions in the Galilee, Beisan and Mt. Tabor, and its only positive results were the fortification of Caesarea and the founding of Athlit (Château Pélerins). The remnants of this Crusade joined the daring attempt to attack Egypt (the Fifth Crusade). Fear of the Crusaders prompted the Muslims to destroy their fortresses at Tibnīn, Banias, Belvoir (Kawkab al-Hawā), Safed, Mt. Tabor, and Jerusalem simultaneously.

The Crusaders now awaited the arrival of Frederick II, emperor of Germany and king of Sicily. His departure was delayed until 1228, when, meanwhile excommunicated by the Pope, he reached Acre. In the interim, the Crusaders had captured parts of Sidon, built the walls of Caesarea, and fortified Qalʿat al-Qurayn (Montfort). As a result of his connections with Al-Malik al-Kāmil, the sultan of Egypt, Frederick succeeded in acquiring the Crusaders' territorial sovereignty without entering battle. Sidon (with the exclusion of Beaufort), Tibnīn, Sepphoris, Nazareth, Lydda, Ramleh, Bethlehem, the Ramleh-Jerusalem road, and Jerusalem itself – excluding the Temple area, which remained under Muslim jurisdiction – were transferred to the Crusaders. The kingdom now included two enclaves connected to the coastal region: Nazareth and Jerusalem. Frederick proclaimed himself king of Jerusalem and then left the country. Frederick's excom-

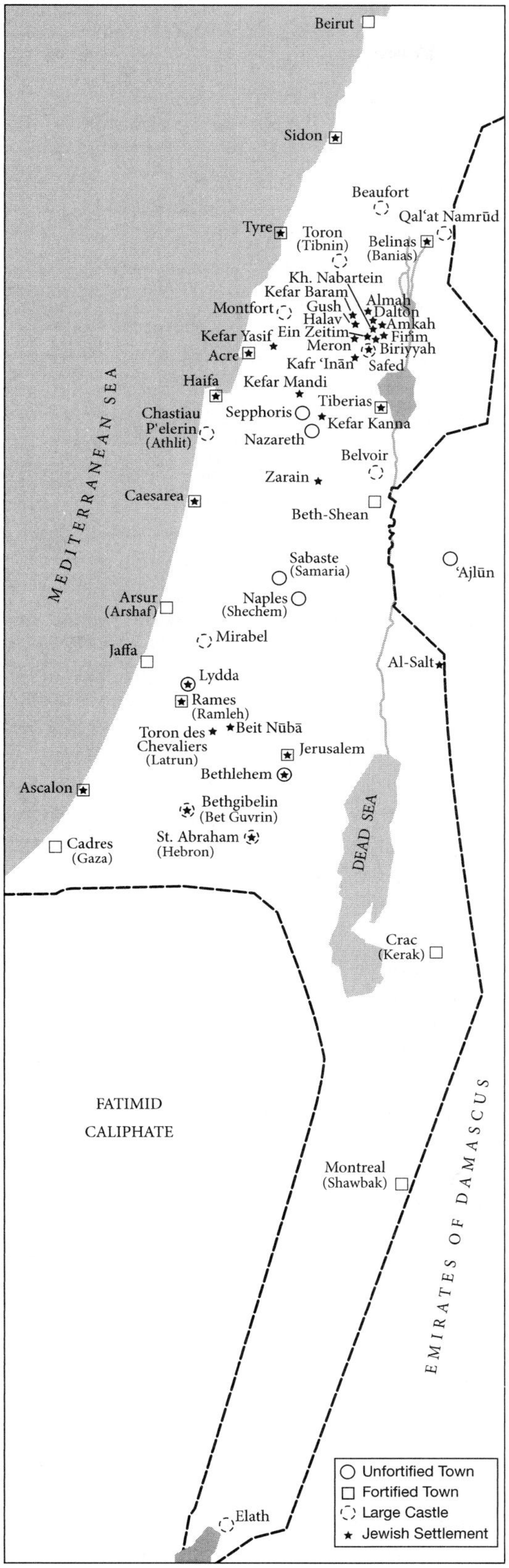

Map. 2. The Crusader kingdom at its greatest extent (1187 C.E.).

munication, self-coronation, and departure from the country brought about civil war, with the opposition to Frederick under the leadership of the House of Ibelin. The war raged intermittently from 1231 to 1243 and depleted the strength of the kingdom of Jerusalem. The Italian communes and military orders carried out their own policy, and the country remained bereft of a true ruler.

The Crusaders' attempt to reconstruct the ruins of Ashkelon terminated with their defeat in the battle of Gaza (November 1239). Meanwhile, the sultan Ismail of Damascus convinced them to enter into a treaty with him against Ayyub, ruler of Egypt and stipulated he would return to them Beaufort (Qalʿat al-Shaqīf), Safed, and Tiberias in Galilee. During the period of mutual political intrigues, Egypt called upon the assistance of the Khwarizmian Turks, who were then in flight from the Mongols. They overran the country, captured Jerusalem from the Crusaders (August 1244), and dealt them a crushing blow at the battle of Hirbiya (Forbie) near Gaza (October 1244), later destroying Galilee. Jerusalem, which was annexed to Egypt, and Judea and Samaria, which were annexed to Transjordan, were never again returned to the Crusaders. Later still (1247), the Egyptians also captured Tiberias and Ashkelon.

The days of the Crusader coastal kingdom were now numbered by the rise of the Mamluks in Egypt (1250), which brought to power a strong military class. With the appearance of a new factor in the Middle East – the Mongols, whose commander (Hulagu) conquered Baghdad in 1258 – it appeared that a Mongolian-European Christian pact that would help the Crusaders withstand the Muslims (rumors circulated that there were numerous Christians among the Mongols) was in the offing. The Crusaders, however, did not exploit the presence of the Mongols and adopted a neutral stance in the severe clash between the latter and the Mamluks of Egypt. In 1260 the Mongols suffered a blow in the battle of Gaza and later a crushing defeat at ʿAyn-Jālūt (En-Harod), which routed their army. A result of the neutral stance of the Crusaders was that they now faced Baybars, the great ruler of Egypt, who slowly but surely captured one fortress after another. Once again the remnants of the Kingdom of Jerusalem did not cooperate with each other and made separate treaties with the conqueror, in order to preserve their meager possessions. Eventually Acre, the center of the kingdom, fell, after a period of siege (April–May 1291), to Al-Malik al-Ashraf the Mamluk. The last fortress, that of Atlit (the Castle of the pilgrims), was abandoned soon after. The period of the Crusades thus came to a close in Palestine.

THE JEWISH POPULATION. During the period of Crusader conquests, the Jews cooperated with the Fatimid forces and the urban Muslim population. Rumors of the murder and pillage perpetrated by the Crusaders upon the Jewish communities in the Rhine area reached the East and gave rise to messianic expectations, which were in turn nourished by the naive belief that the First Crusade served only to gather the nations of the world into the Holy Land in order to destroy them in war ("the war of *Gog and Magog"). Christian sources from that period first mention Jews in connection with the defense of Jerusalem. The Jewish quarter, founded in the 11th century in the northeastern section of the city (between Damascus Gate and the Valley of Jehoshaphat), was the first to be attacked and invaded by the troops of Godfrey of Bouillon. Only a very few survived the terrible carnage and the burning of the synagogues (together with those who sought refuge within them). The Jews are mentioned again in connection with the defense of Haifa in 1100. The Jewish community there enjoyed special conditions conferred upon it by the Fatimids. It is said that Tancred, who retreated from the walls of Haifa, did not attempt to besiege it again until he was admonished that failure to conquer this city defended by Jews would make a mockery of the God of the Christians. The Crusader armies and the Venetian sailors likewise slaughtered the Haifa community.

Contemporary letters and edicts and fragments thereof discovered in the Cairo *Genizah* (some of which have been published by S.D. Goitein; see bibliography) provide more than a glimpse into the life of the Jewish community in Ereẓ Israel under the Crusader rule; they add much to the (sometimes) later descriptions from the non-Jewish sources. A letter found in the *Genizah* describes the fall of Jerusalem, the ransoming of the captives, and the relief efforts on behalf of the refugees who fled with the Fatimid commander. Leaders of the Jewish community in Ashkelon dispatched the letter to the Alexandrian community, begging it to cover the debts incurred by the Jews of Ashkelon in connection with their relief work. A second letter was written by a pilgrim to Ereẓ Israel, who, it may be presumed, came from the Maghreb (North Africa) or Spain. He proceeded as far as Cairo but could not move to Jerusalem because the Holy City had been captured by the "Franks … who murdered all who were in it – Ishmaelites and Israelites. The few who remained after the slaughter have been captured. Some of those have been ransomed and some are still in captivity." He goes on to express the hope that the sultan will defeat the enemies and he will be able to visit Jerusalem soon. Another letter, written in the winter of 1099/1100 by the *av bet din* of the academy, a scion of the Ben Meir family, deals with ransoming members of his family. The writer regards the conquest as an affliction. Indeed, a long letter sent from Ereẓ Israel to Egypt in the first decade of the 12th century informs that conditions changed for the better for those who remained in the country, and the writer would like to renew business relations with his relative and friend. A letter written (in Tyre) to the *dayyan* of Fostat in 1100 includes a short description of the siege of Beirut as related by a fugitive who left the city by night. It seems that all of the 35 Jewish families who lived there were massacred.

Tyre and Banias in the north and Ashkelon and Rafa in the south, which still withstood the Crusaders, absorbed many of the refugees from the massacred communities, while others fled to Egypt. It may be assumed that the communities located in the agricultural region, such as Galilee, suffered minimally from the Crusader conquests. Despite their generally difficult situation, the Jewish settlements still made their influence felt and instances of conversion to Judaism were recorded, such as that of Obadiah the Norman, who remained for a time at Banias and Tyre (when those cities were in Muslim hands). Once the period of military conquest had ended, the Jewish communities began to reconstruct their lives. Their status was enhanced somewhat by the immigration movement from Europe, which was in turn encouraged by improved maritime transportation between the two areas. The legal status of the Jews under the Crusader code, which did not differ from that of Syrian-Christians and Muslims, also helped renew Jewish life in Ereẓ Israel, for inasmuch as the Muslims constituted the majority of the population and the Crusaders' continued existence depended upon them, the Crusader code was very tolerant with respect to infidels. This was in contrast to the hostile attitude of European Christianity toward the Jews that was taking shape in the 12th century. Only in Jerusalem did the Crusaders revive the Byzantine edict that forbade Jews to live within the holy city, and, indeed, only a few families settled there by special permission of the king of Jerusalem.

Various travelers (including *Benjamin of Tudela) who visited Palestine during the second half of the 12th century left descriptions of the conditions of the Jewish communities there. These descriptions are confirmed by the finds in the Cairo *Genizah*. The most important of these communities was Tyre, which apparently continued to exist even after the Crusader conquest. It was an organized community whose leaders and scholars exchanged letters with Maimonides in Egypt on halakhic matters. Next in importance was the Acre community, whose scholars also maintained contact with Maimonides, and third came the Jewish community in Ashkelon, which may not have been destroyed after the surrender of the city to the Crusaders in 1153. The remainder of the Jewish settlements of the period were very small. There were small communities in the coastal cities of Beirut, Sidon, and Caesarea. The cities of Galilee had only the isolated communities of Tiberias in the 12th century and Safed in the 13th century. A letter that mentions the "regnant Dame" of Tiberias (the allusion being to Eschive, who ruled in Tiberias before 1187) has been found in the Cairo *Genizah*. There were also rural Jewish settlements in Galilee: Gush Ḥalav, Almah, Kefar Baram, Amkah, Kefar Ḥananyah, Kefar Tanḥum, Meron, Dalta, Biriyyah. The small communities of Zarʿin, Nablus, Belt Nuba, and Bet Guvrin were scattered in Judea and Samaria. Although the Jewish community in Ereẓ Israel did not intentionally abandon its former settlements, it increasingly concentrated in the Christian area of the coast cities. This move may have been motivated by economic factors, as opportunities for artisans and tradesmen were more abundant in the ports.

Saladin's conquests and those of his successors, the *Ayyubids and the *Mamluks, diminished the territorial scope of the Crusader kingdom and wakened messianic hopes among the Jews in Europe and the East. An important manifestation of the period was the immigration to Palestine from the Diaspora. Many of the refugees of the Crusades longed to return to the Holy Land. The scant information that has been preserved about the 12th-century immigration deals not so much with actual immigration as with visits to the Holy Land (in the 1260s and 1270s) by travelers such as Benjamin of Tudela, *Pethahiah of Regensburg, and R. Jacob b. Netanel Hacohen. Parallel to the unceasing flow of visitors during the 13th century (Judah *Al-Ḥarizi), a trickle of immigrants began to settle. Furthermore, two rather short-lived spiritual centers were created in Jerusalem and Acre. This new movement was probably encouraged by the Crusaders' inability to defeat Saladin and was likewise sustained by the waves of persecution that plagued European Jewry at that time. The Jewish population in Jerusalem, which was limited to a few families during the Crusader occupation, expanded markedly after Saladin's conquest (1187). According to Judah Al-Ḥarizi, who visited Jerusalem (1218), Saladin immediately published a proclamation calling the Jews from all over the world to come and settle in the capital. In his time the Jerusalem community consisted of scholars from France; a fine congregation from Ashkelon (apparently refugees from the Jewish community destroyed there in 1191), led by a Yemenite "prince"; and a large congregation from North Africa, where there was an increase in persecution at the end of the 12th century.

Sources from the Cairo *Genizah* add interesting details to the observations made by Judah Al-Ḥarizi. The fragments published by Braslavi (*Ereẓ Yisrael*, 4 (1956), 156–9) include the names of other French scholars who lived in Jerusalem during the period. A proclamation by Saladin reducing the custom duties to be paid by non-Muslims by half, mentioned in a letter, was no doubt an invitation for Jewish merchants to settle in the conquered area. A letter from 1214 clarifies some of Al-Ḥarizi's remarks about the Jerusalem community. It expressly mentions the synagogue of the "Son of the Yemeni" and ends with greetings for the "Ashkeloni and Maghrebi elders." The first immigration wave from Europe included the "300 French and English rabbis" who immigrated in 1210–11 and settled in Acre. Among them were learned scholars from the ranks of the tosafists, such as R. *Jonathan ben David ha-Kohen from Lunel and R. *Samson of Sens.

The renewed Jerusalem community was short-lived. During the occupation of Jerusalem by the Christians (1229–39, 1243–44), the Jews were not initially allowed access to the city. In about 1236 a special agreement permitting them to visit the Holy City was arranged; it included a special permit for Jewish dyers to settle in Jerusalem, and their presence in the city is mentioned by Benjamin of Tudela and Pethahiah from Regensburg. It may be assumed that the destruction of the city in 1244 by the Khwarizmian Turks caused the simultaneous demise of its Jewish inhabitants. Naḥmanides' immigration to Jerusalem in 1267 stimulated efforts to revive the community, and many students flocked to him from distant places in the East. He completed his commentary to the Pentateuch in Jerusalem. He left Jerusalem for Acre and his death in 1270 apparently brought the Jerusalem community's revival to a halt. At a later period a legend arose about the "Naḥmanides synagogue" in Jerusalem that attempted to ascribe the revival and uninterrupted existence of the Jerusalem community to Naḥmanides.

The development of the Acre community stood out in contrast to Jerusalem's deteriorated condition. Part of the 1210–11 immigration settled in Acre, and later waves were also absorbed there for the most part. Among its important settlers was R. *Jehiel of Paris, who immigrated after 1257 and apparently succeeded in founding a yeshivah in Acre called "*midrash ha-Gadol*" of Paris. Emissaries from the city collected funds in various European communities. The Acre community also maintained connections with R. Solomon b. *Adret and R. *Meir b. Baruch of Rothenburg and played an important role in the second disputation on the writings of Maimonides. The *nagid* *David ben Abraham, grandson of Maimonides, lived in Acre for a considerable time during his exile from Egypt (1284–89) and there met R. Solomon Petit, the most active opponent of Maimonides' doctrines. David used all his influence to procure the issue of a ban (1287) against Solomon by the *nasi* of Damascus as well as a letter against him from *Samuel ben Daniel ha-Kohen, the *Gaon* of the Baghdad Academy (1288). This controversy confirms the existence of a religious center at Acre. The community was almost completely wiped out during the conquest of the city by Al-Malik al-Ashraf in 1291.

As to the economic activities of the Jewish community at the time, the majority of the Jews were artisans, particularly dyers of woven fabrics (dyeing was then a royal monopoly). Another skill practiced particularly by Jews was the blowing of the famous Tyre glass. They also figured among ship owners, as well as druggists and physicians. In contrast, Jews played a minor role in the great Mediterranean international trade (an Italian monopoly), although there were Jewish merchants and peddlers among the local tradesmen.

[Haïm Z'ew Hirschberg / *Encyclopaedia Hebraica*]

Mamluk Period (1291–1516)

When the country again returned to the total rule of the Muslims, its importance in international politics was lost for hundreds of years. Al-Malik al-Nāṣir Muhammad was ruler in Egypt and his governor, Tangiz, longtime omnipotent ruler in Syria and Ereẓ Israel, maintained order and security in the country and constructed waterways and public buildings. Mamluk rule was undermined after the death of Al-Malik al-Nāṣir, and at the beginning of the 15th century disagreement among the chief ministers led to civil wars that wreaked havoc in the Syrian territories. In the middle of the same century, during the rule of the sultans Al-Malik al-Ashraf Barsbāy (1422–38) and Al-Ẓāhir Sayf-al-Dīn Jaqmaq (1438–53), Ereẓ Israel again enjoyed a short period of respite, followed by the increased disintegration of Mamluk rule.

The two-and-a-half centuries of Mamluk domination in Ereẓ Israel brought about little change in the administration of the country. Syria and Ereẓ Israel were divided into large provinces (*niyāba*), which in turn were divided into districts. Each province was headed by a "deputy king" (*nā'ib*) and each district (*wilāya*) by a governor (*wali*). The province of Safed included the districts of Safed, Nazareth, Tiberias, Tibnīn, Athlit, Acre, Tyre, al-Shāghūr, al-Iqlīm al-Shaqīf, and Jenin. It was, in effect, an enclave in the larger province of Damascus, which included a great part of Ereẓ Israel, i.e., the northern districts of eastern Transjordan (Edrei, ʿAjlūn, al-Balqā', Banias), the Beth-Shean district, and the districts of central and southern Ereẓ Israel (Shechem, Qāqūn, Jerusalem, Hebron, Ramleh, Lydda, and Gaza). Various changes were introduced in the administration of the southern districts in the second half of the 14th century. The status of the governor of Jerusalem was raised, and Hebron was added to his district; a special governor, directly responsible to the government in Cairo, was appointed for Ramleh, and Lydda and Qāqūn were added to his district. Because Gaza periodically became an independent province, the status of this district underwent frequent changes. Eastern Transjordan was under the jurisdiction of a special province, Kir Moab (al-Kerak).

Sources from the 14th and 15th centuries attest that the economic structure of Ereẓ Israel remained essentially unchanged during the last centuries of the Middle Ages. The author-prince Abu al-Fidā', who visited the country in 1312, describes the fruit of Ereẓ Israel as export produce. The geographer Al-Dimashkī and a traveler, Ibn Baṭuṭah, both of the 14th century, report that olive oil and soap made from it were the most important products of Ereẓ Israel. Al-Qalqashandī (15th century) relates that there were sugar plantations in the Jordan Valley, and the Burgundian traveler Bertrandon de la Broquière, who visited in 1432, recounts that cotton was cultivated in the Beth-Shean Valley. When the last vestiges of Crusader rule were eliminated, Ereẓ Israel again had no share in the international spice trade, which in the past had been a source of great profits for its inhabitants.

The Mamluks destroyed Acre, Jaffa, and the other coastal cities for fear that they would be used as aids in renewed Crusades. Jaffa remained in ruins until the end of the Middle Ages, while a small settlement was established in Acre in the 15th century. Tiberias and Ashkelon were also partly in ruins at the end of the Middle Ages. Fabri, who visited Ereẓ Israel in 1480 and 1483, found many places in Jerusalem in ruins. According to Obadiah of *Bertinoro, who reached Jerusalem in 1488, the city contained about 4,000 householders, among whom the 70 Jewish heads of families were the poorest of all, lacking any livelihood (A. Yaari, *Massa'ot Ereẓ Yisrael* (1946), 127). According to information from the period of early Mamluk rule, Ramleh was a large city with a flourishing trade; but visitors to Ramleh from the end of the 15th and to the beginning of the 16th century related that it, too, was progressively declining into ruin. All the sources attest that Gaza was a flourishing trading town, about twice the size of Jerusalem. Gaza, Ramleh, and Nablus (Shechem) were apparently the largest towns in Ereẓ Israel at the end of the Middle Ages.

Ereẓ Israel did not play an important role in Arabic cultural life during the period, but various sources attest that there was no lack of learning and education in its towns. The Mamluk sultans and their ministers continued to establish *madrasas* (schools) for instruction in religion and allocate funds for the maintenance of their teachers and students. The number of *madrasas* established in Ereẓ Israel by the end of the

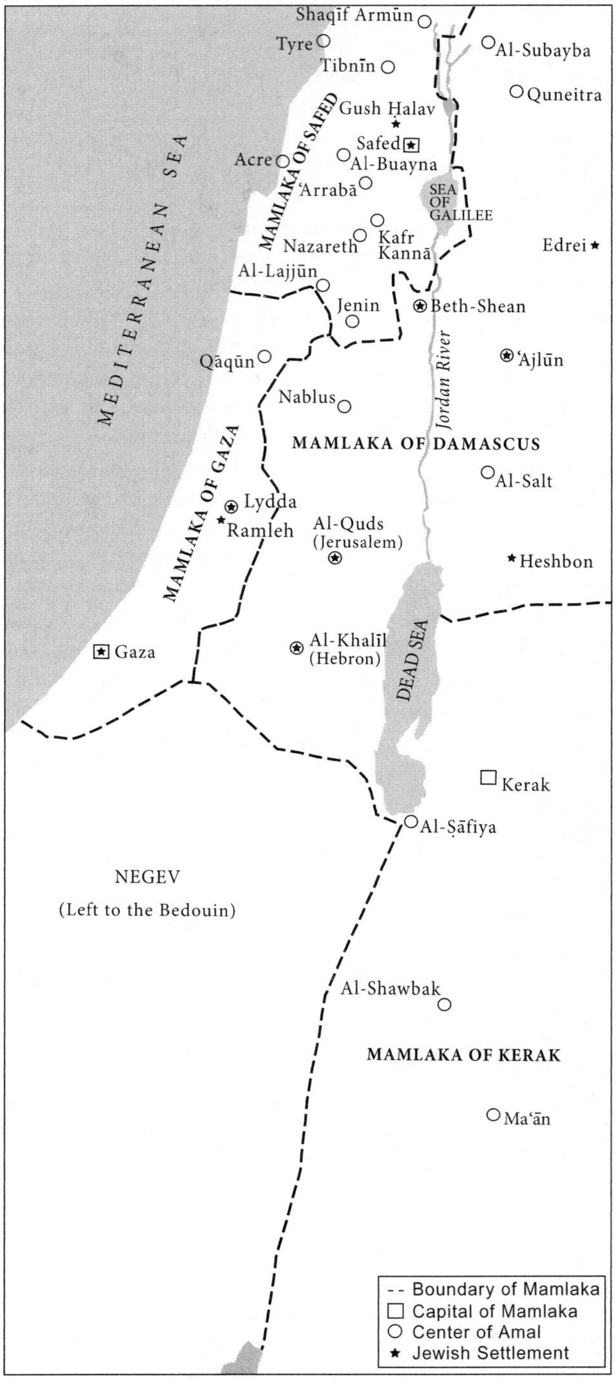

Map 3. The Land of Israel under the Mamluks (14th century C.E.). After Atlas of Israel, *Survey of Israel, 1970.*

Middle Ages reached 50, of which 43 were in Jerusalem. From a religious point of view, the Mamluk period stamped Ereẓ Israel with the characteristic that has distinguished it up to modern times. It became an orthodox Muslim country, while the number of its Shiʿites progressively decreased. Its distance from the ruling centers, on the one hand, and the espousal of religious fanaticism in the *madrasas*, on the other, gave rise to the prominent role played by religion in the daily life. There were periodic complaints by Muslim extremists, which often resulted in lengthy controversies, that the Christians had enlarged their churches in disregard of the Muslim law. Similarly, Jerusalem (from 1473 on) was the scene of a prolonged controversy between the Muslims and Jews over the latter's right to a particular synagogue, which was eventually destroyed by the Muslims (see below). At the same time, the more gifted among the inhabitants would leave Ereẓ Israel for Egypt and Syria. Arabic sources mention a number of Muslim religious scholars who were born or were active in Ereẓ Israel and several local Arabic writers in different areas. Only a few of them, however, were of any significance. Among these, special mention should be made of Mujīr al-Dīn al-ʿUlaymī (1456–1521) who was a judge in Jerusalem and Ramleh and wrote a work on the history of Jerusalem and Hebron.

A number of magnificent buildings were constructed by the Mamluk sultans and their representatives out of a desire to perpetuate their names, even in a forsaken province such as Ereẓ Israel. Fine examples of Muslim architectural art of the period are the tower on the site of the White Mosque in Ramleh, of which only remnants have remained. Others are Bāb al-Qattānīn in the Haram area of Jerusalem ("the cotton-workers' gate"); Qāʾit bāy Sabīl ("the fountain of Qāʾitbāy") on the Temple Mount; and the Tankiziyya *madrasa* near the Western Wall (first half of the 14th century). Also worthy of mention are the Mamluk bridge, the "Jisr Jindās" (second half of the 13th century), which still serves traffic near the town of Lydda.

At the end of the Mamluk period, the security of Ereẓ Israel was undermined, and a worsening of the economic situation ensued. The wars against the Ottomans compelled the Mamluk rulers to seek additional sources of income (e.g., confiscating oil from the farmers in the Nablus district and then forcing the residents of Jerusalem, Hebron, and Ramleh to buy it at exorbitant prices) and to conscript the Bedouin tribes for military service. Such actions caused rebellions among the populace who sometimes even left their permanent places of residence to hide in the mountains and deserts. In the last decade of the 15th century the Bedouins in the Beth-Shean district and Transjordan rebelled. Apart from political and economic upheavals, there were also natural disasters. Arabic sources record the outbreak of plagues in 1438, 1469, 1476, and 1492; a locust plague in 1484, which laid the land waste; and earthquakes in 1458 and 1497. The hardships endured by the people and their dissatisfaction with the authorities gave rise to the general hope that the annexation of Ereẓ Israel to the Ottoman state would result in a change for the better.

JEWISH COMMUNITY. After the wave of bloodshed perpetrated by the Crusaders at the beginning of their conquests, there was a period of respite and gradual recovery among the small and impoverished Jewish communities that managed to survive the difficult times. Gradually, pilgrims began to visit the land and refugees returned to settle there. However, as the Mamluks destroyed the ports that had served the Crusaders as important centers of trade with Europe and the inland towns lost their importance in overland international commerce, the Jews had difficulty in supporting themselves in the large settlements and were scattered in small towns and villages throughout Ereẓ Israel and even Transjordan. R. *Estori ha-Parḥi, a refugee from France (1306) who settled in Beisan during the first half of the 14th century and was the first to study the land, several times makes mention of small Jewish communities in Ereẓ Israel in his book *Kaftor va-Feraḥ*. He even made trips into Transjordan and became acquainted with the communities in Edrei, ʿAjlūn, Salka, Ḥabram (Amrawa). In western Ereẓ Israel he found Jews in Jerusalem (where he lived for some time), Lydda, Ramleh (which he calls Gath), Gush Ḥalav, and Safed. In addition to Rabbanite Jews, he also mentions the Ṣadducees, i.e., Karaites, as well as the Samaritans. He makes special mention of *pilgrimages to Jerusalem from the neighboring countries: Sin (i.e., Syrian Tripoli), Hama, Aleppo, Damascus, Cairo, and Alexandria. There is information from the second half of the 14th century about Jews who lived in Miẓpeh Shemuel (i.e., Nabī Samwīl) near Jerusalem. It is evident, however, that these settlements lacked the economic basis required for peaceful development.

Despite the difficult political and economic conditions in Ereẓ Israel, the Jewish community began to strengthen and consolidate from the beginning of the 15th century, especially in Jerusalem. This caused a reaction on the part of the Franciscan friars, who held the cenaculum above the Tomb of David on Mt. Zion. Properties belonging to the Jewish community were also situated on Mt. Zion. The *Franciscans accused the Jews of having dispossessed them of their share of the tomb, and in 1428 the pope issued an order forbidding the fleets of Italian towns to transport Jews to Ereẓ Israel. The dispute over the ownership of the Tomb of David continued for an extended period (see *Jerusalem) and resulted in great difficulties in Jewish immigration by sea and the renewal of the prohibition against transporting Jews in Christian ships (c. 1468). R. Isaac Sarfati (second half of the 15th century), in a famous letter (whose exact date is unknown), calls on the Jews to settle in Ereẓ Israel, suggesting that they make their way overland for "indeed the way of Turgemah is the way to the land of life, all of it overland until Jerusalem, there is only a passage of six miles through the sea" (A. Jellinek (ed.), *Zur Geschichte der Kreuzzuege* (1854), 20–21). The German traveler Ruter (1479) gives the details of this route: "Following is the description of the overland route from Nuremberg and its neighboring districts to Jerusalem, as described to me by a Jew in Jerusalem who took this road a long time ago. The route can be traveled in great safety. Most of the Jews who come from the lands of Germany to Jerusalem make their way overland ... from Nuremberg to Posen ... Lublin ... Lemberg ... through Wallachin to Chocim (?) ... Akerman (on the shore of the Black Sea) ... Samsun (Turkey) ... Tukat ... Aleppo ... Damascus ... Jerusalem" (J. Braslavsky, *Le-Ḥeker Arẓenu* (1954), 142; R. Roehricht and H. Meisner (eds.), *Deutsche Pilgerreisen nach dem Heiligen Lande* (1880), 112–3). This description explains the presence of settlers from Central and Southern Europe in Jerusalem.

The suffering of the Jews of Spain and the Balearic Islands at the end of the 14th and the beginning of the 15th century, even before the expulsions in 1492 and 1497, increased the immigration from hostile countries. Members of their communities could be found in the major cities of Ereẓ Israel even before the Ottoman Turks conquered it. It appears that some of these settlers were Marranos. Obadiah of Bertinoro explicitly states that he found Marranos in Jerusalem and Hebron who had "returned to the fold" (the Spanish refugees in Safed will be discussed below). Many of the details about the population at this time are known from the letters and travelogues of Italian Jews who were then living in Ereẓ Israel: R. *Elijah of Ferrara (1435); R. *Meshullam of Volterra and R. Joseph de Montagna (both 1481); R. Obadiah of Bertinoro and his anonymous disciple (1490–95); R. Israel of Perugia (1517–23); R. Moses *Basola (1521–23). In addition to the settlements already noted, mention should also be made of Kefar Kannā (near Nazareth), where about 38 families lived. R. Obadiah records that 70 families were living in Gaza. According to R. Joseph de Montagna (A. Yaari, *Iggerot Ereẓ Yisrael* (1943), 91) in 1481 there were 300 Jewish families in Safed, more than four times the size of Jerusalem's Jewish population. A "letter about the matter of *shemittah* from the sages of Safed to the rabbis of the holy yeshivah of Jerusalem" from 1504 has been preserved and shows that even before the great influx of refugees from Spain into Safed, there were revered scholars in the town, headed by R. Perez Colombo (for Safed, see also Yaari, *ibid.*, 152), and R. Joseph Saracosti (of Saragossa), teacher of David ibn Abi Zimri.

According to the detailed description by Obadiah of Bertinoro, the economic situation of the Jews of Jerusalem was severe. The heavy tax burden led the wealthy and the scholars of the community to leave the city. Out of 300 Ashkenazi and Sephardi families, only 70 of the poorest remained, of whom only the artisans – strap makers, weavers, or smiths – and traders in spices and medicines made a scant living. The burden of taxes and levies, to the extent that Torah scrolls and religious objects had to be sold, was connected with fines and bribes that the community had to pay in order to save the synagogue (named after Naḥmanides, near the Ḥurvah Synagogue) from the Muslims, who destroyed it in 1474 (see *Jerusalem).

In view of the poor moral and economic situation, the *nagid* Nathan *Sholal also left Jerusalem and returned to Egypt, where he met Obadiah of Bertinoro. Nevertheless, Obadiah praises the relations between Muslims and Jews in Jerusalem and emphasizes that in all his travels he did not come across Muslim hostility toward the Jews. According to him, if there had been a wise Jew possessing political acumen in Ereẓ Israel, he could have been "a minister and judge both for the Jews and for the Ishmaelites" (Yaari, *ibid.*, 128). Obadiah also reveals some of the ignorance and crudeness rampant in Jerusalem in his time. Learning had decreased in these generations, and the scholars who are still remembered are very few. At the beginning of Mamluk rule, Tanḥum b. Joseph ha-Yerushalmi (d. 1291 in Cairo), an exegete and grammarian who wrote his works in Hebrew, lived in Jerusalem. He also composed a lexicon to Maimonides' *Mishneh Torah*, of which only the introduction is extant. The importance of R. Estori ha-Parḥi's work *Kaftor va-Feraḥ* lies not only in the geographic-historical information it contains, but also in the opinions and decisions on the *mitzvot* of Ereẓ Israel discussed therein. R. Elijah of Ferrara (settled in 1435) disseminated the teachings of Maimonides, the Mishnah, and the Talmud with *tosafot* in Jerusalem and was also appointed a *dayyan* and received questions from Cairo, Alexandria, and Damascus. Obadiah of Bertinoro, according to his own account, served as a gravedigger, for there was no one to perform the rites of burial. He was, in effect, the rabbi of Jerusalem – where he also wrote his commentary to the Mishnah. Two Sephardi pupils studied with him regularly, and there were two Ashkenazi rabbis in the city. According to the testimony of his anonymous pupil, the situation in Jerusalem greatly improved because of Obadiah's activities.

The system of *takkanot* in Jerusalem continued after Obadiah's death (c. 1500) and lasted until the Ottoman conquest. The extant version of the *takkanot* was preserved by R. Moses Basola (d. 1572) who copied them from the calendar of the synagogue in Jerusalem. One of the most important *takkanot* was that according to which scholars were exempt from taxes, even if they were wealthy, except for the head tax. In matters of controversy their cases would be brought to the court of the *nagid* in Egypt. This *takkanah* was apparently first formulated by the *nagid* R. Isaac *Sholal (nephew of R. Nathan Sholal) in 1509.

Isaac Sholal went to Jerusalem a short while after the Ottoman conquest of Cairo. R. Abraham ha-Levi had settled there even earlier and had been known before his immigration as an outstanding scholar and kabbalist. The expansion of the Ottoman Empire in the time of Selim I indicated to him the forthcoming downfall of the "Edomite" kingdom, and he prophesied the coming of the messiah in 1530 or 1531.

[*Encyclopaedia Hebraica*]

Ottoman Period

THE GOLDEN PERIOD OF OTTOMAN RULE (1517–1574). Selim I (1512–20), who manifested the same qualities as his grandfather, Muhammad (II) the Conqueror, did not continue his predecessor's attack on Europe. He was "a man of the Eastern front," as one historian describes him, and during his rule the Ottoman territories were doubled through conquests in Asia and Africa. His first campaign was waged against the Persian shah Ismail I, founder of the Safawid dynasty. After defeating him in 1514, Selim pretended he was preparing for a second military campaign against Persia and complained that the Mamluk sultan was conspiring against him together with the "infidel" Safawids, who belonged to the Shiʿite sect. Selim apparently received authoritative reports about the decline of the government in Egypt and intended to entice the Mamluks into leaving their country, extending far from their supply bases in Africa, and attacking him in Asia. This stratagem succeeded: in May 1516 the aged Mamluk sultan Qanṣūh al-Ghawri went to Syria to fight against Selim and in the battle that broke out on Aug. 24, 1516, in the Valley of Dābiq (near Ein Tāb) in northern Syria, the Egyptians were decisively defeated. As a result, Selim gained all the large cities of northern Syria: Aleppo, Ḥama, Homs, and Damascus. From Damascus, Selim sent out commanders to take control of the neighboring districts. Druze chiefs and Bedouin sheikhs from all over Syria arrived there to swear allegiance to the new ruler and the great vizier Sinān Pasha, who left Damascus to conquer Gaza. Even before the end of 1516, the entire country was apparently under Selim's control. At the beginning of 1517, when Selim embarked on his campaign against Egypt (of which he gained control after a military victory), he visited Jerusalem.

At the beginning of the rule of Selim's son, *Suleiman (I) the Magnificent (the Law Giver in Arabic) (1520–66), the wali of Syria and Ereẓ Israel, Jan-Birdi al-Ghazālī, rebelled against him, believing the time had come to overthrow the yoke of Ottoman rule and establish a sovereign kingdom in Syria and Ereẓ Israel. Some scholars maintain that he exploited the ferment among the population that resulted from the poor economic situation. However the wali was killed by the Ottomans, and his head was sent to Constantinople. Calm was restored in the rebellious districts, the roads that had been impassable during the war were again safe, and the movement of trading caravans to Egypt was renewed. A letter by R. Israel of Perugia (written shortly after the conquest) indicates that the Jerusalem community suffered from the general disorder that resulted from the rebellion (A. Yaari, *Iggerot Ereẓ Yisrael* (1943), 177). Subsequent to the rebellion, all native-born walis were removed from their posts, and thereafter all responsible positions in the government were held only by Ottomans. The military and civilian administration was established according to the Ottoman system evolved by Suleiman the Magnificent. The conquered territories were divided among the Ottomans as military feudal states, and the feudal lords were required to join the battle as cavalry, bringing with them auxiliaries in proportion to the size of their states. The cavalries of the entire region were united under a standard (Turk. *sanjak*, Ar. *liwāʾ*) and in battle were under the command of the *sanjak bey* (Turk. "lord of the standard") or the *mir-liwāʾ* (same in Ar.). This commander was at first appointed from among the cavalry. The external symbol of his position was a banner, with a golden ball on top and a horsetail below it.

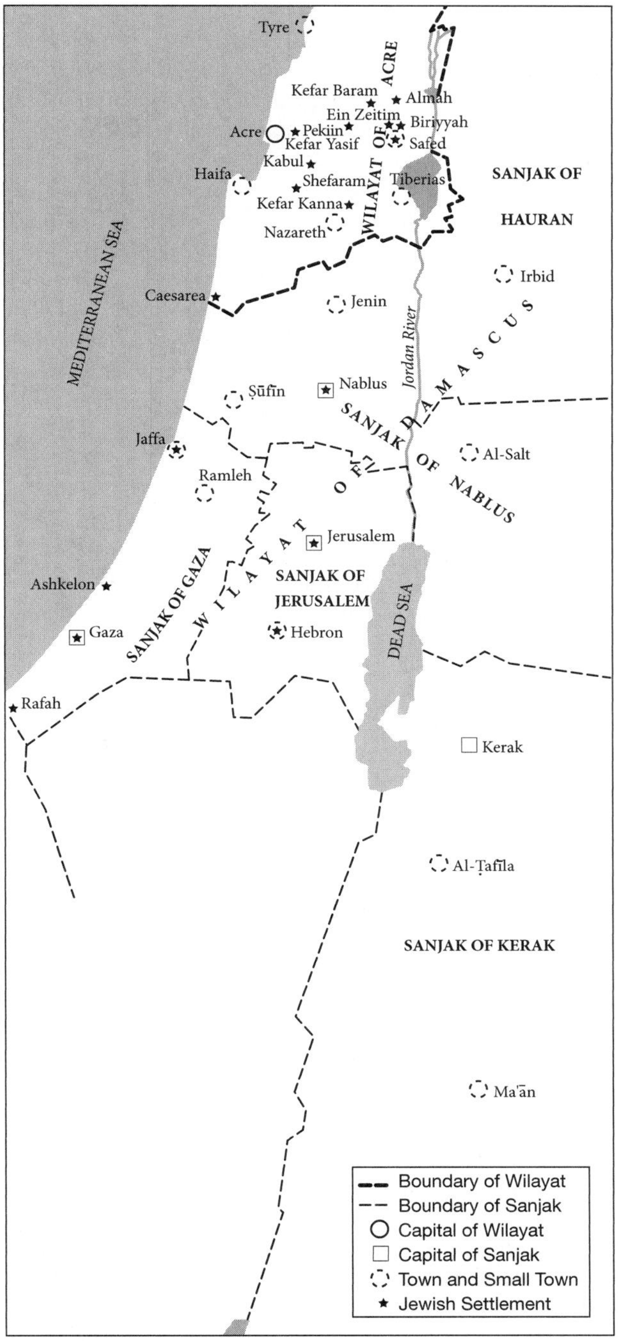

Map 4. The Land of Israel under Ottoman rule (17th century C.E.*). After* Atlas of Israel, *Survey of Israel, 1970.*

With the growth of the Ottoman Empire and its expansion beyond the regions of Anatolia, it was necessary to adapt the administrative organization to the new conditions. The number of the sanjaks increased, and it was useful to appoint deputies to the sultan with a rank higher than that of the *sanjak bey.* They were placed in charge of an area including a number of sanjaks and served as intermediaries between the highest authority and the districts. The first 50 years after the conquest of Ereẓ Israel were the decisive years in the evolution of the new organizational framework of the empire. The organizational framework of the *iyāla* (i.e., the authority) or the *wilāya* or vilayet (the "rule" of the district) was probably also established then.

Ereẓ Israel was divided into four sanjaks: Jerusalem, Gaza, Nablus, and Safed. Each sanjak was an organizational, military, economic, and judicial entity. For practical purposes the sanjak was divided into a number of rural regions (*nāḥiya*). In the sanjak of Jerusalem there were two regions: Jerusalem and Hebron. The sanjak of Gaza was at first divided into three regions: Gaza, Ramleh, and Lydda, but according to the second *deftar* (assessment), Lydda was joined to the Ramleh region. In the sanjak of Nablus (Shechem) there were four regions: Jebel Shāmī (the northern mountain, i.e., Mt. Ebal), Jebel Qiblī (the southern mountain, Mt. Gerizim); Qāqūn, and Banī Saʿab. The *deftar* of 1533–39 also mentions the region of Marj Bani ʿAmir (Valley of Jezreel), but according to the *deftar* of 1548/49 this was annexed to the Tiberias region. In the sanjak of Safed there were at first six regions: Safed, Tibnīn, Tyre, Shaqīf, Acre, and Tiberias; later Tyre was annexed to Tibnīn.

The constitution of the province of Damascus, which included Ereẓ Israel, was established in the *qanun-name* of Suleiman (1548). In contrast to the disorganization and lack of security that characterized the end of the Mamluk period, Ereẓ Israel now enjoyed a secure rule and regulated organization. The improvement in the general condition was also manifested in agriculture, which was improved where it previously existed but was not expanded into desolate areas. Censuses conducted during the first 50 years after the conquest show that the population of Ereẓ Israel doubled, reaching approximately 300,000, and only a fifth to a quarter of the population lived in the six towns: Jerusalem, Hebron, Gaza, Ramleh, Nablus, and Safed. The remainder were primarily farmers living in villages, and some were Bedouin and seminomad who worked the land only seasonally and temporarily. The Bedouin also engaged in collecting a variety of plants for medicine, resin, and the burning of the kali, using its ashes for the manufacture of soap. The major agricultural products of the field were wheat, barley, maize, and different strains of beans (which served as food for man and beast (vetch)), vegetables, cotton, and sesame. The orchards produced dates, figs, pomegranates, berries, olives, apples, pears, and nuts. Fruit was also used for fruit honey. The Jews and Christians produced grape wine, as well as grape honey, which were permitted for the Muslims. The sources also make frequent references to beehives. Cattle breeding was undertaken mainly by the Bedouin, as well as by the fellahin and the residents of urban settlements. There were many jamus (buffalo) in the area of the Ḥuleh swamps, and fishing was popular in the settlements near the Ḥuleh and Lake Kinneret, as well as a few points on the shores of the Mediterranean (Acre, Jaffa).

The growth of the population, the expansion of cultivated lands in villages and the outskirts of cities, and the cultivation of orchards and olive trees led to the expansion of agriculture. There was an increase in the number of oil presses for the production of olive and sesame oils and for extracting fruit juices for the preparation of fruit honey. Together with oil production came the manufacture of soap, which was well known for its quality throughout the Middle East. The windmills operated regularly. Apparently at the initiative of the Jewish immigrants, new branches of industry were established in Safed, e.g., the manufacture and dyeing of cloth and felt. Information about these fields is also supplied by the tax lists in the canuns and the *deftars* of private censuses of the centers of these industries and the countries to which the products were exported. Especially noteworthy were the taxes that were levied on olive oil produced in Jerusalem and Ramleh and on the soap from Jerusalem exported to Egypt. The soap factory in Hebron was the property of the *waqf.* The center of the weaving and cloth dyeing industry was in Safed and its environs, although dyeing was also carried out in Kafr Kann, Nablus, and Gaza. In addition, there were tanneries in Nablus and Ein Zeitim. The fact that a special tax was levied on berry trees indicated that they were apparently cultivated for the feeding of silkworms. In fact, silk spinners are mentioned in a number of places. With the expansion of the cultivation of cotton in Ereẓ Israel, spinning began in Majdal, Lydda, Nablus, and Acre. Apart from the crafts undertaken by the Jews during the period of Mamluk rule, the Christians in Jerusalem, Bethlehem, and neighboring villages engaged in the home manufacture of religious objects (from wood and shells), which were sold to pilgrims on their visits to Ereẓ Israel or exported for sale abroad.

New Developments in the Jewish Communities. The writings of R. Moses Basola (who visited Ereẓ Israel in 1521/22) testify that Jerusalem grew in his time as a result of the Spanish immigration. According to his estimate the Jews of Jerusalem numbered about 300 families, not including widows, who numbered no more than 150 and were not subject to taxes, thus enjoying a comfortable income. About 200 people were supported by charity from public funds and from funds collected in the Diaspora. From 1502 to 1524 the community was headed by the *nagid* R. Isaac Sholal. The detailed Ottoman *deftar* of 1525–26 dealing with the *jamʿāti yahudyin* (the Jewish community) contains a detailed listing of 199 names of householders, excluding bachelors, and it can be assumed that not all of Jerusalem's Jewish residents were included in this census. The community was then composed of four groups: (1) the Ashkenazim, numbering 15 families descended from the Ashkenazim who had lived there since the time of Maimonides, joined by immigrants from Europe (the Italians were counted together with the Ashkenazim at that time); (2) the Sephardim, refugees of the expulsion who were the majority in the city; (3) immigrants from North Africa, known as Maghrebis; and (4) *Mustaʿrab (the Moriscos), longtime residents, descendants of the local inhabitants who had never left Ereẓ Israel. Among the *dayyanim* and scholars, including members of all the communities, there were often differences of opinion regarding the arrangement of prayers, the synagogue, etc. According to R. Israel Ashkenazi, after the conquest spiritual hegemony passed from the Mustaʿrabs and Maghrebis to the Sephardim.

In the center of the country there was still a Jewish settlement in Nablus, and in the south there were settlements in Hebron and Gaza. The community of Safed comprised more than 300 householders, whose economic situation, according to R. Moses Basola, was good. There were three synagogues: a Sephardi, a Mustaʿrab, and a Maghrebi. With the aid of the Jews of Egypt, the Jews of Safed managed to survive the difficult transition period of Mamluk retreat and Ottoman conquest. Jews also lived in the villages of Galilee: Ein Zeitim (four householders); Birya (Biriyyah, 19 families); ʿAlmāh (18 families); Peki'in (33 householders); Kafr Kannā (40–50 families); Kefar Ḥananiah (14 families); and Kefar Yasif, Shepharam, and Kābūl. It is estimated that there were about 1,000 Jewish families (i.e., 5,000 persons) in Ereẓ Israel at the beginning of the Ottoman conquest. The transition period gave rise to messianic hopes among the Jews of both Ereẓ Israel and the Diaspora. In 1523 David Reuveni and Shelomo (Solomon) Molcho arrived in Jerusalem bringing tidings of the forthcoming redemption. When he was in Portugal (1526), David Reuveni asked the king John III: "Help us and let us go out to battle against the provoking Suleiman and take the Holy Land from his hands" (Joseph ha-Kohen, *Emek ha-Bakha*, ed. by M. Letteris (1895), 113). Such hopes, as well as the improvement in the economic situation, gave rise to increased immigration, especially among the refugees from Spain. A few of them went to Jerusalem, whose population, according to official Turkish *deftars*, increased from approximately 200 families in 1526 to 338 families in 1554. R. Levi b. Ḥabib also settled there and cared for the spiritual and material needs of the community. Among the great teachers who lived for a long or short period in Jerusalem were R. *David ibn Abi Zimra (c. 1485; died in Safed, c. 1575) and R. Bezalel *Ashkenazi, a native of Jerusalem (beginning of 16th century) who headed the yeshivah in the city.

The majority of the new immigrants settled in Safed, which developed into an important commercial and industrial town. According to R. David de Rossi, who settled in Safed in 1535: "Whoever saw Safed ten years ago and sees it again now is amazed, for the Jews are constantly coming in and the clothing industry is expanding daily.... There is no *galut* here like in our country [Italy] and the Turks respect the important Jews. Here and in Alexandria [cf. Egypt], those appointed over the taxes and incomes of the king are Jews" (A. Yaari, *Iggerot Ereẓ Yisrael* (1943), 184, 186–7). In the middle of the 16th century, the Jews of Safed apparently numbered 10,000, i.e., the majority of the Jewish population of Ereẓ Israel was concentrated in Safed and its environs – Ein Zeitim, Birya, and other villages in Galilee. During the 16th century Safed became known as a large and important center of Torah and teaching. In 1524 R. Jacob (I) *Berab settled there and sought to renew the system of *ordination, which had not been used for hundreds of years. His plans aroused the violent opposition of the sages of Jerusalem, especially R. Levi b. Ḥabib, guardian of the spiritual and material needs of that community. They argued, inter alia, that the renewal of ordination required the authorization of all the scholars of Ereẓ Israel. Nevertheless, R. Jacob (I) Berab ordained four of the great scholars of his day, who were his students and colleagues: R. Joseph *Caro, author of the *Shulḥan *Arukh*; R. Moses *Trani (the Mabbit); R. Abraham *Shalom; and R. Israel di *Curiel (1538). Furthermore, these four ordained a number of their own disciples. This attempt to renew ordination and reinstate the full authority of the *battei din* of Ereẓ Israel ultimately failed, but the spiritual influence of the scholars of Safed continued, as evidenced by Caro's *Shulḥan Arukh*, which has been accepted by the Jewish world.

Safed became the center of mysticism during this period. In fact all the great halakhic scholars who lived there at the time studied Kabbalah and the Zohar. *Maggid Mesharim*, dialogues between the author and the mystical inspiration (*Maggid*) who guided him, was written by R. Joseph Caro. Before the arrival of R. Isaac *Luria (ha-Ari) in Safed (1569?), mystical scholars and formulators of new methods, such as R. Moses *Cordovero and R. Solomon *Alkabeẓ, author of the Sabbath hymn *Lekhah Dodi*, became known there. The system of practical Kabbalah established by Luria soon acquired many adherents throughout the Diaspora. His teachings were disseminated by his outstanding disciple, R. Ḥayyim *Vital, and other disciples known as "gurei ha-Ari."

The yearnings for redemption and messianic hopes which increased during this period, especially among the Spanish refugees, found ultimate expression in the bold attempt by Doña Gracia Mendes *Nasi and her nephew Don Joseph *Nasi, the wealthy Marrano statesman and Jewish leader, to rebuild Tiberias from its ruins. Don Joseph and Doña Gracia leased from the sultan the area of Tiberias, which was then desolate. Joseph sent his representative Joseph b. Ardict, or Joseph Pomar (presumably identical to Joseph Cohen, his secretary at about this time), to deal with the settlement of Jews in Tiberias. The area, intended to become a city, was surrounded with a wall (1564). As there are but few sources, it is difficult to determine whether Don Joseph intended to establish a Jewish state in Ereẓ Israel or create a limited haven for the Spanish refugees and derive economic benefit from the establishment of a new economic center in which wool and silk cloth would be manufactured. Whatever the original intent, the rebuilt Tiberias began to attract settlers from near (even from Safed) and far (Yemen). At the end of his life, Don Joseph displayed less enthusiasm in dealing with Tiberias. After his death, Solomon *Abenaes received new rights over Tiberias from the sultan Murad III and erected a number of buildings in Tiberias. Finally, however, the plan to reconstitute the city disintegrated and was abandoned because of various political and economic factors.

In connection with these messianic trends and hopes during the time of Sultan Suleiman, when Ottoman rule was at its peak, Christian priests in Syria, still adhering to Crusader ideas, suggested to Emperor Charles v that he conduct a campaign to regain the *holy places. This plan was never realized. Once again, during the rule of Selim II, the Greek patriarch Sophronius (1570) asked the German kaiser to deal mercifully with Jerusalem by renewing Christian rule there.

BEGINNINGS OF THE DECLINE. During the rule of Murad III (1574–95), his son Muhammad III (1595–1603), and succeeding sultans – Ahmed I (1603–17), Mustafa I (1617–18; 1622–23), and Murad IV (1623–40) – the Janissary army lost the strict discipline instituted by Selim I and became a constant source of danger to the sultan by its frequent rebellions and exaggerated demands over salaries and various grants. The situation in the political center was quickly reflected first on the borders of the desert through signs of overthrowing the yoke of the empire. Sheikhs and small princes began to entertain a hope of rebuilding from the ruins wrought by the Ottoman rulers. Prominent among the emirs of the *Druze who ruled in Lebanon was the Maʿan family, whose head, Fakhr al-Din II (1590–1635), conquered the Safed region and ʿAjlūn in eastern Transjordan while Muhammad III's army was engaged in battles with the Persians. Fakhr al-Din successfully uprooted the robbers who had spread throughout the land, and he turned Galilee into a tranquil and secure area. The same period saw the growth of the idea to establish an independent Christian Crusader state in Syria, Ereẓ Israel, and Cyprus. Fakhr al-Din utilized this idea to expand the scope of his influence in Ereẓ Israel with the help of the Christians. He occupied territories in the area of Jenin, came close to Mount Carmel, and signed agreements with the Bedouin in the mountains of Hauran. This activity aroused a violent reaction from the Turkish throne. In 1613 the great vizier Mansur instructed the wali of Damascus, Ahmad al-Ḥāfiẓ, to engage Fakhr al-Din in battle. The Druze emir passed on the administration of his political affairs to his brothers and left for Italy, where he spent a number of years in the courts of the prince of Tuscany and other rulers; he visited the knights of Malta and returned to Lebanon in 1618. Immediately upon his return, he renewed his efforts to regain all the territories lost while he was in exile. Eventually, he conquered the sanjaks of Safed, ʿAjlun, Shechem, and Gaza. At that time the sultan had no statesman or commander who could instill fear into the Druze emir, who even dared to renew the plan for establishing a Christian state in Ereẓ Israel through negotiations with the representatives of the king of Spain.

The expansion of the Maʿan family's rule over almost the entire area of Ereẓ Israel led to clashes with other local rulers, especially the members of the Ṭarbāyā. According to tradition, they received the Jenin region from the conquering Sultan Selim and expanded their sphere of influence gradually to Haifa, along the seacoast, and up to Gaza, sometimes even enforcing their rule over certain areas in Galilee. The al-Furaykh family, a Bedouin family from the Lebanon valley, established their rule by force in Safed, Nablus, and ʿAjlun. Under their influence, the wali of Damascus, Ahmad Kūtshuk ("the Small") was ordered by the central authorities to wage battle against Fakhr al-Din whom the *kapudan pasha* (commander of the fleet), Jaʿfar, was ordered to besiege from the sea, thus preventing Christian boats from rendering assistance. Fakhr al-Din attempted to conciliate the wali of Damascus by giving him Sidon (Saida) and Beirut, and in the meantime he sent Bishop Maroni to Italy to seek aid. Disappointed by his allies, he decided to surrender to the Ottoman rulers. In 1634 he was imprisoned in Constantinople and a year later was killed together with his two sons, who had been taken captive with him. His death, however, did not terminate the Druze's attempts to gain control of Ereẓ Israel. The settlements in Galilee, especially Safed and Tiberias, suffered from the renewed attempts by several Druze emirs to reconquer the region.

The total defeat of the Maʿan family did not improve the situation in the country. The gradual decline of the Ottoman Empire was reflected in repeated rebellions by the Janissaries, the increasing burden of taxes, and the loss of large areas in Europe. Clearly the general situation had a negative influence on the population of Ereẓ Israel in general and on the Jews in particular.

Jewish Population. During the last quarter of the 16th century the security situation of Ereẓ Israel deteriorated. Safed and Galilee suffered particularly from robbery raids by Bedouin and Druze tribes eager for the wealth of this industrial commercial town. Several sources give evidence that such acts were repeated several times. An Ottoman decree of 1576 ordered the expulsion of 500 or 1,000 wealthy Jewish families of Safed, forcing them to move to Cyprus. This decree was annulled later, but the very existence of the order undermined faith in the authorities. Safed began to be depleted of its wealthy residents, a phenomenon that sometimes took on the form of actual flight. The scholars also began to abandon the town, including R. Joseph Trani (son of R. Moses Trani, in 1599), who went to Constantinople. R. Ḥayyim Vital moved to Damascus. R. Isaiah ha-Levi *Horowitz (kabbalist, author of the famous moralistic work *Shenei Luḥot ha-Berit*) decided not to settle in Safed and went to Jerusalem in 1621.

Although Safed was not totally abandoned, as was the case with Tiberias (where not one Jew remained by the end of the 17th century), the decline was evident.

A short time after R. Isaiah Horowitz' arrival in Jerusalem, the community was harmed by the greed of a Bedouin sheikh, Muhammad ibn Farukh, who achieved the position of *sanjak bey* of Jerusalem (1625) and began to tyrannize the population, and especially the Jews, through the imposition of heavy taxes. After a year of persecution, the pasha in Damascus finally dismissed ibn Farukh, but the heavy debts remained in force and many emissaries went out to the Diaspora to collect funds to save the community. The situation was not as favorable as envisioned by R. Isaiah Horowitz, but Jerusalem was rebuilt to some extent, as were other communities in the south – notably Hebron, in which a few of the disciples of R. Moses Cordovero and R. Isaac Luria settled.

During periods of trouble in Jerusalem, Hebron and Gaza served as a temporary refuge from persecution and oppression. The number of Jerusalem's residents increased especially after the decrees of 1648, when some Jewish war refugees from the Ukraine arrived in Ereẓ Israel. The rulers of the city exploited the situation by imposing a heavier burden of taxes on the Jews, especially affecting the poor. Many awaited aid that was usually sent regularly by the Diaspora communities. When this assistance did not arrive in time and was insufficient, emissaries would be sent abroad to arouse the sympathy of the Jews. One of these emissaries was *Shabbetai Ẓevi, who left Jerusalem shortly after his arrival there in order to collect funds in Egypt (1664). On his way to Egypt he stopped in Gaza. The Gaza community was very important at that time because the city was regarded as the capital of the Negev and Sinai and was a large commercial center and a stopping place on the route between Africa and Asia. It was an asylum for Jewish refugees because it enjoyed an independent administration and was also even a refuge in times of plague. In the 16th–17th centuries there were outstanding scholars there. Shabbetai Ẓevi also made the acquaintance there of *Nathan of Gaza. It was in Gaza that Shabbetai Ẓevi saw his visions, and the city became an important center for the dissemination of Shabbeteanism.

Jerusalem, which was then the center of most of the scholars of Ereẓ Israel and even attracted some of the great scholars from the countries of the East, again took over the spiritual leadership, which it had relinquished during the previous century to Safed. Despite the difficult material situation and the harsh attitude of the local rulers, in the 17th century the Jewish population succeeded in consolidating its position in Jerusalem and in the entire southern section of the country.

NEW DEVELOPMENTS IN THE 18TH CENTURY. At the turn of the century, during the reign of Mustafa II (1695–1703), there was a change in the political status of the Ottoman power in Europe. The Treaty of Karlowitz (Jan. 26, 1699) forced the sultan to make many territorial concessions in his border regions. Russia demanded, inter alia, control of the holy places in Jerusalem and all Orthodox Christians in the Ottoman Empire, be they Greeks, Serbs, Bulgarians, or others. This control was expected to provide personal immunity and exemption from taxes and Muslim jurisdiction. With the decline in the military power of the Janissaries, the central authority was compelled to allow its walis to conscript soldiers in another way, in order to put them to use locally. Thus cavalry and infantry troops, composed of Albanian, Bosnian, and Maghrebi mercenaries, were founded. Their salaries were derived from the incomes of government estates and special taxes levied on the population, usually without basis in religious tradition and regarded as illegal by religious scholars. These private armies were one of the sources of the anarchy in Turkey during the 18th century. The walis used them for the purposes of tax collection and expanding their rule at the expense of weaker neighboring provinces.

At the beginning of the 18th century, Ẓāhir al-Omar, a local Bedouin ruler, received the *iltizām* (the right to levy taxes) for most of the districts of Galilee (in the regions of Nazareth, Tiberias, and Safed) from the tribe of Zaydān. He very soon overcame some of his opponents and extended his rule over the district of Tiberias, where he fortified himself as the tax farmer of the pasha of Sidon. In 1742 the pasha of Damascus was ordered by the sultan to fight against Ẓāhir. This episode was described in Hebrew by the son-in-law of R. Ḥayyim *Abulafia, who rebuilt the Jewish community in Tiberias (1740). The attack on Tiberias failed, and in 1743 the pasha tried again. A short while later he died. Thereafter Ẓāhir was able to overcome his remaining opponents and annexed their estates (such as Shepharam) to his territories. He then turned to the sea and conquered Acre. His control of Acre and Haifa (and economically also of Dar-Ṭanṭūra) brought him in direct contact with the traders and agents of Europe who had established bases in the coastal towns to conduct trade with inland regions.

Ẓāhir formed an alliance with the ruler of Egypt, Ali Bey, and the Russian fleet, which arrived in the Mediterranean to the surprise of the Ottomans. In 1771 almost the entire country was under his control, and his Egyptian allies captured Damascus. Ẓāhir captured Gaza, Lydda, Ramleh, and Jaffa, but the Egyptian commander joined the sultan's army, regaining what Ẓāhir had captured and perpetrating a massacre in Jaffa (1775). The Ottomans attracted to their side Ẓāhir's mercenary forces, who betrayed their master and murdered him (1775). On the same day the sultan's army captured Acre and Ahmad Pasha al-Jazzār ("the Butcher") was appointed *sanjak bey* of the Sidon area.

Ahmad Pasha was wali of the Sidon area, whose capital he transferred to Acre, for 29 years (1775–1804). He also became the ruler of the Tripoli area and in 1790–99 and 1804 was the wali of Damascus. He organized a private army of Albanians, Bosnians, Maghrebis, and Bedouin and fortified the walls of Acre, and the value of these fortifications was proven during Napoleon's siege.

Napoleon's invasion of Egypt in 1798 came as a complete surprise for Istanbul, which had considered him an ally when he was conquering Malta and putting an end to the activities of the pirates. At the beginning of 1799, Napoleon's army was advancing toward Ereẓ Israel. He attempted to bribe Ahmad al-Jazzār into joining his side, but the pasha refused to receive Napoleon's delegation. The French then conquered Gaza, Ramleh, Lydda, and Jaffa without difficulty, but had to unleash a fierce attack on Jaffa because of the presence of a large garrison there. Most of the city was destroyed during and after the siege. The population welcomed the conquerors, for Napoleon had incurred their affection through various promises and a humane attitude. Napoleon's army did not turn to Jerusalem because he was interested only in strategic conquests that would open the way to the centers of the Ottoman Empire (for the international constellation, see The Land of Israel in International Affairs). The French conquered Haifa and then besieged Acre. The English fleet came to the aid of al-Jazzār and remnants of the Ottoman army engaged the French in battle but were ambushed near En-Harod by the French general J.G. Kleber. This victory opened the way to Safed, but the opportunity was not exploited. In contrast, Acre defended itself, and Napoleon could not destroy its fortifications because the British fleet destroyed his navy and he lacked heavy cannons. In the meantime, plagues broke out in the French camp, and the famous commander was forced to retreat with his army to Egypt and from there he returned to France.

The situation of the farmers who worked the lands of the government was, at the beginning of Ottoman rule, not unfavorable. The "miri," or the land of the emirate that was taxed, was not a burden on the fellahin, while the land was populated and they benefited, directly or indirectly, from profits made through international trade. With the impoverishment of the Ottoman Empire, however, the tax burden increased and the people began to abandon the villages for the towns. The various payments demanded from the villages became an intolerable burden in the absence of working hands. Furthermore, the Bedouin harassed the villagers in the plains and the valleys and robbed them of the fruits of their labors, which was an added reason to abandon the fertile lands.

According to the French traveler C.F. de Volney (in 1783–85), the decisive majority of the population were fellahin. Nevertheless, this traveler, and others who visited the country, noted the strange contrast between the fertility of the land and the poor state of the few farms. This was the situation in the southern plain (between Gaza and Ashkelon and Hebron) and in the area between Bethlehem and Jerusalem. The broad Acre plain and the region around the Kinneret, which were known for their abundance of water, were overgrown with reeds. The naturalist T. Shaw (1722), who investigated the flora and fauna of North Africa and the Middle East, records that the soil of many valleys was fertile and good. He mentioned that if the land had been cultivated as in the past, it would have yielded a larger crop than the best lands on the shores of Syria and Phoenicia. According to him, cotton grown in the valleys of Ramleh, Jezreel, and Zebulun was of a better quality than that cultivated near Sidon or Tripoli. It was difficult to find beans, wheat, or other grains superior to the produce sold regularly in Jerusalem. The desolation about which travelers sometimes complained was not a result of the natural character of the country, but rather of the sparseness of the population and the indolence of the inhabitants.

Ẓāhir al-Omar attempted to improve the condition of agriculture in Galilee. He encouraged the fellahin to work their lands by granting loans and he especially tried to protect them from bandits. He favored the settlement of Jews and they re-established themselves in Peki'in, Shepharam, and Yasif. In contrast, a traveler accuses Ahmad al-Jazzār, Ẓāhir's successor in Galilee, of not being concerned with the development of agriculture in the Acre plain, which remained a swampland.

Reconstruction of the Jewish Community. The messianic ferment that increased in the Diaspora at the end of the 17th century was connected with increased immigration to Ereẓ Israel. At the beginning of the 18th century it was headed by *Judah Ḥasid and Ḥayyim *Malakh, both Shabbeteans – the former covertly and the latter overtly – who arrived in Jerusalem at the end of 1700 at the head of a convoy organized in Europe. Before their arrival, the Jewish community of Jerusalem numbered 1,200, of whom 200 were Ashkenazim weighed down by a burden of debts. Of the people who left with this convoy, which took two routes (one through Venice and the other through Istanbul), about 500 died on the way and only about 1,000 reached Jerusalem. Its leader, Judah Ḥasid, died almost immediately after the convoy's arrival, and conflicts arose with the veteran settlers, who were opposed to the Shabbatean movement. The new arrivals were a heavy burden on the Ashkenazi community, for the Arabs had lent money to the members of the convoy and now demanded reimbursement from the veteran Ashkenazim. They appealed to the *Council of the Four Lands for the aid of the Polish communities in their battle against the Shabbateans and sent emissaries to Frankfurt and Metz, where financial help for the poor of Ereẓ Israel was concentrated. Help did not arrive, due to political reasons unconnected with Ashkenazi Jewry. The Arab creditors broke into the Ashkenazi synagogue on a Sabbath (Nov. 8, 1720), set it on fire, and took over the area, which they held until 1816. For several years after the burning of the synagogue, Ashkenazi Jews, who were recognizable by their dress, could not settle in Jerusalem for fear of being held for the old debts. Those who dared to do so a generation later had to disguise themselves as Jews from Oriental communities. The European immigrants settled mainly in Hebron, Safed, and even Tiberias.

At that time the Jews lived mainly on charity received from abroad and, in a few cases, on income from businesses in their lands of origin. Any slight change in the situation of the contributors, or any delay in sending aid, could bring disaster upon the poor. The extreme poverty led R. Moses b. Raphael Mordecai *Malkhi, a scholar and famous physician in Jerusalem (end of 17th century), to speak out against the immigration of very poor people, arguing that Ereẓ Israel needed immigrants who could be self-sustaining. In order to supervise the distribution and use of funds and also facilitate the payment of the numerous debts burdening the Jerusalem community, the "officials for Jerusalem" in Istanbul, sent a special *parnas* to act as a kind of administrator for the community and take care of Jewish pilgrims. For those Jews who wanted to devote themselves to the study of the Torah, yeshivot were established in Jerusalem, where outstanding scholars studied. Ḥayyim Joseph David *Azulai, R. Sar Shalom *Sharabi, and R. *Abraham Gershon of Kutow (brother-in-law of Israel b. Eliezer Baal Shem-Tov) were in the yeshivah Beth-El, where kabbalistic studies were also pursued.

The Jews of Hebron suffered because of constant civil wars between the Arabs of Hebron, who belonged to the

Qays faction (of north Arabian origin), and those of Bethlehem, who belonged to the Yemen faction (from south Arabian tribes). The Istanbul officials extended their activities to include Hebron, whose situation had been aggravated by debts owed by the community. Ḥayyim Joseph David Azulai went to Western Europe in 1753 and in 1773 on behalf of the Hebron community. Another emissary was Ḥayyim Isaac *Carigal, who reached North America. In the 1880s the number of the Jews in the city of the patriarchs reached about 300.

The community of Gaza was smaller than that of Hebron and suffered from repeated incursions made by the various armies. It was decimated after the conquest of the town by Napoleon (1799), and in 1811 no one remained there. Many Ashkenazim from Poland and Lithuania settled in Safed and Tiberias, which were centers of Ḥasidism from the second half of the 18th century, establishing a new link with the greatest Diaspora community of the time. Immigrants from Eastern Europe thus settled Galilee and Tiberias, which had been almost depleted of inhabitants during the 17th century. Tiberias was rebuilt by R. Abraham *Abulafia (1740) with the help of the sheikh Ẓāhir al-Omar. After the *Ḥasidim came a wave of their opponents, disciples of R. *Elijah, the *Gaon* of Vilna. According to tradition, the *gaon* himself wanted to immigrate but halted his journey in the middle. In 1770–72, his most important disciples, R. Ḥayyim of Vilna and R. *Israel b. Samuel of Shklov, arrived and a few years after his death many of his disciples, called *perushim*, immigrated. The immigration of the *perushim* was brilliantly described by R. Israel of Shklov.

1800–1917. The beginning of this period saw the end of the district system of administration, during which time Ereẓ Israel displayed all the characteristics of a neglected province of a disintegrating empire but after 1840 there was a turn for the better. The population increased appreciably. The administration of the country was changed and there was an increase in Western influence, resulting from the revolution in means of communication, which brought the Ottoman Empire closer to Europe. The increased rivalry among the European powers turned Ereẓ Israel into a focal point of the "Eastern problem."

According to estimates, which tend to be exaggerated, the number of the inhabitants in Ereẓ Israel in 1800 did not exceed 300,000. The number of Jews apparently did not exceed 5,000, most of whom were Sephardim. Most of the Jewish population was concentrated in the "Four Holy Cities," Jerusalem, Safed, Tiberias, and Hebron. The Christians, who apparently numbered about 25,000, were scattered over a wider area. Their main concentrations – in Jerusalem, Nazareth, and Bethlehem – belonged primarily to the Greek Orthodox, Greek Catholic, and Roman Catholic Churches. The remaining inhabitants were Muslims, almost all of them of the Sunni sect. As more Jews immigrated to the country, the size of the Jewish population doubled by about 1840, with the Christian and Muslim elements unchanged. Between 1800 and the end of 1831, Ereẓ Israel was divided into two Ottoman vilayets (pashaliks). The borders of these changed from time to time, but in general the eastern central mountain region from north of Nablus to south of Hebron (including Jerusalem) belonged to the vilayet of Damascus (al-Shām) and Galilee and the Coastal Plain, to Khan Yunis, belonged to the vilayet of Acre. The coastal region from Khan Yunis to Caesarea was divided into three *nāḥiyāt* (sub-districts): Gaza, Ramleh, and Jaffa. Most of the Negev was at that time under the vilayet of Hejaz, centered in Medina, in the Arabian Peninsula.

The structure of the Ottoman state should not be analyzed from a Western point of view. Even during its zenith, no attempt was made to Ottomanize non-Turkish conquered regions. The children of ruling groups often married local women and assimilated into the local population. Thus local traditions and officials were maintained in Ereẓ Israel and a subject of the Sultan had to maintain his prime allegiance not to the imperial government, but to the religious group or the social class into which he was born. The Christians and Jews, as members of special millets, even had limited direct contact with the Ottoman government. Even the head tax, which exempted one from military service, was collected by means of the millet. Only those non-Ottoman subjects belonging to the Sunni sect of Islam could identify to some extent with the higher (though only nominal) function of the sultan: the defense of the Muslim faith against apostasy.

The vague connection between Ahmad al-Jazzār and the supreme authority continued during the rule of Ahmad's successors – Suleiman, Ismail, and Abdallah (1804–32), who were less active and cruel than he. Of a similar nature were the relations between the supreme authority and the pashas who ruled in Damascus and Gaza. Public welfare had no significance in the view of the rulers, who regarded as their prime function the collection of taxes derived from three major sources: the "miri" land tax (from Muslims); the "kharj," head tax; and customs. When these sources proved insufficient, various crop taxes were levied arbitrarily on Muslims and non-Muslims alike.

At the beginning of the 1780s, Ramleh and Acre derived their income from the sale of raw cotton and plain cotton cloth to the French traders in the Levant. Clothes, dyes, sugar, and coffee (from the West Indies) were bought from the French traders. These traders, however, disappeared from the country after the French Revolution and returned only after the Napoleonic wars. The (British) Levant Company, which filled the gap created by the disappearance of the French traders, was not interested in the cotton of Ereẓ Israel. When the French traders returned to the East after 1815, they did not succeed in reestablishing their former trade connections. In 1821, when the long-fibered strain of cotton was introduced into Egypt, the manufacture of cotton in Ereẓ Israel became relatively useless, except during the U.S. Civil War, when it enjoyed a brief revival. Acre and Ramleh never regained their primary position in the economy of the country. In 1825, when the concession to the Levant Company and privileges granted the Trade Bureau of Marseilles were abolished, the way was opened for free trade.

The period of Egyptian rule in Syria and Ereẓ Israel, which lasted nine years (1832–40), marked the peak of provincial government. This was the first time that an independent pasha had rebelled against the Sublime Porte, conquered territories from other pashas, and compelled the sultan to admit the "legality" of his conquests. Nevertheless, after consolidating his position in Syria and Ereẓ Israel, *Muhammad Ali, the pasha of Egypt, agreed to pay to Sultan Mahmud II the "accepted quota" of the tax (1834). Ibrahim Pasha (stepson of Muhammad Ali), who successfully conducted the military campaign, became the general ruler of the conquered area and established his residence in Damascus. The whole of Ereẓ Israel, whose northern border reached Sidon, now became one district. The few forests remaining in the valleys and on the mountain slopes in central Ereẓ Israel were cut down to supply wood for Muhammed Ali's fleet. Ibrahim Pasha forced the Muslim farmers to join the Egyptian army. Rebellions, which occurred in most of the towns, were put down by force and law and order established. Swiftly executed punishments halted the incursions of the Bedouin. Even a blood revenge feud between the Qays and the Yemen factions was put down and travelers from Jaffa to Jerusalem no longer had to pay taxes to the Circassian sheikhs of *Abu Ghosh. Attempts were made to eradicate bribery in the courts, institute a fair division of taxes, and avoid discrimination against the Jews in favor of the Muslims.

For more than a decade before Egyptian rule in Ereẓ Israel, Protestant missionaries from Britain and the United States tried to obtain permission to establish regular institutions in Jerusalem and other parts of the country. These attempts met with the strong opposition of the provincial rulers and their representatives. Ibrahim Pasha allowed the missionaries not only to preach but even to establish schools. The Egyptian period also saw the beginning of extensive activity in biblical geography and archaeology, especially by the U.S. scholar Edward *Robinson. Moreover, in 1838 the Egyptian government permitted Britain to open a regular consulate in Jerusalem; previously, consular representations were limited – apart from ephemeral French attempts in Jerusalem in 1699–1700 and 1713–15 – to the coastal towns (Acre, Haifa, Jaffa) and Ramleh, and even in these places the powers would appoint local agents as their representatives. Twenty years later, all the important Western nations, including the United States, were represented in Jerusalem by regular consular delegations.

The intervention of the European powers in 1840–41 in the Egyptian-Ottoman conflict forced Ibrahim Pasha and his forces to leave Ereẓ Israel and Syria, which returned to the direct control of the Ottoman Empire. Egyptian rule did not last long enough to have any lasting influence, but thousands of Egyptian farmers who had settled in the southern parts of the country remained there after the retreat of the Egyptian Army. The Qays and the Yemen factions again caused disturbances in the rural areas and the people of Abu Ghosh reinstated the collection of taxes from travelers (lasting until 1846). Former pashas, however, were not returned to their posts and a new administration was established on the basis of strict centralization.

The increasing administrative changes were finally expressed in the Vilayet Law of 1864, which unified the whole provincial administration into one framework. Most of Ereẓ Israel was covered by the sanjaks of Nablus (which, until 1888, included the area of Balqā', east of the Jordan) and Acre, which were part of the vilayet of Beirut, and the independent sanjak or mutaṣariflik of Jerusalem (previously part of the vilayet of Damascus), which was now placed directly under the authority of Istanbul. Each district was divided into sub-districts (Ar. *qaḍā'*, plural *aqḍiya*) and each *qaḍā'* into subdistricts (Ar. *nāḥiyāt*). The provincial administration was composed of a strict hierarchy of Ottoman officials: *mudīr* (head of a *nāḥiya*), *qāymaqām* (head of a vilayet). Each official was subordinate to the head of his administrative region, while the Wali was subordinate to the ministry of the interior in Istanbul (established in 1860). A council (*majlis*) representing all sectors of the population, both Muslim and non-Muslim, aided Ottoman officials of every grade who headed an administrative unit. This administrative system, of course, did not terminate all corruption and abuse or institute representative rule, but it greatly curtailed the arbitrary actions of the provisional rulers and even granted the various religious communities a small measure of influence in public affairs.

Missionary organizations, representing almost every sect in Western Christianity, increased quickly after the departure of the Egyptians. They were concentrated mainly in Jerusalem, which had, toward the end of the 19th century, the greatest proportion of missionaries per capita of any city in the world. Some of the missionary groups developed an increasing number of educational, medical, and charitable institutions. The number of those converting to the new faith, even among Eastern Christians, was negligible, but the establishment of schools and clinics by Protestant missionaries stimulated the Latin and Greek Orthodox communities, as well as the Ottoman government and even the Jewish community, to establish similar institutions.

Political considerations led to increased rivalry among the missionary groups from various countries. The great European powers, which made attempts to gain areas of influence in every part of the Ottoman Empire as potential holding points in a future division of the empire, exploited the missionary activities of their subjects in Ereẓ Israel for the advancement of their political aims. Austria-Hungary, France, Prussia, and Russia rendered financial assistance to missionary activities. After the signing of the Treaty of Kutchuk-Kainarji (1774), Russia claimed the right to protect the Arabs who belonged to the Greek Orthodox Church and even granted its protection to the Greek Orthodox patriarchate in Jerusalem. The czarist government, which was aided by the Russian Orthodox Company for Palestine and the delegation of the Russian church in the country, contributed funds for the establishment of schools, churches, and hostels. France, claimed similar rights in relation to the Roman Catholic community, institutions, and holy places. The Pope reinstituted the Roman Catholic patriarchate in Jerusalem in 1847. The status of France as the protector of Roman Catholicism in the Ottoman Empire was officially confirmed in Article 62 of the Treaty of the Congress of Berlin (1878). This status, however, aroused increasing rivalry on the part of other Catholic countries. In 1841 the Protestant missions of England and Prussia established a joint bishopric in Jerusalem, which the Germans stopped supporting in 1881.

The activities of the Protestant powers within the Ottoman Empire were conducted under less favorable conditions than those of Russia and France since the former had no millets in Ereẓ Israel to "adopt" for religious reasons. Thus, during the Ottoman-Egyptian War of 1839–41, Britain became the "defender" of the Jewish and Druze communities in Ereẓ Israel, as a sort of countermove to France's identification with the Christian Maronite community of Lebanon. One of the causes for the outbreak of the Crimean War (1853–56) was the conflicting claims of France and Russia to the guardianship of the holy places. After 1868 the German *Templer movement established settlements in Jaffa, Sarona, Haifa, and Jerusalem, reaching over 500 in the course of time. The Templer settlements, which continued to expand, later supplied William II with the means of political penetration. Of the U.S. groups of Millennarians who lived in Artas (near Bethlehem) in 1852, in Jaffa in 1866/67, and in Jerusalem in 1881, only the last remained. This was called the "American Colony," although after 1896 it comprised more Swedes than American subjects. Archaeological investigation of the biblical period expanded. A U.S. naval unit headed by Lt. W.F. Lynch explored the Jordan and the Dead Sea. The *Palestine Exploration Fund, established in 1865, completed a survey map of the area west of the Jordan, before embarking on the exploration of ancient sites. The American Palestine Exploration Society, which was short-lived (1870–81), concentrated on eastern Transjordan.

With the appearance of steam boats in the Middle East in the 1830s, regular communications between Ereẓ Israel and Europe were established for the first time. In 1837 Austria and France gained licenses to operate postal services in the Asian provinces of the Ottoman Empire. The Turkish-Tatar postal messengers, who traveled between Istanbul and the capitals of the provinces at approximately six-week intervals, were finally replaced in the mid-19th century by an Ottoman service which, although more frequent, was no less confused. In 1865 telegraphic communications were set up in Jerusalem and other important towns of Ereẓ Israel with the capital of the empire and Europe. Three years later the provincial administration completed the first road in Ereẓ Israel (between Jerusalem and Jaffa) that was suitable for wheeled carriages. Improvements in transportation and communications led to an increase in the number of pilgrims and tourists, who brought new sources of income. By 1880 the population of Ereẓ Israel had increased appreciably, reaching 450,000, of which 24,000 were Jews and 45,000 were Christians. Jerusalem, which had expanded beyond the walls of the Old City following the Crimean War, became the largest town in the country. Its population was estimated as at least 25,000; more than half of them were Jews.

See also the Land of Israel in International Affairs, in *Israel, State of: History.

The Jewish Population. In the history of the Jews of Ereẓ Israel there is a distinct contrast between the periods 1800–40 and 1841–80. In the first 30 years of the 19th century the corruption of Ottoman rule reached heights of perversion. The eight years of the Egyptian conquest (1832–40) were a kind of transition period. After 1840 the Jews were drawn into international conflicts connected with the Eastern problem, but began to enjoy the protection of Western powers. Their numbers increased considerably, as did their economic and cultural influence, although Napoleon's campaign in Egypt and Ereẓ Israel and his call to Eastern Jewry to come to his aid and thus pave the way for the political renaissance of Ereẓ Israel – if such a proclamation was indeed made – made little impression on the Jews of the country. The restraining influence of Ḥayyim Salim *Farḥi, scion of an ancient Jewish family from Damascus, was felt in the country for 20 years. As the financial official and general adviser of Aḥmad al-Jazzāār and his successors in the pashalic of Damascus, Farḥi somewhat eased the lives of not only the Jews, but the Muslims and Christians as well. After 20 years of rule he was murdered in 1820 by Abdallah Pasha, whom Farḥi had aided in his rise to the status of governor.

At that time most of the Jews of the country lived in the four holy cities: Jerusalem, Safed, Tiberias, and Hebron. Although they were sustained by funds from the **ḥalukkah*, they labored under a heavy yoke of taxes imposed by the Ottoman officials. Thus J. Conder wrote in 1831: "The extortions and oppressions were so numerous that it was said of the Jews that they had to pay for the very air they breathed." Nevertheless, the population continued to increase, especially as a result of immigration from Europe. This flow increased with the introduction of steamboat transportation on the Odessa-Jaffa and other routes. The age-old attraction of Ereẓ Israel, which was then felt especially among Eastern European Ḥasidim, brought a constant stream of ḥasidic settlers to Jerusalem and other holy cities. The first Ashkenazi community was established in Hebron in 1820 by Ḥabad Ḥasidim influenced by Ber, the son of R. Shneur Zalman of Lyady. Jaffa, which had been rebuilt by the Ottoman ruler Mohammed Abu Nabut in 1800–20, attracted a considerable number of Jews from 1830 on. The development of the community, interrupted by the bad earthquake of 1837, was renewed after 1839 and especially after the establishment of the rabbinate in 1841. Most of the Jaffa Jews came from North Africa; in 1857 there were only three Ashkenazi families there. In 1874 their number increased to 20, and the total Jewish population of Jaffa numbered 500. Safed, which competed with Jerusalem for spiritual hegemony, suffered greatly in the earthquake of 1837, when some 2,000 Jews lost their lives, and never regained its former position of leadership. The first Hebrew printing press in Ereẓ Israel, which was established there in 1831, moved to Jerusalem after nine years.

Egyptian rule did not greatly ease the burden of taxes, but Muhammad Ali's efforts to institute Western methods opened the way for vital internal and external changes. Although the promises in the sultan's decree of 1839 to grant equal rights to members of the three faiths – Jewish, Christian, and Muslim – were never fulfilled, there was a considerable improvement in the situation of the Jews. The high-flown proclamations of the Ottomans, such as that of 1841 ("Muslims, Christians, Israelites, you are all the subjects of one ruler, you are all the sons of one father"), also had some influence on the status of the oppressed minorities. Of similar significance was the fact that the Western powers, in their struggle for the hegemony of the Middle East, displayed a certain interest in the Jews of Ereẓ Israel. According to the system of *Capitulations (agreements granting special rights to foreign powers in the Ottoman Empire), the Western consuls in the country "protected" the interests of their citizens. Great Britain, and often Russia as well, became (for the reasons mentioned above) the patrons of the Jews of Ereẓ Israel. Britain intervened on behalf of Jews who were Ottoman subjects, but primarily on behalf of Jews from European countries when their own consuls refused to provide assistance. This was so not only during dramatic events, such as the *Damascus Affair of 1840 and the Christian massacre in Syria in 1860, but even under normal conditions. The British government even ventured, in connection with the Damascus Affair, to suggest that the sultan allow the Jews of the "*raʿāyā*" class (non-Muslim subjects of the sultan) to address their complaints against local Ottoman authorities to him through the mediation of the British consuls.

Although the Ottomans rejected this suggestion, the British consular authorities found opportunities to intervene on behalf of the Jews. In 1849 R. Isaiah *Bardaki, the leader of the Russian Jews of Jerusalem, requested that the British consul in Jerusalem grant protection to Jews who had become stateless as a result of discriminatory legislation in Russia. Thirty years later Russia relented in its hostile attitude toward the Jews of Ereẓ Israel and even granted them some protection, while persecuting the Jews in Russia itself. Laurence *Oliphant reflected: "Had Russia encouraged Jewish immigration to Ereẓ Israel and protected the immigrants, she could have had an excellent pretext for political interference in the country."

The idea of establishing a Jewish state or, at least, an autonomous Jewish settlement under supreme Ottoman control became a subject for serious discussion. In 1839, during the second of his visits in Ereẓ Israel, Sir Moses *Montefiore opened negotiations with Muhammad Ali to gain a charter for Jewish settlement in Ereẓ Israel in return for a large loan to Egypt. These negotiations failed, however, because of the downfall of Muhammad Ali, in 1841. The idea of establishing a Jewish buffer state between Egypt and the rest of the Ottoman Empire, however, gained supporters during the conflict between the two powers. The first who advocated this solution was Rev. Wilson Filson Marsh. A detailed plan for Jewish settlement was advanced at that time by Abraham *Benisch, a Bohemian Jew who became editor of the London *Jewish Chronicle*. The memorandum he composed on the question was made available to the Foreign Office by the British consul in Jerusalem, William Young, and gained the support of Montefiore and other British Jewish leaders. Similar plans, though less detailed, were offered at that time on the European continent. The idea was supported by English notables such as Col. Charles Henry Churchill (1840–56), Col. George Gawler (1845), Laurence Oliphant (1879), and others.

Relations between Jews and non-Jews in Ereẓ Israel were not at all amicable. Religious disputes were always common and the Jews were in a state of conflict with the missionaries, who were prohibited by law to convert Muslims, although the London missionary society for the dissemination of Christianity among Jews usually fought for the rights of Jews in Ereẓ Israel. This group was supported by British consuls such as James *Finn, whose autobiographical account, *Stirring Times* (1878), is an important source of information. Although contemporaries often remarked that missionary progress in Ereẓ Israel was slow, Ludwig August Frankel, who visited Jerusalem in 1856, found 131 converts there. According to the estimation of Goodrich-Freer, no fewer than 523 Jews converted in 1839–96, and the expenses for baptizing one Jew amounted to £1,000. In their battle against the missionaries, the Jews often came into conflict with the British and other consuls.

There were also serious internal conflicts within the Jewish community itself. Recipients of *ḥalukkah* funds often complained about discrimination, real or imagined, in their treatment by the *ḥalukkah* officials. The Jews of Germany and Holland were the first to establish a separate *kolel* for themselves, known as "Kolel Hod" (Holland-Deutschland), which served as a model for *kolelim* established by other factions of the community. By the beginning of the 20th century, there were 30 such *kolelim*. This division aroused internal controversies and also damaged the work of the **meshullaḥim* (see *Sheluḥei Ereẓ Israel) sent to collect money for the welfare funds. In 1886 the Ashkenazi *kolelim* in Jerusalem organized a general council under the leadership of Meir *Auerbach and Samuel *Salant.

Although the authority of the Ashkenazi rabbis was solid within their own community, they did not enjoy the legal recognition accorded the Sephardi *ḥakham bashi*, as most of the Ashkenazim were foreign subjects. The first Sephardi chief rabbis, including Solomon Moses *Suzin (in the time of Muhammad Ali), Jonah Moses *Navon (1836–40), and Judah Navon (1840–41), lacked governmental recognition, but from the time of Ḥayyim Abraham *Gagin (1842–48), the *ḥakham bashi* received an official status by governmental appointment, or rather by the sultan's confirmation of his election by the Sephardi community of Jerusalem. After Gagin, the post of *ḥakham bashi* was held by Isaac Kovo (1848–54), Ḥayyim Nissim *Abulafia (1854–61), Ḥayyim David *Ḥazzan (1861–69), and Abraham *Ashkenazi (1869–80) who came from Larissa, Greece.

The number of Ashkenazim gradually exceeded the Sephardim in most of the communities of Ereẓ Israel, and while the old settlements grew from decade to decade, new ones were established. Nablus, the old center of Samaritanism, began to attract Jews when it became a trading center. In 1864 there were in Nablus about 100 Jews, 150 Samaritans, 600 Christians, and 9,400 Muslims. According to Ludwig August Frankl, there were about 100 Jews in the renewed community of Haifa in 1856. The influence of the Jews grew, especially in Jerusalem, which came to have a Jewish majority. When the Old City could no longer contain them, the Jews set up the first suburb outside the walls in 1860 (Mishkenot Sha'ananim, established by Sir Moses Montefiore). During the twenty succeeding years they established more than ten additional suburbs, including Naḥalat Shiva (1869) and Me'ah She'arim (1872), which became the nucleus of the New City.

The economic situation of the Jews of Ereẓ Israel remained generally unchanged, despite several attempts to settle some Jews on the land and teach them useful trades. In 1839 and again in 1849 Montefiore responded to requests by the Jews of Ereẓ Israel to implement far-reaching plans to settle Jews on the land. Montefiore, together with the Rothschilds of Paris, who worked mainly through their adviser, Albert Cohen, and other European philanthropists, helped to establish a Jewish hospital in Jerusalem (1854) and supported the Laemel school, founded by Frankl in 1856 to teach Jews professions and to remove Jewish children from the mission schools. Since the teaching methods of this school were new from several points of view, and since European languages were also taught there, it met with the fierce opposition of extreme Ashkenazi Orthodox Jews and their supporters in the Diaspora, so that Frankl had to turn over the administration of the school to Sephardim, who were more tolerant.

The process of the Jewish community's transformation into a productive factor did not cease but rather increased in pace. Even the missionaries thought of establishing an agricultural settlement for apostate Jews. In 1861 the first land purchase by Jews for agricultural purposes in modern times was made by the Yehuda family at Moẓa. Finally, in 1870, the *Alliance Israélite Universelle established the *Mikveh Israel agricultural school near Jaffa. Agricultural settlements were established at *Moẓa (1873), Petaḥ *Tikvah (1878), and Jauni (Rosh Pinnah), which, although they were abandoned after a short time, opened the way for future development and were reestablished later. In 1881 the U.S. consul wrote that about 1,000 Jews in Ereẓ Israel earned their livings through agricultural labor, and therefore many of them were no longer "paupers and beggars." On the other hand, the appearance of the first Hebrew journals – *Ha-Levanon* in 1863 and **Ḥavaẓẓelet* in 1870 – attested to the expansion of the cultural horizons. In this way the population became ready to open its gates to new immigrants, ways of life, and ideas, which were brought to Ereẓ Israel by the *Ḥibbat Zion movement.

[Haïm Z'ew Hirschberg]

BIBLIOGRAPHY: ARAB PERIOD: Mann, Egypt; Z. Ankori, *Karaites in Byzantium* (1959), 3–25; S. Klein, *Toledot ha-Yishuv ha-Yehudi be-Ereẓ-Yisrael* (1935); M. Assaf, *Toledot ha-Aravim be-Ereẓ-Yisrael*, 1 (1935); S. Assaf and L.A. Meyer, *Sefer ha-Yishuv*, 2 (1942); B. Klar, in: S. Yeivin and H.Z. Hirschberg (eds.), *Ereẓ Kinnarot* (1951), 90–117; Abramson, *Merkazim* (1965), 25–33; R. Hartmann, *Palaestina unter den Arabern 632–1516* (1915). **ADD. BIBLIOGRAPHY:** S.D. Goitein, *Palestinian Jewry in Early Islamic and Crusader Times in the Light of the Geniza* (1980). CRUSADER PERIOD: B.Z. Dinur, in: *Zion* (Me'asef), 2 (1927), 38–66; Dinur, Golah, 2 pts. 1–2 (1931–36); Y. Prawer, *Mamlekhet Yerushalayyim ha-Ẓalvanit* (1946); idem, in: *Zion*, 11 (1946), 38–82; Prawer, Ẓalbanim (includes bibliography). **ADD. BIBLIOGRAPHY:** J. Prawer, *The History of the Jews in the Latin Kingdom of Jerusalem* (1988). MAMLUK PERIOD: M. Assaf, *Toledot ha-Aravim be-Ereẓ-Yisrael*, 2 (1941); Ashtor, Toledot, 3 vols. (1944–70); M. Gaudefroy-Demombynes, *La Syrie à l'époque des Mamlouks d'après les auteurs arabes* (1923). OTTOMAN PERIOD: Ben Ẓvi, Ereẓ Israel (includes bibliography). **ADD. BIBLIOGRAPHY:** Y. Ben Arieh, *The Rediscovery of the Holy Land in the Nineteenth Century* (1983²); idem, *Jerusalem in the Nineteenth Century* (2 vols, 1984, 1986). JEWISH COMMUNITY IN EREẒ YISRAEL: B.Z. Gat, *Ha-Yishuv ha-Yehudi be-Ereẓ Yisrael…* (1963, includes bibl.: 347–52); N. Sokolow, *History of Zionism* (1918); J. de Haas, *History of Palestine…* (1934); S.W. Baron, in: *Jewish Studies in Memory of George A. Kohut* (1935), 72–85; idem, in: JSOS, 2 (1940), 179–208; A. Revusky, *Jews in Palestine* (1936); G. Kressel (ed.), *Netivot Ẓiyyon vi-Yrushalayyim, Mivḥar Ma'amarei A.M. Luncz* (1970).

STATE OF ISRAEL

HISTORICAL SURVEY: THE STATE AND ITS ANTECEDENTS (1880–2006)

Introduction

It took the new Jewish nation about 70 years to emerge as the State of Israel. The immediate stimulus that initiated the modern return to Zion was the disappointment, in the last quarter of the 19th century, of the expectation that the advancement of European civilization would solve the "Jewish question." In Central and Western Europe, the hopes of the Jews to be not only formally emancipated but really absorbed as equals in their respective "host" nations were shattered by waves of social and intellectual antisemitism. In Eastern Europe, particularly in the Russian Empire and Romania, not only did the technical formalities of emancipation seem to be unobtainable, but Jews repeatedly served as the scapegoats of the reactionary regimes in murderous pogroms initiated and organized by the authorities themselves.

In the second half of the century, the traumatic experiences of Jewish intellectuals in East and West produced a movement based on the reaffirmation of Jewish identity, mostly in a secular, nationalist form (e.g., Leon *Pinsker and, later, Theodor *Herzl), and the conviction that the Jewish question would remain insoluble unless the Jewish masses moved out and settled in an autonomous Jewish state to form an independent nation. This rational approach of the intellectuals at first did not necessarily regard Ereẓ Israel as the most desirable territory for the purpose of nation building, particularly in an era when many new nations had emerged on other continents in seemingly empty territories.

The modern Jewish nationalism of the intellectuals soon merged with another powerful trend, deeply rooted in the traditionalist Jewish masses, mainly in Eastern Europe. The latter intuitively sought ways and means of preserving Judaism and Jewish tradition in spite of the rapid disintegration of the self-contained Jewish societies in the ghetto, or shtetl, which were beginning to break up under the impact of the new scientific, urbanized civilization. For the masses of Jewry, any country outside Ereẓ Israel would always be *galut* (exile) even if its population should prove to be predominantly Jewish; a Jewish national renaissance was conceivable only if it was consciously rooted in the Hebrew language and Jewish culture and aimed at the revival of Jewish nationhood in Ereẓ Israel.

The merging of the two trends – the rationally intellectual and the emotionally traditional – gave birth not only to *Zionism as an organized political effort, but also to the beginnings of the pioneering movement of the late 19th century, which laid the foundations, on the soil of Ereẓ Israel, for the economic, social, and cultural rebirth of the Jewish nation. The land itself seemed eminently suitable for the purpose: a marginal province of the weak Ottoman Empire, sparsely inhabited by a population consisting of various religious groups and seemingly lacking any national consciousness or ambitions of its own; a motherland waiting to be redeemed from centuries of neglect and decay by its legitimate sons.

The rebirth of the nation began almost simultaneously from two ends, in Ereẓ Israel itself and in Eastern Europe. Tiny groups of "rebels" against the old *yishuv*, mainly in Jerusalem, decided to break out of the stifling confines of the idle **halukkah* regime and create a national renaissance by tilling the ancestral soil "with their own hands" and reviving the Hebrew language, as the living vernacular of a modern nation, instead of merely a sacred tongue and an inter-community lingua franca. At the same time, small groups of Jewish youth (mostly students) in the Russian *Pale of Settlement and in Romania were so deeply disenchanted with the idea of attaining security, dignity, and equality in any Diaspora country that they decided not to join the mass emigration of Jews overseas, nor to participate in revolutionary endeavors in the countries where they lived, but to make themselves into pioneers in the establishment of the first modern Jewish villages in Ereẓ Israel, which would eventually serve as the cornerstone of an independent, "normal" Jewish nation.

The efforts of this First Aliyah to create new agricultural settlements under a corrupt, hostile regime and in a malaria- and robber-infested environment might have ended in both economic and social failure. The pioneers were in imminent danger of economic collapse from sheer inexperience and complete lack of capital, and, by employing cheap Arab labor, they might have become a thin stratum of "colonists" whose land was in fact tilled by non-Jewish hands. The first danger was averted in time by the philanthropic aid of the Russian *Ḥibbat Zion movement and Baron Edmond de *Rothschild, and later by the more modern methods of the Zionist Organization. The second was eventually avoided by the Second Aliyah, a wave of several thousand new Jewish pioneers who arrived in Ereẓ Israel after the abortive Russian revolution of 1905, determined to create a Jewish working class and to "conquer" by their labor not only the soil but also labor itself, including all manual aspects and forms of it, to ensure the creation of a new Jewish society with a full-fledged productive, self-sufficient structure, rather than an "unproductive," Diaspora-like community.

Some of the men who led this movement (e.g., David *Ben-Gurion and Izhak *Ben-Zvi) lived to see their dream fulfilled in the form of the independent Jewish state. Many despaired of the difficult economic and health conditions and returned to Russia, but a sufficient number of them persisted and remained to lay the foundations of a new, productive, and Hebrew-speaking Jewish society. A few years after their arrival, they established the first clandestine armed self-defense organization (Bar-Giora, later *Ha-Shomer) and the first collective workers groups and "self-labor" settlements. This endeavor, though still very small in size, was large enough to become the focus of a wide Hebrew educational network and a mass movement in world Jewry and to fulfill an important role in the political events during World War I that led to the *Balfour Declaration and the international recognition of the Jewish people's right to establish its National Home in Palestine.

In spite of the more favorable conditions of the British period (1917–48), as compared with the Ottoman era, the fundamental moving forces of the First and Second Aliyah did not change much. Mass immigration, as distinct from the *aliyah* of pioneering groups and individuals, occurred mainly when the condition of Jewish communities in the Diaspora became economically or physically unbearable. The Soviet regime, which cut the Jews of Russia off from the rest of the Jewish people, deprived the reviving nation in Palestine of its main human reservoir; but Jews from Poland, the Baltic states, Romania, and Central Europe exploited almost every conceivable opportunity, "legal" or "illegal," to settle in Palestine, particularly after the closing of the gates to the United States in 1924.

Meanwhile, the "self-labor" principle of the Second Aliyah stimulated the creation of a widespread network of mutual aid institutions combined in a powerful labor federation (the *Histadrut), which enabled the Jewish workers to maintain a bearable standard of living even under adverse conditions. The collective and cooperative settlements of the labor pioneers, as well as urban centers built by Jewish labor with middle-class capital and initiative, soon created a belt of continuous Jewish settlement increasingly resembling a nucleus of national territory. The Hebrew educational system raised a generation of tens and later hundreds of thousands of native-born young people (the "sabras") for whom language, historical tradition, native soil, and national allegiance became one harmonious whole. To protect the *yishuv*'s physical security and prevent pogrom-style Arab violence, a clandestine nationwide defensive militia, the *Haganah, was established. Gradually, self-governing institutions emerged, gaining partial official recognition (such as *Keneset Israel, municipal councils, etc.) and partly serving the Jewish population by mutual consent (e.g., the Jewish magistrates' courts (*batei-mishpat ha-shalom*), voluntary taxes, etc.), which enhanced the independent national character of the expanding community.

After a brief honeymoon, illuminated by the illusion of British benevolence in the beginning of the 1920s, the essential principle of the nation building process remained unchanged: only what the Jews created themselves, despite the unfriendly regime and the hostile environment – by their own initiative, with their own physical efforts, defending themselves with their own arms, at the cost of their own blood – gradually made the new Jewish nation a reality. This principle remained valid during World War II and its aftermath. The new nation was still too small and dependent to save European Jewry during the Nazi *Holocaust, but it made serious efforts to do so. It also prepared itself for all-out self-defense in case of a Nazi conquest of Palestine and, when this danger was averted, for a systematic struggle for national independence against British opposition and Arab violent aggression by "illegal" mass immigration, rapid enlargement of the settlement network, armed sabotage, and so forth.

The establishment of the State of Israel in 1948 was an historic breakthrough into international recognition and national sovereignty, but in historical perspective it proved to be only a "great leap forward" and not the terminal point in the process of nation building. The main developments since the establishment of the state have been the accelerated growth of the population, mainly through the ingathering of the exiles – paradoxically, from those countries which were, or became, Israel's declared enemies (i.e., the Arab countries and those of the Soviet Bloc, including latterly the former Soviet Union itself); the systematic settlement of empty spaces, particularly in the south; economic development through modernization of agriculture, industrialization, and application of modern science; the implementation of genuine democracy on all levels of government and the protection of civil liberties, in spite of an almost permanent military emergency; and pragmatic, compromise solutions for explosive internal problems, such as the antagonism between religious and secular concepts of Jewish nationhood, the strains and stresses between Jews of European origin and those from the "Oriental" countries, and the conflict between the socialist, cooperative, and egalitarian trends of the labor movement and the need to attract private capital and introduce incentives for economic efficiency. An outstanding success was the maintenance of a highly efficient citizen's army, free of militarist trappings, preserving the old spirit of a people's militia and also serving for collective agricultural pioneering and other pacific purposes.

The central and dominant problem however, proved to be more and more the antagonism between Israel and the Arab world, which ostensibly centered on the plight of the Palestinian Arab refugees, who had fled en masse from the territory of Israel during its *War of Independence. Almost immediately, but particularly from the middle 1950s, the great powers began to exploit this antagonism in their own interests, reinforcing its destructive features instead of working toward constructive solutions, until the *Six-Day War (1967) created an entirely new territorial and political situation, fraught with the danger of a new "round" but also opening perspectives for Arab-Israel peace. This situation placed Israel more firmly at the center of world Jewry's attention and devotion than ever before. In the immediate postwar period the two greatest Jewish communities, in the United States and the Soviet Union, which in the recent past had seemed to be irretrievably on the road to complete assimilation, also began to stir toward Jewish revival. While in the United States, after a short spurt of immigration, it became clear that large-scale *aliyah* was not to be expected, massive *aliyah* from the former Soviet Union would become the miracle of the 1990s. Thus, from several scores of pioneers at the outset of the Zionist enterprise, the revived Jewish nation in Ereẓ Israel numbered in the early 1970s over 2.5 million people and in the early years of the 21st century edged toward 5.5 million, poised to become the largest Jewish community in the world.

However, the euphoria of the Six-Day War was relatively short-lived, unleashing processes that would agitate Israel's national life in the coming decades. The nation's pent-up energies, confined within narrow physical borders and a culture of economic austerity for 20 years, burst forth in a recrudescence of economic activity that created new wealth and new inequalities. A new political regime under Menaḥem Begin hastened the demise of the old-style socialism that had dominated the country for so many years and accelerated the transformation of Israel into a modern Western consumer society. Politically, the country underwent severe polarization as the right and left, hawks and doves, became hardened in their respective positions, while the trauma of the *Yom Kippur War initiated a tortuous process that saw peace treaties signed with Egypt and Jordan and years of unabated Arab terrorism destroying innocent lives.

Israel at the outset of the 21st century stood at a new crossroads, facing challenges that only the resiliency and moral fiber of its people might meet. The challenge of the new millennium was to recapture the sense of a common past and a common destiny that had always sustained the nation.

The Land of Israel in International Affairs, 1798–1923

After the Crusades, the European powers attached no great significance to the Land of Israel, and its conquest by the Ottoman Turks reduced its importance still further. The name "Palestine" had only a historical, archaeological, or antiquarian connotation; it did not denote any clearly defined political entity, or even a separate administrative subdivision of the Ottoman Empire. The country was part of the empire; sometimes it was regarded as a part of Syria. As far as international affairs were concerned, it was no more than a remote territory, a bone of contention among unruly pashas and a prey to Bedouin banditry. Although certain European commercial interests, such as the Levant Company, did pay some attention to it at one period, their operations were designated to extend to the Ottoman Empire as a whole, and Palestine did not play a special role in their plans; nor has this competition been shown to have had any appreciable effect on the policies of the powers.

NAPOLEON'S CAMPAIGN. This situation underwent a drastic change when *Napoleon made his surprising move to land an expeditionary force in the East and succeeded in conquering Egypt (1798; see above), followed by an invasion of Palestine in 1799. The invasion, after initial success, was frustrated by the failure of his efforts to take Acre. The reasons that presumably prompted Napoleon to undertake this campaign are of great significance, for they were the same that were henceforth to induce all major European powers to vie with one another for influence in the area.

The predominant consideration was the territory's geographical position at the crossroads of the three commercial and strategic routes of the modern world, which link the Atlantic Ocean and Mediterranean Sea with the Indian and Pacific Oceans, the Mediterranean with the Persian Gulf, and the Eurasian continent with Africa. When Ottoman rule in Asia entered into a decline at the end of the 18th century, every power felt obliged to deny exclusive control of the crossroads to any of its rivals. For Napoleon, the country was of equal importance for both defense and attack: its conquest would enable him to defend Egypt against Anglo-Turkish attempts to wrest it from his hands and provide him with a springboard for campaigns directed at Anatolia and Istanbul, the Persian Gulf, and India.

Another factor that was to enter into the considerations of every power planning to replace the Ottoman Empire in the control of the area was the presence of ethnic and religious minorities that would presumably be prepared to accept the protection of a European power. At the time of Napoleon's campaign in Palestine, the idea of establishing a Jewish state in the area was mooted in Paris. During the siege of Acre Napoleon was said to have issued a proclamation to the Jews, apostrophizing them as "rightful heirs of Palestine" and calling upon them "to take over that which had been conquered" (some scholars, however, regard the proclamation as apocryphal). Napoleon was known to have had plans for fomenting unrest among the Druze and Maronites in the north and exploiting the existence of Christian and Muslim holy places for his purposes.

MUHAMMAD ALI'S CAMPAIGNS. For these and other reasons the future of Palestine became an issue of general European importance during the wars conducted by Muhammad Ali, who was sent to Egypt by the sultan in 1800 in order to reorganize Egypt after Napoleon's failure. Muhammad Ali sought to base his rule in Egypt on the innovations introduced by the Napoleonic conquest. In order to realize his ambition to create a ruling dynasty in Egypt and ward off a possible direct attack by the Ottoman forces, he dispatched Ibrahim, his stepson, to Palestine and Syria. In 1832–33 Ibrahim overran both territories, and for the next seven years the area remained in the hands of Muhammad Ali. The Egyptian regime brought many changes to Palestine. A central government ruled the country, law and order were established, and tens of thousands of Egyptians migrated to Palestine and established a chain of settlements along the coastal plain from Gaza and toward the Sea of Galilee. The non-Muslim residents of Palestine were able to act more freely. Some synagogues and churches were built and a British consulate, the first European consulate in Palestine, was opened in Jerusalem.

Failure of the Ottomans to push the Egyptians out of Syria in 1840 brought the European powers back to the area. It was at this point that Britain (under Lord Palmerston) and, to a lesser degree, Austria decided that it was in their interest to shore up the sultan's tottering power. From their point of view, it was a timely decision, for otherwise there was a danger of Russian hegemony over the Ottoman Empire or of France – an ally of Muhammad Ali – gaining control of the Mediterranean. Furthermore, by this time Syria and Palestine had become a factor in their own right in the policy pursued by the powers. The growing significance of modern means of transportation – steamships and railroads – lent significance to an area that served as a crossroads and control of which would facilitate the construction of interoceanic canals and intercontinental railroads. Palmerston already recognized this. The possession of Palestine would secure control of the Suez route, which was in use even in those pre-canal days (the early steamers preferred to cruise along the Mediterranean coast rather than risk the stormy passage around the Cape of Good Hope, transferring their cargoes overland across the Suez Isthmus to be shipped to their destination through the Red Sea and the Indian Ocean – the traditional route since early historical times). The eastern Mediterranean coast was also regarded as the proper place for the terminal of a land route – a railroad leading to Iraq and the Persian Gulf; in fact, the vision of such a route was to have an ever-increasing effect upon the imperialist policies of Britain and France.

From the French point of view, these considerations required the extension of Muhammad Ali's domain in Syria as far north as possible; the British, on the other hand, were interested in pushing him back as much as possible toward the Nile Valley and denying him access to the main lines of communication to the Persian Gulf. In 1840, when Muhammad Ali, with French support, rejected a demand that his rule be restricted to Palestine, the other powers, led by Britain, intervened by force of arms and compelled him to give up Syria, including Palestine, and restrict himself to Egypt. The Ottoman

Empire paid back the European powers by changing its attitude toward the non-Muslim inhabitants of the Empire as a whole, but this was mainly applied in Palestine.

PROTECTIVE RIGHTS. In the following two decades, Palestine retained a place in international affairs due to its importance for those powers that wanted the right to protect one or the other of the religious minorities in the decaying Ottoman Empire. Russia had long had such rights, confirmed in the Kutchuk-Kainarji Treaty of 1774 (Article 7), over Orthodox Christians in Turkey and the Orthodox Christian holy places in Palestine. France's rights to protect the Catholics (Latins) and their holy places, which had their roots in the age of the Crusades, were confirmed by Capitulations (privileges for the foreigners). Britain and, to some extent, Prussia sought to counter these advantages by extending their protection to the insignificant Protestant minority (which accounts for the creation of the Jerusalem bishopric in 1841). Palmerston and his successors also sought to extend unofficial British protection to the Jewish minority. Under the pressure of the European powers, the Ottomans first allowed the non-Muslim citizens of the Empire to buy and own land and buildings, later extending the right to everyone, including foreigners. This allowed the Europeans and Americans to put up new churches, hospitals, schools, and other buildings in the main towns of Palestine from 1840 on. During the 1860s Christian groups built new agricultural settlements in Palestine. An American group established the American colony near Jaffa in 1866, while a larger group of Germans built three German colonies in Haifa, Jaffa, and Jerusalem. Later on they built new settlements in the Coastal Plain (Sarona), Lower Galilee, and near the Jaffa–Jerusalem road. The Jewish immigrants of the 1880s were also able to establish the first moshavot (agriculture settlements) as a result of this process. Throughout the 1840s and 1850s, fierce competition ensued among the powers to improve their position as protective powers. The struggle was carried out mainly through their consular representatives in Jerusalem, which was an ideal arena in which to press their claims; their real purpose, of course, was to give the powers exercising these rights a hold on the Ottoman Empire that they could exploit whenever its collapse would lead to the ultimate disposition of its territories. It will be recalled that the contradictory claims of Russia and France with regard to the holy places were the direct cause of the outbreak of the Crimean War.

THE STRUGGLE OVER COMMUNICATIONS. Developments in Egypt between 1860 and 1890 again put the emphasis on the control of communications. The Suez Canal was opened in 1869 and France's hegemony in Cairo assured her control of the new waterway. This was a situation that the British felt they could not tolerate; in 1878 Britain took over Cyprus and finally, in 1882, it took Egypt by military conquest, ousting the French and maintaining its position for many decades to come. The two powers now switched roles: it was Britain that now aspired to extend its influence to the north, by way of Palestine and southern Syria, while France, which had struck roots in the Lebanon and in central and northern Syria, sought to confine British influence to Egypt.

In the last decade of the 19th century, when the advance of capitalism and industry played an increasingly important role in general political developments, the competition between the European powers (Britain, France, Imperial Germany, Italy, Austria-Hungary, Imperial Russia) for influence in Syria and Palestine was concerned with religious and cultural hegemony as well as with economic and financial issues. Traditional British-Ottoman friendship had turned into enmity as a result of the British occupation of Egypt and the ascendancy of German influence over the Sublime Porte at the turn of the century. In spite of the Entente of 1903, relations between Britain and France in the Middle East continued to be competitive, rather than friendly. To guard against the possibility of an Ottoman attack upon Egypt, with the possible support of Germany or France, Kitchener, the British commander in Egypt, thought it imperative to establish a buffer state under British protection in the area adjacent to Egypt, between Acre and Aqaba.

These strategic considerations played a dominant role in the struggle between Britain, France, and Germany over railroad construction in the area. The German plans provided for the construction of a railroad link leading from northwest to southeast, from Constantinople to Alexandretta and thence to the Persian Gulf. This plan for a Baghdad Railroad threatened British interests in the Persian Gulf and clashed with two other plans: a British proposal for an east-west route from Baghdad to Haifa (the Willcocks Plan) and a French proposal for a railroad linking Alexandretta or Homs with Baghdad. Another project, in which the Germans took an active part, was that of the Hejaz Railroad (Damascus to Mecca), which competed with the French-built north-south railroad (Aleppo to Mezerib). Of special significance was the Haifa-Darʿa section of the Hejaz Railroad, which competed with the Beirut-Damascus section of the French railroad and came in place of the British Willcocks Plan. Furthermore, the Hejaz Railroad represented a strategic threat to British interests in Egypt, an aspect borne out by the Ottoman demand that the Germans and the French extend their railroad lines to Rafa and construct a line from Maʿan to Akaba (which would have created a direct link between the Mediterranean and the Red Sea and threatened the Suez Canal's monopoly).

By 1912 the struggle among the powers had become sharp enough for the French upper chamber to adopt a resolution emphasizing French interests in Syria (including Palestine). Although the British foreign secretary, Sir Edward Grey, publicly declared that Britain would follow a "hands-off" policy in Syria, he soon modified his statement by denying any intention to recognize exclusive French rights in the area. Moreover, the British representatives in Cairo did not feel committed by his declaration.

In 1914, on the eve of World War I, the Germans settled their differences with the other two powers by two railroad conventions that were to divide the Asian part of the Ottoman

Empire into British, German, and French spheres of economic interest. The German-French convention granted the Germans economic supremacy in Anatolia, northern Syria, and Mesopotamia, while French economic interests would predominate in central and southern Syria, up to the Egyptian border (i.e., the area served by the French railroads and the Hejaz line). The Anglo-German convention, which divided Mesopotamia into German and British spheres of influence, acknowledged the supremacy of British economic interests in the area lying to the south of Beirut and west of Amman as well as in the desert lying between Transjordan and Iraq (this would have enabled the British to build a Suez-Akaba-Kuwait-Barash railroad as compensation for the Willcocks scheme). It should be noted that in the German agreement with the French, Palestine was recognized as lying within the French sphere of interests, while in the German-British agreement it appears as part of the British sphere; thus the Germans succeeded in settling their own differences with the British and the French and simultaneously planted the seeds of contention between the two powers with regard to the future status of the country.

THE AQABA INCIDENT AND THE SINAI BORDER. The Aqaba incident of 1906 is a striking illustration of the importance the British attached to the whole area even before World War I. (It also led to the delineation of the eastern border of Sinai, which eventually became the boundary of Mandatory Palestine.) The peace agreement with Muhammad Ali (1841) had left him, in addition to Egypt, an area in the Sinai Peninsula from the town of Suez to a spot south of Gaza, on the Mediterranean coast, and several fortified cities on the Red Sea coast on the route to Mecca. In 1892, ten years after the British conquest of Egypt, the Ottomans demanded the return of Sinai and the Hejaz cities. Sir Evelyn Baring (later Lord Cromer) rejected the Ottoman demand, and eventually a compromise was achieved by which the Hejaz cities were placed under Ottoman rule, while the Sinai Peninsula was to remain Egyptian territory. In the course of the negotiations, it transpired that the borders in the Sinai Peninsula were under dispute. The Ottomans claimed that the Egyptian border extended from Rafah to Suez. Baring claimed that southern Sinai also belonged to Egypt and that the new border should be a straight line from Rafah to Aqaba. The Ottomans refused to accept this demand.

The controversy played a certain role in the negotiations between Theodor *Herzl and Joseph Chamberlain in 1902–03 concerning Jewish settlement in northern Sinai, which Chamberlain was inclined to believe would help to ward off a possible Ottoman attack and might eventually lead to the inclusion of Palestine in the British sphere of influence. Baring, however, would not hear of this plan, preferring the local Bedouin as instruments of British policy.

As a result of this "Bedouin policy," the British seized an area of Ottoman territory near Aqaba in 1906, although there was no doubt that their action was a flagrant violation of Ottoman sovereignty. The Ottomans charged that this was part of an attempt to extend the Egyptian border at their expense. The tension soon turned into a full-fledged crisis. An Ottoman compromise proposal, which would have divided the Sinai Peninsula in such a manner as to leave both banks of the Gulf of Suez in Egyptian hands and both banks of the Gulf of Aqaba Ottoman, was rejected. The British regarded the issue important enough to warrant an ultimatum to Istanbul, to which the sultan submitted in September 1906. The new Ottoman-Egyptian border now became a line extending from Rafa to Ṭaba and underwent no further change until 1948. Thus the first boundary of modern Palestine was established.

THE *SYKES-PICOT AGREEMENT AND THE MCMAHON – HUSSEIN CORRESPONDENCE. World War I further exacerbated, rather than reduced, differences among the Allies. The railroad agreements with Germany had left the future of Palestine a matter of controversy between Britain and France, and in the very first months of the war the two powers reiterated their interests in the area so as to lay the foundations for the claims they would submit when victory had been achieved. Between November 1914 and March 1915, the British cabinet held several sessions devoted to the subject, finally resolving that, at the very minimum, British interests required the internationalization of Palestine if exclusive British control could not be obtained. The French raised their claims to supremacy in Syria and Palestine in the legislature and in the press; they also asked for Russian support in exchange for French support of Russian claims on Constantinople. The Russians in their turn asked for the exclusion of the Orthodox Christian holy places (in Galilee as well as in Jerusalem) from French control, and the French countered by offering, as a maximum concession, the internationalization of the Jerusalem-Bethlehem area, provided the rest of Palestine became French. Both the Russians and the British refused to accede to this proposal, and in July 1915 the British cabinet came to the conclusion that the best way to counteract French demands was to obtain Russian agreement for a joint Anglo-French-Russian regime in Palestine after the war. The Russians appear to have agreed to this plan.

When the Syrian and Hejazi leaders of the Arab revolt, with British encouragement, raised their claims to the area (as reflected in the Hussein-McMahon correspondence – see next paragraph), it was decided to appoint a mixed Anglo-French commission to submit an agreed plan for the postwar partition of the Ottoman Empire. The commission was appointed in the fall of 1915, with Sir Arthur Nicholson – shortly afterward replaced by Sir Mark Sykes – as the British representative and Charles François Georges-Picot (the former French consul to Jerusalem) for France. The recommendations of the commission, as accepted by the powers, became known as the Tripartite (*Sykes-Picot) Agreement of 1916. It provided for joint Anglo-French-Russian-Italian and Arab control of all parts of Palestine containing holy places. This included the area between a line running from the Dead Sea to Rafah in the south to a line running from the northwest corner of the Sea of

Galilee toward Ras el-Naqura on the Mediterranean shore in the north. The Jordan River was to be the eastern boundary of this area, safeguarding the interests of the European powers as well as those of all religions. France got the rule over the area north of Nazareth and the Sea of Galilee (Lake Kinneret – i.e., northern Galilee and Safed), together with the Lebanon. Britain got the control over Haifa Bay (with the towns of Haifa and Acre) to satisfy the requirements of the British navy and to serve as the terminal of the Baghdad Railroad. The agreement also defined the incorporation of Transjordan and the Negev into an Arab State under British protection, as a corridor between British bases in Egypt and those in southern Iraq, and the creation of a French-protected Syrian-Arab state, including the Hauran.

Meanwhile, Sir Henry McMahon, the British high commissioner in Cairo, had been negotiating with Hussein ibn Ali, the sharif of Mecca, for his assistance in the war against the Ottoman Empire in return for a British promise to support his bid for the restoration of the caliphate. On behalf of his government, Sir Henry McMahon agreed to support Arab independence within the boundaries proposed by Hussein, who asked for all the Arab areas of the Ottoman Empire south of the Taurus Mountains, with two provisos: first, "The two districts of Mersina and Alexandretta and portions of Syria lying to the west of the districts of Damascus, Homs, Hama, and Aleppo, which cannot be said to be purely Arab, and should be excluded from the limits demanded"; secondly, the undertaking to support Arab independence was given only "... for those frontiers wherein Britain is free to act without detriment to the interests of her ally, France...". The term "Syria" was often regarded, particularly by Arabs, as including Palestine and the "district" or vilayet of Damascus extended to the whole of Transjordan. The first proviso, as well as the second, therefore, according to British sources, clearly excluded the whole of western Palestine. This was subsequently verified by Sir McMahon himself and by a British government committee that examined the correspondence. On the other hand, the Arabs claimed that the letters spoke of excluding the cities of Aleppo, Hama, Homs, and Damascus; thus, as Palestine lay south of Damascus, it was not excluded from the Hussein demand and the area of Palestine was promised to the Arabs.

In order to provide a counterweight to French protection of Catholics and Russian protection of Orthodox Christians in the proposed jointly administered area, the British, in 1916, recommended that the Allies permit Zionist settlement in Palestine (presumably under British protection), an idea that had been discussed by the British cabinet as far back as 1914.

THE ZIONIST CLAIMS. When the Zionist leadership heard of the truncation of the Land of Israel envisaged by the Sykes-Picot Agreement, Chaim *Weizmann dispatched a strong protest to the British Foreign Office. In Weizmann's opinion the realization of Zionist goals required that the whole of the Land of Israel be placed under British protection. Eventually, Britain also came to the conclusion that British control of the entire area of Palestine would serve her interests in Egypt and Mesopotamia, and this realization gave added impetus to the British plans for the conquest of the country by her forces alone. Zionist pressure and the wish to win over the Jews of Russia (after the revolution of February 1917) and those living behind enemy lines (Germany, Austria-Hungary) to Britain led to the *Balfour Declaration, which promised the help of Britain in establishing a Jewish National Home in Palestine. This Declaration made no attempt to establish the exact boundaries of the National Home, which later led to much discussion about the limits of the Jewish National Home.

World War I ended with the British conquering Palestine (1917–18). During the war the Zionists had won French support for their aims, mainly through the efforts of Nahum *Sokolow. A month after the war had ended, in December 1918, the French Premier Georges Clemenceau, who was indifferent to Middle East affairs and wholly absorbed in the problem of Germany, gave his consent to British rule over the entire area of Palestine "from Dan to Beersheba" (no more precise definition being given) in exchange for British support of French territorial claims concerning its boundary with Germany. The Zionist leaders, having coordinated their territorial demands with those of Emir Feisal, Hussein's son (which eventually led to the Weizmann-Feisal accord), presented their demands to the Council of Ten at the Paris Peace Conference in February 1919. They called for the borders of Palestine to run from a point on the Mediterranean coast south of Sidon along the foothills of the Lebanon up to Rāshiya (thereby including most of the Litani valley and all the sources of the Jordan), proceeding further east along the Hermon ridge, and then southward parallel to and west of the Hejaz Railroad down to the Gulf of Aqaba. Such an arrangement would have given both Palestine and the Arab state access to the Transjordan section of the Hejaz Railroad. In the south, the Zionists asked for a boundary which would be agreed upon with the Egyptian government. It took 70 years to realize this wish, as Israel and Egypt only agreed on their common border in 1979.

The borders of Palestine were also the subject of an exchange of notes between Britain and France in September 1919 and June 1920 and of discussions by the foreign ministers of the two powers in December 1919 and June and December 1920. Both parties attached great importance to this question, and at one point the French, incensed at British opposition to their Syrian plans, demanded a return to the Sykes-Picot Agreement with its provisions for a truncated Palestine. In the end, the British only partly succeeded in getting the Zionist border proposals accepted and agreed to a narrow interpretation of the agreement they had reached with Clemenceau in 1918. As a result, a boundary agreement was signed between France and the United Kingdom on December 23, 1920. In it the border outlined in the Sykes-Picot Agreement was extended as far as "Dan" only, i.e., including the Safed district and a narrow corridor (the Galilee panhandle) northward, containing Lake Ḥuleh and Metullah as well as half of the Golan Heights but only half of the Sea of Galilee. Details of the border were fixed by a special demarcation commission that functioned from 1920 to 1923, and its final version was amended to include both banks of the Ḥuleh, the Jordan River, and Lake Kinneret (the Sea of Galilee) in Palestine, but left the Golan with Syria. Efforts by the Zionist leaders to obtain more favorable borders, including the water sources in the north and the extensive uncultivated areas in the east, had been frustrated by the compromise between the powers. This final version was ultimately ratified by the League of Nations *Mandate for Palestine.

[Uri Ra'anan / Gideon Biger (2nd ed.)]

Boundaries

BOUNDARIES OF MANDATORY PALESTINE. *In the South.* The formation of the frontiers of Israel actually began with the delimitation and demarcation of the boundary between Egypt (then under British protection) and the Ottoman dominions in 1906. In 1841, after Muhammad (Mehemet) Ali had been pushed back into Egypt, an Ottoman firman (royal decree) fixed the boundary as a straight line connecting the northern outskirts of Suez, at the northern tip of the gulf of that name, with a point southwest of Gaza, near the small village of Rafah, on the Mediterranean. This boundary gave Egypt a triangular area in northern Sinai, which included the entire Mediterranean coast of the peninsula. A few years after the British took control of Egypt in 1882, a dispute broke out over the actual position of the boundary. The British were very unhappy about the Suez-Rafa line, which gave the Ottomans easy access to the Suez Canal (opened in 1869), especially its southern end. They put forward various claims and proposals aimed at pushing the boundary as far eastward, away from the canal, as possible. The dispute reached its climax early in 1906, when the British sent forces to occupy the vital positions in the Sinai Peninsula and at the head of the Gulf of Aqaba. The crisis, which brought the two countries to the verge of war, was settled when the Ottomans were forced to agree to draw the boundary along a line from Rafa to a point on the northern shore of the gulf three miles west of Aqaba village. The British demand for the Rafa-Aqaba line was based on a detailed survey of northern and eastern Sinai. It gave them, as controllers of Egypt, the entire width of the Sinai desert as a natural barrier between Ottoman territory and the Suez Canal, and left them in control of nearly all the main water resources in eastern Sinai, as well as the roads and tracks connecting the Gulf of Aqaba with the Mediterranean Sea.

The demarcation of the boundary was carried out under very difficult conditions, at the height of the summer, and the boundary as marked out on the ground deviates slightly from the line laid down in the agreement – due mainly to mistakes in survey and measurement in the extremely rugged terrain, and partly to the insistence of the Ottoman delegation. Thus the line reached the Gulf of Aqaba near Bir Ṭaba, five miles southwest of the point designated in the agreement, leaving the entire northern shore of the Gulf on the Ottoman side. It should be pointed out that in 1906 this was formally only an administrative line and not an international boundary. It was agreed at the time between the Ottomans and the British that the Sinai Peninsula would continue to form part of the Ottoman Empire, though it was under Anglo-Egyptian administration. This border, 135 mi. (224 km.) long, was adopted in 1919 as the boundary between Egypt and British-mandated Palestine. Except for its northern section (the southern border of the Gaza Strip) it also became the armistice demarcation line between Egypt and Israel during the period 1949–67. It was actually abolished after the occupation of Sinai by Israel in the Six-Day War but the peace agreement between Egypt and Israel, signed in 1979, established this line as the agreed international boundary between them.

In the North. The next stage in the formation of the modern boundaries of Israel came with the delimitation and demarcation, in 1922–23, of the boundary between British-mandated Palestine and the French-mandated territories of Syria and Lebanon. The starting point for the delimitation of this boundary was the Sykes-Picot Treaty of 1916 (see also the Land of Israel in International Affairs, above). According to the treaty, the northern boundary of Palestine was to be a line from the Mediterranean coast a short distance north of Acre to a point on the northwestern shore of Lake Tiberias (Lake Kinneret). The area south of this line was to come under an international regime, except for a British enclave around the Bay of Acre, while the area to the north was assigned to the French.

Toward the end of World War I and during the two years which followed, there was much political activity around the question of the final location of this boundary. Strenuous efforts were made by the Zionist movement to induce the British and French governments to move it much further north, so that it would correspond to the northern frontier of the biblical Land of Israel and bring the whole of Galilee within British-mandated territory. At one stage the Zionist movement pressed for a northern boundary which would run from the outskirts of Sidon (Saida) eastward to the northern foot of Mount Hermon, to encompass most of the valley of the Litani and all the headwaters of the Jordan (see *Zionist Policy).

After lengthy discussions and much lobbying, an agreement was reached and embodied in the Franco-British Convention of Dec. 23, 1920. The boundary between Palestine and Syria-Lebanon was to be a line starting on the Mediterranean coast about 1.2 mi. (2 km.) south of Rosh ha-Nikrah (Ras al-Naqura) where the present Israel-Lebanese border reaches the sea, and running eastward along the watershed between the Fāra Hindāj wadis (now Naḥal Dishon) and Qarqara (now Naḥal Beẓet) in the south, and the al-Dubba al-Ayyūn and Zarqāʾ valleys to the north. Then it was to run along the watershed between the head-streams of the Jordan and the river Litani (Qāsimiyya) up to Metullah. The northwestern part of the *Ramat ha-Golan was to be included in Palestine: from Metullah the boundary was to run along the track leading to Banias and Kuneitra, leaving the track on the French side of the border. Further south the boundary would follow the bed of Wadi Masʿadiyya and one of its tributaries to the northern shores of Lake Kinneret a short distance southeast of the entry of the Jordan, cut across the lake to Samakh (Ẓemaḥ), leaving the eastern half of the lake on the French side of the frontier, and run south to the valley of the Yarmuk river, which it would then follow eastward.

Even before the conclusion of the agreement, the actual border line between the areas under British and French military occupation did not conform with the Sykes-Picot line of 1916. The British extended their control over considerable areas further north, up to a line running from al-Zīb (Keziv) on the Mediterranean coast to the northern shore of Lake Ḥuleh, and later up to the northern fringe of the Ḥuleh Valley. While a Franco-British commission was at work on the exact delimitation of the boundary (1921–22), further negotiations and bargaining between the two governments led to the acceptance of significant changes. The British gave up the area allotted to them in the Golan Heights in return for complete control of the river Jordan and Lake Tiberias. The work of this commission led to the final demarcation of the northern and northeastern boundary of Palestine, which later became the border of Israel (in the northeast up to June 1967).

Between the Mediterranean coast and Metullah there were only minor deviations from the December 1920 agreement, extending the area of Palestine northward by 1–3 mi. (2–5 km.), with a total gain of nearly 70 sq. mi. (200 sq. km.), containing 20 Arab villages. From Metullah to the eastern shores of Lake Kinneret the boundary gave the British full control of the main sources of the Jordan and the entire area of Lake Ḥuleh and Lake Kinneret. The border line ran a short distance east of the Jordan (in some sections only 160 ft. (50 m.) away), so that both banks of the river were inside Palestine, thus giving the British sole ownership of the river and its lakes. This was done with future development possibilities in mind, to enable the British to harness the waters without having to obtain French approval. Along the northeastern shores of Lake Kinneret the boundary ran only 33 ft. (10 m.) from the edge of the lake, thus avoiding the division of six Arab villages and their lands between two states, while leaving the entire lake inside Palestine. It was only about halfway along the eastern shores of the lake that the boundary left the shore and climbed up the steep western slopes of the Golan Heights and ran southward, along the top of the escarpment, to the valley of the Yarmuk near the spa of al-Ḥamma (Ḥammath Gader). Here the boundaries of Syria, Western Palestine, and what was later Transjordan met.

In the final stage of the commission's work the French demanded that the boundary should be moved about three-quarters of a mile (1,300 m.) westward, with its extreme northeastern point near the village of Banias, so as not to cut the main track connecting the Golan Heights with the Lebanon and the Mediterranean coast. This meant that the Banias springs, one of the main sources of the Jordan, would pass from the British to the French controlled area. It was agreed to concede the French request temporarily and leave the final settlement in this section to further negotiations. As the matter was not subsequently raised, the Banias springs remained on the Syrian side of the boundary until June 1967. The section of the northern boundary running between the Mediterranean at Rosh ha-Nikrah and a point 4.4 mi. (7 km.) southeast of Metullah (total length 49 mi.; 78 km.) is the Israel-Lebanese border, while from Metullah roughly southward to the bed of the Yarmuk River – 50 mi. (80 km.) – it was the Israel-Syrian border (until June 1967).

In the East. The boundary between Palestine and Transjordan was first officially delimited in a memorandum submitted by the British government to the League of Nations in September 1922, in the following words: "A line drawn from a point two miles west of the town of Akaba, on the gulf of that name, up the center of the Wadi Araba, the Dead Sea, the river Jordan to its junction with the river Yarmuk; thence up the center of that river to the Syrian frontier." In fact, the boundary ran (1922–48) along the river Yarmuk from al-Ḥamma to its junction with the Jordan and then along the Jordan to the Dead Sea. Being in control of both Palestine and Transjordan, the British placed the boundary at these rivers and in the middle of the Dead Sea as they thought that by these, the two separate states they wanted to establish in that area – Jewish Palestine and Arab Transjordan, would have to cooperate in using the water of the rivers and the minerals of the Dead Sea. After cutting across the middle of the Dead Sea it was assumed to run in the wide bed of the Wadi Araba (Naḥal ha-Aravah) to a point near Be'er Menuḥah. From there to the coast of the Gulf of Akaba the actual position of the boundary was not clear, but this was of little significance during the British Mandate, especially since the region was uninhabited except for a few hundred Bedouin. It was only when it was decided to grant Transjordan independence (1946) that the demarcation of this part of the boundary was undertaken. It was done, however, only partially – at the southern end – by the time the British Mandate over Palestine came to an end, and the full demarcation of the boundary in the Arabah was only carried out in 1950 by the Israel-Jordan Mixed Armistice Commission. In 1994, the peace agreement between Israel and the Hashemite Kingdom of Jordan adopted this line, with some small modifications, as the international boundary between them.

PARTITION PLANS. Two plans to partition Palestine were produced in the course of efforts to settle the Jewish-Arab conflict over the country: the first by the British Royal Commission (the Peel Commission) in 1937, and the second by the United Nations Special Committee on Palestine – UNSCOP – in 1947. The Peel Commission proposed the following boundary for the Jewish State to be established according to its scheme: "Starting from Ras al-Naqura[Rosh ha-Nikrah on the Mediterranean coast]it follows the existing northern and eastern frontier of Palestine to Lake Tiberias [Kinneret] and crosses the Lake to the outflow of the river Jordan whence it continues down the river to a point a little north of Beisan[Beth-

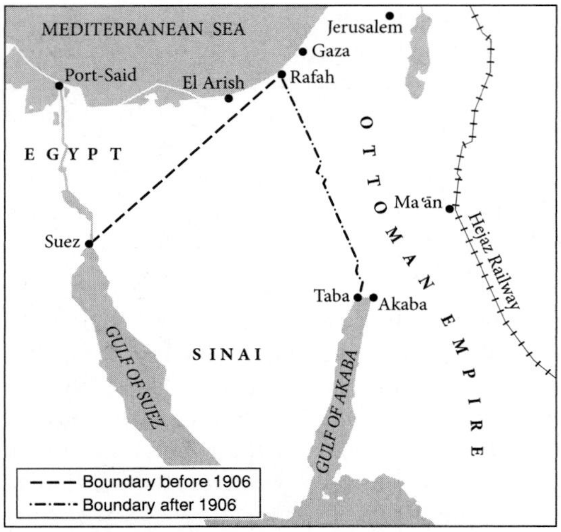

Map 1. Turko-British agreement, 1906.

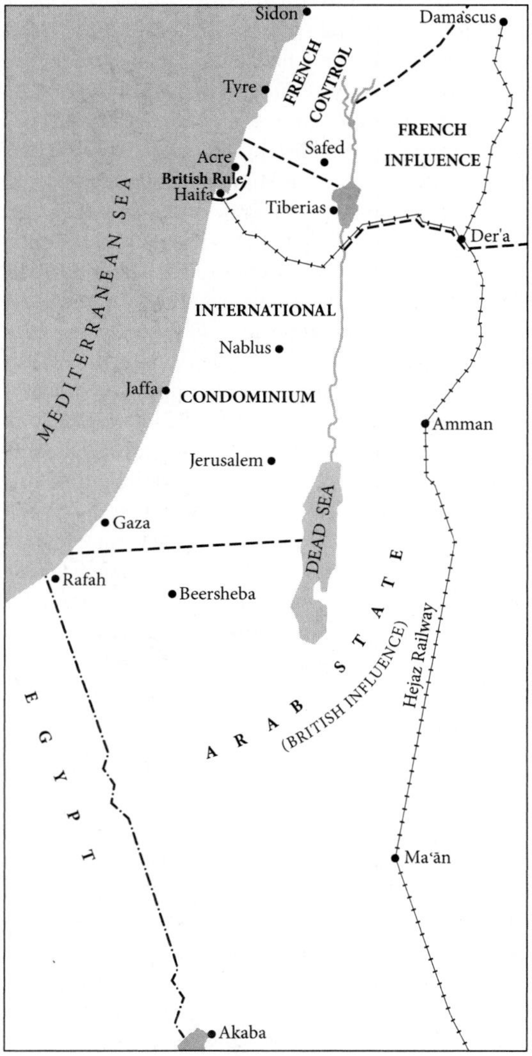

Map 2. Sykes-Picot agreement, 1916.

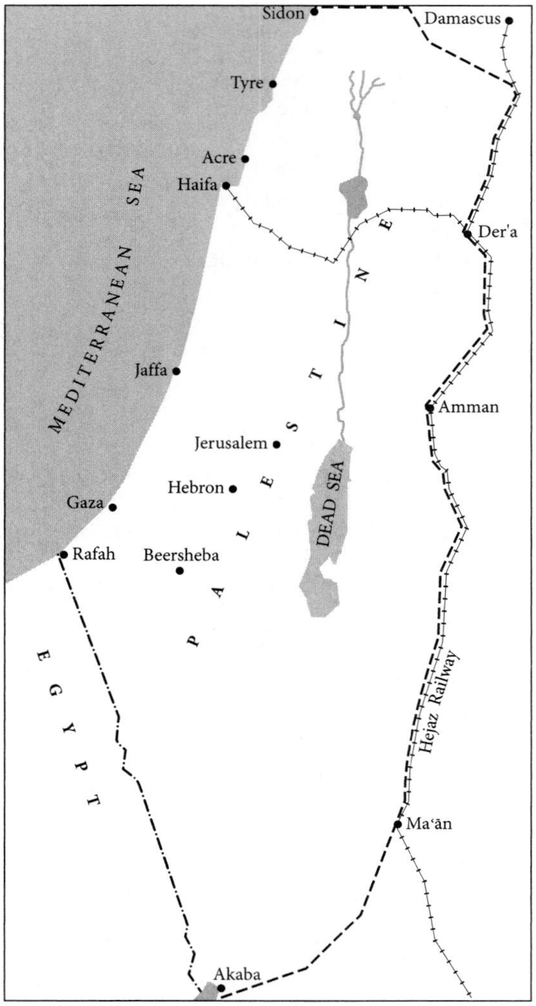

Map 3. Zionist Movement frontier proposals, 1919.

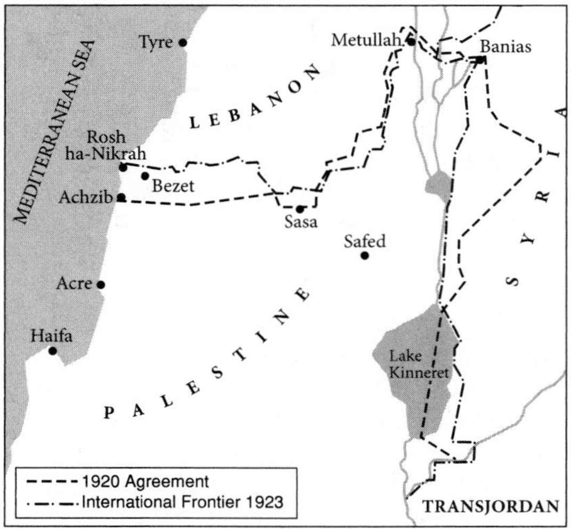

Map 4. Franco-British agreements, 1920–23.

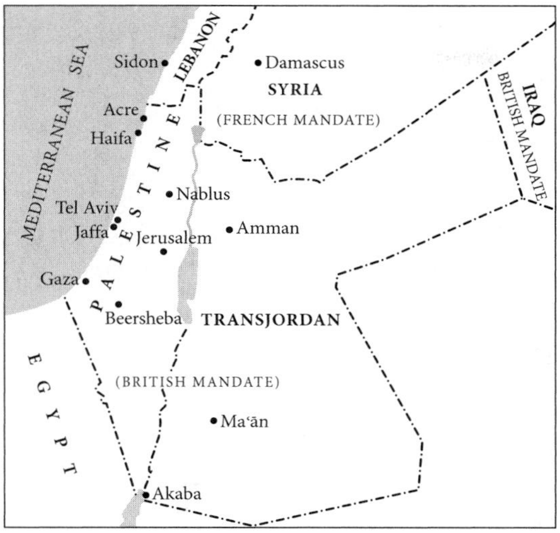

Map 5. The British Mandate, 1922.

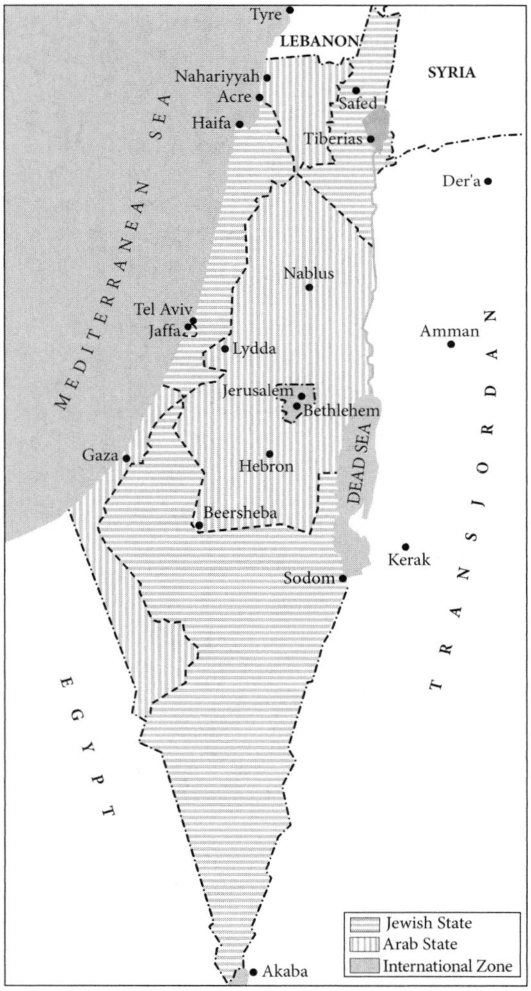

Map 6. UNSCOP partition plan, 1947.

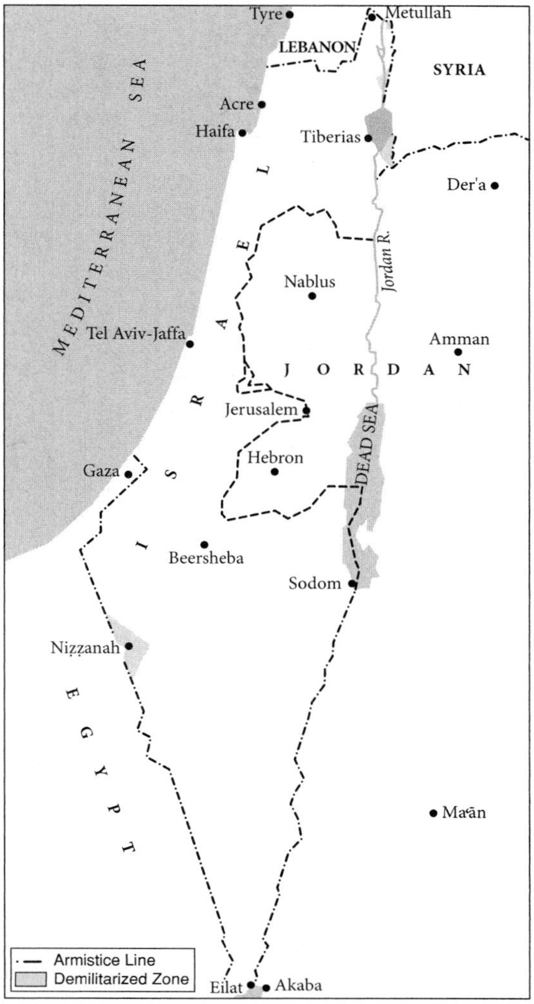

Map 7. Armistice demarcation lines, 1949.

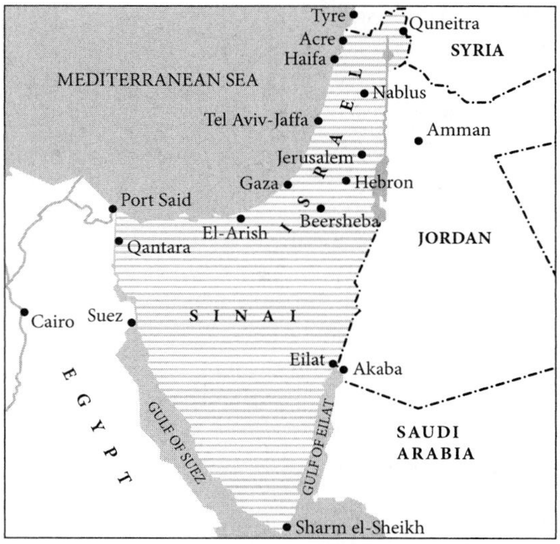

Map 8. Israel and its neighbors, after the Six-Day War. Shading indicates area within 1967 cease-fire lines.

Shean]. It then cuts across the Beisan Plain and runs along the southern edge of the valley of Jezreel and across the Plain of Jezreel to a point near Megiddo, whence it crosses the Carmel ridge in the neighborhood of the Megiddo road[the Wadi Āra (Naḥal Iron) road of today]. Having thus reached the Maritime Plain the line runs southward down its eastern edge, curving west to avoid Tulkarm, until it reaches the Jerusalem-Jaffa corridor near Lydda[Lod]. South of the corridor it continues down the edge of the plain to a point about 10 miles south of Reḥovot, whence it turns west to the sea." This partition plan gave the Jews the entire area of Galilee (within the boundaries of the British Mandate), the upper Jordan Valley as far as Beth-Shean, the valley of Jezreel, most of the Carmel range, and the Coastal Plain as far as 3 mi. (5 km.) south of the present port of Ashdod. The Jewish State was thus allotted about 20% of the area of Mandatory Palestine. Jerusalem and its environs, including Bethlehem, with a corridor leading to the coast comprising Jaffa, Ramleh, and Lydda, remaining under British Mandate, while the rest of the country (about 75% of its area) would become an Arab state. The Woodhead Commission, appointed in 1938 to study the possibility of implementing this scheme, also considered two alternative plans, but came to the conclusion that partition was impracticable and the British government decided to drop it.

The UNSCOP plan was much more complicated and less clearly defined in so far as boundaries were concerned. It proposed that the country be divided into seven segments. The Jewish state and the Arab state were to consist of three segments each, while the seventh segment, including the Jerusalem-Bethlehem area, would come under international control. The Jewish state was to get the eastern part of Galilee; the Jordan Valley from the northern end of the country to a point about 10 km. south of Beth-Shean; the plain of Jezreel; most of the Carmel range; the Coastal Plain from a short distance south of Acre to about 4.5 mi. (7 km.) south of the present port of Ashdod; the eastern part of the Coastal Plain from the latter point to the vicinity of Beersheba; the western and southern parts of the plain of Beersheba, and most of the Negev (with the exception of its northwestern part). Nearly 60% of Palestine was assigned to the Jewish state, but over half of this area was the uninhabited, semidesert Negev. The northern segment (Galilee) of the Jewish state connected up with the central segment (Coastal Plain) only at one point, near Afulah. Similarly, the central and southern (Negev) segments met near Be'er Toviyyah. It was not, however, intended that the partition should be actually implemented according to the border lines specified in the UNSCOP plan, but that they should constitute the basis for negotiations between Jews and Arabs, which would lead to the exchange of areas and the agreed delimitation of more practicable boundaries. The resolution passed by the UN General Assembly on Nov. 29, 1947, which called for the partition of Palestine, made minor changes in these boundaries.

See also *Palestine, Partition Plans.

THE ARMISTICE DEMARCATION LINES – 1949. The de facto boundaries of the State of Israel were delimited after the War of Independence (the 1948 war) in a series of armistice agreements signed with the neighboring states in 1949 on the basis of the position of the front lines between the opposing armies on the day the cease-fire came into force. The armistice lines were later demarcated where they did not coincide with the boundaries of the British Mandate or where demarcation had not been carried out by the British. It was stated in the agreements (e.g., article 5, par. 2 of the agreement with Egypt) that the armistice demarcation lines were not to be regarded as territorial or political boundaries and that the rights and claims of the parties were unaffected. However, since the agreements forbade any acts of hostility or penetration across the lines, they served, in practice, despite repeated violations, as Israel's boundaries until the *Six-Day War of 1967.

The boundary between Israel and Lebanon remained unchanged and was identical with that of Palestine under the British Mandate. Israel handed back to Lebanon a strip north and west of the Palestine-Lebanon border occupied by its forces during the fighting.

In the Israel-Syrian armistice demarcation lines there were only minor de facto changes from the mandatory boundaries. The Syrians occupied during the War of Independence and held until June 1967 the small areas east of Jordan, east of Lake Kinneret, and in the Yarmuk valley which belonged to Palestine during the British Mandate, a total of some 9 sq. mi. (25 sq. km.). Following the signing of the armistice agreement the Syrians withdrew from small areas west of the Jordan (in the Mishmar ha-Yarden area) and near the eastern and northeastern shores of Lake Kinneret. The agreement provided for the formation of demilitarized zones along most of the demarcation lines. These were the occasion for much friction and numerous incidents – mainly due to Syrian interference with Israeli development works and the cultivation of lands by Israeli farmers in the zones. The actual position of the Syrian forces prior to the Six-Day War became the basis of their demand for the withdrawal of Israel from Syrian territory occupied during the war.

Various parts of the long armistice line between Israel and the Kingdom of Jordan were drawn in three different ways. Two parts of the line coincided with the boundaries of Palestine during the mandatory period: the section running along the Yarmuk to its confluence with the Jordan and then along that river to a point approximately 2.5 mi. (4 km.) southeast of Tirat Ẓevi, and the section running across the middle of the southern part of the Dead Sea and all along the Arabah.

Secondly, a line was drawn between the positions held by each side when the fighting stopped, dividing up the no-man's-land. Along two sections, in the valley of Aijalon (Latrun area – from the Budrus to Qaṭanna) and in Jerusalem, no agreement could be reached on the division of no-man's-land. As a result, there were two parallel demarcation lines enclosing strips about 300–4,000 ft. (100–1,200 m.) wide, which citizens of each side could enter only with the consent of the other side.

Thirdly, there were places where the line agreed upon involved the exchange of territory. These were mainly areas required by Israel to maintain communications (mostly railway lines) and areas handed over to the Jordanians in exchange. Israel received a strip up to 3 mi. (5 km.) wide along the eastern fringe of the Sharon Valley, so that the railway from Lydda to Haifa, except for a section of 2 mi. (3 km.) on the outskirts of Tulkarm, was in Israeli territory. The same applied to a narrow strip in the Judean highlands, along the Jerusalem-Lydda railway. In return, the Jordanians got small areas in the Hebron region of the Judean Highlands.

The armistice demarcation line (later called the Green Line because of its color on the agreed maps) left the mandatory boundary along the river Jordan southeast of Tirat Ẓevi and turned westward into Naḥal Beẓek and up the eastern slopes of Mount Gilboa. It then ran along the top of the eastern and northern slopes of the Gilboa and cut across the southern corner of the Jezreel Valley in a westerly direction, leaving the southern tip of the valley on the Jordanian side of the border. The boundary then turned southwest and crossed the southern part of the Carmel range, running parallel with the Naḥal Iron (Wadi ʿĀra) road 2–2.5 mi. (3–4 km.) to the southeast. It then followed the eastern fringe of the Coastal Plain southward to the valley of Aijalon, where it turned eastward near Latrun into the Judean Highlands, running north of the Jerusalem-Sha'ar ha-Gai (Bab al-Wād) road to the northern outskirts of Jerusalem. It then turned south, dividing the city between Israel (western and southern parts) and Jordan (the Old City and the eastern and northern parts). The armistice agreement provided for two small enclaves in the Jerusalem area: one under Israel control, on Mount Scopus, about a kilometer to the north of the city, and the other, under UN control, about half a kilometer south of the city on Government House hill. Israel kept a police garrison in its part of the Scopus enclave, which was relieved once in two weeks by a convoy under UN supervision. On the southern outskirts of Jerusalem the boundary turned southwest, first running parallel to the railway and south of it and then descending to the western slopes and foothills of the Judean Highlands, which it followed southward to a point about 10 mi. (16 km.) northeast of Beersheba. From here the boundary turned east and then northeast, leaving the southern reaches of the Judean Highlands on the Israel side of the border, and reaching the Dead Sea about 2 mi. (3 km.) north of En-Gedi. This section of the line (the Green Line) marked the area which was occupied by Israel in the Six-Day War and (along with the Gaza Strip) was regarded by the Palestinians as the territory earmarked for their independent state. Opposite En-Gedi, in the center of the Dead Sea's western shore, the line joined the mandatory boundary, with which it was identical down to the Gulf of Eilat (Akaba).

The Israel-Egyptian armistice coincided with the Palestinian-Egyptian boundary, as demarcated in 1906, from the shores of the Gulf of Eilat to a point about 4.5 mi. (7 km.) south of Rafa, about 7.5 mi. (12 km.) from the Mediterranean coast. From this point it turned northward and ran almost parallel to the Mediterranean coast, at a distance 4–7.5 mi. (6–12 km.) from the coast to the vicinity of Beit Ḥānūn (northeast of Gaza), where it made a sharp turn westward and reached the coast. This part of the lines, from Rafa to the coast near Beit Ḥānūn, enclosed the Egyptian-held area known as the Gaza Strip. It followed the front line on the day the cease-fire came into force, with minor rectifications in addition to the division of no-man's-land. The agreement also provided for a demilitarized zone around Niẓẓanah (ʿAujā al-Ḥafīr), a frontier post on the Israel side of the boundary and a strategic position on the road from Beersheba to Isma'iliya on the Suez Canal. This triangular enclave, which was under Israel administration, had a base 22 mi. (35 km.) long along the Israel-Sinai boundary with a vertex 7.5 mi. (12 km.) to the east, inside Israel. Niẓẓanah was the seat of the Israel-Egyptian mixed armistice commission and the UN Truce Supervision Observers during the period 1949–56.

The total length of the armistice demarcation lines, the de facto boundaries of Israel during the period 1949–67, was approximately 771 mi. (1,239 km.): 118 mi. (190 km.) along the Mediterranean; 51 mi. (82 km.) with Lebanon; 48 mi. (77 km.) with Syria; 382 mi. (614 km.) with Jordan, including 73 mi. (118 km.) along the Jordan river and 33 mi. (53 km.) along the Dead Sea; 7 mi. (11 km.) along the Gulf of Eilat; 128 mi. (206 km.) with the Sinai Peninsula, and 37 mi. (59 km.) along the Gaza Strip.

CEASE-FIRE LINES – 1967. The Six-Day War of June 5–10, 1967 ended with the acceptance by Egypt, Jordan, Syria, and Lebanon of the Security Council's call for a cease-fire. Israel declared that the armistice regime had collapsed as a result of repeated Arab violations, and that she would maintain the cease-fire lines, which were determined by the positions held by each side when fighting stopped on June 10/11, until the establishment of agreed, secure and recognized borders as part of a permanent peace settlement with her neighbors.

The cease-fire line between Israel and Egypt ran along the Suez Canal from its southern end to Ras el-ʿEsh (about 10 km. from the northern end) and from there due north to the Mediterranean – a total of 112 mi. (180 km.).

The Israel-Jordan cease-fire line was identical with the 1949 armistice line from the shores of the Gulf of Eilat to a point halfway across the Dead Sea opposite En-Gedi. From here it left the armistice line and ran northward across the center of the Dead Sea to the entrance of the river Jordan and then along the course of that river to its confluence with the river Yarmuk, which it followed to a point about a kilometer east of its confluence with Wadi al-Ruqqād. The total length of the Israel-Jordanian cease-fire lines was 298 mi. (480 km.). The Israel-Syrian cease-fire line started from the valley of the Yarmuk, a short distance east of the entry of Wadi al-Ruqqād. For about 3 mi. (5 km.) it followed the eastern edge of the narrow, deeply incised, valley of the wadi, then it crossed to the western side of the valley and ran along the head of the escarpment overlooking it to a point about 2.5 mi. (4 km.) east of the village of Khasfin. From here to the eastern outskirts of the abandoned village of Rafid it ran straight northeast, made a sharp turn to the west and then to the north near Rafīd, and continued in a general northerly direction to the southern slopes of Mount Hermon, passing about 2 mi. (3 km.) east of Kuneitra and 2 km. east of Majdal Shams. The cease-fire line then climbed to the peaks of the southern ridge of Mt. Hermon 7,500 ft. (2,300 m.), where it turned southwestward down the western slopes of the Hermon, reaching the upper Jordan valley east of the village of Ghajar, south of which it met the Israel-Lebanon boundary. The total length of the Israel-Syrian cease-fire line was 50 mi. (80 km.). The Israel-Lebanon boundary remained unchanged except for an added stretch at its extreme east, where Israel held former Syrian areas bordering on Lebanon, which brought the total up to 63 mi. (102 km.). The peace treaties with Egypt (1979) and Jordan (1994) established with some minor modifications the mandatory boundaries between those countries and Mandatory Palestine as the international boundaries between the independent states of Israel and Egypt and between Israel and Jordan. The withdrawal of Israeli forces from Lebanese territory in spring 2000 reestablished the Israel-Lebanon line as an active boundary although Lebanon did not accept it as an international boundary.

[Moshe Brawer / Gideon Biger (2nd ed.)]

1880–1948

UNDER OTTOMAN RULE, 1880–1917. In the last 50 years of Ottoman rule over the Land of Israel, the decaying empire was partly opened to the growing political and economic influence of the European powers in the country. The Sultan Abdul Ḥamid II (1876–1908) tried to preserve his position by increasing the number of officials and strengthening the police forces, encouraging the emigration of loyal elements and settling them in areas inhabited by the rebellious Bedouin, and playing on the differences between the powers. In 1900 Beersheba was rebuilt and became the seat of government offices and a police garrison, and in 1908 ʿAwjā-Ḥifīr (*Niẓẓanah) was also made into an administrative center, the first step taken to get the Negev under control. Another important factor in strengthening law and order was the building of new gravel roads. New wagon ways from Jerusalem to Jaffa, Nablus, and Hebron were constructed as gravel roads in the 1880s. Important rail links were established: a concession for the Jerusalem-Jaffa line was awarded to Yosef *Navon, of Jerusalem, but the railroad was eventually built by a French company in 1890–92. Another railroad, the Haifa-Edrei line, linking up with the Hejaz Railroad (Istanbul-Damascus-Medina), was built by German engineers and completed in 1906.

In 1878, on the conclusion of the Balkan War, a special law was enacted to encourage the immigration of Muslims and their settlement on lands owned by the sultan, providing for 12 years' exemption from taxes and military service. As a result Moroccans settled in Lower Galilee, Circassians from the Caucasian Mountains settled in Galilee, and Bosnians settled in Caesarea. Concurrently, severe restrictions were imposed on the purchase of lands by foreign nationals, and the construction of dwellings and business premises on foreign-owned land was forbidden without a permit from Istanbul. At the same time, the European powers were increasing their foothold in the country, utilizing the Capitulations regime. Following the British occupation of Egypt in 1882, the Ottoman Empire based itself primarily upon its friendship with Germany, which was highlighted by an official visit in 1898 by Kaiser William II and his Kaiserin. They made a triumphant entry into Jerusalem, where the Kaiser received *Herzl. The influx of Europeans (of various types – settlers, monks, pilgrims, tourists) forced the Ottoman government to ensure law and order in order to deprive the foreign powers of a pretext to interfere in its internal affairs. The result was a considerable improvement in public security.

The Jewish Community. In 1880 the total number of Jews in the country was 20–25,000, two-thirds of whom were in Jerusalem, where they constituted half the population. There were smaller communities in the three other "holy cities" – Safed (4,000), Tiberias (2,500), and Hebron (800) – and two more recently established ones in Jaffa (1,000) and Haifa (300). The Sephardim were the older part of the Jewish population and also absorbed immigrants from North Africa, Bukhara, Persia, etc. The Ashkenazim were mostly of East European origin and were divided into *Ḥasidim and their opponents, the Perushim. Most of the Jews subsisted on *ḥalukkah* donations from Jews abroad that amounted to over £100,000 a year. Among the Sephardim the money was distributed by the community leaders, the recipients being mainly talmudic scholars and widows and orphans; among the Ashkenazim, the funds were administered by the *kolelim* (charitable organizations based largely on the origin of the beneficiaries), of which the largest were those of Vilna, Zamut, Grodno, Warsaw, Volhynia, Austria, Hungary, and Chabad Ḥasidim. There were considerable numbers of artisans, unskilled laborers, and small shopkeepers who led a life of poverty and want. Although the Jews were a recognized community and the Sephardi chief rabbi in Jerusalem (the *rishon le-Zion*) enjoyed official status, their status was low; Many Jews, especially among the Ashkenazim, sought the protection of foreign consuls, who readily gave it in order to extend their influence.

The great majority of the Jews were strictly orthodox and accepted the authority of the rabbis, who were opposed to all modern trends and resisted the winds of change that were blowing in from Europe. The help of Jewish philanthropists abroad was readily accepted as long as it did not involve any change in the traditional way of life. Thus free housing was constructed for scholars and the poor, as well as hospitals and yeshivot, but any attempts to establish modern schools or to train people for productive employment in agriculture and handicrafts was met with fierce resistance by the leaders of the *ḥalukkah* regime. Nevertheless, even among the "old *yishuv*" (as the pre-Zionist Jewish community came to be called), there were some who called upon the Jews to earn their living by their own labor. These included the editors of the first newspapers to be published in Jerusalem, notably I.D. *Frumkin of *Ḥavaẓẓelet* (reestablished in 1870), and the founders of the first settlements in 1878 – Gei Oni near Safed and Petaḥ Tikvah near the Yarkon River. At the beginning of the 1880s there was a group of men in Jerusalem who made strenuous efforts to bring about a renaissance of Jewish life; the leading figures among them were Y.M. *Pines (who had settled in the country in 1878), Ze'ev *Herzberg (1877), Eliezer *Ben-Yehuda (1881) and two natives of Jerusalem, David *Yellin and Yosef *Meyuḥas. They also encountered strong opposition from the *ḥalukkah* trustees.

The international conferences and negotiations which followed the 1878 Balkan War were accompanied by renewed proposals for the creation of a Jewish state in the Land of Israel, especially from British visionaries. An outstanding example was Laurence *Oliphant's plan, proposed in his book *The Land of Gilead* (London, 1880), after a visit to the country in the previous year, for large-scale Jewish settlement to the east of the Jordan under the sultan's patronage; Oliphant went so far as to negotiate with the sultan on his plan.

Beginnings of the First Aliyah. A new period in the life of the Jews in the Land of Israel opened in 1882 as a result of the 1881 pogroms in Russia, the persecution of the Jews in Romania, and the rise of the *Ḥibbat Zion movement, whose members were known as Ḥovevei Zion. A considerable wave of *aliyah* set in, which brought to the area about 30,000 Jews between 1882 and 1904. Among the newcomers was a small group of young people, members of the *Bilu movement, who aimed at creating political and economic conditions for the large-scale settlement of East European Jews, and groups of people with small amounts of capital who wanted to settle on the land. Within a year or two a number of agricultural settlements were established in Judea (*Rishon le-Zion, *Ekron, *Gederah, and *Petaḥ Tikvah, which was revived by the new arrivals), the coastal hills (*Zikhron Ya'akov), and Upper Galilee (*Rosh Pinnah and *Yesud ha-Maalah). These villages, known as moshavot, would have collapsed at the outset, however, had it not been for the help extended to them by Baron Edmond de *Rothschild of Paris (known as *Ha-Nadiv ha-Yadu'a*, "the well-known benefactor"), who took most of them under his wing. He established a large administrative apparatus, consisting of managers, agronomists, doctors, teachers, etc., which operated along philanthropic lines from 1883 to 1899. The settlers were completely dependent upon the Baron's officials, from whom they received monthly allowances, and were not permitted to show any initiative. The officials created a type of farmer whose plantations depended on the work of hired laborers, and there was much waste and corruption. It must be stated, however, that they also acquired large tracts of land in Judea, the coastal hills, and Galilee, established new settlements (Metullah, Bat Shelomo, Shefeyah, Mazkeret Batyah, Be'er Toviyyah), and tried to foster industry (wine making, silk manufacture, and a glass factory in Tantura). Independent Jewish settlements were built in 1890 in Ḥaderah and Reḥovot. During this period of direct assistance, the Baron invested £1,600,000 sterling in the settlements. In 1900 he entrusted them to the *Jewish Colonization Association (ICA), which he continued to support. ICA introduced new methods aimed at helping the settlements to achieve independent status as quickly as possible. New villages, in which the farmers worked their own land, were established by ICA in Lower Galilee, (Sejera, Mesḥa, Milḥamiyyah – later Menaḥemiyyah, Yavneel, and Bet Gan).

Government Restriction on Aliyah. The Ottoman government soon recognized that the new *aliyah* was of a different character from its predecessors and regarded it as a source of political danger. As early as June 1882, a law was enacted prohibiting the settlement of East European Jews in the country. The intervention of various Jewish personalities and organizations, and diplomatic pressure (such as that of U.S. Ambassador Oscar Straus in 1887) were of no avail. Although the Ottoman government was forced to permit the temporary stay of pilgrims and tourists, a law passed in 1901 provided for the deposit of their travel documents with the authorities upon arrival in exchange for a permit of pilgrimage covering a stay of three months (the "red slip"). This did not bring Jewish immigration to a stop, and the immigrants remained in the country, avoiding expulsion by baksheesh (bribery) or by seeking the protection of foreign consuls. The ban on immigration was only one of the obstacles to Jewish settlement, however. There were also some restrictions in the 1880s on the purchase of land, and the ban on the construction of buildings in new settlements without a special permit from Istanbul. Throughout the period of Ottoman rule, these measures hampered Jewish land settlement, which was only a very minor trickle in the tremendous stream of migration that took three million Jews to various parts of the world, mostly to the United States.

In 1890 and 1891, increased persecution of Jews in Russia stimulated a new wave of *aliyah*, including groups of well-to-do Jews. It was in this period that the villages of Reḥovot and Ḥaderah were established, and there was a rush to buy land, resulting in speculation and a steep rise in prices. A special delegation from the Ḥovevei Zion in Russia, headed by Vladimir (Ze'ev) *Tiomkin, came to the country to rectify the situation, but did not succeed. The Ottoman government took determined steps to stop Jewish immigration; the great awakening ended in a crisis, and many left the country. For the next decade the major problem confronting the leaders of the *yishuv* was that of hundreds of Jewish laborers waiting for the opportunity to settle on the land. In 1896 a small group of them settled in Metullah and Be'er Toviyyah, but many had to leave.

Many of the newcomers, including Jews from Oriental countries (Yemen, Bukhara), as well as Eastern Europe, made their homes in the cities. By the beginning of the 20th century, Jerusalem had a Jewish population of about 30,000 and the *ḥalukkah* regime was still in force, but new quarters were established outside the Old City, including the Bukharan quarter, Battei Ungarn, and Bet Israel. The Midrash Abrabanel library, later the nucleus of the National and Hebrew University Library, was founded in 1892. In Safed (which had a population of 6,600 at the time), Tiberias (3,200), and Hebron (1,500), the traditional way of life was also kept intact. In the coastal towns, however, a more productive society came into being, and under the influence of the new immigrants and the workers in the nearby villages, many people began taking up trades and commerce. Near Jaffa two new Jewish quarters were founded, Neveh Ẓedek (1887) and Neveh Shalom (1890). In 1891 a mixed Ashkenazi-Sephardi community council was formed in Jaffa, which had a total Jewish population of 3,000. In Haifa, with some 1,500 Jews, the first Jewish quarter was founded in 1891. Together with the 6,000 farmers living in 20 villages, the new *yishuv* now numbered some 10,000, 20% of the Jewish population.

The Clash Between the Old Yishuv and the New. It was this period that witnessed the first struggle over the spiritual character of the *yishuv*. The first clash occurred in 1889, the Jewish year 5649, which was a sabbatical (**shemittah*) year. The Jerusalem rabbis demanded that the farmers let their fields lie fallow during the year and promised to support them from *ḥalukkah* funds, but the settlers refused, quoting rulings of leading Russian rabbis permitting them to work in the *shemittah* year. Among the immigrants who arrived in 1890–91 were a substantial number who were not prepared to follow the old ways, and the rabbis complained of "young men dancing with maidens." When the first Hebrew play, *Zerubbavel* by M.L. *Lilienblum, was staged in Reḥovot in 1890, the performance was stopped by the Ottoman authorities, who had received word that the play called for insurrection against the established government. Eliezer Ben-Yehuda and the newspaper he had founded in 1884 (*Ha-Ẓevi*) roused the ire of the *ḥalukkah* trustees. In 1894 they denounced him to the Ottoman authorities, alleging that he was inciting the Jews to rebellion; he was sentenced to a year's imprisonment and released only after intervention by the Baron's officials. This incident caused a deep rift between the old *yishuv* (joined by some of the newcomers, such as Y.M. Pines and Z. *Jawitz) and the new one, headed by the disciples of *Aḥad Ha-Am. The issue was the character of the *yishuv*, its way of life, and the education of its youth. The controversy spread abroad and might well have done harm to both sides, but fortunately, a kind of armistice was reached in 1897. As a result the secular, nationalist elements of the *yishuv* achieved the right to lead their own way of life, side by side with the strictly religious circles.

It was during this period, too, that the modern Hebrew school was created. The first stage, in which Jewish studies, as well as the Hebrew language itself, were taught in Hebrew, was introduced by Ben-Yehuda, David Yellin, and Nissim Behar. The second stage – the teaching of general subjects in Hebrew – was first introduced in the villages in 1889–92. In the latter year, a teachers' assembly was held for the first time to fix the Hebrew terms to be used in mathematics and the natural sciences as well as to formulate a uniform curriculum for the village schools. The Hebrew Teachers' Association was founded in 1903, eventually becoming a major factor in the country's school system.

In spite of these advances, the new *yishuv* faced a profound moral crisis at the beginning of the 20th century. It was obvious that any rapid development depended upon its political status. This had also been a basic premise in the program of Theodor Herzl, who had started his political activities by attempting to persuade the Ottoman government to grant the Zionist Organization a charter for the settlement of the Land of Israel. Herzl and the political Zionists were critical of settlement methods employed by their predecessors, regarding them as "infiltration" and pointing out their inherent political risks. After several years of fruitless negotiations, Herzl despaired of ever obtaining the Sultan's agreement to his proposals and was ready to entertain the British government's proposal to support a Jewish settlement project in East Africa, known as the *Uganda Plan. It is indicative of the state of mind of the new settlers in the Land of Israel at this time that many of them, including Ben-Yehuda, supported this plan, thus admitting, in effect, that for political and other reasons there was no real prospect of a substantial Jewish settlement in the homeland. This moral crisis led to some emigration of workers, settlers, and even young people born in the settlements. In 1903 the Ḥovevei Zion, headed by Menahem *Ussishkin, called a general meeting in Zikhron Ya'akov at which they proposed the creation of an executive committee to represent the entire *yishuv*, but in the prevailing atmosphere of despondency this proposal fell on deaf ears.

Beginnings of the Second Aliyah. A new wave of immigration – the Second Aliyah – commenced in 1904 and continued until the outbreak of World War I. Again, this was only a small part of a great movement of Jews from Eastern Europe caused by repeated pogroms and the general impoverishment of the Russian Jews. It is estimated that some 40,000 new settlers went to the Land of Israel in this period. Although many returned to Russia or emigrated to other countries, the newcomers, together with natural increase, brought the Jewish population to 85,000 (about 12% of the total) for the country in 1914. The Second Aliyah was not of a uniform character. Some of the newcomers joined the old *yishuv* and settled in the "holy cities," especially in Jerusalem, which at this time contained about half the Jewish population of the country. Here they built new quarters, such as Zikhron Moshe, Romemah, and Ahavah. Others belonged to the middle class, most of whom came with their families as Zionists seeking a full Jewish national way of life for themselves and their children. Some of them made their homes in the towns or the established rural settlements.

The moshavot, especially those in the south, did not take long to overcome the crisis which had marked the early years of the century. In addition to grapes, they began to grow almonds and citrus fruits and established marketing cooperatives: Hitaḥdut ha-Koremim – the Viticulturists' Association – and Pardes – the Citrus-growers' Association. They also attracted Jewish investments from abroad and a special society – Aguddat Neta'im – was set up to prepare plantations for sale to such investors. In the Diaspora, Jewish societies were formed to establish their own *aḥuzzot* ("estates") in the country (Migdal, Poriyyah, Saronah, Ruḥamah, Karkur). The new settlers also introduced an enterprising spirit into the towns. It was on their initiative that the modern garden suburb of *Tel Aviv was founded on the outskirts of Jaffa in 1909 and reached a population of 2,000 by 1914. In Haifa, the Jewish population rose to 3,000. There were also beginnings of new industry, such as the Stein Iron Works in Jaffa and the Atid Oil Factory in Lydda and Haifa.

Labor and Defense Problems. A difficult social problem confronting the new *yishuv* was that of the Arab labor on which Jewish agriculture was based. It was natural for the Jewish settlers to employ Arabs: their wages were low and they made few demands on their employers. The Zionist Movement, however, both in the Land of Israel and abroad, regarded this practice as running counter to one of its major aims – the transition of the Jews to productive labor – and as a potential danger to the political position and security of the Jewish population. An associated problem was that of protection of life and property in the Jewish villages, which were entrusted to local Arab, Circassian, or other strong men. These problems were of particular interest to the young people of the Second Aliyah, who had experience of the revolutionary movement and Jewish self-defense in Russia and regarded themselves as pioneers of the Zionist Movement. Both their political parties – Po'alei Zion and Ha-Po'el ha-Ẓa'ir (see Israel, State of: *Political Life and Parties) – considered it their major task to achieve the employment of Jewish labor in the Jewish sector of the economy and to create a Jewish working class on the land. To tackle the problem of security, a small group of former members of the Jewish self-defense organization in Russia met in 1909 and established the *Ha-Shomer (Watchman) Society, which soon made a good name for itself and took over the responsibility for security in many of the villages in Galilee and Judea. Their work also served to raise the prestige of the Jews in the eyes of their Arab neighbors.

A partial solution to the problem of Jewish agricultural labor was provided by the success of a mission undertaken in 1911 by S. *Yavne'eli, who visited Yemen and called upon the Jews there to settle in the Land of Israel. Thousands of Yemenite Jews heeded his call, establishing their own quarters in the vicinity of the large villages and working in the Jewish plantations and orchards. Among the methods used to facilitate the employment of Jewish labor in the villages was the establishment of labor exchanges, workers' kitchens, and a medical insurance fund (Kuppat Ḥolim). Another was the founding of workers' settlements (*moshevei po'alim*) in which the worker was provided with a small plot of land that enabled him to set up his own auxiliary farm (Ein Gannim, Naḥalat Yehudah).

A more radical change in the status of the labor movement and its methods of operation took place in 1908, when the Zionist Organization started its settlement activities by establishing the Palestine Office in Jaffa under the direction of Arthur *Ruppin. In the initial stage, the workers were employed at the "national farms" (Ben Shemen, Ḥuldah, Kinneret, etc.) established on land purchased by the *Jewish National Fund and managed by agronomists. As a result of controversies between managers and laborers, the work on some of these farms was entrusted to groups of workers on their own responsibility. The first such experiment was made at Deganyah (founded in 1909); this was the beginning of the *kevuẓah* (see *kibbutz), which eventually became the major type of settlement sponsored by the Zionist Organization. In 1911 the workers began to organize in regional federations in Galilee and Judea, and a national health insurance fund was established in 1912. Gradually the organized workers of the Second Aliyah made their imprint upon the *yishuv* and laid the foundations of the labor movement (see Israel, State of: *Labor), which was to become, for about 60 years, the predominant force in the country.

Cultural Development. It was in the period of the Second Aliyah that the Hebrew language and culture took root in the country. Hebrew daily newspapers made their appearance (*Ha-Ẓevi*, edited by Ben-Yehuda, in 1908, and *Ha-Ḥerut*), and Hebrew periodicals published by the labor movement (*Ha-Po'el ha-Ẓa'ir* and *Ha-Aḥdut*) exerted a considerable influence on Jewish youth in the Land of Israel and abroad. Hebrew authors and thinkers, such as J.H. *Brenner, C.E. *Gordon, J. *Fichman, D. *Shimoni, S.Y. *Agnon, and M. *Smilansky settled in the country. Hebrew became the daily language of an ever-increasing number of workers, teachers, and young people. In 1904 the German-Jewish Hilfsverein founded a teachers' seminary in Jerusalem, and in 1905 the Herzlia Hebrew Gymnasium (high school), which was to serve as a model for Hebrew secondary schools all over the world, was established in Jaffa. In 1906 the *Bezalel School of Art, headed by Professor Boris *Schatz, opened in Jerusalem. The foundation stone of a college of technology, the *Technion, was laid in Haifa in 1912. This precipitated a dispute between the Hilfsverein, which wanted the language of instruction in the *yishuv*'s first institution of higher learning to be German, and the Hebrew-speaking public in the country with their supporters abroad, who insisted on Hebrew. This "language war" led to a revolt by the teachers of the Hilfsverein schools and the establishment of a national Hebrew school network, which in 1914 encompassed 3,200 pupils (see Israel, State of: *Education).

At the end of the Second Aliyah period, there were 40 moshavot with a population of 12,000 and landholdings of

409,000 dunams (about 102,000 acres). Of these, 24 had been created or supported by Baron Edmond de Rothschild. Together with the newcomers in the towns, especially in Jaffa and Haifa, the new *yishuv* accounted for a third of the total Jewish population, and it was by far the most active and dynamic section.

Awakening of Arab Nationalism. General developments in the Ottoman Empire in this period also had their effect. While the revolt of the Young Turks (1908) did not fulfill the hopes placed on it by some Zionist leaders (such as Aḥad Ha-Am, Jacobus *Kann, and Vladimir *Jabotinsky) and members of the *yishuv*, it made it possible to campaign openly for the support of public opinion in Istanbul and in the Land of Israel. One of the most important results of the revolt, however, was the rise of separatist movements among the Arabs, who interpreted the new *hürriyet* (liberty) as freedom to realize their national aspirations. The pioneers of this Arab nationalism were mostly Syrians and Lebanese – some of them Christians. The movement also developed in the Land of Israel, where Arab newspapers (*al-Karmil* in Haifa and *Filasṭīn* in Jaffa) were founded and engaged in systematic incitement against Jewish immigration and settlement. In the elections to the Turkish parliament in 1908, the Arabs succeeded in preventing the election of a Jewish deputy to represent the Jerusalem district. In Istanbul, the Arab members of parliament denounced Jewish settlement in the Land of Israel and described the Zionist Movement as a danger to the Ottoman Empire. Arab officials tried to obstruct Jewish land purchase and settlement (as in the *Merḥavyah affair).

Some attempts were made by Zionist groups to establish contact with Arab nationalists, and upon the initiative of Ḥayyim *Margolis-Kalvaryski, an ICA official, a meeting took place between Nahum *Sokolow of the Zionist Executive and Arab leaders. There was the danger, however, that such contacts would arouse suspicions on the part of the Turks, who regarded Arab nationalism as a separatist movement and – perhaps for that reason – showed some signs of an improved attitude toward the *yishuv* in 1913–14 (such as the abolition of the "red slip"; see section in Israel, State of: Historical Survey, Arab National Movement).

World War I. World War I caused general havoc and destruction in the country and had a disastrous effect upon the *yishuv*. In the first three years of the war, the Land of Israel served the Ottoman Empire and her allies as a base for their attempts to launch an attack upon the Suez Canal and Egypt, and, together with Syria, it had to provide the supplies required by the 4th Turkish Corps. In addition to large-scale recruitment, the population suffered from heavy taxes; compulsory labor service on road building, railroads, and tree cutting; and the confiscation of property, such as horses, wheat, and piping. In the fourth year of the war, the front reached the Land of Israel. The presence of large military forces brought various contagious diseases in its wake; in addition there were natural calamities, such as the locust invasion of 1915–16. On October 31, the inflation of the Turkish currency sealed the ruin of the economy, and by the end of 1917 the country faced starvation.

The Jewish population, whose economy depended largely upon the transfer of funds from abroad – especially the old *yishuv*, which was not properly organized to meet an emergency – was exposed to great hardship; in 1917 thousands in Jerusalem and Safed died of starvation. The new *yishuv* was slightly better off; its economic affairs were handled by an emergency committee representing all sections and institutions – the Zionist Executive, ICA, the Alliance Israélite Universelle, the moshavot, the Tel Aviv Committee, the workers' parties, and so forth. A decisive role in alleviating the plight of the Jews was played by the money and food shipped by American Jewry on American naval vessels.

Anti-Jewish Measures. There were also disasters of a political nature. On the eve of its entry into the war, the Ottoman government had abolished the Capitulations regime, jeopardizing the civil status of the many Jews who had enjoyed the protection of foreign consuls. The attitude of the Ottoman military administration, headed by Jemal Pasha, to the Jews was ambivalent. On the one hand, there was the centuries-old tradition of regarding the Jews as a pro-Turkish element, augmented by political considerations, such as the alliance with Germany and Austria and the influence of America; on the other hand, the spirit of independence displayed by the new *yishuv* and its intimate connections with the Zionist Movement made its loyalty to Turkey suspect in the eyes of the rulers. At the outbreak of the war, the authorities confiscated arms from the settlers in the moshavot and in Tel Aviv. A grave problem concerned inhabitants, including Jews, who were nationals of enemy states, especially Russia. The Ottomans asked them to become Ottoman citizens, promising not to draft them into the army for one year. On Dec. 17, 1914, 700 foreign Jews who refused to become Ottoman citizens were detained in Jaffa and deported to Egypt on an Italian boat. This act was followed by a mass exodus of foreign Jews, which continued throughout 1915, in the course of which 11,300 (over an eighth of the entire Jewish population) left the country, mainly by American and Italian boats. Most of them stayed in refugee camps in Egypt, and about 500 enlisted with Joseph *Trumpeldor in the Zion Mule Corps, which fought on the Allied side in the Gallipoli campaign against the Ottomans.

In their efforts to prevent further deportations and the emigration of Jews, the leaders of the *yishuv* managed to persuade the authorities to facilitate the acquisition of Ottoman nationality by waiving the fee and exempting the new Ottoman subjects from military service for a year. Another demonstration of the *yishuv*'s loyalty to the regime was the enlistment of dozens of students of the Hebrew secondary schools and their enrollment in the Istanbul officers' school in 1916. In the spring of 1915 the policy of the Ottoman military administration toward the Jews took on a more definite shape. Zionism, the Zionist flag, the Jewish National Fund stamps, etc., were all outlawed. Several of the active Zionist leaders, especially former delegates to Zionist Congresses, leaders of Ha-Shomer, those who had been active in land purchases, etc., were deported. Two notable deportees were David Ben Gurion and Izḥak Ben-Zvi. On the other hand, there was a more favorable attitude to those who remained. Jemal Pasha even invited some of the Jewish leaders who had no direct connections with the Zionist movement (e.g. Albert *Antebi, Aaron Aaronsohn, Meir *Dizengoff, and Menasheh Meyerowitz) to participate in various projects launched by the government.

In the spring of 1917, when the battlefront was drawing near, the evacuation of the civilian population was taken in hand, and all the inhabitants of Jaffa (about 40,000 of them) including the Jews of Tel Aviv were deported. The Jews found shelter in the moshavot in Galilee and Samaria. A further plan to deport the residents of Jerusalem and the moshavot themselves was dropped after an appeal to Istanbul. The organization of aid to the refugees in their camps was one of the finest chapters in the history of the *yishuv*, but hundreds died of starvation, disease, and cold. In September 1917, when the secret *Nili intelligence ring was uncovered, widespread searches were instituted and hundreds of people were jailed – most of them were deserters from the Turkish army and only a few were in fact members of Nili or of Ha-Shomer. The leadership of the *yishuv* made great effort to ease the lot of these "Damascus prisoners," as they came to be called.

On Oct. 31, 1917, the British opened an unexpected offensive and took Beersheba, going on to Gaza (Nov. 7) and Jaffa (Nov. 16). On Dec. 11, 1917, General Allenby entered Jerusalem and Ottoman rule over the Holy City came to an end 401 years after it had started in 1516. The British advance spared the *yishuv* further persecution and saved it from extinction by starvation and disease. A small part – the inhabitants of Samaria and Galilee – were to endure nine more months of Ottoman rule, until the north was occupied by the British in September 1918. The Jewish population had been reduced by hardship, expulsion, and emigration to 57,000.

The conquest of the south of the country coincided with the issue of the Balfour Declaration "of sympathy with Jewish Zionist aspirations," which was issued by the British foreign secretary on November 2, with the approval of the cabinet (see *Balfour Declaration for full text). The principles of the declaration were approved by the Allied governments and the United States (first unofficially by President Wilson and, on June 30, 1922, by a resolution of Congress). Thus the Land of Israel, under the name of Palestine, reappeared on the world political map, and the small *yishuv*, as the nucleus of the Jewish national home, assumed a significant role on the international scene.

UNDER BRITISH RULE, 1917–1948. The military administration established in Palestine after its occupation by the British forces (Occupied Enemy Territory Administration – OETA) was manned by military men and experts on Arab affairs. Prominent among the occupying troops was the *Jewish Legion, consisting of two Jewish battalions: the 38th ("London") battalion of the Royal Fusiliers and the 39th ("American"). Their arrival caused a great stir among the Jewish workers and the youth, who called for the creation of a third, Palestinian battalion. Negotiations with the British authorities led to the establishment of the battalion, which attracted 850 local Jewish volunteers, in June 1918. In the final attack on the Turkish positions, the 38th and 39th battalions participated in the capture of the Jordan crossings. After the war, when the demobilization of the war-weary troops was speeded up, the three Jewish battalions played an increasingly important role in the occupying forces. At the end of 1919 the Palestinian battalion was renamed the First Judeans, with the seven-branched *menorah* as its emblem. The existence of the battalion was widely regarded as tangible evidence of British intention to carry out the Balfour Declaration.

Arab Nationalist Agitation. The end of the war was followed by great agitation among the Arab nationalists, who declared the Land of Israel to be "Southern Syria" and demanded its incorporation into a large Arab state with its center in Damascus. The British military administration showed no sympathy with the Balfour Declaration; during the years 1918 and 1919 it was not officially published or referred to in Palestine. The Zionist Commission consisting of Jewish representatives from Britain, France, and Italy (joined later by American and Russian members), headed by Chaim *Weizmann, that went out with British government sanction in March 1918 met with many difficulties due to the hostile attitude of many of the men on the spot. Weizmann succeeded, however, in reaching some measure of understanding with the Emir Faisal, who headed the Arab movement at the time. On Jan. 3, 1919, the two men signed an agreement that spoke of "the closest possible collaboration in the development of the Arab State and Palestine" and of measures "to encourage and facilitate the immigration of Jews into Palestine on a large scale." The agreement, however, was repudiated by the Arab nationalists. In April 1920 the Jewish settlements in Upper Galilee were attacked by Arabs, and *Tel-Ḥai and other places were abandoned after an incident in which Joseph Trumpeldor and others were killed. In March 1920 anti-Jewish riots broke out in Jerusalem. The military authorities gave the Arabs a free hand, while arresting the Jewish defenders, led by Vladimir Jabotinsky, who were sentenced to long terms of imprisonment.

Samuel Becomes High Commissioner. The policy of the military administration in Palestine, however, was not supported by Whitehall. On April 24, 1920, the Supreme Council of the Peace Conference at San Remo resolved that the Mandate over Palestine be conferred on Britain, charging her with the establishment of a national home for the Jewish people as laid down in the Balfour Declaration. The frontiers were to be negotiated between Britain and France; as subsequently delineated they included Transjordan (see section in Israel, State of: Historical Survey: Land of Israel in International Affairs and Frontiers). OETA was abolished and Herbert Samuel, a Jew and a Zionist, was appointed high commissioner, arriving on July 1, 1920.

Samuel tried to facilitate Jewish immigration and at the same time to appease the Arabs. He lent his aid to the pioneering immigrants – the *ḥalutzim* – who began to arrive in large numbers at the end of 1919 and gave orders for them to be employed on road projects in the north. He also made Hebrew an official language, side by side with Arabic and English. As a concession to the Jews who wanted the country to be called by its historic name, Ereẓ Israel, the initials (א״י) were added in parentheses to the Hebrew form of the name Palestine. On the other hand, the best government-owned lands in the Beth-Shean Valley were distributed among the Bedouin (who did not know what to do with them and later sold them to the Jews, at a high price). A compromise was reached with the military authorities providing for the creation of one Arab and one Jewish battalion for the defense of the country. To placate Arab nationalist opinion, Samuel appointed Hajj Amin al-*Husseini, who had been sentenced in absentia to 15 years' imprisonment for his part in inflaming the 1920 riots, as mufti of Jerusalem in 1921. In the following year, Husseini was elected president of the Supreme Muslim Council and used these positions of great influence and power to whip up opposition to the *yishuv*.

In the early part of 1921 there were important developments in regard to Transjordan. *Abdullah, a brother of Faisal, invaded the territory with a band of Beduins in order to help his brother, Faisal, who had been pushed out of Damascus by the French in the summer of 1920. (According to recent opinion by prearrangement with, or at least with the connivance of, the British.) On March 27 he was recognized by Winston *Churchill, the British colonial secretary, as emir, with a British advisor and a subvention from Britain. Subsequently, Transjordan was excluded from the area to which the Balfour Declaration applied and was thus closed to Jewish settlement. In May 1921 an outbreak of violence in Jaffa was followed by large-scale attacks on Reḥovot, Petaḥ Tikvah, Ḥaderah, and other places. Forty-seven Jews were killed and 140 wounded; Arab casualties were 48 dead and 73 wounded, mostly due to action by British troops. These disturbances demonstrated the ability of the Arab national movement to inflame the Arab masses and revealed the relative weakness of the *yishuv*. Samuel began to backtrack: he ordered a temporary halt of immigration and entered into negotiations with the Arab Executive Committee.

The Churchill White Paper. The outcome of these negotiations was a White Paper issued by Churchill on June 22, 1922. It gave a restrictive interpretation of the Balfour Declaration, which it said "did not contemplate that Palestine as a whole should be converted into a Jewish National Home" and introduced the principle of "economic absorptive capacity" as the yardstick for Jewish immigration. A system of immigration certificates was adopted, under which people with capital (at first £500, later £1000) could enter Palestine with their families without any restriction while the number of workers without capital to be admitted would be determined by a half-yearly schedule to be fixed by the government after negotiations with the Zionist Executive. The White Paper also stated, however, that the Balfour Declaration was not subject to change and that the Jews were in Palestine "as of right and not on sufferance" (see *Palestine, White Papers).

On July 22, 1922, the League of Nations Council confirmed the Palestine Mandate, citing the Balfour Declaration in the preamble and recognizing "the historical connection of the Jewish people with Palestine, and… the grounds for reconstituting their National Home in that country." The Mandate provided for the recognition of the Zionist Organization as the "*Jewish Agency" to advise and cooperate with the administration "in such economic, social and other matters as may affect the establishment of the Jewish National Home and the interests of the Jewish population in Palestine."

A step designed to appease the Arabs was the plan for a legislative assembly. Although it was to have only limited powers, the Arabs were to have the majority on the basis of their numerical strength. (According to a census taken at the end of 1922, there were 83,794 Jews, about 11% of the total population of 757,182.) The Arabs, however, boycotted the elections to the assembly, and the plan was abandoned (1923). The Arab Committee also rejected Samuel's proposal for the establishment of an "Arab Agency" similar to the Jewish Agency. In the end, a colonial regime was established, headed by the high commissioner and senior officials, almost all British.

The 1921 disturbances also brought about a change in security policy. The plan for locally recruited battalions was abandoned and a British gendarmerie, made up of British soldiers (the "Black and Tans") who had been demobilized after suppressing the Irish rebellion was established. The Jewish villages were provided with sealed armories containing rifles and ammunition, which they were permitted to open only in case of emergency. In April 1925 Lord Balfour attended the opening ceremony of the *Hebrew University in Jerusalem; his visit caused no disturbances, indicating that Pax Britannica prevailed. This situation continued under the next high commissioner, Lord Plumer (1925–28) and encouraged the government to reform the security forces with a view to reducing their high costs. The British gendarmerie was disbanded in 1926, and some of its members were absorbed into the Palestine Police. In addition, the Transjordan Frontier Force, consisting almost entirely of Arabs, was established, and the sealed armories were withdrawn from most of the moshavot. The policy followed by both Samuel and Plumer was to regard the maintenance of law and order, by political and military means, as the prime responsibility of the government, leaving the Jews to build the National Home through their own institutions and with their own resources – by immigration, settlement on the land, the development of industry and commerce, and so forth. Politically the period 1921–29 presented the Jewish people and the Zionist movement with a great opportunity.

The Third Aliyah. The immigration of the period 1919–23 (the Third Aliyah) was of a special character. The driving force behind it was the *He-Ḥalutz movement, which had risen in Eastern Europe, inspired by the Second Aliyah and the emissaries from Ereẓ Israel (notably Joseph Trumpeldor) and impelled by the sufferings of the Jews during the war and the postwar pogroms. Most of the newcomers were young people of strong Zionist convictions who had been influenced by the profound changes and revolutionary upheavals that had taken place in their countries of origin. Many were graduates of the He-Ḥalutz movement in Russia and Poland and *Ha-Shomer ha-Ẓa'ir (in Galicia). In December 1920 they cooperated with the men of the Second Aliyah in founding the *Histadrut, the General Federation of Jewish Labor, which declared as its aim the creation of a new Jewish working society in the Land of Israel (see also Israel, State of: *Labor, section on Jewish Labor Organizations).

The *yishuv* was small and impoverished and, from an economic point of view, incapable of absorbing the tens of thousands of new immigrants. For the first year or two they were employed on public works, mainly road building in the north. It was while working on the roads that various people banded together to form collective settlement groups such as the *Gedud ha-Avodah and the kibbutzim of Ha-Shomer Ha-Ẓa'ir. In 1920 the Jewish National Fund completed the purchase of 50,000 dunams of land in the Jezreel Valley – the "Emek," which was used for large-scale settlement. Some of the newcomers, as well as Second Aliyah veterans, were settled in the villages established in the Emek, which included kibbutzim and kevuẓot (En-Harod, Tel Yosef, Geva, Bet Alfa, Ḥefzi-Bah, Ginnosar as well as Kiryat Anavim near Jerusalem), and moshevei ovedim (Nahalal, Kefar Yeḥezkel). Others worked on construction sites in the cities, where a large part of the building was done by the Histadrut's Public Work Office (later reorganized under the name of *Solel Boneh). There was also a renewed attempt to introduce Jewish labor into the moshavot, where groups of workers sought employment with the Jewish farmers and prepared themselves for their own settlement on the land. In 1923 a severe economic crisis hit the *yishuv,* mainly affecting the newcomers. Thousands were unemployed and 3,200 people left the country, as against a total influx of 8,200 in the course of the year.

In all, the Third Aliyah brought in some 35,000 immigrants: 53% from Russia, 36% from Poland, and the rest from Lithuania, Romania, and other East European countries, apart from 800 from Western and Central Europe (Germany, Austria, Czechoslovakia, Hungary, etc.). The Jewish population reached 90,000 and the *yishuv* underwent a profound change, growing not only in size but also in quality. The new *yishuv* was now in the majority and the old *yishuv*'s efforts to resist the onset of modern trends were doomed to failure. For example, the attempt to deny women the right to vote in the elections to the Jewish community's representative institutions was defeated. Extremist elements in the old *yishuv* tried to combine as a political force and, in cooperation with the Arabs, oppose the new Jewish immigration; the attempt came to a tragic end with the assassination of their leader, Jacob de *Haan.

The thousands of new *ḥalutzim* also added considerable strength to the *Haganah, the self-defense organization formed in June 1920, when the riots in Jerusalem and Jaffa had demonstrated that the *yishuv* could not rely on the British authorities for their security. Members of the Third Aliyah continued to play an important role in the following years, as in the settlement of the Kishon region (1927) and the Ḥefer Plain (1933). Another feature of this period was the introduction of industry. The Silicate Brick Factory was founded in 1922, followed by the salt works at Athlit, the Grands Moulins flour mills, the Shemen edible oil factory, the Nesher cement works, etc.

The Fourth Aliyah. In the middle of 1924 a new wave of immigration, the Fourth Aliyah (1924–28), set in. It was different in social composition from its predecessor. There was a drop in the inflow of *ḥalutzim*, mainly because of the ban on departure from Soviet Russia. On the other hand, there was a rise in the immigration of middle-class people – shopkeepers and artisans – mostly from Poland. This was the result of two developments: the economic crisis in Poland and the economic restrictions imposed on the Polish Jews (hence the name "Grabski Aliyah" after the Polish finance minister); and the severe limitations on immigration to the United States, introduced in 1924 (when only 10,000 Jews emigrated to America, as against 34,000 who went to Palestine). Most of these newcomers, having no desire to change their way of life, settled in the towns, primarily in Tel Aviv, which had the special attraction of being an all-Jewish city. They invested some of their scanty capital in workshops and factories, small hotels, restaurants, and shops, but most of their investments were made in building. In 1925, when the Fourth Aliyah was at its height, 45% of Tel Aviv's labor force was employed on construction, and the city's population grew to 40,000. Haifa also developed (the Hadar ha-Carmel quarter being founded) and some progress was made in Jerusalem. The Slobodka Yeshivah was established in Hebron and the Nur match factory in Acre. The American Zion Commonwealth Company purchased land in the heart of the Jezreel Valley, where it planned the establishment of a central town, Ir Yizre'el ("Jezreel Town") later called Afulah.

There was also significant rural development in the Coastal Plain. The area under citrus cultivation was trebled within a few years, and new villages, based on citrus growing, were founded: Magdiel, Herzliyyah, Binyaminah, Pardes Ḥannah, a group of settlements in the Tel Mond area, in addition to Ra'anannah (founded in 1921). A new town, Netanyah, was founded in the Sharon Valley. In the new villages, the farmers employed Jewish labor for the most part. An interesting episode was the arrival of hundreds of ḥasidic families, headed by their rabbis, and their settlement on the land at Kefar Ḥasidim, near Haifa. In the course of two years, over 62,000 newcomers made their homes in the Land of Israel. It appeared that in addition to the settlement of *ḥalutzim*, financed by national capital, a way had been found to attract the Jewish middle class to agricultural and urban settlement, based on the import of private capital.

Crisis and Recovery 1926–1929. A downward turn came in the spring of 1926, when a severe economic crisis set in. Worsening economic conditions in Poland caused a cessation of the flow of capital from that country, and as a result, the great construction boom came to an end. In 1927 over 5,000 people left the country and only 2,300 came, while unemployment reached 7,000 in the summer of that year. The crisis, which lasted for two years and plunged many middle-class families into penury, was a severe political blow to Zionism and the labor movement. Thousands of workers subsisted on a dole from the Zionist Executive; Solel Boneh was temporarily dissolved; Gedud ha-Avodah, the pioneering labor organization established by the Third Aliyah, split into rightist and leftist factions and some of its members demonstratively went back to the Soviet Union, where they joined the Jewish agricultural settlement project in the Crimea.

The first signs of economic recovery came in 1929, when immigration was renewed. New hopes were aroused by the creation of the enlarged Jewish Agency, through which non-Zionist circles – notably a group of outstanding American Jews – were to associate themselves with the Zionist Organization's constructive work in Palestine. Despite the crises of 1923 and 1927, the balance for the ten years 1919–29 was positive. The population of the *yishuv* had almost trebled, reaching a total of 160,000. Over 1,200,000 dunams (300,000 acres) had been acquired, and an almost uninterrupted chain of towns and villages stretched from Metullah in the north to Be'er Toviyyah in the south. Hebrew had become the living tongue of the *yishuv* and its schools. A significant Hebrew literature, press, and theater (Habimah and Ohel) had come into being. The Hebrew University was opened in 1925 and the Haifa Technion had been officially inaugurated. The *yishuv* was recognized in 1927 as a corporate entity, *Keneset Israel, with its democratic institutions: Asefat ha-Nivḥarim (Assembly of Deputies); and *Va'ad Le'ummi (National Council), elected by the Assembly. Keneset Israel represented the entire Jewish population, except for the extreme Orthodox faction (see *Governance, the section on Jewish Communal Organizations, and *Political Life and Parties).

The Zionist Executive, with funds supplied by Jews abroad through the *Keren Hayesod, financed immigration, supported the Hebrew school system (the government spent most of its education budget on Arab schools), fostered agriculture, industry, and commerce, and coordinated the public health activities of the *Hadassah Medical Organization, Kuppat Ḥolim, and other bodies. Together with the Va'ad Le'ummi, it represented the Jews vis-à-vis the administration and performed, as far as the Jewish population was concerned, a large part of governmental functions. Thus the *yishuv,* as the vanguard of Jewry, was more than a local community; it had become the nucleus of the Jewish state-in-the-making.

Violence and Political Struggle, 1929–31. During the preceding ten months there had been minor disputes between Jews and Arabs about the Jews right to pray at the Western ("Wailing") Wall of the Temple Court in Jerusalem. These arguments were exploited by the mufti of Jerusalem, Hajj Amin al-Husseini, to foment religious hatred by accusing the Jews of designs upon the Muslim Holy Places in the city. On August 23, an Arab mob tried to attack the Jews in Jerusalem; the attacks were repeated on the following days, but were repulsed by the Haganah. (See also *Jerusalem; *Western Wall.) The violence spread to other parts of the country. On the Sabbath, August 24, the Arabs of Hebron fell upon the small defenseless Jewish community in the town, who belonged mainly to the old *yishuv,* and slaughtered some 70 men and women. Old people and infants were butchered, the survivors, numbering several hundred, being evacuated to Jerusalem. Attacks on Tel Aviv and the Jewish quarters in Haifa were repulsed, but on the fifth day of the riots an Arab mob killed 18 Jews and wounded many more in Safed before the Jews could take refuge in the police headquarters while the mob ransacked and burned the Jewish quarter. In Be'er Toviyyah all the settlers held out in a cowshed while the attacking mob plundered and destroyed the village. Huldah, too, was destroyed after the Jewish defenders had held out for many hours against thousands of Arabs and were evacuated by a British army patrol. Many of the attacks on Jewish settlements were repulsed, however. Before a week had passed, large detachments of British troops were brought in and order was restored, but the Arab nationalists had achieved their aim: the problem of Palestine had once again become the subject of political discussion.

A parliamentary commission of inquiry headed by Sir Walter Shaw, was sent to inquire into "the immediate causes" of the outbreak, but exceeded its terms of reference by dealing with questions of major policy. It found that the fundamental cause of the riots had been "the Arab feelings of animosity and hostility to the Jews consequent upon the disappointment of their political and national aspirations and fear for their economic future." Accordingly, the commission proposed restrictions on Jewish immigration and the purchase of lands from the Arabs. A minority report, by Harry Snell, the Labor Party representative, criticized government policy and the Arab attitude. In 1930, a British expert, Sir John Hope-Simpson, reported that "with the present methods of Arab cultivation" there was "no margin of land available for agricultural settlement by immigrants." In October of the same year, the colonial secretary, Lord Passfield (Sidney Webb) issued a White Paper further whittling down the meaning of the Balfour Declaration and the Mandate and foreshadowing fresh restrictions on Jewish immigration and settlement. Chaim *Weizmann, in protest, announced his resignation as chairman of the Jewish Agency, and prominent British statesmen denounced the new policy. Under the pressure of public opinion, the prime minister, Ramsay MacDonald, published a letter to Weizmann in February 1931 reinterpreting the White Paper in such a manner as to nullify its restrictions and make it possible to continue the upbuilding of the Jewish National Home. At the end of 1931 a new high commissioner, General Sir Arthur Wauchope, was appointed. A man of wide erudition and great vision, he showed understanding and sympathy for Jewish efforts in Palestine (see *Palestine, Inquiry Commissions, and *Palestine, White Papers).

The Fifth Aliyah Reaches Its Peak. The next four years were of decisive importance for the development of the *yishuv*. The Fifth Aliyah had begun with a small trickle in 1929, but in 1933, when Hitler rose to power in Germany, the trickle became a flood, and 164,267 Jews entered the country legally in the period 1933–36, while thousands of refugees came as "illegal" immigrants (the *yishuv* regarded British restrictions on *aliyah* as arbitrary and a violation of the Mandate). By the spring of 1936 the Jewish population in Palestine was close to 400,000 – some 30% of the total. The immigration was accompanied by a large influx of capital from Germany, as well as other countries. In these four years of "prosperity," private investment by Jews came to £31,570,000 sterling, over half of which was invested in construction, some £6 million in citrus culture and other forms of agriculture, and £7 million in industry. There was also a considerable rise in the amounts invested by the national funds.

The Fifth Aliyah also settled mostly in the cities and towns. Over half the newcomers made their homes in Tel Aviv, which by 1936 had become the largest city in Palestine with a population of 150,000 and a budget exceeding that of the 22 other municipalities put together. In Haifa, the construction of the country's first modern port by the British authorities was completed in 1933, and its Jewish population was trebled, reaching 50,000, about half the population of the city. Its Jewish quarters were built on the slopes of Mount Carmel, as well as on the sandy terrain in the north of the city (Kiryat Ḥayyim and the other *kerayot*). In Jerusalem a great building boom was initiated by former residents of the Old City, who left after the 1929 riots, and was continued by well-to-do immigrants, including German Jews, who expanded the Reḥaviah quarter. The development of the city was also greatly facilitated by the completion of the water supply line, based on the Rosh ha-Ayin springs. In 1936 Jerusalem had a Jewish population of 76,000 – 60% of the city's total population.

Progress in Industry and Agriculture. In the cities and their environs, modern industry came into being, based mainly on the production of food, textiles, and building materials. The Levant Fair, first held in Tel Aviv in 1932, and again in 1934 and 1936, helped to promote domestic and foreign trade. Two key companies, the Palestine Electric Corporation and the Palestine Potash Company, the concessions for which had been allotted by the British to Jews in the 1920s, were now working at full capacity, employing thousands of Jewish and Arab workers. There was a steady expansion of citrus culture: tens of thousands of dunams were planted and exports rose from 2½ million cases in 1931 to 15,300,000 in 1939, half of it from Jewish citrus groves. Agricultural settlement, however, lagged behind. After the 1929 riots, the settlements which had been hit were rehabilitated with the help of the Emergency Fund collected in Jewish communities abroad. About 20 new villages were established in the Ḥefer Plain, between Ḥaderah and Netanyah (Kefar Vitkin, Aviḥayil, Givat Ḥayyim, Ma'barot, etc.). New moshavim and kibbutzim based on the small budgets provided by the Zionist funds and on work in the citrus groves were also set up near the established moshavot.

Internal Changes and Controversies. There were also changes in the organizational structure of the *yishuv*. In 1932 the Hebrew school system was transferred from the Zionist Executive to the Va'ad Le'ummi, making the *yishuv* responsible for its own education. At the time the system included some 20,000 children, the number increasing to 100,000 by the establishment of independence (1948). It was divided into three "trends": general, religious, and labor. The status of the Haganah also underwent a significant change. The 1929 riots had demonstrated the organization's importance and thousands joined its ranks. A national leadership accepted by all sections was now a necessity, and in 1931 agreement was reached on the establishment of a National Command, consisting of three Histadrut delegates and three representatives of the non-labor sector. The Haganah developed into a nationwide underground organization, with branches in all Jewish towns and villages, running training courses for instructors, accumulating arms in its secret stores, and creating the beginnings of a military industry.

The labor movement played a central role in the life of the *yishuv*. In 1937, the Histadrut had a membership of 100,000 – about a quarter of the Jewish population, and there was a large labor party, *Mapai, which had been established by a merger of the main labor parties in 1930. The Histadrut's economic enterprises and social services made an important contribution to the transformation of the *yishuv* into a "state-on-the-way." Its kibbutzim and moshavim helped, not only to grow food, but also to widen the map of Jewish settlement and establish bases for defense. Solel Boneh, the cooperatives for industry, housing, transport and finance, and marketing agencies like Tnuva and Hamashbir, consolidated the *yishuv*'s economic base. The Histadrut's school system, labor exchanges, and social services – notably Kuppat Ḥolim – fulfilled quasi-governmental functions.

This organizational unity of labor was not matched by a similar concentration of non-labor forces (such as the Farmers Union, the Citzens' Bloc in Tel Aviv, etc.); all they had in common was fear of domination by the "left." At the beginning of the 1930s, the *Revisionist movement came into existence as a result of the differences between Weizmann and Jabotinsky over the policy of the Zionist Organization. Jabotinsky and his adherents engaged in a campaign designed to confront the power of the Histadrut and established a rival *Histadrut ha-Ovedim ha-Le'ummit (National Labor Federation). Revisionist-minded workers and immigrants competed for jobs and sometimes acted as strikebreakers. There was bitter tension between the two camps, which reached its climax in June 1933, when Chaim *Arlosoroff, one of the foremost labor leaders, was assassinated and members of the Revisionist movement were wrongly accused of the murder. The labor movement obtained key positions in the Jewish Agency, the Va'ad Le'ummi, and the Haganah, and remained the major political force in the *yishuv*.

Growth of the Arab National Movement. Among the Arab population there were also far-reaching changes. Jewish mass immigration benefited the Arabs in various ways: their economic situation improved, thousands of them found employment in the Jewish sector, and the land of the fellahin rose in value. Government revenue, supplied largely by the Jews, was used to create a public health service and a progressive school system for the Arabs. The prosperity of the Palestine Arabs became the envy of their brethren in Transjordan; in 1933, Emir Abdullah, the British-appointed ruler, and the Transjordanian tribal chiefs entered into secret negotiations with the Jewish Agency on the possibility of a large-scale Jewish immigration into their area, but the talks were nipped in the bud by British disapproval.

At the same time, however, the rise in Jewish strength and influence was accompanied by the growth of the Arab national movement. The 1929 disturbances had enhanced the prestige of the mufti of Jerusalem and made him the leading Arab figure in Palestine, and a Muslim conference that he called in 1931 added to his standing. In 1932 an Arab political party, Istiqlāl (Independence) came into being, headed by veteran leaders like ʿAwnī ʿAbd-al Hadī and supported by many of the younger generation. An extensive daily press, predominantly nationalist – even fascist – in character, was established and indulged in daily diatribes against the Jews. In 1931 a terrorist organization led by Sheikh ʿIzz al-Dīn al-Qassām was formed in Haifa and from time to time murdered individual Jews. The Arab nationalists tried to prevent Jews from purchasing land by intimidating prospective Arab sellers; they fomented land disputes and turned them into political issues, as in the case of the prolonged dispute between Jews and Bedouin over the Ḥefer Plain (1930–33).

In October 1933 the Arab Executive Committee called for demonstrations throughout the country against growing Jewish immigration. The demonstrations, which were directed against the British authorities, were firmly suppressed by the police and the military; some of the demonstrators were shot to death and others wounded. As a result the committee, which had shown itself as lacking in resolute leadership, lost its influence and disintegrated, giving way to political parties combining modern elements with the old feudal type of leadership. Terrorism also was renewed, and in November 1935 Sheikh ʿIzz al-Dīn al-Qassām's band was trapped by police on Mt. Gilboa and wiped out. The Arab nationalists glorified the fallen terrorists as martyrs for their country. Tension rose steadily. In October over 500 barrels containing arms for the Haganah had been seized in Jaffa port, and the Arab parties declared a general strike in protest against the acquisition of arms by Jews.

External events added to the growing tension. The Italian-Ethiopian war revealed the weakness of British policy; there were riots and strikes in Egypt and Syria, where Britain and France had to make concessions. The British government decided that the time had come to appease the Arab nationalists in Palestine as well. In December 1935 High Commissioner Wauchope revived the old plan for a legislative council, with limited powers, to consist of 14 Arabs, seven Jews, and seven British government officials and business representatives. This time it was the Jews who rejected the proposal, fearing that it would obstruct Jewish immigration and settlement in that tragic hour for European Jewry, while some Arab leaders favored acceptance. When the plan came up for discussion in the British Parliament, it was severely criticized, and the government decided to withdraw it. Instead, the Arabs were invited to send a delegation to London for political negotiations.

The Arab Revolt. On April 19, 1936, riots broke out in Jaffa. The funeral in Tel Aviv of two Jews killed by Arab terrorists had been turned into a demonstration, which was followed by the murder of two Arabs by Jews. It took the government two days to quell the riots. Sixteen Jews were killed and many wounded and Jewish property was ransacked and set ablaze, especially in the border area between Jaffa and Tel Aviv. The Arabs proclaimed a general strike and an assembly of Arab parties in Nablus elected an Arab Higher Committee, headed by the mufti. The committee announced that the strike would go on until the government fulfilled three demands: the stoppage of Jewish immigration; the prohibition of the transfer of land to Jewish ownership; the establishment of "a national representative government." Thus began the three-year period of disorder and violence known as the Arab Revolt.

The strike lasted for nearly six months, coming to an end on Oct. 12, 1936, in response to an appeal by the heads of Arab states. It failed to achieve its aims and the Arab Higher Committee's attempt to organize civil disobedience, based upon a strike of Arab civil servants and police, was not successful either. Shortly after the outbreak of the strike, a campaign of terror was initiated, beginning with the burning of Jewish property and going on to the murder of Jewish passersby and attacks on Jewish settlements, which were repulsed by the Haganah, and upon Jewish interurban transport. Eighty Jews fell victim to the terror in the period of the strike. In the hill regions armed bands of terrorists, with the support of the Arab population and the clandestine assistance of senior Arab officials and police officers, tried to attack Jewish settlements and convoys, as well as British police and army detachments. In August efforts were made to create a cohesive force out of the various terrorist bands, and a former Ottoman Arab army officer, Fawzī al-Kaukji, was invited to undertake the task. By then the British had brought in large military forces and launched a large-scale attack upon the terrorists, using planes and light tanks. When the general strike came to an end, Kaukji left the country.

The Partition Proposal. The British government was not prepared to meet the demands of the Arab Higher Committee and sent out a royal commission, headed by Lord Peel, to institute a thorough inquiry into the problems of the country. The commission heard a host of witnesses – British, Jewish, and Arab – and published its findings at the beginning of July 1937. These included a revolutionary proposal: to partition Palestine into two states: a Jewish state, which would consist of the whole of Galilee and the coastal strip, up to a point south of Reḥovot; and an Arab state, which would comprise Samaria, Judea, and the entire Negev. Jerusalem and its environs, linked to the coast at Jaffa by a corridor, was to remain in British hands, for the supervision of the Holy Places (see *Palestine, Inquiry Commissions; *Palestine, Partition). The British government announced its readiness to carry out the partition plan, but opinions were divided among both Jews and Arabs. Weizmann, David Ben-Gurion, and Moshe Shertok (later *Sharett) supported the plan, while Ussishkin, Jabotinsky, and Berl *Katznelson opposed it. Among the Arabs it was Emir Abdullah who favored partition, hoping to incorporate the Arab portion into his kingdom and thus create a large Arab state which would cooperate with the Jewish state in economic affairs. In any event, the Arab Higher Committee rejected the plan and insisted on the fulfillment of its own demands.

After the end of the general strike, an uneasy calm had prevailed, sporadically broken by outbreaks of Arab terror, but in September 1937, two months after the publication of the commission's report, the disturbances were renewed. At the end of the month the British district commissioner in Galilee, Andrews, was murdered; the government retaliated by disbanding the Arab Higher Committee, arresting its leaders, and expelling them to the Seychelles Islands; but the mufti escaped to Syria, from where he continued to direct the terror. The armed bands resumed their operations on a large scale, although no attempt was made to organize them into a unified military force. Their leaders took control of large areas and instituted a regime of terror against their Arab opponents. Attacks upon the Jews were also stepped up: 415 Jews were killed by the terrorists in the period 1937–39, over half of them between July and October 1938. Nevertheless, the terrorists failed, with very few exceptions, to break into Jewish towns or villages.

In the summer of 1938 the Arab Revolt reached its climax. Terrorist bands captured police stations and broke into Arab towns; for a short while, in October, they held the Old City of Jerusalem (except for the Jewish quarter), though they were easily driven out by British military forces. Then, however, the Revolt began to decline. The British had concentrated large forces, about 16,000 troops, to combat the terrorist bands. The Arab population had also wearied of the murder and blackmail perpetrated by the terrorists, who had been responsible for more Arab than Jewish and British victims. "Peace bands" set up among the Arabs received arms from the British and joined the fight against the terrorists. By the spring of 1939 the Revolt had come to an end.

The 1939 White Paper. At the end of 1938, however, British policy underwent a significant change. After the Munich agreement between Britain, France, Italy, and Nazi Germany (1938), the British came to the conclusion that the Arab world had to be appeased, whatever the price, lest it join Britain's enemies in the event of a world war. On Nov. 9, 1938, the government announced the abandonment of the partition plan and invited Jewish and Arab leaders, including representatives of the Arab states, to a round-table conference in London. The Arab refused to meet the Jews, and in fact there were two conferences, the British meeting separately with Arabs and Jews. No agreement was reached at these talks. On May 17, 1939, the British colonial secretary, Malcolm MacDonald, published a new White Paper that went a long way toward accepting Arab demands. Immigration was to be restricted to 10,000 a year for a period of five years, bringing the Jewish population to a third of the total, after which further immigration would depend upon Arab consent. As a special gesture, 25,000 additional immigration certificates were promised for Jewish refugees in Europe. The sale of land to Jews was to be severely restricted. Finally, the White Paper provided for the establishment within ten years, circumstances permitting, of an independent Palestine state, which would maintain strategic and economic links with Britain.

The British government immediately began to apply the White Paper policy. A reduced immigration schedule was issued for the period May–September 1939. For the six months October 1939 to March 1940 – after the start of World War II – no immigration certificates at all were allotted for Jews on the ground that there had been a large influx of "illegal" immigration. In February 1940 the Land Transfer Regulations envisioned in the White Paper were duly enacted, dividing the country into three zones: Zone A (the hills of Judea and Samaria, Western Galilee and the Northern Negev) in which the sale of land to Jews was completely prohibited; Zone B (Jezreel Valley, Eastern Galilee, and most of the Coastal Plain) in which the sale of land required the approval of the high commissioner; and Zone C (the coastal strip from Zikhron Ya'akov to a point north of Reḥovot, as well as urban areas) in which no restrictions applied. Thus it seemed that the Arab national movement had scored a significant achievement. Yet for the extremists among them, headed by the mufti, this was not enough. By this time, they had tied themselves to the enemies of Britain, mainly to Nazi Germany, in the hope that with their help they would be able to destroy the *yishuv.*

Jewish Defense and Resistance. The three years of the Arab Revolt had been a severe test for the *yishuv,* but despite the uncertain political and security conditions, it grew in numbers, and a total of 60,000 legal and "illegal" immigrants (the latter known in Hebrew as *ma'pilim*) entered the country during the period. Although some branches of the Jewish economy suffered from the Arab boycott, others were strengthened by it. The moshavot now employed Jewish labor, and Jews filled jobs abandoned by the Arabs in ports, quarries, etc. Thousands of people were employed by the various bodies set up for the *yishuv*'s defense. There was a rise in the income of the national funds and a spectacular growth in agricultural settlement, which absorbed many of the new immigrants. In growing measure, the *yishuv* was able to supply its own vegetables, fruit, eggs, and other food. In summer 1936 a port was constructed in Tel Aviv as a result of the strike in Jaffa port, thus opening a Jewish door to the world.

The paramount problem was security. The Haganah developed into a military force that bore the responsibility for the *yishuv*'s safety, and a general staff was set up. From the beginning of the riots, the Jewish Agency had called for self-restraint (*havlagah*) by the *yishuv*, as well as self-defense (*hagannah*): no blind revenge or indiscriminate killing but appropriate defensive measures, including active operations against terrorist bands. All the Jewish villages were fortified with barbed-wire fences, strongpoints, and searchlights; wherever necessary they were reinforced with fighting men. Inter-settlement communications were ensured by armed escorts for individual vehicles and convoys and by the construction of new roads. Ambushes were set outside the settlement perimeter for marauding gangs who sought to destroy the crops.

Through the Jewish Agency, close – albeit unofficial – links were established between the Haganah and the British security forces. A force of Jewish special police (also known by the Arab-Turkish term *Ghafirs*) equipped with uniforms and arms by the police (some of its members received regular pay) guarded railroads, air-fields, and government offices. The Jewish Settlement Police (JSP) was set up to protect the Jewish villages and comprised, by the end of the period, ten district battalions, with mobile patrols equipped with armored cars and Lewis guns. The creation of these forces was tantamount to de facto legalization of the Haganah, to which most of the men belonged.

During this period, the Haganah also formed "field companies" (*peluggot sadeh*), which were trained for action against the terrorists beyond the perimeter of the settlements, and by the summer of 1938 held a continuous line along the borders of the Jewish areas, preventing the incursions of terrorist bands. In cooperation with the British Army, Special Night Squads (SNS) were established, consisting of regular British troops and members of the Haganah. Commanded and trained by Capt. Orde *Wingate, they used guerrilla tactics against the Arab terrorists and succeeded in clearing them out of a wide area in Eastern Galilee.

Agricultural settlement, which had not been halted by the disturbances, was stepped up further when the Royal Commission made its proposal for the partition of the country, for it was clear that the borders of the Jewish state would be determined by the extent of Jewish settlement. Some 50 new settlements, most kibbutzim, were established in areas where no Jewish settlements had previously existed: in the Beth-Shean Valley, Mount Carmel, Western Galilee, etc. In the initial stage, these *stockade and watch-tower settlements were organized as armed camps in hostile territory, and the members, all belonging to the Haganah, lived like soldiers until the Arabs around had become used to their presence. The Arab terrorists repeatedly attacked these outposts, e.g., Tirat Ẓevi in February and Ḥanitah in March 1938, but failed to dislodge them. The high costs of security were met by a voluntary tax, *Kofer ha-Yishuv*, which the Jewish population imposed upon itself.

Throughout this period the Haganah continued to strengthen its underground forces. Arms manufacture was developed under a secret agreement with Polish governmental circles. *Ḥalutzim* were given military training before emigration, and large quantities of light arms were purchased. The Jewish Agency's *havlagah* policy was opposed by the *Irgun Ẓeva'i Le'ummi (IẒL), a group which had seceded from the Haganah and was associated with the Revisionists. The IẒL engaged in terrorism against Arab civilians, which increased in scope in the summer of 1938 after the British had hanged one of its members, Shlomo *Ben-Yosef, who had taken part in an abortive attack against an Arab bus near Rosh Pinnah. The majority of the *yishuv* opposed their methods.

The worsening situation of the Jews in Europe brought about a renewal of "illegal"*immigration, known as Aliyah Bet ("Class B Immigration"), which was organized by He-Ḥalutz and the Revisionist movement. After the annexation of Austria and Czechoslovakia by Nazi Germany (1938–39), Aliyah Bet swelled with its own momentum and became a significant factor in immigration: by the outbreak of World War II, 15,000 Jews had entered the country in this manner. An underground body, known as the Mosad and linked to the Haganah, was set up at the end of 1938 to organize and coordinate the clandestine influx. The anti-Jewish switch in British policy at the end of 1938 caused great bitterness in the *yishuv*, exacerbated by the severe measures employed against the "illegal" boats, some of which were fired on and forced back into the open seas with their human cargo. From time to time strikes and protest demonstrations were held. On May 17, 1939 – the date on which the White Paper was published – a general strike was called and mass demonstrations took place in all Jewish towns and villages. The Haganah formed a special unit to attack telephone lines, railroads, and other government property.

War Breaks Out – Repression Continues. The outbreak of World War II raised expectations of a change in British policy, in view of the *yishuv*'s readiness to cooperate in the fight against the common enemy, as reflected in the immediate registration of 136,000 volunteers, almost the entire Jewish population between the ages of 18 and 50, for national service. It was hoped that the White Paper policy would at least be suspended for the duration of the war. These hopes, however, were soon disappointed. The Mandatory government, headed by the high commissioner Harold MacMichael (1938–44) persisted in its campaign against the refugee boats arriving from Europe. When it became apparent that the internment of the refugees would not stop the flow, the government decided to deport them. In November 1940 the first deportation ship, the *Patria*, was about to sail for *Mauritius with 1,700 people aboard when it was sabotaged by the Haganah to prevent its departure. By a tragic mischance the boat sank and 250 refugees were drowned in Haifa Bay. Soon afterwards, the government deported another group of 1,645 refugees to the island. In February 1942 the *Struma*, carrying refugees from Romania, was turned back by the Turkish authorities when the British government had made it clear that the Jews would not be permitted to land in Palestine. The ship foundered in the Black Sea and 770 refugees lost their lives.

The beginning of the war also coincided with the introduction of repressive measures against the Haganah. In October 1939, 43 of its members, some of whom had served with the SNS during the Arab Revolt, were arrested while participating in an officers' training course and sentenced to five years' imprisonment. Searches for arms were conducted in many Jewish villages. The Jewish Agency's demand for the formation of Jewish military units was rejected: only a few hundred specialists were taken on to bring the British units up to strength, and several companies of the Auxiliary Military Pioneer Corps were formed, the first of these being sent to the front in France. In May 1940, after the Haganah-organized demonstrations and riots in protest against the Land Transfer Regulations, the British military commander demanded the surrender of the Haganah's arms. The first months of the war also caused a severe economic crisis, as a result of the sudden rupture of foreign trade.

The Yishuv and the War Effort, 1940–1942. Some changes took place after Italy's entry into the war in June 1940. The arms searches and arrests were halted and relations between the British authorities and the *yishuv* took a turn for the better. The Middle East became a huge military base. Volunteer men and women were accepted for service and transportation units in the British army which gradually became Jewish units also included women with, for the most part, Jewish officers in command. They rendered important service in Libya, Egypt, Ethiopia, Greece (where a thousand Jewish volunteers were taken prisoner by the Germans), and Crete. In September 1940 a new stage was reached with the formation of Palestinian Jewish and Arab companies of the Buffs, a British infantry regiment, which were to do garrison duty in Palestine; by the end of 1942 the Jewish companies had become three Jewish infantry battalions. Jews also served in antiaircraft units in Haifa and Cyprus. By the end of the war 26,620 Jews from Palestine had joined the British forces, including 4,000 women in the ATS and the WAAF.

The later war years brought about a radical change in the Jewish economy. The isolation of the Middle East from Europe facilitated a great economic advance, based largely on the requirements of the large military forces in the area. There was a significant increase in agricultural production and food processing and a considerable expansion of industry – especially in metals. Jewish scientists and technicians made important contributions to the supply of the forces' needs. There was a glaring contrast between the Jewish participation in the Allied war effort and the attitude of the Arabs, most of whom were indifferent to the outcome of the war, while a substantial number, headed by the exiled mufti, favored an alliance with the Nazis. The mufti and some of his aides went to Germany in 1941, participated in the plans for the destruction of European Jewry, and did all in their power to help the German propaganda machine.

In November 1942 the Zionist General Council approved the *Biltmore Program, which had been formulated earlier in the year by the American Zionist movement on David Ben-Gurion's initiative. It urged "that the gates of Palestine be opened, that the Jewish Agency be vested with the control of immigration into Palestine and with the necessary authority for the upbuilding of the country, and that Palestine be established as a Jewish Commonwealth integrated in the structure of the new democratic world." In the period 1941–42 there was a change in the British attitude toward the Haganah. In May 1941 the Haganah established the *Palmaḥ which in a short time became its regular full-time force. As the German threat to the Middle East became more acute, the Haganah was called in to assist in the invasion of Syria. A joint plan, the "Palestine Scheme," was prepared with the British for the creation of a resistance movement in case Palestine was occupied by the Germans, and hundreds of members of the Palmaḥ were trained by British officers in sabotage and commando tactics.

Relations Deteriorate Again, 1943–1945. When the war front receded at the end of 1942, however, relations between the British and the *yishuv* took a turn for the worse. This was a reflection of the struggle that was being waged between the makers of British Middle East policy and pro-Zionist elements in Britain. The British encouraged the creation of the *Arab League, in which all the Arab states took part and which at its first conferences (October 1944–March 1945) pledged its members to defend the rights of Palestine Arabs. On the other hand, the British Prime Minister Winston Churchill, the British Labor Party, and various British statesmen had promised a change in British policy in favor of the Jews at the end of the war. To many observers, the first sign of such change seemed to be the establishment of the *Jewish Brigade Group in 1944. It consisted of Jewish infantry, artillery, and service units from Palestine and took part in the final battles of the war on the Italian front in the spring of 1945. At the same time, however, the Palestine government stepped up its campaign against the Haganah. Political trials were staged at which the organization was accused of acquiring arms from British arsenals, and searches were made for arms in the kibbutzim, meeting with passive resistance on the part of the members, as at Ramat ha-Kovesh.

At the beginning of 1944 the IẒL, headed by Menahem *Begin, embarked upon a series of armed attacks on government and police installations in order to exert pressure upon the government to change its policy. In October of that year 251 men suspected of belonging to Jewish terrorist organizations were deported to an internment camp in Eritrea. Relations between the British and the Jews were seriously impaired by the murder of Lord Moyne, the British minister of state in the Middle East, on Nov. 6, 1944, by members of *Loḥamei Ḥerut Israel (Leḥi, called by the British the "Stern Gang") – an underground group that had seceded from IẒL in 1940 – which, from the beginning of the war, had adopted a violent anti-British attitude and even sought contact with the Italians and Germans. This act stood in contrast with the general policy of the *yishuv*, which hoped that the end of the war would bring about a better understanding with the British, and the Jewish national institutions called upon the dissident organizations to put a halt to their activities. When the IẒL refused, the Haganah took repressive measures against it in what was euphemistically called the "Saison." There was an impassioned controversy in the *yishuv* over the surrender to the British authorities of some IẒL members arrested by the Haganah.

It was not until the end of 1942 that the *yishuv* became aware of the appalling tragedy of European Jewry, and great efforts were made to help and rescue the Jews of Europe. The British, however, regarded these efforts as a violation of the White Paper policy and did all they could to obstruct them. Eventually a way was found to transfer several thousand Jewish refugees who had reached Istanbul to Palestine. Another project – to drop Haganah parachutists into occupied European countries, where they would rouse Jewish youth to resistance against the Nazis – was severely restricted in scope by the British. Only 32 such volunteers reached various European countries in the period 1943–44, and seven of them lost their lives.

Throughout the war years agricultural settlement continued to grow. Forty new villages were established in various parts of the country; among them were Bet ha-Aravah in the Dead Sea area, Kefar Eẓyon in the Hebron Hills, ten settlements in the southern Shephelah, and three (Revivim, Gevulot, and Bet Eshel) in the northern Negev; which inaugurated Jewish agricultural settlement in that area.

Postwar Disappointment. When the war came to an end, the *yishuv* expected a radical change in British policy. Above all, it expected the gates of the country to be reopened to large-scale Jewish immigration. A few hundred thousand European Jews had survived the Holocaust in German labor camps, in the forests and other hiding places, or as refugees in the eastern parts of the Soviet Union. As they had lost their families and were unable to go back to the scene of their tragic experiences, they made their way to the *Displaced Persons camps established by the Allies in Germany, Austria, and Italy. Essentially, this was a spontaneous mass movement, but it was guided and organized by the *Beriḥah ("Flight") organization, a clandestine body headed by emissaries from Palestine. The DP's received aid from general refugee agencies (UNRRA and later IRO) and Jewish organizations (the *American Jewish Joint Distribution Committee and a delegation from the *yishuv*), but their main goal was to leave Europe at the earliest possible moment and settle in the Land of Israel. The problem of the refugees troubled the military authorities in Europe, and in August 1945 President Truman appealed to the British prime minister, Clement *Attlee, to permit the immigration of 100,000 Jews into Palestine.

The election victory of the British Labor Party, which had always adhered to a pro-Zionist policy, increased hopes for a favorable change in the political position of the *yishuv*, but it soon became clear that a positive solution to the Palestine problem was still far away. Anti-Zionist forces exerted great pressure on the British government to prevent any deviation from the White Paper policy, and it was obvious that Attlee and Ernest *Bevin, the new foreign secretary, intended to maintain, or even intensify, the anti-Zionist line. In order to demonstrate its refusal to accept this state of affairs, in the fall of 1945 the *yishuv* organized the Jewish Resistance Movement, which was run by the Haganah in cooperation with the IẒL and Leḥi. The movement carried out its first operation on Oct. 10, 1945, when a Palmaḥ unit attacked the Athlit internment camp and liberated the 208 "illegal" immigrants who were held there. The Mosad, in turn, renewed the organization of clandestine immigration from Europe. A few boats got through, but the British soon tightened security measures along the coast using all available means, including aerial patrols and coastal radar installations. On Nov. 22, 1945, a boat named *Berl Katznelson* was intercepted, and thereafter most of the refugee boats were apprehended on the high seas and their passengers interned. Each such event caused an uproar in the country and strengthened the *yishuv*'s determination to offer active resistance to the government's policy.

On Nov. 1, 1945, the Jewish Resistance Movement showed its strength by launching a major attack on railroads all over the country and sinking several coastal patrol launches. A fortnight later the British foreign secretary Ernest Bevin, in a long-awaited statement, in effect repudiated his party's pro-Zionist commitments. He announced the despatch of an Anglo-American Commission to Palestine and Europe to inquire into the problem of Jewish refugees. In the meantime, Jewish immigration would continue at a rate of 1,500 per month, beyond the limit laid down in the White Paper, but the "illegal" immigrants would be deducted from the quota.

Struggle and Repression, 1946–1947. The *yishuv* entered upon a long struggle against the British. "Illegal" boats continued to arrive. Two of them, the *Dov Hos* and the *Eliyahu Golomb*, with 1,000 passengers aboard, were ready to sail from the Italian coast at La Spezia when the British military authorities tried to prevent their departure. This attempt, and the ensuing hunger strike by the refugee passengers, roused world opinion, and the British were forced to let them in. Palmaḥ,

IẒL, and Leḥi units continued their attacks upon British police posts, coast guard stations, radar installations, and airfields. There were also frequent violent clashes between the security forces and Jewish demonstrators. This was the atmosphere in the country when the Anglo-American Commission arrived, after visiting the DP camps in Europe. Its report, submitted to the two governments on May 1, 1946, recommended the speedy admission of 100,000 Jewish refugees (see *Palestine, Inquiry Commissions). The British government rejected this recommendation and the Resistance Movement responded on June 17 by blowing up the bridges linking Palestine with the neighboring states.

The government reacted to this attack on June 29, 1946 ("Black Saturday"), by arresting the members of the Jewish Agency Executive who were in the country at the time, sending military forces to dozens of settlements suspected of harboring Palmaḥ units, and conducting exhaustive searches for arms caches, discovering a large one at Yagur. Similar searches took place in the following days and it was obvious that, apart from looking for arms, the military were also trying to do extensive damage. Thousands of persons suspected of being members of the Palmaḥ were interned in camps at Rafa. There was also a further aggravation of the policy towards the "illegal" boats, all refugees apprehended on their way to Palestine being taken to Cyprus and interned there. Tension reached new heights when, on July 22, 1946, the IẒL blew up the central government offices in the King David Hotel in Jerusalem and 91 people were killed – government officials and civilians, Britons, Jews, and Arabs. The Jewish Agency ordered a halt in the armed operations against the British, but IẒL and Leḥi refused to obey.

The government's aim had been to break up the Haganah and bring about the formation of a new, more moderate Jewish leadership, but it soon realized that this objective could not be achieved. In November 1946, the interned Jewish leaders were set free. At the beginning of 1947 negotiations were opened with Jewish and Arab representatives, to whom the British government submitted a new proposal (the Morrison-Grady Plan) providing for the division of Palestine into three sectors, Jewish, Arab and British (the latter including Jerusalem and the Negev), with the British retaining supreme control for another four years. Both Jews and Arabs rejected this proposal, and in February 1947 the British government announced that it was handing over the Palestine problem to the United Nations.

Throughout 1947 tension continued to rise and there was no end to the acts of terror. The IẒL and Leḥi now attacked the military, in addition to government installations. Their most spectacular operation was the liberation of some of their comrades by a daring attack upon the Acre fortress prison. The government's response was further repressive measures and the execution, by hanging, of seven IẒL and Leḥi men, to which the IẒL retaliated by hanging two British sergeants who had fallen into their hands. The transfer of refugees in Haifa port to the British boats, which were to take them to Cyprus, was accompanied by passive resistance and mass demonstrations; on several occasions, special Palmaḥ units succeeded in sabotaging the boats. In July 1947, when the *Exodus 1947* arrived in Haifa with 4,500 refugees aboard, the government decided to force it to return to its French port of departure. There, however, the refugees refused to disembark, and the British took the boat to Hamburg in their occupation zone, where the passengers were forcibly taken off and returned to the soil of Germany. The *Exodus* affair had a profound effect on world public opinion and reinforced the British decision to give up the Mandate. The feeling that a decisive hour was fast approaching impelled the *yishuv* to step up its settlement activities. The establishment of 11 new settlements in the Negev in a single night (the night after the Day of Atonement, Oct. 15, 1946), was to be decisive in securing the inclusion of the Negev in the area allotted to the Jewish state. By the end of 1947 the Jewish population in Palestine was 630,000 – about a third of the total.

The UN Recommends Partition. In May 1947 the Palestine problem came before a special session of the UN General Assembly. To the surprise of all, the Soviet delegate, Andre Gromyko, expressed his government's support for the right of the Jews to establish their own state in Palestine. An international committee, the United Nations Special Committee on Palestine (UNSCOP), was appointed to study the problem and submit recommendations for a solution. After investigating the position in Palestine and in the DP camps, the committee unanimously resolved that the Mandate should be terminated. The majority recommended the partition of Palestine into two independent states – Jewish and Arab – joined by an economic union, with Jerusalem and its environs as an international zone, while the minority proposed the establishment of a federative binational state. On Nov. 29, 1947, the General Assembly accepted the majority recommendation by a vote of 33 to 13 with 10 abstentions. The Jewish state was to consist of Eastern Galilee, the northern part of the Jordan Valley, the Beth-Shean and Jezreel Valleys, the coastal strip from a point south of Acre to a point south of Reḥovot, and the whole of the central and eastern Negev, including Umm Rash Rash (later Eilat) on the Red Sea. Jerusalem and its environs were to have an international regime; the remaining parts of the country were to form the Arab state. The British government announced that it would not cooperate in the execution of the partition plan and would withdraw British civilian staff and military forces by May 15, 1948. The *yishuv* received the news of the impending withdrawal with immense satisfaction; the Palestine Arab leaders and the Arab states announced their rejection of the UN decision and their determination to solve the problem by force (see *Palestine, Inquiry Commissions, and *Partition Palestine).

The Fighting Begins. On the morrow of the UN vote, there were outbreaks of Arab violence. On November 30 a bus was fired on and five Jews were killed. The Arabs proclaimed a general strike and the next day an Arab mob attacked the

Commercial Quarter, a mixed Jewish-Arab neighborhood in Jerusalem adjoining the Old City. The British police stood idly by, while the Haganah was unprepared, and within a few hours the quarter went up in flames. The riots soon spread to all parts of the country. At first they were similar in character to the 1936–39 Arab Revolt, except that now the Jews were alone in facing the armed Arab bands. The Arabs began to organize under local leaders such as ʿAbd al-Qādir al-Husseini in the Jerusalem hills. The Arab states, as yet unable to intervene directly because of the presence of British forces, gave the Palestinian Arabs financial support and encouraged the infiltration of Arab volunteers, which the British did nothing to prevent. Some of the volunteers were organized in the Liberation Army, commanded by Fawzī al-Kaukji (see under Israel, State of: Historical Survey, 1880–1948, from the section The Arab Revolt onwards). The *War of Independence had, in effect, begun.

The defense of the *yishuv* became the sole responsibility of the Haganah. In addition to ensuring the safety of the Jewish population in town and country, it had to keep communications open. Special difficulties were encountered in maintaining contact with isolated Jewish villages, such as those in Upper and Western Galilee and in the Negev, and the four villages of the Eẓyon Bloc in the Hebron Hills. A crucial problem was contact with Jewish Jerusalem, besieged by Arab bands who tried to cut if off from the rest of the country. There were heavy casualties in the fight for the maintenance of communications during the early months of the fighting; serious losses were sustained, for example, by the convoys to Ben Shemen, the Eẓyon Bloc, Yeḥi'am, and, above all, to Jerusalem. Strict rationing of food and water had to be introduced in the capital, which also suffered from large-scale bomb outrages, such as the Ben-Yehuda Street explosion and the blowing up of the *Palestine Post* premises, perpetrated by Arabs with the aid of British army deserters. At the beginning it was the Palmaḥ units, already trained and mobilized in three brigades, that bore the brunt of the struggle. In the course of the riots and the war, six more brigades were set up: Golani and Carmeli in the North; Alexandroni, Kiryati, and Givati in the coastal area; and Eẓyoni in Jerusalem. Air, naval, and artillery forces were created from scratch. General mobilization of all able-bodied men was ordered, and by the time the State of Israel was declared (May 14), 51,500 people were serving in the Jewish armed forces. The major problem confronting the *yishuv* was the lack of arms, which prevented the proper development of operations. It was not until the beginning of April that large consignments arrived, mainly from Czechoslovakia, bringing about an immediate and radical improvement in the armament situation.

Preparations for Independence. In this initial period, when the very existence of the *yishuv* was at stake, the world had grave doubts as to the Jews' ability to hold out. On March 19, 1948, the United States withdrew its support of the Partition Plan and proposed instead a UN Trusteeship over Palestine to last until Jews and Arabs reached agreement. The U.S. State Department brought pressure to bear on the Jewish Agency and the *yishuv* to postpone the establishment of independence, but the Zionist General Council decided in the middle of April to go ahead with all preparations to set up the Jewish state on the departure of the British. A People's Council of 37 members, representing all parties and sections, and a People's Administration of 13, headed by David Ben-Gurion, were set up to act as an unofficial provisional legislature and government.

At the same time there was a radical change in the course of the fighting. The Haganah seized the initiative, rapidly establishing its hold on the entire area allotted to the Jewish state and ensuring its territorial continuity. On April 3, 1948, in Operation Naḥshon – the first in which a full brigade was employed – the road to Jerusalem was cleared by occupying Arab villages and areas on both sides of the road, and large convoys of food and reinforcements were rushed through to the beleaguered city. On April 9, a combined IẒL and Leḥi group attacked the Arab village of Deir Yasīn, west of Jerusalem, and many of its civilian inhabitants were killed – an event which greatly served Arab anti-Jewish propaganda and increased the panic among the Arab population. Kaukji's forces launched a major attack upon Mishmar ha-Emek (April 4), aiming at a breakthrough which would clear the way to Haifa, but were completely routed. On April 11 Safed was cleared of Arab forces. On April 14, Arab terrorists ambushed a convoy of Jewish doctors, nurses, and teachers on their way to the Hadassah hospital in Mt. Scopus – 78 persons were killed. Jewish forces took Tiberias on April 18 and on April 22 the Haganah, after a brief battle with local Arab forces, occupied the whole of Haifa.

Hundreds of thousands of Arabs fled from the areas occupied by the Jewish forces. The mass flight was encouraged by the Arab leadership, which spread atrocity stories about the behavior of the Jewish forces and their intentions toward the Arab inhabitants. On the eve of the British departure, the Haganah seized most of New Jerusalem, but the Jewish quarter in the Old City was cut off and besieged by the Arab legion, a Jordanian force commanded by British officers. The Legion attacked the Eẓyon Bloc with its tanks and overran it on May 13. On the same day Jaffa surrendered to the Haganah after the attack on the town by the IẒL. By the middle of May, the *yishuv* had suffered about 2,500 fatal casualties, almost half of them among the civilian population.

On May 14, 1948, the day preceding the end of British rule, the People's Council convened in the Tel Aviv Museum and approved the Proclamation of Independence, which declared the establishment of the State of Israel.

[Yehuda Slutsky]

From Independence to the Six-Day War

THE END OF THE MANDATORY REGIME. The Declaration of Independence began by explaining the justification for the establishment of the Jewish State at that moment of history. It recalled the shaping of the Jewish people and their culture in the Land of Israel, their unbroken attachment to the land in dispersion, and their return in recent generations to found a thriving and self-reliant society. The right of the Jewish people to national restoration in their land, the declaration continued, was voiced by the First Zionist Congress, acknowledged in the Balfour Declaration, confirmed in the League of Nations Mandate, and now irrevocably recognized by the United Nations. "By virtue of our natural and historic right and of the resolution of the General Assembly of the United Nations," the People's Council proclaimed the establishment of "a Jewish State in the Land of Israel – the State of Israel." From the concluding moment of the Mandate, at midnight on May 14/15, 1948, the council was to act as the Provisional Council of State and the 13-member People's Administration as the provisional government. The declaration concluded by proclaiming the basic principles on which the State of Israel was to be founded, undertaking to cooperate with the United Nations in carrying out the resolution of Nov. 29, 1947, calling upon the Arabs in Israel and the neighboring states to cooperate with the independent Jewish nation in its land, and appealing to the entire Jewish people to join forces with the State of Israel in its constructive efforts.

At the same meeting the council resolved by acclamation that all legal provisions deriving from the 1939 White Paper – particularly the restrictions on Jewish immigration and land purchase – were null and void. Subject to this decision, the law presently in force would remain valid until amended, with such changes as followed from the establishment of the state and its authorities. The provisional government was empowered to enact emergency legislation. At midnight, a few hours later, the last British high commissioner, Sir Alan Cunningham, left Haifa on board a British destroyer. The Mandate was over. At 00:11 A.M. on May 15, U.S. President Truman recognized the provisional government "as the de facto authority of the new State of Israel." Three days later the Soviet Union (as well as Guatemala) granted the new state de jure recognition. During the first month of its existence, nine more countries recognized Israel: five Communist, three Latin American, and South Africa.

THE ARAB STATES JOIN IN THE ATTACK: MAY 15–JUNE 11, 1948. During the night of May 14/15, Tel Aviv was bombarded by Egyptian planes. The attempt by the Arab states to crush Israel at birth had begun. Ben-Gurion, who was in charge of defense, and Ya'-akov *Dori (Dostrovosky), the Haganah chief of staff, could look back on substantial military achievements. Four of the towns with mixed Jewish-Arab population were in Jewish hands; Acre was encircled; Jewish Jerusalem held out, and some of its adjacent Arab quarters had been taken. The Haganah held crucial strong points on the road to the capital from Tel Aviv. About 100 Arab villages had fallen; western and eastern Galilee were cleared of enemy forces; the roads to the north and the Negev were open. Local Arab armed contingents had been crushed, and Kaukji's Liberation Army had suffered severe reverses. Israel had 30,000 fully armed men in the field; the IẒL and Leḥi forces were placed under Haganah command, though both maintained their autonomy in Jerusalem. To reinforce the three Palmaḥ and six other brigades, artillery units were being organized around nuclei of World War II veterans. With the aid of Jewish volunteers from abroad (*Maḥal), Israelis who had served with the RAF, and pilots trained by the Palmaḥ, the tiny air force was expanded. A small navy, similarly manned, had also been founded. Two more brigades – the 7th, consisting mainly of new immigrants, and Oded, made up mainly of men from the Palmaḥ and the kibbutzim – were set up. On May 26 the provisional government issued an ordinance establishing the Israel Defense Forces – Ẓeva Haganah le-Israel (the second word in the name marking the nexus between the IDF and the pre-state militia) and forbidding the maintenance of any other armed force. On the other hand, the exhausted Israel forces, which at first did not have a single tank, fighter plane, or field gun and had suffered heavy casualties, faced fresh, organized troops, equipped with tanks, artillery, and fighting craft. In the north, the Syrians invaded in two columns, one advancing down the Jordan Valley toward Deganyah and the other in Eastern Galilee in the direction of Mishmar ha-Yarden. The former offensive was repulsed, but the other column succeeded in taking Mishmar ha-Yarden on June 10, a day before a truce was declared. The Lebanese, after linking up with Kaukji's irregulars, were content to help him maintain a large pocket in Central Galilee.

In the center, the Transjordanian Arab Legion, which, despite repeated British promises, had not been withdrawn before the end of the Mandate, had taken up positions in and around Jerusalem and together with Iraqi troops, in the "Triangle" area marked by the Arab towns of Nablus, Jenin, and Tulkarm. They hoped, after a speedy victory, to advance to the lowlands, forestalling the Egyptians, who were attacking from the south, by taking the Coastal Plain and the Syrians by occupying Haifa. The Legion reached *Latrun, on the road to the capital, took up positions in the Old City, cut off Mount Scopus, and threatened the Jewish quarters in the north of Jerusalem.

Units of the Harel Brigade penetrated through the Zion Gate and made contact with the defenders of the Jewish Quarter of the Old City, but they were unable to hold out against superior forces and left the Old City. The Jewish Quarter surrendered on May 25. No Jews were left in the Old City, and the Jewish Quarter, with its ancient synagogues and places of learning, was almost completely demolished. The Legion troops could make no further progress, however, and contented themselves with indiscriminate bombardment of the Jewish areas, in which 170 civilians were killed and over 1,000 injured. The Israelis' attempts to lift the siege were unsuccessful, but at the beginning of June they succeeded in bringing up supplies and reinforcements along a makeshift track in the mountains, named the "Burma Road" in recollection of *Wingate's exploits in World War II.

The Iraqis took little part in offensive operations but were able to prevent the fall of Jenin. The Egyptians, however, were more successful. They advanced with a rapid pincer movement through mainly Arab territory, one arm advancing northward along the coast, while the other moved northeast, through Beersheba and Hebron, to southern Jerusalem. The western arm, after being held up by the desperate resistance of the Jewish villages of *Yad Mordekhai, *Kefar Darom and *Nizzanim, was halted by Israeli forces north of the Arab village of Isdūd (Ashdod). The eastern arm split the Negev and cut off its 28 Jewish villages, but it was unable to subdue them.

The first Messerschmidts of the infant Israel air force were assembled only on May 29, with others arriving at the rate of one or two a day. A direct confrontation with the superior Arab forces was out of the question, but they carried out a variety of operations, cooperating with the ground forces, flying in supplies to isolated outposts, bombarding Amman and Damascus, and attacking Egyptian troop-carrying ships. Some of the refugee boats, which had brought "illegal" immigrants, were hurriedly repaired and fitted with antiquated cannon; one of them, the *Eilat*, took part in the battle against Egyptian troop carriers off the Gaza Strip.

On May 20 the UN General Assembly appointed Count Folke Bernadotte as mediator for Palestine to ensure the maintenance of essential services and the protection of the Holy Places and to promote a peaceful solution to the conflict. At the same time, the Security Council called on the parties to cease fire. Israel agreed, but the Arabs refused. On May 29, the day after the mediator's arrival in the Middle East, the council again called for a cease-fire – this time for a period of four weeks – and after bargaining over details and several postponements, the truce went into force on June 11. Israel was in control of eastern and western Galilee, the Jezreel Valley from Haifa to the Jordan River, the coastal strip to a point north of Isdod, a corridor from the coast to Jerusalem, and a large pocket in the heart of the Negev, not including Beersheba.

ORGANIZING THE STATE: MAY 1–JULY 7, 1948. In the midst of battle, the infant state had to improvise the machinery of government. Law and order in the Jewish areas, transport and communications, purchase and distribution of supplies, social services, and the like had been organized on a voluntary basis by the People's Administration during the chaotic last days of the Mandate, but there was only the nucleus of a civil service, consisting of the staffs of the Jewish Agency and the Va'ad Le'ummi and the Jewish officials in the British administration. At its first regular meeting the Provisional Council of State elected Chaim *Weizmann as its president. The administrative headquarters of the government were set up in the rural surroundings of Sarona, a suburb of Tel Aviv evacuated by the German *Templer settlers who had been deported during the war. On May 19 the council adopted the Law and Administration Ordinance, which laid down, in broad lines, its own powers as the legislature and those of the provisional government, thus establishing a rudimentary constitution. Other laws were concerned with weekly and annual days of rest for Jews and non-Jews, the tenure of civil servants and police officers, and the operation of the courts. There was now no bar to the arrival of immigrants. At the end of July the minister of immigration announced that over 25,000 had arrived, mainly from the camps in Cyprus and the Displaced Persons' camps in Europe, although the British and American authorities were making it difficult for young men of military age to leave in case they should strengthen Israel during the truce period.

The truce brought advantages to both sides. While the Arabs were able to rest and reorganize their troops, the Israelis also had a valuable breathing space for redeployment, training, and planning. At the beginning of June the newly formed government faced a critical internal challenge to its authority. Although IZL had undertaken to stop all independent arms purchases, it was learned that a ship called the *Altalena* (the literary pseudonym of Vladimir Jabotinsky) was on its way from France carrying not only 900 immigrants, but also 250 light machine guns, 5,000 rifles, and a large quantity of ammunition. The government demanded that the ship, with its cargo, be placed unconditionally at its disposal, but the IZL leaders refused. On June 20, when the ship approached the shore at Kefar Vitkin, soldiers were sent to prevent the arms and ammunition from being unloaded and a battle developed with IZL adherents, including two companies who had left their army posts. The IZL contingent surrendered, but the ship succeeded in escaping and reaching Tel Aviv, where another skirmish took place between IZL members and a Palmah detachment. The army shelled the ship, and most of the immigrants barely succeeded in jumping into the shallow water before it blew up and sank. The incident left a deep deposit of bitterness but made it clear that no sectional armed force competing with the IDF would be tolerated (see *Irgun Zeva'i Le'ummi).

As the end of the truce approached, efforts were made to extend it: on July 1 Count Bernadotte invited Arabs and Jews to meet for negotiations at Rhodes, and on the 7th the Security Council called on the parties to renew the truce. The Arabs refused, though agreement was reached in Jerusalem on the demilitarization of the Mount Scopus area, including the Hebrew University, the Hadassah Hospital, the Augusta Victoria building, and the Arab village of ʿIsawiyya.

TEN DAYS' FIGHTING: JULY 8–18, 1948. On July 8 the Egyptians renewed their attacks in the south with a view to sealing off the Negev. Now, however, Israel's strong points were fortified and its forces much better trained and armed. Mobile commandos, "Samson's Foxes," inflicted heavy casualties and captured valuable supplies, including armored vehicles. In ten days the Egyptian attack was shattered, with the loss of 740 killed, 1,000 wounded, and 200 prisoners.

On July 9, with the official expiry of the truce, the IDF launched a strong offensive, led by tanks and armored cars, aimed at repelling the threat to Tel Aviv and driving at the Latrun-Ramallah road. On July 11 Lydda was taken, and Ramleh surrendered next day. The Arab Legion counterattacked but was driven back, losing 600 killed and 250 wounded, and on the 16th the objective was achieved. At the same time, the Israelis attacked in Lower Galilee, taking Nazareth and driving most of Kaukji's forces back to Lebanon. In the Jerusalem sector, the Israelis, who could now bombard Legion posts all along the front, broke the Egyptian line in the south and took ʿAyn Karm (Ein Kerem) on the western outskirts of the city. An attempt to take the Old City, however, was unsuccessful. On the night of July 16/17 IDF forces broke in from Mount Zion, while IẒL and Leḥi contingents breached the New Gate, but they were forced to withdraw a few hours before the second truce went into effect in the city. During the "Ten Days" the Egyptians bombarded Tel Aviv and the Negev villages, but the Israelis had acquired a number of "flying fortresses," which attacked Cairo on their way to Israel, carried out many operations in support of the ground forces, and bombed Damascus twice. Twelve enemy planes were shot down, bringing Arab losses from the beginning of the invasion to 34.

On July 15 the Security Council adopted a strongly worded resolution noting the Arabs' rejection of appeals for the extension of the truce, determining that the situation constituted a threat to peace, ordering a cease-fire "until a peaceful adjustment of the future situation of Palestine is reached," and declaring that failure to comply would be a breach of the peace and might involve sanctions under Chapter VII of the UN Charter. The cease-fire was to take effect in Jerusalem on July 17 and in the rest of the country on the next day. This time it was the Arabs who willingly accepted the cease-fire, since the Israel forces were on the offensive. Israel agreed with some reluctance, for, although it had achieved considerable gains, the Syrians still held Mishmar ha-Yarden in the north; Jerusalem was still split, with Mount Scopus an enclave in Arab-held territory; the main road to Jerusalem was blocked at Latrun; and the Egyptians held strategically important positions in the Negev.

POLITICAL AND INTERNAL PROBLEMS: JUNE–NOVEMBER, 1948. Since the beginning of the first truce, the mediator had been trying to work out a solution to the dispute. He did not consider himself bound by the partition plan, which he thought was favorable to the Jews, and tried to find ways of satisfying the demands of the Arabs. On June 27, after consulting separately with representatives of the two sides, he proposed a union of two states (neither completely independent) – one Jewish and one Arab – the latter to comprise Transjordan and part of Western Palestine. After two years Jewish immigration was to be subject to the approval of the UN Economic and Social Council, while the Arab refugees were to be repatriated and their property restored. In an appendix he suggested territorial changes in the partition plan: Transjordan to get Jerusalem (with autonomy for the Jewish population) and most or all of the Negev; Israel to get western Galilee; Haifa port and Lydda airport to become free zones.

Almost all of Bernadotte's proposals were completely unacceptable to Israel, and the Arab League refused to consider anything less than an Arab state in the whole of Western Palestine, with protection for the Jewish minority. After the second truce came into operation, the Arabs still refused to start negotiations and there was a halt in efforts to find a solution. With Arab troops still occupying key positions, the Israel government regarded the indefinite continuance of the truce as highly dangerous. The Arabs committed repeated breaches of the ceasefire, such as the blowing up by the Arab Legion of the pumping station at Latrun, which was to supply water to Jerusalem. Internally, there was uncertainty about the status of Jerusalem, where IẒL and Leḥi units were still in existence.

The economic situation was critical. The burden of the war effort was heavy, and costs were high because of restricted imports, world price increases, and labor shortages due to general mobilization. The cost-of-living index stood at 344 points at the end of July 1949, compared with 280 in November 1947. Although the Haifa refineries had been reopened on July 22, there was a shortage of fuel and the licenses of nonessential civilian vehicles were revoked. Immigrants were still pouring in, however, and as young men were called up the new-comers took their places in office, shop, field, and factory. Thousands of families were accommodated in houses abandoned by Arab refugees, and dozens of new villages were founded, many of them kibbutzim settled by groups for whom no land had been available under the Mandate. On August 17 the minister of finance, Eliezer *Kaplan, announced that the Palestine pound would be replaced by the Israel pound, a new currency with the same exchange value, issued by the Anglo-Palestine Bank.

At the end of August the Zionist General Council met in Tel Aviv to discuss the changes in the structure and functions of the Jewish Agency necessitated by the establishment of the Jewish state. Obviously, the Agency could no longer deal with such matters as defense and relations with foreign governments. Some of its leading members were now ministers responsible to the Israel legislature, and the American Zionists demanded complete separation between the Agency Executive and Israel government. Ultimately, compromises were reached: the Agency would concentrate on immigration, absorption, settlement, youth work, and information; as land purchase was no longer a problem, the Jewish National Fund would devote itself to afforestation and land amelioration. The Agency Executive was enlarged by the co-option of Mapam and Revisionist representatives: 11 were to sit in Jerusalem, seven in New York, and one in London. Kaplan retained his place on the executive as a link with the government.

To regularize the position in Jerusalem, the government placed the Israel-held area under Israel law and appointed Dov *Joseph as military governor. The city's economy had been badly injured by the siege, supply difficulties, and the transfer of government departments to Tel Aviv. On September 17 Count Bernadotte and his assistant, Col. Sarraut, were assassinated in Jerusalem. An unknown organization called the Fatherland Front, generally considered to consist of ex-members of Leḥi, claimed the credit. The government arrested some 200 men and decided to impose strict discipline over all sectional forces. An ultimatum was issued to IẒL to disband immediately and hand in all its arms.

A few days after the murder, Bernadotte's last report to the United Nations was published. It called for the replacement of the truce by a permanent peace, or at least an armistice, and made new territorial proposals: to give the Negev to the Arabs and Galilee to the Jews; to place Jerusalem under international supervision; to join the Arab area with Transjordan; and to permit the refugees to return to their homes. The report was well received in Washington and London, but Israel rejected most of its proposals.

Ben-Gurion had already raised the problem of the separate command of the Palmaḥ, which dealt with recruitment, training, supplies, and even operational matters. The Palmaḥ enjoyed the political support of Mapam, the United Workers' Party: of its 64 senior officers, 60 were associated with that party. Ben-Gurion, while deeply appreciating its spirit and achievements, insisted that the general staff must have complete and unified control of all units. The Palmaḥ and its supporters argued that it fulfilled a vital function and that unified control was assured, through the subordination of its command to the IDF general staff. After prolonged and at times heated debates over the question, which was even discussed by the Histadrut, the government decided on November 7 to dissolve the separate Palmaḥ command and transfer its functions to the appropriate departments of the general staff. Its three brigades continued to exist and played an outstanding part in the IDF's operations until the end of the fighting.

LAST BATTLES: OCTOBER 1948–JANUARY 1949. In the middle of October, fighting broke out again in the Negev. Despite the rulings of Ralph Bunche, who had succeeded Bernadotte as mediator, the Egyptians refused to allow the Israelis to send supplies to their villages and outposts. On October 15, after notifying the UN observers, a convoy was sent down to the Negev; when it was attacked by the Egyptians, the Israel forces opened a general offensive in the area, known as Operation Ten Plagues. In five days the road was cleared, Beersheba taken, and the Egyptians hemmed in around Faluja. The air force played an important part in the campaign by bombarding the Egyptians in the Faluja pocket, while the small boats of the navy harassed them, prevented supplies and reinforcements from arriving by sea, and sank the Egyptian flagship, the *Faruk*. At the same time, a number of posts commanding the railroad to Jerusalem were taken and an attack was launched at the remnants of Kaukji's forces in Galilee, which did not recognize the cease-fire. Operations in the north were completed at the end of the month with the capture of several Lebanese border villages.

The fighting was not yet over, however. The Egyptians held out in the Faluja pocket and threatened Israel villages and communications in the Negev. On November 9 the formidable fortress at Iraq-Suweidan, which had withstood seven attacks, was taken. On November 23 Israel forces advanced from Beersheba to take the desert crossroads at Kurnub and Ein Huṣb, which controlled the road to the Dead Sea Works at Sodom. At the beginning of December the Egyptians took a number of strong points as preparation for a renewed advance on Beersheba, but on the 22nd the Israel forces started a large-scale offensive that turned the Egyptian flank by advancing with an armored column into Egyptian territory from Niẓẓanah (ʿAuja al-Ḥafir) and taking the northern Sinai crossroads at Abu-Aweigila and the airfield at the coastal town of El-Arish. The Israelis withdrew from Sinai under pressure from the powers and the United Nations, but started to advance toward Rafa, the border town on the coast. On Jan. 7, 1949, after the Egyptians agreed to open negotiations for an armistice, the final cease-fire was called.

The War of Independence was, in effect, over, although it was not formally ended until the signature of the Armistice Agreement with Syria in July 1949. The fighting had been spread over a period of more than 13 months, including 61 days of continuous combat. Israel had paid a heavy price: 4,000 soldiers and 2,000 civilians killed. The financial cost was also heavy: about 500 million dollars. The Jewish state, however, was now a definite fact, created by the effort and sacrifice of its people with no effective assistance from the United Nations, which had called for its establishment. On Ben-Gurion's insistence, it had been decided not to specify boundaries in the Declaration of Independence, and Israel did not feel bound by the partition map, which the UN mediator had ignored. It held an area of almost 8,000 sq. mi., compared with some 6,200 sq. mi. within the boundaries delineated in the partition plan, including the whole of Galilee; a coastal strip reaching down to some 27 miles north of the Sinai border, narrowing to six miles north of Tel Aviv and broadening into a corridor from the coast to Jerusalem; and the whole of the Negev. Western Jerusalem was firmly in Jewish hands. The establishment of an Arab state and the internationalization of Jerusalem had been frustrated by the Arab attacks and the occupation (later turned into annexation) by Transjordan of the Arab-inhabited eastern parts of Palestine, later called the West Bank (including East Jerusalem), and the Egyptian occupation of the Gaza Strip, which was also earmarked for the Arab state. This, however, did not prevent the Arabs, in later years, from repeatedly demanding a return to the boundaries laid down in the General Assembly resolution of Nov. 29, 1947.

THE FIRST ELECTIONS: NOVEMBER 1948–AUGUST 1949. While sporadic fighting was still going on, and before the de facto boundaries of the new state had been settled, steps were taken to put the regime on a firm footing of democratic consent. On Nov. 8, 1948, an all-day curfew was proclaimed and, while the entire population remained in their homes, a census was carried out. The population of the areas then under Israel control was found to be 782,000–713,000 Jews and 69,000 Arabs (after the conclusion of the Armistice Agree-

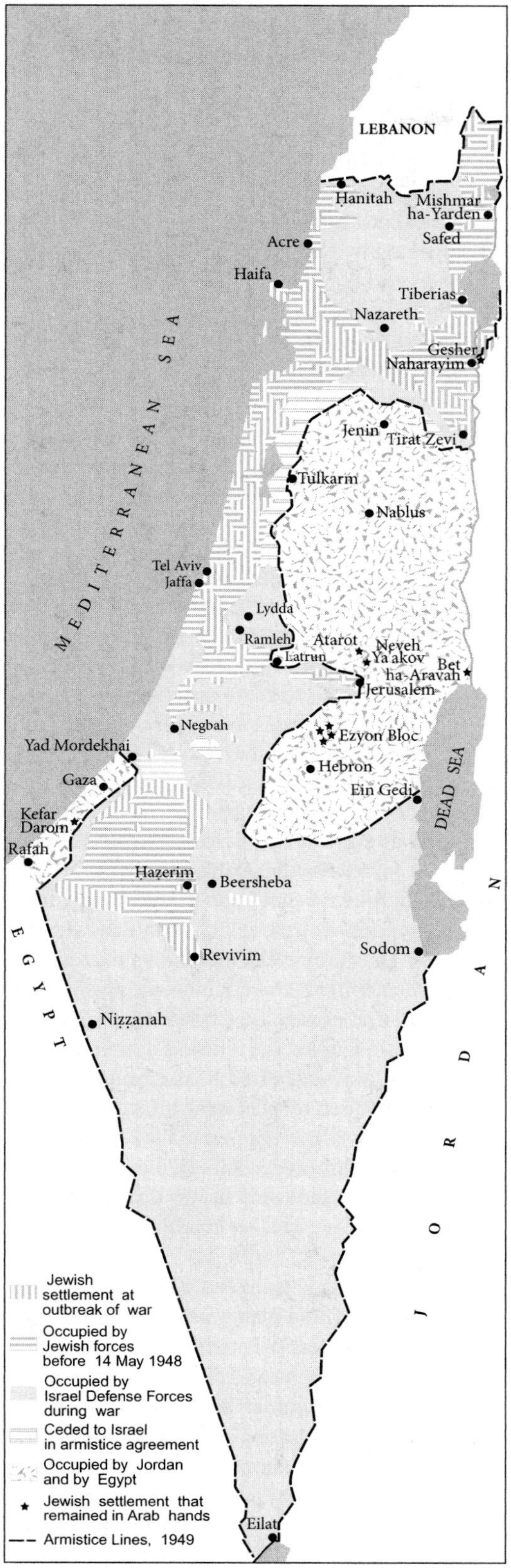

The Israel War of Independence, 1948–49. Based on Atlas of Israel, *Survey of Israel, 1970.*

ments and the readmission of Arabs separated from their families, the number of Arabs rose to about 120,000). Of this number, 506,567 had the right to vote. There was no time to divide the country into constituencies, and the elections were held by the proportional representation system in force for the Zionist Congresses and the Elected Assembly of Keneset Yisrael. The number of seats was fixed at 120, like the membership of Keneset ha-Gedolah, the Great Assembly that functioned after the ancient return from Babylon.

The elections were held on January 25; almost 87% of the electors – 440,000 – went to the polls, including over 73,000 votes cast at special polling stations for soldiers. The results showed a considerable degree of political continuity. The largest party in the Assembly was Mapai with 46 seats, followed by Mapam, the United Workers' Party, with 19 and the United Religious Front (Mizrachi, Ha-Po'el ha-Mizrachi, Agudat Israel, and Po'alei Agudat Israel) with 16. The Revisionist Party was replaced by the Ḥerut movement, founded by the IẒL, which obtained 14 seats. The various middle-class parties coalesced into two groups: General Zionists with 7 and Progressives with 5. The Communists and the communal list of the Sephardim had 4 seats each. There was also an Arab party, the Nazareth Democratic List, with 2 seats; other Arab votes went to various Jewish lists, especially Mapai and the Communists. The Fighters' List (Leḥi), WIZO (Women Zionists), and the Yemenite Federation received one seat each.

The first meeting of the Assembly was held in Jerusalem as a sign of Israel's determination that the Holy City should be the capital of the Jewish state. It was opened at the headquarters of the Jewish Agency, by Chaim Weizmann as president of the Provisional Council of State.

The 114 members who were present made the declaration of allegiance, and four committees were elected to make arrangements for the continuation of the Assembly's work. The first session also elected Yosef *Sprinzak as speaker, and the second elected representatives of Mapam and the United Religious Front as his deputies.

On February 16, the Assembly adopted the Transition Law as a provisional constitution, outlining the functions and procedures of the legislature, the election and powers of the president, the formation of the government, and its relations with the Assembly, which was to be called the Knesset. On the same day it elected Weizmann president, and he was installed on the 17th. The provisional government thereupon submitted its resignation to the president, as provided by the Transition Law, and, after consultations with representatives of all the parties, he called upon Ben-Gurion to form a new cabinet. The first regular government, which obtained a vote of confidence on March 10, was based on a coalition between Mapai, the United Religious Front, the Progressives, and the Sephardim. With the exception of the last, who split up subsequently between Mapai and the General Zionists, these parties constituted the nucleus of almost all subsequent Israel cabinets up to 1977. Contrary to expectations, the Knesset did not proceed immediately to draft a formal constitution. After lengthy discussions and debates, it was decided in June 1950 to enact a number of separate "Basic Laws," which would ultimately be combined to form the constitution. (See also Israel, State of: *Political Life and Parties) Israel's debt to the man who proclaimed the vision of the Jewish state was recognized when, on Aug. 17, 1949, the remains of Theodor Herzl were brought by air from Vienna and reinterred in Jerusalem on a hill renamed Mount Herzl.

ISRAEL JOINS THE FAMILY OF NATIONS: JANUARY–JULY 1949. Negotiations for an armistice between Israel and Egypt started on the island of Rhodes on Jan. 13, 1949, under the auspices of Ralph Bunche. At first the mediator met the representatives of each side separately; when there were signs of progress, the parties held informal meetings; and when agreement was reached, the representatives met under his chairmanship to affix their signatures.

The *Armistice Agreement with Egypt, signed on February 24, gave the entire Negev, down to the border with Sinai, to Israel but left the *Gaza Strip under Egyptian occupation. A demilitarized zone was established around ʿAuja al-Ḥafir (Niẓẓanah) and also on the Egyptian side of the line, in the same area. To ensure de facto control over the Negev, two infantry columns were sent out at the beginning of March 1949 in Operation Uvdah ("Fact"). On March 10 the advance party reached the abandoned police post at Umm Rash Rash on the Gulf of Akaba, ensuring Israel's outlet to the Red Sea and restoring the biblical name, Eilat.

Under the agreement with Lebanon, signed on March 23 at Ras al-Naqura (Rosh ha-Nikrah), the former international frontier was specified as the armistice line, Israel forces withdrawing from the Lebanese villages they had occupied.

The agreement with Jordan, signed on March 4 after a month's negotiations, established a winding border 530 km. (330 miles) long. It left under Jordanian occupation the thickly populated hill country of Judea and Samaria (called the "West Bank" after its annexation by Transjordan), including East Jerusalem, and ran through the Dead Sea down the Mandatory eastern border of Palestine to the tip of the Red Sea (the Gulf of Akaba), about three miles west of Akaba Port. It was agreed that the Arab Legion should replace the Iraqis in the "Triangle" area.

Under the agreement with Syria, which was not signed until July 20, the Syrians withdrew from the areas they had occupied west of the international frontier and Israel agreed, in return, that the areas should be demilitarized and the Arabs who had abandoned them during the fighting be permitted to return. Thus Israeli control over Lake Kinneret and Lake Ḥuleh was assured, but the demilitarized zones were a frequent focus of friction during the following years. Iraq did not conclude an armistice agreement with Israel. See also Israel, State of: *Historical Survey, section on Frontiers.

Although the agreements specifically reserved to the parties the right to make territorial claims in the future, it was stated in each case that the agreement was concluded "in order to facilitate the transition from the present truce to permanent peace in Palestine" (preamble), that "No aggressive actions by the armed forces – land, sea, or air – of either Party shall be undertaken, planned or threatened against the people or the armed forces of the other" (Article 1), and that "No warlike act or act of hostility shall be conducted from territory controlled by one of the Parties… against the other Party" (Article 2). The armistice lines thus constituted de facto boundaries as long as they were respected by both sides, and, despite repeated violations, they served as such until the Six-Day War of 1967. A United Nations Truce Supervision Organization (UNTSO), composed of soldiers from various countries under the command of a chief of staff, and four Mixed Armistice Commissions (MACS), each with Israel and Arab representatives under an UNTSO officer as chairman, were set up to supervise the execution of the agreements and consider complaints. In default of unanimity, the UN chairman acted as an arbiter.

On Dec. 11, 1948, the UN General Assembly recommended (Resolution 194 [III]) that "the Governments and authorities concerned" should "seek agreement by negotiations conducted with a view to a final settlement of all questions outstanding between them," that "the refugees wishing to return to their homes and live in peace with their neighbors should be permitted to do so at the earliest practical date," and that a Palestine Conciliation Commission, consisting of U.S., French, and Turkish representatives, be set up to bring the parties together. When the commission met at Lausanne on April 26, 1949, the Arab delegations insisted on the return of all Arab refugees as a precondition to negotiations, while Israel was prepared to discuss the problem only in the context of comprehensive peace negotiations. Israel later offered to admit 100,000 refugees as part of a comprehensive peace settlement, but the Lausanne talks made no progress and were broken off in September. An Economic Survey Mission headed by Gordon R. Clapp, appointed by the PCC, suggested constructive schemes to employ the refugees in their new locations, but the proposal was rejected by the Arabs, and the United Nations confined itself to relief work through the Relief and Works Agency (UNWRA), appointed in 1949. Meanwhile, Israel had been steadily winning its place in the family of nations. Within a year of its establishment it was recognized by over 50 states, and on May 11, 1949, it was admitted as a member of the United Nations.

The question of Jerusalem, which was to have been internationalized under the partition plan, was still on the agenda of the United Nations and was debated by the General Assembly toward the end of the year. A surprise coalition of Muslim, Catholic, and Communist states voted on Dec. 9, 1949, in favor of internationalization. Israel categorically rejected the proposal and on December 13 the Knesset decided to hold its sittings in Jerusalem as the capital of Israel (it had been meeting in Tel Aviv) and speed up the transfer of government offices from Tel Aviv. The UN Trusteeship Council, which was entrusted with the preparation of a constitution for the international regime on the city, found that the scheme was impracticable, and after the 1950 Assembly had failed to pass any resolution on the subject by the required two-thirds majority, the proposal was, in effect, dropped (see section on Jerusalem in Israel, State of: Historical Survey, Foreign Policy and International Relations).

THE INGATHERING OF THE EXILES BEGINS: 1948–1951. The early years of statehood witnessed the beginnings of the realization of an ancient dream: the *ingathering of the exiles. By the end of 1948, with the state barely six months old, over 100,000 Jews had arrived – the number the Jewish leaders had pleaded with the Mandatory government to admit into undivided Palestine. The right to *aliyah*, implicitly recognized by the annulment of all Mandatory restrictions on immigration, was explicitly proclaimed by the *Law of Return (July 5, 1950), the first clause of which read: "Every Jew has the right to come to this country as an *oleh*" (defined in a footnote as: "a Jew immigrating to Israel for settlement").

Most of the survivors of the Nazi Holocaust were eager to leave Europe. The Displaced Persons' camps were emptied. At first only Czechoslovakia, Bulgaria, and Yugoslavia let their Jews go, but Poland, Romania, and Hungary followed suit later. In addition, there was a great mass migration from North Africa and the Middle East, where the Zionist movement had hardly existed. Thousands came from Turkey and Iran, Morocco and Tunis, Algeria and Libya. By the end of 1951, almost all the Jews of Yemen and Iraq had been brought over in dramatic airlifts. The arrival of these Oriental Jews, most of them deeply pious and with distinctive, centuries-old traditions and customs, brought back into the mainstream of Jewish life communities that had lived on the margin of the great 19th-century Jewish political, cultural, and religious movements. The confrontation between the Ashkenazim from Eastern and Central Europe, who had played the main role in building the National Home, and the Oriental communities, which differed widely in language, outlook, and manners, had profound implications. The flood gathered strength in 1949, when almost 240,000 *olim* arrived, and slackened only slightly in the two following years, when the influx totaled 170,000 and 175,000, respectively. In three and a half years, by the end of 1951, the Jewish population had been doubled by the arrival of over 684,000 immigrants – one-third more than came in the 70 years of pre-State Zionist *aliyah*. The newcomers were divided almost equally between Ashkenazim and Orientals, whereas before 1948 almost 90% had come from Europe.

The handling of this tempestuous flood was a task of staggering dimensions for a small nation still at war, with an untried administrative machine. Efforts were made to get the construction of housing started, using various methods of prefabricated and accelerated building. But the pace inevitably fell short of the needs: in the years 1948–51, 78,000 dwellings, comprising 165,000 rooms, were completed – a remarkable achievement for a country with a population of 1,500,000 at the end of the period, but still only one room for every four newcomers.

A considerable proportion of the new arrivals had, therefore, to be content with temporary accommodation. By the summer of 1949, almost 100,000 persons were living in camps, receiving their meals from central kitchens and supported almost entirely by public funds. Life under such conditions was demoralizing, and it was not always easy to induce the camp residents to move out and become self-supporting. Few of the immigrants knew enough Hebrew to communicate with the authorities and understand what was going on. Most were penniless and unfit – sometimes unwilling – to work with their hands in field or factory. There was a danger that the result would be the creation of not a homogenous nation, but two Israels: one consisting of mainly Ashkenazi veterans, who held positions of power and influence and understood the new society because they had built it, the other mostly underemployed, undereducated, and underprivileged Orientals. It was therefore decided to transfer the immigrants to transitional camps or quarters (**ma'barot*) where, though the accommodation was still primitive, each family could look after itself and find work in the neighborhood. By the end of 1951, about 400,000 of the new immigrants had found permanent housing, though 250,000 were still living in 123 *ma'barot* and ten immigrants' camps.

Settlement on the land, one of the great ideals of Zionism, was now an urgent necessity to solve a triple problem: the overcrowding in the camps and *ma'barot*, the need to till large areas of cultivable land abandoned by Arab refugees, and the shortage of food for the growing population. Although there were some experiments in the cultivation of large stretches by public or private management, which gave the newcomers their first taste of manual labor, the Jewish Agency, which was responsible for new settlements, adhered to the principle of enabling small groups to form autonomous, self-supporting farm villages. While 79 kibbutzim were founded during the first year and a half – more than half as many as during the previous 40 years – the great majority of the newcomers were sent off to establish moshavim, in which each family was responsible for its own holding in a cooperative framework, with guidance and help from the Agency. Thus, in 1949 and 1950, 126 moshavim were established – many on the sites of *ma'barot* or abandoned Arab villages – almost trebling the number of moshavim. An intermediate type was the work village (*kefar avodah*), where the newcomers were employed, generally by the Jewish National Fund, on afforestation or land amelioration. Altogether 345 new villages of all types were established during 1948–51, compared with 293 during the previous seven decades. They filled up gaps in all parts of the country, not only in the Coastal Plain but also in areas where only isolated groups had lived before: Upper Galilee, the Judean Hills, and the arid Negev.

A feature that assumed greater psychological significance in later years was the small proportion of immigrants from Western Europe and the Americas, the main centers of the Zionist movement. Ben-Gurion, in particular, challenged the right of the Zionist to claim a privileged status when so few of them were prepared to carry out their ideals in practice (see also Israel, State of: *Aliyah and Absorption).

ECONOMIC AND SOCIAL PROBLEMS: 1949–1953. Mass immigration, though welcomed as the fulfillment of one of Israel's basic aspirations, aggravated the economic difficulties. The defense burden and the cost of feeding and housing large numbers of unproductive immigrants intensified inflationary tendencies inherited from the Mandatory period. Taxation was high and productivity low; the rate of exchange, which kept the Israel pound on a par with the pound sterling, discouraged foreign investors, and there was a shortage of imported raw materials. Dov Joseph, the minister of supply and rationing, introduced a strict austerity regime: basic foodstuffs were doled out in small quantities month by month and, later, clothing and footwear were rationed too; the economy of the household was dominated by the ration book. Those with relatives or friends abroad could receive food parcels or foreign-currency "scrip," which was exchanged for food; others resorted to a flourishing black market. There was serious unemployment, which had to be mitigated by expensive and unproductive public works, since there was no unemployment insurance. The austerity policy, however, succeeded in conserving resources and lowering prices: the cost-of-living index fell from 493 points at the beginning of 1949 to 378 a year later.

Israel could not bear these burdens unaided. Funds from the *United Jewish Appeal in the United States and similar efforts by Jews abroad helped to support the newcomers, but much capital was needed for housing and development. A $100,000,000 loan from the American Export-Import Bank in January 1949 was followed by a series of grants-in-aid from the U.S. government and technical assistance under "Point 4" administered by a U.S. Operations Mission in Israel. In 1950 the Law for the Encouragement of Foreign Investment was passed. In the same year a conference of Jewish communal leaders and businessmen from the United States, Britain, and South Africa launched a drive for the sale of State of Israel *Bonds, the proceeds to be used for development and immigrant housing.

In 1951 the World Zionist Congress met in Jerusalem for the first time and pledged continued assistance to Israel in the common task of settling and integrating the immigrants. Uneasiness was expressed, particularly by the General Zionists and the Ḥerut-Revisionist Union, at the decline in the status of the Zionist Organization, which Ben-Gurion and the Israel government were accused of belittling and neglecting. In November 1952, after discussions between the Jewish Agency Executive and the government, the Knesset passed the World Zionist Organization Status Law, which recognized the organization as "the authorized agency which will continue to operate in the State of Israel for the development and settlement of the country, the absorption of immigrants from the Diaspora, and the coordination of the activities in Israel of Jewish institutions and organizations active in those fields." A "Covenant," regulating the cooperation between the two bodies, was concluded by the government and the Executive of the Zionist Organization and the Jewish Agency.

In September 1952, after a virulent controversy (see Israel, State of: *Political Life and Parties), an agreement was signed with the German Federal Republic for payment to the State of Israel, which had taken in hundreds of thousands of homeless refugees, as the representative of the Jewish people, of DM3,000,000,000 ($715,000,000) as partial reparations for material losses suffered by the Jews under the Nazi regime. In addition, DM450,000,000 was to be paid to the Conference on Jewish Material Claims, representing Diaspora Jewry, and individuals who had suffered under the Nazis were to receive personal restitution.

Despite difficulties and periodical crises, there was considerable progress. One of the first legislative acts of the Knesset (Aug. 1, 1949) was to pass the Compulsory Education Law, which, though not abolishing the party "trends," brought them under state control. Economic policy was adapted to the changing circumstances: strict controls on imports were eased and premiums were introduced to encourage exports. Funds from abroad were invested in irrigation, and settlement and the building of new villages, loans to industry, road building, and large-scale development schemes like the drainage of the Ḥuleh. *El Al, the Israel National Airline, was established, and a beginning was made with the expansion of the four small ships owned by *Zim, Israel Navigation Co., into a national merchant marine. Government geologists went out to map the mineral deposits of the Negev, and government companies were set up to exploit phosphates, copper, and other resources. A beginning was made with labor legislation, providing for a 47-hour work week, a weekly rest day, and an annual 14-day paid vacation. In 1951 the Equal Rights for Women Law was passed. In November 1952 President Chaim Weizmann died and in the following month Izhak Ben-Zvi was elected as his successor.

Nevertheless, the population felt the strains of shortages, high prices, and government restrictions. The General Zionists, as the mouthpiece of middle-class discontent, registered significant gains in the municipal elections in November 1950. There were disagreements between Mapai and the religious parties over religious education and the recruitment of girls for army or civilian national service. A controversy over an attempt to introduce non-party religious education in the *ma'barot* led to the resignation of the cabinet in February 1951 and premature elections in July of the same year. While Mapai and the religious parties retained their strength, the General Zionists trebled theirs (largely at the expense of Ḥerut), and after an unsuccessful attempt by Mapai to govern with the support of Mizrachi and Ha-Po'el ha-Mizrachi alone, the cabinet was reconstituted, the General Zionists receiving four ministries (including the important ones of Commerce and Industry and the Interior). Economic difficulties, reported by newcomers to their friends and relations abroad, were largely responsible for a sudden and drastic drop in *aliyah*: only 24,000 arrived in 1952 and 11,000 in the following year.

The conclusion of the reparations agreement with West Germany, the success of the UJA and similar appeals and the Bond Drive, the U.S. government grants-in-aid, and the long-term loans obtained from U.S. and international sources allowed Israel to look forward with some confidence to a decade of relative financial security. In 1952 a "New Economic Policy" was instituted to reduce inflationary pressures and cover the gap in the foreign-trade balance. Many controls were removed and prices were allowed to rise to an economic level; the consumers' price index rose by 50% during the year. The government undertook to cut its expenditures, balance the ordinary budget, and stop inflationary expansion of the currency. A beginning was made with the devaluation of the Israel pound to a more realistic level by the institution of three exchange rates, ranging from $2.80 to $1 per Israel pound for different kinds of imports and foreign-currency transactions. Advantage was taken of the introduction of new currency notes to impose a 10% compulsory loan on cash and bank balances. The new policy slowed down consumer spending, construction, and public works, and, consequently, led to a drop in production and a rise in unemployment during 1953. However, these effects were regarded as temporary difficulties involved in the transition to a healthier basis for the economy.

In July 1953 the "trend" school system was abolished by the passage of the State Education Law, under which the general and labor trends were amalgamated as the state education system and the Mizrachi trend became the state religious system, both under the control of the Ministry of Education and Culture. The Orthodox Agudah trend remained independent, but was subsidized from state funds. The fourth trend was the Arab trend, also under the Ministry of Education.

The close of a period of struggle and stress was marked by the temporary resignation of Ben-Gurion from the premiership in December 1953 and his replacement in the following month by Moshe Sharett as prime minister and Pinḥas *Lavon as minister of defense. The reason Ben-Gurion gave for this step was the strain of the accumulated tension of the past two decades, but it was generally believed that he felt a need for a fundamental reappraisal of the nation's problems. In a lengthy essay on "Jewish Survival," published in the *Government Year Book* for 1953/54, he discussed the clashes between religious and non-religious elements, the fragmentation of political life, the confrontation between Ashkenazim and Orientals, the need for a revival of the pioneering spirit, and the problematic relationship between Israel and Diaspora Jewry, especially in Western Europe and America, where the Zionist Organization was relatively strong but the will to *aliyah* was weak. In his retirement, at the new kibbutz of Sedeh Boker in the Negev, he tried, by precept and example, to stimulate the will to voluntary pioneering effort, particularly among the youth as well as settling the Negev

THE WAR ON THE BORDERS: 1950–1955. On May 25, 1950, the United States, Britain, and France, in a tripartite declaration on the Middle East, stated that they would take action if necessary to prevent any violation of frontiers or armistice lines by any state in the area. Arms supplies to Middle East countries, the declaration said, would be governed by their needs for internal security, legitimate self-defense, and their role in the defense of the area. For several years, however, it was chiefly the Arabs who received Western arms, while Israel had to rely mainly on semi-obsolete equipment from various sources.

There was no progress toward the "permanent peace" envisaged by the armistice agreements. In June 1950 the members of the Arab League concluded a collective security agreement against "the Zionist danger" and "Jewish expansionist aspirations." The Arab states continued to regard themselves as at war with Israel, refusing to recognize it or to negotiate a peaceful settlement of outstanding problems. They replied to Israel's calls for direct negotiations with, on the one hand, a refusal to recognize its right to exist, and, on the other, demands for "the implementation of UN resolutions," which they interpreted as meaning the unconditional repatriation of all Arab refugees and the restriction of Israel to the boundaries drawn in the 1947 partition plan. The very existence of Israel was regarded as "aggression," and its destruction became a fundamental aim of Arab national policy. Sometimes indirect terms were used, such as "the restoration of the stolen rights of the Palestinian people," "the liberation of Palestine," the reconquest of the "stolen territory," or "the liquidation of Zionist aggression," but it was frequently stated in the plainest terms that the aim was a "second round" in which Israel would be destroyed and its people "pushed into the sea." The Arab League established a ramified boycott organization to dissuade businessmen in other countries, by economic pressure, from trading with Israel or investing in her economy. Egypt denied passage through the Suez Canal and the Straits of Tiran to shipping and cargoes belonging to, or bound for, Israel.

It was impossible to protect every kilometer of the long and winding borders by sentries or patrols. Border violations by Arab infiltrators bent on plunder, shooting by trigger-happy Arab soldiers, mine-laying on Israel roads and tracks, and, later, armed incursions by trained and organized bands, were almost daily occurrences. In the period 1951–56 over 400 Israelis were killed and 900 injured as a result; there were 3,000 armed clashes with Arab regular or irregular forces inside Israel territory, and some 6,000 acts of sabotage, theft, and attempted theft were committed by infiltrators. UNTSO was powerless; the Mixed Armistice Commissions could do no more than register complaints, appeal for restraint, or, at best, pass resolutions of censure. The Security Council took no action to rectify the situation, and Israel had to look to its own defenses. The Defense Service Law, passed in September 1949, provided for two years' compulsory service in the armed forces for men and women, with reserves training up to the age of 49. In an emergency the reserves could be summoned to their units in a matter of hours. Reprisals against Arab attacks were carried out from time to time, but, although they may have discouraged even graver violations of the Armistice

Agreements and at certain periods induced the governments concerned to restrain infiltration for a while, they did not put an end to the chain of violence. As each reprisal was a reaction to a series of attacks, it was generally on a larger scale, and since these operations were carried out by IDF units, they were immediately censured by the MACs and often by the Security Council.

The trouble with the Syrians was mainly over the demilitarized zones, for they objected to Israel's development work there, arguing that Israel was violating the armistice agreements and changing the geography of the area. At the beginning of 1951, when Israel started work on the *Ḥuleh drainage scheme near Mishmar ha-Yarden, there were several exchanges of fire. In March, seven Israelis were killed in the al-Ḥamma area and the Israel air force bombarded two Arab villages in reprisal. On May 19, after General Riley, chief of UNTSO, had failed to obtain agreement, the Security Council ordered Israel to stop the works on Arab-owned land in the zones. A new dispute broke out at the beginning of September 1953, when the Israelis started work in the demilitarized zone south of the Ḥuleh on the first stage of a major project to channel part of the Jordan waters to the Negev. The Syrians protested, and General Bennike, the new UNTSO chief, ordered Israel to suspend the work until agreement was reached with Syria. Under international pressure, Israel ultimately complied while the Security Council was considering the matter. In January 1954 a proposal calling for a compromise between Israel and Syrian interests was blocked by the Soviet veto in the Security Council, and Israel revised its plans in order to keep the works out of the demilitarized zone.

Meanwhile, in October 1953, U.S. President Eisenhower sent a special envoy, Eric Johnston, to the Middle East to present proposals for a constructive solution of the water problem to the governments of Israel, Syria, Lebanon, and Jordan. Johnston submitted a plan prepared by Gordon Clapp, chairman of the Tennessee Valley Authority, for the utilization of the Jordan and Yarmuk waters by the four countries for agricultural development and refugee resettlement on the basis of mutually agreed quotas. In 1955 a Unified Water Plan, which assured each country of the quantities of water claimed by its experts, was accepted by the parties on the technical level, but the Arab League, meeting in October, refused to give political approval. Israel stated, however, that it would not utilize more than the quantities of water allotted in the plan. Repeated Syrian attacks on Israeli fishing in Lake Kinneret led to further Israel reprisals in December 1955, in which the Syrians suffered about 100 casualties.

A serious dispute with Jordan over the blocking of the road to Eilat by Legion forces in November 1950, followed by three murders by infiltrators in and around Jerusalem and an Israeli reprisal, was settled in February 1951, the Jordanians agreeing to cooperate to stop infiltration. Secret peace negotiations took place with King *Abdullah, but hopes were shattered when a Palestinian assassinated him in Jerusalem on July 20. The position deteriorated. The Jordanians refused to carry out their undertaking in Article 8 of the Armistice Agreement to negotiate arrangements for Israel's use of the Latrun road to the capital and access to Jewish holy places in Jerusalem and the Jewish institutions on Mount Scopus. In January 1953 the Jordanian prime minister announced the annulment of the agreement to prevent infiltration and there were numerous attacks by infiltrators and Jordanian troops on Israel civilians and soldiers. In June 1953 the Jordan government renewed the agreement for the prevention of infiltration, but the attacks continued.

At first ordinary Israeli army units carried out reprisals, but it soon became clear that these troops, consisting mainly of inexperienced draftees – many of whom were newcomers – were unsuitable for such commando-type raids. A special body of volunteers, called Unit 101 (later merged with the paratroops) was formed for the purpose. One of its raids, on the Arab village of Qibya, in which 45 houses were blown up and heavy casualties were caused to civilians hiding in them, was severely censured by the Security Council (Oct. 15, 1953).

Israel initiated an attempt to obtain agreement on a modus vivendi by invoking Article 12 of the Armistice Agreement, under which either party could summon a conference to consider the working of the agreement. At the end of the year, the UN secretary-general issued invitations for such a conference at Israel's request, but Jordan refused to attend. The vicious circle of repeated Arab attacks, reprisals by Israel, and international condemnations of Israel continued throughout 1954; outstanding examples were the killing of 11 passengers in an Israel bus at Ma'aleh Akrabim ("Scorpions' Ascent") on March 17, the killing of three Jews in the Jerusalem corridor on May 9 and of three more in the same area on June 19, and a three-day outbreak of shooting by Legionaries from the Old City wall later in the month. In the following year much of the infiltration was carried out by bands organized by the Egyptians in the Gaza Strip and sent into Jordan to operate from there.

Egypt took the lead in the Arab boycott by banning Israel shipping and the passage of "contraband goods" or "strategic goods" (later extended to include foodstuffs) through the Suez Canal. This practice was defined by General Riley, the chief of UNTSO, in a report to the Security Council as "an aggressive action," and the Council called on Egypt on Sept. 1, 1951, to terminate the restrictions. The resolution stated that "since the armistice regime… is of a permanent character, neither party can reasonably assert that it is a belligerent" (Paragraph 9). Egypt ignored the resolution, and cargoes destined for Israel were confiscated from Norwegian, Greek, and Italian ships trying to pass through the canal. In September 1954 an Israeli vessel, the *Bat Gallim*, and its cargo were confiscated at the entrance to the canal and the crew was imprisoned for three months. In 1949 Egypt occupied the uninhabited islands of Tiran and Sanafir in the Red Sea at the entrance to the Gulf of Akaba; later it established a garrison at Sharm el-Sheikh, interfered with Israeli and international shipping to and from Eilat, and banned Israeli planes from the airspace over the gulf.

On Aug. 18, 1952, Ben-Gurion welcomed the Egyptian officers' revolution led by General Nagib and declared that there was no reason for any antagonism between the two countries. But there was no improvement in relations under Nagib or his successor, Gamal Abdal *Nasser. Sporadic incidents on the Gaza Strip and Sinai borders, which claimed a score or more casualties – seven or eight fatal – in each of the years 1951–53, became more serious and frequent in the last quarter of 1954. Tension was increased by the trial in Cairo of 11 Jews charged with belonging to a "Zionist espionage and sabotage group." Two were executed on Jan. 31, 1955, and the rest were sentenced to long periods of imprisonment. On February 2, Pinḥas Lavon resigned due to disagreements with the prime minister arising out of a dispute over the responsibility for an ill-advised security operation. Ben-Gurion returned from Sedeh Boker to take up the post of defense minister under Sharett's premiership.

Toward the end of February, Egyptian saboteurs, known as *fedayeen* ("suicide fighters"), penetrated deep into Israel territory, and on the 28th a clash between Israeli and Egyptian forces on Israeli territory opposite Gaza developed into the fiercest battle since the War of Independence. The fight was carried over into the Strip; in an Israeli attack on an army camp near Gaza, 38 Egyptians were killed and 44 wounded. The Anglo-American-Iraqi Baghdad Pact had just aroused Nasser's anger against the West, and he turned to the Soviet Bloc for weapons to strengthen his forces. At the end of August came the first reports of an Egyptian deal with the Soviet Union for the supply, through Czechoslovakia, of large quantities of modern heavy arms. Meanwhile the Arab attacks were stepped up; many of them were carried out by *fedayeen* recruited and trained by the Egyptians but operating mainly from the Gaza Strip and Jordan, as well as from Syria and Lebanon. Israel's proposals for a high-level meeting with Egyptian representatives, as well as for the erection of a security fence along the border and other methods of reducing tension, were rejected.

Although Israel had, in principle, followed a policy of non-identification with either of the two world blocs, the sympathies of its leaders and most of its people were undisguisedly on the side of the West, where Jews could organize political and financial support for Israel and *aliyah* was unfettered. In 1952, after the *Slansky trial in Prague, the Israeli minister to Czechoslovakia had been declared *persona non grata*, and in February 1953, after a bomb placed by a fanatic exploded in the courtyard of the Soviet Embassy in Tel Aviv, the U.S.S.R. had broken off diplomatic relations. Although relations were restored a few months later, continued Soviet support for the Arabs at the United Nations indicated a distinct change in the atmosphere, and the Soviet arms deal though a shock, was not altogether a surprise. On Sept. 27, 1955, Nasser broadcast an announcement of the deal; two days later it was reported that large quantities of tanks, artillery, jet planes, and submarines were already on their way to Egypt and that Syria was also getting generous supplies of weapons from the East. Although the Western powers expressed grave concern at this development, they gave no clear reply to Israel's appeals for arms to redress the balance, and the United States warned against any "hasty action." A wave of anxiety swept the country; Israelis from all walks of life came forward spontaneously with donations of cash and jewelry for the purchase of arms.

On October 17 Egypt and Syria signed a military pact. The Syrians renewed their attacks on Israel fishing boats on Lake Kinneret (Sea of Galilee), and an Israeli reprisal was followed by Egyptian attacks in the south. Foreign Minister Sharett went to Paris and Geneva, where the Big Four foreign ministers were meeting, but his talk with Molotov of the U.S.S.R. was fruitless, and only France responded sympathetically to Israel's request for arms. The Egyptians had encroached on the demilitarized zone at Niẓẓanah and attacked an Israel police post, and their planes repeatedly violated Israel airspace. In retaliation, the Israel army attacked an Egyptian military camp at Kuntilla in Sinai. Presenting his new cabinet to the Knesset on November 2, Ben-Gurion announced his readiness to meet Egyptian and other Arab leaders at any time to discuss a settlement, but warned that "if the armistice lines are opened for the passage of saboteurs and murderers – they shall not be closed again to the defenders." The same night Israel forces ejected the Egyptians from Niẓẓanah, inflicting heavy casualties. Egyptian attacks multiplied all along the front: there were four or five incidents a day, and the activities of the *fedayeen* from the Gaza Strip and Jordan were stepped up. Typical *fedayeen* tactics were also used in attacks from Lebanese territory.

On August 26 U.S. Secretary of State John Foster Dulles had suggested territorial changes as part of a possible Arab-Israel settlement. The idea was echoed in a speech at the Guildhall, London, on November 9 by the British foreign minister, Sir Anthony Eden, who suggested a compromise between the Arab demand for a return to the partition plan boundaries and Israel's insistence on the borders demarcated by the Armistice Agreements. On Nov. 15 Ben-Gurion categorically rejected any idea of truncating Israel's territory; Eden's approach was also rejected by Egypt. France agreed to supply Israel with a number of military jet planes, but continued to sell arms to Egypt, while the U.S. and Britain went on sending armaments to Lebanon, Iraq, and Jordan.

THE SINAI CAMPAIGN AND AFTER: 1956–1959. As 1956 opened, the war clouds were visibly gathering. On January 2, Ben-Gurion warned the Knesset of "the danger of the approaching attack from Egypt, and perhaps not only by it." While the U.S.S.R. virulently denounced Israel, the Western powers sponsored a Security Council resolution censuring her for a reprisal operation against Syrian posts that had fired on fishermen in Lake Kinneret. The U.S. still refused to sell arms to Israel, but consented to France supplying her with advanced Mystère aircraft. On February 13 the Soviet Foreign Ministry declared that the U.S.S.R. could not remain indifferent to developments in the Middle East and warned the Western powers against unilateral action in the area. UN Secretary-General Dag Hammarskjöld paid several visits to the Middle East in unsuccessful attempts to achieve a settlement. The dismissal of General Glubb, the British commander of the Jordanian Arab Legion, was followed by an increase in Egyptian influence in Jordan. Israel speeded up the building of shelters, the training of civil defense personnel, and the fortification of border villages. At the end of April, after artillery duels on the Gaza Strip border and widespread *fedayeen* attacks, Hammarskjöld announced agreement on a general, unconditional cease-fire between Israel and its neighbors, but the arms race continued. Jordan agreed to facilitate the operation of *fedayeen* from its territory and the Arab countries competed in threats against Israel.

For some time there had been differences between Sharett, who favored greater trust in the UN and international opinion, and Ben-Gurion, who emphasized the need for Israel to rely first of all on its own strength. In June, feeling that complete harmony between prime minister and foreign minister was essential in view of the growing dangers, Ben-Gurion replaced Sharett with Golda *Meir. Attacks from Jordan continued throughout July; at the end of the month, after Egypt nationalized the Suez Canal, there were a number of incidents on the southern border as well. The clashes continued in the following months and rose to a peak in October, while international tension grew over the future of the canal. On October 13 the Security Council called for "free and open transit through the Canal without discrimination" and declared that its operation "should be insulated from the politics of any country," but Nasser announced that no Israeli ships would be allowed to pass. Two days later Ben-Gurion told the Knesset that Israel was being subjected to a guerilla war conducted by bands of *fedayeen* organized, equipped, and trained mainly in Egypt and recalled the right to self-defense guaranteed by Article 51 of the UN Charter. He also said that Israel reserved freedom of action if the status quo were violated by the entry of troops from Iraq (which had not signed an Armistice Agreement with Israel) into Jordan. On October 25, after an election victory for pro-Nasserist elements in Jordan, that country joined the Egyptian-Syrian military pact against Israel. Abu-Nawar, commander of the Arab Legion, declared, "We and not Israel will fix the time and place of the battle."

The growing attacks on Israel and the threat of a concerted offensive from the north, east, and southwest coincided with growing apprehension in Britain and France over the threat posed by unfettered Egyptian control of the Suez Canal to their communications and interests. Thus Israel's danger was matched by the opportunity. Ben-Gurion paid a secret visit to France in October to ask Prime Minister Guy Mollet for help. Large quantities of French heavy armaments were sent to Israel and unloaded in secret. On October 27 Ben-Gurion submitted to the cabinet a proposal for a large-scale operation to demolish the bases of the *fedayeen* and the Egyptian army in the Sinai Peninsula and the Gaza Strip and to occupy the shore of the Gulf of Akaba in order to safeguard navigation (even if, as he expected, Israel was compelled by international pressure to evacuate the territory occupied).

Orders were given for the mobilization of the reserves, and on October 29 Israel troops moved into Sinai, taking a number of vital positions near the Negev-Sinai border. On the next day an airborne battalion was dropped near the Mitla Pass in west-central Sinai, and a mechanized column reached the same point on the night of October 30–31, capturing vital points in the heart of the peninsula, outflanking the Egyptian positions in its northeast, and threatening the Suez Canal. At the same time another column thrust toward the same point from the northeast. Israel fighter planes established air superiority over the combat areas.

On the afternoon of October 30, Britain and France had issued an ultimatum calling on both sides to stop fighting and withdraw to ten miles on either side of the Suez Canal. The same evening they vetoed a U.S.-sponsored resolution in the Security Council calling for immediate withdrawal of Israeli troops. Israel accepted the Anglo-French demand, but since Egypt rejected it, the advance continued. On the next morning British and French bombers began a systematic bombardment of military targets in Egypt. Israeli infantry and armor, supported by the air force, continued to move southward into the peninsula, westward toward the canal, and north toward the Egyptian lines of communication with the Gaza Strip.

On November 1, Israel forces took Rafa and El-Arish on the Mediterranean coast, and the Egyptian high command ordered a general retreat, which soon turned into a rout. During the next two days the armored spearheads of the IDF halted ten miles from the canal and the Gaza Strip was taken. Meanwhile a reserve infantry brigade had been moving down the western shore of the Gulf of Akaba, and a pincer movement, threatening the last remaining positions, was completed by a southward advance along the eastern shore of the Gulf of Suez. On November 2 the UN General Assembly, in an emergency session, called for an immediate cease-fire and prompt withdrawal of forces. Israel agreed to the cease-fire the next day, provided Egypt reciprocated. On November 5 Israel occupied Sharm el-Sheikh, and the campaign was over.

The Assembly resolved on the establishment of a UN Emergency Force "to secure and supervise the cessation of hostilities." Israel declared that Egypt's hostile acts had "undermined the peace" and "destroyed the armistice agreement" and called for direct peace negotiations. There was no response to this call. Instead, the United Nations, backed by strongly worded letters from U.S. President Eisenhower and Soviet Premier Bulganin, applied intense pressure on Israel for unconditional withdrawal. Ben-Gurion replied on November 7 that troops would be withdrawn on the conclusion of satisfactory arrangements for the deployment of the UN Emergency Force.

During the next three months Israel fought a stubborn political rearguard action to safeguard free navigation in the Gulf of Akaba and ensure that, in return for the withdrawal of its forces, the Gaza Strip would not be used again as a spearhead for attack. Gradual evacuation started late in November and continued pari passu with efforts to obtain the safeguards required. The withdrawal was completed in March, despite considerable misgivings in Israel and vigorous denunciations of the government by Ḥerut, Aḥdut ha-Avodah, and other opposition parties, which charged it with "wasting the fruits of victory." The UN Emergency Force was stationed in the Gaza Strip and at Sharm el-Sheikh, and a number of the foremost maritime nations, headed by the United States, declared their support for freedom of navigation in the Straits of Tiran and the Gulf of Akaba. Israel, for its part, made it clear that any interference with free navigation in the straits or the gulf would constitute a casus belli. As a result of the Sinai Campaign, Israel secured a considerable degree of quiet on its southwestern borders and free access to Eilat, its outlet for trade with West Africa and Asia – gains that were preserved for ten years.

A tragic incident had occurred on the day the Sinai Campaign began. A strict curfew had been proclaimed on part of the eastern border and 43 Arab villagers, returning from the fields to the village of Kafr Qasim after the start of the curfew, were shot and killed by a Border Police patrol. Compensation was immediately paid to the families, and the men responsible were placed on trial. At a special Knesset session on December 12, Prime Minister Ben-Gurion expressed profound concern at this "flagrant violation" of the sacred principle of the sanctity of human life. Sentencing two officers, one corporal, and five privates to periods of imprisonment ranging from 7 to 17 years in October 1958, a military court emphasized that a soldier was not obliged to obey a manifestly unlawful order and would be held criminally responsible if he did. The principle having been established, it was widely felt that allowance should be made for the tension under which the men acted; the sentences were reduced on appeal and the one officer still in prison at the end of 1959 was granted presidential clemency.

While there was comparative quiet on the Gaza Strip and Sinai borders for several years after the Sinai Campaign, tension broke out from time to time with Jordan and, even more sharply, with Syria. Toward the end of 1957 Jordan tried to obstruct communications with the Israeli enclave on Mount Scopus, and in May 1958 a UNTSO officer and four Israel policemen were killed by Jordanian fire. UN Secretary-General Hammarskjöld discussed the problem with the Jordanian and Israel governments and three times sent special representatives to deal with it, as well as paying a personal visit to the area; but Jordan refused to fulfill its obligations under Article 8 of the Armistice Agreement. At the end of 1958 and the beginning of the following year there were a number of serious incidents in the north in which Israeli settlements were machine-gunned and shelled by the Syrians. Israel appealed to the Security Council but without result. In the spring of 1959 Egypt again interfered with ships carrying goods for Israel through the Suez Canal.

More important, however, were the long-term implications of the situation, particularly in view of Soviet arms supplies to Egypt and later, to Syria. With the failure of British and French intervention in Suez, the United States began to take a more active interest in the Middle East. The Eisenhower Doctrine, approved by the U.S. Congress in March 1957, authorized the President to extend "assistance against armed aggression from any country controlled by international Communism." Despite the opposition of two coalition parties, Mapam and Aḥdut ha-Avodah, the government, in effect, acceded to the doctrine on May 21, but the Israeli statement made no mention of Communism and expressed opposition to "aggression from any quarter against the territorial integrity and political independence of any country." On October 21 Ben-Gurion told the Knesset that "almost a fundamental transformation" was taking place in the Middle East: "The forces contending in our area are not so much the forces of the area itself, but the world blocs of the East and the West."

In February 1958 the United Arab Republic was established by the union of Egypt and Syria and a short-lived Iraqi-Jordanian union was concluded. Israel made considerable efforts to keep the local balance of power in its favor, which could only be done by obtaining more arms from the West. Relations with France in this sphere became even closer; the United Kingdom sold Israel submarines; and the United States also began to be cooperative. Despite the opposition of the left-wing members of the coalition, which led to two cabinet crises in 1958–59, military supplies were also bought from West Germany. In 1958 first approaches were made to the European Economic Community to obtain a trade agreement. Despite this leaning toward a Western orientation, relations with Poland steadily improved and those with other Communist countries remained, on the whole, correct.

At the same time efforts were made to foster technical and economic cooperation with the developing countries in Asia and Africa that were achieving independence from colonial rule. The first country to enter into joint projects of this kind with Israel was Burma, as early as 1954; the second was Ghana, in 1957. Although Israel was accused of collaborating with imperialism in the Suez crisis, the Sinai Campaign brought its problems and the importance of its role to the attention of many countries – particularly in Asia and Africa – that had known little or nothing of Jewish history and the achievements of the Jewish state. In 1958 the Foreign Ministry set up an International Cooperation Division. Leaders of the emergent nations visited Israel, many of them even before their countries achieved independence, to study her social structure and methods of building a new society and economy through vocational training, cooperative enterprise, agricultural settlement, education, and industrial development. It was largely through the international cooperation program that Israel began to extend relations with Asian and African countries, which, it was hoped, might ultimately help in Israel's efforts to achieve peace with its Arab neighbors (see also section on Foreign Policy and International Relations in this entry).

CONSOLIDATION AND DEVELOPMENT: 1954–1959. The second half of Israel's first decade was marked by social consolidation and rapid economic progress. The great majority of the new immigrants, who came mainly from Eastern Europe and North Africa, found homes and jobs, learned the elements of the Hebrew language and the ways of the country, enhanced their skills, and improved their standard of living, although there was still a disturbing gap between the newcomers from the Oriental countries and the mainly Ashkenazi veterans. The large-scale capital imports were used to mechanize agriculture and increase its efficiency; expand roads, telecommunications, and electricity supply; enlarge the merchant fleet and the national airline; modernize the Dead Sea potash works and exploit Negev copper, phosphates, and other minerals; and develop industries, many in partnership with foreign investors.

Despite occasional governmental crises, there was a high degree of political stability. In 1954 Aḥdut ha-Avodah seceded from Mapam and in the following year Mizrachi and Ha-Po'el ha-Mizrachi merged to form the *National Religious Party; otherwise the political structure remained unchanged. The Second and Third Knessets completed their statutory terms. Mapai lost five seats in the 1955 elections, largely due to the economic difficulties that still afflicted considerable sections, but remained the backbone of the cabinet and was able to form an administration with a sound parliamentary majority by replacing the General Zionists with Mapam and Aḥdut ha-Avodah. In 1959, after a period of relative border tranquility following the Sinai Campaign and a general improvement in living standards, it more than recouped its electoral losses. In 1958 the first basic (constitutional) law, dealing with the composition and powers of the Knesset, was passed.

The increased foreign-currency resources at the disposal of the economy helped to moderate inflationary pressures. The three exchange rates were reduced to two (IL1.000 and IL1.800 to the dollar) at the beginning of January 1954 and then to a single stable rate of IL1.800 in July 1955. The curve of consumer prices, which rose by some 20% in each of the years 1953 and 1954, gradually flattened out until, in 1959, there was hardly any rise. National income grew from IL1,000,000,000 in 1950 to almost IL3,000,000,000 in 1958 (both at 1956 prices), i.e., from IL790 to nearly IL1,500 per capita. The gross national product grew by around 10% a year, a figure almost unequaled in any other country. While foreign-currency controls were eased, the public sector (government, local authorities, Jewish Agency, and Histadrut) had a very strong influence on the economy, being directly responsible for about one-fifth of the employment and of the national product. The government extracted some 30% of the national income in the form of taxes and, through incentives to investors and control of the development budget, was able to direct most of the long-term capital investment into socially and nationally desirable channels.

A vast expansion of agriculture made the austerity of the early years a memory of the past. By the end of the first decade, self-sufficiency was achieved in the supply of eggs and poultry, dairy products, vegetables, and fruit. This was accomplished by establishing new villages and consolidating existing ones, improving crop yields by mechanization and better methods, extensive land reclamation and soil conservation, and better utilization of water for irrigation. During the ten years 1948/49 to 1957/58, the area under cultivation grew by about 150% – from 400,000 to 1,000,000 acres – while the irrigated area rose more than fourfold to over 300,000 acres. About 70% of the vegetables, 30% of the poultry, and 45% of the milk were produced by new immigrants' villages established during the decade. The drainage of the Ḥuleh swamps, completed in 1957, reclaimed 15,000 acres of high-quality farmland. The Jewish National Fund and the government afforested some 50,000 acres – four times as much land as during two generations of Zionist settlement – and planted trees along almost 500 miles of highway.

The main road network was expanded from about 1,000 mi. to 1,860 mi.; in 1957 the 147-mile first-class road from Beersheba to Eilat was completed, providing a good road link between the Red Sea and the Mediterranean for the first time in history. The railroad was extended to Beersheba and the rolling stock was dieselized. Haifa port was modernized and a start was made with the utilization of Eilat. The merchant fleet grew to 41 vessels, with a total deadweight of 280,000 tons. El Al carried 70,000 passengers in 1,240 flights in 1958, compared with 15,500 in 475 flights in 1950. About IL260,000,000 was invested in expanding electric generating capacity, which rose more than fivefold to 350,000 kilowatts, consumption rising almost sixfold to 1,400 million kwh.

The output of industry was doubled during the decade, reaching almost IL3,000,000,000 in 1958; so was the number of employed, which came to some 160,000. Industrial exports increased from $18,000,000 in 1950 to $81,000,000 in 1958, including $33,000,000 worth of polished diamonds, four times as much as in 1950. Special inducements, including government loans and tax reliefs, were held out to foreign and local investors prepared to help in the dispersal of the population by setting up enterprises in the new development areas. Up to the end of 1958, IL226,000,000, including IL136,000,000 from the development budget, was invested in 366 undertakings to these areas. During the same period 832 undertakings were approved under the Law for the Encouragement of Capital Investment, involving $192,000,000 of foreign and IL 194,000,000 of local capital, as well as IL242,000,000 in government loans. About IL140,000,000 were invested by the state in the exploitation of minerals, including copper, phosphates, potash, and bromine; a new potash plant, replacing the works at the northern end of the Dead Sea destroyed in the War of Independence, was completed at Sodom in 1956. In September 1955 oil was struck at Heleẓ near Ashkelon, and about 100,000 tons, almost 10% of the country's consumption, were pumped in 1958. Two gas wells, with an output of 1,000,000 cu.ft. per day, were sunk.

In 1958, when there were widespread celebrations to mark the country's tenth anniversary, the population passed the 2,000,000 mark; over 1,800,000 were Jews, constituting 15% of world Jewry, as against less than 6% in 1948. The Jewish population had grown since independence by over 1,160,000 or 179%. Over 940,000 immigrants had come in and 105,000 had left, leaving a migration balance of almost 840,000, which accounted for 72% of the growth (the remaining 28% resulted from natural increase). The non-Jewish, mainly Arab, population had grown by 61,000, of which over 95% was due to natural increase.

Toward the end of 1954 a new "ship to settlement" policy was introduced. Instead of the immigrants being housed temporarily in camps or *ma'barot*, they were sent directly from the ship or plane to a new village or "development town" where housing was ready and work available in the neighborhood. A regional settlement scheme for populating large, sparsely inhabited areas was initiated. Clusters of 5–8 villages were focused on a rural center, with an elementary school, cultural facilities, a dispensary, and farm-service institutions. The scheme was first carried out in the Lachish area, with 54 villages by 1959 and the "county town" of Kiryat Gat, where a secondary school, shopping facilities, and industrial plants were located. A social advantage of this arrangement was that immigrants from a particular country – sometimes even a district or town – could be concentrated in a fairly homogeneous village, obviating the friction that often arose between communities of different cultural backgrounds, while the process of merging and integration proceeded when the villagers and their children met in the rural or urban centers and their schools.

Out of a civilian labor force of some 700,000 the daily average of unemployment registered at the labor exchanges was 9,300 – 1.4% of the total. Some 150,000 homes were built for the newcomers during the period, and 45,000 families moved from the *ma'barot* to permanent housing, though 20,000 families (about 110,000 souls) were still to be rehoused. The great majority of the newcomers had thus been provided with the fundamental necessities of integration: homes and jobs. A high proportion, approaching one half, had learned new skills: 106,000 unskilled and semi-skilled adult workers had attended vocational training courses run by the Ministry of Labor, the Histadrut, the municipalities, and voluntary organizations; average output per worker had been raised by about 50%. An entire new farming class, mainly smallholders, had risen, learning to till the soil by practice, example, and the teaching of Jewish Agency instructors. Practically all the children of the immigrants, like those of the veteran population, went to school. When they were called up for military service, the army taught the rudiments of the language, the national culture, and general knowledge to those who had not completed their education; for young newcomers the period of national service was decisive in preparing them for integration and citizenship.

Gradually, the immigrants started to find their way in social and political life. They grew somewhat more independent in their dealings with the authorities and began to learn the techniques of self-government in the village councils, factory and shop committees (the basic cells of the trade-union movement), local political party branches, and local authorities. They played only a minor role in national politics, however. Seeking their votes, the parties placed representatives of the various communities on their election lists, but these were more often veterans of the same origin as the newcomers rather than recent immigrants. At every parliamentary election, independent immigrants' lists, claiming to represent Sephardim or other communal groupings, were submitted, but none of these managed to return any candidates after 1951.

There was still a considerable backlog in the complete absorption and integration of the immigrants, however. The houses built for them during the mass influx were small, often hopelessly inadequate for the many large families. While the immigrants were improving their skills, the veterans were making even faster progress and still largely monopolized senior administrative and managerial posts. Elementary education was free and universal, but standards were lower in the new immigrant areas, where it was difficult to obtain good teachers, and the children did not receive the full benefit, since the home made little or no contribution to the learning process. The major educational effort during the decade had to be devoted to the basic tasks of building schools and providing teachers for the vastly increased school population (in the school year 1958/59 there were over 550,000 pupils and students, compared with 130,000 in 1948/49). Toward the end of the period, special efforts were initiated to bring up the educational standards in immigrant areas. In the secondary schools, scholarships were offered by the state, the Histadrut, and public bodies, and requirements for admission were modified in the case of children from immigrant areas and the Oriental communities. There was a gradual improvement in the percentage of children born in Asia and Africa receiving post-primary education; between 1956/57 and 1958/59, while 71% of the secondary-school population was born in Israel in both years, the percentage of the foreign-born who came from Asia and Africa rose from 36% to 43%.

Perhaps the most serious aspect of the communal problem was the psychological one. To many of the newcomers from North African and Middle Eastern countries, the wide gap between the status, educational achievements, and social conditions of the Ashkenazi and Oriental communities appeared to be due, not only to objective circumstances, but also to favoritism on the one hand and deliberate discrimination on the other. In July 1959, passions erupted into rioting in the Haifa slum quarter of Wadi Salib, the new township of Migdal ha-Emek, and Beersheba. In the last two places, the trouble arose over employment difficulties; in the first – a former Arab neighborhood inhabited largely by North African immigrants who had drifted to the town from various places of prior settlement – the riots, which started with a café disturbance, assumed serious proportions. But in the parliamentary elections that followed in November, the communal lists received comparatively little support and, on the whole, the new immigrants continued to support the established parties. The success of Mapai, which gained seven seats, was thought to be due not only to Ben-Gurion's enhanced prestige after the Suez Campaign and the general rise in the standard of living, but also to a backlash generated by fear of communal fragmentation and the desire for a strong government (see also Israel, State of: *Population, section on Intercommunal Problems).

Another focus of controversy was the place of religion in the country's life, particularly where legislation or administrative action was concerned. From time to time there were heated arguments – sometimes accompanied by street demonstrations – over public Sabbath observance, complaints of discrimination against state religious schools, and such matters as mixed bathing in a Jerusalem municipal swimming pool. The fanatical *Neturei Karta group in Jerusalem often took the lead, more moderate religious circles following suit to avoid losing support. The non-Orthodox community was also concerned with the place of Jewish tradition in the country's life. In 1957 the minister of education and culture, Zalman Aranne, initiated a "Jewish Consciousness" program in the state (non-religious) schools. It aimed at laying greater stress on the Jewish cultural heritage and spiritual values, stimulating the study of Diaspora Jewish history and contemporary Jewry, and inculcating respect for Jewish religious observance and a feeling of responsibility toward the nation in Israel and abroad. People from all sections cooperated in disseminating a knowledge of the Bible through study circles and conventions, in which the prime minister played a prominent role, and there was an unprecedented, almost universal, interest in the World Bible Contest held in Jerusalem in 1958. In 1958 a heated controversy arose over the ruling of the minister of interior, Israel Bar-Yehudah of Aḥdut ha-Avodah, that a person declaring in good faith that he was a Jew by nationality should be so recorded in the Population Register and that minors should be registered according to the declaration of their parents. The National Religious Party objected to anyone being registered as a Jew by nationality unless he was recognized by rabbinical law as a Jew by religion (i.e., born of a Jewish mother or converted according to the *halakhah*) and resigned from the government in protest. A cabinet committee appointed to reconsider the question invited Jewish scholars and religious leaders the world over to express their opinions, which were overwhelmingly in support of the halakhic ruling. The matter was left in abeyance until March 1960, when Ḥayyim Moshe *Shapira, the NRP leader who had rejoined the cabinet as minister of the interior, issued new regulations in keeping with the rabbinical interpretation. The problem came to the fore again in 1970, when the validity of these regulations was challenged in the High Court.

The shadow of the Nazi Holocaust dominated a *cause célère* that aroused bitter feelings in the late 1950s and precipitated a cabinet crisis. In 1955 Malkiel Gruenwald was charged with criminally slandering Israel *Kasztner, then a government official and a candidate for the Knesset on the Mapai list, by accusing him of having collaborated with the Nazis in Hungary during World War II. The Jerusalem District Court found that Gruenwald's charges were, on the whole, justified and acquitted him. The state appealed, but in March 1957, while the appeal was pending, Kasztner was murdered by three young men, who were imprisoned for the crime. At the beginning of the following year the Supreme Court reversed the lower court's findings, clearing Kasztner of most of the accusations against him.

Higher education was considerably expanded with the financial aid of Jewish benefactors abroad. At the end of the decade there were about 10,000 students at the Hebrew University, the Technion (Israel Institute of Technology, Haifa), Tel Aviv University (founded in 1956), and the Bar-Ilan religious university (opened in 1955), compared with 1,500 in 1948. Cut off from its original buildings on Mount Scopus, the Hebrew University opened a new campus in western Jerusalem in 1958. Fundamental and applied research at the Weizmann Institute of Science, founded in 1949, and other institutions was achieving a growing reputation abroad, as evidenced by research grants from the United States and other countries.

Israel took second place in the world for the number of titles published (1,210 in 1958) in proportion to the population, as well as for book imports per head. The *Academy of the Hebrew Language, founded in 1953 to succeed the Va'ad-ha-Lashon ("Language Council"), conducted research and issued authoritative rulings on grammar, terminology, and spelling. The conclusions of Israel scholarship were embodied in new editions of the Bible, the Talmud, and outstanding works of rabbinic literature, as well as encyclopedias of various types, notably the comprehensive Encyclopedia Hebraica. *Archaeology received a new impetus with the achievement of independence and the discoveries made in establishing new villages and digging foundations for new buildings. Seven of the *Dead Sea Scrolls were acquired for the nation, and Israeli scholars, speaking Hebrew as a living language and intimately familiar with the Holy Land, made distinctive contributions to their study.

The established repertory theaters, *Habimah, *Ohel, and the *Cameri, as well as many smaller companies, presented world classics, recent successes, and a smaller number of original works. The *Israel Philharmonic Orchestra, with its 22,000 subscribers (a world-record percentage of the population), the Kol Israel (State Broadcasting Service) Orchestra, and others reached a high standard, and large audiences attended regular music and dance festivals. Israel artists and composers worked in a variety of styles, and some achieved international recognition. There were 18 morning papers – 11 of them in Hebrew – and two afternoon papers, both Hebrew, as well as 320 other periodicals in 12 languages.

The Arab and Druze communities shared in the general rise in living standards. They benefited from universal, free primary education, the national insurance scheme, the legal protection of women and children, and the improved social welfare and health services provided by the state authorities and the Histadrut. Local government was gradually extended to Arab areas; roads were built and water, electricity, and sanitation facilities installed. As a result of irrigation, reclamation, and improved farming methods, the output of Arab agriculture increased sixfold during the decade. Arabs voted in parliamentary elections: 91.2% of them went to the polls in 1955 and 88.4% in 1959 – a higher proportion than among the Jewish electors. There were eight Arabs in the Third Knesset and seven in the Fourth, five of whom represented Arab lists associated with Mapai. In the predominantly Arab-inhabited areas, close to the low and winding borders, military government was in force to prevent espionage and infiltration; residents had to receive permits from the military governors to leave, and others required permits to enter. The system, which was a cause of deep dissatisfaction among the Arabs, was severely criticized by opposition parties, who accused Mapai of exploiting it to ensure political domination over the Arab inhabitants, and the regulations were gradually eased over time (see *Israel, State of: Arab Population).

ECONOMIC ADVANCE AND POLITICAL REALIGNMENT: 1960–1966. The seven years that followed the 1959 elections, in which Ben-Gurion seemed to have reached the zenith of his popularity and power, were marked by continued economic progress – especially in the development of industry – on the one hand, and a series of political crises that transformed the party map of Israel, on the other. While the immediate issue in the internal struggle within Mapai seemed, on the surface, to be the Lavon Affair, there were deeper issues involved. Israel was developing into a modern, mainly urban and industrial, society. Living standards – in housing, household equipment, education, and entertainment – were rising to levels that would have been regarded as unreasonably luxurious by the early pioneers. The electric refrigerator and the gas stove were replacing the ice-box and the kerosene cooker; the veteran population was well on the way to West European standards, and the new immigrants were hot on their heels. The egalitarianism which had reigned – in theory, at least – in the Histadrut and the public service was being challenged. Most of the political leaders had won their spurs in trade-union activity and agricultural settlement; now new strata of administrators, scientists, and businessmen, concerned more with practical affairs than with ideologies, were arising. Professional men and senior officials demanded salaries in keeping with their skills and experience. Younger men, with some encouragement from Ben-Gurion, were breaking into the ranks of the top leadership. Even in the kibbutzim, new problems were arising – some as a result of restitution payments made by Germany to individual members.

The political controversies of the period (treated in greater detail in Israel, State of: *Political Life and Parties), may be divided into three phases. In the second half of 1960, Pinḥas Lavon claimed that new evidence, recently disclosed, proved that he had not been responsible for the security "mishap" that had led to his resignation. In the meantime, he had been appointed secretary-general of the Histadrut, but his further progress in the political field was blocked by the memory of the old affair. Lavon's efforts to clear his name developed into a virulent controversy with Ben-Gurion and his supporters, which came to a climax with Mapai's decision to depose Lavon from his Histadrut post.

At the same time a second focus of controversy emerged: the decision of a cabinet committee clearing Lavon, which Ben-Gurion denounced as a misuse of authority and a miscarriage of justice. When Ben-Gurion resigned and no solution to the subsequent crisis could be found but premature Knesset elections, his party again rallied round him and helped him reform his government after the elections. Ben-Gurion, however, had not given up his struggle to rectify the "miscarriage of justice," and in 1963, shortly before submitting his final resignation as prime minister, he commissioned a new inquiry into the background of the affair.

In 1963 President Ben-Zvi died and was succeeded by Shneour Zalman *Shazar.

Levi *Eshkol, nominated by Ben-Gurion as his successor, at first proclaimed a policy of continuity, but his personal style and inclinations, as well as his associations with the veteran leadership, soon found expression. He displayed a more friendly attitude toward the Zionist Organization, which he assured of full state backing and cooperation in its work in the Diaspora, as well as in Israel, and adopted a more conciliatory tone toward the opposition, placating Ḥerut by authorizing the reinterment in Israel of its deceased leader, Jabotinsky (who had requested in his will, written in the 1930s, that his remains should be transferred to Palestine only "by order of that country's eventual Jewish government"). Eshkol was more restrained in his public references to Arab leaders and to the Soviet Union, though speculations as to a new trend in foreign relations were not justified by any substantive change in policy. At the same time there was no advancement for the Ben-Gurionist "young guard"; the veterans were firmly in the saddle, and the attempt to conclude an alliance with Aḥdut ha-Avodah was widely believed to be motivated not only by the long-standing aspiration for labor unity, but also by the Mapai leaders' desire to establish a counter-weight to the challenge from within their own party.

The third phase started toward the end of 1964, when Ben-Gurion renewed his demand for a judicial inquiry into the actions of the 1960 cabinet committee. The pent-up antagonisms came to the surface and a heated controversy broke out, reaching a climax shortly before the 1965 elections with a split in the party and the establishment of a break-away list, *Rafi (Reshimat Po'alei Yisrael – Israel Labor List), headed by Ben-Gurion, Moshe *Dayan, and Shimon *Peres. The partial healing of the 1944 rift in Mapai by the establishment of an "Alignment" with Aḥdut ha-Avodah was thus achieved only at the expense of a new breach, which was closed only after the Six-Day War.

There were also other changes in the party map. In 1961 the General Zionists and the Progressives united to form the Liberal Party, but the new body disintegrated in 1965, when the General Zionist section merged with Ḥerut to form *Gaḥal (Gush Ḥerut Liberalim – Ḥerut-Liberal Bloc), while most of the Progressives established the Independent Liberal Party. In the latter years the Communists split into a mainly Jewish section, which kept the old name, Maki (Miflagah Komunistit Yisre'elit – Israel Communist Party), and a mainly Arab section, Rakaḥ (Reshimah Komunistit Ḥadashah – New Communist List), with strong Nasserist sympathies.

Controversies over religious matters arose from time to time during the period. It took three years before agreement could be reached on the procedure for electing the Ashkenazi and Sephardi chief rabbis after the death of Rabbi Herzog in 1959 and the expiry of Rabbi Nissim's term in the following year. Between 1962 and 1964 there were repeated demonstrations and sit-down strikes by immigrants of the *Bene Israel community from India in protest against difficulties in getting rabbinical approval to marry with other Jews because of doubts as to the validity of their marriage and divorce procedures in their country of origin. In 1964 there were controversies over the proposal to install an "international" (non-kosher) kitchen on the Zim liner SS *Shalom* and the problem of supervising *kashrut* at the large regional slaughterhouse at Kiryat Malakhi. Considerable feeling was aroused over the case of the ten-year-old Yossele Shumacher, who was withheld from his parents by extreme religious groups associated with his grandfather in order to assure his receiving a rigidly Orthodox education and was ultimately found in 1962 by the Israel Secret Service in New York, where he was being kept under cover. A League for the Abolition of Religious Coercion was established and occasionally clashed with religious zealots.

Religious life flourished, however, with little connection with such controversies. About one-third of the children attended state and other religious schools; in 1968 there were 250 yeshivot, with 18,000 students, mostly in Jerusalem and Bene Berak, constituting the greatest center of Jewish rabbinic learning in the world. A new generation of Israel-born religious youth, recognizable by their knitted skull-caps, were growing up in their own youth movements and a wide network of religious kibbutzim and moshavim. Sabbath and festivals were not only observed in the home but also, as official public holidays, were marked by the closing of shops, factories, offices, and public institutions.

A profound impression was made on the country by the trial of Adolf *Eichmann, who had been the main organizer of the Nazi extermination program. His apprehension in Argentina by Secret Service volunteers was announced on May 23, 1960, and he was indicted under the Nazis and Nazi Collaborators (Punishment) Law, 1950. He was put on trial in Jerusalem on April 11, 1961, and sentenced to death on December 15; on May 31, 1962 – two days after the rejection of his appeal to the Supreme Court – he was executed – the first and only death penalty carried out under Israel law. The trial brought home to the consciousness of the public, particularly the youth and the Oriental communities, the horrors of the Holocaust and its significance in modern Jewish history. It also emphasized the role of Israel as a Jewish state where, for the first time since the beginning of the Exile, a Jewish court could mete out justice for crimes against the Jewish people.

Despite the political, religious, and other controversies, most of the second decade was a period of rapid economic development. During the period 1960–65, the gross national product increased by an average of about 11% a year. Exports were almost doubled, reaching a total of $406,000,000 (50% of imports) in 1965. The domestic market for locally grown food was approaching saturation point; with the rise in the standard of living, further increments in personal incomes were being spent mainly on manufactured goods. Farmers, therefore, concentrated on growing more variegated crops, specialization, and increasing efficiency by mechanization and other means. Exports of fresh agricultural produce totaled $86,000,000 in 1965, of which $71,000,000 was citrus. New crops were introduced: cotton, supplying almost all the local demand; groundnuts, mainly for export; and sugarbeets, processed in local refineries. The national water carrier, which brought the upper Jordan waters through Lake Kinneret down to the Negev, was completed and went into full operation in 1965. As conventional water resources were now almost fully exploited, attention was focused on the desalinization of sea and brackish water, various methods being closely studied and tried out. U.S. President Johnson and Prime Minister Eshkol agreed in 1964 to study the feasibility of erecting a joint atomic-power and sea-water desalinization station, but difficulties in producing water at an economic price delayed execution of the project.

The greatest growth was in industry, which had now become the main instrument for absorbing the immigrants and reducing dependence on external resources by replacing imports and stepping up exports. Industrial production totaled IL 6,900,000,000 in 1965 and employed 236,000 hands. The growth was more rapid in new industries, like metals and machinery, chemicals and fertilizers, copper and phosphates, and electronic equipment, than in the established ones, such as food, textiles, and building materials. Israel now manufactured products like paper, tires, radios, and refrigerators, which had had to be imported in the previous decade. Israel Aircraft Industries, Lydda, which had started as the Bedek works for maintenance and overhaul, was now the country's largest industrial organization, manufacturing small military and civilian planes. As Jaffa and Tel Aviv ports were inadequate to handle the greatly increased trade, a new deepwater port was built at Ashdod and started operations at the end of 1965. A new harbor at Eilat was inaugurated in the same year. The merchant fleet grew to over 100 ships, with a deadweight capacity of some 1,100,000 tons, and El Al carried over 300,000 passengers in 1965 – over six times as many as in 1960. Widespread improvements in technical, financial, and administrative skills helped to raise productivity. The government directed extensive resources – in some years two-thirds of the development budget – to industrial development. Its influence was not always exerted on purely economic grounds. To promote the dispersal of the population and provide employment for newcomers, investors were often induced to erect their plants in *Kiryat Shemonah, *Beth Shemesh, or *Dimonah instead of Tel Aviv or its environs, where they could have operated more profitably. For the sake of self-sufficiency the Histadrut was helped to expand its "Steel City" at Acre, and private entrepreneurs were aided in setting up paper mills at Ḥaderah, though it might have been cheaper to import the paper and the finished steel.

Prices had risen considerably since the exchange rate of IL1.80 to the dollar was fixed, and government efforts to direct investment into socially and politically desirable channels had led to the proliferation of subsidies, preferential loans, tax reliefs, administrative restrictions on imports, and other inducements and pressures. The result was that the average effective rate of exchange in 1961 was about IL2.70 to the dollar, and for some protected or subsidized products as high as IL6.00 or IL8.00 per dollar. Budgetary deficits in 1960 and 1961, as well as a considerable influx of personal restitution payments from Germany, which grew from $26,000,000 in 1960 to $110,000,000 in 1961, added to the inflationary pressures.

In February 1962, a second "New Economic Policy" was announced. It was based on devaluation to the rate of IL3.00 per dollar and the gradual reduction or annulment of discriminatory subsidies, levies, premiums, etc., in order to put production on an economic basis, expose local industries to competition from imports, make exports more profitable, and compel manufacturers to increase efficiency. The policy was not consistently applied, however. Concessions were made to various groups of producers, as well as to mortgagees whose payments were linked to the value of the dollar. Inflationary pressures continued: prices started rising in 1963 at the rate of some 7% per year, and wage increases in the private sector were followed by a considerable rise in civil service salaries, a by-product of the introduction of a uniform grading system. Average nominal hourly wages rose by 17% in 1964 and again in 1965. The adverse trade balance (goods and services) grew to an average of some $500,000,000 in the years 1962–65. This was the price for the continued rise in the national product, a 6–7% annual growth in national income per capita, and a state of full employment.

After the 1965 elections the government took steps to cool down the overheated economy, raising taxes and cutting down its expenditures. Several important public works projects, such as the national water carrier and the building of Ashdod port, had been completed. A drop in immigration from an average of about 60,000 a year in 1961–64 to 30,000 in 1965 and 16,000 in 1966 led to a decrease in the demand for housing and a slump in the building and ancillary industries. The government's measures of economic restraint succeeded in stabilizing prices, keeping imports stationary, and reducing the adverse trade balance by some $75,000,000 in 1966, but only at the cost of an economic recession and a considerable rise in unemployment, to the level of 30,000. After 15 years of almost continuous expansion, the national product in effect did not increase at all during the year. The government hoped that a wage freeze, increased productivity, and the transfer of labor and resources to production for export would, in the long run, put the economy on a sounder footing, but the economic difficulties had a depressing effect on public morale. It was in an atmosphere of gloom and uncertainty that the threat to national survival, in the early summer of 1967, galvanized the nation into a new upsurge of energy and confidence, which encompassed all spheres of national life.

Education continued to expand: in the 1966/67 school year there were some 750,000 pupils and students, including about 120,000 in post-primary schools and 30,000 in the universities. A graded fee system was introduced by stages in the post-primary schools: those who passed a uniform examination in the basic subjects were subsidized, partially or wholly, in accordance with family income and circumstances. About 70% of pupils continued their studies after the age of 14: half in academic high schools and the rest in agricultural or vocational secondary schools. Special efforts were still needed to equalize the educational opportunities of children whose parents had come from Asia and Africa, only about 25% of whom received post-primary schooling. Measures taken in new immigrant areas included free kindergartens for three-and four-year-old children; a longer school day; separate grouping of children in the higher grades of the primary school according to attainments in Hebrew, mathematics and English, enabling them to progress at the rate best suited to their abilities in each subject; and the establishment of an Israel Education Fund through which donors from abroad helped to build comprehensive and other schools in the development areas. The Hebrew University and the Technion continued to expand, with 12,000 and 5,000 students, respectively; Tel Aviv University, which became an independent institution in 1961, had 8,000, and Bar-Ilan 3,500. The nuclei of two more universities at *Beersheba (from 1970 the University of the Negev) and *Haifa (from 1969 the University of Haifa), were established under the supervision of the older institutions.

More and more, Israel was becoming a world Jewish center. In addition to the Zionist Organization, which held its quadrennial congresses and the annual meetings of its General Council in Jerusalem, many Zionist and other Jewish organizations held their conventions in Israel. Thousands of young people attended study institutes and youth-leaders' courses organized by the Jewish Agency or came for periods of work in kibbutzim. The Jewish Agency also conducted courses for teachers and communal leaders, and rabbinical seminaries and other Jewish institutions abroad arranged their own courses in Israel. Ties between Israel and the Diaspora were reinforced by a growing network of family and other personal relationships: a high proportion of the thousands of Jewish tourists had relatives and close friends in Israel. The ideal of the "spiritual center" enunciated by Aḥad Ha-Am was taking shape, although there were those who pointed to evidence of cultural and sociological divergences between the "sabras" growing up in Israel and young Jews in the Diaspora.

There was a steady expansion in the scope, and improvement in the cordiality, of Israel's foreign ties during the period. In 1967 Israel maintained diplomatic relations with 98 countries, with permanent missions in 78 of them, compared with 55 countries and 38 permanent missions in 1958. The number of countries with diplomatic missions in Israel increased from 43 to 58, seven others having non-resident representatives. The only significant exceptions were the Arab and some Muslim countries and a few others, like India, closely associated with them. Relations were particularly close with the United States, the British Commonwealth countries, West European states (like France, Holland, and the Scandinavian countries), and some of the countries of Latin America and Africa. Although the U.S. Operations Mission in Israel was withdrawn in 1962, as Israel could no longer be considered an underdeveloped country, American aid, in the form of government and other loans and the sale of agricultural surpluses, continued. In view of the flow of Soviet jet bombers and missiles to Egypt, U.S. President Kennedy stated in May 1962 that, if necessary, America would take measures to prevent or halt aggression in the Middle East, and in September 1962 the United States, for the first time, publicly agreed to supply arms to Israel by selling Hawk ground-to-air defensive missiles. President de Gaulle maintained France's policy of cordial support and, on the occasion of visits by Ben-Gurion in 1961 and Eshkol in 1964, publicly referred to Israel as "our friend and ally." French Mystère jets constituted a major part of Israel's air-strike force. The international cooperation program was expanded to cover Latin American and some Mediterranean, as well as African and Asian, countries.

Relations with the German Federal Republic aroused considerable difficulty and controversy. Israel was represented by a mission at Cologne, which, while primarily concerned with trade, also performed consular and informative functions. Deliveries under the reparations agreement were duly completed, totaling over $400,000,000 in the ten-year period ending 1962. After a meeting between Ben-Gurion and Chancellor Konrad Adenauer in New York in March 1960, West Germany began to give Israel secret military aid and there were discussions on the possibility of large-scale economic assistance after the end of reparations. Leading individuals and various groups from Germany visited Israel; trade relations developed and there were some cultural exchanges. These trends were criticized by some survivors of the Holocaust and others as "treason to the memory of the victims of the Nazis." Ḥerut and left-wing critics accused the government of giving the stamp of Israel approval to German efforts to attain respectability and of endangering Israel's relations with the Soviet Union. Ben-Gurion replied that only a racist outlook could justify a boycott of Germans as such and that Israel needed German aid and support to safeguard her security. In 1963 there were reports that German scientists were helping Egypt to develop weapons of mass destruction, and Israel demanded that the German government put an end to their activities. Another crisis arose in 1965, when West Germany succumbed to Arab pressure by ending military assistance to Israel, but offered, in compensation, to establish full diplomatic relations and consider extended economic aid. The crisis was resolved when the first German and Israel ambassadors presented their credentials in the respective capitals in August; agreement on a German loan of DM160,000,000 was concluded in May 1966.

The Soviet Union continued to denounce Israel and Zionism, rejecting charges of cultural and other discrimination against Soviet Jews and appeals to permit them to settle in Israel, at least if they had relatives there. There was no response to Israel's efforts to improve economic and cultural relations, apart from isolated exchange visits by sports teams, musicians, etc. In reply to a Soviet note on the denuclearization of the Mediterranean area in 1963, Israel declared that the immediate danger arose out of the conventional arms build-up of the Arab states, which was openly directed against Israel. In May 1964 Prime Minister Eshkol repeated an assurance given by Ben-Gurion in December 1960 that "nuclear development in Israel is designed exclusively for peaceful purposes" and declared that the government "has not taken the initiative in introducing new arms or new types of arms – either conventional or non-conventional – to the Middle East." There was growing concern about the U.S.S.R.'s supply of arms to Egypt and Syria and its use of the veto in the UN Security Council to prevent the adoption of any decision unfavorable to the Arabs.

For a decade after the Sinai Campaign there was no large-scale outbreak of hostilities between Israel and the Arabs, but neither was there a decline in tension. Arab hatred of Israel was continually fanned by teachers, journalists, and politicians; incessant declarations of undying hostility came from leaders of both "progressive" and "conservative" Arab states. Ben-Gurion repeatedly stated that Israel was prepared for complete disarmament in Israel and the Arab countries under mutual supervision and proposed a joint American-Soviet guarantee of the territorial independence of all Middle East states, but there was no response to either proposal.

Nasser made no secret of his refusal to acquiesce in the continued existence of Israel. In June 1962, for example, he spoke of his people's "determination to liquidate one of the most dangerous enclaves opposing the struggle of our peoples." In the main, however, especially after the beginning of his involvement in the Yemen toward the end of 1962, he stressed that a long period of preparation would be required before the final clash. Apart from occasional flare-ups on the border with Jordan, most of the attacks came from Syrian positions on the Golan Heights overlooking the demilitarized zones and Lake Kinneret. An Israeli reprisal operation in 1962 drew the usual Security Council condemnation, but a resolution condemning the killing of settlers in border villages in the following year was vetoed by the Soviet Union.

The Arab summit conferences in Cairo and Alexandria, in January and September 1964, decided to intensify the struggle against Israel by diverting the headwaters of the Jordan River to frustrate Israel's water-development plans, setting up a unified Syrian-Lebanese-Jordanian military command, and establishing a Palestinian Liberation Organization, headed by Aḥmad Shukeiri, with an "army" composed of Arab refugees. On January 20 Prime Minister Eshkol pointed out that Jordan, Syria, and Lebanon were drawing considerable quantities of water from the Jordan-Yarmuk system and that Israel was taking no more than her share in accordance with the Johnston Plan. "Israel will oppose unilateral and illegal measures by Arab countries and will act for the preservation of her vital rights," he declared. In the spring of 1965 Israel artillery, returning Syrian fire, damaged preliminary works in connection with the diversion scheme.

In the same year a new Palestinian terrorist organization, al-Fataḥ, began operations on a considerable scale, sending small bands of terrorists from bases in Syria, Lebanon, and Jordan into Israel to sabotage railroads and other installations and blow up homes and public buildings. Israel warned that it would hold its neighbors responsible for attacks initiated from their territories and carried out reprisals in Jordan and Lebanon. The seizure of power in Syria by an extreme wing of the Baath Party, with pro-Communist leanings, was followed by more frequent shooting at Israeli farmers and army patrols and greater encouragement for al-Fataḥ operations. Syrian Premier Yusuf Zu'ayin warned: "We shall set the entire area afire and any Israeli movement will result in a final resting place for Israel." Israel Foreign Minister Abba Eban told the Security Council in October 1965 that armed infiltrators organized in Syria had committed 61 outrages on Israeli territory since January. He declared that Israel had no interest in the social philosophy or international orientation of the Syrian regime and emphatically denied allegations that Israel was planning to overthrow it. Further attacks took place while the Council was deliberating, but a motion "inviting" Syria to stop sabotage incursions from her territory was vetoed by the Soviet Union.

In default of international action, Israel took steps to strengthen her defenses. On November 8 Prime Minister Eshkol announced that the period of compulsory service for men, which had been reduced to 26 months in 1963, would be restored to 30 months. On November 13, the day after three Israeli soldiers were killed and six wounded by a land mine near the armistice line in the Mt. Hebron area in Jordanian territory, a strong Israeli force crossed the armistice demarcation line and, after evacuating the residents, blew up 40 houses in es-Samu and two other villages where marauders had found shelter; 15 trucks carrying Arab Legion reinforcements were also destroyed. The Security Council unanimously (except for one abstention) censured Israel for the raid.

The Six-Day War and After: 1967–1970

Israel celebrated her 19th Independence Day on May 15, 1967, with a modest military parade in Jerusalem, from which aircraft, armor, and artillery were excluded in compliance with the 1949 Armistice Agreement with Jordan. Three and a half weeks later, after the *Six-Day War, the situation in the Middle East had been radically transformed: the Egyptian, Jordanian, and Syrian armies had been shattered; Israel was in control of territories stretching from the Golan Heights to Sharm el-Sheikh and from the Suez Canal to the Jordan River; and a new upsurge of national energy and confidence had been matched by a wave of concern and devotion that swept over world Jewry, engulfing hundreds of thousands who realized, when the Jewish state was in peril, how much its survival meant to them. This feeling affected Jews in all countries, including both the youth and the most assimilated.

Tension on the Syrian frontier had risen steadily during the early months of 1967, despite a special series of meetings of the Israel-Syrian MAC to discuss practical arrangements for securing a peaceful atmosphere on the armistice demarcation line. Israel repeatedly complained to the UN Security Council and warned that she would take all measures necessary to protect the lives of her citizens. On April 7, after heavy shelling of border villages by Syrian tanks and heavy artillery, Israeli aircraft went into action and shot down six Syrian Mig 21s.

Radio Moscow accused Israel of attacking Syria in the service of American "reactionary and imperialist circles" that were plotting to prevent the consolidation of the "progressive" Syrian regime. While terrorist raids into Israel continued, the Soviet Union told the Egyptians that Israel was concentrating "huge armed forces" near the Syrian border. Dmitri Chuvakhin, the Soviet Ambassador to Israel, refused an invitation from Prime Minister Eshkol to verify, by personal inspection on the spot, that the allegation was unfounded. Israel immediately denied the Soviet allegations and as UN Secretary-General U Thant stated on May 19, "reports from UNTSO observers confirmed the absence of troop concentrations and significant troop movements on both sides of the line."

Meanwhile, on May 14, Nasser had begun openly dispatching large numbers of Egyptian troops into Sinai. Eshkol told the Israel government that the Egyptian troop movements, apparently, had more demonstrative than practical significance, but ordered part of the reserves mobilized as a precautionary measure. On May 16 Cairo Radio declared: "The existence of Israel has continued too long. We welcome the Israeli aggression, we welcome the battle that we have long awaited. The great hour has come. The battle has come in which we shall destroy Israel." On the same day Egypt demanded the withdrawal of the UN Emergency Force (UNEF) from the Gaza Strip and Sinai borders and Sharm el-Sheikh, and when U Thant replied that any such request would be regarded as a demand for its complete withdrawal, officially requested the evacuation of the force. On May 19 the UNEF commander, General Rikhye, told Israel that the force would cease to function the same day. U Thant flew to Cairo on May 22; on the next day Nasser announced his intention to block the Straits of Tiran to Israeli ships and others carrying "strategic cargoes," and Eshkol immediately declared that any interference with freedom of passage in the Gulf of Akaba and the straits constituted "an act of aggression." On May 26 Nasser declared: "Sharm el-Sheikh means a confrontation with Israel. After having taken this step we must be prepared to wage total war on Israel." The Security Council met on May 24 but could not agree on any action. On May 25 Foreign Minister Eban left for Washington, London, and Paris to ask for support and, specifically, measures to lift the blockade in the straits. Only four out of a score of maritime powers that had announced their support for free passage in 1957 were willing to cooperate. Neither Britain nor France was willing to stand by the 1950 Tripartite Declaration. The French spoke of the need to examine the legal position on free passage through the Straits of Tiran, and General de Gaulle warned Eban that he would oppose whichever side struck first.

Under the looming shadow of war, the country was preparing for the worst. The organization and training of the reserves units was being brought up to concert pitch, while older men and women and schoolchildren helped to keep services going. Many worked overtime without pay to get in the harvest, keep up supplies, and fill export orders. After a day's rush on groceries, the government announced that ample supplies of food were available and kept the warehouses open until late at night so that shops could replenish stocks. The country anxiously awaited a government decision to end the uncertainty, and army leaders pressed for action.

A cabinet meeting on May 27 decided to make another effort to avert war. In a broadcast to the nation on the next day, Eshkol said that further diplomatic measures were to be taken to safeguard free passage in the Straits of Tiran and that "lines of activity" had been laid down "for the purpose of removing the military concentrations from Israel's southern border, protecting our sovereign rights and security on the borders and averting aggression, so that we shall not have to act in self-defense with military force." Widespread demands were made for the establishment of a government of national unity to fortify public confidence and, specifically, for the appointment of Moshe Dayan as minister of defense. On May 30, King Hussein of Jordan placed his forces under Egyptian control. Egyptian, Saudi Arabian, and Iraqi troops were sent to Jordan, and Iraqi, Algerian, and Kuwaiti forces to Egypt. On June 1 Dayan was co-opted to the cabinet as defense minister and three days later Menaḥem Begin, the Ḥerut leader, and Yosef Sapir, the Liberal leader, as ministers without portfolio. On June 3 Radio Cairo quoted an order of the day by General Murtaji, commander of the Egyptian Forces in Sinai, hailing "the Holy War through which you will restore the rights of the Arabs which have been stolen in Palestine and reconquer the plundered soil of Palestine." On the next day, Iraq followed Hussein's example.

Surrounded by Arab forces that were liable to attack at any moment, Israel could delay no longer. On the morning of June 5 the Israel air force attacked the airfields of Egypt, Jordan, Iraq, and Syria, destroying 452 planes – 391 of them on the ground – in under three hours and achieving complete superiority in the air. As the attack was nearing completion, the southern command moved against the Egyptian armies massed on the Negev border. One divisional task force broke through heavily defended positions on the coast and reached El-Arish by the evening. A second advanced toward the main Egyptian positions around Abu Aweigila, opposite Niẓẓanah, while a third moved through the sand dunes further north to the Egyptian rear. At the same time, Gaza was attacked from the south. On the second day of fighting, the Israeli forces advanced toward the Egyptian second line and concentrated most of their armor in the heart of Sinai. On the third day, Israeli tanks carried out a large-scale encirclement operation, closing up all avenues of escape for the Egyptian armor and compelling it to engage in frontal combat. In one of the largest armor battles in history, with over 1,000 tanks participating on both sides, the Egyptian power was shattered, and on June 8 the Israeli forces had reached the Suez Canal and were moving south along the eastern shore of the Gulf of Suez. Meanwhile the Gaza Strip had been taken, Israeli naval forces had captured Sharm el-Sheikh, and parachute troops landed there were moving northward to link up with the armor. By dawn on Friday June 9, Israeli forces were encamped along the canal and the Gulf of Suez. The Egyptians had had over 400 tanks destroyed and 200 captured, losing more than 10,000 men and 12,000 prisoners.

On the morning of June 5 Israel had notified King Hussein, through the UNTSO chief of staff, that if his forces kept the peace Jordan would be immune from attack. Nevertheless, almost immediately Jordanian forces opened fire all along the armistice line, occupied UN headquarters in East Jerusalem, and indiscriminately shelled the Jewish areas in the west of the city. Israel's central command counterattacked, concentrating on the hills round the city. By the next day, after bitter fighting that lasted throughout the night, the garrison on Mount Scopus had been relieved and the whole of Jerusalem outside the Old City was in Israel's hands. At the same time the northern command attacked the Jordanian forces in Samaria (the northern part of the "West Bank"), while central command forces, which had taken the strong points on the hills to the north of the Jerusalem Corridor, moved eastward to cut the road from the city to the north. By June 7 Israel was in control of Nablus, Ramallah, Jericho, and Bethlehem. It was now possible to start the historic battle for the Old City, which was taken by a paratroop unit breaking in through St. Stephen's (Lions) Gate in hand-to-hand fighting to avoid any damage to the holy places. By the evening the whole of Samaria and Judea were in Israel's hands.

In the north, the Syrians had been shelling Israel towns and villages from their heavily fortified positions on the Golan Heights. With the fighting over in the south and the center, the Israel air force opened fire on the gun positions, and at noon on June 9 the infantry and armor attacked. After fierce fighting, in which one position after another was taken in close combat, the Israel forces reached the town of Kuneitra, on the main road to Damascus, at 2:30 P.M. on the 10th.

The Security Council, which met on almost every one of the six days of fighting, called for a cease-fire on June 6, 7, and 9. With the acceptance of the cease-fire by Israel, Egypt, Jordan, Lebanon, and Syria, the Six-Day War came to an end. Israel casualties were 777 killed and 2,586 wounded; the Arabs had lost some 15,000 men, hundreds of tanks, and the bulk of their air forces. Israel held 26,476 sq. mi. of territory previously in Arab hands: 444 sq. mi. on the Golan Heights, 2,270 sq. mi. in Judea and Samaria, 140 sq. mi. in the Gaza Strip, and 23,622 sq. mi. in Sinai. A Soviet-sponsored proposal to condemn Israel as the aggressor and demand immediate withdrawal from all occupied territories was rejected by the Security Council on June 14, and three similar proposals were turned down by the General Assembly on July 4.

When Defense Minister Moshe Dayan paid his first visit to the Old City of Jerusalem on June 7, he said: "We have unified Jerusalem, the divided capital of Israel. We have returned to the holiest of our holy places never to depart from it again." On the same day, Prime Minister Eshkol assured the heads of all the religious communities that they would retain control of their holy places, the chief rabbis being in charge of the Western Wall of the Temple Court (the "Wailing Wall"). On June 27 the minister of the interior, under a law passed by the Knesset the day before, issued an order extending the limits of Jerusalem and the jurisdiction of Israel law to the eastern part of the city. At noon the next day the 19-year-old barriers between East and West Jerusalem were removed; henceforth the 66,000 Arabs (54,000 Muslims and 12,000 Christians) and 195,000 Jews of Jerusalem were free to mingle as citizens of one city.

Military government was established in the areas administered under the cease-fire agreements, but the existing local authorities and officials were left free to operate without interference, except where security interests were concerned. Schools were reopened with the same staffs, curricula, and textbooks, apart from the revision or replacement of those containing incitement against the Jews or Israel. A small number of Israel officials, seconded to central and regional military government headquarters, helped to improve services, introduce modern agricultural methods, and stimulate industrial development. The courts were reopened, with the same judges and staffs administering the law previously in force; Israel military courts dealt only with offenses against security. An "open bridges" policy was instituted: West Bank Arabs moved freely to and fro across the Jordan and sold their produce in the Arab countries; residents of the Gaza Strip could travel for the first time to the West Bank and further afield; high school graduates could take Egyptian matriculation examinations and go to study in Egyptian and other Arab universities. Some 200,000 Arabs fled eastward across the Jordan River during the fighting or left to join their families afterward. The applications of 21,000 to return were approved, but by the end of August 1967 only 14,000 had done so. Further applications for the purpose of family reunification were considered on their merits. Relatives and friends of West Bank residents were allowed to come for prolonged visits each summer. Thousands of Arabs worked inside Israel's pre-1967 borders: in March 1970, 18,000 from the West Bank and 6,600 from the Gaza Strip were thus employed through the labor exchanges. Many of the refugee camps were connected with the electricity network; refugees, especially in the Gaza Strip, were a high proportion of those who worked in Israel, earning considerably increased wages (see also Israel, State of: *Arab Population).

Nevertheless, the Arabs of the areas, the great majority of whom had close relatives in Jordan and other Arab countries, regarded themselves as closely connected with the Arab world and, although there was a widespread desire for peace, looked forward expectantly to the withdrawal of Israel forces and the end of Israel rule. In the early months after the war, there were political demonstrations, and some of the young people cooperated with the terrorist organizations. In the Gaza Strip, particularly in the refugee camps, grenades were repeatedly thrown at army patrols and at Arabs "collaborating" with the authorities by going out to work in Israel. Stern measures were taken by the security forces against anyone using violence or harboring terrorists, and the great majority of the population kept the peace and denied shelter to armed infiltrators.

Israel ignored a Security Council resolution of May 21, 1968, calling for the annulment of measures taken to change the status of Jerusalem, but expressed recognition of universal spiritual interests in the city and readiness to guarantee the immunity of the holy places of all faiths. A fire in the al-Aqṣa Mosque in Jerusalem on Aug. 29, 1969, was exploited by Arab propaganda to rouse anti-Israel sentiment in the Muslim world and get a censure resolution passed in the Security Council (September 15), although the arsonist, an Australian named Michael Rohan, was immediately apprehended and found to be suffering from paranoiac schizophrenia. Almost none of the East Jerusalem Arabs applied for Israel citizenship, but they were automatically entitled to vote in municipal elections and 7,000 of them did so in 1969 – more than in the last elections to the city council under Jordanian rule.

The weeks of tension preceding the Six-Day War led to an unprecedented awakening among Jews abroad, especially the youth. Thousands of young volunteers invaded Israel missions and Jewish Agency offices, clamoring to be allowed to help in the emergency; many made their own way to Israel by any available plane. While they arrived too late to fight, they worked in fields and orchards, helped the army clear up the debris of battle, and began the reconstruction of the Hebrew University and Hadassah Hospital buildings on Mount Scopus. About 30% of them stayed and others established *aliyah* groups on their return abroad. The Zionist movement issued a call for *aliyah*, and the 27th Zionist Congress, meeting in Jerusalem in June 1968, adopted a new "Jerusalem Program" calling for *aliyah* from all countries. For the first time there was a large influx of immigrants from the West. The task of fitting absorption machinery to their needs became a matter of urgency, and a Ministry of Immigrant Absorption, headed by Deputy Prime Minister Yigal Allon, was set up for the purpose. Donations by Diaspora Jewry reached unprecedented levels, rising from $50,000,000 in 1966/67 to $350,000,000 in 1967/68. The Jerusalem Economic Conference, attended in April 1968 by over 500 prominent Jewish businessmen and economists from abroad, set up a network of regional and trade subcommittees to organize practical measures for increasing investments, establishing new undertakings in Israel, and enhancing efficiency.

The war had raised far-reaching problems of policy for Israel's leaders and public. The new situation and the entry of Moshe Dayan into the cabinet helped heal the rift in the labor movement: in January 1968 Mapai, Aḥdut ha-Avodah, and Rafi merged to form the *Israel Labor Party, which established an "alignment" with Mapam a year later (for other political developments, see Political Life and Parties). It was clear that a new and critical stage had been initiated, and might determine the destiny of Israel for many years to come. All but a tiny minority agreed that the 1949 armistice lines were dead and buried and that united Jerusalem and the Golan Heights, which had threatened the Jewish villages below for two decades, must not be given up. Apart from these points, however, there were deep differences, cutting across party lines, as to the map of the future. Gaḥal and some members of the Labor and National Religious parties believed that Israel must hold on to the boundaries achieved in June 1967 in order to fulfill the ideal of *Ereẓ Yisrael ha-Shelemah* ("The Undivided Land of Israel") as the national homeland of the Jewish people, with the Sinai Peninsula as a buffer against any further threat from Egypt. Others, including Rakaḥ, some individuals, and small groups, mostly left-wing, called for the return of all the occupied territories as the price of peace. The majority of the Labor Party, Mapam, and the Independent Liberals, as well as many members of the religious parties, were prepared to give up most of the territories in return for definitive peace treaties with Egypt and Jordan.

There was also the problem of the political attitude to be adopted toward the former Palestinian Arabs in the administered territories. The official policy was that peace could be concluded only with the government of Jordan, and that the relations between the former Palestinians and King Hussein were an internal matter of no concern to Israel. Others advocated an attempt to reach a settlement with the population of the West Bank, perhaps on the basis of setting up a separate Palestinian state in the area. Voices were also raised in favor of an attempt by Israel to solve the problem of the refugees under its rule, but the majority view was that large-scale schemes would only arouse antagonism and that the best policy was to improve the employment and social conditions of the refugees as part of the measures for increasing prosperity in the administered areas in general.

The government decided, in view of the differences of opinion within it and the fact that no Arab country was ready to negotiate, that there was no need to take any decisions on boundaries unless and until definite proposals would have to be submitted at the peace conference table. Various interim government pronouncements were summarized, however, in an "unwritten doctrine" adopted, mainly in response to pressure from Dayan, at the first Labor Party convention in August 1969. According to this program, advocacy of which was optional for party spokesmen, the Gaza Strip, as well as the Golan Heights and the whole of Jerusalem, should remain under Israel rule; there should be a territorial link with Sharm el-Sheikh to safeguard freedom of shipping from and to Eilat, and the Jordan River should be Israel's "security border." Under the last head, which was in keeping with the "Allon Plan" proposed by the deputy prime minister, most of the West Bank could be reunited politically with Jordan, but no Arab military forces would be permitted east of the Jordan River.

There was some controversy over the question of Jewish settlement in the administered areas. While the maximalists advocated the establishment of villages and urban quarters wherever possible, as an expression of Jewish rights in the whole of Ereẓ Israel and in order to strengthen Israel's hold on the areas, other circles objected on the ground that such settlement could prejudice peace negotiations. General opinion supported government policy to give priority to settlement required mainly for security reasons. A number of *Naḥal outposts – some of which were later converted into civilian villages – were set up on the Golan Heights, along the Jordan Valley, and on the northern Sinai coast. Two of the villages in the Eẓyon Bloc, destroyed during the War of Independence, were resettled. Most controversial was the beginning of the establishment of a Jewish quarter on the outskirts of Hebron, first on the independent initiative of a religious group and later with government assistance. The building of new quarters in East Jerusalem and the rehabilitation of the Jewish Quarter in the Old City met with virtually unanimous approval in Israel.

Meanwhile, the quest for a solution was proceeding, to the accompaniment of renewed fighting from time to time on various sectors of the cease-fire lines. Immediately after the Six-Day War, Israel called for direct peace negotiations. There were hopes that the Arabs might now be ready to discuss some form of peace or coexistence with Israel. These soon disappeared, however, after the Soviet Union undertook to rehabilitate the Egyptian and Syrian armies, initiating a vast airlift of planes, tanks, and other equipment to replace their losses and sending in thousands of Soviet advisers and experts. The Khartoum Arab Summit Conference in August 1967, at which Saudi Arabia, Libya, and Kuwait promised Egypt and Jordan generous subsidies, resolved that there would be no peace with Israel, no negotiations with Israel, no recognition of Israel, and no compromise at the expense of "the rights of the Palestinian people." Yasser Arafat, leader of al-Fatah, was elected head of the Palestine Liberation Organization, which was subsidized by the Arab governments and provided with facilities to operate from Syrian, Jordanian, and, later, Lebanese territory.

The cease-fire lines were much easier to defend against the threat of a large-scale assault than the armistice lines, with the Suez Canal and the Jordan River as "anti-tank ditches" and the increased warning time available before Egyptian aircraft could approach the populated areas. It was not long, however, before the cease-fire lines were under attack. On the Suez Canal, which Nasser blocked immediately after the war, the Egyptians fired at Israel positions from time to time and the Israelis replied in kind. Land, sea, and air clashes culminated in the sinking of the Israel destroyer *Eilat* on October 21 and the shelling of oil installations in the town of Suez a day later. Al-Fataḥ detachments, trained and organized in Syria, tried to cross the Jordan to carry on the war. Most were intercepted on or near the cease-fire line, but some sabotage was done, especially in Jerusalem and some of the border villages.

The Security Council met again and this time arrived at a decision. On Nov. 22, 1967, after several alternative drafts had failed to win agreement, the Council unanimously adopted a British-sponsored resolution (no. 242, 1967), which emphasized "the inadmissibility of the acquisition of territory by war and the need to work for a just and lasting peace in which every state in the area can live in security." Such a peace should provide for "(I) Withdrawal of Israeli armed forces from territories (the French and Russian traslations had "the territories") occupied in the recent conflict; (II) Termination of all claims or states of belligerency and respect for and acknowledgment of the sovereignty, territorial integrity and political independence of every state in the area and their right to live in peace within secure and recognized boundaries free from threats or acts of force." The resolution further affirmed the necessity "(a) for guaranteeing freedom of navigation through international waterways in the area; (b) for achieving a just settlement of the refugee problem; (c) for guaranteeing the territorial inviolability and political independence of every state in the area, through measures including the establishment of demilitarized zones." The secretary-general was asked to designate a special representative "to establish and maintain contacts with the states concerned in order to promote agreement and assist efforts to achieve a peaceful and accepted settlement in accordance with the provisions and principles in this resolution."

Foreign Minister Eban declared that Israel would "respect and fully maintain the situation embodied in the cease-fire agreements until it is succeeded by peace treaties between Israel and the Arab states ending the state of war…" President Nasser, speaking on November 23, reiterated the "noes" of Khartoum and declared: "Israel's withdrawal from all the occupied areas is not a matter for negotiation." Later, Jordan and Egypt announced their acceptance of the resolution, but insisted on "implementation" by Israel's withdrawal to the boundaries existing on June 4, 1967, as a *sine qua non* of any settlement. They also made it clear that, even after a settlement, they would recognize the right of the Palestinians to continue their struggle for "the liberation of Palestine." Syria refused to have anything to do with the resolution, while al-Fataḥ opposed any agreement whatsoever, calling for the "liberation of Palestine" by force. The Israel representative told the UN on May 1, 1968, that Israel accepted the resolution as a means "for the promotion of agreement on the establishment of a just and lasting peace." As the resolution did not call for withdrawal from "all the territories" or even "the territories," Israel emphasized that the "secure and recognized boundaries" must be determined by negotiation; while they would not be identical with the cease-fire lines, there would be no return to the prewar boundaries, which, Israel spokesmen declared, would be a constant temptation to renewed hostilities. Furthermore, no territory would be evacuated until the conclusion of a peace treaty covering all the points at issue. Gunnar Jarring, Swedish ambassador in Moscow, who was appointed by UN Secretary-General U Thant as his representative, paid repeated visits to Jerusalem, Cairo, and Amman as intermediary between the governments, but there was no change in the irreconcilable attitudes of the two sides.

Meanwhile, the military situation deteriorated on both fronts. Explosive charges planted by infiltrators on the outskirts of villages and in Jerusalem, Tel Aviv, and other places killed and injured civilians and did damage to property. Along the Jordan River, mine-laying; firing at Israel forces by Palestinian irregulars, often with support from Jordanian military posts; shelling of Israel villages, especially in the Beth-Shean and Jordan valleys; and attempts by al-Fataḥ and other detachments to cross the river were almost daily occurrences. By constant vigilance, patrolling, and pursuit, the Israel forces severly hampered the activities of the infiltrators and inflicted heavy casualties on them: up to the end of 1970, 1,828 were killed and 2,884 captured. Al-Fataḥ bases in Jordan were attacked, compelling the terrorists to scatter; after the largest such operation, at Karama on March 21, 1968 – in which Israel losses were heavier than in any other such action – Israel was censured by Security Council. In 1969 the Palestinian guerrillas operated increasingly from bases in Lebanon, which were also attacked by Israel forces. Border villages and towns like Kiryat Shemonah and Beth-Shean were indiscriminately bombarded with Soviet "Katyusha" rockets. Large sums were spent on building shelters, in which the village children regularly spent their nights. Men in the reserves were called up for longer periods, and at the beginning of 1969 compulsory army service was extended from 30 to 36 months for men.

The Popular Front for the Liberation of Palestine (PFLP), a Marxist rival of al-Fataḥ, specialized in the hijacking of aircraft and attacks on the offices of El Al and other Israel institutions abroad. On Dec. 28, 1968, two days after an armed attack on an El Al plane at Athens airport, an Israel commando unit destroyed 14 Arab aircraft at Beirut, where the terrorists had their headquarters. The Security Council censured Israel for the raid, though throughout this period it did not condemn Arab attacks on Israel or (apart from general appeals for the observance of the cease-fire) call for them to be halted or prevented. The PFLP's operations culminated in the hijacking of five international aircraft in August 1970 (in the case of one, an El Al plane, the attempt failed) and the holding of passengers for ransom to obtain the release of Arab terrorists held in Switzerland, Germany, and Britain. This act was one of the factors in the outbreak of the Jordanian civil war, which reduced the pressure on Israel's eastern front during the last part of the year, when the Palestinian organizations seemed to be devoting most of their energies to the struggle against King Hussein.

The most serious military threat came from Egypt. Apart from several sporadic flare-ups, the Suez Canal zone was quiet for a time; in fact, it was frequently visited by tourists from the Israel side. On April 10, 1968, however, Nasser declared: "The Arab nation has decided to embark on the path of struggle and war. We have reequipped our armed forces, so that we may stand firm, later we will move to the containment of Israel and, after that, to the eradication of the aggression." In September and October the Egyptians heavily bombarded Israel positions on the canal, taking the troops by surprise and inflicting heavy casualties. Israel artillery replied, doing serious damage to the towns on the western side, and carried out commando raids deep into Egyptian territory. Israel built a series of bunkers and fortifications, heavily protected, along the length of the canal. In the second week of March 1969, the Egyptians heavily bombarded what they called the "Bar-Lev Line" (after the Israel chief of staff), and on March 30 Nasser announced that Egyptian troops would no longer be bound by the cease-fire. "We ask every soldier at the front to account for his action if he sees the enemy and does not fire at him," he said. On May 1 he announced that 60% of the "Bar-Lev Line" had been destroyed and that the attacks would continue until its destruction had been completed. Egyptian patrols were also sent across the canal, but were repulsed with heavy losses. On July 23 Nasser declared: "Now, brethren, we begin the act of liberation… We are now in the midst of a long, drawn battle… to wear down the enemy." Israel replied to this war of attrition with further commando raids on targets ranging from the Upper Nile Valley to the west coast of the Gulf of Suez and repeated air strikes at Egyptian antiaircraft batteries and posts. Forty-seven Egyptian aircraft were shot down in 1969, and it became clear that Israel had the mastery of the skies.

The cost of military operations, the building of fortifications and shelters, the maintenance of large numbers of men under arms, the purchase of large quantities of military equipment, and the expansion of local arms manufacture, as well as a massive housing program to meet the needs of increased immigration, had a threefold effect. There was a sharp upward trend in economic activity, which started in the second half of 1967 and continued in the succeeding years; the state budget swelled and the government had to take more money from the public in taxes and loans; and there was a drastic worsening in the balance of payments, leading to a drop in foreign-currency reserves (see Israel, State of: *Economic Affairs, section on Economic Development). Full employment and rising prices led to pressures for wage increases, which were partially restrained by a "package deal" between the government, the Histadrut, and the employers' associations in 1970, providing for moderate wage rises (partly in the form of government bonds), coupled with stabilization of prices and taxes. The balance of the agreement was somewhat upset toward the end of the year by a tax increase, mainly in indirect taxes, which necessitated some rise in prices, and salary claims by professional men, port workers, and others, many of them supported by strike action. In view of the strain on the government's finances, the Jewish Agency took over a larger part of the responsibility for social services and support for higher education. Appeal funds totaled about $250,000,000 in each of the years 1968/69 and 1969/70.

In 1970 the Israel air force stepped up its attacks on the Egyptian army camps near Cairo and other towns along the Nile in an attempt to compel the Egyptians to observe the cease-fire. In March it became known that the Soviet Union had come to Egypt's rescue by installing SA3 missiles, which had to be manned by Soviet crews, and providing Soviet pilots to fly operational missions in the canal zone. Until then the Soviets had confined themselves to the function of "advisers" to the Egyptian army, although these were to be found on a low tactical level, as well as at headquarters, and were known to have played an active part in the planning and execution of military operations. On April 18 Israel aircraft were challenged by Russian-flown Egyptian planes, and it was clear that Soviet involvement in the war had reached an advanced stage. Israel decided to refrain from further deep air penetration in order to avoid a dangerous clash with the Soviets, but replied to the Egyptians' spring offensive with heavy air bombardments of their lines close to the canal in order to prevent the rebuilding of their antiaircraft defenses, which might have enabled them to neutralize Israel's air power and, later, to make an attempt to cross the canal in force. In July the Soviet SA3 missiles went into operation for the first time against Israel planes. Israel stated that, while not wishing to clash with the Soviets, she would repel any attempt to make her withdraw from the Suez Canal line without a peace settlement and called upon the United States to deter the Soviets from active involvement in the war. At this stage, an American peace initiative produced a new situation.

Since early in 1969 Four-Power talks – between the U.S., the U.S.S.R., Britain, and France – and Two-Power talks, between the two superpowers, had been proceeding in an effort to agree on "guide lines" for Ambassador Jarring's mission. Israel expressed serious reservations about these talks, in which it could only rely on qualified American support while the Arabs were assured of out-and-out Soviet backing and general support from France, with Britain's attitude, at best, uncertain. Israel contended that a settlement would only be reached by agreement between the parties to the dispute and repeatedly called on the Arab states to enter into peace negotiations in which each side would be free to make any proposals it pleased. On October 1 Prime Minister Golda Meir responded affirmatively to a reported hint by Egyptian Foreign Minister Mahmud Riad that his country might be prepared to accept "something like the Rhodes formula of 1948–49" for indirect negotiations, but the proposal was disavowed by the Egyptian government spokesman. Detailed U.S. proposals for a settlement with Egypt and Jordan, announced by U.S. Secretary of State Rogers in December 1969, were rejected by the Israel government and the Knesset, as they would only permit "insubstantial changes" in the pre-1967 borders. Continual efforts were made to obtain further arms from the United States, which had become Israel's only supplier of military aircraft, as 50 French Mirages, ordered and paid for before the Six-Day War, were held up and a complete embargo on military supplies, imposed by President de Gaulle after the raid on Beirut airport, was being maintained by his successor. In December 1968 it was announced that President Johnson had agreed to supply Israel with 50 Phantom planes, but Israel now asked for 25 more Phantoms and 100 Skyhawks in addition. No public reply was given, but American spokesmen indicated that the United States would not allow the arms balance to be disturbed to Israel's disfavor.

On June 19, 1970, Secretary of State Rogers proposed that discussions on the establishment of a just and lasting peace should be held between Israel and Egypt and Jordan, respectively, under the auspices of Ambassador Jarring. The discussions should be based on "mutual acknowledgment" by the parties "of each other's sovereignty, territorial integrity and political independence," and on "Israeli withdrawal from territories occupied in the 1967 conflict" in accordance with Security Council resolution 242. To facilitate agreement, the cease-fire with Egypt should be renewed for a period of three months at least. On August 4 Israel accepted the American proposal, making it clear that she regarded the original Security Council cease-fire resolution as still binding, that the object of the discussions would be to achieve "an agreed and binding contractual peace agreement," that Israel armed forces would be withdrawn only to "secure, recognized and agreed boundaries to be determined in the peace agreements," and that each party would be free to present its proposals on the matters under discussion. The decision was taken after receiving assurances from the United States that the cease-fire would include a standstill in a zone extending 30 mi. (50 km.) on either side of the Suez Canal, in which both parties would refrain from changing the military status quo by stationing additional missiles or other installations. Gaḥal, while accepting the cease-fire proposal, would not agree to negotiations on withdrawal from the territory of Ereẓ Israel, and its six ministers resigned from the cabinet, with effect from August 6.

The renewed cease-fire went into effect on August 7, but on its very first day Israel intelligence discovered that a number of missile sites in the standstill zone west of the canal had been moved forward, and further violations of the agreement were discovered on succeeding days. After several days the violations were confirmed by the United States from its own intelligence sources. Israel charged that a complete new electronic defense system, consisting of SA2 and SA3 missile batteries, had been erected up to within 6 mi. (10 km.) of the canal, capable of striking at Israel aircraft up to a distance of 20 mi. (30 km.) east of the canal and providing cover for Egyptian artillery, which could inflict heavy damage on Israeli positions as a preliminary to an attempt to cross the waterway. Defense Minister Dayan and army spokesmen, however, stated that Israel's armed strength had increased during the cease-fire and expressed their confidence that any renewed Egyptian attack would be doomed to failure.

The Israeli government, while appointing Foreign Minister Eban as the Israeli representative to the Jarring talks and UN Ambassador Tekoah as his deputy, declared that the immediate and massive violation of the cease-fire standstill agreement cast doubt on Egypt's readiness to observe any agreement to which she might set her hand. It therefore decided on September 6 to suspend participation in the Jarring talks until the missiles were withdrawn and the status quo ante in the canal zone restored. The United States showed understanding for Israel's reluctance to continue the talks in the circumstances and pressed the Soviet Union and Egypt to rectify the position in the Canal zone. These efforts were unsuccessful and there was no apparent change in the situation after the death of Nasser on September 28 and the election of Anwar Sadat to succeed him. The United States tried to induce Israel to return to the talks, however, and President Nixon asked Congress to appropriate $500,000,000 in credits for the supply of arms to Israel to neutralize the Egyptian build-up. At the end of the year, after intensive negotiations with the U.S. administration, the Israeli government decided that conditions had been created that would justify the reopening of the Jarring talks, and the decision was approved by the Knesset on December 29.

Toward the end of the year public opinion in Israel was deeply moved by the plight of Jews in the U.S.S.R. and their open demand for the right to *aliyah*. Mass demonstrations were held at the Western Wall in Jerusalem in the second half of December, during the trial of Jews in Leningrad on charges of planning to hijack a plane in order to leave the Soviet Union. After a statement by the prime minister on behalf of the government, the Knesset called on friendly nations and world public opinion to press for the removal of the restrictions on the freedom of Soviet Jews to leave the U.S.S.R. and settle in Israel.

[Misha Louvish]

From the Yom Kippur War to the First Intifada

With the relaxation of military tension and the cessation of almost all military activities along the borders from 1971 to 1973, the period was marked by a greater concentration on domestic problems. In spite of the border tranquility, however, security expenditure kept rising due to the need to finance costly and modern weapons, about one-third of the budget being earmarked for defense. The growing budget, shortage of labor, influx of foreign capital, and spiraling wage demands resulted in rising inflation. The continued economic boom resulted in conspicuous consumption, including massive foreign travel, and stressed the growing social inequality.

This inequality was at the root of growing discontent among the lower income strata, predominantly Oriental Jews, living in urban slums or in development towns, with large families, and inferior education. This gave rise to a group of young people known as the Black Panthers who organized demonstrations in Jerusalem and Tel Aviv calling attention to their plight and demanding housing for young couples, better schools, and job opportunities. The initial reaction of the Labor Government was to dismiss the entire affair, and the prime minister termed them "not nice," a phrase that was to cost Labor heavily in the elections of 1973 and, more particularly, of 1977.

After some consideration, however, the government did begin to deal more urgently with social needs, and increased budgets for education, housing, and social welfare were allocated. In June 1973, the Prime Minister's Committee on Disadvantaged Youth, consisting of 126 experts, issued its report, which revealed that in the late 1960s there were some 160,000 disadvantaged children in Israel from the point of view of parents' income or educational status and substandard housing. Of them 25,000 were disadvantaged in all three criteria. On the eve of the Yom Kippur War, the cabinet decided to establish a Youth Authority consisting of representatives of ministries dealing with social affairs. Additional budgets were allocated for housing, education and social services, but the ambitious plans fell victim to the Yom Kippur War and the need to finance massive rearmament in its wake.

Between 1971 and 1973 a wave of strikes hit Israel, chiefly in the public service sector, causing hardship and resulting, usually, in wage rises. In some cases the strikes were called without the knowledge or agreement of the Histadrut, in others against its wishes, and it lost out to works committees who were highly critical of the government policies, which, they claimed, favored the rich. The secretary-general of the Histadrut, Yiẓḥak *Ben-Aharon, was also outspoken in his criticism of the policies of Finance Minister Pinḥas *Sapir, charging him with giving preference to industrialists, investors, and the newly rich, but ignoring tens of thousands of families in poverty.

The major preoccupation of the government on the eve of the 1973 elections consisted in the security situation, which seemed better than ever, social problems, and the future of the Administered Areas, which was the focus of a major debate in the Alignment. The discussion on the territories took first place in the minds of the Israeli leaders, and as elections drew near Minister Galili issued a document for approval by the Labor Party designed to placate Defense Minister Dayan and determine Israel's policy in the areas in the next four years. This was to include continued development of the services, new settlements, the continuation of the open bridges policy, the expansion of plans for Arab refugee resettlement, the continuing development of the Jerusalem area as well as the purchase of land in the areas. Among the areas to be developed was the Rafiaḥ Salient, to include a new city, Yammit, and a deep water port. The Galili Document became part of the Labor election platform.

Another important political development took place in July 1973, when General Ariel *Sharon, recently demobilized from the IDF, was able to bring about a new political bloc called the Likud, consisting of Ḥerut, the Liberals, the Free Center and the State List. General Sharon was co-opted to the Likud list of candidates for the Knesset.

There was no abatement in the struggle against Arab terror during the 1971–73 period, with Israel scoring major successes but also suffering tragic setbacks, such as the massacre committed at Lod Airport in May 1972 by a group of Japanese terrorists, who killed over 25 people in cold blood. In September of that year the PLO captured and killed eleven Israeli athletes and trainers, the bulk of the Israeli team for the Munich Olympic Games. The tragedy raised serious questions in Israel regarding the protection of the team and led to the appointment of an inquiry committee and a tightening up of security measures. Successful operations by Israeli agents in Europe and in Beirut nipped in the bud many planned PLO attacks and saved countless lives.

THE YOM KIPPUR WAR AND ITS AFTERMATH. On the eve of the *Yom Kippur War the mood of Israel was mixed. Supreme confidence reigned with regard to security matters, but serious questions were raised regarding the country's goals, and there was growing disenchantment with its aging leaders, who, it was claimed, were beginning to lose touch with the new realities. Whatever achievements had been attained in the previous 25 years, all of them under Labor rule, were clouded by a sense of loss of direction, a drift towards the unknown, and open dissension in matters such as religion, social progress, relations between Israeli Jews and Israeli Arabs, Israel and the Diaspora, and even the arrival of Soviet immigrants, a miracle in itself, ran into difficulties in their absorption.

The buildup of Syrian and Egyptian forces during the month of September 1973 had been noted by Israel but written off as routine maneuvers. Few imagined that the Arabs would dare challenge Israel's military supremacy. Israel's overconfidence and its misreading of Arab intentions and capabilities were a recipe for military disaster. Only hours before the Arab attack was launched did it become clear that the armies of Syria and Egypt were massing for war. Immediately Israeli reserve units were called up, but by then it was too late.

At 2 P.M. on October 6, Yom Kippur, three Syrian divisions accompanied by 1,400 tanks rolled into the Golan Heights while 70,000 Egyptian troops crossed the Suez Canal and quickly overran Israel's entire line of defense. The Syrians advanced toward Rosh Pinnah and the Sea of Galilee while the Egyptians established three major bridgeheads on the Canal. On the Syrian front Israeli counterattacks brought a halt to the Syrian advance by October 8. Two days later the Syrians were in retreat and on October 11 Israeli forces moved into Syrian territory and established a line of defense 20 miles from Damascus.

The Egyptians had dug in along the Canal and only resumed their advance on October 14. By that time Israel had massed its reinforcements and these were able to block the Egyptian advance. On the night of October 15, under General Sharon, Israeli forces crossed the Canal and within days managed to surround the 20,000-man Third Egyptian Army. Fighting ended on October 24 with the Egyptians still entrenched on the east bank of the Canal while Israel maintained its stranglehold on the Third Army on the west bank.

The Yom Kippur War changed everything. Despite the fact that Israel won the most impressive military victory in her history, the shame and humiliation of the surprise attack by the Syrians and the Egyptians and the staggering number of casualties (over 2,500 dead) stunned the country. Serious doubts were sown in the minds of people regarding the capability of Israel's leadership. Demands were made for a thorough investigation of the events that led to the war and the shortcomings and blunders that found Israel unprepared. Israel's growing international isolation, serious economic problems, its almost total dependence on the United States for military, political and economic aid, and internal disarray, all led to the rise of a number of protest movements that demanded an immediate change in the government. The cabinet appointed a commission of inquiry in November 1973 headed by the president of the Supreme Court.

The 1973 elections, postponed from October to December 31, 1973, were held in this atmosphere. Labor won 51 seats, remaining the strongest and largest party. Likud increased its strength to 39 and became the major opposition party. The religious parties held their ground, as did the Communists. A new group, called the Citizens' Rights Movement, won three seats. Prime Minister Meir reformed her cabinet, but following the publication of the Agranat Commission Report on the events that preceded the Yom Kippur War, which led to the resignation of the Chief of Staff David Elazar, the removal of the director of military intelligence, and the commander of the Southern Front, but found no fault in the conduct of Defense Minister Dayan, Mrs. Meir resigned on April 11, 1974. She remained as caretaker prime minister during the negotiations with Syria for a disengagement agreement, while the Labor Party chose Yitzhak *Rabin over Shimon Peres as its candidate for the office of prime minister. He presented his new cabinet to the Knesset in June.

Rabin, born in Jerusalem in 1922, was the first prime minister born in the country, thus bringing to an end the rule of the "founding fathers." He did not include in his cabinet Abba Eban or Moshe Dayan, and Pinḥas Sapir chose to become chairman of the Jewish Agency. Rabin's policy was concentrated on the rehabilitation of the IDF, a slow progress towards peace with Egypt in a series of limited agreements, while re-building the shattered Israeli economy and, above all, the morale of the people and their self-confidence. Following the 1975 Interim Agreement with Egypt, the failure to reach an agreement with Jordan, and the continued civil war in Lebanon, Rabin felt that he could concentrate more on domestic matters, which had been neglected because of the war and its aftermath. He was unable, however, to exert leadership in this sphere and the old problems that plagued Israel before the war resurfaced. Labor relations deteriorated and strikes, especially in the public services, were endemic. The Israel pound was devaluated constantly and inflation rose at an alarming rate. Nevertheless, in 1976 the economic policies of the government were able to reduce Israel's chronic balance of payments deficit. Social tensions continued, but there was little the government could do to divert funds into social services, owing to the need for a crash program of re-arming and of purchasing the most modern and sophisticated American weapons.

Rabin was also being challenged by *Gush Emunim, a group that demanded large scale Israeli settlement in Samaria. In November 1975 it defied the government by settling in Kaddum. It was supported by Menaḥem Begin and the NRP, and Rabin surrendered to pressures and agreed to allow the settlers to move to a nearby army camp. Other attempts made to settle in other parts of Samaria and in Judea were thwarted by the IDF.

At the end of 1975 there was already open criticism of the leadership of Rabin, not only among the opposition and coalition parties, but even in the governing party itself. An invitation to Golda *Meir to join the "Leading Forum" of the Labor Party was regarded as a sign of weakness of Rabin's position. It transpired that the most vehement critics against the government came from the "dovish" circles of the Alignment itself, the most prominent among whom were the former Foreign Minister Abba *Eban and Yiẓhak Ben-Aharon. In the middle of May 1976 an unsuccessful attempt was made within the Labor Party to bring about reconciliation between Rabin and Defense Minister Peres who was challenging the prime minister.

The prestige of the Labor Party in general and that of Rabin in particular, was hard hit when it became known that Asher Yadlin, who had been nominated as governor of the Bank of Israel and was one of the central figures of the Labor Party and chairman of the Kuppat Ḥolim of the Histadrut, was being investigated by the police following rumors of his having been involved in foreign currency violations and illegal business transactions. Yadlin was subsequently found guilty of receiving a bribe, tax evasion, and illegal land transactions and sentenced to a 5-year prison term.

A NEW POLITICAL ERA. At the end of May 1976 Prof. Yigael *Yadin announced his intention of forming a new political party, which was formed in November, under the name "The *Democratic Movement for Change" (DMC). Among the basic principles of his program was his belief in a "Jewish democratic Israel," that Judea-Samaria could not remain under Israeli rule, and that the new party would be willing to conduct negotiations with the PLO, if the latter recognized Israel's right to exist. He maintained, however, that Israel should not be obliged to return to the pre-1967 borders, that important strategic positions must be retained, and opposed the establishment of another state "between the desert and the sea." Yadin also called for a change in the electoral system of Israel.

The year 1976 ended with a government crisis. A delay in the arrival of new American planes involved the desecration of the Sabbath at the official reception. The *National Religious Party protested, and on December 14, 1976, a Knesset session was devoted to this incident and, although a vote of no-confidence against the government was defeated, most of the N.R.P. members abstained.

This unprecedented action by a coalition party made Rabin decide on December 19 to remove the N.R.P. from the government, a step that would involve early national elections. He presented his resignation of the government to President Ephraim Katzir on the following day but continued to serve, in accordance with the law, as head of an interim government until the elections, which were fixed for May 17, 1977. In March 1977 the Labor Party convention chose Rabin as its candidate for the office of prime minister by a narrow majority. In the elections the Likud increased its representation to 43, while two seats were gained by Shlomẓion, which joined the Likud immediately after the elections.

The Alignment declined from 51 members to 32, and the Democratic Movement for Change won 15 seats. An analysis of the voting trends indicated that members of the Oriental communities and the younger voters tended to vote more for the Likud. Younger voters with higher education tended more to vote for the DMC.

The decline in the relative power of the Alignment had started in 1969 when it gained 56 mandates, but, as stated, only 51 in 1973, and 32 in 1977. Part of this continual decline stemmed from basic causes that were exacerbated, while others were due to special factors. The accumulation of opposition to any government with the passage of time is normal in any democratic society, but added to it were the effects of the Yom Kippur War which had not been properly reflected in the 1973 election because of the shock effect.

Additional factors were added in 1976 and 1977, among them the revelations of corruption in the upper echelons of government, the revelation of an illegal foreign currency account held abroad by Prime Minister Rabin and his wife, the treatment in the media of the foreign currency accounts of Abba Eban, for which, however, it was revealed that he had a permit, the suicide of Minister Avraham Ofer, the struggle between Rabin and Peres, the deterioration of labor relations with the approach of the elections, and the declaration of the president of the U.S.A. favoring a "homeland for the Palestinians" a short time before the elections in Israel. In addition there were the report of the state comptroller on the Defense establishment and the tragedy of a helicopter crash virtually on the eve of the elections.

The *Begin government took office on June 20, 1977, with the participation of the Likud, the NRP, and the support of Agudat Israel, Poalei Agudat Israel, and M.K. Flatto-Sharon; on October 24, 1977, the DMC joined the government.

Prior to that, on June 21, 1977, elections were held for the Histadrut. The results established a kind of balance to those of the Knesset elections. Apparently some of the voters in these elections refrained from voting against the Alignment and "balanced" their Knesset vote by continuing to give their support to the Alignment in the Histadrut. The results of the Histadrut elections were Alignment (EMET), 54.6%; Likud (MAḤAL), 28.8%; and the DMC, 8.2%.

The first few months of the Begin administration were marked by a cabinet led by a strong leader who insisted on unity and discipline in the ranks of the ministers. But after six months, following the visit of Sadat to Jerusalem and the beginning of the 16-month-long negotiating process for an Israel-Egypt *peace treaty, cracks appeared. The prime minister was totally absorbed in foreign affairs; the economic ministers were soon facing major problems of spiraling inflation, shortage of housing, and strained labor relations. The Histadrut had almost no common language with the Likud government and at times urged workers to make radical wage demands. Most hurt by the inflation were those who voted for the Likud, the Oriental Jews who, at the lowest levels of Israeli society, were expressing disenchantment with the government and its lack of coherent economic and social policies.

By the end of 1978, while Israelis appreciated the historic breakthrough in the Camp David Agreements, there was growing apprehension over the social and economic costs of peace with Egypt and the need to evacuate all of Sinai, including its 20 settlements and all its military installations. Personal rivalry among cabinet members, constant open bickering and the leaking of secrets, brought a serious deterioration in the stature of the cabinet and damaged the standing and reputation of the prime minister.

In December 1978 the era of the Founding Fathers came to an end with the death of Golda Meir, who had led Israel during one of its most trying times – the Yom Kippur War. Scores of world leaders attended her funeral in Jerusalem. Israel figured on the world scene when Prime Minister Begin shared the Nobel Peace Prize with President Anwar Sadat. The early months of 1979 were devoted to the conclusion of the negotiations for an Israel-Egypt peace treaty, which was finally signed after dramatic round the clock talks in Jerusalem, Washington and Cairo, and a flying visit by President Carter to the area. The historic occasion of the signing of the Peace Treaty on March 26, 1979 was impressively celebrated throughout the country. Mr. Begin was the focus of admiration and congratulations for his role in achieving this historic breakthrough. In April 1979 he paid a two-day visit to Cairo for the purpose of cementing the relations between the two countries.

The peace treaty, however, could not cover up the growing difficulties of the Begin government, which was constantly plagued by internal dissent and rift. The splits in the cabinet grew worse when Dr. Yosef Burg, the minister of interior and police, was appointed chairman of the Ministerial Committee for the conduct of the Autonomy talks. As a result Foreign Minister Dayan tendered his resignation in October 1979. He was succeeded by Knesset Speaker Yitzhak *Shamir, a Ḥerut loyalist who had abstained in the voting on the peace treaty with Egypt, Shamir being succeeded as speaker by the Liberal MK Yitzhak Berman. In May 1980 Defense Minister Ezer Weizman resigned following disagreements over cuts in the defense budget and continued bickering with the prime minister over relations with Egypt. In October 1980 Justice Minister Shmuel Tamir resigned as well. He felt that three ministers could not represent his shrunken party, the Democratic Movement, in the cabinet when its entire strength in the Knesset amounted to four members.

In November 1979 Finance Minister Ehrlich was replaced by Yigael Hurwitz, the former minister of industry, commerce and tourism, who resigned in September 1979 because of his opposition to the Camp David Agreements. Mr. Hurvitz vowed to curb inflation, balance the budget and increase exports. (For details see Israel, State of: *Economic Affairs.) The mood of the country as a result of the economic situation was further dampened by the increase in the percentage of drop-outs among emigrants from Soviet Russia and in emigration from the country (see Israel, State of: *Aliyah and Absorption 1971–1981).

The inflationary spiral was also fueled by the evacuation from Sinai and the new deployment of the IDF in the Negev, where two airbases were built by American companies. The almost clockwork operation of the evacuation from Sinai (see Israel, State of: *Defense Forces, 1971–1981) was conducted by the army alone and did not disrupt the civilian economy.

Growing unrest in the administered areas marked the year 1980. This followed the Camp David Agreements and the refusal of Jordan and the Palestinians residing in Judea, Samaria and the Gaza region to become involved in the negotiations leading to their autonomy. In separate incidents, two Arab mayors were attacked by unknown assailants and seriously injured, while the murder of six Israelis in Hebron in May 1980 was followed by the expulsion of the mayors of Hebron and Halhoul, an act that was later upheld by the Israeli Supreme Court. The unrest, expressed mostly in strikes by students, resulted in harsher Israeli measures which led to increased disquiet. The coexistence policy adopted by Defense Minister Dayan in the late 1960s and followed by his successors Peres and Weizman was apparently coming to an end. But living standards in the areas continued to improve as did the economy there.

The feeling of isolation was increased by the annual UN General Assembly discussions, where Israel was the focus of some 50 percent of the debates and was roundly censured. Hopes that the Israel-Egypt Peace Treaty would ease the situation and at least restore relations with some African and Asian nations did not materialize. On the contrary, after the passage of the Jerusalem Law in October 1980, all the embassies that still resided in Jerusalem moved to Tel Aviv.

In the last quarter of 1980, for the first time in the history of Israel, a member of the cabinet was charged with a criminal offense when Religious Affairs Minister Abu-Hatzeira was accused of taking bribes. His Knesset immunity was lifted and he prepared to face a trial. The affair rocked the National Religious Party and further weakened the standing of the Begin government.

The dominant issue in 1981 was the elections for the Tenth Knesset held on June 30. Bitterness, animosity, and violence, chiefly between the two large blocs – the Labor Alignment and the Likud, marked the election campaign. They campaigned on the slogan of who would offer effective leadership, economic programs, the continuation of the peace process, social progress, reduction of tensions between secular and religious, Sephardi and Ashkenazi, young and old, veteran and newcomer, urban and rural settlers, Arab and Jew, and even men and women. Part of the campaign was focused on the retention of the administered territories, championed by the Likud, Teḥiyyah, and part of the National Religious Party. The prime minister dominated the scene and led his Likud party to a second term in office.

In foreign policy, the major initiatives of Israel were undertaken at the end of the year and included the signing of a Memorandum of Understanding on Strategic Cooperation with the United States on Nov. 30, the passage of the Golan Heights Law on December 14, and major efforts to renew ties with the African continent. The initiatives were sponsored by the prime minister and the defense and foreign ministers, who formed an inner "leading team" which determined major policy issues.

The decision of the defense minister to substitute military government with civilian administration in the West Bank and Gaza sparked unrest in those areas, which resulted in stern measures being taken against rioters and the closure, for two months, of Bir Zeit University near Ramallah.

Immigration declined drastically and sank to a low of 11,500, the lowest figure since 1953. Emigration rose and was estimated at 20,000. The Jewish population of Israel grew by only 1.5 percent in 1981 and reached 3.29 million. The major reason for the decline in immigration was the Soviet Union's decision to sharply curtail exit permits for Jews and the very high rate of drop-outs in Vienna (85 percent on the average).

Labor unrest continued and was expressed by many strikes, the most prominent of which was in the national airline, which almost led to the closure of El Al. At year's end the Histadrut attempted to reassert its declining authority when it forced the defense minister to freeze the planned reorganization of his ministry.

The death of Moshe Dayan on October 16 deprived Israel of one of its most colorful personalities, soldier and statesman, who had led Israel in war and peace.

FROM THE LEBANESE WAR TO THE FIRST INTIFADA. In a broad perspective of Israeli history, the decade of the 1980s was a period of internal strife, growing dissent over major issues such as the war in Lebanon, an era of economic reverses, serious decline in immigration but ending with a major influx, especially from the Soviet Union, and finally – the *intifada*, which brought Israel to face a renewed outburst of Palestinian nationalism.

The Lebanese War, which started on June 6, 1982, was long in the planning and was expected by many Israelis, who felt that the northern border area could not be left exposed to terrorist attacks emanating from the mini-PLO state which had emerged in southern Lebanon. Initially, there was little public debate on the wisdom of the invasion. It was assumed that it would amount to a brief operation lasting less than a week, with few casualties, and covering a limited area, not dissimilar to other operations taken in the past. The Israel Defense Forces (IDF) planners, and above all the key figure pushing for war, Defense Minister Ariel Sharon, based their plans on a number of assumptions. They assumed that the United States would not oppose a brief operation, and that the Soviet Union would not get involved. They assumed correctly that apart from Syria, no other Arab state would intervene. They thought that Israel would need some five to seven days to complete the destruction of the mini-PLO state. They assumed that the Lebanese Christian forces would participate alongside Israel and that once the aims would be achieved, a central and effective government would be installed in Beirut which would sign a peace treaty with Israel. Sharon thought that the destruction of the PLO bases in Lebanon would allow him to deal more effectively with the Palestinians in the West Bank and Gaza. He also thought that in the future Israel and Syria would have to collaborate on deciding the future of Lebanon. Most of these assumptions proved to have been correct.

There were also a number of dissenting voices. The defense minister was warned by both the Mossad and Army Intelligence (*Aman*) that the Christian forces were an unreliable element, more of an armed militia than a trained and disciplined fighting army. Israeli planners did not understand the nature of Lebanon and its society, being more of a tribal and communal nation than a unified one. Above all, the planners failed to gauge the reaction inside Israel to a prolonged war which would demand a high number of casualties, and would give the IDF a new role – that of a police force in a neighboring country. The official aims, contained in the government's announcement of June 6, 1982, were the moving of the Northern Galilee settlements out of PLO artillery and katyusha range, the removal from Lebanon of external forces, and the restoration to that country of a centralized authority which would sign a peace treaty with Israel. It called on Syria not to participate in the war and promised not to attack its troops in Lebanon.

Within five days, most of the military aims were achieved. The IDF expelled the PLO units from southern Lebanon and destroyed the mini-state it had created there. But this was done with a higher casualty rate than anticipated, and with Syrian involvement. Superior Israeli military technology resulted in the destruction of over 100 Syrian jet fighters and a vast number of Syrian missile batteries on Lebanese territory. By the fifth day Israeli military units reached the edge of Beirut. It was then that the United States ordered Israel to cease fire, claiming that it had far exceeded its limited territorial war aims by moving farther north than the 40 kilometers it spoke of initially. Israeli Premier Menaḥem Begin had to accept a cease-fire, which actually never came into being as Palestinian troops continued to fight, as did the Syrian army, now threatened in its positions along the strategic Beirut-Damascus highway. By the end of the first week, public opinion in Israel was aroused. Questions were being asked about the true agenda of the government, the real war aims, the growing number of casualties, and above all how long the IDF intended to stay in Lebanon and in what role. During June, July, and August 1982, while diplomats tried to hammer out an agreement which would remove the PLO from Lebanon and bring about a new order in that country, Israeli troops continued to shell Muslim West Beirut, cutting off water, power, and food. The aerial and artillery bombardment of West Beirut aroused growing international criticism and created hostile world public opinion. In Western media, Israel was portrayed as an aggressor fighting helpless civilians, creating a new refugee problem, this time in Lebanon. Feeble Israeli efforts to explain the true causes of the war and the need to remove the PLO threat to Israel fell on deaf ears. Growing dissent inside Israel was also reflected in the Western media. It became clear that Israel was becoming mired in the Lebanese bog with few considering how to extricate the IDF from that country. Prime Minister Begin argued that the achievements in Lebanon erased the shame of the Yom Kippur War, but that did not convince many Israelis of the need to remain in that country for any length of time.

Protracted negotiations led to the removal of both the Syrian army and the PLO from Lebanon. Israel was instrumental in getting the Christian forces leader Basheer Gemayel elected as president of Lebanon. But on September 1, 1982, Israel suffered two major setbacks. The first was the announcement of Gemayel, in a meeting with Prime Minister Begin, that he did not intend to sign a peace treaty with Israel, because he was first and foremost an Arab. The second was the proclamation of the "Reagan Plan" for a Palestinian settlement, which called on Israel to withdraw from most of the territories it held, and return them to Jordan in the context of a peace treaty. There was to be no Palestinian state, but Jordan would grant special status to the West Bank and Gaza. The situation of Jerusalem would have to be negotiated in the future. Begin, who had no prior notice of the plan, rejected it outright, saying it was not even a basis for negotiations. It looked as though the war in Lebanon had yielded little apart from securing northern Galilee and destroying the PLO as a military force and an important element in the Arab world. The assassination of Basheer Gemayel shortly before his inauguration (September 14, 1982) was the signal for a vicious reprisal by his Christian forces on Palestinians living in two refugee camps in Beirut – Sabra and Shatilla. With the IDF standing by not far from the camps, and unaware of the magnitude of the massacre which lasted three days (September 17–19, 1982), some 400 Palestinians – men, women, and children – were massacred before the IDF put an end to the killing. A clamor went up in Israel to establish a commission of inquiry to investigate the events in the camps. The demand, backed by a demonstration organized in Tel Aviv by left wing parties and groups in Israel, reputedly attracted some 400,000 people, the largest ever held in Israel. When Begin still resisted, he was confronted with a threat by President Navon to resign his office. Finally, the prime minister relented and a commission was constituted headed by Supreme Court President Justice Kahan. While it began its work, tempers cooled and the country awaited two decisions – the verdict of the commission and a political decision on how long and within which borders the IDF would remain in Lebanon.

The government decided to order the IDF to remain in Beirut until an agreement could be worked out with the new Lebanese government headed by Amin Gemayel, the brother of the late Basheer Gemayel. As time went on, the IDF became involved in local communal strife in Lebanon. The Kahan commission issued its report in February 1983. It found the IDF indirectly responsible for the massacre, calling for the resignation of the defense minister and senior army officers. Ariel Sharon had to leave his post but remained in the government as minister without portfolio. Senior officers also had to leave, among them the director of military intelligence. Others, including the chief of staff, did not have their term of duty extended.

On May 17, 1983, after long and difficult negotiations with the participation of U.S. Secretary of State George Shultz, Israel and Lebanon signed an agreement, which fell short of a peace treaty. It ended the state of war, recognized Israel's need to have a security zone in southern Lebanon under its control, called for an Israeli diplomatic presence in Beirut, and demanded the withdrawal of all foreign troops from Lebanon, which meant in effect Syrian troops. The agreement was hinged on this withdrawal. When Syria announced that it would not withdraw its troops, the agreement became a dead letter. Nine months later the Lebanese parliament failed to ratify it and the agreement in effect lapsed. For the next two years, the IDF sought ways to extricate itself from Lebanon, finally withdrawing under orders from the National Unity Government which came into being in 1984. By the summer of 1985, the Lebanese episode ended, leaving Israel in a security zone in southern Lebanon, the PLO re-established in Tunisia, the Syrian army in Lebanon, and Israeli public opinion highly uncertain whether the toll of three years in Lebanon – 659 dead and thousands wounded – had been worthwhile.

In 1983 Israel faced an unprecedented economic threat, caused by the over-valuation of bank shares, inflated by the banks themselves. When the public began to unload these bank shares, there was a danger that the Israeli financial institutions would collapse and that overseas investors and depositors would remove billions of dollars, leaving the Israeli economy in the lurch. In October 1983 the Tel Aviv stock market was closed for 17 days and the government decided to buy the bank shares at a cost to the Israeli taxpayer of some 7 billion dollars. By late 1983 inflation in Israel reached the figure of 200% annually and by 1984 it had amounted to 448%. Inflation was destructive for the country's economic growth, morale, overseas investments, and labor relations. Even the resignation of Finance Minister Yoram Aridor, whose policies brought Israel to the brink of economic disaster, did not alleviate the situation. It took the Government of National Unity's rescue plan (July 1985), which froze prices and wages and put in a mechanism of retrenchment to save the situation. Within a year, the rate of inflation was down to 20%. The plan was made possible by the cooperation of the government, the Histadrut (Trade Union Federation), and the Manufacturers' Association. The three factors realized that with no serious action, Israel's economy would literally collapse. Prime Minister Peres engineered the rescue operation, with the help of Finance Minister Yitzḥak Modai and the Histadrut leadership. The Israeli public, asked to make sacrifices in lowering its standard of living, agreed once it saw a coherent economic policy.

The Government of National Unity (see Israel, State of: *Political Life and Parties) brought about three major achievements – it extricated Israel from Lebanon, it rescued its economy, and it restored public confidence in the economy and the leadership. It failed to attract a mass wave of immigration, and the decade of the 1980s up to 1989 saw an average of some 12,000 immigrants a year, while the number of emigrants leaving Israel reached similar figures. The gates of the Soviet Union were closed and immigration from the free world dwindled. The outstanding exception was the airlift of 17,000 Ethiopian Jews to Israel in 1984. The Jewish Agency decided to transfer to the government much responsibility in the area of immigrant absorption, previously under its domain. The peace process was virtually at a standstill because of the vast chasm between the views of the Likud and those of Labor (see Israel, State: *Foreign Relations).

The absence of meaningful progress towards peace, the growth of a generation of young Palestinians who knew nothing else but Israeli occupation, an economic recession in the oil-producing Arab states which drastically reduced flow of funds to the areas held by Israel causing serious economic hardship, and above all resentment of the prolonged Israeli presence on the one hand and the impotence of the PLO and the Arab governments to change the situation, all this erupted in late 1987 in an uprising called the *intifada* ("shaking off"). A series of demonstrations in the Gaza Strip on December 9, 1987 signaled the beginning of the *intifada*, led by young men in their early twenties, asserting themselves against both Israel and their elders. Starting with demonstrations, throwing stones, burning tires, the aims of those involved in the *intifada* were to call attention to the plight of the Palestinians, to the prolonged occupation in all its ramifications, to focus on the Palestinization of the conflict, to force the Arab states to take notice, to move the rest of the world to take action, and to make the Israel public and government take decisions on future policies. The major achievement of the *intifada* in its first four years was mainly in the area of public relations. Israel's image in the Western media plunged dramatically. The *intifada* leaders forced the PLO to follow its lead. The leaders of the *intifada* hurt the Israeli economy by calling on Arabs in the areas to boycott Israeli goods. The *intifada* helped to precipitate the decision of the U.S. government to recognize the PLO in December 1988, after the latter announced the creation of a Palestine State in the 1947 partition borders, the acceptance of Israel, and what appeared to be a renunciation of terror. The U.S then embarked on a dialogue with the PLO. The *intifada* created major problems for Israel, whose army now had to deal with civil unrest, the mass demonstrations manned by women and young children. This time, unlike the years that followed the 1967 war, the bulk of the Palestinian Arab population seemed to support the uprising, as did a growing number of Israeli Arabs.

Faced with a new type of war, the IDF had to consider the ethical and moral issues involved in fighting against civilians. It was initially thought that if the *intifada* leaders would be caught and deported or imprisoned, the wave of attacks would die down, but this was not the case. As the *intifada* spread from Gaza to the West Bank, it began to claim Israeli lives, both civilian and military. By early 1993, some 160 Israelis had lost their lives. In that period over 1,600 Palestinian Arabs were killed, the majority at the hands of other Arabs who had accused their victims of collaborating with Israel. The IDF found itself having to fight what was essentially an unpleasant, at times "dirty," war. On the whole it succeeded, but there were cases of torture, unnecessary shooting and killing and a number of Israeli officers and soldiers were court-martialed for using illegal force. These were highly publicized in Israel and abroad, where the issue of human rights was prominent in the headlines and Israel was often the object of criticism.

The impact of the *intifada* on Israelis was at first marginal, but as time went on it became central. There was a feeling of a loss of personal safety, and as more acts of terror were committed in Israeli cities, Israelis realized that they were facing a new breed of Palestinians, some of whom were even prepared to engage in suicide attacks. The Gulf War and the resultant peace process put the *intifada* on the back burner for a time, but it remained a major problem for all Israeli governments, which feared that if not dealt with properly, the allegiance of the Palestinians would move from the PLO to the *Hamas (Islamic fundamentalists) who opposed the peace process, negotiations with Israel, and called for the elimination of the Jewish state. By 1991 the areas held by Israel were the arena for a fight for the hearts, minds, and souls of the Palestinians between the PLO and the Hamas movement. There was also a growing demand in Israel for unilateral withdrawal from the Gaza Strip and gradual disengagement from the West Bank as well. The reliance on some 120,000 laborers from these areas meant that their absence could cause havoc to Israeli agriculture, housing construction, and many services. Measures were undertaken to replace Palestinians by Israelis, but there was the need to find employment for Palestinians, as long as they remained an Israeli responsibility. Massive unemployment in the areas could result in an explosion, it was argued.

By the end of the 1980s, the continued *intifada*, the wave of immigration from the Soviet Union, and the end of the Cold War brought about the need for Israel to reconsider many of its social, political, and economic institutions. Many of them had served the country well in its formative years, but no longer provided answers to the complex issues of the final decade of the 20th century. It was widely agreed that reforms were sorely needed in the Histadrut, government corporations, political parties, the electoral system, and government control of many aspects of the life of its citizens; there was need to reconsider the relations between the secular majority and the Orthodox minority. Questions dealing with the nature of Israeli politics and the ties between big business and government had to be considered. But momentous events awaited the country.

[Meron Medzini]

The Road to Oslo and After

THE 1990 NO-CONFIDENCE VOTE. Unlike the post-1984 Knesset election situation, following the 1988 elections Prime Minister Yitzhak Shamir could have formed a narrow coalition of all the right-wing and religious parties. Shamir, however, had preferred to form a "national unity" government with Labor and other political parties.

On March 15, 1990, Shamir's government failed in a no-confidence vote in the Knesset, and became the only cabinet in Israel's history to be dismissed in this way, with 60 MKs voting against it, 55 for, and five abstaining. This followed a political maneuver which was later described as "the dirty trick" by former Prime Minister Yitzhak Rabin. Although officially the crisis began with the dismissal of Peres from the cabinet by Prime Minister Shamir, on March 13, the maneuver was actually planned by Labor leader Peres and Shas leader Aryeh *Deri, who hoped to form a new government under Peres as the new premier.

On March 20 President Chaim *Herzog asked Peres to try to form the new government. By April 11, just hours before the planned Knesset vote of confidence for the new government, it became clear that Peres' efforts had failed and that he could not mobilize a Knesset majority to support his new government. Herzog granted Peres further time to secure a majority, but on April 25 Labor conceded defeat. As a result, on April 27, President Herzog invited Acting Prime Minister Shamir to form the new government. Shamir succeeded in his efforts and his new government won a vote of confidence of 62 to 27 from the Knesset, with one abstention, on June 11. The Shamir government, officially Israel's 24th, was supported by the Likud, a few MKs who had previously defected from the Likud, the religious parties, and the extreme right wing parties. A number of Likud members who had previously challenged Shamir's leadership supported the new government. These included Deputy Prime Minister and Minister of Foreign Affairs David *Levi, Housing and Construction Minister Ariel Sharon, and Finance Minister Yitzhak Moda'i (who had previously defected from the Likud with a few other MKs to form the "Party for the Advancement of the Zionist Idea").

The failure of Peres and the success of Shamir demonstrated that most politicians belonging to the religious parties normally preferred participation in a Likud-led government to participation in a Labor-led government. Prior to the 1977 upheaval, religious parties had joined Mapai/Labor-led governments, but all this had occurred when the Likud or its forerunners could not possibly have formed a majority coalition even with the full support of all the religious and right-wing parties.

IMMIGRATION. During 1990 over 200,000 immigrants arrived in Israel. During the following decade almost one million people immigrated to Israel and became Israeli citizens. Almost 90 per cent of the immigrants came from former republics of the Soviet Union. Between 1990 and 2003 another 50,000 or so immigrated from Ethiopia. This wave of immigrants was almost equivalent – in total numbers – to the huge wave of immigrants that flooded Israel after its birth and marked a significant shift from the decline in immigration during the 1980s, during which only 153,833 arrived. The main cause for the huge immigration was the collapse of the U.S.S.R. The new citizens of Israel changed its demography and its political profile significantly. The very high economic growth rate during the 1990s is also partially attributable to the huge immigration to Israel.

THE 1991 GULF WAR. The first Gulf War marked another strategic shift in the political environment of Israeli politics caused by global developments. In January and February of 1991, during the Gulf War, Iraq launched more than 40 SCUD missiles at civilian target in Israel. Israelis, who feared that some of these missiles would carry chemical warheads, were forced to wear gas masks during the attacks. The government faced a severe "retaliation dilemma." On the one hand, the U.S. supplied Israel with Patriot missiles to protect Israelis from these attacks, but it also pressured Israel not to intervene in the war in any active manner. On the other hand, Israel's ability to deter potential aggressors, which marked Israeli defense strategy for years, became questionable. The enthusiastic support of Saddam Hussein by the Arabs, such as PLO leaders, Jordanians, and residents of the West Bank, convinced many Israelis – including dovish left-wing politicians – to adopt more hawkish positions. At the time, it seemed that the government's relatively moderate policies during the war, coupled with the reactions of various Arab parties, significantly increased the popularity of the right-wing parties in general and the Likud in particular.

THE MADRID CONFERENCE. On October 30, 1991, Israel attended the Madrid Peace Conference, which was co-sponsored by the U.S. and the U.S.S.R. In their letter of invitation Presidents Bush and Gorbachev established a framework for both bilateral negotiations between Israel and Arab parties and multilateral talks. It seems that developments in the USSR and the Soviet bloc, the massive immigration to Israel, and the Gulf War were among the causes for participation of even hardline Arab parties in the conference. One innovative element of the talks was the presence of a Palestinian delegation, which was considered part of a "joint Jordanian-Palestinian delegation." In fact, the Palestinians participating in the conference could have been regarded as semi-official representatives of the PLO. The acceptance of such a formula by Shamir and his relatively hawkish government signified a deviation from the past as talks with PLO representatives not only contradicted an explicit Knesset law but had also caused the dismissal of former Labor Minister Ezer *Weizman from the government by Prime Minister Shamir on December 31, 1989. It is also interesting to note in this context that Peres had been officially dismissed by Shamir in March 1990 following "unauthorized" talks he held with King Hussein of Jordan in London.

Shamir's decision to take part in the Madrid Conference increased the tension between the Likud and the small hawkish parties, Teḥiyya, Tzomet, and Moledet. Within a few weeks after the conference it became clear that Knesset elections would take place at a date earlier than that required by the law.

THE 1992 BASIC LAWS AND THE "CONSTITUTIONAL REVOLUTION." The Knesset decided to dissolve itself and to hold early elections for the Thirteenth Knesset on June 23, 1992. But prior to these elections many politicians believed that major changes should be made in the constitutional framework.

In March 1992 the Knesset passed three new basic laws: Basic Law: Freedom of Occupation; Basic Law: Human Dignity and Freedom; and Basic Law: the Government.

Basic Law: Freedom of Occupation was the most sublime of all Israeli laws from the formal point of view since it was protected by both a "limiting clause" and a "majority shield." The first protection was guaranteed by Article 4: "There shall be no violation of rights under this Basic Law except by a law befitting the values of the State of Israel, enacted for a proper purpose, and to an extent no greater than is required." The second protection was guaranteed by Article 7: "This Basic Law may not be amended except by a Basic Law passed by a majority of Knesset members." Basic Law: Human Dignity and Freedom was protected only by a limiting clause (Article 8) and Basic Law: the Government was protected only by a majority shield (Article 56).

It should be mentioned that other Israeli Basic Laws, with the exception of a few specific articles (most famous of which is Article 4 of Basic Law: the Knesset, pertaining to the system of elections and stipulating that it can only be amended by a majority of Knesset members, i.e., 61), are neither protected by a limiting clause nor by a majority shield. Nevertheless, in a number of cases, the Supreme Court under the leadership of its president, Aharon *Barak, ruled that all Basic Laws take precedence over regular Knesset laws. These rulings and the special formal status given to the 1992 Basic Laws gave the Court almost unlimited power to exercise judicial review.

The main idea behind another new Basic Law: the Government, which replaced the 1958 version of Basic Law: the Government, was the adoption of direct election of the prime minister. A major motivation behind this innovation, which significantly changed the basic nature of Israeli parliamentary democracy, was the dissatisfaction with a number of untoward developments associated with the "dirty trick" of March 1990. Nevertheless, the implementation of this law was delayed until the elections to the Fourteenth Knesset, and the 1992 elections were held, as usual, for the Knesset only. A third version of Basic Law: the Government, which abolished direct elections of the prime minister, as a result of variious unresolvable complications in the system, was passed by the Knesset in March 2001. In the meanwhile, Binyamin *Netanyahu (1996), Ehud *Barak (1999), and Ariel Sharon (2001) had been elected by direct vote.

In 1994 a major development in the battle over judicial review took place when the Knesset rephrased Basic Law: Freedom of Occupation, stating that basic human rights would be honored in accordance with Israel's Declaration of Independence – thus giving the Declaration a legal status that took precedence over Knesset laws. In should be noted in this context that the Declaration of Independence determines that the State of Israel will be based on foundations of "freedom, justice, and peace, according to the vision of the prophets of Israel," and that it will provide "absolute equal social and political rights" to all its citizens.

THE 1992 ELECTIONS. The elections to the Thirteenth Knesset ended in an upset. The Labor Party recaptured the pivotal (middle) position in the Knesset. For the first time since the 1973 Knesset elections, Labor and the more "dovish" parties gained a majority – together controlling 61 out of the 120 seats. It is interesting to note that more votes were given to the right wing and religious parties, which together controlled only 59 seats, than to the left-wing parties. This occurred mainly because of a slight change in the electoral procedure: the threshold was raised from 1.0 per cent to 1.5 per cent of the valid votes. As a result 5.0 per cent of the valid votes went to parties that did not pass the threshold, as compared with 2.4 per cent in 1988. More votes were given to unsuccessful right-wing parties (such as Teḥiyya) than to unsuccessful left-wing parties (such as the Progressive List), and therefore these votes were lost to the right.

Ten lists of candidates won representation in the Thirteenth Knesset: four "left-wing" parties – Labor (44 seats), Meretz (12), Ḥadash (3), and the Arab Democratic Party (ADP) (2); three right-wing parties – Likud (32), Tzomet (8), and Moledet (3); and three religious parties – NRP (6), Shas (6) and Yahadut ha-Torah (4).

Public opinion polls conducted at the beginning of the campaign indicated a convincing lead for the Likud over Labor. Therefore, it is plausible to assume that developments during the campaign persuaded a decisive number of voters to change their votes. One such major event was the nomination of the popular Yitzhak Rabin instead of the unpopular Shimon Peres as Labor leader. Rabin's popularity inthe general public exceeded his popularity in his own party: In Labor's primaries almost 60 per cent preferred other candidates for the premiership. Rabin was considered as a relatively hawkish leader of Labor whose record as chief of staff of the Israeli Defense Forces (IDF) was emphasized by his party to offset its dovish image, as the Palestinian Intifada (uprising) that had started in late 1987 continued to claim a heavy toll.

The Likud, which had reached the peak of its popularity toward the end of 1991 with Israel's participation in the Madrid Peace Conference, suffered a sharp decline in its popularity, especially due to severe internal dissent that made a bad impression on the electorate.

Nine per cent of eligible voters were immigrants, most of whom had come to Israel from the U.S.S.R. (and its successor republics). The new immigrants played a major role in the elections. According to several public opinion polls, turnout among immigrants resembled that of veteran voters. Approximately half of the immigrants supported Labor. In the following elections most immigrants had a change of heart and supported right-wing parties. Apparently, the 1992 immigrant vote resulted from absorption difficulties, while in later elections, right-of-center political views dictated their voting behavior.

Following the Likud's defeat in the 1992 general elections, Moshe *Arens, who was considered by many as a potential successor to Prime Minister Shamir, tendered his resignation from the Knesset. Shamir himself announced that he did not intend to continue leading the Likud. Consequently, the Likud held "primaries" to choose its new leader on March 24, 1993. The winner was Binyamin ("Bibi") Netanyahu, who was supported by 52 per cent of the 145,000 Likud members who cast votes. David Levi came second with 26 per cent, while Binyamin *Begin (15 per cent) and Moshe *Katzav (7 per cent) shared the remaining votes.

RABIN'S GOVERNMENT. After the 1992 elections Labor held negotiations with almost all the other parties which had had seats in the Knesset. Rabin presented his government – Israel's 25th – to the Knesset on July 13, forming a coalition with Meretz and Shas that controlled 62 of the Knesset's 120 seats. In the vote of confidence, Ḥadash and the ADP also supported the government. On the date of its investiture there were 13 Labor members in the cabinet, three Meretz members, and one Shas member. Rabin held, in addition to his position as prime minister, the portfolios of Defense and Religious Affairs. Shimon Peres, the second senior member of the cabinet, held Foreign Affairs.

Although Meretz and Shas could have been considered as the closest possible allies to Labor on questions related to the Arab-Israeli conflict, one of the main problems of Rabin's coalition was the constant tension between the anti-clerical Meretz and the ultra-Orthodox Shas on matters concerning religious affairs. Many of these clashes involved Meretz leader and Minister of Education and Culture Shulamit *Aloni and Shas leader and Minister of the Interior Aryeh *Deri. In December 1992, following another crisis, both Meretz and Shas were appeased by Labor: Meretz was given an additional seat in the cabinet and Shas was given control of the Ministry of Religious Affairs when one of its MKs was made deputy minister there.

Both Minister of the Interior Aryeh Deri and Deputy Minister of Religious Affairs Raphael Pinḥasi had been under investigation since 1990 on suspicion of corruption. Nevertheless, when Attorney General Yosef Ḥarish presented a draft of the indictment to the prime minister on June 20, 1993, Deri followed the instructions of Shas spiritual leader Ovadiah *Yosef and refused to resign. He and the three deputy ministers of Shas did resign on September 12, 1993, following a ruling of the Supreme Court ordering the dismissal of Deri and Pinḥasi. These resignations came into effect on September 14, a day after Israel and the PLO signed the famous Declaration of Principles (the first Oslo agreement; see below) in Washington, D.C.

Although Rabin's government became a minority government following the defection of Shas, it continued to enjoy the support of two parties which were not formal members of the coalition: the Communist-led Ḥadash and the ADP. Thus, Rabin continued to enjoy the support of 62 MKs. Furthermore, two MKs who defected from Raphael *Eitan's right-wing Tzomet Party joined the government as a minister and deputy minister in January 1995.

The main threat to the stability of the government was a result of its policies concerning the Arab-Israeli conflict. More than a third of Labor's parliamentary faction joined a group called "the Third Way." The Third Way opposed both the "ultra-dovish" positions of certain Labor leaders and the "ultra-hawkish' positions of various Likud leaders. It claimed that while Israel had to make major concessions in order to promote the peace process, Rabin's government was taking too many risks without an adequate response from the Arab partners to negotiations. The Third Way focused its criticism on the declarations made by the minister of foreign affairs and other dovish Labor leaders about the future of the Golan Heights. Peres repeatedly expressed his opinion that the Golan is "Syrian soil" and that no peace could be achieved without Israel's withdrawal from the Golan. Towards the end of 1995 it became clear that two Third Way Knesset members would defect from Labor and run their own party in the 1996 Knesset elections.

THE OSLO PROCESS. U.S. Secretary of State James Baker visited Israel immediately after Rabin's cabinet took office. This demonstrated the joint efforts by the U.S. and Israel to continue the bilateral and multilateral negotiations between Israel and its Arab counterparts as agreed to at the Madrid Conference. The peace talks were resumed in Washington D.C. on August 24, 1992. No practical agreement between the parties was reached, but a dramatic development took place in a completely separate negotiating channel.

After months of secret talks, most of which had been held in Oslo under the auspices of Norwegian Minister of Foreign Affairs Johan Jorgen Holst, Israel and the PLO reached an agreement concerning a Declaration of Principles – also known as "the first Oslo agreement" – signed between the parties in the presence of U.S. President *Clinton on September 13, 1993.

Many Israelis had been ready to negotiate with the PLO, at least according to the "formula" proposed by two members of the first Rabin cabinet (in 1974), Victor Shemtov and Aharon Yariv. The formula asserted that Israel would negotiate with "any Arab partner who recognized the right of Israel to exist and who was not involved in terrorism." The PLO, however, had not demonstrated a clear readiness to accept the Shemtov-Yariv formula, although the first steps towards such an end were made by it already in 1988. One reason for the declared readiness of the PLO to conduct negotiations with Israel in 1993 was its relative weakness as a result of its support of Iraq during the Gulf War, the consequent halt of financial aid from the Arab oil monarchies, the collapse of the Soviet Union – the other main sponsor of the PLO – and the growing popularity of groups competing with the PLO, including those inspired by fundamentalist Islamic beliefs.

The September 13 Declaration of Principles was preceded by an exchange of letters between Arafat, Rabin and Holst (September 10). In his letter to Prime Minister Rabin, Chairman Arafat accepted the principles of the Shemtov-Yariv formula and agreed to amend the Palestinian Covenant, which called for the violent extermination of the State of Israel (or any other "Zionist entity in Palestine"). In his letter to Foreign Minister Holst, he also promised to encourage Palestinians in the Gaza Strip and the West Bank to stop the violent *intifada* begun in 1997. In his reply to Arafat, Rabin recognized the PLO as the representative of the Palestinian people and welcomed its participation in the peace process.

Article I of the Declaration of Principles stated that: "The main aim of the Israeli-Palestinian negotiations in the current Middle East peace process is, among other things, to establish a Palestinian Interim Self-Governing Authority, the elected Council of the Palestinian People in the West Bank and the Gaza Strip …." A common reference to the declaration as the "Gaza-Jericho" agreement derives from Article XIV, which confirmed Israel's intention to withdraw from most of the Gaza Strip and the Jericho area.

One of the most vocal critics of the Israeli-PLO negotiations was the new leader of the Likud, Binyamin *Netanyahu.

The Oslo process continued in spite of an anti-Palestinian terrorist attack in Hebron and in spite of terrorist attacks against Jews in Israel and in other countries. On February 2, 1994, a Jewish settler, Dr. Baruch Goldstein, opened fire on Arab worshippers inside the Tomb of the Patriarchs (Ibrahimi Mosque) in Hebron – a site sacred to both Moslems and Jews. Goldstein killed 29 worshippers before he himself was killed. The unprecedented attack was strongly denounced not only by the president and the prime minister but also by all leaders of the Knesset factions and by the leaders of the Jewish settlers in the occupied territories.

On October 19, 1994, a bus was blown up in the middle of Tel Aviv, killing 22 civilians and injuring 47. More than 40 lost their lives in the explosion of the the Jewish community center in Buenos Aires on July 22, 1994, and more than 20 were killed in Panama on July 19, 1994, in the explosion of a plane carrying many Jewish businessmen.

The continued bilateral Palestinian-Israeli negotiations led to a number of agreements between Israel and the PLO.

On May 4, 1994, Prime Minister Rabin and Chairman Arafat signed in Cairo an agreement on the Gaza Strip and the Jericho area. This agreement followed Article XIV of the Declaration of Principles (see above). The Cairo agreement consisted of 23 articles, four annexes, four accompanying letters, and six maps. During the ceremony, Prime Minister Rabin discovered that Chairman Arafat had deliberately neglected to sign the map of the Jericho area. This endangered the completion of the ceremony, which continued only after Arafat finally added his signature to the document.

The Cairo Agreement established a "Palestinian Authority" (PA), which "has, within its authority, legislative, executive and judicial powers and responsibilities." It was also agreed that "in order to guarantee public order and internal security of the Palestinians of the Gaza Strip and the Jericho Area, the PA shall establish a strong police force." Article XVIII stated that "both sides shall take all measures necessary in order to prevent acts of terrorism, crime and hostilities directed against each other, against individuals falling under the other's authority and against their property, and shall take legal measures against offenders."

On September 24, 1995, Foreign Minister Shimon Peres and Chairman Yasser Arafat initialed in Taba the Israeli-Palestinian Interim Agreement on the West Bank and the Gaza Strip, also known as the "Oslo B Agreement." This agreement was signed by Prime Minister Rabin and Chairman Arafat in Washington, D.C., on September 28, 1995. In the detailed 315-page document, Israel agreed that the Palestinians would gain full control of the six largest towns of the West Bank and civic authority and responsibility for public order in 440 Arab villages. The agreement transferred powers and responsibilities from Israel to an elected Council and elected Ra'is (President) of an Executive Authority. Chapter 1 of the agreement dealt with "the Council. Chapter 2 dealt with "redeployment and security arrangements." Chapter 3 dealt with "legal affairs," Chapter 4 with "cooperation," and Chapter 5 with "miscellaneous provisions." The document included seven annexes and nine maps.

Supporters of the Rabin government praised the agreement as a major step toward real peace between the Palestinians and Israel. They claimed that Israel had made only necessary concessions while preserving its option to reconsider the situation if the Palestinians did not fulfill their part of the agreement.

Critics claimed that the PLO would be generously rewarded in spite of the fact that it did not intend to give up its dream of eliminating the State of Israel voiced in its Covenant. They also doubted whether the PLO would fulfill its promise to change the Palestinian Covenant.

THE PEACE WITH JORDAN. When the secret negotiations between Israel and the PLO became public, King Hussein of Jordan expressed his dissatisfaction with the fact that the parties to the Madrid framework were holding their direct bilateral talks under cover. But soon enough he willingly participated in bilateral talks with Israel and on September 14, 1994 – a day after Israel and the PLO singed their Declaration of Principles – Israel and Jordan signed a "common agenda" for negotiations.

As was the case in 1993, the Israel-PLO Cairo agreement was followed by an Israel-Jordan agreement. On July 25, 1994, Prime Minister Rabin and King Hussein of Jordan signed the Washington Declaration in which they announced the termination of the state of belligerency between their two countries. President Clinton of the U.S. witnessed the declaration.

On October 26, 1994, the prime ministers of Israel and Jordan, Yitzhak Rabin and Abdul Salam Al-Majali, signed at the Aravah border crossing the Treaty of Peace between the State of Israel and the Hashemite Kingdom of Jordan. President Clinton also signed the treaty as a witness. The audience at the ceremony was addressed by King Hussein of Jordan, Prime Minister Rabin, Russian Foreign Minister Kozyrev, U.S. Secretary of State Christopher, Israeli Minister of Foreign Affairs Peres, and U.S. President Clinton. The exchange of instruments of ratification of the treaty by King Hussein and Prime Minister Rabin took place on November 10, 1994. The peace treaty included 30 articles, five annexes, and agreed minutes. In the preamble to the treaty the parties expressed their desire "to develop friendly relations and cooperation between them."

Unlike the case of the agreements with the PLO, almost all the leaders of the Likud supported both the Washington Declaration and the Treaty of Peace, and in the Knesset 105 members voted to confirm the agreement. Even vocal opponents of the government like Reḥavam Ze'evi, leader of the extreme Moledet Party, refrained in a Knesset speech from opposing the idea of peace with Jordan but criticized details of the treaty and reminded members of Jordan's past involvement in anti-Jewish and anti-Israeli policies, e.g., Jordanian support of Iraq during the Gulf War. It should be noted in this context that in 1994 it became publicly known that Prime Minister Shamir and King Hussein had held secret talks during the Gulf War in which they coordinated positions.

THE ASSASSINATION OF YITZHAK RABIN. On the evening of November 4, 1995, Yitzhak Rabin was assassinated. It was the first assassination of an Israeli cabinet member since the establishment of the State of Israel. Only once prior to Rabin's assassination had a Knesset member been assassinated. Rabin was shot in the back upon leaving a mass peace rally in Tel Aviv in which both he and Peres had participated.

Several gestures made by the generally restrained Rabin during the rally had been unprecedented. He had embraced his onetime arch-rival Peres and joined in during the singing of "The Song of Peace." The bloodstained text of the lyrics was later found in his pocket.

The murderer, Yigal Amir, a 25-year-old religious extremist and student of law at Bar-Ilan University, expressed his satisfaction when he learned of the results of his act. A comprehensive investigation by the police and a judicial commission of inquiry headed by a former president of the Supreme Court, Meir Shamgar, concluded that no organization had stood behind the crime. Yigal Amir's brother Hagai and two friends were also indicted for their previous knowledge of Amir's plans and for the help they gave him. The investigation suggested that security measures had not been adequate and several officials, including the head of the General Security Service, were forced to resign.

The emotional reaction to the assassination threatened to tear the Israeli public apart. Many, including Rabin's widow, blamed the leaders of the right wing parties for creating the atmosphere that had made Amir's crime possible. Some suggested that the crime was the result of declarations made by extremist rabbis blaming Rabin for his "cooperation with the enemy." Consequently, a number of rabbis were investigated by the police. The leaders of all right-wing political parties and movements, including the leaders of the settlers in the occupied territories, and all prominent religious leaders, strongly condemned the crime.

Rabin's funeral was attended by a number of world leaders, including President Clinton of the United States, Prime Minister Chernomyrdin of Russia, Prime Minister Major of the United Kingdom, Chancellor Kohl of Germany, and President Chirac of France. A number of representatives of Arab countries, including a few who had never visited Israel before, also attended. King Hussein of Jordan said in his eulogy that Rabin died "as a soldier of peace." Other prominent Arab representatives were President Mubarak of Egypt and government ministers from Oman and Qatar.

Prior to the assassination it seemed that public support for Labor was on the wane, but according to public opinion polls conducted after the assassination, in November and December, it was the popularity of right wing leaders and right wing political parties that dropped considerably while the popularity of Shimon Peres and Labor reached a peak. This led to speculation that Peres, who succeeded Rabin as prime minister, might call early elections.

PERES' GOVERNMENT. Two weeks after being named acting prime minister, Shimon Peres completed the formation of a new government – Israel's 26th.

The parliamentary basis of the new government was similar to Rabin's. Most of the ministers continued to hold the same portfolios. Nevertheless, a number of changes in the composition of the cabinet are notable. Peres took the portfolios of prime minister and defense minister, previously held by Rabin. Peres added two new ministers to his cabinet. He asked Rabbi Yehudah Amital to join the government as a minister without portfolio. Amital, who had established a yeshiva in the West Bank, was the leader of the Meimad movement – a moderate religious group that had been established by former members of the National Religious Party (NRP) and that had participated unsuccessfully in the 1988 Knesset elections. Amital's nomination was intended to signal that in spite of Rabin's assassination, religious Jews and settlers in the occupied territories should be regarded as an integral part of the nation. The other new minister was Ḥaim *Ramon, who rejoined Labor and was named minister of the interior. He gave up his position as secretary general of the Histadrut. Amir *Peretz, Ramon's partner in the leadership of the Ram Party, became the new secretary general. Ramon had defected from Labor and established Ram in his successful 1994 attempt to capture the leadership of the Histadrut. Ehud *Barak, former chief of staff of the IDF, who had been appointed by Rabin as a minister of the interior in July 1995, became minister of foreign affairs.

Paradoxically, Peres, who had challenged Rabin's leadership so many times in the past, was regarded now as the late premier's closest friend and ally. Given the new circumstances, many observers argued that Peres was not only the most senior and experienced Israeli politician but also that his leadership was unshakable. Apparently, some of these observers overlooked the dissatisfaction with various government policies and the lack of popularity from which Peres perennially suffered. Nevertheless, Peres decided to call early elections for May 29, 1996.

On January 20, 1996, Palestinians living in Jerusalem, the West Bank, and the Gaza Strip elected the 88 members of the Palestinian Council and the Ra'is (president) of the PA, using a procedure agreed upon by Israel and the PLO in the September 1995 Interim Agreement. Arafat received 88.1 per cent of the vote. The candidates of Arafat's Fataḥ group won an impressive majority in the Council, with little strong opposition to the Oslo process.

On April 24, 1996, the Palestinian National Council (PNC), the quasi-parliamentary supreme body of the PLO, voted to amend the Palestinian Covenant (the quasi-constitution of the PLO) by removing all clauses calling for the annihilation of Israel. Some Israelis criticized the nature of the PNC move, claiming that it did not meet the obligation undertaken in the Interim Agreement and in the letter sent to Rabin by Arafat on September 9, 1993. The critics emphasized that the PNC had not actually amended the Covenant but instead decided in principle that changes would be made, without specifying concrete clauses and concrete dates.

During the last week of February and the first week of March 1996, a series of suicide attacks on Israeli civilian targets shocked the country. The largest number of victims died in attacks carried out in Israel's largest cities, Jerusalem and Tel Aviv. Most of the attacks were carried out by the extreme Islamic group Hamas. As a result, the Peres government decided to impose almost total closure of the West Bank and Gaza Strip until after the May elections. The closure had a serious impact on the Palestinian economy.

Following attacks on Israeli soldiers in the "security zone" in southern Lebanon and the firing of Katyusha rockets into Israel by the paramilitary *Hizbollah organization, the government decided to launch a military operation, "Grapes of

Wrath," in Lebanon. The operation commenced on April 11, 1996. On April 18, a large number of Lebanese civilians were killed by artillery shells near the village on Qana. Prime Minister Peres blamed Hizbollah, stating that its strategy was to fire rockets and initiate other attacks while "hiding behind Lebanese civilians." The Qana incident provoked severe criticism of the government and its policy in Lebanon. Many Arab supporters of Peres declared that they would not support him in the May elections. On election day, however, over 95 per cent of Arab voters who participated in the elections supported Peres. Operation Grapes of Wrath ended in an "understanding" announced simultaneously in Jerusalem and Beirut on April 26, 1996.

THE 1996 ELECTIONS. In the May 29 elections the new electoral and institutional procedure that derived from the 1992 Basic Law: the Government, was implemented. Simultaneously with the elections to the Fourteenth Knesset the voters also elected the prime minister of Israel directly. According to the new law, in order to win a candidate had to have over half the valid votes. In the event that no candidate had an absolute majority, a second round, in which only the two leading candidates participated, would take place. A second round was not necessary in the 1996 elections, as there were only two candidates in the race: Shimon Peres of Labor and Binyamin Netanyahu of the Likud.

According to all public opinion polls, Peres led the race through the entire campaign. Nevertheless, following the wave of terrorist attacks on Israeli civilians in February and March, the gap between the two contestants narrowed to only a few points. Peres continued to lead until election day. Immediately after the closing of the polling booths, the two Israeli television networks declared Peres the winner on the basis of their exit polls. It only became evident that Netanyahu was the new prime minister of Israel four days later, when the count of those who voted in "double envelopes" (mainly IDF soldiers) was completed. Netanyahu won by a margin of 50.5 to 49.5 per cent of the valid votes. It should be mentioned, however, that 4.8 per cent of the votes were invalid. It seems that many voters preferred to express their dissatisfaction with both candidates by casting invalid ballots. Hence, Netanyahu actually got only 48.1 per cent of the total votes.

A primary aim of those who supported the new electoral system was to reduce the dependency of the prime minister on the small parties and individual members of the Knesset. But the law stated that although "the prime minister serves by virtue of his being elected," he must present his government to the Knesset. "Should the Knesset reject the prime minister's proposals for the composition of the government, it will be regarded as an expression of no-confidence."

Almost all the small parties called upon their supporters to split their vote, telling them which candidate to vote for as prime minister. The small centrist parties did not endorse any of the candidates but stressed the need to support their own parties in the Knesset elections "in order to ensure that the elected prime minister will not become a captive in the hands of extremists in his bloc." In fact, the strength of the two large parties decreased dramatically, and the dependence of the newly elected prime minister on the small parties increased. Furthermore, in an early stage of the campaign, two small parties, Tzomet and Gesher, promoted their respective leaders, Raphael Eitan and David Levi, as possible candidates for the premiership. In order to increase the odds of being elected, Netanyahu agreed to join forces with both these parties at the price of giving their Knesset candidates relatively high places on the joint list. It is quite evident that Netanyahu would have had no real chance of being elected in the first round if Levi and/or Eitan had run as independent candidates.

In spite of Netanyahu's victory, the Likud-Gesher-Tsomet list came only second in the Knesset race, winning 32 seats compared with Labor's 34. The religious parties – Shas, NRP, and Yahadut ha-Torah – won 10, 9, and 4 seats, respectively. The anti-clerical and dovish Meretz Party won 9 seats. Two new parties, the "Russian" immigrants party, Yisrael ba-Aliyah, led by former dissident Natan *Sharansky, and the Third Way, led by former Labor member Avigdor Kahalani, won 7 and 4 seats respectively. The Communist-led Ḥadash party won 5 seats, the Arab Democratic Party (ADP) 4, and the extremist Moledet 2.

Prior to the elections, Labor had enjoyed a "blocking majority" of 61 together with its government coalition partner, Meretz, and with the support of Ḥadash and the ADP. In spite of the dramatic increase in the representation of the latter two, the entire "dovish" bloc dropped to only 52 seats, leaving the center in the hands of parties like the Sephardic-religious Shas, the ultra-Orthodox Yahadut ha-Torah, the centrist Third Way, and the new immigrants party, Yisrael ba-Aliyah. The Likud was placed by most observers to the right (i.e., being more hawkish) of these parties. Right of the Likud were the third religious party, the NRP, and Moledet.

NETANYAHU'S GOVERNMENT. Netanyahu's coalition (the 27th government of Israel) rested on 66 Knesset members. All the center and right-wing parties except Moledet participated in it. One of the cabinet members, Minister of Justice Ya'akov Ne'eman, was not affiliated with any of the political parties. When the attorney general ordered a police investigation into allegations that Ne'eman had obstructed court proceedings, he was forced to resign (August 8, 1996). Later he was acquitted.

Although many had argued prior to the elections that Netanyahu was not committed to the peace process in general and to the Oslo process in particular, his government decided within weeks of the elections to continue the negotiations with the PA. Only one minister, Binyamin Begin, voted against this decision. An initial meeting between Netanyahu and Arafat took place on September 4, 1996.

On September 23, 1996, the Hasmonean Tunnel at the ancient Western Wall was opened in the Old City of Jerusalem. On September 24, Yasser Arafat called on Palestinians to strike and demonstrate against this opening of the tunnel. Muslim leaders claimed that the tunnel ran underneath the Temple Mount and that it would undermine the foundations of the Dome of the Rock and the Al-Aqsa Mosque built on the Mount. In fact, the tunnel did not run beneath the Temple Mount. The restoration of the tunnel by archaeologists had been going on since 1987. On September 25, violence erupted in the West Bank and the Gaza Strip. Attacks by Palestinian civilians and Palestinian police (who used weapons supplied by Israel) on Israeli soldiers and Israeli settlers left 15 Israeli soldiers and at least 50 Palestinians dead. These clashes were the most serious since the signing of the Declaration of Principles in September 1993.

On January 16, 1997, Binyamin Begin resigned from the cabinet in protest against the agreement between Israel and the PA for the withdrawal of the IDF from the Arab part of Hebron.

The most dramatic political scandal of 1997 was known as the "Bar-On for Hebron deal." According to a TV news report, Shas ministers had voted for the IDF pullback in Hebron in return for the nomination of Roni Bar-On, a criminal attorney, to the post of attorney general. According to the TV report Bar-On, who was forced to resign the post only two days after being named to it, was expected to arrange a plea bargain for the indicted Shas leader, Aryeh Deri. After an investigation, both Netanyahu and Justice Minister Tzachi Hanegbi were exonerated.

On March 12, 1997, a Jordanian soldier opened fire at schoolgirls who were visiting the "Island of Peace" located on the Jordanian side of the Israel-Jordan border. Seven girls died in the attack. On March 15 King Hussein came to Israel to make condolence calls to each of the seven mourning families.

During 1997 and 1998 the Netanyahu government as well as the Likud party suffered a number of major internal crises. It seemed that the stability promised by those who had supported direct elections of the prime minister was far from being achieved

One of the most important developments in the Palestinian-Israeli conflict was the agreement reached between Arafat and Netanyahu at Wye Plantation in October 1998. Both leaders, in the presence of President Clinton and the ailing King Hussein of Jordan, signed the agreement in the White House on October 23. According to the agreement, Israel was to transfer control over 13 per cent of the West Bank to the civil control of the PA as well as military control over an additional 14 per cent of the West Bank in which the PA already enjoyed civil control. In return, the Palestinian National Council (PNC) of the PLO was to revoke the articles in the Palestinian Covenant that called for the extermination of the State of Israel. The hardliners in Netanyahu's coalition opposed the agreement and his coalition became even less stable.

On December 21, 1998, the Knesset decided to have early elections "within six months" instead of the elections that should have taken place towards the end of 2000. A week later it was agreed that the new elections would be held on May 17, 1999.

THE 1999 ELECTIONS. Netanyahu's position prior to the 1999 elections grew weaker and weaker. His government had already lost its Knesset majority in December 1998. On January 23, 1999, Netanyahu decided to dismiss Defense Minister Yitzhak Mordechai following Mordechai's negotiations with the leaders of the new Center Party. Later, Mordechai was chosen as the Center's leader and its candidate for the premiership.

Already on June 3, 1997, Ehud Barak had been elected as the new chairperson of the Labor Party and its candidate for the premiership. Barak decided to call the Labor party "Yisrael Aḥat" ("One Israel") to give it a semblance of broad appeal and reach out for the religious and working class vote, which had been moving away from the party. David Levi's Gesher and Meimad joined forces with Labor in the creation of the new list.

The most dramatic events of the 1999 campaign took place in its last two days. Three candidates for the premiership: Azmi Bishara of Balad, Yitzhak Mordechai of the Center Party, and Binyamin Begin of National Unity decided to withdraw their candidacies, leaving only Likud's Netanyahu and Yisrael Aḥat's Barak in the race.

Barak won the election by an impressive majority of 56.1 to 43.9 per cent. Nevertheless, it appeared that among Jewish voters alone the elections ended in a virtual dead heat. In Jerusalem, the capital and largest city, Netanyahu won the race by a margin of 64.5 to 35.5 per cent.

Netanyahu resigned his position as Likud leader on May 18. He also resigned from the Knesset a few weeks later. The Central Committee of the Likud appointed Ariel Sharon as its new leader on May 27 after he defeated Jerusalem's Mayor Ehud *Olmert, and MK Meir Shitrit in party elections with 53 per cent of the vote

The elections to the Fifteenth Knesset marked a further fragmentation of the party system. Fifteen parties won seats in the new Knesset. The total of the two big lists of candidates combined, which had reached a peak of 95 seats in 1981, dropped to just 45 in the 1999 Knesset elections. As in the 1996 elections, there is no doubt that one of the reasons for this phenomenon was the new electoral system and the split vote it encouraged, as many voters felt free to support a small party in the Knesset elections while voting for the candidate of a big party for prime minister.

The Likud won just 19 seats. Labor remained the biggest party, but even bolstered by its partners in Yisrael Aḥat it dropped to 26 seats. Shas impressively won 17 seats. It was followed by Meretz (10), Yisrael ba-Aliyah (6), Shinu'i (6), the new Center Party (6), NRP (5), Yahadut ha-Torah (5), the Moslem Ra'am (5), the hawkish National Union (4), the new Russian immigrant party Yisrael Beitenu ("Israel Our Home") (4), Ḥadash (3), the nationalist Arab Balad (2), and Am Eḥad ("One Nation") led by Histadrut General Secretary Amir Peretz (2).

The unexpected success of Shas is attributed to three factors: First, disappointed with the Likud's performance, many former Sephardi Likud supporters voted this time for Shas. Second, many voted Shas as a protest following the conviction of Shas leader Aryeh Deri by the Jerusalem District Court on March 17, 1999. The court had found Deri guilty of bribery, fraud, and breach of public trust. Eliyahu Yishai was appointed as the new leader of Shas on September 27, 1999. Third, Yisrael ba-Aliyah directed its blatant anti-clerical campaign against Shas, using insulting slogans which could have been interpreted as anti-Sephardi. Many voters believed that supporting Shas on election day was the proper response to these attacks.

BARAK'S GOVERNMENT. The Fifteenth Knesset was split between 60 MKs who leaned toward Barak in their preference for a prime minister (i.e., the MKs of Yisrael Aḥat, Meretz, Shinu'i, the Center Party, Ra'am, Ḥadash, Balad, and Am Eḥad), and 60 MKs who probably preferred the Likud's leadership (i.e., the MKs of the Likud, Shas, Yisrael ba-Aliyah, NRP, Yahadut ha-Torah, National Union, and Israel Our Home). Nonetheless Barak had a number of options to form his government. After conducting negotiations with most of the parties, he formed a coalition including Yisrael Aḥat (with representatives of Gesher and Meimad in addition to those of Labor), Shas, Meretz, the Center Party, Yisrael ba-Aliyah, the NRP, and Yahadut ha-Torah. The structure of the coalition proved to be fatal, especially because of the policy distances between some of its members on questions of state and religion as well as on issues related to the Arab-Israeli conflict.

Following the formation of his government (Israel's 28th), Barak gave priority to the peace process. He promised, on several occasions, "to achieve peace with Israel's neighbors within a year." Criticized for his "zigzagging" policies on many issues, Barak proved to be very determined and very consistent on the issue of peacemaking.

On the evening of the Sabbath, Friday, August 27, 1999, the government authorized the transport of a 260-ton electric turbine. This led to threats from the two ultra-Orthodox religious parties to leave the coalition. Following the movement of a second turbine a few weeks later, Yahadut ha-Torah decided to cease its participation in Barak's coalition.

The turbine incidents were followed by a number of clashes between the largest ultra-Orthodox party, Shas, and Meretz. Strangely enough, Meretz decided to leave the government in June 2000 in order to ensure that Shas remained in the coalition. Meretz believed that Israeli-Palestinian negotiations were moving in a promising direction and did not wish to spark a government crisis.

In his 2000 negotiations with the Syrians in Washington, D.C., and with the Palestinians in Camp David, under the auspices of President Clinton of the United States, Barak expressed his readiness to carry out an almost 100 per cent withdrawal from all the territories occupied by Israel since the 1967 war. In May he ordered the Israel Defense Forces to withdraw from the "security zone" in Lebanon on a unilateral basis.

Most "right-of-Labor" politicians were opposed to the major concessions Barak was apparently ready to make to the Palestinians. In fact, even a number of relatively dovish figures, including Shimon Peres, criticized Barak for going too far, especially with regard to future arrangements in Jerusalem. It was against this background that the four Shas ministers and the Yisrael ba-Aliyah minister left the coalition on July 11, 2000. They were followed by the NRP minister, whose resignation came into effect on the following day, and by the defection of David Levi, the Gesher minister of foreign affairs, who left the coalition on August 4. Thus the government shrank to a twelve-minister cabinet, supported by only 30 MKs.

It was against this background that early elections looked inevitable. Barak once again demonstrated his skill at "zigzagging." He made a "secret" agreement with the Likud that would have guaranteed a relatively stable "national unity" government, but then retreated and decided to postpone its implementation. When it became clear that the Knesset was about to call early elections, Barak objected. Then he surprised even the members of his own party, declaring in December that he had no objections to simultaneous Knesset and prime ministerial elections. A few days later, he handed in his resignation to the president. According to Basic Law: the Government, when the prime minister resigned, Knesset elections were not necessary, only "special" prime ministerial elections. Barak's resignation conceivably came in order to block former premier Netanyahu from participating in the coming elections. As mentioned, Netanyahu had resigned from the Knesset following the defeat of the Likud in the 1999 elections. The Basic Law allowed only MKs to be candidates in "special" elections. Barak, however, declared almost immediately that he had no objections to changing the law so that Netanyahu could run against him. But it soon became clear that the candidates would be Labor's Barak and the Likud's Ariel Sharon.

THE 2001 ELECTIONS AND THE FIRST SHARON GOVERNMENT. On February 6, for the third time, Israel went to the polls to elect a prime minister by direct popular vote. Unlike the 1996 and 1999 elections, the Knesset was not elected at the same time.

In a reversal of his 12 per cent 1999 victory, Barak now lost to Sharon by twice that margin: 62.4 per cent of the valid votes were vast for Sharon and 37.6 per cent went to Barak. Barak not only lost the election but the vote of every sector that had supported him in 1999.

The turnout in 2001 was the lowest in Israel's history – 62.3 per cent. The biggest decline was in the Arab sector, which dropped to 25 per cent of what it had been in 1999. In the 15 elections held between 1949 and 1999, the average Arab turnout had been 78 per cent. Now, after giving Barak almost 95 per cent of their vote in 1999, most Arab voters felt they could neither support Barak nor Sharon and the Arab turnout dropped to less than 20 per cent. The background to this extreme expression of alienation was rooted in the fact that 13 Israeli Arabshad been killed by police fire in the October 2000 riots that broke out in support of the Palestinian cause following the beginning of the "second *intifada*"(see below).

Before presenting his government (the 29th government of Israel) Sharon insisted that the entire system of direct election of the prime minister must be scrapped and the old, purely parliamentary system restored. The Knesset acceded to his demand on March 7. Later that day Sharon presented his government to the Knesset. The government consisted of seven parties, controlling over 70 seats in the Knesset. These included the three biggest parties, Likud, Yisrael Aḥat and Shas alongside four smaller parties, National Union, Yisrael Beitenu, Yisrael ba-Aliyah, and One Nation. The two senior representatives of Labor in Sharon's cabinet were former prime minister Peres, who served as minister of foreign affairs, and Labor chairman Binyamin Ben-Eliezer, who served as minister of defense. Most of the more dovish Labor leaders remained outside the government. Sharon wanted to include Barak, but opposition within Labor made such a partnership impossible and Barak retired from active political life "for the time being." Two MKs of the Center Party joined the cabinet in August 2001. In October, Cabinet Minister Rehavam Ze'evi was shot dead in a Jerusalem hotel by terrorists. Two days earlier, Ze'evi had been one of two ministers who had handed in their resignations from the government because of their opposition to what they regarded as too moderate a government response to terrorism encouraged by the PA.

In the first few months after Sharon's government took office, Israel found itself in embarrassing international situations more than once. Thus, in July 2001, the Brussels Public Prosecutor's Office announced that it had opened an investigation of Sharon for alleged crimes against humanity in the massacre of Palestinian civilians by Lebanese Christian militiamen in the refugee camps of Sabra and Shatilla in September 1982. Early in September 2001, Israel and the United States decided to withdraw from the World Conference Against Racism, Racial Discrimination, Xenophobia and Related Intolerance (WCAR), convened in Durban, South Africa, in protest against the virulent anti-Israel language of its draft resolutions. It would seem, however, that the atmosphere changed dramatically following the attack on America on September 11, 2001. The attack demonstrated to many that Israel was in the forefront of the war against a dangerous combination of terrorism, Islamic fundamentalism, and weapons of mass destruction.

Despite the violenceof the Palestinian-Israeli conflict, Sharon continued to work toward the establishment of an independent Palestinian state within the framework of a peace agreement. Many in his party opposed this policy. Thus, on May 12, 2002, the Likud Central Committee rejected Sharon's request to postpone its vote on a binding resolution against the creation of a Palestinian State "west of the Jordan River."

The National Unity government was quite popular according to most public opinion polls, and the circumstances created by the terrorist war against Israel might have enabled the two big parties to continue their cooperation. Nevertheless, when the minister of finance, Silvan *Shalom, presented in October 2002 his budget proposal for 2003, the Labor Party decided to pull out of the government because of the allocations to settlements in the occupied territories. It would seem, however, that a major reason for this decision was the leadership struggle within Labor that pitted the chairman, Ben-Eliezer, against a popular challenger, Haifa's Mayor Amram *Mitzna, whose campaign called for Labor's withdrawal from the coalition. Sharon could still muster a bare majority and remain in office, but he too had party problems, mainly concerning an expected challenge for party leadership by former prime minister Binyamin Netanyahu. On December 5, 2002, Sharon formally announced his decision to dissolve the Knesset and early elections were called for January 28, 2003.

Following Labor's withdrawal Sharon named the popular former chief of staff of the IDF, Shaul *Mofas, as defense minister, and Netanyahu as minister of foreign Affairs.

On November 19 Mitzna won the Labor Party primaries, defeating Ben-Eliezer, and on November 28 Sharon won the Likud primaries, defeating Netanyahu.

THE TERRORIST WAR. The results of Barak's negotiations with Arab partners had been far from being promising. No new agreement was achieved between Israel and any of its Arab partners. Furthermore, in late September 2000 the Palestinians used a visit of Likud leaders headed by Ariel Sharon to the Mount Temple as a pretext for a new wave of violence. It seemed that the withdrawal from Lebanon was interpreted by a number of leading Arab elements as a proof that Israel could be defeated though attrition. The extreme Hamas, Islamic Jihad, Palestinian secular movements, and PA elements joined forces in large-scale terrorist activity against Israelis. At times it looked as if this new *intifada* was initiated and orchestrated by Arafat. At times it looked as if Arafat had lost control of the situation. In any case, the term *intifada* (i.e., uprising) was misleading. The vast majority of terrorist acts were either initiated by Arafat and elements within his organization, Fatah, or by those belonging to the Moslem fundamentalist organizations, Hamas and Islamic Jihad.

Almost from the beginning of the new wave of violence, various international attempts were made to get the parties to the negotiation table. Thus, on April 30, 2001, the Sharm el-Sheikh Fact-Finding Committee headed by George J. Mitchell, former majority leader of the U.S. Senate, published its report on the new Intifada. On June 14, 2001, a Palestinian-Israeli Security Implementation Work Plan, better known as the Tenet Plan, laid out a six-stage timetable for the parties. At the end of 2001 and the beginning of 2002, former U.S. Army general Anthony Zinni tried to mediate between Israel and the Palestinians. On April 30, 2003, the United States, the European Union, the United Nations, and Russia ("the Quartet") published a "Road Map" for a Permanent Two-State Solution to the Israeli-Palestinian conflict. The aim of the plan was to reach a final and comprehensive settlement of the Israeli-Palestinian conflict by 2005. All these efforts proved fruitless.

On January 4, 2002, the IDF captured a 4,000-ton freighter in the Red Sea carrying 50 tons of weaponry, including tons of explosives, rockets, missiles, long-range mortars, mines, etc. The captain of the ship confessed that the PA had hired him and that the shipment was organized and financed by it.

One of the most decisive terrorist attacks took place on March 27, 2002, when 250 Passover guests at the Park Hotel in Netanya were the victims of a suicide bomb carried by a Hamas terrorist. Twenty-nine people were killed and 140 injured. Following the Park Hotel attack, the government decided to carry out "a wide-ranging operational action plan against Palestinian terror," known as Operation Defensive Shield. During the operation, Israel recaptured most of the territories previously controlled by the PA. The most highly publicized action took place in Jenin. Palestinian spokesmen and activists all over the world claimed that Israel had carried out a massacre in the city in which between 1,000 and 5,000 Palestinian civilians were murdered. In fact, 52 Palestinians – most of them terrorist fighters – were killed in Jenin. In one incident during the battle, 13 IDF soldiers were killed when they were ambushed from civilian residences by Palestinian fighters. Documents captured during Operation Defensive Shield proved that the PA, Iran, Iraq, and Saudi Arabia were directly involved in terrorist activities. Furthermore, money provided to the PA by donors such as the European Union and the U.S. had been allocated to finance terror and incitement.

The international dimension of anti-Israel terrorism was underscored on November 28, 2002, when 13 people were killed in Mombasa, Kenya, in an Israeli hotel. Simultaneously, two missiles were fired at an Israeli passenger jet flying from Mombasa but missed their target. The political bureau of Osama bin Laden's al-Qaeda network claimed responsibility for these attacks.

Between the beginning of the "Second Intifada" and the end of 2004 approximately 22,000 attacks on Israeli targets were carried out. Most devastating were the approximately 130 attacks carried by suicide bombers. Over 1,000 Israelis – 70% of them civilians – were killed and over 7,000 injured. The peak in the number of casualties was reached in March 2002, when 135 Israelis were killed. Towards the end of this period, the number of successful attacks and the number of casualties decreased considerably. This was caused mainly by different preventive measures taken by Israel. Thus, over 400 suicide attacks were prevented.

One significant preventive measure was the construction of an "anti-terrorist" fence intended to serve as a physical barrier against terrorist attacks. Arab countries and the Palestinian leadership protested, calling it a "a unilateral step on Arab soil" worsening the living conditions of Palestinians.

On November 11, 2004, the president of the PA, Yasser Arafat, 75, died in a military hospital outside Paris after being flown there from his Ramallah Headquarters. Mahmoud Abbas ("Abu Mazen"), one of the founding fathers of the Fatah and the PLO, succeeded Arafat as interim president. Abas opposed many of Arafat's policies, including the decision to initiate the new wave of violence in September 2000. Hence, he was considered a more moderate potential partner to talks with Israel. Nevertheless, many noted his basic hardline positions and questioned his ability to confront militant Palestinian leaders and organizations. Abas was formally elected as president in general elections held on January 9, 2005.

THE 2003 ELECTIONS. In the January 28, 2003, elections to the Sixteenth Knesset, 13 parties won seats, down from 15 in 1999. For the first time since 1981, the strength of the two biggest parties combined increased. These developments can be attributed in part to the abrogation of direct election of the prime minister and the return to a regular parliamentary system. Voters could no longer split their votes between the candidate of a large party for the premiership and a small party in the Knesset ballot, as so many had in 1996 and 1999. The turnout was the lowest in the history of Knesset elections: only 67.8 per cent.

The most important outcome of the elections was the unquestioned success of the Likud, which won 38 seats – twice as many as Labor's 19 seats. Immediately after the elections, the two MKs of Yisrael ba-Aliyah joined the Likud.

It would seem that Sharon attracted many middle-of-the-road voters, as he projected a position more dovish than any of those previously held by Likud leaders. On the other hand, Labor moved away from the center with Mitzna's repeated calls to negotiate with Arafat, despite the continued terrorism. Mitzna also proposed unilateral withdrawal from the territories if such negotiations failed, and pledged not to sit in a government with the Likud.

Another dimension of the electoral campaign was religion. This placed the anti-clerical Shinu'i, with its 15 seats, on one end of the political spectrum and the ultra-Orthodox Shas (11 seats) and Yahadut ha-Torah (5 seats) on the other. The third religious party, the hawkish NRP, gained 6 seats, balancing the 6 seats of the dovish, anti-clerical Meretz.

The hawkish National Union–Yisrael Beitenu bloc won 7 seats. Three parties won 3 seats each, the Communist-led Ḥadash, Amir Peretz's One Nation Party, and the nationalist Arab Balad. The Islamic Ra'am dropped to 2 seats. On May 4, 2003, Labour's new leader, Mitzna, resigned.

THE ECONOMY. During the 1990s Israel's economy was marked by consistent growth in gross domestic product (GDP) and by a steady rise in GDP per capita. Both indicators reached a peak of around 7.5 per cent in 2000. The early 2000s were marked by clear signs of recession. Both the GDP and the GDP per capita showed a negative growth. The decline in economic activity affected employment. Thus, while unemployment was less than 9 per cent up to the first half of 2001, it climbed to almost 11 per cent in the second half of 2003. At the same time the number of foreign workers in Israel increased to approximately 300,000 towards the end of the 1990s. The deterioration of the economy produced a number of large-scale anti-government demonstrations – some of which were organized by the Histadrut under the leadership of Peretz.

There were a number of reasons for the slowdown of the economy. The four most significant were: global developments and especially the global crisis in the high-tech industry; the considerable decrease in immigration, especially when compared with the early 1990s; government spending policies; the impact of terrorism, with such consequences as a sharp drop in tourism. The recession in areas under the control of the PA was by far more severe.

After the elections of 2003, there seemed to be strong evidence of a growing number of positive economic indicators, such as renewed economic growth and low inflation rates. It seemed that these developments had been partly caused by global developments, by the failure of the terrorist war against Israel, and by new government policies initiated by Netanyahu, who became minister of finance in Sharon's second government.

SHARON'S SECOND GOVERNMENT. Following the 2003 parliamentary elections, Sharon tried to get Labor to join his coalition. But when Labor demurred he formed a coalition with Shinu'i, the NRP, and the National Union-Yisrael Beitenu bloc. The new government (Israel's 30th) was approved by the Knesset on February 27, 2003. In his new cabinet, Netanyahu became minister of finance, switching places with Silvan Shalom, who became minister of foreign affairs. Sharon apparently believed that Netanyahu, a graduate of the Massachusetts Institute of Technology in business administration, was better qualified to oversee Israel's problematic economy.

A number of scandals rocked the political scene during Sharon's second term. These included police investigations of a number of ministers, including the prime minister and his sons, resignation of a Shinu'i minister who apparently tried to incriminate another Shinu'i minister, and resignation of a Likud minister from his post (but not from the government) following publication of the state comptroller's report and possible indictment for politically motivated appointments.

The most prominent issue in Israeli politics in 2004 and 2005 revolved around Prime Minister Sharon's disengagement plan. Sharon's plan was presented to the public for the first time in December 2003. The main assumption behind the plan was that in the absence of any serious partner to peace talks on the Palestinian side, and following the construction of the security fence, it was in Israel's political and security interest to withdraw from the Gaza Strip and dismantle the 21 settlements there (*Gush Katif) as well as four settlements in northern Samaria (the northern part of the West Bank).

The conflict surrounding the disengagement plan shook Sharon's leadership. On May 2, 2004, Sharon was defeated in an internal Likud referendum on the disengagement plan by a margin of 60 percent to 40 percent. Following this defeat, Sharon revised the plan slightly. On June 6, 2004, the cabinet approved the revised plan by a vote of 14 to 7. This result was made possible, among other reasons, by the dismissal of the two National Union–Israel Beitenu ministers. Five of the 13 Likud ministers and the two NRP ministers voted against the Plan. Two members of the NRP left the coalition in June 2004. The other four NRP members left in November 2004. The future of the government looked quite gloomy. But on October 28, the Knesset approved the disengagement plan by a 67–45 vote. This was followed by the dismissal of hawkish Minister Landau of the Likud. However, 17 of the 40 Likud MKs had voted against the plan. On November 3 the Knesset approved a bill to compensate the approximately 8,000 settlers who would be evacuated from the Gaza Strip and northern Samaria according to the disengagement plan. A war of nerves now commenced between the Gush Katif settlers and their supporters and government authorities, including demonstrations, clashes with police and the army, and organized disruptions of the country's daily life by the more extreme elements among the opponents of disengagement.

With the government losing its majority in the Knesset, Sharon and Finance Minister Netanyahu mobilized the support of the ultra-Orthodox Yahadut ha-Torah for the 2005 budget bill in return for government financial support to a number of ultra-Orthodox institutions. Shinu'i declared that it would not support the budget bill under these conditions. Following a humiliating defeat in a Knesset vote on the budget, Sharon dismissed all five Shinu'i ministers on December 4. Sharon's government survived, however, as a result of an agreement with the Labor Party. On January 10, 2005, eight Labor MKs received ministerial portfolios. The budget was approved in March 2005.

[Abraham Diskin (2nd ed.)]

THE 2006 ELECTIONS. The dismantlement of the Gush Katif settlements was carried out as scheduled in the summer of 2005. However, opposition to Sharon within the Likud and the threat that he would be deposed as party chairman by the Likud Central Committee led him to bolt the party and form a new political entity, the Kadimah Party, joined by senior ministers from both the Likud and the Labor party, including Shimon Peres. In January 2006, with elections two months away, Sharon suffered a massive brain hemorrhage and was incapacitated. He was replaced by Ehud *Olmert, who subsequently led Kadimah to an election victory with 29 seats in the Knesset. Negotiations began immediately with Labor, the next largest party with 19 seats and now led by Amir *Peretz, to form a coalition government. In the meanwhile Hamas had won an unexpected victory over the PLO in the Palestinian parliamentary elections, creating a new reality and making future relations with the Palestinian Authority problematic. Olmert's avowed intention was to establish Israel's final borders during his term of office, if necessary unilaterally. Among other declared aims in the coalition agreement were a rise in the minimum wage to $1,000 a month, guaranteed pensions for all citizens, a broader spectrum of medicines to be covered by the National Health Insurance Law, and full implementation of the civil rights of minority groups.

RENEWED FIGHTING. The new government was soon tested. Palestinian rocket attacks on Sederot and other Negev settlements were capped on June 25 by the abduction of an Israeli soldier from an army outpost. Israel responded with air strikes and the movement of ground forces into the Gaza Strip for the first time since the evacuation of the previous summer. On July 12 Hizbollah struck in the north, attacking an Israeli patrol on Israel's side of the Lebanese border. Three Israeli soldiers were killed and another two were taken captive. The fighting rapidly escalated as Hizbollah indiscriminately fired rockets into Israel's northern settlements, including Haifa, and Israel launched massive air strikes into Lebanon aimed at Hizbollah strongholds and staging areas which at the same time caused extensive damage throughout the country as well as a high death toll among Lebanese civilians and mass flight from South Lebanon. As Israelis too fled the north or huddled in shelters, Israeli special forces began crossing the border to hunt down rocket launchers, meeting stiff resistance. Though by and large Hizbollah was condemned as the aggressor by the international community and Israel's right to self-defense was affirmed, many decried what was seen as the use of excessive force by Israel and diplomatic efforts to bring the fighting to a halt intensified. Many, however, also saw Israel as a surrogate for the West in the war against terrorism and made it clear that they would not regret Hizbollah's destruction. However, progress on the ground was slow as the highly trained and disciplined Hizbollah fighters stood fast, and as the fighting dragged on criticism of both the army and government was heard in Israel, though the country remained united in its determination to deal Hizbollah a crippling blow. In the meantime a draft resolution calling for a cease fire was produced by France and the United States as Israel called up its reserves and expanded its ground operations in an effort to reach the Litani River about 18 miles (30 km.) north of Israel's border. The resolution was adopted by the Security Council of the United Nations on August 11 and went into effect on August 14. Among other things it called for the Lebanese army, bolstered by a beefed-up UNIFIL force of up to 15,000 men, to occupy South Lebanon and arms shipments to Hizbollah to be halted. However, it did not assure the dismantling of Hizbollah or the return of the abducted Israeli soldiers. The extent to which the resolution satisfied Israel's expectations, coupled with questions about the performance of the army and government, now became the subjects of increasing public debate.

The toll in the Israel-Hizbollah fighting up to the cease fire was 117 Israeli soldiers and 41 civilians killed. Around 1,000 Lebanese civilians were also killed. Nearly 4,000 rockets had been fired into Israel and 7,000 targets in Lebanon had been hit by Israel's air force in over 15,000 sorties.

Foreign Policy and International Relations

FOREIGN POLICY. *The United Nations Decision.* Although the United Nations did not have the machinery or the power to implement the General Assembly resolution of Nov. 29, 1947, and the State of Israel was established by the efforts of the *yishuv* with the support of the Jewish people, the new state ascribed considerable importance to the fact that its creation was based on the UN decision. The Proclamation of Independence, recalling the Assembly resolution, declares: "This recognition by the United Nations of the right of the Jewish people to establish their own state is irrevocable"; the establishment of the Jewish state is proclaimed "by virtue of our natural and historic right and of the resolution of the General Assembly of the United Nations"; and a later paragraph declares, "The State of Israel will be prepared to cooperate with the organs and the representatives of the United Nations in carrying out the General Assembly Resolution of Nov. 29, 1947, and will work for the establishment of the economic union of the whole Land of Israel."

Care was thus taken to emphasize that the Jewish people's decision to establish the Jewish state was in keeping with the UN's historic ruling. For this reason, and because of violent Arab opposition, one of Israel's main objectives was to achieve international recognition. The first encouraging responses came from the U.S. government, which granted de facto recognition a few hours after the declaration of independence, and from the Soviet Union and Guatemala, which granted de jure recognition three days later. By the end of its first year, following the young state's success in defeating the Arab attack, establishing its legal institutions, and holding general elections to the first Knesset, Israel was recognized by 55 states (the vast majority of those existing at the time, with the exception of the Arab and a few other Muslim countries), and on May 11, 1949, Israel was accepted as a member of the United Nations. Thus the struggle for international recognition was crowned, on the whole, with success, though the effort to establish normal diplomatic relations with all states was much more prolonged and has not yet been completed.

Efforts Toward Peace. The second, even more important, aim of Israel's foreign policy was to bring the war to an end and establish permanent peace with the Arab peoples and states. At first Israel hoped to receive UN support for this aim. It responded to the UN call for a cease-fire and was prepared to cooperate with the UN mediator. However, the first mediator, Count Folke Bernadotte of Sweden, failed in his efforts at mediation and exceeded his powers by proposing a solution of his own to the Palestine problem that was incompatible with both the Assembly decision and the new situation created after the war and was quite unacceptable to Israel. The second mediator, Ralph Bunche, confined himself to actual mediation and succeeded in bringing about negotiations between the two sides, ending with the signature of the Armistice Agreements.

Faithful to the spirit of the Security Council resolution and the uniform text of the preamble to all the agreements, Israel regarded the Armistice Agreements as a transitional stage between truce and permanent peace. It was generally assumed that the armistice period would be brief and would be spent mainly in peace negotiations – an assumption confirmed by the fact that the agreements laid down a procedure for their amendment in case they were not replaced by peace treaties within a year. It was on this assumption, too, that Israel agreed to certain provisions that were not perfectly clear, in order not to hold up the signature of the agreements. Events, however, developed in the opposite direction. The Armistice Agreements were not the starting point for progress toward peace but marked the end of a brief period of goodwill. They were followed by a renewed deterioration in the situation, the gradual erosion of their significance, and Arab threats of an approaching "second round." Nor was any progress achieved at the meetings of the UN Palestine Conciliation Commission, which consisted of representatives of the United States, France, and Turkey. The disappointing experience of the P.C.C. strengthened Israel's conviction that only through direct negotiations would it be possible to achieve peace, or even partial solutions to specific problems.

The principle of direct negotiations has been the cornerstone of Israel's policy ever since, and the Israel government has always tried to secure the support of other countries for it. However, just as the Arab countries were not prepared for progress from armistice to peace, they were equally unprepared for direct negotiations with Israel. The armistice regime was undermined over the years under the pressure of the Arab doctrine and practice of belligerency against Israel. During the Sinai Campaign (1956), Israel declared that in view of Egypt's continual violations of the Armistice Agreement, Israel no longer recognized its existence, and all the Armistice Agreements became null and void as a result of the *Six-Day War in June 1967. Even if they had been strictly observed, however, they left many basic questions unsolved, notably those of the frontiers, the status of Jerusalem, the refugee question, and the problem of Arab economic and political warfare against Israel.

Borders. The Armistice Agreements expressly stated that the demarcation lines laid down in them were not on any account to be regarded as political or territorial frontiers, but as a result of the long period during which the agreements remained in force and the failure to replace them with peace treaties, the demarcation lines were generally identified with the frontiers of the state. Israel repeatedly declared that it was prepared for peace talks without prior conditions, but also made it clear that it regarded the existing lines as a basis for negotiations on permanent frontiers despite their unsuitability for effective defense. David Ben-Gurion and Moshe Sharett stated on several occasions that in a peace treaty Israel would be ready to recognize these borders as frontiers fixed "for a hundred years." The Arabs argued, on the other hand, that there could be no negotiations as long as Israel did not "comply with UN resolutions," i.e., withdraw to the boundaries laid down in the 1947 partition scheme and agree to the return of the refugees. However, they gave no undertaking to sign peace treaties on the basis of these borders. The Soviet Union also referred to Israel's frontiers in terms of the 1947 partition borders.

Israel declared that a return to the partition borders was unacceptable. The partition proposal was based on the assumptions that the two peoples would accept the proposed solution and agree to live in peace, that an Arab state would rise in Palestine side by side with the Jewish state, and that the two would form an economic union. All these assumptions had been refuted by Arab belligerency. Nor were the Western powers prepared to identify the armistice lines with political borders. John Foster Dulles, the U.S. secretary of state, made this clear in a speech in New York on Aug. 26, 1955, and British Foreign Secretary Anthony Eden, in his Guildhall address on Nov. 9, 1955, called for a compromise between the partition borders and the status quo. Both were thinking mainly of territorial concessions by Israel in the Negev, which would facilitate the creation of a land bridge between Egypt and Jordan. It was only after the Sinai Campaign and the withdrawal of the Israel forces from the areas occupied during the fighting that pressure for frontier changes died down and the powers reconciled themselves, in practice, with Israel rule over the areas delimited in the Armistice Agreements. In the absence of any Arab will for peace, however, these lines were never secure borders, and the entire armistice regime collapsed in the crisis of 1967.

As a result of the Six-Day War, the territory under Israel's control now comprised the whole of western Ereẓ Israel, including those areas in Judea and Samaria that had been under Jordanian rule since 1948, the Gaza Strip, the Sinai Peninsula up to the Suez Canal, and the Golan Heights. Israel stated that it would not withdraw from these areas, whose boundaries were determined by the cease-fire agreements of June 10, 1967, until peace treaties were concluded that would assure her of agreed and secure frontiers. The government of Israel also made it clear that it did not regard the previous armistice demarcation lines as secure frontiers and would not return to the boundaries that existed before the Six-Day War. In its acceptance of the American peace initiative in the middle of 1970, the Israel government expressed readiness for withdrawal "to secure and recognized borders" as part of a permanent peace settlement, without specifying which territories it would be prepared to evacuate in return for peace. The attitude of the Arabs and their supporters, on the other hand, was that Israel must evacuate all the territories occupied in the June 1967 war. According to some other states, the principle of secure boundaries implied that the frontiers must differ from those that existed before the war, "without reflecting the weight of conquest" (see also Israel, State of: Historical Survey, The Armistice Demarcation Lines, in the Frontiers section).

Jerusalem. According to the partition scheme, the city of Jerusalem and its environs were to constitute a *corpus separatum*, administered by the United Nations under a special international regime as part of the economic union. During the first ten years of the international regime, the UN Trusteeship Council was to consider the problem in the light of the experience gained in the meantime. The Jewish Agency agreed to the internationalization proposal in 1947 under protest, since it was an inseparable part of the partition plan, but the Arabs categorically rejected it. Jerusalem became the scene of bitter fighting, which the UN was unable to prevent. In the armistice agreement with Transjordan, the demarcation line bisected the city, the Old City and the eastern neighborhoods being held by Jordan and the New City by Israel. Mount Scopus constituted an Israeli enclave; Article 8 of the agreement provided for free Israeli access to the Jewish institutions (the Hebrew University and the Hadassah Hospital) on Mount Scopus and to the Western ("Wailing") Wall. The UN, however, did not abandon the idea of internationalization, and on Dec. 9, 1949, the General Assembly decided that Jerusalem would be placed under a permanent international regime, calling upon the Trusteeship Council to complete the preparation of a constitution for the city. Israel vigorously opposed the idea, since it had been proved to be impracticable, would be a denial of the basic rights of the Jewish population, and would imperil their safety. It was prepared to agree to "functional" internationalization, i.e., the establishment of an international regime for the holy places alone. In reaction to the Assembly resolution, Israel decided to establish its capital in Jerusalem and transfer the Knesset and most of the government offices to the city. The transfer was completed in a few weeks (though the Foreign Ministry did not make the move until 1953 and the Ministry of Defense remained housed in Tel Aviv).

The Trusteeship Council soon arrived at the conclusion that the Assembly plan for territorial internationalization was impracticable. At the autumn 1950 Assembly, Sweden proposed the revision of the previous decision and its replacement by functional internationalization, but the proposal did not receive the necessary two-thirds majority. A Belgian proposal to reiterate the previous decision met with the same fate. On the plane of UN resolutions, therefore, a dead end had been reached, but the 1949 resolution remained formally in force. Accordingly, many countries refused to recognize Jerusalem as Israel's capital or to transfer their missions to it; their representatives sometimes even boycotted official ceremonies there. In the course of time, however, more and more countries acquiesced to the situation, and in 1970, 22 states maintained their diplomatic missions in Jerusalem, while 25 still kept them in the Tel Aviv area, and nine had nonresident missions.

In the Six-Day War, after the Jordanians had started a heavy bombardment of Jewish Jerusalem and occupied the headquarters of the UN Truce Supervision Organization in the zone between the armistice lines, heavy battles developed, and by the third day of the war (June 7) the whole of the city was in the hands of the Israel Defense Forces. Under an amendment to the Municipalities Ordinance passed by the Knesset on June 27, the city was reunified on the following day. In July 1967 the General Assembly adopted two resolutions calling on Israel to annul the steps taken to unify the city, and a similar resolution was adopted in 1968 by the Security Council. However, Israeli public opinion was united in its determination to preserve the unity of Jerusalem as Israel's capital.

Throughout the existence of the armistice regime, Jordan had refused to comply with Article 8 of the agreement, despite all the efforts of Israel and the United Nations. Israeli Jews were not permitted to approach the Western Wall, and the Hebrew University and Hadassah buildings on Mount Scopus were derelict and only Israel police guards, relieved every two weeks by UN convoys, were permitted to protect them. Extraordinary efforts by Dag Hammarskjöld, then secretary-general of the UN, were required in 1958 to obtain permission for the removal of the university's books and collections, and the Jews returned to the Western Wall, the Old City, and Mount Scopus only after the Six-Day War. On July, 27, 1967, a few weeks after the end of the fighting, the Knesset enacted the Law for the Protection of the Holy Places and Israel protected the holy places of all faiths, in close cooperation with their religious leaders.

The Arab Refugee Problem. More than any other aspect of Arab-Israel relations (apart from military clashes), it was the Arab refugee problem that occupied international public opinion in the period between the establishment of the state and the Six-Day War. As early as Dec. 11, 1948 – prior to the signing of the Armistice Agreements – the UN General Assembly adopted a resolution dealing with the question, among others. The Arabs insisted upon the right of the refugees to return to their homes and made no attempt to conceal their hope and intention of using the masses of returning refugees as a force to bring about the destruction of the State of Israel. Israel pointed out that it was not she who had created the problem, but rather the Arab leaders, who had urged the Arab masses to leave the area that was to become the Jewish state; that Israel could not be expected to absorb a hostile population: that, on the other hand, Israel had provided a home for hundreds of thousands of Jews from Arab countries and thus an exchange of population – albeit unplanned – had in fact taken place.

When the Palestine Conciliation Commission began its work, Israel declared its readiness to take the far-reaching step of permitting the return of 100,000 refugees; this offer, however, was withdrawn when the Commission failed to bring about a meeting of the two parties. However, Israel did confirm its willingness to pay compensation for the property the refugees had left behind, irrespective of and before the conclusion of peace, provided the Arabs would put an end to their economic warfare against the state. This offer met with no response from the Arab states, who continued to insist upon the refugees' right to return to their homes; nor did they respond to the unilateral steps like the unfreezing of refugee bank accounts in Israel banks. Thus the debate was repeated year after year, the Arabs attacking Israel and the latter claiming that it was not the fate of the refugees with which the Arab states were concerned, but rather the destruction of Israel (see Israel, State of: Historical Survey, section on Arab Refugees).

Boycott and Blockade. Arab political warfare against Israel was accompanied by economic warfare: not only did the Arab states impose a boycott on Israel and its products, but they also attempted to strangle its economy by persuading other countries not to maintain economic relations with Israel. The Arab boycott organization boycotted companies that had established enterprises in Israel, invested there, or entered into partnership with Israeli firms, and blacklisted ships that called at Israel ports and even airlines running regular flights to Israel. At first the boycott registered some success, but as time went on its effect wore off as a result of Israel's economic growth and the determined action taken by some countries against the activities of the boycott offices. Only firms for whom trade with the Arab countries was of overriding importance gave in to Arab threats and refrained from setting up commercial ties with Israel. Thus the boycott ceased to be an effective weapon (see also *Boycott, Arab). Much more serious was the effect of the maritime blockade. From the very beginning the Suez Canal was closed to Israel shipping and even to ships of other nations bound for Israel ports, and as a rule cargoes en route to Israel were confiscated, although in 1951 the Security Council ruled that this practice was illegal and called upon Egypt to desist from it. Egypt paid no heed to the call. Moreover, at the beginning of the 1950s, Egypt closed the Tiran Straits to Israel shipping and to foreign ships bound for Eilat. As a result of the Sinai Campaign, freedom of passage was established in the Tiran Straits and maintained by the presence of the UN Emergency Force. It was the expulsion of that force by Egypt and the reimposition of the blockade of the straits in May 1967 that were the direct cause of the Six-Day War.

From War to Peace. The period 1970–73 was marked by almost full observance of the cease-fire along Israel's entire frontier. Israel agreed to return to the talks with Gunnar Jarring, the UN emissary, on Dec. 28, 1970, and Jarring returned to Israel in another attempt to break the deadlock. On Feb. 8, 1971, he requested Israel to commit itself to complete withdrawal to the Mandatory border and Egypt to enter into a peace agreement with Israel. Israel maintained that it was desirous of negotiating an agreement on secure and recognized borders but refused to agree in advance to withdraw to the old border, while Egypt insisted that it would consider peace with Israel only if the latter would implement Resolution 242 in all its parts. Egypt saw no need for negotiations as it felt the resolution could be automatically implemented. This Israel refused to accept, with the result that the stalemate continued and the Jarring mission was suspended.

Efforts were now directed towards reaching a partial solution for the re-opening of the Suez Canal. Israel had put forward a proposal to this effect in 1968 and on February 4, 1971, President Sadat returned to the idea, but linked a partial Israeli withdrawal from the east bank of the Canal with an overall withdrawal. Israel was willing to accept the re-opening of the waterway and this was the focus of the talks held during the visit, in May 1971, of the U.S. Secretary of State William Rogers. The talks failed, however, as Egypt insisted that the partial withdrawal be tied to a timetable for full withdrawal; Israel retorted that the interim agreement should remain unlinked with the fundamental issues. The U.S. government argued that the interim solution was a step in the right direction. In the course of 1971–1973 fruitless negotiations continued on this proposal.

Meanwhile there were important developments in the other Arab states. Jordan, which had succeeded in removing the PLO threat already in September 1970, expelled the remnants of the PLO forces in summer of 1971 and they went to Syria and Lebanon. The latter country became the staging area and base of operations against Israel and Israeli personnel and installations abroad.

Preventive Israeli counter-action in Lebanon hurt terrorist plans and was able to reduce their operations effectively. But the PLO continued to attack Israeli targets and forced Israel to devote manpower and an increasing budget to fight off this type of warfare, which was aided and abetted by most of the Arab states.

In 1971–73 Egypt was already making preparations for war. Its relations with the Soviet Union were often strained because of Russia's refusal to supply it with advanced weapons. Sadat had hoped that war threats would bring American pressure on Israel to withdraw. Instead, U.S. policy of rapprochement with both China and detente with the U.S.S.R., as well as the end of the Vietnam War, ushered in a new era of strengthening its friends and seeking diplomatic solutions for conflicts. The U.S. and Russia sought to avoid another war in the Middle East and in two Nixon-Brezhnev summit meetings, both super-powers appealed to Israel and Egypt to renew the Jarring mission and seek a peaceful settlement of the Israel-Arab conflict. The U.S. continued to arm Israel and provide it with economic aid. Israel and the U.S. cooperated in bringing an end to the Syrian invasion of Jordan in September 1970 and the relations between the two were very close. The new situation lulled Israel into a false sense of security. Sadat was determined to demonstrate that a limited war would be the only means of destroying the existing status quo which, while comfortable for Israel, was becoming unbearable for Egypt. He felt that only a war would force the U.S. to pressure Israel and would leave the Soviet Union no other option but to aid Egypt.

There was little diplomatic activity in 1973, and Israel's major concern was the fight against terrorism. But in May 1973, Egypt and Syrian forces made threatening moves and a state of alarm was declared in Israel. It proved, however, to have been false, and this strengthened Israel's feeling that there would be no imminent war. By late summer 1973, while Israel was engaged in an election campaign, Egypt and Syrian forces were deployed in battle positions. In late September Egypt informed the Soviet Union of its intention to attack, and on Oct. 6, 1973, as Israel was observing the Day of Atonement, Egypt and Syria struck (see *Yom Kippur War).

As a result of the war, Israel became isolated in the world. The majority of the African states suspended diplomatic ties with it; the European nations issued pro-Arab statements, the oil embargo was effective in frightening them to submit to Arab demands. The U.S. felt that the time was ripe for a major diplomatic offensive to break the deadlock that had led to the war. Israel and the U.S. now agreed that, before proceeding to negotiations, the first move should be the stabilization of the cease fire that was being repeatedly violated by all sides. U.S. mediation secured the signing of the Six Point Agreement on November 1, 1973, negotiated directly by Israeli and Egyptian officers. The agreement dealt with exchange of prisoners, the lifting of the naval blockade from the Straits of Bab el Mandeb, supply convoys to the encircled Third Army, and a UN presence. The point dealing with withdrawal of forces to positions they held on October 22 was not implemented. The U.S. having gained the confidence of Egypt, was determined to proceed directly to talks, but was desirous of maintaining the overall initiative in its own hands. It was thus decided to call for a peace conference in Geneva to establish a mechanism for the negotiations. At the request of the U.S., Israel agreed in advance to enter into talks for a disengagement of forces agreement, and was able to gain an American agreement not to include the PLO in the conference. Israel refused to commit itself in advance to disengagement on the Golan front, with the result that Syria boycotted the conference which opened on December 21, under the chairmanship of UN Secretary-General Waldheim, with the participation of Israel, Egypt, Jordan, the U.S., and the U.S.S.R. The main tangible result of the conference was the decision on a consensus basis to order an Israeli-Egyptian military working group to reach a separation of forces agreement. This was achieved on Jan. 18, 1974, after ten days of shuttle diplomacy by Secretary Kissinger, when the agreement was signed by the chiefs of staff of the IDF and the Egyptian Army. Even before this agreement was concluded and implemented, preparations were under way for a similar Israel-Syria agreement. This was part of a new American strategy of a "step-by-step" approach to the solution of the Arab-Israel conflict. The U.S. realized that the time was not ripe for an overall settlement in view of Israel's refusal to withdraw to the June 1967 lines and the inability of the Arabs to conceive of peace relations between them and Israel. Hoping to utilize the situation to improve America's standing in the Arab world, remove the Soviet influence, and secure the flow of oil to the West, the U.S. was able to persuade Israel and Syria to agree to reach an agreement, but a month of shuttle diplomacy by Secretary Kissinger between Jerusalem and Damascus failed to achieve it. The agreement was finally signed in Geneva on May 31, 1974. New cease fire lines and buffer zones were established and areas of limitation of forces and armaments were agreed upon, to be supervised by UN forces whose mandate was to be renewed periodically by the Security Council.

The Rabin government, which took office on June 3, 1974, was determined not to negotiate with the PLO and in July issued a statement to the effect that Israel was willing to negotiate an agreement with Jordan based on the existence of two states, Israel and a Palestinian-Jordanian state to the east. American efforts to secure Israel-Jordan talks failed in the summer of 1974. The PLO was gaining momentum; it was recognized by the UN General Assembly as the spokesman for the Palestinians and later, in the Arab summit conference at Rabat in October 1974, as the sole legitimate representative of the Palestinians to set up a national authority in areas that would be given up by Israel. This effectively removed Jordan from the scene and thus left Egypt as the only candidate for further negotiations.

Talks between Israel and the U.S. were renewed in the fall of 1974, after the resignation of President Nixon and the accession of President Ford. They focused on another agreement with Egypt. By then Dr. Kissinger had established close working relations with President Sadat, and Egypt pinned high hopes on him. In late 1974 and early 1975 Israel announced its willingness to withdraw from the Mitla and Gidi passes in Sinai and even from the Abu Rodeis oilfields in return for an Egyptian declaration of nonbelligerency. In March 1975 Kissinger undertook another shuttle trip, but on March 24 had to admit failure, as Egypt refused to agree to the Israeli demands. The U.S. blamed Israel for the failure of the talks, but a few weeks later, when cooler counsels prevailed, the parties resumed the talks which lasted all that summer and were crowned with an Israel-Egypt agreement signed on September 1, 1975. The agreement involved Israeli withdrawal further east, the establishment of a new buffer zone that included the Mitla and Gidi passes, electronic surveillance stations by both Israel and Egypt, supported by a U.S. surveillance team to supervise the movement of forces in this area, a UN presence and a new limited forces zone.

Israel was able to win from the U.S. commitments not to recognize the PLO, to coordinate in advance with it new political initiatives such as a Geneva Peace Conference, the sale of additional weapons, financial aid, and assurances on the supply of oil. This was considered a major achievement for the Rabin government, which now felt that it could devote more attention to the home front, having satisfied most of the U.S. demands. No progress was made with either Syria or Jordan. The cease fire lines, however, remained quiet, and in 1976, for the first time in its history, there were no Israeli casualties along the borders. The civil war in Lebanon gave Israel a respite and brought it closer to Christian Lebanese elements, which were fighting both Palestinian elements and the Syrian army. In 1976 Israel could therefore feel that its position was strong. Civil war in Lebanon kept the Arab world focused on that country, Egypt was satisfied with the Interim Agreement, while Syria was occupied with Lebanon. The U.S. was engaged in an election campaign and the European States, while not happy with the political situation in the Middle East, nevertheless granted Israel the status of an Associate Member of the Common Market. Israel did not fare well in the UN however. In a series of General Assembly resolutions, the PLO was recognized, as stated, as the sole and legitimate representative of the Palestinians. The "legitimate and just demands" of the Palestinians were also recognized and in November 1975 Zionism was branded as a form of "racism and racial discrimination." In the U.S., too, there were voices calling for a reappraisal of the U.S. position on the Palestinians. In a series of documents, the State Department slowly focused the Arab-Israel conflict on the Palestinian issue and suggested the possibility of a separate Palestinian state, in order to prepare public opinion, to mollify Egypt, and to keep the peace initiative in the Middle East in American hands. These moves alarmed Israel as they went counter to the understanding reached in September 1975.

In 1974–1977 terrorist activities continued, the targets being mainly civilians. On May 15, 1974, PLO terrorists attacked a school at Ma'alot killing 27 people, mostly children and teenagers. Other attacks were on a Tel Aviv hotel in March 1976, Zion Square in Jerusalem in July 1976, and on Israeli installations abroad. The Israel air force often bombed terrorist bases in Lebanon, thus keeping down the number of planned attacks.

The main efforts following the signing of the Israel-Egypt peace treaty were to promote the normalization of the relations between the two countries. For that purpose, joint committees, consisting of Foreign Ministry and IDF officers and their Egyptian counterparts negotiated a series of agreements dealing with the opening of the land border at El-Arish for civilian traffic, the inauguration of direct flights between Tel Aviv and Cairo, the creation of telephone and telex linkage, and arrangements for tourism. Simultaneously, the IDF began its withdrawal from Sinai. The first part was completed, according to the agreement, by January 26, 1980, and on that date, the Israel ambassador to Egypt and the Egyptian ambassador to Israel presented their credentials and the respective embassies were opened. President Sadat visited Beersheba in May 1979 and Haifa in September, while Prime Minister Begin held talks with Sadat in Alexandria in July 1979 and met with the Egyptian leaders in Aswan in January 1980. Among other visitors to Egypt were the deputy prime minister, and the ministers of defense, foreign affairs, agriculture, commerce and industry, and senior civil servants. There were considerably fewer high-level visitors from Egypt to Israel.

The normalization proceeded very slowly although a series of agreements were initialed, among them on tourism, communication, civil aviation, agriculture and trade. There arose serious difficulties however in the actual implementation of these agreements, with Egypt raising many bureaucratic difficulties, including a long wait for entry visas for Israeli tourists. Some progress was made during the visit of President Navon to Egypt in November 1980. He addressed the Egyptian ruling party leadership, held lengthy talks with editors, writers and professors, as well as political figures. Speaking in fluent Arabic, his visit was a definite turning point in the relations with Egypt.

There was no progress in the talks on the institution of autonomy in the West Bank and Gaza, due to serious disagreements between Israel, on the one hand, and Egypt and the U.S. on the other. The latter felt that Israel must withdraw its military forces from the territories, give up its control over public land and water resources, halt Jewish settlement, include East Jerusalem in the autonomous area and grant the franchise not only to Arabs living in East Jerusalem but even to Palestinians living in the East Bank of the Jordan. Israel objected and the talks stalled. Efforts by Special Ambassador Sol Linowitz of the U.S. to find a formula that would satisfy the conflicting stand of the parties failed.

Even the involvement of President Carter in the process did not help. The U.S. presidential elections froze the negotiations, the progress of which was hampered by the refusal of Jordan and the local Palestinians to participate in the talks.

In other matters affecting foreign affairs, the peace treaty failed to improve Israel's standing in the third world. Not a single African country which had suspended diplomatic relations with Israel in 1973 made an overt effort to restore them. They continued to vote against Israel in the UN and in other international forums. The nine European members of the Common Market all but opposed the Camp David Agreements and the peace treaty. In a series of resolutions, chiefly that of Venice of June 1980, they proposed their own plan providing for total Israeli withdrawal to the 1967 lines, the establishment of a Palestinian state, and the creation of a European military force to oversee the borders of Israel. These were rejected out of hand by Israel, which charged Europe with tampering with the peace treaty.

Developments in the Middle East, chiefly the invasion of Afghanistan by Soviet forces and the Iran-Iraq war, deflected attention from the immediate Arab-Israel conflict and somewhat eased the pressure off Israel. Nevertheless, it did not prevent the UN General Assembly from passing, in December 1980, a series of violently anti-Israel resolutions which were approved by a massive majority. Among them were calls for amending Resolution 242, for immediate and total Israeli withdrawal from all the territories including East Jerusalem and the halting of settlements. There was a demand that the Security Council impose economic sanctions on Israel.

Following the adoption of the Jerusalem Law in the fall of 1980, all the remaining embassies moved from Jerusalem to Tel Aviv in protest. Turkey reduced the number of its diplomats in Israel and demanded a similar reduction by Israel. Threats were made in an effort to dissuade Israel from annexing the Golan Heights.

Relations with the United States were marked by many areas of agreement, among them the Camp David Agreements, the peace treaty, the need to maintain a balance of power in the region, the need to keep Jerusalem united (but not as Israel's capital with Israeli sovereignty over the entire city). There were agreements concerning water rights and freedom of navigation and the U.S. continued to remain the major arms supplier to Israel, but differences of opinion loomed over such issues as the future of the Palestinians, the future borders of Israel, the problem of Jerusalem, Israel's activities in southern Lebanon, Israeli settlements in the territories, American arms sales to Saudi Arabia, Jordan and Egypt, and the preference accorded to Egypt in the American strategic thinking for the Middle East. There was concern at the end of 1980 that the newly elected President Reagan might want to make some changes in the Camp David Agreements that could pave the way to a Palestinian state in the West Bank and the Gaza Strip.

Israeli foreign aid continued, especially in Latin America, and a large number of trainees from developing countries continued their studies in Israeli institutions.

The year 1981 witnessed Israel's continued isolation in the world, its growing dependence on the U.S., and gnawing doubts about the future of the peace treaty in the wake of the Sadat assassination on October 6. While plans for the final withdrawal from Sinai were being prepared, the government came under increasing pressure from various groups in Israel to reconsider its commitments under the 1979 peace treaty. There were, however, a number of agreements signed between Israel and Egypt that led many Israelis to hope that Egypt would honor its commitments after Israel returned all of Sinai.

Relations with the European nations remained chilly, and were exacerbated by verbal attacks by Prime Minister Begin who, during the heat of the election campaign lashed out against Chancellor Schmidt of Germany, Chancellor Kreisky of Austria, Prime Minister Thatcher of Britain, and other European leaders. They responded to the attacks and relations soured. Israel continued to oppose the Venice Declaration of the "Nine" and conditioned the participation of the forces of four European nations in the international peace keeping force in Sinai to a European proclamation that the force would observe the implementation of the Israel-Egypt peace treaty, and not the Venice Declaration. At year's end there was no certainty that the Europeans would participate in the force. Relations with France improved somewhat in December following the visit to Israel of Foreign Minister Cheysson. But the Golan Law chilled the ties again.

Improved ties with some African nations were reported in November, following a secret visit to Zaire, Gabon, and the Central African Republic by Defense Minister Sharon and the signing of agreements for the sale of Israeli weapons. But hopes for the early resumption of diplomatic ties were dashed after the passage of the Golan Law in December 1981.

Relations with the United States were mostly strained during 1981. The U.S. did not hide its hope that Israel would have a new government after the June 30 elections. However, when Mr. Begin was returned to power, he paid an official visit to Washington where he was greeted warmly by President Reagan. During this visit the ground was laid for the signing of an Israel-U.S. memorandum of understanding on strategic cooperation, designed to coordinate actions against the Soviet Union or forces directed by that power in the region. The agreement was signed by Defense Minister Sharon and Secretary of Defense Caspar Weinberger in Washington at the end of November. Following the Knesset law annexing the Golan Heights on December 14, the U.S. suspended the meetings of the joint U.S.-Israel working teams designed to give the agreement contents, and linking them with progress in the autonomy talks, continued quiet in Lebanon, and other issues. Israel retorted by declaring that the memorandum of understanding was frozen for the time being. This, together with the U.S. displeasure over the Israeli bombing of an Iraqi nuclear facility near Baghdad on June 7 and the bombing of the PLO headquarters in Beirut a month later, and the passage of the bill to sell U.S.-made AWACS and other advanced equipment to Saudi Arabia, considerably soured the relations between the two countries.

By the end of 1981, strenuous efforts were being made by both Israel and the U.S. to restore their dialogue and improve relations. Yet, a residue of bitterness remained and the formerly pro-Israel U.S. public opinion was slowly turning against Israel. U.S. Jewry was also asking questions as to the wisdom and timing of certain Israeli moves.

The decade of the 1980s began with Israel's international standing and image seriously tarnished by the war in Lebanon, and ended, in 1991 and 1992 in a major breakthrough on the international arena, the beginning of a peace process, and the acceptance of Israel by major powers which had traditionally shunned it, among them China and India. Israel also resumed diplomatic ties with nations which had broken them in 1967 (Eastern European nations) and in 1973 (most of the African nations). In spite of repeated periods of strain, Israel-American relations remained very friendly and a close strategic cooperation marked the ties in many spheres. There was also a noted improvement in Israel's economic performance. Two rescue operations which brought to Israel over 30,000 Ethiopian Jews, and the beginning of massive immigration from the Soviet Union restored Israel to its proclaimed role as a haven for oppressed Jews.

The peace process which began in 1977 following Egyptian President Anwar Sadat's visit to Jerusalem, the Camp David Accords (1978), and the Israel-Egypt Peace Treaty (1979), was halted when Egypt suspended the talks on the implementation of the Camp David interim autonomy regime for the West Bank and Gaza (1981). Shortly after that President Sadat was assassinated in Cairo. His successor, Hosni Mubarak, was busy building his own regime and waiting for the last Israeli soldier and settler to evacuate Sinai. This was done on April 26, 1982. Two months later, the Israel Defense Forces (IDF) entered Lebanon to destroy the PLO power base there, to seek the creation of a unified central government in Lebanon, and sign a peace treaty with it. Above all, Israel wanted to protect Galilee from PLO attacks that stemmed from Lebanon despite a cease fire agreement which was brokered by the United States in July 1981. The war in Lebanon generated much ill-will for Israel in the international media. Exaggerated reports on the number of Lebanese and Palestinian civilian casualties as well as physical destruction of cities and refugee camps placed Israel on the defensive. Domestic Israeli opposition to the war also helped Israel's detractors to portray that country as an aggressor. The siege of West Beirut and the massacre in the Sabra and Shatilla camps carried out by the Phalange (Christian Lebanese Forces) resulted in an outcry against Israel. Egypt withdrew its ambassador from Tel Aviv, and the Security Council adopted a number of condemnatory resolutions. When the dust settled down, it was American diplomacy which once again was instrumental in arranging for an agreement to end the state of war between Israel and Lebanon and create a security zone for Israel in southern Lebanon. It even called for the establishment of diplomatic ties between Jerusalem and Beirut. When a peace treaty was actualized, although it fell short of the one Prime Minister Begin wanted, it was an important milestone. It was based on the assumption that all foreign forces, among them the Syrian forces, would leave Lebanon. When this did not happen, it was clear that the agreement was invalid. Nine months after it was signed (January 13, 1984), the Lebanese parliament failed to approve it and it lapsed.

For the next two years, 1983 and 1984, Israel sought ways to maintain a military presence in Lebanon, while keeping the number of its casualties to the minimum and attempting to refrain from becoming involved in ethnic strife. The government of Yiẓḥak Shamir, which took office in September 1983 following the resignation of Prime Minister Begin a month earlier, sought ways and means to extricate the IDF from Lebanon, but felt that it could not do so unless peace was ensured for Galilee. Meanwhile there was no progress on the negotiations for autonomy for the Palestinians. Relations with various European and Latin American nations soured as a result of Israel's Lebanese involvement. The Government of National Unity, which came into being in September 1984 under Shimon Peres, placed as its central foreign policy objectives the continuation of the peace process, consolidation of the peace with Egypt, and withdrawal of the IDF from Lebanon, while insuring the security of the northern settlements. The government would also strive to restore links with the Soviet Union and African and Latin American states that had suspended such ties. At the top of the agenda was the fostering and deepening of the relations of friendship and understanding with the U.S.

The first priority was the withdrawal of the IDF from Lebanon. This was achieved in three stages in the course of 1985, leaving a security zone in southern Lebanon manned by pro-Israeli Southern Lebanese Army units. Parallel to this track, efforts were made to settle outstanding issues with Egypt. The issue of Taba, a small border area which was a thorn in the ties between the two nations, was resolved in 1988 after years of protracted negotiations and international arbitration when Israel agreed to turn Taba over to Egypt, which reappointed its ambassador to Tel Aviv. However, efforts to inject some warmth into Israel-Egyptian relations were, on the whole, unsuccessful. Egypt preferred to maintain a cold peace between the two governments and objected to attempts to create people-to-people ties. The military arrangements of the peace treaty were usually adhered to by both parties.

The major difficulty was over the Palestinian issue. Prime Minister Peres sought to break the stand-off, but was unable to convince his Likud partners over the modalities and procedures required to achieve progress. While Labor and Likud agreed that in the future, under any circumstances, the Jordan River must be Israel's security border in the East, Jerusalem must never be divided or placed under foreign rule and would remain Israel's capital, there would be no Palestinian state between the Mediterranean Sea and the desert, there would be no negotiations with the PLO, and the Israeli settlements in the territories would remain under Israeli jurisdiction, there were disagreements on how to proceed. Peres hoped that Israel would be able to negotiate with local Palestinian leaders who would be part of the Jordanian-Palestinian delegation but would not include Arabs from East Jerusalem and the Palestinian diaspora. He was not averse to an international "event" or "happening" to mark the opening of the negotiations, before moving on to face-to-face talks with the Arab states and the Palestinians. The aim of the talks would be to implement the autonomy regime for a five-year transition period. Various contacts between Israeli leaders and King Hussein of Jordan convinced Peres that Jordan would accept such an arrangement, which was finally agreed upon in a secret meeting in London between Peres and Rabin and King Hussein (April 11, 1987).

The agreement, however, was not accepted by the Likud, which vetoed it in the inner cabinet. The Likud's position consisted of vehement opposition to an international event of any sort, to the participation of the European Economic Community and the United Nations, to Soviet involvement, and even to American mediation. The Likud objected to the concept of "Land for Peace" which Labor was prepared to follow, and championed the concept of "Peace for Peace." An important event took place in July 1986, when Premier Peres paid an official visit to Morocco as guest of King Hassan II. While no concrete results were achieved, here was another Arab state that was prepared to deal openly with Israel. A major role was played by the United States in efforts to resume the stalled peace process. The Reagan Administration, mainly in the person of Secretary of State George Shultz, devised many formulae to close the gap between the Israeli and the Arab positions. But it was evident that King Hussein could not make an independent move without the approval of Syria and the PLO. Syria, still heavily dependent on the Soviet Union for military, economic, and political support, adhered to the Soviet line that called for the resolution of the Arab-Israel conflict on the basis of various United Nations resolutions through an international conference chaired by both the Soviet Union and the United States. In the second half of the 1980s there was little pressure on Israel to make concessions to the Arabs. The Middle East was wracked by the Iraq-Iran war, the military situation along the Israel-Lebanon border was quiet, the peace treaty with Egypt was working, and the Palestinians in the areas were relatively quiet. In 1988 both Israel and the United States held elections, and the issue of the peace process was shelved for the duration of the election campaigns. The onset of the *intifada* (Palestinian uprising) in December 1987 and the decision of the Reagan Administration to enter into a dialogue with the PLO in December 1988 placed Israel in a difficult position, forcing its government to come up with a new peace plan. This initiative, announced on May 14, 1989, called for negotiations with Palestinians for an interim agreement based on the Camp David autonomy plan. At the end of a five-year transition period, discussions would be held for the final resolution of the issues. The U.S. welcomed the plan as a very useful step, but both the PLO and King Hussein rejected it. In an effort to move the process forward, U.S. Secretary of State James Baker devised a five-point plan in October 1989 calling for Israeli-Palestinian dialogue in Cairo. The next problem was how to put together a list of Palestinian delegates acceptable to all. Shamir objected to East Jerusalem and "Palestinian Diaspora" delegates while Peres was prepared to be more conciliatory on the issue. The problem brought down the government of National Unity in March 1990. There was little movement while Shamir constituted his new government, and when the parties were ready to state their positions, the Iraqi dictator Saddam Hussein had invaded Kuwait (August 2, 1990) plunging the Middle East into a major crisis which dwarfed the Arab-Israel conflict.

As the United States began to build its anti-Iraqi coalition, which included Syria, Egypt, Saudi Arabia, and the Gulf States, Israel feared that Washington would link the resolution of the Iraqi crisis to that of the Arab-Israel conflict and would make concessions at Israel's expense to maintain its war coalition. In a number of high level meetings in Washington between Prime Minister Shamir, Defense Minister Arens, and senior members of the Bush administation, agreement on military and strategic cooperation was reached and greater coordination arranged. Israel was assured that no deals would be made at its expense. Meanwhile, the PLO lost much credibility in the West when it openly supported Iraq's invasion of Kuwait. The PLO was joined by Yemen, Libya and Algeria. Palestinians in the territories, then in the third year of the *intifada*, also hoped for an Iraqi victory. King Hussein quietly supported Iraq, although he was warned by Israel that entry of Iraqi forces into Jordan would be seen by Israel as a *casus belli*. Israel began to realize that war was imminent and took measures to prepare its civilian population for such an eventuality.

The allied victory over Iraq ushered in a new era for the Middle East. Futhermore, the collapse of the Soviet Union deprived Syria and other Arab states of their military, political, and economic backer, leaving the United States as the sole super power in the region. New thinking was the order of the day. For the Arabs, it was evident that the main threats to their stability and political regimes were Iran, Iraq, and Islamic fundamentalism, leaving Israel as their fourth perceived danger. It was also clear to them that another Middle Eastern war would be fought with non-conventional weapons, unleashing mutual destruction. The Middle East had entered into the era of a regional balance of terror. The United States sought to reorganize the defense of the Middle East and of its own economic and strategic interests, insuring an uninterrupted supply of oil and helping its allies thwart the dangers of Islamic fundamentalism. Israel emerged from the war bruised, sustaining 39 Scud missile attacks from Iraq, which caused few casualties but much damage in the greater Tel Aviv and Haifa regions and paralyzed the country for some three weeks. Israel's economic vulnerability and dependence on the U.S. were exposed. For the first time in its history it did not engage in preventive war or a pre-emptive strike or retaliatory action, acceding to the request of the United States not to become militarily involved in the war. It allowed the stationing on its territory of American, Dutch, and German soldiers who were manning Patriot anti-missile missiles. The Palestinians emerged from the war badly hurt. Some 350,000 Palestinians were expelled from Kuwait in the wake of the war; the PLO was totally discredited in the West; Palestinians in the areas who supported Iraq were in despair. The Soviet Union, preoccupied with its own internal affairs, was content to let the United States manage the restructuring of the Middle East peace process as long as it was kept in the picture formally as an equal partner.

Between March and October 1991, Secretary of State James Baker visited the Middle East eight times in order to prepare the ground for the resumption of the peace process. The breakthrough came when in July, Syria agreed to attend a peace conference and negotiate directly with Israel. It was agreed that a Palestinian delegation would formally be part of the Jordanian delegation. The U.S. and the Soviet Union would be co-chairmen of the peace conference which was to commence in a ceremonial event and continue in a series of bilateral and multilateral talks. The latter would deal with issues of water, refugees, disarmament, economic development, and environment. The bilateral talks were to focus on borders (withdrawal), the nature of peace, security arrangements, and economic issues. The letter of invitation to the Madrid Peace Conference (October 30, 1991) spelled out the terms of reference under which the Palestinian issue would be discussed; at its core was the creation of a five-year autonomy regime. A final settlement and the issue of Jerusalem were not to be discussed at this stage. Eight rounds of talks took place in Washington in the course of 1991 and 1992, which defined the issues but did not achieve any concrete results. The peace process, however, had become a reality in the Middle East.

Parallel to this development, there was a major improvement of Israel's international standing. Already in the 1980s relations were resumed with a number of African nations starting with Zaire and the Ivory Coast. As Eastern Europe freed itself from Soviet domination in the late 1980s, Israel resumed diplomatic relations with Poland, Hungary, Bulgaria, Czechoslovakia, and on the eve of the Madrid Conference with the Soviet Union. Israel conditioned UN participation in the peace process on the revocation of the infamous General Assembly Resolution 3379 (Zionism = Racism) and this was done on

December 16, 1991. On the Asian continent, full diplomatic ties were established with China and India, an embassy was opened in South Korea, and there was a major improvement in Israel-Japan relations, with more Japanese companies defying the Arab economic boycott and selling directly to Israel. Contacts with Vietnam were entered into while the Israeli ambassador was also named ambassador to Outer Mongolia. The breakup of the Soviet Union into the 16 republics of the Commonwealth of Independent States resulted in the establishment of Israeli diplomatic representations in the Ukraine, Belarus, and the Baltic States, Kazakhstan, and Kirghizia in addition to the Russian Republic.

Relations with the United States were on the whole close and friendly. Israel and the United States agreed on certain principles, among them: the peace process would be based on Resolutions 242 and 338; the PLO would not take part; there would be no Palestinian state; Jerusalem would not be divided again; Israel would only be asked to withdraw from the areas in the context of a peace treaty; close military and strategic cooperation would continue; Israel would be entitled to economic and military aid; and the regional balance of power would be maintained in such a manner to insure Israel's qualitative edge. There were also agreements on freedom of navigation and Israel's water rights. But there were also a series of disagreements, among them: Israel's eastern borders, the future of the Golan Heights, and the resolution of the Palestinian issue (the favored American position was the return of the West Bank and Gaza to Jordan and the granting by Jordan of a special status to these areas). There was constant disagreement over the future of Jerusalem, with the U.S. opposed to Israeli sovereignty over Jerusalem. There were arguments over American arms sales to Arab states and Israeli arms sales to various nations, over Israel's nuclear development, over Israel's presence in Lebanon, and over whether Israel or Egypt should play a greater role in the American planning in the Middle East. The main disagreement was over the key issue of the meaning and nature of Israel's security and who would determine its needs. On a number of occasions there was much strain in the personal relations between President Bush and Prime Minister Shamir, considered by the United States as an "ideological" leader, meaning inflexible and rigid. A major problem occurred in December 1988, when the U.S. decided to recognize the PLO and enter into a dialogue with this terrorist organization. This dialogue, however, was suspended in June 1990 when the PLO refused to denounce a terrorist attack on Israel which had been foiled by the IDF. There were also disagreements on the interpretation of the Camp David Accords, the meaning of the balance of power, and the nature of the autonomy plan.

While Israel became an associate member of the European Economic Community and maintained growing economic ties with the nations of Western Europe, there were serious disagreements on the peace process. The EEC's traditional position called for an international peace conference, the creation of a Palestinian state in the areas, and the redivision of Jerusalem. There were constant arguments over the role played by certain European countries in the arming of Iraq and the building of its war machine. The EEC never failed to condemn Israel for its behavior in the areas, and the criticism grew stronger as the *intifada* broke out and Israel took stern measures.

The traditional friendly ties between Israel and the Latin American continent continued, with Israel extending much technical assistance to various states and training a growing number of students from that continent. Similar close relations were maintained with Australia and New Zealand, even while disagreeing on the resolution of the Arab-Israel conflict. President Herzog of Israel traveled extensively during his two terms of office to the U.S., Canada, Britain, France, Holland, Belgium, Poland, Czechoslovakia, Romania, various South American nations, Spain, Australia and New Zealand, Singapore and Sri Lanka.

Jewish communities worldwide continued to be Israel's most loyal and trusted allies. They were thrilled when Israel airlifted Ethiopian Jews in two daring operations (Moses in 1984 and Solomon in 1991),airlifted the Jewish community of Albania (1992), and had begun the herculean task of absorbing the hundreds of thousands of Jews who had begun to stream to its shores from the Soviet Union, once the gates were opened in October 1989. Between that date and April 1993, some 425,000 Jews arrived in Israel from the former U.S.S.R. Israel was instrumental in getting the Syrian government to allow the emigration of hundreds of the previously besieged members of the Syrian Jewish community and to start the process whereby the remnant of the Jews of Yemen were reunited with families overseas. Yet there were also ongoing debates on the centrality of Israel in Jewish life and on organizational frameworks in which to achieve common goals. The Jewish Agency for Israel continued to be the most effective body for the implementation of the immigration and absorption process, combining in it the Zionist (mainly Israeli) element with the New Zionists (mainly fund raisers) from the diaspora.

One of the major consequences of the peace process, started at the Madrid Peace Conference in October 1991, was the dramatic change in Israel's international position and the network of its diplomatic ties. Before that conference, Israel maintained diplomatic and consular relations with 91 nations, the majority in Europe, North, Central, and Latin America, few in Africa, Asia, and the Far East. Most of the African nations had suspended diplomatic ties with Israel just prior, during, and after the 1973 Yom Kippur War, citing the Arab oil boycott, economic inducements and threats made against their rulers by terrorist Arab groups as the main reasons for doing so. Of the Communist bloc nations, only Romania retained diplomatic ties with Israel after the break of June 1967, when all Eastern European nations followed the Soviet Union and broke off diplomatic ties with Israel.

By early 1995 Israel maintained diplomatic relations with 153 countries (out of the 185 United Nations members), and was represented by an ambassador, minister, or consul, resident and non-resident, in over 100 capitals.

Many factors brought about this development, the origins of which were in the 1980s, but the bulk occurred after the Madrid Peace Conference and were accelerated after the signing, in September 1993, of the Israel-PLO Declaration of Principles.

Resentful over Arab unwillingness to carry out promises made in 1973, mainly in the economic sphere, a number of African leaders reached the conclusion that breaking ties with Israel was counter-productive and brought no appreciable gains. On the contrary, their efforts to obtain economic help were often frustrated by the absence of ties with Israel, a fact cited to them on a number of occasions by international financial organizations. Israel was not there when needed to support their applications for loans and loan guarantees.

Among the first nations to resume ties with Israel in the early 1980s was Zaire. It was followed by the Ivory Coast, Togo, and Kenya. Another reason given by African nations was the change in Israel's relations with South Africa, the end of military ties between both nations since 1987, and, finally, the collapse of the apartheid regime in South Africa and the ascendance of the African National Congress.

In the case of Eastern Europe, the accession of Mikhail Gorbachev to power in 1985, and his decision to pursue a policy based on *perestroika* and *glasnost*, meant that he required vast economic aid from the West to shore up the foundering Soviet economy. He understood that in order to obtain help from the West, and chiefly from the United States, he would have to change the traditional Soviet attitude to Jewish emigration and to Israel. The issue of better relations with the West was linked to freedom of emigration and the restoration of ties with Israel. Israel indicated that it would be prepared to restore diplomatic ties only on condition that the gates of the Soviet Union be opened for Jewish immigration. Arrangements were made to facilitate emigration, first through third countries (such as Hungary, Poland, and Romania), and from 1991 direct to Israel.

Israel and the Soviet Union began negotiations on improvement of relations in the mid-1980s. Russian diplomats admitted to their Israeli counterparts that their decision to break off ties in 1967 had been erroneous and self-defeating. These talks culminated with the decision to re-establish consular relations in 1989. By then, on the eve of the collapse of the Berlin Wall and the bloodless revolutions in all Eastern European nations, it had become evident to the leaders of these countries that in order to bolster their legitimacy, mainly to Western public opinion, they would have to resume ties with Israel. This was done by Hungary, Poland, and Bulgaria even before 1991. President Herzog, Prime Minister Shamir, Finance Minister Peres, and other senior Israeli officials visited the capitals of Eastern Europe, and agreements were signed in various spheres. To some leaders in Eastern Europe, diplomatic ties with Israel was one of the symbols of their release from the Soviet yoke. Poland, Hungary, and Romania facilitated Jewish immigration to Israel. This was done in spite of Arab protests and threats.

In October 1989 the Soviet Union agreed that Jews leaving that country for Israel must go there. Those wishing to travel to other countries had to obtain entry visas to those countries prior to departure. By 1990 more than 200,000 Russian Jewish immigrants had arrived in Israel. Talks were held for the restoration of full diplomatic relations. Israel made it clear to the Soviet government that it could serve as a co-sponsor of the Madrid Peace Conference only if it restored full diplomatic relations, so that there would be symmetry in relations between Russia, Israel, and the Arabs. The Russians agreed, and a day before the opening of the Madrid Peace Conference, both nations announced in Jerusalem the resumption of full diplomatic relations.

The breakup of the former Soviet empire resulted, among other things, in the creation of 15 independent republics called the Commonwealth of Independent States, established in 1992. The leaders of these new republics assumed, rightly or wrongly, that Israel was a very important "door opener" to the West. It was believed that Israel exercised vast influence on the American government and that its contacts, direct or through American Jews, could be used to obtain assistance. Shortly after obtaining their independence, the following republics established full diplomatic ties with Israel: Armenia, Azerbaijan, Belarus, Georgia, Kazakhstan, Kirghizstan, Lithuania, Moldavia, Tadjikistan, Turkemanistan, the Ukraine, and Uzbekistan. Israeli embassies were opened, Jewish immigration was permitted, and Jewish Agency emissaries and teachers were allowed to work in those countries with no hindrance. The ties with all of these republics grew considerably warm in the course of visits of senior officials, and the signing of cooperation agreements in the fields of science, technology, agriculture, and education. Israel did exercise some influence in helping these nations obtain assistance from the west. But early high expectations that Israel could do the impossible were not realized, and there was some disappointment as the economic conditions of a number of these republics verged on collapse.

While the Soviet Union disintegrated, it had little time or inclination to deal actively with the affairs of the Middle East. It failed to prevent the Gulf War and played a small role in that conflict. The major role in the Arab-Israel peace process was left to the United States. But when the Yeltsin regime began to consolidate its hold on Russia in late 1991, Russia served notice that it had a large interest in the affairs of the Middle East and that it intended to play a part in the evolution of the peace process. Russia also announced on a number of occasions that it saw itself as the traditional defender of the interests of the Eastern (Greek) Orthodox Church in the Holy Land and was entitled to be consulted on the future of Jerusalem.

Two other countries in Eastern Europe, Yugoslavia and Czechoslovakia, also disintegrated. Israel re-established diplomatic ties initially with the Czech republic and later with Slovakia. In the former Yugoslavia, it maintained ties with Serbia and Slovenia. Full diplomatic ties were established with Albania. These enabled the rescue of the tiny Jewish community in that country and their transfer to Israel in 1992.

On the African continent, where Israel had 28 diplomatic missions prior to the break of 1973, more nations requested resumption of relations, arguing that there were no longer any impediments for normalization of ties. Among the African nations which resumed ties with Israel after October 1991 were Angola, Benin, Botswana, Burkina Fasso, Cape Verde, Equatorial Guinea, Eritrea, Gabon, Gambia, Ghana, Guinea Bissau, Lesotho, Madagascar, Mauritius, Mozambique, Namibia, Nigeria, Rwanda, Sao Tome, Senegal, Seychelles, Sierra Leone, Uganda, Zambia, and Zimbabwe. Israel and Ethiopia resumed full diplomatic ties in 1990 and this was of vast significance when "Operation Solomon," which saw the airlifting of 14,500 Ethiopian Jews to Israel, was carried out in May 1991. By 1995 Israel maintained diplomatic ties with 36 nations on the African continent (including Egypt and Morocco). Once again hundreds of African trainees were going to Israel for a variety of courses and Israeli experts were again working in many African nations. In 1994 Israel sent a medical team to help ease the plight of refugees in Rwanda following the civil war in that country.

An even more dramatic change occurred on the Asian continent. Contacts with the People's Republic of China had been maintained since the late 1970s, but they were covert. By 1989 China agreed to the setting up in Beijing of an Israeli scientific mission, the nucleus for an embassy. Full diplomatic relations were established in January 1992 during the visit to China of Foreign Minister David Levy. Subsequent high level visits included the visit of Prime Minister Rabin (in October 1993), Foreign Minister Peres, and other Israel officials. From the Chinese side, the vice premier and foreign minister visited Israel. A growing number of Israeli firms are now represented in the two main Chinese centers – Beijing and Shanghai.

China was followed by Mongolia and later by the three republics of former French Indo-China – Vietnam, Laos, and Cambodia. These three sought Israel's help to obtain aid from the West. An Israel embassy was reopened in Seoul in 1992 (it had been closed in 1978 due to budgetary considerations). Similarly, an Israeli consulate general was reopened in Hong Kong in 1987 to facilitate ties with China. There is an Israeli economic office in the Republic of China in Taipei. Israeli offers to sell arms to Taiwan were criticized by Beijing. In 1993 Israel sought to establish direct links with North Korea in order to persuade that country not to sell missiles and nuclear technology to Syria and Iran. The United States objected to these efforts and they were suspended at Washington's request.

There were also changes in ties with some Muslim nations in Asia. On his way home from China in October 1993, Prime Minister Rabin made a stop in Jakarta for talks with Indonesia's President Suharto. There were also attempts to establish contacts with Malaysia, one of whose ministers visited Israel unofficially in 1994. All this resulted in growing numbers of Indonesian and Malaysian tourists to Israel and Israeli nationals were also able to visit Indonesia.

For many years ties with Japan remained formal and cool. At the end of the Gulf War they warmed up considerably. Japan abandoned its policy of accepting the Arab economic boycott on Israel and trade between the two nations rose. Prime Minister Rabin led a large trade mission to Japan (and South Korea) in December 1994. More Japanese firms were investing in Israel and opening offices in Tel Aviv. Asia became the third major export market for Israeli goods, accounting for some 20% of total exports. El Al, the national air carrier, inaugurated direct flights from Ben Gurion Airport to Delhi, Bombay, Bangkok, Hong Kong, and Seoul. Thousands of Asian workers, mainly from Thailand and the Philippines, were working in Israel.

India, which had followed a pro-Arab policy since it recognized Israel in 1950, realized the new international trends and established full diplomatic ties with Israel in early 1992. Commercial and military contacts were considered and there were high levels visits, including one of Foreign Minister Peres in May 1993.

The peace process brought about a revolutionary change in Israel's position in the Middle East. In early 1995 Israel and Jordan opened their respective embassies in Amman and Tel Aviv. In October 1994 Israel opened an office of interests in Rabat, Morocco, and a Moroccan official opened a similar office in Tel Aviv. Talks were held about the opening of a diplomatic representation in Tunisia. Israeli officials visited Tunisia, Oman, and Qatar. Relations with Turkey also warmed up considerably and culminated with the visit to Israel of Prime Minister Cellar in early 1995. Turkey was keen on increasing its economic ties with Israel. By 1994 it had become the favorite vacation spot for Israelis due to low prices and close proximity to Israel. In 1994, some 400,000 Israelis vacationed in Turkey. Cypriot President Glafcos visited Israel in 1994 to further cement ties between the island republic and Israel. Ties with Greece, which had been maintained on the level of a diplomatic mission, were raised to full ambassadorial level. Greece was seen to be displaying a far more evenhanded policy in the Middle East than in the past.

In its relations with the countries of Western Europe, mainly with the members of the European Union (formerly European Economic Community), Israel sought to bring about an improvement in its 1975 trade agreement with the Common Market and to coordinate more closely activities in the area of internal security and the anti-terrorist struggle. The growing threat of Islamic fundamentalism, which menaced not only Israel but a number of Moslem countries and European nations, became an international concern. An agreement between the police forces of Israel and Italy was signed in Rome in 1994, and similar agreements were being projected with other countries. On the European continent itself, the warm ties with Germany continued with periodic visits of heads of state and ministers. Germany supported Israel's stance on its agreement with the European Union and continued to provide Israel with an annual grant. In May 1995 Chancellor Kohl paid a visit to Israel in which he apologized on behalf of the German people for the Holocaust.

Relations with France remained cordial in spite of a fundamental disagreement between Israel and France (under President Mitterrand) over the issue of a Palestinian state which France favored. A new and warm spirit was injected into the ties between Israel, Spain, and Portugal. This was apparent during the visit to Israel of King Juan Carlos and Queen Sophia of Spain (October 1993) and of Prime Minister Rabin to Spain (February 1994). Mr. Rabin was also Israel's first prime minister to pay an official visit to Portugal.

Ties with the Benelux and Scandinavian countries improved vastly. Norway was the host for the secret Israel-PLO negotiations and the agreement was signed initially in Oslo. Rabin, Peres, and Arafat were awarded the 1994 Nobel Peace Prize which was presented in Oslo in December 1994. Ties with Britain improved when Britain lifted its arms embargo against Israel and supported its stance in the EU. Mr. Rabin visited London twice and John Major was in Israel in March 1995.

Another important dividend of the peace process was the signing on December 31, 1993 of the Israel-Holy See Basic Agreement, which heralded diplomatic relations between Israel and the Vatican, and also had enormous significance in terms of the relations between the Catholic Church and the Jewish people. Embassies were established in July 1994. The Vatican's rights and privileges in its property in Israel, including churches, schools, hospitals, and orphanages, were guaranteed by Israel.

The Israel-Holy See agreement had important consequences for Israel-Latin America relations. The relations had always been cordial and warm, and the only Latin American countries that had suspended ties with Israel were Nicaragua and Cuba. Nicaragua restored them, while Israel expanded its diplomatic presence in that continent by opening missions in the Caribbean area. In Buenos Aires, the Israel embassy was blown up in 1992 with many casualties.

The new regional and international realities were also partly reflected in the voting pattern in the United Nations. During the annual deliberations of the General Assembly, some 20 resolutions dealing with the "Palestine" question are generally discussed. Most of them are anti-Israel, many of them repetitive, and all of them irrelevant to the events in the region. Many countries justified their anti-Israel votes by arguing that they did not matter and that what counted were the bilateral relations. Israel usually countered by saying that this was a formal declaration of a political stand. From 1991 there was toning down of the anti-Israel resolutions and the Assembly began to take note of the peace process. But on the whole, even while paying lip service to the process, it did pass anti-Israel resolutions, although with a growing number of abstentions. Thus, for example, in December 1994 the Assembly, in the resolution termed "The Situation in the Middle East," called on Israel to unilaterally withdraw from the Golan Heights. The resolution was adopted by a vote of 77 in favor, 2 against (Israel and the United States), with 70 abstentions (including Russia). In the past the majority of the UN members voted against Israeli nuclear armament. In the vote taken in December 1994 on a resolution which singled Israel out by calling on nations to renounce nuclear weapons, 60 countries voted in favor, 4 opposed and 100 abstained. One resolution, dealing with the future status of the territories, which was approved by 147 nations, contradicted the Israel-PLO Declaration of Principles. But this did not seem to deter those who voted in favor.

Israel's key partner remained the United States. That nation played a crucial role in the peace process. While it pressed Israel not to become actively involved in the Gulf War, it helped defend Israel and provided it with economic and military aid to offset the damage. The Bush and later Clinton administrations were determined to pursue the peace process and exerted much effort in doing so. Washington pushed Israel and Syria to move towards the Madrid peace conference, gave assurances to Israel that its interests would not be harmed, and while initially refusing to grant the Israeli request for a ten billion dollar loan guarantee, did so in the summer of 1992, after the accession to power of the Rabin government.

The United States hosted the bilateral talks which followed the Madrid meetings. Although not crowned with much success, they nevertheless provided a framework for some progress and paved the way for the Israel-PLO agreement and the Israel-Jordan peace treaty.

The warm ties with the United States were evident mainly in strategic cooperation, placing at Israel's disposal new military technology, helping Israel develop new weapons systems, and above all in maintaining its military qualitative edge, so that it could take risks for peace. The annual three billion dollar military and economic loans and grants were maintained, in spite of fears that, they, too, might be cut due to budgetary considerations. The United States' support for Israel was seen in the Arab world as a major factor in changing their traditional thinking of dealing with Israel on the battlefield to dealing with Israel across the negotiating table. The United States played a key role in the Israel-Jordan treaty, a lesser role in the Israel-PLO agreement, and a major role in the negotiations between Israel and Syria. Those required a number of shuttle trips undertaken by Secretary of State Warren Christopher and his peace team. President Clinton visited Israel and witnessed the signing of the Israel-Jordan Peace Treaty on October 26, 1994. Prior to that he witnessed in White House ceremonies the signing of the Israel-PLO Declaration of Principles and the Israel-Jordan Washington Declaration (July 25, 1994). The United States also suggested to many nations that had suspended ties with Israel that it would be useful if they resumed them. There was no change in the American policy regarding Jerusalem. The city should remain united but not entirely under Israel sovereignty. Congressional attempts to legislate the moving of the American Embassy from Tel Aviv to Jerusalem by 1999 ran into opposition from the Clinton administration (and partly the Israel government). Both did not want to jeopardize the situation prior to the talks on the final status of the holy city.

In the mid-1990s, Israel's international position was highly positive, its reputation soaring, its trade growing, and its advice sought by many world leaders. It had come a long way since its isolation in the wake of the Yom Kippur War. However, its new position would see many ups and downs in the post-Oslo period as events continued to take their bloody course and exact their toll on human lives.

For a fuller discussion of the post-Oslo period see "The Road to Oslo and After" above. For Israel and the United Nations, see *United Nations.

[Meron Medzini]

INTERNATIONAL AID AND COOPERATION. Through its international cooperation program of technical assistance, Israel helped many other developing countries find solutions to their economic, social, and educational problems. Israel's contribution is based on its own recent and continuing experience in developing human and material resources. The history of the program began in 1954, when Israel entered into a number of joint projects with Burma under the guidance of its ambassador, David Hacohen. In March 1957, when Ghana became independent (the first sub-Saharan African country to achieve this status in the post-World War II period), Israel answered her request for technical cooperation. In the following year, the program was formally launched with the establishment of the International Cooperation Division within the Ministry for Foreign Affairs, on the initiative of Golda Meir, then foreign minister.

In 1961 an agreement was signed between Israel and Brazil, on the proposal of the Brazilian government, for cooperation in agricultural and water development, mainly in North Brazil. In 1963 Venezuela and Israel started a scheme for the adaptation of Israel's regional development methods under the guidance of planners from the *Lachish regional development scheme. These two projects were followed by the spread of cooperation with Israel to most of Latin America. Meanwhile, several South and Southeast Asian countries invited Israel's cooperation in development, as did several countries closer to Israel: Iran, Turkey, Cyprus, Greece, and Malta. In several instances, public and private, commercial organizations in Israel were asked to carry out projects, but generally, the International Cooperation Division itself carried out schemes through associated governmental and public agencies. By the end of its first decade of activity in 1968, the International Cooperation Division had sent 2,562 experts to development projects in 64 countries in all continents, and had trained 10,569 men and women from 82 countries in Israel. About $60,000,000 was spent on the program from Israel government funds during that period.

Agriculture accounted for more than half of all development projects in which Israel has engaged, with youth organization and training in second place and health programs third. Science and technology comprised a larger share of the total program each year. Half of all projects were undertaken in Africa, but Latin America's share was increasing steadily. Approximately 450 Israelis served abroad each year in more than 150 projects. In addition, about 100 Israelis served as experts on schemes financed by the United Nations. Israel commercial corporations engaged in development abroad employed an additional 400 Israelis in their undertakings. More than a thousand men and women from developing countries graduated from middle- and high-level courses in Israel each year. Courses were usually from four to six months in duration and were held in a variety of languages, principally in English, French, and Spanish. Regular courses were held in cooperation at the Afro-Asian Institute and the Center for Latin American Cooperation Studies in Tel Aviv; in agriculture at the Ruppin Institute, near Netanyah; and in community development at the International Center for Community Development, Haifa. Courses were also held from time to time at a number of other locations. The *Hebrew University, together with Hadassah and separately, as well as the Haifa *Technion, held regular higher-level courses. In addition, lower and middle-level courses were held in the developing countries and graduated more than a thousand trainees each year.

From its inception through the early years of the 21st century, 200,000 men and women had participated in the program's training courses in Israel and abroad and over 10,000 Israeli experts had been dispatched to foreign countries. In the post-Oslo era Israel looked to develop similar partnerships with its neighbors.

[Benad Avital]

Arab Refugees

During the fighting in Palestine that followed the adoption of the *United Nations Partition Resolution of Nov. 29, 1947, and the growing anarchy that accompanied the British withdrawal from Palestine, hundreds of thousands of Arabs abandoned their homes and fled to neighboring Arab countries and to parts of Palestine later occupied by Jordan and Egypt. The refugee problem was thus born out of the unsuccessful Arab attempt to frustrate the UN Partition Plan by force, to prevent the emergence of a Jewish state, and to occupy Palestine at the end of the British Mandate. This political background explains the stubbornness of the question. Though substantially absorbed in fact, the refugees remain permanent wards of the United Nations, and it seems clear that only an Israel-Arab peace settlement can resolve this problem.

ORIGINS OF THE PROBLEM. On Feb. 16, 1948, the United Nations Palestine Commission (appointed to supervise the partition plan) reported to the Security Council that "powerful Arab interests both inside and outside Palestine are defying the Nov. 29, 1947, resolution of the General Assembly and are engaged in a deliberate effort to alter by force the settlement envisaged therein." On April 10, 1948, the Commission reported that "… armed Arab bands from the neighboring states have infiltrated into the territory of Palestine, and, together with local Arab forces, are defeating the purpose of the partition resolution by acts of violence." By that time fighting had swept through the country.

During April the tide turned in favor of the *Haganah, especially in mixed towns such as Haifa, Safed, and Tiberias. The morale of the Arab population sank, and an exodus started into surrounding Arab territories with the encouragement of the Arab leadership, who did not want their people to remain under Jewish control and promised that they would soon return behind the victorious Arab armies. In Haifa, for example, the local Arab National Committee refused to sign a truce and insisted on the evacuation of their community despite an appeal by Shabbetai *Levi, the Jewish mayor. The exodus was accelerated by rumors, spread by the Arabs, of Jewish atrocities. The heavy civilian casualties suffered by the Arabs during an attack by the *Irgun Ẓeva'i Le'ummi on the village of Deir Yasīn near Jerusalem were extensively publicized as a massacre and added to the panic.

On May 15, with the end of the Mandate and the withdrawal of the British forces, the State of Israel was proclaimed. The regular armies of the neighboring Arab states crossed the borders and the residents of many Arab villages were evacuated by their leaders. During the fighting of the next few months, the flight continued into the Arab-held areas of Judea and Samaria (later annexed by Jordan as the "West Bank") across the river into Transjordan, into the *Gaza Strip, and, to a smaller extent, into Syria and Lebanon.

UNITED NATIONS ACTION. Initial efforts to give the Palestine refugees emergency relief were made by voluntary organizations. In December 1948, the General Assembly endorsed a nine-month relief program to be supervised by the secretary-general. At the same session, Resolution 194 (III) was adopted on Dec. 11, 1948. It called upon the states involved in the Israel-Arab conflict to negotiate a peace settlement and established a Palestine Conciliation Commission (consisting of the United States, France, and Turkey) to assist them in doing so. Paragraph 11 of that resolution stated, in part, "Those refugees wishing to return to their homes and live at peace with their neighbors should be permitted to do so at the earliest practicable date" and "…compensation should be paid for the property of those choosing not to return…" Paragraph 11 remained a bone of contention thereafter. The Arab side maintained that it conferred on the refugees a free and unconditional choice between repatriation and compensation. The Israel side argued that the refugee question could not be taken out of the general context of peace; that no return was "practicable" until normal conditions were restored; that only the government of a sovereign state could "permit" entry into the territory of that state; and that political, economic, and security conditions, such as the readiness of the refugees "to live at peace with their neighbors," had to be taken into account. In the negotiations which the Conciliation Commission tried to promote, the refugee problem was treated as one element in a general peace "package."

By 1949, it was already clear that no immediate peace settlement was likely and that more long-range plans would be required for the refugees. The emphasis shifted to their economic absorption in the region as a whole, though the phrase "without prejudice to paragraph 11…" was formally repeated in resolutions. The Conciliation Commission had appointed a United Nations Economic Survey Mission for the Middle East, headed by Gordon Clapp of the Tennessee Valley Authority. The 1949 General Assembly endorsed a three-pronged program recommended by the Clapp Mission: the termination of direct relief within a year, the absorption of the refugees through public works projects, and the transfer of responsibility to the host governments at an early date. As an instrument for carrying out this program, the Assembly set up the United Nations Relief and Works Agency for Palestinian Refugees in the Near East (UNRWA). At the next Assembly, in 1950, the objective was defined as "reintegration of the refugees into the economic life of the Near East," and a three-year program was adopted envisaging the expenditure of $50 million for relief and $200 million for reintegration. UNRWA's original mandate was, therefore, to rehabilitate the refugees and take them off the relief rolls as soon as possible.

THE NUMBERS OF THE REFUGEES. Great difficulty was experienced throughout in reaching a reliable figure for bona fide Arab refugees. It is generally agreed that the figures were inflated at the outset and became more so in the course of time. First, there had been an influx of migrant labor from surrounding Arab countries during the Mandatory period, owing to the tempo of Zionist development. A substantial part of the refugee exodus in 1948 was, therefore, a return to home territory. In a 1949 report on the refugees, the secretary-general pointed out that the rolls had been compiled in a haphazard way and included large numbers of local unemployed or poor persons and nomadic Bedouin tribesmen.

The Clapp Mission estimated that at least 160,000 non-refugees had managed to get onto the relief rolls. Taking Mandatory census figures as a starting point and deducting from them the Arabs who remained in Israel and the indigenous population of the districts occupied by Arab forces (East Jerusalem, the West Bank, and the Gaza Strip), it may be deduced that the total number of bona fide refugees did not exceed a few hundred thousand. UNRWA adopted the following working definition of a refugee:

"… a person whose normal residence was Palestine for a minimum of two years immediately preceding the outbreak of the conflict in 1948 and who, as a result of that conflict, lost both his home and his means of livelihood…" However, UNRWA took over the existing rolls from voluntary agencies without revising them in accordance with the above definition.

In subsequent years the figures became even more unreliable through fraudulent birth registrations, failure to report deaths, and the lack of adequate means for determining family income or physical presence in the area. Thousands of ration cards were acquired by merchants who collected the supplies. Under pressure from the contributing countries, United Nations resolutions repeatedly called for rectification of the rolls, but the host governments were unwilling to cooperate for fear of stirring up trouble in the camps. To the tables in the annual UNRWA reports, a prudent footnote was added that "the above statistics are based on the Agency's registration records, which do not necessarily reflect the actual refugee population." In 1968 the UNRWA registration records contained over 1,300,000 names. Of these, only a little more than 800,000 had ration cards. Of the rest, some received medical education services without rations and others no assistance at all, depending on the degree of self-support. The distribution of the 1968 total by areas, according to UNRWA statistics, was as follows (in thousands): West Bank 245, Gaza Strip 265, East Jordan 494, Lebanon 166, Syria 150, UAR 3.

EXCHANGE OF MINORITIES. The upheaval of 1948 brought about not one population movement, but two, in opposite directions. Following the establishment of the State of Israel, the Jewish minorities started leaving the Arab countries for reasons of political, economic, and often physical insecurity. The majority of them found refuge in Israel. What happened from 1948 onward was in effect a spontaneous and unplanned population exchange, in roughly equal numbers – about half a million or a little more each way. Today, with natural increase, the Jews who reached Israel from the Arab countries constitute a group of nearly a million. This exodus never became a United Nations question and no UN agency was set up to deal with it, because these Jewish refugees became completely absorbed into the life and economy of Israel. Israel spokesmen in the United Nations debates stressed that this exchange of population had to be accepted as a reality, as had happened in certain situations elsewhere, and it could not be put into reverse. The future of the Arab refugees lay in their final absorption into the Arab world, and not in their repatriation to their original homes. Some 40,000 of them were actually repatriated to Israel in the first few years after the 1948 war, for family reunion or hardship reasons.

ATTEMPTS AT RESETTLEMENT. In the period 1950–5, UNRWA initiated a variety of self-support programs, and two major land-settlement projects were planned: one in the northern Sinai and the other in the Yarmuk-Jordan River Valley. The Sinai project was based on an agreement between UNRWA and the Egyptian government, by which a large area in northwest Sinai would be reclaimed with Nile water to be syphoned under the Suez Canal. According to the plan, some 10,000 refugee families from the Gaza Strip would eventually be engaged in agriculture, and another 2,000 families supported by ancillary services and trades. Engineering and economic studies were carried out, and a comprehensive plan drawn up, but the project came to naught when the Egyptian government changed its mind about making water available.

The plan for the development of the Yarmuk and Jordan valleys aimed at the irrigation of about 125,000 acres to provide a living for between 100,000 and 150,000 people. Under its agreement with the Jordan government, the Agency was to provide $40 million out of the Rehabilitation Fund for this project. Some of the preparatory work was carried out, but UNRWA withdrew from the project when the division of the Jordan basin waters became caught up in Security Council debates, followed by the abortive efforts of the United States to promote a regional plan.

In the next few years, the Agency's small-scale self-support measures also withered away. After a decade of existence the Agency had lost its original rehabilitation purpose and had settled down as a self-perpetuating relief operation, with registration rolls that swelled steadily from year to year. The original working definition was extended to include children born after 1948, and by the 1960s a third generation began to appear. By 1969, children and young people far outnumbered the original refugees, and the registered total included about 500,000 infants and children under the age of 15. The constructive side of UNRWA's work remained its education and vocational training services. With the technical assistance of UNESCO, the Agency developed an elementary school network parallel to that of the host governments and provided grants for secondary and higher education. As a result, thousands of youths from refugee families were absorbed locally or found employment further afield in oil-producing countries, such as Kuwait and Saudi Arabia.

"IMPLEMENTING PARAGRAPH 11." By 1959, it was clear that the economic approach, through planned refugee absorption projects, had not solved the problem. The General Assembly launched an effort to reach a political accord limited to the refugee question, taken out of the context of the general Israel-Arab conflict. The Palestine Conciliation Commission, which had abandoned its peace-making efforts by 1951, was now instructed to find ways "to implement paragraph 11" of the 1948 Resolution. In due course, the Commission appointed Joseph E. Johnson, president of the Carnegie Endowment Fund in New York, as its special representative for this purpose. After two years of discussions with the governments concerned, Dr. Johnson submitted a set of proposals based on a "preference" to be indicated by each refugee and referred to the government concerned. A United Nations Rehabilitation and Compensation Fund would be established, and Israel would make an "adequate contribution" to it in lieu of direct compensation. These proposals proved unacceptable to the governments concerned and were shelved. In the General Assembly debates on the annual UNRWA reports, Arab spokesmen developed the thesis that this was not a humanitarian problem concerning displaced persons, but a national problem concerning a displaced people seeking national self-determination. The refugee problem appeared too deeply imbedded in the basic political conflict to be settled as a separate issue.

DE FACTO INTEGRATION. In the course of time, the refugees became in fact economically absorbed to a much greater extent than was revealed in UNRWA statistics or admitted by Arab governments. Such integration was inevitable, since they were living among their own Arab brethren without any barrier of race, religion, language, culture, or way of life between them and their environment. This process was entirely in accordance with the general pattern of the refugee problems caused by wars and upheavals in the contemporary world. Since the end of World War II alone, some 50 million persons were displaced in Europe, Asia, and Africa and were finally absorbed into countries with which they had national, racial, or religious affinities.

In a special report on the refugees submitted in 1959, Secretary-General Dag Hammarskjöld called for intensified investment and development in the Arab countries in order to accelerate what he called the "integration de facto" of the refugees in productive life. He stated that

> The unemployed should be regarded not as a liability, but, more justly, as an asset for the future; it is a reservoir of manpower which in the desirable general economic development will assist in the creation of higher standards for the whole population of the area.

The Secretary-General's views came under political attack from the Arab States, and the report was shelved. The extent to which unplanned absorption was actually taking place, however, was acknowledged in the 1964 annual report of a new commissioner-general of UNRWA. Dr. Michelmore estimated that not more than 40–50% of the registered total were destitute or nearly destitute, about 30–40% were partially self-supporting, and 10–20% securely reestablished. In the same year, Dean Rusk, the U.S. secretary of state, in testifying before the Senate Subcommittee on Refugees, estimated that "there are almost half a million refugees who have registered refugee status but who in fact have jobs – some of them at some distance from the camps, living reasonably normal lives."

In his 1967 report, the commissioner-general stressed the social and economic progress the refugees had made, though he admitted that it had not been possible to reflect the extent of this rehabilitation in UNRWA's published statistics. Even the minority who lived in camps came and went as they pleased and found work in adjacent towns and farming areas. Dr. Michelmore put on record that some of these camps had become thriving villages. The hard core of the refugee problem remained the Gaza Strip, where the refugees outnumbered the local population, and where the economic opportunities were too limited for their full absorption.

THE ABANDONED PROPERTY. The immovable property abandoned in Israel by the refugees was vested in an official custodian. In subsequent years this property, particularly large tracts of agricultural land, became integrated in Israel's economic development and absorbed by its expanding population under appropriate Knesset legislation. This was done without prejudice to the Israel government's offer to pay compensation to the original owners, as part of an agreed settlement of the refugee problem as a whole. In reaffirming this offer at the United Nations, Israel's spokesmen added that any settlement of compensation claims should also take into account Jewish property that had been taken over by Jordan in the 1948 war, as well as a huge amount of property confiscated in Iraq, Egypt, and elsewhere and belonging to Jews from those countries now settled in Israel.

With the cooperation of the Israeli authorities, an office set up by the Palestine Conciliation Commission embarked on the formidable task of compiling an inventory and making an evaluation of all immovable property that had belonged to the Arab refugees. This program took 12 years to complete and the voluminous records that were compiled have remained stored at UN Headquarters in New York, pending a settlement. In the meantime the Israel government released and paid out frozen refugee bank accounts in the sum of $11 million and handed over all the valuables left behind in safe deposit boxes. From 1960 onward, each General Assembly Session was presented with Arab proposals for the appointment of a United Nations custodian to take over the abandoned property and to make available to the refugees revenue from the properties, alleged to total scores of millions of dollars a year. The Arab delegations argued that this revenue would make it unnecessary for the refugees to be maintained on international charity. The Israel reply was that appointing such a custodian would violate sovereignty, that there was no legal basis or precedent for it, that it was beyond the competence of the General Assembly, and that the alleged revenue was nonexistent. The proposals were invariably defeated.

THE ISRAEL-HELD TERRITORIES. As a result of the *Six-Day War (1967), Israel found itself in control of two territories – the West Bank and the Gaza Strip – containing hundreds of thousands of refugees falling under UNRWA's mandate. On June 14, 1967, immediately after the cease-fire, an agreement was signed between the Israel government and UNRWA by which the Agency was invited to continue its operations in these territories with the full cooperation and assistance of the government. In subsequent annual reports, the commissioner-general confirmed that this cooperation was effective. The financial cost of the UNRWA operation to the Israel taxpayer is considerable. In the year ending June 30, 1968, it came to about $3½ million: $2½ million as the Israeli contribution to services for the refugees; $700,000 for port services, transportation, storage, etc.; and a cash contribution of IL 1 million. In addition, the refugees benefited indirectly by the maintenance of public services and economic activity in the territories, the government budget for which amounted to IL140 million per annum.

A joint technical study of the numbers of refugees in these areas was undertaken by Israel and UNRWA officials.

The UNRWA statistics were checked against the results of the census carried out in the territories in September 1967 and the identification cards issued to the inhabitants. The Agency adjusted its figures downward, but they remained somewhat above the levels of the Israel census, which indicated the presence of 207,000 refugees in the Gaza Strip (out of a total population of 360,000), and 105,000 in the West Bank (out of 600,000 plus). The census statistics on housing standards and possession of household goods showed that while the living conditions of the refugees in the camps were not as good as those of the average town population of the areas, they were better than those prevailing in the Arab villages.

THE 1967 DISPLACEMENT. During and after the Six-Day War, there was another large-scale population movement – mainly from the West Bank into East Jordan, and also including over 100,000 from the Golan Heights into Syria. UNRWA reports quoted a Jordanian figure of 400,000 persons alleged to have crossed from the West Bank, including over 100,000 UNRWA registered refugees. According to Israel's estimates, the total was little more than half that figure. A limited number had fled during the 72 hours of hostilities on this front, mainly from the Jericho camps. In addition, the Jordanian lists were presumed to include other groups: local residents left destitute by the war; inhabitants of the eastern side of the Jordan Valley who had moved further inland because of continued border clashes; persons from the West Bank who were already residing in East Jordan before the war; and a steady migration across the bridges that continued for a long period after the cease-fire, for family, income, and other reasons. The policy of the Israeli authorities was neither to encourage nor to prevent their departure.

In the summer of 1967, the Israel government initiated a repatriation scheme with the assistance of the International Red Cross Committee. Under this project 14,000 persons returned from Jordan to their homes in the West Bank and another 7,000 permits were issued but not utilized. After that, a return in small numbers continued under a family reunion scheme. Speaking before the General Assembly on Oct. 8, 1968, Foreign Minister Eban undertook that the processing of applications for the uniting of families would be intensified, and the 7,000 unused permits from the 1967 repatriation project would be made available to other would-be returnees. International concern focused on the plight of the displaced persons in Jordan, particularly some 80,000 of them who were housed in tented camps under winter conditions. The Israeli government was urged to lift restrictions on their return, and in December 1968 the General Assembly adopted a resolution to this effect. The Israel delegation voted against it and maintained that the extent and rapidity with which a return could be facilitated had to be considered in the light of current political and security conditions, which remained disturbed as a result of border warfare and terrorist activity promoted from Jordan.

INCITEMENT IN SCHOOL TEXTBOOKS. For a number of years prior to the Six-Day War, Israeli representatives in the United Nations debates had complained about the fact that textbooks used in the UNRWA/UNESCO schools were indoctrinating the minds of a whole generation of refugee children with hatred, revenge, and incitement to war. After the Six-Day War, the textbooks in the non-refugee government schools now in areas under Israel rule were revised or replaced. As regards the refugee schools, the matter was referred to UNESCO. A three-man committee of experts was appointed to examine the textbooks and found that most of them needed to be revised or replaced. The Syrian government withheld its cooperation, while the Jordanian government rejected the committee's findings on the ground that refugee children were entitled to be taught about their political claims to Palestine. Israel found the expert recommendations generally acceptable.

THE REFUGEE PROBLEM AND PEACE. The resolution unanimously adopted by the Security Council on Nov. 22, 1967, called for the establishment of "a just and lasting peace" between Israel and the neighboring Arab States. As "a just settlement of the refugee problem" was one of the elements in the resolution, it therefore tacitly abandoned the earlier hopes of resolving the problem as a separate issue, and again placed it in the framework of an overall Israel-Arab peace settlement. In his statement to the General Assembly of Oct. 8, 1968, outlining nine principles for peace, the Israel foreign minister proposed that

> A conference of Middle Eastern States should be convened, together with the Governments contributing to refugee relief and the Specialized Agencies of the United Nations, in order to chart a five-year plan for the solution of the refugee problem in the framework of a lasting peace and the integration of refugees into productive life. This conference can be called in advance of peace negotiations.

There was no response to this proposal.

In the later debate on the UNRWA Report, the Israel delegation also proposed that a refugee program should include a Reintegration and Compensation Fund, and reaffirmed the willingness of the Israel government to give substantial financial support to such a Fund. The practical aspects of a solution would take a number of years and very substantial funds, but should not be unduly formidable once the political and psychological roadblocks had been removed. Until there was a peace settlement, the best hope for the refugees lay in stimulating the process of spontaneous economic absorption, especially for the younger persons who had acquired education and skills.

[Michael Comay]

Arab National Movement

THE RISE OF ARAB NATIONALISM. Arab nationalism – as opposed to ethnic self-awareness – did not appear until the end of the 19th century; it was the claim to political rights for the Arabs on the basis of their existence as a separate group that turned mere self-awareness into nationalism in the modern sense. Arab consciousness is of long standing and was based primarily on three factors: the belief in a common descent from Arabian tribes that engulfed the Middle East and North Africa in the seventh century; the existence of literary Arabic; and the special position of the Arabs in Islam. Until the end of the 19th century, however, this consciousness was devoid of all political implications. The religion of Islam provided the source for political organization, government administration, and the legitimacy of rule; the various Muslim empires were the political framework of Islam from the first Caliphate up to the Ottoman Empire.

The wavering of Arab allegiance to the Ottoman Empire may be traced to various sources. The reforms instituted in the empire in the course of the 19th century brought about a substantial change in its traditional Muslim image. The reformist central government sought to impose a Western-style administration and law upon a society that was neither interested in nor ready for modern innovations. The local leaders of Arab provinces reacted vehemently against the secular aspects of the reforms, especially the attempts to place non-Muslims on an equal footing with Muslims. The feeling that Islam was in danger was further heightened by the confrontation with the culture, material progress, and military and economic power of the West. Muslim leaders believed that in order to stand up to the spiritual and military challenge posed by the Christian West, Islam had to regain its pristine strength. Originally, Islam had been Arab in its leadership, predominant culture, and prevailing social and administrative institutions. Thus, the desire to restore its pristine glory resulted in a reassessment of the place of the Arabs in Islam and the conclusion that this aim could be achieved only by reestablishing the Muslim Caliphate in its original form, under the leadership of a descendant of the Prophet's tribe. This conclusion was the origin of the political-religious demand for a change in the status quo prevailing in the Ottoman Empire.

In the course of time, this aim received a tremendous impetus from a variety of other sources. The second and third generation of Ottoman reformers – the Young Turks – sought a new and more forceful ideological basis for the preservation of the tottering empire. The process of Westernization brought them into contact with a concept that appeared to be the key to the success of Western civilization – the concept of nationalism. For a while they vacillated, unable to decide the nature of their nationalism: Pan-Ottoman, pluralist, and liberal, in which all citizens of the empire would participate on the basis of equality and fraternity in a common fatherland – and therefore a nationalism that would be more aptly described as patriotism – or a restricted Turkish nationalism, in which the decisive criterion would be ethnic and linguistic and which would transform the Muslim and supernational Ottoman Empire into a single nation-state, in which the Turks would impose their will, language, and characteristics upon all the other groups. Slowly but surely the Young Turks adopted the second alternative – the liberal, Central-European type of nationalism – and proceeded with efforts to bring about the Turkification of the entire empire. Their aim became noticeable on the eve of World War I and was among the factors responsible for the emergence of a parallel, diametrically opposed, Arab nationalism. Once the Muslim character of the empire was put in question and an attempt made to turn the empire into a Turkish one, it became inevitable that the consciousness of the existence of a separate Arab entity should be transformed into a political attitude (which regarded the Arab entity as the only possible basis upon which a political framework could be established). This cultural and ideological development, however, was confined to educated members of the social elite. The general population continued to regard Islam and the Ottoman Empire as the principal frameworks of its identity. In the years before World War I, only a few hundred activists and political thinkers were converted to the new ideology of Arab nationalism.

PALESTINIAN OPPOSITION TO ZIONISM. Palestine, in the borders defined by the British Mandate, did not yet exist as a separate administrative entity. The Acre and Nablus districts were part of the province (vilayet) of Beirut while the district (sanjak) of Jerusalem, because of its religious and international significance, came under the direct supervision of the Ottoman Ministry of the Interior.

The Arab movement, based primarily upon the awareness of common language and common descent, was by its nature all-embracing and unaffiliated with any particular region of the empire. Nevertheless, there were areas that played a more prominent role in this development. Damascus played a leading part as a seat of Muslim scholarship and the home of Arab families claiming descent from the Prophet, and it became the center of the Arab movement in the prewar years. (The term "Syria" was sometimes used to refer to the vilayet of Damascus, which also included Transjordan, and sometimes to comprise the whole of Palestine, as well as modern Syria and Lebanon.) During World War I, and especially toward the end, Mecca became the center of the movement, due to the desire to defend and strengthen the position of the Hashemite family of Hussein Ibn Ali as the emirs of Mecca. These developments, however, had little impact on Palestine. Only an insignificant number of Palestinian Arabs took part in the movement. It was only toward the end of the war that the attitude of the Arab population in Palestine underwent a change, as a result of the sufferings caused by the war and the intolerable repression carried out by the Turkish government, which saw its very existence hanging in the balance.

Other developments, concerned primarily with Palestine itself, played a greater role. The establishment of the special district of Jerusalem endowed the social elite of that city with a higher status, comparable to that of the capitals of the adjoining provinces of Damascus and Beirut. In general, the rise of the local elite to positions of leadership in society, religion, and administration was a central feature of life in the area in the 19th century. The local leadership group that came into being was a breeding ground for the activists in the movement for Arab awakening; simultaneously, however, a social stratum was created that had regional, economic, and social interests, rather than Pan-Arab aims. The establishment of the special sanjak of Jerusalem – which comprised the southern half of Palestine – also marked the beginning of a process by which Palestine came to be regarded as an entity in its own right. Opposition to Zionism and the British Mandate completed this process and gave it a political character.

As early as the end of the 19th century, the Arab population of Palestine began to pay attention to a new phenomenon: the immigration and settlement of Jews, while some of the veteran Jews were leaving the walled-in quarters in the cities, buying land, building housing estates, and entering new trades and professions. The Arabs also became aware of the new type of Jew that was entering the country, so different from the Jew that the Arabs had known. Instead of remaining secluded in his corner and accepting his inferior status in Muslim-Ottoman society, the new Jew was proud and self-confident. He was also foreign – in language, manners, and mores – and often also alien to the traditional religious atmosphere prevailing among the population. Gradually, both the local Arab leaders and the Ottoman officials came to suspect that the newly arrived Jews had political ambitions and that they had come to the country in order to establish a Jewish state.

It was not surprising, therefore, that from the beginning Jewish settlement met with opposition from both the local Arabs and the Ottoman administration. While at most times this opposition was dormant, there were many instances when it was expressed publicly. The opposition of the local population was direct, taking the form of sporadic attacks, usurpation of lands, and the like; it is doubtful whether this opposition had any political connotations. In 1891, however, nine years after the beginning of the First Aliyah, the first sign of political opposition to Zionism made its appearance. Jerusalem notables – both Muslim and Christian – called upon the Ottoman administration to prohibit the immigration of and the sale of land to Jews. This request was repeated time and again; local spokesmen demanded the enforcement of the restrictions against the entry of the Jews, which had been enacted, but not always observed.

Appeals to the Ottoman administration were not the only form of political opposition. After the 1908 revolution of the Young Turks, the first Arab newspapers made their appearance in Palestine. Some of these supported the Young Turks and others were followers of the liberal opposition (the Entente Liberale Party), but they were all united in their opposition to Zionism. They claimed that Zionism was a danger to the country and called upon both the population and the administration to put an end to it. A similar attitude was also expressed in the first books on the Arab question that began to appear at this time, such as *Le Réveil de la Nation Arabe dans l'Asie Turque* by Negib Azoury (Paris, 1905). Officials of the Ottoman administration who were imbued with the new spirit of nationalism did all they could to put obstacles in the way of Jewish immigration and land purchases. One well-known example was Shukrī al-ʿAsalī, the Kaimakam (subdistrict commissioner) of Nazareth, who in 1910–11 tried to prevent the purchase of the al-Fūla lands (the present Afulah-Merḥaviah area) by Jews. (For Zionist efforts to contact Arab nationalist leaders, see *Zionist Policy.)

THE STRUGGLE AGAINST THE MANDATE. The opposition to Zionism made further advances when the British conquered the country in 1917–18. The severance from the Ottoman Empire was a fact. Beginning in October 1918, a semi-independent Arab regime, under Faisal Ibn Hussein, gradually established itself in Damascus. Palestine, on the other hand, was administered by the British occupation forces. While Syria appeared to have excellent prospects of achieving independence, reports came into Palestine concerning promises made to the Jews by the British (see *Balfour Declaration). The Turkish regime, which was in the process of retreating from Palestine, took care to give these reports wide dissemination, adding exaggerated stories concerning the insolence displayed by Jews in the areas taken over by the British. In November 1918, the British and French governments – partly in order to counteract Turkish propaganda – promised the inhabitants of Syria and Iraq that they would be free to choose their own form of government. This move caused the Arab leaders in Palestine to feel that they were excluded from the promise and would thus be subject to a special regime that would strive for the realization of the Balfour Declaration. At the time, both Jews and Arabs understood the Declaration to have more far-reaching implications than were intended by the British government.

Against this background, the political organization of Palestinian Arabs began to develop. The first political societies were established toward the end of 1918: the Muslim-Christian Society, the Arab Club, and the Literary Club. In January 1919 representatives of these societies met for their first countrywide conference and adopted resolutions defining Palestine as "Southern Syria" and declaring their aim to have Palestine annexed to the Faisal regime in Damascus. The representatives of the Jerusalem leadership, who had the most to gain from an independent or semi-independent, separate Palestinian regime, were not pleased with the results of the conference. Nevertheless, the belief that union with Syria was the best guarantee for the suppression of Zionism prevailed at the conference and it continued to prevail as long as Faisal's star was on the rise. In March 1920, when Faisal was crowned king of all of Syria (including Lebanon and Palestine) and was at the height of his career, enthusiastic demonstrations of support took place in the towns of Palestine; the Nebi Mūsā celebrations in Jerusalem in April 1920 were turned into a manifestation of pro-Faisal feelings and became the occasion for anti-Jewish riots.

In July, however, the Arab Hashemite regime in Syria collapsed under French pressure and the Palestinians were left on their own. Although Syrian exiles tried to continue their struggle for the reestablishment of an all-Syrian kingdom in cooperation with the Palestinian leaders, the latter consistently refused to join them in their work. The Palestinians saw their main interest in the organization of the Arab rank and file for the campaign against Zionism. In December 1920 they convened the "Third" Palestinian Conference (the first conference was held in January 1919; the second had been scheduled to take place in May 1920, but was prohibited by the British military government), at which the Palestine Arab leaders defined their future policy. It was to consist of two basic demands: absolute rejection of Zionism and the establishment of a local government in Palestine, to be elected by the prewar inhabitants of the country. No mention whatsoever was made of union with Syria. In order to realize its aims, the conference elected an executive committee under the chairmanship of Mūsā Kāẓim al-Husseini.

The executive committee based itself upon the Muslim-Christian Societies and found its support among the urban elite of landowners, clergy, merchants, and a few modern intellectuals. As a rule, the committee was dominated by the same elements that had earlier withheld support from the idea of union with Syria. The modus operandi that the committee employed consisted of the formulation of demands, the presentation of protests, and the organization of strikes. It rejected violence and did not lend support to the riots of May 1921, which were organized by the remnants of more extremist organizations that had campaigned for union with Syria in 1919–20 and had received moral and financial support and arms from the Hashemite regime in Damascus. Until the summer of 1922 the committee sought to prevent the confirmation of the Mandate on Palestine by the League of Nations, and until 1923 it persisted in its efforts to have the terms of the Mandate amended. The committee's petitions and the talks held by its delegations in London and Geneva uniformly stressed its opposition to the Zionist connotation of the Mandate, i.e., the promise to help in the establishment of a Jewish National Home in Palestine and the recognition of Hebrew as an official language and of the Zionist Organization as an official body (the Jewish Agency) authorized to advise the Mandatory government on matters pertaining to the establishment of the National Home.

This policy also guided the committee's attitude toward the Zionist movement. The committee refused to recognize Zionism as a legitimate partner in Palestine and would not negotiate with Zionist representatives. During the visit of the first Palestinian Arab delegation in London (August 1921–July 1922), when negotiations with the British government came to a deadlock, the Colonial Office sought to arrange a meeting of the delegation with the leaders of the Zionist Organization. At first, the Arabs refused even to meet with the Zionists, but eventually they agreed to an informal meeting with Chaim Weizmann, which took place in December 1921. The outcome was completely negative, as the Palestinians did not budge from their stand that Zionism had no rights whatsoever in Palestine and persisted in their refusal to negotiate with Zionist representatives. This meeting, however informal, was the only one to take place between Weizmann and the leaders of the Palestine Arab national movement.

The Arab leaders in Palestine also refused to have anything to do with the attempts made in 1922 by Syrian leaders living in Egyptian exile to reach a settlement with the Zionists. The Syrians were prepared to recognize the rights of the Jews to a National Home in Palestine in return for Jewish support of their struggle for independence. Such an agreement, however, would have necessitated a break with Britain, and therefore the Zionist movement was not inclined to accept it. Equally important, however, was the fact that the Palestinian Arab leaders flatly rejected the idea of such an arrangement and refused to accede to the Syrians any right to decide that fate of their country for them, as they had similarly rejected the agreement reached between Faisal and Weizmann three or four years before (see Chaim *Weizmann). Furthermore, the entire affair caused great bitterness against the Syrians and thus reinforced the trend toward Palestinian separatism and abandonment of the concept of all-Syrian Arab unity. For many years, preoccupation solely with the affairs of Palestine became a principle of the Palestine Arab movement and its various organizations.

THE QUESTION OF LOCAL SELF-GOVERNMENT. When they failed in their demands for the abolition of the pro-Jewish provisions of the Mandate, the Palestinian Arabs adopted a policy of noncooperation with the Mandatory government in matters related to the establishment of organs of self-government, as set forth in the Mandate and the Palestine Constitution (1922 Order-in-Council). Toward the end of 1922 and the beginning of 1923, they campaigned against participation in the elections for a legislative council and succeeded in preventing the establishment of this body (which was to have been made up of the high commissioner, ten government officials, and twelve locally elected representatives – eight Muslims, two Christians, and two Jews). In the course of 1922 they also rejected the establishment of a Consultative Council, to be made up of appointed members, and of an "Arab Agency," which was to concern itself with safeguarding the "civil and religious rights" of the non-Jewish population in accordance with the Balfour Declaration and the terms of the Mandate.

At the end of 1923, when the ineffectiveness of this policy became clear, a new force, which advocated more moderate methods, came to the fore. It argued that in order to achieve the expulsion of Zionism from Palestine, the Arabs should cooperate with the Mandatory government and thus attain their goal by influencing government institutions through day-today contact. This group centered around the Mayor of Jerusalem, Rāghib Bey al-Nashāshībī. The Nashāshībī family was involved in a feud with the al-Husseinis (who were in control of the executive committee and the Supreme Muslim Council), and the quarrel between the two families now found its expression in political antagonism. The committee's failure to bring about the abrogation of the pro-Zionist provisions of the Mandate made it possible for Nashāshībī 's supporters (the opposition) to increase their influence and standing. There was a perceptible abatement of anti-Zionist fervor, the committee's work came to a standstill, and in the 1927 municipal elections the opposition scored a decisive victory.

In 1928, after a lapse of five years, the Seventh Palestinian Conference was convened to decide upon a new policy. The resolutions adopted by the conference emphasized the need for a local government, responsible to an elected parliament; opposition to Zionism was mentioned only indirectly by confirming the resolutions passed by previous conferences. A moderate atmosphere prevailed at the conference, the result of the realization that the Arabs had made a mistake in rejecting all the British proposals made in 1923 concerning the establishment of a self-governing body. This line was taken by both the opposition and the executive committee and its supporters. The Seventh Palestinian Conference took place at a time when Zionist settlement had for two years been facing the most severe crisis it had yet undergone. In 1927 more Jews left the country than entered it, and those that did come met with intolerable conditions. Many Palestinian Arabs thought that the Zionist vision was about to evaporate. Accordingly, they thought it preferable to adopt a practical line and not insist on the abrogation of a policy that they thought had in fact failed.

At the beginning of 1929, on the basis of the resolutions adopted by the conference, the executive committee approached the high commissioner with a proposal to establish a "local government." In June of that year, an agreement was reached between the Mandatory government and the leaders of the two factions, Mūsā Kāẓim al-Husseini and Rāghib Bey al-Nashāshībī, on the establishment of an appointed legislative council. The Arabs were now ready to accept an even more moderate form of the arrangement they had rejected in 1923. Other developments, however, foiled the plan. In August 1929 a clash over the *Western Wall was followed by a wave of Arab violence against the Jews, and under the circumstances the British government felt that the time was not ripe for concessions on matters of local administration.

The following year, however, the British government sought to appease the Palestinian Arabs by restricting immigration and the sale of land to Jews (the "Passfield White Paper," October 1930 – see Palestine *White Papers). But when this policy encountered vehement opposition and worldwide protests from Zionist and pro-Zionist circles, the British government, in effect, reversed its policy in a letter from Prime Minister Ramsay MacDonald to Weizmann in February 1931. The government did not give up the idea of finding a way to appease the Arabs, however, and toward the end of 1931, when complete calm had been restored, it again broached the idea of a legislative council. Although the executive committee continued to press for a "local government," it did not appear too difficult to bridge the gap between the British proposal and the Arab demand. Once again, however, the Zionist Movement took issue with the British government and the renewed plan for a legislative assembly was again shelved.

The Zionist Organization declared its unalterable opposition to a local governing body that would give constitutional expression to a minority status for the Jews of Palestine. Its adamant resistance strengthened the hand of those members of the British government who were reluctant to run the risk of establishing a self-governing body in a country in which there were several hostile communities. The plan was not officially revived until the end of 1935, when the representatives of the local population were invited to participate in discussions for its enactment. The reaction of the Arabs was mixed: although they did not totally reject the plan, they did not display any enthusiasm over it, hoping to obtain more by hard bargaining. Jewish opposition was absolute, and all the supporters of Zionism in Britain acted against the proposal. Members of Parliament also had their doubts about its merits and many thought that Palestine, with its host of problems, was not yet ready for self-government. These doubts were strengthened by Zionist resistance, and, when the plan came up for discussion in the House of Commons in February 1936, there was hardly a member who was ready to support it. Thus the plan was finally buried.

The defeat of the plan for a legislative council may have been the spark that set off the "Arab Rebellion" of 1936–39. The roots and motives of the rebellion, however, lie in the early years of British rule.

THE RISE OF HAJJ MUHAMMAD AMIN AL-HUSSEINI. When the British first occupied Palestine, they were faced with a problem that they had to solve immediately, i.e., the organization of Muslim religious life. The severance of Palestine from the Ottoman Empire had left the Muslim community courts and the administration of the *waqf* (religious foundations) without leadership and supervision. These establishments were put under the temporary supervision of the military government, but it was clear that, as a Christian power, the British government would seek to rid itself of this function. At the same time, the British began to enhance the status of the mufti of Jerusalem, Kāmil al-Husseini, appointing him president of the Muslim Court of Appeals. They treated him as the head of the Muslim community of Palestine, although there was no historical or religious basis for this attitude. The result was that when Muslim religious life was organized in the course of 1921, and the Supreme Muslim Council was established (January 1922), the mufti of Jerusalem was elected, as a matter of course, to stand at its head.

In the meantime, however, events had taken a new turn. In March 1921 Kāamil al-Husseini died. He had done all he could to help the British regime, and it had in turn strengthened his position. After his death there were many candidates for the post of mufti of Jerusalem. The al-Husseini family and its supporters closed ranks in support of the candidacy of Hajj Muhammad Amīn al-*Husseini, who lacked the proper religious qualifications, but in the period 1919–20 had come to the fore as a skillful political leader and organizer and was in the forefront of the campaign for union with Hashemite Syria.

He was also one of the instigators of the anti-Jewish riots in Jerusalem of April 1920 and was sentenced *in absentia* to 15 years in jail; in the autumn of that year, however, he was pardoned by the high commissioner, Sir Herbert *Samuel, and returned to Jerusalem.

Now the high commissioner was faced with the demand to appoint him mufti of Jerusalem. Above all, the high commissioner wanted to ensure that the bloody riots that had taken place in Jerusalem would not be repeated during the Nebi Mūsā celebrations in April 1921. He also looked for ways and means to appease the anti-Zionist feelings that prevailed among the Arabs of the country. He came to the conclusion that appointing the leader of the extremist elements to a prestigious religious and public position would assure his proper behavior. Furthermore, Hajj Amīn al-Husseini himself stated in a talk with the high commissioner (as recorded by the chief secretary of the Palestine government) "that the influence of his family and himself would be devoted to maintaining tranquility in Jerusalem, and he felt sure that no disturbances need be feared this year."

Thus in May 1921 Amīn al-Husseini was appointed mufti of Jerusalem and in January of the following year, with the support of the Mandatory government, was elected president of the Supreme Muslim Council. On the whole, peace reigned until 1929. Amīn al-Husseini made good use of this period to reinforce his position and turn the Supreme Muslim Council into a stronghold of his supporters and sympathizers. The council became a government-within-a-government, and the Mandatory authorities did not interfere with the administration of the *waqf* (which yielded a yearly income of £60,000 at the time) and the Sharīʿa courts. Moreover, the Mandatory government favored the strengthening of the Supreme Muslim Council, which thus became – in fact if not in theory – a counterpart to the Zionist Organization and the outstanding representative body of the Palestinian Arabs, thereby creating a measure of balance between the two communities.

From the outset al-Husseini spared no effort to enhance the status of Jerusalem in the eyes of the Muslims. He initiated an impressive project to renovate the city's two principal mosques (Dome of the Rock and al-Aqṣā), after conducting a campaign for contributions throughout the Muslim world. One of the principal themes he used in the campaign was the allegation that the area in which the mosques were situated (known to the Jews as Har ha-Bayit, the Temple Mount, and to the Muslims as al-Ḥaram al-Sharīf) was threatened by the Zionists, who were planning to rebuild the Temple on the site. Amn al-Husseini alleged that the efforts of the Jews to obtain clear and unequivocal rights to pray at the Western ("Wailing") Wall were in fact the beginning of an attempt to take over the entire area. The Muslim authorities pointed to the provision of the Mandate for the safeguarding of the status quo of the Holy Places that existed under the Turkish regime and contended that according to that status the Jews had had no clear rights at the Western Wall. Technically there were grounds for such a contention; in fact, however, the Jews had been praying at the Western Wall both before and during the Turkish regime, although there was no regular synagogue on the spot. The restrictions imposed by the Turks were often circumvented by paying off the local officials.

The constant friction concerning Jewish rights at the Western Wall caused a series of clashes during the 1920s which culminated in the anti-Jewish massacres in *Hebron and *Safed in August 1929. Against this background, the Palestine problem ceased to be an issue of local interest and began to engage the attention of the Muslim world. Amīn al-Husseini encouraged this development and, toward the end of 1931, convened a world conference of Muslims to discuss "the defense of the Holy Places." On the basis of this issue Amīn al-Husseini became the chief spokesman of the Palestinian Arabs. He proved himself the most extreme and consistent foe of the Jews and overshadowed all the other Arab leaders. His rise was facilitated in large measure by the helplessness displayed by the executive committee and its leaders, who were only able to issue anti-Zionist protests, and had even failed in preventing the sale of land to Jews. Furthermore, the same leaders who demanded the passage of a law prohibiting the sale of Arab land to Jews were not averse to making such sales themselves.

Thus, at the beginning of the 1930s, the mufti and his followers began to attack the executive committee and its outdated methods. Under the pressure of these attacks, the committee made a final attempt to organize anti-British riots in October 1933, but retreated in the face of sharp government reaction. The committee members came to realize their impotence, and the death of the chairman, Mūsā Kāẓim al-Husseini, in March 1934 also marked the committee's downfall. Amn al-Husseini rose to leadership with the support of a younger and more extreme generation of activists, who were prepared to solicit aid for their struggle from Arabs outside Palestine and even non-Arab Muslims. They organized scout groups and young Muslim clubs and, from 1934–35 onward, attempted to thwart "illegal" Jewish immigration and the sale of land to Jews. The president of the Supreme Council used the prestige of his office and the power of religious functionaries to intimidate the Arabs who would not comply with his policy.

All his efforts, however, were of no avail. These were the years in which Jewish settlement was expanding at an unprecedented rate. The enlargement of the *Jewish Agency through the adhesion of non-Zionist Jews in 1929 enabled the Zionist Organization to extricate itself from its financial difficulties. The Nazi rise to power in 1933 and the wave of antisemitism that spread through Eastern Europe resulted in a tremendous growth in Jewish immigration. In 1935, no fewer than 61,500 Jews entered Palestine legally. Palestinian Arabs calculated that if this rate continued, it would take the Jews only 12 years to achieve a majority in the country.

The militant Muslim youth, who saw in Hajj Amīn al-Husseini their leader and savior, felt that Jewish immigration and settlement had to be prevented by the use of force. The first group of fighters had been organized as early as 1931 under the leadership of a Haifa Muslim cleric, Sheikh ʿIzz al-Dīn al-Qāsim. The failure of the plan for a legislative council at the beginning of 1936 served the Palestinian Arabs as a sign that they would not achieve their aim with the help of Britain and that the only choice left to them was to take the law into their hands.

ARMED STRUGGLE AND ITS OUTCOME. The first stage of the "Arab Revolt" was a six-month strike, which began in April 1936. Although there were Arab attacks upon Jews and British soldiers and installations during this period, the emphasis was on the general strike and political action by the leaders. The strike ended in October in response to an appeal by the Arab kings, which was welcomed both by the British (who had in fact inspired the appeal) and by the Palestinian Arabs (who had by now tired of the strike). The appeal marked the first intervention in Palestinian affairs by non-Palestinian Arabs – a development that was destined to become a central feature of the entire problem. The end of the strike was followed by the appointment of the Peel Commission, which eventually recommended the partition of the country (see *Palestine, Partition Plans). The plan was turned down by the Arabs; the Jews did not receive it with great enthusiasm; and in the end it was cancelled by the British, upon the recommendation of the Woodhead Commission.

After the publication of the Peel Commission's proposals, the Palestinian Arabs renewed their struggle, terrorism becoming its principal expression. The terror campaign had several aspects: it was directed against the Jews, against the British, and, internally, against Arabs – opponents of the mufti, who were not prepared to offer blind obedience to his leadership and his methods. In 1937 there were even contacts between some Palestinian Arab and Jewish leaders in an attempt to arrive at a political solution to the problem. The first such contacts were made in 1934 on the initiative of David Ben-Gurion, then a member of the Zionist Executive and from 1935 its chairman. No results were achieved and no way found to remove the main stumbling block – the issue of unrestricted Jewish immigration. Although some Arab leaders were prepared to agree to limited immigration, which would raise the proportion of Jews among the population to a maximum of 40%, the Jewish Agency was adamant in refusing to accept minority status for the Jews. In return for the uninterrupted flow of Jews into the country, the Jewish leaders were ready to have Palestine join a Pan-Arab confederation or even federation; for the majority of the Palestinian Arab leaders, however, Arab unity was not an end in itself but only a means in their struggle against Zionism, and the Jewish Agency's readiness to join a wider Arab framework made no impression on them. Significantly, the only Palestinian Arab leader who was at least prepared to discuss such a proposal was ʿAwnī ʿAbd al-Hādī, of the Istiqlāl Party, who advocated Arab unity for its own sake.

Militarily, the "revolt" of 1936–39 ended in defeat, but it brought the Palestinian Arabs a political reward – the 1939 White Paper (see Palestine, *White Papers) – which was in effect an abrogation of the policy formulated in the Balfour Declaration. Ostensibly, Britain had reached the conclusion that the Jewish National Home had become a reality and that by enabling some 450,000 Jews to establish a social, cultural, and political framework in Palestine under conditions of semi-autonomy, the British government had fulfilled its obligation under the Balfour Declaration. This change in policy was rooted in the realization that war with Nazi Germany had become unavoidable and that it was therefore necessary for Britain to secure friendship, or at least a passive attitude, from the Arabs. No concessions had to be made to the Jews, whose support in the struggle with the Nazis was not in the slightest doubt.

Although preparations for World War II brought forth the White Paper policy, the war itself and its tragic consequences for the Jews deprived this policy of the foundations upon which it had rested. Many Palestinian Arab leaders supported the Nazis, and Amn al-Husseini and his associates spent the war years in Berlin and Rome taking part in the Nazi war effort and trying to induce the Muslim population in the occupied territories (Bosnia and the Crimean Peninsula) to collaborate with the Germans. The situation of the Jews was quite different. The war affected them more severely than any other people, and they contributed their utmost to the Allied victory. In these circumstances, the attempts of the British Labor movement to follow, in one way or another, the policy laid down in the White Paper, faced strong opposition from public opinion in the Allied countries. At the same time, the Palestinian Arabs were in great difficulty. Although the "Arab Revolt" had earned them the White Paper, their terror campaign had brought internal dissension to an unprecedented pitch. It took the intervention of the Arab League to establish the Higher Arab Committee in 1945 as the representative body of Palestinian Arabs, and the League even had to appoint its members. Moreover, Palestinian Arab leadership bore the stigma of collaboration with the Nazis, and in the United Nations (which was founded by the anti-Axis nations and in 1947 became the arena for the political struggle for Palestine) the representatives of a people that had fought against the Nazis and had been their principal victim had a tremendous moral and political advantage over Nazi collaborators.

Against this background, the independent Arab governments and the Arab League gradually assumed the task of representing the Palestinian Arabs, while the Arab Higher Committee played a purely negative role, opposing every compromise offered by Britain in 1946 and preventing the Arab League from accepting any solution that did not recognize Palestine as a purely Arab country in which the Jews had no political rights whatsoever. Even individual civil rights, according to the Arab Higher Committee, were to be given only to those Jews who had settled in the country before World War I.

Although the Arab Higher Committee realized that its radical goals could be achieved only by the force of arms, its preparations for the eventuality of war were highly inadequate. No countrywide military organization was established among the Palestinian Arabs, the standard of combat training was low, and it appeared that the committee was relying on volunteers from the neighboring countries and the regular Arab armies. On Nov. 29, 1947, when the UN General Assembly voted to partition Palestine into an Arab state and a Jewish state, the Arab Higher Committee announced its resistance to the resolution and its determination to prevent its implementation by force, but its capacity to carry out the threat was severely limited. Until May 15, 1948, when the regular Arab armies invaded Palestine, the *yishuv* succeeded in defending its territory and even in occupying several important Arab towns and rural centers. The invading irregular Arab troops did not succeed in changing the situation.

The Palestinian Arabs from 1948

The military intervention by the Arab states, the establishment of the State of Israel, the Egyptian occupation of the Gaza Strip, and the annexation of Samaria, East Jerusalem, and the Hebron area by Jordan all had a far-reaching effect upon the subsequent history of the Arab National Movement in Palestine. Palestinian Arabs no longer existed as a political entity. Those who remained in Israel became Israel citizens; those who were under Jordanian rule were given Jordanian nationality; and only in the Gaza Strip was there an insignificant remnant of Palestinian Arab political existence. In addition, hundreds of thousands of the Palestinian Arabs had become refugees, and as a result many of their social institutions were destroyed: villages were uprooted and families torn apart, regional institutions ceased to exist, and it seemed as though the voice of the Palestinian Arab had been silenced.

It took the Arabs who had remained in Israel several years to recover from the shock of defeat. Many believed that the newly established Jewish state was a passing episode and passively waited for the neighboring Arab states to restore the status quo ante. When the Israel Arabs realized that the State of Israel was a permanent feature in the Middle East, two groups developed among them: one accepted the existence of Israel and tried to find a way of leading a peaceful life in the democratic framework of the country, while the other refused to accept the Jewish state and joined anti-Zionist groups to lead a political struggle for equal rights and the return of all Arab refugees and abandoned Arab property. The first group cooperated with the government in their daily lives, devoted themselves to their economic advancement (in which they enjoyed government assistance), and cast their votes in municipal and Knesset elections for lists linked with Mapai, the largest Jewish party. The second group expressed its attitude mainly by supporting the Communist Party or, at times, purely Arab nationalist organizations. Most of the Arab population, however, vacillated between the two trends, and the fact that many Arabs supported Mapam – a leftist, though Zionist, party – was a characteristic expression of the prevailing condition.

In the Gaza Strip, the refugees preserved their Palestinian identity but had no leadership of their own. The difficult conditions in which they lived under Egyptian rule – hundreds of thousands of refugees crowded into a small area and practically not allowed to leave – precluded their social and economic integration and added to their implacable hatred of the Jews and of Israel.

In Jordan, on the other hand, there was a more complex development. A considerable part of the Palestinian population was unhappy about their incorporation as the "West Bank" of the Jordan Kingdom. The supporters of Amīn al-Husseini and many of the young people who had been influenced by the extreme nationalistic ideology of the revolutionary Baʿth Party and the Arab Nationalist organization were in violent opposition to the annexation and it was years before they came to accept it. Until the late 1950s, Jordanian rule on the West Bank was based upon the rivals of al-Husseini, i.e., the supporters of Rahib Bey al-Nashāshībī. In the 1960s, however, the situation changed, largely as the result of the economic advance in Jordan during this period. The cultivation of new lands, the beginnings of industrial development, the increase in trade, and the expansion of education, and other services all required skilled manpower, which the Palestinians were able to supply. Many left for the East Bank, where most of the development was taking place, in order to benefit from the favorable economic conditions there. They were successful in business and assumed important positions in the administration of the country. In fact, from the social and economic aspect, it was Jordan that was being "Palestinianized," rather than the opposite.

The refugees were also affected by this process. Many of them left the refugee camps, found a livelihood in new branches of a budding economy, and in fact were no longer refugees. This process was further accelerated by the growth of an "Arab America" along the Persian Gulf and in Saudi Arabia. Tens of thousands of Palestinians were employed in these areas and were able to make their families independent of the UNRWA rations. Various observers have estimated that on the eve of the Six-Day War at least half of the refugees in Jordan had, from a practical point of view, ceased to be refugees. Nevertheless, this development did not result in a mitigation of the Israel-Arab conflict. The Arab states, which were at all times at odds with one another, exploited the refugees' plight for political ends and tried to outdo one another in adopting extremist stands. Arab solidarity induced them to sustain the urgency of the "Palestine problem," but, with the exception of Jordan, they did nothing to improve the refugees' sorry lot.

At the beginning of the 1960s, when Egyptian-Iraqi tension was particularly acute, the idea of a "Palestine Entity" was again raised, with Egypt and Iraq vying with each other for the sponsorship of the plan and both using it in their attacks upon Jordan. As a result of various inter-Arab developments, the first Arab summit conference, held in January 1964, passed a resolution calling for the unification of Arab efforts on behalf of Arab Palestine. The groundwork was also laid for a Palestine Conference, which was held in May 1964 on the Mount of Olives in Jerusalem and established the Palestine Liberation Organization, with Ahmad Shukeiry as its head. The effectiveness of the organization was limited, for it had come into existence as a result of inter-Arab political maneuvers, each Arab state having its own interpretation of the organization's meaning and purpose. Its leaders were appointed by the Arab League, and the participation of Palestinians in its activities was limited.

Eventually of greater importance for the renewal of the idea of a "Palestine Entity" after the 1967 war was the al-Fataḥ organization, which originally came into being in 1965, largely as the result of inter-Arab quarrels. The revolutionary Baʿth regime in Syria, established in 1963, sought to appear as the outstanding champion of the Palestinian cause and the most extreme in its hatred of Israel. It had not taken part in the establishment of the Palestine Liberation Organization and regarded al-Fataḥ as an excellent weapon to use in its attacks upon the other Arab States. Al-Fataḥ developed the ideology of a "people's war" that would bring about the destruction of Israel, and the Baʿth regime was eager to lend it support and assistance. The increasing terrorist activities from Syrian territory, carried out by al-Fataḥ, created ever-growing tension which finally led the Arab states into a new war against Israel in June 1967, but the outcome of the war was a bitter disappointment to those who had been its prime instigators.

Al-Fataḥ appeared, therefore, as a new version of a Palestinian Arab body, no longer willing to accept Pan-Arab custodianship of Palestinian Arab affairs. This was borne out by the events after June 1967. While in the past Palestine Arab terror organizations had served only as a tool in the hands of Arab rulers, they were now largely independent bodies that from time to time were even able to exert pressure upon Arab governments, particularly in Jordan and Lebanon. Although the terrorist organizations continued to receive financial aid and arms from Arab States (Saudi Arabia, Kuwait, Egypt, and Syria), their leadership was largely independent. Their members were Palestinians first and their Pan-Arab ideology receded. In light of this revival of Palestinian Arab Nationalism, the theory so widely accepted in the 1960s that Pan-Arab ideology had won out over particularist trends lost much of its validity.

The Arab National Movement in Palestine began as a force opposed to Zionism. When it failed in its efforts to stem the realization of the Zionist aim, it turned to the Arab states and to the Muslim world for help. Various developments during the 1940s resulted in the almost complete removal of an independent Palestinian Arab element from the political arena. Yet almost 20 years later, it appeared that the shock and paralysis that the Palestinian Arabs had suffered as a result of their defeat in 1948 was wearing off, and Palestinian Arabs were reappearing upon the political scene. This development was enhanced by the disappointing failure of the Egyptian-Syrian union (in 1961), by the outcome of the Algerian war, and also by the trend of successful "people's wars" and guerrilla tactics in other parts of the world. However, the revitalized Palestinian Arab nationalism, even after adopting a leftist style, remained characterized by unmitigated hostility to Israel, absolute refusal to accept its existence and recognize the right of the Jews to a state of their own, and hatred of Jews, which was virtually indistinguishable from antisemitism.

SINCE THE SIX-DAY WAR. The Six-Day War was a decisive turning point for the Palestine national movement. On the one hand, the Palestinian nationalists' hopes of drawing the Arab states into all-out war with Israel were realized, but on the other, the war resulted in a resounding victory for Israel. The strategy of the al-Fataḥ had been based on the theory that an independent "popular war" would provoke or even compel Israel to initiate retaliatory and preventive action and this, in turn, would lead to a new war, in which the growing power of the regular Arab armies would achieve victory.

As a result of the Six-Day War, however, not only was "Palestine" not "liberated," but Israel now occupied the entire area usually defined as Palestine. The Gaza Strip and the West Bank, which had been under Arab control until June 1967, now came under Israeli rule. About 1,000,000 additional Palestinian Arabs came under Israel's military administration, bringing the total under Israeli rule, together with the Arabs living in Israel since the establishment of the State, to about 1,400,000. This situation had important new aspects, which the Palestinian guerrilla organizations, under the leadership of Yasser Arafat, tried to exploit to their advantage. In the political arena, the Israeli occupation of the whole of Ereẓ Israel reopened the debate about the rights of Jews and Arabs in Ereẓ Israel. The existence of close to one-and-a-half million Palestinian Arabs under Israel authority reawakened a question that had been all but dormant since 1948: the political definition of the Palestinian Arabs. As a result of Israel's conquest, which united the Arabs of the Gaza Strip, the West Bank, and Israel under one government, it was possible, for the first time since 1948, to relate to the Palestinians as a single political body.

After the traumatic shock had passed, the first question marks about the continuation of the struggle began to appear. On June 23, 1967, the central committee of al-Fataḥ met in Damascus and discussed the continuation of the struggle. One opinion called for concentration, in the meantime, on preparations and the building of an underground resistance movement in the territories occupied by Israel. Arafat and his supporters were in favor of the immediate transfer of the activities of the organization from Syria and Jordan to the occupied territories in order to start a "popular liberation war" as soon as possible, in the belief that this time the war would succeed, as it would be based upon much greater popular support then in the past. Arafat's view prevailed, and the leaders began to implement their mission immediately. Hundreds of guerillas, under Arafat's leadership, began to penetrate the occupied territories and set up networks (based upon cells), disseminate propaganda, and carry out the first acts of sabotage.

These efforts ended in failure, however, as the Israel authorities succeeded – through a combination of liberal treatment of the local population and efficient security intelligence – in dislocating the networks and exposing the majority of their members, thus forcing the handful of guerrillas that were not caught (including Arafat) to fall back to the East Bank.

Henceforth, al-Fataḥ gradually adopted a new form of fighting. Its forces concentrated close to the cease-fire lines on the Arab side, along the eastern Jordan Valley and the Lebanese border, whence they fired upon Israel border settlements and sometimes attempted to cross over to lay mines and attack Israel Defense Force (IDF) patrols or passing civilian traffic. Counteraction by the IDF, however, forced the guerillas to withdraw from the Jordan Valley into the interior of Jordan, as they could not withstand IDF raids and the Israel air force attacks. The Hashemite government in Jordan was less than enthusiastic over this development, but it did not do much to prevent it, for fear of being branded as a traitor to the Palestinian cause. Thus al-Fataḥ succeeded in establishing itself deep in the Kingdom of Jordan, with refugee camps as natural bases for its activities.

Although these developments did not lead to military victories for al-Fataḥ, it achieved important successes in the political and propaganda spheres. To the world at large it often succeeded in presenting its efforts as a war of national liberation against a foreign, colonialist conqueror. Within the Arab world, al-Fataḥ became the most outstanding Palestinian organization, overshadowing, and finally gaining control over, the Palestine Liberation Organization. The dubious personality of Aḥmad Shukeiri, head of the PLO, was exposed during the Six-Day War by his flight from Jerusalem and his stand after the war contradicting ideas he had voiced a few days before it. Although he tried to return to the arena of the struggle, Shukeiri could not be trusted, and toward the end of 1967 he was forced to resign as the head of the PLO, Yaḥya Ḥammuda, a lawyer from Ramallah, taking his place. Ḥammuda attempted to make the PLO into a roof organization for all the guerrilla organizations and even established the "Popular Liberation Forces" as the guerrilla arm of the PLO. Al-Fataḥ, however, was willing to join the roof organization only as its decisive power. It agreed to participate in the Palestinian National Conference that convened in Cairo in May 1968, where it won a representation of 38 members (out of 100) on the Palestinian National Council elected at the conference. Even this situation, however, did not satisfy al-Fataḥ, which aspired to a more powerful position. At the following meeting of the council in February 1969, al-Fataḥ and its supporters achieved a majority, Arafat being elected chairman of the organization in place of Ḥammuda.

The council meeting in May 1968 also drafted a Palestinian National Covenant to serve as an ideological basis for the struggle against Israel. The document declared that the Palestinians will struggle for the liberation of all of Palestine, according to the borders in effect during the British Mandate and that the country belongs to the Palestinians alone (Article 6). It stated that "Jews who were living permanently in Palestine until the beginning of the Zionist invasion will be considered Palestinians." In another article, the "Zionist invasion" was said to have started in 1917. Only those Jews who lived in the country before 1917 would, therefore, be considered Palestinians and would be permitted to live in "liberated Palestine."

At the same time, the Palestinian organizations tried to present their struggle as a progressive, humane, and anti-imperialist one. It was difficult to reconcile this attempt with the general spirit of the National Covenant. Shortly after the meeting of the council, therefore, the organizations began to disseminate the idea that the Palestinians were fighting for the establishment of a "democratic and multi-racial Palestine," which would have room for the Jews living in Israel. It was impossible, however, to reconcile this slogan with the terms of the covenant. Some members of the Palestinian organizations attempted to reopen the question at later meetings of the council, but the majority refused to return to it and continued to maintain both aspects of the paradox – the "progressive" slogan and anti-Jewish article – simultaneously. There is also a contradiction between the slogan and Article 1 of the convention, which states that "Palestine is… [an] integral part of the Great Arab Homeland and the People of Palestine are part of the Arab Nation." If the guerrilla organizations took the slogan of a "democratic and multi-ethnic Palestine" seriously, they would have had to take into consideration the fact that today the number of Jews in "Palestine" is greater than the number of Arabs; and if every Jew in Israel were to become a citizen of a "democratic and multi-racial Palestine," it would be difficult to see how the people of such a state could be part of the "Arab Nation."

These contradictions are the expression of the general confusion among the Arabs over their national identity. Should they formulate their political frameworks on the basis of the borders established after World War I? Or perhaps the wider area in which the Arab-speaking peoples live is a more proper framework? Can a common written language bridge the economic, social, and dialectical differences that exist within the great expanse called the Arab world? This search for identity is not confined to the Palestinians alone, but is one of the basic phenomena of Arab life.

The attitude toward this key question contributed substantially to the division among the Palestinians. On the side of al-Fataḥ were the organizations politically connected with the Baʿth Party and unquestionably loyal to the aim of Arab unity. But the split within the Baʿth Party itself brought about the establishment of a number of organizations: The Arab Liberation Front, affiliated with the Iraqi Baʿth Party; the Pioneers of the Popular War of Liberation, called al-Saʿeka and affiliated with the Syrian Baʿth Party; and smaller organizations established by people who were affiliated with the Baʿth but preferred to remain independent. An interesting development took place in the "Arab Nationalist Movement" (al-Kawmiwoun al-Arab). This organization was established during the early 1950s by two Palestinian physicians, George Habash and Wadʿa Haddad (both Greek-Orthodox Christians) in order to work toward Arab unity and thus revenge the defeat of 1948 (their motto was "Unity, Freedom, and Revenge!"). They gradually began to look upon *Nasser as the personality who would realize their goal, and when he turned to the left they followed him. In the 1960s, however, they began to become more leftist than Nasser and despair of the hope that Arab unity would bring about the destruction of Israel. In 1966 the organization decided to adopt the policy of a "popular war" to liberate Palestine without waiting for the realization of Arab unity.

Immediately after the defeat in June 1967, the heads of al-Kawmiwoun al-Arab amalgamated with the Popular Front for the Liberation of Palestine (PFLP), which began to advance a Marxist-Leninist ideology and a strategy of exhibitionist terrorism against Israel (sky hijackings, etc.). Because of its leftist position, the PFLP avoided participation in the Palestinian National Council. In contrast to al-Fataḥ, the PFLP also claimed to operate against "reactionary" elements in all the Arab states and was not content with the struggle against Israel alone.

Within the PFLP, an extreme left-wing branch developed and progressively began to emphasize the notion of a comprehensive social revolution. This branch, under the direction of Nayef Hawatmeh, began a struggle for the control of the Front, and in February 1969 broke away from it to create the Democratic Popular Front for the Liberation of Palestine. It accused the leader of the PFLP of fascism, chauvinistic nationalism, and betrayal of Marxism-Leninism. In its founding platform the DPFLP stated that the solution to the Palestinian problem was "a popular democratic Palestinian state in which all citizens will enjoy full religious and cultural rights and constitutional and social equality." This was the first Arab publication in which the Jews of Israel were not considered as only a religious community, but also as a collective body with its own culture. A year later Hawatmeh raised the possibility that the solution to the Palestinian question could be found through the establishment of a federation, on the lines, perhaps, of Czechoslovakia and Yugoslavia, containing a Palestinian Arab component and an Israeli one, with the stipulation that the Israeli element must liberate itself from the Zionist ideology. This ideological development was restricted to the DPFLP, whose influence was minimal. The other organizations, despite the divisions between them, were united in their denial of national and cultural rights, as distinguished from religious rights, to the Jews of Israel.

The establishment of the Palestinian guerrilla organizations in Jordan brought to the fore the question of their relationship to the Hashemite government. In contrast to the PFLP, al-Fataḥ preferred not to interfere in Jordan's internal affairs. It wanted to concentrate its energies against Israel, with Jordan, as a pro-Western state, providing it with immunity against fierce Israel counterattacks. It was difficult to implement this approach, however. As a result of the growth in the numerical strength of al-Fataḥ, the refugee camps and many areas in Jordan were, in effect, removed from the scope of Jordanian rule. From time to time clashes took place between armed Jordanian forces and members of the guerrilla organizations. It appeared that al-Fataḥ was gradually gaining ascendency over the Jordanian government and was turning the kingdom into a large anti-Israel base, without wishing to control the country's internal affairs. Though the Hashemite authorities tried to avoid clashes with the Palestinian organizations, a bitter clash took place between them and the Jordanian army in June 1970. At that time King Hussein restrained his forces and gave in to the organizations on every point connected with their position in Jordan, but in September 1970 there were fierce battles in which the guerrilla organizations were dealt a severe blow. The hijacking of American passenger planes to Zarqā, and the guerrilla control of Irbid, the second-largest city in the country, was viewed by the king and his army as a grave threat to their rule and position. The confrontation proved again that the military strength of the guerrilla organizations had been exaggerated and deflated the popularly held image of the Palestinian "revolutionary" movement.

This defeat at the hands of the Arab "reactionaries," added to the failure of terrorist tactics to force Israel to withdraw from territories occupied during the Six-Day War, exposed the weakness of the Palestinian national movement. In one unexpected area, however, it had some success. If it had seemed, up until 1967, that the Arabs of Israel were reconciled to their problematic position as citizens of the State of Israel, the appearance of a Palestinian factor, since 1967, led to the emergence of small guerrilla groups affiliated with Palestinian organizations among the Arabs of Israel. Israeli Arabs found themselves faced with a multiple dilemma: not only were they torn between two types of identity – pan-Arab and Palestinian – but they also had to reconcile that identity with the obligations involved in Israeli citizenship.

For subsequent developments, see *Palestine Liberation Organization.

[Yehoshua Porath]

BIBLIOGRAPHY: THE LAND OF ISRAEL IN INTERNATIONAL AFFAIRS. E.L. Woodward and R. Butler, *Documents on British Foreign Policy, First Series*, 4 (1952), 241–634; W.W. Gottlieb, *Studies in Secret Diplomacy During the First World War* (1957); E. Kedourie, *England and the Middle East: the Destruction of the Ottoman Empire, 1914–1921* (1956), index; *Agreement between H.M. Government and the French Government Respecting the Boundary Line Between Syria and Palestine…* (1923); H.F. Frischwasser-Ra'anan, *Frontiers of a Nation* (1955); J. Nevakivi, *Britain, France and the Middle East* (1969), index s.v. *Palestine*; D. Barzilai, in: *Zion*, 33 (1968), 3–4. BOUNDARIES. H.F. Frischwasser-Ra'anan, *Frontiers of a Nation* (1955); E.L. Woodward and R. Butler, *Documents on British Foreign Policy*, First series, 4 (1952), 241–634, 1275–8; *Agreement between His Majesty's Government and the French Government Respecting the Boundary Line between Syria and Palestine* (1923); M. Brawer, *Gevul ha-Ẓafon shel Ereẓ Yisrael u-Farashat Kevi'ato bi-Tekufat ha-Mandat* (1969); Y. Karmon, *Kavvei Hafsakat ha-Esh shel Yisrael* (1968). 1880–1948. J.C. Hurewitz, *The Struggle for Palestine* (1950); Esco Foundation for Palestine, *Palestine, A Study of Jewish and British Policies*, 2 vols. (1947); Royal Institute of International Affairs, *Great Britain and Palestine 1915–1945*

(1946[3]); C. Sykes, *Cross Roads to Israel* (1965); *Palestine Royal Commission Report* (1937); Palestine Government, *A Survey of Palestine* 2 vols. (1946) and Supplement (1947); F.F. Andrews, *The Holy Land Under Mandate*, 2 vols. (1931); J. Marlowe, *Rebellion in Palestine* (1946); idem, *The Seat of Pilate* (1959); Joseph, *British Rule in Palestine* (1948); H.L. Samuel, *Memoirs* (1955); N. Bentwich, *Palestine* (Eng., 1946), incl. bibl.; idem, *Mandate Memoirs 1918–1948* (1965); F.H. Kisch, *Palestine Diary* (1938); R. Meinerzhagen, *Middle East Diary 1917–1956* (1959); R. Storrs, *Orientations* (1937); [King] Abdullah, *Memoirs* (1950); G. Antonius, *The Arab Awakening* (1938); M.E. Abcarius, *Palestine Through the Fog of Propaganda* (1946); M. Assaf, *Toledot Hitorerut ha-Aravim be-Ereẓ Yisrael u-Veriḥatam* (1967); A. Cohen, *Israel and the Arab World* (1970); N. Lorch, *The Edge of the Sword* (1961; repr. 1991); Dinur, Haganah; E. O'Ballance, *The Arab Israeli War 1948* (1956); J. Kimche, *Seven Fallen Pillars* (1953); R.D. Wilson, *Cordon and Search* (1949); D. Ben-Gurion, *Medinat Yisrael ha-Meḥuddeshet*, 2 vols. (1969); Y. Bauer, *From Diplomacy to Resistance: A History of Jewish Palestine 1939–1945* (1973); Michael J. Cohen, *The Origin and Evolution of the Arab-Zionist Conflict* (1987); Yosef Gorny, *Zionism and the Arabs 1882–1948* (1987); B. Wasserstein, *The British in Palestine* (1978); Y. Porath, *The Emergence of the Palestinian – Arab National Movement 1918–1929* (1974). THE STATE OF ISRAEL: 1948–2005. *Government Year Book* (1950–); Israel Central Bureau of Statistics, *Statistical Abstract of Israel* (1949–); D. Ben-Gurion, *Medinat Israel ha-Meḥuddeshet*, 2 vols. (1969); idem, *Israel, Years of Challenge* (1964); J. Dunner, *The Republic of Israel* (1950); G. de Gaury, *The New State of Israel* (1952); N. Bentwich, *Israel Resurgent* (1960); D.R. Elston, *Israel – the Making of a Nation* (1963); idem, *No Alternative, Israel Observed* (1960); T. Prittie, *Israel: Miracle in the Desert* (1967); M. Louvish, *The Challenge of Israel* (1968); W.Z. Laqueur, *The Road to Jerusalem, the Origins of the Arab-Israeli Conflict 1967* (1968); idem, *The Israel-Arab Reader, A Documentary History* (1969, 1970); N. Safran, *From War to War – The Arab-Israeli Confrontation 1948–1967* (1969); idem, *The United States and Israel* (1963), incl. bibl.; J. Kimche, *Both Sides of the Hill* (1960); J. Kimche, D. Bawly, *The Sandstorm, the Arab-Israeli War of 1967* (1968); B. Rivlin, J.S. Szyliowicz (eds.), *The Contemporary Middle East* (1965), 257–545; E. Nussbaum, *Israel* (Eng., 1968); M. Samuel, *Light on Israel* (1968); H.M. Kallen, *Utopians at Bay* (1958); W.R. Polk, D.M. Stamler, E. Asfour, *Backdrop to Tragedy, The Struggle for Palestine* (1957); Y. Freudenheim, *Government in Israel* (1967); O. Kraine; *Government and Politics in Israel* (1961), incl. bibl.; J. Badi (ed.), *Fundamental Laws of the State of Israel* (1961); idem, *The Government of the State of Israel* (1963); A. Zidon, *Knesset, The Parliament of Israel* (1967); M. Louvish (ed.), *Facts About Israel* (1971), incl. bibl.; idem, *The Challenge of Israel* with bibl.; D. Willner, *Nation-Building and Community in Israel* (1969). **ADD. BIBLIOGRAPHY:** G. Wigoder (ed.), *The New Encyclopedia of Zionism and Israel* (1994); N. Lucas, *The Modern History of Israel* (1974); H.M. Sachar, *A History of Israel From the Rise of Zionism to Our Times* (1976); Vol. 2, *From the Aftermath of the Yom Kippur War* (1987); J. Talmon, *Israel Among the Nations* (1982); S. Hattis Rolef (ed), *Political Dictionary of the State of Israel* (1993[2]); A. Sela, *Continuum Political Encyclopedia of the Middle East* (2002[2]); M. Avi-Yonah, *History of Israel and the Holy Land* (2001[2]); M. Gilbert, *History of Israel* (1998); A. Diskin, *The Last Days in Israel: Understanding the New Israeli Democracy* (2003). **WEBSITES:** www.mfa.gov.il; www.knesset.gov.il. FOREIGN POLICY AND INTERNATIONAL RELATIONS. W. Eytan, *The First Ten Years, A Diplomatic History of Israel* (1958); A. Eban, *Voice of Israel* (1957); E.B. Glick, *Latin America and the Palestine Problem* (1958); E. Stock, *Israel on the Road to Sinai 1949–56* (1967); N. Safran, *The United States and Israel* (1963); M. Sharett, *Israel in a World of Transition* (1958); idem, *Be-Sha'ar ha-Ummot* (1956); W. Laqueur, *The Struggle for the Middle East* (1969); M.E. Kreinin, *Israel and Africa; A Study in Technical Cooperation* (1964); L. Laufer, *Israel and the Developing Countries* (1967) includes bibliography; H.S. Aynor, *Notes from Africa* (1969); R. Weitz, *Rural Planning in Developing Countries* (1965); M.J.J. Frank, *Cooperative Land Settlements in Israel and Their Relevance to African Countries* (1968); W. Frankel, *Israel Observed: An Anatomy of the State* (1981); C.C. OBrien, *The Siege* (1986). ARAB REFUGEES. D. Kaplan, *Arab Refugees: An Abnormal Problem* (1959); see also the Annual Reports of the Commissioner-General of UNRWA to the General Assembly, the Progress Reports of the Conciliation Commission for Palestine, the Special Reports submitted by Secretary-General Trygve Lie in 1949 and by Secretary-General Dag Hammarskjold in 1959, and the records of the annual General Assembly debates on the UNRWA reports. ARAB NATIONAL MOVEMENT. N. Mandel, *Turks, Arabs and Jewish Immigration into Palestine, 1882–1914* (1965); P. Graves, *The Land of Three Faiths* (1922); J. Marlow, *The Seat of Pilate* (1959); N. Barbour, *Nisi Dominus* (Eng., 1946); B. Erskine, *Palestine of the Arabs* (1935); J.C. Hurewitz, *Struggle for Palestine* (1950); G. Antonius, *The Arab Awakening* (1938, 1965); Y. Harkabi, *Fedayeen Action and Arab Strategy* (1968); A. Cohen, *Israel and the Arab World* (1970); M. Assaf, *Toledot Hitorerut ha-Aravim be-Ereẓ Yisrael u-Veriḥatam* (1967); E. Elath, *Haj Mohammed Amin El-Husseini* (Heb., 1968); Y. Shimoni, *Arviyyei Ereẓ Yisrael* (1947); Ben-Gurion, *Pegishot im Manhigim Arviyyim* (1967).

POPULATION

THE JEWISH POPULATION

Growth by Aliyah

In 1882 the Jewish population of Ereẓ Israel numbered some 24,000, roughly 5% of the total, and about 0.3% of the world Jewish population. Since then there has been an almost continuous flow of *aliyah*, which brought in roughly 3,467,000 persons over a period of 120 years and created Israel's Jewish population of 5,094,200 persons at the end of 2002 – 76.8% of the total of 6,631,100. At the end of 2003 the total population reached 6,748,000, with the lowest increase of 117,000 persons (1.8%) in one year since 1990. In the year 2000 the population increase was 2.2%; in 2001, 2.2%; and in 2002, 1.9%. The reason for this decline was the emigration of *olim* (immigrants).

This large movement may be divided into three distinct periods. The first (a) was during the last years of the Ottoman regime, when immigration totaled 55,000 to 70,000. The average in the years of the First Aliyah (1882–1904) was about 1,000 a year, rising in 1904–14, the period of the Second Aliyah, to about 3,000 a year. During 1882–1914, a little less than 3% of the enormous numbers of Jews who migrated overseas, mainly from Eastern Europe, went to Ereẓ Israel. The second (b) was during the British Mandatory regime (1919–48), when *aliyah* totaled about 485,000, some 16,000 per year on the average. The peaks were in 1925 (34,000 – 285 immigrants per 1,000 of the country's Jewish population) and 1935 (66,000 – 206 per 1,000). During this period, *aliyah* constituted some 30% of the total Jewish overseas migration. The third period (c) was after the establishment of the State of Israel, when over 2,930,000 went to the new state between May 1948 and the end of 2002, or some 55,000 per year. Of these, some 687,000 immigrated between 1948 and 1951, the peak being in 1949, when about 240,000 arrived – about 266 per 1,000 of the Jewish population. A second great wave of immigration took place in the 1990s, mostly from the former Soviet Union (see below).

There were considerable fluctuations. Immigration tended, on the whole, to increase from period (a) to (b) and to (c), but within each period the curve of immigration was characterized by a wave-like rise and fall. (For figures see *Israel, State of: Aliyah and Absorption.) Waves in immigration were largely due to the interplay of a variety of changing political, economic, social, and ideological factors in the Land of Israel and the various countries of the Diaspora: the influence of Zionism, religion, *ḥalutziyyut*, socialist ideas, and the attraction of the independent Jewish state; the work of Jewish institutions in propagating ideologies, organizing *aliyah*, and helping the newcomers; policies regarding emigration in general, and Jewish emigration in particular, in various countries; changing immigration and absorption policies, as well as political and economic conditions, in the land of Israel and in other countries absorbing Jewish immigration. In the later Ottoman period, immigrants came from many countries, but in the Mandatory period and since the achievement of independence, practically every Jewish community in the Diaspora was represented. While some attraction to Israel seemed to be generally felt throughout the Jewish world, the intensity of participation, as measured by the yearly rates of immigration to Israel per 1,000 Jewish inhabitants of each country, varied considerably between different parts of the world and for each region in different periods. The table on the following page shows the immigration from each of the main Diaspora regions in the various periods between 1919 and 2003, as well as the percentage of immigration from the two regions (Asia and Africa; Europe and America) in each period.

From the end of 1989 a large wave of immigration began arriving in Israel (mostly from the states of the former U.S.S.R.). Within three years (1990–1992) some 450,000 immigrants entered Israel. (In the wave which arrived in Israel after the establishment of the state in 1948 and which was designated a "mass immigration," 690,000 arrived within three and a half years.) They constituted some 10% of the Jewish population. This mass immigration came after a decade of low-level immigration in which 15,000 immigrants on the average arrived each year.

As stated, this large wave – 1990 – 185,000; 1991 – 148,000; 1992 – 65,000; 1995–1996 – 119,000; 1997–1998 – 102,000; 2002 – 19,300 – came mostly from the various regions of the U.S.S.R. By comparison, in the 1970s the total number of immigrants arriving from Russia was 155,000. The second large group came from Ethiopia, from where some 27,000 arrived in 1990–1992 (of whom 15,000 arrived in a special operation, "Operation Solomon," within one day). In the 1980s some 15,000 arrived from Ethiopia; 46,800 immigrated since 1990.

Smaller groups of immigrants arrived from various countries in America (U.S., Argentina, and some other Latin American countries) and Western European countries.

The immigrants of the 1990–92 wave reflected the characteristics of the Russian immigrants. The proportion of females was 53% (similar to that found within the 1970 immigrants). The percent of females was much higher in the older age groups where it reached 61% (in the ages 65 and over).

The age structure of the 1990–92 immigration was characterized by a low percentage of children and a relatively high percent of older persons in comparison to the age structure of the Jewish population in Israel, and even compared to the 1980 immigration.

The immigration of 1990–92 included a high percent of those with high-level education (e.g., those with 13 years of schooling or more comprised 50% of those 15 and above, and those with 16 years and over 11%). A very high proportion of those in academic, scientific, professional and technical fields was found in this immigration.

The number of physicians and dentists who arrived in the 1990–92 immigration was 12,000 and the number of engineers and architects was 45,000.

Like immigration, emigration (*yeridah*) also displays wavelike fluctuations, which are, to a certain extent, connected with waves of *aliyah*, since the former is, to a certain degree, due to a backflow of the latter. However, since the 1960s emigration of veteran foreign-born and Israel-born adults has also been noticeable, probably largely due to economic factors. Bachi has estimated in a very rough way that at the end of 1975 some 11% of the Israeli population (including both emigrants and their descendants) resided abroad. This Israeli Diaspora may have been as large as some 370,000, mostly in Northern America and Western and Central Europe. A rough estimate at the beginning of the 21st century put the figure at over half a million.

The Growth of the Jewish Population

The most immediate demographic effects of *aliyah* were as follows. Between 1882 and 1914, the Jewish population increased by 61,000 (from 24,000 to 85,000). Immigration roughly accounted for this increase, while emigration and natural increase probably canceled each other out. Immigration failed to bring a sizable proportion of the Jewish people to the country and did not succeed in reducing the absolute size of the Diaspora (in 1914 only 0.6% of world Jewry lived in the land of Israel). It did succeed, however, in creating a nucleus of population that was able to survive the expulsions and emigrations, diseases, and famine brought on by World War I (during which the Jewish population was reduced to some 57,000) and served as a basis for further development. During the Mandatory period, the Jewish population of Palestine increased by about 566,000 (from 84,000 according to the census of 1922 to 650,000 on the eve of independence), 71% of the growth being due to immigration and 29% to natural increase. At the end of the period, the Jews of Palestine constituted 5.7% of world Jewry.

During the period between May 1948 and the end of 1970, the Jewish population increased by 1,910,000, of which about

62% was due to the immigration balance and 38% to natural increase. At the end of 1970, the Jewish population of Israel (2,559,000 persons) constituted over 18% of world Jewry.

In the period 1971–1978, the population of Israel as a whole continued to grow, though at an average yearly rate of 27 per 1,000, which was less than in 1961–1970 (35 per 1,000) and much smaller than in 1948–1960 (81 per 1,000). The lower rate of growth was due mainly to a relatively low level of Jewish immigration and decline of the natural increase.

In 2002 the Israeli population numbered nearly 6.7 million persons. Within the period 1983–2002, it increased by 2.5 million (by 38%; an average annual growth rate of 2%). The increase of the population was very uneven. While the first seven years of the period (1983–1989) witnessed a slow growth (1.7% per year), the growth rate in the next three years (1990–1992) was much larger (4.4% per year, adding 200,000 each year) and between 1993 and 2002 was 2.7% per year.

These large differences in growth relate to a Jewish population, which increased in 1983–2002 by 1,681,700 (an average of 5.5% per year) and reached 5,094,200 by the end of 2002. In the period 1983–89 the annual growth attained 1.5%, while in the period 1990–2002 the average growth rate reached 2.4%.

The large differential growth is attributable wholly to the mass immigration which began arriving in Israel at the end of 1989 and brought within three years 450,000 immigrants, so that natural increase (the difference between the number of births and deaths) which contributed 92% of the Jewish population increase in the period 1983–89, contributed only 27% in this later period.

During the period between May 1948 and the end of 2002, the Jewish population increased by 4,335,500, of which about 62% was due to the immigration balance and 38% to natural increase. At the end of 2002, the Jewish population of Israel (5,094,200 persons) constituted over 38% of world Jewry and was exceeded in size only by the Jewish community of the United States (see *Demography). The population increase varied considerably from year to year, largely due to the fluctuations in *aliyah*.

Composition According to Place of Birth

Mainly as a consequence of changing sizes and origins of immigration and of differentials of fertility (which will be discussed below), the composition of the Jewish population according to country of birth has changed considerably in the course of time, but has always been extremely heterogeneous. The following are some of the main aspects of this phenomenon:

PROPORTION OF FOREIGN-BORN. With increasing rates of immigration, the proportion of persons born abroad increased from approximately 42% of the Jewish population in 1916–18 to 58% in 1931 and 64.6% in 1948, and decreased to 37.2% at the end of 2002. The percentage of foreign-born was higher in the adult age-groups, which is exceptional, even in countries of large immigration. If conditions in Israel had been different and a considerable part of the immigrant population had not identified itself strongly with the new country, such high percent ages of foreign-born citizens could have produced a very unstable society, since the majority of the people acquired their cultural background in foreign countries.

Jewish Immigrants to Israel by Continent of Birth, 1882–2004

	Absolute Numbers			Percentages		
Period	Asia and Africa	Europe and America	Total[1]	Asia and Africa	Europe and America	Total
1882–1919[2]			65,000			
1919–May 14, 1948[2]	44,809	385,066	452,158	10.4	89.6	100.0
May 15, 1948–1969	696,670	577,605	1,294,026	54.7	45.3	100.0
May 15, 1948–1951	330,456	334,971	684,201	49.7	50.3	100.0
1952–1954	39,978	11,187	51,193	78.1	21.9	100.0
1955–1957	110,714	49,630	160,961	69.1	30.9	100.0
1958–1960	25,926	46,460	72,393	35.8	64.2	100.0
1961–1964	133,561	86,748	220,323	60.6	39.4	100.0
1965–1969	56,035	48,609	104,955	53.5	46.5	100.0
1972–1979[3]	38,729	228,459[4]	267,188	14.4	85.6	100.0
1980–1989[3]	43,097	110,267[4]	153,364	28.1	71.9	100.0
1990–2001	108,236	951,348[4]	1,060,091	10.2	89.8	100.0
2002–2004	19,345	58,380[4]	77,733	29.5	70.5	100.0

Source: Statistical Abstract of Israel, Central Bureau of Statistics, Jerusalem.
1 Including unknown origin.
2 Palestine.
3 Including potential immigrants.
4 Including Oceania.

GROWING DIVERSIFICATION OF FOREIGN-BORN. Whereas in the last years of the Ottoman period and the first part of the Mandatory period three-quarters of the foreign-born were East European (Russians, Poles, Latvians, Lithuanians, and Romanians, who constituted the backbone of the Zionist enterprise), their proportion in the foreign-born population rapidly decreased, falling to 26.9% by 2002. Central Europeans (Germans, Austrians, Czechs, Slovakians, Hungarians), once a small minority, reached the considerable proportion of 18.4% in the period of Nazi persecution, but they decreased to less than 2.9% by 2002. All Europeans taken together dropped from 76.4% of the foreign-born in 1948 to 24% in 2002. On the other hand, those from Asian countries increased from 12.5% in 1948 to 13.3% in 2002, while the African communities grew from 2.6% to 16.1% (of which four-fifths came from Morocco, Algeria, and Tunisia) in the same period.

These changes have been accompanied by a deep change in stratification according to ages. While people of European origin still constitute the majority of the middle aged and the old, the largest group in the younger, productive ages is of Asian and African origin. Among the children, the native-born ("sabras") constitute the majority. Considering together those born abroad and their children, in 2002 Jews of Asian and African origin constituted 29.5% of those whose origin was known, while people of European and American origins constituted 41.1%. The increasing variety in the composition of the Jewish population confronted the State of Israel with very complex problems arising from the need to give everyone a common cultural, political, and linguistic basis and from the lower educational standards of the Asian and African newcomers.

Distribution of Immigration and Population by Sex and Age

Unlike most international migration processes due mainly to economic factors, modern *aliyah* was in general well balanced in regard to sex. Only in very difficult periods, as for instance in the first waves of 1919–23 and among the "illegal" immigrants in the 1940s, did the proportion of men considerably outweigh that of women. Accordingly, the distribution of population by sexes was also generally well balanced and subject only to minor fluctuations: the percentage of males at different times was the following: 1922 – 52.3; 1931 – 50.5; 1936 – 50.0; 1940 – 50.5; 1948 – 51.7; 1961 – 50.7; 1969 – 50.3; 2002 – 51.2. The age structure of the *aliyah* in the Mandatory period differed from that of the period of independence. Due to selection, the former was extremely abnormal in age distribution; it included a very high proportion of young people and was strongly at variance with the age distribution of the communities of origin (the Jewish population in Europe was largely characterized by a high proportion of old people). In the first phases of the Mandatory period, the Jewish population of Palestine reflected these characteristics and presented a typically strong swelling of the age pyramid in the very young age groups. The high proportion of people of young working age was presumably a considerable asset for the economic, social, and political development of the Zionist enterprise. In the long run, however, the situation was considerably changed by the aging of the young immigrants; the low fertility of the Europeans, then constituting the large majority of the population, which set in motion a general process of aging, and the inadequate influence of the smaller, new immigration waves in rejuvenating the population. The population therefore became more regular in its distribution and lost much of its young character.

During the period of statehood, a considerable part of the *aliyah* was nonselective and reflected the structure of the communities of origin. This *aliyah* had a much higher proportion of children, a somewhat higher proportion of old people, and a higher proportion of those in dependent ages to those in working ages. Unlike the immigration of the Mandatory period, it contributed to a leveling-out of the age distribution of the population. It widened the base of the age pyramid and the high fertility of the Oriental immigrants checked or offset the aging of the population, particularly that of the population in the working ages. As a consequence of all these processes, the Jewish population of Israel is today more regular in its age distributions than in the past; it is younger than many Western populations, but older than Eastern populations. Due to fluctuation in the number of births in the last decade, the percentage aged 15–19 is higher than the 0–14 age bracket and a much higher percentage than in the following brackets.

At the end of 2002, 1.88 million (28.4% of the population of Israel) were children under 15; 61.8% were in the ages 15–64; and 9.9% were older people (aged 65 and over).

The age distribution in 2002 differs from that of a decade earlier in a decrease in the proportion of children, and a small increase in the proportion of older people. These changes were influenced by the age structure of immigrants who arrived in 1990–1992, who had a lower fertility and so a lower proportion of children and a higher proportion of older persons. The proportion of those 65 and over in the veteran population, had the immigration not taken place, would not have changed to any significant degree up to 2010.

The process of aging which the Jewish Israeli population underwent brought the proportion of those 65 and over from 4.0% in 1948 to 7.2% in 1970, 9.7% in 1980, 10.5% in 1990, and 9.9% in 1992. Within this older group the proportion of 75 and over, from among those 65+, was 25% in 1970 and 32% in 1980, 41% in 1992, and 45.7% in 2002.

Considerable differences in the age structure of the Jewish and Arab communities persist; to a large extent as a result of fertility differentials. The proportion of children was 41% among Arabs compared to 25.4% among Jews in 2002; the proportion of those aged 65 and over was 3.9% in the Arab population compared to 11.4% among Jews.

The decrease in the proportion of children found in both the Jewish and Arab population was counterbalanced by the increase in the proportion of those aged 25 and over (mostly in the age group 25–44).

Large differences in the age structure were found between various localities in the country. Tel Aviv-Jaffa and Haifa cities have an older population (16–17% of the population were aged 65 and older), while Jerusalem had a younger population (7.6% aged 65 and over). A similar rate is found in smaller towns and in rural areas. This is a result of the structure of the population in various localities. In localities with a larger proportion of those originating in Asia and Africa, or a large proportion of Orthodox population, the age structure was younger (a larger proportion of children and a smaller proportion of older people).

Marriages, Births, Deaths, and Natural Increase

The study of the vital statistics of Israel's Jewish population is of interest from many points of view. While it has been established and expanded mainly by immigration, its future development, in the long run, will largely depend on the reproductive capacity of the immigrants and their descendants. Since Israel is a new and small country, the enlarging of its population may be of importance in order to provide a sufficiently large and differentiated basis for its economy and social structure. The demographic situation of the Jews of Israel may be significant in the light of the demography of world Jewry, which emerged from the Holocaust extremely reduced in numbers, and the fact that demographic trends in considerable parts of the Diaspora, such as aging of the population, low fertility rates, and losses due to intermarriage, are producing further population decreases. From a scientific point of view, the analysis of the evolution of marriage habits, fertility, mortality, and health standards among the various groups of the Jewish population in Israel is of interest within the larger framework of modern demographic evolution in general and that of the various branches of world Jewry in particular. Demographic patterns in the Diaspora differ considerably in relation to general environment, cultural development, degrees of religious conservatism, and assimilation of Jews into different social classes. In very broad terms, it appears that in many Asian and African communities the old Jewish customs of universal, early, and endogamous marriage, accompanied by high fertility, still tended to prevail until recently. Mortality rates had begun to fall considerably, creating a comparatively large reproductive force. On the other hand, European Jews, particularly in Central Europe, have in general had comparatively low marriage rates, rather high marriage ages, and generally increasing rates of exogamous marriage. Fertility has decreased (mainly among Central European Jews) to such an extent as in many cases to be well below replacement level, despite the generally favorable age-specific mortality rates among Jews as compared with those of non-Jews in the same countries (see *Demography). The following are some of the main features of the vital statistics of the Jewish population of Israel.

MARRIAGE AND DIVORCE. Marriage in Israel is almost exclusively endogamous within the Jewish community. Marriage is almost universal in all groups of the Jewish population: the percentage of single persons at the end of the fertility period is generally small. Only recently has there been some tendency toward increased rates of celibacy among Jewish women. In addition, the generally favorable age structure and the influx of unmarried immigrants – who often appear to postpone marriage before immigration and are afterward eager to marry – have contributed to generally high crude marriage rates among the Jewish population in Israeli during periods of heavy immigration. Average age of Israel brides at first marriage was 25.9 in 2001, which is low by European standards, but higher than that found in Oriental countries. The propensity to marry has continued to be comparatively strong in three population groups – the Jews, the Moslems and the Druze – and weak among the Christians. In 2000 the proportion of Jewish women reaching the age of 45–49 without having been married was 6%. Age at marriage tends to become more uniform than in the past among the various groups of the population of Israel. Early marriages which were frequent in the past among the Moslems, the Druze and among Jews of certain Asian and African origins have become by far less frequent.

Among Jews, preference in marriage between people of same origin still constitutes a rather general feature, but this tendency is clearly decreasing in the course of time; it decreases among people born abroad, with length of stay in Israel, and it is weaker among people born in Israel than among foreign born. Data shows that homogamy (tendency to marry people of equal origin) was comparatively higher – within each class of length of stay – among people born in certain Asian and African countries, such as Yemen, India, Iraq, Iran, Morocco and Libya, where the Jewish communities were on the whole more traditional and less "modernized."

Among those of European origin, homogamy by country was generally much lower. However, those Jews of Romanian, Polish, Bulgarian, and Greek origin had a higher homogamy rate than those from Central Europe and other Western countries. Among Jews marrying a partner originating from a country different from their own, there is still some tendency to prefer a marriage mate originating from a country where customs, culture or language are equal or similar to those of one's own country. Among such areas of marriage preference the following may be quoted: Eastern European countries; Central Europe; former French North Africa; Latin America; Anglo-Saxon countries; and the Sephardi community. The frequency of marriages between people of African or Asian origin and those of European origin is gradually increasing.

DIVORCES. Divorce rates, which had decreased in the 1950s and 1960s, have shown a tendency to increase since then. On the basis of the 1972 census it has been calculated that the average yearly number of divorces per 1000 married persons was, among the Jews of Israel, about four and in 2001 about nine. These rates are higher than those prevalent in many other countries, but lower than those found in the U.S.A., and among various Scandinavian, Central European, Balkan, and Muslim populations. Probability of divorce reaches a maximum two years after marriage and then declines slowly. The propensity to divorce decreases with increasing number of children. However, the percentage of divorced couples with children has increased in the course of time. Divorced people have a high tendency to remarry. Actually, divorced men marry more than bachelors or widowers of same age and divorcées marry more than spinsters and widows. This feature is not peculiar to Israel and is sometimes interpreted as showing that divorce is generally less a repudiation of marriage as such, than an expression of dissatisfaction with a particular marriage partner. This may be connected also with the likely fact that some divorces are obtained to marry somebody else. However, divorced people have also a particularly high propensity to divorce again.

FERTILITY. Patterns of fertility differ among various Jewish population groups far more than marriage patterns. Fertility may be indicated by the average number of children born per woman in the entire reproductive period – about 15–49 (it must be remembered that an average of more than two children per couple is necessary for ensuring adequate reproduction, as some children die before reaching maturity). From the scanty statistical material available it appears that at the beginning of the 20th century, Jews in the Land of Israel still had a rather high fertility. However, in the 1920s and 1930s fertility fell rapidly (1927–29, 3.57 children per woman; 1935–38, 2.54; 1939–42, 2.33. This decrease was due to the rapid spread of birth control (by contraception and abortion), mainly among the Jews of European origin, who constituted the great majority of the Jewish population. Limitation of births was particularly strong in periods of political or economic difficulties, like that of the Arab riots (1936–39) and the beginning of World War II. In the late 1940s there was a "baby boom" among European Jews in Palestine, comparable with that which developed at the time in many Western countries; many of the births may be considered as "delayed" from previous bad times.

Total Fertility Rates (average number of children per woman)

	Jews born in				Non-Jewish population		
Years	Israel	Asia-Africa	Europe-America	Total	Muslims	Christians	Druze
1955–59	2.79	5.40	2.53	3.56	8.17	4.56	7.21
1960–64	2.73	4.79	2.38	3.39	9.23	4.68	7.49
1965–69	2.83	4.35	2.59	3.36	9.22	4.26	7.30
1970–74	3.05	3.92	2.83	3.28	8.47	3.65	7.25
1975–79	2.91	3.40	2.80	3.00	7.25	3.12	6.93
1980–84	2.82	3.09	2.76	2.80	5.54	2.41	5.40
1985–89	2.82	3.14	2.66	2.79	4.70	2.49	4.19
1990–94	2.72	3.33	2.14	2.62	4.67	2.18	3.77
1995–99	2,93			2.62	4.67	2.56	3.24
2004	2.90			2.71	4.36	2.13	2.66

Source: Statistical Abstract of Israel 1995, No. 46; 2005, No. 56.
Data for the five year periods are arithmetical means.

In 1949–50 the fertility of European Jews reached the top level of 3.24. Later, however, it declined again (1960–63, 2.4; 1965, 2.6; 2002, probably in connection with the recession, 2.64). In 1968–69, after the end of the recession, it somewhat increased, possibly also due to a change in public opinion in regard to the fertility problem. However, in general, the fertility of European Jews in Israel was not much higher than the minimum reproduction level. Fertility differentials were not large among European Jews. The main factors of differentiation were religious outlook (among religious women, particularly those observing the injunction of the *mikveh* or ritual bath, there was considerably higher fertility and less contraception and induced abortion than among others); work (working women had less children than others); place of residence (women in Tel Aviv and Haifa had lower fertility than in other towns), the highest fertility being found in Jerusalem, with its large proportion of religious people, and the kibbutzim; education (the higher the education, the lower the fertility); length of stay (the veteran settlers and the second generation have a somewhat higher fertility than new immigrants).

Jews of Afro-Asian origin somewhat reduced their fertility during the Mandatory period, mainly in places and among strata having more contact with European Jews. However, their average fertility remained higher than that of European Jews. Mass immigration brought many large families not accustomed to birth control, which considerably increased the fertility of Asian-African Jews. However, in the course of time, birth control spread among them, especially among the younger generation. Differences in fertility in this group were very large; as among the Europeans, religious outlook and work played some part, but the main differentiations are related to length of stay in the country, education, and place of residence. In the higher educational levels and in certain places, such as the kibbutzim, the differences by origin almost disappeared, while women living in more secluded places, like the moshavim, had a very high fertility rate.

On the whole, the fertility of people of Asian or African origin was still rather high, and due to their large proportion among women in the reproductive ages, the average fertility of Jews in Israel was considerably above reproduction level. However, the fertility of Jews of Asian-African origin continued to decrease in the period after the Six-Day War. This decrease was connected with spreading knowledge of, and the actual use of, contraceptive methods among this group of the population, as indicated above. This rapid evolution is accelerated by increasing levels of education, a larger proportion of working women, growing secularization and increasing contacts with other population groups.

In consequence the fertility of Jews born in Asia and Africa is lower in Israel than it was in the countries of origin, and it is lower in Israel among those born in Asia and Africa than among those born in Israel from parents of Asian-African origin.

Among those of European origin the opposite evolution has taken place. Fertility is higher in Israel than in the countries of origin and it is higher among Israelis born of European origin than among immigrants from Europe. The fertility of people of European origin (first and second generation) is still lower than that of those of Asian-African origin. However, in the late 1960s and early 1970s it tended to increase to some extent and to remain at a more sustained level than in previous periods. Among groups of European origin, the kibbutz population had a more considerable upsurge of its birth rate. Various demographic, political, psychological, economic and social explanations of the increase of fertility rates among people of European origin during the late 1960s and early 1970s may be proposed. In the late 1970s a tendency toward decline of fertility appeared again also among those of European origin.

Among the non-Jewish population a growing tendency toward control of births and reduction of fertility is also noticeable. These tendencies are strong in the Christian population which is more urbanized and has a higher educational level. They have started later and are less pronounced in the Moslem and Druze populations.

Considerable changes have also occurred with regard to abortions. In Mandatory Palestine regulations concerning abortions were very rigid and heavy penalties were laid down both for the woman procuring her own miscarriage or for any person procuring it. Although these regulations remained theoretically in force in Israel, they were not applied in practice. Abortions were very largely performed, generally by physicians, but almost without any public control. In 1966 penalties against the woman were abolished, and those against persons procuring abortions were mitigated. However, growing uneasiness was felt with regard to the discrepancy between written law and actual practice, and in 1977 a law was passed declaring abortions performed outside hospitals to be unlawful and fixing norms for cases which can be permitted in public hospitals by special committees. Those norms permit abortions for social reasons.

The practice of abortion seems to have been in the past widespread among European women, but to have then declined (probably with the wider spread of birth control) mainly among women of a higher educational level. Later, use of abortion increased among women of Asian-African origin, but also apparently declined. Abortion is practiced to a lesser extent among religious women than among non-religious. Legal abortions stood at 12.4% of live births in 2002 compared with a peak of 16.1 in 1984.

In Table: Total Fertility Rates, fertility has been measured by using – in order to enable comparison – the same method employed in the initial section on fertility above.

A total of 139,535 babies were born in Israel in 2002 (of whom 94,327 were Jewish). The last two decades saw a continuous decrease in the birth rate: from 24.6 births per 1,000 population in 1983 to 22.6 in 1988 and 21.2 in 2002. However, the rate in 2002 was still higher than that found in most developed countries (in 1989 the average birth rate for Europe was 12.9, for North America 15.0) but much lower than developing countries (the average in Africa – 45, Asia – 28).

The number of children per woman (at the end of her fertility period = "total fertility") was estimated as 3.21 in 1983, falling to 3.06 in 1988 and 2.64 by 2002. This number reflects large differences in fertility of the various communities in Israel. The birth rate (per 1,000 population) was 19 for the Jewish population compared to 37 among the Muslim population. The "total fertility rate" was 2.64 for the Jewish population, 4.58 for the Muslim population, 2.77 for the Druze population, and 2.29 for the Christian population.

The fertility of the Muslim population declined from 5.4 in 1983 to 4.53 in 1988, but later increased to 4.58 by 2002.

In the Jewish population large differences in fertility still exist between the various communities. The number of children of an Asian-born mother was 40% higher than of a European-born mother (for an African-born mother higher by 66%). But differences among mothers born in Israel of various origins were much lower.

A very distinct change in fertility for European-born mothers was noticed in the period from 1989 to 1992: a decline in total fertility from 2.6 to 2.05. This was caused by the very low fertility level of immigrants from the former Soviet Union who arrived in the large immigration wave of 1990–92 (total fertility for this group 1.5 children).

The decrease in fertility occurred for mothers of practically all levels.

MORTALITY. Before World War II health conditions were favorably affected by the fact that most of the immigrants came from Europe, where the Jews, in general, had lower age-specific mortality rates than non-Jews in the same localities, and that candidates for *aliyah* were generally selected. On the other hand, the change in environment, the transition to harder work, and the presence of an Arab majority with a high mortality rate may have been adverse factors. Since World War II further adverse factors have been operative, i.e., the mass immigration of people who underwent persecution and suffered in the concentration camps and of unselected Oriental immigrants with low health standards. Large-scale medical services, voluntary health insurance for the majority of the population, an exceptionally high proportion of physicians in the population, preventive services, and supervision of most mothers and children have acted as very favorable factors throughout the Mandatory and statehood periods. On the whole, the double challenge of bringing European immigrants to a prevalently Oriental country (up to 1948) and bringing Oriental immigrants to a prevalently European country (after 1948) has been met with considerable success. Life expectancy has steadily increased – from 54 in 1926 to 77.4 for men and 81.6 for women in 2001, and mortality has decreased at all age levels, especially among children and young people. The infant mortality rate, which in 1924 was ranked in the middle of the world list, decreased at so rapid a pace that in 1947 it was lower than that of 89 countries and higher only than that of four and had reached the record low level of 29.2 per 1,000; with mass immigration, it rose again to 51.7 per 1,000 in 1949, but afterward began to drop again and stood at 5.6 per 1,000 births in 1995 and 4.7 in 1999 for Jews. This level was found in countries having the lowest infant mortality rate in the developed countries. The wide gulf between the mortality of children of Asian and African immigrants and that of children of European origin has been bridged to a considerable extent, and the life expectancies of these two main groups of population are now quite close. For Muslims the decrease in infant mortality was from 21.3 to 13.1.

The total number of deaths from all causes was 35,348 in 1995 (i.e., 7.1 per 1,000 population). The major causes of death were similar to those found ten years earlier: heart conditions and cerebrovascular diseases were responsible for 40% of all deaths and cancers, 20%.

Intermarriage Between Groups of Different Origins

The Central Bureau of Statistics of Israel publishes yearly data on marriages according to country of birth and length of stay in Israel of the bride and groom, and particularly detailed data on this point were collected in the censuses of 1989 and 1995. The figures show that the tendency to marry people of the same origin (endogamy) is still very considerable in Israel. However, endogamy differs from group to group: it is lower in smaller than in larger groups; it is lower among people having higher educational standards and in such places as kibbutzim, where the members are more integrated into the life of the community. The most relevant feature found is that endogamy decreases with the length of stay in Israel. Where both husband and wife are new immigrants, endogamy by place of birth is found to be very high, but it is generally low in marriages between veteran residents and practically vanishes among veterans belonging to smaller groups. This finding and the general decrease of endogamy in the course of time show that there is a clear tendency toward a systematic lowering of marriage barriers between different origin groups. About 70% of marriages are still between couples of the same continent of origin, not because of preference for mates from the same community but mainly because of preference for a given level of education and the availability of single people of different ages in different countries.

Geographical Distribution of the Population

One of the most well known characteristics of modern Israel is the "return to the soil" – the establishment of hundreds of villages and the creation of a rural population, which are almost unknown in the Diaspora. Nevertheless, the Jewish population has been largely urban. With increasing mechanization and efficiency in Jewish agriculture, the proportion of people living on the land has been decreasing (17.3% in 1959; 10.8% in 1969, and 8.8% in 2002). Moreover, the share of the rural population in moshavot and moshavim has tended to increase, while that in the kibbutzim has decreased. Due to industrial development in urban areas the two large conurbations of Tel Aviv and Haifa contained, respectively, 54.7% and 18.4% of the total Jewish population at the end of 2002. Great efforts have been made by the authorities to prevent the over-rapid development of these areas and the over-concentration of the population in the coastal strip. This has been done by policies designed to increase the rural population, particularly in border areas, and by establishing "development towns" (mainly in the southern and northern districts). Some of the main developments in the geographical distribution of the population are shown in the following three tables: Jewish Population in Israel by Type of Settlement; Population and Settlements in Israel by Size of Settlement; and Jewish Population of Israel by District and Sub-District, showing the proportion of Jewish population living in each subdistrict.

Jewish Population in Israel by Type of Settlement, by percentage (1945–2003)

	1945	1948	1954	1961	1969	1983	1994	2003
Urban Population	84.6	83.9	76.1	84.6	89.2	90.2	90.5	91.2
Towns	64.3	64.4	64.5	69.7	73.2	–		
Urban settlements	20.3	19.5	11.6	14.9	16.0	–		
Rural Population	15.4	16.1	23.9	15.4	10.8	9.8	9.5	8.8
Villages	3.2	3.5	4.0	4.5	1.7	–	–	–
Moshavim	5.2	4.4	7.3	6.4	5.1	4.5[2]	3.9[2]	4.2
Kibbutzim	6.3	7.9	5.0	4.0	3.4	3.4	2.8	2.1
Other	0.7	0.3	7.6[1]	0.5	0.6	1.9	2.8	2.5
Total	100.0	100.0	100.0	100.0	100.0	100.0	100.0	100.0

1 Including immigrant transit centers.
2 Including collective moshavim.

Population (in thousands) and Settlements in Israel by Size of Settlement (1953–2002)

	1953		1969		2002	
Size of Settlement	Settlements	Population	Settlements	Population	Settlements	Population
5,000–9,999	20	139.9	21	148.6	49	341.2
10,000–19,999	9	135.7	23	306.4	40	562.2
20,000–49,999	10	269.5	16	506.0	45	1,375.5
50,000+	3	651.5	10	1,441.1	9	647.2
100,000–199,999	—	—	—	—	8	1,374.8
200,000+	—	—	—	—	4	1,523.2
Living outside settlements	—	—	—	3.9	—	
Other	—	—	—	—	—	—
Bedouin tribes	—	20.1	—	36.8	—	n.a.
Total	42	1,216.7	69	2,442.8	155	5,828.1

Source: Statistical Abstract of Israel, Central Bureau of Statistics, Jerusalem.

The distribution of the population is marked by the following characteristics. Within the extremely irregular boundaries of Israel (within the 1949 armistice demarcation lines), the population is highly concentrated in certain areas, such as the Coastal Plain, and there is a very low density in the southern areas, which are largely desert. However, in the course of time there has been some tendency to modify these characteristics. The actual distribution has become a little less concentrated than it was in 1948. Population dispersal has increased, and the center of gravity has shifted considerably to the south (toward the Tel Aviv conurbation and southern development towns and zones). These changes have largely been due to the policy of attracting new immigrants to the development zones on the periphery of the country by providing housing and labor facilities in those regions. This policy has had a particularly strong effect on new immigrants from Asia and Africa.

Jewish Population of Israel by District and Sub-District[1] (1948–2003)

	Population (thousands)					Percentages				
District and Sub-District	Nov. 8, 1948	May 22, 1961	Dec. 31, 1969	Dec. 31, 1994	Dec. 31, 2003	Nov. 8, 1948	May 22, 1961	Dec. 31, 1969	Dec. 31, 1994	Dec. 31, 2003
Jerusalem district	**84.2**	**187.7**	**237.6**	**473.2**	**560.5**	**12.0**	**9.7**	**9.5**	**10.7**	**10.9**
Northern district	**53.4**	**194.3**	**244.6**	**458.7**	**516.4**	**7.6**	**10.0**	**9.8**	**10.3**	**10.0**
Safed sub-district	8.9	42.6	51.4	73.8	79.8	1.3	2.2	2.1	1.7	1.5
Kinneret sub-district	14.4	35.4	38.0	60.0	63.8	2.1	1.8	1.5	1.3	1.2
Jezreel sub-district	24.1	66.6	87.7	163.0	184.5	3.4	3.4	3.5	3.7	3.6
Acre sub-district	6.0	49.7	67.5	148.5	172.5	0.8	2.6	2.7	3.3	3.3
Golan sub-district					15.8					0.3
Haifa district	**147.7**	**322.3**	**386.3**	**562.6**	**608.4**	**21.1**	**16.7**	**15.5**	**12.7**	**11.8**
Haifa sub-district	116.4	257.6	311.9	430.2	438.8	16.6	13.3	12.5	9.7	8.5
Ḥaderah sub-district	31.3	64.7	74.4	132.4	169.6	4.5	3.4	3.0	3.0	3.3
Central district	**106.2**	**380.1**	**48.24**	**1,071.8**	**1,391.8**	**15.2**	**19.7**	**19.4**	**24.1**	**26.9**
Sharon sub-district	26.5	85.1	106.1	209.8	261.9	3.8	4.4	4.3	4.7	5.1
Petaḥ Tikvah sub-district	45.9	131.8	171.5	392.2	492.8	6.6	6.8	6.9	8.8	9.5
Ramleh sub-district	1.8	63.9	74.7	133.9	212.2	0.2	3.3	3.0	3.0	4.1
Reḥovot sub-district	32.0	99.3	130.0	335.9	425.0	4.6	5.2	5.2	7.6	8.2
Tel Aviv district	**302.1**	**692.6**	**852.5**	**1,115.4**	**1,095.4**	**43.2**	**35.9**	**34.1**	**25.1**	**21.2**
Southern district	**6.0**	**155.3**	**292.5**	**632.6**	**766.6**	**0.9**	**8.0**	**11.7**	**14.2**	**14.8**
Ashkelon sub-district	4.8	76.4	139.2	313.2	399.7	0.7	3.9	5.6	7.1	7.7
Beersheba sub-district	1.2	78.9	153.3	319.4	366.9	0.2	4.1	6.1	7.2	7.1
Judea, Samaria, and Gaza[3]					**226.3**					**4.4**
Not known	**17.1**	—	—	—	—	—	—	—	—	—
Total	**716.7**	**1,932.3**	**2,496.4[2]**	**4,441.1**	**5,165.4**	**100.0**	**100.0**	**100.0**	**100.0**	**100.0**

Source: Statistical Abstract of Israel, Central Bureau of Statistics, Jerusalem.

1 According to the boundaries of the sub-districts in the years listed.
2 Including Israel residents in the Administered Territories.
3 Following the disengagement from Gaza in Aug. 2005, the approx. 8,000 Jewish residents of the Gaza region were dispersed elsewhere in Israel.

These developments have been strengthened by the fact that there are more of the more prolific elements in the peripheral zones, while a higher proportion of the less fertile sections of the population and the older age groups is to be found in the central areas. Natural increase is therefore higher in peripheral zones and lower in the center, which increases population dispersal. These developments are offset, to some extent, by the effects of internal migration, as recent immigrants move mainly from the periphery to the center. Since the settlement of new immigrants in development areas has been the main factor in population dispersal, the latter has increased more in the periods of considerable immigration.

As new immigrants in the more peripheral areas have been largely of African and Asian origin, there has been a certain tendency toward regionalization. The immigrants of European origin, especially the veterans, are more concentrated in the large conurbations and the older settlements of the Coastal Plain, the Jezreel Valley, etc., while there is a higher proportion of people of African-Asian origin in the southern and northern regions. This regionalization explains the peculiar distribution of the population according to social, economic, and cultural characteristics (such as concentration of veteran immigrants in the central part of the country and dispersion of more recently arrived persons over more peripheral regions), higher educational standards and better economic conditions along the Mediterranean coast, and so on.

[Roberto Bachi / Elisha Efrat (2nd ed.)]

The Communities of Israel

In 2002, Jews constituted 76.8% of the total Israeli population. Most of the others were Arabs and Druze. These were divided by religion as follows: Muslims – 15.5% of the total Israeli population, Christians – 2.1%, and Druze and others, 5.6%.

The percent of the Jewish population declined from 84% in 1980 to 81.5% in 1989 (owing mostly to the large differences in the rate of natural increase of Jews and Arabs). The large immigration from Russia in 1989–1991 caused the proportion of Jews to increase to a smaller extent to 81.9% by the end of 1991.

Jews in Israel Born Abroad According to Native Countries and Periods of Immigration

Countries	Until 1918	1918–38	1939–47	1948 and unknown date	Total no. of immigrants
Yemen and Aden	1,800	8,510	5,676	316	16,302
Syria and Lebanon	459	4,243	5,850	237	10,789
Turkey	399	4,897	4,042	1,214	10,552
Iraq	470	5,272	2,983	277	9,002
Iran	563	2,833	423	97	3,916
The rest of Asia	38	1,451	645	717	2,851
Egypt	152	2,061	2,165	251	4,629
Morocco, Tunisia and Algeria	468	506	534	3,823	5,331
Libya	7	297	439	507	1,250
Asia and North Africa	4,356	30,070	22,757	7,439	64,622
Rest of Africa excluding South Africa	10	170	164	67	411
Soviet Asia	428	3,035	378	261	4,092
Europe, America, South Africa, and Oceania	7,478	211,424	96,334	76,347	391,783
Unknown	56	576	362	665	1,695
Total	12,328	245,265	119,995	84,979	462,567

THE VARIOUS JEWISH COMMUNITIES. The large immigration which arrived in 1989–1991 brought some important changes in the size of the various communities of Israel. The proportion of the "Israeli-born" population, which increased continuously in the previous decades and reached 64% of the total Jewish population in 1989, declined to 60.5% in 1991 (37% of this group were second generation Israeli-born, i.e., born to fathers who were born in Israel). The Israeli-born population was composed of 55% young persons (less than 20 years old), while only less than 1% were aged 65 and over.

The immigration of 1989–91 – which brought mostly immigrants from the former Soviet Russia – increased the proportion of those born in Europe, after a long-term reduction in their proportion. The proportion of those born in Europe and America among the total population decreased from 25% in 1981 to 20% in 1989, but by the beginning of 1992 the proportion returned to 25%. The Asian and African communities born abroad declined continuously from 20% of the total population in 1981 to 16% in 1989 and 15% in 1992.

Use of Languages and Literacy

From statistical data on the use of languages in Israel, collected at the population censuses in 1916–18, 1948, and 1961 and in various sample surveys, two dominant features of the linguistic situation in Israel are obvious: the amazing variety of languages brought by the immigrants from the countries of the Diaspora; and the important role played by the Hebrew language. The revival of Hebrew began at the end of the 19th century, when the majority of immigrants still spoke Yiddish, while the minority generally spoke Ladino or Arabic. At the end of the Ottoman period, Hebrew had succeeded in winning over some 34,000 (40% of the total Jewish population), mainly among the younger generation in "modern" localities (e.g., the new settlements and Tel Aviv). At the close of the Mandatory period, almost all those born in the country were Hebrew speakers, and those born abroad who had arrived before the age of 20 were found to use Hebrew almost to the same extent. At higher ages, it was found that the adoption of Hebrew diminished in speed and intensity in proportion to the age of the immigrants upon arrival. By 1948, 511,000 persons, 75% of the total, used Hebrew as their only or principal language. After the establishment of the State of Israel, the percentage of newcomers who knew Hebrew before arrival was far lower than that of pre-state immigrants, who were largely preselected and ideologically motivated. This decreased the proportion of Hebrew speakers in the period of mass immigration. Subsequently, however, the use of Hebrew again largely increased. The following table shows the changes in numbers and proportions of Hebrew speakers in the course of time. In 1966 they constituted some 70% of adults and there is no doubt that they were the overwhelming majority among the children.

Persons Speaking Hebrew as Only or First Language Among the Jewish Population (Israel), 1914–66

	Age 12 and over Total	Age 2 and over*	Age 2–14*	Age 15 and over*
1914[1]	34,000[2]	40.0[2,3]	53.7[2,3]	25.6[2,3]
1948	511,000	75.1	93.4	69.5
1950	679,000	60.0	80.3	52.0
1954	861,000	60.9	83.9[4]	52.8[5]
1956	—	—	—	58.4[5]
1961	1,391,400	75.3	92.8	67.4
1966	—	—	—	69.3[5]

* Rates per 100 of the Jewish population.
1 Palestine.
2 Aged one year and over (estimate).
3 Excluding Jerusalem.
4 Aged 2–13.
5 Aged 14 and over.

Before statehood, the Jewish population was characterized by the low proportion of illiterates. This was due to the high educational level of the immigrants, who were largely of European origin, and to the fact that most of the Jewish population saw to the education of their children, although it was not compulsory at the time. Only among women in the higher age groups was the proportion of illiterates considerable. With mass immigration from Asia and Africa, the proportion of illiterates increased considerably, mainly in the higher age groups and especially among women. Due to the efforts made by the State of Israel in the educational field, the situation has improved in the course of time. The following table shows the classification of the Jewish population by number of years of schooling according to continent of birth, sex, age, and period of immigration. The higher standards of those born in Israel, Europe, and America, as compared with those of people born in Asia and Africa, are immediately seen.

Percentages of Israel Population Aged 15 and Above, by Population Group, Number of Years of Schooling, Sex, Age, and Continent of Birth, 1961–2004

	Number of Years of Schooling							
	0	1–4	5–8	9–10	11–12	13–15	16+	Median
	Jewish Population 2004							
Total	2.4	1.1	7.1	9.8	36.8	23.3	19.5	12.6
Sex								
Males	1.5	1	6.9	10.5	37.6	22.5	20	12.6
Females	3.3	1.2	7.3	9.1	36	24.1	19	12.6
Age								
15–17			2.2	43.7	53.5			11.2
18–24	0.2	0.2	1.1	3.4	63.9	27.6	3.6	12.4
25–34	0.5	0.3	1.8	3.9	33.2	30.7	29.6	14
35–44	0.8	0.2	2.5	7.4	36.9	25.2	27.1	13.3
45–54	1.1	0.5	7	9.6	31.7	24.5	25.5	13
55–64	3.3	1.4	13	10.1	25.7	22.5	24	12.7
65+	10.6	5	22.5	11.4	20.5	16.7	13.2	11
County or continent of birth								
Israel		0.4	2.9	8.4	44.8	23.6	19.8	12.7
Asia and Arica		12.3	12.5	12.7	39.2	14.7	8.6	11.6
Europe and America		1.3	5.2	11.6	29.2	29.2	23.5	13.3
	Jewish Population 1961–1994							
1961	12.6	7.5	35.4	34.6		6.3	3.6	8.4
1970	9.3	6.3	31.7	39.7		8.1	4.9	9.3
1975	7.6	4.3	25.5	18.8	26.1	10.7	7.0	10.3
1985	5.0	3.1	17.3	16.6	33.6	14.2	10.2	11.5
1994	3.4	2.0	10.8	12.6	37.3	19.3	14.6	12.1
	Non-Jewish Population 1961–2004							
1961	49.5	13.9	27.5	7.6			1.5	1.2
1970	36.1	13.7	35.1	13.0	1.7		(0.4)	5.0
1975	22.9	12.9	38.0	12.6	9.1	3.1	1.4	6.5
1985	13.4	7.7	32.0	19.3	19.2	5.9	2.5	8.6
2004	6.4	4.4	19.0	18.7	32.9	10.4	8.0	11.1

Source: Statistical Abstract of Israel, Central Bureau of Statistics, Jerusalem.

The Regional Distribution of the Population

In 2002, the distribution of the population of Israel by the various regions of the country was very similar to that of a decade earlier, although some differences can be traced, brought about mostly by the dispersion of the large wave of immigration that arrived from the end of 1989 onwards.

At the beginning of 2002, 70% of the population resided in the various sub-districts along the coastline of Israel. (These include the sub-districts of Acre in the north through Haifa District, Central and Tel Aviv Districts, and down to Ashkelon sub-district in the south.) This is similar to the proportion in 1983. Some small increase is found in the part of the population living in the peripheral area in the North and the South and the population living in Judea and Samaria and the Gaza Regions on the other side, but the population of the Tel Aviv and Haifa Districts grew at a slower rate than other districts. (Tel Aviv District population increased in the period 1983 to 2002 by 15.8%, Haifa by 45.8%, while other areas grew by 27 to 30 percent.)

The large immigration which arrived from 1989 did reside to a larger extent in the Haifa and the Northern Districts, and to a smaller extent in the Jerusalem, Tel Aviv, and the Central Districts, compared to the veteran part of the Jewish population in these regions. Thirty-three percent of the immigrants (of the 1990–91 wave) resided in Haifa and Northern Districts compared to 25% of the Jewish population. The percent of immigrants entering the Tel Aviv and Central Districts was 46% (compared to 51% of the population). These movements continued the trend of decrease in the part of the Jewish population of the Tel Aviv District (in 2002, 21.5% of the population compared to 30% in 1983 and 43% in 1948). Data on internal migration of these new immigrants show that the Northern, Southern, and Central Districts did gain on balance from their movement.

As the regional distribution of the Arab population did not change to an important extent, the part of the Jewish population in the Northern District was 50.3% in 1992 compared to 48.4% in 2002.

The population of Israel is an urban population. Only 8.4% live in the small localities of less than 2,000 persons while 43.7% (50% of the Jewish population) reside in 13 localities of 100,000 persons or more. This is very similar to the distribution a decade ago. The three large cities (Jerusalem, Tel Aviv-Jaffa, and Haifa) continued the decline in their proportion of the population, while the population of towns of 100–200,000 inhabitants increased. These localities are Ḥolon – population 165.8 thousand; Petaḥ Tikvah – 172.6; Bat Yam – 133.9; Rishon LeZiyyon – 211.6; Netanyah – 164.8; Be'ersheva – 181.5; Ramat Gan – 122.6; Bene Berak – 138.9.

The largest city of Israel was Jerusalem with 680,000 at the end of 2002 (of whom 459,000 were Jews), followed by Tel Aviv-Jaffa with 360,000, and Haifa with 270,800. If the population of the whole conurbation of Tel Aviv is added a total is reached of 1.5 to 1.8 million, depending on how the boundaries of the metropolitan area are defined. The population of the Haifa conurbation is 971,000.

Within the rural area, the population of the moshavim and the kibbutzim grew at a slower rate than did the total Jewish population, so that the percent of the population residing in moshavim declined within a decade from 4.5% to 4.1% and that of the kibbutzim from 3.5% to 2.1%.

HUMAN RESOURCES

In 2002 the labor force of Israel (i.e., those employed and those unemployed seeking work) numbered about 2.5 million. In the decade from 1982 to 1992, the labor force grew by some 480,000 (i.e., by more than a third or 3.0% per annum). Parallel to the population change, the labor force grew at a slow pace in the period 1982 to 1989 (by 2.3% yearly), and at a much higher rate in the period of the mass immigration (by 4.9% per year).

This decade marked a high increase in unemployment compared to that of the employed. While in 1982 the rate of unemployment (unemployed as a percent of the labor force) was 5%, it increased to 6.4% in 1988 and increased sharply up to 10% in 2002. This was caused partly by the entry into the labor force of a large number of new immigrants who were still looking for a job in the first stages of their stay in the country.

The main trends regarding labor force participation found in the 1970s continued through the 1980s and the beginning of the 1990s. The major development is the continuous increase in the participation of women in the labor force; from 36% of the women aged 15 and over in the labor force in 1982 to 48.4% in 2002, with women constituting 42% of all the labor force. Another continuous trend was the decrease in the labor force participation of men, mostly in the retirement and pre-retirement ages. The participation of men aged 55–64 in the labor force declined from more than 80% in 1982 to 65.9% in 2002, and of those aged 65 and over from 28% to 15.4%. Smaller declines are also found in age 35 and over. Thus, the labor force has become more feminine and of a younger age. The continuous increase in the proportion of those aged 35–44 in the labor force was related to the changes in the age structure and to the decline in participation in other ages.

The labor force is of a higher level of education. Thus persons who had 13 years and over of schooling constituted 28% of the labor force in 1982 and 38% in 2002 (17% had 16 years and over of schooling). The high level of education of the mass immigration which arrived from 1990 contributed to this trend.

The average number of hours worked by the employed population was 36.0 per week. No important trend changes were noticed in the decade 1982–2002.

The large increase of the employed population between 1982 and 2002 was absorbed in the various branches of the economy in similar proportions. Some differences were noticed; a continued decrease in the proportion of those employed in agriculture and industry; the proportion working in construction increased as activity in this branch grew in 1990–91 owing to the large-scale building for immigrants. In addition to the Israelis employed in the construction industry, some 70,000 workers from Judea and Samaria and the Gaza Region were employed in this branch in Israel. The proportion of those working in commerce, business, and personal services continued its growth.

The occupational distribution of the employed population did undergo some changes: the percent of those in scientific and academic (8.2%, 1982; 8.9%, 1991), professional and technical (14.6%, 1982; 16.8%, 1991), managerial/administrators (4.2%, 1982; 5.1%, 1991; 7.3%, 2002;), clerical (18.5%, 1982; 16.5%, 1991; 17.0%, 2002), sales (7.5%, 1982; 8.7%, 1991), and service workers (12%, 1982; 13.2%, 1991; 18.5%, 2002) rose, while those in agricultural (5.2%, 1982; 3.4%, 1991), skilled (25.1%, 1982; 23.7%, 1991; 20.3% 2002), and other occupations declined.

Some 81% of all employed persons in 1992 were wage and salary earners, 14% were employers, self-employed persons and members of cooperatives, 4% were kibbutz members, and 1% were unpaid family workers.

The Israeli Household

The average Israeli household (i.e., the group of people living regularly in the same apartment and sharing common meals, including households of one person) consisted in 2002 of 3.37 persons (3.4 persons in the Jewish household and 5.5 persons in the Arab household).

There were in Israel in 2002, 1.85 million households (1.56 million Jewish). The typical household (68.3% of all households) consisted of a couple with or without children, and in some of them also additional members; 17.6% were households of one person (i.e., widows living alone, young persons living on their own outside their family, etc.), 4.6% were one-parent households with children. Other households consisted of various other structures.

The long-term trend of a slow decrease in the size of the average Israeli household was not found in the 1990s. This trend was reversed in the Jewish population, and a small increase was registered in the Jewish population. This resulted from the entrance of immigrants in 1990–92 in larger households. Though immigrants from Russia came in small nuclear families, some proportion of the families lived together in the same household (i.e., a couple with a parent or parents of the husband or wife).

The proportion of single-member households, which increased continuously up to 1989 (15% of Jewish households in 1981 and 17% in 1989) decreased somewhat (17.6% in 2002), as did larger households of 5 members and over (from 27.2% in 1989 to 24.7% in 1997). Large differences in the size of households were found between households of various communities. The average household of those born in Africa in 1997 was 3.54, in Asia 3.17, and in Europe and America 2.80. The household of those born in Israel was 3.65, resulting from the young age structure of this group.

HOUSEHOLD FORMATION AND DISSOLUTION. The number of marriages and their frequency continued decreasing in the 1980s, as formal marriage was postponed, by some one year for grooms and brides who married for the first time. This occurred as cohabitation of younger men and women continued increasing. The decrease in the marriage rate was found in all age groups but especially in the younger age groups.

The dissolution of families by divorce increased to a small extent. One of every nine marriages contracted in Israel was broken by divorce. The divorced couple was married on the average for 11.5 years and had 1.8 children on divorcing.

[Moshe Sicron]

JEWISH COMMUNITIES ("EDOT")

Jews who went to Erez Israel from a particular geographical region, country, or sometimes town or district often brought with them a characteristic cultural heritage, comprising language (in some cases specifically Jewish, like *Yiddish, *Ladino, *Judeo-Arabic, *Judeo-Persian, Georgian, or Kurdish *Aramaic), religious rites and customs, habits, and traditions. They are sometimes referred to, figuratively, as modern "tribes" (*shevatim*). Members of such a group, known as an *edah* (plur. *edot*), usually established their own synagogues, burial societies (see **ḥevra kaddisha*), and mutual aid or charitable organizations, built their own quarters or (in modern times) settled in the same villages, and tended to support each other in local or, to a smaller extent, national politics. The term *edot* often applies specifically to those groups of immigrants who came from, or trace their origin to, the Islamic countries ("Oriental" immigrants). The *edot* preserved their identity, to a greater or lesser extent, for several generations, their members tending to marry within the *edah*, and the tensions between them were of some importance in the history of the *yishuv* and the State of Israel (See *Israel, State of: Population, section on Intercommunal Problems). There are no accurate statistics on the sizes of the various *edot*, as census figures specify only countries of origin and language groups, which are not identical with community membership.

Communal separatism is particularly recognizable in the composition of the populations of neighborhoods and various streets in Jerusalem, in which about 100 quarters were founded up to the establishment of the State of Israel – most of them on a communal basis – and also in greater Tel Aviv, Haifa, and some other towns. The attempt to mix various communities in the new-immigrant moshavim after the creation of the State of Israel was generally unsuccessful. It was abandoned in the 1950s, after which most of the new settlements were established on a more-or-less homogeneous basis from the point of view of origin and social mores. In the kibbutzim the percentage of non-Ashkenazim is small, but in many of them youth groups composed of immigrants from Asia and Africa have been successfully absorbed.

The Ashkenazi Community

This is the largest and, socially, politically, and economically, the most important and influential community in the country. The Ashkenazim consist of Jews of European origin and their descendants, including most of North and South American Jewry. Most Ashkenazi families spoke – or at least understood – Yiddish at some point in their history. Ashkenazim first went to Erez Israel as individuals or as families from the 13th century onward, and, at the latest by the middle of the 15th century, founded their own community in Jerusalem. In the 18th century it numbered a few hundred souls, but ceased to exist, temporarily, after the first quarter of the century. In Safed, however, there was an Ashkenazi community from the 16th century, and it grew particularly after the ḥasidic immigration in 1777. Some of the newcomers moved to Tiberias, and it was from those two towns that the Ashkenazi community in Jerusalem was revived. In 1816 the *Perushim*, the opponents of the Ḥasidim, organized their own community in Jerusalem.

According to a census held in 1839 on behalf of Moses *Montefiore, the number of Ashkenazim in the country was 1,714 – 26.2% of the total Jewish population. In the next 75 years, until the outbreak of World War I, when the Jewish population grew to about 85,000, most of the immigrants who created the "old *yishuv*" were Ashkenazim. In 1876/77 they numbered 6,800 in Jerusalem – 43% of the city's Jewish population; two-thirds of them were *Perushim* and the rest Ḥasidim. By the time of the First Aliyah (1882), they constituted half of the 25,000 Jews in the country, and for many years afterward the proportion of Ashkenazim among the immigrants was on the increase. It is estimated that in 1895 they numbered 25,800 – 63% of the 40,700 Jews; in Jerusalem they constituted 15,000 out of 28,000 Jews, in Safed 4,500 out of 6,600, in Tiberias 1,600 out of 3,200, and in Jaffa 1,700 out of 3,000. The overwhelming majority of the 2,200 Jews in the new agricultural settlements were Ashkenazim.

According to the 1916–18 census, Ashkenazim accounted for 60% of the 56,700 Jews left in the country after the hardships of World War I. They constituted the majority (about 85%) of the immigrants from the end of the war until the creation of the State of Israel (1948). At the time of the declaration of the state, more than 80% of the 650,000 Jews in Israel were Ashkenazim, but since then their proportion of the total population has been steadily on the decrease, due to the increased immigration from Asian and African countries and the comparatively low Ashkenazi birthrate. In the 1961 census, community of origin was not recorded, but on the basis of the information on country of origin and father's country of origin, it may be estimated that Ashkenazim constituted 52.5% of the population; by 1965 they had declined to less than half the total.

In 1948, 46.8% of the Jews speaking foreign languages spoke Yiddish as their sole language or as the first after Hebrew. By 1961 the proportion had decreased to 22.7% (273,615 persons). Other languages spoken by Ashkenazim were German (73,195), Romanian (69,945), Polish (51,760), English (46,615), Hungarian (43,245), Russian (21,255), Czech and Slovak (4,095), Dutch and Flemish (1,530); smaller groups spoke French, Spanish, Serb, Bulgarian, Portuguese, Danish, and Swedish.

The Sephardi Community

The Sephardim in the strict sense of the term, that is, those speaking Ladino or their descendants, have the longest continuous history in the country, the origin of the community dating back to the 15th or early 16th century. It assimilated the Portuguese Jews, expelled a decade or two earlier, who are mentioned by the 16th-century travelers, the remnants of the Byzantine Jews, and, at a later period, the *Musta'rabs (Arabic-speaking Jews) and Jews from other communities, including some Ashkenazim. Individual Jews of Spanish origin were living in Ereẓ Israel as far back as the 11th century, but there was little immigration in medieval times, and, moreover, few of the Jews expelled from Spain and Portugal at the end of the 15th century made their way to Ereẓ Israel because of the insecure conditions in the country. By the end of the 15th century, however, there were many Sephardim in Safed and in 1509 there was a separate Sephardi community in Jerusalem. The flow of immigration increased after the Ottoman conquest, the immigrants receiving aid from their brethren who had settled in Turkey. The Sephardi community of the 16th century developed a flourishing social and cultural life; it included many famous talmudic scholars and served as a center for learning for the whole of the Diaspora. In the census of 1839 Sephardim were incorporated with the Jews from the Oriental communities, but on the basis of the country of origin of Jews born abroad, it can be estimated that at least half of the total were Sephardim. With the creation of the post of **ḥakham bashi* (chief rabbi) of Jerusalem by the Ottoman authorities in 1842, this honored post was always occupied by a Sephardi.

During the 19th century, there were no organized groups of Sephardi immigrants, but there was increased Sephardi immigration in some years, e.g., after the liberation of Greece in 1829 and of Bulgaria in 1878. By 1877 there were 5,970 Sephardim (not including the Maghrebis – immigrants from North Africa) in Jerusalem, and it appears that 5,500 of this number, 40% of the Jewish population of the city, were descendants of exiles from Spain. Most of them were employed in various branches of commerce, but a few families from Bulgaria settled on the land at Hartuv. There was little Sephardi immigration in the 20th century until 1948, and the Sephardim, therefore, did not found their own quarters in Jerusalem like the other communities. Until 1920, however, when the Ashkenazi chief rabbinate was established, it was the *ḥakham bashi* (also styled *rishon le-Zion*) who was the official religious head of the entire Jewish community. In Jerusalem, the Sephardi community maintained its own community council and *ḥevra kaddisha*. In the 1961 census, 63,000 persons, including some Ashkenazim from South America, entered "Spanish" as their sole or second language; 31,535 spoke Bulgarian; 7,750 Turkish (young people who had been educated in state schools in their country of origin); and 2,635 Greek.

The Italian Community

Visitors and individual settlers came from Italy in all periods and Italian Jews in Jerusalem are mentioned until close to 1870. It was only after Mussolini's anti-Jewish measures in 1938, however, that significant numbers settled in Palestine, when about 500 Italian Jews, including a high proportion of scientists and technological experts, arrived. A number of synagogues have been fitted out with *Sefer Torah* arks and other furnishings transferred from disused synagogues in Italy. According to the 1961 census, 5,300 persons spoke Italian, 1,650 as their first or only language. This figure, however, may have included some Jews from Libya (Tripolitania).

Jews from the Maghreb

This term includes all the Jews of North Africa, with the exception of Egypt. Jews from the Maghreb had come to Ereẓ Israel as far back as the 11th century, though mostly as individuals, and in 1218 *al-Ḥarizi mentions a *Maghrebi community in Jerusalem. Immigration increased after the defeat of the crusaders, and individual Maghrebi Jews settled in Jerusalem throughout the centuries. In 1509 there was a Maghreb community in Safed as well. From the second third of the 19th century onward, immigration from the area increased, mostly from *Morocco, with smaller numbers from Tunisia. For a time there was also immigration from *Algeria, but it dwindled with the spread of French culture in that country. Jews from these countries were the founders of the Jewish communities in Jaffa, where 18% were of Maghreb origin in 1905, and in Haifa. In the first half of the 20th century there was a decline in the proportion of educated and professional men among the immigrants from this area. Before World War I there were an estimated 2,000 Maghreb Jews in Jerusalem. During the British Mandate period there was hardly any immigration to Palestine from these countries, but since the middle 1950s Jews from the Maghreb have constituted a high proportion of the immigrants. In 2002 there were 163,000 Jews who were born or whose parents were born in Morocco, 41,200 from Algeria and *Tunisia, and 18,800 from *Libya, almost the entire Jewish community of which settled in Israel. Many of them were among the 122,250 persons who in 1961 recorded Arabic as their first or only language. Of the 24,300 who spoke only, or mainly, French, the majority were from Algeria and Tunisia; the majority of the 43,000 who gave it as their second language were Moroccan. Many Jews from Libya also spoke Italian. Some Berber-speaking Jews from the Atlas mountains settled in the Adullam region. The Maghreb community in Jerusalem has its own *ḥevra kaddisha*.

Iraqi (Babylonian) Jews

It is customary nowadays to describe the Arabic-speaking Jews from southern and central *Iraq, and even from parts of northern Iraq (Mosul), as "Iraqis," but their community and *ḥevra kaddisha* in Jerusalem, unlike that in Ramat Gan, are still called "Bavlim" – Babylonians. Until the middle of the 19th century, very few immigrants came from that part of the world because of the long and dangerous journey. With the introduction of steamships, which traveled down the Tigris River through the Persian Gulf and the Red Sea to Ereẓ Israel, immigration from Iraq increased. In the 30 years preceding World War I, there was a small community of Iraqi Jews, with three synagogues, which printed its own books in Hebrew with translation in Iraqi Jewish Arabic and booklets in the same dialect. In 1916 the community had 371 members. Between the two world wars, the Zionist idea flourished in Baghdad and Hebrew teachers were sent there from Palestine, but they were expelled in 1935 with the growth of the Arab national movement. Their ties with the *yishuv* were renewed during World War II, when many Jews served in the British forces in Iraq or went there to help in the transfer of refugees from the U.S.S.R. and Persia. In 1951 almost the entire Jewish community was forced to leave (*Israel, State of: Aliyah and Absorption), thus virtually liquidating the oldest Jewish community outside Israel. In 2002, 171,700 Jews were registered as of Iraqi origin, among them 2,000–3,000 of Kurdish extraction. The Iraqi community in Israel includes people from all strata of society and of all educational levels.

Jews from Aleppo

Throughout the ages, there had been immigration from *Aleppo, which was an important Jewish economic and scholastic center. Most of the immigrants, however, assimilated with the Musta'rabs and later with the Sephardim. In 1862 they founded the synagogue of Aram Zoba (Aleppo) in the Old City of Jerusalem, and by 1908 eight more synagogues had been founded in the quarters outside the Old City. The second and third generations of the Aleppo community included large numbers of traders and distinguished scholars. It is difficult to estimate the number of Jews of Aleppan origin. In the 2002 census they were recorded with the 36,900 from Syria and Lebanon.

Yemenites

Few Jews from *Yemen settled in Ereẓ Israel before the 19th century. Noteworthy among them were R. Solomon *Adani in the 16th century and R. Shalom *Sharabi in the 18th. The travels of R. Jacob *Saphir and the Orientalist Joseph *Halevy in Yemen may have stimulated Yemenite Jews to go to Ereẓ Israel, and in 1882 a few hundred of them joined together and made their way to Jerusalem with only the clothes on their backs. The help extended to them by the Jews of Jerusalem and the Diaspora did little to alleviate their distress. In 1885 Ashkenazim active in the community purchased a tract of land for them in the village of Silwān, south of Jerusalem, which was extended over the years. In 1908 it contained five synagogues, as the Yemenites in Ereẓ Israel split into two groups: one following the traditional Yemenite (*Baladī*) version of the prayers, which goes back to the Middle Ages, and the other following the "Syrian" (*Shāmī*) rite, that of the Sephardi communities (with many deviations). In addition, special houses of prayer had to be established for the devotees of the Zohar and the Kabbalah and their opponents (the "Dor De'ah"); the Yemenites also had prayer houses in the Old City and 14 small ones in the poorer quarters of Jerusalem outside the walls. The Yemenites' reputation as diligent farm workers suggested the idea of bringing more of them to Ereẓ Israel and the plan succeeded through the efforts of Shmuel *Yavnieli, an emissary of the Palestine Office in Jaffa. Three convoys arrived in 1908/09 and settled in the large moshavot of Judea and Samaria, where special neighborhoods were established for them.

The Yemenite Jews separated themselves from the Sephardim and established a separate community with a rabbi, *bet din*, ritual slaughter facilities, and cemetery plots of their own. They were outstanding for the level of their religious Jewish scholarship and their devotion to the Torah. In spite of the smallness of the community, they printed their special prayer book (*tiktāl*), R. *Saadiah Gaon's translation of the Pentateuch (*Sharḥ*), and other religious books. They still preserve their traditional pronunciation and melodies in prayer and the reading of the Torah (together with the Aramaic Targum), the *haftarot*, and the Five Scrolls.

In 1916 it was estimated that there were 4,058 Yemenites in Palestine: 1,636 in Jerusalem, 859 in Jaffa, 943 in the moshavot in Judea and 620 in Samaria and Galilee. Almost all the Jews in Yemen were transferred to Israel during "Operation Magic Carpet" (1949–50), and many were absorbed in villages and development towns. In the 1961 census close to 120,000 people born in Yemen and Aden, or whose father was born there, were registered and at the end of 2002 the estimated Yemenite population of Israel was 146,000. The veteran members of the community have risen in the social scale and their characteristic leanness has gradually disappeared with the improvement of nutritional standards (although the adoption of the Israel diet has made them susceptible to certain illnesses from which they were previously virtually immune).

Georgians

(in the vernacular, Gurjim). The first Jews from *Georgia (Heb. *Geruzyah*) arrived in Ereẓ Israel in about 1860, after the development of steamboat transportation. By 1862 they had established a house of prayer in the Old City of Jerusalem and before 1914 had five more in their quarters near the Damascus Gate (abandoned in the riots of 1929) and in the Simeon ha-Ẓaddik quarter in the north of the city. After the disturbances of 1936 they dispersed throughout Jerusalem. They spoke Georgian in the Diaspora and are the only Oriental Jewish community that did not employ Hebrew letters to write their vernacular. No scholars from Georgia settled in Ereẓ Israel, but once in the country some members of the community turned to the study of the Torah. The Georgians succeeded in commerce, and some grew wealthy. In 1916 there were 420 Georgian Jews in Jerusalem and 19 in Jaffa. As Russian nationals they were forced to leave the country during World War I, but after the war most of them returned. Since 1916 they have not been registered as a special community in the censuses. Since the establishment of the State of Israel, their language has been growing extinct and their unity as a community has been disintegrating. After the Six-Day War there was a reawakening among Georgian Jews of the desire to go to Israel. Several groups of them are settled in Lydda, Kiryat Malakhi, and other places.

Persians

It appears that the first Persian-speaking Jews who settled in Jerusalem after the destruction of the Second Temple were *Karaites, who came in the middle of the ninth century. In 1839 14 Persians were registered in Safed. In about 1815 the *Perushim* in Jerusalem were said to have hired an ʿAjami ("foreigner" in Arabic, i.e., a Persian) to complete their *minyan*. The first Persian house of prayer in Jerusalem was founded in 1895 in the Shevet Ẓedek quarter (near Maḥaneh Yehudah) and eight more were established through 1908. In the same year, 80 Persian pupils studied in two *talmud torah* schools in Jerusalem. In 1916 120 Persians were registered in the city: it appears that many more of them registered as Sephardim. Before the end of the 19th century Jews came to Ereẓ Israel from *Isfahan and, especially, *Meshed, and the numbers grew after the establishment of the State of Israel. The Jews from Meshed, who were descendants of forced converts to Islam, were known as *Jadīd al-Islām* "neo-Muslims." They were the richest of the Persian community and created international commercial ties in the export of rugs. Since the Ottoman period they have had two synagogues in the Bukharan quarter of Jerusalem and others lived in some of the poorer quarters. During the Mandate and after the establishment of the state, the educated and affluent among them scattered throughout the new quarters of the city. Two communities, the "Persian" and the "Iranian," were registered during the Mandate period, because of an internal dispute, but this distinction later disappeared. Jews from Afghanistan are also counted among the Persians. In 2002 about 135,400 people were of Iranian extraction, 84,600 of whom were born in the country. More than 37,000 of them spoke Persian, and for 16,370 it was their only tongue or their first language after Hebrew (see *Iran).

Bukharans

This term is used to denote Jews who speak a Persian dialect and whose land of origin is *Uzbekistan. In 1827 the first Bukharans set out for Ereẓ Israel and reached Baghdad, but it is not known if any of them actually arrived in Ereẓ Israel. After *Bukhara was conquered by the Russians, individual Bukharans settled in Ereẓ Israel in 1868 and in the middle of the 1870s a number of Bukharan families were living in Jerusalem. Following R. Yaakov *Meir's journey to Bukhara in 1882 as an emissary for charitable institutions, hundreds of affluent families settled in Ereẓ Israel, and in 1892 they established a quarter in Jerusalem ("Street of the Bukharans"), which was uncommonly spacious and elegant for the period. In most of the families some of the members kept up their businesses in Bukhara while others lived in Jerusalem and were supported by the profits of the family business (in some instances, the members abroad and in Ereẓ Israel changed places every few years). In 1908 the Bukharans had 17 beautiful synagogues in Jerusalem, and the number had grown by 1914. During this period the affluent members of the community had books printed in their native language and in Persian, which they understood. During World War I some of the Bukharans fled and some remained in a state of poverty and deprivation. The Communist authorities in Uzbekistan confiscated the property of the Jews, and those who succeeded in returning to Ereẓ Israel supported themselves by renting out houses. In the census of 1961, 2,300 people were registered as "Bukharan"-speaking, but only 660 entered the language as their only or first tongue.

Dagestanis

A few hundred Jews from Dagestan, who speak Tat (an Iranian dialect), settled in Ereẓ Israel at the beginning of the 20th century: some in Be'er Ya'akov, which was established by them, and some in Jerusalem. Their courage and command of weapons won them a reputation in Ereẓ Israel and in the Diaspora, and some of them were outstanding in *Ha-Shomer. As Russian nationals they were also affected by the expulsion at the outbreak of World War I, but some of them returned during the Mandate period, especially to Tel Aviv, where they lived in the "Caucasian" Quarter. Some of those born in Ereẓ Israel do not speak the language used by the community in the Diaspora.

Krimchaks

The Krimchaks are Rabbanites (in contradistinction to the Karaites) from the *Crimea who speak "*Judeo-Tatar"; their *aliyah* may have had some connection with R. Hezekiah *Medini. Before 1915 they had a small community in Jerusalem and published books and pamphlets in their native tongue, apparently for export. They also departed during World War I and in 1916 there was only one family left. After the war a few returned and established their own synagogue in Tel Aviv.

Kurds

During the 19th century, individuals from the cities and townships of *Kurdistan settled in Ereẓ Israel, and at the beginning of the 20th century, a few hundred more followed. Their language, mistakenly called "Kurdish," is a modern Eastern Aramaic and they consequently called themselves Targum Jews. They lived in some of the poorer quarters in western Jerusalem in huts constructed from discarded kerosene cans, boards, and the like (known as the "Tin Quarter," now called Shevet Ẓedek), although stone houses were later constructed. In 1908 they built their own synagogue. Physically powerful and trained for physical labor over the generations, the Kurds were dominant among the porters in the large cities. Some of them helped the Europeans of the Second Aliyah to establish settlements in Lower Galilee. The conquest of Iraq by the British liberated the Jews in the mountains of Kurdistan from their subservience to local feudal lords, but few of them left their villages. With the call to settle in Israel in 1951, however, they abandoned their property and moved to Israel *en masse*. Most of them settled on the land and their youth adjusted to the Israel way of life.

In 1916 174 Kurds were registered in Jerusalem and 222 in Galilee (together with the Urfalis, see below). In 1916, 8,560 Kurdish-speaking residents were recorded, and 3,920 entered

Kurdish as their only language or first language after Hebrew. The Kurds have their own *ḥevra kaddisha* in Jerusalem.

Close to the Kurds from the point of view of language (but not in life style) are the Jews of Persian *Azerbaijan, most of whom settled in Ereẓ Israel after World War I (immigrating via various countries) and established synagogues in Jerusalem, Tel Aviv, and other places. Exact population figures are not to be had. Most of the older generation deal in commerce, while the youth are employed in technical trades.

Urfalis

The Urfalis and residents of the other cities of Upper Urfa (in southern *Turkey) speak Arabic. Jews from this area began to settle in Jerusalem at the beginning of the 20th century; their first house of prayer was established in 1904. In 1916 206 of them were registered in Jerusalem and a few more in Galilee (together with the Kurds). Settlers from two towns in the mountains north of Urfa (*Jarmuk and Siverek), who came with the Urfalis, were registered in 1916 and during the Mandate period as a separate community. In 1916 there were about 200 of them in Jerusalem, where they had a special synagogue. In the same year there were several settlers from Diyarbakir, who were joined by others from the same place during the 1920s in the wake of the Kurdish revolt in their area of Turkey. They also established a synagogue in Jerusalem.

Musta'rabs

This term denotes Jews who adopted the language and life style of their Arab neighbors, and some of whom, it appears, were descendants of families that never went into exile. Over the years, most of the *Musta'rabs were absorbed into the Sephardi community in the broad sense of the term, and only a few families remained in *Peki'in. In the 20th century, even those families, except for one clan, dispersed in Galilee and Samaria.

Karaites

As early as the middle of the ninth century C.E., a movement to settle in Jerusalem and mourn the destruction of the Temple arose among the *Karaites in Babylon and Persia. In the first generation of the tenth century, the Karaite community in Jerusalem was stronger and larger than the Rabbanite one, but the crusaders destroyed it in 1099. In 1540 Karaites settled for a short period in Hebron. In the middle of the 18th century some settled in Jerusalem and established a synagogue, which continued to exist (but never had a *minyan* of worshipers) until the fall of the Old City in 1948. After the establishment of the State of Israel, about 2,000 Karaites went from Egypt to the new state and settled mainly in Ramleh, Ashdod, Beersheba, and the moshavim of *Maẓli'aḥ, near Ramleh and *Ofakim in the northern Negev. The determination of their status, as Jews according to *halakhah* or as a separate religious community, aroused difficult problems.

Indian Jews

After the establishment of the State of Israel, members of two closely knit communities went from *India: the *Bene Israel, who speak Marathi, and the Jews from *Cochin, who speak Malayalam. Through 1954, 1,200 of the Bene Israel settled in Israel, and in 1965 their number had grown to 7,000. Because of their remoteness from the Jewish world and their ignorance of rabbinical laws of marriage and divorce, the halakhic problem of recognizing their right to marry within the Jewish community arose on their arrival. In 1970, there were about 3,400 Cochin Jews in Israel, many of whom settled in development towns and moshavim established by them in the Judean Mountains.

[Abraham J. Brawer]

INTERCOMMUNAL PROBLEMS

A basic factor in the relationship between the "communities" (*edot*) in Israel is the long-standing dominance of the Ashkenazim in the economic, social, cultural, and political spheres. As a result, the various *edot* did not undergo a process of mutual acculturation: instead, the non-Ashkenazi communities tended to assimilate with the Ashkenazi community and adopt its values and way of life. To the extent that the process of assimilation was impeded, inter-community tension developed and was made much more acute by the fact that the distinctions between the communities were largely superimposed on the existing economic and educational stratification: on the whole, the Ashkenazim were better educated and more prosperous, while there was a higher proportion of poverty, under-education, and illiteracy among the Sephardim and other Oriental communities, particularly the new immigrants from African and Asian countries. The closing of the gap between "the first Israel" and "the second Israel" became a central problem. The alleviation of intercommunal tension through the "integration of the exiles" (*mizzug galuyyot*) became a major aim of national policy. At the same time, the opinion was widely held that the tension would be alleviated with the disintegration of the communities themselves and the disappearance of communal allegiances, and that as long as the communities themselves continued to exist there would not be a sense of a united people in Israel. This process of disintegration, however, proved a much more lengthy and complicated process than was initially envisaged.

During the period of the British Mandate, when a large Ashkenazi majority was created by the mass *aliyah* from Europe and the comparatively small *aliyah* from Asian and African countries, intercommunal tension was expressed primarily in the relations between various Ashkenazi groups, such as "Russians." "Poles," and "Galicians," but especially between these three groups together (Eastern Ashkenazim) and those from central Europe (Western Ashkenazim). This situation even led to the crystallization of specific political groups (such as the Aliyah Ḥadashah Party established by immigrants from "Central Europe" – actually from Germany).

The sting of this tension became blunted, however, during the first few years after the founding of the state due to the arrival of thousands of immigrants from the Islamic countries, as the differences between the newcomers and the Ashkenazim obscured the much finer distinctions between the groups within the Ashkenazi community. Among the Ashkenazi community no one group was outstandingly superior in the economic, political, and educational spheres: immigrants from Eastern Europe had molded the main institutions of the country and its pre-1948 ethos and they were dominant in the political leadership of the Zionist Organization, the *yishuv*, and afterward of the state and in their contribution to the shaping of social values. Immigrants from Germany were distinguished in the liberal professions and economic life and those from Western Europe and America were prominent in the technological and scientific developments after 1948. The confrontation between Ashkenazim and non-Ashkenazim, on the other hand, took place under conditions of obvious inequality.

Until the establishment of the new *yishuv*, the communal frameworks were accepted as the basis of public life and there was no conscious aspiration to merge the *edot*. This aim was a product of the modern nationalist movement and the new *yishuv*, and since the builders of the new *yishuv* were Ashkenazim, the idea of "merging" was conceived as the assimilation of non-Ashkenazim to the way of life and value system of the Ashkenazim. At the same time the secular character of the new *yishuv* widened the gap between the two groups by undermining the religious base common to Jews of all communities.

Under the Ottoman regime, the Jews of the new *yishuv* did not hold commanding economic and political positions in the life of the community: indeed, these hardly existed at all until the institution of the Mandatory regime. When the new *yishuv* acquired such positions during the 1920s, political and communal organizations began to develop among the Sephardim, but they reflected, for the most part, the aspirations of affluent businessmen and products of a Western education, themselves candidates for rapid assimilation to the Ashkenazi way of life.

The problem of intercommunal relations became of central importance with the large immigration after the establishment of the state, which created a situation of numerical equality between Ashkenazim and non-Ashkenazim. The immigrants from Islamic countries, especially from areas that had had all but no contact with Europe (such as Yemen) or countries from which it was mainly the poorer strata who came without the communal leadership (such as Morocco), quickly became an economic, social, and especially cultural proletariat in Israel. They felt uprooted in their new surroundings, where the dominant social forces demanded that they abandon their traditions and culture and assimilate unconditionally into modern Israeli society, which was basically Western. Consciously or unconsciously, the authorities and the prevailing public opinion in the country tended to regard the older generation of new immigrants from Islamic countries as a lost generation that would eventually die off, and their main concern was to help the younger generation throw off the burden of its paternalistic traditions. Israel society, however, was successful in many instances only in shattering the patriarchal family structure, which was the principal framework of the immigrants from Islamic countries, and thus destroying old values without simultaneously transferring its own value system as an integral part of the newcomer's personality. In effect, this resulted in the creation of a segment of society that was socially displaced, living on the fringes of two cultures and attracted to the glittering commercial aspects of modern materialistic culture.

However, manifestations of intercommunal tension and bitterness did not come about principally as a result of cultural deprivation, but because of discrimination affecting the immigrants personally. Basically, this discrimination was a consequence of culture deprivations; but this was not the major complaint of the immigrants from Islamic countries. Their complaint was that their absorption into Western society was not being sufficiently accelerated, that they were being prevented from enjoying its social and material fruits to the same extent as the Europeans, and that prejudice was being displayed toward them. The non-Ashkenazim developed psychological sensitivity toward what the Ashkenazim said and did, and this sensitivity sharpened intercommunal tension.

Most of the communities that came from Islamic countries did not develop a leadership that could serve as their spokesman (with the exception, to a certain degree, of the Yemenites – some of whom were considered veterans – and Jews from Iraq, who came *en masse* together with their communal elite). Manifestations of bitterness by "the second Israel" generally took the form of outbursts – sometimes violent – by individuals; there were very few mob outbreaks, the most serious of which occurred in 1959, especially in the Wadi Salib quarter of Haifa. However, attempts to establish political parties on a communal basis proved failures. Almost all the political parties made a habit of including in their election lists a token number of candidates from the "Oriental" communities and every government had one or two members from these communities.

In the 1960s there was a slackening in intercommunal tensions. This was partly a result of the integration of children of all the communities in the school system. In the early years of the State it was felt that a common education would eliminate differences, but cultural deprivation was perpetuated even under equal educational facilities. Factors at work here were differences in home background and tradition (Oriental families did not have the same tradition of sacrificing everything for their children's education), in living conditions (Oriental families could not provide the same atmosphere for study), the Western outlook of the schools and the teachers, and the concentration of better teaching facilities in the large cities (whereas the Oriental communities were largely in the development areas). There was thus a high dropout rate among pupils of Oriental origin.

However, steady progress was evidenced, for example, by the fact that whereas 13% of secondary school pupils in

1956 were from Afro-Asian origin, the percentage increased to 26% in 1961/62 and 42.6% in 1969/70 – though in the 12th (highest) grade the percentage in the latter year was still only 30.2%. Conscious efforts were made to help such children, not only by special tuition and scholarships, but even by lowering pass standards for children of Afro-Asian background so as to encourage them to continue their education. The rate of intermarriage between Ashkenazi and Sephardi-Oriental communities has risen less sharply than was forecast in the early years of the State but it has nevertheless shown a consistent increase. In the late 1960s, 17% of all Jewish marriages were between the two groups. In addition, army service, in which members of all communities meet under conditions of equality, also helped to blur intercommunal distinctions and the common experiences of the Six-Day War and its aftermath had a powerful influence in the same direction. In 1971, however, there was some recrudescence of intercommunal tension.

Attempts to draw parallels with community problems in other countries are misleading. There are no racial distinctions between the *edot* in Israel; there is a feeling of common national (and, obviously, religious) affiliation; there is no legal discrimination against the members of any community; and no one in Israel is interested in perpetuating the gap between the communities. On the contrary, every effort has been made to work toward the fullest integration. Basically, the communal problem in Israel is only the outcome of a sudden confrontation of two cultures, the first sure of itself and the second in a stage of decline, and of the high correlation between communal affiliation and social and educational attributes. These factors reinforce each other, it is true, but the weakening of one also tends to weaken the other. The sense of communal affiliation is on the decrease among those born in Israel; and immigrants from Islamic countries are rising in social status, being exposed to the dominant culture in the country, and in integration with the Ashkenazim without feeling it necessary to create a parallel leadership of their own.

[Aharon Amir]

Tensions between Jews from African-Asian countries and the Ashkenazi elements in Israel continued from 1970. They were expressed in the early 1970s with the emergence of a group calling themselves the Black Panthers who demanded better jobs and educational opportunities for Jews from Islamic countries. The election in 1977 of Menaḥem Begin and the Likud Party helped change the image of these Jews in their own eyes, since many of them supported the Likud against the Labor Party, which was accused of not doing enough to close the ethnic gap. Mr. Begin launched a program called "Project Renewal" designed to rehabilitate 160 distressed neighborhoods throughout Israel with world Jewry aid. The plan was on the whole a success. For a while it seemed that tensions were abating, and that those "Oriental" Jews had finally found their niche in Israeli society. This was illustrated by the growing number of such Jews in the Knesset, government, top army ranks, and the professions. Almost half of the members of the cabinet came from such families who had grown up in development towns. There was a marked improvement in housing solutions and educational opportunities.

This changed, however, with the onset of the massive immigration from the former Soviet Union, especially that beginning in 1989. This brought to Israel some one million immigrants up to 2002, many of whom were highly trained, educated, and skilled. The attention of Israel was now focused on their immediate absorption. This was seen by many "Oriental" Jews as being accomplished at their expense. The feeling was rife that the Russian immigration, with its tremendous potential, had once again pushed down the eastern Jews to the lower rungs of Israeli society with little chance of breaking out of what they considered to be a vicious circle. They accused both the Likud and Labor governments of not paying enough attention to their plight.

Although some of the resentment was imaginary, much of it was real and based on statistics such as poverty lines, slum areas populated by these Jews, and massive unemployment mainly in development towns populated by this segment of Israeli society. There was no appreciable rise in the number of eastern Jews graduating from universities or finding jobs other than as industrial workers.

The anger was seen in the rise of new political parties based solely on ethnic (and religious) lines in the case of Shas and neighborhood lines in the case of the David Levy faction in the Likud, seen as a counter-balance to the possibility of a "Russian" political party. While the two major political blocs assigned spots in their Knesset slates to eastern Jews, this was not enough to assuage the frustration felt mainly by the second and third generation trying to break out of what they considered a gridlock. By 2002 the ethnic element was seen to be playing an important role in national politics, but at a lower priority than the peace process which seemed to absorb the almost total attention of the government, another cause for resentment and bitterness.

[Meron Medzini]

THE NON-JEWISH POPULATION

Ottoman Period

Although no detailed statistical data are available for the Ottoman period, it is possible to sketch the main demographical characteristics of the non-Jewish population in the 19th century and the beginning of the 20th century. Economic standards were, on the whole, very low, the population living largely on primitive agriculture. Urban development was limited; only a small part of the Muslim population lived in the towns, and in the few larger ones the proportion of Christians and Jews was considerable. As health services were almost nonexistent in most of the country and the government took very little interest in the health and welfare of the population, it may be assumed that mortality was high and offset the high birthrate to a considerable extent. Under those conditions, the population increased slowly. A rough estimate for the year 1914 indicates that the total population of the area that later became Palestine under the British Mandate was 689,000; 604,000 non-Jews and 85,000 Jews.

British Mandate Period

During this period demographic conditions changed quickly. In the first year of British administration, the situation of Muslims in Palestine was more or less similar to that of other countries in the Middle East, such as Egypt. Mortality was still high; malaria still predominated in certain regions of the country; trachoma was widespread; and epidemics of typhoid, measles, etc. were frequent. Child mortality was particularly high in 1927–29; for example, 41% of Muslim children died before reaching the age of five.

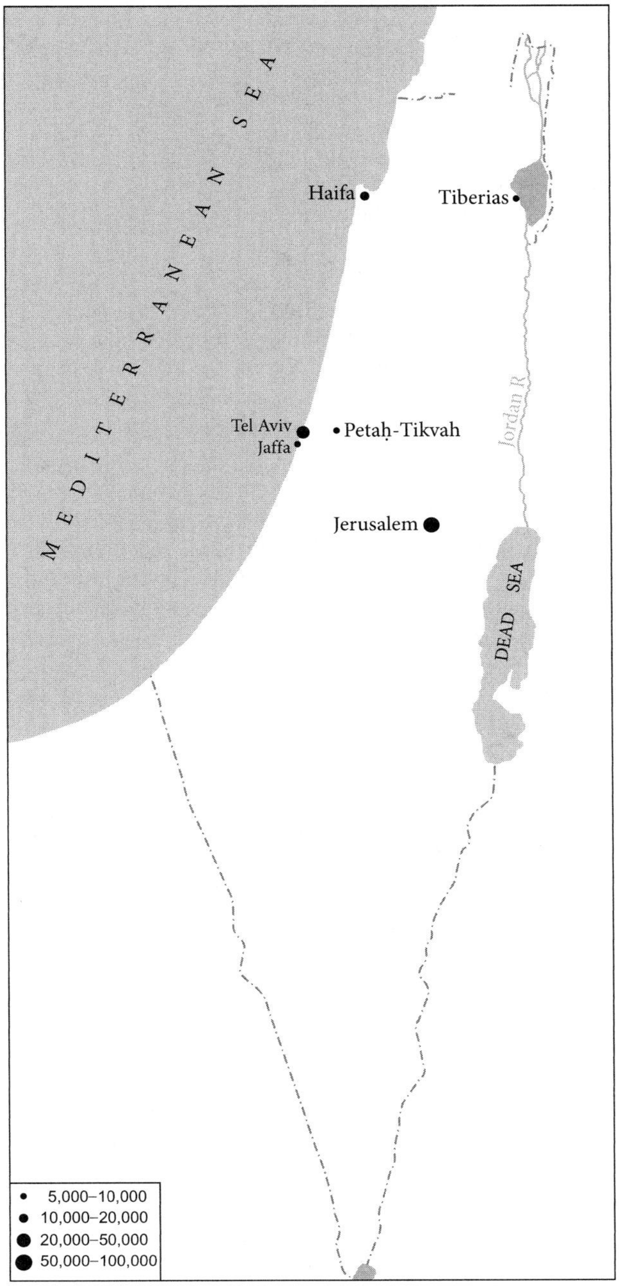

Map 1. Settlements with Jewish population numbering over 5,000, Nov. 1931.

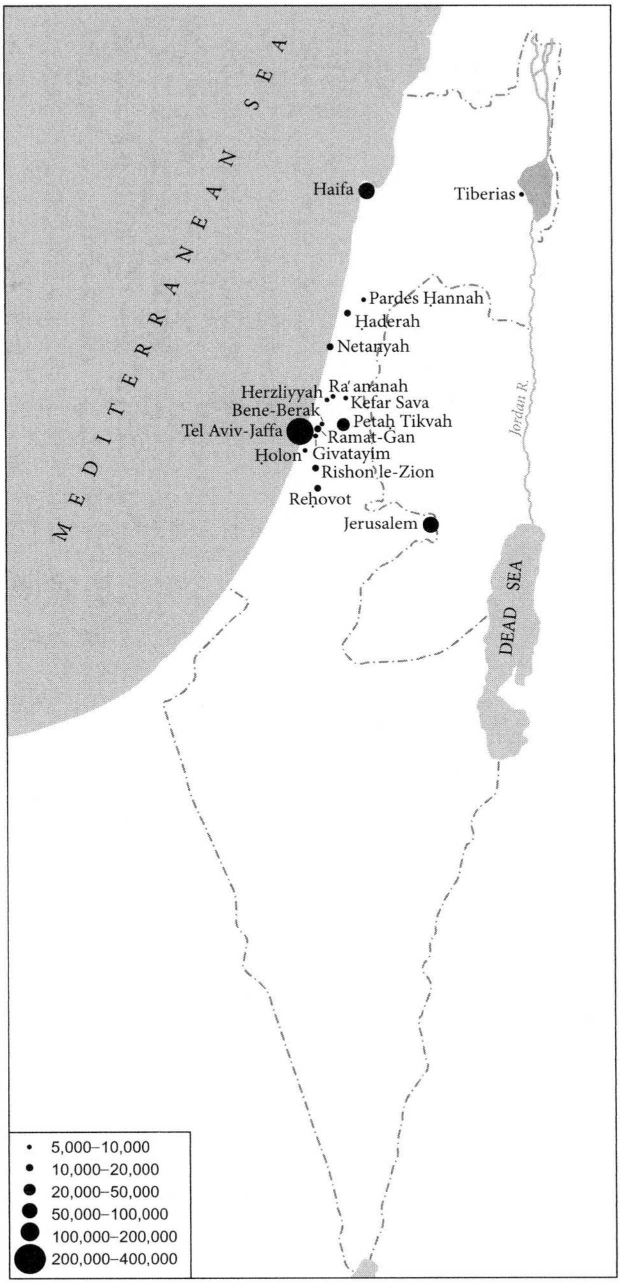

Map 2. Settlements with Jewish population numbering over 5,000, Nov. 1948.

With improving health conditions, better security, economic development, and improved communications, however, mortality quickly decreased: the death rate of Muslims dropped from 30 per thousand in 1924–28 to 21 in 1939–41, while the average life expectancy increased from about 37 in 1926–27 to 47 and the child mortality up to the age of five fell to 29%. In the later years of the Mandate, mortality is known to have continued to decrease, but no reliable data are available (as the village heads who were responsible for reporting were also responsible for food distribution and were thus interested in concealing deaths). The fall in mortality was particularly marked in areas where the Arabs lived in closer contact with the Jewish population and could enjoy the services of Jewish physicians and medical institutions, as well as the benefits of more rapid economic development.

Marriages during the Mandatory period were practically universal among the Muslim population and were contracted at a very young age. Remarriages of divorced and widowed persons were also frequent. Nuptial mores were on the whole very favorable to fertility, which was high, as measured in terms of children per woman in the entire productive span, and tended to increase during the period, due probably to improved health and economic conditions. Among the Muslim population, the fertility rate was 6.1 children per woman in 1927–29, 7.6 in 1939–41, and 8.1 in 1942–43. Among the Christians, marriage was less universal and fertility was lower on the average.

Although no data are available on internal migration, it is known that a considerable movement took place toward the Coastal Plain, which developed more quickly under the impact of Jewish enterprise. The towns that increased their non-Jewish populations most were Jaffa, Haifa, and Gaza. In the interior of the country there was a very considerable development of the non-Jewish population only in Jerusalem; Hebron and Nablus each passed the 20,000 mark toward the end of the Mandatory period. On the whole, Judea and Samaria remained predominantly rural, having an urban population of less than 25% throughout the Mandatory period. Emigration from Palestine was, on the whole, very limited, while in periods of more intense economic development there was some immigration, mainly to find work, from neighboring countries. Under the impact of the large and growing natural increase, the main feature of the demographic evolution of non-Jews in the Mandatory period was the very considerable increase in population: the non-Jewish population almost doubled itself between 1922 and 1948. This corresponds to an average increase of 2.5% per year, which was exceptional at the time for underdeveloped countries.

In the State of Israel: 1948–67

The tension in the late months of 1947 and the beginning of 1948, followed by the invasion from Arab countries and the War of Independence, brought about dramatic changes in the political and demographic situation. The territory of Mandatory Palestine was divided into three parts. In the part that passed under Israel rule, the non-Jewish population was drastically reduced by the flight of Arabs, who took refuge in various Arab states. The number of Palestinian Arab refugees has been assessed at different levels by different research workers, institutions, and political agencies. The difficulty in establishing the true figures stems from lack of accurate data for the end of the Mandatory period (the last census taken by the British authorities was in 1931), the fact that applicants for assistance from the United Nations Relief and Works Agency included many who were not refugees, and the inability of the UNRWA to keep accurate records of deaths, migration, and so on. Despite the difficulties, however, it may be roughly reckoned that the Arab population before the disturbances of 1947–48 and the war of 1948 in the part of Palestine that passed under Israel rule was of the order of magnitude of 750,000. It is known that after the departure of the refugees about 156,000 Arabs remained in Israel.

The economic and social conditions of Israel's Arabs improved quickly and the death rate decreased to the same level as that of the Jewish population. Marriage among Muslims remained practically universal although a little more delayed than during the Mandatory period, and remarriage

Non-Jews in Israel by Religion (1922–2002)

	Oct. 23, 1922[1]	Nov. 18, 1931[1]	Dec. 31, 1949[2]	May 22, 1961[2]	Dec. 31, 1969[3]	1994[3,4]	2002
Muslims	589,177	759,700	111,500	170,830	314,500	766,400	1,038,300
Christians	71,464	88,967	34,000	50,543	73,500	154,500	140,400
Druze and others	7,617	10,101	14,500	25,761	34,600	90,400[5]	355,400
TOTAL	668,258	858,768	160,000	247,134	422,600	1,011,300	1,534,100

Source: Statistical Abstract of Israel, Central Bureau of Statistics, Jerusalem.

1 Palestine.
2 Israel.
3 Israel including East Jerusalem.
4 Average.
5 Druze only.

Non-Jewish Population of Israel by District and Sub-District[1,2] (1948–2003)

	Population (thousands)					Percentages				
District and Sub-District	Nov. 8, 1948	May 22, 1961	Dec. 31, 1969	Dec. 31, 1994	Dec. 31, 2003	Nov. 8, 1948	May 22, 1961	Dec. 31, 1969	Dec. 31, 1994	Dec. 31, 2003
Jerusalem district	**2.9**	**4.2**	**76.6**	**172.8**	**251.7**	**1.8**	**1.7**	**18.1**	**16.8**	**16.1**
Northern district	**90.6**	**142.8**	**202.7**	**468.1**	**611.0**	**58.1**	**57.7**	**48.0**	**45.4**	**39.3**
Safed sub-district	1.9	3.0	3.9	8.4	15.3	1.2	1.2	0.9	0.8	1.0
Kinneret sub-district	5.1	7.9	10.9	22.4	32.2	3.3	3.2	2.6	2.2	2.1
Jezreel sub-district	34.9	53.5	75.0	168.1	228.0	22.4	21.6	17.8	16.3	14.7
Acre sub-district	48.7	78.4	112.8	252.4	335.5	31.2	31.7	26.7	24.5	21.5
Haifa district	**27.4**	**48.0**	**68.8**	**159.5**	**237.5**	**17.6**	**19.4**	**16.3**	**15.5**	**15.3**
Haifa sub-district	9.1	18.6	24.8	53.1	90.8	5.9	7.5	5.9	5.2	5.8
Ḥaderah sub-district	18.3	29.4	44.0	106.4	148.7	11.7	11.9	10.4	10.3	9.5
Central district	**16.1**	**26.9**	**39.1**	**101.4**	**185.1**	**10.3**	**10.9**	**9.2**	**9.8**	**11.9**
Sharon sub-district	10.4	17.4	24.7	57.2	84.2	6.6	7.0	6.8	5.5	5.4
Petaḥ Tikvah sub-district	3.0	4.7	7.3	21.8	45.4	1.9	1.9	1.7	2.1	2.9
Ramleh sub-district	2.6	4.4	6.7	20.6	34.5	1.7	1.8	1.6	2.0	2.2
Reḥovot sub-district	0.1	0.4	0.5	1.9	21.0	0.1	0.2	0.1	0.2	1.4
Tel Aviv district	**3.6**	**6.7**	**8.0**	**25.4**	**68.9**	**2.3**	**2.8**	**1.9**	**2.5**	**4.4**
Southern district	**15.4**	**18.6**	**27.5**	**102.2**	**202.0**	**9.9**	**7.5**	**6.5**	**9.9**	**13.0**
Ashkelon sub-district	2.4	0.3	0.4	8.1	34.2	1.6	0.1	0.1	0.8	2.2
Beersheba sub-district	13.0	18.3	27.1	94.2	167.7	8.3	7.4	6.4	9.1	10.8
Total	**156.0**	**247.2**	**422.7**	**1,030.4**	**1,556.2**	**100.0**	**100.0**	**100.0**	**100.0**	**100.0**

Source: Statistical Abstract of Israel, Central Bureau of Statistics, Jerusalem.

1 According to the boundaries of the sub-districts in the years listed.

2. Excluding Golan Heights, Judea, Samaria, and Gaza.

was still frequent. The fertility rate remained extremely high (eight or nine children to each woman on the average). Only among the Christian Arabs have signs of increasing birth control appeared in recent years. Emigration was practically nil. Under the impact of all these facts, the natural increase of Arabs in Israel has been very high by international standards, and the Arab population doubled itself between 1948 and 1967.

Table: Non-Jews in Israel by Religion gives some details on the changes in the non-Jewish population of Israel classified by religion. Its structure by sex is well balanced and the age structure is very young. Table: Non-Jews in Israel by District shows the geographical distribution of the non-Jewish population by regions. While the Muslim population has largely retained its rural character, the Christian population is largely urban. On the whole, the geographical distribution of the non-Jewish population is very different from that of the Jews; but there is an increasing intermingling of the two populations, as many non-Jews, while still residing in their areas, go out to work in Jewish towns and villages.

Population of the "West Bank" and Gaza Strip Between the Two Wars

The population of Judea and Samaria (called "the West Bank" under Jordanian rule) increased very considerably in 1948 due to the large influx of refugees, but the population increase was very limited in the period between 1948 and 1967. Fertility was high (more or less on the level of eight children per woman), but mortality declined very little, and it may be reckoned to have been almost three times that of the Arabs in Israel at the end of the period. The West Bank remained prevalently rural and largely underdeveloped. Consequently, a considerable emigration developed toward Amman and other more developed regions of the East Bank, the Arab oil states (such as Kuwait, Iraq, and Saudi Arabia), and, to some extent, to overseas countries. As a consequence of the Six-Day War there was a considerable efflux of refugees, mainly from the Jericho region. As a result of all these factors, the population of the West Bank after the Six-Day War was probably only a little larger than it had been in 1948.

The population of the Gaza Strip increased very considerably in 1948 owing to the mass influx of refugees, who were largely settled in refugee camps. This increased still further the non-rural character of the population.

Natural increase in the Gaza Strip was probably similar to that of the West Bank, but emigration was smaller, and the total increase of population was therefore higher. Due to these factors the density of population in the Gaza Strip is very high compared with that of the West Bank.

Population of Administered Territories, 1967–2002

In 1967 and 1968 there was considerable emigration from these territories, mainly toward Jordan and other Arab states, which has brought about some decline in the population. This move-

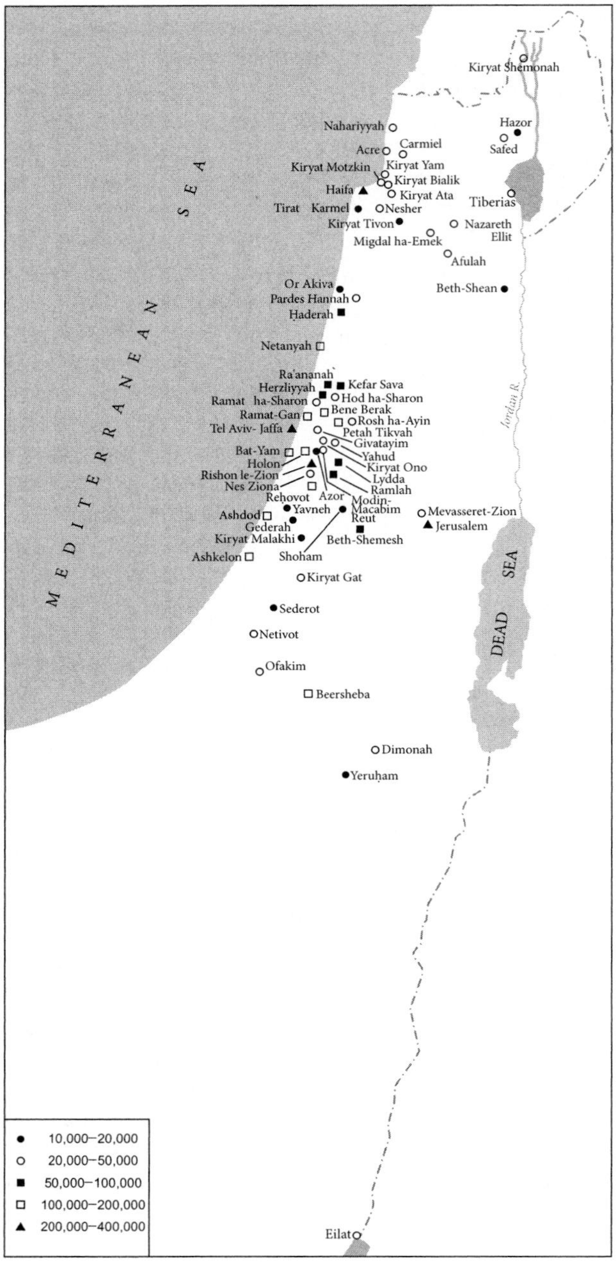

Map 3. Settlements with Jewish population numbering over 10,000, 2004.

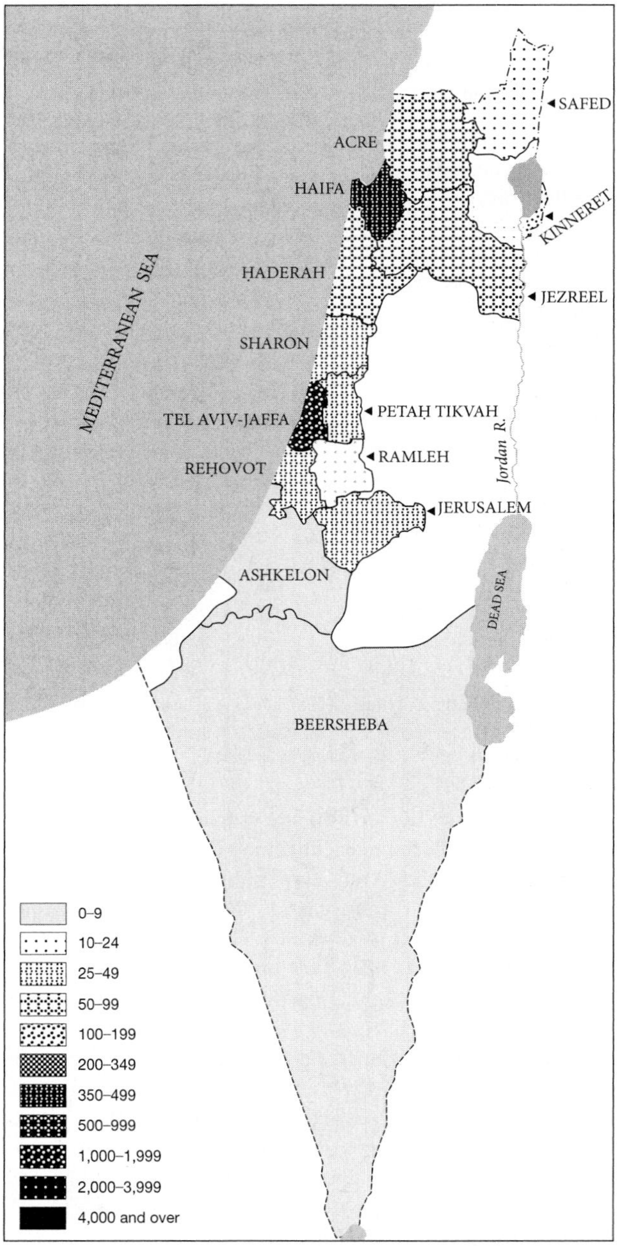

Map 4. Israel population density per sq. km. 1948. The sub-district boundaries are those of 1969. Based on data from Statistical Abstract of Israel, *1970.*

ment has practically stopped, however, and the population has begun to increase, due to a considerable excess of births over deaths. At the end of 1969 the population of Judea and Samaria was 601,000 and of the Gaza Strip 337,000.

The economic condition of the population of the administered territories has very considerably improved. This, and the extended network of medical and social services explain the quick reduction of its mortality during the period under survey. As fertility has remained high, the natural increase has grown. Despite some emigration from Judea and Samaria in the past few years, the size of population has increased considerably, from 581,700 at the beginning of 1969 to 699,600

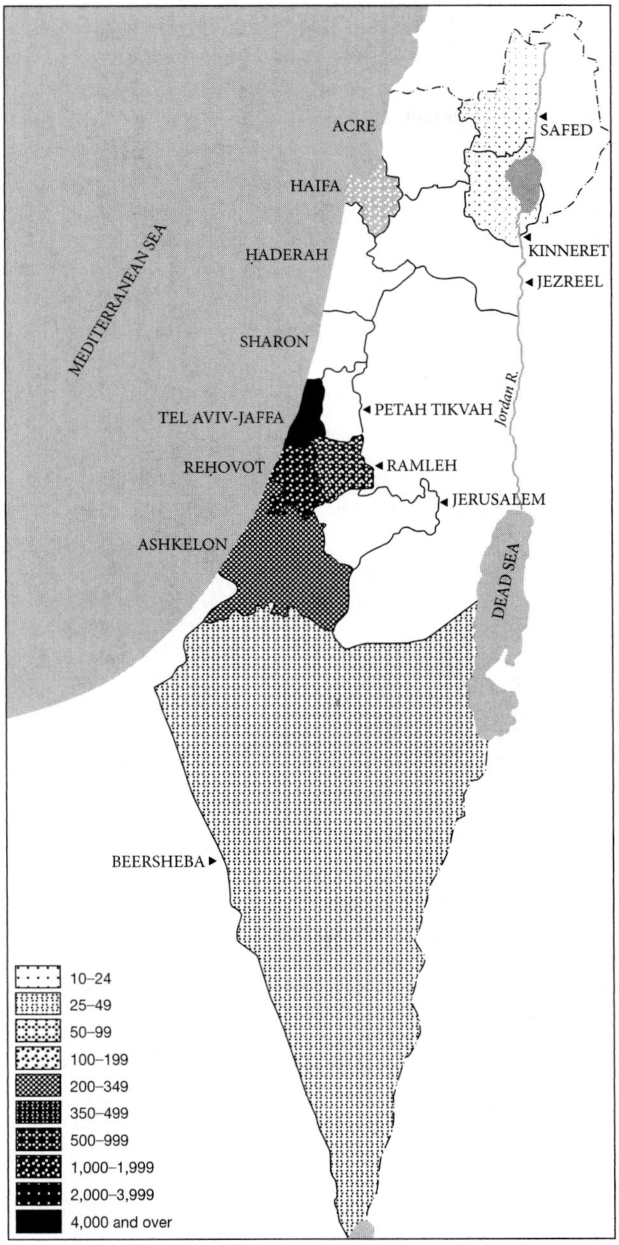

Map. 5. Israel population density per sq. km. 2004. The sub-district boundaries are those of 1969. Based on data from Statistical Abstract of Israel, *2005.*

at the end of 1980 in Judea and Samaria, and from 355,900 to 431,500 in the Gaza Strip and Northern Sinai.

The number of Jews living in the administered territories was estimated at the end of 1977 as 4,400 in Judea and Samaria, 3,500 in the Gaza Strip and Sinai and 3,000 in the Golan Heights. In 2002 it was estimated that 203,700 lived in the administered territories, about 7,000 of them in the Gaza Strip (evacuated by the Israelis in 2005).

[Roberto Bachi]

BIBLIOGRAPHY: JEWISH AND NON-JEWISH POPULATION: *Census of Palestine* (1931, 1933); *Survey of Palestine*, 3 vols. (1946); *Statistical Abstracts of Palestine* (1936–45); Israel, Central Bureau of Statistics, *Statistical Abstracts of Israel* (1950–2003); idem, *Special Publications*, nos. 36 and 53 (Registration of Population Nov. 8, 1948); no. 194 (Marriages of Jews in Israel 1947–62); no. 242 (Projection of the Population in Israel up to 1985); no. 268 (Vital Statistics 1965–66); no. 262 (Internal Migration of Jews in Israel 1965–1966); no. 276 (Demographic Characteristics of the Jewish Population in Israel 1965–67); idem, *Publication* no. 42 (Main Data of the Census 1961); nos. 36 and 39 (Census 1961, Families in Israel); R. Bachi, in: *Proceedings, World Population Conference* (1954); idem, in: *Challenge of Development* (1958), 41–80; idem, in: JJSO, 8 (1966), 142–9; idem, in: *International Symposium on Automation of Population Register System, Proceedings* (1967); idem, in: *Sydney Conference of the International Union for the Scientific Study of Population* (1967); R. Bachi and J. Matras, in: *Milbank Memorial Fund Quarterly*, 40 (1962); R. Bachi, *Ha-Nohag ba-Nissu'in u-va-Yeludah be-Kerev ha-Shekhavot ha-Shonot shel ha-Yishuv ve-Hashpa'ato al Atido* (1944); *Din ve-Ḥeshbon shel ha-Va'adah li-Ve'ayot ha-Yeludah Muggash le-Rosh ha-Memshalah* (1966); D.H.K. Amiram and A. Shachar, *Development Towns in Israel* (1969). R. Bachi: *The Population of Israel* (1977); appeared also in the international series of Population Monographs of CICRED, Paris; idem, *Population Trends of World Jewry* (1976); official publications of the Central Bureau of Statistics, Jerusalem, and especially: *Statistical Abstract of Israel; Population and Housing 1972 Census Series; Monthly Bulletins of Statistics.* JEWISH COMMUNITIES AND INTERCOMMUNAL PROBLEMS: I. Ben-Zvi, *The Exiled and the Redeemed* (1961); idem, *Israel under Ottoman Rule 1517–1917* (1960), also in: L. Finkelstein, *The Jews*, 1 (1960³), 602–89; D. and M. Hacohen, *Our People* (1969); A.M. Luncz, *Jerusalem*, 1 (Eng., 1882), 20–114; H. Mizraḥi, *Yehudei Paras...* (1959); R.H. Hacohen, *Avanim ba-Ḥomah* (1970); A. Ben-Jacob, *Yehudei Bavel...* (1965); idem, *Kehillot Yehudei Kurdistan* (1961); idem, *Yalkut Minhagim: Miminhagei Shivtei Yisrael* (1967); D. Bensimon-Donath, *Immigrants d' Afrique du Nord en Israel. Evolution et Adaptation* (1970); S.N. Eisenstadt, *Israeli Society* (1967), incl. bibl.; S.N. Eisenstadt, R. Bar Yosef and Ch. Adler, *Integration and Development in Israel* (1970), incl. bibl.; M. Sicron, *Immigration to Israel 1948–1953* (1957); A.A. Weinberg, *Immigration and Belonging* (1961); J. Shuval, *Immigrants on the Threshold* (1963). **ADD. BIBLIOGRAPHY:** S. DellaPergola, "The Global Context of Migration to Israel," in: E. Leshern and J. Shuval (eds.), *Immigration to Israel* (1998); idem, "World Jewish Population 2001," in: *American Jewish Year Book*, 101 (2001); E. Deritz and Baras (eds), *Studies in the Fertility of Israel*, Institute of Contemporary Jewry, Hebrew University (1992); Z. Soleel, *Migrants from the Promised Land* (1986); M. Sicron, *"Ukhlusiyyat Yisra'el – Me'afyenim u-Megamot,"* in: *Demografiyyah* (2004); S. DellaPergola, *"Demografiyyah Yehudit, Uvdot, Sikkuyim, Etgarim,"* in: Report of the Jewish People Policy Planning Institute (2003); Israel Central Bureau of Statistics, *Sikrei Ko'aḥ Adam* (2001, 2003); idem, *Indikatorim le-Mispar Toshevei Yisr'ael be-Ḥul* (1992); idem, *Zirmei Hagirah shel Yisra'elim le-Ḥuẓ le-Areẓ;* R. Lamdani, *Ha-Yeridah mi-Yisra'el*, in: *Ra'yon le-Kalkalah*, 20:116 (1983); Ministry of Health, *Beri'ut be-Yisra'el – Netunim Nivharim* (2001); E. Sabbatello, *"Ha-Yeridah min ha-Areẓ u-Tekhunoteha,"* in: *Ba-Tefuẓot u-va-Golah*, 19 (1978).

ISRAEL PLACE LIST (2004) – PLACES OF JEWISH HABITATION IN ISRAEL AND THE ADMINISTERED TERRITORIES

A – Amana
G – Gadna
H – Herut
H – Histadrut
HH – Ha-Ichud ha-Kehilati
HI – Hitahadut ha-Ikkarim
IH – Ihud Hakla'i
IK – Ihud ha-Kevuzot ve-ha-Kibbutzim
KA – Ha-Kibbutz ha-Artzi (Ha-Shomer ha-Za'ir)
KD – Ha-Kibbutz ha-Dati
KM – Ha-Kibbutz ha-Me'uhad
M – Mapam
MH – Hamerkaz ha-Hakla'i
OZ – Ha-Oved ha-Ziyyoni
PAI – Po'alei Agudat Israel
PM – Ha-Po'el ha-Mizrachi
TKM – Tenua Kibbutzit Mehuhedet
TM – Tenu'at ha-Moshavim

NOTES:
Geographical Region: The sign "67+" indicates a settlement beyond the pre-1967 borders.
Year of Founding: Where the year is not indicated, the settlement is ancient.
Form of Settlement: Only the present form of settlement is given.
Affiliation: Only the present affiliation is given.
Municipal Status: RC – the settlement is represented in the regional council indicated.
(RC) – the settlement belongs to the area of the regional council, but is not represented in it.
No. of Inhabitants: The sign .. indicates that the population figures are not available.

Name	Geographical Region	Year of Founding	Settlement Form	Affiliation	Municipal Status	No. of inhabitants 31 Dec. 2004
Acre (Akko)			Town		municipality	45,553 thereof 11,810 non-Jews
Adamit	Western Upper Galilee	1958	Kibbutz	KA	RC Sultam Zor	106
Adanim	Southern Sharon	1950	Moshav	RC	RC Ha-Yarkon	428
Adderet	Judean Foothills (Adullam Region)	1961	Moshav	TM	RC Matteh Yehudah	513
Addirim	Jezreel Valley (Taanach Region)	1956	Moshav	TM	RC Ha-Gilboa	222
Adi	Western Lower Galilee (Shefaram region)	1980	Urban Community		RC Jezreel Valley	1,705
Adora	Southern Hebron Mountains; 67+	1983	Rural Community	H	RC Hebron Mountain	186
Afek	Acre	1939	Kibbutz	KM	RC Na'aman	429
Afik	Golan Heights; 67+	1967	Kibbutz	IK	RC Golan	235
Afikim	Kinneret Valley	1932	Kibbutz	IK	RC Jordan Valley	985
Afulah (Ir Yizre'el)	Jezreel Valley	1925	Urban Settlement		local council	38,864
Agur	Southern Judean Foothills	1950	Moshav	TM	RC Matteh Yehudah	331
Aḥi'ezer	Coastal Plain (Lod Region)	1950	Moshav	PM	RC Lod Plain	1,285
Aḥihud	Acre Plain	1950	Moshav	TM	RC Na'aman	678
Aḥisamakh	Coastal Plain (Lod Region)	1950	Moshav	TM	RC Modi'im	1,076
Aḥituv	Central Sharon	1951	Moshav	TM	RC Ḥefer Plain	775
Aḥuzzam	Southern Coastal Plain (Lachish Region)	1950	Moshav	OZ	RC Lachish	411
Aḥvah	Southern Coastal Plain		Urban Community		RC Naḥal Sorek	246
Ale Zahav	Samaria; 67+	1982	Rural Community	H	RC Samaria	429
Alfe Menashe	Samaria; 67+	1983	Urban Community		local council	5,433
Allonei Abba	Southern Lower Galilee	1948	Moshav Shittufi	OZ	RC Kishon	317
Allonei ha-Bashan	Golan Heights; 67+	1981	Moshav Shittufi	PM	RC Golan	251
Allonei Yiẓḥak	Manasseh Hills	1949	Youth Village	OZ	(RC) Manasseh	208
Allon ha-Galil	Jezreel Valley (Shefaram region)	1980	Urban Community	TM	RC Jezreel Valley	899
Allonim	Jezreel Valley	1938	Kibbutz	KM	RC Kishon	537
Allon Shevut	Hebron Hills; 67+	1971	Rural Center	PM	RC Etzyon Bloc	3,229
Almagor	Kinneret Valley	1961	Moshav	TM	RC Jordan Valley	219
Almah	Eastern Upper Galilee	1949	Moshav	PM	RC Merom ha-Galil	727
Almog	Dead Sea Region; 67+	1977	Kibbutz	IK	RC Megilot	142
Almon	Southern Samaria; 67+	1982	Rural Community	A	RC Matteh Benjamin	739
Alumim	Northwestern Negev (Besor Region)	1966	Kibbutz	PM	RC Azzatah	380
Alummah	Southern Coastal Plain (Malakhi Region)	1965	Rural Center		(RC) Shafir	531

Name	Geographical Region	Year of Founding	Settlement Form	Affiliation	Municipal Status	No. of inhabitants 31 Dec. 2004
Alummot (Bitanyah)	Kinneret Valley	1941	Kibbutz	IK	RC Jordan Valley	251
Amaẓyah	Lachish (Adoraim) Region	1955	Moshav Shittufi	H	RC Lachish	137
Amir	Ḥuleh Valley	1939	Kibbutz	KA	RC Ha-Galil ha-Elyon	552
Amirim	Eastern Upper Galilee	1950	Moshav	TM	RC Merom ha-Galil	469
Amkah	Acre Plain	1949	Moshav	TM	RC Ga'aton	549
Ammi'ad	Eastern Upper Galilee (Hazor Region)	1946	Kibbutz	IK	RC Ha-Galil ha-Elyon	426
Ammikam	Iron Hills (Northwestern Samaria)	1950	Moshav	H	RC Allonah	509
Amminadav	Jerusalem Hills	1950	Moshav	TM	RC Matteh Yehudah	611
Ammi'oz	Northwestern Negev (Besor Region)	1957	Moshav	TM	RC Eshkol	224
Amukka	Upper Galilee	1980	Community		RC Merom ha-Galil	211
Ani'am	Golan Heights; 67+	1978	Moshav Shittufi	TM	RC Golan	379
Arad	Northeastern Negev	1961	Urban Settlement	–	local council	23,477
Arbel	Eastern Lower Galilee	1949	Moshav	TM	RC Ha-Galil ha-Taḥton	333
Argaman	Lower Jordan Valley; 67+	1968	Moshav	H	RC Jordan Valley	166
Ariel	Central Samaria; 67+	1978	Urban Settlement		municipality	16,414
Arsuf	Sharon	1995	Urban Community		RC Ḥof ha-Sharon	127
Arugot	Southern Coastal Plain (Malakhi Region)	1949	Moshav	TM	RC Be'er Tuviyyah	731
Aseret	Coastal Plain (Reḥovot Region)	1954	Rural Center	–	RC Gederot	1,099
Asfar (Meiẓad)	Etzyon Bloc; 67+	1983	Rural Community	PAI	RC Etzyon Bloc	275
Ashalim	Central Negev	1976	Moshav Shitufi	IK	RC Ramat ha-Negev	233
Ashdod	Southern Coastal Plain	1955	City		municipality	196,903
Ashdot Ya'akov	Kinneret Valley	1933	Kibbutz	IK	RC Jordan Valley	552
Ashdot Ya'akov	Kinneret Valley	1933	Kibbutz	KM	RC Jordan Valley	350
Ashkelon	Southern Coastal Plain	–	City		municipality	105,088
Ateret	Western Samaria; 67+	1981	Rural Community	A	RC Matteh Benjamin	350
Athlit	Carmel Coast	1904	Urban Settlement		local council	4,438
Avdon	Western Upper Galilee	1952	Moshav	TM	RC Ma'aleh ha-Galil	474
Avi'el	Northern Sharon (Ḥaderah Region)	1949	Moshav	H	RC Allonah	417
Avi'ezer	Judean Foothills	1958	Moshav	PM	RC Matteh Yehudah	513
Avigedor	Southern Coastal Plain (Malakhi Region)	1950	Moshav	TM	RC Be'er Tuviyyah	646
Aviḥayil	Central Sharon	1932	Moshav	TM	RC Ḥefer Plain	1,133
Avital	Jezreel Valley (Taanach Region)	1953	Moshav	TM	RC Ha-Gilboa	439
Avivim	Eastern Upper Galilee	1960	Moshav	TM	RC Merom ha-Galil	443
Avnei Eitan	Golan Heights; 67+	1978	Moshav	PM	RC Golan	337
Avnei Ḥefeẓ	Samaria; 67+	1990	Urban Community	A		1,038
Avtalyon	Northern Lower Galilee	1987	Urban Community	HH	RC Misgav	311
Ayanot	Coastal Plain (Rishon le-Zion Region)	1930	Agricultural School	–	–	388
Ayyelet ha-Shaḥar	Ḥuleh Valley	1918	Kibbutz	IK	Ha-Galil ha-Elyon	1,271
Azaryah	Judean Foothills	1949	Moshav	TM	RC Gezer	753
Azor	Coastal Plain (Tel Aviv Region)	1948	Urban Settlement		local council	9,993
Azri'el	Southern Sharon (Kefar Sava Region)	1951	Moshav	PM	RC Hadar ha-Sharon	515
Azrikam	Southern Coastal Plain (Malakhi Region)	1950	Moshav	TM	RC Be'er Tuviyyah	1,020
Baḥan	Central Sharon	1953	Kibbutz	IK	RC Ḥefer Plain	246
Balfouriyyah	Jezreel Valley	1922	Moshav	TM	RC Yizre'el	293
Barak	Jezreel Valley (Taanach Region)	1956	Moshav	TM	RC Ha-Gilboa	251
Baram	Eastern Upper Galilee	1949	Kibbutz	KA	RC Merom ha-Galil	462
Bareket	Coastal Plain (Petaḥ Tikvah Region)	1952	Moshav	PM	RC Modi'im	1,124
Bar Giora	Jerusalem Hills	1950	Moshav	H	RC Matteh Yehudah	378
Barkai	Iron Hills (Northwestern Samaria)	1949	Kibbutz	KA	RC Manasseh	341
Barkan	Western Samaria; 67+	1981	Urban Community	H		1,215

Name	Geographical Region	Year of Founding	Settlement Form	Affiliation	Municipal Status	No. of inhabitants 31 Dec. 2004
Bat Ayin	Etzyon Bloc; 67+	1989	Rural Community	A	RC Etzyon Bloc	796
Bat Hadar	Southern Coastal Plain	1995	Urban Community		RC Ḥof Askhelon	378
Bat Ḥefer	Central Sharon	1996	Urban Community		RC Ḥefer Plain	5,081
Bat Shelomo	Manasseh Hills	1889	Moshav	HI	RC Ḥof ha-Karmel	387
Bat Yam	Coastal Plain (Tel Aviv Region)	1926	City		municipality	130,389
Be'eri	Northwestern Negev (Eshkol Region)	1946	Kibbutz	KH	RC Eshkol	759
Be'erotayim	Coastal Plain (Ḥefer Valley)	1949	Moshav	TM	RC Ḥefer Plain	583
Be'erot Yiẓḥak	Coastal Plain (Petaḥ Tikvah Region)	1948	Kibbutz	PM	RC Modi'im	416
Be'er Orah	Southern Arabah Valley	1950	Youth Camp	G	(RC) Ḥevel Eilot	
Beersheba (Be'er Sheva)	Northern Negev	(1948)	City		municipality	184,500
Be'er Tuviyyah	Southern Coastal Plain (Malakhi Region)	1930	Moshav	TM	RC Be'er Tuviyyah	769
Be'er Ya'akov	Coastal Plain (Lod Region)	1907	Urban		local council	8,906
Beka'ot	Northern Jordan Valley; 67+	1972	Moshav	IH	RC Jordan Valley	152
Beko'a	Judean Foothills	1951	Moshav	TM	RC Matteh Yehudah	492
Ben Ammi	Acre Plain	1949	Moshav	TM	RC Ga'aton	461
Benayah	Southern Coastal Plain (Reḥovot Region)	1949	Moshav	TM	RC Brenner	770
Bene-Berak	Coastal Plain (Tel Aviv Region)	1924	City		municipality	142,334
Benei Atarot	Coastal Plain (Petaḥ Tikvah Region)	1948	Moshav	TM	RC Modi'im	600
Benei Ayish	Southern Coastal Plain (Reḥovot Region)	1958	Village	–	RC Ḥevel Yavneh	7,659
Benei Darom	Coastal Plain (Reḥovot Region)	1949	Moshav Shittufi	PM	RC Ḥevel Yavneh	332
Benei Deror	Southern Sharon	1946	Moshav Shittufi	TM	RC Hadar ha-Sharon	1,117
Benei Re'em	Coastal Plain (Reḥovot Region)	1949	Moshav	PAI	RC Naḥal Sorek	978
Benei Yehuda	Golan Heights; 67+	1972	Rural Community		RC Golan	971
Benei Zion	Southern Sharon (Herzliyyah Region)	1947	Moshav	IH	RC Ḥof ha-Sharon	835
Ben Shemen	Coastal Plain (Lod Region)	1921	Youth Village		(RC) Modi'im	628
Ben Shemen	Coastal Plain (Lod Region)	1952	Moshav	TM	RC Modi'im	584
Ben Zakkai	Southern Coastal Plain (Reḥovot Region)	1950	Moshav	PM	RC Ḥevel Yavneh	624
Berakhah	Samaria; 67+	1983	Urban Settlement	A		970
Berekhyah	Southern Coastal Plain (Ashkelon Region)	1950	Moshav	TM	RC Ḥof Ashkelon	893
Beror Ḥayil	Southern Coastal Plain (Ashkelon Region)	1948	Kibbutz	KM	RC Sha'ar ha-Negev	459
Berosh	Northern Negev (Gerar Region)	1953	Moshav	TM	RC Benei Shimon	209
Bet Alfa	Harod Valley	1922	Kibbutz	KA	RC Ha-Gilboa	556
Bet Aryeh	Western Samaria; 67+	1981	Urban Settlement		local council	3,446
Bet Arif	Coastal Plain (Lod Region)	1951	Moshav	TM	RC Modi'im	547
Betar Illit	Judea; 67+	1985	Urban Settlement		municipality	24,895
Bet Berl	Southern Sharon	1947	Educational Center	H	(RC) Ha-Sharon ha-Tikhon	250
Bet Dagan	Coastal Plain (Lod Region)	1948	Urban Settlement		local council	5,352
Bet El	Northern Judea; 67+	1977	Urban Community		RC Matteh Benjamin	4,763
Bet Elazari	Coastal Plain (Reḥovot Region)	1948	Moshav	TM	RC Brenner	989
Bet Ezra	Southern Coastal Plain (Malakhi Region)	1950	Moshav	TM	RC Be'er Tuviyyah	918
Bet Gamli'el	Coastal Plain (Reḥovot Region)	1949	Moshav	PM	RC Ḥevel Yavneh	830
Bet Guvrin	Southern Judean Foothills	1949	Kibbutz	KM	RC Yo'av	239
Bet ha-Aravah	Dead Sea Region	1980	Kibbutz	TKM	RC Megillot	69
Bet ha-Emek	Acre Plain	1949	Kibbutz	IK	RC Ga'aton	447
Bet ha-Gaddi	Northern Negev (Gerar Region)	1949	Moshav	PM	RC Azzatah	642

Name	Geographical Region	Year of Founding	Settlement Form	Affiliation	Municipal Status	No. of inhabitants 31 Dec. 2004
Bet Ḥagai	Southern Hebron Mountains; 67+	1984	Rural Community	A		429
Bet ha-Levi	Central Sharon (Ḥefer Plain)	1945	Moshav	TM	RC Ḥefer Plain	551
Bet Hanan	Coastal Plain (Rishon le-Zion Region)	1930	Moshav	TM	RC Gan Raveh	537
Bet Hananyah	Northern Sharon (Ḥaderah Region)	1950	Moshav	TM	RC Ḥof ha-Karmel	607
Bet Ḥashmonai	Judean Foothills	1972	Rural Community		RC Gezer	914
Bet ha-Shittah	Harod Valley	1935	Kibbutz	KM	RC Ha-Gilboa	871
Bet Ḥerut	Central Sharon (Ḥefer Plain)	1933	Moshav	TM	RC Ḥefer Plain	651
Bet Ḥilkiyyah	Coastal Plain (Reḥovot Region)	1953	Moshav	PAI	RC Naḥal Sorek	438
Bet Hillel	Ḥuleh Valley	1940	Moshav	TM	RC Ha-Galil ha-Elyon	577
Bet Ḥoron	Northwestern Judea; 67+	1977	Rural Community		RC Matteh Benjamin	825
Bet Kamah	Northern Negev (Gerar Region)	1949	Kibbutz	KA	RC Benei Shimon	220
Bet Keshet	Eastern Lower Galilee	1944	Kibbutz	KM	RC Ha-Galil ha-Taḥton	254
Bet Leḥem ha-Gelilit	Southern Lower Galilee	1948	Moshav	TM	RC Kishon	617
Bet Me'ir	Judean Hills	1950	Moshav	PM	RC Matteh Yehudah	561
Bet Neḥemyah	Northern Judean Foothills (Lod Region)	1950	Moshav	OZ	RC Modi'im	689
Bet Nekofah	Jerusalem Hills	1949	Moshav	TM	RC Matteh Yehudah	433
Bet Nir	Southern Coastal Plain (Lachish Region)	1955	Kibbutz	KA	RC Yo'av	279
Bet Oren	Mount Carmel	1939	Kibbutz	KM	RC Ḥof ha-Karmel	306
Bet Oved	Coastal Plain (Rishon le-Zion Region)	1933	Moshav	TM	RC Gan Raveh	313
Bet Rabban	Coastal Plain (Reḥovot Region)	1946	Yeshivah	KD	RC Ḥevel Yavneh	586
Bet Rimon	Central Lower Galilee	1977	Kibbutz	KD	RC Lower Galilee	250
Bet-Shean	Beth-Shean Valley	–	Urban Settlement	–	local council	16,039
Bet She'arim	Jezreel Valley	1936	Moshav	TM	RC Kishon	508
Bet-Shemesh (formerly Hartuv)	Judean Foothills	–	Urban Settlement	–	municipality	61,931
Bet Shikmah	Southern Coastal Plain (Ashkelon Region)	1950	Moshav	TM	RC Ḥof Ashkelon	684
Bet Uzzi'el	Judean Foothills (Lod Region)	1956	Moshav	PM	RC Gezer	484
Bet Yannai	Central Sharon (Ḥefer Plain)	1933	Moshav	IH	RC Ḥefer Plain	395
Bet Yehoshu'a	Southern Sharon (Netanyah Region)	1938	Moshav	OZ	RC Ḥof ha-Sharon	744
Bet Yiẓḥak (Sha'ar Ḥefer)	Central Sharon (Ḥefer Plain)	1940	Rural Settlement	–	RC Ḥefer Plain	1,606
Bet Yosef	Beth-Shean Valley	1937	Moshav	TM	RC Beth-Shean Valley	348
Bet Zayit	Jerusalem Hills	1949	Moshav	TM	RC Matteh Yehudah	1,191
Bet Zera	Kinneret Valley	1927	Kibbutz	KA	RC Jordan Valley	721
Bet Ẓevi	Carmel Coast	1953	Educational Institute	–	(RC) Ḥof ha-Karmel	510
Beẓet	Acre Plain	1949	Moshav	TM	RC Sullam Ẓor	332
Binyaminah (Givat Ada)	Northern Sharon (Ḥaderah Region)	1922	Urban Settlement	–	local council	9,765
Biranit	Western Upper Galilee	1964	Rural Settlement	–	(RC) Ma'aleh ha-Galil	
Biriyyah	Eastern Upper Galilee	1945	Rural Settlement	–	RC Merom ha-Galil	780
Bitan Aharon	Central Sharon (Ḥefer Plain)	1936	Moshav	IH	RC Ḥefer Plain	633
Bitḥah	Northwestern Negev (Besor Region)	1950	Moshav	TM	RC Merḥavim	683
Biẓẓaron	Southern Coastal Plain (Malakhi Region)	1935	Moshav	TM	RC Be'er Tuviyyah	900
Boẓrah	Southern Sharon (Kefar Sava Region)	1946	Moshav	IH	RC Ḥof ha-Sharon	745
Burgetah	Central Sharon (Ḥefer Plain)	1949	Moshav	TM	RC Ḥefer Plain	890
Bustan ha-Galil	Acre Plain	1948	Moshav	IH	RC Ga'aton	433
Caesarea	Northern Coastal Plain	1977	Urban Settlement		local council	4,022

Name	Geographical Region	Year of Founding	Settlement Form	Affiliation	Municipal Status	No. of inhabitants 31 Dec. 2004
Dafnah	Ḥuleh Valley	1939	Kibbutz	KM	RC Ha-Galil ha-Elyon	551
Daliyyah	Manasseh Hills	1939	Kibbutz	KA	RC Megiddo	738
Dalton	Eastern Upper Galilee	1950	Moshav	PM	RC Merom ha-Galil	698
Dan	Ḥuleh Valley	1939	Kibbutz	KA	RC Ha-Galil ha-Elyon	408
Daverat	Jezreel Valley	1946	Kibbutz	IK	RC Yizre'el	278
Deganim (Merkaz Shapira)	Southern Coastal Plain (Malakhi Region)	1948	Rural Center	–	(RC) Shafir	2,910
Deganyah (Deganiyyah) Alef	Kinneret Valley	1909	Kibbutz	IK	RC Jordan Valley	560
Deganyah (Deganiyyah) Bet	Kinneret Valley	1920	Kibbutz	IK	RC Jordan Valley	540
Dekel	Western Negev	1982	Moshav	IH	RC Eshkol	95
Devir(ah)	Northern Negev (Beersheba Region)	1951	Kibbutz	KA	RC Benei Shimon	373
Devorah	Jezreel Valley (Taanach Region)	1956	Moshav	TM	RC Ha-Gilboa	227
Dimonah	Negev Hills	1955	City	–	municipality	33,676
Dishon	Eastern Upper Galilee	1953	Moshav	OZ	RC Ha-Galil ha-Elyon	390
Dolev	Northern Judea Mountain	1983	Rural Community	A	RC Matteh Benjamin	963
Dor	Carmel Coast	1949	Moshav	TM	RC Ḥof ha-Karmel	341
Dorot	Southern Coastal Plain (Ashekelon Region)	1941	Kibbutz	IK	RC Sha'ar ha-Negev	457
Dovev	Eastern Upper Galilee	1963	Moshav	TM	RC Merom ha-Galil	430
Efrat	Etzyon Bloc; 67+	1980	Town		local council	7,273
Eilat (Elath)	Southern Negev	1951	Town	–	municipality	44,538
Eilon	Western Upper Galilee	1938	Kibbutz	KA	RC Sullam Ẓor	631
Eilot	Southern Arabah Valley	1962	Kibbutz	KM	RC Ḥevel Eilot	270
Ein Ayyalah	Carmel Coast	1949	Moshav	TM	RC Ḥof ha-Karmel	703
Ein Gev	Kinneret Valley	1937	Kibbutz	IK	RC Jordan Valley	520
Ein ha-Emek	Manasseh Hills	1944	Rural Settlement	–	RC Megiddo	625
Ein ha-Ḥoresh	Central Sharon (Ḥefer Plain)	1931	Kibbutz	KA	RC Ḥefer Plain	721
Ein ha-Mifraẓ	Zebulun Valley	1938	Kibbutz	KA	RC Na'aman	670
Ein ha-Naẓiv	Beth-Shean Valley	1946	Kibbutz	KD	RC Beth-Shean Valley	510
Ein ha-Sheloshah	Northwestern Negev (Besor Region)	1950	Kibbutz	OZ	RC Eshkol	333
Ein ha-Shofet	Manasseh Hills	1937	Kibbutz	KA	RC Megiddo	720
Ein Hod	Mount Carmel	1954	Artist's Village	–	(RC) Ḥof ha-Karmel	472
Ein Iron	Northern Sharon (Ḥaderah Region)	1934	Moshav	TM	RC Manasseh	414
Ein Karmel	Carmel Coast	1947	Kibbutz	KM	RC Ḥof ha-Karmel	401
Ein Sarid	Southern Sharon (Kefar Sava Region)	1950	Rural Settlement	–	RC Hadar ha-Sharon	1,180
Ein Shemer	Northern Sharon (Ḥaderah Region)	1927	Kibbutz	KA	RC Manasseh	761
Ein Vered	Southern Sharon (Kefar Sava Region)	1930	Moshav	TM	RC Hadar ha-Sharon	1,006
Ein Ya'akov	Western Upper Galilee	1950	Moshav	TM	RC Ma'aleh ha-Galil	544
Ein Zivan	Golan Heights; 67+	1968	Kibbutz	KM	RC Golan	214
Ein Ẓurim	Southern Coastal Plain (Shafir Region)	1949	Kibbutz	KD	RC Shafir	537
Eitan	Southern Coastal Plain (Lachish Region)	1955	Moshav	PM	RC Shafir	363
Eitanim	Jerusalem Hills	1952	Hospital	–	(RC) Matteh Yehudah	200
Elad	Eastern Sharon	1988	Urban Settlement		local council	22,600
Elazar	Etzyon Bloc; 67+	1975	Moshav	PM	RC Etzyon Bloc	993
Eli	Samaria; 67+	1984	Urban Settlement	A	RC Matteh Benjamin	2,308
Eli'ad (El Al)	Golan Heights; 67+	1968	Moshav	PM	RC Golan	247
Elifaz	Arabah Valley	1982	Kibbutz	TKM	RC Eilot	45
Elifelet	Eastern Upper Galilee (Hazor Region)	1949	Moshav	TM	RC Ha-Galil ha-Elyon	476

Name	Geographical Region	Year of Founding	Settlement Form	Affiliation	Municipal Status	No. of inhabitants 31 Dec. 2004
El-Rom	Golan Heights; 67+	1971	Kibbutz	TKM	RC Golan	267
Elishama	Southern Sharon	1951	Moshav	TM	RC Ha-Yarkon	875
Elkanah	Northern Samaria; 67+	1977	Urban Settlement		local council	2,983
Elkosh	Western Upper Galilee	1949	Moshav	TM	RC Ma'aleh ha-Galil	354
Elon Moreh	Samaria; 67+	1979	Urban Community	A		1,152
Elyakhin	Central Sharon (Ḥefer Plain)	1950	Rural Settlement	–	RC Ḥefer Plain	2,561
Elyakim	Manasseh Hills	1949	Moshav	TM	RC Megiddo	637
Elyashiv	Central Sharon (Ḥefer Plain)	1933	Moshav	HI	RC Ḥefer Plain	452
Emunim	Southern Coastal Plain (Malakhi Region)	1950	Moshav	TM	RC Be'er Tuviyyah	694
Enav	Samaria; 67+	1981	Rural Community	A	RC Shomron	468
Enat	Coastal Plain (Petaḥ Tikvah Region)	1925	Kibbutz	IK	RC Mifalot Afek	655
En-Dor	Eastern Lower Galilee	1948	Kibbutz	KA	RC Yizre'el	723
En-Gedi	Dead Sea Region	1953	Kibbutz	IK	RC Tamar	584
En-Harod	Harod Valley	1921	Kibbutz	IK	RC Ha-Gilboa	549
En-Harod	Harod Valley	1921	Kibbutz	KM	RC Ha-Gilboa	763
En-Tamar	Dead Sea Region	1982	Moshav	TM	RC Tamar	149
Erez	Southern Coastal Plain (Ashkelon Region)	1949	Kibbutz	IK	RC Sha'ar ha-Negev	324
Eshar	Central Lower Galilee	1989	Community		RC Misgav	392
Eshbal	Central Lower Galilee	1979	Kibbutz	TKM	RC Misgav	54
Eshbol	Northern Negev (Gerar Region)	1955	Moshav	TM	RC Merḥavim	244
Eshel ha-Nasi	Northern Negev (Besor Region)	1952	Agricultural School –		(RC) Merḥavim	397
Eshkolot	Southern Hebron Mountains; 67+	1982	Rural Community	A	RC Hebron Mountain	231
Eshtaol	Judean Foothills	1949	Moshav	TM	RC Matteh Yehudah	778
Even Menaḥem	Western Upper Galilee	1960	Moshav	TM	RC Ma'aleh ha-Galil	301
Even Sappir	Jerusalem Hills	1950	Moshav	TM	RC Matteh Yehudah	630
Even Shemu'el	Southern Coastal Plain (Lachish Region)	1956	Rural Center	–	RC Shafir	516
Even Yehudah	Southern Sharon (Netanyah Region)	1932	Rural Settlement	–	local council	8,991
Even Yiẓḥak (Galed)	Manasseh Hills	1945	Kibbutz	IK	RC Megiddo	401
Evron	Acre Plain	1945	Kibbutz	KA	RC Ga'aton	702
Eyal	Southern Sharon (Kefar Sava Region)	1949	Kibbutz	KM	RC Ha-Sharon ha-Tikhon	387
Eẓ Efrayim	Samaria; 67+	1985	Urban Settlement		RC Shomron	627
Ezer	Southern Coastal Plain (Malakhi Region)	1966	Rural Center	–	(RC) Be'er Tuviyyah	970
Ga'ash	Southern Sharon (Herzliyyah Region)	1951	Kibbutz	KA	RC Ḥof ha-Sharon	507
Ga'aton	Western Upper Galilee	1948	Kibbutz	KA	RC Ga'aton	41
Gadish	Jezreel Valley (Taanach Region)	1956	Moshav	TM	RC Ha-Gilboa	275
Gadot	Eastern Upper Galilee (Hazor Region)	1949	Kibbutz	KM	RC Ha-Galil ha-Elyon	371
Galon	Southern Judean Foothills	1946	Kibbutz	KA	RC Yo'av	307
Gan ha-Darom	Coastal Plain (Reḥovot Region)	1953	Moshav	IH	RC Gederot	352
Gan ha-Shomron	Northern Sharon (Ḥaderah Region)	1934	Rural Settlement	–	RC Manasseh	638
Gan Ḥayyim	Southern Sharon (Kefar Sava Region)	1935	Moshav	TM	RC Ha-Sharon ha-Tikhon	666
Gannei Am	Southern Sharon (Kefar Sava Region)	1934	Moshav	–	RC Ha-Yarkon	235
Gannei Tikvah	Coastal Plain (Petaḥ Tikvah Region)	1953	Urban Settlement	–	local council	11,970
Gannei Yehudah	Coastal Plain (Petaḥ Tikvah Region)	1951	Moshav	IH	RC Mifalot Afek	
Gannei Yoḥanan (Gannei Yonah)	Coastal Plain (Reḥovot Region)	1950	Moshav	TM	RC Gezer	593

Name	Geographical Region	Year of Founding	Settlement Form	Affiliation	Municipal Status	No. of inhabitants 31 Dec. 2004
Gan Ner	Gilboa Mountain	1987	Urban Settlement		RC Ha-Gilboa	2,599
Gannot Hadar	Southern Sharon (Netanyah Region)	1964	Rural Settlement	–	RC Ha-Sharon ha-Ẓefoni	498
Gan Shelomo (Kevuẓat Schiller)	Coastal Plain (Reḥovot Region)	1927	Kibbutz	IK	RC Brenner	411
Gan Shemu'el	Northern Sharon (Ḥaderah Region)	1913	Kibbutz	KA	RC Manasseh	829
Gan Sorek	Coastal Plain (Rishon le-Zion Region)	1950	Moshav	TM	RC Gan Raveh	323
Gan Yavneh	Coastal Plain (Reḥovot Region)	1931	Rural Settlement	–	local council	13,970
Gan Yoshiyyah	Central Sharon (Ḥefer Valley)	1949	Moshav	TM	RC Ḥefer Plain	561
Gannot	Coastal Plain (Lod Region)	1953	Moshav	IH	RC Emek Lod	480
Gat	Southern Coastal Plain (Lachish Region)	1942	Kibbutz	KA	RC Yo'av	378
Gat Rimmon	Coastal Plain (Petaḥ Tikvah Region)	1926	Rural Settlement	–	RC Mifalot Afek	201
Gazit	Southeastern Lower Galilee	1948	Kibbutz	KA	RC Yizre'el	570
Ge'ah	Southern Coastal Plain (Ashkelon Region)	1949	Moshav	TM	RC Ḥof Ashkelon	534
Ge'alyah	Coastal Plain (Reḥovot Region)	1948	Moshav	TM	RC Gan Raveh	1,095
Gederah	Coastal Plain (Reḥovot Region)	1884	Urban Settlement	–	local council	13,643
Gefen	Southern Judean Foothills	1955	Moshav	PM	RC Matteh Yehudah	315
Gelil Yam	Southern Sharon (Herzliyyah Region)	1943	Kibbutz	KM	RC Ḥof ha-Sharon	321
Gerofit	Southern Arabah Valley	1963	Kibbutz	IK	RC Ḥevel Eilot	325
Gesher	Kinneret Valley	1939	Kibbutz	IK	RC Jordan Valley	472
Gesher ha-Ziv	Acre Plain	1949	Kibbutz	IK	RC Sullam Ẓor	663
Geshur	Golan Heights; 67+	1971	Kibbutz	KA	RC Golan	192
Ge'ulei Teiman	Central Sharon (Ḥefer Plain)	1947	Moshav	PM	RC Ḥefer Plain	298
Ge'ulim	Southern Sharon	1945	Moshav	TM	RC Ḥefer Plain	749
Geva	Harod Valley	1921	Kibbutz	IK	RC Ha-Gilboa	548
Geva Binyamin (Adam)	Judea; 67+	1984	Rural Community	A	RC Matteh Benjamin	2,032
Geva Karmel	Carmel Coast	1949	Moshav	TM	RC Ḥof ha-Karmel	704
Gevaram	Southern Coastal Plain (Ashkelon Region)	1942	Kibbutz	KM	RC Ḥof Ashkelon	307
Gevat	Jezreel Valley	1926	Kibbutz	KM	RC Kishon	664
Gevim	Southern Coastal Plain (Ashkelon Region)	1947	Kibbutz	IK	RC Sha'ar ha-Negev	363
Gevulot	Northwestern Negev (Besor Region)	1943	Kibbutz	KM	RC Eshkol	233
Gezer	Judean Foothills	1945	Kibbutz	IK	RC Gezer	356
Gibbethon	Coastal Plain (Reḥovot Region)	1933	Moshav	–	RC Brenner	279
Gidonah	Harod Valley	1949	Rural Settlement	–	RC Ha-Gilboa	168
Gilat	Northern Negev (Gerar Region)	1949	Moshav	TM	RC Merḥavim	826
Gilgal	Lower Jordan Valley; 67+	1970	Kibbutz	KM	RC Bikat ha-Yarden	164
Gilon	Lower Galilee	1980	Rural Community	H	RC Misgav	952
Gimzo	Judean Foothills	1950	Moshav	PAI	RC Modi'im	190
Ginnaton	Coastal Plain (Lod Region)	1949	Moshav	TM	RC Modi'im	648
Ginnegar	Jezreel Valley	1922	Kibbutz	IK	RC Yizre'el	442
Ginnosar	Kinneret Valley	1937	Kibbutz	KM	RC Jordan Valley	488
Gita	Galilee	1980	Urban Community	MH		225
Gittit	Lower Jordan Valley; 67+	1973	Moshav	H	RC Bikat ha-Yarden	161
Givat Adah-Binyaminah	Northern Sharon (Ḥaderah Region)	1903	Rural Settlement	–	local council	
Givat Avni	Lower Galilee	1991	Urban Settlement		RC Lower Galilee	2,010
Givat Brenner	Coastal Plain (Reḥovot Region)	1928	Kibbutz	KM	RC Brenner	1,186
Givat Ela	Jezreel Valley	1988	Urban Community		RC Jezreel Valley	1,680
Givat ha-Sheloshah	Coastal Plain (Petaḥ Tikvah Region)	1925	Kibbutz	KM	RC Mifalot Afek	428

Name	Geographical Region	Year of Founding	Settlement Form	Affiliation	Municipal Status	No. of inhabitants 31 Dec. 2004
Givat Ḥayyim	Central Sharon (Ḥefer Plain)	1932	Kibbutz	IK	RC Ḥefer Plain	805
Givat Ḥayyim	Central Sharon (Ḥefer Plain)	1932	Kibbutz	KM	RC Ḥefer Plain	919
Givat Ḥen	Southern Sharon	1933	Moshav	TM	RC ha-Yarkon	336
Givat Ko'aḥ	Judean Foothills	1950	Moshav	TM	RC Matteh Yehudah	478
Givat Nili	Northwestern Iron Hills	1953	Moshav	H	RC Allonah	445
Givat Oz	Jezreel Valley	1949	Kibbutz	KA	RC Megiddo	344
Givat Shapira	Southern Sharon	1958	Moshav	IH	RC Ḥefer Plain	168
Givat Shemu'el	Coastal Plain (Petaḥ Tikvah Region)	1942	Urban Settlement	–	local council	17,409
Givat Ye'arim	Jerusalem Hills	1950	Moshav	TM	RC Matteh Yehudah	993
Givat Yeshayahu	Judean Foothills (Adullam Region)	1958	Moshav	OZ	RC Matteh Yehudah	363
Givat Yo'av	Golan Heights	1968	Moshav	TM	RC Golan	398
Givat Ze'ev	Judea Mountains; 67+	1983	Urban Settlement		local council	10,635
Givatayim	Coastal Plain (Tel Aviv Region)	1922	City	–	municipality	47,948
Givati	Southern Coastal Plain (Malakhi Region)	1950	Moshav	TM	RC Be'er Tuviyyah	752
Givolim	Northern Negev (Gerar Region)	1952	Moshav	PM	RC Azzatah	268
Givon Ḥadashah	Judean Hills; 67+	1980	Urban Community		RC Matteh Benjamin	1,179
Givot Bar	Northern Negev	2003	Urban Community		RC Beni Shimeon	66
Givot Zaid	Jezreel Valley	1943	Rural Settlement	–	RC Kishon	
Gizo	Judean Foothills	1968	Rural Settlement		RC Matte Yehudah	190
Gonen	Eastern Upper Galilee (Hazor Region)	1951	Kibbutz	IK	RC Ha-Galil ha Elyon	310
Goren	Western Upper Galilee	1950	Moshav	TM	RC Ma'aleh ha-Galil	425
Gorenot ha-Galilee	Northwestern Upper Galilee	1980	Regional Center		RC Ma'ale Yosef	174
Ha-Bonim	Carmel Coast	1949	Moshav Shittufi	TM	RC Ḥof ha-Karmel	271
Hadar Am	Central Sharon (Ḥefer Valley)	1933	Rural Settlement	–	RC Ḥefer Plain	460
Ḥaderah	Northern Sharon (Ḥaderah Region)	1890	Town	–	municipality	75,283
Hadid	Northern Judean Foothills	1950	Moshav	PM	RC Modi'im	556
Ḥad Nes	Golan Heights; 67+	1989	Rural Community	H	RC Golan	439
Hagor	Southern Sharon (Kefar Sava Region)	1949	Moshav	TM	RC Mifalot Afek	615
Ha-Gosherim	Ḥuleh Valley	1949	Kibbutz	KM	RC Ha-Galil ha-Elyon	508
Ḥafeẓ Ḥayyim	Southern Coastal Plain (Reḥovot Region)	1944	Kibbutz	PAI	RC Naḥal Sorek	429
Ha-Ḥoterim	Carmel Coast	1948	Kibbutz	KM	RC Ḥof ha-Karmel	499
Ḥaifa	Mt. Carmel and Zebulun Valley	–	City	–	municipality	268,251 thereof 25,065 non-Jews
Ḥalamish	Southern Samaria; 67+	1977	Rural Community		RC Matte Benjaim	931
Ḥaluẓ	Lower Galilee	1985	Urban Community	MH	RC Misgav	352
Ḥamadyah	Beth-Shean Valley	1942	Kibbutz	IK	RC Beth-Shean	343
Ha-Ma'pil	Northern Sharon	1945	Kibbutz	KA	RC Ḥefer Plain	496
Ḥamrah	Lower Jordan Valley	1971	Moshav	–	RC Bikat ha-Yarden	125
Ḥanitah	Western Upper Galilee	1938	Kibbutz	IK	RC Sullam Ẓor	440
Ḥanni'el	Central Sharon (Ḥefer Plain)	1950	Moshav	TM	RC Ḥefer Plain	774
Ha-Ogen	Central Sharon (Ḥefer Valley)	1947	Kibbutz	KA	RC Ḥefer Plain	538
Ha-On	Kinneret Valley	1949	Kibbutz	IK	RC Jordan Valley	170
Har Adar	Judea	1986	Urban Community		local council	2,074
Har Amasa	Judean Desert	1983	Rural Settlement		RC Tamar	
Ḥarashim	Upper Galilee	1980	Rural Settlement		RC Misgav	179
Harduf	Jezreel Valley	1982	Kibbutz	TKM	RC Jezreel Valley	385
Harel	Judean Foothills	1948	Kibbutz	KA	RC Matteh Yehudah	146
Har Giloh	Judea Hills	1973	Rural Community			371
Ḥaruẓim	Southern Sharon	1951	Rural Settlement	–	RC Ḥof ha-Sharon	662
Hashmonaim	Judea	1985	Rural Settlement	A	RC Matteh Benjamin	2,235
Ha-Solelim	Western Lower Galilee	1949	Kibbutz	OZ	RC Kishon	697

Name	Geographical Region	Year of Founding	Settlement Form	Affiliation	Municipal Status	No. of inhabitants 31 Dec. 2004
Ḥavaẓẓelet ha-Sharon	Central Sharon (Ḥefer Plain)	1935	Moshav	IH	RC Ḥefer Plain	286
Ha-Yogev	Jezreel Valley	1949	Moshav	TM	RC Yizre'el	543
Ḥaẓav	Southern Coastal Plain (Malakhi Region)	1949	Moshav	TM	RC Be'er Tuviyyah	880
Ḥaẓerim	Northern Negev (Beersheba Region)	1946	Kibbutz	IK	RC Benei Shimon	795
Ḥaẓevah	Central Arabah Valley	1965	Moshav	TM	RC Tamar	419
Ḥazon	Eastern Lower Galilee	1969	Moshav	PM	RC Merom ha-Galil	358
Ḥaẓor Ashdod	Southern Coastal Plain (Malakhi Region)	1946	Kibbutz	KA	RC Be'er Tuviyyah	535
Ha-Zore'a	Jezreel Valley	1936	Kibbutz	KA	RC Megiddo	917
Ha-Zore'im	Eastern Lower Galilee	1939	Moshav	PM	RC Ha-Galil ha-Taḥton	424
Ḥaẓor ha-Gelilit	Eastern Upper Galilee (Hazor Region)	1953	Urban Settlement	–	local council	8,431
Ḥefẓi-Bah	Harod Valley	1922	Kibbutz	KM	RC Ha-Gilboa	393
Ḥeleẓ	Southern Coastal Plain (Ashkelon Region)	1950	Moshav	TM	RC Hof Ashkelon	433
Ḥemdat	Lower Jordan Valley	1980	Rural Community	A	RC Bikat ha-Yarden	120
Ḥemed	Coastal Plain (Lod Region)	1950	Moshav	PM	RC Emek Lod	551
Ḥerev le-Et	Central Sharon (Ḥefer Plain)	1947	Moshav	IH	RC Ḥefer Plain	727
Hermesh	Northern Samaria	1982	Rural Community	H	RC Shomron	229
Ḥerut	Southern Sharon (Kefar Sava Region)	1930	Moshav	TM	RC Hadar ha-Sharon	1,028
Herzliyyah	Southern Sharon	1924	City	–	municipality	83,638
Ḥever	Jezreel Valley (Taanach Region)	1958	Rural Center	–	(RC) Ha-Gilboa	382
Ḥibbat Ẓion	Central Sharon (Ḥefer Plain)	1933	Moshav	HI	RC Ḥefer Plain	458
Hila	Upper Galilee	1980	Rural Community		RC Ma'ale Yosef	490
Ḥinanit	Western Samaria; 67+	1981	Rural Community	MH	RC Shomron	707
Ḥispin	Golan Heights; 67+	1974	Regional Center		RC Golan	1,262
Hod ha-Sharon	Southern Sharon (Kefar Sava Region)	1924	Urban Settlement	–	municipality	41,746
Hodiyyah	Southern Coastal Plain (Ashkelon Region)	1949	Moshav	TM	RC Hof Ashkelon	544
Ḥofit	Central Sharon (Ḥefer Plain	1955	Rural Settlement	–	RC Ḥefer Plain	753
Ḥoglah	Central Sharon (Ḥefer Plain)	1933	Moshav	TM	RC Ḥefer Plain	487
Ḥolon	Coastal Plain (Tel Aviv Region)	1933	City	–	municipality	165,778
Ḥoreshim	Southern Sharon (Kefar Sava Region)	1955	Kibbutz	KA	RC Mifalot Afek	224
Hosa'aya	Jezreel Valley	1981	Urban Settlement	PM	RC Jezreel Valley	1,328
Ḥosen	Western Upper Galilee	1949	Moshav	H	RC Ma'aleh ha-Galil	657
Ḥukkok	Eastern Lower Galilee	1945	Kibbutz	KM	RC Jordan Valley	266
Ḥulatah	Huleh Valley	1937	Kibbutz	KM	RC Ha-Galil ha-Elyon	368
Ḥuldah	Judean Foothills	1930	Kibbutz	IK	RC Gezer	313
Idan	Aravah Valley	1980	Moshav	TM	RC Mid Aravah	232
Ilaniyyah	Eastern Lower Galilee	1902	Moshav	IH	RC Ha-Galil ha-Taḥton	477
Immanuel	Samaria; 67+	1983	Urban Settlement		local council	2,585
Itamar	Samaria; 67+	1984	Rural Community	A	RC Shomron	600
Jerusalem	Jerusalem Hills	–	City	–	municipality	706,368 thereof 37,061 non-Jews
Kabri	Acre Plain	1949	Kibbutz	KM	RC Ga'aton	756
Kadarim	Upper Galilee	1980	Kibbutz	TKM	RC Upper Galilee	117
Kadimah-Ẓoran	Southern Sharon (Kefar Yonah Region)	1933	Urban Settlement	–	local council	15,709

Name	Geographical Region	Year of Founding	Settlement Form	Affiliation	Municipal Status	No. of inhabitants 31 Dec. 2004
Kadoorie	Eastern Lower Galilee	1931	Agricultural School	–	(RC) Ha-Galil ha-Taḥton	200
Kaḥal	Upper Galilee	1980	Moshav	TM		353
Kalanit	Upper Galilee	1981	Moshav	PM	RC Merom ha-Galil	222
Kalyah	Dead Sea Region; 67 +	1968	Kibbutz	IK	RC Megillot	260
Kammon	Bet-Hakerem Valley	1980	Rural Community		RC Misgav	553
Kanaf	Golan Heights	1991	Moshav	TM	RC Golan	285
Kannot	Southern Coastal Plain (Malakhi Region)	1952	Agricultural School	–	(RC) Be'er Tuviyyah	284
Karmei Yosef	Judean Foothills	1984	Moshavah	HI	RC Gezer	1,873
Karmei Ẓur	Etzyon Bloc; 67+	1984	Rural Community	PM	RC Etzyon Bloc	665
Karmel	Southern Hebron Mountains; 67+	1981	Moshav	A	RC Hebron Mountain	319
Karmi'el	Western Lower Galilee	1964	Urban Settlement	–	municipality	43,507
Karmiyyah	Southern Coastal Plain (Ashkelon Region)	1950	Kibbutz	KA	RC Ḥof Ashkelon	302
Karnei Shomron	Western Samaria; 67+	1978	Urban Settlement		local council	6,170
Kaẓir-Ḥarish	Iron Valley	1982	Urban Settlement		local council	3,669
Kaẓrin	Golan Heights; 67+	1977	Town		local council	6,357
Kedar	Judea Mountains; 67+	1985	Rural Community	H	RC Etzyon Bloc	658
Kedmah	Southern Coastal Plain (Malakhi Region)	1946	Rural Settlement	–	(RC) Yo'av	90
Kedummim	Central Samaria; 67+	1977	Urban Settlement		local council	3,010
Kefar Adummim	Judean Desert; 67+	1979	Rural Community	A	RC Matteh Benjamin	2,006
Kefar Aḥim	Southern Coastal Plain (Malakhi Region)	1949	Moshav	TM	RC Be'er Tuviyyah	467
Kefar Aviv	Coastal Plain (Reḥovot Region)	1951	Moshav	IH	RC Gederot	606
Kefar Avodah	Southern Sharon (Herzliyyah Region)	1942	Educational Institution	–	(RC) Hadar ha-Sharon	400
Kefar Azar	Coastal Plain (Tel Aviv Region)	1932	Moshav	TM	RC Ono	545
Kefar Azzah	Southern Coastal Plain (Ashkelon Region)	1951	Kibbutz	IK	RC Sha'ar ha-Negev	690
Kefar Barukh	Jezreel Valley	1926	Moshav	TM	RC Kishon	263
Kefar Bialik	Zebulun Valley (Haifa Bay Area)	1934	Moshav	IH	RC Zebulun	783
Kefar Bilu	Coastal Plain (Reḥovot Region)	1932	Moshav	TM	RC Gezer	1,041
Kefar Bin Nun	Judean Foothill	1952	Moshav	IH	RC Gezer	398
Kefar Blum	Ḥuleh Valley	1943	Kibbutz	IK	RC Ha-Galil ha-Elyon	497
Kefar Dani'el (Bet Ḥever)	Coastal Plain (Lod Region)	1949	Moshav Shittufi	TM	RC Modi'im	268
Kefar Eẓyon	Hebron Hills; 67 +	1967	Kibbutz	KD	RC Etzyon Bloc	416
Kefar Galim	Carmel Coast	1952	Agricultural School	–	–	272
Kefar Gidon	Jezreel Valley	1923	Moshav	PAI	RC Yizre'el	199
Kefar Giladi	Ḥuleh Valley	1916	Kibbutz	IK	RC Ha-Galil ha-Elyon	489
Kefar Glickson	Northern Sharon (Ḥaderah Region)	1939	Kibbutz	OZ	RC Manasseh	285
Kefar Ḥabad	Coastal Plain (Lod Region)	1949	Moshav	–	RC Emek Lod	4,538
Kefar ha-Ḥoresh	Southern Lower Galilee	1933	Kibbutz	IK	RC Kishon	421
Kefar Ḥananaya	Upper Galilee	1990	Urban Settlement	PM	RC Merom ha-Galil	373
Kefar ha-Makkabbi	Zebulun Valley (Haifa Bay Area)	1936	Kibbutz	IK	RC Zebulun	295
Kefar ha-Nagid	Coastal Plain (Rishon le-Zion Area)	1949	Moshav	TM	RC Gan Raveh	936
Kefar ha-Nasi	Eastern Upper Galilee (Hazor Region)	1948	Kibbutz	IK	RC Ha-Galil ha-Elyon	490
Kefar ha-No'ar Ha-dati	Zebulun Valley (Haifa Bay area)	1937	Agricultural School	–	RC Zebulun	571
Kefar ha-Rif	Southern Coastal Plain (Malakhi Region)	1956	Moshav	IH	RC Yo'av	586
Kefar ha-Ro'eh	Central Sharon (Ḥefer Plain)	1934	Moshav	PM	RC Ḥefer Plain	421

Name	Geographical Region	Year of Founding	Settlement Form	Affiliation	Municipal Status	No. of inhabitants 31 Dec. 2004
Kefar Ḥaruv	Golan Heights; 67+	1974	Kibubtz	IK	RC Golan	239
Kefar Ḥasidim Alef	Zebulun Valley (Haifa Bay area)	1924	Moshav	–	RC Zebulun	570
Kefar Ḥasidim Bet	Zebulun Valley (Haifa Bay area)	1950	Rural Settlement	–	RC Zebulun	188
Kefar Ḥayyim	Central Sharon (Ḥefer Plain)	1933	Moshav	TM	RC Ḥefer Plain	467
Kefar Hess	Southern Sharon (Kefar Sava Region)	1933	Moshav	TM	RC Hadar ha-Sharon	1,037
Kefar Ḥittim	Eastern Lower Galilee	1936	Moshav Shittufi	TM	RC Ha-Galil ha-Taḥton	369
Kefar Jawitz	Southern Sharon (Kefar Sava Region)	1932	Moshav	PM	RC Hadar ha-Sharon	481
Kefar Kisch	Eastern Lower Galilee	1946	Moshav	TM	RC Ha-Galil ha-Taḥton	298
Kefar Maimon	Northern Negev (Gerar Region)	1956	Moshav	PM	RC Azzatah	213
Kefar Malal (formerly Ein Ḥai)	Southern Sharon (Kefar Sava Region)	1922	Moshav	TM	RC Ha-Yarkon	447
Kefar Masaryk	Zebulun Valley (Haifa Bay area)	1938	Kibbutz	KA	RC Zebulun	597
Kefar Menaḥem	Southern Coastal Plain (Malakhi Region)	1937	Kibbutz	KA	RC Yo'av	462
Kefar Monash	Central Sharon (Ḥefer Plain)	1946	Moshav	TM	RC Ḥefer Plain	705
Kefar Mordekhai	Coastal Plain (Reḥovot Region)	1950	Moshav	IH	RC Gederot	487
Kefar Netter	Southern Sharon	1939	Moshav	–	RC Ḥof ha-Sharon	619
Kefar Pines	Northern Sharon (Ḥaderah Region)	1933	Moshav	PM	RC Manasseh	946
Kefar Rosenwald (Zarit)	Western Upper Galilee	1967	Moshav	TM	(RC) Ma'aleh ha-Galil	241
Kefar Rosh ha-Nikrah	Acre Plain	1949	Kibbutz	IK	RC Sullam Ẓor	535
Kefar Ruppin	Beth-Shean Valley	1938	Kibbutz	IK	RC Beth-Shean Valley	417
Kefar Rut	Judean Foothills	1977	Moshav	TM	RC Modi'in Region	221
Kefar Sava	Southern Sharon	1903	Town	–	municipality	79,771
Kefar Shammai	Eastern Upper Galilee	1949	Moshav	PM	RC Merom ha-Galil	304
Kefar Shemaryahu	Southern Sharon (Herzliyyah Region)	1937	Rural Settlement	–	local council	1,790
Kefar Shemu'el	Judean Foothills	1950	Moshav	OZ	RC Gezer	581
Kefar Silver	Southern Coastal Plain (Ashkelon Region)	1957	Agricultural School	–	(RC) Ḥof Ashkelon	322
Kefar Syrkin	Coastal Plain (Petaḥ Tikvah Region)	1936	Rural Settlement	–	RC Mifalot Afek	963
Kefar Szold	Ḥuleh Valley	1942	Kibbutz	KM	RC Ha-Galil ha-Elyon	413
Kefar Tapu'aḥ	Samaria; 67+	1978	Rural Community	A	RC Shomron	593
Kefar Tavor	Eastern Lower Galilee	1901	Rural Settlement	–	local council	2,375
Kefar Truman	Northern Judean Foothills	1949	Moshav	TM	RC Modi'im	515
Kefar Uriyyah	Judean Foothills	1944	Moshav	TM	RC Matteh Yehudah	424
Kefar Veradim	Upper Galilee	1993	Rural Community		local council	5,406
Kefar Vitkin	Central Sharon (Ḥefer Valley)	1933	Moshav	TM	RC Ḥefer Plain	1,545
Kefar Warburg	Southern Coastal Plain (Malakhi Region)	1939	Moshav	TM Be'er Tuviyyah	RC	781
Kefar Yeḥezkel	Ḥarod Valley	1921	Moshav	TM	RC Ha-Gilboa	641
Kefar Yehoshu'a	Jezreel Valley	1927	Moshav	TM	RC Kishon	707
Kefar Yonah	Southern Sharon	1932	Rural Settlement	–	local Council	12,351
Kefar Zeitim	Eastern Lower Galilee	1950	Moshav	TM	RC Ha-Galil ha-Tahton	479
Kela Alon	Golaln Heights	1984	Rural Community		RC Golan	58
Kelaḥim	Northern Negev (Gerar Region)	1954	Moshav	IH	RC Merḥavim	265
Kelil	Western Upper Galilee	1979	Rural Community	IH	RC Matteh Asher	255
Kemehin	Central Negev	1988	Moshav	TM	RC Ramat Negev	161
Keramim	Northern Negev	1980	Kibbutz	KA	RC Benei Shimeon	75
Kerem Ben Zimrah	Eastern Upper Galilee	1949	Moshav	PM	RC Merom ha-Galil	401
Kerem Maharal	Mount Carmel	1949	Moshav	TM	RC Ḥof ha-Karmel	425

Name	Geographical Region	Year of Founding	Settlement Form	Affiliation	Municipal Status	No. of inhabitants 31 Dec. 2004
Kerem Shalom	Northwestern Negev (Besor Region)	1956	Kibbutz	KA	RC Eshkol	
Kerem Yavneh	Coastal Plain (Reḥovot Region)	1963	Educational Institution (Yeshivah)	PM	RC Ḥevel Yavneh	335
Kesalon	Judean Hills	1952	Moshav	IH	RC Matteh Yehudah	325
Keshet	Golan Heights; 67+	1974	Moshav	PM	RC Golan	501
Keturah	Arabah Valley	1973	Kibbutz	IH	RC Eilot Region	435
Kevuẓat Yavneh	Coastal Plain (Reḥovot Region)	1941	Kibbutz	KD	RC Ḥevel Yavneh	1,052
Kidmat Ẓevi	Golan Heights; 67+	1985	Moshav	HI	RC Golan	341
Kidron	Coastal Plain (Reḥovot Region)	1949	Moshav	TM	RC Brenner	1,067
Kinneret	Kinneret Valley	1908	Kibbutz	IK	RC Jordan Valley	625
Kinneret	Kinneret Valley	1909	Rural Settlement	–	local council	503
Kiryat Anavim	Jerusalem Hills	1920	Kibbutz	IK	RC Matteh Yehudah	307
Kiryat Arba	Hebron Area; 67+	1972	Town		local council	6,651
Kiryat Ata	Zebulun Valley (Haifa Bay area)	1925	Town	–	municipality	48,930
Kiryat Bialik	Zebulun Valley (Haifa Bay area)	1934	Urban Settlement	–	municipality	36,755
Kiryat Ekron	Coastal Plain (Rehovot Region)	1948	Urban Settlement	–	local council	9,719
Kiryat Gat	Southern Coastal Plain (Lachish Region)	1954	Urban Settlement	–	municipality	47,820
Kiryat Ḥaroshet	Zebulun Valley (Haifa Bay area)	1935	Rural Settlement	–	local council	
Kiryat Malakhi	Southern Coastal Plain (Malakhi Region)	1951	Urban Settlement	–	municipality	19,391
Kiryat Motzkin	Zebulun Valley (Haifa Bay area)	1934	Urban Settlement	–	municipality	39,526
Kiryat Netafim	Samaria; 67+	1983	Rural Community	PM	RC Shomron	419
Kiryat Ono	Coastal Plain (Tel Aviv Region)	1939	Urban Settlement	–	municipality	24,791
Kiryat Shemonah	Ḥuleh Valley	1950	Urban Settlement	–	municipality	22,006
Kiryat Tivon	Southern Lower Galilee (Tivon Hills)	1937	Urban Settlement	–	local council	13,567
Kiryat Yam	Zebulun Valley (Haifa Bay area)	1946	Urban Settlement	–	municipality	39,976
Kiryat Ye'arim	Jerusalem Hills	1952	Educational Institution	–	(RC) Matteh Yehudah	249
Kishor	Central Upper Galilee	1980	Kibbutz and Rural Community		RC Misgav	71
Kissufim	Northwestern Negev (Besor Region)	1951	Kibbutz	KM	RC Eshkol	170
Kokhav Mikha'el	Southern Coastal Plain (Ashkelon Region)	1950	Kibbutz	TM	RC Ḥof Ashkelon	531
Kokhav ha-Shaḥar	Northeastern Judea; 67+	1977	Rural Community		RC Matteh Benjamin	1,365
Kokhav Ya'akov	Judea; 67+	1985	Urban Community	A	RC Shomron	4,389
Kokhav Yair (Ẓur Yigal)	Eastern Sharon	1981	Urban Community		local council	11,802
Komemiyyut	Southern Coastal Plain (Malakhi Region)	1950	Moshav	TM	RC Shafir	246
Koranit	Northwestern Lower	1982	Rural Community		RC Misgav	627
Korazim	Upper Galilee	1983	Moshav	HI	RC Mevo'ot Ḥermon	430
Lachish (Lakhish)	Southern Coastal Plain (Lachish Region)	1955	Moshav	TM	RC Lachish	480
Lahav (Ẓiklag)	Northern Negev (Beersheba Region)	1952	Kibbutz	KA	RC Benei Shimon	393
Lahavot ha-Bashan	Ḥuleh Valley	1846	Kibbutz	KA	RC Ha-Galil ha-Elyon	437
Lahavot Ḥavivah	Northern Sharon (Ḥaderah Region)	1949	Kibbutz	KA	RC Manasseh	257
Lapid	Judean Lowland	1996	Urban Settlement			2,228
Lapidot	Central Upper Galile	1978	Moshav	TM	RC Ma'ale Yosef	161
Lavi	Eastern Lower Galilee	1949	Kibbutz	KD	RC Ha-Galil ha-Taḥton	671
Lavon	Lower Galilee	1980	Rural Community		RC Misgav	183
Liman	Acre Plain	1949	Moshav	TM	RC Sullam Ẓor	593
Li On	Judean Foothills (Adullam Region)	1960	Rural Center	–	(RC) Matteh Yehudah	
Livnim	Upper Galilee	1982	Rural Community	TM	RC Merom ha-Galil	402

Name	Geographical Region	Year of Founding	Settlement Form	Affiliation	Municipal Status	No. of inhabitants 31 Dec. 2004
Lod (Lydda)	Coastal Plain (Lod Region)	–	Town	–	municipality	66,572 thereof 14,661 non-Jews
Lod Airport	Coastal Plain (Lod Region)	(1961)	Airport and Industrial Area	–	–	
Loḥamei ha-Getta'ot	Acre Plain	1949	Kibbutz	KM	RC Ga'aton	468
Lotan	Aravah Valley	1983	Kibbutz	KM	RC Eilot	188
Lotem	Lower Galilee	1978	Kibbutz	TKM	RC Misgav	430
Luzit	Southern Judean Foothills	1955	Moshav	TM	RC Matteh Yehudah	341
Ma'agen	Kinneret Valley	1949	Kibbutz	IK	RC Jordan Valley	338
Ma'agan Mikha'el	Carmel Coast	1949	Kibbutz	KM	RC Ḥof ha-Karmel	1,331
Ma'aleh Adumim	Judea Desert; 67+	1977	Urban Settlement		municipality	28,923
Ma'aleh Amos	Etzyon Bloc; 67+	1981	Rural Community	H	RC Etzyon Bloc	319
Ma'eleh Efrayim	Eastern Samaria; 67+	1970	Urban Settlement		local council	1,456
Ma'aleh Gamla	Golan Heights; 67+	1976	Moshav	TM	RC Golan	306
Ma'aleh Gilboa	Mt. Gilboa	1962	Kibbutz	–	(RC) Beth-Shean Valley	256
Ma'aleh ha-Ḥamishah	Jerusalem Hills	1938	Kibbutz	IK	RC Matteh Yehudah	340
Ma'aleh Levonah	Samaria; 67+	1983	Rural Community	A	RC Matteh Benjamin	514
Ma'aleh Mikhmas	Judean Desert; 67+	1981	Rural Community	A	RC Matteh Benjamin	1.055
Ma'aleh Shomron	Samaria; 67+	1980	Rural Community	H	RC Shomron	549
Ma'a lot-Tarshiḥah	Western Upper Galilee	(1957)	Urban Settlement	–	municipality	20,991 thereof 4,447 non-Jews
Ma'anit	Northern Sharon (Ḥaderah Region)	1942	Kibbutz	KA	RC Manasseh	467
Ma'as	Coastal Plain (Petaḥ Tikvah Region)	1935	Moshav	TM	RC Mifalot Afek	652
Ma'barot	Central Sharon (Ḥefer Plain)	1933	Kibbutz	KA	RC Ḥefer Plain	751
Mabbu'im	Northern Negev (Gerar Region)	1958	Rural Center	–	RC Merḥavim	1,012
Ma'gallim	Northern Negev (Gerar Region)	1958	Rural Center	–	(RC) Azzatah	1,395
Magen	Northwestern Negev (Besor Region)	1949	Kibbutz	KA	RC Eshkol	449
Magen Shaul	Jezreel Valley (Taanach Region)	1976	Moshav	TM	RC Ha-Gilboa	249
Maggal	Northern Sharon (Ḥaderah Region)	1953	Kibbutz	IK	RC Manasseh	509
Magshimim	Coastal Plain (Petaḥ Tikvah Region)	1949	Moshav	IH	RC Mifalot Afek	699
Maḥanayim	Eastern Upper Galilee (Hazor Region)	(1939)	Kibbutz	KM	RC Ha-Galil ha-Elyon	354
Maḥaneh Yisrael	Coastal Plain (Lod Region)	1950	Rural Settlement		(under liquidation)	
Malkishu'a	Mount Gilboa	1976	Rehabilitation Institution		RC Beit Shean Valley	92
Malkiyyah	Eastern Upper Galilee	1949	Kibbutz	KM	RC Ha-Galil ha-Elyon	323
Manarah	Eastern Upper Galilee	1943	Kibbutz	KM	RC Ha-Galil ha-Elyon	241
Manof	Northwestern Lower Galilee	1980	Rural Community	IH	RC Misgav	556
Manot	Western Upper Galilee	1980	Moshav	TM	RC Ma'aleh Yosef	335
Ma'on	Southern Hebron Mountain; 67+	1981	Rural Community	A	RC Hebron Mountain	308
Ma'or	Northern Sharon (Manasseh Region)	1953	Moshav	TM	RC Manasseh	742
Ma'oz Ḥayyim	Beth-Shean Valley	1937	Kibbutz	KM	RC Beth-Shean Valley	566
Margaliyyot	Eastern Upper Galilee	1951	Moshav	TM	RC Ha-Galil ha-Elyon	367
Masad	Lower Galilee	1983	Rural Community	MH	RC Lower Galilee	342
Mashabbei Sadeh	Negev Hills	1949	Kibbutz	KM	RC Ramat ha-Negev	450
Mashen	Southern Coastal Plain (Ashkelon Region)	1950	Moshav	TM	RC Ḥof Ashkelon	651
Maslul	Northwestern Negev (Besor Region)	1950	Moshav	TM	RC Merḥavim	343
Massadah	Kinneret Region	1937	Kibbutz	IK	RC Jordan Valley	289
Massu'ah	Lower Jordan Valley; 67+	1970	Moshav	OZ	RC Bikat ha-Yarden	140
Massu'ot Yiẓḥak	Southern Coastal Plain (Malakhi Region)	1949	Moshav Shittufi	PM	RC Shafir	539
Matan	Southern Sharon	1997	Urban Settlement		RC Southern Sharon	2,900

Name	Geographical Region	Year of Founding	Settlement Form	Affiliation	Municipal Status	No. of inhabitants 31 Dec. 2004
Matat	Northwestern Upper Galilee	1979	Rural Community		RC Ma'ale Yosef	182
Mattityahu	Judan Hills; 67+	1981	Moshav	PAI		1,347
Matta	Judean Hills	1950	Moshav	TM	RC Matteh Yehudah	528
Mavki'im	Southern Coastal Plain (Ashkelon Region)	1949	Moshav Shittufi	TM	RC Ḥof Ashkelon	225
Ma'yan Barukh	Ḥuleh Valley	1947	Kibbutz	IK	RC Ha-Galil ha-Elyon	252
Ma'yan Ẓevi	Mt. Carmel	1938	Kibbutz	IK	RC Ḥof ha-Karmel	488
Mazkeret Batyah	Coastal Plain (Reḥovot Region)	1883	Rural Settlement	–	local council	7,822
Maẓli'aḥ	Coastal Plain (Lod Region)	1950	Moshav	TM	RC Gezer	1,126
Mazor	Coastal Plain (Petaḥ Tikvah Region)	1949	Moshav	TM	RC Modi'im	970
Maẓẓuvah	Western Upper Galilee	1940	Kibbutz	IK	RC Sullam Ẓor	441
Mefallesim	Southern Coastal Plain (Ashkelon Region)	1949	Kibbutz	IK	RC Sha'ar ha-Negev	458
Megadim	Carmel Coast	1949	Moshav	TM	RC Ḥof ha-Karmel	743
Megiddo	Jezreel Valley	1949	Kibbutz	KA	RC Megiddo	326
Meḥaseyah	Judean Foothills	1950	Rural Settlement	–	RC Matteh Yehudah	
Meḥolah	Lower Jordan Valley; 67 +	1968	Moshav	–	RC	360
Mei Ammi	Samaria (Iron Hills)	1963	Kibbutz	KA	Bikat Ha-Yarden	
Me'ir Shefayah	Mt. Carmel	(1923)	Agricultural School	–	RC Ḥof ha-Karmel	417
Meishar	Coastal Plain (Reḥovot Region)	1950	Moshav	IH	RC Gederot	501
Meitar	Northern Negev	1987	Urban Settlement		local council	6,515
Meitav	Jezreel Valley (Taanach Region)	1954	Moshav	TM	RC Ha-Gilboa	347
Mele'ah	Jezreel Valley (Taanach Region)	1956	Moshav	TM	RC Ha-Gilboa	329
Melilot	Northern Negev (Gerar Region)	1953	Moshav	PM	RC Azzatah	248
Menaḥemiyyah	Eastern Lower Galilee	1902	Moshav	IH	local council	1,080
Menuḥah (Vardon)	Southern Coastal Plain (Malakhi Region)	1953	Moshav	TM	RC Lachish	351
Me'onah	Western Upper Galilee	1949	Moshav	TM	RC Ma'aleh ha-Galil	511
Merav	Bet Shean Valley	1987	Kibbutz	KD	RC Bet Shean Valley	366
Merḥav Am	Central Negev	2002	Urban Settlement		RC Ramat Negev	99
Merḥavyah	Harod Valley	1922	Moshav	TM	RC Yizre'el	658
Merḥavyah	Harod Valley	1911	Kibbutz	KA	RC Yizre'el	724
Merom Golan	Golan Heights	1967	Kibbutz	KM	RC Golan	411
Meron	Eastern Upper Galilee	–	Moshav	PM	RC Merom ha-Galil	794
Mesillat Zion	Judean Foothills	1950	Moshav	TM	RC Matteh Yehudah	692
Mesillot	Beth-Shean Valley	1938	Kibbutz	KA	RC Beth-Shean Valley	401
Metullah	Eastern Upper Galilee	1896	Rural Settlement	–	local council	1,490
Mevasseret Zion (Ẓiyyon)	Jerusalem Hills	1951	Urban Settlement	–	local council	21,734
Mevo Beitar	Jerusalem Hills	1950	Moshav Shittufi	H	RC Matteh Yehudah	292
Mevo Dotan	Northern Samaria; 67+	1977	Rural Community	A	RC Shomron	287
Mevo Ḥammah	Golan Heights; 67+	1968	Kibbutz	IK	RC Golan	325
Mevo Ḥoron	Judean Hills; 67 +	1969	–	PAI	–	827
Mevo Modi'im	Judean Foothills	1964	Kibbutz	PAI	RC Modi'im	152
Meẓadot Yehudah	Southern Hebron Mountain	1983	Moshav	A	RC Hebron Mountain	425
Meiẓar	Golan Heights	1981	Kibbutz	TKM	RC Golan	44
Meẓer	Northern Sharon (Ḥaderah Region)	1953	Kibbutz	KA	RC Manasseh	382
Midrakh Oz	Jezreel Valley	1952	Moshav	TM	RC Megiddo	483
Midreshet Ruppin	Central Sharon (Ḥefer Plain)	1948	Seminary	–	–	
Migdal	Kinneret Valley	1910	Rural Settlement	–	local council	1,470
Migdal ha-Emek	Southern Lower Galilee	1952	Urban Settlement	–	local council	24,760
Migdalim	Samaria; 67+	1983	Rural Community	A	RC Shomron	151
Migdal Oz	Etzyon Bloc; 67+	1977	Kibbutz	KD	RC Etzyon Bloc	313
Mikhmannim	Lower Galilee	1980	Rural Community		RC Misgav	270

Name	Geographical Region	Year of Founding	Settlement Form	Affiliation	Municipal Status	No. of inhabitants 31 Dec. 2004
Mikhmoret	Central Sharon (Ḥefer Plain)	1945	Moshav and Educational Institution	TM	RC Ḥefer Plain	1,056
Mikveh Yisrael	Coastal Plain (Tel Aviv Region)	1870	Agricultural School	–	–	747
Misgav Am	Eastern Upper Galilee	1945	Kibbutz	KM	RC Ha-Galil ha-Elyon	242
Misgav Dov	Coastal Plain (Reḥovot Region)	1950	Moshav	H	RC Gederot	529
Mishmar Ayyalon	Judean Foothills	1949	Moshav	M	RC Gezer	406
Mishmar David	Judean Foothills	1949	Kibbutz	IK	RC Gezer	234
Mishmar ha-Emek	Jezreel Valley	1926	Kibbutz	KA	RC Megiddo	922
Mishmar ha-Negev	Northern Negev (Gerar Region)	1946	Kibbutz	KM	RC Benei Shimon	581
Mishmar ha-Sharon	Central Sharon (Ḥefer Plain)	1933	Kibbutz	IK	RC Ḥefer Plain	459
Mishmar ha-Shivah	Central Coastal Plain (Lod Region)	1949	Moshav	–	RC Emek Lod	677
Mishmar ha-Yarden	Eastern Upper Galilee (Hazor Region)	(1949)	Moshav	H	RC Ha-Galil ha-Elyon	445
Mishmarot	Northern Sharon (Ḥaderah Region)	1933	Kibbutz	IK	RC Manasseh	253
Mishmeret	Southern Sharon (Kefar Sava Region)	1946	Moshav	TM	RC Hadar ha-Sharon	618
Mivtaḥim	Northwestern Negev (Besor Region)	1950	Moshav	TM	RC Azzatah	314
Mizra	Jezreel Valley	1923	Kibbutz	KA	RC Yizre'el	710
Miẓpeh	Eastern Lower Galilee	1908	Rural Settlement	–	RC Ha-Galil ha-Taḥton	150
Miẓpeh Aviv	Lower Galilee	1981	Rural Community		RC Misgav	636
Miẓpeh Netofa	Lower Galilee	1979	Cooperative Settlment		RC Lower Galilee	572
Miẓpeh Ramon	Central Negev Hills	1954	Urban Settlement	–	local council	4,631
Miẓpeh Shalem	Dead Sea Region; 67 +	1970	–	–	–	
Miẓpeh Yeriḥo	Dead Sea Region	1978	Rural Community	A	RC Matteh Benjamin	1,469
Modi'in (Makkabim-Re'ut)	Central Israel	1996	Urban Settlement		municipality	53,079
Modi'in Illit	Judea Hills	1996	Urban Settlement		local council	27,386
Moledet (B'nai B'rith)	Southeastern Lower Galilee	1937	Moshav Shittufi	TM	RC Ha-Gilboa	192
Moran	Northern Lower Galilee	1976	Kibbutz	KM	RC Misgav	124
Moreshet	Northwestern Lower Galilee	1981	Rural Community	IH	RC Misgav	879
Moẓa Illit	Jerusalem Hills	1933	Rural Settlement	–	RC Matteh Yehudah	827
Moẓa Taḥtit	Jerusalem Hills	1894	Rural Settlement	–	(RC) Matteh Yehudah	
Na'aleh	Southwestern Samaria	1988	Rural Community		RC Matteh Benjamin	600
Na'an	Coastal Plain (Reḥovot Region)	1930	Kibbutz	KM	RC Gezer	1,169
Na'aran	Lower Jordan Valley; 67 +	1970	–	–	–	
Naḥalah	Southern Coastal Plain (Malakhi Region)	1953	Moshav	TM	RC Yo'av	385
Nahalal	Jezreel Valley	1921	Moshav	TM	RC	926
Naḥalat Yehudah	Coastal Plain (Rishon le-Zion Region)	1914	Rural Settlement	–	local council	
Naḥaliel	Southwestern Samaria	1984	Rural Community	PAI	RC Matteh Benjamin	282
Naḥal Golan	Golan; 67 +	1967	Kibbutz	IK	–	..
Naḥal Oz	Northwestern Negev	1951	Kibbutz	IK	RC Sha'ar ha-Negev	285
Naḥam	Judean Foothills	1950	Moshav	PM	RC Matteh Yehudah	
Nahariyyah	Acre Plain	1934	Town	–	municipality	49,306
Naḥsholim	Carmel Coast	1948	Kibbutz	KM	RC Ḥof ha-Karmel	392
Naḥshon	Judean Foothills	1950	Kibbutz	KA	RC Matteh Yehudah	380
Naḥshonim	Northern Judean Foothills	1949	Kibbutz	KA	RC Mifalot Afek	305
Naomi	Lower Jordan Valley	1982	Moshav	TM	RC Bikat ha-Yarden	127
Nataf	Jerusalem Corridor	1982	Rural Community			390
Natur	Golan Heights; 67+	1980	Kibbutz	KA	RC Golan	

Name	Geographical Region	Year of Founding	Settlement Form	Affiliation	Municipal Status	No. of inhabitants 31 Dec. 2004
Naẓerat Illit	Southern Lower Galilee	1957	Urban Settlement	–	municipality	43,939 thereof 4,848 non-Jews
Negbah	Southern Coastal Plain (Malakhi Region)	1939	Kibbutz	KA	RC Yo'av	387
Negohot	Southern Hebron Mountain; 67+	1982	Rural Community		RC Hebron Mountain	135
Neḥalim	Coastal Plain (Petaḥ Tikvah Region)	1948	Moshav	PM	RC Modi'in	1,946
Nehorah	Coastal Plain (Lachish Region)	1956	Rural Center	–	RC Lachish	1,121
Ne'ot Golan	Golan Heights; 67+	1968	Moshav	HI	RC Golan	291
Ne'ot ha-Kikar	Northern Arabah Valley	(1970)	Moshav Shittufi	–	RC Tamar	226
Ne'ot Mordekhai	Ḥuleh Valley	1946	Kibbutz	IK	RC Ha-Galil ha-Elyon	481
Ne'ot Semadar	Arabah Valley	1982	Kibbutz	TKM	RC Eilot Region	157
Nes Harim	Jerusalem Hills	1950	Moshav	TM	RC Matteh Yehudah	554
Nesher	Zebulun Valley (Haifa Bay area)	1925	Urban Settlement	–	municipality	21,174
Nes Ẓiyyonah	Costal Plain (Rishon le-Zion Region)	1883	Urban Settlement	–	municipality	27,830
Neta'im	Coastal Plain (Rishon le-Zion Region)	1932	Moshav	TM	RC Gan Raveh	479
Netanyah	Southern Sharon	1929	City	–	municipality	169,415
Netiv ha-Gedud	Lower Jordan Valley	1976	Moshav	TM	RC Bikat ha-Yarden	132
Netiv ha-Lamed He	Southern Judean Foothills	1949	Kibbutz	KM	RC Matteh Yehudah	402
Netiv ha-Shayyarah	Acre Plain	1950	Moshav	TM	RC Ga'aton	444
Netivot	Northwestern Negev (Gerar Region)	1956	Urban Settlement	–	municipality	23,654
Netu'ah	Western Upper Galilee	1966	Moshav	TM	(RC) Ma'aleh ha-Galil	256
Ne'urim	Central Sharon (Ḥefer Plain)	1953	Educational Institution	–	(RC) Ḥefer Plain	561
Nevatim	Northern Negev (Beersheba Region)	1946	Moshav	TM	RC Benei Shimon	627
Neveh Ativ	Golan Heights; 67+	1972	Moshav Shittufi	OZ	RC Golan	167
Neveh Daniel	Etzyon Bloc; 67+	1982	Rural Community	PM	RC Etzyon Bloc	1,225
Neveh Efrayim (Monosson)	Coastal Plain (Petaḥ Tikvah Region)	1953	Rural Settlement	–	local council	
Neveh Eitan	Beth-Shean Valley	1938	Kibbutz	IK	RC Beth-Shean Valley	147
Neveh Ḥarif	Arabah Valley	1987	Kibbutz	TKM	RC Eilot Region	62
Neveh Ilan	Jerusalem Hills	(1946)	–	–	–	324
Neveh Mivtaḥ	Southern Coastal Plain (Malakhi Region)	1950	Moshav	TM	RC Be'er Tuviyyah	486
Neveh Shalom	Judean Mountains	1983	Rural Community		RC Matteh Yehudah	180 thereof 92 non-Jews
Neveh Ur	Northern Beth-Shean Valley	1949	Kibbutz	KM	RC Beth-Shean Valley	416
Neveh Ziv	Western Upper Galilee	1989	Rural Community		RC Ma'ale Yosef	368
Neveh Yam	Carmel Coast	1939	Kibbutz	IK	RC Hof ha-Karmel	201
Neveh Yamin	Southern Sharon (Kefar Sava Region)	1949	Moshav	TM	RC Ha-Sharon ha-Tikhon	1.048
Neveh Yarak	Southern Sharon (Herzliyyah Region)	1951	Moshav	TM	RC Ha-Yarkon	938
Neẓer Sereni	Coastal Plain (Rishon le-Zion Region)	1948	Kibbutz	IK	RC Gezer	523
Nili	Western Samaria	1981	Rural Community	A	RC Matteh Benjamin	829
Nimrod	Golan Heights; 67+	1981	Rural Community		RC Golan	
Nir Akiva	Northern Negev (Gerar Region)	1953	Moshav	TM	RC Merḥavim	225
Nir Am	Southern Coastal Plain (Ashkelon Region)	1943	Kibbutz	IK	RC Sha'ar ha-Negev	298
Nir Banim	Southern Coastal Plain (Malakhi Region)	1954	Moshav	TM	RC Shafir	588
Nir David	Beth-Shean Valley	1936	Kibbutz	KA	RC Beth-Shean Valley	530

Name	Geographical Region	Year of Founding	Settlement Form	Affiliation	Municipal Status	No. of inhabitants 31 Dec. 2004
Nir Eliyahu	Southern Sharon (Kefar Sava Region)	1950	Kibbutz	IK	RC Ha-Sharon ha-Tikhon	341
Nir Ezyon	Mt. Carmel	1950	Moshav Shittufi	PM	RC Ḥof ha-Karmel	830
Nir Gallim	Southern Coastal Plain (Yavneh Region)	1949	Moshav Shittufi	PM	RC Ḥevel Yavneh	563
Nir Ḥen	Southern Coastal Plain (Lachish Region)	1955	Moshav	TM	RC Lachish	341
Nirim	Northwestern Negev (Besor Region)	1949	Kibbutz	KA	RC Eshkol	356
Nir Moshe	Northern Negev (Gerar Region)	1953	Moshav	TM	RC Merḥavim	343
Nirit	Southern Sharon	1982	Urban Settlement		RC Southern Sharon	1,068
Nir Oz	Northwestern Negev (Besor Region)	1955	Kibbutz	KA	RC Eshkol	368
Nir Yafeh	Jezreel Valley (Taanach Region)	1956	Moshav	TM	RC Ha-Gilboa	377
Nir Yisrael	Southern Coastal Plain (Ashkelon Region)	1949	Moshav	OZ	RC Ḥof Ashkelon	650
Nir Yiẓḥak (formerly Nirim)	Northwestern Negev (Besor Region)	(1949)	Kibbutz	KA	RC Eshkol	570
Nir Ẓevi	Coastal Plain (Lod Region)	1954	Moshav	IH	RC Emek Lod	1,005
Niẓẓanah	Central Negev	1980	Educational Center			142
Niẓẓanei Oz	Southern Sharon (Kefar Yonah Region)	1951	Moshav	TM	RC Ha-Sharon ha-Ẓefoni	759
Niẓẓanim	Southern Coastal Plain (Ashkelon Region)	1943	Kibbutz	OZ	RC Ḥof Ashkelon	360
No'am	Southern Coastal Plain (Lachish Region)	1953	Moshav	PM	RC Shafir	404
Nof Ayalon	Judean Lowland	1994	Rural Community		RC Gezer	2,377
Nofekh	Coastal Plain (Petaḥ Tikvah Region)	1949	Rural Settlement	–	RC Modi'im	341
Nofim	Samaria; 67+	1987	Rural Community		RC Shomron	414
Nofit	Western Lower Galilee	1987	Rural Community			2,291
Nogah	Southern Coastal Plain (Lachish Region)	1955	Moshav	TM	RC Lachish	332
Nokedim	Etzyon Bloc; 67+	1982	Rural Community	A	RC Etzyon Bloc	674
Nordiyyah	Southern Sharon (Netanyah Region)	1948	Moshav Shittufi	H	RC Ha-Sharon ha-Ẓefoni	2,104
Odem	Golan Heights; 67+	1976	Moshav Shitufti		RC Golan	93
Ofakim	Northwestern Negev (Besor Region)	1955	Urban Settlement	–	municipality	24,017
Ofer	Mount Carmel	1950	Moshav	TM	RC Ḥof ha-Karmel	367
Ofra	Northeastern Judea; 67+	1973	Rural Community	A	RC Matteh Benjamin	2,264
Ohad	Northwestern Negev (Besor Region)	1969	Moshav	TM	(RC) Eshkol	219
Olesh	Central Sharon (Ḥefer Plain)	1949	Moshav	TM	RC Ḥefer Plain	744
Omen	Jezreel Valley (Taanach Region)	1958	Rural Center	–	(RC) Ha-Gilboa	449
Omer	Northern Negev (Beersheba Region)	1949	Rural Settlement	–	local council	5,995
Omeẓ	Central Sharon (Ḥefer Plain)	1949	Moshav	TM	RC Ḥefer Plain	403
Orah	Jerusalem Hills	1950	Moshav	TM	RC Matteh Yehudah	876
Or Akiva	Northern Sharon (Ḥaderah Region)	1951	Urban Settlement	–	municipality	15,772
Oranim	Southern Lower Galilee (Tivon Hills)	1951	Kibbutz Seminary	–	RC Zebulon	211
Or ha-Ganuz	Upper Galilee	1989	Rural Community		RC Merom Galilee	364
Or ha-Ner	Southern Coastal Plain (Ashkelon Region)	1957	Kibbutz	IK	RC Sha'ar ha-Negev	382
Orot	Southern Coastal Plain (Malakhi Region)	1952	Moshav	TM	RC Be'er Tuviyyah	407
Or Tal	Golan Heights; 67+	1978	Kibbutz	KM	RC Golan	258
Or Yehudah	Coastal Plain (Tel Aviv Region)	1950	Urban Settlement	–	municipality	30,071
Oshrat	Western Galilee	1983	Rural Community		RC Matteh Asher	567
Otniel	Southern Hebron Mountain; 67+	1983	Rural Community	A	RC Hebron Mountain	692

Name	Geographical Region	Year of Founding	Settlement Form	Affiliation	Municipal Status	No. of inhabitants 31 Dec. 2004
Ovnat	Judea Desert	1983	Rural Community			
Ozem	Southern Coastal Plain (Lachish Region)	1955	Moshav	TM	RC Lachish	541
Pa'amei Tashaz	Northern Negev (Gerar Region)	1953	Moshav	TM	RC Merḥavim	311
Palmaḥim	Coastal Plain (Rishon le-Zion Region)	1949	Kibbutz	KM	RC Gan Raveh	401
Paran	Arabah Valley	1972	Moshav	TM		374
Pardes Ḥannah-Karkur	Northern Sharon (Ḥaderah Region)	(1913)	Urban Settlement	–	local council	29,32
Pardesiyyah	Southern Sharon	1942	Rural Settlement	–	local council	6,073
Parod	Eastern Upper Galilee	1949	Kibbutz	KM	RC Merom ha-Galil	254
Pattish	Northern Negev (Besor Region)	1950	Moshav	TM	RC Merḥavim	671
Pedayah	Judean Foothills	1951	Moshav	TM	RC Gezer	539
Peduyim	Northern Negev (Besor Region)	1950	Moshav	TM	RC Merḥavim	316
Peki'in Ḥadashah	Western Upper Galilee	1955	Moshav	TM	RC Ma'aleh ha-Galil	328
Pelekh	Central Upper Galilee	1980	Kibbutz	IK	RC Misgav	
Pene Ḥever	Southern Hebron Mountain; 67+	1982	Rural Community	A	RC Hebron Mountain	377
Perazon	Jezreel Valley (Taanach Region)	1953	Moshav	TM	RC Ha-Gilboa	309
Peri Gan	Western Negev	1981	Moshav	OZ		125
Pesagot	Judea Mountains; 67+	1981	Rural Community	A	RC Matteh Benjamin	1,388
Petaḥ Tikvah	Coastal Plain (Petaḥ Tikvah Region)	1878	City	–	municipality	176,230
Petaḥyah	Judean Foothills	1951	Moshav	OZ	RC Gezer	689
Peẓa'el	Lower Jordan Valley; 67 +	1970	Moshav	–	–	215
Porat	Southern Sharon (Kefar Sava Region)	1950	Moshav	PM	RC Hadar ha-Sharon	974
Poriyyah (Kefar Avodah)	Eastern Lower Galilee	1955	Moshav	–	RC Jordan Valley	303
Poriyyah (Neveh Oved)	Eastern Lower Galilee	1949	Rural Settlement	–	RC Jordan Valley	890
Ra'anannah	Southern Sharon (Herzliyyah Region)	1921	Urban Settlement	–	municipality	70,503
Rakefet	Lower Galilee	1981	Rural Community	TM	RC Misgav	701
Ramat David	Jezreel Valley	1926	Kibbutz	IK	RC Kishon	253
Ramat Efal	Coastal Plain (Tel Aviv Region)	1969	Rural Settlement	–	RC Ramat Efal	2,762
Ramat Gan	Coastal Plain (Tel Aviv Region)	1921	City	–	municipality	127,394
Ramat ha-Kovesh	Southern Sharon (Kefar Sava Region)	1932	Kibbutz	KM	RC Ha-Sharon ha-Tikhon	595
Ramat ha-Sharon	Southern Sharon (Herzliyyah Region)	1923	Urban Settlement	–	municipality	35,850
Ramat Magshimim	Golan Heights	1968	Moshav Shittufi	PM	RC Golan	483
Ramat Pinkas	Coastal Plain (Tel Aviv Region)	1952	Rural Settlement	–	RC Ono	521
Ramat Raḥel	Jerusalem Hills	1926	Kibbutz	IK	RC Matteh Yehudah	312
Ramat Raziel	Judean Hill	1948	Moshav	H	RC Matteh Yehudah	425
Ramat Yishai	Southern Lower Galilee (Tivon Hills)	1925	Rural Settlement	–	local council	5,419
Ramat Yoḥanan	Zebulun Valley (Haifa Bay area)	1932	Moshav	IK	RC Zebulun	721
Ramat Ẓevi	Southwestern Lower Galilee	1942	Moshav	TM	RC Ha-Gilboa	400
Ramleh	Coastal Plain (Lod Region)	–	City	–	municipality	63,46 thereof 13,311 non-Jews
Ram On	Jezreel Valley (Taanach Region)	1960	Moshav	TM	RC Ha-Gilboa	596
Ramot	Golan Heights; 67+	1970	Moshav	–	RC Golan	472
Ramot ha-Shavim	Southern Sharon (Kefar Sava Region)	1933	Moshav	IH	local council	1,139
Ramot Me'ir	Coastal Plain (Lod Region)	1949	Moshav Shittufi	TM	RC Gezer	496
Ramot Menasheh	Manasseh Hills	1948	Kibbutz	KA	RC Megiddo	464
Ramot Naftali	Eastern Upper Galilee	1945	Moshav	TM	RC Ha-Galil ha-Elyon	459

Name	Geographical Region	Year of Founding	Settlement Form	Affiliation	Municipal Status	No. of inhabitants 31 Dec. 2004
Rannen	Northern Negev (Besor Region)	1950	Moshav	TM	RC Merḥavim	374
Regavim	Manasseh Hills	1948	Kibbutz	KM	RC Manasseh	256
Regbah	Acre Plain	1946	Moshav Shittufi	TM	RC Ga'aton	579
Reḥan	Northwestern Samaria; 67+	1977	Moshav	OZ	RC Shomron	148
Reḥov	Beth-Shean Valley	1951	Moshav	PM	RC Beth-Shean Valley	308
Reḥovot	Coastal Plain (Reḥovot Region)	1890	City	–	municipality	101,873
Re'im	Northwestern Negev	1949	Kibbutz	KM	RC Eshkol	332
Rekhasim	Zebulun Valley (Haifa Bay area)	1957	Urban Settlement	–	local council	8,272
Reshafim	Beth-Shean Valley	1848	Kibbutz	KA	RC Beth-Shean Valley	344
Retamim	Negev Hills	1983	Moshav	TM	RC Ramat Negev	196
Revadim	Southern Coastal Plain (Malakhi Region)	1948	Kibbutz	KA	RC Yo'av	319
Revaḥah	Southern Coastal Plain (Lachish Region)	1953	Moshav	PM	RC Shafir	738
Revayah	Beth-Shean Valley	1952	Moshav	PM	RC Beth-Shean Valley	225
Revivim	Negev (Southern Beersheba Basin)	1943	Kibbutz	KM	RC Ramat ha-Negev	660
Rimmonim	Northeastern Judea; 67+	1977	Rural Community		RC Matteh Benjamin	536
Rinnatyah	Coastal Plain (Lod Plain)	1949	Moshav	TM	RC Modi'im	795
Rishon le-Zion	Coastal Plain (Rishon le-Zion Region)	1882	City	–	municipality	217,366
Rishpon	Southern Sharon (Herzliyyah Region)	1936	Moshav	TM	RC Ḥof ha-Sharon	823
Roglit	Judean Foothills (Adullam Region)	1958	Moshav	HI	RC Matteh Yehudah	
Ro'i	Lower Jordan Valley; 67+	1976	Moshav	TM	RC Bikat ha-Yarden	115
Rosh ha-Ayin	Coastal Plain (Petaḥ Tikvah Region)	1950	Urban Settlement	–	municipality	36,284
Rosh Pinnah	Eastern Upper Galilee (Hazor Region)	1882	Rural Settlement	–	local council	2,298
Rosh Ẓurim	Etzyon Bloc; 67+	1969	Kibbutz	KD	RC Etzyon Bloc	298
Rotem	Lower Jordan Valley	1983	Rural Community	RC	Bikat ha-Yarden	
Ruḥamah	Southern Coastal Plain (Ashkelon Region)	(1944)	Kibbutz	KA	RC Sha'ar ha-Negev	389
Sa'ad	Northwestern Negev (Gerar Region)	1947	Kibbutz	KD	RC Azzatah	555
Sa'ar	Acre Plain	1948	Kibbutz	KA	RC Ga'aton	388
Safed (Ẓefat)	Eastern Upper Galilee	–	Town	–	municipality	27,327
Sal'it	Samaria; 67+	1977	Moshav	H	RC Shomron	443
Samar	Arabah Valley	1976	Kibbutz	IK	RC Eilot Region	211
Sansna	Southern Hebron Mountain	1998	Rural Community		RC Hebron Mountain	179
Sapir	Arabah Valley	1979	Rural Settlement			314
Sarid	Jezreel Valley	1926	Kibbutz	KA	RC Kishon	600
Sasa	Eastern Upper Galilee	1949	Kibbutz	KA	RC Merom ha-Galil	372
Savyon and Ganei Yehudah	Coastal Plain (Tel Aviv Region)	1954	Rural Settlement	–	local council	3,233
Sedeh Boker	Central Negev Hills	1952	Kibbutz	IK	RC Ramat ha-Negev	441
Sedeh Boker (Midrashah)	Central Negev Hills	1965	Educational Institution	–	RC Ramat ha-Negev	
Sedeh David	Southern Coastal Plain (Lachish Region)	1955	Moshav	OZ	RC Lachish	406
Sedeh Eli'ezer	Ḥuleh Valley	1952	Moshav	OZ	RC Ha-Galil ha-Elyon	599
Sedeh Eliyahu	Beth-Shean Valley	1939	Kibbutz	KD	RC Beth-Shean Valley	669
Sedeh Ilan	Eastern Lower Galilee	1949	Moshav	PM	RC Ha-Galil ha-Taḥton	354
Sedeh Moshe	Southern Coastal Plain (Lachish Region)	1956	Moshav	TM	RC Lachish	337
Sedeh Naḥum	Beth-Shean Valley	1937	Kibbutz	KM	RC Beth-Shean Valley	351
Sedeh Neḥemyah	Ḥuleh Valley	1940	Kibbutz	IK	RC Ha-Galil ha-Elyon	392
Sedeh Niẓẓan	Northwestern Negev (Eskhol Region)	1973	Moshav	TM	RC Eskhol	275

Name	Geographical Region	Year of Founding	Settlement Form	Affiliation	Municipal Status	No. of inhabitants 31 Dec. 2004
Sedeh Uzziyyah	Southern Coastal Plain (Malakhi Region)	1950	Moshav	OZ	RC Be'er Tuviyyah	1,234
Sedeh Warburg	Southern Sharon (Kefar Sava Region)	1938	Moshav	IH	RC Ha-Sharon ha-Tikhon	1,036
Sedeh Ya'akov	Jezreel Valley	1927	Moshav	PM	RC Kishon	861
Sedeh Yiẓḥak	Northern Sharon (Ḥaderah Region)	1952	Moshav	M	RC Manasseh	491
Sedeh Yo'av	Southern Coastal Plain (Malakhi Region)	1956	Kibbutz	KA	RC Yo'av	199
Sedeh Ẓevi	Northern Negev (Gerar Region)	1953	Moshav	IH	RC Merḥavim	222
Sedei Avraham	Western Negev	1981	Moshav	TM		171
Sedei Ḥemed	Southern Sharon (Kefar Sava Region)	1952	Moshav	TM	RC Ha-Sharon ha-Tikhon	641
Sedei Terumot	Beth-Shean Valley	1951	Moshav	PM	RC Beth-Shean Valley	418
Sederot	Southern Coastal Plain (Ashkelon Region)	1951	Urban Settlement	–	municipality	19,968
Sedom (Sodom)	Dead Sea Region	–	Industrial Site	–	–	
Sedot Mikvah	Southern Judean Foothills	1955	Moshav	TM	RC Matteh Yehudah	
Sedot Yam	Northern Sharon (Ḥaderah Region)	1940	Kibbutz	KM	RC Ḥof ha-Karmel	672
Segev	Western Lower Galilee	1953	Rural Settlement	–	–	911
Segullah	Southern Coastal Plain (Malakhi Region)	1953	Moshav	TM	RC Yo'av	342
Senir (Ramat Banias, Kefar Moshe Sharett)	Ḥuleh Valley	1967	Kibbutz	KA	RC Upper Galilee	384
Sha'al	Golan Heights; 67+	1976	Moshav Shitufi	H	RC Golan	230
Sha'albim	Northern Judean Foothills	1951	Kibbutz	PAI	RC Gezer	1,232
Sha'ar Efrayim	Southern Sharon (Kefar Yonah Region)	1953	Moshav	TM	RC Ha-Sharon ha-Ẓefoni	1,074
Sha'arei Avraham	Coastal Plain (Reḥovot Region)	1958	Educational Institution	–	(RC) Naḥal Sorek	
Sha'arei Tikvah	Western Samaria; 67+	1983	Urban Community		local council	3,685
Sha'ar ha-Golan	Kinneret Valley	1937	Kibbutz	KA	RC Jordan Valley	500
Sha'ar Ḥefer (Beit Yiẓḥak)	Central Sharon (Ḥefer Plain)	1940	Moshav	IH	RC Ḥefer Plain	1,606
Sha'ar Menasheh	Northern Sharon (Ḥaderah Region)	1949	Rural Settlement	–	(RC) Manasseh	1,164
Shadmot Devorah	Eastern Lower Galilee	1939	Moshav	TM	RC Ha-Galil ha-Taḥton	402
Shadmot Meḥolah	Lower Jordan Valley	1979	Rural Community	PM	RC Bikat ha-Yarden	517
Shafir	Southern Coastal Plain (Malakhi Region)	1949	Educational	–	RC Shafir	440
Shaḥar	Southern Coastal Plain (Lachish Region)	1955	Moshav	TM	RC Lachish	485
Shaḥarut	Arabah Valley	1985	Rural Community	IH	RC Eilot	105
Shaked	Northern Samaria; 67+	1981	Rural Community	H	RC Shomron	509
Shalvah	Southern Coastal Plain (Lachish Region)	1952	Moshav	PM	RC Shafir	
Sham'a	Hebron Mountain	1989	Rural Settlement		RC Hebron Mountain	344
Shamir	Ḥuleh Valley	1944	Kibbutz	KA	RC Ha-Galil ha-Elyon	553
Sharonah	Eastern Lower Galilee	1938	Moshav	TM	RC Ha-Galil ha-Taḥton	468
Sharsheret	Northwestern Negev (Gerar Region)	1951	Moshav	PM	RC Azzatah	283
Shavei Shomron	Central Samaria; 67+	1977	Rural Community		RC Shomron	539
Shavei Zion	Acre Plain	1938	Moshav Shittufi	IH	local council	640
She'ar Yashuv	Ḥuleh Valley	1940	Moshav	OZ	RC Ha-Galil ha-Elyon	342
Shedemah	Coastal Plain (Reḥovot Region)	1954	Moshav	IH	RC Gederot	410
Shefayim	Southern Sharon (Herzliyyah Region)	1935	Kibbutz	KM	RC Ḥof ha-Sharon	935
Shefer	Eastern Upper Galilee	1950	Moshav	–	RC Merom ha-Galil	252

Name	Geographical Region	Year of Founding	Settlement Form	Affiliation	Municipal Status	No. of inhabitants 31 Dec. 2004
Shekef	Lachish Region	1982	Moshav	H		468
Shekhanya	Northwestern Lower Galilee	1980	Rural Community	IH	RC Misgav	545
Shelomi	Acre Plain	1950	Rural Settlement	–	local council	5,384
Sheluḥot	Beth-Shean Valley	1948	Kibbutz	KD	RC Beth-Shean Valley	400
Shetulah	Western Upper Galilee	1969	Moshav	TM	RC Ma'aleh ha-Galil	230
Shetulim	Southern Coastal Plain (Malakhi Region)	1950	Moshav	TM	RC Be'er Tuviyyah	1,492
Shezor	Western Lower Galilee	1953	Moshav	TM	RC Merom ha-Galil	359
Shibbolim	Northwestern Negev (Gerar Region)	1952	Moshav	PM	RC Azzatah	316
Shilat	Northern Judean Foothills	1977	Moshav	TM		360
Shilo	Samaria; 67+	1979	Rural Community	A	RC Matteh Benjamin	1,825
Sho'evah	Judean Hills	1950	Moshav	IH	RC Matteh Yehudah	468
Shokedah	Northwestern Negev (Gerar Region)	1957	Moshav	PM	RC Azzatah	187
Shomerah	Northwestern Upper Galilee	1949	Moshav	TM	RC Ma'aleh ha-Galil	306
Shomrat	Acre Plain	1948	Kibbutz	KA	RC Ga'aton	348
Shomriyyah	Western Negev	1984	Kibbutz	KA		75
Shorashim	Lower Galilee	1985	Rural Community	TM	RC Misgav	250
Shoresh	Judean Hills	1948	Moshav Shittufi	OZ	RC Matteh Yehudah	469
Shoshannat ha-Amakim	Central Sharon (Ḥefer Plain)	1951	Rural Settlement	–	(RC) Ḥefer Plain	537
Shoshannat ha-Amakim (Ammidar)	Central Sharon (Ḥefer Plain)	1956	Rural Settlement	–	RC Ḥefer Plain	
Shoval	Northern Negev (Gerar Region)	1946	Kibbutz	KA	RC Benei Shimon	566
Shuvah	Northwestern Negev (Gerar Region)	1950	Moshav	PM	RC Azzatah	356
Sifsufah	Eastern Upper Galilee	1949	Moshav	TM	RC Merom ha-Galil	
Sitriyyah	Coastal Plain (Reḥovot Region)	1949	Moshav	TM	RC Gezer	907
Susia	Southern Hebron Mountain; 67+	1983	Rural Community	A	RC Hebron Mountain	663
Tal El	Lower Galilee	1980	Rural Community	HH	RC Misgav	888
Talmei Bilu	Northern Negev (Gerar Region)	1953	Moshav	HI	RC Merḥavim	323
Talmei Elazar	Northern Sharon (Ḥaderah Region)	1953	Moshav	HI	RC Manasseh	662
Talmei Eliyahu	Northwestern Negev	1970	Moshav	TM	RC Eskhol	194
Talmei Yafeh	Southern Coastal Plain (Ashkelon Region)	1950	Moshav Shittufi	OZ	RC Ḥof Ashkelon	133
Talmei Yeḥi'el	Southern Coastal Plain (Malakhi Region)	1949	Moshav	TM	RC Be'er Tuviyyah	591
Talmon	Northwestern Judea Mountain	1989	Rural Community	A	RC Matteh Benjamin	1,760
Tal Shaḥar	Judean Foothills	1948	Moshav	TM	RC Matteh Yehudah	817
Ta'oz	Judean Foothills	1950	Moshav	PM	RC Matteh Yehudah	441
Tarum	Judean Foothills	1950	Moshav	PM	RC Matteh Yehudah	471
Te'ashur	Northern Negev (Gerar Region)	1953	Moshav	TM	RC Benei Shimon	301
Tefaḥot	Upper Galilee	1980	Moshav	PM	RC Merom Galilee	265
Tekoa	Etzyon Bloc; 67+	1975	Rural Community		RC Etzyon Bloc	1,179
Tekumah	Northwestern Negev (Gerar Region)	1949	Moshav	PM	RC Azzatah	446
Tel Adashim	Jezreel Valley	1923	Moshav	TM	RC Yizre'el	580
Telalim	Central Negev	1980	Kibbutz	TKM		277
Telamim	Southern Coastal Plain (Lakhish Region)	1950	Moshav	TM	RC Lachish	579
Tel Aviv-Jaffa	Coastal Plain (Tel Aviv Region)	1909	City	–	municipality	371,439 thereof 5,399 non-Jews
Tel Kazir	Kinneret Region	1949	Kibbutz	IK	RC Jordan Valley	233
Tel Mond	Southern Sharon (Kefar Sava Region)	1929	Rural Settlement	–	local council	8,288
Tel Yiẓḥak (includes Neveh Hadassah)	Southern Sharon (Netanyah Region)	1938	Kibbutz	OZ	RC Ḥof ha-Sharon	699

Name	Geographical Region	Year of Founding	Settlement Form	Affiliation	Municipal Status	No. of inhabitants 31 Dec. 2004
Tel Yosef	Harod Valley	1921	Kibbutz	IK	RC Ha-Gilboa	372
Tene	Southern Hebron Mountain	1983	Rural Community	A	RC Hebron Mountain	538
Tenuvot	Southern Sharon	1952	Moshav	TM	RC Ha-Sharon ha-Ẓefoni	650
Tiberias (Teveryah)	Kinneret Valley	–	Town	–	municipality	39,944
Tidhar	Northern Negev (Gerar Region)	1953	Moshav	TM	RC Benei Shimon	225
Tifraḥ	Northern Negev (Besor Region)	1949	Moshav	PAI	RC Merḥavim	1,287
Timmurim	Southern Coastal Plain (Malakhi Region)	1954	Moshav Shittufi	OZ	RC Be'er Tuviyyah	644
Timrat	Jezreel Valley	1983	Rural Community		RC Jezreel Valley	1,699
Tirat ha-Karmel	Carmel Coast	1949	Urban Settlement	–	municipality	18,862
Tirat Yehudah	Coastal Plain (Petaḥ Tikvah Region)	1949	Moshav	PM	RC Modi'im	734
Tirat Ẓevi	Beth-Shean Valley	1937	Kibbutz	KD	RC Beth-Shean Valley	641
Tirosh	Southern Judean Foothills	1955	Moshav	PM	RC Matteh Yehudah	
Toḥelet	Coastal Plain (Lod Region)	1951	Rural Settlement	–	RC Emek Lod	
Tomer	Lower Jordan Valley; 67+	1978	Moshav	TM	RC Bikat ha-Yarden	296
Tushiyyah	Northwestern Negev (Gerar Region)	1958	Rural Center	–	RC Azzatah	748
Tuval	Central Upper Galilee	1980	Kibbutz	IK	RC Misgav	187
Vardon	Northern Negev	1968	Rural Community		RC Yoav	379
Vered Yeriḥo	Jericho Region; 67+	1980	Moshav	IH		161
Udim	Southern Sharon (Netanyah Region)	1948	Moshav	IH	RC Ḥof ha-Sharon	742
Urim	Northwestern Negev (Besor Region)	1946	Kibbutz	IK	RC Merḥavim	403
Ushah	Zebulun Valley (Haifa Bay area)	1937	Kibbutz	IK	RC Zebulun	348
Uzzah	Southern Coastal Plain (Lachish Region)	1950	Moshav	PM	RC Shafir	496
Ya'ad	Northwestern Lower Galilee	1975	Moshav	TM	RC Misgav	556
Ya'af	Southern Sharon	1974	Rural Community		RC Southern Sharon	129
Ya'arah	Western Upper Galilee	1950	Moshav	TM	RC Ma'aleh ha-Galil	538
Yad Binyamin	Coastal Plain (Reḥovot Region)	1949	Rural Center	–	RC Gan Raveh	390
Yad Ḥannah (Me'uḥad)	Central Sharon (Ḥefer Plain)	1950	Kibbutz	KM	RC Ḥefer Plain	116
Yad Hannah (Semol)	Central Sharon (Ḥefer Plain)	1950	Kibbutz	–	RC Ḥefer Plain	
Yad ha-Shemonah	Jerusalem Hills	1978	Moshav Shituffi			85
Yad Mordekhai	Southern Coastal Plain (Ashkelon Region)	1943	Kibbutz	KA	RC Ḥof Ashkelon	724
Yad Natan	Southern Coastal Plain (Lachish Region)	1953	Moshav	OZ	RC Lachish	294
Yad Rambam	Coastal Plain (Lod Region)	1955	Moshav	PM	RC Gezer	892
Yafit	Lower Jordan Valley; 67+	1980	Moshav	TM	RC Bikat ha-Yarden	101
Yagel	Coastal Plain (Lod Region)	1950	Moshav	TM	RC Emek Lod	668
Yagur	Zebulun Valley (Haifa Bay area)	1922	Kibbutz	KM	RC Zebulun	1,116
Yahel	Aravah Vaelley	1976	Kibbutz	TKM	RC Eilot	196
Yakhini	Northwestern Negev	1950	Moshav	TM	RC Sha'ar ha-Negev	432
Yakir	Western Samaria; 67+	1981	Rural Community	A	RC Shomron	960
Yakum	Southern Sharon (Herzliyyah Region)	1947	Kibbutz	KA	RC Ḥof ha-Sharon	537
Yanuv	Southern Sharon (Kefar Yonah Region)	1950	Moshav	TM	RC Ha-Sharon ha-Ẓefoni	753
Yardennah	Beth-Shean Valley	1953	Moshav	TM	RC Beth-Shean Valley	440
Yarḥiv	Southern Sharon (Kefar Sava Region)	1949	Moshav	TM	RC Ha-Sharon ha-Tikhon	713
Yarkonah	Southern Sharon (Kefar Sava Region)	1932	Moshav	TM	RC Ha-Yarkon	312
Yashresh	Coastal Plain (Lod Region)	1950	Moshav	TM	RC Gezer	692
Yas'ur	Zebulun Valley (Haifa Bay area)	1949	Kibbutz	KA	RC Na'aman	266
Yated	Western Negev	1981	Moshav	TM		178

Name	Geographical Region	Year of Founding	Settlement Form	Affiliation	Municipal Status	No. of inhabitants 31 Dec. 2004
Yavne'el	Eastern Lower Galilee	1901	Rural Settlement	–	local council	2,747
Yavneh (Jabneh)	Coastal Plain (Reḥovot Region)	1950	Urban Settlement	–	municipality	31,830
Yaziz	Southern Coastal Plain (Lachish Region)	1950	Moshav	TM	RC Lachish	778
Yedidah	Judean Hills	1964	Educational Institution	–	(RC) Matteh Yehudah	162
Yedidyah	Central Sharon (Ḥefer Plain)	1935	Moshav	TM	RC Ḥefer Plain	540
Yeḥi'am	Western Upper Galilee	1946	Kibbutz	KA	RC Ga'aton	348
Yehud	Coastal Plain (Petaḥ Tikvah Region)	(1949)	Urban Settlement	–	municipality	25,124
Yeroḥam	Central Negev Hills	1951	Urban Settlement	–	local council	8,749
Yesha	Northwestern Negev (Besor Region)	1957	Moshav	TM	RC Eshkol	155
Yesodot	Judean Foothills	1948	Moshav Shittufi	PAI	RC Naḥal Sorek	377
Yesud ha-Ma'aleh	Ḥuleh Valley	1883	Rural Settlement	–	local council	1,219
Yevul	Western Negev	1987	Moshav	IH		149
Yifat	Jezreel Valley	(1926)	Kibbutz	IK	RC Kishon	750
Yiftaḥ	Eastern Upper Galilee	1948	Kibbutz	IK	RC Ha-Galil ha-Elyon	477
Yinnom	Southern Coastal Plain (Malakhi Region)	1952	Moshav	TM	RC Be'er Tuviyyah	867
Yiron	Eastern Upper Galilee	1949	Kibbutz	KM	RC Merom ha-Galil	351
Yish'i	Judean Foothills	1950	Moshav	PM	RC Matteh Yehudah	553
Yitav	Southeastern Samaria; 67+	1976	Kibbutz	KM		141
Yiẓhar	Samaria; 67+	1983	Rural Community	A	RC Shomron	534
Yizre'el	Mt. Gilboa	1948	Kibbutz	IK	RC Ha-Gilboa	464
Yodefat	Western Lower Galilee	1960	Kibbutz	–	RC Na'amon	369
Yokne'am	Jezreel Valley	1935	Moshav	IH	RC Megiddo	1.050
Yokne'am (Illit)	Jezreel Valley	1950	Urban Settlement	–	local council	17,787
Yonatan	Golan Heights; 67+	1976	Moshav Shituffi	PM	RC Golan	344
Yoshivyah	Northwestern Negev (Besor Region)	1950	Moshav	PM	RC Azzatah	
Yotvatah	Southern Arabah Valley	1951	Kibbutz	IK	RC Ḥevel Eilot	601
Yuval	Ḥuleh Valley	1952	Moshav	TM	RC Ha-Galil ha-Elyon	359
Yuvalim	Lower Galilee	1987	Rural Community	IH	RC Misgav	999
Ẓafririm	Southern Judean Foothills (Adullam Region)	1958	Moshav	TM	RC Matteh Yehudah	275
Ẓafriyyah	Coastal Plain (Lod Region)	1949	Moshav	PM	RC Emek Lod	622
Zano'ah	Judean Foothills	1950	Moshav	PAI	RC Matteh Yehudah	404
Zavdi'el	Southern Coastal Plain (Malakhi Region)	1950	Moshav	PAI	RC Shafir	414
Ẓe'elim	Northwestern Negev (Besor Region)	1947	Kibbutz	IK	RC Eshkol	434
Zeitan	Coastal Plain (Lod Region)	1950	Moshav	TM	RC Emek Lod	845
Zekharyah	Southern Judean Foothills	1950	Moshav	TM	RC Matteh Yehudah	669
Ẓelafon	Judean Foothills	1950	Moshav	TM	RC Matteh Yehudah	582
Zeraḥyah	Southern Coastal Plain (Malakhi Region)	1950	Moshav	PM	RC Shafir	
Zeru'ah	Northwestern Negev (Gerar Region)	1953	Moshav	PM	RC Azzatah	246
Ẓerufah	Carmel Coast	1949	Moshav	TM	RC Ḥof ha-Karmel	765
Ẓeviyyah	Central Lower Galilee	1979	Rural Community	KM	RC Misgav	282
Zikhron Ya'akov	Mt. Carmel	1882	Urban Settlement	–	local council	15,659
Zikim	Southern Coastal Plain (Ashkelon Region)	1949	Kibbutz	KA	RC Ḥof Ashkelon	347
Zimrat	Northwestern Negev (Gerar Region)	1957	Moshav	PM	RC Azzatah	253
Ẓippori	Western Lower Galilee	1949	Moshav	TM	RC Kishon	498
Zivon	Upper Galilee	1980	Kibbutz	KA	RC Upper Galilee	92
Ẓofar	Arabah Valley	1975	Moshav		RC Mid Aravah	332
Ẓofit	Southern Sharon (Kefar Sava Region)	1933	Moshav	TM	RC Ha-Sharon ha-Tikhon	811

Name	Geographical Region	Year of Founding	Settlement Form	Affiliation	Municipal Status	No. of inhabitants 31 Dec. 2004
Ẓofiyyah	Coastal Plain (Reḥovot Region)	1955	Educational Institution	–	(RC) Ḥevel Yavneh	
Zohar	Southern Coastal Plain (Lachish Region)	1956	Moshav	IH	RC Lachish	344
Ẓorah	Judean Foothills	1948	Kibbutz	IK	RC Matteh Yehudah	705
Ẓovah	Jerusalem Hills	1948	Kibbutz	KM	RC Matteh Yehudah	583
Ẓufim	Samaria; 67+	1989	Rural Community		RC Shomron	1,048
Ẓukim	Arabah Valley	1983	Rural Community		RC Mid Aravah	
Ẓur Hadassah	Jerusalem Hills	1960	Rural Center	–	(RC) Matteh Yehudah	3,623
Ẓuri'el	Western Upper Galilee	1950	Moshav	PAI	RC Ma'aleh ha-Galil	302
Ẓur Moshe	Southern Sharon (Kefar Yonah Region)	1937	Moshav	TM	RC Ha-Sharon ha-Ẓefoni	1,904
Ẓur Natan	Southern Sharon	1966	Kibbutz	KA	(RC) Ha-Sharon ha-Tikhon	224

ALIYAH AND ABSORPTION

GENERAL SURVEY

Introduction

Aliyah, "ascension" or "going up," is the coming of Jews as individuals or in groups, from exile or diaspora to live in the Land of Israel. Those who "go up" for this purpose are known as *olim* – a term used in the Bible for the children of Israel who went up from Egypt (Gen. 50:14 and Num. 32:11) and, at a later period, for the exiles who returned from captivity in Babylon (Ezra 2:1, 59 and Neh. 5–6). The call of Cyrus – "Whosoever there is among you of all His people – his God be with him – let him go up..." (Ezra 1:3; II Chron. 36:23) – has been used as a watchword for *aliyah*. It was *aliyah* that re-created the Jewish commonwealth in the Land after the Babylonian Exile, provided the community with some of its prominent spiritual leaders during the Second Temple and subsequent periods, preserved and repeatedly renewed the Jewish presence in Ereẓ Israel during the periods of Byzantine, Arab, Mamluk, and Ottoman rule, and reestablished the State of Israel in modern times.

Motives for Aliyah

The following were the principal motives that led individuals and groups to leave the Diaspora to settle in Ereẓ Israel at various periods:

1) The divine commandment (*mitzvah*) to go to Ereẓ Israel and settle there. There is a dispute about this precept in the Talmud (Ket. 110–111a), where both advocates and opponents of *aliyah* are presented. The Tosafists (see **Tosafot*) stated that the precept was no longer in force (see Tos. to the passage beginning "If the husband desires to go up..." – Ket. 110b), and *Maimonides did not include it in his list of *mitzvot*. *Naḥmanides was the first to maintain that settlement in Ereẓ Israel was a commandment fixed for posterity. This assertion aroused controversy throughout halakhic literature. The dispute was revived with the appearance of the Ḥovevei Zion (see *Ḥibbat Zion), who advanced the commandment to go to Ereẓ Israel, in addition to national and social factors, as a reason for settlement. In the heat of the argument a new position was formulated by some of the orthodox, who argued that not only is it not a *mitzvah* to go to Ereẓ Israel but it is even forbidden, as it contradicts the oath sworn by the Jews: "That Israel shall not go up [all together as if surrounded] by a wall," and that "they shall not rebel against the nations of the world" (Ket. 111a).

2) The desire to study the Torah in Ereẓ Israel, where the Sanhedrin and the great academies were to be found. *Aliyah* for this purpose occurred mainly in the tannaitic and part of the amoraic periods, and has recurred in modern times with the increase in the number of important yeshivot in Ereẓ Israel. There have been cases of entire yeshivot moving to Israel.

3) The belief that one who is buried in Ereẓ Israel has many privileges (TJ, Kil. 9:4, 32c; Gen. R. 96), which led many elderly people to come to Ereẓ Israel in order to die there. This belief existed during the time of the Temple, although it was attacked by some of the talmudic sages (Gen. R. 96:5). Characteristic of this outlook in later generations were the statements of Solomon Shlomel (Dreznitz), a disciple of Isaac *Luria and author of *Shivḥei ha-Ari* ("He who was privileged by God to fix his home in Ereẓ Israel is blessed, and blessed is he who can attain the World to Come"; *Ha-Me'ammer*, ed. A.M. Luncz, 3 (1919), 294).

4) The belief that only in Ereẓ Israel can one fulfill the *mitzvot* of the Torah. This was the watchword of the Karaites in the ninth to 11th centuries, and was stressed by religious groups during the period of the Ḥovevei Zion movement.

5) The persecution of the Jews in Europe. Beginning with the 13th century, Jewish refugees, in order to escape persecution in Europe, began to go to Ereẓ Israel since it was not under Christian rule. There are several questions in the

halakhah concerning those who vowed in times of stress to emigrate to Ereẓ Israel and broke their vows when the trouble had passed.

6) The messianic factor and the anticipation of redemption. Emigration to Ereẓ Israel would help to bring the advent of the Messiah nearer. The following statement of Raphael Mordecai Malki (late 17th century) is characteristic of this approach: "It is a known fact that the Messiah son of Ephraim does not come and is not revealed before 100 or 200 people (as in Jerusalem today), but before thousands and tens of thousands." The emigration of kabbalists after the expulsion from Spain in 1492 was considered to be due to messianic motivations – a letter dated 1521 announces that signs of the redemption are at hand (*Ha-Me'ammer*, 196–201). So are the *aliyyot* of the disciples of *Elijah the Gaon of Vilna and the *Ḥasidim, though the messianic factor in the ḥasidic *aliyah* is a subject of dispute among contemporary historians, some of whom think that it was motivated by the desire to win Ereẓ Israel for Ḥasidism.

7) The curing of illness and barrenness.

8) National and social factors – see *Historical Survey, Introduction, and also Modern Aliyah, below.

Difficulties

Many difficulties stood in the way of those coming to Ereẓ Israel. Transportation was arduous and irregular. Many of the ships which set sail for Ereẓ Israel were dilapidated and they sometimes sank with all their passengers. *Menahem Mendel of Vitebsk, leader of the ḥasidic *aliyah* of 1777, boasts that only one ship sank on his voyage. In addition there were cruel captains and pirates, who sometimes murdered their passengers or sold them into slavery. Large ransoms often had to be paid by various Jewish communities. As a result of these difficulties, there arose the halakhic question of whether it was permissible, for reasons of safety, for a convoy to continue its journey through the desert on the Sabbath. In addition to the many difficulties encountered by the travelers on arrival, there were the harsh political and economic conditions in Ereẓ Israel itself. Despite this, *aliyah* encompassed all currents of Judaism and all Diaspora communities.

From the Second Temple to Ḥibbat Zion

During the time of the Second Temple there were many immigrants to Ereẓ Israel. A famous example is the *aliyah* of Hillel, who went from Babylonia (Pes. 66a) poor and without means, and later became the head of the Sanhedrin (Suk. 20a), founding a long line of *nesi'im* (see **nasi*). One of the high priests appointed by Herod was Hananel ha-Bavli, i.e., of Babylonia. *Aliyah*, mainly from Babylonia, did not cease after the destruction of the Second Temple (70 C.E.). Sources cite many immigrant scholars who achieved a prominent place in the Jewish community of Ereẓ Israel. In the third generation of *tannaim* after the destruction of the Temple (110–135 C.E.), Hanan ha-Miẓri ("of Egypt"; Yoma 63b) and Yose b. Dormaskos, who went from Damascus (Sif. Deut. 1), are mentioned. The next generation (135–170 C.E.) included R. Johanan ha-Sandelar of Alexandria (TJ, Ḥag. 3:1, 78d) and R. Nathan ha-Bavli, who was the son of the exilarch in Babylonia. Among the fifth generation of *tannaim* are (170–200) R. Ḥiyya the Great, the disciple and colleague of Judah ha-Nasi (Er. 73a), and Issi b. Judah (Pes. 113b), both of whom emigrated from Babylonia, and Menahem the Gaul (i.e., France; TJ, Ber. 4:4, 8b).

Aliyah from Babylonia did not cease in the amoraic period, despite the fact that the great centers of Jewish scholarship were located there. Of the first generation of *amoraim* (220–250), R. Ḥanina b. Ḥama, a disciple of Judah ha-Nasi and one of the greatest *amoraim* in Ereẓ Israel, emigrated from Babylonia (TJ, Pe'ah 7:4, 20a). In the second generation (250–290), Eleazar b. Pedat, *rosh yeshivah* in Tiberias (Ḥul. 111b), R. Zakkai (TJ, Shab. 7:1, 9a) and R. Ḥiyya b. Joseph (Ḥul. 54a), who emigrated from Babylonia, and Ḥinena Kartigna'ah (of Carthage; TJ, Shab. 16:2, 15c) are mentioned. The latter attests emigration from Africa. Two *amoraim* called Rav Kahana also emigrated from Babylonia (Zev. 59a). There was a particularly large *aliyah* among the third generation of *amoraim* (290–320), some of the immigrants forming the leadership of the Jewish community in Ereẓ Israel. Prominent among them were: R. Abba (Ket. 112a); R. Avina (TJ, Shev. 4:2, 35a); R. Oshaiah and his brother Hananiah (Sanh. 14a); R. Assi, the colleague of R. Ammi, who was *rosh yeshivah* of Tiberias (MK 25a); R. Zera, a central figure of both Talmuds (Ket. 112a); R. Ḥiyya b. Abba (Shab. 105b); and R. Ḥelbo (Yev. 64b; TJ, Ta'an. 2:1, 65a); R. Yudan of Gaul (Lev. R. 20:4); R. Jeremiah, who later became *rosh yeshivah* at Tiberias (Ket. 75a); R. Samuel b. Isaac (TJ, Ber. 3:5, 6d); R. Samuel of Cappadocia in Asia Minor (Ḥul. 27b); R. Simlai (TJ, Pes. 5:3, 32a); and others. In the fourth generation (320–350) the well-known immigrants included: Ray Huna b. R. Avin (TJ, RH 2:2, 59a), R. Haggai (MK, 25a), R. Yudan of Cappadocia (TJ, Ber. 3:1, 6a), and R. Kahana (TJ, RH 2:6, 59b). Constantine the Great's proclamation of Christianity as the official religion of the state in 323 and his persecution of the Jews in his dominions initiated the decline of Jewry in Ereẓ Israel. In this period – the fifth generation of *amoraim*, in which the Jerusalem Talmud was completed – the stream of immigrants from Babylonia stopped almost completely. The statements of the *amora* R. Abiathar (250–290 C.E.), who opposed the *aliyah* of Jews who left their families behind without a livelihood (Git. 6b), attest that the flow of *aliyah* was coming to an end. In 520, Mar Zutra, a descendant of the exilarchs in Babylonia, settled in Tiberias and was appointed head of the academy. Because the times were not conducive to *aliyah*, only individuals came.

There is little information on *aliyah* in the next few centuries, in which the Muslim conquest took place (636–38), but the *aliyah* of R. Aḥa of Shabḥa, one of the greatest Babylonian scholars, who came in about 750, is well known and other disciples probably immigrated with him. The Karaites, who proclaimed to their faithful: "Be assembled in the holy city and gather your brethren," began their *aliyah* as early as the ninth century. Among them was the author *Daniel b. Moses al-Qūmisi. A Karaite legend attributes the beginnings of their community in Ereẓ Israel to the founder of the sect, *Anan b. David. In the tenth century a cultural efflorescence took place among the Karaites in Ereẓ Israel, among whom were Sahl b. Maẓli'aḥ and Salmon b. Jeroḥam, and the Karaite community spread to Ramleh. In the 11th century important arrivals included Solomon b. Judah, from Morocco, head of the Academy in Jerusalem and Ramleh (1025–1051), and the *nasi* Daniel b. Azariah, a scion of the exilarchs of Babylonia. From the 12th century, testimonies of travelers and not of immigrants have been preserved; the political situation under the Crusaders did not facilitate *aliyah*. According to a famous legend (now known to be untrue) *Judah Halevi went to Ereẓ Israel in 1141 and was killed at the gates of Jerusalem. In 1165 Maimon b. Joseph, the father of Maimonides, went there with his sons, but left after six months. In the late 12th century more Jews from North Africa arrived as a result of the persecutions there during the Almohad regime. Benjamin of Tudela found approximately 1,000 Jewish families during his stay in Ereẓ Israel (c. 1170). Ten years later, Pethahiah of Regensburg mentioned a much smaller number. According to Judah Al-Ḥarizi, who traveled to Ereẓ Israel in 1218, Saladin invited the Jews to settle in the land in 1190, after his victory over the Crusaders. Al-Harizi stated: "From the time when the Ishmaelites [Arabs] occupied the land, Jews settled there" (*Taḥkemoni*, ed. A. Kaminka (1899), No. 28, p. 245).

Persecution of Jews in Europe also contributed to *aliyah*. The most important immigration of this wave was that of the "300 French and English rabbis" who went to Ereẓ Israel in 1210–11. According to an anonymous source: "The king honored them greatly and built synagogues and academies there… A miracle occurred when they prayed for rain and were answered, and, thus, they sanctified God's name" (*Shevet Yehudah*, ed. Azriel Shochat (1947), 147). There are many opinions as to the causes of this *aliyah*. Horodezky holds that it resulted from spiritual pressure – the decline in Torah study in France; in contrast, Dubnow believes that it stemmed from severe economic oppression (*Divrei Yemei Am Olam*, pt. 5, p. 15). A new and improbable view has been advanced: that the purpose was to establish a Sanhedrin – in accordance with Maimonides' opinion that the establishment of a Sanhedrin is a condition for redemption. In about 1260, there were more *olim* from these countries, including Jehiel b. Joseph of Paris, whose yeshivah in Acre was called by the name of his town, Midrash ha-Gadol de-Parisi. The most important *aliyah* in this century was that of *Naḥmanides in 1267. Since his arrival, settlement is said to have been continuous in Jerusalem; hence his title "*Avi ha-Yishuv*" ("Father of the Community"). In the late 13th century, *aliyah* ceased as a result of the fierce battles between the Crusaders and the Muslims. The expulsion from France (1306) led R. *Estori ha-Parḥi, the first Jew to write a geography of Ereẓ Israel, to come to the Land in about 1322. Many came from Spain and Germany in the 14th century, as stated in a letter from a disciple of Naḥmanides: "At present many have arisen willingly to emigrate to Ereẓ Israel" (S. Assaf, *Yerushalayim, Koveẓ shel ha-Ḥevrah la-Ḥakirat Ereẓ Yisrael ve-Attikoteha*, A.M. Luncz (1928), 51). Among those who came from Spain was the well-known kabbalist R. Shem Tov b. Abraham Gaon, who wrote his *Keter Shem Tov* in Ereẓ Israel. In the 15th century Jewish pilgrims and prospective *olim* had to fight against a new obstacle: an order by Pope Martin v (1428) forbidding Italian ships to transport Jews to Ereẓ Israel. This decree remained in force for only a very brief period but it was renewed toward the end of the century, and led to many wanderings in order to circumvent the sea routes, if possible – for instance, as suggested by R. Isaac Ẓarefati in a letter to the Jews, via Turkey (see Historical Survey, above). A number of Italian Jews went to Ereẓ Israel in the 15th century and made their mark on the Jewish community. Among them were *Elijah of Ferrara, who wrote a letter of great importance for the history of *aliyah* in the late 14th and early 15th centuries (first published by Eliezer Ashkenazi in *Divrei Ḥakhamim* (1849), 61–63), and members of his family. The Ashkenazi Joseph da Montagna came from Italy via Venice and was appointed *dayyan* in Jerusalem at the end of 1481. Isaac b. Meir Latif apparently came from Ancona in about 1480.

Immigrants from Mesopotamia, Persia, India, China, Yemen, and North Africa are also mentioned in this century. Yemenite Jews came in caravans from Aden and Turkey, e.g., R. Abraham B. Solomon Treves of Constantinople. The increase in *aliyah* between 1488 and 1495 is attested by the fact that in 1495 it was difficult to find a place to live in Jerusalem. The most important of the Italian scholars who immigrated to Ereẓ Israel was R. Obadiah of *Bertinoro, who arrived in 1488 after three years of wandering. In his letters he writes about other *aliyyot* from Italy and under his influence the number of immigrants increased. In a letter written in 1495, an anonymous student of his praises his master's manifold activities in Jerusalem and he tells of immigrants from Italy and Sicily, some of whom had drowned. After the Turkish conquest (1516), many Jews from the Orient, Sicily, Italy, France, and Germany, as well as refugees from the Spanish and Portuguese expulsions, immigrated to Ereẓ Israel. One of them was R. Isaac *Sholal ha-Kohen, the last *nagid* of Egypt, whose *aliyah* (1517) was of great importance in the development of the Jewish community in Jerusalem. The immigration of Spanish Jews with their characteristic laws, manners, language, and customs had an important impact on the community. Some of them settled in Jerusalem – the most important being the kabbalist *Abraham b. Eliezer ha-Levi and *Levi Ibn Ḥabib – but most of them settled in *Safed, notably Joseph Saracosti, Jacob *Berab, Joseph *Caro, Moses *Cordovero, Moses *Galante, and *David b. Abi Zimra. The immigrants to Safed also included a considerable number from Italy, who even established an independent "Italian community." The extent of the increase of *aliyah* to Safed is attested by the fact that its population numbered 10,000 in the mid-16th century, while according to the Yemenite traveler *Zechariah al-Ḍāhiri, it numbered 14,000 in 1567. A great role in *aliyah* was played by the immigrants from North Africa. Among important immigrants from North Africa were Issachar ibn Susan, who went to Ereẓ

Israel in about 1527: Aaron b. Abraham *Ibn Ḥayyim, author of *Korban Aharon*; and R. Solomon ibn Ẓur. The flourishing of the Kabbalah in Safed contributed to additional *aliyah*, which continued throughout the 16th century, from France, Germany, Italy, and other European countries, as well as from North Africa and the Orient. The immigrants from Europe included: R. Ephraim b. R. Judah, son-in-law of R. Solomon *Luria, who headed the Ashkenazi community in Jerusalem; R. Solomon Shlomel of Dreznitz (Moravia); R. Judah of Ofen (Buda), and his brother-in-law R. Jacob Zak, father of Ẓevi Ashkenazi ("Ḥakham Ẓevi"). Ofen (Buda) served as a gathering place for Jews from France and Germany, who could travel from there in convoy via Turkish territory. Simeon Bak went in 1582 and R. Masʿud Saggi Nahor (*Azulai) went from North Africa. Important newcomers were R. Bezalel *Ashkenazi, author of *Shitah Mekubbeẓet*, who arrived in 1588 and became head of the community in Jerusalem, and R. Isaiah ha-Levi *Horowitz (author of *Shenei Luḥot ha-Berit*), who came in 1621 and became head of the Ashkenazi community in Jerusalem, whose members were "multiplying greatly, literally by hundreds, and constructing great buildings" (letter to his sons). In the early 17th century a renewed *aliyah* of Karaites began, but the persecutions of Ibn Farukh (1625–27) slowed down the influx. Nevertheless, immigrants continued to arrive; among them was Abraham *Azulai, author of *Ḥesed le-Avraham*.

Shabbateanism (see *Shabbetai Ẓevi) stimulated a new wave of longing for *aliyah*. Rumors of vast *aliyyot* spread everywhere; there were rumors of "80 ships" from Amsterdam and "400 families ready to depart" from Frankfurt. However, this enthusiasm died out with the apostasy of Shabbetai Ẓevi. The only great *aliyah* that occurred as a result of Shabbateanism was that led by R. *Judah Ḥasid and Ḥayyim *Malakh (both crypto-Shabbateans) at the turn of the 17th century. There was no *aliyah* like it for many generations before or after it until modern times. In its beginnings the group numbered only 31 families, but more joined it along the way. The enormous influence of the emissaries of the immigrants, who assembled at Nikolsburg (Mikulov) for departure is attested by an eyewitness, the German author J.J. Schudt (*Juedische Merckwuerdigkeiten*, 2 (Frankfurt on the Main, 1714), 58). On its arrival the convoy numbered about 1,500 – some said 1,700. There was a serious setback, however, when R. Judah Ḥasid died immediately after the group's arrival in Jerusalem and the lack of sources of livelihood, illness, and anti-Shabbatean persecutions contributed to the dispersal of the new arrivals. The *aliyah* of R. Abraham Rovigo from Modena, Italy, in 1702, with a convoy of 25 persons was also influenced by Shabbateanism.

But these were not the only convoys. According to one emissary, the Jewish community in Jerusalem numbered 10,000 persons in 1741. Ḥayyim *Abulafia came from Smyrna in 1740 and reestablished the yeshivah in Tiberias. Moses Ḥayyim *Luzzatto and his family arrived in 1743, although his activities in Ereẓ Israel were less important than his work in the Diaspora. There was an important *aliyah* of Turkish Jews at the time, including Gedaliah Ḥayyun, who founded Beth El, the *bet ha-midrash* of the kabbalists in Jerusalem, and the Rosanes, Gabbai, Naḥmias, and Pardo families. There were also Shalom *Sharabi, a Yemenite immigrant, who held a position of prominence in Jerusalem, and Eleazer Rokeaḥ, the rabbi of Amsterdam, who settled in Safed. R. Ḥayyim b. *Attar, author of *Or ha-Ḥayyim*, went from Salé (Morocco) in 1741 and established a yeshivah in Jerusalem. Nathan *Bordjel, author of *Ḥok Nathan*, went from Tunis. An organized *aliyah* of proselytes, who settled in Safed and even sent a special emissary abroad, also took place in the 18th century.

The end of the 18th century marks the beginning of the *aliyah* of Ḥasidim, who made it a principle of their teachings. Ḥasidic legend describes at length how *Israel Ba'al Shem Tov, the founder of Ḥasidism, longed to immigrate to Ereẓ Israel in order to meet with R. Ḥayyim b. Attar, and even made attempts to fulfill this wish, but was compelled to reconsider. His disciples, however, did everything to carry out their master's will. Thus, R. Abraham Gershon of Kutow (Kuty), the Ba'al Shem Tov's brother-in-law, immigrated with his family, and many Ḥasidim from Galicia and Volhynia followed him. The first organized *aliyah* of Ḥasidim took place in 1764, led by the Ba'al Shem Tov's disciples Menahem Mendel of Peremyshlyany, who settled in Jerusalem, and *Naḥman of Horodenko in Tiberias. An *aliyah* of great value to the community in Ereẓ Israel took place in the spring (Adar) of 1777, 14 years after the first; it was led by *Menahem Mendel of Vitebsk and Abraham of Kalisz, whose convoy numbered 300 persons. They left Galatz, Romania, in small boats for Constantinople and from there they sailed to Acre. The voyage lasted four months, and the convoy endured much hardship. They settled in Safed, where they met with many difficulties and most of them moved to Tiberias. This *aliyah* was rightly regarded as having revived Galilee and laid the basis for Jewish settlement there. Many of the leaders of the ḥasidic *aliyah* are worthy of mention: *Jacob Samson of Shepetovka; *Ze'ev Wolf of Zbaraz (Zbarazh); *Jacob b. Aaron the Great of Karlin; Issachar Dov Baer of Zloczow, author of *Bat Eini*; David Solomon of Soroki, author of *Levushei Serad*; *Ḥayyim b. Solomon of Czernowitz, author of *Be'er Mayim Ḥayyim*; and Aryeh Leib of Woloczyska, author of *Ahavat Shalom*. More Ḥasidim came in subsequent generations, notably Abraham Dov of Ovruch in 1832, who headed the ḥasidic community of Safed, and Israel *Bak, who brought his publishing house with him from Volhynia in 1831. The Ḥabad Ḥasidim formed another organized *aliyah*, consolidating the Ashkenazi community in Hebron, which was first organized by Ḥabad Ḥasidim from Safed and Tiberias. Ḥasidim have continued to come up to the present day.

At the same time the *Perushim*, the disciples of Elijah the Gaon of Vilna, also organized an *aliyah*, establishing a community in Jerusalem. The Gaon of Vilna is reported to have made many efforts to go to Ereẓ Israel himself but did not meet with success. The first *Perushim* arrived as early as 1722, led by R. Israel of Shklov, but their impact was not noticeable and they did not even have a *minyan*. A second group, headed by *Menahem Mendel of Shklov, arrived in 1808. Later, Saadiah b. Nathan Nata of Vilna and Nata b. Menahem Mendel of Shklov arrived. Menahem Mendel of Shklov and R. Israel of Shklov are rightly considered the fathers of their community in Jerusalem because of their initiative and powers of organization. Among other members of the community were Hillel Rivlin, scion of the prominent *Rivlin family; R. Abraham Solomon Zalman *Ẓoref; R. Shemariah Luria, a man of means who arrived with a convoy of 40 persons: R. Joseph Sundel of *Salant, the spiritual father of the *Musar movement; and R. Samuel *Salant, his son-in-law, who officiated as the city rabbi in Jerusalem for many years. It is of interest that these *aliyyot* included not only scholars but also artisans.

In 1830 the *aliyah* from Germany began, led by Moses Sacks, the first who thought of large-scale productivization of the Jewish community in Ereẓ Israel. The German immigrants included Jehoseph *Schwarz (arrived in 1833), the author of *Tevu'ot ha-Areẓ*, the most thorough work on Ereẓ Israel since the 14th-century *Kaftor va-Feraḥ*, and R. Eliezer Bergman. A notable *aliyah* came from Holland, which eventually merged with the German *aliyah* to form a joint community known as *Kolel* 'HOD' (Holland-Deutschland). There was also a sizable *aliyah* from Hungary, which was inspired by R. Moses *Sofer, the author of *Ḥatam Sofer*, and played an important role in Jerusalem, though it consisted mostly of individuals, largely youths. Noteworthy are R. Israel Ze'ev Horowitz, Abraham Sha'ag, and Akiva Joseph Schlesinger. As they increased, they formed a separate *kolel*, as did the Polish immigrants. In the 19th century sizable *aliyyot* took place from the Oriental countries as well, including Turkey, North Africa, Iraq, Persia, Bukhara, Kurdistan, Afghanistan, the Caucasus, and Yemen (see *Israel, State of: Population, section on Jewish Communities (*Edot*)).

[Itzhak Alfassi]

Modern Aliyah, 1880–1948
(See Table on following page.)

THE FIRST ALIYAH. The beginnings of the modern Jewish return to the Land of Israel, which laid the foundations for the establishment of the State of Israel, were due to a combination of three causes: the age-old devotion of the Jews to their historic homeland and the hope of messianic redemption; the intensification of the intolerable conditions under which Jews lived in Eastern Europe; and the efforts of an active minority convinced that the return to the homeland was the only lasting and fundamental solution to the Jewish problem (see *Zionism).

In the early 1880s the growing oppression of the Jews assumed acute forms in several Eastern European countries: the pogroms and repression that followed the assassination of Alexander II of Russia; the restriction of Jewish autonomy in Galicia; the pogroms and the restrictions imposed on Jewish trade in Romania; and the Tisza-Eszlar blood libel in Hungary. A spontaneous mass migration movement was the result: between 1880 and 1900 over a million Jews fled from persecution and poverty to the United States. The hopes of the *Haskalah movement for a normalization of the Jewish position through education and enlightenment had been shattered; the Jewish masses were on the move.

Simultaneously with this headlong flight to the New World, another Jewish migration movement, infinitesimally smaller but radically different in character, arose. A handful of young men felt that it was not enough to run away from persecution; the time had come to take the first step toward a fundamental solution of the Jewish problem: the return of the Jews to the Land of Israel. This vital first step must be to go up to live in the Promised Land and cultivate its soil. Branches of the new *Ḥibbat Zion movement sprang up all over Eastern Europe, especially in Russia, though they had to meet in secret and their members ran a risk of arrest. The best-known section of the movement, *Bilu, defined its aim as "the political, economic, and national-spiritual revival of the Jewish people in Syria and Ereẓ Israel." On July 7, 1882, a small group of 14 – including one woman – landed at Jaffa and made its way to the *Mikveh Israel training farm, founded in 1870, where it was given work. Further contingents followed, bringing the number of settlers up to over 50. The unaccustomed work was hard, the pay was wretched, and the novices were treated with contempt by the farm manager. Some of the Bilu'im moved to Jerusalem, where they formed a short-lived cooperative carpenters' workshop. Others received a plot to cultivate in Rishon le-Zion, but the crops were poor. Hopes that the Ḥibbat Zion movement abroad would help them buy land for a settlement of their own were disappointed, and the movement began to disintegrate. The Bilu'im were saved by Yehiel Pines, who bought 800 acres of land in the southern Shephelah, where they founded the village of *Gederah, and appealed to Ḥibbat Zion abroad to defray the cost.

Meanwhile, Ḥibbat Zion had been organizing groups to settle in Ereẓ Israel. In January 1882, a conference at Focsani, Romania, had decided to send out representatives to buy land, to be followed almost immediately by the first group of *olim* (sing. *oleh*), who would settle in the country. The Turkish government immediately ordered the cessation of Jewish immigration, and efforts to secure the withdrawal of the ban by appeals to Laurence *Oliphant and by representations at Constantinople were unsuccessful. The pioneers were undeterred, however; by 1884 six settlements had been established (including Gederah), and *Petaḥ Tikvah revived. Four were supported by Baron Edmond de *Rothschild, the other three being the responsibility of Ḥibbat Zion. In the same year the first international conference of Ḥibbat Zion, with 35 delegates from Russia, Romania, Germany, Britain, and France, met at Katowice and established a provisional central committee in Odessa. The number of societies reached close to 100, with 14,000 members who collected about 30,000 rubles a year, as well as 20,000 rubles from various campaigns. Ramified propaganda was carried out in many parts of Europe and in America.

In these early beginnings, many of the characteristic features of modern *aliyah* were already present in embryo. Like the later Zionist movement, Ḥibbat Zion consisted of three main strata: a large periphery of uncommitted sympathizers; smaller groups of organized members, who propagated the idea and collected funds for practical work; and a still smaller nucleus, without whom nothing could have been done, who followed the principle of *hagshamah aẓmit* ("personal implementation"), to use another term that was current at later stages. Some of those who contributed to the cost of the work did so out of belief in the aims of the movement; others, as in later years, were moved by purely philanthropic motives, or a mixture of the two. There were also rudimentary arrangements in the country to help the newcomers: the Mikveh Israel farm helped to train them; local Jewish leaders cooperated with Ḥibbat Zion missions; Baron de Rothschild sent out officials to administer his benefactions; in 1891 an abortive attempt was made to set up an executive of Ḥibbat Zion in Jaffa, headed by Vladimir *Tiomkin.

Although the seeds of later developments were there, their growth at first was painfully slow. The entire effort would have collapsed but for the benevolence of Rothschild, whose money not only bought land and implements, built homes, and purchased the crops, but also erected synagogues and schools, hospitals and old-age asylums. His administrators, many of whom were corrupt, kept the settlers on a tight rein, however, and stifled any signs of independence. The advent of Theodor *Herzl and the founding of the *World Zionist Organization in 1897, while arousing a tidal wave of enthusiasm in the Jewish world, had little effect at the time in the Land of Israel itself, as the new movement devoted most of its energies to political work in the hope of obtaining a charter for the establishment of a Jewish autonomous territory. The idealism of the settlers was withering away under the pressure of the difficult conditions; most of the new villages employed cheap Arab labor, and the enterprise, started with such high hopes, was producing not a self-reliant community of cheap cultivators, but a class of colonists, with the shallowest of roots in the soil, which was still – even when owned by Jews – being tilled mainly by the native Arab population.

By 1903, the end of the First Aliyah period, a score of new villages had been founded, 350,000 dunams (almost 90,000 acres) of land had been purchased, and some 10,000 Jews had settled in the country, over half of them on the soil. There were also beginnings of urban settlement, especially in Jaffa, where 3,000 newcomers had made their homes. Hebrew was beginning to be a spoken tongue once again, and the first Hebrew elementary schools had been established, though French culture, propagated by the Alliance Israelite Universelle and the Rothschild administration, was widespread. On the whole, however, the pioneering drive had been exhausted and a period of stagnation had set in.

Immigration to Israel, 1882–May 14, 1948

Year	Immigrants[1]	Rate[2]	Year	Immigrants[1]	Rate[2]
1882–1914	55–70,000		1934	45,267	177
1919	1,806	32	1935	66,472	208
1920	8,223	135	1936	29,595	80
1921	8,294	115	1937	10,629	27
1922	8,685	104	1938	14,675	36
1923	8,175	91	1939	31,195	72
1924	13,892	146	1940	10,643	23
1925	34,386	285	1941	4,592	10
1926	13,855	93	1942	4,206	9
1927	3,034	20	1943	10,063	20
1928	2,178	14	1944	15,552	30
1929	5,249	34	1945	15,259	28
1930	4,944	30	1946	18,760	32
1931	4,075	24	1947	22,098	36
1932	12,553	69	Jan. 1– May 14, 1948	17,165	73
1933	37,337	177			

1 Including immigrants without visas and tourists who settled.
2 Immigrants per 1,000 of the Jewish population.

THE SECOND ALIYAH. The depression caused by the stagnation of the first settlements, the controversies in the Zionist organization over the *Uganda Scheme, and the death of Herzl in 1904 were followed by a new upsurge of pioneering fervor which produced the Second Aliyah. The first impetus of the new wave came from the Kishinev pogroms of 1903 and the others that followed two years later. The impotence of the great Russian community in the face of these savage mob attacks shocked thousands of young Jews into a new determination to build a Jewish homeland. Many of them were imbued with socialist ideals and, sorely disappointed by the failure of the 1905 Revolution, decided that they must create their own revolutionary movement on the basis of national revival.

These young men and women were guided not only by a more conscious and consistent national ideology, but also by the ideal of laying the foundations for a workers' commonwealth in the Land of Israel. Naḥman *Syrkin had already advocated an organic synthesis of Zionism and Socialism. The Socialist-Zionist philosophy of the *Po'alei Zion movement, formulated by Ber *Borochov, was founded on a Marxist analysis of the Jewish problem that led to the conclusion that social and economic forces were working for the Socialist-Zionist solution. Others, under the influence of A.D. *Gordon's philosophy of labor, founded the *Ha-Po'el ha-Ẓa'ir movement, which emphasized the importance of physical labor, rather than the socialist reorganization of society, as the foundation of national revival. Both parties added to the idea of personal participation in the building of the homeland the concept of *avodah aẓmit* ("personal labor"; see *Israel, State of: Labor, section on Ideology of Labor).

Among the youth organizations set up at this time was one called *He-Ḥalutz ("The Pioneer") in Romania – the first to use the name. Unlike their elders, its members were not content to make propaganda, collect funds, and prepare for an undefined future. They organized only to make preparations for the journey; once a group, usually consisting of young people from the same town, had gone out, it would make way for another, which would go through the same process. In 1905 a He-Ḥalutz society was set up in the United States, and in 1911 Joseph *Trumpeldor tried to establish a countrywide organization in Russia with a detailed plan for organized training in the Diaspora and activity in the Land of Israel, but the project was dropped when he himself left Russia to settle.

The pioneers of the Second Aliyah were also much more self-reliant than their predecessors. As there was no possibility of exercising political influence on the government of the country, the parties engaged in practical work, looking after the housing, employment, and, later, the health and welfare of the newcomers. The Zionist Organization had also started practical work in the Land of Israel. The *Jewish National Fund was founded in 1901, and two years later the Anglo-Palestine Company (later the Anglo-Palestine Bank) was established in Jaffa as a subsidiary of the *Jewish Colonial Trust; in 1908 Arthur *Ruppin set up the Palestine Office in Jaffa. The workers, however, were far from passive. In 1907 Joseph *Vitkin issued a call for more pioneers, which, coming from one of those who had led the way, had greater force than the exhortations of Zionist leaders in the Diaspora. The workers fought not only for better conditions, but also for the right to employment on the Jewish farms, and in 1909 it was their initiative that led to the establishment of the first *kevuẓah* (see *Kibbutz Movement), the harbinger of a new type of social unit. They were also active in the beginnings of Jewish self-defense (see *Ha-Shomer) and the introduction of Hebrew into all spheres of life. By the beginning of World War I the *yishuv*, 85,000 strong, was a source of inspiration to the movement abroad and a magnet for further *aliyah*.

THE ESTABLISHMENT OF HE-ḤALUTZ. The Third Aliyah, which started in 1919, was partially a continuation of the second, which had been interrupted by the war. A renewed impetus, the result of the Bolshevik Revolution and the postwar pogroms and excesses in the Ukraine, Poland, and Hungary, coincided with a renewed hope, inspired by the *Balfour Declaration and the British conquest of Palestine. The westward road to the United States was still open, and most of those who chose the Land of Israel did so out of Zionist convictions. In 1915–16 David *Ben-Gurion and Izhak *Ben-Zvi, exiled from the Land of Israel by the Turks, had founded a He-Ḥalutz organization in the United States, which merged with the movement for joining the *Jewish Legion. A larger and more lasting pioneering organization arose in Russia after the February Revolution of 1917. A national council of He-Ḥalutz groups in Russia met in January 1918, and the first conference of the Russian He-Ḥalutz movement took place a year later in Moscow under Trumpledor's leadership. He-Ḥalutz gave the underlying principles of the previous *aliyah* movements a more definite and consistent form. Its members belonged to the World Zionist Organization, accepted its authority, and took part in its activities, especially the work of the Jewish National Fund. It was not a party body, though it regarded itself as a part of the Jewish labor movement, and its members in the Land of Israel helped to forge the degree of labor unity which led to the establishment of the Histadrut (see *Israel, State of: Labor).

He-Ḥalutz set up a network of training centers in the Diaspora in which its members studied the ideals of the movement, learned Hebrew and its literature, and gained experience in manual labor and farming. Some groups found employment with non-Jewish farmers; others set up their own training farms. To some extent, this stage was regarded as a regrettable necessity in the absence of immediate facilities for *aliyah*, but it ensured that the young men and women arrived not as complete novices, but equipped with a consistent social philosophy, some experience of living in communes, and at least some rudimentary skills. Even while in the Diaspora, they submitted themselves to the democratic discipline of the movement and were ready to set out for the Land of Israel whenever called upon to do so. Contact was maintained with those who had gone on ahead through emissaries (*sheliḥim*) from Palestine who knew the conditions and spent several months or years in the Diaspora as instructors and leaders. The training farms and communes also performed a valuable function as centers of attraction for youth, who could thus see the principles of the movement put into practice even in the Diaspora.

There were also two other main pioneering organizations: *Betar, affiliated to the *Revisionist organization, and He-Ḥalutz ha-Mizrachi. A non-party religious pioneering body, *Baḥad (Berit Ḥalutzim Datiyyim – "League of Religious Pioneers"), was founded in Germany and later spread to Britain and other countries.

THE ZIONIST MOVEMENT AND ALIYAH. When the Zionist movement started to rebuild its organization immediately after World War I, *aliyah* and settlement were, of course, among its major concerns. The Central Office established in London had sections for immigration and agricultural settlement. The 1920 London Conference, held instead of a regular Zionist Congress, decided that the Jewish National Fund should safeguard Jewish labor on its land and assist the settlement of Jewish agricultural workers on their own farms. A Central Immigration Office was to be opened in Palestine without delay, with Palestine Offices in all countries from which *Ḥalutzim* might come. Each office was to be controlled by a committee representing the local Zionist parties in proportion to their size. They were to give preference to candidates for *aliyah* who had been trained as farm workers or artisans, could speak Hebrew, and were physically fit.

The contributions of Diaspora Jewry to the cost of immigration and settlement were to be channeled through a new agency, *Keren Hayesod, the Foundation Fund, which was to be an instrument of voluntary self-taxation on the principle of the biblical tithe (though this quota was not actually reached in practice). The 12th Zionist Congress in 1921 resolved that Palestine Offices should be set up in the chief ports of embarkation – Trieste in Italy and Constanta in Romania – as well as the principal lands of emigration, and undertook to subsidize the vocational training of the *ḥalutzim*. Of the executive of 13, six members were to sit in Jerusalem and take charge of affairs in Palestine. Thus the World Zionist Organization, with its democratically elected and controlled legislative and executive organs, representing Jews throughout the world who were devoted to the idea of national revival, established the machinery for financing, fostering, and controlling *aliyah* and settlement as the basic methods for establishing the Jewish National Home.

Aliyah, however, was now also a major issue in the relations between the Zionist movement and the non-Jewish population of Palestine, in the policy of the British government and its administration in the country, and, through the League of Nations *Mandate, in international affairs. Although Winston Churchill as colonial secretary rejected Arab demands in 1920 for the stoppage of Jewish immigration, *aliyah* was in fact suspended temporarily after Arab attacks on Jews in 1921. The Churchill White Paper of 1922 (see *White Papers), while affirming that Jewish immigration must continue, stated that it "cannot be so great in volume as to exceed whatever may be the economic capacity of the country at the time to absorb new arrivals" and that "the immigrants should not be a burden upon the people of Palestine as a whole."

THE MANDATORY POWER AND ALIYAH. The Mandate for Palestine recognized the Zionist Organization's right to advise and cooperate with the administration in matters affecting the establishment of the Jewish National Home and the interests of the Jewish population and instructed the administration to "facilitate Jewish immigration under suitable conditions and… encourage… close settlement by Jews on the Land," adding the limitation: "while ensuring that the rights and position of other sections of the population are not prejudiced." This reservation, as well as the phrase "under suitable conditions" was frequently cited in later years by the British as justification for severe restrictions on Jewish immigration, which hampered the development of the Jewish National Home. Arab pressure for the stoppage of *aliyah*, reinforced by repeated and violent attacks on the Jews and the restrictions imposed by the British in response to this pressure from time to time, constituted a leading, perhaps the major, theme in the political history of Palestine throughout the Mandatory period.

In September 1920, shortly after the establishment of the British Civil Administration in Palestine, an Immigration Ordinance was issued authorizing the Zionist Organization to bring in 16,500 immigrants per annum, provided that it be responsible for their maintenance for one year. About 10,000 were admitted in the first 12 months, but new regulations were issued in June 1921 specifying the categories of immigrants to be allowed to enter. The main classes were: persons of independent means, professional men, persons with definite prospects of employment, and small tradesmen and artisans with a capital of £500. Other applicants, apart from tourists, had to be approved in each case by the Immigration Department of the Palestine government. After the publication of the 1922 White Paper, permits were granted to groups of artisans and laborers selected by the Zionist Organization's Palestine Offices, the number of permits being fixed every three months by the government after negotiations with the Zionist Executive. A new Immigration Ordinance, issued in 1925 and amended in 1926 and 1927, defined the rights and functions of the Zionist Executive in regard to the Labor Schedule, which was drawn up for a six-month instead of a three-month period on the basis of an estimate of the demand for labor. It provided for the admission of the following categories:

A.
(i) Persons in possession of not less than £1,000, and their families.
(ii) Professional men in possession of not less than £500.
(iii) Skilled artisans in possession of not less than £250.
(iv) Persons with an assured income of £4 per month.

B.
(i) Orphans destined for institutions in Palestine.
(ii) Persons of religious occupation whose maintenance was assured.
(iii) Students whose maintenance was assured.

C. Persons who had a definite prospect of employment.

D. Dependent relatives of residents in Palestine who were in a position to maintain them.

While the Zionist Executive had to be constantly on the watch to ensure what it regarded as a fair interpretation of these definitions, the most serious differences with the administration arose over category C, which was the only one allowing for the admission of workers without means or capital of their own. As the time came round for the issue of each half-year quota, the Executive would submit a detailed estimate of the demand for labor in the existing economy and in enterprises to be set up with its aid or by private enterprise, but these were invariably slashed by the administration. The result was often a shortage of Jewish labor, which hampered economic development and caused a drift from the countryside to the towns in search of better-paid employment.

The *ḥalutzim* were the outstanding element in the 35,000 immigrants of the Third Aliyah (1919–23). They did not merely find their places in the existing economic social structure or act as passive recipients of aid from the Zionist institutions; they were a creative force, which transformed the character of the *yishuv* and played a prominent part in its leadership. Together with their predecessors of the Second Aliyah, they founded the Histadrut, the comprehensive countrywide labor organization; played a leading role in the creation of the *Haganah defense organization; provided workers for the construction of housing and roads and the beginnings of industry; strengthened the foundations of Jewish agriculture;

and expanded the map of Jewish settlement by establishing many kibbutzim and moshavim. To a large extent, they not only integrated themselves, but also prepared the way for others to follow.

RISE IN MIDDLE-CLASS ALIYAH. The drop in the influx of *ḥalutzim* in 1924, mainly due to Soviet restrictions on the work of He-Ḥalutz, was compensated for by a considerable increase in middle-class immigration, bringing the influx up from some 8,000 in each of the years 1920–23 to almost 13,000 in 1924 and 33,000 in 1925. This was the start of the Fourth Aliyah. About half the *olim* in the two latter years came from Poland, where many Jews were impoverished by an economic crisis and the anti-Jewish policy of Grabski, the finance minister (after whom this wave was often referred to as the "Grabski Aliyah"), while severe restrictions were imposed on immigration into the United States. Most of these newcomers had a little capital of their own, which they invested in small enterprises and construction of housing in the towns.

In 1926, however, the unorganized influx was halted by a severe economic crisis, and of the 13,000 who arrived in 1926 more than half left the country. These were known as *yoredim* ("descenders" – in contrast to *olim*). In the following year there was an even more serious decline to 3,000 immigrants, with nearly twice as many *yoredim*; in 1928 the number of arrivals and departures was about the same – some 2,000 – and it was not until 1929 that the balance was restored, with over 5,000 *olim* and about one-third as many emigrants. This was a striking illustration of the close connection between conditions in Palestine and the rate of *aliyah*. For over a year the Zionist Executive had to pay out "doles" to the unemployed, and it was not until public works had been initiated by the government and some municipalities, and the Zionist Executive, with special funds raised in America and Britain, had started works of its own, that unemployment was reduced and the "dole" system abolished. Despite the setback, the Fourth Aliyah made an important contribution to the development of the *yishuv*, particularly in modern urbanization and the establishment of industry.

ASSISTANCE IN ABSORPTION. While the entire structure of the Jewish community in Palestine and the development of its economy was designed to facilitate the absorption of the immigrants into its cultural, social, and economic life, the Immigration Department of the Zionist Organization (later, of the *Jewish Agency) undertook special measures to help the immigrants find their way. Those who had nowhere to go on arrival were generally accommodated in hostels or transit camps. If their destination was a *Youth Aliyah center, a kibbutz, or a moshav, they usually stayed a few days for registration and medical examination; if they were going to the moshavot or the towns, they might stay longer. The Jewish Agency provided the immigrants with health services for an initial period through the Histadrut's *Kuppat Ḥolim or its own medical department. If in need of help, they were provided with bedding, clothing, and financial aid. The Jewish Agency built houses for the newcomers and subsidized various cooperative and private housing schemes. It set up small cooperative workshops for handicapped or elderly immigrants and contributed to the cost of the social welfare services of the *Va'ad Le'ummi and the municipalities. It also subsidized Hebrew classes for immigrants run by the Va'ad Le'ummi, the labor organizations, and the immigrants' associations. The latter played an important role in the integration of the newcomers by dealing with special cases, acting as liaison with the Jewish institutions, and supplying loans, housing grants, etc.

The vital importance of *aliyah* for the individuals concerned, as well as for the movement as a whole, gave rise to frequent controversies. The Revisionists and other parties complained of discrimination against their members in the allocation of immigration certificates by the Zionist Palestine Offices. Various groups and individuals resorted to a variety of methods to overcome the British restrictions on *aliyah*, which were regarded as violating intrinsic Jewish rights. Many entered as tourists and remained without permission when their legal period of stay was over. To enable penniless immigrants to enter as "capitalists," they were provided with fictitious deposits of £1,000; formal marriages were arranged to enable two to enter on one certificate; some succeeded in crossing the border surreptitiously from Lebanon, Syria, or via Transjordan. In 1934 the first attempt was made to send over an immigrant ship without the permission of the authorities. In Palestine, Jews, including some in the British government service, regarded it as a national duty to help these immigrants. It is estimated that some 50,000 arrived in such ways between 1920 and 1937. The British government made strenuous efforts to prevent this *"illegal" immigration and from time to time deducted the estimated number of "illegals" from the regular immigration quotas.

POLITICAL STRUGGLE FOR ALIYAH. The establishment in August 1929 of the enlarged Jewish Agency (based on Article 4 of the Mandate, which called upon the Zionist Organization to take steps "to secure the cooperation of all Jews who are willing to assist in the establishment of the Jewish National Home") extended the responsibility for the Jewish enterprise in Palestine in principle to Jewry as a whole. A brilliant array of distinguished Jews from Europe and the Americas took part in its founding conference, at which a joint Executive was elected under the presidency of Chaim Weizmann. The expected expansion was held up, however, by the outbreak of Arab violence in the following month and the political struggle of the next two years. *Aliyah* was the major practical issue of this struggle and the touchstone of Britain's capacity to carry out the fundamental provisions of the Mandate. The Zionist Organization had accepted the principle that immigration should be regulated according to the economic absorptive capacity of Palestine, while conducting a continuous struggle with the administration over the interpretation and implementation of the principle. But when Lord Passfield, the British colonial secretary, imposed political restrictions on *aliyah*, as well as limitations of Jewish land purchases, in surrender to Arab violence, the Zionist Organization and the *yishuv* regarded this as a blow to the future of the Jewish National Home, and Weizmann resigned from the presidency of the Zionist Organization in protest. The struggle against the Passfield White Paper was ultimately crowned with success, however, and the MacDonald letter of February 1931, which effectively nullified the White Paper restrictions, reestablished the political conditions for further development and progress.

It was none too soon. Dark clouds were gathering over European Jewry. The worldwide economic crisis was having an increasing effect on the Jews of Eastern and Central Europe; antisemitism was spreading and sharpening; the star of Hitler was in the ascendant in Germany; and at the same time immigration restrictions in the countries not so severely affected were tightening. For millions of Jews in Eastern Europe, in the poignant words of Weizmann's address to the Peel Commission in 1936, the world was divided into "places where they cannot live" and "places which they cannot enter." The only place of refuge was Palestine, where a Jewish community of over 200,000 (in 1933) was ready to welcome them.

IN THE SHADOW OF NAZISM. Between 1933, the year of Hitler's rise to power, and 1936, 164,000 *olim* arrived in Palestine; 24,000 of them were citizens of Germany, in addition to nationals of other countries and "stateless" individuals who had been living there. About a quarter of the immigrants arrived with "capitalist" immigration certificates and the £31,570,000 brought in during the period by private investors was about ten times as much as the total contributed by fund-raising organizations.

Almost a quarter of this sum came through a special arrangement between the Jewish Agency and the German authorities for the transfer (*Haavara) of German-Jewish capital. Under this agreement, emigrants from Germany obtained their first £1,000 in cash so that they could get their immigration certificates and deposited the rest of their assets with a clearinghouse in Berlin; the sterling equivalent was recovered after arrival from a second clearinghouse in Palestine, to which Jewish merchants made their payments for goods imported from Germany, while the German exporters were paid in Berlin. Moneys collected for the Jewish national funds and various other remittances to Palestine were also transferred through Haavara. The arrangement was fiercely criticized as a breach of the worldwide Jewish boycott of German goods, but it was strongly defended on the grounds that it was the only way to salvage the property of German Jews. The 19th Zionist Congress, which met at Lucerne in 1935 and which paid special attention to the plight of German Jewry, approved the agreement but ruled that it be placed under the control of the Executive.

In 1933 a new type of immigration, called *Youth Aliyah, was started to enable boys and girls to be looked after in educational institutions and villages in Palestine. The government issued special immigration certificates for them on the basis of guarantees given by the Jewish authorities. The work was largely financed by *Hadassah and organized by its leader, Henrietta *Szold. Up to the outbreak of the war, 5,000 young people were saved in this way (70% of them from Germany, 20% from Austria, and the rest from Czechoslovakia, Poland, and Romania); another 15,000 were brought over to Britain and the Scandinavian countries.

The German and Austrian Jews made an important contribution to the progress of the *yishuv*. They constituted the first large-scale influx from Western and Central Europe, and their skills and experience raised business standards and improved urban amenities. A relatively high proportion of them practiced medicine or one of the other professions, and they provided a majority of the musicians who formed the new Philharmonic Orchestra, as well as a considerable part of its audiences.

The flood tide of immigration was again halted, however, in 1936, when the Arab revolt began. One of its major demands was the stoppage of Jewish immigration, and the Peel Commission (see *Palestine Inquiry Commission), while proposing the partition of Palestine and the establishment of a Jewish state, also recommended that the government should fix a "political high level" of 12,000 Jewish immigrants a year for the next five years, irrespective of the country's economic absorptive capacity. In August 1937, a new Immigration Ordinance was issued empowering the high commissioner "temporarily" to fix a maximum aggregate number of immigrants for any specified period, as well as the maximum number to be admitted in any category. For the eight-month period up to March 1938, not more than 8,000 Jews were to be allowed in. From March 31, 1939, the ordinance was given general validity, despite the increasing intensity and range of the persecution of the Jews in Europe. The Zionist movement bitterly protested against the imposition of the "political high level" and denounced it as a violation of one of the most fundamental provisions of the Mandate.

The sufferings inflicted on the German Jews by the Nazi regime attracted worldwide attention, and in 1938 President Roosevelt called an international conference at *Evian to seek homes for the refugees. The dismal failure of the conference, which was not allowed to consider Palestine, showed that no one was ready to welcome them but the *yishuv*. The Jewish Agency submitted to the conference a plan for the rapid and constructive absorption of 100,000 refugees in Palestine, but the Jewish National Home was not permitted to perform its most vitally important function at the very time when it was most desperately needed. Immigration had dropped from some 27,000 in 1936 to 9,400 in the following year, and, although it rose slightly to 11,200 in 1938 and 13,700 in 1939, it was far too little to save the Jews of Europe. The British *White Paper of 1939 went a long way to meeting Arab demands for the artificial limitation of Jewish immigration, which was regarded as the major instrument for establishing the Jewish National Home, and envisioned the stoppage of its future development by making further immigration at the end of the five years dependent on Arab consent. The *yishuv*, supported by Jews in the Diaspora and many non-Jewish sympathizers, denounced the White Paper as a betrayal of Britain's obligations under the Mandate. The organization of "illegal" immigration was intensified, and more and more refugee ships made their way to Palestine.

"ILLEGAL" ALIYAH. "Illegal" ships had been dispatched by He-Ḥalutz, bringing pioneering youth, and later by the Revisionists and some individuals, who brought out large numbers of Central and East European Jews, sometimes in collusion with their governments. It was known in the *yishuv* as "Aliyah Bet" ("B Aliyah"). At first this activity was frowned upon by the Jewish authorities, but in 1938, when British restrictions were maintained despite the growing and urgent needs, the underground Mosad le-Aliyah Bet ("Institute for Aliyah Bet"), headed by Shaul *Avigur, took the lead on behalf of the Haganah and the Jewish Agency. Between July 1934 and the outbreak of war in September 1939, 43 ships succeeded in disembarking over 15,000 refugee passengers on the shores of Palestine. The *yishuv* and the Zionist movement did not regard these Jews – most of whom were refugees from poverty, persecution, and, as the event showed, death – as "illegal immigrants"; for them the Mandatory government's attempts to stop them entering the Jewish National Home were illegal. They were referred to as *ma'pilim* ("trail-blazers" or "daring pioneers").

Of the Jews trapped in Europe by the outbreak of war in September 1939, only a few thousand managed to escape the impending catastrophe. It was desperately difficult to get ships, fuel, supplies, and crews willing to risk the voyage in wartime conditions. Legal immigration had declined to a trickle, and those who landed without getting permission in advance, which was seldom possible, were still treated as illegal immigrants. The British navy kept constant watch. Some of the refugee boats were fired on as they approached the coasts. Some were turned back: three of these sank, and only the human cargo of one of them (the *Pancho* in May 1940) was saved from drowning; the passengers on the others were interned in camps or deported to British colonies. The refugees were embarked at ports in the Balkan countries, and some of them landed at Constantinople, whence they made their way by land to Palestine. Twenty-one boats in all completed the voyage, carrying some 15,000 refugees, whose numbers were deducted from the official quotas. There was also some "illegal" immigration overland by Jews from Iraq, Syria, and Lebanon across the northern border.

In the summer of 1943, after the world had learned of the Nazi Holocaust, the British government instructed its embassy in Turkey to give entry permits to Palestine to Jews who succeeded in escaping from Nazi-occupied Europe. The emissaries of the Haganah, including those who were parachuted into enemy territory, did all they could to facilitate the flight of the refugees. From the beginning of 1944 they were assisted by the United States, which set up the War Refugee Board for the purpose. Altogether, some 61,000 persons entered Palestine, with or without immigration certificates, during the years 1940–45.

THE POSTWAR STRUGGLE. After the war, when the British maintained the White Paper policy despite the pressure of the survivors of the Holocaust in the *displaced persons' camps in Europe, *aliyah* became, even more than before, the major practical preoccupation of the Zionist movement. The urgent problem of the survivors, which could not be solved anywhere but in Palestine, aroused the movement and the *yishuv* to greater exertions and stiffened their determination to fight the British policy of continued restrictions. At the same time it was a striking demonstration to the world of the central importance of the Jewish National Home for the Jewish people and the inadequacy of the Mandate, as interpreted by the British government, to provide an answer. The arrival of the refugee boats and the treatment of their passengers by the British did more than anything else to arouse world sympathy for the Zionist cause. The demand for the admission of 100,000 Jews, supported by U.S. President Truman and later by the Anglo-American Committee on Palestine, was a major focus of the Zionist struggle. The visits paid by the UN Special Committee on Palestine to the DP camps and the determination expressed by the survivors of the Holocaust to accept no solution but *aliyah* were major factors in persuading the members of the committee that the Mandatory regime must be ended and a Jewish state established. (As this phase of the struggle for *aliyah* was of such central importance in the history of the *yishuv*, it is described in greater detail in the Historical Survey.) Between August 1945 and May 1948, 65 refugee boats, all but one of which were brought by the Mosad, arrived, with almost 70,000 immigrants on board, bringing the total of Aliyah Bet since 1934 to over 100,000, of which some 80% had come in the Mosad's ships.

During the entire period of the Mandate, some 483,000 Jews had settled in Palestine – almost six times the size of the Jewish population at the beginning of the period. Almost 88% had come from Europe, where the Zionist movement was strong and the pressure of persecution was great, including 39.6% from Poland, 14.2% from Germany and Austria, 12.2% from the Soviet Union, Lithuania, and Latvia, and 4.1% from the Balkan countries. Less than 2% came from the Americas, and some 10.4% from Asia and Africa, which for some time had been outside the mainstream of the development of Zionism.

[Misha Louvish]

In the State of Israel

"INGATHERING OF THE EXILES" BEGINS. With the departure of the British and the assumption of sovereignty by the independent State of Israel, the nature of *aliyah* was radically transformed. The first of Israel's aims, as defined in the *Declaration of Independence, was: "The State of Israel shall be open to Jewish immigration and the ingathering of the exiles." The first act of the newly constituted Provisional Council of State was the abolition of all previous restrictions on Jewish immigration: the only limitations henceforward were to be the readiness of Jews to come, their freedom to leave, and the facilities for transporting them; absorptive capacity was taken for granted. The way was open for the realization of the prophetic dream of the *ingathering of the exiles, i.e., the return to the homeland of all Jews who were willing and able to come and the transfer of complete Jewish communities within a short space of time. This national purpose was given legislative expression in the *Law of Return 1950, which granted every Jew the automatic right to become an *oleh*, i.e., to settle permanently in Israel, and the Citizenship Law, 1952, which enabled every *oleh* to become a citizen as soon as he set foot on Israel soil. At an early stage, it was decided that immigration and absorption should be the joint tasks of the State of Israel and Jewry in the Diaspora. The World Zionist Organization, represented by the Jewish Agency, was therefore charged to encourage and organize immigration and assist in the absorption of the immigrants in close cooperation and coordination with the Government of Israel. The terms of these responsibilities and functions were set down in the World Zionist Organization-Jewish Agency Status Law, 1952, which recognized the Zionist Organization-Jewish Agency as representing Diaspora Jews in all matters concerning immigration and absorption. In 1954 a Covenant was signed by the government and the Agency, further defining the latter's functions and methods of coordinating their activities.

Between May 15, 1948, and the end of 1970, over 1,300,000 Jews – twice as many as the Jewish population at the end of the Mandate – settled in Israel. (See tables: Immigration to Israel, 1948–1970; Immigration to Israel, 1971–2004; Immigrants and Potential Immigrants to Israel by Period of Immigration and Country of Birth, 1919–2004.) They started coming as soon as the State was established. First to arrive were the 25,000 "illegal" immigrants detained by the British in Cyprus: within a few short weeks, they were all brought over. During May–August 1948, while the War of Liberation was raging, 33,000 immigrants came in; then the pace quickened and 70,000 arrived during September–December, mostly survivors of the Holocaust from the displaced persons camps in Germany, Austria, and Italy. In the next four months, January–April 1949, the number of immigrants reached 100,000. In all, 203,000 Jews from 42 countries arrived in the first year of independence. This mass immigration continued until the end of 1951. During this period entire Jewish communities were transplanted to Israel, producing drastic changes in the map of Diaspora Jewry. More than 37,000 of Bulgaria's 45,000 Jews came; 30,500 of Libya's 35,000; all but about 1,000 of the 45,000 in Yemen; 121,512 of the 130,000 in Iraq; two-thirds (103,732) of Polish Jewry; and one-third (118,940) of the Jews in Romania. The DP camps in Europe could be closed because their inmates had gone to Israel. This mass immigration was marked by unexpected and dramatic events, when the Jewish Agency had to improvise the movement of tens of thousands of people within a very short time and in adverse conditions. These migrations were organized as special operations, planned and executed by special emissaries. The most dramatic were Operation Magic Carpet, for the Yemenite Jews, and Operation Ezra and Nehemiah, which brought over Iraqi Jewry.

Thousands of Yemenite Jews, gripped by messianic enthusiasm, had been making their way south on foot, carrying their scanty belongings, to the British colony of Aden. On the establishment of independence, Jewish Agency representatives started negotiations with the imam of Yemen, the local sultans and sheikhs, and the British authorities, and in May 1949 agreement was reached. Although the Jews of Yemen were not forced to leave, almost the entire community made the long and arduous trek to Aden, whence they were brought to Israel in an intensive large-scale airlift. About 47,000 were thus transported "on eagles' wings" (Ex. 19:4) and by the end of 1950, when the operation was concluded, only a few hundred remained.

In March 1950, the Iraqi government suddenly enacted a "Special Law Authorizing the Emigration of Jews" providing they renounced their citizenship in writing. Those above the age of 20 were permitted to take out a sum equal to some $16 each; young people up to 20 and children up to 12 could take only $10 and $6 respectively. Many Jews had to sell their property in haste for pitiful sums not in any proportion to its real value, but they could not take out the proceeds. The Jewish Agency immediately made emergency arrangements to move the Iraqi Jews to Israel. They were flown to Cyprus and then brought to Israel by air or sea, the whole operation being completed within 18 months.

All in all, 684,201 immigrants – more than the entire Jewish population the day independence was proclaimed – came between May 15, 1948, and the end of 1951. (See Table: Mass Immigration to Israel, May 1948–December 1951.)

ABSORBING THE FIRST WAVE. *Aliyah* was the lifeblood of the new state, but it was only the beginning of the process of integrating veterans and newcomers from a hundred countries into one nation. The second stage was *kelitah* ("absorption"), a word that denoted a multitude of tasks: collecting the immigrants at the port or airfield; providing them with food and lodging; building temporary and permanent housing; finding employment; expanding health services; organizing education. Complete absorption was a task that affected all areas of the country's life and demanded massive financial participation by Diaspora Jewry through the Jewish Agency. In one year the Agency's staff had to transport 200,000 immigrants from the point of arrival to their new homes. In the first place, most of them were taken to Sha'ar ha-Aliyah ("Gateway of Aliyah"), near Haifa, a converted British army camp, where they were registered, medically examined, inoculated and vaccinated, classified, and sent on to their destinations. An average of 1,000 a day passed through Sha'ar ha-Aliyah at peak.

At first large numbers were accommodated in dwellings abandoned by the Arabs who had fled during the War of In-

Mass Immigration to Israel, May 1948–December 1951

All Countries	**684,201**
Eastern Europe	
Romania	118,940
Poland	103,732
Bulgaria	37,231
Czechoslovakia	18,217
Hungary	13,631
Yugoslavia	7,595
Soviet Union (Lithuania, Latvia)	4,698
Total	304,044
Western Europe	
Germany	8,856
France	4,008
Austria	2,994
Greece	2,005
Britain	2,143
Italy	1,415
Belgium	1,108
Netherlands	1,102
Spain	412
Sweden	429
Switzerland	386
Other European Countries	147
Total	25,005
Asia	
Iraq	121,512
Turkey	34,213
Iran	24,804
Aden	3,155
India	2,337
China	2,167
Cyprus	136
Yemen	45,199
Other Asian Countries	3,700
Total	237,223
Africa	
Morocco	30,750
Tunisia	13,139
Algeria	1,523
Libya	30,482
South Africa	584
Ethiopia	83
Egypt	16,508
Other African Countries	108
Total	93,177
Western Hemisphere	
United States	1,909
Canada	233
Argentina	1,134
Brazil	442
Other Latin American Countries	870
Total	4,588
Australia	171
Unregistered	19,993

dependence. A national housing corporation, *Amidar, was set up in 1949, and by the end of 1951 28,000 homes had been built (see *Israel, State of: Housing). At the same time prefabricated huts were imported from Sweden. Some went to villages of various types and a number were received by relatives, who helped them to find housing and employment. All these expedients, however, were not sufficient to accommodate the influx and many of them had to be sent to camps – some converted from British army quarters – where they were fed and looked after until homes and work could be found for them. Those who needed to know Hebrew to work in their professions were sent to *ulpanim, special language courses using intensive modern methods, the first of which was set up in 1949.

More than two-thirds of the 393,197 immigrants who arrived during two critical years, from May 1948 to May 1950, were settled in towns and villages: 123,669 were accommodated in houses abandoned by Arabs and 53,000 in permanent housing in towns and villages; 36,497 were helped by relatives to find homes and work; 35,700 settled in newly established moshavim and 16,000 in kibbutzim; and 6,000 children were placed in Youth Aliyah institutions (see section on Youth Aliyah, below). Less than one-third – 112,015 persons – remained in immigrant camps and temporary housing, while no information was available with regard to 9,596.

As the pressure of immigration increased, the camps were filled to capacity. The overcrowding and enforced idleness, without work for the adults or decent conditions for their families, were demoralizing and it became urgently necessary to find better methods of dealing with those for whom permanent housing was not yet available. The immediate solution, devised in 1950, was the **ma'barah*, the transitional camp or quarter, in which the newcomers were provided with work and made responsible for looking after themselves. Some of the large camps were closed down; others were converted

Main Periods of *Aliyah* from Asian countries

Country	Main period of *Aliyah*	Number of Immigrants to Israel	Jewish Population in 1945
Turkey	1919–1950	37,000	80,000
Lebanon+Syria	1950–1955	12,000	25,000
Iraq*	1950–1951	106,662	90,000
Iran	1950–1965	18,000	50,000
Afghanistan	1950	1,200	5,000
China	1949	5,000	9,000
Manchuria	1949	1,000	10,000
Japan			2,000
Philippine Islands	1950–1955	22	1,000
Pakistan	1949–1953	1,500	1,500
India	1950–1955	4,000	30,000
Indonesia	1950	20	2,000
Yemen	1948–1950	43,000	45,000
Aden	1950	2,825	6,000

* Iraq served as an assembly center for immigrants from other places. The high emigration figures do not indicate that all the Jews left Iraq in this period.

into *ma'barot* by closing the communal dining hall and providing each family with facilities for buying and cooking its own meals. In addition, *ma'barot* were specially built near the towns or in other places where work was available in the neighborhood. At first some of them consisted of tents, but these were soon replaced by canvas-walled huts or tin shacks. In each *ma'bara* there were wooden huts for the labor exchange, clinic, school, and kindergarten. The construction of a large *ma'barah* took not more than a few weeks and thus thousands of immigrants were given temporary shelter within a short period. By May 1952 there were 113 *ma'barot* with a population of 250,000.

Jewish Immigrants to Israel[1] by Origin, May 1948–1967

Year	Number	Percent born in Europe, America, or Oceania
May–Dec. 1948	101,828	87.3
1949	239,576	53.7
1950	170,249	50.9
1951	175,249	29.2
1952	24,369	29.6
1953	11,326	28.4
1954	18,370	13.9
1955	37,478	8.6
1956	56,234	13.8
1957	71,224	57.6
1958	27,082	55.3
1959	23,895	66.3
1960	24,510	70.5
1961	47,638	52.9
1962	61,328	22.6
1963	64,364	31.8
1964	54,716	58.3
1965	30,736	53.6
1966	15,730	57.7
1967	14,327	38.2

1 Including tourists settling.

For those who could not as yet find employment, special relief-work projects were organized in afforestation, clearing and reclamation of land, weed-removing and other agricultural work, and road construction. Many such schemes were carried out by the *Jewish National Fund, which specialized in afforestation and land reclamation, the government, road making, etc., and private employers, who were subsidized to encourage them to "make work." Although the projects were often artificial from the purely economic point of view, they provided the unskilled with opportunities to earn an income and accustomed them to manual labor. In each *ma'bara* there were social workers to handle the individual problems of the immigrants: from the repair of leaking huts and contact with the labor exchange to the running of the local kindergarten and school, the provision of facilities for learning Hebrew, maintenance of sanitary conditions, and full medical and social welfare services. Ninety clinics were established in the *ma'barot*, employing more than 100 doctors and 300 nurses.

Meanwhile, there had been an enormous advance in the establishment of new villages: kibbutzim, mainly manned by young people who had been denied the opportunity to settle on their own because of the White Paper restrictions and the shortage of land, and moshavim, the form favored by the great majority of the newcomers. In 4½ years, up to the end of 1953, 345 new villages – 251 moshavim and 96 kibbutzim – with a population of over 20,000 families, were founded – more than in the preceding 70 years. The new settlers cultivated 1,048,000 dunams (262,000 acres) of land, of which 130,000 dunams were irrigated and 53,000 were planted with orchards and vineyards. Their livestock consisted of 660,000 poultry, 22,000 sheep, and 21,000 head of cattle, including 8,000 milch cows. With the aid of Jewish Agency instructors in each village, the apprentice farmers were rapidly increasing their skills, expanding production, and beginning to make a significant contribution to the replacement of imports by home-grown food (see also section on Settlement, below).

Jewish Immigration to Israel by Origin and Some Demographic Characteristics, May 1948–1967

	Total	Europe, America, Oceania	Asia, Africa
Females (percent)	50.0	50.8	49.3
Age distribution (percent)			
0–14	31.3	21.7	39.6
15–29	26.5	23.2	29.2
30–44	20.0	25.0	15.7
45–64	17.7	24.1	12.3
65 and over	4.5	6.0	3.2
Average Number of Persons per Family Unit, 1952–1967	2.9	2.3	3.7
Occupational distribution of earners, 1965–1967 (percent)			
Industrial, building, transport, and services	54.5	50.3	59.8
Managerial, administrative, and clerical	15.4	17.7	12.5
Professional and technical	15.1	21.8	6.7
Mercantile	8.2	5.6	11.4
Unskilled	4.8	3.4	6.5
Agricultural	2.0	1.2	3.1

LULL IN IMMIGRATION. Following the peak, a regression set in: in the years 1952–54 the total number of immigrants was only 51,463. The main reason was the economic recession, which compelled the government to impose a strict austerity regime and reduced the standard of living of the greater part of the population. There was mass unemployment and housing conditions for the immigrants were woefully inadequate. In addition, there was a significant increase in emigration: veteran Israelis and new immigrants were tempted to emigrate to affluent countries, and at times the number who left was higher than the total of those who came in. The lull was used to overhaul the machinery and methods of immigration and absorption. Instead of sending the new arrivals to *ma'barot* or camps, they were taken directly from the ships to homes ready for them and in a few days they were able to go out to work. A start was made with the establishment of new "development" towns, some with the *ma'barot* in the Negev and Galilee as nuclei. Thus *Yeroḥam was originally a *ma'bara*; the Bet She'arim *ma'barah* became the town of *Migdal ha-Emek; and the one at Ḥalsa became *Kiryat Shemonah. Other towns were established from the start on a permanent basis, e.g., *Dimonah, *Kiryat Gat, and *Beth-Shemesh, while existing towns, like *Afulah and *Safed, were given "development" status.

NEW METHODS OF ABSORPTION. In 1955 mass immigration was renewed and from 1955 to the end of 1957 most of the immigrants came from Morocco, Tunisia, and Poland. During these years immigration totaled 162,308, as against 51,463 during the slack period of 1952–54. Immigration from Morocco was stimulated by the surge of nationalism which swept that country in 1954 and was further intensified after it achieved independence in March 1956: during these three years 70,053 Moroccan Jews arrived. Following a similar surge of nationalism and the achievement of independence by Tunisia in 1956, 15,267 Jews came from that country during the same period. The political situation in Poland, and particularly the influx of Polish Jews and their families expatriated from the U.S.S.R., also led to a considerable rise in Jewish emigration: 34,426 in the years 1955–57. Following the Hungarian revolution in 1956, thousands of Jews succeeded in fleeing to Austria, whence the Jewish Agency brought over 8,682, and after the Sinai Campaign in the same year 14,562 Egyptian Jews reached Israel.

The absorption of immigrants during this period was facilitated by the country's economic recovery. There was a considerable growth in industry and agriculture and new development projects increased absorptive capacity. The ship-to-settlement method was put into general use; immigrants founded villages and towns in the regional settlement areas, like the *Lachish area, in the south, with its central town of Kiryat Gat, and the *Taanach area, in the Jezreel Valley, where *Afulah was the urban center.

From 1958 to 1960 immigration slowed down again: the total during this period was 72,781. The largest group came from Romania (27,697) and the total from Eastern Europe was 41,702. During these years there was an increase in the number of professional men among the immigrants: doctors, engineers, economists, and teachers – a trend which had started in 1956. In order to cope with immigrants of this type, the Jewish Agency set up a network of hostels where they could stay with their families in small flats for periods of up to six months, while learning Hebrew and looking for suitable work and housing.

The ulpanim, run jointly with the Ministry of Education and Culture, which was responsible for the teaching, were expanded. Besides the resident ulpanim, which had boarding facilities, there were non-resident ulpanim in the cities, which also catered to part-time students and provided evening classes. Ulpanim were also held in the kibbutzim, where the immigrants put in half a day's work and studied half a day. These schools were described in a UNESCO report as an "excellent institution for adult education." In addition, hundreds of Hebrew courses were run by municipal authorities and voluntary organizations.

After the 1958–60 lull, immigration swelled again from 1961 to 1964, when a total of 215,056 immigrants arrived. There was great disappointment, however, in 1961 and 1962, when most of the 130,000 Algerian Jews who were French citizens, rooted in French civilization, and wished to benefit from the generous assistance given by the French government, opted against *aliyah* when Algeria achieved independence. The great majority settled in France; only 7,700 came to Israel.

During this period the liquidation of the *ma'barot* was speeded up, as more permanent housing schemes were started in all parts of the country. By the end of 1964 only 2,350 families and 980 single persons remained in them; ultimately, only a few who refused to be transferred to permanent homes were left.

YOUTH ALIYAH. Youth Aliyah was an important factor in the absorption of the immigrants. It looked after their children in special educational institutions and in kibbutzim, as well as organizing the immigration of children in advance of their parents. Its aims were: to rescue boys and girls from countries where their physical welfare or cultural identity as Jews was threatened; to help them to adjust to their new home by overcoming physical, emotional, and social handicaps; to raise their cultural standards, and develop their intellectual potentialities. Youth Aliyah provided its wards, in addition to a complete education, with clothing, social and medical services, vocational training; guidance in free-time recreation; psychological guidance and care; religious teaching for children of religious families; and recreation camps. Its educational program was based on the *ḥevrat no'ar* ("youth group") and included study and work on the land in a youth community, guided by *madrikhim* ("youth instructors") and teachers. Special day centers were set up in several new development towns, where adolescents were given vocational training as well as general education. Youth Aliyah graduates also benefited from scholarships for higher education and professional training. The newcomers from Yemen and Iraq, from Persia and Tunisia, differed from their predecessors, and Youth Aliyah had to learn by trial and error how to cope with the new problems. In the course of time, it had to turn its attention to new-immigrant families with poor home conditions which were not conducive to the educational development of the children. Besides, Israel itself was changing: it was becoming more industrialized, and greater technical skill, instead of being the prerogative of the few, was now a necessary part of the equipment of any wage earner, so Youth Aliyah had to adapt its educational program to these changing needs. Since the 1960s some 12,500 children have been under Youth Aliyah's care every year: about 3,000 in kibbutzim; 6,000 in children's and youth villages; 500 in special rehabilitation institutions; and about 3,000 attending day centers in the towns. From its inception in 1934, after the rise of the Nazis in Germany until the end of 1969, Youth Aliyah brought up over 120,000 children and young people. One out of every 20 Jewish citizens of Israel has received his education in Youth Aliyah. As of September 1996, Youth Aliyah became a division of the Israel Ministry of Education.

EDUCATIONAL AND YOUTH WORK. The Zionist Organization's educational work among youth and adults in the Diaspora was of considerable long-term importance for *aliyah*, especially from Western Europe and the Americas. The Youth and He-Ḥalutz (Pioneering) Department maintained contact with Zionist and, later, other Jewish movements in the Diaspora (as well as the pioneering youth movements in Israel), providing them with emissaries, guidance, educational material, training facilities, and financial support. Its Institute for Youth Leaders from Abroad in Jerusalem, established in 1946, offered a year of study and work, including five months' study of Hebrew language and literature, Judaism, geography of Israel, the history of Zionism and of Jewish settlement in the Land of Israel, and youth leadership methods, and five months' work and continued study at kibbutzim. In addition, thousands of young people attended the department's annual six- to eight-week Summer and Winter Institutes in Israel. Two departments were set up for education and culture in the Diaspora, one general and one for Torah education and culture. They organized short seminars for teachers in Israel and abroad and set up two permanent centers in Jerusalem for the training of Diaspora teachers: the Ḥayim Greenberg Institute in 1955 and the Rabbi Ze'ev Gold Institute, for religious teachers, in 1957. These and other schemes helped to foster closer links between Israel and the Diaspora, disseminate knowledge of Judaism, strengthen commitment to Israel and the Jewish people, and stimulate the desire for *aliyah*. Up to 1967 over 30,000 persons spent some time in Israel under one of these schemes, and it is estimated that at least one-third of the participants returned eventually as *olim*.

WESTERN IMMIGRATION. The overwhelming majority of the immigrants in the mass-immigration period came from what have been called "lands of stress," who were motivated not only by the positive pull of the free, sovereign Jewish State, but also by the push of various negative factors. Such were the survivors of the Holocaust who wished to have nothing more to do with Europe, the Jews in certain countries where the defeat of Nazism had failed to stamp out traditional, endemic antisemitism, and the Jews in the Arab and Muslim countries. By the early 1970s, in addition to the 3,000,000–4,000,000 Jews of Soviet Russia, from which there had never been more than a small trickle of Jewish immigration for family reunion, only about a quarter of a million Jews remained in the "lands of stress."

From 1965 to 1967 there was a decline in the rate of immigration: in 1965 the total fell to 33,098; in 1966 there were only 18,510, and in 1967, 18,065. Many came from *Latin America at that period. A number of these people found it hard to settle, in view of the economic recession and other causes, and went back. The Jewish Agency devoted much thought and resources to the requirements of "free" immigration – that is, the immigration of Jews who are free to leave, if they wish, and settle in Israel out of positive motives. The small numbers who came from the "lands of stress" during this period also required, and received, individual treatment.

Immigration to Israel, 1948–1970*

Year	Immigrants[1]	Tourists Settling[2]	Temporary Residents[3]	Returning Residents[4]	Total
May 15–Dec. 31, 1948	101,819	9			101,828
1949	239,076	502			239,578
1950	169,405	808			170,213
1951	173,901	1,228			175,129
1952	23,375	994			24,369
1953	10,347	979			11,326
1954	17,471	899			18,370
1955	36,303	1,175			37,478
1956	54,925	1,309			56,234
1957	71,100	1,491			72,591
1958	26,093	1,163			27,256
1959	23,045	908			23,953
1960	23,643	1,023			24,666
1961	46,650	1,067			47,717
1962	59,600	1,855			61,455
1963	62,156	2,278	2,031		66,465
1964	52,456	2,523	1,867		56,846
1965	28,795	2,235	2,068		33,098
1966	13,610	2,348	2,552		18,510
1967	12,275	2,194	3,587	393	18,449
1968	18,156	2,547	8,404	1,964	31,071
1969	23,207	2,260	12,628	2,374	40,469
1970	22,470	[5]	15,460	4,111	42,041
Total	**1,309,878**	**31,795**	**48,597**	**8,842**	**1,399,112**

Source: Statistical Abstract of Israel, Central Bureau of Statistics, Israel
* Empty spaces denote absence of information.
1 Until 1956 Jews only.
2 Until 1965 Jews only.
3 Figures for temporary residents arriving before 1963 are not available.
4 In the years 1967–1970 returning residents were given some immigrants' privileges.
5 For 1970, tourists settling were counted in the figures for immigrants.

Immigration to Israel, 1971–2004

Year	Immigrants	Year	Immigrants
1971	41,930	1988	13,034
1972	55,888	1989	24,050
1973	54,886	1990	199,516
1974	31,981	1991	176,100
1975	20,028	1992	77,057
1976	19,754	1993	76,805
1977	21,429	1994	79,844
1978	26,394	1995	76.361
1979	37,222	1996	70,919
1980	20,428	1997	66,221
1981	12,599	1998	56,730
1982	13,723	1999	76,766
1983	16,906	2000	60,192
1984	19,981	2001	43,580
1985	10,642	2002	33,567
1986	9,505	2003	23,268
1987	12,965	2004	20,898
Total 1971–2004			1,601,169
Total 1948–2004			3,000,281

A first step in this direction was taken in 1965, when the Agency started setting up hostels – actually small-scale hotels – where newcomers could stay for six months, or even a year, while they studied Hebrew at special ulpanim, looked for jobs, decided where they wanted to live, explored possibilities, and became familiar with the conditions of life. Now more of these hostels were set up and the existing ones improved and enlarged. Then the concept was broadened and "absorption centers" were established, each containing all the services and facilities – residential, social, and cultural – that the new immigrants required until they could move into permanent housing. Special personnel helped them to adjust to the new environment, choose schools, and find employment and housing.

To encourage immigration from the free countries it was necessary not only to "process" immigration, but also to further the idea of *aliyah* and encourage prospective immigrants by facilitating their absorption. This kind of immigration was marked by its individualistic character. Each immigrant was moved to *aliyah* by his own reasons and each had his specific potentialities and needs. In addition to his positive inner motivations, he also had to know that he could find in Israel a job in keeping with his training and experience, housing that reasonably approximated what he was used to, and suitable schooling for his children. Immigrants of this type were easily discouraged by bureaucratic inefficiency and the need to make the rounds of Agency and government offices. Those who gave up the struggle and went back deterred others from making the attempt. Most newcomers from the West came in the first place as "temporary residents," changing their status to that of immigrants only when they were assured of successful integration. The government and the Jewish Agency, therefore, had to make special efforts to provide suitable facilities and minimize the "run-around" to which the immigrants objected. Various schemes were initiated by groups of immigrants who set up housing estates in Israel with the Agency's assistance. Some of these were organized by ḥasidic rabbis who lived in the United States and wished to transplant their communities to Israel. The first, Kiryat Tsanz, near Netanyah, was the blueprint for similar projects in other parts of the country (see also *Israel, State of: Religious Life.).

IMMIGRATION AFTER THE SIX-DAY WAR AND DURING THE 1970S. A significant breakthrough in immigration from the West came after the Six-Day War in 1967. The unprecedented rallying of material and moral support for Israel during the crisis embraced many Jews in the Diaspora who had long since renounced any interest in and concern for things Jewish. It had a particularly cathartic effect on Jewish youth, and over five thousand volunteers went to Israel during May–June 1967 to help in any way they could. By the beginning of 1968, the total number of volunteers from abroad was 7,500, of whom 4,500 went for short periods of up to four months and the rest for six months to a year. They hailed from 40 countries, mainly from Britain (1,900), Latin America (1,500), South Africa (850), France (800), the United States (750), Canada (300), and Australia and New Zealand (275).

More than 4,700 worked in kibbutzim; 450 in moshavim; 1,200 as civilian auxiliaries attached to the Israel Defense Forces; more than 200 in the reconstruction of the University and Hadassah Hospital buildings on Mount Scopus in Jerusalem, and 150 in archaeological excavations; others worked in their own professions, including 225 doctors and nurses, and 100 teachers, youth-group leaders, and social workers, or in land reclamation. The majority received instruction in Hebrew.

About 1,800 remained – as students, or working in their professions or in kibbutzim with a view to permanent settlement. From 1968 volunteers came at a steady annual rate of about 1,800 under various schemes. The largest was Sherut la-Am ("Service to the People") – a year's voluntary service in kibbutzim and development areas. It was estimated that about a third of the volunteers remained in Israel after their year's service, while many of the others eventually returned as immigrants.

There was also a considerable overall increase in *aliyah* from western countries. On July 10, 1967, the Israel government and the executive of the Zionist Organization and the Jewish Agency issued a "Call to Aliyah" appealing to the Jewish people the world over to come to Israel and build the land. During the second half of 1967 there was a visible rise in the rate of immigration; in 1968 the total increased to over 30,000 and in each of the years 1969 and 1970 to over 40,000. To cope with the new mood and the new absorption requirements it was necessary to introduce radical changes in the immigration machinery. Thus, in 1967, the three Agency departments involved – Immigration, Absorption, and Economic – were merged into one and a joint Government-Agency Authority on Immigration and Absorption was set up to centralize planning and execution of policy. The Authority worked out various proposals, later passed into law, for special facilities for new immigrants in the spheres of customs, taxation, housing, school and university tuition fees, etc. New absorption centers, hostels, and kibbutz *ulpanim* were set up all over the country. At the beginning of 1970 there were 14 absorption centers, with a capacity of 4,000 beds; 13 hostels, with 2,500 beds; 6 students' hostels, with 1,700; and 64 kibbutz *ulpanim* with 2,250. Since these facilities were intended for half-yearly periods, their annual capacity was double these figures.

In June 1968 the 27th Zionist Congress in Jerusalem decided to found the Aliyah Movement, organized in local circles or countrywide movements in the Diaspora. Each member committed himself to settle in Israel within three years of joining, but many came within a short period and the membership was in constant flux, members leaving for *aliyah* and others taking their places. In May 1970 there were 125 *aliyah* circles in 22 countries with a total membership of over 15,000, the largest being in the United States (4,000), France (4,000), Argentina (1,400), South Africa (1,000), Britain (900), and Brazil (900).

With the rapid increase in immigration from the West, absorption became an issue that more directly involved several government agencies, in housing, employment, and other services. It was therefore decided in 1968 to set up a Ministry of Immigrant Absorption. It was agreed that, in the main, the Agency should handle immigration while the Ministry would deal with absorption, but the Agency also continued to be directly responsible for the absorption of needy immigrants and refugees, and operated the hostels, absorption centers, and *ulpanim*. The work was coordinated by the Authority, whose joint chairmen were the minister of immigrant absorption and the chairman of the Agency Executive, with a coordinating committee meeting once a week. One of the objects of the new arrangements was to cut down on the bureaucratic procedures of absorption which had often come under criticism, especially by newcomers from the West.

Facilities and concessions available to immigrants in 1970 included: interest-free loans to cover passage and part of shipping costs; exemption from customs and purchase tax on personal and household effects and factory or farm equipment; exemption from purchase tax and reduction in customs on automobiles; exemption from registration fees and part of property tax on purchasing house or business premises; preferential treatment in obtaining employment; partial exemption from income tax and capital gains tax; the right to hold foreign currency for ten years and to redeem State of Israel bonds; accommodation in absorption centers, hostels, and *ulpanim*; housing on easy terms or assistance in purchase or renting of housing; loans for establishment of businesses; free health assistance through a sick fund for six months; various concessions in national insurance benefits; free secondary schooling and university education; and exemption from travel tax. Most of the concessions were available for three years from the date of immigration and also applied to temporary residents.

The government and the Agency established a Student Authority to assist the greatly increased number of students – many of them originally volunteers – who wanted to study in Israel after the Six-Day War. During the academic year 1969–70 there were 7,000 students and 1,500 yeshivah students from abroad in Israel. Over 5,000 of them, who came as immigrants or intended to settle, received assistance and services from the authority: guidance, grants, Hebrew study in *ulpanim*, and support for special preparatory courses. It also helped the universities build additional dormitories and lecture rooms.

From 1971 to 1973 there was an increase in *aliyah* compared with the previous years, the number being 42,000 in 1971; 56,000 in 1972; and 55,000 in 1973. As a result of the Yom Kippur War, however, there came a considerable drop and the figures for 1975–76–77 were: 20,281, 19,745, and 21,420, respectively. Of the 56,000 in 1972, 13,000 were from the Soviet Union.

From the U.S.S.R. The Six-Day War was also followed by the intensification of Jewish consciousness and devotion to Israel among Soviet Jews – partly, it seems, as a reaction against official support for Arab hostility to Israel and partly due to renewed pride in Israel's achievements. In previous years a few Jews had been allowed to leave the U.S.S.R. to join relatives in Israel, but the Knesset, the government of Israel, and representative Jewish institutions everywhere had always demanded that all Jews who wished to leave the Soviet Union and settle in Israel be permitted to do so.

In 1969 and 1970 there was a new development: scores of Soviet Jews publicly declared, in letters to the Israel government and international organs signed with full names and addresses, that they regarded Israel as their historic homeland and demanded recognition of the right to *aliyah*, invoking the Declaration on Human Rights which explicitly guarantees the right of every man to leave any country, including his own. Those who were allowed to leave – often after years of effort – reported that there was a widespread awakening among the younger generation, many of whom were studying Hebrew and hoping to come to Israel. Toward the end of 1970 the severe sentences imposed, after a trial in Leningrad, on a number of Jews accused of planning to hijack a Soviet plane aroused intense indignation among Jews everywhere and widespread support for the Soviet Jews' right to settle in Israel. In 1970 almost 1,000 Jews were permitted to leave the U.S.S.R. for Israel; in 1971 the pace of *aliyah* increased, despite the obstacles raised by the authorities and the holding of further trials of Jews who wanted to go to Israel.

There was a melancholy last act to the tragedy of Polish Jewry. After the Six-Day War the Polish government unleashed an antisemitic campaign against the small Jewish community that still remained, but allowed them to leave. Of the 20,000 Jews who lived in Poland, about 11,500 left by May 1970, but only 3,500 of them went to Israel.

[Zvi Zinger (Yaron)]

Immigrants and Potential Immigrants[1] to Israel by Period of Immigration and Country of Birth, 1919–2004

Country	Period of Immigration									
	1919–Nov. 14 1948	Nov. 15 1948–1951	1952–1960	1961–1964	1965–1971	1972–1979	1980–1989	1990–2001	2003	2004
Eastern Europe	299,719	310,560	98,425	75,507	61,230	164,002	48,955	862,456	10,084	8,390
Bulgaria	7,057	37,260	1,680	460	334	118	180	3,999	57	72
USSR (former)	52,350	8,163	13,743	4,646	24,730	137,134	29,754	844,139	9,816	8,067
Hungary	10,342	14,324	9,819	1,115	1,486	1,100	1,005	2,444	49	113
Yugoslavia (former)	1,944	7,661	320	101	221	126	140	2,029	12	3
Poland	170,127	106,414	39,618	4,731	9,975	6,218	2,807	3,064	24	15
Czechoslovakia (former)	16,794	18,788	783	905	1,849	888	462	527	36	15
Romania	41,105	117,950	32,462	63,549	22,635	18,418	14,607	6,254	90	105
Western Europe	75,439	20,899	7,789	5,069	19,852	19,165	21,640	24,265	1,906	2,055
Italy	1,554	1,305	414	221	719	713	510	656	17	34
United Kingdom	1,574	1,907	1,448	1,260	5,201	6,171	7,098	5,365	274	309
Austria	7,748	2,632	610	297	724	595	356	368	8	8
Belgium	–	291	394	225	887	847	788	1,053	86	102
Germany	52,951	8,210	1,386	796	2,379	2,080	1,759	2,442	92	99
Holland	1,208	1,077	646	353	1,117	1,170	1,239			
Greece	8,767	2,131	676	166	348	326	147			
France	1,637	3,050	1,662	1,192	6,858	5,399	7,538	11,986	1,299	1,403
Nordic Countries[2]	–	85	131	119	767	903	1,178	1,145	30	34
Switzerland	–	131	253	218	668	634	706	981	76	51
Spain	–	80	169	222	184	327	321	269	24	15
Asia	27,651	230,823	32,326	17,882	32,094	17,198	12,320	75,712	3,068	2,718
India	–	2,176	5,380	2,940	10,170	3,497	1,539	2,055	158	94
China	–	504	217	40	56	43	78	277	8	8
Iraq	–	123,371	2,989	520	1,609	939	111	1,325	26	19
Iran	3,536	21,910	15,699	8,857	10,645	9,550	8,487	4,326	133	160
Turkey	8,277	34,547	6,871	4,793	9,280	3,118	2,088	1,311	68	53
Yemen[3]	15,838	48,315	1,170	732	334	51	17	686	4	12
Africa	2126	93,038	143,380	116,424	47,816	18,729	28,539	55,622	3,871	4,559
Ethiopia		10	59	23	75	306	16,965	45.131	3,027	3,701
Algeria[4]	9944	3,810	3,433	9,680	3,177	2,137	1,830	1,682	180	238
South Africa	259	666	774	1,003	2,780	5,604	3,575	3,283	82	112
Tunisia	[5]	13,293	23,569	3,813	7,753	2,148	1,942	1,607	263	228
Libya	873	30,972	2,079	318	2,148	219	66	94	–	–
Morocco	–	28,263	95,945	100,354	30,153	7,780	3,809	3,276	283	151
Egypt, Sudan	–	16,024	17,521	1,233	1,730	535	352	202*	15*	14*
America and Oceania	7,189	3,317	12,523	9,925	30,299	43,099	37,818	39,682	4,083	3,035
U.S.A.	6,635	1,711	1,553	2,102	16,569	20,963	18,904	17,512	1,445	1,578
Canada	316	236	276	241	1,928	2,178	1,867	1,963	150	163
Argentina	238	904	2,888	5,537	6,164	13,158	10,582	11,248	1,345	484
Brazil	–	304	763	637	1,964	1,763	1,763	2,356	207	234
Mexico	–	48	168	125	611	861	993	1,049	67	52
Chile	–	48	401	322	1,468	1,180	1,040	683	104	55
Columbia	–	–	–	126	289	552	475	657	74	79
Venezuela	–	–	–	109	188	245	180	418	60	78
Uruguay	–	66	6474	726	1,118	2,199	2,014	983	375	85
Unregistered Central America[6]	–	17	43	18	111	104	8	824	83	70
All Countries	412,124	658,654	294,486	224,825	191,402	262,297	149,280	1,060,091	23,268	20,898

Source: Statistical Abstract of Israel, 1995, Jerusalem.
Hyphens indicate unavailability of information.
* Includes Sudan.
1 Since the establishment of the State of Israel (5.15.48), includes tourists who changed their status to immigrants; as from June 1969, includes tourists who changed their status to immigrants or potential immigrants. As of 1970 excludes immigrating citizens.
2 Finland, Sweden, Norway, Denmark.
3 Including South Yemen and the former state of Aden.
4 Including Tunisia.
5 Included in figure for Algeria.
6 Honduras, Nicaragua, Guatemala, Costa Rica, El Salvador, Haiti, the Dominican Republic, Puerto Rico, Jamaica, Panama.

The *aliyah* from the U.S.S.R. in 1972 was the beginning of the massive immigration of Jews from the U.S.S.R. Although Russia continued to be a primary source for *aliyah*, there were worrying factors which began with the Yom Kippur War and have since worsened. The percentage of dropouts continued to rise and reached 50.4% in 1977 compared with 49.5% in 1976, 36% in 1975, and 19% in 1974, and continued to increase. In addition, there was also a rise in the emigration of Russian *olim* from Israel in 1976 as compared to previous years, and it reached 10% for the immigrants of 1973, though it must be added that 1973 was the peak year of Russian *aliyah* – 33,477.

Immigrants from the U.S.S.R. can be divided into three categories:

1) European Ashkenazi Jews who had been Soviet citizens since the October Revolution of 1917. These Jews involuntarily underwent a forced, intensive process of assimilation. Their culture was Russian and their attachment to Judaism weak. The national reawakening among Russian Jewry in the wake of the Six-Day War, which is gauged primarily by their desire to settle in Israel, affected only limited circles, mostly among the social elite, while the masses were not attracted.

2) Ashkenazi Jews from regions annexed to the U.S.S.R. during World War II: the Baltic States, Belorussia and Western Ukraine (previously East Poland), Transcarpathia (originally part of Czechoslovakia), and Northern Bukovina and Moldavia (which belonged to Romania). Before the annexation of these areas to the U.S.S.R., and the sufferings of their Jewish communities during the Holocaust, they were the very heart of Eastern European Jewry, and Jewish life flourished there. The survivors of the Holocaust who returned there after the war, in contrast to the veteran Soviet Jews who also came to these regions, continued to lead a full and dedicated Jewish life with no tendency to assimilate.

The same is generally the case with their children brought up under the Soviet regime who, in spite of having had no formal Jewish education, absorbed their Jewishness from the warmth of their parents' home. It is natural that the national reawakening attracted these Jews in large numbers and that they were, in fact, the pioneers of the struggle for the right to settle in Israel after the Six-Day War.

3) Non-Ashkenazi Jews living in the southern republics in the Caucasus and Central Asia. The three communities in this category are: the Georgian Jews, the Bukharan Jews, and the Mountain Jews, the Tats, of the Caucasus.

The members of these communities, although Soviet citizens ever since the victory of the Bolshevik revolution, have remained faithful to Judaism both religiously and nationally. They speak their own national dialects and have not assimilated culturally or linguistically. They meticulously observe some of the practical commandments, especially in the sphere of family life, such as circumcision, religious weddings (in addition to civil marriages according to the law of the land), and Jewish festivals, especially the Day of Atonement.

The 1970 U.S.S.R. population census showed that 90% of Russian Jewry belong to the first group (Ashkenazim who are long-standing Russian citizens), while the remaining 10% is divided equally between the two other groups.

Whereas, however, in the years 1971 and 1972 the Georgian Jews comprised more than one third of all the immigrants, and in 1972 they constituted 34% of all immigrants, there has been both an absolute and relative reduction in the years following, and in 1977 they were only 5% of all the Russian *olim*, the total of which was only about a quarter of the 1973 figure – the peak year.

The number of Bukharan *olim* declined from 3,750 in 1973 to only 380 in 1976, but rose to 760 in 1977. The *aliyah* of Mountain Jews from Dagestan and Azerbaijan in the Caucasus began in significant numbers only in 1974, when 1,570 emigrated to Israel, reaching its peak in 1975 with 2,270 *olim*, constituting 27% of all Russian *olim* in that year, but in 1976–77 this *aliyah* also decreased.

Since the scope of *aliyah* from the European sectors of Russia, according to its pre-World War II borders, was stable throughout the whole period under discussion, it is reasonable to assume that this stability reflects the Soviet policy of a fixed yearly quota in relation to *aliyah* from these areas, and the reduction of *aliyah* during 1975–77 by about a quarter each year, as compared to the peak year 1973, is the result of a drastic decrease in the *aliyah* of the non-Ashkenazic communities in these years. Since the Russian authorities adopted a relatively liberal attitude to this *aliyah*, it would seem that the main reason for the reduction is to be found with these Jews themselves, due probably to the defamation of Israel's image by Soviet propaganda, and the absorption problems of relatives and friends in Israel, as described in their letters.

It may be said that the absorption of immigrants from the Soviet Union is one of the most difficult and painful processes experienced by any group of new arrivals and that most of the problems have been psychological for both the authorities and the newcomers. It was fortunate that the years of large-scale immigration (1971–74) were a time of comparative affluence and economic prosperity, when there was a large demand for manpower, and the State had sizable resources to finance absorption. The national awakening and the heroic struggle of Soviet Jewry evoked widespread admiration and profound sympathy in Israel. Nevertheless serious misunderstandings arose between the community and the newcomers. It became evident that the favorable conditions were insufficient to bridge the deep gap between the unrealistic expectations of both sides and did not prevent deep disappointment and hostility between both the absorbing and the absorbed.

In spite of all these difficulties, the absorption and integration of Soviet immigrants into the Israel economy, community, and way of life progressed. Their identification with Israel, its problems, and its struggles was increasing. Gradually they were beginning to feel that they belonged, and their children, growing up in Israel, bridge the gap and assuage misunderstandings.

Soviet Jews who Immigrated to Israel (*Olim*) According to Ethnic Composition 1970–79

Ethnic group	Number	Percentage	Relative percentage within Sov. Jewish pop.
Ashkenazi Jews	98,500	64.3	93.5
Georgian Jews	29,600	19.4	2.3
Mountain Jews	9,800	6.4	2.3
Bukharan Jews	15,100	9.9	1.9
Total	153,000	100.0	100.0

Although (according to the Russian population census of Jan. 1979) non-Ashkenazi Jews – Georgian, Bukharan, and Mountain Jews – constitute only 6.5% of Russian Jewry, they continue to comprise, as during the whole decade, a third of all Russian immigrants. Moreover, the proportion of drop-outs among them was minimal.

The issue of the drop-outs and the methods for dealing with it became a disputed issue between the government of Israel and the Zionist Executive on the one hand, and the Jewish organizations – HIAS, JDC, United Jewish Federations, and the welfare funds in the United States – on the other. The disagreement focused on two main issues:

(1) recognition of the drop-outs as political refugees who were therefore eligible to emigrate to countries willing to absorb them, especially the United States;

(2) the generous material assistance given to them to ease their absorption in those countries.

The former wished to nullify the recognition of the drop-outs as refugees on the grounds that an emigrant with an entry permit to Israel who refuses to proceed there is not to be considered as a homeless refugee seeking a haven. They also maintained that the generous assistance given at that time to the drop-outs was an irresistible attraction and constituted unfair competition to the conditions of absorption in Israel.

Those who supported the drop-outs maintained that they are honoring the right of the Jewish emigrant to choose his country of destination. They also claimed that the aid afforded was reasonable and modest, especially since it was covered by the government of the United States to a large extent. They argued that if they would stop dealing with the drop-outs and aiding them, other Jewish and non-Jewish organizations would take their place and alienate the drop-outs even further from Israel and the Jewish people.

From May 1980 on there was a drastic decline in the number of Jews allowed to leave Russia. The exit from Ukrainian cities such as Kiev, Odessa, and Kharkov, among whom the percentage of drop-outs was close to 100% in 1979, was especially restricted. In the first half of 1980 only 570 Jews were allowed to leave Kiev compared with 3,893 in the first half of 1979 (a decrease of 85.3%); from Odessa 441 as against 4,736 (a decrease of 90.6%); from Kharkov, 52 as against 550 (a decrease of 90.5%), respectively. This decline reinforced the arguments of the Zionist representatives who claimed that the drop-outs harm the chances for the exit of other Russian Jews, since the Russians granted exit permits only when they were accompanied by requests from relatives in Israel for entrance permits to it. In the early 1980s the Russians also rejected applications for emigration if the party was not a member of the immediate family.

As a result, a partial agreement was reached between the Zionist groups and HIAS and the JDC that assistance and support be given only to drop-outs joining close relatives, but it was rejected by the United Jewish Federations, the welfare funds, and the leaders of the large Jewish communities of the U.S.A. and at the time of writing no acceptable agreement had been reached.

Moreover the "internal" conflict between the government of Israel and the Jewish Agency which had gone on since 1976, as to who should be responsible to deal with *aliyah* and absorption remained unsettled. The Jewish Agency insisted on the complete application of the recommendations of the Ḥorev Commission (see below) according to which one single authority for *aliyah* and absorption was to come into being, consisting of representatives of the government and the Jewish Agency, in place of the hitherto separate functioning by the Ministry of Absorption and the Department for Aliyah and Absorption of the Jewish Agency. The government suggested in its stead the establishment of one supervisory authority headed by the minister of absorption, which would establish policy, coordinate, and supervise the two existing authorities, which would however continue to exist separately with parallel activities but with a clear division of function and areas of authority.

In the absence of an agreement, the Jewish Agency announced that it would not participate in the budget of the Ministry for Absorption as of January 1981.

Other countries. The figures for *aliyah* from other countries are given in tables on Immigration to Israel.

The political situation in South Africa and Argentina resulted in an exodus of Jews from those countries; only a minority of those leaving came to Israel however, but although the actual numbers are small, they show a relatively significant increase over previous years; from South Africa about 41% over 1975 and 148% in 1977 over 1976, and from Argentina 81% in 1976 over 1975 and 34% in 1977 over 1976.

About a third of all the *olim* had completed higher education at the time of their immigration. Approximately another 10% had post-secondary education. Almost all from North America had more than 12 years of education. Only about 12% defined themselves as religious. About two-thirds of the *olim* had no previous Jewish education, but nearly all the North Americans had received some; 18% of all the *olim* had been members of a Jewish or Zionist organization during the two years preceding their *aliyah*. Almost all the West European and North American immigrants had visited Israel prior to their *aliyah*; naturally, the Russians had not visited Israel before.

White collar workers constituted a large majority of all *olim*. The Israeli economy has suffered for many years from a chronic problem of imbalance between workers in industry versus those in services, with a large excess of white collar workers. It is natural, therefore, that the economy has difficulty in absorbing the work force which comes through *aliyah*, since it suffers from the same imbalances, but even more acutely. Moreover, the economy had hardly grown since the Yom Kippur War.

A well-developed system of courses for professional retraining was set in operation. In 1976, 53 retraining courses were opened with 1,585 immigrants participating, and 50 courses were completed in which 1,376 *olim* took part. In 1977, 80 courses were begun with 2,200 participants, and 55 with 1,520 participants were completed. They were mainly in the fields of bookkeeping, pricing, quality control, teaching, medicine and nursing, engineering and technicians. In addition to these courses, there were preparatory classes for about 1,000 *olim* in 1977 in Hebrew and English, as a step towards the retraining programs.

Until the early 1980s immigrants with academic backgrounds were immediately sent to an absorption center where they studied Hebrew intensively for five hours a day for five months. During this period the immigrants received living expenses and initial arrangements were made for their employment. Grants were also made to academicians, quasi-academicians, or government workers who did not reside in absorption centers, but whose continued attendance at daytime ulpanim was a requirement towards finding employment, and to those who did not require retraining, but who could not be employed because of the freeze on budgets and hiring.

In 1978–79 some 7,000 immigrants arrived from Iran and about 30,000 from the Soviet Union, making up for the decrease in *aliyah* from South Africa and Argentina whose increase in 1976–77, albeit in more moderate dimensions, aroused unfulfilled expectations for increased growth. In 1980 there was a disappointing decrease in *aliyah* from Iran and Russia, and a general drastic decline in the number of immigrants as compared to 1979. In the first eight months of the year only some 15,000 immigrants arrived as compared with 25,000 during the same period of 1979 – a decrease of about 40%.

ALIYAH, 1982–1992. The decade 1982–1992 witnessed both the lowest annual immigration figures and the highest recorded since the first years of statehood. The decade also marked the reopening of the gates of the Soviet Union, a cherished dream, and the completion of the evacuation of Jews from certain countries of stress. Some 573,000 new immigrants arrived in this decade and in many respects revolutionized Israeli society. Between 1989 and 1992 some 476,000 immigrants came, the majority from the former Soviet Union, compared with a yearly average of 12,000 during previous years.

For decades, Israeli governmental and non-governmental bodies had worked for the eventual emigration of Soviet Jews. Massive pressures were exerted by Israel and world Jewry through a variety of organizations and institutions to bring about a change in Soviet emigration policy, and eventually these bore fruit. The Soviet government, in return for winning a most-favored nation status in its trade relations with the United States, began to ease emigration restrictions. In the two decades, 1969–1989, some 190,000 Soviet Jews arrived in Israel, of whom 170,000 remained. However, this period was also marked by a growing number of Soviet Jews opting to drop out on the way to Israel and travel to settle in the United States and to other countries. The percentage of these dropouts reached 90% in the mid-1970s. Since these Jews were leaving the Soviet Union on the basis of a scheme for family reunion in Israel, this trend endangered the operation. Israel found itself confronting a growing number of American Jewish organizations who favored the freedom of choice of Soviet Jewish emigrants to decide their destination. Israel claimed that there was no point in moving Russian Jews from one diaspora to another. The issue was resolved in 1989 in an agreement between Israel, the Soviet Union, and the United States, whereby from October 1, 1989, Russian Jews who wished to travel to the United States (or elsewhere) would have to obtain an entry visa in the embassies of their country of destination in Moscow. The United States established a quota of 40,000 emigrants a year. Those traveling to Israel would get their entry visa in the Israeli consulate in Moscow, which had been reopened in 1988.

The end of the 1980s also marked a massive change in Soviet-American relations with the realization of the Soviet president Mikhail Gorbachev, that his country's economic development would require massive Western, especially American, aid. This meant that he had to reduce elements of friction with the United States, one of them being the issue of human rights in general and Jewish emigration in particular. The end of the Cold War in 1989 brought about radical changes in Soviet emigration policies, which allowed most Jews who so wished to leave for Israel, although restricting the movements of a few hundred whom the Soviet government claimed were in possession of state secrets because of previous employment.

The massive wave began in late 1989 and soon swelled into a human tide. The Jewish Agency, which was responsible for the movement of immigrants to Israel, established transit stations for Soviet Jews on their way to Israel in Budapest, Warsaw, and Bucharest. A few traveled through Prague and Helsinki. These stations played a major role in the transit of Jews who came from the Soviet Union by bus, train, and plane, sometimes in private cars, to Israel. The reestablishment of consular, and later full diplomatic, relations between Israel and the Soviet Union also facilitated the transit of Jews. After 1989 the Jewish Agency was permitted to set up Hebrew classes in various parts of the Soviet Union and send emissaries and teachers to prepare Jews for *aliyah* and to teach them Hebrew, Judaism, and Jewish history.

The Soviet Government estimated in late 1988 that there

Immigrant Population from USSR (Former) Immigrated 1990–2004[1], by Year of Immigration and Age

Age	Thereof Jews	Year of immigration								
		1990–1991	1992–1994	1995–1996	1997–1998	1999	2000	2001–2003	2004	Total
	Thousands									
Total	671.8	312.8	187.9	118.7	101.2	66.8	51.0	66.6	11.0	916.1
0–4	40.0	17.5	11.8	7.8	6.5	3.8	2.9	4.4	1.0	55.7
5–9	39.2	19.1	12.6	6.8	5.4	3.8	2.9	3.4	0.5	54.4
10–14	34.5	14.6	11.3	6.6	6.0	4.2	3.0	3.6	0.5	49.9
15–19	43.1	21.8	12.9	8.0	6.7	4.8	3.5	5.0	1.4	64.1
20–24	48.3	23.7	12.6	7.7	7.9	5.7	4.9	7.5	1.1	71.0
25–29	47.6	21.3	13.4	9.6	9.5	5.5	4.5	6.7	1.0	71.6
30–34	43.7	19.0	14.1	9.8	9.3	6.4	4.8	5.9	0.9	70.2
35–39	36.6	16.2	12.8	8.0	7.2	5.1	3.7	4.3	0.7	57.9
40–44	42.6	21.6	12.9	7.8	6.6	4.6	3.5	4.2	0.6	61.8
45–49	46.2	25.4	12.3	7.2	6.1	3.9	2.9	3.9	0.6	62.3
50–54	45.7	24.7	11.2	6.8	5.6	3.7	2.8	3.8	0.5	59.1
55–59	47.2	24.4	10.7	6.9	5.5	3.7	3.0	3.9	0.6	58.8
60–64	23.9	10.0	5.6	4.0	3.4	2.4	1.9	2.6	0.4	30.3
65–69	43.5	15.9	9.8	7.9	6.4	4.0	3.1	3.5	0.6	51.3
70–74	29.6	10.9	7.9	5.1	3.5	2.1	1.4	1.6	0.2	32.7
75–79	30.2	13.0	8.3	4.5	2.9	1.6	1.1	1.1	0.2	32.8
80–84	19.2	9.0	4.9	2.5	1.7	0.9	0.7	0.7	0.1	20.5
85+	10.9	4.7	2.8	1.6	1.1	0.6	0.4	0.4	0.1	11.7
Median age	40.4	40.8	37.0	36.9	34.6	34.4	34.0	32.3	29.5	36.8
	Thereof: females									
Total	358.9	164.5	99.6	64.3	54.7	36.3	27.7	36.4	6.0	489.5
0–4	19.3	8.4	5.6	3.9	3.1	1.9	1.4	2.2	0.5	27.1
5–9	18.9	9.3	6.0	3.2	2.6	1.9	1.5	1.6	0.3	26.4
10–14	16.8	7.1	5.5	3.3	2.9	2.1	1.5	1.8	0.3	24.4
15–19	21.1	10.6	6.3	3.9	3.4	2.4	1.7	2.4	0.7	31.4
20–24	24.0	11.6	6.1	3.7	3.7	3.0	2.5	4.1	0.6	35.3
25–29	24.0	10.3	6.4	5.0	5.2	3.1	2.6	3.8	0.6	36.9
30–34	22.3	9.3	7.4	5.2	4.9	3.5	2.6	3.2	0.5	36.5
35–39	19.2	8.6	6.6	4.2	3.8	2.6	1.9	2.3	0.3	30.3
40–44	22.6	11.7	6.7	4.2	3.6	2.5	1.9	2.3	0.3	33.2
45–49	24.9	13.7	6.7	4.1	3.4	2.2	1.6	2.2	0.3	34.2
50–54	24.7	13.9	6.2	3.9	3.2	2.1	1.6	2.3	0.3	32.5
55–59	25.9	12.8	5.9	4.0	3.2	2.2	1.8	2.4	0.4	32.6
60–64	13.7	5.3	3.2	2.4	2.1	1.5	1.2	1.6	0.2	17.5
65–69	25.2	8.8	5.9	4.9	3.9	2.4	1.8	1.9	0.3	29.9
70–74	17.3	6.6	4.9	2.8	2.0	1.1	0.7	0.9	0.1	19.2
75–79	18.3	8.1	4.9	2.7	1.8	1.0	0.7	0.7	0.1	20.1
80–84	12.9	6.0	3.3	1.8	1.2	0.7	0.5	0.5	0.1	14.0
85+	7.6	3.2	1.9	1.2	0.8	0.4	0.3	0.3		8.2
Median age	43.0	43.0	39.9	39.8	37.0	35.8	35.3	33.6	30.5	39.4

1 Incl. 109.9 thousand children aged 0–14, born in Israel to mothers who immigrated from USSR (former), by mother's year of immigration.

were some 1.8 million Jews in the country, the Israelis put the figure at 2.8 million. By early 1993, some 420,000 Soviet Jews had gone to Israel, another 150,000 to North America, and some 20,000 to Germany. In April 1993 there were still some 1.7 million Jews in the CIS (Commonwealth of Independent States), a million of whom were holding Israeli documents as a first step towards their immigration. It was assumed that at the current rate of emigration (70,000 a year), some 500,000 Jews would remain in the CIS at the end of the century.

Jewish emigration was a result of both a push and a pull. The push came in 1989 when Jews feared that there might not be much time before the Iron Curtain would slam down again and left en masse. There was genuine fear that the collapse of the Soviet empire would be accompanied by a civil war in which the Jews would be the main victims. They thought that in a period of vast social, economic, and political instability, antisemitism, long ingrained in Russia, would reappear. Moreover the greater democratization allowed in Russia meant that antisemitic propaganda and organizations were also permitted. Chief among these groups was Pamyat, a virulently anti-Jewish nationalist organization. Jews felt that life in the former Soviet Union was becoming intolerable for them. There were limited economic and occupational possibilities. Promotion in the army and government was very limited and there were quotas on the number of Jewish students at universities. Academic and professional promotion was also very slow. Many wanted to reunite with families already in Israel. The majority of the immigrants were not permeated by Zionist or even Jewish sentiments. The majority were secular, some third having married non-Jews. But as the Iron Curtain lifted, more people discovered their Jewishness and wanted to leave, most of them for economic reasons. There were some drawbacks. A number feared that the Jewish state was a theocracy. Being secular, and cut off from Judaism for seventy years, this could have problems, mainly for those with non-Jewish spouses. There was concern over military service, *intifada*, and above all fear that the professionals among them would not be able to find suitable jobs. The last concern proved to be true. A number of Jews chose to remain behind to participate in the building of a new society in the CIS, but many of these became disappointed, especially those who found themselves in the midst of civil war in Moldova, Abkhazia, and Tadjikistan.

From a figure of some 200,000 in 1990, 176,000 in 1991, the numbers dropped to 76,000 in 1992. The task of moving Russian Jews to Israel and settling them there was shared by the *Jewish Agency, representing world Jewry, and the government of Israel. The Agency launched a fundraising campaign called "Exodus" which resulted in over $500 million being raised in three years to help cover the costs of flying the Jews to Israel, bringing their luggage and helping in their initial absorption. The government of Israel provided housing, education, health care, and welfare.

Unlike previous years, when immigrants were directed to absorption centers where they would learn the language before being let out into the Israeli economy and society, the

Immigrant Population from Ethiopia[1] by Period of Immigration and Age

Thousands, end of year	2004				
Age	Born abroad			Born in Israel	Total
	Immigrated since 1990	Immigrated until 1989	Total		
Total	53.4	16.0	69.4	30.8	100,2
0–4	1.4		1.4	9.7	11.1
5–9	3.9		3.9	9.1	12.9
10–14	6.2		6.2	7.7	14.0
15–19	8.6	0.2	8.9	3.0	11.9
20–24	7.5	2.2	9.7	0.9	10.6
25–29	5.8	2,6	8,3	0.1	8.5
30–34	4.1	2.5	6.7	0.1	6.7
35–44	5.5	3.7	9.2	0.1	9.3
45–54	3.9	2.0	5.9	0.1	6.0
55–64	2.8	1.3	4.0		4.0
65+	3.7	1.6	5.3		5.3
Median age	24.4	36.2	27.8	8.1	20.1
Males					
Total	26.7	8.1	34.7	15.6	50.3
0–4	0.7		0.7	4.9	5.6
5–9	2.0		2.0	4.5	6.5
10–14	3.2		3.2	4.0	7.2
15–19	4.6	0.1	4.7	1.5	6.2
20–24	3.8	1.1	4.9	0.4	5.4
25–29	2.9	1.3	4.2	0.1	4.2
30–34	1.9	1.3	3.2		3.2
35–44	2.6	1.8	4.4		4.5
45–54	1.8	1.0	2.8		2.8
55–64	1.3	0.7	2.0		2.0
65+	2.0	0.7	2.8		2.8
Median age	23.9	36.1	27.3	8.2	19.7
Females					
Total	26.7	0.8	34.7	15.2	49.9
0–4	0.7		0.7	4.6	5,5
5–9	1.9		1.9	4.5	6.4
10–14	3.0		3.0	0.8	6.8
15–19	4.1	0.1	4.2	1.5	5.7
20–24	2.7	1.0	4.8	0.4	5.2
25–29	2.9	1.3	4.2	0.1	4.3
30–34	2.3	1.2	3.5	0.0	3.5
35–44	2.9	1.8	4.8	0.0	4.8
45–54	2.1	1.0	3.1	0.0	3.2
55–64	1.5	0.6	2.1	0.0	2.1
65+	1,6	0.9	2.5	0.0	2.5
Median age	24.9	36.3	28.3	8.1	20.6

1 Incl. children born in Israel to fathers who immigrated from Ethiopia.

majority of Soviet Jews were absorbed in what was termed "direct absorption track," in which they were given a yearly allowance to cover costs of housing and subsistence, were told to look for work, put their children into school, and become absorbed almost overnight. This, on the whole, proved successful. By 1993 some 35,000 Soviet Jews had found work in industry, others in professions and trades. A major problem was posed by the large number (over 16%) of immigrants over 65 years old who were no longer productive and became the responsibility of the local and national governments. Another difficulty arose with those immigrants who had to be certified again by Israel before they could practice, among them physicians and engineers. They had to be maintained while studying for their qualifying examinations. Many had to be re-trained as the number of physicians, for example, who came between 1989 and 1993 was 12,000 as against the 16,000 doctors already practicing in Israel. Scientists and academics also found difficulties obtaining suitable jobs. But only 2.8% of the immigrants who arrived since 1989 left Israel. Immigrants continued to arrive even during the Gulf War when Israel was attacked by Iraqi Scuds.

The addition of some 420,000 high-quality immigrants from the CIS had vast strategic implications for Israel. The Jewish population increased by 12% in three years. The quality of the immigrants was remarkable. They raised the cultural level of Israel, in music, arts, literature, and drama. Three new orchestras were created for immigrants. They began slowly to replace some Arabs from the Administered Territories who were working in Israel. Their numbers meant that once again there was a Jewish majority in Galilee. Strenuous Arab efforts to stop this immigration demonstrated that the Arab states realized the magnitude of this immigration and its potential for Israel in the scientific, technological, and military areas. The immigration also had an impact on the peace process. Israel with over 4.4 million Jews was a different country from previously. The new reality was slowly grasped by Arab governments, especially after their efforts to block the *aliyah* failed. Sheer numbers enabled the Israel army to consider reducing the length of military service. Israel's economy received a tremendous boost by the arrival of almost half a million new consumers. In 1992 the country recorded a 6.4% growth in its Gross Domestic Product and a rise in exports.

The major problems accompanying this immigration were in the social sphere. Israeli society welcomed immigrants with open arms. They were absorbed mainly by voluntary organizations, previous Russian immigrants, and local authorities. But there were strains, some of them due to a different mentality. Since most of the immigrants were not motivated by Jewish or Zionist ideology, they had to be re-educated in many ways about the meaning and nature of life in a Jewish State. There was some grumbling among Jews of Asian and African origin who feared that well-educated Russian Jews would get the better positions. The ultra-Orthodox and the Orthodox were dismayed over the prospect of the Russian immigrants voting mainly for secular parties, and affecting their political clout. Inevitably, there was considerable disappointment and disillusionment among many of the newcomers. For all the efforts to help a quick absorption, the country could not cope with many of the problems while the immigrants found themselves in unaccustomed surroundings and faced with a new language which some could not master. It was the economic problems that were uppermost. While the immigrants received grants for their initial period, this ran out and they had to face the challenge of finding work, with the possibilities especially limited in the professions and arts. Many found themselves unemployed and others took menial jobs in order to survive. Some of them organized demonstrations to draw attention to their plight. Reports of these difficulties reaching Russia dampened the enthusiasm of many potential immigrants and were a major factor in the drop in immigration figures from 1990 to 1991 and from 1991 to 1992. But on the whole, the Russian immigrants absorbed themselves well into Israeli society and many were beginning to make meaningful contributions to its economy, science, and technology.

The decade also witnessed the end of a number of diasporas. In two dramatic air lifts, the government of Israel and the Jewish Agency brought to Israel over 22,000 Ethiopian Jews. Some 7,500 were airlifted at the end of 1984 from Sudan in an operation called "Moses." To escape famine Ethiopian Jews walked hundreds of miles to Sudan and from there were taken to Israel with the help of the United States government and air force. Between 1985 and 1991, Israeli emissaries brought thousands of Ethiopian Jews to Addis Ababa to prepare them for immigration. Two days before the final collapse of the Mengistu government, in May 1991, and with the active help of the United States, Israel secured use of the Addis Ababa airport for 36 hours. During this time 41 flights brought to Israel 14,440 Jews in "Operation Solomon." Subsequently the rest of Ethiopian Jewry was brought to Israel and effectively, apart from *Falas Moura*, converts to Christianity, the Jewish community of Ethiopia ceased to exist.

By the end of 1992, Israel airlifted the entire Jewish community of Albania (350 souls) while over a 1,000 Jews were rescued from the civil war which engulfed Yugoslavia. Eventually, the numbers of Jews in distressed countries diminished significantly during the decade under review. In 1948 there were over 800,000 Jews in Arab countries, by 1993 there remained some 60,000 Jews in those countries, the three largest communities being Iran, Turkey, and Morocco with about 20,000 Jews in each.

Immigration from Western countries continued to arrive in a trickle. Some 2,500 Jews came annually from North America, and hundreds from South Africa, Australia, France, and Britain.

[Meron Medzini]

DEVELOPMENTS IN ALIYAH AND ABSORPTION, 1993–2002. From 1993 the rate of *aliyah* to Israel averaged between 5,000 and 6,000 a month, the majority coming from the Commonwealth of Independent States (CIS). As compared to the figures for 1990–1992 (1990 – 199,500 immigrants, of those

184,681 from the former Soviet Union; 1991 – 176,000 and 147,673, respectively; 1992 – 77,00 and 64,790, respectively), the numbers for 1993 showed that some 76,800 immigrated to Israel; in 1994 the number rose to 79,800. Some 76,300 arrived in 1995, 60,192 in 2000, and 33,567 in 2002. Immigrants came mainly from the Ukraine, the Central Asian Republics, and the Caucasus areas, driven by the uncertain local conditions, and civil war, the eroding economic situations and sometimes by fear of antisemitism. There was a marked drop in the number of immigrants coming from the Russian Republic. Immigration remained the sole responsibility of the Jewish Agency, which had some 70 emissaries spread throughout the CIS registering Jews for immigration and processing them for travel to Israel.

A new program designed to bring to Israel high school students started in 1993. Called "Aliyah 16," it sent to Israel thousands of teenagers to complete their studies in Israeli high schools, hoping they would remain in Israel after graduation and bring their families in their wake.

The Jewish Agency was also involved in rescue operations of Jews in such distressed areas as Chechniya and Bosnia. Emissaries risked their lives to bring out hundreds of Jews trapped in civil war situations. In 1994 it was announced that the emigration from Syria had been completed with many going to Israel, including the chief rabbi of Damascus. Some 400 Jews remained in Syria of their own free will. Efforts were made to complete immigration from Yemen and bring the Jews remaining in Ethiopia. Between 1990 and 2001, 2,655 came from Ethiopia.

Once in Israel, the major problems were finding suitable jobs for the large number of professionals, among them thousands of doctors, engineers, scientists, and musicians. Surveys have shown that most immigrants made a positive adjustment to Israel after being there for three or four years. This was illustrated by the number of housing mortgages taken out, cars and durable goods purchased, and small businesses established.

Immigration from Western countries continued at about 6,000 annually, mainly from the United States, Britain, France, and Latin American countries.

[Meron Medzini (2nd ed.)]

HOUSING

TO END OF THE MANDATORY PERIOD. Throughout the history of modern Palestine, the construction of housing played a dominant role in the country's economic life. Before World War I, and up to the early 1930s, industry and agriculture were not on a large enough scale to provide immediate employment for new immigrants, and building was the occupation in which they could be absorbed almost as soon as they stepped off the boat. In 1925 no less than 43% of all Jewish workers were employed in construction, and in 1926-27 the percentage was still 34.2. It was only in the 1930s, after the rapid development of industry and agriculture, that the share of construction in total employment was sharply reduced, declining to 19.4% in 1935 and 11% in 1936. Even so, construction remained an important factor in the economy, and in the period 1932–39 it accounted for as much as 47% of capital investment from Jewish sources.

Jewish Housing Quarters. Even before the period of modern resettlement, Jews tended to leave the traditional confines of the old, established cities in order to establish their own urban quarters. As early as 1860, a group of Jewish inhabitants left the unsanitary and overcrowded Old City of *Jerusalem and took the revolutionary step of moving into a new quarter outside the city walls, Mishkenot Sha'ananim, founded by Moses Montefiore. Later, two other quarters were established: Naḥalat Shiv'ah (1869) and Me'ah She'arim (1874). This trend was continued by the new settlers who came to the towns. At first they found homes in Jaffa, Jerusalem, or another of the existing cities, but after a while they sought to establish more modern and spacious quarters for themselves. Perhaps the most striking example was the founding in 1909 (by a group of Jaffa Jews) of Tel Aviv, which, from a mere suburb, became the country's largest city. New Jewish quarters were also founded in Jerusalem (Beit ha-Kerem, Talpiyyot, Reḥavyah, Kerem Avraham) and Haifa (Hadar ha-Karmel, Har ha-Karmel, Kiryat Ḥayyim, Kiryat Motzkin, etc.). A variety of factors contributed to this trend. In addition to the desire to escape from the primitive conditions of the Arab urban centers, there was the urge to create completely Jewish surroundings; to live among people of the same origin and background, or among equally observant Jews; and to enhance security. Furthermore, the price of land inside the old cities was too high to permit the construction of popular housing on any appreciable scale.

Expansion of Building. Every new wave of immigration resulted in an expansion of building activity. In 1934–35, the record year for immigration in the Mandatory period, housing construction reached unprecedented heights, while at the end of the 1930s, when immigration was curtailed, there was a corresponding decline in building. As a rule, however, the rate of construction lagged behind demand and severe housing shortages arose. A census taken in 1937 disclosed that 40% of Histadrut members had less than one room to accommodate their families, while only 15% lived in two-room apartments. The price of land soon became a severe problem in the new Jewish cities and quarters. This brought about a sharp rise in the cost of rented dwellings, which, it became apparent, could not solve the housing problem. On the eve of World War II the price of a building plot accounted for 30–50% of the capital investment required for housing. Credit was another problem: the rate of interest was high (8–9%) and adequate mortgages were not available, so that the builder had to look for additional finances, which was even more expensive. During the war rents were frozen by law, while prices and building costs kept rising. The controlled rents no longer had any realistic relationship to actual building costs. The result was the introduction of "key money," a large one-time payment to the landlord and the former tenant whenever an apartment changed hands. For the lower-income groups, the war veterans and the refugees from Europe, this payment was too heavy a burden.

Public Housing. As a result of this situation, various forms of public and cooperative housing came to the fore. This was not a new feature; most of the Jewish quarters and towns were founded by building societies. In the course of time, large housing companies were established and sought to lower the costs and lessen the burden upon the individual. They obtained low-cost land from the Jewish National Fund and mortgages from public or semi-public financial institutions on comparatively easy terms; lowered contractors' profits; and introduced more rational and standardized construction methods. The Histadrut played a leading role in this field since its early years (see *Israel, State of: Labor) by building workers' quarters (Shekhunat Borochov, near Tel Aviv, built in 1922, was the first) and in 1935 had founded its own housing company, Shikkun, which built houses for immigrants and, after World War II, for war veterans. In addition, the Histadrut founded Neveh Oved, a housing company for agricultural laborers, and Shikkun Amami, for non-Histadrut low-income groups. Another large housing company was Rassco (Rural and Suburban Settlement Co.), founded by the Jewish Agency, which had been engaged in the settlement of middle-class immigrants on the land and now went in for urban housing as well. Some of the political parties had their own housing companies, and in 1945 the municipalities were also authorized by the government to provide housing. The growing share of public and semi-public housing companies in residential construction after the war is illustrated by the figures for 1945–46, when they were responsible for the construction of 12,742 rooms out of 29,000 built for the Jewish population, or 44% of the total.

IN THE STATE OF ISRAEL. *The Early Years.* Housing was one of the most pressing problems faced by the infant state. While the population doubled by immigration in the first three years (see *Israel, State of: Population), improved housing for the existing population was urgently needed. At the end of 1949, the government established a Housing Division, which became the main agency for immigrant housing, as a branch of the Ministry of Labor and put at its disposal budgetary funds, land in various parts of the country, and the planning facilities of the Government Planning Division. The building-materials industry also adapted itself to the growing needs. Other important factors which facilitated the execution of a great housing program in these years were the training of building workers and the experience gained in earlier periods by public and private construction companies.

The rate of construction grew by leaps and bounds: from 843,000 sq. m. in 1949 to 2,137,000 in 1952. There was a slowdown in 1953, but the rate picked up again the following year and continued to be high for most of 1955. The number of building workers increased considerably, but not sufficiently to meet demand, and there was a scarcity of building materials; consequently, the quality of the houses built in this period was rather low. Housing and public works accounted for 45% of all capital invested in 1949, 44% in 1950, and 70% in 1951. Building on this scale was one of the principal causes of the inflation that marked the Israel economy in this period. The pressing needs forced the government to finance two-thirds of all construction, including practically all immigrant housing, public buildings, and housing for special groups. The government was able to use housing to effect a greater dispersal of the population, resulting in an increase in the percentage of the rural and semi-rural population. Private building, accounting for the remaining third, supplied the needs of the established residents.

A unique aspect of housing in Israel was the fact that only a small percentage was built for rental. This was partly due to the freezing of rents by the Tenants' Protection Law 1954, and although rents were raised from time to time, they did not provide sufficient incentive for investors. Moreover, due to the high cost of building, rentals had to be subsidized if they were not to be too high for the great majority of tenants. In view of the need for economy and the avoidance of inflation, therefore, the government favored apartment purchase wherever possible.

Improved Standards. As the standard of living rose, large sectors of the population sought to improve their accommodations. The average size of publicly built apartments grew from 44.6 sq. m. in 1955 to 77.4 sq. m. in 1968; in 2002 privately built apartments averaged 142 sq. m. The average number of rooms per apartment also grew: from 2.0 in 1955 to 2.9 in 1968 and 4.5 in 2002. There was also a general improvement in the finish of the apartments, as well as planning and environmental services. The owner's share in the financing of construction grew appreciably and a considerable part of the finance was raised by stocks issued by financial institutions.

In 1955 a Saving-for-Housing Scheme was introduced by the government, designed to facilitate saving and the use of the proceeds to finance current construction. By the end of 1967, some 70,000 apartments had been built under this scheme, which from 1961 no longer received aid from the government development budget (except for houses built in development towns). Building was increasingly mechanized: modern equipment made it possible to accelerate the rate of construction and erect high-rise buildings (a matter of necessity in view of the increase in land prices after 1960, especially affecting private housing). Most of the public building in this period was for new immigrants. Almost half of immigrant housing was constructed in the development towns (see below), adding further to the dispersal of the population. In 1961 the Housing Division became a separate ministry. This has facilitated advances in the standard of housing and its planning and adaptation to the general development of the country and its social aims.

Housing for Immigrants. It was immigration that was responsible for the extraordinary dimensions of the housing problem in the State of Israel: in two decades homes had to be built for a trebled population, the newcomers carrying with them the habits and the prejudices of sharply contrasting cultures from East and West. The housing authorities had not only to provide them with a roof, but also to establish the conditions for immigrants from a hundred countries to live harmoniously together and adapt policies to the needs of a rapidly developing modern economy. In the five years 1948–53, during which the population grew by 117%, homes had to be built rapidly with inadequate resources in money, materials, and skilled labor. Inevitably, improvised solutions had to be adopted. Abandoned Arab housing provided a breathing space, but thousands had to be accommodated in camps. The Housing Division of the Ministry of Labor cooperated with the Jewish Agency officials in choosing locations for 123 *ma'barot* all over the country and put up every kind of temporary shelter, using wood, corrugated iron, asbestos boards, and canvas stretched over wooden frames.

The next stage was the erection of permanent housing in the old and new villages, in the suburbs, and on the sites of *ma'barot*. Owing to the tremendous pressure, standards were necessarily low: houses were built of the cheapest materials by methods suitable for the relatively unskilled manpower available. The area of the dwellings ranged from 28 to 54 sq. m.; they were often handed over to the tenants barely finished, without internal doors to the rooms, except for lavatories and bathrooms, and the occupants had to make do with a shower until they could find the money to install a bath. It was only in the second half of the 1950s that some progress in housing standards was possible. In the 1960s, and especially with the growing immigration of Jews from Western countries, standards became, on the whole, reasonably satisfactory.

In the early stages, the immigrants themselves, though unskilled, were given employment in the building of their own homes, and as much use as possible was made of materials available in the neighborhood. Efforts were made to mechanize the building industry. Thirteen plants for the manufacture of prefabricated structures were established, and a degree of mechanization was introduced in conventional building methods. From the establishment of the state until 1970, 40,000,000 sq. m. of housing have been built for the accommodation of immigrants and other social purposes. In addition to dwellings, the state also had to erect in the new villages, towns, and suburbs buildings for public services, such as commercial centers, industrial estates, schools and kindergartens, synagogues, cultural centers, and cinemas.

[Haim Darin-Drapkin and David Tanne]

Slums and Overcrowding. Slums and defective or inadequate housing were created by:

(1) the rapid deterioration of abandoned Arab houses in some of the larger towns and the Jewish quarters constructed before World War I (some of these could be repaired, while others had to be pulled down and the inhabitants rehoused);

(2) the building of small and overcrowded, though generally sound and habitable, apartments in the early years of the state (rooms were added where possible, two adjacent apartments turned into one, and large families transferred to more spacious quarters);

(3) the continued occupancy of some temporary buildings by immigrants (these were gradually transferred to permanent homes and the buildings demolished).

A Slum Clearance and Building Authority was set up under the Clearance and Building Law of 1965 to deal with the legal, social, economic, and planning aspects of the problem. Tasks still to be tackled were: reexamination of housing operations in the past, with a view to correcting planning and other defects of the work done in the early years of the state; more building in the development towns to provide accommodation for the growing population; and speeding up slum clearance.

From 1948 to 1967, 600,000 units of permanent housing were built in Israel, 225,000 by private enterprise and 375,000 by public bodies. In addition, 22,000 dwellings were completed in 1968 and 26,000 in 1969. From 1970 to 2002 around 807,000 permanent housing units were constructed.

[David Tanne]

The problem of housing had become more difficult. In 1976–77 the situation which had arisen in earlier years, of lack of coordination between the apartments available (both number and size) and the demand, continued. Although thousands of apartments were available in the development towns, opportunities of employment in these towns are few and in 1976 alone the Ministry of Absorption returned about 1,000 apartments which could not be used to meet the needs of immigrants. On the other hand, there was a serious shortage of housing in the central areas and at the end of 1976 there was a shortage of 3,000 apartments for the immigrants, which was reduced by only a few hundred by the end of 1977. In 1976, 7,450 apartments were provided for the *olim* and 7,060 in 1977. In addition, in 1976, 2,750 mortgages for a total of IL231 million were granted to *olim* for buying apartments on the open market, and in 1977 there were 3,400 mortgages totaling IL293 million. Thus in 1977 the number of immigrants who preferred to buy apartments themselves with the aid of a mortgage, increased significantly.

About two-thirds of all *olim* in 1976–77 received permanent housing in the central coastal region; 10% in the Jerusalem area, and the remainder in development areas. Two-thirds of the 1977 immigrants were directed to their temporary or permanent residences by the Ministry of Absorption; the others chose by themselves. However, 70% of those who were directed by the Ministry agreed to the choice, while 16% went against their will; the others did not consider the choice important. In 1976, 1,130 immigrants were accepted by kibbutzim and 980 in 1977; 95% of them from Western countries. In 1976–77 immigrants were no longer sent to apartments rented by the Ministry of Absorption; the great majority were sent to other temporary residences, about half to absorption centers, and the remainder to relatives, kibbutz ulpanim, or other transition frameworks.

UNIVERSITY AND YESHIVAH STUDENTS. The diminution of *aliyah* in the past few years was reflected also by a decline in the number of student immigrants. The special administrative body set up to deal with them cared for 5,000 students in 1977 compared with 5,600 in 1976 and 6,200 in 1975. (The number of students under the care of the Student Administration in any year is not identical with the number of immigrant students in that year, because many students are handled for several years. However, there is undoubtedly correlation between the two.) In addition, at the end of 1977 there were 2,000 yeshivah students, also under the care of the administration. Of the students in 1977, 54% were immigrants, 43% potential immigrants, and 3% returning minors; 44% came with their parents. Among East Europeans the percentage is 85% as contrasted to 21% from South America. Of the yeshivah students, 72% came from North America, the great majority from the United States. Almost all of them came alone for a fixed time, after which they intend returning to their country of origin. Despite the fact that yeshivah students usually come only for study, a survey undertaken five years after their immigration showed that about half of the yeshivah students who came in 1969–70 had remained in Israel. There was, however, no similar follow-up for yeshivah students who arrived after those years.

Among the yeshivah students were included 25% who came to study at Torah institutions for women; 53.4% of all the university students in 1977 were females. The Student Administration helped the university and yeshivah students in registering at their educational institute (sometimes while the student was still abroad), in preparation towards their studies, with Hebrew ulpanim, in professional guidance and counseling, with individual and group auxiliary lessons, with cultural and informational activities, and with financial aid.

ORGANIZATION OF ABSORPTION. The diminution in immigration, the growing drop-out rate which increased monthly in 1974–75, and the increased criticism of the various absorption authorities in the Israeli mass media, all prompted the Israeli government and leaders of the Jewish Agency to reassess the issues of immigration and absorption. At the beginning of 1976 the prime minister, Yiẓḥak Rabin, and Yosef Almogi, then chairman of the Executive of the Jewish Agency, appointed a "Public Committee for Studying Issues of Aliyah and Absorption." Gen. (Ret.) Amos Ḥorev, president of Haifa University, was appointed chairman of the committee, and the members were mostly well-known public figures from various sectors of the society and the economy, long-term residents and immigrants. The main suggestion in the report of the committee was to abolish both the Ministry of Immigrant Absorption and the Aliyah and Absorption Department of the Jewish Agency and to set up instead an "Authority for Aliyah and Absorption to be operated by the chairman of the Executive of the Jewish Agency and under its auspices." The practical meaning of this suggestion was to transfer the handling of immigration and absorption to the Jewish Agency, as was the case before the establishment of the Ministry of Immigrant Absorption in the second half of 1968. This suggestion gave rise to considerable controversy between the ministry and the Jewish Agency, the former firmly rejecting it and the latter urging its implementation.

Three well-known Hebrew University scholars, who had undertaken extensive research into absorption, since the establishment of the State – Dr. Rivka Bar-Yosef, Dr. Tamar Horowitz, and Prof. Judith Shuval – sent a memorandum to Yiẓḥak Rabin sharply criticizing the method of operation and the conclusions of the Horev Committee. They alleged that the committee had heard the testimony and opinions of immigrants chosen at random, who were not representative of immigrants as a whole. Those who turned to the committee of their own accord were naturally interested parties or persons of extreme positive or negative opinions. The committee presented the current treatment of immigrants as a series of mistakes and ignored the achievements in several areas. They also felt that the committee ignored the objective reasons for the scant immigration and the absorption difficulties; for instance, the decrease of ideological-national motivation toward *aliyah* among Diaspora Jews, the low quality of life in Israel, the closed nature of Israeli society, the lack of correspondence between the Israel labor market and the occupation of the immigrants, etc. The main thrust of the criticism was that the committee considered the organizational aspect as the root of the trouble, while they felt it was of secondary importance.

[Yosef Litvak]

SETTLEMENT

UNTIL WORLD WAR I. Modern Jewish settlement (*hityashevut*) in the Land of Israel is usually reckoned as beginning with the founding of *Petaḥ Tikvah in 1878 by Jews from Jerusalem, with the aid of a group from Hungary. The Zionist movement initially left urban resettlement almost entirely to private initiative, so that the term *hityashevut* was identified with the establishment of new villages. It is only in recent years that it has been extended to cover the development of new towns and urban areas.

The First Settlements. The impetus to the large-scale renewal of Jewish settlement on the land was given by the First Aliyah. (See Table: Population and Area of the Jewish Settlements of Israel, 1898.) The newcomers founded *Rishon le-Zion, *Zikhron Ya'akov, and *Rosh Pinnah in 1882, *Yesud ha-Ma'alah and *Ekron in 1883, *Gederah in 1884, and *Reḥovot, *Mishmar ha-Yarden, and *Ḥaderah in 1890. They were primarily interested in setting up agricultural communities and tried to establish villages like those they had known in Europe, calling them moshavot. Many obstacles were placed in the way of the settlers by the Turkish authorities, and few of them had the slightest knowledge of farming meth-

Population and Area of the Jewish Settlements of Israel, 1898

Region	Settlement	Inhabitants	Area (in dunams[1])
Judea	Mikveh Israel	225	2,600
	Rishon le-Zion	531	6,800
	Nes Ẓiyyonah	121	1,800
	Reḥovot	281	10,500
	Ekron	150	4,090
	Gederah	69	3400
	Be'er Toviyyah	105	5,630
	Moẓa	15	650
	Hartuv	28	5,000
Samaria	Petaḥ Tikvah	502	13,850
	Ḥadera	870	29,880
	Kefar Sava	153	7,500
	Tanturah and Athlit	1,070	20,000
	Zikhron Ya'akov	–	–
Galilee	Sejerah	–	27,000
	Rosh Pinnah	325	14,000
	Ein Zeitim	51	5,600
	Mishmar ha-Yarden	93	2,380
	Yesud ha-Ma'alah	100	12,500
	Meron	–	2,000
	Maḥanayim	–	8,500
	Metullah	233	12,000

1 Four dunams = one acre.

ods. It was not long before the moshavot were threatened with collapse.

At this stage Baron Edmond de Rothschild stepped in. He made considerable investments in the farms, sent out experts to teach viticulture, and installed his own administrators. The settlements were saved, but at a considerable price: the settlers became completely dependent on outside support and had little say in the management of their holdings. By 1898 there were 22 of the new Jewish villages in the country, most of them based on monoculture, with fruit plantations as their mainstay. In 1900 the *Jewish Colonization Association (ICA, founded in 1891), which at first acted only as a source of credit for the farm communities, took over the management from Rothschild's administration. It developed a wider range of activities, established a training farm for agricultural laborers in *Sejerah (1901) and founded Mesḥa (*Kefar Tavor), Menaḥemiyyah, and *Yavne'el (1902), Beit Gan (1902), and *Mizpeh (1908), based on field crops (cereals).

The Zionist Organization's Role. In 1898, at the Second Zionist Congress, the Zionist Organization recognized the major role of settlement in the national revival, appointing a committee for the purpose. It started real activity, however, only after the foundation of the *Jewish National Fund in 1901 and, in particular, after the establishment of its Palestine Department and Palestine Office, headed by Arthur *Ruppin, in 1907 and 1908 respectively. Many of the newcomers of the Second Aliyah wanted to work on the land; at first they sought employment in the existing villages, which employed Arabs almost exclusively, and then, in 1908, began to found their own settlements. The Zionist organization's first settlement enterprise, in 1908, was the Dalāyikat Umm Jūnī training farm on the Jordan. In the following year the Palestine Office handed over part of the farm at Dalāyika, on the west bank of the river, to a group of workers who set up the first kevuẓah or collective village (see *kibbutz), called *Kinneret. Another group later leased the land at Umm Jūnī, on the east bank, on similar terms; it was later called *Deganyah. A third venture, in *Merḥavyah, based on the cooperative principles of Franz *Oppenheimer, proved a failure.

Starting with field crops, Deganyah and Kinneret gradually added new types of agriculture. Yosef *Busel, one of the founders of Deganyah, suggested diversified farming, combining fruit plantations with field crops and animal husbandry, so that the kevuẓah could pay its way and lay the foundation for permanent settlement. Ruppin and Y.A. *Elazari-Volcani, who was then setting up an agricultural research station at *Ben

Jewish Agricultural Settlement and Population up to the Establishment of the State of Israel

	End of 1900	End of 1914	End of 1922	End of 1941	End of 1944	May 1948
Moshavot						
Settlements	21	32	34	45	44	15[1]
Inhabitants	4,950	11,000	11,540	63,240	76,000	24,160
Moshavim						
Settlements		3	11	94	99	99
Inhabitants		400	1,410	24,820	29,500	30,142
Kibbutzim						
Settlements		4	19	87	111	159
Inhabitants		180	1,190	23,190	33,500	54,208
Others[2]						
Settlements	1	8	7	5	5	4
Inhabitants	260	410	780	1,750	4,000	2,121
Total						
Settlements	22	47	71	231	259	277
Inhabitants	5,210	11,990	14,920	113,000	143,000	110,631

1 Some rural settlements have become urban.

2. Agricultural schools, farms, etc.

Shemen, supported the idea, which gradually gained general acceptance. Settlement progressed slowly but steadily until the end of World War I, spreading to new areas in which the Jewish National Fund had acquired land. The moshavot also donated plots of land for daughter settlements, which were set up in 1912–13 by immigrants from Yemen: Maḥaneh Yehudah on the outskirts of Petaḥ Tikvah, Naḥali'el near Ḥaderah, and Sha'arayim near Reḥovot, "Workers' neighborhoods" – auxiliary farms for farm laborers – were established in Ein Gannim, *Naḥalat Yehudah, and Ein-Ḥai (*Kefar Malal), as well as independent villages like *Gan Shemu'el, founded in 1913. By the beginning of World War I there were 47 Jewish villages in the country, 14 of them supported by the Zionist Organization through the Palestine Office.

UNDER THE MANDATE. *Kibbutz and Moshav.* During World War I settlement activities came to a virtual standstill, but in 1919, after the *Balfour Declaration and the start of the Third Aliyah, activities were resumed by the Zionist Organization's Settlement Department, which replaced the Palestine Office. Much attention was paid to the ideological, as well as the practical aspects of the work. The ideal of the kevuẓah or kibbutz (the latter term was first used for the large settlement of *En-Harod, founded in 1921) was fully defined. In 1920 a renewed attempt was made, on a scientific basis, to settle in the hill areas, with the establishment of *Kiryat Anavim, west of Jerusalem, and *Atarot, to the north of the city. (Previous attempts had been made at Moẓa, in 1894, and Hartuv, in 1895.) Between 1921 and 1923 four kevuzot and three kibbutzim were founded in the Jezreel Valley – Emek Yizre'el, known simply as the Emek – where the first large, continuous stretches of land for settlement had been purchased by the JNF (see Table: Jewish Agricultural Settlement).

At the same time a new type of settlement, the cooperative smallholders' village or moshav, developed out of the workers' neighborhoods, but while the latter were intended as auxiliary farms for farm laborers working elsewhere, the moshavim were designed for independent settlers. This development, suggested by Eliezer *Joffe, was first applied in 1921 at Nahalal, in the Emek.

With the acquisition of additional areas in the Kishon basin, southeast of Haifa, in the Jordan Valley, and on the Coastal Plain, the network expanded. The land remained in the ownership of the JNF, which leased it to the settlers for long terms. The settlements established by the Zionist Organization were based mainly on diversified farming, including fruit plantations, field crops, and livestock. Some private villages, based mainly on citrus, also made headway, and moshavot were founded: *Binyaminah in 1922, and *Pardes Ḥannah and Ramatayim in 1928, mainly by middle-class settlers who raised all or part of the funds by their own efforts, requiring less help from the Settlement Department.

Standardizing Farm Units. As yet there were no well-defined types of farms. The size of holdings was not standardized, and the various villages engaged in different varieties of mixed agriculture, so that income levels varied greatly. To encourage standardization, the Zionist Executive appointed a committee in 1929 to devise a "farm index" for the different parts of the country. It examined the size of holding required for a family's livelihood, the equipment and supplies needed per unit, and the crops and livestock best suited to each area. In irrigated areas, such as the Beth-Shean and Jordan valleys and the Coastal Plain, 25 dunams (6¼ acres) were allotted for each farm unit; in non-irrigated or partially irrigated areas, such as the Jezreel Valley, 140 to 280 dunams (35–70 acres). This was the first step toward overall agricultural planning based on the natural conditions of the country.

As irrigation was extended, Volcani proposed reducing the farm unit to 24–30 dunams, to be made viable by more intensive methods, so as to facilitate the maximum utilization of the limited land resources and maintain the principle of "personal labor" (*avodah aẓmit*), to which both moshavim and kibbutzim adhered. The system also enabled each settlement to become an autonomous unit, almost independent of outside supplies and able, if necessary, to subsist in isolation and withstand a state of siege. Volcani's "organic diversified farm" became the prevalent type in Jewish agriculture during the Mandatory period and the early years of statehood.

The countrywide federations of kibbutzim and moshavim, run by the villagers' representatives, played an important role: they recruited new members, made regulations for the affiliated settlements, and dealt with economic problems. Newcomers were frequently organized abroad as "nuclei" (*garinim*), which could settle as a group immediately on arrival. Sometimes the organizations set up new villages on their own, without initial assistance from the Settlement Department of the Jewish Agency, which took them under its wing at a much later stage.

Special Settlement Projects. Between the early 1930s and World War II, a number of special settlement projects were carried out. The "Thousand Family Project" (which in the end comprised only a few hundred families) was started in 1932 and led to the founding of several villages on the Coastal Plain near Reḥovot – *Kefar Bilu, *Neta'im, *Bet Oved – and in the Sharon region – *Ẓofit, *Kefar Hess, *Rishpon, and others. Immigrants from Germany, starting in 1933, set up villages in the Ḥefer Plain and the Sharon. The Arab riots of 1936–39 inspired a new method of setting up outposts overnight: the *Stockade and Watchtower (*ḥomah u-migdal*) settlements, in order to forestall Arab attacks and official British opposition. The Zionist Organization decided to speed up the pace of settlement and set up strongpoints in areas where Jews had not lived previously, so as to create a new Jewish population map in case partition was adopted. The main areas concerned were the Beth-Shean Valley and upper Galilee. In all, 53 new villages, mostly based on diversified farming, were set up between 1936 and 1939. Despite the White Paper restrictions, the establishment of new villages continued during and after World War II: 94 were founded, almost half of them during the war. After the end of hostilities, there was a renewed effort to extend the area of Jewish settlement, special attention being devoted to the northern Negev, where 11 new villages were set up in a single night (Day of Atonement, 1946). Seven more were set up in 1947, and a provisional pipeline was laid from the center of the country to provide them with water.

IN THE STATE OF ISRAEL. The War of Independence in 1948 provided ample validation of the doctrine that settlement ensures control. Practically all areas in which there were Jewish settlements, however few or isolated, withstood the invading Arab armies and helped to determine the boundaries of the state. Political and economic conditions were completely transformed, and the new situation led to a new settlement policy, much broader in scope, covering wider areas, and founded on new organizational and economic principles. The severe food shortage of the first few years necessitated an immediate increase in farm production. At the same time employment had to be found for the new immigrants, many of whom lacked vocational training. Land was no longer a problem, since there were large unsettled areas within the armistice boundaries, though they were exposed to marauders.

Vast agricultural settlement projects were launched, with the Jewish Agency's Settlement Department still in charge. The department was responsible for the planning, execution, and supervision of the work, including the siting of the villages; the planning of buildings, water supply, and irrigation networks; the provision of equipment, seeds, and livestock; and expert guidance in farming methods and the problems involved in the establishment of self-reliant, socially integrated rural communities. Veteran farmers were sent to live in the villages as instructors and, in the early stages, help the villagers solve their social problems. At first the settlers were employed largely in building or (in the case of abandoned Arab villages) repairing houses, paving roads, and laying pipelines; they were usually provided with outside employment in afforestation and the like until they could live on the produce of their farms. The department's central and regional offices, with their expert agronomists, engineers, and architects, supervised the work of the men in the field and, in conjunction with the Ministry of Agriculture, coordinated the choice of crops and the methods of cultivation in accordance with the climatic and soil conditions in various parts of the country.

In each of the two years 1948–49 and 1950–51, some 100 new settlements were founded, at first mainly in abandoned Arab villages on the Coastal Plain and in the mountains of Jerusalem and Galilee, then in the Negev, the Lachish and Adullam areas in the south, the Taanach area in the eastern Jezreel Valley, and finally in the arid Arabah. Settlements in border areas were sometimes established first as outposts by *Naḥal units of the Israel Defense Forces and some of them later became civilian villages.

Between the end of 1947 (when the UN partition resolution was passed) and 1970, 439 new villages were established, with over 27,000 families living in them, while many existing ones were expanded and new urban communities established.

POPULARITY OF THE MOSHAV. An outstanding feature of this period was the growing popularity of the moshav. Before independence kibbutzim outnumbered moshavim; of the new villages founded subsequently (up to the end of 1970, 309 were moshavim and only 130 kibbutzim). The development is shown in Table: Jewish Agricultural Settlements. The main reason for the shift was the ethnic and social background of the newcomers. Before 1948 most of the immigrants who were of European origin intended from the first to become farmers. The later arrivals, on the other hand, over half of whom came from Asia and Africa, were placed on the land without any prior practical or ideological preparation. The collective structure, making as it does much greater ideological demands on the individual, hardly suited their social background and they preferred the moshavim, which are closer to the ordinary type of village.

Modification of Farm Patterns. Until 1953 most of the new villages were based on diversified farming because of the urgent need for fresh agricultural produce, especially milk, eggs, vegetables, and fruit. The structure of the farms was almost identical with the diversified organic farm type, for which the pattern had been set some 15 years before, and it was only after the beginning of 1953 that certain modifications were introduced. In some of the newly settled regions, the hill areas and the Negev, natural and climatic conditions were not suited to this type of farming. Moreover, production methods had improved and increasing mechanization called for greater specialization. The political conditions which had required small farm units and large settlements crowded into a small space, or autonomous units independent of outside supplies, no longer existed. The diversified farm model was therefore gradually abandoned or modified. Specialized farms were set up according to specific local conditions and domestic and foreign market requirements, the farms in each region now specializing in a particular branch of agriculture. Most of the moshavim established in 1955 – in the Lachish region, for instance – were based on field crops, allowing almost twice as much land per farmer as the diversified farms – some 50 dunams (12½ acres) per unit. Industrial crops for export or for replacement of imports, as well as vegetables for consumption and processing, are grown. Farms suited for growing export vegetables are located in special areas, mainly the Besor region in the western Negev. The diversified farms have also been modified in the direction of greater specialization, most of them being converted into dairy farms, while others concentrate on citrus, vegetables, and similar special products.

Regional Settlement Schemes. The political, economic, and social changes that followed the establishment of the State of Israel have also affected the rural pattern. Instead of each village being a closed, independent economic and social unit, they are integrated in a comprehensive regional structure.

A pattern of this kind was first adopted in the Negev settlements founded between 1951 and 1952, which were clustered around service centers, and was further developed in the Lachish area, settled in 1955. The pattern is based on the comprehensive planning of all the agricultural settlements and urban and rural centers in the area. The villages are placed in clusters of four or five around a rural center which provides the necessary facilities, while a larger town community serves the whole region. Only everyday facilities – kindergarten, food store, synagogue, etc. – are situated within the village itself. Other services, such as schools, shopping centers, sorting and packing sheds, and tractor stations, are located in the rural center, while more widely used facilities are located in the regional town. Since larger populations are catered for, the services are cheaper and more efficient, while civil servants, teachers, technicians, and the like can live in the rural center. Industries, mainly processing plants, are sited in the regional towns, closer to supplies of raw materials, thus reducing transportation costs. Services and industries located in the midst of the rural areas provide jobs for the surplus manpower in the villages, stemming the flow to the towns and preventing the impoverishment and abandonment of the countryside.

The regional structure also facilitates greater integration among settlers from different parts of the world, whose divergent backgrounds make it undesirable to make them live in close proximity. Under the regional system each village can be made up of a single ethnic group, while all the groups use the facilities provided at the rural center, where there is contact with people from the other villages. The result is a gradual process of integration which does not disrupt the life of the individual communities. Steps are being taken to establish rural service centers in areas settled before 1954, when the regional system was introduced.

Regional cooperation has also developed among the kibbutzim, which have begun to set up joint ventures. Here, for ideological and social reasons, the service center is not actually lived in; it contains facilities and plants shared by a number of kibbutzim, but does not constitute a separate village, the staff living in adjacent kibbutzim or coming in from a nearby town. A typical example is the center maintained by the Sha'ar ha-Negev regional council, in which 11 kibbutzim jointly run a refrigeration plant, a poultry slaughterhouse and a cotton gin, besides an amphitheater, sports facilities, a regional school, a regional laundry, and other consumer services.

National Planning. Another direct consequence of statehood is that land settlement has become an integral part of the national physical and economic master plans. Under the Mandatory regime, when there was no overall planning and development, the Jewish Agency's Settlement Department was practically independent. Now settlement is a part of national development, and close coordination is therefore maintained with all the other planning authorities. This considerably facilitates integration of rural and urban development: settlement activities are no longer confined to the rural areas, and every project has to take into account urban developments in the neighborhood. Thus, a development project for the Galilee area, started in 1966, covers the entire region, including, in addition to villages and rural centers, towns like Nazareth, *Karmi'el, and Safed. Joint teams representing the Settlement Department and all the other competent authorities collaborate in the preparation of such projects. In line with this trend, the Jewish Agency and the Ministries of Housing, Labor, and Agriculture set up a Rural and Urban Settlement Study Center to investigate the problems involved and outline suitable methods for new development and the modification of existing settlement patterns. The new regions developed in this way were central Galilee, the Besor Region and the western Negev, and the Arabah.

[Raanan Weitz]

New Settlement Since the Six-Day War and Its Challenges

THROUGH THE 1970S. Since its beginnings Zionism has pursued a twofold objective: restoring Jewish national independence through an ingathering of the exiles in the Homeland, and normalizing the people's social structure through a return to productive occupations, in particular to farming. Experience in the pre-State period had taught that wastelands bought and reclaimed with Jewish effort and settled by Jews reinforce the political claim to the relevant districts of the Land of Israel. Although Zionist philosophy regarded the "conquest of the land" as a purely peaceful endeavor, settlements soon proved to be indispensable for defense against armed attacks. The outcome of the 1948 War of Independence vindicated this policy of land acquisition and settlement which had increasingly been conducted under strategic considerations.

Following the Six-Day War, veteran pioneer farmers were the first to take the initiative for new settlement beyond the "Green Line" (the pre-June 1967 armistice borders). Youth and older members of Ḥuleh Valley kibbutzim volunteered to ascend to the Golan and establish outposts there to prevent the Syrians from returning to their dominating positions which through two decades had been a nightmare for the valley's inhabitants. In July 1967 they set up kibbutz Golan which became later, at a new site, Merom Golan, the region's largest Jewish rural location. Children of *Kefar Eẓyon settlers orphaned in 1948 insisted on renewing the Eẓyon Bloc on the Hebron Hills; in September 1967, the reconstruction of Kefar Eẓyon was begun.

Israeli citizens of various political affiliations united in the summer of 1967 to establish the *Ha-Tenu'ah le-Ma'an Ereẓ Israel ha-Shelemah (Land of Israel Movement), with Y. *Tabenkin as one of the proponents. Among the settlement organizations, *Ha-Kibbutz ha-Me'uḥad was the first to project settlement programs beyond the Green Line. The other associations joined in readily, with only *Ha-Kibbutz ha-Arẓi ha-Shomer ha-Ẓa'ir expressing serious reservations.

The political aspect of settlement beyond the Green Line soon became an issue of considerable discussion. Shades of opinion appeared within the Israel Labor Party, although most members accepted Yigal *Allon's plan which became fully known in 1968. Seeking to combine the indispensable improvement of Israel's military defense with a minimum increase in its Arab population, Allon demanded new settlement in the Golan, the Lower Jordan Valley together with the northwestern Dead Sea shore and parts of the eastern slopes of Samaria and Judea, as well as the northeast corner of Sinai (subsequently called the "Rafiaḥ Salient" and, finally, the "Yammit Region"), and a strip paralleling the gulf shore to connect Eilat with the peninsula's southern tip. He also stipulated minor adjustments to the 1949 lines, so as to include within the territory of Israel the Eẓyon Bloc, the Ayyalon Valley, stretches on the Sharon border, etc., thereby emphasizing that he did not intend foregoing the historical link with the Jewish people's heartland but that political realities dictated the limitation of new settlement to the most vital areas.

The Labor-led government accepted the Allon Plan as a guideline, hinting at it in its directives of December 15, 1969, "to speed up the establishment of security outposts and permanent settlement, rural and urban, on the soil of the homeland." A ministerial committee headed by Y. *Galili decided, in cooperation with the Jewish Agency Settlement Department, on the locations to be settled.

At international forums, Jewish settlement in the administered territories encountered growing criticism. Even friendly Western powers showed little understanding of its vital importance for Israel's security. The American administration was at best prepared to acquiesce in Naḥal settlements which could count as military installations, but not in their being later converted into civilian Jewish villages.

The government at first gave precedence to settlements in the Golan which already at the close of 1967 had four outposts, while elsewhere there existed two isolated footholds in Sinai (Naḥal Yam and Naḥal Sinai), and rebuilt Kefar Eẓyon in Judea. During 1968, the number of Golan settlements rose to ten, and in the Lower Jordan Valley a beginning was made with three outposts. On the eve of the Yom Kippur War (October 1973), the Golan had 17 settlements and the Jordan Valley 12, the Gaza Strip four and Sinai nine (in addition to the two earlier outposts, four settlements in the Rafiaḥ Salient and three along the shore of the Gulf of Eilat); Judea had three villages in the Eẓyon Bloc, in addition to the urban nucleus of Kiryat Arba near Hebron, a field school on Mt. Giloh south of Jerusalem, and several new suburbs of the capital; Mevo Ḥoron in the Ayyalon Valley was founded in what had been neutral territory until 1967.

The Yom Kippur War and the soul-searching which came in its wake produced partly contradictory reactions. On the one hand, the inability of the Golan settlements to stem the Syrian assault, the necessity to evacuate several of them during the fighting and to reconstruct them only after the Israel army had thrown back the aggressors, gave rise to doubts whether in fully mechanized warfare rural settlements could still be regarded as an integral part of Israel's defense system. On the other hand, there arose new circles, both in Israel and in the Diaspora, willing personally to take part in pioneer settlement. Foremost among them were religious youth desirous of ensuring settlement throughout Judea and Samaria. "*Gush Emunim" was founded in February 1974 as their framework.

While the interim agreements with Egypt and Syria were being negotiated, Gush Emunim and others saw as their immediate task the prevention of a withdrawal from any area which had been under Israel's control since 1967. A case in point was Keshet, its name being an acronym of the Hebrew words "Kuneitra shall be ours," in the urban area of this Golan town. After the ratification of the agreement with Syria, Keshet, a moshav shittufi, was transferred southward to Khushniya, to serve as a connecting link between the southern and northern settlement blocs of the Golan. Not far from there, Yonatan, another moshav shittufi, was similarly founded without seeking the previous sanction of the authorities.

Gush Emunim, in contradiction to the Allon Plan, soon concentrated its efforts on establishing nuclei of settlement in the heart of Judea and Samaria. Its discussions with the Labor-led government and with dovish circles coincided with mounting pressure from abroad that settlement beyond the Green Line cease altogether. The Rabin government delegated army units to prevent demonstrative Gush marches and settlement attempts in Judea and Samaria and revised government directives were endorsed by the Knesset on June 3, 1974: "Settlement and establishment of outposts shall continue in accord with the resolutions that will be taken by the Israel Government." On July 31, 1974, Rabin declared in the Knesset: "It cannot be permitted that any group of people take the law in their own hands… every single act of settlement may be carried out only after the Government has approved it, after weighing its security and political aspects… the Government will continue to work for settlement, but also protect the settlement ideal from being exploited for anti-democratic purposes." Spokesmen of Gush Emunim claimed that dovish utterances of Israelis engendered the mounting pressure from abroad and complained that the government dragged its feet in developing centers like Kiryat Arba, Yammit, Ma'aleh (Mishor) Adummim, etc. In the discussions, positions coincided increasingly less with party lines and divided not only the Labor bloc but also the National Religious Party and even the Likkud. However, wishing to avoid an extreme confrontation, in January 1976 the government decided as a compromise, to transfer the would-be settlers of Elon Moreh, west of Shomron (Sebastiye), to the Kaddum army camp.

U.S. pressure in the matter was strongly applied before the May 1977 Knesset elections when Rabin visited Washington. President Carter termed the settlements "illegal" and, later in the year, called the adding of new ones "a defiance." More Gush Emunim settlement attempts were thwarted in the spring of 1977. Prime Minister *Begin, immediately after coming into office, visited the settlers at the Kaddum camp together with Ariel *Sharon, minister of agriculture and chairman of the Ministerial Committee on Settlement, and promised "there will be many (more settlements like) Elon Moreh," i.e., unreserved support of the Gush Emunim program. Following his own visit to Washington in September 1977, however, Begin and his government saw need to restrain the Gush. From the beginning of October temporary solutions were found for six of its groups by permitting them to settle inside army camps (Beth Ḥoron, Givon, Bet El, Neveh Ẓuf, Shomron, Dotan; the idea of drafting the settlers for reserve duty in the army was soon abandoned).

Sharon in his long-range program fully backed settling Judea and Samaria, particularly its western slopes which are less densely populated by Arabs than their central parts, together with the building of two or three highways crossing Judea and Samaria from west to east, also these to be secured by new Jewish towns and villages at strategic points. He based his program on a forecast of two million Jews who would live in the region. In October 1977 his proposal to recognize Gush Emunim as a regular settlement movement entitled to moderate government aid was jointly accepted by the government and the Zionist Organization.

In July 1977 Gush Emunim had published its own 25-year master plan, based on the assumption that even without an increase in births and immigration the Jews of Israel would number 5.5 million at the end of the century and half a million more if there was annual immigration of 20,000; the total Arab population would by then number 2.5 million. The plan was modeled so as to increase the Jewish population of Galilee and the Golan from 450,000 to 800,000, that of Judea and Samaria (including Jerusalem) from 300,000 to 1,050,000, and that of the southernmost Coastal Plain, the Negev and Sinai from 350,000 to 850,000, but with an addition of only 500,000 to the 2 million in the Central Coastal Plain. It saw as goals: the inclusion in Israel both of the hill crests and the Jordan Valley, the bolstering of Jerusalem's dominant position as Israel's capital, the reduction of demographic and ecological dangers by a better regional population distribution, and the improvement of the social structure by a transfer of workers from the service to the productive sector. The Gush plan proposed the establishment within 25 years of two cities of 60,000 inhabitants each, the one Kiryat Arba and another near Nablus, as well as four towns of 20,000 inhabitants, 20 "garden towns" with a population of 10,000 and 125 "community settlements" averaging 1,000–2,000 inhabitants, the latter to be grouped in "clusters" of four to eight around regional centers which would provide higher-grade services. In the long run, some clusters would amalgamate into towns or cities. The "community settlement" (*yishuv kehillati*) was to be organized as a cooperative society imposing on its members duties on the community's behalf, but leaving them free in the choice of their occupation, in the structure of their homes, etc. The plan contained maps and tables detailing location and economic foundations for every suggested settlement.

In the summer of 1978, Defense Minister Ezer *Weizman put forward his ideas with regard to settlement in Judea and Samaria. He opposed small farming communities scattered over wide areas and instead suggested six urban centers to be built on rocky ground with no large Arab population in the vicinity, enumerating Efrat, Givon, and Ma'aleh Adummim as supplementary satellites of Jerusalem, and Neveh Ẓuf, Ari'el (Ḥaris), and Karnei Shomron in western Samaria.

In August 1978 Professor Raanan *Weitz, for many years a member of the Israel Labor Party and head of the Jewish Agency's Agricultural Settlement Department, published his own Outline Plan for Rural and Urban Settlement for the period 1979–1983. Radically opposed to the approach of Gush Emunim, Weitz warned against Israel overreaching itself beyond the available manpower and against mingling Jewish and Arab populations within communities or restricted areas, which experience had always shown to have exacerbated antagonism. Judging it impossible to "judaize" Judea and Samaria, he demanded priority for developing the Yammit Region as a barrier between the Gaza Strip and Sinai, and the Lower Jordan Valley confronting Jordan. His five-year plan allocated 14 supplementary rural settlements to the former region and 17 to the latter, while the Golan, of second priority, was to get 11. Within the Green Line, he placed Galilee first with 20 planned rural settlements and later with 16 others stretched along the borders, while for the western Negev he envisaged 10 settlements, eight for the Aravah Valley, and six for the Negev Hills. Of these 102 localities to be peopled by 9,900 units (families), 60 were to be based mainly on farming, seven on industry and 35 combining both. For urban development, Weitz pointed to the need to bring towns to a "threshold size" beyond which they would expand spontaneously. Until 1983, a total of 11,900 families were to be absorbed in Kaẓrin on the Golan, Ma'aleh Efrayim in the Jordan Valley, Allon Shevut in the Eẓyon Bloc, Yammit, and Sapir in the Aravah Valley. Five existing towns of Galilee were to grow by 13,000 families, and Jerusalem with its suburbs by 23,500. With 13 other development towns within the Green Line reckoned to absorb 20,000 families, the plan foresaw a total of 68,400 families to be absorbed in the urban development sector. Weitz's ideas on strengthening communal cohesion preceded those of the Gush's program.

President Sadat's visit to Jerusalem (November 19–20, 1977) and the announcement of the Israel government's preparedness eventually to restore all of Sinai to Egypt, moved the Yammit Region into the center of attention. Shortly before, in September 1977, Prime Minister Begin, together with Housing Minister Gideon Patt, had visited Yammit and announced the go-ahead for the region's master plan, urging the increase of the town's population within two years from about 1,500 to 30,000. On November 2, Begin had requested membership and a house for himself at Ne'ot Sinai, the region's westernmost settlement. In December 1977, the approval of the government and the Knesset to restoring to Egypt the sovereignty over Yammit drew strong protests not only from Gush Emunim but also from the Labor Party and all settlement associations. Moshe Dayan and Ariel Sharon, visiting Yammit on January 2, 1978, disappointed the settlers in spite of their promise that local settlements would be strengthened and afforded full security by the Israel Defense Forces. Bitterness was aroused by Dayan's statement that "when peace is not achieved because of the settler's opposition, the people will not support them." Simultaneously, JNF work crews acting on government authority started groundbreaking work for eight, and then more, sites for settlement nuclei west and south of the region's existing villages, but were withdrawn after a fortnight. On President Sadat's demand that all Jewish settlements in Sinai be dismantled, Premier Minister Begin replied that Israel might rescind its peace proposal if Cairo did not permit the settlements to remain.

In the same month, Weitz published his Southern Project of 100 new settlements of 100 families each, to engage mainly in glasshouse farming, and 15,000 persons to live in nonfarming communities, which were to be established between Beersheba and Yammit, one third of them beyond the Green Line, even if it came under Egyptian sovereignty.

During 1978 and until the first Camp David Conference, the town of Yammit and the region's villages continued to consolidate their economy and increase their population. Construction of two villages begun earlier was pursued, but no new sites were allocated. After Camp David, the Knesset voted on September 25, 1978, to evacuate the region in the event of the signing of a peace treaty, with all speakers pointing to this as the decision's most painful aspect. On December 11, 1978, Weitz revealed to the Knesset Finance Committee his department's plan for "Pitḥat Shalom" ("Peace Salient") in the western Negev to resettle the Yammit Region inhabitants in 24 new villages of 60 units each, at a cost of $250 million, envisaging for the purpose also the Keturah area of the Aravah Valley, the Negev Hills and the vicinity of Nizẓanah, the latter to be a city which would receive the Yammit inhabitants. These city dwellers, however, like the region's farmers, immediately declared they would by no means resettle anywhere else, and demonstrated their opposition in various ways. The protests culminated in the establishment of a "settlement" by Gush partisans 20 km east of el-Arish on March 20, 1979, the day of the Knesset debate on the signature of the Peace Agreement with Egypt.

Settlement in Judea and Samaria was not directly affected by the negotiations with Egypt. However, some people preparing to join settlements in the Lower Jordan Valley canceled their applications in view of the Yammit developments, although few actual members left villages during 1978. Gush Emunim, on the other hand, claimed that growing numbers wished to join its own existing sites and founded new ones. In July 1978, Sharon reported that, apart from 21 Jordan Valley settlements (by the end of 1976), Kiryat Arba and the Eẓyon Bloc villages, a skeleton network existed in Judea and Samaria comprising 16 settlements and three Naḥal footholds, of which four had been established under the previous government and the remainder since the Likkud had come into power. He announced the intention of doubling the number of families in these places to 1000 within a year.

At the Camp David Conference, the Israeli delegation consented to a temporary lull in the creation of new settlements in the region until the final agreement with Egypt scheduled for mid-December. A Gush group trying to set up camp on a hill near Nablus was expelled by the army (September 17–21, 1978), with Defense Minister Ezer Weizman being present at the tussle. While the Israel government reserved the right of "thickening" existing places, America interpreted the promise of Israel to refrain from further settlement as being unlimited in time. When the date passed without the expected agreement, Premier Begin declared settlement to be renewable. However, until President Carter's visit to Egypt and Israel (March 1979), no further settlements were established in the region.

In a newspaper article in January 1979, Y. Allon refuted the claim that rural settlements were no factor in zonal defense in modern warfare, and criticized the Likkud government for having given up Sinai without attempting to achieve border changes, thereby creating a precedent which could encourage other Arabs to demand, and eventually obtain, Israel's retreat everywhere to the untenable Green Line. He maintained that settlement in selected regions must be given new impetus and villages provided with all the necessary means to throw back even full-scale enemy assaults. In February Y. Galili declared that the Labor Party demanded continued Israeli sovereignty over the Lower Jordan Valley, the Eẓyon Bloc, the southern section of the Gaza Strip, and the Golan, and the adding of settlements in these regions.

In March 1979, when President Carter visited Egypt and Israel, the administered region of Judea and Samaria totaled 49 Jewish-inhabited locations. Of these, 23 were in the Lower Jordan Valley, near the Dead Sea, and on the adjoining hill slopes along the patrol road running from Rimmonim to Ma'aleh Efrayim, which separates them from the region densely inhabited by Arabs. Apart from Ma'aleh Efrayim, designed to serve as a semi-urban center, most settlements, moshavim and moshavim shittufiyyim (except for the southern sector where kibbutzim were prominent), were based principally on export-oriented farming of out-of-season vegetables and flowers.

The Eẓyon Bloc at that date contained the semi-urban center Allon Shevut, three kibbutzim, and one moshav shittufi. The construction of nearby Efrat as an urban community was officially approved in early 1979.

Over the rest of Judea and Samaria, 21 footholds were spread, most of them connected with Gush Emunim. Some of them grew quickly, others numbered only a few inhabitants who continued to maintain their jobs and apartments in the cities. Either Jewish-owned or "dead land" claimed by no one which had always, under Turkish, British, and Jordanian rule, counted as state property, was taken. Therefore, practically all hill settlements covered areas of rocky ground largely unfit for agriculture and were generally compelled to direct their future economy toward non-farming ventures.

Settlements in the Golan totaled 26, including the urban nucleus of Kaẓrin whose first residents moved in in 1977. While the first Golan settlements were kibbutzim and moshavim in the southern and northern sectors where some stretches were reclaimed for farming, the newer ones, largely in the central sector, were often built on permanently uncultivable ground and therefore concentrated on industry and other occupations. Since the early 1970s, the JNF has installed on the Golan plateau storage lakes to retain winter rainwater for summer use.

The Yammit Region (dismantled, evacuated, and ultimately leveled in 1982) and the Gaza Strip had 20 Jewish locations, of which nine were in the Strip. In early 1979 the town of Yammit had over 2,000 inhabitants, most having their place of work in pre-1967 Israel. There were two kibbutzim and 12 moshavim and moshavim shittufiyyim engaged in highly intensive and remunerative cultivation of export crops, some of them employing Bedouin of the vicinity as hired laborers. Water was received from shallow groundwater horizons and larger quantities came from the National Carrier. The settlements in the Gaza Strip, located on sand dunes, were kibbutzim and moshavim concentrating on glasshouse and open-air cultivation of out-of-season crops.

On the shore of the Gulf of Eilat existed three settlements, their economy principally based on tourism.

The task of establishing outposts after 1967 slowed similar activities within the Green Line, but in the early 1970s the urgent need was recognized to renew efforts, principally in mountainous Galilee and in the Aravah Valley.

In Galilee, including the Acre Coastal Plain, the Ḥuleh Valley and the Lake Kinneret shore, the proportion of Jews in the population shrank continually to little over 50% in 1978, and to hardly more than 20% in Galilee's hilly interior as a result of the enormous natural increase of non-Jews and, to some extent, by the migration of Jews to other parts of the country. Led by the New Communist Party, Arabs staged, particularly in 1976, riotous "land days" to protest against alleged expropriation of land from Arabs, although these amounted in Galilee to about 6,000 dunams only, much less than Jewish and state property taken for purposes like housing and other development, and although the development plans were designed to benefit Arab citizens no less than Jews. Non-Jews built thousands of houses scattered over state property or applied it to other use, with the intention both to create for themselves a claim to such land and to obstruct further Jewish settlement and development. In a few instances the Arabs of the Galilee demanded that their region should be severed from the State of Israel.

A Galilee development program had been proclaimed in the mid-1960s by Prime Minister L. *Eshkol, but after the founding of three moshavim, two of them near the Lebanese border, it was no longer energetically pursued. The plan was revived at the beginning of the 1970s with the consolidation and "re-planning" of hill moshavim (both in Galilee and the Jerusalem Corridor), and their infrastructure was broadened, especially by enlarging the poultry branch. Residential and farm buildings zones were separated and room was gained for absorbing more settler families in each village, particularly from the locally born second generation. Work started on the reclamation of land for industrial zones, e.g., Goren near the Lebanese border, Tefen in Central Upper Galilee between Ma'alot and Karmi'el, Segev in northwestern Lower Galilee, and Tur'an on the ridge of the same name further to the southeast. From 1976 onward the novel concept of industry-based villages (*kafatim*), consisting of kibbutzim, moshavim, and "community settlements," began to take shape with the founding of outposts, some of them initially maintained by Naḥal. At the end of 1978 they numbered eight. At the founding ceremony of a ninth, in February 1979, Minister Sharon described this location as the first of 29 temporary footholds in Galilee immediately to be created, in order to guard and prepare land for later permanent settlements to take shape within four to five years. Concurrent with new rural settlement were programs for expanding housing, industrial, and other enterprises of urban and semi-urban centers (Safed, Ma'alot, Karmi'el, Shelomi, Kiryat Shemonah, Ḥaẓor). Road building was started in 1978 to make older and more recent locations more easily accessible and to increase the attraction of their residential and industrial zones. Afforestation and preparation of pasture grounds were speeded up, both for their intrinsic economic and ecological value and the prevention of unlawful encroachment on public lands. These measures, at least as much as they promised to multiply Jewish settlers, benefited Galilee's non-Jews. This was in line with Israel's policy which regards the steep rise in the non-Jews' living standard as an integral part of its development objectives. While there were numerous candidates for farming and other enterprises in independent rural locations there were only few for hired employment in factories, tourist enterprises, etc., and vacancies were readily taken up by the region's non-Jews.

In the Aravah Valley, all settlements must be likened to "artificial oases," won by thorough land reclamation and the exploitation of profound, partly fossil, water reserves. Adding new links to the chain of Jewish villages was essential for Israel's security, because the Jordanian border splits this 180 km.-long desert rift lengthwise. The program gathered momentum after 1968, with eight farming settlements added to the five founded previously. Sapir, a semiurban center, was also under construction. This center promises to increase decisively the region's population and to promote its intensive agriculture actively, e.g., with an airfield for the direct dispatch by freightplanes of the region's produce to European markets, or a turkey slaughtering and packing plant to permit the renewal of this profitable branch which the settlements had been obliged to discontinue temporarily because of the long transport run to central Israel.

Of the settlements founded between 1967 and 1981 in other parts of pre-1967 Israel, some are very close to the Green Line and link up with development endeavors beyond it.

[Efraim Orni]

THE 1980S AND AFTER. Between 1983 and 1992, the size of settlement and its regional distribution depended largely on the influence of the main political parties and their approach to Israel's current situation. The Likud and Gush Emunim (whose settlement association is named Amana) persevered in putting the emphasis on Judea-Samaria (the West Bank) and the Gaza Strip. The Ma'arakh Labor Bloc, on the other hand, insisted on restricting new settlement beyond the pre-1967 areas to the Allon Plan (see above) areas that had been envisaged for development after the Six-Day War. It explained that the peace process had to be kept going without the impediment of settlement in areas closely inhabited by Arabs. When the National Unity government was established in 1985, the Likkud partners had to be content with a compromise that permitted the establishment of only a few new settlements in the Administered Areas.

Foreign powers showed increased interest in the settlements. The U.S. kept repeating its wish that Israel refrain from further settlement in the territories and, especially, from directing new immigrants to them. The U.S.S.R. made full renewal of diplomatic relations conditional upon Israel's readiness for compromise concerning the territories although the relations were eventually restored without any concessions. The Arabs made cessation of settlement part of their conditions in peace negotiations.

Israel's right wing endeavored to make up for the decrease in new foundings by "thickening" the territories' Jewish population through speedy enlargement of existing places, aspiring to obtain appropriate budgets for land purchase, road construction, and other investments. Their success was considerable. In Judea-Samaria and the Gaza Strip the number of Jews rose from 22,800 in mid-1983 to 203,700 at the end of 2002. However, Teḥiyyah and other right-wing parties opposing the National Unity government complained that far from enough was being done for expansion.

Within the pre-1967 boundaries, Galilee and the Negev were the locales for few new settlements. In the Golan Heights no change was made.

Between 1983 and 2002, 105 places were founded: 47 in Judea-Samaria; 13 in the Gaza Strip; 3 in the Golan; 42 within pre-1967 Israel. In fact, however, the total of additions in the period was smaller, because the survey indicates as founding date the year when it recognized a settlement's existence, which is frequently later than when the foundations were laid.

A trend discernible in the 1980s and 1990s was the preference given to the novel forms of "community village" or "private village." Permitting settlers much greater freedom in their occupational and private sphere than do the veteran kibbutz or moshav, the community village not only attracted nuclei of new settlers but also groups which had originally intended to choose one of the traditional forms. Even a number of existing settlements decided, or were considering, to turn themselves into community villages. The designers of the new forms had predicted that they would each contain 200 or more families. While most community villages remained below this size, a few had grown beyond it and become, or were on the way to becoming, urban localities.

Of the sites available for new settlement both within pre-1967 Israel and in the Administered Areas, very few have at their disposal a minimum of cultivable soil. Therefore only a very small number of the new settlements included farming in their economic projection. This was encouraged by the fact that the size of cultivable acreage is no longer seen as decisive for Israel's farming capacity and profitability. Instead, most new places endeavor to promote industry, tourism, and other productive services or are content that most of their members commute to their work places in the country's major agglomerations. Among the settlement sites, those which are easily accessible for commuters have an advantage. Construction of good and easy roads has thus become an integral part of regional development.

[Efraim Orni]

PLANNING: URBAN AND RURAL DEVELOPMENT

THE NATIONAL PLAN. On its establishment the State of Israel set itself two political goals: (a) to bring the maximum number of Jews from the lands of their dispersion back to the country of their biblical origin, and (b) to integrate the newcomers into the framework of the new state. A further basic aim was to develop, populate, and provide employment in the entire territory of the state in order to achieve, in the course of time, a fairly equal standard of living in all parts of the country. It was the task of national, physical planning to give these basic objectives their technical and detailed expression and to point out ways for their realization.

When independent Israel came into being (1948), the greater part of the population was concentrated in the coastal strip and the cities of Tel Aviv, Haifa, and Jerusalem. In view of the large influx of new immigrants and the need to settle the sparsely populated areas, the government adopted a policy for the balanced distribution of the population over the entire country. On the basis of this policy, a national plan was prepared for urban development by the building of new towns and rural development by the expansion of agriculture and the establishment of new villages.

After the first decade and a half of intensive planning and implementation, this situation was altered and progress made towards achieving the desired results. To the three existing major cities, a fourth was added – Beersheba, the capital of the Negev. The three major cities still exceed all others both in size and attraction and are constantly enlarging their conurbations. Free enterprises flourish in these cities and they offer a favorable labor market. Recently, there has been a rapid rise in the price of land and a tendency to use good agricultural land for urban settlement and services is making itself felt. The Coastal Plain is the most favored area of settlement and is even preferred to the capital, Jerusalem. Additional urban conurbations are forming in the Coastal Plain (e.g., Ashkelon, Ashdod, Netanyah, Ḥaderah). Agriculture in the Coastal Plain, which is well irrigated and close to the cities, is in a favored position as compared with other regions.

The waves of immigration since the foundation of the state were perhaps proportionally the largest known in history. For a decade and a half an annual average of 13.5% of the initial Jewish population entered the country. To this must be added the natural increase at the rate of 17 per thousand and an increase in the Arab population at the rate of 42 per thousand. This provided sufficient human material for the expansion of the existing settlements and the establishment of new settlements. About 400 rural settlements have been set up since the establishment of the state and many new cities founded. Galilee, the mountain district of Jerusalem and the Southern Region (the Negev) were populated with urban and rural settlements.

This expansion over the entire territory of the state coupled with the partial implementation of an extensive development program has been accompanied by the usual social phenomena. The economic situation of the major cities and the longer-settled areas is better than that of the newly developed regions. The new immigrants for the most part came to Israel devoid of economic means. They had to be housed and economically integrated at the public expense and the required services had to be provided. They had to bear the strains of a period of initial development which the veteran populations had encountered and overcome several decades before.

A national plan for the entire territory of the country was worked out in detail. It was intended to serve as a guide, and it was estimated that it would remain valid for 15 to 20 years. Major parts of the plan involved decisions and investments which would affect generations to come.

Of primary importance was the part showing the distribution of the population against the background of the new cities which were to be planned and developed. Since the establishment of the state, the Planning Department has on six occasions drawn up general plans showing the desired distribution of the population and from time to time has brought these plans up to date.

The 1957–8 plan, which was worked out on a scientific basis, was submitted to an inter-departmental committee for approval.

The final version of the plan, prepared in 1964, envisaged an estimated population of 4 million.

The main functions of the plan were the following:

a) to provide a balanced framework for the plans of individual settlements;

b) to serve as a guide to the practical measures to be taken towards implementing the distribution of the population, e.g., the geographical distribution of housing units and the siting of industrial enterprises;

c) to guide government offices and other bodies in determining the size and location of institutions and other establishments.

In drawing up the plans, the general aim was to further the process of population distribution – a policy vital to the country's defense and settlement needs and one that is necessary to relieve the mounting pressure on land in the overcrowded coastal strip. On the other hand, the plans did not ignore the existence of factors operating against dispersion and in favor of concentration, some of which are based on legitimate demands – e.g., a concern for the best conditions for those industries which will have to compete in world markets.

A continued distribution of the population and a check on the expansion of the big cities were the main objectives which found expression in the plans. At the same time the proposals were drawn up on a practical scale. They did not seek to impose on the state a burden of special investment which it could not bear. Only the measures to be taken in remote and underdeveloped areas justified exceptional effort and large-scale investment on the part of the State (e.g., in Northern and Central Galilee, the Besor Region, Arad, and the Central Negev).

On the other hand, such steps are not required when the aim is merely to increase the existing population of settlements which are fairly well established or which already have a large population (e.g., Beershebaa, Ashkelon, and Afulah).

Finally, it is important to stress that the urbanization of the Coastal Strip (unless this process is limited to the sand dune areas) is likely to produce results as negative as those caused by the continued expansion of the population in the Haifa and Tel Aviv areas.

The plan for the distribution of an estimated population of 4 million was not tied to any particular year. The date on which Israel's population would reach 4 million depended to a large degree on the rate of immigration, a factor which it was impossible to predict. Nevertheless the plan presumed that the population would reach this figure in 1982. In working out the plan, all those factors which affect the growth of population and which to a certain extent offset one another (e.g., the demographic aspect, the possible size of the agricultural and village population, the estimated occupational structure of the population, the limits to the distribution of industry and the possibilities of absorption in outlying regions of the country) were taken into account.

The plans for distribution of the population indicated the way in which development was to take place in the rural and urban sectors and in the new towns.

In addition to the significant expansion of the few cities existing at the time of the establishment of the State, a large number of new towns have been founded. They may be divided into the following types:

1. Former agricultural settlements which have grown into towns (first Petaḥ Tikvah and Rishon le-Zion, then Nahariyyah, Kefar Sava, and Zikhron Ya'akov).

2. Former Arab towns that were repopulated and considerably expanded (Ramleh, Lod, Bet Shean, Beersheba, and Acre – the area outside the city walls).

3. Completely new cities (Kiryat Shemonah, Ashkelon, Ashdod, Dimonah, Bet Shemesh, and Eilat).

4. Larger Arab villages, which are slowly assuming the character of small towns (Shefaram, Rama, Marar, Taiba, and Tira).

5. Small towns in the Negev (Mizpeh Ramon, Arad, and others).

6. Rural service centers for groups of 5–10 villages, which fulfill the urban needs of the rural sector.

The establishment of satellite towns or single neighborhoods within the major and medium-size conurbations of the Coastal Plain cannot be regarded as the foundation of new towns or as a contribution to the distribution of population. It merely constitutes a shift of emphasis within the existing conurbation.

The areas which were most difficult to settle were those along the frontier, less for security reasons than as a result of the low agricultural quality of soil and their distant position. They were at first settled by kibbutzim at considerable distances from each other. Previously low-populated areas in the mountain regions (e.g., the Jerusalem Corridor and parts of Galilee) were provided with a network of agricultural settlements, backed by small townships (e.g., Bet Shemesh, Ma'alot, Kiryat Shemonah).

Several regions whose soil has been neglected but was naturally of good quality were re-populated under major development projects.

Lachish with its township of Kiryat Gat is the oldest and best known among these. It is followed by the projects for Karmiel, Arad, and Besor. In Galilee and along the southern Coastal Plain (around Ashkelon), equivalent results have been achieved by ordinary government development methods.

The development of the arid Negev region constitutes a special problem. What the area lacks in water and agricultural land is to some extent balanced by its natural resources. Towns of various sizes – Beershebaa as a major city, Eilat as a port city, Dimonah as an industrial center, and four additional smaller townships – were meant to provide for the population of this arid zone once the communications system was fully established.

The broad central strip of the Coastal Plain, from the Carmel down to the Gaza border, offers excellent agricultural soil. The prospering coastal towns as well as the towns which have developed from former rural settlements tend to encroach upon this agricultural land and urbanize it. Since the quantity of good agricultural land in Israel is limited and since in the future it will have to provide food for a far larger population, this trend had to be restricted. Measures were therefore taken to ensure that urban expansion did not proceed at the expense of the country's best nutritional soil.

PLAN FOR JERUSALEM. The plan for Jerusalem, which covered the entire city, is of special interest. In keeping with the topography of the capital, which has profoundly influenced its character, the hilltops and mountain slopes were specified for building purposes, constituting compact neighborhood units, while the valleys were left open as public areas. Special attention was paid to holy places and archaeological sites, and typical quarters of special interest were preserved. The open spaces form a suitable setting for public buildings, mostly on the hilltops, such as the Knesset, the government offices, the University, Herzl's tomb, Yad Vashem (the memorial to the victims of the Nazi Holocaust), and the Hadassah Hospital. A special team of experts, set up by the Ministry of the Interior and the Municipality, prepared plans for areas of special historical and religious importance, including the Old City, the Mount of Olives, and their environs. Special attention was paid to the Old City and very strict regulations laid down to preserve its character.

RURAL PLANNING. Land reclamation, soil improvement schemes, swamp drainage, afforestation, terracing, and cultivation of lands neglected for centuries have all been carried out on a large scale. Flood control, catchment, and diversion of surface water, and extensive tapping of underground water have added thousands of acres of good agricultural land to the total cultivable area. The introduction of scientific methods of research and the mechanization of farming have considerably improved and increased agricultural output.

By 1948, when the State of Israel was established, the rural population numbered some 85,000 in about 320 Jewish agricultural settlements. Though agricultural development was certainly guided by the circumstances of the time, there was no comprehensive planning. On the whole, the development was sporadic, conditioned by opportunity, and uncoordinated. The turning point came in 1948 and only since then could comprehensive development be envisaged. Today agricultural and industrial, rural and urban, and economic and social development are all coordinated, thus ensuring the best results for the national economy.

The planning of agricultural development is now based on soil surveys, on land classification, and on the exploitation of water resources.

The supply of water in Israel is limited. The allocation of water for various uses in accordance with the planned economic development of the country is essential and is strictly enforced. A countrywide water supply grid was planned and established. The total water resources are insufficient for the maximum exploitation of all available agricultural land and for the industrial development envisaged. Schemes for harnessing the waters of the Jordan River and for catching rain water flowing from the hills to the sea are in progress. Research into the desalination of sea water and the purification of brackish underground water is also well advanced.

Planned cultivation, guided by government authorities and backed by research, together with the introduction of new scientific methods and an increase in mechanization, have all improved agricultural production. Once the national needs for fresh agricultural produce were met, a shift to the cultivation of industrial and export crops was encouraged. During the period of 1955–61 agricultural exports increased by 85%. The increase in the cultivation of industrial crops was coordinated with the development of the processing industry.

During the first years of development and under the pressure of mass immigration, agricultural settlements were located where water and good soil were available. Little consideration was given to regional integration. As immigration slackened off, reexamination was possible and further development was based on a comprehensive development plan for each region. Regional development authorities were set up to direct an area's development until economic, social, and administrative maturity was attained.

Since the establishment of the State of Israel, 944 rural settlements have been founded and the rural population has increased from 85,000 to about 476,000. It comprised in 2002 about 8.9% of the total population as compared with 12.7% in 1948. Employed in agriculture in 2002 were some 71,700 persons, as compared with 32,000 in 1948. Agricultural production has been increased and marketing methods improving. The rural community has now attained cultural and material standards comparable to those in the towns.

In the early 21st century, agricultural development has pretty much come to a standstill, as all available water resources having been exploited. Improvement in methods of cultivation and in marketing continue, but the continued exploitation of the high-quality agricultural land available must await further progress in the supply of water.

LEGISLATION. Planning procedures and activities are regulated by the Planning and Building Law, 1965, which is administered by the National Planning Board, six district planning commissions, special planning commissions, and local planning and building commissions. The main function of the National Board is to prepare national outline schemes, approve district outline schemes, and advise the government on all planning and building matters. There is a committee for the protection of agricultural land under the auspices of the National Board. The most important functions of the district planning commissions are to approve local outline schemes and detailed plans, and to draw up district outline schemes. The country is divided into town planning areas, each with a local planning and building commission, which prepares local planning schemes and detailed schemes, issues building permits, etc.

The minister of the interior may, upon the recommendation of the minister of housing, declare by order that any area situated within one district shall be a special planning area. Every such area has a special planning and building commission, which acts, with certain restrictions, as a local and district commission. Other provisions of the law deal with expropriation, compensation, defense installations and obstructions to aviation, non-conforming use, offenses, penalties, and miscellaneous matters. The minister of the interior is charged with the implementation of the law and may make regulations after consultation with the National Board.

ADMINISTERED AREAS. Israel's new geographical goals after 1967 were the occupation, as rapidly as possible, of areas beyond the Green Line by the establishment of numerous settlements; the creation of new security belts beyond the 1967 borders, continued socio-economic consolidation of previously established settlements within these borders; and further expansion of infrastructure.

The ways in which these aims were to be achieved were basically the same as 20 years before. In this period too, border settlements were founded, although the borders were now in the Golan Heights, the Jordan Rift Valley, and the northeast of the Sinai Peninsula. Development districts were set up on the Golan Heights, in the southern Gaza Strip, in the Jordan Valley, and at selected and more restricted spots.

Most of the development took place not within the sovereign domain of Israel, but far beyond it. This new development did not form a continuum with the settlement complexes established during the two previous decades. Moreover, the change in priorities in basic investments and the diversion of resources to the occupied territories left insufficient funds for the socio-economic consolidation of the settlements established in the past. In the 1970s a new settlement geography began to take shape, with comprehensive political and security interests beyond the original borderline. Development priority has also been accorded to Jerusalem over the years, despite the 33 towns founded when the state was established to attract urban settlers and scatter the population. The desire was to transform Jerusalem into a big capital city, for nationalist and religious reasons, although this was not justified on objective geographical grounds.

Instead of solving substantive and physical problems within the territory of Israel, accelerated development activity was being directed to sites outside it. In the wake of the frustrations of the withdrawal from Sinai in 1981, and the enforced territorial shrinkage, the declared policy of the government gave greater impetus to the west-east direction, turning its attention to the occupied territories for reasons of security, strategic depth, and territorial integrity. The three objectives of this expansion were naturally the Golan Heights, the Gaza Strip, and Judea and Samaria. The Golan Heights had a great deal of unoccupied land and a small local population, while Judea and Samaria had both, considerable unoccupied land and a large population. On the Golan Heights the acquisition of physical control had been relatively easy and was already accomplished; in the Gaza Strip there was no possibility of expansion, because there were about a million people in an area of about 363 square kilometers, one of the highest densities in the world. There thus remained one possible objective for expansion – Judea and Samaria. It must be borne in mind that this latitudinal direction was beset with considerable difficulty, facing a million-strong Arab population in dense concentration throughout Judea and Samaria, facing a continuum of villages and towns, facing difficulties in acquiring land, and facing a hostile population that did not make things at all easy for the civil administration in the areas. The latitudinal expansion was based on a number of phenomena characteristic of the Israeli population. The Jewish population has a definitely urban mentality and is therefore primed for non-agricultural settlement with industry and services; it is interested in places of residence with improved environmental quality and without pollution and it is prepared to flee chaotic urban crowding even for places beyond the "Green Line." The motivation derived from the fact that in Judea and Samaria it was possible to find relatively easy solutions to all the glaring defects in Israel's living conditions and for which no reasonable solutions were planned.

However, the authorities made a different response to the new geographical conditions. In their change of direction they disregarded the principles that underlay the upbuilding of the country in the past. There is no doubt that the settlement map of the 1970s and 1980s was influenced primarily by political, military, and security factors, subject to pressure from the United States, Egypt, and Syria which dictated various measures in Israel. Yet there were also various domestic nationalistic motives and political party interests that contributed to the settlement activities and the change of the map of Israel. In the course of the process, various social and economic pressure groups arose which were very interested in having Israel change direction so that they could derive certain benefits.

Thus the 1970s and 1980s differ from earlier decades in the political motivation for settlement, going beyond economic considerations, in mass settlement, rural and urban, public and private, in areas whose ultimate fate was not yet known, involving penetration within a dense Arab population, and in new types of settlement – all this with almost daily political strife. Israel's new borders led to a regrettable diffusion of the new settlements; it created too few consolidated areas like the Golan Heights and the Jordan Valley. In the past the Negev had been the chief focus of settlement, later replaced by Galilee. In the 1970s it was Sinai, the Golan Heights, Judea and Samaria, and the Jerusalem environs. In 1977–91 the right-wing Likud government politicized the settlement of Judea and Samaria in order to change the map of the country within a short period of time and strengthen it towards the east. It is doubtful whether this new map is one which will allow the maintenance of a single national sovereignty and a democratic society.

[Jacob Dash / Elisha Efrat (2nd ed.)]

REGIONAL AND SETTLEMENT PLANNING

Regional planning in Israel has always been a highly centralized activity, formulated through a series of statutory national, district, and local guidelines. The National Council for Planning and Construction prepared occasional outline plans at the country-wide level, and these provide the framework for more detailed district and local plans. The National Council is chaired by the chief planner of the Ministry of Interior and is composed of members representing other government ministries (such as Housing and Construction, Education, Economic Planning) and other major interests (the Committee for Land Preservation, environmental groups, and so on).

In 1985, the National Council for Planning completed the Outline Plan (No. 16) for the Geographical Distribution of Seven Million Inhabitants, expected to occur during the 1990s. This plan replaced the existing Outline Plan (No. 6) for Five Million Inhabitants which had been completed in 1975. The expected distribution of population was divided among the six major administrative districts of the country.

The demographic assumptions behind the plan assumed continued natural growth coupled with significant immigration. While at first these assumptions did not appear realistic, the sudden influx of Russian immigrants between 1989 and 1991 transformed the Seven Million Plan into a realistic indicator of demographic growth for the 1990s.

The urban landscape continued to grow, with some 20 percent of Israel's population residing in the four major towns of Tel Aviv, Haifa, Jerusalem, and Beersheba by the year 2002. Within the Dan Bloc metropolitan region, encompassing Tel Aviv and the surrounding towns from Kefar Sava and Netanyah in the north, to Ashdod in the south and Petaḥ Tikvah to the east, over half of the country's population resided on only 25% of the country's land surface, with 40% of the population within the metropolitan center alone. This was in direct contrast to the peripheral regions, especially the Negev, wherein 11% of the population lived in 60% of the country's land area. Despite government attempts to promote population dispersal, through the granting of tax cuts, cheap mortgages and other benefits, the population showed its preference for the center of the country.

A major change to have taken place within Israel's settlement landscape during the 1980s was the continued transformation of the rural landscape. What had previously been a largely homogeneous settlement pattern, composed of cooperative agricultural communities, such as the kibbutz and the moshav ovedim, now gave way to a more varied pattern. On the one hand, many of the existing agricultural communities underwent functional transformation as many of the residents ceased working in agriculture. This was particularly true of the moshav sector, with inhabitants finding an employment alternative in nearby towns. This was one the results of the severe economic problems which afflicted these communities in the wake of the high inflation of the early part of the decade.

Of greater significance was the founding of over 100 dormitory communities, similar in nature to the exurban commuting villages to be found throughout the Western world. Approximately two-thirds of these new communities were established in the West Bank, many of them by Gush Emunim adherents, this region lying within the natural commuting hinterland of both the Tel Aviv and Jerusalem metropolitan regions. A large number of these exurban communities were also founded in Galilee, mostly in the western Galilee region of Segev. These communities were distinct from the traditional agricultural cooperatives in many respects. In the first place, little – if any – employment takes place within the village itself. Nearly all the working residents commute to the nearby towns for their employment. Moreover, these communities are based on a vision of "Western high-quality of life" living standards characterized by the private construction of large detached houses, giving further evidence of the clear emergence of a growing Israeli middle-class. While the majority of these communities were founded with substantial governmental assistance, private investment was responsible for a minority of cases (approximately 20 communities). The private communities were, on the whole, extremely large from the outset, with some of them (such as Metar in the northern Negev, or Koḥav Ya'ir in the center of the country) reaching 1,000 households (5–6,000 people) by the early 1990s.

The sudden arrival of the mass Russian immigration in 1990 and 1991, resulted in short-term, dramatic changes in both planning and construction. At the national level, the National Council for Planning prepared an Outline Plan for the distribution of population, as expected to take place by 1995 – reaching a total of 6.1 million inhabitants. This plan followed the general trend already noted in the Plan for Seven Million Inhabitants, although it proposed some variations on the detailed patterns of distribution.

The lack of sufficient housing for all of the immigrants led to the granting of emergency powers, designed to shortcut the normal bureaucratic delays encountered in the housing process, to the respective ministries, and in particular to the Ministry of Housing and Construction. Large-scale construction programs were put into effect throughout the country. The varied building programs included the construction of both high and low density neighborhoods, some of which consisted of imported housing units. Some of the smaller development towns underwent substantial population increase – as much as 25–30% – in the space of only one or two years. However, this has resulted in significant municipal and functional problems for the local authorities in their attempt to continue to supply a reasonable level of municipal services.

In addition to the major programs of housing construction, thousands of mobile caravan units were imported in order to provide short-term housing solutions until the solid housing would be completed. The government was conscious of the fact that the large caravan estates which sprang up throughout the country could lead to the development of social and economic conditions similar to those which occurred in the immigrant camps of the 1950s. As a result, the new government of June 1992 declared its intention of evacuating all of these camps within as short a time period as possible and encouraging their residents to move into the permanent housing.

[David Newman]

LAND OWNERSHIP

UNDER OTTOMAN RULE. Until 1858, there were no official title deeds for land in the country. There was a plentiful supply for all who wished to cultivate the land, and no one needed to establish official ownership of a specific plot. In the hills, in particular, there were large uncultivated areas which were used only for spring and pasture. In 1858 the Ottoman government promulgated the ṭābū law, designed to enforce registration and establish ownership for all land. But the obligation was no more than theoretical: only limited areas were registered, and many holders did not register their lands at all, to facilitate evasion of taxes and other imposts. Many peasants recorded the natural boundaries of their land but deliberately underestimated the area – there was no cadastral survey at the time. In return for a few coppers other peasants waived their rights in favor of effendis (rich landlords) in the towns. Lands were sometimes registered in the name of a whole village (mushā'a land) without stipulating the names of the current holders; the area was divided up afresh every year according to the number of members in each family, with a steady decrease in the area of the individual holding. Much land was left uncultivated because it had not been manured for centuries and the exhausted soil afforded inadequate yields, while the burden of taxation and extortion by the authorities and the tax farmers was heavy.

The enforcement of the *maḥlūl* law, under which cultivable land untitled for three consecutive years escheated to the state, led to the concentration of considerable areas in the hands of the government, which, being unable to cultivate them, leased them to urban capitalists for trivial rents. As a result, extensive stretches were concentrated in the hands of individual rich landowners, the sultan (*Jiftlik* land), the state, and the waqf (Muslim public, state, or religious trust), to which land was often dedicated to avoid taxation. At the end of the 19th century, large estates were owned by the state and the sultan at Beersheba and Beth-Shean and in the Ḥuleh and Jordan valleys; by *effendis* and foreigners in the valley of Jezreel, along the coast, and in various villages, and by village communities, charitable institutions and associations.

Jewish land purchases outside the four "holy cities" of Jerusalem, Hebron, Safed, and Tiberias began in 1855 with the acquisition of 100 dunams (25 acres) of citrus groves near Jaffa by Sir Moses *Montefiore. This was followed by the purchase of land at Moẓa, near Jerusalem, in 1859, at Mulabbas (Petaḥ Tikvah) in 1878, and 'Uyūn Qārā (Rishon le-Zion), Zammārīn (Zikhron Ya'akov), and Jā'ūna (Rosh Pinnah) in 1882. By the end of 1882, 22,000 dunams (5,500 acres) of land, mostly rural, were in Jewish possession. Jews bought much land after 1882, mainly from owners of large estates, and owned 418,000 dunams (104,500 acres) at the outbreak of World War I.

UNDER THE MANDATE. There was no considerable change in land ownership during the war, but, after the Allied occupation and the establishment of British Mandatory rule in 1920, the old Ottoman land registries were reopened and transactions renewed. A special Land Court was established, at first in the north, to expedite determination of ownership on the basis of surveys, documents, and prescriptive rights. With increased Jewish immigration, more land was purchased, still mainly from owners of large estates. By November 1947, when the UN decided on the partition of Palestine, Jews had 1,820,000 dunams (455,000 acres) of land, of which 800,000 dunams (200,000 acres) were owned by the Jewish *National Fund (JNF), 450,000 by the *Palestine Jewish Colonization Association (PICA), and the rest by public and private companies and by individuals.

IN INDEPENDENT ISRAEL. The area of the State of Israel, within the Armistice demarcation lines of 1949, was 20,700,000 dunams. Of these, 425,000 were covered by water and of the remaining 20,255,000 dunams the state owned 17,675,000 dunams; the JNF 800,000 dunams; PICA 450,000; Jewish individuals 510,000 dunams; and Arab individuals 820,000 dunams. State lands included 14,500,000 dunams inherited from the Mandatory government (mostly uncultivable land, e.g., the southern Negev), and 3,175,000 dunams abandoned by Arabs during the *War of Independence.

Under a series of laws enacted in 1950 and 1951, the government lands were vested in the State of Israel and administered by the State Property Office; the abandoned lands were vested in the Custodian of Absentee Property, while their administration was handed over to the Land Development Authority; a third category, lands formerly owned by Germans and seized during World War II by the Custodian of Enemy Property, were handed over to the Administrator General. In 1955, the State Properties Division was set up to administer all lands owned or held by the state. Although this step did away with most of the duplication, there was still the question of the land owned by the JNF. By agreement with the JNF and the Zionist Organization, a single Israel Lands Authority to administer both state and JNF lands was set up in 1960 under the Israel Lands Law and the Israel Lands Authority Law, both passed in the same year. The former, which is one of Israel's basic constitutional laws, lays down the principle that state, Development Authority, and JNF lands shall not be sold, with exceptions specified in the law itself. The Israel Lands Authority Council consists of seven government and six JNF representatives, with the minister of agriculture as chairman. Between May 1948 and June 1967 the JNF acquired about 1,500,000 dunams from the Development Authority and a further few thousand dunams from Arabs. PICA transferred most of its holdings to the farmers in its villages and some 120,000 dunams to the JNF. At the beginning of 1968, the state and the Development Authority owned 16,200,000 dunams and the JNF, 2,570,000 – making up 92% of the country's area. The Muslim waqf and Christian churches held 150,000 dunams and private persons (Jews and Arabs), 1,385,000.

[Joseph Weitz]

LAND RECLAMATION

The reclamation of hilly terrain was practiced in the Land of Israel in ancient times. The viticulturist in the hills of Judea prepared his plot by digging and clearing stones before planting his vines (Isa. 5:2). Clearing stones and terracing occupy an important place in the *halakhot* dealing with land in the Mishnah and Talmud. Dry-stone walls (in mishnaic terminology *gappot* (Pe'ah 6:2); in Arabic *sinsala*) prevented the rain from sweeping the soil away into the lowlands and enabled it to be absorbed where it fell. The hill regions remained fertile as long as the terraces remained intact, but when the country was overrun by Bedouin, the walls were neglected and collapsed, so that the soil was exposed to erosion. As the prophet foretold: "The mountains shall be thrown down, and the steep places (Heb. *madregot* – "steps," or "terraces") shall fall, and every wall shall fall to the ground" (Ezek. 38:20).

In the second half of the 19th century some of the ancient terraces were repaired and new ones built. With the start of Jewish settlement in the 1880s, all types of land reclamation were utilized: swamp drainage by planting eucalyptus trees in Petaḥ Tikvah and Ḥaderah, stone clearing, deep plowing and terracing for vineyards and orchards in Zikhron Ya'akov, Rosh Pinnah, and Moẓa. Under the British Mandate the Jewish National Fund sponsored the drainage of 87,000 acres (350,000 dunams) of swamps in the Jezreel, Zebulun, Ḥefer, and Ḥuleh valleys, and the reclamation of 4,000 acres (16,000 dunams) of hilly terrain. In the same period PICA reclaimed the Kabarah swamp and others totaling 37,500 acres (150,000 dunams), while 22,500 acres (90,000 dunams) were reclaimed by other agencies.

The greater part of the uncultivated area in Israel consists of the Judean and Negev deserts, which support only desert vegetation and cannot be utilized even after reclamation unless supplied with water. Most of the other categories may be reclaimed by mechanical means. Hard soil – stony or rocky – or steep terrains, unfit for cultivation even if the earth between the boulders or under the stony stratum is fertile or sustains useful wild plants, is common in hill regions, of which there are about 1,080,000 acres (4,242,000 dunams), apart from deserts. About 48% of this area is cultivable, but some 550,000 acres (2,200,000 dunams) can be utilized only after reclamation by stone clearing, deep plowing – including removal of boulders, embedded rock, or outcrops (and terracing) and construction of stone revetments along the declivities to form terraces and prevent soil erosion. If the ground still harbors superfluous trees and shrubs, these have to be extirpated. Swampland, waterlogged for the whole or the greater part of the year, cannot be utilized for agriculture without draining. Scrub soil, choked with undesirable wild brush or grasses, requires deep plowing and root clearance. Saline soil, common in the Negev, the Aravah, and the Plain of Jericho, is ameliorated by leaching out the salts, which entails the use of 2,000–3,000 cu. m. of water per dunam. Gullied soil, where the earth has been swept away and eroded by flash floods due to unskilled plowing of the slopes, is common all over the country, in particular in the southern and northern Negev. It may be reclaimed by filling in the gullies, leveling, and channeling to divert flood-water runoff. Unstable or sandy soil, such as the coastal dunes or the loess of the western Negev, may be utilized for intensive irrigated farming after amelioration with green and organic fertilizers.

Since the establishment of the state (up to the end of 1966), the Jewish National Fund has reclaimed 76,250 acres (305,000 dunams) in the hill regions, 11,500 acres (46,000 dunams) in the valleys, and 8,750 acres (35,000 dunams) in the Negev and the Arabah, totaling 96,500 acres (386,000 dunams), while some 3,750 acres (15,000 dunams) were reclaimed under private ownership. The land is utilized for fruit farming, vineyards, extensive cultivation of vegetables, and irrigated crops. It has been estimated by J. Weitz that an area of another 125,000 acres (500,000 dunams) can be reclaimed for agricultural use.

[Joseph Weitz]

BIBLIOGRAPHY: ALIYAH: *Seminar ha-Kibbutzim, Ha-Aliyah ha-Rishonah, Goremeha ha-Ra'yoniyyim ve-ha-Re'aliyyim* (1963); B. Habas, *Sefer ha-Aliyyah ha-Sheniyyah* (1947); D. Giladi, *Ha-Yishuv bi-Tekufat ha-Aliyyah ha-Revi'it, 1924–1929* (1968), incl. bibl.; M. Basok, *Sefer ha-Ma'pilim* (1947); H.M. Sachar, *Aliyah...* (Eng., 1961); J.B. Schechtman, *On Wings of Eagles* (1961); S. Barer, *The Magic Carpet* (1957); idem, *From the Ends of the Earth* (1964); M. Sikron, *Immigration to Israel 1948–1953* (1957). ABSORPTION: S. Sitton, *Israël, immigration et croissance 1948–1958...* (1963); H. Isaacs, *American Jews in Israel* (1967); S.N. Eisenstadt et al. (eds.), *Integration and Development in Israel* (1970), incl. bibl. ALIYAH IN THE 1970S: Ministry of Immigrant Absorption, *Immigrant Absorption – 1977* (February 1978); *Immigrant Absorption – 1978* (May 1979); *Immigrant Absorption – 1979* (May 1980); Institute of Jewish Affairs, *The Decline of Soviet Jewish Emigration in 1980*, Research Report 17 (1980); Central Bureau of Statistics, *Immigration Statistics Quarterly* 10 (January–December 1979). SETTLEMENT. A. Bein, *The Return to the Soil, A History of Jewish Settlement in Israel* (1952) incl. bibl.; A. Ruppin, *The Agricultural Colonization of the Zionist Organization in Palestine* (1926); J. Ben David (ed.), *Agricultural Planning and Village Community* (UNESCO, Arid Zone Research, 23 (1964); R. Weitz and A. Rokach, *Agricultural Development: Planning and Implementation* (1968); R. Weitz, *Darkenu ba-Ḥakla'ut u-va-Hityashevut* (1958). RELIGION AND SETTLEMENT PLANNING: L. Applebaum, L.D. Newman, *Between Village and Suburb: New Settlement Forms in Israel* (in Hebrew; 1989); Y. Golani, S. Elidor, and M. Garon (eds.), *Planning and Housing in Israel in the Wake of Rapid Changes* (1992). **ADD. BIBLIOGRAPHY:** M. Benvenisti, *The West Bank Data Project – A Survey of Israel's Policies* (1984); S.B. Cohen, *Geopolitics of Israel's Border Question* (1980); D. Elazar (ed.), *Judea, Samaria and Gaza: Views on the Present and Future* (1982); E. Karsch (ed.), *From War to Peace, Israel: First Hundred Years* (2000); D. Newman, *The Geopolitics of Peacemaking in Israel – Palestine* (2002); S. Roy, *The Gaza Strip Survey* (1980); E. Efrat, *Geography of Occupation – Judea, Samaria and the Gaza Strip* (2002); E. Cohen, *The City in the Zionist Ideology* (1970); Y. Gradus, *Desert Development* (1985); D. Grossman, *Rural Process-Pattern Relationships: Nomadization, Sedentarization and Settlement Fixation* (1992); M. Hill, *Planning in Turbulence: Urban and Regional Planning in Israel 1948–1977* (1978); A. Rokach, *Rural Settlement in Israel* (1978); D. Weintraub, M. Lissak, and Y. Azmon, *Moshava, Kibbutz and Moshav: Pattern of Jewish Rural Settlement and Development in Palestine* (1969); R. Weitz, *The Lakhish Region, Background Study in Regional Planning* (1978). LAND OWNERSHIP: J. Weitz, *Struggle for the Land* (1950); idem, *Bi-Netivai le-Yishuvah shel ha-Areẓ* (1960); A. Granott, *Land System in Palestine* (1952); idem, *Agrarian Reform and the Record of Israel* (1956); A. Bonné, *State and Economics in the Middle East* (1948). LAND RECLAMATION: J. Weitz, *Struggle for the Land* (1950). PLANNING: J. Dash and E. Efrat, *The Israel Physical Master Plan* (1964); A. Sharon, *Physical Planning in Israel* (1952); E. Brutzkus, *Physical Planning in Israel* (1964); E. Spiegel, *New Towns in Israel* (1967); J. Shuval, *Immigrants on the Threshold* (1963); A. Glikson, *Regional Planning and Development* (1955); M.D. Gouldman, *Legal Aspects of Town Planning in Israel* (1966); First World Congress of Engineers and Architects in Israel 1967, lecture by J. Dash; R. Weitz, *Ha-Kefar ha-Yisre'eli be-Iddan ha-Tekhnologyah* (1967); International Federation for Housing and Planning, *Proceedings of the 27th World Congress for Housing and Planning* (1964). **ADD. BIBLIOGRAPHY:** E. Efrat, *Physical Planning Prospects in Israel During 50 Years of Statehood* (1998); idem, *The New Towns of Israel (1948–1988), a Reappraisal* (1989); U. Benziman, *Jerusalem: City Without a Wall* (1973); M. Momarm and A. Weingrod, *Living Together Separately – Arabs and Jews in Contemporary Jerusalem* (1991); A. Sharoni, *Planning Jerusalem* (1973).

HUMAN GEOGRAPHY

In respect of human as well as of physical geography, it is convenient to divide the Land of Israel into four major units:

(1) the Mediterranean Coastal Plain
(2) the hill regions of northern and central Cisjordan (west of the Jordan)
(3) the Rift Valley of the Jordan River and the Dead Sea
(4) the desert regions of the Negev and the Aravah Valley (which are similar to parts of the Sinai Peninsula).

The great variety in natural features (see Physiography in *Israel, Land of: Geographical Survey) entails profound differences in historical evolution, demography, and economic development.

In the light of present-day economic considerations, the Coastal Plain has clear advantages and the deserts of the south come last for human settlement. Throughout most of history, however, security considerations were paramount in determining population density. In most periods, therefore, the hills were preferred to the lowlands. On the hilltops or the upper slopes, even small villages could hope to defend themselves against superior enemy forces; they used the poorest and rockiest ground, while retaining the better soils in the valleys for farming. Their economy being basically autarkic, they depended little on lines of communication. Settlers were repelled from the Coastal Plain and the large valleys of the interior (the Jezreel, Beth-Shean, and upper Jordan valleys), on the other hand, because the international thoroughfare, the Via Maris, ran through this area and provided foreign armies, which would plunder the inhabitants of any territory through which they passed, access to this region. Moreover, the assiduous hill farmer could build his terraces with primitive tools, make cisterns in which to collect his drinking water in winter and store it all year round, and thus draw a livelihood – albeit meager – from the soil. In many parts of the lowlands, on the other hand, which were covered with dense brush or malarial swamps, superior skill and knowledge were required to prepare the ground for habitation and agriculture and develop sources of fresh water. Consequently, successive generations of conquerors and rulers shifted the center of population and administration alternately between the Cisjordanian hills (west of the Jordan River) and the Coastal Plain. Peoples coming from the land side (i.e., mainly from the east), whose achievements in material civilization were inferior (i.e., Israelites, Arabs, Mamluks, and Turks), generally preferred the hills, while those crossing the sea from the west, possessing technical knowhow and a talent for international commerce, like Phoenicians,

Philistines, Hellenes, Romans, Crusaders, or Jews in modern times, preferred the coast.

Only in periods of peak density and cultural achievement did the sedentary population spill over into the poorest areas – the northern and central Negev, the Lower Jordan Valley, the Aravah Valley, and southern Transjordan. As soon as the regime showed signs of weakness and decline, these regions again became the exclusive domain of the Bedouin nomad. The border between the desert and the arable land, though basically determined by climatic variations, oscillated violently with the interplay of human factors. Border peasants, protected by a strong central power, could extend their holdings over marginal lands in the transition zone, and governments sometimes settled active or demobilized soldiers to farm desert outposts. The nomads, on the other hand – dependent on the same transition zone for grazing in the dry season – awaited every opportunity to harass the farmers, tear down the fences and destroy homes, and cut trees for firewood or burn them down to use the ground for pasture. If they met no effective resistance, they penetrated ever deeper into the settled area. It happened repeatedly, however (as in the case of the Israelites), that intruding nomads or semi-nomads gradually became tillers of the soil themselves and later found it necessary to repel fresh Bedouin onslaughts.

As the country lies on the crossroads of three continents and two oceans, its population was in constant flux. Multitudes came and went, not only in the wake of historical events (e.g., the entry of the Israelites, the Muslim-Arab conquest, the Crusaders, or modern Jewish immigration), but even in periods when large-scale movements were hardly in evidence. Thus, for example, Egyptians may be supposed to have settled in considerable numbers during the first half of the 19th century, under the rule of Muhammad Ali. Under the British Mandate, there was again a substantial, though unrecorded and uncontrolled, immigration of Arabs overland from Transjordan, the Hauran, Egypt, etc.

Fundamental changes in the country's population were brought about not only by migration but, perhaps on an even larger scale, by the assumption of new national, religious, or linguistic identities on the part of entire sections of the population. Most of the Philistines, for example, seem to have been gradually absorbed into the Canaanite population, which, in turn, was largely Hellenized after the conquest of Alexander the Great. In both the First and Second Temple periods, a considerable part of the pagan population may be assumed to have adopted Judaism. The nascent Christian faith attracted followers among both pagans and Jews, and the process of conversion was accelerated when Christianity became the Roman, and then the Byzantine, state religion. A solid rural Jewish population existed for centuries, however, during the Roman and Byzantine periods, particularly in Galilee and Judea. While the early Arab rulers did little to promote the adoption of Islam by the indigenous population, Islamization spread before and after the Crusades, which led not so much to conversion to Christianity as to a fierce competition between the various Christian denominations. The group most strongly affected by developments from the early Middle Ages was the Samaritans; once prominent in the central areas, they dwindled to some 400 by the middle of the 20th century. Conversion to Islam, which seems to have engulfed the bulk of the remaining autochthonous Jews from the seventh century, continued among both Samaritans and Christians into the 19th century and later. Of the present Christian population, the majority speak Arabic and regard themselves as Arabs.

Distribution of the Population

After Israel's War of Independence (1948) and the signing of armistice agreements with its neighbors, the State of Israel measured 7,993 sq. mi. (20,700 sq. km.), of which 7,821 sq. mi. (20,255 sq. km.) constituted land surface. East Jerusalem, with an area of 24 sq. mi. (70 sq. km.) was reunited with the rest of the city after the Six-Day War (1967). The areas that came under Israel administration in June 1967 total 26,476 sq. mi. (68,589 sq. km.): the Golan Heights 444 sq. mi. (1,150 sq. km.); Judea-Samaria (the "West Bank"), with the districts of Jenin, Nablus, Tulkarm, Ramallah, Jordan Valley, Bethlehem, and Hebron, 2,270 sq. mi. (5,878 sq. km.); the Gaza Strip 140 sq. mi. (363 sq. km.), and Sinai 23,622 sq. mi. (61,198 sq. km.), with the districts of north Sinai, central Sinai, and Merḥav Shelomoh (the Sharm el-Sheikh region). The entire area governed by Israel from June 1967 thus totaled 34,493 sq. mi. (89,359 sq. km.).

The emergence of the State of Israel led to far-reaching changes in the geographical distribution of the Arabs. With few exceptions, they left those parts of the Coastal Plain, the Foothills and Hills of Judea, the Manasseh Hills, the Ḥuleh and Beth-Shean valleys, etc. that were occupied by Israel forces in 1948–49, and most of the Negev Bedouin left the region when it finally came into Israel hands. In Galilee, however, a considerable part of the non-Jewish population, particularly Druze and Christians, remained, while a larger number of Muslims left. In the small areas added to Israeli territory in 1949 in accordance with the Armistice Agreement with Jordan – notably the east rim of the Sharon Plain and the Iron Valley and Hills – the entire Muslim population remained. Consequently, Upper and Lower Galilee, the Iron Valley and Hills, and the eastern Sharon Plain constitute the main centers of Arab and Druze population inside the pre-1967 armistice lines; to these, East Jerusalem was added after the Six-Day War. Of the 36,800 Bedouin in Israel, most lived in the Arad region east and northeast of Beersheba.

At the end of 1969, the overall population density amounted to 371.9 per sq. mi. (143.6 per sq. km.) as compared with 111.6 per sq. mi. (43.1 per sq. km.) in 1948. As in most countries in the 20th century, rapid urbanization took place. Of Israel's population, 82.5% (89.2% of its Jews) were inhabitants of 26 towns and 50 other urban communities; of the 2,397,200 town dwellers, 2,215,500 were Jews and 181,700 non-Jews. The categories termed "large" and "small" villages, totaling 154, included 98 Arab villages and 56 Jewish moshavot or villages of similar form; the former had 201,800 and the latter 53,300 inhabitants. The 349 moshavim, with 122,700 inhabitants, constituted the largest Jewish rural group, followed by the 230 kibbutzim, with 84,400. There were 22 moshavim shittufiyyim, with 5,200, and 46 farms, institutions, and schools with 12,500. There was a preponderance of moshavim in comprehensive regional settlement areas (e.g., Lachish, Taanach, and Merḥavim) and a concentration of kibbutzim in the Jordan-Yarmuk (Kinneret), Ḥuleh, Beth-Shean, and Harod valleys and in areas near the pre-1967 borders. Of the 26 cities and towns, 18 were exclusively Jewish, two (Nazareth and Shepharam) exclusively non-Jewish, and six others (Jerusalem, Tel Aviv-Jaffa, Haifa, Acre, Ramleh, Lydda) were mainly Jewish but had non-Jewish minorities. Inside the pre-1967 armistice lines, Israel had a total of 877 settled places, 76 urban and 801 rural.

Although the geographer's "law of the primate city" (the tendency of the largest city in a country or region to overdevelop at the expense of the remote areas) is at work in Israel, as in other modern countries, planning and development have succeeded to some extent in counteracting the overriding attraction of the metropolis and influencing the distribution of the Jewish population. In 1936, 78% of Palestine's Jewish population lived in the central part of the Coastal Plain, between Haifa in the north and Gederah in the south; 12% in Jerusalem and the Judean Hills; 9.6% in Galilee and the interior valleys; and only 0.4% in the Negev. This compares with an estimated 63% for the central Coastal Plain in 1968; 9.5% in Jerusalem and the Judean Hills; 11.5% in the South and the Negev (Ashkelon and Beersheba sub-districts); 10% in the northern district; and an estimated 7% in those parts of the Haifa, Ḥaderah, Ramleh, and Reḥovot sub-districts lying outside the Coastal Plain or south of Gederah. After the Six-Day War there was also a steady increase in the growth of the Jewish population in Jerusalem.

In 2002 the main part of Israel's population was concentrated in the districts lying along the coastal strip. Over the years the dispersion of population reached the peripheral areas of the country, while the changes in the rate of dispersion occurred mainly in the Jewish population.

In 2002, 21.5% of the Jewish population lived in the Tel Aviv District; 26.7% in the Central District comprising the central lowlands; 10% in the Northern District lowlands; 14.8% in the South; 11.9% in the Haifa District, and 10.8% in the Jerusalem District.

The period after 1967 was characterized by the rapid settlement of the administered territories in Judea, Samaria, and the Gaza Strip, the establishment of such new towns as *Ariel, *Ma'aleh Adumim, and Efrat, and the building of many new neighborhoods in Greater Jerusalem. Another noteworthy feature was the mass immigration of Russian Jews to Israel in the 1990s and their rapid absorption in all parts of the country.

The Coastal Plain

The lowland strip along the Mediterranean shore is geologically the youngest part of the country. The shoreline is mainly straight with a few promontories and indentations, notably Jaffa Hill; a stretch of the Carmel coast between Dor and Athlit, with diminutive bays and headlands; the slightly protruding Carmel cape at the mountain's northern extremity; and Haifa Bay further north. The straight course of the shoreline is unfavorable to the construction of anchorages and ports and has, through most of the country's history, given little encouragement to the development of seafaring and fisheries. The Coastal Plain narrows gradually from 25 mi. (40 km.) wide in the south (at the latitude of Gaza) to 9–12 mi. (15–20 km.) in the Sharon, a few hundred meters in the northern Carmel coast, and 2.5–3 mi. (4–5 km.) in the Acre Plain south of Rosh ha-Nikrah. It is crossed by numerous watercourses, of which the majority are ephemeral. Of the few perennial ones, the Yarkon River carries the most water. Sands thrown up by the sea form a belt of coastal dunes obstructing the outlet of watercourses and contributing to the forming of swamps, principally in the Sharon and Zebulun valleys, which finally disappeared in the 20th century with intensive Jewish settlement and drainage work. The most characteristic soil of the central Coastal Plain is the "red sand," which combines a coarse, porous texture, easily drained and aerated, with adequate mineral content; it is best suited to the cultivation of the local "Jaffa" orange. Toward the south and Negev, it has an admixture of loess, which is concealed over certain stretches beneath a cover – generally thin – of arid dune sand. The eastern Sharon, the Carmel Coast, and the Acre Plain have mostly heavier soils, and parts of the Zebulun Valley are characterized by black swamp soil.

The climate of the Coastal Plain is influenced by the sea, which reduces temperature spans between day and night and summer and winter. Relative humidity is generally high; in built-up areas, like Tel Aviv, it is an irritant on hot summer days. Annual precipitation increases in general, from south to north: rainfall ranges from 4–6 in. (100–150 mm.) at the southern end of the Gaza Strip to 20–24 in. (500–600 mm.) in the Sharon, the Carmel Coast, and the Zebulun Valley, and somewhat more in the Acre Plain. With the exception of its Negev and Sinai sections, the Coastal Plain forms part of the lowland type of the Mediterranean vegetation zone.

The Coastal Plain, which was prosperous during the period of the Crusades, was laid waste by the Mamluk ruler Baybars to prevent any further Crusader invasions. Of the seaports, all but Jaffa and Acre ceased to exist, and even these retained only a fraction of their former importance. Paradoxically, the destruction was worst in those parts enjoying a relatively humid climate, where impenetrable brush and malarial swamp spread quickly, providing hideouts for highway robbers. At the end of the 18th century, conditions reached their nadir.

From the beginning of the 19th century, villages situated near the western rim of the hills began to cultivate lands in the adjoining plain, and even hill peasants from more remote villages ventured out into the lowlands, at first staying only during the sowing and harvesting seasons but later transforming their temporary huts into permanent dwellings. These became daughter settlements of hill villages and often bore the same names, with the Arabic words *nazla* ("descent" – from the hills) or *khirba* ("ruined place" or "outpost") attached. At approximately the same time, new villages, which supposedly drew many of their inhabitants from Egypt, came into being in the southern Coastal Plain. Jaffa, too, began to expand again, serving as the country's only port for, inter alia, renewed Christian and Jewish pilgrimages. Orange and other fruit groves were planted in the town's immediate neighborhood; Sir Moses Montefiore's aid to the Jewish community included the planting of a citrus grove near Jaffa (today Tel Aviv's Montefiore quarter). In the second half of the 19th and the beginning of the 20th century, the German *Templer colonies were founded, mostly in the Coastal Plain (Sarona near Jaffa, Wilhelma near Lydda, and Neuhardthof and the German Colony near Haifa).

A new era in the history of the area opened with the establishment of the Mikveh Israel farming school in 1870. Then came the attempt by "old *yishuv*" families from Jerusalem to set up Petaḥ Tikvah in 1878 and, finally, from 1882 onward, the founding of the first modern settlements by Jewish pioneers from abroad: Rishon le-Zion, Nes Ẓiyyonah, Gederah and Mazkeret Batyah south and southeast of Jaffa; the new site of Petaḥ Tikvah northeast of the town; and Zikhron Ya'akov on Mt. Carmel north of the Sharon. In the 1890s followed the establishment of Reḥovot and Ḥaderah, and the tentative erection of two settlements further south (Be'er Toviyyah and Ruḥamah). The transition from grain to fruit farming and the larger openings for hired labor entailed therein increased the capacity of the Coastal Plain moshavot to absorb Jewish newcomers, but also stimulated a large-scale migration of Arabs from the hills – and even from beyond the country's borders – and the quick expansion of Arab villages in the area.

In the first decade of the 20th century, citrus groves were planted in the veteran moshavot of the Coastal Plain and Jewish workers' quarters, some of them with auxiliary farm holdings, were established to absorb immigrants from Yemen and elsewhere (Naḥalat Yehudah near Rishon le-Zion; Tirat Shalom, Sha'arayim, and others near Reḥovot; Maḥaneh Yehudah near Petaḥ Tikvah; Naḥali'el near Ḥaderah). The network of villages began to spread in the southern Sharon (Kefar Sava, Kefar Malal, and others). Parallel with this was the accelerated growth of Jaffa, where a sizable Jewish community took root. The Palestine Office of the Zionist Organization opened there under Arthur Ruppin in 1908, and Tel Aviv was founded as a suburb of Jaffa in 1909. On a more modest scale, Haifa took on an urban character: the Hadar ha-Carmel quarter was founded, and the Jewish community of the city began to grow.

In the years following World War I, the settlement network became closer in the southern Sharon (renewal of Kefar Sava, founding of Herzliyyah, Ra'anannah, etc.), the citrus groves expanded, and Tel Aviv became a town on its own. In the beginning of the 1930s a continuous chain of Jewish villages was already in existence in the Sharon, thanks to the acquisition (in 1927/28) of the Ḥefer Plain by the Jewish National Fund (JNF), which had also purchased parts of the Zebulun Valley (Haifa Bay area) and prepared the latter's development according to a master plan, dividing it into industrial, residential, and agricultural zones.

This was followed by the establishment of numerous kibbutzim and moshavim in the Sharon and the Rishon le-Zion–Gederah area, as well as the first Jewish foothold in the Acre Plain (Nahariyyah, 1934; Shavei Zion, 1938). The Petaḥ Tikvah–Ḥaderah road, completed in 1936, was the first fairly long communications line running through an area inhabited exclusively by Jews. Tel Aviv and Haifa became the country's largest cities. The port of Haifa was opened in 1934, and Tel Aviv was permitted to construct an anchorage when the Arab riots paralyzed Jaffa port in 1936. At the same time, the Arab villages in the Coastal Plain, particularly those in the Jaffa-Lydda area, expanded further, thanks to the prosperity brought by Jewish settlement activity. Tulkarm and Qalqīlya, on the eastern border of the Sharon, as well as Majdal (Ashkelon) in the south, became small towns.

The founding of Negbah in 1939 heralded settlement in the southern Coastal Plain and the northern Negev, which was pursued throughout World War II and the 1946/47 struggle with the British authorities; Dorot, Nir Am, Gevaram, Yad Mordekhai and other outposts came into being, and another kibbutz, Beror Ḥayil, was set up in May 1948 during a War of Independence battle on the site. With few exceptions (e.g., Fureidis near Zikhron Ya'akov and al-Mazra'a near Nahariyyah), the Arab villages in the Coastal Plain were abandoned in the 1948 war, generally even before Israel forces occupied them. On the other hand, the population stayed on in the Arab villages of the eastern Sharon (al-Ṭīra, Ṭayyiba, Jiljiliya, Qalansawa, etc.), which became Israel territory in 1949, following the Armistice Agreement with Jordan. At the end of the War of Independence, few Arabs remained in former Arab towns (Acre, Ramleh, Lydda, Majdal) and mixed towns (Jaffa, Haifa), where Jewish immigrants were housed from the end of 1948.

After 1949, several veteran moshavot in the Coastal Plain (Rishon le-Zion, Reḥovot, Petaḥ Tikvah, Netanyah, Ḥaderah, Nahariyyah) acquired city status. New villages, mostly moshavim, were set up in all parts of the area, especially in the Acre Plain, the eastern rim of the Sharon, the Lydda Plain, and the Southern Plain. Settlement in the latter region expanded further, mainly eastward, with the implementation of the Lachish regional development project from 1954. From the middle 1950s, a number of development towns were erected, particularly in the south (Kiryat Gat, Kiryat Malakhi, Sederot, etc.). Simultaneously, the Tel Aviv region became Israel's major conurbation.

In the 1960s Ashdod, Israel's second Mediterranean port, was founded and quickly expanded on the sand dunes near the mouth of Naḥal Lachish. Similarly, other Coastal Plain cities and towns progressed, some reaching populations of 50,000 and over. The population of the Tel Aviv conurbation, together with the "outer ring," exceeded 1,000,000 in 1970.

After 1967 industry and services expanded still further in the Coastal Plain. Haifa and Ashdod ports and Ben-Gurion Airport attained record turnovers. All these entailed a further concentration of population and a further steep increase in population density. At the end of 2002, the inhabitants of the districts lying within the Coastal Plain (including parts of Haifa on Mt. Carmel) numbered nearly 4,648,000, approximately 70% of the total population within the pre-1967 borders. The Tel Aviv conurbation and, to a lesser degree, the Haifa conurbation have naturally formed the major attraction for immigration and internal migration. At the same time, however, there has been a slight but constant displacement of the population center toward the south since the early 1950s. This is due not only to the speedy growth of Beersheba (see below), but also to the successful planning and development of Ashdod, Ashkelon, and smaller urban centers in the southern Coastal Plain and to the sound foundations laid for farming villages.

In 2002 the Coastal Plain was the most densely settled and intensively utilized agricultural region of Israel, and an outstanding example of the impact of agrotechnical changes and the evolution of a region. The most striking changes in land use came through urbanization, mainly after 1967. The most marked urban development took place in rural settlements which also included a stretch of coastline: Ḥaderah, Netanyah, Herzliyyah, and Tel Aviv. Almost all other former agricultural moshavot have become towns based on services and industries, such as Pardes Ḥannah, Ra'anannah, Kefar Sava, and Ramat ha-Sharon.

THE SOUTHERN PLAIN (NEGEV COASTAL PLAIN AND PHILISTINE PLAIN). The Southern Plain extends from the mouth of Naḥal Lachish to the south and southwest to merge, almost imperceptibly, with the Sinai coastal area. In the east, it borders on the southern Judean foothills and, in the southeast, on the Beersheba depression, where again, the transition is hardly noticeable. The parts lying within the pre-1967 borders cover an area of some 560 sq. mi. (1,450 sq. km.), whereas the Gaza Strip measures 140 sq. mi. (363 sq. km.). Of all sections of the Coastal Plain, this has experienced the most thorough transformation since 1948.

The population of the Gaza Strip at least tripled when it was flooded by refugees late in 1948. At the end of 2003, the Strip's sub-districts of Gaza and Khan Yunis had about 1.2 million inhabitants. It had the extremely high population density of 8,262 per sq. mi. (3,305 per sq. km.). The Ashkelon sub-district, evacuated by practically all its Arab inhabitants in the wake of the same events, has been covered by a network of 101 Jewish villages, towns, and cities; it has grown faster in population and density than any other area in Israel, with the exception of the northwestern part of the Beersheba sub-district. Its population rose from 7,200 (4,800 Jews and 2,400 non-Jews) in November 1948 to 426,800 (393,400 Jews and 33,400 non-Jews) at the end of 2002 and the population density of the sub-district increased from 14.0 per sq. mi. (5.8 per sq. km.) to 830.2 per sq. mi. (372.1 per sq. km.).

Concurrently, land use underwent profound changes in the Gaza Strip and the rest of the South, as irrigated fruit orchards and garden and field crops replaced dry farming. While in the Gaza Strip this entailed the drilling of numerous, mostly shallow wells and the over-exploitation of the groundwater table, in the Ashkelon sub-district and the northwestern Negev it was the regional Yarkon-Negev pipeline and, later, the National Water Carrier that made intensification of agriculture possible. In the Gaza Strip and the western part of the Ashkelon district, which have lighter soils, citrus groves took the lead. On the heavier soils further inland, particularly in the central and eastern parts of the Lachish region, preference is given to irrigated field crops (cotton, sugar beets, fodder plants, etc.). In the southernmost reaches (Sha'ar ha-Negev and the Eshkol development region), out-of-season export vegetables and flowers, which are favored by mild winters, have become important since the late 1960s. There were 39 Jewish villages in the northwestern part of the Beersheba district (the Besor region, part of which belongs geographically to the Coastal Plain) and 102 in the Ashkelon district. Most are moshavim, although kibbutzim are preponderant in the zone next to the Gaza Strip. Comprehensive regional planning, facilitated in the Southern Plain by the extensive areas abandoned in 1948, is characterized by clusters of villages around regional centers, which in turn depend on regional towns (Sederot, Kiryat Gat, Kiryat Malakhi). These towns also introduced industry based generally on farm produce. The oil wells of the Ḥeleẓ-Beror Ḥayil area introduced an additional feature (see Oil and Gas in *Israel, State of: Economic Affairs). Ashkelon (founded 1948) and Ashdod (founded 1955) became the sites of large and middle-sized industrial plants. The economic pivot of Ashdod is its port. Ashkelon has also developed recreation and tourism. The erection of the terminal of the large oil pipeline at Ashkelon and the refineries, whose construction began in 1970 at Ashdod, herald a quickened urbanization process in the South.

The 21 Jewish settlements of the *Gush Katif group in the Gaza Strip, established between the early 1970s and the 1990s and reaching a population of around 8,000, were dismantled in August 2005 following an Israeli government decision to withdraw from the area.

JUDEAN PLAIN. The term Judean Plain may be applied to the section lying between a line running east from the mouth of Naḥal Lachish and the bed of the Yarkon River. Together with those parts of the Tel Aviv district and Petaḥ Tikvah sub-district, which, lying north of the Yarkon River belong geographically to the Sharon area, it measures 310 sq. mi. (about 800 sq. km.). It includes the Tel Aviv district, the Reḥovot and Petaḥ Tikvah sub-districts, and most of the Ramleh sub-district. This region was the scene of the earliest modern Jewish settlement (Mikveh Israel, Petaḥ Tikvah, Rishon le-Zion, etc.). Today most of it is occupied by the Tel Aviv conurbation (Tel Aviv-Jaffa, Ramat Gan, Ḥolon, Bat Yam, Bene Berak, Givatayim) and its outer ring (Rishon le-Zion, Reḥovot,

Ramleh, Lydda, Petaḥ Tikvah, etc.). In 2000 it had over 2 million inhabitants in 154 settled places, more than one-third of the country's population. The population density at the end of 2002 was 3,600 per sq. mi. (1,440 per sq. km.). Thanks to a rich groundwater table and the light "red sands" prevalent in the southern and southwestern parts, this is one of the main centers of Israel's citriculture. On the heavier soils between Lydda and Petaḥ Tikvah there are citrus groves and other intensive crops, largely of the truck-farming type. The Judean Plain contains over half of Israel's industrial enterprises as well as the country's most dense communications network. Planning efforts in this area aim largely at preventing it from becoming one shapeless "megalopolis" and preserving a neat separation between residential, commercial, industrial, agricultural, and recreational zones, permitting the cities within the conurbation to merge, with time, into one single social and economic unit, but guarding the independence of the towns in the "outer ring." It is thus intended to keep commuting within reasonable limits and not to complicate the grave traffic problems even further.

The wide areas of the Judean Plain served as the largest receiving ground for new immigrant settlers. They facilitated the adoption of new planning principles which found their successful expression in the Lakhish Planning Region, a model of integrated rural and regional planning which was later adopted in other regions of Israel.

The development towns in the south were created and planned according to the policy of population dispersal. The largest town is Ashdod, which became the central town of the Judean Plain. Ashkelon developed on the abandoned Arab township of Majdal and became an industrial town beside its natural park and resort areas. Minor development towns were developed as intermediate links in the urban hierarchy of the region, such as Kiryat Gat, Yavne, and Kiryat Mal'akhi.

SHARON. The Sharon, extending from the Yarkon River north to Naḥal Tanninim, is Israel's foremost farming area. Administratively, it includes the Sharon sub-district and most of the Ḥaderah sub-district, as well as the northern part of the Petaḥ Tikvah sub-district. The Sharon measures about 330 sq. mi. (860 sq. km.). It has 155 settled places and 267,900 inhabitants (including 11 Arab villages with 70,000 inhabitants), and the population density is 2,423.2 per sq. mi. (969.3 per sq. km.). The western halves of all three sub-districts are characterized by light "red sands," particularly favorable to citriculture, while in the east heavier soils prevail. Water supply is ample throughout the region. The southernmost reaches are included in the Tel Aviv conurbation (Herzliyyah, Ramat ha-Sharon, North Tel Aviv) and its outer ring (Ra'anannah, Kefar Sava, etc.). Netanyah is the urban center for the central Sharon and Ḥaderah for the north. A dense network of Jewish rural agglomerations – mostly moshavim and moshavot, with a smaller number of kibbutzim – covers most of the Sharon. The eastern rim, however, on both sides of the pre-1967 armistice lines, has a predominantly Arab population. Ṭayyiba is the largest village within the former borders, while the towns of Tulkarm and Qalqilya lie beyond them. Besides farming enterprises based exclusively on citrus and villages combining citrus with truck farming (vegetables, dairy cattle, poultry), there are also farms geared to special export crops, such as flowers. There are industrial plants in the major towns and moshavot, as well as in the kibbutzim. Tourism and recreation are catered to by towns and villages near the coast.

CARMEL COAST REGION. Administratively, most of this narrow, elongated area belongs to the Ḥaderah sub-district. With an area of 29 sq. mi. (76 sq. km.), it has 67 settled places (54 Jewish and 13 Arab) with 309,500 inhabitants (including 134,800 non-Jews), and a population density of 1,401 per sq. mi. (541.0 per sq. km.). The region has the advantages of fertile, mostly heavy, alluvial soil and an abundant groundwater reserve, not only facilitating fully irrigated farming but also leaving a water surplus, which is diverted to other parts of the country. In addition to citrus groves, vineyards, deciduous fruit, and field, fodder, and garden crops, there are banana plantations, which benefit from the mild winters and, particularly, from the wind shelter provided by the wall-like slope of Mt. Carmel rising in the east. In addition to 13 Jewish and two Arab villages, a number of settlements on Mt. Carmel (e.g., Bet Oren, Ma'yan Ẓevi) cultivate fields in the Carmel Coastal region. Athlit is the principal agglomeration. The northernmost part, with Tirat Karmel, belongs to the Haifa conurbation.

HAIFA BAY AREA (ZEBULUN VALLEY). Mt. Carmel in the southwest, the Tivon-Shepharam Hills in the southeast, and the hills of Lower Galilee in the east clearly delineate this valley; in the north, the Acre-Aḥihud highway is a recognizable border. It covers an area of some 90 sq. mi. (230 sq. km.). Administratively, its southern part belongs to the Haifa district and the northern one to the Acre sub-district. This area was the object of the first regional planning effort, undertaken with the aid of the British town planner, Patrick Abercrombie, at the end of the 1920s and the beginning of the 1930s, which determined its present physical and habitational characteristics. The coastline was largely transformed by the construction of Haifa port, and later, of the Kishon port. The original partition into an industrial zone in the south, a residential zone – the *kerayot* (pl. of *kiryah*, "township") – in the center, and agricultural area in the north, with further farming land in the eastern part of the region, has been superseded by the expansion of the Haifa-Acre conurbation. One industrial zone stretches from Kishon port, near the southeast corner of Haifa Bay, southeastward to Nesher, along the foot of Mt. Carmel; a second has developed north of the *kerayot* zone, extending along the shore to the southern approaches of Acre and including the "Steel City" complex; Kiryat Ata in the east forms a third industrial nucleus. The residential zone of the "*kerayot*" (Kiryat Ḥayyim, which is within Haifa's municipal boundaries, Kiryat Yam, Kiryat Motzkin, and Kiryat Bialik) has expanded considerably northward, particularly on the east side of the

Haifa-Acre highway, thus leaving to agriculture only the easternmost and southeastern sections of the region, with Jewish villages (Kefar Masaryk, Afek, Kefar ha-Maccabi, Yagur, etc.) and Arab centers (Shepharam, etc.). The Haifa Bay area is Israel's primary center of heavy industry. Agriculture includes intensive field and garden crops. This is the only section of the Coastal Plain where citrus is not grown (see *Haifa).

Within the industrial zone there exists a certain functional differentiation. The old industrial zone between the main and Kishon harbor includes the old Shemen table and cooking oil factory, the power stations, and gas installations. To the east is the area of the chemical and petrochemical industries based on the oil refineries.

The residential quarters have spread out in all directions, while the most important development was in the west towards Bat Gallim, Kiryat Eliyahu, and Kiryat Eliezer.

Owing to the proximity of the Bay and Mount Carmel, Haifa is one of the most beautiful towns of the Mediterranean and in addition enjoys a pleasant climate on the top of Mount Carmel and a diversity of landscape which is matched by a diversity of functions.

ACRE PLAIN. The Acre Plain extends from the Acre-Aḥihud highway north to Rosh ha-Nikrah and the Ḥanitah-Adamit ridge. In the east, the limestone hills of Upper Galilee rise in stark contrast to the fertile, intermediate-to-heavy soil cover of the Plain which, measuring about 45 sq. mi. (some 120 sq. km.), is included in the Acre sub-district. In addition to Acre, Nahariyyah exercises administrative and economic functions as a second center of this region. Apart from highly intensive and almost fully irrigated farming, recreation facilities are important in the region's economy. Industry is principally based on the two towns. There are 17 Jewish and nine non-Jewish villages and the development town Shelomi.

THE HILLS. At least half of Israel's area within the pre-1967 armistice borders, and over 60% of Cisjordan, have a hilly or mountainous topography. Elevations reach 3,380 ft. (1,035 m.) in the Negev (Mt. Ramon), 3,350 ft. (1,020 m.) in Judea (Mt. Ḥalḥul), 3,085 ft. (940 m.) in Samaria (Mt. Ebal), 3,963 ft. (1,208 m.) in Galilee (Mt. Meron), and, outside Israel-held territory, 9,233 ft. (2,814 m.) at the peak of the Hermon block. Apart from the Negev, the hill region proper includes Judea in the south, Samaria in the center, and Galilee in the north. The transition from Judea to Samaria is gradual, but Galilee is clearly separated from Samaria by the tectonic valleys of Jezreel and Ḥarod. The characteristic soil of limestone areas is the reddish-brown, relatively heavy and fertile "terra rossa." The chalk hills have mostly rendzina soils of paler hues which, although inherently poorer, are friable and easy to till; on valley bottoms, they are often enriched with organic matter. Erosion runoff has always been the central problem of hill farming. The streambeds are dry in summer and even in winter carry water only occasionally after heavy rain.

The hill climate differs, generally, from that of the Coastal Plain in sharper temperature differences between day and night and, mainly on hilltops, in perceptibly cooler winters, although even there the summer heat is equal to that of the lowlands, and the *sharav* (ḥamsin) is even more oppressive. Humidity is generally lower in the hills, except in midwinter, and evaporation stronger, but rainfall on the western side of the hills is superior to that on the Coastal Plain. Snow falls in Jerusalem and Hebron on the average once in two or three years, and in the highest parts of Upper Galilee nearly every year, although, as a rule, it remains on the ground for a few hours only. In contrast, the eastern side of the hills descending to the Jordan rift lies in the rain shadow, but the arid zone in Samaria is much narrower than in Judea, and on Galilee's eastern slopes rainfall is everywhere above 16 in. (400 mm.) per year. Deforestation has left few remnants of the original plant cover, belonging to the hill type of the Mediterranean vegetation zone. The eastern side of Judea (the Judean Desert, Wilderness of Judah) and of Samaria belong partly to the Irano-Turanian dry-steppe zone and partly to the Saharo-Arabian desert zone. Of the hill regions west of the Jordan – Judea, Samaria, and Galilee – the lower parts (Shephelah, northern Samaria, Lower Galilee), with their broader intermontane valleys, deeper soils, and easier thoroughfares, have been better endowed for settlement since antiquity than the higher reaches (Judean Hills, southern Samaria, Upper Galilee).

Since the late 18th century, Christian churches and monasteries erected in the hills have contributed to the progress of farming, at least in their immediate neighborhood (e.g., Ein Kerem near Jerusalem, Bi'r Zayt in southern Samaria, Kafr Kannā in Lower Galilee), as well as to the importance of towns sacred to Christianity (Bethlehem, Nazareth). In the 19th century, earthquakes caused ravages at Safed, Tiberias, and Nablus, but in the long run did not impede a certain amount of growth in these centers, paralleling that of other towns in the hills and on their outskirts (Hebron, Ramallah, Tulkarm). For Jerusalem, a new chapter began when Jews and non-Jews founded new quarters outside the city walls. At the end of the 19th century, however, the hills began to cede their dominant position to the Coastal Plain. Although emissaries of early Jewish pioneer groups tried to acquire land for settlement near Hebron and elsewhere in the hills, they were soon discouraged by the high prices of land, the unavailability of sizable holdings, and the restricted possibility of farming on European models. Of the three small Jewish hill settlements established before 1899 – Moẓa, Ein Zeitim, and Hartuv – the two latter existed only intermittently.

A new phase opened in the first decade of the 20th century, when the *Jewish Colonization Association (ICA) founded grain-farming villages in eastern Lower Galilee (Ilaniyyah, Yavne'el, Kefar Tavor, etc.). A few private villages (Mizpah, etc.) were established and a training farm opened at Kefar Ḥittim on JNF land. All these villages, like their few predecessors in the hills, did not develop satisfactorily. Kiryat Anavim, a kibbutz founded in 1920 west of Jerusalem, made the first steps toward modernization of hill farming, and two more small villages, Atarot and Neveh Ya'akov, were set up north of Jerusalem. The next hill settlement, Kefar ha-Ḥoresh, was founded only in 1935 west of Nazareth.

Three out of the four traditional "holy cities," all of them in the Hills, suffered setbacks in the 1930s. The old Jewish community of Hebron ceased to exist after the 1929 Arab riots; the Safed community gradually dwindled; and that of Tiberias stagnated. Only Jerusalem's Jewish population increased vigorously in that period.

Hill outposts were finally established on a planned basis and on a larger scale as *stockade and watchtower settlements: from 1937 in the Manasseh Hills (Ein ha-Shofet, Daliyyah, etc.), with the aim of creating a "settlement bridge" between the Sharon and the Jezreel Valley; in eastern Lower Galilee (Sharonah, Kefar Kisch, etc.), to strengthen the existing network of villages; and, since 1938, near the Lebanese border in western Upper Galilee (Ḥanitah, Eilon, etc.). In the Judean Hills, Kiryat Anavim was joined, in 1938, by Ma'aleh ha-Ḥamishah and, in 1946, by Neveh Ilan. The Eẓyon Bloc was established in the Hebron Hills between 1943 and 1947, but was destroyed in the 1948 War of Independence, when Neveh Ya'akov and Atarot also had to be evacuated. While the 1947 UN partition map allocated practically all the hill regions to the proposed Arab state (with the exception of a narrow strip of eastern Galilee, Mt. Carmel, and part of the Manasseh Hills), the 1949 armistice borders added to Israel the rest of Galilee and the Manasseh Hills, the Jerusalem Corridor, and most of the Shephelah, as well as part of the Iron Hills.

Energetic settlement activity started at the end of 1948 in the Jerusalem Corridor and, to a lesser degree, in Galilee. To overcome the particular difficulties of hill settlement, which requires large investments in land reclamation in the initial stage and a long period of waiting until farming becomes remunerative, the JNF established work villages. Afforestation was carried out on a large scale, transforming the landscape and providing initial or supplementary employment to new settlers in the Hills. In 1955, the development of the Adullam region, south of the Jerusalem Corridor, was commenced as an extension of the Lachish region, and in 1963 another development program was launched in central and northern Galilee. Of the relatively few development towns built in the hills, not all expanded as anticipated. In Galilee, Ma'alot struggled hard to overcome its difficulties and attract industry, while the hope of turning Shelomi into a growing urban center was practically given up. Naẓerat Illit (Upper Nazareth) and Migdal ha-Emek, on the other hand, succeeded after initial hardships, and the progress of Karmi'el, slow until 1967, accelerated after the Six-Day War. Similarly, Beth-Shemesh in the Judean Hills, for a long time problematic, made some progress only after sizable industrial plants were established there in the late 1960s. Of the ancient towns in Galilee, Safed and Tiberias regained their original population figures soon after the flight of their Arab inhabitants, but further growth was slow after the early 1950s. Nazareth, which hardly suffered in the War of Independence, greatly improved its economic situation in the State of Israel and became its primary Arab center. There were record increases (averaging 4% and more annually) in the population of the Arab hill villages of Galilee and the Iron Hills, which greatly broadened their economic foundation.

JUDEA. The parts of the region west of the 1949 armistice lines belong to the Jerusalem, Ramleh, Ashkelon, and Petaḥ Tikvah sub-districts. East Jerusalem was reunited with the capital's western parts in 1967. The remaining area of the former Jordanian Jerusalem district was added partly to the Bethlehem and partly to the Ramallah district. The third district of former Jordanian-held Judea is that of Hebron.

Shephelah (Foothills). In this area, which was completely abandoned by Arabs in 1948 and had only a few small Jewish settlements (Ḥuldah, Gezer, Ben Shemen), resettlement began at the end of that year near the "Highway of Valor" (Kevish ha-Gevurah), built to secure the access to Jerusalem, and in 1949 east of Ramleh and Lydda. The kibbutzim of Netiv ha-Lamed-He and Bet Guvrin were at first solitary outposts further south, but more villages were established as part of the Adullam Project after 1955. At the southern and northern extremity of the area, only isolated villages were founded on the sites of the projected Adoraim and Modi'im regional schemes. While Kiryat Gat, Ramleh, Lydda, and Petah Tikvah, all situated outside the western rim of the Shephelah, have become population centers for the area and exercise economic and other functions, Beth-Shemesh is the only development town in the Shephelah proper. In population density, the Shephelah remains well below the average of central and northern Israel. Farming is mostly of a transition type, with partly intensive field crops located on valley bottoms (Elah, Aijalon, Sorek valleys, etc.) and deciduous fruit orchards and vineyards prominent on higher ground. Afforestation takes up considerable areas.

Jerusalem Corridor. In the part of the Judean Hills proper included in Israel in 1948/49, the first new settlements were founded near the Jerusalem highway, and others were added later further south. The easternmost reaches (Mevasseret Zion, Moẓa, Bet Zayit) have since the late 1960s been gradually becoming suburban extensions of Jerusalem. Farming is based principally on poultry and fruit orchards, the latter planted on laboriously terraced hillsides, but there are also some recreation and tourist facilities.

Hebron and Bethlehem Districts. In the population census held by Israel in 1967, the Hebron and Bethlehem districts had about 180,000 inhabitants, the great majority being Muslim Arabs. The Hebron district had a population density of 290 per sq. mi. (112 per sq. km.) and the Bethlehem district 88 per sq. km.; about half the area of the former and over two-thirds of the latter lie within the uninhabited Judean Desert in the east. Of the 87 Arab villages in the Hebron and the 45 in the Bethlehem district, some of the largest lie, characteristically, near the desert border. Most of the villages have existed for centuries or millennia, but small agglomerations, inhabited by Bedouin in the transitional stage from nomadic to sedentary life, refugees of the 1948 war, and others, came into being between 1948 and 1967 in the southwest corner of the Hebron Hills and east of Bethlehem. The dominant crop is the late-ripening vine; vineyards have spread in the last decades over new hillsides. Wheat and olives are second and third in importance. Hebron and Bethlehem (the latter with its sister towns Beit Jālā and Beit Sāḥūr) are the only urban agglomerations. After the end of 1967, the Jewish *Eẓyon Bloc, destroyed during the 1948 war, with 14 villages, a rural center named Allon Shevut, and the town of Efrat were revived.

The Ramallah District. The Ramallah district numbered some 89,000 inhabitants (1967), with a population density of 298 per sq. mi. (115 per sq. km.). Besides the twin towns of Ramallah and al-Bīra, it had 87 villages, after the inclusion of part of the former Jordanian Jerusalem district. Its northern border coincides approximately with that separating Judea and Samaria. Apart from Ramallah and al-Bīra, where first steps toward industrialization have been taken, the district has a rural economy based on olive groves, other fruit orchards, and field crops – the latter principally in small intermontane valleys like that of Levonah (Marj Lubbān).

SAMARIA. Most of this region lies in what was, after 1967, the Israel-held territory of Judea-Samaria, comprising the three districts of Nablus, Tulkarm, and Jenin. Only the northwestern extension of the Samaria Hills, composed of the three subregions of the Iron Hills and Valley, the Manasseh Hills, and Mt. Carmel, as well as the northern rim of Mt. Gilboa, were part of pre-1967 Israel.

Nablus, Tulkarm, and Jenin Districts. In 1967 the Nablus, Tulkarm, and Jenin districts had a combined population of some 303,000, nearly exclusively Muslim Arabs. At the same date, the population density amounted to 565 per sq. mi. (218 per sq. km.) in the Tulkarm, 355 (137) in the Jenin, and 249 (96) in the Nablus district. Villages are more or less evenly distributed over the region, the eastern slopes descending to the Jordan Rift excepted. In farming, olive groves are dominant on the hillsides, and sheep, goat, and cattle herds constitute important supplementary branches. Small fig orchards thrive on relatively moist sites. Thanks to the numerous intermontane valleys covered with fertile alluvium (Shiloh, Mikhmetat, Dothan valleys, Marj Sānūr, etc.), however, agriculture in Samaria is much more variegated than in Judea, comprising winter and summer field crops, vegetables, watermelons, and so on. In the north, deciduous fruit orchards and some citrus groves have been added since the 1950s. From 1967, farming methods greatly improved under the guidance of Israeli experts and new crops, like cotton, have been introduced. An area apart is the narrow Fāriʿa Valley descending to the Jordan rift, where intensive crops irrigated with the water of the perennially flowing Wadi Fāriʿa include citrus, dates, bananas, and other subtropical and tropical fruit, as well as vegetables, green fodder, and so on. The three district centers – Samaria's only urban agglomerations (two of them, to be exact, lying outside the Hills) – subsist mainly on handicrafts, commerce, and administrative functions, although the process of industrialization, begun on a very modest scale before 1967, was speeded up under Israeli administration. The northern and northeastern edges of Mt. Gilboa, which belonged to Israel prior to 1967, have for the most part become an area of afforestation, and one outpost kibbutz, Ma'aleh Gilboa, has been founded there.

Israel's conquest of Judea and Samaria and East Jerusalem in the 1967 War enabled it to extend its frontiers, to improve its security and strategic position, and to realize what many Jews perceive to be their historical right to "all the Land of Israel." After the Six-Day War in 1967 the territories came under Israeli military administration and the previous orientation to Jordan was partly replaced by linkages with Israel. During the conquest of Judea and Samaria some 250,000 Arabs fled the region. Jerusalem then became a reunified city.

At the end of the Six-Day War Judea and Samaria had approximately 595,000 inhabitants, some 225,000 of them in 12 urban centers. By 2002 the Arab population has increased to over a million. The rural population also underwent intense urbanization and is dispersed in over 400 villages of various size. The main reason for the population expansion is the very high natural increase among the Arabs, approximately 37 per 1,000 annually in contrast with 19 per 1,000 among the Jews. The fertility rate among the Arabs remains seven births per woman, while infant mortality is decreasing. The Arab population is much younger than the Jewish one. More than half the Arabs in the administered territories are less than five years old. This figure promises an even higher population in the future. To this should be added the fact that the Arabs still live together in large families and that their attachment to their land does not encourage emigration.

Jewish settlement in Judea and Samaria after 1967 was undertaken for the most part by the religious right as a religious imperative, under the auspices of such groups as Gush Emunim. Settlement commenced with a return of Jewish inhabitants to their pre-1948 homes in settlements or neighborhoods evacuated in the 1948 war, such as the Jewish Quarter in Old Jerusalem, the Eẓyon Bloc, and Hebron. Settlement was accelerated when the Likud under Menaḥem Begin came to power in 1977. The new government authorized settlements on ideological grounds in locations avoided by Labor governments, because they did not serve a strategic purpose and were positioned in areas of dense Arab population concentration.

A highly significant process was the post-1977 wave of settlement that exploited the spatio-economic potential of the West Bank, namely its proximity to Israeli population centers. In effect, settlers were supplied from four major sources: the Tel Aviv metropolitan area, the city of Jerusalem, Israel's periphery in Galilee and the Negev, and Jews from abroad. Most settlers from the Tel Aviv area moved to settlements in the West Samaria area, while most settlers from Jerusalem moved to a group of settlements around Jerusalem. The Haifa area contributed its part to the settlement of North Samaria, while the Israeli periphery contributed mostly to West Samaria and the Jerusalem area. Jewish colonization of the West Bank was mostly part of the metropolitan expansion of Tel Aviv and Jerusalem. The development eastwards started mainly after 1977 as a consequence of the massive and rapid construction of new settlements on the western fringes of the Samaria mountains. These settlements were constructed as suburbs, without a local economic base, as part of the declared government policy of populating the occupied territories. It involved large-scale government spending on land purchases, the construction of infrastructure, and housing projects, with the whole of the occupied territories accorded the status of a development area, which meant government subsidies for housing and loans to private construction companies and industries willing to relocate. By 2002 around 130 settlements with about 230,000 Jews had been established in the region by the Israeli government. The Jewish population in Judea and Samaria was widely dispersed, in keeping with a policy of occupying as much land as possible. Only a few urban or semi-urban settlements in the region are likely to play a role in the future redelineation of boundaries. Foremost among them are the towns of *Ariel, Emmanuel, Elkanah, and Alfei Menasseh, the town of Ma'aleh Adummim east of Jerusalem with its 25,000 inhabitants, and the Eẓyon Bloc with its 19,000 settlers.

Iron and Manasseh Hills. Of the Iron and Manasseh Hills, belonging partly to the Ḥaderah and partly to the Jezreel subdistrict, the former is predominantly inhabited by Arabs and characterized by partly intensive mixed farming, in which there was considerable progress after 1949. Villages like ʿAra, ʿArʿara, and Umm al-Faḥm much more than doubled their population. Mei Ammi was founded in 1963 as a border kibbutz on the armistice line. Farming in the Manasseh Hills-which contain 11 Jewish villages, mostly kibbutzim, as well as one Arab village – comprises intensive field crops and fruit orchards, milch cows, sheep, poultry, and so on. Most kibbutzim have industrial enterprises to complement their economy. The Manasseh Forest, with over 7,000,000 trees planted by 1970, is the largest in the country.

The main importance of the region lies in its role as the historic transit zone from the Coastal Plain to the Jezreel Valley and on to Transjordan and Damascus. The pass between the Menasseh hills and Iron valley was used throughout history as part of the "Way of the Sea" route and was guarded by the town of Megiddo. Even today the Iron-Megiddo pass is on the main road from the Coastal Plain to the Jezreel Valley and Galilee.

Mt. Carmel. The northwestern extremity of the Mt. Carmel block is occupied by suburbs of Haifa. Large parts of its central and southeastern sections have been declared nature reserves, and the expanses covered with pine woods form the background for the recreation facilities developed at several sites (Bet Oren, Ya'arot ha-Karmel, Nir Eẓyon, etc.). Villages on or near the mountain's western edge cultivate land in the Carmel coastal plain below. On the top of Keren ha-Karmel, at the mountain's southeast corner, a Catholic monastery stands on the spot traditionally held to be the site of the prophet Elijah's contest with the priests of Baal.

The difficult topography of Mount Carmel allowed only a small area to be used for agriculture, so that natural vegetation has been preserved there more than in any other part of the country. All slopes are covered with well-developed Mediterranean scrub, and in favored places natural forests, consisting mainly of pine, have survived. All these areas have now been designated as a nature reserve.

GALILEE. Administratively, the Galilean hill country belongs to the Acre, Kinneret, and Safed sub-districts. The hills proper cover an area of over 700 sq. mi. (approximately 1,815 sq. km.). Their population density amounts to about 344 per sq. mi. (132 per sq. km.). Arabs and Druze are in the majority, with 351,100 out of 685 800 inhabitants.

Lower Galilee. The area south of the Bet ha-Kerem Valley and southwest of the Ammud Gorge falls into two separate parts. The first is western and central Lower Galilee, with the towns of Nazareth and Naẓerat Illit (Upper Nazareth) and a few Jewish rural settlements scattered among many Arab villages, some of which are large. The second part is the exclusively rural southeastern Lower Galilee, characterized by nearly flat basaltic plateaus dissected by deeper gorges, in which Jewish villages constitute the majority. In the west and center, olives, deciduous fruit orchards, and vines are to be found on hillsides, while field crops, primarily wheat, are cultivated in the valleys. The largest intermontane valley, Bikat Bet Netofah, with an open canal of the National Water Carrier running through it, is in some rainy winters partly flooded, and its fertile soil is therefore used mainly for summer crops. Eastern and southeastern Lower Galilee, which before 1948 cultivated grain almost exclusively, have introduced additional crops (e.g., cotton, deciduous fruit, etc.) since Israel's independence.

The Lower Galilee has a normal Mediterranean climate with continental influences and a greater range of temperatures. From the point of view of human settlement Lower Galilee is one of the favored regions in Israel. Human occupation has persisted there throughout history, and most of today's villages are situated on sites which have been continuously occupied since earliest historical times, and in many cases have preserved their biblical or Roman names. The number of historical routes there is greater than anywhere in the country; they usually follow basins or deeply cut valleys.

Upper Galilee. Bordering on the Acre Plain in the west, Lower Galilee in the south, the Ḥuleh Valley in the east and northeast, and Lebanon in the north, Upper Galilee bears a more pronouncedly mountainous character. Its cultivated area therefore constitutes only a small percentage of its total surface, whereas considerable expanses are covered with stunted remnants of natural woods or planted forests. Hill farming, with olives and tobacco prominent in Arab villages and deciduous fruit orchards, vineyards, and poultry in Jewish settlements, is practiced largely on terraced slopes. Among the non-Jewish population, Druze are prominent in the west and center (Yirkā, Jatt, Beit Jann, Ḥurfaysh, etc.), and Christians in the north-center (Miʿilyā, Fassūṭa, Gush Ḥalav, etc.), while the majority of Jewish settlements lie close to the Lebanese frontier. Urban agglomerations are Safed and Ma'alot.

The climate of Upper Galilee is typical Mediterranean, modified by altitude. Precipitation there is the highest in Israel with annual average of 800 mm in the central portion. Settlements in the mountains of Upper Galilee show relative stability over the centuries. There were no periods of great prosperity but neither were there periods of almost complete abandonment. Throughout history major roads have been completely absent from the area, with the international routes circumventing it along the valleys of the west, south, and east. The lack of natural routes in Upper Galilee prevented the formation of a natural urban center. In medieval times Safed became the main urban center, located at the top of an isolated hill a short distance from natural routes.

The Jordan and Dead Sea Rift and Its Jezreel Valley Branch

The outstanding features of the Rift Valley in Israel, which is part of the 4,000 mi. (6,500 km.) Syrian-East African Rift, are its straight north-south course, the precipitous mountain walls hemming it in on both sides, and the thick cover of alluvium, nearly flat on the surface, which conceals the enormous depth of the rift bottom. The rift neatly separates Cisjordan from Transjordan. It falls into five major sections: the upper Jordan Valley, comprising the Ḥuleh Valley and the Rosh Pinnah-Korazim sill; the central Jordan Valley, including Lake Kinneret and its surroundings and the Beth-Shean Valley; the lower Jordan Valley, with the subregions of the Succoth and Peẓa'el (Phasael) valleys and the Jericho Plain (Ha-Kikkar); the Dead Sea and its region; finally, the Arabah Valley, which, at least in aspects of human geography, is closely related to the Negev. The Ḥuleh Valley measures 15 mi. (25 km.) from north to south and 4–6 mi. (6–8 km.) from west to east. The northern rim of the valley is 525 ft. (170 m.) above sea level and the surface of the former Lake Ḥuleh was 220 ft. (70 m.) above sea level. The surface of Lake Kinneret lies some 696 ft. (213 m.) below sea level, the figure oscillating with the seasons and the rainfall. With a capacity estimated at 3,000,000,000 cubic meters, it serves as the National Water Carrier's principal reservoir. Three river terraces may be distinguished in the Beth-Shean Valley, the Jordan meandering on the lowest and the town of Beth-Shean lying on the highest. South of this valley the Samaria Hills approach the Jordan bed, leaving only a narrow passage on its west bank. Further south, the rift widens into the Succoth Valley. Mt. Sartaba separates the Succoth Valley from the still wider Peẓa'el Valley, which, in turn, goes over, south of Wadi ʿAwjā, into the Jericho Plain, where the west-east distance between the slopes of the Judean Desert and the edge of the Moab Plateau is 20 mi. (32 km.) and where the valley bottom lies between 820 and 1,250 ft. (250–380 m.) below sea level. The Dead Sea is an inland lake covering the deepest continental depression on earth: in 1963 its water surface lay 1,308 ft. (398.5 m.) below sea level. The Lashon (Lisān) Peninsula divides the lake into a larger, northern and a smaller, southern basin. The high temperatures and evaporation, as well as the absence of any outlet, explain the extremely high salt content of the sea – the highest of any body of water on earth, attaining 29–32% in the southern basin – and the specific gravity of these waters exceeding that of any other lake.

A side branch of the Rift, composed of the Ḥarod and Jezreel valleys, leads from the Beth-Shean Valley northwestward. The Harod Valley, 11 mi. (18 km.) long and 3 mi. (5 km.) wide, is a narrow corridor separating the Ẓeva'im Ridge in Lower Galilee from Mt. Gilboa in Samaria. Naḥal Harod runs through it from its source at the foot of Mt. Gilboa toward Beth-Shean and the Jordan River. The Jezreel Valley is triangular in shape, its apex pointing south to the town of Jenin.

Soils in the Jordan Rift Valley change from dark, heavy alluvium (partly swamp and peat soils) in the Ḥuleh Valley and alluvium of partly basaltic origin around the northern shores of Lake Kinneret to pale, marly *lashon* soils, predominant from Lake Kinneret southward through the Beth-Shean and Succoth valleys to the Jericho region.

In the past, extensive swamps and waterlogging excluded human settlement from the larger part of the Ḥuleh Valley. In the Beth-Shean Valley, the success of farming was dependent on the readiness of settlers to prevent flooding of fields by spring waters and watercourses; when this was not done, thorny brush spread and soils became increasingly saline. In the lower Jordan Valley, agriculture is essentially oasis farming, of which Jericho is the most striking example. The heavy, alluvial soils of the Harod and Jezreel valleys resemble those of the northern parts of the Jordan Valley, as did, until the recent past, their swamps and their waterlogging problems. All the swamps are now drained.

Going from north to south, the climate of the Jordan Valley becomes progressively hotter and drier. The Ḥuleh Valley has a mean annual temperature of 68° F (20° C); although summer days are frequently oppressive, winter frosts, caused by temperature inversion, exclude subtropical crops but are beneficial to the extensive apple orchards. The Kinneret region has hot summers and mild winters, and the Beth-Shean Valley is characterized by a continental temperature regime, with peak summer heat but not entirely frost-free winters. On the Dead Sea shore, the mean annual temperature soars to 77° F (25° C), with summer maximums frequently exceeding 104° F (40° C). Differences in rainfall are no less extreme: the Ḥuleh Valley's northern rim receives an annual precipitation average of 24 in. (600 mm.); the Kinneret region between 16 and 20 in. (400–500 mm.); the Beth-Shean Valley between 10 and 16 in. (250–400 mm.); and the Jericho region about 4 in. (100 mm.), while at Sodom only 2 in. (50 mm.) are registered. The lower the averages, the more extreme are the fluctuations between one rain year and the next. Evaporation in the Rift is very strong, particularly from Lake Kinneret southward, having a negative influence on the water balance and promoting salination.

Great variety is found in the Rift's flora and fauna. The Ḥuleh Valley belongs to the Mediterranean vegetation zone's lowland type; in the former Ḥuleh swamps there was a dense vegetation grouped around the papyrus reed, which has been partly preserved in the Ḥuleh Nature Reserve; the Kinneret region is of a transition type between the Mediterranean and Irano-Turanian (dry-steppe) vegetation zones, and the Beth-Shean and Succoth valleys are within the confines of the latter zone. The Jericho and Dead Sea regions belong to the Saharo-Arabian (desert) zone; the flood terrace of the lower Jordan River and some other stretches have a halophytic (salt-loving) flora, whereas Jericho, En-Gedi, and some other cases constitute enclaves of the Sudanian (moist-tropical) vegetation zone.

Lines of communication crossing the Rift from west to east were through most of history of greater importance than lengthwise north-south roads. The Jordan Valley's role in prehistory is outstanding; finds from the Paleolithic (Ubaydiyya), the Neolithic (Jericho, Sha'ar ha-Golan), and the Chalcolithic periods (Tulaylāt al-Ghusūl, etc.), have been discovered. In most prehistoric and historic periods, however, habitation was discontinuous in time and space; sections of the valley often had more contacts with the adjoining hill regions than with each other. The decline setting in after the Muslim conquest was, in the initial centuries, less pronounced in the Jordan Valley than in other parts of the country; after the Crusades, however, the Rift Valley remained a total waste, as did the Jezreel Valley. In the 19th century, new Arab villages came into being in the Ḥuleh Valley, many of whose settlers presumably hailed from Egypt.

Some of the earlier Jewish settlements in the country (Yesud ha-Ma'alah, Mishmar ha-Yarden, etc.) were founded in or near the Ḥuleh Valley. In the first decade of the 20th century, Jewish settlement gained a foothold in the Jordan-Yarmuk Plain (Kinneret, Deganiyyah). The Jezreel and Harod valleys became the principal object of pioneering efforts in the 1920s, and in the Beth-Shean Valley the first stockade and watchtower settlements were erected in the 1930s. The lower Jordan Valley, on the other hand, did not come into the scope of Jewish development (with the exception of the Rabbat Ashlag potash works and Bet ha-Aravah) and remained outside Israel's 1948 armistice borders. Between 1951 and 1958, the great Ḥuleh drainage project was carried out, making the lake and swamp disappear and creating conditions for adding new settlements, particularly the town of Kiryat Shemonah and the development town of Ḥaẓor. In the Kinneret region, few new villages were founded after 1948. In the Beth-Shean Valley, the town of Beth-Shean became Jewish, and a few more moshavim and kibbutzim were founded. The Jezreel Valley settlement expanded southward with the establishment of the Taanach village bloc. In the lower Jordan Valley, tens of thousands of 1948 Arab war refugees were housed in camps of mud-brick huts by the Jordanian regime. After the Six-Day War, beginnings were made in intensive farming and in development of tourism in the formerly Syrian Baṭeiḥa Valley, and by 1971 eight *Naḥal outposts had been established in the lower Jordan Valley.

HULEH VALLEY. The Ḥuleh Valley, measuring 93 sq. mi. (240 sq. km.), forms part of the Safed sub-district. It has 23 settlements and 34,100 inhabitants (all Jewish), 21,600 living in Kiryat Shemonah and the rest in kibbutzim and moshavim. The area of the valley, fully and intensively cultivated, is entirely covered with irrigated apples and other deciduous fruit orchards, carp ponds, and field and fodder crops. In addition to the local villages, Galilee hill settlements have been allocated fields in the Ḥuleh Valley. Industry exists in Kiryat Shemonah and in several kibbutzim.

THE KINNERET REGION. The Kinneret region forms part of the Kinarot sub-district. With an area of 59 sq. mi. (152 sq. km.) it has 29 settled places (all Jewish) with a population of 56,700 of whom 39,800 live in Tiberias, where their economy is principally based on tourism and recreation. In the rural sector, the 15 kibbutzim are the predominant element, as this was the area where collective settlement came into being and where important ideological and cultural centers of the kibbutz movement (study centers, museums, etc.) are located. Farming, highly intensive and fully irrigated, specializes in tropical and subtropical species (bananas, date palms, etc.); field and fodder crops, vegetables, dairy cattle, and poultry are also important. In addition to carp ponds, fishing in Lake Kinneret is developed. Industrial enterprises are to be found in some of the Jordan-Yarmuk Plain kibbutzim.

THE BETH-SHEAN VALLEY. The Beth-Shean Valley, with an area of 85 sq. mi. (219 sq. km.), numbers 25,000 inhabitants (all Jewish) in 22 settlements. The town of Beth-Shean (with 15,900 inhabitants) contains the majority of the population. Among the villages, 14 are kibbutzim and five are moshavim. Farming is based on salt-resistant date palms and pomegranates, cotton, and other intensive field crops, and carp ponds (making use of brackish spring water); bananas are not cultivated because of the danger of frost. A number of kibbutzim have industrial plants.

LOWER JORDAN VALLEY AND THE DEAD SEA REGIONS. From 1968 the lower Jordan Valley, together with most of the uninhabited hill slopes at its western side, formed the Jericho-Jordan district of Israel-held Judea-Samaria. In 1968 it had a population of 9,600 Arabs, most of whom lived in Jericho. Few fields are cultivated outside the Jericho oasis and the lower reaches of Fāriʿa Gorge.

The Negev

Covering an area of over 4,600 sq. mi. (some 12,000 sq. km.), the Negev constitutes a challenge to Israel's constructive efforts because of its relative vastness, the potential of its mineral wealth, and its position as a communications link with the

Red Sea and the Indian Ocean. While the desert climate sets it apart from the country's center and north, structurally it continues to the south the division of Cisjordan into the Coastal Plain, the Hill Region, and the Rift Valley to the south. The Beersheba depression, gradually rising eastward from some 300 ft. (less than 100 m.) to 1,650 ft. (500 m.) above sea level, has a thick cover of fine-grained, yellowish-brown loess as its outstanding characteristic, although large stretches in the west and southwest are overlaid by sand dunes. The loess is susceptible to severe gullying by flash floods and to sheet and wind erosion, necessitating special soil conservation measures, e.g., contour plowing and planting of shelterbelts of eucalyptus and tamarisk trees around the fields, to make farming possible. Almost the entire Beersheba region belongs to the drainage basin of Naḥal Besor.

The topography of the Negev Hills is basically determined by parallel folds running from northeast to southwest, the highest elevations lying in the southwest. On the bedrock of the Negev Hills, desert erosion has imposed sharp, angular landscape features, most strikingly exemplified in the three *makhteshim* ("erosional cirques" or "craters"): Makhtesh Ramon, Ha-Makhtesh ha-Gadol (Ḥatirah), and Ha-Makhtesh ha-Katan (Ḥaẓerah). There is hardly any arable soil.

The Eilat Mountains at the Negev's southern extremity, which belongs to the same geological province as southern Sinai, eastern Egypt, Edom, and western Arabia, are fundamentally different from the rest of the Negev. The landscape is of infinite variety, with narrow clefts hemmed in by rock walls rising 1,000 ft. (300 m.) over them, which cut through the granite mountains in various directions. Rock debris fills the gorges, while erosion has sculptured awe-inspiring rock facades, like Solomon's Pillars near Timna, the Amram Columns, etc.

The Arabah Valley, the Rift's southern section in Israel, stretches from the Dead Sea to Eilat over a distance of 105 mi. (170 km.) between the Negev Highlands in the west and the Edom Mountains in the east. Particularly in its south, landscape features typical of the Rift are even more spectacular than anywhere else in the country. A thick cover of alluvium, mostly coarse sand and gravel, everywhere obscures the valley's rock foundations. The Arabah has a number of springs, brackish in various degrees, on its western and, more so, on its eastern side. Deep well drillings, particularly in the Ḥaẓevah area, have yielded water in previously unsuspected quantities.

Only the northwestern corner of the Negev has a climate that can, at best, be described as semiarid; all the other parts are desert proper. While peak temperatures, with the exception of the Arabah Valley, hardly exceed those of other parts of the country, there is a large diurnal span of temperatures, typical of continental climates. Humidity decreases in southern and eastern directions, as does rainfall, which is extremely capricious; entire years may pass without any rain, and a thunderstorm lasting a few hours at a desert spot may yield the total annual average. Only the northern half of the Beersheba region and the highest reaches of the Negev hills belong to the Irano-Turanian dry-steppe vegetation zone. All the rest of the Negev belongs to the Saharo-Arabian desert zone, where the vegetation cover is extremely sparse or totally absent over long distances.

Basically, the Negev always seems to have been the nomad's domain, but other forms of human presence and activity appeared in certain periods, conditioned by the exploitation of minerals, the development and maintenance of lines of communications, and the holding of defense posts of the sown land against the wilderness. While prehistoric artifacts found over wide areas and in considerable number possibly testify to periods of greater rainfall in the earlier Stone Age, it is certain that the impressive achievements of the Chalcolithic period, which included manufacturing near Beersheba (Tell Abu Matar) and copper mining and transporting in the Arabah Valley, coincided with climatic conditions hardly different from those of the present. For a millennium the Negev had no sedentary population after the period of the Nabateans, who made enormous efforts in Roman and Byzantine times to conserve water for farming and town dwelling. Only in 1900 did the Turks decide to build Beersheba as an administrative center. Even in the 1930s, no other towns or villages existed south and east of the Rafa-Gaza-Bet Guvrin-Dhahiriyya-Samūʿ (Eshtemo'a) line. Bedouin, affiliated with five large tribal associations – Tarābīn, al-Tiyāha, ʿAzāzma, al-Ḥanājira and al-Jabārāt – roamed the Negev, mainly subsisting on their goat flocks and camel herds and occasionally, in rainy winters, sowing some wheat or barley.

Early Jewish settlers visualized the Negev as a field for future development. Z.D. *Levontin's plan, around 1882, to found Rishon le-Zion south of Gaza, as well as later attempts at purchasing holdings near Rafa and elsewhere in the northern Negev, came to naught, however, mainly because Bedouin would-be vendors did not have their ownership rights entered in the land registry. In the first decade of the 20th century, the idea of Jewish settlement in the Negev was brought up again, first as a daring plan for a Jewish-Bedouin alliance, then as a project to be assisted by the Turkish authorities, in connection with Herzl's *El-Arish project. After World War I, veterans of the *Jewish Legion tried to settle on state land offered by the British authorities at Arad, but despaired when no water was found. In the 1920s and 1930s, Jewish individuals and groups acquired isolated holdings in the Negev, which were taken over by the JNF and secured and enlarged after the end of the 1930s. This made it possible to set up the three "observation outposts" of Gevulot, Revivim, and Bet Eshel in the spring and summer of 1943, and three years later 11 more villages in the south and Negev, on the night following the Day of Atonement (Oct. 6, 1946). By the outbreak of hostilities after the UN partition resolution of Nov. 29, 1947, the number of Negev settlements had grown to 18, and two pipelines drawn from the Nir Am and Gevaram wells supplied them with drinking water and a limited quantity of irrigation water.

In the years 1949–51, settlement activity was energetically pursued. Fifteen thousand of the Bedouin population, estimated at 50,000 before 1947, remained (their number increased to about 126,100 in 2002, when nearly all of them lived in the Arad region). Whereas farming villages are concentrated northwest of Beersheba, since the 1950s outposts have begun to be established in the Negev hills and the Arabah Valley. Urban nuclei were started in the central and eastern Negev (Yeroḥam, 1951; Miẓpeh Ramon, 1954; Dimonah, 1955; Arad, 1961), and the development of Eilat became feasible after the 1956 Sinai Campaign. In the northwest, Ofakim and Netivot were built as immigrant towns. All these made the Negev an integral part of Israel demographically as well as politically. Beersheba became Israel's sixth-largest city, and mineral quarrying and processing (Dead Sea minerals, phosphates, methane gas, copper, ceramic clays, glass sands, etc.) furnished the basis for industrialization. Important were the traffic arteries that came into being after 1948; previously, the only one was the Gaza-Beersheba-Nizzanah road, with a branch leading up to the present-day Yeroḥam. Among these are the Beersheba-Dimonah-Sodom road (continuing to En-Gedi), the Beersheba-Miẓpeh Ramon-Eilat and Tel Shoket-Arad-Shefekh Zohar roads, and the Sodom-Eilat highway. To these was added the Tel Aviv-Beersheba railroad, which was later continued to Dimonah, Oron, and Ẓefa-Efeh.

The entire Negev is included in the sub-district of Beersheba which extends over 4,956 sq. mi. (12,835 sq. km.). The sub-district has 521,200 inhabitants: 393,100 Jews and 128,100 Arabs. Practically all the latter are Bedouin, living as nomads or in transition to sedentary life, mostly in the area between Beersheba and Arad. The population density has increased from 2.85 per sq. mi. (1.1 per sq. km.) in 1948 to 100 per sq. mi. (40.3 per sq. km.) in 2002.

NORTHWESTERN NEGEV. This region, which includes the Gerar and Besor regions, has an area of 549 sq. mi. (1,423 sq. km.). Farming is almost entirely dependent on irrigation, mainly with water from the National Water Carrier. Out-of-season vegetables for export, flowers, deciduous and subtropical fruit trees, and fodder crops are characteristic. A beginning has been made with auxiliary irrigation to secure the grain harvest in the rain-deficient years. Citrus groves have begun to appear in the northwestern Negev since the 1960s. There are 69 inhabited places in this relatively small area; most are moshavim, grouped in the settlement regions of Benei Shimon, Merḥavim, and Eshkol. The development towns of Ofakim and Netivot are based on various industries. The total population of the region, all of them Jewish, numbers 30,500.

BEERSHEBA REGION, The Beersheba region, measuring 614 sq. mi. (1,589 sq. km.), has only 19 inhabited places, among them the city of Beersheba and the town of Arad, where 206,000 Jewish inhabitants live; the rest of the population are Bedouin. The principal economic activity is industry, concentrated in the two towns and partly based on Negev minerals. Beersheba's academic and research institutes have had a mounting impact on the life of the city and its vicinity. Dry farming (mostly barley and wheat fields) is practiced on relatively small areas. While the Bedouin used to wait until the first rains had come down in promising quantity before sowing, auxiliary irrigation has been introduced with the aid of small storage dams that retain occasional flash-flood waters.

NEGEV HILLS, PARAN PLATEAU, AND ARABAH VALLEY. The vast area, extending over 3,793 sq. mi. (9,823 sq. km.), comprises the Negev Hills, Paran Plateau, and Arabah Valley (including the southern section of the Judean Desert and the west shore of the Dead Sea). It has 16 inhabited places, among them the towns of Dimonah and Eilat and the development centers of Yeroḥam and Miẓpeh Ramon. In addition, there are important mining and industrial sites (e.g., Oron, Ẓefa-Efeh, Timna, Sodom, etc.) with no resident population. Phosphates, copper, clay minerals, and the Dead Sea minerals are extracted and treated. Oasis-type farming is to be found in the Arabah Valley settlements (numbering 17 in 2002), where tropical fruit (dates, mangoes, etc.) and out-of-season export vegetables and flowers are prominent. The region contains 80,600 residents, most of them in Dimonah and Eilat.

Mount Hermon

Mount Hermon is a huge uplifted block, 9,232 ft. (2,814 m.) high, which towers above its surroundings – the Litani (Leontes) and ʿĀyūn (Ijon) valleys in the west, the Ḥuleh Valley in the south, the Golan in the southeast, and the Ghuta (Damascus region) in the northeast – and deeply influences their climate and water economy. Much of the annual precipitation on its highest reaches – over 60 in. (1,500 mm.) a year – largely comes in the form of snow, which remains on the ground for several months. The larger part of the mountain belongs to Lebanon, the northeast is in Syria, and the southeast ridge, Ketef ha-Hermon (the "Hermon Shoulder"), which rises to 7,220 ft. (2,200 m.), came under Israeli control after the Six-Day War. Most of the mountain is uninhabited; a number of villages, peopled mainly by Druze, Alaouites, etc., nestle in protected sites on the lower slopes. Among them is the Druze village of Majdal Shams, the northernmost inhabited place held by Israel, which lies in a secondary valley at a height of 3,940 ft. (1,200 m.) above sea level.

See also Physiography in *Israel, Land of: Geographical Survey and entries on places and regions mentioned in this article.

BIBLIOGRAPHY: E. Orni and E. Efrat, *Geography of Israel* (1971[3]); E. Huntington, *Palestine and its Transformation* (1911); A. Ruppin, *The Agricultural Colonization of the Zionist Organization in Palestine* (1926); A.A. Reifenberg, *The Struggle between the Desert and the Sown* (1950); N. Glueck, *Rivers in the Desert: The Exploration of the Desert* (1959); E. Orni, *Huleh, Background and Development* (1952); idem, *Forms of Settlement* (1963[5]); A. Bein, *The Return to the Soil* (1952); E. Efrat and E. Gabrieli, *Physical Master Plan of the Coastal Strip* (1966); Jewish Agency Agricultural Settlement Dept., *The Composite Rural Structure. A Settlement Pattern in Israel* (1960); A. Granott, *The Land System of Palestine* (1952); idem, *Agrarian Reform and the Record of Israel* (1956); D.H.K. Amiran and A. Shahar, *The Towns of Israel. Principles of Their Urban Geography* (1961); E.

Brutzkus, *Physical Planning in Israel* (1964); J. Dash and E. Efrat, *The Israel Physical Master Plan* (1964); E. Efrat, *Judea and Samaria, Guidelines for Regional and Physical Planning* (1971). **ADD. BIBLIOGRAPHY:** Y. Karmon, *Israel, a Regional Geography* (1971); D. Orman and A. Stern (eds.), *Adam u-Sevivah bi-Drom ha-Shefelah* (1988); A. Oren, *Hityashevut bi-Shenot ha-Ma'avak* (1978); E. Efrat, *Ge'ografiyyah Kafrit shel Yisra'el* (1990); idem, *Arim ve-Iyyur be-Yisra'el* (1988); idem, *Ayyarot ha-Pittu'ah be-Yisra'el – Avar o Atid?* (1987); G. Biger, *Moshevet Keter o Bayit Le'ummi – Hashpa'at ha-Shilton ha-Briti al Ereẓ Yisra'el, 1917–1939* (1983); Y. Ben-Artzi, *Ha-Moshava ha-Ivrit be-Nof Ereẓ Yisra'el 1882–1914* (1988); M. Bror, *Gevulot Ereẓ Yisra'el* (1988); Y. Gradus and A. Stern, *Sefer Be'er Sheva* (1979); A. Degani, D. Grossman, A. Shmueli (eds.), *Ha-Sharon bein ha-Yarkon la-Karmel* (1990); M. Harel and D. Nir, *Ge'ografiyyah shel Ereẓ Yisra'el* (1970); R. Nir, *Ge'omorfologiyyah shel Ereẓ Yisra'el* (1970); R. Kark, *Toledot ha-Hityashevut ha-Yehudit ba-Negev ad 1948* (1978); A. Shmueli, A. Sofer, and N. Kleot (eds.), *Arẓot ha-Galil*; A. Shmueli and Y. Gradus (eds.), *Ereẓ ha-Negev, Adam, u-Midbar* (1979); N. Teradyon, *Me-Ereẓ Kishon, Sefer ha-Emek* (1967); E. Efrat, *Geography and Politics in Israel since 1967* (1978); idem, *Tikhnun Le'ummi u-Pittu'ah be-Yisra'el bi-Shenot ha-Alpayyim* (2003).

[Efraim Orni / Elisha Efrat (2nd ed.)]

GOVERNANCE

Ottoman and Mandatory Periods (1880–1948)

CENTRAL GOVERNMENT. *Ottoman Rule.* At the beginning of the period the Land of Israel was not a political or administrative unit; officially, there was no such entity as Palestine. The Ottoman Empire (see History, Ottoman Period) was divided into vilayets (provinces), each governed by a Turkish vali sent from Constantinople, which were subdivided into sanjaks (districts), each under a mutessarif. Northern Ereẓ Israel formed part of the vilayet of Damascus and, from 1888, of Beirut, while Transjordan belonged to the former. The north of the country comprised the sanjaks of Acre and Nablus, while the south was designated as the independent sanjak of Jerusalem, dependent directly on Constantinople. Sanjaks were further subdivided into *aqḍiya* (equivalent to Israel's *nafot*, or sub-districts), each under a *qaimaqam* (equivalent to *keẓin ha-nafah*, or district officer). The smallest Turkish subdivision was the *nāḥiya*, containing a number of villages, which was equivalent to the area of the *mo'eẓah ezorit* ("rural district") of the State of Israel and was under the jurisdiction of a *mudīr*.

The first Turkish parliament, convened in 1912 in Constantinople, included five delegates from Ereẓ Israel – two each from Jerusalem and Nablus and one from Jaffa. All were Muslims from well-established families. In each vilayet and in the independent sanjak of Jerusalem a *majlis umumī* (popular council) was elected, with one delegate representing every 12,000 male Ottoman taxpayers. Elections were held in Jerusalem only once, in 1910: no Jew was elected, one member was a Christian Arab, and the rest were all Muslim. The councils, which met for 40 days a year under the chairmanship of the vali (or, in Jerusalem, of the mutessarif), had limited advisory powers only. They were, however, suspended altogether at the outbreak of World War I.

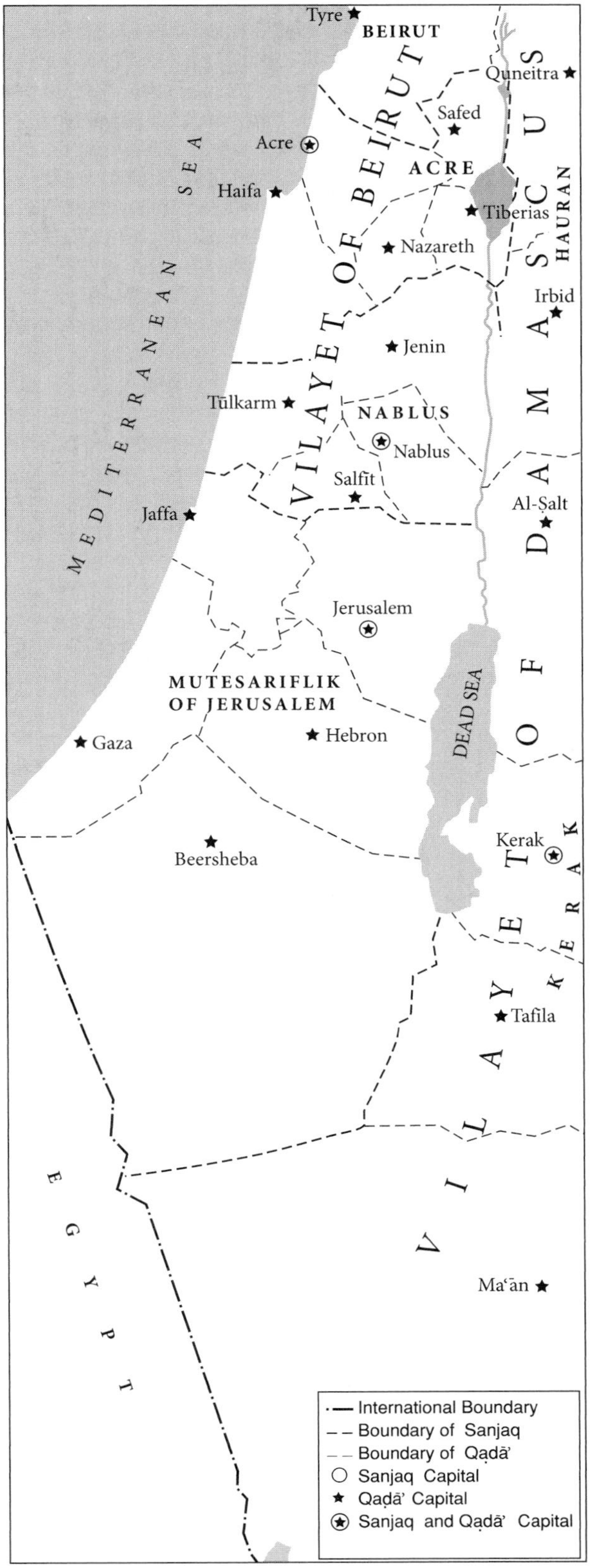

Map 1. Administrative division of Ereẓ Israel at end of Ottoman period, 1910. After Atlas of Israel, *Survey of Israel 1970.*

Map 2. Administrative division of Palestine, 1939. After Atlas of Israel, *Survey of Israel 1970.*

In each *qaḍā*ʾ of Ereẓ Israel (namely Jerusalem, Jaffa, Hebron, Gaza, Nablus, and Acre) a *majlis idara* (administrative council) also functioned, consisting of the local qadi (Muslim judge); the mufti (Muslim jurisconsult); the heads of the local Jewish, Greek-Orthodox, and Armenian communities; Turkish officials from the local departments of finance and public works and from the *qaimaqam*'s secretariat; and some elected members. In Jerusalem Rabbi Ḥayyim *Elyashar was elected.

The country was garrisoned by Turkish troops (one unit was stationed in the Citadel in Jerusalem). Outside the cities a gendarmerie operated, but public security was poor, and blood feuds, sometimes lasting for centuries, were prevalent in the Muslim villages.

British Mandate. From its occupation by British troops in 1917–18 until July 1920. Palestine was under military administration by the so-called Occupied Enemy Territory Administration (OETA "South" – OETA "North" being Lebanon, and OETA "East" Syria and Transjordan). *Mandates were given by the Allied and Associated Powers to Great Britain and France to administer these countries (and Iraq) until self-government became practicable. The operation of all these mandates was under supervision by the League of Nations' Permanent Mandates Commission, to which the two powers reported annually on each territory. The *Balfour Declaration was embodied in the preamble to the Palestine Mandate.

The administration of Palestine did not differ much from that of a Crown Colony. The governor and (titular) commander in chief was called the *high commissioner, who also served as high commissioner for Transjordan with a separate staff in Amman. He was appointed by the Colonial Office and responsible, through it, to the cabinet and Parliament in Britain. During the 28 years of Mandatory government, the following were the incumbents:

1920–25	Sir Herbert (later Viscount) *Samuel
1925–28	Field Marshal Lord Plumer
1928–31	Sir John Chancellor
1931–38	General Sir Arthur Wauchope
1938–44	Sir Harold Mac-Michael
1944–45	Field Marshal Lord Gort
1945–48	General Sir Alan Cunningham

The high commissioner was advised by an Executive Council, consisting of his principal deputy, the chief secretary (from 1920 to 1922 Sir Wyndham *Deedes); the attorney general (from 1920 to 1923 styled legal secretary; until 1931 Norman *Bentwich); the treasurer (afterward styled financial secretary); and, from time to time, one or two other members.

In 1920 Herbert Samuel set up a nominated Advisory Council of ten British heads of department ex officiis, four Muslim and three Christian Arabs, and three Jews. After the signature of the peace treaty between Britain and Turkey at Lausanne in June 1922, the Mandate was formally approved by the League of Nations. The Palestine Order in Council (in effect a constitution) came into force on Sept. 1, 1922, and an attempt was made to replace the Palestine nominees on the Advisory Council by elected members – eight Muslim and two Christian Arabs and two Jews. The elections, however, were boycotted by the Arabs on the principal ground that the preamble to the Order in Council incorporated the Balfour Declaration, which they rejected. An Advisory Council consisting exclusively of nominated British officials was therefore set up.

In 1935–6, Arthur Wauchope tried to establish a Legislative Council of twelve elected (eight Muslim Arabs, three Jews, and one Christian Arab) and fifteen nominated members (five British officials, four Jews, three Muslim and two Christian Arabs, and two representatives of commercial interests). The Jews opposed this attempt, since in their opinion it would have endangered the growth of the Jewish National Home. The plan also aroused strong differences among the Arab leaders.

All civil servants were responsible to the chief secretary, save the chief justice (who dealt directly with the high commissioner), and the government auditor (directly responsible to the colonial auditor in London). The officer actually commanding British troops was responsible to the War Office (from 1924 to 1930, to the Air Ministry). The chief secretary's office, known as the Secretariat, dealt with all correspondence between the high commissioner and the Colonial Office and between the chief secretary and heads of departments and district commissioners.

Administrative districts varied in number between seven in 1920 to two in 1925 and to six in 1939; but there were always 18 subdistricts (based on the Ottoman *qaḍāʾ*). Each district was in the charge of a district commissioner (in place of the former Ottoman *mutessarif*) with a district officer for each subdistrict (in place of the Ottoman *qaimaqam*). The smallest Ottoman unit, the *nāḥiya*, was abolished. All district commissioners were British; at the beginning, so were all district officers, but by the end of the Mandate they were all Palestinians. A new post of assistant district commissioner in charge of one or more subdistricts was created later: at first, all were British; by 1948, several were Palestinian.

In their areas, district commissioners, assistant district commissioners, and district officers represented the Crown. They were primarily responsible for maintaining law and order and coordinating the work of all departmental officers. One of the best-known district commissioners was Ronald *Storrs, in Jerusalem. Legislation under the military administration took the form of proclamations, orders, and notices. From 1920 onward, it was by ordinance, approved by the high commissioner in Executive Council, authorized by the Colonial Office, and formally passed without discussion by the wholly British Advisory Council. There also were subordinate regulations, orders and bylaws. All military and civil legislation up to 1934 was codified by R.H. Drayton, a former solicitor general.

The Palestine Zionist Executive and, later, the *Jewish Agency were recognized under the Mandate as the competent authority in several matters affecting Jewish development and made frequent representations on questions of major policy. After the enactment of the Religious Communities (Organization) Ordinance in 1926 and of the Jewish Community Regulations the following year, the *Va'ad Le'ummi shared with the Agency the responsibility for providing certain services for the *yishuv*, in particular education, health, and social welfare (Va'ad Le'ummi), land development, immigration, settlement, agricultural research, and afforestation (Jewish Agency). Parallel departments – government and Jewish – grew up, facilitating the transfer of authority when Israel became independent.

The Palestine Civil Service in 1948 numbered 10,000, only 250 of whom were British (apart from the British members of the Palestine Police Force, which was not considered part of the civil service). Of the Palestinian civil servants, two-thirds were Arab and one-third Jewish, roughly the demographic ratio. In certain departments (for example, public works), the Jewish proportion was higher; in others (for example, health, curiously enough), it was lower. The proportion of Christian Arabs was much higher than their population ratio and, for lack of suitable education, especially in English, that of Muslim Arabs was much lower.

The budget of the Mandatory Administration rose from under LP2,000,000 (LP1 = £1 sterling) at the beginning to over LP20,000,000 by the end. Even allowing for inflation in World War II, this meant at least a fivefold rise.

The departments at the end of the Mandate fell into the following groups: Secretariat (including Central Translation Bureau, Government Printer, Press Censorship, and Public Information Office); Legal Department (including the offices of the attorney general and solicitor general); Treasury, including the office of the treasurer (later divided into the office of the financial secretary and that of the accountant general), controller of banks, stamp duty commissioners and currency officer (on behalf of the Palestine Currency Board in London); Revenue Departments (Customs and Excise and, later, Income Tax); Security Services (apart from the British forces; including the Transjordan Frontier Force, which protected both Palestine and Transjordan – Palestine paying 6/7 and Transjordan 1/7 of its cost), the Palestine Police Force (including the British Police and Department of Prisons); Land Services (Departments of Surveys, Land Settlement, and Land Registration); Production Services (Department of Agriculture, Department of Forests, Veterinary Department, Cooperatives Department, Development Department, and Department of Commerce); Social Services (Departments of Health, Education, Labor, and Social Welfare); Public Utilities (Departments of Public Works, of Posts, Telegraphs and Telephones, Palestine Broadcasting Service, Palestine Railways, Ports, and Civil Aviation – the Palestine Electric Corporation was a public (concessionary) company, while water supplies were municipal); Wartime Departments, some of which had closed down by the end of the Mandate (War Supply Board, Food Control, Price Control, Heavy Industries Control, Light Industries Control, Salvage, Foreign Exchange Control, Custody of Enemy Property, Road Transport Control, and Imperial Censorship); Judiciary (Magistrates' Courts, District Courts, Land Courts, the Supreme Court, and Municipal Courts; Muslim shari'a (religious) courts, Jewish religious courts, and the several Christian religious courts came under the control of their respective ecclesiastical authorities – see below: Judiciary and Religious Life and Communities); other departments (Antiquities, Immigration, Statistics, Administrator General (public trustee, official receiver, registration of companies, partnerships, trademarks, patents and designs) and Town Planning).

[Edwin Samuel, Second Viscount Samuel]

LOCAL GOVERNMENT. *Ottoman Rule.* The modernization of local government began under the vilayet law of 1864, according to which *nāḥiyas*, or rural districts, were gradually introduced throughout the country. By the end of Ottoman rule many of the *mudirs*, in charge of *nāḥiyas* and controlling the villages comprising them, were local Arabs. Each *nāḥiye* was supposed to have a council, but few were established. The sheikhs who had exercised authority over the *ḥamūlas* (village clans) were replaced by mukhtars (village headmen), two of whom were to have been elected in each village together with a council of village elders – the *ikhtiyāriyya*. But most mukhtars were appointed rather than elected, although consideration was given to the wishes of the local notables. The mukhtar assessed and levied taxes among the villagers, settled disputes, and acted as intermediary in the relations between the provincial administration and the village.

The Jewish villages or moshavot, of which there were 28 by the end of the Ottoman rule, were initially outside this system. They originated their own pattern of self-government, based on Jewish communal self-rule in Eastern Europe, relying on the self-discipline and loyalty of the settlers rather than on any legal powers, and resisting attempts by the Ottoman provincial administration to control them. The ultimate authority in the moshavah was the general assembly, which met several times a year. A village executive committee was elected annually or biannually, and some of the larger moshavot elected village councils, to which the executive committee was responsible. The chairman and other officeholders were elected from among the committee members. In some villages, equal rights were granted, from the start, to all adult members of the community. In others, there were prolonged struggles over political rights between those who owned property in the village and those who did not, mainly the workers. By the end of Ottoman rule, democracy had usually triumphed. Until 1904 the Ottoman provincial authorities paid little attention to the moshavot and their methods of self-government. Then, the four largest were recognized as villages, and those elected by the village council were accepted as mukhtars. By 1914, all moshavot had acquired a similar status.

Municipal government was an innovation of the Ottoman *tanẓīmāt* ("reforms"). In 1863 Jerusalem was made a municipality by special imperial firman ("decree"). Under the 1877 Provincial Municipalities Law, 22 towns and larger villages were given municipal status in the 1880s and 1890s. They were provided with an impressive list of duties and legal powers but, in effect, they were under strict surveillance by the provincial district and subdistrict governors. Municipal staffs were pitifully small and incompetent and their budgets minimal. Only Jerusalem had one or two resourceful mayors, who constructed roads and municipal buildings (including a hospital) and introduced street lighting. Tel Aviv was still a suburb of Jaffa. Under the law, municipal councils (*majlis umumī*) of six to twelve members were to be elected by local taxpayers who were Ottoman subjects; in fact, genuine elections rarely took place. In Jerusalem, Jewish and Christian members sat on the council together with Muslim members. Mayors were appointed by the government, usually for short terms of office.

BIBLIOGRAPHY: M. Burstein, *Self-Government of the Jews in Palestine Since 1900* (1934); A. Heidborn, *Manuel de droit public et administrative de l'Empire Ottoman*, 2 vols. (1908–12); Palestine, Municipal Tax Commission for Jerusalem *Report* (1920); Palestine, Committee on Village Administration and Responsibility *Report* (1941).

[Edwin Emanuel Gutmann]

British Mandate. Municipalities. At the beginning of the Mandatory period there were 22 municipalities in western Palestine: 16 Arab and six (Jerusalem, Jaffa, Haifa, Tiberias, Safed, and Hebron) mixed. Tel Aviv, though administered by an autonomous Jewish council, was regarded as a suburb of Jaffa. In 1926 a Municipal Franchise Ordinance was issued, giving the municipal vote to tenants (males only), even if they held no property, as long as they paid at least one Palestine pound in municipal rates.

A comprehensive Municipal Corporations Ordinance was issued in 1934, authorizing the high commissioner to set up new municipalities or change the boundaries of existing ones on the recommendation of a public committee of inquiry. It prescribed in detail the method of elections, the duties and powers of the councilors and the municipality, sources of revenue (taxes, rates, fees and fines), the procedure for approving the budget, methods of financial control, and the rules for filling major posts, such as those of town clerk, treasurer, town engineer, and medical officer. The procedure for council and committee meetings and the rules for setting up committees were also laid down in detail. The high commissioner retained the right, inherited from the Ottoman rulers, to nominate the mayor and the deputy mayor; bylaws could be passed only on specific subjects listed in the ordinance and subject to the high commissioner's approval. Through the district commissioners, the central government kept the municipalities under strict control.

The ordinance confirmed the unique status of Tel Aviv, which became the world's first all-Jewish city, with the franchise for all residents, men and women – including foreign nationals – who paid as little as LP 0.50 a year in rates. These more democratic provisions were the model for other Jewish councils established later. In Jerusalem, where the Jewish majority had been represented on the municipal council by four members out of 12, there were now six Jewish councilors, four Muslims and two Christians. A Muslim was always appointed by the high commissioner as mayor, however, with a Jew and a Christian as deputies. In 1937 the Jewish deputy was acting mayor for a time, but in the following year another Muslim mayor was appointed.

The first Town Planning Ordinance, issued in 1921, did not repeal any Ottoman law, but stopped the custom of granting immunity from demolition to an unlawfully built house if the builders had succeeded in covering it with a roof. In 1936 it was replaced by a more modern ordinance, which created local town planning committees identical with the town councils and with the mayor as chairman. These were supervised by the District Town Planning Commissions, headed by the district commissioner, on which government departments were represented, and which received general directives from the central Government Planning Division.

Local and Regional Councils. The Local Council Ordinance of 1921 created a new category of elected local authority. While the Jewish rural communities thought the local council had too little power and authority, the Arab villagers regarded its establishment as interference in their ancient way of life and a threat to the social structure of their communities. During the next five years 21 Arab councils, four Jewish, and one German-Christian (Sarona, near Tel Aviv) were set up. The first Jewish local council established under the ordinance was Petaḥ Tikvah, followed during the next two decades by Rishon le-Zion and Reḥovot (1922), Tel Aviv (1923), Ramat Gan and Afulah (1926), Ḥaderah (1935), Bat Yam, Ra'anannah and Kefar Sava (1936), Bene-Berak and Herzliyyah (1937), and others.

In 1941 the 1921 ordinance was replaced by a new, streamlined one, granting the local councils even more powers than the municipalities and authorizing them to act for the public benefit on any matter so long as they did not come into conflict with other legislation. The high commissioner was empowered, by subsidiary legislation, to declare any village a local council or any group of villages a regional council. Two Jewish rural councils, near Ḥaderah and Petaḥ Tikvah, were set up in 1936–37 to protect the agricultural character of these areas.

By the end of the Mandate, in 1948, 11 small Arab towns and large villages, 26 Jewish villages, and Sarona were local councils, and four groups of Jewish villages were combined to form the Emek Ḥefer, Kishon, Nahalal, and Tel Ḥai regional councils. A new source of income was provided for the local authorities in 1945 by the Local Authorities (Business Tax) Ordinance, which allowed them, after passing a bylaw, to tax businesses operating within their boundaries, subject to approval by the high commissioner.

Villages. In 1944, a Village Administration Ordinance was issued, under which small Arab villages were to elect village councils, with tax powers but under closer supervision by the district commissioner and the central government than the local councils. Up to 1948, 24 were gazetted, in an effort to replace the rule of the elders and mukhtars by democratically elected bodies, but most of them existed only on paper, as the villagers were reluctant to depart from their old ways of life.

Local Government and the Development of the Jewish National Home. The tight control of the Jewish local authorities by the central government often led to tension and was criticized by the Peel Commission in 1937 as hampering advance toward self-rule. The Jewish councils cooperated closely with the national authorities of the *yishuv* and were represented at important meetings of the Asefat ha-Nivḥarim (Elected Assembly) and the Va'ad Le'ummi (National Council), which made continual efforts to enlarge their powers and coordinate their activities. The development of Jewish local government was an important factor in justifying the proposal to set up a Jewish state in part of Palestine and in enabling the *yishuv* to establish independence after the British withdrawal.

BIBLIOGRAPHY: M. Gurion (Wager), *Mavo le-Toledot ha-Shilton ha-Mekomi be-Yisrael* (1956/57).

[Yehuda Levanon]

JEWISH COMMUNAL ORGANIZATION (1880–1948). *General Characteristics.* The Jews in the Land of Israel not only had to organize themselves for the purpose of satisfying their religious and cultural needs, but because of the vast difference in culture and standards of living between themselves and the Arab majority, they also had to engage in municipal, political, and economic activities for which the government was nominally responsible. The Ottoman authorities and, from 1918, the British administration performed most of their functions in accordance with the requirements of the Arab majority, while the Turks granted considerable internal freedom to minorities and were usually lax in enforcing law and order. Even before 1918, therefore, the Jewish population assumed some governmental tasks and duties, such as the protection of life and property, the paving of roads and streets, and the administration of justice among its members, while under the British they had, inter alia, to maintain their own educational, social welfare, and health services, apart from those maintained by the government. In addition, the Balfour Declaration and the Mandate conferred upon the Jews certain special rights, not very clearly defined, by virtue of the fact that, although a minority, they were entitled to regard the country as their National Home. This gave an additional impetus to organized Jewish communal life in the land of Israel and endowed the *yishuv* with an importance far transcending its numerical size. The Jewish population also participated, though to a small extent, in some of the general administrative organs (see sections on Central and Local Government, below).

Jewish World Bodies. The communal activities of the *yishuv* were supplemented by the work of world Jewish philanthropic and Zionist organizations, which did not confine themselves to charity, but engaged in agricultural settlement, the maintenance of schools, the provision of health services, and the like. Under the Mandate, in fact, the Zionist Organization and the Jewish Agency undertook a variety of quasi-governmental functions. At the end of the 19th century and the beginning of the 20th, such bodies as the Alliance Israélite Universelle and the Hilfsverein der deutschen Juden were mainly engaged in educational activity, while Baron Edmond de Rothschild and later the Jewish Colonization Association (ICA) also established agricultural settlements and maintained their communal services. In 1924 the activities of Baron de Rothschild and ICA were taken over by the Palestine Colonization Association (PICA).

The major Zionist bodies active in the country were, during the last two decades of the 19th century, the Russian Ḥibbat Zion movement and, in the first half of the 20th, the World Zionist Organization. Through the Zionist Executive – later the Executive of the enlarged Jewish Agency – it carried out extensive activities in the absorption of immigrants, settlement on the land, and the economic, social, and educational progress of the Jewish population, all of which contributed to the rapid development of Jewish communal life.

The Central Jewish Community. Whatever organized communal life existed in Ereẓ Israel prior to 1900 was confined to local communities. Between 1900 and 1917 three ineffective attempts were made to organize a large part or the whole of the *yishuv*. In 1900 representatives of the Jewish villages in Judea met to further their mutual interests; a year later this organization disintegrated. In 1903 a mission sent from Russia by the Ḥibbat Zion movement, headed by Menaḥem *Ussishkin, convened a *Kenesiyyah* (Congress) of 79 representatives, elected by over 2,000 Jewish dues-paying voters, in Zikhron Ya'akov, with a view to founding a national organization of the *yishuv*. The organization did not outlive the year. In 1913 another attempt to establish a general organization also failed.

More fruitful attempts in the same direction were inaugurated at the end of 1917, with the conquest of the country by the British forces, which coincided with the Balfour Declaration. The heterogeneity of the Jewish population and its constantly changing composition were serious difficulties: the formation of a united Jewry proved to be neither easy nor peaceful. There was much opposition and dissension and many obstacles, internal and external, which had to be overcome. The exceedingly diverse social and religious outlooks in the *yishuv* gave rise to a large number of political parties, which also complicated the formation of communal organization.

Between 1917 and 1919 three preparatory assemblies, consisting of delegates from various parties and organizations in the *yishuv*, met to arrange for a Constituent Assembly elected by direct, equal, secret ballot and universal suffrage, including women. The provisional council elected by these assemblies encountered many difficulties. The old *yishuv*, including the ultra-Orthodox and *Agudat Israel, were strongly opposed to uniting with nonreligious Jews. The *Mizrachi and some sections of the *Sephardim objected to giving women the right to vote. Elections to the Constituent Assembly, renamed Asefat ha-Nivḥarim (the Elected Assembly), finally took place in April 1920.

The Asefat ha-Nivharim and the Va'ad Le'ummi. Between 1920 and 1948 the Asefat ha-Nivḥarim was the supreme organ of the *yishuv* in conducting its communal affairs. The elections to this body, originally planned to be held every three years or so, were repeatedly postponed because of the exhausting endeavors to reconcile the dissenting views of the numerous parties, the frequent Arab-Jewish disturbances and consequent unrest, and the protracted negotiations with the Mandatory authorities for the legal recognition of the organized Jewish community.

The first two elections to the Asefat ha-Nivḥarim were held prior to the legal recognition of the status of the Jewish community. Though recognition was given in 1928, it took a considerable time to work out the regulations for the election and the various compromises among the parties. The third election was held on a *curia* basis; every voter could vote only in his own *curia*, Ashkenazi, Sephardi, or Yemenite. The number of members for each *curia* was predetermined: 53 Ashkenazi, 15 Sephardi, and three Yemenite. In the fourth election, election by *curiae* was not strictly adhered to.

Jewish Population (composition by *curiae*, in percentages)

	1918	1928	1943
Ashkenazi	59	71	79.4
Sephardi	33	23	15.9
Yemenite	8	6	4.7

The Asefat ha-Nivḥarim was convened infrequently, for sessions lasting from one to four days, to deal with internal and political issues, organizational matters, and the approval of budgets. The first met three times and the second twice; the third held 18 sessions and the fourth seven. It met for its last working session in October 1947, and the concluding session took place after the establishment of the State of Israel, shortly before the first meeting of the Knesset in February 1949. The Asefat ha-Nivḥarim elected the *Va'ad Le'ummi (National Council or, as referred to by the Mandatory authorities, the General Council), which met several times a year and represented the *yishuv* between sessions of the Asefat ha-Nivḥarim. The membership of the Va'ad Le'ummi during 1920–48 varied from 23 to 42, representing almost all parties in the larger body. It elected an Executive of 6 to 14 members, who headed departments of political affairs, local communities, rabbinate, education, health, social welfare, physical culture, and information. The Va'ad Le'ummi was headed by David *Yellin (1920–29), Pinḥas *Rutenberg (1929–31), Izhak *Ben-Zvi (1931–44), and David *Remez (1944–48), with Ben-Zvi as president.

*The Regulations of the Jewish Community (*Keneset Yisrael).* In 1920 the first Asefat ha-Nivḥarim decided to prepare a draft constitution for the self-government of the Jewish community and to obtain its formal recognition by the British authorities. It took five years to prepare the document and another three for its legal ratification. The long period of preparation was due to internal differences over the rights of women to vote and the nature of the community: whether it should be based on the personal principle (i.e., as in the Diaspora, for the sole purpose of satisfying religious and cultural needs) or on the territorial principle, according to which the communities should also be vested with all municipal rights and duties. In addition, Agudat Israel did its utmost to prevent the establishment of a united Jewish community not based on strictly Orthodox religious lines, even appealing to the Mandates Commission of the League of Nations.

Negotiations with the British authorities were no easier. The Va'ad Le'ummi, following the conceptions recognized under the Turkish regime, advocated obligatory membership: every person born a Jew was to be considered a member of the community unless he declared himself outside the Jewish ranks. It also wanted the organized Jewish community to have the right to levy compulsory taxes to meet the communal requirements of the *yishuv*. The British were accustomed to the idea of national self-government on a territorial, rather than communal, basis, and wanted the *yishuv* to be a voluntary religious community. Finally, compromises were worked out. In 1926 the Religious Communities Organization Ordinance was promulgated, empowering the authorities to approve for each community regulations which went beyond the satisfaction of its religious needs. Almost two years later, on Jan. 1, 1928, the *Official Gazette* published the Regulations of the Jewish Community, which recognized a Community of the Jews in Palestine, as apart from the local communities. Its central organs were granted judicial powers and the right to levy taxes. Membership was automatic for all Jews after a residence of three months, but once a year any person who wished to have his name struck from the register of the community might do so. The territorial principle was partly recognized in the provision that in any Jewish township, village, or quarter where a local council was established, it could also serve as the local community under the regulations.

The regulations provided for lay authorities – the Asefat ha-Nivḥarim, the Va'ad Le'ummi and the local community – as well as religious ones – the Rabbinical Council and the local rabbinical offices. It took two more years for the parties to agree on election regulations, approved and promulgated early in 1930, under which the elections to the Third Asefat ha-Nivḥarim were held in January 1931. The Regulations of the Jewish Community redefined and confirmed the Rabbinical Council as the supreme religious authority of the *yishuv*. The Council consisted of two chief rabbis, one Ashkenazi and one Sephardi, and six additional rabbis, three Ashkenazi and three Sephardi, all elected by an assembly consisting of 71 members, two-thirds rabbis and one-third lay representatives.

The Local Community. The Jewish local community is older than its countrywide counterpart. The newcomers joined existing Jewish communities in the towns and villages or established new ones in order to satisfy their communal religious, social and cultural needs.

In the towns the local communities were not spared the trials that were the lot of the national organization of the *yishuv*. The same conflicting interests of Sephardi and Ashkenazi congregations, ultra-Orthodox and secularists, property owners and workers, and the numerous parties contributed in varying degrees to the friction that plagued the organized local communities in Jerusalem, Jaffa, Haifa, Tiberias, and Safed. Tel Aviv, established in 1909, gained the status of a local council in 1921 and that of a township in 1922 and, being an all-Jewish community, exercised both communal and municipal functions.

Under Turkish rule and, to a lesser extent, under British administration, the rural Jewish communities, first the moshavot and later the kibbutzim and moshavim, had not only to meet the religious and cultural needs of their members, but also to fulfill municipal functions, such as water supply, sewerage, pavement of roads, protection of life and property, and maintenance of educational, social welfare, and health services. These functions, even when not legally recognized, strengthened the corporate life of the rural community, which was regulated by self-imposed rules and financed by self-imposed taxes.

The Regulations of the Jewish Community provided that only one recognized community might be formed in any one place, but the special religious needs of minorities were considered. The community was granted the right to levy taxes and deal with the communal needs of its members. A system of elections was provided for, and the relations between the community and its local rabbinical office were defined. The supervision of the Va'ad Le'ummi over the local councils was officially exerted, even if not always exercised. Both municipal and communal functions were merged in one authority in the Jewish municipalities and local councils in the country. By 1948 there were two such municipal councils (Tel Aviv and Petaḥ Tikvah) and 26 local councils. (See also section on Local Government, below)

Two generations of intensive communal life, both on the local and the national level, contributed a great deal to the maturity of Jewish public life. On the whole, communal activity became gradually more democratic, and the wide experience in self-government thus gained by the *yishuv* served the State of Israel well in setting up its constitutional organs and administrative machinery.

See also *Political Life and Parties.

BIBLIOGRAPHY: M. Burstein, *Self Government of the Jews in Palestine since 1900* (1934); M. Attias (ed.), *Sefer ha-Te'udot shel ha-Va'ad ha-Le'ummi…1918–1948* (1963²); idem, *Keneset Yisrael be-Ereẓ Yisrael: Yissudah ve-Irgunah* (1944).

[Moshé Avidor]

State of Israel

INTRODUCTION. The *Declaration of Independence on May 14, 1948, which declared Israel to be a Jewish state based on universal democratic principles, was accompanied by the establishment of the Provisional State Council as a temporary legislature and the Provisional Government of the newly established State of Israel, which were to be replaced by democratically elected bodies as soon as general elections could be held. Five days later the Law and Administration Ordinance was enacted, which specified the powers and procedures of the two bodies, transformed the system of governance from a colonial system in which all power was vested in the high commissioner, to that of a parliamentary democracy. These provisional institutions consisted mainly of members of the executive bodies of the Zionist Organization and the elected assembly of the *Yishuv*, as well as the heads of several political groups that had not been represented in them. One of the first acts of the Constituent Assembly, which soon changed its name to "the First Knesset," was to pass the Transition Law. In the absence of a constitution, this law provided the basis for the state's governmental system, which was subsequently elaborated and then replaced by additional legislation and amendments, as well as the development of practice and court decisions.

The system that evolved was that of a multiparty parliamentary democracy. At first it was characterized by the predominance of one party, *Mapai, strong governments, administrative centralization, and a large state-run economic sector. However, after 1977 Mapai's successor, the *Israel Labor Party, was no longer predominant, Israel's governments were no longer as strong, and as the years went by the central administration weakened, while large sections of the public sector were privatized. It is only vis-à-vis the local government that the central government in Israel is still omnipotent.

Like the systems of other democratic states, the system of governance in Israel is based on a separation of powers among the Legislature, Executive, and Judiciary, though this separation is not absolute, and there is occasional tension among them (see below). Israel has a president, who is a figurehead without any real power. Its judiciary (see Legal and Judicial System) is independent, and held in high esteem. Though its civil service has undergone a certain measure of politicization, it too is relatively independent.

An overwhelming majority in Israel accepts and respects the system that has evolved. Nevertheless, there are certain groups in the country that question the system's justice and/or legitimacy. On the one hand, there are certain religious circles that refuse to accept the supremacy of the secular state and its institutions, especially when their acts and policies appear to clash with the proscriptions of Jewish law – the *halakhah*. This tendency manifests itself in particular with regard to certain decisions of the High Court of Justice, and issues connected with the future of the territories occupied by Israel in the course of the Six-Day War. On the other hand there are circles among the Arab citizens of the state who would like to change the definition of Israel from a Jewish state to the state of all its citizens, or a bi-national state (see, *Binationalism), a change that if ever introduced would require major changes in its system of governance.

CONSTITUTION AND BASIC LAWS. Israel does not have a comprehensive, formal, written constitution, despite the fact that in the Declaration of Independence it was stated that a constitution was to be prepared by a Constituent Assembly by October 1948. The fact that a constitution has not been written is due primarily to opposition within religious circles to the inclusion of certain human rights issues and to the legal supremacy inherent in such a document over all other laws, both secular and religious.

In pursuance of the Knesset's decision of May 13, 1950, to introduce a constitution by stages in the form of Basic Laws, 11 such laws were introduced by 2004, laying down most of the basic principles of Israel's system of governance (see *Knesset). Though the Basic Laws have not been formally declared as superior to other laws, the High Court of Justice has on a few occasions ruled that provisions in certain ordinary laws are in contradiction to certain Basic Laws, and must therefore be amended. In addition, a few Basic Laws include the provision that certain articles in them can only be amended by an absolute majority (i.e., with the support of at least 61 of the 120 Knesset members), which sets them apart from ordinary laws that can be amended by an ordinary majority.

Though two Basic Laws dealing with human rights were passed in the early 1990s (Basic Law: Human Dignity and Freedom and Basic Law: Freedom of Occupation), in the absence of a complete human and civil rights law it is the judiciary, but particularly the High Court of Justice, that is the main instrument to prevent governmental infringements of these rights.

In the course of the Sixteenth Knesset, efforts were made by the Knesset Constitution, Law and Justice Committee, headed by Knesset Member Mikhael Eitan, with the support of the Israel Democracy Institute, to work out "a constitution by agreement."

THE ELECTORAL SYSTEM. Since Israel is a parliamentary democracy, both the make-up of its parliament and its government are determined by the results of general elections.

Basic Law: The Knesset of 1958 prescribes that elections must be "universal, nationwide, direct, equal, secret and proportional." The Knesset is elected by an extreme form of proportional representation, in which the entire country is regarded as a single 120-member constituency. Seats are distributed according to the percentage of votes polled by each list, limited only by a qualifying threshold that was at first 1%, raised to 1.5% in 1992, and to 2% in 2004. Since the number of seats has remained fixed since the first elections in 1949, but the number of votes cast has risen from 434,684 in 1949 to 3,148,364 in 2003, the number of votes per seat has constantly risen.

Though, as stated above, elections are direct, it is not individual candidates that are elected but lists, each of which is made up of one or more parties (see below). Nevertheless, because many of the parties underwent a process of democratization from the early 1990s, the members of some parties participate in the election of the candidates for their party's list. The members entering the Knesset after elections are determined according to their order in the list on which they ran, on the basis of the number of seats won by it. Should a seat fall vacant due to the resignation or death of a Knesset member, his place is taken by the next candidate on the list.

All resident Israeli citizens are enfranchised at the age of 18. Candidates for election must be at least 21 years old.

Lists represented in parliamentary groups in the outgoing Knesset have a slight advantage over newly formed ones, due to more generous financing arrangements for parliamentary groups already in the Knesset under the amended 1969 Elections Financing Law. This is the main reason why several months before new elections are held one witnesses numerous new parliamentary groups forming in the Knesset by Knesset members breaking off from their previous parliamentary group, for election financing purposes. Most election financing comes from the state budget, but lists may collect contributions from private and corporate bodies for election purposes, within strict limits prescribed by the Law. The state comptroller (see below) is responsible for checking whether the various lists have remained within these limits, and if they have not, they are fined.

To guarantee the utmost fairness, the organization and management of elections are entrusted to a Central Election Committee made up of the representatives of most of the parties, which is presided over by a Supreme Court justice as an impartial chairperson.

Since the current electoral system results in more than 10 lists passing the qualifying threshold in each election, and no list has ever won an absolute majority of the seats in any Knesset (though towards the end of the Sixth Knesset in 1969 the Alignment parliamentary group, made up of the newly founded *Israel Labor Party and *Mapam, briefly had a majority), many proposals have been made to change the electoral system, either to a single-member or multi-member constituency system, or a mixed constituency/proportional representation system, in the hope that such a change would reduce the number of parliamentary groups in the Knesset and increase the stability of Israel's system of government. However, no electoral reform bill has gone beyond first reading in the Knesset.

Though it is argued that strict adherence to parliamentary democracy is incompatible with the use of referenda to decide highly controversial issues, such as electoral reform or withdrawal from territories in Ereẓ Yisrael occupied in the course of the Six-Day War, several attempts were made to introduce a Referenda Law. In 2004 Prime Minister Ariel *Sharon resisted pressure to introduce such a law over the issue of his plan for disengagement from the Gaza Strip and the dismantlement of settlements, since he viewed it as a tactic to delay the implementation of his policy.

POLITICAL PARTIES. The Parties Law of 1992 defines a party as "a group of people who became associated in order to further, in a legal manner, political or social goals, and bring about their representation in the Knesset by means of representatives." Since the Parties Law was passed, all parties must register with the Party Registrar, they must have rules of procedure in accordance with which they operate, and certain institutions that ensure their proper operation. According to the law, a party cannot register if "there is among its goals or in its acts, explicitly or implicitly, one of the following: (1) the rejection of the State of Israel as a Jewish and democratic state; (2) incitement to racism; (3) reasonable basis (to believe) that the party will act as 'camouflage for illegal acts.'" On the basis of Amendment 19 to the Basic Law: the Knesset of 1996, only a party can run in elections to the Knesset.

The parties in Israel are an extremely heterogeneous group of political bodies, whose large number is primarily the result of the electoral system, but also the historical background of the state, and its complex social structure.

Parts of the parties and political blocs in Israel have roots in the pre-state *Yishuv* or World Zionist Organization. These include the Israel Labor Party, the *Likud, the *National Religious Party, and *Agudat Israel. There were parties – such as the *Democratic Movement for Change in 1977, Tami in 1981, and the Third Way in 1999 – that made a brief appearance on the scene against the background of some issue of protest and then disappeared. Among the protest parties *Shas – an ultra-Orthodox Sephardi Party formed in 1984 – was unique, since it survived, and became one of the pillars of the current Israeli party system.

There have been parties with comprehensive ideologies and philosophies, such as *Mapam or the *Liberal Party, or with party platforms that dealt with every political, security, social, and economic aspect of Israel's existence, such as the Israel Labor Party and the Likud, while others have been single-issue parties, such as Teḥiyyah back in the 1980s, whose almost exclusive concern was Jewish settlement in Ereẓ Yisrael, or the Third Way, formed in 1996, which objected to Israeli withdrawal from the Golan Heights. Some parties, such as the Labor Party and the Likud, try to appeal to a wide variety of populations, while others appeal to a specific homogeneous community or sector: Yahadut ha-Torah to the **ḥaredi* population, Yisrael be-Aliyah to new immigrants from the former Soviet Union, and the United Arab List to Israel's Arab citizens.

Frequently the splitting of a parliamentary group in the Knesset (see below) has led to the establishment of a new party – though the "new" parties are occasionally old parties that have reemerged (as in the case of *Aḥdut ha-Avodah-Po'alei Zion, which broke away from Mapam before the 1955 elections, the *Independent Liberal Party – formerly the *Progressive Party – which broke away from the Liberal Party when the latter formed the *Gaḥal bloc with the *Ḥerut Movement in 1965, and Mapam, which broke away from the Alignment in 1984).

While strong charismatic figures have stood at the head of most of the major parties – David *Ben-Gurion at the head of Mapai, Menaḥem *Begin at the head of the Ḥerut Movement (and then Gaḥal and the Likud), Meir *Ya'ari and Ya'akov *Ḥazan at the head of Mapam – these parties survived their departure. However, whenever such charismatic figures have left their base party and tried to form new parties around themselves – as in the case of Ben-Gurion and Rafi in 1965, Ariel Sharon and Shlomzion in 1977, Moshe *Dayan and Telem in 1981, and Ezer *Weizman and Yaḥad in 1984 – they invariably failed, and only Ariel Sharon revived his political career by returning to the Likud.

In the secular parties that emphasize liberalization and pluralism, women have always been present, and their percentage has risen. Two parties have been established and were led by women: Shulamit *Aloni founded the Civil Rights Movement in 1973 and Geula *Cohen founded the Teḥiyyah in 1979. The Israel Labor Party was led by Golda *Meir in the years 1969–74. The *ḥaredi* and Arab parties have never elected women.

Today the parties are much less ideological than they were in the past, and frequently resemble pragmatic pressure groups out to gain as much as they can for their activists and their voters. The problem as seen from the vantage point of the first decade of the 21st century is that unlike the situation in the early days of the state, and perhaps even until the mid-1990s, there is not a single political force – whether in the form of a party or bloc of parties – that commands a stable majority, able to confront the horrendous problems that Israel faces in terms of its economy, its society, its relations with the Palestinians, the Arab states and the Muslim world, and its own identity. Some expect a major implosion (*ha-mapaẓ ha-gadol* – a term coined by Haim *Ramon) that will change the whole party make-up and political structure, but that is all in the realm of speculation.

See also *Political Life and Parties.

The Knesset. The Knesset is a 120-member single-chamber legislature, whose main functions include representation of the citizens of the state, legislation, and supervision of the government. Its members run in elections on lists that are made up of a single party, or several parties, and occasionally also individuals who are not party members. A list that passes the qualifying threshold and enters the new Knesset turns into a parliamentary group. In the course of the terms of all the Knessets except for the Third, parliamentary groups have broken up or united, and the make-up of each Knesset was different at the end of its term from what it had been at its beginning.

It is frequently argued that the Knesset is weaker than the government (see below), but as is true in all democracies, the question is not whether the legislature is stronger or weaker than the executive, but whether the interaction between the two leads to an effective running of the country.

The prime minister, most of his ministers, and all the deputy ministers are members of the Knesset, and a government can be effective only if it is supported by a majority in the Knesset. For the system to run smoothly it is also desirable that the speaker should not only come from the prime minister's party, but that he should sympathize with the government's policies and work in harmony with it. Both in the Fifteenth and Sixteenth Knessets such harmony did not always exist. Another prerequisite for the system to work smoothly is that the chairmen of the Knesset Foreign Affairs and Defense Committee, the Finance Committee, the Constitution, Law and Justice Committee, and the House Committee should come from the coalition benches. The chairman of the State Control Committee must come from the opposition benches. These unwritten rules have, to the present day, been observed.

If the government's majority in the Knesset is extremely large (as in the period 1984–88, when the National Unity Governments led by Shimon *Peres and then Yitzhak *Shamir were supported by over 95 out of the 120 Knesset members) and the opposition is extremely small, the Knesset acts more or less as a rubber stamp. However, when the ratio between coalition and opposition is more balanced, the Knesset is more effective in scrutinizing the work of the government, by amending the bills it proposes, ensuring that ministers report to it and answer questions posed to them, and approving (or rejecting) its policies. If the government does not command a majority in the Knesset, it cannot survive for long, as it must depend on temporary conjunctural coalitions, as occurred in the vote on the removal of all the Jewish settlements from the Gaza Strip and of several settlements in Samaria on October 26, 2004.

Most of the parliamentary work of the Knesset is divided between the plenum, in which all 120 members of the Knesset can participate, and committees, in which a limited number of members participate. This division is especially important in the passage of legislation, where the more detailed work is done at the committee stage, while minor amendments and final approval is in the hands of the plenum. In the past, while the work of the plenum was open and fully reported, the work of the committees usually convened *in camera*, though minutes of Committee meetings were taken and eventually made available to the public. Today committee meetings are much more transparent, and their minutes (except for those of the Foreign Affairs and Defense Committee) are published within a short time after the meetings are held. Both the minutes of the plenum and the committees are published on the Knesset website. All plenum debates and some committee deliberations are broadcast on the Knesset television channel.

One of the difficulties in the smooth functioning of the various types of Knesset committees – permanent committees, special issue committees, and parliamentary inquiry committees – is that since one-quarter to one-third of the Knesset members are ministers or deputy ministers, there are not enough Knesset members left to fully man the committees, and many committees hold meetings with very few members present. Occasionally the chairman is the only member present at a committee meeting. Some have proposed that Israel introduce the so called "Norwegian Law" (called so because of article 62 in the Norwegian Constitution that stipulates that members of the government should resign their parliamentary seats), which would oblige ministers to resign their Knesset seats. Others suggest that quorums be introduced both in the plenum and the committees.

In the past the number of government bills passed was much larger than of private members' bills; today the number of private bills proposed is much larger than that of government bills, and most of the legislation passed is private. In the case of the annual Budget Bill the Knesset has only marginal influence, though there is the habitual last-minute ritual of the Ministry of Finance giving in to the financial demands of minor coalition partners in order to ensure their support. If the Knesset does not pass the Budget Law by March 31 of the financial year for which the new budget applies, new elections must be held. However, the most problematic piece of legislation is what is known as the "Arrangements Law," accompanying every Budget Law since 1985, which enables the government to pass amendments to existing laws, supposedly to facilitate the implementation of the budget, without the Knesset having a real opportunity to properly scrutinize them.

The Knesset dissolves before its four-year term is up under the following conditions: (a) If the Knesset itself decides to dissolve itself before its term is up. In this case a special law is passed, and the third reading requires the support of at least 61 Knesset members; (b) If 61 Knesset members vote for a motion of no-confidence in the government, and the Knesset member proposed by them to form an alternative government fails; (c) If the prime minister decides to dissolve the Knesset, and a candidate proposed by at least 61 Knesset members does not manage to form an alternative government; (d) If the Knesset fails to pass the state budget by March 31 of the year to which the budget applies.

It is the Knesset that elects the president of the state and the state comptroller.

THE PRESIDENT OF THE STATE. The president is the titular head of state, who has primarily ceremonial duties and few powers.

Originally, Basic Law: the State President, which was passed in 1964, stipulated that the president is elected by the 120 members of the Knesset, by secret ballot for a five-year term, which can be prolonged by an additional term (this was after the second president, Izhak *Ben-Zvi, was elected to a third term in 1962). In 1998 the law was amended, so that now the president is elected to a single seven-year term.

The tasks of the president include participation in official ceremonies, including the opening of each Knesset session; official visits in Israel and abroad as the representative of the state; addresses to the public on festive occasions; the granting of credentials to Israeli ambassadors to other countries, and the receiving of the credentials of foreign ambassadors to Israel; receiving the reports from government meetings, and recommending parole, or the reduction of sentences for prisoners.

Except for the period 1996–2001 when the prime minister was directly elected, the president is responsible for consulting all the parliamentary groups elected to a new Knesset with regard to the appointment of a new prime minister, and it is he who calls upon the candidate with the best chances of mustering a stable coalition to form a new government. Should a government resign in the middle of a Knesset term, he has a similar task.

Though the first president, Chaim *Weiẓmann (1948–52), was affiliated on the whole with the General Zionists, his choice as president reflected appreciation for his role in representing the Zionist cause between the two world wars. Izhak Ben-Zvi (1952–63), Shneor Zalman *Shazar (1963–73), Ephraim *Katzir (1973–78), Yitzhak *Navon (1978–83), Chaim *Herzog (1983–93), and Ezer *Weizman (1993–2003) were all Mapai or Labor Party candidates. Israel's eighth president, Moshe *Katsav (2003–), was the first Likud candidate to be elected.

During his tenure of office the president is not expected to take controversial political positions. The only president who blatantly broke this unwritten rule was Ezer Weizman. Navon was the only president who returned to active politics after ending his term.

Should the president of the state be abroad or be temporarily indisposed, it is the speaker of the Knesset who fulfils his functions.

THE STATE COMPTROLLER. The task of the state comptroller is to audit and examine the proper functioning of ministries, the government, local government, the armed forces, all persons and bodies operating on behalf of the State, enterprises, institutions, funds, and other bodies in whose management the government participates, or any body which is financed by the State and is subject to control by law, on the basis of a Knesset decision or government agreement. The control concerns the legality, integrity, proper management, efficiency, and frugality of the audited body's activities and is much broader than what is customary in most other countries. While the comptroller enjoys many of the powers of committees of inquiry, he does not have the administrative power to enforce laws or impose sanctions on the controlled bodies. In his annual and special reports, which deal with a variety of bodies or specific spheres of activity, the comptroller publishes his findings, and may recommend to the state attorney that a criminal investigation be opened, should there be suspicion of criminal wrongdoing. His reports also comment on whether the controlled bodies have paid heed to his findings in previous reports.

Basic Law: the State Comptroller, which was passed in 1988 and amended in 1998, stipulates that the state comptroller be elected for a single seven-year term by the Knesset. He presents his reports to the speaker of the Knesset and the president of the state, and in accordance with the State Comptroller Law of 1958 the Knesset State Control Committee deliberates his reports. Before Basic Law: the State Comptroller was passed the comptroller was appointed by the president of the State, and used to present his reports to the minister of finance.

Since 1971 the state comptroller also serves as ombudsman.

Israel's state comptrollers to date were Siegfried *Moses (1949–61), Yiẓḥak Nebenzahl (1961–82), Yiẓḥak Tunik (1982–86), Ya'akov Meltz (1986–88), Miriam Ben-Porat (1988–98), and Eliezer Goldberg (1998–2005), and Micha Lindenstrauss (2005–). Meltz, Ben-Porat, and Goldberg all served on the Supreme Court before being elected to the job.

THE CENTRAL GOVERNMENT. The government (*memshalah*) is the main policy-making body in Israel. Its make-up and functions were first laid down in the Law and Administration Ordinance (1949). This was replaced by Basic Law: the Government of 1968, which was replaced by a second version of this law in 1992, and a third version in 2001.

Following general elections the president of the state consults with all the parliamentary groups that were elected to the new Knesset, and on the basis of these consultations decides who among their leaders has the best chance of forming a stable government. Should a government resign or be brought down by a vote of no-confidence in the Knesset, it is again the president who calls on the head of one of the groups to form a new government. The designated prime minister has a period of 28 days, which may be further prolonged, in which to form his government. Should he fail, a majority of the Knesset members may ask the president to approach another candidate. So far there have been three occasions on which the person designated by the president failed to form a government. On the first two occasions – in 1951 and 1961 – Ben-Gurion (Mapai) failed to form new governments, and the result was early elections. On the third occasion, after the Twenty-Third Government was brought down by a vote of no-confidence on March 15, 1990, the president called on Peres (Labor) to form a government, and when he failed, turned to Yitzhak Shamir (Likud).

The only period when it was not the president of the state who determined who should form the new government was in the years 1996–2001 when the second Basic Law: the Government was in force, and the prime minister was elected directly by the electorate. Three prime ministers were directly elected: Binyamin *Netanyahu (Likud) in 1996, Ehud *Barak (One Israel) in 1999, and Ariel Sharon (Likud) in 2001.

Since no list in Israel has ever received a majority of the Knesset seats, and since the government requires the confidence of the Knesset in order to survive, all of Israel's governments to the present have been based on coalitions of varying political composition. All the coalitions that have served since the establishment of the State were led either by Mapai or by the Likud. The make-up of Israel's coalition governments has not always been based on ideological cohesion, but on political expediency, with the main goal being maximum political stability. In the years 1967–70, 1984–90, and 2001–2, Israel had National Unity Governments in which both major political parties served together. In the Twenty-First and Twenty-Second Governments, which served in the years 1984–88, the governments were based on parity between the two. The fact that all of Israel's governments have been coalition governments, based on compromise, has meant that the prime minister has never been able to implement his party's platform in full.

The prime minister (*rosh ha-memshalah*, head of the government) is the person who runs the government, and even though he does not always get his way, only he among the government members can decide to break up a government, or recommend that new elections be held. In the years before the lists of the two major parties for the Knesset were elected by their central committees or registered members, the leaders of these parties had much more leverage over their Knesset members and ministers, since the future of the latter's political careers was largely in their hands. However, since the early 1990s, the party leaders, even when they are in the position of prime minister, have much less control over their Knesset members and ministers, since the latter owe their position and power to members of their party's central committee or registered members, and members of the Knesset and even ministers are less afraid to defy the leader of their party than in the past. This was clearly manifested in the Likud in 2004, when the issue of the disengagement from the Gaza Strip and dismantlement of settlements came up both in the government and the Knesset. The direct election of the prime minister was to have strengthened the position of the prime minister vis-à-vis the Knesset, but this system survived for less than five years, for other reasons.

Except for a brief period in the Fifteenth Knesset, there has been no legal limitation on the number of ministers that could serve in the government. In the early governments formed by David Ben-Gurion the number of ministers was 12, and for a certain period the Twenty-Ninth Government formed by Sharon in 2001 had 29. Not all ministers need be members of the Knesset, though most are. The prime minister and deputy ministers must be members. The prime minister may choose a deputy prime minister or deputies. In the event that the prime minister is absent or temporarily indisposed, the deputy prime minister (if such has been chosen) or another designated minister runs the meetings of the government. In the government formed by Ariel Sharon in January 2005 a new position of vice prime minister was created, side by side with the deputy prime minister, in order to resolve a coalition problem. Since Ehud *Olmert already held the position of deputy prime minister, Shimon Peres was given the title of vice premier.

Ministers may hold more than one portfolio, while there may be ministers without portfolio. The number and definition of ministries has changed over the years. At times the creation of a new ministry has reflected changing objective requirements, at times coalition constraints, and at yet others the need to provide a certain prospective minister with a "respectable" portfolio. Thus, for example, in 1990 the Ministry of the Environment was established by removing various functions from other ministries for Roni Milo (Likud), and the same was done in 1996 when the Ministry for National Infrastructures was established in the same manner for Sharon.

The work of the government is governed by several documents. First of all, there are the coalition agreements, signed between the parliamentary group of the prospective prime minister and the other parliamentary groups joining the coalition. Next there are the government guidelines, which indicate the policies that the government intends to pursue in various areas, and are outlined by the prime minister to the Knesset when he presents his government to it and seeks its confidence; a document called "The Procedures for the Work of the Coalition" that outlines how members of the parliamentary groups that are in the coalition are expected to relate to government bills and private members' bills, and other matters connected with coalition discipline; and finally the Rules of Procedure for the Work of the Government, which might vary slightly from government to government. The first three documents are political rather than legal documents, and there are no legal sanctions for their breach. It should be noted that some of the most dramatic steps taken by Israeli governments have run counter to their original guidelines. This was especially notable in the case of the peace treaty signed by Begin in 1979 with Egypt, which involved full Israeli withdrawal from the Sinai Peninsula, and the Declaration of Principles signed by Yitzhak *Rabin in 1993 with Yasser *Arafat, followed by the Cairo and Taba Agreements, which involved Israeli recognition of the PLO and Israeli withdrawal from much of the Gaza Strip and the West Bank in favor of a Palestinian Authority. However, in both cases the documents were brought to the Knesset for approval before they went into force.

The government meets as a rule once a week, on Sundays, to discuss major policy issues and other government business and to approve legislation for submission to the Knesset. Decisions may be taken by majority vote and are then covered by collective government responsibility. All government deliberations are officially secret, but in other than security matters "leaks" to the media are common. At the end of government meetings the government secretary (a political appointee) issues a statement. Government decisions on matters that are not secret have been published, since September 2004, on the website of the Government Office. Before that they could be obtained on request from the Government Secretariat – a professional body that is in charge of providing clerical services to the government and the committees, preparing their agendas, taking minutes at meetings, and circulating decisions.

Much government business is done by permanent or *ad hoc* ministerial committees made up of the ministers directly concerned. Decisions of ministerial committees are usually automatically adopted by the government. In the past two decades it has also become the practice to appoint an inner cabinet to deal with security issues and other sensitive matters. During the office of the two National Unity Governments of 1984–88, the cabinet was made up of 10 members – five from the Alignment and five from the Likud, and no decision could be adopted, unless supported by at least six members. Thus, the decision to leave Lebanon in 1985 was adopted, and approval of the London Agreement, reached between Foreign Minister Shimon Peres (Alignment) and Jordanian King Hussein, was rejected.

Governments in all parliamentary democracies are based on the collective responsibility of all its members, and the prime minister has the right to fire ministers who have voted in the Knesset against government bills or other votes concerning the government's status and policy, or if members of their parliamentary groups did so in the Knesset. It was on this basis that in 1976 Prime Minister Yitzhak Rabin dismissed the ministers from the *National Religious Party, when members of their parliamentary group voted in favor of a motion of no-confidence in the government. In 2004 Prime Minister Ariel Sharon dismissed the ministers from the National Unity Party, not only because they intended to vote in the government against his policy of separation from the Gaza Strip and the removal of the Jewish settlements there, but because he believed they were guilty of incitement against him personally and his policies.

A government continues to serve until a new government is formed, occasionally as a transition government, to which different rules apply than for an ordinary government. The service of a government ends if the prime minister passes away or resigns.

From the First to Eighth Knesset (1949–77, 28 years), 17 governments served. From the Ninth to Sixteenth Knesset (1977–2004, 27 years) 13 served. Nevertheless, the first period, in which Mapai and the Labor Party were predominant, was more stable, and the fact that four different governments served in the course of the Second Knesset merely reflected Ben-Gurion's inclination to try to get his way with problematic coalition partners by resigning and forming a new coalition, frequently with the same make-up as the previous coalition. Since 1977 the make-up of the governments – both in terms of parliamentary groups and personalities – has been much less stable. Whereas in the first period there were several ministers who held particular portfolios in numerous successive governments (for example, Beḥor Shalom Shitrit, who was minister of police from the First to the Thirteenth Governments), in the second period there have been ministries run by several different ministers in the course of a single government (for example, both in the Eighteenth Government led by Menaḥem Begin and in the Twenty-Seventh Government led by Netanyahu, there were three different ministers of finance).

There is never a situation in which there is no government. A government serves until a new one is formed, though after the prime minister has resigned or has passed away, or after new elections have been held, it becomes an interim government until the new government is formed. Only in four Knessets did a single government serve (the Fourth, Seventh, Ninth, and Fourteenth), and of these only two – the Fifteenth

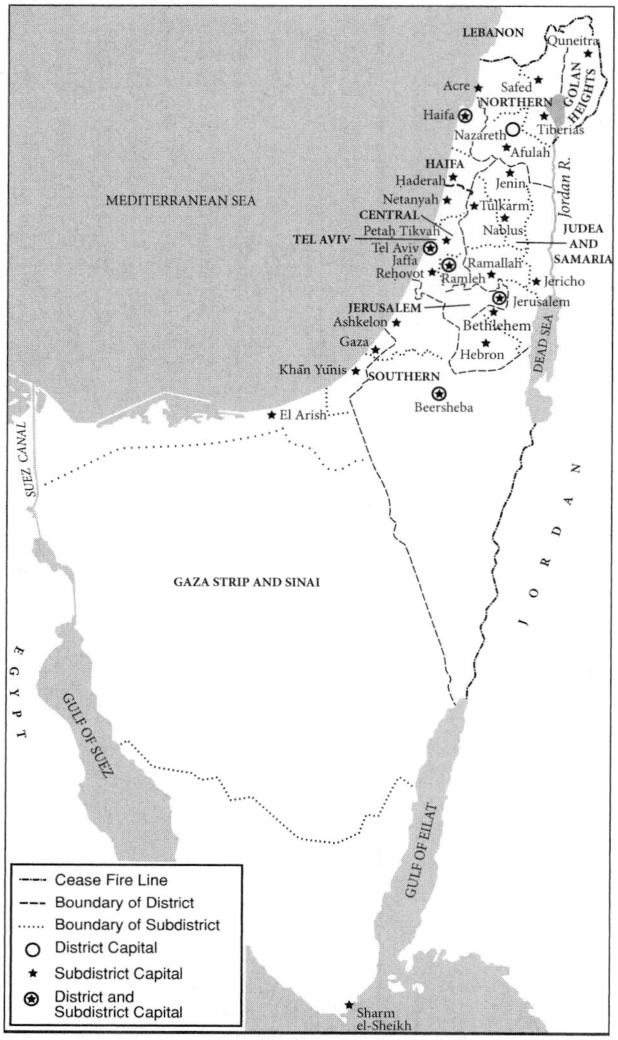

Map 3. Administrative division of Israel and Administered Territories, 1971. After Atlas of Israel, *Survey of Israel 1970.*

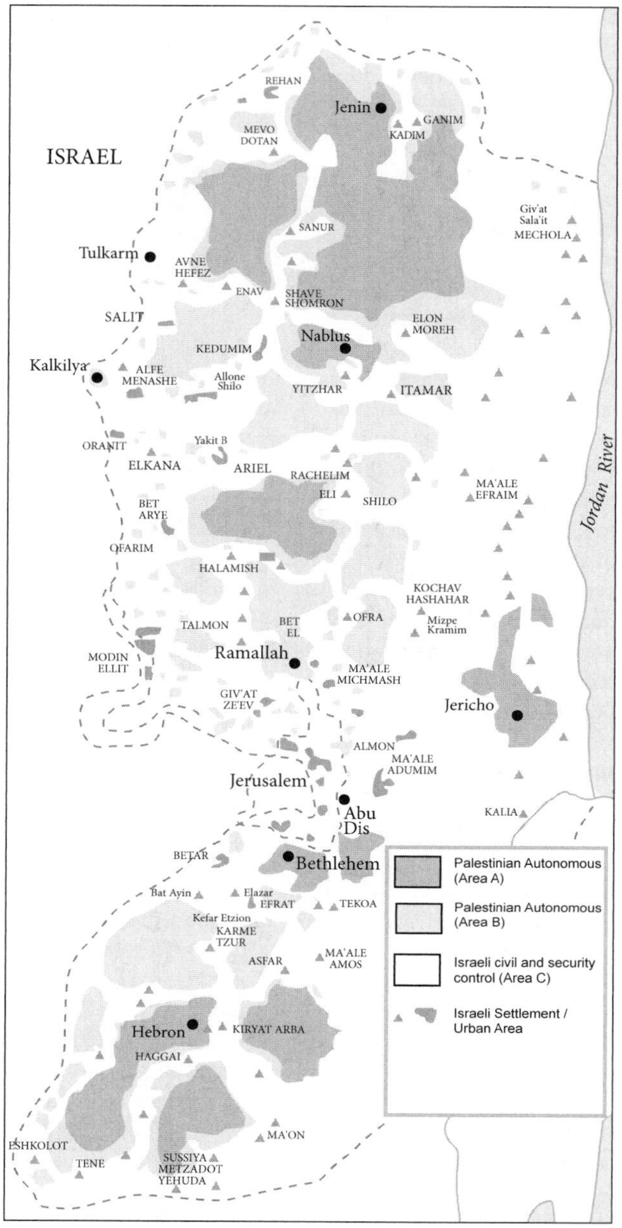

Map 4. Administrative division of Israel and Palestine, 2004.

Government headed by Golda Meir in 1969–73 and the Eighteenth Government headed by Menaḥem Begin (1977–81) – served full four-year terms. There were two governments that came to an end due to the death of the prime minister – the Thirteenth Government, after Prime Minister Levi *Eshkol passed away in February 1969, and the Twenty-Fifth Government, after Prime Minister Yitzhak Rabin was assassinated in November 1995.

See also Political Life and Parties.

THE CIVIL SERVICE. The civil service, in particular its top echelons in key ministries such as the Finance Ministry, has played, over the years, a prominent role in the policy-making system. In the early days of the State much of the civil service was mobilized from the pre-state Va'ad Le'ummi, Jewish Agency, employees in the British Mandatory Government and its armed forces, and the Histadrut. Many of the low-level jobs in the civil service were filled by young persons born in the country and new immigrants. In the early years party appointments for top civil service positions were common, and it was highly unlikely that members of the former dissident groups, the Ḥerut Movement or the Communist Party, would be appointed to any but the lowest positions.

Over the years the Civil Service Commission, which was first situated in the Ministry of Finance and later moved to the Prime Minister's Office, made great efforts to ensure that the civil service enlist new workers on the basis of tenders and that it be run according to a merit system. The main goal of the Civil Service (Appointments) Law of 1959 was to ensure neutrality in the selection of employees at all levels. However, to the present day, many of the tenders are still tailored for specific candidates.

Both the law and the Rules of Procedure in the State Service (*Takshir*), which deals with the status, rights, and duties of state employees, recognize that ministers and director generals should be able to employ their own people in certain positions – especially in their bureaus – considered "trust positions." However, the moment the minister or the director general leaves his position, those installed in the trust positions must leave their positions as well. There are also certain senior posts that are free from tenders, or for which the selection is by means other than tenders, and it is the government's prerogative to decide who should be appointed to them, or to approve them. There are 53 categories of such positions. In addition there are 11 senior diplomatic posts that are political appointments, even though the candidates must be approved by the government after being reviewed by an appointments committee. Since the scandal of the appointment of attorney Roni Bar-On as state attorney in January 1997, a public-professional committee selects suitable candidates for the position from which the government chooses.

Under various laws and the Rules of Procedure in the State Service civil servants are not allowed to engage in any political activities in their place of employment; they cannot be actively involved in party activities or fund raising for political purposes. In addition, civil servants may not engage in private employment unless they have received express permission to do so, and must beware of any conflict of interests. Nepotism is forbidden, as is the receipt of gifts and other benefits, unless expressly permitted. In June 1987 the civil service commissioner published rules of ethics for all state employees, and this in addition to the various laws and the Rules of Procedure in the State Service.

Despite the attempts to run the civil service on the basis of the highest ethical standards, in practice the picture is not always satisfactory. The greatest problem is that of unsuitable political appointments at all levels. The problem intensified after Tami, a Sephardi party headed by Aharon Abuhatzeira, first entered the government in 1981, and later when Shas, a *ḥaredi* Sephardi party, first entered the government in 1984. Both these parties felt that they had a duty to their constituents to redress years of what they viewed as discrimination on ethnic grounds. The problem further intensified after the major parties started to democratize the procedures by which they chose their own candidates for the Knesset in the early 1990s, and politicians became more dependent on members of their parties' central committees or registered party members. The state comptroller (see above) has frequently warned against political appointments that result in unqualified persons being given key jobs, but his special report on political appointments published on August 25, 2004, was the most severe. The state comptroller was especially critical of massive political appointments – to the point of fictitious jobs actually being created for cronies – in the Ministry for the Environment, when Tzaḥi Hanegbi (Likud) headed it in the Twenty-Ninth Government formed by Sharon in 2004. The state comptroller's allegations led the state attorney to recommend that Hanegbi be investigated on possible criminal charges, and Hanegbi – then minister of internal security – voluntarily left his new post to enable the charges against him to be investigated. The Supreme Court has also ruled against political appointments.

It should be noted that the ratio of regular civil servants in the general population fell from around 1.7% in 1952 to around 0.8% 50 years later (these figures include employees in government hospitals but do not include teachers, policemen, military personnel, and many others). This drop resulted from the privatization of certain services previous provided by the government, from the shift of certain services to local government, and since the 1990s from greater use of manpower workers and outsourcing. In general there appears to be a striving for "smaller government," and for certain ministers of finance, like Binyamin Netanyahu, who assumed the post in February 2003, the motivation was not only budgetary but also ideological.

LOCAL GOVERNMENT. The local government system of Israel is still based on the British Mandatory Municipalities Ordinance of 1934, and the Local Councils Ordinance of 1941, as amended by the Law and Administration Ordinance of 1948, with all the powers that had been vested in the high commissioner in this sphere now handed over to the minister of the interior. The minister supervises the activities of the local authorities through six district commissioners and district officers, who operate in 14 subdistricts. If a council's work breaks down through gross inefficiency or chronic dissension among the councilors, the minister may appoint a committee of officials (*va'adah keru'ah*) to administer its affairs until the next elections.

Though in the early years of the State, Knesset members seemed united in the idea of giving local government a suitable position in the Israeli democracy, and passing appropriate legislation to fulfill this vision, in fact no major changes were introduced in the local government system.

Until 1978 municipal elections, first held in 1950, were held for municipal or local councils, and the councilors elected a mayor or head of the local council. From 1955 to 1973 local elections were held simultaneously with elections to the Knesset. Since 1978 mayors and heads of local councils have been directly elected in elections held every four or five years. While the direct election of mayors and local council heads was considered progress in the democratic sense, it has weakened the position of the major parties, increased the number of independent candidates and local lists, and increased the chances of mayors or heads of local councils being elected without enjoying a majority in the council, which has increased the bargaining power of splinter groups and individuals. Until 1989 the Israel Labor Party managed to maintain its hegemony in local government – a hegemony it has since lost.

Until 1996 mayors and local council heads could run for election in the Knesset within the framework of the lists participating in the elections. Already in the elections to the Constituent Assembly several mayors and heads of local councils were elected to the Knesset. Towards the end of the Tenth Knesset the Israel Labor Party forbade its Knesset members to serve simultaneously as mayors, as a result of which two Labor Knesset members resigned as mayors – Jacques Amir in Dimona and Aharon Nahmias in Safad. However, in the elections to the Eleventh Knesset several Labor mayors and heads of local councils were elected to the Knesset and refused to resign. In October 1996 an amendment was introduced to the Law on the Immunity, Rights and Duties of Members of the Knesset, prohibiting Knesset members to serve simultaneously as mayors or heads of local councils. This was part of a decision to prohibit Knesset members to serve in any other position – with the exception of chairmen of one of the trade union associations – while serving in the Knesset, to ensure that they would carry out their duties as Knesset members on a full-time basis. It should be noted that when given the choice between serving in the Knesset or serving as mayors or heads of local councils the choice has almost always been in favor of the former. There are those who feel that this prohibition has weakened local government in Israel, since its heads have been removed from one of the main foci of influence in the country.

There are three types of local authority in Israel: municipalities representing cities and larger towns; local councils representing small towns; and regional councils representing several small settlements of various sizes and types. In May 2004 there were 70 municipalities (compared to eight in 1948), of which 57 were Jewish within the Green Line, three Jewish outside the Green Line, and 10 non-Jewish (Arab, Druze, and Circassian) within the Green Line. There were 142 local councils (compared to 24 in 1948), of which 57 were Jewish within the Green Line, 14 Jewish outside the Green Line, and 71 non-Jewish within the Green Line. Finally there were 54 regional councils (compared to six rural and regional councils in 1948) representing several small settlements of various sizes and types, of which 45 were Jewish within the Green Line, seven Jewish outside the Green Line, and two non-Jewish within the Green Line. In the course of 2003, as part of a plan to increase the efficiency of the local government system, it was decided to reduce the number of small local councils by uniting some of them with each other or with existing municipalities. The plan succeeded only partially, primarily due to pressure from stronger local councils refusing to unite with weaker ones, and pressure from politicians concerned about the loss of jobs at the local authority level.

The local authority provides two types of services: state services, especially in the sphere of education, welfare, and health, and local services, primarily in the spheres of sewage and sanitation, city planning, recreation, sports and cultural activities, and fire-fighting services. The budget of the authorities is divided into the "regular budget," earmarked for current activities, and "extraordinary budgets" for development purposes. The main sources of income are locally collected municipal taxes, various charges for services provided and fees for licenses; income from government allocations for state services (in the case of education and welfare the government covers 75% of costs), and grants, to cover certain budgetary deficits. Towards the end of 2004, of the 266 local authorities, only 15 did not require grants in order to provide their inhabitants with a basic level of services. Since the establishment of the state the scope of services provided by the local authorities has progressively grown, as has their financial dependence on the central government.

Not all the local authorities have demonstrated responsible management, with some actually involved in corrupt practices. Early cases of corruption that reached the courts involved Shmuel Rechtman in Reḥovot in the late 1970s and Aharon Abuhazeira in Ramleh in the early 1980s. In the 1990s and the beginning of the new millennium, such cases were no longer rare. Irresponsible management and corruption were among the reasons why the government has became increasingly wary of covering the deficits of many local authorities, and despite the appointment of several commissions of inquiry (see below), the problem has not been resolved. Already in 1999 only half the local authorities managed to balance their budgets, while the rest had to borrow from the banks. In 2003 only 55 authorities out of 266 were balanced. In 2004 numerous local authorities were unable to pay salaries to their employees for months on end.

Put another way, one might argue that the local government system in Israel is subject to a structural problem, due to the fact that the source of power of the authorities is the local populace but the main source of money to finance their activities, and the main source of decisions affecting them, is the central government. The centralization of the decision-making process is an inseparable part of the Israeli political culture, and it is therefore difficult for the local government to engage in independent activity, while the central government avoids delegating its powers downwards.

Since 1964 six commissions have investigated the situation in the local authorities with the intention of improving the situation. These were the Vitkon Committee of 1964, which investigated the tax system in local authorities; the Kubersky Committee of 1976, which dealt with improving the system of financing local authorities; the Zanbar Committee, which sat from 1976 to 1981 and dealt with the whole system of local government and the relations between the central and local governments; the Harmelech Committee, which sat from 1991 to 1992 and investigated the level of services and budgetary allocations for health and welfare in the local authorities; the Suari Committee, which sat from 1992 to 1993 and dealt with the deficit-covering grants to local authorities; and finally the Shahar Committee, which sat from 1995 to 1998 and dealt with merging some of the smaller authorities and thus reducing their number.

THE SEPARATION OF POWERS. Among parliamentary democracies, such as Israel, the separation of powers among the legislature, executive, and judiciary, even though extensive, is not absolute. Thus, it is not always possible to determine whether the checks and balances that have been installed in the system to ensure that none of the three administrative branches diverges from its legitimate sphere of activity have not themselves created a divergence.

In the case of the Knesset and the government the separation cannot be complete since the prime minister, most of the ministers, and all of the deputy ministers are Knesset members, and though they do not function as ordinary members they do vote in the plenum. Some of those who propose that Israel should adopt the so called "Norwegian Law" do so because they wish to do away with the anomaly created by the existing situation. In addition, the government is responsible for setting much of the Knesset's agenda. Another sphere in which a blurring of the separation of powers occurs between the legislature and the executive is in the case of subsidiary legislation, where the ministries concerned lay down regulations based on the primary legislation, i.e., the laws passed by the Knesset.

As is true in all parliamentary democracies (as opposed to presidential democracies) the Knesset is able to bring down the government by means of a vote of a motion of no-confidence, which since 1996 has required that at least 61 of the 120 Knesset members vote for it. Until 1996 a simple majority of those voting could bring down the government.

As to the separation of powers between the Knesset and the judiciary, in the absence of a constitution, and as a result of the activist inclination of the Supreme Court since the mid-1990s, the courts have on several occasions declared a certain piece of legislation, or certain articles in a law, to be in contradiction to a basic law and consequently unconstitutional. The courts cannot abrogate a law, but they can call upon the Knesset to amend it. One of the proposals made in recent years to deal with this situation was the establishment of a constitutional court which will be separated from the regular judicial system and stop the ordinary courts from meddling in the work of the Knesset.

In the case of the executive and the judiciary, part of the blurring in powers is created by the fact that the attorney general is not only a legal adviser to the government but is also the head of the state's public prosecution. Furthermore, the relationship between the attorney general and the state attorney with the Ministry of Justice is also liable to create a certain blurring of the separation of powers, even though the method by which the attorney general and state attorney are chosen is supposed to ensure their independence within the system. It should be noted that while the activities of the executive are subject to judicial review, this is only true in so far as the upholding of the law is concerned, and the courts refrain from deciding on purely political or military issues.

Though the judges are completely free of the meddling of the legislature in their decisions, two Knesset members and two ministers (the minister of justice and another minister) are members of the committee that selects and promotes judges. The minister of justice chairs the committee.

RELIGION AND STATE. Israel's Declaration of Independence proclaims Israel to be a Jewish State. This was not meant to say that Israel would be Jewish in the sense that Jewish religious law would be supreme in the land as it is in various theocratic regimes, but merely that it would be the State of the Jews, in which all Jews (with few exceptions) would be allowed to settle, in which the official day of rest would be the Sabbath, the official holidays would be the Jewish holidays, and state emblems and symbols would be Jewish.

Though the law in the State of Israel, in all spheres except marriage, divorce, and burial, is the secular law passed by the Knesset, there is no strict separation between religion and the State. Thus, the chief rabbis, municipal rabbis, employees of the religious councils, and their counterparts in other religions are financed by the State. Religious services, in the form of synagogues, *mikva'ot*, and the provision of wedding and burial services, are also the responsibility of the State. In the sphere of weddings and burial services the religious authorities have an almost absolute monopoly that is only very slowly being broken as a result of growing numbers of citizens who are either denied such services (in the case of mixed marriages and persons not considered Jewish by the religious establishment, which is exclusively Orthodox) or demand alternative, non-religious or non-Orthodox services.

But even in the so-called secular law book, there is quite a bit of "religious legislation" – laws that curtail certain activities that touch upon religious beliefs and observance such as the sale of pork, working on the Sabbath, archaeological digs in locations, where there are burial grounds, the performance of postmortems, etc.

It should be noted, however, that there are religious circles in Israel – both in the *ḥaredi* and National Religious camps – that do not accept the supremacy of the laws passed by the Knesset over the *halakhah*, or at least do not accept its supremacy in certain spheres. This is the basis for the opposition of certain circles to the introduction of a secular constitution in Israel and for the rejection by some of government decisions which are felt to be in violation of the *halakhah*, such as the decision to remove Jewish settlements from the Gaza Strip and the West Bank.

[Edwin Emanuel Gutmann / Susan Hattis Rolef (2nd ed.)]

BIBLIOGRAPHY: A. Rubinstein and B. Medina, *Ha-Mishpat Ha-Konstituzi'oni shel Medinat Yisrael*, 2 vols. (1996²); A. Rubinstein, *Ha-Rashuyot ha-Mekomiyot: Be'ayot Merkaziot va-Ḥalufot le-Piteron*, Knesset Research and Information Center (2004).

LEGAL AND JUDICIAL SYSTEM

UNDER THE OTTOMAN EMPIRE (1876–1917)

Judiciary

Throughout the period from the promulgation of the Ottoman Constitution of 1876 until the present time there have been both secular and religious courts exercising jurisdiction in the territory of the land of Israel, but the extent of the jurisdiction of such courts, the qualifications of the judges thereof and of the persons authorized to plead therein, the procedure thereof and the language of pleading therein have varied from time to time.

Under the Ottoman Constitution of 1876 it was strictly forbidden to institute any extraordinary court other than the established courts of justice, but arbitrators might be appointed subject to the provisions laid down by law, and a special high court could be convened by Imperial Irade when necessary to try ministers, members of the Court of Requests or any person who was guilty of an attempt against the person or rights of the sultan or who had attempted to endanger the safety of the state. The constitution also provided that cases under Shariʿa (Muslim religious) law had to be heard by the Shariʿa Courts and civil cases by the Civil Courts.

RELIGIOUS COURTS. Shariʿa Courts were given jurisdiction in matters not within the jurisdiction of the Civil Courts, such as property in waqf (Muslim religious trust), inhibitions and the termination of inhibitions, wills, the appointment and removal of guardians and trustees, and the granting of loans from the estates of orphans and waqf estates. They also had jurisdiction to hear suits to decide the shares of heirs to property and suits relating to estates in which letters of administration had to be taken out, as well as all other suits concerning rights under the Shariʿa law. Where the parties before a Shariʿa Court made a written agreement that a matter in dispute should be dealt with by the Shariʿa Court, although it was within the jurisdiction of the Civil Court, no application could subsequently be entertained in the matter by the Civil Court. The Ministry of Justice in Constantinople exercised administrative powers in regard to the procedure and internal organization of the Shariʿa Courts, the rules of procedure for which were established by law. The Jewish and Christian Religious Courts had jurisdiction over members of their respective communities in matters of personal status.

CIVIL COURTS. Under Regulations of June 30, 1877, courts were divided into two divisions, namely, civil and criminal, in each of which there were courts of first instance and courts of appeal. In addition, there were Peace Courts and Courts of First Instance presided over by a single judge. Courts of First Instance were established in every *qaḍa'* (sub-district) of the empire competent to hear civil actions when the subject matter did not exceed 5,000 piasters or a revenue of 500 piasters per annum without appeal. In cases of higher amounts there was a right of appeal to a Court of Appeal. There were 13 Courts of First Instance west of the Jordan. Commercial Courts were established in important commercial centers; in other places commercial cases were dealt with by the civil courts. In such cases an appeal lay to the Commercial Court in the chief town of the vilayet (province), and from judgments of the latter an appeal lay to the Commercial Court of Constantinople. In each *qaḍā* a Criminal Court, consisting of a president and two members, was competent to deal with contraventions without right of appeal, and crimes subject to appeal to a Court of Appeal. A court of appeal in the principal town of each vilayet was competent to hear appeals from courts of first instance. Such courts were divided into two sections, a civil and a criminal section, and were composed of five or more judges. There were three courts of appeal in Palestine, one in each of the sanjaks (districts) of Jerusalem, Balqa (Nablus), and Acre. Finally, there was a Court of Cassation for the whole empire in Constantinople. It was divided into three sections, a civil section, a criminal section and a Court of Requests.

In the courts that were composed of three or of five judges the president was a professional judge. Not infrequently he had graduated as a clerk or registrar of the courts. The other judges were usually laymen of some local position or apprentices in the judicial service, and it was understood that their function in part was to see that members of their religious community were not oppressed in judgment. Under the constitution of 1876, duly appointed judges who were appointed by the state and held an Imperial Berat were to be irremovable, though their resignation might be accepted; their promotion, transfers, and pensions, and their removal on account of a conviction, were to be subject to a special law, which should indicate the qualifications required. The persons authorized to plead in the courts were the few advocates who had obtained a diploma in the Law School of Constantinople and a few persons who had certificates of practice before the courts in virtue of a long apprenticeship. The language of the courts was Turkish, and their procedure was based on that of the French courts. The position of foreigners was usually safeguarded by the consular authorities of their country until the Ottoman government unilaterally declared the Capitulations abolished at the outbreak of World War I.

Legislation

Under the Ottoman Constitution of 1876 the sultan was empowered to sanction and promulgate all legislation, to make proposals for all kinds of laws, and to safeguard and enforce the rules of the Shariʿa and the laws of the state. Islam was the religion of the Ottoman Empire, but subject thereto the state was required to protect the free exercise of all religions recognized in the empire and the integral enjoyment, in accordance with previous practice, of all religious privileges granted to the various communities, provided that such religions were not contrary to public morals or conducive to the disturbance of public order. All Ottoman subjects were equal in the eyes of the law as regards both rights and duties, except for matters relating to religion. Turkish was the official language of the state.

The parliament consisted of the senate and the chamber of deputies. The president and members of the senate were appointed directly by the sultan for life. They had to be at least 40 years of age and well-known persons who had gained by their acts the confidence and reliance of the public and had a past of honorable government service. Among those eligible for appointment were chief rabbis. The deputies were elected by secret ballot and had to be at least 30 years of age and Ottoman subjects. There was one deputy for every 50,000 Ottoman subjects.

Bills passed and accepted by both houses came into force when approved and sanctioned by an Imperial Irade issued by the sultan. All laws, usages, and customs in force at the time of the constitution remained in force unless and until amended or repealed. Subsequent laws and regulations had to be based on public morals and human relations and on such principles of Muhammadan law and jurisprudence as might be best suited to human intercourse and requirements of the time. This constitution was suspended, however, by order of the sultan a few months after its introduction. It was only put into effect – and then intermittently – after the Young Turk revolution of 1908. Under the Law on the Method of Publishing and Proclaiming Laws and Rules, laws and rules issued under Imperial Irade had to be published without delay in the judicial gazette and inserted in the *dustūr*, the official collection of laws. They then came into operation over the whole of the Ottoman Empire from the date specified in the text or, when no date was specified, 60 days after the date of publication. No law or rule could have retrospective effect, except in cases where a lesser penalty was substituted for a greater.

The Ottoman laws were of three categories: those written originally in Turkish, those written originally in Arabic and translated into Turkish, and those written originally in a European language, mainly French, and translated into Turkish. The most important of those laws written originally in Arabic is the Mejelle, an elaborate code of 1,851 articles containing rules of law and maxims of Muhammadan jurisprudence. It is little more than a Turkish translation from the Arab authorities on Muhammadan law, which is based primarily on the Koran and custom. The substantive part of the Mejelle is arranged in 16 books dealing with: sale, hire, guarantee, transfer of debt, pledges, trusts and trusteeship, gift, wrongful appropriation and destruction, interdiction, constraint and preemption, joint ownership, agency, settlement and release, admissions, actions, evidence and administration of oath, and administration of justice by the court.

French influence reigned supreme in the Ottoman Empire from the early part of the 19th century, when the Turkish sultans, who were the sole legislators, began to carry out the legal reforms insisted upon by the European powers. To save time and trouble they borrowed almost en bloc the principal legal codes of France, such as the commercial, maritime, civil procedure, and criminal codes. This borrowing process continued almost without interruption until Turkey entered World War I. It is therefore impossible fully to understand Ottoman legal principles without a study of French law, and Turkish lawyers and judges frequently consulted French legal textbooks and court decisions on difficult or disputed points of law.

UNDER THE BRITISH MANDATE (1917–1948)

British Military Administration, 1917–1920

One of the first acts of the British Military Administration in the Occupied Enemy Territory of Palestine was to reestablish the courts, reopening them in Jerusalem on July 24, 1918. They reduced their number to two Courts of First Instance in the original occupied territory of southern Palestine, one at Jerusalem and the other at Jaffa, and subsequently, when northern Palestine was occupied in the autumn of 1918, two others, one at Nablus and the other at Haifa, each with a British president and two Palestinian judges. In addition, a Court of Appeal was established for the whole country, composed of two British and four Palestinian judges: two Muslims, one Orthodox Christian, and one Jew. Three of the original judges of that court were taken from the small band of advocates practicing in Palestine, who were of higher caliber than the Ottoman judges. In addition, a number of Turkish judges were appointed for the Peace Courts to deal with the smaller cases. The first head of the legal department of the British Military Administration, known as the senior judicial officer, was a British army officer (Major Orme Clarke) who had been adviser to the Ottoman Ministry of Justice a year before World War I. He was the administrative head of all the judges, clerks, and staff of the Civil Courts and laid the foundations of the Palestine judicial system. He also appointed the judges of the Muslim Religious Courts after consultation with a committee composed of the Muslim members of the Court of Appeal and the inspectors of the Shariʿa Courts. The records of the civil courts, which had previously been kept in Turkish, were, as from the British occupation, kept in Arabic, which was then the predominant language in the country. The privileges of the consular jurisdiction which had been enjoyed by foreigners in Palestine by virtue of the Capitulations were not restored, but provisions were made for trial by British judges of cases in which foreigners were involved.

British Civil Administration, 1920–48

JUDICIAL. The above military system was retained with several modifications by the British Civil Administration. During the first two years (1920–22), the legal secretary, who had replaced the senior judicial officer of the British Military Administration, besides being the legal adviser of the high commissioner, was the administrative head of the courts and responsible for the appointments and dismissals. In 1922 he was replaced as administrative head of the courts by the chief justice of Palestine, who was the head of the judiciary, and he became the attorney general. The Courts of First Instance became District Courts, the Criminal Courts became the Court of Criminal Assize, and the Peace Courts became Magistrates' Courts.

Civil Courts. The Civil Courts established by the Palestine Order-in-Council, 1922, were the Magistrates' Courts, the District Courts, the Court of Criminal Assize, and the Supreme Court. The high commissioner was also empowered, by order, to establish Land Courts, as might be required from time to time. Magistrates' Courts had the jurisdiction assigned to them by the Ottoman Magistrates Law of 1913 as amended by Palestine legislation. District Courts had jurisdiction as Courts of First Instance in all civil matters not within the jurisdiction of the Magistrates' Courts and in criminal matters not within the jurisdiction of the Court of Criminal Assize, and as Appellate Courts from the Magistrates' Courts. Each was composed of a British president and two Palestinian judges. Any two judges of a District Court could sit to try misdemeanors and civil cases, but the full court had to sit to try grave charges and hear appeals. The Court of Criminal Assize had exclusive jurisdiction with regard to offenses punishable with death and such jurisdiction with regard to other offenses as might be prescribed by ordinance. It was composed of the chief justice, or any British judge of the Supreme Court, and the full District Court of the district in which the crime was committed. The Supreme Court, sitting as a Court of Appeal, had jurisdiction, subject to the provisions of any Ordinance, to hear appeals from all judgments given by a District Court in first instance, the Court of Criminal Assize, or a Land Court. Sitting as a High Court of Justice, it had jurisdiction to hear and determine petitions or applications not within the jurisdiction of any other court and necessary to be decided for the administration of justice.

In civil matters when the amount or value in dispute exceeded LP500 an appeal lay from the Supreme Court to His Majesty in Council under Article 44 of the Palestine Order-in-Council. In criminal matters, according to a decision of the Privy Council, an appeal lay to it if it gave leave, but such appeals were very rare. Under Article 45 of the Palestine Order-in-Council, 1922, the high commissioner was empowered by order to establish for the district of Beersheba and other tribal areas separate Tribal Courts, in which tribal custom was applied insofar as it was not repugnant to natural justice or morality. In addition there were Municipal courts and military courts. The former, established under the Municipal Courts Ordinance (of 1928) in certain municipal areas, had jurisdiction to try offenses against municipal regulations and bylaws and certain other offenses, such as town planning offenses committed within the municipal area, while the Military Courts had jurisdiction to try offenses under the Emergency Regulations, 1936 and the Defense (Emergency) Regulations, 1945. There were also numerous tribunals, in many of which a judge presided, established under various laws, as need arose, to deal with special classes of cases, such as those for general claims, shipping, and rents. The civil courts were empowered to exercise jurisdiction in all matters and over all persons in Palestine, but they were expressly precluded from exercising jurisdiction in any proceeding whatsoever over the high commissioner or his official or other residence or his official or other property, and no action could be brought against the Government of Palestine or any department thereof unless with the written consent of the high commissioner previously obtained. During the period of the Mandatory regime, nearly all the Ottoman rules of procedure in civil and criminal cases were replaced by rules based upon those obtaining in England save that no provision was made for trial by jury.

Jurisdiction over Foreigners. Article 8 of the Mandate declared that the privileges and immunities of foreigners, including the benefits of consular jurisdiction and protection as formerly enjoyed by Capitulations or usage in the Ottoman Empire, should not be applicable in Palestine, and Article 9 provided that the Mandatory regime should be responsible for seeing that the judicial system established in Palestine should assure to foreigners, as well as to natives, a complete guarantee of their rights. The Palestine Order-in-Council, therefore, contained special provisions for the exercise of jurisdiction over foreigners. It defined "foreigner" as meaning any person who was a national or subject of a European or American state or of Japan, but as not including native inhabitants of a territory protected by, or administered under, a Mandate granted to a European state, Ottoman subjects, and persons who had lost Ottoman nationality and had not acquired any other nationality, but the definition was altered by the Palestine Amendment Order-in-Council, 1935, to mean a person who was not a Palestinian citizen. Under the provisions, matters concerning foreigners had to be dealt with by a British judge or a majority of British judges. The burden of proof that they were entitled to be treated as foreigners was upon the persons claiming that right. The Order-in-Council also provided that a consul in Palestine might execute such non-contentious measures in relation to the personal status of nationals of his state as the high commissioner with the approval of the secretary of state might from time to time prescribe by regulation. By the Personal Status (Consular Powers) Regulations of Dec. 1, 1922, the high commissioner prescribed such non-contentious measures.

Religious Courts. In matters of personal status, namely, suits regarding marriage or divorce, alimony, maintenance, guardianship, legitimation and adoption of minors, inhibition from dealing with property of persons who are legally incompetent, successions, wills and legacies, and the administration of the property of absent persons, jurisdiction was conferred by the Palestine Order-in-Council, 1922, upon the courts of the religious communities established and exercising jurisdiction at the date of the Order (Sept. 1, 1922), namely the Muslim Religious Courts, the Rabbinical Courts, and the courts of the nine recognized Christian communities: Eastern (Orthodox), Latin (Catholic), Gregorian Armenian, Armenian (Catholic), Syrian (Catholic), Chaldean (Uniate), Greek (Catholic) Malkite, Maronite, and Syrian Orthodox. The Muslim Religious Courts were given exclusive jurisdiction in matters of personal status of Muslims and also exclusive jurisdiction in cases of the constitution or internal administration of a waqf constituted for the benefit of Muslims before a Muslim Religious Court, and there was an appeal from the court of the qadi to the Muslim Religious Court of Appeal, whose decision was final. The Rabbinical Courts of the Jewish community and the courts of the several Christian communities had exclusive jurisdiction in matters of marriage and divorce, alimony and confirmation of wills of members of their community, other than foreigners, and jurisdiction in any other matter of personal status of such persons, where all the parties to the action consented to their jurisdiction. The Rabbinical Courts and the courts of the several Christian communities, also had exclusive jurisdiction over any case as to the constitution or internal administration of a waqf or religious endowment constituted before these courts according to the religious law of the community concerned.

Matters of personal status affecting foreigners other than Muslims were within the jurisdiction of the District Courts, but those courts had no jurisdiction to pronounce a decree of dissolution of marriage. Foreigners could consent to matters of personal status being tried by the courts of the religious communities having jurisdiction in like matters affecting Palestinian citizens, but such courts, other than Muslim Religious Courts, had no power to grant a decree of dissolution of marriage to a foreign subject. Where any action of personal status involved persons of different religious communities, application could be made by any party to the chief justice, who was required, with the assistance, if he thought fit, of assessors from the communities concerned, to decide which court should have jurisdiction. Whenever a question arose as to whether or not a case was one of personal status within the exclusive jurisdiction of a Religious Court, the matter had to be referred to a Special Tribunal composed of two British judges of the Supreme Court and the president of the highest court in Palestine of the religious community concerned, or a judge appointed by him. The chief justice or the senior puisne judge of the Supreme Court, presided over the Tribunal.

The jurisdiction of the Rabbinical Courts and the Christian Religious Courts remained unchanged throughout the period of the Mandatory regime, but that of the Muslim Religious Courts was altered by the Palestine Amendment Order-in-Council, 1939, whereunder they could exercise jurisdiction over Muslims who were foreigners only if, according to their national law, Muslim Religious Courts had jurisdiction over them in matters of personal status. No provision was made in the Palestine Order-in-Council, 1922, for the granting by the courts of orders or decrees in connection with the marriage of persons neither of whom was a Muslim or a member of the Jewish community or of any of the nine recognized Christian communities, or for the dissolution or annulment of such marriages. The Palestine Amendment Order-in-Council, 1939, authorized the making by ordinance of provision for such matters, but no such ordinance was enacted.

Appointment and Qualifications of Judges. Under the Palestine Order-in-Council, 1922, the high commissioner was empowered, subject to the direction of the secretary of state, to appoint, or authorize the appointment of, such public officers of the government under such designations as he might think fit, and to prescribe their duties, and all such officers, unless otherwise provided by law, held their offices until the Order-in-Council was amended in 1939, during the pleasure of the high commissioner and thereafter during His Majesty's pleasure.

Under the Courts Ordinance, every judge of the Supreme Court or of a District Court had to be appointed by the high commissioner and held office during the pleasure of His Majesty. The persons qualified to be appointed as British judges were British judges of any court in Palestine already appointed at the date of the commencement of the Courts Ordinance (Sept. 1, 1924), and any person, being a British subject, who had been duly admitted to practice as a barrister-at-law or advocate in any part of His Majesty's dominions, or in any territory which was under His Majesty's protection, or in any territory in respect of which His Majesty had accepted a mandate from the League of Nations, and who was in any case of not less than three years' standing. Persons qualified to be appointed as Palestinian judges were judges of any court in Palestine already appointed at the date of the commencement of the ordinance, persons who had held office in Palestine as magistrates or junior government advocates or inspectors of the courts for not less than three years in any one of those offices or consecutively in one or any one of those offices, and advocates of Palestine of not less than three years' standing.

Magistrates were appointed by the high commissioner by warrant. Under the Magistrates' Courts Jurisdiction Ordinance the high commissioner was empowered to impose by the warrant of appointment such restrictions or limitations upon the jurisdiction of the appointee as he thought fit, and it was the practice to issue restricted warrants to district commissioners and British district officers, as well as to a number of Palestinian officers who had passed an elementary law examination, to enable them to try minor criminal charges, to issue warrants of arrest, and to release on bail.

The qadis of the Muslim Religious Courts, the president and members of the Muslim Religious Court of Appeal and the inspectors of the Muslim Religious Courts were nominated by the Supreme Muslim Shariʿa Council for approval by the Palestine Government and, after such approval, were appointed by that council, the president and members whereof received salaries from the Palestine government in consideration of their services in connection with the affairs of the Muslim Religious Courts. Under the Jewish Community Rules each Rabbinical Office sat as a Rabbinical Court of First Instance, and the Rabbinical Council was the Court of Appeal in matters in which the Rabbinical Courts had jurisdiction. The judges of the courts of the recognized Christian religious communities were appointed by the heads of the communities.

Qualifications of Advocates. Under the Advocates Ordinance, 1922, licenses to practice as advocate in Palestine were issued by the chief justice, who was advised by a Legal Board appointed by him consisting of at least three members who were officials of the government holding office of a legal or judicial character and not less than two advocates practicing before the civil courts. Licenses were granted either to practice before any civil courts or before any Muslim Religious Court in Palestine. Applicants for a license to practice before any civil court had to satisfy the Legal Board that they had attained the age of 25 (reduced to 23 in 1944), had passed not less than two years' service in a licensed advocates' office, and were adequately qualified by examination as to their knowledge of law. Qualifying examinations were taken by students of the Palestine Government Law School, known as the Jerusalem Law Classes; persons with legal qualifications acquired abroad could take qualifying examinations in Palestine law.

Applicants for a license to practice before the Muslim Religious Courts had to satisfy the board that they were adequately qualified by examination as to their knowledge of Muslim law and were of good character, or that they were so certified by the Supreme Muslim Shariʿa Council. Advocates alleged to be guilty of disgraceful, fraudulent, or unprofessional conduct were subject to Courts of Discipline constituted by, and subject to, the control of the chief justice. Until the ordinance was amended in 1930, no woman could be granted a license to practice as an advocate. That disqualification was removed by the amending ordinance, but a woman holding such a license did not have the right of audience in a Tribal Court or in a Muslim Religious Court unless she was certified by the Supreme Muslim Shariʿa Council to be qualified to practice. Under the Law Council Ordinance, 1938, the Legal Board was replaced by the Law Council, which was composed of not less than six members appointed by the high commissioner of whom not less than four had to be practicing advocates, with the attorney general as ex officio chairman. It was also empowered to inquire into the conduct of advocates and persons permitted to practice before the Muslim Religious Courts.

LEGISLATION. Under the Mandate for Palestine, confirmed by the Council of the League of Nations on July 24, 1922, His Britannic Majesty, who had been selected by the principal Allied Powers as mandatory for Palestine, was given full powers of legislation and of administration in Palestine save as such powers were limited by the terms of the Mandate. Under article 15, the mandatory was required to ensure complete freedom of conscience and the free exercise of all forms of worship for all, subject only to the maintenance of public order and morals. There was to be no discrimination of any kind between the inhabitants of Palestine on grounds of race, religion, or language, and no one was to be excluded from the country on the sole ground of his religious belief. Under article 22 English, Arabic, and Hebrew were the official languages. Under article 21 the mandatory was required to secure the enactment of a law of antiquities based on the rules set out in that article. Such a law – the Antiquities Ordinance – was enacted and is still in force. Under article 7 the administration of Palestine was made responsible for enacting a nationality law, which was to facilitate the acquisition of Palestinian citizenship by Jews taking up their permanent residence in the country.

The Palestine Order-in-Council, 1922, was made by His Britannic Majesty by virtue and in exercise of his powers in that behalf by the U.K. Foreign Jurisdiction Act, 1890 or otherwise, and came into force on Sept. 1, 1922. It provided (article 46) that the jurisdiction of the civil courts should be exercised in conformity with the Ottoman law in force in Palestine on Nov. 1, 1914 (the date when Turkey entered World War I), such later Ottoman laws as had been or might be declared to be in force by public notice, and such orders-in-council, ordinances, and regulations as were in force in Palestine at the date of the commencement of the order (Sept. 1, 1922) or might thereafter be applied or enacted. Subject thereto, and so far as the same should not extend or apply, the jurisdiction of the courts should be exercised in conformity with the substance of the common law and the doctrines of equity in force in England, so far as the circumstances of Palestine and its inhabitants and the limits of His Majesty's jurisdiction permitted and subject to such qualification as local circumstances rendered necessary.

Provision was made for the election of a legislative council in and for Palestine, but the election held was boycotted by the Arabs (see *Governance), and was declared by the Palestine (Amendment) Order-in-Council, 1923, to be null and void. By article 3 of the amending order-in-council the power to legislate in and for Palestine was vested in the high commissioner appointed by His Majesty in council, and it was exercised by him alone throughout the period of the mandatory regime. He was given full power and authority, without prejudice to the powers inherent in or reserved by the Palestine Order-in-Council to His Majesty, and subject to any conditions and limitations prescribed by royal instructions, and after consultation with the advisory council composed of senior government officials, to promulgate such ordinances as were necessary for the peace, order, and good government of Palestine.

However, no ordinance could be promulgated which restricted complete freedom of conscience and the free exercise of all forms of worship, save insofar as was required for the maintenance of public order and morals, or which tended to discriminate in any way between the inhabitants of Palestine on the ground of race, religion, or language; or which was in any way repugnant to, or inconsistent with, the provisions of the Mandate. Furthermore, no ordinance which concerned matters dealt with specifically by the provisions of the Mandate could be promulgated until a draft thereof had been communicated to a secretary of state and approved by him, with or without amendment.

Every ordinance promulgated by the high commissioner was subject to disallowance by His Majesty within one year of the date of its promulgation, while certain classes of ordinance could not be promulgated by the high commissioner unless he had previously obtained instructions thereupon from one of His Majesty's principal secretaries of state. Those included ordinances relating to immigration, divorce, Palestine currency, or the issue of bank notes; ordinances the provisions of which appeared inconsistent with obligations imposed upon His Majesty by treaty or by the Mandate; and ordinances interfering with the discipline or control of His Majesty's forces by land, sea, or air. No ordinance could be promulgated unless a draft had first been made public for one calendar month at least before its enactment, unless immediate enactment was, in the judgment of the high commissioner, indispensably necessary in the public interest.

Article 35 of the order-in-council applied to Palestine the enactments in the First Schedule to the Foreign Jurisdiction Act, 1890, with certain modifications. (Generally speaking, Palestine ordinances were modeled upon English law and cannot be fully understood without a thorough study of its principles and the decisions of the English courts on the English law upon which they were based.) All ordinances were published in English, Arabic, and Hebrew and the Interpretation Ordinance provided that in the case of any discrepancy between the English text and the Arabic or Hebrew text, the English text should prevail. In some ordinances, such as the Bills of Exchange Ordinance, the Partnership Ordinance, and the Bankruptcy Ordinance, 1936, it is expressly provided that they are to be interpreted by reference to the relevant law of England. In the Criminal Code Ordinance, 1936, it is provided that it is to be interpreted in accordance with the principles of legal interpretation obtaining in England, and expressions used in it are to be presumed, so far as is consistent with their context except as may be otherwise expressly provided, to be used with the meaning attached to them in English law and are to be construed in accordance therewith. The Civil Wrongs Ordinance, 1944, must be similarly interpreted, but subject to the Interpretation Ordinance.

For the most part, by the time the Mandate was terminated, Palestine legislation had replaced the Ottoman law which formed part of the law of Palestine on Nov. 1, 1914, when Turkey entered the war, although some important parts of it, including part of the civil law (Mejelle) and the Land Law, were not replaced. Thus, for example, the commercial and criminal law and the law of civil and criminal procedure were replaced by Palestine legislation modeled upon English law adapted to local circumstances. The process started at the very beginning of the mandatory regime and continued with increasing speed throughout the period. On the other hand, in the early days of the Mandate the Palestine courts were very reluctant to apply English judge-made law, although during the second half of the period, in view of certain decisions of His Britannic Majesty's Privy Council, which was an appellate court from the Supreme Court of Palestine, they increasingly introduced English judge-made law into the law of Palestine, and referred more and more in their judgments to English legal textbooks and judicial decisions.

[Henry Eli Baker]

IN THE STATE OF ISRAEL

ISRAEL'S DECLARATION OF INDEPENDENCE. On Friday, 5 Iyyar 5708, May 14, 1948, the establishment of the State of Israel – the Jewish state in Palestine – was proclaimed by the National Council (Mo'eẓet ha-Am). The Council comprised 37 representatives of the Jewish community of Ereẓ Israel (the *yishuv*) and of the Zionist movement. The Mandate over Palestine, which the League of Nations had conferred on Great Britain in 1922, had come to an end. The British Parliament, for its part, had enacted on April 29, 1948, the Palestine Act, by which the jurisdiction of the British Crown over Palestine would cease on May 15, 1948. The Declaration of the Establishment of the State turned the National Council into a provisional legislature called the Provisional State Council, which together with its executive arm, the National Administration (Minhelet ha-Am) served as a provisional government. These were to function until regular authorities were duly elected, in accordance with a constitution which was to be instituted not later than October 1, 1948. The Declaration included the "credo" of the new state:

> THE STATE OF ISRAEL will be open for Jewish immigration and for the Ingathering of Exiles; it will foster the development of the country for the benefit of all its inhabitants; it will be based on freedom, justice and peace as envisaged by the prophets of Israel; it will ensure complete equality of social and political rights to all its inhabitants irrespective of religion, race or sex; it will guarantee freedom of religion, conscience, language, education and culture; it will safeguard the Holy Places of all religions; and it will be faithful to the principles of the Charter of the United Nations.

The development of constitutional law in Israel corresponds to the course which the Declaration of the Establishment of the State of Israel has run to reach its present status in Israel's legal system. In the early days of the State of Israel, the tendency of the Supreme Court was to deny the Declaration any legal force, let alone any constitutional status; the Declaration was regarded as a political instrument to be used on the international level (Ziv v. Gubernik (1948) 1 PD 85). Thus the Supreme Court refused to accept the argument that certain Mandatory Emergency Regulations, empowering the authorities to detain – without due process – a person suspected of acts prejudicial to public safety, contravened the Declaration, wherein human rights and individual liberties were expressly guaranteed (El-Kharbutli v. Defense Minister (1949) 2 PD 5). At a later stage the Supreme Court saw in the Declaration an instrument for the interpretation of statutes. Thus in the landmark decision of the Supreme Court in what was probably Israel's most famous and consequential civil rights case (*Kol ha-Am* v. Minister of the Interior (1953) 7 PD 871, where the respondent had suspended the publication of a newspaper after it published an article which in the minister's opinion was "likely to endanger the public peace," in the language of the Mandatory Press Ordinance), Supreme Court President Agranat declared:

> The system of laws under which the political institutions ... have been established and function are witness to the fact that this is indeed a State founded on democracy. Moreover, the matters set forth in the Declaration of Independence – especially as regards basing the State "on the foundations of freedom" and securing freedom of conscience – meant that Israel is a freedom-loving state. It is true that the Declaration "does

> not include any constitutional law laying down any rule regarding the maintaining or repeal of any ordinances or laws" ... yet insofar as it "expresses the vision of the people and its faith" ... we are bound to pay attention to the matters set forth therein when we come to interpret and give meaning to the laws of the state, including the provisions of a law made at the time of the Mandate and adopted by the State after its establishment; for it is a well-known opinion that the law of a people must be studied in the light of its national way of life. Thus ... we must interpret the term "likely," when we read it together with the other matters stated in (the) section ..., in the sense of "near certainty" ....

A further development in the legal interpretation of the Declaration occurred when the Supreme Court saw in it the source of such human rights and freedoms as those of freedom of expression (Israel Film Studies Ltd. v. Levi Gerri and Film Censorship Board (1969) 23 PD (1) 693), or freedom of worship (Peretz v. Kefar Shmaryahu Religious Council (1962) 16 PD 2101). In the case of Yerdor v. Chairman of the Central Elections Committee for the Sixth Knesset (1965) (19 PD 3, 365) the appellant represented a party list which was refused confirmation by the Elections Committee. Technically, the list was valid, but its platform did not recognize the integrity of the State of Israel nor its existing boundaries. Most of the members in the list were former members of the El Ard group, which had been outlawed by government decree. The Supreme Court dismissed the appeal (by majority decision). In the decision, President Agranat stated that the continuing existence of the State of Israel was the major premise in the light of which all Israeli laws have to be interpreted. This underlying condition was derived from an interpretation of the Declaration of the Establishment of the State of Israel and is considered to be a "fundamental constitutional fact, the existence of which no organ of the State, be it administrative, judicial or quasi-judicial, may deny when it comes to exercise any of its powers." Following this line of reasoning the president arrived at the conclusion that, notwithstanding the candidates' eligibility when treated as individuals, the list of candidates, qua list, had no right to take part in the elections to the Knesset. The Declaration, in effect, received through this decision a supra-constitutional character.

Several attempts were made in the Knesset to confer on the Declaration the status of law, but they all failed. In 1994 the Declaration reached the acme of its legal standing, when a new section was added to Basic Law: Human Dignity and Freedom and Basic Law: Freedom of Occupation. Called "Basic Principles," it read as follows: "Fundamental human rights in Israel are founded upon recognition of the value of the human being, the sanctity of human life, and the principle that all persons are free; these rights shall be upheld in the spirit of the principles set forth in the Declaration of the Establishment of the State of Israel."

Thus the Declaration was now a cornerstone of human rights and freedoms in Israel and part of Israel's emerging constitution. In the draft constitution which the Israel Democracy Institute (a non-government academic organization) has drawn up, the Declaration figured as the preamble to the proposed constitution.

THE LAW OF THE LAND. When the Provisional State Council – the legislature of the new state – convened, its first enactment was the Law and Administration Ordinance, 1948. The term "ordinance" was the Mandatory designation of all primary legislation issued by the High Commissioner in accordance with British royal instructions. The laws which the Provisional State Council adopted continued to be called "ordinances." Early in 1949, when the newly elected Constituent Assembly convened, its first act of legislation was to change its name to "the First Knesset" and its enactments were henceforth to be termed "laws" (*ḥukkim*). Section 11 of the Law and Administration Ordinance, 1948, stated that the law which existed in Palestine on the eve of the establishment of the State of Israel would continue to be in force, subject to any enactments of the new legislature and also subject "to such modifications as may result from the establishment of the State and its authorities."

The law which was in force upon the establishment of the new state comprised remnants of Ottoman law, British Mandatory legislation (incorporatimg a large body of English law) and, in matters of personal status – the law of the various religious communities: Jewish law, Muslim law and Christian law (see above).

It remained for the courts to decide to what extent the law of Palestine was altered as a result of the establishment of the State of Israel. The courts, under the leadership of the Supreme Court, adopted at the outset a conservative attitude in preserving parts of Mandatory legislation, which in later years would hardly be able to stand up to judicial scrutiny, e.g., the Press Ordinance or the notorious Emergency (Defense) Regulations, 1945.

THE QUEST FOR A CONSTITUTION. The Declaration of the Establishment of the State of Israel, in the section immediately following the proclamation of the establishment of the state, clearly expressed the determination of the founders that the duly elected regular authorities of the state should be instituted "in accordance with a Constitution which shall be adopted by the Elected Constituent Assembly not later than October 1, 1948." Indeed, preparations for a constitution were initiated by the Jewish national organizations even before the state was proclaimed. However, it became very clear that a constitution would not be forthcoming. The reason for this, first of all, was the war for the existence of the state, which raged for many months following its establishment. The population was enlisted in the war effort, and thus a Constituent Assembly could not be elected by the date – October 1, 1948 – set forth in the Declaration. Secondly, "the ingathering of the exiles" – the incoming flow of Jewish immigrants from all quarters of the world, especially from Europe and the Arab countries – and the attitude of the religious parties, which objected to any constitution other than the Torah, together made it necessary to back off from the idea of drawing up a constitution.

An expedient was found early in 1949 after the election of the Constituent Assembly. The first law considered by the newly elected Assembly provided for a change in the name of the Constituent Assembly, which thus became the "First Knesset." The change, of course, was not a mere matter of semantics; it meant a departure from the initial determination to base the newly established state on a democratic constitution. This departure was explained at the time with the argument that the existing population of Israel should not impose its ideals on coming generations; and therefore only when more Jewish immigrants came to the country – only then – would the time be ripe for drafting a constitution.

Long and recurrent debates were held, both in the Knesset and in the general public, on the question of whether or not there should be a written constitution. A compromise was reached in the Knesset whereby the constitution would be drawn up chapter by chapter through the enactment of Basic Laws, which in time would be collected into a single document and together form Israel's constitution. The initiator of this compromise was Member of Knesset I. Harari, and the resolution adopted by the Knesset on June 13, 1950, bears his name and is still considered binding. It was not until 1958 that Basic Law: the Knesset, the first of Israel's Basic Laws, was enacted, followed, at a slow pace, by the following Basic Laws: State Lands (1960); President of the State (1964); Government (1968); State Economy (1975); Israel Defense Forces (1976); Jerusalem, Capital of Israel (1980); Judicature (1984); State Comptroller (1988) Human Dignity and Freedom (1992), and Freedom of Occupation (1992). A revised version of Basic Law: the Government was enacted in 1992 and again in 2001: a revised version of Basic Law: Human Dignity and Freedom and Basic Law: Freedom of Occupation was enacted in 1994.

The Basic laws were adopted by the Knesset in the same manner as other legislation, that is to say, in general, by a simple majority. Their constitutional import derived from their content, and, in some Basic Laws or certain provisions therein, the inclusion of "entrenched clauses," which require a special Knesset majority for their amendment. Such an entrenched provision was included in section 4 of the Basic Law: the Knesset, which lays down the principles of the electoral system, and it provides that these may not be changed except by an absolute majority of the Knesset (i.e. at least 61 of 120 members).

In the case of Bergman v. Minister of Finance (1969) (23 (1) PD 693) the petitioner challenged the validity of a law providing for the financing of the expenses of the parties in elections for the Knesset and the local authorities. Financing, according to the law, was to apply only to those parties which had sat in the outgoing Knesset; any new party would be denied financing. Since one of the principles of the electoral system set out in the said section 4 of the Basic Law was that elections should be equal, the Supreme Court ruled that the financing law indeed violated the principle of equal elections and that, since it had not been enacted by an absolute majority, it was inoperative. This decision has been followed in a number of cases in which the Supreme Court has struck down legislation passed with an ordinary majority and which contravened the principle of equal elections.

A modification occurred in 1992 with the enactment of Basic Law: Freedom of Occupation and Basic Law: Human Dignity and Freedom. These Basic Laws contained a "limitating clause," which stated: "There shall be no violation of rights under this Basic Law except by a law befitting the values of the State of Israel, enacted for a proper purpose, and to an extent no greater than required, or by a regulation enacted by virtue of express authorization in such laws." The "values of the State of Israel" mentioned in the limitating clause are those mentioned in the opening sections of both Basic Laws on human rights – "recognition of the value of the human being, the sanctity of human life, and the principle that all persons are free," in conjunction with the overall principles set forth in the Declaration of the Establishment of the State of Israel.

The language of the "limitating clause" is the basis for judicial review of legislation, since it clearly opens all legislation which violates any of the human rights protected by the Basic Laws to the review of the courts. The courts must then decide whether the particular law befits the values of the State of Israel, whether it was enacted for a proper purpose, and whether the violation is proportionate to the benefits of the legislation. The Basic Laws therefore assume the effect of constitutional articles. In 1995 the Supreme Court indeed ruled, in a special panel of nine judges (one member dissenting) that the new Basic Laws are indeed part of the constitution of Israel (CA 6821/93 United Mizrachi Bank Ltd. v. Migdal and Others 49 (4) PD 221). We thus have a judicial proclamation of a constitution, although generally a constitution is enacted by a constituent assembly.

In the case mentioned above, the Supreme Court was asked to declare a piece of legislation to be of no legal force due to its violation of the right to property protected by Basic Law: Human Dignity and Freedom. In that particular case, the Supreme Court did not declare the legislation null and void, but judicial review of legislation has become part of Israel's legal legacy.

In addition, two of the justices in the panel of the Supreme Court expressed the view that all Basic Laws have superior normative status and that all legislation which is substantially inconsistent with them may also be declared invalid. Since that landmark decision, the Supreme Court has shown great reluctance and restraint in using its power to strike down legislative propositions found to be contrary to the limiting clause of the Basic Laws; it has done so – through the early years of the 21st century – in a very limited number of cases.

The above decision furnished a powerful impetus for the demand to adopt a full constitution. In the Knesset, the Constitutional, Legislative and Judicial Committee took matters in hand and initiated a long series of deliberations to promote a draft constitution. The Israel Democracy Institute, a non-government academic organization, undertook the herculean task of preparing a draft constitution, with the aim of rallying, as much popular support as possible. By 2005 this effort was in its final stages. The Institute intended to submit its draft to the Knesset for further and final action.

THE BILL OF RIGHTS. In June 1950, the Knesset adopted the Harari Resolution, according to which Israel's constitution would be built up by the Knesset, chapter by chapter, in the form of Basic Laws. These, according to the decision, would eventually be bound together into one document, the Constitution. As has been already mentioned, the first Basic Law, dealing with the Knesset, was enacted in 1958. After an interval, additional chapters were enacted; the question of a Bill of Rights was sidetracked. One of the main obstacles was the objection of the religious parties to an equality clause, which could jeopardize legislation giving preference to religious laws. This would be problematic, for example, in matters of marriage and divorce, governed in Israel by religious law, which gives men a certain preference over women. The same goes for laws imposing Sabbath observance or those affecting the import and sale of non-kosher meat.

As early as 1949, however, the Supreme Court ruled that there are in existence natural rights, which, though not written in the law books, are recognized by the courts. The specific case dealt with the right of a person to engage in any occupation he chooses, unless prohibited expressly by legislation. The case was later expounded upon, with the Court maintaining that these rights stem from the character of the State of Israel as a freedom-seeking democratic country, where the courts interpret the laws and review administrative action in light of these fundamental rights. Additional rulings of the Supreme Court emphasized the legal existence of freedom of expression, freedom of worship, the right of assembly, freedom of association, and indeed all basic freedoms. Nevertheless, precedence was always given to the enactments of the legislature, even if they were unjust.

In the late 1960s a special subcommittee was set up in the Knesset to prepare a Bill of Rights – Human Rights of the Citizen. The bill was presented in 1973; it passed the first reading but did not proceed any further. In the 1980s an additional attempt was made in the same subcommittee of the Knesset. A new draft was prepared, but it did not win substantial support in the Knesset and the attempt failed.

Early in the 1990s a comprehensive draft Bill of Rights was prepared at the Ministry of Justice under the direction of Dan *Meridor, then minister of justice. This draft tried to incorporate the lessons of previous attempts. It followed the Canadian Charter of Rights and Freedoms, which was part of the Constitution Act, 1982, and which included a "limitating clause" applying to all the rights and freedoms set out in the Charter. The Canadian Charter gave expression to the notion that human rights are not absolute, and they are "subject only to such reasonable limits prescribed by law as can be demonstrably justified in a free and democratic society." Still, the government did not approve the draft owing to the opposition of the religious parties upon which the coalition depended. In 1992, Member of Knesset Amnon *Rubinstein presented to the Knesset, as a private member's bill, parts of the Justice Ministry's draft bill. The first section dealt with human dignity and freedom, the second with freedom of occupation; other parts failed to pass the threshold of enactment. On March 3, 1992, Basic Law: Freedom of Occupation was enacted; two weeks later Basic Law: Human Dignity and Freedom passed its third reading in the Knesset plenary and became law. On March 9, 1994, the revised text of the Basic Law: Freedom of Occupation became law. This text included the "Basic Principles" of the early 1990s Ministry of Justice draft, referring to the values of the State of Israel enunciated in the Declaration of the Establishment of the State of Israel.

The enactment of these two Basic Laws was described by Minister of Justice Meridor and by the president of the Supreme Court, Judge Aharon *Barak, as a "constitutional revolution." The reason for the use of such a radical expression was that the Knesset had, for the first time, placed limitations on itself with regard to the subject matter of the laws it was empowered to legislate (prior to that, such limitations had existed only with regard to the form and procedure of legislation). From now on, the Knesset could limit human rights only "by a law befitting the values of the State of Israel, designed for a proper purpose and to an extent no greater than required."

As mentioned above, these two Basic Laws were declared by the Supreme Court to be of basic constitutional force. They became the basis of the judicial review of legislation. Although not all the fundamental human rights have come to be protected, these laws have had tremendous reverberations in the public and produced widespread enthusiasm for the cause of human rights. There was great confidence that additional Basic Laws protecting more and more fundamental human rights would eventually be enacted. These, together with the existing Basic Laws, supplemented by Basic Law: Legislation, which as of 2005 had not yet been enacted, was expected to set the stage for the completion of the constitution.

THE LAW UNDER THE BRITISH MANDATE. (For a more general survey of the judicial and legislative systems under the British, as well as under the Ottoman Empire, see above.)

When the British administration succeeded the former ruler of Palestine, the Ottoman Empire (in which Palestine was the southern district of the province of Syria), it found a quite elaborate legal system. In keeping with the general 19th century trends, substantial parts of the law were made up of codes – to a large extent based on European codes, mostly French. There was thus a code of commercial law and criminal procedure. The comprehensive Civil Code, the Mejelle, was based on Islamic law. In matters of personal status, mainly family matters, the Ottomans accorded extensive autonomy to the various religious communities; that autonomy was also imposed on the Ottomans by the system of capitulations, where European consuls had jurisdiction in personal matters concerning their nationals.

When the British assumed the Mandate over Palestine, they issued under the King's seal the Palestine Order-in-Council, 1922. Section 46 of this Order defined the sources of the laws which would apply in Palestine. Priority would be given to the enactments of the new legislator, the British High Commissioner, to the Orders-in-Council issuing from the King of Great Britain and to Acts of the British Parliament. Subject to these, the Ottoman laws would continue to apply, as they were in force in Palestine prior to the British occupation. Next in line would come the religious laws. In cases of lacunae in the sources quoted above, the law to be applied was "the substance of the common law and the doctrines of equity in force in England"; these bodies of law were to apply only "so far as the circumstances of Palestine and its inhabitants ... permit."

The British Mandatory administration, in keeping with the policy of Great Britain in administering its colonies, was anxious to introduce into Palestine the essentials of the English legal system. The major judicial officials, judges and lawyers working for the government, were English or had been trained in England. From the constitutional aspect, the English principles of the common law and equity were to prevail in Palestine only in cases where the local law did not seem to offer a solution.

Nevertheless, the courts were most eager to adjudicate on the basis of English law. In view of certain decisions of His Britannic Majesty's Privy Council, which was an appellate court from the Supreme Court of Palestine, the courts increasingly introduced English judge-made law into the law of Palestine and referred more and more in their judgments to English legal textbooks and judicial decisions. Thus extensive legislation based on English law (either codified or common law) was introduced into Palestine with regard to subjects such as companies, cooperative societies, banking, bills of exchange, bankruptcy, patents and copyright. In 1936 a Criminal Code Ordinance was introduced, which, together with legislation on criminal procedure and evidence, based the penal law in Palestine on the same principles obtaining in England. Additionally, the force of precedent – by which decisions of the Supreme Court were binding for all the lower courts – was introduced. One British institution which was not introduced was the jury system. The English administrators believed that the strife which tore the country asunder, with the ever-rising tension between the Jewish and Arab populations, made the system unfit for Palestine (as a matter of fact, the jury system had not been introduced in any of the British colonies).

The latter part of the Mandatory period, beginning in 1936, was marked by severe outbreaks of Arab hostilities against the Jewish population in Palestine, known as the Arab Revolt. At that time the attention of the administration was focused on security and defense measures. The exigencies of World War II and the Jewish effort to secure independence, which continued long after the war had subsided, stimulated a tremendous legal effort to regulate the economy and finance and further develop emergency defense regulations. These culminated in the imposition of martial law over large areas of Palestine and for ever-increasing periods of time. In this regard mention has to be made of the Emergency (Defense) Regulations, 1945, which allowed the British "an impressive array of legal tools of detention, deportation, confiscation, censorship, demolition of houses, restraint of movement, food control, press control, money control, rent control and capital punishment" (Yoram Shachar, "History and Sources of Israel Law," in *Introduction to the Law of Israel*, p.5).

One exception to the general trend described above was the enactment of the Civil Wrongs Ordinance, 1944, which came into force in 1947. This Ordinance codified the law of torts and replaced the provisions of the Mejelle on the subject.

On the eve of the establishment of the State of Israel, the law was engaged to a large extent in emergency legislation. This legislation was directed at the activities of the Arab dissident population, which was bent on thwarting the UN resolution for the partition of Palestine into a Jewish state and an Arab state. On the other hand, the British Mandatory administration was at war with Jewish resistance groups, who strove to drive the British out of Palestine. The organized Jewish population, represented by its elected bodies and the Jewish Agency, was busy setting up the framework for the future army and other branches of government of the forthcoming State of Israel. At the same time, it endeavored to facilitate a massive movement of immigration of Jewish deportees and displaced persons from Europe who had survived the Holocaust, and of Jews from Arab countries in North Africa and the Middle East.

THE LEGISLATIVE PROCESS. The procedure and prerequisites for legislation have not – generally speaking – been laid down by provisions of law. These have been included in the several drafts of Basic Law: the Legislature, which have not succeeded in passing the third reading in the Knesset and becoming law. The legislative procedure is set forth in the Standing Rules which the Knesset has adopted and amended from time to time. A draft of every law submitted to the Knesset for enactment is published in *Reshumot* (the official gazette) either by the government or by a member of the Knesset; a note is attached explaining each proposed section. Over 90% of laws passed by the Knesset were originally introduced by the government, which has evolved a procedure for presenting its draft laws to the Knesset. In recent years the proportion of private members' bills is rising steeply. The initiative for a government-sponsored draft law comes from the ministry concerned with its subject, which prepares the first draft together with an explanatory note. That draft is examined in the Ministry of Justice, which prepares a draft for submission to the cabinet Committee on Legislation, and the draft approved by the committee is submitted to the government for approval. The draft approved by the government is sent by the secretary to the government to the speaker of the Knesset, who has it placed on the table of the Knesset and entered as an item on its agenda.

In accordance with the procedure laid down by the First Knesset and now incorporated in the Standing Rules, each draft law goes through three readings, in addition to the committee stage which follows the first reading. At the first reading of a government-sponsored bill the minister who will be charged with the implementation of the law, if it is enacted, explains the provisions and purposes of the law, and then there is a general debate dealing primarily with its general principles. It is then examined in detail by a standing committee, which prepares the text to be submitted to the Knesset for the second reading. At the second reading the chairman of the committee reports to the Knesset on the draft law and it is put to the vote section by section. At the third reading the final text is voted upon by the Knesset. Subsequently, it is submitted for signature by those persons who by law are required to sign it and it is then published in *Reshumot*.

A private member's bill is submitted to the speaker of the Knesset and has to pass a preliminary stage in the Knesset plenary and, if approved, goes to a standing committee, which may either prepare the text for the first reading in the Knesset or propose that the bill be quashed. If approved in the first reading, the bill follows the same procedure as a government-sponsored bill.

Where a draft law has been referred by an outgoing Knesset to one of its committees after the first reading, the government formed in the incoming Knesset may notify the Knesset in plenary session that it wishes the continuity provisions of the Continuity of Consideration of Draft Laws Law, 1964, to apply to it. If it does so each parliamentary party may propose within two weeks that those provisions shall not apply, giving reasons for the proposal. If no such proposal is submitted, or if the proposal is rejected by the Knesset, then the incoming Knesset must continue the consideration of the draft law from the stage reached by the outgoing Knesset, and it must treat the latter's deliberations on the draft law as if they were its own deliberations.

THE JEWISH ELEMENT IN ISRAEL'S LEGISLATION. The vast majority of the laws passed by the Israel legislature have their counterparts in the legislation of most other countries, but some of them are peculiar to Israel, owing to its being a Jewish state and the realization of the aims of Zionism. Among these are the Days of Rest Ordinance, 1948, proclaiming the Sabbath and the Jewish festivals to be the official days of rest in the country; the Transfer of Herzl's Remains Law, 1949; the *Law of Return, 1950, under which the right of every Jew to settle in Israel is recognized; the *World Zionist Organization – Jewish Agency (Status) Law, 1952, which regulates the status of the World Zionist Organization in Israel and its relationship to the State. The State Education Law, 1953, defined the object of the education provided by the state elementary schools, as follows: "to base elementary education in the State on the values of Jewish culture and the achievements of science, on love of the homeland and loyalty to the State and the Jewish people." In 2000 the Law was revised and the aims of the state education system greatly enlarged. They include: "to implant the principles set out in the Declaration of the Establishment of the State of Israel and the values of Israel as a Jewish and democratic country" and also "to teach Israel's Torah, the history of the Jewish people. Israel's legacy and Jewish customs (*masoret*), to implant awareness of the remembrance of the Shoah and Jewish heroism, and to teach respect for them." Laws relating to Jewish law and religion cover such subjects as *kasher* food for soldiers (1948), Jewish religious services budgets (1949), the Chief Rabbinate Council (1955), the jurisdiction of religious courts in marriage and divorce (1953), *dayyanim* (1955), the prohibition of pig breeding (1962), phylacteries and mezzuzot (prevention of cheating) (1974), the Chief Rabbinate of Israel (1980), prevention of cheating in *kashrut* (1983), Passover prohibition of *ḥameẓ* (1985).

Furthermore, whenever legislation is required on any particular subject, the relevant principles of Jewish law, if any, are examined and, if found suitable, incorporated, for example, the Restoration of Lost Property Law, 1973, the interpretation of which raised the still undecided question in the Supreme Court of whether the language used, which was derived from Jewish law, referred to the substance of Jewish law or was to be interpreted independently from Jewish law (FH 13/80 Hendeles v. Kuppat-Am Bank (PD 35 (2) 785)). With reference to non-Jewish communities, on June 27, 1967, less than two weeks after the Six-Day War, the Knesset passed a law for the protection of all holy places under Israeli jurisdiction.

The Holocaust and its consequences have led to the enactment of laws on the punishment of Nazis and their collaborators (1950), the establishment and administration of the *Yad Vashem Memorial Authority (1953), compensation for those disabled in the war against the Nazis (1954) or by Nazi persecution (1957), Holocaust Memorial Day (1959), and Prohibition of Holocaust Denial (1986).

The Jewish character of the State of Israel first came to the fore in the above-mentioned case of Yerdor v. Elections Committee for the Sixth Knesset (1965), where the Supreme Court invoked the Declaration of the Establishment of the State of Israel. It was 20 years later, in 1985, that the Knesset responded, when a list of candidates was presented to the Elections Committee for confirmation which did not recognize the right of the State of Israel to exist as a Jewish and democratic state. In 1985, Basic Law: the Knesset was amended and a new section, 7A, inserted, by which no list was to participate in Knesset elections if it rejected the existence of the State of Israel as the state of the Jewish people, or rejected the democratic nature of the state or incited to racism. In 2002, section 7A was amended and the cause for disqualification was phrased: "rejection of the existence of the State of Israel as a Jewish and democratic state." A similar terminology was used in the Parties Law, 1992, and again in the human rights Basic Laws.

THE LAW OF RETURN. During the first years of independence most of legislation was concerned with amendments to the Mandatory statutes, in order to adapt them to the new

A Corinthian capital, 4th–3rd century B.C.E., with the head of the god Dionysos, found at Bet She'an. *Photo: Hanan Isachar.*

The Land of Israel offers a fascinating variety of archaeological findings that illuminate the attachment of the Jewish people to its ancient homeland from the birth of the nation in the biblical period through the period of the Second Temple and beyond. They are a part of the Israeli landscape as much as its flora and fauna.

ARCHAEOLOGY

(opposite page) TOP:
Wine press in the antique Nabatean Byzantine town of Shivta in the Negev, 2nd century; Shivta was declared a World Heritage Site by UNESCO in 2005.
Photo: Dinu Mendrea.

(opposite page) BOTTOM:
Mamshit, an antique Nabetean Byzantine town captured by the Romans in the 2nd century C.E., was declared a World Heritage by UNESCO in June 2005.
Photo: Dinu Mendrea.

RIGHT: **One of the twin lions decorating a gateway in the center of Jerusalem, made by Rabbi Simcha Shlomo Janiver-Diskin, a well-known figure in Jerusalem in the late 19th century.**
Photo: Shlomo (Yosh) Gafni, Jerusalem.

LEFT: A capital found at the archaeological park in Ashkelon, one of the five principal cities of the Philistines in Canaan. *Photo: Hanan Isachar.*

(opposite page) LEFT: Finds of everyday objects from the Cave of Letters. Roman period, Naḥal Ḥever, 2nd century C.E. *Collection, Israel Antiquities Authority. Photo © The Israel Museum, Jerusalem, by Moshe Caine.*

(opposite page) RIGHT: Tel Hazor in the Upper Galilee: the Pillared Building, a public storehouse from the 8th century B.C.E. *Photo: Hanan Isachar.*

Jerusalem—Tombs of Absalom, Zechariah, and the Hezir family, 1st century B.C.E.–1st century C.E., on the slopes of the Mount of Olives with the Jewish cemetery. *Photo: Dinu Mendrea.*

Corridor in the Cave of the Sarcophagi shows sarcophagus with lions, from Bet She'arim, late Roman period. *Photo: Dinu Mendrea.*

An overview of the old synagogue near the hot springs at Tiberias, 3rd century C.E. *Photo: Albatross Aerial Photography.*

ABOVE: Animal reliefs from the excavations at Tiberias, 3rd century C.E. *Photo: David Harris.*

Aerial view of the Oven Cave, the Carmel Cave, and the River Cave in Mount Carmel *Photo: Albatross Aerial Photography.*

Bone-reaping hook with deer sculpted head, found in the prehistoric caves of Mount Carmel. Kebara Cave, 10th millennium B.C.E. *Collection, Israel Antiquities Authority. Photo © Israel Museum, by Nahum Slapak.*

An aerial view of the Old City of Jerusalem.
Photo: Albatross Aerial Photography.

An aerial view of Ein Gedi showing the remains of the Byzantine-period synagogue (end of the 4th–7th century C.E.), which is proof that a large Jewish community existed there.
Photo: Albatross Aerial Photography.

circumstances and changing needs. The first major piece of legislation was enacted in 1950; it was The Law of Return, 1950, which guaranteed every Jew's right to immigrate to Israel and become an *"oleh"* (immigrant). That law was complemented by the Citizenship Law, 1952, which awarded Israeli citizenship to every *oleh* (*olim* also have the right to opt out) and regulated the issue of citizenship for Israel's non-Jewish inhabitants. Another complementary law was the Law of Entry, 1952, which regulated the issuing of visas and residence permits to non-Israelis.

The question of "Who is a Jew," for the purposes of the Law of Return, came up before the Supreme Court in 1962 in the case of Rufeisen-Brother Daniel, who was born Jewish but had converted to Christianity and joined a Catholic order (HC 72/62–16 PD 2428). He petitioned the court to have his nationality registered in the register of inhabitants as Jewish, since he felt he still belonged to the Jewish people. The Court denied the petition, reasoning that, in Judaism, nationality and religion come together and cannot be separated.

The question came up again in 1968 in the Shalit case (HC 58/68–23 PD (2) 477), where a Jew and his non-Jewish wife demanded that their children be registered as Jewish, since they were brought up as such (but had not converted to Judaism). In a majority decision, the Court accepted the petition and the children were registered as Jews.

In 1970 the Law of Return was amended to include a definition of "Jew" according to which a Jew was anyone who was born to a Jewish mother or had converted to Judaism and did not belong to another faith.

In yet another case (HC 264/87–43 PD (2) 727) the Supreme Court decided in 1987 that a person who had converted to Judaism need not necessarily have done so according to Orthodox practice. The Supreme Court had a hand in additional developments in this area.

CODIFICATION OF THE LAW. After the establishment of the State of Israel, the binding text of the Mandatory statutes incorporated into the Israeli legal system was their English version; the Hebrew and Arabic official translations were not conclusive. That situation was untenable. In 1952 a huge task was undertaken: the production of an authoritative Hebrew text of the statutes in which all the amendments were to be incorporated. For this task, special committees were set up, headed by judges. The final text was to be authorized by the Constitutional, Legislative and Judicial Committee of the Knesset and published in the Official Gazette – *Reshumot*. Henceforth the "New Version," as it came to be called, would be the only binding text of the law.

In 1964, as amendments to old Mandatory statutes and to Israeli laws proliferated, it became a more and more daunting task to produce an authoritative text of the original statute as amended from time to time. A procedure was therefore introduced whereby special committees were set up to draft a "Consolidated Version" of the laws. The draft could consolidate several statutes, including a "New Version" of Mandatory legislation. In this manner, the laws became more accessible to those who had recourse to them.

A greater and far more ambitious project was undertaken to codify the civil law of Israel and harmonize the provisions included in the various laws comprising the civil law of the State. A special committee of experts was appointed by the minister of justice, headed by the president of the Supreme Court, Prof. Aharon Barak. After years of arduous work and extensive research, the draft Civil Code of Law was delivered and due to be presented to the Knesset for enactment.

REFORM OF THE CIVIL LAW. It was only in the 1960s that a major and formidable effort was undertaken to reform the then existing legislation, which, as has been seen, was mostly Mandatory and even Ottoman. A series of laws was enacted in the field of civil law, which, step by step, replaced the provisions of the Ottoman Civil Code, the Mejelle, with modern legislation, in keeping with the most progressive trends in the Western world. Some of the important laws that were enacted in the field of civil law are Legal Capacity and Guardianship Law, 1962; Standard Contracts Law, 1964; Agency Law, 1965, Inheritance Law, 1965; Guarantee Law, 1967, Pledges Law, 1967, Bailees Law, 1967; Sale Law, 1968, Gift Law, 1968, Land Law, 1969. Transfer of Obligations Law, 1969, Movable Property Law, 1971; Contracts (Remedies for Breach of Contract), 1970; Hire and Loan Law, 1971. Contracts (General Part) Law, 1973; Contract for Services Law, 1974; Insurance Contract Law, 1981, and the Credit Card Law, 1986. In 1995 the Knesset passed the Computers Law, bringing Israeli law into line with the new technology.

The comprehensive Land Law, 1969, replaced nearly all the Ottoman and Palestine legislation relating to land. The comprehensive Planning and Building Law, 1965 replaced the Mandatory Town Planning Ordinance, 1936. In 1975 the Road Accident Victims Compensation Law was passed. In general terms, this law provides that anyone injured in a road accident is automatically entitled to compensation, irrespective of who was at fault. An advance on the compensation is payable within 60 days of a request by the victim of the accident.

The cumulative effect of these laws was revolutionary: they constituted a severing of Israel's link to its immediate legal heritage, which was English law sprinkled with Ottoman laws. Israel emerged at last as an independent nation, capable of formulating its own legal solutions adapted to Israeli society; at the same time, the new legislation brought Israel into line with the most progressive trends of the modern world. At the same time, special efforts have been made to incorporate into Israel's legislation, as much as possible, concepts of Jewish law.

The new civil legislation rendered the Ottoman Mejelle unnecessary, and in 1984 it was abolished, symbolizing the end of an era, which in fact had ended many years earlier.

Another departure from Israel's legal past occurred with regard to its linkage to English common law and doctrines of equity, which were binding in Palestine by virtue of Section 46 of the Palestine Order-in-Council, 1922. That section provided for the application of the English sources of law only in cases of lacunae – i.e., whenever local law was silent on the matter at hand – and even then only to the extent that local conditions allowed. The Courts, however, applied English principles quite freely. It was only in the case of Kochavi v. Becker (11 PD 225) that the Supreme Court of Israel finally had the opportunity to settle a question which had come up before it but had not required adjudication – what effect, if any, did English precedents, laid down after the establishment of the State of Israel, have on the law of Israel? Justice Witkon's reply was:

> To my mind, English precedents can no longer be binding for us, even if they were delivered before the establishment of the state. These precedents have great power to direct us and to persuade us, but they cannot be binding on our courts. Indeed we are free to deviate from them, either on the basis of the express provision of section 11 of the Law and Administration Ordinance, 1948, or on the basis of the mere fact that our courts now operate in a sovereign country which is no longer dependent on the adjudication of a foreign country.

The deputy president of the Supreme Court, the late Justice *Heshin, said:

> It does not stand to reason that a sovereign state, having its own set of laws and its own legal system, should continue to be subjected to the rule of a foreign legal system and to the innovations which its courts produce concerning its legal thought, for the sole reason that in the past, when the two countries were closely linked, one of the countries suckled from various spheres of the law of the other country.

It was only in 1980 that Section 46 of the Palestine Order-in-Council, 1922, was officially and finally repealed, although by that time it had no real legal effect. The occasion was the enactment of the statute entitled Foundations of Law, 1980, which stated the following:

> Where a court, faced with a legal question requiring decision, finds no answer to it in statute law or case law or by analogy, it shall decide it in light of the principles of freedom, justice, equity and peace in Israel's heritage.

A new controversy arose regarding the meaning and relevance of the phrase "the principles of freedom, justice, equity and peace in Israel's heritage." The Supreme Court was divided on the question of whether the phrase allowed the introduction of the provisions of Jewish law – that is, whether the question before the court should be decided according to Jewish law, or whether the principles referred to are those derived from the Jewish heritage that are also accepted universally, since the Bible is also a vital component of Western civilization. As mentioned above, no decision was reached, since each of the opposing views was supported by only one of the judges – Justices Barak and Elon. The president of the Supreme Court, M. Landau, who presided over the bench, decided that the question did not require a decision in the particular case, and thus the link remained unresolved.

CORPORATE LAW. When the State of Israel was established, it inherited the Mandatory Companies Ordinance, 1929, which was an almost exact replica of the English Companies Act, 1929. Many amendments have since been enacted by the Knesset. In 1982 a "New Version" was introduced, in Hebrew, to consolidate the law with its amendments, taking into consideration other pieces of legislation bearing on the subject. However, the basic notions of corporate law remained old-fashioned and unsuitable for a thriving modern economy. Several efforts were made to replace the old ordinance and introduce a new companies law, but these efforts were not successful.

In 1999 a new companies law was enacted on the basis of a draft prepared by Prof. H. Procaccia of the Hebrew University Faculty of Law. The new law reflected the progressive features of corporate law obtaining in the Western democracies.

In 1975 the Knesset enacted the Government Companies Law, which regulates the establishment and functioning of government companies. These controlled a significant part of the country's means of production at the time. Another development in corporate law was the enactment of the Amutot (Non-Profit Associations) Law, 1980, which replaced the Ottoman Law of Association of 1909.

REFORM OF CRIMINAL LAW. In the more than 50 years that have passed since the establishment of the State of Israel, a dramatic change has been effected in criminal law. At the beginning, the Mandatory Criminal Code Ordinance, 1936, was the binding text. It was built along the lines of English criminal law; indeed, one of the provisions of the Code was that for purposes of interpretation, reference was to be made to English law. This provision was abolished in 1972. A long series of amendments was enacted. The most outstanding of them included the following: The Penal Law Revision (Bribery) Law, 1952; The Penal Law Revision (State Security) Law, 1957; The Penal Law Amendment (Deceit, Blackmail and Extortion) Law, 1963; The Penal Law Amendment (Bigamy) Law, 1959; The Penal Law Amendment (Prostitution Offenses) Law, 1962; and The Penal Law Amendment (Prohibited Games, Lottery and Betting) Law, 1964.

In the field of penology, the law was reformed radically. Thus, in 1950, the penalty of whipping was abolished; so was collective punishment (1964). The death penalty for murder was abolished in 1954. In that year, the Penal Law Revision (Modes of Punishment) was enacted, introducing the imposition of conditional sentences of imprisonment, and entirely overhauling the penal system.

In 1977 a "Consolidated Version" of the Criminal Code Ordinance was introduced – in Hebrew – replacing the Mandatory English version. In 1994, the Knesset enacted the Penal Law (amendment No. 39) (Introductory Part and General Part), which entirely reformed the basic notions of the legal elements of crime and criminal responsibility. This law was based on a draft prepared by Prof. S.Z. Feller and Prof. M. Kremnitzer, both from the Faculty of Law at the Hebrew University.

LABOR LAW AND SOCIAL SECURITY. One of the impressive achievements of Israel's legal system was the emergence and development of labor and social security law. It began in the 1950s with the country's socialist agenda to get the workers' unions into the law books. Coupled with this interest was the need to regulate the welfare services offered to the population, a great portion of which consisted of new immigrants who had come destitute from the refugee camps in Europe or from North Africa and the Middle East.

Upon its establishment, Israel inherited a meager fund of legislation on labor and social security. The whole field clamored for reform. A series of laws was enacted in the 1950s, based to a large extent on standards designed by the ILO (the International Labor Organization): Hours of Work and Rest Law, 1951; Night Baking (Prohibition) Law, 1951; Annual Leave Law, 1953, Apprenticeship Law, 1953; Youth Labor Law, 1954; Employment of Women Law, 1954. These laws were all intended to protect vulnerable persons in the workplace. Then came a series of laws intended to safeguard the interests of employees: Sick Pay Law, 1964; Severance Pay Law, 1963; Wage Protection Law, 1958; Employment (Equal Opportunities) Law, 1981 (replaced in 1988); Male and Female Workers (Equal Pay) Law, 1964 (revised in 1996); Male and Female Workers (Equal Retirement) Law 1987; Minimum Wage Law, 1987. Another series of Laws dealt with organizing labor and labor disputes. Thus the Employment Service Law, 1959, set up labor exchanges; the Labor Inspection (Organization) Law, 1954 provided for safety in the workplace; and the Settlement of Labor Disputes Law, 1957, was intended to deal with strikes and lockouts in essential public services.

One outstanding piece of legislation was the Collective Agreements Law, 1957, which consolidated the power of the large labor unions and employers' organizations to sign collective agreements which would be binding for future employees and employers as well.

In 1954 the National Insurance Law came into effect, providing for the payment of pensions to the elderly and to victims of work accidents, as well as allowances for mothers. The National Insurance Institute was established, setting up an impressive array of institutions for the rehabilitation of handicapped persons, professional training, and financial and other care for invalids.

Under the National Health Insurance Law, 1994, the entire population is entitled to receive health care from any one of the four sick funds operating in the country. Everyone is obliged to belong to a sick fund of his choice; the dues are collected by the National Insurance Institute and distributed in a prescribed manner to the sick funds.

The disruption of life caused by a growing number of labor disputes and the special nature of labor relations were the basis upon which the labor tribunals were set up by the Labor Courts Law, 1969. The Law instituted a two-tier system of adjudication: Regional Labor Tribunals and a National Labor Tribunal. The tribunals are headed by career judges, who are appointed, like regular judges, by the president of the State on the recommendation of the Judges Nominating Committee (where the cabinet minister in addition to the minister of justice is the minister of industry, trade, and employment). Alongside the presiding judge there are panels of representatives of the public – laymen with a background in labor relations – who represent employees and employers. They are appointed for a term of three years jointly by the minister of justice and the minister of industry, trade, and employment, after consulting with representative employees' and employers' organizations.

The regional labor tribunals sit as courts of first instance in matters of labor relations and disputes arising from the employee-employer relationship. They also adjudicate in disputes between individuals and the National Insurance Institute. In addition, they sit in criminal cases dealing with offenses related to specific labor legislation.

The National Labor Tribunal sits in panels of three career judges and two lay representatives of the public; in certain matters the panel consists of four lay representatives of the public and three career judges. The National Labor Tribunal hears appeals from the Regional Tribunals. It also sits as a court of first instance in specified matters.

The Labor Tribunals are generally considered to be a great success in settling labor disputes and in reviewing decisions of the National Insurance Institute. Their greatest achievement was the development of labor law and the establishment of an Israeli common law in labor matters.

EMERGENCY LEGISLATION. When the establishment of the State of Israel was proclaimed, Israel found itself from the outset in a state of war with the neighboring Arab countries whose armies had invaded Palestine and were advancing towards Jerusalem, Tel Aviv, and the Galilee to thwart the UN resolution on the partition of Palestine. It was because of this situation that the first enactment of the Provisional State Council, the Law and Administration Ordinance, 1948, side by side with establishing the Council as the legislative authority of the new State, also authorized the Council to declare a state of emergency. In the event of such a declaration, the provisional government was authorized to empower the prime minister or any of the ministers to make emergency regulations to such an extent as he considered desirable for the defense of the state, public security, and the maintenance of supplies and essential services. Such emergency regulations could amend any law, or temporarily suspend its operation, and were to cease to have effect at the expiration of three months, unless their validity was extended or they were replaced by the minister who made them or by an ordinance of the legislature. Immediately after enacting the first ordinance, the Provisional State Council issued a declaration that a state of emergency existed in Israel; the declaration was published in the Official Gazette on May 21, 1948. An extensive set of emergency regulations was drawn up, covering a large part of the economy and all security matters.

The state of emergency which was declared in 1948 was still in force at the beginning of the 21st century, although the legal framework for making such a declaration was now Basic Law: the Government (both in the 1992 version as well as the later version which was enacted in 2001 and came into force in 2003). In the 1948 version, the state of emergency – once declared – would remain in effect until repealed by a declaration of the legislature. Under Basic Law: the Government, a state of emergency can be declared for a maximum period of one year, and the Knesset must review the situation and decide from time to time whether conditions warrant a new declaration of a state of emergency. Under the 1948 provisions, emergency regulations could alter any law or suspend it; the new laws clearly state that emergency regulations cannot prevent recourse to the law courts, or establish retroactive punishment, or permit violation of human dignity (sec 39 (d)). In addition, several Basic Laws include a provision forbidding emergency regulations to alter, suspend, or impose conditions on the operation of any provision of those Basic Laws. Through the years, the broad discretion which the language of the law accorded to the ministers in enacting emergency regulations became more and more limited. In the case of Poraz v. the Government of the State of Israel HCJ, 2994/90-(44 (3) PD 317) the Supreme Court invalidated emergency regulations promulgated by the minister of construction and housing which bypassed existing statutory arrangements for building permits, in part on the ground that it was not necessary to employ emergency powers when it was possible to achieve the same purpose through the ordinary, if slower, legislative process.

It should also be noted that beside the existence of emergency regulations, the Knesset has enacted laws which are in force solely for the duration of a state of emergency, e.g. Supervision of Goods and Services Law, 1957, or Emergency Powers (Detention) Law, 1979, which repealed part of the Mandatory Emergency (Defense) Regulations, 1945, concerning preventive or administrative detention of persons.

THE COURTS OF LAW. *(a) The Supreme Court.* The Supreme Court plays a distinct role in Israeli society and stands out as one of the most important institutions in the State.

Basically, the Supreme Court stands at the head of a three-tier system of adjudication; under it are the district courts and at the lowest level are the magistrates courts. Under Basic Law: Judicature, every decision of a court sitting in first instance is appellable to the higher court. Thus the Supreme Court sits as an appellate court on decisions which the district courts deliver as a court of first instance, and – by special leave – also sits as an appellate court on decisions made originally by magistrates courts. In this capacity, its rulings on legal norms are binding for all the lower courts, according to the principle of the binding precedent which applies in Israel, following the Anglo-American tradition. The greater achievement of the Supreme Court occurred in its other capacity, that of High Court of Justice. In this capacity, the court reviews administrative action and acts as an arbiter between the individual and the state and other public authorities, thus safeguarding the rights of the individual and imposing the rule of law.

As a matter of fact, the powers of the Supreme Court, as set out in the statute, have not changed basically from what they were during the time of the British Mandate. What changed was the gradually broadening scope of both the review of administrative action and the petitioners legally permitted to apply for redress of public grievances. Thus, members of the Knesset, law professors, and civic bodies are generally allowed to present their petitions in matters of general public interest, both when the government has acted and when it has refrained from action. It is in this manner that the Supreme Court entertained a petition against the prime minister for not dismissing a minister and a deputy minister against whom criminal charges had been brought. Similarly, the Supreme Court has entertained a petition against the attorney general for refraining from bringing charges against banks and bankers who were responsible for a disastrous collapse of bank shares in the 1980s.

In its capacity as a High Court of Justice, the Supreme Court has made itself a guardian of civil liberties. Furthermore, the Supreme Court acts as a constitutional court in the sense that it imposes the rule of law on the lawgiver, the Knesset, and that it has ruled that laws which do not conform to provisions of a Basic Law have no legal effect, by reason of unconstitutionality. While it is true that the Court is considered a bastion of the rule of law, some of its decisions have aroused public controversy, and in certain political circles proposals have been put forth to curtail the powers of the Supreme Court. However, the Court generally enjoys deep respect and prestige among large parts of the population.

The Supreme Court is seated in Jerusalem. It is composed of such number of members as the Knesset, by resolution, determines; in December 2003 the number was 15. The Court is composed of the president, the deputy president, and 13 other members. The Court sits in panels of three, and occasionally in panels of five, seven, or an uneven larger number, depending on the importance attached to the forthcoming decision. Whenever a judgment which has been delivered by a panel of three is contrary to existing adjudication or deals in a matter which the Court deems deserving of review owing to its importance, difficulty, or novelty, then there is a "Further Hearing" either on the entire judgment or on parts thereof.

The caseload of the Supreme Court is extremely heavy in view of the statutory right of appeal from decisions of the district courts sitting as first instance. Several commissions have proposed reforming the system to the extent that recourse to the Supreme Court would be discretional. These proposals have not been realized to date; part of the load on the Court has been alleviated by transferring some of its powers to the district courts, in specified administrative matters.

(b) District Courts and Magistrates Courts. The administration of the courts is the responsibility of the minister of justice; in practice, the courts are administered by the director

of courts, who is generally a judge of the rank of president of a district court, appointed by the minister of justice with the consent of the president of the Supreme Court. The courts operate according to the provisions of the Courts Law (Consolidated Version), 1984.

As stated above, the courts operate under a three-tier system, similar to the one used in Mandatory times. The jurisdiction of the magistrates courts is prescribed by the Courts Law: in criminal matters they sit in cases of contraventions and misdemeanors and also in specified felonies. In civil matters, the magistrates courts have jurisdiction where the amount of the claim or the value of the subject matter does not exceed the sum of NIS 2.5 million. They also have jurisdiction in claims concerning the possession, use, or division of immovable property. Usually the court is presided over by a single judge, but in special cases the bench is composed of three judges.

District courts have unlimited jurisdiction to deal with any civil or criminal matter not within the jurisdiction of a magistrates court or any other court or tribunal. As stated above, the district courts have concurrent jurisdiction with the Supreme Court in specified administrative matters. The transfer of jurisdiction to the district courts is gradual; at present not all the district courts have been empowered to act in this field. Judgments given by a magistrates court are appealable to a district court. Judgments given by a district court on appeal are appealable to the Supreme Court by leave to appeal. Judgments given by a district court sitting as a court of first instance are appealable to the Supreme Court. There are five district courts: in Jerusalem, Tel Aviv-Jaffa, Haifa, Beersheba, and Nazareth.

(c) Other Courts and Tribunals. There are also municipal courts, presided over by magistrates. Small claims courts, presided over by magistrates, are empowered to deal with civil claims not exceeding NIS 17,800 in value. These courts, which are not bound by the usual rules of procedure, are required to act in a manner most expedient for a just and speedy determination of the cases brought before them. Advocates may not appear for the parties to litigation in these courts, save by leave of the court and for special reasons. Traffic magistrates, appointed in the same way as judges of a magistrates court, have jurisdiction to try offenses against the Road Transport Ordinance or rules thereunder. A fairly recent innovation was the establishment of family courts under the Family Affairs Court Law, 1995. This Court deals with a variety of family and personal status matters, which previously were under the jurisdiction partly of a district court and partly of a magistrates court. It thus deals, inter alia, with claims for maintenance, parenthood, adoption, inheritance, visitation rights, and cases arising from the operation of the Prevention of Domestic Violence Law, 1991. The family courts are presided over by magistrates court judges. Judgments given by this court as well as those given by the other courts mentioned above are appealable to a district court.

Under the Military Justice Law, 1955, there are various courts martial and a court martial appeal court, which deal with offenses by soldiers and army employees.

There are also numerous tribunals, boards, and committees established under various laws to deal with special classes of cases, over many of which a judge presides. The procedure in these tribunals is regulated by the Administrative Tribunals Law, 1992. The labor tribunals were described above.

RELIGIOUS COURTS. As stated above, upon the establishment of the State of Israel, the law of the new state comprised all sections of the law which had existed on the eve of its establishment. Mandatory law, in its turn, inherited the Ottoman law which had existed prior to the establishment of the British Mandate for Palestine. In Ottoman times all matters of personal status were within the jurisdiction of the religious courts of the various religious communities. These courts are still operating, although several changes were made by the Israeli legislature, particularly as regards the rabbinical courts.

Under the Rabbinical Courts Jurisdiction (Marriage and Divorce) Law, 1953, the rabbinical courts have exclusive jurisdiction in matters of marriage and divorce of Jews in Israel, who are nationals or residents of the state, in any matter connected with a suit for divorce between Jews which has been filed therein, whether by the wife or the husband, including maintenance for the wife and for the children of the couple, and claims for **ḥaliẓah* filed therein by a woman against her deceased husband's brother, including maintenance for the woman until the day when *ḥaliẓah* is given. Furthermore, when a Jewish wife sues her Jewish husband or his estate for maintenance in a rabbinical court, otherwise than in connection with divorce, the plea of the defendant that a rabbinical court has no jurisdiction in the matter may not be entertained, and in matters of personal status of Jews in which a Rabbinical Court has not exclusive jurisdiction under the law, it will have jurisdiction after all the parties concerned have expressed their consent thereto. Upon the coming into force of the Adoption of Children Law, 1960, the adoption of children was excluded from the definition of matters of personal status in the Palestine Order-in-Council; so were successions, wills and legacies upon the coming into force of the Inheritance Law, 1965. Jurisdiction in matters of adoption under the above law is conferred upon Religious Courts, however, if the parents, the adopters, and the adoptee have consented in writing to their jurisdiction, or, in the case of an adoptee not being capable of understanding the matter, or being under the age of 13 years, if a social welfare officer and the attorney general have consented to their jurisdiction. Under the Inheritance Law, 1965, a Religious Court which had jurisdiction in matters of personal status of the decedent may make an order of inheritance or an order confirming a will and determine rights to maintenance from the estate if all the parties concerned according to the law have expressed in writing their consent thereto.

The Druze Religious Courts Law, 1962, established, for the first time in Israel, a Druze Religious Court and a Druze

Religious Court of Appeal. The Druze Religious Court is given exclusive jurisdiction in matters of marriage and divorce of Druze in Israel who are nationals or residents of the state and matters relating to the creation or internal management of a religious trust established before a court under Druze religious law or of a Druze trust established before the coming into force of the Law in accordance with Druze custom otherwise than before a religious or civil court. In matters of personal status of Druze in which a Druze Religious Court has no exclusive jurisdiction under the law, such court will have jurisdiction after all the parties concerned have expressed their consent. The Druze Religious Court of Appeal has jurisdiction to deal with appeals from judgments of the Druze Religious Courts.

Matters of dissolution of marriage, including divorce, annulment of marriage, and recognition of a marriage as void *ab initio*, which are not within the exclusive jurisdiction of a Jewish, Muslim, Christian, or Druze Religious Court, are within the jurisdiction of the District Court or a Religious Court as determined by the president of the Supreme Court in accordance with the provisions of the Jurisdiction in Matters of Dissolution of Marriage (Special Cases) Law, 1969. That law will not apply if both spouses are Jews, Muslims, Druze or members of one of the Christian communities maintaining a Religious Court in Israel. In cases to which the law applies, the provisions of the Palestine Order in Council, prohibiting the District Courts and Religious Courts from granting decrees of dissolution of marriage, will not apply. When a District Court upon which jurisdiction has been conferred under the law deals with the matter, it must do so in accordance with the following order of priority: (1) the internal law of the place of permanent residence common to the spouses; (2) the internal law of the last place of permanent residence common to the spouses; (3) the internal law of the country of the common nationality of the spouses; (4) the internal law of the place where the marriage was celebrated; but it may not deal with the matter according to a law as aforesaid if according thereto different laws are applicable to both the spouses. If there is no law applicable as aforesaid, the court may deal with the matter in accordance with the internal law of the place of permanent residence of one of the spouses as appears to it just in the circumstances of the case, but the consent of the spouses will always be a ground for divorce.

APPOINTMENT OF JUDGES IN CIVIL AND RELIGIOUS COURTS. Under Basic Law: Judicature an entirely new system of appointment was created: all the judges of the Magistrates' Courts, the District Courts and the Supreme Court are appointed by the president of the state upon the recommendation of a Nominations Committee submitted to him by the minister of justice, who is its chairman. The Nominations Committee is composed of three judges, namely, the president of the Supreme Court and two other judges of the Supreme Court elected by the judges of that court for three years; two members of the government, namely the minister of justice and one other member chosen by the government; two members of the Knesset elected by it by secret ballot; and two practicing advocates elected by the Chamber of Advocates. Candidates for appointment may be proposed by the minister of justice, the president of the Supreme Court, or jointly by three members of the nominations committee.

Persons qualified to be appointed as judges of the Supreme Court are persons who have held office as a judge of a District Court for a period of five years, persons inscribed, or entitled to be inscribed, in the Roll of Advocates in Israel and who, for not less than ten years, including at least five years in Israel, have been engaged in any of the following: (1) the profession of an advocate; (2) a judicial or other legal function, in the service of the State of Israel or another service approved by the minister of justice, by regulations, for this purpose; (3) the teaching of law at a recognized university or law school.

Eminent jurists may also be appointed. Persons qualified to be appointed as judges of a District Court are persons who have held office as a judge of a Magistrates' Court for a period of four years, persons inscribed, or entitled to be inscribed, in the Roll of Advocates in Israel and who, continuously or intermittently, for not less than seven years, including at least three years in Israel, have been engaged in one or several of the occupations enumerated above. Persons qualified to be appointed as judges of a Magistrates' Court are those inscribed or entitled to be inscribed in the Roll of Advocates in Israel for not less than five years, including at least two years in Israel.

Similar systems of appointment have been created for judges of the Rabbinical Courts, the Muslim Religious Courts, and the Druze Religious Courts, but no legislation has yet been passed regulating the appointment of the judges of the Christian Religious Courts, who continue to be appointed by the head of the community. Under the Dayyanim Law, 1955, the judges of the Rabbinical Courts, known as *dayyanim* (see **dayyan*) are appointed by the president of the state upon the recommendation of a Nominations Committee submitted to him by the minister for religious affairs. Currently the duties of the minister for religious affairs are performed by the minister of justice. The committee is composed of the two chief rabbis of Israel, two *dayyanim* elected by the body of *dayyanim* for three years, two members of the government, namely, the minister for religious affairs and one other member chosen by the government, two members of the Knesset elected by it by secret ballot, and two practicing advocates elected by the Chamber of Advocates. Persons qualified in accordance with regulations made by the minister with the consent of the Chief Rabbinate Council are eligible for appointment as *dayyanim* if they were so qualified within the two years preceding the appointment. Under those regulations they must have a rabbinical certificate authorizing them to teach and adjudicate (*Yoreh, yoreh, yadin, yadin* – see **semikhah*) issued by an expert rabbi or Torah institute whose certificate is recognized as sufficient by the Chief Rabbinate Council, be 30 years of age, be or have been married, and have a character and mode of life which befit the status of a *dayyan* in Israel. In addition, a *dayyan* of a Rabbinical Court must have passed examinations held on behalf of the Chief Rabbinate Council or be exempted therefrom, while a *dayyan* of the Rabbinical Court of Appeal must have been a *dayyan* of a Rabbinical Court for at least three consecutive years, or be known as an illustrious Torah scholar (*gadol ba-Torah*) according to a majority of the members of the Council of the Chief Rabbinate Council including the two chief rabbis. The subjects of the examination for *dayyanim* are (1) general knowledge of the Talmud and the **Posekim*; (2) thorough knowledge of the *Shulḥan Arukh, **Even ha-Ezer* and **Ḥoshen Mishpat*; (3) drafting of a judgment in a hypothetical case with reasoned findings of fact and decisions of substantive law; (4) knowledge of the rules and procedure based upon the **Halakhah*.

Under the Qadis Law, 1961, the judges of the Muslim Religious Courts, known as qadis, are appointed by the president of the state upon the recommendation of a Nominations Committee submitted to him by the minister for religious affairs. The Nominations Committee is composed of two qadis elected by the body of qadis for three years, two members of the government, namely, the minister for religious affairs and one other member chosen by the government, three members of the Knesset, including at least two Muslims, elected by the Knesset by secret ballot, and two advocates, including at least one Muslim, appointed by the Chamber of Advocates. Persons qualified to be appointed as qadis are Muslims who have had suitable training in Shariʿa Law, whose way of life and character befit the status of a qadi in the State of Israel and who are at least 30 years of age and are, or have been, married.

Under the Druze Religious Courts Law, 1962, judges of the Druze Religious Courts, known as qadis *madhhab*, are appointed by the president of the state upon the recommendation of a Nominations Committee submitted to him by the minister for religious affairs. The Nominations Committee is composed of the chairman of the Druze Religious Council constituted by rules made by the minister for religious affairs under the Religious Communities (Organization) Ordinance, the president of the Druze Religious Court of Appeal, or, if he serves also as the chairman of the Druze Religious Council, a qadi *madhhab* elected by the body of qadis *madhhab* for three years, another qadi *madhhab* similarly elected, the minister for religious affairs and the minister of justice, two Druze members of the Knesset (or other Druze, if there is only one Druze member of the Knesset or none) elected by the Knesset by secret ballot, and an advocate elected by the National Council of the Chamber of Advocates for three years. Persons qualified to be appointed as qadis *madhhab* are Druze who have had a suitable training in Druze religious law, whose way of life and character befit the status of a qadi *madhhab* in the State of Israel and who are at least 30 years of age and are, or have been, married. As from July 9, 1964, no person may be appointed as a judge, *dayyan*, qadi, or qadi *madhhab* of the courts to which the above laws apply, unless he is an Israel citizen. If the candidate for appointment has also another nationality and the laws of the state in which he is a national enable him to divest himself of such nationality, he will not be appointed until after he has done everything necessary on his part in order to divest himself thereof.

Every person appointed as a judge, *dayyan*, qadi, or qadi *madhhab* must, before assuming his office, make before the president of the state a declaration whereby he pledges himself to bear allegiance to the State of Israel, to dispense justice fairly, not to pervert the law and to show no favor, while every judge must also pledge himself to bear allegiance to the laws of the State of Israel. Every judge, qadi, and qadi *madhhab* in judicial matters is expressly declared by the law applicable to him to be subject to no authority other than that of the law, while under the Dayyanim Law, 1955, every *dayyan* in judicial matters is expressly to be subject to no authority other than that of the law according to which he judges. The reason for the difference in wording as regards the *dayyanim* is to make it clear that only the laws concerning the legal system of the *dayyanim*, including those laws which restrict the jurisdiction of the *dayyanim* and no other laws, bind the *dayyanim* in judicial matters.

An additional safeguard for the integrity of the judges is stated in section 10 of Basic Law: the Judicature, where the salaries and pensions of the judges are provided for. The Basic Law declares that no decision should be made to reduce only the salaries of judges.

Every judge, *dayyan*, qadi, and qadi *madhhab* will hold office from the day of his declaration of allegiance and his tenure will end only upon his death, resignation, retirement on pension, or removal from office by virtue of the law applicable to him. He may resign his office by submitting a letter of resignation to the appropriate minister, and his tenure of office will terminate upon the expiration of three months from the submission of the letter of resignation, unless the minister has consented to a shorter period. He may retire on pension if he has attained the age of 60 after having held office for 20 years, if he has attained the age of 65 after having held office for 15 years and if he so requests and his request is approved by the appropriate Nominations Committee. A magistrates court judge may retire on pension if he has attained the age of 50 after having held office for 20 years, or if he has attained the age of 55 after having held office for 15 years. Every judge must retire if the appropriate Nominations Committee, on the strength of a medical opinion, decides that, owing to his state of health, he is unable to continue in office, or on attaining the age of 70 years, unless he is a chief rabbi of Israel or a senior presiding *dayyan*, in which case he must retire on pension on attaining the age of 75 years.

Every judge, *dayyan*, qadi and qadi *madhhab* is subject to the jurisdiction of a Court of Discipline constituted under the law applicable to him. The Court of Discipline for judges consists of five members, including three judges of the Supreme Court, as the president of the Supreme Court may in respect of each case prescribe, and its members are appointed in respect of each case by the body of the judges of the Supreme Court. Similar provisions apply, *mutatis mutandis*, to *dayya-*

nim. The courts of discipline for qadis and qadis *madhhab* consist of three members: the president of the Shariʿa Court of Appeal or the Druze Religious Court of Appeal, as the case may be, or the qadi or qadi *madhhab*, as the case may be with the greatest length of service, an advocate appointed for each case by the National Council of the Chamber of Advocates, and one member appointed for each case by the minister of religious affairs. The minister of justice may submit a complaint against a judge, and the minister for religious affairs against a *dayyan*, a qadi or a qadi *madhhab*, to the competent Court of Discipline on one of the following grounds: (1) he has acted improperly in carrying out his functions; (2) he has behaved in a manner unbecoming his judicial status in the State of Israel; (3) he has been convicted of an offense which in the circumstances of the case involves moral turpitude; (4) the Nominations Committee has found that he obtained his appointment unlawfully.

The Court of Discipline must submit its findings, whether favorable or unfavorable, to the appropriate minister; if it finds that the person concerned is unworthy to continue in his functions, the minister must submit its findings to the president of the state, who must remove him from office. Criminal proceedings may not be brought against a judge, *dayyan*, qadi or qadi *madhhab* save by the attorney general before a District Court composed of three judges. The salaries and other payments to be made to a judge, *dayyan*, qadi and qadi *madhhab* during and after his period of tenure, including those to be made to his dependents after his death, are fixed by resolution of the Knesset or by the Finance Committee of the Knesset if so authorized by the Knesset.

THE BAR. The Chamber of Advocates Law, 1961 established a self-governing integrated bar, administered by institutions elected democratically by the body of advocates. This is the only profession enjoying autonomy: other professions are controlled by the government. Under that law a person may not practice the profession of an advocate in Israel unless he is a resident of Israel, is 23 years of age, has qualified as an advocate by passing the prescribed examinations and serving one year as a law apprentice, and has been accepted as a member of the chamber. Law apprenticeship may be served with a judge of the Supreme Court or a district court or with a magistrate of at least five-years' standing, a court martial judge who is a jurist of at least five years' standing, or a member of the Chamber of Advocates who is of five years' standing or holding a post in the Government Legal Service prescribed for that purpose by the minister of justice. At the end of the period he must undergo written examinations of the Chamber of Advocates in practical subjects and an oral examination conducted by examining committees composed of three members each, namely, a judge, as chairman, and two advocates, one of whom is a member of the Legal Service.

Advocates are subject to the jurisdiction of Disciplinary Tribunals composed solely of advocates as prescribed by the Chamber of Advocates Law, 1961. From a judgment of a Disciplinary Tribunal the accused advocate, the prosecuting chamber, and the attorney general, may appeal to the National Disciplinary Tribunal; there is an additional appeal to the Supreme Court. There are about 33,000 members of the Chamber of Advocates, not all of them necessarily in actual legal practice.

THE ATTORNEY GENERAL. The attorney general occupies one of the most important senior positions in the administration of the country and is one of the pillars upon which the rule of law is upheld within the government framework. Based on the Mandatory model, the attorney general is a professional jurist. In 1997 the minister of justice appointed a public committee to examine the proper method for appointing the attorney general and subjects related to his post. The committee was headed by retired president of the Supreme Court Meir Shamgar, who, before being elevated to the Bench, occupied the post of attorney general. With him were three former ministers of justice and a renowned law professor. The report, submitted in 1998, describes the duties of the attorney general as follows:

(1) He is the head of the public prosecution. In this capacity he is responsible for applying the penal law in the State, including appearance in the law courts, either in person or through his representatives.

(2) He represents the State in non-criminal litigation, namely in civil suits as well as administrative, fiscal, and labor relations litigation and in any other representation in non-criminal matters.

(3) He gives legal advice to the government and other public officials.

(4) He gives legal advice and assistance to the government in general and to the minister of justice in particular in preparing legislation to be submitted to the Knesset and oversees its proper integration in the law of the land. Likewise he examines private-member bills submitted to the Knesset.

(5) He represents the public interest and upholds the law in a variety of additional subjects specified in provisions of the law.

The attorney general is appointed by the government for a single term of six years.

THE STATE COMPTROLLER. The office of the state comptroller was established by law in 1949. In 1988 Basic Law: the State Comptroller was enacted. Section 2(a) charges the comptroller with the duty to "carry out inspection of the assets, finances, undertakings, and administration of the state, of government offices, of every enterprise, institution or public corporation of the state, of local authorities, of bodies or other institutions subject to inspection by this Law." The office of state comptroller is the most effective instrument for review of public administration.

The state comptroller is elected by the Knesset for a tenure of seven years, which may not be renewed, and is empowered to request all information from the public body being audited. The comptroller's reports are presented to the Knesset, where they are discussed by its Public Audit Committee. The comptroller thus serves as the long arm of the Knesset for the efficient review of the administration and as a main source of information necessary for the Knesset's control over government activities.

The state comptroller also serves as the public complaints commissioner (Ombudsman), and decides authoritatively on thousands of complaints from citizens against state and government agencies, government corporations, and local authorities. In addition, the state comptroller inspects the finances of the political parties and their campaign accounts. The publication of the yearly comptroller reports is covered extensively by the media. The state comptroller enjoys enormous public prestige. (See also Israel, State of: Political Life and Parties.)

[Henry Eli Baker / Shlomo Guberman (2nd ed.)]

POLICE. The establishment of the Israel Police preceded that of the State itself. At the end of 1947, after the United Nations partition decision, the Mandatory police began to break up. Non-Jewish constables were withdrawn from the coastal area; only about 700 Jewish policemen and a little inferior equipment were left. The most serious problem was the shortage of men to fill command and technical posts, most of which had been held by British officers. Second in urgency was the need to change the character of the Police, which, especially in the few preceding years, had been more military than constabulary, into the kind of force normal in a democracy, dedicated only to ensure the rule of law and the public welfare. At the end of 1948, the Police had a strength of 1,882.

Three stages of development may be distinguished. The first was organization and recruitment. This was not easy, for the army demanded first choice of men and material. Nevertheless, within two years 3,497 men had joined, and equipment was assembled from whatever source, regardless of uniformity. In organization and methods, new forms had to be found to fit new needs. Mass *aliyah*, unemployment, and a flood of new legislation naturally enlarged the scope of police work. Relations between the people and the Police were not good, partly because of the aftereffects of the Holocaust and of two wars, and the suspicions of newcomers from eastern European and Arab lands where the policeman was suspect and disliked. Policemen often found themselves confronted by angry demonstrators in front of Government or public offices; the men were pressed into service day and night, with inadequate compensation. The growing manpower, with a large turnover, was also troublesome. In the second stage, fall-out was heavy, but these were years of natural selection, which strengthened those who stayed on, contributed to their professional specialization and built up a cadre of experts and officers. By the second half of the 1950s long-range planning was feasible and different techniques could be tried out in organization and command, in criminal investigation and traffic control. Some of these were borrowed, but most were the fruit of the force's own ideas and experience. This was a period of ever-increasing traffic and accidents, security problems complicated by border infiltration, and more crime. In the third stage administration and organization were stabilized and efficiency was steadily increased.

A task unknown to most other police forces is the guarding of the cease-fire lines against infiltration and attack from the neighboring countries. This was done by the Frontier Guard, in cooperation with the army. After the Six-Day War, the Israel Police was also responsible for law and order in the areas administered under the cease-fire agreements. Local Arab policemen, 90% of whom served under Jordanian and Egyptian rule, were recruited and retrained for the purpose. Increasing terrorist attacks led the government to give the police responsibility for internal security in 1974. This involved the creation of a Civil Guard joined by tens of thousands of citizens to patrol neighborhoods as well as the creation of an Anti-Terrorist Unit and Bomb Disposal Division. Beginning in the late 1970s, rising crime also led to the creation of such units as the National Serious Crimes Investigation Unit, the National Fraud Unit, the Internal Investigations Unit, the Headquarters Staff Work Unit, Tel Aviv District's Central (Serious Crimes) Unit, etc.

The police faced many challenges and crises in the course of its history. Over 50 were killed in 1982 and 1983 bombings in Tyre during the Lebanese War. The two Intifadas severely taxed its resources and during rioting in the North of Israel in October 2000, 13 Israeli Arab citizens were killed and hundreds wounded in a police action that drew heavy criticism. In August 2005 the police joined the army in the evacuation of the *Gush Katif settlements, an operation which won it much praise for the restraint and patience shown in dealing with the angry settlers.

The Israel Police is controlled by national headquarters in Jerusalem and commanded by the Inspector General. In 2005 the strength of the force was around 25,000 in six districts, 10 subdistricts, and 80 police stations.

WEBSITE: www.police.gov.il.

POLITICAL LIFE AND PARTIES

Introduction

It was largely due to the existence of the pre-state political parties, which had conducted intensive political activities for almost half a century within the framework of the **yishuv*, under the British Mandate for Palestine, that upon gaining its independence in May 1948 the State of Israel was able to embark immediately on the establishment of an orderly and democratic parliamentary system. After the first *Knesset elections in January 1949, before the *War of Independence was formally over, the main concern of the parties was to gain governmental and municipal power, though most of them also continued their activities on the world Zionist scene, and for a certain period maintained independent social and economic services. The *Histadrut, which remained an important power center until the mid-1990s, was another forum in which many of the political parties, but especially the labor parties, vied for control.

Since its establishment Israel has always had coalition governments, which except for one brief period in the early 1990s, always included at least four coalition partners. The main reason for this phenomenon is Israel's electoral system, which has led to a multiplicity of parties entering the Knesset, and none ever winning a majority of the Knesset seats, which is a prerequisite for forming a government in a parliamentary system (see *Governance).

The political history of the State of Israel may be divided into two periods. The first lasted from the establishment of the state until the political "upheaval" of 1977, in which *Mapai (until 1968) and the *Israel Labor Party thereafter were predominant and headed all the coalition governments formed. The second began in 1977, when the *Likud gained power for the first time and remained the predominant political party for the majority of the time, except for the years 1984–88 when the political bloc which it led was equal in size to that led by the Labor Party, and the years 1992–96 and 1999–2001 when the Labor Party managed to establish coalition governments, which excluded the Likud.

It should be pointed out that since its establishment, all of Israel's presidents but one (Chaim *Weizmann), all of Israel's prime ministers, and all but two of the speakers of the Knesset (Nahum Nir for part of the Third Knesset, and Avraham *Burg in the Fifteenth Knesset) have been members of the ruling party at the time.

In the early period Israel had a strong central government, with a relatively small number of ministers, a large public economic sector (either state- or Histadrut-run), and a relatively egalitarian society, in which the Histadrut and the kibbutzim were viewed – in Israel and abroad – as symbols of communalism. Despite the famous religious "status quo," Israel was predominantly secular, and despite the heterogeneous make-up of its population, relatively homogenous in its social values and culture. In this period occurred all but one of the major wars in which Israel participated, and only at its end did some minor steps in the direction of peace materialize.

In the second period, the government weakened, to a point that in 1992 a attempt was made to change the system of government in order to strengthen the prime minister and his government (see below), state control over many spheres of life gradually decreased, Israel moved from a predominantly social democratic to a predominantly neoliberal economy, and by the beginning of the 21st century ranked high among the Western democracies in terms of economic and social polarization within its society and emphasis on individualism. In this period the Histadrut greatly weakened, as did the kibbutzim, and it was now the settlements beyond the Green Line that gained predominance as symbols of the new Israel. The heterogeneity of Israeli society became much more visible, and the role of religion grew. In the second period Israel fought only one major war (the *Lebanese War), though it faced two major Palestinian uprisings. A significant peace process began with the peace treaty that was signed with Egypt in 1979, which was followed by the Oslo process, peace with Jordan (1994), and the establishment of formal relations with several additional Arab states.

The political map of Israel changed significantly during the first 56 years of its existence, even though there are still several parties today – the Likud, the Labor Party, the *National Religious Party, *Agudat Israel, and Ḥadash – whose origins can be traced to the pre-state period. In general one may speak of a movement from left-wing to right-wing predominance, even though on many (though not all) issues the differences between the political right and left have become blurred. Whereas until the *Six-Day War of June 1967 Israel's main concern was its physical survival, since then it has been the borders and nature of the state.

Since its establishment, the population of the State of Israel has grown more or less sixfold, mostly through immigration, and parties based on "ethnic" origin have existed, but they have usually been relatively insignificant. Over the years the religious representation in the Knesset has grown, but the greatest changes have been in the strengthening of **Ḥaredi* religious parties at the expense of "Zionist" religious parties and the growing role played by the religious parties – until the Sixteenth Knesset – as "balancers" in the political game.

As to the Arab representation in the Knesset, this has changed both in size, quality, and nature, but except for one Arab deputy minister in the course of the Thirteenth Knesset, Arabs have not been admitted to the government, and their percentage in other power centers, the judicial system and the civil service has remained much below their percentage in the population. Whereas in the first Knesset Arab representation was through the Israel Communist Party and traditional family (*hamulah*)-based parties supported by Mapai and later the Alignment (see below), by the end of the 20th century the Arab representation in the Knesset was more nationalistic, radical, and independent.

[Susan Hattis Rolef (2nd ed.)]

Early Parties, 1900–1918

The first parties in the new *yishuv* were founded in the first decade of the 20th century by newcomers belonging to the Second Aliyah. *Ha-Po'el ha-Ẓa'ir ("the Young Worker," as distinct from the "old workers" of the First Aliyah, most of whom had become overseers or private farmers), led by Yosef *Aharonovitz, Yosef *Vitkin, and Yosef *Sprinzak, was founded in 1905. *Po'alei Zion, a Socialist Zionist party which originated in Russia, Austria, and other countries, was established in the Land of Israel in 1906. Among its leaders were Izhak *Ben-Zvi, David *Ben-Gurion, and Yiẓḥak *Tabenkin. Its aim was "to create a Jewish society based on socialist foundations in the Land of Israel," and the method it envisaged was "an unremitting class struggle." Ha-Po'el ha-Ẓa'ir rejected the class struggle on the ground that the Jewish society and economy in Palestine were still in the precapitalist stage. "Our interest – to create a Jewish center in the Land of Israel – and the class struggle are a contradiction in terms," wrote Aharonovitz. The first article in the Ha-Po'el ha-Ẓa'ir program called for "the conquest of all branches of work" (Hebrew *kibbush avodah*, meaning that Jewish workers should do even menial work themselves, not leaving manual effort to non-Jews). A group of nonparty workers, notably Berl *Katzenelson and David *Remez, opposed the division into two parties and called for labor unity.

The parties engaged in practical work as well as theoretical discussion. New arrivals in Jaffa often found that they had to choose between two hotels, one for each party. But there was little difference in their day-to-day lives and their practical approach to problems. Both groups tried to remove the obstacles to Jewish immigration, win rights of employment for Jewish workers in the Jewish farms and orange groves, and improve working conditions.

At its first conference in Jaffa, at the beginning of 1907, Po'alei Zion proclaimed its aspiration for "political independence for the Jewish people in this country," and decided to send an independent faction of delegates to the Zionist Congress. It was associated almost from the first with the Po'alei Zion world movement, whereas Ha-Po'el ha-Ẓa'ir established ties with the *Ẓe'irei Zion movement in the Diaspora only in 1913.

In 1908 a controversy broke out in Ha-Po'el ha-Ẓa'ir on the question of how to encourage the workers to remain on the land. At a special conference Vitkin called for the establishment of workers' smallholdings near the moshavot to enable them to become independent cultivators instead of mere agricultural laborers. The "conquest of labor," he declared, must be accompanied by the "conquest of the soil." He was opposed by Aharonovitz, who believed that the only way to increase the Jewish population was to create an agricultural proletariat, working as wage earners on private farms, and leave the "conquest of the soil" to the Zionist Organization. The issue was ultimately decided by the exigencies of life: members of Ha-Po'el ha-Ẓa'ir were among the founders of *Deganyah, the first kevuẓah, and *Nahalal, the first moshav, while Po'alei Zion, despite its class-war doctrine, devoted most of its energies to constructive activities, including the establishment of labor exchanges, cooperative groups, and mutual aid institutions.

A bureau of the religious *Mizrachi Party, which had been a part of the World Zionist Organization since 1902, was set up in the Land of Israel in 1912, but did not become active until after the end of World War I. Its labor wing, *Ha-Po'el ha-Mizrachi, was founded in 1922. The basic principle of the movement was: "The Land of Israel for the People of Israel in accordance with the Torah of Israel." The non-Zionist Orthodox *Agudat Israel, which opposed the secular organization of the *yishuv*, was also established in the Land of Israel in 1912, simultaneously with the founding of its parent world organization.

Steps Toward Labor Unity

Toward the end of World War I, the nonparty labor group led by Berl Katzenelson appealed for an end to the rivalry between the two workers' parties, so that labor could exert its full influence in the development of the *yishuv*. It called for the establishment of an all-inclusive labor organization which would be a trade union as well as a political party, establishing settlements and cooperatives, helping new immigrants, and providing social services for its members. At a unity conference in February 1919, Po'alei Zion and the nonparty group, with the support of a majority of the Agricultural Workers' Federation, formed *Aḥdut ha-Avodah ("Unity of Labor"). Ha-Po'el ha-Ẓa'ir refused to join, mainly because the new organization described itself as "a branch of the socialist labor movement in the world." To an attack on these grounds by A.D. *Gordon, Joseph Ḥayyim *Brenner replied that although the critics rejected socialism, they followed its principles in daily life. Ha-Po'el ha-Ẓa'ir also believed in building up small, closely knit communes, while Aḥdut ha-Avodah aimed at developing a mass movement.

To diminish the growing rivalry between them, Joseph *Trumpeldor, a leading figure of the Second Aliyah, proposed the establishment of a neutral, independent trade union federation to which both would be affiliated. His initiative bore fruit after his tragic death, when the organization he envisaged, the Histadrut, was established at a labor movement conference in Haifa in December 1920. The 4,433 registered members elected 38 delegates from Aḥdut ha-Avodah, 27 from Ha-Po'el ha-Ẓa'ir, 16 from the New Immigrants list representing *He-Ḥalutz, *Ha-Shomer ha-Ẓa'ir, and others, and six from the extreme leftist Mifleget Po'alim Soẓialistim ("Socialist Workers' Party"), nicknamed "Mopsim," which had split off from Po'alei Zion when Aḥdut ha-Avodah was formed.

Immediately after the end of World War I, preparations were made for the establishment of an autonomous, democratically elected body to organize the *yishuv* and represent it in dealings with the authorities. A provisional committee held three sessions in 1918 and 1919, the first representing only Tel Aviv and its surroundings, the second Jerusalem as well, and the third consisting of delegates from all parts of the country. On April 19, 1920, elections were held to an Asefat Ha-Nivḥarim (Elected Assembly). In addition to the workers' parties and Mizrachi, a variety of communal, religious, vocational, and local groups sought representation and nineteen lists of candidates were submitted. Each list received one delegate for every 80 votes polled; 77% of the electors voted and 314 delegates were elected. Aḥdut ha-Avodah, with 70 delegates, was the largest group; next came the Sephardi Union with 54, Ha-Po'el ha-Ẓa'ir with 41, the Farmers' Union with 16, the Progressive Party (Mitkaddemim) with 13, the Yemenites with 12, two Mizrachi lists with a total of 11, and 11 other groups with a total of 46 places. An additional 51 delegates were chosen at separate polls by Orthodox men, who refused to participate in elections in which women had the franchise.

At the Assembly's first session, in October 1920, the 20 factions combined into three wings: right, consisting of the Oriental Jews and the religious groups; left, composed of the two labor parties; and center, consisting of the other groups.

The Assembly elected a Va'ad Le'ummi (National Council) of 36, comprising Aḥdut ha-Avodah 8, Sephardim 6, Ha-Po'el ha-Ẓa'ir 5, Orthodox 5, Progressives 3, Farmers 2, Yemenites 2, Mizrachi and Clerks 1 each. Meir *Dizengoff, Vladimir *Jabotinsky, Haim Margolis-Kalvaryski, and David *Yellin were elected on a personal basis. The Va'ad Le'ummi was headed by a presidium of three, assisted by an executive council whose membership varied from 7 to 14.

The second session of the first Assembly, which was scheduled for May 1921, did not take place until the following March, because of the May riots and their aftermath, the categorical refusal of the Orthodox delegates to participate as long as women were allowed to vote, and the Sephardim's and Farmers' objections to the proposed self-taxation system. Further negotiations with these groups, as well as fruitless attempts to obtain official recognition by the Mandatory government, held up the convening of the third session until June 1925. Despite prolonged efforts to solve the problem of women's suffrage, the Orthodox and Mizrachi delegates did not attend the second and third sessions, and it was not until the eve of the next elections that the Mizrachi agreed to participate, with the Orthodox maintaining their boycott.

At the elections to the second Assembly, held on December 6, 1925, the Palestine branch of the Revisionist Organization, led by Jabotinsky, made its first appearance in the politics of the *yishuv*, gaining 15 seats out of 201. The labor parties increased their relative strength, while the middle class and the religious Jews became even more fragmented than before. Aḥdut ha-Avodah had 54 seats, Ha-Po'el ha-Ẓa'ir 30, Sephardim and Oriental groups 19, five Mizrachi lists together 19, the Women's Equal Rights Association 13, and the Agricultural Bloc 9. A "working-class" list, with 6 seats, reflected the influence of the Palestine Communist Party (PKP), which had been formed illegally in 1921 by members of the "Mopsim" and other groups. The Yemenites, alleging discrimination, boycotted the elections, but were later permitted to elect 20 additional delegates of their own. The second Assembly elected a Va'ad Le'ummi of 38: 18 representing the United Bloc (Mizrachi, Sephardim, Yemenites, Farmers, and others), 9 for Aḥdut ha-Avodah, 5 for Ha-Po'el ha-Ẓa'ir, and 2 each for Women, Revisionists, and the Democratic group.

Strengthening of the Political Parties

The high commissioner's ratification of the regulations for Keneset Yisrael, officially recognizing its representative bodies, the Asefat ha-Nivḥarim and the Va'ad Le'ummi, was announced on Jan. 1, 1928, but it took more than two years to draft the election rules and to prepare a register of all the members of the Jewish community as prescribed by the regulations. The total number of Assembly members was fixed at 71, with the electors divided into three colleges, or curiae: Ashkenazim, with 53 delegates, Sephardim 15, and Yemenites 3. Each elector was allowed to vote only in his own college.

In 1930 Aḥdut ha-Avodah and Ha-Po'el ha-Ẓa'ir merged to form Mapai (Mifleget Po'alei Ereẓ Israel – "Palestine Labor Party"), which immediately became the strongest political force in the *yishuv*. The Left Po'alei Zion and Ha-Shomer ha-Ẓa'ir remained outside the merger.

At the elections to the third Assembly, on Jan. 5, 1931, Mapai, with 27 delegates, together with 4 Sephardi Labor, was by far the strongest party. The Revisionists, with 16, including 5 Sephardim, also increased their strength considerably, followed by the Sephardim (general) with 6, Mizrachi and Ha-Po'el ha-Mizrachi 5, and General Zionists 4. The Farmers refused to participate in the elections when their demand for three guaranteed seats was refused and the Communists did not win a place. In the 23-member Va'ad Le'ummi, Mapai had 11 members, Sephardim 4, Mizrachi 3, General Zionists 3, Women 1, and Yemenites 1. The Revisionists refused to join the Va'ad Le'ummi because of dissatisfaction with the Assembly's political decisions, but were given 5 seats in the following year, leaving Mapai with 10 seats and the three other main parties with 2 each.

The third Assembly lasted for over 13 years, as elections were repeatedly postponed because of recurrent Arab violence, continuous political tension, and then the outbreak of World War II. With the growth of the *yishuv*, the parties in Palestine, especially Mapai, became the dominant influence in the Jewish Agency. Chaim *Arlosoroff, named head of the Jewish Agency political department in 1931, was succeeded, after his assassination in 1933, by Moshe Shertok (*Sharett). David Ben-Gurion became chairman of the executive in 1935.

While the Jewish Agency was responsible for major political affairs, politics played a prominent role in most of the Assembly's 18 sessions. Jewish Agency representatives reported regularly to the Assembly and the Va'ad Le'ummi, political resolutions were generally drafted in close cooperation between the two bodies, and representations to the British authorities were often submitted jointly. Other issues were defense against Arab violence; the utilization of national funds; the allocation of immigration certificates; education; trade union policy and the right to strike; the role of the Histadrut in the establishment of new settlements and economic enterprises; and the activities of local authorities and local councils.

Most political parties not only worked in the Va'ad Le'ummi, the Jewish Agency, the local authorities, and the Histadrut but also established agricultural settlements, schools, housing projects, industries, transport, and service cooperatives, and other constructive enterprises, either independently or through affiliated economic bodies. Almost all the parties organized their own youth movements. Conflicting party influences were also apparent in the ranks of the Haganah.

The most outspoken opposition to the official policies of the Jewish Agency and the *yishuv* came from the Revisionists, who called on the Zionist movement to proclaim the establishment of a Jewish state on both banks of the Jordan as the ultimate aim of Zionism. They accused Chaim Weizmann and his labor supporters of compromising with the British government, alleged that the Executive discriminated against middle-class immigrants and businessmen, opposed the "trend" system in education (see Israel, State of: Education, 1918–1948), and demanded compulsory arbitration in labor disputes. Tension mounted after the murder of Arlosoroff in 1933, when two Revisionists were accused of the crime. An agreement reached in the following year by Ben-Gurion and Jabotinsky on a modus vivendi in labor relations was rejected, after a referendum, by the members of the Histadrut. Controversy grew still more heated after the majority of Revisionists left the World Zionist Organization in 1935, and a minority, refusing to leave, founded the *Jewish State Party.

Revisionist criticism of Labor's economic and social policies was, on the whole, supported by the right wing of the General Zionists. In 1935 the General Zionists split into the Federation (Hitaḥadut) and the Union (Berit) of General Zionists, known respectively as the A and B Factions. The A group, with Weizmann as its leader, cooperated with Labor. So did Mizrachi and Ha-Po'el ha-Mizrachi, though they frequently opposed Mapai on religious and educational issues. On the left, Ha-Shomer ha-Ẓa'ir, which gradually became more active as a political party, demanded joint organization of Jewish and Arab workers and greater efforts to reach an agreement with the Arabs, while also endorsing the principle of immigration to the full economic absorptive capacity of the country. Despite party differences, there was a large measure of common ground on such practical issues as immigration, settlement on the land, defense, and opposition to the restrictive policies of the Mandatory government. An exception was the anti-Zionist Palestine Communist Party, which made largely unsuccessful efforts to recruit Arab members and in 1936–39 openly supported the Arab revolt and Arab terrorism against the Jews. In 1939 it split up into separate Jewish and Arab groups.

The 1937 Peel Commission's proposal for the *partition of Palestine into two states, Jewish and Arab, and a British zone, aroused controversy that largely cut across party lines, particularly in Mapai and in both factions of the General Zionists. While the majority in these parties was prepared, in principle, to consider partition, Berl Katzenelson of Mapai and Menaḥem *Ussishkin of the General Zionists B were categorically opposed. The Revisionists were against partition on political grounds and the Mizrachi on religious grounds, while Ha-Shomer ha-Ẓa'ir advocated the establishment of Palestine as a binational state. The latter joined forces on the issue of Arab-Jewish relations with a small nonparty group, founded as *Berit Shalom ("Peace Alliance") in 1925 and later called Kedmah Mizraḥah (from 1936), the League for Jewish-Arab Understanding (from 1939), and Iḥud (from 1942). Among its leaders were *Rabbi Binyamin (Radler-Feldman), Haim Margolis-Kalvaryski, Judah L. *Magnes, and Martin *Buber. Bitter, occasionally violent, controversy arose over defense policy during the Arab riots of 1936–39. The Revisionists rejected the Haganah's policy of *havlagah* ("restraint"); their members were the backbone of the *Irgun Ẓeva'i Le'ummi, which carried out reprisals against the Arabs and engaged in guerrilla activity against the British forces.

During World War II, after the abandonment of partition by the British and the adoption of the White Paper Policy, opinion in the Zionist movement crystallized around the *Biltmore Program. This plan, calling for the establishment of Palestine as "a Jewish Commonwealth integrated in the structure of the new democratic world," was approved by the Inner Zionist General Council on Nov. 10, 1942, by 21 votes to 4, with 3 abstentions. The program was supported by Mapai, the General Zionists, and Mizrachi, and opposed by Ha-Shomer ha-Ẓa'ir, which called for political parity of Jews and Arabs, and by the Left Po'alei Zion. The abstentions came from representatives of Si'ah Bet (the "B Faction" of Mapai), who insisted on a demand for Jewish rights in the whole of Palestine.

A new party, Aliyah Ḥadashah, mainly representing recent immigrants from Germany and Central Europe, founded in 1942, favored a continuation of the British Mandate and a further attempt to reach an agreement with the Arabs (see *Independent Liberal Party). The struggle conducted within Mapai by Si'ah Bet for the right to fight for its independent left-wing views on social policy came to a head at the Mapai

Representation of Parties in the Elected Assemblies, Palestine.

	First	Second	Third	Fourth
Date of elections	**April 19, 1920**	**Dec. 6, 1925**	**Jan. 5, 1931**	**Aug. 1, 1944**
Number of electors	28,765	64,764	89,656	300,018
Percentage of votes cast	77%	57%	56%	67%
Number of lists represented	20	25	14	18
Composition of Delegates:				
Aḥdut ha-Avodah	70	54	—	63[6]
Ha-Po'el ha-Ẓa'ir	41	30	27[6]	63
Other labor groups	—	6	7[7]	40[9]
Sephardim	54	19	6	—
Other Oriental communities	18	21[3]	3	6
Orthodox	51[1]	—	—	—
Mizrachi groups	11	19[4]	5	24
Other religious groups	2	—	—	3
Revisionists	—	15	16[8]	—
Farmers	16	9	—	—
Women's groups	5	14	3	4
General Zionists	—	—	4	7
Other Groups	46[2]	34[5]	—	24[10]
Total	314	221	71	171

1 Elected at separate polls
2 Eight lists.
3 Including 20 Yemenites elected at separate polls.
4 Five lists.
5 Eleven lists.
6 Mapai.
7 Including four Sephardi Labor.
8 Including five Sephardi Revisionists.
9 Ha-Shomer ha-Ẓa'ir – 21; Le-Aḥdut ha-Avodah – 16; Popular Democrats (Communists) – 3.
10 Including 18 Aliyah.

conference at Kefar Vitkin in October 1942, with a majority decision to prohibit factions within the party. In May 1944 Si'ah Bet formed a new party, Ha-Tenu'ah le-Aḥdut ha-Avodah (see *Aḥdut ha-Avodah, second entry), which amalgamated with Ha-Shomer ha-Ẓa'ir and the Left Po'alei Zion in January 1948 to form *Mapam (Mifleget ha-Po'alim ha-Me'uḥedet, "United Workers' Party").

The fourth Asefat ha-Nivḥarim was elected on August 1, 1944. The Revisionists, General Zionists B, and Sephardim boycotted the elections because their demands for changes in the electoral system were refused, while Agudat Israel maintained its ban. However, 67% of the vastly increased electorate of 300,000 went to the polls (see Table: Parties of Elected Assemblies).

Labor continued to dominate the Va'ad Le'ummi: of 42 members, 15 were from Mapai, and eight from the other two left-wing parties, while Izhak Ben-Zvi and David Remez were elected president and chairman respectively. During the subsequent period, major political and defense issues overshadowed all others. Interparty conflict was reflected in the dissensions between the Haganah, which was controlled by the Jewish Agency, and the largely Revisionist Irgun Ẓeva'i Le'ummi. Left-wing predominance in the *Palmaḥ, which was part of the Haganah, also gave rise to occasional disagreements.

When the Palestine problem was submitted to the United Nations (1947), however, the majority of the *yishuv* and the Zionist movement was united in support of the demand for the establishment of a Jewish state, even in part of the country, though the Revisionists pressed for their maximalist program and Ha-Shomer ha-Ẓa'ir continued to advocate a binational state. After the UN Special Committee on Palestine (UNSCOP) issued its report recommending the establishment in Palestine of both a Jewish and an Arab state, almost all parties (including the Communists after the U.S.S.R. had expressed its support for partition) collaborated in the effort to carry out the transition to independence.

[Misha Louvish]

Transition to Statehood and to First Elections

On April 12, 1948, the Zionist General Council laid the foundations for the self-governing institutions of the Jewish state by appointing a provisional legislature, called Mo'eẓet ha-Am (People's Council), and an executive called Minhelet ha-Am (People's Administration). Seats were allocated on the basis of the existing relative power of the parties. The 37 members of the People's Council consisted of the 14 members of the Executive of the Va'ad Le'ummi (National Committee), the 11 members of the Jewish Agency Executive from the **yishuv*, and 12 delegates from parties not represented on either. Its party makeup was 10 from Mapai, six General Zionists, five from *Ha-Po'el ha-Mizrachi and *Ha-Mizrachi, five from *Mapam, three from *Agudat Israel, three Revisionists, and one each representing the Communists, *WIZO (Women's International Zionist Organization), *Aliyah Ḥadashah, the Sephardim, and the Yemenites. Chaim *Weizmann was the president of the Council and its 38th member. For the first time, Agudat Israel and the Communists were represented on the governing bodies of the Yishuv.

On May 14, the People's Council and the People's Administration became respectively the Provisional Council of State and the Provisional Government of the independent State of Israel. The Revisionists and Communists were in opposition.

The Provisional Government set the basic pattern for Israel's future coalition system. Until the eve of the *Six-Day War in June 1967 all political parties from the General Zionists in the Center to Mapam on the Left were welcome to join the coalition. The *Ḥerut Movement, established by Menaḥem *Begin in June 1948 as the successor to the Revisionist Party, and the Communists, were excluded. Towards the elections to the Constituent Assembly, which were to be held in February 1949, a few of the veteran leaders of the Revisionist Party decided not to join the Ḥerut Movement and to submit their own list.

The General Zionists split in August 1948. One group retained the original name while the other, together with Aliyah Ḥadashah and *Ha-Oved ha-Ẓiyyoni, formed the new Progressive Party.

During the War of Independence of 1948–9, internal political problems remained more or less in the background, though the Ḥerut movement denounced Ben-Gurion's measures against the IẒL (*Irgun Ẓeva'i Le'ummi), especially in connection with the *Altalena* affair, measures that were also criticized by the General Zionists and Mizrachi, while Mapam was disturbed by the disbandment of the *Palmaḥ high command.

The First Knesset, 1949–1951

The elections to the Constituent Assembly, which soon was renamed "the First Knesset," were held on January 25, 1949, and the first meeting of the Assembly was held 20 days later, on February 14, 1949.

Table 1. Results of the elections to the Constituent Assembly

Electorate:	506,684
Valid votes cast	434,684
Qualifying threshold (1%)	4,346
Votes per seat	3,592

The first elections were held for a Constituent Assembly that was to act as a parliament but also to prepare a constitution for the state. The Constituent Assembly held its first meeting in Jerusalem on February 14, 1949 – *Tu bi-Shevat* – and two days later changed its name to the First Knesset.

The First Knesset elected Joseph *Sprinzak as its speaker, and Dr. Chaim *Weizmann as the first president of the state.

For several months the Knesset held its meetings in Tel Aviv. This was due both to the security situation and the fact that the status of Jerusalem as the capital of the State of Israel had not yet been finalized. The Knesset formally moved to Jerusalem in the middle of December 1949, and in March

Table 2. Results of the elections to the Constituent Assembly by party

Name of list	Number of valid votes	% of total votes	Number of seats	1st Govt.	2d Govt.
Mapai	155,274	35.7	46	X	X
Mapam	64,018	14.7	19		
United Religious Front*	52, 982	12.2	16	X	X
Ḥerut Movement	49,782	11.5	14		
General Zionists	22,661	5.2	7		
Progressive Party	17,786	4.1	5	X	X
Sephardim ve-Edot Mizraḥ	15,387	3.5	4	X	X
Maki (Communists)	15,148	3.5	4		
Minority List associated with Mapai	7,387	1.7	2	X	X **
Fighters List	5,363	1.2	1		
WIZO	5,173	1.2	1		
Yemenite Association	4,399	1.0	1		

* A list combing all four religious parties: Ha-Mizrachi, Ha-Po'el ha-Mizrachi, Agudat Israel, Po'alei Agudat Israel.

** Members of the coalition, but not the government.

Table 3. Members of the First Government (formed on March 10, 1949)

Ministerial Position	Name (party)
Prime Minister and Minister of Defense	David Ben-Gurion (Mapai)
Agriculture (from 1.6.50) and Supply & Rationing	Dov Yosef (Mapai)
Education & Culture	Shneur Zalman Shazar (Mapai)
Finance and Trade & Industry	Eliezer Kaplan (Mapai)
Foreign Affairs	Moshe Sharett (Mapai)
Health, Immigration and Interior	Ḥayyim Moshe Shapira (URF)
Justice	Pinḥas Rosen (Progressive)
Labor & Social Security	Golda Meir (Mapai)
Police	Beḥor Shalom Shitrit (Sephardi)
Religions and War Victims	Yehudah Leib Maimon (URF)
Transportation	David Remez (Mapai)
Welfare	Yiẓḥak Meir Levin (URF)

1950 settled in the Arazi-Frumin building on King George Street in Jerusalem, where it was to remain until August 29, 1966.

Soon after the elections, President Weizmann called upon the leader of Mapai, David Ben-Gurion, who had headed the provisional government, to form the first government of the State of Israel. Ben-Gurion was chosen by the president both because Mapai was the largest parliamentary group in the Knesset and because no other group was able to form a coalition commanding a majority in the Knesset, as was to remain the case until after the elections to the Ninth Knesset in 1977.

It took Ben-Gurion one and a half months to put together his first government. From the start he excluded the Herut Movement and the Communists as potential coalition members, for ideological reasons. Though the two labor parties – Mapai and Mapam – together held 65 seats in the Knesset, Ben-Gurion, taking a more statist (*mamlakhti*) approach, preferred to set up a coalition with the United Religious Front, the Progressive Party, the Sephardim, and the Arab lists associated with Mapai (though the latter did not receive seats in the government itself).

In addition to urgent security matters, the new government's attention was focused on the very difficult economic situation and on immigration absorption. The Knesset, on the other hand, had its hands full with adapting some of the Mandatory legislation to the needs of the independent Jewish state while passing new laws at an average rate of 7.5 bills per month. In addition to the laws concerned with the country's system of government and legal system, one of the important laws to be passed was the first version of the *Law of Return, passed in July 1950, which recognized the right of every Jew to settle in Israel.

Though the Proclamation of Independence had assigned to the Constituent Assembly the task of passing a constitution, it soon became apparent that this was an impossible mission, due to differences of opinion with the religious parties regarding the nature of such a document. In June 1950 the Harari resolution was passed, which stipulated that the Knesset would concentrate instead on the passing of Basic Laws, each of which would deal with a specific issue regarding the democratic system of government. Once work on the Basic Laws was completed, they would be combined into a constitution. It should be noted that even by the Sixteenth Knesset, work on the Basic Laws had not yet been completed, largely due to religious opposition to basic laws dealing with human rights as envisioned by the secular society, and a Basic Law on legislation that would declare the constitutional legislation to be supreme.

The economy, as run by the Mapai-led government, was highly centralized, with most agriculture in the hands of the collective kibbutzim and the cooperative moshavim. The Histadrut was not only a very powerful trade union association but controlled a large section of the country's industry, financial institutions, retail outlets, and health services. Though there was a growing sector of private industry, much of the industry in the country was state- or Histadrut-owned and run. The General Zionists and Ḥerut Movement both urged greater freedom for private enterprise, and denounced the austerity policy – the *Ẓena* – associated with Minister of Supply and Rationing Dov *Yosef. From the left Mapam criticized Mapai's policy of wage restraint and actively supported demonstrations by the unemployed.

There were also difficulties within the coalition. The Compulsory Education Law of September 1949 confirmed the division of the educational system into four streams: general, labor, national religious, and *ḥaredi*. A crisis soon developed since the religious bloc was dissatisfied with the fact that the children of religious immigrants in the transit camps (**ma'barot*) were receiving a nonreligious education.

It was against this background that Ben-Gurion submitted his first resignation in October. In the new government formed on November 1, the Ministry of Supply and Rationing no longer existed, its functions being taken over by the Ministry of Agriculture and the Ministry of Commerce and Industry – the latter in the hands of Ya'akov Geri, who was not a Knesset member. While the party make-up of the new government remained the same, the ministers on behalf of Mapai were shuffled.

Table 4. Members of the Second Government (formed November 1, 1950)

Ministerial Position	Name (party)
Prime Minister and Minister of Defense	David Ben-Gurion (Mapai)
Agriculture	Pinḥas Lavon (Mapai)
Education & Culture	David Remez (Mapai) (d. 5.19.51)
Finance	Eliezer Kaplan (Mapai)
Foreign Affairs	Moshe Sharett (Mapai)
Health, Immigration and Interior	Ḥayyim Moshe Shapira (URF)
Justice	Pinḥas Rosen (Progressive)
Labor & National Security	Golda Meir (Mapai)
Police	Beḥor Shalom Shitrit (Sephardim)
Religions and War Victims	Yehudah Leib Maimon (URF)
Trade & Industry	Ya'akov Geri (not an MK)
Transportation	Dov Yosef (Mapai)
Welfare	Yitzḥak Meir Levin (URF)

Growing dissatisfaction with the policy of rationing resulted in some losses to Mapai in the municipal elections of November 1950, in favor of the General Zionists. On February 14, 1951, the General Zionists presented a motion for the agenda regarding education in the immigrant camps and *ma'abarot*, and the education streams. When a vote took place on this motion, the government lost, with 49 members of the Knesset voting against the government and 42 voting in favor. Even though this was not formally a vote of no confidence, Ben-Gurion viewed it as such, resigned and called for new elections.

On the eve of the new elections a major strike broke out amongst the seamen employed by the publicly owned ZIM shipping company. The strike, which was finally broken up by force, lasted for half a year. Though it broke out against the background of pay and work condition claims, it was fueled by political tension between supporters of Mapai, which represented the establishment, and Mapam, which represented a radical position.

The Second Knesset, 1951–1955

The elections to the Second Knesset were held on July 30, 1951, and the first meeting of the Knesset was held 52 days later, on September 20, 1951.

In the elections to the Second Knesset, the General Zionists increased the number of their seats from 7 to 20 (which soon rose to 23, when the Sephardi and Yemenite parliamentary groups joined them). This increase took place largely at the expense of the Ḥerut Movement, which went down from 14 to 8 seats, and the labor parties Mapai and Mapam, which together went down from 65 to 60 seats – Mapam losing to Mapai, and Mapai losing to the General Zionists.

Table 5. Results of the elections to the Second Knesset

Electorate:	924,885
Valid votes cast	787,492
Qualifying threshold (1%)	7,874
Votes per seat	5,692

Table 6. Results of the elections to the Second Knesset by party

Name of list	Number of valid votes	% of total votes	Number of seats	3d Govt.	4th Govt.	5th Govt.	6th Govt.
Mapai	256,456	37.3	45	X	X	X	X
General Zionists	111,394	16.2	20		X	X	
Mapam	86,095	12.5	15				
Ha-Po'el ha-Mizrachi	46,347	6.8	8	X	X	X	X
Ḥerut Movement	45,651	6.6	8				
Three minority lists associated with Mapai	32,288	4.7	5	X*	X*	X*	X*
Maki (Communists)	27,334	4.0	5				
Progressive Party	22,171	3.2	4		X	X	
Agudat Israel	13,799	2.0	3	X			
Sephardim ve-Edot Mizraḥ	12,002	1.8	2				
Po'alei Agudat Israel	11,194	1.6	2	X			
Ha-Mizrachi	10,383	1.5	2	X	X	X	X
Yemenite Association	7,965	1.2	1				

* Members of the coalition but not the government.

The Second Knesset once again elected Joseph Sprinzak as its speaker. It took Ben-Gurion two months to form a new government. The Third Government included the same groups that had participated in the Second Government, less the Progressives. The General Zionists who conditioned their joining the government on their receiving the Ministry of Commerce and Industry, did not join the new government, though together with the Progressives they did join the Fourth Government, formed about a year later.

During the term of the Third Government the emotionally charged issue of *restitution payments from Germany came up against the background of the country's desperate foreign exchange situation. In January 1951, the government decided to make a claim for reparations from Germany for Jewish property lost during the Nazi period. In September West German Chancellor Konrad *Adenauer announced that the German Federal Republic was prepared to open negotiations on the subject with representatives of the Jewish people and the State of Israel. On January 9, 1952, Ben-Gurion made an announcement in the Knesset to that effect. Not everyone in Israel viewed this decision favorably, and the leader of the Ḥerut Movement, Menaḥem Begin, led a mass demonstration in protest. The crowd made its way toward the Knesset build-

Table 7. Members of the Third Government (formed October 8, 1951)

Ministerial Position	Name (party)
Prime Minister and Defense	David Ben-Gurion (Mapai)
Deputy PM	Eliezer Kaplan (Mapai) (from 6.25.52 to his death on 7.13.52)
Agriculture	Levi Eshkol (Mapai) (until 6.25.52)
	Perez Naftali (Mapai)
Commerce & Industry	Dov Yosef (Mapai)
Education & Culture	Benzion Dinur (not an MK)
Finance	Eliezer Kaplan (Mapai) (until 6.25.52)
	Levi Eshkol (Mapai)
Foreign Affairs	Moshe Sharett (Mapai)
Health	Joseph Burg (Ha-Po'el ha-Mizrachi)
Interior and Religions	Ḥayyim Moshe Shapira (Ha-Po'el ha-Mizrachi)
Justice	Dov Yosef (Mapai) (until 6.25.52)
	Ḥayyim Cohen (not an MK)
Labor	Golda Meir (Mapai)
Police	Beḥor Shalom Shitrit (Mapai)
Postal Services	Mordechai (Max) Nurock (Ha-Mizrachi) (from 11.3.52)
Transportation	David Zvi Pinkas (Ha-Mizrachi) (d. 8.14.52)
	David Ben-Gurion (Mapai)
Welfare	Yitzḥak Meir Levin (Agudat Israel) (until 9.18.52)
Without Portfolio	Perez Naftali (Mapai) (until 6.25.52)
Without Portfolio	Pinḥas Lavon (Mapai) (from 8.17.52)

ing, breaking some windows and clashing with the police. For his part in the demonstration Begin was suspended from participation in Knesset sittings for several months. However, with the support of the Progressives, the Knesset Foreign Affairs and Defense Committee finally authorized the government to open negotiations, which commenced in March 1952 and were concluded in September.

Added to the reparations crisis was the growing dissatisfaction of the two *ḥaredi* parties, Agudat Israel and Po'alei Agudat Israel, with the government's education policy and the proposal to institute national service for religious girls who had been exempted from military service. On September 19 their representatives in the coalition resigned, leaving the government without a majority in the Knesset. When Ben-Gurion failed to bring the General Zionists into the coalition immediately, he resigned, and in December formed a new government, with the participation of the General Zionists and the Progressives, but without the *ḥaredi* parties.

The coalition agreement of the new government provided for the abolition of the "streams" in the national education system (dividing them into national and religious sections), for income tax reforms, and for a liberalization of export regulations. Mapam was not invited to join the coalition. This was partially due to its position regarding the *Slansky Affair in Prague, in which a Mapam member – Mordekhai Oren – had been implicated. Mapam did, however, finally support the

Table 8. Members of the Fourth Government (formed December 24, 1952)

Ministerial Position	Name (party)
Prime Minister and Defense	David Ben-Gurion (Mapai)
Agriculture	Perez Naftali (Mapai)
Commerce & Industry	Perez Bernstein (General Zionists)
Development	Dov Yosef (Mapai) (from 6.15.53)
Education & Culture	Benzion Dinur (not an MK)
Finance	Levi Eshkol (Mapai)
Foreign Affairs	Moshe Sharett (Mapai)
Health	Yosef Sapir (General Zionists) (until 12.29.53)
	Yosef Serlin (General Zionists)
Interior	Israel Rokach (General Zionists)
Justice	Pinḥas Rosen (Progressive)
Labor	Golda Meir (Mapai)
Police	Beḥor Shalom Shitrit (Mapai)
Postal Services	Joseph Burg (Ha-Po'el ha-Mizrachi)
Transportation	Yosef Serlin (General Zionists (until 12.29.53)
	Yosef Sapir (General Zionists)
Welfare and Religions	Ḥayyim Moshe Shapira (Ha-Po'el ha-Mizrachi)
Without Portfolio	Pinḥas Lavon (Mapai)
Without Portfolio	Dov Yosef (Mapai) (until 6.15.53)

election of the Mapai candidate for president of the State – Izhak *Ben-Zvi – to succeed Chaim Weizmann, who had passed away in November 1952.

The Fourth Government passed the law for free compulsory education, approved by the Knesset on August 15, 1953. Under the new system only Agudat Israel was permitted to maintain an independent school system, which was to receive state assistance.

In November 1953, Ben-Gurion unexpectedly announced his desire to retire from the premiership for personal reasons, explaining that he needed a rest after 23 years of incessant political activity. He proposed that Levi *Eshkol replace him as prime minister and that Pinḥas *Lavon replace him as minister of defense. But after Eshkol refused the premiership Mapai nominated Moshe *Sharett for the post. In keeping with his call for the settlement of the Negev, Ben-Gurion established his new home in Kibbutz Sedeh Boker. His last action before retirement was to appoint Moshe *Dayan as IDF chief of staff.

As prime minister in the Fifth Government, Sharett continued to hold the Foreign Affairs portfolio, while as proposed by Ben-Gurion, Lavon became minister of defense.

Beneath the surface this partnership did not work, owing to disagreements between Sharett and Lavon over defense policy. The prime minister complained that he was not consulted in advance about reprisal attacks across the borders. Then came the infamous *Esek Bish* (lit. "bad business"), involving a botched-up security operation in Egypt, which resulted in the arrest of 13 Egyptian Jews, of whom one committed suicide and two were executed following a trial in Cairo. A committee of inquiry, made up of the president of the Su-

Table 9. Members of the Fifth Government (formed January 26, 1954)

Ministerial Position	Name (party)
Prime Minister and Foreign Affairs	Moshe Sharett (Mapai)
Agriculture	Pereẓ Naftali (Mapai)
Commerce & Industry	Pereẓ Bernstein (General Zionists)
Defense	Pinḥas Lavon (Mapai) (until 2.21.55) David Ben-Gurion (Mapai)
Development	Dov Yosef (Mapai)
Education & Culture	Benzion Dinur (not an MK)
Finance	Levi Eshkol (Mapai)
Health	Yosef Serlin (General Zionists)
Interior	Israel Rokach (General Zionists)
Justice	Pinḥas Rosen (Progressive)
Labor	Golda Meir (Mapai)
Police	Beḥor Shalom Shitrit (Mapai)
Postal Services	Joseph Burg (Ha-Po'el ha-Mizrachi)
Transportation	Yosef Sapir (General Zionists)
Welfare and Religions	Ḥayyim Moshe Shapira (Ha-Po'el ha-Mizrachi)
Without Portfolio	Zalman Aran (Mapai)

preme Court, Isaac *Olshan, and former Chief of Staff Ya'akov *Dori, established to investigate the affair, failed to reach any conclusions. Though Lavon refused to take responsibility for the affair, he was forced to resign in February 1955, and was replaced by Ben-Gurion, at Sharett's request. The "Lavon Affair," as the *Esek Bish* came to be known, continued to bedevil Israeli politics for another decade, and was the first of many occasions on which no one in authority was willing to take responsibility.

Sharett resigned on June 29, 1955, against the background of a vote of no-confidence concerning the Kasztner Affair (see *Kasztner, Reszo Rudlof), presented to the Knesset by the Ḥerut Movement and the Communists, in which the General Zionists abstained. Since the General Zionists refused to resign from the government, Sharett resigned, forming the short-lived Sixth Government – a minority government – without the General Zionists and the Progressives.

Throughout the term of the Second Knesset the labor movement underwent several major personal and ideological upheavals. In addition to Ben-Gurion's temporary withdrawal, towards the end of the Knesset's term Mapam broke up again into two parties: Mapam and *Aḥdut ha-Avodah-Po'alei Zion, while the *Ha-Kibbutz ha-Me'uḥad settlement movement split in two, with several individual kibbutzim breaking up. Ha-Kibbutz ha-Me'uḥad was now associated with Aḥdut ha-Avodah-Po'alei Zion, while *Iḥud ha-Kevuẓot ve-ha-Kibbutzim was associated with Mapai (*Ha-Kibbutz ha-Arẓi continued to be associated with Mapam).

It is worth noting that in this period, while the kibbutzim formed no more than 3 percent of the population, close to 20 kibbutz members were members of the Knesset – over 15 percent of the total.

Table 10. Members of the Sixth Government (formed 29 June, 1956)

Ministerial Position	Name (party)
Prime Minister and Foreign Affairs	Moshe Sharett (Mapai)
Agriculture and Commerce & Industry	Pereẓ Naftali (Mapai)
Defense	David Ben-Gurion (Mapai)
Education & Culture	Benzion Dinur (not an MK)
Finance	Levi Eshkol (Mapai)
Health and Development	Dov Yosef (Mapai)
Interior	Israel Rokach (General Zionists)
Justice	Pinḥas Rosen (Progressive)
Labor	Golda Meir (Mapai)
Police	Beḥor Shalom Shitrit (Mapai)
Postal Services	Joseph Burg (Ha-Po'el ha-Mizrachi)
Transportation	Zalman Aran (Mapai)
Welfare and Religions	Ḥayyim Moshe Shapira (Ha-Po'el ha-Mizrachi)

The Second Knesset dealt extensively with foreign policy issues, many debates dealing with the government's growing Western orientation. Those who had hoped that Israel would be able to remain neutral were disappointed by the fact that it was not invited to participate in the 1955 Bandung Nonaligned Conference.

The problem of Arab infiltrators from Jordan and the Gaza Strip frequently came up in the Knesset, and the debate on the issue came to a peak after the attack on a bus at Ma'aleh ha-Akrabim in the Negev in March 1954, in which numerous civilians were killed. The detention of the freighter *Bat-Galim* by the Egyptian authorities in September 1954, and the denial of passage to Israeli ships and cargoes destined for Israel though the Suez Canal, engaged the attention of the MKs as well as Israel's representatives to the UN.

The essence of Israeli democracy and the relations between religion and state were frequently raised by Knesset members in the course of the debates on various issues, especially in connection with three "religious" laws adopted on August 26, 1953: the Anatomy and Pathology Law, the National Service Law, and the Rabbinical Courts Jurisdiction (marriage and divorce) Law.

In September 1954, the Mapai Central Council adopted Ben-Gurion's proposal to press for the replacement of the proportional representation electoral system by a single-member constituency system. What Ben-Gurion had hoped to achieve was a reduction in the number of parties elected to the Knesset, which would have simplified the task of forming governments in Israel. It was claimed at the time that by "gerrymandering" the constituencies, Mapai would actually be able to win an absolute majority in the Knesset. However, the proposed system was never adopted by the Knesset.

The Third Knesset, 1955–1959

The elections to the Third Knesset were held on July 26, 1955, and the first meeting of the Knesset was held 20 days later, on August 15, 1955.

Table 11. Results of the elections to the Third Knesset

Electorate:	1,067,795
Valid votes cast	853,219
Qualifying threshold (1%)	8,532
Votes per seat	6,938

Table 12. Results of the elections to the Third Knesset by party

Name of list	Number of valid votes	% of total votes	Number of seats	7th Govt.	8th Govt.
Mapai	274,735	32.2	40	X	X
Ḥerut Movement	107,190	12.6	15		
General Zionists	87,099	10.2	13		
National Religious Front (National Religious Party)	77,936	9.1	11	X	X**
Aḥdut ha-Avodah-Po'alei Zion	69,475	8.2	10	X	X
Mapam	62,401	7.3	9	X	X
Religious Front (*Ḥaredi* parties)	39,836	4.7	6		
Maki (Communists)	38,492	4.5	6		
Three minority lists associated with Mapai	37,777	4.4	5	X*	X*
Progressive Party	37,661	4.4	5	X	X

* Members of the coalition but not the government.
** Left the government on July 1, 1958.

In the elections to the Third Knesset Mapai lost 5 seats, 4 of which went to Mapam and to Aḥdut ha-Avodah-Po'alei Zion, which ran for the first time as an independent list. Within the center-right political camp, the General Zionists lost 7 seats to the Ḥerut Movement.

At its first meeting, the Third Knesset elected Joseph Sprinzak (Mapai) for a third term as its speaker. After his death in January 1959, Naḥum Nir of Aḥdut ha-Avodah-Po'alei Zion was elected to succeed him, defeating Mapai's candidate.

It took Ben-Gurion three months to form a new government, but he finally managed, for the first time, to bring all three labor parties into the coalition.

In the speech in which he presented his new government and its program to the Knesset, Ben-Gurion emphasized the gravity of the security situation, and especially the problem of the *fedayeen* infiltrations from the Gaza Strip and the major arms deal signed between Egypt and Czechoslovakia with the blessing of the Soviet Union, and this after it had been Czechoslovakia that had supplied Israel with arms during its War of Independence, then too with Soviet blessings. In the following year Ben-Gurion was to hold negotiations with France and Great Britain for collaboration in what was to become known abroad as the Suez Operation and in Israel as the *Sinai Campaign.

Table 13. Members of the Seventh Government (formed November 3, 1955)

Ministerial Position	Name (party)
Prime Minister and Defense	David Ben-Gurion (Mapai)
Agriculture	Kadish Luz (Mapai)
Commerce & Industry	Pinḥas Sapir (Mapai)
Development	Mordekhai Bentov (Mapam)
Education & Culture	Zalman Aran (Mapai)
Finance	Levi Eshkol (Mapai)
Foreign Affairs	Moshe Sharett (Mapai) (until 6.19.56) Golda Meir (Mapai)
Health	Israel Barzilai (Mapam)
Interior	Israel Bar-Yehudah (Aḥdut ha-Avodah-Po'alei Zion)
Justice	Pinḥas Rosen (Progressives)
Labor	Golda Meir (Mapai) (until 6.19.56) Mordekhai Namir (Mapai)
Police	Beḥor Shalom Shitrit (Mapai)
Postal Services	Joseph Burg (NRP)
Transportation	Moshe Carmel (Aḥdut ha-Avodah-Po'alei Zion)
Welfare and Religions	Ḥayyim Moshe Shapira (NRP)
Without Portfolio	Perez̦ Naftali (Mapai)

While Ben-Gurion's acrimonious exchanges with the leader of the Ḥerut Movement, Menaḥem Begin, became increasingly bitter, differences of opinion between the prime minister and Moshe Sharett over the coordination of defense and foreign policy finally led to Sharett's replacement as minister for foreign affairs by Golda *Meir. Mordekhai *Namir, who had served as secretary general of the Histadrut, replaced Meir as minister of labor, while Namir was replaced in the Histadrut by Pinḥas Lavon in June 1956.

On the eve of the Sinai Campaign 49 Israeli Arab villagers were shot dead by border policemen at Kafr Kassem for breaking a curfew of which they were not aware. The persons responsible for the massacre were put on trial and given prolonged prison sentences. However, even though Ben-Gurion referred to the event as one that "struck a blow at the most sacred principles of human morality," all those imprisoned had their prison sentences reduced.

Israel's military success in the Sinai Campaign, which had commenced on October 29, 1956, though greatly dependent on the coalition with France and Great Britain, increased Ben-Gurion's popularity while turning Chief of Staff Moshe Dayan into a national hero. Mapam had disapproved of the operation, but remained in the cabinet. The Ḥerut Movement strongly supported Ben-Gurion's move, but following Ben-Gurion's decision to give in to international pressure and withdraw from the Sinai Peninsula, the Gaza Strip, and Sharm el-Sheikh following the war, it accused him of defeatism and of squandering the military gains.

In May 1957 a violent strike broke out at the Ata textile factory, due to the owner's refusal to accept an agreement signed between the Histadrut and the Manufacturers Association. The government refused to back the workers' militant position. However, it was over the question of Israel's endorsement of the Eisenhower Doctrine, which called for U.S. assistance to any country threatened by Communist aggression, that a crisis broke out in the coalition in that very same month. Aḥdut ha-Avodah-Po'alei Zion and Mapam argued that Israel should not adopt such a pro-American position. These two parties advocated a more neutral policy, not only for ideological reasons but also because they feared it might negatively affect the chances of Jews to leave the Soviet Union. However, when Ben-Gurion's policy came up for a vote in the Knesset on June 3, both parties abstained rather than vote against the government. The Ḥerut Movement and the General Zionists also abstained, but for the opposite reason, because they felt that Israel's support for the American policy should be stronger.

On October 28, 1957, Izhak Ben-Zvi was reelected by the Knesset for a second term as president of the state. The following day a mentally disturbed person threw a hand grenade into the Knesset plenary hall, which wounded Prime Minister David Ben-Gurion and several ministers.

A new government crisis broke out in December 1957 against the background of Israel's relations with West Germany, when it became known that Dayan had visited Germany to discuss arms purchases. The plan fell through as a result of pressure by Aḥdut ha-Avodah-Po'alei Zion and Mapam, but the whole episode led Ben-Gurion to tender his resignation on December 31. His new government, formed a week later, had the same party make-up as the previous one, but only after Aḥdut ha-Avodah-Po'alei Zion and Mapam undertook to uphold coalition discipline and cabinet secrecy.

On February 12, 1958, the Knesset adopted the first Basic Law – Basic Law: the Knesset. The new law included an article that stated that it could only be amended by an absolute majority of the MKs. Nevertheless, it was not given superior status to ordinary laws.

A General Zionist proposal to institute an electoral system containing elements of both proportional and constituency representation – a proposal which was to be put forward on numerous occasions in the future – was rejected.

As in previous Knessets, the religious parties frequently raised the issue of the nonobservance of the Sabbath in the State of Israel, while Knesset members from the Communist Party frequently raised the issue of the military administration and movement restriction to which the Arab and Druze citizens of Israel were still subject.

A new coalition crisis, this time involving the NRP, erupted over regulations issued by the minister of the interior defining a Jew for the purposes of the population register. The NRP objected to the definition's diverging from the halakhic definition, and its two ministers resigned from the government when the regulations were approved by the Knesset on June 29. However, their resignation did not cause the government to lose its parliamentary majority.

No sooner was this crisis over than a new government crisis broke out over the sale of Israeli arms to West Germany, which Aḥdut ha-Avodah-Po'alei Zion and Mapam objected to. When the two parties voted in the Knesset against a motion approving the transaction, Ben-Gurion demanded the resignation of the ministers who had voted with the opposition, and when they refused, submitted his resignation. An attempt by Ben-Gurion to form an alternative government with the General Zionists and the NRP failed, leading to new elections.

Table 14. Members of the Eighth Government (formed January 7, 1958)

Ministerial Position	Name (party)
Prime Minister and Defense	David Ben-Gurion (Mapai)
Agriculture	Kadish Luz (Mapai)
Commerce & Industry	Pinḥas Sapir (Mapai)
Development	Mordekhai Bentov (Mapam)
Education & Culture	Zalman Aran (Mapai)
Finance	Levi Eshkol (Mapai)
Foreign Affairs	Golda Meir (Mapai)
Health	Israel Barzilai (Mapam)
Interior	Israel Bar-Yehudah (Aḥdut ha-Avodah-Po'alei Zion)
Justice	Pinḥas Rosen (Progressives)
Labor	Mordekhai Namir (Mapai)
Police	Beḥor Shalom Shitrit (Mapai)
Postal Services	Joseph Burg (NRP) (until 7.1.58) Israel Barzilai (Mapam) (from 11.24.58)
Religions	Ḥayyim Moshe Shapira (NRP) (until 7.1.58) Ya'akov Moshe Toledano (not an MK) (from 12.3.58 until 11.30.59)
Transportation	Moshe Carmel (Aḥdut ha-Avodah-Po'alei Zion)
Welfare	Ḥayyim Moshe Shapira (NRP) (until 7.1.58) Pereẓ Naftali (Mapai) (from 1.25.59)
Without Portfolio	Pereẓ Naftali (Mapai) (until 1.25.59)

In the course of the election campaign serious riots by immigrants from North Africa broke out in the Wadi Salib quarter of Haifa, in the development town of Migdal ha-Emek, and in Beersheba, against the background of claims of discrimination and hardship. This was the first open protest by immigrants of Muslim country origin against the Mapai-Ashkenazi establishment, but the latter failed to read the writing on the wall. Among the "new faces" introduced by Mapai into its list prior to the elections to the Fourth Knesset, none were of representatives of the new immigrants.

The Fourth Knesset, 1959–1961

The elections to the Fourth Knesset were held on November 3, 1959, and the first meeting of the Knesset was held 27 days later, on November 30, 1959.

Table 15. Results of the elections to the Fourth Knesset

Electorate:	1,218,483
Valid votes cast	969,337
Qualifying threshold (1%)	9,693
Votes per seat	7,800

Table 16. Results of the elections to the Fourth Knesset by party

Name of list	Number of valid votes	% of total votes	Number of seats	9th Govt
Mapai	370,585	38.2	47	X
Ḥerut Movement	130,515	13.5	17	
National Religious Party	95,581	9.9	12	X
Mapam	69,468	7.2	9	X
General Zionists	59,700	6.2	8	
Aḥdut ha-Avodah-Po'alei Zion	58,043	6.0	7	X
Religious Front (*Ḥaredi* parties)	45,569	4.7	6	X
Progressive Party	44,889	4.6	6	
Three minority lists associated with Mapai	34,353	3.5	5	X*
Maki (Communists)	27,374	2.8	3	

* Members of the coalition but not the government.

Mapai emerged from the elections to the Fourth Knesset with 47 seats – the largest number of seats that it had ever received in an election. It gained three of its seats at the expense of Aḥdut ha-Avodah-Po'alei Zion and another three at the expense of the General Zionists, who lost two additional seats to the Ḥerut Movement.

Mapai's strong position was due to the rapid rise in the standard of living, and the almost total cessation of border incidents on all fronts. The port of Eilat was able to develop, while friendly relations had been forged with several Asian and new African countries. None of the "ethnic" lists, representing "Oriental" immigrants, that participated in the elections managed to pass the qualifying threshold, and this despite the ethnic awakening that had occurred in the aftermath of the Wadi Salib riots.

The fourth Knesset elected Kadish *Luz as its third speaker. Ben-Gurion's new government included three new Mapai Knesset members, two of whom were to become household names: Abba *Eban, who had recently returned to Israel after eight years as ambassador to the U.S. and the UN, former Chief of Staff Moshe Dayan, and Giora *Josephthal, who had served as treasurer of the Jewish Agency. Shimon *Peres, who had served as director general of the Ministry of Defense and was largely responsible for promoting the close relations with France, was appointed deputy minister of defense.

The NRP rejoined the Coalition, after a satisfactory arrangement was reached regarding the registration problem of the previous government. Aḥdut ha-Avodah-Po'alei Zion was represented in the new government by Yiẓḥak *Ben-Aharon, who was also to become a household name over the years.

One of the new government's first tasks was to arrange for the election of the chief rabbis, but due to political controversies the election did not take place for another five years, with the post of Ashkenazi chief rabbi remaining vacant following the death of Chief Rabbi Isaac Halevi *Herzog on July 25, 1959.

Table 17. Members of the Ninth Government (formed December 17, 1959)

Ministerial Position	Name (party)
Prime Minister and Defense	David Ben-Gurion (Mapai)
Agriculture	Moshe Dayan (Mapai)
Commerce & Industry	Pinḥas Sapir (Mapai)
Development	Mordekhai Bentov (Mapam)
Education & Culture	Zalman Aran (Mapai) (until 5.10.60) Abba Eban (Mapai) (from 8.3.60)
Finance	Levi Eshkol (Mapai)
Foreign Affairs	Golda Meir (Mapai)
Health	Israel Barzilai (Mapam)
Interior	Ḥayyim Moshe Shapira (NRP)
Justice	Pinḥas Rosen (Progressives)
Labor	Giora Josephthal (Mapai)
Police	Beḥor Shalom Shitrit (Mapai)
Postal Services	Benjamin Minz (Torah Religious Front) (from 7.17.60 until 5.30.61)
Religions	Ya'akov Moshe Toledano (not an MK) (until 10.15.60)
Transportation	Yiẓḥak Ben-Aharon (Aḥdut ha-Avodah-Po'alei Zion)
Welfare	Joseph Burg (NRP)
Without Portfolio	Abba Eban (Mapai) (until 8.3.60)

A lengthy dispute over the claims of the secondary school teachers for salary increases, and recognition of their separate union, led to the resignation, on April 24, 1960, of Minister of Education Zalman Aran, who was eventually replaced by Abba Eban on August 3.

In May the Religious Front presented a motion of no confidence in the government over the question of how many Jews had left Egypt at the time of the Exodus. Prime Minister David Ben-Gurion made it clear that "the Knesset cannot decide on issues of history and faith." Two months later, on July 18 Benjamin *Minz – a member of Po'alei Agudat Israel in the Religious Front – was appointed minister of postal services. Since Rabbi Minz had not received the blessing of the spiritual leaders of the Religious Front, his agreement to assume the post created a crisis within the Religious Front, which split, with Agudat Israel and Po'alei Agudat Israel forming two separate parliamentary groups. It should be noted that after this event and until the Sixteenth Knesset, no Ashkenazi *ḥaredi* MK ever again considered joining a government in a full ministerial post, though several were appointed as deputy ministers.

Toward the end of 1960, the Lavon Affair, which had taken on the shape of a personal vendetta by Ben-Gurion against Lavon, once against shook the Israeli political scene. On January 30, 1961, the Knesset rejected a motion of no confidence in the government against the background of the affair by 77 votes to 26, but in the debate, Mapam, Aḥdut ha-Avodah-Po'alei Zion, and the Progressives severely criticized Ben-Gurion's conduct, leading him to submit his resignation on the following day. Ben-Gurion proceeded to get the Mapai Central Committee to vote in favor of the removal of Lavon from his post as secretary general of the Histadrut. However, when President Ben-Zvi called on Ben-Gurion to form a new government, Mapam, Aḥdut ha-Avodah-Po'alei Zion, and the Progressives refused to serve under him, while the NRP was unwilling to remain Mapai's only coalition partner. Since Mapai refused to put forward a new candidate for the premiership, the Knesset decided on March 13 to dissolve itself and call for new elections.

Prior to the new elections the General Zionists and the Progressives united into a single parliamentary group, which called itself the Liberal Party.

In the interim period between the announcement of new elections and their actually taking place, the trial of Nazi war criminal Adolf *Eichmann, who had been abducted from Argentina in May 1960, began.

The Fifth Knesset, 1961–1965

The elections to the Fifth Knesset were held on August 15, 1961, and the first meeting of the Knesset was held 27 days later, on September 9, 1961.

Table 18. Results of the elections to the Fifth Knesset

Electorate:	1,274,280
Valid votes cast	1,006,964
Qualifying threshold (1%)	10,070
Votes per seat	8,332

Table 19. Results of the elections to the Fifth Knesset by party

Name of list	Number of valid votes	% of total votes	Number of seats	10th Govt	11th Govt	12th Govt
Mapai	349,330	34.7	42	X	X	X
Ḥerut Movement	138,599	13.8	17			
Liberal Party	137,599	13.6	17			
National Religious Party	98,786	9.8	12	X	X	X
Mapam	75,654	7.5	9			
Aḥdut ha-Avodah-Po'alei Zion	66,170	6.6	8	X	X	X
Maki (Communists)	42,111	4.2	5			
Agudat Israel	37,178	3.7	4			
Two minority lists associated with Mapai	35,376	3.5	4	X*	X*	X*
Po'alei Agudat Israel	19,428	1.9	2	X**	X**	X**

* Members of the coalition but not the government.
** Held post of deputy minister.

Though Mapai tried to ignore the Lavon Affair during the election campaign, the other parties and several academics denounced Ben-Gurion's behavior as a danger to democracy. Mapai ended up losing five seats and its affiliated Arab parties one. The new Liberal Party, which had been formed by the merger of the General Zionists and the Progressives on the eve of the elections to the Fifth Knesset, gained three seats, totaling 17, equaling the Ḥerut Movement.

The Fifth Knesset reelected Kadish Luz as its speaker. The negotiations for a new government, conducted by Levi Eshkol on behalf of Ben-Gurion, were prolonged and difficult, due to the insistence of the other potential coalition members that Mapai, with its reduced strength, should no longer hold a majority of the seats in the cabinet. Finally Aḥdut ha-Avodah, the NRP, Po'alei Agudat Israel, and the Arab parties joined the coalition. Of the latter two, the first appointed a deputy minister while the latter declined to receive a ministerial post. Two changes took place in the Eleventh Government: after minister of housing and development Giora Josephthal passed away he was replaced by Yosef *Almogi, while after Minister of Transportation Yiẓhak Ben-Aharon resigned due to differences of opinion with his colleagues in Aḥdut ha-Avodah over his advocacy of unification among the three labor parties, he was replaced by Israel Bar-Yehudah.

Table 20. Members of the Tenth Government (formed November 2, 1961)

Ministerial Position	Name (party)
Prime Minister and Defense	David Ben-Gurion (Mapai)
Agriculture	Moshe Dayan (Mapai)
Commerce & Industry	Pinhas Sapir (Mapai)
Education & Culture	Abba Eban (Mapai)
Finance	Levi Eshkol (Mapai)
Foreign Affairs	Golda Meir (Mapai)
Health and Interior	Ḥayyim Moshe Shapira (NRP)
Housing and Development	Giora Josephthal (Mapai) (until 8.23.62) Yosef Almogi (from 10.30.62)
Justice	Dov Yosef (not an MK in the Fifth Knesset)
Labor	Yigal Allon (Aḥdut ha-Avodah-Po'alei Zion)
Police	Beḥor Shalom Shitrit (Mapai)
Postal Services	Eliyahu Sasson (not an MK in the Fifth Knesset)
Religious Affairs	Zeraḥ Wahrhaftig (NRP)
Transportation	Yiẓhak Ben-Aharon (Aḥdut ha-Avodah-Po'alei Zion) (until 5.28.62) Israel Bar-Yehudah (Aḥdut ha-Avodah-Po'alei Zion) (from 5.28.62)
Welfare	Joseph Burg (NRP)
Without Portfolio	Yosef Almogi (Mapai) (until 10.30.62)

Though Ben-Aharon was not immediately successful, his advocacy of unity was eventually to bear fruit (see below).

During this period there was considerable controversy over the continuation of the strict Military Administration under which the Arab and Druze citizens of the country lived, imposed soon after the establishment of the state. Ḥerut leader Menaḥem Begin was one of the strongest advocates of its abolition, just as he had fought against the continued application of the Emergency Regulations which Israel had inherited from the British Mandatory Government. Begin was supported in his fight against the Military Administration by the Liberals, Mapam, partially by the NRP, and of course by the Communists and Arab parliamentary groups. Attempts to bring about the abolition of the Military Administration were defeated narrowly both in 1962 (though on that occasion the Druze were exempted) and 1963. It was finally abolished in 1966.

President Izhak Ben-Zvi, who had been elected for a third term, passed away on April 23, 1963, and was succeeded by Zalman *Shazar, who defeated the opposition's candidate Perez̦ Bernstein of the Liberal Party.

Ben-Gurion submitted his resignation on June 16, 1963. Formally he resigned on personal grounds, but in fact it was due to the Lavon Affair, of which he refused to let go. On Ben-Gurion's recommendation, Levi Eshkol was nominated by Mapai as his successor. Eshkol completed the negotiations for the formation of the Eleventh Government, with the same party make-up as the previous government, in one week. He was replaced in the Ministry of Finance by Pinḥas Sapir. Abba Eban became deputy prime minister.

Table 21. Members of the Eleventh Government (formed June 26, 1963)

Ministerial Position	Name (party)
Prime Minister and Defense	Levi Eshkol (Mapai)
Deputy Prime Minister	Abba Eban (Mapai)
Agriculture	Moshe Dayan (Mapai) (until 11.4.64) Chaim Gvati (not an MK in the Fifth Knesset) (from 11.9.64)
Housing and Development	Yosef Almogi (Mapai)
Education & Culture	Zalman Aran (Mapai)
Finance and Commerce & Industry	Pinḥas Sapir (Mapai)
Foreign Affairs	Golda Meir (Mapai)
Health and Interior	Ḥayyim Moshe Shapira (NRP)
Justice	Dov Yosef (not an MK in the Fifth Knesset)
Labor	Yigal Allon (Aḥdut ha-Avodah-Po'alei Zion
Police	Beḥor Shalom Shitrit (Mapai)
Postal Services	Eliyahu Sasson (not an MK in the Fifth Knesset)
Religious Affairs	Zeraḥ Wahrhaftig (NRP)
Transportation	Israel Bar-Yehudah (Aḥdut ha-Avodah-Po'alei Zion)
Welfare	Joseph Burg (NRP)
Without Portfolio	Akiva Govrin (Mapai) (from 12.1.63)

Eshkol's style was very different from his predecessor's, and he was more conciliatory towards the Ḥerut Movement, finally enabling the former Revisionists to bring the remains of Ze'ev *Jabotinsky to Jerusalem. Eshkol was also more open to criticism on foreign affairs issues, especially in reference to the Soviet Union.

Though Eshkol considered his government "a government of continuity," tensions developed between those members of Mapai who remained loyal to Ben-Gurion, and the rest. When a strong minority of Ben-Gurion loyalists in the Mapai Central Committee tried to get Eshkol to hold a new inquiry on the Lavon Affair, he resigned as prime minister with the demand that the party stop interfering with the decisions of the government. The party reacted by calling upon him to form a new government, which he presented to the Knesset on December 23, 1964.

Table 22. Members of the Twelfth Government (formed December 22, 1964)

Ministerial Position	Name (party)
Prime Minister and Defense	Levi Eshkol (Mapai)
Deputy Prime Minister	Abba Eban (Mapai)
Agriculture	Chaim Gvati
Commerce & Industry	Pinḥas Sapir (Mapai) (until 5.23.65) Haim Zadok (from 5.23.65)
Development	Yosef Almogi (Mapai)* Haim Zadok (Mapai) (from 5.31.65)
Education & Culture	Zalman Aran (Mapai)
Finance	Pinḥas Sapir (Mapai)
Foreign Affairs	Golda Meir (Mapai)
Health and Interior	Ḥayyim Moshe Shapira (NRP)
Housing	Yosef Almogi (Mapai)* Levi Eshkol (Mapai) (from 5.31.65)
Justice	Dov Yosef) (not an MK in the Fifth Knesset)
Labor	Yigal Allon (Aḥdut ha-Avodah-Po'alei Zion)
Police	Beḥor Shalom Shitrit (Mapai)
Postal Services	Eliyahu Sasson (not an MK in the fifth Knesset)
Religious Affairs	Zeraḥ Wahrhaftig (NRP)
Transportation	Israel Bar-Yehudah (Aḥdut ha-Avodah-Po'alei Zion) Moshe Carmel (Aḥdut ha-Avodah-Po'alei Zion) (from 5.30.65)
Tourism	Akiva Govrin (Mapai)
Welfare	Joseph Burg (NRP)

* Left Mapai to form Rafi.

Moshe Dayan had resigned as minister of agriculture before the new government was formed, and was replaced by Chaim *Gvati. Ben-Gurion loyalists objected not only to Eshkol's policy over the Lavon Affair but also to an agreement he had reached with the leader of Aḥdut ha-Avodah, Israel *Galili, on the formation of a joint list for the elections to the Sixth Knesset.

The clash between Eshkol's and Ben-Gurion's supporters came to a head at the Mapai Convention of February 1965, following which Eshkol called upon those ministers who supported Ben-Gurion's positions to resign. As a result, Minister of Housing and Development Yosef Almogi and Deputy Minister of Defense Shimon Peres resigned their posts. Haim *Zadok joined the cabinet on May 23 as minister of commerce and industry and development, while Eshkol assumed the position of minister of housing. Minister of Transportation Israel Bar-Yehudah was succeeded, after his death, by Moshe Carmel.

On June 29 Ben-Gurion announced that he intended to run at the head of an independent list for the elections. Two weeks later seven Mapai MKs, headed by him, formed a new parliamentary group – Reshimat Po'alei Yisrael – or as it came to be known: *Rafi.

Significant political changes were also taking place in the opposition, when in May 1965 the Ḥerut Movement and the Liberal Party (minus seven former members of the Progressive Party) formed a new political bloc and parliamentary group called *Gaḥal (Gush Ḥerut Liberalim). The former Progressives now formed a new party and parliamentary group called the *Independent Liberal Party.

In August Maki (the Israel Communist Party) split in two. The new party called itself Rakaḥ, which consisted mainly of Arabs (the main exception being Meir *Vilner), while Maki remained predominantly Jewish.

It should be noted that in the course of the Fifth Knesset the government's new economic policy, introduced by Pinḥas Sapir after becoming minister of finance, which dealt with the stabilization of the market by means of price stability and the setting of a single exchange rate for the currency, came under harsh criticism from the opposition. Furthermore, growing awareness of the issue of discrimination on ethnic grounds resulted in frequent questions to ministers and motions for the agenda. The end of the Eichmann trial, the affair of the German scientists working on Egypt's rocket project, and the establishment of diplomatic relations with West Germany also raised storms.

The Fifth Knesset held several serious debates around the issue of religion and state, as a result of violent events against this background.

The Sixth Knesset – 1965–1969

The elections to the Sixth Knesset were held on November 1, 1965, and the first meeting of the Knesset was held 21 days later, on November 22, 1965.

Table 23. Results of the elections to the Sixth Knesset

Electorate:	1,449,709
Valid votes cast	1,206,728
Qualifying threshold (1%)	12,067
Votes per seat	9,881

In the elections to the Sixth Knesset the Alignment of Mapai-Aḥdut ha-Avodah received 45 seats – four more than the combined pre-election strength of its constituents after Rafi had broken away from Mapai. Rafi increased its representation to 10 MKs. An interesting addition to the Knesset was Ha-Olam ha-Zeh Ko'aḥ Ḥadash, headed by Uri *Avneri, editor of the weekly *Ha-Olam ha-Zeh*. This was the first time that a radical protest list had gotten elected to the Knesset. In the Jerusalem municipal elections, Teddy *Kollek of Rafi, who was to remain in office for 27 years, was elected mayor with the support of Gaḥal and the religious parties.

Table 24. Results of the elections to the Sixth Knesset by party

Name of list	Number of valid votes	% of total votes	Number of seats	13th Govt	14th Govt
Alignment	443,379	36.7	45	X	X
Gaḥal	256,957	21.3	26	X*	X
National Religious Party	107,966	9.9	11	X	X
Rafi	95,328	7.9	10	X*	X
Mapam	79,985	6.6	8	X	X
Independent Liberals	45,299	3.8	5	X	X
Agudat Israel	39,795	3.3	4		
Two minority lists associated with the Alignment	39,464	3.3	4	X**	X**
Rakaḥ (New Communist Party)	27,413	2.3	3		
Po'alei Agudat Israel	22,066	1.8	2	X**	
Ha-Olam ha-Zeh Ko'aḥ Ḥadash	14,124	1.2	1		
Maki (Communist Party)	13,617	1.1	1		

* Joined the government on June 4, 1967.
** Members of the coalition but not the government.

The Sixth Knesset reelected Kadish Luz as its speaker for the third term, while President Zalman Shazar was elected for a second term.

Golda Meir, who was suffering from ill health, was not a member of the Thirteenth Government, and she was replaced in the Ministry for Foreign Affairs by Abba Eban. Haim Zadok resigned in November 1966 from the Ministry of Commerce and Industry over differences of opinion with the minister of finance, and was succeeded as minister of commerce and industry by Ze'ev *Sherf. Beḥor Shalom Shitrit, who had been minister of police since Ben-Gurion's first government, resigned in November, and was succeeded by Eliyahu Sasson, whose position as the minister of postal services was taken over by Israel Yeshayahu, the first minister of Yemenite origin.

When Eshkol introduced his new government, nothing indicated that this would turn into a historical government – historical in that it was to see Israel through its most brilliant and fateful military victory since its War of Independence, and historical in that for the first time in Israel's history, Menaḥem Begin was invited to join a government.

The new government was soon confronted by a deep economic recession. For the first year and a half of the Sixth Knesset's term, Rafi frequently joined Gaḥal in criticizing the government's economic policy, which, they claimed, had led to the recession. Rafi and Gaḥal also accused Eshkol and Eban of unfounded optimism in foreign and security affairs.

In 1966 the military administration to which the Arab population of Israel had been subjected since the state's establishment was finally removed.

At the end of March 1967 Shmuel *Tamir, and another

Table 25. Members of the Thirteenth Government (formed January 12, 1966)

Ministerial Position	Name (party)
Prime Minister	Levi Eshkol (Alignment-Labor Party-Alignment*) (d. 2.26.69)
Deputy PM and Absorption	Yigal Allon (Alignment-Labor Party-Alignment*) (from 7.1.68)
Agriculture	Haim Gvati (Alignment-Labor Party-Alignment*) (resigned from the Knesset)
Commerce & Industry	Haim Zadok (Alignment) (until 11.22.66) Ze'ev Sherf (Alignment-Labor Party-Alignment*) (from 11.22.66)
Defense	Levi Eshkol (Alignment-Labor Party-Alignment*) (until 6.5.67) Moshe Dayan (Rafi-Labor Party-Alignment*) (from 6.5.67)
Development and Tourism	Moshe Kol (Independent Liberal) (resigned from the Knesset)
Education & Culture	Zalman Aran (Alignment-Labor Party-Alignment*)
Finance	Pinḥas Sapir (Alignment-Labor Party*) (until 8.5.68) Ze'ev Sherf (Labor Party-Alignment*) (from 8.5.68)
Foreign Affairs	Abba Eban (Alignment-Labor Party-Alignment*)
Health	Israel Barzilai (Mapam-Alignment*) (not an MK)
Housing	Mordekhai Bentov (Mapam-Alignment*) (resigned from the Knesset)
Information	Israel Galili (Alignment-Labor Party-Alignment*) (until 6.5.67)
Interior	Ḥayyim Moshe Shapira (NRP)
Justice	Ya'akov Shimshon Shapira (Alignment-Labor Party-Alignment*) (not an MK)
Labor	Yigal Allon (Alignment-Labor Party*) (until 7.1.68) Yosef Almogi (Labor Party-Alignment*) (from 7.8.68)
Police	Beḥor Shalom Shitrit (Alignment) (until 1.2.67) Eliyahu Sasson (Alignment-Labor Party-Alignment*) (from 1.2.67)
Postal Services	Eliyahu Sasson (Alignment) (2.1.67) Israel Yeshayahu (Alignment-Labor Party-Alignment*) (from 1.2.67)
Religious Affairs	Zeraḥ Wahrhaftig (NRP)
Transportation	Moshe Carmel (Alignment-Labor Party-Alignment*) (not an MK)
Welfare	Joseph Burg (NRP)
Without Portfolio	Israel Galili (Alignment) (until 6.5.67)
Without Portfolio	Menaḥem Begin (Gaḥal) (from 6.5.67)
Without Portfolio	Yosef Sapir (Gaḥal) (from 6.5.67)
Without Portfolio	Pinḥas Sapir (Labor Party-Alignment*) (from 8.5.68)

* The first Alignment was between Mapai and Aḥdut ha-Avodah. Mapai, Aḥdut ha-Avodah, and Rafi formed the Labor Party on Jan. 23, 1968. The Labor Party and Mapam formed the second Alignment on Jan. 28, 1969.

two Ḥerut Movement members of Gaḥal, broke away to form the Free Center parliamentary group. The main reason for the secession was criticism of Begin's leadership.

The threat posed by Egyptian troop concentrations in Sinai in May 1967, and what appeared to many as indecisiveness on Eshkol's part and servility to the gentiles on Eban's part, led to a widespread demand for the establishment of a National Unity Government. Begin proposed that Ben-Gurion return to the premiership in order to reassure the public or, alternatively, that the defense portfolio be given to Moshe Dayan. Eshkol preferred Yigal Allon – Dayan's lifelong political rival – as defense minister, but Dayan was a favorite with the NRP and a large section of Mapai, while Allon happened to be abroad when the crisis began, so Dayan was finally chosen. Begin and Yosef Sapir of Gaḥal were also added to the Government on June 5 – the first day of the war, when the government held its meeting in the Knesset air-raid shelter due to Jordanian shelling of the area of the government compound. Immediately after the fighting ended Prime Minister Levi Eshkol announced the unification of Jerusalem, and the Knesset added to the Government and Legal Procedures Ordinance article 11(b) regarding the application of the Israeli system of justice, jurisdiction, and administration to the territories of Ereẓ Israel liberated, held, or occupied – depending on one's ideological point of view.

In 1968 a wave of airline hijackings and terrorist attacks inside Israel began, which was to bedevil Israeli politics for many years to come.

In the course of the negotiations on the enlargement of the government in May, Peres, on behalf of Rafi, had proposed that Mapai and Rafi reunite. Half a year later, on January 21, 1968, the two parties, together with Aḥdut ha-Avodah, jointed together to form the Israel Labor Party. In the institutions of the new party Mapai received 57% of the seats, while Rafi and Aḥdut ha-Avodah received 21.5% each. Ben-Gurion refused to join the new party, and remained in the Knesset as a single MK. Golda Meir was elected secretary general of the Labor Party but was later replaced by Pinḥas Sapir.

To compensate Allon for his failure to appoint him minister of defense, Eshkol appointed him deputy prime minister in addition to giving him the Ministry of Immigrant Absorption. Almogi of Rafi replaced Allon in the Ministry of Labor. After being appointed secretary general of the Labor Party Sapir remained in the government as minister without portfolio, and was replaced in the Ministry of Finance by Sherf, who now held the two central economic positions in the government.

On January 20, 1969, before the approaching elections to the Seventh Knesset, a new Alignment was formed between the Labor Party and Mapam, despite the opposition of Rafi. For the first and only time in the history of Israel a single parliamentary group held an absolute majority in the Knesset – 63 seats.

Once Jerusalem had been reunited and the euphoria

of the Six-Day War started to subside, serious debates began regarding the appropriate policy that should be followed to make the most of the military victory. Though Eban had informed the UN in February 1968 that Israel accepted UN Security Council Resolution 242, this fact was only made public in August 1970. In the meantime various policies and plans started to be debated, including the Allon Plan, which called for an Israeli withdrawal from most of the West Bank and Gaza Strip and the incorporation of these territories in a Jordanian-Palestinian state, and Dayan's policy of integrating the territories occupied during the war into the Israeli economy but keeping Israel and the territories functionally separate.

The sudden death of Levi Eshkol on February 26, 1969 resulted in Golda Meir's reentering active politics after being chosen by the Labor Party as his successor. Meir's new government had a similar makeup to Eshkol's, and only the foreign affairs and security chapter in the government's guidelines was redrafted in agreement with Gaḥal.

Table 26. Members of the Fourteenth Government (formed March 17, 1969)

Ministerial Position	Name (party)
Prime Minister	Golda Meir (Alignment)
Deputy Prime Minister and Absorption	Yigal Allon (Alignment)
Agriculture	Chaim Gvati (Alignment) (not an MK)
Defense	Moshe Dayan (Alignment)
Development and Tourism	Moshe Kol (Independent Liberal) (not an MK)
Education & Culture	Zalman Aran (Alignment)
Finance and Commerce & Industry	Ze'ev Sherf (Alignment)
Foreign Affairs	Abba Eban (Alignment)
Health	Israel Barzilai (Alignment) (not an MK)
Housing	Mordekhai Bentov (Alignment) (not an MK)
Interior	Ḥayyim Moshe Shapira (NRP)
Justice	Ya'akov Shimshon Shapira (Alignment) (not an MK)
Labor	Yosef Almogi (Alignment)
Police	Eliyahu Sasson (Alignment)
Postal Services	Israel Yeshayahu (Alignment)
Religious Affairs	Zeraḥ Wahrhaftig (NRP)
Transportation	Moshe Carmel (Alignment) (not an MK)
Welfare	Joseph Burg (NRP)
Without Portfolio	Menaḥem Begin (Gaḥal)
Without Portfolio	Israel Galili (Alignment)
Without Portfolio	Pinḥas Sapir (Alignment)
Without Portfolio	Yosef Sapir (Gaḥal)

The issue of the disappearance of Yemenite children in the early years of the state came up for the first time in this period, and a commission of inquiry was set up to deal with it. The problem of elected representatives changing political allegiance in return for material gain – which was referred to as *kalanterism*, after a certain Raḥamim Kalanter, who had changed sides in the Jerusalem municipality in return for such benefits – was also an issue that came up for debate in the Knesset.

Other issues over which there were deep differences of opinion were the implementation of a national health insurance system, demanded by Gaḥal on the one hand and Uri Avneri on the other, and the issue of organ transplants, raised by the religious parties.

Towards the end of the Knesset's term, Rafi considered seceding from the Labor Party and running separately in the elections to the Seventh Knesset, but was finally pacified when it was agreed that the former members of Rafi would be allowed to nominate their own candidates to the Labor Party list and as ministers in the government that would be formed after the elections. Ben-Gurion decided to run in the elections within the framework of a new list – Ha-Reshimah ha-Mamlakhtit (the State List).

The election campaign preceding the elections to the Seventh Knesset was comparatively subdued, one of the reasons for this being a new Election Financing Law that limited spending on the campaign. For the first time TV was used for electioneering, while the role of mass public rallies was reduced.

[Misha Louvish / Susan Hattis Rolef (2nd ed.)]

The Seventh Knesset, 1969–73

The elections to the Seventh Knesset were held on October 28, 1969, and the first meeting of the Knesset was held 25 days later, on November 17, 1969.

Table 27. Results of the elections to the Seventh Knesset

Electorate:	1,758,685
Valid votes cast	1,367,743
Qualifying threshold (1%)	13,677
Votes per seat	11,274

Table 28. Results of the elections to the Seventh Knesset by party

Name of list	Number of valid votes	% of total votes	Number of seats	15th Govt
Alignment	632,035	46.2	56	X
Gaḥal	296,294	21.7	26	X*
National Religious Party	133,294	9.7	12	X
Two minority lists associated with the Alignment	44,989	3.5	4	X**
Agudat Israel	44,002	3.2	4	
Independent Liberals	43,933	3.2	4	X
State List	42,654	3.1	4	
Rakaḥ (New Communist Party)	38,827	2.8	3	
Po'alei Agudat Israel	24,968	1.9	2	
Ha-Olam ha-Zeh Ko'aḥ Ḥadash	16,853	1.4	2	
Free Center	16,393	1.2	2	
Maki (Communist Party)	15,712	1.1	1	

* Left the government on 6.8.70.
** Members of the coalition but not the government.

Table 29. Members of the Fifteenth Government (formed December 15, 1969)

Ministerial Position	Name (party)
Prime Minister	Golda Meir (Alignment)
Deputy PM and Education & Culture	Yigal Allon (Alignment)
Agriculture	Chaim Gvati (Alignment)
Commerce & Industry	Yosef Sapir (Gaḥal) (until 8.6.70)
	Pinḥas Sapir (Alignment) (from 9.1.70 until 3.5.72)
	Haim Bar-Lev (Alignment) (from 3.5.72)
Communications (formerly Postal Services and Transportation)	Shimon Peres (Alignment) (from 9.1.70)
Defense	Moshe Dayan (Alignment)
Development	Ḥayyim Landau (Gaḥal) (until 8.6.70)
	Chaim Gvati (Alignment) (from 9.1.70)
Finance	Pinḥas Sapir (Alignment)
Foreign Affairs	Abba Eban (Alignment)
Health	Chaim Gvati (Alignment) (from 12.22.69 until 7.27.70)
	Victor Shemtov (Alignment) (from 7.27.70)
Housing	Ze'ev Sherf (Alignment)
Immigrant Absorption	Shimon Peres (Alignment) (from 12.22.69 until 7.27.70)
	Natan Peled (not an MK)
Interior	Ḥayyim Moshe Shapira (NRP) (d. 7.16.70)
	Joseph Burg (NRP) (from 9.1.70) (resigned from the Knesset)
Justice	Ya'akov Shimshon Shapira (Alignment) (until 6.13.72 and from 9.12.72 until 11.1.73)
Labor	Yosef Almogi (Alignment)
Police	Shelomo Hillel (Alignment)
Postal Services	Elimelekh Shimon Rimalt (Gaḥal) (until 8.6.70)
Religious Affairs	Zeraḥ Wahrhaftig (NRP)
Tourism	Moshe Kol (Independent Liberal) (resigned from the Knesset)
Transportation	Ezer Weizman (Gaḥal) (until 8.6.70)
Welfare	Joseph Burg (NRP) (until 9.1.70) (resigned from the Knesset)
	Ya'akov Mikhael Hazani (NRP) (from 1.9.70)
Without Portfolio	Israel Galili (Alignment)
Without Portfolio	Shimon Peres (Alignment) (until 22.12.69)
Without Portfolio	Israel Barzilai (Alignment) (d. 6.12.70)
Without Portfolio	Victor Shemtov (Alignment (until 7.27.70)
Without Portfolio	Menaḥem Begin (Gaḥal) (until 8.6.70)
Without Portfolio	Arye Dulzin (Gaḥal) (not an MK)

In the elections to the Seventh Knesset, the new Labor-Mapam Alignment lost the overall majority it had commanded in the Sixth Knesset when it was first formed, but nevertheless won an impressive victory – 56 seats, more than any list had ever received in an election – and together with the two minority lists, it controlled half the Knesset seats.

Gaḥal maintained its strength with 26 seats, even though the Free Center, which had broken away from Gaḥal, received two. The National List, headed by Ben-Gurion, received 4 seats, while the National Religious Party received 12. Ha-Olam ha-Zeh Ko'aḥ Ḥadash doubled its strength, but before long split in half.

In the negotiations for the new government, Gaḥal demanded representation in proportion to its Knesset strength and greater influence over the government's basic principles. In protest against the appointment of the six Gaḥal ministers, of whom four were given portfolios, at first Mapam refused to play an active role in the government, and its two ministers remained without portfolio.

Despite the changes in the government, there was no significant break with the past.

Against the background of a continued wave of airline hijackings and terrorist attacks by Palestinian terrorists, in the condemnation of which nearly all the parties joined, there were several peace initiatives – one on behalf of the UN (the Jarring mission) and another led by the U.S. (the Rogers Plan) – on which opinions in Israel were divided. The willingness of the Labor leaders to respond favorably to the second Rogers Plan for negotiations with Egypt resulted in Mapam's finally accepting ministerial responsibilities on July 27, 1970, and in Gaḥal's decision to resign from the National Unity Government, on August 6, even though its Liberal wing believed this to be a mistake. The departure of Gaḥal from the government led to a redistribution of seats among the remaining coalition members, and two portfolios formerly held by Gaḥal – Transportation and Postal Services – were united in the Ministry of Communications under Shimon Peres.

Pinḥas Sapir, who had returned to the Ministry of Finance in the new government, now also assumed the Commerce and Industry portfolio, while Chaim Gvati added the Development portfolio to the previously held Agriculture.

Gaḥal's return to the opposition, in addition to reducing the number of ministers in the government, rejuvenated Israel's parliamentary life. Even though the NRP remained in the government, some of its younger members started to express opposition to the Alignment's declared willingness to consider withdrawal from part of the territories occupied during the Six-Day War in return for peace, marking the beginning of the NRP's gradual shift to the right, and the beginning of the end of its 20-year "historic coalition" with the labor camp.

However, even within the Alignment there were differences of opinion on the issue of the future of the territories, with certain sections of the Labor Party – especially former members of Rafi, and some former members of Aḥdut ha-Avodah (with the marked exception of Yigal Allon) – taking a more hawkish position. Though Allon's Plan – which advocated the return of most of Judea and Samaria, as well as the Gaza Strip to Jordan, leaving the Jordan Valley and Eastern Mountain Range, as well as Gush Eẓyon, the Latrun corridor, and several other areas in Israeli hands – was never formally accepted by the government, it did constitute the basis for Israel's new settlement map in the course of the Seventh and Eighth Knessets. At the same time Dayan, who had started implementing his "open bridges" policy soon after the Six-Day War, developed the concept of the "functional partition."

Nevertheless, at this point, with a prosperous economy and no real prospects for serious negotiations with Israel's neighbors due to the three "noes" of the 1968 Khartoum Arab Summit Conference, the position of the Alignment, and its various components, seemed strong and stable, and as in the past, Gaḥal, and its components, seemed no closer than in the past to unseating the labor camp from power.

The appearance of the Black Panther protest movement in 1970, which held a series of violent demonstrations in Jerusalem, should have lit a red light for the Alignment. But instead of reacting to growing dissatisfaction and disaffection by Israeli citizens of Sephardi origin, who were demanding their fair share in the booming economy, Golda Meir brushed the Black Panthers off as being "not nice," alluding to the criminal records of some of them. Nevertheless, the Knesset dealt extensively with the subject of economic gaps in society, and the term "poverty line" came into use.

Other issues on the political agenda in the course of the Seventh Knesset were the amendment of the Law of Return, which defined a Jew for the purpose of the right of return as "anyone born to a Jewish mother or who has converted, and is not a member of another faith"; the absorption of a wave of immigration from the Soviet Union, which was followed in the Soviet Union itself by the persecution of Jews who identified with Israel; the immigration to Israel of the leader of the *Jewish Defense League rabbi Meir *Kahane, who was to radicalize right-wing politics in Israel, and the attempted immigration to Israel of Meyer *Lansky, one of the Jewish heads of organized crime in the U.S., who sought asylum but was refused entry.

The outbreak of the Yom Kippur War on October 6, 1973, came to Israel as a total surprise, despite early warning signals. The surprise was the outcome of what might be described as cockiness resulting from overconfidence, and a mistaken concept that the neighboring states would not dare attack Israel. Though with the help of U.S. supplies Israel managed to emerge from the war, after close to three weeks of fierce fighting, in a favorable strategic situation, the war had been extremely costly in human lives, economic resources (Israel's enormous national debt dates from that time), and public loss of faith in the political and military leadership.

Though the political consequences of the war did not manifest themselves immediately, there is no doubt that the consequences of what came to be known as the *meḥdal* – the failure – was a major contributor to the election upset (*mahapakh*) three and a half years later. The convening of the Geneva Peace Conference towards the end of December, with the participation of Egypt and Jordan but the marked absence of Syria, did not help in any way to mitigate the sense that an earthquake had occurred.

Elections to the Eighth Knesset were to have been held in November 1973, but were put off to December 31 due to the outbreak of the war.

After retiring from the army as a brigadier general in June 1973, Ariel (Arik) *Sharon actually considered joining the Labor Party, but finally decided to join the Liberal Party within Gaḥal, and was instrumental in getting the Ḥerut Movement, the Liberals, the Free Center, and the State List (without Ben-Gurion, who resigned from the Knesset in May 1970) to form the *Likud. However, before entering the politics arena as an active player, Sharon returned to active service during the war, strengthening his reputation as a brilliant tactician with serious disciplinary problems.

The Eighth Knesset, 1973–77

The elections to the Eighth Knesset were held on December 31, 1973, and the first meeting of the Knesset was held 21 days later, on January 21, 1974.

Table 30. Results of the elections to the Eighth Knesset

Electorate:	2,037,478
Valid votes cast	1,566,855
Qualifying threshold (1%)	15,668
Votes per seat	12,424

Table 31. Results of the elections to the Eighth Knesset by party

Name of list	Number of valid votes	% of total votes	Number of seats	16th Govt	17th Govt
Alignment	621,183	39.6	51	X	X
Likud	473,309	30.9	39		
National Religious Party	130,349	8.3	10	X	X*
Religious Torah Front	60,012	3.8	5		
Independent Liberals	56,560	3.6	4	X	X
Rakaḥ (New Communist Party)	53,353	3.4	4		
Two minority lists associated with the Alignment	39,012	2.4	3		X**
Civil Rights Movement (CRM)	35,023	2.2	3		X***
Moked	22,147	1.4	1		

* Joined the government on 30.10.74.
** Members of the coalition but not the government.
*** Left the coalition after the NRP joined.

The full political repercussions of the Yom Kippur War were not to be felt until the elections to the Ninth Knesset. Nevertheless early signs of what lay ahead could be discerned in the results of the elections to the Eighth Knesset. The Labor Alignment lost five of its seats and now had 51, while the Likud received 39 seats. The Alignment lost three of its seats to the new Citizens' Rights Movement (Ratz), established by Shulamit *Aloni, who had left the Labor Party due largely to her personal rivalry with Golda Meir. The new party, besides being more dovish than Labor, advocated a strong human and civil rights agenda. But what was more significant was that the Alignment lost two seats to the Likud.

It took Golda Meir over two months to form a new government, with the participation of the NRP and the Independent Liberals. The distribution of seats in the new Government was almost identical to that at the end of the Fifteenth Government, with the new addition of Yitzḥak *Rabin, who had recently returned from serving as Israel's ambassador to Washington, as minister of labor.

Table 32. Members of the Sixteenth Government (formed March 10, 1974)

Ministerial Position	Name (party)
Prime Minister	Golda Meir (Alignment)
Deputy PM and Education & Culture	Yigal Allon (Alignment)
Agriculture	Chaim Gvati (Alignment)
Commerce & Industry and Development	Ḥaim Barlev (Alignment)
Communications	Aharon Uzan (Alignment) (not an MK)
Defense	Moshe Dayan (Alignment)
Finance	Pinḥas Sapir (Alignment)
Foreign Affairs	Abba Eban (Alignment)
Health	Victor Shemtov (Alignment)
Housing	Yehoshua Rabinowitz (Alignment)
Immigrant Absorption	Shelomo Rosen (Alignment) (not an MK)
Information	Shimon Peres (Alignment)
Interior	Joseph Burg (NRP)
Justice	Ḥayyim Yosef Zadok (Alignment)
Labor	Yitzḥak Rabin (Alignment)
Police	Shlomo Hillel (Alignment)
Religious Affairs	Yiẓḥak Rafael (NRP)
Tourism	Moshe Kol (Independent Liberal) (resigned from the Knesset)
Transportation	Aharon Yariv (Alignment)
Welfare	Ya'akov Mikhael Hazani (NRP)
Without Portfolio	Israel Galili (Alignment)
Without Portfolio	Gideon Hausner (Independent Liberal) (resigned from the Knesset)

However, a month after establishing her government, on April 11, 1974, Golda Meir resigned, following the publication of the interim report of the *Agranat Commission, which had investigated the background to the outbreak of the Yom Kippur War. Meir resigned despite the fact that the report had exonerated her from any responsibility for the war's failures, placing the full blame on the military.

It was only on June 3 that a new government was finally established by the political novice Yitzhak Rabin, who was chosen by the Labor Party as Meir's heir, after a political contest between him and Shimon Peres. Rabin's advantage was that his name had not been associated in any way with the Yom Kippur War. Three of the veteran Labor leaders – Moshe Dayan, Abba Eban, and Pinḥas Sapir – were left out of the new government, with Peres becoming defense minister, Yigal Allon foreign minister, and Yehoshua Rabinowitz finance minister. The fact that Rabin was the first Israeli-born prime minister, with another Israeli-born cabinet member, Allon, responsible for foreign affairs, seemed to herald a new and optimistic era of Israeli politics. The presence in the government, at its inception, of Shulamit Aloni, side by side with the Independent Liberals, and the absence of the NRP, also appeared to promise a new direction.

However, soon the NRP joined, Aloni left, and the government proceeded on a bumpy, unstable road that led to the election upset of 1977.

Table 33. Members of the Seventeenth Government (formed June 3, 1974)

Ministerial Position	Name (party)
Prime Minister	Yitzḥak Rabin (Alignment)
Deputy PM and Foreign Affairs	Yigal Allon (Alignment)
Agriculture	Aharon Uzan (Alignment) (not an MK)
Commerce & Industry and Development	Ḥaim Barlev (Alignment)
Communications	Yitzḥak Rabin (Alignment) (until 3.20.75) Aharon Uzan (from 3.20.75) (not an MK)
Defense	Shimon Peres (Alignment)
Education & Culture	Aharon Yadlin (Alignment)
Finance	Yehoshua Rabinowitz (Alignment)
Health	Victor Shemtov (Alignment)
Housing	Shelomo Rosen (Alignment) (from 1.16.77)
Immigrant Absorption	Shelomo Rosen (Alignment)
Information	Aharon Yariv (Alignment) (until 2.4.75)
Interior	Shelomo Hillel (until 10.29.74) Joseph Burg (NRP) (from 10.30.74 until 12.22.76) Shelomo Hillel (from 1.16.77)
Justice	Ḥayyim Yosef Zadok (Alignment)
Labor	Moshe Baram (Alignment)
Police	Shelomo Hillel (Alignment)
Religious Affairs	Ḥayyim Yosef Zadok (Alignment) (until 10.29.74) Yiẓḥak Rafael (NRP) (from 10.30.74 until 12.22.76) Ḥayyim Yosef Zadok (Alignment) (from 1.16.77)
Tourism	Moshe Kol (Independent Liberal) (not an MK)
Transportation	Gad Yaacobi (Alignment)
Welfare	Victor Shemtov (Alignment) (until 10.29.74) Ya'akov Mikhael Hazani (NRP) (from 10.30.74 (d. 7.2.75)) Yitzḥak Rabin (Alignment) (from 7.7.75 until 7.29.75) Joseph Burg (NRP) (until 11.4.75) Zevulun Hammer (NRP) (until 12.22.76) Moshe Baram (Alignment) (from 1.16.77)
Without Portfolio	Israel Galili (Alignment)
Without Portfolio	Gideon Hausner (Independent Liberal) (not an MK)
Without Portfolio	Shulamit Aloni (CRM) (until 11.6.74)

The Rabin government had to contend with a major foreign debt, created as a result of the Yom Kippur War, but despite generous U.S. economic and military aid, the rate of inflation started to rise sharply, and to the anti-Alignment protest movements that emerged against a political background was added social unrest against an economic and social background.

The shuttle diplomacy of U.S. Secretary of State Henry *Kissinger led to disengagement agreements with Egypt and Syria in 1974, and another interim agreement with Egypt in 1975 that involved the principle of "territories in exchange for peace." An initiative by Allon to continue this process *vis-à-vis* Jordan with the "Jericho Plan" came to naught after the results of the Rabat Arab Summit Conference of October 1974, which declared that only the PLO could negotiate a settlement for Palestine. However, what seemed to some a welcome development in the Arab-Israeli conflict also sharpened the political divide in Israel regarding the future of the territories occupied by Israel in the course of the Six-Day War, between those willing to give up territories for peace and those opposed.

The emergence of *Gush Emunim and the sharp turn to the right among the younger leaders of the NRP must be seen against this background. The growing number of Palestinian terrorist attacks on Israeli territory and against Israeli targets, Israel's growing isolation in the international arena, which reached its peak with the 1975 UN General Assembly Resolution 3379 that equated Zionism with racism, and the decision of the Soviet Union to once again close its gates to emigration to Israel contributed to the gradual movement of Israeli public opinion to the right.

The killing of six Israeli Arabs by Israeli security forces on March 30, 1976, in the course of "Land Day" demonstrations, proclaimed by the Arab community to protest against the confiscation of Arab land by the state, was to have a profound effect on political developments among Israeli Arabs.

Several financial scandals connected with senior members of the Labor Party – the first involving Asher Yadlin, who had been a candidate for the position of governor of the Bank of Israel and ended up in prison; the second involving Minister of Construction and Housing Avraham Ofer, who committed suicide before charges were brought against him; and the third involving a bank account held by Rabin's wife in the U.S. in contravention of Israel's foreign currency laws, and which ultimately resulted in Rabin's resignation from the premiership – added to a sharp decline in Labor's popularity.

In fact, the government resigned on December 22, 1976, before the bank account scandal became known, against the background of the abstention of the NRP in a vote on a motion of no confidence, brought by Agudat Israel in connection with the alleged breach of the Sabbath caused by a ceremony held at an air force base, and the removal of its ministers from the government that followed.

In 1976, in preparation for the elections to the Ninth Knesset, various protest movements and individual politicians who had left the labor movement, on the one hand, and the Likud, on the other, formed a new party under the leadership of Yigael *Yadin, which called itself the *Democratic Movement for Change (DMC, popularly known as "Dash").

In the course of the Eighth Knesset there were also early attempts by the government to enact two central Basic Laws, Basic Law: Legislation and Basic Law: Human Rights, but both efforts were cut short due to the opposition of the religious parties.

The Ninth Knesset, 1977–81

The elections to the Ninth Knesset were held on May 17, 1977, and the first meeting of the Knesset was held 27 days later, on June 13, 1977.

Table 34. Results of the elections to the Ninth Knesset

Electorate:	2,236,293
Valid votes cast	1,747,820
Qualifying threshold (1%)	17,478
Votes per seat	14,173

Table 35. Results of the elections to the Ninth Knesset by party

Name of list	Number of valid votes	% of total votes	Number of seats	18th Govt
Likud	583,968	33.4	43	X
Alignment	430,023	24.6	32	
Democratic Movement for Change	202,265	11.6	15	X*
National Religious Party	160,787	9.2	12	X
Hadash	80,118	4.6	5	
Agudat Israel	58,652	3.3	4	X**
Flatto Sharon	35,049	2.0	1#	
Shlomzion	33,947	1.9	2	X***
Maḥaneh Sheli	27,281	1.6	2	
One minority list associated with the Alignment	24,185	1.4	1	
Po'alei Agudat Israel	23,571	1.3	1	
Civil Rights Movement	20,621	1.2	1	
Independent Liberals	20,384	1.2	1	

\# Received sufficient votes for two seats, but did not have additional members on his list.
* Joined the government on Oct. 24, 1977. After the DMC fell apart in 1978, most of its members went into opposition.
** Did not hold a ministerial post.
*** Joined the Likud on July 5, 1977.

The elections to the Ninth Knesset produced what came to be known as the *mahapakh* or "big upset." The Alignment lost 19 seats and was now left with 32, while the Likud gained four and went up to 43. Most of the remainder of the former Alignment votes went to the DMC, which obtained 15 seats. Soon after the election Moshe Dayan left the Alignment to join the new government formed by Menaḥem Begin and remained in the Knesset for a time as an independent MK. Shlomzion, a party formed by Sharon just before the elections against the background of disagreements within the Likud, gained two seats, and soon joined the Likud.

The main reasons for Labor's defeat were a late reaction to the Yom Kippur War; a general feeling that the movement had been in power for too long, and was both no longer in touch with popular feelings and showing clear signs of corruption; a full-scale revolt by the movement's former Sephardi voters – many of them of the second generation of immigrants from the Muslim countries; and growing dissatisfaction with Labor's economic policy, with the central role played by the state and the Histadrut. However, until after the elections to the Tenth Knesset in 1981, many Labor leaders were inclined to see the defeat as a mishap, or temporary setback – not a change in political trends.

Other noteworthy election results were the gains of Ḥadash, which received five seats. Ḥadash, formed in the course of the Eighth Knesset, was now made up of the Communist Party and the colorful Charlie Bitton of the Black Panther movement, who had held talks with several of the Zionist parties before deciding to opt for Ḥadash. Flatto Sharon, a Polish Jewish businessmen and fugitive from French justice, won enough votes for two seats, but did not have a second member on his list. Later on Sharon was to stand trial on charges of having bribed voters.

While the DMC's electoral success was impressive, the new party's main success was in significantly weakening the Alignment. However, the Likud, under Menaḥem Begin, managed to rally a coalition of 61 MKs, even before the DMC decided to join the government, and within a year the new party broke up into a number of parliamentary groups and individual MKs, while two of its MKs joined the Alignment.

The Ninth Knesset elected Yitzhak *Shamir from the Likud as its speaker, and afterwards when he was appointed minister for foreign affairs, Yiẓhak Berman. The Knesset also elected Yitzhak *Navon of the Labor Party as president of the state.

It took Begin just over a month to form his government. This was to be a new government in more senses than one. It was the first government without any of the labor parties, even though Moshe Dayan, as an individual, agreed to assume the post of minister for foreign affairs. Most of the ministers had never held ministerial posts, despite the brief participation of Gaḥal in the National Unity Government of 1967–70. Simḥah *Ehrlich, of the Liberal branch of the Likud, became minister of finance and embarked on a policy of liberalization. The two religious parties in the coalition – the NRP and Agudat Israel – which gave Begin his parliamentary majority without the DMC, were also able to bring about changes in the famous "religious status quo," through the introduction of amendments in the Anatomy and Pathology Law, the Abortion Law, and the regulations relating to the service of women in the IDF. Agudat Israel refused ministerial posts in the government, but received the chairmanships of two important Knesset committees: Finance and Labor, and Welfare.

Paradoxically, it was this government that was to sign the first peace treaty between Israel and an Arab state. Though the first steps towards a rapprochement with Egypt had been taken by the Rabin government, it was the Begin government that hosted Egyptian President Anwar *Sadat, who delivered a speech in the Knesset on November 20, 1977. Dayan and Ezer Weizman, who became minister of defense in the new government, played a central role, together with Begin, in first attaining the Camp David Accords of September 1978 and then the Israeli-Egyptian peace treaty of March 1979.

Table 36. Members of the Eighteenth Government (formed on June 20, 1977)

Ministerial Position	Name (party)
Prime Minister	Menaḥem Begin (Likud)
Deputy PM	Simḥah Ehrlich (Likud)
	Yigael Yadin (DMC) (from 10.24.77)
Agriculture	Ariel Sharon (Likud)
Commerce & Industry and Tourism	Yigael Hurwitz (Likud) (until 10.1.78)
	Gideon Pat (Likud) (from 1.15.79)
Communications	Menaḥem Begin (Likud) (until 10.24.77) (with Transportation)
	Meir Amit (DMC) (until 9.15.78) (with Transportation)
	Yitzḥak Modai (Likud) (from 1.15.79 until 12.22.80)
	Yoram Aridor (Likud) (from 1.5.81) (with Finance)
Construction & Housing	Gideon Pat (Likud) (until 1.15.79)
	David Levy (Likud) (from 1.15.79)
Defense	Ezer Weizman (Likud) (until 5.26.80)
	Menaḥem Begin (Likud) (from 1.28.80)
Education, Culture & Sport	Zevulun Hammer (NRP)
Energy & Infrastructures	Yitzhak Modai (Likud)
Finance	Simḥah Ehrlich (Likud) (until 11.7.79)
	Yigael Hurwitz (Likud) (until 1.13.81)
	Yoram Aridor (Likud) (from 1.21.81) (with Communications)
Foreign Affairs	Moshe Dayan (Single MK) (until 10.23.79)
	Menaḥem Begin (Likud) (until 3.10.80)
	Yitzhak Shamir (Likud) (from 3.10.80)
Health	Eliezer Shostak (Likud)
Immigrant Absorption	David Levy (Likud)
Interior and Police	Joseph Burg (NRP)
Justice	Menaḥem Begin (Likud) (until 10.24.77)
	Shmuel Tamir (DMC) (until 8.5.80)
	Moshe Nissim (Likud) (from 8.13.80)
Labor and Welfare	Menaḥem Begin (Likud) (until 10.24.77)
	Israel Katz (not an MK) (from 10.24.77)
Religious Affairs	Aharon Abuhaẓeira (NRP)
Transportation	Menaḥem Begin (Likud) (until 10.24.77) (with Communications)
	Meir Amit (DMC) (until 9.15.78) (with Communications)
	Ḥayyim Landau (Likud) (not an MK) (from 1.15.79)
Without Portfolio	Ḥayyim Landau (Likud) (not an MK) (from 1.10.78 until 1.15.79)
Without Portfolio	Moshe Nissim (Likud) (from 1.10.78 until 8.13.80)

The Peace Treaty with Egypt, which was based on a complete withdrawal of Israel from the Sinai Peninsula, was not accepted by some Likud members, but was approved by the Knesset with a large majority, due to the support of the Alignment. However, the signing of the treaty led to the departure of two members from the Likud – Geulah *Cohen and Moshe *Shamir – who formed a new parliamentary group, Teḥiyyah-Banai, to the right of the Likud.

While the new government pushed forward the achievement of peace in the south, it also engaged in a military operation in the north – the Litani Operation of March 1978, led by Chief of Staff Mordechai (Motta) *Gur – the goal of which was to hit the Palestinian terrorist organizations that had gained a controlling foothold in Southern Lebanon. The Litani Operation was in reaction to a terrorist attack along Israel's coastal road carried out by Palestinians who had come from Lebanon.

As minister of agriculture, Ariel Sharon played a major role in promoting Jewish settlement in Judea, Samaria, and the Gaza Strip. A permanent settlement was set up at Elon Moreh, Bet Hadassah in Hebron was occupied, and the number of Jews in the territories rose to around 8,300. The polarization of Israeli society against this background started to manifest itself, with the Peace Now movement being established in 1978 and the so-called "Jewish Underground" in 1980.

Despite its promising beginning, Begin's coalition proved to be extremely unstable. After the DMC fell apart, some of its former members, including Minister of Justice Shmuel Tamir, left the government. Dayan and Weizman also left the government, because of their dissatisfaction with the lack of progress in the negotiations for the establishment of autonomy for the Palestinians, which had been included in the Camp David Accords. Dayan was replaced in the Ministry for Foreign Affairs by Yitzhak Shamir, while Begin replaced Weizman. Changes also took place in the Ministry of Finance, when a massive deterioration in Israel's balance of payments and rising inflation forced Ehrlich to resign. After his resignation Yigael Hurwitz became Minister of Finance, with a declared economic policy of "not a penny to spare." Hurwitz then resigned when his policy did not gain the government's support, and he was replaced by Yoram Aridor, who embarked on what could be called election economics. These were just a few of the changes that took place in the government. By December 1980 the government's majority in the Knesset had shrunk from 76 to 63.

In the Labor Party, in 1979 Yigal Allon decided to challenge Shimon Peres' leadership. However, Allon passed away suddenly in February 1980, and the challenge to Peres' leadership reverted to Yitzhak Rabin, who in 1979 had published a book in which he referred to Peres as a "tireless schemer." The contest, which took place in December 1980, ended with Rabin suffering a bitter 71–29 defeat, and Peres being reconfirmed as the party's chairman and candidate for prime minister.

In the course of the Ninth Knesset an unprecedented number of new parliamentary groups was formed, and of MKs changing their allegiance – some as many as three times.

Early in 1981 the Knesset voted to hold early elections on June 30. The election campaign was accompanied by a good deal of verbal and physical violence. In addition to Minister of Finance Aridor's raising salaries and keeping prices down by lowering customs duties, the decision to bomb the Iraqi nuclear reactor Osiraq, a month before the elections, was also viewed as an election ploy.

The Tenth Knesset, 1981–1984

The elections to the Tenth Knesset were held on June 30, 1981, and the first meeting of the Knesset was held 20 days later, on July 20, 1981.

Table 37. Results of the elections to the Tenth Knesset

Electorate:	2,490,014
Valid votes cast	1,937,366
Qualifying threshold (1%)	19,373
Votes per seat	15,312

Table 38. Results of the elections to the Tenth Knesset by party

Name of list	Number of valid votes	% of total votes	Number of seats	19th Gov't.	20th Gov't.
Likud	718,941	37.1	48	X	X
Alignment	708,536	36.6	47		
National Religious Party	95,232	4.9	6	X	X
Agudat Israel	72,312	3.7	4	X*	X*
Ḥadash	64,918	3.4	4		
Tami	44,466	2.3	3	X	X
Teḥiyyah	40,700	2.3	3	X**	X
Telem	30,600	1.6	2	X	X
Shinui	29,837	1.5	2		
Civil Rights Movement	27,921	1.4	1		

* Did not hold a ministerial post.
** Joined the coalition on July 26, 1982.

Despite the fact that the opinion polls had predicted that the Alignment would be victorious in the elections to the Tenth Knesset, the Likud emerged from the elections as the largest parliamentary group with 48 seats to the Alignment's 47. The Alignment had hoped for an upset vistory of its own but it failed to materialize. Since the results were close, one may assume that what finally made the difference were the successful attack on Iraq and Aridor's election economics, but the Alignment had begun to realize that the results of the elections to the Ninth Knesset were not simply a temporary setback. For the sake of parliamentary convenience, Shulamit Aloni, with the CRM's single seat – down from three – joined the Alignment for the duration of the Tenth Knesset.

Four new lists – Shinui, Telem, Teḥiyyah, and Tami – entered the Knesset. All four lists were formed by members of the Knesset who had broken away from other parliamentary groups in the course of the Ninth Knesset. Shinui, led by Prof. Amnon *Rubinstein, was the only parliamentary group that had broken away from Dash and survived, receiving two seats. Telem, headed by Moshe Dayan, who had left the Alignment soon after the previous election, also received two seats. Dayan was to pass away soon after the elections. Teḥiyyah, led by Geula Cohen, who had broken away from the Likud, fared better with three seats, as did Tami, an ethnic party formed by Aharon Abuhaẓeira, who had broken away from the NRP after being acquitted of criminal charges that had been leveled against him in 1980. Abuhaẓeira felt that his former colleagues – predominantly Ashkenazi – had not stood by him because of his Moroccan ethnic origin.

The NRP, which had always received 10–12 Knesset seats, now fell to six. It lost some of its Sephardi voters to Tami, while Teḥiyyah gained some of its right-wing voters.

Table 39. Members of the Ninteenth Government (formed on August 5, 1981)

Ministerial Position	Name (party)
Prime Minister	Menaḥem Begin (Likud)
Deputy PM	Simḥah Ehrlich (Likud) (d. 6.19.83)
Deputy PM	David Levy (Likud) (from 11.3.81)
Agriculture	Simḥah Ehrlich (Likud) (d. 6.19.83)
	Menaḥem Begin (Likud) (from 6.19.83)
Communications	Mordekhai Ẓippori (Likud)
Construction & Housing	David Levy (Likud)
Defense	Ariel Sharon (Likud) (until 2.14.83)
	Moshe Arens (Likud) (not an MK) (from 2.23.83)
Education, Culture & Sport	Zevulun Hammer (NRP)
Energy & Infrastructures	Yiẓhak Berman (Likud) (until 9.30.82)
	Yitzhak Modai (Likud) (from 10.19.82)
Finance	Yoram Aridor (Likud)
Foreign Affairs	Yitzhak Shamir (Likud)
Health	Eliezer Shostak (Likud)
Industry & Trade	Gideon Pat (Likud)
Interior and Religious Affairs	Joseph Burg (NRP)
Justice	Moshe Nissim (Likud) (from 8.13.80)
Labor and Welfare and Immigrant Absorption	Aharon Abuhaẓeira (Tami) (until 5.4.82)
	Aharon Uzan (Tami) (from 5.4.82)
Science & Development	Yuval Ne'eman (Teḥiyyah) (from 7.26.82)
Tourism	Gideon Pat (Likud) (until 8.11.81)
	Avraham Sharir (Likud) (from 8.11.81)
Transportation	Ḥayyim Korfu (Likud)
Without Portfolio	Mordekhai Ben-Porat (Telem) (from 7.5.82)
Without Portfolio	Sarah Doron (Likud) (until 10.19.82)
Without Portfolio	Yitzhak Modai (Likud) (until 10.19.82)
Without Portfolio	Ariel Sharon (Likud) (from 2.14.83)

The Tenth Knesset elected Menaḥem Savidor of the Likud as its speaker. It was also to elect Chaim *Herzog of the Labor Party as president of the state.

It took Begin three weeks to form his new government. In many respects it resembled the makeup of his previous government at the end of its term of office, with one significant change: Ariel Sharon was appointed minister of defense, despite some misgivings on Begin's part. Of the new parties Tami and Telem joined the coalition when it was formed, while Teḥiyyah joined in July 1982. A novelty in this government was the large number of deputy ministers, whose number now reached 11. This was to become a regular feature in Israel's governments, which were to become increasingly large, thus leaving fewer of the Knesset's 120 members to perform parliamentary work.

The new government followed its predecessor in making major concessions to the religious parties in the sphere of religious legislation, such as an amendment to the Law of Return on the issue of Who is a Jew, the suspension of El Al flights, and drastic limitations on the granting of work permits on the Sabbath and religious holidays, increased funding for yeshivot and religious institutions, and amendments to the laws dealing with *kashrut*. Efforts by the new government to bring about administrative changes in the ministries met with labor unrest and sanctions. Whereas during the first Likud-led government few personnel changes were made in the civil service, now there were many new political appointments – a sign that the Likud had gained confidence as a ruling party.

In the political sphere, the new government remained committed to the peace treaty with Egypt, and Sharon – one of the architects of Jewish settlement in the territories occupied in the course of the Six-Day War – oversaw the dismantlement of the remaining Jewish settlement in the Sinai, including the town of *Yammit. In the course of the Tenth Knesset no progress was made regarding autonomy for the Palestinians, as agreed in the Camp David Accords. However, a new experiment was made, led by the head of the Civil Administration in the territories, Menaḥem Milson, to create an alternative leadership to the PLO, in the form of the village leagues. Settlement activities in Judea and Samaria continued with vigor, and at the end of 1981 the Knesset passed a law to extend Israeli law to the Golan Heights. Seven Alignment MKs voted in favor of the new law.

Half a year later, in June 1982, Minister of Defense Ariel Sharon convinced the government to invade Southern Lebanon in order to oust the PLO, which had created bases there from which it attacked Israel, though the official pretext for what was called "Operation Peace for Galilee" was the attempted assassination of the Israeli ambassador to London, Shlomo Argov.

In its first stage, as long as the operation was limited to a 25-mile (40 km) strip in Southern Lebanon, there was broad Israeli consensus in favor of its goals. However, Sharon was determined to continue advancing, and went on to capture most of the Lebanese capital of Beirut and other strategic positions. A debate was later to develop as to whether Sharon had duped Begin into approving his more ambitious plans, which included the installation of a government in Lebanon that would be friendly to Israel and which would sign a peace treaty with it. However, the massacre by members of the Lebanese Christian Phalange in the refugee camps of Sabra and Shatila in September 1982 following the assassination of newly elected Lebanese President Bashir Jumayyil resulted in a major public outcry in Israel. A mass demonstration, reportedly attended by 400,000 in Tel Aviv, which was organized by the *Peace Now movement and supported by the Alignment, the CRM, and Shinui, called for Sharon's resignation and was followed by the appointment of a National Commission of Inquiry headed by Supreme Court Justice Yiẓḥak Cohen, to investigate the responsibility for the massacre. The Commission exonerated the army from direct responsibility for the massacre, but found that Sharon had not acted to prevent it, and called for his resignation. In a Peace Now demonstration calling for the implementation of the Commission's recommendations, a hand grenade was thrown into the crowd by a right winger, killing one of the demonstrators and wounding several, including future member of the Knesset Avraham *Burg.

Sharon resigned from the Ministry of Defense in the middle of February 1983 and was replaced by Moshe Arens, an aeronautics engineer who was not a member of the Knesset. Six months later Begin resigned. The reasons for the resignation were his beloved wife's death, failing health, and distress over developments in the war in Lebanon, especially the large number of Israeli casualties.

Surprisingly, Begin's resignation, after nearly 40 years of leading the IZL, the Ḥerut Movement, Gaḥal, and the Likud, was not followed by a power struggle in the Likud, and Yitzhak Shamir – a former leader of Leḥi (*Loḥamei Ḥerut Israel) and of Begin's generation – was accepted by all the groups within the Likud as the heir apparent, despite his much more subdued and passive political style.

The government that Shamir formed in October 1983 was almost identical to Begin's second government.

Table 40. Members of the Twentieth Government (formed on October 10, 1983)

Ministerial Position	Name (party)
Prime Minister and Foreign Affairs	Yitzhak Shamir (Likud)
Deputy PM and Construction & Housing	David Levy (Likud)
Agriculture	Pessaḥ Grupper (Likud)
Communications	Mordekhai Ẓippori (Likud)
Defense	Moshe Arens (Likud) (not an MK)
Education, Culture & Sport	Zevulun Hammer (NRP)
Energy & Infrastructures	Yitzhak Modai (Likud)
Finance	Yoram Aridor (Likud) (until 10.15.83) Yigal Cohen Orgad (Likud) (from 10.18.83)
Health	Eliezer Shostak (Likud)
Industry & Trade	Gideon Pat (Likud)
Interior and Religious Affairs	Joseph Burg (NRP)
Justice	Moshe Nissim (Likud)
Labor and Welfare and Immigrant Absorption	Aharon Uzan (Tami)
Science & Development	Yuval Ne' man (Teḥiyyah)
Tourism	Avraham Sharir (Likud)
Transportation	Ḥayyim Korfu (Likud)
Without Portfolio	Mordekhai Ben-Porat (Movement for Social Renewal) (until 1.31.84)
Without Portfolio	Sarah Doron (Likud)
Without Portfolio	Ariel Sharon (Likud)

The new government had to contend with the complications of the war in Lebanon, growing hostility abroad, growing dissension at home, the collapse of the shares of all Israeli banks except the First International Bank, and a deteriorating economic situation, with an inflation rate that reached three-digit figures. To save the banks from insolvency, the state became their *de facto* owner – a strange twist of events for a government that advocated a free economy and privatization. To deal with the mounting inflation, Minister of Finance Yoram Aridor came up with a "dollarization" plan that would turn the U.S. dollar into the official currency of Israel, and this because, due to the hyperinflation, most prices in Israel were in any case being quoted in dollars. However, the plan was generally received with ridicule, Aridor was forced to resign and was replaced by Yigal Cohen Orgad.

Two major economic projects (*ex post facto*, both found to be beyond Israel's economic means) were launched in the course of the Tenth Knesset: the Mediterranean-Dead Sea Canal for the generation of electricity and desalination and the Lavi fighter plane. It was also at this time that members of the extreme right "Jewish Underground," led by Yehudah Etzion, which had planned terrorist attacks against Arabs and the blowing up of the mosques on the Temple Mount, were apprehended, and the No. 300 bus affair, in which the General Security Service was responsible for killing two Palestinian terrorists after they had been caught, took place. The latter two events had significant, long-term political implications.

The Eleventh Knesset, 1984–88

The elections to the Eleventh Knesset were held on July 21, 1984, and the first meeting of the Knesset was held 23 days later, on August 13, 1984.

Table 41. Results of the elections to the Eleventh Knesset

Electorate:	2,654,613
Valid votes cast	2,073,321
Qualifying threshold (1%)	20,733
Votes per seat	16,786

Tami joined the Likud in August 1988 and Ometz joined the Likud in September 1988.

Even though the Alignment emerged from the election with a larger number of seats than the Likud – 44–41 – neither side could muster a majority to establish a government without the other. The result was a decision to establish a National Unity Government, with the novel idea that in the first two years Shimon Peres would serve as prime minister, with Yitzhak Shamir as vice premier and foreign minister, and in the following two years they would switch places. It took the two parties 54 days to reach an agreement on all the details of this unique coalition scheme, with the idea of rotation of the premiership at its center. Sharon was appointed minister of industry and trade, from which position he continued to encourage Jewish settlement in Judea, Samaria, and the Gaza Strip.

Table 42. Results of the elections to the Eleventh Knesset by party

Name of list	Number of valid votes	% of total votes	Number of seats	21st Govt	22d Govt
Alignment	724,074	34.9	44*	X	X
Likud	661,302	31.9	41	X	X
Teḥiyyah-Tzomet	83,037	4.0	5		
National Religious Party	73,530	3.5	4	X	X
Ḥadash	69,815	3.4	4		
Shas	63,605	3.1	4	X	X
Shinui	54,747	2.7	3	X	X***
Civil Rights Movement	49,698	2.4	3		
Yaḥad	46,302	2.2	3	X**	
Progressive List for Peace	38,012	1.8	2		
Agudat Israel	36,079	1.7	2		
Morashah-Po'alei Agudat Israel	33,287	1.6	2	X	
Tami	31,103	1.5	1		
Kach	25,907	1.2	1		
Ometz	23,845	1.2	1	X	X

* Mapam left the Alignment and formed its own parliamentary group in opposition, and Yossi *Sarid left the Labor Party and joined the CRM in opposition, so that soon after the elections the Alignment was left with only 40 seats.

** Yaḥad joined the Alignment and ceased to exist as a separate parliamentary group.

*** Left the government on May 25, 1987.

The six members of Mapam, who opposed the idea of the National Unity Government, formally left the Alignment on October 22, 1984, and formed their own parliamentary group. On the same day MK Yossi Sarid also left the Labor Party to join the CRM, which had received three seats, while Yaḥad – a party formed by Ezer Weizman after he had sat out the elections to the Tenth Knesset and which had also received three seats – formally joined the Alignment.

Of the 13 smaller lists that had entered the Knesset in addition to the Likud and the Alignment, six joined the coalition, in which the right-wing-religious bloc had a majority.

In this Knesset *Shas, the *ḥaredi* Sephardi Party whose spiritual leader was Rabbi Ovadiah *Yosef, was first elected to the Knesset. The party, which was supported by the spiritual leader of the "Litvak" *ḥaredim*, Rabbi Eliezer Menaḥem *Shach, was formed against the background of the dissatisfaction of the Sephardi rabbis with the status of their followers in the Ashkenazi *ḥaredi* parties. The appearance of Shas halved the strength of Agudat Israel from four to two members.

Two other religious parties elected to the Eleventh Knesset were Morashah-Po'alei Agudat Israel with two seats and the extreme right wing party of Rabbi Meir *Kahane – Kach – which won one seat. Kach had failed to pass the qualifying threshold in the two previous elections, and in the course of the Eleventh Knesset legislation was passed which would exclude Kahane – who advocated a transfer of the Arabs from Israel and proposed several racist bills that the Knesset Presidium refused to place on the Knesset agenda – from running in future elections. At the other end of the political spectrum, a new radical Arab-Jewish party – the Progressive List for Peace – received two seats. Its two representatives were Mohammed Mi'ari, who back in 1964 had been a member of the El Ard movement, which was banned from participating in the elections to the Sixth Knesset, and reserve Major General Matityahu (Matti) Peled, who had been one of the Israeli personalities to hold talks with representatives of the PLO in the course of the late 1970s.

Table 43. Members of the Twenty-First Government (formed on September 13, 1984)

Ministerial Position	Name (party)
Prime Minister	Shimon Peres (Alignment)
Vice Premier and Foreign Affairs	Yitzhak Shamir (Likud)
Deputy PM and Construction & Housing	David Levy (Likud)
Deputy PM and Education & Culture	Yitzhak Navon (Alignment)
Agriculture	Arie Nehamkin (Alignment)
Communications	Amnon Rubinstein (Shinui)
Defense	Yitzhak Rabin (Alignment)
Economics & Inter-Ministerial Coordination (changed name to Economics and Planning)	Gad Yaacobi (Alignment)
Energy & Infrastructures	Moshe Shahal (Alignment)
Finance	Yitzhak Modai (Likud) (until 4.16.86)
	Moshe Nissim (Likud) (from 4.16.86)
Foreign Affairs	Yitzhak Shamir (Likud)
Health	Mordechai Gur (Alignment)
Immigrant Absorption	Ya'akov Tzur (Alignment)
Industry and Trade	Ariel Sharon (Likud)
Interior	Shimon Peres (Alignment) (until 12.24.84)
	Yiẓhak Ḥayyim Peretz (Shas) (from 12.24.84)
Justice	Moshe Nissim (Likud) (until 4.16.86)
	Yitzhak Modai (Likud) (from 4.16.86 until 7.23.86)
	Avraham Sharir (Likud) (from 7.30.86)
Labor & Welfare	Moshe Katzav (Likud)
Police	Haim Bar Lev (Alignment)
Religious Affairs	Shimon Peres (Alignment) (until 12.23.84)
	Joseph Burg (NRP) (from 12.23.84 until 10.5.86)
	Zevulun Hammer (NRP) (from 10.7.86)
Science & Development	Gideon Pat (Likud)
Tourism	Avraham Sharir (Likud)
Transportation	Ḥayyim Korfu (Likud)
Without Portfolio	Moshe Arens (Likud)
Without Portfolio	Joseph Burg (until 12.23.84)
Without Portfolio	Yigael Hurwitz (Ometz)
Without Portfolio	Yiẓhak Ḥayyim Peretz (Shas) (until 12.18.84)
Without Portfolio	Yosef Shapira (not an MK)
Without Portfolio	Ezer Weizman (Alignment)

The Eleventh Knesset elected Shlomo Hillel from the Alignment, as its speaker. Despite the fact that 15 parties were elected to the new Knesset, the work of the Knesset ran relatively smoothly, as the government enjoyed the support of over 95 MKs. However, the vast size of the coalition damaged the democratic fabric of the Knesset, and its Rules of Procedure had to be amended to enable the opposition, which numbered fewer than the mandatory 30 members required to call a special session during the recess, to function properly.

One of the first decisions of the government was for a three-stage withdrawal of the IDF from Lebanon. This decision, taken in January 1985, was only made possible because Likud Deputy Prime Minister and Construction and Housing Minister David *Levy voted on this issue with the Alignment. Due to the inability to reach an agreement with Lebanon, and its patron Syria, guaranteeing that it would maintain quiet along Israel's border, Israel decided to remain in a security zone in Southern Lebanon and support the local Christian militia known as the South Lebanese Army (SLA). Israel was to remain in Southern Lebanon for another 15 years.

Another urgent issue dealt with by the National Unity Government was the economic crisis that had led to a three-digit rate of inflation. The Economic Stabilization Plan, prepared by Minister of Finance Yitzhak *Modai with the full support of the prime minister, which *inter alia* involved extremely high interest rates, managed to contain the inflation, but at the cost of a sharp rise in unemployment and a serious financial crisis that was a deadly blow to many private and public companies, including the Histadrut-owned holding company Koor, small private businesses, and kibbutzim, moshavim, and many private farms.

In response to a proposal by the Knesset State Control Committee, the government also appointed a National Inquiry Commission, chaired by Supreme Court Justice Moshe Bejski, to investigate the crash of the bank share market that had occurred during the term of the previous government. The Commission published its very grave conclusions in April 1986, and the government set up a ministerial committee to deliberate its recommendations.

Even though Modai's economic policy was generally considered very successful, his sharp tongue caused a falling out with Peres and several other ministers, and on April 16, 1986, he was forced to switch places with Minister of Justice Moshe Nissim. Before finally being forced to resign from the government in July, after once again falling out with Peres, Modai dealt with the GSS affair (Bus No. 300) that had taken place during the term of the previous Knesset (see above).

The *Pollard Affair hit the headlines in November 1985, when Jonathan Pollard, a Jewish U.S. naval intelligence employee, was caught spying for Israel. The Israeli Embassy in Washington, D.C., refused to give Pollard sanctuary, even though it had been Foreign Minister Yitzhak Shamir's adviser on terror who had taken Pollard on when Shamir was prime minister. The government washed its hands of the affair, and cooperated with the U.S. in its investigation, much to the chagrin of several members of the Knesset.

Two months before the rotation, following a deal between the Alignment and the Likud, two significant amendments were passed by the Knesset to the Penal Law and to the Order for the Prevention of Terror. The first made racial incitement a criminal offense, while the second prohibited unauthorized meetings by Israeli citizens with representatives of terrorist organizations.

Despite misgivings on Peres' part, the rotation in the premiership took place as planned on October 20 and a new government was formed, with only minor personal changes.

Table 44. Members of the Twenty-Second Government (formed on October 20, 1986)

Ministerial Position	Name (party)
Prime Minister	Yitzhak Shamir (Likud)
Vice Premier and Foreign Affairs	Shimon Peres (Alignment)
Deputy PM and Construction & Housing	David Levy (Likud)
Deputy PM and Education & Culture	Yitzhak Navon (Alignment)
Agriculture	Arie Nehamkin (Alignment)
Communications	Amnon Rubinstein (Shinui) (until 5.26.87)
	Gad Ya'akobi (Alignment) (from 6.9.87)
Defense	Yitzhak Rabin (Alignment)
Economics and Planning	Gad Ya'akobi (Alignment)
Energy & Infrastructures	Moshe Shaḥal (Alignment)
Finance	Moshe Nissim (Likud)
Foreign Affairs	Yitzhak Shamir (Likud)
Health	Shoshana Arbeli Almoslino (Alignment)
Immigrant Absorption	Ya'akov Tzur (Alignment)
Industry and Trade	Ariel Sharon (Likud)
Interior	Yiẓhak Ḥayyim Peretz (Shas) (until 1.6.87)
	Yitzhak Shamir (Likud) (from 1.6.87)
Justice	Avraham Sharir (Likud)
Labor & Welfare	Moshe Katzav (Likud)
Police	Haim Bar-Lev (Alignment)
Religious Affairs	Zevulun Hammer (NRP) (from 10.7.86)
Science & Development	Gideon Pat (Likud)
Tourism	Avraham Sharir (Likud)
Transportation	Ḥayyim Korfu (Likud)
Without Portfolio	Moshe Arens (Likud) (until 9.4.87 from 4.18.88)
Without Portfolio	Mordechai Gur (from 4.18.88)
Without Portfolio	Yigael Hurwitz (Ometz)
Without Portfolio	Yitzhak Modai (Likud)
Without Portfolio	Yiẓhak Ḥayyim Peretz (Shas) (from 5.25.87)
Without Portfolio	Yosef Shapira (not an MK)
Without Portfolio	Ezer Weizman (Alignment)

Soon after Shamir became prime minister, the controversy with Egypt over the fate of Taba, just south of Eilat, was handed over to international arbitration, despite objections in the Likud. The arbitrators decided, just before the elections to the Twelfth Knesset, that Taba belonged to Egypt.

On April 11, 1987, Peres, as foreign minister, reached a secret agreement in London with King Hussein of Jordan for the holding of a peace conference, with the goal of reaching a comprehensive peace agreement between Israel and its neighbors and resolving all aspects of the Palestinian problem. However, when the agreement, of which Peres had not informed Shamir in advance, was brought to the 10-member cabinet (in which the Likud and the Alignment were equally represented) in the beginning of May, there was a tie vote and the agreement was not approved. Seven months later the Intifada broke out, which led to an "iron fist" policy by the IDF, which was led by Minister of Defense Yitzhak Rabin. One of the consequences of the outbreak of the Intifada was the decision of Arab MK Abdel Wahab Darawshe, to leave the Labor Party and form his own parliamentary group – the Arab Democratic Party.

Several months before the elections to the Twelfth Knesset, the Ḥerut Movement and the Israel Liberal Party united into a single party called the Likud.

The Twelfth Knesset, 1988–92

The elections to the Twelfth Knesset were held on November 1, 1988, and the first meeting of the Knesset was held 20 days later, on November 21, 1988.

Table 45. Results of the Elections to the Twelfth Knesset

Electorate:	2,894,267
Valid votes cast	2,073,321
Qualifying threshold (1%)	20,733
Votes per seat	16,786

Table 46. Results of the elections to the Twelfth Knesset by party

Name of list	Number of valid votes	% of total votes	Number of seats	23rd Govt	24th Govt
Likud	709,305	31.1	40	X	X
Alignment	685,363	30.0	39	X*	
Shas	107,709	4.7	6	X	X
Agudat Israel	102,714	4.5	5	X	X
Civil Rights Movement	97,513	4.3	5		
National Religious Party	89,720	3.9	5	X	X
Ḥadash	84,032	3.7	4		
Teḥiyyah	70,730	3.1	3		X**
Mapam	56,345	2.5	3		
Tzomet	45,489	2.0	2		X***
Moledet	44,174	1.9	2		X****
Shinui	39,538	1.7	2		
Degel ha-Torah	34,279	1.5	2	X	X
Progressive List for Peace	33,279	1.5	1		
Arab Democratic Party	27,012	1.2	1		
The Party for the Advancement of the Zionist Idea#	0	0	0		X

\# Broke away from the Likud.
* Left the government on March 15, 1990.
** Left the government on Jan. 21, 1992.
*** Left the government on Dec. 31, 1991.
**** Joined the government on Feb. 5, 1991 and left it on Jan. 21, 1992.

As in the case of the Eleventh Knesset, so in the Twelfth 15 lists were elected, and the steady decline in the number of members elected on the Likud and Alignment lists continued. A new right-wing party, Moledet, led by former Major General Rehavam *Ze'evi, which advocated voluntary transfer of the Arab population from Ereẓ Israel, emerged, gaining only two seats, but enjoying greater legitimacy than Kach owing to the makeup of its membership. The three Zionist parties left of the Alignment – the CRM, Shinui, and Mapam (which ran on its own for the first time since the elections to the Sixth Knesset) – together gained 10 seats, and towards the end of the term of the Twelfth Knesset merged into a single parliamentary group, though for the time being the three parties continued to exist separately outside the Knesset. For the first time the *ḥaredi* "Litvaks" ran in the election as a separate list from Agudat Israel, on a list called Degel ha-Torah. Though the changes from the Eleventh Knesset did not seem too great, this time the right-wing-religious bloc was markedly stronger than the left-wing-Arab bloc.

The new Knesset elected Dov Shilansky from the Likud as its speaker.

It took Likud leader Yitzhak Shamir close to two months to form his new government. Even though he could have formed a right-wing-religious government, Shamir preferred to continue his coalition with the Alignment. Within the Alignment – now made up exclusively of the Labor Party – there were those who objected to entering a new National Unity Government under worse conditions than the two previous governments. One of those who fought against the entry into the government was the secretary general of the party, Uzi Baram, who before the elections had tried to get former President Yitzhak *Navon elected as Labor's leader in place of Peres. But the majority decided in favor of joining the government. While Yitzhak Rabin continued to hold the Ministry of Defense, Peres now assumed the thankless task of minister of finance. Ariel Sharon was once again appointed minister of industry and trade.

As the Intifada continued, and became increasingly more violent and vicious, the United States showed renewed interest in actively trying to find a settlement to the Palestinian problem, indicating that the PLO could be a party to such a settlement if it were to agree to recognize Security Council Resolutions 242 and 338 and depart from the path of terror. On May 14, 1989, the Israeli government, not willing to consider any dealings with the PLO, came out with a peace initiative of its own. At the center of the plan was the opening of talks with Palestinians from the territories – not representatives of the PLO – with the idea of the holding of elections there to choose leaders with whom Israel could negotiate an interim self-government plan. The idea of holding elections in the territories had originally been broached by Rabin before the elections, and the fact that it was adopted by the Likud and the Alignment together was seen as a positive development.

However, soon opposition to the plan emerged within the Likud, led by Sharon, David Levy, and Yitzhak Modai.

Table 47. Members of the Twenty-Third Government (formed on December 22, 1988)

Ministerial Position	Name (party)
Prime Minister	Yitzhak Shamir (Likud)
Second to the Prime Minister and Finance	Shimon Peres (Alignment) (until 3.15.90)
Deputy Prime Minister and Construction & Housing	David Levy (Likud)
Deputy Prime Minister and Education & Culture	Yitzhak Navon (Alignment) (until 3.15.90)
Agriculture	Avraham Katz Oz (Alignment) (until 3.15.90)
Communications	Gad Ya'akobi (Alignment) (until 3.15.90)
Defense	Yitzhak Rabin (Alignment) (until 3.15.90)
Economics and Planning	Yitzhak Modai (Likud, after 3.15.90 the Party for the Advancement of the Zionist Idea)
Energy & Infrastructures	Moshe Shaḥal (Alignment) (until 3.15.90)
Environment	Roni Milo (Likud) (until 3.7.90)
	Rafael Edri (Alignment) (until 3.15.90)
Foreign Affairs	Moshe Arens (Likud)
Health	Ya'akov Tzur (Alignment) (until 3.15.90)
Immigrant Absorption	Yiẓḥak Ḥayyim Peretz (Shas)
Industry and Trade	Ariel Sharon (Likud) (until 2.20.90)
	Moshe Nissim (Likud) (from 3.7.90)
Interior	Aryeh Deri (Shas) (not an MK)
Justice	Dan Meridor (Likud)
Labor & Welfare	Yitzhak Shamir (Likud) (until 3.7.90)
	Roni Milo (Likud) (from 3.7.90)
Police	Haim Bar-Lev (Alignment) (until 3.15.90)
Religious Affairs	Zevulun Hammer (NRP) (from 12.27.88)
Science & Development	Ezer Weizman (Alignment) (until 3.15.90)
Tourism	Gideon Pat (Likud)
Transportation	Moshe Katzav (Likud)
Without Portfolio	Ehud Olmert (Likud)
Without Portfolio	Mordechai Gur (until 3.15.90)
Without Portfolio	Rafael Edri (Alignment) (until 3.7.90)
Without Portfolio	Moshe Nissim (Likud) (until 3.7.90)
Without Portfolio	Avner Ḥai Shaki (NRP) (from 12.27.88)
Without Portfolio	David Magen (Likud) (from 3.7.90)

As practical steps were taken by the new Bush Administration and Egyptian President Hosni Mubarak to implement the plan, major differences of opinion appeared between the two main coalition partners, with Labor warmly supporting Baker's five points and Mubarak's ten points while the Likud hemmed and hawed.

Led to believe by Shas that it would support an alternative government to the one led by Shamir, Peres embarked on what Rabin was later to term "the stinking ploy." The Labor ministers all resigned from the government on March 13, 1990, the resignation going into effect on March 15, when a vote on a motion of no confidence in the government was brought to the Knesset and passed thanks to the absence of five of the six Shas MKs. This was the first and only time that a government in Israel was brought down by a vote of no confidence. Peres was then summoned by the president to form a new government, but in the end he failed. A new right-wing-religious government was finally formed by Shamir in the middle of June, not before some extreme cases of individual MKs switching sides in return for promises of office or other emoluments.

On March 15, 1990, the day of the vote of no confidence, five members of the Likud – all former members of the Liberal Party – broke away from the Likud to form a new parliamentary group called the Party for the Advancement of the Zionist Idea. In Shamir's new government, formed on June 11, 1990, Modai, the leader of the new group, was appointed minister of finance, but not before demanding a scandalous financial guarantee that Shamir would stick to his agreement with him.

At first two of the parties to the right of the Likud – Teḥiyyah and Tzomet – joined the new government, and in the beginning of February 1991, Moledet joined as well, despite opposition by several Likud MKs, including Menaḥem Begin's son, Ze'ev Binyamin *Begin, who felt that the policies advocated by Ze'evi with regard to the Arabs were unacceptable.

Table 48. Members of the Twenty-Fourth Government (formed on June 11, 1990)

Ministerial Position	Name (party)
Prime Minister and Environment and Jerusalem Affairs and Labor & Welfare	Yitzhak Shamir (Likud)
Deputy Prime Minister and Foreign Affairs	David Levy (Likud)
Deputy Prime Minister and Industry & Trade	Moshe Nissim (Likud)
Agriculture	Rafael Eitan (Tzomet) (until 12.31.91)
Communications	Rafael Pinḥasi (Shas)
Construction and Housing	Ariel Sharon (Likud)
Defense	Moshe Arens (Likud)
Economics and Planning	David Magen (Likud)
Education Culture & Sport	Zevulun Hammer (NRP)
Energy & Infrastructures and Science & Technology	Yuval Ne'eman (Teḥiyyah (not an MK) (until 1.21.92)
Finance	Yitzhak Modai (Party for the Advancement of the Zionist Idea; after 3.3.92 the New Liberal Party)
Health	Ehud Olmert (Likud)
Immigrant Absorption	Yiẓḥak Ḥayyim Peretz (Shas)
Industry and Trade	Moshe Nissim (Likud)
Interior	Aryeh Deri (Shas) (not an MK)
Justice	Dan Meridor (Likud)
Police	Roni Milo (Likud)
Religious Affairs	Avner Ḥai Shaki (NRP)
Tourism	Gideon Pat (Likud)
Transportation	Moshe Katzav (Likud)
Without Portfolio	Rehavam Ze'evi (Moledet) (from 2.5.91 to 1.21.92)

One of the issues that the new government had to deal with soon after it was formed was the flood of immigrants that started to arrive from the former Soviet Union. The main problem faced by the government was housing, which was the responsibility of Ariel Sharon, who was appointed minister of construction and housing in the new government. A new concept of "direct absorption" was introduced in an attempt to do away with some of the bureaucracy associated with immigrant absorption. Another major immigration feat directed by the new government was "Operation Solomon," which took place on May 24, 1991, and involved flying 15,000 Ethiopian Jews directly from Addis Ababa to Israel in a single day.

The new government strongly promoted a policy of further economic liberalization and privatization, and one of its notable achievements was ending the monopoly on radio and television broadcasts of the Israel Broadcasting Association.

Following the Gulf War, in which, at the behest of the U.S., Israel remained passive, even though it had suffered at least 40 direct hits by Iraqi SCUD missiles, the peace process was given a new impetus and changed course, with the Madrid Conference at its center.

The Conference convened in the Spanish capital at the end of October 1991 and was followed by bilateral talks between Israel and its neighbors, as well as multilateral talks on specific issues. Israel conditioned its participation on the Palestinians not being represented by the PLO but by representatives of the West Bank and Gaza Strip, who formed part of a joint Jordanian-Palestinian delegation. Though all the other delegations to the Conference were headed by foreign ministers, Israel's delegation was headed by Prime Minister Shamir, who refused to commit Israel to any territorial concessions or to discuss the establishment of a Palestinian state. All Israel was willing to discuss was an autonomy plan for the Palestinians. Israel's most eloquent spokesman at the Conference was the deputy minister in the Prime Minister's Office, Binyamin *Netanyahu, who had been elected to the Twelfth Knesset on the Likud list after a successful term as Israeli ambassador to the UN.

Following Israel's policy of constraint in the course of the Gulf War, and the Madrid Conference, a significant improvement occurred in Israel's international status, with numerous states reestablishing diplomatic relations with it, or – like China and India – establishing relations with Israel for the first time. The 45-year Arab boycott (which had been declared by the Arab League in 1946) was also implemented now less rigorously, and the U.S. involvement in the peace process intensified. However, towards the end of this period the tension between Israel and the U.S. grew against the background of Washington's making a grant of $10 billion worth of American loan guarantees for the absorption of immigrants conditional on Israel's stopping all settlement activities in the territories.

Despite the impressive achievements of the government in the foreign arena, Shamir's government faltered as a result of the opposition of the three right-wing parties – Tzomet, Teḥiyyah, and Moledet – to the Madrid process. All three left the government in the course of December 1991 and January 1992.

In the last few months of its existence, the Knesset passed several important pieces of legislation. In March 1992 the Knesset passed two Basic Laws dealing with civil rights – Basic Law: Freedom of Occupation and Basic Law: Human Dignity and Freedom. Other important legislation addressed the problem of members of the Knesset who for personal political gain deserted their parties and changed sides, and the problem of political instability, both of which led to growing public cynicism and disaffection with the political system. The latter problem was addressed by means of a new version of Basic Law: the Government, which introduced the system of the direct election of the prime minister. The new law, which was to go into effect only in the elections to the Fourteenth Knesset in 1996, had been introduced by four members of the Knesset from four different groups: Ariel Lynn of the Likud, David Libai of the Labor Party, Amnon *Rubinstein of Shinui, and Yehoash Tzidon of Tzomet.

One of the manifestations of the political instability and disaffection in this period was the increase in the number of petitions to the High Court of Justice – some of them presented by members of the Knesset – in connection with the work of the Knesset.

Left without a Knesset majority for his government after the departure of Tzomet, Teḥiyyah, and Moledet, Shamir called for early elections. Prior to the elections Yitzhak Rabin decided once again to contend for the Labor Party leadership, winning in primaries held for the first time in the Labor Party, with just over the mandatory 40 percent of the vote, over Peres, Ora Namir, and Yisrael Kessar. Primaries were also held in the Labor Party for its list to the Thirteenth Knesset.

The Thirteenth Knesset 1992–1996

The elections to the Thirteenth Knesset were held on June 23, 1992, and the first meeting of the Knesset was held 20 days later, on July 13, 1992.

Table 49. Results of the Elections to the Thirteenth Knesset

Electorate:	3,409,015
Valid votes cast	2,616,841
Qualifying threshold (1.5%)	39,253
Votes per seat	20,715

In the elections to the Thirteenth Knesset, the Labor Party under the leadership of Rabin won an impressive victory, increasing its Knesset representation by 50 percent – from 30 to 44 seats. Meretz also managed to increase the number of its seats from 10 to 12, while the Likud suffered a bitter defeat, losing eight of the 40 seats it had held in the Twelfth Knesset. While some of the Likud votes undoubtedly went to Labor, some former Likud voters opted this time for Tzomet, which quadrupled its strength from two to eight seats. While the left made real gains in the election, the defeat of the right was, in fact, marginal, and it might well have won the elec-

Table 50. Results of the elections to the Thirteenth Knesset by party

Name of list	Number of valid votes	% of total votes	Number of seats	25th Govt	26th Govt
Labor	906,810	34.7	44	X	X
Likud	651,229	24.9	32		
Meretz	250,667	9.6	12	X	X
Tzomet	166,366	6.4	8		
National Religious Party	129,663	5.0	6		
Shas	129,663	4.9	6	X*	
Yahadut ha-Torah	86,167	3.3	4		
Ḥadash	62,545	2.4	3	#	#
Moledet	62,269	2.4	3		
Arab Democratic Party	40,788	1.6	2	#	#
Yi'ud	0	0	0	X**	X

* Left the government on September 14, 1993.
** Broke away from Tzomet on Feb. 7, 1994 and joined the government on January 9, 1995.
\# Supported the government from outside the coalition.

tion had it not lost several tens of thousands of votes cast for several right-wing splinter groups that did not pass the 1.5% qualifying threshold. The Ashkenazi *ḥaredi* Party, *Yahadut ha-Torah*, which was made up of Agudat Israel and Degel ha-Torah, lost three seats, while the Sephardi *ḥaredi* party, Shas, kept its strength at six.

It took Rabin three weeks to form a new coalition, and he was able to present his new government at the first meeting of the Thirteenth Knesset, in which Shevaḥ Weiss was elected speaker of the Knesset. The coalition was made up of Labor, Meretz, and Shas, which together commanded the support of 62 members of the Knesset and was supported by an additional five MKs from Ḥadash and the Arab Democratic Party, who did not join the coalition, but reached an agreement with Labor.

Table 51. Members of the Twenty-Fifth Government (formed on July 13, 1992)

Ministerial Position	Name (party)
Prime Minister	Yitzhak Rabin (Labor) (assassinated on 11.4.95)
Second to the Prime Minister and Foreign Affairs	Shimon Peres (acting Prime Minister from 11.5.95)
Agriculture & Rural Development	Ya'acov Tzur (Labor) (not an MK)
Communications	Moshe Shaḥal (Labor) (until 6.7.93) Shulamit Aloni (Meretz) (from 6.7.93)
Construction & Housing	Binyamin Ben-Eliezer (Labor)
Defense	Yitzhak Rabin (Labor) (assassinated on 11.4.95) Shimon Peres (Labor) (acting from 11.5.95)
Economics and Planning	Shimon Sheetrit (Labor) (until 6.18.95) Yossi Beilin (Labor) (from 6.18.95)

Table 51 continued

Ministerial Position	Name (party)
Education & Culture	Shulamit Aloni (Meretz) (until 5.11.93) Yitzhak Rabin (Labor) (until 6.7.93) Amnon Rubinstein (Meretz) (from 6.7.93) (the Ministry changed its name to Education, Culture and Sport)
Energy & Infrastructures	Amnon Rubinstein (Meretz) (until 6.7.93) Moshe Shaḥal (Labor) (until 1.9.95) Gonen Segev (Yi'ud) (from 1.9.95)
Environment	Ora Namir (Labor) (until 12.31.92) Yossi Sarid (Meretz) (from 12.31.92)
Finance	Avraham Beiga Shoḥat (Labor)
Health	Haim Ramon (Labor) (until 2.8.94) Yitzhak Rabin (Labor) (from 2.8.94 until 6.1.94) Efraim Sneh (Labor) (from 6.1.94)
Immigrant Absorption	Yair Tsaban (Meretz)
Industry and Trade	Micha Harish (Labor)
Interior	Arie Deri (Shas) (until 5.11.93) Yitzhak Rabin (Labor) (from 5.11.93 until 6.7.93) Aryeh Deri (Shas) (from 6.7.93 until 9.14.93) Yitzhak Rabin (Labor) (from 9.14.93 until 2.27.95) Uzi Baram (Labor) (until 6.7.95) David Libai (Labor) (until 7.18.95) Ehud Barak (Labor) (from 7.18.95) (not an MK)
Jerusalem Affairs	Yitzhak Rabin (Labor) (until 12.31.92 when Ministry was canceled)
Justice	David Libai (Labor)
Labor & Welfare	Yitzhak Rabin (Labor) (until 12.31.92) Ora Namir (Labor) (from 12.31.92)
Police	Moshe Shaḥal (Labor)
Religious Affairs	Yitzhak Rabin (Labor) (until 2.27.95) Shimon Sheetrit (Labor) (from 2.27.95)
Science & Technology	Amnon Rubinstein (Meretz) (until 12.31.92) Shimon Sheetrit (Labor) (until 6.7.93) Shulamit Aloni (Meretz) (from 6.7.93) (Ministry changed name to Science and Arts on 8.1.93)
Tourism	Uzi Baram (Labor)
Transportation	Yisrael Kessar (Labor)
Without Portfolio	Shulamit Aloni (Meretz) (from 5.11.93 until 6.7.93)
Without Portfolio	Aryeh Deri (Shas) (from 5.11.93 until 6.7.93)

In the economic sphere, the Labor-led government, with Avraham Beiga *Shoḥat as minister of finance, did not withdraw from the basically liberal policy of previous governments and affirmed the idea of privatization in principle. It should be noted that the most successful process of privatization had been carried out in the previous few years within the framework of the Histadrut-owned industrial conglomerate Koor by Benny *Gaon.

While Labor did not stop allocating funds to the Jewish settlements in Judea, Samaria, and the Gaza Strip, and to the yeshivot, it did pay greater attention to the development towns and the Arab sector. At the beginning of 1995 the government decided not to introduce a tax on stock market earnings, which Shoḥat had prepared. A watered-down version of this law was finally introduced in the course of the Fifteenth Knesset.

The first year of the coalition's existence was riddled with internal bickering between the *ḥaredi* Shas and the secular Meretz. One of the main foci of tension was Shas's objection to Shulamit Aloni's position as minister of education and culture, and some of her outspoken remarks that offended its leaders. A compromise was finally reached in June 1993, when Aloni was replaced in the Ministry of Education and Culture by Amnon Rubinstein, also from Meretz, while a new portfolio of Science, Arts and Communications was concocted for Aloni. The Ministry of Interior, originally given to Aryeh *Deri of Shas, saw numerous changes of minister – at first due to the Shas-Meretz imbroglio and later, after Shas had left the coalition, due to various internal Labor constraints.

A significant development in the course of the Thirteenth Knesset, which had both political and economic implications, was an upheaval in the Histadrut, which had been controlled by the Labor Party, and its predecessors, Ha-Po'el ha-Ẓa'ir and Mapai, since its establishment in 1920. Though the Histadrut started losing power in the 1980s, largely because of the financial difficulties of Koor, the kibbutzim, and the Kupat Ḥolim health fund, it was still considered one of the important power centers of the Labor Party. In the beginning of February 1994, Minister of Health Haim *Ramon resigned his position due to opposition in the Labor Party to his National Health Insurance Bill, which involved the separation of Kupat Ḥolim from the Histadrut. In April, perceiving the weakness of the official Labor candidate, Haim Haberfeld, for the position of secretary general of the Histadrut in the forthcoming elections, Ramon decided to run for the position, at the head of his own list. In the elections held on May 10, Ramon won an impressive victory. Even though he was temporarily suspended from the Labor Party, Ramon finally managed to get his National Health Insurance Law through the Knesset on June 15, 1994, and was eventually reinstated in the Labor Party.

Around the time that Ramon left the government, three members of Tzomet broke away from it to form Yi'ud, and in January 1995 one of the three, Gonen Segev, joined the government as minister of energy and infrastructure.

The first year of the Labor-led government did not seem to bode well for the peace process. In December 1992, the government decided to expel over 400 *Hamas and Islamic Jihad activists to Lebanon, and the Washington talks that followed the Madrid Conference came to a standstill. However, at first unknown to the Israeli public and even the American government, secret negotiations were held with PLO representatives in Oslo. The Oslo process, which had begun as a private initiative, with the direct involvement of Deputy Minister of Finance Yossi *Beilin, finally became in May 1993 an official process, backed by both Prime Minister Rabin and his deputy and foreign minister, Shimon Peres. When news of the forthcoming agreement became known at the end of August 1993, the Israeli public was taken by surprise by the sudden willingness to recognize the PLO and hand over to it control over Gaza and an area around Jericho in the first stage and the rest of the major Palestinian towns in the second stage. Nevertheless, at this stage there was no talk of the dismantling of settlements.

On September 13 Rabin and Yasser *Arafat signed the Declaration of Principles (DoP) in Washington and addressed letters to President Clinton in which Israel recognized the PLO and the PLO recognized Israel. Shas left the government the following day. Nevertheless, the Accords were approved by the Knesset on September 23. The vote took place in the form of a vote on a motion of no confidence in the government, in which 61 MKs supported the government (Labor, Meretz, and the Arab parties), 50 voted against it, eight members abstained, and one stayed away. The eight who abstained were five of the six members of Shas and three members of the Likud.

The Agreement with the Palestinians was followed on October 26, 1994, by the signing of a peace treaty with Jordan, with which *de facto* relations had existed for many years. This agreement involved only minor territorial changes and was approved by the Knesset on October 25 by a majority of 105, with the three Moledet MKs voting against, six members abstaining, and six absent.

While the initial public reaction to the Oslo Accords was relatively mild, the signing of the second stage in the process – the Taba Agreement of September 28, 1995, which involved Israeli withdrawal from all the major towns in Judea and Samaria, except Hebron, and the holding of elections in the West Bank and Gaza Strip for a Palestinian self-governing authority – was met with a wave of demonstrations against the government and its policy. Some of these demonstrations, organized by various right-wing groups and frequently attended by leaders of the Likud, were accompanied by violence and incitement against the government in general and Rabin in particular. Even though several members of the Likud had abstained in the vote on the DoP and were willing to keep an open mind on the whole process, the Likud as a whole was opposed to it. The Likud's campaign against the Oslo process was led by its new leader, Binyamin Netanyahu, who had been elected in primaries in March 1993.

At the end of a counterdemonstration by supporters of the peace process, held at Kikar Malkhei Yisrael (now Rabin Square) in Tel Aviv on November 4, 1995, Prime Minister Yitzhak Rabin was assassinated by Yigal Amir, a Jewish assassin who acted independently. The event caused deep shock throughout the country, and was almost unanimously condemned by everyone, including some of Rabin's most bitter opponents. Eighteen days after the assassination Shimon Peres formed a minority government that was nevertheless approved by the Knesset. Ramon was now reinstated as minister of the interior.

Table 52. Members of the Twenty-Sixth Government (formed on November 22, 1995)

Ministerial Position	Name (party)
Prime Minister	Shimon Peres (Labor)
Minister in PM's Office	Yossi Beilin (Labor)
Construction & Housing	Binyamin Ben-Eliezer (Labor)
Agriculture & Rural Development	Ya'akov Tsur (Labor) (not an MK)
Communications	Shulamit Aloni (Meretz)
Defense	Shimon Peres (Labor)
Education, Culture & Sport	Amnon Rubinstein (Meretz)
Energy & Infrastructures	Gonen Segev (Yi'ud)
Environment	Yossi Sarid (Meretz)
Finance	Avraham Beiga Shoḥat (Labor)
Foreign Affairs	Ehud Barak (Labor) (not an MK)
Health	Efraim Sneh (Labor)
Immigrant Absorption	Yair Tsaban (Meretz)
Industry and Trade	Micha Harish (Labor)
Interior	Haim Ramon (Labor)
Internal Security	Moshe Shaḥal (Labor)
Justice	David Libai (Labor)
Labor & Welfare	Ora Namir (Labor) (until 5.21.96 – appointed ambassador to China)
Religious Affairs	Shimon Sheetrit (Labor)
Science & Arts	Shulamit Aloni (Meretz)
Tourism	Uzi Baram (Labor)
Transportation	Yisrael Kessar (Labor)

Table 53. Results of the Elections to the Fourteenth Knesset

Electorate:	3,933,250
Valid votes cast	2,973,580
Qualifying threshold (1.5%)	44,604
Votes per seat	24,779

Table 54. Results of the elections to the Fourteenth Knesset by party

Name of list	Number of valid votes	% of total votes	Number of seats	27th Govt
Labor	818,741	27.5	34	
Likud-Gesher-Tzomet	767,401	25.8	32	X
Shas	259,796	8.7	10	X
National Religious Party	240,271	8.1	9	X
Meretz	226,275	7.5	9	
Yisrael be-Aliyah	174,994	5.8	7	X
Ḥadash	129,455	4.4	5	
Yahadut ha-Torah	98,657	3.3	4	X
The Third Way	96,474	3.2	4	X
United Arab List	89,514	3.0	4	
Moledet	72,002	2.4	2	

Table 55. Direct election of the prime minister May 29, 1996

Candidate	Votes	Percentage
Binyamin Netanyahu	1,501,023	50.5
Shimon Peres	1,471,566	49.5

Though the shock of Rabin's assassination made it seem unlikely that Peres would lose the approaching elections, in which for the first time the prime minister was to be elected directly together with the Fourteenth Knesset, there were several factors working against Labor. The first was a rise, in the course of March 1996, in the number of terrorist attacks carried out by members of the Hamas and Islamic Jihad, starting in March 1996. The second was the departure from the Labor Party of two of its members – Avigdor Kahalani and Emanuel Zissman – against the background of Labor's willingness to withdraw from the Golan Heights within the framework of a peace agreement with Syria. In March 1996, the two set up a new parliamentary group called The Third Way, which formally opposed any Israeli concessions on the Golan.

However, towards the end of the Knesset's term the Likud too lost two of its members – David Levy and David Magen – who in March 1996 broke away to form an ethnic party with a social orientation, called Gesher.

The Fourteenth Knesset – 1996–99

The elections to the Fourteenth Knesset were held on May 29, 1996, and the first meeting of the Knesset was held 19 days later, on June 17, 1996.

In the elections to the Fourteenth Knesset the Likud, running in a single list with Tzomet and Gesher, received only 32 seats, compared to the 40 that the Likud and Tzomet had received in the Thirteenth Knesset. Labor, losing 10 of the seats it had originally held in the Thirteenth Knesset, received 34, but since Binyamin Netanyahu received close to 30,000 votes more than Shimon Peres in the direct elections for the prime minister, it was he who formed the new government.

One of the unforeseen results of the direct elections for prime minister, which gave the voters a double vote – one for a Knesset list and one for prime minister – was a further weakening of the two main parties, which together received only 66 seats compared to the 76 that they had received in the Thirteenth Knesset. This resulted from the splitting of votes between the two big parties on the prime minister vote and the smaller parties on the Knesset vote.

The religious lists together increased the number of their seats from 16 to 23. Shas gained four additional seats, the NRP gained three, and Yahadut ha-Torah kept its four. The Arab parties – Ḥadash and the United Arab List (UAL) – together increased their strength from five to nine seats. For the first time, members of the more moderate faction in the Muslim Movement entered the Knesset, within the framework of the UAL.

Amongst the new lists, running for the first time, the new immigrant list Yisrael be-Aliyah, led by Natan *Sharansky, received seven seats. Yisrael be-Aliyah, representing immigrants from the former Soviet Union, was the first Ashkenazi ethnic party to emerge since the foundation of the state, when the pre-state Aliyah Ḥadashah ran as the Progressive Party. The Third Way received four seats.

The Fourteenth Knesset elected Dan Tichon of the Likud as its speaker. Netanyahu presented his government – made up of all the right-wing and all the religious parties, which together controlled 66 Knesset seats – on the morrow of the new Knesset's first sitting. Yitzhak (Itzik) Mordechai was appointed minister of defense and David Levy minister for foreign affairs. Ariel Sharon was not included in Netanyahu's original distribution of portfolios, but three weeks after the government was formed, the Ministry of National Infrastructures, given powers that in the past had been vested in various other ministries, was created for Sharon.

Table 56. Members of the Twenty-Seventh Government (Formed on June 18, 1996)

Ministerial Position	Name (party)
Prime Minister and Construction & Housing	Binyamin Netanyahu (Likud-Gesher-Tzomet)
Deputy PM, Agriculture & Rural Development and Environment	Rafael Eitan (Likud-Gesher-Tzomet, from 3.4.99 Tzomet)
Deputy PM, Tourism and in charge of Arab Sector	Moshe Katzav (Likud-Gesher-Tzomet)
Deputy PM and Foreign Affairs	David Levy (Likud-Gesher-Tzomet) (until 1.6.98)
Deputy PM and Education, Culture & Sport	Zevulun Hammer (NRP) (d. 1.20.98)
Communications	Limor Livnat (Likud-Gesher-Tzomet)
Defense	Yitzhak Mordechai (Likud-Gesher-Tzomet) (until 1.25.99) Moshe Arens (Likud) (from 1.27.99) (not an MK)
Education, Culture & Sport	Zevulun Hammer (NRP) (d. 1.20.98) Yiẓḥak Levy (NRP) (from 2.25.98)
Energy & Infrastructures	Yiẓḥak Levy (NRP) until 7.8.96)
Finance	Dan Meridor (Likud-Gesher-Tzomet) (until 6.20.97) Ya'akov Ne'eman (from 7.9.97 until 12.18.98) (not an MK) Meir Sheetrit (Likud) (from 2.23.99)
Foreign Affairs	David Levy (Likud-Gesher-Tzomet) (until 1.6.98) Binyamin Netanyahu (Likud-Gesher-Tzomet) (from 1.6.96 until 10.13.98) Ariel Sharon (Likud-Gesher-Tzomet) (from 10.13.98)
Health	Tsaḥi Hanegbi (Likud-Gesher-Tzomet) (until 11.12.96) Yehoshua Maẓa (Likud-Gesher-Tzomet) (from 11.12.96)
Immigrant Absorption	Yoel-Yuli Edelstein (Yisrael be-Aliyah)
Industry and Trade	Natan Sharansky (Yisrael be-Aliyah)
Interior	Eliyahu Suissa (Shas) (not an MK)
Internal Security	Avigdor Kahalani (Third Way)

Table 56 continued

Ministerial Position	Name (party)
Justice	Ya'akov Ne'eman (until 8.10.96) (not an MK) Tzaḥi Hanegbi (Likud-Gesher-Tzomet) (from 4.9.96)
Labor & Welfare	Eliyahu Yishai (Shas)
National Infrastructures	Ariel Sharon (Likud-Gesher-Tzomet) (from 7.8.96)
Religious Affairs	Binyamin Netanyahu (Likud-Gesher-Tzomet) (until 8.7.96) Eliyahu Suissa (Shas) (from 8.7.96 until 8.12.97) (not an MK) Zevulun Hammer (NRP) (from 8.22.97, d. 1.20.98) Yiẓḥak Levy (NRP) (from 2.25.98 until 9.13.98) Eliyahu Suissa (Shas) (from 9.13.98) (not an MK)
Science	Ze'ev Binyamin Begin (Likud-Gesher-Tzomet) (until 1.16.97) Binyamin Netanyahu (until 7.9.97)
Science and Technology	Mikhael Eitan (Likud-Gesher-Tzomet) (from 7.9.97 until 7.13.98) Silvan Shalom (Likud-Gesher-Tzomet) (from 7.13.98)
Tourism and in charge of Arab Sector	Moshe Katzav (Likud-Gesher-Tzomet)
Transportation	Yiẓḥak Levy (NRP) (until 2.25.98) Shaul Yahalom (NRP) (from 2.25.98)
Without Portfolio	Shaul Amor (Likud-Gesher-Tzomet) (from 1.20.99)

The new system was designed to strengthen the power of the prime minister at the expense of the Knesset, but this goal was not achieved, because of the weakness of the prime minister's own party. The new system was also to have reduced the horse-trading that traditionally took place before the formation of each new government. But instead, it increased the number of such deals, since now each of the candidates for prime minister tried to gain the support of the smaller lists for his candidature before the elections, and once one of the candidates was elected, he still had to negotiate terms with each potential coalition partner. The new system also further weakened party discipline in the Knesset. Party discipline had started to weaken following the introduction of primaries for the selection of the Knesset lists in the big parties. Members of the Knesset, who had gotten on their parties' lists after being chosen by the members of their parties, now felt greater loyalty to those who had voted for them than to the leadership of their parties.

Netanyahu's government was characterized by a succession of scandals, some around his own political style, some around controversial decisions, such as the appointment of attorney Ya'akov Ne'eman, who was not a member of the Knesset, as minister of justice, the appointment of Tzaḥi Hanegbi as Ne'eman's successor, and the appointment of attorney Roni

Bar-On as state attorney. Ne'eman resigned when a police investigation was launched against him, which did not prevent his being appointed minister of finance, and once again resigning when he was indicted (though he was subsequently acquitted). Tzaḥi Hanegbi was also investigated, but the state attorney did not object to his appointment as minister of justice. Bar-On's curious appointment as state attorney in January 1997 lasted for just one day. Though Bar-On's credentials as an attorney were not denied, he was not viewed as having the appropriate background and experience for the job, and was perceived as the candidate of certain public and political figures, including former Minister of the Interior Aryeh Deri, against whom a police investigation was underway on suspicion of misappropriating funds. Bar-On was later elected to the Sixteenth Knesset on the Likud list.

Even though Netanyahu had opposed the Oslo process from the beginning, he continued to fulfill Israel's obligations under the Taba Agreement, and in the Protocol Concerning the Redeployment in Hebron of January 15, 1997, reached an agreement with Arafat on an Israeli withdrawal from the Arab parts of Hebron and a continued withdrawal from additional territories in the West Bank, in return for a Palestinian undertaking to complete the process of amending the Palestine National Covenant and to fight terror. The new agreement was passed by the Knesset, with the support of the opposition, by a vote of 87 in favor, 17 against, one abstention, and five members absent. On October 23, 1998, Netanyahu signed the Wye River Memorandum, dealing with steps to facilitate the implementation of the Taba Agreement. This agreement was approved by the Knesset in a vote of confidence in the prime minister on November 17, 1998, again with the support of the opposition, by a vote of 75 in favor, 19 against, nine abstentions, and 17 members absent.

On June 3, 1997, a year after the elections, former Chief of Staff Ehud *Barak, the most highly decorated Israeli officer in the history of the state, who had been elected to the Fourteenth Knesset, was elected in primaries as leader of the Labor Party after he defeated MKs Dr. Yossi *Beilin, Prof. Shelomo Ben-Ami, and Dr. Efraim Sneh with around 50% of the vote.

Throughout the term of the Fourteenth Knesset the *ḥaredi* parties bitterly attacked the judicial system in general, which in the eyes of these parties had an anti-religious bias, and the president of the Supreme Court, Aharon *Barak, in particular, for his activist approach to the functioning of the Court.

In the course of the Fourteenth Knesset there were numerous changes within and among the parliamentary groups, which besides creating an atmosphere of instability at the time, were to bring about changes – some temporary, some more permanent – in the Israeli political map. Among the more significant changes were the following:

Two Knesset members broke away from Yisrael be-Aliyah to form a new immigrant group to its right; Ze'ev Binyamin Begin and two additional members left the Likud to form a group to its right, taking the name Ḥerut; while one member of Tzomet joined Moledet. Prior to the elections to the Fifteenth Knesset and in their aftermath, all these various groups to the right of the Likud started to merge into what was to finally emerge as the National Union.

Several members of the Labor Party, the Likud, and Tzomet left their parliamentary groups to form the new Center Party, with ambitions to become a new political force in the center of the political map. The Center Party was led by Itzik Mordechai, who resigned from the Likud and his post as minister of defense. Another center party that reemerged in the course of the Fourteenth Knesset was Shinui, which was reinstated as an independent political group by Avraham Poraz after he left Meretz and was joined by a member who left Tzomet.

Finally, three members, headed by the chairman of the New Histadrut, Amir *Peretz, left the Labor Party to form a new workers group with a social agenda, under the name Am Eḥad.

Despite frequent changes of ministers in the Ministry of Finance, the government's policy was generally based on budgetary constraint, for the purpose of containing the rate of inflation, while the Bank of Israel implemented a high interest rate policy. The combination of these two policies led to a slowdown in the economy, and bitter criticism of the government's policy by the opposition. The main reason for the calling of early elections to the Fifteenth Knesset was the government's difficulty in getting the budget approved by the Knesset.

The Fifteenth Knesset, 1999–2003

The elections to the Fifteenth Knesset were held on May 17, 1999, and the first meeting of the Knesset was held 21 days later, on June 7, 1999.

Table 57. Results of the Elections to the Fifteenth Knesset

Electorate:	4,285,428
Valid votes cast	3,309,416
Qualifying threshold (1.5%)	49,672
Votes per seat	25,936

In the direct elections for prime minister Ehud Barak, the newly elected chairman of the Labor Party, won an impressive and clear-cut victory over his rival from the Likud, Binyamin Netanyahu. However, despite the fact that the Labor Party had run in a single list with David Levy's ethnic party Gesher and the moderate religious party Meimad, One Israel, as the list was called, received only 26 seats in the Fifteenth Knesset – eight seats less than Labor had received in the Fourteenth. The Likud also crashed, receiving only 19 seats compared to 32 in the previous Knesset. Thus, One Israel and the Likud together commanded together only 45 seats in the Fifteenth Knesset compared to 66 in the Fourteenth Knesset. Soon after his defeat, Binyamin Netanyahu resigned from the Knesset and the leadership of the Likud, and was replaced by the veteran Ariel Sharon.

Shas emerged as the big winner of the elections, increasing its representation from 10 to 17, largely at the expense of the

Table 58. Results of the elections to the Fifteenth Knesset by party

Name of list	Number of valid votes	% of total votes	Number of seats	28th Govt	29th Govt
One Israel (Labor-Gesher-Meimad)	670,484	20.2	26	X	X#
Likud	468,103	14.1	19		X
Shas	430.676	13.0	17	X*	X##
Meretz	253,525	7.6	10	X**	
Yisrael be-Aliyah	171,705	5.1	6	X*	X
Shinui	167,748	5.0	6		
The Center Party	165,622	5.0	6	X	
National Religious Party	140,307	4.2	5	X***	X
Yahadut ha-Torah	125,741	3.7	5		X
United Arab List	114,810	3.4	5		
The National Union	100,181	3.0	4		X###
Ḥadash	87,022	2.6	3		
Yisrael Beitenu	86,153	2.6	4		X
Am Eḥad	66,143	1.9	2		X####
Balad	66,103	1.9	2		
Gesher	0	0	0	X	X#####

* Left the government on July 11, 2000.
** Left the government on June 24, 2000.
*** Left the government on July 12, 2000.
\# Left the government on November 2, 2002.
\## Left the government on May 23, 2002 and returned on June 3, 2002.
\### Left the government on March 14, 2002.
\#### Left the government on February 22, 2002.
\##### Broke away from One Israel and left the government on August 4, 2000; rejoined the government on April 8, 2002 and left on July 30, 2002.

Table 59. Direct election of the prime minister May 17, 1999

Candidate	Votes	Percentage
Ehud Barak	1,791,020	56.1
Binyamin Netanyahu	1,402,474	43.9

Likud. Though Shas had emerged as a Sephardi *ḥaredi* party, and most of its Knesset representatives were *ḥaredim*, the vast majority of its supporters were traditional in religious outlook, attracted to Shas because of the sense of pride and power that the party bestowed on them. The Center Party, which everyone expected to become a new and more successful version of Dash, disappointed with only six seats. Shinui, with a new leader – journalist and TV personality Yosef (Tomi) *Lapid – and an agenda clearly calling for a reduction in the power of the religious parties, received votes that the Center Party had hoped to get. On the extreme right two lists – the National Union and Yisrael Beitenu – received four seats each. Yisrael Beitenu, which had started off as a predominantly Russian new immigrant party to the right of Yisrael be-Aliyah and was led by a former member of Prime Minister Netanyahu's staff, Avigdor Lieberman, soon merged with the National Union – a list made up of three small parties: Moledet, Tekumah, and Ḥerut. Two parties that vanished from the political map were Tzomet and The Third Way.

The Fifteenth Knesset elected Avraham Burg from the Labor Party as its speaker. Burg, who had not received a ministerial appointment in Barak's government, had contested Barak's candidate for speaker, Shalom Simhon, in the One Israel parliamentary group, and won. In the course of his term he insisted on his right to carry out an independent policy. The Knesset also elected Moshe *Katzav of the Likud as Israel's eighth president. Katzav defeated Labor candidate Shimon Peres.

Barak had hoped to form a government rapidly, but it took him almost two months to put a coalition together. Owing to the weakness of One Israel, and seeking to form as broad and stable a government as possible, Barak finally put together an unlikely coalition. The coalition was joined by Meretz from the left, the Center Party, two religious parties – Shas and the NRP – and Yisrael be-Aliyah. Altogether, the new coalition was supported by 70 MKs but was to prove to be fickle and unstable, and this largely due to the fact that Meretz – abhorred by the religious parties – was the most influential coalition partner, and the fact that the religious parties and Yisrael be-Aliyah felt that Barak was willing to make too many concessions to the Palestinians.

Table 60. Members of the Twenty-Eighth Government (Formed on July 6, 1999)

Ministerial Position	Name (party)
Prime Minister and Defense	Ehud Barak (One Israel)
Deputy PM and Communications	Binyamin Ben-Eliezer (One Israel)
Deputy PM and Transportation	Yitzhak Mordechai (Center Party) (until 5.30.00)
Deputy PM and Foreign Affairs	David Levy (One Israel) (until 8.4.00)
Minister in PM's Office	Haim Ramon (One Israel)
Minister in PM's Office for Social Issues and Dispersions	Michael Melchior (One Israel)
Agriculture & Rural Development	Ḥayyim Oron (Meretz) (8.5.99–6.24.00) (resigned from Knesset) Ehud Barak (One Israel) (until 8.5.99 and from 9.24.00)
Construction and Housing	Yiẓḥak Levy (NRP) (until 7.12.00) (resigned from Knesset) Binyamin Ben-Eliezer (One Israel) (from 10.11.00)
Education	Yossi Sarid (Meretz) (until 6.24.00) Ehud Barak (from 9.24.00)
Environment	Dalia Itzik (One Israel)
Finance	Avraham Beiga Shoḥat (One Israel)
Foreign Affairs	David Levy (One Israel) (until 8.4.00) Shelomo Ben-Ami (One Israel) (from 11.2.00)
Health	Shelomo Benizri (Shas) (until 7.11.00) Roni Milo (Center Party) (from 8.10.00)
Immigrant Absorption	Ehud Barak (One Israel) (until 8.5.99) Yuli Tamir (One Israel) (from 8.5.00) (not an MK)

Table 60 continued

Ministerial Position	Name (party)
Industry and Trade	Ran Cohen (Meretz) (until 6.24.00) Ehud Barak (One Israel) (from 9.24.00)
Interior	Natan Sharansky (Yisrael be-Aliyah) (until 7.11.00) Haim Ramon (One Israel) (from 10.11.00)
Internal Security	Shelomo Ben-Ami (One Israel)
Justice	Yossi Beilin (One Israel) (resigned from Knesset)
Labor & Welfare	Eliyahu Yishai (Shas) (until 7.11.00) Ra'anan Cohen (One Israel) (from 8.10.00)
National Infrastructures	Eliahu Suissa (Shas) (until 7.11.00) Avraham Beiga Shoḥat (One Israel) (from 10.11.00)
Regional Cooperation	Shimon Peres
Religious Affairs	Yiẓḥak Cohen (Shas) (until 7.11.00) Yossi Beilin (One Israel) (from 10.11.00) (resigned from Knesset)
Science	Ehud Barak (One Israel) (until 8.5.99)
Science, Culture and Sport	Mattan Vilnai (One Israel) (from 8.5.99) (resigned from Knesset)
Tourism	Ehud Barak (One Israel) (until 8.5.99) Amnon Lipkin-Shaḥak (Center Party) (from 8.5.00)
Transportation	Amnon Lipkin-Shaḥak (Center Party) (from 10.11.00)

When Barak began his term as prime minister, there was still great optimism in most parts of the public regarding the chances that the peace process would enter its third and final stage, leading to the establishment of a Palestinian state. There was also optimism regarding progress on the Syrian front. However, the only political move that Barak succeeded in implementing was a unilateral withdrawal from Southern Lebanon, which he had promised in his election campaign. Despite the far-reaching territorial concessions that Barak was willing to make to the Palestinians, including the subject of Jerusalem and involving over 90 percent of the territory of the West Bank and Gaza Strip, negotiations with Arafat in Camp David in July 2000, under the auspices of President Clinton, came to naught. Between June and August 2000, all of Barak's coalition partners except the Center Party left the government, while the Center Party was on the verge of disintegration, partially due to charges of sexual harassment brought against its leader, former Minister of Defense Itzik Mordechai, which caused him to resign from the government and then from the Knesset.

Following a provocative visit to the Temple Mount by Opposition leader Ariel Sharon on September 28, 2000, the second Intifada broke out in October. Sharon's visit was, however, merely a pretext. The decision of the Palestinian leadership to embark on a violent road was apparently a strategic one. Violence also erupted in October in the Israeli Arab sector, resulting in 13 Israeli Arabs being killed.

Having lost his parliamentary majority, and with growing economic difficulties resulting from the world economic crisis and the Intifada, Barak decided to call for new elections for prime minister, but not for the Knesset. Barak, who faced Ariel Sharon in these elections, suffered a stinging defeat, losing close to half the votes he had received 19 months earlier.

Table 61. Direct election of the prime minister February 6, 2001

Candidate	Votes	Percentage
Ariel Sharon	1,698,077	62.4
Ehud Barak	1,023,944	37.6

Not long after the election Barak followed Netanyahu's footsteps and resigned his Knesset seat and the Labor leadership, though not before considering joining the government Sharon was about to form.

It took Sharon one month to form his government. He convinced Labor-Meimad (after Gesher had left One Israel) to join, appointing Shimon Peres as foreign minister and Binyamin (Fuad) *Ben-Eliezer as minister of defense. In addition to Labor-Meimad, all the religious parties, all the right-wing parties, and Am Eḥad joined the coalition. The government was so big that it was necessary to add a table in the Knesset plenary hall to accommodate its ministers.

Table 62. Members of the Twenty-Ninth Government (formed on March 7, 2001)

Ministerial Position	Name (party)
Prime Minister	Ariel Sharon (Likud)
Deputy PM and Finance	Silvan Shalom (Likud)
Deputy PM and Construction & Housing	Natan Sharansky (Yisrael be-Aliyah)
Deputy PM and Interior	Eliyahu Yishai (Shas) (until 5.23.02 and from 6.3.02)
Deputy PM and Foreign Affairs	Shimon Peres (Labor-Meimad) (until 11.2.02)
Agriculture & Rural Development	Shalom Simḥon (Labor-Meimad) (until 11.2.02) Tzipi Livni (Likud) (from 12.17.02)
Communications	Reuven Rivlin (Likud)
Defense	Binyamin Ben-Eliezer (Labor-Meimad) (until 11.2.02) Shaul Mofaz (Likud) (not an MK) (from 11.4.02)
Education	Limor Livnat (Likud)
Environment	Tzaḥi Hanegbi (Likud)
Foreign Affairs	Shimon Peres (Labor-Meimad) (until 11.2.02) Binyamin Netanyahu (Likud) (from 11.6.02) (not an MK)
Health	Nissim Dahan (Shas) (until 5.23.02 and from 6.3.02)
Immigrant Absorption	Ariel Sharon (Likud)
Industry and Trade	Dalia Itzik (Labor-Meimad) (until 11.2.02) Ariel Sharon (Likud) (from 11.2.02)
Internal Security	Uzi Landau (Likud)
Jerusalem Affairs	Eliyahu Suissa (Shas) (until 5.23.02 and from 6.3.02)

Table 62 continued

Ministerial Position	Name (party)
Justice	Meir Sheetrit (Likud)
Labor & Welfare	Shlomo Benizri (Shas) (until 5.23.02 and from 6.3.02)
National Infrastructures	Avigdor Lieberman (National Union) (until 3.14.02)
	Efi Eitam (NRP) (from 9.18.02) (not an MK)
Regional Cooperation	Tzipi Livni (Likud) (until 8.29.01)
	Roni Milo (Center Party, then Likud) (from 8.29.01)
Religious Affairs	Asher Ohana (Shas) (until 5.23.02 and from 6.3.02) (not an MK)
Science, Culture and Sport	Mattan Vilna'i (One Israel) (until 11.2.02)) (not an MK)
Social Coordination	Shmuel Avital (Am Eḥad) (until 2.22.02)
Tourism and in charge of Arab Sector	Rehavam Ze'evi (National Union) (murdered 10.17.01)
	Binyamin Elon (National Union) (10.31.01–3.14.02)
	Yiẓhak Levy (NRP) (from 9.18.02 (not an MK)
Transportation	Efraim Sneh (Labor-Meimad) (until 11.2.02)
	Tzaḥi Hanegbi (Likud) (from 12.15.02)
Without Portfolio	Dani Naveh (Likud)
Without Portfolio	Salah Tarif (Labor-Meimad) (until 1.29.02)
Without Portfolio	Ra'anan Cohen (Labor-Meimad) (until 8.18.02)
Without Portfolio	Dan Meridor (Center Party) (from 8.29.01)
Without Portfolio	Tzipi Livni (Likud) (8.29.01–12.17.02)
Without Portfolio	David Levy (Gesher) (4.8.02–7.30.02)
Without Portfolio	Efi Eitam (NRP) (4.8.02–9.18.02) (not an MK)
Without Portfolio	Yiẓhak Levy (NRP) (4.8.02–9.18.02) (not an MK)

The most urgent task of the new government was to pass the 2001 budget. Sharon also insisted on the immediate cancellation of the direct elections of the prime minister, which had decimated the power of the two major parties. Another important bill that the Knesset passed soon after Sharon was elected was one known as the "Tal Law," which tried to contend with the problem of military service for *ḥaredi* youth – an issue that was causing increasing bitterness and mutual recriminations between the religious and secular parts of Israeli society.

As the Intifada became progressively more violent, with suicide bombers committing increasingly frequent acts of terror, the IDF reacted with growing ferocity. On October 17, 2001, Minister of Tourism Rehavam Ze'evi was murdered by Palestinian terrorists in a Jerusalem hotel. Though international efforts were underway to try and stop the escalating violence, little progress was made.

The cost of fighting the Intifada and the deterioration in Israel's international standing – both diplomatically and economically – continued to exacerbate the economic situation, with growing rates of unemployment and failed businesses. At the same time the cutback in Palestinian workers employed in Israel greatly increased the number of foreign workers, both legal and illegal, from Eastern Europe, Southeast Asia, and Africa, performing jobs that Israelis would not take.

Within the Labor Party a leadership contest between Burg and Binyamin *Ben-Eliezer in December 2001 ended in a very narrow victory for the latter, and accusations of fraud. Eleven months later, a leadership contest between Ben-Eliezer and Amram Mitzna – a former major general and mayor of Haifa – ended in a conclusive victory for the latter. Two weeks before Mitzna's victory, and with growing differences of opinion with the Likud on economic and social issues on the one hand and on relations with the Palestinians on the other, Labor-Meimad decided to leave the government.

By the end of the term of the Fifteenth Knesset, of the six members of the Center Party, the party's leader had been forced to resign from the Knesset, one member joined Labor-Meimad, two returned to the Likud, and another – Dan *Meridor – rejoined the Likud but formally remained in the Center Party parliamentary group with another member for technical reasons. However, while at the end of the Knesset, technically speaking the Center Party still existed, to all intents and purposes it had suffered the same fate as Dash 24 years earlier.

From a political point of view, the term of the Fifteenth Knesset was one of the most complex and unstable that Israel had ever known. It was the second Knesset – the first being the Eleventh – in which two governments served with prime ministers coming from different parties. The difference was, however, that while in the Eleventh Knesset there was a National Unity Government with a rotation agreement between the leaders of the two major parties, this time each of the two prime ministers had been elected directly. As a result of the growing weakness of the government, a peak number of private members, bills were put to a vote – 4,236, of which 239 were adopted. In the same period only 162 government bills were passed and 39 committee bills. After no Parliamentary Inquiry Committees had been established in the Fourteenth Knesset, no fewer than nine were appointed in the Fifteenth. In the course of this Knesset 19 members had resigned – the largest number in the course of a single Knesset.

The Sixteenth Knesset, 2003–2006

The elections to the Sixteenth Knesset were held on January 28, 2003, and the first meeting of the Knesset was held 20 days later, on February 17, 2003.

The elections to the Sixteenth Knesset were once again held on the basis of the old system, without elections for the prime minister. The Likud, doubling the number of its voters, also doubled the number of its seats, and was soon joined by Yisrael be-Aliyah, which suffered a bitter defeat, gaining only two seats. Yisrael be-Aliyah, which had lost two members to the Right in the course of the Fourteenth Knesset, and two members to the Left in the course of the Fifteenth Knesset, appeared to have lost its *raison d'être* as a new immigrants party. The leader of Yisrael be-Aliyah, Natan Sharansky, immediately resigned his Knesset seat, but joined Sharons' new government as minister responsible for Jerusalem affairs. Labor-

Table 63. Results of the Elections to the Sixteenth Knesset

Electorate:	4,720,075
Valid votes cast	3,148,364
Qualifying threshold (1.5%)	47,226
Votes per seat	25,138

Table 64. Results of the elections to the Fifteenth Knesset by party

Name of list	Number of valid votes	% of total votes	Number of seats	30th Govt.
Likud	925,279	29.4	38	X
Labor-Meimad	455,183	14.5	19	X#
Shinui	386,535	12.3	15	X****
Shas	258,879	8.2	11	
National Union	173,973	5.5	7	X**
Meretz	164,122	5.2	6	
Yahadut ha-Torah	135,087	4.3	5	X##
National Religious Party	132,370	4.2	6	X***
Ḥadash	93,819	3.0	3	
Am Eḥad###	86,808	2.8	3	
Balad	71,299	2.3	3	
Yisrael be-Aliyah	67,719	2.2	2	X*
United Arab List	65,551	2.1	2	

* Merged with the Likud on March 10, 2003.
** Fired from the government on June 6, 2004.
*** Joined the government on March 3, 2003, left the government on November 11, 2004.
**** Left the government on December 4, 2004.
\# Joined the government on January 10, 2005.
\## Joined the coalition on March 30, 2005.
\### Merged with Labor-Meimad on May 23, 2005.

Meimad, under Mitzna, suffered a bitter defeat, going down to 19 seats – the same number that the Likud had received in the previous elections. Shinui, which campaigned against what it considered the excessive strength that the *ḥaredi* parties had gained over the previous decade, was the great success story of the elections to the Sixteenth Knesset, repeating the success of Dash in 1977, with 15 seats, taking votes away from both Labor-Meimad and Meretz. Even though Yossi Beilin and Yael Dayan joined the Meretz list after failing to be elected to realistic places on the Labor list, Meretz suffered a bitter defeat and lost four of its ten seats. For the first time since it entered the Knesset in 1984, Shas lost seats, going down from 17 to 11, most of which returned to the Likud.

The Sixteenth Knesset elected Reuven (Ruby) Rivlin from the Likud as its speaker.

Sharon formed his new government on February 29, 2003. He had hoped to form a coalition with Labor-Meimad and Shinui that would not have to rely on the religious and extreme-right parties. But even though Shinui leader Tomi Lapid did his utmost to convince the Labor Party to join a secular government headed by Sharon, Mitzna preferred to remain in Opposition, and Sharon formed a government that included Shinui, the NRP, and the National Union, leaving Shas and Yahadut ha-Torah outside. In May 2003 Mitzna resigned from the Labor Party leadership, and once again Shimon Peres assumed the leadership as a caretaker, promising to step down later on prior to a future leadership contest.

Table 65. Members of the Thirtieth Government (Formed on February 28, 2003)

Ministerial Position	Name (party)
Prime Minister	Ariel Sharon (Likud))
Vice Prime Minister and Minister of Industry, Trade and Labor	Ehud Olmert (Likud)
Vice Premier and Minister for Regional Cooperation	Shimon Peres (Labor-Meimad) (from 10.1.05)
Deputy PM and Foreign Affairs	Silvan Shalom (Likud)
Deputy PM and Minister of Justice	Yosef Lapid (Shinui) (until 4.12.04)
Minister in the PM's Office	Gideon Ezra (Likud) (until 31.8.04)
Minister in the PM's Office	Uzi Landau (Likud) (until 28.10.04)
Minister in the PM's Office	Tsaḥi Hanegbi (Likud) (from 6.9.04)
Minister in the PM's Office	Mattan Vilnai (Labor-Meimad) (from10.1.05)
Agriculture & Rural Development	Israel Katz (Likud)
Communications	Ariel Sharon (Likud) (until 17.8.03) Ehud Olmert (Likud) (29.9.03–10.1.05) Dalia Itzik (Labor-Meimad) (from 10.1.05)
Construction and Housing	Efi Eitam (NRP) (3.3.03–10.6.04) Tzipi Livni (Likud) (acting minister 31.8.04–10.1.05) Yitzhak Herzog (Labor-Meimad) (from 10.1.05)
Defense	Shaul Mofaz (Likud) (not an MK)
Education, Culture and Sport	Limor Livnat (Likud)
Environment	Yehudit Na'ot (Shinui) (until 17.10.04) Ilan Shalgi (Shinui) (17.10.04–4.12.04) Shalom Simḥon (Labor-Meimad) (from 10.1.05)
Finance	Binyamin Netanyahu (Likud) (until 9.8.05) Ehud Olmert (Likud) (acting minister from 9.8.05)
Minister in the Ministry of Finance	Meir Sheetrit (Likud) (until 5.7.04)
Foreign Affairs	Silvan Shalom (Likud)
Health	Danny Naveh (Likud)
Immigrant Absorption	Tzipi Livni (Likud)
Interior	Avraham Poraz (Shinui) (until 4.12.04) Ofir Paz-Pines (Labor-Meimad) (from 10.1.05)
Internal Security	Tsaḥi Hanegbi (Likud) (until 6.9.04) Gideon Ezra (Likud) (from 6.9.04)
Jerusalem Affairs	Natan Sharansky (not an MK) (3.3.03–4.5.05)
Justice	Tomi Lapid (Shinui) (until 4.12.04) Tzipi Livni (Likud) (from 10.1.05)
National Infrastructures	Yosef Paritzky (Shinui) (until13.7.04) Eliezer Sandberg (Shinui) (19.7.04–4.12.04) Binyamin Ben-Eliezer (Labor-Meimad) (from 10.1.05)

Table 65 continued

Ministerial Position	Name (party)
Religious Affairs	Ariel Sharon (Likud) (until 31.12.03, when Ministry was abolished)
Science & Technology	Eliezer Sandberg (Shinui) (until 19.7.04) Ilan Shalgi (Shinui) (24.7.04–29.11.04) Victor Bralovsky (Shinui) (29.11.04 – 4.12.04) Mattan Vilnai (Labor-Meimad) (28.8.05)
Tourism	Binyamin Elon (National Union) (until 6.6.04) Gideon Ezra (Likud) (4.7.04–10.1.05) Avraham Hirshson (Likud) (from 10.1.05)
Transportation	Avigdor Lieberman (National Union) (until 6.6.04) Meir Sheetrit (Likud) (from 4.7.04)
Welfare	Zevulun Orlev (NRP) (3.3.03–11.11.04)
Without Portfolio	Haim Ramon (Labor-Meimad) (from 10.1.05)

One of the characteristics of the Sixteenth Knesset was the entry of a large group of new members to the Knesset both on the Likud and Shinui lists. While those of Shinui were mostly professionals, many of whom had been active in Shinui for many years, those of the Likud were relatively young, with little previous political experience, and strongly committed to those who voted for them in the Likud Central Committee rather than the old-time leadership. Soon a succession of political scandals broke out among both new and old members of the Likud, some bordering on criminal acts, involving election financing, cronyism, and double voting in the Knesset plenum. A police investigation concerning Sharon's 1999 election finances implicated his two sons, MK Omri Sharon and Gilad, but since both chose to remain silent, the investigation dragged on, and only in the summer of 2005 was it decided that charges would be brought against Omri. As a result of the disinclination of the Knesset House Committee to lift the immunity of Knesset members at the request of the state attorney, the Knesset amended the law in July 2005 to facilitate the procedure.

In terms of the peace process with the Palestinians no progress was made until the death of the chairman of the Palestinian Authority, Yasser Arafat, in November 2004, and the IDF continued to act vigorously to prevent acts of terror being committed by Palestinians inside Israel, including the assassination of Palestinians known to be involved in acts of terrorism as planners and perpetrators, and the construction of a security fence to separate Israel from the West Bank. The latter policy was strongly criticized by the international community, primarily due to the delineation of the fence east of the Green Line.

As minister of finance, Binyamin Netanyahu devised a new economic policy designed to pull the Israeli economy out of the deep crisis it had goten into as a result of the world economic slump, the bursting of the hi-tech bubble, and the ongoing *Intifada*. The crisis reduced economic growth to an all-time low, led to unprecedented levels of unemployment that crossed the 10% line, and brought the annual inflation rate down to 1–2%. In his effort to encourage economic growth Netanyahu followed a policy of drastic budgetary cuts, including a steep reduction in all welfare payments, and policies designed to bring the chronically unemployed back to work. Though the policy brought about an improvement in the performance of the economy on the macro level, it caused a good deal of social distress, resulting in numerous strikes and demonstrations, most noteworthy that by single mothers as personified by Vicki Knafo in May 2003. In 2004 efforts also began to cut down on the number of illegal foreign workers in Israel, estimated to have reached 100,000–200,000. Netanyahu initiated major reforms in the banking, tax, pensions, local government, and sea port systems.

In December 2003 Sharon officially announced his policy of unilateral Israeli disengagement from the Gaza Strip, and the dismantlement of all the Jewish settlements there, as well as several settlements in Northern Samaria. The plan was first debated in the Knesset the following month. There were those who argued that Sharon proposed his revolutionary policy in order to divert attention from the criminal investigations being carried out against him. However, the timing of the move could be laid to a combination of American pressure for some Israeli move *vis-à-vis* the Palestinians following the toppling of Saddam Hussein's regime in Iraq, the stalemate with the Palestinians as the second *Intifada* entered its fourth year, and growing international criticism of Israel for constructing the security fence to protect itself against Palestinian suicide bombers. Within the government the plan enjoyed the enthusiastic support of Shinui only. The plan was also fully supported by the Israel Labor Party and Yaḥad from the Opposition. Though a majority of the Likud ministers and the majority of the Likud Knesset members also supported it, within the Likud Central Committee a majority objected to the plan. A group of rebels from within the Likud joined the settlers, Mo'eẓet Yesha (the formal leadership of the settlers in Judea, Samaria, and Gaza), the National Union, and the National Religious Party in placing growing pressure on the Government and the Knesset to reject the plan. This pressure manifested itself in mass demonstrations and, as time went on, clashes with the security forces.

In order to reduce opposition to the plan within the government, Sharon fired the ministers from the National Union in June 2004. Efi Eitam, still formally leader of the NRP, resigned soon thereafter, and together with MK Yitzhak Levy established a new parliamentary group that eventually joined the National Union. The remainder of the NRP remained in the government until November 2004, but then resigned as the disengagement plan was approved by the Knesset and Sharon refused to consider a referendum on the issue. Netanyahu tried, together with a few other Likud ministers, to lead a rebellion against Sharon during the Knesset vote on the implementation of the plan in October 2004, but his attempt failed and he ended up voting for it.

Shinui, which continued to support the disengagement plan, left the government in November 2004, due to Lapid's objection to the proposed increase in financial allocations to the religious parties in the 2005 budget. Left with a minority government, Sharon finally reached an agreement with the Labor Party, which entered the government in January. Besides Peres, who became vice premier and minister for regional cooperation, Labor's two most senior ministers were two of its younger leaders, elected by the party's Central Committee: Ofir Paz-Pines and Yitzhak Herzog. Nevertheless, since the Likud rebels continued to vote against the government on most issues, the government now depended in many votes on Shinui, Yahad, and even the Arab parties.

On August 9, 2005, on the eve of the implementation of the disengagement plan, Netanyahu resigned from the government dramatically, claiming that he did not want to be associated with this act, even though he admitted that there was no chance of preventing it. Netanyahu was replaced in the Ministry of Finance by Ehud *Olmert.

Despite clashes between the settlers, who were to be removed from their homes, and groups of radical youngsters who had joined them before the removal, on the one hand, and large contingents of policemen and soldiers, on the other, the fear of major violence and fatalities in the course of the disengagement did not materialize, and the removal of the settlers, followed by the destruction of their homes, was completed within a week in the middle of August 2005.

[Susan Hattis Rolef (2nd ed.)]

The 2006 Elections

Though Prime Minister Sharon's popularity in the world soared as a result of the disengagement, and he enjoyed extensive support within the Israeli population at large, within the Likud his popularity sank. In November 2005, faced with the threat of being deposed as party chairman by the Likud Central Committee, Sharon dissolved the Knesset, quit the Likud, and formed Kadimah, a new political party. He was joined by Tzipi *Livni, Shaul *Mofaz, Meir *Sheetrit, Gideon Ezra, and Tzaḥi Hanegbi from the Likud and Shimon Peres, Haim *Ramon, and Dalia *Itzik from the Labor Party. Previously, Amir Peretz had defeated Peres in the contest for the Labor Party chairmanship, and in December Binyamin Netanyahu was elected to the Likud chairmanship in place of Sharon.

Sharon suffered a massive brain hemorrhage in early January 2006. Ehud Olmert became acting prime minister. Elections were held on March 28, 2006, with a low turnout of 3,186,739 voters (63.5%). Kadimah received 29 seats and Olmert was invited by the president to form the new government. Labor received 19 seats, the Likud 12, Shas 12, Yisrael Beitenu (led by Avigdor Lieberman) 11, and the pensioners' party, Gil, a suprising 7 seats, seen as reflecting a protest vote among disaffected younger voters.

ADD. BIBLIOGRAPHY: Knesset website, www.knesset.gov.il; A. Arian (ed.), *Elections in Israel: 1969* (1972); *1973* (1975); *1977* (1980); *1981* (1983); A. Arian and M.L. Shamir (eds.), *Elections in Israel: 1984* (1986); *1988* (1990); *1992* (1995); *1996* (1999); *2003* (2005); G.S. Mahler, *Bibliography of Israeli Politics* (1983); A. Arian, *Politics in Israel: The Second Generation* (1989); *Ha-Enziklopedyah ha-Ivrit – Medinat Yisrael* (1993); S.H. Rolef, *The Political Dictionary of the State of Israel* (1993²); A. Diskin, *Ha-Beḥirot la-Kenesset ha-12* (1990); idem, *Ha-Beḥirot la-Kenesset ha-13* (1993); A. Diskin and M. Hofnung (eds.), *Ha-Beḥirot la-Kenesset u-le-Rashut ha-Memshalah 1996* (1997); S.H. Rolef, *Leksikon Politi shel Medinat Yisrael* (1998); Y. Schatz, *Leksikon ha-Medinah: Ezraḥut, Ḥevrah, Kalkalah* (1998); A. Carmel, *Ha-Kol Politi: Leksikon ha-Politikah ha-Yisraelit* (2001); J. Mendilow, *Ideology Party Change and Electoral Campaigns in Israel 1965–2001* (2003).

DEFENSE FORCES

Ottoman and Mandatory Periods (1878–1948)

The development of the self-defense force of the *yishuv* was an influential part of the history of Jewish settlement in Ereẓ Israel. In the last quarter of the 19th century, when the first Jewish agricultural settlements came into being, the Turkish regime was hostile toward them. The internal security of the village areas left much to be desired, and the safety of the settlers depended on the good graces of the local strong man – the Bedouin or village sheikh. The Jewish settlers had to cope with border friction, disputes on water rights, and intrusions on their crops and property. Their choice was either to fight for their rights or be left to the mercy of their neighbors. As a result, individuals and groups of young people organized to fight for these elementary rights. This was the period of the first watchmen (*shomerim*), typical of whom was Abraham *Shapira, head watchman of Petaḥ Tikvah, who became well known among the Arabs by guarding the village and its fields with the help of the young settlers and hired Bedouin. After some time, guard duty in most of the settlements became the task of local Arab strong men, who undertook to protect them by sending their men to guard Jewish life and property.

HA-SHOMER. The immigrants of the Second Aliyah, which began in 1904, were critical of the early settlers and well aware of the dangers involved in employing non-Jewish watchmen. The young newcomers had been influenced by the ideas of the Zionist Movement and modern Hebrew writers. Many of them had been through pogroms and had learned the arts of self-defense in Russia. They saw the settlers' dependence on outside armed forces as a fundamental defect. Israel *Shochat, one of the first to consider the idea of a Jewish armed force, pointed to various Middle East minorities, such as the Druze and Circassians, who had won their right to exist by proving their bravery against their attackers. Shochat came to the conclusion that a group of Jewish fighters should be created to win the respect of their neighbors and raise the prestige of the *yishuv*'s fighting ability. He therefore established *Ha-Shomer in 1909. Within a period of four to five years, Ha-Shomer had taken over the guard duty of all the Jewish settlements in Lower Galilee, as well as of several of the larger settlements in Samaria and Judea. During the same period, guard duty in several other settlements was also assumed by young Jews. The image of the Jewish fighter was thus created.

Ha-Shomer's principle was to employ Jewish watchmen only; its methods called for a small body of professional watchmen who would study Arab methods of fighting and try to outdo their enemy in organizational ability, discipline, and force of arms. In 1913 Shochat presented a memorandum to the Zionist Organization proposing the establishment of a countrywide organization for the defense of the settlements that would incorporate every male capable of bearing arms. The men of Ha-Shomer were to head the organization, train the members, and be responsible for the security of the arms depots. Ha-Shomer was thus the first stage in the development of the *yishuv*'s military force.

THE JEWISH LEGION. During World War I the idea of the *Jewish Legion was born. Its main protagonist, Vladimir *Jabotinsky, envisaged the Legion (which was established during the war years) as helping the British army to conquer Palestine and, on the conclusion of the war, serving as the garrison of the country. It was also to ensure the security of the Jewish settlements by serving as a concrete symbol of the political status of the Jewish National Home. After the *Balfour Declaration (1917), the opposition of the Arab National Movement (see *Israel, State of: Historical Survey, section on the Arab National Movement) to Jewish immigration and settlement became increasingly stronger. The riots that took place in Palestine in the years 1920–21 strengthened recognition of the need for an independent Jewish force.

The *yishuv* learned its first lesson when faced with the problem of defending settlements in northern Upper Galilee, which was under French rule at that time. As a result of the Arab uprising against the French, the settlements were in danger, and the Jewish authorities were inclined to transfer the settlers to the area under British occupation. This suggestion was indignantly rejected by Ha-Shomer, which sent reinforcements of men and ammunition to the besieged villages and entrusted the organization of the defense to Joseph *Trumpeldor. The stand against the Arabs at *Tel Ḥai in March 1920, during which Trumpeldor and several of his comrades fell in battle, became a symbol of Jewish resistance both in Ereẓ Israel and in the Diaspora. It also established a new principle in the *yishuv*'s defense policy – "No Jewish settlement is to be abandoned for any security consideration whatsoever." The second lesson was derived from the 1920 Passover riots in Jerusalem. Jabotinsky headed a self-defense organization that he had established openly and, he assumed, legally, demanding arms from the British authorities. When the riots broke out in Jerusalem, however, the British prevented this defense force from entering the Old City. Jabotinsky and 20 of his men were arrested and sentenced to long prison terms. The rioting continued for several days before the British army restored order to the city. To ensure its security the *yishuv* needed an autonomous force, independent of any foreign power. Consequently, Ha-Shomer decided to disband and an *Aḥdut ha-Avodah conference held at Kinneret in June 1920, attended by a group of ex-Battalion soldiers led by Eliyahu *Golomb and Dov *Hos, established the *Haganah ("Defense") organization. The third lesson came in May 1921 with the outbreak of bloody riots that spread from Jaffa to the Jewish villages in Judea and Samaria and included the murder of Jews and attempts to break into their villages. The attacks were vigorously repulsed by local defense forces with the help of the British army. The participation in the defense of Tel Aviv of a unit of Jewish soldiers that was to have been the nucleus of a renewed Jewish Battalion led the British to disband the unit and cancel the plan to revive it. These events strengthened the view that the *yishuv* could rely on neither a foreign army nor a Jewish Legion under a foreign command whose policy was guided by extraneous military and political considerations.

HAGANAH – EARLY DAYS. During the first nine years of its existence, the Haganah was a loose organization of local defense groups in the large towns and in several of the settlements. Although it enjoyed Zionist sympathy it received no material support from the Zionist Organization, which regarded the Haganah as a local version of the self-defense organizations of Eastern Europe. Jabotinsky, who felt very strongly about the security problems of the *yishuv*, held to the idea of the Legion, and at first regarded the Haganah not only as a poor substitute, but as an irresponsible security factor likely to cause political harm. The Haganah's development was dealt a serious blow by the withdrawal of the ex-members of Ha-Shomer because of a disagreement on administrative policy. These men established an independent arms depot and a training center within the framework of the *Gedud ha-Avodah ("Labor Legion").

The Arab riots of August 1929 changed the attitude of the *yishuv* and the Zionist Organization toward the Haganah. It had become evident that the bloodiest anti-Jewish riots and the heaviest looting had occurred in those places where there was no Haganah (such as Hebron) or where the Haganah was weak (as in Safed). The Jewish population of Jerusalem, Tel Aviv, Haifa, and several of the settlements had been saved by the stand of the Haganah forces – limited as they were. Following the riots, the Haganah went through a difficult organizational crisis, which was climaxed by the establishment of a countrywide supreme command in which the labor and non-labor sections were accorded equal representation. During this crisis a group of local commanders seceded and established the *Irgun Ẓeva'i Le'ummi (IẒL – "National Military Organization"), consisting mainly of right-wing and *Revisionist elements.

In the period from 1931 to 1936, the Haganah became a large organization encompassing nearly all the youth and adults in the settlements as well as several thousand members from each of the cities. It initiated a comprehensive training program for its members, ran officers' training courses, and established central arms depots into which a continuous stream of light arms (rifles and pistols) flowed from Europe. Simultaneously, the basis was laid for the underground production of arms (Ta'as), the first product of which was the hand grenade.

This period saw the crystallization of two additional principles that brought the Haganah even closer to becoming a national army. The first was the principle of a single defense organization, subject to a single and central command, which inevitably entailed opposition to the existence of dissident groups. The second principle was the recognition of the authority of the *yishuv*'s political leadership, i.e., the *Jewish Agency and the *Va'ad Le'ummi.

During the riots that broke out in April 1936 and the three years of the Arab revolt that followed, the Haganah played a central role in the life of the *yishuv*. Although the British administration did not officially recognize the organization, the British Security Forces cooperated with it by establishing an armed civilian militia. One of the largest units of this force was the Jewish Settlement Police (JSP), with branches in all the villages and city suburbs. Thousands of Haganah members were sworn in as "Supernumerary Police," received uniforms and arms from the administration, and were trained under the supervision of British army and police officers. Other police units were established to guard the railroads, airfields, government offices, and various installations. With the increasing intensity of the Arab revolt, Jews were incorporated into British army units to fight the marauding Arab bands. In the summer of 1938 Special Night Squads (SNS) were established under the command of Captain Orde *Wingate, who trained them in the methods of guerilla warfare. The JSP became a militia of 12 battalions, including mobile defense units equipped with armored vehicles and machine guns.

The British administration attempted to make the establishment of the police units conditional upon the surrender of all illegal arms. However, this condition was resolutely rejected by the Haganah command, who saw these legal units as only one aspect of its activities. The Haganah continued to develop as an autonomous force and stepped up the local manufacture of arms as well as the purchase of arms from abroad. The latter was further increased by a secret agreement between Haganah representatives and Polish government circles. At the outset of the riots, the Haganah's aim was the fortification of the settlements. Barbed-wire fencing and concrete outposts were erected and trenches were dug. As the riots continued it became clear that it was also necessary to guard traffic on the roads and workers in the fields, as well as crops and orchards outside the limits of the settlements. Yiẓhak *Sadeh played an important role in the establishment of mobile units, which quickly became field squads (*peluggot sadeh*). The Arab revolt threatened to slow down Jewish settlement, and it fell to the Haganah to safeguard newly established settlements. To this end, the *Stockade and Watchtower type of settlement was evolved.

One of the most serious questions that faced the Haganah at the outbreak of riots was that of "restraint" (Heb. *havlagah*). Attacks by Arab bands on unarmed men, women, and children aroused a desire for revenge; some Jews began to feel that Arabs interpreted the lack of any Jewish reaction as weakness and that the *yishuv* should adapt its behavior to the "Arab mentality." But the Jewish Agency decided on a policy of restraint on both ethical and political grounds, and the Haganah accepted its authority on this question. A formula was eventually worked out that allowed for limited retaliatory actions sanctioned by the Haganah command. In the spring of 1937, the IẒL split, and a section of its members returned to the ranks of Haganah. The other section, mainly under the influence of the Revisionist movement, maintained a dissident armed force subject to the authority of Jabotinsky. The IẒL did not accept the policy of restraint and, from the summer of 1938, developed methods of mass retaliation against the Arab population.

HAGANAH IN THE STRUGGLE FOR INDEPENDENCE. In September 1939 a General Staff of the Haganah was established under the political direction of the Jewish Agency through the head of the Haganah command. The Haganah's administration was systematically overhauled; countrywide defense plans, training methods, armament plants, and methods for acquiring arms were developed and expanded. The first chief of staff was Ya'akov *Dori. The Arab revolt was the testing ground for the Haganah's fighting capacity. It was during this period that many men who were to be Israel Defense Forces (IDF) commanders – such as Yigal *Allon, Moshe *Dayan, and Moshe *Carmel – received their first taste of warfare. As a result of the British government's anti-Zionist policy (expressed in the *White Paper of 1939), the Haganah took upon itself the additional task of fighting the White Paper regime. It supported organized *"illegal" immigration and organized demonstrations against the White Paper and the 1940 Land Laws. Opinion was divided as to whether the Haganah should limit itself to its former tasks or should become the spearhead of the political struggle. In fact, the Haganah did become actively involved in the struggle in all its forms, although at times within frameworks established for specific purposes, such as the organizations for "illegal" immigration (Ha-Mosad, 1939–48 and *Beriḥah, 1945–48), which did not act under the direct supervision of the Haganah command.

During World War II, the Haganah acted in accordance with the policy laid down by David *Ben-Gurion, "to fight the war as if there were no White Paper, and to fight the White Paper as if there were no war." From the summer of 1940, the Haganah also headed a movement of volunteers from which Jewish units were formed for service in the British Army (these units took part in campaigns in the Middle East, North Africa, Greece, and Italy), as well as the Jewish battalions that led to the creation of the *Jewish Brigade in 1944. Haganah members strove to add national character to the Jewish units and to have them commanded by Jewish officers, many of whom were Haganah men. For Haganah members, British army service meant not only participation in the fight against the Nazis, but also first-class military training. They learned methods of organization and command of large armed units, as well as branches of warfare that could not be taught in an underground framework (for example, the use of heavy artillery). The Haganah cooperated with British intelligence units and sent its men on various commando missions, such as the attempted sabotage of the Syrian oil refineries, in which 23 men were lost, in 1941. Another example of this cooperation was the dropping of some 30 Jewish parachutists behind enemy lines in Europe.

The Haganah further strengthened its independence during the war by establishing its own intelligence service which systematically followed all developments in the Arab community, the British administration, and the Jewish dissident groups (IẒL and *Loḥamei Ḥerut Israel (Leḥi)) that affected the *yishuv*'s security. Haganah members were divided into two main forces, one in charge of the defense of the settlements and the other trained for active warfare in all areas of the country. A systematic program of training was instituted for the youth of the country both in the legal framework of Ḥagam (intensified physical education), and the illegal one of *Gadna (youth battalions). In 1941 the Haganah's first mobilized regiment, the *Palmaḥ, came into being. Its men were mobilized for a two-year period and quartered in various work camps all over the country, where they underwent military training and simultaneously earned their keep by working in nearby kibbutzim and villages.

The war years saw many open clashes between the Haganah and the British Mandatory authorities, when the latter carried out searches for arms, as well as arrests and trials of Haganah members. In the final years of the war, the Haganah was faced with a difficult task: it was asked by the Jewish Agency to intervene and prevent IẒL sabotage of British installations, which was not in accord with Jewish Agency policy at that time. The mission (called "*ha-sezon*"), executed in conjunction with British police, was distasteful to those who participated in it. At the end of the war, when it became clear that the British government had no intention of altering its anti-Zionist policy, the Haganah began an open, organized struggle against the British Mandatory rule in the framework of a unified Jewish Resistance Movement (*Tenu'at ha-Meri ha-Ivri*), consisting of Haganah, IẒL, and Leḥi. "Illegal" immigration was intensified by the establishment of Haganah branches in the Jewish DP camps, and the Beriḥah was organized, bringing refugees from Eastern Europe to the camps in Central Europe and Italy. Haganah members accompanied the immigrant boats as sailors and organizers on their way to Ereẓ Israel and the camps in Cyprus. The systematic sabotage of all British army and police installations in Palestine began with the countrywide sabotage of the railroad network in November 1945 and reached its climax with the "Night of the Bridges" in June 1946, when all the bridges on the country's borders were blown up. On "Black Saturday" (June 29, 1946) and thereafter, countrywide searches were carried out by the British armed forces, one of the purposes of which was to disable the Haganah by arresting Palmaḥ members and uncovering its arms caches. When the Jewish Agency gave orders to limit the extent of the struggle, the IẒL and Leḥi again broke away from the Jewish Resistance Movement.

In the spring of 1947, David Ben-Gurion assumed the task of preparing the Haganah for the possible showdown with the armed forces of Arabs in Palestine and those of the Arab states. Plans were laid for full-scale mobilization of the *yishuv*, the founding of an air force, and the expansion of arms manufacture and acquisition. An important step in this direction was the purchase in the U.S. of machinery for the production of ammunition and explosives. In the first months of the War of Independence, the Haganah became the regular army of the State of Israel. Complete mobilization was declared; seven divisions were organized by fusing British army experience and Haganah fighting practices; and the Palmaḥ was expanded into three brigades. A large armaments industry was created and heavy arms and planes were acquired. An air force and a navy came into existence. After lengthy discussions the members of IẒL and Leḥi were incorporated into the Haganah's forces.

In the spring of 1948, the Haganah went over from defensive to offensive warfare, occupying areas essential for the *yishuv*'s security: "Operation Naḥshon" opened the road to besieged Jerusalem, while other operations liberated Tiberias, Haifa, Safed, Jaffa, and other areas. On May 26 the Provisional Government of Israel decided to transform the Haganah into the regular army of the State, to be called "Ẓeva Haganah le-Israel" ("Israel Defense Forces"). During the 70 years prior to the establishment of the State, a Jewish fighting force had come into being, the image of the Jewish fighter had been created, and a fighting tradition developed.

[Yehuda Slutsky]

Israel Defense Forces

The Israel Defense Forces (abbr. IDF; Heb. צְבָא הֲגַנָּה לְיִשְׂרָאֵל; Ẓeva Haganah le-Israel; abbr. צה"ל, Ẓahal) were established on May 26, 1948, by the provisional government of the State of Israel, and on May 31, 1948, the first official oath-taking ceremony took place. It is unique in the armies of the world in the degree to which it has succeeded in eliminating distance between itself and the people that it serves; indeed it is an organic part of the people. This closeness results from the fact that the IDF is essentially based on reserve service of the civilian population. Accordingly, and primarily due to this reason, it has not developed into a standard professional army but has retained more of the pre-state character of a popular militia. Because of its popular character and the fact that the youth of the country, without exception, have to pass through its ranks, the IDF has proved to be one of the most important factors in effecting the integration of the various cultural elements of the population of Israel. In the early days of the state, the IDF probably had more influence in this respect than any other single element, and today it is on a par with the school system in bringing about national integration. It has taken an active part in the educational integration of the new immigrants in the country by conducting intensive courses to raise all ranks to a minimum educational standard and by allocating women teachers to immigrant villages with a view to raising the standard of education there. The army continues to supply these services as well as providing additional facilities for more advanced education of its officers and men up to and including university education. In times of national stress (not only military) the IDF has been in the forefront. The great waves of immigration in the early 1950s, which posed major organizational problems, were successfully absorbed with the help of the army, which also assisted in conducting welfare activities in the immigrant camps.

TERMS OF SERVICE. From its inception, Israel established a system of compulsory military service that requires both men and women of certain ages to report for varying periods. Men aged 18–55 (inclusive) and women aged 18–38 (inclusive) – Israel citizens and permanent residents of the country – were liable for service. The law governing military service is the Security Service Law, 1959. The IDF comprises three types of service: conscript service, reserve service, and regular service. Men aged 18–29 (inclusive), women aged 18–26 (inclusive), and licensed medical practitioners aged 18–38 (inclusive – both men and women), were deemed liable for conscript service. From the late 1960s, the period of service for conscript males aged 18–26 was 36 months and for males aged 27–29, 24 months; new immigrants aged 27–29 served 18 months. The period of service for women was 24 months, later reduced to 21 months. The minister of defense is authorized to recognize service in the Border Police as military service within the framework of the law.

On conclusion of his conscript service, every soldier is assigned to a reserve unit. Within the framework of the law, a reservist could be called for service one day per month or alternatively three days per three months. The law set out maximum periods of service as follows: men in the rank of private (*turai*) and lance corporal (*turai rishon*) aged 18–39 (inclusive) 31 days per annum, and those aged 40–54, 14 days per annum. Corporals (*rav turai*) and above could be asked to serve an additional seven days to the above periods. Privates and lance-corporals of the women's forces were liable for 31 days per annum and corporals and above for an additional seven days service per annum. Men aged 45–54 were liable for service only in the Civil Defense organization (later replaced by the Homeland Command), unless their rank was that of second lieutenant (*segen mishneh*) and above or the reservist's specialization was a required one, as determined by the minister of defence in accordance with the regulations of the law.

In addition to the monthly and annual reserve service, every reservist is liable for what is known as "Special Service." The minister of defense may, if he is satisfied that the defense of the state so requires, mobilize any reservist for conscript or reserve service in such locations and for such periods as his order specifies. This order can be a general one or can refer to specific units or specific persons. In the event that such an order is issued, the minister of defense is required to bring it to the knowledge of the *Knesset Foreign Affairs and Defense Committee as soon as possible. The committee may or may not approve the order with or without changes, or may bring it before the Knesset. It lapses within 14 days if not approved by the Foreign Affairs and Defense Committee or by the Knesset before the conclusion of the stated period. Such an order, extending service for men to 36 months, was issued in January 1968.

Mothers and pregnant women are exempt from national service within the framework of the Security Service Law. Married women are exempt from conscript service but not from reserve service. The law provides for the exemption of women from service on the basis of religious reasons.

The tendency in the early 2000s was to cut back on reserve service, for which purpose the appropriate legislation was being drafted.

COMPOSITION OF THE IDF. The IDF is composed of three elements: regular officers and NCOs; the standing army, which is composed of the regular officers, NCOs, and conscripts; and reserve forces, which are mobilized at any given time. Officers and NCOs may volunteer for regular service in the armed forces after they have completed their conscript service. They can commit themselves for varying periods ranging from one to five years. Their conditions of service, rates of pay, and so on are linked to those prevailing in the government civil service. The mandatory age of retirement is 55, but regulars who have completed a minimum of ten years' service and have reached the age of 40 may be authorized by the chief of staff to retire on partial pension, based on the payment of 2% per annum of service and related to their last rank.

ORGANIZATION OF THE FORCES. The IDF is subject to the orders of the government of Israel and carries out its policy. The minister of defense is responsible to the government and issues the instructions of the civilian authority to the armed forces. A special ministerial defense committee deals in detail with defense problems on behalf of the Cabinet. Military matters in the Knesset are dealt with, usually in closed session, by the Foreign Affairs and Defense Committee, which also deals, jointly with the Finance Committee, with budgetary matters related to the armed forces. The Ministry of Defense includes the minister of defense's personal staff and is divided into departments dealing with the following subjects: procurement of weapons and equipment; research and development; military industries; the aircraft industries; and manpower problems, such as rehabilitation, disabled ex-servicemen, responsibility for service widows and orphans, and military cemeteries; building and properties; sales; data-processing units; foreign aid; youth and *Naḥal division; *Gadna division; public relations; *shekem* ("canteen services"); soldiers' welfare committee; legal advice; and financial control. The senior military authority is the chief of staff, who commands all the armed forces. The chief of staff is appointed by the minister of defense, after advising the government. The period of service of the chief of staff is usually three to four years.

The IDF is an integrated organization controlling the land, sea, and air forces. Operationally, the armed forces are divided into three regional ground commands, Northern, Central, and Southern, in addition to the air force and the navy. The commanders of the air force and the navy are at the same time senior advisers to the chief of staff in their respective functions. The chief of staff heads the General Staff, which functions in the general headquarters of the IDF. This organization is responsible for carrying out the security policy of the State of Israel and for controlling the IDF in times of war and peace. On occasion there has been a vice chief of staff. Failing such an appointment, the chief of the General Staff Branch replaces the chief of staff in his absence.

The General Staff is divided into four branches. The General Staff Branch, headed by a major general, who is the senior of the chiefs of branch, is responsible for coordination with the General Staff and for the operational control of the armed forces, including training, planning, operations, and research and development. The Intelligence Branch, headed by a brigadier or major general, is responsible for the collection, collation, and dissemination of all military, political, and economic information that might be of interest to the General Staff for the purpose of planning and operations. It is also responsible for security within the armed forces, censorship, the official army spokesman, liaison with foreign attachés, and the appointment of Israel military attachés abroad. The Manpower Branch, headed by a brigadier or major general, is responsible for the mobilization of the manpower required by the IDF, for the assignment of men to units, for planning and control of manpower, education, personal services, discipline, information, religious and medical services, etc. The Quartermaster General Branch, headed by a brigadier or major general, is responsible for the organization of the supply of equipment, arms, food, clothing, housing, etc., for the maintenance of emergency stores, and for the readiness of all administrative emergency organizations falling within its area of responsibility.

In addition to the regional commands and the air force and navy, the commanders of which hold the rank of major general and control all the forces within their particular command, there are a number of specific commands.

Naḥal is a special organization, unique to the IDF. Its initials stand for No'ar Ḥaluẓi Loḥem ("Fighting Pioneer Youth"). New settlement was considered important in Ereẓ Israel from a security point of view, especially in the border areas. With this consideration in mind, a special corps was established that combined military and agricultural training and also engaged in the establishment of new settlements along the borders. Upon conclusion of military service, those Naḥal soldiers who wished to return to civilian life did so, while others remained and continued to live in the kibbutz. As long as a new settlement was not self-supporting, it remained within Naḥal, under military discipline and tied organically to the army. When the settlement developed and began to be self-supporting, it was transferred by the army to the civilian authority and became a civilian village. Starting in the 1980s, however, a transition began toward regular service in the infantry within the Naḥal framework, which in 1999 became part of the Central Command. About 10 percent of Naḥal soldiers continued to serve in settlement frameworks.

Gadna, the abbreviation for Gedudei No'ar ("Youth Battalions"), dealt with premilitary training of Israel youth in and out of school. The organization was essentially educational in nature, although it provided its members with some basic military training in various arms. Members of Gadna assisted in afforestation projects, archaeological excavations, and border kibbutzim. Gadna was designed to develop a spirit of constructive patriotism and to identify the army primarily with construction and not with destruction. In the early 1990s it merged with the Education Corps (see below).

The Training Command sets the training objectives of the General Staff and controls and operates all the military schools and training bases within the IDF.

The Armored Command is directly under the command of the General Staff. It is entrusted with the task of developing the armored strength of the IDF and its doctrine, training programs, and equipment.

Ḥen (Ḥeil Nashim; "Women's Corps") was essentially an auxiliary military organization supporting the armed forces in many fields. It supplied women for duties in communications, hospitals, teaching duties, and many other headquarters functions, and thus relieved the men of the country for active combat. In 2004 the corps was abolished as women sought to become fully integrated in the army, including combat service.

A special arrangement to accommodate modern Orthodox religious soldiers is *hesder* service, which combines regular army service with yeshivah study over a period of four years in which those in the program serve actively for 16 months. Another religious framework, created in 1999, is known as Naḥal Ḥaredi, in which ultra-Orthodox soldiers serve in a special battalion which enables them to adhere more easily to their religious way of life. In 2005 it numbered around 1,000 soldiers.

THE MINORITIES IN THE IDF. Members of the minorities may, under certain circumstances, volunteer for service in the IDF and in the Border Police. The Border Police Force is completely integrated between Jews and *Druze, and many Druze have attained officer rank. The Druze community is now liable for conscription into the IDF in the same manner as members of the Jewish community. Until a few years ago this community was permitted to volunteer for service, but at the specific request of the Druze community itself the National Service Law imposing conscription was applied to its members. Bedouin and members of the Christian Arab community may volunteer for service. The IDF includes a Minorities Unit in which Druze and Christian Arabs serve. A certain percentage of members of the unit are Jewish, and the unit has served with distinction in many border operations.

ARMY CORPS. Troops serving in the IDF are assigned to various army corps, which are responsible for the professional and technical training of officers and the enlisted men and the development of equipment and the doctrines of the various arms. These corps include the air force, navy, infantry, armor, artillery, engineers, paratroops, signals and communications, intelligence, ordnance, supply, medical, military police, general service corps, and homeland. The formations directly under the General Staff are the regional commands, the navy and the air force, and the armored forces. The basic formation in the IDF is the brigade group. Any number of brigade groups can be combined under the command of divisional groupings in time of war.

REGIONAL DEFENSE. The static defense of the country is based on a regional defense system that is controlled by a special staff in the headquarters of the regional command. Various border villages are trained as defensive localities. The villages are controlled by an area headquarters, which in turn is under command of a district headquarters, which is controlled by the special staff for regional defense in command headquarters. The purpose of this organization is to ensure that the armed forces will be relieved of the task of static defense and will be thus free to engage the enemy in battle. The air force is responsible for the entire air defense of the country, and the navy is responsible for all aspects of coastal defense.

TRAINING. The armed forces support a training establishment that provides for every form of training in all arms of service, from the initial training of a private up to and including Command General Staff School. A number of army personnel are sent abroad annually for training. The basic theme of the training given to the personnel of the IDF emphasizes the necessity for personal initiative and the importance of the officers and NCOs displaying personal example in leadership. Great emphasis in all facets of leadership training is placed on this point and on the fact that the officer must always lead his men into battle. In fact, these values have developed into a living tradition of which the IDF is very proud. The IDF assists the training of armies in Asia, South America, and Africa, particularly in fields such as commando and parachute training and specific programs such as Naḥal and Gadna.

EDUCATION IN THE FORCES. The IDF exercises a profound educational influence not only on the youth during their national service but also on those who come in contact with the army during periods of reserve duty. Owing to the close relationship between army and people, which became even closer during the years of almost continuous military activity following the Six-Day War, each had a considerable influence on the other. The IDF's educational work is of particular importance for new immigrants, for whom it is often a basic training in citizenship.

There are three main branches under the control of the Chief Education Officer: Instruction, Education, Entertainment. The primary responsibility for regular educational and cultural activity rests on officers and NCOs, who are trained for the task at the Military College of Education and the Educational Training Institute respectively, and provided with topical printed material. The IDF publishes an illustrated weekly of current events *Ba-Maḥaneh*, and runs a radio program, Gallei Ẓahal, which "sandwiches" news, information, reportage, and comment between layers of popular music and entertainment. Both are served by army reporters with the troops.

All soldiers who do not have a basic knowledge of Hebrew must study the language in the normal course of their training and service, as well as at special intensive courses. Those who have not completed elementary education (eight years' study) attend three-month courses in Hebrew, history, geography, civics, arithmetic and geometry, nature study, and army history at the Army Education School (the Marcus Camp) at the end of their national service, receiving certificates recognized by the Ministry of Education and Culture. Optional post-primary courses, mainly for regular army men, prepare them for the official matriculation certificate. There are also correspondence courses, which can be taken during periods of active service. In the late 1970s a new framework was created, the Center for the Advancement of Special Populations, to help disadvantaged recruits. Hundreds of women NCOs were deployed as instructors. In the 1980s a Corps Training School was established to train its educational leadership. In 1993 the Corps merged with Gadna as the integration of Russian and Ethiopian immigrants became a first priority.

The IDF publishes a wide variety of brochures and books on various regions and sectors, Diaspora Jewry, history of Israel, etc., and a series of low-priced, small paperbacks of Hebrew and translated fiction, called "*Sifriyyat Tarmil*" ("Knapsack Library"). Soldiers in camps and at the front are supplied with daily newspapers, books, games, radio and, wherever possible, TV. Films are shown about twice a week and civilian entertainers perform frequently for soldiers at the front, sometimes in the framework of reserve service.

ARMS PURCHASE AND MANUFACTURE. From the early days the IDF was dependent to no small degree for arms supplies on foreign sources. The story of "*Rekhesh*" – as the "acquisition" of arms was called from the clandestine Haganah period and immediately after the establishment of the State – is a thrilling one. The first major arms purchase directly affecting the future army of Israel was that from Czechoslovakia in 1948, which included rifles, machine guns, and, later, Messerschmitt fighter planes. At the same time arms were purchased in France and from the surplus markets of the United States as well as those of many other countries. Until the British left the arms were smuggled into Palestine despite a British embargo. Supplies continued to arrive after the establishment of the State, primarily from the military surplus markets of the world.

In 1952, Israel formally signed an agreement with the United States government allowing for reimbursable military aid under Section 408E of the Mutual Security Act, but the U.S. remained a very small supplier. Israel's first jet aircraft, Meteors, were supplied by Britain, which also became in due course a major supplier of naval equipment, primarily destroyers and submarines. The 1950s saw the development of a special relationship between Israel and France, which became Israel's major arms supplier, providing aircraft, armor, and artillery. France remained Israel's main supplier of arms – above all, of modern jet aircraft – until June 2, 1967, when an embargo on the sale of arms to Israel was imposed by General de Gaulle.

The United States involvement in the supply of arms to Israel grew in the 1960s, with the supply, first, of Hawk ground-to-air missiles and, later, of Patton M48 tanks, which together with British-supplied Centurion tanks constituted Israel's armored force. The United States became a major supplier of aircraft to Israel only after the Six-Day War and following the French embargo. U.S. supplies, which included F-4 Phantom fighter bombers and A-4 Skyhawk fighter bombers, were designed to offset the massive supply of arms by the Soviet Union to the Egyptian and Syrian forces.

From the earliest days Israel made efforts to develop her own arms industry and in the course of years a major industry, capable of supplying most of the small arms and ammunition requirements of the IDF, as well as other types, was established. Parallel to this, Israel Aircraft Industries was established with a large electronic manufacturing component capable of assembling jet trainers and maintaining all the types of aircraft in service in the Israel Air Force.

UNIFORMS. The first IDF uniforms (1948) were to a large degree identical with those of the British army during World War II, though the symbols of rank were different. Over the years, the IDF developed uniforms that specifically answer to its needs, but influences of style from Western armies (Britain and the United States) are still noticeable. The basic colors of the winter uniform – dark khaki (army), blue-gray (air force), and dark blue (navy) – are of "Anglo-Saxon" origin, as are the beige and white of the summer uniforms (British origin). The official dress uniform has been influenced to a large degree by the United States; the cut of the daily uniforms and caps, however, generally follows the British model: the black and red berets of the IDF follow the example of the British armored and paratroop corps, while the combat helmets follow the American model. The IDF nonetheless aims toward developing an original style of uniform, especially for the women soldiers. The symbols of rank for NCOs are mostly original (straight horizontal stripes in place of the angular stripes in Britain and America); in the lower ranks of commissioned officers, American influence is felt somewhat; and in the higher ranks (major and up), British influence is distinguishable.

CAMPAIGNS. The IDF came into being during the Israel *War of Independence (1948), when seven Arab armies combined to invade the newly created state. A number of outstanding battles were fought, particularly those leading to the defeat of the Egyptian army in the Negev desert and in Sinai, the defeat of the Arab armies in Galilee, and the defense of Jerusalem. The armistice agreements concluded with Israel's neighbors in 1949 were not followed by the hoped-for peace, however, and from 1953 Israel was beset by Arab marauder activity designed to kill and sabotage within the country. As a result, a number of successful retaliatory actions were mounted by the IDF, with the Paratroop Corps in the lead, against Egypt, Syria, and Jordan. This state of affairs culminated in the *Sinai Campaign of 1956, in which the IDF defeated the Egyptian army in the Sinai Desert and cleared the whole of the Sinai Peninsula.

In the following years the IDF was again called upon to engage in a number of retaliatory and defense operations until the outbreak of the *Six-Day War in June 1967. In less than a week the IDF destroyed the enemy air forces, defeated the Egyptian, Jordanian, and Syrian armies, and occupied the whole of the Sinai Peninsula, the Gaza Strip, Judea and Samaria on the West Bank of the Jordan, and the Syrian mountains known as the Golan Heights. Subsequently the IDF was engaged in defending the cease-fire lines and protecting the country against attempts at terrorist infiltration.

[Chaim Herzog]

The victory in the Six-Day War fostered a feeling of invincibility in the country that was to have dire consequences. Harboring a spirit of vast confidence in its ability to predict and stem any attack on Israel, the IDF was taken completely by surprise in the *Yom Kippur War under a combined attack by Egyptian and Syrian forces that initially drove the IDF from its positions on the Suez Canal and Golan Heights. Though it ultimately succeeded in driving Egyptian and Syrian forces back, the Yom Kippur War was a marked watershed in the development of the IDF. As a result of the report of the Agranat Commission a number of senior officers were dismissed and David *Elazar, the chief of staff, submitted his resignation. His successor Major General Mordecai ("Motta") *Gur undertook the slow but steady rehabilitation and rearming of the forces, an unprecedented expansion in the size of the army, navy, and air force, and the absorption of vast amounts of new weapons, most of them from the United States. The IDF was also busy withdrawing to new lines in the wake of the disengagement agreements with Egypt and Syria, the Interim Agreement with Egypt and the Israel-Egypt Peace Treaty of March 1979.

From 1975 the IDF had been engaged in helping the Christian militia forces in southern Lebanon defend themselves against the PLO. Following a murderous terrorist attack on an Israeli bus in March 1978, the IDF launched an invasion into southern Lebanon that brought it to the banks of the Litani. The campaign lasted some days, but did not produce the anticipated results and the army withdrew in June 1978 after the arrival of a United Nations force (UNIFIL). The conduct of the campaign was the subject of criticism by the Israel State Comptroller in his 1979 report. The term of office of General Gur terminated in April 1978 and he was replaced by Major General Rafael *Eitan, a veteran combat officer, who set out to tighten army discipline and instituted various austerity measures.

Israel's military industry produced various types of modern weapons for internal use and for export. Among the latest items manufactured in Israel were the Merkavah ("Chariot") tank, the Gabriel missile carriers, and the Wasp torpedo boats. Other rockets and missiles have won renown at home and abroad. The main activities in 1979 and 1980 were continued military operations against the PLO in southern Lebanon, growing efforts to stem disturbances in the West Bank, and the growth of the IDF, primarily in modern equipment. The signing of the Israel-Egypt Peace Treaty resulted in a massive re-deployment of the forces which were withdrawn from Sinai to the Negev. Operation "*Rimon*" was the code given to the removal from Sinai of tens of thousands of tons of materials, equipment, camps, water, and power lines and almost a million mines were lifted without mishap. The whole operation was carried out meticulously according to the pre-determined time schedule.

The peace treaty, however, did not bring in its wake the anticipated reduction in the defense budget. On the contrary, due to the uncertainties along Israel's Eastern border, the Iraq-Iran war, the support given by Jordan to Iraq, and the threat of a Syrian-Jordanian war, the IDF had to maintain a high degree of alert along that border. Nevertheless, the Finance Ministry was demanding a major reduction in the defense budget in view of the serious economic situation. These demands were resisted first by Minister Ezer Weizman, and after his resignation, by Prime Minister Begin, who took over the Defense portfolio. The discussions concerning the establishment of a Field Forces Command, that started in 1979, which elicited many arguments pro and con, among the Israeli generals, had not been concluded as of 1980.

Israel's arms industries continued to mount their export drives, and it was estimated that in 1980 they would sell equipment abroad to a value of $125 m.

Tension continued along the Israel-Lebanon border in the early part of 1981. In July the Israel air force carried out massive bombing raids on PLO headquarters in Beirut and on supply depots, installations, and offices in other parts of southern Lebanon. Massive destruction was reported. In the Beirut raid, scores of civilians were killed and wounded leading to a Security Council condemnation of Israel. From July 12 to 24, the entire northern part of Israel, from Nahariyyah to the Syrian line, came under heavy PLO shelling, bombing, and firing. Thousands of artillery and mortar shells, as well as Katyusha and other types of rockets were fired indiscriminately, resulting in heavy damage and loss of lives in over 30 Israeli towns and settlements. Israel retaliated in kind and the situation deteriorated. A cease-fire was arranged on July 24 through the mediation efforts of U.S. envoy Philip Habib, who enlisted Saudi Arabia to help persuade the PLO to accept the cease-fire. Cross-border shelling ceased, but the PLO reportedly bolstered its artillery power and strengthened its armed units which at the end of 1981 numbered some 20,000 men.

The IDF continued its orderly withdrawal from Sinai and its new deployment in the Negev. In November 1981 one of the two U.S. built air-bases was handed over to the Israel Air Force and became operational.

At the end of the year, Defense Minister Ariel Sharon announced his plan to reorganize the Defense Ministry in order to bring about better control and greater efficiency. This led to a work conflict with the civilian workers of the ministry. Major changes were also announced in the high command of the IDF with the retirement of two generals and study leaves for two others. The term of office of Chief of Staff Raphael Eitan was extended to an unprecedented fifth year.

The next decade was marked by four major events. The first was the war in Lebanon (1982–85); the second was the slow withdrawal from Lebanon (1985); the third was the outbreak of the first Intifada (1987); and the fourth, Israel's experience during the 1991 Gulf War.

The decision to go to war in Lebanon was the result of many factors, among them the desire to put an end to the emerging PLO mini-state in Southern Lebanon and the destruction of the PLO forces, headquarters, and supply depots strewn throughout Southern Lebanon. There was a feeling that once the PLO would disappear from the Middle Eastern scene, Israel would find it easier to negotiate with Palestinian leaders in the territories under its control who would be free to deal directly with Israel. There was hope that war in Lebanon would bring about Israel-Syria negotiations over the future of that country. Above all, there was the desire to free Galilee from the constant threat of shelling and attacks by PLO elements. There was also the aspiration to bring about the creation of a central government in Lebanon, which would be able to demand the withdrawal of Syrian forces from Lebanon and eventually sign a peace treaty with Israel.

The shooting of the Israel ambassador, Shelomoh Argov, in London by members of the Abu Nidal terrorist group on June 2, 1982, served as the reason for Israel to enter Lebanon on June 6, 1982. Announcing the military action and the code-name "Peace in Galilee," Israel said it was aimed at clearing a zone of 40 miles from its borders from the PLO. It stated that if Syrian forces would remain neutral, Israel would not attack them. Within one week, Israeli forces occupied most of Southern Lebanon, reaching the outskirts of Beirut. Hopes that the Lebanese Christian forces under the command of Basheer Gemayel, with whom prior coordination existed, would join the war did not materialize. The IDF did engage Syrian troops in various parts of Lebanon, culminating in the destruction of Syrian anti-aircraft missiles and the shooting down of close to 100 Syrian jet fighters and bombers. When a cease-fire was proclaimed on June 11, the Israel Defense Forces (IDF) deployed along the Beirut Damascus road and inside Beirut. It had captured vast quantities of PLO equipment, including tanks and artillery. To induce Yasser Arafat, trapped in West Beirut, to leave the city, the IDF began to besiege West Beirut. During June, July, and August sporadic fighting continued in Lebanon while Israeli and American diplomats sought a diplomatic solution that would enable the PLO to depart from Lebanon. An arrangement was reached in late August and the PLO withdrew on September 1, moving its headquarters to Tunis. Technically the war aims were achieved.

However, already in mid-June, there was growing dissent in Israel over the continued war in Lebanon and over its final aims. For the first time during the war, Israelis were questioning its aims and the real intent of the political leadership. The public was shocked when elements of the Lebanese Christian forces carried out a massacre of hundreds of Palestinians in two refugee camps Sabra and Shatilla in Beirut on September 16–18. A demonstration in Tel Aviv, with an estimated 400,000 protestors, forced the government to appoint a commission of inquiry. The final report of the Kahan Commission did not blame the IDF for the massacre, but found it indirectly responsible for not anticipating the consequences of the Christian forces' entry into West Beirut. It recommended the removal of the defense minister and other senior officers from their posts. By then, there had been over 200 Israeli casualties in Lebanon. The impact of the war on the morale of the IDF was highly negative. A new chief of staff, General Moshe Levy, replaced General Rafael Eitan in April 1983 and began to plan a slow disengagement in Lebanon. A political agreement entered into with Lebanon on May 17, 1983, enabled the IDF to start a slow withdrawal south. In the next two years the IDF remained in Southern Lebanon, becoming embroiled in ethnic conflict there, and the number of its casualties mounted. The Shamir government insisted on remaining in Lebanon until a political settlement would be worked out, refusing to admit that the war in Lebanon was erroneous and yielded few benefits. In retrospect it can be seen that the war did destroy the PLO infrastructure in Lebanon, dealt a massive blow to the Syrian army, and resulted in the PLO losing its predominant position in Palestinian politics. But the PLO was replaced in Southern Lebanon by Shi'ite forces whose attacks on the IDF caused many casualties and hastened the decision to withdraw from that country.

The decision was made by the Government of National Unity on January 14, 1985. The withdrawal was carried out in three stages and by the summer of 1985 IDF units were deployed in the newly created Security Zone north of the Israel-Lebanon border. Between 1982 and 1985 Israeli casualties in Lebanon reached 651 dead and thousands wounded.

During the next two years, the Israel defense establishment, under Defense Minister Yiẓhak Rabin, learned the lessons of the war in Lebanon, created the Territorial Forces Command, deepened strategic cooperation with the United States on many levels, and modernized the IDF's equipment. In the ongoing war against terrorism, the IDF carried out a daring aerial attack on the PLO headquarters in Tunis on October 1, 1985.

Chief of Staff Moshe Levy completed his term of office in 1986 and was replaced by General Dan Shomron who continued to modernize the force and prepare it for any eventuality. Israel's main threat was seen to be from Syria, then busy building its own forces and seeking strategic parity with Israel. The continued Iraq-Iran war, a working peace with Egypt, and friendly relations with Jordan gave Israel a respite, and it could concentrate its efforts on stemming terrorist attacks against its own territories and against Israeli citizens and facilities overseas. Many achievements were recorded in that struggle.

At the end of 1987 the IDF was plunged into another, and wholly new, arena. On December 9, 1987 Palestinian Arab rioting erupted which soon developed into an uprising known as the Intifada. It was led by young Palestinians who despaired of the prolonged Israeli occupation, the political deadlock, their own frustrations with both the local Palestinian leadership and that of the PLO, and their despair over the failure of the Arab states to resolve their plight. The IDF now had to deal with civil disobedience, initially with stones and sticks, and since 1991 with growing cases of shooting and stabbing of Israeli civilians and soldiers in the West Bank and the Gaza Strip as well as inside Israel. Young Israeli recruits faced young Palestinians armed with stones, sticks, knives, and firearms. It was a new kind of struggle for which the IDF was not prepared. Soon moral and ethical dilemmas arose. When can a soldier fire on Arabs? Should he carry out what he may consider an illegal order? There were a number of cases in which IDF soldiers were court-martialed for illegal actions, including the killing of innocent bystanders. The Israeli settlers in the areas accused the IDF of not being effective enough in protecting them and their settlements from attacks. Tension rose between the IDF and the settlers. The IDF sought to minimize the attacks on Israelis, but were unable to stem the growing tide of killing of Palestinians by terrorists who accused them of collaborating with Israel. Between January 1991 and April 1993, 151 Israeli soldiers and civilians were killed in the Intifada, while 1,500 Palestinians were killed by their own brethren.

The IDF, under the command of General Ehud Barak (chief of staff from April 1990), insisted that the solution to the Intifada must be a political and not a military one. But it did employ various methods to combat the Intifada, among them deportation (including the mass deportation of 415 *Hamas (Muslim fundamentalists) activists in December 1992), blowing up of homes of terrorists, curfews on selected areas, and occasionally the sealing off of the entire territories from Israel. By early 1993 it appeared that the Intifada had assumed new dimensions, focusing more on killing of Israelis in the hope that public opinion would force the Rabin government to decide on unilateral withdrawal from the territories in general and from the Gaza Strip in particular.

The 1991 Gulf War caught Israel unprepared for Scud missile attacks against major urban centers. For the first time in its history, Israel did not mount a pre-emptive strike at enemy targets, neither did it retaliate after it was attacked. By so doing, Israel adhered to an American request not to become involved in the war against Saddam Hussein. In return it received additional U.S. military aid and weapons. During the war there was close cooperation between the Israel and American high commands, and Israel was given advance warnings of incoming Scuds. By sheathing its sword, Israel won international support and praises.

The Gulf War ushered in the era of missile warfare into the Middle East. It became obvious that another war would be fought with non-conventional weapons. Israel, in close cooperation with the United States, began developing its Arrow anti-missile missile, which underwent successful preliminary tests in 1992 and was due to be operational in the mid-1990s. One of the lessons drawn by the IDF resulted in the establishment of the Home Front Command, to deal specifically with civil defense, as clearly the next war would not differentiate between soldier and civilians. The IDF came under much criticism from the state comptroller for failure to provide the population with proper gas masks and other means of defense. Another consequence of the war was that with the diminution in Iraq's aggressive potential, Iran became considered as the major threat to Israel and to regional stability. Iran was the main backer of the Ḥamas, the fundamentalist Islamic group which opposed peace negotiations and a peace treaty with Israel. Reports of an Iranian nuclear weapons program meant that Israel had to find the adequate answer for the threat. Islamic fundamentalism had become the main danger to the governments of Israel, Egypt, Syria, and Saudi Arabia, as well as Algeria and Morocco. The IDF was poised at the end of 1992 to deal with continued Intifada, the consequences of a peace process, and preparations for a possible future war that could utilize nonconventional weapons. In spite of the end of the Cold War and the disappearance of the Soviet Union as a major factor in the Middle East, certain Arab states that previously relied on the U.S.S.R. for their armaments now sought weapons elsewhere and began to purchase surplus Soviet equipment and new weapons produced by China and North Korea. The arms race in the region continued despite efforts to stem it and talk about arms reduction within the framework of the Madrid peace process.

While the Israel Defense Forces were not involved in the 1993 secret negotiations that led to the Oslo Accords and the Israel-PLO Declarations of Principles, they became intimately involved in the negotiations for their implementation. Thus the IDF played a key role in the planning and execution of the withdrawal from Gaza and Jericho in May 1994 and in drawing up plans for re-deployment in the West Bank. At the same time, it continued to train its soldiers in the latest weapons systems, acquire modern military technology, and adjust its size and philosophy to the emerging peace process in the Middle East. While the threat from the immediate neighboring countries receded gradually, with Israel and Syria holding negotiations for the future of the Golan Heights, Iraq and Iran loomed high as Israel's major strategic threats. The growing possibility of both these countries acquiring nuclear capability in addition to the development of other non-conventional weapons, forced the IDF to devise new strategies to deal with this threat.

The IDF continued to fight an almost daily war of attrition in Southern Lebanon against *Hizbollah terrorists who were armed and funded by Iran and tacitly aided by Syria. This was reflected in daily clashes causing casualties on both sides. Growing violence and the shelling of Israeli settlements in Galilee forced the IDF to launch, in July 1993, Operation Accountability, during which time Lebanese civilian population abetting Hizbollah was driven north. The United States arranged an understanding whereby Israeli settlements would not be shelled. This arrangement, which had the tacit support of Syria, seemed to work, but did not prevent clashes in the Security Zone in Southern Lebanon.

Lt. General Amnon Likpkin-Shahak was appointed chief of staff on January 1, 1995, replacing Lt. General Ehud Barak. The new deputy chief of staff was Major General Matan Vilnai. Both had to deal increasingly with problems of how to keep the IDF out of Israeli politics, a growing number of training and other accidents, and the eroding image of the IDF, an organization which previously was above national debate. They were also charged with the task of building a smaller, more compact, highly modern and efficient army. Whereas in 1985 the defense budget was some 45% of the national budget, in 1995 it dropped to some 25%, reflecting the new national realities and priorities.

[Meron Medzini (2nd ed.)]

The War against Terrorism

Many important military and political events occurred during the post-Oslo period, but the focus of the period was the violent conflict between Palestinian terrorist groups and the Israeli army. Terrorist groups operated with the support of Yasser *Arafat. The beginning of this period was marked by mixed feelings of apprehension, doubts, and hopes that the peace process would bring an end to the protracted Israeli-Palestinian conflict. These hopes, which were accompanied by political measures, gave Europe and the United States confidence that a stable peace would finally be achieved in the Middle East. The Oslo Accords were seen as a milestone in achieving a settlement between the Palestinians and Israel. It was hoped that a peace treaty between the Palestinians and Israel would achieve stability in the Middle East. This was especially true after a peace treaty that was signed between Egypt and Israel (1981) and between Jordan and Israel (1994). However, these hopes were shattered. Instead of the Accords being implemented, hostile Palestinian terror activity broke out. Between 1995 and 2000, relations between the *Palestinian Authority (PA) and Israel were characterized by a lack of good faith and by instability. As time went on, it became clear to the State of Israel that the PA was not capable of implementing the agreement. This was due to the fact that the PA was incapable of preventing terrorist attacks against Israeli citizens. According to the agreements, Arafat had undertaken to prevent all terrorist activity, but as time went on it became clear that not only was he not preventing terror activity but he was supporting it. The trust between the Israelis and the Palestinians evaporated, and it became impossible to implement the other agreements after the Oslo Accords.

In September 2000, MK Ariel Sharon made a highly publicized visit to the Temple Mount. The visit aroused great anger among the Palestinians, who saw it as a threat to their control of the al-Aqsa mosque there, and brought on the beginning of the so-called al-Aqsa Intifada. The violence sparked by Sharon's visit became the moving force in the Palestinian war of terror. It escalated into a hostile conflict between the IDF and terrorist groups operating from the Gaza strip, Judea, and Samaria against the citizens of Israel. Instead of promoting the Oslo Accords, the IDF was forced to take military action against terrorist groups. The mission of the IDF was to fight and eliminate terrorist activity in order to restore security and peace to the citizens of Israel. The 1995–2005 period was characterized by the integration of political and military activities in which the prime minister and the chief of staff were involved.

The IDF, as the operative arm, which works under political directives, had become the main body fighting Palestinian terror. This was especially true because of the phenomenon of "suicide bombers." The situation in this period created instability in Israeli society. The ordinary Israeli citizen felt less secure, and the future of the Oslo Accords was cast into doubt. The lack of stability in the political sphere caused a split in Israeli society. This is reflected in the fact that during this period there were five different governments. For the first time in Israel's history a prime minister was assassinated as a result of the mounting tension. The IDF's response to Palestinian insurgence terror was Operation Defensive Shield, which began on March 29, 2002. In a matter of days the IDF had taken control of all the cities of the West Bank, in order to wipe out terrorism and prevent the suicide bombings. By the middle of 2004, the IDF found itself in control of all of the West Bank and the Gaza Strip. For the first time since the beginning of the Intifada, there was a sharp decline in the amount of terrorist activity. However, in spite of the fact that the IDF had left Lebanon (2000), Israel still faced a threat from Hizbollah on the northern border, and the threat from the West Bank and Gaza Strip remained potentially explosive. In August 2005 the IDF withdrew from the Gaza Strip as well, after dismantling the Israeli settlements there (see *Gush Katif).

1995–2000. Many events preceded this period both in the political and military arena. In September 1992 the first Oslo Accords were signed. It was emphasized in this agreement that the Palestinian Authority recognized Israel's right to exist and took responsibility for preventing terrorist attacks against Israel and its citizens. Israel recognized the fact that the establishment of the Palestinian Authority would be the first step towards the establishment of a Palestinian state. The obstacles that remained in implementing these agreements were the status of Jerusalem, the refugee problem, and the future borders of the Palestinian state. Parallel to the Oslo Accords, Hizbollah continued its terrorist activities along the northern border. After the IDF redeployed in 1985 along the security strip in south Lebanon, the army continued fighting terror with the cooperation of the residents of south Lebanon. As a result of Hizbollah's increased terror activity, the IDF stepped up its defensive activity in the security zone. This activity included patrols, ambushes, and raids to eliminate the terrorist leaders, with the massive use of aircraft, tanks, and artillery. From 1991 Hizbollah began to launch Katyusha rockets against Jewish settlements along the northern border, especially Kiryat Shemonah. After a massive attack of Katyusha rockets, Israel responded with a campaign called Operation Accountability (*Din ve-Ḥeshbon*) commencing July 23, 1993. During this campaign, the Israeli Air Force attacked Hizbollah strongholds, Shi'ite villages, and the cities of Tyre and Sidon. Fifty terrorists were killed and 3,000 citizens fled to the capital city of Beirut. After six days of fighting, both sides agreed to prevent attacks from their sides of the border. Between 1991 and 1995, 6,532 terrorist operations were carried out against the Israeli army in which 77 soldiers were killed and 392 wounded. Parallel to the terrorist activity on the northern border, Palestinian terrorist organizations began to attack civilian targets in Israel's big cities. The Hamas, the Islamic Jihad, and later the Tanzim (al-Aqsa Brigades) began to use suicide bombers. The first suicide bombing occurred on April 16, 1993, when a car driven by a suicide bomber exploded near a group of soldiers in the vicinity of Beit El. From April 1993 to December 2000, hundreds of terrorist acts took place inside Israel, 20 of which were by suicide bombers. The main suicide bombings took place in Tel Aviv, Jerusalem, Netanyah, and Afulah. In these bombings, 240 people were killed. Yitzhak Rabin, as prime minister, Ehud Barak, the chief of staff, and Amnon Lipkin-Shahak as his deputy, realized that terrorism had become a strategic threat to the existence of Israel. For the first time, fundamentalist Islamic Palestinian terror was defined as the main threat to Israel's existence. The IDF began to prepare for a war against terror, especially against the suicide bombers. On February 25, 1995, Dr. Baruch Goldstein, a resident of Kiryat Arba, entered the Cave of the Patriarchs in Hebron with a semi-automatic weapon and killed 29 Palestinians praying in the mosque. In addition, another 101 Arabs were wounded. This event increased the tension between the Palestinian Authority and the State of Israel. On May 4, 1994, the Cairo Agreement was signed between the PA and the government of Israel. This was a continuation of the Oslo Accords. According to this agreement, the Israeli government agreed to turn the control of the Gaza Strip and Jericho over to the PA. The continuation of suicide bombings proved to the Israeli government that Yasser Arafat was not capable of preventing terror attacks. This meant that Arafat was not able to fulfill the main condition of the Oslo Accords. As a result of the terror activity a large segment of Israeli society opposed the Oslo Accords. In spite of the great opposition to the Oslo process, Israel signed another interim agreement with the PA called Oslo B. On September 28, 1995, Rabin and Yasser Arafat signed the agreement with the backing of the U.S., Russia, the European Union, President Mubarak of Egypt, and King Hussein of Jordan. Ehud Barak, the chief of staff, had reservations about the agreement because he did not believe that the PA would be able to carry it out. Under the direction of Rabin the army began to plan its redeployment in Judea and Samaria. The redeployment was carried out by Central Command headquarters of the IDF. It was based on the Oslo B agreement stipulating that the IDF was to withdraw from all the major cities in Judea and Samaria and to transfer control to the PA. The redeployment plan was called *Keshet Ẓeva'im* ("Colors of the Rainbow"). In order to ensure security in Judea and Samaria, the IDF set up headquarters outside the cities. Division headquarters in Judea and Samaria now had under its authority six new brigade headquarters, dozens of battalion headquarters, and dozens of company headquarters. The new deployment expressed itself in the division of responsibility between the IDF and the PA according to Oslo B. The major Palestinian cities were defined as Area A in which the PA was responsible for security and civilian administration. The areas outside the Palestinian cities, which included most of the Palestinian villages, were defined as Area B. In these areas, administrative authority was in the hands of the PA but security was the responsibility of the IDF. The rest of the area was defined as Area C and under the full control of Israel. The deployment of the IDF was based on three important principles: securing the main roads for Israeli settlers; the protection of settlements; and continuing anti-terrorist activities. The IDF began to patrol the main arteries of Israeli transportation. In order to increase security on these roads, access to some of them was denied to the Palestinians. To ensure the security of the settlers, every settlement was given military reinforcement. In addition, patrol roads, security fences, watchtowers, and sometimes even tanks were positioned in the periphery of the settlements. To control the movement of the Palestinians, the IDF deployed over a hundred checkpoints along the main roads of Judea and Samaria. The Ministry of Defense even invested money in armored buses for schoolchildren as well as armored ambulances and had armored convoys accompany them.

In October 1994, a peace treaty was signed between Jordan and the State of Israel. This treaty changed the perception of security along their common border. Division and brigade commanders began to have regular meetings. A hotline was set up between the two armies to coordinate military activities along both sides of the border. In spite of the improved relations, Jordanian-Palestinian soldiers fired upon Israeli patrols along the border. When in May 1996 a group of terrorists killed three Israeli soldiers, Israeli and Jordanian soldiers worked together in Jordanian territory to eliminate the terrorists. The political conflict within Israeli led to the assassination of Prime Minister Yitzhak Rabin on November 4, 1995, at a mass rally in support of the Oslo agreement. After this terrible event, Shimon Peres became prime minister. Terrorist activities including suicide bombings continued. On February 25, 1996, a suicide bomber blew himself up on a bus in Jerusalem killing 26 people. Along with Palestinian terrorist activity, the Hizbollah continued its operations along the northern border, which included a massive attack of Katyusha rockets against Israeli settlements. At the beginning of 1996, as a result of the rocket attacks, the settlements on the northern border had become in effect hostages of the Hizbollah. In response, the IDF undertook Operation Grapes of Wrath (*Invei Za'am*) in southern Lebanon. The aim of this operation was to eliminate Hizbollah strongholds, to destabilize civilian life, and to put pressure on the Lebanese government to put an end to Hizbollah activities.

In this operation, the IDF used all of its forces, which included massive airpower, tanks, artillery, and the navy. During the course of the operation, 770 Katyusha rockets fell on Israel. Twenty-four citizens were wounded and three were killed. In the midst of Israel's massive artillery attack, a Lebanese village, Kefar Kana, was mistakenly hit and approximately 100 people were killed. Another hundred were injured. Under the auspices of the Security Council, an understanding was reached between Israel, Lebanon, and Syria under which Lebanon and Syria would prevent the launching of Katyusha rockets against Israel. In this operation the IDF demonstrated its tremendous capability in coordinating naval, air, and ground forces. Palestinian terror activity, parallel to the terror activity of the Hizbollah, forced the army to change its deployment and methods of warfare against terror. This was especially true as far as the suicide bombers were concerned. To achieve this aim, the IDF increased its forces, set up new military units, and increased the cooperation with the regular and border police in fighting terror.

In May 1996, Benyamin Netanyahu (Likud) was elected prime minister of Israel, and Yizhak Mordecai was appointed minister of defense. At the end of September, in spite of the objections of the General Security Service, Netanyahu ordered the opening of the northern gate of the tunnel leading to the Western Wall of the Temple Mount in Jerusalem. This led to violent demonstrations in which 15 Israeli soldiers were killed, as well as 60 Palestinian soldiers and policemen. As a result, a summit meeting was held with Netanyahu, Arafat, King Hussein, and President Clinton participating. This summit led to the signing of the Hebron Agreement on January 17, 1997. By the end of the month, the IDF had withdrawn from most of Hebron, except for Kiryat Arba, the Cave of the Patriarchs, and the Jewish Quarter (Bet Hadassah).

Suicide bombings carried out by so-called *shahidim* (martyrs) continued. In the summer of 1997, two suicide bombings took place in which 21 Jerusalemites were killed. The terrorist activities of the Islamic Jihad and the Hamas caused the IDF to increase its presence in the main city centers. Netanyahu ordered the Mossad to eliminate Halad Mashal, one of the leaders of the Hamas. The attempt to assassinate him in Amman failed, and proved to be a great embarrassment for Israel. To improve relations, Israel agreed to Jordan's request to release Palestinian prisoners. Among them was Sheikh Ahmad Yassin, the leader of the Hamas in Gaza.

In February 1997, while transporting soldiers from Mahanaim in northern Israel to south Lebanon, two helicopters collided while flying above the settlement of She'ar Yashuv. Seventy-three fighters, officers, and crew were killed. It was the worse air disaster in the history of the Israeli Air Force. As a result, the air force commander decided to appoint a senior officer as coordinator of helicopter units. In addition, as part of the preparation of Israel's defense against future threats, the Israel Space Agency began a program to launch space satellites. In coordination with NASA, an Israeli astronaut began his training in Houston, Texas, in 1998.

On October 23, 1998, President Clinton organized the Wye Summit, whose purpose was to implement the Oslo Accords. It was agreed that the IDF would continue withdrawing from Judea and Samaria. In addition, an international airport was to be built in Gaza. As part of the agreement, the Palestinian National Council undertook to abolish sections of the Palestinian Convention that called for the destruction of the State of Israel. In July 1998, Shaul Mofaz was appointed chief of staff of the IDF. On July 6, Ehud Barak was elected prime minister. He also held the portfolio of minister of defense. In his election campaign, Barak had promised to pull all Israeli forces out of Lebanon.

On May 24, 2000, the IDF withdrew from southern Lebanon. This was a unilateral decision not coordinated with the Lebanese or Syrian governments. This overnight withdrawal left the Israeli government and the army with two difficult problems. The first was the inability to support the soldiers of the South Lebanese Army. The second was the fact that the IDF did not have the time to build an electronic fence along the border. It took a year to complete the job, during which time the army had to patrol the border. The Northern Command of the IDF was redeployed along the international border. Its operations were integrated with the air force, intelligence, and special units. The redeployment along the international border now legitimized Israel's response to any attacks of Hizbollah. On May 7, 2000, three Israeli soldiers were abducted by the Hizbollah. In the ensuing investigation conducted by the IDF a brigade commander was dismissed from his post and the advancement of a division commander was held up.

Barak's attempts to reach an agreement with the Syrians (on the Golan Heights) and the Palestinians (Judea and Samaria and Gaza) brought him face to face with Arafat and Clinton at Camp David in July 2000. In spite of the fact that Barak had agreed to give up 90% of Judea and Samaria, and even to give up sovereignty over the Arab neighborhoods in East Jerusalem, the summit failed. Clinton's compromise proposals of December 2000, did not overcome the impasse between Arafat and Barak.

On September 28, two months before this proposal, Barak had given permission to Knesset member Ariel Sharon (Likud) to pay a publicized visit to the Temple Mount. His visit caused an outbreak of Palestinian violence that led to the involvement of the IDF and the Border Police. As a direct result of the Palestinian riots, disturbances broke out among Israeli Arabs a month later. Thirteen Israeli Arab citizens were killed. The riots on the Temple Mount, the identification of the Israeli Arabs with the Palestinians, and the failure of the Camp David summit led to the outbreak of the Al-Aqsa Intifada. This was characterized by Palestinian insurgency accompanied by intensive terrorist activity. The last few months of 2000 saw an increase in Palestinian terror attacks, Hizbollah terror, and especially the involvement of Israeli Arabs in terrorist activities within Israel. Israel reinforced its forces in Judea, Samaria, and Gaza and along the northern border. Arafat's inability to prevent terror against Israel and his rejection of Barak's proposal at Camp David brought about a change in his strategy. Seeking the involvement of the international community by maintaining the volatile situation, Arafat began to give secret support to terrorist groups. Consequently he began to be viewed by the Israeli and the American governments as irrelevant to the peace process. The suicide bombings moved the IDF to plan a military operation that would destroy the terrorist infrastructure and its leaders. The Israeli government instructed the IDF to plan this campaign to restore security to Israeli citizens.

2001–2005. On March 7, Ariel Sharon was elected as the prime minister of a national unity government and Binyamin Eliezar became minister of defense. During this period the suicide bombings continued. From December 2000 until April 2004, 541 civilians and soldiers were killed. As part of their policy, the terrorist organizations attempted to eliminate Israeli leaders. On October 17, 2001, the minister of tourism, Rehavam *Ze'evi, was assassinated in a hotel in Jerusalem. On March 27, 2002, on the night of the Passover *seder*, a suicide bombing in the Park Hotel in Netanyah killed 30 civilians and wounded over a hundred. The prime minister, the minister of defense, and the chief of staff decided to take a drastic step in the war against terror. The ensuing military action was named Operation Defensive Shield (*Ḥomat Magen*), with the following aims:

a) The IDF was to take over and control the cities and villages that had become havens for terrorists;

b) To arrest and capture terrorists and the leaders behind them;

c) To confiscate all weapons;

d) To eliminate terrorist installations, laboratories for making bombs, weapon-making factories, shelters for terrorists, and anyone carrying weapons who was endangering the security of Israel.

Between January and March 2002, the IDF had worked systematically to destroy the terrorist infrastructure. In March and April 2002, a decisive blow was struck in Operation Defensive Shield, and from June 2002 until May 2003 the IDF completed its control of Judea and Samaria. From the middle of 2003 until 2004, the IDF had stabilized its control of Judea and Samaria. Although according to the Oslo Accords some of these areas were in Area A, they returned to full control of the Israeli army. Operation Defensive Shield, which had begun on March 29, 2002, officially ended on May 10, 2002. Infantry and tank units from the regular forces and the reserves participated in this operation.

To improve its control over the forces in Judea and Samaria, a new divisional headquarters was set up which took over the responsibility for Bethlehem and Hebron. The takeover of Palestinian cities was carried out in a relatively short time, and with the exception of Jenin was carried out with virtually no casualties. In Jenin 27 soldiers were killed, 14 of them in the refugee camp. In Ramallah, Arafat and his command were trapped in the *Mukata* (the central command of the Palestinians in Ramallah). In Bethlehem, a number of terrorists took refuge in the Church of the Nativity and were forced to leave the country after an agreement. Alongside of Palestinian terror, the Hizbollah continued its attacks with the support of Syria and Iran. From the time the IDF withdrew from Lebanon in May 2000, until July 2004, numerous attempts to attack Israeli soldiers and settlements took place along the northern border. During this period, 14 attempts were made by the Hizbollah to infiltrate Israel. As a result of these activities, 13 soldiers and six civilians were killed. In addition, 54 soldiers and 14 civilians were wounded.

In June 2002, the American administration proposed its roadmap for peace in the Middle East. Because of its distrust of Arafat the Israeli government was not willing to implement the roadmap. This was the reason it began to erect a fence between Israel and the Palestinians. The area on both sides of the fence included advanced technological early warning systems to prevent Palestinian terrorists from infiltrating into Israel. In the first stage, 132 kilometers were built and another 150 were being planned. The fence more or less followed the pre-Six-Day War "green line." Thanks to the fence terrorist attacks decreased by 75% in January–July 2004 in comparison with the same period the year before. Together with the IDF's activity along the security fence, the army began to eliminate terrorist leaders in Gaza, and Judea and Samaria. Israel's success in killing the chief terrorist leaders, and the lack of experience of their successors, contributed to the decline in terrorist activity. In these killings the IDF integrated intelligence, advanced technology, and helicopters.

In February 2003, the space mission of the American spaceship *Columbia* failed. The first Israeli astronaut, Col. Ilan Ramon, was killed in this mission. This disaster was a serious setback to Israel's space program and curtailed Israeli-American cooperation in space. Israel's space activity had become an important part of the state's national security.

In March 2003, the American army invaded Iraq in order to bring down the regime of Saddam Hussein. This was the end result of the terrorist attack by Al-Qaeda in New York on September 11, 2001. After the United States took over Iraq and had captured Saddam Hussein, terrorist activity against American soldiers in Iraq escalated.

The success of the terrorists in Iraq encouraged Palestinian terror groups to increase their activity in Israel. In the beginning of 2004, Hamas escalated its activities in the Gaza Strip. As a result, the IDF made strikes in Gaza and killed Sheikh Yassin and Aziz El Rantisi. These men had been the most prominent among Hamas leaders in encouraging terror attacks against Israel. After the murder of Tali Hatuel and her four daughters in Gush Katif in March 2004, the IDF intensified its operations against terrorists in Gaza. During these operations, two armored vehicles loaded with explosives blew up and 13 Israeli soldiers were killed. In consequence, the IDF began a campaign to destroy the terrorist infrastructure in Rafah and in particular the tunnels used for smuggling explosives from Egypt to the Gaza Strip. In this campaign 40 terrorists were killed and 56 houses were demolished. The campaign enabled the army to control the Philadelphi Corridor, thus creating a buffer zone that separated Egyptian territory from the Palestinians.

The terrorist groups in Gaza felt limited in their capability to infiltrate Israel and launch mortars and Kassam rockets. To upgrade the level of their attacks on Israel, the Palestinians tried to obtain weapons from outside sources. An example of this was the ship *Karin A* that tried to smuggle weapons from Iran to Gaza. This ship was captured by the Israeli Navy. It was then that the IDF realized that Al-Qaeda and Hizbollah were working hand and hand with the Palestinians.

The escalation of terrorist activities and the inability of the PA to advance the peace process led Prime Minister Sharon to announce a plan for unilateral withdrawal from Gaza. On April 28, 2004, this plan was made known to the public. The main idea of this proposal was to break the political stalemate with the PA and to minimize the friction with the Palestinians. The implementation of this plan would bring Gaza under Palestinian control and give a chance to the PA to prove their ability to prevent terrorist activities. On August 22, 2004, the disengagement task force was set up. A year later, in August 2005, the IDF together with the police, removed the settlers of Gush Katif in the Gaza Strip from their homes, for the most part meeting with passive resistance, and then proceeded to dismantle the settlements.

In this period, based on intelligence reports, the IDF redefined the threats against the security of the State of Israel. These were as follows:

a) The escalation of Palestinian terror through the use of long-range rockets on Israeli aircraft.

b) Hizbollah activities on the northern border launching hundreds of rockets on Israeli settlements.

c) The threat from Syria that could develop into a war of attrition along the Lebanese border and on the Golan Heights. In addition, there was the threat of the use of Scud missiles against Israeli targets in the center of the country.

d) The ability of Iran to launch Shihab missiles on Israeli targets in the center of the country, and the possibility that they would develop nuclear capabilities within a short time.

Along with these threats, Egypt and Saudi Arabia were amassing ballistic missiles. The Middle East was becoming a "powder keg" and this was endangering the security of Israel. The reality of this strategic situation forced Israel to develop advance response systems that would ensure Israel's military superiority and its deterrent ability. The increase in Israel's military strength between 1995 and 2005 occurred in its naval, land, and air forces.

The Israel Space Agency, with the aim of maintaining a military advantage, developed a satellite system in this period. Its purpose was to gather intelligence and serve as a means of communication. In this period the satellites *Shavit*, *Ofek*, and *Amos* were launched. In spite of the *Columbia* disaster, cooperation between the Israel Space Agency and NASA continued. The Israel Aircraft Industry continued to be the main arm in developing advanced military weapons. In land combat, new technologies were developed. These included new means of artillery and an advanced tank Merkavah 4. In Operation Defensive Shield the concept of "limited confrontation" (guerrilla war) began to evolve. To improve means of combat, the IDF began equipping its soldiers with new guns (the Tavor) and began using lightweight armored jeeps. New anti-tank missiles and advanced night-vision binoculars were developed. The air force equipped itself with new helicopters (Blackhawk and Apache), and new aircraft (the F-15i and F-16i). These new fighter jets enabled Israel to reach enemy targets up to 4,000 kilometers away (covering all of the Middle East). The navy acquired three new submarines (Dolphins) that enabled it to operate anywhere in the Middle East. Moreover, the navy developed missile carriers that increased its ability to deter enemy threats. Israel's experience in the Gulf War (1991) led the IDF to develop a defensive ballistic missile system in cooperation with the United States. As a part of its Arrow missile system a special radar device was created to act as an early warning system. In this period (2000–5), after a number of successful test launches the Arrow became an important factor in the defense of Israel. In addition, rockets and long-range missiles were developed for the land, air, and naval forces. In order to deal with new terrorist threats, Israel's intelligence capabilities were upgraded. New means of gathering intelligence were developed. This included unmanned aerial vehicles (UAV).

In spite of the IDF's great military strength, it had to deal with the phenomenon of soldiers' refusal to serve in protest against the Israeli occupation. In this period the number of young people refusing to serve in the army increased. In 2004, pilots and officers in special units published a letter in which they declared their refusal to serve in Judea, Samaria, and Gaza. In the 2005 evacuation of Gush Katif there were also isolated instances of refusal to carry out orders, but the extent of such incidents, at both ends of the political spectrum, were far rarer than had been feared.

In addition to the strategic cooperation between Israel and the United States, Israel advanced its military cooperation with Turkey and India. Israel helped these countries to upgrade their tanks, aircraft, and military technology.

As a result of terror activities all over the world, regular armies have begun to fight militant groups or even individual terrorists. This type of asymmetric combat is what characterizes the period. The greatest fear of the enlightened world is that fundamentalist Islamic groups will gain control of weapons of mass destruction. The threat is one which Israel deals with as well. In order to maintain national security, the State of Israel must remain superior in its deterrent systems and continuously improve its deterrent capabilities. Stability in the Middle East will only be achieved when peace agreements are signed between Israel and Syria, and Israel and the Palestinians. Until that time the Israel Defense Forces must meet all actual and potential military challenges. (For the clashes between Israel and Hizbollah in Lebanon in summer 2006, see *Israel, State of: Historical Survey.)

[Gideon Netzer (2nd ed.)]

BIBLIOGRAPHY: OTTOMAN AND MANDATORY PERIODS. E. Golomb, *History of Jewish Self-Defense in Palestine 1878–1921* (1946); M.P. Waters (pseud.), *Haganah* (1945?); M. Pearlman, *The Army of Israel* (1950), chs. 1–8; E. Dekel, *Shai: The Exploits of Haganah Intelligence* (1959); M. Mardor, *Strictly Illegal* (1964); Dinur, Haganah. ISRAEL DEFENSE FORCES. Y. Allon, *The Making of Israel's Army* (1969); idem, *Shield of David* (1970); S. Peres, *David's Sling* (1970). **ADD. BIBLIOGRAPHY:** C. Herzog, *The Arab-Israel Wars: War and Peace in the Middle East from the War of Independence through Lebanon* (1983); Z. Schiff, *A History of the Israeli Army, 1870–1974* (1974). **WEBSITE:** www1.idf.il.

ECONOMIC AFFAIRS

THE PRE-MANDATE (LATE OTTOMAN) PERIOD

Geography and Borders

In September 1923 a new political entity was formally recognized by the international community. Palestine, or Ereẓ Israel as Jews have continued to refer to it for 2,000 years, officially began its existence as a territory ruled by Britain under a mandate from the League of Nations. Since 1917, Britain had ruled the area as an occupier of territory belonging to a defeated enemy (the Ottoman Empire), and since 1920, under the terms of a mandate assigned by the post-World War I San Remo Conference and ratified by the League in July 1922.

The 27,009-square-kilometer area of Mandatory Palestine stretched from the shore of the Mediterranean Sea east to the Jordan River and the Dead Sea, and to the Aravah Valley to the Gulf of Eilat (Akaba). It was in this territory that Britain had promised the Zionist movement, in the words of the *Balfour Declaration of November 2, 1917, to allow the "establishment in Palestine of a national home for the Jewish People." This language was incorporated into the League Mandate, which also provided for the establishment of the *Jewish Agency. In order to accommodate the British commitment to the Zionists, the Palestine Mandate alone, unlike the other Middle East mandates of the League to the British and French, did not provide for the eventual self-rule and independence of the local population, which at the time was 90 percent Palestinian Arab.

The September 1923 borders of Palestine differed from those of the 1920 mandate, which included the almost 90,000 square kilometers east of the Jordan River. That area remained part of the British Mandate until its independence in 1946, but was split administratively by Britain from Palestine in May 1923 and ruled autonomously as the Emirate of Transjordan. The Mandate was divided in this way in part as the result of the British government's decision, proposed in the Churchill White Paper of 1922, to exclude the area east of the Jordan from the scope of the Balfour Declaration.

The borders shared by Mandatory Palestine with two other newly established political entities – Lebanon and Syria to the north and northeast, both under a League mandate to France – were the result of lengthy negotiations, from 1916 through 1922, between Britain and France. The final border settlement was part of a comprehensive agreement that also involved the creation of Iraq (as a British mandate) and the splitting of its spoils. These included, among other things, the allocation of shares of the Iraq Petroleum Corporation, which held exclusive oil concessions in that territory.

Palestine's border with Egypt, which left the Sinai Peninsula on the Egyptian side, was set along a virtually straight line from Rafa on the Mediterranean to Akaba on the Red Sea. The British, in occupation of Egypt since 1882, had imposed this line on the sultan in 1906 as a border between the two districts, which were both nominally part of the Ottoman Empire.

These borders had great significance for future developments, and not only because of the small size of the Jewish state as it emerged 25 years later. The country is located in a semi-arid zone abutting the desert, and the location of the northern and northeastern borders determined the available water supply, which in turn determined the eventual development and structure of its farming sector.

The Genesis of the Jewish Resettlement Effort

For centuries, the area that formally became known as Palestine in the early 1920s had been an outpost of the declining Ottoman Empire. It had a Jewish community of fewer than 10,000 – in 1800 it was less than three percent of the population. A total of 275,000 people lived in that geographical area by that time, and the very small Jewish communities were in the four "holy cities" of *Jerusalem, *Hebron, *Tiberias, and *Safed, and focused primarily on Torah study and religious activities. For their livelihood, these communities relied almost exclusively on contributions from Jewish communities in the Diaspora.

The late 18th- and 19th-century Industrial Revolution in Western and Central Europe that sparked unprecedented economic growth in those countries ultimately spilled over in the closing decades of the 19th century to Europe's fringes, including the eastern shore of the Mediterranean among other places. It brought in its wake a major transformation in travel and trade in the form of railroad and steamship transport. The construction of the Suez Canal (opened 1869) was a clear expression of that process, which was also stimulated by the growing interest in the area by the European powers and competition among them for a stake there. It put the "Holy Land" on the tourist and pilgrimage maps of Europe, as well as on the political maps of its major powers.

ALIYAH AND THE TRANSFORMATION OF THE SOCIAL STRUCTURE OF THE YISHUV. The emergence of the Zionist Movement (see *Zionism) in the closing decades of the 19th century, and the spread of its message among the rapidly growing Jewish communities in Eastern and Western Europe was, of course, closely linked to the economic growth and political expansion occurring at the time in Europe, which contributed to the mass emigration of Jews from Eastern Europe, mainly from the Russian Empire, which at that time had barely initiated its industrialization drive, to Central and Western Europe, and beyond the Atlantic to the United States. A small portion of this mass emigration, reacting to the first pogroms in southern Russia in the 1880s and inspired by the Zionist notion of a "return to the land of the Patriarchs," reached Palestine. These immigrants to Palestine marked the beginning of the First Aliyah of 1882–1903. The Hebrew term *aliyah*, dating from the Second Temple period and referring to the pilgrimage to Jerusalem on the three Jewish festivals, was soon adopted to describe the waves of Zionist immigration to Palestine.

The impact of the first stage of that flow appears already in the population data of 1890, which provides the first reliable estimate of Palestine's population: in the 1880s, the Jewish community grew by 80 percent to 43,000, or about eight percent of the total population, compared to a negligible percentage at the beginning of the nineteenth century and just five percent in 1882, when the first wave of Zionist immigration began to reach the country.

Table 1 offers a first glimpse of the rapidly changing structure of the Jewish community in response to the First Aliyah, 1882–1903, when there was an annual average of 1,000–1,500 immigrants during the 20-year period between 1882 and 1903. This shows in terms of change the size of the Jewish population in Jerusalem and in the three other holy cities (Hebron, Tiberias, and Safed, not shown) as a proportion of the total Jewish population. In 1882 the Jewish community in Jerusalem plus 3,000–4,000 Jews living in the three other holy cities consisted of about 20,000 people, of a total of 24,000. Yet during the short eight-year interval between 1882 and 1890, the proportion fell from 71 percent to about 58 percent of the total Jewish community. These figures underline the predominance through 1882 of the old *yishuv* (Jewish community in Palestine) – the mission of which, as conceived by its members, was to maintain the presence of Jews in Jerusalem in the vicinity of Judaism's holiest site, the Temple Mount, and its Western Wall, the Kotel. Among this sector of the community, the study of the Talmud in the yeshivah was deemed the only worthy activity, a belief that precluded its members from engaging in economic activity. The 1890 population figures show that this sector was still the majority of the Jewish population. However, these figures also indicate that within a very short period – just eight years – its share of the population was significantly reduced.

Table 2 shows the gross and net immigration figures through 1947, the last year before the establishment of Israel.

THE FIRST AGRICULTURAL SETTLEMENTS: 1882–1902. The establishment of *Mikveh Israel as an agricultural boarding school near Jaffa in 1870 signaled a change in the Jewish community's attitude toward the modern world, marking the beginning of its adaptation to the urban-industrial economy rapidly spreading outward from Europe. A full decade passed before Karl *Netter was able, with financing from and on behalf of the *Alliance Israélite Universelle, the organization set up by Jewish notables in France, to transform the school into a functional operation. Under its influence, and following the example of Petaḥ Tikvah (the first modern Jewish settlement, founded in 1878 by an enterprising group from Jerusalem), six agricultural settlements were established near Jaffa and in the eastern Galilee in the first half of the 1880s, populated

Table 1. Population in Mandatory Palestine and Its Major Towns[1]

	1882 (1)	1890 (2)	1914 (3)	1922 (4)	1931 (5)	1939 (6)	1944 (7)	1947 (8)
Population: Total	(500,000)	532,000	689,000	768,000	1,036,000	1,505,000	1,748,000	1,970,000
Jews	24,000	43,000	94,000	85,000	175,000	449,000	536,000	630,000
Arabs[2]	476,000	489,000	595,000	683,000	861,000	1,056,000	1,212,000	1,340,000
Major towns:								
Jerusalem: Total	31,000	42,000	70,000[3]	63,000	91,000	–	152,000	–
Jews	17,000	25,000	45,000	34,000	51,000	–	92,000	–
Arabs	14,000	17,000[4]	25,000	29,000	40,000	–	60,000	–
Jaffa: Total	11,000	23,000	46,000	50,000	55,000	–	94,000	–
Jews	1,000	3,000	13,000	9,000	8,000	–	28,000	–
Arabs	10,000	20,000	33,000	41,000	47,000	–	66,000	–
Haifa: Total	6,500	8,700	20,000	25,000	50,000	–	129,000	–
Jews	500	1,700	3,000	6,000	16,000	(48,000)	66,000	–
Arabs[5]	6,000	7,000	17,000	19,000	34,000	–	63,000	–
Tel Aviv	–	–	1,500	15,000	47,000	(160,000)	166,000	–

Notes:
1. Figures rounded to the nearest one thousand.
2. The dominant component of the Arab population was Muslims. The total number of Arabs includes Muslims, Christians, and a minuscule group of "others." Christians were about 15 percent of the Arab community in 1922, 11.4 percent in 1931, and almost 12 percent in 1944.
3. The estimate refers to 1910.
4. The population figure refers to 1886–87.
5. The relative size of the Christian and Muslim communities in Haifa was altogether different from that in the total Arab population in Mandatory Palestine. In 1922 Christians were about 40 percent of the Arab population of Haifa; while their share of the total Arab population declined during the Mandatory period, in 1944 the Christian community in Haifa grew to about 43 percent of the total Arab population in that town.

See Bibliography for main statistical sources.

Table 2. Aliyah – Immigration, Net Immigration, and Immigration Ratios[1]

Wave of Immigration	Period	Immigration (1)	Net Immigration (2)	Ratio – %[2] (3)
First Aliyah	1882–1903	20,000 – 30,000		
Second Aliyah	1904–1914	35,000 – 40,000		
Third–Fourth Aliyah	1919–1931	117,000	87,000	(92.0)
Fifth Aliyah	1932–1939	248,000	229,000	80.0
Postwar Aliyah	1940–1947	101,000	92,000	–
Total	1922–1945	407,000	396,000	73.0
Total	1919–1947	466,000	408,000	–
Arabs	1922–1945	–	49,000[3]	8.5

Notes:
1. Figures are rounded to the nearest one thousand.
2. Ratio of net immigration to the corresponding increase of the Jewish population in the relevant time interval.
3. Upper round estimate.

It was the revival of immigration during the single decade of the Second Aliyah, from 1904 to 1914, which finally changed the balance between the old and the new *yishuv* in favor of the latter. Using the same yardstick – the population of the Jewish community in Jerusalem as a proportion of the total Jewish population – the share of the old *yishuv* was already only 48 percent by 1914. This figure does exclude the old *yishuv* communities in the three other Holy Cities, but implicitly includes the whole Jewish population of Jerusalem in the old *yishuv*. Yet, already by that time a significant number of Jerusalem's Jews were productively employed in trades and services, and they considered themselves members of the Zionist movement. This was true, to an even greater extent, of the Jewish communities in *Jaffa and its new Jewish suburb *Tel Aviv, in *Haifa, and in the rural settlements (Table 3). A 60–40 percent ratio of new *yishuv* to old *yishuv* would thus better approximate the comparative size of these two components of the Palestine Jewish community by 1914. The new *yishuv* was by that time clearly in the vanguard of Zionist-inspired activity. Its mission according to the Zionist vision and design was nothing less than creating the economic and political infrastructure of the future Jewish state in Palestine.

by new immigrants from czarist Russia and Romania. These colonies represented an attempt to implement the notion of the "Resettlement of the Land of the Patriarchs" articulated by the new Zionist organizations then surfacing throughout the Russian *Pale of Settlement, following a wave of pogroms in 1881. One of the six settlements was *Gederah, established on the southern coastal plain in 1884 by *Bilu, an organization of Jewish students in Russian universities.

The founding of these rural settlements naturally required substantial capital investment. The first stage of the settlement process involved the acquisition of land. through 1918 this had to be done under the Ottoman land code, which endowed vague property rights in land in most areas subject to its jurisdiction and which did not maintain a systematic method of land registration and property rights. The latter were of a bewildering variety, the legacy of the semifeudal system that had existed for ages. On top of that was the hostility of the Ottoman authorities to Jews' acquisition of land, which raised the cost of purchasing real estate.

With limited means at their disposal, these six settlements, with a population of about 500 (Table 3), soon came to grief. Their survival, and indeed the entire resettlement effort, would soon have collapsed but for the appearance on the scene in 1883 of Baron Edmund *Rothschild. For the ensuing two decades Baron Rothschild offered encouragement, financial support, and expertise to the resettlement effort. His funding of that experiment, which helped increase the number of these settlements to 22 by 1900 (Table 3) was 20 times greater than the funds channeled for that purpose by the other Jewish organizations as "grants in aid" to the resettlement drive.

The teething problems of that experiment were not due only to the shortage of funds to finance the buildup of capital stock. There was also the pioneers' lack of experience and know-how in farming. Furthermore, the French farm experts hired by Baron Rothschild to guide the settlers knew little of local conditions, including the native climate, soil, and pests specific to Palestine.

Given their experience and the vision of Baron Rothschild, who was aware of the biblical image of the "land of corn and wine," their choice of crops focused inevitably on high-cost and time-intensive grapes as the main product of these settlements. Viniculture did not provide year-round employment. Maintaining this kind of farming operation entailed hiring seasonal labor, which in practice meant indigenous Arabs paid the prevailing low wage. Furthermore, though each farming household had its own plot, it had to follow the instructions of an administrator put in charge of the settlements by the Baron, thus eroding personal responsibility and enterprise among the settlers. To absorb the output of these vineyards Rothschild built two major wine cellars, one in *Rishon le-Zion for the southern settlements and the other in *Zikhron Ya'akov for the northern settlements. Subsidized by his funds, these first two industrial enterprises in Palestine paid above European market prices for the grape crop. Europe was the inevitable destination of their output.

These pioneer agricultural settlements experienced severe problems in their early years. The acquisition of farming know-how through "learning-by-doing" required time. And so did the emergence of entrepreneurs and entrepreneurial knowledge, and the accumulation of equity by farm households. These were evidently the necessary conditions for freeing settlers from the shackles of the Baron's bureaucracy and the benefit of his funding.

In spite of these tribulations, the groundwork of the resettlement movement was laid in the last two decades of the 19th century. This is evident in the number of Jewish rural settlements, which expanded to 22 by 1900, as Baron Rothschild wound up his organization, granting the settlers the land and the two wine cellars and other elements of infrastructure set up by him, thus putting the settlements on an independent footing. By that time, they had a population of 5,000, or ten times the number of settlers in 1882. There was a similar expansion by this time of Jewish-owned land, half of which was in rural areas (Table 3), although the total amount was negligible; indeed it was small even in proportion to size of the Jewish population, which had grown to 50,000.

Despite their shortcomings, the efforts of the first wave of settlers opened the way for things to come. They led to the emergence of a community of experienced farmers and agricultural entrepreneurs and taught some highly significant lessons to Zionist leaders just as the *World Zionist Organization, established in 1897, was coming into its own. They suggested that a near-European living standard was a necessary condition for the survival of Jewish farming in Palestine, and that this required not only substantial capital investment, but also the diversification of the prevailing agricultural economy – the single-crop farming pursued, by and large, by the first generation of Jewish settlements. By the turn of the century these settlements resembled the European colonies in southeast Asia and Africa with their monocultural plantations producing commercial crops for world markets and exclusively dependent on indigenous seasonal labor. The dominance of Arab workers in the Jewish settlements reproduced the situation in the European colonies.

These features were of course inconsistent with the grand scheme formulated by the World Zionist Organization under the leadership of Theodor *Herzl (1897–1904). Its declared ultimate objective – the establishment of a Jewish State in Palestine – was a response to rising overt antisemitism in Europe and the increasing poverty of Jewish communities, especially in Eastern Europe, which had hardly been touched by the Industrial Revolution but were experiencing a population explosion. These conditions induced mass emigration. In pursuit of its ultimate goal, Zionism envisioned the immediate building up of a self-sustaining economy in Palestine, offering a reasonable standard of living as a necessary condition for inducing a significant fraction of the huge Jewish emigration from Eastern Europe to move to Palestine rather than to Western Europe and to the United States. The Zionists called, therefore, for a major revision of the Palestine resettlement strategy.

THE SECOND ALIYAH AND THE NOTION OF MIXED FARMING. The Second Aliyah started in 1904, in response to another set of pogroms in Russia in 1903–04. In the succeeding decade, ending with the outbreak of World War I in 1914, it brought about 40,000 Jewish immigrants to the shores of Palestine. This was indeed only a small fraction of the Jewish emigration from Eastern Europe during that decade, about three percent, but it was substantially larger than the total inflow of the First Aliyah of 1882–1903 (Table 2).

Table 3. Jewish Agriculture Settlements, Rural Population, Farm Output, and Land Possession, 1882–1947

			Output[2]			Land (In Thousands of Dunams[3])		Irrigated Area (In Thousands of Dunams)		
Year	Rural settlements (1)	Rural population[1] (2)	Total (3)	Mixed farming (4)	Citrus (5)	Total (6)	Rural (7)	Citrus groves (8)	Mixed farming (9)	Total (10)=(8)+(9)
A. Jewish Sector									–	–
1882	6	500	–	–	–	23	–	–	–	–
1900	22	5,000	–	–	–	218	114	–	–	–
1914	47	12,000	–	–	–	418	230	–	–	–
1921	–	–	80	79	80	–	–	–	–	–
1922	79	15,000	100	100	100	575	387	10	–	–
1931	129	38,000	445	277	678	1,008[4]	–	70	13	83
1935	–	–	646	469	890	–	–	153	16	169
1936	199	89,000	846	481	1,349	1,232	626	155	–	–
1939	254	–	1,248	622	2,112	–	–	156	46	202
1941	259	113,000	–	–	–	1,544[5]	1,318[5]	131	77	208
1945	–	–	–	–	–	–	–	120	95	215
1947	308	153,000	–	–	–	1,660	1,380	120	115	235
B. Arab Sector										
1922	–	478,000	100	100	100	–	–	19	–	–
1931	–	577,000	141	131	355	–	–	52	–	–
1935	–	–	218	122	841	–	–	125	–	–
1939	–	–	244	136	966	–	–	143	–	–
1944	–	788,000	–	–	–	–	–	–	–	–

Notes:
1. Rounded to the nearest thousand. Figures for the Arab sector include nomads.
2. Real farm output.
3. Rounded to the nearest thousand dunams.
4. The figure refers to 1942.
5. The figure refers to 1933.

Students and other young people, many inspired by the socialist ideology spreading at that time in the Jewish communities of Eastern Europe and which they attempted to wed to Zionism, were the dominant group in this wave of immigration. Their arrival in Palestine had an immediate effect on the old settlements, and particularly on the direction and features of the resettlement process. It soon led to a major transformation in the structure of Jewish agriculture, particularly the employment of Jewish labor. The slogan *"avodah ivrit"* ("Jewish labor"), so much a part of the vocabulary of the post-1903 Socialist Zionist immigrants, reverberated for the next three decades in the politics of the Yishuv, and inspired the restructuring of Zionist settlement policy.

The *Palestine Office set up by the World Zionist Organization in 1908 in Jaffa, under the direction of a new immigrant, Arthur *Ruppin, adopted *avodah ivrit* as its guiding principle. Ruppin identified the reliance of the late 19th-century settlements on Arab labor as their Achilles' heel, particularly as it limited their capacity to absorb new immigrants. The employment of Jewish labor was accordingly specified as the instrument to promote Jewish economic viability and growth. The Palestine Office proceeded to implement the *avodah ivrit* strategy in its chosen first line of activity, forestation, which soon became one of the symbols of the Zionist resettlement effort. With the modest funds at its disposal it initiated the planting of the Herzl Forest in *Ben Shemen and Huldah in 1908, relying exclusively on Jewish labor, as insisted on by the vociferous claims of Jewish workers, whose ranks were by that time swelled by newcomers of the Second Aliyah.

Furthermore, to promote the success of the new immigrants who out of ideological conviction volunteered to go into agriculture, the Palestine Office determined that it should provide basic training in farming. This decision led to the establishment of Ben Shemen, one of the first settlements founded and financed by the Zionist organizations, as an agricultural experiment and training facility.

A second foundation of the resettlement strategy adopted by the Palestine Office was the promotion of mixed farming, involving grain, fodder, vegetable, dairy and poultry production. This kind of agriculture promised a balanced year-round demand for labor and correspondingly stable employment and income throughout the seasons, unlike single-product plantation farming. The Palestine Office launched an experiment along these lines in two new settlements in the north, Kinneret and Deganyah, established in 1908 and 1909 respectively.

Table 3a. Socioeconomic Composition of Jewish Rural Settlements

Year	Private Enterprise[1] (1)	Cooperatives – Moshavim (2)	Collectives – Kibbutzim (3)	Others[2] (4)	Total (5)
1922	64	2	12	1	79
1931	82	10	30	4	126
1936	76	70	48	5	199
1947	60	117	124	7	308

Notes:
1. Though private farm settlements were still established over time, many of the older settlements grew rapidly and were transformed into urban entities in which manufacturing and services dominated occupation more and more. With some lag this was formally recognized by the authorities, which designated them urban settlements. Hence the reduction of the number of private rural settlements from 1930 onwards.
2. Agricultural school (Mikveh Israel, Kadoorie, etc.).

These two settlements opened the door to another venture, which dominated Zionist resettlement policy for decades to come. Deganyah soon became the forerunner of settlements based on the "self-labor" principle: it was to be manned by a group of Jewish workers and run as an autonomous economic entity – operating as a collective of its members. These settlements were allocated land and provided with basic capital – equipment, working capital, and housing – in the form of loans and credit from the Zionist authorities. Running production activity on their own, they were required to pay rent and to repay their debt, including interest, on a long-term schedule. The land was nationalized, the property of the Keren Kayemet Leyisrael (*Jewish National Fund), set up by the World Zionist Organization to purchase and own property. It was to be leased to its cultivators in perpetuity.

The requirement to pay rent and repay loans and credit allocations with interest was a major incentive for agricultural settlements to move into mixed farming, since this structure, involving immediately marketable products in urban markets, offered a cash flow which could provide a current income and the means to meet financial commitments. Thus efficient production made feasible by self-employed labor would assure the settlements' financial viability. The rapid expansion of urban markets, which was indeed a fact of life in the decade preceding the outbreak of World War I, was of course a prerequisite for the success of this strategy.

A score of older late 19th-century settlements in the coastal plain north and south of Jaffa adopted a diversification strategy on their own, in response to market signals. This transition from viniculture dominance was accelerated by the emergence at the turn of the century of a highly profitable new branch of agriculture, the citrus industry, which benefited from rapidly expanding European markets, which were made more easily reachable by the contemporary steam revolution in the shipping industry, and the much greater frequency of landings in the Port of Jaffa. A simultaneous expansion of almond growing was another component in the move towards diversification. Thanks to the differing times of high season in these three branches, this diversification in the older settlements enabled a much more balanced demand for labor, which offered more leeway for the employment of Jewish labor. The introduction of almond and citrus growing required huge investments, and a longish gestation period, before the first crops, and an even longer interval before they reached their peak productivity levels. The older settlements, some of which had been around for as long as two decades, had by this time nurtured a group of entrepreneurs with sufficient capital and collateral to obtain bank credit on their own, allowing them to embark on these new ventures. Similarly, the rapid expansion of the urban Jewish community in Jaffa and vicinity, with its fast-growing market for fresh food, offered an incentive to farmers in the old settlements to move into dairy and vegetable farming. Thus private agricultural enterprise was encouraged to implement the same diversification strategy, though with a different structure offering employment to high-wage Jewish labor, promoted by the Palestine office in its own settlements.

The mixed farming concept adopted in practice by both old and new settlements in the first decade of the 20th century; the high cost of Jewish labor, which encouraged the use of labor-saving devices; and a choice of crops and products that did not involve labor-intense cultivation inevitably imposed a highly significant requirement – the use of irrigation as a major farm input. Palestine's short winter season, the moderate rainfall in that season even along the coastal plain and in the northern part of the country and much more so in the semi-arid areas in the south and southeast, imposed this requirement. It was a necessary condition for high yields per unit of land and labor, generating correspondingly high incomes approaching European standards. The development of irrigation in the Jewish sector, which in the last decades of the Ottoman period involved drilling wells all over, soon became a hallmark of the Zionist resettlement effort.

The 25 Jewish agricultural settlements established between 1900 and 1914, increasing the total to 47, meant first and foremost a significant spatial expansion (Table 3). It involved penetration into new regions. Northeastern Galilee, lower Galilee, and the northern Jordan Valley appeared on the map of Jewish settlements. The number of settlements along the southern coastal plain, north and south of Jaffa, was significantly increased. The result was an increase in rural Jewish population. This grew 140 percent to 12,000 between 1900 and

1914 (Table 3). This rate was indeed significantly greater than that of the overall Jewish population, which grew by around 90 percent to approximately 94,000.

The rural demographic expansion affected the older settlements, several of which, with populations over 1,000, had already acquired some urban features. The focus of their contributions to production and employment, however, was still agricultural. The market-driven diversification, providing for increases both in demand and in seasonal stability of demand for labor, was absorbing a growing number of Jewish workers. As the dominant contributors to the Jewish sector's farm production, these settlements became the main battlefields of the struggle for *avodah ivrit*. This struggle, which started in the previous decade, continued through the mid-1930s, at which time it disappeared from the political agenda.

THE DEVELOPMENT OF THE URBAN SECTOR. Though the economic performance of Jewish agricultural settlements was significant, whether compared with 1880, when they started, or with 1900 when they moved into their second stage, they still accounted for only about 13 percent of the Jewish population at the outbreak of World War I in 1914. In that period of a little over three decades, which might be called the "warm-up" period of the "Return to Zion," the urban Jewish population increased six times more, in absolute terms, than the agricultural settlements' population. With an 87 percent share in 1914, urban Jews were evidently the dominant group within the Jewish population of Palestine.

These aggregates, however, offer a skewed perspective of the process, in which the dynamic element consisted of immigrants who established the urban version of the Zionist Return to the Land of the Patriarchs, and who established the commercial and industrial infrastructure of a modern economy. By 1914 this element was seemingly more than half of the total Jewish population, which by that time was already close to 100,000 (Table 1). Together with the 12,000 Jews in the rural settlements (Table 3), these made up the new *yishuv*, about two thirds of the total Jewish population. The static element of the urban population was the old *yishuv*, in 1914 still about a third of the total.

The rapid growth of both the Jewish and the total population of Jaffa is evidence of the formation of a modern economy. Arthur Ruppin's 1907 estimate of Jaffa's Jewish population in 1882 put it at 1,000. In 1914, Jaffa's Jewish population was already 12,000, and its Jewish suburb, Tel Aviv, founded in 1909, had by that time a population of 1,500. The Jaffa-Tel Aviv urban center already had a Jewish population of slightly more than the total population of the Jewish agricultural settlements. The Jewish population of Haifa, and perhaps a third of the Jewish population of Jerusalem, were by that time involved in economic activity – commerce, finance, even manual labor – and were thus an active component of the new *yishuv*.

The emergence of Jaffa as the hub of urban development in Palestine in the last decade of the 19th century signaled a growing linkage of that territory with the European economy. The opening of the Jaffa–Jerusalem single-track railroad in 1892 enhanced Jaffa's standing as Palestine's main port, depot, and leading commercial center and contributed to the rise of commercial and quasi-industrial activity. The growth of shipping services serving, among other activities, the increasing tourist traffic reflected the growing interest of the European powers in the territory, highlighted by the visit of the German Kaiser in 1899. The rapidly growing Jewish community was inevitably the vanguard of the expanding commercial, financial, and administrative activity. The main office of the Anglo-Palestine Bank opened in Jaffa in 1903, followed by the establishment of the Palestine Office of the World Zionist Organization in 1908. The presence of these commercial and financial services made Jaffa the urban center for the Jewish agricultural settlements, most of which were located in the coastal plain in Jaffa's periphery.

The rapid increase of the Jewish population of Jaffa, from a negligible fraction of the total in the early 1880s, to more than a quarter of the town's population by 1914 (Table 1), led in 1907 to an initiative to establish a modern Jewish suburb. In response to the proposal of a group of 60 families, the Zionist organization decided to grant the members of that group credit to finance the purchase of the land north of the city. The actual funds came from the Anglo-Palestine Bank and had to be repaid at the market rate of interest. Though an ad hoc decision, this transaction nevertheless set a precedent: Zionist resettlement policy applied not only to the agricultural sector, but also, occasionally, took into account the requirements of the urban sector as well.

The planned suburb of Jaffa, established in 1909, and with a population of 1,500 in 1914, was the kernel of Tel Aviv, which soon after World War I became the leading center of the Jewish resettlement effort. Though the Zionist Organization did provide the financial launching pad for that initiative, urban resettlement activity was on the whole initiated, financed, and run by private enterprise. It received only marginal financial support, seed money, from the Zionist organization. For better or for worse, the urban sector proved to be, already in its early stages, and even more so later on, the dominant factor in Jewish resettlement of Palestine.

The Arab Sector: Demography, Farming, and Urbanization

In the early 1880s the Arab population consisted of a dominant Muslim community and a much smaller group of Christians, totaling slightly less than half a million people. By 1914 it had grown to approximately 600,000, suggesting an average annual growth rate of about 0.7 percent, not significantly different from that suggested (on the basis of a rough estimate of the population for 1800), during the first 80 years of the 19th century (Table 1).

The breakdown in Table 1 of the main Arab population in the urban centers in 1890, to which the population of Nazareth and three other small Arab towns should be added, suggest that about ten percent of the Arab population lived in towns. This means that approximately 90 percent of that population lived in rural areas, eking out a meager living from the land by farming.

Traditional agriculture as practiced for a millennium – dry farming exclusively dependent on the rainfall during a short winter season – provided for the livelihood of this population living in small, almost self-sufficient villages, using and exchanging currency only infrequently. Grain provided the staple food, and a few sheep and goats per family supplied milk and meat. Olive trees and grapes exclusively dependent for water on rainfall provided cash crops. These were grown mainly in the mountainous areas of Galilee, Samaria, and the Judean hills. The payment of heavy taxes in cash was required from the middle of the 19th century onward and made cash crops necessary. The sale of these crops – olive oil and grapes, in particular – provided one of the main economic links with the market towns near clusters of these small villages.

From 1800 on the Ottoman administration attempted to establish registration of land titles. The last vestiges of the feudal system were indeed eliminated during the second quarter of the 19th century. Nevertheless, the traditional periodic redivision of land among members of the clan living in each of these villages did not disappear as Jewish immigration gained momentum in the 1880s. The periodic redivision of fallow land reduced the incentive of the peasants to make improvements, with long-lasting effect on fertility. It also made it quite difficult to purchase landed property subject to the redivision rule.

Nevertheless, that rather stagnant feature of the Arab sector was subjected to meaningful challenge and change in the three decades from the 1880s onward through the outbreak of World War I. By that time the effects of the industrial revolution in Europe began to penetrate the stagnant system. The rising flow of tourists and pilgrims, the establishment of several German agricultural colonies, and the initiation of Jewish economic activity (the latter two involving capital imports) all helped to provide markets for the cash crops of the Arab *fellah* (peasant). Furthermore, the Jewish settlements began to offer seasonal employment, providing a rising flow of cash income. Thus the Arab farm sector was pulled more and more into the market orbit.

This process also reflected the emergence of a new agricultural enterprise, initiated by Arab landlords – citriculture. By the turn of the century the Jaffa orange, a mutation which had first appeared in an orange grove in the vicinity of that town in the 1840s, made its entrance into European markets as a specific and superior orange brand. It was the enterprise of Arab growers that initiated the rapid expansion of orange plantations in the 1890s; Jewish entrepreneurs soon followed. Increased shipping services in the Jaffa port reflected the importance of the Jaffa orange as the dominant export of the country, as it remained for four decades to come. The all-out expansion of the citrus groves and the corresponding growth of exports occurred later, though, after World War I.

These developments fostered the transformation of Jaffa into the major commercial and financial center of the Arab sector of Palestine in the ensuing decades, through 1914 and beyond. Simultaneously it became the leading location of the slow but significant process of Arab urbanization. This increased the Arab urban population from some eight to ten percent at the beginning of the 1880s to about 15 percent of a much larger total in 1914. Jaffa was the vibrant center of that process. Its Arab population grew by more than three times in that formative interval, while the total Arab urban population a little more than doubled. The rising importance of Jaffa as a center of Arab population and economic activity in that 40-year period was underlined by the drastic change in the ratio of the Arab population of Jerusalem and Jaffa. in the early 1880s, the Arab population in Jerusalem was 40 percent larger than Jaffa's; by 1914 Jaffa took a clear lead over Jerusalem (Table 1). This was an omen of things to come in the postwar period.

THE MANDATORY PERIOD, 1918–1948

Palestine as a Unique Political and Economic Entity

The immediate effect of World War I on Palestine was the transfer of the territory from the authority of the dismembered Ottoman Empire to that of the British Empire. The transfer involved radical changes in the institutional and legal structures, as well as in the economic arrangements, within which the affairs of the territory would be carried on.

First was the establishment of a unitary political authority for the entire territory (there was no such authority under the Ottomans; the territory incorporated into Mandate Palestine was part of several Ottoman provinces). The British established a Palestine government with a high commissioner, responsible to the Colonial Office in London, as its head. An administration divided into departments of state (customs and excise, public works, education, immigration, law, and an independent judicial system staffed by British judges with a sprinkling of locals) were the skeleton of that government. The British government sought and received formal approval for these arrangements at the San Remo Conference of 1920 and the League of Nations in 1922, in the form of a mandate. The population of Palestine was not consulted.

A second highly significant change was the legal definition of the borders of the territory approved by the League of Nations' Mandatory committee, which had formal authority over the ultimate disposition of the territory (see Geography and Borders, above).

The text of the League's Mandate to Britain included in its preamble the language of the Balfour Declaration of November 2, 1917, in which the British government stated that "His Majesty's Government views with favour the establishment in Palestine of a national home for the Jewish People." The Zionist movement interpreted that statement as an implied commitment to free immigration of Jews into the territory, as well as an implied promise to make available uncultivated state land to the newcomers. Since Palestine had a total population of less than 800,000 in 1922, of whom some 160,000 lived in urban areas, the Zionist leadership presumed initially that plenty of such land was potentially available even within the 27,000 square kilometers allocated to Palestine under the terms of the Churchill White Paper of 1922 (that is, after it had been separated from Transjordan). This was, however, never the perception of the British officials running the Palestine government; land belonging to the public domain was never made available to Jewish settlers. Yet the acquisition of land by purchase was made much more feasible legally than it had been during Ottoman times.

An immediate measure implemented by the government was the census of 1922, which offered a reliable source of demographic information, including data on the national and religious composition of the population, and of its location. Another was the beginning of a process of land registration, specifying legal ownership of real estate in the urban and rural areas. This process, which was to facilitate real estate transactions, was not completed for the whole territory by the end of the Mandatory period.

The establishment of the British Mandatory government had several beneficial economic effects. Three features of the new political entity had immediate and far-reaching long-term significance for the running of its economy. First, the adoption of the Palestine pound as the local currency. Second, the creation of a unitary customs area within the borders of the British Mandate (thus including Transjordan). Third, the maintenance of a policy of "free trade."

The Palestine pound offered a stable monetary and financial anchor for the economic system. Though formally issued by the Palestine Currency Board (located in London), it was similar to its predecessor – the Egyptian pound, adopted as Palestine's currency temporarily in 1918 – in its relationship to the British pound sterling. It was fully backed by sterling, and the one-on-one exchange rate with the British pound underlined its prestigious status. The creditability endowed by this status and the stable exchange rate regime of sterling with other major world currencies facilitated the flow of capital imports, and was a major support of economic growth.

The second feature, the creation of a territorial customs zone, was curious in that Transjordan, the territory east of the Jordan River, which was included in the British Mandate for Palestine, was governed separately from Palestine but was included in the Palestine customs zone. Likewise, it shared the same currency, the Palestine pound, until 1948. Transjordan was excluded from the provisions of the Balfour Declaration and thus from Jewish immigration (see Geography and Borders) and its direct economic impact. In view of its minuscule economic capacity during the Mandate period, this did not make a meaningful difference to the economy of Palestine.

The distinctive feature of the policy on import duties adopted by the Mandatory government was its focus on revenue. Fiscal considerations were almost the exclusive criterion applied by the Department of Customs and Excises in its setting of duty rates on imports; these were thus quite low – a comprehensive standard rate of 12 percent *ad valorem*. In the two prewar decades these import duties provided about 50 percent of total government tax revenue. The standard rate was raised to 15 percent in the war years. A low income tax, applicable only to very high-income brackets and to incorporated business, was also imposed in 1941.

Finally, the third feature was the Mandatory Government's free-trade policy. It adamantly refused to impose protective duties even in the worldwide depression of the 1930s, though all other governments – including Britain and its Empire – resorted to such tactics. It thus did not relent under the pressure of the Jewish community, represented by the Jewish Agency, to impose some protective duties to support the recently established domestic (Jewish) industries from the dumping tactics employed by virtually every state. Free trade and free capital mobility within a fixed exchange-rate regime with sterling were the operating rules of Mandatory Palestine's external economic relations for two decades through the outbreak of World War II.

The Emergence of the Jewish Economy, 1920–1931

IMMIGRATION AND THE DEMOGRAPHIC BALANCE. The 1920s may be identified as the time of the emergence of the Jewish economy, a development triggered primarily by increased immigration. Though much smaller than hoped for by the Zionist leadership, the numbers still signified a major change and a correspondingly significant shift in the balance of the national composition of Palestine's population. During the 12-year period starting in December 1919 with the arrival of the ship *Roslan* from Russia with almost 700 immigrants and ending in 1931, gross immigration was close to 120,000. This was twice the total number of immigrants to Palestine in the more than three decades of the prewar period from the early 1880s through 1914 (Table 2). In the 1920s, it amounted to about 18 percent of total Jewish emigration in that period, a significantly higher proportion than in the pre-World War I decades (in both periods the United States was the dominant destination of Jewish emigrants). Note also that net immigration figures in Table 2 indicate that close to one quarter of the immigrants to Palestine during the 1920s left for other destinations.

This inflow of immigrants had a clear-cut impact on the national composition of Palestine's population. The 1922 census estimates suggest that Jews were about 11 percent of the total population of Palestine. The 1931 census data indicates that the Jewish population had again grown substantially, to 17 percent of the total (Table 1).

This change in the population balance was even more significant in the main urban areas. Thus Tel Aviv's population was about 30 percent of Jaffa's in 1922; by 1931 it had grown to 85 percent of a greatly increased Jaffa population. Furthermore, the Jewish share of the population of the whole Tel Aviv-Jaffa conurbation had grown from 37 percent in 1922 to 54 percent in 1931. The population balance in Jerusalem and

Haifa moved in a similar direction. Only in Haifa was the Arab population still the dominant community in 1939; the Jewish population, which had been growing rapidly, was about one third of the total.

LAND AND THE RESETTLEMENT PROCESS. Most of the growth of Jewish population – 90,000 between 1922 and 1931 – occurred in the urban centers, with Tel Aviv as its focus. Yet the major resettlement effort implemented by the Zionist authorities was designed to establish a significant Jewish foothold all over Palestine as soon as possible. To implement that policy most of the resources at the disposal of the Zionist Organization were directed to the rural sector.

This effort shows in terms of population and the number of settlements. Rural population grew by 2.5 times in the 1922–1931 decade, by more than 3 times compared to 1914, the benchmark figure for measuring the post-Balfour Declaration resettlement effort. The comparison of the growth of the whole Jewish population between 1914 and 1931, which did not quite double during that period, is meaningful in that context (Tables 1 and 3).

The effort in terms of the number of settlements, which rose from 47 in 1914 to 129 by 1931, is even more stunning (Table 3). The number itself suggests a major extension of the geographical presence of Jewish settlements in that period, which might be thought of as the time of the "coming out" of the Jewish presence in Palestine. The penetration into the Jezreel Valley – the formation of two groups of agricultural settlements in its eastern and western parts, and of a small urban center, Afula, in the middle – was the vanguard of that effort.

The necessary condition for the success of this effort was the acquisition of large blocks of land in what was a marshy, malaria-ridden (and thus effectively unpopulated) area in 1920–21. The process of land acquisition shows clearly in the land ownership columns of Table 3: the figure for 1922 indicates an expansion of rural land ownership of almost 70 percent by Jewish entities – private entrepreneurs and households, corporate firms, and, mostly, the Jewish National Fund (Keren Kayemet), the land purchasing and holding corporation created and owned by the World Zionist Organization. In the ensuing decade through 1931, Jewish land purchases accelerated; the total amount of land owned by Jews increased by 75 percent, indicating that the rate of increase of rural land possession by Jews was significantly higher. The Haifa bay area and the Hefer Valley in northern coastal Sharon Plain were the focus of the land acquisition effort in the 1920s. later moves to acquire land, particularly the penetration into the Beit She'an Valley and the northeastern and western Galilee, implemented in the 1930s, were inspired by the realization that the allocation of noncultivated "crown" land to Jewish settlers, as envisioned by the Zionist leadership in the early 1920s, was not going to happen.

The drive to acquire land was maintained in the 1930s, though land prices rose rapidly as a result of that very process. The efforts of private entrepreneurs to acquire land in the coastal plain were induced by the high profitability of the thriving citriculture industry from the 1920s through about the early 1930s, and by the acceleration of urbanization resulting from the increase in Jewish immigration in that decade. Thus, though land purchases by the Jewish sector emerged as a major political issue, and were finally restricted by law in 1940 (reflecting the change in British policy expressed in the White Paper of 1939, abandoning partition as a viable future for Palestine, and regarded by Zionists as an official abandonment of the Balfour Declaration commitments), the amount of land owned by the Jewish sector still grew by 50 percent in the decade ending in 1941. Growth was even greater in the rural areas (Table 3). The highly significant feature of the process in that period and through the war years was the penetration into the Negev, the southern and arid part of Palestine, during the war years and in the face of the Land Transfer Regulations of 1940, which restricted land purchases by Jews. This high-priority effort was implemented by the Jewish National Fund.

The 1947 figure for the total land holdings of the Jewish sector suggests that these grew by about four times during the three decades of the British Mandate. A comparison for rural land holdings based similarly on the 1914 data suggests an almost sixfold increase during the period (Table 3). The spread of these rural holdings through 1941 was almost everywhere, exclusive of the Negev; during the war years it was mostly in the Negev. Yet the total of Jewish land holdings on the eve of independence was only about six percent of the total land area of Mandatory Palestine.

This level of acquisition would not have been achieved without the purchase of land by the Jewish private sector, especially for citrus plantations but also for housing and for commercial and industrial use in urban areas. The entries in Table 3 for citrus plantations, whose area grew by 15 times between 1922 and 1939 – a private sector activity absolutely dominated by the profit motive – offer a clear indication of their contribution to the Jewish land acquisition drive. This drive was a joint effort of the Keren Kayemet and the private sector, which financed its acquisitions in significant part by capital imports. Yet it was the "national sector," whose behavior was not subject to profit considerations, that led the way; its share of land ownership in the Jewish sector increased from about 10 percent in 1920 to about 50 percent in the closing years of the Mandate. Land acquisition policy was obviously designed to serve as the springboard of the resettlement process.

PROSPERITY AND DEPRESSION IN THE 1920S. The employment, capital stock, and national product columns in Tables 4 and 5 indicate vigorous growth in the 1920s through 1931. Employment in the Jewish economy grew by 2.4 times, more than the corresponding growth of population. Due to the substantial growth of the annual investment flow, the capital stock at the end of the period was more than three times greater than at the beginning. This also meant that the capital-labor ratio

Table 4. Patterns of Employment, Labor Force, Capital Stock, and Investment, 1922–1947[1]

Year	Arab Economy				Jewish Economy					Government
	Employment (1)	Net Fixed Capital Stock (2)	Net Investment (3)	Net Capital-Labor Ratio (4) [=(2)/(1)]	Labor Force (5)	Employment (6)	Net Fixed Capital Stock (7)	Net Investment (8)	Net Capital-Labor Ratio (9) [=(7)/(6)]	Capital Stock (10)
1922	100	100	100	100	100	100	100	100	100	100
1931	117	126	317	108	244	240	319	272	133	215
1935	131	157	826	120	489	491	655	1029	134	365
1936	–	–	–	–	588	579	817	790	141	–
1938	–	–	–	–	635	616	1,039	443	169	–
1939	144	195	257	135	684	665	1,109	341	167	541
1941	–	–	–	–	756	746	1,223	144	164	652
1943	–	–	–	–	793	804	1,289	191	160	–
1945	178	239	319	134	877	889	1,359	319	153	717
1947	–	256	–	–	951	963	1,542	1,104	160	7,393

Noes:
1. Figures are rounded to the closest digit. Capital Stock figures refer to the beginning of the year. Capital Stock and Investment figures refer to net investment and net fixed reproducible capital stock.

Table 5. Indices of National Product Aggregates and National Sector Ratios, 1922–1947[1]

Year	NDP (Net Domestic Product)			NNP (Net National Product)		NNP Per Capita		Jewish-Arab Ratios (%)[2]	
	Arab (1)	Jewish (2)	Palestine (3)	Arab (4)	Jewish (5)	Arab (6)	Jewish (7)	NNP (8)	NNP Per Capita (9) [=(7)/(6)]
1922	100	100	100	100	100	100	100	22.8	191.1
1931	140	413	197	143	436	113	204	69.6	344.7
1935	237	1,109	418	246	1,182	175	295	109.6	321.4
1936	227	1,039	395	229	1,039	159	244	112.0	292.5
1939	231	927	376	229	1,023	148	190	101.7	245.6
1941	273	1,157	456	271	1,274	165	216	107.6	249.1
1945	386	1,758	670	384	1,937	207	283	115.1	261.7
1947	488	2,225	848	485	2,452	245	323	117.4	252.6
Average Annual Growth Rates (%)									
1922–1931	3.8	17.1	7.8	4.1	17.8	1.4	8.2		
1931–1935	14.1	28.0	20.7	14.5	28.3	11.6	9.7		
1935–1939	-0.6	-3.9	-2.7	-1.8	-4.3	-4.2	-11.6		
1935–1947	6.2	6.0	6.1	5.8	6.3	2.8	0.8		
1939–1947	9.8	11.6	9.8	11.4	10.7	6.5	6.9		
1922–1947	6.5	13.2	8.9	6.5	13.7	3.6	4.8		

Notes:
1. Index figures are rounded to the relevant digit. The percent in columns (8) and (9) are rounded to the first decimal point.
2. Ratios of Jewish NNP and NNP per capita to Arab NNP and NNP per capita respectively.

was 40 percent higher than in 1922, an increase that generated an almost 80 percent rise in average labor productivity during that period (Table 6). These increases in the major inputs – labor, capital, and land, the last relevant mainly to farm production – and the corresponding increases in productivity generated a more than fourfold increase of the Jewish sector's national product. Thus, though population increased by about two times during that period, the much greater increase in production per capita allowed for a higher standard of living for the Jewish population. This highly significant performance was a feature of the Jewish economy of Palestine even during the last years of this decade (1929–31), in which occurred the advent of the disastrous worldwide economic depression of the 1930s.

Though that final outcome was highly impressive, the going during that decade was not smooth. Its ups and downs were directly linked to the immigration waves of the Third and Fourth Aliyah, which peaked in 1922 and 1925 respectively. The first of these two peaks reflected the entry of 9,000 immigrants in that single year. The second marked the arrival

Table 5a. Ratios of NNP to NDP by National Sectors, 1922–1947 (%)[1]

1922–1931	1922	1931	1935	1936	1939	1941	1945	1947
Arab Sector	102.5	104.3	106.2	103.5	101.6	101.5	102.0	102.0
Jewish Sector	89.4	94.6	95.3	97.0	98.6	98.4	98.5	98.6

Note:
1. Net National Product and Net Domestic Product at 1936 prices.

of 34,000 Jews in Palestine, an event unheard of in the four decades of the Zionist experiment since the early 1880s. This single-year inflow was equal to the total inflow during the entire pre-World War I decade of the Second Aliyah.

These peaks and the following troughs had their inevitable counterparts in terms of employment and unemployment and the level of economic activity. The ups and downs were related to rising waves of immigrants and corresponding waves of increased investment, followed by their significant decline. Thus employment in the Jewish sector was almost 10 percent higher in 1924 than in 1923, and at its peak in 1926 about 65 percent higher than in 1923, a rate that could not be sustained. Corresponding to the ensuing decline in employment, the unemployment rate shot up from a negligible figure at the top of the prosperous year 1925 to almost 7.7 percent in 1927. The inevitable effect of that was a major wave of emigration, almost 75 percent of the (decreased) inflow of new immigrants in 1926–27 (Table 2). It was the collapse of investment, in housing in particular, which generated the cyclical downspin: investment in buildings in 1926 was down to less than one half the 1925 rate, and in 1927 it decreased further to just 20 percent of the peak level. Total investment returned to the 1925 level only after five years in 1930–31. The net product of the Jewish sector, though, kept growing throughout the 1920s, as did the product per capita, which after a short two-year interval of minor decline, passed the previous 1925 peak by 1928, even though the Jewish population grew by 14 percent in the interval.

Both population and product per capita kept growing through 1931, with the latter showing a high annual average growth rate of 8.2 percent (Table 5) in spite of the impact of a "classic" economic recession (1926–27). The well known negative effects of such downturns had in that case a twist specific to the activities in the Jewish sector: it reduced considerably the inflow of immigrants, and owing to a surge of emigration, particularly in the second half of the decade, net immigration was slightly negative in 1927 and 1928. This occurred at a crucial juncture in the Arab-Jewish confrontation and the emerging change of heart of the British government, highlighted by its attempt to impose restrictions on Jewish immigration and land purchase at the turn of the 1930s.

STRUCTURAL CHANGES: AN INTERIM SUMMARY. These developments were not accidental. They were directly linked to the changing demographic balance and economic power, which were the hallmarks of developments in the first decade of the British Mandate through 1931. The growth of the *Yishuv*'s population to 175,000 by 1931 meant that its share of Palestine's population expanded from 11 percent in 1922 to 17 percent in 1931 (Table 1). This also involved a highly significant and much greater spatial distribution by way of the increase in the number of Jewish settlements since the end of the war (Table 3). The most significant development, probably not fully comprehended by contemporaries, was the dramatic change in the economic performance of the two sectors, measured in terms of national product aggregates. The NNP estimate for 1922 suggests that the NNP of the Jewish sector was about 23 percent of that of the Arab sector. Both sectors expanded in that decade, but the disparity between them (the Jewish sector grew by an almost 18 percent average annual growth rate, while its Arab counterpart grew by only about 4 percent annually) had an inevitable cumulative effect: by 1931 the Jewish sector's national product was already about 70 percent of that of the Arab sector (Table 5).

Table 6. Capital Per Unit of Labor and Net Domestic Product per Employee and Real Wages, 1922–1947[1]

	Capital Per Unit of Labor (P£)			NDP Per employee (P£)			Real Wages	NDP per Employee
Year	Arab Sector[2]	Jewish Sector	Ratio	Arab Sector[2]	Jewish Sector	Ratio	Jewish Sector	
	(1)	(2)	(3) [=(2)/(1)]	(4)	(5)	(6) [=(5)/(4)]	(7)	(8)
1922	115	191	1.66	34	57	1.7	100	100
1931	123	249	2.02	43	102	2.4	157	179
1935	137	255	1.86	62	137	2.2	172	240
1939	155	308	1.99	55	92	1.7	149	161
1941	–	308	–	–	101	–	114	177
1945	159	295	1.86	74	129	1.7	207	226
1947	–	308	–	–	151	–	248	265

Notes:
1. Figures in columns (1), (2), (4), and (5) are in constant 1936 prices in Palestine pounds. Figures in columns (7) and (8) are indices with 1922 = 100.
2. The Arab labor input series used for the estimate are the Metzer (1998) series of the Arab labor force. This series, the only available one, offers a reasonable approximation for the labor input generating (domestic) product in view of the still highly self-sufficient character of the dominant Arab farming sector; thus the relatively small size of the wages and salary earning groups.

Table 7. Employment and Unemployment by Economic Branch, 1922–1947

Year	Employment (in thousands)					Employment: 1922 = 100					Unemployment Rates (%)
	Total	Agriculture	Manufacturing	Construction	Services	Total	Agriculture	Manufacturing	Construction	Services	
	(1)	(2)	(3)	(4)	(5)	(6)	(7)	(8)	(9)	(10)	(11)
A. Jewish Sector[1]											
1922	29,800	7,957	4,977	3,963	12,903	100	100	100	100	100	1.5
1931	68,900	17,983	13,987	5,994	30,963	231	226	281	151	240	3.1
1935	139,500	34,736	28,040	–	–	468	437	–	–	–	1.2
1936	154,300	–	–	–	–	518	–	–	–	–	3.0
1939	167,000	37,074	37,909	5,010	87,007	560	466	762	126	674	4.3
1941	187,500	–	–	–	–	629	–	–	–	–	2.7
1945	232,700	30,018	71,904	10,026	120,742	781	377	1445	253	936	0.2
1947	246,800	–	–	–	–	828	–	–	–	–	0.3
B. Arab Sector[2]											
1922	194,000	127,070	9,312	3,492		100	100	100	100	100	–
1931	227,000	143,464	18,614	5,221		117	113	200	150	110	–
1935	255,000	–	–	–	–	131	–	–	–	–	–
1939	280,000	162,960	21,000	3,920		144	128	226	112	169	–
1945	345,000	188,025	30,360	17,250		179	145	326	493	201	–

Notes:
1. Employment data in the Jewish sector refers to Jewish and Arab labor in that sector. Unemployment rates refer to Jewish unemployment as a percentage of the Jewish labor force.
2. Employment in Arab sector is based on Metzer labor forces estimates.

The comparative growth of national product, of course, had an impact on the patterns of product per capita. Even though the Jewish population grew much more rapidly, Jewish product per capita, which was nearly twice that of its Arab counterpart in 1922, nevertheless leapt to a ratio of 3.5 in 1931 (Table 5). This huge gap was not maintained in the second half of the 1930s and in the 1940s because of the much more rapid increase of the Jewish population. But the ratio at which it settled in the late 1930s – about 3.5 – afforded an altogether different living standard for the Jewish than for the Arab population and the setting of altogether different socioeconomic patterns for the two societies.

The result of the robust economic performance by the Jewish sector in that decade was a highly significant change of structure. One aspect of it was the rapidly changing comparative economic status of the two national sectors described above. Of even greater significance were the rapid urbanization of the Jewish sector, involving the emergence of an industrial manufacturing sector and an extensive commercial sector, and the reorientation of Jewish agriculture in both its branch composition (product mix) and its socioeconomic form of organization. Both of these were linked to the resettlement effort, which really came into its own in the Mandatory period.

This process pushed the old *yishuv* into a small and relatively declining demographic niche. It became a kind of backwater component of the Jewish national entity, which was forging ahead with the Zionist project. The mechanism of that process shows in the increased number of Jewish settlements, which in the 13 years from the end of the war almost tripled, and more than tripled in terms of the size of the rural population (Table 3). Their very number suggests the penetration of these settlements into locations everywhere, from Galilee in the north and along the central coastal plain to the vicinity of Jerusalem and south toward the line separating the semi-arid and arid zones of the Negev from the rest of the country. Their contribution to production shows in the growth of farm output by more than five times in the 1921–1931 period (Table 3), with corresponding growth of net Jewish farm product by almost 4.7 times in the 1922–31 interval (Table 8).

This growth involved significant changes in the composition of the branch structure of Jewish agriculture and in the techniques of running and managing it. The new settlements set up by the Zionist Organization adopted *ab ovo* the mixed farming strategy, with fruit plantations and vineyards as part of the mix but neither dominant. The composition of the mix was designed to offer a year-round comparatively balanced demand for labor to assure a steady flow of income to the cultivators.

Irrigation, tractor-driven farm machinery, and improved plant varieties as well as high capital-labor ratios were to serve as the instruments of a meaningful move toward European living standards. The Zionist (later Jewish Agency) authorities would provide financing for the acquisition of these resources and for the cost of purchasing the land. The cultivators would lease the nationalized land for low rents and would repay the long-term credits allocated to them to pay for the investment in capital stock – housing, machinery, and plan-

Table 8. The Industrial Pattern of Real Net Domestic Product, 1922–1947[1]

Year	Agriculture			Manufact.	Construct.	NDP
	Citrus (1)	Other (2)	Total (3)	(4)	(5)	(6)
A. Jewish Economy						
1922	100	100	100	100	100	100
1931	956	222	466	449	222	413
1935	2,157	353	951	1,111	1,330	1,109
1936	1,471	409	759	1,134	1,031	1,039
1939	1,296	446	699	1,143	286	927
1941	–	–	588	1,688	478	1,157
1945	–	892	1,499	3,062	872	1,757
1947	–	–	1,999	2,932	1,539	2,225
B. Arab Economy						
1922	100	100	100	100	100	100
1931	552	102	121	290	257	140
1935	1,066	141	180	444	535	237
1936	880	134	176	421	514	227
1939	647	156	177	482	165	231
1942	–	–	293	683	873	318
1945	–	–	381	764	524	386
1947	–	–	–	–	–	488

Note:
1. Nominal Product (value added) series for each of the branches and for total product deflated by price indices. Deflation for the Jewish sector series in terms of cost of living index in Jewish markets. Deflation of the Arab sector series: the Metzer deflator of Arab material output.

tations. They would also pay (low) interest charges on the outstanding debt.

These settlements were established by groups of pioneers inspired by socialist Zionist ideology following the maxim of "self-labor": this excluded the option of hired workers, and involved by definition adherence to the rule of *avodah ivrit*. The first of these groups, which would soon be organized as legal entities, surfaced in the early 1920s from the "floor" – by the initiative of their members. these self-initiated groupings – there were two types, the kibbutz and the moshav, based on collective and cooperative principles respectively – soon formed the vanguard of the resettlement effort and were at its core for the next four decades. There were already 11 kibbutzim and 2 moshavim in 1921, at the very infancy of the movements; by the end of their formative decade, in 1931, the kibbutz movement counted 30 settlements, and the moshav 10, in locations all over the country, from Galilee and the Jezreel Valley in the north along the coastal plain to the Jerusalem district.

The mixed farm output figures for 1931 (Table 3) indicate that within that decade real output expanded 2.8 times and the corresponding farm product by a lower factor, 2.2. These imply very high growth rates indeed, about nine percent annually, and an even higher figure for mixed farm output (Table 8). This expansion of production was, of course, due not only to the production lines set up in the nascent collective and cooperative settlements, but reflected the vigorous growth of production in the older rural settlements, about 40 in number, already in place by 1914. Rapid urbanization (see below) provided expanding markets for vegetables, dairy products, and poultry from the prewar settlements and postwar private-sector settlements. The latter multiplied in the 1920s and early 1930s in the vicinity of the Tel Aviv-Jaffa urban center. The growth of the Jewish rural population by 2.5 times in the 1922–31 interval, reflecting an almost 11 percent annual growth rate (compared to the 8.4 percent annual rate of the total Jewish population) suggests the extent of new employment resulting from expanding farm production.

This expansion occurred not only in mixed farming, as the farm output and net production figures indicate: total Jewish farm output grew by almost 4.5 times through 1931 while its mixed farming component grew by only 2.8 times. The difference between these two figures is of course the tremendous expansion of citriculture in the two interwar decades. The rapidly increasing demand for Jaffa oranges in Europe in the 1920s generated prices that were highly profitable. Expectations of high profit in the 1920s encouraged private entrepreneurs, Jewish and Arab, to expand citrus orchards rapidly. entrepreneurs in the older settlements and the new private enterprise settlements of the 1920s and early 1930s moved en masse into this line. The Jewish orchard area, which in 1922 was still almost the same as its prewar size, expanded from 10,000 dunams to 70,000 in the decade ending in 1931 (Table 3).

The citrus boom offered rapidly rising employment opportunities, manned to a significant extent by Arab workers, and thus to a sharpened struggle for *avodah ivrit*. However, it had a positive effect on the Jewish labor market too: this is clearly suggested by the more rapid growth of the rural population than of the total Jewish population in the 1922–31 period. The citrus boom generated a structural change in the economy of the older settlements, particularly those located in the citrus growing belt along the central coastal plain. It also encouraged the acquisition of urban features by some of these older settlements, involving rapid expansion of the commercial, financial, and technical service center in the Tel Aviv-Jaffa conurbation and in the Haifa and Haifa Bay area. The commercial and service sectors of the Jewish economy were effectively manned by Jewish workers only, and thus profit considerations were in these activities fully consistent with the *avodah ivrit* principle.

The rapid process of urbanization with Tel Aviv as its center of gravity was primarily the product of the crest of the Fourth Aliyah and the building boom it generated in the mid-1920s. Tel Aviv's population, which was 15,000 in 1922, more than doubled within three years; in 1925 it was already 34,000. With the Jewish population of Jaffa at about 8,000, Jews were by that date already the dominant community in the Tel Aviv-Jaffa conurbation. Though the focus of urbanization in that period was Tel Aviv, the process occurred all over: the Jewish population of Haifa grew by 2.7 times to 16,000 in 1922–31, and that of Jerusalem grew by 50 percent.

With net Jewish immigration of about 90,000 in the 1922–31 period, and an expansion of Jewish urban population in the three main towns – Jerusalem, Tel Aviv, and Haifa – by about 60,000 in 1922–31, to which figures in several small urbanizing settlements near Tel Aviv could be added, the main structural transformation of the Jewish community of Palestine was clearly a robust process of urbanization. This was closely linked to another major change, the emergence of manufacturing industry and its transformation into the major component of the Jewish economy (see below, The Economics of the Fifth Aliyah, 1932–1939/The Advent of Manufacturing).

The Arab Sector: Demographic Growth and Economic Expansion, 1920–1947

DEMOGRAPHICS. One of the significant features of the development of the Arab sector of Palestine was the demographic revolution to which it was subjected through the Mandatory period. This shows clearly in the rapid acceleration of population growth during that period. Population data for the period of 1890–1914 suggests that even at that late stage of the Ottoman period, the annual average growth rate was about 0.8 percent, effectively similar to the 0.7 annual average for the 19th century. Yet the 1922–1931 population growth rate based on census data and much more reliable than the population estimates through 1914 leapt at once to an average annual rate of 2.6 percent: the annual average for the entire period of the Mandate (1922–1947) was 2.7 percent.

A comparison with the Egyptian annual population growth rate is suggestive. That stood at 1.5 percent in the two decades ending in 1947 and 1.3 percent annually in the three decades between 1917 and 1947, coinciding almost exactly with the three decades of Mandatory rule. The much higher growth rates of Palestine's Arab population reflected improving living standards and health services (producing in particular a dramatic reduction of child mortality), as well as immigration, from Syria in particular and also from Egypt. These developments were clearly due to the highly significant transformation of the Arab economy, involving a rapidly rising national product, which allowed for the notable increase in the standard of living.

THE ECONOMIC AGGREGATES. The patterns of national and per capita product demonstrate this performance, in absolute and comparative terms. They had surfaced already in the 1920s, as shown by the annual average growth rate of national product for 1923–1931, which was 4.1 percent. It accelerated in the 1930s and in spite of a politically imposed standstill in 1936–39, during the Arab Revolt, the Arab sector's national product grew almost fivefold, at an annual average rate of 6.5 percent, in the 25 years ending in 1947, the last full year of the Mandate. The per capita product, which reflects the correspondingly rapid growth of population, grew at a lower rate of about 2.5 times through those 25 years, at an annual average rate of 3.6 percent (Table 5).

This was undoubtedly a good performance by international standards in those years, and even better in comparison to the performance of the neighboring Arab states.

Arab immigration into Palestine from the neighboring countries, quite visible in the marketplace at that time, was close to 50,000 during the 25 years ending in 1947. This inflow, which provided about 7.5 percent of the increase in the Arab population (Table 2), offers quantitative evidence of the significantly better performance of the Arab economy in Mandatory Palestine than the economies of the neighboring Arab countries.

The robust performance of the Palestinian Arab economy in the aggregate was in the 1920s and through 1936 linked directly and indirectly to the outstanding economic growth of the Jewish sector, which in the 1920s through 1931 grew at an annual average rate of about 18 percent. During the war and its aftermath of 1940–47, in which the Arab sector's national product grew even more rapidly at an annual rate of close to 10 percent, it was the British army demand for labor and goods that generated the booming prosperity of Palestine's two national sectors through 1945. This prosperity was sustained in the ensuing two years by the release of the suppressed inflationary pressures accumulated during the war.

ARAB-JEWISH ECONOMIC LINKS. The means by which the Jewish sector's economy had a direct impact on the Arab sector's was the employment of Arab wage labor by Jewish enterprises. The indirect means by which the very rapid growth of the Jewish economy pulled the Arab economy in its wake was its purchasing on capital and current accounts. The latter involved purchases of consumer goods and of inputs such as stone for the building industry. Purchases on capital accounts involved primarily the acquisition of land.

An estimate of the direct impact of the payment of wages to Arab labor by Jewish employers is presented in Table 5a, which reproduces the ratios of net national product to net domestic product in each of the national sectors. This table expresses the increment of wage income earned by Arab labor in the Jewish economy; on the Arab sector line, it is added to the domestic product generated by the Arab economy; on the Jewish sector line, it is deducted from the domestic product generated by the Jewish economy. The ratios for the Arab sector through the 25 years of the Mandatory period are consistently above 100 percent in this series, while that of the Jewish sector is less than 100 percent all the way through 1947. At the height of the boom in 1935, wages paid by Jewish enterprises added six percent to the Arab GDP, suggesting that through the entire first half of the 1930s, the average income added to the domestic product of the Arab economy by employment in the Jewish sector topped 4 percent of GDP.

The Arab boycott against the rapidly expanding Jewish political and economic entity in the spring of 1936, which also involved mass demonstrations that devolved into armed riots against Jewish targets and later clashes with the British army and the Haganah, began in 1936 and continued through early 1939. These events shattered the direct economic link with the Jewish sector almost completely. A fraction of the exogenous wage income, mainly from government and military employment, survived; it revived and grew in the war years, as more and more Arab wage labor was drawn into the market.

The comparisons of national to domestic product in Table 5a indicate that Arab wage labor in the Jewish sector was of much lower significance during the war years than it had been in the 1920s through 1935. The severance of the direct links between the national sectors, initially generated by politics in 1936–39, though not complete, became permanent during the war due mainly to two economic factors: the collapse of the citrus industry – the main employer of Arab labor in the Jewish economy – at the outbreak of the war reduced its demand for labor almost totally; and the corresponding rise of manufacturing industry to be the dominant economic sector of the Jewish economy. Manufacturing required different kinds of labor than farming, insuring that the post-1936 labor situation remained the status quo. By 1945 only 1.2 percent of the Arab labor force was employed in the Jewish economy (Tables 5 and 7).

Indirect links between the two national sectors, however, remained strong. The growth of the Jewish economy inevitably had a highly significant indirect effect on the Arab economy, through their trading links. The demand for goods spilling over from the Jewish sector generated a lively Arab export trade, generating higher output and correspondingly higher productivity and income. Another link between the sectors was land purchase, through which funds flowed from the Jewish to the Arab sector. These financed investment (in citriculture, in particular), which generated employment and growth as well.

The significant positive effect of Jewish activity on the Arab economy can easily be substantiated by the aggregate data at our disposal. The world economy plunged into depression and crisis from 1930 onwards. This should have affected the Arab economy negatively, or at least arrested its growth rate. Yet in that very period, through 1935, the growth rate of the Arab economy as expressed in terms of NNP leapt to an annual average of more than 12 percent, stimulated by the rapid growth of the Jewish economy. Similarly, the direct effect of the Jewish economy on its counterpart can be seen in employment figures: close to five percent of the Arab labor force was employed in the Jewish sector by 1935, compared to three percent in 1931 and an even lower rate in the 1920s.

The succeeding period 1936–39 provides the obverse image of these developments: the reduction in the inflow of Jewish immigrants imposed by the British government in response to the Arab uprising, and the correspondingly lower capital inflow (lower by 50 percent), led to a recession. Jewish sector national product was 13 percent lower in 1939 than in 1935. The Arab sector's NNP also fell, though not as much; it declined by only seven percent, mainly due to a major reduction of employment in the Jewish sector. Thus, Palestine's recession was a special case, due largely to the 1936–39 hostilities, just at the time the world economy was recovering from the worst of the crisis. these developments hit the more industrialized and market-oriented Jewish economy more seriously. Its Arab counterpart followed in the same direction, though at a significantly slower pace (Table 5).

URBANIZATION, WAGE LABOR, AND INDUSTRIALIZATION. Through the three decades of the British Mandate the Arab sector had undergone a process of urbanization, involving the emergence of manufacturing, industry, growing intensity of commercial and financial activity, and inevitably a population dependent on wage labor.

The urbanization process was visible yet slow. Table 3 suggests that the rural population grew significantly in absolute terms, including a still nomadic group (which however declined in number). In the 22 years ending in 1944 the rural Arab population grew by more than one third. This estimate is based on reliable data – the first (1922) and second (1931) censuses. The rural share of the total Arab population had been declining slowly but consistently, from about 70 percent of the total in 1922 to 67–68 percent in 1931, and 64–65 percent in the very last years of the British Mandate. This process involved a corresponding increase of urban population to almost 35 percent of the total.

Yet this figure seemingly understates the thrust of Arab urbanization, since it is affected by the population figures of Jerusalem. Jerusalem had been the religious center of the Palestinian Arab community for centuries. In the Mandatory era it soon emerged as its political center also, though it lost its priority in demographic terms. Jerusalem was out of the main areas of Arab demographic and economic expansion, which focused on the two ports of Palestine, Jaffa and Haifa. This shows clearly in the population data. Between 1922 and 1944 Jerusalem's Arab population grew by approximately 50 percent; that of Jaffa, already by 1914 larger than Jerusalem's, by more than 60 percent; that of Haifa, where the new deep-sea port opened in 1931, by over 200 percent, growing larger than Jerusalem's in the 1930s (Table 1).

Jaffa and Haifa were undoubtedly the centers of gravity of the Arab sector's economic development, and thus also the centers of the industrialization process. They were inevitably the location in which manufacturing, industry, and commercial and financial services expanded most rapidly, generating a long-term process of modernization. Among other things, this was manifested in the rapid growth of wage labor relative to self-employment, the dominant economic category in a traditional farming society, including its urban component.

The robust expansion of production reflected rising employment and a much higher investment rate, which contributed to a continuous increase of the Arab capital stock at a rate higher than the increase of employment. This process was slow in the 1920s; by 1931 the Arab capital stock was 26 percent higher than in 1922. Yet employment grew at a lower rate in that period, which meant that the capital labor ratio in 1931 was eight percent higher than in the early 1920s. Conterminously with the all-time high spurt of investment in the Jewish sector from 1932 to 1935, the Arab sector investment rate leapt as well. Thus, toward the end of the Mandate period the

Table 9. Employment, Domestic Product, and Relative Labor Productivity, 1922–1945 (%)[1]

	Arab Sector			Jewish Sector		
	NDP (1)	Employment (2)	RLP[2] (3) [= (1)/(2)]	NDP (4)	Employment (5)	RLP[2] (6) [= (4)/(5)]
1922						
Agriculture	39.4	65.5	0.602	12.9	26.7	0.483
Manufacturing	5.2	4.8	1.083	19.7	16.7	1.180
Construction	1.8	1.6	1.125	12.5	13.3	0.940
Services	53.6	28.1	1.907	54.9	43.3	1.268
Total	100.0	100.0	1.000	100.0	100.0	1.000
1931						
Agriculture	33.9	63.2	0.536	14.6	26.1	0.559
Manufacturing	10.7	8.2	1.305	21.4	20.3	1.054
Construction	3.2	2.3	1.391	6.7	8.7	0.770
Services	52.2	26.3	1.985	57.3	44.9	1.276
Total	100.0	100.0	1.000	100.0	100.0	1.000
1935[3]						
Agriculture	32.0	56.8	0.563	12.3	24.9	0.493
Manufacturing	10.3	7.4	1.391	21.9	20.1	1.090
Construction	–	–	–	–	–	–
Services	–	–	–	–	–	–
1939						
Agriculture	30.1	58.2	0.517	9.7	22.2	0.437
Manufacturing	10.8	7.5	1.440	24.2	22.7	1.066
Construction	1.3	1.4	0.929	3.9	3.0	1.300
Services	57.8	32.9	1.757	62.2	52.1	1.194
Total	100.0	100.0	1.000	100.0	100.0	1.000
1945						
Agriculture	38.9	54.5	0.714	10.7	12.9	0.829
Manufacturing	10.3	8.8	1.170	33.1	30.9	1.071
Construction	2.4	5.0	0.480	6.0	4.3	1.395
Services	48.4	31.7	1.527	50.2	51.9	0.967
Total	100.0	100.0	1.000	100.0	100.0	1.000

Notes:
1. Employment refers to persons employed in each of the national sectors. Thus, Arabs employed in the Jewish sectors are included in its employment.
2. Relative Labor Productivity (RLP) is the ratio between domestic product and total employment in each economic sector. Aggregate relative productivity is equal to unity (1.000) by definition.
3. Figures for agriculture and manufacturing are percentages, which together with figures for construction and services, for which no separate data is available, total 100 percent.

capital labor ratio was higher by one third than at its beginning (Table 4). This, of course, explains the major improvement of labor productivity – by 1931 it had already improved by 26 percent; in 1945 it was more than two times higher than in 1922 (Table 6). It explains the significant rise of real income per capita and of real wages (Table 5).

The performance of the Arab sector suggested by the aggregate factor inputs, by output and by national product figures, are, however, (weighted) averages of the inputs and of the output and product (value added) of several economic branches. The employment and domestic product series of Table 9 illustrate the dominance of agriculture throughout the Mandatory period. These demonstrate a rather slow process of changing economic and social structure.

Agriculture was indeed the dominant branch in terms of employment throughout the three Mandatory decades. Yet its share in employment declined from about two thirds of the labor force in 1922 to around 55 percent towards the end of that period. The corresponding rise of employment in manufacturing and construction from 7 percent in 1922 to 13–14 percent in the late 1930s and mid-1940s were the obverse of the relative decline of agriculture. Yet these figures do not demonstrate fully the highly significant social change – the emerging importance of the wage-earning strata in Palestinian Arab society. The rise of the citrus industry, a farming branch, had a similar effect in agriculture to that generated by the rise of manufacturing and construction – a significant transition to wage labor. Its major impact on that score is suggested by the tenfold increase of output in citriculture between 1922 and 1935, while that in all other farm branches increased only 40 percent or so (Table 3). The subsequent decline of Arab net product between 1935 and 1939 (Table 5) did not reflect, however, a decline of physical output of citrus products and thus of wage employment: it reflected the collapse of prices in the export markets.

The Arab manufacturing and construction employment figures of Tables (7) and (9) do not represent Arab wage labor employed in the Jewish sector, by the Mandatory government, and in the war years by firms working for the British army. Employment in the Jewish sector increased from two percent of the Arab labor force in 1922 to close to five percent at its peak in 1935, after which it declined significantly. Yet this slack was easily absorbed by the late 1930s and even more so in the war years by wage employment in military-sponsored projects. This of course suggests that the proportion of wage earners in the material production branches of the Arab economy and engaged by these "other" labor markets increased by more than the figure suggested in Table 9. These suggest that this increased from 6.4 percent of total employment in 1922 to almost 14 percent in 1945. If the government, military, and Jewish sectors are added, the figure for the end of the Mandate period appears closer to 20 percent. To this should be added wage employment in services, which suggests that at the end of the Mandatory period in the late 1940s, wage and salary employment was already about 35–40 percent of total Arab employment.

The modernization process of the Arab economy and society, showing in terms of urbanization and the emergence of a major population of wage labor, inevitably involved industrialization, underlined by the comparative growth of manufacturing industry. Even at its peak in 1935, affected by high prices in foreign citrus markets, Arab farm net domestic product was only 80 percent higher than in 1922. In the same period the product of Arab manufacturing increased by about 350 percent; the construction boom involved an even greater leap to an all-time high (Table 8). Manufacturing industry started indeed from a low base: the workshop employing a small number of workers was the prevalent feature of that sector in the early 1920s. The soap industry in Nablus, based on a local raw material, olive oil, was a case in point. Urbanization and growth led to the emergence of manufacturing establishments focusing on the production of consumer goods. Flour mills, cigarette factories, and small textile establishments appeared in the later 1920s and 1930, and so did larger manufacturing establishments, supplying raw materials such as stone, bricks, and lumber to the building industry, which was expanding in the mid-1920s and again in 1932–1935, thanks to a building boom in both national sectors. "Exports" to the Jewish construction market were a dominant component of the demand for quarry output. In the four years ending in 1935 the net product of Arab manufacturing grew accordingly by much more than 50 percent. Agricultural product started to grow again during the war years. Yet by 1945 Arab manufacturing product was almost eight times greater than in 1922, while increase in farm production was less than half of that. This applied similarly to the comparative growth of employment in the two branches (Table 7).

THE RESTRUCTURING OF THE FARM SECTOR. Agricultural employment and product grew substantially in absolute terms through that period. It was clearly citriculture, however, that was the backbone of the Arab agricultural sector through 1939. While between 1922 and 1939 total Arab farm output grew just over twofold, the output of citrus grew by almost eight times and that of noncitrus output, which was subject to cyclical yield features, rose by about only 1.6 times. In its peak year, 1937, noncitrus farm output was almost two times higher than in 1922. The growth rate in terms of value added was similar.

With the closure of foreign markets during World War II, the citrus industry effectively disappeared from the map. Yet the other components of Arab agriculture, lagging through 1939, benefited from the booming food markets, civilian and military, in Palestine and the Middle East. Net farm product of the Arab sector, effectively the noncitrus branches, more than doubled during the almost six years of the war. This was evidently a much better performance than that shown during the 17-year period ending with the outbreak of the war (Table 8).

Peasant dry farming was the hallmark of Arab agriculture at the advent of the Mandatory period. For the highly self-sufficient farm population, grain growing provided the basic food requirements, with livestock output also mainly for home consumption. This pattern changed substantially during the period of the Mandate. While Arab rural population grew by about 65 percent, the area under grain cultivation grew by only 13 percent; grain output even declined in the 1930s. Yet the area allocated to vegetables, tobacco, olives, and other fruit grew by 5 to 6 times, and the output of vegetables, largely cash crops, increased eightfold and that of fruit fourfold. The mixed farming output obviously responded to the pull of the markets, through the war years especially.

Thus, though land under cultivation hardly increased, farm employment rose by 14 percent and the intensification of cultivation due to a fourfold increase in the area of irrigated land allowed an increase of mixed farm output that compensated for the collapse in citrus production. Yet the use of mechanical equipment in farming was still small. This is underlined by a simple statistic: out of 500 tractors operating in Palestine in the early 1940s, Arab farmers owned and used only 50.

The dominant factor of Arab peasant farming in the three decades of the Mandate, and particularly from the 1930s onward, was clearly its move into the market system. It heralded the disappearance of subsistence farming and its replacement by cash crop production, complemented by seasonal employment in the rapidly expanding Arab and the Jewish citrus industry. In the war years, employment in military projects served as a substitute for the loss of citrus industry employment.

The Economics of the Fifth Aliyah, 1932–1939

IMMIGRATION, LEGAL AND ILLEGAL, AND PALESTINE'S DEMOGRAPHIC STRUCTURE. The Jewish population, which was

175,000 at the end of 1931, grew to 650,000 at the time of the Declaration of Independence on May 15, 1948. Thus, during that short interval of some 16 years it grew by about 3.5 times (Table 1), at an average annual rate of 8.2 percent. Although this rather unusual growth of population reflected natural population growth rates in situ, it was dominated by a wave of Jewish immigration in the first half of the 1930s, peaking in 1935 (Table 3). During these four years, more than 160,000 immigrants arrived in Palestine, a figure almost equal in size to the total Jewish population of 1931. That high annual average of about 40,000 was cut drastically to about 21,000 in the next four years, through 1939. In the six war years and the two years immediately thereafter through 1947, this low immigration rate was reduced even more, to an annual average of about 12,000, close to the rate prevailing in the first years of the Mandate through 1931.

A highly significant feature with important implications for the size of the Jewish community in Palestine was the rate of emigration, a common phenomenon of countries absorbing significant numbers of immigrants. In the 1920s this was quite high: emigration was on average 25 percent of the total immigration inflow between 1919 and 1931. In the 1930s this rate was down to only about eight percent, a decrease reflecting the hostile attitude of governments of the time toward Jewish refugees – underlined by the attitude of the participants of the 1938 *Evian Conference on refugees. The emigration rate was similarly about nine percent from 1940–47.

The immigration inflow was not smooth, nor was the outflow of emigration. Ups and downs were due mainly to political factors in Europe on the one hand and the changing policies of the Mandatory government on the other. The short-lived surge of the Fourth Aliyah of 1924–27 was clearly a response to the economic crisis in Poland. It was also affected by the drastic limitations on immigration to the United States imposed by the Immigration Act of 1924, which effectively closed the United States as a destination of immigrants from Eastern Europe, thus redirecting Jewish immigration toward Palestine.

In the 1920s, the first decade after the Balfour Declaration, Palestine was on the whole an open destination to Jewish immigrants, even though Churchill's 1922 White Paper imposed conditions of "economic absorption capacity" for the allocation of immigration certificates to workers, i.e., to potential Jewish immigrants who could not prove ownership of a required minimum (£1,000) of liquid funds. Immigrants who did have such funds, the so-called "capitalist immigrants," were automatically allocated entrance permits for themselves and their families, and work permits. For immigrants in the "workers" category there was a quota. Its size was to be negotiated every six months by the representatives of the Zionist authorities and the Immigration Department of the Mandatory government. These entrance permits – "certificates," as they were known in the Jewish community – were put at the disposal of the Zionist Organization and allocated by its Palestine Office to Jewish applicants, mostly in Europe. In the 1920s most of these permits were allocated to applicants in Eastern European countries; from the early 1930s on, those in Germany, Austria, and Czechoslovakia were given priority.

In the negotiations over the size of the six-month quota of labor entrance permits, differences between the optimistic estimates of the so-called "economic absorption capacity" of Palestine, offered usually by the representatives of the Jewish Agency, and the more conservative estimates of the director of the Immigration Department, were inevitably the rule. In

Table 10. The Banking System in the Mandatory Era

	Number of Institutions[1]	Deposits		Credit		Ratios to Totals (percent)			
						Deposits		Credit	
		Total	APB[2]	Total	APB	APB	Foreign[3]	APB	Foreign
	(1)	(2)	(3)	(4)	(5)	(6)	(7)	(8)	(9)
1920	5	–	–	–	–	–	–		
1931	75[4]	–	100	–	100	–	–		
1932	91	–	120	–	106	–	–		
1935	–	–	437	–	256	–	–		
1936	134	100	447/100	100	225/100	37.1	27.4	25.3	19.1
1940	97	93	97	85	126	39.1	40.2	37.3	13.6
1944	91	419	558	125	116	49.4	20.8	23.4	10.3
1946	–	573	726	282	379	47.0	17.5	34.0	11.1

Notes:
1. Includes banks and cooperative credit institutions.
2. APB is the Anglo-Palestine Bank (Bank Leumi after independence), owned by the Zionist Organization and the dominant bank in the country. According to the Mandatory classification of banking institutions, it was identified as a foreign bank since it was incorporated in Britain. There are two index number series representing APB deposits and credit, with benchmarks in 1931 and 1936 respectively, because of changes in classification of debit and credit items in the bank's balance sheet.
3. Other foreign banks were dominated by two institutions: the British Barclays Bank, agent of the Palestine Currency Board and the government of Palestine's banker, and the Ottoman Bank. The balance to 100 percent in columns 6–7 and 8–9 respectively represent the share of other local banking institutions, dominated by the Jewish banking sector.
4. The figure refers to 1930.

Table 11. The Jewish Economy: Net Product, Investment, and Capital Imports

	1936 Prices (P£, in thousands)					Ratio (%)		
			Capital Imports[2]					
	NNP	Net Investment[1]	Private	Public	Total	Net Investment / NNP	Capital Imports / NNP	Capital Imports/ Investments
	(1)	(2)	(3)	(4)	(5)	(6) [=(2)/(1)]	(7) [=(5)/(1)]	(8) [=(5)/(2)]
A. Jewish Economy								
1922	1,549	796	2,477	678	3,155	51.4	203.7	396.4
1925	3,001	1,992	4,944	998	5,942	66.4	198	298.3
1926	3,143	1,289	3,589	1,208	4,797	41.0	152.6	372.1
1928	3,839	1,440	1,623	1,265	2,888	37.5	75.2	200.6
1931	6,761	2,168	2,446	1,059	3,505	32.1	51.8	161.7
1935	18,309	8,191	9,630	942	10,572	44.7	57.7	129.1
1936	17,464	6,285	5,875	1,204	7,079	36.0	40.5	112.6
1938	15,342	3,526	4,781	1,646	6,427	20.0	41.9	182.3
1939	15,843	2,712	4,569	1,818	6,437	17.1	40.6	237.4
1941	19,732	2,204	1,850	1,478	3,328	11.6	16.9	151
1945	30,004	2,536	2,100	2,281	4,381	8.5	14.6	172.8
1947	37,974	8,791	1,550	1,678	3,228	23.2	8.5	36.7
1922–1929	23,385	9,116	23,279	8,637	31,916	39.0	136.4	350.1
1930–1939	130,269	44,621	54,219	11,788	66,007	34.3	50.1	150.0
1940–1947	216,932	27,983	16,950	15,636	32,586	13.0	15.0	116.4
Total	370,586	81,720	94,448	36,061	130,509	22.1	35.2	159.7
B. Arab Economy								
1922	6,796	362	–	–	–	5.3	–	–
1925	7,789	403	–	–	–	5.2	–	–
1928	7,835	762	–	–	–	9.7	–	–
1931	9,709	1,149	–	–	–	11.8	–	–
1935	16,694	2,982	–	–	–	17.9	–	–
1936	15,581	2,642	–	–	–	17.0	–	–
1939	15,584	929	–	–	–	6.0	–	–
1941	18,430	1,698	–	–	–	9.2	–	–
1945	26,075	1,964	–	–	–	7.5	–	–
1946	30,062	2,036	–	–	–	6.8	–	–

Notes:
1. Net investment in fixed reproducible capital stock.
2. The capital import figures are the sum of unilateral transfers and capital account funds of Jewish immigrants, firms, and private investors, according to the balance-of-payments data.

spite of a short-lived attempt by the British government in 1930 to withdraw from its commitment through 1935, the pace of Jewish immigration was more or less determined by the number of European Jews wanting to emigrate to Palestine. The upsurge of the Fourth Aliyah in 1924–27 was determined by economic and political pressures in Eastern Europe. What could be described as the pre-state wave of mass immigration in 1932–36, which brought almost 200,000 Jews to Palestine, more than doubling the size of the Jewish population within those five years, was evidently the all-out economic crisis in Europe which had led to the rise of the rabidly antisemitic Nazi government of Germany. Its influence in such areas as the elimination of the civil rights of Jewish citizens radiated to Eastern European governments, particularly those of Poland and Romania, which had been long pursuing more covert antisemitic policies of their own, generating a "pushing out" effect on the Jewish communities in those states.

The political dominance of Hitler's Germany in Europe, demonstrated by the appeasement embodied in the Munich Agreement of 1938, led finally to the desperate attempts of Jews to emigrate from Europe to almost any destination open to them. This should have led to another wave of mass immigration to Palestine, given the closed-door policies of the United States, Canada, Australia, and South American coun-

Table 12. Main Items of Palestine's Balance of Payments: 1922–1947[1] (P £ Million)

	Current Account			Unilateral Transfers				Capital Account					Errors and Omissions
	Credit[2]	Debit	Net	Credit				Credit	Debit				
				Immigrants[3]	Donations[4]	Other[5]	Net	Private[6]	Banks[7]	Government[8]	Board[9]	Net[10]	
	(1)	(2)	(3)	(4)	(5)	(6)	(7)	(8)	(9)	(10)	(11)	(12)	(13)
1922–39	60	171	-111	75	25	9	109	26	6	2	9	9	7
1940–47	309	313	-4	35	40	11	86	-10	48	9	35	-102	20
1922–47	369	484	-115	110	65	20	195	16	54	11	44	-93	13

Notes:

1) Because of the major inflationary developments during the war years prices rose by 144 percent, at an annual average of about 14 percent in the seven-year period ending in 1946; as a result the nominal Palestine pound figures of this table for that period are not comparable at all to the figures from 1922 to 1939. On the other hand, the stable prices in the 1930s and the comparatively small value of the balance-of-payment flows in the 1920s suggest that the figures for the 1920s are quite comparable to those of the 1930s.
2) The credit figures refer to exports plus receipts from transactions with the British army. These were only P£8 million in 1922–39, but P£180 million in the 1940–47 war years, about 60 percent of Palestine's "export" trade in those years.
3) Funds transferred by Jewish immigrants.
4) Funds transferred by Jewish institutions, donated by communities in the Diaspora.
5) Funds transferred by non-Jewish foreign institutions and by the Palestine government.
6) Capital imports by Jewish private entities.
7) Liquid funds, effectively secondary reserves of the banking system transferred to and held mainly in London.
8) Palestine government funds transmitted mainly to the Crown agent in London.
9) The sterling collateral of the Palestine Currency Board for the outstanding balance of Palestine pounds in circulation.
10) The net figures in the capital account. (12) = (8) – [(9) + (10) + (11)].

tries which were linked to the high unemployment rates in those places.

Palestine immigration data, however, indicates that this was not the case. In the 1936–39 period, Jewish immigration was cut by an annual average of more than 50 percent compared to 1932–35. The same holds true for the entire war period through 1947, even though Jews in eastern and southern Europe, desperate to save their lives from 1935 onward, were looking for havens to escape to. If an open door to Palestine, or at least the relatively liberal immigration policy through 1935, had continued, this option would have been used by many more Jewish refugees in 1936–39. Indeed about a million Jews living in Romania and the Balkan countries could have made use of such an option as late as 1941 and even 1942. More than 100,000 Jewish refugees attempted to make it to Palestine as illegal immigrants in the immediate aftermath of the war in 1945–47.

The reduction of Jewish immigration to Palestine from 1936 on was the result of the policy of the British government, in breach of its 1922 commitment to the League of Nations. It was made in response to the Arab uprising of 1936–39, and during the war years, particularly from 1942 onward, reflecting a cynical reading of the expected relative political power of the Arabs and the Jews in the postwar era. The British Foreign Office, headed by Foreign Secretary Anthony Eden, advocated this policy. The first attempt to adopt such a policy came in 1930–31 from the Labour government's colonial secretary, Lord Passfield (Sidney Webb), but at that time it was revoked by Prime Minister Ramsay MacDonald before being implemented. In 1937, when only 10,000 immigrants were allowed into Palestine, it was finally implemented on the spot on grounds of insufficient "economic absorption capacity." The representative of the Mandatory government argued that a very low base reading of the absorption capacity was warranted, apparently in view of the recession phase of the business cycle, a well-known feature of market economies. In the wake of the roaring Fifth Aliyah-driven prosperity of 1932–35, a short downturn of the level of economic activity was indeed in the offing.

This justification for limiting Jewish immigration was soon superseded. The British government adopted the policy announced in the White Paper of 1939, revoking the commitment to "facilitate Jewish immigration" (and to the eventual partition of Palestine that had been its official solution for the growing strife between the Jewish and Arab communities). The White Paper envisioned an independent Palestinian state after a period of ten years. During this time Jewish immigration would be limited to a quota of 75,000, who would be allowed to enter within five years, after which Jewish immigration would end. It also limited drastically the area of Palestine where Jews would be allowed to purchase land. This policy was adamantly pursued by the Conservative government in power, and later by the coalition government through the years of the war. It was also adopted by the postwar Labour government, which used the British Navy to pursue ships loaded with European Jewish refugees attempting to make it to Palestine illegally. They caught most of the ships while still on the high seas. The refugees were held in camps on Cyprus until the emergence of the state of Israel in 1948.

About 120–150,000 *ma'pilim* (*"illegal" immigrants) made it to the shores of Palestine – i.e., without an entry permit. Transport was organized and financed by the Zionist authorities and Jewish organizations. Some 20–25,000 of these illegal immigrants arrived before the war, between 1934, when the first ship from Europe, the *Welos*, made it to a hidden landing spot, and 1940. About 100,000 were involved in the illegal immigration drive during the war years and especially in the all-out efforts to breach the British embargo after the war. *Ha'palah* was the Hebrew term coined for that entire campaign. This operation was part of the last stage of the struggle for the establishment of the state of Israel, and involved in 1941 and 1942 two accidents that cost hundreds of refugees their lives.

Nevertheless, the Aliyah brought close to half a million immigrants to Palestine during the three decades of the Mandatory period. As is true of mass migrations to any country, some of the immigrants – after 1930, very few – returned to their home countries or went to other destinations. Estimates of Jewish immigration to Palestine for 1936–45, during which the preliminary stage of the illegal immigration effort took place, suggest that about 20 percent of the total of 130,000 immigrants in that period came illegally. They arrived by ship from Europe or through the northern land border with Lebanon and Syria. Those who arrived via the latter route were mostly from the Jewish communities of Iran, Iraq, and Syria.

In the 1920s, the Zionist movement faced an uphill struggle with the Jewish communities in Europe to convince them to use the opportunity of the "free Aliyah" option available in those years and follow the Zionist message of the Return to the Land of the Patriarchs. From the mid-1930s onward the struggle was with the British government, which attempted to implement a closed-door policy while hundreds of thousands of Jews were by that time knocking on the gates. The half a million immigrants who made it to Palestine during these three decades changed the demographic landscape and thus the economic and inevitably the political structure of Palestine. The Jewish community was only 11 percent of the total population in the first Mandatory census of 1922. At the second and final Mandatory census in 1931, it was already about 17 percent. in the following four years, with the mass immigration of 1932–35, it grew to 27 percent of the total population. By May 1948, at the time of the declaration of statehood, the Jewish population was about one third of the total of about two million people living in Palestine.

THE BREAKTHROUGH IN THE JEWISH ECONOMY, 1932–1939. *Labor Force, Employment, Investment, and Capital Stock.* The almost 250,000 Jewish immigrants of the 1930s, two-thirds of whom had arrived by 1935 before the British government began to implement the closed-door policy, represented a major enlargement of the Jewish labor force. By the end of 1935 the labor force was two times greater than in 1931. The significant reduction in immigration reduced its rate of expansion in the next four years through 1939 to only 40 percent, but this meant that by the outbreak of the war it was still close to three times greater than at the beginning of the decade. Employment grew correspondingly by two times through 1935, but at a significantly lower rate than the growth of the labor force in the second half of the 1930s, reflecting the downturn in the business cycle and rising unemployment. Though the rate of unemployment increased to 4.2 percent, employment in the Jewish sector was by 1939 still higher by about 25 percent than in 1935 (Tables 4 and 7).

This rising trend of employment and of production would have been impossible without a major increase of the capital stock of the Jewish economy and the buildup of the infrastructure of Palestine – the "Government Capital Stock" (roads, railroads, ports, telephone and radio facilities, etc.), in the terms used in Table 4. The Jewish sector investment figures show the extraordinary bulge of investment in 1935, which represents the peak of the rising trend of investment from 1932 onward. Though declining afterward through 1939, the lowered investment level of that year was still higher than investment levels in each year previously through 1931.

This means that capital stock kept accumulating through the second half of the 1930s, though at a significantly lower rate than in the 1931–35 interval. The major upswing of the Jewish economy within these four years involved an expansion by more than two times of the reproducible net capital stock of the Jewish economy; at the end of the 1930s it was more than three times greater than at its beginning. The expansion rate of the infrastructure capital stock (the so-called Government Capital Stock) was lower, though it still grew by a factor of 2.5 in the 1930s. The highly significant more rapid increase of the capital stock than of the labor force and employment meant that the capital-labor ratio and the capital-employment ratio, displayed in Table 4, rose at a very high rate of 20 percent in the 1920s, and kept rising in the 1930s at an even higher rate. This pattern was maintained even though, with the growth of immigration, the Jewish labor force and employment grew at a much higher rate than in the 1920s.

Furthermore, the levels of education and expertise displayed by the immigrants of the 1920s and especially the 1930s reflected the state of the art in the industrial countries from which they came and contributed immensely to the human capital of the Jewish community. This feature, among others, underlines the considerable relative decline of the old *yishuv* component of the community. It can also be seen in the establishment of a comprehensive elementary school system, financed and run by the Jewish sector's own political authorities, even though there was no legal enforcement of attendance. A significant secondary school system, initially small in terms of attendance rates of the relevant age group, assured the education of the coming generations.

Production and Living Standards. The expansion of the labor force and of employment, and even the higher growth of capital stock, supported by rising productivity show inevitably in rising production and living standards. The 1939 national product was 2.3 times greater than that of 1931, on the eve of the arrival of the Fifth Aliyah. This means that Jewish national product grew at the enormous annual average of 11 percent through these eight prewar years (Table 5).

The national product of 1939 was indeed significantly smaller than the all-time high of 1935, to which it had risen at a spectacular rate in the four-year period since 1932. This was an expression of the major slowdown of the economy, related to the outbreak of the 1936 Arab revolt, and particularly to the recurring prewar political crises in Europe. These had started with the breach of the Versailles Treaty by Hitler's Germany and Mussolini's invasion of Abyssinia toward the end of 1935, followed by the Anschluss in Austria and the succeeding Munich Crisis, both in 1938, and finally the outbreak of the war in 1939. The specific domestic reason for the downturn of the Palestine economy in the second half of the 1930s was the major reduction by about 50 percent of the inflow of Jewish immigrants and the corresponding reduced inflow of Jewish capital imports – effectively the total capital inflow into the Palestinian economy. This inflow was lower by about 23 percent in the four-year period 1936–39, relative to the all-time high in the preceding four-year period, with investment following suit.

Living standards measured in terms of per capita product, or of real wages, rose at a significantly lower rate than that of total product. At the height of prosperity in 1935, before the emergence of the 1936–40 slowdown, per capita product was higher by 45 percent than in 1931, and real wages grew by close to 10 percent (Tables 5 and 6). These very rapid rising trends were achieved even though the Jewish population grew in these four years by two times, and the labor force by a similar factor. The ensuing slowdown changed the direction of these two indicators of the Jewish sector's average living standards. But by the depth of the depression in 1939, which can be seen in the 4.3 percent unemployment rate (Table 7), per capita product and real wages were about 90 percent and 50 percent higher, respectively, than they had been in 1922. This means that per capita product and real wages had risen at an annual average of 3.8 percent and 2.4 respectively since the early 1920s. This was thus quite a performance in view of the world economic crisis of the 1930s, and the weak, or at best mediocre, performances of the European economies in the late 1920s, with the Mandatory power, Britain, itself in the doldrums.

THE JEWISH AND ARAB ECONOMIES: COMPARATIVE TRENDS AND LINKS. Measures of living standard (product per capita), and productivity (product per employee), which grew by annual averages of 3.8 and 2.8 percent respectively through 1939 (Tables 5 and 6), suggest that during the first two decades of the Mandate the Jewish economy made a major stride into industrialization. The growth of its real economic aggregates, in particular labor force, capital stock, national product, and trade, as well as the considerable and highly significant capital imports, suggest that the Jewish economy at the outbreak of World War II was an altogether different entity than at the advent of the Mandate era.

This conclusion is underlined by the comparative trends in the products of the two national economies. The Jewish national product was less than one quarter of the Arab national product in 1922; by 1935 it was already greater, and about 53 percent of the total product of Palestine, even though the share of the Jewish population was only 27 percent at that time (Tables 5 and 6). The economic slowdown of the late 1930s inevitably had a greater impact on the comparatively more industrialized and urban Jewish economy than on the Arab, still dominated by its farming sector. Thus, by 1939 the ratio between the two economies' products equalized somewhat, with the Jewish share slightly above 50 percent, while its share of the population had reached 30 percent.

These differences between national product and population ratios also show in per capita national product ratios. The advantage of the Jewish sector, indicating a much higher average living standard, emerges already in the 1922 figures; the Jewish per capita product was almost two times greater than its Arab counterpart. This soared to a ratio above three during the first half of the 1930s. The slowdown of the late 1930s and the continuing, though much lower, Jewish immigration, reduced somewhat the gap between the two economies' per capita products to a factor of about 2.5 through the last decade of the Mandatory era.

The gap between the national product and per capita figures for the two economies was greater in terms of domestic product, which relates more to productivity, than in national product, which offers a better index of living standards. This is because the Jewish economy offered employment to Arab labor, while Jewish workers were not willing to work for the wages prevalent in the Arab sector. Another feature of this relationship that boosted the net product of the Arab economy was the sale of Arab farm produce to Jewish urban populations. An estimate of the quantitative effect of that linkage on Arab gross domestic product and net national product is unavailable.

The outbreak of the Arab rebellion in 1936 led to a widespread severing of links between the two economies. Most importantly, it reduced the employment of Arab labor, both in absolute terms and, even more, relative to total employment in the Jewish economy. The war, which after 1939 shut off the main export markets of Palestine's citrus industry, prevented a major revival of employment of Arab labor in the Jewish economy during what was a relatively peaceful time in Palestine. At its peak in 1935 the share of Arab labor of employment in the Jewish sector was 8.4 percent; by 1945 it had fallen to only 1.7 percent, involving only about 1.2 percent of the total Arab labor force. These developments – the Arab rebellion and the impact of war conditions – show clearly in the NNP to NDP ratios of Table 5a. By 1939 the direct contribution to Arab net national product by employment in the Jewish sector was down from 6.2 in 1935 to only 1.6 percent. This ratio was effectively maintained through the end of the Mandate period.

These figures indicate that although the severance of the economic links between the Arab and Jewish economies in Mandatory Palestine became permanent only with the outbreak of the Israeli War of Independence in December 1947, it had already become a fait accompli over the preceding decade, starting in 1936.

The Business Cycle of the 1930s. The rapid transformation of the Jewish economy into industrialization was demonstrated by the duration and intensity of the business cycle to which it had been subject in the 1930s: the effects of this cycle characterized the performance of Palestine's economy as a whole, though they were not as great on the Arab economy. At the very time at which the world's economy plunged into the disastrous economic crisis of the 1930s, the Jewish economy of Palestine, and that of the country as a whole, benefited from overall prosperity and full employment. In spite of a growth in the size of the labor force of the Jewish sector by about 32 percent between 1929 and 1933 the unemployment rate was less than one percent (Table 7), and the national product had grown by close to 145 percent. That rising trend continued through 1935, at which time the wave of mass immigration peaked, with net domestic product almost four times higher than in 1929. Palestine's national product grew inevitably at a lower rate, yet still by a robust rate of about 2.6 times, which indicates a prosperous six-year period through 1935 for Palestine's economy as a whole (Table 5).

In market economies, the "prosperity stage," a term that undoubtedly applies to the Jewish economy of the early 1930s, in a business cycle is usually followed by a recession. This is true especially in a case in which the rising trend of economic activity is as vigorous as it was in the first half of the 1930s in Palestine: an annual average growth rate of 28 percent in the NDP of the Jewish economy in 1931–35, and of 12 percent in Palestine's economy as a whole.

A declining rate of investment is usually the trigger for a slowdown. This was indeed the case in Palestine; that leading economic determinant of a downturn in industrialized economies surfaced at the peak in 1935. The key branches involved were those which had prospered most during the rising pattern of the 1928–35 cycle – the building and citrus industries. At the aggregate level, total investment still increased in the Jewish sector in 1935 to its peak for the entire decade (Table 4): but its rate of increase in that year was only 12 percent, much lower than the almost 50 percent rate of the preceding year, 1934, and even lower than that of 1932. A similar pattern was followed by the building industry; the peak of investment in housing for the decade was reached in 1935 as well. The slowdown of the Jewish population growth rate, which had doubled in the four years from 1932 to 1935, inevitably reduced the increase in demand for living space, with a corresponding lag effect on investment in housing, and thus on the level of activity in the building industry.

A similar development was facing the dominant agricultural branch, and the mainstay of Palestine's exports, the citrus industry. Jewish sector investments in that branch peaked in 1934; investments were lower by about 16 percent in 1935 and by 1937 were only 50 percent of what they had been in 1934. They collapsed altogether in the successive prewar years. Arab peak investment in that branch lagged by two years; its peak was reached in 1936. Yet owing to the dominance of Jewish sector investments, the tide for the citrus industry as a whole, both in terms of investment and of planted area, was turned

Table 13. Monetary Aggregates and Prices, 1922–1947

Year	Monetary Aggregates			Prices		
	Currency[1] (1)	Demand Deposits (2)	Money: M1 (3) [=(1)+(2)]	Jewish Markets[2] (4)	Palestine[3] (5)	Wholesale Prices[4] (6)
Indices: 1931=100						
1922	–	–	–	156	164	174
1927	64	(75)	–	132	143	143
1929	94	–	–	117	125	130
1931	100	100	100	100	100	100
1935	285	325	310	111	99	106
1936	249	326	298	108	105	110
1939	370	319	348	111	109	111
1941	581	479	516	165	168	187
1945	2,104	1,905	1,976	319	256	352
1946	1,886	1,943	1,921	337	266	366
1947	1,830	–	–	342	–	–
Average Annual Rates of Change (percent)						
1927–1931	15.7	12.8	–	-1.5	-2.3	-2.1
1931–1939	17.8	15.6	16.8	1.3	1.1	1.3
1939–1946	26.2	29.4	27.6	17.2	13.6	18.5

Notes:
1. Currency in circulation.
2. Cost of living index in Jewish markets.
3. Weighted cost of living in Jewish and Arab markets.
4. Wholesale price index applies to the entire economy.

by the end of 1934, at the peak of Palestine's prosperity. This significant reduction in investment was a lagging response to market signals: the decline of orange prices in the main European export markets. This trend emerged from the beginning of the decade: by 1934 they were 10 percent lower than in 1931. They declined significantly further, in 1936, even though exports of competing Spanish oranges declined abruptly due to the outbreak of the Spanish Civil War.

The slowdown of the flow of investment in the two leading branches of the economy, the building industry (in the Jewish sector in particular) and citriculture, was triggered by market signals. Inevitably its effects led to a downturn of the business cycle beginning early in 1936. Yet the severity of the downturn, the awareness of which surfaced only later in that year – Jewish NDP declined by 6.3 percent – was due to ominous political developments. The world political crisis, which began late in 1935 with the Italian invasion of Ethiopia, and led finally to the outbreak of World War II in 1939, inevitably had a negative effect on Palestine's economic activity. Its direct impact was compounded by the outbreak of the Arab revolt in April 1936, involving initially a boycott of the Jewish economy, supported by violence against Jews and later by an armed insurgency against the British army. The political response of the British government to that challenge was a drastic curtailment of Jewish immigration (see Immigration, Legal and Illegal, and Palestine's Demographic Structure above). This entailed an inevitable slowdown of Jewish capital imports (by 25 percent), and affected consumption immediately (Table 13). Capital imports were, of course, the main source of investment finance, which declined consequently, and together with lower consumer expenditures, reduced aggregate demand.

Thus, following the 6.3 percent decline of Jewish domestic product in 1936, the three succeeding years through 1939 saw a further cumulative decline of 16.4 percent from what had been an extraordinarily high domestic product in 1935. In terms of national product, which netted out wages paid to Arab workers, the rate of decline was lower, about 13.4 percent. That loss of national product entailed a corresponding reduction of per capita product by 35 percent from 1935, reflecting also the continuing growth of Jewish population due to immigration, which temporarily rose again in 1939, and natural increase (Table 5).

The Jewish economy's per capita product for 1939 was thus down by 35 percent from that of 1935, and regained only toward the end of the war. Similarly, real wages in 1939 were down by 13 percent from 1935, indicating the strain in the labor market. This showed in terms of the growth of unemployment: the rate in the Jewish sector, only about one percent in 1935, rose to 4.3 percent in 1939. This significant growth in unemployment resulted not only from the downturn of the business cycle but from the growth of the Jewish labor force by about 50 percent in the second half of the 1930s, owing to the immigration of about 100,000 additional immigrants.

The social and economic implications of this situation soon led to the establishment of the rudiments of a social security system – unemployment benefits in particular – run by the *Histadrut (the general federation of Jewish labor, founded in the 1920s as a means to establish the institutions of a Jewish national economy; see below, The Histadrut and the Economics of the Yishuv) with significant funding from the Jewish Agency. This added a second welfare state element to its first pioneering effort, the compulsory "sick fund" which all members of the Histadrut had to join; indeed it provided coverage to members only. Reorganized in the 1930s, it was financed almost exclusively by union membership fees, with some support from the Jewish Agency, though none from the Mandatory government. The virtual welfare state, which by the late 1930s was well established, was for the benefit of the Jewish community only. It is another indicator supporting the claim that the Jewish community – the *yishuv* – of close to 450,000 people by that time, was by then already a socioeconomic entity belonging to the industrialized group of countries. In more than one sense, this emerging character was an expression of the Fifth Aliyah's influence.

THE ADVENT OF MANUFACTURING. *The Buildup of Infrastructure: Power, Communities, and Ports.* The history of manufacturing in Palestine emerges only in the Mandatory period. This is underlined by the fact that electricity generation on a commercial scale began only in 1923 by the Palestine (later Israel) Electric Corporation, which received in September 1921 exclusive concessions to exploit the Yarkon and Jordan rivers for irrigation and electricity and which eventually supplied electricity to the whole country excluding Jerusalem. It was Pinchas Rutenberg whose enterprise, stamina, and persistence overcame the major political obstacles and financial risks involved in the founding of this basic infrastructure facility. The PEC was rightly identified as a Zionist undertaking, even though it was a corporation whose shares were traded on the London Stock Exchange and paid dividends to shareholders.

Electricity consumption by manufacturing industries was only one million kilowatt hours (KWH) in 1926. It grew to 20 million in 1938 and to 86 million KWH in 1947, the last full year of the Mandate. This clearly warrants tracing the first steps of manufacturing to the early 1920s. Although the employment and product figures for 1922, presented in Tables 7 and 8, refer to manufacturing as one of the three standard branch breakdowns for analysis of economic structure, the approximately 4,000 employees classified as working in the "handicraft and manufacturing" branch of the Jewish sector (Table 7) that year were working in handicraft workshops – small entities having not more than two or three hired employees, offering services to urban consumers and businesses. This was equally true of the Arab sector, in which at that time the number of employees in handicrafts was lower than in the Jewish sector.

The development of manufacturing and large-scale irrigation in Jewish agriculture, and thus the economic growth of the country as a whole, were interwoven with that of the production capacity of PEC. Its first diesel generator power station, set up in Tel Aviv in 1923, had a capacity of 750 kilowatts. By 1926 its generating capacity was 2,250 KW; in 1932, after the opening of its major hydroelectric project (Jordan-Kinneret) its capacity was increased to 16,200 KW; on the eve of the war in 1938 it was already at 63,000 KW; and in 1947, at the end of the Mandatory period, it was 75,000 KW. The running of the system, the continuing expansion of generating capacity, and the extension of the electricity network across the country required the building up and training of a sizable labor force, supported by a rapidly expanding group of specialists, including engineers, accountants, and managers.

The PEC, the railroad system, and the Public Works Department, which was in charge of building and maintaining the road network (the latter two were departments of the Mandatory government), provided the basic necessities for the rapidly expanding economic infrastructure. The major demand for their services was generated by the rapid growth of Jewish manufacturing industries and the Jewish sector as a whole. Large enterprises employing sizable staffs are a typical feature of an evolving industrial system, and in the 1930s the PEC had more than 1,000 on payroll and the railroad and the works department even more – a sign of Palestine's industrialization by the outbreak of World War II in 1939.

The Emergence of Manufacturing. A manufacturing industry involving state-of-the-art machinery and technology, a significant number of employees, a relatively high capital-labor ratio, requiring heavy long-term capital investment and producing for the mass market, began to appear in Palestine in the 1920s. This industry depended on the existence of a modern infrastructure of transportation and communication facilities, electric power, and a modern port (the deepwater port of Haifa opened in 1931). The proliferation of manufacturing firms in a significant variety of economic areas was quite clearly the dominant activity in the Jewish economy from the mid-1920s onward. It accelerated during the highly prosperous first half of the 1930s, through 1935, and declined during the downturn of the business cycle in the second half of that decade, which were years of consolidation. It reaccelerated strongly during the war years and in the war's aftermath through 1947.

This pattern can be discerned in the manufacturing employment, net product, and output figures in Tables 7 and 8. Employment in 1931 was 2.8 times higher than that of 1922, and real product (and output) of industry had almost trebled. The rapid expansion during the high tide of the Fifth Aliyah years of 1932–35 shows in terms of a roughly 2.5 times growth of net manufacturing product and output during that very short period, an incredible average annual growth rate of about 25 percent. The abrupt downturn of the cycle between 1936 and 1939 is demonstrated by the very slight growth rate of manufacturing product at an annual average of only about one percent for that period. The growth of employment and of capital stock slowed down too, but not by that much. Thus during the decade of the 1930s, ending with the outbreak of the war in 1939, employment in manufacturing grew at an annual average of about 11 percent and net product by about 13 percent (Tables 7 and 8). This means that by the end of that decade and in spite of the downturn of 1936–39, the Jewish economy's manufacturing sector (essentially, by that time, the whole of Palestine's manufacturing sector), was an altogether different and much larger entity than at the beginning.

This can be seen in the number and size of the manufacturing establishments, the kinds and quality of equipment used, the technologies of production, and the diversity of the industrial branches in which they specialized. The number of handicraft and manufacturing establishments, fewer than 2,000 in 1922, grew only to about 2,500 in the decade ending in 1931. By 1935 they were already twice that number – more than 5,000. The number of manufacturing establishments grew rapidly and by the end of the war in 1946 amounted to about 7,000.

An indicator of the rising capital vs. labor intensity and particularly the transformation of manufacturing technology is the rapid increase of the average horsepower of the machinery in use in manufacturing establishments. This was negligible in 1922 (800 HP), about 6,000 in 1930, and 40,000 by 1939. The far-reaching transformation undergone by the technology of production in the 1930s is also suggested by the data on the import of industrial machinery in the 1930s; in the peak year, 1935, the value of these imports was six times higher than in 1932, the year in which these imports increased 40 percent. This corresponded to the increase in Jewish immigration of the Fifth Aliyah.

The immigration inflow of Jews from Germany, which soon turned from a trickle into a flood, also brought a major increase in private capital imports, but only in the form of goods. This was the only way in which the German emigrants were allowed to transfer capital, under the *Haavara agreement of 1933 with the German government (see below). These imports of German equipment and raw materials were the point on which that agreement hinged. Due to the restrictions on immigration imposed by the British from 1936 onward, the flow of capital transfers in general slowed from its 1935 peak. Yet from 1936 through 1939 the import of machinery was still sustained on a level of three to four times that of 1932. This circumstance had a far-reaching impact on the technology, capacity, and volume of production of Jewish manufacturing industry later on. Only after the outbreak of the war, though, was the capacity fully utilized (see above, The Business Cycle of the 1930s).

Clearly the 1920s were the infancy period of manufacturing in Palestine, and the 1930s saw its emergence as a major component of the Jewish economy – effectively, of the economy of the whole of Palestine. This reading of the events is sustained by the data on the average number of workers per establishment, which grew from only 2.6 in 1922, to 5.1 in 1937, and to about 10 by the end of the war. The 1930s averages reflect the appearance of factories of significant size. There were 50 or so firms that employed more than 50 workers; 13 of them even employed more than 100 workers, or about 25 percent of the total employment in manufacturing in 1937. Almost all of these firms were founded only in the 1930s. Two such firms, the Potash Corporation, established in 1929, and the Palestine Electric Corporation were the only business establishments that employed more than 1,000 workers by that time.

The small size of the markets in an economy with a population of less than one million in the 1920s was of course a major constraint on the establishment of manufacturing capacity in Palestine. The only enterprises free of this constraint were those that could produce for export. A case in point was the Potash Company, based on the exclusive concession for Dead Sea minerals acquired by Moshe Novomeisky, a pioneer of the Palestine chemical industry. Its first output came in 1935, and it soon employed several hundred workers, reaching almost 1,000 by 1939; it continued to grow rapidly through the war years. But the dominant group of industrial firms, most of which were established in the 1930s, produced for domestic markets, where they were subject to competition from imports.

In the 1930s, the era of the worldwide economic crisis, governments imposed tariffs to protect their home markets, and assisted domestic firms in dumping their goods on foreign markets. The Mandatory government, which according to paragraph 18 of the Mandate was not allowed to impose discriminatory tariffs, was reluctant to interfere with free trade principles in support of local industry, even though Palestine, as an open market, suffered from dumping and universal (nondiscriminatory) tariffs would have been allowed. This passive attitude was underlined by the British refusal to allow Palestine to join the Imperial preference system established for the Empire in 1931, which offered a modicum of protection to those within. This arrangement thus discriminated against Palestine's exports, yet offered free access to its markets. Another reason for the British reluctance to impose tariffs on imports of manufactured goods was partly political – their expected effect on prices. Such a measure, it was thought, would offer support to a sector of the economy dominated by the Jewish firms, while forcing consumers, most of whom were Arabs, to pay higher prices.

Under these constraints manufacturers could face the competition of imports only if they operated in industries in which distance, and thus transportation costs, and local tastes and style preferences, offered "natural" protection. Construction materials such as cement, stone, and sand, which involve heavy transportation costs per unit of value, fall clearly into this category. This rule applied similarly to major consumer goods, particularly fresh food products, clothing, and furniture. Thus, the major manufacturing enterprises established in the mid-1920s, such as the Nesher cement factory, which for the next seven decades of the 20th century monopolized the domestic market, and the Shemen oil factory, belonged clearly to that category. The latter, though, soon had to face domestic competition from new enterprises that appeared in the 1930s.

The breakthrough of manufacturing occurred with the advent of the Fifth Aliyah in the 1930s. It shows in a twofold increase in manufacturing employment within a period of only four years by 1935 (Table 7), and in a similar increase in the total capital stock of the Jewish economy (Table 4). It was in this decade that Dead Sea potash manufacturing began, and similarly the textile, clothing, and shoemaking industries were established. Several manufacturing firms, competing with each other, appeared in the textile and clothing industries. The new enterprises of the 1930s founded by manufacturers who had been running similar firms in Central Europe followed the trail opened by manufacturers who had arrived from Poland with the Fourth Aliyah in 1924–25, who had been running what was considered at that time the Jewish textile industry in Lodz. Several firms producing chemicals, pharmaceuticals, cigarettes, and chocolate were founded in the late 1930s, as the flow of Jewish capital imports, which rose rapidly (Table 11), provided the financing, and immigrants, especially from Central Europe, provided the expertise and enterprise.

By the outbreak of the war, the Jewish sector had accordingly established a meaningful manufacturing industry. It was heavily oriented toward consumer goods and housing – about three-quarters of the gainfully employed in manufacturing worked in these sectors. It already included, however, some enterprises with significant spare capacity in the metal, machinery, and electrical equipment industries. Yet, though growing rapidly in terms of employment, capital stock, and production – employment grew at an annual average of 13 percent in the eight years ending in 1939 (Table 7), and net product of manufacturing by a similar rate – a meaningful portion of the existing capacity which had been created in the second half of the 1930s was not being utilized. That excess capacity and the high unemployment rate, 4.3 percent, reflected market demand constraint: inability to compete with imports. It made available a production potential, however, that could be used given higher demand.

URBANIZATION AND SOCIOECONOMIC STRUCTURE. The industrialization process initiated in the 1920s, and accelerated as the Fifth Aliyah progressed in the 1930s, entailed simultaneously a clear-cut process of urbanization and a structural change in the Jewish economy, and thus in the economy of Palestine as a whole. As in any country undergoing industrialization, manufacturing activity in Palestine was located mainly in urban centers, and inevitably stimulated the expansion of those centers. The great increase of Tel Aviv's population – actually the emergence of the Jaffa-Tel Aviv conurbation stretching, initially, towards the north, was part of this process. By 1939 the population of Tel Aviv and the Jewish population of Jaffa together were already 175,000. By this date the several urban centers between Tel Aviv and Petaḥ Tikvah to the north already totaled close to 20,000 people. This means that at the outbreak of the war the Jaffa-Tel Aviv conurbation contained a population of around 200,000 Jews, about 45 percent of the Jewish population of Palestine. The official 1944 estimate in Table 1 suggests that by that time the population of that area was about 250,000. During the last decade of the Mandate through 1947 it was thus the center of gravity of the Jewish population, and even more so of the Jewish community's economy, especially manufacturing industry.

Haifa and its Jewish satellite suburbs emerged in the 1930s as a similar northern urban center for the Jewish population. Though smaller than Jaffa-Tel Aviv, it was a mixed town with an Arab population similar in size. The completion in the early 1930s of Haifa's deepwater port, the only one in Palestine; the building of Iraq Petroleum's major pipeline, terminating at Haifa, in the mid-1930s; and finally the opening in 1939 of the IPC Refinery, whose capacity was many times larger than Palestine's own requirements, made Haifa a hub of major Jewish and Arab manufacturing activity. Jewish entrepreneurs and the Zionist authorities had discovered its potential by the mid-1920s, when private entrepreneurs located two major factories (the Nesher cement factory and the Shemen Oil and Food Products firm) in the Haifa Bay area, and the Jewish National Fund participated in 1935 in the purchase of a major tract of land there to serve as a manufacturing zone. By 1939 this zone was home to many Jewish manufacturing. Haifa and its satellite suburbs in the Haifa Bay area had by 1939 a Jewish population of 48,000 (Table 1).

No significant development of Jewish manufacturing took place in Jerusalem. But the growth of the Jewish population to some 80,000 by 1939 involved mostly those belonging to the new *yishuv*. Its labor force was employed in commerce, services, and public sector employment – the Jewish Agency and its subsidiaries – and finally in Palestine Mandatory and municipal government. The old *yishuv*, sticking to its traditional mission of maintaining a presence near the holy sites and engaging in Torah study at the yeshivot, became a proportionately declining component of the Jewish community.

The major structural change generated by the appearance of manufacturing industry and its growing impact on the Jewish economy and on Palestine's economic system as a whole is demonstrated by the figures in Table 9. The contribution of "handicraft and manufacturing," at that time entirely in handicraft workshops, to Jewish national net product in 1922 was somewhat less than 20 percent, and accounted for about 17 percent of employment in the Jewish economy. A decade later, reflecting the effects of the Third and Fourth Aliyah, the contribution rose slightly to 21 percent of the total net product, and employment in manufacturing rose too, to about 20 percent of the total. The 1930s and the war years, especially the latter (see the figure for 1945 in Table 9), brought a major increase: manufacturing employment rose to close to 31 percent of the total in the Jewish economy.

The contribution of agriculture followed an opposite trend: employment fell drastically, to 13 percent of total employment in the Jewish economy, while relative contribution to Jewish NDP fell only slightly, to roughly 11 percent of total product in 1945, compared to 13 percent in 1922. These figures indicate that labor productivity in Jewish farming, which in 1931 was only about one half of that of manufacturing, improved considerably: in 1945 it was up to about 77 percent. The effective disappearance of the citrus industry during the war contributed to this pattern. The major improvement in absolute and in relative terms of labor productivity in farming is a clear expression of the success of the mixed farming strategy adopted by the rapidly growing Jewish self-employed farming community.

The population figures in Table 1, supported by information about Jewish suburbs in the Tel Aviv and Haifa area and several newly urbanized centers, indicate that by 1939 about 80 percent of the Jewish population was living in these conurbations. They had become the Jewish population's centers of gravity as well as of manufacturing, by then the dominant sector of the economy, developments that had obvious political ramifications. The basic socioeconomic character of the Jewish community, which would have to fight for its survival in the War of Independence, was in place by the beginning of World War II.

AGRICULTURE AND THE MAJOR ZIONIST RESETTLEMENT EFFORT. *The Evolving Map of Jewish Settlement Blocs.* Industrialization and urbanization, which inevitably entailed also the rapid expansion of the service sector, dominated the Jewish economy in the 1930s and through World War II. Yet it was the Zionist resettlement effort that was at the core of the drive to establish a Jewish polity and was the focal point of the political and armed clashes with the Arabs. This effort also involved a political struggle with Britain, the Mandatory power, which in attempting to accommodate the national rights of the Palestinian Arabs, was gradually withdrawing from its commitments to the Zionists embodied in the Mandate (see above, Palestine as a Unique Political and Economic Entity).

The expansion of the Jewish settlement effort resulted in a growing number of settlements over an expanding geographical area and of an increase in rural population. The impact of this increased significantly over time. Thirty-nine new Jewish settlements appeared on the map of Palestine in the decade ending in 1931. Within the next five years through 1936, there were more than twice that many – a total of 89. In the so-called *stockade-and-watchtower settlement drive, launched in December 1936 – the name referred to the defensive measures necessitated by the attacks on Jews and Jewish settlements during the Arab Revolt of 1936–39 – 82 new settlements were established, most of the them by 1939.

In the immediate aftermath of the war, the number of settlements grew again and finally reached a total of almost 300 (Table 3). Most of the 22 new settlements founded in that final period of the Mandate came into being during 1946–47, when a campaign was launched to settle the arid southern region hitherto hardly touched by the Zionist settlement drive – the Negev.

Eleven of these settlements, or rather outposts – nuclei of settlements – were quickly set up at the conclusion of Yom Kippur, in early October 1946. The timing was designed to surprise the British authorities, whom it was feared would attempt to prevent the establishment of a Jewish foothold in the Negev. The political future of the area was then under discussion at the United Nations. Two more outposts, the last two settlements founded in the Mandate era, provided a link between the western Negev group of settlements established in 1946 and Revivim in the east. Revivim was the oldest of these outposts, set up in 1943 as a foothold and an agricultural experimental station. These last two settlements were set up on November 19, 1947, just ten days before the final vote in the United Nations General Assembly on the proposed UN Special Committee on Palestine (UNSCOP) partition plan calling for the establishment of two states, one Jewish and one Arab, in Palestine. This move underlined the strategic target of the Resettlement effort, which had been underway for about 70 years – to lay claim to the maximum territory for the intended Jewish State.

In the 1920s, though, the locations of the approximately 50 settlements set up between 1921 and 1931 were not chosen primarily for political reasons. They reflected more the availability of land in large blocs for sale by absentee Arab landowners. The bloc technique had nevertheless been consistently pursued ever since, based on considerations of economies of scale. Common provision of services to and purchase of goods for several settlements as a unit cut the cost of technical support and advisory services, purchase of materials and supplies, marketing of products, schooling, and health services for these small rural entities. The relevance of defense considerations grew over time and from the late 1920s was inevitably high on the settlement planning agenda.

The colonizing of the Jezreel Valley in that decade with about 20 settlements in its eastern and western sections, with a small town, Afula, in its center, was the first example of that policy. The bloc settlement technique is also evident in the mostly private enterprises set up in the 1920s in the citriculture belt of the central coastal plain. This did not exclude the establishment of isolated settlements also. Yet, the deliberate effort to establish a formidable Jewish presence in strategic locations all over Palestine became Zionist policy in the 1930s, as the Arab political pressures expressed by the 1929 riots and the 1936–39 uprising induced the British government to withdraw stepwise from the Balfour Declaration, and even from the more restricted 1922 Churchill White Paper commitment to the Zionist cause. This policy required large-bloc land acquisitions allowing the implementation of the stockade-and-watchtower policy, in the northeastern and northwestern Galilee, the Beit She'an area and the mid-Jordan Valley.

Not all the 55 settlements founded from December 1936 through 1939 were located in these three clusters of stockade-and-watchtower settlements (such as Ḥanitah, established in March 1938 on the Lebanese border in the western Galilee). The two settlements set up in the mountains near Jerusalem to increase the hitherto small Jewish presence along the winding road up to Jerusalem from the coastal plain were a case in point. During World War II, the bloc-forming strategy was maintained, but shifted location towards southern Palestine. Most of the approximately 20 settlements set up between 1940 and 1945 were located in the southern coastal plain penetrating east along the edge of the arid Negev. These settlements served as the springboard for the last resettlement campaign of the Mandatory era, culminating in the 1946–47 effort to establish outposts in the Negev.

Production, Productivity, and Living Standards. The expansion of the rural population by about ten times to 153,000 between 1922 and 1947 (Table 3) and the accompanying growth of employment were the results of the resettlement effort. The corresponding increases in output and national product were just as great. The output figures, available only through 1939, indicate a growth of mixed farming output by more than six times and a tremendous 20-fold expansion of citrus output. Total agricultural production of the Jewish economy grew by 12.5 times between 1922 and 1939 (Table 3). National product figures, which are available for a longer period, through 1947, indicate that net farm product grew by approximately 20 times during those 25 years at an average annual rate of close to 14 percent, a somewhat higher rate than in the 1920s and 1930s.

The closing of shipping routes at the outbreak of the war dealt the citrus industry a severe blow. Yet this very development, which also reduced the competition of imports, generated a prosperous market, invigorated by the British army's demand for the output of domestic mixed farming: the net product figures, the only series available for the War and the postwar years (Table 8), indicate that mixed farm product grew by two times during the six-year period of the war, at an average annual rate of 12 percent. This represents a significant acceleration compared to the 1922–39 period, when growth, though robust, was only 9 percent (Table 8).

This performance is quite interesting in view of the employment data, which indicates a reduction of employment in Jewish farming by significant factor of 20 percent between 1939 and 1945 (Table 7). This reflects mostly and perhaps exclusively the drastic reduction in employment in the highly labor-intensive citrus industry. Most, if not all, of the reduced labor input was thus due to the reduction in the number of hired Arab laborers in the Jewish economy. Jewish farm employment was hardly affected. These figures suggest that the growth of net farm production in the Jewish economy by two times during the war years was created by the same level of, or at most by a small increase in, labor input. This of course means that average labor productivity in farming soared upward during these years, carrying per capita income in that branch with it. The real wage and per capita income for the whole economy, which grew by almost 40 percent in the 1939–45 period, offers supporting evidence for the growth of mixed farming productivity (Tables 5 and 6).

Mixed Farming, Citriculture, Capital Investment, and Irrigation. The performance of Jewish agriculture during the period of the Mandate through 1947, which in the longer run assured the viability of the farming entities set up by the resettlement process, would not have succeeded without heavy capital investment. This allowed major expansion of irrigation, acquisition of state-of-the-art farm machinery, and heavy expenditure on research leading to the development of crop varieties adapted to the climate and specific soil conditions.

The rising capital-labor ratios – capital grew at an annual rate of 11.6 percent while labor at 8.8 percent (Table 4) – were reflected materially in the workshop and in the field (these figures apply to the Jewish economy as a whole, and therefore to manufacturing as well). They clearly reflect developments in the Jewish agricultural sector, one of the most important of which was the mechanization of cultivation. Between 1920 and 1940 Palestine's tractor fleet grew from zero to 500; 450 of these were owned and operated on Jewish farms (because of the war these could not be added to through 1946). Similarly, animal husbandry underwent a major transformation owing to the adoption of modern breeding techniques; average milk production per cow increased by 40 percent in the short period from 1937 to 1941, and grew further through 1947.

Dairy production requires year-round fodder growing. Thus, like poultry, vegetable, and fruit production, the main elements of Jewish mixed farming were from their very beginning highly dependent on irrigation. For citrus cultivation as well, which was not a component of mixed farming but was conducted on monocultural plantations, irrigation was the necessary condition for its existence. The development of water-extraction and water-saving technology was accordingly a life-and-death issue for the Zionist resettlement endeavor. The extension of the irrigation of land was therefore given top priority, and became a symbol of the whole project.

The rapid expansion of the citrus industry in the 1920s and its acceleration in the first half of the 1930s was fully consistent with the rationale of the resettlement policy. High prices in the dominant British market and in other European markets in the 1920s and early 1930s promised high profitability from investment in citrus groves. Citriculture thus attracted a major portion of Jewish capital imports and of funds at the disposal of Jewish entrepreneurs to investment in that branch, which imposed the necessity of digging wells to tap into groundwater. The expansion of the area of citrus groves by about seven times in the decade through 1931, and by more than two times in the short 1931–35 period – thus by 16 times altogether between 1922 and 1935 – meant, of course, a corresponding extension of the irrigated area of the Jewish farming sector.

Though 1935 was the peak year of Jewish immigration and prosperity, the collapse of orange prices in export markets that year effectively stopped for good the further expansion of citrus groves. Prices were already lower by 10 percent in 1931, and by 16 percent in 1932–34, compared to the peak price years of 1926–29. Though further planting was halted by 1936, the cumulative expansion of the area of groves, which peaked in 1939 (Table 3), meant that by the outbreak of the war, about 77 percent of the irrigated area held by the Jewish sector was in citrus groves. These were almost exclusively located along the central coastal plain where access to groundwater was easy and the soil composition was optimal for this crop.

The expansion of mixed farming was linked with the resettlement plan from the very beginning. From the 1920s onward, it was the declared strategy of the Jewish Agency's Settlement Department, the successor to the Zionist Organization's Palestine office, which had been directing settlement operations since 1908. Mixed farming was designed first of all to offer a European standard of living to the settlers. Its viability, with its output of dairy products, poultry, vegetables, deciduous fruit and grapes, was dependent on the rapid expansion of domestic urban markets. Owing to shorter growing periods these products were definitely less capital intensive than the citrus industry, yet nevertheless required substantial capital investment per unit of labor. To assure year-round production and a steady flow to markets, irrigation facilities were required.

The settlement drive of the 1930s and the 1940s thus entailed a major extension of irrigation facilities. Though some settlers who decided to move into farming, mainly immigrants from Germany who began arriving in the mid-1930s, could provide a significant portion of the cost of setting up their settlements, the funds for capital investment for most of the mixed farming settlements were provided by Zionist institutions from contributions collected all over the globe, and by the banking system. The bank credits were guaranteed by the Settlement Department.

The mixed farming resettlement strategy took its first steps in the 1920s. Toward the end of that decade, in 1929, the irrigated area used for mixed farming was 12,000 metric dunams, about 25 percent of the irrigated area at the disposal of Jewish farming entities. This was expanded by 25 percent through 1935–36, but the area of citrus groves grew by 240 percent in the same period, which reduced the share of irrigated land devoted to mixed farming to only ten percent of the total. At this point, the citrus plantations in the Jewish sector – though not in its Arab counterpart – stopped producing commercially for almost two decades. Yet the expansion of mixed farming, and correspondingly the irrigated area devoted to it, expanded rapidly. By 1939 the area of irrigated land used for mixed farming was almost three times greater than in 1935, and thus close to a quarter of the total at the disposal of Jewish agriculture. By 1947, in the wake of the major resettlement effort, supported by the conversion of 10–15 percent of the citrus area to vegetable and fodder growing, irrigated land used for mixed farming was greater by 150 percent than in 1939. Almost 50 percent of the total irrigated area was by that time devoted to mixed farming. The rest was in citrus groves, the intense cultivation of which was revived late in 1945 in response to the postwar revival of European markets.

In the long run, the viability of the settlements' pursuit of mixed farming depended on the availability and expansion of markets for their produce. Output grew by about six times in the 1920s and 1930s, at an average annual rate of about 11 percent from 1922 to 1939. This, however, was a significantly lower growth rate than that of the output of the Jewish citrus industry, which depended exclusively on export markets; citrus production grew by 21 times during the same period. It was, of course, the rapid growth of the Jewish urban population and its rapidly rising per capita income that provided the expanding domestic markets for food products. The importance of these markets is underlined by the data for the war and postwar periods. The rate of growth of the Jewish population declined, though the population and its per capita income kept growing significantly. But the war provided a new group of customers – British and other Allied military personnel; effectively all the markets under the canopy of the Allied Middle East Supply Center. The war also eliminated competition from foreign food imports to Palestine's domestic markets. These prospering markets absorbed the output of the mixed farming sector, which during the six years of war grew by two times at an average annual rate of more than 12 percent. It was this development that assured the viability of the rural settlements and allowed the settlers a reasonable standard of living. The settlements constituted an economically viable Jewish presence everywhere in Palestine north of Beersheba, the whole settled part of mandatory Palestine.

The Economic and Political Rationale of the Irrigation Drive. The expansion of domestic food markets was the crucial element in the success of the mixed farming strategy. The conception of that strategy, however, as the pioneers of the Second Aliyah (1903–14) arrived in Palestine, was linked to the idea of *avodah ivrit*. The pursuit of that agenda from the very start by the Zionist Organization's Palestine Office (founded April 1908) and its successor from the 1920s on, the Settlement Department of the Zionist Authority (from 1929 the Jewish Agency), was based on this consideration, along with the need to assure the long-term economic viability of the rural settlements. This entailed the establishment of farming communities able to provide year-round full employment and income sufficient for a near-European standard of living. Multi-branch mixed farming, which required irrigated land, met these needs.

By the 1930s price considerations led to an even greater emphasis on investment in irrigation. Palestine's population was about 700,000 in 1920, about 1 million in 1931 and 1.5 million by 1939, and the population growth led inevitably to rising land prices. In Palestine this fact had a special twist, because the dominant feature of the land business was the acquisition of land by Jews from Arab sellers. The continuing purchase of land that increased Jewish land holdings from a minuscule fraction to six percent of Palestine's total land area – 12 percent of the northern, non-arid, part of the country – raised average land prices threefold between the early 1920s and the middle 1930s. The rapidly rising seller's market in the 1920s and early 1930s suggested that the substitution of water for land area, that is, a widespread extension of irrigation, was a highly rational business proposition for the buyers. This was noted succinctly by Arthur Ruppin, the grand resettlement operator, in a review of his 25 years with the Zionist Organization in Palestine: "The more water the settler has, the less land he needs."

Political considerations as well offered support for this development in the resettlement strategy. The acquisition of land by Jews was used as a major propaganda device by the Arab leadership to generate pressure on the British government to withdraw from its commitment, embodied in the League of Nations Mandate, which incorporated the language of the Balfour Declaration, to support "the establishment in Palestine of a national home for the Jewish people." The Arabs finally prevailed on this score: the 1939 White Paper restricted the rights of the Jews to acquire land in most of Palestine's territory. A rapid extension of irrigation was an obvious response suggested by the economic and political conditions. Though expansion of the area under citrus cultivation stopped in 1936, Jewish settlement efforts in the last decade of the Mandate still focused on the extension of irrigation to accommodate the expansion of mixed farming. Between 1935 and 1947, irrigated land cultivated by the mixed farming sector grew sevenfold, and in the twilight of the Mandate period was almost similar in size to that under citrus, and, as noted above, a significant amount of citrus-growing land was converted during the war years to vegetable and fodder production (Table 3).

Schemes to allow major extensions of irrigation, thus increasing the absorption capacity of Palestine for Jewish immigration, were at the top of the Zionist agenda in the late 1930s and 1940s. The technical issues involved extracting groundwater through wells and pumping and distributing it from small rivers and springs located mostly in the north of the country. The significant increase in the irrigated area of Palestine in the Mandatory period to about 400,000 dunams by 1945 was achieved mostly on an ad hoc basis by local private enterprise and the Jewish Agency's Settlement Department. By the mid-1930s, though, the Settlement Department initiated an irrigation project in the Jezreel Valley involving, for the first time, several settlements. In 1936 it founded the Mekorot Water Company to build that project and run the system. That firm and its control of Israel's water system became a fact of public life after 1948.

Yet intensive study of the water problem by local "watermen" and invited foreign experts from the United States, involving a comprehensive vision of the system as a whole, began only during the war period. One of these experts – W.C. *Lowdermilk, an American soil conservationist – presented in 1945 a conceptual outline for a comprehensive national water grid drawing water from the Jordan in the north of the country and linking it with underground reservoirs in the center, to irrigate the arid and empty Negev in the south, comprising about 50 percent of the area of Palestine. This grand design, which presumed the creation of an integrated national water supply system, fired the imagination of the Zionist leadership, but was anathema to the Arab leadership, and inevitably beyond the horizon of practical politics of the British administration. It had to wait for the emergence of Israel as an independent state for its implementation.

The Unique Socioeconomic Structure of the Jewish Farm Sector. The convincing performance of the farm sector, measured in terms of production, productivity, and income, is suggested by the much more rapid rise of output and product than of employment: product per farm employee increased by two times in the decade ending in 1931, and by 1945 was four times higher than in 1922. The growth of product by two times between 1939 and 1945 was especially impressive, since it occurred at a time when the citrus industry had disappeared effectively from the product side of the equation during the war. Furthermore, it was achieved with a 19 percent lower labor input (Tables 7 and 8). It reflected the success of the mixed farming component of Jewish agriculture, which responded to the pull of the markets.

The kibbutz and the moshav, the collective and cooperative settlements that emerged in 1921, dominated this sector. The founders of the two movements were imbued with Socialist Zionist notions already in the air among second Aliyah immigrants in the pre-World War I period. They were reinforced by the new immigrants of the Third Aliyah (1919–23), who carried the message of the postwar western European social democratic movement. These immigrants joined with the veterans of the Second Aliyah in building the Tiberias-Ẓemaḥ road, the first public works project of the nascent Mandatory government in 1920. In the labor camps set up along the route, they organized groups of pioneers who approached the Zionist authorities with a proposal to found farm settlements that would implement Zionist ideas of national land and self-labor. The latter condition meant, of course, the implementation of the Zionist *avodah ivrit* principle, since it excluded by definition the employment of hired (Arab) labor. The self-government feature of these settlements, which they proposed as well, meant that they would be managing the economic activities of the settlements on their own account.

These principles were fully consistent with the notions adopted by the Zionist movement before the war: the ownership of land by the Jewish National Fund, the movement's land purchase and ownership corporation (established in 1901), and the principle of *avodah ivrit*. The socialist principles of the proposed settlements – the self-labor rule and the collective or cooperative principles of running the settlements adopted by the kibbutz and moshav movements – were inconsistent neither with the Zionist message nor with its strategy of resettlement. Indeed, they were fully in line with the latter.

The two movements did differ on a crucial feature of the organization of the settlements, the management of production, and thus correspondingly on the principle of income distribution. The moshav adopted the family model, which meant that the basic social cell, the family, would control its own production and benefit from the income. It would, however, strictly adhere to cooperative marketing of output and cooperative purchase of consumer goods and supplies and equipment required for production, a policy entailing cooperative ownership of major farm machinery. Mutual help in the case of calamities was enshrined in the operating rule of these producer and consumer cooperatives. The initial endowment of land and of capital funds to each family was of course to be equal.

The kibbutz model, in contrast, was a collective. As a collective entity the kibbutz was conceived as operating as a unitary multi-branch firm, with full collective command of the labor and equipment at its disposal, and most income distributed in kind on the basic principle of equality. This initially involved the severance of the direct link between a member's contribution to production and his real income. Among the leadership of the Zionist movement, business-minded opponents of this kind of organization argued that this feature of the kibbutz would have a negative effect on effort, and thus on the efficiency of production, which would soon destroy that utopian project. In spite of the heated debate on the subject, particularly in the 1920s, the political leadership of the Zionist movement stuck to the policy it adopted in the early 1920s to rely on the kibbutz movement, inspired indeed by socialist principles, as the battering ram of the resettlement effort. They claimed that only time would prove whether the opponents or the supporters of that social experiment were right. In 1946 Martin Buber, a professor of sociology at the Hebrew University and a veteran Zionist leader from Germany, described the maturing movement at that time as an "experiment which has not failed."

In more than one sense, the socioeconomic experiment involving the two movements, which survived a very difficult initial period in the 1920s, proved to be a roaring success toward the end of the Mandate period. By that time, roughly from the mid-1930s on, the two movements were an integral component of the Zionist consensus. This shows in their expansion in geographical and demographic terms and in the growth of their production, productivity, and real income, especially during World War II. Only 12 kibbutzim and two moshavim, effectively all post-World War I founded, were on the map in 1922, with a total population not much beyond 1,000. By 1931, there were 30 kibbutzim and 10 moshavim, with a population of close to 3,000 and 2,000 respectively. Ten years later, in 1942, there were 90 moshavim and 86 kibbutzim with almost equal populations totaling 51,000, or about ten percent of the Jewish population. By 1945 kibbutzim and moshavim, distributed throughout the country, numbered 101 and 96 respectively, with a total population in both of about 65–70,000, or some 12 percent of the Jewish population (see Table 3a).

The temporary eclipse of the citrus industry during the war, which led to the abandonment of about 20 percent of the plantation area and its conversion to mixed farming, dramatically affected employment in that sub-branch. This correspondingly reduced the contribution to employment and to farm product of the private farm settlements, which included almost all the pre-World War I moshavot and most of the moshavot founded in the 1920s and early 1930s, which specialized in citrus growing. farm employment figures for 1945 indicate accordingly that during the war years farm employment declined in absolute terms: about 13 percent of the employed persons in the Jewish economy as a whole were engaged in farming activity (Table 7). Only about one-third of these had been employed in the farming activity of the moshavot, with the traditional private enterprise-employee relationship, i.e., wage labor. Two thirds of farm employment – about 8.5 percent of total employment in the Jewish economy, in that period – was engaged in the socialist-inspired and -run settlements (Table 3a). This means that the increase in farm output and product – by two times, or an average annual rate of 12 percent in the six years of the war through 1945 – was to a significant extent due to the performance of these entities. The major increase in relative labor productivity in farming, by more than 80 percent (Table 8) in the decade from 1935 to 1945, can be ascribed to a considerable extent to these settlements, run on the basis of collective and cooperative principles.

This outstanding performance during the war years was shared by the private mixed farming enterprises active in the moshavot, most of which were located in the central coastal area. Their activities during the war met the market's rapidly rising demand for vegetables, dairy products, poultry, deciduous fruit, and grapes, and were evident in the conversion of 20 percent of the land under citrus cultivation to mixed farming. The relative decline of farm employment in the private-enterprise settlements reflects, on the one hand, the temporary eclipse of the labor-intensive citrus industry in which they specialized between the World Wars, and on the other, more importantly, the process of urbanization (including the establishment of manufacturing enterprises) that had been occurring in the older settlements since the early 1930s. This process gathered momentum in the second half of that decade and remained strong through 1947. At least five of the pre-World War I agricultural settlements had populations of 1,000 by the outbreak of World War II. Several more were approaching 5,000 and more by that time. This meant that though farming activity was not completely eliminated in these moshavot, manufacturing and services became more and more the focus of their economic activity. Thus Netanyah, located on the central coastal plain, became from 1940 on the center of the transported diamond industry (see below, The Rise of the Manufacturing Industry, 1936–1947). The urbanization process of these settlements was after a longish period formally recognized by the Mandatory government, which granted them municipal status. The gap between the ratio of population in these "individualist" private-enterprise settlements, which was 50 percent of Jewish farm population in 1942, and that of their employment of Jewish farm labor, which was only 30 percent, is explicable in these terms.

The Histadrut and the Economics of the Yishuv

The two socialist-inspired settlement movements – the kibbutz and the moshav (see above, The Unique Socioeconomic Structure of the Jewish Farm Sector) – were components of the economy operating under the canopy of the *Histadrut, the General Federation of Hebrew Workers of Ereẓ-Israel, established in 1920. In contrast to the traditional European labor federation model, the Histadrut was not conceived as an assemblage, or congress, of trade unions, in which individual workers belong not to the federation but to the member unions, with the federation as an umbrella organization. Histadrut membership was personal; its members belonged to it directly, and in the case of married couples each adult of the family was a member, even if one of them was not part of the labor force. Unions operating in specific industries such as construction, office work, etc., were indeed established, but these were run as subsidiaries of the parent organization.

The adjective "general" in its name was designed to highlight its all-embracing structure, indicating its function as a direct representative of the interests of all workers in town and country, in private enterprises, in the public sector, and in self-employment (the last taken to include membership in the kibbutzim and moshavim). But "general" also represented much more than that; the Histadrut was conceived to embrace not only the traditional functions of unions as representatives of workers in the struggle over wages and work conditions, but those of a quasi-state institution providing social welfare services such as medical and unemployment insurance.

Furthermore, it was also, as a quasi-state institution, to serve as the promoter and owner of an enterprise sector: the establishment of the Workers' Bank in 1921 and a building and public works contracting firm were among the first, but not the only, such enterprises founded by the Histadrut at that time, as the Third Aliyah was reaching Palestine. The Zionist authorities provided some of the equity finance required to set up these two firms. the contracting firm was known as *Solel Boneh ("Road Construction and Building"); its mission was to take on contracts in these areas, offering employment and training in building skills to new immigrants particularly. The building boom of the Fourth Aliyah, starting in 1924, was a major lift to Solel Boneh, which by that time had acquired standing both in the construction and road building industries and with suppliers and banks.

Yet at the height of the crisis of 1926, in the wake of the Fourth Aliyah downturn that began in 1926, Solel Boneh had to declare bankruptcy. This required financial support from the Zionist authorities' meager and declining cash flow. These funds were destined to offer not only (very low) unemployment benefits, but also cash payments to settle a fraction of Solel Boneh's debts. The conservative credit policy of Bank Hapoalim, withstanding the pressure from the Histadrut leadership to increase credit facilities to the collapsing company, allowed it to outlive the major economic crisis of 1926–28. This saved the honor of the labor movement, which by that time was subject to bitter criticism from the supporters of private enterprise among the Zionist leaders. The collapse of Solel Boneh, which led to the tapping of the meager financial resources of the movement, provided a new stimulant to their approach.

At that juncture it led to a redirection of the Histadrut business sector toward cooperative enterprises, in the services in particular. The cooperative bus firms that emerged in the late 1920s and the late 1940s by 1947 dominated the public transportation market after their amalgamation into three major firms. These firms represented one of the dimensions of business activity emerging at that time under the aegis of the Histadrut.

As the rising tide of immigration of the Fifth Aliyah entered Palestine, the building boom of the early 1930s led to the revival of Solel Boneh as a contracting firm in the building trade. Its management had absorbed the lessons of the late-1920s collapse and the firm thus survived robustly the downturn of the late 1930s, acquiring experience and capacity that was put at once into well-paid service as the demands of the war economy grew from 1940 on. The liquidity of the banking system and the very low interest rates prevailing in the Sterling bloc (see below, The Monetary and Financial System) offered liberal credit to Solel Boneh's rapidly increasing project portfolio. From 1941 on these included major building projects ordered by the British military all over the Middle East, including Iran. It was in these years that Solel Boneh emerged as the leading contracting firm in Palestine and vicinity. It soon moved into manufacturing, acquiring from private entrepreneurs in the early 1940s profitable firms such as Nesher, the cement monopoly; Palestine's only glass producer, Finizia; and the Vulcan iron casting firm, all of them located in the Haifa Bay area, the center of Palestine's heavy industry. The broad scope of Solel Boneh's manufacturing interests soon led to the establishment of a manufacturing subsidiary corporation, Koor. For four decades after Independence, the Koor conglomerate dominated manufacturing in Israel, as did Solel Boneh the building industry until its second collapse in the mid-1980s.

Through the mid-1930s the focus of the Histadrut as a union was the *avodah ivrit* agenda, the struggle for the exclusive right of Jewish workers for employment in the Jewish sector of Palestine's economy. Indeed, the ventures of Histadrut into the urban business sector, through both the direct ownership of Solel Boneh, and the promotion of cooperative ventures, some in manufacturing, had the same goal as its rural enterprises, the kibbutzim and moshavim: to provide exclusive employment openings in the Jewish economy to Jewish workers. This does not mean that the Histadrut was not engaged in the traditional business of a workers union, the struggle for employment and better work conditions and wages. Its employment mission was carried out by establishing a system of labor exchanges under its canopy. The unemployment problem and the wage issue finally rose to the top of the agenda in the second half of the 1930s, as the Arab strike and uprising severely eroded the direct links between the two national sectors, eliminating almost completely *avodah ivrit* as a relevant issue. From then on the Histadrut, which had started out with 4,500 members in 1921, had 28,000 in 1930, and by 1939 some 100,000, put an increasing focus on typical trade union issues. During the high inflation, full-employment war years, the maintenance of real wages surfaced inevitably as a major issue. The pressure of the Histadrut led initially, in 1940, to a countrywide agreement with the Jewish Manufacturing Association on a uniform cost-of-living allowance, and eventually to the setting up of a Mandatory government committee on wages, on which the Histadrut was represented. Its recommendation to adopt a technique of automatic periodic cost-of-living adjustments (COLAS) was implemented in 1942.

Government sponsorship of the COLA agreement between the Histadrut and the Manufacturing Association was the first step on the long winding road of price linkages that led ultimately to comprehensive indexation and prevailed for the ensuing five decades in Mandate Palestine and in Israel. It gave the Histadrut major leverage on the operations of the economy in the long run. In more than one sense it represented the political power with which it was endowed by its membership: in 1947, 27 years after its establishment, its membership comprised around 66 percent of the labor force. Its operations as a trade union, as the umbrella of the kibbutzim and moshavim, and its control of major holding companies in the building trade and in manufacturing, with the main sick fund and other welfare state services subject to its control and guidance, made it to a significant extent the executive organ of the Zionist movement in its endeavor to establish a Jewish polity in Palestine.

The Monetary and Financial System

The introduction by the British army in 1918 of the Egyptian pound as the legal tender of Palestine, replacing the confusing mix of monetary units used in the last years of the Ottoman rule, was undoubtedly the first and most significant reform implemented by the Mandatory power. The Egyptian pound, issued by a Currency Board controlled by the British government, was of course a full-blooded fiat of the British pound sterling. Its circulation in Palestine, and that of its replacement (in 1927), the Palestine pound, issued by the newly established Palestine Currency Board, meant effectively that it was sterling that provided the lifeblood of the monetary and financial system of the country for the three decades of British rule through 1948.

The modus operandi of the Currency Board was simple. It set the official rate of exchange of the Palestine pound with sterling at 1:1, and was ready to sell Palestine pounds for the presented value of the sterling, or to purchase Palestine pounds, at that effective rate. There was accordingly a free market in sterling for the Palestine currency, which meant that Palestine was on a sterling base throughout the three decades through February 1948. Sterling, and therefore the Palestine pound, was on the gold standard between 1925 and 1931, hence on a fixed exchange rate with the dollar and other major currencies, and on a flexible exchange rate regime with these currencies as sterling went off gold in 1931.

The rules also meant that the government of Palestine could not borrow from the Currency Board, which prevented it from inflating the currency. (It could borrow in the British capital market, but this option was only marginally used – the Mandatory government had on the whole a balanced budget.) The inflationary option was of course open to the British government, since it could use sterling to buy Palestine pounds for its use, and its budget, authorized by the U.K. Parliament, could involve deficit financing. That option was never used, however, during the two decades before the outbreak of the war in 1939. This meant that the money supply – the number of Palestine pounds in circulation – was, during that time, demand-determined. It was set by the cumulative requirements of private households and commercial firms and other enterprises – in other words ultimately by the "needs of trade." There was no inflation of the currency in the two decades between the wars, and the Palestine pound was regarded justifiably as a stable and highly reliable currency.

The banking system provided another component, which in developed and rapidly developing countries is an important part of the (M1), defined as the sum of currency at the disposal of the (non-banking) public and current account deposits in the banking system. In the mid-1920s even the Jewish banking sector deposit data indicate that banks were not yet a significant factor in the financial system. The Arab banking sector was in its infancy throughout the Mandatory period. The share of deposits in Arab banks in the total for Palestine in 1938 was only two percent; it grew to seven percent by the end of the war in 1946. For those same dates the share of deposits in Jewish banks was 76 and 79 percent of the total, respectively. Foreign banks, dominated by the Palestine branches of two major banking institutions, the Ottoman Bank and Barclays, held 22 percent of total deposits in 1938. This ratio declined to only 14 percent in 1946.

The dominance of Jewish banking in terms of outstanding credit was even more significant. By 1936, the Anglo-Palestine Bank had a greater credit portfolio than all the branches of foreign banks. In 1946 the credit allocated by it was three times greater than the total of all other foreign banks. The contribution of Arab banks to outstanding bank credit was five percent at most; this means that the commercial bank credit market was ruled by the Jewish banking sector. In the 1940s it accommodated 85 percent of outstanding credit (Table 10).

The story of the financial sector of Palestine is therefore the story of the Jewish banking sector. This story begins with the Anglo-Palestine Bank, set up in 1903 by the World Zionist Organization, which owned its voting shares. By 1920, at the advent of the Mandatory period, it was one of the five banking institutions operating in the country. A decade later, in 1931, the banking system already had 75 institutions, more than half of them cooperative credit associations, set up exclusively in the Jewish sector and of minuscule size even in aggregate terms. Only two of the 75 were Arab banks. Somewhat fewer than 10 of these institutions were branches of foreign banks proper, and these were dominated by major banking institutions – Barclays and the Ottoman banks. The rapid rise in the number of banking institutions in the 1920s, and the surge in the number of banks and cooperative credit associations to 134 by 1936 took place almost entirely in the Jewish sector of the economy.

The rapid expansion of the financial sector with its increase in the number of banking institutions was the result of developments in the larger economy. The very high growth rate that accompanied the absorption of the Fifth Aliyah into the Palestine economy – 170 percent in terms of the Jewish national product during the four-year period 1931–35 – of course affected the financial sector. The corresponding increase of debt held by the Anglo-Palestine Bank grew by almost 160 percent, and the more than fourfold increase in its deposits reflected the very rapid growth of the real economy (Tables 5 and 10). These figures represent only the rapidly rising volume of business in one of the approximately 130 banking institutions operating in Palestine at this date. However, with the financial flagship of the Zionist movement holding more than one-third of the deposits and an even greater proportion of the outstanding debt held by banking institutions in the country in 1936, this statistic undoubtedly offers a reasonable approximation of developments in the financial sector as a whole.

The proliferation of banking institutions in this period was not due only to the outstanding growth rate of the real economy. It reflected also the huge capital imports belonging to the immigrants, particularly from Germany and central Europe: the tide of private capital imports peaked in 1935 at a level four times higher than in 1931, and more than two times higher than the previous peak of 1925, which was linked to the arrival of the Fourth Aliyah, mainly from Poland. Indeed, the 1935 capital inflow was the all-time high of the private and total Jewish capital inflow during the three decades of the Mandatory period (Table 11). And this inflow accompanied a significant group of immigrants whose expertise was in the field of banking. The natural inclination of these immigrants was to use their own capital to open a bank in the new country. In view of the effective absence of banking legislation – until 1936 there were hardly any legal requirements, such as a government license or minimum equity requirements – they could simply proceed to do so if they chose. Only a small number of the more than 50 new banks that opened between 1931 and 1936 belonged to these immigrants with expertise and capital of their own; several were quite successful and became household names in the Jewish community. But many soon went out of business, as the 1940 entry in Table 10 indicates.

The 1936 and 1937 banking legislation, which required of banking institutions a government license, minimum capital stock, regular publication of financial statements, personal probity on the part of directors, and which established a government bank supervision department, soon led to the elimination of the more flimsy institutions. But the main reason for the disappearance of a significant number of banks by 1940 – about one-quarter of their number in 1936 – were economic and related to political developments on a world scale rather than specific developments in Palestine's economy.

The immediate causes of the closing of most of these institutions were three runs on the banks – late in 1935 and in the summers of 1938 and 1939. The first run was in response to the Ethiopian crisis, the second reflected the uncertainty related to the Munich crisis that led to the disintegration of Czechoslovakia and Hitler's dominance of Europe, and the third was caused by the Polish crisis immediately preceding the outbreak of the war on September 1, 1939. On the whole, however, the Jewish banking sector survived these three crises very well, even though Palestine had no central bank to act as a lender of last resort. After the second run in 1938, the Palestine government adamantly refused to offer any help, even though a third run was anticipated, and indeed soon occurred as the Danzig crisis gathered momentum. What the Jewish banking community asked the government to do was just to offer a guarantee to the three major foreign banks operating in Palestine – the Jewish Anglo-Palestine Bank, Barclays bank, which was the agent of the Palestine Currency Board and had been earning a hefty income in that capacity, and the Ottoman Bank. This guarantee was to be implemented if and when these banks were called on to rediscount financial assets submitted by other local banks in the case of a run in response to another war scare.

The Jewish banking system survived that run, as it did the two previous, due, among other things, to the special discount facility offered by the Anglo-Palestine Bank, even though it had no government guarantee. The willingness and ability of the APB to act as lender of last resort was, of course, due to its status as the oldest and most important financial institution of the Jewish economy and its function as the umbrella for the Jewish business and financial sector for more than three decades. Its total assets at the end of the 1920s were four times greater than the total value of the assets of the next five largest Jewish banks, and its deposits in 1936 were somewhat larger than the total deposits of all domestic (Jewish and Arab) banks; by 1940 that ratio was even higher.

Its managing director, the grand old man of the Jewish financial community, E.Z. Hofien, could venture into such stormy seas due to a highly conservative credit policy modeled on the traditional pattern of the British banking system. Even though the World Zionist Organization owned the controlling shares of the bank, its management had the freedom to pursue traditional banking policy, which requires the maintenance of high liquidity ratios and protection of the institution's solvency. This allowed APB to plunge into the cold water of the second half of the 1930s to sustain the liquidity of deserving Jewish banks, a move which could be regarded as noblesse oblige. The attitude of the APB management was also affected by the fact that the strain in the financial markets on the eve of the war also reflected the general downturn of economic activity since 1936, involving rising unemployment.

The banking legislation initiated in 1936 shrank significantly the number of banking institutions. Those eliminated, however, were almost exclusively small and ephemeral; those that remained constituted a robust and profitable system. The prosperous economy of the war years bringing a flood of liquidity, high profits for businesses, and rapidly rising real incomes sustained the profitability of the banking system. This applied of course to APB whose share of the business grew to almost 50 percent of the total deposits in the entire banking system of Palestine and to about one-third of the commercial credit (Table 10). This gap between the bank's share of deposits and its share of credit indicates a huge increase in its portfolio of financial investments. The currency controls imposed at the outbreak of the war meant that the excess liquidity was channeled exclusively into British government gilt-edged bonds, turning APB effectively into a trustee of what was soon identified as the Jewish economy's ownership of Palestine's sterling balances. The low two percent interest rate of the war years, a highly inflationary context, meant that the profitability of this investment portfolio was quite low. It provided, however, a large pool of potential liquidity for the bank, which sustained the viability of the state of Israel at a crucial time as it emerged from the 1948 War of Independence.

The Balance of Payments and Jewish Capital Imports

STRUCTURAL FEATURES OF PALESTINE'S BALANCE OF PAYMENTS IN THE INTERWAR DECADES AND THE WAR PERIOD. The outstanding performance of the Jewish sector of the economy during the Mandatory period – its net national product grew by 10 times between 1922 and 1939, and by almost 25 times in the 25 years between 1922 and the end of the Mandatory period (Table 5) – would have been inconceivable without a rapid expansion of the investment flow. The expansion of capital stock by 11 times through 1939 and 15 times for the 25 years ending in 1947 (Table 4) indicate that though the rates of investment over time were subject to significant cyclical variation, this was indeed the case (Table 4). But these huge rates of investment, which through 1936 involved ratios of 35 percent or higher of the net national product of the Jewish economy (and even at the bottom of the cycle in 1939 were still 17 percent of NNP), were not, indeed could not have been, financed by domestic savings. They were inevitably financed predominantly by capital imports associated with the waves of immigration.

Balance-of-payment data offer insight into this phenomenon and on the composition of Palestine's foreign trade and capital flows during the Mandate. These data, however, reflect the economy as a whole and thus also the Arab and government of Palestine sectors, which also grew and maintained flows of investment that expanded capital stocks. These are shown in Table 4, and indicate that net capital stock of the Arab economy grew by 2.5 times through the 25 years ending in 1947, at an average annual rate of 3.8 percent. Investment in infrastructure by the government expanded at a more rapid pace – 7.4 times during the same period, less than half the rate of Jewish capital stock. Yet by and large the government investments were financed by taxation: Palestine government capital imports were very small indeed and constituted only a small fraction of the financing of the country's infrastructure (Table 12).

The Arab economy undoubtedly financed its investment from domestic savings and, to a significant extent, from the substantial sums received from the sale of land to Jewish private entrepreneurs and to the Jewish National Fund.

Unilateral transfers, displayed in the balance-of-payments data (Table 12), reflect accordingly almost entirely Jewish sector inflows. The capital account credit figures also refer almost entirely to the Jewish sector. The flows of the government of Palestine and Palestine Currency Board appear on the debit side of the capital account. These are quite similar in volume to the credit figures in column 6 in the unilateral transfers section, which refers to inflows from non-Jewish sources. These figures indicate that the government of Palestine's contributions to the inflow of resources during the Mandatory period was negligible.

The balance-of-payment figures underline the major difference between the periods (prewar through 1939; war and aftermath, 1940–47) in Palestine's external economic relations. Palestine's current account dominated by trade flows was in substantial deficit in terms of the economic aggregate figures in the interwar years. The import flow was huge, about 45 percent of Palestine's GDP (Gross Domestic Product), while its exports were only about 13 percent. This means that the P£111 million deficit on the current account for that entire period amounted to about 32 percent, almost a third, of Palestine's GDP, a world record. The inflow of Jewish immigrants' funds on capital account, plus the flow of contributions of the Zionist and other Jewish organizations all over the world, effectively provided the funds required to pay for the huge net imports in the interwar period. Similarly, private Jewish firms and immigrants effectively provided the total inflow of funds on capital account, P£26 million in the interwar period. A major portion of this was the capital transferred under the *Haavara Agreement, which between 1933 and 1938 allowed the transfer of Jewish immigrants' private capital from Germany only in the form of goods, which were subsequently sold and therefore reconverted into capital.

These funds allowed the banking system, dominated by the Anglo-Palestine Bank, to invest its excess financial resources in London, to accumulate sterling reserves to sustain their liquidity and offer coverage for their rising current account deposits. A fraction of these funds also provided the required cover for the expansion of the monetary base – reflecting the rapid income-driven increase in the demand for currency. This feature can be inferred from the Currency Board debit balance for 1922–39 of £9 million in the capital account section of Table 12.

The structure of the balance of payments for the 1940–47 period, the years of the war and its immediate aftermath, was an altogether different story. The net current account of the country in the 1940–47 period, minus P£4 million, indicated that the huge deficit in Palestine's current account disappeared altogether, due mainly to the huge expansion of its export business. These "exports" were mainly goods and services provided to the British and allied armies in Palestine and the Middle East. The unilateral transfers account – about 87 percent of its total of P£86 million was from Jewish sources – contributed a major inflow of funds. Yet though the average yearly inflow of these funds, in nominal terms, was approximately two times greater than it had been in the interwar period, its real value, owing to major wartime inflation, was significantly smaller. The major difference was the reduction of such transfers (leading to the collapse of the nominal value, and thus even more the real value, of immigrants' funds (column 4)) reflecting of course the reduction of immigration and the abject poverty of most of those refugees who did arrive. Even so, this positive inflow financed almost entirely the major deficit on Palestine's capital account, which effectively meant an accumulation of sterling balances – a nominal debt of the U.K. government to banks, firms, and households holding currency balances. The P£10 million debit in place of the P£26 million positive private sector capital account figure from the interwar period (Table 12) actually represented investments in British funds – presumably gilt-edged bonds – by Palestine's banking system, businesses, and households. This was the only avenue open to them in view of the currency controls imposed at the outbreak of the war. It can be inferred that most of these funds originated in the Jewish sector, given the dominance of the real Jewish economy by that time in terms of GNP per capita (Table 5), and even more so its dominance of the small capital market of Palestine in those days.

The huge cumulative debit of the banking system in the balance-of-payments account in that period reflects of course the wartime inflationary developments and represents the acquisitions of sterling reserves by the banks to back their inflated current account debits. The same feature is exhibited by the huge debit flow of the Palestine Currency Board, representing its purchase of sterling-denominated gilt-edged bonds, the backing for the (inflated) increase of currency required by the public. These two outflows of nominal finance created the so-called "sterling balances" of Palestine – a nominal debt of the United Kingdom. When Palestine's sterling balances were finally released, as they were between 1949 and 1951 according to agreements between the United Kingdom and Israel, the ownership of these balances by predominantly Jewish economic entities – households, commercial business firms, and the banking system – was finally established.

JEWISH CAPITAL IMPORTS AND GROWTH. This survey of the structure of Palestine's balance of payments identifies the major contributions of unilateral transfers and capital imports to the workings of Palestine's economy during the three decades of the Mandate. These two major inflows of resources were indeed directed to the Jewish sector, providing it with the means for an all-out investment effort generating very rapid growth. Yet the benefit of this was inevitably transmitted to the Arab sector too, directly and indirectly, and to the cash flow of the Mandatory government, which gained from the rising income-induced expansion of tax revenue. The outstanding average annual growth rate of the domestic product of the economy of Palestine as a whole, which was about 9 percent (Table 5) for the 25-year period through 1947, is an obvious case in point.

The overall contribution of capital imports to the fabulous growth rate of the Jewish economy (an annual average of close to 14 percent during the Mandate period) is underlined by the investment and capital import figures presented in Table 11. The high investment-national product ratios are the evidence: the close to 40 percent ratios in the figures for the 1920s, and the roughly 35 percent in the 1930s – the latter reflects the leap by 3.5 times of national product in that decade – could not have been sustained from domestic savings for two consecutive decades. Investment ratios in the 1940s were lower (though not low in comparison with the ratio of Arab investment in Palestine or with conventional peacetime ratios in the major economies). These much lower ratios were due to wartime government controls imposed on investment, in housing in particular. The effect of the abolition of controls after the war shows clearly in the 23 percent investment ratio of 1947.

Investment ratios even on the order of those of the 1930s could not have been sustained by domestic savings rates. Investment rates beyond 20 percent of national product are not sustainable for such long periods even in rich economies. The capital import figures, dominated by the transfer of funds by the private sector, offers an explanation for the extraordinary investment ratios displayed in the figures for the interwar period. The capital import ratio series of Table 11 show that the inflows of these foreign resources were year-in and year-out in the 40–50 percent ratio. The very high ratios of the 1920s do not indicate higher inflows in absolute terms; the capital inflows of the 1930s were on the whole greater. The ratios of the 1920s are high because of the low absolute value of net national product in that decade.

In other words, the inflow of these funds provided full financial backing to the investment effort of the Jewish sector, and even a substantial surplus that could be used for other purposes. Yet since the net investment figures in Table 11 represent net fixed reproducible capital in 1936 prices, a major component of investment in the Jewish economy is not included: the cost of land purchased from Arab owners. These purchases were indeed an investment from the point of view of the Jewish sector, but not from that of Palestine's economy as a whole. Thus, a fraction of the difference between the approximately P£66 million inflow of Jewish capital imports in the 1930s and the approximately P£45 million in investments accounted for in the investment series of fixed reproducible capital stock, was the cost of the acquisition of land. For the whole 25-year period for which data are available the size of the gap between the total Jewish capital import and investments was greater – close to P£50 million, in 1936 prices, about 37 percent of the total capital inflow (Table 11).

The second component for which this P£50 million difference provided backing was monetary liquidity – primarily the acquisition of Palestine pounds currency balances. The total net debit figure of the Palestine Currency Board in the capital account section of Table 12 indicates that these were P£44 million (Table 12). Yet the Arab sector, too, held a fraction of these balances. The figures thus exaggerate the investment of the Jewish economy in the accumulation of a currency balance – which probably was not much more than half of the P£44 million total, and perhaps even less than that. The cumulative building up of inventories was of course another form of investment not recorded in the fixed reproducible capital stock data. It had been absorbing a fraction of the extra resources provided by the capital imports.

The debit entry of the banking system in the balance-of-payments record (Table 12), which reflects the acquisition of its secondary liquid reserves in London accumulated during these decades, was a foreign financial investment that provided the backing for the customer deposits in Palestine's banks. These funds were part of the monetary liquidity of the economy. In this case as well, and owing to the substantial size of British banks, the P£54 million cumulative debit items for banks in the capital account data in Table 12 do not represent a financial investment of the Jewish banking system only. A significant fraction of that figure represents an investment of the foreign banks, and a much smaller one of the Arab banks. Nevertheless, it explains a sizable fraction of the gap between the P£130 million Jewish capital imports and the fixed reproducible investment in the Jewish economy.

These data underline the strategic function of capital imports in the growth of the Jewish economy and that of Palestine as a whole during the Mandatory period. The huge inflow of Jewish capital imports provided the necessary backing for the investment flow that was crucial for generating the 14 percent average annual growth rates of the Jewish economy, and the corresponding nine percent rates for Palestine's economy as a whole. Furthermore, even the much lower investment rate of the Arab economy, which grew at an annual rate of 6.5 percent, would not have been realized but for the funds provided by the Jewish capital imports used to purchase Arab-owned land.

It was thus the total Jewish capital imports that had spurred the Palestine economy to the production potential it had arrived at on the eve of the war. And it was this material potential and the human capital element, dramatically increased by the immigrants, that made it feasible for Palestine to serve as the locus of the Middle east supply system set up by the British and allied forces during the war. It provided in more than one sense the infrastructure of the Middle East war effort.

Money, Prices, and War Finance

MONETARY AND PRICE DEVELOPMENTS IN THE INTERWAR DECADES. A survey of the data suggests that the history of money, prices, and rates of economic activity for the three decades of the Mandate can best be understood as falling into two subperiods: the two interwar decades, and the years of World War II and its immediate aftermath, 1940–47.

Even though the 1920s and 1930s were on average decades of very rapid growth, they were also years of declining prices in the first of the two decades, and of stable prices in the second (Table 13). This was the case even though in the second half of the 1920s, for which only currency-in-circulation data are available, the monetary expansion was quite robust: significantly beyond 12 percent, as the only available indicator, the currency expansion rate of about 20 percent between 1927 and 1929, suggests. The growth rate of the money supply (Table 13) in the 1930s at an average annual rate of about 17 percent, with prices hardly budging until the outbreak of the war, indicates that stable prices were the rule. This was the case even though in the full-employment economy of the early 1930s real growth accelerated immensely. It declined somewhat after 1935, yet the average annual NDP growth rate was still close to nine percent for the decade ending in 1939 (Table 5).

The high growth rates of the money supply – about 17 percent annually for the 1927–39 period (16 percent in the 1930s, based on more reliable data) – did not generate price inflation because they were demand-determined: the increased supply of money provided the liquidity required by the very rapidly growing economy (nine percent in the 1930s, somewhat higher than in the 1920s). The major monetarization process to which the Arab economy was subject during that period, as more and more of its production was transmitted to the market, also contributed significantly to the increase in demand for money, inevitably in the form of currency rather than current account deposits.

Thus, with an effective free-trade regime maintained by the Mandatory government, prices were on the whole determined by world markets. Prices were declining significantly in the sterling and sterling-linked economies in the 1920s; in Palestine they stabilized after the floating and depreciation of sterling in 1931, and in the wake of the worldwide economic crisis and deflation of the early 1930s. Even in the full-employment environment between 1928 and 1935, prices hardly budged. The supply of money was accordingly a dependent variable, expansion of which was determined by the growth of the economy and the monetarization process. Its expansion was a response to these rather than a proactive move by government intended to affect the level of prices.

BRITISH WAR FINANCE AND THE INFLATION OF PALESTINE'S MONETARY AGGREGATES. World War II, however, created an altogether different trade and monetary regime. From September 1939 on it severed lines of communication with Europe and North America and later with Southeast Asia. Shipping space restrictions reduced transport to and from the western and southern hemispheres too, before being interrupted almost completely when Japan entered the war in December 1941. This meant that imports to Palestine were soon reduced to a trickle. Exports – primarily, of course, citrus – also shrank to almost nothing with the closure of European markets.

These war-imposed developments eliminated at once the severe competition from imports to which domestic, almost entirely Jewish, manufacturers and mixed farm producers had been subject in the interwar years. It also meant that Palestine's prices were no longer determined by world markets. It was the rapidly expanding aggregate demand that, from the outbreak of World War II through the end of the Mandate, not only set quantities (as it had before the war), but also determined the level of prices in Palestine's economy, a variable it could hardly have affected earlier.

The factor on which the trend of aggregate demand during the war years depended was, of course, British (and later Allied) military demand. Purchases for military purposes shot up from about three percent of Palestine's gross domestic product in 1937–38 to 22 percent in 1940, a year at the end of which Palestine's economy was operating at close to full employment. The peak of military demand in terms of Palestine's economic capacity was reached in 1941 at 38 percent of GDP. The military still absorbed about 16 percent of GDP in 1945, although military operations were focused from 1943 on southern and western Europe and not the Middle East.

The huge demand generated initially by the need to supply an army of several hundred thousand soldiers located in the Middle East command, which stretched from Iraq to the western border of Egypt, had to be financed. The source of that finance was primarily the United Kingdom budget. The payment instrument was, of course, Palestine pounds, which the U.K. treasury purchased from the Palestine Currency Board by submitting sterling – strictly according to the Board's operating rule. Formally, this procedure involved a deficit in the U.K. budget and not that of the government of Palestine, which on the whole maintained a balanced budget. In any case, it could not "borrow" from the Palestine Currency Board – that is, the Board could not print money.

This constraint did not apply, however, to the U.K. government, which could borrow sterling from its central bank, the Bank of England, and convert it into Palestine pounds to pay for the goods and services its military purchased in its mandatory dependency. The British government did not make use of this tactic during the interwar decades, neither in Palestine nor in other colonies or countries subject to its control, but that inevitably changed during the war. In theory, recipients of Palestine pounds had a claim on U.K. resources, since the Palestine pound was convertible into sterling. In practice this was impossible, owing to wartime currency controls. The only alternative, used by the Palestine Currency Board and the Palestine banks, was to acquire gilt-edged (non-price indexed) bonds, which represented a U.K. debt. These were the so-called "sterling balances" accumulated during the war. Palestine's sterling balances accumulated during the war, like those of other members of the sterling bloc, were frozen immediately at the end of the war. This prevented their use by creditors in Palestine to pay for imports of goods and services from Britain in the postwar period, unless released by the British Treasury.

SURGING WAR INFLATION, 1940–1947. This borrowing by the British government to finance bulging aggregate demand, leading by 1941 to overemployment in Palestine's economy (Table 7), was inflationary by definition. The inflationary effect shows clearly in the monetary series of Table 13. The currency data, which does not represent the whole money supply, but is available from 1927 onward, offers the first evidence of monetary inflation, one of the most significant features of the war years. In the 12 years between 1927 and 1939, currency circulation increased by approximately 5.8 times, at an average annual rate of 15.7 percent. It expanded at 26 percent annually during the seven years ending with 1946, and at an annual rate of 34 percent during the six years of the war. Reliable money supply figures are available only from 1931 on, but these tell the same story: money supply grew by an average annual rate of 34 percent in the six war years through 1945 and at a rate close to 28 percent in the seven years of war and its immediate aftermath through 1946 (Table 13). The annual rate of expansion of the money supply (M1) in the 1930s was roughly 17 percent.

With the monetarization process in the Arab sector close to completion and the gap between the expansion of the money supply on one hand and the growth of national product and income on the other at 10 percent, major inflation was inevitable. It began in 1940; the 1941 price index indicates an annual average rate of price inflation of 22 percent during these two war years. In 1945, after six years of war, the average annual price inflation was lower, but still more than 15 percent. And even though it was significantly reduced in 1946 and 1947, as the data for the Jewish markets in Table 13 indicate, the average annual inflation rate of 15 percent for the 1940–47 period had an inevitable effect on the workings of the economy, particularly on inflationary expectations, inherited by Israel in 1948.

Manufacturing and the Transformation of the Economic Structure, 1937–1947

Inflation was indeed an important feature of the war period and its immediate aftermath. It was not, however, the only significant process with long-term implications. The real economy of the Jewish sector underwent a significant change in structure during the war years, a process that had already begun to emerge in the second half of the 1930s.

THE 1936–1940 RECESSION. Economic processes during the war actually had their origins in the prewar period, and were of course affected by the context in which they began to evolve. A main feature of that context was a significant recession that started in 1936, whose impact was felt primarily by the Jewish economy. The 1936 domestic national product had fallen by six percent from the very high peak of 1935 (which had risen by about 13 percent from 1934). It further eroded somewhat through 1939 to the 1934 level. The trough of the cycle was reached in 1938. Yet in spite of the downturn, total employment in the Jewish economy increased every year through 1939; only employment in the construction industry declined (Table 7). This means that the depression was mainly an income depression, explicable by a significant negative development: the drastic fall of the prices of Palestine's main export, citrus: these were down by 30 percent by 1939. With citrus exports accounting for about 10 percent of the Jewish GDP, the price collapse had an unavoidable effect on incomes, although citrus production was in 1939 more than two times its level in 1935.

The other main source of weakness during the prewar period was the building industry, in the wake of the end of the immense building boom of 1932–35. The net product of that industry in 1939 was about only 20 percent of its 1935 peak (Table 8). Thus, while employment in the citrus industry was at least maintained through the summer 1939, employment in the building industry declined almost at once and was clearly a drag on the labor market by 1936. The unemployment rates in Table 7 show a rise in the Jewish labor market from a negligible figure in 1935 to 4.3 percent in 1938 and 1939. In comparative terms, with unemployment rates of those years in the nine-to-ten percent range in Britain and other western European countries, and at even higher rates in the United States, a rate of 4.3 percent was seemingly quite reasonable. such a retrospective reading of the situation applies particularly to the Jewish community, which continued to absorb immigrants at rates not much below the average of the wave of 1932–35. Indeed immigration in 1939 surged again, to 31,000.

This, however, was not the view of contemporaries, as the political annals of the period indicate. The situation in 1936–40 was perceived as a major crisis. The struggle to get hired for "a day's work," as the Hebrew idiom of those years had it, particularly in the Tel Aviv conurbation which "grew on yeast" in the 1930s, was bitter indeed. However, by late 1940, and particularly from 1941, the employment problem disappeared for almost an entire decade.

The weak labor market, which shows in the unemployment figures, can be seen in the wage series too. Real wages declined by almost 13 percent between 1935 and 1939, not only because of low demand, but also because of the continuous growth of the labor force (and the population as a whole), which in part reflected the continuing flow of immigration. Declining income, in terms of per capita product, was even more severe: Jewish per capita product declined by 17 percent during the same period.

THE RISE OF THE MANUFACTURING INDUSTRY, 1936–1947. The strains in the economy in the second half of the 1930s did not prevent the significant reordering of economic priorities. It was the rise of manufacturing industry that generated a major change in the structure of the production sector. This shows clearly in terms of that sector's employment and contribution to net product during that period, which accelerated during the war. It had grown only somewhat more rapidly in terms of employment and production than agriculture in the first half of the 1930s. In 1935 Jewish manufacturing employment was 80 percent of that of agriculture. By 1939, the figures were even; in spite of the slowdown, employment in manufacturing had grown by 35 percent between 1935 and 1939. By 1945 it employed 72,000, almost twice as much as in 1939 and more than twice the number employed at that time by agriculture (Table 7).

The product figures reveal a similar development. Though the rising trend of manufacturing product (value added) did slow down between 1935 and 1939, it still kept growing. Due to the downturn in the citrus markets (though not in the markets for mixed farming products), the product of agriculture as a whole was down by 26 percent (Table 8). During the war years the net product of manufacturing expanded by an annual average of almost 18 percent even though net investment slowed down. By 1945 it was the dominant sector of the Jewish economy, generating one-third of its net national product and responsible for 31 percent of its total employment, three times more than agriculture. The 1935–45 (or –47) decade accordingly saw a major restructuring of the Jewish economy. Though Zionist ideology and policy still insisted on the priority of agriculture, developments in the economy were attracting Zionist attention to manufacturing.

The surge of growth in manufacturing product was possible because of the existence of excess capacity in the wake of the major investment flow in the second half of the 1930s, which was accelerated by the highly significant contribution of the flow of private capital imports in the form of German equipment and machinery (the only form allowed to Jewish immigrants from Germany). The huge increase in military procurement provided the demand; procurement increased from about three percent of national product in 1938 to 22 percent of GDP in 1940. The peak in absolute terms and relative to NNP was reached in 1941, at 38 percent of national product. Military procurement then declined, although it was still a major component of aggregate demand, as the theater of war moved away from the Middle East. Yet that decline in the last two years of the war, to below 17 percent of GDP, did not reduce manufacturing product. Production continued to grow though 1945 and stayed almost at this peak through 1947 owing to two new demand factors that appeared during the war (Table 8).

One of these was the demand for substitutes for the producer and consumer goods that Palestine had been importing before the war, especially those from Europe. The nascent manufacturing sector in the metals and machinery, electrical equipment, textile, and clothing industries could hardly compete without tariff protections against cheap prewar imports from established industries in developed countries (which maintained their own protective tariffs), and Palestine was not allowed to join the British Imperial Preference System instituted in 1931. The second new source of demand was the economies of the Middle East, in countries where the British (later Allied) Mid-East Procurement Center in Cairo operated, and which, like Palestine, were cut off from their traditional import linkages.

The impact of the expansion of manufacturing activity during the war years is underlined by the data on the growth of electricity use by manufacturing; use grew by almost three times between 1939 and 1946. The Iraqi pipeline transporting crude oil to Haifa, the Haifa refinery that opened in 1939, and finally the heavy prewar investment in generation and transmission capacity made by the Jewish Palestine Electric Corporation (using German equipment imported under the Haavara Agreement) allowed this rapid expansion of electricity generation during the war years. The direct pipeline link from the Iraqi oilfields and the capacity of the Haifa refinery allowed Palestine to avoid energy rationing, a prevalent feature of war economies.

All types of manufacturing activity increased during the war, in response to strong domestic and foreign demand generated by rapidly rising income in Palestine and other Middle East countries. Yet three industries in particular benefited most from the vigorous expansion of these markets. One of these was the diamond industry, which "made Aliyah" – that is, it "immigrated" to Palestine in response to the outbreak of war in Europe. The others – metals and machinery, and electrical and optical equipment – benefited from the war effort, which generated specific demand for their output.

Diamond polishing in Palestine started from scratch in 1939, and by 1943 offered employment to almost eight percent of workers employed in manufacturing in the Jewish economy. In the interwar period this industry had been mainly located in its traditional centers, Belgium and the Netherlands, manned predominantly by Jewish workers and entrepreneurs. Its raw material supply came mainly from South Africa and its primary market was the United States. The two last features, and the fact that Palestine, like South Africa, belonged to the sterling bloc, were highly beneficial to the British economy, which in the war was very short of dollar export revenue. British interest coincided in this case with both the interest of the Jewish operators in that industry in fleeing Nazi-occupied Europe and the Zionist effort to foster immigration to Palestine. It was inconsistent with the major effort, fostered by the British Foreign Office and implemented by the Mandatory government, to restrict Jewish immigration to Palestine. The diamond industry case was from the point of view of the British the exception that proved its (policy) rule.

The relatively simple machinery required for diamond processing and polishing, which could be produced in Palestine, facilitated the forced and rapid transfer of the industry. In more than one sense it involved mainly the transfer of expertise – i.e., human capital at the disposal of the Jewish immigrants. The rapid expansion of output, which provided the entire supply of industrial diamonds for the Middle East, and exported 80 percent of its product, mainly to the jewelry business in the United States, required extensive training of locals. This was soon successfully accomplished. Though its comparative contribution to manufacturing employment declined significantly after the war, the diamond industry survived in Palestine even as the traditional centers of the industry in Belgium and the Netherlands were revived after the war. Israel became one of the major centers of that industry, in trading and polishing, in the second half of the 20th century.

The second industry that expanded vigorously during the war was metal and machinery. It was converted to war production, supplying, among other things, almost all the antitank mines and spare parts for vehicles and ships required in the Middle East. The third, a related precision instruments and optics industry, was a by-product of this development and initially produced exclusively for military requirements. This complex of industries soon provided, in the immediate aftermath of the war, the foundation of what was initially the illegal small-arms industry of the Haganah, and after independence provided the basis for Israel's defense industry. A chemical industry based on the Dead Sea Potash Works, established in the early 1930s, and the beginning of a pharmaceutical industry also emerged in the late 1930s. In the last years of the war they employed about 10 percent of the labor force in manufacturing.

Neither of these industrial complexes, which took shape by the late 1930s and emerged as highly significant components of the Jewish economy's manufacturing capacity, could have emerged without a substantial group of highly trained and experienced workers. In the 1930s this was provided mainly by the stream of immigrants from Germany and Central Europe, which included a significant share, 15 percent, of university graduates: engineers, medical doctors, chemists, etc. These immigrants initially faced severe absorption problems; it was hard for them to find work in their fields of expertise. The outbreak of the war soon resolved their employment problems. The demand for their know-how grew immensely as communications and trade links with Europe and America were disrupted and the British and Allied military supply system in the Middle East had to rely more and more on domestic resources. They were soon reinforced by Hebrew University of Jerusalem and Haifa Technion (the Israel Institute of Technology) graduates, who began moving into the market for highly trained labor.

The rising incomes across the board generated, inevitably, increasing demand for consumer goods such as food and textiles. In the prosperous years of the war and its aftermath these grew, too, in terms of employment and production. However, the growth was at significantly lower rates than in producer goods. Expansion of demand was felt in the Arab manufacturing sector too. Between 1939 and 1945 its employment grew at an average annual rate of six percent and its product by about eight percent, although this was less than half the corresponding annual growth rates of the Jewish sector. Furthermore, while Jewish manufacturing was undergoing a major structural change, Arab manufacturing expanded along traditional consumption goods lines.

Although the citrus industry was in the doldrums, the Arab labor force benefited from the conditions of overemployment of the war years and moved into the openings in its own manufacturing sector, military building projects in particular. This reduced significantly its direct linkage with the Jewish economy, which in 1935 had been employing a meaningful share of Arab labor in citriculture and construction. These years thus saw the beginning of the end of the one-way labor market links between the two distinct economic sectors that had begun with the Arab uprising of 1936.

War Prosperity, Inflation, and the Short-Term Peace Reconversion

In terms of the unemployment rate, which rose to 5.7 percent in 1940, the first year of the war seemingly belongs to the period of the economic slowdown. But with employment in the Jewish economy expanding by almost six percent in that year, the labor market had been improving considerably. The rise of the unemployment rate was due mainly to the almost eight percent increase in the size of the labor force, reflecting, with a lag, the surge of Aliyah in 1939. By 1941 unemployment disappeared from the economic scene for the next seven years.

With unemployment at less than three percent in 1941, and close to zero in the six succeeding years through 1947, the labor market showed the exploding economic prosperity of these years. The relief on the employment front reflected primarily the booming war-induced domestic aggregate demand described above. It was also due to the substantial voluntary recruitment into the British army: the 27,000 Jewish volunteers serving in the Jewish brigade and other Jewish units were about 11 percent of the labor force in 1945. The most interesting feature of the postwar labor market shows in the unemployment data of 1946 and 1947; in these two years, though all the Jewish soldiers had been released from service and rejoined the labor market, and there had been 41,000 new immigrants, the unemployment rates were 0.2 and 0.3 percent in 1946 and 1947 respectively (Table 7). The markets, including the labor market, evidently operated in boom conditions at that time, which were also years of all-out struggle with the British government for "free Aliyah" as well as the illegal immigration drive carried out by the Zionist Organization. These struggles were supported emotionally, politically, and financially by the remaining Jewish communities all over the globe.

Prices, wages, and incomes responded to the war boom immediately. Prices rose at once – by the end of 1940 these were already 20 percent higher than in 1939, and by 1941 they were 49 percent higher than on the eve of the war. Nominal wages also rose, though initially at lower rates: almost seven percent in 1940 and about 14 percent in 1941. Thanks to price inflation, these figures actually represented a highly significant reduction of real wages, as can be seen in the real wage figures in Table 6. If initially, in the still weak labor market of 1940, workers and the population at large were subject to a temporary "money illusion" by the booming labor market, the severe erosion of real wages from 1941 led to a corrective arrangement: an official committee representing labor, industrial employees, and the Palestine government recommended in 1942 that wages be linked to the cost of living, with periodic adjustments to match changes in the cost-of-living index. This recommendation was immediately adopted, initiating the era of price indexation, which turned out to be a major institutional device affecting the workings of the Palestine, and later Israeli, economy for almost six decades to come.

Its immediate effect was an effective upward adjustment of real wages. By 1943 these were approximately back to the level of 1939, but now in the context of overemployment, thus reflecting a major increase in income of the entire labor force. It was increasing productivity that sustained that pattern and allowed real wages to climb further. By the end of the war these were 40 percent higher than at the previous (accidental) peak of 1935. The net domestic product per employee figures in Table 6 exhibit the rising average product of labor and indicate a robust 40 percent rise in labor productivity by 1945 from 1939. These figures explain the factors supporting the highly significant performance of the Jewish economy in terms of real wages during the six years of the war.

The economics of the last two years of the Mandate period were of special significance, particularly in the political context of that period. These were years of confrontation with the British government, which stuck to the policy articulated in the 1939 White Paper, abandoning some of Britain's commitments under the 1922 League of Nations Mandate. Yet these two years of confrontation, which involved clashes with the British army and navy, mainly related to the Zionist-organized illegal immigration of Jewish refugees, were years of roaring prosperity in Palestine, and correspondingly also of declining inflation. Price inflation was down to an average of three to four percent, and national product grew at an average annual rate of 12.5 percent. Correspondingly, per capita product in the Jewish sector grew at a somewhat higher rate due to a lower rate of population increase (Table 5). This performance, reflecting a significant increase of labor productivity in the Jewish economy, was expressed in an outstanding leap of real wages by a 9.4 percent average annual rate.

These highly beneficial developments in terms of price inflation, production, and corresponding income growth and thus overall economic welfare were due to an exogenous postwar factor that supported the maintenance of high aggregate demand yet generated downward pressure on prices. This was, of course, the reopening of communications and transport links with Europe and across the Atlantic and the Indian Ocean, allowing both the revival of citrus production and export and reopening Palestine to a flow of imports. The citrus exports – at a lower level of production than before the war, owing to the conversion to other uses of about 20 percent of the prewar growing area – offered a significant net contribution to exports representing a meaningful increase of net national product, in 1947 in particular. The imports were sufficient to generate downward pressure on domestic price levels.

The postwar high domestic aggregate demand, even though military procurements had been cut drastically, was primarily due to the instantaneous revival of the building industry. After six years in which building for civilian purposes was legally prohibited, and a full decade of a depressed Jewish building industry, the Jewish population – 20 percent larger in 1945 than in 1939 – was eager for an expansion of living space. The much higher per capita incomes and especially the accumulated savings from the war years provided the financing for a major building boom. The war-inherited inflationary expectations were of course also relevant, and suggested to many households the wisdom of an immediate move into the housing market. The building industry revival offered a substitute market for the cement and stone industries just as military procurements were disappearing. Its upturn of activity, and its traditional role in Palestine as the leading branch in the business cycle, provided the stimulus for a major revival of domestic demand. That logic applied similarly to the Arab building sector, which also rebounded sharply in the immediate aftermath of the war. The employment data of Table 7, which indicates a twofold increase in employment in construction in the Jewish sector and an increase of more than four times in the Arab sector, underlines this retrospective reading of events.

These prosperous economic conditions contributed undoubtedly to the morale and steadfastness of the Jewish population in the political struggle with the British between 1945 and 1948 for unrestricted immigration and the establishment of a Jewish state. Thus successful economic performance at this last stage of the Mandate offered the Jewish community a material base for the crucial stage of that effort.

IN THE STATE OF ISRAEL

The Israeli War of Independence, set off by an Arab attack on a Jewish bus on November 30, 1947, in response to the United Nations decision on the Palestine partition plan the previous day, followed by violence against Jews and Jewish property in Jerusalem and all over the country, raged on and off in 1948 between temporary UN-imposed armistices. March 10, 1949, the date when Israel Defense Force units reached Eilat, on the shore of the Red Sea, marked the end of the war.

The four armistice agreements of 1949 – the last signed with Syria in July, following earlier agreements with Egypt, Lebanon, and Jordan in February, March, and April respectively – constituted a crucial geographical and demographic watershed for the emerging Jewish state. These agreements defined the armistice lines, known as the "Green Line," – effectively, an international border – with the four neighboring Arab states. These gave effective political control to Israel over 20,770 square kilometers of the 27,009 sq km area of Mandatory Palestine – about 77 percent of its total area.

The immediate demographic impact of the war, confirmed in practice by the armistice agreements, was also highly significant. A major share of the Arab population – about 500–550,000 – that had been living in the area on the Israeli side of the 1949 Armistice lines escaped during the hostilities to areas behind the lines of the Arab forces. Those refugees who lived in the north, in Haifa and Galilee, went – temporarily, as they believed – to Lebanon and Syria. Those in the central and southern part of Palestine crossed into the Jordanian-held areas later known as the West Bank and the Egyptian-held territory soon known as the Gaza Strip. This meant that at the end of the hostilities only about 150,000 Arabs and 15,000 Druze remained within the Green Line.

On the other hand, from May 15, 1948, onward, the Zionist demand for "free Aliyah" could at last be realized. Thus, from May 15 to the end of 1948, about 100,000 immigrants arrived in Israel. A similar number arrived in the following two quarters through mid-1949 – the total for that whole year amounting to some 240,000. This meant that the Jewish population, which was almost 650,000 at the declaration of Independence, grew to almost 900,000 within one year (Table 14).

These two factors, geography and demography, inevitably determined the economic agenda of the nascent state.

Free Aliyah and Demographics, 1948–2005

THE FIVE WAVES OF IMMIGRATION. The drastic transformation of the demographic structure within that single year was an expression of the initial stage of the first wave of mass immigration, which arrived between May 15, 1948 and the end of 1951. It represented the "free Aliyah" policy adopted by the government, for which the Zionist movement had been struggling for three generations.

Its implementation at that rapid pace also reflected the availability of candidates for immediate immigration to the emerging Jewish state. First there were the approximately 100,000 illegal immigrants whom the British had deported to Cyprus between 1945 and May 1948, and held in detention camps there. Another reservoir of potential immigrants was the population of European Jewish refugees still living in displaced persons camps run by the Allied Military Government in Germany in 1948, three years after the end of World War II. Almost all of the 200,000 immigrants to Israel through the end of 1949 from Europe (and America) shared this experience. Though the flow from Europe continued (at a significantly lower rate), the focus of the effort in 1950 shifted to Yemen and in 1951 to Iraq. Almost all of these two ancient Jewish communities, comprising 70–80,000 and over 100,000 respectively, with roots going back to the era of the Talmud and the Mishna, went to Israel in 1950 and 1951.

That first wave of mass immigration of 1948–51, which involved a gross immigration flow of almost 700,000 (more than the Jewish population at the time of independence) subsided in 1952. This was not accidental. Though the emptying of Jewish refugee camps all over Europe and the almost com-

Table 14. Population in Israel: Selected Years[1]

Year	Population (Thousands)				Population Growth (1950=100)				Ratio
	Jews[2] (1)	Arabs[3] (2)	Druze (3)	Total (4)	Jews (5)	Arabs (6)	Druze (7)	Total (8)	Jews[4] (9)
1947	630	–	–	–	52	–	–	–	–
1948	650[5]	–	–	–	54	–	–	–	–
1949	717	–	–	873	63	–	–	–	82.1
1950	1,203	152	15	1,370	100	100	100	100	87.8
1955	1,591	180	19	1,790	132	118	127	131	88.9
1960	1,911	216	23	2,150	159	142	153	157	88.9
1967	2,384	–	–	2,776	198	–	–	203	85.9
1970	2,582	404	36	3,022	215	266	240	221	85.4
1980	3,283	588	51	3,922	273	387	340	286	83.7
1990	3,947	792	83	4,822	328	521	553	352	81.9
2000	5,181	1,081	104	6,369	431	711	693	465	81.3
2003	5,447	1,188	111	6,748	453	782	740	493	80.7
Average Annual Rates of Change = (Percent)									
					Jews	Arabs	Druze	Total	
1947–2003		–	–	–	3.9	–	–	–	–
1950–2003		–	–	–	2.9	4.0	3.8	3.1	–
1950–1970		–	–	–	3.9	4.5	4.5	4.0	–
1970–2003		–	–	–	2.3	3.5	3.5	2.5	–

Notes:
1. Year-end population figures rounded to the nearest one thousand.
2. The estimate for the Jewish population from 2000 on includes population belonging to the groups classified in the official statistics as "religious unclassified" and "non-Arab Christians." In 2003 the former group included 255,000 people and the latter 27,000.
3. Includes Muslims and Arab Christians.
4. As a percent of total population.
5. Estimate of Jewish population on May 15, 1948.

Table 15. Immigration to Israel: 1948–2003

Year	Immigrants (Thousands)		Immigrants Per Thousand Residents	Immigrants by Continent (Percent)[1]			
	Total	Yearly Average		Asia	Africa	Europe, America, Oceania	Total
	(1)	(2)	(3)	(4)	(5)	(6)	(7)
1948–2003	2,951	54	–	13	17	70	100
1948–1951	687	196	180	36	14	50	100
1952–1960	294	33	18	13	50	37	100
1961–1967	289	41	17	10	46	44	100
1968–1979	405	34	9	11	8	81	100
1980–1989	154	15	4	9	15	76	100
1990–1993	529	132	38	–	–	–	–
1990–1999	956	96	18	–	–	–	–
2000–2003	161	40	6	–	–	–	–
1990–2003	1,117	80	–	1	5	94	100

Note:
1. Immigrants by last continent of residence.

plete transfer of the Jewish communities of Iraq and Yemen were highly successful, the major slowdown in 1952 reflected a deliberate, though not officially stated, policy of the Israeli government to shelve temporarily its efforts to encourage, organize, and finance immigration. This was due to the immense strain imposed on the nascent economy of Israel by the first post-independence immigration wave. The all-time high rate of 180 immigrants per 1,000 residents during the 44-month period from May 1948 to December 1951 (Table 15) offers a quantitative indication of that strain.

The absorption organization for new immigrants run by the Jewish Agency almost collapsed under the weight of the numbers; its capacity to provide shelter, food, and medical services (mainly in abandoned British army camps) was pushed to the limit. With its foreign currency reserves drying up, and a major balance of payments current account deficit, the government's ability to provide housing and assure medium-term absorption of the newcomers into the labor force was overwhelmed; the major problem was the need for employment. The economics of absorption thus suggested the absolute necessity of a temporary lull in the inflow. The average yearly number of arrivals, which was 196,000 during that first post-independence wave and which was never repeated in the ensuing five decades, underlines the economic strain to which the system was subjected (Table 15).

The second wave of immigration, after a three-year lull in which the average annual inflow was only 17,000, started in 1955 and ran through 1957. It involved an average annual rate of 55,000. As did the first, it required the allocation of resources for the immigrants' initial absorption and integration, but it imposed an altogether smaller strain on the emerging, still fragile, economic system. This is suggested by the figure of 33 immigrants per thousand residents during this period; for the whole of the decade after the end of the post-independence wave of immigration, from 1952 to 1960, it was only 18 per thousand residents. This was less than one-tenth the size of the first wave (Table 15).

The timing of this second wave was set almost exclusively by the political conditions and considerations of the regimes ruling the countries of origin of these immigrants. Primarily they were Tunisia, Algeria, and Morocco in North Africa (1955–56) and Poland (1956–57) in Eastern Europe. The Algerian war, which by that time was peaking, created the incentive for the Jewish community to emigrate. Covert consent of the governments of Morocco and Tunisia, which were by that time independent states, made emigration organized by the Jewish Agency feasible. In Algeria, at that time still under the control of France, the operations of an Aliyah organization were of course legal. In Poland, a post-Stalinist upheaval bringing a change of the leadership of the ruling Communist party, using overtly antisemitic media propaganda, induced most of the remnants of the Jewish community to take the option the authorities opened of immigration to Israel. By the mid-1950s, after almost a decade of independence, a convincing economic performance, and a much more stable inflow of unilateral receipts from abroad, allowing a formidable current account deficit, the policy of encouraging emigration to Israel and using every political loophole abroad to facilitate it was again given top priority by the government.

The third wave of Aliyah of the early 1960s through 1965, averaging again somewhat more than 50,000 immigrants annually, was also dominated by political upheavals in North Africa, and the covert consent of the Moroccan government to the operation of a Jewish *aliyah* organization offering Jews facilities and expenses to move, semi-legally, to Israel. The fourth, post-Six-Day War wave of immigration, with an average inflow of 45,000 through 1974, was undoubtedly generated by the identification of Jewish communities worldwide with Israel and its victory against all odds. This burst of identification and enthusiasm included even Soviet Jewry, which for almost five decades was perceived by Zionists as a "lost tribe." With Zionism an anathema to the Communist regime, and the universal ban on foreign travel for Soviet citizens, Jewish immigration to Palestine had been virtually stopped since around

1920. Due largely to foreign pressure, the conservative Brezhnev regime allowed an exception to the universal foreign travel ban and even more so on emigration. This was made only for Jews applying to immigrate to Israel. The application procedure and the secret criteria on the basis of which applications were granted or rejected imposed considerable danger on the applicants. Yet many Jews did take the risk. This resulted in an inflow of about 30,000 immigrants annually from the Soviet Union in the early 1970s (1971–74 approximately) before the policy changed and reduced permits to a trickle.

In the post-Yom Kippur War period through the mid-1980s, the so-called "lost decade" ("lost" economically), immigration reached record lows (see below, The Evolution of the Jewish Demographic Structure). The annual average was 18,000 for the 15-year period ending in the late 1980s. The rate of inflow was only four per 1,000 residents (Table 15), which means that for that rather long period *aliyah* had only a minor impact, if any, on the economy. Net immigration was even lower. Emigration was quite small from the 1980s on, but it usually increased during economic slowdowns such as this.

The revival of sustained economic activity began sometime around 1987–88, in the wake of the 1985 stabilization policy (see below), but only gained real momentum from 1990 onwards, as the unexpected mass immigration following the relaxation of the Soviet Union's emigration policies after 1988 began to flow into Israel, from December of that year onward. Within its first 43 months through the mid-1993, over half a million immigrants arrived – not many fewer than the 690,000 who arrived in the first post-independence wave of mass immigration of 1948–51. Though the annual average of immigrants was lower, about 130,000 compared to 200,000 for the first wave, and considerably lower per Israeli resident, 38 compared to 180, an inflow of more than 500,000 immigrants into a country with a population of about 4.5 million, and a Jewish community of 3.7 million, did of course have a significant and immediate economic impact. In the short run it first affected, inevitably, aggregate demand. In the longer run, it made a major contribution to the national product. The very large influx of immigrants of the early 1990s was not sustained throughout the decade. From 1993 to 2000, it ranged from 60–70,000; in the ensuing period through 2005 it was about 30,000. Yet in the closing of the decade of the 20th century and through 2005, about 1.15 million immigrants came to Israel, which by the end of 2005 had a population of about seven million, with a Jewish (and Jewish-affiliated) community of some 5.5 million.

THE EMIGRATION (YERIDAH) EFFECT. These immigration figures and the total immigration data of Table 15, which indicate the total number of immigrants between 1948 and 2003 was close to 3 million, are of course gross figures. Net immigration was inevitably lower; Israel, as is any country absorbing significant immigration, is subject to emigration too. Its incidence among new immigrants is, as elsewhere, higher than that among the longer-established population.

Owing to Israel's inability to agree on a legal definition of "emigrants," the statistics on emigration (in Hebrew parlance *yeridah*, a semiderogatory expression) are rough estimates. The best estimate of emigration in the 1990s, the era of the second mass immigration, was about seven percent of the total number of newcomers. Since the option of returning to the country of origin or moving to another destination was severely limited in the late 1940s and through the 1950s, the emigration rate during the first mass immigration was clearly lower. Between the late 1960s through the 1980s, immigration rates were much lower and options to emigrate were rapidly increasing. These rates, which of course include the emigration of older immigrants and native Israelis as well, were undoubtedly higher than the seven percent of the 1990s. This applied particularly to periods of economic slowdown, for example the second half of the 1980s. All in all the available consensus estimate of emigration from 1948 through 2003 puts it at about 450–500,000. This means that the average emigration rate was about 15 percent of the total immigration inflow (Sicron 2004).

THE PATTERN OF DEMOGRAPHIC BALANCE. The impact of *aliyah* on the demographic balance, a highly sensitive issue from the very beginning of Zionism in the last quarter of the 19th century through the early 21st century and beyond, is indicated in the population data in Table 14. Israel's total population increased 7.7 times in the 55 years between the end of 1948 through 2003, at an average annual rate of 3.8 percent, and Jewish population grew at the same rate. The latter rate was 3.9 percent, based on the rough mid-1948 estimate of the Jewish population.

These were evidently very high population growth rates. An inevitable highly significant economic implication of these very high growth rates was scarcity of land, for the population as a whole and for the Jewish population in particular. The settlements established beyond the Green Line since 1967 do not make a meaningful difference on this account. Yet in spite of the dire predictions of British experts in the early 1930s about the depressant implication of growing land scarcity, which would erode the living standards of the Palestinian Arab population in particular, the living standards of the Arab community of Israel, about one million by 2003, had improved by an order of magnitude even though the land area at the disposal of Israeli Arabs had not grown since 1949. This holds, of course, for the Jewish population too, though Israel, with an area of only about 80 percent of Mandatory Palestine, had by 2004 a population of about 7 million, compared to one million in 1930 when these predictions were made. Indeed Arab population in Israel alone was in 2003 some 20 percent larger than the Arab population of Mandatory Palestine in 1931 (Tables 1 and 14). This of course underlines the fact that land is only one of the relevant factors of production, even in the case of the farming industry.

The demographic balance, which in the seven decades of the pre-state Zionist resettlement effort was a crucial political issue, was at the turn of the 21st century still a highly sensitive subject. Its quantitative dimensions are displayed in Table 14, in terms of the ratio of Jews to the total of Israel's population. The figure for the end of 1948, which represents the initial universal population registration implemented on November 11 of that year (before the end of the war) indicates an 82.1 percent ratio of Jewish population to the total, which at that date was less than one million. The first mass immigration changed that ratio; it peaked at about 89 percent toward the mid-1960s, when Israel's population was 2.5 million.

However, the much lower immigration rates even during the peaks of subsequent immigration waves through 1989 did not overcome the major fertility gap between the Arab (majority Muslim) population and the Jewish population. Jewish total birth rates, which were 3.56 children in the 1950s, declined over the decades to 2.73 in 2001–05. Even the recent low rates are indeed very high compared to those elsewhere in the industrial world, even those of the 1950s, and particularly at the turn of the millennium, when in some industrialized countries birth rates had collapsed to a figure below 1.0. However, Jewish birth rates paled in comparison to the total birth rate of the Israeli Muslim Arabs which were a record even in the Arab world of the 1950s and remained so around the year 2000. (They were as high as 9.23 in the 1960s.) They then declined considerably to 4.5 in 2003. The birth rates of the small Christian Arab communities were for several decades considerably lower than those of the Jewish community.

With such comparative birth rates, the low *aliyah* influxes of the late 1950s through the late 1980s could not overcome the declining trend of the ratio of Jewish population to the total. By 1988, before the arrival of the next, unexpected mass immigration, the Jewish population's share of the total declined to 81.7 percent. That next mass immigration, and the reduction of the Muslim-Jewish birth rate gap from 5.84 in the 1960s to 2.05 in the 1990s and to less than 2 by 2003, halted the decline. The Jewish share of the total population hovered in the 81 percent range from 1990 to 2003.

THE EVOLUTION OF THE JEWISH DEMOGRAPHIC STRUCTURE. The demographic structure of the Jewish community, which in the Mandatory period was dominated by immigrants from European countries, was subject to a significant change during the nearly six decades of the state of Israel's history. This had a direct long-run bearing on the productivity and on the quality of its labor force

According to the rough classifications of immigrants by previous continent of residence, in the successive waves of immigration from 1948 through 1967, about 50 percent of the immigrants were from Asia and Africa through 1960 and close to 60 percent in the 1961–67 period (the Asia-Africa category refers effectively to immigrants from Arabic-speaking countries stretching from Yemen to Iraq and through North Africa). That pattern changed from the 1970s on, since almost all Jewish communities in those countries had by that time already left, mostly to Israel, while the Communist regimes of Eastern Europe, including the Soviet Union, liberalized emigration rules for Jews who wanted to move to Israel. The collapse of the Soviet Union in the early 1990s changed the rules of the game altogether, an opportunity seized by most members of the Jewish community, generating the 1990–2000 mass immigration that brought over a million new immigrants to Israel. Immigrants in the European-American category were accordingly about 59 percent of the 1968–89 "low immigration" period, and close to 94 percent of the immigration avalanche in the 1990s and later. The overall average of European-American immigrants from 1948 through 2003 was about 70 percent of the total, including about 7.5 percent from the Americas, North and South.

The evolution of the social and cultural mosaic of Israel's Jewish community was of course affected by the rapidly growing number of its native-born members; they were 35 percent in 1948 and about 64 percent in 2003. Second generation native Israelis were somewhat less than seven percent in 1948, and more than 30 percent by 2003. What complicates the sociological features even more, and thus the economic implications of the evolving communal structure of the Jewish population, is of course the prevailing widespread intermarriages between members of distinct Jewish communities. This has been loosening significantly the traditional cohesion of these communities, which, separated by history and geography, have found themselves together in Israel. A process of integration into a cohesive entity was of course a high priority for Zionism – the so-called "melting pot," in Zionist parlance. That process has gained considerable momentum, as the rising rate of intermarriage indicates. It was quite high by the 1990s – about 33 percent of marriages.

The immediate implication of the changing mosaic of the intermixed Jewish communal structure had an obvious effect on its comparatively high birth rate. It indeed was lower than that of the Arab Muslim population, which still has Third World features in this sphere. Yet Jewish total birth rates in the range of 2.66–2.73, as they were in the 2000–04 period, are sky-high compared to the comparable rates characteristic of the industrialized world. They were even higher (in the 3.0–3.56 range) from the 1950s through the 1970s. These rates would have been lower if most of the Oriental Jewish community had not immigrated to Israel since 1948. The available data indicates that immigrants from Asia, and particularly from North Africa, had significantly higher birth rates than those of immigrants from Europe and native Israelis. The opposite is true of the immigrants from the Soviet Union in the 1990s; the birth rate among that group was significantly less than two.

Total birth rates were also affected by religious observance. The Orthodox and "traditional" section of the Jewish community had, and has, higher birth rates than the secular group. The behavior of the latter is more in line with that of the industrialized societies of the West. It was, however, still higher by a meaningful margin than that prevalent in the industrialized countries through 2004. The higher birth rates of

Oriental Jews reflect the much higher ratio of Orthodox and traditional observant Jews in that community. Nevertheless, though still higher than that of the European-American section of the Jewish community, an interesting phenomenon over time was the pattern of their obvious and consistently declining birth rates toward the relatively stable overall norm maintained in the late 1990s and into the first decade of the new century. This is evidently another manifestation of the melting pot process which has developed within the Jewish community over almost six decades.

ALIYAH AND HUMAN CAPITAL. Human capital, the accumulation of which is of major significance in the process of economic growth, was another subject affected by the waves of immigration. The pre-state level of that factor was quite adequate, comparable to that of the highly industrialized countries of Western and Central Europe. It was undoubtedly significantly improved by the pre-state Fifth Aliyah of 1932–39, which included a relatively high number of university personnel, medical doctors, architects, and engineers, and made a major contribution towards the emergence of the industrial society of the Jewish community of Palestine. Among other things it enabled the Jewish community to make a crucial contribution to the 1939–45 war effort.

The major mass immigration of the late 1940s and early 1950s could not improve matters on that score. Even maintenance of the previous average level was a problem in view of the composition of the newcomers. The European immigrants who came to Israel were Holocaust survivors, and most of them were young people for whom school attendance had merely been a dream for those years. The immigrants from the Arab countries, about one half of the total, came from what in those decades were Third World environments, which could hardly provide a meaningful preparation for life in an industrial society.

It was thus not an accident that the very first law adopted by the Knesset was the law mandating nine years of compulsory education from kindergarten through elementary school. This assured the continuation of the effectively universal primary education system that the Jewish community had maintained in the Mandate period. The government also immediately channeled major resources into secondary schools and higher education. By the early 1960s secondary education was already universal. The two academic institutions established in the early 1920s, the Hebrew University of Jerusalem and the Technion – Israel Institute of Technology, together had only about 1,600 students in the shortened 1948–49 academic year, which started in April 1949 after the cessation of hostilities. By 1960 the number of students totaled 10,000 at these institutions and Tel Aviv University, which had also opened by that time. The number of university students was close to 40,000 by the outbreak of the Yom Kippur War in 1973, when seven universities were operating, and 125,000 by 2003. In that year there were also some 68,000 students enrolled in first- and second-degree programs in the academic colleges.

The effort to increase training, know-how, and experience during these years was mainly domestic, financed by the public sector. It was supported by significant direct contributions from Jews in the Diaspora, who financed mainly the infrastructure of the rapidly expanding and growing number of institutions of higher education. Furthermore, the immigrants of the 1970s and 1980s were better educated and had mostly come from modern industrial societies. But with *aliyah* low for about 15 years after the Yom Kippur War – the number of immigrants per resident was down to around four per resident (Table 15) – the impact of the better-educated new arrivals could not make a major difference on the stock of human capital. It improved with the rapidly increasing flow of graduates from universities and other institutions of higher education.

This changed as the mass immigration of the 1990s began arriving in Israel. The relatively high number of scientists and experienced engineers, and the impressive array of teachers, nurses, and other trained professionals arriving in that decade (mostly from the former Soviet Union), were reminiscent of the composition of the Fifth Aliyah. Furthermore, elementary and high school-age immigrants arriving with their parents also had a strong educational background.

Most significant was the very size of that immigration, which added more than 20 percent to the size of the population within somewhat more than a decade. Thus, on top of its contributions to the highly sensitive demographic balance of the state at the turn of the century, it undoubtedly increased significantly the stock of human capital – one of the array of factors of production, and a vital component of the labor force. The expected long-run benefit of this feature could not be fully expressed within the short period of just over a decade. Its expected impact in the longer run is obvious.

The Resettlement Saga of the State Years, 1948–2005

The dominating challenges for the leadership of the nascent state in its first decade were its control of population entry into Israel, which involved highly significant though not absolute control of the *aliyah* flows surveyed above, and its control of the land. Most of this latter was uncultivated state land, but it included a significant area hitherto cultivated by the rural Arab population of about 350–380,000, who left their homes during the 14 months of active hostilities between November 1947 and January 1949, and sought refuge in the Jordanian-held sector of Palestine, in Lebanon and Syria, and in the Gaza Strip, occupied by Egypt. These refugees also left housing, most of which was of very poor standards compared to that prevalent in industrialized countries. The 150–200,000 refugees from urban areas – Jaffa, Haifa's Arab neighborhoods, the mainly Arab southwestern sections of Jerusalem, and several much smaller urbanized centers, also left empty housing. A highly significant portion of this housing was used for new Jewish immigrants.

ALIYAH AND MAKESHIFT HOUSING. Of the roughly 200,000 immigrants who arrived within the first year of independence, and the approximately 700,000 in the ensuing 43 months through 1951, only a small number had relatives or others who could help them find housing and offer them support as they began their absorption into Israeli society. Groups organized by the kibbutz movement or the Youth Aliyah Organization would direct some to specific kibbutzim prepared to take them in, but most had no alternative but to rely on makeshift arrangements made by the official absorption organization run by the Jewish Agency. During the first 43 months of the mass immigration phase this organization directed new arrivals to the recently emptied housing in Arab towns and Arab neighborhoods of mixed towns (Jerusalem, Haifa, Safed, and Tiberias). These urban locations offered some basic infrastructure in addition to housing. Other newcomers were sent to Jewish urban centers, which could offer infrastructure, but initially only very limited housing. This process required the virtually overnight erection of campuses of temporary housing – tents and corrugated sheet metal huts for thousands. Former British army camps located in or near these towns, Haifa and Jerusalem in particular, were also used for this purpose. These were the so-called *ma'abarot*, a new Hebrew term invented to specify the transitional nature of these arrangements: temporary neighborhoods for new immigrants.

THE EXPANSION OF JEWISH PRESENCE: SETTLEMENTS, NUMBERS, LOCATION, AND STRUCTURE. The figures shown in Table 16 indicate that by 1952, four years after independence, population in Jewish rural settlements was already about 250,000 – almost 100,000 more than in 1947. Allowing for natural growth, rural settlements therefore had absorbed 70–75,000 of the new immigrants – about ten percent of immigrants who had arrived during the period of what could be described as the genesis of the Jewish state. This process involved the creation of 277 new settlements during the four years after May 1948.

In terms of the number of settlements established, the period from May 1948 through the end of 1952 compares to the 70 years of Zionist resettlement starting with the foundation of Petaḥ Tikvah in 1878, a period within which 308 rural settlements were created. During the war, Arabs destroyed nine in locations outside the Green Line.

Though effectively part of the process of providing housing to new immigrants, this all-out effort was focused on the traditional Zionist objective – extending the Jewish presence everywhere in Ereẓ Israel. This was inhibited by British policy, which over the three decades of the Mandate first slowed the resettlement effort and after the 1939 White Paper attempted to stop it altogether.

The Armistice agreements signed between February and July 1949 meant not only the end of the Mandatory legal restriction on the acquisition of land by Jews, but also led to the transfer of Crown land, which effectively included the entire area of the Negev – about half the area of the state – to the ownership of the state of Israel. On top of that, the state took effective possession of land owned and cultivated by the Arab refugees from the rural areas, including a substantial portion of the Arab citrus groves in the coastal plain, all of which, except for the Gaza Strip, was inside the Green Line. These areas, most of which were used for dry farming of field crops, including other fruit groves, were taken under the management of the so-called Custodian of Absentee Property, serving ostensibly as the legal representative of the original property owners. These areas, too, were immediately available for cultivation at no immediate cost to the resettlement authorities, comparable to Crown land. The state of Israel thus acknowledged implicitly the titles of the original Arab owners of this land, as well as of the urban real estate which was similarly placed under the management of the Custodian of Absentee Property. Conceivably the value of these properties would eventually be negotiated at a future peace conference.

This implicit capital commitment to the absentee owners involved of course no immediate payment for the use of these properties. Nor was any cost involved for the use of cultivable state (formerly Crown) land not previously used for farming. Thus in contrast to the pre-state situation in which a major portion of Jewish capital imports had to be allocated for the purchase of land, this cost item was wiped out (although there was an ostensible conceptual commitment to payment in the future). This meant that whatever resources were immediately available for the resettlement effort could be devoted to capital investment, which among other things involved land improvement and the extension of irrigation – major inputs in agricultural production.

The high priority given to the major resettlement effort that was launched in 1948, while the war was still going on, was underlined by the establishment of 37 settlements between May 15 and the end of that year. These were more than ten percent of the number of settlements established during the previous 70 years. The urgency of this move derived from the belief that the borders of the state could be assured only by the Jewish spade.

Though reflecting the traditional priority given by the Zionist movement to agriculture, economic considerations at the time supported such a policy, not only in Israel, but everywhere. The post-World War II environment, which still involved at that time rationing and price controls (over consumer goods and food in particular), in all western European countries, led to the universal rise of state agricultural policy across Europe (still in force six decades later in the European Union). In Israel, with mass immigration the dominant feature in the 1945–51 period, and the young state's foreign currency reserves at low levels, universal rationing and price controls were also the rule. Promotion of farm production was in these circumstances evidently of the highest economic priority, and fully in line with developments elsewhere.

Finally, the direction of a substantial group of the new immigrants to rural resettlement allowed controlled provision to them not only of housing in the new settlements, but also of an allocation of capital investment in the form of land,

Table 16. Rural Settlements, Populations and Cultivated Area

	1947	1948–49	1952	1961	1972	1983	1995	2003[1]
A. Jewish Sector								
1. Rural Settlements								
a. Total[2]	299	–	628	708	692	878	955	940
b. Kibbutzim	138	–	217	228	226	267	269	266
c. Moshavim	69	–	261	366	374	448	454	451
d. Moshavot	59	–	68	70	44[4]	68	80	71
e. Communal and Institutional Localities[3]	33	–	82	44	48	95	152	152
2. Population (Thousands)	135	–	256	298	255	330	423	481
a. Kibbutzim	(40)	–	69	77	89	115	125	116
b. Moshavim	35	–	79	124	130	150	173	223
c. Moshavot	46	–	72	86	23[4]	40	50	55
d. Communal and Institutional Localities	14	–	36	11	13	25	75	87
3. Cultivated Area (Thousands of Dunams)								
a. Total	1380	1310	2960	3180	3405	3056	3071	3804
b. Irrigated	235	292	638	1331	1707	2079	1824	1770
c. Citrus	120	125	135	339	425	394	276	184
d. Other Plantations	–	275	208	302	289	385	386	464
4. Planted Forests	62	53	148	326	536	678	856	971
B. Arab and Druze Sector								
1. Rural Localities	–	–	102	101	90	91	40[5]	33
2. Population (Thousands)[6]	–	–	132	184	206	200	86	81
3. Cultivated Land (Thousands of Dunams)	–	340	590	850	760	719	599	533
a. Irrigated	–	8	12	29	58	75	83	93
C. Total Cultivated Area								
1. Cultivated Area[7]	–	1600	3550	4150	4165	4300	4300	4337
2. Irrigated	–	300	540	1360	1765	2194	1943	1863
3. Citrus	–	184	135	340	426	400	277	184

Notes:

1. The figures for settlements and population are for 2003; the entries for cultivated areas in sections B and C are for 2002.
2. The difference of nine settlements between the figures for 1947 in tables 3 and 16 reflects the number of Jewish settlements destroyed in the war and located beyond the Green (Armistice) Line.
3. Through 1972, and excluding 1952, the category includes rural educational institutions, which operate as separate settlements. In 1953 it also included so-called "labor villages," a kind of settlement converted later to a cooperative settlement, or abolished altogether, and also private ranches.
   A new type of settlement, which surfaced in the mid-1970s, the so-called "communal locality," is included in this category from 1983 onwards. It reflects the reclassification of settlements by the CBS. This type of settlement is located in rural areas, and is small – several hundred housing units at most. Its residents are not involved in farming; they practice urban occupations mostly in an urban center in the vicinity.
4. The significant reductions of the number of Moshavot between 1961 and 1972, which affected the corresponding population figures, reflects the granting of legal urban status to a significant number of older settlements that had over 2,000 residents. These were thus classified as urban localities by the Central Bureau of Statistics and included in its urban category of settlements.
5. The significant reduction of the number of Arab rural localities is due to the reclassification of localities with populations of 2,000–9,999 as urban entities. The total number of non-Jewish localities, rural and urban, was 110 in 1950 and 122 in 2003.
6. The population figures for Arab rural localities include the Bedouin (nomadic and later semi-nomadic) tribes. Their population was about 30,000 in 1952 and by 2003 was close to 60,000.
7. Israel's total cultivated area figures in Part C also include the areas of planted forest, and the irrigated area figures include the areas of fishponds. These two items are not included in the corresponding entries in Part A-3 or the relevant lines of Part B

farm equipment, and circulating capital, and an immediate opening to productive employment. The integration of all these elements into effective new production units providing adequate real income of course required guidance – on-the-spot instruction for the newcomers, who were not only new immigrants, but also new to agriculture. This service was provided to settlements of new immigrants by a small group of veteran farmers operating as coaches, who volunteered to stay temporarily in the new settlements.

This stage of the resettlement saga, which nearly doubled the number of rural settlements within four years, began only late in 1949. But by the end of 1948 there were the 37 new settlements – 27 kibbutzim and ten moshavim. these had been founded by groups of veterans – graduates of the local youth movements, second-generation members of the settlement movement – who had been serving in the army and had been released from active service during the period within which the last three major campaigns of the war were still being fought, suggesting the sense of urgency with which the state viewed the establishment of these settlements. The supply of this kind of settler, however – young, Mandatory Palestine-educated, graduates of the Jewish school system and youth movements – was limited. Thus, of the roughly 80 kibbutzim added to the 138 already existing in 1947, 67 were already operating by the end of 1949, and only 16 new ones were added in the succeeding three years.

This situation prevailed among the moshavim also. Only a handful of the 67 cooperative settlements established in 1949 were manned by veteran youth; the others were populated by new immigrants, most of whom were not ready to attempt a collective form of life (nor had they an inkling of how to do so). This applies even more to the approximately 70 moshavim established in 1950. Thus, of the over 150 newly established cooperative settlements dotting the map of Israel by the end of 1952, most were comprised of new, post-War of Independence immigrants (Table 16). The new immigrants' share of the total number of Jewish settlements was significantly lower, perhaps 140 of the approximately 540 (excluding the institutional and communal localities) on the ground by the end of 1952. They already made up more than 25 percent of the Jewish rural population, however, which within these four stormy years grew by almost 100,000 to 250,000.

This was not the end of the resettlement saga, which established new settlements all over, with a focus on border areas. It involved the opening of a major new development in the arid, and effectively empty, half of the state – the northern part of the Negev near Beersheba, which was intended to become a major urban center. Another focus of resettlement activity was the Jerusalem corridor, where less than a handful of Jewish settlements existed during the Mandate. The attempted Arab siege of Jerusalem through July 1948, facilitated by the absence of Jewish settlements along the road to the city, was the backdrop of the decision to grant priority to the establishment of settlements in this area at the very beginning of the resettlement campaign through 1952.

The resettlement process, which also involved the establishment of several towns, continued through the coming decades as well. Yet the figures on rural settlements from 1952 on indicate a highly significant reduction in the rate of creation of new rural settlements from 1953 to 1961; their number increased 13 percent to 708 (Table 16), but this has to be compared to the 100 percent increase in the number of settlements within the first four years of the new state. The curve in the trend declined significantly after 1960 and effectively flattened from the late 1980s onward.

Between the census years 1961 and 1971 Jewish rural populations even declined. This development, however, was not due to net migration from the settlements; it reflected rather the growth of the older and larger settlements, which in terms of population and economic activity had been transformed into urban localities and acquired the legal status of towns. Hence the reduction in the number of moshavot (the "individual enterprise" settlements) to only 44 by 1972 (Table 16). From then on, through the following three decades the curve of rural settlements turned upward again, as did rural population, which kept growing at an average annual rate of two percent.

The 1970s signified a major turning point in the resettlement strategy. The target, increasing the number of Jewish settlements, did not change at all. In the almost four decades between the Six-Day War and 2004, the traditional establishment of settlements in the Negev and Galilee, the Golan Heights (captured in 1967 and annexed to Israel), the lower Jordan Valley and Judea and Samaria (the West Bank) was still going on. In many of these new establishments production activity would focus on agriculture. This shows in the growth of the number of kibbutzim, moshavim, and moshavot (Table 16) through 1995, which did stop in the following decade. Yet total rural population still kept growing significantly in the following eight years at an average annual rate of 1.6 percent, due to the emergence of a new type of rural settlement, the "communal settlement." This type of settlement, which emerged in the 1970s both within the Green Line and in the West Bank, was not conceived as an agricultural production entity. Placed within at most an hour's driving distance from a major urban center, this type of settlement was designed as a bedroom community, whose residents would work in the nearby urban center. Some business ventures – high-tech or semi-high-tech industrial activities predominating – were established in some of these communities. And of course the option of working from home, at least part-time, was in the age of the personal computer undoubtedly quite prevalent. The social and economic character of these communal settlements were governed by the rules of their legal form of organization as a nonprofit association. This feature allowed the community to exercise control over the choice of candidates for membership. The location and small size of the communities, with hundreds of units at most, sustained their rural features.

The emergence of this novel type of community in the second half of the 1970s gathered momentum in the coming decades; 103 out of a net addition of 224 rural settlements through 2003, almost one half, were communities of this type. These also accounted for the surge in the rural population from its low point in early 1972. A parallel feature of these developments was the effect of emigration from the existing cooperative settlements, reflecting among other things the increase in mechanization and labor-saving technology. Veteran settlers had been selling their patrimonies to newcomers of the communal village type, and the second generation of settlers, who had had the benefit of Israel's higher education system, joined in and though staying in the villages went into high-tech or other business ventures unrelated to farming.

The emerging pattern of rural settlement in the closing decades of the 20th century and in the first decade of the 21st has thus severed the more than 100-year (since 1869) association of the Zionist movement with agricultural ventures. This was indicated in the farm employment figures: in 2003–04, it was about 30 percent lower than its all-time high in 1960, and 15 percent lower than in 1970. Agricultural product, though, was higher by more than five and three times respectively (Table 17).

Table 17. Farm Production, Employment, Capital Stock and Water Usage[1] (1950 = 100)

	1949	1950	1952	1960	1965	1970	1973	1980	1990	2000	2003
1. Net Product	80	100	144	367	507	664	782	1,238	2,087	3,230	2,049
2. Citrus:											
a. Output[2]	101	100	128	226	325	468	625	571	558	264	187
b. Exports[2]	–	100	97	238	–	488	–	510	276	170	72
3. Farm Employment	50[3]	100	130	165	158	140	128	118	103	123	118
4. Water Usage	77	100	141	319	330	376	390	372	366	343	308[4]
5. Gross Capital Stock	–	100	132	291	443	517	584	730	719	613	616
6. Tractors[5]	26	100	–	286	–	629	–	1,030	1,054	–	–

Notes:
1. Data apply to the whole farming sector.
2. Output and exports in physical terms (tons).
3. The estimate of farm employment refers to 1947.
4. The figure is for 2002.
5. Tractors used in farming only.

Table 18. Resources, National Product, Consumption, and Investment, Total and Per Capita, 1947–1974[1]

Year	Total						Per Capita[3]			Ratio Res/GNP
	Resources[2]	GDP		Consumption		Gross Investment	GDP	Consumption		
		Total	Business	Private	Public			Private	Public	
	(1)	(2)	(3)	(4)	(5)	(6)	(7)	(8)	(9)	(10)
A. 1950 = 100										
1947	–	–	50	–	–	–	109	–	–	–
1950	100	100	100	100	100	100	100	100	100	1.31
1951	121	130	130	122	121	118	113	106	105	1.21
1954	136	160	155	157	146	95	128	126	117	1.11
1955	160	177	175	169	170	104	135	129	130	1.09
1960	225	278	290	256	236	159	177	163	150	1.06
1965	364	445	442	406	379	264	235	214	199	1.07
1967	387	460	432	423	555	171	227	208	273	1.06
1970	563	644	656	540	869	366	291	244	393	1.14
1973 (Sept.)	724	840	888	694	869	603	–	–	–	–
1973	768	843	858	680	1245	531	345	279	510	1.19
1974	794	889	889	732	1282	511	356	293	513	1.17
B. Annual Average Rates of change (%)										
1950–54	7.9	12.5	11.8	11.9	9.9	-12	6.4	5.9	4.0	–
1954–73 (Sept.)	9.3	9.2	9.7	8.2	10.0	10.4	–	–	–	–
1954–73	9.5	9.1	9.4	6.7	12.2	9.5	5.4	4.2	6.6	–
1950–73	11.3	19	10.0	19.2	10.6	9.2	6.7	5.5	9.0	–

Notes:
1. Figures are rounded.
2. Resources for domestic use: GNP plus Import surplus.
3. Derived from series in columns (2) and (4), (5) and the corresponding population series of Table 14, column (8).

THE PERFORMANCE OF AGRICULTURE. The identification of resettlement and agriculture, the policy pursued during the first decade of independence, had been closely linked in Zionist ideology and in practice. In that first decade in particular, this link was also fully consistent with the needs of the markets: the domestic market for fresh food and the foreign market for Israel's major export item in those days, citrus fruits. Universal rationing and price controls on food meant that from the very first day of independence, the domestic markets for food, fueled by the immense requirements of arriving immigrants in the first wave of mass immigration, were sellers' markets, with supply lagging behind increasing demand. This applied to British and continental markets for Israeli citrus in that decade too.

The expansion of farm output required, of course, corresponding growth in inputs – cultivable land, irrigation, capital stock, labor, and know-how. Cultivable land was not a constraining element in the first decade, and particularly in the first years after independence. This was can be seen in the expansion of the cultivated area of Jewish settlements by more than two times between 1948 and 1952 (Table 16). The 1952 figure includes 300,000 dunams in the Negev, about ten percent of the cultivated area, used for farming. Irrigated areas expanded by approximately the same ratio.

Farm output depended on the contribution of the Arab sector, thus on the amount of land at its disposal, but not exclusively. By 1948–49 and in the 1950s, when the Arab population lived predominantly in rural villages, cultivated land at its disposal was 21 percent of the total. By 1952, due to an agreed border adjustment implemented late in 1949 that added to Israel a group of villages in the fertile eastern section of the Sharon plain, that area grew substantially by about 74 percent. Its relative share in the total declined somewhat later, yet it was still 14 percent of the total area cultivated by Jewish farmers in 2003. The irrigated area at the disposal of Arab farmers, though, was initially minuscule – only about two percent of that at the disposal of Jewish farmers. By 2003 it was only five percent of that total. The Arab land input was accordingly most meaningful in production by dry farming techniques.

The major increase of output and product required a corresponding increase in the water supply to agriculture, which was implemented in that period. Water usage in farming approximately doubled during the short period between 1949 and 1952. A rough estimate for farm employment suggests that it increased by more than land and water usage. In any case the more reliable estimate for expansion of employment in farming for the 1950–52 period is quite consistent with the former figure. Though no estimate for the capital stock in agriculture in the period of the Mandate is available, the 32 percent increase in gross stock within two years (Table 17) speaks for itself. A proxy for that highly significant factor of production in Jewish sector farming – the number of tractors used, which grew almost fourfold between 1948 and 1950 – underlines the massive increase of capital stock which occurred in that brief period. Correspondingly, the capital-labor ratio in Jewish farming rose considerably.

The rapid expansion of these inputs focused initially on mixed farming and thus soon relieved the shortages on the domestic fresh food market. The rapid growth of production shown in the output and net product figures for 1950–52 (Table 17) relieved the shortages in the domestic markets by 1954–55. Even though Israel was again involved in a war, the 1956 Suez-Sinai campaign, rationing disappeared altogether from the system by the second half of the 1950s. Indeed, toward 1960, surpluses appeared in some farm products. the massive increase in farm output at an average annual rate of 13 percent for the decade of the 1960s was also due to the renewed focus on the foreign market for citrus, which shows by the more than twofold increase in the planted area of citrus compared to 1952. This reflected the very high priority given to exports, and to the state of the European markets, which in the 1950s offered generous, and for most of the 1960s adequate, rates of return on capital invested in what had been since the Mandatory period the traditional export of Palestine.

By the 1970s, however, Israel's domestic food market, like the European markets, was subject to pressure from Third World agricultural exports. Its expansion rate in that decade declined to only about five percent. From the 1980s onwards the expansion of demand declined further to two to three percent, similar to the growth rate of the population. This development squeezed rewards in agriculture to labor and capital, as is suggested by, among other things, the lower rate of growth of net product than of output.

IRRIGATION AND ITS NATURAL CONSTRAINT. Farming industry patterns of return were also affected by costs. This is highlighted by the peak in water usage in farming in the 1970s, and the corresponding peak in irrigated and total cultivated land a decade later. All this after a massive increase of both cultivated and irrigated land by almost threefold and sevenfold respectively during the four decades through the mid-1980s. Water usage in farming grew almost fivefold between 1949 and the mid-1970s after almost three decades of rapid expansion.

Water usage was of course limited effectively by natural constraint; Israel's water extraction from the flow of renewable fresh water sources peaked in the late 1970s. Thus, the growth of population and of water use by manufacturing forced the national water system to impose a reduction of the fresh water quota for agriculture. Seawater desalination was an option by that time, but at a very high cost that precluded its use for farm production (see below).

The great expansion of water usage and of irrigated areas in the Jewish farm sector, and also in the Arab sector – total usage went up fivefold between 1949 and 1973 – was supported by highly subsidized water prices. The growing shortage of water led among other things to the creation of sewage water treatment projects. Ultimately, however, despite the subsidies and the political clout of the Jewish farming community the price of water for farming was raised over time; since the 1970s, by about two and a half times, which in turn has affected farming costs and particularly the costs of water-intensive products – with citrus groves a striking example.

Another feature which in the longer run has affected farming costs was the rapidly rising cost of labor, reflecting the rising pattern of real wages, in the wake of rising labor productivity in competing branches; farming could not lag far behind. Wages increased by 44 percent in the 1950s, and by 1970 were twice as high as they had been in 1950 (Table 19). The citrus industry, for instance, which is both labor- and water-intensive, was therefore subjected to a significant squeeze on profitability from 1972 onward.

One way to reduce the impact of rising costs was to change the composition of the branch mix in farming. Thus in the early 1960s kibbutzim phased out vegetable growing due to its high labor intensity. Another device, which the collec-

Table 19. Labor Force, Employment, Capital Stock, Real Wages, and Productivity[1], 1950–1975

	Labor		Capital Stock[2]		"Other"			
Year	Labor Force (1)	Employment (2)	Housing (3)	"Other" (4)	Capital Stock / Labor Ratio (5) [=(4)/(1)]	Real Wages (6)	TFP[3] (7)	Unemployment Rate (%) (8)
A. Indices, 1950=100								
1950	100	100	100	100	100	100	100	11.2
1954	135	140	204	198	147	116	114	9.2
1955	138	144	228	219	159	122	125	7.4
1960	161	177	370	384	238	144	154	4.6
1965	199	224	584	664	334	182	172	3.6
1967	203	210	650	746	367	200	173	10.4
1970	219	243	826	948	433	208	218	3.8
1973	245	275	–	1231	502	219	256[4]	2.6
1975	251	289	1329	1450	577	191	254	3.1
B. Average Annual Rate of Change (%)								
1950–54	7.8	8.8	19.5	18.6	–	10.1	–	–
1954–73	3.1	3.6	–	10.1	–	6.7	–	–

Notes:
1. Index numbers rounded to the closed digit.
2. Reproducible Capital Stock. The "other" Capital Stock figures refer to private sector machinery and production facilities inclusive of structures.
3. TFP is Total Factor Productivity of the private sector exclusive of the contribution of housing.
4. Throughout September 1973, before the outbreake of the Yom Kippur War.

tive settlement movement attempted to avoid, was to employ "available cheap labor." This option came about after the 1967 Six-Day War in particular, which opened the Israeli unskilled labor market to Palestinian workers from the Gaza Strip and the West Bank. In the wake of the political developments of the late 1980s, security considerations reduced the employment of these workers – the farming and building industries were allowed to hire foreign contract labor from Southeast Asia, China, and Eastern Europe as substitutes.

The drastic reduction of the size of the citrus industry – the area under citrus cultivation was cut by 50 percent during the closing quarter of the 20th century (Table 16) – is a clear expression of the process of branch mix restructuring in Israeli agriculture at the aggregate plane. It was clearly propelled by the rising costs of labor and water, and accelerated by the rapid urbanization of the coastal plain, the historical location of citrus plantations since early in the century. Yet the comparison of the rate of decline of land under citrus, and the output of that branch (Tables 16 and 17) between 1970 and 2000, shows that output declined much less than area. This indicates, of course, substantial rising productivity.

This was indeed typical of agriculture as a whole, which also adopted the strategies of employment of cheap foreign labor and elimination of labor- and water-intensive crops. Mechanization of all stages of production from field and orchard through packing and transportation to markets was also adopted by all branches of agriculture. These strategies were supported by close linkage to the extensive agricultural counseling service run by the Ministry of Agriculture, which spread knowledge about new plant varieties and cultivation techniques developed by its agricultural experimentation stations.

An outstanding example is the major increase in the efficiency of water use, initiated in the late 1960s and spread rapidly in the following decades. This involved the transformation of irrigation technique from sprinkler technology, which first appeared in the 1930s, to drip technology based on plastic pipes below the surface of the soil, which more recently is computer- rather than human-controlled. The latter development allows timing the irrigation for nighttime, which reduces evaporation, thus saving water per unit of output. The water-saving features of the Israeli farming industry show already in the first stage of development of Israeli farming in the quarter-century between 1948 and 1973, when farm product increased almost tenfold while water usage increased only fivefold. This was the era of sprinkler irrigation technology which, in the citrus industry in particular, replaced the previous primitive flooding technique.

Yet the major accomplishment in that area occurred in the following three decades through 2003, when farm output and net product kept growing, though at a much lower rate than previously, while water usage declined. Output and net product increased by 2.4 and 2.3 times respectively between 1973 and 2003 while water usage was over 20 percent lower. This reflected the fact that 60 percent of the irrigated area had installed computerized water-saving drip technology over that period. The natural supply constraint (see above) reflected in declining water quotas (vigorously criticized by farmers) and a 150 percent increase in the (still subsidized) price of water for farming pushed the farming community to move in that direction. The same was true of the rise of the cost of labor, since the new irrigation technology also allows for significant labor savings.

THE CHANGING STATUS OF AGRICULTURE. The pattern of rising farm output and net product suggests an outstanding performance; in the somewhat more than five decades through 2004, net product grew at an average annual rate of 6.9 percent. This average obscures the significant changes which had transformed the farming industry, nor does it reveal the major change it had undergone over time in its status in terms of economic aggregates: its comparative demands upon the available economic resources and its contribution to national product and exports.

The changes in the pattern of farm output and net product over time, however, suggest insights about some of these features. The leap suggested by the product figures of 1950 compared to those of 1949 reflect the return to normal economic activity – the end of hostilities and the major release of manpower from the army after the signing of the armistice agreements in 1949. Yet the output figures for 1955, which indicate that total farm production had approximately doubled, and even more the data for 1960, showing that agricultural output was close to four times greater than it had been a decade before, means that by then Israel's farm industry had overcome the extreme scarcity of fresh food of the first years of independence. Driven by the still reasonably good European export markets for citrus, the expansion of the major export industry of the Mandate era was given high priority. Its reconstruction proceeded at a rapid pace; the area of citrus orchards peaked by the early 1970s at a level 3.5 times higher than in 1947. Correspondingly, citrus output was more than six times higher in 1973 and exports about five times higher than in 1950.

Yet though farm output and net product grew rapidly, they did not maintain the outstandingly high growth rate of the economy as a whole during the 1950s. From then through the first years of the 21st century growth rates of farm output and product declined to two to three percent annually, much lower than national product growth rates. This is a clear indicator of a structural change, underlining the transformation of farm production to meet the requirements of the domestic market. Moreover, the demand of foreign markets for citrus exports, which remained stable approximately through the 1970s, declined from the 1980s; by 1990 they were only about 50 percent of what they had been in 1980, and following the downward pressure of prices, exports, and thus total output, collapsed from 1990 on (Table 17).

Overall agricultural exports did not, however, decline along with those of citrus. These were still somewhat higher in absolute value terms in 2003 than in 1980 and previous decades. This was due to a change in the composition of farm exports. New products, flowers in particular, whose export to Europe was made feasible by air transportation from the early 1970s on, made the difference. These grew fortyfold through 2003. Though still growing in absolute terms, farm export growth lagged substantially in comparison to manufacturing exports, which grew tenfold from the early 1970s. This just underlines the growing domestic orientation of the farm industry in the closing decades of the 20th century.

The rapid erosion of the status of agriculture is demonstrated in terms of its relative contribution to employment and domestic product, shown in Table 27. In the 1950s and early 1960s agriculture offered employment to about 17 percent of the total work force. That figure was down to under nine percent by the 1970s, followed by a rapidly declining trend in the following decades to just two percent or so at the turn of the century. The trend was even stronger and more rapid in the Jewish sector labor force. The Jewish farm industry employed an ever-growing number of Palestinian workers after 1967; after the outbreak of the Palestinian Intifada (uprising, literally "shaking off") in 1987, their number declined, but they were replaced by a substantial influx of workers recruited from Southeast Asia.

The domestic product figures follow a similar trend. Farm output and domestic product grew throughout the 50-year period. Product was eight times greater after about 25 years in 1973, and 18 times greater in 2003. Yet the economy as a whole expanded at a more rapid pace. Agriculture held the line in the 1950s – its net product in 1960 was still close to 13 percent of the total, as it was in 1950; yet it declined to seven percent of the aggregate net product by 1970, followed by a rapid decline to about 1.5–2 percent 30 years later, in the first decade of the 21st century.

These data offer the best insight on the background of the change in strategy of the resettlement effort begun in the 1970s and accelerated in the 1980s. While still adhering to the resettlement goal of setting up rural Jewish settlements all over, the strategy employed to achieve this objective was changed. Resettlement, which for about a hundred years was closely linked with its historical twin, agricultural production, was diverted elsewhere. New rural settlements were designed exclusively around alternative production branches; manufacturing and later high-tech service centers served as their production infrastructure. The emergence of the automobile as a cheap, universal method of transportation made this change feasible. in response to demand, making use of their varied geographical locations, more and more older settlements also followed this pattern, in order to offer alternative employment for the younger generation.

THE ARAB RURAL ECONOMY. The product and net output figures of Table 17, and thus the industrial breakdown of employment and national product, refer to the Israeli economy as a whole, the Arab sector's contribution included. This applies also to the variable inputs of Table 17, gross capital stock, tractors, and water usage. Only specific data for inputs – cultivated and irrigated land – and implied figures for employment over time suggested by the rural population data are available. The absolute level of the output and product figures described above represent accordingly the contribution of the Arab sector inputs to farm product. Yet relationships between input and output studied with reference to the Jewish sector refer to the linkage between changes in inputs over time and the corresponding changes in outputs for this sector too. And the changes were quite similar in the two sectors. Both were subjected to a process of urbanization and correspondingly to a reallocation of labor from farm employment to other branches, and both increased substantially the area under irrigation. The latter expanded indeed by a much higher factor than the irrigated area of Jewish agriculture; the rates of expansion were about twelvefold and sixfold for the Arab and Jewish sectors respectively between 1948–49 and 2003 (Table 16). The area under irrigation in the Arab sector was, indeed, initially negligible. This indicates that the Arab rural sector, which emerged after the armistice agreement with Jordan of March 1949, had effectively no citrus plantations from the time of independence.

The dramatic increase in land cultivated by Arab farmers in Israel, by more than 70 percent as suggested by the difference between the figures of 1952 and 1948–49, occurred in the 1949–50 season. It reflected the agreement in the armistice on the Green Line, which transferred the so-called "little triangle" in the eastern coastal plain to Israeli territory. Otherwise, the pattern of the increase over time in the cultivated area is similar to the pattern followed by the Jewish sector, and it also began to decline in the late 1970s, a process that accelerated in the 1980s.

This is demonstrated by the abrupt decline of the number of rural localities and of the rural population due to the rapid growth that transformed rural localities – initially de facto, later de jure – into urban localities. It also involved a transition of a major share of the Arab labor force into nonfarm activities: the building industry, manufacturing, and services, involving the erosion and finally the elimination of almost the last vestiges of rural self-sufficiency and the transition to farm production for the market. The rapid rise of irrigated areas, from a negligible two percent of the total area cultivated by Arabs in the early 1950s, to about 17 percent (Table 16) is an obvious example of this transition. The structural change the Arab farm sector had undergone was highlighted by the specialization of the Arab sector in the cultivation of several crops, strawberries and vegetables, which are cash crops par excellence. This process, which involved integration into the market system of an industrializing society, and a major improvement in educational standards involving universal compulsory elementary school education, and from the 1970s also secondary education, inevitably had far-reaching implications; it was expressed by a major rise in Arab rural living standards.

A Generation of Rapid Growth, 1948–1973

Though punctuated by two wars and periods of economic strain, the first 25 years of Israeli independence were the heyday of economic growth. Rapid growth was indeed produced by all industrial economies in those decades. The Western European economic system in particular, emerging from the catastrophe of World War II, grew at very high rates in the first two decades following the war. Yet the nine percent growth rate of GDP for the close to two decades ending at the outbreak of the Yom Kippur War in October 1973, for which the data on economic aggregates is more reliable, puts Israel at the top of the world's growth league in this era (its performance was even better for the period 1950–73); effectively, for the whole of the 25-year period from the May 1948 Declaration of Independence through the Yom Kippur surprise. The figures for the longer period, in which growth rates were even higher, imply an annual average growth rate of ten percent, made feasible by a more than sixfold expansion of investment (Table 18). The per capita figures for GDP, affected by the very rapid growth of population, indicate much lower expansion factors. GDP per capita grew about 3.5 times compared to that of 1950. This allowed an increase of living standards, in terms of per capita private consumption expenditure, by approximately three times between 1950 and 1973 (Table 18), an average annual increase of over six percent.

Yet that growth was not a smooth process. The tremendous strains imposed on the economy at the very early stages of independence are underlined by the ratio of resources available for domestic use to GNP in 1950; resources allocated to private consumption expenditures, public sector consumption, and gross investment for the economy at large were 31 percent higher than national product. The difference between these two figures was provided by the import surplus, representing the major deficit on the current account of balance of payments. This enormous deficit had to be financed somehow. From 1949 through 1951, this meant the complete running down of Israel's meager international reserves; the country was scraping the bottom of the barrel by the end of 1951.

The major improvement here, showing in the much lower ratio of resources to GNP in 1954 (1.11), was implemented by a major change in economic policy, labeled the New Economic Policy of 1952 (see below, The New Economic Policy (NEP), 1952–1954). The persistent reduction of Israel's dependence on a net inflow of real resources to sustain the level of welfare of the Israeli polity is visible through the 1967 Six-Day War and its immediate aftermath. From that point on the tide turned, and by 1973, in the wake of the Yom Kippur War, the dependence of the economy on foreign resources to maintain its level of welfare in terms of consumption and investment expenditure increased again: it leapt to 19 percent of GNP from significantly below ten percent, where it had been hovering since 1955 (Table 18).

In the early 1970s Israel's economy was generating a national product seven to eight times higher than in the early 1950s, maintained by a population of more than three million compared to the 1.4 million of the early 1950s. This turnabout had a major impact on the economy and on society in the following decade through 1985, known later as the so-called "lost decade."

STRUGGLE IN THE FIRST STAGE, 1948–1954. The major strain imposed on the economy by the first stage of the struggle to absorb the postwar mass immigration shows in terms of the aggregates: consumption expenditures, private and public, grew approximately at the same rate of growth as national product between 1950 and 1954. The rate of expansion of resources at the disposal of the economy – the growth of which was significantly lower than the growth of national product, depending as it did on the size of the import surplus that could be financed – imposed accordingly a constraint on the level of investment. Since mass immigration was still at its height in 1951 consumption expenditure, both private and public, kept growing through 1954, though at a reduced rate. Investment thus had to decline; it was lower by 15 percent in 1953 and by five percent in 1954 than in 1950 (Table 18).

But investment was the crucial ingredient that not only provided the resources to increase rapidly the stock of housing, a vital necessity when the Jewish population more than doubled between May 1948 and the end of 1951, and kept growing at a slower rate through 1954. More than half the new immigrants were at that time still living in abandoned British army camps and corrugated iron sheds put up at the outskirts of urban areas. Investment in the capital stock of production branches to achieve rapid increases in employment and housing was a high-priority requisite for the absorption process. The 11 percent unemployment rate of 1950 and the 9.2 percent rate of 1954 are a capsule expression of the two main issues of that time, housing and employment (Table 19).

The consumption expenditures for 1954, which show that average per capita private consumption was 26 percent higher than at the peak immigration year of 1950, indicates a significant improvement on this score. This shows similarly in terms of housing stock, which increased by two times within these four years, and in terms of the unemployment rate, still towering at 9.2 percent, but already two percentage points lower than in 1950, even though the labor force had increased by 35 percent in that short period.

TOWARD THE FULL EMPLOYMENT THRESHOLD AND BEYOND. It took more than a decade, through the four peaceful post-Suez (1956) years to 1960 before the expansion of employment caught up with population growth. An unemployment rate of 4.6 percent for 1960 put the economy on the threshold of full employment, the dominating economic feature of all the industrialized economies of these decades. This was achieved even though the labor force of 1960 was 20 percent greater than that of 1954, in the wake of a significant increase of *aliyah* from 1955 onward. The rapid expansion of the labor force and employment was still at a significantly lower rate than the accumulation of capital stock. Capital stock – the stock of the production branches plus infrastructure (roads, electricity, etc.) – which had expanded by almost four times between 1950 and 1954, had accumulated at a very rapid pace of about 12 percent annually between 1954 and 1960. The capital-labor ratio, which grew by 42 percent between 1950 and 1954, expanded accordingly by another 60 percent in the ensuing six years through 1960 (Table 19). The rapidly rising total factor productivity (TFP), which was more than 50 percent higher in 1960 than a decade before, led to a somewhat lower yet still highly significant increase of real wages and contributed to the expansion of national product over and above the rates of growth of capital and labor.

The growth of national product by close to three times in the 1950–60 decade, and by 73 percent in the six years from 1954 to 1960, and a corresponding though slower growth of per capita GDP, allowed a significant improvement in living standards. Per capita household consumption expenditures in 1960 averaged more than 60 percent higher than in 1950, and were about 30 percent higher than in 1954. Housing standards, too, were in much better shape. With a housing supply greater by 3.7 times in 1960 than in 1950, and by 80 percent than in 1954, dwelling space per capita did not only increase at a higher rate than total population, it outpaced the growth of the Jewish population, which grew by 59 percent in that period.

These two indicators, the highly significant improvement of housing standards and the increase in per capita consumption expenditures dominated by nonhousing components, are a clear expression of a promising performance. An obvious indicator of what had been going on in the field of housing was the almost complete elimination of the ma'barot, the immigrant housing camps that had sprouted all over during the 1950s. This followed the provision of housing – austere, but permanent, newly built or renovated – for all newcomers.

GROWTH AND GROWTH PAINS: WADI SALIB. These figures are averages, however, and do not indicate the rising inequality in Jewish society, with a dividing line running effectively between "oldtime" settlers, specifically 1948 settlers, and new immigrants. This rift came into the open in the July 1959 riots in Wadi Salib, a dilapidated downtown Haifa neighborhood with rundown housing that had been a poor Arab neighborhood, a slum, in Mandatory times. The residents were immigrants from the Maghreb, the Arab countries of North Africa. The outburst had, therefore, an ethnic component reflecting the immigrants' sense of being discriminated against by the European Zionist establishment. Yet it had undoubtedly a solid economic cause: these people faced poor employment and economic opportunities, while the new immigrants from European countries were already being absorbed quickly into society. The outbreak of these riots was a complete surprise to the community at large and to the political establishment in particular. In their wake the Israeli political agenda was reset, with priority given to economic development and especially more even income distribution, with a focus on the large Jewish immigrant community from Arab North Africa.

Yet, in spite of this worrisome incident at the turn of the 1950s, the 1960s, effectively through the Yom Kippur surprise of October 1973, were a period of robust economic growth and rapidly rising living standards. The decade was punctuated by the policy-designed slowdown of 1966–67 (see below,

The Mid-1965-to-Mid-1967 Slowdown), clearly displayed in the 10.4 percent unemployment rate of 1967 (Table 19) and rapidly fading away in the aftermath of the June 1967 war. The growth process in that decade-plus period had finally transformed the branch structure of the economy (Table 27) and generated economic benefits all over. Private consumption expenditures per capita were more than 30 percent higher in 1965 than in 1960; by 1973 they were 71 percent higher, having grown at an annual average of more than five percent during what had been labeled the "seven good years" between the Six-Day War and the outbreak of the Yom Kippur War. Though evidently not evenly distributed among the various population strata, an expansion rate of private per capita consumption expenditures at these huge annual rates could not but filter down to the lowest income groups. Public consumption expenditures for welfare state benefits – education, health, social security – had a similar effect.

The increase of living standards over time was evidently constrained by the corresponding trends of national product and the import surplus, the sum of which had been determining the level of resources available for spending on investment. One of the most important developments from the mid-1950s through most of the 1960s was the meaningful reduction of the contribution of import surplus. This meant a reduction of dependence on foreign real resources to sustain the level of spending on consumption and investment in the domestic economy, and thus sustain welfare levels. By 1960 the ratio of resources to domestic product, which was as high as 1.31 in 1950, was down to 1.06 in 1960, and effectively stayed at that level through 1967. This suggests that the allocation of resources for consumption and investment in the Israeli economy of the 1960s required a real boost from abroad of only six percent, compared to the 31 percent required for that purpose in 1950, over and above the resources generated by domestic production. And this six percent excess over GDP of real resources had a reliable foreign financial backing through this period from the contribution of Jewish communities abroad, U.S. foreign aid, and German reparations (which ended in 1966), as well as Germany's personal restitution payments to individual Israeli residents, the flow of which even increased later on.

THE "SEVEN GOOD YEARS" AND THE MORTGAGE ON THE FUTURE. The impact of growth on rising welfare shows in a rapid rise of per capita private consumption expenditure in the 1960s, particularly during the "seven good years" between the Six-Day War and the Yom Kippur surprise attack against Israel. This was a period of full employment, and from 1970 on, overemployment – in more than one sense, years of exploding prosperity. The 11 years of relative peace along the borders between 1956 and 1967, allowing rather stable defense expenditures in terms of a rapidly rising GNP (Table 20), led to a significant improvement in public sector finances; this was expressed in the closing years of the 1950s by a major reduction in government deficit. Current expenditure on income account flows (excluding capital account operations) even had a slight surplus. Between 1960 and 1965, there was even into substantial surplus (Table 23).

This feature is underlined by the gross savings ratios of the economy at large presented in Table 20. These represent an estimate of the total of private sector and government savings. Thus from 1960 through 1965 domestic savings provided three-quarters of the resources required for investment, compared to one-quarter in the early 1950s, and somewhat more than half in the second half of the 1950s. The balance of the resources required for the major increase of investment during this period was provided by the import surplus, the ratio of which to GNP was comparatively low. Furthermore, this vital component of the total resources at the disposal of the economy had by that time sound backing, even though by the mid-1960s U.S. economic aid was terminated after Israel

Table 20. Domestic Use of Resources and Investment Import Surplus Saving Ratio (%)

Year	Consumption					Ratio to GNP (%)		
	Private	Public						
	(1)	Total (2)	Defense[1] (3)	Gross Investment (4)	Resources[2] (5)	Gross Investment (6)	Import Surplus (7)	Savings (8)
1950	38	30	7	32	100	42	31	11
1952	43	31	6	26	100	30	15	15
1954	44	33	6	23	100	26	11	15
1955	42	34	6	24	100	26	9	17
1960	44	33	7	23	100	24	6	18
1965	43	32	8	25	100	27	7	20
1967	42	44	16	14	100	15	6	9
1970	35	45	21	20	100	23	14	9
1973	32	47	24	21	100	25	19	6
1975	33	47	26	20	100	23	17	6

Notes:
1. The total public sector consumption expenditures (column 2) include defense expenditures (column 3). The figures in columns 1, 2, and 4 thus add up to 100 percent.
2. Total resources at the disposal of the economy for domestic uses, which are the sum of GNP and Import Surplus.

Table 21. Foreign Trade and Balance of Payments, 1949–1975 ($ Million)

Year	Goods and Services								1990 Dollar Prices[1]			
	Export (1)	Import (2)	Deficit (3) [=(2)–(1)]	Net Unilateral Transfers (4)	Net Foreign Interest Payments (5)	Capital Imports (6)	Long-Term Foreign Debt (7)	Foreign Currency Reserves (8)	Deficit: Goods and Services (–) (9)	Net Unilateral Transfers (10)	Foreign Debt (11)	Net Foreign Interest Payments (12)
1949	43	263	220	118	–	–	–	–	1,202	645	–	–
1950	46	328	282	90	1	107	–	–	1,552	483	–	6
1952	86	393	307	191	–	115	–	(30)[2]	1,398	942	–	–
1955	144	432	288	210	20	76	419	50	1,387	990	2,043	100
1960	336	682	346	311	51	107	599	213	1,472	1,291	2,645	223
1965	711	1,234	523	341	57	175	1,214	643	2,034	1,295	1,556	226
1967	949	1,480	531	522	–	–	1,556	715	1,710	2,042	5,842	–
1970	1,374	2,657	1,283	668	126	682	2,622	459	3,952	2,039	8,397	405
1973	2,654	5,325	2,671	2,190	–	–	4,830	1,809[3]	7,742	6,447	14,218	–
1975	3,687	7,536	3,849	1,770	388	1,033	7,617	1,184	8,511	3,289	17,371	887

Notes:
1. In terms of U.S. cost-of-living index.
2. Foreign currency reserve of 1954.
3. At the end of September 1973 reserves were 1,264 million dollars.

Table 22. Main Sources of Unilateral Transfers and Long-Term Capital Imports, 1950–1975

Year	Unilateral Transfers					Transfers Plus Credit[1]					
	Immigrants and others[2] (1)	World Jewry (2)	U.S. Government (3)	German Government[3] (4)	Total (5)	Immigrants and others (6)	World Jewry[4] (7)	U.S. Government[4] (8)		German Government (9)	Total (10)
A. $ Million											
1950	20	90	–	–	110	20	111	(45)	45	–	176
1955	35	83	21	106	245	35	131	(23)	44	106	316
1960	37	124	14	174	349	37	205	(21)	35	174	451
1965	99	206	5	130	440	99	338	(52)	57	129	623
1970	173	290	3	202	668	173	426	(343)	346	202	1,147
1975	263	506	642	359	1,770	256	595	(1,212)	1,854	359	3,064
B. Components of Transfers and of Long Run Capital Imports (Percent)											
1950	18	82	–	–	100	11	63	26		0	100
1955	14	34	9	43	100	11	41	14		34	100
1960	10	36	4	50	100	8	45	8		39	100
1965	22	47	1	30	100	16	54	9		21	100
1970	26	43	(0)	31	100	15	37	30		18	100
1975	15	29	36	20	100	8	19	61		12	100

Notes:
1. Includes American aid and long-term credits from U.S. government agencies; in 1950 from the Export-Import Bank only. The entries in brackets represent the capital account component of U.S. aid; it involved long-term credits from the U.S. government and government agencies.
2. Includes funds of immigrants and other Israeli individuals.
3. Includes reparation payments to the state of Israel, and personal restitution payments to Israeli citizens.
4. Includes contributions from the United Jewish Appeal in the U.S. and from other Jewish community appeals worldwide, plus the annual gross inflow of the Independence Loan Fund initiated in 1951 in the U.S. and later expanded to Jewish communities in other countries. Column 2 entries refer to contributions only.

was officially classified as a "highly successful graduate" of its aid program; German reparations too, which flowed into the coffers of the government, came to their planned end. Slowly rising levels of United Jewish Appeal funds, and personal restitution payments to Israeli residents, which grew for several decades, provided most of the funds required to pay for the import surplus of those years.

Though robust growth and rapidly rising living standards made feasible by an avalanche of investment starting from a cyclical trough in 1967 were maintained through the "seven good years" between the two wars, the financial infrastructure of investment was subjected to a severe shock in the wake of the Six-Day War and succeeding war of Attrition (1968–70). It was rocketing defense expenditures that made the differ-

Table 23. Public Sector Fiscal Indicators: 1949–1974[1] Ratios to GNP (%)

Year	Expenditures[2]	Tax Revenue[3]	Unilateral Transfers[4]	Absorption[5]	Deficit (–) / Surplus (+)	Net Public Debt		
						External	Domestic	Total
	(1)	(2)	(3)	(4)[=(2)+(3)]	(5)[=(4)–(1)]	(6)	(7)	(8)
1949–1951	50.7	12.8	6.5	19.3	-31.4	–	–	–
1952–1955	38.3	17.4	9.4	26.8	-11.5	–	–	–
1956	31.2	21.7	5.6	27.3	-3.9	–	–	–
1956–1960	33.7	27.9	6.7	34.6	0.9	–	–	–
1960–1965	29.2	29.0	5.7	34.7	5.5	–	–	56.5
1966	33.8	30.8	2.7	33.5	-0.3	13.3	33.8	47.1
1967–1969	43.3	33.1	4.5	37.6	-5.7	19.6	35.7	55.3
1970–1973 (Sept.)	59.6	45.3	4.0	49.3	-10.3	–	–	–
1973 (Sept.)	46.7	37.6	4.5	42.1	-4.6	–	–	–
1970–1973	62.6	44.2	6.5	50.7	-11.9	27.3	43.3	70.6
1973	73.6	43.7	15.5	59.2	-14.4	21.8	52.8	74.6
1974	74.9	47.2	8.0	55.2	-19.7	23.6	59.8	83.4

Notes:
1. The indicators refer to the "Great Government," i.e., to the fiscal cash flow of the government, the Jewish Agency, the municipal governments, and the nonprofit institutions benefiting from the government budget (universities, etc.) and receiving domestic donations and donations from abroad, mainly from Jewish communities in foreign countries.
2. Includes expenditures abroad – mainly for defense imports and net interest payments on foreign debt.
3. Includes tax revenues, receipts on interest accounts and receipts on property income accounts. From 1960 on, the revenue flow includes "virtual" receipts on civil services pension accounts.
4. Unilateral transfers of donations from abroad, flowing into the coffers of the government, the Jewish Agency and linked institutions, universities, etc., from sources such as the UJA, Universities Appeal, German reparations, and U.S. government foreign aid grants.
5. Unilateral transfers by public sector entities from donations collected abroad and foreign government grants are treated as equivalent to tax revenue, since these do not increase the national debt.

ence: they leapt from 8.5 percent of GNP in 1965 to 17 percent in 1967 (and from eight to 16 percent in terms of resources; see Tables 18 and 20), and much more in absolute terms. By 1970 these were about 24 percent of GDP. Through boosting aggregate demand and growth this imposed a major burden on the budget, and on the balance of payments, which was subjected to an avalanche of defense imports. The balanced government budget between 1957 and 1966 was by 1967, and even more so by 1970 and later, a lost cause. The deteriorating fiscal situation shows clearly in terms of government consumption expenditures, which by 1967 were almost 50 percent higher than in 1967, and by September 1973 were again higher by almost 60 percent, in real terms, than the 1967 budget, which had to cover expenditures of the Six-Day War.

The inevitable spurt in the budget deficit eroded Israel's savings rate; it was cut in half at once from 20 percent of GNP in 1965 to nine percent in 1967, declining further to six percent of GNP by 1973. The increasing rate of investment, which despite these fiscal pressures was maintained between the wars, required accordingly a substitute for the flow of domestic savings: a rapidly increasing import surplus, which was indeed achieved. But it had to be financed by borrowing abroad. in view of the huge resources required, Israel had no option but to approach the U.S. government, which indeed was forthcoming; its aid, however, was in credits, thus increasing the state's foreign debt substantially (Table 22). An increased flow of donations from Jewish communities in the Diaspora as well as funding on capital account by means of the purchase of State of Israel Bonds and direct investment in Israeli business were the other options pursued in these circumstances.

The booming economy of the almost seven interwar years, involving overfull employment between 1970 and (October) 1973, rode on a rapidly increasing total national debt. Net debt was 47 percent of national product in 1966 and rose rapidly in 1973 to 75 percent of GNP, which had in that time almost doubled. National debt in absolute (real) terms had accordingly nearly tripled. Correspondingly, the foreign debt, a component of the total national debt, rose by somewhat more than three times in nominal dollar terms (Table 23). This ominous development would figure as a major constraint on the economy in the forthcoming decade (1974–85) later referred to as the "lost decade."

THE ROLE OF INPUTS: LABOR, CAPITAL STOCK, AND PRODUCTIVITY. The growth performance, within the first 25 years of statehood, was set by the rate of expansion of primary inputs at the aggregate plane: the labor force and employment, the accumulation of human and real capital stock, and their interaction subject to improving entrepreneurship. Finally, public sector attitudes and policy had a major impact on the economy as a whole, particularly in the first decade, when comprehensive controls, including through the 1952 universal rationing, were still the order of the day. Currency control, though more relaxed than in the first decade, was still the practice by 1973 and continued for more than another decade.

The free *aliyah* policy inevitably had a major impact on the expansion of the labor force. Between 1950 and 1970 population and the labor force grew effectively at the same rate (Tables 19 and 14). Yet the size of a labor force suggests only its potential as a factor of production. Its effective contribution to the growth of output and national product depends on the state of employment, and also on its quality – a highly educated and trained labor force makes an obvious difference, in industrialized economies in particular. The pre-state Jewish population had a comparatively high education standard, quite comparable to that of industrialized Central and Western Europe and North America. About one third of the labor force had high education qualifications. This proportion declined during the 1950s. In 1947 the median number of years of schooling of immigrant males in the age range of 14+ was 9.9 years; it was down to 7.3 by 1954. The efforts put into education from the very beginning – the first law passed by the Knesset early in 1949 was the Compulsory Education Law – showed results in the statistics after a decade. By 1960 the median figure of years of schooling of the same age group of males was part of the way back toward the higher standard: it was 8.2 years. The effort to improve the qualifications of the labor force was implemented at all stages – primary, secondary, and higher education. Two higher education institutions, the Hebrew University of Jerusalem and the Technion-Israel Institute of Technology in Haifa, had fewer than 2,000 students in 1949–50, and awarded 193 degrees that year. By 1959–60 Israel already had four university-level institutions, with 9,300 students; 1,237 degrees were awarded in that academic year. By 1974–75, there were seven institutions of higher education with 52,000 students, and 8,800 degrees were awarded. By that time, Israel had certainly overcome the decline in the average qualification of its labor force that occurred in the 1950s, in the wake of mass immigration.

Employment opportunities, however, were the most significant immediate constraint on the potential contribution of the labor force to production. Employment through 1954 grew at a rate higher than the growth of the labor force; this reduced the unemployment rate, dominated by the new immigrant group, to 9.2 percent from the very high 11.2 percent in 1950. The struggle to absorb newcomers into productive activity was one of the main priorities of that decade. By its end, that effort was on the threshold of success, as the 4.6 percent unemployment rate of 1960 suggests. The threshold was finally crossed at the very beginning of the 1960s. The 3.6 percent unemployment rate of 1965 is a clear indicator of the prosperous years of the first half of that decade. The engineered slowdown of 1966–67 (see below, The mid-1965-to-mid-1967 Slowdown) generated a significant reversal to 10.4 percent. The slowdown was short-lived, however, interrupted by the outbreak of the Six-Day War. By 1968 the system was already back to full employment levels. Indeed, the 15 percent increase in employment, two times higher than the growth of the Israeli labor force by that time, could not have been implemented without the appearance of a new economic factor: Palestinian workers from the occupied territories. Employers eagerly hired them at a time of overfull employment, which was the state of the labor market and the highly prosperous economy between 1970 and October 1973.

The hiring of Palestinian workers from the West Bank and Gaza Strip reflected the preference of individual employers, in agriculture and the building trades in particular. The tightening labor markets in the closing years of the 1960s, and the much lower wage rates at which these workers could be hired, were incentives. But policy considerations of the government, supported by public opinion, were also in favor of the practice. Employment in the Israeli economy was undoubtedly beneficial to the unskilled and semiskilled laborers who dominated the labor force from the territories. Wages offered by the Israeli employers, though low in Israeli terms, were undoubtedly much higher than the alternatives in the West Bank and Gaza Strip. The response to the demands of the Israeli market was therefore rapid and highly significant in quantitative terms. By 1973, six years after the opening of the border allowing free movement across the lines, close to one-third (31.5 percent) of the total employment of residents from the territories was in Israeli enterprises and municipalities. These workers' comparatively high earnings raised substantially the living standard of the lower income strata of the territories' population in absolute terms, and undoubtedly also in relative terms compared to that of the middle class.

Yet, though Israeli employment of Palestinian workers was soon a major share of employment for the territories, it was only 5.6 percent of total employment in the Israeli economy at that time. The immediate short-run effect on the workings of the economy was accordingly considered beneficial by the political establishment. Political considerations clearly suggested that this "natural" business driven development was highly beneficial politically, as an effective instrument serving peace and stability in the short run, and rapprochement in the long run. The long-run effects of the employment of these workers at the lowest unskilled and semiskilled levels, particularly in the building trades and agriculture, on the wages and employment of low-skilled Israeli labor in the same industries, was not considered, or at least was not considered highly relevant. In the long run, however, it had a major impact on relative wages in the Israeli economy: it reduced the wages of low-skilled workers. This led to a biased income distribution, increasing the spread between the lowest tenth percentile of wage earners and those in the higher brackets. It soon induced an outflow of Israeli workers from these jobs, in the building trades and agriculture especially.

The performance of the economy in these 25 years, during which the growth rate of the economy was on average ten percent a year, was of course conditioned by the increase of the real reproducible capital stock of the production branches. This increase over time is displayed in the "Other" Capital Stock figures of Table 20. In the 23 years through 1973 it grew at an annual average of 11.5 percent. The growth rate was even greater at the very beginning; it was close to 19 percent in the 1950–54 interval, and in the 10 percent range in the following two decades though 1973.

These very high growth rates were achieved by an all-out investment effort, made feasible mainly by government control of the real resources acquired abroad – the import surplus – and the highly significant share of that inflow in the total of the resources at the disposal of the economy. Investment in the early years of the Israeli economy was accordingly very high: it absorbed between one-third and one-quarter of the total resources, which of course implies much higher ratios to national product (Tables 19–20). In spite of the major strain of mass immigration in these years, investment in infrastructure was a very high priority. Thus, the major water projects of 1950–54 – the such as the Yarkon Project providing water to the Negev and Jerusalem – absorbed ten percent of total investment (including housing) in 1950–54, which was close to three percent of GNP.

These very high investment rates in the production branches soon generated rates of expansion of capital stock significantly over and above the high growth rates of the labor force and of employment. The rising capital-labor ratio figures of Table 19 offer insight into the long-run implications of this process on productivity and on the pattern of real wages. The corresponding productivity figures (Total Factor Productivity, TFP), which represent a weighted average of the productivity curve over time, attributed to the two factor inputs – capital and labor – suggest that in the 1950–55 period, factor productivity increased by 25 percent. This means that national product increased by 25 percent more than can be attributed to the expansion of the weighted average of these two factors of production. In the five-year period preceding the war through 1973, the rate of increase of productivity was lower, in the 20 percent range per period. Yet the per capita GDP growth, which was close to 3.5 times during that 24-year period from 1950 to 1973, would not have been realized but for the increase of weighted factor productivity by approximately 2.5 times during the same interval.

The obvious economic implication of rising factor productivity is a feasible increase of the rewards – real wages – as well. This process shows clearly in the real wage figures for that period, covering the span of a generation. The rise of real wages by 2.2 times during the 1950–73 period, an average annual rate of close to seven percent, could not have been achieved without the rising capital-labor ratios, by a factor of five, and the simultaneous rising factor productivity, which implies rising average labor productivity too. The real wage pattern displays accordingly a highly important feature of the growth process: the real wages that rose rapidly even in periods of high unemployment such as 1950–55 and 1966–67 (Table 20) served as a vehicle to spread the benefits of growth widely – hired workers were increasingly a dominant group of income recipients.

On the other hand, the productivity and wage rate figures display and explain another interesting feature: between 1950 and 1955, when productivity rose more rapidly than it did for the next 18 years, wages, at least through 1954, increased more than total factor productivity. This means that no reward was left to the other factor of production – capital and those who provided it, in those years effectively the government. In 1955, a year of transition (see above, The Histadrut and the Economics of the Yishuv), things improved only marginally in that regard. Yet even in this year of recovery, unemployment was still high – 7.4 percent of the labor force, an improvement compared to the 11 percent of the early 1950s. the benefit of the very rapidly rising wages went, of course, only to the employed section of the population, which by that time included a substantial component of post-1948 immigrants. The ranks of the unemployed, however, were dominated by post-1948 immigrants, and they obviously did not benefit from the wage increase. With unemployment still about seven percent in 1957 the inevitable social tension and resentment among the immigrants in the second half of the 1950s clearly prepared the way for the 1959 Wadi Salib riots (see above, Growth and Growth Pains: Wadi Salib), even though unemployment was down to 5.5 percent in that year.

A similar feature, a significantly higher increase of real wages (owing to the success of the Histadrut Labor Federation in pushing them up) than total factor productivity, is visible in the data for 1965 through 1967, with a corresponding leap of unemployment after about six years of nearly full employment (Table 19). The slowdown of these two years, mid-1965 to mid-1967, was due, among other things, to the same feature – the rise in real wages, over and above the rise in labor productivity.

Nevertheless, the rapidly rising employment and corresponding rise of real wages linked to rising factor productivity allowed a major improvement in the welfare of a widening segment of society. This effect may be attributed to, among other factors, the rapid increase of "other" capital stock (the stock of the production branches) as well as to the increased stock of housing, which had undoubtedly a major effect on the welfare of society. The high priority the government gave to housing, which required a major fraction of investment resources, can be seen in the capital stock figures for the period. In the first years through 1955 the stock of housing grew at a higher rate than that of the production branches. This relationship reversed in the late 1950s. Yet even the 1970 and 1975 figures in Table 19 indicate that investment in housing did not lag far behind investment in infrastructure and the production branches.

There was, however, another silent, unmeasured factor that contributed to the pattern of rising national product, and thus of measured productivity improvement in terms of TFP: the accumulation of so-called "human capital," a term that surfaced in the growth literature of the 1960s. Basically, human capital is know-how, expertise, skill, acquired through education in schools, universities, training institutions, and on-the-job training (the last, though, usually also requires some previous formal training or education).

Accumulating human capital involves costs, and in industrial societies these can be heavy in view of the length of the learning process. Secondary school graduates spend 12 to

13 years studying, and those with a higher education close to two decades. These costs are measurable, but measurement of the stock of human capital offers conceptual and technical difficulties. A technique to overcome these problems, involves the use of proxy indicators, such as years of schooling of the labor force, and/or the quantitative expansion of the population of students. For the first decade through 1960, the number of students is the only available measure. From then on, better data on years of schooling and median years of schooling are available.

Thus, in the school year 1959–60, the number of students in the Jewish school system from kindergarten to university was 4.2 times greater than in 1950, and the number of students in universities 4.7 times greater. The much smaller Arab education system grew by almost the same factor. Yet Arab students at universities were at that time still a very small number. In the same period 20.1 percent of the Jewish population had 0–4 years of schooling, a similar number had 5–8 years of schooling, and only 9.9 percent of the Jewish labor force had post-secondary or higher education. The median figure for years of schooling was 8.4 years. The significance of these figures, which suggest a much higher stock of human capital even at this stage, can be seen by a comparison to the data on the Arab population. Its median was 1.2 years of schooling in 1961, with 63.4 percent in the 0–4 years bracket.

Within one decade, by 1970, the standard of education of the post-15-year-old group – effectively the whole labor force – had improved considerably. The more drastic change occurred in the Arab population. The median years of schooling of the Jewish population rose to 9.3 years, and 11.8 percent of the labor force had a post-secondary or university education, while almost 40 percent had secondary education. Correspondingly, the median years of schooling of the Arab population rose to five years and 13 percent had 9–10 years of schooling. By 1975, the median years of schooling were 10.3 and 6.5 years for the Jewish and Arab communities respectively.

These figures suggest a drastic change in the stock of knowledge of the labor force. It was already visible clearly by 1960, and supports the proposition that the rapid accumulation of human capital was a significant factor explaining rapid productivity enhancement, and thus growth of product per capita, and rising welfare.

The Balance-of-Payments Constraint

The outstanding performance of the economy in the long run, involving a 5.5 percent annual rate of increase of private per capita consumption expenditure for a generation, meant that by 1973 this expenditure was 2.5 times higher than in 1950. This is also true of public sector expenditure, which had to finance a heavy burden of defense and welfare-state spending. It required very high rates of investment, and thus a diversion of available resources to the buildup of capital stock: infrastructure, housing, and the equipment and structures used by the production branches.

This effort is demonstrated by the investment figures displayed in Table 20, which show the value of the annual flows of investment in terms of resources and GDP. Investment was above 40 percent of national product through 1951; it declined to what was still a very high percentage of GDP in 1952, and after 1954 settled to still comparatively high rates of 25 and 20 percent for the following decades. These very high rates of investment were not and could not have been financed by domestic production, as indicated by the corresponding rates of saving, which were in 1950 11 percent of GDP, and thus provided resources for only one-quarter of real capital formation in that year. The contribution of domestic savings improved later; by the mid-1950s savings contributed about one half the resources channeled into investment, and in the first half of the 1960s the contribution of savings rose further, to about 75 percent of investment. Yet this trend, which pulled the economy toward "economic independence" (the declared objective of the economic agenda of those years), turned abruptly downwards toward the 50 percent range in the prosperous years of 1967–73, which was, however, a period of combat and exploding defense spending.

The balance of resources required for these very heavy investment expenditures were provided by the huge import surplus. With its exports of goods and services less than 20 percent of its imports between 1948 and 1951 (Table 21), Israel was down to the last dollar of its foreign currency reserves. By that time the government was desperate to raise cash to pay for a tanker of crude oil to fuel the economy's electricity generation capacity. The balance of payments was clearly the dominant constraint on the activities of the system. Things improved on the foreign currency front thanks to the New Economic Policy (see below, The New Economic Policy (NEP), 1952–1954). By 1955 exports covered one third of the cost of imports of goods and services plus net foreign interest payments, which were significant due to the rising foreign debt that had been accumulating since 1949. In 1960 and through the mid-1970s, the much greater and robust economy improved its balance-of-payments current account. Exports in that period financed imports plus interest payments within a range of 45–55 percent of that total. However, even a 50 percent gap here, particularly in an economy which by 1973 generated a national product eight times greater than that of 1950, meant that the foreign payments balance was still of major relevance. It had indeed been the Achilles' heel of the system during the entire 25-year period since 1948. To finance year in and year out such unusually high foreign debt, quite out of line with those prevailing in older industrialized economies, was therefore always at the top of the economic, and thus the political, agenda. Its seriousness was underlined by the contemporary political discussion over the (quite popular) notion of economic independence.

Table 21, Foreign Trade and Balance of Payments, and Table 22, focusing on unilateral transfers and the capital account of the balance of payments, offer insight into the strategy by which successive Israeli governments attempted to maintain simultaneously high rates of investment and private and public sector consumption expenditures requiring resources significantly greater than those generated by domestic production. The thrust of their economic policy required mobilization and control of large balances of foreign finance. It depended on a major and reliable inflow of unilateral receipts, which do not create foreign debt, and from late 1949 on, long-term foreign credits, which do accumulate foreign debt. The dominant share of debt during these 25 years was credits to the government or to public sector utilities, such as the nationalized electricity utility being a case in point. The low credit rating and tight exchange controls prevailing through the early 1970s and later precluded significant private venture capital imports.

Unilateral receipts, which consisted originally only of contributions from Jewish communities abroad, were supplemented from 1952 through 1965 by U.S. government grants, and from 1953 through 1965 by West German reparations. From 1954 on German restitution payments to Israeli citizens, which increased in volume through the turn of the 21st century, were another component of unilateral payments.

The annual totals of these flows of unilateral transfers, which grew persistently over time in real terms, were clearly the mainstay of foreign finance, which made the comparatively large, and sometimes very large, input surplus feasible. Their ratio to the deficit on trade and services plus net foreign interest payments was about 55 percent through 1955. This declined later, but on the whole was still in the 40–45 percent range through 1975 (Table 21).

The balance of the funds required to even out foreign payments consisted of long-term capital imports, which in the 25 years through 1973 were predominantly on government accounts. The first attempt to obtain long-term foreign credits was confined to the U.S. In 1949, the U.S. government-owned Export-Import Bank approved two major loans of $135 million to the Israeli government. These loans were to finance purchases of American products, equipment, and raw materials for the Israeli economy. the immediate contribution of these funds to the capital stock and production facilities of the economy is suggested by the fourfold increase in the number of tractors used in Israeli farming within one year from 1949 to 1950 (Table 17). These funds were used across the board – to purchase equipment for public transportation and for manufacturing industry too.

The second avenue of entrance into the capital market was the setting up of the State of Israel Bonds organization in the U.S. This was later expanded to other industrialized countries in which substantial Jewish communities were living. Since these bonds carried similar rates of return to those of U.S. government bonds of the same term, their sales, which for years was more or less confined to members of the Jewish community, were effectively promoted as quasi-donations. By the early 1960s, after the buildup of foreign currency reserves from virtually zero in 1951, Israel's improved credit rating initiated an inflow of short- and medium-term Jewish capital from other countries, in Latin America in particular, involving government guarantees and denominated in U.S. dollars. These funds were mainly used to increase substantially the foreign currency reserves, thus improving Israel's credit significantly in the post–Six-Day War period (Table 21).

The Table 22 figures showing the sources of unilateral transfers and the sum of transfers and capital imports offer an insight into the considerations leading to a policy that relied on a huge import surplus to sustain a major investment effort during these 25 years. Note first that transfers through 1970 grew threefold in real dollar terms, while GDP grew almost sevenfold. In 1973, transfers significantly outpaced the growth of GDP. This year, similar to 1967, was indeed an exception that proved the rule: in these two years, which were years of full-scale war, transfers grew by almost 80 percent and 100 percent respectively compared to the preceding years. It was the generosity of the Jewish communities abroad that made the difference owing to the special circumstances of these two years.

These exceptions help to identify the assumption underlying the policy. This was that Israel could rely in the long run on the generosity of the Jewish communities of the world to provide a substantial flow of donations through the United Jewish Appeal. And indeed, a stable, slowly rising flow of financial resources have been put at the disposal of Israel's public sector entities. In the 1950s and through the mid-1960s there were two other stable and quantitatively predictable sources of unilateral transfers: U.S. government foreign aid, of which Israel was a recipient through 1965, and German reparations payments, whose annual level was determined in the 1951 Reparations Agreement. Another source of unilateral finance was German restitution payments to individual Israeli citizens. By the mid-1950s these were still small, but toward the late 1950s and even more in the 1960s and later these rose to a significant flow. Finally, there were the funds of immigrants, linked to the waves of immigration. These were negligible in the age of the first, poverty-stricken mass immigration of the early 1950s and through the mid-1960s, but rose in the later decades.

Table 22 offers an outline of the relative contributions of the major sources of unilateral transfers. In the years of mass immigration through 1951 the source of these funds was almost exclusively Jewish communities abroad; they provided 90 percent of the flow in 1950. By 1955 the West German government provided more than 40 percent of these funds, rising to 50 percent by 1960, as the personal restitution payments began. The German share was reduced to 30 percent by 1965, as the reparations commitment was phased out. U.S. aid provided close to ten percent in the 1950s and was also phased out by 1965. It came back with a bang after the Yom Kippur War. In any case, over these 25 years, world Jewry contributed year in and year out about 30–45 percent of unilateral transfers, a reliable flow of resources that sustained Israel's economic activity.

Capital imports – in practice, mainly foreign credits granted to the government of Israel or subject to government guarantee – were throughout that period another major source of funds used to finance a meaningful chunk of Israel's major import surplus. The two U.S. Export-Import Bank loans of $100 million and $35 million in 1949 were a case in point. A significant portion of U.S. economic aid in the 1950s and effectively the whole of it between 1965 and 1973 was in the form of long-term credits at low interest rates, funded by programs such as the Agricultural Surplus Program, designed to promote U.S. farm exports. Because of its volume, which increased considerably from 1970 on to support the purchase of major weapons systems by Israel, the sum of the foreign support of Israel's import surplus was made up of somewhat different elements from that of the transfers alone. In the crucial mass emigration era, U.S. government aid was 25 percent of that total, declining in the late 1950s to ten percent, and leaping to 30 percent of total transfers plus the capital imports component of Israel's balance of payments, as the War of Attrition along the Suez Canal and the Jordanian border peaked in the late 1960s and early 1970s. Yet the mainstay of the economic support was still world Jewry, though its share declined over time. It was about 64 percent of the total in the 1950s and 37 percent in 1970. Germany's relative contribution changed similarly *pari passu* (Table 22, section B).

The major import surplus maintained for these 25 years, which were the gestation period of the Israeli economy, was, as noted, a crucial element of the economy's transformation into a vibrant, rapidly growing system, almost fully industrialized, by around 1970. Its maintenance at high ratios in terms of the economy's aggregates depended crucially on the availability of these three finance flows, provided by world Jewry, by the U.S. government (directly and indirectly), and by the German government, year in and year out for a generation. For better or for worse, the balance of international payments served as a kind of regulator for the net inflow of foreign resources into the system. Israel's economic policy captains had of course only partial control of the size and the timing of the inflow of these resources. U.S. commitments, for instance, were annual, on the basis of its budget years; the contributions of world Jewry were for better or worse the result of the decisions of a multitude of individuals. Even the German commitments, particularly after the completion of the Reparations Agreement in 1965, were to a great extent subject to the decisions of Israeli households. It was in this sense that the balance-of-payments constraint affected behavior, at the level of the policymakers in the first instance, and by the public at large. Events in the external economic front were accordingly a key control instrument of the economy.

The Dominant Role of Fiscal Policy

The public sector had the dominant role in managing the economy because it controlled both the available resources and the instruments of policy. The public sector – that is, the "great government," defined as the government of Israel, the Jewish Agency, municipal authorities, and nonprofit institutions financed substantially by government funds – (1) was the pipeline through which most of the available foreign currency was channeled into the economy, supported by tight currency controls; (2) promoted and enabled the resettlement effort; (3) allocated resources for investment and determined the branch composition of capital formation generated by this investment; and (4) managed immigrant absorption. These functions have been outlined in previous sections. In what follows the focus is on the traditional functions of fiscal policy and measures of fiscal performance, offering a glimpse of the considerations that shaped Israeli policy, its scope and objectives, its successes and failures, and its critical turning points, over the first 25 years of statehood.

The public sector expenditure figures in Table 23 offer clear evidence on the scope of the "great government." At the very beginning, in the first three years after independence, total public sector spending was 51 percent of GNP. The highly significant reduction of its scope to 38 percent in 1952–55 is, among other things, a clear expression of a crisis situation, a crucial turning point along a bumpy road. This budgetary measure of the scope of government was reduced in the following rapid-growth decade through 1966 to about 30 percent of GNP, quite in line with the level of government expenditure in the industrial nations of Western Europe. In more than one sense, the Israeli economy was part of the post-World War II trend among these nations in which the scope of the public sector increased with major extensions of the welfare state.

Yet the expenditures from 1967 through the seven good years until the Yom Kippur surprise attack indicate another crisis situation. Expenditures leapt first to 43 percent of GNP in 1967–69, 10 percentage points higher than in 1966. This reflects mainly a much higher defense budget, due to and in the wake of the Six-Day War. The second even higher spurt in expenditures in 1970–73 to 63 percent of GNP reflects the cost of the War of Attrition, the rebuilding of the Suez Canal defense line, and later the cost of the Yom Kippur War, attributed to 1973. Defense expenditures in that year were about 29 percent of national product (Tables 18 and 20). The 75 percent of GNP fiscal expenditures of 1974 underline the burden the defense budget had imposed on the system from 1966 onward. The political crisis had had an explosive impact on the economy. Defense expenditures of about ten percent of GNP were the rule from 1960 to 1966; they rose to 20 percent of GNP on average from 1973 through 1976.

This does not suggest, however, that the rapid rise of the scope of government, as measured by public sector expenditures, was exclusively due to the defense burden. The decades between 1954 and the Yom Kippur War were an era of a rapidly expanding welfare state. The National Insurance Institute, created in 1954, served initially as a public sector instrument of the absorption process. Compulsory payroll and self-employment contributions to the universal insurance service were initially, through the 1960s, higher than the benefits paid to the insured. Entitlements were only 1.6

percent of GNP in 1957. But these grew rapidly, as more and more programs were added to the system. By 1970 benefits paid out were 5.2 percent of GNP, and by 1974 8.7 percent, which meant that social security benefits were already more than ten percent of total budget expenditures. Adding the cost of health and elementary, secondary, and higher education, we see that by 1970 at least 35 percent of the exploding budget expenditures of the 1970s were allocated to welfare state services.

The huge scope of government expenditures in terms of the initial production capacity of the economy, and the large scope later on in the post-1954 decades, required corresponding revenue. Yet tax revenues through 1951 were minuscule compared to expenditures. To these should be added the income from unilateral transfers flowing exclusively into public sector coffers – mainly to the Jewish Agency, which was put in charge of the initial absorption of immigrants in the era of mass immigration, and of the resettlement effort. Through 1951 these unilateral receipts consisted entirely of contributions from Jewish community appeals abroad; the 6.5 percent of Israel's GNP that these appeals infused into the system at this time could be conceived as a self-imposed tax on Jews all over the world. This infusion of resources was highly significant. Yet, though adding it to the meager tax revenue of that age increased the cash flow into the public sector by 50 percent, to 19 percent of GDP on average in the three fiscal years 1949–51, the public sector still generated a huge deficit, about 31 percent of GNP (Table 23). The gap in the cash flow was covered by the classical technique adopted by governments in this predicament everywhere – printing money.

The mechanics of that process and the impact on price levels of this way of evening out the government cash flow are discussed below (see The Monetary Infrastructure and Suppressed Inflation). The relevant feature in the fiscal context suggested by the data is that the three-year average through 1955 shows a drastic reduction of the fiscal deficit to 11.5 percent of GDP. Furthermore, in the following year, the year of the Suez/Sinai Campaign, the budget deficit was down to less than four percent of GNP. In the following decade, in 1966, it was pulled effectively into the black (Table 23).

The year 1952 was a critical turning point in the realm of government finances. the new Economic Policy (NEP) announced in the Knesset by Prime Minister David Ben Gurion on February 9, 1952, was based on the premise that the necessary condition for stable economic progress was to put government finances on a firm basis. This meant an immediate reduction of the current budget deficit to a reasonable level. The rapid growth of national product and the reduction of rising public sector expenditures below the rate of growth of GNP, indicated by the 38 percent ratio for 1952–55 (compared to 51 percent in 1950), made the difference.

The end of the first wave of mass immigration in 1951 helped to make this achievement more feasible. It was helped, however, by a highly significant boost on the revenue side. Note first the major relative increase of unilateral receipts, reflecting the appearance of U.S. economic aid in the form of grants starting in 1952, and German reparation payments in 1953 (Table 23). Though Israel's robust economic growth soon reduced their ratio from nine percent of GNP to 5–6 percent, these offered a stable source of revenue for more than a decade through 1965.

The further, though relatively small, reduction of the growth of public sector expenditure, which kept it within the 30 percent range through 1966, contributed to the maintenance of fiscal discipline during this period. But the real revolutionary development in the fiscal dimension of the economy occurred on the revenue side of government finances. The revenue system inherited from the Mandatory government was designed within the conceptual framework of the British colonial tradition, which, in line with the "free trade" concept, also envisioned a small government. In any case, the Mandatory model of government did not envision a government attempting to promote growth and construct a welfare state. Thus, for the first two decades of the British rule of Palestine, no comprehensive income tax was instituted.

The small ratio of tax revenues to GNP inherited from the Mandatory government reflected accordingly the absence both of the legal framework and of the experienced revenue administration required to provide significant revenues to government. These were built up during the 1950s. By 1956 the tax system collected revenues on the order of about 22 percent of GNP. By the 1960s, supported by revenue from compulsory payments to the National Insurance Institute, tax revenues amounting to 30 percent of GNP was quite comparable to those collected in the older industrial economies. In the early 1970s through 1973 tax revenues moved to very high absorption rates – 45 percent of GNP, comparable to those collected by the "high-revenue" systems of the Scandinavian countries. These rates were implemented by a major increase of compulsory National Insurance Institute payments and higher effective real income tax rates. This performance of the revenue system was a major factor in keeping tight fiscal discipline between 1955 and 1966. It thus effectively obviated the need for the government to resort to the printing press at the Central Bank.

Yet 1967 was another turning point for public sector finances: they started to move in the opposite direction. The slight 0.3 percent deficit of 1966 was caused by the severe macroeconomic slowdown, which involved a high unemployment rate. But the leap to an average annual fiscal deficit rate of 5.7 percent of GDP in the 1967–69 period was of an altogether different significance. That deficit rate was not due to failure on the revenue side; tax revenue rose considerably to 33 percent of GNP (Table 23) as a result of rapidly rising incomes and the increasing efficiency of the tax administration. The response of the Jewish communities worldwide to the 1967 Six-Day War and the subsequent War of Attrition generated a significant rise of unilateral transfers to 4.5 percent of GNP. What made the difference was rapidly mounting defense costs, which increased government expenditures by ten percentage points to 43 percent in the closing years of the 1960s.

Since the leap in government expenditures and the corresponding rise of aggregate demand were initiated at the bottom of the cycle, showing a 10 percent unemployment rate by mid-1967, the rapidly rising demand was initially absorbed by the rapid expansion of production; national product rose at an annual average of almost 14 percent in 1968 and 1969. This was facilitated by a rapid reduction of unemployment and underutilized manufacturing capacity. The inflation of expenditure thus initially pulled the wheels of the economic system forward. But toward the end of 1969, the economy was clearly on the threshold of full employment. With an unemployment rate of 4.5 percent in 1969, even though a massive inflow of Palestinian workers had already been pulled into the economy to sustain a 13 percent expansion of employment, it was at that time quite clear that by 1970 at the latest the economy would have crossed the threshold of full employment.

This eventually called for fiscal restraint, at least from 1970 on. An attempt at restraint along the revenue route was indeed implemented; owing to the significant rise of rates of social security contributions in that year, and of other tax rates, government revenue leapt from 33 to 45 percent of GNP in the 1970–73 interval. But the spurt of expenditures easily overcame the effort of restraint on the revenue side of the fiscal balance. The very high expenditure levels, averaging almost 60 percent of GNP between 1970 and September 1973 (just before the Yom Kippur War), meant that the inflationary impact of the fiscal policy could not be contained. To even out its cash flow the Treasury had no option but to use its credit facility at the Bank of Israel to print money.

The overfull employment level, underlined by the unemployment rates of 2.7 and 2.6 percent in 1972 and 1973, and the employment of a quantitatively significant group of Palestinian workers, meant that the public sector deficit of 10.3 percent of GNP from 1970 through September 1973, just before the outbreak of the war, generated heavy inflationary pressures. And indeed, this reversal, from more than a decade of tight fiscal restraint to the exploding budget deficits of the early 1970s, could not but provide the fuel for rapid inflation. This rose to double-digit rates from 1970 on. In the three prewar quarters of 1973, it was already running at an annual rate of 21 percent (Table 25).

Table 24. Monetary Aggregates and Interest Rates, 1948–1974

Year	Money Supply M1	Outstanding Credit Balances: Banks[2]	Outstanding Credit Balances: Total[3]	Bank of Israel[1]: Government Net Liabilities[4]	Bank of Israel[1]: Discounts	Interest Rates (%): Free Credit Nominal	Interest Rates (%): Free Credit Real	Interest Rates (%): Develop Credit[5] Real	Interest Rates (%): Makam Discount Rate[6] Nominal
	(1)	(2)	(3)	(4)	(5)	(6)	(7)	(8)	(9)
Indices: 1954=100									
1948	29	–	–	20	–	–	–	–	–
1950	54	–	–	59	–	–	–	–	–
1951	69	40	40	91	–	–	–	–	–
1952	74	87	–	91	–	–	–	–	–
1954	100	100	100	100	–	–	–	–	–
1955	120	111	120	–	100	7.9	3.0	–	–
1959	208	227	240	239	214	9.5	7.8	–	–
1960	253	286	286	263	363	9.5	5.9	–	–
1965	571	554	734	119	888	8.8	1.6	0.87	–
1966	575	686	877	201	1,667	8.5	0.6	4.9	7.70
1969	850	1,780	1,967	1,929	5,241	11.0	6.8	–	6.30
1970	911	2,123	2,497	2,690	6,417	18.4	7.8	-1.0	7.75
1973 (Sept.)	1,915	3,040	3,726	–	–	–	–	-13.8	8.50[7]
1973	2,115	4,063	5,062	3,502	17,895	20.5	-4.6	–	8.50
1974	2,496	–	–	5,624	30,491	24.6	-20.2	-30.2	9.25

Notes:

1. Selected Bank of Israel assets.
2. End-of-year balances. The entries in Banks, column 2, include the "free" credit and "directed" (BOI-subsidized) credit of the commercial banking system.
3. Total, column 3, also includes the balances of the government's highly subsidized "development budget" credits, for which the banks served as a conduit only, receiving fees for the service of distributing to and receiving payments from beneficiaries.
4. For the period 1948–December 1954, government net liabilities were with the Issue Department of Bank Leumi, which served as the currency board of the state before the establishment of the central bank.
5. Interest rates charged for investment credits financed by the government development budget (by "Pamela deposits") and not from commercial bank sources.
6. Makam (Hebrew acronym for short-term loan) bonds used as an instrument for policy and not as finance for government cash flow.
7. Discount rates in 1971 and 1972 were also 8.5 percent.

Table 25. Prices, Wages, and Exchange Rates, 1948–1974[1]

Year	Prices				Nominal Wages	Rates of Exchange[2]	
	Consumer C.O.L	GNP Implicit	Import Prices			Official	Effective Imports[3]
			I£	Dollar			
	(1)	(2)	(3)	(4)	(5)	(6)	(7)
A. Indices 1954=100							
1948	42.1	–	–	–	29.4	18.5	21.5[4]
1950	39.0	46.1	22.3	–	33.6	19.8	22.3
1951	46.9	53.5	–	–	43.1	19.8	22.3
1952	78.1	74.6	44.7	–	73.1	19.8	44.7
1954	100.0	100.0	100.0	100.0	100.0	100.0	100.0
1959	122.1	138.0	133.5	98.0	139.2	100.0	144.1
1960	126.3	142.2	138.2	98.0	156.1	100.0	149.2
1961	137.3	154.5	138.2	95.1	171.7	100.0	153.8
1962	151.8	167.1	153.0	93.1	193.0	166.7	173.8
1966	192.1	227.5	169.9	100.0	332.7	166.7	179.8
1967	192.5	231.8	174.2	100.0	334.0	194.4	184.3
1969	203.5	238.4	205.6	102.9	369.6	194.4	211.3
1970	244.5	263.9	217.3	103.9	402.9	194.4	221.3
1973 (Sept.)	346.5	408.4	(273.7)	113.7[5]	663.1	233.4	(225.0)[5]
1973	361.5	493.0	–	145.6	681.4	233.4	–
1974	564.7	666.6	–	200.2	927.9	333.4	–
B. Average Annual Rates of Change (Percent)							
1949–1951	3.7	–	–	–	13.6	2.3	–
1952	66.5	39.4	–	–	–	0.0	103.2
1951–1954	28.7	23.2	–	–	32.4	71.6	65.7
1954–1959	4.1	6.6	5.9	–0.5	8.4	0.0	7.6
1959–1966	6.7	6.5	3.5	0.3	12.1	7.5	3.2
1961	9.0	8.9	0.0	–3.0	10.0	0.0	3.6
1962	10.2	8.2	10.7	–2.7	12.4	66.7	13.0
1966–1969	2.0	2.4	6.6	1.0	3.6	5.3	5.5
1970–1973 (Sept.)	15.2	14.7	–	–	16.9	5.0	–
1973 (Sept.)	21.2	–	–	–	24.1	0.0	–

Notes:
1. End prices exchange rates and nominal wages.
2. Exchange rate on the U.S. dollar.
3. Effective exchange rates for imports involve the official exchange rate of the Israeli Pound (I£) plus several "disguised" impositions such as an across-the-line charge of a duty rate, etc.
4. The entry is for 1949.
5. The entry refers to the end of 1972.

The Monetary Infrastructure and Suppressed Inflation

THE EMERGENCE OF THE ISRAELI POUND. One of the first demonstrations of sovereignty made after the Declaration of Independence was the replacement of the Palestine pound (P£) with an Israeli currency. The Mandatory Palestine pound served as legal tender for more than two decades through August 16, 1948, when the Israeli government concluded an agreement with the Anglo-Palestine Bank to issue the Israel pound (I£), as it was named, and confer on it the status of legal tender. The conversion rate of a Palestine pound to an Israel pound was set at 1:1. That established a de facto exchange rate for the new currency, since the nominal value of the Palestine pound was identical to that of the British pound sterling (the exchange rate between them was 1:1). This meant that the Israel pound had, initially, the same nominal exchange rate as the British pound with the U.S. dollar and other currencies.

Neither the date of issue of the Israeli currency, nor the choice of a Currency Board to execute that function, nor the decision to locate the Department of Issue within the Anglo-Palestine Bank, were matters of chance. The exchange rate set for the Israel pound was also not plucked from thin air. All these decisions had well-founded reasons. The three months' delay of the transition to a national currency was imposed by a major foreign policy constraint, set by the United Nations decision of November 29, 1947 to establish two states within the area of Mandatory Palestine, the economies of which were to be linked by a customs union and a single currency. An immediate issue of an Israeli currency would have been inconsistent with this decision.

The implementation of the new currency was accordingly delayed until almost the last minute, even though it generated strain in the markets due to shortages of currency for transactions. This was clearly demonstrated by the appearance of substitutes – municipal coupons, etc. The unilateral exclusion of Palestine from the sterling bloc in February 1948, a clearly hostile move by the British government, and the closing of the Barclays Bank offices in beleaguered Jerusalem, which had been serving as the agent of the London-based Mandatory Issue Department, technically prevented even the use of foreign exchange to acquire Palestine pound notes from March 1948 on. In any case, the closing of the Mandatory Issue Department's Agent's offices offered a political opening for a move by Israel, which could also refer to the declared refusal of the Arab side to proclaim its independent state. In view of the urgent need for circulating money, and even more to provide the government with the required liquidity for its day-to-day operations, the government decided to take the plunge.

Since the creation of a central bank was of course an impossible feat within the first three months of independence, the currency board device was the obvious option. It suggested continuity with the previous system in the provision of monetary liquidity. Furthermore, the establishment of the Israeli Issue Department within the Anglo-Palestine Bank (APB) – the largest banking institution of Mandatory Palestine and the long-standing Zionist flagship in the realm of finance, with over 40 years of experience and presence in Palestine – followed in a sense the classical British Bank Act of 1844. It established the Issue Department as a distinct legal entity, the profits and losses of which were revenue or debit charges on the government budget. According to the covenant between the government and the APB, two representatives of the government were appointed as (minority) members of the management committee of the Issue Department. In a separate letter attached to the covenant, but not published, APB agreed that with regard to two subjects – the volume of credit allocated to the government, and the setting of its rate of discount, the management of the department "could take into consideration the point of view of the government." The covenant, which granted a monopoly for issuing currency to the APB – soon to change registration from a British to an Israeli banking corporation and adopt the Hebrew name Bank Leumi le-Israel (National Bank of Israel) – was set to last three years. Though the length of that term was a bone of contention in the negotiations, the Issue Department stayed in place for more than six years within Bank Leumi, until it was moved to the Bank of Israel, which opened its gates on December 1, 1954.

Though formally similar to its predecessor, the Mandatory Issue Department, the set of assets that it could purchase in return for its issue of currency – the only liability it could create – indicates that it was an altogether different kind of "money-creating" institution. Whereas the Mandatory entity was allowed to purchase sterling only in return for issuing Palestinian currency, and hold its reserves only in gilt-edged British government securities, the Israeli institution was empowered to own a portfolio of "domestic" assets, besides foreign currency. These included short-term Treasury bills and, following the amended legislation of 1949, Land Issue bonds (long-term government debentures), and also "commercial paper."

The last option, however, was never used. The first two, which in practice amounted to the granting of credit to the government, were soon made use of by the Treasury. To reduce the risk of an inflationary impact due to the Issue Department's legal obligation to finance the cash flow of the government, the Board of Directors of APB requested a clear legal restriction on its ability to extend credit to the government. The August 1948 legislation, which made the covenant law, included accordingly the requirement of a minimum of 50 percent foreign currency reserve against the only liquid liability of the Issue Department – the outstanding nominal balance of Israeli currency. The June 1949 amendment to the original 1948 legislation, which added Land bonds – soon to surface in the money market as an asset legally similar to foreign currency – effectively neutralized the foreign currency reserve restriction, which, however, remained in the law.

The money supply figures offer the rationale for this amendment to the original legislation designed to restrict the money supply, only one year after its enactment. Currency in circulation at the end of 1948 had increased at an annual rate of more than 100 percent, and the supply of money by 70 percent, within the seven or so months of independence, including the last quarter of that year after the successful completion of the one-month trial (mid-August to mid-September) during which the population exchanged its Mandatory currency for Israel pounds. The rapid rise in monetary liquidity continued in 1949, the first full year of the new monetary regime. The outstanding balance of currency increased in that year by 60 percent and the supply of money by almost 40 percent. All in all the money supply during the three years between the end of 1948 and the end of 1951, a period of mass immigration, grew at an annual average of about 34 percent (Table 24). This meant eventually a major inflation of the money supply.

This development was triggered by the huge deficit, the average of which was 31 percent of GNP during the 43 months through the end of 1951, in spite of the highly significant inflow of unilateral transfers from the donations of Jewish communities abroad. To even out its cash flow the Treasury sold Treasury bills to the banking system, thus borrowing at an interest rate of about 2.5 percent. These rates charged by the banks were based on the commitment of the Issue Department, made upon its opening, to purchase any quantity of Treasury bills offered to it at a discount rate within the range of 1.3–1.7 percent.

These very low interest rates were quite similar to the comparable rates in the industrialized countries at the time. Such rates were the subject of dispute between managements of central banks and national treasuries, but were still prevailing in Western Europe and North America. The discount rate range set by the management of the Issue Department was therefore not out of line with what was acceptable elsewhere at that time. Yet as in the case of the exchange rate of the Palestine pound with the Israel pound, set at 1:1 in August

1948, the discount rate, though facilitating the acceptance of the new currency and thus seemingly reasonable in the very short run, created major economic problems later.

The complication that triggered these problems involving the exchange rate and the discount rate (and thus the cost of bank credit) was the difference between inflation rates in Palestine and those in Britain and the United States. the inflation rate during the war was much higher in Palestine than in Britain. In Palestine prices rose by about three times between 1939 and 1947 (Table 13). In Britain during the same period they rose by approximately 80 percent. Since British inflation was higher than American during the war and its aftermath, the gap between Palestine's rate of inflation and that of the U.S. was even greater.

The choice of 1:1 as the rate at which Palestine currency was converted into Israeli currency (and was thus the exchange rate with sterling as well) – involved therefore a highly significant overvaluation of the Israel pound in relation to sterling, and an even greater overvaluation against the U.S. dollar. This choice offered therefore an implicit subsidy to imports and penalized exports. The difference between the average annual rates of inflation between 1939 and 1947 in Palestine (about 15 percent) and Britain (about half that) meant that inflationary expectations in Israel, still involved in a shooting war in 1948 and later subject to an avalanche of mass immigration, were much higher than in the U.K. The inevitable consequence of an interest rate for bank credit lower than the inflation rate (in line with the Issue Department's discount rate) was a strong and accelerating demand for credit by businesses and households. The highly liquid banking system was able to provide credit at low rates, in view of the low discount rate set by the Issue Department for treasury bills, which allowed banks to resupply their reserves when required, at low cost. This soon created an all-out inflation of the money supply, shown by the M1 figures in Table 24.

SUPPRESSED INFLATION, 1948–1951. The expansion of the money supply by more than by two times between the end of 1948 and 1951, at an annual average rate of 34 percent, could not but generate a major increase in the price level, though resources grew substantially too. The estimate for the growth of resources for domestic uses during the same period put the annual average rate of increase at 15–20 percent at most. Comparison with an inflation of the quantity of money by 34 percent annually suggests severe price inflation. Yet the price data in Table 25 does not, apparently, warrant the conclusion suggested by economic theory. Indeed, the data indicate that prices even declined somewhat between 1948 and 1950, and that the significant 1951 increase reflects the worldwide Korean War inflation effect of that year, which inflicted a major cost shock on the world economy, since it raised commodity prices all over the globe. However, even this shock, which also affected Israel in 1951, meant that during the first three full years of independence since the beginning of 1949, the annual average increase in prices was apparently within the three-to-four percent range. This was quite similar to the rate of price inflation to which industrial countries were subject in that postwar period.

Yet an inspection of the price data of Table 25 suggests immediately that this very low reading of the inflationary environment in Israel at that period is facile. This is the clear message to be read in the rise of the cost of living by almost 67 percent in 1952 and a further 19 percent in 1953. The price readings for the pre-1952 years, like those in its aftermath, were official prices of a price-controlled economic system subject to tight rationing. The price controls were inherited from the Mandatory period and were inevitably extended during the 14 months of active combat through the first quarter of 1949. The immediate impact of the mass immigration on the limited resources of the economy, involving in these years a huge import surplus (Table 18), financed, among other methods,

Table 26. Manufacturing, Employment, Capital Stock, Product, and Productivity, 1954 = 100

	Employment	Capital Stock	Manufactured Product	Factor Productivity	
				Manufacturing	Business Sector
	(1)	(2)	(3)	(4)	(5)
1950	74	54	80	117	88
1954	100	100	100	100	100
1955	102	115	111	106	110
1960	134	260	193	115	135
1965	183	390	362	153	151
1970	213	488	580	203	191
1973	231	639	757	228	223
1975	239	740	810	226	222
1980	244	1,038	962	235	232
1985	258	1,316	1,153	250	248
1990	264	1,550	1,270	256	272
1995	340	2,113	1,824	280	295
2000	356	3,106	2,414	312	280
2004	336	3,732	2,288	288	273
2005	–	3,866	–	–	–

Table 27. Structure of Civilian Employment and of Domestic Product, 1950–2003

Year	Agriculture (1)	Manufacturing (2)	Construction and Public Utilities[1] (3)	Public and Commercial Sector (4)	Others (5)	Total (6)
A. Employment (%)						
1950	17.3	21.2	10.7	(16.0)	(34.8)	100
1960	17.1	23.2	11.5	17.5	30.7	100
1970	8.8	24.3	9.5	24.0	33.4	100
1980	6.4	23.7	7.4	29.6	32.9	100
1990	4.2	21.7	6.2	29.6	38.3	100
2000	2.2	18.0	6.2	32.3	41.3	100
2003	1.8	16.4	6.4	33.5	41.9	100
B. Net Domestic Product (%)						
1950	11.8	28.4	10.2	21.1	28.5	100
1960	11.7	23.8	9.5	18.7	36.3	100
1970	6.9	25.7	13.6	20.3	33.5	100
1980	6.6	20.9	11.4	24.4	36.7	100
1990	3.3	22.1	8.2	24.0	42.4	100
2000	1.5	17.6	7.0	23.7	50.2	100
2003	1.7	15.3	7.3	25.5	50.2	100

Note:
1. Includes employment and product in electricity generation and distribution in the national water supply system.

by drawing on the last dollar of international reserves in 1951, led inevitably to the extension of the scope of rationing early in 1951. While European economies were at that time rapidly getting rid of the shackles of World War II-era rationing, in what the Labour government of Britain described in 1951 as a "bonfire of controls," the Israeli government felt that it had no option but to make a major move in the other direction. It attempted to increase the scope and tighten the regime of supply and rationing – the name of the ministry which later became the Ministry of Trade and Industry – by extending rationing from food to clothing, involving a point coupon book issued to every resident.

The tight and tightening rationing regime supported by price controls was, however, subject to rising pressure from the government deficit of those years (see above, The Dominant Role of Fiscal Policy), which forced the government to print money to sustain its cash flow. This rapidly inflated the volume of currency in circulation – the monetary base – and on top of that allowed an expansion of bank credit, and thus a corresponding increase of the money supply. With the money supply expanding by 138 percent between 1948 and the end of 1951, and official prices rising by only 11 percent, even an annual average 20 percent increase of resources in the economy could not have withstood the immense pressure of that avalanche of money flowing into the pockets of households and businesses during this period.

The success of the price controls and rationing inherited from the British depended inevitably and crucially on the acceptance and support of public opinion, which began to erode by mid-1950. Prime Minister David Ben-Gurion thus put his prestige on the line in a radio address, and appealed to the public to avoid resorting to, and to fight the appearance of, black markets. The increased purchasing power put into the pockets of the populace later on eroded the support of public opinion and burst the price control dam, and black markets spread rapidly. When an early election was called for June 1951 to settle a sensitive dispute over education between the religious and secular segments of the population, the main issue of the campaign turned out to be rationing and price controls.

A small liberal party, advocating the virtues of a market economy and calling for the abolition of controls, succeeded in tripling its parliamentary representation, while left-wing parties lost power. The political turn of the tide, and the growing understanding in political circles, supported by the minister of finance and top Treasury officials, that controls, and the overvaluation of the Israeli currency, are "anti-production" devices, suggested the scrapping of the supply and rationing policy. This position was strongly supported by the agricultural settlements, whose memberships were predominantly supporters of the ruling Labor Party. The major resettlement effort during these three years had generated by 1951 a substantial increase of output, but price controls prevented farmers benefiting from the sellers' market still dominating the produce markets. They could do that only by selling on the black market, which they were reluctant to do, even though they did not avoid these markets altogether. With the election campaign out of the way by midsummer, a reformulation of economic policy involving a dramatic departure from the supply and rationing/suppressed inflation model was put into practice.

The New Economic Policy (NEP), 1952–1954

The alternative model – the New Economic Policy model inaugurated formally on February 9, 1952 in the prime minister's statement in the Knesset – was much more market-oriented. It was obvious that the necessary condition for reform was a reasonable fiscal stance. Budget deficits of the size allowed during the first 44 months of independence were not a viable option any more, especially in the context of a stabilization policy. Yet, the absorption of mass immigration and the resettlement drive, which required an all-out effort to provide housing and urgent infrastructure investment in water and irrigation, roads, school facilities, etc., required a flow of investment resources beyond the small capacity of the Israeli economy to provide. The population figures alone suggest the nature of this constraint. The national product of a Jewish population of about 650,000 by mid-1948 could not have provided the resources for the investment required for a Jewish population of 1.4 million in 1951. This meant that to sustain the investment flow even at the level of 1950, a substantial import surplus was essential. Foreign finance to pay for it was equally essential.

By the end of 1951 Israel's foreign currency reserves, consisting effectively of sterling balances accumulated during World War II through 1947, which had financed partially the capital formation since 1949, were exhausted. During 1951, the Israeli government, with the full support of the Jewish leadership in the U.S., made a successful effort to set up the framework for a stable flow of foreign finance. This involved three new sources of finance, in addition to the annual contribution of United Jewish Appeal (UJA) funds of $90–100 million (current) dollars, which had already been flowing for several years. The first of these was an expected flow of about $65 million annually for 12 years from the West German government under the Reparations Agreement. This agreement was concluded in 1952 after a major, soul-searching and highly divisive political dispute that split Jewish public opinion all over the globe, and led to riots in the streets of Jerusalem in January of that year as the Knesset debated the issue. The submission of a claim for reparations was finally approved by a small majority; the agreement was finally signed in September and the flow of funds started in 1953.

The success of the Jewish leadership in including Israel among the recipients of American economic aid, involving grants, long-term loans, and credits under the U.S. farm surplus program, ensured a second stable source of about 40–50 million current dollars for more than a decade from 1952 onward. Though not formally a long-term commitment, and thus needing renewed Congressional approval annually, it was nevertheless, and rightfully, conceived as a stable source of funds. The third new source for funds on the capital account was the State of Israel Bonds organization supported by the Jewish communities in the U.S. and later in Canada (and over time in other countries with sizable Jewish communities). To avoid competition with the United Jewish Appeal, which collected contributions, and to underline its character as a businesslike organization, the Israel Bonds organization was designed to sell long-term (ten-year) government of Israel debentures carrying an interest rate similar to that of U.S. government long-term debt. This rate did not compensate, of course, for the major difference between the financial risk involved in bonds of the government of Israel and that of U.S. government debentures. The sale of these bonds was accordingly based on campaigns similar to those run by the UJA. The first campaign was inaugurated with a coast-to-coast appeal led personally by David Ben-Gurion in the winter months of 1951. These bonds soon provided a flow of close to $50 million annually. However, they involved the creation of long-term foreign debt to be repaid after 10 to 15 years. Yet what counted most in the formulation and implementation of the NEP was immediate liquidity considerations, for which the Israel Bonds funds were on an equal footing with German reparations and U.S. government aid.

The New Economic Policy was based on the assumption that a flow of roughly 150 million (current) dollars from these three sources was assured. This meant that together with an annual inflow of about $90–100 million of U.S. funds, a cash inflow of about $200–250 million annually could be counted on for investment allocation. On the basis of this assumption, even though the German Reparations Agreement had not been finalized by that time, it was possible to nail down the basic premise of the New Economic Policy: fiscal rectitude. The program committed the government to avoid budget deficits; the regular budget would be covered by tax revenue and the substantial development budget by the flow of funds from abroad.

The monetary dimension of the program committed the government to stop immediately the sale of Land Bonds and Treasury bills to the banking system and to the Issue Department to sustain its cash flow. This meant that the government was to stop forthwith printing money to finance its expenditures, as it had been doing since August 1948.

Though the respective fiscal policy and the corresponding restrictive monetary policy were to serve as the foundation of the policy, what conquered the headlines and public opinion as NEP came into the open in February 1952 was the immediate major devaluation of the Israeli currency: it was to be devalued by threefold, though that move was to be tempered initially by maintaining the previous rate of exchange for the import "essentials" (crude oil, food, and feed grains), and an intermediate rate for the import of other raw materials. That three-tier exchange rate system was eroded over time by moving more and more import items into the higher rate. When the process was finalized late in 1954, and the two lower exchange rates were eliminated, the top rate was again devalued by 80 percent. Thus, by 1955 the official exchange rate of I£1.8 to US$1.00 was higher by five times than the November 1949 rate in which Israel followed the U.K. devaluation of sterling against the dollar at the same rate of about 44 percent.

What was not revealed at the official introduction of the NEP, nor in the government response to the debate in the Knesset made by Eliezer Kaplan, the first minister of finance, who prepared the program, was the last item of the NEP program: a 10 percent tax (formally a non-price-linked loan) on money – that is, on cash and demand deposits. The delay in implementing that important component of the program was caused by a technicality: the implementation of the tax on currency required an exchange of old for new banknotes. The new notes, carrying the new Hebrew name of the issuing bank, Bank Leumi, instead of its former name, the Anglo-Palestine Bank, were not ready for distribution. In any case, the delay was fortunate since the implementation of NEP was expected, and indeed proved, to be a complicated and painful exercise.

One feature of the pain was the necessity to cut government expenditure significantly. The prime minister, who also served as minister of defense, decided to support the commitment to a balanced budget with a 20 percent cut in the defense budget. This led to the resignation of the chief of staff. A related move designed to lower expenditure was the termination of the postwar wave of mass immigration by the end of 1951. Though not actually a drastic move – it was more a passive response to the situation in the countries of origin of potential immigrants – it was still important to the success of the policy. This move was not publicized at the time. The major slowdown in the inflow of immigrants allowed accordingly a slight reduction of the absorption budget.

Yet besides the pain indicated by the rise of unemployment – in 1953 the rate rose again to 11 percent, and was still 9.4 percent in 1954 when the NEP was considered an outstanding success – it was the price explosion that imposed universal pain on households. This was not accidental; on the contrary, the leap of prices (67 percent in 1952, 19 percent in 1953) was part of the disinflation policy. It was this price explosion, combined with the 10 percent tax on money finally imposed in June 1952, that reduced at one go the purchasing power of the Israel pound, and thus the real quantity of money, which had expanded tremendously under the suppressed inflation policy though 1951. Though never stated in so many words by the prime minister or the finance minister, the adoption of the NEP meant the virtual abandonment of the supply and rationing policy pursued through 1951, thus allowing greater market control of the economy.

The first two years of the process was a bitter pill for the economy, and strained the tolerance of the political community and that of the beleaguered new finance minister, Levi Eshkol, who took over from the ailing Kaplan in the summer of 1952. Employment in 1953 was lower than in 1952; the rising unemployment led to a virtual freeze of GNP growth and of the volume of real resources in the economy. Prices rose steeply, as noted above. And the final adjustment of the exchange rate, to a level 80 percent higher than the top rate of February 1952, was about to be implemented through 1954. Under the open inflation of the NEP this was expected to raise prices further.

Yet the economic aggregate and price data for 1954 suggest that the difficult surgery of the NEP had seemingly succeeded, and the sick body of the economy was undoubtedly on the road to recovery. After almost two years of stagnation GNP shot up by about 20 percent, corresponding to the growth of employment by four percent. This reduced the unemployment rate to a still high, but significantly lower, 8.9 percent. Price inflation was down to 7.5 percent. With the government deficit of 1954–55 down to 7.5 percent of GNP it was also clear that a major fiscal improvement had been achieved (Table 23).

These results showed even more strongly in the 1955 data. With inflation down to about 5 percent and GNP starting its rapid, decade-long growth process at an annual rate of 12 percent, employment higher, and the unemployment rate at 7.4 percent, it was clear by that time that the operation had succeeded and the patient had survived. This was clearly felt among most of the population; the per capita product and private consumption expenditures were higher by 35 and about 30 percent respectively than in 1950, only five years before.

The now more regular pulse of the state also showed in what was popularly considered the measure of well-being, the rate of immigration. down to only 11,000 in 1953, it was up to 38,000 in 1955, signaling the beginning of the second wave of mass post-independence Aliyah. It lasted for a decade through 1965, and brought half a million immigrants to Israel.

The Bank of Israel (BOI) and Macroeconomic Policy, 1954–1973

THE CREATION OF A CENTRAL BANK. The last quarter of 1954 marked not only the end of the NEP, by that time already perceived as a highly successful operation. It also marked the establishment of the Bank of Israel (BOI) as the state's central bank. Its incubation period was longer than expected, so the length of service of the Issue Department at the Bank Leumi, initially set for only three years, was extended to more than six years, until December 1, 1954, at which date the Bank of Israel opened for business.

The 1954 Law of the Bank of Israel was prepared by a committee that had the advice of a panel of five (Jewish) experts, who also scrutinized the final results. one member of the panel was a top executive of a major commercial bank in the U.K., another was a member of the Board of Governors of the Central Bank of Canada, and the three others included a leading academic monetary economist in the U.S., the first director of research of the International Monetary Fund, and the secretary of the United Nations Economic Affairs Committee. The law was, of course, significantly affected by the Keynesian worldview, which dominated economic thought in the immediate aftermath of World War II. It gave the bank the classical function of central banks, making monetary policy. It provided its management with the conventional instruments of central banking, forged in the 19th century and developed in the first decades of the 20th.

The Bank's management was accordingly empowered to set minimum commercial bank reserve ratios, and to run a discount window. Through its discount rates it would have the ability to regulate the volume of currency in circulation and affect the volume of current account deposits, the two components that make up the money supply (M1). The Bank, as an institution of governance, worked in tandem with the Treasury, which in accordance with the traditional division of labor in industrialized economies, made fiscal policy.

Coordination of macroeconomic policy, the sum of these two elements (monetary and fiscal), has always been a problem for governments, and Israel's was no exception. The problem soon surfaced in the 1950s and 1960s, and focused on the inevitable issue – the momentum of growth versus price stability. The BOI Law indeed specified the two targets the Bank was to aim at: it was "to ensure the external and domestic stability of currency" and simultaneously ensure "a high level of production, employment, national income and investment."

Price stability and growth were accordingly set on an equal footing as the targets of monetary policy. But policies pursuing these two targets cannot necessarily be compatible over time. The Treasury, representing the political community, would usually focus on full employment and growth, which are not always consistent with price stability. The inflationary experience of Israel through 1951, which forced the economy to go through the drawn-out agony of the New Economic Policy, was an obvious example, just at the time the BOI commenced operations.

The task of guiding the economy along a path of virtue – growth and stable prices – was therefore considered of paramount importance by the first governor of the bank, David *Horowitz, who remained at the helm for 17 years through 1971. His freedom of action, when he believed a situation required restrictive policy such as higher interest rates and slower expansion of the money supply, was constrained by several features of the Bank of Israel Law. The most important of these was the section that allowed credit accommodation of the government by the central bank. It did involve a constraint: the volume of such an accommodation was not to exceed 20 percent "of the size of its budget." The level of such a credit was thus practically set by the decision of the Knesset's Finance Committee – a representative of the political authority, that is, the government itself. That section of the law was formulated in a "permissive" sense: the central bank was "permitted" to make an accommodation, yet not "required" to respond positively to an application for such accommodation.

The Bank of Israel's preliminary decision to change the minimum liquidity ratio required approval by the government. In practice this meant that the approval of the Ministerial Committee of Economic Affairs, of which the Bank's governor was a nonvoting member, could be delayed, partially eroded, or not forthcoming at all. Finally, the ability of the bank to have an "open market" policy, by means of which it could set its discount rate, was effectively limited owing to the shortage of financial instruments such as traded government bonds. An option to overcome this constraint was available under to a specific section of the law, but it too required government approval, which was not forthcoming for more than a decade, until 1966. The Bank's management's freedom of action to implement a restrictive monetary policy on its own volition was therefore quite limited.

Another constraint on the Bank of Israel's degree of freedom was the Ottoman-era law that put a ceiling on the legal nominal rate of interest that creditors, and thus the banking system, could charge for credit. The rate maintained through the Mandatory period was nine percent, a ceiling that was not relevant between 1920 and 1939, an era of declining, and in the late 1930s, stable, price levels. It would, however, have been an effective limit on the ability of BOI to restrict monetary expansion, even in the later 1950s, when the annual average price inflation was in the four-to-five percent range.

The only weapon entirely at the disposal of the Bank of Israel's management, through 1973 and later, was the requirement stated in section 35 of the law that "at whatever date the outstanding volume of means of payment had risen by 15 percent or more over and above its volume in the last 12 months, the governor of the bank has to publish a 'Report on the Expansion of the means of Payments.'"

This reference to the governor in person, rather than to the central bank management, underlines another inherent structural weakness of Israel's central bank through its first 50 years of existence. The BOI Law does not mandate the institution of a board of governors or a committee to be in charge of monetary policy. The only decision-making authority of the central bank is, under the law, the governor of the bank himself. He had a seven-member advisory committee with which he could consult, and a larger advisory council of 15 (including the seven advisory committee members) was also a component of the management structure. But these two bodies were entitled only to advise the governor. The actual decisions on monetary policy were his and his alone. Without the support of a board, the governor, when meeting with his counterparts from the government – the minister of finance and the members of the Ministerial Committee of Economic Affairs – was indeed going alone into the negotiating chamber.

THE BANK OF ISRAEL'S DEBUT. Despite the inherently weak position of the leadership of the institution formally charged with managing the monetary dimension of the economy, the Bank of Israel's performance in the following decade through 1965 was reasonable. During this period, Israel absorbed another half million immigrants; its population grew by 52 percent, its GDP grew by almost 10 percent annually and its per capita GDP increased by an average of 5.7 percent annually (Table 18). And this was achieved at a modest annual average rate of inflation of 5.5 percent, a rate which was not altogether out of line with inflation rates in Western European industrialized countries.

The money supply figures grew at a seemingly high annual average rate of 17 percent, a rate somewhat higher than the 15 percent at which the law required the governor to issue a formal warning – the required "report on the Expansion of the Means of Payment." Yet with GDP growth at almost 10 percent annually, and an extensive monetarization process going on both in the Arab sector of the economy, whose linkage with markets accelerated in that period, and among the substantial population of immigrants who had to acquire quickly domestic means of payment, demand for money in real terms grew on average of 13–14 percent annually. Thus, money supply grew by only a few percentage points, more rapidly than demand for it. The expansion of the money supply beyond the demand for it was accordingly minor for most of those years, with some exceptions mainly towards the end of the period. This indeed reflected fiscal discipline, maintained on the whole throughout that decade, even though Israel was again engaged in a war, the Suez/Sinai Campaign, late in 1956, following increasing tensions and military activity along the borders in 1955. The budget deficit of 1956 was only four percent, and through the following decade there were small surpluses (Table 23). The cash flow on income account of the government was accordingly evened without exceptional applications for central bank credit accommodation i.e., printing money.

Indeed, during its introductory period, through about 1960, the central bank was hardly called upon to exercise monetary restraint. Furthermore, its success in persuading the Treasury and the government to raise the legal ceiling on interest rates allowed it a greater degree of freedom in the making of monetary policy. The low inflation rates of the closing years of the 1950s (in the range of three to four percent), the higher ceiling on interest of 10 to 11 percent, and the elimination of a legal requirement to consider cost-of-living data in setting interest rates, made the difference.

Yet by late 1960, the Bank called for restrictive monetary action, due to the rise of the money supply in that year at a 22 percent annual rate, generated by an unexpected significant increase in West German personal restitution payments, converted into Israeli currency. The advisory bodies of the Bank approved the governor's proposal to raise the banks' minimum legal reserve ratio, designed to restrain their capacity to expand their current account deposits. This would have restrained the expansion of the money supply. Yet government approval of this proposal was not immediately forthcoming. It was delayed by six months, and when it finally came, the ministerial committee approved a smaller increase than the Bank had proposed. Furthermore, the ministerial approval included another erosion of the proposed restriction: it increased the quota of subsidized credit that the banking system was requested to allocate to privileged borrowers in farming and manufacturing.

In more than one sense this was the pattern of the ministerial committee's actions for the next 25 years, whenever the central bank proposed to make a restrictive monetary move. The next incident came soon: the rise of inflation in 1961 at an annual rate of nine percent, compared to the three percent average annual rate in the previous three years, and the rapidly rising restitution payments, data on which was known to the BOI by mid-1961, suggested the need for a further tightening of monetary policy. This was even more urgent in view of the discussion going on at that time between the Treasury and the Bank about a further significant devaluation of the currency. That move was necessitated by the cumulative rise of prices since 1954, the date of the last change in the nominal exchange rate.

This BOI proposal for another raise in the liquidity ratio was also delayed, and the amount of the raise shrunken. It was implemented only a year later, in the third quarter of 1962, after the February devaluation of that year – clearly another critical juncture for the Israeli economy. The devaluation had therefore taken place in an inappropriate monetary environment. Delay in the decision-making mechanism had given the political community the ultimate power in monetary matters.

THE 1962 DEVALUATION. The decision to raise the nominal exchange rate from I£1.8 to I£3 to the dollar, made on February 9, 1962, was not the result of an immediate balance-of-payments crisis, as such a hefty change might suggest. On the contrary, since the receipts of unilateral payments alone covered 80 to 90 percent of the import surplus at that time, there was no short-term foreign payments problem. The corresponding rise of net capital imports easily covered the difference between these two flows, and even allowed a significant increase of foreign currency reserves (Table 21). In 1960, reserves were seven times greater than they were in 1954, and in 1961 alone these increased by 27 percent, while GNP grew by about ten percent, the "standard" rate for that decade. This growth performance involved, among other things, a lower contribution of the import surplus to the economy – its share was down to only six percent of GNP (Table 18) – and ample reserves, which in 1954, 1960, and 1961 were a reasonable three months' worth of imports.

The decision to make the move on the exchange rate was reached after a lengthy debate in which Minister of Finance Levi Eshkol and the governor of the Bank of Israel, supported by academic opinion, were in favor of that move, and the minister of trade and industry was adamantly against it. It reflected purely long-run considerations. It was first of all the import surplus, down indeed to six percent of GNP in 1960 (higher in absolute terms), that was the concern of Treasury officials. The rising flow of unilateral transfers, the level of which was quite close to the value of the import surplus in the early 1960s, served as a medium-run insurance policy. Its importance was enhanced by the corresponding long-term capital imports, which were also rising. Yet it was also obvious that a growing economy, wedded to rapid growth, as in the Israeli case, would require a corresponding increase of imports. Even if imports and exports grew at a similar rate, the gap between them in absolute terms would get larger, requiring expansion of foreign financing – transfer payments and/or capital imports. Yet by the turn of the 1960s the grant element of U.S. aid was already phasing out, and the total of grants and long-term credits was down. Thus, even optimists who presumed that U.S. aid, in the form of long-term credit, would continue beyond 1965, thought that it would not grow in absolute terms. The predictions on German transfers, which in 1960 provided 50 percent of the unilateral receipts (Table 22), were even worse.

According to the 1952 agreement reparations would end by 1965, which meant that approximately one half the foreign currency flow from West Germany would be cut. On the assumption that individual restitution payments would continue to grow and partially compensate for the loss of reparations payments, total German transfer payments would be lower by perhaps 25–30 percent.

This reading of the situation suggested that a highly optimistic estimate of the future balance of payments would assume that the flow of transfers plus capital imports would be maintained at the approximate levels of the 1960s. Yet rapid growth required corresponding growth of imports, which would soon generate a threatening payment gap unless Israeli exports grew at a more rapid pace than imports. Devaluation of what was clearly the nominally overvalued Israeli currency was accordingly the cure prescribed by rational economic analysis.

This reasoning was supported by the relation between the nominal and effective exchange rates. The effective rate was the sum of the nominal exchange rate and the various (and differing) subsidies paid by the state to exporters of goods – citrus exporters, for instance, were paid a different, lower, subsidy for each dollar of foreign currency submitted to authorities, than, among others, exporters of manufactured goods. On the other hand, domestic producers were protected by high duties, by specific impositions over and above the nominal prices that importers had to pay for the foreign currency they required to pay for imports. These impositions were differential too and discriminated between types of product, location of plants, etc. Finally, some domestic products, textiles in particular, were protected by quotas. Thus, though the nominal exchange rate was frozen at its 1954 level, the effective exchange rate – the one that was actually in effect and generated the behavior and decisions of exporters and importers, and thus ultimately of producers and consumers in the domestic market – did change over time.

The data on the effective rate in Table 25, which represents an average of the great number of differential rates, indicates that by 1959 the effective exchange rate on imports was 44 percent higher than in 1954. In the next two years through 1961 it rose to a premium of 54 percent over and above the nominal rate set in 1954 and frozen since then. The corresponding 1961 average effective exchange rate for exports was higher by 45 percent. This nine percent gap between the effective exchange rates averages on imports and exports indicates discrimination in favor of industries selling in domestic markets over export industries. These figures reflect averages; within each of these two groupings, exports and imports, differing subsidies or impositions were assigned to specific enterprises, based on development policy. This practice generated a host of specific rates, which had accumulated haphazardly over time.

Furthermore, though by 1961 imports had the benefit of the average 54 percent higher rate of exchange and exports received a premium of 45 percent on the nominal exchange rate of foreign currency at conversion, unilateral transfers and capital imports were converted at the nominal rate. Since prices, though lagging behind the rate of increase of the effective exchange rate, were still 37 percent higher than in 1954, this meant that the real value of transfer payment funds and capital imports account was eroded by this rate, at least if the funds were converted at the official rate.

Those bearing the burden of the erosion were accordingly those who received funds on unilateral transfer and capital account. They included first of all the public sector, the government, whose real foreign receipts therefore shriveled. To maintain its level of expenditure, it thus borrowed from the central bank, from the banking system, and by issuing price- and foreign exchange-linked bonds. This option was of course not open to private sector recipients of transfers, particularly households receiving German restitution payments and immigrants who had been bringing in their own funds, nor to private sector capital imports. Any policy intended to encourage these inflows, rather than to discourage their transfer, needed to eliminate the effective confiscation of significant portions of these funds through conversion at the nominal rate of exchange. A compensating device was therefore soon invented: another "unofficial" rate of exchange, implemented by means of a complicated capital market device, which was soon applied to private capital imports too. this was added to what was called in the market vernacular of the early 1960s "the set of *one thousand exchange rates*."

The price and cost structure, and thus the allocation of resources, was soon adapted to the differential exchange rate, the impact of which is necessarily strong in small, comparatively open economies like Israel's. This, however, led to a growing distortion of the structure of the economy that reduced efficiency and eroded growth. The complicated set of exchange rates, which in practice involved several prices for the same item, a given unit of foreign currency, was wide open for abuse, and some of the abuses made headlines. The long-term distorting effect of the multi-exchange rate system, which had been growing over time with the additions to the sets of rates, prompted the eventually successful argument made by the academic economists: that there must be an immediate major adjustment to the nominal exchange rate and that all (or at least most) of the industry-specific and product-specific rates accumulated over time must be abolished. The two ministries responsible for quotas, import impositions, and export subsidies, the Ministry of Trade and Industry and the Ministry of Agriculture, were against the devaluation policy, and the Ministry of Finance and the Bank of Israel, supported by the academic economists, were in favor.

Given the differences between the nominal and the effective exchange rates, the 67 percent nominal rate devaluation announced in February 1962, exactly a decade after the initiation of the New Economic Policy, though seemingly very high, was not what appearances suggested. The effective exchange rate of imports in 1961 was already 154 on the 1954 100 base, and the export rate was at 145 on the same base. The cost effect in the markets of the official increase of the nominal exchange rate by 67 percent was accordingly nine percent at most. Weighted to account for import goods, the price effect could not have been more than about five to six percent even if no other factors were involved. Moreover, domestically the cost effect of the devaluation was at least partly compensated for by the elimination, or at least reduction, of some of the impositions that previously substituted for a higher formal exchange rate. Furthermore, due to the downward world market trend, dollar import prices declined by almost three percent in 1962, pushing the cost effect of the devaluation to at most two to three percentage points. On the other hand, the positive effect on exports should have been significantly greater, since the rate of nominal devaluation was about 15 percent higher than the effective export exchange rate of 1961. Thus even the elimination of some export subsidy items from the register in response to the devaluation should still have increased export profitability by some eight to ten percent.

Yet the long-term beneficial effects of the devaluation still hinged on the macroeconomic environment in its aftermath. The rapid growth process, reflecting robustly growing aggregate demand, is not friendly to the simultaneously cost- and demand-boosting effect of devaluation. With an unemployment rate of 4.6 percent in 1960, declining to 3.6 percent in 1961, in spite of a significant rising wave of immigration, the economy was clearly operating at full employment capacity. In these circumstances, a boost to exports to reduce the expansion, in absolute terms, of the imports surplus, which was the main immediate target of the devaluation, required a highly restrictive monetary policy, with higher interest rates, to reduce the demand on resources for domestic use – for investment and consumption.

This policy, however, was not forthcoming, due to the adamant refusal of the government to allow the BOI to pursue it. In the short run the rate of inflation increased considerably in the wake of devaluation: following the leap of inflation to nine percent in 1961, annual rates of inflation in 1962–65 ranged from 8.2 to 9.6 percent, on the verge of double digits. This was quite out of line with Israel's experience in the second half of the 1950s, and of course with contemporary rates of inflation in industrial countries. These rates, which inevitably reflected and affected the pattern of nominal wages, rose by an annual average of 12 percent between 1960 and 1965. This process rapidly eroded the higher post-devaluation real rate of exchange as well as the feasibility of hitting the original target – the reduction of the import surplus relative to GNP.

THE MID-1965-TO-MID-1967 SLOWDOWN. The reckoning of performance early on in 1965 suggested that the prediction of a slower rate of increase of unilateral transfers was right (Table 12). Yet the targeted improvement of the import surplus was not achieved – it increased not only in absolute (real) dollar terms, it grew at an even higher rate than the rapidly growing domestic product, to seven percent of GNP in 1965 compared to its six percent level since 1960. This suggested that the worries about the longer-run ability of the economy to finance the deficit on the current account of the balance of payments were justified. High inflation rates in the full-employment economy persisting for the fourth year by 1965 were another feature that required a response. This situation led to the decision of the Finance Ministry, never stated officially, to attempt to slow down the economy by employing the fiscal tools at its disposal. The slowdown was to be implemented by reducing the size of the development budget used to finance the government's infrastructure investment (cheap credits for business-sector investments in production branches and cheap mortgage credits for housing). The curtailment of the flow of mortgage finance reduced the scope of immigrant and public housing projects, which led to a slowdown in the building industry – the business cycle's leading branch – by mid-1965.

The completion of several major projects made this strategy feasible with hardly any public outcry or political fuss. The completion of the National Water Carrier in 1964 led to the reduction of expenditures on the water system from about 1.2 percent of GDP in the 1960–64 period, to 0.6 percent in 1966. The completion of the Ashdod port project, the country's second deepwater port, which was absorbing a similar fraction of resources; the end of the reconstruction of the Dead Sea Potash Works; and of a major defense project that occurred at about the same time, reduced immediately and significantly the demand for labor, equipment, and raw materials, and of course financing. What the decision on the slowdown amounted to was postponing the start of work on other major projects that were indeed in the pipeline.

The effect of these measures was eventually felt in 1966; the unemployment rate of that year, before the downward pressure on the price level, rose from 3.6 to 7.4 percent. It increased further in the first prewar quarters of 1967 to 10.4 percent of the labor force. This very rapid and substantial deterioration of economic performance reduced the inflation rate early in 1967 from the almost eight percent rate of 1966 almost to zero. The major downturn of 1966 through the first quarter of 1967 was expected by the authorities. They were thus already inclined to initiate fiscal re-expansion to reduce the impact of the slowdown. The unexpected outbreak of the Six-Day War in June 1967 engendered of course an immediate reversal of the economic cycle, which soon turned vigorously upwards.

THE "SEVEN GOOD YEARS" AND THE DEMISE OF MONETARY CONTROL, 1967–1973. The vigorous rise of aggregate demand in the third quarter of 1967 was fed by the dramatic surge in defense expenditures. Domestic defense expenditures were 6.9 percent of a depressed GNP in 1966, higher by only one percent than in 1965. These however averaged almost 13 percent in the six-year period of 1967–72, in which national product grew by leaps and bounds: the GNP of 1972 was almost 80 percent higher than that of 1966. Thus by the outbreak of the October 1973 war, domestic defense expenditures in real terms were close to three times higher than they were before the Six-Day War. These expenditures were generating direct public sector demands for supplies and labor across the board; the size of the standing army, inclusive of reserves, grew significantly. A major fraction of the defense expenditure was channeled to defense industries, whose scope of activity and demand for resources grew astoundingly in that period. Employment in the defense manufacturing sector in 1972 was 2.5 times its size in 1966, and involved 20 percent of employment in manufacturing.

That all-out defense effort showed immediately as it surfaced in the fiscal balance, which for a decade between the Sinai Campaign of 1956 and the Six-Day War of 1967 was not running a deficit on its regular budget expenditures; for most of these years it was even in surplus. Only in 1966 did a slight deficit surface, which was in any case quite warranted economically in view of the slowdown of that year. Yet in the three years from 1967 to 1969 a highly significant deficit averaging 5.7 percent of GNP appeared. And in those three years and the three quarters of 1973 before the unexpected outbreak of the Yom Kippur War, the fiscal rectitude pursued since 1952 collapsed altogether. The annual average deficit of 10.3 percent of GNP is the obvious illustration.

This, however, did not result from Treasury negligence on the revenue front. On the contrary, tax revenue actually leapt from the 31 percent of GNP in 1966 to 45 percent on average for 1970–September 1973. That very high absorption rate, and its overall increase, reflected also the very rapid growth of national income. First of all, however, it was an expression of expanding tax legislation, which among other things significantly increased National Insurance Institute rates. Furthermore, the tax absorption effort also benefited at this stage from the inflationary increase of income, since income tax exemptions were not calibrated to inflation. It was also supported by a meaningful growth of unilateral transfers. These grew significantly in absolute terms: from the trough of 2.7 percent of GNP to four, even 4.5 percent of Israel's much higher GNP of the early 1970s. It reflected also the return of U.S. aid in the form of grants, paying mainly for defense imports from the U.S., and of course the major increase in donations from Jewish communities abroad.

Yet this major rise in public sector revenue could not cope with the flood of rising expenditures. This pattern was not due only to the all-out expansion of defense expenditures. It was also due to a substantial simultaneous increase of the scope of the welfare state, and of the role of the National Insurance Institute, in particular. Its canopy was significantly increased by the widening of the child allowance program and several other small programs in the early 1970s. Nevertheless, through 1972, after a hefty increase in payroll contributions in 1970, it was still paying its way – in 1965 its revenue from contributions was still 30 percent higher than the flow of its benefits. Yet by 1973 its flow of receipts was lower than the benefits, which amounted to roughly two percent of GNP. Substantial increases of expenditure in other welfare state budgetary items, such as education and health, were also implemented in those years, thus contributing to the dangerous increase in the budget deficit.

The overall expansionary fiscal policy characterizing the seven good years called evidently for a restrictive, and after 1970 highly restrictive, monetary policy. The Bank of Israel's failure to convince the minister of finance, and thus the Ministerial Committee of Economic Affairs, to restrict the monetary avalanche in the wake of the 1962 devaluation shows clearly in the interest data for that period. Instead of rising, interest rates continued to decline, even after the devaluation of 1962–65, though monetary policy in the wake of such a move in a full-employment context requires the very opposite.

The post-Six-Day War expansionary fiscal policy began late in 1967, leading to a rise in aggregate demand. A countervailing restrictive move by the central bank was again the order of the day. At this juncture, the BOI was much better equipped to follow along a restrictive policy on its own volition and the timing of its management's choice. This was due to a contract signed with the Treasury in April 1966, in the altogether different very high-unemployment context of that time, with nobody expecting a war within a year. According to this document, the Treasury put at the disposal of the BOI a significant quota of short-term Treasury bonds, or *Makam* (the Hebrew acronym for "short-term loan"). The central bank was allowed to sell or buy them in the money market at discount rates and timing determined by itself. This meant of course that the BOI was handed the option, which it did not have previously in 1961–65, to run open market operations. The Treasury agreed not to use the proceeds of Makam sales deposited at the BOI for its cash flow. It nevertheless still kept ultimate control of the open market operations, since BOI could not sell more than the allocated quota. Thus, on the volume of sales, the Treasury still had the size of the quota as a control mechanism. In 1966 and the prewar quarters of 1967 the Treasury did not bother to control the volume of open market purchases, since these were of course expansionary monetary moves.

Moving into the arena in the recessionary third quarter of 1966, the BOI was initially purchasing Makams rather than selling. By the beginning of 1968 the economy was on the road to recovery. Employment was nine percent higher than in 1967, and the unemployment rate was down to 6.4 percent. The very great expansion of money in 1967 – by 26 percent pushing interest rates downward – was by that time in the sights of BOI management. Its open market desk thus entered the money market vigorously on the selling side, raising the discount rate in 1969 to 6.3 percent from the lowest rate of the series, 5.8 in 1968. The abolition of the legal ceiling for the nominal interest rate in 1970 offered leeway for further restrictive moves, reflected in Table 24 in a further rise in the discount rate to 7.75 percent.

Yet this proved to be too little too late. The final attempt to restrain monetary inflation was made in 1971, when the discount rate was raised to 8.5 percent after a struggle with the Treasury, which was unhappy even with the 1970 adjustment. The interesting feature of this process in which the BOI attempted to implement a restrictive monetary policy was the growing reluctance of the political community represented by the Ministerial Committee of Economic Affairs to allow it to proceed. Yet the data for two subperiods of the seven good years between the wars indicate clearly that the policy of the Ministry of Finance was a crucial mistake. In the first subperiod, embracing the three years from 1967 through 1969, when the BOI was allowed to pursue a restrictive monetary policy, the money supply grew by only about 14 percent, not significantly beyond the growth of demand for liquidity generated by the 10-to-11 percent growth of GNP supported by a monetarization process. During this period, in which by 1969 the economy was operating at the threshold of full employment, and in which there was even a small devaluation against the dollar, prices rose by an annual average of only two percent. Yet as the economy clearly passed the brink of full employment and moved into a period of overfull employment – the unemployment rate was down to 3.8 percent in 1970, and was only 2.7 percent in 1972, even though Palestinian workers were already employed all over – a highly restrictive policy was evidently called for.

At this juncture, however, the BOI was unable to turn the screws tighter. The inevitable result of the expanding fiscal deficits of these years, not countervailed by restrictive monetary moves, was a monetary explosion. The annual average expansion of the money supply in the 45 months between January 1970 and September 1973 was 31 percent. This explosion carried prices to an annual 11 percent inflation rate in 1970, where it hovered though 1972. In the last nine months prior to the Yom Kippur War, inflation in Israel was running at 21 percent annually. This clearly signified a major failure of macroeconomic policy. And it preceded the outbreak of the unexpected war, and thus could not be attributed to it.

The Manufacturing Drive and the Restructuring of the Economy, 1954–1973

The price explosion during the 45 months from 1970 through September 1973, with inflation rising to an even higher double-digit rate for the fourth year running, might suggest a reversion to the environment of the early 1950s; the 1973 prewar inflation rate, 21 percent, was similar to the inflation rate of 1953. Yet the economy of 1973 was altogether different, and not only because of its size. At the outbreak of the war Israel's GNP was more than seven times greater than that of 1950, and more than five times greater that that of 1954, but no less significant was the far-reaching structural change the economy had undergone during these two decades. The most outstanding feature of that change was of course the rise of manufacturing. In terms of its product, it grew to almost ten times its 1950 level, and 7.5 times its 1954 level (Table 26). This means that manufacturing product was growing at an annual average rate of more than 11 percent, outpacing the very rapid growth of GNP, which was around nine to 10 percent in that period.

By the early 1970s manufacturing was the main production branch in terms of inputs (capital stock and employment) and product. In 1970 24 percent of the total labor employed in that full-employment period, and almost 26 percent of national product, were in manufacturing (Table 27). The growth of capital stock clearly outpaced the expansion of employment in that branch, which meant a rising capital-labor ratio. This trend accelerated significantly from the 1960s through the early 1970s, when the highly capital-intensive defense industries surged dramatically.

Israeli industry of the 1950s was still in its early phase. The identification of manufacturing as the growth branch par excellence was made only later, after the 1956 Suez/Sinai Campaign, toward the end of the first decade of independence. Although traditional Zionist policy had identified the resettlement process with the establishment of agricultural settlements, by this time even its most fervent supporters were coming to accept that this had to change. A market constraint imposed by the limitations of demand for farm products (resulting in overproduction of some that had been in short supply just a few years before), and a supply constraint imposed by the natural limitations of the availability of water, both suggested that these settlements were close to the maximum employment that could offer a decent living standard. This led to a new consensus on the policy of economic development, designed to maximize the absorption of immigrants: priority shifted to the development of manufacturing industry.

This shift first appeared in the late 1950s in the program for the Lachish region, in the center of which was to be built a major urban center based on manufacturing, the new town of Kiryat Gat. It was planned as the location of a new major textile manufacturer, Polgat (an acronym formed from the name of the entrepreneur who was to build and run this entity, and the name of the town). A similar industrial hub, based on a textile combine, was to be built in the new town of Dimonah in the arid, empty eastern Negev. Three other new immigrant towns, Kiryat Shemonah in Galilee, and Sederot and Ofakim in the western Negev, were to follow the same model of manufacturing base and service center for new farm settlements, which toward the end of the 1950s had already been operating for several years.

This shift of priorities toward manufacturing shows clearly in the input and production data of Table 26, which record features of manufacturing industry, and in Table 17, which documents inputs and product in agriculture through the 1970s. Initially, farming production grew at a much higher rate than manufacturing. By 1954 manufacturing product was 25 percent greater than in 1950, while that of farming grew by 80 percent – reflecting the booming sellers' market for fresh food in the first decade of the state. But by 1962 manufacturing had drawn even with farming in terms of product growth, and from that point onwards it was always ahead.

This was due to the growth of inputs. Until approximately 1955, when Pinhas Sapir, the new minister of trade and industry, announced the industrialization drive, the expansion of employment in the two branches was similar. After a decade, by the mid-1960s, the growth of employment in manufacturing (and handicrafts) overtook by a significant measure that of agriculture. By 1970, the growth of farm employment has stopped, while manufacturing employment kept growing. This was the end of the story; agriculture, which employed a significant share of the labor force – 17.3 percent of the total in 1950 – and maintained that share through 1960, was down to only nine percent by 1970, while manufacturing employment expanded at a more rapid pace than total employment between 1950 and 1970, when almost 25 percent of total employment was in manufacturing and handicrafts.

The comparative trends of investment and thus capital stock follow a similar pattern. Both branches had had the benefit of a major investment drive, generating corresponding expansion of their capital stock. Yet by 1960 capital stock at the disposal of manufacturing was almost five times greater than a decade before, while that in farming, which also grew very rapidly, was less than three times its 1950 size.

The comparative factor productivity of manufacturing displays an interesting feature. While that for the whole business sector increased significantly between 1950 and 1955, reflecting the success of agriculture and other industries on this score, that of manufacturing declined. This was of course the period of mass immigration, during part of which the economy was under the supply and rationing regime. The price upheaval of 1952 might have distorted the complicated productivity estimates for the period, thus exaggerating the erosion of productivity in manufacturing. But by 1965, at the end of a decade of rapid growth, manufacturing drew even with the business sector as a whole in terms of productivity, and from that point on kept ahead (Table 26). Since the productivity measure for the whole business sector is heavily affected by that of manufacturing, due to its significant weight in the total, this suggests of course that its performance on that score had been much better than that of several other manufacturing sub-branches.

As is the case in any industry, manufacturing consists of a variety of types of activity. Thus any industrialization drive orchestrated by the government would require a decision about focus. The protected domestic market, short of basic manufactured consumer goods, was at this juncture the obvious priority for manufacturing activity. The obvious lines of business for development were food processing, textiles and clothing, and of course building materials, which in 1952 accounted for 17, 23, and 8 percent respectively of total employment in manufacturing. To these, metal machinery and electronic equipment, lines that had expanded rapidly during World War II, and by 1952 accounted for 23 percent of total employment in manufacturing, might be added.

The establishment of major textile works and food processing factories was therefore at the heart of the first industrialization drive in the latter half of the 1950s. This choice reflected not only market considerations; resources were also relevant. There was a shortage of private entrepreneurs and private investment capital, as well as of managerial experience and general know-how. The low capital intensity of these industries, which meant that they offered a high number of employment openings per unit of capital investment, made them better able to accommodate the shortage of investment funds. They also required a less highly skilled labor force, so that they could more easily employ immigrants who lacked industrial experience.

Furthermore, in these two lines managerial skills and know-how were available. Two major private-enterprise textile conglomerates had been established in the Jewish community of Mandatory Palestine in the 1930s, and textiles and clothing had been primarily Jewish industries in prewar Eastern Europe (and in South America, where many Jewish entrepreneurs had fled), whence came most of the new immigrants. Thus, the effort to persuade Jewish entrepreneurs to invest in the textile industry, which also would receive government funding, was high on the agenda. It did generate a response; the Polgat conglomerate of Kiryat Gat was one example.

These traditional manufacturing activities, operating in the protected domestic market of the late 1950s and early 1960s, could not offer much potential for export penetration into the markets of major industrialized economies. Others could; by the early 1960s, Israel had a pioneering pharmaceutical industry. It had been established in the early 1930s; the academically trained and technically skilled manpower required for it was provided in that decade by immigrants from Germany and several other Central and Eastern European countries. It bloomed during the war years, when the Middle East was cut off from European and North American supplies. This situation provided it with the war-protected British military market and those of other Middle Eastern countries. Consequently, it could already hold its own in postwar foreign markets. The same was true of the chemical industry, which, after the reconstruction of the Dead Sea Potash Works, the first stage of which was completed in the late 1960s, developed rapidly.

Yet the real breakthrough of Israel's manufacturing industries into the world market occurred with the emergence of the high-tech electronics industry in the 1960s. This date is highlighted by the fact that the Central Bureau of Statistics 1960 Yearbook had no entry for electronics in its manufacturing industry tables. Yet in the Yom Kippur War, the Kfir fighter jet produced by Israel Aircraft Industries (IAI), a government-owned corporation employing close to 10,000 workers, was already engaged in combat with the Egyptian and Syrian armies. The major components of this fighter jet, though not its engine, were produced by IAI or its subsidiaries; its highly advanced state-of-the-art electronics were designed and produced in Israel. This aircraft symbolized the entry of Israeli manufacturing into the era of high-tech. If textiles were the focus of the first stage of the industrialization drive of the late 1950s and early 1960s, the rapidly expanding defense industries were the engine of the second stage in the late 1960s and through the early 1970s.

Employment in this industrial complex, by that time mostly owned and run by the government, grew by 4.4 times between 1960 and 1972, while that of manufacturing as a whole grew only twofold. Thus, by 1973, about 20 percent of industrial employment was offered by defense industries. Furthermore, since the capital intensity of the production of the sophisticated components of these industries was and is much higher than in other manufacturing sub-branches, the capital stock of the former necessarily expanded at an even higher relative rate. The expansion of manufacturing in the two decades from 1954 to 1973, and its conversion into the major industrial branch in terms of employment, capital stock, production, and from the 1960s onwards, exports, was to a great extent due to the performance of the defense industries.

Exports were undoubtedly a highly meaningful expression of the structural change the Israeli economy had undergone in the 25 years between the Declaration of Independence and the Yom Kippur War. In 1950 the dollar value of industrial exports (exclusive of diamonds) was only about 50 percent of the value of farm exports; by 1970 industrial exports were more than three times greater than farm exports. This, of course, underscores the major transformation of the real dimension of economic activity. In 1950 agriculture was still employing 17 percent of the labor force, compared to 21 percent in manufacturing and handicrafts, and agricultural production was almost 12 percent of net national product. That of manufacturing was 28 percent. By 1970 agriculture was down to only 8.8 percent of total employment while manufacturing employed close to 25 percent of the labor force. By that date, the contribution of agriculture to the NNP was down to 6.9 percent, while that of manufacturing was about 26 percent (Table 27). Israel's socioeconomic structure had been transformed and now exhibited the characteristics of a highly industrialized economy, in which urban manufacturing and services dominated.

ECONOMIC SLOWDOWN, REVIVAL OF ALIYAH, AND THE EMERGENCE OF HIGH-TECH, 1974–2004. The three decades in which Israel's economy moved into its maturing stage between the early 1970s and the first years of the 21st century through 2004 were on the whole significantly affected by war and war-generated strains. It was the Yom Kippur War and its immediate political aftermath that set the economic agenda at the beginning of that period, soon followed in the early 1980s by the 1982–84 Lebanon campaign, which involved an occupation of a significant slice of south Lebanon. The outbreak of the first Palestinian Intifada late in 1987 shifted the focus from the armies of neighboring Arab states to a struggle with Palestinian resistance, which on and off after several short pauses in the 1990s, was restarted on a full scale late in 2000.

This had of course far-reaching domestic political implications and inevitably affected the economy. Soaring defense expenditures that through the whole of the 1970s required the allocation of resources of an order of 25–30 percent of national product imposed a heavy burden on the economy at large, and also on the fiscal system, which almost collapsed under the strain.

Yet in spite of these challenges to the system and populace, the overall economic performance was seemingly reasonable. GDP was higher by more than three times in 2004 than it was in 1973, and the product of the business sector even grew

Table 28. Resources, National Product, Consumption, and Investment: Total and Per Capita[1], 1970–2004

Year	Resources[3]	GDP		Consumption		Gross Investment	Per Capita[2]			Ratio of: Resources / GNP
		Total	Business	Private	Public Sector		GDP	Consumption Private	Consumption Public	
	(1)	(2)	(3)	(4)	(5)	(6)	(7)	(8)	(9)	(10)
A. 1973 = 100										
1970	73	76	76	79	70	69	84	87	77	1.14
1973	100	100	100	100	100	100	100	100	100	1.19
1975	107	110	109	108	113	101	105	103	108	1.17
1980	115	128	125	134	100	83	109	115	85	1.04
1985	131	149	150	168	104	83	116	131	81	1.03
1989	158	172	179	221	98	94	126	161	72	1.04
1990	172	184	194	233	106	117	128	162	74	1.07
1995	251	247	279	340	115	221	147	202	68	1.09
2000	301	309	361	430	134	246	162	225	70	1.06
2004	309	321	371	479	141	191	156	233	68	1.05
B. Average Rate of Change										
1970–73	10.9	9.4	9.4	8.1	12.6	13.1	5.9	4.6	9.1	–
1973–85	2.3	3.3	3.4	4.4	0.3	-1.6	1.2	2.2	-1.8	–
1985–2004	4.6	4.1	4.9	5.6	1.6	4.5	1.6	3.0	-0.9	–
1985–1989	4.7	3.7	4.5	7.1	-1.5	3.2	2.1	5.3	-2.9	–
1989–2004	4.6	4.2	5.0	5.3	2.5	4.8	1.4	2.5	-0.4	–

Notes:
1. Entries are rounded to the nearest digit.
2. Derived from series in columns 2, 4, and 5, and the corresponding population data from Table 14, column 8.
3. Resources for domestic use = GNP plus import surplus (imports less exports).

by about 3.7 times. Correspondingly, private consumption expenditure grew by almost five times in these three decades, benefiting of course from the much lower expansion rate of public sector consumption expenditure. The latter grew by only 40 percent through 2004, due to the relatively stable, in absolute terms, defense expenditures. From the early 1990s on these required, therefore, only about eight to nine percent of a significantly greater GNP. The overall growth figures could not match, of course, the average nine to 10 percent growth rate of the 1948–73 period, but they still allowed a reasonable 1.4 percent annual per capita growth rate (Table 28), even though population increased rapidly, by industrial countries' standards, at 2.5 percent annually.

There was a rapid population increase in the last decade of the 20th century, due to mass immigration from the Soviet Union and, after 1991, its successor states, whose Jewish population had been released from the restrictions imposed by the Soviet state until 1989. About a million people arrived in this immigration (Table 15), lifting *aliyah* from the nadir of the 1980s and making a major change in the demographics of the Jewish population, which grew to about 5.6 million by the end of 2005 (when the total population reached almost seven million).

This growth of course affected the performance of the economy. The familiar lag in economic absorption of the immigrants had a depressant effect on per capita product, though inevitably less of one on per capita consumption. The twofold population increase in the three decades through 2003, an annual growth rate of 2.4 percent (an unusually high rate compared to other industrialized countries), offers a partial explanation of the "meager" (by its historical standards) 1.4 annual average increase in Israel's per capita GNP. It was far off the phenomenal 5.5 percent corresponding growth rate during the 25-year period ending with the Yom Kippur War (Table 18).

The comparatively very high demographic expansion also offers a partial explanation of the decline of Israel's comparative per capita product from the levels reached early in 1990, it was about 70 percent of that of the United States and about 80–85 percent of the European Union average, and declined to somewhat more than 50 percent of the U.S. and E.U. figures by 2000. For better or worse, the Israeli economy, with a population of about seven million and generating a national product more than three times its size of the early 1970s (with corresponding growth of its exports and imports) was by 2005 an entirely different enterprise than in the early 1970s. Yet though it had clearly crossed the threshold of industrialization in the interval, the progress toward that target was sloppy. The period through the mid-1980s was trying indeed, but performance and well-being improved significantly from the 1990s onwards.

The "Lost Decade": War Expenditures and Inflation, 1974–1985

THE GROWTH RECORD. The drastic decline of the growth rate of national product in the so-called "Lost Decade" (economists' name for the interval between the Yom Kippur War in October 1973 and the start of the highly restrictive Economic Stabilization Policy on July 1, 1985) can be seen in the data of Table 28. The national product of that twelve-year period grew at a rate of 3.3–3.4 percent for total and business sector products respectively, only about one third of the very high growth rate, in the range of nine to 10 percent, over the 25-year period through 1973. Per capita GDP grew at an annual rate of only 1.2 percent, about one fifth of the performance in the previous period. The growth rate of private consumption expenditure, an indicator of current living standards, expanded at less than 50 percent of the growth rate prevailing in the 1948–73 period, the so-called formative period of the state.

This decline of growth performance in the later 1970s and 1980s was not unique to Israel. Mediocre performance, even dismal in some cases, as in Britain, was universal from the 1970s on throughout the industrialized countries, which had been driving the world economy in the postwar era. Low or flat output growth and higher rates of inflation led to the emergence of a new economic term, "stagflation," a shorthand expression for the two dominant economic phenomena of these years, stagnation and inflation. The simplistic and popular explanation for these features, which were indeed visible everywhere, attributed them to the so-called "energy crisis," which became the subject of headlines after the OPEC oil cartel's price hikes, the first of which was implemented on October 19, 1973, while the Yom Kippur War was still being fought. The initial quadrupling of oil prices, followed by further hikes in the 1970s through the early 1980s, at which time prices finally collapsed, undoubtedly had a significant impact on the workings of the major economies. Yet the widespread malaise of the 1970s was clearly also affected by the exhaustion of the postwar reconstruction efforts of the Western and even Eastern European economies, which had been going on from the end of World War II until 1970.

The seeds of rapid worldwide inflation were generated by the full employment U.S. economy of the 1960s, which had been pursuing a significant war effort in Vietnam while financing a major Cold War defense budget, and simultaneously implementing President Johnson's War on Poverty programs. The so-called Vietnam inflation was a fact of life in the U.S. by 1968. Given the dominance of the U.S. economy in the world at large, this could not but generate an inflationary impact on the other industrialized and fully employed economies of that era. The sudden price explosion of crude oil, and thus of energy generally, added of course to the conflagration.

THE SLOWDOWN OF ALIYAH AND THE EFFECTS OF SLUGGISH INVESTMENT. These developments had of course an immediate impact on the Israeli economy, which by 1970 had crossed the threshold into a full-employment environment, and from around 1971 moved into overfull employment. Yet structural factors specific to Israel, as well as short-run domestic developments, go a long way to explain the weak economic performance during that decade. The meaningful slowdown

Table 29. Labor Force, Employment, Capital Stock, Real Wages, and Productivity[1]

Year	Labor		Capital Stock[2]		"Other" Capital-Labor Ratio[3]	Real Wages	TFP[4]	Unemployment Rate (Percent)
	Labor Force (1)	Employment (2)	Housing (3)	"Other" (4)	(5) [=(4)/(1)]	(6)	(7)	(8)
A. 1973=100								
1970	89	85	78	77	86	91	86	3.8
1973	100	100	100	100	100	100	100	2.6
1975	102	102	154	118	116	95	100	3.1
1980	117	115	196	154	132	116	104	4.8
1985	129	124	251	182	141	123	111	6.7
1989	143	135	–	202	141	149	116	8.9
1990	147	139	298	207	141	148	121	9.6
1995	187	183	371	265	142	153	132	6.3
2000	217	218	–	391	180	178	126	8.8
2004	238	227	–	469	197	171	122	10.4
2005	(243)[5]	(237)	–	(481)	(198)	–	–	9.0
B. Average Annual Rates of Change (Percent)								
1973–85	2.1	1.8	7.9	5.1	–	1.7	0.9	–
1985–90	2.6	2.3	3.4	2.6	–	3.8	1.7	–
1990–2004	3.5	3.6	–	6.0	–	1.0	(0)	–

Notes:
1. Indices rounded to the nearest digit.
2. The "Other" Capital Stock series refers to reproducible capital stock in production branches.
3. Capital-labor ratios refer to the ratios of "Other" Capital Stock (column 4) to the labor force.
4. Total Factor Productivity refers to business sector productivity.
5. Entries in brackets are preliminary estimates.

of *aliyah*, which had been a major engine of growth for the 25 years through 1973, had undoubtedly a considerable effect on the growth pattern. Though specific to Israel, this factor was imposed by an external authority, the Soviet Union, through its policy on emigration: the flow of Jews from the Soviet Union, which between 1969 and 1973 reached 40–50,000 annually, was reduced to a trickle by 1974. Immigration thus plunged to an annual average of only 19,000 during the ensuing 15 years through 1988.

Thus, with the housing industry, the traditional leading sector of a rising economic cycle, in the doldrums, investment was low. Though the economy did grow, it was sluggish during the lost decade; the rate of growth declined successively year in and year out. Gross investment in 1985 was 83 percent of the level it reached in 1973. It revived in the second half of the 1980s, yet by 1989, in the wake of the 1985 Stabilization Policy, and before the surge in *aliyah*, it was still only at 94 percent of the 1973 levels, when GDP had been only 60 percent of what it was in 1989 (Table 28). Reflecting the dismal economic environment of the lost decade, investment in the production branches was similarly continuously lower in these years than in 1973. Its revival began only in the early 1990s, when the economy changed track (see below, The Resurrection of Growth and Restructuring).

Similarly to the reduction of the growth rate of the labor force to an annual rate of two percent during the lost decade, half what it was in 1970–73, the much lower investment rates reduced the growth rates of the capital stock of the production branches (see the figures for "other" capital stock in Table 29). The slower expansion of capital stock and of the labor force, and the state of the markets, negatively affected the productivity pattern of the economy, with an inevitable negative impact on national product. This shows in the total factor productivity data, implying lower labor productivity measurers (Table 29). TFP stopped growing altogether between 1973 and 1975, and during the lost decade grew on average at only half the rate that had prevailed in the "seven good years" between 1967 and 1973.

DISMAL FISCAL FUNDAMENTALS, 1973–1985. The strangulation of growth and the rapidly increasing inflation were due to the expansionary fiscal policy supported by a permissive monetary stance. Undoubtedly the expanding, indeed exploding, defense expenditures were the cause of fiscal expansion from 1967 on. Defense expenditures did indeed shoot up in 1967; at the end of that year these were higher by almost 80 percent than in 1966, when nobody expected an actual war. At the end of the War of Attrition along the Suez Canal in the summer 1970, defense expenditures were twice the level of 1967 in real terms. The Yom Kippur War generated a further expansion, so that at the all-time high in 1975 they reached a level never reached again through 2005; in real terms these were 55 percent higher than in 1970, thus more than five times the 1966 level in real terms.

The burden that expenditures of this magnitude imposed on the economic system is underlined by the ratios of these rising defense expenditures of domestic resources, shown in the Table 20 data which allow a comparison with defense expenditures before 1967. In one year, from 1966 to 1967, defense expenditures leapt from eight percent to 16 percent of total resources in the economy for domestic use. By 1970 defense expenditures required 21 percent of the same total. This rise reflected the 1968–70 War of Attrition and the threatening strategic environment of the Cold War, in which the Arabs had the political and military backing of the Soviet Union.

This rapid increase of defense expenditures, not only in absolute terms, but also relative to the production capacity of the economy, was subjected to another upward push by the Yom Kippur War and its aftermath; defense expenditures rose to a record high of 26 percent of resources. Since in those years resources included a substantial component of import surplus financed by unilateral transfers, including donations from world Jewry, U.S. government grants, and foreign credits, the ratios of defense requirements to production capacity, and thus to the taxing capacity of the government, offer a more meaningful picture of the tremendous burden defense imposed on the economy. The ratios of defense expenditures to domestic resources displayed in Table 30 show that these were about 21, 24, and 26 percent of Israel's GNP in 1970, 1973, and 1975 respectively. This of course means that if foreign finance had not been available, the public sector would have been required to impose taxes at these levels just to finance defense. Civilian public sector services – education, health, welfare, and roads – would accordingly have required additional taxes.

It was at this juncture, at the beginning of the 1970s, in which welfare state long-term trends and short-run political considerations imposed a further squeeze on the strained fiscal system. The social security system, which started in 1954, had been providing a net contribution to the cash flow of the government, though at declining rates, through 1972. This was due to the youth of the population, which meant that old-age benefits required a lower outflow of payments than the inflow of payroll contributions to the National Insurance Institute. Twenty years after the system began the age structure effect reduced this surplus. Furthermore, child allowances, introduced in the 1960s, were initially negligible, but substantially increased in the early 1970s, reflecting the priorities of the political community at this stage. Thus, between 1965 and 1975 the cost of old-age benefits rose by more than one percent of GNP, and the cost of child allowances grew by more than 1.5 percent of GNP. Hence, despite a major hike in payroll contributions in the early 1970s, before the war, the National Insurance Institute, which had a surplus cash flow of 0.6 percent of GNP in 1970, had a negative cash flow of two percent of GNP from 1973 onward, increasing over time.

To cope with these rapidly rising expenditures, the Treasury attempted persistently to raise tax revenues. Both rapidly rising national income and extensions of the scope of tax legislation contributed to the effort. Thus, between 1967 and 1969, tax revenues grew by 10 percentage points to 33 percent of GNP. In the almost four years before the Yom Kippur War, the rate of increase of tax revenue was significantly greater. By 1970 tax revenue was about 42 percent of GNP compared to only 31 percent in 1966, and by the outbreak of the war it rose to 44 percent (Tables 23 and 33). Furthermore, unilateral transfers, reflecting the contributions of world Jewry and U.S. defense and economic aid (which resumed in 1970 in the form of long-term loans and in 1973 as grants as well), rose very significantly (Tables 22 and 32), thus contributing to government revenue absorption. Yet the leap of absorption, defined as the sum of tax revenue, donations, and grants, was not enough, and could hardly have been large enough to countervail fully the avalanche of expenditures.

Table 30. Components of Domestic Use of Resources and Investment Import Surplus and Savings Ratios, 1970–2003

Year	Consumption Expenditures (%)					Ratios to GNP (%)		
	Private (1)	Public[1] Total[2] (2)	Defense (3)	Gross Investment (4)	Resources[3] (5)	Gross Investment (6)	Import Surplus (7)	Gross Savings (8) [=(6)–(7)]
1970	35	45	21	20	100	23	14	9
1973	32	47	24	21	100	25	19	6
1975	33	47	26	20	100	23	17	6
1980	40	44	21	16	100	17	4	13
1985	45	41	19	14	100	14	3	11
1989	52	33	13	15	100	16	4	12
1990	50	33	12	17	100	18	7	11
1995	50	28	9	22	100	24	9	15
2000	53	27	8	20	100	21	6	15
2003	56	29	9	15	100	15	5	10

Notes:
1. The totals of public sector consumption expenditures do not include direct public sector investment or benefits paid out by the National Insurance Institute.
2. The total public consumption expenditures include the corresponding defense expenditure figures.
3. The entries in columns 1, 2, and 4 total 100 (percent), i.e., the total resources in the economy for domestic use.

Table 31. Foreign Trade and Balance of Payments (in $ Millions), 1970–2004

Year	Goods and Services									At 2000 Constant Dollar Prices[1]			
	Export (1)	Import (2)	Deficit (3) [=(1)-(2)]	Net Foreign Interest Payments[2] (4)	Unilateral Transfers[3] (5)	Current Account (6) [=(3)-(4)+(5)]	Net Capital Imports[4] (7)	Net Foreign Debt (8)	Foreign Currency Reserves (9)	Deficit Goods & Services (10)	Unilateral Transfers (11)	Foreign Debt (12)	Net Foreign Interest Payments (13)
1970	1,178	2,585	-1,407	136	668	-875	682	2,622	459	5,206	2,472	9,710	503
1973	2,420	4,959	-2,539	209	2,197	-551	984	-3,283	1,809	8,126	7,032	10,507	669
1975	3,687	7,536	-3,849	718	1,770	-2,797	1,033	7,617	1,184	11,303	5,198	22,367	1,917
1980	9,791	13,567	-3,776	1,875	2,967	-2,664	1,207	11,640	3,394	7,117	5,592	21,940	5,007
1985	10,125	11,706	-1,581	2,382	4,997	1,034	94	18,574	3,720	2,307	7,290	27,099	3,475
1989	16,088	17,692	-1,604	2,212	4,876	815	88	15,665	5,331	2,071	6,297	20,231	2,857
1990	17,522	20,434	-2,887	2,204	5,906	1,060	-207	15,122	6,316	3,588	7,340	18,795	2,739
1995	27,988	37,058	-9,070	2,020	7,004	-4,086	2,231	19,217	8,309	9,940	7,676	21,061	2,213
2000	45,727	46,551	-824	7,202	6,483	-1,543	455	3,151	23,164	824	6,483	3,151	7,202
2004	50,376	52,048	-1,672	4,022	6,199	505	523	11,867	26,632	1,541	5,713	10,937	3,707

Notes:

1. Derived by applying the U.S. GDP implicit price deflator.
2. This series includes also net wage payments to foreign workers – workers from the Palestinian Authority included. These received the bulk of wages paid to foreign workers in the late 1970s and early 1980s, and only 10 percent of that total from the year 2000 onwards.
3. Net unilateral transfers.
4. Long- and medium-term capital imports.

Table 32. Main Sources of Unilateral Transfers and Long-Term Capital Imports, 1970–2004

Year	Unilateral Transfers[1]					Transfers Plus Credits[1]				
	Immigrants & Others[2] (1)	World Jewry (2)	US Government (3)	German Government (4)	Total (5)	Immigrants & Others (6)	World Jewry (7)	U.S. Government (8)	German Government (9)	Total (10)
A. $ Million										
1970	180	290	3	204	677	180	(131) 421	(339) 342	(40) 244	1,187
1973	386	742	805	264	2,197	386	(359) 1,101	(238) 1,043	(38) 302	2,832
1975	250	511	973	359	2,093	250	(310) 821	(797) 1,770	(68) 427	3,268
1980	601	460	1,495	468	3,024	601	(424) 884	(1,368) 2,863	(127) 595	4,943
1985	275	570	3,843	334	5,022	275	(525) 1,095	(5) 3,848	(138) 472	5,690
1989	1,092	706	2,727	544	5,069	1,092	(825) 1,847	(0) 2,727	(140) 684	6,350
1990	1,142	961	3,163	620	5,886	1,142	(728) 1,531	(0) 3,163	(62) 682	6,518
1995	2,523	1,206	2,679	856	7,264	2,523	(1,113) 2,319	(0) 2,679	(98) 954	8,475
2000	1,460	1,252	3,157	614	6,483	952	– –	(0) 3,157	(40) 654	–
2004	1,244	1,241	2,648	943	6,076	1,244	– –	(0) 2,648	(38) 981	–
B. Components of Transfers and Long-Run Capital Imports (%)										
1970	27	43	0	30	100	15	35	29	21	100
1975	12	24	46	18	100	8	25	54	13	100
1985	5	11	77	7	100	5	19	68	8	100
1990	19	16	54	11	100	18	23	49	10	100
1995	35	17	37	11	100	30	27	32	11	100
2000	16	21	53	10	100	–	–	–	–	–
2004	20	20	44	16	100	–	–	–	–	–

Notes:

1. The figures in brackets in columns 7, 8, and 9 refer to the flow of credits – Israel Bonds funds in the World Jewry entries in column 7, and credit funding by the U.S. and German governments in the entries in columns 8 and 9. The second figure in each column is the total of these credit figures and the Jewish contributions, U.S. government grants, and German reparations displayed in columns 2, 3, and 4.
2. Net transfers.

The balanced budget of the first half of the 1960s, which was initially in surplus on current account and effectively balanced in 1966, disappeared from the horizon for two decades through 1985. In 1967–69 the public sector was already running a significant deficit of 5.7 percent of national product. In 1970 the deficit run by the government was already beyond

Table 33. Public Sector Fiscal Indicators: Ratios to GNP (Percent), 1970–2004[1]

Year	Expenditures[2] (1)	Tax Revenue[3] (2)	Unilateral Transfers[4] (3)	Absorption[5] (4)	Deficit(-) Surplus(+) (5) [=(4)-(1)]	Net Public Debt External (6)	Domestic (7)	Total (8)
1970	58.9	42.7	3.9	46.6	-12.3	28.1	35.2	63.3
1973	73.7	43.5	16.5	60.0	-13.7	–	–	–
1975	80.1	47.1	12.0	59.1	-21.0	14.8	60.1	74.9[6]
1980	74.0	50.2	11.8	62.0	-12.0	–	–	–
1984	72.3	41.2	16.6	57.8	-(14.5)	–	–	170.9
1985	67.7	47.5	21.2	68.7	1.0	50.8	110.4	161.2
1989	58.4	44.6	8.4	53.0	-5.4	25.5	107.6	133.1
1990	57.5	44.0	8.7	52.7	-4.8	19.3	98.4	117.7
1995	54.8	46.1	4.5	50.6	-4.2	16.7	68.7	85.4
2000	50.4	43.7	4.7	48.4	-2.0	3.3	69.8	73.1
2004	51.6	43.0	3.4	46.4	-5.2	3.5	82.3	85.8
1974–77	–	–	–	–	–	–	–	113.4
1978–80	–	–	–	–	–	–	–	140.4
1981–83	–	–	–	–	–	–	–	170.9

Notes:

1. The indicators refer to the fiscal cash flow of the "great government," i.e., the government, the Jewish Agency, the municipal governments, and the nonprofit institutions benefiting from the government budget (universities, etc.), which also received domestic and foreign donations, mainly from members of Jewish communities abroad.
2. Includes expenditures abroad, mainly for defense imports and net interest payments on foreign debt.
3. Includes tax revenues, receipts of interest on development budget credits endowed to business and households (for housing), foreign receipts on interest earned by the Bank of Israel on its foreign currency revenues, and receipts on property income account. From 1960 on, the revenue flow included "virtual" receipts on civil services' pension accounts.
4. Unilateral transfers of donations from abroad, flowing into the coffers of the government, the Jewish Agency and other World Zionist Organization institutions, universities, etc., from sources such as the UJA, university appeals, yeshivah appeals, German reparations, and U.S. government foreign aid grants.
5. Unilateral transfers of public sector entities from donations collected abroad and foreign government grants are treated as equivalent to tax revenue, since these do not increase the national debt.
6. The figure refers to 1974.

12 percent of GNP and in the wake of the war it grew further, to its all-time high of 21 percent of product. The reduction of defense expenditures during the next decade through 1984 allowed correspondingly lower deficits, but these persisted beyond the 12–15 percent range (Tables 23 and 33). To even out the cash flow, the government resorted to the age-old device that governments have always used during periods of war and crisis – the printing press. Fully in line with the 1954 Bank of Israel Law, the central bank accommodated the cash flow requirements of the public sector, reflecting of course the dismal imbalance of fiscal fundamentals that surfaced in the wake of the Six-Day War in 1967, and began to generate rapid inflation. It was beyond 10 percent annually from 1970 onward.

The lag in the appearance of price inflation for three years in spite of deterioration of the fiscal fundamentals from 1967 onwards is quite explicable. The vigorous fiscal expansion, followed by a revival of investment in the second half of 1967 after the Six-Day War, occurred in the context of a depressed economic environment. The peak 10 percent unemployment rate of 1967 and the following two years of about 7.5 percent, and inevitably a corresponding underutilized capital stock, indicate the level of excess capacity. The significant average of budget deficits for the three years through 1969 of 5.7 percent of national product generated rising aggregate demand, which had first of all a quantity effect – it could be and was met by rapidly rising production. The price effect, which coincided with an upturn from a major depression, was accordingly very small, even though a devaluation of 17 percent against the dollar (the same rate as the British pound, also devalued that year) was implemented in November 1967.

These years were thus a period of rising product and incomes, at average rates beyond 10 percent, and of comparatively stable prices. Yet the unemployment rate of 3.8 percent in 1970 (even though immigration was rising rapidly from 1969 onward) and the influx of Palestinian workers from the territories who were rapidly increasing the domestic labor supply suggest that by that time the economy had crossed the full-employment threshold. This is highlighted by the unemployment rates in the range of two to three percent in 1972 and 1973 (Table 29), indicating that by that time the economy was already at overfull employment.

Highly restrictive fiscal measures were required, supported by a restrictive monetary policy, to avoid inflation in 1970, and even more so in the succeeding years through the outbreak of the October 1973 war. Yet neither of these policy measures were forthcoming. The budget deficit of 1970, at the very high level of 12 percent of GNP, and the average from 1971 through the nine prewar months of 1973 beyond 10 percent, more than twice its annual level in 1967–69 (Tables 23 and 33), underlines its impact on the inflationary developments which soon affected the economy and society as a whole. In view of the fiscal expansion, which was accommodated, rather than countervailed (see below, The Sterilization of Monetary Policy), the 22 percent annual inflation rate of the nine prewar months of 1973 (Table 36) was, of course, no surprise. That major prewar turn-up of inflation could not be attributed to the unexpected war, nor to the environment of foreign markets, in which inflation also was rising at the time. The most inflationary industrial economy of 1973, Britain's, was undergoing only single-digit inflation.

The immediate impact of the war, which generated a skyrocketing budget deficit of 21 percent of GNP in 1975, added of course to the conflagration (Table 33). Inflation was already running at 40 percent in that year, and in 1976. After a failed attempt to liberalize currency controls late in 1977, inflation took off at 50 percent and soon, towards the end of 1979, crossed the triple-digit mark. It finally accelerated to 400 percent in 1984.

The reduction of defense expenditures in the second half of the 1970s, after a temporary increase in 1981–82 linked to the invasion of Lebanon, made the significant reduction of the budget deficit from the 21 percent of 1975 to the 12–14 percent range of the early 1980s feasible. At such deficit levels, which inevitably required corresponding central bank credits to even out the government's cash flow, a reduction of inflation running at rates beyond 100 percent annually was of course impossible. Government effort to reduce the size of the gap involved the impositions of ever-higher tax rates. These succeeded indeed in pushing tax revenue temporarily to a record high of almost 50 percent of GNP by 1980, which supported the reduction of the deficit to the 12 percent range.

Yet real tax revenue was lower by nine percent of GNP in 1984 than it was in 1980. And this was not due to a reduction of tax rates: it reflected, rather, the dynamic effect of inflation – which by that time was beyond 100 percent annually for the fifth year – on the fiscal fundamentals. These were eroded by the so called "Tanzi Effect," which describes a feature of the behavior of taxpayers and tax transmitters (employers deducting income tax and social security contributions, businesses charging purchase taxes) in economies in which inflation runs at about three percent or more per month. Since, owing to administrative constraints, it is feasible to collect tax revenue only once a month, or at most every 15 days, taxpayers, even law-abiding taxpayers, pay only on the very last day.

Table 34. Monetary Aggregates, 1970–2005

Year	Money Supply		Outstanding Credit Balance[1]		Bank of Israel	
	M1/GDP (Percent) (1)	M1 (2)	Total (3)	"Free" (4)	Government Net Liabilities (5)	Discounts[2] (6)
A. Indices: 1970=100; 1985=100						
1970	17.7	100	100	100	100	100
1973 (Sept.)		193	176	178	–	–
1973	18.8	219	192	181	130	279
1975	17.6	313	427	299	310	659
1980	6.3	1,991	892	891	1,292	9,100
1984	3.8	7,881	–	–	9,084	35,848
1985	3.6	28,170	3,104[3]	30,020	28,756	47,644
1985	–	100	100	100	100	100
1989	5.6	535	369[3]	458	51	95
1990	5.8	702	464	–	81	0
1995	5.3	1,720	1,466	–	22	0
2000	5.6	2,555	3,287	–	(–)[4]	0
2004	7.4	3,954	4,580	–	(–)	0
2005	8.7	4,483	–	–	–	0
B. Annual Rates of Change (%)						
1970–1973 (Sept.)	–	27.0	22.8	23.3	–	–
1973–1985	–	51.5	52.8	51.3	–	–
1985–1989	–	52	–	–	–	–
1989–2000	–	15.3	22.0	–	–	–
2000–2004	–	11.5	8.6	–	–	–
2000–2005	–	11.9	–	–	–	–

Notes:

1. Outstanding balances of the banking system.
2. The figures reflect "directed (subsidized) credit" in terms of foreign currency only, endowed by the central bank. This way of promoting exports was phased out after 1985 and effectively eliminated by 1990.
3. The figures for 1985 and 1989 include the "directed credits" endowed to specified beneficiaries. By 1990, that category of bank credit was finally eliminated, so that totals down the road reflect the so-called "free credit" category of the previous decades.
4. From 2000 on the government had a net credit position with the BOI.

Table 35. Interest Rates and Inflation Rates, 1970–2005

Year	Band of Israel Rates				Banking System			
					Overdraft Rates		Short-Term Deposits	
	Makam[1] (1)	Monetary Loans (2)	Term Deposits (3)	BOI Rate[2] (4)	Nominal (5)	Real (6)	Nominal (7)	Inflation Rates (8)
1970[3]	7.75	–	–	–	17.83	7.0	–	10.1
1973 (Sept.)[3]	8.50	–	–	–	20.5	-1.5	12.0	22.3
1975	9.25	–	–	–	29.4	4.8	–	23.5
1980	–	–	–	–	176.2	18.6	78.0	132.9
1984	–	–	–	–	–	–	406.0	444.9
1985(a)[4]	–	–	–	–	444	12.2	–	385
1985(b)[4]	20.0[5]	25.3[6]	–	20.8[7]	328	33.3	163.0	221
1989	17.5	13.8	–	14.5	34.3	11.3	11.6	20.7
1990	16.5[8]	15.1	–	15.3	29.6	10.2	13.2	17.6
1995	14.5	15.6	14.1	15.6	22.4	13.2	13.3	8.1
2000	8.8	13.0	9.4	9.8	10.1	10.1	8.0	0.0
2004	4.8	–	4.4	4.4	10.2	8.9	3.1	1.2
2005	5.2	–	–	3.9	9.6	7.0	2.8	2.4

Notes:
1. The role of Makam as an instrument of policy was revived in 1986. The rates are for Makam bonds with a life of one year.
2. BOI "bank rate" average for the year. The BOI rate emerged in 1994 as an instrument of monetary policy.
3. The figures for 1970 and 1973 (Sept.) are debit interest rates on "free credit" in the commercial banking system. From 1975 onward these rates were charged by the banks on approved overdraft facilities.
4. 1985(a) refers to the six months, January–June, of that year, before the implementation of the 1985 economic stabilization policy; 1985(b) refers to the second half of this year, July–December, when the stabilization policy was in effect.
5. The figure is for 1986.
6. The figure is for 1987, in which year this BOI monetary instrument was introduced.
7. The figure is for 1988.
8. The figure is for 1991.

In an economy in which inflation had been running at more than six percent per month (just beyond 100 percent annually), taxpayers of all sorts thus make an average of three percent on the flow of taxes passing through their hands. Their gain is of course an equivalent loss to the state's revenue. With very high tax rates, as these usually are, and indeed were in Israel in the late 1970s and early 1980s – marginal income tax rates were 60 percent or more for comparatively low incomes – attempts to overcome this perfectly legal praxis was and is an exercise in futility. The drastic decline of tax revenue from 50 percent to 41 percent between 1980 and 1984, the five years in which inflation was continuously beyond the 100 percent annual rate, was undoubtedly due to the Tanzi effect. It did start before that, as inflation rose towards the 40–50 percent rate. it involves some learning by doing, and requires some time, but when it finally takes hold, as it clearly did in Israel by the early 1980s at the latest, the only way to overcome it is to stop, or at least reduce significantly, the rate of inflation. That was the line adopted by the government as the July 1985 stabilization policy was implemented.

GALLOPING INFLATION, 1974–1985. When the Yom Kippur War occurred in October 1973, Israel had already been subject for almost a year to an inflation rate topping 22 percent (Tables 25 and 26), a fact that was of great significance later on. When the resulting war-generated leap of the budget deficit occurred, simultaneously with the energy crisis resulting from an approximately fivefold increase in the price of oil, the momentum of inflation increased at once to about 57 percent in 1974. The average inflation rate for the four years, 1974–77, was 40 percent (Table 36). This was more than four times the rate of inflation in the industrialized countries, which rose in these years of stagflation to an average of approximately 10 percent.

An economy subject to inflation rates of 40 percent over four years was vulnerable to any shock, external or domestic, that would accelerate the rate of price inflation even further. And such shocks were not long in coming. The first was a clearly domestic affair: the summer election of 1977, which led to the demise of the three-decades-long Labor party-dominated governing coalition. The Likud-dominated coalition adopted the proposals made by Simcha Ehrlich, its finance minister, a member of the Liberal Party faction within the Likud, to signal that its economic policy would represent a new departure. The minister's first strategic move involved the relaxation of the strict currency control regulations originally introduced by the British in 1939 and maintained by every Israeli government. This involved an initial substantial devaluation and the institution of a relatively flexible exchange rate. The budget deficit for 1977, though lower than the all-time high of 1975 (21 percent of GNP), was still in the 15–16 percent range. A substantial devaluation of the currency and the floating of the exchange rate with a budget deficit of this order was a ques-

Table 36. Prices, Wages, and Exchange Rates, 1970–2004

Year	Consumer Prices (1)	Dollar Import Prices (2)	Nominal Wages: Total (3)	Nominal Wages: Israeli Workers (4)	Exchange Rates[1]: Nominal (5)	Exchange Rates[1]: Real (6)
A. 1970=100						
1970	100	100	100	100	100	100
1973 (9)	163	140	166	168	120	86
1975	342	200	317	320	203	59
1977	685	212	622	629	440	64
1980	4908	364	4,132	4,162	2,157	44
1984	329,370	302	–	–	182,571	55
1985 (6)	646,196	–	–	–	–	–
B. 1985=100						
1984	–	100	–	–	42	–
1985	100	100	100	100	100	100
1989	195	127	311	310	131	105
1990	230	136	354	352	137	103
1995	408	140	664	658	209	103
1998	524	126	902	894	277	113
2000	531	125	1,046	-1,033	269	108
2002	573	123	–		316	114
2004	569	131	1,057[2]	1,053[2]	296	121
C. Annual Average Rates of Change (Percent)						
1969–1973 (Sept.)	13.8	8.7	16.2	16.5	4.7	–
1973 (9)	22.3	–	–	–	–	–
1973–1977	39.6	–	39.1	39.1	38.3	–
1977–1984	141.6	6.9	–	–	136.6	–
1979	111.4	–	–	–	–	–
1985–1995	15.1	3.4	20.8	20.7	7.6	0.3
1998–2004	1.4	0.7	3.21	3.31	0.1	1.1

Notes:

1. The index numbers for the real exchange rates for Part A (1970–1985) were estimated on the basis of the corresponding entries of nominal exchange rates and prices. Since they do not refer to the foreign price inflation, they exaggerate the degree of the real depreciation of the Israeli currency. This was, however, of minor effect owing to the very great spread between Israel's and foreign inflation rates between 1970 and 1985. The figures for real exchange rates for 1985–2004 were standardized with reference to foreign price inflation; hence their significance is not fully equal to the respective ratios of Israel's price and nominal exchange rates in Part B.
2. The figure refers to 2003.

tionable operation in the first place. A delay, to allow time for the reduction of the deficit below perhaps 10 percent of GNP, might have been well advised. The Bank of Israel indeed advised that there be an immediate, thus simultaneous, reduction of the deficit at least.

Though the finance minister accepted the BOI's proposal, agreeing that this requirement was a condition for success, the prime minister and the government were reluctant to agree to the deep cut of expenditures that this would have required. The liberalization was thus implemented in November 1977, without the support of a significant cut in the fiscal deficit. The immediate price effect of an approximately 50 percent devaluation of the currency was a similar leap in the inflation rate in 1978. By 1979 the economy moved into galloping inflation beyond the triple-digit threshold, which forced the Treasury to reverse its relaxation of currency controls, and also brought about the resignation of Mr. Ehrlich.

With inflation running beyond 100 percent annually (about 6.5 percent per month) for more than six years starting in early 1979, feeding inflationary expectations among all economic entities – businesses, households, the banking system – the economy soon lost its bearings. The rising frequency of cost-of-living wage supplements contributed to that development, and to the disappearance of the so-called "nominal anchor." This phenomenon is underlined by the rapid decline of nominal money balances relative to the level of national product. In the Israeli case it shows in the decline of the M1/GDP ratio from close to 18 percent, where it stood in the early 1970s, to only 6.3 percent as Yigal Hurwitz took over the Finance Ministry late in 1979 (Table 34). His attempts to reduce the fiscal deficit, which earned him the nickname "I have not" (and his headline statement addressed to all "madmen – climb down from the roof") came to nothing. In the absence of support from the prime minister and members of the government, Mr. Hurwitz resigned, and the third finance minister in this government, Yoram Aridor, was appointed several months before the election campaign in 1981. His attempt to focus on the bubble component of the inflation, without, at least initially, addressing the component driving the inflationary process – the budget deficit – came to nothing by the summer of 1983. His secret plan to dollarize the system – to substitute the U.S. dollar for the shekel (which had become the country's new unit of currency in 1980 as part of the devaluation of the currency) as the legal tender of the country, thus forcing fiscal discipline on the government, was leaked. This, combined with the bank shares crisis (see below, The Bank Shares Crisis, 1983), led to his resignation in October 1983 and the appointment of Yigal Cohen-Orgad, the fourth finance minister of the Likud government in its seventh year.

In the remaining eight months before the July 1984 election, the Treasury focused on the state of the balance of payments. This required, of course, real devaluations of the currency, involving a further push on the price accelerator. The price level thus rose at an annual rate of more than 300 percent in that short time, which also meant that for the seven years between 1977 and 1984, Israel's annual average inflation rate was more than 140 percent. It also meant that prices in the autumn of 1984, as a new national unity government received its vote of confidence in the Knesset, were 3,300 times higher than in 1970, when the great inflation took off.

The latter figure suggests the effects of the galloping inflation that had accelerated over time and in 1984 was heading toward hyperinflation. It generated havoc not only in the fiscal domain but all over the production sector, and had a major impact on income distribution. It was obviously at the root of the very poor growth performance during the lost decade. This highly dangerous economic situation, if not the result of the 1984 summer election (a tie), called for the establishment of a national unity government, conceived as the only instrument that could face the simultaneous economic and political crises: the former, galloping inflation and a decade of very poor growth; the latter, the 1982 invasion of Lebanon that mired the Israel Defense Forces in the occupation of southern Lebanon.

THE STERILIZATION OF MONETARY POLICY. Monetary policy requires that as economies move into a full-employment environment, the central bank, responsible for the maintenance of price stability, should begin putting on the brakes. The operational implications of this rule require accordingly the raising of the interest rate, designed to reduce the injection of liquidity into the system. This restrictive move might be supported by an attempt to reduce the expansion of bank credit by raising legal minimum reserve ratios. The reduction of monetary expansion – the rate of growth of money – is the target of both instruments.

The money supply figures in Tables 34 and 24 indicate that in the 45 months through October 1973, in the full- and overfull-employment economy, the money supply (M1) expanded at 27 percent annually, much more than the corresponding increase of demand, in the 12–14 percent range, which reflected mainly the real growth rate of national product. Insight into the significance of that rapid monetary expansion can be found in the expansion of the money supply between 1966 and 1969: it was roughly 14 percent, similar to the very rapid rate of growth of national product during these years, in an economy that had been approaching the full-employment threshold it crossed by early 1970. The rather stable price level in that period, which rose at an annual rate of only two percent (Table 25) in that first half of the "seven good years" period, compared to inflation rates beyond 10 percent from 1970 on and 22 percent in the first nine prewar months of 1973, is accordingly easily explicable in terms of the comparative rates of monetary expansion.

The post-Yom Kippur War inflation rates, initially 40–50 percent and moving into triple-digits by 1979, consequently square with the severe average inflation rate of the money supply, about 52 percent annually from 1974 through July 1985 (Table 34). Rates of this order of magnitude for more than a decade suggest, of course, a collapse of monetary control. This inevitably raises questions about the policies pursued by the Bank of Israel. The monetary data in Table 34 indicate that these were fully accommodative.

Though accommodation was its practice, it clearly did not represent the preferences of the BOI's management. Indeed, at the very beginning of the inflationary process, early in 1970, the BOI proposed publicly to initiate immediately restrictive moves. With the 1966 Makam (short-term loan) agreement with the Treasury, which enabled the central bank to implement a restrictive open market policy, still in force, BOI proposed to raise the discount rate at which these bonds were sold to the public in 1970. This conventional move, implemented by central banks in the industrialized countries on similar occasions, was designed to stem the inflation of the money supply generated mainly by the government deficit, financed by borrowing from the central bank. The case in point for restrictive monetary moves was the full employment environment, which by that time was a fact of life. The BOI also proposed to raise simultaneously the legal minimum reserve ratio to reduce the expansionary momentum of commercial bank credit.

In order for the Bank to make these restrictive moves, government approval was required under the 1954 BOI Law, and this was not forthcoming. Only after a 20-month delay, in August 1971, did the Ministerial Committee on Economic Affairs approve the BOI proposal to raise the discount rate on Makams to a range of 8.5–9 percent. By that time inflation was already running at an annual rate of 12 percent; it was the second year in which it was beyond 10 percent. This meant, of course, that the purchase of bonds at this rate would involve a negative rate of return for the buyer. The delay of the approval, and the level to which the rate was belatedly, raised signified the demise of restrictive open market operations by BOI, and thus of effective restriction of monetary expansion.

The government was a bit more permissive with respect to the second instrument, the minimum legal reserve ratio, which the BOI also proposed to use. Though the Ministerial Committee never agreed to the proposed full measure of restraint, the BOI was permitted to raise the legal minimum ratios, thus reducing the impact of the so-called monetary multiplier. But the restrictive moves, already constrained by the range within which the value of this instrument could be reduced, were inevitably too little and too late. The central bank was unable to operate restrictively on the open market, and was injecting liquidity into the system between 1970 and 1973, at a juncture at which its mission should have been exactly the opposite, to drain liquidity from the system. The struggle against inflation was accordingly lost at the very beginning, in the early 1970s, when inflation was still running at annual rates of only 10–23 percent.

It was of course the 1954 BOI Law that handed the ultimate power of monetary control to the political community, represented by the government. This law, legislated in the post-World War II era of the early 1950s, in which the modus operandi of the industrialized economies differed altogether from that of the 1970s onward, was in fact the legal basis of Israel's monetary control in that period. The political community did not cherish inflation, which it considered a highly unfortunate development, showing clearly in the frustrating per capita national product growth rate of only 1.2 percent between 1973 and 1985. Yet short-term political considerations pushed it toward ever-growing fiscal deficits. At the takeoff point of inflation in 1970–73 it was the cost of the War of Attrition, and the cost of rebuilding the Suez Canal defense line afterward. Furthermore, from 1969 on the increase of immigration to 40–50,000 annually, fed mainly by the first wave of immigration of Jews from the Soviet Union after 50 years of closed gates, inevitably required a major increase in the absorption budget. Nobody in his political senses, government or opposition, would dare to question these expenditures. Finally, increased National Insurance Institute transfer payments, by almost three percent of GNP, within these four years through 1973, imposed a further burden on government revenue. A significant portion of these expenditures was clearly inspired by the political considerations of the ruling Labor party, expecting a serious challenge from the leading opposition party, the Likud.

An attempt to finance the increasing expenditures (from 43 percent of GNP in 1967–68 to almost 60 percent of a higher GNP in 1973) was made; tax revenue was raised from 43 percent of GNP in 1967–69 to 45 percent in 1970–73 (9) (Table 23). But this did not close the gap between expenditure and tax revenue, which was about 17 percent of GNP. Unilateral transfers from abroad – world Jewish community donations and U.S. government grants added four percent of GNP to fiscal absorption – reduced the fiscal gap to a still enormous 13 percent of GNP (Table 23).

This was the background that led the finance minister, clearly representing the government's attitude, to reject the BOI's persistent proposals to let it implement a meaningful restrictive monetary policy during that crucial takeoff period, 1970 through October 1973, of the Great Inflation. The simultaneous rising (Vietnam) inflation in the U.S. and similar developments in western European countries involving inflation rates of 5–10 percent, only served to support the Treasury in its running argument with the BOI on the adoption of restrictive moves. It maintained that the rising pattern of the price level reflected mainly the rising costs of imports, and that Israel's 11–12 percent inflation of 1970–72 was thus not out of line with developments in the world economy. The leap to the 22 percent inflation rate of the three prewar quarters of 1973 was, like the war, clearly not expected by the political community. Whether having expected that price explosion, the ruling political forces would have avoided the sterilization of monetary policy they effectively imposed in 1970, or would at least not have implemented the expansionary welfare state policy that added three percentage points of GNP to the government deficit by 1973, is anybody's guess.

The 1985 Economic Stabilization Policy

THE ISSUES AND THE PROGRAM. It took nine months after its inauguration before the national unity government tackled inflation with a comprehensive plan. The priority it gave Lebanon, and other foreign policy issues involving life and death, is understandable. However, it was obvious that withdrawal from Lebanon would contribute to the solution of the economic dilemma, since it would allow a substantial reduction of defense expenditures. Instead, the government worked out with the Histadrut, representing workers, and the Israel Manufacturers Association, representing the manufacturing industry and business in general, a series of three-month package deals freezing prices, wages, and taxes. These did not commit the government to freeze the real rate of exchange, leaving it free to raise the nominal rate by an amount higher than the expected rate of price inflation, generating a "cost push" effect.

In any case, these deals – there were three of them – between October 1983 and June 1984 failed dismally. They reduced inflation rates somewhat for the first month of each of the three periods, but these rose soon afterwards. The inflation rate of about 20 percent per month in April 1985, implying an annual rate of 850 percent, on the verge of hyperinflation, suggested the inevitable demise of the package deals exercise, pegged among other things to price linkage techniques that had been developed and even extended into the tax system through the early 1980s. In 1982 the price linkage device still allowed an increase of real wages, but it failed to do so in 1983. Similarly, the dynamics of triple-digit inflation rates had been rapidly eroding tax revenues too. The labor unions and the government understood by that time that the protective shield against inflation that the price linkage technique had provided for a decade had been shredded to pieces. Production and commercial businesses lost their bearings as rapid changes in relative prices resulting from accelerating inflation made it impossible to calculate price-cost relationships realistically. This of course affected profitability and calculations of resource allocation.

By mid-1985, it was clear that only a comprehensive reform, whose implementation would require toil and tears, and whose success would be visible only after a longish interval, could make the difference. The immediate goal of such a program would be twofold: (1) to rapidly reduce inflation rates to 10–20 percent per annum; and (2) to reduce the deficit on the current account of the balance of payments to a sustainable level. The rock-bottom base of such a program required getting the fiscal domain of the economy into reasonable shape. The condition for success was accordingly the immediate elimination of the budget deficit, which in 1984 was more than 14 percent of GNP and by June 1985 was running at the same level. In view of the already very high tax rates, which were a heavy burden on those paying the full rates but which also provided numerous loopholes to businesses and household entities belonging to one group or another, it was clear that raising taxes was not a meaningful option for the purpose.

The only means that could promise a major and immediate reduction of the deficit was therefore on the expenditure side of the equation. The IDF withdrawal from Lebanon that was gradually implemented in 1985 offered significant and genuine savings. But the main channel for an immediate reduction of expenditures was provided by a single item: government subsidies to essentials, mainly domestically produced food items, which involved by that time an expenditure flow of almost six percent of GNP. More than two thirds of the subsidies were eliminated at once, thus reducing the deficit by about four percent of GNP, on the morning of July 1, 1985. The remaining subsidies were to be eliminated over the following six months.

The immediate direct consequence of that move, apparent only on August 15 when the consumer price index for July was published, was a 27.5 percent price leap. Thus the elimination of subsidies seemed to be another step in the inflationary pattern, but it was actually exactly the opposite. It did, however, have an immediate adverse affect on labor, since in one go it reduced real wages and severed the automatic wage-price linkage, a structural feature of Israel's labor market since 1943, when it was introduced by the Mandatory authorities. An agreement with the Histadrut annulling the automatic monthly cost-of-living adjustments was part of the labor market component of the 1985 stabilization program.

The actual steps toward reducing the budget deficit were preceded by an important amendment to the 1954 Bank of Israel Law. This amendment, known popularly as the "No Printing Law," forbid the BOI from granting credit to the government, which meant that the government would be unable to proceed as before and even out its annual cash flow by "printing money." This seemingly technical legal device served as the foundation of later fiscal policy, and as the control lever for monetary policy. Its passage was a condition set by the U.S. for a special stabilization grant of $1.5 billion, about 1.5 percent of GNP. This inflow, and an increased flow of contributions from world Jewish communities, on top of the reduction of subsidies and defense spending, resulted in an immediate hefty reduction of the budget deficit on the order of 9–10 percent of national product.

The achievement of the second goal of the policy, the rapid improvement in the balance of payments, posed a dilemma for the government. An improvement in the balance of payments required of course a significant devaluation – a significantly higher price for foreign exchange, and therefore for imports, in real terms – and the prevention of the erosion of the new rate in the longer run. This would lower the cost of exports and improve the profitability of the export trade, as well as of import-competing domestic products, but the rise in the prices of imports was inconsistent, from the point of view of the man in the street, with the promised all-out fight against inflation. Indeed, the roughly 31 percent devaluation of the currency that was part of the initial implementation of the stabilization policy on July 1, 1985, contributed significantly to the 27.5 percent rise in prices of that month. This increase was indeed more than expected by the Treasury and the planning committee, and also by the Histadrut, which had agreed to the elimination of the price-wage linkage in return for a permanent future compensation agreement. The agreed rate of compensation in real terms thus turned out to be lower than the rise of prices in July alone; price increases later on reduced real wages even further.

To face and overcome the apparent, though not actual, inconsistency of a major increase in the price level with an inflation-reduction program, the program included a highly publicized so-called "nominal anchor." This was the devalued nominal exchange rate, set at 1.5 New Israeli Shekels (NIS) to the dollar (New Shekels had replaced old shekels as part of the devaluation). The government committed itself to maintain that rate as long as nominal wages did not rise above a prescribed and tightly set limit. Accordingly, foreign currency for current account transactions – for imports and even for foreign travel – would be made available on demand to all and sundry at that nominal fixed exchange rate. Exporters and transmitters of funds on unilateral transfers and capital accounts would receive the same exchange rate. This meant the elimination of the multiple exchange-rate system that had been maintained for decades.

The transparency of this commitment was assured by the fact that foreign currency transactions could be made every day, six days a week. The long-term credibility of the commitment was based on the significant monetary reserves at the BOI, and even more on the support of the U.S. government for the stabilization policy, underlined by its commitment to grant Israel $1.5 billion within two years. The first part of that sum was made available immediately at the inauguration of the program. Furthermore, importers, other businesses, and households had accumulated substantial stocks before the expected inauguration of the program, which everybody knew would involve a devaluation; this amounted to implicit help for the maintenance of these commitments.

The novelty of the stabilization program was symbolized by the notions introduced into the economic and political vocabulary at that time – transparency and credibility. The success of the program was tightly pegged to the credibility of the government's commitment, which could be gauged by the daily information on the rate of exchange. The fact that this information was publicly available every day was accordingly of great significance. To satisfy the political needs of the Histadrut and some of its vocal supporters in the government, a freeze on prices was declared and some taxes slightly raised at the advent of the policy. Yet no control system to enforce the price ceiling was set up beyond the usual very slow-working sanction of a legal proceeding against violations of the price freeze.

Yet a highly restrictive economic mechanism to hold the line on prices was immediately put into effect: monetary policy, to be run by the BOI. It was resurrected now after having been put in cold storage in 1970 (see above, The Sterilization of Monetary Policy). The effective freedom given to the central bank to engage in a restrictive monetary policy was not stated openly in the document summarizing the measures required by the stabilization policy (approved in a night session of the government on June 30–July 1, 1985). The only reference to the monetary dimension spelled out in that document was to bank credit: during the first month of the program, the nominal volume of bank credit was to grow at a rate lower by 10 percent than the price rise during that month. And this volume (i.e., the volume of bank credit on August 1) would be frozen as a nominal quota to serve as the credit ceiling for the next three months.

It was understood that the two quantitative instruments available to the BOI – the legal minimum reserve ratio and the credit quota mentioned explicitly in the program document – would affect interest rates, pushing them upward. Since this development was a condition of success, the BOI was not required to prevent it. The freedom of action granted to the BOI in the money market gave it the ability to raise interest rates to as high as the traffic would bear.

PERSEVERANCE IN IMPLEMENTATION. A well-known immediate post-devaluation effect is the reflow of money that had been "parked" temporarily abroad in expectation of the devaluation. When this parked money flowed back to Israel in 1985, it generated a very high liquidity in the banking system and in the economy in general. Thus, though nominal interest rates were raised, these did not square with the actual leap of the price level by 27.5 percent in July, which was higher than had been expected. This meant that the real interest rate in July may even have been negative, since the banks estimated the probable price hike within a range of 17–20 percent at most.

This changed quickly from August on, however, as the BOI raised the required minimum reserve ratios three times in July, with a fourth and last rise to 50 percent on August 1. Simultaneously, it raised its monetary loan (discount window) rate forcing bank lending rates upward for overdraft facilities. These averaged almost 97 percent in real terms in the first quarter after the inauguration of the stabilization policy, and were even higher – 118 percent – in the next, the last quarter of 1985. The average real interest rate for all bank credit was 12 percent in July–September 1985 and 15 percent in October–December. These rates were allowed to decline substantially in 1986 and 1987, as the success of the stabilization policy became apparent, but were still maintained within a relatively high range. The post-stabilization policy positive real interest feature of commercial bank credit, representing the tight environment of the money market as a whole, was accordingly the real negation of the money-market dimension of the economy before 1985, and particularly since 1970. During this period, zero and even negative real interest rates on bank credit were the effective rule.

To close the loop of the stabilization program, an agreement on income policy was reached several days after the opening move of July 1. The automatic wage-price linkage would be scrapped, and nominal wages would be adjusted upward with a lag, at a rate significantly lower than the initial (unknown at the time) July price shock. In the wake of the nominal permanent upward adjustment of wages, a freeze of three months would follow before negotiations on a new cost-of-living contract were to start. The immediate result of this three-party agreement was a substantial cut in real wages. It involved an immediate cut of 14 percent in the real wages of civil servants, and about seven percent for employees in the business sector. The real wage level in the business sector was restored only after more than a year, toward the end of 1986. Three years were required, through 1988, before the real wage level in the public sector was restored to its 1984 level. This development offered highly welcome support for the necessary reduction of government expenditure and thus of the deficit, the prerequisite for getting inflation down and improving the balance of payments – the twin goals of the program.

The rise in the price level in July 1985 was expected, though not its exact rate. Though apparently inconsistent with the inflation reduction goal, it actually served this goal with the implementation of the other components of the program, leading to a declining pattern of inflation in the somewhat longer term. This first manifested itself in the August 1985 price index, which rose by only 3.9 percent compared with the 27.5 percent of June, and the 15–19 percent range in the two first quarters of 1985. But there had been such monthly ups and downs, and this rate was not identified at the time as an omen of success.

The political community, usually focused on the short term, and some of the planning committee were hoping against hope that the inflation target of 15–20 percent annually (one to two percent monthly) would be reached within three to four months. In the event it was about seven to eight months. By mid-January 1986 when the December price figures appeared, they indicated that price inflation in the last quarter of 1985, the second quarter since inauguration of the stabilization policy, was at a monthly average of 2.2 percent (an annual rate of close to 30 percent). It was still off the (officially undeclared) target, and far above inflation rates in the industrialized countries, but it registered as a success in Israeli public opinion. It still required the maintenance of stringencies through 1986, a year in which the 1985 price and wage freezes were repealed. An average inflation rate of somewhat less than 20 percent was reached in 1986 and maintained through 1989 (Table 36), and there was a major improvement of the goods and services account – by the end of 1985, and in 1986 as well, the dollar deficit was down by more than 50 and 20 percent respectively (Table 31) – so it could be said that the twin goals of the stabilization policy had clearly been met. The goods and services deficit in 1985, which was less than half that of 1980 and allowed the current account of the balance of payments to move into surplus for the first time in the state's history, was in a sense the epitome of that success.

This performance on inflation and the balance of payments was accomplished with a temporary small increase of unemployment, to 7.1 percent in 1986 from 6.7 percent in 1985. The employment constraint – the requirement to minimize the employment effects of the restrictive moves required to implement the stabilization policy – was thus met even in the first stage of the program. With unemployment down to 6.1 and 6.4 percent in 1987 and 1988 respectively, the economy was clearly operating on the threshold of full employment, with a robust balance of payments and inflation down to an annual rate of 15–20 percent. This meant that the mission to restore economic stability seemed to have been successfully completed by around 1988.

MAJOR FISCAL AND MONETARY RESTRAINT. This in any case was the sense of the country, as macroeconomic activity yielded to the highly restrictive measures of fiscal and particularly monetary policy, the major instruments of the stabilization policy. This policy, particularly its monetary policy component, changed the rules of the economic game, affecting households and business, the latter in particular. The fiscal discipline imposed by the stabilization policy showed results almost immediately. By the fourth quarter of 1985, only six months after the policy went into effect, the budget was in the black. The surplus of one percent of GNP for the full fiscal year 1985 (Table 33), compared to the deficit of more than 14 percent in 1984 and an average deficit of more than 12 percent for 1980–84 represented a revolution. Indeed, in the two decades through 2004, the budget deficit effectively never exceeded five percent, and on average was in the range of two to three percent of GNP.

On the whole the Treasury kept aloof from the Bank of Israel's efforts to rein in the monetary and financial markets, a departure from its behavior before 1985. At most the minister himself, or usually one of his lieutenants, would make a critical comment on the "high" interest rate set by the central bank, even though the BOI Law, which aside from the "no printing" amendment of 1985, had not been changed, granted the government veto power with regard to the instruments used by the BOI to determine its interest rates.

The revolution in monetary policy and its impact on the macroeconomy started on the very day the stabilization policy was inaugurated. Its highly restrictive impact showed in the towering real interest rates on overdraft facilities, which rose to nearly 300 percent annually in the first quarter the policy was in effect. These sky-high real interest rates were reduced in the following quarter and after. The approximately 20 percent per annum real interest rate on overdrafts which was still in force after 18 months of the stabilization policy, in the last quarter of 1986, underline the vigor with which monetary policy had been employed to support the disinflation effort. These very high interest rates for overdrafts, which admittedly involved only a small portion of the volume of commercial bank credit (and which for more than a decade through 1985 had been in the negative to zero range), raised the average cost of total bank credit to positive real rates. These were in the three to four percent range by the end of 1986 and had been much higher late in 1985.

During the period of accelerating inflation, businesses had accumulated large amounts of stock, a highly profitable operation as inflation continued to rise. The very high interest rates in the last quarter of 1985 forced them to liquidate these stocks. This liquidation began in the last quarter of 1985, as more and more major store chains started "sales" campaigns. It was this development that finally broke the back of inflation. Maintenance of high real interest rates during the stabilization effort, which were lowered as inflation declined to the 15–20 percent range, was the guiding principle of the BOI in the 1990s. This led on several occasions to criticism from the political community and business leaders, in the production branches especially. Yet on the whole, despite public opinion and political criticism, the BOI stuck to its guns and proceeded with its stringent policy.

The implementation of this policy required, however, the creation of instruments for manipulating the money and capital markets. The BOI began late in 1985, introducing a novel instrument, the monetary loan, auctioned to the banking system weekly. Its effectiveness depended, of course, on demand for reserves by the banking system, and thus ultimately on demand for credit by its customers. Initially the BOI encouraged the need of the banks for reserves by drastically raising reserve ratios, which it could do freely thanks to the hands-off policy followed by the Treasury. Thus, within one month, July 1985, the BOI raised the reserve requirements for commercial banks two times, from 35 percent at the end of June to 50 percent on August 1. Demand for bank reserves got another upward push from the major increase in prices in July.

Another turn of the screw that forced the commercial banks to look for money to bolster their reserves was the campaign launched by the BOI, with silent support from the Treasury, to eliminate entirely within three years the highly subsidized so-called "directed credit." During the "lost decade" this involved at least 30–35 percent of total credit accommodated by the banking system. The simultaneous reduction by the Treasury of long-term business and household "development budget" credit backed by government deposits with the banking system served the same purpose.

To establish the BOI interest rate as "the controlling device of the interest rate structure of the economy," the central bank needed flexible instruments in the money market. The Treasury, which in 1985 and 1986 was focusing on the stabilization policy, agreed to renew the Makam contract of 1966 with the BOI. It had been frozen effectively in the early 1970s, as the Treasury in those days refused adamantly to sanction an increase in the discount rate at which these certificates were sold, which the double-digit inflation rate of these years called for. This had neutralized the relevance of monetary policy as a macroeconomic control mechanism for 15 years through 1985.

Under this contract the BOI was allocated a quota of Makam bonds, which it could use at will, setting the discount rate at issue according to its reading of the state of the markets. To strengthen its grip on the market and reduce its dependence on the attitude of the political community represented by the government, the BOI with at least no formal protest by the Treasury, introduced the monetary loan, mentioned above. In response to the banks' demands, BOI would accommodate them by offering "monetary loan" credits to bolster their reserves. The loans were auctioned at a competitive weekly bidding, thus setting the discount rate for that week. The monetary loan instrument increased the clout of the BOI in managing monetary policy since it was not constrained by a Treasury quota, as it was for Makam bonds. By varying the size of the weekly auctions according to its judgment, the BOI could manipulate the discount rates for these assets. If the state of the economy – the inflation rate in particular, the rate of exchange, and sometimes also the general level of activity – required restriction, the BOI would reduce the quantity offered at auction, which would push the rate upward. If an expansionary move were warranted, it would increase the size of the loan.

Armed with these two instruments, the Makam bond (not fully in its control) and the monetary loan, BOI began to intervene in the money market in 1986. The outstanding balances of Makam bonds and the monetary loan in 1987 indicated that by that time its intervention was quite forceful. Hence by 1987 at the latest the BOI's interest rate, set for every forthcoming month on the last Monday of the previous month, became headline news. It was the basis for the setting of the debit and credit interest rates by the banking system, the cornerstone of the interest rate structure of the economy.

Resurrection of Growth and Restructuring

STABILIZATION AND SLOWDOWN. The shakeup prompted by the stabilization policy was, of course, not confined to stopping the onslaught of inflation and reducing of the balance-of-payments deficit. The immediate reduction of inflation to annual rates of 15–20 percent from close to hyperinflationary levels within the short period of six to eight months, and the prospects for continuing this pattern thereafter, which by mid-1986 seemed excellent, suggested that a revolutionary change in the rules of the game had occurred. This was underlined by the dramatic change in the cost of money; real interest rates, which rose sky-high as the stabilization policy went into effect, were reduced. Yet still the average real interest rate on commercial bank credit between 1986 and 1989 was somewhat above 10 percent; for the 15-year period through July 1985 these rates were at best close to zero. For many major manufacturing enterprises and for the farming entities with large quotas of subsidized credit, these rates were negative during the entire period through 1985.

Economic activity was sustained with little rise in unemployment in 1986, and unemployment rates in the two succeeding years were lower than in 1985 (Table 29). National product in the 1985–89 interval grew at an average rate of 4.4 percent, a whole percentage point more than the average rate in the last decade. Investment was revived meaningfully after its drastic decline in 1984 and 1985, and private consumption expenditure bloomed. The stabilization policy, the model for a number of similar policies instituted at about the same time in South America, was soon hailed as a success in view of its rapid salutary effects on inflation and the balance of payments.

A shakeup nevertheless occurred in 1989 in the wake of the collapse of several major firms. These enterprises were mainly, though not exclusively, components of the so-called Histadrut Production Group, created and run by the labor federation for several decades, which had benefited from significant "development budget" credits and commercial bank "directed credits." As interest rose on the directed credits, both the cash flow and the profit margins of these firms collapsed, putting them under severe strain. The reduction of the flow of "development budget" credits imposed a similar strain on firms benefiting from those. Business entities in the farming sector were subjected to similar strains. The financial squeeze imposed from mid-1985 onward led ultimately in 1989 to bankruptcies across the board, and to a significant economic slowdown involving a leap of unemployment to almost nine percent and an absolute decline of investment (Table 29). This component of aggregate demand, usually a leading indicator of the economic cycle, was already slumping by 1988; it thus predicted the downturn of activity.

The slow growth of national product, only 1.4 percent in 1989, was frustrating, and business GDP did even worse soon after. These developments were seen as a clear omen of a drawn-out slowdown, generated by the highly restrictive fiscal and monetary policies, by that time in place for more than three years. With a real interest rate of about 12 percent on overdraft facilities in 1989 (Table 35), and a similar, though somewhat lower, 10 percent average rate on total bank credit, the immediate future seemed quite bleak to entrepreneurs in the summer months of that year. The Treasury, which ran a low fiscal deficit, and the BOI, which ran a tight shop, considered that slowdown as the inevitable price which had still to be paid to maintain the low inflation rate which only a few years earlier was verging on hyperinflation. By the autumn of 1989, therefore, the immediate future did not seem bright at all either to the man in the street or the man in the government ministry (whether political or administrative), and inevitably not to the entrepreneur in the business sector.

PROSPERITY FOLLOWING THE SECOND MASS ALIYAH. Comparison of the main economic indicators – national product, investment, private consumption, and employment – in 1989 and 1990 might suggest that a magician's wand had changed the economic scene at once. The 1.4 percent national product growth rate of 1989 was replaced by an approximately seven percent rate in 1990. Investment, which had declined in 1989, leapt 25 percent in 1990; employment grew three percent. Indicators across the board, excluding the unemployment rate, were on the rise.

The magician's wand that abruptly cut off the declining trend, and improved the mood all over, was the unexpected turn of events in the Soviet Union; its collapse generated the second mass immigration to Israel of the 1990s. The almost 200,000 immigrants who arrived in Israel in each of the years 1990 and 1991 set the pattern for the forthcoming decade, in which more than one million arrived. By the end of this decade, the flow had added more than 25 percent to the Jewish population, and almost 20 percent to the total population of the country.

It was undoubtedly investment that restarted the growth of the economy. With roofs overhead the first necessity for the new immigrants, public sector housing was initiated by the government and financed by the budget. Initially it absorbed the major share of resources poured into capital formation. The production branches which in 1989 had excess capacity, and which were to absorb the rapidly expanding labor force, came later. Farming was of minor relevance at best; though employment in that branch improved somewhat in the 1990s, its total employment in 2004 was lower in absolute terms than two decades previously, in 1985. And in any case, the labor absorbed in farming in these decades was unskilled and poorly trained, mostly foreign workers from Third World countries. The new immigrants, and the domestically highly educated newcomers to the labor force, were therefore not candidates for low-level farm employment.

The growing labor force was accordingly absorbed mainly into manufacturing, including high-tech lines that had been emerging in the late 1980s, in the wake of the personal computer revolution. These followed the path that was blazed by the growth of Silicon Valley. Figures for employment in manufacturing, which grew by almost 20 percent in the 1990s, underline this feature (Table 39). Trade and services too expanded vigorously; employment in these areas grew by almost 130 percent in the 1990s. This meant that in the last decade of the 20th century and the early years of the 21st, when the economy began growing again, there was a far-reaching intersectoral and interbranch restructuring. Agriculture, which in 1990 still claimed more than four percent of total employment and contributed more than 3.3 percent of GNP, was down to the minuscule requirement of about two percent of the labor force, and contributed a mere 1.5 percent of GNP. The relative standing of manufacturing declined somewhat as well. Employment in manufacturing declined from about 22 percent of the total in 1992 to 18 percent in 2000, and a similar decline of its comparative contribution to national product occurred. Nevertheless, it remained the leading unique sector, whose performance set the pace of the economy. The public sector and "other" service sector expanded both in terms of their employment ratios and their contributions to national product (Table 27).

Yet the most significant restructuring occurred within branches: following the worldwide pattern, in farming (see above, The Changing Status of Agriculture) and in manufacturing, whose restructuring had a profound effect on the pattern and performance of the economy as a whole (Table 39; see also below, The Evolution of Manufacturing and the High-Tech System, 1973–2005).

Table 37. Banking System Aggregates, 1950–2004

Year	Banking System				Ratios (Percent)			Two Major Banks Ratio[2]	
	Banking Corporations (1)	Offices (2)	Employment 1970=100 (3)	Automatic Teller Machines (ATMs) (4)	Deposits/ GNP (5)	Balance Sheet/ GNP (6)	Employees/ Total Employment[1] (7)	Credits[2] (8)	Deposits[2] (9)
1950	108	204	–	–	–	–	–	–	–
1967	45	760	77	–	8.3	75.0	1.3	–	–
1970	42	812	100	–	10.5	89.5	1.5	–	–
1975	30	967	154	–	6.7	158.7	2.0	–	–
1980	30	1,099	226	214	4.5	279.5	2.6	–	–
1985	30	1,103	235	540	5.9	279.7	2.5	–	–
1990	29	1,038	212	587	8.1	163.7	2.1	–	–
2000	23	1,032	236	1,322	9.1	135.7	1.5	84.1	69.7
2004	18	951	222	1,406	10.5	137.1	1.3	79.1	68.1

Notes:
1. Ratio of the number of employees in the banking system to total employees in the economy.
2. Ratios to totals in the banking system of credits accommodated to the public by the two dominant banks, Bank Hapoalim and Bank Leumi.

Table 38. Selected Capital Market Indicators, 1960–2003[1]

Year	Market Value of Securities 1990=100		Rates of Return 1979=100		Value of Turnover[2] 1990=100	Capital Issues[3] 1985=100		
	Bonds (1)	Shares (2)	Bonds (3)	Shares (4)	(5)	Shares (6)	Government Bonds (7)	Corporate Bonds (8)
1960	–	–	–	150	–	–	–	–
1970	–	–	–	100	–	–	–	–
1974	–	–	–	81	–	–	–	–
1977	–	–	–	46	–	–	–	–
1979	–	–	100.0	100	–	–	–	–
1980	–	81	107.7	163	–	–	–	–
1982	–	–	189.6	437	–	–	–	–
1985	–	–	92.1	149	27	100	100	100
1990	100	100	109.2	208	100	912	328	511,739
1995	133	298	110.2	343	140	1,297	541	–
2000	148	538	130.5	600	471	5,555	581	518,800
2003	210	574	158.5	658	666	1,286	1,169	1,105,496

Notes:
1. At constant prices of 1979 (columns 3 and 4); 1990 (columns 1 and 2); and 1985 (columns 6, 7, and 8).
2. At the Tel Aviv Stock Exchange.
3. Net shares sold and net government and corporate bonds issued on the Tel Aviv Stock Exchange.

Table 39. Traditional and High-Technology Branches in Manufacturing Industries: Production and Employment by Technological Intensity and Educational and Skill Levels of Employees, 1990–2004

Year	Manufacturing Industry		High-Technology Branches		Medium High-Technology Branches		Medium Low-Technology Branches		Low-Technology		Textiles	Elec-tronics	Skill Endowment of Labor		Wage Ratios: Skilled / Unskilled	Wage Ratios: High Educ. / Others
	Prod.[1] (1)	Employ.[2] (2)	Prod. (3)	Employ. (4)	Prod. (5)	Employ. (6)	Prod. (7)	Employ. (8)	Prod. (9)	Employ. (10)	Prod.[3] (11)	(12)	Skilled (13)	Higher Educ.[4] (14)	(15)	(16)
Indices: 1990, 1994=100 Percent of Total																
1990	75.4	85.5	–	–	–	–	–	–	–	–	100.0	100.0	–	–	–	–
1994	100.0	100.0	100.0	100.0	100.0	100.0	100.0	100.0	100.0	100.0	129.0	170.6	–	–	–	–
1995	108.4	103.8	107.1	102.1	103.7	102.9	115.3	108.3	106.0	102.1	134.7	179.0	18.7	35.9	2.63	1.68
2000	133.4	103.2	187.5	126.7	115.6	99.7	121.7	106.5	101.8	87.9	124.5	332.0	25.4	43.8	2.38	1.75
2003	124.0	93.9	169.2	117.5	109.5	89.7	119.9	100.1	96.2	81.2	111.2	229.0	28.6	46.9	2.37	1.87
2004	132.5	95.0	194.6	122.8	109.8	87.8	123.9	100.1	98.3	81.7	102.3	278.0	–	–	–	–

Notes:
1. Columns 1, 3, 5, 7, 9, 11, and 12 refer to production in the relevant branches.
2. Columns 2, 4, 6, 8, and 10 refer to employment in each branch.
3. Employment in textiles in 2004 was down to 63 percent of the number employed in 1990; employment in electronics and telecommunications equipment was 78 percent higher in 2004 than in 1990.
4. Workers with 13 years and more of schooling.

In spite of the slowdown of 2001–03, the 15 years through 2005, which began as the first wave of the new mass *aliyah* arrived in Israel, was on the whole an era of substantial growth. The stabilization policy of 1985–89, which had succeeded in pulling Israel from the quagmire of (almost) hyperinflation-cum-stagnation and a hopeless foreign payments position, prepared the infrastructure for the revival generated by the unexpected flow of immigrants. The GNP grew at an annual rate of 4.2 percent, one percentage point higher than the annual average during the lost decade; this meant that by 2005 Israel's GNP was almost two times greater than in 1989. The most significant feature of this growth, however, was that the engine powering the economy was the business sector. Its annual average growth rate, in terms of its product, was five percent, which meant that business product grew by 2.2 times during these years. This also indicated that the process had been eroding the traditional role of the public sector in the production dimension of the economy.

This growth performance was led by a major upturn of investment through the decade ending in 2000. After a hiatus in 2001–03, resulting from the global, and Israeli, downturn of the high-tech led business cycle, investment levels turned upward again, pushing beyond their peak of 2000. Thus, by 2004–05 the nonhousing capital stock of the economy was about 2.4 times greater than in 1989. The labor force and employment grew at similar rates through the 1990s. In the wake of the recession through 2003, employment growth lagged by about four percent compared to the expansion of the labor force; this lag was almost eliminated by 2005, as the level of activity revived. Thus, both were about 70 percent greater by 2004–05 than at the advent of the mass immigration of the 1990s.

With the nonhousing capital stock increasing by 140 percent during the same period, this means that capital intensity in production measured by capital-labor ratios rose substantially by about 40 percent during the 15–16 year period through 2004–05. This of course was another significant feature of the period, which had been reducing the demand for unskilled labor. But correspondingly, the treading of the economy along this path meant rising factor productivity (Table 29) and thus rising per capita product; this grew by almost one quarter during that period, allowing significantly rising living standards. In terms of private per capita consumption expenditures, average living standards increased by 45 percent during that period.

The resources for that highly significant performance by an economy continuously absorbing immigration, which increased population by 20 percent, were not provided only by the growth in production. They also came from a small decrease in public sector consumption expenditures. This saving shows clearly in significantly lower per capita public sector consumption expenditures in 2004 than in 1989, and reflects a decline in the defense budget in absolute terms, and particularly in relative terms as a ratio of GDP (Table 28). This reduction in defense spending was implemented even though for most of that time, between 1988 and 2004, the mass resistance of Palestinians in two Intifadas, and the unstable political equilibrium in the Middle East that involved two wars in Iraq, still required a major defense budget.

The declining pattern of defense expenditures from 13.5 percent of GNP in 1989 to about eight percent from 1995 through 2003 (Table 30) indeed made a difference. Yet even these much lower requirements were three to four times higher in terms of GNP ratios than those typical of the industrialized Western European countries, and were even greater than those of the United States. Thus, though an average growth rate of GDP in the range of 4.3 percent annually in the 15 years through 2005 is seemingly quite reasonable, Israel's comparative level of per capita product declined. By the mid-1990s it was already close to 60 percent of that of the U.S. and around 70 percent of the average for the European community, the standard of measurement for the Israeli populace. These ratios were somewhat lower by the end of the following decade. One of the reasons for this disappointing pattern was clearly the defense burden imposed on the productive performance of the economy, and the other was of course the much more rapid population growth than that of the western and northern European countries in particular.

GROWTH AND INCOME DISTRIBUTION. Another feature retarding the growth of national product in this period was the initially low and even decreasing rates of participation in the labor force. This was due to socioeconomic developments encouraged by the growing political clout of the extreme Orthodox sector of the Jewish community, and to the still pre-industrial social features of Arab Muslim communities, which involve comparatively rapid demographic expansion. These two groups share a common feature – they have large families. This means that by definition, the participation rates of their members in the labor force are lower; female employment is quite limited and children, who of course affect the average level of per capita product, do not participate in the labor force at all.

Related aspects that reduced significantly the participation of Orthodox Jewish males in the labor force, and thus in income-generating employment, were the considerable increase in child allowances and the much more generous public sector contributions to financing yeshivot. Yeshivot pay is low but meaningful for the students who make Torah study their life's occupation, thereby keeping them out of the labor force for life, and reducing the contribution of their community to national product. The expanding funding of both large-scale child allowances, linked to the number of children in a family and rising significantly with each successive child, and the yeshivot and their students, had of course implications on welfare state spending and thus on public finance. It also negatively affected income distribution. Whatever the level of social security allowances, and it was a heavy and rapidly growing fiscal burden, a growing number of families in which males avoided the labor force altogether were not experiencing rising real family income.

Economic growth in the 1990s was linked to the high-tech production sector, and capital investment and employment in this sector mushroomed, generating a rapidly increasing demand for highly skilled, and highly paid, workers. This demand, and the decline of low-technology industries such as textiles, which had to compete with growing imports from Third World countries, depressed relatively, as they did in all industrialized countries, the wages and incomes of low-skilled workers. In business sector employment, though not in public sector employment, the demand for low-skilled employees even declined. The pressure on both the level and the terms of employment of low-skilled workers was increased from 1990 onward. This was also due to the shortsighted policy of government, which relented to the pressure of entrepreneurs in farming and the building industry in particular, to allow the employment of foreign workers on a temporary (visa) basis, as substitutes for Palestinian workers, whose employment increased rapidly from the 1970s, but from 1988 onwards were increasingly excluded from the Israeli labor market due to security considerations. At the all-time high, around 1987, Palestinian workers accounted for about seven percent of the total employment in the Israeli economy. At the record high, in the highly prosperous year 2000, the share of non-Israelis employed in the Israeli economy was 12 percent, of whom only one third were Palestinians, and the balance legal and illegal foreign workers. This of course means that the share of non-Israelis employed in low-skilled work was much higher, probably 30–35 percent.

This onslaught of foreign workers inevitably generated a significant pressure on the wage rates of low-skilled Israeli workers. Data on pretax and pre-transfer payments (mostly social security benefits) for the late 1990s thus indicate a significantly growing dispersion of wage income of the Israeli employees. The steeply rising income tax rates, which exclude about half of all employees from income taxes altogether, helped to reduce significantly the post-tax and transfer payments gap between the high-wage employees and the unskilled low-wage employees. Transfer payments, particularly the rising, generous child allowances and the so-called guaranteed income benefits paid to low-income families, were the instruments used for that purpose. These increased National Insurance Institute benefits threefold in terms of their ratio to GNP between 1989 and 2000, and thus more than that in real terms; they reduced further disposable income inequality.

Thus, the post-tax, post-transfer payments income distribution inequality grew somewhat over the period of the 15 years in which growth provided for an increase of average per capita GDP by more than 25 percent, close to 1.5 percent annually. The rising inequality in disposable incomes was contained due to the highly progressive income tax structure, which excluded about half the wage-earning population from income tax liability in the first place, and the expanding transfer payment policy pursued by the five governments running the country during that period.

THE DECLINING ROLE OF GOVERNMENT AND THE FADING OF DIRIGISME. This policy had of course an inevitable expansive effect on the scope of fiscal policy. In spite of that expansion, "smaller government" policy was, by and large, implemented through 1989, as the sine qua non of the disinflation policy. The inflation rate was indeed contained within the prescribed 15–20 percent annual rate through 1989, which meant that the preliminary goal of the policy was reached (Table 35). This applies even more to its twin goal, reducing the balance-of-payments deficit; the balance of payments was in surplus on current account from 1985 through 1990, a development unheard of for almost four decades since independence (Table 31). This success on the foreign front put the economy on the threshold of a new economic era.

Israel's rating in the international financial arena, and thus on the world capital market, has improved continuously ever since. The apparent domestic political cost of this policy was a tight lid on the size of the fiscal deficit; in the introductory 1985–89 period, the public sector budget even had a small surplus, though in the last year of the period it ran an exceptionally large deficit of 5.4 percent of GNP (Table 33). This deficit was in contrast not only to the preceding budgets since 1985 but to the succeeding budgets for the next 15 years through 2005, and was due to the slowdown of that year that reduced tax revenues substantially. The tight fiscal ship mandated by the stabilization policy was accordingly maintained with an approximately three percent average annual deficit, the range set by the 1994 Maastricht Convention as the standard for members of the European Union.

The low-deficit rule put Israeli governments during the two decades of 1985–2003 into a tightening corner. At a given structure of tax legislation, a reduction of the rate of inflation from very high to low rates improves the real tax revenue of the government (the Tanzi effect in reverse). This phenomenon indeed occurred in 1985; tax revenues increased at one go by more than six percentage points of GNP (Table 33), making an immense immediate difference to government finances at that crucial time. The withdrawal from Lebanon that began late in 1984, and the ongoing Iran-Iraq War of 1980–88, allowed a substantial cut in defense spending from close to 20 percent of GDP in 1985 to about 14 percent in 1989. This sustained the effort to maintain fiscal discipline at the crucial first stages of the stabilization process (Table 30). The growth process, involving an annual average of six percent GNP growth between 1990 and 1995, while defense expenditures were approximately stable in absolute terms, meant that the latter's share of GDP declined to the range of eight to nine percent, approximately where it remained through 2005.

However, this release of resources from the defense budget was to a great extent absorbed by other public sector expenditures. The most significant of these were welfare state cash benefits, dominated by social security benefits; these increased in the two decades through 2004 by two percentage points, to 8.2 percent of GDP. With the corresponding cash benefits channeled to an absorption "basket" for new immigrants and handicapped victims of Nazi persecution among others, total welfare state cash benefits were about 10 percent of GDP in the early years of the 21st century. Thus, from 1990 on welfare state cash benefits rather than defense costs were the largest item of public sector expenditure. This huge order of magnitude in terms of production capacity is similar to that of the leading industrialized states, even though Israel's per capita GNP was in the first decade of the 21st century only about 55–65 percent of that of these states. It also explains the permanent pressure on fiscal policy to maintain an even keel, in accordance with the EU's 1994 Maastricht Convention on fiscal conduct that Israeli governments have chosen to abide by, though of course it does not apply to Israel at all.

This meant that public sector revenues had to be adapted to the rapidly rising requirements of the social security system. Moreover, the burden imposed on the revenue system to assure the maintenance of the budget discipline was even greater than that imposed by rising social expenditures. This was due to the pattern of the flow of unilateral transfers from abroad received by public sector entities. In the two decades through 2005 these came from two sources: donations from world Jewish communities and a major annual grant from the U.S. government. The latter was fixed in terms of nominal dollars and was the dominant component of the flow; it was 87 percent of the total in 1985, and 68 percent in 2004. It declined in nominal terms from 1990 onward, and much more in real terms.

The Jewish component of that flow increased in nominal terms by more than two times in these two decades, and by about 50 percent in real terms. But this did not compensate for the decline in the U.S. contribution to Israel's public sector budget (Table 32). The real and relevant dimensions of these features are underlined by the pattern of relative contributions to revenue absorption displayed in Table 33. Unilateral transfers were about 29 percent of the total absorption by the public sector in 1985. These rose to 31 percent in 1994, supporting one of goals of the stabilization policy, the elimination of the huge budget deficit. By 1989 the contribution of transfers to absorption was almost down to 16 percent, and in 2004 to about seven percent.

World Jewish donations and U.S. grants contributed only 3.4 percent of GNP to the revenue flow of Israel's public sector in 2004, compared to 21 percent in 1985. U.S. grants were 2.3 percent and the contributions of world Jewry added approximately another one percent. This drastic downward trend of revenue from foreign sources was perhaps the most important piece of news for foreign capital market operators.

The long-run implications of that development were of course highly favorable, particularly the steep decrease of the dependence of Israel's fiscal stability on U.S. funding. But it inevitably shaped tax and revenue policy during these decades, since total expenditure in terms of GDP neither could nor was intended to be reduced at the same rate at which the flow of U.S. grants, in real terms, was declining. This meant that Israel had to substitute tax revenue for the grants, so one of its defining features during that decade was still its traditional "great government" aspect – a high-expenditure, high-tax economy.

Expenditures and tax revenues as a share of GDP indeed declined during these decades expenditures were almost 68 percent and revenue 48 percent, respectively, of GDP as the stabilization policy took effect. Though much lower in relative terms 20 years later, expenditures crossed just under the benchmark of 50 percent of GDP in 2005, and tax revenue was in the 43 percent range; these ratios were still higher than the rates in most E.U. member states, and even more than those of North America.

Prior to the 1990s Israel had a *dirigiste* economy. This pattern changed as the claims of the public sector on economic resources, though still very large, declined, so that by the turn of the century *dirigisme* could no longer be said to characterize the way the economy was run. The growing divorce from direct involvement of the government, as the representative of the political community, in the management of economic activity at the microeconomic level was initiated by the 1985 stabilization policy, which effected a departure of the Treasury and the other economic ministries – the Trade and Industry, Agriculture, and Tourism in particular – from day-to-day involvement in the monetary dimension of the economy. It involved not only the effective freeing of the Bank of Israel to determine interest rates and reserve requirements according to its own judgment, but dictated the neutral stance of the Treasury toward the abolition of "directed credit," which in 1985 was about 35 percent of outstanding commercial bank credit (50 percent in the farming community). This of course increased very significantly the leverage of the interest rate policy of the central bank, simultaneously eliminating the involvement of the government in the allocation of bank credit. This change, which occurred slowly but continuously over about four years through 1989, weaned businesses, including agricultural entities, off cheap subsidized credit. The transition was difficult and led among other things to the bankruptcy of firms that had been household names for more than a generation. The change from a system of subsidized credit to high market interest rates imposed an especially heavy burden on the farming community, which had largely been financed by "directed credit" as part of the Zionist resettlement drive. many settlements, moshavim and kibbutzim, could not hope to repay their accumulated debt in the new economic circumstances. All this was part of the redirection of the economy from its *dirigiste* tradition, and was implicit in the 1985 decision to grant effective freedom to the central bank to manage monetary policy.

The 1985 rules in the foreign exchange market, in particular the setting of the dollar exchange rate as the nominal anchor of the economic system, establishing a single exchange rate for all transactions, constituted of course a major anti-*dirigiste* move even though this was not their immediate objective, which was to simplify the currency control system established by the British in 1939. This very simplification immediately reduced the involvement of the authorities in the micromanagement of foreign exchange. The success of the first stage of the stabilization policy, which reduced inflation to an annual range of 15–20 percent through 1994, led to the reduction of more layers of currency control, which among other things, led later to the elimination of income tax regulations discriminating between domestic and foreign investments. This change was completed only after the turn of the century. It was the last vestige of currency control.

A related process with a similar effect – the reduction of government involvement in the management of production – was the slow but determinate reduction of trade barriers that had been launched in the 1970s. Israel, as a member of the World Trade Organization (WTO), but especially after 1970s–80s trade accords with the European Community and the U.S., persistently pursued a policy of slowly reducing protective import quotas and duties. This process was effectively completed by the late 1990s, reducing significantly the option of protectionist moves by government ministries.

PRIVATIZATION. Privatization, which surfaced as a concept and operational economic target in the 1990s, was not an invention unique to Israel. This notion had been spreading in all the major industrialized economies, with Britain spearheading it in the last two decades of the 20th century. It suggested a feasible reduction of the direct involvement of government in the running of the economy, with a focus on one sector, public utilities, traditionally under the public sector canopy. These were the electricity, water supply, and communications systems and the railroads and broadcasting networks. Almost all of these entities operated in markets in which the technology of production and/or distribution had traditionally offered major advantages to firms with monopoly power.

In the Israeli case this notion had a special twist, since it was initially applied in 1989 to the the banking system, almost entirely nationalized by accident in 1983 in the wake of what became known as the Bank Shares Crisis, an event linked to the triple-digit inflation that dominated the economy for almost five years. To overcome the financial crisis (see below, The Bank Shares Crisis, 1983) the government committed itself to supporting bank share prices by purchasing (through the Bank of Israel) bank stock in the market at a declared minimum price. These purchases cost the BOI an enormous sum, about four percent of GNP, an inflationary move in itself in the context of triple-digit inflation. The longer-run effect of the support policy was state ownership – the effective nationalization of almost the entire banking system by the end of 1983.

With the stabilization policy of 1985 having substantially achieved its goals, the government in power set up a task force in 1988 within the empty shell of an existing government corporation; its unique mission was to reprivatize the banking system as soon as possible. Thus, privatization of banking was a consensus policy from the very beginning. Two small banks were indeed sold in the early 1990s. Yet it required close to a decade, through 1995, before a meaningful move – the privatization of one of the two dominant banks, Bank Hapoalim, could be implemented. Progress afterward was slow, and only in 2005 did the sale in an auction of a substantial portion of Bank Leumi stock, with an option for for a further purchase, and the sale of the controlling interest in the Israel Discount Bank, the third largest, take place.

The difficulty of implementing this reprivatization was not due to political opposition or opposition from the commercial banking system. It was inherent in the small scope of the domestic capital market and the significant size of the banks, two large and one medium-sized. The purchase of a controlling interest in any of them would require a huge fraction of total financial investment. It was only the the inflow of foreign financial resources from 1991 on that enabled a deal requiring an investment of the magnitude involved in the purchase of Bank Hapoalim.

This new foreign investment had far-reaching significance. With the success of the 1985 stabilization policy the capital inflow improved to several hundred million dollars annually, but never crossed the 500 million line before 1991. The rapid and steady elimination of currency control regulations from the early 1990s, supported by the dipping of the inflation rate into single digits in the first half of that decade and declining further toward price stability in the second half, finally made the difference. The average annual inflow of foreign capital funds in the 1992–99 interval leaped to almost five billion dollars annually, with an all-time high of 12 billion dollars in the high-tech bubble year of 2000. After the bubble burst, through 2005 the average foreign investment inflow returned to the $5 billion annual average. That major inflow of foreign private capital, at an average of four to five percent of GDP, created a total transformation of Israel's capital market. Among other things it opened the gates for privatization.

In more than one sense the Bank Hapoalim case provided the opening for privatization supported by foreign funds. Yet even in that case a significant fraction of the cost of the purchase was provided to the group of domestic and foreign entrepreneurs who purchased the controlling interest in the bank by Bank Leumi, the still-nationalized second-largest bank. Several of the smaller banking institutions were privatized as well in the 1990s, with much smaller hurdles of financing required that could be raised in the home market by domestic tycoons. The privatization of the banking system was almost completed by 2005, 23 years after the accidental nationalization: controlling interests in Bank Leumi, the Zionist financial flagship established in 1903 and almost equal in size to Bank Hapoalim, and in the Israel Discount Bank, were finally sold. They were acquired by foreign investors with funds raised in foreign capital markets.

Privatization was not confined to the financial sector. Indeed, the real sectors, in the utilities and manufacturing, had been proceeding rapidly along this route since the early 1990s. The process was facilitated and encouraged by two technical revolutions: the communications revolution, which allowed the building of wireless telephone systems, and the PC revolution, which provided the bedrock for the high-tech industry. These offered a convenient opening for the move to restrict the monopoly power of major firms.

Though it was the government-owned telephone company, Bezeq, that first ventured into the cellular telephone business, its traditional monopoly on that popular means of communications was soon challenged by two private-sector corporations, which were granted licenses to operate in that field. Bezeq's monopoly on international telephone communications was similarly abolished, by permitting other companies into the field by the early 1990s. the sale of Bezeq itself to private entrepreneurs, completed in 2005, symbolized clearly the government's adoption of the idea of privatization fostered in the 1970s and 1980s in Britain, which said that even classic utilities with justified monopoly power would offer better service to the economy as private businesses.

The high-tech revolution in Israel was started within the nationalized defense industry and in the army's intelligence and technology unit. These employed highly educated, trained, and experienced personnel. The adoption of outsourcing by the IDF and the defense industries in the late 1980s soon led to the setting up of small independent civilian groupings, manned by veterans of the army and the defense industries, working by contract on projects, mainly research, for their erstwhile employers. As their numbers grew, several of these converted to private startups financed by venture capital.

The interesting feature of that development is clearly that it was led by veterans of IDF technology and communication units and the research departments of the national defense industries who decided to adopt the Silicon Valley model for their private business ventures. Many of these soon succeeded and by the 1990s and the turn of the century had made major contributions to Israeli manufacturing, its export volume, and its standing in the high-tech world. Indeed, the avalanche of foreign funds in 2000, as the global bubble inflated, was linked to Israel's by then Silicon Valley-like status.

This is not to say that the government sector was and is not still indirectly involved in the promotion of the high-tech industry. Intel, a major international corporation in that field with a significant and growing presence in Israel since the 1980s in both research and production, is a case in point. Its application for an income tax allowance for its major investment in a new production facility, which will employ 1,000 workers in addition to the 6,000 it already employs, was granted in 2005. But this still indirect government involvement is minuscule in relative terms compared to the situation during the first three decades of statehood through the early 1980s. The rapid expansion of the economy, novel technologies of production and communications, and the post-1990s rising inflow of foreign capital – a flow inherently and instantaneously linked to the mood swings of the major world capital markets – eroded the *dirigiste* features of the Israel economy, inherited from the World War II British model. What was left of that structure in the first decade of the 21st century was the high net national domestic debt, along with comparatively large public sector expenditures and tax revenue, in terms of national product.

The Balance-of-Payments Revolution, 1985–2005

The major transformation the economy had undergone in the two decades through 2005 – a major transition to a free-floating exchange rate, a major inflow of foreign capital, privatizations and the shedding of *dirigisme*, and meaningful growth – was inherently linked to a revolutionary change in the balance of payments. A meaningful indication of that change, which offered a kind of insurance policy to international ratings agencies and thus to foreign investors, was the rise in the level of foreign currency reserves. These were only about $3.7 billion in 1985. One of the twin goals of the stabilization policy of that year was an immediate improvement of the balance of payments. Reserves in 1995 were more than two times as great, by 2000 they were already $23 billion, and they continued to grow rapidly through 2005 (Table 31).

What counted for the state's macroeconomic policymakers was the number of months' worth of imports for which the available reserves were able to pay. By the end of 1984 reserves were not scraping bottom, as in the mid-1950s when there was usually enough for only a few weeks, but they were down to only 2.4 months' worth. The stabilization policy improved this. at the end of 1989 there were enough for 3.6 months, and by the end of the 1990s, the decade in which the balance of payments disappeared from the headlines, there were enough reserves for six months' worth of imports. The figure continued to climb through 2005.

What was a more crucial test for the rating agencies, and thus for the foreign investment banks that opened branches in Tel Aviv through this decade, was of course the ratio of foreign currency reserves to foreign debt. This measure underlined the revolutionary change the system had undergone in the two post-stabilization policy decades. At the end of 1985, six months after the inauguration of the policy, Israel's foreign currency reserves were equal to 29 percent of its total foreign debt. By 1989 this ratio improved to about 34 percent of the debt, which was long-term and thus did not impose an immediate threat to the reserves. Within a decade, however, the situation was completely reversed; by 2000 reserves were more than seven times greater than foreign debt. It settled at more than two times the level of debt in 2004, in the wake of a considered move by the government to convert a portion of the bulging domestic debt into a $10 billion loan covered by a U.S. government guarantee, which would reduce its cost.

What counted even more with rating agencies and thus with foreign investors was Israel's robust economic performance during the summer of 1998, in the crisis that involved the collapse of the currencies of the so-called "Asian Tigers," the major South American economy, and Russia. With the Israeli exchange rate effectively, though not formally, fully flexible, the Bank of Israel did not intervene in the exchange market; it allowed the exchange rate to bear the burden of withdrawals, as foreign and domestic investors sold their shekel assets and purchased foreign currency. The depreciation of the shekel vis-à-vis the dollar was indeed significant – 18 percent in 1998, compared to eight percent in 1997 and even lower rates before that (e.g. 1.8 percent in 1994). When the storm was over by 1999, the dollar value of the shekel was restored, and in the prosperous high-tech bubble year of 2000 the shekel appreciated by close to three percent. Thus, the flexible exchange rate – and domestic prices strongly linked to it – absorbed effectively the tremendous pressure from the exchange markets on the so-called emerging economies. Dollar reserves even grew slightly in 1998 and stayed put in 1999, at which time the world crisis condition was over.

But for the Israeli economy, which only within the previous decade had eliminated currency controls altogether, this was undoubtedly a test of maturity from the point of view of foreign observers. Thus, even though the last vestige of indirect control, differential income tax rules applying to the capital market, was eliminated only at the end of 2004, the 1998 incident settled the main issue. Israel's foreign exchange market, and thus its capital market, was given a passing grade with honors. The ensuing avalanche of foreign investment through 2005, years in which the state had to withstand a series of terror attacks, proves the point.

The success in the capital account stakes had by that time a sound basis in the "real foreign front," expressed in terms of the trade account, and summarized in terms of the current account data. That transformation occurred in 1985, when after 37 years of statehood Israel's current account was in a small surplus, contributing to the accumulation of reserves. This reflected the drastic reduction of the deficit in the trading and services account, a process that had been going since the 1960s. By 1985 that deficit was still close to four percent of GNP, to which should be added a similar percentage for the interest charges on the foreign net debt, totaling approximately eight percent of GNP. The improvement in the trade and services account, through greater expansion of exports than of imports, brought the deficit on it within the range of one percent of GNP from 2000 on. The somewhat lower ratio of charges on foreign debt meant that a deficit of four to five percent on these two accounts was easily met by the flow of unilateral payments, which were in the six-to-seven percent range from the late 1980s on (Table 31). Of these only 35–40 percent were from Jewish sources – world Jewry and immigrants – and most of the rest from U.S. government grants, financing mainly U.S.-produced weapon imports. Still, the balance of payments, which for almost four decades was a headache for Israeli governments, disappeared as a pressing economic issue, and no longer made headlines.

Monetary Policy and the Effective Independence of the Bank of Israel, 1985–2005

THE POST-STABILIZATION REVIVAL OF MONETARY POLICY. The success of the stabilization policy in dealing with the twin problems of the balance of payments and inflation, which was finally settled in the second half of the 1990s as the economy achieved price stability, would not have been possible but for the steadfast restrictive monetary policy pursued during these two decades. The monetary orders of the 1985 program were issued by the working party operating under the authority of the Prime Minister's Office and the Treasury. These decreed that the strict nominal quota on bank credit be in force through about six months. The Bank of Israel executed the order, which resulted in sky-high real interest rates through a longer period than had been hoped for. Early in 1986, however, it reduced the inflation rate to a moderate range of 15–20 percent, the short-term target of the policy (see above, The 1985 Economic Stabilization Policy). The BOI, through its newly established monetary department, was to run the monetary show continuously; initially to preserve what had been gained, and later to push the system toward lower inflation rates, ultimately to reach the goal of price stability. The central bank thus took the 1985 orders as a license to execute a highly restrictive monetary policy through two decades. The Treasury at times responded with nonsympathetic noises at greater or lesser volume, but little effective interference.

Carrying out this policy required the creation of suitable instruments for the purpose. At the very beginning, July 1985, the BOI used the only instruments it then had and lifted the required minimum reserve ratios twice to the unheard-of ratio of 50 percent, which it maintained for more than seven months. This forced the banks to maintain a large gap between debit and credit interest rates, which in turn encouraged the appearance of credit gray markets. But the reserve ratio was a blunt instrument in the first place; it could affect only one component of the money supply, the current account deposits, at the cost of reducing the efficiency of the commercial banks as business enterprises. It was an inefficient instrument for the regulation of the money supply, since it could affect only the size of the multiplier, but not the more crucial component of the money supply, its multiplicand, the monetary base.

The "no-printing" amendment, which removed from the 1954 BOI Law the obligation of the Central Bank to respond to the government's application for credit, increased the degree of freedom of the central bank in applying a restrictive monetary policy. It eliminated the power of the Treasury to increase the size of the monetary base, thus to expand the supply of money by borrowing from the central bank, i.e., printing it. Though operationally only a preventive rule, it increased the relative power of the BOI to run the show.

Yet credit accommodation to the government was not the only way expansion of the monetary base could be accomplished; balance-of-payment inflows inclusive of the proceeds of government borrowing abroad were a case in point. To deal with such events it was obvious that the BOI was in need of the same kinds of instruments available to every central bank in the industrialized world. An obvious candidate for that purpose was the Makam debenture – a short-term Treasury bond. According to the defunct 1966 contract between the Bank of Israel and the Treasury, Makam bonds were allocated to the central bank to serve that very function, as an instrument to affect the size of the monetary base. The death knell of its successful service in that capacity in 1967–69 was sounded in 1970, when the Treasury adamantly refused to sanction the raising of the discount rate on Makam debentures as a means of controlling the double-digit inflation rate which by the end of that year was a fact of life. This of course meant the demise of monetary policy as a macroeconomic control mechanism for the next 15 years, through 1985.

The radical change of heart at the Treasury in 1985, with its unique focus on the success of the stabilization policy, led to a renewal of the 1966 contract with the BOI. According to the understanding between them, the BOI was again allocated a quota of Makam bonds, which it could use according to its own judgment. Thus by selling or buying according to its own readings of the preferred pattern and level of discount rates in the money market, it had the freedom to navigate the credit and financial markets and simultaneously support the exchange rate, the nominal anchor of the economy.

The Bank soon began to use the Makam instrument, as the 1986 entries for outstanding balances of Makam bonds on its balance sheet indicate. To strengthen its grip on markets and reduce its dependence on the political attitudes and decisions of the government, the BOI, with at least no formal protest from the Treasury, put in 1986 a second instrument into its arsenal: the so called "monetary loan." This instrument, which was not subject to a Treasury quota, would be used by the commercial banks to bolster their reserves whenever these were close to the legal minimum. It was to be auctioned weekly by competitive bidding, thus setting the discount rate for that loan accommodation. This instrument offered much greater flexibility to the BOI to influence the structure of interest rates, since it was not constrained, as was the Makam bond, by a quota that had to be negotiated with the Treasury. Thus, during the crucial years (1986–89) when runaway inflation was finally contained and brought down to a 15–20 percent annual rate, the outstanding monetary loan was greater than the outstanding balance of Makam debentures. This instrument increased significantly the clout of the BOI in the application of its highly restrictive monetary policy, showing in terms of close to 12 percent real interest rates on overdrafts in 1989 (Table 35). Finally, it succeeded in establishing the Bank's priority in this field, since by varying the size of the auction of the weekly monetary loan, according to its own judgment and discretion, it did push the structure of interest rates towards the 1985 goal.

Yet to fix interest rates in the monetary and financial market by maneuvering on the supply side, rising demand by the banking system for reserves (base money) was required. During the stabilization interval through 1989 this was "naturally" provided by the inflationary process still running at 15–20 percent; to sustain the provision of the volume of credit in real terms to the economy, the nominal credit volume had to grow *pari passu* with the rising price level. A real expansion of commercial bank credit, required by growth, therefore necessarily involved the expansion of bank reserves. Thus, in these crucial years when sustaining the success of the stabilization policy required staunch support on the monetary front, the strengthening of the grip of the central bank on money and finance by means of the "monetary loan" instrument was vital.

The strengthening grip of the BOI on the monetary dimension of the economy gained further support from the abolition of the "directed credit." The gradual abolition of that highly subsidized credit quota, which by 1985 made up about 35 percent of total bank credit, was begun by the BOI with the silent support of the Treasury, even though it imposed hardships on those who had received such credit, particularly those who had a much greater component of cheap credit at their disposal than average. The obvious rationale for this process was the abolition of the dual price system for money, which offered growing benefits to its privileged recipients the higher the inflation rate, and inevitably generated a credit black market. The elimination of "directed credits," led later to the collapse of several major household-name firms, even though it was a gradual, drawn-out process. That gradual implementation was accomplished by moving bank clientele from the cheap credit tranche to the full-priced component at the expiration dates of credit instruments. Since the interest rate subsidy was mainly based on the lower legal minimum reserves that the banks were required to maintain for that purpose, the conversion of credit from subsidized to nonsubsidized required, accordingly, higher reserves per unit of credit. This generated growing demand for bank reserves, hence supported the BOI's effort to gain control of the money market by manipulating the supplies of base money by means of its two newly acquired instruments, the Makam bonds and the monetary loans to commerical banks.

By affecting the the monetary balance by intervening in the money market with these instruments, the BOI could make a liberalizing move with what had hitherto been its only instrument of control over the supply of money, the legal minimum reserve ratio, which determined the size of the money multiplier. The all-time high, a huge 50 percent reserve requirement imposed on the banking system on August 1, 1985, in support of the stabilization policy, was reduced four times in succession in 1986 and 1987 to only 30 percent. Toward the end of 1989 the minimum legal reserve ratio was down to a new all-time low of 15 percent, a ratio never dreamt of for over 40 years. By the mid-1990s it was down to six percent, and to even lower rates for very short-term credit. Reserve ratios were thus rapidly downgraded as an instrument of monetary policy and by the 1990s were effectively excluded from the arsenal of monetary controls.

THE BANK OF ISRAEL ACQUIRES THE MONETARY REINS. The success of the first stage of the stabilization policy, shown by its reaching its two goals – moderate, stable inflation in the 15–20 percent range, and a significant improvement in the balance of payments (Tables 36 and 31) – was of course not the end of the story. Israel's success, in contrast to the dismal failure of Argentina and Brazil, which launched their stabilization programs at approximately the same time, was an argument in favor of the Israeli model. Its success in maintaining the level of economic activity despite its drastic monetary measures was discussed all over the world.

Yet these moderate inflation levels, which through 1988 kept the level of unemployment at an acceptable level, still did not compare favorably with the disinflation programs of the industrialized countries, which had been launched somewhat earlier, and pulled inflation down to mid-single-digit rates by the early 1990s. To maintain the improvement in the real exchange rate, which was necessary to keep the current account of the balance of payments in good shape, there was no option but to adjust the nominal exchange rate, the nominal anchor of the economy since 1985, and devalue the currency against the dollar. The devaluation was implemented early in 1987 after 18 months in which the exchange rate was kept stable in line with the commitment made at the launching of the stabilization policy. Another devaluation, induced in part by speculation against the shekel facilitated by the liberalizing of currency controls in 1987, was implemented in 1988, and another in June 1989, generating a cumulative rate of devaluation of 30 percent within 48 months.

The economic rationale of these developments can be inferred from Table 36, which shows that domestic prices rose by almost two times between 1985 and 1989. Given the much lower inflation ratios in the major industrial countries, these small devaluations still allowed an improvement of five percent in the real exchange rates, its ultimate target. Inflation at annual rates of 15–20 percent, though quite moderate by the standards of the lost decade, still forced the hand of the authorities, who had to allow rises in the nominal exchange rate in order to prevent the erosion of the real exchange rate and avoid its negative effect on the balance of payments.

Both the BOI management and the Treasury were by that time aware that the very success of the stabilization effort posed a dilemma for economic policy. The credibility of the policy was inevitably put to a severe test, since it was pegged to the nominal anchor, the exchange rate. The commitment of the authorities to the exchange rate of 1.5 New Israeli Shekels per dollar made in July 1985 was indeed officially qualified by the condition referring to the real wage rates. Since these rose rapidly, even though unemployment rates were still in the 6–7 percent range and increased to almost nine percent in the wake of the 1989 slowdown, the authorities indeed formally had a case for the devaluation. But the credibility of government commitments depends much more on the actual everyday features, than on qualifying statements made years ago, which after the passage of some time only experts are aware of, if anyone.

The credibility issue was directly linked to the dollar exchange rate as the nominal anchor of the system; its 30 percent rise in the four-year period through 1989 was seemingly inconsistent with the role it fulfilled for several years. The obvious response to the exchange rate problem was to increase its flexibility, thus allowing it to move within a range rather than a point fixation. Such a move would definitely reduce the danger of speculative attacks on the shekel in the short run (which occurred in 1988), offer a better adaptation of the exchange rate to the differential inflation rates of trading partners in the medium run, and a better response to differences in the interstate pattern of rising productivity in the long run.

The move to a flexible exchange rate even within a narrow range would, however, erode its function as a nominal anchor for the system, an essential ingredient of the disinflation process since 1985. A move toward price stability, to perhaps a one to three percent annual average inflation rate, at that time the standard for the major economic powers, from the "moderate" 15–20 percent rate at which the economy was stuck for five years through 1990, would require such an anchor. This meant, of course, that allowing growing flexibility of the exchange rate, the purpose of which was to provide stability to the foreign exchange market, which is so crucial in small open economies such as Israel's, was inconsistent with the nominal anchor role assigned to the dollar exchange rate in 1985. A move to a flexible exchange rate regime would require, therefore, a substitute nominal anchor.

The first moves toward a flexible exchange rate were implemented in 1989, at which time a narrow horizontal range was established within which the rate would be allowed to fluctuate according to supply and demand in the market. This model endowed the central bank with the function of regulating the exchange market by means of its stock of foreign exchange reserves, and the relevant price instrument, the interest rate. The degree of freedom of the BOI as an operator in the exchange market was soon considerably increased as the narrow range within which the exchange rate would be allowed to fluctuate was considerably widened in 1992 from a six to a ten percent range (plus or minus five percent from the targeted middle rate of the range). Furthermore, since the ongoing inflation in 1990–91 was still running at an 18 percent rate (Table 35), the midline targeted rate, and thus the upper and lower bands of the range, identifying the highest and lowest rates at which BOI intervention in the market was prescribed, were to slope upwards. This upward slope, an admission that moderate inflation was still a fact of life, required therefore, a device allowing the maintenance of the real exchange rate. To maintain at least the real rate of 1990, the slope of the midline and thus of the upper and lower lines of the band limiting the range within which the exchange rate would be allowed to fluctuate, was set as the difference between Israel's inflation rate and the inflation rate of several major economic powers – the U.S., the European Community, etc. A good omen that appeared as the new system of exchange rate management was established in 1992 was the significant plunge of the inflation rate from 18 percent in the opening years of the 1990s, to only 9.4 percent. The economy thus moved to a single-digit inflation rate after an interval of more than two decades.

The definite move to a flexible exchange rate in 1992, accompanied by the widening of the exchange rate range to 10 percent, eroded of course by definition its role as a nominal anchor for the system. Following the technique taken up by more and more European members of the OECD from proposals discussed in the academic literature, Israel adopted the so-called "*inflation target*" rule. The authority deciding on, and publicizing, that target would be, as everywhere, the government, which of course was advised by the BOI. In the summer of 1991 deliberations about the forthcoming budget were linked with the formulation of an inflation target. The BOI suggested the adoption of a multiperiod declining *inflation target*, as a signal of the long-term trend of the policy. This proposal was not accepted by the government in power, facing an election campaign by the middle of 1992. The inflation target adopted for 1992, 14–15 percent, was indeed lower than the current rates at the time of deliberations, which were in the 17–18 percent range. This target signaled that the government, and hence its budget for the forthcoming year, was bent on attempting to reduce inflation gradually. If credible, it would notify business and labor unions, households and entrepreneurs how to adapt their plans to that price signal.

Adoption of this strategy was of course a political decision influenced by the advice and prodding of the BOI to adopt a lean fiscal policy and tough inflation targets. It was the government's responsibility, subject to parliamentary approval. But the day-to-day handling of both the foreign exchange rate and domestic money and financial markets was to be the realm of the BOI. This division of labor is and was the traditional model for central banks and treasuries in the major economic powers, identified by OECD membership. The BOI charter of 1954, and circumstances specific to Israel, limited the freedom of action of the central bank, and the Treasury made the full use of the power granted to the government by law, particularly from 1970 onwards. At that time, this led to the demise of monetary policy for 15 years to come through 1985. It was the stabilization policy in 1985 that effectively gave a new lease on life to monetary policy. Its scope was gradually but persistently expanded over longish intervals, during which stringent policy was required to secure the contemporary moderate level of inflation.

The BOI could implement that policy, which among other things eliminated the "directed credit" over time, allowing, ultimately, the widening of the impact of any monetary move initiated by BOI across the board, to the whole volume of commercial bank credit, because of the neutral stance taken by the Treasury and the finance ministers of three successive governments, even though they were of rival parties. This increased significantly the efficiency of monetary policy and by the same token the clout of the central bank and of the interest rate it set to regulate the markets: the so-called BOI interest rate, a term and a concept hammered into the psyche of the financial markets by the early 1990s, and that of the public by around 1994.

The crucial point at which the BOI interest rate became headline news, as it was announced on the last Monday of the month, was late in 1994. At that time the BOI, which was already paying attention to the government's inflation target, yet focusing on the pattern of the exchanges, changed tack. It decided to focus directly on the inflation rate as its guiding principle for monetary policy, letting the rate of exchange, which could fluctuate within a significantly widened range of 14 percent (±7 percent of the targeted mid-rate), find its own level. The healthy status of the balance of payments backed up this meaningful new departure (Table 31), which put the focus of monetary policy in the next decade on the inflation rate rather than on the exchange rate. The specific occasion was highly relevant to the about-turn. Presuming that the decline of the inflation rate to 9.4 percent in 1992 suggested that it would remain near 10 percent in 1993, and assuming a reasonable state of the balance of payments, the central bank responded with a significant 4.5 percent reduction of its marginal monetary loan interest rate from 16 percent in 1991 to 11.4 percent in 1993. This, however, resulted in a zero real rate of interest at the unexpectedly higher inflation rate of 1993.

This relatively expansionary monetary policy coincided with a major wave of mass immigration, with inflows of 75–80,000 annually, and contributed to the high rate of growth – seven percent in 1994. Inflation, however, reaccelerated to an annual rate of 14.5 percent. At this rate of inflation, the BOI marginal real rate of interest on the monetary loan set early in 1994 was negative, and the inflation target for that year, set by the government in 1993 at eight percent, was well under the actual rate. The hand of the BOI's management was thus forced. At the risk of a public confrontation with the Treasury, the central bank immediately jacked up its rate by two percentage points to 13.5 percent, and kept raising that rate though 1996, by a total five percentage points. Its success in pulling inflation down to the 10 percent range, and thus within the official inflation target of 8–11 percent set by the outgoing government in 1995 for 1996 and 1997, spoke for itself. This stiff monetary policy did lead, however, to a publicized clash with the Treasury, which complained of its negative effect on the level of economic activity and the ensuing slowdown in growth that was a fact of economic life through 1999.

THE STRUGGLE FOR PRICE STABILITY. The BOI succeeded in tightening the money market and jacking up interest rates due to the novel monetary reins which it had invented and perfected in the late 1980s and 1990s: the monetary loan, which emerged in 1986–87; and the reverse of that instrument, the "fixed-term commercial banking system deposit" with the central bank, put into service in 1996. The latter was the product of the success of BOI's monetary policy, as the growing foreign confidence in the stability of the economy led to a 33 percent increase in foreign currency reserves between 1990 and 1995, and a trebling of these reserves in the next five years through 2000 (Table 31). The massive capital inflow increased the liquidity of the banking system, releasing its dependence on the BOI's monetary loans. In response, the central bank turned the tables and instead of providing liquidity to the system, it drained liquidity from it by offering them a highly competitive rate for term deposits, set in the weekly BOI auctions.

These developments increased to a very great extent the effective independence of the central bank, though not its legal status, enshrined in the 1954 BOI Law. The government, effectively the Treasury, had the legal option to prevent the implementation of the use of the monetary loan instrument when it came on line in 1985, and really took off in 1987, at which time the BOI was run by one governor; it similarly had the option to prevent the use of the fixed-term commercial bank deposit instrument when this was "invented" by a different governor in 1996. These two devices were introduced and used by four BOI governors between 1985 and 2005 to overcome the constraint which, until 2002, the Treasury had imposed by means of the Makam quota, the technically preferable instrument for open market operations. The political urgency that required the success of the stabilization policy might have been the reason why the finance minister in 1985 and 1986, or the prime minister of the day, turned a blind eye to what might have been understood by them as minor technical matters. The data for 1987, in which the outstanding monetary loan had not only expanded by four times in one year, but was already greater than the total of outstanding Makam debentures, might have drawn the attention of the new finance minister at that time. Yet even though he was presumably aware that the increasing use of that instrument by the BOI reduced the effective restrictions of the Treasury on monetary policy, he chose not to intervene. He adopted that attitude even though it was obvious that the BOI's use of that instrument was designed to circumvent the veto power of the Treasury on the scope of the BOI's open market policy by means of the Makam quota, hence on its power to affect the monetary and financial markets as a whole.

Almost a decade later, when the fixed-term bank deposit was introduced, initially as a supplement and soon effectively as a major substitute for the monetary loan instrument, it was already too late to use the legal power still available to the Treasury to prevent the introduction of that new instrument. Such a move would have led to the resignation of the BOI governor, the third in succession since the launch of the stabilization policy, and would have been considered by the international rating agencies, and so by potential foreign investors, as an attempt to turn the clock back from the strategy of pursuing price stability by opening the economy, which by 1995 was clearly experiencing an upsurge of private capital inflow. This flow was greater by seven times compared to the level of 1990 and by 17 times compared to that of 1985.

The focus on price stability as the guiding principle of BOI policy from 1994 on created growing tensions with the Treasury, supported by the political establishment, and was not popular with public opinion. The open clash of 1995–96 with the finance minister, that continued with his successor in the next government, controlled by the rival political party, is understandable in terms of the declining level of economic activity and rising unemployment to almost nine percent in 1999 (Table 29). Yet the BOI, using as its guiding principle the government's declared inflation target, which from 1993 on was in the upper single-digit range, raised its marginal interest rate by five percentage points within less than three years, between 1994 and 1996. This move succeeded indeed in reaching the price target, locking Israel's inflation rate at ten percent from 1995 through 1998, and leading the system to price stability from 1999 on.

Furthermore, though Israel's outstanding performance in 1998 – as the collapse of their currencies plunged into financial crisis first the "Asian tigers" and soon the major countries of Latin America and Russia as well – was clearly due to the measures initiated in 1994 by the BOI, this did not preclude another highly public dispute with the Treasury in 2001. It was the granting of effectively full flexibility to the exchange rate and the clear downward trend of prices toward stability that in 1998 allowed Israel to ride almost unscathed through the storm, and to be the recipient of an avalanche of capital imports in the year of the global high-tech bubble of 2000 (Table 31).

Though the admittedly quite restrictive monetary policy pursued by the BOI in the second half of the 1990s proved highly successful, this did not prevent scathing attacks on BOI policy from the finance minister and Treasury officials in 2001 as the high-tech bubble burst and economies everywhere, including Israel, experienced a decline in economic activity. In the Israeli case, this decline was smaller than in other places. It involved an absolute decline of GNP by approximately one percent in 2001, which was indeed a major contrast to the eight percent growth rate of the bubble year of 2000. The absolute decline of GDP was even worse than the frustrating three percent growth rate of the three preceding years, 1996–99, when Israel's prices stabilized. In view of the zero rate of inflation in 2000, the BOI interest rate was reduced by three percentage points in 10 steps, even though GNP growth accelerated to eight percent in that bubble year. In response to the bursting of the bubble in 2001, it was moved a further 2.4 percentage points in seven steps to an all-time low rate of 5.8 percent from December of that year.

Yet the finance minister of the new government formed at the beginning of that year mounted a public campaign against the "high-interest-rate policy" of the BOI, and even submitted a proposed bill to the government to amend the BOI Law of 1954 to revoke the power of the BOI's governor to set the central bank interest rate and give it to a committee made up of a Treasury representative and several political personalities. This proposal to erode the authority of the central bank over monetary policy was not only inconsistent with the trend elsewhere in the industrialized world, it was also inconsistent with the conclusions of the Levin Committee, whose mandate was to consider the Bank's role and recommend changes in the BOI Law. The committee's report of 1998 proposed that the BOI's management, structure, and authority be remodeled along the lines of the Bank of England and the European central banks, to increase, not erode, its independence. Price stability was to become its statutory priority.

This all-out political pressure on the governor of the bank led in December 2001 to an understanding with the prime minister that involved an immediate cut of the BOI interest rate by two percentage points to 3.8 percent. The quid pro quo was the government's consent to two proposals that had been advocated for many years by the BOI. The government agreed to the complete abolition of the exchange rate range, legally allowing it to float freely; and secondly, the government agreed finally to allow the BOI complete control over Makam bond issues, which meant the abolition of the Treasury quota. The BOI of course had its devices for circumventing the quota – the monetary loan and its reverse counterpart, the commercial bank term deposits – but these instruments were technically clumsier.

This deal, made in the last week of 2001, was in appearance a complete victory for the government; the quid pro quo items were mentioned by the media, if at all, as technicalities of minor significance. To the public it seemed that in the struggle between the central bank and the Treasury, which had the support of the political community and the media, the BOI had got the worst of it. Yet within three months, in March 2002, the BOI raised the interest rate back to 4.4 percent; in June the rate was 7.1 percent; and in July 2002, seven months after the "victory" of the Treasury, the interest rate was 9.1 percent, higher by more than three percentage points than it had been at the time of the BOI's "capitulation" in December 2001.

Nobody dared to raise his voice against these stringent moves. The reason for this change of tune by the political and business communities was the very developments the BOI had predicted would occur in response to the rapid reduction of the interest rate, even though the economy had then been in a slump. The dollar rate of exchange leapt ominously to a 34 percent an annual rate in the first two quarters of 2002, with a strong and immediate effect on prices, as would be expected in a small economy like Israel's. Prices in those two quarters rose at an annual rate of 13 percent, in contrast to the stable price pattern that had emerged from 1999 on; the inflation rates in the years 1999, 2000, and 2001 were 1.3, zero, and 1.4 percent respectively. The inflation rate in 2002 in the wake of the Treasury's "victory" of December 2001 was 6.5 percent.

Within three months, in March 2002, the governor of the BOI felt free to begin the series of major hikes that pushed the BOI interest rate to 9.1 percent. These developments suggested that the Treasury's victory had proven hollow. In view of this, the political and the business communities kept quiet, even though the moves by the central bank were highly restrictive, and did not oppose the very high nominal and real July 2002 interest rate, in an economy which was in recession.

The successive hikes in the interest rate succeeded by the summer of 2002 in stanching the outflow of funds, and thus stabilized both the exchange rate and the price level at approximately the peak they had then reached. The year-end result of what could retrospectively be described as a laboratory experiment in populist political intervention in monetary and financial policy was a bulge in the curve describing the declining pattern of inflation from 1998 on. The 6.5 percent inflation rate of 2002, in the wake of a 10 percent or so surge in the dollar exchange rate, thus proved to be only an interruption on the road of price stability, the threshold of which the economy had passed by the end of the 20th century (Table 36).

The most significant result of the 2002 learning-by-doing experiment was the clear demonstration of the BOI's effective, though not legal, independence. As of 2006 a revision of the 1954 BOI Law to put the central bank in a 21st-century legal framework similar to those of the central banks of the major economic powers is still pending.

The 2002 incident, though costly – the unnecessary leap in inflation and the exchange rate involved a real cost to the economy – earned the BOI its spurs. It demonstrated the clear benefit of the division of labor in the guidance of the macroeconomy, allowing the central bank to operate as the arbiter of the monetary dimension of the economy. This was admitted by the new finance minister who moved into the Treasury when a new government came to power in January 2003, and the international financial community, represented in a sense by the rating agencies, of course understood the incident in that the same way. The bank's new status also offered greater transparency in and credibility for Israel's surging capital market, which came into its own only in the wake of the 1985 stabilization policy and acquired world significance in the later 1990s.

Though the 1954 Bank of Israel Law had not been changed by 2006, the central bank's role in the formation and running of macroeconomic policy had nevertheless undergone a revolution originating in the 1985 stabilization policy. It was implemented in stages, as the Bank's management, run by four successive governors between 1985 and 2004, acquired more and more freedom of action to manage monetary policy according to their own reading of events at home and abroad. Wielding instruments forged between 1985 and 1995 to control the monetary base, having gradually convinced successive governments to repeal currency controls, the last vestiges of which were finally abolished in 2005, and in view of the full flexibility of the exchange rate effective from 1998 (formal agreement on which was reached only in December 2001), the independence of the central bank as the institution managing monetary policy was effectively accomplished by the first years of the 21st century. Legislation to formalize it, however, is still pending.

Furthermore, in more than one sense, the achievement of price stability was a clear reflection of the *effectiveness* of the central bank's independence. This process was inherently linked with developments in the foreign currency arena: a major structural change represented by the complete abolition of the vestiges of currency control in 2005 and the partial withdrawal of the government from the running of the pension system through privatization. The privatization of the unintentionally nationalized banks was of course a component of that structural change.

The Banking System

A CENTURY OF GROWTH AND PERFORMANCE. From its very beginning, the Jewish resettlement effort in Palestine, led by the World Zionist Organization from the last years of the 19th century, was integrally linked with banking. The establishment of the Jaffa branch of the Anglo-Palestine Corporation, later renamed the Anglo-Palestine Bank in 1903, embodied this linkage. Its legal framework as a corporation registered in England, with a London office, rooted it in conservative British banking traditions and techniques, which became the foundation of its behavior as a financial institution.

The appearance of Britain as the mandatory power after World War I led to a rapid expansion of the banking system involving major banks like Barclays and the Ottoman Bank, which opened branches in Jerusalem and were soon followed by others. In 1920 there were just five banks in Palestine, with a total of eight branches; by 1930 there were 32. The Fifth Aliyah from the early 1930s on generated a flood. In 1936, there were a record-high 75 commercial bank main offices and several also had a number of branches. To this should be added the cooperative credit societies established mostly by the Jewish labor movement, over 100 by 1936. A number of Arab banks and foreign establishments, mainly branches of British banks, also operated in Palestine. Banking, though, was on the whole mainly a Jewish affair. When an inevitable shakeup occurred in the economic downturn after 1936 through the prewar world political crisis, the very small fry, effectively all Jewish banking establishments, disappeared. By the outbreak of World War II, the number of commercial banks was down to 33, and by 1948, upon the declaration of the state, there were only 23, plus 70 local cooperative credit societies.

The major Jewish banking institutions in the Mandatory period mixed conservative English banking traditions with the continental European concept of a versatile structure, allowing them to own firms in the real sectors of the economy. This structure and practice meant that in spite of three runs on banks between 1936 and 1939 generated by the several stages of the prewar crisis, none of the major Jewish banks collapsed, even though there was no central bank to sustain liquidity in times of financial stress. And when after the second Munich Crisis of 1938 that induced the second bank run, the application of the Jewish banking community for a Palestine government guarantee for credit from major *foreign* banks was rejected, it was the flagship of Zionist finance, the Anglo-Palestine Bank, which provided the liquidity to Jewish banks at its own risk, thus preventing their collapse.

It was this historical role that led the management the Anglo-Palestine Bank (renamed Bank Leumi in 1951) to make practical moves designed to prepare the issue of an Israeli currency, even before the November 29, 1947, UN decision about partition. In the winter of 1948, months before the Declaration of Independence, the chairman of the bank, Siegfried *Hoofien, ordered banknotes from an American printer to replace the Mandatory Palestine pound. This was the Palestine pound with the mark of the Anglo-Palestine Bank. The bank also absorbed the cost of that order, though there was no commitment by the Zionist authorities before May 15, 1948, or from the Israeli government for three months after that, that it would declare these banknotes legal tender.

Yet it was this anticipatory act, whose risk was borne by the Anglo-Palestine Bank, which allowed, on August 16, 1948, the signing of a covenant between the bank and the state of Israel setting up an Issue Department as a discrete entity within the bank, authorized to issue the legal tender of the state. The availability of the new notes flown in from the U.S. allowed the immediate conversion of the Mandatory notes, a process successfully completed within one month by the end of September 1948. The emergence and acceptability of the new legal tender provided a basic requirement of the monetary system of the state of Israel, allowing an easy overnight transformation of the banking system.

There were 108 banking corporations in Israel in 1950 (Table 37), reduced to fewer than 50 in 1967, when the banking system had adjusted to the post-World War II situation and the second decade of independence. This apparently major reduction reflects mainly the process of consolidation to which the cooperative credit societies, local banking institutions mostly with single offices, had been subjected. Considerations of economy of scale and rapidly rising real wages had led to the steady absorption of these small cooperatives, mostly creations of the Histadrut, by Bank Hapoalim, the major financial institution of the labor movement; several independent credit societies were absorbed by Bank Leumi. This two-decade-long process thus concentrated the banking system into several major groupings. This is demonstrated by the share of the three largest banks in terms of their numbers of offices, employment, and deposits. Their share of the number of offices was about 14 percent in 1951 and 22 percent a decade later in 1961; their share of employees was 46 percent in 1951 and 56 percent a decade later. These three banking conglomerates held 58 percent of total deposits with the banking system in 1951 and 64 percent a decade later in 1961.

These data underline a dominant feature of the system, its oligopolistic structure, which continued to strengthen over time. This shows clearly in terms of the continuous decline in the number of banking corporations through 2004. They numbered only 40 percent of what they had in 1967, though employment in the system increased almost threefold and deposits, another measure of nominal scope, grew more than nominal GNP (Table 37). Deposits in real terms grew by more than sevenfold at an annual rate of 5.5 percent for these 37 years.

The two largest Israeli banks – giants in Israeli terms – which had absorbed the bulk of the smaller institutions, expanded much more rapidly than the third largest during the closing decades of the 20th century. Thus, in the early years of the 21st century, these banking corporations, Bank Hapoalim and Bank Leumi, held approximately 70 percent of the total deposits, and accommodated close to 80 percent of total credit to businesses, households, and public sector entities. This process apparently suggests growing monopolistic power for these institutions. However, other developments in the financial sector worked in the opposite direction from the 1990s on.

The Jewish economy of Palestine was clearly a monetary economy from the very beginning, hence the very extensive and highly solvent, liquid, and reliable banking system inherited from the Mandatory years. The high liquidity maintained by banks during World War II sustained their ability to stand the stress of the transition period of the War of Independence, even though there was no legal minimum reserve ratio, and bank supervision set up late in the 1930s was effectively in its infancy at independence. The shell of the Bank Supervision Department set up by the Mandatory government moved initially to the Treasury. When the central bank, the Bank of Israel, was established in 1954, it was moved to there. The first instructions regarding legal minimum reserves were issued in 1951, and were hardly relevant since by that time the banks maintained higher reserve ratios than those required. The rationale for government intervention on this matter reflects consideration for the safety of the banking system, but for more than a generation, between roughly 1960 and 1989, the very high reserve ratios imposed by the Supervisor of Banks were used as instruments of monetary policy, and not to sustain bank liquidity.

These very high reserve ratios had, however, a significant affect on the banking system and on Israel's financial markets. The very high reserve ratio created a large gap between credit and debit interest rates, and thus induced the creation of a (nonbank) credit graymarket, the so-called "bill intermediation market." It was designed to circumvent the legal interest rate ceiling (10 to 11 percent in the late 1960s) set under the 1957 Interest Rate Ceiling Law. It soon became a major "free" credit market, in which the commercial banks participated in the guise of intermediaries between specific lenders and specific borrowers. In the mid-1960s this grew into a major credit market, even though the legal camouflage of the "intermediation" device was quite flimsy. It took a first-instance District Court verdict that questioned the legality of the debt created by these so-called "arbitration" deals to force the Treasury to eliminate the interest rate ceiling in 1970. This also eliminated that market overnight.

A substitute for the interest rate ceiling, designed to offer cheap bank credit to preferred sectors in the form of subsidized "directed credits," was put into operation immediately. The subsidy was partially directly financed by the BOI; it had to buy a set quota of promissory notes from these privileged credit recipients at low discount rates. The commercial banks financed a greater quota of these subsidized credits in return for lower minimum reserve requirements for outstanding "directed credit" balances.

Aside from the subsidized "directed credit" tranche, the government was involved in the micromanagement of bank credits financed by the development budget. These were allocated from balances of government "deposits for credit allocation" with the commercial banks, according to government instructions, at interest rates set by the authorities. The banks acted only as administrators of these loans, for set fees.

The close involvement of public sector authorities in the workings of the banks involved the BOI's power to set minimum reserve ratios, and the supervisory responsibility of the supervisor of banks; the direct involvement of the Treasury in the provision of commercial bank credit resources; and the indirect involvement of the Treasury through its maintenance of interest rate ceilings through 1970. Different ministries participated in the allocation of "directed credit" balances and development credits to privileged business entities. The ministries of Agriculture, Trade and Industry, and Tourism were involved in determining the size and allocation of development credits. All this had a major impact on the structure of the banking system. Its oligopolistic nature, which increased over time through 1985, was undoubtedly strengthened because of it.

The growth of the economy of course required an expansion of the capacity of the banking system to offer credit accommodation. This in turn increased the claims of the system on resources. These claims can be seen in the increasing number of bank offices and rising employment in banking entities (Table 37). In the two decades from 1950 to 1970 the number of banking offices grew about fourfold: though no employment data for 1950 is available, employment grew undoubtedly at a lower rate. This clearly shows from a comparison of the number of bank offices and the employment data that could be compared for the almost four decades through 2004. Even in the pre-personal computer age, increase in the volume of banking business allowed the introduction of more and more labor-saving equipment, reducing the intensity of employment.

Nevertheless, the employment data and the ratio of banking sector employment to total employment in the economy suggest some highly interesting features the banking system had to face over time. The very rapid increase in employment from 1970 on, and its effective peak at the end of the lost decade in 1985, was a clear product of rising inflation and its acceleration to the verge of hyperinflation by early 1985. The leap in employment in the banking sector to 2.5–2.6 percent of total employment in the economy is an expression of what in the vernacular is described as the "flight from money" in periods of rapid inflation. That feature shows in the decline in the ratio of the money supply (M1) to GNP from the about 19 percent at the beginning of the lost decade in the early 1970s, to only 3.6 percent in 1985, and in its slow turnaround that year as inflation was arrested (Table 34). The process of "flight from money" occurs when there is an increase of the number of transactions per unit of production – the so-called velocity of circulation of money. In a fully monetarized economy, which Israel was by this stage, this inevitably increases the scope of banking activity over what is warranted by the growth of the economy. This rapidly rising pattern of velocity occurred in Israel even though the 1970s was a decade of computerization, and requirements for manpower were being reduced in the banking and financial sector.

The dramatic change in this situation, as seen in the decline of banking offices and employment during the two decades through 2004, while banking activity grew by more than GNP – four times in terms of deposits and credit accounts – reflects the decline of inflation-induced activity on the one hand, and technological change – the rise of the PC –on the other. The latter is demonstrated by the threefold increase in the number of automatic teller machines (ATMs) between 1985 and 2004 (Table 37).

The Bank Shares Crisis, 1983

In the 1983 Bank Shares Crisis, almost the entire banking system was nationalized, unintentionally. This incident, a highly significant occurrence in a capital market still almost in its embryonic stage in the 1980s, was effectively an expression of an approaching explosive economic crisis caused by triple-digit inflation rather than a problem of the banking system as such. There was no run on the banks, neither before the crisis climaxed, nor during the attempts to find a solution (which entailed closing the stock exchange for several weeks), nor in the aftermath following the settlement and the resumption of trading in bank shares.

The crisis originated in the policy of the large banks of manipulating the prices of their shares in the market, and figures as one of the historic accidents of both the banking system and the capital market. It exploded in October 1983, as the four major banking corporations, which represented more than 90 percent of banking activity, decided to stop "managing" the prices of their shares, a policy they had been following with success on a significant and increasing scale since 1979. The point of that process was to prevent a significant decline of the real, not just the nominal, price of these shares. This required a pool of shares managed by the banks, and the financial resources to enter into the market on the demand side when necessary. A decline in the market price of a bank's shares below the target was accordingly countered by the pool's buying up shares in the market, thus increasing the number of shares at its disposal. A rise of prices beyond the target price would be met by sales from the pool, which reduced the strain on the liquidity of the banks. As long as these price fluctuations approximately evened out within a short time, the technique did not pose a danger to the banks' liquidity position.

The policy of the banks' share pool managements was to assure rates of return on these securities similar to those of government bonds, which were price-linked – a unique advantage among investment instruments – and thus offered a significant real return. The policy was clearly successful between 1979 and 1982. The results were soon visible in the real rates of return, as well as the rising number of bank shares in the new issue market and their relative value in the secondary market, the stock exchange, where bank shares had become a popular investment vehicle even for households. Within one year, by the end of 1980, bank share prices had risen by 40 percent in real terms. Two years later, by the end of 1982, they were 140 percent higher than they had been at the end of 1979. The whole stock market rose at these inconceivably substantial rates during that time, but it was clearly the bank sector shares that led the way. This is clearly shown by the rising volume of new issues of bank stock, 74 percent of new issues in 1980. The share of the total value of bank shares traded in the secondary market, the stock exchange, was similar. The share of bank stock in the total value of the portfolio of financial assets held by the public rose to one-third by that time; it was 10 percent in 1979. This pattern of stock prices in general, and specifically of those of banks, was the result of almost a decade of high double-digit inflation and several years of triple-digit inflation. The price management of their shares by the banks contributed significantly to that process; otherwise the dollar value of their shares would not have risen by about 4.5 times within less than five years as it did. This pattern of bank share prices soon generated an increasing divergence between the dollar market value of the outstanding bank shares, and the adjusted value of the net worth of each of the share price managing banks. This ratio diverged little from unity at the end of 1978, but it had reached between 2 and 3 on the eve of the collapse of the bank shares market in the first week of October 1983.

The major macroeconomic significance of the strain in the capital market that emerged early in 1983 and the related collapse of the bank share market in October is illustrated by two figures. The outstanding value of the bank share portfolio was about one-third of GDP on the very eve of the collapse of the market. It was down to 20 percent of GDP by the end of 1983. It was only because of the direct intervention by the government, which entered the market to buy shares at a cost equal to four percent of GDP, that the price collapse was not much worse.

These orders of magnitude indicate that ownership of bank shares as financial assets was by that time popular and widespread even among ordinary households, and explain the political rationale of the attempt of the government to stem the crisis. The economic rationale for government intervention was fear that a collapse of the price of bank shares would generate a shock in the financial markets overall. This reading of the situation seemed likely given the showing in terms of major price declines of nonbanking stock since January 1983. In these circumstances a run on the banks was thought quite possible. What caused particular anxiety at the Treasury was the danger that even a minor run, which could be countered with support from the central bank if confined to domestic currency deposits, would have led to a widespread withdrawal of foreign currency deposits. Since by that time foreign currency deposits were 40 percent of total deposits with the commercial banks, this would have meant a complete exhaustion of Israel's foreign currency reserves.

The settlement, followed by an immediate reopening of the stock exchange and a resumption of trading in bank stock, committed the government to purchase bank shares offered for sale later at a minimum price of no less than 75 percent of the market price at the time trading had been stopped in October 1983. This amounted to a maximum loss of 25 percent for bank shareowners, who were able to sell immediately at market prices. For many, particularly those who purchased their shares through the end of 1982, this involved no loss at all, or at most, a much smaller loss. Nevertheless, many decided to sell at once, forcing the intervention of the BOI. The state, in other words, through the central bank, bought the banks – almost the entire banking system had been effectively nationalized. The cost to the government was high; the cost of the shares it had acquired was two to three times greater than the adjusted net worth of the banks. The settlement ended the immediate crisis in the capital market, but it had a decade-long negative effect on the propensity of people to enter the Israeli stock market.

A Revitalized Banking System, 1985–2005

Though it was the management of the major commercial banks that led to the shares crisis, the government did not even consider getting involved in running the banks. The managements stayed on, and the government, which had underwritten the value of bank shares, set up a legal structure – an empty shell of a government-owned corporation – that allowed the bank managements to run the banking system without its interference, and even to co-opt new directors if and when required. Though it took more than a decade before the sale of the first major bank, and two decades before most of the commercial banking system was reprivatized, the involvement of government and the BOI in the actual running of the system declined rapidly and significantly after the implementation of the 1985 stabilization policy. This was primarily due to the rapid elimination of the "directed credit" tranche, which excluded the involvement of the economic ministries in the allocation of bank credit, thus leaving allocation of credit resources to the discretion of the banks.

This trend gained support as the banks were allowed to reduce the highly stringent reserve ratios as these were gradually eliminated as instruments of monetary policy. This process, which was implemented between 1987, when minimum required reserve ratios were still 38 percent, and 1994, when these were down to six percent, allowed a major reduction in the "interest gap" – the difference between debit and credit interest rates. This in turn encouraged rapid growth of deposits, showing clearly in the deposit-GNP ratio in Table 37: deposits were only 5.9 percent of GNP in 1985, 8.1 percent in 1990, and 10.5 percent in 2004. The return of the public into the nonprice- (or exchange rate-) linked bank deposits supported rapid expansion of bank credit – the main business of banks. The expanding monetary loan, which was indeed used by the BOI as an instrument of monetary policy, offered nevertheless growing flexibility for the management of credit policy, since banks could acquire reserves, if they preferred to do so, in the weekly auctions of the central bank, or reduce the balance of their debt to the central bank. Furthermore, the interest rates set for these bank deals at the discount window of the central bank served as an efficient index to the cost of finance that banks would charge, or pay to debtors and depositors, respectively.

These features, and the revival of economic growth as the last decade waned, as well as increasing momentum of the 1990s' mass immigration, explain the rapid expansion of bank credit in real terms of about 11 percent annually, and the somewhat lower rate of expansion of seven percent in the 2000–04 period (Tables 34 and 35). Indeed, the 1990s were the heyday of the commercial banks. Instead of the fluctuating rates of return on capital of somewhat less than five percent in the four years through 1990, they made 7.2 percent in the first half of the 1990s, and 10.7 percent in the second half, which included the high-tech bubble year of 2000. The strong demand for credit, with the banks dominating the market, since at that time even major private firms could not yet go to the bond issue market to finance their activities, offered a bonanza to the banks. A case in point was the privatization of the largest bank in the country, Bank Hapoalim, bought in 1995 by a group of major domestic and foreign financiers. To finance a significant share of the cost of the purchase, these leading figures in the business and finance community had to apply to the second largest of the five major banking corporations, Bank Leumi, in which the government still had a controlling interest.

Indeed, the dominant position of the banks as a group in the finance market exhibited highly significant monopolistic features, owing to the size of the two largest, Bank Hapoalim and Bank Leumi, which between them were responsible for more than 60 percent of business volume. The growing impact of the banking system on the economy as a whole even as the state financial dimension of the system declined meant more restricted competition in the financial sector due to the banking oligopoly. This pattern is clearly demonstrated by the rapid decline of the share of government in commercial bank credit. It was 50 percent in 1986, just as the stabilization policy was taking effect, was down to 38 percent in 1990, and below 20 percent by 2000.

The impact of banking on the economy, however, did not result only from the banks' clout in the allocation of credit. Most institutional investors – pension funds, provident funds, and of course mutual funds – were subsidiaries of banks, run as distinct legal entities. A group of private brokers had been operating on the stock exchange for decades, but the scale of their business compared to the brokerage and other capital market facilities offered by the banks was tiny. The challenge to competition in the financial and capital markets was that the supermarket feature of the banking system, benefiting from economies of scale due to the spread of their branches across the country, handed them potential customers on a platter. This feature had been criticized already in 1986.

The committee investigating the bank share fiasco of 1983 referred to that feature in its report. Among other problems it pointed to the inherent conflict of interest involved in the dual functions of banks as owners of mutual, pension, and provident funds; for these they were marketers and sellers, while for the public – private households in particular – they were serving as investment advisors, telling them what to buy. One of the main recommendations of that committee was to require the complete divestment by banks of these entities, and also partial divestment of firms operating in the production sector of the economy. The latter reform, restricting the holding of equity in firms operating in the real sector of the economy to 20 percent of total stock, was implemented only after a decade in the mid-1990s. The recommendation on divesting financial subsidiaries was met with total resistance from the banks. The two decades since 1985 were of course the period in which the capital market really took off. The banks, which historically had funded the capital market and nurtured it through good and bad through the 1980s, felt that this reform was a challenge to their profitability and to their standing in the economy.

Their resistance thus bought them another decade as the effective moderators of the capital market. It took, of course, another committee in 2005 to recommend implementing the 1985 recommendation, before the banking system gave in by late 2005. The interesting feature in that context was that though the recommendation of the Bachar Committee allowed several years for the process of divestment, the banks, which were fighting tooth and nail in 2005 against the reform, took advantage of the boom in Israel's capital market since 2004 and almost completed the process of divestment within one year. They, of course, immediately reaped the benefit from the major capital gain, which the state of the market at that time allowed.

The Reemergence of a Capital Market, 1985–2005

The position of the banking system on the so-called Bachar Reform – named after the director general of the Treasury who chaired the 2005 Bank Reform Committee – was not affected only by profit-and-loss considerations. It reflected also an emotional aspect: the conviction of the upper and mid-level managers that the reform would exclude them from their "creation," the Israeli capital market. This was indeed started and nurtured by the banks. It first appeared in the mid-1930s in a room at the Anglo-Palestine Bank in which a very small number of securities were traded once a week. Yet even after independence, the Tel Aviv Stock Exchange, which was by that time a unique legal entity with a small membership, was of minor significance. The largest group of securities traded were government price-linked bonds with a sprinkling of rate-of-exchange-linked bonds and other bonds carrying a government guarantee, such as those of the government-owned Israel Electric Corporation and a number of similar entities.

The ups and downs of the pre-1985 stabilization policy small capital market can be traced in the rates of return columns of Table 38. The drastic decline of the market in the early 1960s shows in the rates of return on shares, which were lower by one-third in 1970 than in 1960, even though the market had been moving away from its slump in the wake of the post-Six-Day War period.

The inflation-induced upturn in the market, and its short era of glory that ended with the Bank Shares Crisis of 1983, is expressed in the more than fourfold increase of the rates of return on shares between 1979 and 1982. This explosion of the stock market pulled in its wake the government bond market in which rates of return grew correspondingly by 80 percent. The Bank Shares Crisis can be discerned in the collapse of the rate of return figures: the entry for 1985 is one-third of its level of 1982, even though the government guaranteed a floor price for bank shares. Indeed, the dismal state of the capital market in 1985 shows clearly in the government bond market, in which rates of return were at their lowest in 1985: price- (or rate-of-exchange-) linked bonds were down 15 percent compared to 1982 (Table 38).

The depressed state of the bond market during the early stages of the stabilization policy was of course also due to the highly restrictive monetary policy run by the BOI in that period. Though a quite reasonable explanation for the expert observer, what counted initially for public opinion, and particularly for the small private investor, was of course not the sophisticated explanations on the state of the economy, but the dismal experience of 1983 and its aftermath.

The post-stabilization policy period, the 1990s in particular, when the policy's success (and the new rules for fiscal and monetary policies) were finally absorbed, signified an altogether new departure for the capital market. What made the difference was of course the renewal of growth supported by the dismantling of currency control, which required two decades before it was finally completed. This process could be implemented only on the basis of the fiscal discipline pursued by the governments in office from 1985, and the rapidly increasing independence of the central bank, in the 1990s in particular, with its full commitment to price stability within a market economy.

The value of turnover data in Table 38 underlines the revival of activity on the Tel Aviv Stock Exchange, which increased by about four times by 1990, through the stabilization period and its aftermath, and the very rapid expansion of activity from the mid-1990s, when most of the currency control regulations, though not all, had faded away. The post-1995 upward surge of activity, showing an almost fivefold expansion of turnover, and corresponding rising activity in the new issue market, underline the rapidly rising scale of activity and the environment of rising real rates of return in which this occurred.

The data that best demonstrates the major turn of the tide in Israel's capital market are those reflecting the inflow of foreign investment into the economy. In 1985–90 the annual inflow was about $200–300 million annually. It gained a new lease on life after 1990. By 1995 the inflow was $2.3 billion. In 2000, the year of the high-tech bubble, it leapt to $11.5 billion. It settled down at about $6 billion a year between 2001 and 2004.

Not all of this flow was transmitted via the capital market; a portion of it was direct investment in the real sector of the economy. Yet in the late 1990s and in the 2000–04 interval about 80 percent was transmitted through this channel. The growing interest and confidence of foreigners in the Israeli capital market followed the return of the Israeli public to the capital market, after the lessons it learned in the wake of the bank shares fiasco of 1983.

The stabilization policy was the watershed that separates two altogether different environments: the scope of the capital market and, especially, its impact on and relevance to the economy. This is clearly indicated in terms of the value of turnover in the stock market, which grew by almost seven times between 1990 and 2003, responding to the gains of investors: real rates of return on shares grew on average by 9.2 percent annually, and returns in the less risky bond market were almost three percent at an annual average. Yet the clearest structural alteration in the capital market was the appearance of the corporate bond market. The capital issues columns of Table 38 indicate the appearance of this altogether new market component, which appeared before 1990 but did not really flourish until after 2000. Until 1985 corporate bonds simply could not compete with government bonds. Though government bond issues grew by 11 times since 1985, the order of magnitude of the expansion of the volume of corporate bonds is several times greater. This represents a development that affects not only the capital market, but the power of the banking system to set debit interest rates for major debtors, who had now acquired a direct entrance into the capital market.

In the new era, in which by 2005 exchange controls had been completely abolished, events in the stock exchange were to a very great extent affected by developments in the major world capital markets – New York, London, Frankfurt, and the East Asian centers. Another highly relevant feature was the process of major withdrawal of the Israeli state from the capital market. This was possible because of the small budget deficits run by the government for two decades, and by the privatization drive, which provided resources to reduce the foreign national debt to a negligible size by 2003 – smaller than the foreign exchange reserves at the disposal of the BOI. By 2002 it also involved the release of pension and provident funds from compulsory investment in nontradable government securities. This forced these major institutional investors into the private capital market. It offered an opening for the development of a corporate bond market, which for the four decades of the state through the late 1980s did not exist (Table 38).

The final major reform of the capital market, implemented late in 2005, forced on the reluctant bank system the divestment of their investment subsidiaries: pension, provident, and mutual funds, which dominated trading in the stock exchange. The move was conceived as a reform that would substantially strengthen competition in the capital market, now also subject to competition from abroad. This linkage with the world capital market was strengthened by the Israeli economy's safe passage through the world financial crisis of 1998, under the strict and restrictive management of the BOI. It made a major contribution to Israel's ratings on foreign capital markets and also to the self-confidence of its monetary management.

The Evolution of Manufacturing and the High-Tech System, 1973–2005

In the three decades from the Yom Kippur War through 2003, the manufacturing industry grew rapidly. Its product was three times greater than in the early 1970s, capital equipment grew by almost six times, and employment by 50 percent, thus involving a rapidly increasing capital intensity and rising productivity. This allowed the payment of higher real wages, which rose correspondingly by more than 70 percent (Tables 26 and 29). Indeed, the major orientation of manufacturing lines of activity on the protected domestic market still offered through the mid-1970s leeway for rising productivity due to the economics of scale. With a national product more than three times greater in the early years of the 21st century than in the early 1970s (Table 28), and a population more than two times greater (Table 14), the economics of scale, supported of course by rising capital investment, allowed even the traditional industries – textiles and clothing, food processing – to face the challenge of rising imports. More and more of these were indeed penetrating into the Israeli market after trade agreements made with the U.S. and the European Common Market (later the European Community), and also in response to the World Trade Organization agreement, which naturally also covered the exports of developing economies. The inherent feature of all of these agreements was the establishment of a requirement that customs duties, quotas, and other devices designed to protect domestic industries be gradually eliminated. This process, from which consumers benefited, generated pressure on domestic manufacturers, which had either to raise productivity and reduce costs, or phase out the production lines in which it had been engaged.

The significant growth of manufacturing as the mainstay of the production sector indicates that it succeeded in facing the changing world trade environment. This success, however, required a major restructuring. The beginnings of this had already appeared in the late 1960s and early 1970s, leading to a major development of the pharmaceutical industry (including the emergence of Teva as a brand name on the world market), and of an array of defense industries. By the late 1970s and particularly in the 1980s, these were competing in the American and European markets for major contracts in several areas of manufacturing activity: pharmaceuticals, advanced electronics, and optics. By the 1990s the Israeli defense industries had put into orbit the first Israeli-made satellite riding on an Israeli-made missile. In the 1980s there was even begun a major project to produce a fighter aircraft. Limited by the requirements of the IDF, however, the unit cost of that plane, a prototype of which was indeed produced, was too high to continue. The project was thus shelved and the costs written off.

Yet the experience of the manpower employed in that project and many other defense industry lines provided the sophisticated and highly trained personnel who soon moved into high-tech research and development. This emerged in Israel in the late 1980s and flourished in the early 1990s. It carried revolutionary developments in its wake in two areas – the high-tech industry and the capital market. Mirroring developments in California's Silicon Valley and in some major European economic powers, it took a decade before its presence was recognized.

The statistics of production and employment in the high-tech technology branches, indeed the breakdown of manufacturing industry by sub-branches, presented in Table 39 did not yet appear in the CBS Annual of 2000. The breakdown by type of industry involving high-tech is thus available only from 1994 onward. The available data nevertheless demonstrate the revolution in the structure of industry of the 1990s. Employment in manufacturing as a whole grew by only about 10 percent between 1990 and 2004. On the basis of 1994, the first year for which sub-branch statistics are available, employment in 2004, which was a year of slowdown, was even five percent lower. The rising capital intensity of manufacturing overall, and rising productivity, still allowed an increase of manufacturing product in 2004 by about one-third over 1994, and by 75 percent over 1990. Yet this performance, which reflects an average for manufacturing industries as a whole, was far off the performance of the high-tech branches. Employment in these leading branches grew by 23 percent in the decade through 2004, and product grew by almost two times, even though the high-tech bubble of the late 1990s had burst by 2000. (The effect of the burst bubble in terms of lower employment and product is quite visible in the entry for the year 2003 of Table 39.)

The other end of the manufacturing branch spectrum is visible in the textiles production figures: production in 2004 was down by 20 percent from 1994, and similar to its level in 1990. The electronics branch, on the other hand, which includes plants belonging to high- and medium-tech sub-branches, increased output by almost three times. This suggests that the shedding of labor, visible in the manufacturing industry as a whole, was effectively the dominant feature of the low-tech branches, some of which were fading out altogether – sewing workshops being the obvious example.

These developments had social consequences, as is suggested in the skill endowment columns of Table 39, which reflect human capital, and the corresponding wage ratio figures. Both the skill endowment and the high-education components of the manufacturing labor force increased substantially. This is a measure of supply and demand simultaneously. The slight reduction in the wage ratio for skilled and unskilled workers suggests that the increased demand for skilled labor was met by a substantially increased supply, reflecting the comprehensive system of extension studies offered to the Israeli labor force both at the plant and branch levels. On the other hand, the rising pattern of the ratio of wages paid to highly educated workers represents, to a very great extent, the absorption of the rising classes of university-educated students by the high-tech branches that cannot operate without them. These fields pay high salaries, based on their short-run profitability, yet apply the rules of hiring and firing, and do not abide by industry-wide agreements, which as a method of setting wage rates offer employment security too. The rising pretax and pre-transfer payments income inequality that this feature entails has become a major social and political issue in the 21st century.

This rapid rise of high-tech entities, some of which are now household brands in the United States and most industrialized countries, reflects the surfacing of a multitude of small groups of enterprising, usually quite young people with an idea, which might or might not offer a new way of doing things. These are the well-known "startups," which need risk capital. This means that venture capital firms and high-tech start-ups are in a sense Siamese twins. The success of nurturing high-tech enterprises is crucially linked to the availability of venture capitalists raised in a high-tech environment and ready to face the risks.

The availability of an exciting capital market was therefore the sine qua non for the surfacing of Israel's high-tech industry. On the other hand, the very emergence and availability of a multitude of entrepreneurial talent and a highly educated labor force contributed to the expansion of the capital market and its role in forging industrial growth. This underlines the requirement of open lines of communication on capital account transactions, allowing free mobility of foreign and domestic capital into and out of the system. The process, which on the one hand led to price stability, and on the other hand reduced, and finally eliminated, administrative restrictions on the free flow of funds was vital to the rapid expansion and success of high-tech.

BIBLIOGRAPHY: The Pre-Mandate and Mandate Period 1880–1948: R. Nathan, et al., *Palestine: Problem and Promise* (1946); K. Navrazk, *The Mandate and the Economy of Palestine* (Heb., 1946); *UN Economic Survey Mission for the Middle East,* Reports 1 and 2, 1947; J. Metzer and O. Kaplan, *The Jewish and Arab Economy in Mandatory Palestine* (Heb., 1990); J. Metzer, *The Divided Economy of Mandatory Palestine* (1998). STATISTICAL SURVEYS: Palestine Office of Statistics, *Statistical Abstract of Palestine (1936–45)*; The Jewish Agency of Palestine, Economic Department, *Economic Facts and Figures* (1949). THE STATE OF ISRAEL: A. Bein, *A History of Zionist Resettlement* (Heb., 1954); A.L. Gaathon, *Capital Stock, Employment and Output in Israel 1950–1959* (1961); idem, *Economic Productivity in Israel* (1971); N. Halevi and Klinov-Malul, *The Economic Development of Israel* (1968); D. Patinkin, *The Israeli Economy in the First Decade*, 1965; H. Ben-Shahar, *Interest Rates and the Cost Capital in Israel* (Heb., 1965); D. Horowitz, *The Economics of Israel* (Heb., 1967); H. Givati, *A Century of Settlement, Parts I–II* (Heb., 1981); Y. Ben-Porat, *The Israeli Economy Maturing Through Crisis* (1986); H. Barkai, *The Genesis of the Israeli Economy* (Heb., 1990); M. Bruno, *Crisis, Stabilization and Economic Reform*, (1993). MONEY AND INFLATION: Foreign Exchange Rates, IMF, *International Financial Statistics* (1948–2005); H. Barkai, *The Lessons of Israel's Great Inflation*, 1995; L. Leiderman (ed.), *Inflation and Disinflation in Israel* (1999); A. Ben-Bassat (ed.), *From Government Involvement to Market Economy 1985–1999* (2001). WATER AND IRRIGATION: *Thirty Years of Mekorot* (Heb., 1967); Y. Kislev, *The Water Economy of Israel* (2001). MONETARY BANKING AND HISTORY: N. Gross, E. Kleinman, et al., *From Mandate to State: A Banking Institution of a Rejuvenated Nation: the Seventy-Five Years of Bank Leumi Leisrael* (Heb., 1977); M. Heth, *The Banking Institutions in Israel* (Heb., 1966); idem, *Banking in Israel (Parts I and II)* (Heb., 1994); N. Liviatan-H. Barkai, *The Bank of Israel: Fifty Years of Struggle for Monetary Control* (Heb., 2004). MISCELLANEOUS: M. Sicron, *Demography: The Population of Israel, Characteristics and Patterns* (Heb., 2004); N. Halevi, *Import Policy and Trade Liberalization of Manufacturers* (Heb., 1994). MAIN STATISTICAL SOURCES: Central Bureau of Statistics, *Statistical Abstracts of Israel* (1949/50–2004); Bank of Israel, *Annual Reports* (1955–2004); Bank of Israel Supervisor of Banks, *Annual Reports 1965–2004*;

[Haim Barkai (2nd ed.)]

LABOR

Jewish Labor Organizations

IN THE PRE-STATE PERIOD. Since the last decades of the 19th century, a number of sporadic labor associations have arisen in agriculture and in the printing, clothing, and building trades, as well as groups limited to a particular locality or place of work. The *Teachers' Association was founded in 1903, but its aims were only partially those of a trade union. The first abiding Jewish trade union organizations in Ereẓ Israel were the two regional associations of agricultural workers founded in Galilee and Judea in 1911. In 1913 a clerical workers' union was set up. In 1919 a railroad workers' union, including both Jews and Arabs, was founded; it later took in the postal and telegraph workers.

Founding of the Histadrut. The founding of the *Histadrut, the General Federation of Labor, in 1920, was not primarily the result of the development of these early trade unions, but rather the outcome of strongly held ideas about the unity of the Jewish workers in Ereẓ Israel and their mission in the building of the country as a workers' commonwealth. *Aḥdut ha-Avodah, founded in 1919 (see Israel, State of: *Political Life and Parties), aimed at establishing one body, organized on a trade union basis, which would deal with all the interests of the workers including ideological and political activities. However, it did not achieve the support of all the workers, especially those in the *Ha-Po'el ha-Ẓa'ir party, which rejected its socialist definitions. The newcomers of the Third *Aliyah, belonging to the *He-Ḥalutz, Ẓe'irei Ẓion, and *Ha-Shomer ha-Ẓa'ir movements, who arrived in 1919 and 1920, were opposed to the authority of both Ha-Po'el ha-Ẓa'ir and Aḥdut ha-Avodah, which had set up competing labor exchanges, contracting companies, and medical services and each of which claimed to represent the workers, especially in the vital area of agricultural settlement.

Joseph *Trumpeldor's appeal (at the beginning of 1920) for the unification of the workers to deal with their common interests and the threat by a conference of ḥalutzim, which met on Mount Carmel in autumn 1920, to set up a separate workers' organization pushed the parties into agreement on the convening of a general conference of workers in December 1920. Eighty-seven delegates, representing 4,433 voters, participated. (Aḥdut-ha-Avodah had 37 delegates, Ha-Po'el ha-Ẓa'ir 26, "newcomers" 16, pro-Communist 6, and others 2.) The very fact that delegates were chosen by general elections (although they were held on a party-list system) constituted an agreement to establish a general organization, and not just an interparty coordinating body, as Ha-Po'el ha-Ẓa'ir wanted, but there was much controversy at the founding conference over the character of the organization. The leaders of Aḥdut ha-Avodah (Berl *Katznelson, Shemuel *Yavne'eli, and others) wanted to endow it with the widest possible powers in political activities, cultural affairs, and defense, while Ha-Po'el ha-Ẓa'ir, led by Yosef *Sprinzak, wanted to preserve the power of the parties. The differences were resolved by a compromise: the founding conference decided to establish the General Federation of Jewish Workers in Palestine (Ha-Histadrut ha-Kelalit shel ha-Ovedim ha-Ivriyyim be-Ereẓ Israel), which, according to its constitution "unites all workers in the country who live on the fruits of their own labor without exploiting the labor of others, for the purpose of arranging all the communal, economic, and cultural affairs of the working class in the country for the building of the labor society in the Land of Israel." With the founding of the Histadrut, the He-Ḥalutz Organization in Palestine announced its dissolution. *Gedud ha-Avodah, the Labor Legion, which had been set up in 1920 to carry out pioneering tasks on a cooperative basis, joined the Histadrut but later developed into an opposition group.

Early Activities. In the early years, the Histadrut devoted itself to creating work and encouraging immigration by building up an independent labor economy. Agricultural settlement was to be the highroad to this goal, but the shortage of national lands and public funds for the purpose, which delayed the start of the Zionist Organization's operations, pushed the workers into public works and building. The Histadrut set up an Immigration and Labor Center, which received immigrants and tried to find them work on a contract basis – groups of workers undertaking jobs and sharing the proceeds. The contracting offices which the different parties had set up before the establishment of the Histadrut were unified into the Office for Public Works and Building, which received government and other contracts. Cooperative contracting seemed the right way not only to build an independent labor economy, but also to compete in the unorganized labor market.

Within the framework of the Histadrut's Office for Public Works and Building, various subcontracting groups from different backgrounds, organized according to different principles, were formed. Some came from the youth movements and some from particular cities abroad, while other groups were organized ad hoc for the purpose of a particular job. Some worked as partnerships, while others divided up the income either in equal parts or with higher shares for the skilled workers. Some of these groups became well enough organized to be ready to establish agricultural settlements. The Histadrut was careful to keep all these groups open to new immigrants and tried to limit the advantages of the skilled workers.

In the organization of its basic units, the Histadrut gave preference to "*kibbutzei avodah*" and "*ḥavurot*" (collective work groups), which undertook subcontracting jobs, the urban cooperatives, which were regarded as stages on the road to an independent workers' economy, and trade union organizations, which were seen as a correlative to the capitalist economy. Of the trade unions themselves, the Histadrut favored those set up on an industrial, rather than a narrow craft basis, despite the very small scope of industrial enterprise at the time. The industrial basis was regarded as a safeguard against separatist tendencies among the skilled workers and as training for the running of industries in the future. In accordance with this policy, a National Union of Public Works and Building Employees was established in 1922; it was also intended to exercise democratic control over the Office of Building and Public Works. There was opposition to this policy from the skilled workers, as well as from the Communists and other left wing adherents, who regarded the building of a workers' economy as utopianism and exploitation of the workers. Bank ha-Po'alim (the Workers' Bank), which was founded in 1921, was intended to be the credit institution for the Office of Public Works and for the contracting groups; its long-range goal was to help to build the independent labor economy. The basic capital of LP 50,000 was invested by the Zionist Organization, which bought the founding shares. A Histadrut delegation which went to America to raise money from the half million Jewish workers there in the summer of 1922 did not succeed in its mission, due to anti-Zionist opposition. The supply organization, Hamashbir, which furnished the workers of the Office with consumer goods on credit, was also included within the framework of the Histadrut. Medical aid was provided by Kuppat Ḥolim (the Workers' Sick Fund), which had been founded in 1913, split in 1919, and was reformed.

Labor Economy versus Class Struggle. At the Second Convention of the Histadrut, which took place in February 1923, the debate between the advocates of the independent labor economy and those who defended purely trade union interests continued. The former view was favored by the great majority of the 130 delegates, representing 6,581 voters. Aḥdut ha-Avodah, which had 69 delegates, more than half the total, regarded it as a Palestinian form of the class war and Ha-Po'el ha-Ẓa'ir, with 36, as the Jewish national way to the building of a people's socialism and a just society. The left-wing opposition, on the other hand, argued that this was "the socialism of poverty" and demanded a class-war policy which would assume the evolution of a capitalist economy and the adaptation of the immigrants to its existence. At that conference, the Histadrut completed its constitution and decided to join the Trade Union International in Amsterdam, against the opposition of the left, on the one hand, and Ha-Po'el ha-Ẓa'ir – which opposed all international ties – on the other.

From 1922 to 1927 the policies of the Histadrut, under the vigorous leadership of David *Ben-Gurion, were guided by three central principles: the building of the Land of Israel as a socialist economy under workers' control; maximum economic self-sufficiency, the workers supplying their own needs in order to accumulate capital; and the syndicalist idea of identity between management and labor. These aims found expression in the legal-economic framework set up by the Histadrut to safeguard its social principles and run the labor enterprises which were under the control of the workers. *Ḥevrat ha-Ovedim, the General Cooperative Association of Jewish Labor in Palestine, which was identical in membership with the Histadrut and the legal owner of its assets, ensured its influence in its subsidiary companies by means of founders' shares. One of the subsidiaries was Nir, the Cooperative Society for Agricultural Settlement, which was established to control and develop the workers' agricultural settlements, and to whose members its shares were sold. A second was *Solel Boneh, the Cooperative Society of Jewish Workers for Public Works, Building, and Industry. By means of preference shares without voting rights, the two companies were able to raise external capital.

The grandiose plans of Ḥevrat ha-Ovedim, which was licensed by the authorities in 1924, were only partially realized, however. Solel Boneh over-expanded its activities in order to give as much employment as possible and went bankrupt in 1927; its failure caused difficulties for Hamashbir, which had given it credit in kind. The Zionist Organization did not recognize Nir as the representative of the agricultural settlements in signing contracts, and there was also internal criticism of excessive control over the individual settlements. For all practical purposes the Histadrut remained in control only of its central institutions, and not of the cooperatives or the communal settlements. During the economic recession of 1923, large-scale public works were stopped, investment and credit were severely limited, and unemployment rose to 1,500–2,000. These developments increased the Histadrut's responsibilities in the distribution of work and assistance, and its leadership proposed the building of the economy by the workers' own resources as a defense against the retreat from Zionism. The planting of tobacco in the villages marked an improvement in the employment situation in 1924. The idea of moving to the countryside suited the aspirations of many workers at that time, and collective contracting groups began to form in the villages. Later on, in 1925, the urban employment situation picked up with the beginning of the Fourth Aliyah.

The leaders of the Histadrut regarded the building of a workers' commonwealth as first and foremost a question of agricultural settlement. There were still groups of workers – some of them formed before World War I – that had been supported by the Palestine Office of the Zionist Organization and wanted to settle on the land. The decisions of the London Conference in 1920 favoring settlement on Jewish National *Fund land by self-employed farmers or groups suited the principles of the workers. The Histadrut represented the candidates for settlement in contacts with the Zionist institutions, which left the choice of the social form of each settlement up to the settlers themselves. Gedud ha-Avodah adopted the idea of the "large commune" conceived by Shelomo *Lavi. Workers' groups from the youth movements or from particular cities also formed collective settlements. Some workers formed organizations for cooperative smallholders' settlements (moshavei ovedim). Groups of all these types settled in the Jezreel Valley in the early 1920s.

In 1923 *En-Harod, the first "large" kibbutz, split away from Gedud ha-Avodah in a dispute over economic autonomy, and in 1927 formed the *Ha-Kibbutz ha-Me'uḥad (United Kibbutz) movement. In the same year *Ha-Kibbutz ha-Arẓi (Countrywide Kibbutz) of Ha-Shomer ha-Ẓa'ir settlements was founded. Gedud ha-Avodah split; some of its members became Soviet-oriented communists and left the country for the U.S.S.R., while the others joined Ha-Kibbutz ha-Me'uḥad. The kibbutz movements represented their settlements in dealing with the Histadrut, while the latter's Agricultural Center presented to the Zionist Organization on behalf of the settlers matters dealing with priorities in allocation of land, budgeting, and development of various branches of farming. It also protected the social structure of the settlements – especially in periods of economic difficulty, mediated in disputes between settlements, and looked after agricultural training – especially of women in special training farms. In 1926 it founded an Office for Agricultural Contracting.

Organization in the Cities. Despite the emphasis on the building of an independent agricultural economy, the Histadrut did not neglect job opportunities in the cities. It set up labor exchanges which fixed conditions and priorities for applicants for employment. With the development of industry, in addition to building, and the creation of regular jobs, the trade unions began to develop at the expense of the labor communes of the earlier period. The idea of combining the labor commune with workers' neighborhoods and small auxiliary farm plots or other forms of cooperative economy was not realized on a large scale. The Jewish National Fund did not supply the land, nor the Zionist institutions the funds, for this purpose. The independent workers' economy was limited for the most part to the countryside. Despite the absence of legislation or regulation and the competition of cheap labor, the Histadrut gained many achievements, including recognition of its right to represent the workers in collective bargaining, the conclusion of wage agreements, and the beginnings of social benefits. On the question of allocation of work only through the labor exchanges, the Histadrut ran into opposition from religious workers who did not belong to it (some of whom formed *Ha-Po'el ha-Mizrachi in 1923) and employers who, on one occasion, in 1925, announced a lockout. These conflicts brought on the intervention of the British police. The Va'ad Le'ummi tried to mediate on behalf of the *yishuv*, but ran into difficulties, partly because of the absence of a representative employers' organization. The main Histadrut institution in the towns was the local labor council, which, in practice, set up the various trade unions and coordinated the activities of the other Histadrut institutions in the locality. Elections to the councils were held on a personal basis, which led to complaints of discrimination from the smaller parties, and at the Third Convention proportional representation was introduced.

The ramified activities of the Histadrut swelled the size of its staff and led to complaints of bureaucracy. To bridge the gap between members and officials, the family wage system, under which all the Histadrut's employees were paid on the same scale, wages depending only on whether the official was married and the number of his children, was adopted at the Second Convention. Breaches of the system in the direction of professional scales were condemned at the Third Convention, and a watchdog committee was set up.

Despite its very limited funds, the Histadrut did not abandon its activities in the field of education and culture, which were conducted both by central institutions and local branches with the idea of creating a "workers' culture." These activities included instruction in Hebrew, publications, libraries, theater (see *Ohel), periodical literature, and, from 1925, the daily newspaper *Davar. From 1923 an autonomous "workers' trend" in the Hebrew educational system began to take shape. To overcome the effects of the split in the Jewish labor movement in the Diaspora, the Histadrut tried to set up an organization which would unite all groups supporting labor in Palestine, and the Labor Palestine Committee was founded in 1923. The Palestine Workers' Fund (Kuppat Po'alei Ereẓ Israel – Kapai), which had been founded before World War I by the World Union of *Po'alei Zion, was transferred to Histadrut authority in 1927.

New Policies After the Third Convention. The Histadrut's membership grew more rapidly than the economy as a whole, or even than the number of workers, but it did not succeed in taking in the religious workers: a section of Ha-Po'el ha-Mizrachi joined in 1925 but left again in 1927. The growth of the Histadrut was noticeable at its Third Convention, which took place in 1927, at the height of an economic crisis, when it had 22,500 members – a fivefold increase since 1920, though the Jewish population of the country had only doubled in the period. The majority of the membership, nearly 70%, was urban. Of the 201 delegates, Aḥdut ha-Avodah had an absolute majority with 108, and Ha-Po'el ha-Ẓa'ir had 54.

Communist influence made itself felt, mainly among the unemployed, and the Zionist parties combated it not with the ideal of an independent workers' commonwealth, but by a many-sided policy of activating all public and economic factors. The Histadrut leadership called on the Mandatory Government to adopt a policy of aid and encouragement to agriculture and industry, and urged the Zionist Organization to conduct its settlement activities with a view to establishing productive enterprises. The advantages of private capital investment were recognized, and willingness was expressed to conclude collective agreements on working conditions. The economic institutions of the Histadrut were reorganized, maintaining their autonomous character, and a Control Commission was set up. The convention defined its policy towards Arab workers as the establishment of autonomous trade unions allied with the Histadrut in a federation to be called the Alliance of Palestinian Workers (Berit Po'alei Ereẓ Israel). In view of the economic crisis and the financial retrenchment carried out by the Zionist Organization, the Histadrut leadership agreed in the late 1920s to the enlargement of the *Jewish Agency, in the hope of raising larger sums for agricultural settlement, and decided to seek a more influential role in the Zionist Organization.

In 1928 the employment situation began to improve and there was a shift in the structure of the economy, followed by a change in the structure of the Histadrut. The leading source of employment was no longer building, but large national industrial enterprises like the electric station at Naharayim, the Dead Sea Works, and the Athlit quarries. About 20% of the workers employed in building Haifa port were Jewish. There was development in medium-sized industries, handicrafts, services, and particularly transportation. Many found employment in the large citrus-based moshavot. The 1929 Arab riots also had the effect of increasing the use of Jewish labor, even if only for a short period. As a result, the Building Workers' Union decreased in size, and trade unions based on regular membership and more skilled workers developed. There was an improvement in labor relations and efforts were made to sign collective agreements.

The Histadrut intensified the struggle for Jewish labor in the moshavot, despite the opposition of the left wing (Ha-Shomer ha-Ẓa'ir and Left Po'alei Ẓion) who were against the demand for 100% Jewish labor; a Histadrut company for agricultural contracting (Yakhin) was set up. The workers in the villages for the most part regarded hired labor only as a stage on the way to independent settlement; some of them organized themselves into groups ready to set up kibbutzim or moshavim. The Jewish National Fund bought land in the Kishon region and the citrus areas for the scheme to settle 1,000 wage-earners' families on the land (Hityashevut ha-Elef; see Israel, State of: *Aliyah, Absorption, and Settlement, section on Settlement). As the *Keren Hayesod's funds were not sufficient, these settlements were financed partly by workers' savings and partly by Histadrut investment, in the main through the Nir Company. The Histadrut's Agricultural Center determined the order of priority for settlement, had a say in the apportionment of land, and exercised a considerable degree of authority.

Expansion of Activities and Influence. In the early 1930s the Communist challenge to the Histadrut, which had been based on unemployment and the failure to develop an independent socialist economy, weakened. *Mapai, the Palestine Labor Party, founded in 1930 by the unification of Aḥdut ha-Avodah and Ha-Po'el ha-Ẓa'ir, was supported by some 80% of the membership, and there was no longer any large opposition party. The minority parties, Ha-Shomer ha-Ẓa'ir and Left Po'alei Ẓion, concentrated on the demand for class militancy in the *yishuv* and in the Zionist movement, and for closer cooperation with the Arab workers. The leadership rejected any limitation of Jewish workers to skilled occupations and stood firmly on the need to penetrate all branches of the economy, state and private Jewish. In the Jewish-owned economy it demanded the employment of Jewish labor only, as the Arab workers had ample scope in the governmental services and also in Arab enterprises which were closed to Jews.

The Histadrut was strengthened by the immigration of members of Ḥe-Ḥalutz, which, since its Third Convention in Danzig, regarded itself as a source of reinforcements for the ranks of labor in Palestine. The growing influence of the Histadrut parties in the Zionist Organization had the effect of increasing immigrant quotas and allocations for agricultural settlement. Opposition to the status of the Histadrut in the *yishuv* in those years came from the Revisionist workers' organization, *Histadrut ha-Ovedim ha-Le'ummit, the National Labor Federation, founded in the spring of 1934, which opposed the integral character of the Histadrut and its control over labor exchanges and job opportunities. The Histadrut leadership rejected all demands for the limitation of its all-inclusive character, and was ready to agree in principle to a labor exchange not exclusively run by the Histadrut only on condition that a single body would be responsible for the organized allocation of work, and that the Histadrut's influence in the representation of the workers not be weakened. In the early 1930s there were violent clashes over these controversies. In the autumn of 1934 Ben-Gurion and Vladimir Jabotinsky, the Revisionist leader, reached agreement on avoidance of violence and the regulation of the relations between the two federations, but the agreement was rejected by a Histadrut referendum. The development of joint labor exchanges began in the second half of the 1930s and continued all through the 1940s, ending only with the establishment of state labor exchanges in independent Israel.

Despite the contraction of the Histadrut's comprehensive economic ambitions, it continued, with some success, to strengthen the labor-owned enterprises, although most of the Jewish sector of the economy was based on private capital. The labor economy was reorganized in 1924–34 according to directives laid down at the Third Convention. These demanded that the economic institutions be put on a sound financial basis; that each enterprise operate on a scale appropriate to its own economic, financial, and organizational capacity; that a regularly constituted authority should be developed for each enterprise, participating in its management and responsible for the economic consequences of its activities; and that each enterprise have complete internal financial autonomy within the framework of the overall authority and control of Ḥevrat Ovedim.

Contracting ceased to be the central branch of the labor sector. Solel Boneh was replaced by a Public Works Center under the control of the Histadrut Executive Committee, while contracting offices were set up under the local labor councils. Solel Boneh was reestablished in 1935 and absorbed the local contracting offices between 1937 and 1945. Some of its veteran employees were granted permanent status and special privileges. Bank ha-Po'alim expanded its turnover and capital through deposits and sale of shares. In 1926 Tnuva was established to market agricultural produce and took over the sales department of Hamashbir. It was divided into regional branches – Haifa, Tel Aviv, and Jerusalem – and was under the control of the settlements that sold their produce through it. In 1928 the Cooperative Center was founded to organize the cooperatives in manufacturing and crafts, transport, and other services; the transport cooperatives were particularly successful, but Histadrut control was fairly lax. In 1930 Hamashbir was reorganized as Hamashbir Hamerkazi, a cooperative wholesale society with defined functions, and was placed under the authority of the kibbutz movement and consumers' cooperatives in the towns and moshavim. A Housing Center was set up in 1930 with all its shares held by Ḥevrat Ovedim. In 1935 it became Shikkun, Workmen's Housing Ltd. It represented tenants' cooperative societies in their dealings with the Jewish National Fund, acquired and developed land, and prepared building plans. The building was done on public land and the apartments were cooperatively owned.

Problems of Prosperity. Between 1927 and 1933 the proportion of urban to rural workers shifted to the advantage of the countryside: the percentage of town workers fell during the period from 70% to 56.9%. The period of prosperity from 1933 to 1935 increased the demand for labor and stepped up wages, but led to developments which the leadership regarded as dangerous and incompatible with labor principles: for example, the renewed concentration of workers in the building trade and in the cities, with a decline in economic activity in the rural areas; employment of hired labor by cooperatives and contracting groups; letting and selling of apartments built with public funds at inflated market prices. There were complaints about the rise of a privileged bureaucracy, isolated from the public it served. All of these questions were taken up at the Fourth Convention of the Histadrut in 1933–34. The number of Histadrut members had risen to 33,815; 22,341 participated in the elections. Of the 201 delegates, 165 belonged to Mapai. The Histadrut leadership regarded the expansion of the labor market through private capital investment and increased demand as a desirable but economically unstable phenomenon, while the status of hired labor (as against labor economy) and the rise in workers' consumption were seen as socially undesirable. It was believed that the Histadrut should concentrate its efforts on stepping up savings during the period of prosperity in order to invest the proceeds in the building of an independent workers' economy, especially in agriculture. Since 1928 the Histadrut had been trying to build up its own credit facilities for agricultural settlement by selling shares in Nir. In 1934 it was decided to reorganize Nir as a limited company in order to secure funds from the private market.

The emphasis on increasing immigration and work on the land brought a renewed struggle for the employment of Jewish labor in the moshavot and citrus groves. The Histadrut called on the workers to go to the villages despite the higher wages in the towns, and demanded that the grove owners provide them with employment. Efforts by the Zionist Organization to mediate did not help very much, but the outbreak of the 1936 Arab riots completely changed the situation. Under Katznelson's leadership, the Histadrut began to widen its cultural activities and its work among the youth, laying greater emphasis on its ideological character. In 1934, after Ben-Gurion had joined the Jewish Agency Executive, he was succeeded as secretary-general by David *Remez.

Enhanced Role in National Leadership. The Arab revolt of 1936, which transformed the life of the *yishuv*, also had an important influence on the activities of the Histadrut. Its political and communal activities widened: it had a political office in London to foster relations with the British Labor Party and the Trade Union International, and its representatives gave evidence before the Peel Commission. In its political appearances the Histadrut attacked the Communist interpretation of the Arab revolt as the uprising of an oppressed people against colonialist domination, emphasizing the progressive structure of the new Jewish society and the economic advantages accruing to the Arabs from Jewish settlement. Its support, as a workers' organization, for increased immigration, despite unemployment, was of great importance.

In the Jewish community itself, the Histadrut used its moral authority and its organizational and economic resources to strengthen the defense of the settlements and road communications, but it opposed retaliation against Arab civilians as practiced by the "dissident" underground organization *Irgun Ẓeva'i Le'ummi (IZL). In the united *Haganah (defense) organization, which was based from 1937 on parity between labor and non-labor, the Histadrut represented the labor sector. Its authority over the pioneering and settlement organizations made it a leading factor in the establishment of the stockade and *watchtower settlements, while members of He-Ḥalutz and the Histadrut took the initiative in setting up the organization for clandestine *"Illegal" immigration. Although more men had to be employed in defense – as policemen and watchmen and in building fortifications – 1936–40 was a period of recession and unemployment. Building activity slowed down and the demand for labor fell, despite the growth in citrus cultivation. The Histadrut established a Work Redemption Fund to which every worker contributed several days' pay to support the unemployed. Public works were started through public companies established in partnership with the Jewish Agency. Expansion into new fields, such as fishing and shipping, was encouraged. In that period the organizational structure of the Histadrut was strengthened. In 1937 it introduced the "unified tax" – a single membership fee to cover the cost of organization, mutual aid, and health services – thus integrating trade union membership with membership of Kuppat Ḥolim.

In the late 1930s, the Mapai leadership tried to achieve unity with Ha-Shomer ha-Ẓa'ir and its urban partner, the Socialist League, hoping to avoid ideological and political controversies that would weaken the Histadrut's capacity for common political action. The ideological conflicts were already too deep, however. Ha-Shomer ha-Ẓa'ir regarded the Histadrut as an organization dedicated to the class struggle and refused to accept national authority in labor affairs. It wanted to establish joint Arab-Jewish trade unions and believed that the Zionist goal could be achieved by class partnership with the Arab workers in the framework of a binational state, which would accept the Zionist demand for free immigration. It also developed a leftist orientation in international affairs. It strongly opposed any ideological or cultural activity on the part of the Histadrut. Although the Histadrut had established a publishing house, Am Oved, in addition to its daily organ,

Davar, Ha-Shomer ha-Ẓa'ir set up its own publishing house, Sifriyyat ha-Po'alim, and newspaper *Al ha-Mishmar*.

The period of World War II presented the Histadrut with difficult problems, both as a labor organization and as a Zionist body. At the beginning of the war period, the employment situation worsened because of a decline in investment and building, a shortage of raw materials and industrial goods, and marketing problems, especially in citrus. In November 1939 there were 18,000 unemployed; in January 1941 there were still more than 10,000. Only in 1941 did the tide begin to turn, owing to recruitment to the armed forces, which reduced the numbers looking for work, and increased economic activity, first in building army camps, bridges, and fortifications, and later in the economy as a whole. The scarcity of imported goods created favorable conditions for the development of local agriculture and industry, while the British Middle East Supply Center regulated the supply of raw materials.

The war situation changed the character of trade union activities. In 1943 the Mandatory government issued a decree forbidding strikes and introducing compulsory arbitration. The rise in the cost of living made it necessary to adjust wages, which were linked to the cost-of-living index. During these years the trade unions achieved seniority payments, annual vacations, and employers' contributions to Kuppat Ḥolim for their members. Trade-union negotiations became more centralized, with the development of larger enterprises and the growth of the Manufacturers' Association. The trade unions developed in different directions and along flexible lines on countrywide industrial and craft foundations; in all cases care was taken to preserve the authority of the center over the sectional organizations.

The Zionist character of the Histadrut and its organizational and economic power made it the center for discussion and decisions on the *yishuv*'s war effort. The Histadrut supported enlistment in the British army, with emphasis on the defense of Palestine by Jewish units. The entry of the Soviet Union into the war, in June 1941, overcame the hesitations of some of the pro-communist groups about the war. The Histadrut's control over the labor market made it easier for it to put pressure on those who shirked enlisting. It also agreed to demands, strongly supported by the left groups, to recruit members for the Haganah and the *Palmaḥ. The kibbutzim and other settlements were put at the disposal of these units as places of work and bases for military exercises. The Histadrut also developed and encouraged independent activity in the rescue of European Jewry and "illegal" immigration.

The great possibilities for marketing and investment during the war increased the strength of the Histadrut's economic sector, whose long-range aims had been curtailed since 1927. Initiative, technical and management capacity, and capital, which had accumulated in the contracting and supply companies, were invested in industry. Enterprises were also set up in partnership with private capital on a 50–50 basis. At first Solel Boneh and Hamashbir took up branches closest to their own field of operations – building materials and food products – and then expanded into other areas. The management of the enterprises became more and more independent of the central institutions of Ḥevrat Ovedim, and the Histadrut's control over the cooperative sector was weakened. Efforts to renew Nir ha-Shittufit to take the initiative in labor settlement did not succeed: the kibbutz movements preferred their own separate funds. On the other hand, the Histadrut's credit and social insurance institutions developed successfully.

Controversies and Splits. The war period created political and ideological problems which led to disagreements and splits in the Histadrut. In the elections to the Fifth Convention in 1941, 88,198 members voted out of the total eligible membership of 105,663. Out of 392 delegates, Mapai had 278 and Ha-Shomer ha-Ẓa'ir and the Socialist League 77. A non-socialist group, *Ha-Oved ha-Ẓiyyoni, returned 14 delegates. At the convention, which met in 1942, there were outstanding differences between the left, which believed that Zionism might be realized with the support of world Communism, and the majority in Mapai, which stood first and foremost for the enhancement of the *yishuv's* own strength. The definition of Zionist aims in the *Biltmore Program (1942), which demanded the establishment of Palestine as a Jewish commonwealth, sharpened the controversy. Ha-Shomer ha-Ẓa'ir continued to support the binational solution and the disagreement came to a head over the question of the instructions to be given to the Histadrut delegation to the conference of the World Federation of Trade Unions, in which the Soviets participated, in 1945. These controversies weakened the Histadrut's capacity for political action, but it was united in its opposition to the 1939 White Paper and to the "dissident" underground organizations (IẒL and *Loḥamei Ḥerut Israel).

Both prewar unemployment and wartime prosperity aroused tensions within the Histadrut over such matters as the relations between workers and unemployed, hired labor in the contracting companies and the cooperatives, and conflict between the bureaucracy and the membership. In 1944 Mapai split, and a minority group, Siah Bet (B Faction), later Ha-Tenu'ah le-Aḥdut ha-Avodah, adopted an independent stance in the Histadrut. It called for more "class independence" and opposed Ben-Gurion's program, which had been followed since the beginning of the 1930s, of emphasizing the Histadrut's leading role in the *yishuv* and the Zionist movement, even to the extent of giving up separate labor activities.

The elections to the Sixth Convention in 1944, in which 106,420 of the 151,860 eligible voters participated, showed that Mapai still had a majority, though a much reduced one: 216 out of the 401 delegates. Ha-Shomer ha-Ẓa'ir and Left Po'alei Zion had 83 delegates, Ha-Tenu'ah le-Aḥdut ha-Avodah 71, and Aliyah Ḥadashah, a new non-socialist group (mainly immigrants from Germany and Austria) and Ha-Oved ha-Ẓiyyoni 12 each. The Mapai leadership tried to win greater support among the urban workers and achieved a decision to set up national unions of factory, transport, and building workers, in addition to the existing national unions of agricultural, clerical, engineering, railroad, and postal workers. They also tried to reduce the influence of the left-wing parties on the pioneering and youth movements in the Diaspora and succeeded in getting the Histadrut to decide on a united pioneering movement under its sponsorship. The period between the end of World War II and the War of Independence was not, as some had feared, one of economic depression. Investment capital and increased consumption raised the demand for labor and enhanced the power of the Histadrut. During the struggle against British rule and the War of Independence, the economic and organizational strength of the Histadrut provided a solid basis for the military strength of the Haganah.

[Israel Kolatt]

IN INDEPENDENT ISRAEL – 1948–70. The achievement of independence obviously necessitated a reconsideration of the role of the Histadrut in national life. Some thought that the State could now perform most of the functions the labor movement had assumed during the Mandatory period and that the Histadrut should become purely a trade-union body, dealing only with wages and working conditions. The great majority of its leading members, however, believed that it should continue to combine the defense of the workers' standard of living with the provision of social services, the building of a labor economy, and cultural activity. According to this view, which was held by Mapai and Mapam (founded in 1948 by the union of Ha-Shomer ha-Ẓa'ir, Left Po'alei Zion, and Aḥdut ha-Avodah), its centralized structure must be preserved in order to prevent particularist tendencies and exorbitant claims by pressure groups, to influence the allocation of the labor force to those places and trades in which it was required by national needs, and to mobilize public capital and labor potential in development areas which did not attract private enterprise.

In an address to the Eighth Convention of the Histadrut in 1956, David Ben-Gurion expressed this view:

During the period of the British Mandate, the Histadrut fulfilled governmental functions in the consciousness of a historic function and in the absence of Jewish governmental organs. On the founding of the state, the continuation of these functions is a superfluous burden on the Histadrut and a serious injury to the state… The Histadrut is not a rival or competitor of the state, but its faithful helper and devoted support. The labour movement, therefore, has a dual additional aim after the rise of the state:

(a) to mold the character of the state and make it fit to carry out to the full the mission of national and social redemption, and to strengthen and organize the workers for this purpose; and

(b) to initiate pioneering activities in the educational, economic, and social spheres which cannot be carried out by compulsion, law, and the governmental machine alone.

Thus, while the Histadrut's school system and the labor exchanges it ran in cooperation with the other labor federations were taken over by the state, the labor economy in agriculture, industry, and services, and social-welfare agencies, such as Kuppat Ḥolim and the provident and pension funds, were considerably expanded. At the same time, the Histadrut continued to carry out its trade-union functions, coordinating the wage claims and policies of the various sections and reorganizing its structure by establishing additional national trade unions. In several of the enterprises for which it was jointly responsible together with the Jewish Agency, such as the *Mekorot Water Corporation and *Zim Israel Navigation Company, the government supplied a steadily increasing share of the development capital and took over a larger part of the control.

The membership of the Histadrut has risen much faster than the growth of the population: from 133,140 (not counting housewives) at the beginning of 1948 to 448,390 in 1958 – 68% of the labor force – and 722,249 in 1969 – 78% of the labor force. Together with housewife members, the total grew from 180,600 in 1948 to 988,207 in 1969. The "population" of the Histadrut (including members' families) increased sixfold during the same period: from 267,912 to 1,631,607; with the religious labor federations, the total was 1,827,300 in 1969 – 64.4% of the country's population.

Political Forces in the Histadrut. In the elections to the Seventh, Eighth, and Ninth conventions of the Histadrut, held in 1949, 1956, and 1960, Mapai kept its absolute majority with 57.6%, 57.4%, and 55.43% of the total vote. In 1949, Mapam had 34.43%, and when Aḥdut ha-Avodah seceded from it, the two left-wing parties together had 27.15% in 1956 and 30.95% in 1960. There was thus no serious challenge to the traditional view of the Histadrut's structure and functions, which was supported by all three parties. The small Ha-Oved ha-Ẓiyyoni (Progressive) and General Zionist Workers factions, which were in favor of limiting the Histadrut's activities, obtained less than 9% of the votes between them at their peak and, although represented in the federation's executive organs, had little influence on its policies. Mapam, Aḥdut ha-Avodah, and the Communists (who rose from 2.63% in 1949 to 4.09% in 1956 and dropped again to 2.80% at the Ninth Convention), however, hindered Mapai's efforts to ensure wage restraint by proposing higher rates of increase than the majority thought practicable and conducting sporadic agitation among the workers outside the framework of the Histadrut's governing institutions.

At the Tenth Convention, in 1966, there were three new features in the political set-up. Mapai joined with Aḥdut ha-Avodah to form the Alignment (Ma'arakh), which gained only a bare majority, 50.87%. *Rafi, which had broken away from Mapai under Ben-Gurion's leadership, also contested the elections, gaining 12.13%. Perhaps the most significant new departure, however, was the *Ḥerut Movement's decision to take part in the Histadrut elections despite its close association with the *Histadrut ha-Ovedim ha-Le'ummit, National Labor Federation, to which many of its members belonged. Together with its Liberal partners in the Ḥerut-Liberal Bloc (*Gaḥal), it formed the Blue-White Workers' Association (Iggud Ovedim Tekhelet-Lavan), which emerged as the second-largest group with 15.21%, Mapam (without Aḥdut ha-Avodah) obtaining 14.51%. However, Rafi, although many of its members believed in the absorption of Kuppat Ḥolim into a state health service and were not very enthusiastic about the labor economy, did not press its views; at the beginning of 1968 it merged with Mapai to form the *Israel Labor Party and thus joined the Alignment.

All the country's political parties, except the religious ones, took part in the elections to the 11th convention in 1969, at which the Israel Labor Party combined with Mapam in a more comprehensive Alignment, obtaining 62.11% of a reduced poll. The Ḥerut-Liberal Bloc increased its strength to 16.85%, and the Independent Liberals (formerly Ha-Oved ha-Ẓiyyoni) improved to 5.69%, while Ha-Oved ha-Dati, which had formed a part of the 1965 Alignment, gained 3.06% and the two Communist lists 4.04% between them. The presence of representatives of the Free Center, a splinter group which had broken away from Ḥerut (1.99%) and Ha-Olam ha-Zeh (1.33%) reinforced the Gaḥal challenge to the leadership – without, however, undermining the Alignment's control.

The post of secretary-general of the Histadrut, which is one of major influence in national affairs, was held by a succession of personalities of ministerial caliber: Pinḥas *Lavon (1949–51 and 1956–59), Mordekhai *Namir (1951–56). Aharon *Becker (1959–70), and Yiẓḥak *Ben-Aharon (from 1970). The last belonged to the Aḥdut ha-Avodah wing of the Israel Labor Party; all the others were members of Mapai.

The Labor Economy. The labor economy expanded rapidly during the first decade of the state, the numbers employed rising from 60,000 in 1949 to 174,000 in 1960, i.e., from about 6% to 9% of the population and almost 25% of the labor force. During the second decade, its growth was slower: in 1969 it employed 215,000, about 22% of the labor force; there were plans, however, for a renewed drive in the field of industry. Labor enterprises thus played a notable part in the provision of employment for new immigrants. In agriculture there was a considerable increase in the number of kibbutzim and an even larger one in the moshavim, the numbers employed in Histadrut agriculture rising to 74.7% of the national total in 1968. The Histadrut also played a large part in establishing industries in the new villages and towns and in extending transport, marketing, and shopping services to the development areas, especially in the early years, before government incentives to private industry began to take effect. Its role was conspicuous in construction, road building and other public works, harbor expansion and construction, and the extension of the area under citrus, previously the preserve of the private farmer, in which the share of the labor settlements grew to about 50%. *Solel Boneh, the biggest Histadrut enterprise, was reorganized in 1958, despite some opposition, on the initiative of Pinḥas Lavon. It was divided into a Building and Public Works Company, with over 22,000 employees and a turnover of IL 462,000,000 in 1969, an Overseas and Harbors Works Company, operating in Africa, Asia, and the Middle East, with a turnover of IL 138,000,000, and Koor, an industrial holding company, with factories employing 12,000 and a turnover of IL 700,000,000. *Tnuva, which handles over two-thirds of all farm produce and is increasingly active in exports, had a turnover, counting subsidiary food industries, of IL 690,000,000 in 1969. Hamashbir Hamerkazi had about 550 affiliated cooperative enterprises, with a total turnover of some IL 413,000,000, and its industries employed 1,750 workers with a turnover of IL 118,000,000 (all figures for 1969). The Cooperative Consumers' Alliance had some 1,500 branches all over the country, including supermarkets in the large towns. Producers' cooperatives did not expand in the same degree, except for the passenger-transport companies, *Egged and Dan. Bank Hapoalim became the third-largest bank in the country with 150 branches (see Israel, State of: *Economic Affairs, section on Banking). Hundreds of cooperative housing societies raised the standards of workers' housing and enabled thousands of wage-earners to buy their own homes.

The kibbutzim, moshavim, and industrial and service cooperatives were troubled by the problem of hired labor, which was incompatible with their basic socialist principles. Rapid expansion made it impossible for their owner-members to dispense with the employment of outside labor, which aroused serious questions of social inequality. The problem was raised frequently at conferences of the Histadrut and its constituent bodies, and efforts were made to work for a solution by mechanization, automation, and assistance to hired workers to become full members of the cooperatives.

In 1955 the Histadrut decided on the establishment of joint management-labor advisory councils in some of its enterprises, but little was done by the managers to put the decision into effect. With the expansion of the centrally run concerns, which employed tens of thousands of workers, it was felt that they were beginning to lose their specific character as labor enterprises and that the employees saw little difference between them and private plants. The 86th Council of the Histadrut, in 1964, decided that the principle of workers' participation in management should be put into practice in the labor industries. A central department for labor participation, consisting of representatives of Ḥevrat ha-Ovedim and the Trade Union Department, was set up to carry out the decision. Workers' representatives were to be elected to the management of each plant to serve for not more than three years running. In these plants, the workers were also to receive a share in the profits. The tenth convention of the Histadrut in 1966 confirmed the decision, declaring: "The place of the Histadrut economy in the building and development of the country largely depends on the identification of the worker with his enterprise, and his participation in the responsibility for its management and maintenance." Up to 1970, joint management had been established in 15 enterprises.

Wages Policy. The structure of employment in the Israeli economy has had an important influence on the Histadrut's wage policy. About half the wage earners – the highest percentage in any country outside the Communist world – are employed by the public sector: the civil service, local authorities. Jewish Agency and its institutions, Histadrut enterprises, and so forth. In addition, a large part of industry and agriculture is subject to government influence through subsidies, loans, licenses, and various incentives. Thus, some three-quarters of the workers are employed in undertakings over which some measure of public control is exercised in the national interest. In the public and semi-public sectors, a responsible labor organization like the Histadrut cannot be concerned merely with increasing the amount the worker takes out of the undertaking in the form of wages at the expense of the employer's profits, since exorbitant demands may have to be met, in the last analysis, from the pocket of the local taxpayer or the contributor to pro-Israel funds from abroad.

Furthermore, some 90% of wage earners are organized in the Histadrut or the religious labor federations which cooperate with its trade union department. The Histadrut also has a central strike fund, which can assist the workers in an authorized trade dispute even in a weakly organized sector. This gives it a much greater bargaining power than exists in other countries, even in times of slack employment, and certainly in normal times, when there is no significant shortage of jobs. Moreover, it does not represent a downtrodden class, but one of the major elements in the building of the country, whose representatives not only wield considerable power in the trade-union field and control an important sector of the economy, but, through the labor parties, have held a dominant position in parliament and government throughout Israel's history.

This massive power implies a great responsibility, to which the Histadrut's leadership has always been acutely sensitive. Its power has enabled it to lie down and, to a large extent, to enforce, an all-inclusive wage policy covering all industries and services, but lack of restraint in exercising it might have been disastrous to the economy. The Histadrut's wage policies have, therefore, always been based on the assumption that, while using its power to maintain and improve the workers' standard of living, organized labor must share in the responsibility for the future of the economy, since no one is more interested in its stability and progress.

C-o-L Allowances and Labor Contracts. At its seventh convention, in May 1949, the Histadrut decided to press for the maintenance of the cost-of-living allowance system, in order to preserve the real value of wages, while supporting the introduction of methods conducive to greater productivity, such as the institution of work norms with premiums for output above the norm, while assuring the worker of a fair minimum wage. In 1951, the cumulative cost-of-living allowances were merged with the basic wage, and the Histadrut demanded wage increases of 10–15%. In 1953 it was decided not to claim a further increase in the basic wage; pay was to rise only in accordance with increases in the cost of living and by increased premiums earned by greater productivity, with exceptions in backward undertakings. The same general policy was maintained in the following two years.

In 1955 the government appointed a committee headed by Israel Guri, chairman of the Knesset Finance Committee, to consider salaries in the civil service and public institutions, particularly the claims of senior administrative officials and members of the liberal professions, that the differentials between their pay and that of lower-grade employees had been narrowed by the effect of the cost-of-living allowances. The committee recommended a general pay increase, with increased differentials for higher and academic grades, and its recommendations were carried out.

In 1956 the Histadrut decided that, in view of the grave security situation, one-third of the increases granted to the senior civil servants should be frozen for the time being, while other workers should get a graduated increase of 5–15%. The full rates were paid in 1957, and the frozen amounts were repaid during that and the two following years. In January 1957, the basic wages were again consolidated with the accumulated cost-of-living allowance, and it was decided that collective agreements between workers and employers be signed once in two years. In 1958 there was no change in basic wages, but seniority increments were raised, employees belonging to the professions were given a special annual grant to cover the cost of professional literature, and the wages of professional and administrative staffs were increased to cover overtime payments.

In 1959 and 1960 a number of changes were instituted: the addition of another grade at the top of the scale in industry and construction; higher family allowances for industrial workers; a special holiday allowance to cover hotel or recreation home expenses; an increase of 2% in employers' contribution to building workers' pension funds; and the preservation of seniority allowance on promotion for civil servants (who had previously started at the basic salary for the new grade).

At the ninth convention, in the latter year, it was decided in principle that further general increases in wages should be linked with rises in the net national product, and in 1962 the Histadrut established an independent institute, staffed by economists and statisticians, to produce objective figures on the level of national productivity which would serve as criteria for future wage policy.

In 1961 the problem of salaries in the public service again became acute. In the course of time, special salary scales had been instituted for employees belonging to various professions: physicians, technicians, engineers, journalists, social workers, and so forth. There were 20 different scales, resulting in many inconsistencies and frequent claims by those who felt themselves unfairly treated in comparison with members of other professions. Toward the end of 1961, the government appointed another committee, headed by the governor of the Bank of Israel, David *Horowitz, to propose a reform of the system. In the meantime, administrative staffs were paid advances on account of the wage increases expected after the conclusion of the committee's work. The Horowitz Committee reported in 1963, recommending the institution of a single scale for the entire civil service, with the exception of teachers, regular army, police, and prison staffs, and drafted conversion tables for the transfer of all employees to the new scale. The government and the Histadrut, however, felt that automatic conversion would perpetuate the inequalities between the various scales, and it was decided, instead, to carry out a comprehensive job evaluation, so that each employee's grade should be decided according to the work he was doing. The determination of the grades of the various classes of employee was a prolonged process, lasting several years. Owing to pressures exercised by staff representatives and the grant of an 18% increase to professional workers in 1965 in order to keep up differentials, the total civil service wage bill increased by one-third.

In 1963 it was decided to make no change in the existing labor contracts, in order to support the government's policy of economic stabilization following the devaluation of the Israel pound in 1962, but in 1964 the Histadrut decided, in view of a rise in productivity, that wages should be raised by 3% in that and the following year. In addition, family allowances of IL 6 per month for each of the first three children were instituted through an equalization fund (the fourth and subsequent children were already covered by the family allowance scheme of the National Insurance Institute; see Israel, State of: *Health, Welfare, and Social Security, section on Social Security). In 1965 these allowances were taken over by the Institute and financed by a levy on employers of 1.8% of wages. In 1966 the existing labor contracts were further renewed without change for a period of two years.

In view of the burden of increased defense expenditure after the *Six-Day War (1967), the Histadrut made no further wage claims when these agreements expired, so that wages were largely frozen for a period of two years. In 1970 it was felt that complete restraint could no longer be justified and that increased productivity during the past four years warranted a wage increase of some 8%. However, in view of the security situation and the drastic increase in the adverse balance of payments, a package deal was concluded between the Histadrut, the government, and the employers' organizations, providing for a 4% rise in the cost-of-living allowance and another 4% wage increase to be paid in government bonds, while the government undertook not to raise taxes and the employers not to increase prices, as well as to invest a further 4% of wages on government bonds. A committee representing the three parties was appointed to supervise the implementation of the agreement.

Strikes. During the past decade the Histadrut's centrally imposed wages policies were under constant pressure from various groups of workers who felt that they were entitled to higher wages and, in most cases, manned services, where a stoppage would produce considerable inconvenience to the public, such as the ports, the posts, or electricity supply. The tendency toward decentralization, as well as the strong loyalties of the workers to their directly elected local or sectional committees at the expense of their allegiance to the more distant central organs of the Histadrut, made wildcat strikes easy to call and difficult to control. In 1967–1971, the majority of the labor disputes, claims, and stoppages – many of which took the form of slowdowns, working to rule, or similar measures – were not officially recognized. Attempts by the Histadrut and local labor councils to impose discipline were generally unsuccessful, and most of the unofficial disputes ended in compromises, which gave the strikers at least part of their demands.

There were considerable and irregular fluctuations in strike statistics over the period. The number of strikes rose from 45 in 1948 to a peak of 90 in 1955, fell to 46 in 1958 and 51 in 1959, rose to 135 in 1960 and reached a peak of 288 in 1965 and 286 in the following year, falling in 1967 to 142 and in 1968 to 101. The number of strikers during the years 1949–56 varied between 7,308 in 1950 and 12,595 in 1952; it fell in 1957 to 3,648 and rose slightly during the following two years; it increased in 1960 to 14,420 and climbed steeply to a peak of 90,210 in 1965, falling again to 25,058 in 1967 and 42,176 in 1968. The number of days lost by strikes during the period varied from a low point of 31,328 in 1959 to a peak of 242,699 in 1962, going down to 58,286 and 73,153 in 1967 and 1968 respectively. A more significant index of the number of days lost per thousand wage earners showed no consistent trend. The figure was 281.0 in 1949 and 235.1 in 1966, going down to 68.7 in 1959 and rising to 392.7 in 1957 and 447.3 in 1962. In 1967, the index fell to 99.5, rising slightly to 112.6 in 1968. In 1969 there was a slight increase in the number of strikers (44,500) and a considerable one in days lost (102,000). The year 1970 was a particularly bad one, with repeated disputes in the ports (especially in the new port of Ashdod), and prolonged strikes by nurses and secondary school teachers: 114,900 persons struck, and 390,000 days' work were lost.

Reliable statistics on the proportion of authorized to unofficial strikes are available only since 1960. Between that year and 1965 the percentage of strikers participating in authorized strikes varied from 5.5% to 19.3%, but it rose during the three subsequent years to 30%, 55%, and 69% respectively. Similar tendencies are shown by the figures for the number of days lost. In 1969 40%, and in 1970 44% of the strikes were authorized by the Histadrut. Most of the strikes during the years 1965–70 were in the public sector (excluding Histadrut concerns), the percentage varying from 39.5% in 1967 to 50% in 1965, 52.5% in 1968, 60% in 1969, and 55% in 1970. (No statistics on this point are available for earlier years.) Figures classifying strikes according to branch of economy show that in most years until 1964 the number of strikes and days lost were greatest in industry, followed by the public services, but from 1965 the public services were hardest hit by strikes.

Social Services. While the total population increased about fourfold in the 20 years 1948–68, the number of persons insured in Kuppat Ḥolim grew more than sixfold: from 307,623 to 1,968,302, including members of the religious labor federations and certain other categories outside the Histadrut. The main increase took place in the years of mass immigration, as the great majority of the newcomers joined. In 1948, 35.3% of the total population and 43% of the Jewish population were insured with Kuppat Ḥolim; by 1968 these percentages stood at 70% and 82% respectively. It played an important part in providing remedial and preventive medical treatment for the new immigrants, established hundreds of clinics in new towns and rural centers, and taught the elements of hygiene to newcomers from backward countries. (See also Israel, State of: *Health, section on Kuppat Ḥolim)

In the early years of statehood there were a large number of small provident funds, reaching 328 in 1953, with 60,000 members, through which workers saved a regular percentage of their wages, with parallel contributions from the employers. The funds provided small loans and other services from time to time, with a lump sum payable upon retirement. This system was found to be unsatisfactory, and measures were taken to amalgamate small funds into large ones, which would provide pensions instead of lump sum payments. The first of these funds was that for Histadrut employees, founded in 1954. The largest is Mivtaḥim, which provides pension, holiday, and other payments for a large variety of workers, including casual laborers. There are also funds for clerks and officials, employees of Histadrut industries, members of cooperatives, agricultural workers, and building workers. Mivtaḥim and the last two funds also cover payments for holidays, work accidents, rehabilitation, where necessary, and so forth. Pension rates are raised in accordance with the rise in the cost-of-living and keep pace with wage increases. At the end of 1968 the total membership of the funds was over 350,000, together with their families about half the population of the country, and their accumulated capital amounted to more than IL 20,000 million. The funds are under treasury supervision, and 80% of their capital must be invested in government-recognized securities. Most of the remainder is invested in securities issued by Gemul, the Histadrut investment company. Of the remaining 20%, about half is used for cheap loans to members for housing and so forth. The operations of the funds not only constitute a valuable local service but are of considerable economic importance as a method of saving and a source of capital investment.

International Affiliations. When the World Federation of Trade Unions was founded after World War II, the Histadrut cooperated fully with it, but when Communist influence grew in the WFTU and it was left by many Western trade union federations, who formed the International Confederation of Free Trade Unions, the Histadrut, after heated debate, joined the latter in May 1950. The Histadrut maintains close ties with the member federations of the ICFTU and sends experienced trade unionists to advise on labor organization, particularly in Asia and Africa. Its representatives also play an important role in the 15 international federations representing specific trades. Many delegations and groups of students, particularly from developing countries, have come to Israel to study the Histadrut's methods and achievements. The trade unions in these countries are interested in the Histadrut's unitary structure, its success in integrating members with varied cultural and educational backgrounds, and its prominent role in national life. Its Afro-Asian Institute has become an important international center for labor studies.

The Histadrut also belongs to the International Cooperative Alliance, which represents cooperative movements in both Western and Communist countries, and Israel's cooperative economy has aroused widespread interest. Despite Israel's small size, Histadrut representatives play a prominent part in the work of the International Labor Office and are regularly elected to its governing body. The Histadrut's influence in all branches of the international labor movement is an asset of considerable political importance for Israel.

Educational and Cultural Activity. The Compulsory Education Law, 1949, maintained the "trend" system, under which the Histadrut was responsible for one of the four school networks. The Labor "trend," which was controlled by the Histadrut's Educational Center (Merkaz le-Ḥinnukh), aimed at "molding a self-reliant pioneering Jewish personality, imbued with the Zionist-Socialist ideal" and "imparting to the child the values of the labor movement in the country and a sense of participation in the fate of its people." It established new schools in many immigrant centers and in 1953 had some 900 schools and kindergartens, with over 3,000 teachers and 60,000 pupils, out of 3,210 institutions, 15,304 teaching posts, and 320,361 pupils in the entire Jewish educational system.

In 1953, when the Knesset passed the State Education Law (see Israel, State of: *Education), the labor schools were merged with those of the "general trend" to form the nucleus of the state educational system and ceased to be organized in a separate framework. However, the influence of its principles may be seen in the clause of the State Education Law which prescribes that state education shall be based, inter alia, "on training in agricultural labor and handicrafts; on fulfillment of pioneering principles; on the aspiration to a society built on liberty, equality, tolerance, mutual aid and love of fellowman."

The Histadrut's Cultural Department provides a variety of services for members in town and country. These include: lectures, films, publications and periodicals; organized trips; courses in Hebrew and geography, Bible, music, dancing, and the arts; clubs and libraries; educational books and materials; theater performances for immigrants; libraries for schools in immigrant centers, in cooperation with the Presidential Residence Fund; educational circles for the parents, and schools for trade union leaders. Volunteers were organized during the mass immigration period to help newcomers by teaching Hebrew and other subjects. In addition, the local labor councils engage in similar activities on their own initiative, and there is a wide network of cultural committees in towns and villages. There are special departments for the kibbutzim and the moshavim.

Arab Workers. In the early years of statehood the Palestine Labor League continued to perform trade union functions on behalf of Arab workers, with the close cooperation of the Histadrut. Labor organization was stepped up in the Arab sector; Arabs could now find employment in the Jewish economy, receiving the same pay and conditions as Jewish workers, and the labor exchanges assured them of participation in the fair division of work. In November 1952 the Histadrut Council decided to open the Trade Union Department at all stages to Arab workers on the basis of complete equality, and grant them full rights in provident funds and other Histadrut mutual-aid institutions. At the end of 1953 a special section for Arab workers was established in the Trade Union Department. Trade union branches were established in Arab centers and, in mixed places of work, joint workers' committees were elected by Arab and Jewish workers.

In February 1959 the Histadrut Council decided on the admission of Arabs and members of other minority communities as full members. With the assistance and advice of the Histadrut, agricultural, industrial, consumers' and housing cooperatives were established in Arab centers. Kuppat Ḥolim opened general and mother-and-child clinics in Arab villages and towns. The Histadrut, especially through its youth and women's movements, maintains clubs and cultural activities in the Arab areas. Arab membership of the Histadrut grew from 6,427 (9,956 including housewives) in 1958 to 31,254 (50,446 including housewives) in 1969. The number of Arab members and dependents increased in the same period from 21,534 to 118,098 – 29% of the Arab population, compared with 10.1% in 1958.

After the reunification of Jerusalem, the Histadrut started to organize the workers among the 65,000 Arabs in the eastern part of the city. Under Jordanian rule, most of them had been badly paid and exploited, and the few trade unions had little influence. Despite the opposition of some Arab notables, about 5,000 workers joined the Histadrut, which tried to equalize their pay with that of the Jewish workers. Most of the Arab employers resisted the efforts, but compromises were reached with the hoteliers and some others. In 1970, there were 2,000 Jerusalem Arabs working for Jewish employers.

Kuppat Ḥolim opened a branch in East Jerusalem, which, after initial difficulties in finding Arab doctors and nurses and overriding the reluctance of Arab women to go to Jewish doctors, won acceptance. Arab trade unionists in Jerusalem took part in Histadrut courses on labor relations and submitted their candidacy in Histadrut elections. The Histadrut's work in the city was regarded as a significant contribution to understanding between Jews and Arabs.

The Women's Labor Movement. All women members – including housewives – are entitled to vote in the elections to *Mo'eẓet ha-Po'alot, the Women Workers' Council, which thus has a membership of almost half a million – 46% of the total. Housewives are organized in Irgun Immahot Ovedot, the Working Mothers' Organization, with branches all over the country. The women's movement has made an important contribution to the integration of the immigrants by teaching the women Hebrew, introducing them to the life of the country, and helping to look after the children. It has also done much to improve the status and conditions of Arab women. Its projects in Israel are assisted by the sister movement abroad, *Pioneer Women.

Youth and Sport. In 1959 *Ha-No'ar ha-Oved combined with the school youth movement, Ha-Tenu'ah ha-Me'uḥedet, to form a single organization of working and student youth. It has more than 100,000 members: some 40,000 of them, aged 14–18, in trade sections, which function as a kind of junior Histadrut, and the rest, aged 10–18, in groups for recreational and educational activities. The *Ha-Shomer ha-Ẓa'ir youth movement (with 13,000 members) and Dror-Maḥanot ha-Olim (5,000), affiliated to *Ha-Kibbutz Ha-Me'uḥad, are also, like their parent bodies, within the framework of the Histadrut.

*Ha-Po'el, with 85,000 members in 600 branches all over the country, is the largest sports organization in Israel, engaging in 17 types of sport. Its representatives play a prominent part in the governing bodies of the various sports, such as the Football Association (see also under *Sport). The Histadrut youth and sports movements have done much to bring new immigrants and their children into the mainstream of Israel life.

See also: Youth Movements in Israel, State of: *Education, Kuppat Ḥolim under Israel, State of: *Health

[Moshe Allon]

Ideology of Labor

Labor was one of the central themes, both ideologically and organizationally, which occupied the attention of the Jews at the beginning of their resettlement in the 1880s. Its ideology was developed by a number of leaders and thinkers, such as Ber *Borochov, Nachman *Syrkin, A.D. *Gordon, Joseph Ḥayyim *Brenner, Joseph *Trumpeldor, Berl *Katznelson, and David Ben-Gurion, on the basis of Zionist-Socialist analyses of the Jewish problem and the experience gained in the process of resettlement. For specific historical, religious, and social reasons, the occupations of the Jews in the Diaspora had been limited, for the most part, to finance, commerce, teaching, medicine, and law. Few were to be found in the basic sectors of the economy, such as agriculture, industry, transportation, and mining. The desire to renew the political life of the Jewish people in its historic homeland through the creation of a society in which Jews themselves would carry out all the organizational and economic functions required for its maintenance was thus combined with the concept of *kibbush ha-avodah* ("the conquest of labor"). This meant the establishment of a national economy with a varied and all-embracing productive and organizational framework, and the spiritual vocational and educational preparation of Jews to engage in all the occupations required in such an economy. *Kibbush ha-avodah* was linked with the ideal of *ḥalutziyyut* ("pioneering"), which inspired the individual not only to advocate and support the national revival, but to be ready himself to settle in the homeland as a *ḥalutz*, or pioneer, prepared to do any kind of work, however arduous, unaccustomed, or dangerous, that might be required at the time, to build this new national society (see *He-Ḥalutz).

At first, organized attempts were made to develop the basic, productive branches: agriculture, construction, and handicrafts. Settlement on the land, which was intended to create the agricultural base for the Jewish community in Palestine, was the central sphere of activity in the "conquest of labor" in the first 50 years of renewed national life. Later, in the 1920s and 1930s, construction and handicrafts developed, and so, to a certain extent, did administration, public services, and light industry, which were further expanded by the large wave of Jewish immigration from Germany that followed the Nazi assumption of power in 1933.

The advent of World War II and the increased demand of the Allies for industrial products led to the development of heavy industry, including metals, textiles, and food processing. There was also a considerable technical advance in construction and road building, as a result of army orders, both in Palestine and in other places. At the same time there were significant changes in labor relations and the beginnings of labor legislation.

This process received a great impetus by the establishment of Israel in 1948. Large investments in the development of agriculture, services, administration, industry and mining, construction, sea, air, and land transportation, and all the occupations connected with national defense, widened the productive framework and increased the variety of work available. Labor relations, social conditions, and labor codes were partially transferred from the voluntary to the governmental level.

These events determined the stages of development and affected the status of labor. In the first stage, that of settlement on the land, there was a close identity between ownership and work. Jewish immigrants established villages and cultivated the land on their own farms. At this stage there was no substantial body of hired Jewish laborers, and the wage labor needed in agriculture came from the neighboring Arab villages. This division between Jewish employers, and Arab proletarians aroused the ideological opposition of young immigrants who came from Eastern Europe in the wake of the abortive revolution and the pogroms in 1905–06, especially in the Russian-ruled areas of Poland and Romania. Belonging to a class whose social and economic foundations were crumbling, influenced by revolutionary workers' movements, as well as the Zionist ideal, and having absorbed socialist principles on the role of labor in production and of the workers in society, these pioneers fought for the right to work on the Jewish farms. They regarded their own transformation into manual workers as a part of the social and national revolution of the Jewish people and as a precondition for the creation of a self-sustaining Jewish society and economy.

At this stage, which continued until the beginning of the 1920s, this Jewish working class was only a small part of the small Jewish community of about 60,000. It lacked vocational training and practical experience, but it had a highly developed working-class consciousness and struggled to develop a modern labor policy, achieve as high a wage level as possible, and establish labor relations similar to those accepted in Western countries. In fact, the theory of an ideological and trade union struggle preceded the development of the means of production in the Jewish community. The Jewish workers who came to the Land of Israel after the failure of the Russian Revolution in 1905, the immigrants of the Second Aliyah, regarded it as their mission to achieve a Zionist solution to the Jewish problem through immigration to the Land of Israel, building up a Jewish economy, and establishing progressive social patterns, and they saw the organization of labor as a basic part of that mission.

With the establishment at the beginning of the Second Aliyah of workers' political parties that carried out some trade union functions, as well as political activity, and the establishment, in December 1920, of the Histadrut (see above), which combined trade-union functions with social-welfare services and independent cooperative and workers' enterprises, a new stage was reached, both from an organizational point of view and from the angle of labor's influence in the Jewish community. In many respects the political and trade-union organization of the workers ran ahead of national, social, and economic development. In fact, the established standards and practices in labor relations, wages, and social conditions inside the *yishuv*, although based on voluntary agreements, largely determined the conditions of production.

The organizational structure, practices, and ideology of the Jewish labor movement were, therefore, from the very beginning on a standard characteristic of the advanced industrial countries. The Histadrut, which absorbed the bulk of the immigrants and represented the vast majority of the organized workers, even went beyond that stage by assuming many functions not normally accepted by trade-union organizations in other countries. It saw as its task the practical implementation of social and economic programs that other labor movements regarded as long-term political and social goals. These programs included setting up new villages (moshavim and kibbutzim), industrial and service undertakings, workers' cooperative and contracting enterprises, and public services whose guiding principle was the idea of *avodah aẓmit* ("self-labor" or "personal labor," i.e., that a man must live by the fruits of his own labor without exploiting the labor of others). This concept was the guiding principle in the determination and implementation of the Histadrut's labor policies.

The ideological principles, trade union policy, and organizational patterns of Israel labor were laid down and assumed the force of binding customs in the life of the *yishuv* during the British Mandatory regime (1918–48), when the level of governmental services was largely determined by the condition and needs of the backward Arab population. In the course of that period they reached a standard that was high even in comparison with those achieved by workers' movements and trade unions in Western countries. With the establishment of the State of Israel and the institution of its governmental laws and institutions, under labor political leadership, a new phase in labor relations began. The voluntary social achievements of the *yishuv*, which had been enforced by collective agreements between the Histadrut and the Manufacturers' Association (organized at the end of the 1920s), became part of the state labor code and the pattern of the country's life.

Labor Relations

LABOR LEGISLATION IN THE MANDATORY PERIOD. Due to established custom in colonial territories and because of the possible effects on the Arab and governmental economies, the British Mandatory authorities were in no hurry to enact labor laws. For many years, in fact, they left almost unchanged the situation which they had inherited from the Ottoman Empire, in which relations between employer and employee were regulated by a section of the Mejelle which dealt with lease contracts (see *Legal and Judicial System). During the first 20 years of the Mandate, only a handful of labor laws were enacted: the Mining Ordinance (1925), which regulated safety conditions and prohibited, inter alia, the employment underground of women or children under 14, ordinances prohibiting the use of matches made with white phosphorus (1925), and a law enjoining the fencing of machinery (1928). Article 21 of the Criminal Code, concerning intimidation in labor disputes, the Defense (Trade Disputes) Order (1942), and the Defense (War Service Occupations) Regulations (1942) were concerned solely with meeting emergency needs.

An important, if belated, step was the establishment of a Department for Labor Affairs in 1943, largely under pressure of economic developments during World War II. As if to make up for the backwardness in this field that had marked the period of British rule, the department set to work with dispatch in the few years left before the end of the Mandate, paying more attention to the advanced needs of the Jewish economy. The Accidents and Occupational Diseases Ordinance (1945), which provided for compulsory notification of accidents at work, or occupational diseases which caused more than three days' absence, marked a considerable advance, as did two other ordinances issued in the same year concerned with employment of women and children, which greatly improved health conditions at work. The Factories Ordinance (1946), which established standards of safety and hygiene, was a very important and progressive addition to Mandatory labor legislation. Three other ordinances that would also have improved the Mandatory labor code were issued in 1947, but never came into effect. They were the Trade Boards Ordinance, which was to set up machinery for establishing minimum wages and working conditions in backward industries; the Industrial Courts Ordinance, for the settlement of labor disputes through conciliation and arbitration; and the Trade Union Ordinance, to regulate the legal status of workers' and employers' organizations.

VOLUNTARY AGREEMENTS DURING THE MANDATORY PERIOD. While the Mandatory government concentrated most of its attention on safety conditions, the Jewish community had a large measure of internal autonomy in its labor relations. In the absence of adequate legislation, it established practices and customs which, though voluntary, were firmly adhered to, as attempts to violate them were frustrated by the pressure of the organized community, which was led by the labor movement. This autonomy was reinforced by a High Court ruling to the effect that accepted custom in labor relations was legally binding. An eight-hour work day, annual vacations, severance pay, allocation of work through labor exchanges according to agreed priorities, rest on the Jewish Sabbath and festivals, recognition of the trade unions, collective bargaining, and collective agreements became established practice.

In the early years, labor relations in the Jewish community were concerned mainly not with wages and working conditions, but with the employment of Jewish labor in the citrus groves, which was the main source of employment. Wages and working conditions were practically stable, with slight variations, from the beginning of the Mandate until the outbreak of the World War II, so far as Jewish workers organized in the Histadrut were concerned, and were not, therefore, a serious cause of labor disputes. Tension in the labor sphere was due mainly to unemployment and charges of unfair distribution of the available jobs.

The Histadrut, the General Federation of Jewish Labor, was the largest and most influential workers' organization, but there were also two others, organized along political and ideological lines. The demonstratively secular character of the Histadrut at the time, both in outlook and in practical programs, led to the formation of a religious workers' organization, *Ha-Po'el ha-Mizrachi, which later joined the Histadrut's medical-insurance fund and trade union department, while maintaining its separate framework for other affairs. There was also the National Labor Federation (*Histadrut ha-Ovedim ha-Le'ummit), organized in 1934 under the aegis of the Revisionist Party, which opposed the Histadrut's socialist outlook and some of its trade union principles – especially the use of the strike weapon. From the beginning it had its own trade union department and medical-insurance fund.

In 1925 the Zionist Executive in Jerusalem intervened in a dispute between Ha-Po'el ha-Mizrachi and the Histadrut, when the contracting company of the former engaged workers without using the Histadrut's labor exchange. This intervention, which was intended to avoid direct interference by the Mandatory government, created a precedent. In the early 1930s the number of labor disputes increased as a result of the growth in the numbers of wage earners and of plants. In the course of a full-scale debate on the problem at the Zionist General Council in 1934, there was a demand for the conclusion of labor contracts which should assure fair labor conditions for the workers "within the economic possibilities of the economy" and, on the other hand, "a reasonable level of output, especially from the agricultural laborer." The meeting decided that the agreements should be based on

(1) reasonable working conditions for the employees and adequate productivity;

(2) obligatory resort to arbitration;

(3) the establishment of labor exchanges on a basis of parity between workers and employers, the chairman and secretary being agreed upon by both sides;

(4) the establishment of a labor exchange center under the *Va'ad Le'ummi to supervise the local exchanges and appoint the chairman and secretary wherever the two sides failed to agree.

At the same time, the Labor Department of the Jewish Agency began to concern itself actively in labor disputes. This department, which was headed by Yiẓḥak *Gruenbaum, with representatives of the Histadrut and Ha-Po'el ha-Mizrachi, was the highest authority in all such matters from its foundation in 1935 until the establishment of the state. During this period it dealt with more than 2,500 disputes, for the most part concerning collective agreements, and through its decisions it set the seal of approval on working conditions and practices worked out by collective agreements. Among other things, it developed a system for the resolution of labor disputes by arbitration or the good offices of the department, which was also recognized as a court of appeal.

LABOR LEGISLATION IN THE STATE OF ISRAEL. The emergence of Israel as an independent state in 1948 marked a turning point in the approach to labor relations. The Mandatory government had not had time to put the Industrial Courts Ordinance (1947) into effect; nor did the Provisional Government of Israel in its early days find time to breathe life into this stillborn enactment. In practice, the procedures and customs which had been accepted amongst the Jews of Palestine remained in force. The government set up a Labor Relations Department in the Ministry of the Interior, which inherited the functions of the Labor Department of the Jewish Agency and, after the elections, to the First Knesset was transferred to the Ministry of Labor.

Before long the government submitted to the Knesset the first labor law: the Ex-soldiers (Reinstatement in Employment) Law (1949), which was aimed at alleviating the difficulties caused by conscription for the War of Independence. It was followed by a lengthy series of labor laws, many of which gave legal force to procedures already established by custom and agreement within the Jewish community. They dealt, inter alia, with hours of work and rest (1951), annual leave (1951), employment of youth (1953), apprenticeship (1953), employment of women (1954), enforcement of collective agreements (1957), settlement of trade disputes (1957), penalties for excessive delays in payment of wages (1958), labor exchanges (1959), severance pay (1963), equal pay for men and women (1964), and labor tribunals (1969).

LABOR EXCHANGES. Under the employment Services Law (1959), employers must engage employees, and employees must accept employment, through the state labor exchange. There are exceptions for the civil service above a certain grade, managerial staff, posts requiring higher education or special training, and persons employing a spouse, parent, child, grandchild, brother, sister, or cousin. The manner in which applicants are referred to jobs is laid down in special regulations which generally take into account the nature of the occupation, the type of work, social condition, disablement, recent demobilization from the armed services, etc. The law prohibits any discrimination on the basis of sex, age, race, religion, nationality, party allegiance, etc. This law legalized the situation which was achieved in the pre-state period by a long struggle on the part of the workers, who established their own labor exchanges in order to prevent unorganized labor and protect new immigrants against closed-shop tendencies that might develop in particular occupations or localities.

Anyone seeking employment is registered at the labor exchange nearest his home. His trade or profession and grading are registered on the production of recognized certificates or on the basis of an examination by a qualified authority. He (or she) must reregister daily or at longer intervals according to his trade or profession. The labor exchange receives requests for staff, allocates them among the registered job seekers, and provides vocational counseling for those who lack skills or wish to change their occupation. Its services are given free of charge. There are 15 regional exchanges, divided into 164 branches and sections, as well as 41 branches in Arab areas and 68 branches for young people aged 14–18. Professional men and women are served by a special exchange with branches in Jerusalem, Tel Aviv, Haifa, and Beersheba. There is also an exchange for seamen in Haifa as well as special provisions for domestic servants, with seven branches in the large cities.

COLLECTIVE AGREEMENTS. Labor relations in Israel are based upon a system of collective agreements, or labor contracts, which is recognized in the Collective Agreements Law (1957). These agreements, which are signed by an employer or employers' association on the one hand and the representative of the trade union on the other, lay down conditions of work, including wages, social benefits, working hours, shifts, and labor relations, as well as rules of conduct and discipline, engagement of staff and the termination of employment, negotiation procedures, the settlement of disputes, and the rights and obligations of the parties. Collective agreements may be "special," applying to a particular enterprise or employer, or "general," applying to the whole or part of the country or to a specific type of work.

Collective agreements were to be registered by the chief labor relations officer at the Ministry of Labor. The representative organizations conclude skeleton agreements, which are adapted to conditions in each industry by subsidiary agreements negotiated between the trade union or labor council concerned in each case and the appropriate section of the employers' organization. The minister of labor is empowered to issue an order extending the application of the general collective agreement to employees or employers who are not organized in a trade union or employers' organization. In general, collective agreements are negotiated every two years by the Histadrut and the Manufacturers' Association, which was established in 1924. In 1964, a roof organization called the Coordinating Committee of Economic Organizations was set up to represent the various employers' organizations in agriculture, industry, commerce, etc.

The Trade Union Department of the Histadrut speaks for about 90% of the workers, including, by agreement, members of Ha-Po'el ha-Mizrachi and *Po'alei Agudat Israel, the labor wing of *Agudat Israel. It consists of representatives of the national trade unions, but in determining its policies it is guided not only by the immediate needs of the workers but also by the long-term interests of the national economy. Histadrut ha-Ovedim ha-Le'ummit, which is in favor of compulsory arbitration in labor disputes, has its own trade unions and does not cooperate with the department. In each town there is a directly elected labor council (*mo'eẓet po'alim*), which deals with local matters.

THE WORKERS' COMMITTEE AND THE LOCAL LABOR COUNCIL. The basic unit of trade union representation is the workers' committee (*va'ad ha-ovedim*), which is elected by all the workers (whether they belong to the Histadrut or one of the smaller federations) in each factory, office, shop, etc. It consists of three to nine members, depending on the size of the enterprise, elected every two to three years. Theoretically, voting is on an individual basis, but in practice the workers usually support the candidates nominated by their own parties. Labor councils are elected in each town by proportional representation in the same way, and at the same time, as the national convention of the Histadrut, lists of candidates being submitted by the political parties. The workers' committee, together with the local labor council, represents the workers in all matters connected with the labor contract and protects the rights specified in the contract or the regulations founded on it, as well as rights laid down by law. It discusses with the management any questions of labor conditions or discipline that may arise from time to time and has equal representation on productivity committees. It also organizes mutual aid projects and serves as a channel for information from the management on the position of the enterprise, production plans, technological changes, and so forth. A representative of the local labor council may be invited in advance to join in the discussion of particularly important matters; in any case, he is called in when the workers' committee fails to reach agreement with the management. The committee reports regularly to general meetings of the workers, to which it may submit matters of special importance for a decision by majority. Any decision involving a strike must, according to the regulations, be taken by secret ballot and be approved by the labor council.

WAGES. Wage rates and payments for social benefits in the various branches of the economy are fixed in the annual or biennial labor contracts, in accordance with the wages policy laid down biennially by the Trades Union Department of the Histadrut through negotiation between the trade unions and the employers' organizations. Changes generally take the form of wage increases and higher cost-of-living allowances.

During the British Mandatory regime, the agricultural laborer's wage was generally taken as a basis, the Jewish worker's earnings usually being some 25% higher than the Arab's. In many Jewish public services, such as the Zionist Organization, the Histadrut, the schools, and the health services, the "family-wage" system was in force. Under this system, all employees earned more or less equal wages (with differentials of 20–50% for various professional standards), supplemented by allowances for dependents. During World War II there was a sharp rise in prices, due to the decline in the exchange rate and increased demand for consumer goods and services, coupled with an increased demand for labor for the developing industries and services for the British army. There was a growing need to adjust wage rates to the changing price level. The solution was found in the system of cost-of-living allowances, under which the nominal wage was raised at fixed intervals in accordance with the rise in the cost-of-living index.

After the establishment of the State of Israel the system at first remained in force in the main branches, but the development of the economy, which called for more skill and managerial responsibility, led to the abolition of the "family" system and demands for higher differentials. Up to the economic recession which started in 1964/65, the system of cost-of-living allowances, adjusted annually, had a great influence on wage levels. From 1965 onward, however, both wage rates and differentials began to rise, largely as a result of regrading in the civil service and the pressure of professional men's organizations.

In the biennial negotiations between labor and employers, on which the government exercises an indirect but powerful influence, general wage increases are based on the average rate of increase in output, with adjustments according to the situation in different industries and the state of the labor market. In many enterprises workers receive premiums in return for output in excess of the accepted norm. This system is encouraged by the trade unions, the employers' associations, and the government. There is a growing use of scientifically measured norms, the contribution of technological progress to productivity being taken into account in order to encourage the introduction of automation.

See also section on Jewish Labor Organizations.

SOCIAL BENEFITS AND DEDUCTIONS FROM WAGES. The net wage received by the worker consists of the gross wage paid by the employer minus income tax and other deductions. The gross wage includes: basic salary in accordance with accepted wage rates; cost-of-living allowance, fixed by agreement between the Histadrut and the employers in accordance with the annual fluctuations in the consumer's price index, which is determined by the government's Central Bureau of Statistics; seniority increment for each year of employment in a given enterprise – ranging from IL 5 to IL 15 per annum up to a fixed "ceiling" of years of service or total increment; allowance for a wife, laid down in the labor agreement; children's allowances for the first three children, paid out of an equalization fund financed by the employers collectively through the National Insurance Institute (allowances for the fourth and subsequent children come directly from national insurance – see Social Security and Welfare).

The following deductions are made from the salary: income tax, national insurance contributions (see Social Security and Welfare), and pension fund contributions; in many concerns, by custom or agreement, deductions are also made at source for Histadrut membership fees (covering trade union and Kuppat Ḥolim), municipal rates, and contributions to national institutions. The employer's contribution for social benefits includes: basic pension – 11% of gross wage, excluding overtime and bonuses (with 5% more paid by the employee); comprehensive pension – 11% of gross wage (with a further 5% from the employee); parallel fee – 2.7% of wages, paid by the employers to the medical insurance fund; vacation pay – 4% of wage to cover paid holidays for those employed less than 75 consecutive days (workers with permanent status receive their wages without interruption throughout the vacation period); vacation expenses – cost of accommodation in a recreation home for a certain number of consecutive days at an agreed rate per day, as fixed in the labor contract; sick leave, up to one month per year – the right being cumulative within limits laid down in the labor contract. Salary for a "13th month" is paid in some undertakings and offices. In some offices or institutions, generally in the academic professions, there is a special payment, up to an agreed maximum, for professional literature. Some employers make a monthly deposit to meet the cost of severance pay. In certain posts, mainly managerial, the employer provides a car and pays for upkeep and fuel up to a fixed number of kilometers. He may pay the cost of a home telephone, the employee making a fixed contribution to cover the cost of his private calls.

Permanent status may be granted under the terms of the labor contract after a trial period of six months, which may be extended by prior notice for a further six months. An employee with permanent status may not be dismissed without the agreement of the workers' committee, and only in accordance with an agreed order of priority. In some academic posts senior employees are given a sabbatical year with pay. In case of bankruptcy, employees are guaranteed priority over other creditors for the payment of their wages up to a sum of IL 2,100, as well as severance pay up to IL 1,050 per employee.

INSPECTION, SAFETY, AND HYGIENE. Many factors increased the danger of work accidents after the establishment of the state: the rapid development of industry, construction, and transportation; the expansion of the electricity network; automation and the use of more sophisticated equipment; and the employment of new immigrants and untrained workers. To meet the situation, a considerable body of safety legislation, along the lines of international conventions, was enacted in a short time to comply with local needs. The powers and scope of the factory inspectorate were extended in the Labor Inspection (Organization) Law of 1954, which also established the Safety and Hygiene Institute, jointly run by the Ministry of Labor, the employees, and the employers' organization, for the prevention of industrial accidents by research, guidance, and publicity. Regulations have been issued specifying safety measures required in various occupations. Industrial injuries compensation is provided through national insurance.(See Table: Work Days Lost.)

HOURS OF WORK AND REST. The standard working day in Israel consists of eight hours and the working week of 47 hours. If more than eight hours are worked, whether for unforeseen reasons or under an official overtime permit, each of the first two hours in excess of eight is regarded for wage purposes as an hour and a quarter, and every additional hour as one and a half hours. Every employee is entitled to 36 hours rest per week. The weekly holiday day is Saturday for Jews, Friday for Muslims, and Sunday for Christians. Religious holidays recognized by the government are rest days for workers of the religion concerned, and national holidays are rest days for all workers. Work on the weekly rest day is allowed by special permission of the Ministry of Labor if it is essential for the defense of the state, the safety of the person or of property, the prevention of serious injury to the economy, the maintenance of a continuous work process, or the supply of the essential needs of the public or part of it. A general permit of this kind may be granted by a committee composed of the prime minister, the minister of religious affairs, and the minister of labor. For wage purposes, each hour worked on the day of rest is regarded as not less than one and a half hours.

ANNUAL VACATION. Under the Annual Leave Law (1951), every employee is entitled to an annual vacation with pay totaling at least 12 days, not including weekly rest days and national and religious holidays. Shift workers receive four additional days. Every employee must be given an annual vacation of at least seven consecutive days; in certain occupations, specified in the regulations, a longer period is obligatory. Collective agreements also provide for longer vacations for workers in certain posts, whether at higher levels of responsibility or in certain occupational grades. Day laborers who are constantly changing their place of work receive a cash payment in lieu of vacation. This is paid through a special fund to which the employer contributes 4–5% of wages.

An employee is entitled to accumulate vacation periods, with employer's consent, up to a stipulated maximum (65 days for civil servants) and during a stipulated period in accordance with the labor contract. By mutual agreement an employee may receive a cash payment in lieu of vacation in excess of the seven obligatory days. The dates of the vacation for each employee are fixed by the management in consultation with the workers' committee, taking the wishes of the employee and the needs of the enterprise into account. The following are not included in the vacation period, but are stipulated in collective agreements: sickness during the vacation, if the employee informs the employer within 24 hours; periods of reserve duty or military service; days of mourning, i.e., seven days from the death of a member of the family, in accordance with religious custom; special leave of one day for a son's or daughter's wedding or the birth of a child, and three days for the employee's own wedding. Jewish religious holidays are New Year (Rosh Ha-Shanah) two days, Day of Atonement one day, Sukkot two days, Passover two days, and Shavuot one day, as well as Independence Day and two optional days. For civil servants, the latter may be chosen from the eve of the Day of Atonement, Hoshana Rabba (7th day of Sukkot), the Tenth of Tevet, Purim, the eve of Passover, Martyrs' and Heroes' Remembrance Day, Israel Defense Forces Remembrance Day, Lag ba-Omer, the first of May, 17th Tammuz, and the Ninth of Av.

Under most labor contracts employees are entitled to an annual allowance sufficient to pay for seven days' accommodation in a recreation home or inexpensive hotel, on condition that he takes at least ten consecutive days' vacation during the same year. This right is acquired after three years' service to the same employer (two years for employees under 18). Day workers are entitled to allowances for four to ten days, depending on seniority and other factors, in return for a contribution of 0.5% of wages to a special fund, matched by a similar contribution from the employer. Permanent employees are entitled to paid sick leave usually up to 30 days per year, which may be accumulated on terms laid down in the labor contract. Employees are insured through the insurance funds and are entitled to up to seven months' sick leave per year.

EMPLOYMENT OF WOMEN. Women have the right to work, without discrimination, at equal pay for equal value of work in the same jobs as men, so long as they can do the job in accordance with their physical capacity without impairing their health. Jewish women played a prominent part in the work of the pioneers, in settlement on the land and the "conquest of labor," in the Jewish underground defense forces, and in political effort. The government makes special efforts to increase the share of women in the labor force. The role of women is particularly important in the liberal professions and primary, secondary, and higher education, in administration, in retail distribution, in industries such as food processing, textiles, and electronics, and in various agricultural jobs. Women are constantly penetrating into vocations once regarded as male preserves.

In 1969 women constituted 31.5% of the labor force, which is lower than in most developed industrial countries. The reason is that a large portion of the Jewish population came from Muslim countries, where it was not customary for women to work outside the home. Among the second generation there is a growing tendency to go out to work, which is more marked where the educational level is higher. The fact that girls aged 18–20 (with the exception of those excused on religious grounds) serve in the armed forces increases their readiness to seek work on the completion of their service. The minister of labor is empowered by law to prohibit or restrict the employment of women in a particular job or industrial process which may seriously impair their health. Women may not be employed on night shift, with the exception, under certain conditions and subject to the minister of labor's approval, of work in managerial posts, the customs, telephone exchanges, the police, airline stewardesses, hospitals, newspapers, hotels and restaurants, places of entertainment, etc. By law, a working mother is assured 12 weeks' maternity leave, beginning six weeks before the birth, if the mother chooses, as well as to a maternity grant from the National Insurance Institute. She is also entitled to be absent from work during pregnancy and breast-feeding, or up to one hour's leave per working day for the purpose of breast-feeding.

EMPLOYMENT OF JUVENILES. The employment of, or peddling by, children under 14 is forbidden, but they may be employed in art or entertainment with the approval of the minister of labor. The employment of young persons (aged 14–18) is forbidden in any place which is likely to have an undesirable effect on their physical, emotional, or moral development, such as hotels, cafés, dance halls, mental institutions, mines, abattoirs, various types of manufacture, and so forth, as specified in a list of occupations published by the ministry. Young workers must undergo medical examination before starting work and at six-month intervals, depending on the nature of the job, up to the age of 21. They may be employed for no more than eight hours per day and no more than 40 hours per week, and those under the age of 17 must not be employed at night without the approval of the minister of labor.

According to the law, every young person aged 14–18 in employment must be enabled by his employer to learn a trade, and the employer must not make deductions from his earnings for absence for the purpose of attending recognized lessons. Guidance in the choice of a trade by a qualified vocational counselor must be provided. The Apprenticeship Law (1953) empowers the minister of labor to define certain trades as apprenticeship trades, in which the employment of young persons is prohibited unless they are learning the trade through an approved program of study. During his training, the apprentice is paid in accordance with the collective agreement for the trade. For 1–1½ days per week he is required to attend a special school for apprentices, where he studies the theoretical aspects of his trade and continues his general education. After three years' apprenticeship, he generally receives a trade certificate. In 1970 there were 23 such schools, attended by about 15,000 apprentices; a total of some 50,000 apprentices had qualified since the passing of the law.

DISMISSALS. Labor contracts usually obligate the employer to consult the workers' committee and receive its consent before dismissals are carried out. Grounds for dismissal may be low output, infractions of discipline, sabotage, unjustifiable absence, or unpunctuality. Most labor contracts call for at least two weeks' notice of dismissal. When staff has to be reduced, it is generally stipulated that the last-in-first-out rule be observed, with certain exceptions: for instance, relative levels of skill and social circumstances, such as size of family, are also taken into account. A dismissed employee is entitled to severance pay if he has worked for the same employer for at least one year without interruption, or in two consecutive years in the case of seasonal employees. An employee who resigns is not entitled by law to severance pay, but in many cases he receives it by agreement with the employer. Resignation due to impaired health, change of residence due to marriage, a move to an agricultural settlement, or the resignation of a mother within nine months of the birth of a child for the purpose of looking after the child, or when she has adopted a child, are regarded as equivalent to dismissal for the purpose of severance pay. Severance pay is also awarded in case of resignation due to proven and substantial worsening of working conditions or special circumstances connected with labor relations. The rate of severance pay laid down by law is one month's wages for every year of employment on monthly salary by the same employer, and two weeks' wages for every year during which a worker has been employed on a daily basis. In general, a month's salary, for the purpose of calculating severance pay, is the salary of the last month, but with regard to the years before 1964 there is a special basis for calculation which is specified by law.

VOCATIONAL TRAINING. From the early days of Zionist pioneering, when Jewish traders, shopkeepers, and students tried to turn themselves into farmers, vocational training in the widest sense of the term (then called in German *Umschichtung*) was a fundamental part of the national goal. (Various aspects of the question during the Ottoman and Mandatory periods are dealt with in the section on Aliyah and Absorption.) In independent Israel the vocational training system was built on the foundations established by the Jewish Agency and other voluntary bodies. It started by extending the apprenticeship system and setting up various courses for adults. Later, adult vocational centers were established throughout the country and furnished with up-to-date equipment. The network of vocational schools grew with the help of *ORT (Organization for Rehabilitation and Training), which established well-equipped vocational high schools and also engaged in the training of apprentices.

Vocational high schools are owned and run by public bodies and supervised by the Ministry of Education and Culture. In 1970 there were 278 such schools with 51,000 pupils, run by: ORT-Israel – 84 schools with 13,000 pupils; the Amal network of the Histadrut – 25 schools and 5,250 pupils; local authorities – 94 schools with 15,000 pupils; Youth Aliyah – 22 schools and 32,000 pupils; Agudat Israel – 24 schools with 2,000 pupils; the Working Women's Council (Mo'eẓet ha-Po'alot) – 25 schools and 1,000 pupils; Mizrachi Women's Federation – four schools and 1,540 pupils; WIZO – three schools and 1,250 pupils; the Hadassah Organization – two schools with 900 pupils; and other bodies with 30 schools and 5,600 pupils, most of them learning clerical skills. Students receive both vocational and general education for three or four years, leading to a recognized trade certificate. There are also vocational schools attached to specific industries, the curriculum including practical work on the factory floor. Courses are held for adolescent drop-outs (aged 14–18) from the high schools, the curriculum being devised to enable them to serve in the army in their trades, thus extending their period of training (for apprenticeship training, see above, section on Employment of Juveniles).

For adults, the Ministry of Labor runs specially equipped training centers, some established with outside assistance (e.g., technical aid from the U.S. government, the UN, and the International Labor Office), giving 3–18-month courses depending on the trade. In 1970 there were 22 of these, with about 12,000 trainees. In addition, on-the-job training has been used to deal with the huge number of unskilled adults among the immigrants. The trainee is taught by a skilled tradesman until he is fit for normal employment, and the employer receives a subvention from the government in return for the training. Special attention is devoted to the training of tradesmen to the levels of practical engineer, instructor technician, and foreman, which provide a link between the graduate engineer and the artisan. The shortage of staff at these intermediate levels is one of the more serious defects in Israel's labor force. To fill this gap, the Government Institute for Technical Training has been set up jointly by the Ministries of Labor and Education and Culture, with the technical aid of the International Labor Organization. The institute runs day and evening courses, directly and through the Technion, the universities, and the ORT network. About 6,000 tradesmen attend courses each year. The aptitudes and inclinations of young workers are examined in special vocational guidance centers. There are also diagnosis and observation centers to guide handicapped persons in the choice of a vocation.

ARBITRATION AND MEDIATION. Labor contracts contain provisions for settling differences, generally by agreed arbitration. Sometimes the parties agree on a single arbitrator and sometimes an arbitration court, consisting of one representative each of employees and the employer, and a third person agreed upon by both sides, is set up. This procedure is normally used in disputes over the interpretation of clauses in the labor contract, but not where a new demand is made. Where agreed arbitration is not used, or where the issue is not dealt with in the labor contract, the good offices of the chief labor relations officer at the Ministry of Labor, whose powers are derived from the Settlement of Trade Disputes Law (1957), are invoked. His authority applies to disputes between employers and employees, between an employer and a trade union, or between one trade union and another, but not to disputes between individuals. Either party to a dispute may notify the chief labor relations officer, but in the event of a threat to strike, or to impose a lockout, the party which makes the threat must make the notification.

The officer may mediate in person or appoint a mediator; in general, he prefers the two parties to settle the dispute themselves. Each party must give reasoned replies to the claims of the other side and appear before the mediator at his demand. The parties are not compelled to accept the mediator's proposals, but any signed settlement, whether reached by the parties themselves or in response to the mediator's proposals, has contractual force. The same applies to the ruling of an arbitrator or arbitration commission nominated by the chief labor relations officer when the labor contract provides for agreed arbitration.

There is no compulsory arbitration law in Israel. Attempts to introduce such a law have never secured a majority in the Knesset. Opponents of compulsory arbitration argue that it restricts the freedom of the workers to fight for their interests, that in a democratic country there cannot be control of wages without parallel control of profits, and that, in any case, compulsory arbitration cannot be effectively enforced. Proposals to introduce compulsory arbitration in essential services have also been rejected for the same reasons, as well as because of the difficulty of defining essential services.

STRIKES AND LOCKOUTS. The right to strike is recognized in Israel: strikers and employers imposing a lockout enjoy immunity under the Collective Agreement Law (1957) and the Civil Damages Ordinance. According to the Histadrut's rules, strikes must have the approval of its competent authorities, but wild-cat strikes are not infrequent.

Most strikes are over claims for pay rises and break out before the signature of a new labor contract. The number of strikes over dismissals, the transfer of enterprises, or non-recognition of labor unions is relatively small; such issues are usually settled through the arbitration machinery specified in the labor contracts. About 60% of the strikes which took place in the decade ending in 1969 were over pay and related issues, 20% over delays in the payment of wages, 10% over dismissals, and 10% over the signing of agreements and the recognition of trade unions; very few were over classification, transfer of factories, and other matters. Strikes are not more frequent in Israel than in other industrialized countries, but in view of the military and economic pressures to which Israel has been subject for a long time, they constitute a grave economic and social burden.

According to an amendment to the Settlement of Trades Disputes Law, passed in 1969, employees or employers must give 15 days' notice to the chief labor relations officer at the Ministry of Labor and to the other party of their intention to declare a strike or a lockout as the case may be, in order to enable the two parties to settle the dispute through direct contact or the chief labor relations officer to attempt to settle it by mediation. Labor contracts include provisions for the settlement of disputes through accepted forms of arbitration. In the great majority of cases, agreements for the settlement of disputes also settle the issue of strike pay. The Histadrut has a strike fund from which grants or loans are made to workers who are on a recognized strike. Neither strikes nor lockouts are regarded in law as a breach of contract, and those responsible are not, therefore, liable for damages – except in cases of sabotage.

UNEMPLOYMENT AND UNEMPLOYMENT INSURANCE. Fluctuations in the dimensions of immigration and the rate of economic growth, as well as the changing security situation, have led to a varying incidence of unemployment from time to time. A further cause of periodic unemployment has been the dependence of a large part of the Israel economy on construction, which is affected by fluctuations in supply and demand. To alleviate unemployment, the government initiated public works financed from the public purse, such as afforestation, land reclamation, drainage, archaeological excavations, and road construction and maintenance. Relief work of this kind was allocated to the unemployed, each applicant receiving 12–24 days' work per month-depending on the number of persons he had to support. Wages were linked with those of agricultural laborers. Special programs, with five hours' work a day five times per week, were instituted for those with limited ability to work.

Total unemployment figures include both those actually unemployed and those employed on relief work. Two sets of data are published:

(a) manpower surveys, covering a statistical sample of those who make up the civilian labor force aged 14 and over, which define as unemployed those who did not work at all during the week to which the survey related; and

(b) the daily average of unemployed, which is calculated by dividing the total number of unemployment days during the month among those who registered as work seekers at the labor exchanges at least once a week, by the number of working days in the month.

The first set of data includes those who do not normally work; the second covers only those registered at the labor exchanges.

In 1965 it was decided that unemployment grants should be made from the public purse to those unemployed who, for one reason or another, could not be employed even on relief work. The grants, made to persons registered at the labor exchange who had been unemployed for at least 34 days, were the equivalent of 15 days' pay per month at IL 7 per day for a single person, 19 days' pay at IL 8 for a married man without children, and, according to a sliding scale, up to 24 days' pay at IL 10 per day for a man with eight dependents or more. Proposals for the institution of unemployment insurance, financed partly by contributions from workers and employers, were under consideration in 1970.

LABOR COURTS. The Labor Courts Act, establishing a separate judicial network for matters related to labor, came into force in 1969. These matters include labor laws, social conditions, and national insurance questions. The labor courts are empowered to adjudicate claims between employer and employee, disputes arising out of a special collective agreement, touching on the maintenance, applicability, implementation or infraction of the agreement, claims of an employee against a trade union, and any matter related to the National Insurance Law. The claims may relate to trade disputes, employment services, reinstatement of demobilized soldiers, compensation to employees on reserve duty, severance pay, delayed payment of wages, etc.

There is a national labor court, which is also a court of appeal, and four regional labor courts. Each regional labor court is composed of one judge and two lay members, one representing the employees and the other the employers. The national labor court is composed of three judges and one or two representatives each of labor and employers, depending on the case. The labor courts are not bound by the rules of evidence, except in special cases, and are empowered to use the procedure which they regard as best suited to serve the ends of justice. Parties may be represented by appointees of employers' organizations or trade unions, who need not be lawyers.

PENSIONS. There are three types of retirement-insurance schemes:

(a) The national insurance old-age pension (see Israel, State of: *Health, Welfare, and Social Security, section on Social Security and Welfare).

(b) Budgetary insurance entitles the employee to a pension on reaching retirement age (and in certain circumstances at a lower age) equal to 2% of his salary for every year worked, after not less than ten years' service. When an employee has started work after reaching the age of 40, the competent authority may increase his pension in accordance with customary or agreed rules. In this type of scheme, which is in force in the civil service, the employee makes no contribution to the cost of the pension.

(c) There are two types of insurance through pension funds. "Basic insurance" covers pension for the insured person, partial pension and a lump sum for his heirs, mutual life insurance for pensioners and active members of the fund, withdrawal grants, and loans to members. "Comprehensive" pension insurance provides, in addition, full pension for survivors and a full or partial disablement pension.

Contributions vary from 7.5–10% of wages for basic pension, 4–5% coming from the employee and the rest from the employer, and 13.5–16% for the comprehensive pension, the employee paying 4–5% and the employer the rest. Retirement age is 65 for a man and 60 for a woman, or earlier in certain occupations. If an employee continues to work beyond the retirement age, he receives a higher pension on retirement, up to 70% of his salary. The qualifying period of membership is ten years. Accumulated rights may be transferred from one pension fund to another under special conditions laid down in the regulations. An employee who stops working before reaching retirement age is entitled to a severance grant, which includes the accumulated total of his contributions and those of the employer, plus accumulated interest and linkage increments (related to changes in the rate of exchange or the cost of living). Alternatively, if he has at least ten years' contributions to his credit, he may opt to receive the grant on reaching retirement age or continue to pay his contributions in order to receive a full pension. Surviving dependents are entitled to payments ranging from 20% of the deceased's pension for an orphan who has lost one parent to 60% for a widow. Surviving relatives of a member of the fund who dies before acquiring pension rights receive a bereavement grant. A person holding comprehensive insurance for not less than three years is entitled to a disability pension, provided he began to work before the age of 55 (50 for a woman). The pension for a totally disabled person who is unable to work two hours per day is 50% of wages, plus 5% for every dependent (up to a maximum of 20%), plus 1% for every year of service. A partially disabled person receives a pension calculated on the basis of the percentage of disablement.

The Histadrut maintains seven pension funds: for employees of Histadrut institutions, industrial workers, building workers, workers in Histadrut enterprises, agricultural workers, office workers, and workers in cooperatives, excluding transport. There are also company insurance funds in banks, private companies, etc. The pension ranges from 35–40% of the last salary, on the completion of ten years' insurance, up to a maximum of 70% on the completion of 32–35 years.

[Zalman Heyn]

Employment

Successive waves of immigration generally brought with them periods of considerable unemployment and a legacy of underemployment, from which, even in the changed circumstances of the 1960s, it was difficult to escape. Stress was laid on the need to build up the goods-producing sectors – agriculture, industry, and building. In the early days, the development of agriculture was the central Zionist theme, although it is doubtful whether employment in agriculture ever reached 20% of the Jewish labor force. Industrial development began on a serious scale only during World War II, and received special attention after 1955. Because of the lack of previous agricultural and industrial training of most of the immigrants, and the limited growth of the goods-producing sectors, Israel always had a service-based economy.

As late as 1955, 46% of the Jewish labor force was employed in the goods-producing sectors (a proportion slightly higher than that in the United States, the most service-oriented economy in the world, and much lower than in Western Europe). Within the service sectors, the proportion of Jews employed in public and government services was 22%, by far the highest in the world. Whereas in most countries underemployment tended to be concentrated in agriculture, in Israel it tended to be concentrated in public and government services. The unemployment rate, traditionally high in Israel because of unrestricted immigration, reached a peak of about 10% in 1953, but dropped to 7% in 1955.

Between 1955 and 1965, while the Israel gross national product expanded at a real annual rate of 10%, the structure of employment in Israel underwent radical changes. The proportion in the goods-producing sectors actually advanced slightly, from 48.4 to 48.9% (this includes the Israel Arabs). Employment in agriculture, following world trends, declined over the decade, but relative gains in industrial and construction employment more than offset this. Small relative declines in commerce and private services were only partially offset by a relative expansion in public services. The slight rise of employment in goods-producing sectors was contrary to world trends: in Western Europe the proportion employed in the goods-producing sector fell to 50–55%. As Israel living standards neared European levels during this decade, the broad distribution of the labor force between economic sectors began to resemble that of Western Europe. By 1965 the distribution of the labor force by economic sectors had begun to approach normalcy, though some sharp differences were still evident. The proportion of the labor force in industry, despite the rapid absolute and relative rise, was still low compared to Western Europe, as was the proportion in commerce. On the other hand, comparatively large proportions were still engaged in construction and in public services.

The picture of total employment had also changed over the decade. From 1955 to 1960 unemployment fell steadily, from 45,500 to 34,000, or from 7.2 to 4.6% of the labor force. Thereafter, the number of unemployed tended to remain stable, though, because of increased employment, the percentage dropped. The unemployment rate fluctuated only between 3.3 and 3.7% from 1961 through 1965. This rate was considerably lower than that prevailing elsewhere. During the early 1960s, Israel enjoyed its first sustained period of full employment. The residual unemployment was essentially of a frictional character. Indeed, in 1964, a peak year, there were large numbers of unfilled jobs.

The proportion of the total population of working age in the labor force declined slightly over the 1955–1965 decade, but this decline was purely demographic. The number of people in the 14–17 age group and over 55 years of age expanded significantly over the period. This offset increased labor force participation by specific age groups, though differently for men and women. Between 1955 and 1965, labor force participation of male youths aged 14–17 grew: it grew substantially for those over 55 years of age. Thus, while in 1955 it could be argued that male labor force participation was low by western European or American standards, by 1965 it was quite normal.

The labor force participation rates of women also advanced rapidly during the same decade. Despite the unfavorable demographic development, the participation rate grew from 26.5% in 1955 to 30.3% in 1965. But, despite this increased rate, the overall level was generally below that in the United States or Western Europe. The 1965 employment rate for women up to the birth of their first child was comparable to that in other countries. Thereafter, particularly after the age of 35, the rate was much lower, i.e., fewer married women with children tended to return to the labor force as compared to other advanced countries. This is due to the extremely low labor force participation of Jewish women originating from Islamic countries. These women had many children, lived in traditional style, and had few labor market skills. Daughters of these immigrant women are, however, adapting more to western work and childbearing patterns, and the problem appears to be simply generational.

The economic and employment growth patterns were abruptly halted by the recession of 1966–67. During this period, employment declined, especially in industry and building, and unemployment soared briefly over the 10% mark. After the Six-Day War a very rapid recovery set in with a trend to return to full employment. There was, however, a further relative shift to services caused mainly by a decline in building employment and a further decline in agricultural employment.

With the approach of the 1970s, Israel's capacity for economic growth tends to be limited largely by manpower shortage. Immigration is still relatively small, and manpower reserves have been drained. The important tasks are to reduce frictional unemployment and to utilize underemployed manpower by increased training in needed skills.

[Herbert Allen Smith]

Developments in Employment and Labor, 1970–1980

EMPLOYMENT. In the period from 1970 to 1978, the Israeli civilian labor force grew, on the average, by 3% per annum, reaching 1,318,100 persons in 1980, and the demand for workers also increased steadily. Out of the total civilian labor force in 1980 approximately 1,254,000 were employed, while the remainder, 63,600, were unemployed.

The unemployment rate, i.e., the number of unemployed persons as a percentage of all persons in the labor force declined from 3.8% in 1970 to 3.6% in 1978, but increased to 4.8% in 1980. Of particular significance during the period was the increased participation of women in the labor force. Their percentage grew, on the average, by 5% annually, whereas the number of men rose by a mere 2%.

Employment of residents of the Administered Areas in Israel also rose significantly during this period, from approximately 21,000 in 1970 to close to 70,500 in 1980, an average of 16% per annum. The majority of these workers have found employment in Israel in construction, manufacturing and agriculture.

Data from the national Employment Service also reflect the rising demand for labor in Israel's economy. Through 1978 the number of job seekers (monthly average) declined during the period under review by 3% per annum, while the number of job openings (monthly average) declined by 2%. As a result, the number of jobs for which no workers were found had doubled.

WAGES. The average real wages of workers rose by 22% during the period under review. The highest rise was in the economic branch of electricity and water – 74%, and the lowest in the building trade, only 7%.

The rise in industry was greater than that in public services, which increased by only 12% as compared with 29% in industry. From this it would appear that the standard of wages in the industrial sector was 10% higher than in the public service sector, which was a reversal of the trend of the previous decade.

Although the average real increase in wages in the financing and business services economic branch was 22%, a breakdown of the branches reveals that whereas in banking, insurance and property the increase was 32%, in other business services it was only 6%.

The situation changed again somewhat in 1979 as a result of significant increases in salary in the industrial sector and an even greater increase in the public sector, which also received the differences in pay for 1978 retroactively.

The demands of the workers for nominally significant pay increases were affected by the increased rate in the rise of prices at the end of 1978 for the late, partial compensation given through the cost-of-living raise and by the erosion of disposable income because of only partial adjustments in the income tax brackets.

By the end of the year the rapidly increasing rate of inflation had eroded the real gain in salary, despite the fact that the nominal salary continued to increase quickly. The constantly increasing consumer prices resulted in the real salary of employed workers increasing during the year by 3.7% over all the economy and close to only 1% in the industrial sector.

LABOR REIATIONS. The period 1971–1979 can be divided into three main sub-periods which were influenced by three factors extraneous to labor relations: the Yom Kippur War and the rise in the cost of raw materials and in that of oil in the world.

The period January 1971–September 1973 was one of economic growth; October 1973–December 1974, the period of war and emergency, 1975–1979, a slowing down in economic activity.

The first period was characterized by a flourishing and developing economy. There was a demand for workers which could not be met and which led to pressure in the labor market, which was accompanied by an inflationary process. An attempt was made to restrain the rise of wages by collective wage through "package deals," i.e., agreements between the government, the Histadrut, and the employers on limited wage increases, the employers on their part undertaking not to raise prices. The function of the government was price control and an undertaking not to increase municipal taxes.

The "package deals" entered into in 1970 were still in force in 1971, but the rise in prices, with a concomitant increase in the medium of circulation at a time when wage increases were restricted by the package deals, brought about strong pressure in the form of strikes and labor disputes – especially in the public sector – to increase salaries. The strikes, called while the agreements were still in force, were confined to small groups who did not receive the authorization of the Histadrut. They amounted to 169 strikes, involving 88,265 workers with 178,612 days of work lost, and encompassed 58% in the public sector, 25.4% in the private and 9% in that of the Histadrut.

A similar deal was signed in 1972 for the years 1972–73, but the gap between the increase in prices and of goods, which became greater as a result of the devaluation of the currency in August 1971 and the growing inflation in the second half of 1972, had the effect of drawing out the negotiations and the abandonment of the framework of these agreements, with the result that the signing of many of the agreements did not take place until the second half of 1972, and in some cases 1973. The number of strikes and of workers involved was almost identical with that of 1971, but the number of work days lost increased to 235,058. Similarly, although there were only 96 strikes in 1973, they encompassed 122,345 workers, and 375,020 work days were lost.

In 1974 the state of emergency which continued after the Yom Kippur War and the fact that a considerable number of workers were still mobilized, was not conducive to strikes. During the war the labor agreements were extended for a period of three months, and in most branches they were further extended on the termination of this period, the parties involved agreeing to an increase in basic wages of IL50–IL80, while the minimum wage and the cost-of-living increment were increased.

There was a rapid return to the pre-war situation in the second half of 1974 which found its expression in the relative rise in the number of strikes. The majority of strikes were in the public sector such as El Al, the Dead Sea Works, and the ports. Signs of the third period, 1975–78, became evident. As the agreements previously entered into were due to lapse in 1976 – in January in the private sector and in April in the public – the number of strikes in 1975 (118) returned to that of the pre-war period, although the number of work days lost were fewer. In the second half of 1975 the reform in the income tax regulations, the main item of which – insofar as it affected workers – was that all income, including side benefits, was liable to taxation, had its effect upon the labor situation, causing strikes and labor disputes.

The year 1976 saw the signing of labor agreements. In the private sector, they were signed in February and included an increase of 6% for that year and an additional 3% for 1977, but in the industrial sector a larger increase was agreed upon. The agreements in the public sector, which were not signed until April, provided an increase of 2.5% for 1976 and a similar further increase for 1977. The gradual abolition of special increments was also agreed to, as a result of which strikes and sanctions on the part of those affected took place, causing a considerable loss of working days. In view of the realization that the increments granted did not keep pace with the continuous inflation, steps were taken particularly, but not solely, in the public sector to obtain higher wages than were provided for in the collective agreement, and were reflected in the larger number of strikes (50) in the third quarter of the year.

In the light of these many labor disputes in the public sector, negotiations were instituted between the Histadrut and the government for the establishment of an agreed arbitration body, which was set up in February 1977.

The results of the elections to the Ninth Knesset in 1977 had considerable influence on labor relations, and the price increases, which reached 30%–40%, gave rise to the feeling in the public sector that the increases in wages granted in the labor agreement of 1976 were not commensurate with them. The approaching elections afforded the workers in this sector an opportunity to apply pressure on the government to obtain increases. Forty percent of the strikes and 75% of the working days lost occurred in the first quarter of the year preceding the election. The steep rise in the number of working days lost was caused by the large labor groups involved, such as the Treasury officials, the Transport Ministry, the Bank Leumi, and the institutes of the representative workers' organizations.

In 1978, for the first time in three years, there was a marked increase in employment in the industrial sector without a corresponding slowing down in the employment in the public sector. The collective negotiations on labor agreements took place against a background of galloping inflation.

The still further increases which were anticipated during the year gave rise to the need for the working out of an agreed policy on wages between the employer, the government and the Histadrut, in order to render possible the conducting of negotiations in the industrial and public sectors, and the date for the coming into effect of the agreements was postponed to April.

In the industrial sector a collective agreement was signed on March 20, and on its basis individual agreements were entered into in various economic branches, and undertakings, but in a number of cases they were accompanied by labor disputes, particularly in the industrial undertakings connected with the public sector.

In the public sector the negotiations were protracted for a long time, during which prices rose and corresponding situations were established which arose from decisions arrived at through arbitration. The agreements in the public sector were not concluded until November, after which various trade unions joined in them, but as a result of the slow pace of the negotiations, agreements signed at the beginning of 1979 granted higher increments to some of the workers in the public sector and brought about added demands, from organizations which had already signed agreements, for the reopening of negotiations.

These protracted negotiations were accompanied by considerable unrest, particularly in the public sector and large unions. The steep increase in days of work lost was due to the strikes of the teachers' unions in which no less than 500,000 days were lost, but it should be pointed out that most of them were subsequently made up. Sixty percent of the strikes were without the approval of the Histadrut.

The year 1979 was also a restless year in labor relations, despite the fact that, with the introduction of the new economic policy towards the end of the year, there was a noticeable decline in the number of strikes.

In the course of the year there were 116 full strikes in which 529,362 working days were lost, representing an increase of 39% in the number of strikes compared with the previous year, but the number of work days lost was only half of that of the previous year.

There were also 98 partial strikes (i.e., sanctions of different types). The majority (52%) were in the public sector, most of them (52%) of which were for wages and benefits which included demands for new classification of scales.

In 1980 there was a sharp drop in the number of full strikes (84) and partial strikes (54); the number of work days lost was half that of 1979.

The breakdown of the strikes 1971–78 reveals a number of tendencies or characteristics of strikes in Israel:

1. Although the number of strikes remained more or less constant, the number of workers involved and working days lost rose steadily (with the exception of 1974). Even taking into consideration the increase in the number employed, there were larger groups participating in strikes (for example, 88,265 in 1971 and 250,420 in 1979, although for 1980 the number of strikers was 91,451).

2. The majority of strikes took place in the public sector, to which can be added those included under "others" which include doctors, nurses, engineers, teachers with a sharp drop in the other two, the smallest number being in the Histadrut sector.

3. The proportions of distribution of strikes among the various economic branches changed each year. Whereas in 1971, 44.6% of strikes were in the public services, in 1978 it went down to only 20%, while in transport and communications it rose from 14.3% to 36.5%. In industry the strikes were connected with the signing of collective agreements.

4. Some 50%–60% of the strikes were unauthorized. It also reveals a slight increase in the number of lockouts by employers.

LEGISLATION. *The Settlement of Labor Disputes – Law of 1957.* In 1972 this law was amended with the aim of preventing strikes – including slowdowns – during the period covered by agreements. The law defines as unprotected any strike in the public sector where a collective agreement applies, except for strikes not connected with wages or social conditions and which received the authorization of the Histadrut. The same applied to strikes even when the agreements had lapsed if they had not been authorized by the Histadrut. In these cases the workers were not protected and they could be charged with invoking monetary damage.

In 1977 another amendment was adopted which defined a partial, non-protected strike. In brief it may be stated that it provided for partial payment of wages for partial work, i.e., if the workers instituted sanctions, the employers were entitled to apply to the labor courts, and if they decided that the workers were indeed instituting slowdowns, they would be entitled only to partial wages. The amendment was an attempt to grant the employer in the public service a deterrent against such workers after prolonged use on their part of this weapon.

The Law of Collective Agreements – 1957. A number of amendments were enacted to this law also in 1976. One provided for the setting up of committees to supervise the implementation of extended provisions in general collective agreements given by the minister of labor and social affairs.

Despite the fact that, as a result of these instructions, non-organized workers were granted the privileges which had been achieved between the Histadrut and the employers, there was no guarantee that these workers would receive the privileges granted them by the extended provisions. The supervisory committee was set up in order to ensure that they should receive the amendment authorized them to make a list of all the undertakings subject to the law and ensure adherence to them. Each such committee was composed of representatives of the Ministry of Labor and Social Affairs, representatives of the Histadrut and of the employers. A further amendment made it obligatory upon the employer to pay a fee for organizational technical work to the employers' organization, which is a party to the extended collective agreement.

Additional amendments made at the same time granted the right of inspecting collective agreements legally registered, and it was also laid down that an extension order relating to the cost of living allowance, price increase compensation or minimum wage could go into effect from a date up to three months prior to the date of publication.

[Nurit Nirel]

The 1980s and After

With the rise of the Likud to power in 1977 and the acceleration of processes that would alter the economic profile of the country, great changes occurred in the labor sector as well – both institutionally and in the condition of the individual worker. The very rapid transformation of the economy from socialist to capitalist lines in the 1980s in the midst of runaway inflation left the two cornerstones of the socialist economy – the Histadrut and the kibbutz – literally reeling. The Histadrut would be forced to sell off its economic holdings to survive and be divested of its Kuppat Ḥolim health care system under the new State Health Insurance Law, as well of management of its pension fund, thus losing its standing as an economic giant and, in health care, one of its main attractions as a labor union. Membership consequently dropped from 1.5 million in the mid-1980s, 75% of the labor force, to around 700,000 (around 30%) in the early 2000s. Though the Histadrut continued to operate as an ordinary labor union, it was now perceived as being controlled by a few powerful company unions (Bezek, the Electric Corp.) and its strike activity was mainly confined to the public sector. The decline of the kibbutz was also symptomatic of the country's transformation. Caught up in the speculative fever of the 1980s and crushed by spiraling interest rates in the accompanying inflation, many found themselves on the brink of bankruptcy. At the same time, internal pressures weighed in to bring about far-reaching social and economic changes that in effect ended collective life. Among these changes were differential salaries, outside employment for members, privatization of services, and nonmember housing, making the kibbutzim resemble ordinary communities.

The demise of socialism and the special ethos that had characterized the country in its formative years under a Likud government that promoted free enterprise and private initiative, and ironically derived a good deal of its support from low-income voters, together with a broad range of additional factors that affected the labor sector – the failure of traditional industries, rising unemployment, the influx of foreign workers, a welfare system that undermined the work ethic, and then cutbacks in welfare spending that caused hundreds of thousands to slip below the poverty line, a persistent recession tied to the second intifada and global economic conditions – all combined to undercut the status of working men and women. Perhaps nothing was more symptomatic of Israel's new economic spirit than the Basic Law: Freedom of Occupation passed by the Knesset in 1992 and interpreted by the clas-

Employment in Israel by Economic Sector (1955–1991/92)

	Percentage distribution by economic branch								
Year	Agriculture	Industry and mining	Construction	Utilities	Commerce	Transportation	Public services	Private services	Total employment
1955	17.6	21.5	9.3	2.0	13.5	6.6	21.2	8.3	585,700
1960	17.3	23.2	9.3	2.2	12.3	6.2	22.0	7.5	701,800
1965	13.0	25.4	10.5	1.8	12.6	6.9	22.6	7.2	879,200
1969	10.5	26.2	8.2	1.9	12.9	7.7	24.2	8.4	945,800
1991/92	3.4	21.4	6.6	1.1	24.0	6.3	29.6	7.5	1,583,000

Source: Labor Force Surveys, Central Bureau of Statistics.

sically liberal Barak Supreme Court as protecting the right of employers to fire workers, but not of workers to work.

The upshot of Israel's new economic reality is that the gap between rich and poor has been steadily growing. At the beginning of 2006 average income in the upper 10% bracket was 12 times higher than in the lower 10% bracket and accounted for 27.8% of national income. Half the country's wage earners, with incomes of up to a little over $2000 a month, accounted for less than 20% of national income.

In 2006 Israel had a labor force of around 2.5 million, representing about half its working age population, a percentage considerably lower that in the developed nations of the OECD. Unemployment was somewhat over 10%, with the rest of the nonworking population not part of the work force. Nonparticipation in the work force was particularly marked among those with little education, Arab women, ultra-Orthodox men, and residents of provincial areas.

The labor force was employed in the following sectors: public services (31.2%), manufacturing (20.2%), finance and business (13.1%), commerce (12.8%), construction (7.5%), personal and other services (6.4%), transport, storage and communications (6.2%), and agriculture, forestry and fishing (2.6%).

[Fred Skolnik (2nd ed.)]

See also *Israel, State of: Economic Affairs.

BIBLIOGRAPHY: JEWISH LABOR ORGANIZATIONS: W. Preuss, *The Labour Movement in Israel* (1965³); F. Zweig, *The Israeli Worker…* (1959); N. Malkosh, *Histadrut in Israel* (1962²); I. Sobel, in: W. Galenson (ed.), *Labor in Developing Economies* (1963), 187–250; M. Braslavsky, *Tenu'at ha-Po'alim ha-Ereẓ-Yisre'elit*, 4 vols. (1955–63), includes bibliography; P. Merḥav, *Toledot Tenu'at ha-Po'alim be-Ereẓ Yisrael…* (1967); G. Kressel, *Ha-Histadrut, Madrikh Bibliografi* (1970); Ha-Histadrut ha-Kelalit shel ha-Ovedim ha-Ivryyim be-Ereẓ Israel, *Ḥukkot ha-Histadrut* (1952); idem, *Ha-Histadrut mi-Yom Kum ha-Medinah* (1969–), statistics; S. Kurland, *Cooperative Palestine* (1947); G. Muenzer, *Labor Enterprise in Palestine* (1947); Z. Even Shoshan, *Toledot Tenu'at ha-Po'alim be-Ereẓ-Yisrael*, 3 vols. (1955–66). LABOR RELATIONS. Y. Gothelf, *Ba-Derekh 1965* (1965); A. Doron, *Tenu'at ha-Avodah ha-Yisre'elit – Avar ve-Atid* (1966/67); I. Ben-Aharon, *Be-Fetaḥ Temurah* (1968²); Y. Yagol, *Temurot be-Tenu'at ha-Po'alim ha-Ivrit* (1958); A. Manor, *Mahut ha-Histadrut* (1957²); Y. Sprinzak, *Mesimot, Al Be'ayot ha-Histadrut* (1968). See also section on Jewish Labor Organizations. EMPLOYMENT: Israel, Ministry of Labor, Manpower Planning Authority, *Annual Reports* (Heb. and Eng., 1964–); Israel, Central Bureau of Statistics, *Statistical Abstract of Israel* (Heb. and Eng., 1950–); The Israel Institute of Productivity, *Productivity in Israel*, (October 1979); Annual Reports of the Department of Labor Relations of the Ministry of Labor: *Statistical Abstract of Israel*, Annual Report.

RELIGIOUS LIFE AND COMMUNITIES

Jews

UNDER OTTOMAN RULE. The Jews of the pre-Zionist old *yishuv*, both *Sephardim (from the Orient) and *Ashkenazim (of European origin), dedicated their lives to the fulfillment of religious precepts: the study of the *Torah and the meticulous observance of its commandments; prayer at the holy sites for the coming of the Messiah and interment of their remains in the Holy Land to await his advent. They lived apart – mainly in the holy cities of Jerusalem, Hebron, Safed, and Tiberias – under the authority of their rabbis and religious courts (*battei din*, see *Bet Din), which dealt with civil disputes as well as problems of *halakhah*, with their own autonomous educational, charitable, and social institutions. Many of the most renowned Jewish religious scholars of the time were to be found in the old *yishuv*. Indeed, religious learning was so widespread that even the humblest possessed a basic knowledge of the Torah, if not more.

Communal Organization. While the *yishuv* was still very small, Ashkenazim and Sephardim prayed together and occasionally intermarried. As the number of Ashkenazi immigrants increased, however, the two communities moved apart, while the Ashkenazim were divided among themselves according to their respective lands of origin. Social and political conditions under Ottoman rule militated against the participation of the Jewish population in the economic life of the country. Moreover, many of the immigrants were elderly people who had come to the Holy Land to be buried there, and there was a high proportion of widows and orphans. Hence, the old *yishuv* had to depend for its sustenance upon contributions from abroad, known as **ḥalukkah*.

Accordingly, in every community there were subcommunities called *kolelim* (or *kolelot*), each with its *va'ad*, (committee), which distributed the funds received from its place of origin. This was the only form of communal organization that existed at the time. At the turn of the century, there were Sephardi *kolelim* of Jews from North Africa, Georgia, Persia, Aleppo, Iraq, Bukhara, Daghestan, Afghanistan, and Yemen. The Ashkenazim were even more fragmented. They were not only divided into *Ḥasidim and *Perushim* (descendants of disciples of *Elijah of Vilna), but subdivided into over 30 *kolelim*, which maintained the only registers of births and deaths, marriages and divorces. Each *kolel* kept to itself; each prospered or declined in proportion to the support it received from its parent community in the Diaspora. Although the total amount contributed may have been increased by the splintering, the resultant dissension impeded the development of the *yishuv*.

Aware of the neglect of the common good caused by the proliferation of the *kolelim*, and influenced by the dominant personality of R. Samuel *Salant (see below), rabbis and communal leaders of the Jerusalem Ashkenazi community established in 1866 an overall committee of all *kolelim*, which they named Keneset Yisrael. Its functions were: to handle the affairs of the Ashkenazim in Jerusalem, especially the payment of taxes to the government; to distribute *ḥalukkah* funds to families not belonging to any of the *kolelim*; and to provide help in special individual cases. Its income was derived from funds collected in countries not connected with any specific *kolel*, such as the United States, Great Britain, and South Africa.

The supervision of *sheḥitah* (ritual slaughter) to ensure perfect *kashrut* was a matter of great concern, as in any Orthodox Jewish community. At first, complete control was in the hands of the Sephardim, but in 1864 the *ḥakham bashi* (chief rabbi) was persuaded to allow the creation of a separate *sheḥitah* board for the Ashkenazi community in Jerusalem. The fees paid for its certification became an important source of revenue for the Ashkenazi rabbis and other religious functionaries. In the other cities Sephardim and Ashkenazim also kept their *sheḥitah* separate.

Like the *kolelim*, the voluntary burial societies became more and more fragmented as time went on. At first all interments took place in the ground owned by the Sephardim on the Mount of Olives, but in 1858 the Ashkenazim acquired their own section on the mount and established a separate burial society. Important as a source of revenue from legacies and the sale of plots, the burial societies became the adjuncts of the various *kolelim*, and to this day there is a multiplicity of such societies in Jerusalem.

The Rabbinate and its Courts. Supreme religious and judicial authority was vested in the *ḥakham bashi* of Jerusalem, also entitled *rishon le-Zion*, who was elected by the leaders of the local Sephardi community. On the recommendation of the *ḥakham bashi* of the Ottoman Empire, he received a firman from the Sublime Porte appointing him official representative of the Jewish community of the Holy Land in its dealings with the government, and investing him with authority over all Jewish spiritual and religious affairs. He and his courts had exclusive jurisdiction in matters of matrimony, personal status, charitable trusts, certification of wills, and legacies of all Jewish Ottoman subjects. His investiture was marked by a solemn ceremony conducted in the R. Johanan b. Zakkai Synagogue in Jerusalem. In the discharge of his functions, he was assisted by two committees: one consisting of Sephardi rabbinical judges, for religious affairs; the other, composed of lay communal leaders, for dealing with the government, etc.

The office was held by Raphael Meir *Panigel (1879–93) and then by Jacob Saul b. Eliezer Elyashar (1893–1906). R. Elyashar's death was followed by a virulent controversy over the succession. When R. Ya'akov *Meir, who, in addition to his rabbinic knowledge, had studied languages and sciences on his own, was elected by a majority, the conservative section of the community vigorously opposed him, and he consequently left the country and accepted the post of chief rabbi in Smyrna. In 1907 the more progressive element elected R. Eliyahu-Moshe *Panigel, who had studied for a while at the modern Laemmel school, but he was forced to resign in 1908 and was replaced by R. Naḥman Batito, who held the office until his death in 1915. In the following year R. Nissim Yehudah Danon was elected, but he relinquished his post in 1918, and no further appointment was made until the official establishment of the Chief Rabbinate in 1921.

The Ashkenazim, who for the most part were foreign nationals, conducted their own rabbinic courts and maintained their own educational and philanthropic institutions. In practice, the large *kolelim* were autonomous, and the *ḥakham bashi* made no effort to interfere. R. Samuel Salant was recognized as the undisputed head of the Ashkenazi community in Jerusalem for almost 70 years (1841–1909), as it grew from 500 to 30,000 souls, though he refused to accept any formal appointment. His enormous erudition and piety earned him the deference of the Sephardim as well. He curbed dissension and also the opposition of the old *yishuv* to the new. As he became weakened by advancing age, he appointed R. Eliyahu David *Rabinovich-Teomim (known as "the *ADeReT*") in 1901 to assist him as head of the *bet din* of the Ashkenazi community of Jerusalem, but the latter died in 1903. On the death of R. Samuel Salant in 1909, R. Ḥayyim Berlin assumed the title and held it until his death in 1915. No new appointment could be made during World War I. In 1895 R. *Shneur Zalman of Lyady, who had settled in Jerusalem, founded, together with local ḥasidic dignitaries, a ḥasidic *bet din* in the city, which functioned in harmony with that of the Ashkenazi majority. In the Sephardi communities, too, separate rabbinic courts emerged for the Moroccan and Yemenite communities. In Safed, Tiberias, and Hebron, the Ashkenazi and Sephardi rabbinates conducted their respective religious courts.

Decisions in all matters, civil and religious, public and private, were rendered in accordance with the law of the Torah. The litigants willingly submitted to the verdicts of the *battei din*; very rarely was it necessary to compel a recalcitrant to comply with a court order by withholding his *ḥalukkah* allotment or imposing some other penalty. Deviations from orthodoxy could be punished by the imposition of the **ḥerem* ("ban"), which was invoked against many prominent rabbis and notable persons. In 1886 R. Naphtali Herz ha-Levi Weidenbaum was sent from Jerusalem to be rabbi of the growing community in Jaffa. In 1890, the Ashkenazim elected a community council, which was joined by the Sephardim and which conducted its deliberations in Hebrew.

In 1904, R. Abraham Isaac ha-Kohen *Kook was appointed rabbi of Jaffa and the surrounding Jewish villages. His was the first appointment made independently of Jerusalem, though he still received his modest salary from Keneset Yisrael, supplemented by fees from the Rishon le-Zion wine cellars for his certificate of *kashrut*. His appointment created a veritable revolution in Jewish religious life. He was the first outstanding rabbi in Ereẓ Israel who was a Zionist. His strong character, rabbinic erudition, and mastery of philosophic and mystic teachings enabled him to pursue his own independent course. Holding that even the least religious of the new settlers had been motivated by deep, subconscious religious impulses to become pioneers in the Land of Israel, and that secular Zionism would therefore ultimately become religious, he treated the nonobservant with respect and affection, proffering them his warm friendship. To the new *yishuv* he was an inspiration, and even the most doughty anti-Zionists among the old had to treat him with respect. R. Ben-Zion Meir Ḥai *Ouziel, appointed Sephardi chief rabbi of Jaffa in 1912, was also an avowed Zionist. Having gone abroad to attend a world conference of *Agudat Israel in 1914, Rabbi Kook was prevented from returning to Jaffa by the outbreak of World War I.

Education. The *yeshivot were of the same pattern as their Diaspora counterparts, except that in the Holy Land heads of families and even the elderly continued to study and draw students' stipends in addition to their regular *ḥalukkah* allocations. In the earliest-founded villages, the farmers' sons would study Torah in the evenings, generally with the local **shoḥatim* as teachers. Between 1900 and 1905 a few more progressive *ḥadarim* were founded, and R. Zerah Braverman, head of the Me'ah She'arim Yeshivah, together with his associates, established *talmud torah*s where secular subjects were taught in conformity with the spirit of Jewish tradition (see also Israel, State of: *Education).

Shemittah. A new issue erupted as the result of the existence of Jewish farming villages. The *sabbatical year (*shemittah*) 5649 (1888/89), when Jewish law required farmers to leave their fields fallow, was approaching. The question arose as to whether they must actually abstain from cultivating their fields or could evade the prohibition by the legal device of having the land "sold" formally to a non-Jew. The Jerusalem rabbis adamantly opposed the formal sale of the land. Some of the settlers abstained from all work, some relied on the rabbinically prepared bill of sale, and others openly defied the *shemittah* laws. The debate was acrimonious and prolonged, growing more intense from one sabbatical year to the next. For the year 5670 (1909/10), Rabbi Kook himself arranged the bill of sale and the conflict reached its peak. The Ashkenazi rabbis of the old *yishuv* endeavored to enlist support all over the world against anything but the complete cessation of all work on the land, although Rabbi Kook pleaded that such rigid adherence to the restrictions would threaten the very existence of the Jewish villages.

UNDER THE BRITISH MANDATE. *The New Yishuv Expands.* From 1919 onward the texture of the *yishuv* began to change, as large numbers of immigrants streamed in; ten or fifteen years later the new *yishuv* had, in numbers, overtaken and surpassed the old. Many of the middle-class families who arrived from eastern Europe were religious, some Ḥasidim. They gravitated toward Tel Aviv and Haifa, where they founded their synagogues and other religious institutions in the traditional mode. They differed from the old *yishuv*, however, in their positive attitude to organized communal life and their western clothing. Many of them filled the ranks of the Orthodox Agudat Israel movement and established its educational system. The Yemenite immigrants who flocked to the newer settlements, especially to Jaffa and Tel Aviv, were deeply religious in outlook and feeling. A considerable number of German Jews who arrived during the 1930s were observant Jews; they established synagogues and religious institutions of their own and made their contribution to religious education.

The Chief Rabbinate. With the end of Turkish rule, the office of *ḥakham bashi* ceased to exist. Furthermore, there had been no president of the Ashkenazi *bet din* of Jerusalem from 1915. On the initiative of Chaim *Weizmann and communal leaders the office of the Rabbinate of the Jewish Community in Jerusalem was established with the participation of Sephardi and Ashkenazi rabbis. Its budget was covered by the Zionist Commission with funds provided by the American Jewish *Joint Distribution Committee. The British authorities granted some measure of recognition, and the rabbinate functioned both as a court of first instance and as a court of appeal. The Va'ad Kelali (Jerusalem community council) convened a national conference of rabbis and heads of *kolelim*, yeshivot, and other institutions, which invited Rabbi Kook, who was about to return to the country, to become president of the *bet din* and chief rabbi of Jerusalem. His former antagonists bitterly opposed the nomination, but he accepted the position. Rabbi Kook's prestige and influence extended far beyond the area of his jurisdiction.

Some of the rabbis of Jerusalem, led by R. Yiẓḥak Yeruḥam Diskin and R. Yosef Ḥayyim *Sonnenfeld, regarded the newly inaugurated rabbinate as a Zionist institution and a disaster for religious Jewry. They went so far as to designate the anniversary of its founding a day of fasting and prayer. They therefore organized their own Ashkenazi council, which later became the *Edah ha-Ḥaredit* ("Orthodox Community") of Agudat Israel, with its own *bet din* (today more or less identical with the *Neturei Karta, who do not recognize the State of Israel). In 1920 the first British high commissioner, Sir Herbert *Samuel, appointed a committee headed by Norman *Bentwich, the attorney general, to consider the creation of a united Chief Rabbinate for the entire country. The committee recommended that a board of 71 electors, of whom two-thirds would be officiating rabbis and one-third laymen, elect a Chief Rabbinate Council for Palestine. This body would consist of Sephardi and Ashkenazi chief rabbis as joint presidents, three Sephardi and three Ashkenazi rabbis as members, and three laymen in an advisory capacity. The Rabbinate would function both as a court of first instance and as a court of appeal. A committee met early in 1921 to arrange the election. It drew up a list of 88 officiating rabbis (59 of them from Jerusalem) and 34 laymen. Later that year, the electors assembled in Jerusalem under the presidency of R. Yehudah Leib Fishman (*Maimon). After prolonged discussion, particularly over the proposal for lay counselors, the elections took place on February 23, and the council was elected, with R. Kook and R. Ya'akov Meir as chief rabbis (The Sephardi chief rabbi retained the title of *rishon le-Zion*). The government immediately recognized the council and any *bet din* sanctioned by it as "the sole authorities in matters of Jewish Law" and undertook to execute through the civil courts judgments given by its *bet din*. The appointment of *ḥakham bashi* was declared to have lapsed. In 1922 the jurisdiction of the Chief Rabbinate was defined by the Order-in-Council. Section 53 of the order stipulated: "The Rabbinical Courts of the Jewish Community shall have:

(a) exclusive jurisdiction in matters of marriage and divorce, alimony and confirmation of wills of members of their community other than foreigners…

(b) Jurisdiction in any other matter of personal status of such persons, where all the parties to the action consent to their jurisdiction.

(c) Exclusive jurisdiction over any case as to the constitution or internal administration of a Wakf or religious endowment constituted before the Rabbinical Courts according to Jewish Law."

In 1928, when the government finally approved the Regulations of the Jewish Community Keneset Yisrael, the Chief Rabbinate Council was recognized by it as the supreme religious body of the Jewish community.

The Chief Rabbinate was not recognized by the religious zealots of Jerusalem. Nonreligious Jews set up their own Courts of Peace (*battei mishpat ha-shalom*), which followed a combination of civil and Jewish law. Although the Mandatory authorities and their High Court of Justice tended to restrict the jurisdiction of the Rabbinate, it regulated a number of matters that had been neglected. It supervised, for example, compliance with the biblical precepts concerned with the cultivation of the soil, such as the separation of tithes (*ma'aser*) from agricultural produce, and the proper observance of the laws of **orlah* and *kilayim*. With the decline of the craft of the scribe in Eastern Europe, all manner of individuals in Jerusalem began to engage in the writing of scrolls of the law and the texts for **tefillin* and **mezuzot*. By its certification stamp, the Rabbinate was able to assure purchasers that the articles were produced in conformity with the prescriptions of Jewish religious law. The Rabbinate also arranged for the immigration of some 3,000 rabbis from Europe above the regular immigration quota.

The Chief Rabbinate Council was enlarged by the cooption of a number of renowned religious scholars. The first incumbents were succeeded by Chief Rabbis Isaac Halevi *Herzog (1936–59) and Ben-Zion Meir Ḥai Ouziel (1939–54). During their tenure, relations with the lay authorities were harmonious and fruitful. R. Herzog played a leading role in the relations between the Jewish population and the Mandatory government. He frequently appeared on behalf of the *yishuv* before the high commissioner and the various commissions appointed to investigate the situation in Palestine. Together with his colleague, R. Ouziel, he initiated cooperation between scientists and rabbis in seeking technological solutions to halakhic problems. He hailed the emergence of the new State of Israel as the beginning of the ultimate redemption.

Local Rabbinates. According to the regulations of Keneset Yisrael, the *battei din* and communal rabbis appointed by a local community and sanctioned by the Chief Rabbinate were recognized as official rabbis and served as the religious representatives of the community in its relations with the governmental district authorities. The local rabbinates served as courts of first instance, and their offices worked harmoniously with the committees of the local communities. With the increase in the population of Jaffa and, later, in Tel Aviv, hundreds of synagogues, houses of study (*battei midrash*) and yeshivot were established and many district rabbis were appointed. *Battei din* with limited jurisdiction were set up to deal with divorce, *kashrut*, etc. The two local chief rabbis were R. Solomon *Aronson and R. Ouziel. Rabbi Aronson was succeeded, on his death in 1935, by R. Moshe Avigdor *Amiel, a leader of the World Mizrachi movement, and R. Ouziel was followed, on his appointment as joint chief rabbi of Palestine in 1939, by R. Moshe *Toledano, a native of Tiberias. In Haifa R. Yehoshua Kaniel, of Jerusalem, was appointed in 1922 to the *bet din* and later became the Ashkenazi chief rabbi of the city. Among the Sephardi chief rabbis of Haifa were R. Eliahu Reine (1923–43), R. Nissim Ohanah (1943–66), and Rabbi Eliahu Bakshi-Doron (1975–1993).

THE KEHILLOT (COMMUNITY COUNCILS). A single community council had served both the Ashkenazim and Sephardim of Jaffa and continued to function for both towns when Tel Aviv was founded. At first it drew its income from *sheḥitah* fees; only in 1919 was a small, direct tax levied, yielding LP 500–1,000 per annum from 1919 to 1925. A joint council was elected in Haifa in 1908 and conducted its operations energetically from its inception. The other communities, however, lacked resources and could not control the local institutions or provide adequate communal services; for generations they had been accustomed to rely on outside support from the *ḥalukkah* or other forms of financial aid. In Jerusalem the first community council was elected in 1918, and similar bodies came into being in Tiberias, Safed, and Hebron in 1919. It was only after the regulations governing the *kehillot* were finally approved by Keneset Yisrael in 1928 that the community councils began to increase their activities. They determined the number of rabbis to be appointed and set up their own *sheḥitah* boards, later called religious councils, which organized and supervised religious facilities and services: *sheḥitah*, synagogues, ritual immersion pools (**mikva'ot*), interments, the separation of tithes from agricultural produce, etc. Where not less than three-quarters of the local population were Jewish, the municipal authority, according to an act of 1921, also performed the functions of the community council or *kehillah*.

Only in 1932, after protracted negotiations with the existing council in Jerusalem, did elections for a new council finally take place there. Several years had to pass before the Jerusalem community council embraced all public services: welfare, culture, education, etc.; its religious council was responsible for *sheḥitah*, *kashrut*, burials, and so forth. In 1929, the Va'ad Le'ummi, the executive organ of Keneset Yisrael, resolved that the community council of Tel Aviv and Jaffa should amalgamate with the Tel Aviv municipal council, which, as Tel Aviv was a totally Jewish city, could fulfill the functions of both bodies. The community council refused to accept the decision, however, and held its own elections in 1933. Its activities were limited to religious services and in 1939 it was absorbed by the municipality. The community council in Haifa was founded in 1931. In Safed elections for the community council took place in 1932 and in Tiberias in 1934. The Jews of Hebron, who were evacuated after the Arab massacre of 1929, returned in 1931 and elected their community council, but were obliged to leave again in 1936 on account of Arab violence. By the beginning of the 1940s, community councils had been set up in Petaḥ Tikvah, Bene Berak, Ramat Gan, Netanyah, Ḥaderah, Reḥovot, and Bat Yam; in other localities, local committees were recognized as community councils, while in some places religious councils were also established.

Education and Settlement. In 1920 the Mizrachi combined its schools with some other religious ones under a supervisory committee headed by R. Ouziel. This religious network, which consisted of 15 primary schools and eight kindergartens, with 2,137 pupils (compared with 6,622 in the general schools), became a part of the Zionist school system with an inspector of its own, and, after prolonged negotiations, was granted autonomy within the system (see Israel, State of: *Education). The Mizrachi "trend" grew rapidly: in 1928 it had 61 schools and 5,774 pupils. In 1948, there were 26,654 pupils in the Mizrachi trend – about one-fifth of the total; 7,253 in Agudat Israel schools; some 3,000 in those of the old *yishuv*; 2,000 in private schools; and 4,000 in yeshivot.

Modern secondary yeshivot were founded by the religious youth movements: *Bnei Akiva (the first at Kefar ha-Ro'eh in 1940); No'ar Mizrachi (the first at *Pardes Ḥannah in 1945) and Ezra, the youth movement of *Po'alei Agudat Israel.

Apart from the religious pioneering youth movements, which established collective and cooperative settlements, Ḥasidim from Poland arrived in the 1920s, during the Fourth Aliyah, and participated in the "return to the soil." Although they had never worked with their hands before, they stood up to their knees in the marshes, their caftans tucked in at the waist, devoting themselves with ḥasidic fervor to what they regarded as a sacred task: draining the swamps of the Holy Land. In 1924 they founded the first religious moshav, *Kefar Ḥasidim, in the valley of Zebulun. *Bene-Berak, near Tel Aviv, was founded in 1925 by another group of Ḥasidim from Poland. It was planned as a moshav, but in the course of time it became a city with a large religious majority and many yeshivot.

IN THE STATE OF ISRAEL. Religious Jewry – with the exception of the ultraorthodox Neturei Karta – played its full part in the struggle for statehood: yeshivah students fought with the *Haganah and other underground organizations; bearded and sidelocked Jews helped to build the emergency "Burma road" to besieged Jerusalem in 1948. Agudat Israel, which had refused to join the institutions of Keneset Yisrael and the Jewish Agency, was represented in the provisional council of state and the provisional government. The mass immigration of the first few years contained a high proportion of religious Jews – especially from the Oriental countries. Hundreds of synagogues were built, and refugee scholars from Europe set up yeshivot bearing the names and continuing the traditions of those destroyed by the Nazis.

At the first elections to the *Knesset, the four religious parties – Mizrachi, Ha-Po'el ha-Mizrachi, Agudat Israel, and Po'alei Agudat Israel (see Israel, State of: *Political Life and Parties) – formed the United Religious Front, which joined the first coalition government after its demands on religious questions, such as the deferment of yeshivah students and the exemption of religious girls from the military service, had been met.

Article 2 of the government's statement of Basic Principles, presented to the Knesset on March 8, 1949, reads:

> The state will provide for the public religious needs of its inhabitants but will prevent coercion in matters of religion. The Sabbath and the Jewish holy days will be fixed days of rest in the State of Israel. The right of non-Jews to their Sabbath and days of rest will be safeguarded.

These principles were restated and rephrased by later governments. From 1959 they were supplemented by the obligation to "guarantee religious education to all children whose parents so desire" and to "maintain the status quo in the state in religious matters," thus confirming an unwritten agreement which had been in force since the establishment of independence.

One of the reasons why the Knesset did not immediately proceed to enact a comprehensive written constitution was the opposition of the religious parties. In the debate on the subject in 1950, they objected to a constitution which did not clearly express the religious character of the Jewish people; the Agudat Israel representatives declared that "Israel's Torah is her constitution" and no other was needed.

Ministry of Religious Affairs. The powers of the Mandatory high commissioner in matters of religion were transferred to the minister of religious affairs, who was responsible for the administrative aspects of the Chief Rabbinate and the rabbinical courts, the religious councils and religious committees, and the appointment and maintenance of local rabbis. The ministry deals with *kashrut*, yeshivot, synagogues, *mikva'ot*, the supervision of burials, and the provision of ritual appurtenances and sacred books. It is responsible for the arrangements at the Western Wall and supervises the activities of the Sabbath Observance Council and Keren Yaldenu ("Our Child's Fund"), which counteracts the use of material inducements by missionary organizations. The ministry also provides religious services for Karaites and Samaritans, Muslims, Christians, and Druze.

Rabbinical Courts and the Chief Rabbinate. In 1953 the Knesset passed the Rabbinical Courts Jurisdiction (Marriage and Divorce) Law, which gave the Chief Rabbinate and the religious courts sanctioned by it exclusive jurisdiction of all matrimonial cases, including alimony and support of children, for all

Jewish residents, including foreign nationals. Jews may marry only by the traditional ceremony (*ḥuppah ve-kiddushin*) after the marriage has been duly registered with the rabbinate, and only rabbis approved by the Chief Rabbinate may conduct marriage ceremonies. Rabbinical courts also have jurisdiction in matters of trusteeship, confirmation of wills, etc., where the parties involved accept their authority. Attempts have been made to legalize civil marriages by appeals to the High Court of Justice, and some people get around the law by civil marriage abroad (particularly in nearby Cyprus). A certain status has, however, been accorded by law to "common law wives." Rabbinical judges (**dayyanim*), who have the same status as judges of district courts, are appointed by the president of the state on the recommendation of a special committee and take the oath of allegiance in his presence.

Sephardi Chief Rabbi Ouziel died in 1954, and in the same year the minister of religious affairs promulgated new regulations for the election of the chief rabbis and the Chief Rabbinical Council. Rabbi Yiẓḥak *Nissim was elected *rishon le-Zion* and Sephardi chief rabbi for a five-year term in 1955. On the death in 1959 of Ashkenazi Chief Rabbi Herzog and the approaching end of Chief Rabbi Nissim's term of office, arrangements had to be made for new elections. After a lengthy controversy over the composition of the election arrangements' committee and of the electoral college, new regulations were issued by the minister of religious affairs in 1963, increasing the number of electors from 75 to 125. Rabbi Nissim was reelected and R. Issar Yehudah *Unterman was elected Ashkenazi chief rabbi.

The Chief Rabbinical Council has departments for *kashrut*, supervision of *scribes (*soferim*), and committees for marriage licenses; confirmation of rabbinical ordination (*semikhah); precepts specific to the Holy Land; and responsa on matters of *halakhah*. The chief rabbis preside over the *Bet Din Gadol* (Rabbinical Supreme Court), which hears appeals from decisions of the district rabbinical courts in Jerusalem, Tel Aviv, Haifa, Petaḥ Tikvah, Reḥovot, Tiberias, Safed, Beersheba, and Ashdod-Ashkelon. Regulations governing the election of local rabbis were issued by the minister of religious affairs in 1966.

Religious Councils. Under the Religious Services Budget Law (1949), which was given its final form in 1967, every local authority is required to appoint a religious council consisting of religious individuals that will provide all public religious facilities for the local population. The composition of each religious council must be ratified by the minister of religious affairs. Forty-five percent of the members are nominated by the minister, 45% by the local authority, and 10% by the local rabbinate. Any deficits in the operation of the religious council are covered by the local authority (two-thirds) and the government (one-third). In 1970, 185 such councils were in existence and their combined budgets totaled IL 28,500,000.

Education. Under the "trend" system, which was incorporated in the Compulsory Education Law of 1949, the state took over the responsibility for providing religious education at the option of the parents. At the beginning of the year, the Agudat Israel network had been recognized as a fourth trend, so that there was now a choice of two types of religious school – Mizrachi and Agudat Israel (in addition to *talmud torah* and other schools outside the state system) – as alternatives to the general and labor trends. To cater to the numerous religious families among the new immigrants, especially from the Muslim countries, a religious subtrend (Reshet Dati) of the labor network was developed by Ha-Oved ha-Dati, but was frowned on by the religious parties. There was considerable difficulty in implementing the parents' rights to choose between the four trends in the immigrants' camps, particularly among the newcomers from Yemen and the other Oriental countries, who could not be expected to understand the differences between the various types of school. Besides, the Mizrachi and Agudat Israel argued that the Reshet Dati was being elevated to the status of a fifth, unauthorized, trend. At first it was agreed, as a compromise, that the Ministry of Education and Culture should run religious classes for the Yemenites, while in the other camps the parents would choose between religious and general classes, but the agreement broke down when the minister of education and culture, David *Remez, refused to apply it to the **ma'abarot* (transitional settlements). The controversy led to a cabinet crisis in February 1951 and a premature general election.

The problem was solved by the passing of the State Education Law (1953), which abolished the trend system and instituted two types of schools, state and state religious, both under the control of the ministry. The Agudat Israel system remained independent. By this time, the Mizrachi trend had more than doubled in size, with almost 55,000 pupils. It became the nucleus of the state religious system, which was also joined by the schools of the Reshet Dati and a few of the Agudat Israel ones. The law provided that the system should have no connection with any party, communal, or other nongovernmental body and that the schools should be religious in their curriculum and way of life. An autonomous wing for state religious education was established in the ministry, with power to supervise the religious aspects of the schools' work and ensure that teachers, inspectors, and headmasters were satisfactory from the religious point of view. Defining the goals and attitudes of state religious education, a brochure published by the ministry in 1953 stated:

In Israel a religious kindergarten, primary school or secondary school is an institution which aims at the religious personality. It does all the work which a kindergarten or an elementary school has to do in general, but does it in such a manner, with modes of presentation and interpretation of common subject matter, and with classroom and school life organized in such a way, that the pupil may be expected to grow into maturity imbued with ideas, principles and values that mark him as an observer, in deed and in creed, of the Jewish religion.

In 1968–69 the primary schools of the state religious system had 109,358 pupils, over 28% of the total in Jewish schools, in 363 institutions with 4,062 classes (29% and 30% of the total, respectively).

More intense religious study was pursued in 26 yeshivah high schools, where students spend the majority of their day in the study of Talmud and also study secular subjects for the matriculation examination; there were also 15 vocational and agricultural yeshivah high schools; and four schools for girls in the Bnei Akiva movement.

Hundreds of yeshivot had been established by 1970: *yeshivot ketannot*, for students aged 14–15; yeshivah high schools, described above; *yeshivot gedolot* (for those aged 18–25); and *kolelim*, for married men, some of which gave training for *dayyanim* in rabbinical courts, while others encouraged research in specific fields. In 1969/70, there were 62 *yeshivot ketannot*, with over 4,000 students; 26 yeshivah high schools, with 4,235 students; 15 vocational and agricultural yeshivot, with 2,355 students; 66 *yeshivot gedolot* with 5,350 students; and 96 *kolelim*, with 2,900 students – a total of over 20,000 students, including 800 from abroad. In 1969 the Ministry of Religious Affairs allocated IL 2,400,000 toward the maintenance of yeshivot. After the Six-Day War, new yeshivot were established in the Old City of Jerusalem, Kefar Eẓyon, and Hebron.

In *Bar-Ilan University students are required, in addition to the regular curriculum, to take a number of courses in Judaic studies and to conform to religious standards. The Jerusalem College for Women, established in 1964, provided a three-year course, and its graduates were recognized as having the equivalent of a B.A. degree for high school teaching purposes. The type and intensity of the religious training was similar to that of the yeshivah. There was also a religious technical college in Jerusalem, which provided intensive talmudic training, in addition to the study of technical subjects.

Agudat Israel schools, which preferred to stay out of the state system and established its Ḥinnukh Aẓma'i (Independent Education), were recognized and supervised (though not controlled) by the state, and 85% of their costs was met from the state budget. The system opened in 1953/54 with an enrollment of 16,000; in 1969/70 it had 228 schools with over 31,000 pupils. Religious education, in the aggregate, covers some 35% of the pupils in Jewish schools.

Ḥasidic Settlement. Soon after Israel became independent, the rabbi of Lubavitch, the head of the *Chabad Ḥasidim, who lived in the United States, urged some of his followers, originally from the Soviet Union, to settle in Israel. They founded *Kefar Ḥabad, the Lydda Yeshivah, and a number of other institutions. Other ḥasidic leaders have followed in their wake. R. Yekutiel Halberstam, the rabbi of Klausenburg, founded the Kiryat Zanz quarter in *Netanyah and a quarter in Jerusalem; the rabbi of Vizhnitz founded a quarter in Bene-Berak and the rabbi of Bobova one in Bat Yam; the rabbi of Sasov established Kiryat Yismaḥ Moshe and Rabbi Shemuel Ehrenfeld, Kiryat Mattersdorf. Even the rabbi of Satmar, the leader of the Neturei Karta, an inveterate opponent of the "Zionist state," built quarters for his followers in Jerusalem and Bene-Berak.

Various Religious Trends. A number of groups, some of them loosely organized, tried to work out the implications of modern conditions, particularly the revival of statehood, in the sphere of Jewish religious thought and practice. They expressed their views on public platforms, in the press, and in periodicals devoted to religious study and thought. Some religious intellectuals, like Yeshayahu *Leibowitz and Ernst *Simon, maintained that the *halakhah* was created to meet the needs of Diaspora life and must therefore be adapted to the new exigencies and opportunities of Jewish sovereignty. The Movement for Torah Judaism, headed by Ephraim *Urbach, worked for the regeneration of religious life on a nonparty basis within the framework of the *halakhah*. Both groups had some influence in academic circles, especially among student groups like the Yavneh Association, which sought to harmonize the achievements of science and technology with Jewish religious principles and called on the rabbinate to march with the times. There were also various unattached scholars and thinkers, like Samuel Hugo *Bergmann and Dov *Sadan, who tried to establish religious ideas on philosophical, scientific, or mystical foundations.

The radio helped increase interest in the Jewish religious heritage by regular daily Bible readings and commentaries, talks on the Talmud and the Midrash, and discussions on religious problems; there were weekly television programs for the end of the Sabbath and special features for festivals. The Bible Study Association held well-attended conventions, arranged study groups, and issues publications in which religious and nonreligious scholars combine to cast light on the Scriptures. There were various schemes to encourage and facilitate systematic study of a daily page of Talmud, or paragraph of the Mishnah, by disseminating, in pamphlet form, selections from talmudic material and rabbinic commentaries. Religious ceremonials associated with family occasions, such as circumcision, bar mitzvah, marriage, and interment and mourning, are observed by the vast majority, even of those who would not define themselves as "religious."

Controversy over Religious Questions. Though the nonobservant majority regard religion as a matter for the conscience of the individual and resent administrative or legislative restrictions imposed on religious grounds, no *Kulturkampf* developed in the first 20 years of Israel's existence. The observant did, however, manifest a tendency to isolation, some of them concentrating in predominantly religious areas. Controversies flared up from time to time over the application of religious laws and principles to matters in the public domain. Examples are: complaints of inadequate provision for religious education, partially resolved by the appointment of a National Religious Party member as deputy minister of education and culture; licenses for Sabbath work in factories; road traffic on the Sabbath, particularly in the vicinity of religious quarters in Jerusalem; *kashrut*, e.g., the controversy over the proposal to install two kitchens, one non-*kasher*, in the Zim liner *Shalom*; *autopsies, which were sanctioned by the more Orthodox only in rare cases and which, in the view of moderate religious circles, were performed too frequently and with inadequate safeguards; the refusal of the rabbinate to recognize divorces issued by Conservative rabbis in America; the Chief Rabbinate's directives on marriages with members of the *Bene Israel community from India; and the inauguration of television broadcasts on the Sabbath.

The most prolonged controversy has been that over the question of "Who is a Jew?" i.e., how should Jewish "nationality" (*le'om*) be defined for the purpose of the population register? The argument led to a cabinet crisis in 1958 and broke out again in 1970, after the Supreme Court ruled by a majority that a Jewish father, married to a non-Jew, was entitled to have his children registered as Jews "by nationality." The Knesset thereupon passed a law providing that only persons recognized as Jews by the *halakhah* (i.e., children of a Jewish mother or those converted to Judaism) may be registered as Jews by nationality, but amended the *Law of Return to extend the privilege of automatic citizenship to the non-Jewish spouses and close relatives of Jewish immigrants. The controversy was reopened in mid-1970, however, over the recognition of conversions to Judaism performed by Reform and other rabbis not recognized by the Chief Rabbinate.

The Six-Day War and its aftermath intensified the feelings of the Orthodox. The Western Wall draws worshipers at all hours of the day and night, and the crowds swell to tens of thousands on outstanding dates in the Jewish religious calendar. Orthodox Jews were in the forefront of the establishment of yeshivot and synagogues in the Old City of Jerusalem, the resettlement of the *Ezyon area, and the reestablishment of a Jewish community in *Hebron.

[Mordechai Hacohen]

SABBATH AND JEWISH HOLIDAYS IN MODERN ISRAEL. The outstanding feature of the Jewish Sabbath and festivals in Israel is their public character. Even before the establishment of the State of Israel, shops, offices, factories, and most restaurants in Jewish towns and areas were closed; most public transport was suspended, and there was a pervading atmosphere of calm and repose. In Tel Aviv the Oneg Shabbat ("Joy of the Sabbath") meetings, founded by Ḥ.N. Bialik, drew large audiences. Observance was no longer, as in the Diaspora, hampered by the influence of the environment, but open and unrestrained.

In the State of Israel this trend became even more explicit. There is a virtual standstill in labor and trade on Sabbath and holy days: no newspapers are published; bus transportation is mostly suspended; no trains run; government offices and places of amusement are closed. Synagogues are full of worshipers and crowds stroll at their leisure in the streets and gardens. On the other hand, there are many taxis and private cars on the road; the television and radio operate; football and other matches are watched by large crowds of enthusiasts; privately organized trips by bus and truck take thousands of holidaymakers to the beach and countryside.

Some traditions observed in the Diaspora by only the most conscientious, however, are part and parcel of the national scene in Israel. Thus, on the Day of Atonement broadcasting stops and there is virtually no vehicle to be seen in the streets. The traditional booths are seen everywhere during the Feast of Sukkot – in the courtyards or on the balconies or roofs, of even non-religious homes. On Simḥat Torah and the following evening, the Scrolls of the Law are carried in procession through the streets by dancing and singing worshipers. Mass pilgrimages to Jerusalem, especially, since 1967, to the Western Wall, have become a traditional feature at Passover, Shavuot, and Sukkot, the pilgrim festivals of ancient times. On Ḥanukkah, the Feast of Lights, eight-branched candelabra blaze over public institutions and glow in every home. Young torch-bearers carry the light from the birthplace of the Maccabees in Modi'in to the president's residence in Jerusalem. At dusk on the eve of the fast of the Ninth of Av, restaurants, cafés, kiosks, and places of entertainment shut down to mark the anniversary of the destruction of the First and Second Temples. Tens of thousands walk to the Western Wall to chant the *kinot* ("dirges").

Minor festivals hardly observed in the Diaspora have been revived; they include Tu bi-Shevat, the New Year of Trees, on which thousands of trees are planted, and Lag ba-Omer, on which tens of thousands assemble in *Meron, the traditional resting-place of R. *Simeon b. Yoḥai, and bonfires lit by youngsters all over the country illuminate the skies at night. During the Purim holiday brightly costumed children parade the streets and transform it into a kind of popular carnival. Efforts have been made to evolve ways of celebrating Yom ha-Aẓma'ut (*Independence Day) along Jewish traditional lines: special synagogue services are held, and several collections of prayers and songs have been published for the purpose. However, usages for converting the day into a full religious festival have not yet been universally accepted.

Public Services. Vital public services and utilities, such as power stations, water-pumping installations, telephone exchanges, and police services, continue to function on the Sabbath. Religious leaders and members of the Association of Religious Scientists are seeking technical ways and means of avoiding violation of the Sabbath. Some religious kibbutzim have developed automatic irrigation systems and milking machines for the purpose. The idea of using non-Jewish labor on the Sabbath has evoked much discussion and has met with considerable opposition. In many instances, the principle of **pikku'aḥ nefesh* ("saving of human life"), which permits work on the Sabbath, has been applied; thus the supply of electric power and water to hospitals enables their use *post factum* in private homes. One extreme religious group does not, however, take advantage of this provision for non-urgent purposes.

In the Army. Rules for the observance of the Sabbath and festivals, as worked out by the chief chaplaincy of the *Israel Defense Forces, are laid down in the standing orders of the general staff. They take into account the need for the army to be permanently alerted against potential attack. On Sabbaths and festivals all work ceases, except for duties which are essential for security. Leave is so timed that no soldier need travel on the Sabbath on his way home or on returning to his base. The chaplaincy, under Rabbi Shlomo Goren, produced a unified prayer book for Ashkenazim and Sephardim. It deals with the elucidation of the religious law to meet every situation or eventuality. For example, on Rosh Ha-Shanah those in positions near the enemy lines are exempt from the injunction to listen to the sound of the *shofar* if there is a danger that the enemy may hear it. During actual fighting on the Day of Atonement a soldier in battle must break his fast as soon as he feels that hunger is affecting his fighting capacity; in hot areas, like the Arabah, he must drink water. On Sukkot, those in outlying posts near enemy lines are exempt from the duty of dwelling in a *sukkah* by day and by night. On Ḥanukkah soldiers having no candles or suitable oil may light the *menorah* with rifle or lubricating oil.

New Patterns. In the course of time new patterns of festival observance emerged in the collective agricultural settlements, both religious and secular. In the nonreligious villages they were almost entirely transformed into nature festivals, and religious aspects were given a secular interpretation, while the religious settlements added modern nuances to old traditions. In the secular kibbutzim, the reaping of the *omer* is celebrated on the second day of Passover and the bringing of the *bikkurim* ("firstfruits") is observed on the eve of Shavuot. The religious settlements, however, feared that a revival of ancient custom in this form might be regarded as a transgression of the *halakhah*, which forbids "the bringing of the offering outside the precincts of the Temple area." In all kibbutzim, both religious and nonreligious, the *seder* is celebrated as a large communal festivity, but while the religious kibbutzim keep to the traditional text of the *Haggadah*, the nonreligious ones have introduced alterations in the traditional text and added modern literature and pieces of a topical nature.

The Legal Framework. Under the British Mandate, attempts to promulgate a countrywide Sabbath law applying to the Jewish population were unsuccessful. Consequently the religious representatives in the Jewish townships and municipalities pressed for local legislation. In 1948, on the eve of the establishment of the state, such bylaws, varying from one place to another, were in force in 42 towns and localities. One of the first legislative acts of the Provisional State Council after independence was aimed at safeguarding the social aspect of Sabbath and festivals throughout the country. This was the Days of Rest Ordinance of June 3, 1948, which prescribed the Sabbath and the Jewish festivals as regular days of rest, while assuring non-Jews of the right to observe their own Sabbath and festivals.

The Hours of Work and Rest Law of 1951 grants every employee at least 36 continuous hours of leisure each week. For Jews this weekly rest period coincides with the Sabbath, and a similar rest is prescribed on the Jewish festivals. This law, however, does not cover cafés, the self-employed, or cooperative enterprises, including public transport. These are regulated by municipal ordinances, which are not uniform. While cafés are open on the Sabbath, for instance, in Tel Aviv, they are closed in Jerusalem. In both cities the buses do not operate, while in Haifa they run on a limited schedule. In some townships with a mainly religious population, certain streets or quarters are closed to all road transport on Sabbath and festivals. The Council for the Sabbath, which operates within the framework of the Ministry of Religious Affairs, and local groups endeavor to have the existing laws enforced, and to have appropriate bylaws introduced in new communities. They also conduct extensive educational activity and press for further legislation.

The law grants the minister of labor authority to permit work on the Sabbath in enterprises regarded as vital to national security or the economy, or installations like blast furnaces or cement kilns which require continuous operation. The issue of licenses to work on Sabbath is subject to approval by a committee consisting of the prime minister, the minister of religious affairs, and the minister of labor.

[Benjamin Zvieli]

DEVELOPMENTS IN THE 1970S. Synagogue attendance grew considerably from 1970 to 1980. Compared with some 6,000 Orthodox synagogues in 1970, there were in 1980 approximately 8,000, and they existed even in some secular veteran kibbutzim, such as En Ḥarod.

The rise in population, due largely to immigration and the development of new townships, created a shortage of places of worship. In 1978 there was a shortage of 600 synagogue buildings, and temporary places of worship were established in huts, basements, shelters, schools, and private houses. These were being replaced by permanent houses of worship with the assistance of the Ministry of Religious Affairs, the Ministry of Housing, the Jewish Agency, religious organizations, and other agencies. In order to facilitate, and economize on, the erecting of new synagogues the Ministry for Religious Affairs prepared 12 standard models of synagogue buildings.

A chain of 30 Young Israel synagogues was set up. More than 40 synagogues were established by the Wolfson Trust and others were under construction. The old Ramban (Nahmanides) synagogue in the Old City of Jerusalem was restored, following the renewal of the Sephardi Great Synagogue named after Rabban Johanan Ben Zakkai, which includes four synagogues in a single large block.

The Western Wall itself served as a large synagogue at which services were held continuously throughout the day and night. It was estimated that the Wall was visited by two million people annually, naturally with especially large attendances on festivals and days of remembrance. The celebration of bar mitzvahs at the Wall became commonplace, including boys who come from abroad.

A new and modern prayer book (*siddur*) of both the Ashkenazi and Sephardi rites was published, in which all the omissions and alterations of the text in the Diaspora editions, due to censorship, were restored; it includes new prayers, e.g., for Remembrance Day, for Independence Day and Jerusalem Day, and for the welfare of the State of Israel, etc. A series of *maḥzorim* (prayerbooks for the Jewish holidays) in the format of the *siddur* has also appeared.

Translations of the *siddur*, the Bible, and the Passover Haggadah into Russian were published to serve the needs of the new Russian immigrants.

Publication. The publication of numerous books on biblical and halakhic subjects is a prominent feature of Israel religious life. Important projects, such as the complete Jerusalem Talmud, the *Enẓiklopedyah Talmudit, Oẓar ha-Posekim*, and the special edition of the new biblical commentary *Da'at Mikra* by the Rabbi A.I. Kook Institute, continued through the 1970s. The ancient manuscript of the Bible from Aleppo, the so-called *Keter* (of the tenth century) was published, and additional volumes of the new Talmud edition accompanied by a modern commentary by Rabbi A. Steinsalz appeared.

Since the establishment of the State of Israel, both chief rabbis served jointly, both as presidents of the Supreme *bet din* and as chairmen of the Chief Rabbinate Council, and candidates for appointment as *dayyanim* (judges in religious courts) have had to be approved by both. Under a new law enacted in 1980, however, the two chief rabbis would henceforth hold one of these offices in rotation for five years, while their term of office was increased from five to ten years. The Chief Rabbinate Council (Moeẓet ha-Rabbanut ha-Rashit), the representative rabbinical body in Israel, was enlarged from 12 to 16 members.

At the end of the 1970s there were about 500 officiating rabbis in Israel, 210 of whom were entitled to perform and register the marriage ceremony.

Rabbinical courts functioned in nine places throughout the country, besides the Supreme *bet din*, the seat of which is in the Old City, Jerusalem. Those courts were served by 90 *dayyanim* (judges).

There was a Religious Council (Mo'eẓah Datit) in practically each town and settlement, whose duty was to supervise religious matters in the local community. The functions of the Religious Councils were supervised by a special department in the Ministry of Religious Affairs.

New types of yeshivot emerged. An interesting new development was the establishment of a number of yeshivot for "penitents" (**ba'alei teshuvah*), i.e., people who were hitherto estranged from Jewish observance and practice and had now accepted its responsibilities, and they also included synagogues. In addition, together with the traditional advanced yeshivot, a number of yeshivot for juniors, as well as high school yeshivot which combine secular education with Torah studies, were established, while several *yeshivot hesder*, where students combine military service with intensive Torah studies, made their impact on Jewish youth. Ulpanim were established for girls, in which extensive study of Torah and a high standard of general studies prepare them for their future role in Israel society.

[Benjamin Zvieli]

NON-ORTHODOX CONGREGATIONS. *Conservative Judaism.* The first Conservative congregation in Ereẓ Israel, called Emet ve-Emunah, was founded in 1937 in Jerusalem by newcomers from Germany and headed by Rabbi Kurt David Wilhelm, who was authorized to perform marriages by Chief Rabbi Kook. Rabbi Wilhelm was succeeded by R. Aharon Philipp (1948–70), who was also authorized. In 1970 there were also Conservative congregations in Ashkelon, Haifa, Netanyah, and Tel Aviv, of which the first two had recent arrivals from the United States as rabbis. These congregations were a part of the Conservative World Council of Synagogues, forming a separate branch. The teaching arm of Conservative Judaism, the *Jewish Theological Seminary of America, maintained a student center in Jerusalem, and Conservative youth groups conducted summer educational programs in Israel.

At its convention in Jerusalem in 1970, the second to be held in Israel, the World Council of Synagogues urged the Israel authorities to grant full recognition to Conservative rabbis in all spheres of religious life. The convention recognized the importance of "fostering a greater climate of understanding, awareness, and commitment among our communities toward the serious problems facing Israel" and resolved to encourage *aliyah*, visits by students, and other forms of direct contact with Israel.

Developments in Conservative Judaism in the 1970s. By the close of the 1970s Israel had 35 Conservative congregations, of which nine were in Jerusalem. There was also a national youth movement consisting of 23 youth groups in various cities.

The Center for Conservative Judaism in Jerusalem maintains a youth hostel, conducted along traditional religious lines, and a religious educational program for university youth (Beit Atid). In 1978, the synagogue of the center reorganized as a membership congregation which included approximately 200 families. In the same year, a national organization, Hatenuah Le'yahadut Mesortit, was established. The organization represented the United Synagogue of Israel and the Israel Branch of the Rabbinical Assembly, which numbered 100 Conservative rabbis who had taken up permanent residence in Israel. Both bodies were associated with the World Council of Synagogues, the international arm of the Conservative movement. From 1968, the biannual conventions of the World Council took place in Jerusalem.

While the impulse for the establishment of Conservative congregations in Israel came initially from immigrants from the United States, they also attracted a growing number of immigrants from other countries, as well as those Israeli-born. Thus, for example, the congregation in Ashkelon, Nezach Yisrael, included in its membership 20% native born Israeli families; 20% immigrants from English-speaking countries; 23% of eastern European origin, 18% from South America, 12% of western European origin, and 7% Russian immigrants.

Rabbinical students of the Jewish Theological Seminary of America were now required to spend one year at the American Student Center (Neve Schechter) established in Jerusalem as part of their pre-rabbinic training, and in 1978, a school known as Midreshet Yerushalayim opened which offers a one-year program of Jewish study for non-theological students. In addition, the center maintains an institute, known as Machon Chai, in which courses in Judaism are offered to high school students.

In 1976, the World Council of Synagogues officially joined the World Zionist Organization, thus broadening to a considerable extent the direct involvement of the Conservative movement in Zionism.

[Theodore Friedman]

Progressive Judaism or Reform Judaism. Progressive or Reform Judaism was introduced into Israel in 1957 at the initiative of the Israel Committee of the Central Conference of American Rabbis. After a visit by Rabbi Herbert Weiner, a founding committee was established in Jerusalem under the chairmanship of Shalom Ben-Chorin. The services were held first in an apartment and later in a public hall until, in 1962, the congregation moved into its own synagogue, the Har-El. Congregations were also established in Tel Aviv, Haifa, Ramat Gan, Kefar Shemaryahu, Nahariyyah, Upper Nazareth, Beersheba, and Natanyah, as well as a second congregation in Jerusalem at the *Hebrew Union College. In 1959 the Progressive community joined the World Union for Progressive Judaism, which sent rabbis to serve it.

The Progressive congregations in Israel were organized in the Va'ad Arẓi (National Board), which worked with the Israel Committees of the World Union for Progressive Judaism and the Union of American Hebrew Congregations. Four full-time rabbis constituted the Mo'eẓet ha-Rabbanim ha-Mitkaddemim – Maram (Council of Progressive Rabbis), which discussed policy on liturgy, *halakhah*, and public issues. The movement published its own prayer book, the first issued by the Reform movement entirely in Hebrew, and a *maḥzor* for the High Holidays. The main differences between these services and the traditional ones were that men and women prayed together and that congregational singing was accompanied on the organ. The Leo Baeck School in Haifa (founded in 1939), with 700 primary and 250 secondary pupils, and the Hebrew Union College Biblical and Archaeological School, Jerusalem, founded in 1963, were affiliated to the WUPJ.

The Progressive movement in Israel had no official status. Its rabbis were not entitled to perform weddings, grant divorces, or carry out conversions. The Biennial Conference of the WUPJ, held in Jerusalem in 1968, demanded "full and unreserved recognition of the religious rights of all Jews in Israel who are not Orthodox, and the complete and uncompromising accordance to them of all privileges, prerogatives and services presently enjoyed by the Orthodox Jewish Community of the Jewish State." As first steps the Conference urged that: 1) Progressive Jews in Israel be allowed to marry those registered in the Rabbinate as eligible for marriage; 2) anyone converted to Judaism by Reform or Liberal rabbis anywhere be recognized by Israel as Jews and admitted to Israel under the Law of Return; 3) Progressive congregations in Israel receive full support and aid from the Ministry of Religious Affairs. The amendments to the Law of Return and the Population Registry Law passed by the Knesset on March 10, 1970, which did not define the term "conversion," implicitly conceded the second claim in regard to conversions carried out abroad. The minister of justice stated subsequently, however, that in Israel the position was governed, in his view, by the Mandatory Ordinance of 1927, which required the consent of the Chief Rabbinate to conversions to Judaism.

[Schalom Ben-Chorin]

During the 1970s significant developments took place within the Israeli Progressive Movement, and in the programs of World Progressive Judaism in Israel: (1) Rabbinical Conferences – The Central Conference of American Rabbis became the first rabbinical group from the United States to convene its annual meeting in Israel, in 1970, and for a second time in 1974. Yom ha-Aẓma'ut was declared an official religious holiday and a special service drawn up and included in the regular liturgy of the Reform Movement. (2) Rabbinical Training – Both the Hebrew Union College-Jewish Institute of Religion and the Leo Baeck College in London adopted a policy requiring every student for the rabbinate to spend his first year in Israel in an intensive Hebrew ulpan program, and the former embarked on a program for the training of Israeli rabbis at its Jerusalem campus. All candidates were required to obtain an M.A. degree at The Hebrew University in addition to their rabbinic studies, and the first student was ordained in the summer of 1979. (3) Education – The Leo Baeck School, a secondary school in Haifa, which combines a solid program of secular studies with a liberal orientation in Jewish studies, erected a magnificent new campus; (4) Youth Programs – An Israeli youth movement was established and a national youth center opened in Jerusalem; (5) Kibbutz Movement – Kibbutz Yahel, the first Progressive Jewish collective settlement, was established in 1976; (6) Affiliations with the World Zionist Organization – In 1976 the World Union for Progressive Judaism became the first international Jewish religious organization to affiliate with the World Zionist Organization, and was followed by affiliation with the Conservative and Orthodox religious movements; and (7) Advocacy of Jewish Religious Pluralism – The Progressive Movement continued to advocate the creation of conditions conducive to Jewish religious pluralism in Israel, as well as to oppose successfully all attempts to amend the Law of Return to the detriment of the non-Orthodox movements, and sponsored a resolution adopted by the 29th World Zionist Congress calling for religious pluralism within the World Zionist movement and the State of Israel "to implement fully the principle of guaranteed religious rights for all its citizens, including equal recognition of religious authorities and equal governmental support for all religious movements within Judaism."

[Richard Hirsch]

Other Trends. Another non-orthodox manifestation in Israel's religious life was represented by the Jerusalem congregation Mavakkeshei Derekh (which was unaffiliated with any trend). This grew out of a series of national meetings (in 1962 ff.) between city and kibbutz intellectuals who were trying to find a new way of expressing their religious beliefs in the context of the new situation emerging from the realities of the State of Israel, which they saw as a potential religious force in world Jewry and not only in Israel. The emphasis was not so much on *halakhah* as on Judaism as a communal force. Its prayer service represents the consensus of the group and is built around the reading of the Torah and study (see *Conservative Judaism).

DEVELOPMENTS THROUGH THE EARLY 1990S. Jewish religious institutions continued to be linked to political developments, with a drop in the influence of the modern Orthodox and a parallel rise in the ultra-Orthodox (*ḥaredi*) community. Politically, the *National Religious Party, which spoke for modern Orthodoxy, declined sharply from the 1960s, when it had 11 or 12 representatives in the Knesset. In the 1984 elections, this party won four seats, in 1988, five, and in 1992, six. In contrast, the parties to the religious right of the NRP, which had had six seats in the 1960s, won eight seats in 1984, 13 seats in 1988, and ten in 1992.

The modern Orthodox camp, and in particular, the National Religious Party, had become identified with *Gush Emunim, the movement favoring Jewish settlement of the entire Land of Israel, and in particular, the Administered Territories. The religious obligation to retain all of the Land of Israel was associated with a belief in the potential arrival of the Messiah. The most extreme form of this messianism found expression in movements aimed at restoring a Jewish presence on the Temple Mount, either in addition to, or in place of, the Muslim shrines occupying the site. One small group of extremists was arrested while planning to destroy the mosques there. A group known as the Faithful of the Temple Mount, which had previously attempted unsuccessfully to conduct public Jewish prayer on the Temple Mount, organized a "cornerstone-laying" ceremony with a block of stone weighing several tons, but was barred from the area by the police. Another organization, the Jerusalem Temple Institute, occupied itself with creating ritual objects and garments to be used in the Temple upon its restoration.

A relatively small number of Orthodox leaders tried to disassociate themselves from this trend, by organizing, in 1982, *Netivot Shalom, a religious group loosely identified with the Israeli peace movement, and founding Meimad, a moderate religious party, in 1988. Although Meimad won considerable sympathy in left-wing non-Orthodox circles, it failed to garner even the minimum of votes needed for one seat in the Knesset.

Political developments in the ultra-Orthodox camp were highlighted by the fragmentation of *Agudat Israel, which had formerly been its sole political representative. *Shas, a Sephardi ultra-Orthodox movement, combined religious fervor with bitterness over the discrimination and wrongs of the past. The party participated in the 1983 Jerusalem municipal election and then went on nationally to become the dominant ultra-Orthodox voice. Seeking votes outside the traditional ultra-Orthodox strongholds, Shas brought a new flavor to the local political scene, especially in the 1988 elections when the secular public was bemused to see a television election advertisement in which a group of black-clad rabbis pronounced a formula releasing voters from promises to vote for other parties.

Degel ha-Torah, organized in 1988, was an Ashkenazi split-off from Agudat Israel. Despite the desertions, Agudat Israel enjoyed considerable success in this election, thanks to the support of the Chabad Ḥasidim, who had previously refrained from supporting any party. The change was a result of the bitter attacks by Degel ha-Torah's leader, Rabbi Eliezer Schach, head of the anti-ḥasidic camp, on Chabad's Rabbi Menachem Mendel Schneerson, the Lubavitcher Rebbe, a fellow nonagenarian. Rabbi Schach, who enjoyed an adulation from his followers not unlike that bestowed on ḥasidic rebbes, became the object of harsh criticism in the wake of the 1988 elections, when he ruled out any coalition with Labor because of the lack of religious observance in kibbutzim, whose very Jewishness he questioned.

An apparent victory for the NRP was the election, in 1983, for a ten-year term, of Ashkenazi Chief Rabbi Avraham *Shapiro and Sephardi Chief Rabbi Mordechai *Eliahu, both identified with the nationalist-religious ideology of the NRP. Rabbi Shapiro, in particular, was the principal of the Merkaz ha-Rav yeshivah, the ideological cradle of Gush Emunim. However, the chief rabbinate became more alienated from the secular Jewish majority, while in Orthodox circles, an increasing public looked to the ultra-Orthodox *ḥaredi* rabbis for spiritual leadership.

The challenge to the chief rabbis was especially effective from Rabbi Ovadiah *Yosef, Eliahu's predecessor, who continued to be regarded by many as the rightful leader of Sephardi Jewry. Yosef, the spiritual mentor of Shas, challenged a halakhic ruling by Shapiro and Eliahu that it was impermissible to give up any part of the Land of Israel, even for the sake of peace. Yosef ruled that territorial concessions were permissible to prevent bloodshed.

Another challenge to the chief rabbis concerned the observance of the sabbatical year, during which it is forbidden to work the land of Israel. Prior to the sabbatical year which began in October 1986, the chief rabbis, following a precedent set by their predecessors, ruled that in order to promote Jewish settlement, it was permitted, and even desirable, for Jewish farmers to nominally "sell" their land to a non-Jew and continue to work it. The *ḥaredi* rabbis ruled that one could not eat produce grown as a result of such a ruling and succeeded in convincing the Ministry of Commerce and Industry to import grain, so bakeries would not use that grown locally. This incident highlighted a tendency by food producers to seek *kashrut* certification from *ḥaredi* institutions, although legally, only the official rabbinates were empowered to issue such certification.

In the schools, a growing number of parents preferred the *ḥaredi* schools to the modern Orthodox State Religious system. Even within the State Religious system there was a tendency to extremism, with the establishment of new schools to cater to a more religiously strict public, and many existing schools opted for separate classes for boys and girls. Part of the success of the *ḥaredi* school networks could be attributed to the increasing funds allocated to them as the price for government coalitions. Especially remarkable was the flourishing of *ḥaredi yeshivot*, where a growing number of adults studied religious subjects full-time. It was estimated that there were more yeshivah students than ever before in Jewish history.

The growth of the *yeshivot* became a source of contention with the secular majority, many of whom were unhappy at the government subsidies which went to such institutions. Both the secular and many modern Orthodox objected to the fact that in a country in which universal military service was the rule, the yeshivah students received automatic deferment, often until an age at which they were no longer fit for military service. At one point it was estimated that some 20,000 young men were enjoying such deferment.

The question of public Sabbath observance continued to be an issue, with a tendency for some public desecration of the Sabbath, despite repeated protests and demonstrations. In particular in Jerusalem, for the first time, several cinemas began to have Friday night showings, and a large number of pubs, discotheques, and cafes opened their doors on the Sabbath.

There were acrimonious disputes in Jerusalem over the issue of the exhumation of the bones of Jews. According to the ultra-Orthodox interpretation, land even suspected of containing Jewish remains should remain untouched, so as to facilitate resurrection of the dead. This interpretation led to considerable conflict between Atra Kadisha, an organization devoted to preserving Jewish burial sites, and archeologists and civil engineers. In 1982 and 1983, Atra Kadisha led public protests against the archeological excavations at the City of David. According to Atra Kadisha, the site contained a medieval Jewish cemetery. The archeologists, who denied this, succeeded in completing the excavations. In 1992, a number of tombs from the Second Temple period were uncovered during construction of a major highway interchange at French Hill, and a large burial area which archeologists insisted was Christian, because of the presence of Christian symbols, was uncovered during construction of the Mamilla project. Archeologists removed and then, following violent protests, returned for burial, the bones and sarcophagi of one tomb from French Hill. At Mamilla, the builders removed the bones and bulldozed the burial area in the dead of night. The young demonstrators who reacted introduced a new level of violence into religious-secular disputes, violently confronting the police, stoning cars, and burning garbage dumpsters.

The immigration of Jews, both from Ethiopia and from the former Soviet Union, presented a challenge to the religious establishment. The Ethiopian Jews (see *Beta Israel) were intensely observant, but their practice differed considerably from normative Judaism. When large numbers began to arrive as a result of Operation Moses in 1984, the chief rabbis ruled that they would have to undergo a symbolic conversion ceremony before they could be married. In protest over what they saw as a questioning of their Jewishness, the Ethiopian Jews objected to the ruling and held a sit-in strike for a month, across from the offices of the chief rabbis. Although the Ethiopian Jews garnered considerable public sympathy and support, they were unable to win over the chief rabbis, who eventually circumvented the issue by allowing a rabbi sympathetic to their cause to register their marriages. In 1992, the Ethiopian Jewish community was again unsuccessful in a confrontation with the chief rabbinate, this time in a bid for the community's traditional religious leaders, the *qessim* (Amharic: *qessotch*), to be allowed to perform marriages and carry out divorces in Israel.

Yet another religious dilemma faced the Ethiopian Jewish community after Operation Solomon, the mass airlift in which the bulk of Ethiopian Jewry was brought to Israel in May 1991. Remaining in Ethiopia were thousands of *Falash-Mura* (*falas moura*), Jews who had become estranged from the Jewish community and in many cases had converted to Christianity. Although the *qessim*, for the most part, regarded these people as renegades, to be abandoned, most members of the community in Israel agitated for them to be returned to Judaism and brought to Israel. The government eventually decided that close relatives of those living in Israel could be brought in as a humanitarian gesture.

A different type of problem resulted from the mass immigration from the former Soviet Union. Although some of the immigrants from the Baltic states and Central Asia had some basic knowledge of Judaism, many of the others were almost totally ignorant of even the most basic elements of Jewish history, religion, and culture. A considerable number of these immigrants were either the offspring of mixed marriages or brought with them non-Jewish spouses. It was not clear how many were actually Jewish according to *halakhah*. During the years that Rabbi Yitzḥak Peretz of Shas was the absorption minister, the ministry embarked on a campaign of "spiritual absorption," introducing the immigrants to the practices of ultra-Orthodoxy, with questionable success. The immigrants studied some essentials about Judaism at the ulpanim in which they learned Hebrew, and a wide variety of public institutions and organizations offered courses in Judaism. Perhaps the most promising indication of the immigrants' desire to return to Judaism was the large number of men who asked to be circumcised.

Non-Orthodox movements continued to make limited progress. Their main success was in barring a change in the Law of Return, which would have, in effect, excluded those converted to Judaism by Conservative and Reform rabbis abroad from recognition as Jews eligible for Israeli citizenship. Although the number of such converts immigrating to Israel was minimal, many Jews abroad, particularly in the U.S., saw this as a crucial issue, in view of the high rate of mixed marriages and the fact that a growing part of the American Jewish community included converts or their children. The failure of the religious parties to gain support on this issue from the other parties was a result of massive pressure by American Jewish organizations.

A related issue was the decision of the Interior Ministry not to register such converts as Jews in their identity cards and in the population registry. After Shoshana Miller, a Reform convert from the U.S., successfully petitioned the High Court of Justice to be registered as a Jew, the ministry continued to try to circumvent the decision. It proposed registering all converts as such in the identity cards, a move that aroused opposition not only from the non-Orthodox, but from the chief rabbis and many other Orthodox rabbis, who pointed out that Jewish law forbade reminding a convert of his or her non-Jewish origins.

In 1992, the first woman rabbi, Naama Kelman-Ezrachi, was ordained by Israel's Reform rabbinical school and, in the same year, the rabbinical school of the local Conservative (Masorti) movement decided to admit women as students in its rabbinical program. In 1986, Leah Shakdiel, an Orthodox schoolteacher, was elected to the religious council of Yeruḥam, the first woman to be elected to such a body, but she did not take her seat until the High Court of Justice ordered the religious affairs minister to validate her election two years later. In 1988, women won the right to serve on the body electing the Tel Aviv chief rabbi.

However, the High Court rejected the petition of another women's group, the Women of the Wall, which included women of all religious streams, who aroused the fury of ultra-Orthodox worshipers when they attempted to read from a Torah scroll at the Western Wall. The Court upheld a Religious Affairs Ministry ruling which forbade them to wear prayer shawls, read from a Torah scroll, or even sing aloud at the Western Wall.

[Haim Shapiro]

THE 1990S AND AFTER. At no time in Jewish history has there been such a great flourishing of religious institutions and Jewish life anywhere in the world as in late 20th century Israel. This is a result of the high birth rate among the religious public, the wave of people returning to religion and traditional roots, government allocations to religious services, the Israeli welfare state enabling thousands of yeshivah students to study for many years, and the exemption from military service for yeshivah students.

In May 2000, the Ministry of Religious Affairs was supporting 196,000 students at yeshivot, *kolelim* (yeshivot for married men), and schools with extended Torah studies. These included 41,000 at *kolelim* and 38,000 at yeshivot for unmarried men over the age of 18. Among the important yeshivot in Israel: the Hebron and Mir yeshivot in Jerusalem, with 4,000 students, and the Ponivezh yeshivah in Bene Berak. Yeshivah study was funded by a number of ministries (Religious Affairs, Education, Welfare), as is the establishment of synagogues (Religious Affairs, Housing and Construction, Interior). Research shows that two-thirds of **ḥaredi* men studying at yeshivot do not work, and, as a result, Menachem Friedman, a researcher studying the *ḥaredi* population in Israel, has called them the "society of scholars."

It is hard to find reliable data on the number of synagogues since these are often private and unfunded institutions, and so it can only be estimated that there are many thousands. According to Ministry of Religious Affairs figures, in 2001 there were no fewer than 750 *mikva'ot* operating in Israel, 400 of them in small communities.

Religious Education. The great flourishing of religious life in Israel is also manifested in the field of education. Between 1989/90 and 2004/5 the share of *ḥaredi* elementary education in the Hebrew elementary education system (grades 1 to 8) increased from 6.5% to 20%. The main reasons for this were the high birth rate in the *ḥaredi* population, the establishment by Shas of its own network of schools, and the establishment of Torah-based schools aimed at bringing secular and traditional Jews back to religion. During the same period, state religious education declined from 21% to 19%.

The majority of *ḥaredi* schools do not belong to the state or state religious education systems and are defined as "recognized but unofficial" or "exempt" (exempt from the Compulsory Education Law). In other words, these are private institutions with only limited state supervision of their educational content.

In the middle of the 1980s Shas established its Ma'ayan ha-Ḥinukh ha-Torani network, competing with the independent education system of Agudat Israel. A large number of its students came from the non-*ḥaredi* Sephardi religious public and the traditional public. The result was that many more students were recruited from state religious and state schools than from the *ḥaredi* schools.

As of the beginning of the 1980s, a split developed in the Ashkenazi *ḥaredi* education system. Many ḥasidic sects established independent educational institutions. Independent *talmud torah* schools attracted pupils from the Lithuanian stream, and as a result, independent education became, to a large extent, a network of schools for girls and schools operating in provincial towns.

Since the 1950s, the *ḥaredi* education track for girls has directed all its graduates towards working as teachers and supporting their husbands studying in the *kolel*, and therefore *ḥaredi* girls of high school age study at teachers seminaries. As of the 1980s, there has been a shortage of teaching positions in the *ḥaredi* sector. The schools employ many teachers in part-time positions, but even this is not enough to solve the women's employment needs, and some seminaries are opening training tracks in other fields, such as computers.

Despite the establishment of Shas schools, the Sephardi *ḥaredi* elite, including senior members of Shas, continue to send their children to the schools, yeshivot, and seminaries of the Lithuanian *ḥaredi* community. Many of these institutions, especially the girls' seminaries, have a quota of between 10% and 30% for Mizraḥi students, which is against Israeli law and has provoked harsh public criticism.

In the 1970s and 1980s the Ashkenazi *ḥaredi* schools cut back their efforts to recruit traditional students from the Mizraḥi communities, among other things due to a fear that these students would have a bad influence on the *ḥaredi* students. At the end of the 1990s special schools were set up alongside Agudat Israel's independent education system, specializing in bringing children back to the religious fold – the Netivot Moshe schools which compete, in practice, with Ma'ayan ha-Ḥinukh ha-Torani; and Shuvu, focusing on immigrants from the former Soviet Union and also providing a high standard of general education. These were established with the support of Agudat Israel in the U.S., which also raises funds for them on a large scale. The main recruitment of students is through the Lev LeAchim organization, and the aim is to use the children to bring the whole family back to a religious way of life.

The Compulsory Education Law in Israel prohibits the state from recognizing institutions which do not teach the foundation curriculum, including basic general studies preparing students for life and work in a modern country. For the first 50 years of the state's existence, this law was not applied, and a large number of *ḥaredi* institutions, in particular boys' schools, offered almost no general studies. Following a petition submitted to the High Court of Justice in 1999 by MK Yosef Paritsky of Shinui, the court instructed the Ministry of Education to implement the law. The ministry began a process of gradual implementation of the curriculum, arousing considerable resistance in the *ḥaredi* public.

Since the 1980s, education in Israel has been characterized by an accelerated process of privatization and a move by the elite from state schools to exclusive schools. Whereas among the secular public this has resulted in the opening of experimental and democratic schools, among the national religious public the result has been the establishment of a Torah-based education system, where there is far greater emphasis on keeping the religious precepts than in state religious schools. At the same time, private schools have opened for the moderate religious public, some of which also include secular students.

Yeshivot. Some of the graduates of *talmud torah* schools and *ḥaredi* schools for boys continue to junior high school or equivalent institutions, and some go straight to *yeshivah ketanah*, which is the *ḥaredi* equivalent of high school. Graduates of *yeshivah ketanah* go on to yeshivah *gedolah* at the equivalent of army age and, after marriage, study in a *kolel*.

Lessons at *ḥaredi* yeshivot focus on the Talmud and its interpretations, and also include subjects such as Pentateuch and Ethics, but do not include general studies. The *ḥaredi* curriculum does not train students for any occupation outside the realm of religion. In the 1990s there began to be institutes offering professional and academic training to yeshivah and *kolel* graduates, in fields such as computers, the law and social work.

The national religious yeshivah study track usually includes a yeshivah high school combining religious and secular studies and preparing students for matriculation and *hesder* yeshivah. The *hesder* yeshivah track lasts five years, three and a half years in yeshiva and a year and a half in the army. In 2000, the Ministry of Religious Affairs supported some 5,000 *hesder* yeshivah students – a thousand students in each year. In other words, unlike *ḥaredi* youth who, almost without exception, attend *yeshivah gedolah*, only a small percentage of national religious youth go on to *hesder* yeshivah.

In the 1990s, a new track was developed for national religious youth in which graduates of religious or yeshivah high schools study for a year in a pre-army *mekhinah* (preparatory course) and then go on to full military service. The *mekhinah* is intended to meet two main challenges: the desire of many national religious young men to serve a full three years rather than the shortened *hesder* service, and strengthening the students' faith and reducing the number who turn away from religion in the army.

Returning to the Religious Fold. During the 1940s and 1950s, the demographic movêment between the *ḥaredi* and secular public was almost exclusively towards the secular. But as of the 1970s the direction has been reversed. Among the reasons for the wave of people returning to religion are the worldwide trend, the moral crisis in Israeli society following the 1973 Yom Kippur War, the failure of secular education, and more. An entire network of organizations has been set up in *ḥaredi* society to bring people back to the fold and absorb them on their return. These include the Arakhim organization, focusing mainly on seminars to bring people back to religion, and the Or ha-Ḥayyim institutes, which operate yeshivot for the newly religious and schools for their children.

A distinction is usually drawn between two types of return to religion. One is the move from a completely secular life, such as on a kibbutz, to an extreme *ḥaredi* lifestyle. This is usually associated with the Ashkenazi public. The other involves the traditional public drawing closer to religion and becoming more religious. This is usually associated with the Mizraḥi sector and apparently accounts for the majority of the newly religious.

During the 1990s, the Ministry of Religious Affairs financed the studies of 43,000 people in institutes aimed at those returning to religious observance – 27,000 men and 16,000 women. According to a survey carried out by the Dahaf Institute for *Yedioth Aharonoth*, 7% of the adult Jewish population, more than 200,000 people, have returned to religion. Whereas in the beginning lectures and seminars were the main means of bringing people back, in the 1990s the *ḥaredi* pirate radio stations and religious schools for secular children also served this purpose.

The Ministry of Religious Affairs. The 1990s were marked by control over the religious establishment moving from the NRP to the increasingly strong religious party Shas. Between 1990 and the end of 2003 the ministry was headed by no fewer than 13 ministers, an average of one minister a year. This power struggle was symbolized more than anything by the period between 1996 and 1999, when it was agreed that both parties would have deputy ministers in the Ministry of Religious Affairs. The position of minister was rotated annually between the parties. During the 1990s the ministry's budget was one and a half billion shekels a year. Although this is a small budget in terms of a government ministry, this ministry had considerable power because it controlled the transfer of thousands of allocations to religious organizations every year, as well as many religious positions – religious judges, rabbis, and so forth.

In the 1980s and 1990s the Ministry of Religious Affairs became a symbol of corruption to the Israeli public. A series of reports by the state comptroller revealed large-scale fictitious reporting and fraudulent expenses. The report submitted by State Comptroller Miriam Ben Porat in 1995 on allocations in the Ministry of Religious Affairs states that: "The picture emerging from this report is very serious, as if ethical values and fundamental principles of truth and integrity have ceased to exist. The ministry has failed in its role of responsibility for allocating public funds."

Demands to dismantle the ministry were brought up again and again. This move was also supported by *ḥaredi* figures, such as MK Moshe Gafni, who felt that the ministry in its then current form was a cause of blasphemy. At the end of 2003 it was dismantled. The majority of its budget, including the yeshivah budgets, was transferred to the Ministry of Education and Culture. Religious services, including the Chief Rabbinate and the religious councils, *kashrut*, and burial services, were placed in the hands of the Prime Minister's Office. As a result, strong criticism was voiced over the fact that the Likud was introducing dozens of political appointees into the religious services. In 2005 religious services in the Prime Minister's Office became the responsibility of a national authority for religious services.

The Chief Rabbinate. At the end of the 20th century and the beginning of the 21st, Israel's Chief Rabbinate lost much of its status and spiritual authority. The *ḥaredi* public took advantage of its political strength to take control of the Chief Rabbinate. The chief rabbis are usually people supported by the *ḥaredim*, despite the fact that the *ḥaredim* do not obey the Chief Rabbinate. These are rabbis who, even in the view of the *ḥaredim*, are not among the first ranks of leadership. The waning of the Chief Rabbinate was symbolized by the abandonment of its home in the Heikhal Shelomo Synagogue in the center of Jerusalem in 1997, and the move to simple offices in the increasingly *ḥaredi* Romema neighborhood. Heikhal Shelomo was considered a symbol of the state rabbinate and an alternative it to the *ḥaredi* rabbinate.

The last two chief rabbis to be perceived as major rabbis in the religious community and as having an influence beyond this community were rabbis Shlomo Goren and Ovadiah Yosef, who served from 1972 to 1983. Goren was chief rabbi of the IDF for many years, and was strongly identified with the army and Israel's wars. Yosef was considered to be the unquestioned spiritual leader of the religious and traditional Sephardi public. The period of their tenure was characterized by numerous squabbles and infighting. In 1983 the two were forced out of office against their will and the status of the Chief Rabbinate began to decline. Not merely did the supporters of Rabbi Yosef continue to call him Rishon le-Zion, the title of the Sephardi chief rabbi, but he continued to be considered the most important Sephardi rabbi, undermining the status of all those who came after him.

Goren and Yosef were replaced by rabbis Avraham *Shapira and Mordecai *Eliyahu. The two were seen as the spiritual leaders of the national religious public, considered to be the hard core of supporters of the Chief Rabbinate. At the same time, they had very limited influence beyond this group. During their tenure the rabbinate moved towards the political right wing.

In 1993 rabbis Israel *Lau and Eliyahu *Bakshi Doron were elected with the support of rabbis from Shas and Yahadut ha-Torah (UTJ), and were seen as subordinate to them. Rabbi Lau was outstanding in the field of public relations, and was very popular among the secular public. Bakshi Doron solved a number of difficult halakhic issues, including reducing to a minimum the list of people prohibited from marrying. In 2003 rabbis Shlomo Amar, also a disciple of Rabbi Yosef, and Yona Metzger were elected to the position. Metzger had previously been a neighborhood rabbi, and there were complaints that he did not have sufficient experience for the position.

Chief rabbis are elected for a period of 10 years. They serve in rotation as president of the Chief Rabbinate Council and president of the High Rabbinical Court. The religious establishment is the last state body in Israel to retain an ethnic structure. There are two chief rabbis, Ashkenazi and Sephardi, and the same is true in a number of towns. The election of *dayyanim* (religious judges) to the High Rabbinical Court also unofficially preserves the ethnic balance. Proposals to elect a single chief rabbi have not been accepted. But in 2000 Minister of Religious Affairs Yossi *Beilin introduced regulations severely limiting the possibility of electing two rabbis in the same town. As a result, today there is only one chief rabbi of Tel Aviv.

Religious Councils. Religious services in Israel's towns and local councils are provided by 133 religious councils, 21 of them regional religious councils. In 2001, they received a budget of NIS 137 million from the Ministry of Religious Affairs. Among other things, the councils provide marriage registration services, *kashrut* supervisors, *mikva'ot*, neighborhood rabbis, *eruvim*, etc. Proposals to reform religious services have been discussed again and again, with the aim of simplifying elections and funding and reducing political influence, but as of the end of 2005 this had not been implemented.

Since the 1990s the religious councils have been in a state of severe crisis, for a number of reasons. The method of funding the religious councils is very complex, with the government funding 40% and the local council providing 60% of their budget. The severe budgetary crisis in the local authorities meant that many of them did not transfer funds to the religious councils, which were then unable to pay salaries and pensions. The religious prohibition against striking religious services such as *mikva'ot* and burial made it very hard for employees of the religious councils to protest effectively. The image of the councils as corrupt and hostile to the secular public also made it very difficult for them to enlist public support.

Another central factor in the crisis in the religious services was the very complex method of appointing members of the religious councils. This method gives representation on the councils to the minister of religious affairs (45%), the local authorities (45%), and the town rabbis (10%), and requires consultation between the three bodies and a reciprocal right of veto. Differences of opinion are passed on for decision by a committee of ministers. As a result, the religious councils are not reconvened on time, sometimes being delayed by many years.

The main issue regarding the composition of the religious councils involves political power struggles. Until 1992 the NRP (National Religious Party) controlled the Ministry of Religious Affairs and had sole control over the religious councils. With the rise to power of Shas, which also took control of the Ministry of Religious Affairs, there began to be serious power struggles between the two parties, which were frequently referred to the High Court of Justice for decision.

In 1987 the High Court of Justice instructed that Leah Shakdiel be appointed to the religious council of Yeruḥam, and ruled that there should be no discrimination regarding the appointment of women to the religious councils. Despite the objections of the religious establishment to this ruling, it came to terms with it, among other things because for the most part the women elected to serve on the councils are religious or traditional and obey the rulings of the rabbis.

During the 1990s the High Court of Justice ruled a number of times that Reform and Conservative Jews should be allowed to be appointed to the religious councils. To prevent the entry of Reform and Conservative Jews to the religious councils of large cities, in some places these councils were not convened for a number of terms.

Religion and State. During the 1980s and 1990s consensus in Israeli society was on the wane, including the sphere of religion and state. The political upset of 1977 that brought the Likud to power also considerably increased the influence of the religious parties and increased ties between religion and state and the funds transferred by the State for religious education, religious services, and religious job slots. Those who support this state of affairs see it as an expression of the Jewish character of the state, while those who object claim that the result is religious coercion and corruption. The fact that religion is identified with infighting, coercion, and corruption has seriously damaged the image of the religious establishment and increased tensions between the religious and secular populations.

Religious budgets have become a central issue in coalition negotiations and the negotiations over the state budget.

Thus, for example, between 1996 and 1999 (during the government of Binyamin Netanyahu, when the religious parties were a central component of the coalition) the budget for yeshivot in the Ministry of Religious Affairs increased from NIS 691 million to NIS 878 million, an increase of 27%. The budget for the Ma'ayan ha-Ḥinukh ha-Torani schools of the Sephardi *ḥaredi* party Shas increased during the 1990s by over 100%, from NIS 12.5 million in 1990 to NIS 137.5 million in 1999, an indication of the growth of this school system and the increasing power of Shas.

Among the struggles that took place at this time with regard to the authority of the religious establishment and public religious adherence were the following: the demand for civil marriage, the fight over non-Orthodox conversion, passage of the law prohibiting the public display of *ḥameẓ* during Passover, the demand that the Chief Rabbinate not take into consideration Sabbath observance and modesty when giving *kashrut* certification, etc. The Supreme Court played a central role in these religious struggles, usually ruling in favor of increased freedom from religion and religious equality, and acquiring the reputation of an anti-religious entity. Among the court's rulings provoking considerable resistance among the religious and *ḥaredi* public were: permitting the import of non-kosher meat to Israel, recognizing the common-law rights of same-sex couples, recognizing Reform and Conservative conversion carried out abroad, etc. This conflict reached a climax when a quarter of a million *ḥaredi* and religious demonstrators held a prayer rally against the Supreme Court at the entrance to Jerusalem.

Since the 1970s there has also been a radicalization in the lifestyle of both sides, religious and secular. The secular lifestyle has become more free, as seen, among other things, in provocative billboard advertisements, entertainment and shopping on Friday nights, the opening of many non-kosher restaurants, etc. The lifestyle of the *ḥaredim* and part of the national religious community has been characterized by the establishment of separate settlements and neighborhoods, and the increasing number of prohibitions in spheres such as women's clothing, *kashrut*, and the use of electronic devices. A national *ḥaredi* group has emerged among the national religious public characterized by zealous observance of religious law. The shared life of secular and *ḥaredi* has become almost impossible.

The Wave of Immigration. The wave of immigration from the former Soviet Union during the 1990s, bringing more than a million immigrants under the Law of Return, created a new phenomenon in Israel. Among the immigrants were 300,000 Russians who were not Jewish. These immigrants, including the non-Jews, were absorbed into Jewish society and created, for the first time in Israel, a significant phenomenon of assimilation and marriage between Jews and non-Jews. Many people, including Prime Minister Ariel Sharon, aimed for mass conversion of the non-Jewish immigrants, but the Orthodox establishment placed obstacles in the way of conversion, by requiring converts to live a religious lifestyle. The result was a relatively limited rate of conversion of fewer than a thousand immigrants from the FSU each year. A particularly thorny issue is created by the fact that the only recognized form of marriage in Israel is religious. As a result, the 300,000 non-Jewish immigrants are not able to realize their right to marry in Israel and have to go abroad for this purpose. Another trend brought by the immigrants is the opening of dozens of non-kosher food stores in all neighborhoods where there are a large number of immigrants, selling pork and ham. In addition, there is a chain of luxury supermarkets by the name of Tiv Ta'am that remains open on the Sabbath and also attracts secular non-immigrants.

Reform and Conservative congregations. A phrase that is considered characteristic of the attitude of non-religious Israelis to the progressive streams of Judaism is: "The synagogue I don't attend is Orthodox." During the 1990s and early 2000s the Reform and Conservative streams made a few significant achievements, but they were unable to change the overall picture. Only a few thousand people belong to the congregations of each of these movements, representing a very small percentage of the membership of Jewish religious congregations in Israel. In 2005 the Reform movement had 26 congregations in Israel and the Conservative movement had 42.

Where they have had greater success is the increasing trend among the secular population to turn to Reform and Conservative rabbis for their religious ceremonies, weddings, bar mitzvahs, and circumcision. Particularly noteworthy in this field is the Beit Daniel congregation led by Rabbi Meir Ezri which, in many respects, has become the religious institution serving the north Tel Aviv elite. In the 1990s the phenomenon of women serving as rabbis also reached Israel. This is still limited to a few individuals, and even the debate over what they should be called in Hebrew – *rava*, *rabbi*, or *rabbanit* – has not yet been settled.

The Reform movement has been very visible in the legal and public battles undertaken by its lobby, the Center for Jewish Pluralism, led for many years by rabbi and attorney Uri Regev. Among other things, petitions submitted by the movement to the High Court of Justice forced the Ministry of Religious Affairs to fund Reform and Conservative religious institutions.

Conversion. The most important battle waged by the Reform and Conservative movements is the one known as "who is a Jew?" In practice, the question is who is a rabbi or who is qualified to carry out conversion, and whether Reform and Conservative rabbis may do so.

This question is of the greatest importance, because Judaism is the only criterion by which someone who is not a family member of an Israeli can obtain citizenship. As a result, conversion courts hold the keys to citizenship in the Jewish state. The Reform and Conservative streams that make up the majority of United States Jewry see the obstacles that Israel places in the path of recognition of their converts as a kind of statement that their rabbis are second-class rabbis.

The battle over the issue of conversion is being carried out in a way that is very characteristic of the religious struggles in Israel, with the Reform and Conservative movements trying to make use of the High Court of Justice, while the Orthodox movements rely on their political power in the Knesset. These battles have two practical aspects. One is registration as a Jew in the Ministry of the Interior – in the population registry and in identity cards. This is largely a symbolic matter and is of particular importance to converts who are in any case entitled to Israeli citizenship (for example, those with a Jewish spouse or Jewish father) and are interested in symbolic recognition of their Jewishness. In order to sidestep the issue of registration, in 2002, then-Minister of the Interior Eli Yishai of Shas decided to cancel the section denoting nationality in the identity card.

The more significant question is recognition of Reform and Conservative converts under the Law of Return, for receiving Israeli citizenship and the broad economic assistance given to new immigrants. In 1989 the High Court of Justice ruled that the state must recognize every conversion carried out in a recognized Jewish community in the Diaspora – Orthodox, Reform or Conservative – and give converts rights under the Law of Return. At the same time, the legal battle over the fate of Reform and Conservative converts converted in Israel is still underway. The fight over "who is a Jew?" reached its peak in 1997, when the religious parties tried to amend the law so as to ensure an Orthodox monopoly over conversion in Israel, and a serious split arose between the government and leaders of the Reform and Conservative movement in the United States. Following this crisis, a committee was set up to examine the subject of conversion, under the leadership of attorney Ya'akov Ne'eman. Due to its inability to reach agreement, the committee's recommendations were never signed. Nonetheless, the government decided to implement some of them. A joint conversion institute was set up for all three streams of Judaism, with graduates undergoing Orthodox conversion.

Marriage. Israeli law does not recognize non-Orthodox marriage and divorce for Jews. However, at the beginning of the 1960s the Supreme Court ruled that, under the international charters signed by Israel, and in accordance with population registration laws, the Ministry of the Interior was obliged to register Israelis married in an official ceremony outside Israel as married. In this way the concepts of "Cyprus marriage" and "Paraguayan marriage" came into being. Paraguayan marriages were performed for many years by mail. This option has been blocked, but even today it is possible to marry with only one of the partners being present. This offers a solution for couples where one partner is unable to leave the country (for example, for fear that a foreign partner will not be permitted to return). The problem of the absence of civil marriage in Israel was considerably exacerbated in the 1990s, with the arrival of some 300,000 immigrants from the former Soviet Union who are defined in Israel as having no religion and are therefore unable to marry in Israel. Some of them return to their country of origin in order to get married. The number of Jewish couples marrying in Israel in 1970 was 24,000, and the same number married in 1990. This shows a decrease in the number of couples getting married, an increase in the age of marriage, and a decreasing willingness to be married by the Orthodox rabbinate. According to the website of the New Family organization, a few thousand Israeli couples get married abroad each year, some because they cannot get married in Israel and others because they do not want a religious marriage ceremony. It is hard to obtain more precise data, among other things because many of the couples that marry abroad are never registered in Israel. Many couples prefer to live together in a common-law relationship without marrying at all.

Divorce and the Rabbinical Courts. Even couples married in a civil marriage service are required by Israeli law to divorce in the rabbinical court. In 2004, 9,650 Jewish couples divorced in Israel. In 2005 the court system included 12 regional courts and the High Rabbinical Court of Appeals. The position of *dayyan* (religious judge) is considered highly desirable in the rabbinic world, because of the high salary, linked to that of regular judges, and because of the considerable prestige. *Dayyanim* are elected by the Committee for the Election of Dayyanim, in which political entities, especially the religious parties, have great influence.

The rabbinical court system is headed by the president of the High Rabbinical Court and the director of the rabbinical courts. The presidency, which is held by one of the chief rabbis, changes hands every five years. The fact that some chief rabbis have very little experience as *dayyanim* and nonetheless are automatically appointed as president of the High Rabbinical Court has aroused criticism. At the beginning of 2004, as part of the dismantling of the Ministry of Religious Affairs, the rabbinical courts were placed under the control of the Ministry of Justice, which thus became the ministry responsible for all the courts in Israel.

The status of the rabbinical court system began to be considerably eroded as of the 1980s. Serious claims were raised against the rabbinical courts, among other things due to the fact that the majority of *dayyanim* are *ḥaredim* and are not familiar with the secular lifestyle, which includes sexual relations before marriage and extramarital relationships. It was also claimed that there was discrimination against women, with unsatisfactory solutions for **agunot* ("chained" women) and women refused a *get* (religious divorce), many delays and absenteeism on the part of the *dayyanim*, limited working hours, etc. In 1995 the Knesset passed a law enabling the religious courts to impose sanctions on husbands refusing to give their wives a *get*, including imprisonment, preventing them from leaving the country, and taking away their driving license.

The establishment of the Family Courts in 1995 made it possible for a large portion of the public to negotiate almost the entire divorce process in an alternative system, coming to the rabbinical courts with a signed agreement. In a letter sent by the director of the rabbinical courts, Rabbi Eliyahu Ben Dahan, to the *dayyanim* in 1998 he warned that "the public is voting against us with its feet." Ben Dahan ended his letter with an appeal to the *dayyanim* to search their souls and improve their service, because "if we do not come to our senses soon, the day is not far off when we will find ourselves doing nothing more than arranging divorce papers."

However, while the secular public is seeking out alternatives to the rabbinical courts, opposition to them actually developed among the religious public. Religious women's organizations began to lead the fight with regard to *agunot*, as well as the demand to improve the attitude of the *dayyanim* towards women and towards the rabbinic pleaders representing them.

Burial. Until the beginning of the 1990s, the Hevra Kaddisha burial societies had an absolute monopoly over Jewish burial in Israel. The most significant entity in this field was the Tel Aviv Hevra Kaddisha, which had a monopoly throughout almost the entire Dan region, in which almost half of Israel's Jewish residents live. Serious claims were made against this burial society regarding the payment of huge salaries and very high pensions. The society underwent a series of crises, the management was changed several times, and salaries were drastically cut. Jerusalem, on the other hand, suffers from a surfeit of ethnic burial societies. According to the data of the Ministry of Religious Affairs, in 2001 there were 600 burial societies operating in Israel.

Under Israeli law, burial is free and the burial societies are funded by the National Insurance Institute. However, the law permits the burial societies to charge a fee for the purchase of burial plots during a person's lifetime, for reserving a plot alongside a spouse, for purchasing a plot in a closed cemetery (in which only a few plots remain), and in other cases. During the 1980s and 1990s there was considerable criticism over the high prices charged by the burial societies for the purchase of plots, often as much as NIS 20,000, and in exceptional cases even NIS 50,000. In July 2001 the Knesset passed a law setting the maximum price for purchasing burial plots in different areas, ranging from NIS 2,000 to NIS 11,000.

At the end of the 1980s a movement for secular burial got underway, in the form of associations called "Menuḥah Nekhonah." Outwardly, the religious establishment did not object to these initiatives, and it was even argued that it was preferable for observant Jews that secular Jews not be buried alongside them. In practice, the religious establishment engaged in foot dragging, and the only association to succeed in starting burial services by 2005 was Menuḥah Nekhonah Beersheba. Secular people wishing to hold non-religious burial services are forced to turn to the kibbutzim that have opened commercial cemeteries.

A serious problem arose in the mid-1990s following the wave of immigration from the former Soviet Union, when no place was found to bury people without a religion and some bodies lay in the morgues for many days. The problem was eventually solved by the allocation of separate plots in Jewish cemeteries for people without a religion, and by burying some of the non-Jewish immigrants in kibbutz cemeteries.

The Jewish method of burial in the earth is very wasteful of space, only allowing for 250 graves per dunam (a quarter acre). In the 1990s the burial societies began making use of a number of methods for high-density burial, in order to save on land use: multi-level burial (Rama burial) with bodies buried in the earth on each level; burial in niches (Sanhedrin burial) in which the graves are in the walls; and so on. The cost of these burial structures is very high, three times higher than open burial. In 2005 a crematorium began operating in Israel for the first time. On the face of it, there was no legal reason why crematoria did not operate in Israel prior to this. It is reasonable to assume that the main obstacle was the fact that the concept of the crematorium is linked in the Israeli consciousness to the Holocaust.

[Shahar Ilan (2nd ed.)]

Christians

TO 1970. In 1970, over 105,000 Christians, representing almost all the principal branches of Christendom, lived under Israeli rule, mainly in Jerusalem, Bethlehem, Ramallah, Nazareth and Galilee, Haifa, and Jaffa. Most of them were town-dwellers and over 80% spoke Arabic. Juridically, most belonged to religious communities enjoying a large measure of autonomy in matters of personal status and led by patriarchs, who were both their high priests and ethnarchs. The "Community" is the ancient framework of the religious minorities in the Muslim world, but its roots go back to pre-Islamic times. The Ottoman government officially recognized a definite number of them, the so-called *millets*. This system was maintained by the British Mandatory power between 1918 and 1948 and still persists in Israel. In a schedule added in 1939 to the Palestine Order-in-Council of 1922, the religious communities are listed as follows: the Eastern (Orthodox), the Latin (Catholic), the Gregorian Armenian, the Armenian (Catholic), the Syrian (Catholic), the Chaldean (Uniate), the Greek (Catholic) Melkite, the Maronite, and the Syrian Orthodox. Neither the Copts and Ethiopians, nor the Anglicans and other Reformed Churches are mentioned in this list. The Church of England and the Evangelical Lutheran Church were subsequently granted official status by the government of Jordan, however, and the Evangelical Episcopal Church was recognized by the government of Israel in 1970.

Each community, as a rule, is headed by a patriarch assisted by a synod. The clergy (sometimes with the assistance of lay assessors) constitute the ecclesiastical courts of first instance; the synods form ecclesiastical courts of appeal. These courts have jurisdiction in certain matters of personal status, such as marriage, divorce, alimony, and confirmation of wills. In other matters of personal status, such as legitimation and adoption, guardianship, maintenance, and succession, their jurisdiction is conditional upon the consent of the interested parties.

The Christian religious communities have their headquarters in Jerusalem, where the most venerated Christian sanctuary is the Church of the Holy Sepulcher. Equally sacred to all Christian communities, it is controlled in practice largely by the Greek Orthodox, Latin, and Armenian patriarchates. The Syrians and the Copts have small chapels within its precincts, while the Ethiopians and Anglicans have the use of chapels in its immediate neighborhood. This situation is the "provisional" result of centuries of struggle among the various churches over the *holy places. Since the question of the holy places has never been solved, the position has been left, by agreement, in *status quo ante*. Other holy places are to be found in Nazareth and Bethlehem, and on the shores of the Sea of Galilee.

THE (GREEK) ORTHODOX. The most ancient ecclesiastical body in the Holy Land is the (Greek) Orthodox patriarchate of Jerusalem, which is probably the closest successor to the original Judeo-Christian community of St. James. A gentile, Greek-speaking, Christian community emerged in the city, then called Aelia Capitolina, before the middle of the second century, and gained importance in the days of Constantine (after the discovery of the holy places). In 451 Bishop Juvenal received the rank of patriarch. The Church of Jerusalem prospered in Byzantine times, decayed under the Arabs, was superseded by a Latin patriarchate during the Crusades, languished in the later Middle Ages, and recovered some strength under the Turks. At the beginning of the present century, however, it numbered a mere few thousand, fighting for the preservation of Orthodoxy in the Holy Land. In 1969 there were some 37,000 Orthodox in Israel and the Israel-controlled territories.

The head of the church is the patriarch, who is assisted by a holy synod of 14 to 18 members. He is also supported by the Brotherhood of the Holy Sepulcher, made up of a hundred monks, almost all of Hellenic origin, which is the dominant factor in the life of the church, and from whose ranks patriarchs, bishops, archimandrites, and other office-bearers are elected. The Orthodox Church of Jerusalem is therefore an Arabic-speaking community led by an almost exclusively Greek-speaking hierarchy. The lower, married, clergy are Arabic-speaking. The Brotherhood enjoys important rights in the chief holy places, and is the sole owner of some. The patriarchate possesses 45 historic monasteries (some dating back to early Byzantine times) and numerous churches. The seat of the patriarch and the headquarters of the Brotherhood is the Convent of St. Constantine and St. Helena in Jerusalem, which also houses a library containing thousands of manuscripts, some going back to the tenth century.

The Orthodox patriarchate of Jerusalem is the only autocephalous church in the country, all others being dependent in various degrees upon supreme hierarchs residing abroad, for example in Rome, Etchmiadzin (Soviet Armenia), Damascus, and Beirut. In Sinai there is a further autonomous (though not autocephalous) Orthodox church: founded in the third century as a missionary outpost, it is today a tiny monastic community, headed by an abbot with the title of archbishop. In 527 Justinian built a fortified monastery there, and in 566 a church in memory of his wife Theodora. In the ninth century, the monastery received the name of St. Catherine. It houses a famous library which includes numerous priceless manuscripts.

Jerusalem is also the seat of two Russian Orthodox missions. One of them represents the Moscow patriarchate; the other, the Russian Church Abroad. Both claim to be the legitimate successors of the ecclesiastic mission established by the Russian Government in the 19th century. The Moscow mission is in possession of the cathedral in Jerusalem and of a few churches in Jaffa, Haifa, Nazareth, and Tiberias, while the other is in charge of eight establishments, including the Church of St. Magdalene in Gethsemane. The mission of the Church Abroad, being out of communion with the patriarch of Moscow, is not recognized by the Orthodox patriarch of Jerusalem. A representative of the Romanian patriarch is in charge of a church and a tiny community in Jerusalem.

THE NON-CHALCEDONIANS. These are the Churches which recognize only the dogmas defined by the first three ecumenical councils.

The Armenians. This group had 72 monasteries in the Holy Land in the seventh century, and its numbers increased considerably under the Arabs and crusaders. As a result, much of Mount Zion became the property of the Armenian Church as early as the tenth century, and many splendid buildings were built there, e.g., the Church of St. Thoros. They prospered during the existence of the Armenian Kingdom of Cilicia, when they enjoyed the support of Armenian kings and princes and received numerous pilgrims. In 1311 (or perhaps 1281) their bishop was raised to the rank of patriarch. In later times they fared less well, losing all but six of their 72 monasteries, but they managed to maintain – against the Greek Orthodox – what they considered their rights in the main holy places. In Mandatory times (1918–48) they formed a prosperous community of some 5,000 souls, with their own churches, schools, and cultural institutions. Many have emigrated (to Soviet Armenia and elsewhere), and today they number over 2,500 in Israel-controlled territories.

The Armenian patriarchate is organized as the Monastic Brotherhood of St. James, composed of nine bishops, 32 archimandrites, and 70 monks. Only 36 serve in Israel; the remainder minister abroad. The head of the brotherhood is the patriarch, the leader of the church, president of all its assemblies, and governor of church property, who also represents his community before the state. He is assisted by a holy synod, which derives its authority from the general assembly of the brotherhood. Supreme in Jerusalem, the patriarch is, however, to some extent dependent on the *Katholikós* of all the Armenians in Etchmiadzin (Soviet Armenia). The patriarchate of Jerusalem is of great significance to the entire Armenian nation, on account of the holy places and the religious and cultural institutions of which it is in charge. The Armenian patriarch enjoys a position similar to those of the Greek Orthodox and Latin patriarchs, with whom he shares the basilicas of the Holy Sepulcher in Jerusalem and of the Nativity in Bethlehem. He also holds in common with the Orthodox the Tomb of the Virgin on the outskirts of Jerusalem. The seat of the patriarchate is on Mount Zion, where the convent, the Cathedral of St. James with its historic treasures, the seminary, and the schools are situated. The library contains some 4,000 manuscripts, mostly of the Cilician period, including the oldest gospel in *erkataguir* characters, probably of the eighth century.

The Syrian Orthodox and Copts. The Syrians have had a bishop in Jerusalem since 1140, the Copts since 1236. The Syrian Orthodox (also called the Jacobites), numbering about 2,000 in what was formerly the whole of Jordan, are headed by an archbishop residing in the monastery of St. Mark. On Christmas, the Syrians and Copts celebrate at the Armenian altars in the Church of the Nativity. On other solemn occasions they officiate in their own tiny chapels in the Church of the Holy Sepulcher.

The Ethiopians. Although they owned a considerable number of chapels and altars in various holy places from the Middle Ages until the first part of the 16th century, the Ethiopians are today confined to the Deir al-Sultan on the roof of the subterranean chapel of St. Helena (in the Church of the Holy Sepulcher), a beautiful church and monastery (Debre Gennet) in western Jerusalem, and a chapel near the Jordan River.

THE CATHOLICS. The Catholic Church is represented in Israel by Latins and Uniates (Melkites, Maronites, Chaldeans, Syrian Catholics, and Armenian Catholics). Each community belongs to an independent jurisdiction, but all depend, severally, upon the Sacred Congregation of the Oriental Churches in Rome.

The Latins. The Latins number more than 24,000 Europeans, Arabs, and others. They are headed by a patriarch, under whose jurisdiction are those Latins living in Transjordan and Cyprus. The Latin patriarchate of Jerusalem, which was founded by the crusaders in 1099, ceased to exist in 1291 but was reestablished in 1847/48. The patriarch is assisted by a coadjutor, two auxiliary bishops and a chapter of canons. Seventy diocesan clergy are in charge of 47 parishes distributed over Israel, Jordan, and Cyprus. A patriarchal seminary was founded in 1853.

Within the Latin community there are more than 40 religious orders and congregations. These include the Salesians with their orphanages and trade schools, the Brethren (*Frères*) with their colleges, the White Fathers and the Fathers of Beth Harram with their seminaries, the Trappists with their abbey at Latrun; the Benedictines with their abbey of the Dormition in Jerusalem, the Dominicans with the École Biblique, also in Jerusalem, the Carmelites, with their sanctuaries on Mt. Carmel, the Assumptionists, with their large organized pilgrimages, the Jesuits with their Pontifical Biblical Institute, and, most important, the Franciscans. There are 25 communities of women with more than 12,000 members and several hundred houses. These include the Sisters of the Rosary (who are of local origin), the Sisters of St. Joseph, the Filles de la Charité, the Carmelite Sisters, the Sisters of Zion, and the Poor Clares.

Most of these religious "families" went to the Holy Land during the last 120 years, but the Franciscans had arrived centuries before the other orders. For more than 500 years (since 1333), their "Custody of the Holy Land" was the sole agency in charge of Catholic interests in Palestine and the Near East. They endeavored to regain rights of worship and possession in the major sanctuaries, rehabilitated abandoned shrines, attended to numberless pilgrims, and ministered to the tiny "Latin" communities that sprang up around their convents. In 1848, they surrendered some of their functions and prerogatives, but not the most important, to the restored patriarchate. With over 400 members drawn from 28 nations, they are still the guardians of the most important Catholic sanctuaries. While sharing, under the status quo, the Church of the Holy Sepulcher and the Grotto of the Nativity with the Orthodox and the Armenians, they hold in exclusive possession sacred sites in Nazareth, Cana, Capernaum, Tabor (all in Galilee), Gethsemane, Bethany, and Bethpage (all near Jerusalem), and Mt. Nebo. With worldwide Catholic aid, they have erected many churches and chapels, notably the monumental Basilica of the Annunciation in Nazareth, completed in 1967. Their Studium Biblicum is now a section of the theological faculty of the Pontifical University of St. Anthony in Rome. The numerous religious, cultural, educational, and welfare activities of the Latin Church in Israel, Jordan, and Cyprus are supervised by the apostolic delegate, representing the Holy See.

The Uniates (the Oriental churches in communion with Rome). The Uniates are represented in Israel by comparatively small communities, except for the strong Melkite community. The Maronites number about 3,000, for the most part near the Lebanese border; the Chaldeans and the Syrian and Armenian Catholics are a mere handful. Though all Uniate patriarchs reside in the Arab countries, their jurisdiction is recognized in Israel, where they are represented by patriarchal vicars in Jerusalem. None of the Uniate churches has rights in the principal Holy Places.

The Melkites are a most significant community. They are 26,500 strong: 23,500 in their diocese of Acre and Galilee and smaller numbers in Jerusalem and in the Israel-controlled territories. Under the guidance of their former archbishop, Georges Hakim (from 1967 Patriarch Maximus v of Antioch), they made great strides, increasing numerically, building numerous churches, establishing schools and seminaries, and integrating into the country's economic and social life. Arabic of speech, Byzantine of rite, and Catholic in church allegiance, they feel that they can play an important role in inter-church, and perhaps intercommunal, relations.

ANGLICANS AND PROTESTANTS. Reformed Christianity came to the Holy Land some 150 years ago. One of its aims was missionary work among Jews and Muslims, but most of its converts came from the (Greek) Orthodox. In 1841 an Anglican bishopric was established in Jerusalem in cooperation with Prussian Lutherans, the first incumbent being Michael Solomon *Alexander, a convert from Judaism. The original accord between the English and the Germans broke down in 1881, and the bishopric was reconstituted in 1887 on a solely Anglican basis, the Lutherans carrying on independently.

Anglicanism prospered, especially in the Mandatory period, but by 1948 most of its English-speaking adherents left the country. Today the Evangelical Episcopal Church, some 3,000 strong, is overwhelmingly Arabic-speaking. The bishopric was raised to archiepiscopal rank in 1957, and the Anglican archbishop in Jerusalem presides over a synod composed of the bishops of Egypt and Libya, Sudan, Iran, and Jordan. In 1970 the church was recognized by the Israel government as a separate religious community. The Anglicans have no rights in the Church of the Holy Sepulcher, but they enjoy the privilege of occasionally celebrating in the nearby (Greek) Orthodox chapel of St. Abraham. The archbishop's own cathedral is the Collegiate Church of St. George in Jerusalem, consecrated in 1898.

German Lutherans established schools, hospices, and hospitals in the Holy Land, the best-known being the Augusta Victoria Hospice (now a hospital) on Mount Scopus, the Hospice of the Order of St. John in Jerusalem, the

Talitha Kumi School at Bayt Jālā near Bethlehem, and the German Evangelical Institute for Archaeological Research in the Holy Land. Despite setbacks as a result of the two world wars, the Lutherans have reestablished themselves. Led by a *propst*, residing in the building of the Church of the Redeemer in the Muristan area of the Old City, they now form the Evangelical Lutheran Church numbering about 1,500, mostly Arab.

Non-German Lutheran institutions include the Swedish Theological Institute in Jerusalem, the Swedish school and hospital in Bethlehem, the Finnish Missionary School in Jerusalem, and the Scandinavian Seamen's Church in Haifa. Reformed Christianity is also represented by a number of minor Protestant groups and agencies which, being mostly of foreign and recent origin, do not enjoy the status of official communities, although of course they have complete freedom of worship. These include Presbyterians, Baptists, Pentecostalians, the Society of Friends (Quakers), Adventists, and Brethren.

[Chaim Wardi]

DEVELOPMENTS AMONG THE CHRISTIAN COMMUNITIES IN THE 1970S. Despite some emigration, the Christian population of Israel and the administered areas rose from 105,000 in 1970 to over 120,000 in 1980. The 1970s were marked by manifold activities and developments in the Christian Churches, especially in Jerusalem. In addition, an unprecedented number of congresses and colloquies, seminars and study tours were conducted in Israel by Christian organizations and groups from all over the world, while local ecclesiastics represented their Churches in many overseas forums.

In addition to *Christians News from Israel* published by the Ministry of Religious Affairs, which provides a comprehensive survey of Christian life in Israel, the various communities published their own periodicals and bulletins. They included *Nea Sion* (Greek Orthodox), *Sion* (Armenian), *Terra Sancta* and *Christian Information Centre Bulletin* (Franciscan), *Jerusálem* (Latin), *Proche-Orient Chrétien* (White Fathers), *Ar-Rabita* (Greek Catholic), *Aram* (Syrian Orthodox), *Envangelische Gemeinde Jerusalem* (Lutheran), *Ha-Yahad* (Baptist), and *UCCI News* (United Christian Council in Israel). The Jerusalem Post also published a regular column, *Oekomenikos* on Christian life and developments in the country.

Holy Places. A number of major holy places, a focal point of Christian religious life, were renovated, among them the Tomb of Mary at the church in Gethsemane and the Cenacle (Room of the Last Supper). Restoration of Christianity's most venerated shrine, the Basilica of the Holy Sepulcher, entered its final stage after nearly two decades of intensive work. The Greek Orthodox and Armenian Patriarchates of Jerusalem and the Franciscan Custody of the Holy Land, the three major communities with rights of property and worship in the Basilica, embellished their respective sections and were sharing equally in the restoration of the foundations and facade, the parvis and portals, the Stone of Unction, and the floor and dome of the Rotunda. Despite the traditional sensitivity in inter-Church relations, the work in the Basilica were carried out in a spirit of cooperation, predicated on a strict adherence to the precepts of the status quo and, where agreement between the communities proved impossible, repairs were financed and executed by the Ministry of Religious Affairs, acting as a neutral agent. The ministry likewise undertook improvements at the room of the Last Supper, contested by the Moslems and Franciscans since the sixteenth century, and at Deir el-Sultan in the Basilica of the Holy Sepulcher complex, the object of a century-old conflict between the Coptic and Ethiopian Churches. The latter dispute was taken up in 1971 by a Ministerial Committee of the government which sought to move the sides towards an agreed solution. The question of ownership of the holy places and properties of the Russian Orthodox Church has been the subject of two lawsuits lodged in Israeli courts by the Russian Orthodox Church Outside Russia: one contests the control of Russian church property in pre-1967 Israel by the Moscow Patriarchate's Russian Orthodox Mission; the other seeks to annul a transaction of 1965, by which the Government of the Soviet Union sold Russian property, mainly real estate in the "Russian Compound" in Jerusalem, to the Israel Government.

Religious Life. The 1970s saw the construction and the refurbishing of tens of churches and monasteries throughout the country. The Greek Orthodox Patriarchate renovated many of its more than 50 historic monasteries and churches and built new shrines in Jericho and Shepherds' Field, near Bethlehem. The Armenian Patriarchate was putting up a magnificent new shrine on Mount Zion incorporating archaeological remains which were excavated in 1971–72 and span two and a half millennia. Among the new Catholic sanctuaries and religious institutions were an open-air basilica on the Mount of Olives, commemorating the mystery of the Ascension, a Byzantine style church being built at Tabgha to enshrine the celebrated mosaic pavement and the other remains of the $4^{th}/5^{th}$ century basilica that stood on the traditional site of the multiplication of the loaves and fishes, a church in Zababadeh in the West Bank, and a retreat house of the Sisters of St. Joseph in Abu Ghosh (Kiryat Ye'arim). The Franciscans repaired many of the shrines in their charge. The Greek Catholic (Melkite) community consecrated new churches in towns and villages in Galilee, and restored others in Jerusalem and the West Bank. The other Uniate Churches have also been active in this respect: in Jerusalem, the Maronites readied a renewed center and chapel, and the Syrian, Armenian, and Chaldean Catholics extensively renovated their respective houses of worship. There was a new Ethiopian convent in Bethany, and the small Church of the Romanian Orthodox Mission in Jerusalem was beautified. Also in the capital, the Lutheran Church of the Redeemer and St. Paul's (Anglican) Church were completely refurbished. The Church of the Latter-Day Saints (Mormons) and an ecumenical Christian group each developed a memorial garden on the Mount of Olives, offering local residents and visitors of all faiths and denominations verdant retreats for meditation and private prayer.

In 1975 the new premises of the 140-year-old Armenian theological seminary for the training of priests for the whole Armenian Church were opened during the visit to Jerusalem of the supreme head of the Armenian Church. Distinguished alumni of the seminary, among them the Patriarch of Istanbul and the Primates of Egypt, Europe, Australia and America, gathered in Jerusalem for a world congress on the contemporary situation and mission of the Armenian Church. The school of the Greek Orthodox Patriarchate, which prepares aspirants to the Brotherhood of the Holy Sepulcher, is housed in the renovated Holy Trinity monastery on Mount Zion. Catholic clergy were trained at theological academies in Jerusalem, Beit Jala, and Cremisan.

Major organizational changes in the Anglican and Lutheran churches granted a far greater degree of local autonomy than heretofore, and for the first time each was headed by an Arab bishop.

Practical steps were taken towards liturgical renewal. The Latin Patriarchate played a central role in the promulgation of catechisms and translations into Arabic of new liturgical texts. For the first time, the Syrian Orthodox Church in Jerusalem published an edition of the eucharistic liturgy in which the Syriac text in the ancient Aramaic characters is accompanied by an Arabic transcription and translation. The Armenian Patriarchate completed the translation of the New Testament into modern Western Armenian. The United Christian Council in Israel, comprising nineteen Protestant and Anglican Church representations, published several liturgical and scriptural works.

A number of the more than 40 Catholic religious orders and congregations celebrated the centenary of their presence in the Holy Land, among them the Rosary Sisters, the Italian Sisters of the Nigrizia, the White Fathers, the Christian Brothers (Frères), the Fathers of the Sacred Heart of Bétharram, and the Fathers of Our Lady of Zion. In addition, some ten new orders have arrived in the last decade.

Among the ranking prelates who came to Israel during the period under review were the Armenian Catholicos, the Orthodox Patriarchs of Russia, Georgia, Bulgaria and Romania, the Patriarch of Ethiopia, the Primate of the Russian Orthodox Church Outside Russia, a large number of Roman Catholic Cardinals and Vatican officials, the Minister General of the Franciscan order, the secretary-general of the World Council of Churches and several successive Moderators of the Church of Scotland. The total of Christian visitors and pilgrims arriving annually has risen from 100,000 in 1969 to 600,000 in 1980. In 1975 it was swelled by many Catholics who included the Holy Land in their Holy Year pilgrimage to Rome.

In 1977 a law passed by the Knesset making it illegal to promise, give, or receive material benefits in exchange for religious conversion caused a concerned reaction from the Christian communities, who felt the legislation might affect religious liberty in general and the functioning of their philanthropic institutions in particular. In reply to a petition submitted to the President of the State by the Greek Orthodox, Latin and Armenian Patriarchs and the Custos of the Holy Land, it was made clear however, that the government had no intention whatsoever of restricting in any way the religious freedom of the Christian, or any other, communities in Israel, or of impeding their pursuit of normal educational, social or philanthropic activities.

The proposed draft of the Basic Law on the Rights of Man studied in the 1970s by the Committee on Constitution, Law and Justice of the Knesset, and particularly the sections dealing with religious freedom, aroused considerable interest among Christian bodies and interfaith groups.

Education. The Church authorities expanded and remodeled many of their 85 schools which had an enrollment of some 20,000, including a large number of Muslims. These schools are directed and, to a large degree, financed, by the various Churches. At the request of the Greek Catholics, however, the government recently assumed the burden of the teachers' salaries in their schools.

There was a marked rise in the number of Christian students, theologians and clergy coming to Israel from all parts of the globe, with an increasing number from the Third World, to participate in courses given by some thirty local religious centers. Among the new programs opened for them in Jerusalem were the sessions of spiritual renewal organized by the White Fathers for members of the Order working in Africa; courses at the Inter-Community Bible Center of Bethesda; the seven-month program of the Dormition Abbey's "Beit Yosef" on Mount Zion, for theology students from West Germany, Austria and Switzerland; courses at Ratisbonne monastery directed by the Congregation of Our Lady of Zion and the Fathers of Zion; the study project for Mormon students from Brigham Young University in the United States; the annual seminars for Dutch and Belgian theologians; and the one-year program at The Hebrew University which is sponsored by West German Protestant Churches. The Institute of Holy Land Studies (Protestant), St. George's College (Anglican), and the renovated Swedish Theological Institute (Lutheran) expanded their existing study programs. An Ecumenical African Institute for Biblical Studies was set up in Jerusalem to help African clergymen and theologians explore the sources of their Christian faith. At the new Mater Ecclesiae Center in Tiberias, nuns from Asia and Africa attend six month sessions of spiritual renewal.

Many of these projects benefited from a close cooperation between local Christian and Jewish scholars. A most significant example was the program initiated in 1975 by the prestigious Pontifical Biblical Institute (Jesuit), which brought students from Africa, Asia, Europe and the Americas under the tuition of scholars from The Hebrew University of Jerusalem. These studies constitute a basic part of the three-year course at the Pontifical Biblical Institute in Rome leading to

Licenciate in Sacred Scripture, which prepares priests as instructors in Catholic seminaries throughout the Christian *oecumene*.

A Dominican scholar in Jerusalem, who was consultant to the Vatican Commission for Religious Relations with the Jews, was appointed head of the philosophy department at The Hebrew University of Jerusalem.

Social and Cultural Activities. The Christian Churches were attentive to the social and cultural needs of their communities and, during the 1970s, a number of new institutions and services were added to the scores already existing.

In Bethlehem, the ultra-modern Caritas Baby Hospital and the Ephpheta Institute for deaf-mute children were opened under Catholic patronage; the unique Institute of Medical Genetics and Twin Studies, on Mt. Olives, staffed by the recently arrived Congregation of the Handmaids of the Sacred Heart, was steadily being developed, while, nearby, the Polish Sisters of Saint Elizabeth established an orphanage for girls. The Lutheran World Federation and Catholic Relief Services instituted a number of new projects, several of them in cooperation with the Ministry of Social Affairs and the Military Government in the West Bank. The Greek Orthodox and Armenian Patriarchates opened new health centers in Jerusalem. In Haifa, homes for the aged were inaugurated by the Greek Catholics and the Lutherans.

Community centers were set up by the Greek Orthodox in a number of towns. The Greek Catholics opened such centers in villages in Galilee and instituted mobile library services in that area.

Two major cultural institutions being developed in the capital have won wide acclaim. For the first time, the accumulated art treasures of the centuries-old Armenian community in Jerusalem were put on permanent display to the public in a forty-room museum which was opened in 1979 in the Armenian Quarter of the Old City. The exhibits include ritual objects, illuminated manuscripts, icons, painted tiles, copper work, mosaics and tapestries. The Notre Dame of Jerusalem Center, which was formally decreed a "Pontifical Institute" in 1978, is to include a hostel for pilgrims, an arts and crafts pavilion where Christian artisans will have facilities for creating and displaying their works, and a large meeting-hall electronically equipped for simultaneous translations for the use of local Catholic communities and pilgrim groups.

A number of Christian clergy were awarded the title of "Distinguished Citizen of Jerusalem" (*Yakir Yerushalayim*) for their contributions to the spiritual and cultural life of the capital.

Ecumenical and Interfaith. Several new ventures were helping the cause of positive relations and cooperation among the various Christian communities. Foremost among them was the Ecumenical Institute for Advanced Theological Studies at Tantur, near Jerusalem, inaugurated in 1972. It provided a place where Christian theologians from all over the world could come together to pursue their own research and to participate in a community dedicated to the recovery of Christian unity through theological study, in the environs in which the Church first came into existence. The Institute seeks also to take advantage of its location in the midst of Jewish and Muslim cultures. In 1979 the Institute launched a major project of research and reflection of Christianity in the Holy Land.

A different undertaking is the Christian Information Center which opened its doors in 1973 in the Old City of Jerusalem. The Center gathers and dispenses information on behalf of all the Christian Churches. The ecumenical spirit is also evident in the increasing participation by Christians from all denominations in the annual Week of Prayer for Christian Unity, and in the activities of the Ecumenical Theological Research Fraternity in Israel.

Reference has already been made to the cooperation between Christian and Jewish scholars in Israel. Christian involvement in groups such as the Israel Interfaith Committee and the Rainbow Group is also noteworthy, as are the "Hope" seminars initiated in 1973, and the appearance, in 1972, of a semi-annual bulletin of religious thought in Israel, *Immanuel*, published by the Ecumenical Fraternity. Two significant interfaith symposia were organized in 1980, one on the occasion of the 15th centenary of the birth of St. Benedict, the other commemorating Armenian Martyr's Day and entitled "Genocide and Collective Responsibility."

Initiatives of another kind are the interfaith Neve Shalom center on land near Latrun, and Nes Amim, a Protestant moshav (co-operative farm village) in Western Galilee, which in 1975 inaugurated a new center to house seminars and study projects which further its ideal of promoting understanding between Jews and Christians through constructive co-existence. A second Protestant moshav, Yad ha-Shemonah, was under development near Abu-Ghosh by a group from Finland. An international Christian "embassy" was opened in Jerusalem by evangelical Christians who wish to demonstrate and promote Christian support for Israel.

In the main, Christian involvement in interreligious activities in Israel remained limited, and was primarily the province of western Christians. The political situation, the lack of a tradition of pluralism among Oriental Churches, and the essential western character of interreligious contacts in Israel tended to minimize the participation of the predominantly Arab indigenous Churches.

Generally speaking, the Churches continued to follow a policy of neutrality in the political realm. In internal matters, such as religious life, administration, culture and education, they maintained their traditional independence.

[Daniel Rossing]

THE 1980S AND AFTER. According to the Central Bureau of Statistics, the estimated Christian population of the State of Israel at the end of 1991 was 128,000, compared with 94,170 Christian inhabitants counted in the 1983 decennial census. Estimates vary greatly regarding the extent to which this number has been augmented by Russian and Ethiopian Christians who arrived in Israel with the most recent waves of immigration from those countries. On the other hand, Christian sources note that in the face of continuing political tension and an uncertain future in the Middle East, a growing number of Christian families in Jerusalem and the Territories have now chosen emigration to the West.

The various strands – Christian, Israeli, Arab, Palestinian – intertwined in the identities of Christians in the land, have been colored by political conflicts in the area during the past decade. The civil and religious strife in Lebanon and renewed contact with fellow-Christians there in the wake of the 1982 War in Lebanon, stirred, especially among Christians in Galilee, stronger feelings of identity with their particular Christian community. The protracted *intifada*, on the other hand, has induced many Christians living in Jerusalem and the Territories to accentuate their Palestinian identity and advocate solidarity with their Muslim neighbors, despite, or perhaps because of, rising Islamic fundamentalism. In the latter circumstance, some Christians have begun to formulate a Palestinian Christian "theology of liberation," designed to strengthen local Christians in their Palestinian context and identity. Church leaders in Jerusalem on their part have issued with increasing frequency joint public statements and pastoral letters expressing their deep dismay over the suffering of their faithful. Israel government officials in turn have accused Church leaders of being one-sided in their political positions, and fault them for their failure to speak out on Palestinian violence and their refusal to publicly acknowledge recurrent instances of Muslim extremism directed against their members and institutions.

The sensitive situation of the Christian communities in the present political climate was brought to the fore in 1990 by the St. John's Hospice Affair. Over the past decade, Muslims have continued without opposition to purchase, lease, or rent many properties in the Christian Quarter of Jerusalem's Old City. However, when a group of Orthodox Jews managed, with assistance from the Ministry of Housing, to sub-lease and subsequently take up residence in a building in the vicinity of the Holy Sepulcher owned by the Greek Orthodox Patriarchate, Christians felt obliged to protest loudly in order to avert Muslim accusations of collusion with Zionist designs. The initial support for the Christian side which was forthcoming from many Jewish circles weakened significantly when the Greek Orthodox Patriarch of Jerusalem, Diodoros I, traveled to Rome to enlist the support of the pope, and to Damascus where President Assad readily offered his help to defend the Christians of the Holy Land.

In line with a process of indigenization in evidence throughout the Catholic world, for the first time in the history of the Latin Patriarchate a local Arab Christian, Monsignor Michel Assad Sabbaḥ, took office as Latin Patriarch in Jerusalem in January 1988. During the past decade his Church and the various Uniate Catholic communities have dedicated a significant number of new houses of worship and refurbished many of their older churches and convents throughout the country. The spiritual life of the local Catholic Church has been strengthened by the arrival of 11 additional religious orders and congregations, and by the publication of a new missal and lectionnaire in Arabic in accord with the liturgical reforms recommended by the Second Vatican Council.

Through official visits to the leaders of Orthodox Churches abroad, and by hosting them in Jerusalem, the Greek Orthodox patriarch of Jerusalem has attempted to reassert the centrality of Jerusalem as the "Mother" Church of the Christian oecumene. For the first time in several centuries, representatives of Orthodox Churches from throughout the world gathered in Jerusalem in October 1986 at his initiative to discuss issues of world peace. The patriarch has also labored to more effectively capitalize on the extensive real estate holdings of his Church, in order to generate the funds required for an ambitious project of renovation of the Patriarchate's historic shrines and convents throughout the country. The Palestinian laity of his community, both in Israel and in Jordan, have lobbied ever more forcefully for a greater say in the affairs of the Patriarchate and for the redirecting of its resources to educational and welfare projects for their benefit.

In February 1990, Yegishe Derderian passed away after 30 years of service as Armenian Patriarch during which the Jerusalem Patriarchate played a central role in the religious and cultural life of the Armenian diaspora. Under the leadership of his successor, Archbishop Torkom Manoogian, renewed access to the Armenian homeland has brought benefit to the community, but also the burden of the tragedies and tribulations of their fellow-Armenians living there.

The religio-political divide within the Protestant communities in the country has widened during the last decade. Among those who deeply identify with Jews, whether as an affirmation of the Jewish roots of their faith or with an aim to pave a path for missionary inroads, western evangelical circles close to the International Christian Embassy have been ever more vocal in their political support for the State of Israel, at times in ways which have irritated the indigenous Churches. On the other hand, most Arab Protestants and many of the expatriate Christians who work among and empathize with them, have adopted a much more critical posture vis-à-vis the State of Israel and endeavor to distance themselves from any religious or political links, past or present, with Israel.

Holy Places. Significant progress has been made in the restoration of major Christian shrines throughout the country. Renovations in the Church of the Holy Sepulcher have continued, although in parts of the basilica progress is still impeded by age-old disputes concerning the Status Quo. The three principal communities – Greek Orthodox, Armenian, and Latin – have completed most of the works of restoration and beautification in the sections of the shrine held respectively by them, and have finally jointly agreed concerning the embellishment of the ceiling of the dome of the Rotunda, darkened for decades by the ugly scaffolding left in place pending the outcome of their deliberations. The Civil Administration in Judea and Samaria has repeatedly patched the roof of the Basilica of the Nativity in Bethlehem but has not been able to achieve agreement among the Churches concerning the major repairs called for since the days of the British Mandate. The annual general cleaning of that shrine has become in recent years the scene of altercations between the three main communities. Both the Egyptian and Ethiopian governments have continued to actively press for a resolution of the long-standing Coptic-Ethiopian dispute over Deir al-Sultan, the monastery on the roof of the Holy Sepulcher, which would favor their respective countrymen.

Among other holy places which have been reconstructed or undergone repairs are the Church of the Multiplication of the Loaves and Fishes at Tabgha, the traditional house of St. Peter in Capernaum, over which a controversial octagonal "memorial" structure has been erected, and the Tomb of the Virgin near the Garden of Gethsemane. The Cenacle on Mount Zion, traditional site of the Last Supper, has been refurbished by the present caretaker, the Ministry for Religious Affairs, and the East Jerusalem Development Corporation has esthetically renovated the Via Dolorosa. The traditional place of the baptism of Jesus at Qasr al Yahud, located in a closed security zone along the Jordan River southeast of Jericho, remains inaccessible to the general public, but in recent years the Civil Administration in the Administered Territories has made arrangements for an annual Catholic pilgrimage to the site, and for the Orthodox celebration of the Feast of Epiphany there. The Government Tourist Corporation has developed baptismal facilities for the convenience of pilgrim groups along the Jordan river just south of the Sea of Galilee.

Education, Social, and Cultural. Nearly all the Christian schools in the State of Israel, with the exception of those in East Jerusalem, have in the course of the last decade received official recognition from the Ministry of Education and Culture and now benefit from extensive funding from the state budget, which has made it possible for them to expand and improve their programs. Christian schools in the Territories have been severely affected by the civil unrest and repeated closures during the Intifada. However, there too Christian educational activities have continued to expand, for example through additional facilities inaugurated at Bethlehem University and at the Salesian Technical School in Bethlehem, as well as through a new theological seminary opened in the village of Beit Sahour by the Greek (Melkite) Catholic Church.

The dozens of study frameworks available to Christians from abroad have been augmented by the Vatican-sponsored Centre Chrétien des Etudes Juives opened in Jerusalem in 1987 at the Monastery of Saint Pierre de Sion (Ratisbonne). The new graduate institute is run under the academic direction of the Institut Catholique de Paris, and, like many other Christian study programs in Israel, benefits from close collaboration with The Hebrew University. Among Jewish educational institutions in the capital which have developed special study programs for Christians are the Shalom Hartman Institute for Advanced Jewish Studies and the Melitz Centers for Jewish-Zionist Education.

A protracted controversy surrounding the construction of a new Mormon Church-affiliated Brigham Young University study center on Mount Scopus was defused by a written undertaking of officials of the Church that the center's staff and students will scrupulously refrain from any missionary activity in the country.

The local Churches, with the financial support of western coreligionists, have devoted increasing attention to the social and cultural needs of their communities. The Greek, Armenian, and Coptic Orthodox, as well as the Latin, Syrian, Greek, and Maronite Catholics, have all established additional community and retreat centers or expanded existing facilities.

Several Churches have initiated much-needed housing projects for Christian residents. Christian medical services have been expanded and improved, *inter alia*, at the Caritas Baby Hospital and the Holy Family Maternity Hospital in Bethlehem and at the Scottish Hospital in Nazareth. Historical museums have been opened to the public in Jerusalem by the Latins, Armenians, Greek Orthodox, and Greek Catholics. During the past decade many of the Christian hospices have been renovated and modernized to meet the needs of today's pilgrim.

The Jerusalem Municipality has honored several Christian personalities with the title "Distinguished Citizen of Jerusalem" and, in January 1987, the Knesset paid special tribute to "Righteous Gentiles" living in Israel.

Ecumenical and Interfaith. Ecumenical and interfaith activities in Israel have continued to attract primarily persons of Western background. Attempts to involve representatives of the dominantly eastern or Arab Christian population have met with little success. Ecumenical contacts among local Christians have focused mainly on discussion of political rather than theological issues. Steps were taken to establish an Arab Christian-Muslim dialogue, but significant progress was impeded by difficulties, magnified by present political realities, in coming to grips with the less than happy history of Muslim-Christian relations in the region.

The opening of formal talks between representatives of the Vatican and the Government of Israel in 1992 was received with mixed emotions by many Christians in the country. There is, on the one hand, deep apprehension that official Vatican recognition of the State of Israel might imperil their fragile relations with their Muslim neighbors, and on the other, the cautious hope that formal agreements between the State and the Vatican will clarify and even enhance their position in local society. Both the Government and the Vatican have stressed that the outcome of the talks will in no way prejudice the existing Status Quo in the Holy Places, and that any rights and privileges which might be secured by the Catholic Churches and institutions would be extended to other Christian communities in the country as well.

The most noteworthy event of the decade was Pope John Paul II's millennium visit to Israel in 2000, with tens of thousands of Christian pilgrims coming in his wake. The pope celebrated mass at the Church of the Holy Sepulcher, as well as in Nazareth, and visited Yad Vashem.

At the beginning of 2005 there were 117,000 Christians in Israel, constituting 2% of the population. The demographic balance between Muslim and Christian Arabs has changed in mixed towns. In Nazareth, for example, the biggest Arab city in Israel with a population of 62,000 in 2002, the balance went from near parity to a 67% percent majority for the Muslims, their new-found hegemony creating tensions, as in their attempt to build a mosque near the Church of the Annunciation.

The internal breakdown of the Christian community in Israel is as follows: 37% Greek Catholic, 30% Greek Orthodox, 23% Latin Catholic, 5% Maronite, and 5% others.

[Daniel Rossing]

Muslims

UNDER TURKISH RULE. Islam drew no distinction between "church" and state, for the latter had both political and religious functions. The Muslims of the Holy Land, therefore, saw no reason to organize as a community. They felt that they were the state, and the government should put their needs first. It was the non-Muslims who needed communal organizations recognized by the authorities and enjoying internal autonomy to protect their interests. The Muslims were almost all Sunnites, most of them, especially in the villages, belonging to the Shāfiʿī school, though the Shariʿa (Muslim religious) courts were conducted according to the Ḥanafi school, prevalent in the towns. Religious life in the countryside followed tradition, receiving inspiration and content from the mosques and the tombs of holy men. In some of the villages, especially the district of Samaria, renowned for its religious fervor, orders of zealots developed which maintained *zawāyā* (small prayer houses) as meeting places for their adherents. Traditional religious education was given in both town and village, the imam serving as teacher, in addition to his other duties. These classes were replaced in the course of time by more modern schools, which were taken over by the British Mandatory government. The pilgrimage to Mecca was the aspiration of all, even the poor making great efforts to get there despite the expense and danger involved, and the return of a pilgrim was a major event. Sufi orders maintained *zawāyā* and *takāyā* (hostels) in Jerusalem, where lodgings were provided for pilgrims on their way to Mecca and bread and soup for the poor, drawing their revenues from waqf (religious trust) funds and contributions from the pilgrims. Such institutions were founded by immigrants from North Africa, India, Bukhara, and Afghanistan.

However, the charitable and educational institutions which the Egyptian rulers had founded in the Ayyubid period, especially in Jerusalem around the Al-Aqṣā Mosque, were in a state of progressive decline. They depended for their maintenance on the waqf revenues, estimated to total 40,000 Turkish pounds, which the government sent to Constantinople, instead of devoting them to the purposes for which they were destined. This was one of the grounds for the dissatisfaction expressed in the Arabic newspapers that started to appear after the revolt of the Young Turks in 1908. Articles were published denouncing the neglect of educational and religious establishments, which was said to have led to a religious and spiritual decline. The writers demanded that the government use the income from the charitable trusts for the maintenance of the institutions and the establishment of new ones, such as a college for religious studies and a vocational school for the children of the poor, aid for the distressed and indigent, and the preservation of the Muslim holy places, some of which were beginning to pass into Christian hands. Fears were expressed for the future of the younger generation, many of whom were being educated in schools run by foreigners, whose teachings were not compatible with Ottoman loyalty or the principles of Islam.

These demands fell upon deaf ears – Turkey was too preoccupied with her wars to pay attention to them. One new religious institution, al-Madrasa al-Ṣalāḥiyya, a training college for religious functionaries, was opened in Jerusalem during World War I in order to counteract the influence of religious leaders in the service of the British, but was shut down when the war ended.

UNDER BRITISH RULE. The passage from four centuries of Ottoman rule to the rule of a Christian government did not, at first, present serious problems for the Muslims. The experienced officials of the British military administration, transferred from Egypt to deal with civilian affairs, did much for religious life. Festivals were celebrated with great splendor under the patronage of the British authorities; plans were prepared for the repair of the Al-Aqṣā Mosque, and the expenses of the annual pilgrimage to Nebi Mūsā (the reputed tomb of the Prophet Moses) were borne by the government. In 1921 the Palestine Administration set up the Muslim Higher Council, a secular body, which managed the religious and judicial affairs of the community, ran the charitable trusts, and was responsible for maintaining mosques. Subject to government approval, it appointed religious judges and functionaries, as well as inspectors and other officials. The Council did little, however, to further religious life. Its attempt, in 1922–23, to set up a secondary school in Jerusalem to train religious functionaries was a failure. The only institution of the kind was the al-Jazzār school in the mosque of that name in Acre.

During the period of British rule, however, nationalist trends, previously not in evidence, came into prominence, working in close alliance with religion. From its inception, the Muslim Higher Council introduced the religious element into the Arabs' political struggle against the Jews. Mass celebrations of Islamic festivals became political demonstrations, often ending in violence. The younger generation was inflamed by religious fanaticism and incited to attack the Jews. Delegations were sent to all Islamic countries to warn the faithful of the danger of Jewish domination over the Al-Aqṣā Mosque, the third in importance in the Muslim world. As a result of the efforts of the mufti of Jerusalem, Hajj Amim *al-Husseini, a Muslim Congress was held in Jerusalem in 1931, which helped to weld Muslim solidarity while furthering the mufti's political ambitions.

The Council was widely criticized in the Muslim community for its commercial enterprises, the preferential treatment of the favored few, the neglect of the villages and their religious functionaries, and the failure to build new mosques and further post-primary education. After the Arab revolt of 1936–39 some of the council's members were dismissed, and it passed to government control. Several groups and institutions freed themselves from its domination and there was a revival of interest in religious life and education. In Haifa, for example, the improving economic situation and the desire to compete with local Christian institutions stimulated the Muslims to establish their own charitable trusts and educational institutions. After World War II a number of societies and clubs were set up to intensify devotion to Islam and reform Muslim social life on the basis of Islamic principles. The Muslim Brotherhood, founded in Egypt, established a few branches in Palestine.

UNDER ISRAELI RULE. The end of the British Mandate saw the complete collapse of Muslim public life. Most of the religious leaders, who had played a prominent part in political activity, fled the country. The religious judiciary crumbled and the charitable trusts were abandoned. Great difficulty was experienced in finding replacements for religious judges and functionaries, especially in the towns, and the whole system of Shariʿa courts had to be reconstructed, with the aid of Sheikh Ṭahir al-Ṭabarī, the only qadi who remained. For the first time in the history of the relations between Judaism and Islam, Jewish authorities had to be responsible for organizing Muslim religious life.

The Israeli government, through the Ministry of Religious Affairs, took steps to restore the institutions of the Muslim community. Shariʿa courts were set up in Jaffa, Acre, Haifa, Nazareth, and Ṭayyiba (for the central region, where Muslims are numerous) and religious functionaries appointed under the authority of the qadis to mosques in towns and villages. Muslim advisory commissions were set up in Jaffa, Ramleh, Lydda, Haifa, and Acre to look after holy places and promote religious and welfare services. The revenues of the waqf properties, which were administered by the Custodian of Absentee Property, were used to finance the work of the commissions in religious education, health, and welfare, as well as the repair of mosques and the erection of new ones. The management of the holy places was entrusted to the Muslim Department of the Ministry of Religious Affairs, and the government assumed responsibility for the salaries of religious judges and functionaries. By a law of 1965, the Custodian of Absentee Property was empowered to release waqf properties, the fruits of which were destined for religious purposes, education, and welfare to committees of trustees, which replaced the advisory commissions, appointed wherever there were waqf properties and Muslim communities.

The adaptation of Muslim life to the laws of the land was a relatively smooth process. There was understanding, on the whole, for the laws that made primary education compulsory for girls as well as boys, fixed the minimum age of marriage for girls at 17, gave women equal rights, prohibited bigamy and regulated divorce. These were not found to be in conflict with Muslim doctrine; the Israel Supreme Court ruled, for example, that polygamy is not obligatory under Islam.

There were about 100 mosques in pre-1967 Israel, over 20 of which had been built after 1948 – notably the Mosque of Peace in Nazareth, the first to be erected to serve the city's 16,000 Muslims. Many mosques were restored with the government's assistance: for example, it contributed over IL 100,000 to repair the mosque of al-Jazzār in Acre. Some 200 religious functionaries receive monthly government stipends. The four Shariʿa courts (the one at Jaffa also has authority over Jerusalem), exercise exclusive jurisdiction over members of the community in matters of personal status, such as marriage, divorce, and inheritance.

The Circassians are one of the minority communities in Israel, adhering to the Muslim faith and numbering about 3,000. When their country, Cherkessia, was subjugated by Russia in 1864, a mass emigration to Turkey took place, some of the refugees later settling in Galilee, where they now inhabit two villages, *Kafr Kama and *al-Riḥaniyya. Circassian (Adyghe) was an unwritten language when they emigrated, and though they still speak it, the language of instruction in their schools is Arabic. Wishing to overcome this drawback, they applied to the Israel Ministry of Education for assistance, and Professor J.C. Catford of the University of Michigan, a specialist in Caucasian and general linguistics, agreed to come and help them learn the Cyrillic orthography now used for their language in the U.S.S.R. He completed a six-week course in Kafr Kama in August 1973. Owing to the absence of teachers and materials, however, it was found impossible to implement this arrangement and, in 1978, following recommendations by a committee appointed by the Ministry of Education, it was decided that all subjects in the school in Kafr Kama would be taught in Hebrew, a measure which was to be extended to al-Riḥaniyya, too. A specialist appointed by the Ministry was to prepare a curriculum and texts in Circassian history and culture. The Circassians are conscripted for service in the Israel Defense Forces and serve in the Israel police.

There are some 600 members of the Aḥmadiyya sect in Kabābīr near Haifa; they conduct missionary activities. Acre is the center of the Shādhiliyya movement of Sufis, the founders of which are buried in the sect's *zāwiyā* in the town.

Religious life follows its traditional path, Fridays and the festivals of Islam being recognized as official holidays for Muslims. The government of Israel declared its readiness to facilitate pilgrimages to Mecca, but the Arab states refused to cooperate. The Arabic station of the Israel Broadcasting Authority broadcasts daily readings from the Koran, as well as prayers and sermons on Fridays and Muslim festivals. Religion is taught in primary and post-primary schools; the teachers are specially trained and religious textbooks compiled. The popular traditional festivities, such as the pilgrimages to the tombs of Sayyidunā Ali near Herzilyyah and Nabī Ṣāliḥ at Ramleh, have been revived. For the first time in the history of the Muslims in the Holy Land, a regular government publication is issued (by the Muslim Department of the Ministry of Religious Affairs) containing the decisions of the courts and views on major Muslim religious problems.

After the Six-Day War. The reunification of Jerusalem after the 1967 war enabled all Muslims in Israel, for the first time since 1948, to pray at the Al-Aqṣā Mosque, since previously, as Israelis, they could not cross the armistice lines. However, the qadis of the Shariʿa courts in East Jerusalem, who continued to receive their salaries from the Jordanian government and obeyed its political directives, remained unwilling to come to an arrangement with the Israeli authorities on the regulation of matters of Muslim personal status. Other Muslim religious officials were paid by the waqf. The qadi of Jaffa, who had authority over Jerusalem, appointed three marriage registrars for the Muslims of the Holy City, who celebrated about 700 weddings for couples from Jerusalem up to 1970. The Shariʿa court in Jaffa also dealt with about 200 cases submitted by Jerusalem Muslims.

The situation in the Israel-administered areas of Samaria and Judea, where the waqf administration looked after mosque repairs and paid the religious functionaries, was somewhat similar, while in the Gaza Strip the latter, as well as the qadis, received their stipends from the government of Israel. In all the areas the Shariʿa courts continued to function in the same way as under Jordanian or Egyptian rule. The Israeli authorities provided facilities for Muslims from the administered areas to go on pilgrimage to Mecca, but the Arab governments concerned still refused to extend the privilege to Muslim citizens of Israel.

Despite the continued lack of religious leaders of stature, Islam serves as a general unifying factor in the Arab Muslim community. However, the practice of religion among them, as among other communities, is on the decline, particularly among the intellectuals and the city workers. This is due to the advance in education, the rise in the standard of living, the change in the status of women, the modernization of the towns and the countryside, and contact with new ways of life and thought, which have weakened the bonds of tradition and patriarchal discipline.

[Jacob Yehoshua]

Religious Life in the 1970s. Considerable improvement was made in everything pertaining to the religious life of the Arabs in Israel during the 1970s. The following areas are of note:

(1) The Haj – Although as early as 1959 the Government of Israel granted permission for Israeli Arabs to make the pilgrimage to Mecca, on the sole condition that Saudi Arabia guarantee their safety, it was not until 1978 that the necessary permission was granted by Jordan (for transit) and by Saudi Arabia. The minister of religion sent his greetings to the 2,700 pilgrims who took advantage of this permission and expressed the hope that they would pray in Mecca for peace in the Middle East.

(2) The Shari'a (Muslim Courts of Law) – These courts were established in Acre, Haifa, Jaffa, Nazareth, Taibeh and Beersheva, but the last was subject to the jurisdiction of the Kadi of Taibeh, and that of Haifa to Acre. The Arabs of East Jerusalem were subject to the jurisdiction of Jaffa, and they had three officials authorized by the Court of Jaffa to deal with registration of marriages. For the first time the Supreme Shari'a of Appeals was established in Jerusalem which had two permanent Kadis.

The Shari'a Courts have a wider jurisdiction than the Rabbinical Courts.

(3) Mosques – Considerable work has been done with regard to the repair and extension of existing mosques, and the erection of new ones, both in the cities and in Arab villages. Subventions were granted both by the Wakf and the Ministry of Religions, but considerable contributions were made by the local inhabitants, and the erection of the mosques in the villages of Iksal and Makre cost 4 million lira.

The Bedouin, who are gradually turning to permanent settlement, established mosques in their settlements; one was established in Bir el Maksur in the Galilee, and another in Shaval in the Negev. Extensive work was also done in the repair and establishment of cemeteries.

(4) Religious Officials – Imams, conductors of religious services and marriage officers, unlike the kadis, were recognized as permanent government employees under Turkish rule and during the period of the British Mandate, but since the establishment of the State they have been in receipt of increasing stipends by the government. Their request, however, for recognition as government employees had not yet been acceded to as of 1980.

(5) Freedom of Religion – The contacts established after the Six-Day War between the Muslims of Israel and those of the West Bank and Gaza, who were much more meticulous in their religious observance and more under the influence of their religious leaders, brought about a change in the religious atmosphere of the Muslims in Israel. Through the leaders of the local councils they have stated that they will continue to be loyal to their nationality and, at the same time, they will make every effort to revive their traditional culture and language, as loyal citizens of Israel, and will cooperate with its institutions and citizens. Although a request by the Muslim authorities to the government, after the establishment of the State, to be permitted to continue their previous practice of punishing Muslims who flouted the religious restrictions applying to the month of Ramadan, was refused, a similar request from the Shari'a courts in the West Bank was being increasingly acceded to. The communications media devoted

considerable time to Muslim religious programs, particularly during the month of Ramadan.

There was a noticeable tendency on the part of Muslims in Israel to demonstrate to their coreligionists in the West Bank that their religious loyalties are no less than theirs, and this constitutes the stimulus behind their demands for a better religious education, the training of religious ministrants, and the erection of mosques. The Muslim religious quarterly which was distributed among religious leaders and Orientalists in the various universities, and which reflected all the development in the religious life of the Muslims and the decisions of the Shari'a courts, ceased publication after 15 years with the retirement of its editor, the director of the Muslim Department of the Ministry of Religious Affairs.

The Muslims, who constitute 80% of the Arabs of Israel, suffer from a severe lack of religious officials. The Ahamadiah School, attached to the al-Jazzar mosque in Acre, which trained the secondary officials referred to above, was closed in 1948 for lack of students, and the closing of the gates of the religious universities in Egypt to Israeli Muslims brought about a diminution in the supply of higher ranking officials. A religious college established in Hebron after the Six-Day War, supported by the Ministry of Religions, attracted a considerable number of students. Similar institutions exist in East Jerusalem and Gaza, but the lack of religious officials is still sorely felt, and at a conference of local heads of councils of the Triangle held in February 1979, a demand was put forward for the establishment of an institution for their training. The Arab department of the Ministry of Education took steps in recent years to deepen religious education among Muslims, and a special department for this purpose exists in the Teachers' Training College in Haifa.

A number of laws were passed by the Knesset regulating the personal status of Moslems.

A law, promulgated in 1972, granting subsidies from the National Insurance to divorced or deserted Muslim wives, after a decision of the Shari'a courts, was enthusiastically received, and the Kadi of Nazareth stated that it was unique in the Muslim world.

Two other laws, however, were received with reservations. The one gave an option to couples to divide assets acquired after their marriage either equally, in the case of divorce, according to civil law should the couple so desire, or according to Muslim law which does not recognize such a right; and the second law accorded the same choice with regard to inheritance.

Dr. Subhi Abu Gosh, the director of the Shari'a courts, declared that all the laws promulgated by the State since its establishment, such as that of equal rights for women, of the prohibition of bigamy, minimum age of marriage, divorce by mutual consent, etc., had paved the way for these new laws.

The Muslim religious authorities have one grievance, however. The rabbinical courts have the right to permit a married man to take a second wife in exceptional cases, provided the decision to that effect by the Beth Din receives the approval of the two Chief Rabbis, whereas in the case of the Shari'a courts this permission is specifically confined to cases of mental illness on the part of the first wife, or absence of the wife for a continuous period of at least seven years. The Muslim authorities demand the same exemptions as those granted by the rabbinic courts. In point of fact, however, in practice, under no circumstances do the Chief Rabbis grant permission for a Jew to take a second wife where there is any possibility of him living with two wives, and confine it to mental cases or desertion by the wife, as is the case with the Shari'a courts.

The 1980s and After. Since the establishment of the State of Israel, the Muslim religious institutions have changed considerably. Due to the growing number of the Muslim population (over 19% of the total population in 2005, constituting 82% of Israel's Arab population), many needs and problems have emerged. Some of these problems have been solved, while others still await solutions.

The Muslim courts, called Shari'a courts after the name of the Muslim law, are located in areas which are heavily inhabited by Muslims. There are seven regional courts covering all the areas in Israel which are inhabited by Muslims: Acre, Haifa, Nazareth, Jaffa, Taibeh, Jerusalem, and Beersheba.

There is also the Shari'a Court of Appeal, which according to the law is located in Jerusalem. According to the law, every kadi is automatically considered a member of the Court of Appeal; however, it is possible to hold the sessions of the Court of Appeal with only two members present.

Shari'a courts implement the Shari'a law, the dominant law in those courts, and have the sole authority to deal with matters of personal status, according to articles 51 and 52 of the Palestine Order in Council of 1922.

These matters include marriage, divorce, custody, maintenance, and other personal issues. Israeli law has narrowed the courts' authorities in specific issues such as inheritance, where the law gives parallel authority to the Civil District Court. The Shari'a Court is not allowed to deal with cases of inheritance unless all beneficiaries sign an agreement for that matter.

The Israeli law prohibits Muslim men to divorce their wives without their consent. Moreover, it prohibits bigamy and the marriage of under-age girls (those under the age of 17 years). Should such violations take place, although they are permitted by the Shari'a law, it is the kadi's responsibility to notify the authorities. These laws, in addition to the Law of Equal Rights for Men and Women of 1951, have caused dramatic positive changes in the status of Muslim women.

The increase in the Muslim population and the growth of religious movements among Muslim youths has led to a noticeable increase in building houses of worship for religious services. New mosques have been constructed and old ones have been renovated or expanded. In the mid-1990s there were around 250 mosques in Israel, four times as many as in 1967. The budget needed for such enterprises comes, mainly, from contributions of local Muslim organizations and individuals, in addition to a sum of money donated by the Ministry of Religious Affairs. Another source of support is the revenues of the Muslim Waqf (religious trust).

In several towns (such as Jaffa, Ramleh, Lydda, Haifa and Acre) the government has appointed special committees, in order to administer the Waqf's properties in these places, to collect the rentals, and to spend them on religious projects, mainly maintenance of mosques. The most famous project, with which the Waqf committee of Jaffa was involved was the reconstruction of Hassan Bey Mosque. Hundreds of Muslim functionaries are working in the religious sphere of life in addition to the kadis and the clerks of the Shari'a courts. This group includes: Imams – conductors of religious services; Muezzins – those who call for prayers; and Ma'zuns – writers of marriage contracts. The first two groups (about 270 persons) were not considered as government officials and were deprived of all kinds of social benefits such as pensions, widows' allowances, clothing, recreation, etc. After a lengthy struggle in 1981, 214 functionaries achieved the status of state employees with all the mentioned benefits. The third group, composed of writers of marriage contracts, are appointed by the kadis each in his own region and have no rights whatsoever. The income of this group is gained by collecting fixed fees upon writing of the marriage contract from the partners concerned.

Until 1978, Muslims in Israel were denied the right to fulfill the fifth religious pillar of Islam – the Hajj, i.e., the pilgrimage to the holy places of Mecca and Medina in Saudi Arabia. In 1978 an unwritten agreement between Israel, Jordan, and Saudi Arabia made possible the carrying out of the Hajj for thousands of Muslims in Israel.

The mass media in both Israel and the neighboring Arab countries broadcast special programs on various religious occasions such as Ramadan – the month of fasting, *'id al-Fitr*, the feast which marks the end of Ramadan; *'id ad-Adha* the feast of sacrifice; the Prophet Muhammad's Birthday; the Hijra New Year and other occasions. The Friday prayers are usually broadcast live by these stations.

[Awni Habash]

Bahāʾī Faith

The Bahāʾī Faith is a world religion whose center is in Ereẓ Israel. Named after its founder, Bahāʾ Allāh ("The Splendor of God"), Bahaism developed out of the Bābī, a Ṣufi (Muslim mystical) movement, which was founded in 1844 in Persia. It upholds the unity of God, enjoins its followers to search after truth, and advocates promotion of unity and concord among peoples. It maintains equality of rights for men and women, prohibits monasticism, advocates an auxiliary international language, and has abolished priesthood. The faith inculcates the principle of the oneness and wholeness of the entire human race.

Sayyid Ali Muhammad, the founder of the Bābī movement, was born in Shiraz, Persia, between 1818 and 1821 and was brought up as a member of a Shīʿ-Ṣufi sect. Some Shīʿītes and the Ṣufis believe that in each age there is a man, called the Bāb ("Gate"), who initiates in the secrets of the faith. To the Bābīs he is the "Gate" to the knowledge of divine truth. In 1844 Ali Muhammad proclaimed himself the Bāb of his time and was accused of heresy. He was arrested and shot in Tabriz in 1850. His body was interred by his followers in a secret tomb in Teheran.

In 1852 an attempt on the life of the Persian shah, Nāṣir al-Dīn, was followed by severe persecution of the Bābīs, which led the Bāb's successor, Mirzā (Persian, "prince") Yaḥyā, and the latter's stepbrother, Mirzā Ḥusayn Ali (b. 1817), to flee to Baghdad. In 1863 the Turkish government, at Persia's request, exiled Mirzā Yaḥyā to Cyprus. Mirzā Ḥusayn Ali proclaimed himself the successor to the Bāb under the name Bahāʾ Allāh. The government exiled him to Adrianople (1864) and later to Acre, which he reached in 1868, accompanied by about 70 of his family and followers. It was he who turned the faith into a universalist ethical religion, of which he became the leader. In 1899 he had the body of Ali Muhammad, the Bāb, transferred from its tomb in Teheran to Acre. The Bahāʾ Allāh died in 1892, and his tomb in the village of Mazraʿa (near Acre) in a building at Bahjī (Persian, "garden") became a shrine that the Bahāʾīs regard as the holiest place in the world.

Bahāʾ Allāh's eldest son, ʿAbbās Effendi, became the leader of the faith under the name of ʿAbd al-Bahāʾ ("the Servant of Bahāʾ"). After transferring his residence to Haifa, he set out on travels to North Africa, Europe, and the U.S. ʿAbbās Effendi arranged for the interment of the Bāb's body in a shrine in Haifa on Mount Carmel. ʿAbd al-Bahāʾ (ʿAbbās Effendi) died in 1921 and was interred in the same shrine.

The great mausoleum (Maqām-i Aʿla), which is a landmark in Haifa, was only completed in 1953. ʿAbd al-Bahāʾ was succeeded by his eldest grandson, Shoghi Effendi Rabbānī (1897–1957), who, as guardian of the Bahāʾī faith, resided in Haifa.

The faith spread all over the world; Bahāʾīs reside in over 11,000 localities in over 200 countries, with around six million adherents in 2005. The spiritual and administrative center of the Bahāʾī World Faith is the Universal House of Justice (erected in 1963 in Haifa), comprising, in the Holy Land nine members, known as Hands of the Cause.

Bahaism was favorably disposed to Zionism, believing that the return of the Jews to their land was foretold in the writings of Bahāʾ Allāh and ʿAbd al-Bahāʾ. On June 30, 1948, Shoghi Effendi wrote to Prime Minister Ben-Gurion expressing "loyalty and best wishes for the prosperity of the newly proclaimed State of Israel" and recognizing the significance of the ingathering of the Jews in "the cradle of their faith."

Druze

The Druze (in Arabic Durūz, sing. Durzī, derived from al-Darazī, one of the founders of the sect) are a religio-political community inhabiting parts of Syria, Lebanon, and Israel. The Druze are set apart from other groups primarily by their adherence to a separate religion. Their language is Arabic and in overall cultural and social patterns they are not appreciably different from the villagers and mountaineers among whom they live. The factors keeping them apart include the effective prohibition against intermarriage with other communities, the non-admission of converts, a number of individual customs, a long history of armed conflict against intolerant rulers and rival groups, and a strong sense of communal separateness and group solidarity. Their population in the early 21st century has been estimated at around 1 million, living mainly in Syria (the great majority in the Jebel el-Druz Province), Lebanon (mostly in the provinces of Mt. Lebanon and al-Biqāʿ), Israel (in 18 villages, mostly in Upper Galilee, some also in Lower Galilee and Mt. Carmel), and Jordan. In June 1967 several Druze villages of the Golan (province of Quneitra), totaling about 6,000 inhabitants, came under Israel rule. By the early 21st century they had grown to over 15,000. In 2005 the total Druze population of Israel was around 113,000.

HISTORY. The Druze religion has its roots in Ismailism, a religio-political movement which, after years of underground activity, founded the Fatimid Caliphate in the tenth century. The Druze community originated in the reign of al-Ḥākim bi-Amr-Allah (996–1021), the sixth Caliph of the Ismaʿili Fatimid dynasty. Active proselytizing to the new creed was brief and had lasting results only in some of the remoter parts of the caliph's domains. Since about 1050 the community has been closed to outsiders. It has not moved far from the regions where the original conversions were made.

The first testimony on the Druze in non-Arab literature occurs in the book of travels by *Benjamin of Tudela, who toured Syria about 1167. Little is known of the history of the Druze until the Ottoman conquest of Syria (1516). On that occasion, the Emir Fakhr al-Dīn, of the house of Maʿan, helped the sultan Selim I, who confirmed him as Emir of the Druze. They lived in southern Lebanon and northern Palestine, in many of the villages where they are still found, and were a separate, "unbelieving," and warlike community. Their sheikhs and emirs had evidently succeeded in gaining a certain amount of local autonomy, especially on Mt. Lebanon, for, from the Ottoman conquest of Syria and Palestine, there gradually emerged a sort of semi-autonomous emirate that was based, in large measure, on Druze military power and feudal organization. This emirate was centered in Mt. Lebanon. Until the 18th century relations between Lebanese Druze and their neighbors, especially the Maronite Christians, were tolerably good, but they later deteriorated. Civil strife between Druze and Maronites lasted until 1860, when the bloody events of that year ended in an intervention by the great powers and, eventually, in the special autonomous administration of Mt. Lebanon within the Ottoman Empire. The net result of the complex political settlement was a defeat for the Druze, who have never since regained their ascendancy in the Lebanon region.

The main center of the community after 1869 passed to Mt. Hauran, where a Druze settlement had been established approximately one hundred years earlier by immigrants from Lebanon; Mt. Hauran then became known as Jebel el-Druze ("Mountain of the Druze"), a name that had formerly been synonymous with Mt. Lebanon. There the Druze were governed, largely by the emirs of the al-Aṭrash house, as a semi-autonomous community until the end of Ottoman rule in 1918. In 1921 the French tried to set up an autonomous Druze state under French mandate, but this failed and, in 1925, the Druze rose against the French, spearheading a general Syrian uprising.

In Galilee there probably were Druze settlements as early as the 11th or 12th century, and the presence of such settlements is clearly documented from the 13th century on. The Galilean Druze seem always to have kept close contact with the other branches of the community, especially those of Mt. Hermon and southern Lebanon, but do not seem to have participated as a group in the events which called the attention of the world to their brethren. During the British Mandate over Palestine they refrained, by and large, from taking part in the Arab-Israel conflict, and, during the 1948 War of Independence, turned this watchful neutrality into active participation in fighting on the Jewish side. Druze have since then served in the Israel Defence Forces, at first as volunteers and later within the framework of the regular draft system. Many Druze also serve in the Israel Border Police. They thus opted squarely against the mainstream of Arab nationalism and for integration in Israel.

Since 1957 the Druze have been given official recognition in Israel as a separate religious community. In 1962 the Knesset set up official Druze communal courts, which had previously functioned without official sanction. The spiritual leadership of the community is in the hands of its sheikhs from the various centers of Druze population.

RELIGION. The Druze religion, which Druze call *Dīn al-Tawḥīd* ("unitarianism" or "monotheism"), is based on principles derived essentially from Ismailism (Ismāʿīliyya), some of which originate in Neoplatonism and are common to a number of gnostic sects. It includes belief in a deity that operates in the world through a system of five cosmic principles, or "emanations"; belief in periodic human manifestations of the deity and the emanations; and esoteric interpretations of the "revealed" religions whose recognized prophets (e.g., Moses, Jesus, Muhammad) were the bearers of esoteric truths only. The inner meaning of these prophets' mission, in each case, is secretly propagated to a select group by an incarnation of the first cosmic principle, or "Universal Mind." During the time of Moses, that incarnation was Shuʿayb, or *Jethro, Moses' father-in-law; Druze pay homage to his putative grave near Hittim in Galilee. The Druze have few ceremonials or rituals and initiate only a very few members of the community into the precepts of the religion, which are not published or discussed in the outside world at all. Though their religion has its roots in a form of Islam, they are not Muslims.

Further Information on the Druze Religion. Until 1973 the basic principles of the Druze faith were kept a closely guarded secret, but in July of that year the Israel Ministry of Religious Affairs published a pamphlet, written by Nissim Dana, director of the Druze Division of the ministry, which for the first time outlined the three principles of the Druze faith. They are: guarding one's tongue; protecting one's brother; and belief in one God. Publication of the pamphlet was originally approved by the Druze religious leaders, but they later withdrew their sanction.

The first principle obliges a member of the faith to be courteous, honor his promises, and keep secrets; the second principle calls on the Druze to help each other when in trouble; and the third states that they must strive to do God's will, lead a modest life, refrain from pleasure-seeking, and accept both the good and the bad in life with good grace.

The basic element in the Druze faith, according to the author, is the belief in seven prophets – Adam, Noah, Abraham, Moses, Jesus, Muhammad, and Muhammad ibn Ismail. Individual prayer, as practiced by the three other monotheistic religions, is unknown among the Druze. Their prayer-rooms are bare of decorations and furniture, except for cupboards, low stools, and carpets, on which the devout sit when they study their holy scriptures. Women are not excluded from religious duties, and some are known to have risen high in the religious hierarchy. Smoking, alcohol, and the eating of pork are banned, as is a certain plant named *melouhiya*, which is a staple vegetable in Egypt.

According to the pamphlet, the Druze believe in reincarnation – the soul of a dying man reentering the body of a child born at the same moment. They also believe they are descended from the tribes of Reuben, Gad, and the half-tribe of Manasseh, who lived east of the Jordan. On ordination, a graduate of the Druze community's Religious College in Lebanon is given a white garment which strikingly resembles the *tallit (Jewish prayer shawl).

BIBLIOGRAPHY: JEWS. A.M. Luncz, *Lu'aḥ Yerushalayim*, 13 vols. (1896–1916); idem, *Yerushalayim*, 20 vols. (1882–1916); D.N. Brinker, *Lu'aḥ Yerushalayim*, 11 vols. (1941–1952); Israel, Government Year Book (1950–), Ministry of Religious Affairs, Reports; I. Gan-Ẓevi (ed.), *Ha-Madrikh le-Yisrael ha-Datit…* (1968); Ha-Maḥlakah le-Ḥinnukh ve-Tarbut ba-Golah, *Dat Yisrael u-Medinat Yisrael* (1951); N. Kraus (ed.), *The Encyclopedical Religious Yearbook* (Heb. and Eng., 1962); N. Bentwich, in: A.J. Arberry (ed.), *Religion in the Middle East…*, 1 (1969), 59–118; J. Badi, *Religion in Israel Today…* (1959); H. Weiner, *Wild Goats of En-Gedi* (1963[6]); E. Goldman, *Religious Issues in Israel's Political Life* (1964); Mizrachi World Center, *Religion and State in Israel* (1965); M. Ostrovsky, *Irgun ha-Yishuv be-Ereẓ Yisrael* (1942); Y. Even-Ḥen, *Ha-Rabbanut ha-Rashit le-Yisrael be-Avar u-va-Hoveh* (1964); Z. Warhaftig, *Baa'yot ha-Dat be-Yisrael* (1966); S.Z. Abramov, *Perpetual Dilemma, Jewish Religion in the Jewish State* (1976); S. Herman, *Jewish Identity* (1977). **ADD. BIBLIOGRAPHY:** M. Friedman, "The Haredi Society – Sources, Trends and Processes" (1991), 80–86; The Committee for Reaching an Appropriate Settlement Regarding the Enlistment of Yeshiva Students, report (April 2000), 15–30; A. Dayan, *As an Overwhelming Spring* (1999), 22–44; I. Shahar, *Haredim Ltd.* (2000), 15–21, 151–60, 205–17. **WEBSITES:** State Comptroller's Report 94, No. 45, pp. 236 – 269; 2002 State Budget, chapter: The Ministry of Religious Affairs, on the Ministry of Finance website: http://www.mof.gov.il/; 2006 State Budget, chapter: The Ministry of Education, Culture and Sport, on the Ministry of Finance website: http://www.mof.gov.il/; The website of the National Authority for Religious Services: http://www.religions.gov.il/; The website of the rabbinical courts: http://www.rbc.gov.il/; The Kadishanet website: http://kadishanet.co.il/.SABBATH AND JEWISH HOLIDAYS: *Sefer ha-Mo'adim, Parashat Mo'adei Yisrael, Erkam, Gilluyeihem ve-Hashpa'atam…*, 8 vols. (1956–67). NON-ORTHODOX CONGREGATIONS: S. Ben-Chorin, in: *Journal of Central Conference of American Rabbis* (June, 1962), 3–11; J. Kaufman, *ibid.* (Jan. 1963), 3–9. CHRISTIANS. C. Copp, *Holy Places of the Gospels* (1963); C. Wardi (ed.), *Christians in Israel. A Survey* (1950); L.G.A. Gust, *Status Quo in the Holy Places* (1930); S. Colbi, *Christianity in the Holy Land* (1969); B. Bagatti, *L'Eglise de la Gentilité en Palestine* (1968); idem, *L'Eglise de la Circoncision* (1965); B. Collin, *Les Lieux Saints* (1948); N. Moschopoulos, *La Terre Sainte* (1957); Israel Ministry of Religious Affairs, *Christian News from Israel* (1949–). MUSLIMS. A. Cohen, *Israel and the Arab World* (1969); A.L. Tibawi, *Arab Education in Mandatory Palestine* (1956), index; Y. Waschitz and M. Zubi, in: *Ha-Mizraḥ he-Ḥadash*, 15 (1965), 85–92; A. Yinnon, *ibid.*, 57–84; 16 (1966), 349–80; *Israel Government Year Books*. BAHAI FAITH. J. Ferraby, *All Things Made New; A Comprehensive Outline of the Bahai Faith* (1957); *The Bahai Faith 1844–1963, Information Statistical and Comparative (pamphlet), with addendum to 1964; The Bahā'ī World*, vol. 13 (1954–63), 1970, edited by the Universal House of Justice, an authoritative source for the history of the Faith. DRUZE. Sprengling, in: AJSLL, 56 (1939), 388–414; EI[2], 2 (19622), 136–7, 631–4; H. Blanc, *Ha-Deruzim* (1958); M. von Oppenheim, *Vom Mittelmeer zum Persischen Golf*, 1 (1899), 110 ff.; E.N. Adler, *Itinerary of Benjamin of Tudela* (1907), 20 (Heb. sect.), 18 (Eng. sect.); H.Z. Hirschberg, *Religion in the Middle East*, 2 (1968), 330–48.

EDUCATION

Pre-State

1880–1914. Education in the small *yishuv*, which numbered about 25,000 in 1880, largely resembled the traditional types prevailing in Jewish communities elsewhere. The Jews of East European origin maintained the traditional ḥeder, talmud torah, and yeshivah, where Yiddish was the language of instruction; the Sephardi and Oriental Jews sent their boys to the *kutub*, where they studied in Ladino or Arabic. A little Hebrew was taught, mostly as the sacred tongue. Few girls, if any, attended the schools. Several attempts to establish modern schools were made in the second half of the 19th century. In 1856 the Laemel School was founded in Jerusalem by a wealthy Austrian Jewish family to provide secular and religious education in German; its "modernity" aroused much opposition. In 1864 the Evelina de Rothschild School for girls was opened in Jerusalem; in the 1870s it was transferred to the ownership of the *Anglo-Jewish Association, changing its medium of instruction from French to English. In 1870 the *Alliance Israélite Universelle established the first agricultural school in the country – *Mikveh Israel.

The Philanthropic School Systems. Toward the end of the 19th century and at the beginning of the 20th, a number of schools were established by European Jewish philanthropic organizations, while the Anglo-Jewish Association continued to expand the Evelina de Rothschild School. The Alliance Israélite Universelle established schools using French as the medium of instruction in Jerusalem, Jaffa, Tiberias, and Safed, and later in Haifa. The German-Jewish *Hilfsverein der Deutschen Juden (known as Ezra), formed in 1901, soon outdid the Alliance: by 1913 it was maintaining 27 schools in the country, ranging from a kindergarten to a teachers' training college. German was the chief language of instruction, but Hebrew was being taught by competent teachers. The *Jewish Colonization Association (ICA) maintained some of the schools in the villages, and early in the 20th century the Ḥovevei Zion in Russia helped to support some educational institutions.

Hebrew Education. The First Aliyah (see *Israel, State of: Historical Survey, section Modern Aliyah, 1880–1948), in the 1880s, brought to the newly established villages, as well as to Jerusalem and Jaffa, Jews who believed in a national revival and wanted Hebrew to be the language of instruction in the schools they established for their children. In the early 1880s, Eliezer *Ben-Yehuda started teaching Hebrew as a modern language in an Alliance school in Jerusalem. Other teachers bravely ventured into new territory by teaching arithmetic, geography, and other subjects in Hebrew, undertaking the difficult task of devising terminologies and preparing textbooks as they went along. It was in the new villages that Hebrew teaching and Hebrew speech in daily life spread more quickly. Young teachers fired by Ben Yehuda's example taught Hebrew as a living tongue in the village schools, and general subjects were also taught in Hebrew. The establishment of Hebrew kindergartens – the first in *Rishon le-Zion in 1898 – contributed greatly to the spread of spoken Hebrew at home and in the street.

The Second Aliyah, which started in 1904, gave a further impetus to the growth and extension of Hebrew education. In 1906 a group of young teachers, aided by the Ḥovevei Zion in Russia, established in Jaffa the first Hebrew secondary school, the Gymnasia Herzlia, which moved to Tel Aviv in 1909. This daring venture roused enthusiasm in the country and among Zionists abroad, especially in Russia, hundreds of whom sent their children to study in it. In 1908 the Hebrew Secondary School was founded in Jerusalem, and in 1913 the Reali Secondary School was opened in Haifa. In 1906 the *Bezalel School of Arts and Crafts, the first essay in secondary vocational education, was established in Jerusalem.

The Teachers' Association. There was a growing need for some national body to give guidance to individual teachers and schools in methodology and terminology, syllabuses and curricula. Toward the end of the 19th century, in the absence of an organized Jewish community in the Land of Israel, the Hebrew teachers made several attempts to organize themselves. In 1903 Menaḥem *Ussishkin, on a mission to the country on behalf of Ḥovevei Zion, convened a conference of teachers at Zikhron Ya'akov, which laid the foundation for the Hebrew *Teachers' Association. This association, especially in its early years, did a great deal to strengthen Hebrew education, drawing up syllabuses, publishing textbooks and educational material for teachers, improving the status of teachers, and organizing refresher courses and in-service training. It exercised many functions that were later assumed by the organized community, and, after 1948, by Israel's Ministry of Education and Culture.

The constantly growing importance of Hebrew in education, as well as the strength of the Teachers' Association, became apparent in the autumn of 1913, during what was known as the "*Language War." The question arose as to what language should be used in the technical institute (*Technikum*) due to be opened in Haifa. The institution, sponsored by the Hilfsverein, was financed by contributions from its own funds, Zionist sources, and American Jewish donors. The Hilfsverein insisted that German be used, whereupon the Zionist members of the institute, headed by *Aḥad Ha-Am, resigned and a storm of protest swept the *yishuv*. The teachers rose up in arms: most of those in the Hilfsverein schools resigned, and their association, with the assistance of Zionist bodies, opened 11 parallel Hebrew schools, creating the nucleus of a national Hebrew school system headed by a board of education. The "Language Conflict" marked the beginning of the end of the Hilfsverein's educational work in the Land of Israel; when the country was conquered by the British in 1917–18, their schools, being enemy (German) property, were handed over by the military authorities to the Zionist Organization.

UNDER BRITISH RULE (1918–1948). *Development of a National System.* During the 30 years of British rule in Palestine, a Jewish school system was created and developed mainly by the efforts of the Jewish community itself. Throughout the period there were two parallel school systems, Arab and Jewish. The Arab school system was taken over by the British authorities from the Turkish rulers, substituting Arabic for Turkish as the medium of instruction, and was maintained mainly by the government. These schools were attended largely by Muslim children, Christian Arab children receiving their education mostly in denominational or missionary schools. The Jewish schools were by and large the responsibility of the Jewish community, although some of them were private or were supported by Jewish bodies abroad. The Mandatory government's Department of Education, which fully controlled the Arab school system, maintained only nominal supervision over the Jewish schools. There was no law of compulsory education during the Mandatory period, and only about half the Arab children attended school for four years or more. The Jewish community, however, succeeded in providing almost universal schooling for its children. The Jewish school population grew almost tenfold during the Mandatory period and totaled nearly 100,000 in 1948.

From the Jewish Agency to the Va'ad Le'ummi. The Jewish national school system, born in 1914 after the "Language Conflict," was administered by a Jewish Board of Education, which controlled some 40 kindergartens and schools by 1918 and over 100 in 1920. From the beginning of the 1920s the Zionist

Executive (from 1929 the *Jewish Agency) maintained and administered these schools. At first it contributed some 90% of the cost and aimed at bringing all the Jewish schools under its management. Before long, however, financial difficulties forced the Zionist Executive to curtail its educational budget, which was constantly reduced and by 1932 was only 42% of the system's expenditure.

Gradually, the financial responsibility for the maintenance of kindergartens passed into the hands of local bodies; secondary schools mostly fended for themselves by introducing high tuition fees, and the vocational schools secured assistance either locally (for example from the *Histadrut) or from Jewish bodies outside the country, such as *ORT and *WIZO. The Zionist Executive's financial responsibility was limited mainly to the elementary schools and the teachers' training colleges. Not infrequently, financial difficulties caused delays in the payment of salaries to teachers, which brought about teachers' strikes, sometimes for several weeks.

The view gained ground, in Zionist circles as well as in the *yishuv* itself, that the financial and educational responsibility for the school system ought to be transferred to the organized Jewish community in Palestine. In the later 1920s the Jewish population gradually assumed greater financial responsibility for the education of its children, both by paying tuition fees and by self-taxation. It was therefore accepted as a logical and natural development that control of Jewish education in the Land of Israel was formally transferred, in the autumn of 1932, from the Jewish Agency to the *Va'ad Le'ummi, the Jewish National Council. The Jewish Agency continued to be represented on the governing body of the educational system and to contribute annually to its budget, although its share in the late 1930s was less than 8% of the total.

Administration of the Jewish National School System. In the years 1932–48, the national school network continued to expand under the control of the Va'ad Le'ummi, despite the general weakness of its authority and the poverty of the financial resources it could devote to education. Another factor contributing to the lack of unity in the educational system was the growing assumption of responsibility for the control of education by the Jewish local authorities and especially by the political parties and bodies, through the "educational trends" (see below). Four bodies were involved in the administration of the Jewish national system of education in this period: the Va'ad Le'ummi, which exercised supreme authority over major policy and approval of budgets; the executive committee of the school system, which took administrative and financial decisions – it had six members: three, including the director of Jewish education, appointed by the Va'ad Le'ummi, and one representative each of the Jewish Agency, the Tel Aviv municipality, and the central administration of the Jewish settlements; the Education Committee (Va'ad ha-Ḥinnukh), appointed biennially by the Va'ad Le'ummi, consisting of 13 members representing various political and educational trends (including three teachers and one person nominated by the Hebrew University), which dealt with educational matters and functioned only in an advisory capacity; and the Department of Education, consisting of the director of education and the chief inspectors of the three "educational trends," which was the executive body administering the current work of the school system.

The School System: Structure and Content. The Jewish school system in the Land of Israel in 1918–48 included kindergartens, elementary and secondary schools, and teacher-training colleges. The kindergartens, for the three-to-five age group, were highly popular and well developed. Most of them were maintained by local authorities and women's voluntary organizations; others were run privately by their teachers. They fulfilled an important social function by enabling mothers to go out to work as well as the educational function of preparing the children for school. Moreover, they played a significant part in welding together the heterogeneous Jewish population, with its divergencies of language, culture, and modes of life. The toddlers introduced the Hebrew language into their homes, as well as often unfamiliar habits of hygiene and the taste for new foods. In its own special way the kindergarten became an important instrument of adult education in the broadest sense, particularly among the mothers. Elementary schools, consisting of eight grades, were attended between the ages of 6 and 14. They were open six days a week, the first four grades studying four hours daily, and the higher grades five to six hours, in one session. Schools in the kibbutzim had both morning and afternoon sessions. From the very beginning, Jewish educators had to cope with the difficult task of coordinating and integrating Hebrew and general subjects in the curriculum. About one-third of teaching time was devoted to Hebrew subjects, which included on the average four to five periods of Bible a week in all grades. The rest of the time was devoted to general subjects, including arithmetic, history, geography, science, art, singing, physical education, handicrafts, gardening, and in the four upper classes, English. In the religious schools more periods were devoted to Hebrew subjects.

Most of the Jewish secondary schools followed the Central European pattern. They comprised 12 years of study, the first eight of which paralleled the elementary school. As they charged considerable tuition fees, attendance was restricted, and many pupils joined them only in the ninth year of study, after completing eight grades in the elementary schools. Although financially independent of the Va'ad Le'ummi, the secondary schools accepted its educational supervision and presented all their graduates for final examinations conducted by its Department of Education. These examinations were responsible for the development of a more or less uniform curriculum for Jewish secondary schools throughout the country. The kibbutzim and moshavim, however, maintained their own secondary school system which did not prepare its pupils for final examinations or diplomas. These secondary schools also combined Jewish and general studies. In the two upper classes, pupils could choose between programs emphasizing humanistic or scientific studies. In addition to English, they had to take a second foreign language: Arabic or French.

The teacher-training colleges were usually based on five or six years' study, the first three or four paralleling the upper grades of the secondary schools and the last two offering mainly pedagogical training. One section trained kindergarten teachers and the other elementary school teachers. Secondary school teachers were usually university trained.

The Va'ad Le'ummi controlled, financially or educationally, two-thirds of the Jewish schools in the country. The rest were very varied: eight Alliance Israélite Universelle schools with about 3,000 pupils, where Hebrew and French were the media of instruction; the Evelina de Rothschild School in Jerusalem, with Hebrew and English as languages of instruction; a number of vocational schools maintained by voluntary bodies; *talmud torah* institutions and yeshivot of the Orthodox religious type, some using Yiddish; and the nucleus of a network of Orthodox elementary schools controlled by *Agudat Israel. In addition, both the *Hebrew University in Jerusalem and the *Technion opened their gates for regular studies in 1925 as autonomous institutions.

The Educational "Trends." When the Va'ad Le'ummi assumed control of the national school system in 1932 it was already divided into three "trends": General, Mizrachi, and Labor. Between 1918 and 1920 the national school network was unified, but it included some schools, comprising about 20% of all the pupils, which were specifically religious in character. In 1920 the London Zionist Conference decided to recognize two categories of Jewish national schools in Palestine: schools of a general character, designated as belonging to the General Trend; and religious schools, which were included in the Mizrachi Trend, named after and affiliated to the religious Zionist movement.

The General Trend tried to combine national and general progressive values in its education. While maintaining a positive attitude toward Jewish religious tradition, it left religious observance to the individual pupils, in accordance with the desires of their parents. The schools of the Mizrachi Trend, while providing a general education, laid emphasis on religion, and their principals, inspectors, and teachers were observant Jews. In the early 1920s the Jewish labor settlements, both kibbutzim and moshavim, began to organize their own schools, which combined general education with labor ideology and new approaches to educational methods. Such schools were soon established by labor circles in towns as well, and in 1926 the Zionist Organization accorded them a recognized status as the Labor Trend, affiliated to the Histadrut, which by 1938 was included in the administrative network of the Va'ad Le'ummi education system. Each of the three trends, while forming part of the national system, enjoyed considerable autonomy in drawing up the curriculum and appointing teachers and inspectors. Each was led by a school council of ten to twelve members (including parents, teachers, and inspectors) headed by a chief inspector selected by the trend, who represented it in the Department of Education. The chief functions of the council were to protect the interests of the trend, nominate inspectors, hear their reports, and appoint representatives on various educational bodies. Toward the end of the Mandatory period, 53% of the pupils belonged to the General Trend, 24% to the Mizrachi, and 23% to the Labor Trend.

The Orthodox schools of Agudat Israel, as well as the yeshivot and other non-Mizrachi religious institutions, including those of the old *yishuv*, remained outside the national system and formed de facto a separate trend, in which secular subjects were eliminated or drastically reduced. Toward 1948 about half of them were maintained and controlled by Agudat Israel and the other half by the old *yishuv* and others. Together their pupils numbered about half as many as those in the Mizrachi schools.

While the variety of curricula and the freedom of each trend to try new experiments was all to the good, the splitting up of the national system into three separate groups, to a large extent separately administered, was not always beneficial to education, particularly since not only the Mizrachi and Labor trends were backed by political bodies but the General Zionist parties also assumed some sort of responsibility for the General Trend, and rivalry among the trends was sometimes instigated and abetted by the sponsoring parties. This situation became anomalous in the early years of statehood, when political parties supported "their" trends in an effort to attract more pupils from children of newly arrived immigrants who knew little or nothing about the differences between them, believing that by placing a child in one of the schools of its "trend" it would thereby also gain its parents' votes at election time.

Relations with the Mandatory Government. Up to 1922, the British administration gave no financial assistance to the Jewish schools in the country, which were considered "private schools." At first the Zionist Executive was satisfied with this situation, for many Jewish leaders and educators preferred to have an autonomous educational system, without government interference. The British administration, with limited resources at its disposal, was content to deal with the education of the Arab children; even then it could not meet more than about one-fifth of their needs. As the enrollment in Jewish schools grew and the Zionist Executive began to find it difficult to meet all its financial obligations to its education system, it requested the support of the British administration, which made small annual grants to the Jewish schools in the years 1922–26. The Jewish authorities asked for a grant based on the number of Jewish pupils at school and for an allocation per pupil equal to the cost of an Arab pupil in the government schools. The government objected, as this would have entailed allocating to the Jewish schools nearly half the educational budget, whereas the Arabs constituted about five-sixths of the population. In 1927 the government decided to allocate the money in proportion to the size of the Arab and Jewish populations. In 1933, it adopted a new formula, dividing the grant in proportion to the total numbers of Jewish and Arab children between the ages of five and fifteen in the country, as officially estimated. Thus, while government grants for education increased almost every year, they averaged only about 10% of the Jewish educational budget.

The Mandatory government's Education Ordinance of 1933, regularizing the administration of schools, recognized the Va'ad Le'ummi schools, heretofore technically "private," as "public." The ordinance referred to the "Hebrew Public System" as paralled to the "Arab Public System," which was under direct government control. When the government increased its grant to Jewish education in 1927, it insisted on formal approval of its budget, improvements in its administration, and the participation of a government representative in an advisory capacity on the executive committee of the Jewish national system. The government Department of Education, which had a small Jewish inspectorate for Jewish schools, interfered little in their affairs, although from time to time it offered suggestions for administrative and structural reforms. In 1945, at its initiative, a government commission was sent out from England to examine the administrative machinery of the Va'ad Le'ummi education system and its report, published in 1946, proposed far-reaching reforms. This report was still under discussion when the Mandate ended.

Budget and Finance. With the reduction in the contribution of the Jewish Agency to the maintenance of education, the *yishuv* itself had to assume ever greater financial responsibilities for the school system. While in the early 1920s it provided only 10–20% of the funds required, its share rose by 1933 to about 80%. A striking feature was the large percentage of school costs paid by parents. Only the kibbutzim and the moshavim provided free education. To these must be added the Tel Aviv community, which found it possible to abolish elementary school fees by defraying the cost of schooling out of the municipal budget. Only a small registration fee was demanded of parents and this, too, was remitted in whole or in part in needy cases.

On the Eve of the Establishment of the State of Israel. The Jewish national education system under British rule had many weaknesses: it controlled only 65% of the Jewish schools; it was never accorded full legal recognition; it constantly had to contend with financial difficulties; and the trend system enfeebled its administrative unity. Nevertheless, it not only grew tenfold during the period from 1918 to 1948 but also developed the attributes of a state system of education. The national system embraced kindergartens, elementary and secondary schools, trade and agricultural post-secondary institutions, and teacher-training colleges. It included special schools for handicapped children, school luncheons, health services, school clubs, and extracurricular activities. A great deal of attention was paid to curricula and methods of teaching. Rules were laid down for teachers' terms of service, and the Teachers' Association grew into a powerful professional body. In addition to the network of schools maintained or supported by the Va'ad Le'ummi, there were numerous private and semi-private schools, a system of evening schools for working youth maintained by the Histadrut, and a large number of evening courses for adults in which newcomers learned Hebrew and adults could pursue further knowledge in the sciences, humanities, and foreign languages. The State of Israel thus inherited a network of schools which could be easily converted into a state school system.

[Moshe Avidor]

In the State of Israel

The establishment of the State of Israel in 1948 greatly changed the country's Jewish community as well as the Zionist organization and movement. When Israel attained independence 650,000 Jews were living in Palestine and immediately masses of immigrants flooded the new state. In 44 months, up to the end of 1951, the pre-State Jewish community absorbed 684,000 new immigrants from 50 different countries – more people than its original number. First came about 300,000 Holocaust survivors from Europe and then mostly immigrants from Arab countries in Africa and Asia, some of them driven out of their homes and arriving with their entire communities. The total number of the latter reached 500,000 people before the end of the first decade of Israel's independence.

The population of immigrants consisted of mostly poor families with many children. This had a direct and strong impact on the educational system, since there was an intimate relationship between society and the schools: the educational system was oriented toward responding to the needs arising from social processes.

Formation of the Educational System in the Independent State of Israel. Most basic structural and normative characteristics of the Israeli educational system, still operative in the present day, were formed in the first years of the State's independent existence. The Compulsory Education Act was passed in 1949 and the State Education Act was enacted in 1953. During those years education in the newly established State was a matter of sharp political division and confrontation, the outcome of which determined the character and structure of the educational system in the coming years. The public and political debate found expression in issues of structure, authority, and procedures; however, its underlying motif was a struggle over the ongoing application of the "ideological socialization" approach. It meant that the educational system was to be used as means of socialization into the Zionist ideology, or, more precisely, the Zionist ideology as interpreted by the ruling elite.

The Social and Political Atmosphere of the First Years. Until 1953 Israel had four separate educational systems affiliated with different sectors. That was the legacy that pre-independence Jewish society in Palestine brought into the sovereign State of

Israel. The social and political atmosphere in which the ideologically divided system operated had, however, changed. The mass immigration brought in tens of thousands of children whose education had to be administered by the State. The establishment of state administration caused the different parties to fight for government power positions and struggles of the same nature intensified among the educational sectors. The major issue was who would educate the new immigrant children, with each ideological-political party striving to bring more children into its education system. The power struggles over education of the immigrant children were very sharp, often deteriorating to violence, and even brought about appointment of a State investigation committee. The first elected government in Israel fell over this issue; in all those squabbles, however, the preferences of the children's parents were the last to be heard.

Alongside the ideological-political rush for power positions in the state administration a new school of thought emerged at the time, closely associated with the personal and strong leadership of the first prime minister, David Ben-Gurion. This school of thought asserted that the sovereign state as a modern democracy should monopolize authority over certain particularly important functions: the armed forces, and education of the young toward becoming future members of society. This doctrine, which came to be called "Sovereignty" (the Hebrew term "*Mamlakhti'ut*" being a derivative of "*melekh*," a sovereign king), was applied very strenuously by Ben-Gurion in the organization of the armed forces. He intended to do the same in the educational system, in view of the enormous task of educating the large masses of immigrant children who now populated the country.

This educational philosophy is closely related to the "melting pot" philosophy for absorbing waves of immigration. It asserted that new immigrants should go through a process of re-socialization, at the end of which they would become absorbed in the native society as equal members of the Israeli collective. The educational meaning of this philosophy coincided with the "sovereign" state-organized educational system. It claimed that only the state can educate immigrant children to become well integrated as its future citizens, and not their parents, whose integration in a new country is far more difficult, burdened with economic and other survival problems. Another product of the "educating state" idea was to hold the value of patriotism higher than all others.

The Compulsory Education Act. The first statutory change was the Mandatory Education Act adopted by the Knesset on September 21, 1949. It fixed nine years as the length of compulsory education between the ages of 5 and 13, i.e., one year of kindergarten and eight years of elementary schooling. It established that those years of education would be free for all children, and that children would be able to enroll in any of the four segmented educational networks approved by the Ministry of Education. Proponents of the unified national education system claimed that that legislation fostered the disintegration of society into ideological-political factions, as it obligated all parents to enroll their children in one of the four ideological-political networks of schools. Indeed, the immediate effect of the Compulsory Education Act was conflicts between the different networks over enrollment of children in their schools. The law effectively stated that parents should make the decision which school their children would attend free of any coercion or enticement. In practice, however, many complaints were filed in the Ministry of Education, against the "Workers Education Network" operators in particular, regarding cases of pressure, threats, extortion, and enticement of principals and parents with the aim of getting them to transfer children into schools of a particular network of educational institutions.

The Compulsory Education Act stated that it would not be applied in the transit camps (**ma'barot*) of new immigrants, but that the minister of education would be authorized to make the education arrangements there. In the immigrant camps a separate educational system was established, called "Uniform Education." The Uniform Education schools intended to give immigrant children a general education with a political or cultural orientation. They followed the "melting pot" philosophy, which had as its aim the melding of immigrants into one social and cultural fabric.

The National Education Act. Prior to the 1951 general elections the dominant and ruling party, *Mapai, proposed to dismantle the segmented education networks and institute a single national system that would end the debate over the education of immigrant children once and for all. Mapai won the elections and some other political parties supported the idea of unified national education as well, but the National Education Act was ratified only two years after the elections, in August 12, 1953. It determined that the ideologically distinct school networks would be dismantled and in their place two educational systems would be instituted: National and National-Religious (as the religious parties demanded), and that the Agudat Israel (ultra-Orthodox) school sector would continue its independent existence with state funding while retaining its pedagogic and curricular autonomy.

The National Religious educational system was the direct descendant of the Mizrachi network and it incorporated also the institutions of the smaller Religious Worker sector. The National System was the unification of the Workers Education Network and the non-religious General Education Network, each of them losing its unique ideological character in the process.

ESTABLISHING NORMS IN THE EDUCATIONAL SYSTEM. *The right to free elementary education.* In the first five years of Israel's independence a number of normative principles were established, and in the coming years they had a lasting effect on the educational system for better or for worse. The Compulsory Education Act institutionalized the right of all children in Israel to elementary education regardless of the economic conditions of their parents. In order to actualize this norm, the Compulsory Education Act encompassed two additional principles: state funding of education on the elementary level (a principle significantly eroded in later years) and legal authorization of the state to impose the compulsory education laws on reluctant parents. The Compulsory Education Act established the liberal social norms that contributed to the fact that the rate of illiteracy in Israel is among the world's lowest.

The educational system as an agent of national socialization. The objectives of the National Education Act were less social than national. It intended to enhance national solidarity in Israel and facilitate the cultural integration of the masses of new immigrants. That law fixed the responsibility of the state for the contents of education to ensure that they were compatible with the state's interests.

The educational system as agent of absorption of immigration. The social-political circumstances that surrounded the legislation of the National Education Act also established the principle by which the educational system serves as an agent of integration of Jewish immigration. The national interest, as represented by the parliamentary majority (the coalition government at the time) was well served by the law that ensured the state's control over the socialization of its new citizens, immigrants, and the young generation.

Additionally, the Labor Movement, the dominant element in the educational system, determined the content of the socialization processes that the immigrant children were made to experience. These contents promoted secularity, a negative outlook on *galut* (exile, Diaspora) existence, Western civilization ("modernity"), and socialism. The immigrants were placed in an inferior position relative to the native or veteran Israelis and were required to shed their old cultural skins and put on the new, better one. In terms of identity, the educational system presented an ideal Israeli model that was completely alien to most immigrants, and demanded of them to adapt. Paradoxically, the educational experience of new immigrants in Israel created a dichotomy: the educational system did indeed facilitate the integration of immigrant children into Israeli society but simultaneously created in them and in their parents residual layers of alienation.

Differentiation and gaps between immigrant and native-born children. The Compulsory Education Act had additional effects. As mentioned, one of its outcomes was the establishment of the "unified education" system in the immigrant camps, separate from the sectoral schools that existed at the time. This was the beginning of differentiation between immigrant children and native children in the educational system. That differentiation continued in the immigrant transit camps that were hastily constructed around the country. Geographic separation of the new immigrants caused separation and differentiation among schoolchildren too. New immigrants were then transferred to new housing units in proximity to old settlements, but even then schools were mostly separate or there were separate classes for immigrant children. In the 1951–52 school year, the educational system in Israel had 80,000 immigrant children; three out of four of them went to schools where all the students were new immigrants and another 9,000 attended separate classes for immigrant children in the General Education sector. The educational reality prevented all contact between new immigrant and native children in contrast to the "melting pot" ideal. The distinction between what has become known as "the First Israel" and "the Second Israel" was thus reinforced and perpetuated for years to come.

Differentiation and gaps between the Jewish and Arab educational systems. The principle of state-supervised compulsory and free education for all children had an impact on education in the Arab minority sector as well. At the outset of Israeli independence the Arab educational system was in very poor shape, with few educational institutions (under the British Mandate in Palestine many Arab children had studied at schools administered by the British). The Compulsory Education Act applied to the Arab minority sector brought tens of thousands of Arab children into the system, while the educational infrastructure of facilities, buildings, equipment, curricula, textbooks, and qualified teachers was very limited. The Compulsory Education Act was not fully applied within the Arab minority sector; many children were left out of school. The reasons for this were the poor conditions of learning and teaching facilities as well as difficulties in administering the education tax.

The institutionalized centrality of Zionist socialization in the national educational system determined the marginality of Arab education in the State of Israel. The official policy in the Arab sector was created by the security establishment and focused on neutralization of opposition and facilitation of loyalty to the State. The educational materials were purged of Arab national contents while religious and cultural-ethnic themes were accentuated.

Differentiation between secular and religious education. The National Education Act legalized the politically biased character of the Israeli educational system and made permanent its division into secular and religious education systems that grew wider apart with the coming years. The control of the National Religious Educational System by Mizrachi (later the National Religious Party) caused it to become more and more independent with the years while the autonomy of the ultra-Orthodox educational system, which was practically complete from the beginning, became ever more uncontrollable by the state.

EDUCATIONAL POLICY. Israeli policy makers for education now encountered a situation in which the population included masses of immigrants from the Islamic countries in Africa and Asia. This situation required that the system grant equal educational opportunity, facilitate social-economic mobility, and serve as the crucible for forging one nation out of people of many different ethnic backgrounds. Problems in attaining such goals were exacerbated by the fact that there existed a high correlation between the country of origin of the new immigrants and basic social variables such as education level, number of children in the family, and socio-economic status (generally low). However, the educational system had a strong belief, rooted in the Jewish and Zionist traditions, in both its responsibility and ability to fulfill its educational, social, and national tasks.

The suddenly realized dream of the Ingathering of the Exiles required that educational policy make it its first objective to establish an adequate and equal educational environment for all the children of Israel. The inequalities in learning potential between various groups of students were discerned from the very beginning and the system coped with them in various ways in order to narrow the gaps. In the first 30 years, the educational policy chosen toward that end was integrative, with many shifts and changes. In the first decade the egalitarian ideology was dominant; in the second decade the emphasis of policy shifted to individual potential, based on the idea of affirmative action. Only in the third decade, after the egalitarian and the affirmative action policies failed to produce the desired results, was the policy of integration adopted. Beginning with the fourth decade of the State's independent existence educational policy in Israel became pluralistic, with school autonomy and students' choice of schools and courses. Educational policies over the years reflected the dominant cultural and ideological trends as they shifted from strong socialist sentiments, aspirations for cultural integration, and high levels of communal solidarity, to capitalism, individuality, and legitimization of multiculturalism. In the following sections the educational policy will be described separately for each of the decades.

The Policy of Equality: 1st Decade. The principle of equality in the educational system was applied, in accordance with policy, in all areas:

Making schools equal for all the children of Israel

One curriculum for all

Teaching procedures and teaching accessories equal for all classes of the same age level

One standard for the number of students in a classroom

Identical textbooks

Formally equal training for all teachers

Equal allocation of resources

Even before the end of the first decade, the policy of equal education was failing. A nationwide survey in the mid-1950s indicated clearly that the equalization objective was not attained. The failure was apparent in three areas:

Low levels of learning achievement.

Poor achievement of students at all levels of learning aptitude, including those with normal learning potential.

Correlation between low learning achievement and ethnic origin.

The Policy of Affirmative Action: 2nd Decade. The unsatisfactory results of state-administered education in the first decade were a cause of concern for the system's leadership and led it to adopt a new policy by the end of the 1950s. It became known as the policy of Affirmative Action. The minister of education in the 1960s, Zalman Aran, referred to this policy once as "educational favoritism." The idea was to institute "reverse-discrimination" or "corrective discrimination" that would intentionally create better educational conditions for underprivileged children. "Eligible for Affirmative Action" became the new key concept in education and it was applied to elementary schools (not to individuals) on the basis of definite criteria. Schools in Israel were thus classified in three categories: First, Second, and "Eligible for Affirmative Action." The eligibility of a school for affirmative action was established on the basis of three criteria: the percentage of ethnically "Eastern" ("Sephardi," not "Ashkenazi") children at the school; the mean level of learning achievement; and the level of physical infrastructure of the school: buildings, facilities, equipment, including the professional level of teachers. According to data of the Ministry of Education in 1970 about one-third of children in elementary schools attended schools that were eligible for affirmative action.

The affirmative action policy produced some educational success, notably in learning reading skills; however, its main goal of narrowing the differences in learning achievement and consequently closing social gaps was not attained.

Social Integration and the Reform in Education: 3rd Decade. The parliamentary commission that decided on a new policy aimed at narrowing the social gaps in education (the Rimalt Commission) set three major goals: upgrading the level of teaching and learning achievement; narrowing the educational gaps among children in Israel and creating conditions for all children to become integrated socially and economically; and creating frameworks that would become meeting grounds for children of parents from all countries of origin, in integrated regional schools. In these frameworks, the committee saw the feature of "national and educational value in itself."

The social program launched was called "the Integration Program," and its main objective was creating ethnically integrated classrooms. The Integration Program was grounded in the Zionist social ideology that had as its national goal ethnic integration of all tribes of Israel in order to prevent the ethnically based polarization of society. The integrated classroom had to include high-aptitude learners (labeled now "Privileged"), most of whom happened to be from middle-class Ashkenazi families, and low-aptitude learners (defined as "Underprivileged"), who were mostly of Eastern origin and children of lower class and lower-middle class families. The suggested optimal ratio of Privileged vs. Underprivileged children in an integrated unit was 60–70 per cent and 30–40 per cent respectively.

The educational program of the integrative social policy was called the "Reform in Education." Its structural aspect was that instead of the 8–4 grade division between elementary school and high school, the division now became 6-3-3, and thus junior high school classes came into being in Israel. The heterogeneous classes planned by the integration program were intended for the junior high school level (grades 7–9). The Reform in Education brought the ninth year of schooling into the framework of the law of compulsory free education for all.

The answer to the question, "to what extent did Integration contribute to the cohesion of the Israeli society," remains unresolved.

Autonomy in Education: 4th Decade. Autonomy could be accomplished only if the national educational administration transferred power and authority over education to the jurisdiction of schools, communities, and the local authorities.

Designers and planners of autonomy in education assumed that local people would be better able to cope with their communities' specific problems, including such perennial problems in education as the low learning achievement of students living in poor areas and problems of social disintegration. It was assumed that in granting autonomy to communities the overall goals of the national educational system would be better served. That new policy became known as "School Autonomy" or "Autonomy in Education."

The range of autonomy in schools includes its organizational structure, distribution of resources, curriculum and teaching methods, evaluation of students' achievement, and partnership with the community to meet its goals. Autonomy in education is synonymous with pedagogic independence granted to schools so that they can develop their particular character and take local initiatives. In this framework, the autonomous school could develop its own pedagogic philosophy, structure, and planning of teaching, and its internal mechanisms of evaluation and feedback.

Community schools. The policy of school autonomy allowed schools to take their own educational approach and led to the development of Community Schools. This model became quite widespread, currently with over 500 such schools in the country.

Community schools began to operate in Israel in 1978 on an experimental basis. The educational philosophy behind that project was that a school needs to be autonomous in choosing its pedagogic methods and has to perform more tasks than the traditional socialization and imparting of knowledge to its students. The school is a part of the community: it should strive to make elements of community life present in the school and elements of school life present in the community. This would constitute a fertile ground for the growth of social and cultural values that enrich the intellectual and spiritual world of students, parents, and the entire community. The planning of community schools in Israel was oriented toward two broad objectives: one was improvement and enrichment of the educational level of schools through contact with adult members of the community; the second was to provide an agency that would answer social and cultural needs of the community by organizing various activities.

Free Choice in Education: 5th Decade. The educational philosophy of free choice was adopted in Israel in the 1990s, after the educational system had already followed the policies of equality, affirmative action, integration, and autonomy. The free-choice trend in education could be regarded in association with a renewed rise of capitalism in the 1980s that generated a stronger demand to satisfy the particular interests of the wealthier classes.

Free choice is thus becoming an ever-more dominant guiding principle in the Israeli educational system, as part of the general processes of liberalization. It is closely associated with the autonomy in education policy and its derivative, the special-interest school.

Summary: Education and Society in Israel. The turning point in Israeli education occurred after the state become sovereign and its charismatic leader at the time, David Ben-Gurion, called upon it to become an agent of radical change from the former language, culture, and values of the Jews who immigrated in masses to begin a new life as citizens of their new homeland, which was struggling to survive. It seemed imperative then that they adapt to the culture and social values of the new society. The radical aspect of this supreme goal and its effect on education in Israel must be kept in view: the educational system was charged with a mission of radically changing the immigrant children and thus effecting a profound change in an entire population.

The Israeli educational system has had the intention and strong motivation to influence social integration. The changing policies it followed were not sufficient to close the educational gaps between Jews of Ashkenazi and "Eastern" descent. There occurred a certain narrowing of differences in learning achievement; however, they still exist as a challenge to Israeli society and its educational policy makers.

THE STRUCTURE OF THE SCHOOL SYSTEM. Not just the essential educational rationale and policies were formed in the 1950s but also the system's organizational structure. This included division into grades and branching into academic and non-academic tracks, work procedures, lines of authority, and links between different organizational units all the way from the individual classroom teacher up to the director-general and the minister of education.

Centralized Administration and Supervision. The basic premise has been that the State is responsible for providing every child with an acceptable level of basic education. Based on this obligation it has been understood that beyond all particular changes and variations the State has, by the agency of its Ministry of Education and Culture, a decisive role in administering the education system and guiding it. The functions of the Ministry of Education cover budgetary, curricular, and operational aspects of the education system's activities. The Ministry itself is monitored by the parliamentary Committee of Education. The main tasks of the Ministry of Education are defined as implementation of the Compulsory Education Law, financing the system, which includes construction of school buildings and of other educational facilities; administrative, curricular, and didactic supervision of the functioning of the system; and employing of teachers up to the 9th grade.

In addition to the Ministry of Education, the Ministry of Welfare covers some areas of the educational system's operations, such as remedial learning services, day care centers, training of personnel, boarding schools, and institutions for handicapped children.

The Ministry of Education is structured according to three formal principles. One is division between sectors of the Israeli population. The most obvious division is between the Arabic and Hebrew educational systems, which in practice are two separate systems under the administrative umbrella of the Ministry of Education. Hebrew education is divided into separate systems of schools, the National and the National-Religious. Thus, in effect, Israeli education is divided into three separate networks, the National, the National-Religious, and the Arab. External to the official system there exists also the "Independent" network of schools of the ultra-Orthodox Jews, associated with the ultra-Orthodox and religious political parties. The "Independent" network is based on existing legislation and is financed by the State; however, the extent of the Ministry's involvement in its operations is almost nil. Yet another independent system, "El ha-Ma'ayan," was initiated in the 1970s. It is nationally Jewish, religiously Orthodox, and ethnically Eastern, associated with the Orthodox non-Ashkenazi political party Shas. Recent years have also seen the establishment of schools called "Mofet," whose prime movers have been immigrants from the former Soviet Union and which include the teaching of Russian culture and intensive teaching of the physical sciences. That network has not been officially recognized, but it too gets financial support from the Ministry of Education. The Ministry of Education maintains a unified Pedagogic Department and the religious schools have representatives in all its other departments as well.

The second basic structural principle of the educational system is a division of the Ministry's units that operate in three separate areas: administrating educational personnel; organization and financing; and supervision in the areas of pedagogy and curriculum.

The third principle concerns routine operations of the educational system. It operates in six districts: North, Haifa, Center, Tel Aviv, Jerusalem, and South. On this regional level it coordinates its operations with the educational departments of local authorities that have a substantial role in routinely managing the system.

The Education Budget. In 2003, Israel spent 10% of its GNP on education, the highest percentage in the world, including rich countries like the U.S., France, Spain, Sweden, Japan, and the U.K. The expenditure per student is close to the average of OECD countries: \$3,483 in primary level classes in Israel vs. \$3,595 in OECD and \$4,777 in secondary classes in Israel vs. \$4,971 in OECD.

The high level of national spending on education includes nevertheless a growing share of private spending. This is an indication that private educational services substitute for and supplement the public services.

Gradation and Tracking in the Educational System – An Overview. From the beginnings, the compulsory education system included free kindergarten and eight years of free schooling. The system also included four grades of secondary education that was not free, in three tracks of specialized teaching and learning: academic, technological (at that time called "vocational"), and agricultural. The reform in education in 1968 changed the system to six elementary school years, three junior high school years, and three high school years. Most schools shifted to the 6–3–3 setup though some retained the old 8–4 division. In the 1970s, free compulsory education was extended to include two years of preschool (ages 4–5) and ten years of schooling.

The national school system includes formal and informal educational frameworks. Formal education includes two years of preschool, elementary grades 1–6 or 1–8, junior high school grades 7–9, high school grades 10–12, and "Comprehensive" school grades 7–12. High schools have three tracks: Academic, Technological, and Agricultural, with a small proportion of boarding schools. In 2004 a new reform was under consideration, which aimed to eliminate the junior high school division. It has not been put in practice yet.

In addition, the national school system covers special education institutions and special schools for exceptionally talented students. Academic-level education also falls under the auspices of the national system, including eight graduate and postgraduate level universities, public and private undergraduate colleges, and teachers' colleges. In recent years, foreign colleges and universities awarding first and second academic degrees opened affiliates in Israel; however, the Israeli Ministry of Education has no direct authority over these institutions of academic studies. Frameworks of informal education that are supported by the Ministry of Education include some extracurricular activities in regular schools which go under the name of "Social Education" – art projects, sports, educational TV, and youth organizations.

Kindergarten Education. The first kindergarten in Israel was open in 1898, in one of the first Jewish settlements, Rishon le-Zion, and since then preschool education has been considered an integral part of the system. The insistence on preschool education is based on the premise that many learning problems originate in environmental-social deprivation. Preschools allow the system to supervise and control at an early stage some aspects of the child's close environment. Therefore, preschool curricula attempt to upgrade the child's level of aptitude in learning and in social behavior as a means of closing social and educational gaps.

Day care centers and kindergartens in Israel serve children of 2–6 years of age. Children aged 3–6 fall under compulsory education in kindergartens operated by the local authorities and subject to professional supervision by the Ministry of Education. The day care centers for the 2–4-year-olds are predominantly private. Some belong to women's organizations or the local authorities. Most are supervised by the Ministry of Education. Some day care centers operate until late afternoon and admit infants 6 months old and children until school age. The preschool system, like the school system, is divided into general secular, general religious, ultra-Orthodox, and Eastern-Orthodox kindergartens. Naturally, on this level too the Jewish and the Arab preschools are separate. The national aspect of preschool education in Israel finds expression in compulsory free education for all children age 4–6; in subsidized tuition for ages 3–4; in national curricula; and in implementation of supervision and control laws that apply to all children from the age of two. The system creates conditions that make the rate of attendance at the preschool level very high.

Public kindergartens in 2003 were attended by 313,000 children out of 1,946,000 in the whole system (about 16%), 245,000 of them in the Hebrew sector and 68,000 in the Arabic sector. In the compulsory kindergartens (for age 5) there were 126,000 children, 96,000 in the Hebrew and 30,000 in the Arabic sector (figures of the Central Bureau of Statistics).

Nowadays the emphasis in preschool education is on literacy, appreciation of culture, computer literacy, beginning of scientific-technological education, as well as facilitation of creativity and learning-related activities and games with the participation of the child's parents. The pedagogic goal is to plant the seeds of knowledge and scientific interest, to acculturate children to the quick pace of technological change and sophistication as early as at the preschool age; further, to facilitate good and close relations between preschool teachers and parents, based on the premise that this is an important factor in the child's well being, and to facilitate the child's psychological and social development. On the basis of this educational policy, preschool children in Israel are introduced to computer games and to curricula in different areas of knowledge.

Primary Education. Primary education, more than any other level of the system, experienced two major shakeups in its formative years in the early 1950s. One was the transition from independent, ideologically uniform systems to State supervision and control. The second was separation of the religious and the secular schools. The second development was the less significant, as the separation between independently operating systems of secular and religious education existed already in the pre-State area. The greatest effect of the change was in the secular independent schools, because two different systems, the "General" (ideologically middle-class) and the "Workers" (ideologically socialist) school systems were made into one. The other shakeup was caused by the influx of immigrant children at that time, affecting mostly the elementary schools, which had to shoulder the heaviest share of the burden. As pointed out above, the immediate results of these historic events were a disproportionate and rapid growth of the educational system and de facto separation between immigrant and native-born children which resulted in two qualitatively unequal kinds of schools. This, in turn, contributed to the widening of the gap in learning achievement between students along the lines of native-born vs. immigrants (a variable that disappeared with the passing of years) and of ethnic origin (a variable that still affects learning results).

Until the reform of 1968, elementary schools consisted of eight grades. The legislated reform changed it into six grades. In the early 21st century, over three decades later, one-third of elementary schools still operated according to the old eight-grade structure. Elementary schools are the biggest section of the system in terms of numbers of students, classrooms, teachers, and teaching hours. They operate six days a week, about 200 school days a year, four to eight classroom hours a day, depending on the designation and level of a classroom and a school. One of the outstanding features of the Israeli elementary school is that almost all teachers are female. According to figures of the Central Bureau of Statistics, the number of primary level students in 2003 was 776,000 out of the system's total of 1,946,000 (40%); 572,000 of them were attending Hebrew schools and 204,000 Arabic schools.

In lower grades of elementary schools one teacher teaches many different subjects in her capacity as homeroom teacher (called the class's "educator"). In grades 4–6, the division of classroom sessions into separate subjects is instituted and more teachers teach in each homeroom class. The Ministry of Education tries to introduce the separation of content areas taught by specialized teachers earlier and, at the same time, to require teachers of the lower grades to specialize in teaching two subjects. It also wishes to upgrade the level of math and English teachers to bring elementary school teachers up to the level of secondary school teachers and thus upgrade the quality of teaching in the lower grades.

Most elementary schools have libraries, psychological counseling services, and truant officers. Many are equipped with computers as learning aids. Supervision by the Ministry of Education is administered by a supervisor who has responsibility for teacher placement, supervision, and evaluation. Teachers of particular subjects have professional supervisors as well. Teaching is done in homeroom classes and in equalized-level classes with students from different homerooms, selected according to their learning aptitude in certain subjects (mostly English and arithmetic). The schedule is fixed; students have practically no choice of programs. The basic curriculum is designed by the Ministry of Education but schools have a measure of autonomy in balancing different subject areas and adding their own programs. The Ministry of Education regularly administers nationwide learning achievement surveys in arithmetic, reading comprehension, and English.

Primary level education is the receptor of a large part of innovation and pedagogic initiative, both organizational and curricular. Over the years, schools on this level have been established with designated specializations in art, nature, ecology, as well as open schools, ideologically oriented schools, community schools, and autonomous-democratic schools. Elementary schools have launched new teaching methods such as learning in small groups, coordinated teaching, independent research groups, learning in media centers, and more. Innovative changes include the schools' own curriculum design and alternative achievement evaluation methods.

Parents of elementary school children have limited possibilities of influencing curriculum, methods, or personnel placement in schools. The system, however, encourages parents to take part in extracurricular activities, mostly by way of the PTAS ("Parents' Committees"). This becomes one of the major ways in which inequality among various schools is generated: schools in which parents are relatively wealthy can afford much more in the way of enrichment programs, equipment, and extracurricular projects than schools in poor neighborhoods. Moreover, registration bylaws were formerly more strictly imposed, so that parents could not register their children in any school they chose but had to register them in their registration area. Today parents have more freedom to choose the school they consider the best for their child in or outside their area.

Learning Achievement in Elementary Schools. In 1963, Israel was found on top of the list among 12 leading industrialized nations, based on identical achievement tests in mathematics and science administered in elementary schools. This result was generated in an Israel still absorbing immigrants and having economic problems. Thirty-five years later, in the late 1990s and based on international TIMSS-R testing, Israel was ranked no. 39 among 53 nations in achievement in mathematics and science. The gap between top achievers and bottom achievers among Israel's children was greater than in 49 of the nations that participated in the test. In reality, the figure is much worse, since it does not include students of the ultra-Orthodox schools whose achievement in these subjects is extremely low. The top students in Israel were ranked 35th among the 53 nations.

In 2003, based on a PIRLS test in reading comprehension administered to fourth graders, Israeli children were ranked 23rd in the 53-nation sample.

In 2003, the results of a PISA test administered in 40 countries by OECD, the organization of industrialized nations, to 15-year-old students, were published. The students were tested in reading comprehension, mathematics, and science. Israel was ranked no. 30 in reading comprehension, no. 31 in mathematics, and no. 33 in science (Ben David, 2003). Those results prompted the minister of education to launch yet another educational reform, with the stated goal of improving learning results (on the recommendations of the Dovrat Committee, which issued its Report in 2005 – partially implemented and in many quarters criticized for its emphasis on organizational rather than substantive reform).

Secondary Education. The Israeli education system intends to accommodate diverse populations of students and succeeds in providing most children with 12 years of schooling. In this, it differs significantly from pre-independence days, when secondary education was accessible to only a small segment of the general population and most students failed the entrance examinations. In 1948, only 12% of the Jewish young were actually learning in secondary schools. In 2003, 96.3% of children 15–17 years of age received 9 to 12 years of schooling (97.2% of the Jews and 93.3% of Arabs); 90.8% of Israelis 18–24 years of age had finished secondary school (95.1% of Jews and 75.6% of Arabs).

In reality, wide gaps in learning achievement in elementary schools (or, at the latest, in junior high schools) constitute a barrier on the way to a high school. The stated goals and policy of the Israeli educational system, however, aim at overcoming this barrier and enabling practically all students to get 12 years of schooling. To that end, the Israeli Knesset (Parliament) enacted a law in 1979 granting free education to all up to the age of 16. The idea was also to alleviate the tight financial situation of secondary schools. The Free Education Act had some effect on secondary school attendance, lowering the dropout rates in senior classes, in particular with students of Eastern ethnic origin and, among them, in particular, boys in academic secondary schools. In the year 2003–4, 282,143 students attended Hebrew secondary schools; 65.6% of them were in the National Secular system, 16.8% in the National Religious system, and 17.6% in the ultra-Orthodox system. The number of students in Arabic secondary schools has been 62,142 (5,494 of them Druze).

In light of its ideology and stated goals, the national educational policy was to establish varying types of schools with courses of study for students of widely differing scholastic levels. The leaders of the national educational system have believed in providing an equal opportunity for all children in Israel to get secondary education. Tracks of available courses include academic high schools that prepare students to take the matriculation examinations for post-secondary education and offer a wide range of subjects. There is also the Comprehensive High School, in which some students take the academic track (for matriculation) and others take the non-academic track (vocational, technological); agricultural and technological secondary schools also offer academic courses along with the specifically vocational ones. Critics of this educational policy claim that although the number of students in secondary schools is consistently rising, the ethnically Eastern Jewish students are directed to the vocational tracks and the Ashkenazis to the academic tracks. The differentiation in courses of study constitutes, in the view of critics, a discriminatory practice that sustains the ethnic division in the educational system and preserves class differences as well as the power of the ruling Ashkenazi elite. These critics see the Israeli educational system as stratified by class.

Hebrew high school seniors in Israel (12th grade) currently number 82,805. According to track, 50,357 learn in academic schools, 25,661 in technological schools, and 1,021 in agricultural schools. Arab high school seniors number

14,331, 9,631 in academic and 4,449 in technological schools or courses.

In 2002, 21,600 students (6.6%) dropped out of grades 9–12 in junior high and high schools. The proportion of dropouts in Hebrew schools was 5.6% and in Arabic schools it was 11.1%. Demographically, most dropouts were boys, children of parents with a low education level, children of single mothers, and new immigrants living five years in Israel or less.

Junior High Schools. In 1968, the Israeli Knesset passed legislation on a reform in the structure of the educational system. The Ministry of Education accordingly restructured the elementary and secondary schools and created junior high schools for grades 7–9. Reform in education had two main goals: integration across all social groups and strata and raising the learning achievement level of underprivileged students. The integration policy was put into practice by dividing the country into "educational regions" which did not necessarily include geographical proximity or continuity but were socially heterogeneous. The students in each of the schools in an "educational region" had to come not from one but from different socio-economic groups. Graduates of elementary schools, without selection, were enlisted in junior high schools in the same "educational region" in order to ensure social integration of all students. Classes in those schools became heterogeneous in terms of learning aptitude and achievement; however, they were being subdivided into homogenous higher- and lower-level learning groups, particularly for basic subjects like English and mathematics. This arrangement undermined, to a great extent, the integration reform. Beyond that, in areas where all the population was demographically homogeneous integration was difficult to institute. The political division of the national educational system into the secular and religious makes integration still more difficult, since in the national-religious system there is a relatively dense concentration of underprivileged students.

Twenty-seven years since its inception, the structural reform of the Israeli educational system is applied to 65.5% of the Jewish students, 73.9% in the national secular schools, 58.9% in national-religious schools, and 70.9% in Arab schools. Many junior high schools are not administratively separate but operate within Comprehensive Schools that include also upper secondary school grades.

In 2003–4, 189,006 students were registered in Hebrew junior high schools and 64,999 in Arabic junior high schools. The percentage of registered students on that level, out of the total age group has been 73% in both sectors. The Dovrat Commission appointed by the Ministry of Education in order to draft and recommend a reform aimed at improving learning achievement suggested eliminating junior high schools altogether; so far only a few local governments have begun to implement this recommendation.

Academic Secondary Schools. In 1995–96, 50% of students in grades 10–12 were registered in academic high schools and 43% in technological-vocational schools. The proportion of academic and non-academic students in secondary schools has changed significantly since the early days of statehood in both Hebrew and Arabic schools. The proportion of academic students declined sharply and then increased slightly. This was mainly due to a policy that focused on the development of technological-vocational tracks of study as an alternative for underprivileged students. It should be noted that although the proportion of academic students in Arabic secondary schools is markedly higher than in Hebrew secondary schools, the proportion of Arab students who graduate and pass the matriculation examination is much lower than in Hebrew schools.

Matriculation examinations and certificates. Up until the 1960s, academic secondary schools in Israel were selective, had strict scholastic achievement requirements for admission, and admitted only those who qualified. From the mid-1960s, the Ministry of Education facilitated the way of more students to secondary education. Comprehensive schools were established; vocational and technological tracks of study were opened for students whose chances of passing the matriculation examinations were low. As technological education began to develop dynamically and the academic secondary school did not keep up with developments, it was labeled as old fashioned and its image suffered. In the 1970s, the Ministry of Education, to prevent a further deterioration of the academic school's prestige, initiated changes that made curricula more flexible in comparison with its former rigid learning tracks. The newly introduced concept was "learning modules." In addition to improving the image of academic secondary schools, it intended to enable more students to pass the matriculation examinations. Learning modules were defined in volume as three weekly teaching hours per year and a distinction was made between compulsory and elective modules. Students thus were given a choice of subjects and of the level of learning in each module. The matriculation examinations were changed to accommodate the learning module system, which included both compulsory and elective subjects on different levels.

The process of opening the curriculum to choice and flexibility and the cutback in high school years (three years instead of four with the establishment of junior high schools) contributed to the expansion of specialized high schools and courses, and to a corresponding contraction in basic studies for all students. Many schools offered courses that were not formerly available in secondary education. As a result, the Matriculation Departments in the Ministry of Education had to produce each year hundreds of matriculation examination questionnaires in dozens of subject areas and at different levels.

In the second half of the 1970s, the matriculation system came under mounting public criticism. The gist of the criticism was that the system promoted social selectivity and served as a gatekeeper for institutions of secondary education. Critics claimed that the matriculation system worked mostly against students of low socio-economic status who could not even enter the tracks of study that led to matriculation. Another line of criticism concerned the integrity and fairness of the examinations in such an intricate and complicated system. A public committee was appointed in 1979 to examine the matriculation system and make recommendations. It did not suggest significant changes but recommended preserving the existing structure of the system; criticism continued after the committee published its report. Many critics pointed out that the matriculation examinations, which serve as a mechanism of selection for admission to colleges and universities, turned the academic high school into "matriculation factories" and actually impaired effective teaching and learning. High schools became known and valued only by the performance of their graduates in matriculation examinations, which resulted in much greater competition among schools. In order to keep their position in this competition, some schools adopted a policy of dismissing students who were capable of remaining in school, and wanted to remain, but could not reach the levels of achievement that the school administration demanded.

Matriculation examinations were reformed in 1994–95. The number of compulsory subjects of examination was reduced from seven to four by means of an annual lottery; subjects that the lottery eliminated were to be graded by the school's teachers. The reduction in the number of examinations was intended to allow more students to get the matriculation certificate as well as to help schools teach for broader and deeper knowledge rather than, as the critics claimed, being "matriculation factories." The lottery system came under criticism as not being dignified and because of the concern that important subject like Bible and English would not be taught intensively enough during the school year. The minister of education eliminated the lottery system in 1997–98 but the reform in matriculation examinations – four subjects instead of six – has remained.

Having its students eligible for the matriculation certificate has become a major goal of the Israeli educational system. In the Hebrew academic high schools, 89.7% of the students took the examinations but only 67.3% passed. In technological schools, 77.7% were examined and only 47.8% got the certificate; the rates in agricultural schools were 84.2% and 46.1%, respectively. In Arabic academic high schools, 94.7% of the students were examined and only 58% qualified; in Arabic technological schools 76.5% were examined and 38.2% qualified.

There is big gap in the proportion of Jewish and Arab students who get the matriculation certificate, and the gap is slowly widening. In the Arab sector, the lowest qualification rate is in Muslim schools whereas the rates in Christian Arab schools are the same as in Hebrew schools. In the Hebrew sector, a gap between Eastern and Ashkenazi students still exists; however, it is slowly being narrowed.

A statistically high probability of getting the matriculation certificate correlates with the socio-economic status of students and their parents. In 2003, it was found that in communities with a high socio-economic profile, two-thirds of high school graduates pass the exams and get the certificate. In communities of low socio-economic profile, like the Jewish "development towns" in the provinces and most Arab towns, the proportion of students who pass the matriculation examinations upon graduating from high school was about 40%.

These data indicate that Israeli secondary education did succeed in having more students learn 12 full years. Increase in the number of students who tried to get the matriculation certificate was slower, and many of those who are examined do not get the minimum passing grades in all of the required subjects. The social class factor significantly affects the chances of a student to matriculate.

The Policy of "a Second Chance." The certificate of matriculation in Israel is a crucial factor in determining the educational and occupational destiny of a person. This certificate is the necessary – but not always sufficient – passport to academic studies. In view of its importance, the educational system in Israel allows students a second chance to pass the examinations and get the certificate. Three alternative types of institutions are certified by the Ministry of Education to teach for that purpose: private morning and afternoon schools, pre-academic preparatory courses, and a "Second Chance" project for underprivileged students. These teaching and learning frameworks accept the many high school graduates who did not qualify for the matriculation certificate. Most students who study with the Second Chance project or the pre-academic preparatory courses get the certificate and are admitted to colleges and universities.

The outcome of the "second chance" policy is reflected in the following statistical data: one-third of all students who failed to matriculate on their high school graduation in 1995 upgraded their grades in the subjects they needed through a "second chance" framework and got their matriculation certificates in or before 2003. Accordingly, the total rate of successful matriculation climbed from 50% on graduation to 59% in 2003. Gaps between different populations in Israel can be observed in this area too: in Hebrew schools, 69% of graduates got the matriculation certificate in 1995, rising to 81% in 2003 – an increase of 17%; in Arabic schools, the rate climbed from 49% to 61% – an increase of 25%. In Hebrew schools, ethnic differences could still be noted: the rates for students of Eastern origin climbed from 61% to 74%; for students of Israeli origin, from 72% to 83%; and for students of European and American origin the rates were 75% and 86%, respectively.

The Comprehensive School. Comprehensive schools embody the egalitarian ideal of education and equal educational opportunity for all. The terms "comprehensive" in this context can be understood in two ways. One is that education has to include all members of society regardless of race, ethnicity, religion, gender, or class. Another meaning is that education needs to encompass and include the variety of human interests and talents and facilitate the development of each individual's potential. Those ideals are put into practice in comprehensive schools by a policy of general admittance of all children without selection; then, by providing basic education for all, no dismissal of slow students, a wide range of courses and tracks of study, and social integration. Most comprehensive schools have six grades (7–12). The practice of not dismissing students, including those who finished the junior high school grades, requires the comprehensive schools to offer a variety of other than regular academic courses on different levels.

The Comprehensive School in Israel has a long history. Educators in some schools promoted the "comprehensive" idea as early as 1953; however, until 1963 it did not get official attention. In the 1960s new schools were established that were not called "comprehensive" but did made their curriculum flexible, adjusting it to the needs of underprivileged populations and offering both academic and vocational courses. Schools of this type were established mostly in peripheral areas and in communities with a high concentration of new immigrants; in the following years the educational authorities began working out the organizational and pedagogic frameworks for operating this new model. When, in 1968, the Knesset legislated the Reform in Education program and secondary schools were made over to include six grades (7–12), it recommended that they become "comprehensive" and so this educational idea became officially recognized. In the 1970s some of the most prestigious schools in Israel were already among those that had become fully or partially comprehensive. These schools developed school-based curricula in prestigious areas (arts, computer science, etc.) in order to provide incentives for all junior high school graduates to continue their studies in their high schools. After the October 1973 Yom Kippur War the pace of the changeover slowed down markedly, however, beginning in 1988 the comprehensive school movement began intensive development through a new model of educational institution, the Community Education Center.

Community Education Centers are clusters of organizationally unified schools, usually a number of junior high schools and a comprehensive high school in the same area that accepts all the area's pupils after they finish junior high school. The Community Education Center is a comprehensive system with advanced facilities and a wide range of courses and special classes on all levels. It admits pupils from diverse socio-economic and ethnic backgrounds in order to promote social integration. The model has no parallel in the world; it was developed to meet the unique educational needs of Israel's multicultural immigrant society. Since the beginning of the 1990s, close to 20 Community Education Centers have become operational in Israel and new ones are being planned.

The numbers for students learning in Hebrew comprehensive schools show an increase from 30,845 in 1970 to 52,672 in 1980 and 159,864 in 2000. The numbers leveled out in the 2000s, the figure for 2004 being 153,645. In Arabic comprehensive schools, the number was 5,100 in 1980, 28,195 in 1990, 30,420 in 2000, and 31,377 in 2004. In Hebrew education, there was massive growth in comprehensive schools between 1970 and 2000, then a slow decline. In Arabic education, the massive growth occurred between 1980 and 1990, and then continued slowly to 2004.

In 1978, 1986, and 1990, comprehensive schools were nationally surveyed. The results indicated that the extent of their being "comprehensive" is not yet complete. Admission policies were found to be less selective than those of the academic secondary schools; however, some selective mechanisms were still being used. The choice of courses and tracks of study has been more diversified but not always able to meet the students' preferences (the assignment of students to courses is less often their choice and more often the school's decision). Most students do earn the national matriculation certificate or get the school's graduation certificate; however, their range of mobility between classes and courses is limited, and it opens mainly in the less advanced direction. The survey found that privileged pupils were not negatively affected by attending comprehensive schools, most of them taking the high-prestige courses and passing the matriculation examinations. However, underprivileged pupils benefited less in comprehensive schools in spite of studying a full 12 years and, in lesser proportions, getting the matriculation certificate. In addition, the survey revealed that the comprehensive school had not narrowed the gap in learning achievement across ethnic lines. The hope of accomplishing integration did not really materialize. Integration seems to occur more readily in extracurricular activities, in particular when many schools are rather homogenous in their ethnicity and class composition.

Vocational-Technological Education. A vocational or technological school differs from an academic school in that, besides teaching general academic subjects, it trains students for future work in a specific profession. Until 1953 vocational education in Israel was supervised by the Ministry of Education. Later it came under the administrative authority of the Ministry of Labor and the Ministry of Education supervised only its academic courses. In 1959, vocational schools again came under the auspices of the Ministry of Education. The Ministry of Labor has been responsible only for industrial schools that operate in certain industrial plants.

Students in vocational schools study for three or four years; graduates of five-year courses in some schools obtain upon graduation a technician's degree and certificate, and graduates of six years of vocational education can obtain the professional degree of practical engineer. The tracks of study are divided between technical and non-technical courses. Technical courses are predominantly for boys and non-technical courses are predominantly for girls. Courses teach professions and train for vocations that differ in their relative occupational prestige: metalworkers, mechanics, electricians, electronics technicians, computer technicians, fashion designers, office workers, and the like. The largest organizations of vocational schools in Israel are the school networks of *ORT and Amal.

Up until the 1960s, vocational education of Jewish youngsters was relatively small in proportion to general academic education and it was non-existent in the Arab sector. Beginning with the 1960s, it expanded rapidly in the Jewish sector and in the Arab sector parallel expansion occurred only in the 1980s. The massive expansion is attributed to the dual function of vocational education. On the one hand, its aim is practical, training a skilled workforce for specific occupations. On the other hand, it serves the pedagogic ideal of secondary education for all, including the disadvantaged, being an alternative to academic education. The policy that facilitated the expansion of vocational education resulted in the establishment of vocational-technological schools in areas with a high density of Eastern Jewish communities, notably in the "development towns" in the periphery. The trend affected both the National and National-Religious categories of schools. It turned Israel into one of the countries with the highest proportion of secondary vocational schools at a time when in the rest of industrialized world the share of vocational education dropped steeply in comparison with the rest of secondary education.

Technological schools in Israel developed from the 1960s mostly as alternative institutions of learning for pupils who were not found admissible to regular academic schools. Until the end of the decade, students at vocational-technological schools were not directed to take the matriculation examinations. With the idea of attracting good learners to technological schools, their curriculum was modified to contain four unequal-level tracks. One track led to matriculation; another track led to a professional occupational degree (a license to practice a profession on a certain level) and partial matriculation (not all compulsory subjects included). This modification gave more hours in academic subjects to students following studies on these tracks. Technological-vocational education thus opened itself to high-ability students and turned out to be a track of studies promising greater opportunity for educational, economic, and social mobility.

Rapid technological and scientific advancement demanded scientists and skilled workers in science and industry, and technological education lagged behind. In 1992, a committee was appointed to examine the educational system in areas of science and technology and make recommendations in order to organize technological education for the 21st century. The committee found that scientific and technological knowledge of most graduates of technological schools is insufficient and often outdated. Its central recommendation was to strengthen the theoretical basis of studies in science and technology while doing less practical work in all courses, including courses in which many pupils are slow learners. Another recommendation referred to the need for teachers to upgrade their knowledge of science and technology.

The high proportion of vocational or technological education in Israel relative to other developed countries has been a subject of ongoing concern; however, most criticism was not about the numbers but about its effect on social stratification and mobility. As it turns out, most of the Jewish pupils in technological education are ethnically Eastern. In 2003, 6,439 pupils of Eastern origin were enrolled in technological schools or courses, a full 48% of all Eastern students; 31.3% of them obtained a certificate. The 1,457 pupils of European-American ("Ashkenazi") origin enlisted in technological courses in 2003 constituted only 23.9% of all Ashkenazi students and 35.4% of them obtained the certificate. The figures indicate that the population of students in the technological educational track in Israel is clearly Eastern. Vocational education had as one of its primary objectives to admit slower pupils, usually those who come from underprivileged family backgrounds. This fact as well as the fact that even after most courses were open to matriculation many students in technological schools were not ready for the matriculation examinations turns technological education, for its mostly Eastern students, into an obstacle on the way to the college-level and university education that is the key to upward social mobility. At the same time, the merits of technological education should not be underestimated. It improved the general education level of the young population and enabled most to complete 12 years of study in the national school system.

Boarding Schools. The concept of boarding schools in Israel denotes institutions with students living in a semi-autonomous community of children. They spend most of their time living in a community of peers. Israeli boarding schools are divided into a number of categories: agricultural, vocational, pre-military vocational, military, religious "yeshivot," kibbutz educational institutions, and boarding schools for gifted children.

There exist two opposing philosophies regarding the educational goals of boarding schools. One approach regards the school as an extension of an alternative society, isolating and protecting the children from the outside world and the values that the school rejects. That boarding school wants to develop in students the skills to cope in the outside world in their own way rather than adapting to it. The other philosophy regards the boarding school as an "open house": it educates the young in harmony with the prevalent values in the outside world and prepares its students to become a productive part of it. Both philosophies are applied in Israeli boarding schools, including some compromises between them. The educational impact of boarding schools on their students is seen in such features as a value-oriented curriculum, institutional "totality" and consistency of the educational environment, intensive socialization processes, social isolation, and selection of students.

Historically, boarding schools in Israel developed in line with the Zionist ideology and its pioneering spirit that legitimized education outside the family home. They were established as "Youth Villages" or agricultural schools (farming was specifically a Zionist form of pioneering, directly opposed to Jewish family traditions). Another trend was sending children from towns to be educated in the "Youth Community" of a kibbutz collective village. The boarding school movement peaked in the days prior to the establishment of the State of Israel, when they were a powerful tool in the socialization of the "New Jew" as a member of the new Jewish society in the Land of Israel, a "Sabra." That educational ideal required that a person be distanced as far as it may from the immigrant or Diaspora type and instead live naturally in a free and independent Jewish society. Boarding schools thus served as a means of early socialization of the young to elite groups (many of Israel's political and cultural leaders were graduates of boarding schools, including Yitzhak *Rabin, Shimon *Peres, and the writer Dahn *Ben-Amotz). Boarding schools served to absorb immigrant youth, to socialize them into the new country and integrate many of the war orphans during and after World War II. Later they took in immigrant children from the Muslim world. In those early years, boarding schools were not at all selective in admitting children. They saw their role in re-educating the immigrant young and shaping them as much as possible toward becoming, like the native-born children, equal members of the new Israeli society.

During the 1950s, Youth Villages and some of the Agricultural Boarding Schools underwent changes. The structural changes involved all schools that became nationally administered. Educational policy changed from an ideological-pioneering emphasis to individual and practical achievements according to the pupil's needs. In the days before independence, boarding schools served the collective Zionist ideology and national needs. After the founding of the State of Israel, they became part of the national educational system. Their function as absorption and socialization centers for immigrant children continued, but the role of education in answering specific individual needs became equally important, such as teaching an occupation or opening avenues of upward social mobility for graduates. These changes in boarding schools have mirrored the overall changes in the Israeli society.

Beginning with the 1970s, some of the boarding schools served as centers of education for underprivileged children in need of assistance in developing their learning potential. Those children have been mostly of homogeneous social profile: Eastern ethnic origin, children of parents of low socioeconomic strata. This change produced a negative image for boarding school education, except for the yeshivas and premilitary boarding schools that prepared their graduates to become career officers. From the 1980s, boarding schools have admitted many immigrant children from Ethiopia and from the former Soviet Union – actually returning to their traditional role in the pre-State and early statehood days.

Enrollment and registration of students in boarding schools is carried out through the agency of the Ministry of Welfare, Ministry of Education, and Youth Aliyah (an organ of the Jewish Agency). The authorities may direct a child to a boarding school for reasons of the child's welfare and growth, which could be in jeopardy in his or her family environment, under difficult socio-economic conditions and as a function of time in Israel. The educational results meet expectations: the achievement level of new immigrant and other graduates of boarding schools has been higher than that of children of the same social groupings in regular schools.

Although boarding schools did well in integrating immigrant children in Israel, the number of children registered in them has dropped since the 1980s. In 1984–85, 11.6% of all secondary school students in Israel were in boarding schools. In 2002–3 their number dropped to 7.9% (37,893 students). It needs to be noted in this context, that in general-secular boarding schools most students are offered vocational courses while in the general-religious boarding schools most courses are academic.

Agricultural Education. Agricultural education has accompanied Jewish-Zionist settlement in Ereẓ Israel since its very beginnings. The first agricultural school, *Mikveh Israel, was established in 1870 near Jaffa. Agricultural education in the early days was a direct extension of the Zionist movement in its drive to reclaim, settle, and work the land. Farming schools were educating the young to undertake this national effort. The mainstream of the Zionist movement, the Labor Movement, made its greatest effort in what it considered the most important task in building a nation, creating an agricultural infrastructure. That was the heyday of farming schools; they attracted many young people who were the elite of the native-born Israelis from villages and cities. Schools of agriculture were considered elitist, and a spearhead of Zionist national education. Farming was considered a highly important subject of study in all elementary and secondary schools.

With the passing of the years, agricultural education sharply declined. This can be explained by the fact that agriculture in Israel slowly but steadily lost its appeal as a way of life and as a profitable or prestigious occupation. First, the ideology that idealized working the land as the noblest national occupation waned in the first two decades of independence. Secondly, the share of agriculture in the Israeli economy became much smaller while industry and services expanded as a result of both government policy and market trends. Thirdly, the rapid growth in the number of agricultural settlements established soon after the War of Independence to populate all parts of the country with Jews and settle new immigrants resulted in agricultural surpluses and diminished profitability. Finally, advanced technology lowered the demand for workers in agriculture. All those factors brought about a sharp decline in the social and occupational status of farming and, concurrently, a decline in the status of agricultural education. Farming schools, formerly breeding grounds for future national leaders, became boarding schools for the least advanced pupils. Farming education became a form of occupational rehabilitation for troubled youth. The general decline of agricultural education is reflected in student enrollment. It went down from 9.1% in 1959–60 to 2.7% of secondary school pupils in 2002–3. From the 1980s, agricultural schools became boarding schools for immigrant children. In the Arab population, agricultural education went through a similar process. The rates were 4.8% of all students in 1959–60 and 1.4% in 2002–3. It has been assumed that, in addition to the factor of general economic modernization, as in the Jewish sector, the decline in agricultural education among Arabs, who traditionally constituted a predominantly agricultural society, had two additional causes. One was scarcity of arable land as family plots were subdivided among heirs, as well as through land appropriation by the government. Second, later legislation abolished the War Emergency status under which a military government had confined Arabs to their village areas, opening the Jewish job market to Israeli Arabs.

Special Education. Special Education is a separate branch of the national educational system serving mentally or physically impaired children 3–21 years of age (children younger than three in need of special care are the charge of the Ministry of Health and the Ministry of Welfare). "Special children" are children with irregular health, mental, or educational conditions, like mental retardation, emotional disturbance, learning disability, emotional and social neglect, physical impairment, or chronic disease. The "special" child's condition impairs his or her intellectual, psychological, or social development and requires special treatment in education and care.

Special education institutions differ from regular schools in their size, curriculum, pedagogic methods, and psychological approach. Their educational efforts are directed to suit each particular condition of the child and the educational environment is designed for coping with various problems of the pupil population. Special education schools also include special courses that combine academic learning with learning vocational skills and educational-correctional institutions for minors who cannot be accommodated in other institutions or who are directed there by a court order.

Educational, social, and moral considerations made the educational system in the 1990s adopt a policy of integrating as many special children as possible in regular classes and schools. This new policy required reorganization – instituting separate special education frameworks in schools alongside the regular classes – but also budgetary changes. Integration of special children in regular schools has been accomplished in recent years. It is done in special classes of various kinds such as remedial learning, special care classes, integrated classes, and therapeutic centers which pupils attend several hours a day, or in learning specific subjects.

In 1995, special education children constituted 3.3% of all school children 5–18 years of age. The special education budget was 8% of the total national education budget. The data provided by the Central Bureau of Statistics indicate that in the half century prior to the 2000s the proportion of special education institutions relative to regular Hebrew schools declined from 19% to 2.5%. In Arab education, the opposite trend is in evidence: it climbed from 0.6% to 6.7%. The reduction in the proportion of special education schools in Hebrew education is understood as being the result of integration in regular schools. In Arab education, the change reflects a general upgrade in educational services that include attention and care for the special children.

Teacher education for special children is done in separate courses in teachers' colleges. Admission procedures for these courses are more demanding than for others; special education teaching in Israel is generally credited with a higher occupational status than regular teaching. In universities, special education is taught in separate departments in schools of education.

Special education in Israel is grounded in legislation. The Special Education Act was legislated in 1988 and applied since January 1989. It clearly establishes the State's responsibility in caring for special children; the right of any special child to receive free special education; the obligations of local authorities; authorization of parents and their representatives to take part in decision making before assignment of their child to special education; and the duties of parents as partners in the care, rehabilitation, and education of their child. The Special Education Act reflects the efforts Israel has made in becoming a modern welfare state since the 1980s. Political pressure from interested parent groups contributed to the legislation that gave parents a standing in decision making concerning the educational alternatives for their special children. Among special education pupils are children of upper and middle class parents who have an interest in placing them in regular schools. These parents, belonging to the more politically influential groups of society, succeeded in bringing about maximum integration of special children in regular Israeli schools. In contrast, parents of the same groups whose children are normal have been applying pressure from the 2000s for pluralism in education that would bring about greater segregation of special children in separate frameworks of teaching and learning.

Higher Education. Higher education in Israel began with the cultural aspirations of Zionism to make the Jewish community in Palestine a cultural center for world Jewry and create a new Jewish culture with the Hebrew language as its living core. The Hebrew University established in Jerusalem in 1925 was intended to actualize the Zionist program of creating an education and research center not just for the Jewish community in Palestine but also for the entire Jewish world. The Haifa High School of Engineering ("Technion"), also opened in 1925, was intended to serve a Zionist goal as well, that of producing Jewish engineers and architects for building the physical infrastructure of the Land of Israel. Both the Hebrew University in Jerusalem and the Haifa Technion could be regarded as an expression of the intention on the part of the Jewish community in Palestine to establish and maintain its higher education institutions on the European model.

Since the establishment of the State of Israel in 1948, six additional universities have been established. Bar-Ilan University in Ramat Gan was inaugurated in 1955 with the intention to serve the Jewish religious population. Tel Aviv University was established in 1956. Haifa University and Ben-Gurion University in Beersheba opened in 1972. The Weizmann Institute of Science was established before Israel's independence as a research institute only, but in 1958 it became an academic institute that confers degrees in physical and natural sciences. The last of the universities is the Open University (UWW), admitting students since 1976.

Unlike other universities, the Open University admits all applicants and has no admission procedures. Students study off-campus with much independence. This makes the Open University a very prominent example of the equal opportunity in educational principles. It opens its gates to students who failed the matriculation examination, older students who begin their studies after being established economically, full-time working students, and students from depressed neighborhoods and equally depressed "development towns" in the country's periphery.

Alongside the universities Israel has regional colleges with academic courses accredited by the Higher Education Council. Colleges confer first academic degrees in courses offered in cooperation with a university. The Ministry of Education and Higher Education Council support the colleges in order to enable more students to get their first academic degree – a policy in line with the general educational policy of providing an equal opportunity to get an academic degree for the greatest part of the population. Tuition is equal in all universities and its share in the total budget of academic institutions is generally dropping. An amendment to the Higher Education Council Act of 1995 allows colleges to grant first academic degrees, in order to facilitate the arrival of more high school graduates at institutes of higher education. Some colleges in Israel operate as annexes of foreign universities, though their degrees are accredited only by the Ministry of Labor, not by the Ministry of Education. Options for getting a bachelor's and master's academic degrees in Israel have been widened. With higher education becoming more democratized in general, the number of academic degree holders in Israel is increasing, but so is the criticism of academic standards.

Universities, colleges, and annexes of foreign universities in Israel are considered academic institutions. In addition to these, the higher education system includes specialized schools in various professional domains that certify their graduates as teachers, technicians, welfare assistants, and paramedical practitioners, and in administration, business, music, and performing and visual arts. Some of those schools are accredited by the Higher Education Council and confer B.A. or B.Sc. degrees to students in their respective fields of study.

An additional higher education institution is the pre-academic preparatory school that operates under the auspices of academic institutions in cooperation with the Ministry of Defense. Those schools were established to give a second chance to army veterans who had not completed their matriculation studies when in high school, so that they could resume their studies and make it to college. Beginning in the 1990s, half the preparatory school students were of Eastern ethnic origin. Some of these schools prepare their students for the matriculation examinations; others teach toward passing the entrance examinations to universities or colleges.

The Higher Education Council (HEC) is authorized by law to serve as the repository of budgets from the government and the Jewish Agency for institutions of higher education. The direct authority of managing public monies budgeted for higher education is in the hands of the Planning and Budgeting Committee of the HEC. The HEC approves the budget of the universities and allots the funds. It licenses the opening of new institutions of higher learning, gives accreditation to their degrees, and approves the opening of new departments in existing institutions. It also allots funds for teaching positions among academic personnel and supervises academic standards.

As in other countries, higher education in Israel is a major channel of social mobility. The national value of equal educational opportunity is realized in higher education by the system's effort to lower the barriers of admission in order to ease the way for more people. Stringent admission procedures are applied only in some schools or departments that are considered prestigious and where the number of applicants far exceed the institution's capacity. The prestige or desirability of schools leading to various professional degrees changes with social and economic developments. However, demand for or surplus of professionals in specific areas has never been a factor in the admission policies of higher education institutions in Israel; the policy has always aimed at enabling the most people to be admitted and get their degrees. Academicians have no special privileges in army service. Apart from a very limited number of students who learn in a framework called "Academic Reserves" for degrees in areas that are in demand in the army, university studies are not considered a reason to postpone one's army service. High school graduates have to serve their term in the army before they can turn to academic study. For that reason, Israeli students are 2–3 years older than students in other countries.

Higher education in Israel is not free. Scholarships are scarce, given to outstanding students. Tuition costs and other issues of cost, such as the cost and conditions of dormitories, were subject to a number of clashes between student organizations and academic authorities. In the late 1990s, they flared up again and even led to some violence.

The number of graduates who get their degrees is steadily rising in all universities. The annual rate of increase from 1979–1980 to 1992–93 was 3.8% and from 1989–90 to 2002–3 it was 4.7%.

The following figures apply to the 2003–4 academic year: 52.7% of all undergraduate and graduate students study in universities, 30.4% in colleges, and 16.9% in the Open University (UWW). 79.8% of undergraduates in Business Administration and Management and 71.8% of undergraduates in Law study in accredited academic colleges. 93.5% of undergraduates in Physics, Natural Sciences, and Agriculture; 88.1% of undergraduates in Medicine and Paramedical Sciences, as well as 82.7% of undergraduates in Humanities study in universities.

In 2003, the total number of undergraduate and graduate students in Israel was 228,695. In the seven universities the number of registered students was 120,552 (52.7%), 76,581 of them undergraduates. In academic colleges the number of students was 69,420 (30.4%), 68,115 of them undergraduates. An additional 38,723 students (16.9%) enrolled in the academic department of the Open University, 37,406 of them undergraduates.

Between 2000 and 2003, the number of undergraduate students in both universities and accredited academic colleges increased by an average annual rate of 4.4%. The growth occurred mainly in colleges, by an average annual rate of 8.6%; in the universities, it was up by a 1.1% annual average. The proportion of students learning in colleges is still growing.

The proportion of undergraduate students enrolled in various academic fields of study varies widely between the universities and the colleges. As mentioned, 79.8% of undergraduates in Business Administration and Management and 71.8% of undergraduates in Law study in colleges. The figure for Education is 89.7% in colleges; 55% of all students in colleges study in these three fields of study. In other disciplines, the proportion of university relative to college undergraduates is higher: 82.7% in Humanities; 66.2% in Social Science; 88.1% in Medicine and Paramedical Sciences; 63.3% in Mathematics, Statistics, and Computer Science; 93.5% in Physics, Biology, and Agriculture; and 51.5% in Engineering and Architecture. In all those areas combined, 82.9% of all undergraduates study in universities.

Graduate students in 2003 numbered 37,107 (34,568 of them in universities), an increase of 7.5% in comparison with 2002 and an average annual increase of 5.9% since the year 2000. Doctoral students in the universities numbered 7,944, 7.3% more than the previous year and representing an average increase of 6.1% since the year 2000.

In 2004–5 there was increase in the numbers of students in comparison with 2003–4. 245,000 students were registered in the eight universities, 23 colleges, and 26 teacher colleges. Approximately 191,000 were undergraduates, 43,000 graduates, and 9,000 doctoral students; 47,000 new undergraduates were admitted, 56% of them women. The proportion of women in graduate studies has been 57% and in doctoral studies 52.7%. The proportion of Arab students is on the rise but still low, about 11% of undergraduates and only 5% of graduate students. Most undergraduates study in colleges, 54% vs. 46%

Students in universities and in other institutions of post-secondary learning

Educational Institutions	1989–90	1999–2000	2001–2	2002–3	Annual Change 1989–90 to 1999–2000	Percent 1999–2000 to 2002–3
Total	88,464	199,438	217,906	228,906	8.5	4.7
Universities	67,201	112,987	117,146	120,552	5.3	2.2
Thereof: First Degree	46,519	74,194	75,247	76,581	4.8	1.1
Academic Colleges	3,668	33,709	43,492	48,320	24.8	12.8
Thereof: First Degree	3,668	33,250	42,622	47,015	24.7	12.2
Teachers Training Colleges	4,618	20,004	20,546	21,100	15.8	1.8
Open University	13,007	32,738	36,722	38,732	9.7	5.8
Thereof: First Degree	13,007	32,400	36,110	37,406	9.6	4.9

(Source: Central Bureau of Statistics, 2004)

Distribution of Undergraduate[1] Students by Institution and Field of Study, 2002–3

Field of Study	Teachers Colleges	Academic Colleges	Universities	Total (100%)
Total	21,100 (14.6%)	47,016 (32.5%)	76,581 (52.9%)	144,697
Humanities	-	3,391 (17.3%)	16,241 (82.7%)	19,632
Education and Teacher Training	21,000 (88.7%)	243 (1.0%)	2,457 (10.3%)	23,800
Social Sciences	-	9,480 (33.8%)	18,607 (66.2%)	23,800
Business and Management Sciences	-	8,187 (79.8)	2,072 (20.2%)	10,259
Law	-	8,060 (71.8%)	3,162 (28.2%)	11,222
Medicine	-	-	1,298 (100%)	1,298
Paramedical Sciences	-	901 (14.4%)	5,343 (85.6%)	6,244
Mathematics, Statistics, and Computer Science	-	3,883 (36.7%)	6,705 (63.3%)	10,588
Physical Science	-	-	2,781 (100%)	2,781
Biological Science	-	503 (11.2%)	3,989 (88.8%)	4,492
Agriculture	-	20 (2.5%)	796 (97.5%)	816
Engineering and Architecture	-	12,348 (48.5%)	13,130 (51.5%)	25,478

1 In addition, 37,406 students were registered in academic courses of the Open University, 30,822 in Humanities and Social Sciences, and 6,358 in Mathematics and Natural Sciences.

in universities. The most popular fields of study are Law, Medicine, Paramedical Sciences, Business Administration, Computer Science, Biotechnology, Social Science, and Humanities. The most stringent admission procedures exist in schools of Medicine, Psychology, Law, Engineering, Computer Science, Biotechnology, and Business Administration.

Teacher Training. Teacher training in Israel is carried out separately for elementary school teachers and secondary school teachers. Elementary school teachers are trained in teachers colleges called "seminars," many of which became academic colleges conferring a B.Ed. degree under the supervision of the Ministry of Education. Graduate teachers can resume their studies for an M.A. degree in all universities, pending completion of some additional courses. The transition to the academic level requires teachers colleges to maintain academic standards in admission, teaching staff, and curriculum. This has occurred in line with the national policy of upgrading the level of teachers and teaching in Israel.

In 2003, teacher training in Israel included 21,000 students. The process of bringing teacher training to academic level began in 1971 as an initiative of the then director-general of the Ministry of Education, who appointed a committee to examine the issue of transforming teachers seminars into colleges. This subsequently became a long-range national project under the rubric of "Academic Upgrading of Teaching Personnel in Israel." The stated goal was to allow every teacher employed in the system to gain the first academic degree in 10 years. In 1995, the authorities decided to increase the time for training junior high school teachers. Twenty-six institutions for teacher training operate in Israel; 24 are Hebrew and only two Arabic. In 1979, the total number of teachers seminars was 59, but the "academic upgrading" made it necessary for the small ones to become integrated in larger colleges.

By their essence and legal definition, teacher-training institutions exist in a border area between a post-secondary school and the university. Whereas universities in Israel are academically and organizationally independent, teachers colleges are administered and supervised by the Ministry of Education. They are dependent on the Ministry's approval in making decisions regarding administration or academic changes like, for example, opening new courses or developing curricula in new directions. Their curriculum is academic and professors enjoy full academic freedom; however, their conditions of employment are unlike those in the universities, they are not expected to conduct research, and they are evaluated for the quality of their teaching, not their research.

Teachers for secondary schools are trained in schools of education in the universities. Applicants are generally undergraduate seniors in other university schools. They study two years and graduates get, in addition to their academic degree, a permanent teacher's certificate valid for all schools supervised by the Ministry of Education. Teacher certificate studies in all universities include pedagogic subjects and a limited number of internship hours at a school. The major difference between university teacher training and training in a college is in the time of internship. Universities require only very limited internship (a few hours of practice and teaching of a test lesson) while in teachers colleges it is an integral element of the training course.

Another aspect of upgrading teacher training has been the quality of applicants. In 2003, 94.9% of Jewish teacher training students had held matriculation certificates, compared to 27.8% in 1969–70 and 58.3% in 1979–80. In the Arab sector, 96% of students in 2003 held the matriculation certificate. 15.9% of Jewish students that year were men. The percentage of men in teacher training for Arab schools is declining with the years, from 46.9% in 1969–70 to 22.9% in 1990 and 12.9% in 2003. The figures reflect social developments in Arab society, where women, having gotten a higher education and more independence, turn to professional work as teachers, while men turn to other occupations.

Extracurricular (Informal) Education. Children and young people in Israel take part in various organized activities that are not included in regular school teaching. Those activities are referred to as "informal education," education that is not compulsory. Unlike school, the area, intensity, or character of activity is (or should be) freely chosen by the child. Informal education is associated with activities beyond intellectual learning with emphasis on the development of the child's personality and identity, concern about problems of the adult world, and development of social skills for successful social functioning and social integration.

The Ministry of Education in Israel participates in financing many extracurricular educational activities and organizations. In 2003, informal education was allotted 4% of its budget. The numbers and proportion of children who take part in various informal education activities is difficult to measure, because activities differ widely in their popularity; general estimates are that it engages about 20% of the young 14–17 years of age.

Informal education in Israel originated in youth activism of the Zionist organizations in Diaspora countries, at the turn of the 19th and 20th centuries. This continued with great intensity in the Jewish community in Palestine, before the establishment of the State of Israel. The "Pioneering Youth Movements" in Israel were a direct continuation of such movements in European countries before World War II. They played an invaluable role in mobilizing youth for national pioneering enterprises. They successfully socialized the young generation into the ideology of Zionism and particularly the Labor-Zionist movement, served as hothouses for growing future elites and, mostly, were instrumental in creating the Israeli youth culture. At the center of it they were instrumental in creating the new iconic human prototype, the "Sabra," who is ever ready and able to perform the greatest national feats in conformity with Zionist goals. Youth Movement organizations were very conspicuous in the early days and they created the informal education tradition in Israel.

The prominence and strong positive image of the youth organizations continued into the 1950s; they attracted many children and youth age 10–18 and their ideology, culture, and education continued to be popular. Times were changing, the Israeli government was now the main agent of national enterprise; however, the reality of enormous tasks and little resources in early years left much space for voluntary activities such as the youth movements had undertaken. By the late 1950s, the ideological fervor characteristic of the early years following the War of Independence had waned and this had its negative effect on the popularity of youth movements. Their decline has been steady and continued even after they had changed their character as missionaries for national missions toward more personal character education and youth culture.

According to some social analysts, the youth-movement organizations have not accomplished their educational function because their fixed patterns of action, ideals, and images were bogged down in past reality rather than being meaningful to adolescents in the 1990s. Collectivist-egalitarian values were no longer popular in an Israeli society that had become oriented toward individualistic and materialistic goals, while the patterns of organized educational activities had little chance to compete with the many avenues of entertaining pastimes open to the young in the modern world. The exception were the religious-Zionist youth movements, which operated with renewed fervor mirroring the political struggles surrounding Jewish settlement in Judea, Samaria, and the Gaza Strip and continued to affirm nationalist values.

In the 1960s, new frameworks of informal education were established by state and local authorities, for young people who dropped out of school and for schoolchildren after school hours. Those informal education activities were actually an attempt to fill the gaps that formal education left.

Informal education in Israel currently operates in four main frameworks. The first are the youth-movement organizations. In 2002, 14 youth-movement organizations were registered with the Ministry of Education; they are being budgeted in proportion to the number of their members. The second framework is "supplementary education" which the educational system provides outside of regular school hours. Participation in supplementary education is optional and a matter of choice; the adult personnel is professional, operating under the supervision of the local authority and with the financial assistance of the Ministry of Education. Supplementary education activities take place in various locations, youth centers, community centers, schools, clubs, etc. A third framework of informal education is maintained for young people who are not in school or are employed in a work place and so are in danger of becoming alienated from normative social values. In this framework, activities may take place in "street groups," neighborhood "educational working groups," or boarding schools for youth at risk, that is, potential delinquents.

The fourth framework of informal education is Social Education at school, and it is conceived as semi-formal, in subjects that the curriculum does not deal with sufficiently. "Social Education," which actually means character education or socialization for socially accepted national values, is considered of the greatest importance in Israeli society. In the Ministry of Education there is a Youth Department with separate divisions for Social Education in elementary and secondary schools. Social Education is not a separate unit in schools and does not compete with regular curricular teaching and learning. It comes to complete the range of a school's educational goals in affecting the school's living atmosphere and interrelations by specific activities and structured experiences, student councils, election of students for various roles and positions, and other democratic practices.

[Rachel Pasternak (2nd ed.)]

BIBLIOGRAPHY (all items in Hebrew): H. Adler, "The Role of Education in Ethnic Integration in Israel," in: S.N. Eisenstadt and A. Zlochover (eds.), *Gathering of Exiles, Hebrew University Symposium* (1966), 17–31; M. Al Hadj, *Education of Arabs in Israel: Control and Social Change* (1996); O. Almog, *The "Sabra": A Portrait* (1997); H. Ayalon, "Address of Residence, Ethnic Origin, and Chances a Child Has for Graduation Attending a Regular Academic School," in: *Megamot*, 34:3 (1992-a), 382–401; idem, "Second Opportunity for Whom? – The Private Secondary Schools in Israel," in: A. Yogev (ed.), *Branching Education in Israel* (1992-b), 54–68; H. Ayalon, R. Shapiro, and R. Shavit, "The Educational-Social Position of Alternative Frameworks for Learning Toward the Matriculation Certificate in Israel," in: J. Danilov (ed.), *Educational Policy Planning 1990–1993* (1994), 125–62; J. Bashi, "Elementary Education in Israel," in: W. Ackerman, A. Carmon, and D. Zucker (eds.), *Education in a Newly Forming Society*, vol. 1 (1985), 313–48; M. Chen, A. Levi, and H. Adler, *Process and Outcome in Educational Practice: Contribution of Junior High School to the Educational System* (1978); A. Cohen, *Freedom Education* (1983); Y. Cohen, "Socio-economic Gaps between Eastern and Ashkenazi 1975–1995," in: *Soẓiyyologya Israelit*, 1:3 (1998), 115–34; Y. Dahan and Y. Jona, "Tel Aviv Does Not Believe in Its South," in: *Hed Hakhinukh*, 69:7–8 (1995), 7–8; Y. Dar and N. Rash, "Integration in Education and Learning Achievement: Results of Research in Israel and Hypotheses," in: *Megamot*, 31:2 (1988), 180–207; idem, "Socioeconomic Gaps in Learning Achievement in Junior-High Schools in Israel," *Megamot*, 27:4 (1991), 367–81; R. Elbaum Dror, *Hebrew Education in Eretz-Israel* (1986); C. Frankenstein, "The Parentless School," in: *Megamot*, 12:1 (1962), 3–23. Y. Friedman, *Community School Theory and Practice* (1990); M. Gal, "Informal Education in Israel, in: W. Ackerman, A. Carmon, and D. Zucker (eds.), *Education in a Newly Forming Society*, vol. 2 (1985), 601–66; R. Gavizon and A. Abu Raya, *The Jewish-Arab Breach in Israel: Attributes and Challenges* (1999); R. Gavizon, I. Gerbi, and G. Levi, G. *The Socio-economical Breach in Israel* (2000); A. Goldring, "Designs for Parental Choice of Schools for Their Children" in: J. Danilov and D. Inbar (eds.), *Free Choice in Education in Israel* (1994), 12–34.; I. Hakimi and R. Kahana (eds.), *Education in Boarding Schools in Israel* (1990); Y. Harpaz, *Community Schools: Evolution of an Idea* (1985); F. Heimann, Y. Pozner, and R. Shapiro, "Toward School Autonomy: A Survey of Attitudes about Autonomy in the Israeli Education System," in: R. Shapiro, R. Green, and J. Danilov (eds.), *School Autonomy in Practice: The Lessons* (1994), 187–208; S. Hershkovitz, "Social Aspects of Higher Education," in: S. Guri-Rosenblitt (ed.), *Accessibility of Higher Education: Admission Processes and Social Aspects* (2000); D. Horovitz and M. Lissak, *Community Becoming a Nation: Political Community of the Palestine Jews in Years of British Mandate* (1977); M. Hoshen, "Parental Decisions Regarding the Education of

Their Children: The Geographic Area Aspect," in: J. Danilov and D. Inbar (eds.), *Free Choice in Education in Israel* (1994), 35–62; D. Inbar, "Free Choice in Education: Trends and Strategies," in: J. Danilov and D. Inbar (eds.), *Free Choice in Education in Israel* (1994), 97–116; H. Ish Shalom and M. Shemida, *Social Reform in Israel and Other Nations – Secondary Education for All: Structure, History and Functioning Patterns* (1993); Y. Kashti and J. Sagi, "Rebelliousness and Colonization in Adaptation of Youth to Boarding School Living: A Case Study," in: *Iyyunim be-Minhal ve-Irgun ha-Ḥinukh*, 14 (1987), 63–82; *Knesset Protocols*, vol. 2, 1949; V. Kraus, "Social Ranking of Professional Occupations in Israel" (doctoral diss., Hebrew University of Jerusalem, 1977); V. Lavie, *Differences in Resources and Achievement in Arabic Education in Israel* (1997); Lissak, M. (1999), *The Big Wave of Immigration in the 1950s: Failure of the Melting Pot* (1999); J. Navon, *Patterns of Expanding Educational and Occupational Opportunities: The Ethnic Aspect* (1987); National Statistics Bureau (selected years), *Israel Statistics Annual*; N. Nir-Yaniv, *Forty Years of Kindergarten in Israel: Practice and Challenge* (1990); E. Peled, "Educationally Neglected Children of Eastern Ethnicity and the Policy of Their Education in the Pre-Independence Years," in: *Iyyunim be-Ḥinukh*, 34 (1982), 115–38; Y. Peres and R. Pasternak, *Community in Education Between Success and Failure* (1993); M. Raziel, "Closing the Gap in Learning Achievement Between Pupils of Eastern and Ashkenazi Ethnicity: An Overview Analysis," in: *Megamot*, 38:3 (1997), 349–66; S. Reshef and Y. Dror, *Hebrew Education in the "National Home" Days 1919–1948* (1999); J. Schwartzwald, "As a Foreign Implant?: Religious Pupils of Eastern Origin in Wealthy Junior High Schools," in *Iyyunim be-Ḥinukh*, 19 (1978), 107–22; idem, "Self-Concept in Junior High Pupils: Its Meaning for Religious School Education," in: *Megamot*, 24:4 (1979), 580–88; idem, "Ethnic Integration in Separate Conditions: The National-Secular vs. the National-Religious Schools," in: J. Amir, S. Sharan, and R. Ben Ari (eds.), *Integration in Education* (1985), 100–20; M. Smilanski, "The Social Aspect of the Educational System's Structure," in: *Megamot*, 8:3 (1957); J. Shapiro, *Elite with No Heirs* (1984); R. Shapiro and R. Shavit, "Introduction," in: R. Shapiro and R. Shavit (eds.), *Schools and Their Communities* (1995), 7–18; Y. Shavit, "Tracking and Expansion of Teaching Hours in Hebrew and Arabic Education in Israel," in: A. Yogev (ed.), *Branching Education in Israel* (1992), 69–79; State of Israel (selected years), D. Shprintzak, E. Bar, and D. Peterman, *The Education System Reflected in Statistical Figures* (Ministry of Education, Department of Economics and Statistics); State of Israel: Ministry of Education, *Tomorrow 98': Report of the High Commission for Scientific and Technological Education* (1992); State of Israel: The Knesset (1971), *Report of the Parliamentary Commission of Inquiry into the Elementary and Secondary Education in Israel* (1971); S. Svirski, *Not Backward but Backwardized: Eastern and Askenazi Jews in Israel* (1981); idem, *Israeli Education: The Realm of Separate Study Courses* (1990); idem, "'There you'd meet many immigrants of your age'…: Schools, Army and Socialization of the Israeli Prototype," in: S. Svirski (ed.), *The Seeds of Inequality* (1995), 71–117; idem, "'Progress in own tempo and be integrated': The separate tracks of study in Israel," in: S. Svirski (ed.), *The Seeds of Inequality* (1995), 118–65; S. Svirski, *Eligibility for Matriculation Examination by Place of Residence 1997–1999* (2000); S. Svirski and B. Svirski (1997), "Higher Education in Israel," in: *Meida al Shivyon*, 8; S. Tsartsur, "On the Problems of Educating a Foreign Minority in Its Own Country," in W. Akerman, A. Carmon, and D. Zucker (eds.), *Education in a Newly Forming Society* (1985), 473–525; Z. Tzameret, *The Days of the Melting Pot: The Inquiry Committee on Education of the Immigrant Children 1950* (1993); idem, *Balancing on a Narrow Bridge: the Formation of the Education System in the Big Wave of Immigration Days* (1997); S. Weil, *Ethnographic Dynamics in Israeli Community Schools* (1985); D. Weintraub and V. Kraus, "Social Differentiation and Place of Residence," in: *Megamot*, 27:4 (1982), 367–81; E. Yaar, "Private Investment as a Springboard to Socio-economic Mobility: An Additional View on Ethnic Stratification in Israel," in: *Megamot*, 29:4 (1986), 393–412; A. Yogev and H. Ayalon, "The Free Secondary Education Act and Equal Opportunity in Education: Social and Economic Aspects," *Riv'on le-Kalkalah*, 131 (1987), 873–83; A. Yogev, "High School and Future: Change Processes and Shaping of Policy," in: J. Danilov (ed.), *Educational Policy Planning 1989* (1990), 29–49.

HEALTH SERVICES

Before Statehood

At the beginning of the 19th century, the Land of Israel (Ereẓ Israel) was ridden with disease. Wide areas were infested with malaria; enteric fever, dysentery, and trachoma took a heavy toll; and infant mortality was very high. There was an improvement under the British Mandatory administration (1922–48), but, due to budgetary restrictions, its earlier efforts were concentrated almost exclusively on malaria control. Its elementary preventive and curative health services, moreover, were mainly intended for the Arab population, and the Jews had to build up their own. Their efforts were spearheaded by two voluntary organizations: *Hadassah, the Women's Zionist Organization of America, and *Kuppat Ḥolim, the medical insurance fund of the *Histadrut.

In 1913 Hadassah had sent two American-trained nurses to do pioneer work in the Old City of Jerusalem; they were followed in 1918 by the American Zionist Medical Unit. From these modest beginnings grew a countrywide network of diagnostic, preventive, and public health services and teaching and research institutions. In 1918–19 modern hospitals were opened in Tiberias, Safed, Jaffa, Haifa, and Jerusalem. The first Jewish nursing school was opened in Jerusalem by Hadassah in 1918. A network of mother-and-child care stations was established in many parts of the country, while school hygiene and lunch programs were initiated in Jerusalem. Most of these were handed over, at different stages, to the municipalities or to the Jewish authorities and, later, to the government of Israel. This also applied to the hospitals, except the one in Jerusalem, which in 1939, in partnership with the Hebrew University, became the country's first university hospital.

Whereas Hadassah began its services in a town, the initial aim of Kuppat Ḥolim ha-Kelalit (General Health Fund) was to bring medical care to the villages. However, its curative services – clinics and hospitals – soon spread to the towns as well, playing a vital role in the development of Jewish medical care. It set up an organizational system aiming to ensure that medical services were available to all its members according to need, no matter where they lived, with premiums based on income.

By the time the State of Israel was proclaimed in 1948, health standards among both Jews and Arabs had risen enormously. Malaria and TB had been wiped out; all children were inoculated against smallpox and typhoid; and infant mortality was low, even by international standards. The Mandatory government's Department of Health was succeeded by a ministry, but existing health services had to be taken over as they stood and gradually adapted to the changing needs. Owing to the conditions prevailing at the time, more radical planning for the future had to be postponed.

Immigration Problems

On the whole, there was a serious deterioration in the health of the population after 1948. Among the hundreds of thousands of immigrants were many whose health standards were low, and a high proportion suffered from contagious diseases, some of which, like trachoma, had been eliminated in Ereẓ Israel. For example, thousands of Yemenite Jews were stricken by tuberculosis within months of their arrival, and tens of thousands more, who hailed from other Eastern countries, lacked the most elementary knowledge of hygiene. Problems were enormous, and immediate solutions had to be found. The new Ministry of Health had to start from scratch, recruiting medical personnel previously employed by various Jewish public institutions and voluntary organizations. The ministry was faced with the dual task of detecting and treating all cases of infectious diseases among the newcomers while protecting the health of the existing population. Since there had been neither time nor opportunity to examine the immigrants in their countries of origin, this had to be done thoroughly on their arrival. Arrangements for such examinations were set up in the transit camps. Serious cases were immediately hospitalized, putting considerable pressure on the country's limited hospital resources, while milder cases were treated on the spot. Health services, such as mother-and-child care stations and general clinics, were set up in the immigrant camps and *ma'barot* by Kuppat Ḥolim ha-Kelalit and the Ministry of Health. Women's voluntary organizations, like *WIZO (the Women's International Zionist Organization), opened crèches and kindergartens in them.

The slowdown in immigration between 1952 and 1954 gave the Ministry of Health breathing space and enabled it to organize on a more permanent basis. By the time large-scale immigration was resumed in 1954, the reception of the newcomers had undergone a radical change. Health examinations took place before their departure for Israel, and healthy arrivals were taken immediately to permanent accommodation. A small number of would-be settlers had their entry deferred if their health fell far below the required standard.

Health of the Population

The state of health of the Israeli population compares favorably with Western standards. Life expectancy at birth in 2000 was 76.6 for males and 80.4 for females. Life expectancy for Israeli males is among the highest in OECD countries while for women it is in the low middle range. In the last two decades of the 20th century life expectancy increased by 4.8 years for males and 5.0 years for females. The crude birth rate in 1995–2000 was 21.7 per 1,000. The crude death rate was 6.1 per 1000. The infant mortality rate was 5.4, per 1,000 live births in 2000.

The leading causes of death at the beginning of the 21st century were heart diseases, malignant neoplasms, cerebrovascular diseases, diabetes, and accidents. Among women, breast cancer was the leading cancer ailment, accounting for approximately 30% of all cancer morbidity and 20% of cancer mortality. Among men the leading cancers were prostate cancer (in Jewish men) and lung cancer (in Arab men). The cancer with the highest mortality was lung cancer for both Jewish and Arab men (National Cancer Registry, www.health.gov.il).

The Ministry of Health

In addition to being the supreme authority in all medical matters, the Ministry of Health operates as the licensing body for the medical, dental, pharmaceutical, nursing, and paramedical professions and is responsible for carrying out all health legislation passed by the Knesset. It is the policy of the ministry to step in where no services are furnished by nongovernmental institutions to assure the provision of adequate medical care throughout the country. It is, in addition, Israel's principal public health agency. It has two main divisions: curative services and preventive and promotive public health services. The former is responsible for the licensing and supervising of nongovernmental medical institutions and operates all government hospitals (general, mental, tuberculosis, and other long-term illnesses). The division for public health services coordinates the six district and 14 subdistrict health offices. It maintains its own public and preventive services and supervises those of nongovernmental institutions, operates mother-and-child care centers and school health services, and is responsible for industrial hygiene, water purity, milk and food supplies, and prevention of air pollution by industry, motor vehicle exhausts, and radiation.

Health Insurance

Israel's population is covered by a compulsory health insurance law, which is operated by the four non-profit health insurance funds (*kuppot ḥolim*). The insured are entitled to free treatment in clinics, at home, or at the physician's residence, free hospitalization, dental and optical care at reduced rates, medicines, facilities for convalescence, and so forth. The law established a range of services equal for all. In addition, people can purchase supplementary services via the health insurance funds or private insurance companies.

[Malka Hillel Shulewitz / Shifra Shvarts (2nd ed.)]

The following were the principal health insurance funds in 2000:

KUPPAT ḤOLIM HA-KELALIT. Kuppat Ḥolim ha-Kelalit, the first health insurance institution in Israel, was founded in 1911 by a small group of agricultural workers and taken over in 1921 by the Histadrut (Federation of Labor). It is the largest countrywide fund of its kind, with its own medical institutions and a staff of 30,000 (in 2000), including 5,000 doctors and 10,000 nurses. Over 50% of the population is insured with Kuppat Ḥolim, which covers inhabitants of town and country, manual laborers and professional people, salaried and self-employed, Israel-born, veterans, and new immigrants.

Its countrywide organization (1,200 primary care clinics in 2000) enables it to extend its services to the most outlying areas. It provides medical care in its own clinics and has its own laboratories, pharmacies, and convalescent homes. Hospitalization, the largest item, is provided in its own hospitals, situated in rural and development districts, as well as in urban areas, or at its expense in other hospitals. These have outpatient clinics for consultation and the follow-up of discharged patients, as well as nurses' training schools, and some of them have centers for postgraduate medical training and research.

Until 1994 a Histadrut member was automatically a member of Kuppat Ḥolim and his insurance premiums were included in his membership dues, which were fixed according to income. Members of certain other workers' organizations, such as *Ha-Po'el ha-Mizrachi and *Po'alei Agudat Israel, were also insured with Kuppat Ḥolim. Between 1948 and 1994, its membership, including dependents, increased tenfold: from 328,000 to 3,600,000.

Kuppat Ḥolim grants medical care to insured breadwinners and their families (covering industrial injuries and chronic illness), as well as convalescence and sick pay. It provides the services of general practitioners, specialists, and nurses in clinics and at the patient's home, hospitalization in its own and other hospitals, X-ray treatment, physiotherapy and medical rehabilitation, and laboratory tests; medicaments and medical appliances come from its own pharmacies. Preventive medical services include mother-and-child care, industrial medicine, and health education. Eyeglasses and dental treatment are provided at moderate charge. Kuppat Ḥolim ha-Kelalit provided medical services for new immigrants from the day of their arrival, with no qualifying period. During the period of mass immigration, newcomers ignorant of the elementary rules of health and hygiene were instructed in its clinics and mother-and-child centers. In January 1995 the affiliation of Kuppat Ḥolim ha-Kelalit to the Federation of Labor ended with the enactment of Israel's health insurance law, and Kuppat Ḥolim became an independent organization.

[Izhak Kanev / Shifra Shvarts (2nd ed.)]

KUPPAT ḤOLIM LE-OVEDIM LE'UMMIYYIM. Kuppat Ḥolim le-Ovedim Le'ummiyyim (Sick Fund for National Workers) was founded in 1933. Its services in 2000 encompassed about 10% of the Israeli population. Although it is linked to the National Labor Federation (*Histadrut ha-Ovedim ha-Le'ummit), members of the sick fund are not obliged to belong to the federation. Its main feature is the free choice of a doctor by the patient, in addition to the maintenance of dispensaries and arrangements for hospitalization for the insured in government and other hospitals.

KUPPAT ḤOLIM ME'UḤEDET (AMAMIT). Kuppat Ḥolim Me'uḥedet (Amamit) ("Popular Sick Fund") was founded in 1931 on the initiative of Hadassah, mainly for farmers in villages not affiliated to the labor movement. It serves about 11% of the Israeli population (2000). In the larger centers members are free to choose their doctor; in smaller places the fund employs doctors for the insured. It has arrangements for the hospitalization of its members in government and other public hospitals. In 1974, Kuppat Ḥolim Amamit merged with Kuppat Ḥolim Merkazit to become Kuppat Ḥolim Me'uḥedet.

KUPPAT ḤOLIM MACCABI. Kuppat Ḥolim Maccabi (Maccabi Sick Fund), the second largest health fund in Israel (2000). Maccabi was founded in 1941 and serves about 24% of the population. Most of its members live in urban areas, smaller towns, and rural localities. They are free to choose their doctors; hospitalization is arranged with government and other hospitals.

THE NATIONAL HEALTH INSURANCE LAW. In January 1995, the implementation of the National Health Law revolutionized Israel's health system. All Israelis can now affiliate with the health insurance funds of their choice with premiums charged in proportion to income. The premiums are collected and then distributed by the National Insurance Institute among the Israeli health insurance organizations according to the number of insurees and according to the special needs of particular population groups. The law established a range of services equal for all. People can supplement these services via the health insurance funds or private insurance companies

MOTHER-AND-CHILD HEALTH SERVICES. The objective of these services is to provide for prenatal, natal, and postnatal care for every mother and full preparation for the birth of every child; protection and promotion of health for every child from birth to adolescence; and the detection and rehabilitation of handicapped children. Health protection includes routine immunization. Every child is vaccinated against smallpox, and a triple vaccination against diphtheria (mortality from which has virtually vanished), tetanus, and whooping cough is automatically given to over 80% of children from age three months upward, as is immunization against measles. Following a serious polio epidemic that started in 1950, the Salk vaccine was administered to all children between six months and four years from 1956 and the Sabin vaccine has been in use since 1961. As a result, cases of the disease in Israel are very rare, though the public health problem of rehabilitating patients from previous years remains.

One of the characteristics of Israel's mother-and-child care services has been their flexibility, in response to the demands of a constantly developing society. The scope of the services also aims at promoting the healthy growth and development of the family as a unit, and, since the family is bound up with the neighborhood in which it lives, the centers have undertaken to serve the surrounding community. In addition to coordination between preventive and curative services, several family health centers assume full responsibility for promotive, preventive, and curative services for all members of the family. In two Arab villages (Ṭayyiba and Ṭīra) they also provide lying-in facilities. In 2000 a network of 800 mother-and-child care centers dotted the country (in contrast to 120 in 1948). Of these, 520 were run by the Ministry of Health and by Kuppat Ḥolim ha-Kelalit, the remainder being the responsibility of the Jerusalem and Tel Aviv municipalities. Three were still retained by the Hadassah Medical Organization in Jerusalem (including a family and community health center) as part of its teaching framework.

SCHOOL HEALTH SERVICES. Health services for children of school age, originally started by Hadassah in the early 1920s, are provided by the Ministry of Health for 66% of the pupils who benefit, and local authorities for 20%, while Kuppat Ḥolim looks after the remainder. The work is done by school health teams, consisting of a physician and a public health nurse, special attention being given to the requirements of handicapped children. The control of infectious diseases through immunization is continued in this older age group, with the addition of the BCG vaccination in the seventh grade. There is also considerable activity in the field of health education.

HOSPITALIZATION. Though Kuppat Ḥolim is responsible for 50% of the population, it provides only 30% of the country's acute hospital beds, which are available primarily for its own members, and it pays for the treatment of members in other hospitals. Government, Hadassah, municipal, private, and mission hospitals accept all fee-paying patients and take turns in admitting emergency cases immediately (on days set by the Ministry of Health), financial adjustments being made afterward. In 2000 there were 48 general hospitals in the country with over 14,000 beds (2.2 beds per 1,000 population). There were also over 272 chronic disease hospitals providing 18,200 beds (2.9 beds per 1,000 population), and 21 psychiatric hospitals with approximately 5,500 beds (0.9 beds per 1,000 population).

A reduction in the average period spent in the hospital has led to better utilization of beds. This has been due to the combination of up-to-date medical skills, the establishment of more special departments, and the development of laboratory facilities. Nevertheless, the availability of beds still falls far short of the country's requirements, particularly in relation to chronic patients. In order to remedy the situation, a master plan for the construction of hospitals was worked out by the Hospital Planning Unit of the Ministry of Health.

All Jewish births and 95% of non-Jewish births take place in hospitals. Jewish women in Israel have always preferred hospital to home confinements, but Arab women, as well as many of the new immigrants, were not accustomed to this. To lower child mortality, which was higher among women who chose to deliver their babies at home, and to induce mothers to avail themselves of the advantages of delivery under safe conditions, the National Insurance Law of 1953 stipulated that the maternity grant is payable only to mothers confined in the hospital or who arrived at the hospital within 24 hours after the delivery.

MEDICAL PERSONNEL. There were 26,000 licensed doctors in Israel at the end of 2000: one for every 370 persons (and the supply of specialists in Israel does not lag behind that of other progressive countries). This is the highest ratio in the world, but many of the doctors are in the higher age groups. Over two-thirds of Israel's doctors graduated abroad. It was therefore necessary to equalize the various levels of training gained in different countries by additional training for the immigrant physicians. In partnership with Kuppat Ḥolim, the Hebrew University and Hadassah Medical School established in 1962 the Institute for Postgraduate Training, which specializes in short-term refresher courses. A second medical school was opened at Tel Aviv University in 1965, a third in Haifa in 1969, and the last in 1973 at Ben-Gurion University of the Negev in Beersheba.

Most doctors are salaried full-time staff in hospitals and other institutions; few are in private practice. All are members of the Israel Medical Association, which has adapted Hebrew terminology to the needs of contemporary medicine, set up libraries and information services, and, through its Scientific Council, laid down qualifications for specialization. Since 1980, following the initiative of Kuppat Ḥolim ha-Kelalit and the Ben-Gurion University Medical School, the Israel Medical Association started the family medicine track in medical specialization. In 2000, there were already over 800 family physician specialists working in primary care in Israel.

In 2000 there were about 30,000 nurses in Israel, 70% of them registered nurses and 30% practical nurses. From the mid-1990s, Israel suffered a shortage of nurses in the health care system. The practical nursing route was established in order to cope with the nurse shortage and to offer new immigrants with a nursing background a chance to work in the health system. Practical nurses can become registered nurses by passing the Israel Ministry of Health licensing tests. There are 40 nursing schools in Israel, almost in every general hospital. The diploma of registered nurse is awarded after a three-year course, according to standards set by the Nursing Department of the Ministry of Health. By the year 2000 almost all nursing schools in Israel upgraded their studies to a university level with a B.A. in nursing – a four-year program. In 1968 a University School of Nursing affiliated to the Faculty for Advanced Studies in Medicine of Tel Aviv University was inaugurated, leading to a B.A. degree. Schools of occupational therapy, physiotherapy, and X-ray and laboratory techniques function in different parts of the country. The Hebrew University's course for the M.A. in Public Health provides training in administration. There is a dental school at the Ein Kerem Medical Center and also at Tel Aviv University.

In 1994, following the recommendations of the Netanyahu Committee for the health care system, Ben-Gurion University opened a bachelor and postgraduate program for health administration, both managed jointly by the Ben-Gurion University School of Management and the Faculty of Health Sciences. In 1998 Ben-Gurion University opened the first school for emergency medicine to fill the need for paramedics in the civilian and military sectors. The need was felt due to the increase in terrorist attacks in Israel from the mid-1990s. In 2000 Ben-Gurion University opened the second school of public health in Israel, which has about 50 graduates every year. In 2003 Haifa University established a new Faculty for Health and Society.

HOSPITAL EMERGENCY SERVICES. Israel's security situation demands a well-planned emergency system that can be speedily put into operation. The effectiveness of this advanced planning was put to the test during the Six-Day War (1967) when the main hospitals – Soroka University Medical Center in Beersheba, Sheba (Tel ha-Shomer) Medical Center, Rabin Medical Campus (Beilinson), and Hadassah Ein Karem Medical Center – were ready to receive the wounded immediately after hostilities broke out. Beds, operating and laboratory facilities, and equipment were available underground, and casualty teams worked around the clock. The use of helicopters to facilitate the speedy transport of the wounded to the hospitals and the remarkably high standards of preparedness and treatment saved many lives. During the succeeding years of almost continuous border warfare, the hospitals continued to maintain this degree of preparedness.

[Malka Hillel Shulewitz / Shifra Shvarts (2nd ed.)]

Medical Research

Medical research in Israel has a long-standing tradition dating back to before the establishment of the state. Its contribution is undoubtedly a significant factor in the high standards of medical care in the country. The areas in which Israel exhibits particular competence today include genetics, cancer research, immunology, autoimmune diseases, diabetes, neurology, cardiovascular conditions, gene therapy, bone marrow transplantation, and stem cell research.

The first steps towards establishing medical research institutions in Palestine were taken before World War I, with the creation in Jerusalem of the Nathan Straus Health Center and Dr. Beham's Pasteur Institute. The Institute of Microbiology (Parasitology), founded in 1924 at the Hebrew University, with its departments of biochemistry and bacteriology and hygiene, founded two years later, served as the basis for the first Medical Center on Mount Scopus. In 1927 I.J. Kligler opened the Malaria Research Station at Rosh Pinnah, which initiated research, control, and supervision of anti-malarial projects in all areas of Jewish settlement and in the adjacent Arab villages.

Research in general, including medical research, can be placed in three broad categories: basic, strategic, and developmental and evaluative. Each of these categories covers, in varying degrees, the full spectrum of health and medical research: namely biomedical, clinical, public health, health economics, health policy and health services, and each of these categories maintains its own balance between advancement of knowledge and application.

BASIC RESEARCH. This category of research is initiated by the researcher (curiosity-driven) and generates new knowledge on questions of scientific significance.

STRATEGIC RESEARCH. This category can be initiated by researchers, the health system, or the health industry. It generates new knowledge to answer specific health needs and problems.

DEVELOPMENTAL AND EVALUATIVE RESEARCH (APPLIED RESEARCH, INCLUDING CLINICAL TRIALS). This category is mainly initiated by industry, but can also be sponsored by research institutions and government. It evaluates products (vaccines, drugs, diagnostics, prostheses, or equipment), interventions (public or personal health services), and instruments of policy that improve existing options.

Support of research in Israel comes from several sources: the Israeli government, European Community (EC), National Institutes of Health (NIH), international and national nongovernment organizations (NGOs), international and national private foundations, charitable organizations, and private donations. The Israeli government supports research via different ministries and international agreements. The most important source of government support of basic research comes from the Israel Science Foundation (ISF), whose funds are budgeted by the Finance Ministry and channeled via the Budgeting and Planning Committee of the Council for Higher Education of the Ministry of Education. The Ministry of Science and Technology (MOST) supports both basic and strategic research and the Ministry of Commerce and Industry supports for the most part R&D by industry. Under bilateral agreements the Israeli government allocates matching research funds to the U.S.-Israel Binational Science Foundation (BSF) and the German-Israeli Foundation for Scientific Research and Development (GIF). These granting agencies support competitive grants in the different areas of scientific research that also include medical research. Medical research is also supported by organizations such as the Israel Cancer Society (ICA), the Israel Cancer Research Fund (ICRF), the Juvenile Diabetes Foundation (JDF), etc.

Most medical research in Israel is performed at its four medical schools: the Hebrew University (HU), Tel Aviv University (TAU), Ben-Gurion University (BGU), and the Technion, and their affiliated hospitals. Medical research and research in disease-linked life sciences are performed in the relevant faculties of the above universities and at Bar-Ilan University, which does not have a medical school, and the Weizmann Institute of Science. It is noteworthy that in two of the four medical schools more than 90% of the clinical researchers are from the respective hospitals. At BGU more than 90% of the clinical researchers are from the Soroka Medical Center and at HU more that 90% are affiliated with Hadassah University Hospital. For the most part, the number of investigators at a specific hospital is relative to the size of the hospital and the closeness of the affiliation with its medical school.

Several government ministries have chief scientists whose responsibility is to support and administer research and development grant programs in their respective fields.

The office of Chief Scientist established in the Ministry of Health in 1970 is a pivotal factor at the crossroads of research in biomedical science and the pursuit of disease-oriented clinical research and development. Its aims are (1) to promote, assist, and undertake basic, applied "disease-oriented" and clinical research in the health sciences; (2) to promote and support research in hospitals and universities; and (3) to encourage young physicians to do research.

Efforts are made to assist investigators working in peripheral hospitals situated far from the major centers of medical research in Israel and to assist young investigators taking their first steps in research.

[Bracha Rager and Benny Leshem (2nd ed.)]

Services for the Arab Population

When the Ministry of Health was established, a special division was set up to serve the Arab and Druze communities. In 1952, however, with their progressive integration into the structure of the state, the division was abolished. The ministry set up clinics and mother-and-child health centers in Arab areas. An Arab officer is attached to the Regional Services Administration of the ministry to act as a liaison between the head office and the field units. Many Arabs and Druze have joined Kuppat Ḥolim, which has set up clinics in many villages. Integrated preventive and curative services are available at six health centers, in addition to general clinics and mother-and-child centers, covering more than 80% of Israel's Arabs. Case-finding activities are conducted among the Bedouin tribes in the Negev to combat tuberculosis, trachoma, and ringworm. The incidence of these once-prevalent diseases has decreased considerably, thanks largely to a mobile unit that regularly visits Arab villages and Bedouin encampments examining children and others. This service facilitates the early diagnosis and treatment of these diseases where they still exist. Eighty-four percent of Arab women now have their babies in hospitals, and the supervision of the mother-and-child centers is highly valued. Until 1994 about 87% of the Arab population were insured in the public health sector in Israel, mainly in Kuppat Ḥolim ha-Kelalit. Since 1995 all Arab citizens in Israel are entitled to equal health services under the Health Insurance Law. The extension of health coverage to the entire Arab population led to expansion of primary health services within the Arab villages in the north of Israel and also in the south in the Bedouin community. The major part of the Arab population chose to stay with Kuppat Ḥolim ha-Kelalit and only few moved to Macccabi and the smaller Me'uhedet and Le'ummit health insurance funds.

[Malka Hillel Shulewitz / Shifra Shvarts (2nd ed.)]

IN THE ADMINISTERED TERRITORIES. Immediately after the Six-Day War, a civil administration to deal with health services was attached to the military government in the areas administered under the cease-fire agreements. It faced two major problems: first, the low standard of health among large sections of the population in comparison with that prevailing in Israel, as well as higher infant and maternal mortality rates and inadequate inoculation rates, particularly against such serious diseases as polio; and second, the exodus of medical and paramedical personnel, which continued in 1967–68. This movement ceased in 1969, however, and a reverse trickle started. The situation was further relieved by the participation of Israel personnel, and joint efforts led to an overall improvement. In addition, Israel's health services were opened to residents of the administered territories when they required specialized treatment (including hospitalization) unavailable in their own places of residence. Following the signing of the Oslo Accords in 1994, responsibility for health care was gradually transferred to the *Palestinian Authority.

[Malka Hillel Shulewitz]

BIBLIOGRAPHY: B. Rosen, R. Goldwag, S. Thomson, and E. Mossialos, in *The European Observatory on Health Care Systems*, 5:1 (2003); S. Shvarts, *The Workers' Health Fund in Israel, Kuppat Ḥolim, 1911–1937* (2003); S. Shvarts, in *Social History of Medicine*, 11:1, 73–88; S. Brammli-Greenberg and R. Gross, *The Private Health Insurance Market in Israel* (2003).

SOCIAL SECURITY AND WELFARE

SOCIAL POLICY

In the first three decades of statehood through the end of the 1970s Israel acquired the basic features of a modern welfare state. This meant that Israel succeeded in developing a broad network of social services that included comprehensive service systems in health, education, housing, social security, and the personal social care services. Combined with other social and economic policies the country was committed to maintaining and improving the standard of living of the population. All these policies brought about a far-reaching transformation of Israeli society.

Since the 1980s Israel's social policies have undergone a significant change. The change occurred in the nature of its welfare regime and also involved structural and political changes with reference to the government's role in ensuring the welfare of the population and maintaining welfare and social security services.

In terms of its welfare regime the major trend was to depart to a great extent from the European model with regard to welfare policy and social protection and move towards a more American model. The European model to which Israel adhered for many years is based on a high degree of social solidarity and mutual obligation among the different sectors of the population. It is also geared to prevent growing social inequality and the existence of wide social gaps. In contrast, the trend prevalent in Israel since the 1980s tended more towards the American model of a limited government role in providing social services and social protection to the entire population, leaving citizens more dependent on market forces and the uncertainty evolving from it.

The main trend that dominated Israeli social policy from the late 1980s was thus to reduce state involvement in the provision of welfare, to cut government spending on social welfare and social security, and to introduce changes in the existing social security and welfare programs that will have a long-term impact on the government's commitment to reducing social welfare spending.

This trend became more dominant in the years 2000–2004, when the government embraced a program of radical reform and restructuring of the welfare state. A combination of ideological, political, economic, and demographic factors played an important part in this policy shift and were mostly related to the changing patterns of the demographic balance of power in Israeli society. The main characteristic of the policies adopted was an extensive retrenchment in welfare and social security programs and a further reduction in collective responsibility for the well being of the population.

SOCIAL SECURITY

The core of the Israeli welfare state is its social security system, which includes a wide range of national insurance schemes and a range of non-contributory income maintenance programs. The entire system is maintained by the National Insurance Institute, an autonomous state agency operating under the supervision of the Minister of Welfare.

The national insurance schemes developed since the 1950s became the major instrument ensuring the social security of large portions of the population. They include old age and survivors insurance, maternity, unemployment, work injury, and general disability insurance, a national health insurance program, and some additional minor social insurance-based schemes. Demographic changes, such as the growth of the elderly population, the size of the children's population, and the composition of the immigrant groups, have been a critical factor in the growth of the system.

Old Age and Survivors Insurance

Old age and survivors insurance is the largest national insurance scheme. Nearly 40 percent of all national insurance benefits are paid out by this scheme. All the residents of Israel (with a few exceptions) are covered by this scheme and have to pay premiums until retirement. The age of absolute entitlement to an old age pension is 70 for men and 67 for women. Until the recent retrenchment measures the absolute entitlement age for women was 65 only. Men from the age of 67 to 70 and women from the age of 64 are entitled to a pension conditional on an income test when their incomes are below a defined threshold.

Latterly, until the reforms, the old age national insurance pensions were of a uniform rate (with some increments) and set at a fixed percentage of the national average wage (16% of the average wage for a single person and 24% for a couple). The pensions were automatically updated every year in line with changes in the average wage. The linking of the pensions to the average wage had a considerable equalizing effect in the sense that they ensured higher earning replacement rates for pensioners with low pre-retirement incomes compared to low income replacement rates for those with high pre-retirement incomes.

The reform adopted severed the linkage of pensions to the average wage and their automatic annual updating. In the future pensions will be updated in line with the price index only. The pensions will thus lose their dynamic feature and will be gradually eroded, leaving the pensioner lagging behind the rest of the population in sharing national prosperity as reflected in the rise in wages.

Children's Allowances

The second biggest program in Israel's social security system, accounting for about 20 percent of all benefit payments, are the children's allowances. Towards the end of the 1990s the program was fully universal in its coverage, i.e., it provided benefits for every child in Israel younger than 18. It consisted of one uniform scheme fully integrated into the direct tax system. In practice the program was built on a credit point system and played a dual role: It served as a tax credit for families with incomes exceeding the tax threshold and was the equivalent of a "negative income tax" for families whose income was below the tax threshold level. The allowances were the dominant and almost only factor taking into account family size in the direct tax system. They were linked to the consumer price index and raised accordingly in January of every year. The value of a credit point in 2000 was equal to 2.5 percent of the average wage.

There were numerous changes and upheavals in the children's allowance payments since the first scheme of large-family allowances was instituted in 1959. The major structural reform introduced in 2003 was its alteration from a system of benefits by which the number of credit points was awarded on an ascending scale which increased steeply from the third child on, to a system of a single flat-rate allowance paid for all children irrespective of the number of children in the family. Children born after July 1, 2003, are entitled only to the new flat-rate allowance. To ease the transformation, which involves substantial losses of income to large families, the change will be phased in gradually over a longer period of time and will be in full operation in 2009.

The chief policy issue involved in the structural change of the children's allowance program arose from the problem of large families in two particular population groups: the ultra-Orthodox Jewish sector and the Arab population. The high fertility rates among these two population groups were seen to have a major effect on the increasing cost of public support for these families. The argument was that the increased benefit rates to large families encouraged the high fertility rates among them. Moreover, by providing them with additional income the allowances supported their voluntary withdrawal from participation in the labor force. The restructuring of the program was thus explained in terms of these wider social and demographic issues and their possible negative effect on the national economy.

Unemployment Insurance

Unemployment insurance was established only after a prolonged debate in 1973. Despite the important task of the scheme in providing an alternative income to the involuntarily unemployed there was strong opposition to its introduction, which came, perhaps paradoxically, from the Israeli labor movement. With the growth of unemployment in the 1990s various amendments were introduced to the scheme to make it more difficult to receive unemployment benefits. The aim of these policies was to strengthen labor market discipline among the working population and to increase the flexibility of the job market. As a result there was a significant reduction of the scheme's capability to provide adequate protection for the unemployed.

Long-Term Care Program

The long-term care program started to operate in 1988. The program covers all residents included in the old age insurance program. The long-term care services are limited to the elderly population. They are provided to elderly persons who are dependent to a great extent or entirely on the help of others to perform essential daily tasks. Entitlement to long-term care under the program is conditional on dependency and income tests. The program has grown rapidly, both in the number of beneficiaries and in expenditure, since it began.

The package of services provided includes personal care at the home of the elderly person or in a day care center, housekeeping help, supply of absorbent materials, laundry services, and the installation of distress alarms. The services are provided by non-profit as well as commercial service organizations licensed for this purpose.

The non-contributory income maintenance programs include the safety-net income support scheme, benefits to the victims of hostile actions, and a range of other minor benefit programs.

Safety-Net Income Support

The safety-net income support scheme has been in operation since 1982. The scheme replaced the earlier system of assistance to the needy through the social welfare bureaus of the local authorities and transferred this responsibility to the national government. The program is by its very nature highly selective and caters to the neediest population groups. The granting of benefits is conditional on strict means and employment tests. Under these conditions the program was designed to guarantee everyone who meets the eligibility criteria a legally defined minimum level of income applied uniformly in every location in the country.

The program has grown greatly since its inception. Although the benefits provided were far less generous than in most European countries, the program nonetheless became, in the years 2002–3, the target of a strong political anti-welfare backlash. It was argued that its benefits were too generous and therefore creating serious disincentives to work. Eventually, in line with the government's retrenchment policies, welfare reform measures were introduced in 2003 that significantly reduced the level of benefits. Under the reform single persons and couples under the age of 25 are no longer entitled to income support. Women with young children aged two years and up are required to report for work as opposed to the previous age of seven and up. In addition, most rebates granted to income-support recipients, such as reduction of medical prescription costs or TV license payments, were canceled. About 70 percent of those receiving income support were affected by these changes.

The Personal Social Services

From the establishment of the state until 1977 the Ministry of Welfare was in charge of operating the personal social services. In 1977 a new Ministry of Social Affairs was established which amalgamated the former ministries of Labor and Welfare. The merger of the two ministries did not produce over the years the expected beneficial results and in 2003 the old Ministry of Welfare was recreated while the Labor part was ceded to the Ministry of Industry and Trade.

The personal social service system includes a wide range of care services that cater to the needs of weak population groups with difficulties in their personal and social functioning. These groups include the disabled; the physically, mentally, and emotionally handicapped; the elderly; young people in distress; battered women and neglected children at risk. This service system is maintained for the most part by the welfare bureaus of the local authorities and their care services are generally provided under the auspices of the social work profession and by professional social workers.

Although the foundations of the system were established as early as the 1930s, its legal base remains somewhat unsatisfactory. The Welfare Service Law of 1958, which defines its operating principles, is mostly outdated and has not kept up with the changes in the field. The main deficiencies are related to the lack of a binding definition of the rights of a needy person to receive services, there are no details as to the package of services that the authorities are required to provide, and there is no clear obligation of the central and local government to fund the services. In times when retrenchment was the dominant theme in the social policies of Israel, the personal social service system was particularly vulnerable and thus seriously hurt by cutbacks in resources for its maintenance.

Voluntary Agencies

The voluntary sector, i.e., private non-profit organizations, plays an important role in Israeli social welfare. The sector is composed of a great many agencies, some of them associated under national women's umbrella organizations like WIZO and Na'amat while others operate independently on the local community level. They provide a wide range of social care services catering to the needs of particularly vulnerable population groups and thus complement the welfare services provided by the state. Their activities are especially important in the field of child welfare, care of neglected and abused children, services to the growing elderly population, and to new immigrant groups, such as the recently arrived Ethiopians.

The role of the voluntary sector gains additional significance in times of government retrenchment in the field of welfare and in the event of cutbacks in social expenditure. The failure of the authorities to meet the increased demand for social services has forced the voluntary sector to shoulder more of the welfare burden. This has become especially evident in the growing number of food banks operated by the voluntary sector on the local community level and the operation of soup kitchens providing meals to the needy.

BIBLIOGRAPHY: A. Doron and R.M. Kramer, *The Welfare State in Israel – The Evolution of Social Security Policy and Practice* (1991); A. Doron, "Social Welfare Policy in Israel: Developments in the 1980s and 1990s," in: *Israel Affairs*, 7:4 (Summer 2001).

[Abraham Doron (2nd ed.)]

CULTURAL LIFE

Introduction

The movement for the return to Zion which emerged as a force at the end of the 19th century was based on a variety of motivations, including the political – the demand for an independent homeland where the Jews could forge their own destiny without dependence on the goodwill of others; the religious – based on the traditional belief in God's promise of the Land of Israel to the people of Israel; and the sociological – which maintained that only in their own land could the Jews revert to a normal occupational structure. In addition, from the early days of the modern movement, stress was laid on the cultural aspect, the argument being that true Jewish creativity would emerge only when the Jew was resettled in his ancient homeland. The spokesman of Cultural Zionism was *Aḥad Ha-Am, and one of his classical statements on the subject was made at a conference of Russian Zionists held at Minsk in 1902. He stressed the need to establish a great academic institution in Ereẓ Israel, emphasized that the Hebrew language was essential in developing the new Jewish culture, and advocated "a concentration of genius and talent in the service of Jewish culture to restore the Jewish people to its rightful place in the comity of human culture." Aḥad Ha-Am spoke of "the spiritual center of our nation which is destined to arise in Palestine in response to the insistent urge of the national instinct," adding, "We dare not neglect to do what is necessary to make Palestine a permanent and freely developing center of our national culture, of our science and scholarship, our art and literature." He envisioned "the larger cultural enterprise on which we shall embark after the establishment of the center in Palestine, when the work of the returned wanderers will serve as the starting point for an advance into higher realms of achievement" (*Aḥad Ha-Am*, translated by Leon Simon (London, 1946), 97–100).

Until the 19th century, Jewish cultural creativity in the Diaspora had been expressed mainly within a religious framework. The bulk of the literature had been on religious subjects, art had been confined to ritual spheres, and musical expression was liturgical. There had been notable exceptions, in particular in periods of freer contacts with the non-Jewish world, but in general the universal aspects of Jewish cultural and artistic talents had been stunted or shunted into a narrow context. Natural development only became possible as a result of emancipation. This was spectacularly evident in the 19th century as Jews in Central and Western Europe moved into those expressions that had hitherto been denied them. Toward the end of the century, a similar, if proportionately more limited, trend became discernible also among eastern European Jewry. This new cultural revival was marked by a strong secular trend, and it was confined to the Ashkenazi sector – no parallel flowering was possible among Sephardi Jewry (except for the few in western lands) or in Oriental communities. It was the strong upsurge of intellectual and cultural creativity in European Jewry which Aḥad Ha-Am sought to attract and harness to the Jewish nationalistic expression within the Zionist movement. Although political Zionism was the dominant motivation in the various *aliyot*, the ideals of cultural Zionism became interwoven in the fabric of Zionist ideology. There were those whose prime reason for settling in Ereẓ Israel was the conscious desire to participate in a new Jewish creativity; but even those coming as the result of other ideals or impetuses subscribed to the cultural ideals.

The first generations of settlers consciously struggled with the interrelations of the different components which they felt would be required for an Israeli culture. On the one hand, it would have to be solidly based within Jewish traditions and the Hebrew language; on the other, it would have to relate to a universal context. In the early decades of settlement, and especially in the first flush of nationalist sentiment, the particularist tendencies were dominant. A marked continuity with the eastern European Jewish tradition was perpetuated in all forms of cultural expression. But in the course of time, more stress was laid on universalism and less on introspection. The first generation was firmly based on its European roots; the second generation was rooted in its experiences in Ereẓ Israel, especially those connected with *aliyah* and the kibbutz movement; the third generation, emerging around the time of the 1948 War of Independence, was dominated by the sabra with his newly found self-confidence; the fourth generation (or the second sabra generation, coming of age around the time of the Six-Day War) was universalistic and outward looking, seeing Israeli culture as one expression of contemporary world culture; the fifth generation is totally attuned to western popular culture and in effect not different from its counterpart in Europe and America.

Against this background, Israeli culture has assimilated a kaleidoscope of varied elements. Jewish traditions, religious and historical, and the Hebrew language constitute the firm foundations – sometimes only subconsciously – of the cultural patterns that have emerged. A colorful originality has been imparted by the diversity of the Jewish elements. Jews arriving from communities in all parts of the world have brought with them both cultural expressions that developed within their own framework and aspects of the majority culture which they had absorbed over the centuries. The intermingling of the Ashkenazi, Sephardi, and Oriental traditions has provided an immense opportunity. This has, moreover, been reflected by the physical location of this new creativity – in a Middle East setting at the meeting point of Europe, Asia, and Africa. The uniqueness of this situation and location prompted the consideration that this was a place where East meets West – to some extent geographically and to a large extent through the composition of population. As a consequence, considerable cultural and artistic activity has been devoted to an attempt to weld Oriental and occidental elements in an endeavor to achieve original concepts. Much of Israel's artistic expression has been characterized, therefore, by this east-west synthesis. However, one element that has as yet made little penetration is that of the Arab world. Especially since the establishment of the State of Israel, cultural developments in Arab countries have been largely sealed off from the Israelis, while achievements among Israel Arabs have been on a limited scale (see Arabic Literature, in Israel, State of: *Arab Population) and have had virtually no influence on the mainstream of Israel culture.

Since the beginning of the 20th century, Israel's culture has developed significantly. From small and sometimes artificial beginnings, achievements have been registered in most spheres, justifying the vision of Aḥad Ha-Am. This has been attested to by international recognition (e.g., the award of the Nobel Prize for literature to S.Y. *Agnon, international prizes for art and music, acclaim for Israel actors and actresses) as well as by the crystallization of distinctive expressions that are especially meaningful both for Israelis and for Jews in other countries.

Hebrew Language

The determination to revive Hebrew as a spoken language was intimately associated with the nationalist revival toward the end of the 19th century. The phenomenon was paralleled in other countries (e.g., Ireland), and the speaking of Hebrew became part of Zionist ideology. Although not spoken as an everyday tongue for some 17 centuries, Hebrew had remained a language of literature and of prayer, never forgotten and always cherished. The tradition of writing in Hebrew was maintained, even though the results were frequently clumsy and artificial. Already in the middle of the 19th century, Hebrew was being spoken in Jerusalem, where it provided a link between the Ashkenazi and Sephardi Jews who had no other language in common. As early as 1855, a meeting of Jewish notables, convened in Jerusalem to discuss the foundation of the first secular school (the Laemel School), held its deliberations in Hebrew.

The tendency, however, was sporadic and ill-defined until the arrival in Jerusalem of Eliezer *Ben-Yehuda in 1881. He had launched his single-minded campaign for the revival of Hebrew as a spoken language while he was still in Europe. In 1879 he had suggested the foundation of a Jewish State with Hebrew as its language and in 1880 published a withering attack on the prevalence of foreign languages and influences in Palestine. At that time the Laemmel School, under Austrian influence, included German in its curriculum, while *Mikveh Israel and other institutions founded by the *Alliance Israélite Universelle fostered knowledge of French and admiration for French culture.

Ben-Yehuda found support in Jerusalem, especially among Sephardi circles, and conducted a campaign for teaching in Hebrew. At first this was greeted for the most part with a reaction of scorn and disbelief. Even scholars who supported the general concept of a Hebrew revival, such as Aḥad Ha-Am and Yehudah Grasovski (*Goor), were not prepared to follow Ben-Yehuda to the extent of using Hebrew as the language for general instruction in the schools. But Ben-Yehuda was adamant, writing: "If we want our people to survive, if we want our children to remain Hebrews, we must train them in the Hebrew language… We must make our sons and daughters forget the corrupt foreign dialects which tear us to shreds." To prove his point, in 1883 Ben-Yehuda accepted a teaching position in a girls' school run by the Alliance in Jerusalem. Although he had to give it up after a few months, he succeeded in that time in introducing the *Ivrit be-Ivrit* ("Hebrew in Hebrew") teaching method. The possibilities of the method were realized by the pedagogical authorities. Apart from the ideological aspect, it had a practical side, in that there were not enough Sephardi pupils to fill the schools and there was a desire to attract Ashkenazi students as well. Ashkenazim, however, would not attend schools where the language of instruction was Ladino or Arabic. Hebrew provided a common tongue through which Jewish children from any origin could be instructed. Ben-Yehuda won over to his point of view a number of influential personalities, notably David *Yellin and Joseph Meyouḥas, and they rapidly succeeded in further spreading the use of Hebrew in schools. By 1888, all subjects were being taught in Hebrew at the school in Rishon le-Zion, which was also the site of the first Hebrew-speaking kindergarten (1898). A meeting of Jewish teachers in Jerusalem in 1892 passed a resolution advocating the exclusive use of Hebrew in schools. When the first high schools were opened – in Jaffa in 1906 and in Jerusalem in 1908 – their language of instruction was Hebrew.

Ben-Yehuda was not satisfied with the growth of Hebrew in the schools alone. He also wanted it to be the general language of conversation among adults. In 1883, together with Jehiel Michael *Pines, he organized a secret society called Teḥiyyat Israel ("The Revival of Israel") whose members swore to speak with one another solely in Hebrew "even in marketplaces and streets, without being ashamed." The following year, he founded the Safah Berurah ("Pure Language") society to disseminate the Hebrew language and its conversational usage. Ben-Yehuda was also disturbed by the fact that his various efforts were only reaching male members of the community. He wanted girls and women to learn Hebrew, so that it would be the language they would talk to their children. His advocacy led to the establishment in Safed of the first girls' Hebrew school in 1891.

The path of the Hebraists was far from smooth, and they met with determined opposition from various quarters. The Orthodox elements in Jerusalem were openly hostile and imposed a *ḥerem*. The officials of Baron Edmond de *Rothschild, who were the products of French culture, feared that the spread of Hebrew would endanger their own influence in the country and objected to changes in the language of instruction in French-speaking schools. Stalwarts of Yiddish and Ladino were apprehensive that the development of Hebrew would lead to the neglect of their languages (as eventually was the result). Moreover, there were objective reasons. The language still lacked the requisite elasticity for instruction. There were no textbooks or reading books in Hebrew. In order to establish recognized standards and bring order into the diversity that had been unleashed, Ben Yehuda organized the Va'ad ha-Lashon ("Language Committee") in Jerusalem (1890). Its task was to determine new usages. But after a year this committee, as well as the Safah Berurah society, went out of existence as a result of internal dissensions. In 1904 it was reorganized under the auspices of the *Teachers' Association. The Committee now consisted of leading philologists and teachers, and their mandate included decisions on the coinage of new terms, the determination of orthography, the preparation of specialized dictionaries, and the standardization of pronunciation. On the last point, the Committee decided that the Sephardi pronunciation should be standard, as this bore the closest resemblance to Hebrew speech in ancient times. School principals and teachers were informed of this decision in 1907.

Ben-Yehuda also started work on his monumental Hebrew dictionary, five volumes of which appeared in his lifetime (the entire 17-volume dictionary eventually extended over 8,000 pages). It covered all subjects comprehensively and was a basic reference work for the developing language. Further pioneer dictionaries in many specialized spheres were issued by the Va'ad ha-Lashon.

Recognition of Hebrew in Ereẓ Israel was not attained without a bitter struggle, known as the Language Conflict, to replace German by Hebrew in the schools of the *Hilfsverein der deutschen Juden and the newly established *Technion (see Israel, State of: *Education, 1880–1914). By the end of World War I, the Language Conflict had receded far into the distance, and the position of Hebrew throughout the country was unchallenged. Already in 1916–18, a census showed that 40% of the Palestinian Jews outside Jerusalem were Hebrew-speaking. The proportion among children was 54%, and in Tel Aviv and in the villages it was 77%.

The Palestine Mandate of 1922 gave Hebrew official recognition as one of the three languages of the country (alongside English and Arabic). It was henceforward used in the administration, on coins, stamps, and so on. Within the Jewish community the use of Hebrew was stressed as a patriotic activity. A youth organization, the Gedud Meginnei ha-Safah ("Language Protection Legion"), was founded in Tel Aviv in 1923 to combat the speaking of languages other than Hebrew (it remained in existence until the late 1930s). By 1948, 80% of the Jewish population spoke Hebrew, and for 54% of them it was their sole language of communication.

Hebrew became the official language of the State of Israel on its establishment in 1948. The mass immigration of the ensuing years posed difficult problems which were met by original approaches. Outstanding among these was the institution of the *ulpan, the intensive Hebrew courses for newcomers to the country which were introduced in various forms. The proportion of Hebrew speakers inevitably dropped somewhat (in 1954 only 53% of the adult population spoke Hebrew), but the figures rose steadily as the newcomers learned the language, and especially as all the children were Hebrew speakers. In 1953 the Ministry of Education established a Hanhalat ha-Lashon ("Language Transmitting") department to work among new immigrants. Special techniques were devised for acquiring the language quickly, including a fundamental vocabulary of 1,000 words that served as the basis for special books, daily newspapers, and radio broadcasts.

In 1954, by act of the Knesset, the Va'ad ha-Lashon became the *Academy of the Hebrew Language, established to determine correct and grammatical Hebrew usages. The Academy works through various committees, each specializing in a particular field, and it has fixed tens of thousands of technical terms. The procedure for determining new words takes two to three years, during which time the various philological possibilities are carefully studied. Sometimes the Academy is overtaken by events, and by the time it has made its decision, the public is using another word which cannot be rooted out. But this is further evidence that Hebrew has become a living language used for everything from football to atomic physics.

Literature

Until the early part of the 20th century, only a few individuals of small significance were writing in Ereẓ Israel. The foundations of modern Israeli writing were laid by a group of literary pioneers from the Second Aliyah including S.Y. Agnon, Moshe *Smilansky, Joseph Ḥayyim *Brenner, David *Shimoni, and Jacob *Fichmann. Until World War I, Hebrew literature was centered in Eastern Europe. After the war and the Russian Revolution, many Hebrew writers found their way to Palestine, so that at the time Palestinian writing was essentially a continuation of the European tradition. In 1921, 70 writers from various parts of the country met in Tel Aviv and founded the Hebrew *Writers' Association, with the declared objective of working together to protect and promote Hebrew literature and spiritual interests. About this time the first literary periodicals made their appearance – *Ha-Adamah*, edited by Brenner, and *Ma'barot*, edited by Fichmann. The 1920s and 1930s witnessed the emergence of Palestine as the dominant center of Hebrew literary activity. In Palestine there was a Hebrew press, Hebrew publishers, and a Hebrew-reading public. Moreover, even when Hebrew writers had lived outside the country, the return to Zion had been one of their basic themes, and, now that they had the opportunity, many of them went to settle in Palestine. The great figures of the early part of the century – *Bialik, Aḥad Ha-Am, *Tchernichowsky – all spent their last years in Tel Aviv, and although this was not the period of their greatest creativity, they exerted a great influence on younger Hebrew writers.

The first generation of writers in the country was European-born and very much European-influenced. Although some of their writings related to the situation in Palestine, their main concern was still with the world they had left. Authors such as Y.D. *Berkowitz, Devorah *Baron, and Asher *Barash continued to write about Eastern Europe. The major writers of this school, S.Y. Agnon and Ḥayyim *Ḥazaz, were deeply rooted in their European background and served as links between the classical writers of the early decades of the Hebrew revival and the Hebrew writers in Israel during the following generations.

For the next generation of writers the center of focus was the Land of Israel, even when they were writing about other parts of the world. Their framework was the period of *aliyah* and, very often, life in the kibbutz. Their attitude to their new land (most of them were born elsewhere) was sometimes one of disappointment, but this generally led to a deeper understanding of the values of the new civilization in which they were participating. Among the outstanding names are Uri Zvi *Greenberg and Avraham *Shlonsky, who found in the Land of Israel the requisite antidote to the rootlessness of the Diaspora. The third generation of writers emerged around the time of the War of Independence (1948). Its key figures (e.g., S. *Yizhar, Moshe *Shamir) were all sabras or had been brought to the country at an early age. This was no longer a "desert generation," but young men for whom Israel was an established fact – to be criticized and fought for, like any other country. The eastern European symbols and even the renewed challenge of immigration played only secondary roles. Strong influences now came in from other literatures, especially western. A fringe group called the "Canaanites" even sought to deny the connection between Israelis and Jews elsewhere. The 1948 war was their great moment, and for a time they coasted on its backwash. But this was replaced by a feeling of emptiness and of searching for new values, leading to experiments in exploring other Jewish communities in Israel or the Jewish past. The subsequent generation – the second sabra generation (of the 1960s) – endeavored to place Israeli culture within a world context and stressed not so much the unique and particularistic aspects of Jewish life and Israel as the universal. This school of writers often identified with the "protest" literature of other countries. Of the writers who began publishing in the 1960s, Amos *Oz and A.B *Yehoshua have emerged as giants, fully engaged in political issues, in addition to producing their highly acclaimed works of fiction. The following generation, writers who were born in the 1960s and 1970s and made their debut in the 1980s and 1990s, examined the basic questions of Jewish-Israeli existence by exposing the collective tensions in individual characters and fates. Among the major concerns repeatedly treated are: the makings of Israeli identity and its relation to Jewish roots and Diaspora experience; the legitimacy and validity of the Zionist vision and the discrepancy between the initial Zionist project and its implementation; the recurrence of war and acts of terror and the inability to solve the over 100-year-old Arab/Palestinian-Israeli conflict in non-violent ways; the changes in the system of political, social and moral values and in the mentality of the Israelis; the long shadows of the Holocaust, the inner world of the survivors, as well as the duty and need to remember; problems of absorption, socio-ethnic difference and discrimination; and last but not least, gender issues, primarily the status of women in Jewish/Israeli life and culture and homoerotic proclivities. Grappling with these issues, writers turned to various genres and narrative modes such as the historical novel, the family saga, realistic allegories, expressionist and surrealist narratives or, more recently, to postmodernist narrative.

Apart from Hebrew writers, there is considerable creative productivity in Israel in other languages, notably in Yiddish. Before World War II, Warsaw, Moscow, and New York were the main centers of Yiddish activity. In Palestine there was still a certain hostility to the language, which, it was felt, constituted a challenge to the Hebrew revival, and little creativity was recorded. However, with World War II the whole picture changed. The European centers were liquidated by Hitler and Stalin and the New York center declined. Immigration brought many of the leading Yiddish writers to Israel and the internal attitude relaxed and became friendly, in view of the Holocaust in Europe, on the one hand, and the secure position attained by Hebrew, on the other. Yiddish writing in Israel can be marked by generations, similar to those in Hebrew literature. The first consisted of the old guard, such as David *Pinski and Sholem *Asch, who passed their last years in Israel. The second generation, led by Avraham *Sutzkever, started its career in eastern Europe but continued in Israel, writing about life in the new country. The third generation was centered on "Young Israel," a modernist group of poets and prose writers, most of whom are kibbutz members, whose work has been greatly influenced by the avant-garde schools of English and French writing.

Subjects on which Yiddish writing in Israel has been outstanding are the European Holocaust (the leading writer on this is K. *Zetnick), and life among new immigrants, both of which have been experienced by many of the Yiddish writers at first hand. Yiddish authors were organized in a Yiddish authors' association with more than 120 members (see *Yiddish Literature).

Libraries

The number of libraries in Israel has been estimated at 700, and the proportion of library books per capita is among the highest in the world. But these facts are misleading, as most of the libraries are professional, and there is a general lag in public libraries. However, municipal attention has been directed to this problem and the gaps are being filled.

The country's major library, both in size and in the scope of its activities, is the *Jewish National and University Library in Jerusalem. The nucleus of this collection was formed in 1892 when the city's B'nai B'rith lodge decided to start a library. In 1895 the Zionist and physician Joseph *Chasanowich decided to transfer his collection of 8,800 books from Bialystok to Jerusalem and donated them to this library. By 1899 there were 15,000 books in this collection and by 1910, 32,000 (of which 10,000 were in Hebrew). In 1920 the library passed into the possession of the World Zionist Organization, and with the opening of The Hebrew University on Mount Scopus in 1925, it was finally housed as the Jewish National and University Library. Between 1948 and 1967 it was cut off from Jewish Jerusalem, where a new library was established. In 1967 the number of books reached 1,500,000. By 2005 it housed around 5 million items.

The other institutes of higher learning have also built up significant libraries. Among other large ones are the central Tel Aviv library, Sha'arei Zion (130,000 volumes), the Schocken Library in Jerusalem (55,000 volumes) specializing in medieval Hebrew poetry and early printings, the Pevsner Library in Haifa (40,000 volumes), the library of Rabbi Yehudah Leib Maimon in Jerusalem (40,000 volumes), and the library of the Central Zionist Archives in the Jewish Agency, Jerusalem (35,000 volumes; see *Libraries).

Theater

The first theater production in Palestine was an amateur company's performance of Abraham *Goldfaden's *Shulamit* in Jaffa in 1894. Eleven years later a dramatic society was founded, also in Jaffa, in which teachers and writers as well as actors participated. Its initial productions were in Yiddish, but Karl *Gutzkow's *Uriel Acosta* was performed in Hebrew.

In 1907 Menahem *Gnessin founded a group called "Lovers of the Dramatic Art" in order to promote the Hebrew theater. They were motivated by the desire to foster theater for the sake of the drama, the language, and as an instrument of general culture. Performances were given in Jaffa and Jerusalem (the latter despite the opposition of religious circles) and were received with widespread interest and enthusiasm by the new Jewish settlement.

Dramatic activities were interrupted by World War I but soon after its conclusion were resumed. The first professional group, the Te'atron Ivri ("Hebrew Theater"), was founded in 1921 by David Davidov (d. 1976) (who had been an actor in eastern Europe before settling in Palestine). The group was a cooperative and every two weeks put on a new production, deriving its repertory from European and Yiddish classics. Despite a variety of difficulties, it continued to perform until 1927. Meanwhile, Menahem Gnessin had established a Hebrew company in Europe and, in 1925, brought this group (Te'atron Ereẓ Yisre'eli – "The Ereẓ Israel Theater") to Tel Aviv. About this time the first satirical theater company, Ha-Kumkum ("The Kettle"), began to perform successfully in Tel Aviv. Even more successful in this genre was Ha-Matate ("The Broom"), which opened in 1928 and continued to perform until 1954.

The *Ohel theater, which began to perform publicly in 1926, grew out of an actors' studio founded the previous year by Moshe *Halevy. Under the auspices of the Histadrut's cultural committee, it was originally a volunteer group whose objectives were the theatrical expression of the ideals of the Jewish workers' movement as well as the creation of an original Hebrew drama. Its repertoire was based on plays of specific Jewish and socialist interest. It ran into increasing financial difficulties, was disaffiliated by the Histadrut in 1958, and eventually disbanded in 1969.

In 1928 the *Habimah group opened in Palestine. This theater had been founded in Moscow in 1917 and had achieved an international reputation. The company had left Russia in 1926 and toured Europe and America until most of the actors decided to go to Tel Aviv (a small group remained in the U.S.). In 1932 they decided to make their permanent home in Palestine, with the declared objective of acting as a cultural bridge between the Jews of Palestine and the Jews of the Diaspora.

The intensive activities in the theater were accompanied by pioneer attempts at writing original Hebrew plays. These often went back to Jewish history for their content, but some of them dealt with the new life in Palestine. Not many of these were successful, and it took some time before the Hebrew drama developed out of its experimental period.

The third major company, the *Cameri Theater (Ha-Te'atron ha-Kameri), was founded in 1944 by a group of actors led by Joseph *Millo. Their aim was to establish a theater in the European tradition, which they felt was lacking in the country. They were critical of Habimah's stylized and dated performances, inspired by the methods taught by Stanislavsky and Vakhtangov some 30 years previously in Russia, and they were out of sympathy with the doctrinaire tendencies of the Ohel repertory. After early experiments with one-act plays and as a children's theater, the company commenced its career as a full-fledged theater in 1945. Its principles included the promotion of a contemporary international repertoire, together with the encouragement of promising Israeli talent. The Chamber Theater pioneered in presenting not only classics but also commercial successes from the Western capitals. Its breakaway from the eastern European influences that had hitherto dominated the Hebrew stage also had its influence on the other companies, and before long the Habimah theater revised its repertoire, adding popular "hits" and plays reflecting local life to its standard classic repertoire. In 1958, on the occasion of its 40th anniversary, Habimah was officially recognized as the Israel National Theater. Both the Habimah and Cameri companies appeared abroad on a number of occasions and received international acclaim.

Another company that later made its mark was the *Haifa Municipal Theater, established under the direction of Joseph Millo. Apart from the major companies, Israel's theatrical life was marked by a plethora of smaller groups. Although generally of limited existence, these have played a role both in developing younger talent and in bringing experimental and avant-garde plays to the Israel public. A trend starting in the early 1960s was the success of the big musical play. This was pioneered by producer Giora *Godik with his productions of *Gevirti ha-Navah* (*My Fair Lady*) and *Kannar al ha-Gag* (*Fiddler on the Roof*), as a result of which original Israel musicals have been successfully presented by Godik and by the major companies (notably adaptations of Yigal *Mossinsohn's *Casablan* and Sammy *Gronemann's *Shelomo ha-Melekh ve-Shalmai ha-Sandelar* ("King Solomon and the Cobbler").

Another popular form of entertainment was the small troupe, presenting songs and sketches. These were initially influenced by army ensembles (the Chizbatron during the 1948 war, the *Nahal group, and those of the various commands). Former members of these groups formed the Baẓal Yarok ("Green Onion") group and its many successor ensembles, composed mainly of the same popular performers in varying combinations. There were scores of amateur theatrical groups throughout the country, many of them on kibbutzim. In addition there were companies performing in several languages other than Hebrew, although generally not of a high standard. The Yiddish theater also proved a disappointment from the artistic aspect. Although up to seven groups have been active at one time, the concentration was on the cheaper manifestations of the Yiddish theater, dominated by operettas and melodramas. The groups were largely made up of newcomers to the country, and their appeal was directed to recent arrivals. No original Yiddish play of merit has appeared in Israel, and for outstanding theatrical experiences in the language Israelis had to rely – apart from the numerous shows put on by Shimon Dzigan – on visiting companies such as those of Ida *Kaminska and Joseph *Buloff.

The Hebrew drama has, however, shown considerable development since the War of Independence. This brought many of the young authors to playwriting and the successes of that time, such as Yigal Mossinsohn's *Be-Arvot ha-Negev* ("In the Steppes of the Negev") and Nathan *Shaḥam's *Hem Yaggi'u Maḥar* ("They'll Be Here Tomorrow"), although inferior as plays, stimulated native drama. Many original plays have been written since that time, generally deriving from contemporary Israel life or from Jewish history.

The turning point in the Hebrew drama's attitude to society was the euphoric mentality that overtook Israel after the sweeping victory in the Six-Day War (1967). This was followed by a period of collective self-reckoning, soul searching, and myth shattering in the wake of the humiliating surprise of the Yom-Kippur War (1973). Whereas Israeli drama before 1967 was basically positive toward the ideal of the "New Jew," post-1967 protest plays adopted an asocial, agnostic, and deconstructive position, in order to warn society against the dangers of a militarist power-cult and the moral deterioration inextricably connected with the occupation of Palestinian-inhabited areas and the subordination of human values to the imperative of territorial expansion. In fact, one may argue that from 1967 to Rabin's murder in 1995 the core of Hebrew drama was politically mobilized, rhetorically militant, and ideologically leftist.

Yehoshua Sobol presented *Ghetto* (1984), which depicted everyday life in the Vilna ghetto in World War II before the uprising there. This presented the *Judenrat* (Council of Jewish Elders) of the ghetto not as villains, but as sober men who were forced to face an impossible situation and to decide who has to die in order to save the lives of others. Understandably, the play was followed by a public discussion, and Sobol was praised by some, but vilified by others as a blasphemer, who was tarnishing the memory of those who perished in the Holocaust.

The next Sobol play touched an even more sensitive nerve. In *The Palestinian* (1985) he retold the Romeo and Juliet story in the Israeli context of an ultra-rightist activist, a follower of Meir Kahane, falling in love with a Palestinian girl.

Other Israeli theaters continued to present the public with a wide choice of repertoire, of classical, modern and commercial plays, but the repertoire of the Haifa Theater set the tone and helped characterize the Israeli theater as intensely political. Even classical plays presented in these years acquired a local, political meaning. *The Trojan Women* by Euripides was presented at the Habimah Theater in 1982 (directed by Holk Freitag) as if it were happening in a refugee camp somewhere in Lebanon. Moliére's *Tartuffe* was presented by the Haifa Theater (adapted by Sobol, directed by Besser, 1985) as an attack on the Jewish clerical establishment; Beckett's *Waiting for Godot* was presented at the Haifa Theater in Arabic (1984, translated by Anton Shamas, directed by Ilan Ronen) as happening on an abandoned building site, with Gogo and Didi as Palestinian construction workers speaking in Arabic, and Pozzo as their Israeli employer who addressed them in Hebrew.

Theater thus became a public forum for discussing political issues, and politicians who preferred to see it as an art-form and entertainment intensified their attacks. The culmination of these conflicting points of view came in 1988, when a new Sobol-Besser production was presented by the Haifa Theater within the framework of "Israeli Play Celebration" for Israel's 40th anniversary. *Jerusalem Syndrome* concerned a group of inmates of an insane asylum enacting the conflicts that preceded the destruction of the Temple, but the stage images reminded the public of scenes from the Intifada (the Palestinian uprising which erupted at the end of 1987). The play got a very mixed reception from the critics, and political activists demonstrated in front of the theater and interrupted the performances with shouts, whistles, and stink-bombs. Sobol and Besser, at that time the artistic directors of the Haifa Theater, resigned from their posts.

In the same month, January 1988, the Cameri Theater of Tel Aviv presented its very professional, impressive, and successful production of the musical *Les Misérables* with an all-star cast, most of them signed especially for this production, and not company actors. This production marked a shift of gears, and the theater in the following years became more of a place of entertainment than a public forum for discussion of ideas. Other theaters followed the Cameri's example: Habimah presented *Cabaret* and *Salah Shabati* (a musical written by Ephraim Kishon), both of which demanded a huge investment, pleased the audiences (not the critics), but created a huge deficit in the theater's budget.

The end of the 1980s and the beginning of the 1990s were difficult years for the Israeli theater. Artistic and managing directors changed posts, marketing wars intensified, deficits soared, and it seemed that the creativity of Israeli playwrights and directors waned. Some of them turned to writing personal stories, some turned to careers abroad. Others continued to portray actual events on stage, but those plays did not create a public debate; they became part of a cultural entertainment, using yesterday's newspaper as a basic material for drama. Plays like *Gorodish* (by Hillel Mittelpunkt, telling a story of a Six-Day War hero who became a symbol of the 1973 war disaster) or *Pollard* (by Motti Lerner, about the American Jew who spied for Israel and was convicted in the U.S.), both of them at the Cameri Theater, became huge commercial hits. But plays rarely – if ever – became a subject for journalistic coverage outside the arts pages.

Another interesting development in the Israeli theater has been its absorption of immigrants from the former U.S.S.R., both as actors and as audiences. Some actors learned Hebrew and found work within the existing companies. Others created a theater of their own, *Gesher* (meaning "bridge"), and started performing in Russian, counting on a Russian-speaking audience. However, they used simultaneous translation into Hebrew and impressed the Hebrew-speaking public (and the critics) by the commitment of their theatrical work. After their first production in Russian (*Rosenkrantz and Guildenstern are Dead* by Tom Stoppard, directed by Yevgeni Arie), they switched into Hebrew and presented *The Idiot* by Dostoyevsky in Hebrew, and continued to impress the audiences with their company spirit and sense of purpose, which has been absent to a certain measure in other Israeli theater companies.

The second substantial reversal in Israeli drama took place in the 1990s and characterizes plays written and performed at the beginning of the third millennium. The interconnected historical and theatrical developments (from the Oslo Peace Accord to Rabin's murder and the second Intifada) produce a complete renunciation of communal ideals, along with their formal objective correlatives.

The idealistic, committed, and selfless Hebrew plays of the early settlement period in Ereẓ Israel have thus reached the extreme opposite pole, as has indeed the entire Zionist ideology which generated them. However, both drama and theater are still engaged in the same quest for social identity.

[Michael Handelsaltz and Gad Kaynar (2nd ed.)]

Music

From the early 1900s the Yishuv in Palestine concerned itself with the organization of its musical life, by establishing schools and performing institutions whose aim was to preserve the rich tradition of European classical music and to create new Israeli classical and folk music, all in providing opportunities for the musicians to practice their art. Their model was essentially European and continued to be developed in the period of statehood. The performing bodies, especially orchestras, which have been central in this respect, required, to maintain themselves, the development of music education, research, and publishing outlets. All these needs were addressed in the period of statehood through official sponsorship and encouragement. Furthermore, the waves of immigration, especially the Fifth Aliyah of the 1930s and the later influx of immigrants from the U.S., Europe, and especially the former U.S.S.R., considerably affected the musical life of Israel and increased the number of performing bodies in the country.

ORCHESTRAS. As early as 1895, a community orchestra was founded in the settlement of Rishon le-Zion, which was a well-organized amateur wind band with a paid conductor. Other settlements followed the model, such as Petaḥ Tikvah and the Jewish community of Jaffa. Orchestral playing got under way seriously in 1927 with the foundation of the Palestine Symphony Orchestra under Fordhaus Ben-Zissi. There was intensive musical activity throughout the country and artists of international renown gave guest recitals. One of them was the violinist Bronislaw *Huberman, who became the guiding spirit in the establishment in 1936 of the Palestine Orchestra (later the *Israel Philharmonic Orchestra), initially composed of refugees from Nazi Germany. The orchestra gave its first concert in 1936 under the baton of Arturo Toscanini. It immediately became one of the pivots of musical life in the country and acquired an international reputation. The Israel Philharmonic Orchestra, with its leader Zubin *Mehta, continued to provide its subscribers with programs, and to make regular concert tours abroad and produce records which help spread its reputation throughout the world.

Another important development took place in 1936, the creation of the Palestine Broadcasting Service by the British mandate authorities (later Kol Israel and then Shiddurei Israel). The composer Karel *Salomon took charge of its musical programs, which included Western classical music, folk and art Jewish music, and special programs of Hebrew Oriental songs led by composer and *ʿud* player Ezra *Aharon. Seven musicians were at the service of the musical programs; in time they became the core for the Jerusalem Symphony Orchestra founded in 1950, which was expanded in 1976. Among its conductors and music directors were G. *Singer, H. Freudental, Lukas *Foss, Mendi *Rodan, G. *Bertini, David *Shalon, and Leon *Botstein. In 1948 the IDF army orchestra was built to play light classical music and occasional music at official events. At the same time the army established a youth orchestra (*Tizmoret ha-Gadna*), which played symphonic music.

The Haifa Symphony Orchestra was founded in 1949. It also has regular series throughout the year. In 2004 the new Haifa Symphony orchestra was established on the initiative of the mayor and enjoys the support of the municipality. It has now as director Noam *Sheriff. The orchestra provides regular annual series of concerts in Haifa and the environment. In 1970 the Kibbutz Chamber Orchestra was established, growing out of the Kibbutz Orchestra; its musical director, Noam Sheriff, was followed by conductors Shalom Ronli-Riklis in 1983–85, Lior Shambadal in 1986–92, and Doron Salomon from 1993. It continues to attract audiences in the kibbutzim as well as in the cities.

The influx of immigrant musicians in the 1970s and 1990s, especially from the former U.S.S.R., made the founding of new orchestras possible. The Beersheba Orchestra was founded in 1974 first under the direction of Avi Ostrovsky, and later with Mendi Rodan as the conductor and musical director; its name was changed to Israel Sinfonietta Beersheba. It continues to perform especially in the South of Israel.

In 1965 Gary Bertini established the Israel Chamber Ensemble and conducted it until 1976; it was taken over by Rudolf *Barshai in 1977 when he emigrated from Russia. Renamed "The Israel Chamber Orchestra," it was enlarged to a body of 45 musicians. Uri Segal became musical director (1982–83) after Barshai left Israel in 1981. Segal was followed by Yoav Talmi (1984–88), and Shlomo *Mintz was appointed its music advisor in 1988.

The Reḥovot Camerata Orchestra led by Avner Biron was founded in 1983 and in 1996 moved to Jerusalem. In 1988 conductor Shimon Cohen founded The Symphony Orchestra Rishon le-Zion, and in 1989 conductor-composer Noam Sheriff was appointed its music director. Since the 1989–90 season it has been the house orchestra of the New Israel Opera, which performs selected pieces from the international repertory at the Art Center in Tel Aviv.

The Ra'ananah Symphonette Orchestra, also consisting of new immigrant musicians, was founded in 1991.

INSTITUTIONS OF EDUCATION. The first music school, the Shulamit Conservatoire, was founded in Jaffa by the German-born singer Shulamit Ruppin in 1910 and maintained a pure German curriculum. The first director was the violinist and conductor Moshe Hopenko. The school stimulated lively interest, with an unexpectedly large enrollment (75 pupils in its first year). Other schools were founded in Jerusalem in 1918 and in Haifa in 1923. In the 1930s, with the Fifth Aliyah, nicknamed the German Aliyah, many prominent musicians came, among them the violinist Emil *Hauser (former member of the Budapest string quartet), who founded the Palestine Conservatoire in Jerusalem in 1933 with a faculty of more than 30 teachers. The comprehensive curriculum of the conservatoire comprised classes for most instruments, composition, history and theory, as well as Arabic *'ud* given by Ezra Aharon, and courses on non-western music given by Edith *Gerson Kiwi. The conservatory was the source of teachers to both Academies of Music in Jerusalem, 1945, and the Tel Aviv Academy of Music, 1946, the leading professional music schools until today. In 1945 the School for Music Educators was established by Leo *Kestenberg, which continues until today under the auspices of the Levinsky College of Teachers. In 1947 the New Jerusalem Conservatory was established which later was united with the Jerusalem music academy. In 1951, the Oranim School for Music Teachers opened and operated for about 40 years.

Next to the Jerusalem Academy of Music and the conservatory, a musical high school was established in 1961. The Tel Aviv musical high school Thelma *Yellin had already opened in 1959.

The Jerusalem Music Center was initiated by Isaac Stern, Pablo Casals, and Teddy Kollek, mayor of Jerusalem, was established in 1973 and opened officially in 1975. Its aim was to create a center of highest professional standards, where outstanding experts would provide master classes and promote Israeli performers and Israeli music.

The pioneering stage of ethnomusicological and historical music research in Israel entered a new phase with the opening of departments of musicology at the three main universities in Israel: the department at The Hebrew University was founded in 1965 by Alexander Ringer, that of Tel Aviv University in 1966 by Eric Werner, and that of Bar-Ilan was opened in 1970 under the guidance of Bathia Churgin.

OPERA. The vision of Israel as a western country can be very well seen through the founding of an opera house in Tel Aviv. In 1923 Mordechai *Golinkin arrived in Palestine and forthwith organized the first opera company, which lasted four years. The opera presented mostly mainstream works such as *La Traviata, Otello,* and *The Barber of Seville*. The performers were immigrants mostly from Russia. Due to lack of funds the opera collapsed in 1927. In 1941 the Folk Opera of Erez Israel was established as a cooperative and premiered one of the first native Hebrew operas in 1945: *Dan ha-Shomer* ("Dan the Guard") by Marc *Lavry. The Opera ceased to exist in 1946 due to financial and technical problems. A permanent opera was eventually established in 1947 as a result of the efforts of Edis *de Philippe. The opera was directed by her until her death in 1978. The New Israeli Opera was founded in 1985 in order to reestablish operatic activity after the Israel National Opera had closed down in 1982. Until 1990 performances were coproduced with the Israeli Chamber Orchestra. Since 1990 the Israel Symphony Orchestra Rishon Le-Zion has taken part in all its productions.

VOCAL ENSEMBLES. Choirs had been formed in many parts of the country and some still continue. Many children's choirs perform and children's choir competitions take place annually. In 1925 Menashe *Ravina arranged the first choir festival. In 1926 Moshe Bik established the Workers Choir in Haifa. The Rinat chamber choir, the Tel Aviv Philharmonic Choir, The Cameran vocal ensemble and other groups were well known and promoted original pieces as well as classical music.

DISSEMINATION AND PRESERVATION OF JEWISH MUSIC. In 1925 the pioneer of Jewish music in the country, Joel *Engel, organized concerts in Tel Aviv. In 1925, Hopenko, Golinkin,

Abileah, and *Rosovski founded the Society for Hebrew Music, which provided monthly chamber concerts.

In 1928 the educator David *Schor founded the Institute for the Dissemination of Music, called the Nigun Society, which included members from the Jewish Folk Music Society. That same year David Schor, along with Shlomo Rosovsky and Menashe Ravina, established the music department of the National Library of The Hebrew University of Jerusalem, which is still the central library of music and holds the largest collection of Jewish and Israeli music in print and in sound. The National Sound Archives, which is now part of the music department of the National Library, was initiated in 1935 by the famous scholar Robert *Lachmann, who came to Jerusalem on the invitation of The Hebrew University and founded there an institute for Oriental music that made ethnographic recordings, especially of Arabic music. Lachmann's studies in Jerusalem during the last years of his life (1935–39) marked the beginning of modern ethnomusicology in Israel.

In 1938 Dr. Sali Levi established in Jerusalem the World Center for Jewish Music in Erez Yisrael to promote new compositions by Jewish composers, and he published a newsletter. The Center ceased to exist in 1940. Both Lachmann's and Levi's archives are at the Music Department of the National Library. Next to the Music Department of the National Library, Israel Adler established in 1964, the Jewish Music Research Center which promotes research and publications on Jewish music.

Publishing houses for Israeli music were established as early as 1949, namely Israel Music Publications under the direction of Peter Gradenwitz. It continued to publish mainly Israeli art music until 2000. The Israel Music Institute was established by the Committee for Culture and Arts to publish scores and later recordings of new Israeli art music. It has been the major publishing house for Israeli art music from1961.

In 1953 the Israeli Composer's League was established to protect the rights of Israeli composers and promote their music. In 1956 Moshe Gorali opened a music museum and library in Haifa. In 1960 he edited a music journal, *Tazlil*, for musical research, which was issued for 20 years.

The Renanot Institute for Religious Music was established in Jerusalem in 1957 to teach and promote traditional Jewish music. It produces books and records; it also organizes a yearly conference on Jewish music.

INTERNATIONAL FESTIVALS, COMPETITIONS, AND CONGRESSES. The biennial Zimriyyah Choir Festival, founded by A.Z. Propes in 1952, attracted a large number of choirs from many countries, which sing together with local groups all over the country in friendly collaboration. Originally conceived as an exclusively Jewish choir festival, it has long since become an ecumenical meeting, with non-Jewish choirs in the majority.

Propes was the initiator of another two events: the Harp Contest, founded in 1959, which was the first of its kind internationally and occupies an important place in the international harp community, and the Israel Festival, founded in 1961. The Israel Festival was discontinued in 1980 for budgetary reasons, but was renewed in 1982. New venues for its activities included local historical sites such as Jerusalem's Sultan's Pool, used for the first time for music performances in 1982, the Roman Amphitheater of Beth Shean, and the citadel of Jerusalem's Old City. It commemorated Stravinsky's centenary in 1982 by performing a number of his works for ballet.

Under the significant name of *Testimonium* (Testimony), a contemporary music festival was conceived and initiated by Recha Freier. The idea behind it was to reveal evidence about the various aspects of the history of the Jewish people and its significance. There have been six Testimonium festivals between 1968 and 1983, at which 35 works of famous international and Israeli contemporary composers were written for those festivals. These works represent a unique synthesis between the reopening of historic events and musical composition.

In 1974 Yaakov Bistritski established the Arthur Rubinstein Piano Competition, which takes place every four years and includes a new Israeli piece each time. Since 1978, a new festival has been added: the Liturgica, Vocal Music from Jerusalem, organized around Hanukkah and Christmas, availing itself of the many choirs coming for the season to Jerusalem (and Bethlehem), presenting programs of music with spiritual content of great interest.

In 1959 the Musical Youth Organization opened a branch of the World Musical Youth Organization, promoting meetings of young musicians from all over the world for the purpose of playing together. The Congress of the Jeunesses Musicales was held in Israel in 1973.

The First World Congress of Jewish Music was held in Jerusalem in 1978, with the participation of many scholars from Europe and the United States. In July 1980, the Festival of Contemporary Music was organized by the local section of the International Society for Contemporary Music, with some 65 works performed in Jerusalem, Tel Aviv, Beersheba, and Kibbutz Shefayim. In 1998 the first international chamber music festival, under the musical direction of Elena Bashkirova was held; the festival takes place every year for ten days, during which musicians from all over the world perform chamber music.

MUSIC BROADCASTING. The music department of the Broadcasting Authority played an important role in promoting local composers and soloists, as well as in the development of musical life in Jerusalem (see also *Music). It records its symphony's concerts as well as chamber music, which promote Israeli premieres and performers. The Broadcasting Authority also played a major role in promoting and performing Oriental music.

In 1948, the Israel Broadcasting Authority started an Oriental ensemble, led by Ezra *Aharon and comprising selected known Jewish artists in their countries of origin; they were joined later on by a few Israeli Arab artists. They performed and recorded Arabic and Jewish Oriental music and appeared in public concerts as well.

Finally, the 21st century is becoming the scene of a more pluralistic attitude to music to include Oriental, classical, and Israeli and popular song in concert, as well as in broadcasting and teaching.

[Ury Eppstein / Gila Flam (2nd ed.)]

Israeli Song

THE FIRST PERIOD – 1882–1904. Israeli song – the song of the people in the Land of Israel – started evolving some 135 years ago. It was first heard in the last decades of the 19th century, when Jewish poets in Europe took to writing songs in Hebrew expressing Zionist themes. There was Naftali Hertz *Imber, Menahem Dolitzki, Mane, and a number of artists who wrote children's songs in Hebrew such as A. Liboushitski and N. Pines. They used ḥasidic melodies, songs in Yiddish – including songs from the *Goldfaden plays – and Romanian, Polish, and Russian folksongs; they also took up themes from Jewish composers such as A.M. Bernstein, P. Minkowski, D. Novkovski, and A. Zonzar (whose song "*Ha-Shoshanah*," published in 1863, is considered one of the first Hebrew songs). Most of these songs reached Ereẓ Israel with the immigrants of the First Aliyah, who then made up new songs such as "*Ḥushu Ahim, Ḥushu*," the work song "*Ya Ḥalili Ya Amali*" and others. This was the beginning of the Hebrew song repertoire.

THE SECOND PERIOD – 1904–1923. This is the time of the Second and Third Aliyah. Because of the shortage of suitable musical material for schools and kindergartens, some music teachers simply composed the songs they needed. Among those teachers mention must be made of Hanina Kratshevski (1873–1926) and A.Z. *Idelson, who were the first composers in the Land of Israel, and the poets Levin Kipnis and Israel Dushman, who wrote the lyrics of "The Ma'pilim Song," "*Poh Ereẓ Ḥemdat Avot*," "*Ḥanukkiyah Ḥanukkiyah*," "*Ha-Ḥaluẓim be-Yad Ḥaruẓim*," "*Ḥad Gadya*," and others.

At the same time there were a number of popular songs whose influence is still being felt in the Hebrew repertoire today. Some of them were Hebrew adaptations of Oriental melodies such as "*Hakhnisini taḥat Kenafeiḥ*," "*Yad Anugah*," "*Bein Nahar Perat*," "*Ani Re'itiha*." These songs were generally characterized by the interval of second or augmented second, slow tempo, and a free rhythmical performance. Another group included songs based on ḥasidic melodies from eastern Europe with short lyrics taken from the biblical books or prayers such as "*El Yibaneh ha-Mikdash*," "*Ve-Taher Libenu*," "*El Yibneh ha-Galil*," "*Ẓibḥu Ẓedek*." It was mainly from these songs that members of the Second Aliyah took the musical themes for Hora and Rondo dancing.

During World War I the *yishuv* in Ereẓ Israel was cut off from all other Jewish centers. Consequently a chasm developed between the repertoire of songs from Ereẓ Israel and Hebrew songs in Europe, because of changes in Hebrew accentuation and in the repertoire itself. Henceforth there was to be a reversal in the process: Ereẓ Israel was no longer importing songs but exporting them to communities abroad.

THE THIRD PERIOD – 1924–1948/9. This period is considered the golden age of songs from Ereẓ Israel. In the late 1920s, composers such as Shalom *Postolski, Yedidia *Admon, Menashe *Rabina, Nahum *Nardi, Sara Levi *Tanai, Moshe Bik (1900–1979), and others started their work. Some of them, who are considered the fathers of Hebrew song, had no musical education at all, and indeed there were those who could not even read or write musical scores. In the beginning they took their lyrics from the works of Bialik and L. Kipnis, and then went on to new poets such as Avraham Broides, Itzhak Shenberg (Shenhar), Sh. Shalom, Emmanuel Ha-Russi, Avigdor Ha-Meiri, David Shimonowich (Shimoni), Anda Amir, Yehiel Heilperin, Raḥel, Lea Goldberg, Miriam Steklis, and others.

Work and the homeland were the main themes of the songs, but there were also songs about the Galilee and the valley, songs about building and creating, songs for the children and for festivals. The 1930s saw the arrivals of composers like Moshe *Wilensky, Daniel *Sambourski, Mark *Lavry, and others, who contributed greatly to the musical scene.

Many composers saw themselves as taking part in the creation of a reemerging Hebrew culture, and their songs as folk songs expressing that culture, even though folk songs are usually derived from anonymous sources. They believed that the Dorian melodic mode, the Yemenite-Oriental trills, and the use of syncopated rhythms in their various forms were the expression of the roots of the New Hebrew song. The themes of the songs served as an historical common link. It was during these years that country and shepherd songs were written, songs for ceremonies and festivals, as well as many of the children's songs. One can hear in some of them the impact of Middle Eastern influence, either through composers originating from that part of the world (Sara Levi Tanai, Nissan Cohen Nelamed, and others) or through the effect of the surroundings on other composers (Y. Admon, N. Vardi, D. Zahavi, A. Amiran, for instance). Attempts to create a "country culture" brought popularity to the composers, essentially in the kibbutz movement (D. Zahavi, M. Shalem, Y. Sharet, S. Postolski and others).

The onset of World War II and subsequent enlistment in British army units of youngsters brought a new trend of Hebrew "army songs" (M. Ze'ira, D. Sambourski, and others). Another theme appeared: the Holocaust of European Jewry and the destruction of Jewish culture. This theme was to become dominant in the next period and bring back to Hebrew song Jewish folk songs – "the songs of the shtetl" – with their melodies in minor tones and, in the wake of the new political orientation, a great number of Russian melodies.

These songs were disseminated orally and in writing. Most publishing houses of the time, which published the songs, were national ones, like that of the Keren Kayemet le-Israel, the educational system, and the Histadrut.

THE FOURTH PERIOD – 1948/9–1967. There was nothing at first to distinguish this from the previous period; however, there soon appeared a melange of varied themes and currents. On the one hand, songs of mourning and sorrow together with victory songs, on the other, a new genre – songs written under the influence of modern "salon" dances such as the tango and rumba, but also waltzes or songs from the pop charts of Europe and the United States. This led to a number of new styles which took shape in the 1950s, such as new versions of country and shepherd songs scanned by exclamation – "Ho, Ho," for instance – which dominated the Hebrew song festivals organized by Kol Israel in the years 1960–67. The melodies were in minor scales and modes, constructed fairly simply, generally with a guitar, accordion, and drum accompaniment. This style was popular among some of the composers of the first period to follow the establishment of the State of Israel: Emmanuel Zamir (1925–1962), Gil *Aldema, Dubi Zeltzer, Amti Neeman (1926–2005), Effi Netzer, Arieh Lebanon, and Yosef Hadar.

New audiences were emerging too: people who danced folk dances, but also new immigrants in camps or development towns. These songs were made possible by the support of the Music Division, the Information Department, the Histadrut, and local authorities.

At the same time the "salon" style, which was flourishing, was being strengthened by the diffusion of international hit parades on radios and records and in movies. This style was characterized by salon rhythms, which were then considered foreign or incompatible with the motives of Ereẓ Israel. The songs emphasized the individual, the "me" which was to flood Hebrew song in the next period.

The best-known composers of that style are Sando Ferro ("*Yafo*," "Josephina Swing"), Tuli Raviv ("*Sekharoret*," "*Al Na Tomar Li Shalom*"), Zvi Gold-Zahavi ("*Arẓenu ha-Ketantonet*"), Ari Tselner ("*Ha-Samba rak ha-Samba*"). Yafa *Yarkoni, Israel Itzhaki, Jetta Luka, and Lilith Nagar were some of the singers who sang these songs.

The year 1951 saw the first appearance of the *Naḥal band, the first of the army bands. Indeed, its success paved the way for the creation of other army bands that were to leave their mark on the Israeli musical scene – both in the style of songs and in their rendition – for more than 25 years. Alexander *Argov, Moshe *Wilensky, Dubi Zelzer, Naomi *Shemer, Arieh Levanon, Nurit *Hirsh, Matti *Caspi, Beni Nagri, Eldad Shrem are among the better-known composers of songs for the army bands.

In the second half of the 1960s there was a change in the accompaniment of the songs: synthesizers, drums, electric guitars, and bass guitars made their appearance. Among those responsible for this sound change in army bands was Yair Rosenblum (1944–1996). Other bands adopted the new style to create something both young and modern similar to what was then popular in the western world where rhythm was becoming more dominant. These changes were instrumental in the appearance of "rhythm bands" and rock bands. It began as an almost underground phenomenon in suburban areas – the Ramleh band and the bands in Misgad Street and in South Tel Aviv.

This was the golden age of the varied vocal ensembles and most specifically of the duos, trios, and quartets such as the Batsal Yarok band, the Tarnegolim, Mo'adon ha-Te'atron, Ha-Tayelet, Gesher ha-Yarkon and well-known duos Ilka and Aviva, Ran and Nama (Nehama *Hendel and Menahem Lezerovich), the Dudaim (Beni Amdurski and Israel Gurion), Ha-Parvarim, Ha-Ofarim, Hedva and David, and more. Great singers of the time were, among many others, Shoshana Damari, Shimshon Bar-Noi, Yosef Goland, Ya'akov Teiman, Israel Itzhaki, Yafa Yarkoni, Jo Amar, Tzadok Savir, Miriam Avigal, Hana Aharoni, Hadassah Sigalov, Aliza Gabai, Gila Edri, Shimon Israeli, Geula Gil, and Freddi Dura.

During the previous period, it was the composer who was responsible for the success of the songs, but now the singers were taking center stage. They were the ones who went looking for material and saw to its diffusion. Nearly all the bands that came into being during this period were using the material of composers who did not belong to the bands.

It was through the Ha-Ḥalonot ha-Gevohim band that rock made its entrance into Hebrew and Israeli songs. Shmulik Kraus, who was a member of the band, composed some of its melodies.

The themes of the songs of that period were taken from current events: the conquest of Eilat, the creation of the Lachish region, absorption of immigrants in the camps, the murder of travelers to Petra, Operation Magic Carpet (mass immigration of the Jews of Yemen), the creation of the new towns of Ashkelon and Dimonah, etc. Hebrew song was still looking for itself, moving from one musical style to another, between ethnic song from the various Jewish communities and song from Europe and the United States, as if it were trying to find its identity but all the time enriching itself toward the future.

THE FIFTH PERIOD – FROM 1967. The Six-Day War (1967) was to be a watershed for Hebrew song. It was followed by an outpouring of patriotic songs not unlike those of Ereẓ Israel. These songs mixed well with the wave of nostalgia that swept the country from the beginning of the 1960s. To this day, old (in new renderings) and new patriotic songs constitute a mainstream known as "Songs of Ereẓ Israel."

With the inauguration of television in Israel, a new dimension – quite unlike what had preceded it – was introduced into Israeli songs. The change was due to the influence of European and American culture, to the methods of diffusion, and to the greater visibility of composers and singers. The various festivals, concerts, and shows of singers and pop and rock bands throughout the world created new possibilities for the artists and performers of Hebrew song. Henceforth it would no longer be a question of "how you sound" but of "how you look."

Because it was now possible to reach hundreds of thousands of viewers and listeners, all parameters underwent change, including style, number of participants, choice of repertoire, and adaptation to the greatest possible number of viewers and listeners (ratings).

During this period, a number of composers were also performing. The dominance of the singer Arik *Einstein for some 35 years led composers such as Shalom *Hanoch, Miki Gavrielov, Yoni Richter, and Itzhak Klepter to unique creative directions. In the early 1970s a new band, Kaveret, appeared on the scene. Though it did not last long, Kaveret was to bring a new sound to Israeli songs. Among the participants in the band – who later kept on writing songs after it broke up, each in his own style – were Danny Sanderson, Ephraim Shamir, Alon Oleartchik, and Yoni Richter.

Shalom Hanoch, Tsvika Pik, Shmulik Kraus, Mati Caspi, Meir Ariel, Yehudit Ravitz, Hava *Alberstein, Dani Litani, Shlomo Gronich, Shlomo *Artzi, and others were representative of a group of composer/performers who either were solo performers or part of groups such as Lul, the Churchills, Ha-Keves ha-Shesh-Esre, etc.

Several specific styles developed after the Six-Day war. One of them was ḥasidic song, led by dancing rabbi Shlomo *Carlebach. The ḥasidic songs festivals held yearly after 1969 had a great influence. The main characteristics of the style are short lyrics taken from biblical and prayer books. Their melodies are mainly in minor scales, having middle to middle + range; they are made of simple and symmetrical structure, their tempo is fixed or uses accelerated movement, and their harmony is mainly based on the basic functions of the scale.

Ethnic influences on Israeli songs were prominent before the creation of the State, but they were centered on Yemenite song. After the Yom Kippur War (1973), but essentially after the political upset of 1977, there was heightened ethnic consciousness, and more weight was given to performers from Oriental communities. In less than two decades the Oriental/Mediterranean style became one of the dominant styles in Hebrew song, characterized by melismatic ornamentation, recurrence of the augmented second, microtonality, and melodic fioritures; they are accompanied by electric instruments (synthesizers), electric guitars and bass guitars, stringed instruments and Oriental instruments such as violin, *'ud* (lute), *qanun* (zither) *darbuka* (goblet drum), as well as Greek instruments such as the *bouzouki*. Avihu *Medina, Moshe Ben Moshe, Boaz Sharabi, Shlomo *Bar, and Yona Roeh are among the leading composers of that style. Among the notable performers in this style are Nissim Seroussi, Zohar *Argov, Eli Louzoun, Haim Moshe, Zahava *Ben, Yoav Itzhak, Margalit Tzanani, Shimi Tavori, Sarit Hadad, Shlomi Shabat, Eyal Golan, and ensembles such as Ẓelilei ha-Kerem, Ẓelilei ha-'Ud, etc.

During the 1990s, some performers/composers set up bands to work with them: Yuval Banai and Machina, Arkadi Duchin and Natasha's Friends," Aviv Gefen and Toyut, Rami Kleinstein and Ha-Mo'eẓah, Shlomo Artzi and his band, Kobi Oz and Tippex, Zeev Nehama and Tamir Klisky with Ethnics and others.

Israeli songs and songs of Ereẓ Israel are performed in Jewish communities throughout the world and for the most part express the solidarity between the Jewish world and Israel. The beginning of television programs in the fifth period helped to introduce Hebrew song among other cultures. From time to time, Israeli performers made it to the top in international song festivals: in two successive years – 1962 and 1963 – songs by Moshe Wilensky "*Stav*" and "*Layla ve-Ashan*" sung by Rivka Raz took first place at the Polish song festival. Hedva and David took first prize in a song contest in Japan with "*Ani Ḥolem al Noemi*." Since 1973 Israel has participated regularly in the Eurovision song contest and has won three times. Ofra *Haza won world fame with her specially adapted Yemenite songs. It is possible that the large diffusion of these songs can be seen as an attempt to merge with the Middle Eastern native culture.

[Nathan Shahar (2nd ed.)]

Israeli Folk Dances

Israeli folk dances represent a special kind of communal and social dance, created by Israelis. Unlike traditional folk dances of most other cultures, which were created years ago in rural areas by anonymous farmers and shepherds, and transmitted from generation to generation, Israeli folk dances can be defined as "contemporary folklore" reflecting social and ideological phenomena.

At the beginning of the 20th century, their main function was to enrich and diversify the rather meager repertoire of social dances of the "Zionist pioneers," who would start and conclude all gatherings with the same "Hora" – a Romanian-influenced dance – and the "Rondo" – a communal series of walking and running and changing forms, including simple dance steps. As time passed there was an increasing eagerness to have original "Ereẓ Israeli" or Hebrew dance for the enhancement of their social and cultural life.

An important development in this respect took place in the 1920s and 1930s with the arrival in the country of the first skilled dancers and professional choreographers; mostly from Germany and Russia, some of them became members of kibbutzim.

Like the many national revival movements in the 19th and 20th centuries that made use of folk music and dance as means of strengthening national pride and identity, the Zionist political movement made a similar attempt, but without having a genuine source of traditional folklore. Being reluctant to rely only on traditional Jewish folklore, they were led to invent a new one compatible with the Zionist ideology, which sought "normality."

The sources from which Israeli dance was drawn were in this phase biblical or ḥasidic, and the traditional dances the immigrants brought with them from their countries of origin. Among the latter, the rich folklore of Yemenite Jews gained particular favor in the belief that they were the genuine heirs of biblical tradition. Another important source of inspiration was the dances of the Arabs and the Druze, and to some degree, the Circassians who live in Israel.

The first original Israeli dance, a solo dance with a shepherd's staff, was created and performed in Tel Aviv in 1924 by Baruch *Aggadati (1895–1976). The Ohel theater company later transformed this dance into a group dance for a performance. Gurit *Kadman, the "mother of Israeli folk dance," revised it and changed its name to "Hora Aggadati," which has continued to be known and danced as such until our day. Kadman created several folk dances and was a leading force in the formation of the "folk dance movement" in Israel. She believed that in order to be a "normal people" we had to create "Israeli folk dances," and that the people of Israel should become a "dancing nation." With regard to creating and spreading folk dances she was of the opinion that one can consider as folk dances those created by individuals, artists, and amateurs, and not according to the traditional processes qualifying the emergence of folk dancers of other nations.

During the 1930s professional dancers and choreographers began to create "pageants" for holiday festivals, trying to revive the old biblical way of celebrating the Jewish holidays as festivals of farmers and shepherds. Lea Bergstein, a member of kibbutz Beit Alfa, established the shepherd's festival, which she created in 1930 to the music of Matityahu Shelem. Later they both moved to kibbutz Ramat Yoḥanan, where they created the "*Omer*" and "*Seder*" (Passover) celebrations, "*Ḥag ha-Bikkurim*" (the festival of the fruits of the season), "*Ḥag ha-Asif*" (Sukkot). Rivka Sturman, a member of kibbutz Ein-Harod, introduced the communal dance *Ha-Goren* ("The Granary"). The steps and the formation of her dances still serve as a basis for many of the new Israeli folk dances.

Other leading dance creators were Yardena *Cohen; Sara Levi-Tanai, who in 1949 founded, along with her leading dancer Rachel Nadav, the Inbal dance theater; Shalom Hermon, who in 1946 created in Tel Aviv the first Hebrew communal folk dance event (*harkadah*) and in 1953 the first folk dance parade in Haifa on Israel's Independence Day. Another great contributor to staging the holiday's festivals was Shulamit Bat-Dori of kibbutz Mishmar ha-Emek. She was a leading director of mass pageants, among them the Daliyyah National Israeli Folk Dance Festivals initiated by Gurit Kadman and the members of Kibbutz Daliyyah.

In July 1944 the first festival took place, in which 14 folk dance groups, 200 dancers, and 3,500 spectators participated. The program included 22 folk dances, of which only eight were created in Ereẓ Israel; the others were folk dances brought to Israel by pioneers from various countries. In this festival Jewish Yemenite dances, the ḥasidic "Sherale," and "Debka dances," performed by Arab and Druze groups, were presented.

The festival was opened with a performance called *Davka* (in spite of), created by Gertrud *Kraus. The festival gave a fresh impetus to the folk dance movement in Israel and was followed by four additional festivals in the amphitheatre of Daliyyah: in 1947, 1951, 1958, and 1968.

The Daliyyah festival also marked the first stage in making Israeli folk dance an established movement through the sponsorship of the national authorities, including first and foremost the Histadrut (Labor Federation), which established a Folk Dance Section in 1952 that became involved in the organization of many dancing projects; then came the establishment of the Inter-Kibbutz Committee of Folk Dance and that of the Ethnic Dance Project in 1971 by the Histadrut and the Ministry of Education and Culture. In the 1980s the Ministry of Education and Culture introduced projects initiated by Shalom Hermon, such as the "dancing school" and "dancing kindergarten," which contributed to the dissemination of folk dances through the educational system.

It should be noted that the Daliyyah festival also gave rise to several regional and national folk dance festivals, as well as to dance groups that emphasized the "theatrical" and "show" elements of the folk dances. However, some of their staged dances became folk dances. The leading figures in this field were Zeev Havatzelet and Yonatan Karmon, who created the "Israeli style" of folk dance performances on stage. In 1988, an annual national Israeli dance festival was initiated in the city of Karmiel and directed for 12 years by the choreographer Yonatan Karmon. This festival, which presents folk and modern Israeli dances, attracts thousands of folk dancers every year, and 250,000 spectators.

There are about 120 performing folk dance groups, including Jewish ethnic and Arab *Debka* dance groups, which present on stage their traditional ethnic dances; many of them represent Israeli dances in international folklore festivals.

Israeli folk dances created by Israelis in Israel and abroad number today more than 4,000. According to a survey conducted by TeleSeker in 1994, there were in Israel about 100,000 people who dance regularly, at least once a week; 100,000 more people dance every 2–4 weeks; and about 200,000 dance from time to time.

It is noteworthy that the first creators of Israeli folk dances were influenced by the works of Rudolf von Laban (1879–1958) of Vienna, a choreographer and dance teacher who devised a theory of movement which still constitutes the basis of modern dance. He felt that the folk dance was disappearing because of the changes brought about by modernity, and that therefore a new way had to be found. The means that seemed to him central in this process of renewal was a "chorus of movements" which combined a speaking chorus group with the simplest dance movements that people could perform without prior technical knowledge.

In spite of the fact, that Israeli folk dances have many sources of inspiration, they have a style of their own. Israeli folk dances were the products of the emerging "Israeli culture" of the Sabras. They symbolized the ideas of collectivism and equality; all were equals in the circles of the dances and their sources, thus a real integration and interaction of cultures and dances was achieved in the dances. Today the folk dances are still popular, but they have lost some of their ideological basis and serve mainly as popular entertainment.

Many of the new dances are still based on the basic steps created in the 1940s and 1950s; but, in comparison to the "old" dances," the "new" underwent many changes due to the processes of urbanization, commercialization of folk dances, the impact of globalization, the development of multi- cultural societies, and the emergence of professional dance instructors who make a living from creating and teaching folk dances.

Some of the "new" dances, of the last 20 years, are beautiful and follow the style of the "old" dances. But many of them are just artificial combinations of steps. These changes reflect the decline of the sense of belonging to a collective expressed in the circle shifted to a feeling of isolation. Many of them lost their ideological basis and became fashionable forms of leisure-time activity, and their melodies are mainly those of "pop" songs. Nevertheless, when dancers are asked, "why do you dance?" they will tell you that it is because they "enjoy dancing"; but many of them would also say: "Because I feel that the dances represent beautiful Israel."

See also *Music; *Dance.

BIBLIOGRAPHY: G. Kadman, *A Dancing Nation* (1969), 86–88 (Heb.); R. Ashkenazi, *The Story of Folk Dances in Dailyyah* (Heb., 1992); Z. Friedhaber, "Israeli Folk Dance between Folklore and Entertainment," in: *Israel Dance*, 2 (Sept. 1993), 59–60; idem, "A Hundred Years of Zionism in Dance," in: *Folk Dance in Israel. Supplement to Israel Dance*, 4 (1997), 3–16 (Heb.).

[Dan Ronen (2nd ed.)]

Art

PAINTING. Except for a few minor manifestations, there was no expression in the field of graphic arts in the 19th century. The beginning of modern art in Ereẓ Israel can be traced back to the activities of Boris *Schatz, who in 1903 met Herzl and propounded his scheme for establishing a Jewish art center in Ereẓ Israel. The plan was developed and approved by the Seventh Zionist Congress in 1905, and the following year Schatz opened the *Bezalel School in Jerusalem. He was breaking completely new ground, apart from which he had to contend with a number of objective negative factors, including the small size of the Jewish population, the paucity of local support, and the forceful hostility of the extreme Orthodox elements.

Schatz had won the support of the Congress on the basis of his program "to establish suitable enterprises and thus provide the Jewish population of Palestine with new ways of sustenance and possibilities of existence." The first group of Bezalel artists and teachers (Schatz, *Lilien, Hirszenberg) felt an immediate need to evolve a national style. They felt that this could only be founded on Jewish tradition and must illustrate Jewish themes from history and folklore, as well as establish close connections with Ereẓ Israel (e.g., pictures of Bedouin). Their aim was to use European techniques to illustrate Jewish traditions, but with the emphasis not so much on the pictorial as on the decorative. Schatz developed painting and sculpture and also promoted handicrafts for both artistic and economic objectives. The early Bezalel group stubbornly opposed the influence of modern art, which they felt as a threat to the Jewish nature of their work. They set up a permanent exhibition of artists connected with their school and working within their tradition.

During World War I most of the teachers were exiled or fled, but they returned soon after the war when new elements began to come to the fore, composed both of recent arrivals and of a younger group of painters who had received their artistic education at Bezalel. These painters also envisioned a national art not based primarily on eastern European traditions. They were dazzled by the land itself, by its color, light, and inhabitants, and were captivated by Oriental and Muslim influences. The organizational milestone at this stage was the foundation of the Association of Jewish Artists (later, the Association of Painters and Sculptors in Israel) in 1920 in Jerusalem. This group held its first display in the citadel of the Tower of David in Jerusalem in 1923, and their annual exhibitions became major events in the cultural life of the country. From 1926 they began to exhibit in Tel Aviv. About 20 to 30 painters participated in the show each year, displaying 100 to 150 works. Among the leaders of this group were Israel *Paldi, Reuven *Rubin, Menahem *Shemi, and Nahum *Gutman, all deeply influenced by trends in other parts of the world, especially Paris, with expressionism as the dominant style. The group came to the understanding that national art cannot be created artificially but must develop organically from within.

A further stimulus to artistic life came with the opening of the Tel Aviv Museum in 1931. The development of the theater turned some of the artists to stage designing. An additional dovetailing with European trends resulted from the immigration of refugee artists from Nazi Germany after 1933. Many of these were mature artists who had made their mark in Europe and were well within the European tradition. Their own enchantment with the School of Paris was conveyed to the painters in Palestine, and Palestine art began to faithfully reflect European models, notably in expressionist, cubist, and other abstract styles. Under the impact of all these forces Israeli art took on more universal proportions. The outstanding expression was the establishment in 1948 of the New Horizons group to promote abstract art and free Israeli art from provincialism. The leaders of this group were Yoseph *Zaritzky and Marcel *Janco, the latter a founder of the Dada movement who had settled in Palestine in 1941.

By the 1950s the artists of Israel reflected all the European styles, and the work was extremely variegated. Apart from the variety in style, diversity also emerged from the multiplicity of ethnic backgrounds, some of the noted artists deriving from the Oriental communities. Intensive art life developed in the country, and important artists' centers were founded in *Safed and Ein *Hod. Some of the younger artists developed in the kibbutzim, where the tendency was to remain closer to their surroundings and be somewhat less abstract than was the general trend. However, one of the significant directions of the 1960s was toward a synthesis incorporating both the influence of western Europe and aspects of Jewish tradition, which had been so stressed by the pioneers of art in the country. The extent to which art is practiced is illustrated by the fact that by the mid-1960s the Association of Painters and Sculptors had more than 400 members (see also *Art).

CRAFTS. Considerable attention has been given to the development of handicrafts and home industries. The Bezalel School trained craftsmen even in its early days, looking to artistic traditions of the Orient as well as the Jewish past, and many of the objets d'art produced have been Jewish ritual objects. The fostering of handicrafts was particularly successful after the period of mass immigration, with each community contributing from its own artistic traditions. Both *WIZO and the government-sponsored Maskit organizations have developed and marketed home-industry products. These have incorporated Yemenite, Persian, North African, and European, as well as Bedouin and Druze styles. The crafts include, notably, ceramics, glass, woven fabrics, mosaics, clothing fashions, and wood compositions.

SCULPTURE. Boris Schatz, himself a sculptor, influenced the early development of the medium in the country. Conditions for sculptors were even less favorable than for painters, in view of the traditional Jewish religious objections. However, despite criticism, Schatz persevered with his own work and with training pupils. Even after World War I, sculpture developed only very slowly, despite the arrival of a number of sculptors in the country. The kibbutzim, in the absence of pressures exerted by religious elements in the towns, pioneered in the commissioning of sculptures. A certain development can be traced in the 1930s, when sculptors proceeded with the execution of work even in the absence of specific commissions. After World War II governmental and official institutions began ordering various types of sculpture. The monuments erected after the War of Independence gave an impetus to the art. Of the towns, Haifa was the most active in siting sculptures in public places.

The outstanding influence in the 1930s and 1940s was Ze'ev *Ben-Zvi. He taught at Bezalel, and his pupils (David *Palombo, Itzhak *Danziger) gained prominence in the 1960s. There is no defined school of sculpture in Israel, even less so than in the area of painting. Sculpture is marked by a variety of styles, influenced by the origin and outlook of the sculptor. Examples from antiquity and archaeology have been strong influences. Abstract sculpture was virtually unknown until the 1960s, but has become one of the popular forms of expression under the influence of the French school in general and expressionism in particular (e.g., the works of Yigal *Tumarkin). New techniques have been employed with the use of new materials, and a further development results from the combination of plastic arts for the adornment of public buildings (see also *Sculpture).

DEVELOPMENTS IN ART THROUGH THE 1970S. Art in Israel in recent years has been characterized by a diversity of trends. In addition to abstract and figurative painting, there is minimal, conceptual or environmental art, portrayal of ecological elements, photography, film and video as artistic media, as well as happenings and performances.

A major figure who has emerged in the abstract field is Moshe Kupferman (b. 1926), member of kibbutz Loḥamei ha-Getta'ot, who studied with painters of the New Horizons group, Streichman and Steimatsky. Spontaneity, expressiveness and chance characterize his art. The grid on his canvas is created simultaneously by means of markings and erasures. In his paintings one can observe several planes.

Geometric abstraction typifies the work of Alima (b. 1932) and the hard-edge compositions of Reuven Berman (b. 1929). The approach of Michael *Gross (1920–2004) approach can be described as abstract minimalism. His work was characterized by reduction and translation of reality into stains and lines. Sometimes he used materials as artistic means – a tree can be represented by a piece of wood attached to the canvas. Gross did not reduce and frame reality, but created abstract equivalents. He also designed sculpture such as the half arch in the Jerusalem neighborhood of Kiryat ha-Yovel, overlooking the Judean Mountains.

Important retrospective exhibitions of Arie *Aroch (1908–1974) were held at the Israel Museum and at the Tel Aviv Museum in 1977–78. These exhibitions emphasized his major influence on Israeli art. In the 1950s his abstract paintings began to reflect his interest, by representing experiences in a child's manner, as can be seen in the scribbles etched into the oil paint. His works include collages of objects which are remote from the present, although they are strikingly modern. The absence of polish gives his work a patina which otherwise is only created with time. One of the artists who was influenced by Aroch is Raffi Lavie (b. 1937) who in turn serves as a source of inspiration and influence to the younger generation. In his abstract paintings he applies, in addition to color and line, collage elements such as faded photographs, in which the patina may have some nostalgic associations. In other paintings he pastes new, shiny photographs on paper. His exhibitions have demonstrated that the *enfant terrible* has turned out to be almost a "classic" figure in the history of recent Israeli art, proving that his artistic values have drawn a relatively large audience. His substantial influence is a result of his teaching in the State Art Teachers' Training College, his encouragement of young artists, and his activities as an organizer in the art world. The group "Ten Plus" was founded by him together with Buky Schwartz, Benni Efrat, Uri Lipchitz, Pinchas Eshet, Siona Shimshi and others as an alternative to the dominating lyrical abstraction prevalent at the time. The group did not succeed in creating a consistent ideology. "Ten Plus" provided a focus for artistic fermentation and served as an organizational framework.

The geometric shapes of Menashe *Kadishman's minimal sculpture reflect the influence of his teacher, the English sculptor, Anthony *Caro. The resistance to gravity and reductive, simple, geometrical shapes are features in his work. Composition is based on the tension between weights, shapes and sizes, as in the yellow painted steel sculpture in the Israel Museum's Billy Rose Art Garden or in the sculpture in the plaza in front of the Mann Auditorium, Tel Aviv. Another aspect of his art is his involvement with nature and landscape as expressed by his varied attention to trees. In addition to painting real trees, he painted metal sheets which were attached to trees in Montevideo and in New York's Central Park (1969), In Jerusalem he created his *Laundry Forest* (1975) in the plaza in front of the Israel Museum. White canvas sheets were cut into shapes of trees and hung, through which visitors had to cross. It suggested the Israeli habit of hanging laundry in the street outside buildings. Thus Kadishman introduced urban landscape into nature.

Buky Schwartz (b. 1932) was also a student of Anthony Caro in London. Schwartz creates large-scale minimal sculpture. In 1969 he designed a memorial for Yad Vashem in Jerusalem.

The sculptor Yeḥi'el *Shemi (b. 1922), a member of kibbutz Kabri, created sculpture from scrap iron, violently torn and welded. Later, he made his sculpture from ready-made standard construction units. He designed some important public monuments such as the welded steel and cement memorial in Achziv (1967) facing the Mediterranean and the monument at Ben-Gurion Airport (1972). He did a sculptural system for the Jerusalem Theater (1970) consisting of three pieces: a relief over the entrance which was designed as an integral part of the wall, a sculpture in the lobby and another in the central plaza. These sculptures help to emphasize the general sculptural quality of the building.

Dani Karavan (b. 1930) designed an environmental sculpture for a memorial in Beersheba and for the *Venice Biennale* in 1976 which was dedicated to peace. A year later he won the Israel Prize and was invited to participate in *Documenta 6* in Kassel. For this exhibition he designed another environmental sculpture made of white cement. The sculpture's shapes invited visitors to climb the tall stairs and penetrate into the sculpture. Peace was again the theme in his large show at the Belvedere in Florence and, at the same time, in Prato's ancient Castello.

Whereas in *Documenta 5*, one of the most important exhibitions for contemporary art, only one Israeli artist was invited to participate, several Israelis were asked to exhibit their work in *Documenta 6*. Among them was Michael Gitlin (b. 1943), who marks space by means of standard wooden sheets painted black and cut by an axe. The breaking lines are not completely straight and reflect an expressive quality. Pinchas Cohen-Gan (b. 1942), whose earlier work focused on political issues, exhibited drawings. Beni Efrat's (b. 1935) contributions were performances and Michael Druks (b. 1940) showed video art. Earlier works by Druks include sculpture of discarded billboards, and a photo-collage of an electric power plant in Tel Aviv whose smokestack (which raised ecological concern in the general public before it was built) was turned to an angle of 45° like a cannon, with possible sexual connotations.

On the works of Joshua Neustein (b. 1940) the fold, the tear and the cut replace the lines and create the composition's structural interrelationships. In a conceptual work, "Jerusalem River" (1970), Neustein, with Georgette Battle and Jerry Marx, used a tape recorder with sounds of flowing water in the Jerusalem mountains in order to create a fantasy river by means of sound. A conceptual work by Neustein with political implications was the marking by dogs of their territorial area in the Golan Heights as a way of defining border lines.

Political involvement by artistic means interested Pinchas Cohen-Gan. In addition to his sensitive drawings, he expressed his political concern by constructing a temporary shelter in a refugee camp in Jericho (1974). A comment on the hostile environment of Israel is the work in which Cohen-Gan created living conditions for fish in the Dead Sea (1972–73) by means of plastic pipes filled with sweet water. In the *9e biennale de Paris* for young artists (1975) he exhibited another political work, "Reconciliation with Asia."

Other artists with varied artistic interests are Micha Ullman (b. 1939), a conceptual artist who also produces video art. Yair Garbuz (b. 1945), who paints and creates assemblages, photographs, films as well as video; Yocheved Weinfeld, Moti Mizrahi and Gideon Gechtman produce interesting body art. The latter used male nudity as opposed to the more conventional use of female nudity. Gechtman artistically expressed personal problems of internal and external pain as a result of an open-heart operation he had undergone and documented on video tape and photographs. The work of the late Yitshak Danziger (1916–77) reflects a serious interest in ecological and landscape problems. Danziger created a relatively limited number of works of art, but most of these serve as milestones in the short history of Israeli art, from his first important works "Shbazia" (1938) and "Nimrod" (1939) inspired by Near-Eastern archaeology to an architectural interest in the Bedouin tent, as can be seen in the "Negev Sheep" (1956). For the Yarkon Park in Tel Aviv, he designed a white cement landscape sculpture which is planted into the ground and integrates with the topography and plants of the park. The ecological concern is expressed in the rehabilitation project for the Nesher quarry near the Haifa-Nazareth road (1971).

The public at large prefers paintings inspired by surrealism. The best representatives of fantastic art in the 1970s are Shmuel *Bak and Yossl *Bergner.

Art Museums and Galleries. The Israel Museum was inaugurated in 1965 and serves as the major center for artistic activities and exhibitions of well-established artists as well as young, unknown, artists. Numerous exhibitions of Israeli and international art are organized annually and are an important source of up-to-date information for artists and the general public. The museum also awards several prizes, among them the Sandberg Prize, a prize for young artists, and a prize for industrial design. The Tel Aviv Museum moved to its new building in 1971, and in 1977 a new director and staff were named. The guiding principles for selecting exhibitions are similar to those of the Israel Museum. One of the innovations is a strong emphasis on photography. Many galleries were opened in recent years, most of them completely commercial ventures. Only a few galleries are willing to take any risks in exhibiting works of art which cannot be sold. The public continues to prefer oil paintings on canvas to prints, but graphics are becoming increasingly popular. Several years after this art form was in demand in the West, printing studios were opened in conjunction with the Artists' Houses in Jerusalem and Tel Aviv as well as the Israel Museum.

Periodicals. Periodicals devoted to art are *Gazith*, founded 1933, edited by Gabriel *Talpir; *Qav*, Journal of Modern Art, 1965–1970, edited by Yona *Fischer and Rachel Shapiro (twelve issues were published); *Ẓiyyur u-Fisul* (Painting and Sculpture Quarterly), founded 1972, edited by Dan Tsalka; *Journal of Jewish Art*, founded 1973, edited by Bezalel *Narkiss, a journal devoted to Jewish art in Israel and abroad. The journal is published and edited in Israel for Spertus College of Judaica Press in Chicago. *Mussag*, founded 1975, edited by Adam Baruch, ceased publication after 13 issues, owing to lack of support.

Art History. The first department in art history to include the history of Jewish and Israeli art among the subjects taught was founded in 1964 by Prof. Moshe Barasch of The Hebrew University in Jerusalem. Since then, departments of art have opened at Tel Aviv University and the University of Haifa. They also include courses in these areas.

[Michael Levine]

DEVELOPMENTS IN ART THROUGH THE 1990S. Israeli art from the 1980s can be characterized by its increasing pluralism and by the expansion of its significant dialogue with major urban centers of international art. Although minimalism and conceptualism were clearly hallmarks of the 1970s, the art scene has grown more complex largely due to the increasing number of artists. One can, however, cautiously generalize art of the early 1980s as more emotional and expressionistic in character, while in the late 1980s and early 1990s, a more intellectual, understated, and intentional approach was discernible.

The undaunted art lover can see in Israel's museums, galleries, and beyond (in out- and indoor monuments, parks, or nature reserves, etc.) a dizzying number of exhibitions. The Gabriel Sherover Information Center for Israeli Art at the Israel Museum records approximately 2,000 per year. Older or established artists are often seen in solo retrospectives, and the younger generation is exposed in group or thematic shows.

Important internal art stimuli during the past decade have included biannual exhibitions for sculpture (since 1988), and photography (since 1986). There were four Tel Hai events for outdoor environmental sculpture (since 1980). There are also prizes awarded by the Tel Aviv Museum of Art, the Israel Museum, Jerusalem, the America–Israel Cultural Foundation, and the minister of education to encourage the young artist. The opening of the Museum of Israeli Art, Ramat Gan, in 1987 added another exhibition space for emerging talent. Smaller museums in Arad, Bat-Yam, Herẓliyyah, Petaḥ Tikvah, and Tefen also contribute to the dynamism.

Not all art in Israel is in the museums. In the field of sculpture, manmade efforts are united with nature's aesthetic in reserves or parks, such as the Desert Sculpture Park on the edge of the Ramon Crater (curated by Ezra Orion). A project that began in the early 1960s but was only realized in the mid-1980s, its object was to add contemporary sculpture along the rim of the cliff which was sculpted by nature itself into geometrical rock formations. Israeli sculptors who worked there in dolomite stone from 1986 to 1988 were Ezra Orion, Dalia Meiri, Noam Rabinovich, Itzu Rimmer, Hava Mahutan, Dov Heller, Sa'ul Salo, Berny Fink, and David Fein. Israel Hadany, whose work can be found in many sculpture gardens and urban spaces, also sculpted a stone monument for the Albert Promenade to counterbalance the natural beauty of Miẓpeh Rimon (1992).

In an effort to bring art to the streets of Tel Aviv, its municipality sponsored a project which brought 15 sculptures to the Tel Aviv-Jaffa area from 1989 to 1992. Participants in the project were Ilan Averbuch, Zadok Ben-David, Gideon Gechtman, Isaac Golombeck, Yaacov Dorchin, Yaacov Hefetz, Dina Kahana-Gueler, Motti Mizrachi, Lawrence McNabb, Sigal Primor, Gabi Klasmer, Zvika Kantor, Yuval Rimon, and Yehiel Shemi.

Dani Karavan's "White Square" environmental sculpture of stone, water, and landscaping was completed in 1988 in the Wolfson Park, Tel Aviv. A homage to the pioneers of the "White City" – Tel Aviv – it was one of four works chosen to represent Israel in the architectural biennale in Venice (1991). (The others were the Sherover Promenade in Jerusalem by Shlomo Aharonson, Zvi Hecker's spiral house in Ramat Gan, and Moshe Safdie's design of the extension of the Hebrew Union College in Jerusalem.)

The international Tel Ḥai Contemporary Art Meeting, a project of the Upper Galilee Regional Council, began in 1980 with the aim of promoting sculpture in nature, installations in interior spaces, and of creating an alternative space to the sociocultural concept of museums. It provided artists with a place of historical meaning and sentimental identity. Three additional Tel Ḥai events (1983, 1987, and 1990) attracted scores of local, and some international, participants.

In the final analysis, however, the museums carry the greatest weight concerning artistic quality. In the past decade homage was paid to solo figures considered to be singularly important and influential artists. Following are short descriptions regarding a limited number of them, chosen because they signify unique trends and/or are of seminal importance throughout the period under discussion.

Moshe Kupferman (b. 1926) was honored with an exhibition at the Israel Museum and Tel Aviv Museum of Art in 1984–85 (curator: Yona Fischer) which surveyed this prominent non-representational artist's work in paint and on paper from 1963 to 1984. Employing purposely limited color palette and formal vocabulary, Kupferman constructs his unique oeuvre by a process combining subtle layering, erasing and recombining color, and adding and subtracting planes and lines. The resulting abstract black-white-violet grid and scaffold compositions formed by decisive strokes of the brush are laden with emotion and expressionism relating to the artist's own outlook on life.

Abstraction in contemporary art has another strong protagonist in Lea Nikel (b. 1918) whose solo exhibition at the Israel Museum in 1985 (curator: Yigal Zalmona) was devoted to her thunderously bright, multicolored canvases. Nikel's paintings are afire with painterly instinct and values, which she has never deserted for any kind of propaganda content in her work.

Philosophical and poetic qualities can be found in the work of the minimalistic sculptor Micha Ullman (b. 1940), who was chosen to participate in the last two Documentas (8 and 9). Ullman's "Containers" were the subject of an exhibition at the Israel Museum (curator: Yigal Zalmona) in 1988. To his simple formal vocabulary of forms (often chairs and pits made of clay, mud, soil), Ullman added massive steel house-like elements ("Day," "Night," and "Havdalah") to express the nuances of concepts like borders, shelter/grave, reincarnation. In his latest work he dealt with negative and positive areas in red sand within a steel and glass vitrine, another variation on the theme of the relationship between the container and the contained.

The versatility of Menashe *Kadishman (b. 1932) spans three decades and three major areas: painting, sculpture, and prints. In the past decade he has dealt with humanistic and universal themes: the sacrifice of man, as portrayed by the Abraham–Isaac/lamb–God story (an example stands in the plaza before the Tel Aviv Museum of Art in corten steel); births: the subject of an exhibition of that title in the Israel Museum in 1990 (curator Yigal Zalmona); nature, focusing on trees – as cotton sheets in the 1970s, and later on in prints and in steel. Examples of the latter are the blue metal tree silhouettes before the Wolfson Towers and near the Knesset in Jerusalem.

Oswaldo Romberg (b. 1938) is an architect-artist-teacher concerned with the language of art. "Building Footprints," a mixed-media installation at the Israel Museum in 1991 (curator: Yigal Zalmona), was another step in his continuing research of prominent art historical paintings and monuments. By isolating their formal and/or color components, Romberg helps the viewer analyze the details of the powerful whole.

Yigal Tumarkin (b. 1933) has been on the map of Israeli art since the late 1950s as a painter, sculptor, and printmaker. A retrospective on his sculpture covered the decades 1957–1992 at the Tel Aviv Museum of Art (curator: Ellen Ginton). It surveyed his artistic growth from his earlier tortured and maimed Grunewaldesque bronze figures, his anti-war mixed media paintings to his most recent period with more abstract/less explicit metal sculptures.

As an artist and teacher at the Bezalel Academy of Art and Design, Jerusalem, Pinchas Cohen-Gan (b. 1942) has played an influential role on the younger generation of artists. Active in different media (painting, printmaking, photography), Cohen-Gan works with conceptual and socio-political content while he varies stylistically from expressionistic to minimalistic. The Tel Aviv Museum of Art (curator: Talia Rappaport) devoted a retrospective "Works on Paper 1969–1992" to him. A stick-like human figure, often running, and a big human head are recurring motifs in his work and hint at the trials of an Everyman in constant search of answers.

In the 1980s, there were a series of historical exhibitions which were critical attempts to understand the roots of earlier Israeli art. These exhibitions may have actually raised questions relating to national identity before they were asked in other fields. The conflict between localism and internationalism, between provincialism and urban centers, between group vs. individual values were relevant to the art arena, as well as reflecting the duality of Israeli society's values.

At the President's House, Jerusalem, an exhibition in 1983 titled "The Archetype of the Pioneer in Israeli Art" (curator Dr. Gideon Ofrat) traced the subject from the early 20th century until the 1980s in two- and three-dimensional works. Artists working in the 1980s and concerned with this vein of ideological expression included the late Abraham Ofek, Naftali Bezem, Yossl *Bergner, Yair Garbuz, Oded Lerer, Motti Mizrahi, and Menashe Kadishman.

Another manifestation of the historical/heroic approach was seen in the graphic work of David Tartakover, who often nostalgically bases his images on idealistic graphics of the Mandate Period. Tartakover also created a series of famous "Tel Avivians," paying homage to local heroes of the first Jewish city in 2,000 years. The name of the exhibition "Produce of Israel" (curator: Izzika Gaon) at the Israel Museum and Tel Aviv Museum of Art, 1983–84, was devoted to many positive aspects of Israeli cultural life.

A few years later, in 1987, "To Live with the Dream" at the Tel Aviv Museum of Art (curator: Batia Donner) presented an analysis of the idealism and the following disillusionments, using documentation from graphic, painting, and sculpture media from the Mandate to post-statehood decades. Stereotypes, cultural heroes, places, cultural symbols, borders, and territory were the sub-topics of the show. (In 1980 an important exhibition titled "Borders" [curator: Stephanie Rachum] also investigated how artists define this concept.)

After the Gulf War in 1991 an exhibition called "Real Time" at the Tel Aviv Museum of Art (curator: Batia Donner) reviewed the patriotic expressions, largely in the graphics medium, seen on billboards, in newspaper advertisements, posters, etc., during the war itself. Many of them used the blue-white motif of the flag as a rallying point. However, this type of expression was as short-lived as the war, and Israeli society quickly returned to normalcy and its ideological problems.

At the Israel Museum in 1991, 24 artists participated in "Routes of Wandering: Nomadism, Voyages and Transitions in Contemporary Israeli Art" (curator: Sarit Shapira). The show dealt with questions relating to the most contemporary version of the pioneer/place/land ideology. Art and philosophy seem to have gone full circle. Deterritorialization has replaced the concept of "place," with borders being burst both conceptually and actually. The show dealt with images relating to means of transportation in Israeli art; maps; and most importantly, the concepts represented by travel and moving around. Some examples of the work on exhibit were Moshe Gershuni's "There," Benni Efrat's 1989 sculpture, "Quests for Air Spring 2037," a bed-shaped cell with a suitcase in it; and Moshe Ninio's "Exit," blurred text on a photograph. The few human figures were generalized and transitory, like Pinchas Cohen-Gan's arrangement of a "Cardboard Box Figure," an image of an anywhere man fleeing.

As previously mentioned, the types of art available reflect the pluralistic approach dominant in Israel's museums and galleries. If one is looking for specific information or documentation of contemporary life, there are few painters working in a realistic style. Outstanding among them are Israel Hershberg, who paints fastidiously hyper-realistic still lifes and interiors; Pamela Levy, who bases her paintings on photographs of leisure time and situations (such as swimming) which she reworks into allegorical and tense situations; David Reeb, also inspired by televised or photographic images of actualia, such as soldiers in action, converts them into compelling paintings freezing significant and formerly fleeting images; and Ivan Schwebel depicts biblical stories by placing his characters in contemporary cityscapes, such as Jerusalem's Ben-Yehudah Street, to give the viewer a feeling that the ancient conflicts are still relevant to our own times.

There is a significant group of artists whose work reacts to the political climate from symbolic, emotional angles. An exhibition in New York's Jewish Museum (curator: Susan Goodman) titled "In the Shadow of Conflict: Israeli Art, 1980–1989" summarized a decade of work along this line with a wide variety of artistic reactions to war, the neither-nor situation, and the dream of peace. Artists included in the show were Arnon Ben-David, Pinchas Cohen-Gan, Yair Garbuz, Moshe Gershuni, Tsibi Geva, Michael Gitlin, Menashe Kadishman, Gabi Glasmer, Moshe Kupferman, Dudu Mezah, Motti Mizrachi, Avner Moriah, Moshe Muller, Joshua Neustein, David Reeb, Yigal Tumarkin, Micha Ullman, and the late Aviva Uri.

Although much is heard of orientalizing music, levantization in the visual arts is rare. The closest to it are the paintings of Tsibi Geva, with their Islamic-inspired style or content: allover patterns with overtones of meanings such as the 'kefiya' paintings or patterns of terrazzo floor tiles; or a series of works which combine names of Arabic words and towns written in Hebrew with illustrations ostensibly drawn by Arab children.

Since 1981 there have been a series of group exhibitions by Jewish and Palestinian artists whose aims were to promote both political and artistic peaceful co-existence by constructing bridges of understanding. Several exhibitions were held at the Artists House and at the "El-Quwaiti" theater in Jerusalem during this period. There were group exhibitions of Palestinian artists in 1988 and 1990 at the Artists House, Jerusalem. In 1992 the group of 12 Palestinian and Israeli Artists (curator: Ariella Azoulai) joined forces again in a show which coincided with the peace negotiations and renewed their commitment to the process. Participating were Moshe Gershuni, Tamar Getter, Pamela Levy, Assad Azi, Arnon Ben-David, David Reeb, Sliman Mansour, Nabil Anani, Taisin Barkat, Kamal Butalah, Khalil Rabel, and Taleb Dweik. Sliman Manzur and Israel Rabinovitz were invited by the Swedish Socialist Party in Stockholm for a joint exhibition, "Out of the Same Earth," which contained a work they created together.

On the international scene, and in Israel as well, compelling work has been based on the written word as the central image. An exhibition at the Janco-Dada Museum, Ein Hod, titled "Imagewriting" (curator: Sara Hakkerts, 1992) investigated how 24 Israeli artists use letters, words, and sentences in their work, and in this way illustrate their points of view about local events. There were very few political statements (with the exception of works by Yair Garbuz, Arnon Ben-David, and Tsibi Geva). Other participants included Nurit Isaac-Polachek, Shaul Bauman, Jenifer Bar-Lev, Eli Gur Arie, Tamar Getter, Michael Grubman, Moshe Gershuni, Elisha Dagan, Svetlana Dubrovsky, Alexander Rudakov, Nurit David, Rachel Heller, Boris Yuchvitz, Pinchas Cohen-Gan, Raffi Lavie, Chaim Maor, Bashir Makhoul, Michal Na-aman, Moshe Amar, and Michal Shamir.

Poetic texts written by Oded Yedaya in white or black ink on black and white photographs were the subject of an exhibition curated by Nissan Peretz at the Israel Museum in 1988. Yedaya's compositions combine figurative elements (images and words) with a strong abstract substructure.

In a solo exhibition at the Tel Aviv Museum of Art, 1992 (curator: Ellen Ginton), dreams were Jenifer Bar-Lev's subject. She interspersed original stream-of-consciousness poems in English with Hebrew biblical texts with a patchwork of painted shapes and/or other materials, like blue jeans or kitsch paintings.

Nurit David and Yocheved Weinfeld are two other artists whose multimedia creations intersperse textual elements with imagery. Zvi Goldstein is another multimedia artist whose texts are integral to his work. His verbal manifestos are of a didactic rather than a personal nature, and he combines them with objects that look as if they belong to a highly technologically advanced culture. These installations deal with the position and options of a third world country.

Recently there have been very personal, humoristic works which contain underlying, serious meanings created by a few mavericks in the art world. Philip Rantzer converts found objects into adult, kinetic toys which provide the museum viewers with a piquant black humor. In his exhibition "Sometimes I Get a Hankering for My Wife" at the Israel Museum in 1992 (curator: Yigal Zalmona), he created a house with his ready-mades and collectibles, running water, and delectable, sundry items such as a breadbox with a small video screen and songs by the Andrews Sisters.

Zvika Kantor uses banal, domestic objects but constructs them out of absurd kitschy materials. An example is his "Duet of Happiness" piano made not for music lovers but for those with a sweet tooth, as it is made only of sugar cubes and chocolate. Dudu Gerstein also makes light colorful and amusing sculpture cutouts, such as a flowering plant, by painting aluminum with duco paint. Elisha Dagan paints wood with industrial paint and makes three-dimensional word sculptures, such as "Oh Baby Wolffff" and "Motherrrr" which can be read by looking down at the generally waist-high structures.

Dr. Gideon Ofrat's choice for Israel's representative to the Biennale was Avital Geva, a conceptual anti-art establishment artist who has chosen not to be exhibited since the early 1970s, when he executed some bold conceptual projects (like the yellow line beginning on the road near his kibbutz, Ein Shemer, and ending at the Israel Museum). Geva has spent the past years experimenting with knowledge in the form of growing tomatoes and fish, and thus studying the artistic process.

Photography clearly influences a number of contemporary artists, who rework it in other media. However, it is also the chosen sole medium for certain artists. There were many exhibitions devoted to young and established photographers concentrating on this art form alone. Notable among them were exhibitions showing the work of Pesi Girsch, Bareket Ben Yaakov, Judy Orgel Lester, and nostalgic shows by the young Gabi Salzberger called "Rusted Pioneers" and homage to the late Alfred Bernheim, all curated by Nissan Peretz at the Israel Museum. At the Museum of Israeli Art in Ramat-Gan there was another homage to the late Alfonse Himmelreich, "Dance Photographs: Mood and Movement," curated by Vivienne Silver in 1987. Moshe Ninio's exhibition titled "Cycle of Days" in 1991 at the Israel Museum (curator: Yigal Zalmona) incorporated mixed media with photography. His blurred, enlarged photographic details printed on metal plates were clearly detached from their original contexts, and the sparse, iconic images resulting were intended to supply new meanings, above and beyond the former content.

Zvi Tolkovsky, a versatile painter and printmaker, organized a quasi-documentary exhibition in 1991 containing photographs and found objects which had been left at the deserted refugee camp of Nueima, at the Israel Museum (curator: Rika Gonen). Displayed like archeological remnants from a forgotten people, the show brought out the poignancy of this relatively recent "tel."

In 1992 Sigal Primor's "The Antarctic Challenge," (curator: Yigal Zalmona) at the Israel Museum moved from Alfred Hitchcock's *Psycho* to the South Pole, and the indefatigable sculptor Ezra Orion celebrated the space year by transmitting a laser beam column to infinity from Israel and international locations.

[Elaine Varady]

Critical post-modernist attitudes, which became quite dominant in Israeli art in the 1980s, express a growing tendency to give voice to the "Other" – artists raised in immigrant families, homosexuals and lesbians, or artists belonging to minority groups. The "Israeli experience," based on a collective, monolithic memory, had fallen apart. The paintings of Yair Garbuz (1945–), David Reeb (1952–), Tsibi Geva (1951–), and Avishai Eyal (1945–), or the photographs of Micha Kirshner (1947–), Michal Heyman (1954–), Shuka Glotman (1953–), and Adi Ness (1966–) are examples of a new critical and deconstructive examination of the Israeli experience, of local history and its visual representations, and of the manipulations of the collective-political memory. Various aspects of the post-modern condition gained in prominence in the course of the last two decades. These include an erasure of the borders separating illusion from reality (art based on the virtual worlds created in the cinema, for instance, as reflected in the paintings of Anat Ben Shaul; the sense of apocalyptic threat expressed in the works of Dorit Yacoby and Moshe Gershuni). The threat of loss of the family home or the national one is given form by the prominence of the "house" motif in the sculptures of Micha Ulman, Philip Renzer (1956–), Gideon Gechtman, and Buky Schwarz (1932–). For more than a decade now, there has been a growing emphasis on the Holocaust as one of the major constituents in defining the Israeli identity, especially on the part of artists such as Yocheved Weinfeld, Simcha Shirman (1947–), Haim Maor, and Uri Katzenshtein (1951–), who are second-generation survivors.

The particular problems of identity and the tensions surrounding the broad concept of the "Israeli experience" largely account for the development in the Israel of recent years of an art that is fully sensitive and attentive to what is happening both in the public sphere and in the private domain, and that has gained a prominent position in the global art scene, as evinced by the interest shown in exhibitions of Israeli art in various venues abroad.

[Haim Finkelstein and Haim Maor (2nd ed.)]

Architecture

Modern architecture in Ereẓ Israel, i.e., from the end of the 19th century, is basically European in style and outlook. This is expressed in the use of new building technology and in the functional approach to planning. The European-type building was first brought to Ereẓ Israel in the later part of the 19th century by settlers of European origin (Jews, and the German Templers) and by consular and missionary circles. They introduced the fashions of their country of origin, while local conditions and influences were scarcely reflected in their constructions. However, in the early 20th century, a first attempt at an individual style was made. This was expressed in the first Jewish housing projects in Jerusalem, in the villages under the auspices of Baron Edmond de Rothschild, and in other moshavot. In town buildings, too, there was the first groping for a style characterized by Muslim, Oriental, and even Assyrian elements (notable examples are the buildings of the Herzlia High School in Tel Aviv and the first Technion building in Haifa). After World War I a number of architects went to Palestine from western Europe and England. A strong influence was exerted by Richard *Kaufman, who stressed the horizontal structure; another group was influenced by expressionism; while the British school used local Arab designs, expressed largely in the buildings of the Mandatory government.

The 1920s saw the first functional buildings (for example, the Jewish Agency building, the Bet ha-Kerem High School, certain kibbutz dining rooms), while particular attention was paid to the designing of kibbutzim.

From 1933, a considerable number of architects went to Palestine from Central Europe, particularly from Germany and Austria. The first modern apartment buildings, built in a European style, date from this period. By this time, also, the Technion was producing many architects, and their common background contributed to a uniformity in style throughout the country. In the 1940s the tendency was toward greater simplicity in architecture, although further experiments were made in applying Oriental aspects.

The establishment of the State of Israel in 1948 enabled the undertaking of large-scale national and regional planning. Under the urgent pressure of mass immigration, however, sacrifices were made in quality, variety of design, and architectural values. Many of the buildings put up hastily were shoddy, and a depressing sameness characterized many of the *shikkunim* ("housing projects"). The Mandatory rule insisting on natural-stone construction in Jerusalem had to be disregarded. It was only when the pace of immigration slackened in the mid-1950s that it proved possible to concentrate again on improving quality and on aesthetic aspects. More attention was now paid to the finish, to externals, and to the development of surroundings of houses. Overall planning, which to some extent had remained on paper, was now implemented. The quick expansion of the towns led to pressure on space, and the high-rise building began to appear in Israel. Many impressive public buildings were erected in various parts of the country, and the style was generally international, rather than specifically Israeli. The reunification of Jerusalem in 1967 presented a new and significant challenge to Israel's architects (see also *Architecture).

Developments in the 1970s. The changes that have taken place in Israeli architecture from the Six-Day War on are a reflection of the changes that took place in Israeli society during the same period – changes in the political, social, economic and psychological spheres.

When a nation's development is stable and gradual, and architectural development parallels that process, architecture develops gradually and over a long period. When a society experiences crises (war, revolution or any traumatic event), they find expression in abrupt changes in architectural development.

Between the years 1948 and 1967, social development in Israel, the consolidation of social classes and social concepts, economic development, formation of life styles and values, all evolved in a gradual and consistent manner. The Six-Day War brought a social and cultural shock in its wake which led to a turning point in social development. As a direct result, architecture took on a new dimension.

The dominant influence on architecture in Israel had hitherto been that of western Europe and America. The way of thinking and concepts of form were adjusted to economic conditions, building techniques and the system of values that characterized Israeli society, and the specific needs of the time.

Generally speaking, one can define Israeli architecture during the years 1948–67 as being neutral, international and lacking any special or national quality relating to a particular locale. It was architecture based on the need to supply physical and economic needs and had very little to do with emotional or symbolic needs.

Before 1967 the need to supply housing on a massive scale predominated, and only relatively minor attention could be paid to the building of public and private services beyond this basic one. As Israel's economy expanded, however, more resources were diverted to such projects.

The Six-Day War broke the natural curve of development, A significant change took place in the psychology of Israeli society and in social and economic development. Economic development accelerated and a large amount of capital became available which immediately affected the building sector. In a short time the economic expansion reached increasingly wider social strata, which led to social changes and created a new social class with a higher income.

These developments created a greater demand for expanded services, both private and public.

In the 1960s changes took place in western culture regarding architectural ideas. These were years of reaction against the previous decade. The architectural ideology of "between the wars," which was applied to building in Europe and the United States during the 1950s, created a specific type of architecture which was the subject of harsh criticism during the 1960s.

This reaction took expression in the form of a search for a new, human scale. Man and his relationship to society became the cornerstone for all architectural theories in the 1960s. The relationship of man to his environment, environmental design as a part of social formation, the place of the individual within the larger context, and providing the individual with the possibility of maintaining his identity vis-à-vis himself and his surroundings became the basic principles of every significant concept in planning.

Social, anthropological and ecological research, which established links between planning and environmental behavior, became the intellectual basis in the search for new solutions in planning. The planner was confronted with the goals of providing the individual with privacy and the opportunity to create his own immediate surroundings, while at the same time providing involvement and strengthening the feeling of community and belonging. Some of the urban and architectural projects of the 1960s and 1970s are applications of the fusion of the social sciences with architecture.

Public participation in the area of physical planning also increased during this period. The Israeli public, which for years had been almost totally inactive in making or influencing planning decisions, became aroused as the first large-scale projects, bearing great impact on their surroundings, were initiated, The construction of the Dan Hotel in Haifa on the skyline of the Carmel range, the demolition of the old Herzlia High School, one of the first public buildings in Tel Aviv, and the erection of Binyenei ha-Ummah, the first large-scale structure built near the entrance to Jerusalem, were the first projects to gain attention. In fact, however, public involvement grew in keeping with the increasingly large scale of building projects. The public became aware of the influence of the physical environment on day-to-day living. In Israel, too, the 1960s were years of criticism after a lengthy period of building. An attempt was made to learn from the mistakes of the past and to find the causal relationship between planning and the various social problems, Israeli society of the 1960s, especially after the Six-Day War, demanded of the planner environmental and social quality, and visual significance in addition to quantitative and physical solutions to the problems at hand.

All these factors – economic and social, psychological and theoretical – were instrumental in creating the architecture of the past decade in Israel. It was designed to deal with a more massive building program, with new symbolic and psychological demands and with new architectural terminology and a new social and urban philosophy. Jerusalem's. historical and international status, its geographical position, the emotional response its evokes, and its resources were diverted to Jerusalem, and the city became the building center of the country. The primary goals in the planning of Jerusalem were to reunify the city, to increase its population substantially, and to convert it into the center of the country's spiritual and public life.

Jerusalem's historical and international status, its geographical position, the emotional response its evokes, and its uniqueness are factors of the first importance in the planning of the city and dictated the approach that architects would have to take in dealing with urban and planning problems.

Because of the need for haste and, at times, even a lack of understanding of the periodic element and the critical factors which determined the architecture of the past, the solutions provided in the new building were exclusively formalistic.

Elements borrowed from the past and the existing environment provided the answer to new and more complex problems with which it was difficult to deal. The use of stone, the arch, the dome, the wall, the roofed passage and the dense infrastructure were elements borrowed from the past, copied and offered as a solution in bridging the gap between the existing and the new, and the answer to the search for a national architecture and a link with the historical environment. The new neighborhoods that were established around the periphery of Jerusalem represent a good example of this – Ramat Eshkol (J. Perlstein); Neveh Ya'akov (Hertz); Gilo (A. Yaski); East Talpiot (D. Best); Ramot (Y. Dreksler, stage A; Y. and O. Ya'ar, stage B). These communities were built immediately after the Six-Day War and include all the problems that plagued the architects of Jerusalem. Each neighborhood was planned in its own unique way, but several elements are characteristic of them all: the use of stone and of visual elements taken from the surrounding environment, the separation of pedestrian and vehicular traffic, and the attempt to create a center especially designed for each particular neighborhood, which would provide the neighborhood with its own unique character and offer a meaningful focal point for its inhabitants.

The architects who designed these buildings contributed their own personal expression of form and spatial conception to the life-style suited to the area. Traditional roofed passageways, terraced housing, arches, domes, compactness, defined interior spaces were all utilized, while at the same time an attempt was made to employ the latest building techniques and modern housing standards.

Outstanding examples of such contributions are to be found in the buildings of Z. Hecker in Ramot, which sought to define new formal spaces, those of A. Sharon in Gilo, which provided a different rhythm to a neighborhood subunit by using open elements, the buildings of M. Lofenfeld and G. Gemerman in Gilo, which addressed themselves to the enclosed street and massive building on a hilltop overlooking Jerusalem, and, finally, those of R. Karmi in Gilo, which were meant to enhance interaction among the residents by establishing various grades of private and public space, and providing many public meeting places.

The confrontation between the old and the new also took place in the heart of Jerusalem – the Jewish Quarter of the Old City. The historical and emotional significance of the old Quarter is paramount; therefore, the desire to restore the existing structures and preserve the ancient character as much as possible affected the solutions open to the team of architects.

The neighborhood of Yemin Moshe (S. Mendel and G. Kertesz) was also restored with the primary aim of preserving, as much as possible, the character of that old quarter. The Hebrew University on Mount Scopus was the largest and most prestigious project in Jerusalem after the unification of the city. A team of architects consisting of R. Karmi, D. Reznik and S. Shaked was set up to design the campus. They strove to accommodate the massive bulk of the university to its location on Jerusalem's sensitive skyline without altering its natural beauty, while, at the same time, enabling the university to function properly and giving it the prominence it deserved.

The faculty buildings include: the Library (Rechter), the Humanities building (R. Karmi), the Social Science building (Eitan), the Student Center and Buber Institute (A. Yaski), the restoration of the Faculty of Law and the Administration building (Rabina), and the Education building (D. Reznik).

In the rest of the country the visual-historical impetus was smaller, the socio-economic transition determining the pace and nature of construction.

The projects increased in scale and were carried out by groups of architects who had to find a common language and to adjust not only to local features but also to each other.

Tel Aviv, which has maintained its place as the economic center of Israel, was transformed into a metropolis of high-rise buildings and suburban settlements.

In housing, a trend developed toward planning for defined social and ethnic groups: when the architect knew beforehand who the future inhabitants of the proposed neighborhood would be, he attempted to offer solutions in terms of the specific needs of the population by consulting its representatives in the various planning stages. In Ḥaẓor in the Galilee, Reznik sought to respond to the communities of the Gur Ḥasidim, as did S. Mendel and G. Kertesz in planning for the Bedouin of Santa-Katarina and Dahab, and Ya'ar in relocating housing in the slums of the Manshiya quarter in Tel Aviv.

The Ben-Gurion University of Beersheba was designed by a team which strove to coordinate the various elements in an overall framework. The planning and coordination was done by a team headed by A. Yaski. The library was designed by M. Nadler, the Humanities building by A. Niv and R. Reiffer, and the Science and Engineering building by A. Yaski.

The planning of Kikar Namir (Atarim) of Tel Aviv and the Marina on an urban scale (Rechter), the changes in Dizengoff Center, the high-rise office buildings, the IBM Center (A. Yaski), Asia House (M. Ben-Horin), and America House (Sharon), were all projects which helped change the face of the city.

Additional buildings worthy of mention are the Hilton Hotel, Jerusalem (Rechter); the Rothschild Cultural Center, Haifa (A. Mansefeld and D. Havkin); the Carmel Hospital, Haifa (Rechter); the Soldiers' Home, Afeka (A. Yaski); the Amal Technological High School, Tel Aviv (R. Karmi); the Safed Hospital (M. Zarḥi), the Municipal Library, Tel Aviv (M. Lofenfeld and G. Gemerman), the Rest and Recreational Home, Zikhron Ya'akov (Rechter), and the new Supreme Court building, Jerusalem (R. Carmi and A. Carmi Melamed).

[Elinor Barzacchi-Komissar]

Galleries and Museums

The country's major museums are comprised in the Israel Museum Association. Foremost among these is the Israel Museum, opened in Jerusalem in 1965. It incorporates the Bezalel Museum, founded by Schatz in 1906 in association with the Bezalel School, but from 1925 to 1965 an independent institution. Its collection includes paintings by Jewish and non-Jewish artists, Jewish ritual art, manuscripts, and a comprehensive art library. The Israel Museum also houses the archeological museum of the government's Department of Antiquities, the Shrine of the Book (which contains the *Dead Sea Scrolls and the *Bar Kokhba letters), and the Billy *Rose Sculpture Garden. In 1967 the Rockefeller Museum (formerly in the Jordanian-held section of Jerusalem) came under Israeli control and was placed under the administration of the Israel Museum. Other members of the Association are the Tel Aviv Museum (including the Helena Rubinstein Pavilion of Modern Art), the Haifa Museum of Modern Art, and the Mishkan le-Omanut (Home of Art) in kibbutz *En-Harod. Smaller archaeological museums include those at Jaffa, with antiquities of the Tel Aviv area; Haifa, which has several, including a sea museum devoted to the history of navigation in the Mediterranean and a prehistoric museum displaying finds from the Carmel region; Acre, where the museum is housed in a Crusader structure; and Beersheba, namely the Negev Museum, situated in a former mosque, as well as many kibbutz and rural museums and those on the sites of excavations (e.g., Megiddo, Hazor, and Tell al-Qasīla on the outskirts of Tel Aviv). Other collections are housed in the Haaretz Museum in Tel Aviv (which includes museums of glass and numismatics), the Museum of Japanese Art on Mount Carmel, the Museum of Ethnology in Haifa, the Glicenstein Museum of painting and sculpture in Safed, the Mané *Katz gallery in Haifa, and the Bat Yam Museum displaying Sholem *Asch's collection of Jewish ceremonial art. The artists' houses of Jerusalem, Tel Aviv, and Haifa provide permanent exhibitions by the artists of the three main cities, and there are many private galleries. In addition to permanent exhibitions, traveling exhibits (organized in particular by the Israel Museum) are widely circulated throughout the country, especially to schools.

Press

PRE-STATE. The modern era of the Hebrew press in Ereẓ Israel began in 1863. As early as 1841, Israel *Bak had established a Hebrew printing press in Jerusalem. Bak, however, belonged to the ḥasidic community, and the *Mitnaggedim* resented their dependence on his press for their printing activities. They therefore sent two members of their community – Joel Moses *Salomon and Michael Cohen – to study printing in Europe, and, on their return, they established a press. In order to keep the press occupied, they founded the newspaper *Ha-Levanon* in 1863. Shortly thereafter, Bak produced a rival paper, *Ḥavaẓelet*. The two Jerusalem newspapers became involved in a campaign of mutual recrimination and were closed down by the Ottoman authorities within a year. *Ha-Levanon was* revived as a newspaper in Paris in 1865, but Bak persisted in his efforts to reopen *Ḥavaẓẓelet* in Jerusalem and eventually succeeded, in 1870.

The Ereẓ Israel press from the very first aired vital problems of the Jewish community, such as agricultural policy, and thus developed political and topical journalism. There was a sharp battle in the Jerusalem press with regard to the charitable funds (**ḥalukkah*), touching on the basic administrative arrangements of the Jewish community. The conflicts between newspapers at times reached such intensity that they were banned.

A new era opened for the press when Eliezer *Ben-Yehuda arrived in Ereẓ Israel in 1881, where he worked on *Ḥavaẓelet*. In 1884 he left to form his own newspaper, *Ha-Ẓevi*, which revolutionized the Jerusalem press by introducing a secular tone and a modern journalistic style. The use of Hebrew as a spoken language was part of his Hebraist ideology: the revived national language would serve to unify all sections of the Jewish community. Ben-Yehuda conceived of the idea of a Hebrew dictionary, containing simple, precise language serving everyday needs. In any case, the existing language employed in the Jerusalem press failed to meet modern needs.

The first agricultural settlements were established in the early 1880s, creating a new Hebrew community different in essence from the "old" *yishuv* in Jerusalem and other towns. In his paper, Ben-Yehuda became the spokesman of this new *yishuv*, while *Ḥavaẓelet* retreated from its Haskalah tendencies and became the mouthpiece of the "old" *yishuv*. Ben-Yehuda's advocacy of the *Uganda Scheme served to alienate many of his supporters. At the turn of the century, his son, Ithamar *Ben-Avi, joined him on the staff of the paper, introducing further modernization, under the influence of the French press, with which he was closely acquainted. Weekly publication proving insufficient; they began publishing *Ha-Ẓevi* as the first daily newspaper of Ereẓ Israel.

The major changes in the country's life brought about by the Second Aliyah (1905–14) were not reflected in Ben-Yehuda's papers, and the newcomers, who advocated immigration to Ereẓ Israel and the development of Jewish manual labor, required a labor press. With meager financial resources they established their own papers, *Ha-Po'el ha-Ẓa'ir* (1908) and then *Ha-Aḥdut*, sponsored by the Poalei Zion Party (1910).

World War I put an end to all these papers, and a new period opened up for the Hebrew press after the war, under the influence of the new wave of immigration (the Third Aliyah), mainly from Eastern Europe.

In 1919, Hebrew writers and journalists, educated in the liberal journalistic tradition in Russia, established the daily **Haaretz* (initially *Ḥadashot ha-Areẓ*), as a continuation of a Hebrew paper initiated by the British military administration. *Haaretz* became a Zionist progressive paper "in the Odessa style," edited by the best of the Hebrew writers, with a minority of local contributors, among them Ben-Yehuda and his son. The local journalists, however, soon found that they had little in common with the "Russian" trend, and established their own paper, *Do'ar ha-Yom* (1919), edited by Ithamar Ben-Avi. In 1923 *Haaretz* moved to Tel Aviv, under the editorship of M. *Gluecksohn. With the transfer of *Haaretz* to Tel Aviv, this city gradually became the center of journalism. Later, in 1937, *Haaretz* was sold to Salman *Schocken, whose son Gershom then became editor.

In 1925 the labor movement decided to publish its own paper, *Davar*. The first editors were Berl *Katznelson, Zalman *Shazar, and Moshe *Beilinson. Published by the Histadrut, it reached many of its members and became the most widely circulated morning paper. The growth in the number of parties led to a parallel growth in the number of papers, as each party was interested in propagating its views through its own organ. Thus the Revisionist party took over *Do'ar ha-Yom* (1928–30); then it published its own newspapers, *Ha-Yarden* (1934–36), and *Ha-Mashkif* (1938–48).

The struggle against the British Mandatory authorities was characterized by frequent seizures or temporary closure of papers, particularly from the 1930s onward. Papers were often obliged to change their names and utilize unexploited licenses. This situation was at its worst in the 1940s, during the closing years of the British Mandate, when an illegal press made its appearance – consisting mainly of wall posters – which represented the underground movements.

A clear distinction began to emerge between the dailies and the weeklies. The latter no longer gave straight news, placing their emphasis on signed articles. A further consequence now was the clearer distinction between the writer and the journalist; hitherto the dividing line had been blurred, but now there emerged the journalist-reporter type, familiar in Western journalism.

Until 1929 all the daily papers apart from *Do'ar ha-Yom* were, of necessity, published at noon, for technical reasons: Reuter bulletins, for example, until then arrived by train from Egypt. The riots of 1929, the Nazi rise to power in 1933, as well as the murder of Arlosoroff in the same year, increased circulation and resulted in the establishment of afternoon papers, which appear at noon. *Haaretz, Ha-Boker,* and *Davar* began to publish afternoon papers, but all these were discontinued upon the appearance of a new type of afternoon paper. The first such paper, founded by Azriel *Carlebach, **Yedioth Aharonoth*, appeared in 1939. After a disagreement over personality and management differences with the publisher, Yehudah *Mozes, Carlebach left the paper in 1947 and founded **Maariv*.

The wave of immigration from Germany, which began in 1933, confronted the Hebrew press with the problem of a readership insufficiently acquainted with the Hebrew language. The result was a new type of paper written in easy Hebrew with vowels; the more difficult words were translated (first into German and later into other languages). Initially, these formed voweled supplements of the established press, but in 1940 the first independent voweled paper, *Hegeh*, was introduced. Many immigrant journalists from Germany took their first steps in Hebrew journalism in *Hegeh*. It ceased publication in 1946, but was renewed in 1951 as *Omer*, published, as its predecessor was, by *Davar*.

[Getzel Kressel and Geoffrey Wigoder]

IN THE STATE OF ISRAEL. The press in the State of Israel was characterized by a number of trends: first, the role of the party political press in political recruitment and its subsequent decline; second, the growth of the independent press, and competition among the popular papers; third, challenges faced by the independent press from radio, television, and the Internet; fourth, the decline of the foreign language press; fifth, greater independence from official pressures.

The first 20 years of the state were characterized by the continuation of a vibrant and lively party political press which owed its origins to the Jewish struggle for independence during the British mandate. The party press declined in the 1960s and 1970s, both as Israel began to enter a period of normalization after the economic and defense struggles which characterized the early years of statehood, and because the independent press offered readers a more diverse and comprehensive coverage. Key party newspapers included *Omer* (Histadrut, 1951–79) and *Lamerḥav* (Aḥdut ha-Avodah, 1954–71), which amalgamated with *Davar* but closed in 1994; *Ḥerut* (Ḥerut, 1948–65) and *Ha-Boker* (published by the General Zionists, 1935–65), which were replaced by *Ha-Yom* (1966–69) after Ḥerut allied itself with the Liberal Party to form *Gaḥal; *Ha-Dor* (Mapai, 1948–55); and *Al ha-Mishmar* (United Workers Party (Mapam), 1943–2005). The daily party press was replaced in some cases by periodical party literature.

The only daily party political press remaining comprised the **ḥaredi* religious press: *Ha-Modi'a*, the organ of Agudat Israel, which represented the ḥasidic wing of Ashkenazi *ḥaredim*, and *Yetad Ne'eman*, the organ of Degel ha-Torah, which represented the Lithuanian wing of Ashkenazi *ḥaredim*. These organs fulfilled extra-party functions providing readers – under the slogan of the "right not to know" – with a censored version of public information which excluded content offensive to *ḥaredi* sensibilities. The rigorous social-religious controls which characterized the Ashkenazi *ḥaredi* establishment failed to stop the growth in the 1990s of a commercial *ḥaredi* weekly press including *Erev Shabbat*, *Yom ha-Shishi*, *Mishpaḥah*, and *Ba-Kehillah*, which applied modern techniques of newsgathering and graphics to newspaper production. *She'arim* (1951–81), organ of the Poalei Agudat Israel closed. *Ha-Ẓofeh* was sold to commercial interests in 2005 but continued to reflect thinking in the National Religious Party. A short-lived attempt by Shas, the *ḥaredi* Sephardi party, to launch a daily, gave birth to *Yom Yom* as a weekly.

The independent press comprised *Yedioth Aharonoth*, *Maariv*, and *Haaretz*. Until the mid-1970s the mid-market, and politically right-of-center, *Maariv* was the most widely circulated daily in Israel. Its position was taken over by *Yedioth Aharonoth*, owned by the Mozes family, which under the banner of "the country's paper" tried to cater to all tastes from right to left, and which, while popular in layout with provocative headlines and human interest stories, also engaged in more serious reporting. *Maariv*, a cooperative controlled by its journalists, was hampered by a cumbersome decision-making process. After *Maariv* was briefly owned by the British media magnate Robert *Maxwell (1988–91), the paper was bought by Ya'akov *Nimrodi, whose son Ofer as the publisher downmarketed the paper in an unsuccessful attempt to compete with *Yedioth Aharonoth*. The rivalry between *Yedioth Aharonoth* and *Maariv* grew so intense that charges of wiretapping in the 1990s by one paper against the other resulted in Nimrodi's being placed on trial and imprisoned.

Haaretz's comprehensive coverage of political, economic, and social affairs and the arts inside Israel and foreign news turned it into the country's quality newspaper read by decision-makers and leaders in the political, economic, and artistic sectors. With the demise of the party political press, *Haaretz* enjoyed a singular role as Israel's elite newspaper. An attempt by *Haaretz*'s publishers to establish a popular newspaper, *Ḥadashot*, in 1984, in order to compete with *Yedioth Aharonoth* and *Maariv*, proved short-lived, and it ceased publication in 1993. The creation of a quality financial daily, **Globes* in 1983, was accompanied by an expansion of economic coverage by the other three newspapers. With the exception of *Globes*, which published in the evenings following the close of the stock market, *Yedioth Aharonoth* and *Maariv* had also become morning newspapers like *Haaretz*.

Forty-two percent of Israelis in 2005 surveyed by TGI Teleseker read *Yedioth Aharonoth* every day, 23% *Maariv*, and 7% *Haaretz*. Readership of the weekend Friday issues of *Yedioth Aharonoth* and *Maariv* was 25% higher than that of their dailies. In the face of the parallel growth in radio and television, newspapers carved themselves a new role of providing background and analysis of breaking news, for which the broadcast media did not have time. The Internet caused a decline of newspaper readership. Israelis used the Internet an average of 6.5 hours a week in 2005 according to TGI; 39% reported that the Internet was their first source of information. The three newspapers, and others, answered the Internet challenge by initiating their own on-line news operations. While *Haaretz*'s was based on the newspaper's existing newsgathering operation, *Yedioth Aharonoth*'s Y-Net and *Maariv*'s Walla had separate newsgathering operations.

A large number of foreign-language newspapers existed in the first decades of the state, fulfilling important informational and acculturating roles for the new immigrants in their new homeland. There were newspapers in English, German, Russian, Polish, Romanian, Yiddish, Spanish, French, Hungarian, and Bulgarian. Key newspapers included *Jedioth Hadashoth* (1936) and *Jedioth ha-Yom* (1936) in German; the **Jerusalem Post* (1932) in English; *L'Echo d'Israel* (1948), *L'Information d'Israel* (1957), and *Le Journal d'Israel* (1957) in French; *Uj Kelet* (1948) in Hungarian; *Israelskie Nowiny I Kurier* (1958) in Polish; *Letste Nayes* (1959) in Yiddish; *Izraelski Far* (1959) in Bulgarian; and *Viata Nostra* (1959) in Romanian. With the exception of a few, most had ceased publication or had become weekly or monthly publications by the end of the 1970s, as most readers turned to the Hebrew media, given the Hebrew media's greater resources and consequent wider coverage. The *aliyah* of hundreds of thousands of Russian Jews in the 1980s and 1990s created a Russian press, but these were more commercial in orientation than the earlier newspapers. Key Russian dailies included *Vesty* (1992; owned by *Yedioth Ahoronoth*), *Vremny* (1991), *Novosty Nedely* (1991), and *Nasha Strana* (1971).

Over the half century since independence, the Israeli Hebrew press became more critical of Israeli officialdom. In the early years, government leaders saw the Hebrew media as channels to generate support for governmental policy, such as through the Editors Committee system, a framework in which Israeli editors were briefed by senior ministers and officials on defense-related matters. But the military intelligence surprise preceding the 1973 war, the 1984 Shin Bet affair involving the No. 300 Tel Aviv–Ashkelon bus hijacking, and a series of Mossad operational failures produced a more critical approach by journalists toward the defense establishment. As Israel's regional and international status improved, and as the standard of living rose, Israelis became less fixed upon the singular goal of national development. Both exposure to the standards of other countries and societies, in particular the United States, and a greater role in public affairs by the Israeli Supreme Court, strengthened demands for official accountability. Yet, both the expansion of governmental public relations in Israel's official bureaucracy since the 1970s, characterized by the public relations work of spokesmen in government ministries and attached to ministers, and a plethora of specialist reporters covering "beats," defined in many cases according to government ministry, created a subtle framework for the transfer of official information into the public sphere.

Local newspapers expanded in the 1980s as *Yedioth Aharonoth, Haaretz,* and *Maariv* established newspapers in different cities and large towns in an attempt to tap local advertisers. *Yedioth Aharonoth* had a chain of 170 local newspapers. News coverage of local developments in the local press have improved public awareness of municipal matters and incrementally moved the public's focus and identity toward the peripheral, local areas, away from the geographical centers of Israeli power. By contrast to the growth in local media, the periodical press (some of which is also owned by *Yedioth Aharonoth, Maariv,* and *Haaretz*) comprising special interest publications – on travel, hobbies, cars, family, television, and food – showed, with the exception of women's magazines and youth magazines, much slower growth, despite rising consumer standards. News magazines, including *Ha-Olam ha-Zeh*, the satirical, sensationalist weekly, and the more sober *Koteret Rashit*, proved to be passing media phenomena as news consumers found their needs fulfilled by the daily press. The far-flung media interests of *Yedioth Aharonoth, Haaretz,* and *Maariv,* which extended also to television, raised questions regarding a danger to press freedom from media concentration.

While there have been Israeli Arab dailies sponsored by political parties, their growth was limited due both to their ideological orthodoxy and to government controls over content. A government and Histradut newspaper *Al-Yawm* (1948–68) was replaced by *Al-Anba*, which had a broader range of non-governmental views. Many Israeli Arabs are exposed to the Israeli Hebrew media. There were a number of Arab commercial magazine initiatives in the 1980s, often tied to a specific local community. Two dailies in East Jerusalem, *Al-Quds* and the defunct *Al-Fajr,* had a wide following among the Palestinian population. A Palestinian press flourished also in other areas, including Gaza and Ramallah, after the creation of the Palestinian Authority in 1993.

The opening of departments of journalism in universities and academic colleges since the 1980s contributed to raising the professional standards of journalists. More than half the country's journalists are women. A minuscule number of Israeli Arab journalists work in the Hebrew press.

Israel is also a major center for foreign news organizations. Three hundred and fifty foreign news organizations have either correspondents posted from abroad or are represented by local journalists, making it the tenth largest foreign press corps in the world, and the largest in the Middle East. Most foreign media come from Western Europe and North America. The media revolution inside the Arab world resulted in nearly 50 Arab news organizations having correspondents in Israel since the 1990s. The considerable foreign coverage that Israel receives, and the sympathy in western liberal opinion for the Palestinians as the underdog in the Arab-Israeli conflict, increased the importance for the Foreign Ministry and the Army Spokesman's Division to brief the foreign media about events and give them access to cover them.

[Yoel Cohen (2nd ed.)]

BIBLIOGRAPHY: PRESS IN PALESTINE: G. Kressel, *Toledot ha-Ittonut ha-Ivrit be-Ereẓ Yisrael* (1964); G. Yardeni, *Ha-Ittonut ha-Ivrit be Ereẓ Yisrael bi-Shenot 1863–1904* (1969); *Sefer ha-Shanah shel ha-Ittona'im, 1941–1968* (1969). **ADD. BIBLIOGRAPHY:** PRESS IN ISRAEL: A. Barness, *The Israel Press* (1961); D. Caspi and Y. Limor, *Ha-Metavvekhim* (1986); idem, *The In/Outsiders* (1999); D.Caspi, *Media Decentralization: The Case of Israel's Local Newspapers* (1986); Y. Cohen, *Focus on Israel: Twenty-Five Years of Foreign Media Reporting* (1994); D. Goren, *Secrecy and the Right to Know* (1979); U. Lebel, *Bitaḥon ve-Tikshoret: Dinamikah shel Yaḥasim* (2005); M. Negbi, *Ḥofesh Ittonut be-Yisrael: Arakhim bi-Re'i ha-Mishpat* (1995); TGI Teleseker survey (2005).

Broadcasting

Local radio began to operate under the British Mandate (1922–48), which established the "Voice of Jerusalem." This official radio station came on the air for the first time on March 30, 1936, and served the Jewish and Arab populations as well as British administration officials. With the establishment of the State of Israel, the name of the radio station was changed to *Kol Israel* (Voice of Israel) and an army radio station, *Gallei Ẓahal* (IDF Radio), was also opened. For many years, these two stations constituted the country's entire broadcasting system – monolithic and government-controlled.

In 1965, the status of state radio underwent a major change. *Kol Yisrael*, by then broadcasting on two wavelengths, became an autonomous body, the Israel Broadcasting Authority. Three years later, when Israel Television was established, it also became part of the Authority.

In 1996 the government declared its intention to privatize public broadcasting as part of a general policy of privatization. Supporters of public radio argued that the stations should be kept free of commercial constraints, in order to guarantee freedom of speech in a democratic society. Subsequently, in the mid-1990s, 15 regional radio stations were added to the *Kol Israel* and *Gallei Ẓahal* national stations.

KOL ISRAEL. The network operates several stations, geared to various audiences. Reshet Alef (first station) broadcasts general, cultural, and children's programs. Reshet Bet (second station) focuses on news and current events. Reshet Gimmel (third station) offers light Israeli music, especially Hebrew songs. Kol ha-Musikah plays classical music, Kol ha-Derekh combines traffic reports and music, and Reka is aimed at new immigrants, broadcasting mainly in Russian and Amharic. Kol Zion la-Golah is beamed to Jewish communities abroad and *Kol Israel* in Arabic is broadcast for Israeli Arabs and listeners in Arab countries.

GALLEI ẒAHAL. *Gallei Ẓahal*, the army radio network set up in 1950, broadcasts on two stations and enjoys great popularity. The first station provides news and talk shows and the second (*Gal-Galaẓ*) offers music and traffic reports. Although funded by the army, it is popular among civilians.

REGIONAL RADIO. The licensed regional radio stations set up in the mid-1990s operate privately. Two of them are aimed at specific audiences: *Radio 2000* for the Arabs of northern Israel and *Kol Ḥai* in central Israel for Jewish religious listeners. Broadcasting Authority licenses are limited to a 4–6-year period. Revenue is from commercials.

UNLICENSED (PIRATE) STATIONS. An unusual phenomenon in Israel is the proliferation of radio stations operating without licenses. The first such station, the Voice of Peace, started broadcasting in 1973 on the model of similar stations in Europe, transmitting mainly from a ship anchored outside Israel's territorial waters. Today, many more such stations operate around the country. Although they are illegal, the authorities tend to be lenient. Some are amateur, others provide ethnic music or religious programs, and some are commercial, funded by advertisements.

BIBLIOGRAPHY: L. Yeḥiel, "The Electronic Media: Television and Radio," at http://www.mfa.gov.il/mfa/mfaarchive.

Television

Local television started fairly late in Israel – in 1968 – mainly out of economic and social considerations. Israel's first prime minister, David *Ben-Gurion, opposed its introduction despite the recommendations of a committee that he himself had set up in 1951. He was put off by the entertainment factor and was afraid that television would promote materialistic and individualistic pursuits among the country's youth. Levi *Eshkol, the minister of finance, thought that television should be kept out of Israel indefinitely because it would create pressures for higher living standards.

Orthodox Jewish circles also opposed television, fearing it would show women in immodest dress and broadcast unsuitable programs. Thus tens of thousands of ultra-Orthodox households do not have television sets. Religious circles also fought against television broadcasts on the Sabbath. In the early days of Israeli television, the Israel Broadcasting Authority (IBA) tended to accede to the demand for a Sabbath blackout. However, with the backing of the Supreme Court, and against the will of Prime Minister Golda *Meir, the IBA decided not to stop broadcasts on Friday evenings.

For many years Israeli viewers had only one channel, broadcasting a few hours for children (Educational TV) in the afternoon and a few hours for adults in evening in black and white. The year 1994 marked a revolution in Israeli television viewing. After more than a quarter of a century of living with its single channel, Israelis were now offered a choice of 40 channels in more than a dozen languages. To the state-owned Channel One were added, gradually, three networks: the commercial Channel Two, the commercial Channel Ten (both financed mainly by commercials) and cable TV, which captured a considerable portion of the national market.

CHANNEL TWO. Starting full operations in November 1993, the network awarded three companies franchises: Tel-Ad, Reshet, and Keshet, each getting two days a week of air time with the seventh day rotated among them. Channel Two has its own news division, shared by the licensees. Broadcasting 22–24 hours a day, it produces 40% of its programs locally, getting high ratings, and thus exerting a great influence on the Israeli entertainment scene.

CHANNEL TEN. On the air since January 2002 after the merger of the winners of the concession (Israel 10 and Eden Broadcasting), the network has been plagued by financial problems, with ratings and revenues not as high as expected. Programming is similar to that of Channel Two.

CABLE TV. The year 1994 also saw the completion of the country's cable TV infrastructure. By mid-1994, some 720,000 Israeli households were able to receive cable television and, in 2004, the average penetration rate was 60 percent. The two major cable companies were Hot and Yes, which started broadcasting in 2002.

The law governing cable TV divided the country into geographical areas, with one licensee per area and revenues provided by user fees. The cable networks offer dozens of channels, some Israeli (although broadcasting many foreign shows) and some foreign, picked up by satellite (including MTV, SKY NEWS, CNN, BBC, and ESPN, as well as channels from Arabic and European countries).

Among the local channels, many are aimed at specific population groups, including Israel Plus (the Russian channel), Tekhelet (national-religious), the Mediterranean channel (aimed at Sephardim), the science channel, and a planned Arabic channel.

EDUCATIONAL TELEVISION. In 1965, Israel became the first country in the world to have educational TV before regular TV. ETV provides not only educational programming but also enrichment programs and broadcasts on current events. It broadcasts on Channels One and Two, as well as on cable TV. Funding is provided by the Ministry of Education and Culture.

VIEWING CULTURE. A study of leisure culture in Israel conducted in the early 1990s showed that Israelis spend about half of their free time in front of the TV. This is somewhat more than the average in Western countries. The preference of the Israel public, confirmed in every survey, is for news programs and news-based talk shows, with the three major networks always ready to interrupt regular broadcasting with breaking stories. Another penchant is the taste for South American melodramas.

Another important influence of television is its rapidly growing share of the advertising market, reshaping the industry.

BIBLIOGRAPHY: Y. Elitzur, "Israeli Television and the National Agenda," at http://www.mfa.gov.il/mfa/mfaarchive; L. Yeḥiel, "The Electronic Media: Television and Radio," at http://www.mfa.gov.il/mfa/mfaarchive; http://www.channel2.co.il/broadcast_channel10.asp.

Film

Though small in scope (an average of 10–15 films a year since 1967 and even fewer before that), the Israeli film industry offers a wide range of styles and genres and has always had substantial audiences in Israel and abroad. In fact, in the 1960s the number of tickets bought in Israel annually was similar to the number in countries over twice its size. Although not artistically acclaimed until recent years, the Israeli film has faithfully mirrored the country's culture and politics.

Israeli cinema began even before the State of Israel was established. Though very few feature films were made before the 1950s, many informational shorts, documentaries, newsreels, and promotional films were produced and funded by various Zionist organizations (Jewish Agency, Jewish National Fund, etc.). These films were made primarily for distribution abroad. One example is *Eretz Yisrael Mitoreret* ("Eretz Israel Awakens"; Ben-Dov, 1923), which tells the story of a wealthy American Jewish cotton broker who decides to return to the land of his fathers after traveling in the country for a month, meeting famous figures from the *yishuv* and visiting various towns and kibbutzim.

The key figures in this early cinema were Baruch Agadati and Nathan Axelrod, both filming from a Zionist perspective emphasizing the building of the land. Both established film companies: Moledet, Carmel, and Geva, which made daily newsreels. Later (in 1958), the Carmel Studio was incorporated into the Herzliyyah Studio.

Key films in the early Zionist cinema are *Oded ha-Noded* ("Oded The Wanderer"; Chaim Halachmi, 1932), *Sabra* (Alexander Ford, 1933), *Land Of Promise* (Yehuda Lehman, 1935), *On The Ruins* (Nathan Axelrod, 1936), *Bet Avi* ("My Father's House"; Herbert Kline, 1947) – all emphasizing the land and nature, all dealing to a certain extent with Zionist pioneers, Jewish labor, and the liberal and humanistic sides of Zionism. One can see the influence of Soviet socialist cinema in the visual style and editing techniques.

During the 1950s the Heroic-Nationalist genre was constructed, following the patterns of the early Zionist cinema. Filming became more organized with the establishment of Israel, and now had both a propaganda aim vis-à-vis foreign audiences and a pedagogic aim for new immigrants, who found the medium easy to understand.

Key films are *Giva 24 Eina Onah* ("Hill 24 Doesn't Answer"; Thorwald Dikenson, 1955), *Ammud ha-Esh* ("Pillar of Fire"; Larry Frisch, 1959), *Hem Hayyu Asarah* ("They Were Ten"; Baruch Dienar, 1959), *Hu Halakh be-Saddot*; ("He Walked in the Fields"; Yosef Milou, 1967), and *Ha-Matarah Tiran* ("Target Tiran"; Rafi Nosbaum, 1968). In these films national issues are at the center of the plot, constituting an axis around which the exploits of the heroes revolve. The tools of the cinematic medium (photography, editing, music, etc.) are used to glorify the idea of building and struggling for the land. In very dynamic scenes we see people plowing, reaping, and dancing the pioneer *hora*, sometimes with the use of montage editing, which make them even more vivid.

But as the country changed, so did its films, with the materialism and individualism of the post Six-Day War period starting to make itself felt. First, popular romantic themes began to creep into the Heroic-Nationalist genre, as in *Kol Mamzer Melekh* ("Every Bastard a King"; Uri Zohar, 1967), and later the national film itself began to give way to two new genres: the Class Cinema and the Personal Cinema, which were dominant in the 1960s and 1970s.

The popular films of the late 1960s and 1970s dealt with ethnic problems between Sephardim and Ashkenazim. These productions, later called "burekas (knish) films," were either melodramas or comedies, all with a happy ending and often involving a "mixed" marriage. Even though received very poorly critically, these films were enthusiastically received by the public. Films like *Sallah Shabbati* (*Kishon, 1964) and *Kazablan* (Frisch, 1964) were huge successes, each with 1.2 million viewers. Films like *Charlie ve-Ḥetzi* ("Charlie and a Half"; Davidson, 1974) and *Ḥaggigah be-Snuker* ("Snookerfest"; Davidson, 1975) are considered cult films, shaping the culture and imbued with nostalgic echoes.

As opposed to the popular Class Cinema, influenced by popular radio and theater shows, Personal Cinema (also called the New Sensitivity) drew its inspiration from European Modernism and the French New Wave. This cinema was acclaimed by the critics but had very limited audiences. Films such as *Ḥor ba-Levenah* ("Hole in the Moon"; Zohar, 1964) and *Mikreh Ishah* ("The Case of a Woman"; Katmor, 1969) were highly sophisticated in plot and filmic expression but were box-office flops. An exception was *Sheloshah Yamim ve-Yeled* ("Three Days and a Child"; Zohar, 1967), Based on a short story by A.B. *Yehoshua, it starred Oded Kotler, who won the Cannes Film Festival award for best actor, and had a large audience.

In the late 1970s, three films foreshadowed the coming political cinema of the 1980s. *Ḥirbet Ḥizah* (Ram Levy, 1978), dealing with the roots of the Israeli-Palestinian conflict, was the first of the "conflict films." *Masa Alunkot* ("Paratroopers"; Judd Ne'eman, 1977), the first anti-heroic war film, set the stage for a dozen more. *Rove Ḥulliyot* ("Wooden Gun"; Ilan Mosensohn, 1978) dealt, for the first time in Israeli cinema, with the shadow cast by the Holocaust on Israeli society and presaged a number of films on the subject.

The Israeli cinema of the 1980s was mostly political, offering a radical critique of Zionism. The loss of political power to the nationalist right-wing parties in 1977 prompted a new moral and political stance among the left-wing cultural elite.

The Israeli cinema reacted to the results of the 1977 elections with a new school of film. The films of the 1980s attacked the Zionist master-narrative that had dominated the cinema of the 1930–50 period. This trend had begun in 1978 with *Ḥirbet Ḥizah*, Ram Levy's television drama (based on a story by S. *Yizhar), and continued to develop in such films as *Ḥamsin* (Daniel Wachsman, 1982), *Me-Aḥorei ha-Soregim* ("Beyond the Walls"; Uri Barabash, 1984), *Ḥiyyukh ha-Gedi* ("Smile of the Lamb"; Shimon Dotan, 1986), *Avanti Popolo* (Rafi Bukai, 1986), and *Saddot Yerukim* ("Greenfields"; Yitzhak Yeshurun, 1989). Not only did these films represent the Arab-Israeli conflict as an uncompromising struggle between two national movements but in some cases judged the entire Zionist enterprise to be misguided.

Films in the 1990s took a different turn, less political, more escapist. Many of these can be termed "Sheinkin films," for the bohemianish street in Tel Aviv, and deal with the problems of young people in a big city searching for meaning. Major examples are *Shuru* (Gavison, 1991) and *Shirat ha-Sirenah* ("Siren's Song"; Fox, 1994), both focusing on the life of career people in their 30s looking to find their way in society. Another direction was seen in films that tried to come to terms with the past and the older generation. *Sheḥor* (Hasfari, 1994), *The New Land* (Ben Dor, 1994), and *Aya – Autobiographiyah Dimyonit* ("Aya – An Imaginary Autobiography": Bat-Adam, 1994) all focus on childhood experiences, the generation gap, and the identity crisis among people of different origins in a new country. Political themes can be traced in films like *Ha-Ḥayyim al pi Agfa* ("Life According to Agfa"; Dayan, 1992), which portrays a self-destructive society.

The most controversial film of this last period was *Jenin, Jenin* (Bakri, 2002), a 54-minute documentary purporting to present Israeli military operations in the West Bank town of Jenin during Operation Defensive Shield. Condemned as a distorted version of events, it was banned by the Israel Film Board, a decision subsequently overturned by the Supreme Court, reasoning that "lies do not justify a ban."

After 2000 one can discern a general period of growth in the Israeli film industry. Due in part to the country's new Cinema Law passed in 2000 and a budget increase for the Israeli Film Fund (from $2.5 million in 2000 to $7 million in 2003), about 12–14 new feature films are getting roughly two-thirds of their budgets funded. Foreign investments are on the rise and local box-office sales jumped from 140,000 in 2000 to 450,000 in 2002.

Although these years were not the most auspicious for Israel economically and politically, the industry has turned out some widely successful films since 2000, including *Yossi & Jagger* (Eytan Fox, 2002), *Kenafayim Shevurot* ("Broken Wings"; Nir Bergman, 2002), *Massa'ot James le-Eretz ha-Kodesh* ("James' Journey to Jerusalem"; Ra'naan Alexandrowicz, 2003), *Ha-Assonot shel Nina* ("Nina's Tragedies": Savi Gavison, 2003), and *Nissu'im Me'uḥarim* ("Late Marriage," 2001) by the Israeli-Georgian filmmaker Dover Kosashvil. Made before the most recent Intifada, these latest Israeli films focus on personal and not national politics, engaging themselves with politics in a metaphorical way – which may be the reason for the films' successes both at home and abroad.

BIBLIOGRAPHY: N. Graetz, *Sippur me-ha-Seratim* (1993); D. Fainaru, "The State of the Arts: Israeli Cinema," at: http://www. Mfa. gov.il/mfa/meaarchive/1990–1999; A. Kaufman, "'Yossi,' 'James,' and 'Broken Wings': Next Generation Israeli Cinema Strikes a Chord Without Politics," at: http://www.indiewire.com/biz/photos/biz_030924israel.jpg; J. Ne'eman, Israeli Cinema of the 1980s & 1990s: A Radical Critique of Zionism, at: http://www.sfjff.org; E. Shohat, *Israeli Cinema* (1989). **WEBSITES:** http://www.sfjff.org/guide/img-guid/IsraeliFilm; Internet Movie Data Base (imdb.com)

[Anat Biger (2nd ed.)]

For sports in Israel, see *Sports.

ARAB POPULATION

GENERAL SURVEY

Under the British Mandate, 1917–48

In 1917, at the time of the British conquest of Palestine during World War I, the country's Arabic-speaking population numbered less than 600,000 persons; in 1947 it was estimated at 1,200,000. This enormous increase, by more than double in 30 years, was accompanied by steady progress in health, education, and standard of living. These achievements were partly due to the more efficient administration introduced by the Mandatory government, which improved security, consolidated land tenure and lessened the power of local autocrats, paid more attention to the needs of the villagers, expanded health and educational services, fostered agriculture, and abolished conscription. In the main, however, Arab progress – far superior to that registered in the neighboring countries, where Britain and France had introduced similar administrations – was connected with the growth of the Jewish community and its efforts to develop the country. This is shown by the comparative vital statistics, percentage of school attendance, and number of doctors, nurses, teachers, and so forth. Tax revenue received from the Jews by the Mandatory government enabled it to improve its health and education services for the Arabs. The Jews introduced better transportation and more modern banking and production methods; they provided an expanding market for Arab agricultural produce, as well as a convenient labor outlet. Their public services, which were partially at the disposal of the Arabs, stimulated them and the government to create similar facilities for the Arab population. Thousands of Arab immigrants, mostly illegal, entered the country throughout the period.

IN THE COUNTRYSIDE. About 67% of Palestinian Arabs worked on the land, the majority living in about 900 villages. Their agricultural methods were primitive: much of the plowing was done with the wooden "nail," unchanged since ancient times: there was little systematic fertilization (natural manure was used for fuel, and chemical fertilizer was rare); no attempt was made to tap water for irrigation; modern methods of marketing, cooperative purchasing, and credit did not take root, while loan sharks held sway over thousands of families. Large stretches of land – according to various estimates 25–30% – were under collective village ownership (*mushʿa*), and since they were periodically redistributed the farmers were not interested in improvements, land amelioration, etc. The ownership of land by the *waqf* (religious trusts) was also regarded as a hindrance to its rational utilization. Nevertheless, the Arab fellahin or peasants were progressing from a natural economy, working only for its own needs without technological and social development, to a more modern economy. Not only landowners, but thousands of fellahin undertook intensive fruit and vegetable growing, using fairly modern methods, as well as poultry and livestock raising. Not only were substantial sums of money pumped into the Arab village – at least part of which was invested in the improvement of economic, housing, and other conditions – but thousands of youths were attracted to the cities and the Jewish settlements, some of them returning to their villages equipped with new ideas and ways.

Although these developments led to the growing disintegration of the rural social structure, the old patriarchal framework still wielded great power. The patriarchal family or group of interrelated families (*ḥamūla*) was still the dominant social unit. It was not the individual who determined his relationship to society, to his neighbors and the government, to organizations and political parties, but the family or *ḥamūla*, the head of which still held absolute sway not only in business, marriage, and family affairs, but even over the lives of its members. Nomadic customs, such as blood feuds and collective family responsibility, survived. The killing of girls or married women by their brothers, husbands, or other relatives for deviation from accepted village morality was a common occurrence.

For the most part, the village *ḥamūla* was bound by a kind of alliance – sometimes through consanguinity or common origin – with others in neighboring villages. Thus, networks of clans arose, connected, in semi-feudal fashion, with urban families or with regional or urban notables. In exchange for protecting the interests of the villagers against rival families, the authorities, the police, and the courts and "arranging" their economic, financial, employment, and public affairs, the village notables and the leading urban families enjoyed the villagers' political loyalty. This was the basis of political life among the Palestinian Arabs. Although the political attitudes and party affiliations of the urban leaders frequently changed, their relationship with the village families remained almost fixed. Hence the "parties" formed in the cities, with the recurrent formation and disintegration of factions, were the concern of limited groups of urban intellectuals and politicians, and their influence on the village masses was negligible.

IN THE CITIES. Of the 30–35% of Palestinian Arabs who lived in the cities, 30–35% were engaged in manual labor, industry, and construction; 15–17% in haulage and transportation: 20–23% in business; 5–8% in the free professions; 5–7% in public services; 6–9% in domestic services and the like; and the rest in miscellaneous occupations. The traditional manufactures of the urban Arabs, including home industry (such as the production of soap, oils, flour, and textiles), were increasingly displaced by new local industries and cheap foreign products. However, side by side with the traditional manufactures, and in great measure deriving from them, a modern Arab industry was developing, especially in textiles and cigarette manufacture. At the end of the period, the number of urban Arabs in steady employment in industry, crafts, public works, construction, and international and Jewish projects was estimated at 25,000–30,000, in addition to a few thousand in home industries. Many were semi-rural transients who later returned to their villages.

A similar development took place in commerce, where, side by side with the traditional small concern, modern Arab wholesale commerce evolved, especially in food marketing. Arabs also played an important role in the import and export trade, as well as in banking. In addition to the international and British banks – which employed many Arab managers and senior officials – and the Jewish banks, there were two Arab ones: the Arab Bank (established 1930) and the Arab People's Bank (established 1940). Although the characteristic features of the urban economy in Arab countries – preference for commerce over industry and the investment of surplus capital in real estate – existed in Palestine, they gradually became less clear and prominent there, doubtless because of the Jewish example. The middle class, including an intellectual stratum, was also more developed among the Palestinians than in other Arab societies. There were three or four dailies (one founded in 1911) during the period, as well as several weeklies and other periodicals, and textbooks and essays were published in Arabic; there was no significant literary work, however. The bulk of their cultural nourishment came from Egypt and, second hand, via Lebanon. Likewise, the Palestinian Arabs scarcely evinced any artistic capacity in theater, music, etc.; here, too, Egypt was the main source of supply.

[Yaacov Shimoni]

DEMOGRAPHY AND VITAL STATISTICS. The first official census in 1922 counted some 752,000 inhabitants, of whom 83,790 were Jews. Of the 668,258 non-Jews, 78% – 589,177 – were Muslims; there were 71,464 Christian and 7,617 Druze and others. In March 1947 the non-Jewish population was given as 1,319,434: 1,157,423 Muslims, 146,162 Christians, and 15,849 others. (The figures for Arabs in 1947 were, apparently, inflated because of the institution of rationing in 1942 and the consequent reluctance to report deaths.) Most of the Christians were also Arabs, but their total included a substantial number of English, other Europeans, and Armenians as well (see Table: Muslim Population in Palestine).

Most of the Arab growth was a result of the extraordinary natural increase, due to the fall in the death rate and the rise in

Population of Palestine, 1922–47

Year	Muslims	Christians	Druze & Other	Jews	Total
1922	589,177	71,464	7,617	83,790	752,048
1931	759,700	88,907	10,101	174,606	1,033,314
1936	862,730	108,506	11,378	384,708	1,366,692
1942	995,292	127,184	13,121	484,408	1,620,005
1947	1,157,423	146,162	15,849	614,239	1,933,673

Muslim Population in Palestine

	Urban		Rural	
	No.	Index	No.	Index
Census 1922	139,074	100	451,816	100
Census 1931	188,075	136	571,637	126
Estimate 1936	229,000	165	619,000	137

fertility, while the birthrate remained stable. Natural increase rose from 23.3 per thousand in 1922–25 to 30.7 in 1941–44 (see Table: Muslim Births, Deaths and Natural Increase, Palestine). Fertility, as measured by the average number of children born to a Muslim mother, rose from 6.1 in 1927–29 to 8.1 in 1942–43. In Egypt, on the other hand, the death rate was 33.7 per thousand in 1924–26 and 30.3 in 1939–41, while the fertility rate in 1940 was 6.4. As the British Mandatory government's *Survey of Palestine* (1946) put it: "The Arabs of Palestine have, during the last two decades, been in an almost unique demographic position. This improvement is particularly noticeable in those sub-districts of the coastal plain which have been the main Jewish immigration areas" (p. 714).

Muslim Births, Deaths, and Natural Increase, Palestine

Years	Births	Deaths	Natural Increase
1922/25	50.2	26.9	23.3
1931/35	50.3	25.3	25.0
1941/44	50.1	19.4	30.7

Improvements in health conditions by the drainage of swamps, better sanitation, and modern medical methods were largely responsible for almost halving the infant mortality rate among Muslim children and raising the average life-span by more than ten years (see Table: Muslim Infant Mortality and Life Expectancy). In 1921 there were 304 government hospital beds in the country, 402 Jewish, and 782 Christian. By 1944 there were 1,377 beds in government and 1,410 in Jewish hospitals. The percentage of malaria patients dropped from 7.17 in 1922 to 0.7 in 1944. In Egypt, by comparison, there was no decline in infant mortality during the period; life expectancy for males rose from 31 to 34.2 between 1917–27 and 1927–37, while for females it actually fell from 36 to 31.5.

Part of the increase in Arab population, however, was due to migration. In the 20 years between 1922 and 1942, 20,015 Muslims, 15,645 Christians, and 336 others (excluding Jews) were officially registered as immigrants to Palestine. Since

Muslim Infant Mortality and Life Expectancy

Years	Child Mortality[1]	Life Expectancy	
	(per 1,000 births)	Male	Female
1926/30	412	37.1	37.9
1936/40	289	46.4	47.7
1941/44	251	49.4	50.4

[1] Deaths per 1,000 in the first five years of life.

there was considerable unrecorded movement of laborers across the borders, especially from Syria, the actual number of immigrants was undoubtedly much larger; it has been estimated as high as 100,000.

EDUCATION. There was also a significant improvement in education. In July 1920 the 171 government schools in the country had 408 teachers and 10,662 pupils, almost half of whom were Arab. In July 1944, as a result of the British drive to improve the system, there were 64,790 Arab pupils in government schools (59,045 Muslims and 5,745 Christians), as well as 39,828 in private schools (17,815 Muslims and 22,013 Christians). To a large extent the increase was due to the construction of new schools in the villages. Education did not reach all the Arabs, however. According to the 1931 census, 85.6% of the Muslims, 76.7% of the Druze, and 42.3% of the Christians over seven years old were illiterate. In 1944 only 34% of the total school-age population was in school. The most deprived were the village girls. While 85% of the Muslim boys and 52% of the girls in the urban areas received some schooling, in the villages the percentages were only 65% for boys and 5% for girls.

The demarcation lines laid down in the armistice agreements with Egypt and Jordan split the Arabs of Western Palestine between three territorial units: the State of Israel; the central hill region of Judea and Samaria, annexed to Transjordan as the "West Bank" of the Jordan kingdom; and the Gaza Strip, under Egyptian occupation.

In the State of Israel, 1948–67

With the flight of thousands of Arabs immediately before and during the War of Independence (see Arab Refugees in *Israel, State of: Historical Survey), some 156,000 were left in Israel in November 1948, out of an estimated 750,000 who lived in the area at the end of 1947. The succeeding 18 years saw a sharp increase in their number: it doubled by the end of 1966, when there were some 312,500, and from 1951 to 1966 they accounted for about 11% of the population. Table: Non-Jewish Population, Israel, 1949–69 shows the Arab and Druze population at the end of each year, in thousands.

The major reason for this growth was the unusually high rate of natural increase, one of the highest in the world, which rose in Israel from 33.7 per thousand in 1950 to 42.8 in 1960 and 43.4 in 1966, falling to 40.8 in 1969. There was a drop in the death rate from 9.48 per thousand in 1950 to 7.5 in 1960 and 5.9 in 1969, and a high birthrate: 56 per 1,000 in 1950, 50.3 in

Non-Jewish Population, Israel, 1949–69 (in thousands)

Year	Muslims	Christians	Druzes & Other	Total	% of Population
1949	111.5	34.0	14.5	160.0	14.9
1950	116.1	36.0	15.0	167.1	12.9
1951	118.9	39.0	15.5	173.4	11.4
1952	122.8	40.4	16.1	179.3	11.0
1953	127.6	41.4	16.8	185.8	11.0
1954	131.8	42.0	18.0	191.8	11.2
1955	136.3	43.3	19.0	198.6	11.1
1956	141.4	43.7	19.8	204.9	11.0
1957	146.9	45.8	20.5	213.2	10.8
1958	152.8	47.3	21.4	221.5	10.9
1959	159.3	48.3	22.3	229.9	11.0
1960	166.3	49.6	23.3	239.1	11.1
1961	174.9	51.3	26.3	252.5	11.3
1962	183.0	52.6	27.3	262.9	11.3
1963	192.2	53.9	28.5	274.5	11.3
1964	202.3	55.5	28.6	284.6	11.3
1965	212.4	57.1	29.8	299.3	11.5
1966	223.0	58.5	31.0	312.5	11.8
1967[1]	286.6	70.6	33.1	392.7	14.1
1968	300.8	72.1	33.3	406.3	14.3
1969	317.0	73.0	34.0	424.0	14.5

1 Including 55,000 Muslims and 12,000 Christians added as a result of the reunification of Jerusalem.

1960, and 46.7 in 1969. The average number of children born to an Arab woman in 1967 was 7.4, while the average Arab family in 1968 consisted of 6.8 persons.

As a result of this unusual rate of natural increase, the Arab population was very young. The median age, which was 17 years in 1955, dropped to 16.3 in 1961 and to 14.8 in 1967. In 1955, 45% of the Arab population was under 15 years old. By 1967 that age group accounted for more than half of the population (50.4%), and almost three-quarters of all the Arabs (74.3%) were younger than 30. Just over half the Israel Arabs are males: according to the 1955 census, 51.5% of the Muslims, 50% of the Christians, and 51.4% of the Druze were males, and this proportion continues to hold.

Other factors also helped to augment the number of Arabs in Israel. While emigration was negligible (less than 6,000 Arabs left Israel between 1949 and 1969), there was a substantial immigration, some 40,000 returning under the "reunion of families" scheme. Border adjustments under the 1949 Armistice Agreements also added some 30,000 Arabs in the "Little Triangle" area, a narrow strip from the Jezreel Valley to Kafr Qassem.

IN THE VILLAGES. The majority of Israel Arabs live in villages, as they have throughout the centuries, but the percentage of rural inhabitants steadily decreased: from about 78% of the Arab population at the end of 1949 to 57% – some 241,000 souls – in 1969. Most of the Arab villages are in the northern section of Israel (Northern and Haifa districts), where almost 80% of the rural Arab population lived in 1969, making up some 67% of its rural population. Of the 98 Arab villages, 40 held 2,000 or more inhabitants each, and 58 less than 2,000. More than a third (36%) of the Arabs lived in the large villages and 11% in the small ones; almost 9% were Bedouin.

While agriculture was still the main occupation, there was been a noticeable drop in the percentage of Arabs working on the land. In 1954 58% of Israel Arabs were engaged in agriculture; by 1964 this figure has decreased to 39% and in 1969 it was only 31.5%. On the other hand, the area cultivated by Arabs in Israel increased from 340,000 dunams (85,000 acres) in 1948/49 to 870,000 dunams (217,000 acres) in 1968/69. The land under irrigation went up from 8,000 dunams (2,000 acres) in 1948/49 to more than 40,000 dunams (10,000 acres) in 1968/69. Of the cultivated area, a little less than half (400,000 dunams) was cultivated by the Bedouin. Almost 90% of the area (apart from that cultivated by the Bedouin) is privately owned.

The government did much to aid the development of the Arab villages. An IL 85,000,000 five-year plan for the purpose was completed in 1967 and a second, to cost IL 115,000,000, was launched. The three main goals have been the intensification of cultivation, diversification of crops, and the extension of land area. The first aim was implemented through a program of increased irrigation, mechanization, fertilization, and disease control; the second through the introduction of industrial crops, such as cotton, ground nuts, and sugar beet; and the third by reclaiming unused land and protecting the soil from erosion and overuse. In addition, access and internal roads were built, loans and technical assistance provided, and electricity and piped water supplied. As a result of these efforts and of the general rise in the country's standard of living, life in the villages improved markedly. At the end of the British Mandate there were only five farm machines in the entire Arab sector; by 1968 there were more than 450 of all types. Before Israel was established hardly a single Arab village had either electricity or running water; by 1968 virtually every village was connected to the national electric grid and every home had running water.

These changes altered many of the traditional aspects of the Arab village. Almost half the members of the Arab labor force now worked outside their regular place of residence, as many of the villagers found employment in the cities, while continuing to live in their villages. Modernization and democratization weakened the hold of traditional institutions, such as the *ḥamūla*, or extended family, which depended upon its economic power, ownership of the land, and influence with the government to maintain control of the village. Now, with outside employment available, compulsory education, and the election of local councils, a leadership more responsive to the wishes of the villagers was created and strengthened.

IN THE CITIES. The major urban centers inhabited by the Israel Arabs include the six "mixed cities" of Acre, Haifa, Jerusalem, Lydda, Ramleh, and Tel Aviv-Jaffa, as well as the two wholly Arab towns of Nazareth and Shepharam. The percentage of Arabs living in cities and towns steadily increased since the end of the Mandate. In 1947 some 25% of all Palestinian Arabs were urban; by 1969 the figure had grown to 43%, totaling 181,700 persons. The population rise in the two wholly Arab towns between 1950 and 1969 is indicative of the general trend. Nazareth's population grew during the period by almost two-thirds: from 20,000 to 32,900, while Shepharam more than doubled its size, from 3,900 to 10,500. Of the total non-Jewish population in Israel in 1969, aged 14 and over, 42.3% belonged to the labor force. Of these 91.4% were employed – the largest percentages, next to agriculture, in construction and industry.

In 1959, the *Histadrut began to accept Israel Arabs individually as full members (prior to that date they were only admitted to its medical insurance fund and to the trade unions). As a result, the number of Arabs paying union dues increased from some 6,000 in 1955 to 50,000 in 1969 and accounted for about half the Arab working population. Membership in the Histadrut, together with labor legislation that prescribes equality between Arab and Jewish workers, improved the conditions of the Arab laborer. Efforts were made to reduce pockets of unorganized and unskilled Arab labor, which did not yet benefit from wage protection and other social benefits.

HEALTH, EDUCATION, AND CULTURE. The sharp decrease in the death rate among Israel Arabs is basically a result of improved health services (see Health Services in *Israel, State of: Health). While the general death rate fell from some 9.48 per thousand in 1948 to 5.9 in 1969, the infant death rate dropped from 48.8 per thousand in 1951 to 40.3.

The Compulsory Education Act of 1949, providing for free and compulsory education between the ages of 5 and 14, and the construction of a school in almost every Arab village completely changed the picture of education for Israel Arabs (see *Israel, State of: Education). In 1958, 57 Arabs were enrolled at the Hebrew University in Jerusalem; the figure had grown to 160 by 1964 and more than 200 in 1969/70. In the latter year, 32 Arab students were enrolled at Tel Aviv University, 45 at Bar-Ilan University, 42 at the Technion, and some 300 at Haifa University.

Regular publications in Arabic included two dailies, two weeklies, and about ten monthlies and quarterlies. Some of these periodicals were affiliated with political parties and some with religious groups, while others were independent. Books in Arabic were widely available, many of them published in Israel by public or private concerns. Some were written by Israel Arabs or translated from other languages, including Hebrew. Works by Arabs in other countries were also available. There was a large central library in Jaffa, with almost 100,000 volumes. Arabic theater performances were held, mainly by amateur companies. Arabic movies and musical performances attracted large audiences. Regular Arabic radio programs put out by the Israel Broadcasting Authority for 14 hours a day included readings from the Koran and church services, as well as news, literary features, music, and items of human interest. Nightly television programs were broadcast in Arabic.

LOCAL GOVERNMENT. The Ministry of the Interior strongly encouraged the formation of local councils in order to raise the level of Arab local government to that of the Jews, to serve as a link between the villages and the government, and to act as a vehicle for economic progress, as part of the program for rural development. In 1948 only three Arab localities under Israel rule were governed by local councils. The municipal council of Nazareth was established in 1935 and that of Shepharam in 1934, while the village council of Kafr Yasīf dates back to 1925. By 1969 there were two Arab municipalities, 45 villages with local councils, and another 23 within larger regional councils. These covered some 80% of Israel's Arabs. Participation in local elections, which was greater than that of either Jews or Arabs in national elections, bore witness to the close relationship between the council and the villagers. Generally the national parties only vied for council seats in the larger localities, such as Nazareth; in the smaller villages the candidates generally represented rival families, clans, or religious communities. The major part of the councils' budgets was raised by local taxes, calculated according to the area of land or number of rooms owned, but the government made substantial contributions, especially for development projects, like the installation of electricity and water lines, or the construction of roads and schools, to which it usually contributed about 50% of the total expenditure.

NATIONAL POLITICS. The Arab community played a full and active role in national politics. Except for the first Knesset election in 1949, the proportion of Arab voters was higher than that among the Jews. Table: Percentage of Electors Voting at National Elections shows the comparison. After the first Knesset, which had only three Arab members, there were at least seven and sometimes eight (Second, Third, and Fifth Knessets). Most of these – two in the First Knesset, five in the Second, Third, and Fourth, four in the Fifth and Sixth, and five in the Seventh – were members of lists associated with, or affiliated to, Mapai (since 1968 the Israel Labor Party) or its alliances with other parties. These lists, which had names like Cooperation and Fraternity or Progress and Development, were generally divided along religious, geographical, and family lines. While the percentage voting for Mapai (Labor) or its affiliated lists dropped from more than 60% in 1949 to 50% in 1965, it nevertheless remained greater than that of any other party and rose to 57% in 1969 for the Labor-Mapam alliance (Ma'arakh).

The Israel Communist Party tried to attract Arab votes by making an Arab nationalist appeal, and provided a legal way of opposing the regime. This was particularly true of Rakaḥ (New Communist List), the larger of the two factions into which the party split in 1965 – the smaller, Maki, being mainly Jewish. Rakaḥ succeeded, together with Mapam, in gaining control of the Nazareth municipal council for a short period, from December 1965 to March 1966 and thereafter remained a strong

Percentage of Electors Voting at National Elections, Jews and Arabs, Israel, 1949–69

Election Year	Arabs	Jews
1949	79.3	86.9
1951	85.5	75.1
1955	91.0	82.8
1959	88.9	81.6
1961	85.6	81.6
1965	87.8	83.0
1969	84.0	82.0

opposition. The strength of the Communists in the Knesset elections was irregular; winning 22% of the Arab vote in 1949 they dropped to 10% by 1959 but went up again to 22.6% in 1965, when they secured 38,800 votes (of which 38,000 went to Rakaḥ), as compared with the Labor affiliated lists' total of 48,000. In 1969 Rakaḥ obtained 34,000 votes to 67,000 for the Ma'arakh and its affiliated lists.

Mapam, the third of the national parties to appeal to the Arabs on a sustained basis, always included an Arab candidate in a prominent place on its list. Its strength gradually increased to 12.5% of the Arab vote in 1959 and fell slightly to 9.2% in 1965.

There were a number of attempts to organize wholly independent Arab parties – the first began immediately after the establishment of Israel – but all have proven unsuccessful. An extremist group, known as al-Ard, was declared illegal by the Supreme Court for opposing the existence of the State of Israel.

The two major national issues which agitated the Israeli Arabs in the first 20 years of statehood were military government and absentee property. Military government was established immediately after the 1948 war to control areas bordering on the Arab states and other sections of the country which the government considered strategically important. These areas included those in which most Israel Arabs lived, with the exception of the mixed cities. Movement was restricted within the areas and passes had to be obtained from the military government for travel to other parts of the country, whether on business, for work or study, or for short visits. Military government was gradually curtailed as security improved and opposition to it grew among Jews as well as Arabs. On Dec. 1, 1966 it was completely abolished. The problem of absentee property arose from the flight of the Arab refugees. In 1950 the government appointed a custodian to handle the property abandoned by those who left the country. Some of the land was used for the settlement of Jewish refugees and the establishment of new towns. However, many Arabs protested against inequities in defining an absentee owner and, in 1953, a Land Acquisition Law was passed. By 1965 the government had restored, exchanged, or paid compensation under this law to two-thirds of the claimants requesting redress.

[Julian J. Landau]

There were also other causes for dissatisfaction among Israel Arabs. Middle East tensions inevitably reacted on the situation within Israel and normal development was seriously hampered by the abnormality of the situation. The slowness of progress toward overall integration caused a certain disillusionment, especially among potentially intellectual circles, some of whom left the country in the hope of making their way successfully elsewhere. And while the Arab minority as a whole remained quiescent even at times of greatest strain, there was an inevitable undertone of identification with Arab national aspirations, which found expression in various ways. Attempts to induce Israel Arabs to cooperate in terrorist activities after 1967 proved far less successful than was at one time anticipated. But the cases that did occur (followed by punishment by the Israel authorities) had an adverse effect on the Jewish-Arab relationship.

Under Jordanian Rule, 1948–67

Under the United Nations partition resolution of Nov. 29, 1947, an Arab state was to be established, side by side with the Jewish state, in Western Palestine. Emir *Abdullah of Transjordan, however, joined the other Arab countries in opposition to partition; on Dec. 2, 1947, both houses of the Transjordanian parliament decided unanimously "to support Arab interests in Palestine," and the Arab Legion played a major part in the operations against Israel. Abdullah's army crossed the Jordan River on May 15, 1948, occupied the hill regions of Samaria and Judea, and set up a civil administration in the area. On May 18, the Legion reached Jerusalem and on the 27th occupied the Old City and part of its environs, but it did not go beyond the area allotted by the UN plan to the Arabs.

In September, Count *Bernadotte, the UN mediator, proposed the unification of the Arab part of western Palestine with Transjordan, but the proposal was rejected by the United Nations. On September 23, an "All-Palestine Government," loyal to Hajj Amīn al-*Husseini, the former mufti of Jerusalem, was set up in Gaza under Egyptian patronage and was soon recognized by all the Arab states, except Transjordan, against whom it was obviously directed. The Transjordanian authorities reacted by calling an assembly at Jericho, which, on October 1, passed a resolution calling for the annexation of "Arab Palestine." This decision was immediately denounced by the *Arab League, which warned Abdullah not to take any action that might lead to the liquidation of the independence of Palestine. On December 13, however, the Transjordanian parliament unanimously approved the Jericho resolution, and a week later the government of Transjordan appointed Sheikh Hassan al-Din Jarallah as mufti of Jerusalem in place of Husseini. In March 1949 a civil administration was set up in the area and in the following month the name of Abdullah's kingdom was changed to the Hashemite Kingdom of *Jordan. From March 1950, Jordanian government publications no longer used the name "Palestine," which was replaced by the term "West Bank" (i.e., the western part of the Jordan kingdom).

On Jan. 1, 1950, the former Transjordanian parliament was dissolved and new elections held on both banks, half the number of deputies – 20 (including three for the Christians) – being allotted to the West Bank. Despite the opposition of the Communists and the ex-mufti's followers, the elections were held on April 11, with a victory for Abdullah's supporters. On the 16th Abdullah appointed a new senate of 20, with eight Palestinian members, and on the 24th parliament confirmed the annexation of the territories west of the Jordan River, which were in the hands of the Legion. The Israel government spokesman described the annexation as "a unilateral step which is not binding on Israel," but Britain recognized the new status of the West Bank on April 27 and announced that the conditions of her alliance with Transjordan would apply to the annexed area. The Political Committee of the Arab League resolved that the annexation was a violation of its decisions, but did not accept an Egyptian proposal to expel the Jordan kingdom from the League. Jordan, which held the part of Jerusalem containing almost all the holy places, opposed the UN resolution on its internationalization.

Abdullah's new subjects were a constant source of trouble. The acquisition of some 900,000 Palestinians (half of them permanent inhabitants of the annexed areas and half refugees from those parts of western Palestine which became Israel) trebled the population of the kingdom and radically undermined its stability. The Palestinians had a much higher level of education, on the whole, than the population of Transjordan and looked down on its Bedouin tribesmen. Their professional men and skilled tradesmen could not find employment, nor their politicians satisfaction for their ambitions, in the primitive Jordanian economy and society. The refugees eked out a bare subsistence in the camps maintained by the UN Relief and Works Agency, and much of its inadequate allotments found their way into the pockets of corrupt local officials. The idle and discontented refugees were like tinder, readily inflamed in any emergency. Many of them blamed Abdullah for failing to prosecute the war against Israel with sufficient energy and denounced him as a tool in the hands of the British, anxious only to expand his kingdom. There were frequent demonstrations in the refugee camps, where Abdullah's secret police repeatedly discovered plots against the regime. Finally, the discontent, fed by the incitement of Egyptian agents and the ex-mufti's Higher Arab Committee, bore fruit; on July 20, 1951, Abdullah was assassinated on the steps of the Al-Aqṣā Mosque in Jerusalem by followers of Husseini.

Palestinians continued to play a prominent part in Jordanian politics during the reign of Abdullah's grandson *Hussein. Mūsā al-ʿAlamī, an opponent of the ex-mufti, headed the Jordanian branch of the all-Arab Baʿth party, but he lost most of his support in the wave of Nasserist enthusiasm that followed the Egyptian officers' revolution in 1952, since he was in favor of union with Iraq. When riots broke out in the refugee camps, with Egyptian encouragement, ʿAlamī's model farm near Jericho was sacked by the demonstrators. The West Bank was also a focus of conflict between Jordan and Israel because of acts of violence committed by Palestinian infiltrators and Israel reprisals, which reached their peak in the attacks on Qibya on Oct. 14, 1953, and Naḥḥālīn on April 29, 1954.

Palestinians also played a prominent part in the three days of continuous demonstrations that followed the arrival in Amman, in December 1955, of General Templer, the chief of the British Imperial General Staff, for the purpose of persuading Jordan to join the Baghdad Pact, and which were followed by the resignation of the government. At the elections in October 1956, it was Suleiman al-Nabulsi, of Nablus (Shechem) who led the pro-Nasser National Socialist Party to victory and, as prime minister of the post-election cabinet, brought Jordan into the Egyptian-Syrian-Saudi Arabian military pact and the joint Egyptian-Syrian command. The Palestinians also played a considerable role in the unrest that threatened to topple King Hussein's throne during the next few years.

With the increasing prosperity that followed the generous American subventions to Jordan, in addition to the aid it received from the United Kingdom, Saudi Arabia, and Kuwait, thousands of Palestinian refugees flocked from the camps into Amman and over 200,000 peasants and refugees from the neglected West Bank crossed the Jordan River. The refugees, as well as the Palestinian intellectuals, began to find places in the Jordanian economy. However, the Palestinians were constantly competing for power with the Transjordanians, who kept the reins firmly in their hands, thanks largely to their predominance in the Arab Legion. The determination of the Arab states to perpetuate the problem helped to keep the Palestinians conscious of their separate character, and the idea of a "Palestine entity" began to be mooted. In 1964 the Palestine Liberation Organization, headed by Ahmad Shukeiri, was set up, and the al-Fatḥ Organization was founded in 1965 to carry on the struggle for "the liberation of Palestine" (see Arab National Movement in *Israel, State of: Historical Survey).

In 1966 the population of the West Bank totaled 860,000, of whom some two-thirds lived in the countryside. About 90% were Muslims, most of them Sunnis. The majority of the 50,000 Christians lived in the Jerusalem district (including Bethlehem) and most of the rest in the Nablus district. According to the UNRWA rolls, which were never rigorously investigated, there were some 435,000 refugees, of whom about 140,000 lived in the camps (see *Israel, State of: Historical Survey (Arab Refugees)). They were regarded as citizens with equal rights, and a considerable proportion of them had their own sources of income in addition to the UNRWA allocations. It was estimated that about 120,000 refugees emigrated from Jordan – most of them from the West Bank – to Arab and other countries, and many of them sent money home to support their families and relations. One of the results of this emigration was a surplus of women in the area. The natural increase was very high, over 4%; the percentage of children below the age of 15 was, consequently, also high – 43%. Participation in the labor force was among the lowest in the world – some 22%. Of those employed, some 37% worked in agriculture, 14.6% in services, 11.6% in industry, and 10.4% in construction.

In the Gaza Strip, 1948–67

In the *Gaza Strip, which was left in Egyptian occupation under the terms of the 1949 Armistice Agreement with Israel, the resident population of 50–60,000 was swamped by the influx of refugees from other parts of the country, variously estimated at between 120,000 and 150,000, while Arab sources claim even higher figures. With a total of 180–200,000 inhabitants, the population density was over 1,400 per sq. mi., among the highest in the world. The refugees were concentrated in 12 camps and settlements, where they were maintained by UNRWA and the Quakers. Unlike Transjordan, Egypt obeyed the Arab League's ban on the annexation of portions of former Mandatory Palestine occupied by Arab states, thus absolving herself of the responsibility for supporting the Strip's inhabitants. The "Palestine Arab Government," established in September 1948 with its "temporary" center in Gaza, soon ceased to operate. The mayor of Gaza's repeated appeals to the Egyptian government to annex the Strip were rejected on the ground that "the independence of Palestine" must be protected.

Until the end of 1953 the Strip was administered as occupied territory. Local authorities continued to operate under Egyptian supervision in the two main towns, Gaza and *Khan Yunis, but the representatives of the rural population had no say in the running of their affairs. The Egyptians did nothing to develop the economy: they protected their own textile industry by withholding raw materials from the Gaza cotton mills, exhausted the Strip's foreign currency reserves, and rigidly enforced customs barriers between the area and Egypt. At the end of 1953 a law was passed to regulate the administration of the Strip. The executive power was in the hands of the governor, who was subordinate to the Egyptian minister of war, and an executive council consisting of heads of departments appointed by the ministry. There was a legislative council, also headed by the governor, consisting of members of the executive council, eight members of local authorities, and six representatives of the professions. The governor could veto any law passed by the legislative council, subject to appeal to the Egyptian minister of war, who also appointed the judges. In 1955 a new constitution was promulgated, providing for the election of the legislative council.

Despite her obligations under the Armistice Agreement, Egypt concentrated armed forces in the Strip, which also served as a major base for infiltrators into Israel and later for the fedayeen (terrorist "suicide squads") under Egyptian command. Israel's retaliatory operations against military targets in the Strip aroused the fury of the populace, particularly the refugees, who rioted against the Egyptian authorities and the UN observers, demanding a free hand to fight Israel. During the Sinai Campaign (1956), the Israel Defense Forces occupied the Strip. The Israel authorities took energetic measures to restore normal life, reconstituting the municipalities and local authorities. Israel withdrew from the Strip in March 1957, however, and the entry of a UN Emergency Force was immediately followed by the return of the Egyptians, severe punishment being meted out to local leaders who had collaborated with the Israelis.

The UN force was stationed mainly along the armistice demarcation line, and there was a considerable drop in the number of border incidents. Its presence helped to mitigate the economic difficulties of the population, but they were still forbidden to leave the area without the Egyptian military governor's permission. On the establishment of the United Arab Republic (1958), the Egyptians promulgated a new constitution for the Strip, providing for an executive council of ten, headed by the Egyptian governor, and a legislative council of 30, including eight Egyptians. At its first meeting, the council expressed a desire to join the UAR, but the Strip continued to be administered as a separate territory. In 1962 a new constitution was promulgated giving the refugees equal rights with the permanent inhabitants. Egypt continued to maintain a "Palestinian" military unit consisting of local inhabitants. As a result of the cease-fire agreement accepted by Egypt after the 1967 war, the Strip was again placed under Israel administration.

Most of the lands owned by the permanent inhabitants of the strip before the War of Independence were on the Israel side of the demarcation line; according to the Clapp Committee, which reported to the UN in September 1949, all the cultivable land in the Strip was already under plow. Hence, food and other goods had to be imported, while the purchasing power of the population was low, due to poverty and unemployment. The major export was citrus, but the economy of the Strip was based mostly on welfare income, mainly from the UN; contributions from relatives abroad; the budget of the Egyptian administration; and the outlays of the UN force – making a total estimated in 1960 at $21,000,000. In 1962 there were 53,000 pupils in primary schools, 14,000 in pre-secondary schools, and 8,800 in secondary and vocational schools. Separate schools for the children of the refugees were maintained by UNRWA. Due to the high rate of natural increase, especially among the refugees, the population grew rapidly and, since few could leave, so did the overcrowding in the area. The Egyptian estimate of the population of the Strip – 454,960 in 1966 – was found to be vastly exaggerated when the Israel authorities carried out a census in September 1967, but even the census total of 356,000 gave a population density of some 2,500 per sq. mi.

After the Six-Day War

As a result of the Six-Day War over a million more Arabs came under Israel rule. Jerusalem was reunified by the Ministry of the Interior's order of June 28, 1967 extending the municipal boundaries to include the eastern part of the city, the population of which were regarded as permanent residents of Israel. Judea and Samaria (the "West Bank"), the Gaza Strip, the Sinai Peninsula, and the Golan Heights were placed under military government.

JERUSALEM. The reunification of Jerusalem added some 67,000 Arabs – 55,000 Muslims and 12,000 Christians – to the Israel Arab community bringing the total up to 392,700, 14.1% of the population at the end of 1967 and 422,700 (14.6%) in 1969. The number of non-Jews in the Jerusalem district increased from 4,800 in 1966 to 76,600 at the end of 1969, i.e., from 1.5% to 18.1% of the Arab population. Out of 39,000 over the age of 14, 14,000 belonged to the civilian labor force. Of these, 13,000 – about 93% – were employed: some 4,600 in various services; 2,400 in commerce, banking, and insurance; 2,900 in industry; 1,300 in transport, storage, and communications; and 1,400 in construction and public works. The number of pupils in East Jerusalem schools increased from 11,894 in 1968/69 to 13,119 in 1969/70: 1,160 in kindergartens, 9,470 in elementary schools, 2,002 in preparatory schools, and 487 in high schools.

JUDEA AND SAMARIA (THE "WEST BANK"). The population totaled 595,000 in the census of September 1967 and 608,000 at the end of 1970. The annual birthrate was estimated at 43, the death rate at 19, and the natural increase at 24 per thousand. There was a great deal of population movement into and out of the West Bank after the 1967 war. Out of some 200,000 who left during or immediately after the war, 14,900 returned, on application, with the approval of the Israel government. In addition, up to the end of 1969, 8,130 were allowed in to rejoin their families. During the same period some 225,000 persons crossed into Jordan for employment or study, with permits allowing them to return; 31,000 came for visits from Jordan or other countries for periods of up to three months; and 42,000 (mainly students) came for summer visits. Of 307,200 residents aged 14 or over, 113,200 were part of the labor force in 1969 (including 87,000 out of the 147,000 males). Over 97% of the labor force was employed: 46% in agriculture; 28% in services, including transportation and commerce; 14% in industry and crafts; and 12% in construction. In 1969/70 a total of 177,400 pupils went to school in Judea and Samaria: some 132,000 to the 681 government schools, another 26,700 in UNRWA institutions, and 18,200 in 119 private schools.

IN THE STATE OF ISRAEL. The Israel government's budget for the region rose from IL 86,000,000 in 1968/69 to IL 94,000,000 for 1970/71. More than half the budget (about 51%) was devoted to social services, including health, education, welfare, and employment. Some 27% was used for economic purposes, such as agriculture and water, traffic, and communications, while the remaining 22% was for administrative, judicial, and police services. As a result of the government's policy of encouraging local authorities, 22 of the 23 municipalities functioning before the war continued to operate, as well as 31 rural councils.

Shortly after the conclusion of the war, trade between the area and Jordan was resumed, and the passage of goods between Israel, the Gaza Strip, and Judea and Samaria was authorized. In 1969, the area had an adverse trade balance of IL 123,400,000 with Israel and IL 17,800,000 with other countries, and a favorable balance of IL 39,900,000 with Jordan.

THE GAZA STRIP AND NORTHERN SINAI. The 1967 census counted 389,700 persons living in the Gaza Strip and northern Sinai. The population at the end of 1970 was 372,000. A natural increase in 1968–70 totaled about 29,000 (27.9 per thousand in 1970); some 47,000 persons must have left the Strip – many of them for the West Bank. About 162,000 persons lived in the town of Gaza, 153,000 in Khān Yunis, and 35,000 in El-Arish. The annual birthrate is estimated at 41, and the death rate at 16 per thousand. In 1968 and 1969 about 3,000 Arabs were permitted to return from Egypt to the Strip in exchange for Egyptian nationals who returned to Egypt. In 1968 some 45,000 traveled to Arab countries on business, or for work or study, but only 9,000 were able to do so in 1969, since the Jordan government closed the bridges in August 1969 to those without official Jordanian documents. Thirty-two percent of the 183,000 residents aged 14 or over were part of the labor force at the end of 1969, and 94.4% of these were employed. Fifty-six percent of those employed were wage earners; average daily wages rose from IL 3.9 in 1968 to IL 5.8 in 1969. About 5,000 went out to work in Israel.

In 1969 the area had an adverse trade balance of IL 27,700,000 with Israel and favorable balances of IL 4,400,000 with Jordan and IL 5,200,000 with other countries.

There were some 105,000 pupils in 191 schools in the area – 83 government institutions and 108 run by UNRWA – in the 1969/70 school year. More than half of the pupils – some 58,000 – attended UNRWA schools. The government budget for the area was IL 53,000,000 in 1969/70 and IL 867,500,000 in 1970/71. In the latter year, 39.9% of the budget was devoted to social services, 31.6% to economic purposes, and 28.5% for administrative expenses. Local income totaled IL 5,500,000 in Gaza, Khan Yunis, El-Arish, and Rafa. The government initiated numerous public works, such as road construction and maintenance.

GOLAN HEIGHTS AND SINAI DESERT. The Golan Heights in the north and the Sinai Desert in the south were, basically, deserted areas after the war. The Golan Heights were almost totally abandoned by the original population of about 90,000 Syrians. Some 6,500 Druzes remained in five villages, which continued to be run by their traditional leaders under the general supervision of the military governor. There were ten schools with 58 classes in the area. The Israel government budget for the Golan Heights was IL 6,000,000 in 1968/69 and IL 9,000,000 in 1969/70.

Southern Sinai was and remains a desert with little possibility of settlement. It is estimated that as many as 50,000 Bedouin roam through it, with some 400 local mukhtars and sheikhs to guide their affairs. The government's budget for the area was IL 1,000,000 in 1968/69 and double that figure in 1969/70.

See also *Israel, State of: Health and Welfare. For Druze, see *Israel, State of: Religious Life and Communities.

[Julian J. Landau]

Developments in the 1970s

ISRAEL. The Arab population of Israel continued to grow during the 1970s. Whereas on the eve of the Six-Day War there were approximately 312,000 Arabs and Druze in Israel, consisting of 223,000 Muslims, 58,500 Christians, and 31,000 Druze, towards the end of 1972, as a result of natural increase and the addition of 55,000 Muslims and 12,000 Christians through the reunification of Jerusalem, the number had grown to 470,000 – about 15% of the population. The Jerusalem Arabs are permanent residents of Israel and entitled, as such, to vote in municipal elections. They have not been compelled to accept Israeli citizenship, though they may receive it on application, but only a few score have opted to do so, the great majority having chosen to retain their Jordanian citizenship. In 1980 the number had grown to 639,000 – 498,300 Muslims, 89,900 Christians, and 50,700 Druze. The population is undergoing a process of urbanization, the higher proportion of city-dwellers rising to some 60%. This population is also considerably younger than its Jewish counterpart (average age 20.9 years, compared with 30.4 in the Jewish sector). About 50% of all Arabs in Israel are 14 years old or under, and this is an indication of the vast potential demographic changes that will develop if the Jewish population continues to stagnate at its present growth rate. The continued improvement of health services in Israel, and the mounting standard of living, make their impact on the life expectancy of the Arab population. In 1976 every Arab newborn had a life expectation of 63 (females, 71.5 years), compared to 64 in Lebanon, 56 in Syria and Jordan, 55 in Egypt, and 45 in Saudi Arabia. The impressive growth of the Arab community in Israel, from a poor peasant society whose leaders had deserted her in the early stages of the War of Independence (1948), into a predominantly urban and modern society, must be attributed, first of all, to the Arab educational system in Israel. Ninety-five percent of all school-age Arab children attend school at present, compared with 38% in the pre-1948 period. A total of 185,000 Arab students attend all levels of schooling, from kindergarten to university. The new generation of Israeli Arabs, who were born and raised under the Israeli system, has produced a new elite of several thousand university graduates and professionals. In the year 1976 alone there were 2,000 registered students in all Israeli universities. In 1948 only two Arab municipalities existed in Israel – Nazareth and Shefaram – and one local council. In the 1970s, in addition to those two municipalities, some 50 local councils were established, duly elected by their population. Despite the process of urbanization, however, the cultivated area in the Arab villages grew 2.6 fold since the establishment of Israel; in real estate terms, from 340,000 dunams in 1948 to 895,000 dunams in 1975, part of which was under irrigation and yielding high crops, thanks to the mechanization and modern agricultural techniques developed in Israel. While in 1950 more than half the Arab manpower was employed in agriculture, only 16% depended for their livelihood on farming in 1976, despite the tremendous increase of cultivated area and productivity. The balance of manpower turned to typically urban occupations, such as construction (24%), services (22%), industry (18%), and other branches of the economy (17%). By 1976 only half the manpower of the Arab settlements was employed locally, while the remainder sought and obtained work outside their localities.

The impact on the Arab village was tremendous: an unprecedented boom in construction, modern furnishing, home appliances, roads, electricity, running water, telephones, health and education services, and banks. By 1976 the Arab population achieved a higher rate of per family income than Jewish families originating from Asia and Africa, and only slightly lower than the overall Israeli average.

Its fundamental malaise, however, the insolubility of its problem as a minority with national ambitions of its own, which run counter to the national aspirations of the host Jewish majority, was not relieved, and was intensified by the agitation against the Peace Treaty with Egypt.

A new phase in the identity crisis of Israel Arabs was marked in April 1976 with the outbreak of what came to be known as the "Day of the Land." What was to be a protest by the Arabs in the Galilee against what they termed "expropriation of their land," grew into the Communist instigated political agitation, where the Arabs' legitimate desire to maintain control of their lands was overshadowed by the irredentist slogan "We shall liberate you, O Galilee!" This outburst, which resulted in loss of life and left an indelible residue in the hearts of Israeli Arabs, was accompanied by concurrent wide-scale demonstrations in the cities of Judea and Samaria, in support of their "oppressed brethren" in Israel proper. These combined disturbances were hailed throughout the Arab world as an "uprising of the Palestinian people" on both sides of Israel's pre-1967 borders, against "Israeli occupation."

This open ideological linkage between Israeli Arabs and the Arabs in the Administered Territories of Judea and Samaria was one of the most dramatic developments since 1976.

The "Day of the Land" brought into the explicit realm thenceforth implicit and latent unity of destiny that the two branches of the same people carried in their hearts. The acclaim it received from other Arabs added to it an aura of an all-Arab national struggle which in turn tended to reinforce the Palestinian and Israeli Arabs in the virulence of their anti-Israeli slogans. More and more Arab-Israeli youth, under the impact of the 1973 war and the prominence of the PLO, coupled with the awakening of the Palestinians in the Administered Territories, were now more inclined than before to throw in their lot with the population of the Territories, under the unifying umbrella of "Free democratic Palestine" in both its political and symbolic meanings.

These trends became manifest in the elections of 1976 in Judea and Samaria, and in the Israeli elections of 1977. In the former, a new and young local leadership rose, which swept aside the traditional patriarchal leadership, and announced in no uncertain terms its sympathy with, if not its formal affiliation to, the PLO. During the 1977 elections, extreme pro-PLO elements among the Arabs either gave their vote to the Rakaḥ party, or altogether boycotted the elections, as Rakaḥ seemed too moderate for them, and not nationalist enough to cope with the mood of the times. Thus, while in the previous elections (1973), some 80% of the Arab-Israeli population cast their votes, this time some 72% only went to the polls, the difference being attributed to the boycott by extremist elements. Rakaḥ gained more votes than in the previous elections, nearly enough to win them a fifth seat in the Knesset.

The "liberal policy" which was devised by the government, and implemented through the Office of the Prime Minister's Adviser for Arab Affairs, far from contributing to the integration of the Arabs in Israeli society, by, for example, an inculcation of Israeli values into the Arab-Israeli population, perpetuated the gap and alienation between them. The fact that the Arabs enjoyed civil rights, such as the right to vote and to higher education, but were exempt from national duties such as military service, created two societies in Israel: Jewish "insiders" and Arab "outsiders." If the acquisition of Israeli citizenship and of civil rights could be made contingent upon the fulfillment of one's national duties on the one hand, and if all channels of national promotion in the army and bureaucracy were open to the Arabs, on the other, only then would conditions be created for a genuine integration. One has to realize, however, that because of the ongoing Arab-Israeli conflict and the national sensitivities involved, the Arabs in Israel, who now felt more and more akin to the Palestinian Arabs in general, would not be made to embrace Israeli values in one stroke. The Arab students' demonstrations on Israeli campuses, and their flat refusal to nightwatch in university dormitories where they are admitted for lodging, were only a few manifestations of these sentiments.

ARABS IN THE ADMINISTERED TERRITORIES. The political turnabout, as expressed in the municipal elections of 1976, made the most dramatic imprint on the West Bank, and by extension on almost all the population of the Administered Territories. The elections of 1976, despite their lower turnout, still gave a strong indication of the transformation that came about in the Territories, under the umbrella of Israeli occupation. The new city councilors were younger, more educated, and more openly inclined to support the PLO than their predecessors. In the West Bank, the mayors enjoyed a higher prestige than ever before, not only because of the disappearance of the intermediary District Commissioners who used to separate them from the central government under Jordanian rule, but also due to their peculiar position as the sole elected representatives of the Arab population in the Administered Territories. Thus, although they were ostensibly leaders on the local level only, and assumed to refrain from national "high politics," they implicated themselves more and or less openly in political matters having nothing to do with such topics as roads, sewers, taxation, and water supply. They, in fact, played the role of intermediaries between the Israeli military governors and the people; they made no secret of their journeys to Jordan, and they took up public positions on matters of major political significance, although they were prohibited from organizing, initiating, or participating in regular political activity, via political parties.

It is true, however, that despite the more extreme anti-Israel stance adopted by the new municipal leadership, life exigencies made the modus vivendi between them and the Israeli authorities imperative. Thus, political utterances apart, the level of acts of terror decreased compared with 1976 and 1977, and the propensity for the continued normalization of daily life in the Administered Territories did not seem to have been adversely affected. Even the events of the Machpelah Cave in Hebron, on Yom Kippur of 1976, in which an Israeli Torah Scroll was torn by an Arab mob, was played down by the then mayor of Hebron, Kawasmeh, his noted anti-Israel positions not withstanding.

Another manifestation of the pragmatic approach of the new leadership of the West Bank was the fact that despite its avowed support of the Palestinian Revolution as the only representative of the Palestinian people, and the implication of their subservient role to the central institutions of the PLO, they continued, nevertheless, to pay homage to King Hussein and to raise funds in the Gulf States, thus exposing the relationship of the Arab population with the anti-revolutionary regimes in the Arab world.

A new element of uncertainty and expectation – if not hope – was injected into this situation upon the visit to Israel of President Sadat, in November 1977. If on the one hand suspicion, skepticism, and sometimes hostility were evinced by the Palestinian public vis-à-vis Sadat, whose dramatic move caused consternation in the Rejection Front in general, and in the Palestinian establishment in particular, on the other hand, new hopes seemed to glitter for other Palestinians who hurried to dispatch successive delegations to Cairo, both to voice their support for his bold initiative and to elicit a pledge that their cause would not be eroded in the process. These delegations represented various strata of the West Bank and the Gaza Strip populations, although the mayors, who are on record as the staunchest proponents of the PLO, obviously refrained from joining them.

Again, as in the case of the Arabs in Israel proper, no clear-cut policy was applied whereby rewards and punishments were meted out to the Arab population of the Territories in accordance with their conduct. Certainly, no one expected them to love or welcome their Israeli occupiers or even to accept their rule on an indefinite basis. But no one could expect Israel either to go out of her way in her policy of "liberalization," of technological development, agricultural advancement, expansion of health and other services, let alone universal suffrage.

A military government is obligated to maintain the laws and the level of services that had existed prior to the occupation, but is under no constraint to improve them at a tremendous cost, only to win ingratitude and hatred. Their universal application turns them into a matter of course, and only elicits more demands for more improvements and creates more expectation for more rights, political and otherwise, which when withheld can only provoke frustration and more enmity.

The best negative example of this is seen in the West Bank election of 1976 in which the base of voters was broadened, compared to Jordanian times, and free campaigning was allowed. But when the results of the vote became known, a great embarrassment, to say the least, befell the Israeli public. The choice was very simple: either one is "liberal," allows free elections, and is prepared to bear the consequences, or one bans the elections altogether as long as military rule obtains. If the elections are truly free, then the first implication is that the voting population wants to rid itself of the military government. To bear the consequences means, in this case, to respond to the sentiments and needs expressed in these elections, i.e., to grant to the population self-rule, by its elected representatives, on the basis of their political platform, and this, in principle, was the idea underlying the peace proposals of the Israeli government.

To sum up, the Arab population of Israel and the Arabs in the Administered Territories gradually drew closer to one another under the impact of rising Palestinian nationalism and the mounting Arab and Islamic self-confidence in the wake of the 1973 War. To contain this political-minded population, as a minority devoid of national rights, under Israeli rule, seemed to become a "mission impossible." The autonomy which was proposed at the Camp David negotiations remained unacceptable to the PLO and leaders of the West Bank Arabs.

[Raphael Israeli]

From the 1980s to the mid-1990s

ISRAEL. In the early 1990s the Arab population of Israel was close to 730,000 (compared to 150,000 when the state was established, and excluding the East Jerusalem Arabs who are not citizens of Israel, estimated in 1993 to number 170,000).

During the 1980s the social and political consciousness of the Israeli Arabs crystallized, having been deeply influenced by pivotal political events in the region: the Lebanon War (1982–83), the Intifada in the Administered Territories (1987 on), and the Gulf crisis and war (1990–91). Despite the high tension these events created in the relations between Jews and Arabs in general, the Israeli Arabs became more integrated and more involved in the life of the state. They were seriously opposed to the war against the PLO in Lebanon, expressed in various ways by solidarity with the Intifada in the Administered Territories, and demonstrated sympathy for Saddam Hussein, but all of this did not lead to deep rifts between them and the Israeli-Jewish establishment. In many ways the opposite is true. Israeli Arabs conducted their political struggle through legitimate channels while emphasizing their being Israeli citizens. Their fight took the form of opposition to government policy and stressing their separate national identity while desirous of striving for principles of equality within the Israeli democratic frameworks.

The nature of the Israeli Arabs' struggles is best exemplified by the Intifada which engulfed the entire area of Judea, Samaria, East Jerusalem, and the Gaza Region, but in which Israeli Arabs did not take part. The manifestations of civil disobedience in the Administered Territories did not appear at all among the Israeli Arabs. Although there were occasional instances of rock throwing or the waving of the Palestinian flag in Arab settlements in Israel, it can still be said that the Israeli Arabs did not participate in the Intifada.

The separate identity of Arab citizens of Israel (from that of the Administered Territories' Arabs) was given expression in the establishment of new public bodies and in the founding of political parties and social movements. In 1982, in the wake of the Lebanon War, a "Supreme Watch Committee" was set up which in the 1980s turned into a quasi-representative body for the entire Arab population of Israel. This grew out of the committee of Arab mayors and gradually took on high political and social standing. Its members were the heads of the Arab locales, Arab Knesset members from all parties, the Arab representatives in the Histadrut, and leaders of various political movements. The committee had no recognized legal standing and reached its decisions most often by general agreement, but it had great prestige and influence. It made the decisions to give assistance of a humanitarian nature to Administered Territory residents and to express identification with their struggle, took decisions on the behavior of the Arab populace on memorial days and on the annual Land Day, and also discussed the issues of readying the Arab public for elections to the Knesset, the Histadrut, and the city and village councils.

While in previous years the Israeli authorities did everything possible to prevent the establishment of separate Arab bodies for fear of the consolidation of Arab nationalism hostile to the state, from the early 1980s on the Israeli regime was tolerant on this issue. The members of the Israeli Arabs' Supreme Watch Committee acted in concert (not officially) with factors within the overall Israeli social and political system.

In contrast to the first decades of the state in which the Israeli Arabs were divided generally into supporters of the Communist party or supporters of Zionist parties, in the 1980s a different party-political structure took shape. The Communist party declined, with the decline of the Communist regimes. Its position was claimed by two movements of an Arab-National nature, namely, "The Progressive List for Peace" (initially a Jewish-Arab party) and the "Democratic List" (led by Abd al-Wahab Darousheh who left the Labor party). A more important change came with the rise of a new powerful factor – the Islamic Movement. This movement did not compete in Knesset elections; its strength was seen in the election campaigns for the local authorities. The Islamic Movement won, among others, the mayoralty of Umm al-Fahm as well as the chairmanship of other councils mainly in the central district bordering Samaria. In Galilee, with its high concentration of Christians, the Islamic Movement had only modest success. The movement rose against the background of the flourishing of similar movements throughout the Arab east. The ideological stances of the Islamic Movement in Israel were more moderate than those of its sister movements in the Administered Territories, the Hamas and the Islamic Jihad, which called for violent struggle against the state.

The 1980s were a time of significant development in the local rule in Israeli Arab villages. Seventeen new authorities (around one-quarter of all Arab authorities in the country) were established. In some places the locality's status was changed and large settlements were recognized as cities. Although the average socio-economic standing of the Arab public was still lower than that of the Jews, there was accelerated development of various public services.

ADMINISTERED TERRITORIES. At the start of the 1980s a gap, which became even wider, opened between the Israeli administration and the Palestinians' leaders and their institutions in Judea, Samaria, and the Gaza Region. Talks about instituting autonomy in the Administered Territories according to the Camp David Accords ceased when no real progress was made. Israel proposed personal autonomy, for the residents only, with no territorial ramifications, while the Egyptian proposals spoke of Palestinian administration which would in effect lead to total Israeli withdrawal from the territories. When Ariel Sharon was defense minister (in the second Likud government elected in 1981), there were many settlement campaigns.

The most prominent change in the Territories in 1981–84 was the emergence of village leagues. The Israeli administration which nurtured them saw these leagues as representing the silent majority of the inhabitants of the villages in Judea and Samaria who ostensibly opposed the preeminence of the PLO-supporting radical city dwellers. The government gave the heads of the leagues and their activists wide authority and budgets, and residents were directed to the leagues in order to obtain permits and recommendations for various petitions to the administration.

The village leagues attracted marginal members of the Palestinian population. Many people saw them as a collection of doubtful individuals collaborating with the Israeli regime. In order to protect the league people, the Israeli administration allowed their leaders to start militias which were given weapons for self-defense by the Israel Defense Forces (IDF). In March 1982 Jordan published an official report according to which membership in village leagues would be considered an act of treason punishable by death. This led to the collapse of the leagues, some of whose major activists had previously been considered traditionally loyal to the rule in Amman. After 1984 the Israel administration gradually ceased supporting the leagues. In the mid-1980s the leagues' activities were greatly reduced, and they are remembered as the only episode in which the Israeli administration tried to encourage a political group in the territories.

The Lebanon War that began in June 1982 with the aim of damaging the PLO organizational infrastructure succeeded in effecting the removal of its headquarters and offices from Lebanon.

The events in Lebanon led to closer relations between the PLO and Jordan as well as to an improvement in the relations between the Administered Territories' residents and the Jordanian government. In Amman the work of the Jordan-PLO committee became regularized, and large sums of money were poured into the territories. The Jordanian Parliament convened in Jan. 1984 for the first time in nine years, with representatives from the West Bank.

In the Administered Territories the Lebanon War gave rise to a gradual increase in disturbances and acts of terror against Israel. Elements in the Israel military tendered the explanation that the retreat from Lebanon under terrorist pressure and attrition had reinforced the feeling among young Arabs that it was possible to fight against Israel using those means. Immediately after two Jews were killed, an underground group of Jewish settlers attacked the Muslim college in Hebron, killing three Arab students and wounding several. The police and security services captured members of a "Jewish underground" who confessed to a number of acts against Arabs, including mayors of cities, and to planning to blow up the Dome of the Rock.

In early 1985 an agreement was signed by which the Popular Front for the Liberation of Palestine–The General Command, led by Aḥmad Jibril, released the few Israeli prisoners of war from the Lebanon War and Israel freed from Israeli prisons 1,150 prisoners convicted of membership in terrorist organizations and of carrying out terrorist acts. Most of the Arabs returned to their homes in the Administered Territories and within Israel and were not deported. The Palestinian public saw this as a great victory.

After the breakdown of an agreement between King Hussein and Arafat in Feb. 1986, the Jordanians increased efforts to acquire influence in the Administered Territories. The Jordan government published a five-year plan for the territories' development while at the same time announcing the closure of the PLO office in Amman.

On Dec. 9, 1987, the popular rebellion, the Intifada ("shaking off"), broke out in the Administered Territories. On that day an Israeli truck ran over four Arab workers from the Gaza Region as they returned from work in Israel. Three days earlier an Israeli merchant had been stabbed to death in Gaza, and a rumor ran among the Arab populace that the traffic accident was really an Israeli act of revenge. During the funerals wild disturbances broke out during which another three Gaza residents were killed.

Besides the broad economic, social, and political circumstances which led to the uprising, there were other contributory developments. During summer and fall 1987 the U.S. government did not succeed in promoting any ideas towards a settlement in the region. In November an Arab summit meeting took place in Amman which disappointed the Palestinians, since it refrained from discussing their issues. At the end of November a young Palestinian coming from Lebanon managed to infiltrate an Israeli army camp near Kiryat Shemonah by use of a glider. He shot and killed six Israeli soldiers before being killed. The Administered Territories populace was thrilled by the success of this suicide mission as well as by the deaths of Israeli soldiers and the escape from prison of a number of security prisoners connected to the Islamic extremists from Gaza.

The first weeks of the Intifada were characterized by spontaneous large-scale outbursts of demonstrations along with commercial and school strikes throughout the territories and in East Jerusalem. No organization or guiding hand was behind this. Handbills were printed daily, slogans were painted on walls, and calls were heard to fight against Israeli rule. Almost daily reports were received of Arabs injured in clashes with Israeli soldiers. World media showed increased interest. Even during the first month Israel security forces arrested hundreds of Arabs suspected of instigating strikes and demonstrations, and on Jan. 3, 1988, expulsion orders against nine Administered Territories activists were issued. The Israeli measures did not lead to any calming down of the situation and the foment in the Administered Territories reached new heights.

During February–March 1988 there were indications of the intent to turn the uprising into organized civil disobedience against Israeli rule. Handbills signed by a body called "The United Intifada Command" began to appear with instructions to the people. Representatives of the different PLO factions and activists from the Islamic movements took part in the Command. Announcements were broadcast on a number of PLO radio stations, and the youths who heard them printed transcripts, photocopied them, and distributed them in cities, villages, and refugee camps.

The civil disobedience which coalesced at the start of the Intifada was organized by activists sympathetic to the PLO with the aim of creating the widest breach possible between the Arab-Palestinian population and the institutions of the Israeli administration. Most of the Administered Territories' educational institutes, including the universities and colleges, were closed by military orders in the middle of the 1988 school year since they were hotbeds for demonstrations, and in effect the educational system was shut down. Heavy pressure was applied on other Arabs employed by the Israeli administration to leave their jobs. Particularly targeted were those who came into contact with the broad public. Workers of the Department of Motor Vehicles, those who check and test drivers and vehicles, were asked to quit. The same was true for workers in taxation departments, in civil courts, and offices in the Israeli administration civil service system. Those who did not quit received threats; stones and Molotov cocktails were thrown at their homes.

One of the areas of civil disobedience intended to lead to a break between the residents and the Israeli regime was the declaration of a boycott on all Israel-made goods. The tradesmen were requested to rid themselves of all products bought or made in Israel for which a local substitute could be found. In addition, the residents were asked to try to avoid turning to the Israeli authorities on any issue whatsoever, to shun the civil courts operating within the framework of the Israel Civil Administration, and to refrain as much as possible from working in Israel and from trading with Israelis.

Unified Intifada Command instructed the residents to institute an austerity regime. It was forbidden to hold weddings with many guests or have other parties. The purchase of luxury items, including new cars, was interdicted. The inhabitants were requested to avoid going out for recreation, to refrain from seeking entertainment, not to eat in restaurants and not to visit the seashore or vacation spots in Israel. In many places Arabs who had private gardens were made to uproot shrubs and flowers and tear out grass in order to make room to plant vegetables for home use to replace the Israel produce.

Storekeepers were ordered to keep their stores closed almost completely and to open them only as directed in the handbills. Gradually an arrangement took shape whereby it was permitted to open businesses for three hours in the morning and only on those days on which there was no general strike. In the afternoons and on the frequent strike days all public institutions, such as municipalities and public transportation, were shut down. Even owners of private cars were told not to drive on the roads.

All of these moves were prompted by "Popular Committees" formed in villages, refugee camps, and urban neighborhoods. Many of the committees were based on youth organization clubs found practically everywhere in the Administered Territories: the (PLO) "Shabiba" and other groups identified with the left-wing Palestinians organizations.

Popular education committees were set up to arrange for school-like frameworks in private houses in place of the closed schools. Hundreds of adjudication committees were set up to which the residents were to turn in place of the courts to settle disputes. The local committees tried to create the impression of creating the structure of an independent Palestinian regime. They set up roadblocks at entrances to villages which they declared "liberated territory."

The Intifada's political effects became more noticeable in summer 1988. At the end of May, U.S. Assistant Secretary of State Richard Murphy, responsible for dealing with the region's affairs, announced that the U.S. would consider opening a dialogue with the PLO on the condition that the organization accept UN resolutions 232 and 338 and condemn the use of terror. At the end of July, King Hussein announced that his country had no claims on the West Bank and was in effect breaking relations with the Administered Territories. Residents of Judea, Samaria, and East Jerusalem, most of whom were still Jordanian citizens, feared that this decision would prove detrimental to them but in actuality it did them relatively little harm. Pension payments to Jordanian civil servants in the territories continued as usual as did export (mainly agricultural produce) from the territories to the eastern side of the Jordan. Administered Territory residents could continue to use their Jordanian passports.

This break was a political victory for the Palestinian national leadership in the Administered Territories and for the PLO command in Tunis, for this was an unequivocal declaration that the PLO institutions were the only and sole representations for territory residents, with no challenge to this from Jordan.

The Jordanian statement and the continued Intifada paved the way for the dramatic decisions by the Palestinian National Council (PNC), meeting in Algiers. Intifada activists applied great pressure to the PLO leaders to transform the successes of civil disobedience into political achievements. On Nov. 15 the PNC declared the "establishment of an independent state" and its acceptance of UN resolution 242. The latter made it possible for Arafat to appear before the UN assembly meeting in Geneva in Dec. 1988. At a press meeting held there he declared that the meaning of the PNC decision was recognition of the State of Israel and demurring from acts of terror. Arafat's statement had been coordinated with the U.S. which announced that the U.S. was opening a dialogue with the PLO. This development was the zenith of the Intifada's political achievements.

In the Administered Territories the Palestinian declaration of independence was accepted enthusiastically and general support was given to the Palestinian leadership's new political line. On December 9, with the first anniversary of the Intifada, sources in the Administered Territories claimed that over the course of the year more than 300 Arabs had been killed and some 20,000 injured. Israel gave similar figures. The number of Arabs arrested or detained in Israeli prisons was close to 12,000.

During the Intifada's second year (1989) cracks and internal dissension began to show. One of the most salient was the phenomenon of intra-Arab murders of people suspected of collaborating with the Israeli rule. The ongoing Intifada pattern yielded great suffering for the Administered Territory residents. The suspension of the education system, lengthy strikes, and severe Israeli punitive measures all led to a lowering of the standard of living across the board. In some places there were residents who refused to comply with the demands of the United Command leaflets and who tried to oppose the young activists' directives.

While in 1988 some 20 suspected collaborators were murdered, in 1989 the victims numbered over 150. In 1990 and 1991, the number of Palestinians killed by security forces declined, while there was a steep increase in those killed by other Arabs as suspected collaborators. By the start of 1992 the number of Arabs killed during the Intifada was 2,000 – 600 of whom had been murdered as suspected collaborators.

The severe hardships suffered by the people led, as early as the second year of the Intifada, to calls for its cessation in return for the start of political negotiations. In early 1989 exploratory moves were made towards creating an Israeli political program which would bring calm to Judea, Samaria, and Gaza. A number of prominent Palestinians in the Administered Territories were informed of the details of the plan fashioned by Defense Minister Yiẓḥak Rabin. It included a proposal to hold general elections in the territories as an initial step towards designating a representation accepted by the Arab presidents. After a series of contacts and recommendations raised by representatives of the U.S. and Egyptian president Hosni Mubarak, sharp differences of opinion broke out within the Israeli government (regarding East Jerusalem residents' participation in the elections in the territories) leading eventually to the dissolution of the National Unity Government.

The atmosphere in the Administered Territories changed from the end of 1989 as the result of the upheavals taking place in Eastern Europe. For nearly 40 years the Communist bloc countries had served as strong political support for sizable parts of the Arab world, including the Palestinians, besides providing aid in the form of money, weapons, military training, and grants to students. As those countries began to collapse, a feeling of dismay and confusion arose among the Palestinians as the Eastern European countries established diplomatic relations with the State of Israel and a large wave of emigration of Jews from the Former Soviet Union was set into motion.

In 1990 calls were heard in the Administered Territories for a return to the "armed struggle" against Israel, that is, acts of terror and the use of firearms. On June 1 terrorist cells belonging to the pro-Iraqi organizations linked to the PLO tried to attack Israeli bathers on the southern shores of the country. In the wake of this (abortive) attempt, the American administration suspended its dialogue with the PLO whose leadership refused to oust from its ranks Abu al-Abbas, the head of the organization taking responsibility for this act.

The Intifada began to lose the public enthusiasm which had characterized its beginning. Mass demonstration ceased. Public opinion and the world media paid attention to happenings in Eastern Europe and largely stopped covering the Middle East. Gradually schooling was resumed on a regular basis, and in the large cities Intifada activists allowed the storekeepers to keep their stores open for longer hours. To a significant degree life returned to what it had been prior to the outbreak of the popular uprising.

On August 2, 1990, a dramatic change occurred with Iraq's conquest of Kuwait. The Palestinian population and its leadership took a stance in favor of Iraq and its ruler Saddam Hussein who, from the outset of the crisis, linked the solution of the problem he had created in the Gulf with a solution to the Palestinian problem. The Kingdom of Jordan with its large Palestinian population also joined the supporters of Iraq.

During the continuing tension in the Gulf, a serious incident occurred in the Old City of Jerusalem. On the broad plaza of the Temple Mount mosques there erupted a demonstration of Muslim worshipers who began to throw rocks on Jewish worshippers at the Western Wall. Israeli soldiers and policemen who broke into the plaza shot 18 Arabs to death and wounded dozens of others. The incident was prompted by rumors concerning the activity of a group of Israelis called the "Temple Mount Faithful" which had demanded over the years removing the control of the mosques to Israeli authorities.

The incident sparked new foment in the Administered Territories. Orthodox Muslim groups, which had organized themselves into the "Islamic Resistance Movement" (whose Arabic initials form "Hamas"), had been prominent. They even published a manifest claiming that all of the country's land was Muslim *hekdesh* (consecrated property) meaning that the very existence of the State of Israel contradicted Islamic teachings. Stabbing attacks on Israelis by Muslim extremists became evermore frequent. In most cases the Administered Territories attackers acted alone, unprompted by any organization and ready to die as a martyr. Attempting to thwart these strikes, Israeli security authorities limited the right of free passage of Administered Territories Arabs into pre-1967 Israel.

The number of Administered Territories inhabitants working in the Israeli economy dropped from 130,000 to 50,000 in the period following, with the average number in the early 1990s being about 80,000. The Israeli public became more fearful of employing Arabs from the Administered Territories as knifing attacks by young Administered Territories Arabs occurred from time to time.

The Administered Territories' economic situation was severely affected by the Gulf War events. Besides limitations on working in Israel, there was an almost complete halt of the transfer of money to the Administered Territories by relatives working in the Gulf oil-producing countries. After the war, there began mass expulsions of Palestinians who had worked in Kuwait. Some 20,000 who had Israeli Military Administration identity cards rejoined their families in the Administered Territories. The great need in Israel for construction workers to erect housing for new immigrants somewhat alleviated the Administered Territories economic distress.

Following the outcome of the Gulf War, political activity in the region aimed at convening a peace conference stepped up. The Palestinian stances in the new world order, after the Soviet Union's collapse and Iraq's defeat, became more flexible and allowed for a compromise with Israeli demands. With American mediation a Palestinian delegation was composed with members from the Administered Territories and quasi-official East Jerusalem advisers.

At the end of Oct. 1991 the Palestinian delegation from the Administered Territories, without PLO representatives, took part in the Madrid peace conference in which delegations and observers from most Arab countries participated. Additional meetings were held throughout 1992 in Washington, Moscow, and other world capitals. The discussions encountered many stumbling blocks. The main demand of the Administered Territories delegates was the cessation of the widespread settlement activity in the Administered Territories sponsored by the Israel government. Opposition to the peace process, rooted in Muslim extremist circles, also developed in the Administered Territories.

[Daniel Rubinstein]

Towards the end of 1995 the number of Israel Arabs was approaching one million. The figure is based on data from the Israel Central Bureau of Statistics which reports on the number of "non-Jews" living within the State of Israel. This figure includes the Arabs living in Jerusalem, numbering some 170,000, the great majority of whom are not citizens of Israel; and members of other communities: about 100,000 Druze; some 160,000 Arab Christians; and the small, non-Arab Christian population, such as the Armenians and the various church-affiliated individuals who reside permanently in Israel. According to the forecast of the Central Bureau of Statistics, the non-Jewish population of Israel was to reach 1.14 million by 2005 when it would constitute some 22% of the Israel population as compared to 18% in the mid-1990s.

Changes occurring among the Arab population of Israel in the first half of the 1990s derived from the political and socio-economic processes taking place in Israel during that period, the most important being the peace process with the PLO and the Arab states begun at the Madrid conference in the fall of 1991.

During the first half of the 1990s there were three types of elections, affording an insight into political and social trends among Israel Arabs: the elections for the 13th Knesset held in June 1992, the municipal elections of November 1993, and the Histadrut elections in May 1994.

The most important of these was the Knesset elections of 1992 which took place in the midst of peace talks started at the Madrid conference. This time the Israel Arab population which, for the most part, traditionally votes for the parties seen as part of the left-wing bloc, and only to a small extent for right-wing parties, played a key role in the political turnover in Israel. After 15 years of Likud rule, partially in conjunction with the Labor party, Labor, under the leadership of Yiẓḥak Rabin, acceded to power. This turnover was possible, among other reasons, because of the Arab votes which went to the left-wing parties (Labor and Meretz), but even more decisively to the fact that two parties, almost all of whose voters are Arabs, held the balance of power when it came to composing the coalition government. The two parties are the Democratic Front for Equality (Ḥadash), at the heart of which is the veteran Communist party, and the Arab Democratic Party (Mada), headed by the former Labor party member Abd al-Wahab Darousheh, which together gained five seats and formed an "obstructive bloc" in the Knesset barring the way to forming any government with the right-wing or religious parties. The Labor party won 44 seats in the Knesset elections, Meretz (made up of Mapam, Ratz, and Shinui) gained 12, Ḥadash, 3, and Mada, 2. This totaled 61 creating for the first time a situation whereby the votes of the Arabs would be the critical in the formation of a government, headed by either Labor or by Likud.

Through a series of parliamentary arrangements, a precedent was established in 1992 whereby there was partial coalition cooperation between the Labor party and Ḥadash and Mada. These Arab parties which in the past had been considered invalid for coalition membership, since they were considered to have a nationalist Arab orientation, became in the Thirteenth Knesset part of the bloc supporting the government. They were not co-opted to the government, but promised to support it, thus enabling Prime Minister Rabin to receive partial support from religious Knesset members (from the Shas party) and a faction which broke away from Zomet (called Ye'ud). Ḥadash and Mada actually had no choice but to support the Labor government led by Rabin, which achieved a certain equilibrium by cooperating with the "obstructive bloc." Although during the Thirteenth Knesset there were instances in which these factions threatened to bring the government down, as of summer 1995 the unity of this bloc was maintained, so that for the first time in Israel's history the Arab voters achieved a position of significant influence over Israeli policy.

The Arab population has always been occupied with two aspects: the national one closely linked to the Arab-Israel conflict and the struggle of Israeli Arabs for equal rights. Regarding the first, most scholars of the Israeli Arab population feel that the contribution of the Israeli Arabs and their Knesset representatives towards the change of the government's attitude toward the PLO is most important. The existence of the "obstructive bloc" made it easier for the government to implement the policy of the Oslo agreement: recognition of the PLO, the withdrawal from Gaza, and the continuation of negotiations with the Palestinian movement. At least in one instance – the attempt by the government to expropriate land in East Jerusalem in May 1995 – the Knesset members of Ḥadash and Mada succeeded in bringing about the cancellation of the expropriation after they proposed a no-confidence vote in the government. This victory was proof of their power and was considered by many as a milestone in the history of Israeli parliamentarism.

Examination of the second topic, the struggle for equality, also reveals important achievements for Israel Arabs during this period. Some of the gains derived from the coalition agreements ensured the existence of the "obstructive bloc." Surveys made in early 1995 showed that there had been an increase of 200% in the allotments granted to Arab municipalities in relation to the period during which the previous government was in power. A significant change occurred in the apportioning of resources to the Arab sector for various educational purposes, and progress was made towards the equality of Arab education with that of the Jewish system. More buildings and classrooms were added, equipment was purchased, and more jobs were allocated. Steps were taken towards equalizing the child allotments paid by National Insurance to those given Jewish families. According to previous legislation, from the 1970s, a family with at least one member defined as a "former army server" receives an addition to child allotments until the child reaches 18. Since the vast majority of Israel Arabs do not serve in the army, they were not eligible for this supplemental payment. In line with the Rabin government policy, it was decided that within three years this gap should be eliminated.

The 1995 surveys also indicated a growing momentum in the level of infrastructure development in the Arab sector, particularly in the paving of roads and in water and sewage systems. In addition, there has been significant advance in the integration of Arabs in government jobs and according to a special government decision Arabs will fill posts in various government offices. Another problem which the Rabin government dealt with was the granting of recognition to a series of Arab villages officially unrecognized and therefore ineligible for government services.

There is still a sizable gap between Arabs and Jews concerning the allotment of resources and government handling of issues in all the areas mentioned, but considerable progress was made towards equality during the first half of the 1990s. Not all of the achievements derive from the significance of the "obstructive bloc" in the Knesset. The decision to make the Arab municipality allotments equal to those of the Jews, for instance, was already taken by the Shamir government in 1991, and even during the Rabin administration the heads of Arab municipalities complained that little progress had been made on this issue. They held a lengthy strike (in July–August 1994) opposite the Prime Minister's Office in Jerusalem. The data also attest to the fact that the rate of economic development and investments in the Arab sector were very low in comparison to the average in Israel. The level of teaching and the pupils' achievements in the Arab schools fell far below the average. Many of the problems with the Bedouin villages in the Negev had not been solved.

The peace process and the security problems which developed after the Oslo agreement led to a series of changes among Israel Arabs. Following terrorist attacks, from 1990 on, the governments of Israel (beginning with that of Shamir and then Rabin's) instituted a policy of implementing a *seger* ("lockout") on residents of the Gaza Strip and Judea and Samaria. Gradually the periods of the "lockouts" grew until they were to a large extent permanent. As part of the security "lockout," residents of Gaza and the West Bank were prohibited from entering the area of Israel proper. Also, to a high degree, it was forbidden to transport produce and merchandise from these Administered Territories to Israel as defined by the Green Line (the pre-1967 borders of the State). This policy led, for the first time since 1967, to a certain break between the Israel Arabs and the Palestinians in the Administered Territories. Moreover, the Arabs of Gaza gained Palestinian autonomy with many of the trappings of sovereignty and the ostensible contrast between them and the Israel Arabs grew, at least regarding their political status.

The physical separation between the Israel Arabs and those in the Administered Territories was accompanied by the consciousness of the Israel Arabs in being separate and their consciousness of being a social unit more closely linked to the State of Israel and cut off from the Palestinian national experience. A number of studies published in Israel in 1994–95 indicated greater integration of the Israel Arabs within the state to the detriment of their attitude on the issue of Palestinian nationality. Despite the internal split among the Israel Arabs, there was almost total unity among them on the Declaration of Principles signed between Israel and the PLO. This support encompassed all of the Israel Arab organizations and parties and stood in contrast to the dissension and disagreements on the agreement with the Palestinians in Gaza and the West Bank. Some commentators deduced from that indications that the Israel Arabs do not consider themselves as directly involved in what takes place on the internal political level of the Palestinian public and its national movement. Representatives of the Israel Arabs often served as advisers and intercessors on problems and disagreements which arose in the Administered Territories, but always as observers from the side and not as those directly involved in the national or party problems in the Administered Territories.

Whereas the 1992 Knesset elections led to a revolution in the parliamentary status of the Israel Arabs, the municipal elections in November 1993 continued conservative trends. The most prominent was that Ḥadash with the veteran communists who had led the Israel Arabs for decades continued to be the leading movement among this population. Ḥadash candidates won in 12 of the municipal elections out of 56 in the Arab sector. The candidates of the Islamic Movement were chosen head of 5 councils. Candidates of the general lists (of the branches of the Jewish-Zionist parties in the Arab sector) won in 15 authorities (12 Labor, 2 Likud, and 1 Meretz). Candidates of the Progressive Movement (led by Muhammad Mi'ari) won in 3 local authorities and Mada candidates won in 6. The others elected elsewhere ran independently, with no link to any party or movement at all.

Within the system of municipal elections, in Israel in general and within the Arab sector in particular, there is great importance to local, family (clan), and personal considerations, and this tendency was reinforced with the institution of the system of direct election of local authority heads. Despite this, a general trend toward changes in the voting patterns could be discerned, and in this case it must be remembered that these elections were the only ones in which the Islamic Movement candidates took part. This movement became very much stronger among the Israel Arab population during the 1980s and achieved striking success in the previous local authority elections in 1989. In the years that followed there was a debate among movement activists as to whether to stand also for Knesset elections, but as the elections for the Thirteenth Knesset approached in 1992 the movement leaders decided not to present candidates. In May 1995 Islamic Movement activists met to discuss possible participation in the Knesset elections, with an eye on the coming 1996 elections. While the movement's leader, Sheikh Abdallah Nimer Darwish, supported the proposal to organize a party slate for the approaching elections, many opposed his proposal and to avoid a split within the movement it was decided not to make up an independent list from the movement. The group's leaders recommended, however, to the political bodies of Israel Arabs to join together in a combined list, and they allowed their supporters freedom of choice over whether to vote and whom to support.

The 1993 municipal elections showed that the dramatic momentum of growing support for the Islamic Movement had been halted. It did more or less maintain its strength, but apparently did not gain new supporters. The party that practically disappeared from the Israel Arab political map was the Progressive Movement for Peace which in previous years had threatened the dominance of Ḥadash (Rakaḥ) over the Arab population. As early as the 1992 Knesset elections, this party failed to pass the minimum percentage for gaining a seat, and in the municipal elections it failed completely. Not one of its candidates became head of a local authority in any Arab settlement and only a few of its people were elected to local councils.

The great success story of the local elections belonged to the candidates of the Arab Democratic Party (Mada), headed by Knesset member Abl al-Wahab Darousheh. In the previous municipal elections in 1989 Mada candidates won in two localities and in 1993, they took six.

The general picture coming into focus from these election results presented the halting of the Islamic Movement and the preservation of the power of the communists (Ḥadash) and the Jewish-Zionist parties. This again demonstrated the retention of the trend towards integration and involvement of Israel Arabs in the general political and social system in Israel. The increase in power of the extremely religious Muslims had threatened the way of life of many of the Israel Arabs who had adapted to a social life that included both men and women, the drinking of liquor at social parties, and other types of behavior forbidden by the extremist believers. Some scholars studying Israel society felt that this threat served as an important factor in the Communist party maintaining its strength (since most of its voters are Arabs), even at a time when most of these parties worldwide declined or disappeared.

The May 1994 elections of the Histadrut, the largest voluntary body in Israel, and their results provided additional proof of the integration of the Israel Arabs into the state, in the era of the peace process. Whereas in the previous Histadrut elections (November 1989) there was a faltering attempt to organize a joint list for all Israel Arabs, in 1994 the candidacy of the Israel-Arab sector was almost totally in conjunction with and involved with the all-Israel system. Some 220,000 Israel Arabs belong to the Histadrut, constituting about 15% of the membership. The percentage of Arabs voting was 55% (somewhat higher than the general average) and the important fact is that 78% of them voted for general (Jewish-Zionist) parties and only 22% for parties considered Arab. As among the Jewish population, so among the Arab, Ḥaim Ramon's list "Ḥayyim Ḥadashim" was strikingly victorious and won 26% of the Arab vote. Mada joined the Labor party in exchange for a promised 3% representation in Histadrut institutions, while Ḥadash, which set up a common list with the remnants of the Progressive List, upon hearing the election results immediately joined the coalition created by Ḥaim Ramon and his colleagues. In 1994, for the first time in Histadrut history, parties like Ḥadash and the Progressive List became part of the coalition guiding this important body. Many among the Arab population took this as a significant achievement for Arab Histadrut members.

[Daniel Rubinstein]

1995 to 2005

DEMOGRAPHY. *Population.* At the beginning of 2005 the Arab population of Israel numbered 1.337 million people (19% of the total population): 1.107 million Muslims (82% of the Arab population), 117,000 Christians (9%), and 113,000 Druze (9%).

The proportion of Muslims in the Arab population increased over the years from 70% at the end of the 1950s to 82% in 2005, the proportion of Christians decreased from 21% to 9%, and the proportion of Druze remained almost unchanged.

The internal breakdown of the Christian community in Israel is as follows: 37% Greek Catholic, 30% Greek Orthodox, 23% Latin Catholic, 5% Maronite, and 5% others.

According to a Central Bureau of Statistics forecast, in 2025 the Arab population is expected to number 2.32 million (33% of the total population), out of which Muslims will comprise 85%, Christians will comprise 7%, and Druze 8%.

Rate of Growth. In 2004, the annual rate of growth of the Arab population was 3.4%: 3.6% amongst Muslims, 1.9% amongst Christians, and 2.4% amongst Druze. This rate is one of the highest in the world, mainly because of the high rate of growth of the Bedouin population in the Negev (southern Israel) – about 5.5% per year. For comparison, the annual rate of growth of the Arabs in Syria and Jordan is 2.8% and in Egypt 2.1%.

Fertility. The total fertility rate among Druze has been declining since the 1960s. At the beginning of the 1960s the average number of births per Druze woman in Israel was 7.5. In 2003, however, the average number of births per Druze woman was only 2.9. This fertility rate is close to that of the Jewish and Christian populations (2.7 and 2.3, respectively), and lower than that of the Muslim population (an average of 4.5 births per woman).

As a result of high fertility rates, the Arab population is very young. Its median age is 19.7: 18.5 amongst Muslims, 22.7 amongst Druze, 27.9 amongst Christians. For comparison, the median age of the Jewish population is 30.3.

The relative proportion of Christians in the total Arab population of Israel has dropped drastically since the 1940s because of the decreasing fertility rate: from about 20% in 1949 to about 15% in 1972, and to less than 9% at the end of 2004.

In 2003, an Arab family totaled an average of 5.4 persons, almost two persons more than a Jewish family. The average number of persons in a Muslim family is 5.7, in a Druze family – 5.0, and in a Christian family – 3.9.

HEALTH. *Life Expectancy.* In 2003 life expectancy of Arab males was 74.6 years and that of Arab females 78.0 years, compared to 77.9 years for Jewish males and 81.8 years for Jewish females. Since the early 1980s, the life expectancy of the Arab population has increased by nearly four years.

Life expectancy of the Arab population in Israel is higher than in the neighboring Arab countries: Lebanon – 71.3 years for males and 74.4 years for females, Syria – 69.8 years for males and 72.1 years for females, Jordan – 68.9 years for males and 71.5 years for females, and Egypt – 65.3 years for males and 68.5 years for females.

Infant Mortality. In 2003 the infant mortality rate of the Arab population was 8.2 deaths per 1,000 live births (in 1980 it was 24.2 deaths per 1,000 live births). The decline in infant mortality resulted mainly from the improvements in environmental conditions, in the living standard, and in the level of education of the population. This rate was much lower than in the neighboring Arab countries, including the Palestinian Authority: 102 deaths per 1,000 live births in Iraq, 38 in Egypt, 27 in Lebanon, 26 in the Palestinian Authority, 22 in Jordan, and 18 in Syria. Nonetheless, the infant mortality rate of the Arab population in Israel was still twice as high as that of the Jewish population.

EDUCATION. In the past three decades the education level of the Arab population rose significantly. In 1970 half of this population had up to five years of schooling. In 2003, half of the Arab population had almost ten years of schooling.

The median number of years of schooling of the Arab population increased from 9 in 1990 to 11.1 in 2003. Among the Jewish population, the median increased from 11.9 to 12.6 during the same period. However, significant gaps between Jews and Arabs still exist. 26% of Arabs aged 25–34 studied more than 12 years, compared to 60% amongst Jews of the same age group.

In 2003 Arab students comprised 8.1% of all university students, 9.8% of the undergraduate students, 5.1% of the master's students, and 3.3% of the Ph.D. students.

The level of education of the Christian community is higher than that of the Muslim and Druze communities. 27% of the Christians have more than 12 years of schooling, with almost no difference between men and women, whereas among Muslims and Druze this rate is 14% (about 16% of the men and about 11% of the women).

As mentioned above, education statistics show wide disparities between Arab and Jewish students. The Arab school system is under-resourced: in 2004, only 7% of the Ministry of Education's budget was allocated to it, while the Arab population comprised 19% of the total population in Israel. The average number of Arab students per classroom is 32, compared to 27 for Jewish students. Disparities also affect funding for auxiliary education services and are reflected in achievements: the dropout rate among students aged 16–17 years is 40% for Arabs students and only 9% for Jewish students. The matriculation success rate of Arab students is 31.5%, compared to 45% amongst Jewish students.

GENERAL TRENDS. *Implications of the Peace Process.* The peace process of the 1990s exerted conflicting influences on the political orientation of the Arabs in Israel. The Palestinization process of the Arabs in Israel was weakened in terms of its external affinity. The recognition by Israel of the PLO and of the legitimate rights of the Palestinian people to self-determination and the establishment of the *Palestinian Authority represented the realization of the national platform of the Arabs in Israel as formulated during the 1970s and 1980s onward.

The Palestinian Authority maintained its link with the Arabs in Israel on various levels, such as the formation of a Liaison Office; hosting delegations of Israeli Arab political figures; visits by Palestinian public figures to Arab communities in Israel; and involvement in elections to the Knesset with the intention of influencing the Arab vote in Israel. However, the leadership of the PLO and the Palestinian Authority essentially maintained the traditional approach of excluding the Arab population of Israel from the peace talks and ignoring their cause.

Israeli Arab intellectuals and political elites reached the conclusion that the real solution to the Arab population's national aspirations was not necessarily found in the establishment of a future Palestinian state. This realization marked the start of a new process of directing the national resources of the Arab population inward, i.e., the localization of the national Palestinian struggle.

Israeli reality was not favorable to the Arabs. The ethnonational structure of the state, and the pronounced preference for the Jewish majority, prompted a policy of built-in discrimination and intentional exclusion vis-à-vis the Arab citizens. In the socioeconomic context, the gaps between Jews and Arabs widened. While Israeli governments from the start of the 1990s declared their commitment to deepening Jewish-Arab equality, in most cases this remained lip service only. In the political context, except for the Rabin-Peres tenure (1992–96), the Arab Knesset members and their parties were systematically sidelined not only by the governmental coalition members of the Right but also of the Left.

The Perceived Contradiction between the Idea of a Jewish and Democratic State. During the period under consideration, political discourse in Arab society focused, among other issues, on what was conceived, from an Arab point of view, as a built-in contradiction between the nature of Israel as a Jewish state and as a liberal democracy committed to the equality of all its citizens. Arab academicians and politicians across the entire political spectrum frequently questioned the viability of the model of "a Jewish and democratic state," pointing to its inherent weakness. The dilemma depicted acutely by them was how the Arab citizen could feel equal and identify with a state whose symbols, flag, and anthem were Jewish, and whose contents and identity were founded on an ethnic Jewish outlook and not on a collective Israeli outlook based on civil equality.

The discourse on the desirable nature of the State of Israel engendered various alternative models for a solution that would respond to and reflect the national needs of the Arab minority and to the built-in conflict between Israel's Jewish aspect and democracy.

Alternative Models. a) A state for all its citizens. The demand to annul Israel's Jewish-Zionist nature and replace it with a "state of all its citizens" model attained wide popularity, and was included in the platforms of most of the Arab parties from the 1990s. Nevertheless, this proposal remained a generalized slogan, without generating in-depth academic or political discussion. Conceivably, some of the politicians who supported it did not actually believe in the possibility of implementing it. Rather, it served them as a tactical means to stir the Jewish public and as a way of expressing the rising tide of rage over the gaps and over the disrespect and disregard of the government. Still, the demand to turn Israel into a "state of all its citizens" took hold among the public at large and was often voiced, albeit without any examination of the price involved in adopting it.

b) Autonomy. Notions of autonomy, endorsed by Arab academicians in the early 1990s, proposed granting the Arabs in Israel personal-cultural autonomy in the areas of education, communications, the use of Arabic, participation in drawing up development plans, the return of confiscated lands, and even the formation of a supreme political representative body by means of elections and territorial autonomy, which would include two regions – the Galilee and the "Triangle" area (in central Israel). These ideas failed initially to attract much support. Few continued to support the demand for territorial autonomy.

During the latter 1990s the demand for cultural autonomy gained popularity in political circles and among educators. Its advocates believed that it could relieve the fundamental problems of the Arab education system by bringing about a shift in the responsibility for Arab education, particularly regarding the question of contents and syllabi, traditionally supervised by the Jewish-controlled Ministry of Education, from Jewish to Arab officials.

c) National institutions. The deep rift in Jewish-Arab relations, caused by the bloody events of October 2000, in which 13 Arab citizens were killed in violent confrontations with the police (see below), as well as the ongoing government policy of neglect and especially the continuous sense of alienation, frustration, and bitterness, prompted some Arab politicians and intellectuals to reexamine the option of independent national institutions for the Arabs. However, public discourse on the institution-building process remained unfocused and has not undergone in-depth ideological exploration. Discussion has referred to "supreme and unified national institutions," "national and representative" institutions, and "constitutional" institutions.

Following the massive shunning of the polls by the Arab electorate in the February 2001 elections for prime minister demands mounted for alternative, non-Knesset representational channels, including a separate Arab parliament. The dogmatic faction of the Islamic movement, led by Sheikh Ra'id Salah, considered establishing an alternative social infrastructure which would be capable of relying on itself (see below). However, supporters of the notion of a separate parliament stressed that their intention was not detachment from the state, or separatism. From their point of view, the Arabs in Israel must set up national institutions for themselves since this was the only integrative way in which they could live in this state. The separatists' opponents, especially the Israeli Communist Party, rejected this line, saying that it served the radical Jewish Right and provided an excuse for the authorities to perpetuate discrimination and deprivation.

d) Bi-national state. Since the late 1990s, the option of a bi-national state has been mooted as an attainable alternative to the existing minority-majority relationship in the State of Israel. Some supporters of this idea restricted their model of a bi-national state to the borders of the Green Line. Accordingly, turning Israel into a bi-national state would involve a constitutional change granting both nations equal legislative status, canceling Israel's Jewish and Zionist character, and transforming Israel into a bilingual and multicultural state. Others suggested that a bi-national democratic state should include granting the Arabs in Israel the right to conduct their own cultural affairs and other matters distinctive to them independently.

e) National minority with collective rights. One of the major changes that the Arab population underwent in the 1990s expressed itself in the political and ideological parlor of the Arab elites. Thus the term "minorities" typically used by Israeli authorities to relate to the non-Jewish population began to be vigorously rejected as symbolizing Israel's intention of fostering internal disunity along the religious-ethnic division lines of the Muslim, Druze, Christian, Circassian, and Bedouin communities. Instead, a perception of the Arabs as a national collective with distinctive linguistic, cultural, and historic attributes has taken hold. The most widespread definition of this change focuses on the demand to recognize the Arab-Palestinian citizens of Israel as a national minority with collective rights. The practical evidence of this change is the demand not only for their due civil rights as individuals, but also for the associative or collective rights due them as a national minority.

Reopening the "1948 Files." a) Restoration of the memory of the Nakba. One of the most impressive aspects of the "return to 1948" phenomenon is the restoration of the collective historic memory of the *Nakba* – the perceived catastrophic loss of Palestine in the 1948 war. This changed reality was molded by three major factors: (1) the emergence of a new generation of Arabs who, unlike their predecessors, chose to highlight their national identity rather than water it down; (2) the implications of the Oslo process and the start of discussions about a permanent settlement, the refugee question, and the right of return; (3) the 50th anniversary celebrations of the State of Israel in 1998, which served as a powerful spur to the process.

Several central motifs recur in the narratives of Israeli Arabs vis-à-vis the significance of the *Nakba* on the emotional-national level. One is the perception of the *Nakba* memory not as a historic event that is over and done with, but rather a tragedy whose consequences continue to this day and whose victims are not only refugees in camps but also the Arab citizens in Israel. Another motif is the desire on the part of the Arabs in Israel for legitimization of the fact that 1948 marked not only a war of independence, sovereignty, and liberation for the Jews but also the terrible tragedy for the Arabs.

In practical terms, particularly following the 50th anniversary of the State of Israel, national-political activity focused on *Nakba* memorial ceremonies held on two dates – 5 Iyyar, the Hebrew date of Israel's Independence Day, and May 15, the date of the establishment of the state in the international calendar and the date assigned as *Nakba* Day. Ceremonies consisted mainly of pilgrimages to the sites of abandoned or destroyed villages, where their histories were recounted.

b) Revival of the displaced persons issue. Another significant manifestation of the trend toward opening the "1948 files" has been the revival, from the early 1990s, of the displaced persons (*al-muhajjarun*) issue, or "refugees in their own homeland" – those Palestinians who remained in Israeli territory during the 1948 war, or who returned after the war, but were unable to return to their original homes and villages, which had been abandoned or destroyed during the war.

The demand for the return of the displaced persons to their villages of origin was renewed following the start of the political process between Israel and the PLO in the early 1990s. The representatives of the displaced persons came to the conclusion that their salvation would not come from the PLO and that the struggle for the right of return would have a better chance if it were waged in Israel, as a sophisticated use of the Israeli judiciary system.

The "internal refugees" in Israel had begun to organize in the early 1990s with the establishment of a Countrywide Committee for the Protection of the Rights of the Displaced Persons in Israel. Activities included organized visits to the sites of the abandoned villages and the preservation of remaining sites and ruins at the villages, especially mosques, churches, and cemeteries.

c) Struggle for land. The acuteness of the land issue intensified during the 1990s, when government inaction and the inability of the Arab local councils to provide solutions to housing distress exacerbated the frustration and evoked rising protest against continuing expropriation of land and demolition of illegal buildings. The Arab sector opted for new initiatives, in an attempt to undermine and eliminate the 1948 land policies. Initiatives by Arab MKs provided one channel consisting of legislative action to annul such institutions as the Jewish National Fund Law.

The judiciary supplied another channel for these attempts with a Supreme Court decision that removed the ban on the purchase of land in Jewish areas by Arab citizens. Such a case was the Katzir-Qa'adan precedent: in March 2000 the Supreme Court ruled that the State must consider favorably the request by 'Adel Qa'adan, a resident of Baqa al-Gharbiyya, to lease a plot of land and build a house in the Jewish settlement of Katzir. The Court stated that the State could not discriminate between Jews and non-Jewish citizens in the allocation of State land.

The Rising Power of the Islamic Movement. a) Activism in the local sphere. The Islamic Movement succeeded in changing the face of Arab village society. Mosque attendance increased steadily; the number of mosques in Israel grew from 60 in 1967, to 80 in 1988, 240 in 1993, and 363 in 2003.

As the socio-economic gaps between Jews and Arabs widened and the secular Arab political bodies failed to improve matters, the Arab community became increasingly eager for some external force to step in and remedy the imbalance. Following the basic ideological tenets of the Muslim Brotherhood, the Islamic Movement filled the void. It provided practical solutions for the deteriorating local conditions, being especially successful in mobilizing the Arab inhabitants for active, Islamic-oriented work in their communities. Muslim volunteers built internal roads in Arab villages, opened kindergartens, libraries, and clinics, and established drug-rehabilitation centers. Indeed, the Islamic Movement found solutions for many of the daily hardships that resulted from the authorities' failure to meet the Arab sector's needs.

This approach proved to be a prescription for success. In the 1998 municipal elections the Islamic Movement won representation in 13 localities, compared to 16 in 1993 and 14 in 1989. In the 2003 municipal elections the Islamic Movement won representation in only nine localities, but it still maintained its power, especially in Umm al-Fahm, where the Islamic Movement's candidate for mayor, Sheikh Hashim Abd al-Rahman, won 75% of the ballots, thus preserving the Movement's dominance in the city since 1989, and also in Nazareth, traditionally under the sway of Christian-Communist power, where the movement's candidate for mayor, Ahmad Zu'aby, won 48% of the ballots.

During the 1990s, The Al-Aqsa Association for the Preservation of the Waqf and the Islamic Holy Sites, established by the Islamic Movement in 1991, mounted a campaign to restore the *waqf* properties to their lawful owners in the Muslim community. In March 2001 the Islamic Movement established a Supreme Muslim Council, intended, inter alia, to serve as the elected Islamic body to which the *waqf* properties would be reinstated.

The success of the Islamic Movement was not only the result of the religious appeal. For many, it was a vote of confidence in a movement that successfully dedicated itself to the social, economic, and cultural advancement of the Arab sector.

b) The split within the Islamic Movement's ranks. The question of whether or not to participate in the Knesset elections aroused an internal controversy within the Islamic Movement's ranks. One of the most important developments prior to the 1996 elections was the Movement's reversal of its long-held position of staying out of Israeli parliamentary elections. In March 1996 the Movement's General Congress endorsed its participation in the Knesset elections within the framework of a unified Arab party headed by an Islamic Movement candidate.

The initiative to reverse the previous decision taken in 1995 came from the group of Islamic leaders associated with Sheikh Abdullah Nimr Darwish, founder of the Islamic Movement in Israel. The motivation for this effort was the desire to unite the fragmented Arab vote and prevent a situation in which, as a result of increased factionalism, Arab representation in the Knesset would be weakened or even eliminated.

This new decision caused an immediate crisis within the Movement. Two of the more radical leaders, Sheikh Kamal Khatib and Sheikh Ra'id Salah, mayor of Umm al-Fahm at the time, announced that they did not view themselves as bound by the Movement's resolution to participate in the Knesset elections, a move which eventually caused a split within the Movement's ranks into two factions: the first, headed by Sheikh Darwish, adopted a more pragmatic view toward integration into Israeli society, including participation in Knesset elections; the second, headed by Sheikh Ra'id Salah, maintained a more dogmatic view.

Representatives of the latter faction argued that the Islamic Movement cannot integrate into the Israeli system, since it is based on a set of Jewish-Israeli laws which stands in complete contradiction to the very essence of Islamic Law. Hence, this faction endorsed the idea of establishing independent institutions for the Arab population in Israel a step further. As part of its social world view, especially in light of the October 2000 events, the dogmatic faction considered establishing an alternative social infrastructure for a community which was capable of relying on itself (*al-Mujtama' al-'Issami*) by means of independent industrial, commercial, and financial institutions, and its own health, security, and education services. However, no significant practical steps were taken to implement these ideas.

In May 2003, some leaders of the dogmatic faction, including Sheikh Salah himself, were placed under arrest on charges of money laundering and the transfer of money to Islamic activists in the West Bank. The faction's press was temporarily closed for what was described as publication of inflammatory material. Eventually, some of the detainees were released in January 2005 and the rest, including Sheikh Salah, were released four months later.

POLITICAL EVENTS. *Elections to the Knesset – 1996, 1999, 2003.* The 1996, 1999, and 2003 election campaigns in the Arab sector were characterized by an electoral shift from the Zionist parties to the Arab parties, mainly because of disappointment with the Zionist parties. The total vote for the major Zionist and Jewish parties declined from 49.3% in 1992 to 32.3% in 1996, 17.3% in 1999, and 18.5% in 2003. The vote for Labor dropped from 20.3% in 1992 to 16.6% in 1996, 7.43% in 1999, and 7.7% in 2003. Meretz declined from 9.70% in 1992 to 10.5% in 1996, 5.02% in 1999, and 4.2% in 2003. The right wing Likud party and the religious Jewish parties dropped from 19.3% in 1992 to 5.2% in 1996, 4.84% in 1999, and 6.6% in 2003. In contrast, the total vote for Arab parties rose from 38.4% in 1992 to 62.4% in 1996, 68.64% in 1999, and 68.8% in 2003.

The strong shift toward the Arab parties reflected the response of the Arab population to the profound change in their platforms, which became more relevant to the Arab electorate than ever before, being less preoccupied with Palestinian issues and the peace process, as in the past, and displaying much more focus on communal issues directly pertaining to the collective rights of the Arab population as a national minority. These platforms became concentrated on the following issues:

1. The need to change Israel's Zionist character so as to transform Israel into a state of all its citizens, with full national rights and cultural autonomy for the Arab minority.

2. A demand to recognize the status of the Arabs in Israel as a national minority.

3. Taking legal measures to ensure equality.

4. Maintaining an aggressive national stance regarding issues of Arab lands.

A typical ritual which repeated itself prior to the election campaigns of 1996, 1999, and 2003 in the Arab sector was the strenuous effort to form a united Arab list which would represent all political forces competing for the Arab vote. Such a list, it was argued, would lead to larger and more effective Arab representation in the Knesset. Some Arab observers argued that the increased political pluralism was devastating in terms of the Arab community's ability to stand behind a clear and unified political message.

In all cases the outcome was the same: the various political parties held talks with each other but to no avail. The efforts to form a large unified list failed to materialize mainly because of personal rivalries, as well as ideological barriers.

Elections for Prime Minister – 2001. Following the announcement of special elections for prime minister in February 2001 a sharp internal debate took place in the Arab sector over the question of whether to participate or boycott the elections. The general atmosphere in the Arab sector was full of frustration and lack of confidence in the Israeli authorities. The boycott idea was broached as a protest against the actions of the Israeli security forces against the Arabs in Israel and those in the Palestinian territories during the October 2000 events (see below), as well as against the ongoing government policy of neglect toward the Arab sector. Another major consideration in favor of the boycott was the realization that the boycott would not affect the representation of Arab parties in the Knesset, since these were not parliamentary elections.

Eventually, the impact of the October 2000 events was decisive: an unprecedented majority of Arab citizens boycotted the prime minister elections, resulting in an 18% turnout of Arab voters – the lowest since the establishment of the state. Most of the voters came from the Druze communities, which traditionally affiliated themselves with the Israeli establishment and the security forces.

The Municipal Elections of 1998 and 2003. The municipal elections in the Arab sector held in November 1998 and October 2003 were characterized by a powerful resurgence of the traditional clan, the *hamula*, at the expense of the Zionist-affiliated party lists (Labor, Likud, Meretz, and the religious parties), which almost totally disappeared from the municipal scene. The influence of the more ideologically orientated Arab-dominated parties was also considerably diminished. The strengthening of the *hamula* framework at the expense of nationalist movements reflected a weakening of the affiliation of the Arab citizens of Israel to the Palestinian national cause and a trend toward deeper integration in Israeli society.

The election campaigns clearly illustrated that the basic loyalty of the Arab citizens was to the family or tribal circle, which provided security and stability socially, economically, and politically. Loyalty to the family took precedence over regional, religious, ethnic, and even political loyalties, systematically overshadowing party allegiance. Ultimately, the municipal elections of 1998 and 2003 illustrated the fragmentation of Arab society in Israel along clan, party, ethnic, and religious lines.

The Al-Aqsa Intifada and the October 2000 Events. Early in October 2000, violent demonstrations swept the Arab communities of the Galilee and the Triangle area as a spin-off of the Al-Aqsa Intifada in the territories, resulting in the death of 13 Arabs and one Jew. These events evoked profound shock in the Israeli public, marking a watershed in Jewish-Arab relations in Israel.

The outburst was the most violent act by the Arab population since the establishment of Israel, involving a level of force never before employed, including the destruction of public buildings, the protracted blocking of major highways, the employment of Molotov cocktails, and even the sporadic use of live ammunition against security forces. The harsh response of the police also marked a significant precedent. The police used tear gas and fired rubber bullets and live ammunition at the Arab demonstrators. As a result, in addition to the 13 Arabs and one Jew who were killed, hundreds of protesters and dozens of police officers were injured. Arab leaders accused the police of employing excessive force in dispersing the demonstrators, using live ammunition and shooting indiscriminately at close range.

Perceiving a threat in MK Ariel Sharon's visit to the Temple Mount on the eve of the Jewish New Year, September 28, 2000, the Arabs of Israel expressed solidarity with their brethren in the territories. Ostensibly many adopted the Islamic movement's call to protect the al-Aqsa mosque, claiming that Israel was trying to exert its authority over the third holiest site in Islam.

The swift response of the Arabs in Israel reflected their sense of identification with the Palestinian cause. Yet, the major cause for the outburst of violence was largely attributable to domestic factors. Signs of rising tension in the Arab sector were already evident during the first half of 2000. Spokespersons of the Arab population pointed out that most of the Arab local councils contended with paralyzing budgetary deficits, the Arab villages had become foci of unemployment, and the problem of the unrecognized villages, especially in the Negev, had worsened. The October 2000 riots reflected the disappointment of the Arabs in Israel with Prime Minister Barak personally and with his government's policies toward the Arab sector generally. While 95% of the Arab electorate had voted for Barak in the personal 1999 elections, many felt betrayed when he declined to invite Arab parties to join his coalition and did little to address the longstanding socio-economic needs of the Arab sector. The uprising represented the culmination of a process of growing alienation and discontent over unfulfilled expectations to attain equality, especially by the younger generation.

The State Commission of Inquiry for the October 2000 Events. Following sustained harsh criticism on the part of the Arab leadership over the killing of the 13 Arab citizens by the police, Prime Minister Barak announced the establishment of a state commission of inquiry to investigate the October 2000 riots, headed by Supreme Court Justice Theodor Orr, with a mandate to examine the behavior of the security forces, inciters, and organizers of the clashes. The decision was welcomed by the Arab leadership.

On September 1, 2003, the Orr Commission published its findings and recommendation. The commission's report identified the following as the root causes of the events:

a) *Government discrimination* – The commission noted that "government handling of the Arab sector has been primarily neglectful and discriminatory ... Evidence of the distress included poverty, unemployment, a shortage of land, serious problems in the education system and substantially defective infrastructure."

b) *Police behavior* – The commission criticized the police for using lethal riot control methods and for its overall attitude toward the Arab minority. In the report, the commission's members noted: "The police must learn to realize that the Arab sector in Israel is not the enemy and must not be treated as such."

c) *Radicalization of the Arab sector* – The commission noted that another cause for the escalation which led to the outbreak of the riots was "the ideological-political radicalization of the Arab sector," which manifested itself in "expressions of identification with and even support of the Palestinian struggle against the state." The commission also blamed the Arab leadership, including some Arab MKs and heads of the Islamic Movement, for failing to "understand that the violent riots ... and identification with armed activity against the state ... constitute a threat against the state's Jewish citizens and substantially damaged the delicate fabric of Jewish-Arab relations in Israel."

[Arik Rudnitzky and Elie Rekhess (2nd ed.)]

POPULAR CULTURE

Backward political and economic conditions under Ottoman rule prevented the emergence of literary or artistic talent among the Arabs, particularly among the rural population. However, there was a widespread popular culture of song, dance, and other entertainment among the fellahin.

IN THE VILLAGES. In the cold and rainy season, when they could not go out to till the fields, as well as on festive occasions, such as circumcisions, betrothals, or weddings, the fellahin vied with each other in showing their skill in singing, dancing, and storytelling. Everyone was expected to know the traditional songs and dances. In the *maḍāfa*, the guest hall in the home of a village notable, the fellahin would assemble to discuss farming, politics, and the latest news, listen to popular legends, or welcome important guests. When a *maddāḥ* (panegyrist) visited the village, the entire population would assemble at the *maḍāfa* to listen to his tales and legends of heroes in poetry and prose rhyme, sometimes accompanied on the one-stringed *rubāba*. The best-known stories of this type were those of ʿAntara ibn Shaddād, the famous sixth-century poet. Popular legendary heroes were Sayf ibn Dhū Yazan, the heroic sixth-century king of South Arabia; Abu Zayd al-Hilālī, with his miraculous adventures; and the members of the heroic Banū Hilāl tribe. Today, most of this folklore has been publicized widely through the theater, television, and books, but it is still recounted by village storytellers.

Public poetry reading is a well-developed feature of rural Arab life, especially at public and family celebrations and the return of the pilgrims from Mecca, as well as on the occasion of deaths or disasters. Local village poets are employed to compose long poems for each special occasion. Those that are especially successful are absorbed into the general cultural life of the rural Arabs; others become part of local tradition. The fellahin poets deal with all aspects of private and public life: marriage, death, love, nature, work, pleasure and amusements, religious life, etc. Numerous types of Arab rural poetry, distinguished by tune and melody, are *mījana, dalʿūna, ʿatāba, ẓarīf al-ṭūl, al-saḥja*, to mention only a few. Popular public poets often perform in pairs. The Asad brothers of Deir al-Asad and the Rināwī brothers of Deir Ḥannā are the best-known contemporary performers.

The fellahin still preserve many customs that have existed in the Middle East for centuries and some of which are reflected in the Scriptures: for example, the pouring of water by the young on the hands of their elders; grinding of corn in hand mills; washing babies in salt water and anointing them with olive oil; and marriages between close relatives. They are fond of games, which may last for hours and generally attract numerous spectators, such as *sija*, which resembles chess; *maqala*, which entails the moving of stones on a special board and involves accurate calculations; and *al-fanājīn*, in which a large number of players try to guess the location of a ring hidden under one of several saucers.

THEATER. A few years after the establishment of the State of Israel, some attempts were made to put on stage shows in Arabic, but they came to naught. It was only in 1965 that Arab theater and dance companies, initiated by individuals and assisted by the *Histadrut Arab Section and the Beit Gefen Center, Haifa, were more or less permanently established. The Beit Gefen Drama School, established in 1963, is directed by Adīb Jahshān. In 1966 it produced Mahmud ʿAbbāsī's *Al-Fidā*ʾ ("The Ransom") with great success under the direction of Abu Farīd. The only company that remained active for a considerable period was the independent Popular Theater, directed by Antuwān Ṣāliḥ of Nazareth, who studied direction in Paris. It presented Strindberg's *The Father* and *The Servant of Two Masters* by Goldini, featuring Yusuf Faraḥ and Adīb Jahshān, who graduated from the Ramat Gan Drama School and gained a considerable reputation. The appearance of actresses in Arab theater shows encountered numerous obstacles, as it was frowned on by Muslim tradition. For a considerable period the Arab theater suffered from lack of feminine participants, and the difficulty was only recently overcome. The best-known Arab actress in Israel was Alīs Abu Samra from Acre, a teacher at the ʿArrāba village who appeared for the Popular Theater and went on tour in the United States. In later years such actors as Muhammad *Bakri, Yusuf Abu Varda, and Makhram Khoury achieved prominence.

MUSIC AND DANCE. Ḥikmat Shāhīn, born in Tarshīḥa, directed the Beit Gefen Music and Dance company. Iskandar Shihāb, of Shepharam, organized a local nonprofessional company. Yusuf al-Khill (from a well-known Arab family of singers and composers) was the director of the Nazareth Roman Catholic Music and Dance company, which was one of the oldest. Suhayl Raḍwān was the director of the Histadrut Dance Company in Nazareth and of the Arab Music School in Haifa. A few dance companies were organized by the Histadrut and private groups in Arab, Druze, and Circassian centers, but do not perform regularly. Later, performances by mixed Arab-Jewish folk dance and music ensembles had popular success. A 1994 production of *Romeo and Juliet* by a troupe of Jewish and Arab actors from Jerusalem, performing in a mixture of Hebrew and Arabic, won national and international acclaim, touring widely abroad.

PAINTING. A few talented Arab painters have gained prominence in Israel recently. The paintings of ʿAbd Yūnis of ʿArʿara, a graduate of the Bezalel School of Arts, have been well received, and he has also done book illustrations. The young Druze painter Abdallah al-Qarā, born in Dāliyat al-Karmil, studied in Paris and exhibited with great success in Israel and the United States, where he resided.

[Mahmoud Abassi]

ARABIC LITERATURE

Throughout the period beginning with the second half of the 19th century and ending with the establishment of the State of Israel (1948) Palestine, a backwater in Arab cultural life, could occupy no significant position in the field of Arab literature, nor play a role comparable to that of Iraq, Egypt, Syria, and Lebanon. This situation changed after 1948, both in the State of Israel and in the area taken over by Jordan, when Arab poetry and prose, mostly with political overtones, emerged as a lively expression of cultural life. The initial development of Arab literature in Palestine was extremely slow and usually imitated literary trends dominant in the neighboring Arab states. Indeed, most Palestinian-born writers and poets flourished and gained fame outside Palestine.

UNDER OTTOMAN RULE: 1880–1918. Though Palestinian Arab literature, however rudimentary, was always nationalist, community differences were especially discernible in the late 19th and early 20th centuries. Muslim writers, mainly influenced by classical Arab literature, tended to emphasize form at the expense of content; the Greek Orthodox were influenced by Russian literature and the Roman Catholics by French. But with the growing prominence of the Palestinian national movement after World War I, these differences gradually disappeared.

During the second half of the 19th century, emphasis was laid on form and linguistic ornamentation. Assonant prose and pseudoclassical poetry were dominant. The sole exception was the work of Muhammad Rūḥī al-Khālidī (1864–1913), Ottoman consul general in Bordeaux and a member of the Ottoman parliament. He was a distinguished literary critic whose field of research and writing was the influence of Arab literature on European literature. The new Ottoman constitution of the Young Turks in 1908, granting cultural freedom to all nationalities within the Ottoman Empire, was a turning point in the development of Arab literature in Palestine. Many newspapers and periodicals appeared, and literary activity was of considerable intensity. Among the foremost writers of the period were Khalīl al-Sakākīnī, Isʿāf al-Nashāshībī, Ḥannā al-ʿĪsā, Khalīl Baydas, and Abdallah Mukhliṣ.

UNDER THE BRITISH MANDATE: 1918–48. After the British conquest of Palestine, Muslim education, extremely rudimentary until then especially in comparison with Christian missionary education, progressed sufficiently to enable Palestinian writers to establish literary societies, regular literary publications, and publishing houses. Many Palestinian Arabs went abroad to acquire education at Arab or European universities. Growing Palestinian Arab nationalism found its expression in poetry directed against both the British and Zionism. Some 200 books in Arabic were published in Palestine during the Mandatory period. This was a marked advance in quantity, though quality still lagged behind Egypt, Syria, and other centers.

The best-known poet of the period was Iskandar al-Khūrī al-Baytjālī, a judge living in Haifa who published six volumes of poetry, some of which contain outspoken criticism of the modernization of Arab society. Wadī al-Bustānī (1886–1954), a Lebanese lawyer who also resided in Haifa, concentrated on the political and social events of the 1918–30 period in his anthology *Filasṭīniyāt* ("Palestine Verses," 1946). Other poets of stature were ʿAbd al-Karīm al-Karmī, Hasan ʿAlāʾ al-Dīn, the poetess Fadwā Ṭūqān, ʿAbd al Munʿim al-Rifāʿī, Burhān al-Dīn al-ʿAbbūshī, Ibrahim ʿAbd al-Fattāḥ, Ibrahim Ṭūqān, and Isḥāq Mūsā al-Husseini.

Ibrahim Ṭūqān and Isḥāq Mūsā al-Husseini, both members of prominent families, occupied important positions in their community. Ṭūqān (1905–1941), born in Nablus and educated at the American University of Beirut, wrote anti-Zionist and anti-British poems along with his colleague and friend Muhammad Hasan ʿAlāʾ al-Dīn. Unsparing in his attacks on Arab land speculators, Ṭūqān praised the Arab rioters and acclaimed organized warfare against Jews. He was considered by many to be the most outstanding Arab poet in Palestine. By contrast, Isḥāq Mūsā al-Husseini, a humanist, directed his efforts at social and moral reform: he demanded improvement in the status of Arab women and called for equality, brotherhood, justice, and mutual tolerance. His allegorical novel *Mudhak Rarāt Dajāja* ("Memoirs of a Hen," 1943), in which he implied that the Arabs should come to peaceful terms with the new Jewish community, drew bitter criticism from Arab nationalists. In short-story writing, Maḥmud Sayf al-Dīn al-Irānī and ʿArif al-ʿAzzūnī were prominent. Both were leftist writers who dealt critically with the political life of the Palestinian Arabs as in al-Irānī's short story "Germs," published in his book *Awwal al-Shawṭ* ("The Beginning of the Race," 1938).

There were two other significant groups. One, which aimed at disproving and counterattacking Zionist claims, included Yusuf Haykal, ʿĪsā al-Safarī, Wadī ʿal-Bustānī, and Saʿīd Basīsā, as well as ʿĀrif al-ʿĀrif, who wrote on tribes and cities in Palestine. The second group devoted itself to improving Arab educational standards by compiling good textbooks. Ahmad Ṣāliḥ al-Khālidī and Khalīl al-Sakākīnī were its most prominent members.

AFTER 1948. With the Arab defeat in 1948, most of the Arab intelligentsia fled the country. They continued their anti-Israel activity outside Israel's borders engendering a new current in Palestinian literature, *Adab al-ʿAwda* ("the Literature of Return"). Fadwā Ṭūqān and Harun Hāshim R̄āsh̄īd were considered the most prominent exponents of this school. The Arab population remaining in Israel after the 1948 war was, in the main, rural. Of the few Arab writers who stayed, most were Communists who, stunned by the Arab defeat, interrupted their literary activities. Two political and social factors, however, advanced and revived Arabic literature in Israel: the Communist Party, and the new Jewish immigration from Iraq (1950–51). Since the British Mandate, some Arab writers had had Communist affiliations, and in 1944 they established the official party organ *al-Ittiḥād* ("The Union") in Haifa.

The tide of Jewish immigration from Iraq included such writers and poets as Shalom Darwīsh, Salīm Shaʿshūʿ, Avraham Ovadya, Mikhael Murād, Shemuel Moreh, Sasson Somekh, David Ẓemaḥ, and S. al-Kātib (Shalom Katav). Eliyahu Agasi and Meir Ḥaddād also belonged to this category, although they had come to Israel much earlier. The best-known novelists of the group were Ibrahim Mūsā Ibrahim and G. Barshan. They published their work mainly in the weekly literary supplements of the daily *al-Yawm* ("The Day," 1948–68) and in the weekly *Ḥaqīqat al-Amr* ("The Truth," 1937–59). However, the role of the Iraqi Jewish writers and poets in the revival of Arabic literature in Israel was necessarily of short duration. Having integrated into Israel's Jewish society, they no longer aimed at pursuing Arabic literature, nor could the Arab literary elite in Israel accept Iraqi Jewish leadership, which they considered alien.

In due course, young Arab poets and writers educated in Israel schools assumed literary leadership. At first, during the early years of the state, their prose and poetry dwelt upon life, love, and nature, and their literary output was weak in form and content. Later, however, such political issues as peace between Israel and her neighbors and Jewish-Arab cooperation in Israel predominated, constituting the subject matter of the periodicals *al-Wasīṭ* ("The Mediator," 1951–53) and *al-Mujtamaʿ* ("Society," 1954–59), both edited by Mīshīl Haddād and Jamāl Qaʿwār.

In 1956 two topics gained prominence in Israel Arab literature: the political and social condition of the Israel Arabs and criticism of the Israel authorities. This literature was influenced by rapid changes in the cultural make-up of Israel Arabs, as the result of such factors as the institution of free, compulsory primary education, the rise in the Arab standard of living, freedom of speech and publication, and the activity of the *Histadrut and various, mainly Jewish, political parties among the Arab population. At first, most of the works of Arab writers in Israel were published from 1953 in the Communist monthly *al-Jadīd* ("Anew"). The situation gradually changed, however, as new journals began regular publication in the late 1950s and in the 1960s. These included *Mapam's *al-Fajr* ("Dawn"), the Histadrut's *al-Hadaf* ("The Aim"), *Anwār* ("Lights"), and *Mifgash-Liqāʾ* ("Encounter"), a bilingual literary magazine in Hebrew and Arabic. Arabic publishing houses inaugurated by Mapam and the Histadrut encouraged greater local activity in all literary genres. Some Arab writers even began writing in Hebrew.

Arab poets in Israel found themselves in the unique position of living in a liberal, democratic state with which, for national reasons, they were often unable to identify. Some of their poetry, which attained high standards, was dubbed by

Arab critics as *Adab al-Muqāwama* ("Resistance Literature"), because it dealt with the plight of the Palestinian refugees and expressed dissatisfaction with the status of the Arab population in Israel, as well as, sometimes, rebellion, vengeance, and hatred of Jews. Some, more moderate, Arab poets, like their Iraqi Jewish colleagues, e.g., Rāshid Hussein and Jamāl Qaʿwār, dwelt on the advantages of Jewish-Arab peace and cooperation. Stylistically, the poetry was simple and easy to comprehend, with intelligent use of colloquial Arabic, proverbs, and folk adages. Prominent works were Mahmud Darwish's *Nihāyat al-Layl* ("The End of the Night," 1967) and Samīḥ al Qāsim's *Dukhān al-Burkān* ("The Smoke of the Volcanoes," 1958), which revealed considerable progress in poetic quality. The poets Rāshid Husseini, Abu Ḥannā, Tawfīq Fayyāẓ, and Ḥannā Ibrahim, all of them nationalists or Communists, also developed a good rhythmic structure, giving expression to themes centered mostly on Arab nationalism. Among the few poets living in Judea and Samaria who continued regular writing and publishing after the *Six-Day War (1967), the foremost was the poetess Fadwā Ṭūqān of Nablus.

FICTION. The Israel Arab short story has failed to equal the attainments in poetry. Mainly influenced by European and Egyptian literary trends, it was realistic in theme and journalistic in style, dealing with the problems of the Arab minority in Israel, the attitudes of the Israel authorities and Jewish population toward the Arabs, the sufferings of the Palestinian refugees, and the Israel military government. Major writers were Najwā Qaʿwār, Faraj Salmān, and Tawfīq Muʿammar. At the same time, under the influence of modern, progressive Jewish society, a number of other writers, such as Qayṣar Karkabī, Ṭaha M. Ali, and Mustafa Murrār, published short stories criticizing outmoded Arab customs.

Attempts to produce an Arab drama of high standard in Israel have so far been unsuccessful, notwithstanding the efforts of Tawfīq Fayyāẓ and Najwā Qaʿwār. The novel, however, has made considerable progress. In 1958 Tawfīq Muʿammar published his first work, *Mudhakkarat Lājiʾ* ("Memoirs of a Refugee"), which deals with the Arab population in Israel after the flight from Haifa in 1948. The most successful novel was ʿAtā Allāh Mansur's *Wa-ʿĀdat Samīra* ("And Samira Came Back," 1962), a realistic, colorful story of a young couple whose marriage fails. Other noteworthy novels were Mahmud ʿAbbāsī's *Ḥubb bilā Ghad* ("Love without Morrow," 1962), Fahd Abu Khaḍra's *al-Layl wa-al-Ḥudūd* ("The Night and the Border," 1964), and M. ʿAbd al-Qādir Kanaʿna's works.

Writers who favor peace, brotherhood, and cooperation with the Jews seem to refrain from giving expression to their ideas as forcefully as the Communists and extreme nationalists, who increasingly cooperate with each other, especially as their numbers have been augmented since 1967 by writers from Judea and Samaria.

[Shmuel Moreh]

1967–1987. Between 1967 and 1987, and particularly after the Six-Day War (1967), the Palestinian-national factor became more pronounced in Israeli Arab literary works. During this period, poets Tawfiq Zayyad (1929–1994), Taha Muhammad Ali (1931–), Samih al-Qasim (1939–), and later Salim Jubran (1941–) and Siham Daud (1952–), whose writing became prominent, focused on themes such as the question of national identity, the renewed interaction with the Arab world and the Palestinian community, the outcome of the wars of 1967, 1973, and 1982, the first Intifada (see below), and the sense of discrimination among the Arab minority in Israel.

A rising sense of solidarity and literary cooperation developed during the 1970s and 1980s between Palestinian writers in Israel and their counterparts in the larger Palestinian and Arab world. Palestinian writers and critics began to publish in Arabic periodicals and newspapers in Israel, such as *al-Jadid*, *al-Mawakib*, and *al-Ittihad*. Conversely, Israeli-Arab writers, such as Samih al-Qasim, Emile *Habibi (1921–1996), Zaki Darwish (1941–), and Riyad Baydas (1960–) published in Palestinian journals such as *al-Karmil*, *Shu'un Filastiniyya*, *Filastin al-Thawra*, and *Balsam*. Thus, Israeli Arab writers won the legitimization they had long expected to obtain.

One literary issue remained unchanged since 1948: the relationship of Israeli Arabs to the land. The emphasis shifted from the role of land as a source of livelihood to land as a focus of national and emotional attachment, as was reflected in the works of Samih al-Qasim, Muhammad Naffa' (1939–), and Riyad Baydas. This trend was strongly reflected in the poetry published following the violent events of "Land Day" on March 30, 1976. In contrast to former years, the land issue has now acquired a new character and became an ethos and a symbol – a national, political, social, and even religious one.

The theme of refugees and infiltrators, which had been central for many Israeli-Arab writers in the 1950s and early 1960s, lost its popularity in the late 1960s, although it still served as the subject of a few short stories after the war of 1967. By the 1970s and 1980s only few writers, like Emile Habibi and Riyad Baydas, still addressed this issue but from a different point of view: the presentation was less ideological and more sentimental and nostalgic.

One of the most prominent phenomena which began to develop during the 1970s and 1980s was the writing of many Israeli Arab writers in Hebrew as well as Arabic. Writers such as Anton Shammas (1950–), Salman Masaliha (1953–), Na'im Arayidi (1948–), Muhammad Hamza Ghanayim (1953–), Siham Daud, Nida Khoury (1953–), and Farouq Mawasi (1941–) became very popular among the Hebrew reading audience. They also translated a significant amount of Arabic literature and fiction into Hebrew, thus contributing to bridge the gap between Jews and Arabs in Israel.

1987–2005. The themes which the literary works of Arab poets and writers dealt with after 1987 continued to range from the narrow circle of socio-economic discrimination against the Arab minority in Israel to the wider issue of the collapse of the Eastern bloc. However, the main topic that preoccupied the literary world of the Arabs in Israel was the Intifada (uprising) in the Gaza Strip and the West Bank and the political developments that followed suit.

After the outbreak of the first Intifada (lasting from 1987 to 1993), the declaration of independence by the PLO (1988), the signing of the agreements between Israel and the PLO (1993–95), and the peace treaty between Israel and Jordan (1994), a sense of euphoria was reflected in the writings of Israeli Arab scholars, who praised the Intifada and enthusiastically supported the Palestinians' aspirations for national independence.

Israeli Arab writers like Riyad Baydas and Samih al-Qasim published their works in a series of Palestinian anthologies called *Ibdaʿat al-Hajar* ("The Stone Creations"), which were brought out by the Association of Palestinian Writers in the Gaza Strip and the West Bank. Similarly, quite a few works written by Israeli Arabs had been published by *Filastin al-Thawra*, published in Cyprus under the auspices of the PLO. The extensive literary activity of Israeli Arabs during the Intifada also found expression in Arab magazines and periodicals in Israel, especially the journal *al-Jadid* and the literary supplement of the daily *al-Ittihad.*

However, a more melancholic trend was reflected in the works of Israeli Arab writers after Prime Minister Yitzhak Rabin's assassination (1995), the rise of the right-wing Binyamin Netanyahu's government in Israel (1996), and especially after the October 2000 events in Galilee (see above). Israeli Arab works were filled with a sense of frustration and despair regarding the chances of realizing the Palestinian community's national aspirations.

The case of Emile Habibi demonstrated the unique and complicated status of the Arabs in Israel during this period. During the late 1960s and early 1970s Habibi became one of the most prominent Israeli Arab writers, who won legitimacy in the Palestinian community and the Arab world and was also praised for his writing skills, which were apparent in his famous novellas *The Optimist* (1984), *Akhtiya* (1986), and *Saraya, Daughter of the Bad Genie* (1991). However, the same Habibi was sharply criticized by many writers in the Arab world, who castigated him for accepting the Israel Prize for literature in 1992. This case demonstrated the ambivalent attitude of the Arab world toward the Arab literary world in Israel.

One trend which became more prominent during the 1990s was the writing of Israeli Arabs in Hebrew only, thus addressing Hebrew readers in general and not only Arabic readers in the Israeli public. One of the best-known Arab writers who represented this trend was Sayid Kashua (1975–), who published two novellas: *Dancing Arabs* (2002) and *Let it be Morning* (2004). These novellas were semi-autobiographical narratives about the struggle of Israeli Arabs in the light of the crisis of assimilation triggered by the October 2000 events.

[Arik Rudnitzky and Elie Rekhess (2nd ed.)]

Bedouin

TO 1970. The penetration of Bedouin into the Palestine area began in the pre-Islamic period, and continued intermittently until the late 19th century. The Bedouin occupied uninhabited arid regions such as the Negev; marshland such as the Ḥuleh Valley and the Ḥefer Plain; the sand dunes of the Coastal Plain; and the rocky hill country of Allonim-Shepharam. Prior to 1948 there were 80,000 Bedouin in the whole of Palestine, 60,000 of them in the Negev. In early 1970 their number in Israel was 36,800, of whom 26,300 were in the Negev.

Bedouin in the Negev. These Bedouin were only semi-nomadic because of the proximity to settled areas. The region over which they spread extended from the Gulf of Eilat in the south to the Hebron mountains in the east and the settlements of the coastal plain in the west. Their concentrations were large, composed of a number of tribes forming a clan, generally related by blood. They engaged in sheep-rearing and desert agriculture. Frequent years of drought led to long periods of wandering and to raids on permanent settlements.

Under Ottoman rule there was hardly any interference in the internal life of the Bedouin save in times of intertribal warfare. Tribal law courts were established by the Mandatory authorities in the early 1920s. The courts, which met every Tuesday in Beersheba, consisted of three sheikhs who acted as judges and were entitled to impose fines up to LP 200 (£200). Each of the parties in the dispute had the right to propose one judge, and the district commissioner appointed the third. After the establishment of the State of Israel, the tribal courts of law were reestablished in 1954. Nine tribal heads were appointed as judges, with the approval of the minister of the interior. Criminal cases were heard in the regular courts. From the late 1950s, the Bedouin increasingly used the regular courts even in cases involving tribal and family matters, and consequently the tribal courts were abolished in 1962.

Bedouin of Northern Israel. These Bedouin originally came from the Syrian and Transjordanian deserts. They were fragments of tribes which split for financial reasons or because of blood feuds, and they settled in uncultivated areas. Unlike the Bedouin of the Negev, their groupings are small, the area of their wanderings contained by rural settlements. The influence of their surroundings has been considerable: some have become cowherds, others small farmers or hired laborers.

Government Activities. Clinics and schools were opened by the Israel government in areas of Bedouin settlement. New economic opportunities were developed for the Bedouin, even among groups that were previously entirely nomadic. This contact with new settlements and enterprises wrought important changes in the Bedouin way of life. Many abandoned sheepherding and camel driving and took employment as building and agricultural laborers or in various services. As a result, the Bedouin gradually exchanged their tents for a more permanent habitation, often huts of tin or wood. The dependence of the individual upon the tribal sheikh also diminished. To encourage the process of permanent settlement, the government set up a number of villages for Bedouin in the north in the early 1960s, and planned three rural settlements in the

Negev. Some of the Negev Bedouin found their main source of livelihood in the Ramleh-Lydda area. Housing quarters built for them in Ramleh were occupied in the mid-1960s.

Bedouin of Judea and Samaria. According to the 1961 Jordanian census there were 14,947 Bedouin in the area west of the Jordan River. The Arab al-Turkumān tribe, which lives in the Dothan Valley, derives most of its income from land cultivation, also raising sheep and cattle. Of the clans living on the edge of the Judean Desert, the largest is the Taʿamra clan. Part of the clan has begun to settle permanently on a wide area of land. They earn their livelihood mainly from sheep rearing, some agriculture, and as hired laborers. The Jordanian government provided a regional school for them.

Bedouin of Sinai. The number of Bedouin in Sinai and the Gaza Strip was estimated at 60,000. The Suez-Wadi Akaba route was traditionally used by pilgrims to Mecca, and many tribes gathered in this area. With the opening of the Suez Canal (1869), however, the tribes moved northward, and El-Arish became the Bedouin center in northern Sinai. Bedouin in the Gaza Strip area herd flocks, practice desert cultivation, and engage in fishing along the coast. The Bedouin in the Sheikh Zuwayd area produce salt from a natural source there. In central Sinai the tribes are still nomadic, raising camels and goats as well as engaging in smuggling, and the law of the desert still prevails. During the 1960s many economic and social changes took place in southern Sinai. The expansion of the manganese mines and oil plants opened up employment opportunities for the Bedouin as hired laborers, and they began to settle in the region. The heads of tribes and others owned cars in which the laborers were taken to work and provisions brought into the desert from the outside. After the Six-Day War (1967), the Israel government employed these Bedouin in relief works.

[Joseph Ginat]

1970–2005. In 2004 the Bedouin population in Israel numbered approximately 220,000 inhabitants: 145,000 in the Negev in Southern Israel; 65,000 in Galilee in Northern Israel; and a small portion, some 10,000, in central Israel.

Since the establishment of the state of Israel, the Bedouin population has increased tenfold: the population in the Negev increased from 15,000 (1948) to 145,000 (2004), and the population in Galilee increased from 6,500 (1948) to 65,000 (2004). With an unparalleled 5.5% annual growth rate, this population doubles itself every 15 years. It is estimated that by the year 2020 the Bedouin population in the Negev will number approximately 300,000. The Bedouin population is also the youngest in Israeli society: About 55% of the Bedouin are younger than 14.

Land Disputes with the State. For most of Israel's history, the Bedouin in the Negev have been engaged in a dispute with the government over possession of land and housing rights. Between 700,000 to 1,000,000 dunams are under dispute. Land possession and ownership among the Bedouin were traditionally determined by internal custom, which did not involve any written deeds of sales or ownerships. Israel, which sought control over the area, did not accept the unwritten understandings between clans as constituting a legal right.

The government followed the following policy guidelines regarding the land issues:

1) Establishment of seven government-planned Bedouin townships since 1968 (see below).

2) Settlement of disputes by compensation and allocation of alternative land.

3) Demolition of illegal housing in encampments (see below, "Unrecognized Villages").

The Urbanization of the Bedouin in the Negev. In the late 1960s and early 1970s the Israeli government initiated a program to resettle the Bedouin population in the Negev in seven permanent townships: Tel Sheva (founded in 1968), Rahat (1972), Ar'ara ba-Negev (1982), Kseifa (1982), Segev Shalom (1984), Hura (1990), and Laqiya (1990). At the end of 2004, these townships had 93,300 residents: Rahat, which is considered the Bedouin "capital" in the Negev, had 37,400 residents; Tel Sheva – 12,500; Ar'ara ba-Negev – 11,700; Kseifa – 9,400; Hura – 8,800; Laqiya – 7,600; and Segev Shalom – 5,900.

These townships rank at the bottom of the government's socio-economic index of localities, making them the poorest in Israel. Some experts studying Bedouin society point out that the planning of the seven Bedouin localities was a failure due to insufficient land allocations, restrictive planning regulations, insufficient local government budgets, absence of government jobs offered for the inhabitants, inferior education and health level as compared to neighboring Jewish localities, and inadequate social and recreational services.

Moreover, in exchange for a plot in one of these townships, the Bedouin were required to settle their claims to expropriated lands. As a result, many of them were reluctant to abandon their traditional lands and therefore refused relocation to these townships.

Bedouin of Galilee. Most of the Galilee Bedouin live in 20 of their own permanent settlements: four of these settlements – Basmat Tab'un, Wadi Hamam, Bir al-Maksour, and Ibtin – were established by the government in the 1960s, and the rest were gradually recognized by the government during the 1970s, 1980s, and 1990s. Some 17,000 Bedouin live in mixed Arab localities (such as the cities of Shefaram and Abu Sinan, which have Muslim, Christian, Druze, and Bedouin communities), and only 3,000 Bedouin live in scattered and rural communities which are unrecognized by the government.

The Unrecognized Villages. The term "unrecognized villages" applies to those Arab communities in the Negev and Galilee that existed before the establishment of the State of Israel, but have never been incorporated into designated planning frameworks and thus remain "unrecognized" for planning and permit purposes.

This means that these villages, which range in size from 500 to 5,000 inhabitants, lack master plans for development, and without such plans, no building permits are granted for any type of construction. These villages lack recognized local governing bodies and receive limited or no government services such as schools, running water, electricity, and sewage and garbage collection. They also lack public services, such as an educational framework for preschool children, elementary and high schools, paved roads, public transportation, telephone connections, and community medical facilities. In the Negev, there are approximately 45 unrecognized villages, none of which are marked on government maps.

There are contradictory estimates regarding the exact Bedouin population of the unrecognized villages in the Negev. While the Ministry of Interior claims that some 55,000 residents live in the unrecognized villages, the Regional Council for the Unrecognized Bedouin Villages in the Negev (RCUV) maintains that these villages have somewhat over 75,000 residents.

The RCUV was established in 1988 as a Bedouin advocacy group, consisting of many local committees representing the Bedouin population in the Negev. Another group which was founded in 1988 is the Association of Forty, which represents the unrecognized villages in Galilee, as well as those in the Negev.

BEDOUIN OF CENTRAL ISRAEL. The Bedouin population in central Israel has emerged from two types of migration waves from the Negev. The first was *pasture migration*, which began in 1957 when the Negev was struck by a six-year drought. This migration led to the establishment of dozens of Bedouin settlements, spreading from Kiryat Gat in the south to Mount Carmel in the north.

The second kind was *labor migration*, especially by Bedouin families that lacked land and livestock and were looking for work. That migration process, which occurred in the period between 1954 and 1970, created Bedouin centers in the mixed Jewish-Arab cities of Ramleh and Lod and in some Arab localities in the Small Triangle area, such as Taybeh and Kafr Qassem.

[Arik Rudnitzky and Elie Rekhess (2nd ed.)]

BIBLIOGRAPHY: ARAB POPULATION: D. Peretz, *Israel and the Palestine Arabs* (1958); W. Schwarz, *The Arabs in Israel* (1959); S. Jiryis, *The Arabs in Israel 1948–1966* (1968); S. Teveth, *The Cursed Blessing* (1970); M. Krajzman, *La Minorité Arabe en Israel* (1968); Y. Ben Porath, *The Arab Labor Forces in Israel* (1966); A. Cohen, *Arab Border Villages in Israel, A Comparative Study of Continuity and Change* (1965); Y. Lifshitz, *Ha-Hitpatḥut ha-Kalkalit ba-Shetaḥim ha-Muḥzakim 1967–1969* (1970); Misrad Rosh ha-Memshalah, Lishkat ha-Yo'eẓ le-Inyenei Aravim, *Ha-Ḥevrah ha-Aravit be-Israel* (1968); Z. Vilnay, *Ha-Mi'utim be-Israel* (1959); O. Standel, *Mi'utim* (1970). ARAB POPULATION: AFTER 1970: A. Har-Even (ed.), *Shivyon ve-Shiluv, Din ve-Heshbon Hitkaddemut Shenati 1993–1994*; S. Osatzky-Lazar and A. Ghanem, *Sekirot al ha-Aravim be-Yisrael*, 11–16 (Sept. 1993–Jan. 1995); O. Masalha, *Ha-Aravim Ezreḥei Yisrael ve-Idan ha-Shalom* (1994); A. Gonen and R. Hamasi, *Ha-Aravim be-Yisrael be-Ikvot Kinun ha-Shalom* (1993). BEDOUIN: E. Marx, *Bedouin of the Negev* (1967), incl. bibl.; C.S. Jarvis, *Yesterday and Today in Sinai* (1933); A. el Aref, *Bedouin Lore, Law and Legend* (1944); idem, *Al-Qaḍa' Bayn al-Badū* (1933); M. von Oppenheim, *Die Beduinen*, 2 (1943), 3–132; Y. Ginat, *Ha-Bedu'im* (Heb., 1966); E. Epstein, *Ha-Bedu'im: Ḥayyeihem u-Minhageihem* (1933); T. Ashkenazi, *Tribus semi-nomades de la Palestine du Nord* (1938); A. Musil, *The Manners and Customs of the Rwala Bedouins* (1928). ARAB CULTURE: Moreh, in: *Middle Eastern Studies*, 3:3 (Apr. 1967); idem, in: *Ha-Mizraḥ he-Ḥadash*, 9 (1958), 26–39; 14 (1964), 296–309; A.L. Tibawi, in: MEJ, 17 (1963), 507–26; Y. Shimoni, *Arviyei Ereẓ Yisrael* (1947), 396–415; Al-Adāb, 16 (1968), no. 4 (a special issue on the literature of resistance); N. al-Din al-Asad, *al-Ittijāhāt al-Adabiyya al-Ḥaditha fi Filasṭin wa-al-Urdun* (1957); idem, *al-Shir al-Hadīth fi Filasṭin wa-al-Urdun* (1961). **ADD BIBLIOGRAPHY:** ARAB POPULATION 1995–2005: Central Bureau of Statistics website: www.cbs.gov.il; *The Arab Population of Israel 2003*, Statistilie no. 50, Israel Central Bureau of Statistics; *The Arab Population in Israel*, Statistilie no. 27, Israel Central Bureau of Statistics (Nov. 2002); E. Rekhess, "The Arabs of Israel after Oslo: Localization of the National Struggle," in: *Israel Studies*, 7:4 (Fall 2002), 1–44; idem, "The Arabs in Israel," in: B. Maddy-Weitzman (ed.), *Middle East Contemporary Survey*, 19 (1995), 375–80; idem, *ibid.*, 20 (1996), 392–400; idem, "The Arabs in Israel," in: B. Maddy-Weitzman (ed.), *Middle East Contemporary Survey*, 21 (1997), 442–49; idem, "The Arabs in Israel," in: B. Maddy-Weitzman (ed.), *Middle East Contemporary Survey*, 22 (1998), 349–55; idem, "The Arabs in Israel," in: Bruce Maddy-Weitzman (ed.), *Middle East Contemporary Survey*, 23 (1999), 322–30; E. Rekhess, "The Arabs in Israel," in: B. Maddy-Weitzman (ed.), *Middle East Contemporary Survey*, 24 (2000), 293–301; *Identity Crisis: Israel and its Arab Citizens*, ICG Middle East Report, no. 25, Amman/Brussels (March 4, 2004); N. Rouhana, N. Saleh, and N. Sultany, "Voting Without Voice: the Vote of the Palestinian Minority in the 16th Knesset Elections," in: A. Arian and M. Shamir (eds.), *The Elections in Israel 2003* (Heb., 2004), 311–48; E. Rekhess, "The Islamic Movement Following the Municipal Elections: Rising Political Power?" in: E. Rekhess and S. Ozacky-Lazar (eds.), *The Municipal Elections in the Arab and Druze Sector (2003): Clans, Sectarianism and Political Parties* (2005), 33–41. ARABIC LITERATURE: A. Elad, Ami, "The Literature of the Arabs in Israel (1948–1993)," *Ha-Mizraḥ he-Ḥadash*, 33 (1993), 1–8; A. Elad-Bouskila (ed.), *The Other Rooms: Three Palestinian Novellas* (2001); A. Elad-Bouskila, *Modern Palestinian Literature and Culture* (1999); M. Ghanayim, "Arabic Fiction in Israel: New Trends and Developments," in: *Ha-Mizraḥ he-Ḥadash*, 33 (1993), 27–45; Sh. Moreh, "The Development of Arabic Poetry in Israel," in: *Ha-Mizraḥ he-Ḥadash*, 33 (1993), 11–26; M. Sen, "Voices in Conflict: The Language of Israeli-Arab Identity," in: *Yale Israel Journal*, 4 (summer 2004), 15–23; S. Somekh, "The Optimistic and the Pessimistic," in: *Ereẓ Aḥeret*, 16 (May–June 2003), 64–67 (Heb.). BEDOUIN: E. Levinson and H. Yogev (eds.), *2004 Statistical Yearbook of the Negev Bedouin* (2004); I. Abu-Saad and H. Lithwick, *A Way Ahead: A Development Plan for the Bedouin Towns in the Negev* (2000); G. Kaufman, "The Bedouin Population in the Galilee: Processes and Changes, from Nomadic Existence to Permanent Settlement, 1963–2002," in: *Bitaḥon Le'ummi (National Security)*, 4 (April 2005), 77–98 (Heb.); Y. Ben-David, *The Bedouin in Israel* (July 1999); Ministry of Foreign Affairs website: www.jewishvirtuallibrary.org/jsource/Society_&_Culture/Bedouin.html; *Second Class: Discrimination against Palestinian Arab Children in Israel's Schools* (Sept. 2001); Human Rights Watch website: www.hrw.org/reports/2001/israel2/ISRAEL0901-03.htm; I. Abu-Saad, "Education as a Tool of Expulsion from the Unrecognized Villages," in: *Adalah's Newsletter*, vol. 8 (Dec. 2004); 'A. Abu-Rabi'a, *A Bedouin Century: Education and Development among the Negev Tribes in the 20th Century* (2001).

WEBSITES: Central Bureau of Statistics website: www.cbs.gov.il; The Association of Forty website: www.assoc40.org.

ISRAEL, family of rabbis, scholars, and emissaries in Jerusalem and Rhodes. MOSES (d. 1740) was an emissary of the Safed and Jerusalem communities from about 1680 to 1740. In 1710–13 he visited Tunisia, Algeria, and Morocco on behalf of Safed and during his travels wrote several responsa. His return trip in 1714 took him to Rhodes where he was elected rabbi. In 1727 the Jews of Constantinople asked Moses to go on a mission in their behalf, and he spent five years in Italy, Holland, and France. While in Italy, he discussed halakhic issues with Jewish scholars there, such as R. Isaac *Lampronti and R. Raphael *Meldola. On completion of his mission he returned to his rabbinical post at Rhodes and spent the last years of his life preparing his responsa for publication. (Part 1 appeared in 1734, part 2 in 1735, and part 3 posthumously in 1742, all in Constantinople under the title, *Masat Moshe*). In 1737 or 1738 Moses moved from Rhodes to Alexandria, Egypt, where he died. His exegetical writings were printed under the title of *Appei Moshe* (Leghorn, 1828). His son, ABRAHAM BEN MOSES (c. 1708–1785), served as rabbi in Canea, Crete, from 1743 to 1755. In 1751 he visited Western European countries, together with R. Mordecai Rubio, on behalf of Jerusalem. In Hamburg, he met R. Jonathan *Eybeschuetz and gave him a letter justifying his stand on the amulets issue. He was later appointed rabbi of Alexandria, where he served until 1766; from there he moved to Leghorn, where he lived for six years, after which he became rabbi of Ancona. Here, in 1775, he welcomed R. Ḥayyim Joseph David *Azulai. He left two sons, MOSES, who took his place as rabbi of Alexandria, and ḤAYYIM RAFAEL, who published his father's works: *Imrot Tehorot* (Leghorn, 1786), a book on *Even ha-Ezer*; and *Beit Avraham* (*ibid.*, 1786), on the *Ḥoshen Mishpat*, to which was appended *Ma'amar ha-Melekh*, on the principle of **Dina de-Malkhuta Dina*. ELIJAH BEN MOSES (c. 1710–1784), born in Jerusalem, grew up in Rhodes, returning to Jerusalem in 1744. In 1763 he went as an emissary to Western Europe, passing through Italy, France, and Holland. During the course of his mission he wrote many responsa. He returned to Rhodes, and in 1772 was appointed rabbi in Alexandria. Elijah was succeeded there by his son, JEDIDIAH SOLOMON who published his father's works: *Kol Eliyahu* (2 parts, Leghorn, 1792–1807), responsa; *Ara de-Yisrael* (*ibid.* 1806), religious laws, alphabetically arranged, printed with his *derashot, Shenei Eliyahu; Maḥaneh Yisrael* (*ibid.*, 1807); *Kisse Eliyahu* (Salonika, 1811), novellae on the *Shulḥan Arukh; Aderet Eliyahu* (Leghorn, 1828), on the *Sefer Mizvot Gadol* of R. *Moses of Coucy; and *Ugat Eliyahu* (*ibid.*, 1830), responsa.

BIBLIOGRAPHY: Frumkin-Rivlin, 3 (1929), 29–31; S. Markus, *Toledot ha-Rabbanim le-Mishpaḥat Israel-Rodos* (1935); Rosanes, Togarmah, 5 (1938), 73–4; M.D. Gaon, *Yehudei ha Mizraḥ be-Erez Yisrael*, 2 (1937), 294ff.; Yaari, in: *Sinai*, 25 (1949), 149–63; Yaari, Sheluḥei, index.

[Avraham Yaari]

ISRAEL, EDWARD (1859–1884), U.S. astronomer and explorer. Israel was born in Kalamazoo, Michigan and studied astronomy at the University of Michigan before volunteering to serve in the Lady Franklin Bay Expedition to Arctic Greenland under the command of A.W. Greely (1882–1884). When relief ships failed to get through to the party in the summers of 1882 and 1883, it sought to return on foot in what became a nightmarish trial of cold, hunger, and reported cannibalism that was survived by only 6 out of 25 men. Israel died and was buried on the way, eulogized for his "unswerving integrity during these months of agony."

BIBLIOGRAPHY: A.L. Todd, *Abandoned: The Story of the Greely Arctic Expedition, 1881–84* (1961).

ISRAEL, EDWARD LEOPOLD (1896–1941), U.S. Reform rabbi. Israel was born in Cincinnati, Ohio, and educated at Harvard University and the University of Cincinnati (B.A., 1917). He was ordained at Hebrew Union College in 1919 and was awarded an honorary LL.D. by Washington College (now University) in 1938. His first pulpit was at Temple B'rith Shalom in Springfield, Illinois (1919–20), followed by Congregation Adath B'nai Israel (Washington Avenue Temple) in Evansville, Indiana (1920–23). In 1923, he was appointed senior rabbi of Har Sinai in Baltimore, Maryland, where he remained for nearly 20 years, until his appointment as executive director of the *Union of American Hebrew Congregations – a position he was tragically unable to fill, owing to his untimely death.

Although a product of classical Reform Judaism, Israel was a leader of the Labor Zionist movement. He was not only an activist on behalf of Jewish settlement of Palestine but also a liberal who championed the rights of American workers. As chairman of the Social Action Committee of the *Central Conference of American Rabbis, he was an outspoken critic of "yellow dog" contracts in American business. He served on the national executive board of the American League for Peace and Democracy, until he resigned in 1936, charging that it (as well as the Advisory Youth Congress, which he quit in 1940) had fallen into Communist hands.

Alarmed by the rise of the Nazis to power, Israel joined with Rabbi Stephen S. *Wise in organizing a boycott of companies selling German imports. He led a demonstration at the Port of Baltimore when the German battleship *Emden* docked there in 1936. One of the first clergymen to deliver addresses and sermons on the radio, his remarks were frequently quoted by President Franklin D. Roosevelt. Popular with all elements of the Jewish community, Israel was elected president of the multi-denominational *Synagogue Council of America in 1940. Dedicated to the ideal of creating unity of Jewish consciousness, Israel died while holding that office. He is the author of *The Philosophy of Modern Mysticism* (1922).

BIBLIOGRAPHY: K.M. Olitzky, L.J. Sussman, and M.H. Stern, *Reform Judaism in America: A Biographical Dictionary and Sourcebook* (1993).

[Bezalel Gordon (2nd ed.)]

ISRAEL, JONATHAN (1946–), British historian. Professor of Dutch history and institutions at University College, London, Israel became one of the best-known contemporary historians of Jewish and world history during the mercantilist period (c. 1550–1750). His work centers on the Netherlands and its trading empire and on the role of the Jews in mercantilism. His best-known books include *European Jewry in the Age of Mercantilism, 1550–1750* (1989) and *The Dutch Republic: Its Rise, Greatness, and Fall, 1477–1806* (1996). From 1990 he was editor of the Littman Library of Jewish Civilization.

[William D. Rubinstein (2nd ed.)]

ISRAEL, KINGDOM OF, the northerly of the two kingdoms into which Solomon's kingdom was divided after the revolt led by Jeroboam against Rehoboam (c. 928 B.C.E.). It is also called the Northern Kingdom, the Kingdom of Samaria, and, in extra-biblical documents, the House of Omri, after the founder of one of its most important dynasties. The Kingdom of Israel was constituted by all the tribes, except Judah and Benjamin. Its capital was Shechem at first and then Samaria (c. 876 B.C.E.). It had two main sanctuaries, one at Shechem, the other at Dan. Although much more important than Judah, Israel did not enjoy the same stability. During the 206 years of its existence, it had ten dynasties, the most important of which were those of Jeroboam, Omri, and Jehu. Israel was almost constantly in a state of war with Damascus. In 722 the Assyrians took Samaria, deported its inhabitants, and put an end to the Kingdom of Israel. The Northern Kingdom is constantly criticized in the Book of Kings because of the sins of Jeroboam and the idolatry of Ahab. The prophets Elijah, Elisha, Hosea, and Amos exercised their ministries in the Kingdom of Israel. After the fall of Samaria, some of its literature was brought south and found its way into the Hebrew Bible.

In the Aggadah

The rabbis, despite their belief in the eternal integrity of the Davidic monarchy and their prayers for its restoration, were not markedly hostile to the ancient Kingdom of Israel that was formed by the secession of ten tribes from Davidic rule after the death of Solomon. Any Jew, regardless of his tribe of origin, was regarded as eligible for the kingship (*Midrash Tanna'im*, p. 104; Hor. 13a). Israelite kings are evaluated by the *aggadah* as individuals, their political role in the maintenance of a dual monarchy being virtually ignored; the only negative point made with some consistency is that the Israelite monarchy was a temporary phenomenon and, for example, did not anoint its kings as the Davidides did (Hor. 11b). In all this, the rabbis faithfully reflect the attitude of I Kings 11:29–39, which tells of Ahijah's prophetic promise to Jeroboam that the latter would rule over Israel as David had ruled over Judah, "but not for all days." A significant exception to this rabbinic posture may be the view of R. Akiva that the ten tribes have no share in the world to come (Tosef., Sanh. 13:12; cf. Sanh. 10:3), which may derive from a harsh attitude toward the secessionists; other interpretations of this teaching are, however, quite possible.

In their discussion of the founding of the Israelite monarchy and the concomitant shriveling of Davidic hegemony, the rabbis focus on the vices and merits of David, Solomon, and Jeroboam, rather than on the broader issues developed in the Bible. Rav declares that David's improper behavior toward Mephibosheth and his readiness to believe *lashon ha-ra* were to blame for the secession (Shab. 56a). *Seder Olam Rabbah* (ch. 15) states that a secession of 36 years was ordained to punish Solomon for his 36-year-long marriage to the daughter of Pharaoh, but that the dual monarchy was extended due to the unworthiness of Asa, king of Judah. Jeroboam is described as a disciple of the prophet Ahijah and a great scholar who merited kingship by virtue of the rebukes he delivered to Solomon over the various excesses connected with the latter's Egyptian marriage. Indeed, so great was Jeroboam's potential that God offered him special rank in paradise if he would abandon his idolatry. Subsequent to his enthronement, however, Jeroboam built two golden calves and directed the people to worship them (I Kings 12:28), becoming for the rabbis (Avot 5:18) the archetypal sinner who leads others into sin; Jeroboam is one of the three kings who is denied the life of the world to come (Sanh. 10:2).

Other kings of the Israelite monarchy are similarly evaluated with regard to their individual achievements: Omri is specially singled out by R. Johanan for having enriched the state through the addition of the city of Samaria, which served thereafter as capital (Sanh. 102b). His son, Ahab, is denied the life of the world to come; the rabbis describe both Ahab's wickedness and also Jezebel's responsibility in leading her weaker husband to sin; some claim he eventually repented of his sins. The military successes of this evil king are credited to the virtue of his people, which refused to inform upon the prophet Elijah when he dwelt in their midst. Just as the rabbis attribute the rise of the Northern Kingdom to the spiritual flaws of the Davidic dynasty, so do they discuss its fall in terms of spiritual failings: when the Assyrians removed the golden calves during the reign of Hosea, that king encouraged his people to renew the pilgrimages to Jerusalem, but to no avail – the Assyrian victory brought about the extinction of the northern state (*Seder Olam Rabbah*, ch. 22).

Rabbinic teachings on the history of the Kingdom of Israel are doubtless compounded of historical insight founded on their own philosophy of history, and exhortation and analysis reflecting contemporary issues and realities.

See also *Jeroboam: in the *aggadah*.

BIBLIOGRAPHY: IN THE AGGADAH: Ginsberg, Legends, 4 (1947[5]), 179–91, 257–66; Alon, Meḥkarim, 1 (1957), 30.

[Gerald Y. Blidstein]

ISRAEL, RICHARD J. (1929–2000), U.S. rabbi. Israel received his undergraduate education at the University of Chicago and was ordained at Hebrew Union College in 1957, having spent a year of study at a yeshivah in Israel, long before study in Israel was a requirement for Reform ordination and long before Reform Judaism was that open to tradition. He then served as rabbi of the Bene Israel Congregation in Bombay, India. For most of his career Israel worked on college campuses as a *Hillel Foundation assistant director; at UCLA and as a director at Yale for 12 years (1959–71). In 1971 he came to Boston as executive director of the Hillel Council of Metropolitan Boston, a position he held for 14 years. He was the director of the Rabbinic Program for the College Campus of the Reconstructionist Rabbinical College. He was also president of the National Association of Hillel Directors and of the Yale Religious Ministry.

In the last years of his life he directed a bureau of Jewish education, the Judaica program of a group of Jewish community centers, and taught at the Jewish communal service program at Brandeis University. He wrote for the *Jewish Catalogue.* A man of diverse interests and talents, his work *The Kosher Pig and Other Curiosities of Modern Life* (1994) is a collection of essays on the challenges of living in the contemporary world as a fully committed Jew. He was also a marathon runner and a beekeeper for three decades, which provided the honey he needed for Rosh Hashanah.

His writing used humor to mask its seriousness. Israel's essays are often pragmatic and nonetheless profound. He offers hints on keeping a skullcap (*yarmulke*) in place on bald heads and writes on the problem of worshipping near people chanting to themselves at different speeds. "It is in the tension between privacy and community," he writes, "that Jewish prayer is located." Other books of his include *Jewish Identity Games: A How-To-Do-It Book* (1978); *The Jewish Mission to the Jews: The Context and Practice of Outreach* (1985); *The Promised land of Milk and Date and Jam: The Problems of Bee-ing in the Bible and Talmud* (1972).

[Michael Berenbaum (2nd ed.)]

ISRAEL, STEVE (1958–), U.S. congressman (D-NY). Born in Brooklyn and raised in Levitown, a Long Island community built on tract land after World War II, Israel attended a local community college and then went to Syracuse and George Washington University, where he received his B.A. (1982). He immediately went to work on Capitol Hill, working for Robert Matsui and later for Richard Otinger. Intrigued by a career in politics, he returned to New York and ran for the Town Council and then, in 1999, for the Congressional seat that Rick Lazio gave up to run against Hillary Clinton. He handily won what had previously been a Republican seat.

His rise to leadership within the Democratic Minority was steady. In his first term, he passed more new measures in the House than any other freshman Democrat, most proudly a bill to accelerate research and treatment of ovarian cancer. In his second term, Israel was quickly tapped for a leadership position as assistant whip. He was one of only two New York members of Congress to serve on the vitally important House Armed Services Committee, and also on the House Financial Services Committee, which oversees efforts to crack down on the international financing of terrorism. He was the founder and chair of the Democratic Study Group on National Security, co-chaired the bipartisan House Cancer Caucus, and co-chaired the bipartisan Long Island Sound Task Force. In his third term, Rep. Israel was appointed to chair the House Democratic Caucus Task Force on Defense and Military, a group of 15 members of Congress who will outreach to the defense community and advise the House Democratic Leadership on military policy.

BIBLIOGRAPHY: L.S. Maisel and I. Forman, *Jews in American Politics* (2001).

[Michael Berenbaum (2nd ed.)]

ISRAEL, WILFRID (1899–1943), Jewish communal figure. He was a member of a German merchant family prominent in Berlin from the mid-18th century. The family engaged in commerce and was active in Jewish affairs and in pioneering in employees' welfare. Their dry goods business, which became one of Berlin's largest department stores, was founded by NATHAN ISRAEL (1782–1852) in 1815 and was sold in accordance with German anti-Jewish regulations in 1939. Wilfrid Israel was active in the all-encompassing Jewish Zentralausschuss fuer Hilfe und Aufbau and Kinder- und Jugend-Aliyah, established following Hitler's rise to power as well as in the *Hilfsverein der Deutschen Juden. Under the political pressure he gave up his commercial enterprise and emigrated to England in 1939, where he became a board member of the *Jewish Colonization Association (ICA) and helped in 1941 create the Association of Jewish Refugees in Great Britain. He was deeply interested in Palestine, especially in the Ben Shemen Youth Village and kibbutz *Ha-Zore'a, established by German Jewish youth, and he made plans to emigrate there. In 1943 he volunteered for a mission to Spain and Portugal to rescue European refugees under Jewish Agency auspices. He died when the plane in which he was returning to England was shot down by the Luftwaffe. His art collection was bequeathed to kibbutz Ha-Zore'a, where it is displayed in the Wilfrid Israel House for Oriental Art and Studies.

BIBLIOGRAPHY: Reissner, in: YLBI, 3 (1958); idem, *Wilfred Israel, July 11th, 1899–June 1st, 1943* (1944). **ADD. BIBLIOGRAPHY:** W.M. Behr, "In Memoriam Wilfrid Israel," in: H.A. Strauss and K.R. Grossmann (eds.), *Gegenwart im Rueckblick* (1970), 296–98; N. Shepherd, *Wilfrid Israel* (1985); idem, *A Refuge from Darkness – Wilfrid Israel and the Rescue of the Jews* (1984).

ISRAEL, YOM TOV BEN ELIJAH (Sirizli; d. 1890), rabbi and *posek*; born in *Jerusalem. His father was the rabbi of the Cairo community, and when he died in 1866, Yom Tov Israel took his place; before that he had held a high official position, as related by Jacob *Saphir in his description of Egypt in 1858. In 1884 Yom Tov Israel returned to Jerusalem and served in the rabbinate until his death. He was the author of *Minhagei Miẓrayim* (Jerusalem, 1873), on Jewish religious customs in Egypt, in the introduction to which he lists all the rabbis who had served in Egypt from the days of *Maimonides up to his own time. Some of his novellae on *halakhah* were published in the collection *Torah mi-Ẓiyyon*. He led the Jerusalem rabbis who in 1888 permitted plowing and sowing in the *shemittah* year (the Sabbatical Year); his decision on this issue was published in *Devar ha-Shemittah* (Jerusalem, 1888).

BIBLIOGRAPHY: Frumkin-Rivlin, 3 (1929), 298; M.D. Gaon, *Yehudei ha-Mizraḥ be-Ereẓ Yisrael*, 2 (1937), 295–6; J.M. Landau, *Ha-Yehudim be-Miẓrayim* (1967), index.

ISRAEL ACADEMY OF SCIENCES AND HUMANITIES, institution whose main functions are to promote work in the sciences and humanities, to advise the government on activities in these fields, and to represent Israel in international bodies and conferences. The academy was founded under a 1961 law. Its seat is in Jerusalem. In 1959 the government appointed 15 leading Israeli scholars as the founding members. The subsequent membership may at no time number more than 25 representatives of the sciences and 25 for the humanities. Accepted applicants are co-opted for life by the existing members. Members who reach the age of 75 are not included in these numbers, although they continue as full members. The academy's president is appointed by the president of the state, on the academy's recommendation, for an initial, renewable, three-year term. Martin *Buber, the first president of the academy (1959–62), was succeeded by Aharon *Katzir-Katchalsky (1962–68) and Gershom *Scholem (from 1968). In 1981 Jacob Ziv was elected president.

Science research projects supported by the academy have included a study of the flora and fauna of the region, and the pre-historical excavations and a geological survey of the Lower Pleistocene of the Central Jordan Valley. In the humanities, the academy supported projects in Jewish history, literature, thought, and religion. In cooperation with the Jewish Theological Seminary of America, it prepared a Concordance to the Jerusalem Talmud, and, in cooperation with the French National Center for Scientific Research (CNRS) of Paris, a survey of Hebrew paleography. Other activities were aimed at strengthening basic research in Israel, including founding and administering the Israel Science Foundation, with an annual budget of $53 million; taking part in the establishment of a new National Research Council (NRC, 2003) and an active Forum for National Research and Development Infrastructure (TELEM); helping initiate the projected five-year, $300 million Israel Nanotechnology Program (INP); and facilitating the participation of Israeli scientists in cutting-edge research at international high-energy physics (CERN) and synchrotron radiation (ESRF) mega-facilities.

[Moshe Avidor]

WEBSITE: www.academy.ac.il.

ISRAEL BEN BENJAMIN OF BELZEC (17th century), rabbi and author. Israel was rabbi in Rubashov, Belzec (c. 1648), and Lublin (c. 1648–50) and was regarded as one of the foremost talmudists of his time. He was the author of *Yalkut Ḥadash* (*Yalkut Yisre'eli*), an alphabetically arranged collection of homilies taken from diverse kabbalistic, aggadic, and midrashic works (published anonymously, Lublin, 1648, and later with an appendix entitled *Shikhḥat Leket*, Wilmersdorf, 1673); and *Tiferet Yisrael*, a collection of sermons delivered between 1632 and 1654 (Ms. Bodleian), including a funeral oration delivered in 1648 for the victims of the *Chmielnicki massacres. According to Jehiel *Heilperin, Israel was also called Jacob, but he should not be confused with Jacob Israels of Temesvár, rabbi of Slutsk, who was a victim of the Chmielnicki massacres of 1648.

BIBLIOGRAPHY: Heilperin, Dorot, 3 (1905), 54; Fuenn, Keneset, 683; S. Nissenbaum, *Le-Korot ha-Yehudim be-Lublin* (1899), 54; S. Wiener, *Kohelet Moshe* (1893–1918), 591 (no. 4825); Neubauer, Cat, nos. 924, 989.

[Joseph Elijah Heller]

ISRAEL BEN ELIEZER BA'AL SHEM TOV (known by the initials of "Ba'al Shem Tov" as **Besht**; c. 1700–1760), charismatic founder and first leader of *Ḥasidism in Eastern Europe. (See Chart: Ba'al Shem Tov Family). Through oral traditions handed down by his pupils (*Jacob Joseph of Polonnoye and others) as well as through the legendary tales about his life and behavior, he became Ḥasidism's first teacher and its exemplary saint. These tales, collected early in *Shivḥei ha-Besht* (Kapust and Berdichev, 1814–15; *In Praise of the Ba'al Shem Tov*, 1970) are also the main source for his biography. It is related that Israel was born in Okop, a small town in Podolia, to poor and elderly parents in hard times aggravated by wars in the region. Orphaned as a child, he later eked out a living first as an assistant (*behelfer*) in a *ḥeder* and later as a watchman at a synagogue. At Yazlovets, near Buchnach, where he was working as *behelfer*, he met and became friendly with young Meir b. Ẓevi Hirsch *Margolioth, later a famous talmudic scholar; Israel was considered by Meir both as colleague and teacher. According to tradition, in his 20s Israel went into hiding in the Carpathian Mountains in preparation for his future tasks. (He was accompanied by his second wife, Hannah, the first having died shortly after their marriage.) There he lived for several years, first as a digger of clay, which his wife sold in town; later he helped his wife in keeping an inn. In about 1730 he settled in Tluste. Israel had one son, Ẓevi, and a daughter, *Adel. His grandchildren were *Moses Ḥayyim Ephraim of Sudylkow and *Baruch of Medzibezh; *Naḥman of Bratslav was his great-grandson.

In the mid-1730s – ḥasidic tradition fixes it on his 36th birthday – Israel revealed himself as a healer and leader. The circles of Israel's followers and admirers widened rapidly. Many people were drawn by his magnetism and the widespread reports of his miracles, and several groups of Ḥasidim which had been formed earlier came under his influence and accepted his leadership and teaching to a greater or lesser degree (see *Ḥasidism; *Abraham Gershon of Kutow, Israel's brother-in-law; *Aryeh Leib of Polonnoye; *Naḥman of Kosov; and *Naḥman of Horodenka (Gorodenka)). Tradition hints that some of the members of these ḥasidic circles were at first repelled by Israel's activity as miracle healer, as a **ba'al shem*, although Israel himself was proud of this work, as demonstrated by his signature "Israel Ba'al Shem of Tlust"

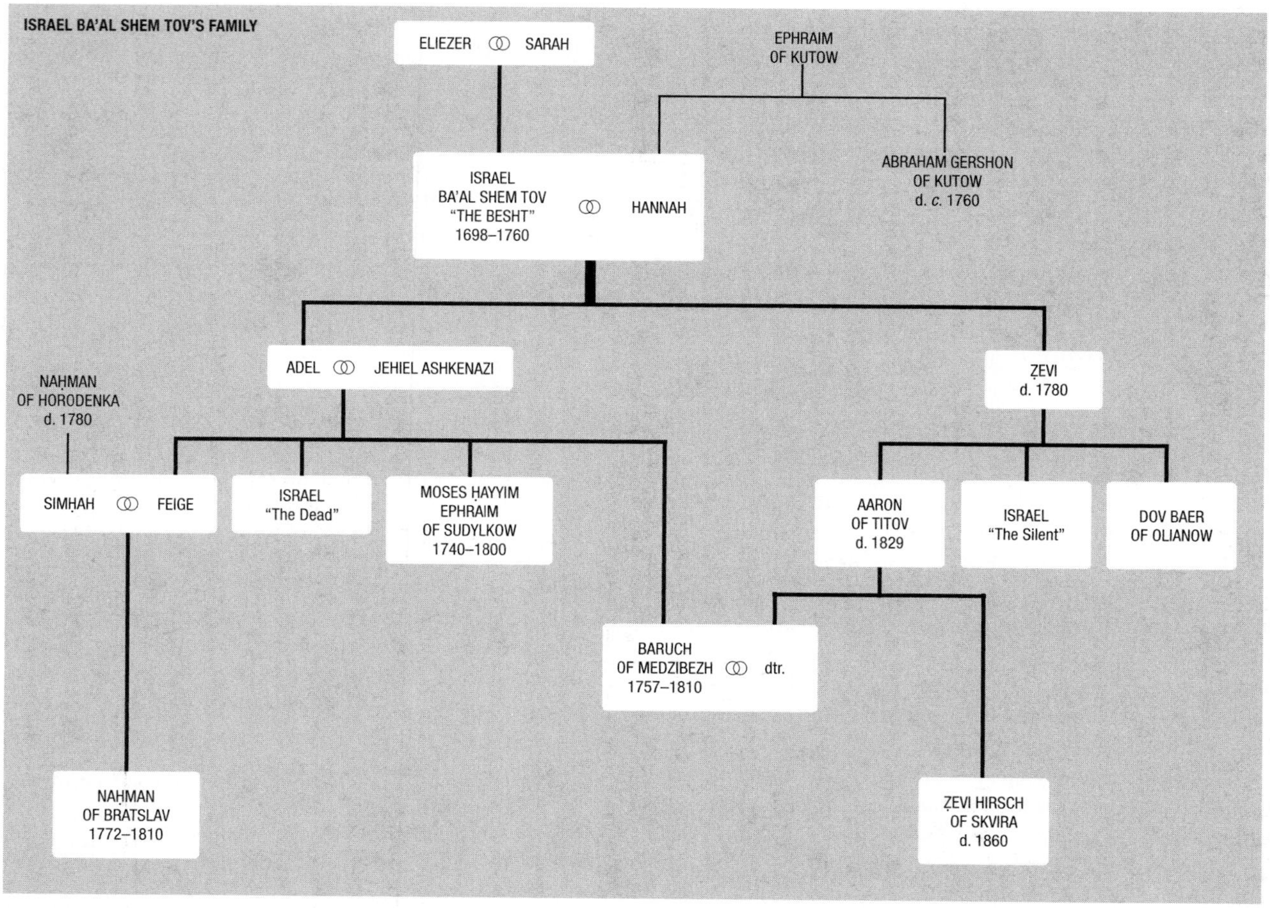

(Responsa *Mayim Ḥayyim* part one, 1858). However, contemporaries who did not belong to his circle regarded this activity favorably, as indicated by the designation of Israel as "the famous *ba'al shem tov*, may his light shine" (Meir Teomim in *Nofet Ẓufim Rav Peninim*, 1772).

For many years Israel planned to go to Ereẓ Israel. Once he had to return when he had already embarked and "he was very sad" (*Toledot Ya'akov Yosef*, Korets, 1780, p. 201). As late as 1751 – only nine years before his death – he wrote to his brother-in-law, "God knows that I do not despair of traveling to Ereẓ Israel; however, the time is not right" (*Ben Porat Yosef*, Korets, 1781).

Israel undertook journeys (*Shivḥei ha-Besht* tells a great deal about his travels and horses) to effect cures, expel demons and evil spirits (*leẓim*), and to win influence. In eulogistic folktales, the tradition of his pupils, and in writings hostile to him (see *David of Makow), the interdependence of his healing work and the charisma of his leadership are clearly apparent. Later ḥasidic tradition, however, tried to deprecate the importance of these healing and magical practices. In tales about him as well as through his teachings, Israel's great personal charm, remarkable magnetism, and ecstatic personality and behavior are revealed. Prayer was his main ecstatic and mystic approach to God, but intellectual study and learning took a secondary place. In specially exciting moments he reached a state of mystical exaltation – *aliyyat neshamah* – of which he gave realistic descriptions. Future events and past personalities, both good and evil, were shown to him in dreams. In traditional tales he is portrayed as engaged in conversation and in meeting with people, even women, individually or in small groups. He is never described as preaching in a synagogue. The traditional picture of Israel, always with his pipe in his hand or mouth, emphasizes the importance of his edifying secular tales. Israel's teachings do not indicate any talmudic scholarship, and his opponents criticized him for the lack of this and for his preoccupation with healing, writing amulets, and his conversation with simple men (see, e.g., David of Makow in PAAJR, 25 (1956), p. 147). Material from the *aggadah* and moralistic and kabbalistic works and traces of an acquaintance with the writings of Saadiah Gaon are evident in his teachings.

Ḥasidic legend made Israel one of the leaders in the disputation with Jacob *Frank in 1759, but his true attitude to this is expressed in the saying attributed to him after the apostasy of the Frankists: "The *Shekhinah* wails and says as long as a limb is attached to the body there is hope for its cure; but when it is severed, it cannot be restored; and every Jew is a limb of the *Shekhinah*" (*Shivḥei ha-Besht*).

Israel and his followers were conscious of his mission as a leader of his people. Many of his dreams and visions, much of what was revealed to him from on high, are related to the actual problems and sufferings of the Jews in his generation. Teaching the importance of charity, he himself gave much, and he helped in ransoming captives and prisoners, a pressing problem in his time. He taught that devotional joy was the proper attitude of the Jew in every moment of his life and in particular in prayer, exemplifying this through his own attitude to life and through his own mode of prayer. His admirers told especially about the light and fire that they imagined emanating from his person, and about his fiery way of reciting his prayers. Opposing too much fasting, he advised against preaching through harsh admonition. Even more than his teachings, his idealized personality became the inspiration for the life, leadership, and aspirations of the Ḥasidim up to the present day. It is typical of ḥasidic appreciation of the personality of its ideal figure that tales related by Jacob Joseph of Polonnoye state that Israel's particular teacher in heaven was *Ahijah the Shilonite, the prophet of the overthrow of a misguided establishment and of a new kingdom in Israel. Whether partly true or wholly legendary, the ḥasidic tale that in his youth Israel miraculously came by "compositions containing secrets and mysteries of the Torah, divine and practical Kabbalah" which had belonged to *Adam Ba'al Shem expresses the awareness that the theoretical roots of Israel's teachings lay in the *Kabbalah; the story also indicates the ḥasidic conviction that his appearance and influence were a mystery and a miracle.

[Haim Hillel Ben-Sasson]

Principal Teachings

R. Israel was aware of his special mission and his charismatic qualities. Despite this he feared failure and once told his grandson, Moses Ḥayyim Ephraim of Sudylkow, "Behold, I swear to you that there is one man in the world who hears Torah from God and the *Shekhinah*, and not from an angel or a seraph, and he does not believe that he will not be pushed aside by God as he can easily be plummetted into the deep abyss of evil" (*Degel Maḥaneh Efrayim*, p. 113). Although the teachings of the Ba'al Shem Tov derive to some extent from the Kabbalah and the frequently employed kabbalistic terminology, the original content of Besht Ḥasidism lies in its emphasis on personal existence and the salvation of the soul of the individual, which must precede the redemption of the world: "For before one prays for general redemption one must pray for the personal salvation of one's own soul" (*Toledot Ya'akov Yosef*). This emphasis on the personal replaced preoccupation with messianism and Israel forbade any attempt at magical activity designed to accelerate the eschatological era. His attitude is made clear in a letter to Abraham Gershon (dated 1751), in which he describes his dialogue with the Messiah during a spiritual ascent on Rosh Ha-Shanah, 1747: "I asked the Messiah, 'When will you come, master,' and he answered me, 'When your learning will be made known and revealed to the world and its source will spread and all can recite *yiḥudim* and experience spiritual ascent as you can…' and I was astonished and deeply grieved by this, and wondered when this would come to pass" (*Ben Porat Yosef*). Though expressing his deep messianic faith and strong messianic longings, this attitude is far from the mystical messianism which had proved so destructive shortly before (see Jacob *Frank; *Shabbetai Ẓevi).

At the core of Israel's teaching is the principle of **devekut* ("adhesion"), although for him the term had far greater emotional content than in its earlier kabbalistic usage. Averring that "faith is the adhesion of the soul to God" (*Toledot Ya'akov Yosef*, p. 23), he demanded that *devekut* exist in all daily acts and in social contacts. Man must worship God and cling to Him not only when practicing religious acts and holy deeds, but also in his daily affairs, in his business, and in social contacts, for when a "man is occupied with material needs, and his thought cleaves to God, he will be blessed" (*Ketonet Passim* (1866), 28a). His belief is linked with the Lurianic doctrine of the raising of the holy sparks (*niẓoẓot*), though he uses this concept with the limited meaning of the salvation of the individual soul alone. Because of his emphasis on the constant possibility of *devekut*, Israel did not advocate withdrawal from worldly life and aloofness from society. Indeed, he emphasized the element of joy in the worship of God and vigorously opposed fasts and asceticism. He warned Jacob Joseph of Polonnoye "lest he bring himself to the danger of many fasts, which contribute to melancholy and sadness" (*Shivḥei ha-Besht*). According to Israel, physical pleasure can give rise to spiritual pleasure, i.e., *devekut*. A physical act can be considered a religious act if the one performing it intends to worship God and the act is performed in a state of *devekut*, an assumption which demands *devekut* on the part of every Jew, not only the spiritual elite. For Israel as well as his disciples, *devekut* – especially during prayer – would often assume a definitely ecstatic character.

The study of Torah is also of prime importance in Israel's teachings, although he did not interpret the traditional ideal of "Torah for its own sake" in its generally accepted sense but understood "for its own sake" as "for the sake of the letter." "Thus I learned from my teacher in this matter" (*Toledot Ya'akov Yosef*, p. 151). Through contemplating the letters of the text which he studies, man opens the divine worlds before him. This belief is based on the assumption that the letters of the Torah evolved and descended from a heavenly source. Therefore one who studies properly, i.e., by contemplating the letters, restores the outward forms of the letters to their spiritual prototypes, their divine source. When the student links the letters of the Torah to their root he himself becomes joined to their higher forms and thus receives mystical revelations. "The desired intention in study for its own sake is for a man to attach himself in holiness and purity to the letters, both actively and potentially; they will make him wise and radiate much light and true eternal life – and he who manages to understand and become attached to holy letters can even tell the future from these letters" (M. Margoliouth, *Sod Yakhin u-Vo'az* (Ostraha, 1794), 6).

Prayer is one of the main stages for the worship of God. Through prayer, a man reaches *devekut* and contact with the divine worlds. As in the study of Torah, so too in prayer the way to *devekut* is through concentration on the mystical meaning of the letters: "According to what I learned from my master and teacher, the main occupation of Torah and prayer is that one should attach oneself to the spirituality of the light of the *Ein Sof found in the letters of the Torah and prayer, which is called study for its own sake" (*Toledot Ya'akov Yosef*, p. 25). However prayer which directs man to the attainment of *devekut* is at times disturbed by undesirable (lit. "foreign") thoughts (*maḥashavot zarot*) and the one who prays must deal with them properly, so that they do not damage his spiritual efforts. Israel's particular way of dealing with "undesirable thoughts" came to be called "the wisdom of the Besht" and caused R. Naḥman of Horodenka to recognize his authority and join his group. Undesirable thoughts were derived from a heavenly source and were understood by Israel as the results of cosmic processes generally associated with the doctrine of the fallen holy sparks in Lurianic Kabbalah. The spark is hidden in the extraneous ("sinful") thought and aspires to rise and be redeemed. This thrust conveys the undesirable thought to the human heart. He who sublimates the extraneous thought helps the spark to return to its divine source. According to some, Israel's teaching contains hints that extraneous thoughts are the final stage in the process of *aẓilut* ("emanation"). They are conceived of mainly in a Neoplatonic form and identified with the *kelippot* ("shells," forces of evil) at the extremity of the emanation. Some undesirable thoughts must be sublimated and corrected; others must be repelled and removed. "If a man wishes to ask, 'how do you distinguish between a thought to be repelled and one to be sublimated?' he should contemplate if correction to the thought entered his mind together with the extraneous thought, and then he will seek to bring it close to him and to sublimate it, and if he cannot immediately correct this thought, then he must remove it" (*Ben Porat Yosef*, p. 39).

The *Ẓaddik*

Two assumptions are basic to Israel's doctrine of the **ẓaddik*: the recognition of the existence of superior individuals whose spiritual qualities are greater than those of other human beings and who are outstanding in their higher level of *devekut*; and the conception of the Jewish community at large and the mutual responsibility of all members of the nation, as "every Jew is a limb of the *Shekhinah*" (*Shivḥei ha-Besht*). In order to fulfill his destiny the *ẓaddik* must at the same time observe the *mitzvah* of *devekut* and maintain contact with the material world through the circle surrounding him, even those who are counted among the sinners. Spiritually alone with God, he is the center of his community. He influences society and is influenced by it: the sins of his contemporaries affect him and lower his stature; his sinful thoughts stimulate others to commit sins. The task of the *ẓaddik* is to teach the people to worship God by means of *devekut* and to cause sinners to repent. The *ẓaddik* descends spiritually to the sinner, associates with him, and by his own ascent raises him and restores him to goodness, aiding him in purifying himself of his blemishes. The process of descent is executed when a weakness occurs in the *devekut* of the *ẓaddik*, but even then *devekut* does not cease and the descent does not signify the *ẓaddik*'s complete severance from the divine source. Indeed, in order that he may rise from the depths and raise the sinner with him, the *ẓaddik* must preserve his *devekut* to God. "When the *ẓaddik* descends from his heights it is an expression of the quality of mercy, in order that he may associate with the masses and elevate them" (*Toledot Ya'akov Yosef*, portion *Va-Yiggash*). Clearly this idea of the descent of the *ẓaddik* recalls Shabbatean notions and some scholars view it as a ḥasidic transformation of the Shabbatean doctrine of the descent of the Messiah.

The *ẓaddik* also engages in the restitution and elevation of the soul of a sinner who has died. It is related that Israel performed special acts to restore the souls of deceased sinners: "There are *ẓaddikim* who raise the wicked from hell during prayer. Thus I have heard in the name of Israel Ba'al Shem Tov" (*Rav Yeivi*, Ostraha, 1808, p. 40). Israel even attempted to restore the soul of Shabbetai Ẓevi, saying that he "had a spark of holiness but was seized by *Samael" (*Shivḥei ha-Besht*), but he was compelled to abandon this attempt because he realized that what holds true for Shabbetai Ẓevi would also be true for Jesus. There is no proof, however, that Israel had Shabbatean tendencies, as some scholars hold. It is known that he severely criticized the book **Ḥemdat Yamim* (Izmir, 1731/32), whose anonymous author was a Shabbatean. On the other hand, it is clear that he had seen Shabbatean writings (although their Shabbatean nature was only revealed later and he was not aware of it). Israel's doctrine of the *ẓaddik* was intended to express a spiritual relationship only and contained none of the later elements of "practical ẓaddikism" (see *Ḥasidism), nor any mention of the later belief that the *ẓaddik* must be supported by his disciples.

Reactions

Israel's reputation spread far from the areas of Podolia and Volhynia where he was active, even to circles unconnected with his religious leadership. That his activity also aroused opposition is evident in *Shivḥei ha-Besht* and hinted at in some of his parables. R. Ḥayyim ha-Kohen Rappaport, the *av bet din* in Lvov, warned his relatives in Buchach not "to turn to the 'witch doctor' who calls himself Ba'al Shem." However, the veracity of the document of excommunication in Ostraha (Ostrog; *Shever Poshe'im Zot Torat ha-Kanna'ut*) is questionable and its relation to Israel Ba'al Shem Tov uncertain.

The Teaching and Legend of the Ba'al Shem Tov

Israel Ba'al Shem Tov did not leave any works either in his own hand or signed by him, nor are there any contemporary portraits of him. However, several letters bearing his name have been published: to Abraham Gershon of Kutow (*Ben Porat Yosef*), to Jacob Joseph of Polonnoye (*Shivḥei ha-*

Besht), to Moses of Kutow (*Buẓina de-Nehora*, 1880), to an anonymous individual (*Shivḥei ha-Besht*), and to R. Meir *av bet din* of Staro-Konstantinov (Responsa *Mayim Ḥayyim*). Various fabrications exist. In 1919 a package purporting to be documents from Israel and his disciples was found in Kherson, U.S.S.R. which had allegedly come from the government archives in Kiev where documents were preserved regarding the trial of Israel of *Ruzhin, charged by the government for instigating the murder of an informer. Apparently, however, all these documents are forgeries or copies of works that had been previously published.

Israel did not put his teachings into writing and even opposed the attempts of others to do so. Only 20 years after his death, his disciple, Jacob Joseph, presented in three of his own works – *Toledot Ya'akov Yosef*, and *Ẓafenat Pa'ne'aḥ* and *Korets*, 1782 – hundreds of sermons and homilies which he had learned from the Ba'al Shem Tov. At the end of *Toledot Ya'akov Yosef* there is a collection of Israel's sayings, and the author comments: "These are statements which I heard from my teacher and I only took down fragmentary notes because I was afraid both of writing everything and also of forgetting it." Other disciples and their disciples included in their works statements which they had heard from him or which had been cited in his name. Aaron b. Ẓevi Hirsch ha-Kohen of Opatow (Apta) claimed to have collected all the statements of Israel which had appeared up to that time in his *Keter Shem Tov* (Zolkiew, 1795), but most of his quotations are from the works of Jacob Joseph. The book *Ẓavva'at ha-Ribash* of Isaiah of Janow (1794) does not include the testament of the Ba'al Shem Tov, but only a selection of his statement, and according to *Shneur Zalman of Lyady, who had collected the statements, did not understand their meaning. Most scholars contend that the work mainly includes teachings of the school of Dov Baer, the *Maggid* of Mezhirech, but this needs further study. The most complete and best anthology of Israel's teachings is *Sefer Ba'al Shem Tov* (Lodz, 1938), edited and arranged by Simeon Menahem Mendel Wodnik.

The legends about the Ba'al Shem Tov have distorted his historical character. Formed even during his lifetime, the stories about his miracles became an integral part of the ḥasidic atmosphere and both increased the admiration for him and stimulated his opponents. Disciples who had come in contact with him and his family were among the first to assert his supernatural qualities. But people who were not among his close associates also at times told of his charismatic personality, even during his lifetime. Thus there developed a literature of *shevaḥim* (lit. "praises"). The first anthology of legends was *Shivḥei ha-Besht*, compiled by Dov Baer b. Samuel of Linits, the son-in-law of Alexander Shoḥat, who served for several years as Israel's scribe. The collection was copied many times and hence was full of errors. Only after the compiler's death was it printed as *Shivḥei ha-Besht* by the publisher Israel Jaffe, a disciple of *Menahem Mendel of Vitebsk and Shneur Zalman of Lyady. Jaffe proofread the anthology, removing distortions which in his opinion resulted from copying. He rewrote the first chapter on R. Israel's birth, youth, and revelation according to the tradition given by Shneur Zalman. Thus Jaffe must be viewed as the second author and editor of the anthology, and his edition, printed in Kopys (Kapust) in 1814, has been accepted as the basic one; all other editions are based on it, with only slight changes. In that year the second book was printed in Berdichev and the third in Laszczów. Similarly, two editions appeared in Yiddish (Ostraha (Ostrog) and Laszców) which differ greatly from the Hebrew edition. The reciprocal relationship between the Hebrew and Yiddish versions of *Shivḥei ha-Besht* has not yet been fully investigated. Later, *Shivḥei ha-Besht* appeared in many versions, in Hebrew, Yiddish, and Ladino. J.S. Bick records an unpublished translation in Polish in a letter to Mendel Lefin. But even Ḥasidim had reservations about the work, especially the strange and unreliable stories which aroused the criticism and scorn of the *Mitnaggedim* and *maskilim*, who used it as a weapon in their war against Ḥasidim. It contains some 230 stories, arranged in series united by common themes, heroes, and motifs. Despite its imaginary-legendary character, historical events are recalled along with undoubtedly reliable traditions. Many of the historical events recalled are confirmed in non-ḥasidic sources.

In the 19th century several collections of legends about the Ba'al Shem Tov, his colleagues, and disciples appeared (also in Yiddish), some of which repeated stories found in *Shivḥei ha-Besht* and some of which contained new tales. Only isolated ones are true. One of the propagators of imaginary legends about Israel and the leaders of early Ḥasidism was Michael Levi Frumkin, also known by the name *Rodkinson, a Chabad Ḥasid who became a *maskil*. However, what is related in *Kevuẓat Ya'akov* (1897) can be accepted as true. Isaac Eizik of *Komarno and the Shneersohn *ẓaddikim* should be included among the ḥasidic masters who cultivated the legends about Israel Ba'al Shem Tov and added new traditions. Many of the stories concerning the Ba'al Shem Tov were retold by Martin Buber (see, for example, his *Tales of the Ḥasidim*, 1 (1961²), 35–86 and *Jewish Mysticism* (1931)).

[Avraham Rubinstein]

BIBLIOGRAPHY: Jacob Joseph of Polonnoye, *Toledot Ya'akov Yosef* (1780); idem, *Ben Porat Yosef* (1781); idem, *Ẓafenat Pa'ne'ah* (1782); idem, *Ketonet Passim* (1866); Moses Ḥayyim Ephraim, *Degel Maḥaneh Efrayim* (1811); Aaron ha-Kohen of Apta, *Keter Shem Tov* (1794/95); Isaiah of Janov, *Seder Ẓavva'ot me-Rabbi Yisrael Ba'al Shem Tov im Hanhagot Yesharot* (1794); idem, *Sefer Katan im Kavvanot ha-Mikveh* (1819); idem, *Likkutei Yekarim* (1792); S.M.M. Wodnik, *Sefer Ba'al Shem Tov* (1938); D. Fraenkel, *Mikhtavim me-ha-Besht ve-Talmidav* (1923); Ch. Bloch, *Kovez Mikhtavim Mekoriyyim me-ha-Besht ve-Talmidav* (1920); M. Mark, *Rabbi Yisrael Baal Shem Tov* (1960); M.L. Rodkinson, *Toledot Ba'al Shem Tov* (1876); I. Schipper, in: *Hadoar*, 39 (1960/61), 27f.; Y. Opatasho, *Mayses fun Rab Yisroel Baal Shem Tov* (1957); S.Z. Setzer, *Rab Yisroel Ba'al Shem Tov* (1919); T. Ysander, *Studien zum bĕst'schen Hasidimus* (1933); G. Scholem, in: *Review of Religion*, 15 (1950), 115–39; E. Eindelman, *Rabbi Yisroel Ba'al Shem Tov* (1961); J.L. Maimon (ed.), *Sefer ha-Besht* (1960); M.J. Gutmann, *R. Yisrael Ba'al Shem Tov* (1922); Y. Twersky, *Ha-Ba'al Shem Tov* (1959); A. Kahana, *R. Yisrael Ba'al Shem Tov* (1900); *Shivḥei ha-Besht* (1815); D. Ben Amos and J.R. Mintz, *In Praise of the Ba'al Shem Tov*

(1970); A. Walden, *Shem ha-Gedolim he-Ḥadash* (1864); M. Bodek, *Sefer ha-Dorot mi-Talmidei ha-Besht* (1865); Ch. Shmeruk, in: *Zion*, 28 (1963); Y. Raphael, in: *Aresheth*, 2 (1960), 358–77; 3 (1961), 440–1; A. Rubinstein, in: *Tarbiz*, 35 (1965/66), 174–91; B. Landa, *Ha-Besht u-Venei Heikhalo* (1961); H. Zeitlin, *Rabbi Yisrael Ba'al Shem Tov* (1910); E. Steinman, *Rabbi Yisrael Ba'al Shem Tov* (1960); Dubnow, Ḥasidut, 41–75, 411–6; A.Z. Zweifel, *Shalom al Yisrael* (1868), 48–60; M. Unger, *R. Israel Baal Shem Tov* (1963); J.I. Schochet, *Rabbi Israel Baal Shem Tov* (1961); H. Rabinowicz, *The World of Ḥasidism* (1970), index; J.G. Weiss, in: JJS, 8 (1957), 199–213; H.H. Ben-Sasson (ed.), *Toledot Yisrael ba-Et ha-Ḥadashah*, 3 (1969), 55–57. **ADD. BIBLIOGRAPHY:** D. Ben-Amos and J.R. Mintz (eds.), *In Praise of the Baal Shem Tov: The Earliest Collection of Legends about the Founder of Hasidism* (1996); M. Rosman, *The Founder of Hasidism: A Quest for the Historical Ba'al Shem Tov* (1996); I. Etkes, *The Besht, Magician, Mystic and Leader* (2004); Y. Buxbaum, *Light and Fire of the Baal Shem Tov* (2005); Z. Gries, *Conduct Literature (Regimen Vitae), Its History and Place in the Life of the Beshtian Hasidism* (Heb., 1989); H. Pedaya, "The Baal Shem Tov, Rabbi Jacob Joseph of Polonoye and the Great Maggid," in: *Daat*, 45 (2000), 25–73 (Heb.).

ISRAEL BEN JOEL (Susslin; 14th century), liturgical poet and talmudist. The *tosafot* of Israel, who lived in Erfurt, are quoted by Jacob b. Moses *Moellin (Maharil), Israel b. Pethahiah *Isserlein and others; a halakhic decision of his appears among the responsa of *Meir of Rothenburg (Budapest edition, no. 1021) and of Moses Mintz (no. 104). Israel also composed an elaborate elegy, which refers to contemporary religious persecutions, mentioning the names of 22 localities, six countries, and 13 rabbis who died as martyrs. His *tosafot* are extant in manuscript form (according to Zunz in Munich Ms. 358, although Steinschneider in his catalog does not list this work; apparently also in Bodleian Ms. Opp. 8).

BIBLIOGRAPHY: Davidson, Oẓar, 3 (1930), 321 no. 280; Fuenn, Keneset, 692.

[Jefim (Hayyim) Schirmann]

ISRAEL BEN JONATHAN FROM LECZYCA (first half of 17th century), kabbalistic author. Israel lived in Leczyca and Shklov, where he acted as rabbi. Around 1650 he had to leave his country and became an exile in Italy. He had friendly contacts with Abraham Joseph Solomon b. Mordecai *Graziano in Modena. Israel published *Or Israel* (Amsterdam, 1657), kabbalistic homilies in the spirit of the *Zohar, in verse form, with ten chapters arranged according to the order of the Ten Commandments. A copy of this book with glosses in the handwriting of Abraham Graziano is in the library of the Academy of Sciences, Leningrad.

BIBLIOGRAPHY: Steinschneider, Cat Bod, 1166, no. 5462; Fuerst, Bibliotheca, 2 (1863), 148; S. Wiener, *Kohelet Moshe*, 1 (1893), 59, no. 472.

[Joseph Elijah Heller]

ISRAEL BEN PEREZ OF POLOTSK (d. about 1785), ḥasidic rabbi, one of the leading disciples of *Dov Baer of Mezhirech. He excelled as a preacher, and as an emissary for his teacher together with Azriel of Polotsk, he won over many Jews to Ḥasidism. After the death of Dov Baer in 1772, Israel settled in Polotsk and with several of the Maggid's disciples helped *Menahem Mendel of Vitebsk to spread Ḥasidism in Belorussia. In the month of Adar 1777, as a result of the persecutions by the *Mitnaggedim in Lithuania and Belorussia, he went to Ereẓ Israel with Menahem Mendel and *Abraham b. Alexander Katz of Kalisk at the head of a group of 300 Ḥasidim. They reached Ereẓ Israel in Elul 1777 and settled in Safed. Because of their economic difficulties, Israel was sent abroad a year later to organize the collection of funds and to arrange for regular maintenance of Ḥasidim who settled in Ereẓ Israel, his qualities as a speaker and organizer making him suitable for this task. His first stop was Constantinople where he collected a considerable sum of money. From there he continued to his native Belorussia where he contacted *Shneur Zalman of Lyady and Issachar Baer of Lubavitch. With them he headed the Ḥasidim in Belorussia when the movement was banned for the second time by the *Mitnaggedim* in 1781. Israel was instrumental in introducing the custom of *ma'amadot* (collection of funds for regular maintenance of Ḥasidim who settled in Ereẓ Israel) among the Ḥasidim. He intended to return to Ereẓ Israel, but became ill and died in Fastov, Ukraine, where he was buried. His detailed letter written in Jassy in Iyyar 1778 to the trustees of the charitable funds in Vitebsk contains important information on ḥasidic settlement in Ereẓ Israel and the situation of the Jews there, and on his visit to and activities in Constantinople. Israel conceived the establishment of a permanent fund for Ḥasidim who settled in Ereẓ Israel. The few teachings attributed to him concern ways of repentance. He did not found a ḥasidic dynasty.

BIBLIOGRAPHY: Dubnow, Ḥasidut, index; Yaari, Sheluḥei, 608–11; idem, *Iggerot Ereẓ Yisrael* (1943), 312–6; I. Halpern, *Ha-Aliyyot ha-Rishonot shel ha-Ḥasidim le-Ereẓ Yisrael* (1946), 20–37; Horodetzky, Ḥasidut, index; W.Z. Rabinowitsch, *Lithuanian Ḥasidism* (1970), index.

[Wolf Zeev Rabinowitsch]

ISRAEL BEN SAMUEL HA-KOHEN (11th century), *Gaon* of the Sura Academy from 1017 to approximately 1033 (succeeded R. *Dosa b. Saadiah). Israel was the son of R. *Samuel b. Hophni and the brother-in-law of R. *Hai Gaon. At the time that his father was *gaon* of the academy, Israel functioned as its secretary. He had close ties of friendship with R. *Abraham b. Nathan (Abraham b. Atta), the leader of the Kairouan community, and at the latter's request composed a book in Arabic, on the obligation of reciting the prayers; only a few fragments of this work have been preserved. Two letters by Israel were found in the Cairo *Genizah*. One is addressed to his own community and emphasized the need of following the Rabbanite tradition of biblical exegesis rather than that of the Karaites. A number of his rulings that have survived were published in B.M. Lewin's *Oẓar ha-Ge'onim* (1, 3, 5, 6; 1928–34) and in S. Assaf's *Teshuvot ha-Ge'onim* (1927). He was succeeded in the gaonate by R. Azariah ha-Kohen (d. before 1038), who was either his brother or his son.

BIBLIOGRAPHY: Poznański, in: REJ, 62 (1911), 120–3; 63 (1912),

318; Marmorstein, in: JQR, 8 (1917–18), 6–8; Mann, *ibid.*, 364–6; 11 (1920–21), 410ff.; Mann, Texts, index; Assaf, in: *Tarbiz*, 2 (1931), 328–30; Abramson, Merkazim, 75–76. **ADD. BIBLIOGRAPHY:** D.E. Sklare, *Samuel ben Hofni Gaon and His Cultural World* (1996), 5, 9–10, 25, 34, 87.

[Abraham David]

ISRAEL BEN SAMUEL OF SHKLOV (d. 1839), talmudic scholar of Lithuania and, later, in Ereẓ Israel, where he was leader of the "*Kolel ha-Perushim," the local community of the disciples of *Elijah b. Solomon Zalman, the Vilna Gaon. Israel was born and brought up in Shklov. Although he studied under the Vilna Gaon for only six months before the latter's death, he was nevertheless entrusted with the preparation of the Gaon's commentaries for publication. In 1809 he joined the third group of the Gaon's pupils, led by Ḥayyim b. Tobiah, that immigrated to Ereẓ Israel and settled in Safed, where there were already 40 families from the two previous groups. Within less than a year of his arrival he was sent by the Kolel ha-Perushim to Lithuania to organize permanent assistance for the immigrants. During the course of this mission, which proved extremely successful, he published the notes of the Vilna Gaon on the tractate *Shekalim* of the Jerusalem Talmud together with a commentary of his own under the title of *Taklin Ḥadtin* (Minsk, 1812). Though caught up in the Napoleonic wars which had meanwhile reached Russia, he succeeded in returning to Safed at the beginning of 1813. In the summer of that year, seeking to escape a plague which broke out in Safed, Israel and his family set out for Jerusalem. His wife died on the journey, his two sons, two of his daughters, and his son-in-law died in Jerusalem, and his father and mother at Safed and only he and his youngest daughter survived. In 1816, after having returned to Safed, Israel was chosen to succeed Menahem Mendel of Shklov, the leader of the Kolel ha-Perushim there, when the latter moved to Jerusalem. Israel served as head of the community, which now numbered 600, first in Safed and later in Jerusalem. He organized assistance from abroad, maintained amicable relations with the ḥasidic and Sephardi communities, represented his community before the authorities, and established good relations with the Arabs. Reports having reached Safed in 1830 of the existence of Jewish tribes in Yemen, he sent a special envoy there to search for remnants of the Ten Tribes. When Israel *Bak opened a Hebrew printing house in Safed in 1832, he entrusted him with the printing of his *Pe'at ha-Shulḥan*, on laws applying in Ereẓ Israel, which had been omitted from the Shulḥan Arukh. The work did not appear until 1836, its printing having been interrupted by an attack by the Arabs of Upper Galilee on the Jews of Safed. Israel organized help for those who had suffered from the attack, which lasted for 33 days and in the course of which much Jewish property was looted. On the first day of 1837 an earthquake killed more than 2,000 Jews in Safed. Israel was then in Jerusalem, and upon hearing of the disaster, he immediately sent help to Safed and letters to Jews abroad soliciting their aid for the stricken. Safed having been reduced to rubble, Israel for the last two years of his life lived, like most of the refugees from the earthquake, in Jerusalem. Louis *Loewe, who met him there, related that on the Sabbath Israel spoke only Hebrew. His health failing, Israel went in 1839 to Tiberias where he died. His grave and tombstone were discovered in Tiberias in 1964. Israel's diary has been partially preserved, as have numerous letters which he wrote to people abroad. They constitute important sources for the history of the Jewish settlement in Ereẓ Israel during the first half of the 19th century.

BIBLIOGRAPHY: Frumkin, in: *Zion*, 2 (1927), 128–48; Frumkin-Rivlin, 3 (1929), 138–57, 164–7; Levy, in: *Sinai*, 5 (1939), 30–37; A. Yaari, *ibid.*, 52–65; idem, *Iggerot Ereẓ Yisrael* (1943), 324–63, 404, 550–1; Yaari, Sheluḥei, 674, 757–9; L. Jung (ed.), *Men of the Spirit* (1964), 61–81.

[Avraham Yaari]

ISRAEL CHAMBER ORCHESTRA (formerly the **Israel Chamber Ensemble**). The Israel Chamber Orchestra was founded in 1965 by conductor Gary *Bertini, to offer a range of music which had not previously been available to the Israeli public, from Baroque to original contemporary works commissioned for Israeli composers. The repertoire includes solo recitals, works for chamber orchestra, and chorale concerts. Orchestra members include many recent immigrants, particularly from the U.S.S.R. and the United States.

Among the outstanding musical directors have been Rudolf Barshai and Luciano Berio. Uri Segal became musical director of the Israel Chamber Orchestra, following a successful career abroad. After winning first prize in the 1969 Mitropoulos Conducting Competition in New York, he conducted major orchestras in New York, England, and then throughout Europe, America, and in New Zealand. Subsequent directors were Yoav Talmi, Shlomo *Mintz, and Philippe Entremont, who served as principal conductor in 1995–98 and was afterwards appointed laureate conductor. Maestro Salvador Mas Conde served as musical director in 1998–2001, succeeded by Noam *Sheriff (2002–5) and Gil Shohat (from 2005), an Israeli composer known for his avant-gardism.

In 1978 the orchestra undertook a project of music education for youth, presenting the first series of special Youth and Family Concerts. Using "special events," commentary, audiovisual media, and actor-mime performances accompanying musical presentation, the programs aim to bring youth closer to music and musical understanding. The orchestra also performs in special locales or atmospheres suitable to the work being performed.

The Israel Chamber Orchestra presents its regular annual concert series performances in Israel and undertakes annual concert tours abroad, especially in Europe and America. Each concert program is recorded and filmed in cooperation with the Israel Broadcasting Authority.

The orchestra continues to expand and diversify, including "New Dimensions" concerts of contemporary music, guest soloists, and conductors, and also places a strong emphasis on opportunities for Israeli soloists and rising young artists.

Numerous well-known artists have performed with the

orchestra, including Mstislav Rostropovich, Vladimir *Ashkenazy, Isaac *Stern, Itzhak *Perlman, Pinchas *Zuckerman, Shlomo *Mintz, Yefim *Bronfman, and Jean Pierre Rampal. Several internationally acclaimed choirs appeared with the Orchestra, such as the Netherlands Chamber Choir, Stuttgart Chamber Choir, Ensemble Vocal de Lausanne, Gulbenkian Choir, Brigham Young University Choir, Toelz Boys Choir, Prague Chamber Choir, and Vienna Sangerknaben.

The orchestra is supported by public and private funds, and a public council serves it in an advisory capacity.

WEBSITE: www.ico.co.il.

ISRAEL EXPLORATION SOCIETY (IES; Heb. Ha-Ḥevrah le-Ḥakirat Ereẓ Israel ve-Attikoteha), society founded in Jerusalem in 1914 on the initiative of I. *Ben-Zvi, Y. *Press, D. *Yellin, A.M. *Luncz, A. *Brawer, and others, on the model of the foreign societies engaged in the exploration of the Holy Land, its history and antiquities. Its original name, the Jewish Palestine Exploration Society, was changed in 1948 after the establishment of the State of Israel. The activities of the Society were interrupted by the outbreak of World War I and were resumed in 1920 with the assistance of A. Masie and N. *Slouschz, under the British Mandatory government. Its first excavations included Absalom's Tomb and a synagogue at Hammath-Tiberias, both by N. Slouschz, and in 1925–27 the Third Wall at Jerusalem was partly cleared by E.L. *Sukenik and L. *A.Mayer. In 1929 B. *Mazar (Maisler) became secretary of the Society and, under its auspices, excavated at Ramat Raḥel (1931) and began uncovering the necropolis of *Bet She'arim (1936). S. *Klein was president of the Society from 1932 until his death in 1940 when he was succeeded by L.A. Mayer (until 1959). From 1933 to 1966 the Society published a quarterly bulletin (BJPES, from 1948, BIES); its other publications were a series of proceedings (*Koveẓ*, 4 vols.) and a library of Palestinology (17 vols.). In 1943 the Society initiated a series of annual conventions. The chairmen of the Society since 1944 have been Y. Ben-Zvi, M. Schwabe, Z. Lif, Y. Yadin, and A. Biran, chairman in 1995. From 1960 B. Mazar was president. With the establishment of the State of Israel the activities of the Society expanded enormously, parallel with the growth of interest in archaeology. It continued the excavations at Beth She'arim and conducted other ones at Tell Qasile, Hazor, *Masada, the Judean Desert caves, En Gedi, *Arad, the Temple Mount, Jewish Quarter and City of David in Jerusalem, Herodion, Aphek, Lachish, Dor, Ẓippori, and other sites. It is presently co-sponsoring the renewed excavations at Tel Hazor. Besides the excavation reports of these and other sites, the Society publishes the Hebrew-English series *Eretz-Israel: Archaeological, Historical and Geographical Studies* (1951–), the Hebrew-language journal *Qadmoniot* (1968–); since 1995, in cooperation with the Israel Antiquities Authority), the Hebrew-language *Studies in the Geography of Israel* (1960–), and the English-language quarterly *Israel Exploration Journal* (1951–). A major reference work jointly published by the Israel Exploration Society and Carta is the four-volume illustrated *New Encyclopedia of Archaeological Excavations in the Holy Land* (1993), which has also appeared in a Hebrew version.

The Society's annual conferences are major events for Israeli archaeologists and the general public interested in the subject. During annual archaeological field trips, members of the Society have visited sites throughout Israel and many neighboring countries. In recent years it has organized and co-sponsored two international congresses devoted to biblical archaeology (1984 and 1990) proceedings of which have been published in two volumes entitled *Biblical Archaeology Today.* In addition to its own publications, the society co-publishes books with the Kibbutz Meuḥad, Mosad Bialik, Yad Ben-Zvi, Magnes Press, and other publishers. In 1989 the IES and its director, Joseph *Aviram, received the Israel Prize.

[Michael Avi-Yonah]

WEBSITE: www.hum.huji.ac.il/ies/.

ISRAEL (ben Samuel?) HA-DAYYAN HA-MA'ARAVI (d. before 1354), Karaite scholar living in *Cairo. Israel, with his pupil *Japheth b. David ibn Ṣaghīr, is reported to have overcome the last vestiges of opposition to the reform of the Karaite law of incest, begun by *Jeshua b. Judah and others in the 11th century, which abolished the catenary theory of forbidden marriages that threatened the physical survival of the Karaites as a group. He was unsuccessful, however, in his attempt to reform the burdensome Karaite law of uncleanness. Israel was a prolific writer in both Arabic and Hebrew. His works include *Shurūṭ al-Dhabāḥah* on slaughtering, abridged in Hebrew as *Hilkhot Sheḥitah* (Vienna, 1830); *Seder Inyan Ibbur* on the calendar (published in J.C. Wolf's *Bibliotheca Hebraea*, 4, 1733); both tracts are said to be parts of a comprehensive code of Karaite law titled *Sefer ha-Mitzvot*; and *Tartīb al-ʿAqāʾid al-Sittah* (ed. by E. Mainz, in: PAAJR, 22 (1953), 55–63) on the principles of faith, translated into Hebrew as *Sheshet ha-Emunot*. He also wrote liturgical poetry.

BIBLIOGRAPHY: Mann, Texts, 2 (1935), index, s.v. *Israel of Maghreb*; L. Nemoy (ed.), *Karaite Anthology* (1952), 235, 378.

[Leon Nemoy]

ISRAEL ḤARIF OF SATANOV (d. 1781), homilist and kabbalist. A famous rabbi of his time, known for his deep knowledge of both *halakhah* and Kabbalah, Israel was a member of the first group of Ḥasidim to follow *Israel b. Eliezer Ba'al Shem Tov, founder of the movement. Israel wrote many works, some of which were lost and others accidentally burned. Only one major work, *Tiferet Yisrael*, a collection of kabbalistic homilies delivered during the years 1747–80, appeared in print. The book was published in Lemberg in 1865 by his grandson, Rabbi Abraham Isaiah Yaffe, who added an introductory note. Another of Israel's writings found in Abraham Yaffe's possession was an interpretation of the Holy Name, a work often quoted in *Tiferet Yisrael.*

Israel was a traditional Lurianic kabbalist, whose concepts of the world, redemption, and ethics were derived from the teachings of that school. His work lays great emphasis on the expectation of the redemption and gives several calculations when the Messiah will come and the process of redemption will begin; the latest date given is 1788. However, this messianic interest did not bring Israel into alliance with the followers of Shabbetai Ẓevi and Jacob Frank, his book rather containing clear polemical expressions opposing the Shabbatean movement. It is probable that Israel was closely connected with Ba'al Shem Tov, but there is no proof that his theology was influenced by the teachings of the new Ḥasidism.

BIBLIOGRAPHY: I. Tishby, in: *Zion*, 32 (1967), 10–15; G. Scholem, in: *Tarbiz*, 25 (1955/56), 432; B. Minz, in: *Shivḥei ha-Besht* (1961), 39–45.

[Joseph Dan]

ISRAELI (Chernomorski), BENZION (1887–1954), pioneer of the Second Aliyah. Born in Glukhov, Ukraine, Israeli settled in Ereẓ Israel in 1906, working in Petaḥ Tikvah and Reḥovot as an agricultural laborer and guard. He returned to Russia for a time and served in the army. Upon his return to Ereẓ Israel he worked on Kinneret Farm and in Sejerah and in Kefar Uriyyah in the Judean Hills. He was one of the founders of the kevuẓah *Kinneret. Together with his friend Noah Naftulski, he devoted himself to the cultivation of bananas in the Jordan Valley. He traveled eight times to Iraq, Persia, and Egypt and after considerable efforts and dangers brought back choice date scions; the date trees in Israel are to his credit. In 1919 he was a member of the central board of the Agricultural Worker's Organization of *Aḥdut ha-Avodah and was active in Ḥever ha-Kevuẓot in promoting the union of the kibbutz movement. In 1941, Israeli joined the Jewish Brigade, in spite of his age, and organized the volunteering for army service in Palestine. With his unit he went to North Africa and the Italian front, and at the end of the war was active in the rescue of the survivors of the Holocaust. He was the prime mover in the establishment of Oholo, an educational institution on the shores of Lake Kinneret. He was killed by a plane which crashed into a crowd during a ceremony to honor the memory of the Haganah paratroopers of World War II at kibbutz Ma'agan. His writings and speeches were edited by S. *Yavnieli (1956).

BIBLIOGRAPHY: S. Stoler, *Masot Benzion Israeli* (1959).

[Abraham Aharoni]

ISRAELI, ISAAC BEN JOSEPH (first half of the 14th century), Spanish astronomer who worked in Toledo. Israeli is best known for his book *Yesod Olam* ("The Foundation of the World") written in 1310, which was considered the most important contribution to Hebrew literature in this field. It dealt with the geometrical problems of the earth in the Ptolemaic system of the universe as revised by al-Biṭsūjī, the seasons, etc., and included astronomical tables. The high esteem in which this book was held over several centuries led to an edition in 1777 being published in Berlin by Jacob Shklover, and a more complete edition, with a preface by David Cassel, was produced in Berlin (1846–48) by B. Goldberg and L. Rosenkranz. There are also commentaries on this work by Isaac *Alḥadib, Judah *Bassan, and Elijah *Mizraḥi. An abridged version in Arabic was written by the author's son, Joseph Israeli b. Isaac, a Hebrew translation of which (under the title *Kiẓẓur Yesod Olam*) still exists. Isaac Israeli is also the author of two other books, still extant in manuscripts, *Sha'ar ha-Shamayim* and *Sha'ar ha-Millu'im*.

BIBLIOGRAPHY: Steinschneider, Arab Lit, 164; idem, *Die Mathematik bei den Juden* (1897), 39; Waxman, Literature, 2 (1960²), 320–1; G. Sarton, *Introduction to the History of Science*, 3 (1947–48), 691–2, includes bibliography; W.M. Feldman, *Rabbinical Mathematics and Astronomy* (1931), 111.

[Arthur Beer]

ISRAELI, ISAAC BEN SOLOMON (c. 855-c. 955), physician and philosopher. Born in *Egypt, Israeli emigrated at about the age of 50 to *Kairouan, capital of the *Maghreb, where ʿUbayd Allāh al-Mahdī, founder of the Fatimid dynasty, appointed him court physician. His renown among his fellow Jews is attested by the fact that *Saadiah Gaon, while still in Egypt, addressed numerous letters to him, consulting him on philosophical and scientific matters. He remained unmarried and is quoted as having referred to his books as more likely to keep his memory alive than children would.

Philosophical Writings

Of Israeli's philosophical writings, the *Kitāb al-Ḥudūd* (*Sefer ha-Gevulim*, "Book of Definitions") is the best known. It was popular among the Latin schoolmen, who knew it in two versions, a Latin translation of the Arabic original by Gerard of Cremona, and an anonymous abridged Latin text (both edited by J.T. Muckle in *Archives d'histoire doctrinale et littéraire du moyen âge*, 12–13 (1937–38), 299ff.). Medieval Jewish writers, too, were familiar with the work. Moses *Ibn Ezra reproduces a few passages from it without naming the source in his *Kitāb al-Ḥadīqa* ("Book of the Garden"), as is most probably also the case with the 11th-century *Ghāyat al-Ḥakīm* ("Aim of the Wise"), known among the Latin schoolmen as *Picatrix*, by a Muslim author in Spain who seems to have used Israeli's work. Isaac ibn *Laṭīf, Abraham *Ibn Ḥasdai, and Isaac de Lattes also mention the book. *Maimonides, in his letter to Samuel ibn Tibbon, lists it among some Neoplatonic treatises described by him as of little merit, whereas Shem Tov ibn *Falaquera remarks: "The books of Isaac Israeli are most useful" (*Sefer ha-Mevakkesh*). The Arabic original of the work was translated into Hebrew twice. Nissim b. Solomon's version was first published by H. Hirschfeld (in: *Festschrift… Moritz Steinschneiders* (1896), Heb. sect. 131–41). Fragments of the second Hebrew version were discovered by A. Borosov and edited by A. Altmann (JSS, 2 (1957), 232–42). The book offers 56 definitions. It opens with an account (based on al-*Kindī) of *Aristotle's four types of inquiry (whether, what, which, why), and an elaboration of al-Kindī's definitions of philosophy. Israeli's dependence on al-Kindī was first noticed by S.M. Stern. There follow definitions of wisdom, intellect, soul, the celestial sphere, the vital spirit, and nature, which reflect the influence of a Neoplatonic pseudepigraphon (ascribed to Aristotle) that is traceable even more clearly in Israeli's other writings, and other definitions, most of them very brief. Israeli's *Kitāb al-Jawāhir* ("Book of Substances") has survived only in fragments of the original Arabic, discovered by A. Borisov and edited by S.M. Stern (JSS, 7 (1956), 13–29). The *Sefer ha-Ru'aḥ ve-ha-Nefesh* ("Treatise on Spirit and Soul"), which may have formed part of a larger work (possibly an exegetical treatise on "Let the waters bring forth abundantly," and is extant only in Hebrew, was published by M. Steinschneider (in *Ha-Karmel* (1871), 400–5). In both works Israeli develops his doctrine of emanation which is derived from the Neoplatonic source mentioned above. A clue to this source is found in another treatise attributed to Aristotle, the *Sha'ar ha-Yesodot le-Aristo* ("Chapter on the Elements by Aristotle"), preserved in a Hebrew Mantua manuscript, but which, following a suggestion by G. Scholem, A. Altmann has established to be a work by Israeli. It incorporates the previously mentioned pseudo-Aristotelian treatise, and refers to its source in the opening sentence ("Aristotle … said"). In his edition of the Mantua text (JSS, 7 (1956), 31–57), Altmann showed that Israeli's metaphysical doctrine throughout his writings is decisively influenced by this source, and he listed a number of parallel texts in other writings (partly already noticed by Scholem and J. Guttmann), which enhanced the significance of the discovery of that source. The relationship between Israeli's source on the one hand, and the parallel texts in Abraham ibn Ḥasdai's *Ben ha-Melekh ve-ha-Nazir* and in the long version of the *Theology of Aristotle* (discovered by Borisov) on the other, has been investigated by S.M. Stern (see A. Altmann and S.M. Stern, *Isaac Israeli, A Neoplatonic Philosopher of the Early Tenth Century* (1958), 95–105, 114–7, and Stern's article in: *Oriens*, 13–14 (1961), 58–120). The conclusion reached by Stern is that there existed a Neoplatonic treatise (termed by him "Ibn Ḥasdai's neoplatonist") which served as a source for the anonymous author of the long version of the *Theology of Aristotle*, Israeli, and Ibn Ḥasdai. A further treatise by Israeli, and the most extensive in scope, is his *Kitāb al-Ustuquṣṣāt* ("Book on the Elements"), of which there is a Latin version by Gerard of Cremona (printed in *Omnia Opera Ysaac*) and two Hebrew translations, one by Abraham ibn Ḥasdai (*Sefer Yesodot*, edited by S. Fried, 1900), and one contained in a Munich manuscript which may have been made by Moses ibn Tibbon. An excerpt from this work and the full texts of all the other treatises by Israeli hitherto mentioned were published in English translation with comments in Altmann-Stern's *Isaac Israeli*.

His Philosophy

The philosophical doctrine of Israeli describes the various stages of being as a series of emanations from the intellect (Plotinus' *Noûs*), while the intellect itself is constituted by the union of first matter and first form (the latter also called "wisdom"), which are "created" by the power and will of God. Israeli thus upholds the notion of *creatio ex nihilo* in the case of the first three hypostases, while adopting the Plotinian concept of emanation for the rest. Both the long version of the *Theology* and Ibn Ḥasdai use a similar phraseology, due no doubt to their common source. The interposition of first matter and first form between God and the intellect is likewise derived from the peculiar variant of Neoplatonic doctrine represented by Israeli's source, and is reflected also in the parallel texts. A somewhat similar interposition occurs in the pseudo-Empedoclean scheme known from the Hebrew fragments of the "Five Substances" (ed. by D. Kaufmann, in: *Studien ueber Salomon Ibn Gabirol*, 1899) where, however, spiritual matter alone intervenes between God and the intellect. From the intellect, three souls (rational, animal, and vegetative) and the celestial sphere (also called "nature") emanate. The process of emanation is, following Plotinus, sometimes described as a radiance, "like the light of the sun, which emanates from its essence and substantiality," but is also viewed as a casting of shadows by the light and as the coming-to-be of progressively denser substances out of these shadows. The celestial sphere is the last of the "simple substances" emanating from the intellect, and holds an intermediate position between the higher world and the sensible world. From the motion of the celestial sphere the four elements come into being, and from them, in turn, arise the composite substances of the sublunar bodies. Man's soul, caught in the embrace of the "shells" and "darkness" of the coarse sensible world, is destined to pursue an upward path leading to union with the supernal light of wisdom. Like al-Kindī and the *Ikhwān al-ṣafā'* (*Brethren of Sincerity), Israeli adopts Proclus' theory of the three stages of purification, illumination, and union. The bliss of the highest stage is, in Israeli's view, tantamount to the bliss of paradise. In this way he links traditional Jewish eschatology with Neoplatonic mysticism. He interprets the notion of hell in terms of the impure soul's inability to penetrate beyond the sphere; it is doomed to remain beneath the sphere and to be consumed by its fire. In his concept of prophecy (treated in his *Book on the Elements* and in the commentary to the *Sefer Yeẓirah* of his disciple, *Dunash ibn Tamīm, who reflects his master's view), Israeli distinguishes between three forms: that of a created voice (*kol*); of spirit (*ru'aḥ*), including vision (*ḥazon*); and of speech (*dibbur*), which designates union with the supernal light and represents the highest rank. The case of Moses is described in terms of this highest stage. The function of prophecy is, however, conceived also in terms of spiritual guidance of the multitude of men, for which reason the divine truths must be couched in imaginative, allegorical form. Israeli's influence on the Neoplatonic trend in medieval Jewish philosophy must not be underrated. He is the father of Jewish Neoplatonism, and his traces can be found in such philosophers as Solomon ibn *Gabirol and Joseph ibn *Ẓaddik. The Gerona school of Jewish mysticism is likewise indebted to him. The Mantua text of Israeli's *Book on the Elements* is quoted in *Azriel of Gerona's commentary on the Aggadot.

Medical Works

Israeli has been classed among the great physicians of the early

Middle Ages. From 875 to 904 he apparently was a successful eye doctor near Cairo. His medical works were translated (or adapted) by Constantine the African (1087) from the Arabic into Latin, and were thus introduced to Europe and included in the Salerno school. Innumerable manuscripts in Arabic, Latin, and Hebrew by various translators testify to their popularity. Among Israeli's medical and quasi-medical writings are books on urine, fevers, the pulse, drugs, and the abovementioned "Treatise on Spirit and Soul" in a half-medical and half-philosophical treatise, probably part of a commentary on Genesis (all printed in *Omnia Opera Isaac*, 1515). A work entitled *Musar ha-Rofe'im* ("Medical Ethics") has also been attributed to Israeli, though his authorship has been doubted by some scholars.

[Alexander Altmann]

Harry A. Wolfson questioned Alexander Altmann's interpretation of Israeli's doctrine of creation in "The Meaning of *Ex Nihilo* in Isaac Israeli," in: JQR, 50 (1959), 1–12 (reprinted in Wolfson, *Studies in the History of Philosophy and Religion*, 1(1973), 222–33) and was answered by Altmann in "Creation and Emanation in Isaac Israeli: A Reappraisal," in: I. Twersky (ed.), *Studies in Medieval Jewish History and Literature* (1) (1979), 1–15. See also G. Vajda, in: P.B. Fenton, *Le Commentaire sur le Livre de la Création de Dunas ben Tamim de Kairouan (xe siècle)* (2002).

[Daniel J. Lasker (2nd ed.)]

BIBLIOGRAPHY: J. Guttmann, *Die philosophischen Lehren des Isaak b. Salomon Israeli* (1911); idem, in: MGWJ, 69 (1919), 156–64; Altmann, in: *Tarbiz*, 27 (1958), 501–7; Plessner, in: KS, 35 (1960), 457–9; H. Friedenwald, *Jews and Medicine*, 3 (19672), 86–88, with list of medical works and bibl.

ISRAELI, ISRAEL (d. 1317), Spanish talmudist. Born in Toledo, Israeli lived there all his life. His family was among the leaders of its community and the names of many scholars in the family, as well as many scribes, are known. Israeli was the brother of Isaac *Israeli, author of *Yesod Olam* and according to him was a pupil of *Asher b. Jehiel (the Rosh) after the latter's arrival in Toledo. Israel was eminent both for his talmudic and secular knowledge. The best-known of his works is his commentary to *Avot* which was largely influenced by Maimonides' method and which in turn was the main basis of the commentary of his grandson, Isaac b. Solomon Israeli, on *Avot* (1965). Various quotations are found in the *Midrash Shemu'el* to *Avot* by Samuel b. Isaac of Uceda. In his commentary Israeli expresses his opinion that the prohibition against the study of "Greek wisdom" was never applied in practice, and that rabbis and teachers are not to be precluded from accepting a salary. This opinion is in direct contrast to the view of Maimonides on this subject. His commentary on the Bible was well known, and Joseph *Naḥmias frequently quoted from it in his various works. Israeli possessed wide general knowledge, as was common among Spanish Jews of the upper classes in his time, and it was he who translated for Asher b. Jehiel various halakhic passages from Arabic to Hebrew. As a result, Israeli became directly involved in one of the most renowned halakhic disputes in Jewish history, which touched upon the authoritative interpretation of the "*Takkanot* of Toledo" (see *Takkanot). These *takkanot*, one of which laid down the manner in which a husband inherited from his wife, differed completely from talmudic *halakhah*, and had been enacted by the leaders of the community a few generations before, and committed to writing in Arabic. When Asher arrived in Toledo, he found to his surprise that the *takkanah* had been extended in practice and interpreted by the Toledo *bet din* far beyond the implication of the original text. He objected strongly and insisted that the scope of the *takkanah* be limited to the minimum implied by its plain language, and beyond that it had to accord with talmudic law. Israeli took a contrary stand. He claimed that since the *takkanah* was written in literary Arabic and not in the vernacular, Asher b. Jehiel, who came from Germany, was not fluent in the language, and could not appreciate the exact meaning of the *takkanah*, nor could he rely upon the Hebrew translation. Israeli even went further and maintained that a *takkanah*, based originally upon reason and logic and not upon the religious halakhic tradition, must of necessity be interpreted in the widest and most rational manner, in the spirit in which it was written, and not in accordance with the traditional methods of interpretation used in *halakhah*. Israeli's claims are preserved, in incomplete form, in the responsa of Asher b. Jehiel (no. 55), and careful reconstruction of his arguments illustrates his broad horizons in Talmud, philosophy, and jurisprudence. It has been conjectured, without basis, that there were two scholars named Israel Israeli, both members of the same family, and that all the above details do not apply to the same individual.

BIBLIOGRAPHY: M.S. Kasher and J.J. Belachrowitz (eds.), *Perushei Rabbenu Yiẓhak b. R. Shelomo mi-Toledo al Massekhet Avot* (1965), 5–13 (preface); Teicher, in: *Essays and Studies Presented to S.A. Cook* (1950), 83–94.

[Israel Moses Ta-Shma]

ISRAEL ISSERL BEN ISAAC SEGAL (end 17th–early 18th century), rabbi (probably in Poland) descended from the family of Moses b. Israel *Isserles. His work *Asefat Ḥakhamim* (Offenbach, 1722) – the printing of which he personally supervised – is a collection of sermons arranged according to the weekly portions of the Torah, with additional sermons for the major festivals. Most deal with ethical problems; some, however, also include halakhic material. After presenting a quotation from the Bible, followed by one from the Talmud or Midrash, Israel usually proceeds to raise problems – which are sometimes quoted from other sources – and to supply their solutions. He quotes not only many ethical works written in Eastern Europe at his time, but oral statements of his contemporaries, including his teacher, R. Abraham *Broda.

BIBLIOGRAPHY: Steinschneider, Cat Bod, 1165, no. 5458; Ben-Jacob, Oẓar, 46, no. 490.

[Joseph Dan]

ISRAELI, SHAUL (1910–1995), Israeli rabbi. A rabbi and Torah scholar, Israeli was born in Slutzk. He came to Palestine during the Mandate period and studied at Mercaz Harav yeshivah. He was the first rabbi of Ha-Po'el ha-Mizrachi settlements, a founder of Yeshivot Bnei Akiva high schools, and a member of the Chief Rabbinate. He published *Ereẓ Hemdaḥ* on religious laws relating to the Land of Israel. In 1987 he founded the Ereẓ Hemdah Institute for the training of *dayyanim*. In 1992 he was awarded the Israel Prize in Jewish studies.

ISRAELIT, DER, leading Orthodox weekly in Germany, founded in 1860 by Marcus *Lehmann, in Mainz. The Hebrew periodical **Ha-Levanon* was published from 1872 to 1882 as the Hebrew edition of *Der Israelit*, and also appeared in Yiddish from 1873 to 1879. From 1883 to 1905 *Der Israelit* appeared twice weekly. It was published jointly with the *Jeschurun*, founded by S.R. *Hirsch, from 1889 to 1891. After Lehmann's death in 1890, successive editors were his son Oskar, his nephew and rabbinical successor Jonas *Bondi, Julius Lorsch, Jacob *Rosenheim, and S. Schachnowitz. Rosenheim, who reorganized the paper financially in 1906 when its offices were moved to Frankfurt, became its principal leader writer. Under Rosenheim *Der Israelit* achieved a high journalistic standard and was widely read not only in Germany but also in Austria, Hungary, and Western Europe. It carried a number of literary and educational supplements, and M. Lehmann's popular stories first appeared in installments in his paper. *Der Israelit* was the organ both of secessionist (Austritt) Orthodoxy in Germany and of *Agudat Israel. The paper's last issue appeared on Nov. 3, 1938.

BIBLIOGRAPHY: H. Schwab, *History of Orthodox Jewry in Germany* (1950), index; *Juedische Presse im 19. Jahrhundert…* (1967), 53f.; J. Rosenheim, *Zikhronot* (1955), 97ff.; J. Bondi, in: *Der Israelit* (Jan. 6, 1910).

ISRAELITE (Ar. **Isrāʾīliyyāt**, "Israelite" tales), name of a type of Muslim literature which deals with two different subjects: (1) stories from the Bible, legends, and other tales as they have been handed down in Jewish literature in the name of figures from the biblical world, scholars, and rabbis, and which are found in the Talmud and Midrashim. The objective of this material in the works of Arab historians, Koran exegetes, and the legends of the prophets is to explain Muhammad's words when their meaning is obscure or opposed to the Bible. The Isrāʾīliyyāt thus served as a channel for the absorption of many legends in the treasury of the historical tales of Islam. The traditionists were generally Jews who had converted to Islam or scholars of Jewish origin. The most famous of these were *Kaʿb al-Aḥbār and *Wahb ibn Munabbih. Beginning at an early date, this fact aroused suspicion and the opposition of the orthodox circles of Islam who sought at least to conceal the identity of the traditionists. (2) The second principal subject of Isrāʾīliyyāt is the lives and deeds of the mystics of Islam, the ancient men of piety who flourished during the period known as that of the *Banū Isrāʾīl* ("the people of Israel").

BIBLIOGRAPHY: Goldziher, in: REJ. 44 (1902), 65; S.D. Goitein, in: *Tarbiz*, 6 (1935), 89–101, 510–22.

[Haïm Z'ew Hirschberg]

ISRAELITISCHES FAMILIENBLATT, leading non-party Jewish weekly in pre-Hitler Germany, founded in 1898 in Hamburg by M. Lessmann, publisher, and M. Deutschlaender, editor. Among the weekly's editors in the 1930s were Julian Lehmann, Alfred Kupferberg (Nehushtan), and Ezriel *Carlebach. The circulation of 25,000 in 1935 increased to 30,000 in 1937. With its numerous supplements – illustrated, literary, and educational – and its full coverage of news from the Jewish world at large as well as every community in Germany, the *Familienblatt* wielded considerable political and educational influence and was a model of Jewish newspaper production. Originally it was the newspaper of the Hamburg Jewish community but in 1935 it was transferred to Berlin, where it became the official organ of the Reichsvertretung der deutschen Juden (Central Organization of German Jews; see *Reichsvereinigung). In the same year the Nazis prohibited the publication of the *Familienblatt* for three months. It permanently ceased publication after *Kristallnacht* in November 1938.

BIBLIOGRAPHY: Edelheim-Muehsam, in: YLBI, 5 (1960), 308–29; EJ, s.v. *Juedische Presse im 19 Jahrhundert…* (1967), 43.

ISRAELITISCH-THEOLOGISCHE LEHRANSTALT, leading Jewish theological seminary in Vienna. The Israelitisch-Theologische Lehranstalt, founded in 1893, served first the Austro-Hungarian Empire and later its successor states. Although efforts to establish a training school for rabbis and teachers of the Jewish religion can be traced to the days of Emperor Joseph II (1786), the impetus to a regular theological seminary did not come until the Viennese community had become one of the largest in Europe, 120,000 in 1880. Then a dramatic controversy over the Talmud between an anti-Jewish Prague professor, August *Rohling, and a staunch defender of Jewish rights, Joseph Samuel *Bloch, demonstrated to Jewish philanthropists in Vienna the importance of Jewish cultural efforts against the rising tide of antisemitism. Led by Wilhelm von *Gutmann, several financiers, aided by a few major Jewish communities and a small government subsidy, helped establish the Lehranstalt. Among the benefactors were also such distinguished Jewish scholars as Adolf *Jellinek, Joshua Heschel *Schorr, and Abraham *Epstein.

From the outset the school could boast of a remarkable array of scholarly luminaries on its faculty and a select, if small, student body. Under the leadership of its long-term rector Adolf *Schwarz, its teachers, including David Heinrich *Mueller, Adolf *Buechler, Meir *Friedmann (Ish Shalom), Samuel *Krauss, and Victor *Aptowitzer, trained a total of 324 students, for the most part recruited from Galicia and other parts of the empire. World War I and the dissolution of the empire caused a major financial crisis, which was only partially alleviated by the efforts of the Viennese chief rabbi Hirsch Perez *Chajes, who succeeded in enlisting the aid of

U.S. philanthropists. The seminary survived under somewhat reduced circumstances until the annexation of Vienna by Hitler in 1938 and the ensuing destruction of all Jewish cultural institutions. Its precious library was confiscated and the collections are now widely scattered. Its alumni, however, continued to serve in high positions in the rabbinate and schools of higher learning in Europe and the U.S. as well as in Israel.

ADD. BIBLIOGRAPHY: P. Landesmann, *Rabbiner aus Wien* (1997).

[Salo W. Baron]

ISRAEL LABOR PARTY (Mifleget ha-Avodah ha-Yisraʾelit), Israeli social-democratic party founded in January 1968 through a union between *Mapai, *Aḥdut ha-Avodah-Poʿalei Zion (which had seceded from it in 1944), and *Rafi (which had seceded from it in 1965). Each of the three components of the new party maintained, at first, a considerable degree of internal cohesion, nominating representatives to the party's governing bodies in the agreed proportion of 57% for Mapai and 21.5% each for the other two.

The Israel Labor Party continued to advocate the traditional economic and social policies of the labor movement in Israel since the foundation of the State, which professed the ideals of egalitarianism and cooperation, a strong public sector in the economy, and substantial government involvement in economic affairs and welfare. Two strong pillars of the party continued to be the kibbutzim of *Ha-Kibbutz ha-Me'uḥad and *Iḥud ha-Kevuẓot ve-ha-Kibbutzim, and the *Histadrut. However, like its predecessors, it did not object to private initiative, and was supported by many industrialists.

By the 1990s its ideological positions on economic and social issues had shifted, to a large extent, from social-democracy to social-liberalism. As a party that from the very start attracted numerous former IDF career officers into its ranks, it was always very security minded, but on the issue of ways of dealing with the Arab-Israel conflict and the territories conquered in the course of the Six-Day War, until the signing of the Oslo Accords in 1993 the party was divided between doves and hawks; between those who believed in territorial compromise and those who sought functional solutions; and later on between those who favored establishing contacts with the PLO and those who believed Israel should try and reach a solution with the Hashemite Kingdom of Jordan. On these issues the party gradually moved to the left, both because its more hawkish elements left it for more rightist parties and because of changing circumstances. Even though its platform for the 1992 elections to the Thirteenth Knesset stated that it objected to talks with the PLO, it accepted the reality of the Oslo Accords of September 1993 and the political process that followed, and finally came to support the establishment of a Palestinian state in the West Bank and Gaza Strip, as long as such a state was established by agreement with Israel and was willing to live in peace with it.

Until the early 1990s the party's leaders were elected by the Central Committee, and the Knesset list was put together by the party leadership. However after its Fourth Conference, held in 1986, the party started to undergo a process of democratization, and since its Fifth Conference, held in 1991, its leadership and list for Knesset elections have been elected by means of primaries in which all the registered members of the Party participate. The Labor Party's chairmen since its establishment have been Levi *Eshkol (1968–69), Golda *Meir (1969–74), Yitzhak *Rabin (1974–77), Shimon *Peres (1977–92), Rabin (1992–95), Peres (1995–97), Ehud *Barak (1997–2001), Binyamin *Ben-Eliezer (2001–2), Amram Mitzna (2002–3), Peres (2003–5), Amir *Peretz (2005–).

Since its establishment the Israel Labor Party has progressively lost strength. When the Labor Party was founded in 1968 it had 63 Knesset seats. In the elections to the Seventh to the Twelfth Knessets (1969–88) it ran in the framework of the Alignment with other parties and groups and received 56, 51, 32, 47, 44, and 39 seats, respectively. In the elections to the Thirteenth and Fourteenth Knessets (1992 and 1996) it ran independently, receiving 44 and 34 seats, respectively. In the Fifteenth Knesset (1999) it ran in a list called One Israel, with Gesher and Meimad, and received 26 seats, and in the elections to the Sixteenth Knesset (2003) it ran in a single list with Meimad and received 19 seats only.

The process of decline began in the aftermath of the Yom Kippur War, leading to Labor's first-ever electoral defeat in 1977. The original reasons for its weakened position were the feeling that it had been in power too long and had grown corrupt and the fact that the second generation of the Oriental community in Israel had turned against it. The process continued as Israeli society shifted to more right-wing and/or more liberal, and/or more religious positions, and with the economic collapse of the kibbutzim and the Histadrut. The direct elections for prime minister in 1996, 1999, and 2001, and the failure of a younger generation of leaders to take control of the Party, further weakened it.

The Labor Party led the governments in 1968–77, 1984–86, 1992–96, and 1999–2001. It also participated in governments led by the Likud in 1986–90 and 2001–2.

In 1969–94 all the secretaries general of the Histadrut were from the Labor Party – Yitzhak *Ben-Aharon (1969–73), Yeruḥam *Meshel (1973–84), Israel *Kessar (1984–92), and Ḥayyim Haberfeld (1992–94). In the Histadrut elections of 1994 Haim *Ramon ran against Haberfeld in an independent list and beat him. He handed over the leadership of the Histadrut to Amir *Peretz in 1995. The latter left the Israel Labor Party in 1999, returning in January 2005 and being elected party chairman in November. In the 2006 elections, Labor won 19 seats and joined Ehud *Olmert's coalition government.

BIBLIOGRAPHY: A. Doron, *Mifleget ha-Avodah ha-Yisraʾelit (Toledot u-Beʿayot)*, (1972); S. Weiss, *Anatomyah shel Nefilah: Mismakh Pnimi*, (1977); Z. Dror, *Mifleget ha-Avodah ha-Yisraʾelit: Sippur ha-Toledot* (1980); Y. Beilin, *Banim be-Ẓel Avoteihem* (1984); idem, *Meḥiro shel Iḥud: Mifleget ha-Avodah ad Milḥemet Yom ha-Kippurim* (1985); B Kornhandler, *Mifleget ha-Avodah mi-Dominantiyyut le-Opoziẓyah* (1992); S. Sheffer, *Yeẓivut ve-Shinui ba-Dimui shel Mifleget ha-Avo-*

dah kefi she-Hu Mitbattei be-Maẓa'eha be-Ḥamesh Ma'arḥot Beḥirot 1973–1988 (1993); M. Bar'eli, *Mi-Tenu'ah le-Manganon: Nitu'aḥ Hitnavvenutah shel Tenu'at ha-Avodah* (1994); B. Caspit, *Hitabbedut: Mifl-agah Mevateret al Shilton* (1996); A. Bar, *Primeris, Beḥirot Makdimot ve-Shitot Aḥerot* (1996); R. Hazan, *The Labor Party and the Peace Process: Positions, Disintegration, Amid Political Cohesion* (1998). A. Diskin, *The Last Days in Israel: Understanding the New Israeli Democracy* (2003).

[Susan Hattis Rolef (2nd ed.)]

ISRAEL MEIR HA-KOHEN (**Kagan**; known as **Ḥafeẓ Ḥayyim**; 1838–1933), rabbi, ethical writer, and talmudist; one of the most saintly figures in modern Judaism. Of humble origin, he was taught until the age of ten by his parents and then went to Vilna where he continued his studies. He did not particularly distinguish himself as a student; nevertheless, he later towered above all his contemporaries in his qualities of religious leadership. While in a yeshivah in Vilna, the Ḥafeẓ Ḥayyim became seriously ill as a result of the very long hours he put in every day studying. This episode had a lifelong affect on him, for he became very sensitive to his students' health, always encouraging them to eat and sleep well. His surname Poupko is hardly known, nor is he referred to by his own name, but he became universally known as Ḥafeẓ Ḥayyim, after the title of his first work. His personality, his piety, his humility of conduct, his integrity of thought and action, together with his books, exercised a tremendous influence on religious leaders, and fascinated the masses, to whom he became the admired master and leader. Hundreds of sayings full of practical wisdom are attributed to him, and hundreds of stories both factual and legendary, all rich in morals, are reported about his life.

He refused to make the rabbinate his calling, and after his marriage in Radun he subsisted on a small grocery store which his wife managed and for which he did the bookkeeping. He also did his own "bookkeeping," maintaining a daily record of his own deeds to assure himself no wrong had been perpetrated by him nor any time wasted. He spent his time either learning Torah or disseminating its knowledge among others, particularly the more simple folk, whom he always encouraged in matters of learning, observance, and faith. The Ḥafeẓ Ḥayyim did not intend to establish a yeshivah. So many students, however, flocked to him that by 1869 his home had become known as "the Radun yeshivah" or as "the Ḥafeẓ Ḥayyim yeshivah." Forty-five years later, the yeshivah moved to a big building of its own and R. Naphtali Trup was appointed its head. For many years it was the Ḥafeẓ Ḥayyim's responsibility to provide for the students, a task in which he was later assisted by his three sons-in-law, leaving him more time for writing, publishing, and distributing his books.

When he was 35 he published anonymously in Vilna (1873) his first book, *Ḥafeẓ Ḥayyim*, devoted entirely to an exposition of the primary importance of the laws of slander, gossip, and tale bearing. Throughout his life, he laid great emphasis on the careful observance of these laws, so generally neglected in spite of the fact that their transgression involves the violation of numerous prohibitions. In 1879 he published another book on the same subject and a third in 1925. He even composed a special prayer to be recited every morning asking for protection from the sins of slander and gossip. According to a popular legend, whenever anyone would gossip in his presence, the Ḥafeẓ Ḥayyim would fall asleep so as not to listen. His best-known and most widely studied work is his six-volume *Mishnah Berurah* (1894–1907), a comprehensive commentary on Shulḥan Arukh, *Oraḥ Ḥayyim* which has been accepted as an indispensable reference book on practical everyday halakhic matters. One hundred years later it is still studied and referred to widely. In 1999, D. Eidenson published a comprehensive index to the *Mishnah Berurah*, titled *Yad Yisrael*.

As early as 1923, the Ḥafeẓ Ḥayyim expressed interest in immigrating to Israel. In 1925, he began to make concrete plans to leave Radun. Rabbi Moshe Blum came to his aid by finding financial assistance, while Rabbi Yosef Ḥayyim Sonnenfeld signed his visa request during Ḥol ha-Mo'ed of that year. In the end the Ḥafeẓ Ḥayyim did not depart, first because of the pressure applied by the leading yeshivah heads, especially Rabbi Hayyim Ozer Grodsensky, and second, because his wife's health prevented her from traveling. In a letter dated 3 Tevet 5686 (1926), the Ḥafeẓ Ḥayyim endeavored to discover the benefactor who anonymously provided the financial assistance so he could return the money.

The Ḥafeẓ Ḥayyim did not publish his books for academic purposes, but rather produced them wherever he saw a need to strengthen some aspect of Jewish life, sometimes intervening in person to reinforce his teaching. Among the 21 books which he published, mention should be made of *Ahavat Ḥesed* (1888) on various types of charity; *Maḥaneh Yisrael* (1881), a code of practical laws for Jewish soldiers (he also endeavored to ensure that when stationed near Jewish communities kosher food was provided for them as well as urging young men to marry early to avoid the draft); *Niddeḥei Yisrael* (1894) to encourage Jews who had emigrated to the West to maintain their religious loyalties; and a variety of books on the observance of the dietary laws, laws of family purity, and the obligation of Torah study; and *Likutei Halakhot* (1900–25), a comprehensive digest of the sacrificial laws found in the Mishnah of *Seder Kodashim*. Since he hoped for and believed in the imminent coming of the Messiah, he emphasized the study of the laws of sacrifices and worship in the Temple and other related subjects. Overall, the Ḥafeẓ Ḥayyim required a stringent halakhic approach to contemporary problems to better maintain and regulate the boundaries between halakhic Judaism and the surrounding secular Jewish society. In addition, the many books that he wrote were in direct response to the educational challenges of his day. He witnessed parents abandoning traditional *ḥeder* schools to send their children to secular schools, a move that would lead to better social and financial security. The Ḥafeẓ Ḥayyim was also very wary of the rise of Communism after World War I.

Throughout his life, the Ḥafeẓ Ḥayyim traveled extensively to muster support for many Jewish causes. He was one of the founders of the Agudat Israel and was one of its spiritual leaders. He was chosen to open the First World Convention of *Agudat Israel (1912). The Ḥafeẓ Ḥayyim's help enabled the many European yeshivot to survive the critical financial problems of the interwar period. Under his aegis, the Va'ad ha-Yeshivot (committee on behalf of yeshivot) was organized and it successfully raised the necessary funds for these schools. After his death, his name was perpetuated by many yeshivot and religious institutions throughout the world which were called Ḥafeẓ Ḥayyim.

BIBLIOGRAPHY: M.M. Yoshor, *Saint and Sage* (1937); idem, in: L. Jung (ed.), *Jewish Leaders* (1953), 459–73; D. Katz, *Tenu'at ha-Musar*, 4 (1957), 1–175; A. Shurin, *Keshet Gibborim* (1964), 115–21; M. Weinbach, *Who Wants to Live* (1968); idem, *Give Us Life* (1969). **ADD. BIBLIOGRAPHY:** Y. London, *"Ha-Ḥafeẓ Ḥayyim ve-ha-Ma'avak al Demuto shel ha-Ḥinukh ha-Yehudi be-Mizraḥ Eiropah"* (diss., Hebrew University, 2002); S. Fishbane, *The Method and Meaning of the Mishnah Berurah* (1991); idem, in: *Judaism* (Fall 1993); M. Yosher, *The Chafetz Chaim: The Life and Works of Rabbi Yisrael Meir Kagan of Radin*, 2 vols. (1984); L. Eckman, *Revered by All: The Life and Works of Rabbi Yisrael Meir Kagan – Ḥafeẓ Ḥayyim* (1974); A. Ben-Natan, in: *Eshel Natan* (1988), 110–15; N. Waxman, in: *Shanah be-Shanah* (1974), 419–32.

[Mordechai Hacohen / David Derovan (2nd ed.)]

ISRAEL MOSES BEN ARYEH LOEB (18th–19th century), talmudist and preacher. His father was a rabbi in Lissa, where Israel received his rabbinical training. At the age of 28, Israel was appointed rabbi in Prandzew, and later served in Zabludow and in Kornik. He carried on correspondence with prominent rabbis and talmudic scholars of his time, including Akiva *Eger, the latter giving his approbations to Israel's single published work, *Rishmei She'elah* (Warsaw, 1811). This work, consisting of his halakhic responsa, was published with an appendix containing some of his talmudic novellae on *Mo'ed Katan*, as well as several homiletical sermons taken from his two unpublished works, *Eshel ha-Sarim* and *Eshel ha-Rashim*.

BIBLIOGRAPHY: J.J. Eisenstadt and S. Wiener, *Da'at Kedoshim* (1898), 237; L. Lewin, *Geschichte der Juden in Lissa* (1904), 261f.

[Elias Katz]

ISRAEL MUSEUM. In 1964 the Bezalel National Art Museum was incorporated into the new Israel Museum. The Israel Museum, situated in the heart of modern Jerusalem, houses a collection of Jewish and world art, the archaeology of the Holy Land, and the Dead Sea Scrolls. The museum was founded to collect, preserve, study, and display the cultural and artistic treasures of the Jewish people throughout its long history as well as the art, ethnology, and archeology of the Land of Israel and its neighboring countries. It also aims at encouraging original Israeli art. The initial IL20,000,000 (about $5,730,000) complex of buildings was designed by the Israeli architects Alfred Mansfeld and Dora Gad and financed by gifts from Israel, the United States, and Europe. The first IL1,500,000 (about $428,570) came from the U.S. government through its Information Media Guaranty Program, and the Israeli government provided the 22-acre plot. In 1996 the exhibition area totaled 17,190 sq. m. (about 20,560 sq. yd.) with an additional 19,110 sq. m. (about 22,850 sq. yd.) for storage, laboratories, workshops, a library, and offices, including those of the Israeli Government Department of Antiquities. The museum has a vast ethnographical collection which contains material representing the art and ethnology of non-Western cultures in addition to Jewish civilization.

The following are the Museum's sections:

THE JUDAICA AND ETHNOGRAPHY SECTION. The Museum has the world's largest collection of Judaica, including two whole 18th-century synagogue interiors. It ethnography collection includes costumes, jewelry, and articles typical of Jewish ritual and daily life in Diaspora communities.

THE ARTS WING. Included in the Arts Wing is the Bezalel Museum of Fine Arts founded in 1906 by Boris *Schatz. It is made up of nine different art departments: European art, drawings and reprints, Israeli art, modern art, contemporary art, design and architecture, photography, Far East art, and the art of Africa, Oceania, and America. The collection also includes period rooms – French, English, and Venetian.

THE SAMUEL BRONFMAN BIBLICAL AND ARCHAEOLOGICAL MUSEUM. Representing periods from prehistoric times to the 15th century C.E., this collection – based on that of the Israel Department of Antiquities (started in 1948) – contains archeological artifacts ranging from an elephant tusk from about 200,000 B.C.E., Chalcolithic clay ossuaries from Azor, highly developed Canaanite pottery, and Hebrew inscriptions and other objects from the Israelite period to representative finds from the Persian, Hellenistic, and Second Temple periods as well as the Roman, Byzantine, and Arabic civilizations. There is a selection of synagogue and church mosaics and a numismatic collection.

THE BILLY ROSE ART GARDEN AND THE LIPCHITZ PAVILION. The Billy Rose Art Garden, designed by Isamu Noguchi, displays 19th- and 20th-century sculpture. Curved retaining walls, made of the rocks from the site, frame the exhibition space for the sculptures displayed in the open air.

The Jacques Lipchitz Pavilion has 140 bronze sketches donated to the Museum by Reuven Lipchitz, the sculptor's brother.

THE SHRINE OF THE BOOK. The Shrine of the Book, designed by the U.S. architects Frederick J. Kiesler and Armand P. Bartos, is the repository for Israel's Dead Sea Scrolls, the Bar Kokhba letters (for details see *Dead Sea Scrolls and *Bar Kokhba), and objects found in the Dead Sea Caves.

YOUTH ACTIVITIES. Within the Israel Museum itself is the Ruth Youth Wing, an active educational department. The wing's area consists of 3,500 sq. m., which is 10% of the entire museum area. It hosts around 300,000 visitors a year.

THE TICHO HOUSE. Formerly the home of Dr. Abraham and Anna *Ticho, located in the center of Jerusalem, the building is now put to multipurpose use exhibiting the works of Anna Ticho and serving as a location for cultural events and a restaurant.

THE PALEY ART CENTER. The Paley Art Center for Youth, located near the Rockefeller Museum, conducts programs for Jerusalem's Arab population and offers various activities in the Arab language.

ROCKEFELLER ARCHAEOLOGICAL MUSEUM. The Rockefeller Archaeological Museum is situated in East Jerusalem, and houses a collection of antiquities revealed by excavations held mainly between the years 1919 and 1948.

WEBSITE: www.imj.org.il.

[Avraham Biran / Shaked Gilboa (2nd ed.)

ISRAEL OF BAMBERG (mid-13th century), tosafist. He studied under *Samuel b. Baruch, whom he succeeded as rabbi of Bamberg. His son was R. Jedidiah of Nuremberg. The *Mordekhai* of *Mordecai b. Hillel mentions Israel's *tosafot* to tractates *Shabbat* and *Avodah Zarah*, which though no longer extant, are quoted by a 15th-century Italian codifier (Ms. Adler 2717, folio 308). In his *Shitah Mekubbeẓet* to tractate *Bava Kama*, Bezalel *Ashkenazi frequently cites the *Tosefot Talmidei R. Yisrael* ("Tosafot of R. Israel's students"). In his *tosafot*, Israel relies primarily on his teacher, and, on one occasion, quotes Eleazar of Erfurt. Benjacob is of the opinion that these *tosafot* were based on *Alfasi and not, as is customary, on the Talmud. There is a difference of opinion as to whether the Israel ben Uri Shraga, whose *tosafot* are also mentioned in the *Mordekhai* to *Shabbat*, can be identified with Israel of Bamberg.

BIBLIOGRAPHY: Benjacob, in: *Devarim Attikim*, 2 (1846), 10; Zunz, Gesch, 40; S. Kohn, in: MGWJ, 27 (1878), 82; A. Eckstein, *Geschichte der Juden im ehemaligen Fuerstbistum Bamberg* (1898), 144f.; Marmorstein, in: *Devir*, 2 (1923), 242, no. 67; Urbach, Tosafot, 443.

[Yedidya A. Dinari]

ISRAEL OF KREMS (fl. mid-14th century), talmudist. He studied together with Abraham *Klausner under Moses of Znaim (Moravia). There is no basis for Graetz's assertion that he is identical to Israel b. Isaac of Nuremberg whom the Elector Rupert appointed in 1407 as *hochmeister* of all the rabbis in Germany. Israel *Isserlein, his great-grandson, relates that his ancestor wrote "glosses to the Asheri." Most scholars therefore assume that Israel is the author of *Haggahot Asheri* printed as notes to Asher b. Jehiel's commentary on the Talmud (Vilna edition), although Steinschneider doubts this. *Haggahot Asheri* is for the most part compiled from the works of 13th- and early 14th-century rabbis who lived in Germany – among these works are Mordecai b. Hillel's *Mordekhai, Haggahot Maimoniyyot*, Isaac of Corbeil's *Sefer Mitzvot Katan*, and Alexander Suesslin Kohen's *Aguddah* – the author usually giving his sources. Some of the glosses are his own, and some refer to the text of the Talmud proper rather than to the commentary of Asher. These glosses are often the sole source for quotations from certain *rishonim*, including, for example, many of the halakhic decisions of *Hezekiah b. Jacob of Magdeburg, and statements of the tosafist, *Isaac of Dampierre.

BIBLIOGRAPHY: Graetz, Gesch, 8 (1900⁴), 102–4; Freimann, in: JJLG, 12 (1918), 304f.; S. Krauss, *Die Wiener Geserah vom Jahre 1421* (1920), 48, 81; Urbach, Tosafot, 208, 366, 442.

[Yedidya A. Dinari]

ISRAEL PHILHARMONIC ORCHESTRA, Israel's major orchestra. The Israel Philharmonic was founded by the violinist Bronislaw *Huberman in 1936 as the Palestine Orchestra, also called the Palestine Symphony Orchestra. Huberman envisaged a Jewish orchestra in Palestine as a rescue operation for musicians persecuted by the Nazis, as well as a contribution to cultural life in Palestine. Early in 1934 he began persuading influential people in Palestine and abroad to invest time and money in the venture. Assisted by conductors Issay Dobrowen and William Steinberg, he selected musicians for the orchestra, mainly from Germany, Poland, Holland, Austria, and Hungary. Some instrumentalists came from the United States, and a few were already resident in Palestine. Arturo Toscanini, the eminent Italian conductor, conducted the first concerts in December 1936, in the three main cities, thereby immediately establishing the international rank of the orchestra. For the Jewish community the influx of so many proficient musicians provided a tremendous cultural stimulus as well as a good symphony orchestra. Besides numerous chamber music concerts and recitals in cities and communal settlements, in farming villages and small towns, the opportunity to study all kinds of orchestral instruments now became available on a large scale (see *Music, in Ereẓ Israel). This led to the discovery and cultivation of talents hitherto dormant in the community. In 1948, after the foundation of the State, the orchestra changed its name to the Israel Philharmonic Orchestra. The musicians formed a cooperative, taking over management and financial responsibility. In subsequent years membership expanded to over a hundred players, of whom an increasing number were born and trained in Israel. From 5,000 subscribers in 1936 the number has grown to over 28,000, necessitating the performance of every program 4–5 times, despite the move to larger concert halls in Tel Aviv and Jerusalem. Together with regular visits to Beersheba, Ein Gev, and other outlying areas, as well as army camps, the number of concerts given each season is around 150 in Israel and another 40 abroad. The income of the orchestra is derived 65 percent from earned income, 20 percent through contributions and gifts, and 15 percent from government and municipal appropriations. Recordings were made for Columbia in 1954–55, and for Decca in 1957–62. In 1967, after the reunification of Jerusalem in the Six-Day War, Leonard *Bernstein conducted Mahler's Resurrection Symphony on Mt. Scopus. In 1969 Zubin *Mehta was appointed music director. Visits abroad included tours to Cairo and military establishments (1942), a tour to the United States (1951), Europe (1955), around the world (1960), Greece

(1959 and 1965), Cyprus (1960), Australia and New Zealand (1966), and a second visit to the United States (1967), and to prestigious European festivals (1971). Between the years 1977 and 1986 the orchestra conducted tours all over the world, including Europe, the U.S., Mexico and Japan. In 1981 Mehta's appointment was extended for life. During these years, the orchestra made recordings for Sony, EMI, Deutsche Grammophon, Teldec, and others. Between the years 1987 and 1996 the orchestra made its first visits to Poland, China, and India. In 1991 the orchestra played in Toledo, Spain, with Placido Domingo, and in 1992 it played in Amsterdam in the presence of the Queen of Holland. During the 1991 Gulf War 1991, Isaac *Stern performed with the orchestra with gas masks unforgettably strewn across the stage. In 1996 the orchestra celebrated Mehta's 60th birthday with a tour of the United States. After the mass exodus from the former Soviet Union many musicians from there joined the orchestra. Both local and foreign conductors, soloists, and composers are presented in the orchestra's programs, the scope of which is further broadened by fully staged operas and large choral works. Into the 21st century, the orchestra's face has changed as the older generation retires and new musicians, mainly from the Young Israel Philharmonic, are recruited. In addition, the orchestra initiates new programs aimed to attract new subscribers, especially young audiences.

BIBLIOGRAPHY: E. Thalheimer, *Five Years of the Palestine Orchestra* (1942); Israel Philharmonic Orchestra Association, *News* (1963–). **WEBSITE:** www.ipo.co.il.

[Yohanan Boehm / Shaked Gilboa (2nd ed.)]

ISRAEL POLICY FORUM (IPF) was established in 1993 by a group of American Jewish leaders who were encouraged by recent developments in the Middle East peace process and discouraged that some of the American Jewish community's most established organizations did not seem to embrace them despite overwhelming evidence from polls that American Jews were supportive. Indeed, IPF's first public act was an advertisement on the op-ed page of *The New York Times* supporting what would soon be known as the "Oslo process."

In its first year, IPF focused primarily on education within the institutional Jewish community. When it became clear that those opposed to the peace efforts both from Israel and within the American Jewish community were going to Capitol Hill to lobby against the policies advanced by the government of Israeli Prime Minister Yitzhak Rabin and U.S. President Bill Clinton, the organization expanded its activities to include advocacy on Capitol Hill.

IPF's activities took on new meaning after the assassination of Rabin and the subsequent election of Benjamin Netanyahu as prime minister. Until that time, American Jews who associated themselves with IPF could also say they were supporting the policies of the government of Israel. Although Netanyahu did follow through with some of the commitments made by his predecessors in the Oslo accords, he did so reluctantly and largely as a result of prodding from Clinton. IPF distinguished itself by mobilizing American Jewish support for Clinton's efforts through its education and advocacy activities. In a September 1997 opinion survey commissioned by IPF, 89% of American Jews agreed that "to be effective and credible to both sides, the U.S. must be even-handed when facilitating negotiations."

Significantly, IPF carved out its unique conceptual niche during the Clinton-Netanyahu years when it asserted that the role of the United States is to serve as both Israel's best friend and ally *and* as a credible mediator in the peace process. In a full page ad, which appeared in *The Washington Post* on the eve of the Israeli-Palestinian Summit at the Wye Plantation in October 1998, IPF proclaimed that "continuing, balanced U.S. diplomacy is needed to keep the peace process moving forward," an important shift from the more traditional view, as articulated in AIPAC's position that there should be "no daylight" between the U.S. and Israel.

When Ehud Barak became Israel's leader, IPF found itself once again more closely identified with Israeli government policies. Barak made a point of meeting with both IPF and the Conference of Presidents of Major American Jewish Organizations on his first official visit to U.S., sending a signal that he was looking for more reliable support from American Jewish organizations than Rabin was able to count on.

IPF was a leading catalyst of "pro-Israel, pro-peace" activities during the period leading up to the failed Camp David II summit. Clinton recognized the central role played by IPF when he unveiled his plan for resolving the Israeli-Palestinian conflict at an IPF gala only weeks before he left office.

The years after Camp David II were challenging to IPF but the organization carried out some important projects nevertheless, such as "Foundations for a Future Peace" by Mideast scholar Stephen P. Cohen. Among the principles it articulated was the prescient point: "Peace must not be perceived as the enemy of religion and traditional faith. If it is, what is now a national conflict will degenerate further into a religious conflict." During the same period, IPF sponsored a task force on U.S. diplomacy in the Mideast, which outlined a regional strategy that would simultaneously address the interrelated issues involving Iran, Iraq, Lebanon and the Israeli-Palestinian dispute.

IPF was the leading Jewish force supporting Ariel Sharon's disengagement plan in 2004 and 2005. After the disengagement, IPF launched a campaign to encourage assertive U.S. efforts to parlay Israel's bold move into a process that would lead to the establishment of a viable Palestinian state living in peace alongside the State of Israel.

[Jonathan Jacoby (2nd ed.)]

ISRAEL PRIZE. The Israel Prize, instituted in 1953, is awarded by the minister of education and culture on the recommendation of judges appointed for each subject for outstanding work in the following fields: Jewish Studies (and Rabbinical Literature), Humanities (and Hebrew Literature), Social Sciences (and Education, Law), Exact Sciences (Mathematics, Physics, Chemistry, and Technology), Science (including Agriculture and Medicine), and Arts and Culture (Painting, Sculpture, Theater, Music, Dance, Architecture, and Media). The prizes are presented at a State ceremony on the night of Independence Day.

In 1972 the government decided to award a special additional prize for outstanding contributions to the advancement and development of society and the State in the public, political, social, settlement, economic, and other spheres. The Israel Prize is considered the most prestigious prize awarded by the State of Israel.

Israel Prize Winners

SCIENCE (INCLUDING AGRICULTURE, MEDICINE)

1953 L. *Halpern (Med.)
1954 M. *Zohary
1954 F.S. *Bodenheimer (Agr.)
1955 I. *Reichert
1955 J. *Bentor
1955 A. *Vroman
1955 N. *Hochberg (Agr.)
1955 B. *Shapiro (Med.)
1955 S. *Hestrin-Lerner (Med.)
1956 M. *Aschner
1956 M. *Winik (Agr.)
1956 C.E. *Wertheimer (Med.)
1957 S. *Hurwitz (Agr.)
1957 S. *Adler (Med.)
1958 L. *Picard
1958 S.E. *Soskin (Agr.)
1958 B. *Zondek (Med.)
1959 E. *Katchalski
1959 M. *Sela
1959 H. *Oppenheimer (Agr.)
1960 I.C. *Michaelson
1961 A. *Katzir
1961 O. *Kedem
1961 J. Van Der *Hoeden (Agr.)
1962 Z. *Saliternik (Med.)
1963 A. *Fahn
1964 M. *Rachmilewitz (Med.)
1965 S. *Stoller (Agr.)
1966 M.R. *Bloch
1967 A.L. *Olitzki (Med.)
1968 E.D. *Bergmann
1968 H. *Oppenheimer (Agr.)
1968 C. *Sheba (Med.)
1969 S. *Lifson
1970 A. De *Vries (Med.)
1971 I. *Arnon (Agr.)
1972 L. *Sachs
1973 H. *Mendelssohn
1973 H. *Halperin (Agr.)
1973 R. *Stein (Med.)
1974 I. *Berenblum
1977 Y. *Efrat (Agr.)
1977 Z. *Avidov (Agr.)
1978 N. Saltz (Med.)
1979 Y.H. Lindner
1984 M. *Jammer
1984 A. *Bondi (Agr.)
1984 S. Rabicovitch (Agr.)
1985 H. *Neufeld (Med.)
1985 B. *Padeh (Med.)
1986 M *Evenari
1986 Y. *Demalach
1988 N. *Goldblum
1990 M. *Prywes
1990 M. *Wilchek
1990 A. *Levitzki
1992 D. *Erlik
1992 I. *Wahl
1994 A. *Hershko
1994 N. *Sharon
1994 E. Svirski (Agr.)
1996 Y. *Stein (Med.)
1996 I. *Chet (Agr.)
1998 Y. *Birk (Agr.)
1998 R. *Rachminov (Med.)
1999 M. *Ravel (Med.)
1999 Y. *Cohen (Agr.)
1999 H. *Sieder
2000 R. *Mechoulam
2001 M. *Eliakim (Med.)
2001 R. *Arnon (Med.)
2001 B. *Ramot (Med.)
2002 A.Ḥ. *Halevi (Agr.)
2002 A. *Yonat
2003 A. *Ciechanover (Med.)
2004 H. *Razin
2005 R. *Zaizov
2005 S. Feldman

ARTS, CULTURE, AND SPORT

1953 Z. *Ben-Zvi
1954 O. *Partos
1955 Z. *Schatz
1956 H. *Rovina
1957 P. *Ben-Haim
1957 D. *Karmi
1958 *Bezalel
1958 *Habimah
1958 Israel Philharmonic *Orchestra
1959 Y. *Zaritsky
1959 Y. *Bertonoff
1960 A. *Meskin
1961 M. *Avidom
1962 A. *Sharon
1963 M. *Ardon
1964 M. *Margalit

1965 M. *Seter
1966 A. *Mansfeld
1966 D. *Gad
1967 M. *Janco
1968 Y. *Danziger
1968 J. *Millo
1968 G. *Kraus
1968 B. *Idelson
1969 S. *Finkel
1970 J. *Tal
1971 A. *Aroch
1972 Y. *Rechter
1973 A. *Elhanani
1973 D. *Krook-Gilead
1973 S. *Levi-Tannai
1973 H. *Meron
1973 R. *Rubin
1974 Y. *Admon
1975 M. *Bernstein-Cohen
1976 M. *Kirschenbaum
1977 Y. *Fischer
1977 D. *Karavan
1977 E. *Cohen
1978 G. *Bertini
1979 O. *Porat
1979 R. Klatzkin
1980 P. *Litvinovsky
1980 Y. *Bergner
1980 A. *Ticho
1981 G. *Kadman
1982 A. *Yaski
1983 N. *Shemer
1983 M. *Wilensky
1983 H. *Hefer
1986 B. *Lishansky
1986 Y. *Shemi
1987 M. *Zohar
1987 L. *Konig
1987 M. *Khouri
1988 A. *Argov
1988 S. *Damari
1990 Y. *Streichman
1991 D. *Bertonoff
1991 Y. *Yadin
1994 H. *Avenary
1994 Y. *Orland
1995 L. *Nikel
1995 M. *Kadishman
1995 D. *Reznik
1996 N. *Aloni
1996 M. *Efrati
1996 A. *Navon
1997 B.Z. *Orgad
1997 A. *Erlich
1997 A. *Heido
1997 H. *Yavin
1997 D. *Rubinger
1998 D. *Ravikovitch
1998 L. *Yahalom
1998 D. *Zur
1998 D. *Rizinger
1998 H. *Levi-Agron
1998 Y. *Arnon
1998 Y. *Banai
1998 Y. *Yarkoni
1999 M. *Golan
1999 D. *Perlov
1999 Y. *Rosen
1999 E. *Roth-Shachamorov
2000 M. *Gross
2000 M. *Bar-Am
2001 B. *Hagai
2002 R. *Carmi
2002 D. *Tratkover
2002 D. *Yudkovsky
2003 Z. *Harifai
2004 Y. *Tomarkin
2004 G. *Almagor
2004 G. *Aldema
2004 Y. *Gaon
2005 A. Libek
2005 O. *Naharin
2005 I. Pinkas
2005 S. Tevet

JEWISH STUDIES (INCLUDING RABBINICAL LITERATURE)

1953 G. *Allon
1954 M.H.Z. *Segal
1955 E.E. *Urbach
1955 Y. *Heinemann
1956 N.H. *Tur-Sinai
1956 Y. *Yadin
1956 Y. *Abramsky (R.L.)
1957 J. *Schirmann
1957 R. *Margaliot (R.L.)
1958 J. *Klausner
1958 B. *Dinur
1958 Y. *Baer
1958 Y. *Kaufman
1958 G. *Scholem
1958 I. *Herzog (R.L.)
1958 J.Z. *Halevi (R.L.)
1958 J.L. *Maimon (R.L.)
1959 S.J. *Zevin (R.L.)
1960 A.C. *Schalit
1961 S. *Goren (R.L.)
1962 H. *Yalon
1963 M. *Kasher (R.L.)
1964 Z. Ben *Ḥayyim
1966 S. *Morag

1966 Y. *Arieli (R.L.)
1968 S. *Yeivin
1968 B. *Mazar
1968 D. *Sadan
1968 M.J. Epstein *Ha-Levi (R.L.)
1968 O. *Hadayah (R.L.)
1969 Y. *Kafaḥ
1970 O. *Yosef (R.L.)
1971 S. *Lieberman
1973 J. Even *Shmuel
1973 Makhon ha-Talmud ha-Yisra'eli ha-Shalem, project of Yad Harav Herzog
1974 S. *Abramson
1976 E.J. Waldenberg (R.L.)
1977 N. *Avigad
1977 M. *Stern
1977 R. *Mahler
1979 M. *Elon
1979 I. *Tishby
1980 J. *Katz
1980 D. *Flusser
1981 A. Sofer-Schreiber
1982 D. *Benveniste
1982 Z. *Vilnay
1982 R. *Amiran
1987 E.Z. *Melamed
1987 A. *Bein
1988 M. *Goshen-Gottstein
1988 A. *Steinsaltz
1990 M. *Weiss
1991 H. *Beinart
1991 N. *Feinbrun-Dothan
1992 S. *Israeli (R.L.)
1992 Y. *Kiel
1992 D. *Sperber
1993 M. *Bar-Asher
1994 M. *Greenberg
1994 M. Weinfeld
1994 C.Z. *Dimitrovsky
1994 E. *Schweid
1995 A. *Funkenstein
1996 Y. *Raẓaby
1996 Ḥ. *Shamruk
1997 Y. *Sussman
1997 J. *Dan
1997 S. *Talmon
1997 J. *Bacrach
1997 H.D. *Halevi
1998 Y. *Bauer
1998 M. *Gil
1999 M. *Idel
1999 M.Z. *Kaddari
1999 M. *Banet
1999 M. *Breuer
1999 A. *Steinberg
2000 M. *Haran
2000 A. *Goldberg
2000 Y. *Frankel
2000 G. *Sarfatti
2001 A. *Ravitzky
2002 S. *Safrai
2003 I.M. *Ta-Shma
2003 A. *Grossman
2004 S. *Yefet
2005 A. Dotan

HUMANITIES (INCLUDING HEBREW LITERATURE)

1953 Y. *Cahan (H.L.)
1953 H. *Hazaz (H.L.)
1954 S.H. *Bergman
1954 D. *Shimoni (H.L.)
1954 S.Y. *Agnon (H.L.)
1955 Z. *Shneour (H.L.)
1955 Y. *Lamdan (H.L.)
1956 G. *Shofman (H.L.)
1956 M. *Yalan-Stekelis (H.L.)
1957 Y. *Lewy
1957 J. *Fichmann (H.L.)
1957 U.Z. *Greenberg (H.L.)
1957 E. *Smoli (H.L.)
1958 M. *Buber
1958 S.Y. *Agnon (H.L.)
1958 Y.D. *Berkowitz (H.L.)
1958 Y. *Cahan (H.L.)
1959 L.A. *Mayer
1959 S. *Yizhar (Yizhar Smilansky)
1959 E. *Fleischer (Y. Goleh) (H.L.)
1961 E.Y. *Kutscher
1961 Y. *Burla (H.L.)
1963 N. *Rotenstreich
1963 E. *Steinman (H.L.)
1965 S. *Zemach (H.L.)
1965 S. *Dykman (H.L.)
1966 H. *Polotsky
1967 A. *Shlonsky (H.L.)
1968 S. *Sambursky
1968 S. *Pines
1968 A. *Hameiri (H.L.)
1969 J. *Prawer
1970 A. *Kovner (H.L.)
1970 L. *Goldberg (H.L.)
1972 D. *Ayalon
1972 Y. *Bat-Miriam (H.L.)
1973 S. *Shalom (H.L.)
1975 S. *Halkin (H.L.)
1976 E. *Mani
1976 G. *Baer
1977 S. *Avitzur
1978 A. *Amir
1978 A. *Even-Shoshan

1978 L. *Kipnis
1978 N. *Gutman
1978 H. Rosen
1981 M.Y. Kister
1982 A. *Gilboa (H.L.)
1982 Y. *Amichai (H.L.)
1982 D. *Ayalon
1983 S. *Friedlaender
1983 A. *Saltman
1984 Y. *Tchernowitz-Avidar (H.L.)
1985 J. *Blau
1985 A. *Sutzkever
1986 A. *Avrech
1986 S. *Rosenfeld
1988 H. *Gouri (H.L.)
1988 M. *Shamir (H.L.)
1989 S. *Werses (H.L.)
1989 I. *Yeivin
1990 N. *Spiegel (H.L.)
1990 Z. *Yavets
1990 M. Altbauer
1992 E. *Habibi
1992 A. *Yeshurun (H.L.)
1993 D. *Miron (H.L.)
1993 G. *Shaked (H.L.)
1993 G. Goldenberg
1993 Y. *Arieli
1993 H. Lazarus-Yafeh
1993 M. *Confino
1993 Y. Harkavy
1995 C. Epstein
1995 N. *Zach (H.L.)
1995 A.B. *Yehoshua (H.L.)
1996 S. *Sandbank
1996 M. *Barash
1996 M. *Piamenta
1996 M. *Sternberg
1998 A. *Oz (H.L.)
1998 E. *Manor (H.L.)
1998 T. *Dotan
1999 H. *Mirski (H.L.)
1999 M. *Yardeni
1999 S. *Moreh
1999 B. *Narkiss
2000 A. *Kahana-Carmon (H.L.)
2000 M. Vizeltir (H.L.)
2000 H. *Daleski
2000 A.H. *Fish
2000 S. *Shaked
2000 Y. *Yovel
2000 A. *Kasher
2001 Ẓ. *Avni
2001 Y. *Braun
2001 H. *Shmueli
2002 A. *Biran (Bergman)
2002 E. *Kishon (H.L.)
2003 Y. *Bar-Yosef (H.L.)
2003 Y. *Hendel (H.L.)
2003 A. *Megged (H.L.)
2003 A. *Amir (H.L.)
2003 S. *Shahar
2004 M. *Brinker (H.L.)
2004 D. *Noy (H.L.)
2004 Z. *Amishai-Maisels
2005 Y. *Orpaz-Averbuch (H.L.)
2005 B.A. Scharfstein
2005 O. Kapeliuk
2005 Y. *Landau
2005 S. Somech

SOCIAL SCIENCES (INCLUDING LAW, EDUCATION)

1953 M. *Dvorzetsky
1953 D. *Feitelson (Ed.)
1954 G. *Tedeschi (Law)
1954 A. *Biram (Ed.)
1956 J.L. *Talmon
1956 N. *Leibowitz (Ed.)
1957 R. *Katznelson (Shazar)
1957 P. *Dykan (Law)
1957 S. *Lehmann (Ed.)
1958 *Youth Aliyah (Ed.)
1960 S. *Rosenne (Law)
1960 A. *Arnon (Ed.)
1962 I. *Kanev
1962 J. *Bentwich (Ed.)
1964 M. *Silberg (Law)
1965 J. *Shuval
1965 *Israel Defense Forces (Ed.)
1965 C. *Frankenstein (Ed.)
1967 B. *Akzin (Law)
1967 A.E. *Simon (Ed.)
1968 D. *Horowitz
1968 S. *Agranat (Law)
1968 J. *Berman (Ed.)
1968 A.M. *Dushkin (Ed.)
1968 S. *Persitz (Ed.)
1970 D. *Patinkin
1971 Z. *Zeltner (Law)
1971 H. *Ormian (Ed.)
1973 S.N. *Eisenstadt
1973 P. *Rosen (Law)
1973 B. *Dinur (Ed.)
1975 A. *Barak
1975 Y. Sussman (Law)
1975 A. *Simon (Ed.)
1977 D. *Amiran
1978 E.L. Gutman
1979 B. *Ben-Yehudah (Ed.)
1979 I.R. Etzion (Ed.)
1980 H. *Cohn

1982 R. *Bachi
1986 S. *Katznelson and Ulpan Akiva
1986 G. Zak and Ha-Kefar ha-Yarok
1987 M. *Yaari
1989 E. *Katz
1989 Wingate Institute
1989 I. *Froman
1991 M. *Landau (Law)
1991 D. *Friedman (Law)
1991 E. *Helfman
1992 M. *Lissak
1992 D. *Navon
1992 R. *Feuerstein
1993 R. Levy
1993 Y. Partos ("Zev")
1994 Y. Oman
1994 M. Bruno
1995 Y. Amir
1995 R. Shapiro
1996 S. *Avineri
1997 Y. *Englard (Law)
1997 Y. *Zamir (Law)
1998 Y. Rosenfeld
1998 A. Levi (Ed.)
1998 E. Marks
1999 Y. *Ben-Arieh
1999 A. Shahar
2001 G. Salomon
2001 Y. *Rand (Ed.)
2001 R. *Ben-Israel (Law)
2001 Y. *Visman (Law)
2002 A. *Koriat
2002 M. *Brawer
2002 M. *Harel
2002 Y. *Frankel
2002 A. *Rubinstein
2002 N. *Rakover (Law)
2003 B. *Manheim
2003 Y. *Liebman
2003 M. *Amir
2003 S.G. *Shoham
2004 A. *Doron
2004 E. Samuel-Cohen
2005 M. Erez
2005 Y. Dror

EXACT SCIENCES

1953 J. *Levitsky
1953 S.A. *Amitsur
1954 F. *Ollendorff
1955 M. *Fekete
1956 A.A. *Fraenkel
1957 S. *Hestrin
1957 D. *Feingold
1957 G. *Avigad
1958 G. *Racah
1958 M. *Reiner
1960 F. *Sondheimer
1962 W. *Low (Z. Lev)
1965 I. *Talmi
1965 A. *de-Shalit
1968 E. *Goldberg
1969 Y. *Ne'eman
1972 D. *Ginsburg
1973 A. *Dvoretsky
1974 R. *Levine
1976 Y. *Rom
1980 C. *Pekeris
1981 Y. Lindenstrauss
1981 I. Piatzky-Shapira
1982 Y. *Yurtner
1987 O. *Harari
1989 H. *Harari
1989 Y. *Aharonov
1991 S. *Agmon
1991 D. *Froman
1993 H. *Furstenberg
1993 S. Alexander
1993 Y. Ziv
1995 M.O. *Rabin
1995 A. *Dostrovsky
1998 S. *Sela
1998 D. *Shechtman
2000 J. *Singer
2000 A. *Pnueli
2001 J. *Imri
2001 S. *Strickman
2002 I. *Willner
2003 A. *Libai
2003 Ẓ. *Ben-Abraham
2004 J. *Bernstein
2004 D. *Harel
2005 Y. Bakenstein

SPECIAL PRIZE.

1972 A. *Harzfeld
1973 S. *Avigur
1973 Pinkas Kehillot Project of *Yad Vashem
1974 S.H. *Bergman
1974 Y. *Alouf
1975 H. *Kagan
1975 G. *Meir
1976 R. *Guber
1976 Y. *Maimon
1976 S. *Holzberg
1976 E. Korin
1977 E. Levitt
1977 A. Yaacov
1977 A. Kalir
1978 R.Y. *Ben-Zvi

1978 M.Z. *Neriah
1979 T. Brody
1979 Y. Yekutieli
1980 Beit Yad Labanim, Petaḥ Tikva, with distinction to B. Oren
1980 Society for the Protection of Nature, with distinction to A. Zehavi, A. Alon, and Y. Sagi
1981 R. *Freier
1981 Kibbutz *Deganyah Alef
1982 C. *Gvati
1983 Z. *Warhaftig
1984 *NAḤAL (No'ar Ḥaluẓi Loḥem)
1984 Development Towns Project
1985 Israel Television Arabic
1986 Y. Sa'id
1986 A. *Hatokai
1988 A. *Eliav
1988 R. *Hecht
1988 T. *Kollek
1989 Y. *Hazan
1989 B. de *Rothschild
1989 *Israel Exploration Society
1990 Sheikh A. *Tarif
1990 R. *Weitz
1990 I. *Pollack
1991 Miriam *Ben-Porat
1991 Stef *Wertheimer
1991 Yeshivot Hesder
1994 "Yad Sarah"
1994 Noga Hareuveni and the staff of Ne'ot Kedummim
1995 Y. *Ben-Aharon
1995 A. *Sereni
1996 M. *Dubois
1996 M. *Shamgar
1997 U. Galili
1997 Y. *Tal
1997 A.E. *Feurer
1998 S. *Stern-Katan
1998 S. *Hillel
1998 H. Israeli
1999 R. Bergman
1999 Y. Vinberg
1999 B. *Kapah
2000 S. *Aloni
2000 A. *Carol
2000 *Ha-Gashash ha-Ḥiver
2001 A. *Eban
2001 M. *Ben-Porat
2001 Y. *Shamir
2002 E. *Hurvitz
2002 *Keren Kayemet le-Israel
2003 G. *Cohen
2003 M. *Amit
2003 *Yad Vashem
2004 Y.D. *Grossman
2004 L. *Van Leer
2004 M. Shnitzer
2005 I.M. Lahuh
2005 *Cameri Theater

ISRAËLS, JOZEF (1824–1911), Dutch painter. Israëls, who was born in Groningen, the son of a money changer, studied first at the Amsterdam Academy, then at the Académie des Beaux-Arts in Paris, where he copied the works of old masters at the Louvre and became acquainted with the School of Barbizon. After returning to Amsterdam in 1847, Israëls earned his living by painting portraits and historical subjects. Among these were scenes from Jewish life and history as well as from Dutch history. In 1855, when for health reasons he went to live at the fishing village of Zandvoort, he turned to the representation of fishermen and country people. His pictures of the Netherlands coast showed the influence of the Barbizon school, while his interiors are reminiscent of the Dutch paintings of the 17th century. His treatment of light is reminiscent of Rembrandt, and so are some of his subjects, particularly his *Saul and David* and *The Jewish Wedding*. In 1871 Israëls moved to The Hague, where he was joined by a number of other painters. This group became known as the "Haagse School" and produced fine, realistic landscapes in which shades of green and a grey sky played a great part. Israëls was thus one of the discoverers of the true Dutch landscape. But he also frequently reverted to Jewish subjects. One of his best-known works is *The Son of an Ancient People* (1889), which shows a forlorn shopkeeper in the Amsterdam ghetto and is filled with that compassion which distinguishes his best paintings. Israëls is considered one of the leading Dutch 19th-century painters.

His son ISAAC ISRAËLS (1865–1934) studied at the Academy in The Hague and then spent some time in Paris, Spain, and England. On his return home he painted mainly portraits and military subjects. However, after a stay in the mining regions of Belgium, he turned to the representation of working-class people. In 1886 he settled in Amsterdam and, in contrast to his father, became a painter of city life. When he moved to Paris in 1903 he saw the work of Toulouse-Lautrec, whose influence can be found in his coffeehouse and cabaret scenes. Handling his brush with great freedom and using strong colors, Isaac Israëls showed great vitality and succeeded in conveying much of the character of his time.

BIBLIOGRAPHY: M. Liebermann, *Jozef Israëls* (Ger., 1922[4]); P. Zilcken, *Josef Israëls* (It., 1910); J.E. Phythian, *Jozef Israëls* (Eng., 1912); M. Eisler, *Jozef Israëls* (Eng., 1924); W.J. de Gruyter, *Catalogue of the Israëls Exhibition in Groningen and Leiden* (1956); C. Wentinck, *Catalogue of the Israëls Exhibition, Amsterdam* (1958).

[Edith Yapou-Hoffmann]

ISRAELSOHN, JACOB IZRAILEVICH (1856–1924), Russian Semitic scholar. Born in Mitau (Jelgava), Latvia, Israelsohn received a traditional Jewish education with secular training in German and Russian. He studied at St. Petersburg

(1876–83), specializing in Arabic, in particular Jewish-Arabic literature. However, he could not get an academic appointment because he was Jewish and had to earn his livelihood as a journalist (writing mainly for *Voskhod*), translator, encyclopedia contributor, secretary to the Jewish community of St. Petersburg, and philanthropy assistant to the Polyakov family in Moscow and later in Kiev. In 1922 he moved to Brussels. Israelsohn assisted D. Chwolson in translating his work from German to Russian, and during a sojourn in France, assisted Joseph *Derenbourg in his research into Judeo-Arabic material. Israelsohn played a very important, behind-the-scenes role in preparing the scholarly aspect of the defense in the *Beilis trial. It was he who induced the Russian Hebraists I. Troitski and P. *Kokowzoff to give evidence as experts. Possibly it was this activity that inclined him toward studying the history of the Jews in Eastern Europe. He was held in high esteem for his modesty, warmth, and kindness.

Israelsohn's publications include a Russian translation, with introduction, of Josephus' *Jewish War* and part of *Against Apion* (1895); an edition of Samuel b. Hophni's Arabic commentary on the end of Genesis (1886); of Yaḥya ibn Bal'am's commentary on Jeremiah (in *Festschrift… A. Harkavy* (1908), 273–308 (Heb. sect.)), cf. A. Marx, in: JQR, 1 (1910/11), 430; and a chapter on Nathan Neta Hannover's life and works in the YIVO publication *Gzeyres Takh* ("The 1648/49 Massacres," 1938).

BIBLIOGRAPHY: B. Dinur, *Bi-Ymei Milḥamah u-Mahpekhah* (1961), 376–8, 393–5, 411; E.E. Friedman, *Sefer Zikhronot* (1926), 372–3; S. Ginzburg, *Historiste Verk*, 1 (1944), 174; 2 (1946), 146, 154; I. Markon, in: *Yevreyskaya Letopis*, 4 (1926), 197.

[Moshe Perlmann]

ISRU ḤAG (Heb. אִסְרוּ חַג), designation for the day following the three *pilgrim festivals. The name is derived from Psalms 118:27: "Bind the sacrifice (*isru ḥag*) with cords, even unto the horns of the altar," which the Talmud (Suk. 45b) interprets: "He who makes an addition (*issur*) to the festival (*ḥag*) is considered to have built an altar and sacrificed on it." Rashi comments that this is understood by some to refer to the day after a festival. In the Jerusalem Talmud the day is known as *bereih de-mo'ada* ("the son of the festival"; TJ, Av. Zar. 1:1, 39b). Liturgically, it has been the custom to treat *isru ḥag* as a sort of minor holiday; no supplicatory and penitential prayers are said, and fasting and funeral eulogies are prohibited.

BIBLIOGRAPHY: Eisenstein, Dinim, s.v.

[Jacob Nacht]

ISSACHAR (Heb. יִשָּׂשכָר), the ninth son of Jacob and the fifth of Leah; eponymous ancestor of the tribe bearing this name. Issachar's birth was considered by Leah to be a sign of divine favor, after a long intermission in childbearing, in reward for having given her handmaid to Jacob (Gen. 30:18). For that reason she called him Issachar, apparently popularly interpreting the name to mean "man of reward." The invariable association with *Zebulun in the order of birth, in the blessings of Jacob and Moses, and in the tribal lists testifies to the proximity of the two tribes and to the close ties between them (Gen. 49:13–15; Deut. 33:18; cf. Num. 1:28–31; Josh. 19:10–23). The boundaries of the tribe may be reconstructed from the description of its neighbors – Naphtali to the north, Zebulun to the west, and Manasseh to the south – and from the list of cities within the territory (Josh. 17:11; 19:17–23; 21:28–29). It may be inferred that the border of Issachar stretched in the north from Mt. Tabor to the river Kishon in the west; in the east it lay along the length of the Jordan from Beth-Shemesh to the edge of Beth-Shean; in the south, it may have traversed the length of the mountains of Gilboa and the ridge of the mountains of Ephraim. The main part of the territory was in a plateau that sloped down to the Jordan Valley and the Valley of Jezreel. This topographical feature found rhetorical expression in the verse, "Issachar is a strong-boned ass, crouching between the saddlebags" (Gen. 49:14).

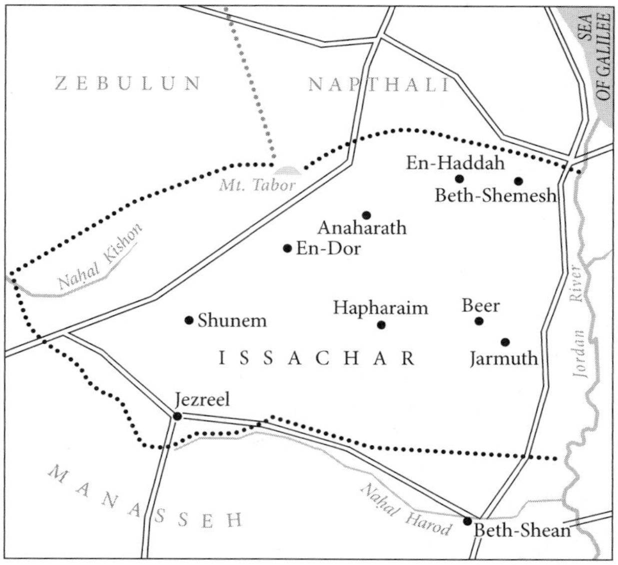

Territory of the tribe of Issachar. After Y. Aharoni in Lexicon Biblicum, *Dvir Co. Ltd, Tel Aviv.*

The territory of the tribe contained 16 cities including Jezreel, Shunem, and Beth-Shemesh. Several cities situated within the borders of Issachar, such as Beth-Shean, En-Dor, Taanach, and Megiddo actually constituted enclaves of the tribe of Manasseh (Josh. 17:11). Apparently, Issachar did not at first drive out the Canaanites since the Manassite cities within its borders remained Canaanite (Judg. 1:27ff.). The silence of the Bible in this regard may possibly hint at the subjection of Issachar by the Canaanites. A similar hint appears in the blessing of Jacob: "He bent his shoulder to the burden, and became a toiling serf" (Gen. 49:15).

In the war against Sisera, the tribe participated alongside Zebulun, and *Deborah the prophetess may herself have come from Issachar (cf. Judg. 5:15). The tribe also produced the judge Tola son of Puah (Judg. 10:1) and Baasha, king of Israel (1 Kings 15:27). In the time of Hezekiah the men of Issachar were among those who went from Ephraim to observe the Passover in Jerusalem (II Chron. 30:18). The territory of Issachar was conquered by Assyria in 732 B.C.E., and annexed to the Assyrian province of Megiddo.

[Samuel Abramsky]

In the Aggadah

The *aggadah* highlights various features of the relationship between Issachar and Zebulun, in which Zebulun the merchant provided for his brother Issachar, thus enabling him to study Torah. The *Testament of Zebulun*, dating from the Second Temple period, praises Zebulun's support of the needy. Issachar is first mentioned as a great scholar and renowned judge by the *tanna* *Eliezer b. Hyrcanus (c. 100 C.E.), whose evaluation was based on I Chronicles 12:33: "And the children of Issachar, which were men that had understanding of the times, to know what Israel ought to do." A homily of an anonymous *tanna* also develops these notions: "'Rejoice Zebulun in thy going out' [Deut. 33:18] – Zebulun was an agent between his brother and other people; he would buy from his brother and sell to others; and buy from other people and sell to his brother; 'And Issachar in thy tents' – these are the *battei midrash* in which Torah matters are debated; 'And of the children of Issachar… their heads were 200' [I Chron. 12:33] – this tells us that the tribe of Issachar produced 200 heads of the Sanhedrin; 'And the princes of Issachar were with Deborah' [Judg. 5:15] – this teaches us that the great *bet midrash* of the future will be in the territory of the tribe of Issachar" (*Midrash Tanna'im…*, ed. D. Hoffmann (1909), 218, no. 18). This brings out the economic partnership of Issachar and Zebulun, the latter buying and selling on behalf of the former. From the last part of the homily it is clear that even before the Sanhedrin was established in Jerusalem there were *battei-midrash* in the territory of Issachar which were renowned for their greatness. It is reasonable to assume that this homily dates either from the period immediately before the Bar Kokhba War or from shortly after, when the Sanhedrin was forced to move from Jerusalem, in the territory of Judah, to Galilee, in the territory of Issachar (cf. Gen. R., ed. Ḥ. Albeck, 197, 1220ff.).

To the theme of the scholar being supported by the merchant, the *amoraim* added several points: "'For he saw a resting place that it was good' [Gen. 49:15] – this refers to the Torah; '… and he bowed his shoulders to bear the weight' [*ibid.*] – of the Torah; '… and he became a servant under taskwork' [*ibid.*] – these were the 200 heads of the Sanhedrin that the tribe of Issachar produced. How did Issachar attain all this? Through the efforts of Zebulun, who traded for him and thus sustained Issachar, who devoted himself to Torah study …" (Gen. R. 98:12). This motif was expanded by *Ḥiyya b. Abba in the third century C.E. When collecting funds for needy scholars (see TJ, Hor. 3:7, 48a; Meg. 3:1, 74a), R. Ḥiyya described the great rewards in store for those laymen who supported poor Torah scholars, using the example of Issachar and Zebulun to lay stress on the obligation.

[Moshe Beer]

BIBLIOGRAPHY: IN THE BIBLE: A. Saarisalo, *The Boundary Between Issachar and Naphtali* (1927); M. Noth, *Das Buch Josua* (1938), 86ff.; Alt, KI Schr, 1 (1953), 193–202; Y. Aharoni, *Hitnaḥalut Shivtei Yisrael ba-Galil ha-Elyon* (1957), 43–48, 98–111, 115–20; S. Yeivin, in: EM, 3 (1958), 944–52; Y. Kaufmann, *Sefer Yehoshu'a* (1959), 207–20, 223–6; Z. Kalai, *Naḥalot Shivtei Yisrael* (1967), 144–51, 164–72, 355–60; W.F. Albright, *Yahweh and the Gods of Canaan* (1968), 230–1; IN THE AGGADAH: Ginzberg, Legends, index; Beer, in: *Sefer ha-Shanah… Bar-Ilan*, 6 (1968).

ISSACHAR, SIMḤAH (15th century), Hebrew poet who lived in the German Rhineland. Issachar was one of the few medieval German poets who wrote secular poetry. He was the first known German author of rhymed prose. A *maqāma* by him was published by A.M. Habermann (see bibliography), its subject being debates between opposites standing before the king on their importance. The debaters are the wise man with the fool, the wealthy man with the poor man, truth with falsehood, the good inclination with the evil, day with night. The sole manuscript contains only five debates, and at the end is marked: "I did not find any more in the copy." It appears, however, that there were additional debates, such as the sick man and his visitor, the dry with the wet, the old man with the youth, beauty with ugliness. As is usual in the *maqāma*, there are more than 20 short rhymed poems; the name Issachar appears in many of them as an acrostic.

BIBLIOGRAPHY: Habermann, in: YMḤSI, 2 (1936), 91–116; Stock, in: KS, 14 (1937–38), 84–86.

ISSACHAR BAER BEN SOLOMON ZALMAN (Klazki; d. 1807), Lithuanian talmudist. The brother of *Elijah b. Solomon Zalman the "Gaon of Vilna," he was also known as Issachar Baer Ashers, in accordance with the custom then prevailing, since his father-in-law was Asher Ginsberg. Issachar Baer wrote a commentary to the Pentateuch entitled *Ẓuf Devash* (unpublished), which is primarily a literal commentary but also includes elucidations of talmudic passages and a commentary on the Shulḥan Arukh, *Yoreh De'ah*. He was also interested in secular learning and in a letter to the Amsterdam rabbi, Saul, dated 1775 (see Horowitz, in bibl.), he asked him to send him the *Nicomachean Ethics* of Aristotle, as well as some kabbalistic works.

BIBLIOGRAPHY: S.J. Fuenn, *Kiryah Ne'emanah* (1915), 205f.; I.T. Eisenstadt and S. Wiener, *Da'at Kedoshim* (1897–98), 208 (first pagin.); D. Maggid, *Toledot Mishpehot Ginzburg* (1899), 60, 69, 104, 226; Z. (H.) Horowitz, *Kitvei ha-Ge'onim* (1928), 5–8.

[Samuel Abba Horodezky]

ISSACHAR BAER BEN TANḤUM (1779–1855), Lithuanian rabbi, known popularly as "Berele Bunes," although his family name was Behagaon. Issachar Baer was born in Orla, Poland, but spent his life in Vilna. In 1817 he was appointed *moreh ẓedek* (scholar in residence) in that city, and delivered discourses on Talmud and *halakhah* in the *bet ha-midrash* founded in 1780 and named after Elijah of Vilna. He annotated the commentaries on Alfasi (published in the Vilna (Romm) edition of the Talmud under the title *Pe'ullat Sakhir*) as well as the Mishnah of the order *Zera'im* with the commentary of *Samson of Sens, and the *Sefer ha-Mitzvot* of Maimonides with the criticisms of *Naḥmanides. He is best known for his *Ma'aseh Rav*, a collection of the religious practices of Elijah of *Vilna (collected by his disciple Saadiah b. Nathan Nata), to which he wrote a commentary also titled *Pe'ullat Sakhir*. This book, first published in Vilna and Grodno in 1832 by his son Mordecai, gained great popularity and has frequently been republished. A note by Mordecai at the end of *Ma'aseh Rav* indicates that his father also had written novellae which had not been published. Issachar Baer frequently gave *haskamot to rabbinical works.

BIBLIOGRAPHY: H.N. Maggid (Steinschneider), *Ir Vilna*, 1 (1900), 41–48; S.J. Fuenn, *Kiryah Ne'emanah* (1915), 215, 277f.; J.L. Maimon (ed.), *Sefer ha-Gra*, 1 (1953), 341f.; B. Landau, *Ha-Ga'on he-Ḥasid mi-Vilna* (1965), 323ff., 328–30; idem, *Hashlamot ve-Tikkunim…* (1967), 384f.

[Abraham David]

ISSACHAR BERMAN BEN NAPHTALI HA-KOHEN (commonly known as **Berman Ashkenazi**; 16th century), commentator on the Midrash. He was born in Sczebrzeszyn, Poland, where he died. The statement in the *Kore ha-Dorot* that he died in Palestine and was buried in Hebron is incorrect. Issachar studied under Moses *Isserles. In 1584 he completed the final recension of his *Mattenot Kehunnah* on the *Midrash Rabbah*. In this commentary, the author made a great effort to correct the text "for the mistakes and errors of the copyists are very many" (introd.). He collated numerous manuscripts of the Midrash and the Jerusalem Talmud; "I ordered the printers not to repeat the previous mistakes in the new book" (commentary to Five Scrolls, first edition, Cracow, 1587–88) and endeavored to arrive at the plain meaning of the Midrash (Eccl. R., no. 12). He looked for persons proficient in foreign languages such as Latin and Arabic to explain foreign words and reveals a knowledge of medicine and astronomy. He was eager to "fit the commentary to the words of the Midrash so that the explanation should correspond to the intention of the saying" (introd.). As a result of its brevity and clarity the *Mattenot Kehunnah* achieved considerable popularity and is included in almost every edition of the Midrash. Issachar is also the author of *Mareh Kohen*, an index to the subjects and biblical quotations in the Zohar (Cracow, 1589; Amsterdam, 1673). The first part was translated into Latin by Christian Knorr von Rosenroth and published in part 2 of his *Cabbala Denudata* (Sulzbach, 1677).

BIBLIOGRAPHY: H. Albeck, *Mavo u-Mafteḥot le-Midrash Bereshit Rabbah*, 1 (1965[2]), 134–6; Reifmann, *Ohel Yissachar* (1887), with annotations by N. Bruell.

[Ephraim Kupfer]

ISSACHAR DOV BAER BEN ARYEH LEIB OF ZLOCZOW (d. c. 1810), rabbi and ḥasidic *ẓaddik*, a grandson of Naphtali b. Isaac ha-Kohen of Frankfurt, author of *Semikhat Ḥakhamim* (Frankfurt, 1704). Rabbi in Zloczow, he was a noted rabbinical scholar who wrote novellae on the Torah and responsa, *Bat Eyni* (Dubno, 1798), in which he discussed halakhic questions with the great scholars of his generation, including Ḥayyim ha-Kohen *Rapoport of Lvov and Ẓevi Hirsch of Zamosc. Issachar was also one of the outstanding disciples of the ḥasidic leader *Dov Baer the *Maggid* of Mezhirech. His work *Mevasser Ẓedek*, first published with *Bat Eyni* and later separately (Lemberg, 1850), is written in the ḥasidic manner and contains the teachings of Ḥasidim such as *Levi Isaac of Berdichev, *Jehiel Michael of Zloczow, and others. Toward the end of his life Issachar settled in Ereẓ Israel and died in Safed. His son-in-law Abraham Ḥayyim of Zloczow succeeded him.

BIBLIOGRAPHY: Frumkin-Rivlin, 3 (1929), 77–8; Y. Raphael, *Ha-Ḥasidut ve-Ereẓ Yisrael* (1940), 139–41.

[Zvi Meir Rabinowitz]

ISSAR JUDAH BEN NEHEMIAH OF BRISK (d. 1876), Lithuanian rabbi. He lived in Szydlowiec, Brest-Litovsk (Brisk), where he was head of the *bet din*, and Siedlce. He immigrated to Ereẓ Israel toward the end of his life and died there. He was the author of *Ezrat Yehudah* (1862), responsa and novellae; and *Neḥamat Yehudah* (1866), comprising two parts – *Igra de-Shemata*, essays on halakhic novellae, and *Igra de-Pirka*, pilpulistic homilies and novellae which aimed at resolving difficulties in Maimonides' code. Some of the responsa in *Ezrat Yehudah* deal with the problem of **agunot* that arose in consequence of the great fire which swept Brest-Litovsk in 1847. He was in correspondence with Joseph Saul *Nathanson (*Ezrat Yehudah*, 59a–b). In his introduction he mentions other works which have not been published.

BIBLIOGRAPHY: A.L. Feinstein, *Ir Tehillah* (1885), 34, 221; L. Ovchinskii, *Naḥalat Avot*, 1 (1894), 22 no. 107.

[Josef Horovitz]

ISSERLEIN, ISRAEL BEN PETHAHIAH (1390–1460), the foremost rabbi of Germany in the 15th century. Isserlein was also called, after the towns in which he resided, Israel Marburg and Israel Neustadt, but he was mainly known as "the author of *Terumat ha-Deshen*," his chief work. Isserlein, the great grandson of *Israel of Krems (author of *Haggahot Asheri*), was born in Regensburg. His father died when Israel was a youth, so he was educated in Wiener-Neustadt in the home of his mother's brother Aaron Plumel (Blumlein). In 1421 his uncle and mother were killed during the Vienna persecutions. After staying for some time in Italy, Isserlein established his residence in Marburg, Styria. In 1445 he returned to Wiener-Neustadt where he was appointed rabbi and *av bet din* of the city and neighborhood. Here Isserlein spent the rest of his life, and through him Wiener-Neustadt became a center of study, attracting a large number of students, many of whom later served as rabbis in various communities. Outstanding scholars and communities addressed their problems to him and accepted his decisions. The most important *posekim* valued his books and highly praised his personality. Moses *Mintz called him *Nesi ha-Nesi'im* ("chief of chiefs"; responsa, no. 12 Salonika, 1802 ed., 10b). Isserlein refused to accept a salary from his community. He opposed those rabbis who tried to dominate their congregants by threats of excommunication. Through his efforts and personal authority he prevented a controversy among the German communities of the Rhine district when Seligman of Bingen attempted to impose various *takkanot* on them enacted on his responsibility, and threatened excommunication of those who did not accept the *takkanot* (see Moses *Mintz).

Isserlein lived a life of piety and asceticism. To some extent he may be regarded as continuing the tradition of the Ḥasidei Ashkenaz of the 13th century. In any case the influence of the *Sefer Ḥasidim* (see *Judah ha-Ḥasid) is recognizable in many of his rulings. One of his intimate pupils, *Joseph b. Moses, noted down in *Leket Yosher* (ed. by A. Freimann, 1903–04) Isserlein's daily behavior as well as what the author heard from him in his discourses. Isserlein's most important work is his responsa *Terumat ha-Deshen*, so called because it contained 354 (the numerical equivalent of דשן) sections. Most of these problems were presented by the author himself in order to investigate, clarify, and give practical halakhic rulings on them. They provide an authentic picture of contemporary Jewish life. In this work Isserlein emerges as an erudite and profound scholar, endowed with a logical mind. He based his decisions on the Talmud and mainly on the works of the French and German scholars. Among Spanish scholars he mentions in particular Isaac *Alfasi and *Maimonides; others, such as *Naḥmanides, he mentions only rarely, and still others, such as Solomon b. Abraham *Adret, not at all. Isserlein sought to restore the study of Talmud and other ancient sources to their former importance, because of a growing tendency to rely mainly upon the *posekim*. He decided in accordance with the view of the earlier authorities rather than the later. He was not deterred by the authority of *Jacob b. Asher, author of the *Turim*, when the latter differed from the *geonim*. Generally speaking, Isserlein adopted a strict line where biblical prohibitions were concerned, but in many matters he inclined toward leniency, particularly in order to establish harmonious relations with the Christians. Of his responsa, which he gave on actual cases, 267 have been preserved and arranged by one of his pupils in a collection, *Pesakim u-Khetavim*, which was published together with *Terumat ha-Deshen* (Venice, 1519, and elsewhere). His other works include *Be'urim* ("expositions") to Rashi's biblical commentary (Venice, 1519, new edition, Jerusalem, 1996); *She'arim*, on the laws of **issur ve-hetter* (published in Jerusalem, 1978), which is mentioned in his *Pesakim u-Khetavim* and also in the *Torat Ḥattat* (Kracow, n.d.) and *Darkhei Moshe* of Moses *Isserles (extracts were published as glosses to the *Sha'arei Dura* (Venice ed., 1548) of Isaac of Dueren). Some *piyyutim* and prayers are also attributed to him. Some of Isserlein's responsa found their way into the collections of responsa by Jacob *Weil and of his pupil Israel *Bruna. Isserlein's works contain valuable material on the general history of the Jews of Germany in the 15th century and in particular on the organization of the communities and their spiritual life.

[Simha Katz]

Female Family Members

All of the known women of Isserlein's family combined serious religious educations with solid business acumen. Since the Isserlein family belonged to the Austrian Jewish social elite of prominent rabbis and bankers, it seems likely that their wives also came from important families. Unfortunately, we do not have any information about their descent. Isserlein's mother (her name is not transmitted) was a very pious woman who was said to have blessed the Creator every morning with the words, "Who has not made me a beast" (LY 1: 7). Following her example, Isserlein did not allow any other form of this blessing. She was murdered, probably at the stake, during the 1421 persecutions of Jews in Vienna, the *Wiener Gesera. Isserlein fasted on the Ninth of Nissan, the anniversary of her death (LY 1: 115). Isserlein made one of his only two documented loans with Roslein, wife and later widow of his paternal uncle, Venzlein of Herzogenburg: in 1415, a Viennese couple pawned their house to them for 66 pounds (Geyer-Sailer, p. 510, n. 1708). Roslein lent money by herself as well (Geyer-Sailer, p. 511, n. 1713).

Isserlein was married to SCHOENDLEIN; highly educated and pious, she must have been of prominent descent. We have no evidence that she herself lent money, but she was very wealthy. For the holidays, she purchased a precious silk *tallit* with ornaments for her husband out of her private property (LY 1: 12). She lived in her own room which she examined personally for *ḥametz* before Passover and her testimony was trusted (LY 1: 80). She and her husband had four sons: Pethahiah (called Kechel), Abraham, Shalom, and Aaron. Isserlein's only daughter, Muschkat, died as a child "in the days of his old age"; perhaps he had remarried after Schoendlein's death (LY 2: 97). Schoendlein managed the yeshivah household consisting of family members, servants, and a number of students who spent the Sabbath with their master. On behalf of her husband, she wrote a responsum in Yiddish to a woman with a *niddah* problem (LY 2:19).

Isserlein's daughter-in-law, REDEL, probably the wife of his son Pethahiah/Kechel, studied with an old married man named Yudel Sofer in the house of the rabbi (LY 2: 37). Redel made minor loans to the prostitutes of Wiener Neustadt, an undertaking that Isserlein did not consider immoral (LY 2:16). He blessed his daughters-in-law on Sabbath eves by putting his hands on their heads (LY 1: 57). In 1442, PLUMEL, daughter of Isserlein's uncle Rabbi Aaron Blumlein and widow of his relative Rabbi Murklein of Marburg, signed a business document with a Hebrew confirmation and her signature.

[Martha Keil (2nd ed.)]

BIBLIOGRAPHY: Berliner, in: MGWJ, 18 (1869), 130–5, 177–81, 224–33, 269–77, 315–23; Guedemann, Gesch Erz, 3 (1888), 14, 18, 23, 29, 85, 87, 93, and passim; Weiss, Dor, 5 (1904⁴), 248–52; S. Krauss, *Die Wiener Geserah vom Jahre 1421* (1920), index s.v.; Tamar, in: *Sinai*, 32 (1953), 175–85; S. Eidelberg, *Jewish Life in Austria* (1962). **ADD. BIB-**

LIOGRAPHY: S. Spitzer, in: *Sinai*, 82:5–7 (1978), 226–36; R. Geyer and L. Sailer, *Urkunden aus Wiener Grundbuechern zur Geschichte der Wiener Juden in Deutschoesterreich* 10, 387, no. 1280; 510, no. 1708; J. Bar Mosche, *Leket Yoshe* (LY), ed. J. Freimann (1903; rep. 1964); M. Keil, "'Maistrin' (Mistress) and Business-Woman. Jewish Upper Class Women in Late Medieval Austria," in: A. Kovács and E. Andor (eds.), *Jewish Studies at the Central European University. Public Lectures 1996–1999* (2000), 93–108.

ISSERLES, MOSES BEN ISRAEL (1525 or 1530–1572), Polish rabbi and codifier, one of the great halakhic authorities. His full family name, Isserel-Lazarus was shortened to Isserles, but he is usually referred to as "the Rema" (acronym of Rabbi Moses Isserles). Isserles was born in Cracow. His father was very wealthy and a talmudic scholar. Isserles was a great-grandson of Jehiel *Luria, the first rabbi of Brisk (Brest-Litovsk). He studied first under his father and his uncle, Moses Heigerlich. His father sent him later to Lublin to the yeshivah of Shalom *Shachna where he studied until 1549, purportedly marrying Shachna's daughter. (Current scholarship has raised a doubt as to whether the Rema's first wife was indeed the daughter of Shalom Shachna.) She died in 1552 when only 20 years old, and in her memory her husband in 1553 built a synagogue, first called the Isserles synagogue and later the synagogue of the Rema, which still exists. Isserles' second wife was the sister of *Joseph ben Mordecai Gershon Ha-Kohen of Cracow, author of the responsa *She'erit Yosef.* Besides Talmud and the codes, Isserles also studied philosophy, astronomy, and history. While still young he was renowned as an outstanding scholar and in 1550 was a member of the Cracow *bet din*. That year his signature appeared on a ruling along with those of Moses Landau and Joseph Katz in connection with the ban against the sale of Maimonides' works issued by the rival of Meir *Katzenellenbogen. Isserles founded a yeshivah, supporting its students from his private means. He gained a worldwide reputation as an outstanding **posek* and all the great scholars of the time addressed their problems to him. Among those who corresponded with him on halakhic matters were Meir Katzenellenbogen and his son *Samuel Judah, Joseph *Caro, Israel son of Shalom Shachna, Solomon *Luria, and his own brother-in-law Joseph Katz. Among his pupils were David *Gans, the author of *Ẓemah David*, whom Isserles encouraged to study history, Mordecai b. Abraham *Jaffe, Abraham ha-Levi *Horowitz, father of Isaiah Horowitz, the author of *Shenei Luḥot ha-Berit*, *David b. Manasseh ha-Darshan of Cracow, *Menahem David of Tiktin, his cousin *Joshua Falk b. Alexander ha-Kohen, Aaron b. Abraham Solnik *Ashkenazi, and Ẓevi Hirsch Elzisher (of Alsace?). Isserles had three brothers, Isaac, Eliezer (son-in-law of Solomon Luria), and Joseph, and one sister, Miriam Bella the wife of Phinehas *Horowitz. He had a son Judah Leib, and two daughters. One, Dresel, became the wife of Simḥah Bunim Meisels, and the other, whose name is unknown, married Eliezer b. Simeon Ginsburg. His great granddaughter, the daughter of his grandson Simeon Wolf of Vilna, married *Shabbetai b. Meir ha-Kohen.

Isserles was of a humble and friendly disposition. This humility is particularly noticeable in his controversy with his older relative Solomon Luria. The dispute arose originally in connection with the question of the defective lung of an animal, but developed into discussions on philosophical topics, Kabbalah, and grammar. Through it was revealed Isserles' self-confidence, for he held to his opinion where he was convinced he was in the right, admitted to any error, and replied with courtesy and humility. Isserles was also a scribe and allegedly wrote a *Sefer Torah* in accordance with the rules contained in an old manuscript which Joseph Caro bought for him in Ereẓ Israel and sent to Cracow. (This last tradition has also been questioned. There is no factual basis for this assertion (see Penkower, *Textus*, 1981)). Isserles died in Cracow and was buried next to his synagogue. Until World War II thousands of Jews from every part of Poland made a pilgrimage to his grave every year on *Lag ba-Omer, the anniversary of his death.

Isserles' Works

His contemporaries considered Isserles to be the "Maimonides of Polish Jewry" and he can be compared with him in his universal outlook, in his attachment to both Talmud and secular knowledge, in his manner of study, in his methodical approach, in his decisiveness, in his character, and in his humility. His works were in the fields of *halakhah*, philosophy, Kabbalah, homiletics, and science. They include the following:

(1) *Darkhei Moshe*, to the *Beit Yosef* of Joseph Caro, notes and supplementary laws, mostly by Ashkenazi scholars, not given in the *Beit Yosef.* Isserles had begun to write a commentary to the *Turim* of *Jacob b. Asher, but while he was engaged in this task the *Beit Yosef* was published. He then wrote his *Darkhei Moshe ha-Arokh* to *Oraḥ Ḥayyim* (Fuerth, 1760) and *Yoreh De'ah* (Sulzbach, 1692). He later abridged it and it was published on all four parts of the *Tur* (Berlin, 1702–03) with the title of the *Darkhei Moshe ha-Kaẓar.* Isserles utilized the *Darkhei Moshe* as a basis for his glosses on the Shulḥan Arukh, the *Haggahot* or *Ha-Mappah*. It contains explanations, supplements, additions, and includes the views of the Ashkenazi scholars ignored by Caro. At times Isserles decided against the view of the Shulḥan Arukh, ruling in conformity with Asher b. Jehiel and his son Jacob, rather than with Isaac Alfasi and Maimonides as does Caro. By spreading his *Mappah* ("tablecloth"), so to speak, over the Shulḥan Arukh ("Prepared Table") – which had codified Sephardi practice – he in fact made that work acceptable to Ashkenazim as well as Sephardim. The *Mappah* was first published with the Shulḥan Arukh in the Cracow edition of 1569–71.

(2) *Torat ha-Ḥattat* (Cracow, 1569), laws of **issur ve-hetter* in accordance with the *Sha'arei Dura* of *Isaac b. Meir of Dueren. This work was criticized by *Ḥayyim b. Bezalel (see below), and Yom Tov Lipman *Heller wrote criticisms (**hassagot*) to it called *Torat ha-Asham*. Isserles was defended by Joseph Saul *Nathanson of Lemberg in his glosses *Torat Moshe.* Isserles himself abridged the book calling it *Torat Ḥattat ha-*

Kaẓar, and Eliezer b. Joshua Shevrashin wrote a commentary to it, *Dammesek Eli'ezer* (Wilmersdorf, 1718).

(3) The Responsa of the Rema (Cracow, 1640) consists of 132 responsa written between 1550 and 1571, 91 by Isserles and the rest by colleagues and pupils.

(4) Halakhic glosses, to *Bava Meẓia* (published in the Amsterdam Talmud 1644–48), to *Niddah* (Ms. Oppenheim), and to the *Mordekhai* of *Mordecai b. Hillel, in which he established the correct readings. These glosses were noted down during the course of teaching and are incorporated in the Romm edition of the *Mordekhai*. He wrote comments on the Rosh of *Asher b. Jehiel and on the *Issur ve-Hetter*, under the title *Yad Ramah* (Lemberg, 1866), and on the *Sheḥitah u-Vedikah* (Cracow, 1557) of Jacob *Weil. *Karnei Re'em*, his glosses to the supercommentary (Venice edition) of Elijah *Mizraḥi to the Pentateuch was published by Solomon Zalman Ḥayyim Halberstamm in the *Meged Yeraḥim* (Lemberg, 1856) of Joseph Kohen Zedek and later in an edition of the Pentateuch (Jerusalem, 1959) together with the commentary *Ha'amek Davar* of Naphtali Ẓevi Judah *Berlin.

(5) His philosophical and kabbalistic works include *Meḥir Yayin* (Cremona, 1559), a homiletical and philosophical commentary to the Book of Esther; *Torat ha-Olah* (Prague, 1570), a philosophic conception of Judaism. In his work he endeavors to give Jewish philosophy and thought a kabbalistic basis and to establish their inner identity, maintaining that they merely used different terminology. He also explains the meaning of sacrifices and the measurements of the Temple and their symbolism. *To'afot Re'em* contains glosses to Maimonides' *Guide of the Perplexed* and the commentaries to it of *Shem Tov ibn Shem Tov and Isaac Profiat *Duran (published by Sirkin in *Oẓar Ḥokhmah* 2–3, 1861–65). In *Darkhei Moshe*, Isserles also mentions his *Yesodei Sifrei ha-Kabbalah*. This work and his commentaries to the Zohar and to the *aggadot* of the Talmud have apparently been lost. He also engaged in the study of general sciences. His glosses on Chapter 18 of the fourth *ma'amar* ("discourse") of the *Yesod Olam* of Isaac *Israeli were published in the *Yuḥasin* (Cracow, 1580–81) of Abraham *Zacuto. He also wrote a commentary on *Mehallekh ha-Kokhavim* ("The Course of the Stars"), a translation by Ephraim Mizraḥi of the *Theorica Planetaram* of Georg Peuerbach.

His Opinions

In philosophy Isserles followed the teachings of Aristotle as he had learned them from the works of Maimonides. He also advanced reasons for the precepts and pointed out benefits accruing from their observance. He dealt with anthropomorphism, maintaining that the phrase "the hand of God" referred to an angel. He accepted the three principles of Judaism propounded by Joseph *Albo in his *Ikkarim*. Although he regarded philosophy and Kabbalah as identical, he preferred philosophy because of its logic. In his *halakhah*, at times, he based himself both on philosophy and on Kabbalah and statements in the Zohar, but where the Kabbalah conflicted with the *halakhah*, he did not accept it. He also endeavored to give a rational explanation of strange *aggadot*. In one of his responsa to Solomon Luria, he admitted that he did not possess an intensive knowledge of grammar, but he had a great love of the Hebrew language and permitted the reading of the secular books of *Immanuel of Rome, military chronicles, etc., on the Sabbath if they were written in Hebrew. His regard for Ereẓ Israel is reflected in a beautiful statement based on the talmudic saying (Kidd. 49b): "ten measures of wisdom descended to the world of which Ereẓ Israel took nine" – "It was for that land that the Torah was primarily given, its natural habitat is there where the very air makes one wise." In *halakhah*, Isserles strove to give to *minhag* (custom) the force of *halakhah* even where it had no halakhic source, and at times accepted a custom as binding even where it conflicted with the *halakhah*. There are also cases where he states that "the custom is a wrong one" or "if I had the power I would abrogate the custom. For it is based on an error and there is no reason to rely on it." The vast majority of the customs he followed were those which developed among Ashkenazi Jewry. Isserles was very frequently lenient "in cases of stress and where considerable financial loss is involved," a leniency seldom shown by previous *posekim*.

These two traits, his attitude to *minhag* and leniency in case of loss, as well as the codification itself in his glosses on the Shulḥan Arukh, gave rise to powerful opposition from great contemporary scholars, particularly from Ḥayyim b. Bezalel who had studied with him under Shalom Shachna.

In the introduction to his *Vikku'aḥ Mayim Ḥayyim*, Ḥayyim enumerates the reasons for his opposition: (1) Codification obliges the rabbi giving a decision to decide the *halakhah* according to the view of the majority; (2) Isserles adopts the lenient view of the *rishonim* against the stringent view adopted by *aḥaronim*; (3) he cites customs of Polish Jewry but pays no attention to those of Germany; (4) the codes cause neglect of the study of the primary sources in the Talmud and *rishonim*, and lead to ignorance; (5) the rabbis will not be listened to because people will rely on published books; (6) just as Isserles disagrees with the rulings and customs of Caro so it is permitted to disagree with him; (7) why should German Jewry abrogate its customs in favor of those of Poland? (8) he did not associate any other scholars in his rulings but decided on his own; (9) if leniency is permitted in cases of considerable loss it will be applied in cases of small loss also; (10) Isserles had been lenient where in accordance with strict law one should be stringent; and (11) once something was forbidden it acquired the force of a custom and could not be abrogated.

Even though Ḥayyim's *Vikku'aḥ Mayim Ḥayyim* was not actually published until long after his death and that of Isserles, their debate reflects a major shift within Ashkenazi Jewry. This period of time witnessed a shift of the center of European Jewry from Germany to Poland. The growing Polish communities were very different from the German ones. In Germany, the Jewish communities were relatively small while enjoying a great deal of autonomy within the larger

German cities and towns. This led to numerous, well-defined, local *minhagim* (customs). In Poland, the Jewish communities were larger, more amorphous, because of the constant influx of immigrants, and less autonomous. Thus, they did not develop individual town customs, but broader, district and country-wide *minhagim*. In abandoning the numerous, Ashkenazi local customs while adopting the Polish ones, Isserles was speaking to a much larger, growing audience. By spreading his *Mappah*, glosses and notes, over Caro's *Shulḥan Arukh*, he was actually binding together all of Ashkenazi (read: Polish) Jewry and enabling their continued halakhic observance. Despite the arguments of Ḥayyim and other contemporary scholars, the rulings and customs of Isserles were accepted as binding on Ashkenazi Jewry and continue to form the basis of Ashkenazi Halakhah to this day.

BIBLIOGRAPHY: A. Siev, *Ha-Rema* (1957); idem, in: *Talpioth*, 4 (1949), 743–58; 5 (1950–52), 244–87 (bibl. of Isserles' works), 649–68; 6 (1953–55), 321–35, 723–9; 9 (1964), 314–42 (bibl. of writings of Isserles); idem, in: *Hadorom*, 21 (1965), 100–21; 25 (1967), 211–9; C. Tchernowitz, *Toledot ha-Posekim*, 3 (1947), index; Nissim, in: *Sinai Sefer Yovel* (1958), 29–39; O. Feuchtwanger, *Righteous Lives* (1965), 79–81. **ADD. BIBLIOGRAPHY:** Y. Ben Sasson, *Mishnato ha-Iyyunit shel ha-Rema* (1984); A. Strikovsky (ed.), *Ha-Shulḥan ve-ha-Mappah* (1988); Y. Hurvitz, *Rabbi Moshe Isserles – Ha-Rema* (1974); Y.T. Langermann, in: *Physics, Cosmology and Astronomy 1300–1700* (1991), 83–98; E. Reiner, in: *Kwartalnik Historii Zydow* 207 (2003), 363–72; J.S. Penkower, in: *Textus*, 9 (1981), 39–128; Y.M. Peles, in: *Zekhor le-Avraham* (1993), 39–41; A. Berger, in: ibid. (1991), 71–77; M. Rafler, in: *Sinai*, 107 (1991), 239–41; Y.M. Peles, in: *Yeshurun*, 9 (2001), 756–67; A. Ziv, in: *Sefer Zikaron le-Shemuel Belkin* (1981), 148–54; Z.A. Sloshatz, in: *Niv ha-Midrashi'ah*, 18–19 (1985), 69–80; G. Goldberger, in: *Sefunot*, 2:4 (1990), 84–89; N. Greenfeld, in: *Moreshet Ya'akov*, 3 (1989), 33–39.

[Shlomo Tal / David Derovan (2nd ed.)]

ISSERLIS, STEVEN (John; 1958–), English cellist. His grandfather was the Russian pianist and composer, Julius Isserlis (the family has also a connection to *Felix Mendelssohn). Isserlis received his training at the International Cello Centre in London (1969–76) and at Oberlin College, Ohio (1976–8). In 1977 he made his London debut and went on to perform as a soloist with the world's leading orchestras and conductors. Isserlis was also active as a recitalist and chamber music performer. As a performer and musician he combined outgoing flamboyance with inwardness and introspection and intellectual, brilliant, adventurous thought. His repertoire embraces traditional cello works; early music played on original instruments, contemporary music, and rarely heard works. He gave first performances of works by Robert Saxton, Elizabeth Maconchy, Howard Blake, and John Tavener, including *The Protecting Veil* (1989, London), of which his recording won a Gramophone Award. Among his recordings are the concertos by Elgar and Barber, Britten's Cello Symphony, and much chamber music. His awards include the Piatigorsky Artist Award (1992), the Royal Philharmonic Society's Instrumentalist of the Year (1993), CBE (1998), and the Stadt-Zwickau Robert Schumann Prize (2000). He writes the sleeve notes for most of his recordings as well as articles for leading newspapers and journals. Among his publications are "Prokofiev's Unfinished Concertino: A Twisted Tale," in: *Three-Oranges* (May 2002, 3:32–33) and his children's history of great composers, *Why Beethoven Threw the Stew* (2001). He also edited and arranged several works. Owing to a strong interest in musical education Isserlis was much in demand for teaching – he was artistic director of the IMS Prussia Cove and was regularly invited to teach at various prestigious academies in the U.S., Europe, and Australia.

BIBLIOGRAPHY: Grove Music Online; Baker's Biographical Dictionary (1997); E. Eisler, "Steven Isserlis: Author, Advocate, Scholar, Sleuth," in: *Strings*, 5:99 (Jan. 16, 2002), 42–53.

[Naama Ramot (2nd ed.)]

ISSERMAN, FERDINAND M. (1898–1972), U.S. Reform rabbi. Isserman was born in Antwerp, Belgium, and immigrated to the United States in 1906. He served in the United States Army during World War I, volunteering for the infantry despite his exemption as a theology student. He received his B.A. from the University of Cincinnati in 1919 and his ordination from Hebrew Union College in 1922. He subsequently earned his M.A. from the University of Pennsylvania (1924). Isserman's first pulpit was as assistant rabbi to Rev. Dr. Harry W. *Ettelson at Rodeph Shalom Congregation in Philadelphia (1922–25), following which he served as rabbi of Holy Blossom Temple in Toronto (1925–29). He made a big impact in that community, leading a campaign against corporal punishment in the city's public schools and organized the first goodwill dinner among Catholics, Protestants, and Jews in Canadian history as well as the first interdenominational Armistice Day service in Toronto. He was also a contributing editor to the *Canadian Jewish News*. In recognition of his work, an interfaith prize bearing his name was established at the University of Toronto.

In 1929, Isserman became rabbi of Temple Israel in St. Louis, Missouri, where he remained until his retirement in 1963. He brought his ecumenical and social activism with him, as well as a passion to fight racism, which he denounced during weekly broadcasts on a leading St. Louis radio station for nearly 30 years. He was chairman of the Inter-Racial Commission of the *Synagogue Council of America; chairman and organizer of the Social Justice Commission of St. Louis (1930–31); founder and vice chairman of the St. Louis Seminar of Jews and Christians (1929–35); vice president of the Missouri Welfare Board; a member of the national executive committee of the National Conference of Christians and Jews; and a member of the boards of the St. Louis Community Chest and the Urban League of St. Louis. As chairman of the Justice and Peace Commission of the *Central Conference of American Rabbis (1942–45), he organized and chaired both the Commission's American Institute on Judaism and a Just and Enduring Peace (1942) and the Institute on Judaism and Race Relations (1945). In 1950, he helped organize the CCAR's Institute on Reform Jewish Theology Today.

In 1933 and 1934, Isserman, as chairman of the American section of the World Union for Progressive Judaism, traveled on fact-finding missions to Europe and Germany, returning to warn Jews and Americans of the dangers of Nazism. He took a leave of absence from his congregation during World War II to serve in North Africa with the First Armored Division and American Red Cross Headquarters. He received citations for his volunteerism from the Treasury Department and the Red Cross.

Isserman was involved in scholarship in Missouri and the Reform movement as well. He served on the Board of Governors of Hebrew Union College (1930–38) and was a member of the board of the Bible College of the University of Missouri. As president of the University of Missouri's Jewish Student Foundation for more than a decade, he was instrumental in building a chapel for Jewish students there. In 1950, he was elected first president of the joint HUC-JIR Alumni Association. In 1967, he was honored with the Religious Heritage of America's Regional Clergyman of the Year Award.

In addition to being an editorial contributor to the St. Louis publication *Modern View* (1929–41), Isserman wrote five books: *Sentenced to Death: The Jews of Nazi Germany* (1933, rev. 1961); *Rebels and Saints: The Social Message of the Prophets of Israel* (1933); *This Is Judaism* (1944); *The Jewish Jesus and the Christian Christ* (1950); and *A Rabbi with the American Red Cross* (1958).

BIBLIOGRAPHY: K.M. Olitzky, L.J. Sussman, and M.H. Stern, *Reform Judaism in America: A Biographical Dictionary and Sourcebook* (1993).

[Bezalel Gordon (2nd ed.)]

ISSUR GIYYORA (i.e., Issur "the Proselyte"; beginning of the fourth century), prominent figure of the amoraic period in Babylonia. He was the father of the Babylonian *amora* R. Mari b. Issur, who inherited the considerable fortune left by his father, of which Rava was the executor (BB 149a). There are conflicting opinions as to the identity of Issur's wife Rachel. Some maintain that she was Rachel the daughter of the famous *amora* Samuel (see Rashi, Ber. 16a; BM 73b; Rashbam BB 149a). A significant remark made by Issur as to what non-Jews thought about the observance of Jewish law has been preserved in the following passage (Av. Zar. 70a): "Rava has said: Issur Giora once told me, 'When we were still gentiles we used to say that Jews do not observe the Sabbath, because if they did observe it how many purses would be found in the streets!'" i.e., a Jew would discard his purse on the onset of the Sabbath, and no other Jew would pick it up.

[Jacques K. Mikliszanski]

ISSUR VE-HETTER, a term designating the totality of halakhic rulings with regard to forbidden foods and related topics. From the second half of the 12th century, however, it came to be used for a specific literary genre dealing with this subject, and from that time books wholly devoted to this topic were produced in great numbers (the *Issur ve-Hetter* of Rashi is not to be included among them, since it belongs to a completely different category; see *Rashi).

The creation of this type of literature is connected with the spread of Jewish settlement in Germany. This gave rise to the development of different customs in various spheres of life, including to no small degree topics of *issur ve-hetter*. There is indeed no doubt that *issur ve-hetter* literature should be regarded as a branch of the more comprehensive literary genre known as *minhagim literature. Research into the *issur ve-hetter* literature is complicated. The authors of many of the books are anonymous or have been erroneously identified; in addition, many glosses and notes were added to the original text of works by copyists and other scholars who wanted to adapt them to the local prevailing custom; a large part of this literature is still in manuscript in different libraries, at times wrongly catalogued. Among the most important works of this subject are the *Sefer ha-She'arim* or *Sha'arei Dura*, called "*Issur ve-Hetter*," by Isaac b. Meir of *Dueren (Cracow, 1534), which is seemingly the earliest work of this type; 36 *She'arim* on laws of *issur ve-hetter* by Israel *Isserlein, apart from his glosses on the *Sha'arei Dura*; the laws of *issur ve-hetter* at the end of the *Minhagei Maharil* (Sabionetta, 1556) which is an abridgment of the *Sha'arei Dura*, as is the *Torat Ḥattat* (Cracow n.d., c. 1570) of Moses *Isserles. The well-known *Issur ve-Hetter he-Arokh* (Ferrara, 1555), attributed in error to Jonah *Gerondi but apparently compiled by Jonah Ashkenazi, a pupil of Israel Isserlein, contains, besides laws on forbidden foods, laws connected with the duty of saving life.

BIBLIOGRAPHY: Ta-Shema, in: *Sinai*, 64 (1969), 254–7.

[Israel Moses Ta-Shma]

ISTANBUL, city in N.W. *Turkey, on both sides of the Bosphorus at its entrance on the Sea of Marmara (for history prior to 1453, see *Constantinople). Constantinople was taken from the Byzantine emperor in 1453 by the Ottoman sultan Mehmed II (1451–81) and became the new capital of his state, known from then on as Istanbul. The Arabs called it *Qusṭanṭīniyya*, and the Jews wrote the name Qustantina (or Qustandina), hence the name *Kushta* in Hebrew. During the Ottoman period three townlets in its vicinity became quarters of Istanbul: Galata, between the Golden Horn and the Bosphorus; Eyüp, at the northwest extremity of the Golden Horn; and Üsküdar (Scutari), on the eastern shore of the Bosphorus. The town occupied a central position on the routes between Asia and Europe and the maritime communications between the Black Sea and the Mediterranean Sea passed through it. It also served as an administrative and commercial center. After World War I the capital of Turkey was transferred to Ankara.

The 15th and 16th Centuries

Immediately after the conquest of the town on May 29, 1453, the armies of Mehmed, II, the Conqueror, perpetrated a massacre of its inhabitants which lasted for several days; they did not, however, according to one opinion, attack the Jewish community, and according to some Ottoman sources (fermans

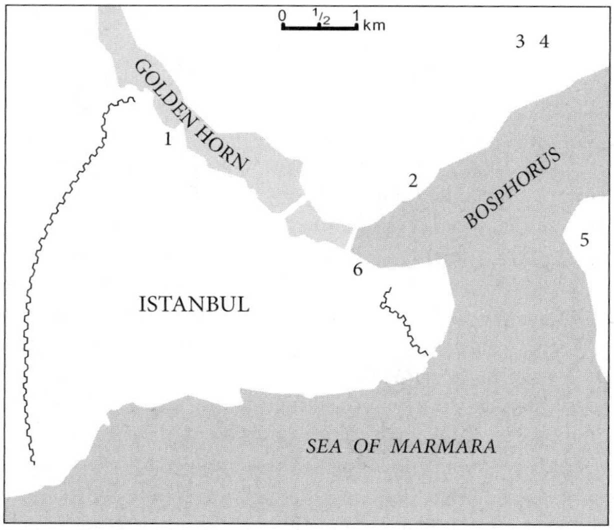

Figure 1. Jewish quarters in Istanbul in the 17th century. 1. Areas designated for Jewish settlement by Sultan Muhammad II in 1453. 2. The Jews' Bath is believed to have been in this neighborhood. 3. Area with a majority of Jewish inhabitants. Don Joseph Nasi's famous residence, Belvedere, was near this quarter. 4. Site of a well-known printing press in the late 16th century. 5. Near there was the Jewish cemetery which, according to the Armenian geographer, Inciciyan, owed its special sanctity to the fact that, lying on the Asiatic side of the Bosphorus, it was not separated by sea from the Holy Land. 6. Jews' Gate, one of the main Jewish quarters, in early Ottoman Istanbul. Some of the Jews transported from Salonika by Muhammad II are said to have been settled here. After U. Heyd, "The Jewish Communities of Istanbul," Oriens, *vol. 6, 1953.*

from the 16th and 17th centuries) the Jews assisted the Ottoman armies in their conquest of the town. Some sources say that the fate of the Jewish residents in the city was not different from that of their Greek neighbors, and Jews who did not run away in time were killed, their women and daughters were raped and their houses were plundered by the Ottoman soldiers. During the conquest the old synagogues of the community in the district of Balat were destroyed. Prior to the siege, the majority of the Jews resided in the area called now Galata, Kasim Pasha and Hasköy. In the census of 1455, which was incomplete, the names of Jews appeared as residents of two quarters: Fabya, near the church of San Fabyan, and Samona, near Karaköy. There was also a Jewish quarter near the church of San Benito, but only a few Jews lived there. The survey of 1472 does not mention even one Jewish household in Galata, and this remained the situation until the middle of the 16th century. In order to renovate the town, populate it, and convert it rapidly into a flourishing and prosperous capital, Mehmed II adopted a policy of transferring Muslim, Christian, and Jewish inhabitants, most of them merchants and craftsmen, from various regions of the empire – principally from Anatolia and the Balkans – to the new capital. All the transferred Jews were Romaniots (see *Romaniot) and were called by the Ottoman authorities "sürgün" (after the Turkish word for "those who were exiled") to distinguish them from the other Jews, principally from Spain, Portugal, Ashkenaz (Germany), and other European lands, who were named "kendi gelen," meaning "those who came of their own free will." The sürgüns also included the survivors and escapees of Jews from the city who resettled in it as sürgün. All the Jewish population of Asia Minor and many communities in Greece, Macedonia, and Bulgaria were deported to Istanbul over a period of 20 years. They paid taxes to the vakif of the Sultan Mehmed II and had a special status forbidding them to leave Istanbul without a license of the Ottoman authorities. There were sürgüns in the 16th century who left the city, and continued paying their taxes in Istanbul. They paid higher taxes than those paid by the kendi gelen directly to the central treasury. The sürgün settled in the vicinity of the commercial complex of Mahmud Pasha. The surveys made for the vakif of Mehmed II in 1535, 1540, and 1545 noted the existence of a congregation named Galata, but it is clear that this congregation must have been located not in Galata and was comprised of Jews whose origin was Galata. Most sürgüns settled in a trapezoid-shaped area formed by Eminönü, Sirkeci, Tahtakale, Mahmud Pasha, and Zeyrek. The 1495 register of the vakif of Mehmed II mentions many locations where Jews were living. In addition to the Edirne (Karaite) quarter near the harbor of Eminönü are Balik Pazari, Zindan Hani, Sari Demir, on the way to Unkapani, Tahtakale, the area near Edirne Kapi, Sirkeci, and locations in the other direction from Eminönü toward Sarayburnu. In 1569 a great fire broke out in the Jewish area, but according to the 1595–97 register of the vakif of Mehmed II, 60 percent of the Jews were still living in the trapezoid. The main settlement was the quarters of Balik Pazari and Babi Orya. There were a few sürgüns who settled in Balat near Egri Kapi, where the Jewish community had its most important cemetery. The congregations there were Okhrida, Yanbul, Kastoria, and Karaferiye. Only 20 percent of Istanbul's Jews resided in Balat at the end of the 16th century. Another place where Romaniots settled after the conquest was in the neighborhood of Samatia (Psamatia) near the Castle of Yediküle on the Marmara coast. The Jews also had an old cemetery in Kasim Pasha, and it is clear that Jews resided in Kasim Pasha and in Hasköy in the middle of the 15th century. Hasköy had been a center of *Karaite Jews at the beginning of the 16th century. Many Ashkenazi Jews settled in this area in the 15th, 16th and 17th centuries. In the middle of the 16th century Portugese Jews settled in Galata. In 1540, 47 Romaniot congregations based on their places of origin existed; each was conducted by an autonomous leadership and had separate institutions. The Ashkenazi, Sephardi and Italian Jews also built separate and autonomous congregations. A few Ottoman censuses make it possible to evaluate the demographic changes in the community of Istanbul in the 15th and 16th centuries. The census of 1477 shows 1,647 Jewish households in Istanbul, forming 11 percent of the total population; in 1489, the number had risen to 2,027 and by the turn of the 15th century we find 3,600 Jews in the city out of 100,000 inhabitants. An Ottoman register from 1535 lists 8,070 Jewish households in the capital. In the middle of that century the

Jewish population rose from some 18,000 persons to nearly 50,000. A *jizya* register of 1542 informs us about 1,490 Jewish householders. A slight growth from 2,645 Jewish *hane* (family) in 1529 to 2,807 *hane* in 1566 is recorded in another survey, and all together we find 1,647 Jewish households in the years 1520–1539 out of a total of 16,326 households. European travelers in Istanbul and Jewish sources give higher figures for the Jewish community of Istanbul.

On the eve of the Ottoman conquest and after it, the community was led by R. Moses b. Elijah *Capsali. The Jews of Istanbul constituted a religious-administrative unit which enjoyed an extensive internal autonomy. The first to represent the Jewish community of Istanbul was the Romaniot Rabbi Moses Capsali. In addition to its religious importance, this function was also of a political nature. Capsali concerned himself with the internal affairs of his community, served as the representative of the Istanbul Jewish congregations before the government, and collected the Jewish taxes. He was named "The leading rabbi" but had difficulty imposing his authority over the congregations of the newcomers, especially the Sephardim. He had disputes with some rabbis and secular leaders from Istanbul and other cities. After his death, around 1498–1500, R. Elijah *Mizraḥi was actually the rabbi bearing the title "the leader Rabbi" of the Romaniot congregations. During his tenure he had grown weak, and, as he states himself, he could not take care of the task because the problems of the congregations were numerous, so the secular affairs of the community were in the hands of a Spanish Jew, *Shealtiel (Salto) who had the office of **kahya*, collected taxes from the Jews and dealt with all their financial matters with the Ottoman authorities. After 20 years of service, Shealtiel was ousted from office by the community leaders on October 19, 1518, after many complaints of bribery and arbitrary taxes were lodged against him by Jews. The community banned him and his sons from holding the position of *kahya* or performing any other function involving contact with the Ottoman authorities. He was returned to office on April 29, 1520, by the leaders of the congregations and R. Elijah Mizrahi. After the death of Shealtiel no successor replaced him. After R. Elijah Mizrahi died in 1526, R. Elijah (son of R. Binyamin) ha-Levi was recognized by all the Romaniot communities, and after his death in 1534 or 1535 R. Abraham Yerushalmi inherited his office in the year 1555. Some of the Romaniot scholars who were forced to leave the city during the conquest later returned. Among them we note R. Mordecai Comitiano and R. Shalom ben Joseph Anavi. Among the Romaniot scholars settling in Istanbul after the conquest we note R. Efraim ben Gershon, R. Meshullam, R. Abbaye, R. Menachem Tamari, and R. Elijah ha-Stipyoni. A few Spanish scholars settled in the city before the expulsion, such as R. Hanokh Saporta of Catalonia and R. Gedaliah ibn Yahya (d. in Istanbul in 1488), the author of *Shalshelet ha-Kabbalah*.

Ashkenazi Jews had already settled in the town before the Ottoman conquest, but their greatest numbers arrived at a later date. Some from Hungary and Austria first arrived during the 15th century in reaction to the enthusiastic appeal which was included in a letter sent by R. Isaac Ẓarfati, an inhabitant of Adrianople (second half of the 15th century), to the Jews of Germany, Austria, and Hungary, in which he described the agreeable, peaceful, and happy life of the Jews of Ottoman Turkey. The proximity to Ereẓ Israel and messianic aspirations also drew many Jews into settling in Istanbul and other towns of the Ottoman Empire. Refugees from Bavaria, who had been expelled by King Ludwig IX, arrived during the late 1460s. The second wave arrived after the conquest of Hungarian territories during the reign of the sultan *Suleiman the Magnificent (1526). For many years the Ashkenazi community enjoyed an independent status. The Ashkenazim continued relations with their coreligionists in their countries of origin, and were slow to assimilate among the Sephardim. In time the differences disappeared. Spanish and Portuguese Jews arrived in the town as a result of the massive expulsions of 1492 and 1497. Among the refugees who came to the capital after 1492 were eminent Torah scholars, rabbis, *dayyanim*, *rashei yeshivot* and authors of significant books. Between 1492 and 1520 there settled in Istanbul R. Abraham Hayyun, R. David Ibn Yahya, R. Isaac ben Joseph Caro, R. Abraham Ibn Ya'ish, R. Judah Ibn Bulat, R. Solomon Taitazak and his famous son Joseph Taitazak, R. Isaac Dondon, R. Solomon Altabib, R. Moshe ben Shem Tov Ibn Habib, R. Solomon Almoli, and R. Jacob Tam ibn Yahya. Other active rabbis in Istanbul in the 16th century were R. Joseph ibn Lev, R. Samuel Ḥakham Halevi, R. Samuel Jaffe Ashkenazi, R. Elijah ben Hayyim, R. Gedaliah Ibn Hayyun. The Italian R. Joshua Soncino served as rabbi of a Spanish congregation.

Strong tensions also existed between the Romaniot scholars who came with the sürgün, and the spiritual leaders of the native Romaniot community over questions of *halakhah* and *minhagim*. Later, disputes occurred about hegemony between Romaniot and Sephardi leaders. The *Karaites in Istanbul were also involved in a dispute between the Romaniot and the Sephardi scholars over the attitude toward them. The Romaniots wanted to follow their tradition to teach the Karaites. At the beginning of the 16th century, the Sephardim were still struggling with the Romaniots over issues such as the right over a proportionate amount of the meat supplied to the Jewish community; they did not recognize the authority of the Romaniot leader rabbi. By the time of R. Elijah Mizrahi's death, the influence of the Sephardi *minhagim* had increased. The Sephardim in town agreed to accept the Romaniot custom considering the *erusin* as *kidushin*, and this decision was upheld in Istanbul for hundreds of years. In the years 1582–1603 the Romaniots were still a majority of the Jews in the city. The Jews of Istanbul established famous yeshivot which were headed by R. Elijah Mizrahi, R. Joseph ibn *Lev, R. Isaac *Caro, R. *Tam ibn Yaḥya, R. *Elijah b. Ḥayyim. The Spanish yeshivot in the city continued the teaching methods of the original Spanish yeshivah. R. Yosef Taitazak was brought from *Salonika to head a Spanish yeshivah supported by wealthy patrons, and in 1554/5 Gracia Mendes appointed the Spanish Salonikan Rabbi Joseph Ibn Lev to head the new yeshivah she founded.

THE ORGANIZATION OF THE KAHAL, AND ECONOMIC AND SOCIAL LIFE OF THE JEWISH COMMUNITY. The refugees founded various *congregations (*kahal-kehalim*) according to their country of origin, the region-province, or the town which they had abandoned. The refugees of Spain, Sicily, and Portugal who arrived in Istanbul founded the congregations called Gerush Sepharad, Cordova, Aragon, Messina, Sicily, and Portugal. These congregations jealously maintained their independence and individuality. Every *kahal* had its own synagogue, rabbi, teacher, *talmud torah, ḥevra kaddisha*, welfare institutions (*hekdeshim*), and various societies, such as *gemilut ḥasadim* ("benevolent society"), *bikkur ḥolim* ("visiting of the sick"), and societies for the support of the yeshivot of Tiberias; in most cases they also had a *bet din*. Moreover, secular affairs were handled by a group of functionaries called *maʿamad*. The members of the *maʿamad* were called *memunnim, berurim*, and *gabbaʾim, tovei hakahal*, or *nikhbadim*. A majority of these persons were important businessmen. They were elected in the presence of all the taxpayers of the *kahal* and administered the affairs of the *kahal* according to established agreements and *takkanot*. These leaders were responsible for the registration of the *kahal* members, and the imposition and collection of taxes, and their transfer to the Ottoman authorities. In every *kahal*, the *ḥakham* (Rabbi) was the spiritual leader of the congregation and headed its law court. Penalties, such as the *ḥerem* and *niddui* ("bans"), were imposed on those who challenged the opinion of the rabbi of the *kahal*. The *takkanot* and agreements on which they based their decisions concerned various matters, especially social and economic ones, such as the prohibition of leaving one *kahal* for another, tax assessments, the appointment of rabbis and Torah teachers and the conditions of their actiivity, the prohibition of wearing expensive apparel and jewels by women, *ḥazakot*. Sephardi congregations did not have a single rabbinical authority over all the rabbis. During the 16th century the new settlers from Europe, especially from Portugal and Italy, founded many new congregations. A significant congregation named "Seniora" was founded by Gracia Mendes in the middle of the 16th century for the *anusim* from Portugal settling in Istanbul. Following disputes in some congregations, there were individuals or groups who preferred to set up new congregations or to join others. The congregations enabled individuals to change their affiliations only before the tax assessment and payment. Great fires that ruined the southern shore of the Golden Horn in 1539 and 1554 caused many Jews to move to areas where they joined congregations whose customs differed from theirs. The 1569 fire in what became Yeni Cami brought many Jews to Hasköy and elsewhere before the famous mosque was built there. Other fires broke out in 1568, 1569, and 1588.

The numerous *kehalim* of the capital had their roof organization, which was known in responsa literature as *Ha-Vaʿad ha-Kolel shel ha-Kehillot*, to which every *kahal* sent its delegate. There were also other institutions in which all the *kehalim* were associated.

The 16th century was thus a flourishing period for the community, and Istanbul became one of the world's most important Jewish centers. Not long after the settlement of the sürgün, the Jews in Istanbul were excelling in traditional fields of big business, especially in commerce, crafts, medicine, and the manufacture of firearms. They were involved in a lucrative trade of cloth and spices, and Jews from Istanbul traveled to trade with centers such as Bursa, Salonika, Caffa, Kilia, and Akkerman, Egypt, Aleppo, Dubrovnik, Venice, and Ancona. In 1514 the Jewish guild of physicians in Istanbul had six members and the Muslim guilds had sixteen members. A considerable number of Jews were involved in tax farming and the farming of mints all over the empire in the second half of the 15th century. Until the end of the 16th century the richest congregations of Istanbul were the Romaniot. Jews of Istanbul were allowed to work in all aspects of economic activity except those performed by the Ottoman administrative-military system of government. Many Jews of Istanbul produced and sold food and wine. There were Jews compelled by the government to bring sheep from Anatolia and the Balkans to Istanbul, causing some of them to go bankrupt. Many Istanbul Jews were engaged in all the various occupations dealing with precious metals and stones. The farming of the minting house of Istanbul was often in Jewish hands in the second half of the 15th century and in the 16th century Many Istanbuli Jews were **sarrafs* (money changers). Other Jews focused on the production of luxury textiles such as silk and also traded in angora wool brought from Anatolia. Many other crafts and occupations were engaged in by Jews in Istanbul; they were, for example, tailors, carpenters, pharmacists, bakers, fishermen, tinsmiths, glassmakers, blacksmiths, painters, bookbinders, and also actors, dancers, and musicians. Many Jews owned shops in the markets of Istanbul. For international trade some of the Jewish merchants of Istanbul used the services of larger entrepreneurs, exporters and importers, and others sent their representatives to other cities. The Spanish Jews in Istanbul had close trading connections with Spanish communities in Italy, Europe, and the Levant. Many Jews in Istanbul became wealthy, and the economic elite in the Jewish community included many Romaniots and Sephardim.

Another significant phenomenon which contributed to the security of the Jewish community was the activism of the court Jews, especially physicians. It is worth noting Jacob (Hekim Yakub) who served as personal physician to Mehmed II until his own death in 1481, and received a tax exemption for himself and his descendants in the Ottoman Empire. Jacob was also a financial adviser to the sultan and his translator, and he seems to also have been a companion to the sultan on every military campaign. Moreover, he maintained close connections with Italian diplomats in Istanbul. Mehmed II appointed this qualified Jew as *defterdar*, the high official in charge of the treasury. Later he converted to Islam at an advanced age and was appointed vizier. Some of his sons remained Jewish and enjoyed the privilege exempting them from all taxes. Jacob's career ended in the early 1480s, and at the same time (c. 1481) the physician Efraim ben Nissim Ibn Sanchi arrived in Istanbul from Portugal. He became a court physician and his son

Abraham also fulfilled the same role in the court. During the 16th century the most significant physicians of the court were the members of the *Hamon family, Joseph and his son Moses of Granada (who served the sultans *Bayazid II, *Selim I, and *Suleiman I, the Magnificent) and the grandson and great grandson, Joseph and Isaac Hamon. There were also prominent Jewish capitalists and bankers who held central positions in the financial areas of the empire – treasury and lease of taxes – and positions of a political nature; their influence at court was beneficial to the Jewish communities of Istanbul and other towns. During the third quarter of the 16th century, the *Mendes family played an important role in the life of the city. This Marrano family from Portugal owned a bank in Lisbon with a branch in Antwerp. After the death of Francesco Mendes, the head of the bank, his widow Gracia (*Nasi) left Lisbon with her young daughter Reyna and her nephew João Micas for Antwerp and from there continued to Venice and Turkey. In Istanbul they openly returned to Judaism in 1553 and João Micas called himself Joseph *Nasi. A short while later, he married Reyna, the daughter of Gracia. There were now ample opportunities available to the Nasi family for financial and commercial activities in the town. Their affairs were not limited to giving credit but also included commercial negotiations with various European countries and competition with the Venetian merchants for the Levantine trade. The friendship of Joseph Nasi with the sultan Suleiman the Magnificent and his son Selim II won him an influence in state affairs which he exploited not only for his own benefit but also for the Jews in general. He made generous donations to the yeshivot of the capital, while at the same time the Mendes family established a large and renowned yeshivah, supporting its students and its head R. Joseph ibn Lev. This yeshivah was named Yeshivat ha-Gevirah after Dona Gracia Mendes, by means of whose financial contributions the novellae and the responsa of R. Joseph ibn Lev, which were debated in the yeshivah, were published. They also supported the Hebrew printing press in the capital (see below). Through its extensive influence Gracia Mendes obtained as a *multazima* (lessee) a concession from the sultan to rebuild the town of *Tiberias, which lay in ruins. Joseph Nasi supported this act, but he and Gracia Mendes did not manage to visit the town. The family assisted in its reconstruction and gave financial support to the yeshivah of Tiberias, which had been reestablished by the *ḥakhamim* of *Safed who had come down to the town. This yeshivah was later supported by Don Solomon ibn Ya'ish of Istanbul whose son Jacob settled there and was known as a pious scholar. During the 16th century a few Jewish women were active in the harems of the sultans by rendering various services. These women had the title **kiera*. The most famous *kieras* were Strongilah, Espiranza Malki, and Esther *Handali. In 1566 R. Moshe Almosnino prepared a list of court Jews in Istanbul who helped him to obtain the Writ of Freedom (*mu'afname*) from the sultan for the Jewish community of Salonika: Joseph Nasi, Judah Di Sigura, Abraham Salma, Meir Ibn Sanji, and Joseph Hamon. Generally those court Jews were very wealthy and attempted to help their brethren in Istanbul and other Ottoman Jewish communities by using their political connections, Sometimes they became involved in internal quarrels of other communities. Gracia Mendes and Joseph Nasi used their status in the Istanbul community and at court, after the burning of the *anusim* in Ancona in the year 1555, to ban the harbor of Ancona and transfer the Jewish Ottoman mercantile representatives to the city of Pesaro. From 1564 R. Shelomo Ashkenazi served as the personal physician of the sultan; he was sent by the sultan Selim II to arrange the peace treaty in 1573 between the Ottoman Empire and Venice. During the reign of the sultan Murad III (1574–95), however, the Jewish community was shaken by a decree ordering the killing of Jews, which resulted from the appearance of men and women in the streets in rich clothing and jewels. As a result of the intervention of the physician R. Solomon *Ashkenazi at court, the decree was mitigated, but Jews were forbidden to wear such apparel. Subsequently, the rabbis of Istanbul and the community leaders reached an agreement that "the women and the girls shall not go out in grandiose apparel, golden jewelry, and precious stones." Bula Ikshati Ashkenazi, the wife of Solomon Ashkenazi was also active as a physician at court at the turn of that century.

Don Solomon Ibn Ya'ish (1520–1603) also had very important political and economic status in Istanbul. He was an active diplomat of the Ottoman Empire after settling in Istanbul in 1580 and was also the farmer of the Istanbul customs. Until his death he served the sultans Murad III (1574–1595) and Mehmed III (1595–1603) and was deeply involved in Ottoman politics.

The 17th Century

The economic and cultural decline of the Jewish community of Istanbul began during the 17th century, together with a general decline of the Ottoman Empire. The great fires which devastated a number of quarters during the 17th century (1606, 1618, 1633) induced the Ottomans to transfer the Jews especially to Hasköy, causing changes in the structure of the *kehalim*. The ancient organization according to origin and synagogue fell into disuse and many Jews joined synagogues near their new residence even if they belonged to another *kahal*. This process was essentially responsible for the fusion of the Romaniots with the Sephardim. From this time onward each individual identified himself according to the quarter or neighborhood he lived in. In 1608, 24 Romaniot congregations existed in Istanbul including 1,152 households, one Karaite congregation with 70 households, 8 Spanish congregations with 539 households, 4 Italian congregations with 209 households, 2 Ashkenazi congregations with 77 households, one Hungarian congregation with 59 households, and two unidentified congregations including 89 households. The total Jewish population was 2,195 households. In the Hasköy cemetery in 1609–1623 the Romaniots were 30.7 percent of the identified stones, the Ashkenazim were 15.3 percent, and the Iberian Jews were 38.4 percent. In the period 1624–1700 the Romaniots were 27.1 percent of the identified stones, the Ashkenazim were 14.2 percent, and the Iberian Jews were 46.3 percent. According to the Ottoman census of 1603–1608, 55.6 percent of the Jews of Istanbul were Romaniots, 5.9 percent were Ashkenazim, and 38.5 percent were Iberian Jews. According to the Ottoman census of 1623, the Romaniots were 57 percent of the Jewish population, the Ashkenazim were 1.5 percent, and the Iberian Jews were 41.5 percent. In 1634, according to one source, there were in the city 2,555 Jewish tax-units. The last census of the century, in 1688, reflects the drastic change in the ethnic groups of the community, especially reflecting the decrease in Romaniot figures over time. There were 3,611 Jewish *jizya* payers, i.e., 18,000 individuals. In Balat there were 1,547 Jewish households; in Galata, 1,033; in Hasköy, 515; and in Orta Köy, 637 households. The Romaniots were only 27.8 percent of the Jewish population, the Ashkenazim were 4.1 percent, and the Iberian Jews were 68.1 percent. Maps describing the Jewish population in the city in the 17th century indicate major Jewish concentrations alongside both the Golden Horn and the Bosphorus. In Orta Köy the Jews were a majority of the local population, and according to the Turkish traveler Evliya Çelebi the same situation existed in Hasköy. In that century there were some wealthy Jews who lived in palaces.

During the 17th century many Sephardi Jews, former *anusim,* and many Italian Jews settled in Istanbul, which assisted the growth of the Sephardi and Italian congregations. In that century the Jewish population became much more integrated and homogenous in its culture, and the majority of its spiritual leaders were Sephardim. "*Va'ad Berurei Averot,*" whose authority was to deal with offenders, was very active in Istanbul. Special appointees to deal with ritual questions (*issur ve-hetter*) functioned in Istanbul from the 17th century until the beginning of the 20th. The appointees issued regulations on many matters relating to *kashrut*, ritual matters, and personal morality. In the community *batei din* functioned in the various districts, and there also existed a supreme *beit din.* In that century every *kahal* had at least one *kahya*, and it is possible that at times there also served one *kahya* of the Romaniots and another of the Sephardim. At the beginning of the century the palace medical staff consisted of 41 Jewish physicians and 21 Muslim physicians. Following the economic decline in the number of Istanbul's Jewish residents, the number of Jewish physicians and advisers at the court fell. By mid-17th century the medical staff was reduced to fourteen Muslim physicians and four Jews only. Still, Jews served at the court of the sultan until the second half of the 18th century and even at the beginning of the 19th. Sultan Ibrahim I (1630–1648) sent a Jewish diplomat, Samuel Markus, to Madrid. The Italian Israel Conegliano (Conian; c. 1650–c. 1717) settled in Istanbul in 1675 and became the physician of Grand Vezir Ḳara Mustafa Pasha and was also consulted by Sultan Mehmed IV (1648–1687).

During the reign of Sultan Murad IV, in 1633, a blood libel against the Jews of Istanbul occurred, saying that they had murdered a Turkish child on the eve of Passover (see *Blood Libels). Following the massacres of 1648–49 in *Poland, the Cossacks, Tatars, and Ukrainians took many Jews into captivity and sold them in Istanbul. The Jews of Istanbul competed with one another in observing the precept of redeeming captives, thus saving thousands of Jews. The community of Istanbul sent a special emissary to Italy and Holland in order to raise funds for the redemption of captives. R. Nathan *Hannover, the author of *Yeven Meẓulah*, who was an eyewitness to the events in Podolia and Volhynia and escaped through Western Europe, writes:

> There was among them [the Jews] a *ḥazzan* and his name was R. Hirsch. When the Tatars came, he began to lament and to intone the El Male Raḥamim [prayer for the departed] in a loud voice over the deaths of our brothers of the House of Israel; all the assembled broke into a great weeping and they aroused the mercy of their captors who comforted them with kind words and said to them: "Be not concerned, you will not lack food nor drink. Tomorrow we shall bring you to your brothers in Constantinople and they will redeem you." In this fashion the Tatars dealt with our brothers of the House of Israel in Istanbul, who redeemed them together with the other captives from Poland – about 20,000 souls – and they spent much money on them.

In the 17th century the Jews of Istanbul lost many of their former professions and were gradually reduced to secondary positions, typically as agents or tax farmers. They suffered further disadvantages, such as growing economic competition with the European-backed Christians and incessant internal disputes. In 1666 *Shabbetai Ẓevi arrived in Istanbul, and the opinion of the Jews of the capital was divided: the majority feared that his appearance would be the cause for actions against Jews in general. Others were attracted by his messianic enthusiasm and went out to meet him in order to pay him homage. The opponents informed the grand vizier of this and he ordered Shabbetai Ẓevi's arrest. The imperial police seized and imprisoned him in Gelibolu. After Shabbetai Zevi's conversion the communal leadership sought to limit the damage within the Jewish communities as much as possible. They did it by calming the people and by attempting to prevent discussion on the subject. The leaders of the Istanbul community decided to neither attack nor prosecute the believers or former believers but rather to ignore them. There is practically no evidence of Shabbateans in Istanbul at the end of the 17th century and during the 18th. A *ḥerem* ("ban") was also issued there against Nehemiah Ḥayon in 1714.

In spite of the economic and political decline of the Jewish community of Istanbul during the 17th century, the community had a considerable elite which included old families such as Ibn Ya'ish, Hamon. Ankawa, Benveniste, Ibn Faraj, Ibn Valiasid, and Zonana. In the middle of the century a difficult dispute about the rabbinate of the Neve Shalom congregation broke out. The quarreling parties involved the Ottoman authorities in this discussion. In the community many scholars were active such as R. Joseph *Trani, R. Isaac ben R. Yom Tov Ibn Faraj, R. Kalev Ben Samuel, R. Aaron Hamon, R. Barukh Ben Hayyim, R. Solomon Caro, R. David Egozi, R. Yom Tob Barbinya, R. Jacob and R. Isaac Elnekave (Ankawa), R.

Yesha'ya Mitrani, R. Moses and R. Joshua Benvinste, R. Moses Shilton, R. Joseph Kazbi and R. David Falcon. R. Joseph Trani from Safed who settled in Istanbul in 1605 was appointed by the wealthy Ibn Ya'ish brothers, head of the Gerush congregation yeshivah. In 1620 he preferred to be appointed *rosh yeshivah* of the wealthy figure Jacob Elnekave, but he continued to visit the former yeshivah in the mornings. R. Joseph Trani was the spiritual leader of the community from 1607 until his death in 1639.

The 18th Century

During the 18th century several fires (in 1704, 1715, 1729, 1740, 1751, and 1756) devastated the Jewish quarters. The greatest of these was in 1740 after which the Jews were not allowed to rebuild their quarter. As a result most of the Jews moved to Ortaköy and Galata. Others settled in Üsküdar, Hasköy, and Piri Paşa. In 1740 the Grand Vizier issued new proclamations regarding the dress of the Christians and Jews, forbidding them to wear certain colors and furs. By then the Jewish community of Istanbul had become more homogenous and better organized. It developed institutions adjusted to the topography, administrative structures, and general character of the city. The local Jewish leaders in each quarter communicated with the quarter's authorities on local issues. In the 18th century the sultans continued to hire Jews as physicians and advisers. The physician Tubias (Toviyyah) Cohen (ca. 1652–1729), a native of Metz, settled in Istanbul and entered the service of Sultan Ahmed III (1703–30) until his retirement and settling in Jerusalem in 1714. Another Jew, Daniel de Fonseca (ca. 1668–ca. 1740), former Portugese *anus,* settled in Istanbul in 1702 and served as a physician and diplomat to the French Embassy, and in 1714 he became the physician of Ahmed III, serving until 1730. Other Jewish court physicians during the reigns of Mahmud I (1730–54) and Osman III (1754–57) were Isaac Çelebi, Joseph the Rofeh, David Halevi Ashkenazi, and Judah Handali. In the second half of the 17th century there was a sharp decline in the number of Jews at the court. According to the inheritance register of the chief rabbi of Galata which was written in 1770, there existed an active *millet yazicisi,* a post unknown before, possible referring to an official, probably a *kahya,* who registered transactions within the Jewish community.

In 1772, up to 300 of Istanbul's 1,500 Jews who could not pay the increased war taxes served instead in the military. Upon Napoleon's invasion of Egypt, Sultan Selim III demanded that the Jews furnish men for the navy, which they did. In 1807 the Jewish community fulfilled among the other citizens the government's order to strengthen the city's defenses. During the Greek war of independence, the Ottomans also drafted non-Christians, including some 500 Jews. In 1772 Mustafa III (1757–74) ground the Jewish community into bankruptcy when he levied great sums to finance a military campaign: 18,000 members of the Jewish community paid jointly 65,000 kuruş. The community's debts amounted to 325,000 kuruş. According to the 1772 budget, 15 percent of Istanbul's Jews were in the lower class of taxpayers, 15 percent in the higher, and the remainder in the middle category. Jews in Istanbul continued to serve as tax farmers, contractors and purveyors for the military, and there were also traders and bankers. In spite of the economic decline of the community in the second half of the century, local Jews still were in prominent positions. Jews in Istanbul were members in mixed guilds until the late 17th century. Much of this changed after the end of the 18th century, when communally-based guilds began to replace mixed ones. The francos who settled in Istanbul during the 18th century had many economic rights, were protected by foreign ambassadors, benefited from preferential taxation in trade, and enjoyed relative independence from the local Jewish community. By the end of the century the Istanbul Jewish community had lost much of its former traditional advantages and was sharply affected by the ongoing decline process in Ottoman society.

Istanbul was one of the most important centers for funds because of its geographic proximity to Ereẓ Israel, and since it was the capital of the central government of Ereẓ Israel, its *ḥakhamim* were spiritually close to those of the Holy Land throughout the Ottoman period. The funds destined for Ereẓ Israel from Eastern Europe also passed through the capital and it was there that the letters and recommendations of the emissaries and their missions were verified, in Istanbul as in many other communities. The "officials for Ereẓ Israel" (*pekidei Kushta*), were active from 1726 until the beginning of the 19th century and the Jewish settlement of Erez Israel was under their patronage. They collected various contributions for the Jews in Ereẓ Israel and transferred them through special emissaries. In 1727 the community of Istanbul imposed a payment of one para per week per person in favor of Jerusalem on all the communities of the Ottoman Empire and later on other Oriental countries and Italy. They also solved problems of the Jerusalem community with the Ottoman government, established many *takkanot,* and forced Jerusalem Jews to act according to the *takkanot*. Other committees of *pekidei Kushta* in Istanbul were economically responsible for *Hebron, Tiberias, and Safed. On some occasions there were also indirect taxes, for example, a tax imposed on the capital in 1763, which consisted of "half a lavan (the Ottoman coin akçe, whose common appellation was *lavan*, "white") on every metro (measure of volume) of wine and beer" in order to save Hebron from its debts. There were special societies, whose members contributed regularly to charities for Ereẓ Israel, the first having been founded during the last third of the 16th century for the benefit of the yeshivah of Tiberias. *Pekidei Kushta* organized the immigration and the Jewish pilgrimage to Erez Israel during the 18th centuries and also helped immigrants from East Europe who passed through Istanbul on their way to Ereẓ Israel. There were many active benevolent societies in the community during the Ottoman era. A noteworthy example is the "Benevolent Society of the Congregation of the Kaïkçis," founded in about 1715 by the Jewish boat owners whose task it was to ferry people from one side to the other on both the Golden

Horn and the Bosphorus. The objective of this union was not a professional one but to provide its members with assistance in times of need. They were later joined by workers from related professions: the *balikçis*, fishermen; the *mayvecis*, fruiterers, who often sailed on boats because of their occupation; and the *mayahaneçis*, wine merchants, the owners of taverns, who used boats in order to convey their goods from the town to the villages. Every member was required to contribute one perutah per week, i.e., an akçe or para, toward the society's fund. The *mayahaneçis* brought four metros (measure of volume in Ladino) free of charge in every boat for the fund. This money was used for supporting the members of the society in difficult times. In order to assure the proper function of the society, the *bet din* of Istanbul appointed two scholars as "supervisors of all the affairs of the society." It appears that the society continued to exist until shortly before World War I.

During the 18th and 19th centuries the study of the Torah decreased and the cultural standard reached such a low point that the majority could not even read the Bible. It was for this reason that books came to be published in Spanish and Ladino (see below, Hebrew Printing). The leading author of the Spanish literature period was R. Jacob *Culi, who was active in Istanbul during the middle of the 18th century and wrote *Me-Am Lo'ez*. *Ladino literature also began to develop at that time and many works were published in this language. Besides Rabbi Culi, R. Abraham b. Isaac Asa, who may be referred to as "the father of Ladino literature," is worthy of note. He translated religious works, the Bible, the *Shulḥan Arukh*, and works of history, ethics, and science into Ladino. In Istanbul during the 18th century the most distinguished intellectual families included the Kimḥi, *Rosanes, and Navon families. R. Ḥayyim Kimḥe and R. Binyamin Kazish headed yeshivot. Some members of the Rosanes family were rabbis, *dayyanim*, and authors, and R. Judah *Rosanes was an author and opponent of the notorious Shabbatean sect. In the 18th century scholarship and intellectual life were in decline. The number of yeshivot declined, but many rabbis were active and compiled significant books, especially responsa and sermons. The dominant *posekim* were R. Efraim Navon (1677–1735), R. Isaac Ben David (d. in 1755), R. Eliezer Yiẓhaki, R. Meir Yiẓhaki (d. in 1753/4); R. Raphael Isaac Yerushalmi (d. in 1782), R. Shabbetai Halevi, R. Samuel Halevi (d. in 1829/1830), R. Isaac Lahmi, R. David Matalon, R. Ḥayyim Moda'i (d. 1793), R. Abraham Meyuḥas (d. c. 1773), R. Judah Meyuḥas, R. Hayyim Jacob Meyuḥas, R. Binyamin Kazish, R. Ḥayyim Kimhe, R. Isaiah Solomon Kimhe, R. Abraham ben Joseph Rosanes (d. 1748), R. Aaron ben Samuel Rosanes (d. 1759), R. Judah ben Samuel Rosanes (d.1727), R. Isaac Rosanes (d. 1748), R. Eliezer ben Nissim Ibn Sanji (d. 1724), R. Ḥayyim Shelomo Sefami, R. Jacob Sasson (d. 1714), R. Moshe Hacohen (d. 1735), R. Elijah Palombo, R. Abraham Ben Avigdor, R. Ḥayyim de Toledo, R. Judah Navon (d. 1761), R. Abraham Anavi (d. 1813), R. Eliyahu Palombo, R. Moshe Frisco (d. 1807), R. Aharon Zonzin, R. Elijah ben Jacob Alfandari (1670–1717), R. Solomon Alfandari (d. 1774); R. Raphael Jacob Assa, R. Michael Ashkenazi, R. Reuven Mizrahi, R, Nissim Samuel Gabbai, R, Ḥayyim Jacob ben Emmanuel Hamon (d. 1788); R. Emmanuel Zonana, R. Yom Tov Elnekave (d. in Koskonjuk, 1786).

The 19th and Early 20th Centuries

In the 19th century there was a general atmosphere of tolerance between Jews and Turks, but relations with Christians were usually bad. On April 27, 1821, The Grand Vizier Benderli Ali Pasha ordered three Jews to take away the body of the executed Greek Patriarch. After they fulfilled the order, a riot led to the injury of an estimated 5,000 Jews. In 1826 several leading Jews in Istanbul who had economic connections with the Janissary corps were executed by an order of the Sultan Mahmud II. In the course of the 19th century the population of Istanbul's Jews remained stable at around 50,000–55,000. This statistic is based upon Ottoman censuses and other sources. In 1830 42,000 Jews lived in Istanbul; between 1881–1882 and 1906, the Jewish population of Istanbul grew by one-third. In the Istanbul census of 1830, almost a quarter of the Jews subject to the *jizya* were placed in the highest or good category, over half were classified as average, and only a fifth were labeled poor.

The Jewish population in 1885 numbered 44,361; in 1893/4, 46,440; in 1906/7, 47,779; and in 1911/12, 53,606 Jews. The Jewish residents lived in 1885 and in 1906/7 in ten districts: Bayezit, Fatih, Cerrah Pasha, Beshiktash and Bosporous to Rumeli Hisar, Yeniköy and Upper Bosporus; Beyoglu and Dolmabahçe, Dolmabahçe to the end of the Golden Horn, Kanlica and Upper Anatolian Bosporous, Üsküdar and Kadiköy. The majority of Jews lived in Fatih (10,133 persons in 1885 and 10,698 persons in 1906/7), Beshiktash (4,581 persons in 1885 and 4,591 persons in 1906/7), Beyoglu and Dolmabahçe (22,865 persons in 1895 and 24,658 persons in 1906/7), and Üsküdar (5,197 persons in 1885 and 4,097 persons in 1906/7). From the middle of the 19th century the Jewish population of Istanbul increased in absolute numbers. According to the 1882 census, there were about 26,000 Jews, and by 1885, the Jewish population had grown to 44,361 persons. In 1914 52,000 Jews were recorded in the city. From then on, the number has been steadily decreasing to about 49,500 in 1945 and about 36,900 in the 1955 census. After the attacks on the Jews of Thrace, thousands of Jews from Kirklareli, Galipolli, Tekirdag and other towns in Thrace fled to Istanbul and remained there. The main reason for the population drop from 1948 onwards is the mass immigration to Israel and other countries, which explains the number of 19,000 Jews in the city in 1988. In 1844 they constituted five percent of the total population. Between 1844 and 1945 their percentage went up and down alternately, stabilizing at 4.9 percent in 1945. In 1882 there was a relative increase to 7 percent of the city population, and in 1927 there was also a relative increase to 8.6 percent of the general population. In 1955 the percentage of Jews in the general population dropped to 2.4 percent, because of the large immigration to Israel in 1948–1952, reaching 0.3 percent in 1988, due to continual emigration and other demographic processes. In 1988 between 18,900 and 19,200 Jews lived in Istanbul. The above data indicate a decrease in fertility and aging as well as erosion in the size of the Istanbul Jewish community. In 1988 Istanbul South and old neighborhoods in the North and Asia sections were emptied of their Jews, while a massive expansion took place in the Jewish neighborhood of the new Istanbul North. Another accelerated trend, which is still continuing, is a return to the new suburbs of Istanbul/Asia, a place offering them better living conditions. Most of the Jews continue to work in Istanbul South and look for work in Istanbul North.

Fires broke out during the 19th century in 1872, 1874, 1883, 1890, 1891, 1894, and 1896. They destroyed c. 2,000 Jewish houses. Fires also broke out in various quarters in the years 1900; 1905, 1908, 1909, 1911, 1912, 1915, 1918, 1921, 1922, 1923, 1924, and 1941. In 1856 Ludwig Frankel pointed out that about half of the Jews were employed as artisans, i.e, makers of cloth, leather, metal products, etc. In 1885 a census showed 31.1 percent of Jewish males classified in commerce, trade, and industry. The vast majority of Jews were, however, unskilled workers, peddlers, or petty-retail traders.

During the first half of the 19th century powerful Jews from distinguished families were prominent. Isaiah Adjiman, Bekhor Isaac Carmona, and Ezekiel Gabbai were the allies of the Janissaries, for whom they acted as bankers and moneylenders, and some of them bore the title Ocak Bazergani. They also held positions of leadership in the community of Istanbul. Jewish physicians began to reappear at the sultan's court. In the late 1830s, the Jewish dentist Jacob Bivaz entered the palace and served there for 30 years. In 1844, Dr. Spitzer, a Moravian Jew, became a physician and adviser to sultan Abdul Mejid (1839–1861). Some Jewish physicians served at the court of Abdul Hamid II, including Elias Pasha Cohen, Isidore Pasha Greiwer, Leon Behar, David Hayun, and Sami Gunsberg. Influence was wielded by Abraham de *Camondo, the representative of a respected family of scholars and wealthy merchants. He was also influential in ruling circles and founded a modern school. Sultan Mahmud II (1808–39) conscripted a unit of 30 Jewish soldiers from Hasköy and 30 from Balat into the army which set out to suppress the revolt in Morea (the Peloponnesus). In 1835 the office of **ḥakham bashi* (chief rabbi) was instituted and R. Abraham ha-Levi was its first incumbent. The office of *ḥakham bashi* gained increased prestige and importance during the 19th century. It also became the focus of an intense power struggle within the Jewish community of Istanbul. During the reign of the sultan Abdul-Mejid I the authorities allowed the admission of Jews into the military school of medicine and the poll tax was abolished (1853). The era from 1839 to 1876 became known as the *tanẓīmāt* period (after the name of the sultan's progressive legislation). As a result of the publication of the *khaṭṭ-i humayun* ("sultanic decree," 1856), the secular leadership began to gain strength at the expense of the religious leadership in various communities, including that of the Jews. In 1840 Moses *Montefiore visited Istanbul. After the foundation of the modern school by Abraham de Camondo, a *Va'ad Pekidim* (*Majlis jasmi*, "Committe of Functionaries") was founded; it was composed of wealthy men and intellectuals of progressive views, under the leadership of Camondo. In 1860 the three members of this body were Carmona, Hamon, and Adjiman. At that time the *ḥakham bashi* was R. Jacob Avigdor. Splits occurred between the progressive-intellectual circles and the conservative-religious Jews within the community. In the course of this conflict the French language was introduced into the school. Missionary schools were opened for Jewish children in Istanbul by the American Board Mission to the Jews, the Church of Scotland Mission, and the English Association for Promoting Christianity among Istanbul Jews, but only a few Jews converted to Christianity. In that century 40 synagogues functioned in the community. All the religious services of the Istanbul community were supplied by ten "*Hashgakhot*."

In the middle of the 19th century the francos in Istanbul such as Jacques de Castro, had come into close contact with European Jewry who were interested in spreading Western culture and education in the community. When Albert Cohn arrived in Istanbul in 1854 as the representative of Baron Rothschild and the Central Consistory, Camondo and other francos and some Ashkenazim were ready to open a modern school. The school was inaugurated in November 1854 and was supported by important Jewish philanthropists.

In 1856 a campaign against Camondo was led by R. Isaac Akrish and R. Solomon Kimḥi, who claimed that the new school encouraged children to convert to Christianity. Thereafter, a *ḥerem* was issued against Camondo, but Isaac Akrish was imprisoned upon the order of the *ḥakham bashi*. He was set free by Sultan Abdul-Aziz and settled in Hebron. The school operated during the years 1858–1889. In 1875 the Alliance Israélite Universelle founded a school in Istanbul. In 1878 Dr. Moshe Alatini founded a modern school for girls in Balat. Madame Fernandez headed a girls' school in Hasköy. Schools were established in Galata and Balat for Ashkenazi boys. In the beginning of the 20th century, 35 percent of the Jewish school-age population in the community attended Alliance schools. There were approximately 1,000 Jewish students who attended English protestant schools in Hasköy and in French Schools in other quarters of the city. Not many Jews joined the modern institutions established by the Ottoman government. Three days after the announcement of the 1856 decree, a blood libel case occurred at Balat, where a mob of Greeks, Armenians and Turks started attacking Jews. Another blood libel broke out in Istanbul in 1874. An order by the name of *ḥakham-khane niẓam namesi* ("Organizational Regulation of the Rabbinate") was issued (1864), which defined the administration of the town's *kehillot*, which was to consist of 12 notables and, among them, four senior rabbis. In 1865 a law was passed which defined the institutions of the community. It was to be headed by the *ḥakham bashi*, a secular council, and a religious council.

The first council included most of the Jewish officials of the government administration, while the second included rabbis. Both were elected for three years. In every quarter there was a local rabbi who headed the synagogue committee, as well as a *kahya* whose duty it was to report births, deaths, and the like to the authorities. There were also three *batei din* which dealt only with matrimonial matters. All other matters were brought before the secular tribunals of the state. The above-mentioned regulations remained in effect until the establishment of the republic, when they were allowed to lapse without being replaced. Groups of Jewish immigrants of Ashkenazi descent from Austria, Germany, Hungary, Poland, Romania, and Russia who arrived in Istanbul in the mid-19th century managed to survive as separate entities, alongside the Ottoman Sephardi community. This statute was recognized by the Ottoman authorities and also by the rabbinate, which signed tax agreements with them regarding burial and ritual slaughter. After 1856 a large number of Karaites from Crimea settled in Istanbul. In 1866, R. Shelomo Kimḥi published a pamphlet against the Karaites, in which he collected all the arguments which had been voiced against them over the generations. The Karaites addressed petitions to the chief rabbi, who ordered the destruction of all the copies which had been circulated. During the second half of the 19th century other disputes broke out in the community. In 1862, following an article in the Ladino journal *Journal Israelite* by its editor Yehezkel Gabbai, in which he attempted to show that not all freemasons were atheists, bans were issued against the newspaper and its editor. This dispute resulted in the resignation of the *ḥakham bashi* Ya'akov Avigdor in 1863. In 1862 the francos established in Şişli a separate Italian Jewish community with its own synagogue, cemetery, and administration. This act caused a deep split in the community of Istanbul. During the reign of Abdul-Hamid II (1876–1909), individual Jews of the town are mentioned as having received decorations and as having held senior positions in the administration. In 1880–1884 the leadership of the community was involved in a deep crisis. In this crisis Abraham Ajiman, David Carmona, the *ḥakham bashi* R. Moshe Ha-Levi, Abraham ben Zonana, Bechor Ashkenazi, and other leaders were involved. A new leadership of the community was established in 1883. The local Jewish press had considerable influence on leadership politics. Jewish religious life in Istanbul suffered a decline, especially from the second half of the 18th century until the beginning of the 20th. During the entire 19th century, up to the beginning of the 20th, 26 authors composed 40 books. These rabbis concentrated on halakhic creativity and attempted to meet the challenges of the problems of their generations and tried to offer the best possible halakhic solutions.

In 1906 a large number of refugees arrived from Russia as a result of the revolution of 1905. The Jewish population of Istanbul grew to 100,000 at the beginning of the 20th century. Shortly following the Young Turk Revolution (1908), Jews appear to have been active in government service in Istanbul. Among them were Emmanuel Shalem, Ezekiel Sasoon, Nissim Russo, Vitali Strumsa, and Samuel Israel. But Jews never became cabinet ministers as did Christians in Istanbul. During the 19th century the Jewish community of Istanbul rebuilt its synagogues. From the second half of the 19th century, newspapers and periodicals began to be published in Ladino. The first periodical appeared in 1853 under the name of *Or Yisrael* and was edited by Leo Ḥayyim de Castro. A soup kitchen and relief and charitable institutions were also established. At the beginning of the 20th century the community organization consisted of two separate councils: the religious council (*bet din*) and the secular council, the latter of which dealt with the administrative and financial affairs of synagogues, schools, hospitals, etc. There were cases of conversion to Islam performed in Istanbul in the 18th and 19th centuries, for example in 1771 the conversion of 14 rabbanites and several Karaites residing in Hasköy was reported to the government by the local kadi. In 1838 and 1839 the local kadi reported the conversion of two Jews. In the 19th century Galata served as a major Jewish residence area, and functioned as a political and cultural center for the entire Jewish community of the Capital. Many businessmen maintained their headquarters in this district. A sizeable number of Jews also moved to new neighborhoods north of Galata (around Şişli) and on the European bank of the Bosphorus (Ortaköy, Beshiktash, Arnavutköy) districts, which underwent a rapid development process at that time, while Balat and Hasköy remained poor. The Asiatic neighborhood of Kuzguncuk, known for the Western orientation of its residents, as well as Haydarpasha, played an important role in the modernization process and the penetration of Western culture into Jewish life. Many of the Jews adopted secularism. Nevertheless, throughout the 19th century there existed in Istanbul the yeshivot of R. Eliyahu Anav (in Balat), R. Joseph Alfandari, R. Joshua Zonzin, Uziel Yeshivah, and Kimhi Yeshivah (in Orta Köy) headed by R. Solomon Eliezer Alfandari. At the end of the century R. Shemarya Gabbai established a yeshivah for R. Refael Bitran in Daj Hamami. The responsa literature and the minutes registers of the *batei din* of the community from the 18th and 19th centuries contain dozens of names of Istanbul scholars in every generation. Almost 100 special *minhagim* of Istanbul Jews were written by the rabbis of the community throughout the Ottoman period.

[Abraham Haim and Yaacov Geller / Leah Bornstein-Makovetsky (2nd ed.)]

Under the Republic of Turkey (from 1923)

The national and secular nature of the Turkish state, which was created by Kemal Ataturk, severely affected the position of the Jews in Istanbul. The laws giving religious autonomy to the Jewish community were allowed to lapse and the *millet* system was abolished. Matters such as personal status (e.g., marriage) were under civil jurisdiction. The community lost the right to levy its own taxes, causing communal institutions to depend for support on voluntary contributions. The measures of secularization affected not only the Jews but, in general, all non-Muslims. In accord with this policy, Turkish became the language of instruction in the schools instead of French (which was used in the *Alliance Israélite Universelle schools throughout the Middle East and North Africa);

the use of French was allowed to continue for a time in the upper grades. The government proscribed the affiliation of any local groups with foreign organizations. Jews, therefore, were prohibited from being represented on such international Jewish bodies as the World Zionist Organization, the World Jewish Congress, and others. In 1932 the schools in Turkey were secularized, in accordance with the character of the state, and religious instruction was prohibited. As other non-Muslim subjects, the Jews of Istanbul were most severely affected by the imposition of the capital levy (*varlik vergisi*) of 1942. In January 1943 the government confiscated the property of those who did not pay as ordered and sent them to labor camps. Some 1,500 Jews from Istanbul were sent to labor camps in Ashkale, and about 40 died there. On the other hand, dozens of Georgian, Kurdish, and German Jewish families which arrived in Istanbul between 1925 and 1950 functioned within the general community's central organizational framework.

Contemporary Period (from 1948)

In 1949 the Turkish National Assembly passed a law which granted the Jewish community autonomy in its internal affairs. This law had been proposed by the Jewish delegate in the house of representatives, Solomon Adato. Religious instruction, which until then had been restricted exclusively to the synagogues, was permitted in schools as part of the normal curriculum. A large number of Jews attended the government schools and continued their studies at the universities. The general educational standard of the Jews of Istanbul was improved as a result of the powerful influence of the Alliance Israélite Universelle. Jewish physicians, lawyers, and engineers of the community played an important role in the life of the country and Jews were also well represented in its commerce. They were rarely employed in the civil services. The number of Jews in Istanbul, estimated at 55,000 in 1948, dropped to 32,946 and 30,831 in the 1955 and 1965 censuses, respectively, as a result of the large-scale emigration to the State of Israel. In 1970 an estimated 30,000 Jews lived in Balat, Hasköy, Ortaköy, and other quarters. The wealthy lived in the Pera and Şişli neighborhoods. The *Haschgaha* in the above-mentioned and six other quarters elects a committee which constitutes the members of the city's general community council. This is comprised of 60 men, including a few members of the Ashkenazi congregation. The general council elects the president of the community and administrative and religious committees. Each congregation also has a rabbi. The council's income is derived from dues, synagogue contributions, and donations. By 1950 the general council numbered only 42 members, since for several years new members were not elected to replace those who had died or emigrated. In 1950, elections were held to fill the 18 vacancies. Samuel Abrevaya was elected president of the community, and held the post until his death in 1953. He was succeeded by Henri Soriano and, later, Israel Menaşe. Until 1953, Istanbul Jewry had no official chief rabbi recognized by the authorities. In that year R. Raphael Saban was chosen. In 1968, the following institutions were supervised by the community's general council: the Or Ḥayyim Hospital (built in 1885); an orphanage; the Ẓedakah u-Marpe charitable organization (founded in 1918), which was responsible for the education of underprivileged students; an old-age home (founded in 1899); a Maḥzikei Torah organization, which provided training one day a week for cantors and *mohalim*; and the Mishneh Torah association, which helped poor students. In 1968 the community also had three elementary schools and a high school. In 1966 the attendance figures at these schools were 950 pupils, most of them poor, since the wealthy Jews preferred to send their children to foreign schools. There were also Jewish youth organizations in Istanbul in 1968, such as Ne'emanei Zion, Amical, and others, some of which undertook a certain amount of Hebrew education. Most of the community members in the 1980s and 1990s worked in the following occupations: light industry, trade, engineering, medicine, law, clerical work, religious services, and various aspects of the technical trade. There are also rich businessmen, such as Jack Kimche, who had an industrial-cum-commercial firm in Istanbul. He simultaneously held a representative position as a member of the Turkish National Bureau of Commerce and Industry. The academic-teaching sphere is still modest among the local Jews.

Among the members of the community in the latter part of the 20th century and into the 21st there is a high level of solidarity. Many of them plan to emigrate and do not establish permanent relations with the majority population. They oppose mixed marriages and live in their own neighborhoods. They establish schools for their children, but the majority of the local Jews send their children to Turkish schools. The Jews of Istanbul under the Turkish republic preserve their religion and avoid involvement in local politics, except for issues that directly affect them as a group. The majority of Istanbul Jews are businessmen, but there are many poor Jews who receive a monthly income from the community. The Jews in the period 1948–1992 still preserved the characteristics of a middleman minority, with its economic and social aspects. The Muslim majority population, as in the previous centuries, still considers the local Jews a foreign minority and not ordinary Turkish citizens. In the riots of 1955 and 1963 against minorities that erupted in Istanbul because of economic conditions, Jews also sustained damage. In the 1960s and 1970s, hundreds of local Jews were caught by the Turkish authorities for smuggling their financial savings to Israel and other countries, and for other crimes: the exchange of money on the black market in Istanbul and Izmir, and the so-called exploitation of the country's resources. However, the reforms of the republican period were adopted voluntarily and readily by the community leadership, and the European day of rest was adopted by the vast majority of community members, to the dismay of their leaders. Adoption of the Swiss civil law permitted marriage between Jews and non-Jews. From the 1960s on, the process of intermarriage increased. In the early 21st century intermarriage was making serious inroads into the community fabric:

in 1990 – 25.8% percent; in 1991 – 39.4%; in 1992 – 42.1%; and in 1993 – 41.9 percent.

In the 1970s and 1980s the Jewish community of Istanbul was involved in certain aspects of Turkish foreign policy, and there were appeals to the community to act in the United States on behalf of its foreign and domestic affairs. The Turkish government also invited community representatives to accompany Turkish personalities on their visits to Israel. In 1992 the community celebration of the Quicentennial of Sephardi Jewry in Turkey was supported by the government. Later the community founded a Jewish school in Ulus, instead of the Jewish school in Galata.

Very few Jews function openly in their political parties in Istanbul, but many more of them provide support and advice behind the scenes.

At the end of the 1980s the secular Council (*Conseil Laïc*, Parliament) ran into problems when the entire work load had to be borne by about six persons. In 1988, a committee was established which proposed a new structure. The membership of the council was expanded from 27 to 41, and that of the Executive Committee to 17. Together they comprised the Senate which also comprised the members of the Vakifs and their leaders, the heads of the communities of Izmir, Ankara, Adana, Bursa, etc. – all in all about 150 members. This body, which is not recognized by the government, meets once every half-year to receive a report. The council elects its president as well as the president of the Executive Committee and the president of the Senate. Since the establishment in 1892 of B'nai B'rith in Turkey, its leaders and their descendants have been active in community life and have been the cultural and intellectual elite of the Istanbul community. In 1994, the organization numbered 335 persons. B'nai B'rith operates a recreational house for poor children in Istanbul and provides scholarships for students each year; other welfare institutions are old people's neighborhood burial societies that were united at the beginning of the 1970s into one *ḥevra kaddisha* serving the entire community; and Barin Yurt, a shelter for the poor, that was opened by the community in 1991.

The weekly *Shalom* is the Istanbul community's only written press. There are 16 synagogues in the city, three of them are open daily; 63% of the Jews attend the synagogue once or twice a year. About 600 students aged 6 to 18 attend Mahazikei Torah, an educational institution that supplements the synagogue. The Istanbul Rabbinate comprises five *dayyanim*, including the president of the Rabbinical Court and the *ḥaham bashi*, who heads this body.

For further information, see *Turkey.

[Hayyim J. Cohen / Leah Bornstein-Makovetsky (2nd ed.)]

Hebrew Printing

From the beginning of the 16th century to the end of the 18th, Istanbul was one of the centers of Hebrew printing. The Ottoman Empire and its capital served as a refuge for Jews fleeing from Spain and Portugal after the expulsions of 1492 and 1497, some of whom brought with them their skill in the new art of printing, as well as manuscripts of great rabbinic writers and Kabbalah writers of the past. Later, Marranos escaping the Inquisition played a similar part. In the Ottoman Empire Hebrew books could be printed and sold freely, without the hindrance of the Christian Church. Books were also printed in Spanish (in Hebrew characters), both original manuscripts and translations from Hebrew and other languages, for which there was a growing demand throughout the Spanish-Portuguese Diaspora.

THE 15TH AND 16TH CENTURIES. The first Hebrew printing press – which was the first printing press in any language in the Ottoman Empire, the first book in Turkish being printed in 1728 – was set up in Istanbul in 1493 by David and Samuel ibn *Naḥmias, exiles from Spain. Their first book was Jacob b. Asher's *Arba'ah Turim*. It was followed a year later by a volume of the Pentateuch with Rashi, *haftarot* with David Kimḥi's commentary, the Five Scrolls with the commentary of Abraham Ibn Ezra, and the Antiochus Scroll. The Naḥmias family were active until 1518. In this early period of Hebrew printing in Istanbul (1504–30) more than 100 books of remarkable range and quality were published, among them Midrashim, the *Aggadot ha-Talmud* (forerunner of Jacob *Ibn Ḥabib's *Ein Ya'akov*), geonic works, Alfasi, *Maimonides' Code – printed for the second time, but on the basis of another manuscript – and his *Sefer ha-Mitzvot* as well as his responsa and letters. Meanwhile, Gershom *Soncino and his son Eliezer had arrived in Istanbul from Italy, and their press published over 40 books between 1530 and 1547, including a Pentateuch with Targum Onkelos, Rashi, and *Saadiah's Arabic and Jacob b. Joseph *Tavus' Persian translations (1545–46), followed by another Pentateuch edition, also with Targum Onkelos and Rashi, and translations into Greek and Spanish, both in Hebrew characters with vowel signs (1547). Eliezer also printed a Hebrew translation, by the physician Jacob Algabe, of the Spanish romance *Amadís de Gaula*, the first secular work in Hebrew to be printed in Istanbul. A former employee of the Soncinos, Moses b. Eliezer Parnas, continued printing on their press after Eliezer's death in 1548, publishing at least five books by 1553. Others active in printing during the period were the *Halicz brothers, printers from Cracow who publicly returned to Judaism in Istanbul after having undergone baptism in Poland in 1537. Between 1551 and 1553 they printed a Hebrew Bible, Isaac of Dueren's halakhic compendium *Sha'arei Dura*, and a Hebrew version of Judith. More important were the activities of Solomon and Joseph, the sons of Isaac *Jabez from Spain, who arrived in Istanbul via Salonika and Adrianople. From 1559 until his death in 1593, Solomon, in partnership with his brother Joseph from 1570, printed such important items as the responsa of R. Elijah Mizraḥi (1559) and R. Joseph ibn Lev (1561) and, in particular, the larger part of the Talmud (1583–93). Eliezer b. Isaac (Ashkenazi) of Prague, a Hebrew printer from Lublin, went to Istanbul in 1575 with his equipment and printed geonic responsa and part of the *Maḥzor Romania*. After a dispute with his partner in this enterprise,

David b. Elijah Kashti, the rest of the *Maḥzor* was printed by Kashti at the press of Joseph Jabez (1575–78). Under the patronage of Reyna, daughter of Doña Gracia and the widow of Joseph Nasi, Joseph b. Isaac of Ashkelon printed some 15 books, one of them in Ladino, of no great distinction, first at the palace of Belvedere at Ortaköy, 1592–94, and later at Kuru Çeşme, 1597–99. Manuscripts from Joseph Nasi's library were published by his interpreter, R. Isaac b. Samuel Onkeneira.

THE 17TH CENTURY. A Marrano, Solomon b. David, revived the trade by printing Rashi's Pentateuch commentary in 1639. He was followed by his son Abraham and son-in-law Jacob b. Solomon Gabbai. They published mainly Sephardi authors, such as the responsa of Joseph b. Moses *Trani (1641). They also published a *Midrash Rabbah* in the same year, a vowelled Mishnah text with the commentary *Kav Naḥat* by Isaac Gabbai (1644–45), and other halakhic, homiletic, and kabbalistic literature.

THE 18TH CENTURY. Hebrew printing during the 18th century in Istanbul was dominated by Jonah b. Jacob Ashkenazi, his sons, and his grandsons, who between 1710 and 1778 issued 188 works, employing at one time as many as 50 workers. Jonah designed and improved his type, and was among those who cast the first Turkish type in 1728. He traveled widely in search of worthwhile manuscripts. He printed such important works as the Zohar (Istanbul 1736–37); the first edition of the famous and influential book *Ḥemdat Yamim* (Smyrna, 1731–32; Istanbul, 1735–72); and a Bible with Ladino translation (in partnership with the Venetian Benjamin b. Moses Rushi). Altogether, his Ladino productions, originals or translations from the Hebrew, brought about a revival of Ladino literature and language.

THE 19TH AND 20TH CENTURIES. Using the remnants of the Ashkenazi press, Elijah Pardo produced six books between 1799 and 1808, among them Rashi's *Pardes* (1802) and the Zohar on Genesis (in installments, 1807–08). Isaac b. Abraham Castro, his sons and his grandsons printed with interruptions from 1808 to 1848, beginning with *Tikkunei Zohar*, rabbinical works, Ladino translations, and polemics against the Christian missions. The Castro press remained active until 1925. The Christian printer Arap Oglu Bogos, commissioned by Jews, printed at least 18 books in Hebrew and Ladino from 1822 to 1827. In the 20th century, with the gradual decline of the Hebrew presses, Ladino literature was eventually published by Christian missionaries; French and English literature in Ladino was published by Greek and Armenian printers. From 1860 to 1940 the Ladino newspaper press, as well as some Jewish printers and publishers, printed mainly Ladino literature.

[Abraham Haim / Yaacov Geller]

BIBLIOGRAPHY: M. Franco, *Essai sur l'Histoire des Israélites de l'Empire Ottoman* (1897), passim; Rosanes, Togarmah; A. Galanté, *Histoire des Juifs d'Istanbul*, 2 vols. (1941–42); Yaari, Sheluḥei, index; U. Heyd, in: *Oriens*, 6 (1953), 299–314; Scholem, Shabbetai Ẓevi, index; Y. Rofeh, in: *Sefunot*, 10 (1966), 621–32; H.Z. Hirschberg, in: *Religion in the Middle East*, 1 (1969), 119–225; D. Jacoby, in: *Byzantion*, 37 (1967), 167–227. HEBREW PRINTING: A. Yaari, *Ha-Defus ha-Ivri be-Kushta* (1967); A. Freimann, in: ZHB, 11 (1907), 30 ff., 49 ff; C. Roth, *House of Nasi, Duke of Naxos* (1948), 173–82, 216–9; S. Assaf, *Mekorot u-Meḥkarim* (1946), 255–6; A.M. Habermann, in: KS, 43 (1968), 163–6; I. Mehlmann, *ibid.*, 577–81; A.K. Offenberg, in: *Studia Rosenthaliana*, 3 (1969), 96–112. **ADD. BIBLIOGRAPHY:** R. Mantran, *Istanbul dans la seconde moitié du XVIIe siècle* (1962); *Areshet*, 5 (1972), 457–93; A. Cohen, *Palestine in the 18th Century* (1973), 249–56; S.J. Shaw, *History of the Ottoman Empire and Modern Turkey* (1977); M. Benayahu, in: *Sefunot*, 11 (1967–1968), 187–230; idem, *ibid.*, 14 (1971–1972), 125–43; A. Schochet, in: *Cathedra*, 13 (1979), 6–9, 15, 30–37; M. Glazer, in: IJMES, 10 (1979), 375–80; S.J. Shaw, in: IJMES, 10 (1979), 266–77; E. Bashan, *Sheviya u-Pedut* (1980), index; M.A. Epstein, *The Ottoman Jewish Communities…* (1980); Y. Barnai, in: *Mikedem u-mi-Yam* (1981), 53–66; C. Issawi, *The Economic History of Turkey*, 1800–1914 (1980); Y. Barnai, in: S. Ettinger (ed.), *Toledot ha-Yehudim be-Arẓot ha-Islam*, 1 (1981); 2 (1986); J. Hacker, in: *A Tale of Two Cities, Jewish Life in Frankfurt and Istanbul*, 1750–1870 (1982), 38–49; idem, in: *Christians and Jews in the Ottoman Empire*, 1 (1982), 117–25; R. Mantran, *ibid.*, 1 (1982), 127–40; P. Dumont, *ibid.*, 1 (1982), 209–42; C.V. Findley, *ibid.*, 1 (1982), 344–65; M. Rozen, in: *Michael*, 7 (1982), 293–430; Y. Barnai & H. Gerber, in: *Michael*, 7 (1982), 206–26; H. Gerber, in: *Pe'amim*, 12 (1982), 27–46; M. Benayahu, in: M. Stern (ed.), *Umma ve-Toldoteha* (1983), 281–87; H. Gerber, *Yehudei ha-Imperiya ha-Otmanit ba-Me'ot ha-Shesh-Esre ve-ha-Sheva-Esre, Ḥevrah ve-Kalkalah* (1983); A. Cohen, *Jewish Life Under Islam* (1984), index; A. Shmuelevitz, *The Jews of the Ottoman Empire in the Late Fifteenth and Sixteenth Centuries…* (1984); Y.R. Hacker, in: *Zion*, 49 (1984), 225–63; J.M. Landau, *Tekinalp, Turkish Patriot* (1984); R. Cohen, *Kushta-Saloniki-Patras* (1984); B. Lewis, *The Jews of Islam* (1984), H. Inalcik, *Studies in Ottoman Social and Economic History* (1985); L. Bornstein-Makovetsky, in: *Shevet ve-Am*, 10 (1985), 101–9; idem, in: *Michael*, 9(1985), 27–54; Z. Çelik, *The Remaking of Istanbul: Portrait of an Ottoman City in the 19th Century* (1986), 9, 21, 26, 38, 40–1; H. Gerber, in: JSS, 10 (1986), 143–54; Y. R, Hacker, in: *Zion*, 52 (1987), 25–44; L. Bornstein-Makovetsky, in: Z. Ankori (ed.), *Mi-Lisbon le-Saloniki ve-Kushta* (1988), 69–95; Y.R. Hacker, in: *Galut Achar Gola, Sefer Yovel Le-Chaim Beinart* (1988), 497–516; S. Sadak, in: *Vidas Largas*, 7 (1987), 33–7; Barnai, in: S. Almog (ed.), *Antisemitism Through the Ages* (1988), 189–94; M.C. Varol, *Balat-Faubourg juif d'Istabul* (1989); L. Bornstein-Makovetsky, in: *The Mediterranean and the Jews: Banking, Finance and International Trade (XVIth–XVIIIth Centuries)* (1989), 75–104; idem, in: *Sefunot*, 19 (1989), 53–122; A. Rodrigue, *French Jews, Turkish Jews, The Alliance Israélite Universelle and the Politics of Jewish Schooling in Turkey, 1860–1927* (1990); Y.R. Hacker, in: *Zion*, 55 (1990), 27–82; E. Bashan, in: *Pe'amim*, 48 (1991), 54–65; Y. Okon, in: *Kiryat Sefer*, 63 (1990–1991), 1341–42; L. Bornstein-Makovetsky, in: A. Haim (ed.), *Ḥevrah u-Kehillah* (1991), 3–24; idem, in: A. Rodrigue (ed.), *Ottoman and Turkish Jewry: Community and Leadership* (1992), 87–122; A. Levi, *Toledot ha-Yehudim ba-Republikah ha-Turkit, Ma'amadam ha-Politi ve-ha-Mishpati* (1992); idem, *The Jews in Palestine in the Eighteenth Century under the Patronage of the Istanbul Committee* (1992); J. Barnai, in: *Ottoman and Turkish Jewry: Community and Leadership* (1992), 174–5; W.F. Weiker, *Ottomans, Turks and the Jewish Polity, A History of Jews in Turkey* (1992); A. Levy, *The Sephardim in the Ottoman Empire* (1992); R. Kastoryano, in: *Ottoman and Turkish Jews, Community and Leadership* (1992), 253–77; I. Karmi, *Jewish Sites of Istanbul* (1992); A. Cohen & E. Simon-Pikali, *Yehudim be-Veit ha-Mishpat ha-Muslemi* (1993), 37–52; A. Levy, in: *Pe'amim*, 55 (1993), 38–56; M. Rozen, *Hasköy Cemetery*

Typology of Stones (1994); E. Benbassa, *Une diaspora sépharade en transition: Istanbul XIX–XXe siècles* (1993); A. Levy, *The Jews of the Ottoman Empire* (1994), 1–150, 425–38; S. Spitzer, in: *Asufot*, 8 (1994), 369–86; J. McCarthy, in: A. Levy (ed.), *The Jews of the Ottoman Empire* (1994), 380, 387; T. Be'eri, in: *Pe'amim*, 59 (1994), 65–76; S. Yerasimos, in: *Turcica*, 27 (1995), 101–30; F. Müge Göçek, in: A. Levy (ed.), *The Jews of the Ottoman Empire* (1994), 705–11; B. Arbel, *Trading Nations, Jews and Venetians in the Early Modern Period* (1995), 13–28; L. Bornstein-Makovetsky, in: M. Rozen (ed.), *Yemei ha-Sahar* (1996), 273–311; M.Z. Benaya, *Moshe Almosnino Ish Saloniki* (1996); A. Levy, in: *Yemei ha-Sahar* (1996); I. Karmi, *The Jewish Community of Istanbul in the 19th Century* (1996); Y.R. Hacker, in: *Zion*, 62 (1997); L. Bornstein-Makovetsky, in: *Michael*, 14 (1997), 139–70; L. Bornstein-Makovetsky, in: *Jewish Law Association Studies*, 9 (1997), 9–18; idem, in: A. Demsky, Y. Reif & J. Tabory (eds.), *These Are the Names, Studies in Jewish Onomastics* (1997), 7–13; idem, in: Y. Bartal & Y. Gafni (eds.) *Eros, Erusin ve-Issurin* (1998), 305–34; M. Rozen, in: *Turcica*, 30 (1998), 331–46; M.M. Weinstein, in: *Studies in Bibliography and Booklore*, 20 (1998), 145–76; Y. Ben-Naeh, in: *Cathedra*, 92 (1999), 65–106; E. Eldem, *The Ottoman City between East and West* (1999), 148, 152, 155–60, 182, 186, 189, 204; L. Bornstein-Makovetsky, *Pinkas Beit ha-Din be-Kushta Pinkas Beit Din Issur ve-Heter, 1710–1903* (1999); C.B. Stuczyncki, in: *Pe'amim*, 84 (2000), 104–24; M. Rozen, in: *Mediterranean Historical Review*, 15:1 (June 2000), 72–93; M. Saul, in: *Turkish-Jewish Encounter* (2001), 129–67; G. Nassi (ed.), *Jewish Journalism and Printing Houses in the Ottoman Empire and Modern Turkey* (2001); M. Rozen, *A History of the Jewish Community in Istanbul, The Formative Years, 1453–1566* (2002); L. Bornstein-Makovetsky, in: M. Rozen (ed.), *The Last Ottoman Century and Beyond* (2002), 83–128; idem, in: *Jewish Law Association Studies* (*The Jerusalem 1998 Conference Volume* (2002), 117–40; S. Tuval, *Ha-Kehillah ha-Yehudit be-Istanbul, 1948–1992* (2004); M. Baer, in: IJMES, 36:2 (2004), 159–81; Y.R. Hacker, in: *Kehal Israel*, 2 (2004), 287–309; Y. Ben-Na'eh, *ibid.*, 341–68; M. Rozen, *The Last Ottoman Century and Beyond, The Jews in Turkey and the Balkans 1808–1945* (2005).

°**ISTÓCZY, GYÖZÖ** (1842–1915), Hungarian lawyer and antisemitic politician. Forced to resign his position as judge because of an irregularity he had committed, he began to develop a persecution mania, claiming that "the Jews" had "framed" him; this seems to have been the origin of his pathological hatred of Jews. In 1872 he was elected to parliament, where, in 1875, he attacked Jewish emancipation on the grounds that it would encourage further Jewish immigration. In 1878 he suggested that the Jews should be transported to Palestine, where their statehood should be reestablished, declaring that "among their [Arab] fellow-Semites the Jews could beneficially employ their manifold talents, and at the same time assist the financial regeneration of the ramshackle Ottoman Empire." In 1880 Istóczy tried to found a German-type antisemitic union and incited college students to anti-Jewish demonstrations. In the same year he founded a monthly paper, *Tizenkét Röpirat* ("Twelve Pamphlets"), which contained the most primitive and virulent anti-Jewish propaganda. He modeled himself on the most notorious German Jew-haters, such as A. *Stoecker and A. *Rohling. He accused the Jews of enslaving the Christian Magyars through usury and the press, calling upon the Hungarians to defend themselves against these dangers. Istóczy and his friends were largely responsible for creating the atmosphere in which the ritual murder charge was brought against the Jews of *Tiszaeszlar in 1882. In 1883 Istóczy founded the Anti-Semite Party, which obtained 17 seats in parliament in 1884. *Tizenkét Röpirat* became the party's official mouthpiece and continued to appear until 1892, but the party itself existed until 1895. After its demise Istóczy retired from active political life and published Hungarian versions of several works of classical literature, such as Josephus' *Jewish War* (1900), *Contra Apionem* (1903), and, in the same year, *Tacitus' "Observations on the Characteristics of the Jews" (from his *Historiae*). Istóczy's translations are, on the whole, unscholarly and clearly show his political bias.

BIBLIOGRAPHY: *Istóczy Gyözö országgyulesi beszédei, inditványai és törvényjavaslata 1872–1896* (1904); L. Venetianer, *A magyar zsidóság története* (1922), 314–7, 324–5; S. Hegedüs, *A tiszaeszlári vérvád* (1966), 20, 31–33; Z. Bosnyák, *A magyar fajvédelem úttöröi* (1942), 29–62 (incl. bibl.); N. Katzburg, *Antishemiyyut be-Hungaryah 1867–1914* (1969).

[Jeno Zsoldos]

ISTOMIN, EUGENE (**George**; 1925–2003), U.S. pianist. Born in New York to parents of Russian-Jewish ancestry who were both professional singers, Istomin first studied with Kiriena Siloti and then at the Mannes College. At 12 he entered the Curtis Institute, where he studied with Rudolf *Serkin and Horszowski. At the age of 17, Istomin won the Leventritt and Philadelphia Orchestra Youth Awards, making sensational debuts with both the Philadelphia and New York Philharmonic Orchestras.

His first recording, which brought him considerable acclaim, was of Bach's D minor Concerto with the Busch Chamber Players.

Starting in 1950, Istomin became a regular participant at the Prades Festival organized by the famous cellist Pablo Casals. His rare combination of virtuosity, poetic insight, and aristocratic style won him international acclaim as a recitalist, orchestral soloist, and chamber musician. Embarking on major tours abroad from 1956, he performed with the world's leading orchestras and conductors. In 1961 he formed a trio with Isaac *Stern and Leonard *Rose with which he made dozens of recordings, including concertos, solo works, and the famous trio's extensive survey of the chamber music literature. Istomin was associated primarily with 19th-century and early-20th-century works. Eminent composers such as Henri Dutilleux and Ned Rorem wrote and dedicated works to him. He was a cultural ambassador under every president from Eisenhower to Reagan. In 1975 he married Marta Casals, the widow of Pablo Casals, and went on to settle in Washington. Later he served on the faculty of the Manhattan School of Music. In 2001, he was inducted into the French Legion of Honor.

BIBLIOGRAPHY: Grove online; MGG²; Baker's Biographical Dictionary (1997); S. Rodd, "Eugene Istomin: Keeper of the Flame," in: *Keyboard Classics & Piano Stylist* 13, 4 (1993) 6–8.

[Naama Ramot (2nd ed.)]

ISTRIA, peninsula in the N. Adriatic. The first Jewish settlement dates to the Middle Ages. In 1380 Jews opened a bank at Capodistria. Later Jews settled at Isola, Pirano, Rovigno, Pola, and Veglia. A number of Jews from Germany settled in Istria in the 1480s, mainly in the cities of Muggia, Pirano, and Parenzo. Under the protection of the republic of Venice, they were permitted to engage in trade and moneylending. The most important bank was probably established in Pirano in 1484. In 1502 the pseudo-messiah Asher *Lemlin appeared in Istria. Jews were expelled from Muggia in 1532. Jewish banks in Istria continued to function with interruptions until the middle of the 17th century, when they were replaced by the **monti di pietà* (church loan banks). By then most of the Jews had left the area, mainly for Trieste and other neighboring communities in Italy.

BIBLIOGRAPHY: Milano, Italia, index; Milano, Bibliotheca, index; Roth, Italy, index; Ive, in: REJ, 2 (1881), 175–98; I. Zoller, *Ricordi di vita ebraica nell'Istria* (1913); idem, in: *Corriere Israelitico*, 51 (1912), 197–9. A. Ive, *Dei Banchi Feneratizi degli Ebrei di Pirano* (1881).

[Daniel Carpi / Samuele Rocca (2nd ed.)]

ISTRUMSA, ḤAYYIM ABRAHAM (18th–19th century), rabbi in Greece, born in *Salonika. He served as rabbi and preacher in Komotini from 1793 to 1801, after which he went to Salonika, preaching mainly in the "Old Castile" and "Old Catalonia" synagogues. Afterward he served as rabbi in the Greek towns of Serres, Larissa, and Kastoria. In 1804 he officiated at the reconsecration of the newly renovated "Old Italian" synagogue in Salonika. Istrumsa was the author of *Yerekh Avraham* (Salonika, 1815), halakhic rulings and a dissertation on the writing of names in bills of divorce, including the halakhic rulings of his grandfather, Daniel; and *Ben Avraham* (*ibid.*, 1826), homilies, responsa, and novellae on the Torah and *Arba'ah Turim*.

BIBLIOGRAPHY: M.D. Gaon, *Yehudei ha-Mizraḥ be-Ereẓ Yisrael*, 2 (1937), 37; Rosanes, Togarmah, 5 (1938), 146.

[Simon Marcus]

ITALIA, SHALOM (c. 1619–c. 1655), engraver, etcher, and draftsman. Probably born in Mantua, Shalom Italia lived in Amsterdam from at least 1641, and was active there for eight and possibly 15 years. Of the ten signed works by him, only two are dated – 1642 and 1649; five other works are ascribed to him. In his early works he signed in Hebrew: "by Shalom Italia" (איטאליאה) but later in Latin: "Salom Italia sculpsit." Most of his copper engravings and etchings were done for scrolls (*megillot*) of Esther, but he also engraved portraits, book illustrations, and a **ketubbah*. The decorations in his *megillot* are in the form of arcades framing the text, with Purim characters between the columns, and scenes from the *megillah* in cartouches at the bottom of the text columns. One of the first *megillot*, formerly in the Rothschild Collection in Frankfurt, was hand drawn, signed, and dated 1649. C. Roth has attributed another fine example, the etched *Howitt Megillah* of about 1647, to Shalom Italia (London Jewish Museum, 35). His best-known portrait, of Jacob Judah Leon *Templo, was not signed by him when it first appeared in 1641, but only in its later version, when it was attached in 1654 to his book on the cherubim. Another portrait, of *Manasseh Ben Israel, was signed and dated 1642.

Also attributed to him are the four crude illustrations to Manasseh Ben Israel's *Piedra Gloriosa* (1655). These unsigned engravings are based on works by *Rembrandt, and if they are by Shalom Italia then it must be assumed that he was still active in 1655. A single engraved *ketubbah* (Israel Museum) signed by him was used in Rotterdam in 1648, but was probably executed before 1641. In tracing the stylistic and technical development of Shalom Italia, M. Narkiss drew attention to the influence of the French artist Daniel Rabel (1578–1637) and the Dutch artist Hans Janssen (active in Amsterdam 1631–33).

BIBLIOGRAPHY: A.D. de Vries, in: *Oud Holland*, 13 (1885), 156; J.S. da Silva Rosa, in: *Maandblad voor de Geschiedenis der Joden in Nederland*, 1 (1947/48), 214–22; S. Kirschstein, *Juedische Graphiker aus der Zeit von 1625–1825* (1918), 9–14; E. Hintze, *Katalog der… Ausstellung "Das Judentum in der Geschichte Schlesiens"* (1929), no. 533; Christie, Manson, and Woods, *The Collection of… Arthur Howitt Sale* (1932), no. 213; A. Rubens, *Anglo-Jewish Portraits* (1935), no. 159; M. Narkiss, in: *Tarbiz*, 25 (1956), 441–51; 26 (1957), 87–101.

[Bezalel Narkiss]

ITALIAN LITERATURE

Influence of the Bible

As in other European cultures, the Bible became known to the Italian literary and cultural world through the Latin Vulgate, which was extensively studied in medieval times and, to a lesser extent, in the humanist period of the 15th–16th centuries. Fragmentary translations of the Bible into Italian, based on the Vulgate, were made in the 13th century. Translations in an entirely separate category were those made by Jews from Hebrew into *Judeo-Italian, written in Hebrew characters. These translations lacked literary or aesthetic value, and were used exclusively by Jews, although they may also have been known to gentiles during the 12th and 13th centuries. They are important for the study of the history of Italian dialects and the phonetics of the Italian language: among them are the translations of the Psalms, Song of Songs, Amos, Jonah, and Habakkuk. Two examples of translation into Italian from the Vulgate are the *Splanamento de li Proverbi di Salomone*, written by Gherardo Pateg (early 13th century), and the *Cantico delle creature*, a free adaptation of Psalm 148 by St. Francis of Assisi. Written in rhythmic prose, the latter constitutes the earliest document of authentic Italian poetry. The piecemeal translations were collected at the end of the 14th century under the title *Biblia volgare*; but the exact development from anonymous and fragmentary manuscripts to the *Biblia volgare* – containing the entire Old and New Testaments and a portion of the Apocrypha – has yet to be explored.

With the advent of Bible criticism, non-Jews, too, began to translate the Bible into Italian from the original tongues (see *Bible, Translations). The work of A. Brucioli and G. Marmochini is representative of Renaissance Bible translation, but the process was abruptly checked by the Counter-Reformation, which prohibited study of the Bible in the vernacular. A translation which continues to enjoy great popularity is that by the Protestant G. Diodati (1607). In a much delayed reaction, the Catholic Church decided more than 150 years later to distribute Archbishop Martini's version (1776–81), which was popular up to the late 19th century. During the Renaissance, Jews also set themselves to making Bible translations in a good literary style. The best-known Jewish translations were those by David min-ha-Tappuḥim (David de *Pomis; Ecclesiastes, Venice, 1571) and Ezechia da Rieti (Proverbs, Venice, 1617).

BIBLICAL THEMES. Italian literature's unique relationship to the Greco-Roman world long restricted the Bible's role in the experience and expression – aesthetic, philosophical, and moral – of Italian writers. Most authors and men of culture were educated along classical lines, which excluded a study of the Bible as literature. *Dante Alighieri, Italy's greatest poet, was a solitary exception. He had a rich and highly original relationship with the Bible, which was one of the two principal sources of his poetry, the other being Vergil's *Aeneid*. Through the Vulgate, Dante acquired a biblical style and infused his *Divine Comedy* with biblical expressions, images, and linguistic patterns. Dante placed the heroes of Israel – the patriarchs, the Hebrew kings, the prophets, Judith, and the Maccabees – in heaven, and made them symbolize and exemplify faith, valor, and humility. Dante believed that the Hebrew Bible was the primary evidence of Divine revelation, teaching faith in one God, and that the Old Testament's authority had not been diminished by the New Testament. During the 14th century, biblical influence can be detected in biographical works and in tales of a moral and didactic type, as well as in religious and mystical literature. This literature, which was only of marginal importance, was mainly inspired by the Psalms, Proverbs, and Ecclesiastes.

The earliest plays on biblical themes, all anonymous, were written in the 15th century, and are a direct continuation of the *sacra rappresentazione* of medieval religious drama. Works of this kind include *rappresentazioni* such as *Caino e Abele, Abramo e Agar, Abramo e Isaac, La regina Ester*, and *Nabuccodonosor*. The Florentine playwright Feo Belcari derived much of his inspiration from these plays. His drama, *La rappresentazione di Abramo e Isaac* (1449), is an attempt at a realistic recreation of the episode of the **Akedah*. After the era of humanism and the Renaissance, it was not until the beginning of the Baroque period, when the Aristotelian principles of unity of time and place in tragedy had been abandoned, that Italian writers returned to the Bible. Under the impact of the didactic and ethical demands of the Counter-Reformation, the Bible became a rich source of inspiration. Baroque writers tended to express their religious emotions in drama or music. Biblical figures and events provided suitable literary material. From the 17th century onward, this trend was particularly evident in Italian drama, which served as a model for the French dramatist, *Racine. Heroism and tragic faith now replaced the old epic and Greek tragedy. Torquato Tasso was the author of *Gerusalemme liberata* (1581), an epic poem dealing with the Crusaders who sacrificed their lives for a religious ideal. After *La reina Ester* by the Genoese poet Ansaldo Cebà (1615), the foremost Italian tragedian inspired by biblical themes was Frederico della Valle, who dramatized *Judith* (1628) and *Esther* (1628). Della Valle had many imitators and followers who combined in their works Baroque taste and the didactic aims of the Jesuits. The favorite biblical characters dramatized in Italy during the 17th and 18th centuries were Joash, king of Judah, David, Saul, Rachel, "mother of the Maccabees," and Judith. Another favorite character, John, appeared in *Giovanni di Giscala* by A. Varano (1754). Pietro Metastasio also treated biblical subjects in his melodramas *La morte di Abele* (1732) and *Gioas, Re di Giuda* (1735), which combine tender music with the conflict between good and evil, as understood by Baroque and Arcadian writers. A fundamental turning point in the conception of biblical tragedy may be seen in the *Saul* (1782) of Vittorio Alfieri, who also wrote the ponderous *Abele* (1796). With characteristic pre-Romantic taste, Alfieri invests Saul's battles and death with the defiant grandeur of an individual who tries to impose his will on friend and enemy alike, even when his own doom has been sealed by divine decree. In the 19th century, the Bible was a source of inspiration for some of the Italian Romantics. However, these writers sought in the Bible the new ideas of human freedom and the principles of absolute justice rather than epic greatness and heroism. Tragic episodes in the Bible were now associated with the historic tragedy of the Jewish people, sometimes punished and persecuted because of their sins, sometimes redeemed. The fate of biblical Israel was identified with that of the Italian nation, downtrodden and oppressed because of its reluctance to revolt and free itself. This trend is exemplified in *La terra dei morti*, a poem by Giuseppe Giusti, where Ezekiel's vision of the dry bones is satirically applied to the situation of 19th-century Italy. Even more than in tragedy, poetry, and prose, biblical influence was dominant in Italian opera, reaching a peak in Giuseppe Verdi's *Nabucco* (1842). Following the unification of Italy, the Bible – a source of inspiration for 700 years – ceased to influence Italian writers to any significant extent. The legacy of the Bible was at best seen in a biblical style of writing and in a richly evocative lyrical expression – prophetic pathos on the one hand, and an absence of rhetoric on the other. However, two novels, both centered on the biblical character of King David, deserve mention for the stature of their authors: *Il pianto del figlio di Lais* (1945) by Riccardo Bacchelli and *Davide: romanzo* (1976) by Carlo Coccioli (this latter based on a reading of the Bible in Hebrew).

The Image of the Jew

Jews and Judaism play a comparatively minor part in Italian literature. The relatively small number of Italian Jews throughout the ages and the classical ties of Italian literature and culture explain the limited role of Jews in Italian intellectual life, particularly during the golden age of Italian literature.

DANTE AND BOCCACCIO. Dante's only allusion to Jews is in his *Divine Comedy*, where he refers to Christianity's origin in the Jewish people. As for the "historical" Jews living after the triumph of Christianity, Dante praised them as exemplary people who, unlike the Christians of his time, remained loyal to their God. Only occasionally do Jews appear as central figures in the Italian prose and fiction of the later Middle Ages. Giovanni *Boccaccio portrayed them sympathetically in two famous stories, demonstrating his tolerant approach to the controversies between the three great religions and using his Jewish heroes to deride the moral corruption of the Catholic Church. Boccaccio's exotic Jew reveals the greatness of the human mind and plays a positive role in the writer's human comedy. The Jew also appears in the early 15th-century version of the *Wandering Jew tale. Here he is a wholly sympathetic character, contrasting markedly with the tragic, guilt-ridden figure of the later German tradition.

MEDIEVAL AND RENAISSANCE STEREOTYPES. A very different attitude is displayed by the 14th century Florentine Franco Sacchetti in his *Trecento novelle*. In the five stories introducing Jewish characters, all the religious prejudice of the medieval Church is brought into play. The Jew is a moneylender, merchant, or swindler whose sole aim is the corruption of the true Christian. It is therefore legitimate to injure and trick him and to rejoice at his humiliation. A similar approach characterizes Ser Giovanni Fiorentino's late 14th-century story of Giannetto in the collection *Il Pecorone*. The Jewish villain's greed and his hatred of Christians lead him to devise a cruel scheme to tear the flesh from a living body. This story was adapted by the English translator William Painter in his *Palace of Pleasure* (1566), a favorite source for many Elizabethan dramatists. According to some scholars, this was the original source of *Shakespeare's Shylock in *The Merchant of Venice*. There were also popular, stereotyped Jews in many anonymous Italian stories of the 15th century, most of which had a didactic and moralizing aim. However, a few of these stories present the Jew as a figure of integrity and pride, commanding respect rather than scorn. With the advent of humanism and the Renaissance, the standardized description of the Jew as merchant and usurer sank to the level of folk-literature. The Jew now figured only in satire and comedy, which gradually blended with the comic stereotype of Italian Renaissance writers. Such was the case with Pietro Aretino, who introduced Jewish secondhand dealers in his comedies *La cortigiana* (1526) and *Il Marescalco* (1533). A Jewish scoundrel, sorcerer, and fortune-teller appears in the comedy *Il negromante* (1520) by Ludovico Ariosto. The intention, however, is not to mock the Jew as a Jew, but to construct a broad satire on human folly victimized by shrewd impostors. In the development of the *commedia dell' arte*, the Jewish moneylender is one of the many comic characters of the Pulcinella and Harlequin type. The best known of these are the character of Manovello (Immanuel) the Jew, and the comic descriptions of ghetto Jews in *Amfiparnaso* (1597) and *Veglie di Siena* (1604) by the Modena composer Orazio Vecchi.

LATER PORTRAYALS. The last stage in the comic description of the Jew is marked by the many stereotypes of Roman ghetto Jews in the comic folk poems written in the 17th-century Roman dialect. G. Berneri's *Meo Patacca* (1695) is the most famous example of this genre. These poems, partly in the tradition of Italian folk theater and partly in that of refined comedy, contain many words borrowed from the Roman variant of Judeo-Italian. The last appearance of the Jew in Roman dialect poetry is the description of Jews and ghetto life in the 50 or more sonnets by the Roman poet Giuseppe Gioacchino Belli. But here, a worn and stereotyped theme is enlivened by penetrating social and anti-ecclesiastical criticism. In contrast to comedy, satire, and popular literature, the refined poetry and *belles lettres* of the Renaissance and Baroque periods lack Jewish themes. Despite the legendary exchange of sonnets between Petrarch and the Jewish poetess Giustina *Levi-Perotti, the Jew finds no place in the poetry, epic, tragedy, or prose of Ariosto, Matteo Boiardo, and Pulci, nor in Baroque and Arcadian poetry, idylls, and pastoral studies (*Favole pastorali*). The one writer to provide an exception to this rule was P.F. Frugoni, in whose *Il cane di Diogene* (1687) the reader finds a Jew who is a strange combination of ritual slaughterer, physician, and sorcerer. Frugoni was a writer far in advance of his time, and his descriptions of a strange and marvelous, but nevertheless believable, world match anything to be found in modern literature. The beginning of Romanticism and national awakening brought about in Italy by the French Revolution sparked a parallel literary revolution. Once modern Italian literature had liberated itself from the classical tradition, writers also began to show interest in the wretched condition of the Jew – bereft of rights, persecuted, the victim of blind prejudice. Some of the greatest Italian poets and authors of the 19th century, such as Vittorio Alfieri, Ugo Foscolo, Giacomo Leopardi, and A. Manzoni, expressed their sympathy for the Jews, took up their cause, and looked upon them as comrades in the struggle against Church despotism and for national liberation and social and economic improvement. The Jew now became a useful subject for polemics in the struggle for civil rights, individual liberty, and freedom of speech. This sympathetic attitude, however, did not give rise to any notable literary works. The real extent of the Jewish tragedy was beyond the comprehension of these writers, who dealt mainly with biblical episodes in which the leitmotifs were freedom and epic heroism. The Jew was never subjected to a searching and universal analysis. The few attempts by authors such as the 19th-century Ippolito Nievo, who wrote the tedious (and unpublished) historical novel *Emmanuel*, and the playwright Achille Torelli, who wrote the drama *L'Israelita* (1841), were unsuccessful. At the same time, the polemical press and the publications of Italy's national liberation movement – primarily through its chief philosopher, Giuseppe Mazzini – were inspired by such general ideas in Judaism as its concept of Divine Unity, its moral values, and its democratic social outlook.

THE 20TH CENTURY. In the 20th century neither Italian prose writers nor poets showed any particular interest in the Jews and their fate. This may be explained by the exiguity of the Jewish nucleus in Italy, the nonexistence of a "Jewish problem" from the unification of Italy until the Fascist persecution, and the scant knowledge of the Old Testament characteristic of Catholic countries. Works like those of Thomas *Mann, inspired by the story of Joseph, would be inconceivable in Italian literature. Only in recent years, in the wake of the tragedy of European Jewry and the birth of the State of Israel, have a few works on such themes appeared, especially documentaries and histories. Great poets of the early 20th century such as Carducci, Pascoli, and D'Annunzio (the last having a Jewish character in his *Più che l'amore*), and major prose writers like Verga and Fogazzaro, have at best shown only casual and marginal interest in Jewish problems. Nor has it been usual for Jewish writers to face Judaism as a separate issue. In some cases, the Jew was chosen as a subject for literary and poetic discussion. One notable exponent of this trend is Luigi Pirandello, whose story *Il presepe* depicts a Jew who marries a non-Jewish girl. *Un goj*, one of Pirandello's short stories, also concerns a Jew. On a lesser plane, Giovanni Papini often presents a biased or distorted picture of Jews and Judaism, as in *Storia di Cristo* (1921), *Gog* (1931), and *Lettere... del papa Celestino VI* (1947). For his part, Alfredo Panzini in his novel *Viaggio con la giovane ebrea* (1935) dwells on the issue of the patriotism of the Jews in their countries of birth in lengthy and somewhat ambiguous dissertations. In the interwar period two novels appeared which dealt with a specific Jewish theme: *Schemagn Israel* (1924), by Luigi di San Giusto, the tragic story of a Jewish family of Trieste during World War I; and *Ebrei* (1930), by Mario Puccini, the tale of a Jewish family in Ancona during the same period. Jewish themes are also used more or less directly in novels such as *La nave degli eroi* (1927) by Clarice Tartufari, *Kaddish* (1930) by Guido Milanesi, *Lilith* (1934) and *Il paradiso perduto* (1935) by Salvatore Gotta, as well as *Mamma* (1959; reprinted in 1961) by Virgilio Brocchi. The end of World War II saw the publication of R.M. Angelis' novel, *Panche gialle* (1945), which tells of the plight of German Jews in 1933. Among works which have drawn inspiration from the Bible are *Giuda* (1922) by F.V. Ratti; *Giobbe, uomo solo* (1955) by G.B. Angioletti; *Giuda* (1917) and *Rosa di Sion* (1918), by Enrico Pea, whose story *Lisetta* (1946) also contains Jewish characters; and two plays by Diego Fabbri, *Processo a Gesù* (1953), and *Inquisizione* (1950). Jews and episodes from Jewish life also appear in and *Il mulino del Po* (1938–40) by Riccardo Bacchelli. Among the works of Marino Moretti is the novella *Tre sorelle* (in the collection *Cinquanta Novelle*, 1962), a revision of *Le sorelle Nunes* (1948). Jewish characters and events connected with Jews are referred to, not always with sympathy or understanding, in various works by Curzio Malaparte (Kurt Erich Suckert) like the quasi-documentary novels *Kaputt* (1944) and *La pelle* (1949). Many works of a documentary character were published in the immediate postwar period. Jewish episodes and characters are also found in *Cortile a Cleopatra* (1931) and *Ballata Levantina* (1961) by Fausta Cialente, as well as in Giuseppe Borgese's novels *Rubé* (1921), *I vivi e i morti* (1923, 1951) and his drama *Lazzaro* (1925), and in A. Gatti's *Ilia ed Alberto* (1931).

The tragedy of the Holocaust again placed the Jews in the center of literary interest. One of the most important novels of postwar Italy is *La Storia* (1974; *History: a Novel*, 1977) by Elsa Morante (whose mother was Jewish, but who did not show any signs of Jewish identity). In this ambitious novel, which explicitly attempted to renew the epic-popular tradition, some of the heroes and minor characters are Jews, or half-Jews, of Rome in the years of World War II and the postwar period. Roman Jews are also present in *La parola ebreo* (1997) by Rosetta Loy, an anamnesis of the antisemitic period in Italy, centered on the indifference of so many Christians. The sociologist Sabino Acquaviva himself tried his hand at the historical novel, with *La ragazza del ghetto* (1996), on a difficult love relation between a Jewess and a Catholic nobleman in the Venice of the 16th century.

Jews and Judaism are equally inconspicuous in Italian poetry, where they obtain no more than a passing reference. In one of her poems, "L'Apparizione" (1918), Ada Negri commemorated the war hero Roberto Sarfatti, son of Mussolini's biographer Margherita Sarfatti, who fell in World War I; but the choice of the theme was anything but deliberate. In contrast, "Dora Markus," a long poem by Eugenio Montale presents a specific Jewish motif. Similarly, the Nobel Prize winner Salvatore Quasimodo touches on Jewish subjects in the poems: "Il mio paese è l'Italia," "Auschwitz," "Alle fronde dei salici," and "Alla nuova luna." Others of his poems are inspired by the Book of Psalms. In Rossana Ombres' verse collection *Le ciminiere di Casale* (1962), the last group titled "Per una nuova sinagoga" is of Jewish interest. A few poems about Jews and the State of Israel were written by Diego Valeri (1887–1975) in 1967 and reprinted in his book *Verità di uno* (1970). In *Poesie e prose* (n.d.) by Egidio Meneghetti various poems in the Venetian dialect, especially "Lager," and "Bortolo e l'ebreeta," are concerned with Jewish motifs. So are "Isacco & Co.," "Ci avevo un gatto e se' chiamava Ajò," and other farcical sonnets in the Roman dialect by Trilussa (Carlo Alberto Salustri) and before him, by the poets G. Belli, whose sonnets contain many Jewish references; and Gigi Zanazzo.

The Jewish Contribution

Jews have spoken and written in Italian since the language began to evolve, yet the Jewish contribution to Italian literature has been limited. In medieval and even in modern times, Jews wrote in their own Judeo-Italian dialect and produced a literature, occasionally of poetic and aesthetic value, unknown to Italian authors and poets. Only recently have scholars begun to study this body of writing. The first text to be recorded in Judeo-Italian, which belongs to the Roman-Jewish-Italian *koiné*, is an elegy, probably written at the end of 12th century or beginning of 13th. The first Jew who made a significant contribution to Italian poetry was *Immanuel b. Solomon of Rome (14th century) who, apart from his substantial writing in Hebrew, produced poetry in Italian according to aesthetic principles of the *dolce stil novo* school. He was a friend of two famous poets, Cino da Pistoia and Bosone da Gubbio, with whom he exchanged sonnets. "Bisbidis" and "Sirventese del maestro di tutte le arti," two humorous poems in which he boasts of his aptitude for all crafts, are well known. In the 15th century, the Hebrew poet and philosopher Moses of Rieti wrote a treatise on science and metaphysics in central Italian and Hebrew letters, *Filosofia naturale e fatti de Dio*, which contains visions and allegories of great literary value.

RENAISSANCE AND BAROQUE WRITERS. Judah *Abrabanel's *Dialoghi d'amore* (1535) was an important contribution to scholarly philosophic prose. Although its unpolished style led some writers to suppose that the original was not written in Italian, the *Dialoghi* is a classic of Italian philosophic literature and greatly influenced 16th-century writing on Platonic love. The work was early translated into Spanish and French and widely emulated. The writer Bembo and the great philosophers Giordano Bruno and Baruch *Spinoza used the *Dialoghi* as a source from which they developed their own theories and systems. Leone da Sommi *Portaleone, who wrote the first treatise on stage production, enjoyed an important role in the history of Renaissance theater. His principal work on the subject is the *Quattro dialoghi in materia di rappresentazione* ("Four Dialogues on the Art of Staging"). Sommi also wrote plays (*Le tre sorelle*, "The Three Sisters," 1993) and epics which were often staged at the court of the dukes of Mantua. Another important work testifying to the activity of Italian Jews in the Renaissance is the *Trattato dell'arte del ballo* (1463; *On the Practice of Art of Dancing*, 1995) by *Guglielmo da Pesaro. Jewish poets, however, devoted most of their work to expounding their Jewish faith in classical Italian in order to widen an understanding of Judaism among the gentiles. These poets even attained some popularity in the gentile world at the time. Johanan (Elhanan) Mordecai Judah Alatrini, perhaps the same as Angelo Alatini (d. before 1611), wrote original poems and sonnets of religious inspiration, collected under the title *L'Angelica Tromba* (1628), and also translated into Italian the *piyyut Barekhi Nafshi* by R. Baḥya b. Joseph. As Angelo Alatini, he wrote *I Trionfi* (1611), a pastoral fable in Arcadian style, with characters drawn from Latin mythology. Earlier, in the 16th century, Eliezer Mazliaḥ b. Avraham Cohen (Lazzaro da Viterbo, c. 1585) and Simone Massarani wrote devotional poetry, the latter publishing a rhymed translation of Judah Al-Ḥarizi's *Mishlei Ḥakhamim (Motti di diversi saggi tradotti da lingua hebraea in volgare*, Mantua 1592). The same Lazzaro da Viterbo (1585), Deborah Ascarelli (1601), Samuel b. Moses Castelnuovo (1609) translated poems and *piyyutim* from Hebrew, including a section of the poem *Mikdash Me'at* by *Moses of Rieti. Intended primarily for the Jewish public, the translations were sometimes written in Hebrew letters and in this case belong to Judeo-Italian rather than to Italian literature. At the end of the 16th century, but mainly in the 17th, scholarly works by Jewish authors were published in Venice. These treatises adhered to the style and conception of the Renaissance, as evidenced in *Discorso intorno all'umana miseria e sopra il modo di fuggirla* (Venice, 1572) by David (b. Isaac) de Pomis, and to early modern European thought, as the two treatises *Socrate, ovvero dell'umano sapere* (Venice, 1651) and *Discorso circa il stato degli hebrei* (Venice, 1638) by Simone (Simḥah) b. Isaac Luzzatto. The treatise by Leone Modena, *Historia de' riti hebraici* (Paris, 1637), a good example of the erudite literary style of the Italian Baroque, was widely published in Italy and abroad (in French, Dutch, Hebrew, and English translation). David de Pomis' Hebrew-Aramaic dictionary, *Ẓemaḥ David* (Venice, 1587), which contains Italian definitions, and Leone Modena's Hebrew-Italian dictionary, *Galut Yehudah* (Venice, 1612), constitute the first Italian works in Oriental studies. In the late Renaissance and during the 17th and 18th centuries, it became customary for Italian Jewish poets to share the style and the subjects of Baroque and Arcadian Italian poetry. Well versed in Italian culture, the principles of rhetoric, and the technique of verse composition, these Jewish writers were fluent in both Italian and Hebrew. Although they did not differ in style from their Italian contemporaries, the Jewish poets lacked their energy and talent but sometimes achieved excellent results. A long line of Jewish poets wrote sonnets, pastorals, occasional poems, canzonets, and madrigals. Poets were common among rabbis, intellectuals, and women, especially in the communities of northern Italy. In Rome, however, there were "poetic academies" and literary circles deeply influenced by Baroque and Arcadian Italian poetry. Judah b. Joseph *Moscato and Azariah De' *Rossi wrote elegies on the death of Princess Margaret of Savoy, and the Venetian poetess Sara Copia *Sullam composed original sonnets, her home becoming a center of cultural and poetic life in Venice. Leone Modena, the brothers Jacob and Emmanuel *Frances, and later Ephraim and Isaac *Luzzatto wrote many occasional poems in Italian. As the Baroque challenged poets to experiment in criticism and cunning poetic invention, it became a literary convention in the 17th century to write poems with double meanings, a technique in which Leone Modena excelled. He and his contemporary Baruch Luzzatto wrote plays; the former re-writing Solomon *Usque's drama *Esther*, (thus continuing a tradition of plays written for the occasion of Purim by Jewish Italian authors (for instance Mordehai Dato, mid-16th century, *La storia di Purim io ve racconto*, written in "ottava rima," i.e., in the poetic form made popular by Ariosto), and writing the pastoral epic *Rachele e Giacobbe*, which has been lost, Luzzatto composing the pastoral epic *L'amor possente* (1631). In honor of the rulers of their time, Deodato (Nethaneel) Segre (17th century) and Israel Benjamin Bassan (1701–1790) composed poems of praise. Segre wrote poems and a book praising the dukes of Savoy (1621), while Bassan composed a series of octaves in Italian and Hebrew in honor of Francis III, duke of Modena (1750), and a series of sonnets, *La Corona estense*, eulogizing the house of Este. Hezekiah Manoah Ḥayyim *Corcos (Tranquillo Vita Corcos) established an academy which taught the Arcadian poetic style. He trained his pupils to recite compositions in Italian on festive occasions, e.g., his *Discorso* (1710), in which he developed the story of Esther and Mordecai. Jacob Josef Saraval, Eliah Ḥayyim Morpurgo, and Benedetto Frizzi were among the outstanding figures of Italian Judaism who wrote Italian works of different kinds in a period when Hebrew was slowly replaced by Italian as the language of scholars. Actually, the European Enlightenment partially broke down the cultural synthesis characterizing the literary style and outlook of Italian Jews. By the end of the 18th century some Jewish poets and writers demonstrated their desire to take part in gentile culture and to be read by a larger public. This process reached its height in the 19th century, when specifically Jewish issues were absorbed in general human problems – the equality of peoples, freedom, and the process of national liberation. Italian Jews saw in this development an opportunity to improve their own inferior condition. It is noteworthy that important teachers of the Italian language and literature at the end of the century were Jewish: Isaac Azulai (alias Joseph Leontini, the son of the well-known H.J.D. *Azulai) was the private teacher of the princess of Prussia and wrote some Italian grammars in German; Filippo Sarchi, the son of Elia Morpurgo, had the chair of Italian in Vienna; the son of a convert to Protestantism, Giovanni (John) Florio (1553–1625) popularized Italian literature in England. But the apostate Lorenzo da Ponte (previously Emanuele *Conegliano), author of the three famous libretti for the Mozart operas *Le nozze di Figaro, Don Giovanni*, and *Cosi fan tutte*, is signally typical of the modern period. A brilliant adventurer who, like Casanova, exemplified the libertine, Da Ponte immigrated to the United States where he made the Italian language and literature popular.

Unlike these two figures, Salomone *Fiorentino and Samuel *Romanelli reveal in their poems and other writings a balance between loyalty to Judaism and active participation in Italian cultural life. Fiorentino wrote sonnets, elegies, and many epic poems (part of his collected poems first appeared in 1801) and won recognition for his style and adherence to the classical tradition, which he infused with new meaning. In many of his poems, Fiorentino was inspired by the Bible and displayed a profound religious feeling. He was the first to translate the Sephardi liturgy into literary Italian (Basle, 1802). Like Fiorentino, Romanelli wrote hymns and songs of praise (*Raccolta di inni e di lodi*, Mantua, 1807) and translated his own plays into Italian from the Hebrew original (*Maḥazeh Shadai* or *Illusione felice, ossia visione sentimentale*, and *Alot ha-Minḥah*, translation appeared with Hebrew original, Vienna, 1793). Romanelli translated Solomon ibn *Gabirol's *Keter Malkhut* into Italian, as well as prayers and *piyyutim*. Many of Romanelli's poems were lost or have remained in manuscript.

THE 19TH AND 20TH CENTURIES. During the 19th century Jewish writers and scholars increasingly participated in the struggle of the Italian Risorgimento. This participation necessarily brought about a dichotomy between the author's Jewish identity and the new ideals of the Risorgimento that laid claim to their entire personality. Graziadio Isaia *Ascoli, the greatest 19th-century Italian philologist and pupil of Isaac *Reggio and Samuel David *Luzzatto, was one of the prominent Jewish scholars of traditional Jewish background who were firmly established in Italian culture, but did not become alienated from Judaism. Others who also straddled two cultures, but who gradually lost their Jewish identity, were the Italian literary scholar, Alessandro (d') *Ancona, the philologists Salomone *Morpurgo and Adolfo *Mussafia, the critics Eugenio *Camerini and Tullo *Massarani, and Erminia Foà Fusinato (1834–1876), who was active as a poet, literary critic, and educator. These subordinated their Jewishness in order to identify completely with Italy's culture and liberalism at the time of her national unification. On the other hand, Graziadio David *Levi was opposed to the loss of Jewish identity, even though he had fought with Mazzini and was later an enthusiastic follower of Garibaldi. A versatile writer, Levi wrote plays, essays, poems, criticism, and hymns. He attempted a synthesis of Jewish and European culture by identifying the essence of Judaism with the principles of 19th-century European liberalism: faith in one God; belief in absolute political justice, entailing national liberation; belief in the unity of mankind expressed in social equality; and the fraternity of nations. Extraordinarily perceptive, Levi sensed the danger of German antisemitism, foreseeing its dire consequences, and also predicted the unification of Europe.

After Italian unification (1870), Jewish authors began writing novels, then an undeveloped genre in Italy. Enrico *Castelnuovo introduced an element of social concern in addition to the usual preoccupation with the romantic and decadent. In his novel *I Moncalvo* (1908), he depicts a Jewish family that has grown rich and, as some members of the family are absorbed into the upper class, the problems resulting from their abandonment of Jewish principles. Although not as prolific as Castelnuovo, Alberto *Cantoni was more original. In a series of short stories and in the novel *L'illustrissimo* (which appeared posthumously in 1906), he combined interesting stylistic experiments with a particular sense of humor which, besides the comic and ludicrous, expressed the absurdity of life and the validity of imagination. His themes and stylistic experiments presage the drama of Pirandello, who regarded Cantoni as his teacher. Jewish contributions to poetry were meager during the period of the Risorgimento and were devoted to spreading the ideals of the national liberation movement. Giuseppe *Revere wrote a subtle collection of poems and was also well known for his historical dramas *Lorenzino de' Medici* (1839) and *I piagnoni e gli arrabbiati…*

(1843). A distinguished representative of the bourgeois theater of the 1890s and early 20th century, Sabatino *Lopez wrote over 70 plays and long dominated Italian drama. Lopez, who had a talent for lucid expression, based his work on the "comic" in human life and remained faithful to the tradition of classical Italian drama derived from Goldoni's comedies. Aldo de *Benedetti, who composed a few sentimental comedies and became known between 1930 and 1938, can be regarded as an epigone of Lopez.

LITERATURE OF CONFLICT. Immediately before and after World War I, Jewish writers expressed a different attitude toward Judaism. Their former faith in Italy's liberation had been undermined at the time that Italian Jews first caught a glimpse of Jewish life abroad. But the depiction of Jewish life in novels remained in the sphere of folklore and impressionism, where old customs and the warmth of Jewish family life were affectionately described. This exotic treatment of Jewish life was aimed at arousing the interest of gentiles without making any ideological or even aesthetic claims. Characteristic of this genre are the novels *Dall' East End al... Cantico dei Cantici* (1910) by Guglielmo Lattes; *Israel, Rachele al fonte* (1923) by E.D. Colonna; *Shylock senza maschera* ("Shylock Unmasked," 1924) by Graziadio Foà; and *Yom ha-Kippurim* (1925) and *Beati misericordes* (1930) by the Zionist author Giuseppe *Morpurgo. In *Yom ha-Kippurim* Morpurgo depicts the crisis of a traditional Jew attracted to liberal western society and raises the issues of mixed marriage and assimilation. The poet Angiolo *Orvieto attempted a different approach to the problem by declaring himself to be simultaneously Italian and Jewish. In addition to his extensive activity as founder and editor of the best Italian literary organs of the early 20th century, he often expressed this dual loyalty. In *Il vento di Siòn* (1928), his main verse collection, Orvieto appears in the guise of a 16th-century Jewish poet who tries in vain to combine his love for Zion and the Jewish people with his love for the beauty of Italy and his native Florence.

After the rise of Fascism, Jewish themes were seldom or only superficially treated. The cultural elite of Italian Jewry was prevented from producing noteworthy prose or poetry because of the superficial principles of aesthetics dictated by the Italian ministry of propaganda and its own isolation from the great European and American literary movements. The few Jewish works published depicted only a stereotyped Jewish character. In the novels *Remo Maun, avvocato* (1930) by A. Grego and *Agenzia Abramo Lewis* (1933) by Alfredo Segre, the Jew is shown as a vacillating character living the homeless life of an adventurer. Whether in the Levant or New York, the Jew is seen as exotic, strange, and cosmopolitan, and his ability to adapt to any given situation is thought to make up for his lack of a firm socio-cultural basis. Certain aspects of the Jewish character described in these two novels reappear in Italian Jewish fiction published after World War II. The once-popular novels of Guido *da Verona and Annie Vivanti *Chartres derived from the decadent atmosphere of the early 20th century and the literary "eroticism" prevalent after World War I. Annie Vivanti's best work, *I Divoratori* (Eng., *The Devourers*, 1910), deals with the problem of the child prodigy whose parents sacrifice themselves for the child's sometimes illusory talents. Da Verona's novels are hedonistic and erotic. Following D'Annunzio and using a rhetorical and inflated style, Da Verona criticized bourgeois marital conventions without, however, basing his criticism on serious analysis of the causes of the collapse of moral values in that society. The erotic novel's decline into cheap pornography is seen in the works of *Pitigrilli (pseudonym of Dino Segre), a Fascist informer, who became a Christian.

In contrast to this marginal literature, a group of writers and poets living in and around Trieste made an important contribution to contemporary Italian literature, suggestive in many ways of the Jewish contribution to Central European and German literature early in the century and between the World Wars. This group also left its mark outside of Italy and was able to transcend the limits of literary fashion because of its pan-European taste and talent for combining diverse and contradictory cultural elements. Foremost among the group's writers was Italo *Svevo (pseudonym of Ettore Schmitz). In his novel *La coscienza di Zeno* (1923; *Confessions of Zeno*, 1930) Svevo analyzed contemporary man, his meaningless life and the incongruity between his limitless aspirations and the limited means for fulfilling them. His techniques include the use of reminiscence, monologue, and psychological introspection, closely resembling those of James Joyce. Joyce was in fact influenced by Svevo, whom he met during his stay in Trieste after 1903. Umberto *Saba, one of Italy's outstanding contemporary poets, expressed the meaninglessness of existence, which for that very reason is rich in deep poetic truth. In some of Saba's poems and short stories there are allusions to his origin and to his experiences as a boy growing up among the Jews of Trieste: in one of them, the main character is Samuel David *Luzzatto, a relative of his mother. Drawing the logical and radical conclusions from the theories of Schopenhauer and Nietzsche, the poet and philosopher Carlo *Michelstaedter anticipated the principal theses of existentialism in his *La persuasione e la rettorica* (1913), which appeared three years after his suicide. Michelstaedter's pessimistic theory, which enjoyed a new vogue after World War II, presents death as the only existential act in which man can attain truth and prove his freedom. The autobiographical novel *Il segreto* (1961) by Anònimo Triestino (pseudonym of Giorgio Voghera, 1908–1999), who was influenced by Svevo's style, centers on the mental problems of a Jewish adolescent whose inhibitions prevent him from revealing his love to a girl of his own age. The boy, intensely introverted, suffers in his relations with friends who are free from the mental anguish typical of a Jewish youth. Voghera is also the author of *Quaderno d'Israele* (1967), *Gli anni della psicanalisi* (1980), and *Carcere a Giaffa* (1985).

THE HOLOCAUST AND ITS AFTERMATH. A total change in the status and ideological stand of Italian Jewish authors took place during and after World War II. Contact with the ideological and aesthetic problems of world literature and the trauma of the Holocaust forced Jewish authors, as it did others, to break conventional frameworks. No longer could they be content with writing commercially oriented literature for the amusement of an old-fashioned reading public. The ideological fight against Fascism and the need actively to seek a total change in social values were now focal to the lives of those who in their youth were rejected and alienated from the literary world. Jewishness as a theme reappears, not as an ideological problem one must take a stand on or solve, but as a human experience lived through in childhood or during persecution and war. Three authors alienated from Judaism and Zionism were Giorgio *Bassani, Natalia *Ginzburg, and Primo *Levi, who combined Jewish family reminiscences and the problems of Jewish alienation in a gentile world with leftist political activity and aspirations. A distinction should be made between the partial Jewish concerns of these three writers and the works of Alberto *Moravia (pseudonym of A. Pincherle) and of Carlo *Levi, which are devoid of any reference to their Jewish origin and show no interest in Jews and Judaism. Moravia and Levi identified with the struggle against Fascism and with the revolutionary-leftist trend of European avant-garde literature before World War II. Moravia, reputedly the most popular contemporary Italian author (especially in English-speaking countries) regarded all manifestations of life as influenced by sensuality and sex. His characters, enveloped in an internal lie, clearly express modern man's alienation from his society and, in particular, his sense of estrangement in the relations between the sexes. The suffering caused by alienation is relieved only by the bitter truth of literary confession. Carlo Levi's *Cristo si è fermato a Eboli* (1945; *Christ Stopped at Eboli*, 1947) describes the horrifying desolation of the underdeveloped areas in southern Italy to which he was exiled by the Fascists. Unlike Moravia, Levi clings to the aesthetic theories of the Marxist left. In travel diaries written later, Levi preached social revolution and loyalty to the struggle of the proletariat against the existing regime. Bassani's principal work, *Il giardino dei Finzi-Contini* (1962; *The Garden of the Finzi-Contini*, 1965), is a lyrical description of Jewish life in an Italian provincial town before its destruction in World War II. Clinging to a noble and ancient tradition, his characters live on their reminiscences. They lack the strength to confront the cruel reality of persecution and are therefore doomed. Many of Bassani's novels and short stories have the Jewish society of his youth as background, but his identification with Judaism is only in the sphere of recollection. He has therefore rightly been called "Proust adapted to Jewish life." Like Bassani, Natalia Ginzburg also wrote about her Jewish home, after she had produced a number of novels influenced by Cesare Pavese. Ginzburg completely broke up the conventional structure of the novel. In her *Lessico Famigliare* (1963), she reconstructed her childhood and the atmosphere of her Jewish home by stressing the function of words and the special family language that united its members. Descriptions of childhood and the atmosphere of the Jewish Levant also inspired Fausta Cialente's novel *Ballata Levantina* (1961; *The Levantines*, 1962).

Primo Levi's work is of a different type. In *Se questo e un uomo* (1947; *If This is a Man*, 1959) and *La Tregua* (1963; *The Reawakening*, 1965) he relates his tragic experiences in a German extermination camp and the hardships of wandering across Russia and Central Europe on his return home. Levi's confrontation with Jewish life and Jewish solidarity is raised to a universal dimension, in which human emotion and understanding bridge the gap between people differing in culture and personality. In *I sommersi e I salvati* (1986; *The Drowned and the Saved*, 1988), more an essay than a novel, Levi goes back again to the Auschwitz experience, drawing pessimistic conclusions from an accurate and crude analysis: if these things happened once, they can happen again.

Centered on the years of the antisemitic persecutions are also *The Parnas, A Scene from the Holocaust* (1979) by the Italian-American psychiatrist Silvano Arieti, on the thrilling and tragic story of the lay leader of the Jewish community of Pisa; and *Per violino solo* by Aldo Zargani (1995; *For Solo Violin. A Jewish Childhood in Fascist Italy*, 2002), the vibrant memories of a "stolen childhood" told by a grandfather to his grandchild. *Storie dell'Ottavo distretto* (1986) is a collection of descriptions of Jewish characters of Budapest, the hometown of the authors, the brothers Giorgio and Nicola Pressburger. A sense of decay pervades all of these stories. The Jewish identity theme is important in *Il principio della piramide* (1989) by Roberto Vigevani (but published under the name Rude Masada), who wrote also *Diario, sogni e allucinazioni di Mansholt Levy* (1979), the sad and comic story of a young Jew from Chicago. Clara Sereni is the author of *Il gioco dei regni* (1993), on her extraordinary family to which belonged the Zionist leader Enzo *Sereni and the Communist leader Emilio Sereni, her father, both important intellectuals. Other novels dealing with the Jewish past are *I giorni del mondo* (1981) by Guido Artom, an account of the Jewry of Asti; *Gli occhi colore del tempo* (1995) by Sergio Astrologo, and *Tutti I giorni di tua vita* (1997) by Lia Levi. *Con le peggiori intenzioni* (2005) by Alessandro Piperno, a bestseller, breaks with the memorialistic gender based on the tragedy of the war, in that it describes a family of Roman Jewish merchants in the 1980s and 1990s, their excesses and their generosity.

Both before and after World War II, Jewish scholars again made important contributions to Italian literary criticism. A literary historian and a subtle critic, Attilio *Momigliano was sensitive to the most delicate nuances of poetry and brought deep psychological insight to his assessment of character motivation. Eugenio *Levi wrote essays on Italian drama and its history and contributed toward a greater understanding of European and American classics in Italy. He also wrote interesting essays on Zangwill, Svevo, and other Jewish writers. Giacomo *Debenedetti advocated a committed literature and breaking away from B. Croce's aesthetic patterns and academic theories. Alienated from Judaism, but persecuted as a Jew, Debenedetti left a moving document, *Sedici Ottobre* (1943), about the deportation of Roman Jews to concentration camps. In the academic world, outstanding literary scholars included Mario *Fubini, who specialized in the study of Italian literature of the 18th and 19th centuries; and Cesare Segre, who made an important contribution to the study of medieval Italian literature. Following the lead of G.L. Ascoli, the philologist Benvenuto *Terracini brought an original approach to the study of language problems. The new method he introduced into the investigation of Italian dialectology established Terracini as one of the greatest contemporary linguists.

BIBLIOGRAPHY: M. Steinschneider, in: *Buonarroti*, 5 (1870); idem, in: MGWJ, 42 (1898), 33ff.; 43 (1899), 32ff.; 44 (1900), 80ff. **ADD. BIBLIOGRAPHY:** U. Cassuto, in: *Festschrift A. Kaminka* (1937), 129–41; G. Romano, *Ebrei nella letteratura* (1979); H.S. Hughes, *Prisoners of Hope* (1983); L. Gunzberg, *Strangers at Home* (1992); R. Speelman, in: *Gli spazi della diversità* (1995), 69–101.

[Joseph Baruch Sermoneta / Giorgio Romano / Alessandro Guetta (2nd ed.)]

ITALIENER, BRUNO (1881–1956), rabbi, author, and historian of Jewish manuscript illumination. Italiener, who was born in Burgdorf, Hanover (Germany), studied at the Jewish Theological Seminary in Breslau and Erlangen University. He served from 1907 to 1928 as rabbi of the Israelitische Religionsgemeinde in Darmstadt. During World War I, he was a German Army chaplain. He was the chief rabbi of the Temple Congregation in Hamburg from 1928 until 1939, when he left Germany because of the Nazi persecution. He settled in London and was rabbi of the Bernhard Baron Center from 1939 to 1941, when he was appointed rabbi of the West London synagogue of British Jews. Italiener continued his communal work after his retirement in 1951 and also continued his scholarly activity, contributing to many learned journals. He was very active in the work of the Reform movement in England. Italiener's main scholarly contribution was his publication of a facsimile edition of the *Darmstaedter Pessach-Haggadah* (1927), which contained a monograph of the history of illuminated *Haggadot*. This work is an important source for the history of Jewish manuscript art. He also contributed many articles and essays on various phases of Jewish letters, including the "*Mussaf-Kedusha*" (in HUCA, 26 (1955), 413–24) and *Waffen im Abwehrkampf* (1920), which was influential in the formulation of programs for the combating of anti-semitism.

[Ruth Ivor]

ITALY. Jews have lived in Italy without interruption from the days of the Maccabees until the present, through a period of 21 centuries. Although they were never subjected to general expulsion, there were frequently partial ones. They often enjoyed good relationships with the rulers and general population or were granted special privileges. They remained few in number, refrained from attracting attention, were intellectually alert, and continued faithful to their traditions. The record of Italian Jewry thus provides one of the most complex and fascinating chapters in the history of the Jewish Diaspora.

The Roman Pagan Era (second century B.C.E. to 313 C.E.)
Probably preceded by individual Jews who visited Italy as traders, a Jewish embassy was dispatched to *Rome in 161 B.C.E. by *Judah Maccabee to conclude a political treaty with the Roman senate. It was followed by others sent by his brother *Jonathan 15 years later, by *Simeon in 139, and by *Hyrcanus I in 133. In 139, either these emissaries or the other Jews living in Rome were apparently accused of conducting religious propaganda among the Roman population and expelled from the city. However, the decree soon became obsolete. Jewish prisoners taken by *Pompey during his invasion of Ereẓ Israel, 63–61 B.C.E., were brought to Italy, but most were probably freed after a short time. *Julius Caesar, who considered that the Jews represented a cohesive element in the Roman world, granted them certain exemptions to enable them to fulfill their religious duties. These exemptions were subsequently confirmed by most of the Roman emperors. Under *Augustus, the number of Jews in the capital increased. In 19 C.E., during the reign of *Tiberius, his minister Sejanus deported 4,000 Jewish youths to Sardinia to fight banditry, ostensibly to punish the Jews for having tried to defraud a woman of the Roman nobility. In fact, this was part of the policy to suppress the Oriental cults, and an edict was also issued ordering the Jews to leave Italy unless they abandoned their religious practices. Tiberius abrogated the measures after Sejanus' execution.

The growing friction between the Jews of Rome and the rising Christian sect led *Claudius to rid Rome of both elements (49–50), but this time also the decree was short-lived. The Jewish struggle in Judea against the Romans ended in 70 with wholesale destruction and massacre and mass deportations of Jewish prisoners, a large number of whom were brought to Italy. According to later sources, 1,500 arrived in Rome alone, and 5,000 in *Apulia. There too they attained freedom after a relatively short time, and many remained in Italy. The emperor *Vespasian prohibited the voluntary tribute of the *shekel that Jews in the Diaspora customarily sent to the Temple and changed it to a "Jewish tribute," the *Fiscus Judaicus, to be paid into the public treasury. Under *Domitian (81–96) the exaction of this tax was brutally enforced. It was mitigated by his successor *Nerva, but the tax was not abolished until two centuries later. The Jewish uprisings against Roman rule which broke out in Judea, Egypt, and Cyrenaica during the reigns of Trajan and Hadrian and culminated in the heroic but vain revolt of Simeon *Bar Kokhba (132–5) are not recorded to have affected the Jews in Italy. *Antoninus Pius (138–61), *Caracalla (211–7), Alexander *Severus (222–35), and probably other emperors displayed benevolence toward Jews. Jews were included in the edict issued by Caracalla in 212 that extended Roman citizenship to all freemen in the empire.

From the end of the second century until the beginning of the fourth, the Jewish settlements in the Diaspora, although proselytizing intensely, did not encounter opposition from the

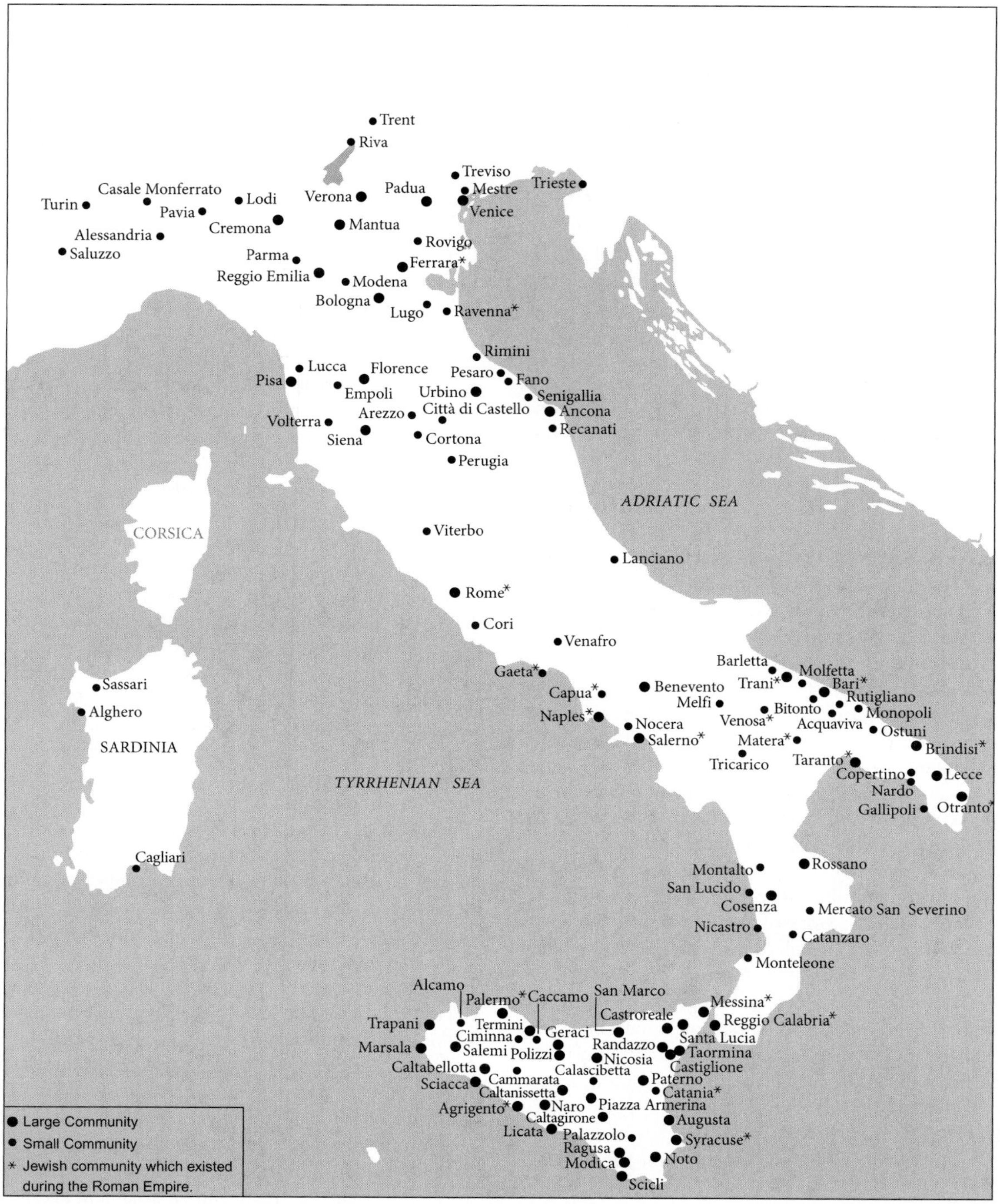

Map 1. Major Jewish communities in Italy, 1450–1550. Based on A. Milano, Storia degli ebrei in Italia, *Turin, 1963.*

Romans, though Septimius *Severus in 204 prohibited conversion to Judaism. The Christian communities, however, which expanded rapidly and proved intransigent, were severely dealt with. The fact that the Jews in Italy were of petty bourgeois or even servile origin, and that they were not infrequently suspected of opposing Roman policy abroad, prevented individual Jews from attaining prominence in economic or social life. It has been estimated that there were 50,000 Jews in Italy during the first century of the empire, of whom over half were concentrated in or around Rome. In the capital, they engaged in humble occupations and lived in the proletarian sections. Cultural standards were not high, although there were painters, actors, and poets. The communities centered on the synagogues, of which 12 are known to have existed in Rome, although not contemporaneously. The ruins of one have been discovered in *Ostia. Their knowledge of Hebrew was rudimentary. The religious convictions and customs of the Jews aroused a certain interest among some sectors of the Roman population and sometimes attracted adherents. This picture emerges from the numerous inscriptions found in the Jewish *catacombs rather than from the evidence provided by the generally hostile Roman intellectuals. Outside Rome the position was substantially similar, as may be deduced from tombstone inscriptions. Initially, Jews settled in the ports: Ostia, Porto, Pozzuoli, Pompeii, *Taranto, and *Otranto. They subsequently spread inland, although it is impossible to state the relative numbers. In the first three centuries of the empire Jews were found in Campania: *Naples, *Capua, and *Salerno; in Basilicata, Apulia, and *Calabria: *Bari, Otranto, Taranto, *Venosa, and *Reggio; and in *Sicily: *Syracuse, *Catania, and *Agrigento. In northern Italy, the presence of Jews has been traced in Civitavecchia, *Ferrara, *Brescia, *Milan, Pola, and *Aquileia. Their occupations may be inferred but are attested only in a few cases. No significant evidence concerning Jewish scholarly and literary activities has been preserved. *Caecilius of Calacte, an orator and literary critic who wrote in Greek during the Augustan period, was highly esteemed, but none of his works is extant. *Josephus composed his major historical works at the imperial court in Rome. It is also known that there was a talmudic academy in Rome which attained distinction in the second century under the guidance of the *tanna* *Mattiah b. Ḥeresh.

Early Middle Ages (313–c. 1100)

The official acceptance by the Roman Empire of Christianity as a religion and its subsequent expansion marked for the Jews the transition from an era of tolerance to one of subjection. The Christians did not aim at the complete suppression of Judaism, with which they acknowledged affinity in certain common origins and religious convictions. They therefore desired the physical preservation of the Jews, but only in the role of spectral witnesses of ancient truths, with limited possibilities of existence. For this reason, from the fourth century onward the *Church Fathers increased their efforts to secure new laws that would restrain the Jews in their religious practices, limit their political rights, and curb them both socially and economically; at the same time, they exerted pressure on them individually to leave their religion. Constantine the Great prohibited conversion to Judaism and debarred Jews from owning Christian slaves. Constantius (337–61) extended the prohibition to the ownership of pagan slaves and prohibited marriages between Jews and Christian women, imposing the death penalty for such cases. Church dignitaries sallied forth to the public squares to preach against the Jews and incite the populace to destroy their places of worship. In 315 Sylvester, bishop of Rome, is said to have sponsored a public debate directed against the Jews; in 388 Philaster, bishop of Brescia, encouraged the populace of Rome to set fire to a synagogue, and *Ambrose, bishop of Milan, praised the population of Aquileia for doing the same, expressing his sorrow that the synagogue in Milan had not been similarly treated. The emperor *Theodosius II prohibited the construction of new synagogues, permitting only those in danger of collapse to be restored but not enlarged. In addition, he debarred Jews from practicing law or entering state employment. The legal codes that bear the names of Theodosius (438) and later of *Justinian (529–34) established a new status for the Jews as inferior citizens. They were obliged to carry out numerous special duties and were excluded from public offices and from several professions.

The disintegration of the western Roman Empire, the weak and remote influence of the eastern one, and the lack of forceful Church leaders, led to continuous changes in the situation of the Jews in Italy, if not always evidenced by the sources. Much depended also on which of the invaders succeeded in gaining the upper hand in the various parts of Italy. King Theodoric the Ostrogoth proved benevolently disposed toward the Jews and, between 507 and 519, intervened on their behalf against their opponents in Milan, *Genoa, Rome, and *Ravenna. The Jews actively sided with the Goths when Naples was besieged by the Byzantine general Belisarius in 536. As a result they were persecuted by the Byzantines when a few decades later they conquered Italy. Among the popes of this period, only *Gregory I (590–604) is significant for Jewish history. He afforded the Jews protection in Rome, Terracina, Naples, Palermo, Ravenna, and elsewhere against vexations at the hands of local bishops, insisting that although he desired the conversion of the Jews, he was opposed to attaining this by violence. The missionary fervor of the eastern emperors was felt in their Italian possessions, especially in the south. The Jews in *Oria, Bari, *Brindisi, Taranto, and Otranto suffered from discriminatory legislation and campaigns of forcible conversion under the emperors *Basil I in 873–4 and *Romanus I Lecapenus in 932–6. About the same period, the population in the south suffered from raids by roving Arab bands from North Africa. In Sicily, the Saracenic conquest (827–1061) brought more stability and proved beneficial to the Jews of the island. Toward the end of the 11th century, there were a few Jews living in northern Italy, mostly in *Verona, *Pavia, and *Lucca, a considerable nucleus in Rome, and numerous groups in the south of the country and in Sicily, totaling a significant number.

Although the course of the political events affecting the Jews in these seven centuries is almost completely unknown, the Venosa tombstone inscriptions, particularly from the fourth and fifth centuries, and the chronicle of *Ahimaaz of Oria, which relates events from the ninth century on, throw some light on the Jews in some centers in the south. The Jewish occupations are hardly mentioned, although it is known that there were Jewish artisans and merchants, and, especially in the south, dyers and silk weavers; Jews not only owned houses in the towns but also engaged in farming. Something more is now known about the state of Jewish culture, especially around the tenth century. Tombstone inscriptions were by now composed in Hebrew, and not in Latin or Greek as previously. There were talmudic academies in Rome and Lucca (connected with the *Kalonymus family) and in the south, in Venosa, Bari, Otranto, Oria, and later in *Siponto. A legend telling of four rabbis from Bari, who, after being taken prisoners at sea in 972, were set free and later established rabbinical schools in Mediterranean cities (see *Four Captives), would seem to show that Jewish scholarship in Apulia had gained a reputation beyond Italy. The scholars whose names are preserved may be taken to represent the schools or literary circles which had formed around them. Of special importance were the liturgical poet *Shephatiah b. Amittai of Oria (ninth century), the astronomer and physician Shabbetai *Donnolo (tenth century), and *Nathan b. Jehiel Anav of Rome (11th century), who composed the *Arukh*. The *Sefer *Josippon*, a Hebrew work based on Josephus' *Jewish War*, was probably written by an Italian Jew in the mid-tenth century.

Later Middle Ages (1100–1300)

Italy in the 13th century shows no change in the distribution of the Jewish population, which remained mainly concentrated in the south of the peninsula. Reports of a considerable Jewish settlement in *Venice are difficult to verify. There were a few dozen Jewish families resident in Pisa and Lucca, and isolated families elsewhere. Only in Rome were there as many as 200 families. The Jews were prosperous and led an active intellectual life. They lived on good terms with their Christian neighbors, including those of highest rank. It is of no great importance that a Roman Jewish family which had adopted Christianity, the *Pierleoni family, produced an antipope, *Anacletus II (1130–38), but it is highly significant that Jehiel *Anav, a nephew of Nathan b. Jehiel, supervised the finances of Pope *Alexander III (1159–81). However, the spirit predominating in the city of Rome must not be confused with that of the Church, which now renewed its efforts to assert its authority.

In this period the Jews of Italy were trapped between two conflicting attitudes manifested by the Church. One is expressed in the *bull first issued by Pope *Calixtus II (1119–24), beginning *Sicut Judaeis*, which afforded the Jews protection from assaults against their persons, property, or religious practices, and from conversionist pressures, which was confirmed repeatedly by succeeding popes. The other aspect, manifestly hostile, was enunciated by the Third *Lateran Council (1179) which forbade Jews to employ Christian servants, and by the Fourth Lateran Council (1215), convened by Pope *Innocent III, which made efforts to have the Jews placed in a position of perpetual serfdom, and meanwhile introduced the regulation compelling Jews to wear a distinguishing *badge on their garments. About 20 years later the Inquisition began to preoccupy itself with the Jews, who were submitted to the mercies of the *Dominican friars. The rabid campaign against the Talmud initiated in France in 1240 was in due course extended to Italy. The practice of compelling Jews to attend conversionist *sermons began in Lombardy in 1278. Jewish life was still centered, however, in southern Italy and in Sicily. According to *Benjamin of Tudela, in the late 12th century there were not fewer than 1,500 Jews in Palermo and about the same number all told in Apulia and the Campania. These reached the height of their prosperity under Frederick II (1212–50), who extended his personal protection to the Jews and secured them the monopoly of the silk weaving and dyeing industries and foreign commerce. He also supported them against the fiscal claims of the bishops, and took a personal interest in promoting Jewish culture. When in 1265 sovereignty of the area passed to the Angevin rulers, the Jews in the south came under the direct influence of the Holy See on which the new dynasty was largely dependent. Under Charles II a *blood libel was raised against the Jews of *Trani and developed into a violent crusade to convert all the Jews in the south, then numbering probably between 12,000 and 15,000. The campaign lasted until 1294; by then about half the Jewish population had been forced to abjure their faith, entire communities had been annihilated, and many of the synagogues, of which there were four in Trani alone, were converted into churches. Most of the Jews who did not submit fled, while others continued to observe their faith in secret.

Jewish intellectual activity in Italy during this period is represented by several scholars, who interested themselves in various fields without predominating in any. In general, their works on philosophy, ethics, philology, and Kabbalah reflect the influences of contemporary Spanish Jewish literature. There were noteworthy talmudic academies in Rome and southern Italy, in particular at Bari and Otranto. Prominent among the scholars in Rome toward the end of the 12th and during the 13th century, were Menahem b. Solomon b. Isaac, a biblical exegete who also probably arranged the liturgy according to the "Roman" or Italian rite; the philosopher and biblical scholar Zerahiah b. Shealtiel *Gracian; and several members of the Anav family (Benjamin and Zedekiah b. Abraham, Jehiel b. Jekuthiel, Benjamin b. Judah), who extended their activities to almost every field of Jewish learning. Outside Rome, there were the philosopher *Hillel b. Samuel of Verona, Isaac b. Melchizedek of Siponto, commentator on the Mishnah, and the halakhist *Isaiah b. Mali of *Trani (the Elder). Several of these at the same time practiced medicine, wrote liturgical poetry, and translated from Latin and Arabic into Hebrew or vice versa. Members of the ha-Meati family, following in the footsteps of the founder of the family Nathan b. Eliezer, distinguished themselves as translators, as also did Jacob *Anatoli of Naples, *Faraj b. Solomon of Agrigento, and *Ahitub b. Isaac of Palermo. In their task of spreading knowledge they received support from the Hohenstaufen and Angevin courts at Naples. *Judeo-Italian began to be spoken by the Jews of southern and central Italy in the early Middle Ages, then by all Italian Jewry, toward the 14th–16th centuries.

The Zenith (c. 1300–1500)

Toward the end of the 13th century and beginning of the 14th, the Jews in Italy embarked on a new sphere of economic activity as small-scale moneylenders (loan bankers). They were driven into this occupation partly because no regular form of financial assistance was available from other sources for small merchants or needy individuals, and partly because of the Church prohibition on lending money for interest by Christians. Many Jews on the other hand had large amounts of liquid capital, realized after they were obliged to leave the south at the end of the 13th century, or when they left Rome, which declined after the Holy See moved to Avignon in 1309. It was in fact from the south and Rome that a phalanx of Jews wishing to establish themselves as moneylenders made their appearance in several towns and districts in northern and central Italy. They were admitted into these localities and openly encouraged by the local rulers, although often received more hesitantly by the general population. At the same time numerous Jews from Germany, and some from France, crossed the Alps to escape persecution and established themselves in towns in the north of Italy, where they opened loan banks.

The 14th and 15th centuries were periods of expansion and consolidation for the Jewish loan bankers. Their activities resulted not in the accumulation of large fortunes in the hands of a few, but in small fortunes in the hands of many, which led to widely spread prosperity. It is difficult to estimate the number of localities in the peninsula in which Jews were living around the middle of the 15th century – possibly 300 or more. However, it is certain that the prosperity resulting from their moneylending activities was of more benefit to the Jews in Rome and in the north than those in the south. These activities brought them into contact with all sectors of the population, both poor and rich, the small shopkeeper and the lord of the town, the illiterate and the scholar. Hence many of these bankers tended to adopt the way of life of the gentile upper classes, or what has been termed the "Man of the Renaissance," with his taste for letters and art, and pleasure in affluent living.

Nevertheless, the Jews of Italy never became estranged from their Jewish intellectual and religious heritage. This was a period of unprecedented cultural activity, and the Jewish scholars, poets, physicians, and codifiers, who at the same time cultivated secular disciplines and languages, are significant more for their number than for individual excellence. Among the most important were the kabbalistic exegete Menahem b. Benjamin *Recanati, the talmudist and biblical exegete *Isaiah b. Elijah of Trani (the Younger), the poet *Immanuel b. Solomon of Rome, who composed in Italian as well as in Hebrew and also wrote biblical commentaries, his cousin, the philosopher and translator Judah b. Moses *Romano, *Kalonymus b. Kalonymus, of Provençal origin, author of the satires *Massekhet Purim* and *Even Boḥan*, and Shemariah b. Elijah of Crete, author of a philosophical commentary on the Bible. Outstanding from the end of the 14th century to the middle of the 15th are the poet and physician Moses b. Isaac *Rieti, author of *Mikdash Me'at*, a poetical work in Hebrew modeled on Dante's *Divine Comedy*, and Obadiah of *Bertinoro, author of the classical commentary on the Mishnah. A few decades later saw the activity of the philosophers Elijah *Delmedigo and Johanan Alemanno, both associated with the humanistic circle of *Pico della Mirandola, the halakhist Joseph *Colon, *Judah b. Jehiel, and David Messer *Leon, father and son, the former a philosopher and the latter a biblical scholar. Of Spanish origin were two of the most outstanding personalities and philosophers of their time, Don Isaac *Abrabanel and his son Judah (Leone Ebreo), author of the famous *Dialoghi d'amore*. In addition, there were the pioneers of Hebrew printing and other Jews who distinguished themselves in medicine, art, and drama.

However, these brilliant economic and cultural achievements did not exclude some darker interludes. Pope *Urban v (1362–70) confirmed the bull giving protection to the Jews, as also did *Boniface ix (1389–1404), who surrounded himself with Jewish physicians. The situation deteriorated after the final condemnation of the Talmud in Spain in 1415 and increasing anti-Jewish activities by the Franciscan friars. Delegates of the Jewish communities assembled in Bologna in 1416, and in Forlì in 1418, to combat these and other dangers. They succeeded in their representations to Pope *Martin v (1417–31), who issued two favorable bulls in 1419 and 1429, and endeavored to control the anti-Jewish preachings of the Franciscans, and especially the activities of their most aggressive representative, John of *Capistrano. However, in 1442, *Eugenius iv introduced harsh anti-Jewish measures which Jewish delegates meeting in Tivoli in 1442 and in Ravenna in 1443 tried unsuccessfully to oppose. In these circumstances, many Jews preferred to move to the territories of rulers who were better disposed, like the Gonzaga in Mantua and the Este in Ferrara. In the following decades the official Vatican attitude again moderated. On the other hand, the Franciscan preachers, often opposed by the civic authorities, violently attacked the Jews and especially Jewish money-lenders, demanding that they should be expelled and their activities replaced by Christian charitable loan banks (see *Monti di Pietà). In order to inflame the populace the friars spread all manner of slanders against Jews, of which the most distressing was the charge of ritual murder in 1475 at *Trent. Other incidents took place elsewhere and were followed by expulsions, generally of a temporary nature.

The Crisis (1492–1600)

Two factors undermined the existence of the Jews in Italy from the end of the 15th and throughout the 16th centuries: the attitude of the Spanish crown toward its Jewish subjects which extended to its Italian possessions, and the confusion caused by the Counter-Reformation struggle in Italy. When the edict of expulsion of the Jews from Spain was issued in March 1492 both Sicily and Sardinia were under Aragonese rule so that the measure was applied there also. Promulgated in May, it was at once implemented, and the process of expulsion was completed by January 1493. In Sicily, 6,300 Jewish-owned houses were confiscated, and a levy of 100,000 florins was imposed. It is calculated that almost 40,000 Jews in all left the country. In Sardinia, the numbers affected were far less. The majority of the exiles went to continental Italy, but a considerable number chose other lands: North Africa, Greece, Turkey, the Levant. The Jews of the two islands were not the only ones to seek shelter in the Kingdom of Naples under the protection of King Ferdinand. They were joined by about 9,000 Spanish Jews. Spanish Jews also received a generally benevolent welcome in other Italian states, and even in the Papal States under Pope *Alexander VI (1492–1503). However, in 1503 the Kingdom of Naples also passed under Spanish rule and in 1510 the expulsion of the Jews was ordered – probably some tens of thousands, though the exact number is difficult to ascertain. The decree was not carried out immediately and 200 wealthy families were formally permitted to remain. In 1515 the edict of expulsion was extended to the *New Christians – that is to Jews who had become converted to Catholicism more or less sincerely and their descendants. In 1515 and in 1520 the quota of tolerated wealthy families was increased, and then lowered again. In 1541 this agreement was definitively abrogated and the law excluding Jews remained in force in southern Italy for over three centuries.

Conditions in central and northern Italy were completely different. In Rome Popes Julius II, *Leo X, *Clement VII, and Paul III, although differing in character, were well-disposed toward the Jews under their jurisdiction. The same applied to the Medici in Florence, the Este in Ferrara, and the Gonzaga in Mantua, who encouraged the activities and talents of their Jewish subjects, both the older inhabitants and the new arrivals. In Venice the senate began to treat the Jews with a little more consideration, although in 1516 Jewish residence was confined to the *ghetto.

The reaction of the Roman Church to the rise of Protestantism reached a climax in the middle of the 16th century. In its efforts to preserve Catholics from all possibility of religious contamination, the Church acted with particular harshness against the Jews. The first blow fell in 1553, when Pope *Julius III ordered that all copies of the Talmud be confiscated and burned throughout Italy, on the charge that it blasphemed Christianity (see *Talmud, Burning of). The attack became more violent under *Paul IV (1555–59). His bull *Cum nimis absurdum* of July 14, 1555, obliged the Jews in the Papal States to lock themselves in the ghetto at night, prohibited them from engaging in any commercial activity except the sale of rags, required them to sell their houses, and submitted them to all the most harassing restrictions enacted during the preceding centuries. At *Ancona, on the pope's orders, 25 Portuguese Marranos found guilty of having returned to Judaism were sent to the stake. Under Pius IV (1559–65) the oppression abated, but rose to even worse excesses under Pius V (1566–72), who expelled the Jews from all of the Papal States, except Rome and Ancona. Some relief was afforded under Sixtus V (1585–90), who permitted Jews to resume their activities in the towns they had recently been forced to leave. However, all vacillation ended with *Clement VIII (1592–1605), who, in a bull of Feb. 25, 1593, reverted to the harsh measures of Paul IV and Pius V and ordered the Jews to leave the papal domains within three months, except Rome, Ancona, and Avignon. For over two centuries this restrictive papal legislation continued to apply to the Jews living in the papal territories, and was adopted with almost no exceptions by the other Italian states. In the meantime, 900 Jews were banished in 1597 from the duchy of Milan, then under Spanish rule.

Jewish cultural and spiritual life did not suffer because of these vicissitudes. Every town of standing had its yeshivah, that of Padua becoming important under Judah and Abraham *Minz and Meir *Katzenellenbogen. Scholars of this period include the philosopher and biblical exegete Obadiah *Sforno; the religious philosopher Jehiel Nissim of Pisa; the grammarians Abraham de *Balmes, Samuel *Archivolti, and Elijah (Baḥur) *Levita; the physician and lexicographer David de' *Pomis; the geographer Abraham *Farissol; the chroniclers Solomon *Ibn Verga, Gedaliah *Ibn Yaḥya, *Joseph ha-Kohen, and the antiquarian Abraham *Portaleone; the scholarly historian Azariah de' *Rossi, author of *Me'or Einayim*; the poet *Moses b. Joab; and the dramatist Judah (Leone) de' Sommi *Portaleone, who wrote in both Hebrew and Italian. In addition, many Jews individually contributed to art, drama, music, and the development of printing. Outstanding in the medical profession were the papal physicians Bonet de *Lattes, Samuel and Joseph *Sarfati, Vitale *Alatino, and Jacob *Mantino; also *Amatus Lusitanus, author of *Curationum Centuriae*, Elijah Montalto, and the *Portaleone family of Mantua, five generations of whom attended on the Gonzagas.

Persecutions (c. 1600–c. 1800)

This period is generally known as the Age of the Ghetto. It logically begins in 1555, when compulsory segregation was imposed by Paul IV, or even with the isolated instance when the Venice ghetto was established in 1516. However, it was at the end of the 16th century that the ghetto became an accepted institution in Italy, from Rome to the Alps. Every ghetto had its individual character. Some were overcrowded and unhealthy like that of Rome, the largest of all; others were more spacious and vivacious as in Venice (long the center of Hebrew printing), Ferrara, and Mantua; some had only a nominal existence, as in *Leghorn. All the ghettos – except that of Leghorn – were locked at night; the houses, even if owned by Christians, had fixed rents (*jus gazaga*; see **Ḥazakah*). Jews who went outside the ghetto were obliged to wear a distinguishing badge on their garments. They could not enter the professions except (with severe restrictions) that of medicine. To travel out of the town they required special permits. Almost everywhere they were compelled to attend conversionist sermons. The police gave adequate protection to the ghetto from concerted attacks, but only reluctantly in cases of individual molestation. There were approximately 30,000 Jews living in Italy in the 17th and 18th centuries, of whom between 4,000 and 7,000 lived in Rome, somewhat fewer in Leghorn, and the others distributed in almost 70 places. The position of the Rome community was the most critical. Conditions had steadily deteriorated through the restrictions on earning a livelihood and the high taxation imposed by the Holy See. From the middle of the 17th century some of the popes (*Innocent x, xi, and xii) attempted to mitigate their lot, but were unable to prevent the community from being declared bankrupt in 1698.

In the 18th century also other pontiffs (Clement xi, *Benedict xiv, *Clement xiv) were moved to sympathy by the desperate plight of Rome Jewry, but any measures they introduced were counteracted by hostile successors. In the first year of his pontificate, Pius vi (1775–99) published an "Edict Concerning the Jews," characterized by utter obscurantism. In the other towns of the Papal States with Jewish communities, Ancona and (from 1598) Ferrara, the pressure upon the Jews was less extreme. Elsewhere, in the 18th century, in small communities – e.g., in Piedmont – Jews who were considered useful to the economy received particular assistance. In Veneto the Jews helped to arrest the decline of the towns where they were living, particularly Venice. In Tuscany, the Jews of Leghorn, who were completely free to utilize their commercial ability, were so successful that the grand dukes of the House of Lorraine, in particular Leopold i (1765–90), began to treat their other Jewish subjects similarly and to improve their conditions. When the French armies entered Italy in 1796–98, the new revolutionary spirit momentarily triumphed: the walls of the ghetto were demolished and the Jews received equal rights. However, with the restoration of the old regimes in 1799, all the new-found liberties were abolished. Napoleon's campaign of 1800 again brought freedom to the Jews, but in 1815 the restoration resulted in a complete and almost general return of the old conditions.

Intellectual life within the ghetto was inevitably inferior to that of the preceding period. Learned Jews were obliged not only to renounce their contacts with the outside world, but also any participation in academic institutions and, hence, pursuit of secular studies. This resulted in a very different literary orientation. Among the authors of Jewish apologetics were Leone *Modena, Simone (Simḥah) *Luzzatto, and Isaac *Cardozo. Controversies arose between the supporters of Kabbalah, Mordecai *Dato, *Aaron Berechiah of Modena, Menahem Azariah of Fano, Moses *Zacuto, and Solomon Aviad Sar Shalom *Basilea, and its opponents, Azariah de' Rossi and Azariah *Figo. Benjamin b. Eliezer ha-Kohen *Vitale and Abraham *Rovigo tended toward Shabbateanism. Joseph *Ergas and *Malachi b. Jacob ha-Kohen were instrumental in transferring the center of kabbalistic theosophy to Leghorn. Besides the emergence of two poetesses in the Italian language, Deborah Ascarelli and Sarah Coppio *Sullam, poetry was represented by Jacob Daniel *Olmo, the brothers Jacob and Immanuel *Frances, and Isaiah and Israel Benjamin *Bassani, father and son. Important as a poet, dramatist, and ethical writer was Moses Ḥayyim *Luzzatto. Salomone *Fiorentino, who wrote poems in Italian toward the end of the ghetto period, was much admired. Talmudic studies attracted such illustrious scholars as Isaac *Lampronti, author of the stupendous compilation *Paḥad Yiẓḥak*; barely less distinguished were Moses Zacuto, Solomon *Finzi, Samuel *Aboab, and Samson *Morpurgo. The polygraph Ḥayyim Joseph David *Azulai also spent much time in Italy. Hence it would be wrong to state that the walls surrounding the ghetto and its high buildings resulted in intellectual darkness. In fact, the contrary is true. Through scrupulous observance of the *mitzvot* and self-imposed regulation, either to supply the communities with necessities or to avoid excesses in entertainment and dress, the ghetto became a hive of activity, necessarily confined but tremendously alive. Many had several synagogues, all well attended, some with fine architecture such as those of Venice, Padua, Pesaro, and the small Piedmontese communities. There was a constant supply of teachers to listen and instruct. Moral and religious observance was strict but not oppressive. A social-service network provided assistance to all those who lived within the ghetto, especially well organized at Venice and Rome. In consequence, when they withdrew at night into the ghetto, the Jews did not have the feeling of living in prison.

Freedom and Equality (1815–1938)

The record of the half century that passed between the reestablishment of many ghettos and their final abolition differed in the various regions. In Tuscany, after the restoration of the grand duchy in 1815, the Jews there were granted relative equality; only the army and public office remaining barred to them. In the duchy of Parma, the most stringent restriction was that prohibiting Jews from residing in the capital. In the Lombardo-Venetian kingdom under Austrian rule, where there were the important communities of Mantua, Venice, Verona, and Padua, and the growing community of Milan, conditions were not particularly irksome. In Naples, where Jews had begun to resettle, the only restriction was that they were not allowed to constitute an official community. Elsewhere, however, their situation was now again deeply humiliating, especially in contrast with the freedom they had tasted. In the duchy of Modena, all the old disabilities were restored. The same applied to the Kingdom of Sardinia, comprising Piedmont and Genoa, where the only relaxation was that the Jewish badge was not reimposed. In the Papal States intolerance increased, until in 1827 Pope *Leo xii even resuscitated the notorious anti-Jewish edict of 1775.

However, those Jews once more living in such sad conditions now no longer had to rely only on the assistance, mainly ineffectual, of their more fortunate brethren. The middle-class Italian population which was struggling to liberate the country from reactionary regimes, especially the *Carboneria* and the *Giovine Italia* movements, had among their aims the elimination of all anti-Jewish discrimination. Distinguished politicians and writers such as Vincenzo Gioberti, Niccolò Tommaseo, Ugo Foscolo, and Cesare Balbo fought for the same ideas. Some expressed these aims in writings which reached a wide public, for instance Carlo *Cattaneo in his *Ricerche economiche sulle interdizioni imposte dalla legge civile agli israeliti* (1837), on the economic restrictions imposed on the Jews, and Massimo d'*Azeglio, *Dell' emancipazione civile degli israeliti*, which appeared at the end of 1847. On their part, the Jews did not wait for their aspirations to freedom to be fulfilled through outside assistance and took an active share in the struggle. The Risorgimento movement, which started in Piedmont in 1820–21, became more daring in Modena in 1831 and culminated in the 1848–49 revolutions in Milan, Rome, and Venice – the last under the leadership of Daniele *Manin. The movement included in its ranks many Jewish volunteers from various parts of Italy. Before the uprising broke out in 1848, even the most reactionary governments hastened to grant the Jews some concessions. Pope *Pius IX (1846–78), having abolished compulsory Jewish attendance at conversionist sermons and other humiliating regulations, admitted Jews into the civic guard; in 1848 he ordered that the gates and walls of the ghettos be demolished in Rome and in other towns of the Papal States. In Piedmont, in June 1848, the House of Savoy introduced into the constitution of the kingdom a provision that established equal civil and political rights for all citizens, without religious distinction.

In some retrogressive centers popular insurrections later broke out, after which, in 1849, two Jews were members of the constitutional assembly of the newly-proclaimed Roman republic, and in Venice two others, Isaac Pesaro and Leone Pincherle, became ministers in the provisional republican government. When, at the end of 1849, some of the ousted rulers returned and attempted to reimpose the humiliating anti-Jewish measures, they succeeded in doing so only on paper because they no longer had the support of wide sectors of the public. The darkest reaction indeed still prevailed in the towns of the Papal States: Rome, Ancona, Ferrara, and Bologna. The Jews here were again confined to the ghettos, although the gates were not locked at night. Jewish students were excluded from the public schools, and Jews were barred from commercial partnerships with Christians. They were subjected to pressures to accept conversion; these culminated in the notorious kidnapping of the child Edgardo *Mortara in Bologna in 1858, and of Giuseppe Coen in Rome as late as 1864. Even in the Lombardo-Venetian kingdom, the Austrian government became hostile to the Jews, who were suspected of holding liberal ideas. Only Piedmont upheld the emancipation of 1848, and as it extended its jurisdiction over the new areas which in 1861 became the Kingdom of Italy, additional Jewish groups were admitted to complete equality. Between 1859 and 1861 Emilia, Romagna, Tuscany, Lombardy, the Marches, and the Kingdom of Naples were absorbed; in 1866 Veneto and in 1870 Rome were incorporated in the new Italian kingdom. Trieste, which remained outside the boundaries of the Kingdom of Italy until 1919, had a large Jewish community under Austrian rule, generally well-disposed toward Jews.

As soon as equality had been extended to the Jews, the fact was accepted by the Italian people, anxious to demonstrate that the previous segregation had been imposed by political and ideological considerations and did not reflect popular feelings. The Jews reciprocated with alacrity. The principle that religion should not be an obstacle, whether in law or in fact, and the total absence of ill feeling or prejudice between Christians and Jews led to two far-reaching consequences. First, Jews felt free to embrace any career – political, military, academic, professional, administrative, or commercial – and to attain the highest positions. Secondly, freedom to associate on equal terms with other citizens encouraged Jews to minimize existing differences – some even concealed their Jewish identity or rejected it. The Jewish population formed 0.15% of the total in 1861 and 0.13% in 1938: yet 11 Jews sat in the chamber of deputies in 1871, 15 in 1874, and nine in 1921; in the senate there were 11 in 1905, and 26 in 1923. In the universities the proportion of Jewish professors was 6.8% in 1919, and 8% in 1938. The proportion of Jews in the liberal professions and public administration was 6.4% in 1901 and 6.7% in 1928. Jews attained outstanding positions in several branches of national life, not only quantitatively but qualitatively. Among many examples were Luigi *Luzzatti, for almost 20 years minister of finance, who became prime minister in 1910; Giuseppe *Ottolenghi, minister of war in 1902–03; Leone *Wollemborg, minister of finance from 1901; after 1923 Ludovico *Mortara was for many years president of the Court of Appeals and, for a time, minister of justice.

In this period, the structure of the Jewish communities changed radically. In 1840 there existed about 70 organized communities, in 1938 only 23. In 1840 Italian Jewry numbered 37,000, in 1931 47,485 (including many newly-arrived immigrants). The distribution of the Jewish population also changed. Many small rural communities disappeared, while medium-sized urban ones suffered through migration to the larger centers. Before the establishment of united Italy, each community had its own administrative and social structure, the central organization imposed by Napoleon lasting for only a short while. A first step toward introducing some measure of coordination among the communities was established by the Rattazzi Law of July 1857. But it was only in 1911 that a "Union of Italian Jewish Communities" (Consorzio delle comunità israelitiche italiane) was set up on a voluntary basis. Finally the law of Oct. 30, 1930, established on an obligatory national basis the Unione delle comunità israelitiche italiane and defined its administrative competence and that of the individual communities. It also defined the prerogatives of the rabbis, including authorization to perform marriages, provided that the relevant articles of the Italian legal code were read. The law laid down that all those considered Jews by Jewish law automatically belonged to the community if they did not make a formal renunciation.

The upheavals which took place in Jewish life in Italy in the 19th century had important consequences on the nature of Jewish scholarship. Isaac Samuel *Reggio (1784–1855), a disciple of Moses *Mendelssohn and of N.H. *Wessely, propagated the view that it was necessary to diverge from rigid orthodoxy and give a wider place to secular studies. These ideas he wished to put into practice in the rabbinical college of Padua (later *Collegio Rabbinico Italiano) founded in 1829. However, when Lelio *della Torre and Samuel David *Luzzatto, one of the great pioneers of the scientific study of Judaism, directed the college, they followed the traditional path, and under their control it became one of the most highly esteemed rabbinical seminaries in Europe. Luzzatto was an outstanding scholar and an acute exponent of vast portions of the Jewish heritage, including the philosophy of religion, history, literature, ritual, and Hebrew linguistics. Luzzatto's death marked the end of the college in Padua; its functions were partly assumed by the rabbinical college of Leghorn, under the direction of Elia *Benamozegh. The Padua college itself, after brief vicissitudes, was transferred to Florence in 1899 under the dynamic Samuel Hirsch *Margulies; after his death in 1922 it relapsed into inactivity, to be resuscitated later in Rome. Among those trained in these institutions were Mordecai *Ghirondi, Marco *Mortara, David *Castelli, Umberto *Cassuto, Dante *Lattes, and Elia S. *Artom. These and other scholars were able to publish the results of their research and studies on general problems in the numerous Jewish periodicals that appeared in Italy from the second half of the 19th century.

[Attilio Milano]

Holocaust Period

From *Mussolini's accession to power in 1922 until late in 1937, the Fascist government did not formally interfere with the social and legal equality enjoyed by Italian Jewry. However, even in its early stages, the Fascist movement showed evidence of intolerance toward minority groups. Some of the party leaders, including Mussolini, made particular mention of the potential danger to national unity inherent in the "alien character" of the Jews, with their international, cosmopolitan contacts. When the Fascist movement came to power, the government gave priority to real or imaginary pragmatic considerations over ideological principles. The government wanted to make use of "international Jewry" in order to strengthen its policies as a whole, and increase its penetration into the Levant in particular. The Fascist government also sought to prevent the Zionist movement from being attached solely to British interests in the Middle East. However, many Fascist leaders feared the fancied political and economic strength of the Jews. The Abyssinian War of 1935, the worsening of relations between Italy and Britain, the attempts at a rapprochement with the Arab nationalists, and, above all, the strengthening of links with Nazi Germany in late 1936 reversed the political considerations which had been paramount until then. Italian Fascism then turned to militant antisemitism. In this, as in other matters, the Fascist government was forced to present a united front with its ally, Germany, and to foster the ideological program and the organizational and legislative network of Nazi racial antisemitism. The change of attitude was heralded by a section of the press which condemned "the Jewish and Zionist danger." Early in 1937, Pietro Orano published his book, *Gli Ebrei in Italia*, stressing the "alien" character of the Jews. The book sparked a vociferous anti-Jewish and anti-Zionist campaign in the Italian press; when the party newspaper, *Il Popolo d'Italia*, joined in, it was clear that the die had been cast. The *Manifesto della Razza* appeared in July 1938, ostensibly the work of a group of scientists but apparently edited by Mussolini himself. The Manifesto asserted the existence of a "pure Italian race of Aryan stock," into which the Jews had never integrated, and called for the implementation of a clear racial policy of a "northern Aryan character." In September, the first two laws against Jews were passed, one forbidding them to study or teach in any school or institution of higher learning, the other ordering the deportation of all Jewish aliens who had found refuge in Italy after 1919. A "department for demography and race" was established to coordinate the policy of racial discrimination in all branches of the government, and to conduct a census of Jews living in the country. On October 7, the Supreme Council of the Fascist Party determined the principles on which detailed anti-Jewish legislation was to be based. This legislation, passed on November 17, 1938, included prohibitions on marriage between Jews and Aryans and decreed severe civil and economic restrictions, such as interdictions against Jews serving in the army, working in the government, municipal service, or any other public institution, or employing Aryan servants, and the confiscation of Jewish property. The law defined a member of the "Jewish race" as a person with one Jewish parent but exempted Jews in special categories, such as recipients of military awards and those who were wounded in World War I. The restrictions gradually grew more severe as decrees or mere instructions from the party secretary were enacted and executed. Jews were forbidden to own radio sets, visit holiday resorts, enter public libraries, publish newspapers, or be partners in business firms with "Aryan" Italians.

The opening of the racial campaign severely affected the small Jewish community, not only from the economic point of view, but also ethically and organizationally. Many Jews, who from birth were accustomed to complete social equality and who regarded themselves as Italians in every sense, found it hard to understand the meaning of the discrimination and persecution to which they were now subjected. Some were unable to stand the test and tried to find a way out by conversion to Christianity. In 1938–39, 3,910 cases of apostasy were recorded, as against 101 in the previous two years. Over 5,000 others preferred to emigrate. The Jewish community in Italy, which according to the official census of 1931 numbered 47,485 persons, was reduced by 1939 to 35,156 persons, or 0.8% of the total population. Nevertheless, Jewish institutions managed to surmount the crisis, organized themselves for efficient action, gave help to the needy and refugees, and established Jewish elementary and high schools.

Italy's entry into World War II as Germany's ally (June 10, 1940) caused no drastic change in the status of most of the Jews. In the early months of the war, 43 concentration camps were set up in Italy for enemy aliens, and several thousand Jews of foreign nationality, as well as about 200 Italian Jews, were interned; however, conditions in the camps were, on the whole, bearable. In May 1942 the government decreed that all the Jewish internees would be mobilized into special work legions in place of military service. This order was only partially carried out, and the number of Jews actually mobilized

Map 2. Major Jewish communities in Italy, 1931 and 1970.

did not exceed 2,000 men. The fall of the Fascist regime on July 25 and Italy's surrender to Germany on Sept. 8, 1943, were turning points. The country was cut in two, with the south in the hands of the Allies, and central and northern Italy under German occupation.

The Italian Jewish community, which for historical reasons was concentrated in Rome and in the north, found itself in the German-occupied area, i.e., the Fascist protectorate called the Italian Socialist Republic, headed by Mussolini. Within an extremely short period of time, these Jews passed from a regime of civil and economic discrimination (September 1938–July 1943), through a brief period of liberty and equality (July 25–Sept. 8, 1943), to find themselves victims of the horrors of the "*Final Solution*," together with thousands of Jewish refugees from France and Yugoslavia who had escaped into Italy during the early years of the war.

At first, the authorities in the Italian Socialist Republic contented themselves with a declaration of principles which defined members of the "Jewish race" as aliens and, for the period of the war, as members of an enemy nation (Nov. 14, 1943). This was followed by an order issued by the Ministry of the Interior that all Jews, without exception, should be interned in special concentration camps and all Jewish property confiscated (Nov. 30, 1943). In the meantime the occupation authorities, through Theodor Dannecker, Eichmann's emissary from the *RSHA's IVB4 office, or through *SS and *Gestapo officers, completely took over the administration of the move to murder Italian Jewry. When the German occupation began, the first outbreaks of violence occurred against Jews in Merano (Sept. 16, 1943) and around Lake Maggiore (Sept. 22, 1943). With a detailed list of names and with the assistance of the Fascist armed forces, the Germans hunted out Jews in the principal towns. In Rome, the Germans surrounded the Jewish quarter and on a single day (October 16) arrested more than 1,000 persons, who were dispatched directly to *Auschwitz; immediately on arrival (October 22 or 23) most of them were murdered. Similar *Aktionen* were held in Trieste (October 9), Genoa (November 3), Florence (November 6), Milan (November 8), Venice (November 9), and Ferrara (November 14). Jews who were caught were at first imprisoned in local jails and later sent to special concentration camps set up in northern Italy, especially in *Fossoli and *Bolzano. When the camps were full, the inmates were sent on to extermination camps, mainly to Auschwitz. It is hard to estimate the exact number of Jews arrested in this early stage, but it may be as many as half the total number of Jews deported from Italy during the German occupation.

A second stage began toward the end of 1943, when Jewish life in Italy went underground and organized Jewish public worship became impossible in the country for the first time in 20 centuries. Numerous Jews managed to cross the border into Switzerland; others found their way through the front line, in spite of many obstacles, to southern Italy, or joined the groups of anti-Fascist partisans in the mountains. However, the great majority preferred to seek sanctuary among the Italian population, in the homes of "Aryan" acquaintances, among peasants and the working classes, and even in Catholic religious institutions. Manhunts were, however, regularly carried out by the German and Fascist police, with the concomitant danger of betrayal by Fascist or avaricious citizens, and the constant need to seek new shelter. However, at the hour of greatest danger, many discovered that the greater part of the Italian people was willing to help the persecuted for humanitarian reasons alone, despite the heavy penalties that they risked by their actions. Of the approximately 2,000 Jews who fought against the German and Fascist forces in the ranks of the partisans, more than 100 fell in battle and five won the highest medals for bravery. Others served in the Allied armies or intelligence services. The number of Jewish victims in Italy is estimated at about 7,750 out of a Jewish population of about 35,000 at the beginning of the German occupation.

[Daniel Carpi]

The arrest, manhunts, and deportations of entire Jewish populations that the Italians had witnessed in western Europe and Greece, the atrocities performed before their eyes in Croatia, and the rumors about events in eastern Europe convinced many Italian soldiers and diplomats that it was their human duty to assist the persecuted Jews regardless of their nationality. What was no less than a rescue operation was then mounted in the region controlled by the Italian army in Dalmatia and Croatia, where 5,000 Jews from the remainder of Yugoslavia had found asylum; in southern France, where more than 25,000 Jews had gathered, mostly refugees from northern France; and in Athens and other parts of Greece in the Italian zone, where there were some 13,000 Jews. Altogether some 40,000 Jewish refugees from various countries found a safe haven in the areas of Italian occupation. (In addition, a few thousand refugees had been permitted to enter Italy itself and gained asylum there.)

Despite repeated protests, in no case did the Italians surrender the Jews to the Germans, the Croatian Ustasha, or the Vichy police. They maintained this position in the face of intense pressure, coupled with demands for extradition made by the Germans at various diplomatic levels and even upon Mussolini himself. At least twice Mussolini succumbed to these pressures and gave orders to surrender the Jewish refugees in the Italian zone of Croatia, but the diplomats and high-ranking military officers around him joined forces to evade implementation of this criminal order. Among those who acquitted themselves honorably in this affair were Deputy Foreign Minister Giuseppe Bastianini and senior diplomats Luca Pietromanchi, Luigi Viau, and Roberto Ducci in Rome; diplomatic representatives Guelfo Zamboni, Giuseppe Castruccio, and Pellegrino Ghigi in Greece; the diplomats Vittorio Zoppi, Alberto Calisse, and Gustavo Orlandini in France; and Vittorio Castellani in Croatia. Among military personnel three generals, Giuseppe Pièche, Giuseppe Amico, and Mario Riatta, merit recognition. Other distinguished figures were Police Inspector Guido Lospinoso, who operated in southern France, where he was assisted by the Jewish banker Angelo Donati and the Capuchin friar Pierre-Marie *Benoît.

Unfortunately, some of the Jews who had found asylum in the Italian occupied zone were arrested by the Germans after September 8, 1943, and were killed in the Holocaust.

[Sergio Itzhak Minerbi (2nd ed.)]

Contemporary Period

Italian Jewry's losses resulting from Fascist persecutions can be estimated at about 40%: by deportations (7,749 dead out of 8,360 deportees, around 16% of the Jewish population in 1938), conversion to other religions (5,705 cases during the period 1938–43, around 12%), and emigration (approximately 6,000 persons, around 13%). Indirect consequences of the persecutions were a drastic decline in the birth and marriage rates, which further aggravated the already precarious demographic conditions of Italian Jewry. In the course of the persecutions, the small communities in particular, which were already declining in numbers, suffered severely. At the end of World War II, 29,117 Jews remained in Italy, and a further 26,300 refugees originating mainly from central and eastern Europe were added to this number. Italy was a main gathering place for the refugees en route to Palestine, and the great majority later reached Palestine, legally or illegally.

Meanwhile, the difficult work of reconstructing the communities was begun, with the help of Jewish international relief organizations. Politically, the Jewish minority in Italy lived under generally good conditions after World War II. The Italian Jews and their institutions enjoyed full rights guaranteed by the Constitution and by the respect of the greater part of the Italian people.

At the end of World War II, a certain number of refugees settled permanently in Italy. Subsequently, immigrants arrived, mainly from Egypt and other Middle Eastern countries and from North Africa, especially following the persecutions of Jews after the *Sinai Campaign in 1956. At the same time, immigration also took place from Hungary and other eastern European countries, although to a smaller extent. Schematically, the following three groups could be distinguished in Italian Jewry: the Jews of Rome, the great majority of whom were born there, who partly still lived in the old ghetto, endowed with a sturdy vitality that could be linked in part to the modest conditions of the community and in part to the survival of strong bonds with Jewish tradition; other Italian-born Jews, widely scattered geographically, with more tenuous links with Jewish culture but steadily growing ties with secular Italian culture, and hence more open to social contacts with non-Jews, mixed marriages, and increasingly rapid assimilation; and Jews born abroad, characterized by greater social cohesion, but inclined to adopt rapidly the habits and customs of the less vital groups of Italian Jewry. According to the results of a statistical inquiry carried out, on a national basis, under the auspices of The Hebrew University of Jerusalem, 12,000 Jewish families were living in Italy in 1965, comprising about 32,000 Jews out of a total population of 52,000,000 (a density of 0.6 per thousand). The geographical distribution of the Jews was 42.2% in Rome; 7% in Milan; 21.8% in the six medium-sized communities of Turin, Florence, Trieste, Genoa, Venice, and Leghorn; and 8.3% in the 15 small communities of Naples, Bologna, Ancona, Mantua, Pisa, Padua, Modena, Ferrara, Verona, Alessandria, Vercelli, Parma, Merano, Gorizia, and Casale Monferrato. Isolated Jews were also spread over more than 200 minor centers.

A few demographic details from the above survey will suffice to indicate the state of decline of the Jews in Italy. The birth rate for the Jews was 11.4 per 1,000 as against 18.3 per 1,000 for the entire population; the fertility rate (children from birth to four years per 1,000 women of age 15–49) was 210 for the Jews as against 360 for the general population; the marriage rate was 4.6% as against 8.0%; the mortality rate in general was 16.1% as against 9.6%; the Jews were considerably older: the average age was 41 years as against 33 years for the total population; finally, the demographic balance of the Jewish population was negative, -4.7%, as against +8.7% for the general population. In contrast to the general population, the Jewish population was almost entirely urban and limited to the regions of the center and north. Its educational level was higher, with a large proportion of university graduates (14% as against 1.4%). The largest concentration in occupational distribution was to be found in the business and services sectors (80.7% of the Jews as against 30.3% of the general population), with a certain representation in industry (18.7% as against 40.6%) and an almost total absence from agriculture (0.6% as against 29.1%). The majority were self-employed, followed by those employed in commerce, in the free professions, and as executives and employees. In Rome, the number of hawkers was considerable.

The central organization of Italian Jewry was the Union of Italian Jewish Communities, which represented Jewish interests vis-à-vis the government. Under the successive presidencies of R. Cantoni, A. Zevi, R. Bonfiglioli, and S. Piperno Beer, the Union intervened on behalf of Italian Jews in the face of antisemitic incidents and acted on behalf of the heirs of the victims of the Holocaust in matters of reparations and compensation. The Union also had a special section for cultural activities, rabbinical activity, on the other hand, being under the supervision of the Italian Rabbinical Council. Each community was responsible for organizing all religious and welfare services and cultural activities, as well as administering its own property. Jewish education was carried out through a system of Jewish schools, recognized by the state, in which the syllabus of the state schools was followed with the addition of Jewish subjects. Such schools existed in seven communities in 1970; in 1965–66 the total number of their students amounted to 1,986. The greatest number of pupils, however, was to be found in the elementary schools; in the higher grades the number of Jewish students attending Jewish schools fell drastically in favor of state schools. Rabbinical training was given at the Collegio Rabbinico Italiano, in Rome, and the S.H. Margulies Rabbinical School in Turin. Finally, a few hundred Jewish students attended technical courses at *ORT.

Among Italian-Jewish publications were *La Rassegna Mensile d'Israel*, a Jewish cultural magazine; *Israel*, a Jewish weekly of moderate Zionist tendencies; its cultural monthly, *Shalom*; and *Ha-Tikvah*, the monthly organ of the Federation of Jewish Youth. In general, assimilation of young Jews, particularly those born in Italy, was very noticeable and was also evident from the data on mixed marriages. In Milan, during 1952–66, 46 out of 100 Jewish bridegrooms married non-Jewish brides, and 26 of the 100 Jewish brides married non-Jews. In 1955 was founded in Milan the institution CDEC (Center of Jewish Contemporary documentation) devoted to the promotion of didactic activities and research on contemporary Italian Judaism, Shoah and antisemitism for researchers, students, and schools. The Italian Zionist Federation encouraged *aliyah*, which, though small in numbers, was well qualified professionally. It also organized various cultural and educational activities concerning Israel, frequently in collaboration with *WIZO (ADEI) and other representatives of world Zionist organizations. Soon after World War II, due partly to the presence of the *Jewish Brigade, many young Italian Jews were imbued with Zionist enthusiasm which led to their participation in the Israel *War of Independence (1948) and in some cases to settlement in Israel. This, however, did not always have strong ideological roots, and as a result a considerable number returned to Italy. During that period also the major part of the population of the Apulian village of *San Nicandro was converted to Judaism under the leadership of D. Manduzio and subsequently settled in Israel.

Jews were more modestly represented in realms of culture and in public life than in the first few decades of the 20th century. It should be noted, however, that many representatives of the Jewish intelligentsia had either left Italy because of the racial laws or perished during the persecutions. Among the Jews who rose to distinction in Italy in the post-World War II period in the humanistic field were the writers C. *Levi, A. *Moravia (Pincherle), G. *Bassani, and P. *Levi; in the field of science, the mathematician G. Castelnuova, president of the Academia Dei Lincei, the physicist E. *Segre, Nobel Prize winner in 1959, and the physicist B. *Pontecorvo, who caused a storm when he defected to the Soviet Union after the war. General G. *Liuzzi was head of the General Staff of the armed forces in the years 1954–59. On the other hand, there was a more modest Jewish participation in Italy's political life as compared with the period before the rise of Fascism. In the legislatures of the Italian parliament there was a succession of Jewish representatives, on the average about ten out of 1,000 deputies and senators in the two houses. Of special note is a leader of the Communist party, Umberto *Terracini of Turin, who was president of the Constituent Assembly in 1947.

[Sergio DellaPergola]

DEMOGRAPHY. At the start of the 1980s there were some 41,000 Jews in Italy, of whom 36,000 were permanent residents, some 2,000 Israeli students, and some 3,000 Russian Jews, most of whom were in Rome awaiting emigration visas to other countries. Of the permanent Jewish population, 14,500 lived in Rome and 9,500 in Milan, while the communities of Turin, Florence, Trieste, Leghorn, Venice and Genoa accounted for 6,000, with the remaining 2,000 in 14 small communities. Two characteristic demographic traits of the community were aging and assimilation. The Jewish birthrate continued to be low while, for the first time, the rate of intermarriage reached a level of more than 40 percent in Rome, and was considerably higher in other towns.

In 1993, the number of Jews officially registered in Italian communities was 31,000, with an estimated additional 10–15,000 unaffiliated. Mixed marriages fell from 50% to 40% in ten years. During the 1980s a number of small communities died out. Rome Jewry was the most homogeneous, made up mostly of families – most of them store owners – who survived the war and a dynamic post-1967 Libyan Jewish community by now well-integrated, although they had their own synagogue. The Milan community was of international origin with groups of Syrian, Iranian, Lebanese Jews and others, each with their own synagogues. Lubavitch families had settled in various cities, attracting some of the youth. Friction arose initially because the Lubavitch rabbis accused the Italian rabbis of laxity in maintaining halakhic standards, challenging Italian Jewry's elastic traditions of accommodating all forms of religiosity under an umbrella definition of Orthodoxy. A *modus vivendi* was found, resulting in greater cooperation. No Conservative or Reform congregations existed in Italy because they are traditionally regarded as a threat to Jewish unity and a step toward assimilation.

POLITICAL EVENTS. Along with the general community, Jews also suffered from the continuing erosion in political stability and public order which characterized Italy during the 1970s, and at least three Jews were abducted and held for ransom. In November 1977 the liberal journalist, Carlo Casalegno, joint editor of *La Stampa* and a good friend of the Jewish community and of Israel, was killed in an ambush in Turin.

Some of the members of the Red Brigade and the NAP (Proletarian Action Group) received their military training in Palestinian terrorist camps in Lebanon.

Despite certain self-defense precautions taken by Jewish institutions, there was a general feeling of frustration and distrust in the Jewish community which stemmed from a ceaseless trickle of antisemitic events, often combining anti-Jewish and anti-Zionist elements and trends. These ranged from a variety of Nazi-Fascist or Marxist-Leninist graffiti to more committed documents by intellectuals and official bodies, to bombs thrown against synagogues (which, however, caused neither casualties nor any considerable damage).

Research on antisemitism in contemporary Italy, directed by Professor Alfonso Di Nola, suggested a possible connection between Italian proletarian, revolutionary and reactionary interests and Arabs terrorist groups. In fact, Arab organizations continued to make Italy one of their European strongholds and acted with increasing effrontery against Israeli interests and property, particularly air transport between the two countries.

The main cause of concern to Italian Jews was the consequences of the radicalization of the political struggle on the general scene. A dangerous political instability prevailed in 1974–75. In this connection it was difficult to disentangle wholly the implication of the Middle East crisis from purely local factors. The Italian mass media, headed by the government-controlled radio and television, adopted an open pro-Arab attitude during the Yom Kippur War. One incident received considerable publicity. A satirical article on Col. Qaddhafi, written by two non-Jews, appeared in *La Stampa*, of which Arrigo Levi – a former volunteer in the Israel War of Independence – had been appointed editor a few months earlier. The Libyan government issued a formal protest, demanding, *inter alia*, the dismissal of the editor and threatening a total boycott of all products of Fiat, which owned the newspaper. Although Levi was allowed to retain his post, the Italian government issued a "balanced statement" on the matter, showing understanding of the Arab position. This was later openly manifested when Italy voted in favor of the admission of the Palestine Liberation Organization as an observer at the UN General Assembly. The resurgent neo-fascism and the anti-Israel tide did not cause any actual direct damage to the Jewish community. Nevertheless, fears for the personal safety of Italian Jewish leaders reached a peak after the arrest in Jerusalem of Greek Catholic Archbishop Capucci. There was evidence of an anti-Jewish mood subtly penetrating into intellectual, cultural, and artistic circles. It could be observed in most Italian universities, including most departments of political science and history, where the Middle East conflict is usually taught, and as a result the academic objectivity and scientific standing of these institutions was slowly being compromised. On the other hand, there were a few positive highlights, such as the courageous stand taken by Chief Rabbi Elio Toaff in a few debates on radio and television, which were widely followed, and the support given Israel by a group of members of the Italian parliament, a delegation of which went on a mission to Israel in 1974. Vigorous and effective pro-Jewish stands were taken in the Jewish and non-Jewish press by such writers as Carlo Gasalegno, Aldo Garosci, Tullia Zevi, Marsimo Della Pergola, Alberto Nirenstein and the editorial board of the Roman Jewish monthly *Shalom* which had favorable repercussions in the country.

In November 1976 an official proposal was published to grant a conditional release to SS Lieut. Col. Herbert Kappler, who had directed the slaughter at the Fosse Ardeatin (near Rome), after 28 years of imprisonment. The reaction in the Jewish community was immediate; they hastened to the military hospital where Kappler was held. Larger demonstrations followed in anti-Fascist circles, and the proposal was eventually dropped. On Aug. 15, 1977, however, Kappler was suddenly abducted by his wife to the townlet of Soltau in West Germany. An immediate request of extradition, submitted by the Italian government, could not be complied with under German constitutional law. For a few weeks there was some tension between the Italian and German governments (the Germans had actually been exerting pressure to obtain Kappler's release), and only his death a few months later brought the case to an end. There were also some expressions of intellectual revisionism which attempted to minimize the extent of the Holocaust, or to find psychological or political Jewish responsibilities for it. Some of the most vociferous theories about "Jewish racism" were heard in 1976 on the occasion of a strike by a leftist union at the Sonzogno publishing house, to prevent publication of the Italian version of a report on the IDF rescue operation at *Entebbe. Nor was the Vatican's position more encouraging; in February 1976, the Vatican delegation at an Islamic-Christian conference held in Tripoli voted in favor of a document stating that Zionism is an aggressive, racist movement, foreign to Palestine and to the whole of the Orient.

During the 1980s the Middle East political situation continued to make itself felt. A Palestinian terrorist attack on the Rome synagogue on October 9, 1982, resulted in the death of a two-year-old boy; 40 Jews were wounded. In October 1985, the Italian cruiser *Achille Lauro* was hijacked and an invalid Jewish passenger, Leon Klinghoffer, shot and thrown overboard. On December 27, 1985, terrorists struck at the El Al counter of Rome's Airport, leaving many dead and wounded. In June 1986, the Italian government signed an agreement with the U.S. for cooperation against terrorism.

The Lebanese war in 1982 and the Intifada in 1987 set off media campaigns against Israel, often tinged with antisemitism. Newborn Italian "Progressive Judaism" movements proposing a two-state solution for Israelis and Palestinians began a constructive dialogue with the traditionally critical Italian Left. An Israeli-Palestinian meeting was held in 1989 by the Milan Center for Peace in the Middle East. Jewish and Italian groups joined Shalom Akhshav in a Jerusalem "Time for Peace" march in 1989.

During the Gulf War, the Italy–Israel Friendship Association staged a 1,000-person Solidarity for Israel demonstration outside Israel's Rome Embassy.

On May 25, 1992, Oscar Luigi Scalfaro was elected president of the Italian Republic only two months after having been nominated the first president of the newly formed Italy-Israel Parliamentary Friendship Association. On March 20, he had defended Israel as "a land for which we Europeans have still not been able to assure the basic requisites of security."

Two Italian Jews were elected to parliament: Bruno Zevi on the Radical ticket in 1987 and Enrico Modigliani, a Republican, in 1992. With Italian support, the European Economic Community lifted the freeze on scientific cooperation with Israel in 1991.

In 1991/2 economic instability and political scandals shook coalition alliance parties and strengthened the newly emerged Northern Lombard League favoring regional autonomy, a stop to immigration, and the expulsion of southern Italian migrants. Italy's extreme-right fringe became more audacious, permitting Fascist salutes and racist slogans. There were antisemitic outbursts in sports stadiums (rival teams being referred to as "Jews"), desecrations of Jewish cemeteries, and violence against foreign immigrants. In June 1992 an international revisionist congress was held in Rome, but Italian authorities blocked further meetings.

A massive *Kristallnacht* anniversary demonstration against antisemitism in Italy's major cities on November 9, 1992, concluded a week of chain reactions to a misleadingly alarmistic report on antisemitism in the weekly *Espresso*. Following the issue, 30 Jewish stores in Rome were plastered with yellow stars with the message "Zionists Out of Italy" and other graffiti proclaimed "Jews – Back to Africa." About 100 Jewish youths then stormed the headquarters of the Fascist "Movimento Politico Occidentale."

At the end of 1992 parliament was debating a bill updating and reinforcing existing laws against antisemitism, neo-Fascism and racism in all its forms.

A record total of Italian tourists, mostly pilgrims, went to Israel in 1992. El Al increased flights and extended coverage to Venice, Verona, and Bergamo. From 1992 all organized pilgrimages included visits to Yad Vashem. In February 1991, Milan's Cardinal Martini led 1,250 pilgrims, traveling in four planes from Milan and two from Rome. The Italian Touring Club published its first "Green Guide" to Israel in 1993.

LEGAL AFFAIRS. A subject of central importance because of its possible impact on communal life was the proposed revision of the Concordat between Italy and the Vatican, in force since 1929. The question of the special role of Catholic religious norms admitted by the Italian Constitution and ordinary law, had a general relevance on the nature of the Italian state, and antagonized both Catholic and secular political forces. The Jews, more particularly, pointed to four areas of inequality in comparison to the Catholic majority, and supported reform of existing legislation:

(a) The Concordat virtually makes Catholicism the official religion of the state, other cults being merely "accepted," and therefore, although formally unequal, are free to organize themselves according to their own principles.

(b) Catholicism has a privileged status in public education.

(c) Although Catholic religious marriages are exclusively regulated by Canon law, they are granted civil validity, while in the case of Jews, religious and civil marriages, though usually performed by the same official in the synagogue, lead to separate jurisdictions in case of controversy.

(d) The Vatican has exclusive property rights and jurisdiction over all catacombs, including Jewish ones. In fact, the Jewish catacombs are closed and inaccessible, and there were fears of their being damaged and despoiled. The Jews asked that these monuments, of the greatest historical and religious importance, be turned over to the Jewish community, which would set up an international committee to supervise maintenance and further research and excavations.

The chance that all these points would be accepted for reformulation was actually remote. Related to revision of the Concordat was a possible reform of the Law of Jewish Communities (1930), under which membership in Jewish communities in Italy is compulsory. Certain Jewish circles advocated a new communal structure, based on voluntary membership. This was opposed by persons fearing it would considerably reduce the financial support to communities, impairing the functioning of their services, particularly of Jewish schools which provide at least a few years of Jewish instruction to about 75 percent of Jewish children in Italy. The largest complex is in Rome with 1,200 children between the ages of 5 and 18.

COMMUNITY LIFE. The Union of Italian Jewish Communities held national congresses in 1982, 1986, and 1990. Tullia Zevi, a journalist from Rome, was elected as the UIJC's first woman president in 1982, a position she still held in 1992. The 1982 keynote address on the importance of historical memory was written by Primo Levi, the distinguished novelist and Auschwitz survivor. The Italian Jewish biologist, Rita Levi Montalcini, co-winner of the 1986 Nobel Prize for medicine, addressed that year's UIJC Congress, which was also attended by the president of the Italian Republic, Francesco Cossiga.

In 1984, the Italian Constitutional Court repealed a 1930 law requiring compulsory membership and taxation of Jews by local communities. This law was successfully contested by a Libyan Jewish immigrant. In 1987, a new *intesa* (agreement) between the UIJC and the Italian government was signed, becoming effective in March 1989 and containing allowances for Sabbath requirements, legalizing rabbinic marriages, and making rabbinic ordination equivalent to university degrees.

Similar *intese* were stipulated with other religious minorities in Italy, and in 1992 negotiations began between the government and the c. 100,000-strong community of Muslim immigrants.

Italy became a state of religious pluralism on February 18, 1984, when a revised Concordat between the Holy See and the Italian Republic abolished Catholicism's privilege of being the "state religion," for the first time in 16 centuries. In December 1992 the UIJC decided to call a special national congress on the possibility of financing the Jewish communities by opting for voluntary contributions from tax payers of "8 per 1000 lire" of their income taxes – a system already adopted by the Catholic Church, Protestants, Seventh Day Adventists, and Mormons.

CULTURE. A large number of new books dealing directly or indirectly with Jewish subjects were published from the 1970s on, showing continued interest in the subject by a wide public. The most interesting new initiative was the series of books of Jewish culture issued by Carucci. They mainly included reprints of scholarly essays by such authors as Elia Benamozegh, Martin Buber, Umberto Cassuto, Dante Lattes; satirical Jewish poetry by Crescenzo Del Monte; translations and exegeses of biblical texts; an d a new demographic, sociological and political analysis of Italian Jewry by Sergio Della Pergola.

Fausta Cialente was awarded the 1976 Strega Prize for her *Le Quattro Ragazze Wieselberger*, including autobiographical flashbacks on Jewish society in Trieste at the turn of the century and in Egypt in the 1940s. The 1977 Portico d'Ottavia Prize was awarded to Richard Rubenstein for the Italian translation of his essay "The Religious Imagination," a psychoanalytical analysis of Jewish sources. Given honorable mention on the same occasion were Gitta Sereny's *In Quelle Tenebre* (a vivid evocation of the Holocaust) and Paolo De Benedetti's *La Chiamata Di Samuele*. A new volume of the scholarly *Yearbook of Jewish Studies* was issued by the Collegio Rabinico Italiano, now a division of an expanding Instituto Superiore di Studi Ebraici which provided a framework for scientific study and research on Jewish subjects. In June 1977 a new cultural popular festival was inaugurated in the area of the old ghetto in Rome, attracting for one day many thousands of Jews and non-Jews to theater, music, sport, and cooking exhibitions. Alberto Vigevani was awarded the literary prize Portico d' Ottavia for a collection of tales, *Fine delle domeniche*, bringing his youthful reminiscences of a vanishing Jewish identity in the assimilated, bourgeois environment of a small Jewish community. Elsa Morante's *La storia*, including vivid flashbacks to the ghetto of Rome during the Nazi occupation, was very favorably reviewed by literary circles and had a great commercial success. Several books were published on the history of local Jewish communities, most noteworthy of which was *Gli ebrei a Perugia* by Ariel Toaff. In 1976 the publication began of the scientific-historical review *Italia – Studi e ricerche sulla cultura e sulla letteratura degli ebrei d'Italia*. An interesting new edition of the Passover Haggadah was issued by the Federation of Jewish Youth in Italy, in which the translation of the traditional text was complemented by modern Jewish prose and partisan songs. Cultural links between Italy and Israel were strengthened after a new cultural agreement between the two countries became fully operative.

In May 1981 a five-day international congress, "Italia Judaica," was held in Bari under the joint sponsorship of the Italian Ministry for the Protection of Cultural Patrimony and Environment and the State Archives; the papers presented covered various aspects of Jewish history and culture in Italy.

JEWISH HERITAGE. Major efforts were made to preserve Italy's vast and precious but rapidly deteriorating Jewish heritage. Private foundations and government sponsorship could only partially cover the enormous costs required for maintenance and restoration.

The National Jewish Bibliographic Center was established in Rome in 1984 and in 1990 a new wing was inaugurated. In 1986 a grant from the Olivetti group permitted work to begin on the collection and preservation of about 25,000 volumes of archival and bibliographical materials from extinct and small communities all over Italy. Other contributions included a donation by Nobel Prize winner Rita Levi-Montalcini. Israeli experts came to help in the framework of Italy-Israel cultural agreements, and Father Pierfrancesco Fumagalli, secretary of the Vatican's Commission for Religious Relations with Jews, himself a specialist in illuminated Hebrew manuscripts, contributed from his expertise. In April 1992 a three-year agreement was made with the musicological departments of the University of Cremona and The Hebrew University for collecting, recording, and transcribing liturgical and other music by Italian Jewish composers for a special section of the Library.

The Vatican transferred the custody of the Roman Jewish catacombs to the Italian state in 1985; but for lack of funds for guards and upkeep, the Villa Torlonia catacombs are not yet open to the public.

The Venice and Rome synagogues were refurbished and the restoration of ancient synagogues and cemeteries in small communities were under way. Excavations in Calabria unearthed a fourth-century synagogue.

In 1990, the Italian government announced plans for renovating the Roman ghetto.

The works of Josef B. Sermoneta and Roberto Bonfil, both professors at The Hebrew University of Jerusalem, best articulate the problem of interpretation of Jewish culture in the Italian Renaissance. Sermoneta ("Aspetti del pensiero moderno nell'ebraismo italiano tra Rinascimento e età barocca," *Italia Judaica*, II, 1986) argued that the familiarity with Italian literary and cultural trends did not entail assimilation: in short, participating in the cultural enterprises of the Renaissance went hand in hand with asserting Jewish uniqueness and spiritual superiority. Bonfil (*Gli ebrei in Italia nell'epoca del Rinascimento* 1991) urged Jewish historians to renounce harmonistic interpretation and to study Jewish history "on its own terms," that is by defining the social status of Jews in Renaissance Italy, and then reconstructing their unique Jewish experience. The studies of David Ruderman, Michele Luzzati and Kenneth R. Stow show many interesting aspects of Italian Jewish history.

Congresses. Among initiatives made possible by renewed Italy-Israel cultural and scientific agreements were five international "Italia Judaica" conferences including in Genoa, 1984, on "Italian Jewry in the Renaissance and Baroque Periods"; in Tel Aviv, 1986, on "Jews in Italy from Ghetto Times to the First Emancipation"; in Siena, 1989, on "The Jews in United Italy 1870–1945"; and in Palermo, 1992, on "Jews in Sicily up to the Expulsion in 1492."

Throughout 1992 Italy commemorated the 500th anniversary of the arrival in Italy of Jews expelled from Spain. A major international congress was held in Genoa. In Ancona, a monument was unveiled to the memory of a group of Marranos burned at the stake in 1556.

Exhibitions. In 1989 a "Gardens and Ghettos" exhibition on Italian Jewish art was shown in New York and Ferrara, and 1992 saw an important exhibition in Rome of all Judaica literature published in Italy from 1955 to 1990.

HOLOCAUST STUDIES. A special commemorative edition of Italy's 1939 racial laws was published in 1989 by Italian authorities in Rome. In Florence, Israeli architect David Cassuto was awarded a silver medal in honor of his father, Rabbi Nathan Cassuto, for moral courage in wartime Italy.

In 1986, RAI-TV produced a series of programs on Nicola Caracciolo's book on Italians and Jews in World War II; in 1987 Susan Zuccotti's *The Italians and the Holocaust* was translated into Italian; in 1991 Liliana Picciotto Fargion's *Libro della Memoria* containing the individual stories of every deportee from 1943 to 1945, published by the Milan Jewish Documentation Center (CDEC), was presented in a solemn public ceremony in Rome.

EDUCATION AGAINST ANTISEMITISM AND ANTI-ZIONISM. In 1992, CDEC, with government sponsorship, inaugurated a

"Videothéque of Jewish Memory," offering 700 selected videocassettes for free loans to individuals and groups. On November 10, 1992, the Italian Ministry of Education made an agreement with the Union of Italian Jewish Communities on the use in schools of audiovisual programs on Jewish history. A course on Israel for high school teachers was held in Bergamo, organized by the Federation of Italy-Israel Friendship Associations.

CATHOLIC-JEWISH RELATIONS. A special document on Ecumenism by the Diocese of Rome in 1983 called for the Church to insure that sermons did not contain "any form or vestige of antisemitism," and called for "a rediscovery of our Jewish roots."

After the revision in 1984 of the Concordat between Italy and the Holy See, Catholicism was no longer a "state religion," and attendance at Catholic religious courses in schools became voluntary.

In 1985 the Vatican's Commission for Religious Relations with Jews promulgated *Notes on the Correct Way to Present Jews and Judaism in Preaching and Catechesis.* These were discussed in the Vatican by a Jewish delegation which was received by Pope John Paul II to mark the 20th anniversary of the *Nostra Aetate* declaration.

On April 13, 1986, John Paul II visited Rome's main synagogue, the first such visit by a pope in history, and addressed Jews as "our cherished older brothers."

In October 1986 the pope invited leaders of the world's main religions to prayer at Assisi. Judaism was represented by ADL Representative Dr. Joseph Lichten and Rome's Chief Rabbi Elio Toaff, who led a study session in front of an ancient synagogue.

In 1987 the pope received Austrian President Kurt Waldheim in private audience, arousing worldwide Jewish protest.

The 1988 the Vatican Document *The Church and Racism* contained the statement "Anti-Zionism serves at times as a screen for antisemitism, feeding on it and leading to it."

On January 17, 1990, the Italian Episcopal Conference celebrated its first annual national day of dialogue with Judaism in parish churches throughout Italy – so far the only national Episcopal Conference to have taken this initiative.

That same year the cult of "Saint Domenichino" (an alleged Jewish ritual murder victim) in Massa Carrara was abolished by the Catholic Church, declared illegitimate, and without any historical foundation.

In November 1990 the Pope declared that "Antisemitism is a sin against God and man," endorsing a statement made by the International Catholic-Jewish Liaison Committee in Prague, in September 1990.

On July 29, 1992, a bilateral permanent working commission was established between "the Holy See and the State of Israel, in order to study and define together issues of reciprocal interest and in view of normalizing relations," according to a joint communiqué. This was described as a first step toward diplomatic recognition.

SOVIET TRANSMIGRANTS IN ITALY. The last groups of Soviet transmigrants left Italy in 1990 after 100,000 had passed through Rome, Ostia, and Ladispoli during the previous two decades. Changed U.S. immigration laws in 1989 and direct processing of visas for Israel in Moscow, ended the flux that had been coordinated by HIAS, the Joint Distribution Committee, the Jewish Agency, and Italian authorities, who had set up schools and social centers, with religious help from the Lubavitch movement.

COMMUNITY LIFE, HISTORICAL MEMORY AND NATIONAL POLITICS IN THE MID-1990S. Two factors permeated Jewish debate in Italy in this period: (1) a series of half-century anniversaries all over the country, commemorating the World War II events related to Italian and international Holocaust history, and (2) the political rise of the "post-fascist" Alleanza Nazionale (AN) party led by Gianfranco Fini.

Meetings, debates, conventions, congresses, ceremonies and colloquiums were held in every region of Italy, organized by local authorities, often in co-operation with Jewish communities, to remember, and also to research and record, the unpublished memories of victims, rescuers, bystanders and all the rest of the generation that lived through the war and are very rapidly disappearing. Scores of new books on Jewish and war history appeared.

In 1994, national elections scheduled for March 27 conflicted with the first day of Passover and were extended to 10 p.m. March 28, after heated protest, to permit Jews to vote. The national elections of March 1994 resulted in a new Conservative conglomerate led by media tycoon Silvio Berlusconi, with a strengthened AN party in its midst.

Fini's courting of the Jewish community, in an effort to facelift his party and whitewash the past, met with consistent refusal by the elected leaders of Italian Jewry, even after the AN passed a motion at its national party meeting in February 1995 condemning antisemitism and calling the Fascist racial laws "an inestimable disgrace."

The quadrennial national Congress of the Union of Italian Jewish Communities (UIJC) held in Rome July 3–5, 1994, passed some significant political and community policy motions.

They expressed "concern over Italy's being the first country in the European Union in which forces having roots in fascism ... have become part of the governmental majority." They warned against "historical revisionism finding legitimization in a "gray area" equating the values of the struggle for liberation and Nazi-Fascism." They stressed Italian Jewry's commitment to the Constitution, individual freedoms, rights of minorities, pluralism, separation between Church and State, and demanded that international Jewish delegations visiting Italy confer with Italian Jewish leaders before scheduling meetings with Italian government officials.

As always, the UIJC Congress stressed its commitment to "the centrality of Israel" and "support for Israel's government."

Economic duress convinced representatives this time to accept the opportunity offered by the government to permit taxpayers to designate eight out of every 1,000 lire to the Jewish community (as many already do to the Catholic Church).

Equating rabbinical degrees from the Rome Rabbinical College with university degrees, and instituting a "laurea" in Jewish Studies at the College was proposed, and later achieved – although at the end of 1995, the latter is still considered an "experimental" degree.

A representative of the Lubavitch movement, which is present in nearly all Italian Jewish communities, was invited to join the Rabbinical Assembly.

Tullia Zevi was elected for her fourth term as president of the Union of Italian Jewish Communities.

At the end of 1995, Italian Jewry was faced with two other milestones in Jewish history: the murder of Yiẓḥak Rabin and the forthcoming trial of Nazi war criminal Erich Priebke, extradited in November from Argentina to Italy, co-responsible, as SS Col. Herbert Kappler's assistant, for the reprisal murder of 335 people, including 70 Jews, in the Ardeatine Caves in Rome in March, 1944.

GENERAL EVENTS. On January 12, 1993, the Ministry of Education introduced the study of contemporary history and the Holocaust into the school system, which previously ended with World War One.

On March 31, 1993, Tullia Zevi won the year's "Courage" prize for "commitment to tolerance and coexistence…." She was named "Knight of the Grand Cross of Merit of the Italian Republic" by the president of Italy, Oscar Luigi Scalfaro.

Nazi skinhead sections were closed down all over Italy as a result of new, stricter laws, but sporadic antisemitic and anti-Zionist incidents continued. On March 19, 1994, masked thugs broke into an exhibition on Israel in Brescia shouting "Zionist assassins," "Intifada," tearing down posters and leaving excrement on the floor.

A 750 lire stamp, issued September 25, 1993, designed by Eva Fischer, commemorated the wartime deportations. Other stamps designed by Ms. Fischer in 1995 commemorated the Montecassino battle and the Ardeatine Caves massacre.

The 50th annual anniversary of the *Jewish Brigade in Italy was celebrated in Piangipane Ravenna with services for those who fell; in Bari, a concert commemorated the landing of the Brigade.

Women increasingly occupy key positions in organized Italian Jewry. In addition to Tullia Zevi, President of the UIJC, women are presidents of five of Italy's 20 Jewish communities: Lia Tagliacozzo in Turin; Dora Bemporad in Florence; Celestina Ottolenghi in Ferrara; Bianca Finzi in Bologna; and Paola Bedarida in Leghorn.

In Spring 1995, Tullia Zevi suggested that European Community funds available to religious communities be used by the UIJC for Jewish monuments, libraries and youth activities, including international exchange.

Synagogues already restored and reopened after many years of neglect include: (a) the 1824 synagogue of Sabbioneta (province of Mantua) designed by Carlo Visioli, reopened 1993 after 10 years of work costing 100 million lire; (b) and the famous 400-year-old synagogue of Casale Monferrato and its 25-year-old museum; (c) the Pitigliano synagogue, which held its last Yom Kippur service in 1959, was festively re-opened to the recorded voice of the community's last cantor, Azeglio Servi; (d) the Pesaro synagogue, whose reconstruction by Italian Fine Arts authorities caused much controversy. The original light blue and gold-starred cupola of the Portuguese community was painted white; the ancient carved wood separation fence of the women's section was replaced instead of being restored; five inlaid wood rectangles in the entrance portals were replaced by six new ones. The 1437 cupola of the Cuneo synagogue, last restored in 1885, needs further reconstruction; 300 million lire more are needed above the 70 million spent (30 Jews have resettled in Cuneo and in 1995 the first bar mitzvah since the war was held.) The Synagogue of Alessandria was damaged by floods and needed repair. The 1875 Ivrea synagogue, falling apart, was handed over to the municipality in exchange for repairs not yet begun.

New Jewish museums opened in Bologna and Ferrara.

Projects under way include the restoration of the ancient Jewish quarter of Salemi, Sicily, made possible through a 50 billion lire grant by UNESCO. A research center, a kosher restaurant and 20 houses for scholars will be built.

Conventions and meetings on the many aspects of Jewish history in Italy took place in many towns, and the boom in Judaica publications continues. These include national, regional and municipal histories of Jewish life, Holocaust studies, and Jewish literature, including contemporary Israeli novelists in translation.

A major Italian Jewish convention, organized by Rabbi Shalom Bahbouth of the Department for Community Assistance (DAC), took place in Jesoli near Venice in 1994 on "Shalom and the Future of the Jewish People."

[Lisa Palmieri-Billig]

1995–2005. Among the main factors permeating Jewish life in Italy was the right-wing Alleanza Nazionale (AN), led by Gianfranco Fini, and the role of Silvio Berlusconi, chief of the Italian parliament since 2002, as well as the subject of the Holocaust, particularly since 2000 when the Italian parliament designated January 27 as Holocaust Remembrance Day, commemorating the liberation of Auschwitz. Efforts were made in the Italian Jewish communities to organize debates, conventions, congresses, ceremonies, and colloquiums, in order to promote the knowledge of Judaism and emphasize the importance of memory within non-Jewish society, though there have been complaints of a lack of activism in the promotion of internal culture, particularly in the small communities. The Lubavitch and Reform movements have been growing in many Italian cities. The Reform movement, called *Lev Cha-*

dash, was an absolute novelty in Italy. Founded in 2001 by a group of Italian Jews disagreeing with the Orthodox establishment in matters of conversion and mixed marriage, it had a great deal of success. In September 2004 Rabbi Barbara Aiello of the United States began her tenure at the Reform synagogue in Milan.

Even if less than in other countries, the risk of a new antisemitism nonetheless grew with a 2003 report showing a majority identifying Jews as the number one danger to world peace. A 2005 poll, under the rubric of "Italian Opinion on the Israeli-Palestinian Conflict and the Mideast Question," showed that a certain movement toward antisemitism, or at least a certain view of events, was emerging among Italians: 11% of those interviewed described themselves as either strongly or fairly strongly in agreement with the proposition that the Jewish Holocaust did actually happen but did not produce as many victims as is usually assumed. In particular, 34.1% of those interviewed described themselves as strongly or fairly strongly in agreement with another proposition, that is, that Jews secretly control economic and financial institutions as well as the media. In addition, 53.7% of Italians were very critical of the Israeli government's handling of the Palestinian question, while 77.8% were against the construction of the security fence that will separate Israelis and Palestinians. Another 35.9% of those interviewed agreed with the statement that the Sharon government was carrying out real genocide and treating the Palestinians the way that Nazis treated the Jews. Furthermore, even as Pope John Paul II and his successor Benedict XVI improved relations with the Jewish world, theological and political problems remained in relations between the Vatican and the Jewish communities concerning Israel.

In 1998 Amos Luzzatto, physician and scholar of Judaism, was elected president of the Union of Italian Jewish Communities. In 2002 Riccardo di Segni, a well-known radiologist and outstanding talmudist and historian, became the Italian chief rabbi, replacing Elio Toaff, who had held the office for 50 years. Riccardo di Segni is the author of numerous articles and books on Jewish culture and thought. He has lectured widely to university audiences, as well as in the community and synagogue. In 2005 Alfonso Arbib, a rabbi and educator of Tripoline origins, became chief rabbi of Milan, replacing Giuseppe Laras, who had held the office for more than 30 years. Among the outstanding scholars and active rabbis in Italy were Scialom Bahbout and Roberto Della Rocca. Scialom Bahbout, physician and researcher at the University La Sapienza of Rome, was the founder and director of Dac (Department for Assistance and Culture of UCEI). He also founded the Italian *bet midrash* Tifereth Yerushalaim in Jerusalem in 2003. Roberto Della Rocca is the director of the Department for Education and Culture (ex Dac) of UCEI, vice president of the Central Conference of Italian Rabbis, and professor of Judaism at the Pontificia Lateranense University in Rome.

Women continued to occupy key positions in organized Italian Jewry. In 2003 Sandra Crema Eckert became president of the Modena Jewish community.

The degree issued by the Collegio Rabbinico of Rome was made equal to the Italian Laurea. Jewish studies (history, philosophy, urban history) have been significantly upgraded in Rome, Venice, Bologna, Naples, Trieste, Pisa, and Milan. Italian-Israeli professors like Roberto Bonfil, Sergio DellaPergola, and Alfredo Mordechai Rabello of The Hebrew University, and Sergio Minerbi of Ben-Gurion University, maintained wide institutional relationships with the Italian academies and government. Also, the relationship between the Italian Jewish communities and the Italian Jews in Israel was quite close and allowed valuable cultural exchanges. In the field of Italian Jewish history, the studies of Michele Sarfatti and Liliana Picciotto Fargion shed new light on the extent of the Holocaust in Italy and Nazi-Fascist persecution. They belong to the CDEC, which continued to promote didactic activities and research on contemporary Italian Judaism, Shoah, and antisemitism for researcher, students, and schools.

Among the outstanding works with an Italian Jewish content was the film *La vita è bella* (*Life Is Beautiful*) in 1997 by Roberto Benigni, who won two Oscars for best foreign film and best actor. The film was considered a masterpiece. It also won the Oscar for original musical score. No other Italian film has received so much international recognition, having also won the First Prize at the 1998 Film Festival at Cannes. Because the protagonist, Guido, is well aware of what is happening but is determined to shield his son from the terrifying reality of the situation in the camps through the invention of an elaborate game, *Life Is Beautiful* came under attack in some circles for mocking the Holocaust.

In Milan, under the supervision of Maria Modena Mayer, professor of Hebrew literature at the Statale University, the Association of Friends of The Hebrew University of Jerusalem (AUG) and the Vigevani Foundation have organized many scientific congresses and colloquiums and given scholarships to Italian scholars and students to study in Israel. Furthermore, in 1996, the Center Judaica Goren-Goldstein was founded in Milan thanks to cooperation between the Cuker Goldstein Goren Foundation and the Statale University in Milan, devoted to teaching Jewish thought and culture. In addition to *La Rassegna Mensile d'Israel*, which continued its activity under the direction of Amos Luzzatto, other journals of Italian Jewish studies were published: *Italia – Studi e ricerche sulla cultura e sulla letteratura degli ebrei d'Italia* (since 1976), *Zakhor* (since 1997), and *Materia Giudaica* (since 1996). There were also well-organized websites: www.morasha.it, giving an overview of Italian Jewry and culture; www.torah.it, which offers the possibility of improving knowledge in Judaic matters; and www.informazionecorretta.com and www.israele.net focusing on information on Israel. The Jewish Giuntina publishing house of Florence produced new books on Jewish history and culture, and translations from the Hebrew, English, and Yiddish of classical Jewish works. The Jewish Belforte publishing house of Leghorn also published books of various kinds on Judaism. Furthermore, the Zamorani publishing house of Turin is devoted to the publication of historical texts. In 2002–3 Pavia University, under the direction of Professor Paola Vita Finzi and Eng. Vittorio Modena, conducted a research project – Israeli Financing Innovation Schemes for Europe (IFISE) – among many European, Italian, and Israeli universities and institutions to arrive at a methodology for the creation of seed and start-up capital sources for high-tech firms in Europe, following the Israeli success stories of Yozma and the Technological Incubators Programs and its application to Italian conditions.

[Robert Bonfil (2nd ed.)]

Relations with Israel

Although Italy was one of the Axis powers during World War II, this fact left no imprint on her relations with Israel. The active help given in Italy to the survivors of the Holocaust from all over Europe – in particular toward their migration to Palestine – and the fact that, even under the Fascist regime, Italy did not participate in the horrors perpetrated by her German ally but rather actually helped in the rescue work, served to place Israel-Italian relations on a regular footing from the outset. When the young State of Israel approached the question of her foreign ties, Italy was among the first countries in which an Israeli diplomatic mission was established. Israel established an embassy in Rome and a consulate-general in Milan (the Israeli ambassador also maintains contact with the *Vatican), and Italy's embassy was located in Tel Aviv. The development of essential ties, however, was quite slow, due mainly to Italy's postwar policy, the principal aims of which were settlements of territorial questions directly relating to her and a return to a position of equality in the family of nations. Over the years, increased contacts and a strengthening of ties was achieved, because of Italy's rising influence in the various European organizations in which Israel was actively interested; the rise in Italy's position as a Mediterranean country, and her anxiety in view of the Soviet Union's increasing penetration into the Mediterranean basin; the decline – from Israel's point of view – in France's influence after her change in policy on the eve of the *Six-Day War (1967); and the great diplomatic ability Italy displayed when an El Al plane was hijacked to Algeria in 1968 (the release of the plane, its crew, and passengers were secured through Italy's intervention), and when a TWA plane was hijacked to Damascus in 1969 and six Israelis were held prisoners after the release of the rest of the passengers.

Objective difficulties existed in some areas, such as that of commercial ties, since the economies of the two countries had a certain similarity in important fields of production (e.g., citrus), and it was therefore not easy to realize their mutual desire to increase trade between the two countries. Italy even placed obstacles in the way of Israel's affiliation with the Common Market because of citrus competition. Italy's active ties with Israel were linked to its general relationship with the Middle East, in which it had important interests. It did not develop a unilateral policy on the question of the Israel-Arab dispute, and its cautious diplomatic initiatives were aimed at advancement toward a negotiated peace.

[Yohanan Meroz]

The significant improvement in relations between Italy and Israel under the Berlusconi government and the historic visit of Gianfranco Fini to Jerusalem in 2003, when he repudiated the Nazi-Fascist Republic of Salò for the first time, are developments at the center of discussion within Jewish communities. In particular, Giulio Terzi di Sant'Agata, Italy's ambassador to Israel during 2001–3, worked to improve these relations between the two states with great success. Meanwhile, the majority of Italian leftists continued to support the Palestinian cause. In 2002 the liberal newspaper *Il Foglio* organized a demonstration in Rome in support of Israel, called Israel Day, with a large turnout of Italian citizens, politicians, and journalists.

[Robert Bonfil (2nd ed.)]

The dominant pattern of an excess of Israeli imports over exports to Italy continued. Thus exports from Italy to Israel rose from $13.6 million in 1960 to $314.9 million in 1980, whereas imports to Italy rose from $10.6 million in 1960 to $285.1 million in 1980. In 2004 exports to Italy stood at $810 million, while imports climbed to $1,566 million. A considerable expansion in the number of tourists from Italy to Israel, which rose steadily from 2,400 in 1960 to 37,000 in 1977 and 55,800 in 1980, indicated the growing interest for the Holy Land among Jews and non-Jews. In 2004, 42,000 Italians visited Israel.

Musical Tradition

The various strata of Italian Jewry and the diverse origins of the Jewish communities are reflected in the variety of their musical traditions. Six stylistic traditions can be distinguished:

(1) The Italian rite (also called *lo'azi, Italki* or *Italyani*) came to the communities of north central Italy in the late Middle Ages. In 1970 it was still in use in "Italian rite synagogues" of Turin, Padua, Mantua, Venice, Ferrara, Alessandria, Ancona and Siena. In Pitigliano, Reggio Emilia, and Florence it ceased some decades earlier. In Milan and Bologna it was adopted in the modern synagogues.

(2) Sephardi rites and chants which came from Spain, either directly or by way of North Africa, to the communities on the west coast, chiefly Leghorn. Their use eventually spread to Genoa, Naples, Pisa, and in the 19th century to Florence (where they replaced the Italian rite and its melodies).

(3) The Sephardi chant, originating partially from Marranos in Spain but mainly from the Balkan Peninsula and the Orient, and received by the communities on the Adriatic coast, chiefly Venice, and later Trieste, Ferrara, and Ancona. In the Venetian "colonies" of Spalato and Ragusa this tradition is extinct.

(4) The rite of three small communities in Piedmont: Asti, Fossano, and Moncalvo (extinct), which were settled by Jews from France in the 14th to 15th century, and called *APAM after their Hebrew initials.

(5) The Ashkenazi rite used by the communities of south-German origin formed in the 16th–17th century at Casale Mon-

ferrato, Padua, Verona, Venice, Gorizia. It is extinct in Rovigo, Vercelli, Modena, Sandaniele del Friuli, and other small centers.

(6) Rome, where until the beginning of the 20th century various congregations had "*Scole*" (synagogues) which, according to their origin, were called Sicilian, Castilian, Catalan, or Italian. In the 20th-century Great Synagogue, inaugurated in 1904, the different musical traditions fused into a single rite, in which the Italian element predominated, but in which the influences of Sephardi chant and ancient and modern Roman Christian liturgy could be discerned.

The most important element common to these different traditions is the Italian pronunciation of Hebrew. Because of the nasalization of the *ayin*, the loss of the *he*, the pronunciation of the *tav* without *dagesh* as *d*, and especially since all the vowels (including the *sheva na* at the beginning and frequently at the end of a word) are fully pronounced, a peculiar sonorousness of musical expression emerged which completely Italianized the tunes, including those of German and Spanish origin. Concomitantly, the chants of Germanic origin underwent a leveling of their pentatonic and characteristically wide intervals, and those of Oriental origin lost such exotic elements as the interval of the augmented second, the plaintive and excessively melismatic turns, and the coloratura passages. The majority of the chants and their style of performance are characterized in all Italian rites by an ecclesiastical solemnity or, at times, by operatic idioms. In the 18th–19th centuries, the singing was also influenced by the "learned" styles of Italian music or by popular songs.

In the synagogues built according to the "Italian plan," i.e., bipolar construction, the *tevah* or *bimah* is situated in an elevated niche, like a counterapse, in the western wall opposite the *aron*; the benches are therefore arranged in two rows along the northern and southern walls and the worshipers are thus able to see the face and gestures of the *ḥazzan*. The singing therefore developed responsorial forms with much public participation. Under the direction of the *ḥazzan*, who became a kind of conductor of this homophonous choir, there was participation even in the recital of the introductory formulae of the *Shema* and the psalms. In the 19th century, with the construction of modern synagogues where the *bimah* is closer to the *aron*, participation by the public was reduced; but following the example of the Reform synagogues in Vienna and Paris, an organized choir (male, sometimes mixed or female) was introduced for which new collections of liturgical chants were composed, even in such small Jewish communities as those in Vercelli, Asti, Trieste, Saluzzo, and Mantua. Those chants were composed mainly in 19th-century idiom, reminiscent of the operatic style of Verdi or Rossini, or based on patriotic songs of the Italian Risorgimento in which the Jews had enthusiastically taken part. This music required the use of an organ; however, after World War II, the organ was abolished in all Italian Jewish communities. It should be noted that the development of "cultured" 19th-century music had its precedents in many Italian cities in the art music composed for synagogue use by Jewish and some non-Jewish musicians during the ghetto period of the 17th and 18th centuries. In the 16th and 17th centuries, Jewish musicians and composers were greatly appreciated by, and enjoyed the favor of, the local rulers. Salomone de Rossi of Mantua, Leone de Modena of Venice, and the Christian Carlo Grossi of Modena are examples of this Jewish-Italian musical symbiosis.

The Italian rite in Rome and in the northern communities possesses its own tradition of biblical cantillation in the reading of the **parashah*, the **haftarah* (including a special "festive" intonation of the *haftarah*), and in the sung rendition of the psalms. This tradition is documented in the notations of *parashah* and *haftarah* tunes published by Giulio *Bartolocci (1693) and in the intonation of the psalms, noted first by E. Bottrigari (1599) and some years later by Jacob b. Isaac Finzi, *ḥazzan* of the Ashkenazi community of Casale Monferrato, according to the tradition of his teacher, R. Abraham Segre (preserved in the Hebrew manuscript, Jews College, London, Montefiore 479, fol. 147b).

In this tradition, only five or six of the main (disjunctive) accents are rendered by musical motives of their own, the subservient (conjunctive) accents being disregarded. The application of the motives does not coincide with the "Tiberian" accentuation system with which the biblical text is provided, implying the existence of an independent system based on an oral tradition. This independent system is related to the old Near Eastern practice of Ekphonesis, an early Byzantine term meaning public reading of the Scriptures. Since the Italian rite derives from the Palestinian which dates from an earlier period than the one in which the Tiberian system of the Masoretic accents became established, it may be proposed that this method of biblical cantillation is equally ancient.

The cantillation is limited to a strictly tetrachordal (four-tone) range, and tends to be syllabic, without melismas, the musical motifs being spread over entire words or groups of words. In the Sephardi and Ashkenazi synagogues of Italy, too, this syllabic rendition prevails in biblical cantillation and even more so in the melodies of the prayers. The medieval and Oriental taste for melismatics is preserved only in some archaic melodies of the APAM rite or in rites of more conservative and isolated centers such as Gorizia (Ashkenazi) and Leghorn (Sephardi). However, there too, cantorial improvisation in the Oriental style is excluded, the melodic formulas for each liturgical ceremony being fixed by tradition in the form of leitmotiv-like systems which are peculiar to each community. Italian rabbis often protested against the melismatic influences of Oriental or Ashkenazi *ḥazzanim* on the repertoire of a community, not only because they wished to keep the local musical traditions intact, but because melismas interrupted or distorted the rendering of the text according to the correct grammatical accentuation.

No liturgical or quasi-liturgical Judeo-Italian vernacular songs are found in the tradition, and perhaps none existed. There are, however, a few exceptions: songs in "Bagitto" (the Jewish Livornese dialect), in Judeo-Corfiote (in Trieste), and in Piedmontese-Jewish, all of which are translations of Hebrew Passover songs, Purim parodies, and the like. Moreover, in the middle of the 19th century, some poems written in Hebrew, with parallel Italian translation, were set to compositions and popular anthems of the Risorgimento to celebrate the emancipation of the Jews.

The hymns of the proselytes of San Nicandro, created between 1930 and 1950, form a separate and peculiar repertoire. The hymns are of biblical inspiration, but the language is the dialect of the Gargano-Puglia region and the melodies are adaptations of regional songs. Women perform the hymns in a kind of primitive polyphony.

The only systematic collection of traditional synagogal melodies for the annual liturgical cycle is Federico *Consolo's *Libro dei canti d'Israele* (1892), containing the Sephardi tradition of Leghorn. A collection of Ashkenazi melodies of Ferrara was made in 1925–35 on the initiative of A.Z. *Idelsohn, but most of the material has been lost. A collection from the present repertoire of the Roman synagogue has been published by A. Piatelli (see bibliography). An early and interesting musical transcription is the "Twelve Biblical Intonations" of the Ashkenazi and Sephardi Jews of Venice. Performed by the gentile composer Benedetto Marcello, they were used by him as a melodic basis for his psalm-paraphrases in the paraphrases, *Estro poetico-armonico* (Venice, 1724–27).

[Leo Levi]

BIBLIOGRAPHY: The history of the Jews in Italy has attracted the attention of a considerable number of scholars. Over 2,000 major and minor historical works have been published of local, regional, or general interest. A complete classified bibliography may be found in: A. Milano, *Bibliotheca historica italo-judaica* (1954), with supplements in 1964 and in: RMI (Nov. 1966). Complete histories are: C. Roth, *History of the Jews of Italy* (1946); A. Milano, *Storia degli ebrei in Italia* (1963); and on a smaller scale, G. Volli, *Breve storia degli ebrei d'Italia* (1961); C. Roth, *Jews in the Renaissance* (1959); and the corresponding work in Hebrew, M.A. Szulwas, *Ḥayyei ha-Yehudim be-Italyah bi-Tekufat ha-Renaissance* (1955); as well as collections of essays by the last-named writers, all dealing with individual aspects of Italian Jewish history. See also bibliographies to articles on specific cities, in particular *Rome, *Leghorn, *Venice, *Florence, and *Mantua. FASCIST PERIOD: J. Starr, in: JSOS, 1 (1939), 105–24; M. Michaelis, in: *Yad Vashem Studies*, 4 (1960), 7–41; D. Carpi, *ibid.*, 43–56; idem, in: *Rivista di studi politici internazionali*, 28 (1961) 35–56; idem, in: *Dappim le-Ḥeker ha-Sho'ah ve-ha-Mered*, 3 (1968); R. de Felice, *Storia degli ebrei italiani sotto il fascismo* (1961): U. Nahon, in: *Scritti… Leone Carpi* (1967), 261–84; R. Katz, *Black Sabbath* (1970). CONTEMPORARY PERIOD: R. Bachi, in: JJSO, 4 (1962), 172–91; Unione delle Communità Israelitiche Italiane, VII Congresso, *Relazione del Consiglio (1966–5726)* (1966); F. Sabatello, in: P. Glikson and S. Ketko (eds.), *Jewish Communal Service* (1967), 107–12; S. della Pergola, in: *Bi-Tefuẓot ha-Golah*, 10:1–2 (1968), 159–77. MUSICAL TRADITION. SOURCES: Jews' College, London, Ms. Montefiore no. 479, fol. 147b: Notation of Psalm intonation by J. Finzi in Casale-Monferrato, 1600; S. Rossi, *Ha-Shirim asher li-Shelomo* (Venice, 1622–23); A. Kircher, *Musurgia Universalis* (Rome, 1650), pt. 1, 64–67; G. Bartolocci, *Bibliotheca magna rabbinica*, 4 (Rome, 1675–93; repr. 1969), 427–41; M. Zahalon, *Meẓiẓ u-Meliẓ* (Venice, 1715); B. Marcello, *Estro poetico-armonico* (Venice, 1724–26); F. Consolo, *Libro dei canti d'Israele* (1892); E. Ventura, et al., in: RMI, 5 (1931), 429–32; A.Z. Idelsohn, in: HUCA, 11 (1936), 569–91; E. Piattelli, *Canti liturgici ebraici di rito italiano* (1967); STUDIES: E. Birnbaum, *Juedische Musiker am Hofe von Mantua* (1893); E. Werner, in: MGWJ, 81 (1937), 393–416; L. Levi, in: *L'Approdo*, 3 (1954), 37–44; idem, in: *Sefer ha-Mo'adim* (1954), 182–6; idem, in: RMI, 23 (1957), 403–11, 435–45; 27 (1961); idem, in: *Yeda Am*, 2 (1955/56), 59–69; idem, in: Centro Nazionale Studi di Musica Popolare, Roma, *Studi e Ricerche* (1960), 50–68; idem, in: *Scritti… G. Bedarida* (1966), 105–36; Adler, Prat Mus, index; idem, in: *Jewish Mediaeval and Renaissance Studies* (1967), 321–64; S. Naumbourg (ed.), *Cantiques de Salomon Rossi* (1877, repr. 1954); F. Rikko (ed.), *Salomon Rossi, Ha-Shirim asher li-Shelomo*, 3 vols. (1967–). **ADD. BIBLIOGRAPHY:** D.A.L. Bidussa, G.L. Voghera. *Oltre il ghetto: momenti e figure della cultura ebraica in Italia tra l'Unità e il fascismo* (2005); R. Bonfil, *Rabbis and Jewish Communities in Renaissance Italy* (Heb., 1979; published for the Litman Library by Oxford University Press, 1990); idem, *Gli ebrei in Italia nell'epoca del Rinascimento* (1991); idem, *Tra due mondi. Cultura ebraica e cultura cristiana nel Medioevo* (1996); E. Capuzzo, *Gli ebrei nella società italiana: comunità e istituzioni tra Ottocento e Novecento* (1999); E. Collotti, *Il Fascismo e gli ebrei. Le leggi razziali in Italia* (2003); S. DellaPergola, *Anatomia dell'ebraismo italiano: caratteristiche demografiche, economiche, sociali, religiose e politiche di una minoranza* (1976); R. De Felice, *Storia degli ebrei italiani sotto il fascismo* (1961, 19884; *Jews in Fascist Italy: A History* (2001)); E.R. Gruber, *Virtually Jewish. Reinventing Jewish Culture in Europe* (2002); B.D. Ruderman (ed.), *Preachers of the Italian Ghetto* (1992); idem, *Essential Papers on Jewish Culture in Renaissance and Baroque Italy* (1992); G. Fabre, *Mussolini razzista: dal socialismo al fascismo: la formazione di un antisemita* (2005); A. Milano, *Storia degli ebrei in Italia* 1963 (rist. 1992); G. Formiggini, *Stella d'Italia Stella di David. Gli ebrei dal Risorgimento alla Resistenza* (1970, repr. 1998); *Italia judaica: gli ebrei in Italia tra Rinascimento ed età barocca*: atti del 2. Convegno internazionale, Genova 10–15 giugno 1984 (1986); *Italia judaica. Atti del III Convegno internazionale* (1989); L. Picciotto Fargion, *Il Libro della memoria. Gli Ebrei deportati dall'Italia (1943–1945). Ricerca del Centro di Documentazione Ebraica Contemporanea* (1991, 2002[2]); M. Sarfatti *Mussolini contro gli ebrei. Cronaca dell'elaborazione delle leggi del 1938* (1994); idem, *Gli ebrei nell'Italia fascista: vicende, identità, persecuzione* (2000); G. Schwarz, *Ritrovare se stessi: gli ebrei nell'Italia postfascista* (2004); A. Stille, *Benevolence and Betrayal: Five Italian Jewish Families under Fascism* (1991); R.K. Stow, *Theater of Acculturation: The Roman Ghetto in the Sixteenth Century* (2000); M. Toscano, *Ebraismo e antisemitismo in Italia: dal 1848 alla guerra dei sei giorni* (2003); C. Vivanti (ed.), *Gli Ebrei in Italia, I. Dall'Alto Medioevo all'Età dei Lumi* (1996); idem (ed.), *Gli Ebrei in Italia, II. Dall'emancipazione a oggi* (1997); K. Voigt, *Il rifugio precario. Gli esuli in Italia dal 1933 al 1945*, 2 vols. (1993 and 1996); M. Michaelis, *Mussolini and the Jews: German-Italian Relations and the Jewish Question in Italy, 1922–1945* (1978); idem, *La Persecuzione degli ebrei durante il fascismo: Le leggi del 1938* (1998); M. Sarfatti: *Le leggi antiebraiche spiegate agli italiani di oggi* (2002); S. Zuccotti, *The Italians and the Holocaust: Persecution, Rescue, and Survival* (1987); *Dalle leggi antiebraiche alla Shoah: Sette anni di storia italiana 1938–1945* (2004); D. Carpi, *Between Mussolini and Hitler: The Jews and the Italian Authorities in France and Tunisia* (1994).

ITELSON, GREGOR (1852–1926), philosopher. Itelson, who was born in Zhitomir, studied in St. Petersburg. He left Russia in 1884 and settled in Berlin. He was interested in the investigation of the philosophical foundations of the sciences and sought to reform the principles of logic. He had a direct influence on the representative philosophical and scientific thinkers of his time. In a particularly significant lecture delivered before the Second Philosophical Congress (Geneva, 1904), Itelson endeavored to liberate logic from its dependence on psychology and restore its lost autonomy by redefining it as "the science of objects in general, existent and nonexistent." This definition was directly opposed to the accepted view of logic as the science of thought. His conception was close to the views evolved at that time by Meinong, Husserl, and Couturat as a result of the influence of Bolzano. Itelson's theories drew him close to "the algebra of logic"; he also tried to find a logical basis for mathematics, which he defined as "the science of ordered objects." During the last years of his life Itelson taught at the Juedische Volkshochschule, Berlin. His extensive library was bequeathed to the Jewish National and University Library in Jerusalem.

BIBLIOGRAPHY: KS, 3 (1927), 242; *Kantstudien*, 31 (1926), 428–30; *Revue de métaphysique et de morale* (1904), 1037ff.

[Samuel Hugo Bergman]

ITHAMAR (Heb. אִיתָמָר; "father of Tamar"?), fourth and youngest son of *Aaron (Ex. 6:23; Num. 26:60; I Chron. 24:1). Another explanation is "Isle of Palms." Akkadian and Ugaritic √ʾ*mr* "see" could result in "He-is-Seen." At first Ithamar served as priest together with all three of his brothers (Ex. 28:1; Num. 3:2–3) while they were all alive, and after the death of *Nadab and *Abihu (Lev. 10:12; Num. 3:4; I Chron. 24:2) with *Eleazar, the other survivor and the designated successor to the high priesthood (Num. 20:28; cf. 25:13; et al.). During the wanderings in the wilderness Ithamar was assigned special duties as leader over all the Levites (Ex. 38:21) and as officer in charge of the *Gershonites (Num. 4:28) and Merarites (Num. 4:33; 7:8) in connection with the Tent of Meeting. The house of Eli apparently traced descent to Ithamar (cf. I Sam. 14:3; I Chron. 24:3; so Yal., Shofetim 68; Jos., Ant., 5:361.

[Nahum M. Sarna]

In the Aggadah

Ithamar was the third person in all Israel to be taught the Torah by Moses (i.e., after Aaron and Eleazar). He sat on Aaron's left while the rest of Israel received instruction (Er. 54b). Ithamar ultimately succeeded Eleazar as high priest (PdRK 37:134) and the office remained in his family for 42 years, until the death of the sons of Eli. God then promised that the post would return to the family of Eleazar through Zadok (a descendant of Phinehas; Yal., Shofetim, 68).

BIBLIOGRAPHY: Westphal, in: ZAW, 26 (1906), 222–5; Meek, in: AJSLL, 45 (1929), 158–60, 165; Moehlenbrink, in: ZAW, 52 (1934), 214–5, 217–9, 225; Meisler (Mazar), in: *Leshonenu*, 15 (1947), 40. IN THE AGGADAH: Ginzberg, Legends, 3 (1925), 134, 144; Y. Ḥasida, *Ishei ha-Tanakh* (1964), 61. **ADD. BIBLIOGRAPHY:** W. Propp, in: ABD, 3:579–81.

ITINERARIES OF EREẒ ISRAEL. Apart from the accounts of their experiences which were recorded by Jewish wayfarers to Ereẓ Israel, which constitute a good part of Jewish travel literature of the Middle Ages, from an early date pious pilgrims set down lists of the places in the country which those who followed them might wish to visit. When in the course of the Middle Ages, presumably under Christian and Muslim influence, significance began to be attached to the intercession of the departed righteous before the divine throne, these came to be considered of importance as places of efficacious prayer. In some cases (e.g., Rachel or the Patriarchs), the place or region of burial was indicated in the Bible; in others, the names of biblical heroes and saints were connected with ancient sepulchers (or in some cases probably to caves which might have served as sepulchers) in the neighborhood of the places with which their life activity was associated. Later on, as talmudic study strengthened its hold, a similar significance began to be attached to the sepulchers or reputed sepulchers of sages of the mishnaic or amoraic period.

Lists of the principal places of pilgrimage in this sense began to be compiled at a relatively early date. The account of Samuel b. Samson (1211) of his travels in the Holy Land is in effect no more than such a travel guide, although couched in the first person. In due course, these itineraries assumed an almost stereotyped form. The title generally given them was "*Iggeret Mesapperet Yiḥusei ha-Ẓaddikim*" ("Epistle Recounting the Ascription of the Righteous") or something similar – they were sometimes accompanied by the form of prayer to be recited over the graves in general or certain individual graves. After the invention of printing these were in due course published, probably for distribution by Emissaries for the Holy Land in the course of their missions – sometimes as broadside sheets. Such publications appeared under various titles such as *Iggeret Mesapperet Yaḥasuta de-Ẓaddikayya di-ve-Ara de-Yisrael* (Venice, 1590, 1599, 1626 (broadside), 1640; Mantua, 1676, appended to the *Ḥokhmat ha-Mishkan* by Joseph Shallit *Richietti, Verona, 1680; and in North Europe in Frankfurt without date, broadside). Under the title of *Yiḥus ha-Ẓaddikim* there is a similar but more ample work by Gershom Scaramella, embodying also prayers and readings at the sacred sites, published by Jacob of Gazzolo at Mantua in 1561 (repr. Venice, 1598). In the Renaissance period, illustrated editions of Christian itineraries to the Holy Land began to be published. Influenced perhaps by this, Italian Jews at this period produced illustrated copies of these itineraries, using as their basis, apparently, a text drawn up about 1537 by an anonymous writer, though the prototype may go back half a century earlier. Normally, a scroll form was used, possibly for display. Each brief paragraph, containing a listing in rough geographical order of places in Ereẓ Israel and of the graves of the righteous or holy sites situated in each, would be followed by a row of colored pictures representing the sites in question. Originally, they were probably drawn from reality, however approximately, but in due course, as a result of more and more recopying, they tended to lose their relation to fact. Thus, for the sake of symmetry, in the conventional representation of Gaza, what had originally been the cupola of a mosque in the center of the town became converted into the city gate! The series would sometimes be introduced by a wholly midrashic representation (bearing no relation whatsoever to actuality) of Jericho within a seven-fold maze. A few sites outside Ereẓ Israel closely connected with Jewish or biblical history (e.g., Cairo, Damascus) would also be included with their synagogues, etc. It is possible that these parchment scrolls were also prepared by emissaries of the Holy Land as gifts to munificent contributors. Illuminated itineraries of this type in scroll form, basically very similar, are in the libraries of the Jewish Theological Seminary of America (Mss. Adler 1641 and 2910) and of the Hebrew University of Jerusalem (Ms. Heb. 8° 1187); others are in private collections. Another, now untraceable, by Uri b. Simeon of Biella provided the crude cuts reproduced by Hottinger in his *Cippi Hebraici* (Heidelberg, 1659). But the usage was protracted long afterwards: a paper and vellum scroll of the sort of Yemenite origin of the late 19th century is in the Lenin State Library in Moscow (Ms. Ginzburg 579). A similar text converted into volume form and copied at Casale in northern Italy in 1598 in the collection of C. Roth was published by him in 1929 in facsimile under the misleading title *The Casale Pilgrim*.

BIBLIOGRAPHY: Sukenik, in: KS, 7 (1930/31), 99–101; Narkiss, in: *Ommanut*, 2 (1941), 7–10; Z. Vilnay, in: *Maẓẓevot Kodesh* (1963²); M. Ish-Shalom, *Masei Noẓerim le-Ereẓ Yisrael* (1965), 3–49; P. Thomsen, *Palaestina-Literatur*, 7 vols. (1908–60), passim; T. Tobler, *Bibliographia geographica Palaestinae* (Ger., 1867).

[Cecil Roth]

ITINERARIUM ANTONINI, Roman roadbook, dating mainly from the early third century C.E. It gives the distances between major cities of the Roman Empire. Though ascribed to the emperor *Antoninus Pius, it is hardly an official publication. It is assigned by some critics to a Christian named Aethicus Ister, but most probably is a composite work by several authors. The work is of value in establishing the sites and names of the following towns in Ereẓ Israel (alternative names in parentheses): Ptolemais (Acre), Sycamina (Haifa), Caesarea, Betar (Bethar), Diospolis (Lydda), Iamnia (Jabneh), Ascalona (Ashkelon), Gaza, Gadara, Scythopolis (Beth-Shean), Neapolis (Nablus), and Elia (Jerusalem).

BIBLIOGRAPHY: O. Cuntz (ed.), *Itineraria Romana*, 1 (1929); Pauly-Wissowa, 18 (1916), 2320–63.

[Louis Harry Feldman]

ITINERARIUM HIEROSOLYMITANUM OR ITINERARIUM BURDIGALENSE (Lat., "Jerusalem itinerary" or "Bordeaux itinerary"), a work, probably written by a Christian c. 333 C.E., describing a route for travel from Bordeaux to Jerusalem, and the return trip from Heraclea (in Thrace) through Rome, and ending in Milan. The author often points out sites of historical and religious significance, especially those in and near Jerusalem. Among the numerous places in Palestine mentioned are Ptolemais (Acre), Sicaminos (Haifa), Mt. Carmel, Caesarea, Isdradela (Yezreel), Scythopolis (Beth-Shean), Sechim (Nablus), Hiericho (Jericho), Bethleem (Bethlehem), Bethasora (Beth-Zur), Cebron (Hebron), Nicopolis (Amwas), and Lidda (Lydda). Though in many ways this *Itinerarium* is very similar to the *Itinerarium Antonini, the precise relationship between the two works is not clear.

BIBLIOGRAPHY: O. Cuntz (ed.), *Itineraria Romana*, 1 (1929), 86–102.

[Howard Jacobson]

ITTAI (Heb. אִתַּי), name of two biblical figures. The etymology of the name is uncertain.

(1) The Gittite, i.e., the man of Gath, leader of a unit of six hundred Gittite mercenaries in David's service. He is specifically referred to as a "foreigner" in II Samuel 15:19, but swears fealty to David in words reminiscent of Ruth's pledge to Naomi. He and his unit joined David on his flight from Jerusalem on the outbreak of Absalom's rebellion (II Sam. 15:18–23), and in the battle with the rebels he commanded one of the three divisions in which David's forces were grouped (II Sam. 18:2, 5).

(2) Also called Ithai (אִיתַי – I Chron. 11:31), son of Ribai of Gibeah, of the tribe of Benjamin and one of David's thirty "mighty men" (II Sam. 23:29; I Chron. 1:31).

BIBLIOGRAPHY: Maisler (Mazar), in: BJPES, 13 (1947), 112; Yeivin, in: Y. Liver (ed.), *Historyah Ẓeva'it shel Ereẓ Yisrael…* (1964), 161–2. **ADD. BIBLIOGRAPHY:** C. Ehrlich, in: ABD, 3, 583.

ITZIG, DANIEL (also called **Daniel Jaffe** or **Daniel Berlin**; 1723–1799), German banker, entrepreneur, and leader of the Berlin Jewish community. The son of a horse merchant, Itzig married into the wealthy Wulff family and began his career as purveyor of silver to the royal mint. This activity reached its peak during the Seven Years' War (1756–63) when *Frederick II gave Itzig and V.H. *Ephraim contracts for financing the war through the issuance of successive series of debased coinage. In 1761 Itzig received the rights of a Christian merchant. After the war he invested his money in manufacturing leather and iron goods, built himself a palace, and established a bank. Itzig was appointed chief representative of Prussian Jewry by Frederick II and in 1787 was head of the commission which prepared suggestions for the improvement of the status of Prussian Jewry. From Frederick William II, whose confidential financier he was, he received, on May 2, 1791, the coveted *Naturalisationspatent*, bestowing full citizenship on him and his entire family. He was the first Prussian Jew to be so honored. In 1797 he was appointed court banker and inspector of road construction. In 1798 *Frederick William III refused the Berlin Jewish community's 1795 request, in which Itzig was first signator, for improved conditions.

In 1761 Itzig envisaged a school for poor children where secular and religious subjects were to be taught. Such a school was set up in 1778 by his son Isaac Daniel. At the request of Moses *Mendelssohn and David *Friedlaender, Itzig's son-in-law, he prevented R. Hirschel *Levin from declaring a ban on N.H. *Wessely's *Divrei Shalom ve-Emet* (1782–85). As conversions to Christianity increased, Itzig stipulated in his

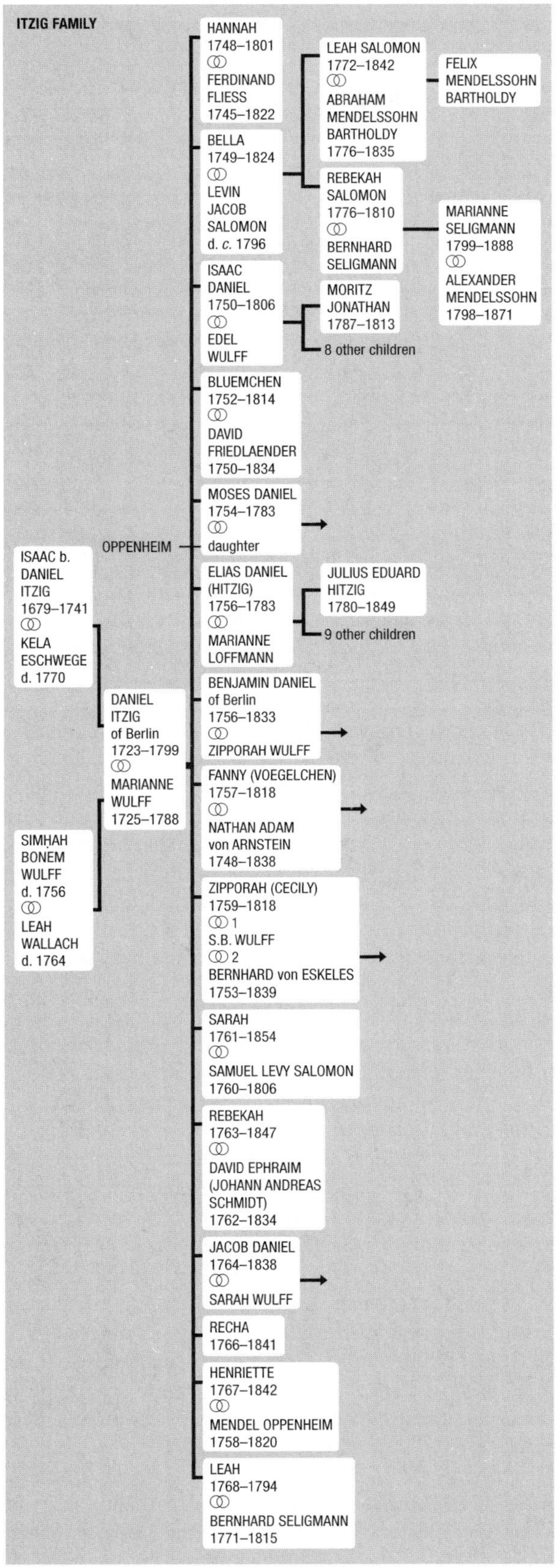

will that any of his descendants who were converted would be disinherited.

Of his five sons, ISAAC DANIEL (1750–1806) was the most talented. With David Friedländer he founded the *Juedische Freischule of Berlin, which he also directed. In 1796 he declared himself bankrupt after the French government defaulted on a payment for 10,000 horses. His son, MORITZ JONATHAN (1787–1813), caused a sensation by publicly thrashing the romantic poet Von Arnim, who had declined Moritz's challenge to a duel for deriding the admittance of Jews to upper classes of society, considering that a Jew was hardly a worthy opponent. Moritz died, a volunteer, at the battle of Lützen. ELIAS DANIEL (1756–1818), son of Daniel, changed his name to Hitzig, "Itzig" being the pejorative nickname applied to Jews. His son, JULIUS EDUARD (1780–1849), was a friend of the romantic authors A. von Chamisso, Z. Werner, and E.T.A. Hoffman, as well as the Berlin police director. The Bible scholar Ferdinand *Hitzig (1807–1875) was a descendant of this family. Of Daniel Itzig's ten daughters, one married David *Friedlaender, another Bernhard von *Eskeles, and a third daughter, Fanny von *Arnstein, presided over the most brilliant salon at the Congress of *Vienna. Virtually none of Daniel Itzig's descendants remained Jews.

BIBLIOGRAPHY: H. Rachel & P. Wallich, *Berliner Grosskaufleute und Kapitalisten*, 2 (1938), index; H. Schnee, *Die Hoffinanz und der moderne Staat*, 1 (1953), 121ff., 169–76; 5 (1965), no. 14, 15, 21, 22; S. Liptzin, *Germany's Stepchildren* (1944), 17–20. **ADD. BIBLIOGRAPHY:** K. Cauer, *Oberhofbankier und Hofbaurat* (1973); O. Stieglitz, *Die Ephraim* (2001), 239–56.

ITZIK, DALIA (née **Ballas**; 1952–), Israeli politician and teacher, Knesset member since the Thirteenth Knesset (1992). Itzik was born in Jerusalem to a non-religious family of Iraqi origin, but was sent to religious schools and attended the Evelyna de Rothschild girls' school. She started her university studies at Bar-Ilan University, but then moved to the Hebrew University of Jerusalem and received a B.A. in literature and history in 1980, and a teacher's diploma from the Efrata Teachers Seminary in Jerusalem. In 1999 she received a law degree from the Interdisciplinary Center in Herzliyyah.

She was one of the founders of the Katznelson School in the spirit of the values of the Labor Movement in Jerusalem, where she taught in 1973–89 and from 1984 to 1989 served as chairperson of the Teachers Association in Jerusalem. In those years she also served on the Administrative Committee of the Broadcasting Authority.

Itzik was elected to the Jerusalem Municipal Council as a representative of Teddy *Kollek's "One Jerusalem" list in 1989, serving as deputy mayor in charge of education. She was elected to the Labor Party list for the elections to the Thirteenth Knesset in the primaries in the Jerusalem region, and was elected to the Knesset. She served on the Knesset Finance Committee (1992–96) and on the Education and Culture Committee (1992–99), chairing the Committee in 1995–96. She was a member of the Committee on the Status of Women

(1996–99) and chairperson of the Special Committee for Research and Scientific Technological Development (1997–99). In the government formed by Ehud *Barak in 1999 Itzik was appointed minister of the environment, and in the National Unity Government formed by Ariel *Sharon in 2001 was appointed minister of industry and trade, until the Israel Labor Party left the government in November 2002. In the Sixteenth Knesset, elected in 2003, she served as chairperson of the Labor-Meimad parliamentary group. She participated in the negotiations leading to the formation of the National Unity Government under the leadership of Ariel Sharon, and in January 2005 was appointed minister of communications. In 2005 she joined Sharon's new Kadimah party and was reelected, becoming speaker of the Knesset in 2006.

[Susan Hattis Rolef (2nd ed.)]

IUDEX JUDAEORUM (Lat. for "judge of the Jews"; Ger. Judenrichter), gentile official in medieval Austria who adjudicated conflicts between Christians and Jews and appeals by Jews against decisions of the *bet din*. The office was established by Duke *Frederick II in the privileges (*Privilegium Fridericianum*) of 1244 (par. 15–18, 22, 27). The *iudex Judaeorum* was appointed by the dukes of Austria. Legal contracts between Jews and gentiles or those pertaining to the inheritance rights of Jews were confirmed by the seal of the *iudex*. The office was reconfirmed by Rudolf IV in 1361. During the 15th century some towns replaced the *iudex Judaeorum* by a court of law composed equally of Christians and Jews.

BIBLIOGRAPHY: J.E. Scherer, *Die Rechtsverhaeltnisse der Juden in den deutsch-oesterreichischen Laendern* (1901), 234–40; A. Rosenberg, *Beitraege zur Geschichte der Juden in Steiermark* (1914), index.

IVANCICE (Czech **Ivančice**; Ger. **Eibenschitz**), town in S. Moravia, Czechoslovakia. According to unattested records Jews built a synagogue there in 956, but documentary evidence of the existence of Jewish settlement begins in 1490, when three Jews of Ivancice signed as guarantors to a financial transaction. In 1608 the community was exempted from paying guard duties but was expected to help to defend the town with the Christian population in emergencies. There were 27 Jewish-owned houses in 1672 and 67 in 1752. The community numbered 533 (living in 72 houses) in 1791, 797 in 1830, 619 in 1869, 400 in 1914, and 141 in 1930 (2.8% of the total population). There was an important yeshivah in Ivancice which had some noted rabbis, including Joseph Rakov (d. 1707), editor of a letter-writing handbook; Nathan Nata Selig of Cracow, the father of Jonathan *Eybeschuetz; Moses Karpeles (1814–28), friend of Moses *Sofer; and Beer Oppenheim (1829–59), one of the first rabbis to combine talmudic with secular scholarship. Ivancice was constituted as one of the **Politische Gemeinden*. In the 1920s it was under the guidance of R. Heinrich *Flesch of Dolni Kounice. After the *Sudetenland crisis (1938) a large refugee camp was opened in Ivancice, which existed until 1942. Under Nazi rule the community was constituted a district-community. In 1942 the Jews from Ivancice were deported to death camps. The synagogue appurtenances were transferred to the Jewish Central Museum in Prague. The synagogue building was demolished in 1950. A religious congregation existed for a short time after World War II. A number of Jewish families are named after the town of Ivancice, in variant spellings.

BIBLIOGRAPHY: B. Wachstein, in: M. Stein (ed.), *Jahrbuch des traditionstreuen Rabbiner-Verbandes in der Slowakei* (1923), 34–66; idem, in: H. Gold, *Juden und Judengemeinden Maehrens...*(1929), 183–92; R. Trpik, *ibid.*, 75–82; Germ Jud, 1 (1963), 94. **ADD. BIBLIOGRAPHY:** J. Fiedler, *Jewish Sights of Bohemia and Moravia,* (1991), 84–85.

[Isaac Ze'ev Kahane]

IVANJI, IVAN (1929–), Yugoslav author and translator. Born in Zrenjanin, Banat, Ivanji survived deportation to Buchenwald and after the war studied and worked in Belgrade. He wrote poems, such as the collection *Živeću uvek prolećem* ("I Will Always Live with Spring," 1950); novels, including *čoveka nisu ubili* ("The Man They Did Not Kill", 1954); short stories, especially for children; and plays for radio. Ivanji also translated German and Hungarian works, and was one of the editors of the annual *Jevrejski almanah*. Later works include *Guvernanta* ("Nurse," 2002), *Balerina* (2003), and *Stubovi culture* ("Pillars of Culture," 2003).

IVANOVO (Pol. **Janów Poleski**; in Jewish sources **Janovi al-Yad Pinsk**), town in Brest-Litovsk district, Belarus. The first Jews settled in Ivanovo during the 1620s. The Jews of Ivanovo were subordinated to the jurisdiction of the community of *Pinsk. Prior to the *Chmielnicki uprising (1648–49) the Jewish population already had community status. The Jews presumably earned their livelihoods from trade, leasing of estate lands, and production of alcoholic beverages. According to the 1765 census there were 422 Jews living in and near the town. At the beginning of the 19th century the Ḥasidim of the *Stolin and Lubieszow dynasties gained adherents among the Jews of Ivanovo, although the majority remained **Mitnaggedim*. In 1847 the 1,283 Jews of the town formed about 56% of its population. The wealthier ones then began to engage in the acquisition and sale of forest products. By 1897 the number of Jews in Ivanovo had increased to 1,875 (about 62% of the total population). In the second half of the 19th century, Jews were engaged in petty trade and crafts, mostly as tailors, shoemakers, carpenters, furriers, etc. Their rabbi was Joshua Aryeh Leib, author of *Mizpeh Aryeh* and son of R. Samuel Avigdor of Karlin. At the beginning of the 20th century Jews established flour mills, a large lumber mill, an oil press, a tannery, and a small electric power station. Zionist societies were active from the beginning of the 20th century. The Hebrew educator and teacher Israel Judah (Jesse) Adler and the Hebrew poet Berl *Pomerantz lived in Ivanovo.

In the early 20th century there emerged a class of Jewish salaried workers employed in construction, carpentry, and the processing of hides, hogs' bristles, and furs. The 1921 census recorded 1,988 Jews (65% of the population) in the town. A great fire which broke out in 1929 destroyed 75 houses belonging to Jews; 120 Jewish families were left homeless. Damage to Jewish property amounted to the sum of 1,500,000 zlotys. In the early 1930s the Jewish quarter was completely renovated. Between the two World Wars a *Tarbut school operated in the town as well as a branch of the Bet Yosef yeshivah of Pinsk (except between 1929 and 1935). A highway running between Pinsk and Brest and passing through the town promoted the export of wood, grain, and cattle to central Poland and the West via Danzig.

Holocaust Period

After two years of Soviet rule, when all Jewish businesses were nationalized and Jewish institutions and organizations were closed, the Germans entered Ivanovo on June 25, 1941. On August 5 an SS cavalry unit murdered around 420 Jewish men. The chairman of the Judenrat, Alter Diwinski (former head of the community), successfully organized the supply of food and medicines to the community; he was later murdered by the Nazis because of his opposition to further "selections" from the Jewish population. A ghetto was established on Passover eve, 1942, where living conditions were extremely difficult – 60 persons to a small house. Outside the ghetto boundaries some 300 youths worked at a lumber mill and 50 others were employed in railroad maintenance. The ghetto was liquidated two days after the Day of Atonement, on September 24, 1942, when most of the Jews in Ivanovo were massacred. Those working at the lumber mill were murdered on September 25, 1942, and 62 artisans were killed in mid-October. A few dozen Jews, mainly young ones, succeeded in escaping to the forests, where they joined partisan units. About 100 Jews survived; all left for the West, most of them for Israel. No Jews were living in Ivanovo after World War II.

BIBLIOGRAPHY: M. Nadav (ed.), *Yanov al-yad Pinsk, Sefer Zikkaron* (1969); S. Dubnow (ed.), *Pinkas ha-Medinah* (1925); Z. Rabinowitz, *Ha-Ḥasidut ha-Lita'it* (1960), 10, 146; B. Wasiutyński, *Ludność żydowska w Polsce w XIX wieku* (1930), 83. **ADD. BIBLIOGRAPHY:** PK.

[Arthur Cygielman / Shmuel Spector (2nd ed.)]

IVANYI-GRUNWALD, BELA (1867–1940), Hungarian painter. Born in Somogysom, Ivanyi-Grunwald began his career as a naturalist but after a visit to Rome in 1904 became an impressionist. He then turned to compositions with mystic figures accentuated by light and shade. For a while he lived among painters in Szolnok where he developed his own style of decorative compositions. It is generally recognized that his teaching influenced a generation of Hungarian painters.

IVGY, MOSHE (1953–), Israeli actor. With more than 44 films to his credit, Ivgy has taken on the late Shaike *Ophir's mantle as Israel's hardest-working actor. As the years went by, he distinguished himself not only as a popular actor but as a talented and versatile one. Born in Morocco as one of seven children, Ivgy moved to Israel as a child. Not accepted at any of Tel Aviv's established theater companies, he founded his own theatrical troupe, The Gypsy Theater, then moved on to film. His Eastern background and low-key persona made him a natural for the many North African characters who began to appear in Israeli films. Soon, Ivgy graduated from sidekick roles to leading-man status. In 2004, he starred in two of Israel's biggest popular and critical hits, Joseph Cedar's *Campfire*, in which he played a lonely Orthodox minivan driver, and Danny Verete's *Metallic Blues*, where he was a car salesman heading for Germany. He has flirted with an international career and appeared in David Mamet's *Spartan*, also in 2004. His films include *Shuroo* (1991); *Cup Final* (1991); *Lovesick on Nana Street* (1995); *Yom Yom* (1998); and *Life Is Life* (2003). He is the father of actress Dana Ivgy.

[Hannah Brown (2nd ed.)]

°**IVO OF CHARTRES** (c. 1040–1115), bishop of Chartres from 1091 until his death. He was proclaimed the patron of barristers because of his contribution to canon law, in particular the *Decretum* which he drew up in 1094. In it Ivo voices the change in the Christian attitude toward the Jews which occurred during the 11th century. The 13th book of the *Decretum* contains a series of texts in which the Jews are proclaimed unfit to testify in court, to fill any public office, and forbidden to appear in public during Easter or to supply medicaments to Christians. Among the prescriptions is one of major importance for the social standing of Jews vis-à-vis gentiles: that which declares them unqualified for military service. This had already appeared in Roman law (Theodosian Code, Novella 3), but Ivo preferred to attribute it to the Church Father *Jerome, to give the maximum theological weight to the social ostracizing of the Jews.

BIBLIOGRAPHY: B. Blumenkranz, *Juifs et chrétiens…* (1960), index; R. Sprandel, *Ivo von Chartres und seine Stellung in der Kirchengeschichte* (1962).

[Bernhard Blumenkranz]

IVORY. The Bible usually designates an elephant's tusk as *shen* (Heb. שֵׁן, lit. "tooth"), a term indicating both raw and finished ivory (e.g., I Kings 10:18; Ezek. 27: 15; II Chron. 9:17). In connection with the importation of this item from distant places, the Bible (I Kings 10:22; II Chron. 9:21; cf. Ezek. 27:15) uses the term *shenhabbim* (Heb. שֶׁנְהַבִּים), from *shen* and *habbim*, plural of *hav*, possibly from Egyptian *3bw*, "elephant." It is possible, therefore, that *shenhav* indicates only the raw material. Because it is as rare as it is beautiful, ivory is used in the Bible to personify human beauty. Thus, "your neck is like an ivory tower" (Song 7:5 [4]); or "his body is ivory work encrusted with sapphires" (*ibid.* 5:14). Since the use of ivory was limited to the very wealthy, the prophets use ivory as a symbol of great wealth (Amos 3:15). The raw materials were brought to Palestine by land or sea from such distant places as India, Upper Egypt, and, to a lesser degree, from Syria and Libya. Considered of great value – in a class with spices, gold, and precious stones – ivory was used for creating tiny art objects, and small but valuable utensils. Objects of ivory have been found in Palestine in a Chalcolithic cave in the Judean Desert (Wadi Ḥever), and small statuettes dating from the same period have been discovered in the northern Negev. Ivory was used to make pendants, small idols, elegant sheaths for swords, cosmetic vessels, and combs, examples of each having been found in excavations at Megiddo, Ḥazor, Samaria, and Tell al-Farica. Carved ivory was also used as a decorative finish for the walls of houses, especially the interior, and as adornments on furniture. Both uses enhanced the beauty of Ahab's palace at Samaria (I Kings 22:39). Thrones, beds, and other furniture might also be thus decorated (e.g., I Kings 10:18; Amos 6:4). Motifs for designs ranged from geometric patterns and shapes from nature – especially those of animals and plants – to mythology and great feats of heroism.

BIBLIOGRAPHY: J.W. Crowfoot and G.M. Crowfoot, *Early Ivories from Samaria* (1938); G. Loud, *The Megiddo Ivories (1939); Y. Yadin et al., Ḥazor,* 1 (1958), pls. cl, cli; 3–4 (1961), pl. ccxl, no. 10.

[Ze'ev Yeivin]

IVY (Mishnaic) (Heb. קִיסוֹס, *kisos*, from the Gr. κισσός), *Hedera helix*, which grows wild in the forests of Israel. It is mentioned in the Mishnah as a plant occasionally grown in a vineyard (Kil. 5:8). Its dense branches are considered a screen (separation) against uncleanliness (Oho. 8:1). It is probable that it was customary to train various clinging plants, including ivy, upon the walls of permanent *sukkot*, with the result that the Mishnah lays it down that a *sukkah* over the roof of which ivy has been trailed is invalid (Suk. 1:4). This may be the source of Plutarch's statement that *sukkot* were made from the branches of vines and ivy, from which he concluded that the Jewish feast of Tabernacles was merely a feast of *Dionysius, to whom ivy was dedicated (*Quaestionum Convivialium*, cap. 4: problem 6, 671 D). However, Tacitus (*Historia* 5:5) had rejected the equation of the feast of Dionysius with Tabernacles, although he remarks that the Jewish priests used to be adorned with ivy wreaths. According to the Book of Maccabees (II Macc. 6:7; cf. III Macc. 2:29) Antiochus Epiphanes forced the Jews to wear ivy wreaths in honor of Dionysius on the feast of Bacchus.

BIBLIOGRAPHY: Loew, Flora, 1 (1928), 219–21; H.N. and A.L. Moldenke, *Plants of the Bible* (1952), index. **ADD. BIBLIOGRAPHY:** Feliks, Ha-Ẓome'aḥ, 142.

[Jehuda Feliks]

IVYE (in rabbinical literature, איווי; Pol. **Iwje**), small town in Grodno district, Belarus. Jews settled there in the first quarter of the 17th century. In 1720 there was already a well-established Jewish community in Ivye, which is often mentioned in the record of the Lithuanian Council with regard to taxation (see *Councils of the Lands). The Jews of the town and its immediate vicinity derived their livelihood from innkeeping, the distillation of brandy, the lease of estates, hawking, and the management of dairies. There were 804 Jews in Ivye in 1847. In 1891, following the outbreak of a fire in which some 100 Jewish houses were damaged, many left the town, and by 1897 only 573 remained (total population 3,653). In this period the Jews were engaged in wholesale trade in grain, flax, and other agricultural products as well as and petty trade, crafts, and some farming. In the mid-19th century, Rabbi Solomon David Grodzenski established a yeshivah in the town. A Ẓe'irei Zion circle was organized in 1917. In 1921, after the town was annexed by Poland, the Jewish population of Ivye numbered 2,076 (c. 76% of the population). It grew to around 3,000 by 1938. During the 1920s a Hebrew *Tarbut school, a national-religious Yavneh school, and a Jewish elementary school for girls were established. From summer 1933 until September 1939 the "Beit Yosef" yeshivah was active. Among the well-known personalities originating from the town were R. Moses Ivyer, a friend of the Gaon of Vilna; Ḥayyim Ozer *Grodzinski; Isaac b. Jacob Ashkenaz, the author of *Berit Olam* (1820); the family of Izhak *Ben-Zvi; R. Isaac Kosovsky, and Shakhne Epstein, who was editor of *Der Emes* in Moscow in the 1930s and in 1942–45 secretary general of the *Jewish Anti-Fascist Committee and editor of *Einikeit*.

[Arthur Cygielman / Shmuel Spector (2nd ed.)]

Holocaust Period

During the period of Soviet rule (1939–41), Jewish communal institutions were dissolved, activity by Zionist parties and youth movements was banned, and the Hebrew Tarbut School became a state school in Yiddish. With the outbreak of war between Germany and the Soviet Union on June 22, 1941, Jewish youths were mobilized into the Red Army; others attempted to reach the Soviet interior. On July 1, 1941, the city was captured by the Germans and one month later, on the Ninth of Av (August 2, 1941), approximately 225 members of the Jewish intelligentsia were murdered. In September 1941 the Jews were concentrated into a special quarter of the town. Jews from the surrounding towns were brought in and the population swelled to around 4,000. On May 8, 1942, the ghetto was surrounded by the German army and police and on May 12 an *Aktion* took place in which about 2,550 people (1,424 women, 500 men, and 626 children and infants) were murdered. Subsequently an underground organization arose, which began to acquire arms, and attempted to make contact with the partisans in the nearby forests. One group left the ghetto and reached the partisan camp of Tuvia Bielsky. At the end of 1942 and the beginning of 1943 the systematic murder continued. On Jan. 20, 1943, 1,100 Jews were transferred to Borisov (near Minsk) and perished there shortly after. In March a small group was sent to the Lida ghetto, in August 70 were transferred to a labor camp near Smolensk, and the last Jews were sent to the Sobibor and Majdanek death camps in September 1943. The city was declared "*Judenrein*." Jewish communal life was not renewed after the war. Most of the survivors left the U.S.S.R. for Poland and went from there to Israel or other countries.

[Aharon Weiss / Shmuel Spector (2nd ed.)]

BIBLIOGRAPHY: S. Dubnow, *Pinkas ha-Medinah* (1925), index; M. Kaganowitz (ed.), *Sefer Zikkaron li-Kehillat Ivye* (Heb. and Yid., 1968). **ADD. BIBLIOGRAPHY:** PK.

IYYAR (Heb. אִיָּר), the post-Exilic name of the second month of the Jewish year. Its pre-Exilic name is Ziv (I Kings 6:1), the shorter equivalent of the targumic Ziv Niẓanayya ("brightness of flowers"). Occurring in Assyrian inscriptions, in *Megillat Ta'anit, and later branches of rabbinic literature, but nowhere in the Bible, Iyyar is held to be etymologically connected with the Hebrew *or* ("light"). The zodiacal sign of this month is *Taurus*. In the present fixed Jewish calendar it invariably consists of 29 days. The first of Iyyar – bound by the same calendric rules as the first of *Tishri – never falls on Sunday, Wednesday, or Friday. In the 20th century Iyyar, in its earliest occurrence, extended from April 12th to May 10th, and, in its latest, from May 11th to June 8th. All of Iyyar falls within the period of the *Omer*, the first of Iyyar being the 16th day of the *Omer*. Historic dates in Iyyar comprise the following: (1) 1st of Iyyar, the anniversary of the first census by Moses in the wilderness (Num. 1:1); (2) 2nd of Iyyar, the commencement of the building of the Temple by Solomon (II Chron. 3:2); (3) 5th of Iyyar, Israel *Independence Day, the anniversary of the establishment of the State of Israel in 5708 (1948); (4) 7th of Iyyar, the *Hasmoneans' dedication of the walls of Jerusalem upon the repair of the breaches by the Greeks (Meg. Ta'an. 2); (5) 10th of Iyyar, the anniversary of the death of *Eli and his sons and the capture of the sacred ark by the Philistines, once observed as a fast (Meg. Ta'an. 13); (6) 14th of Iyyar, the Second (or "Little") *Passover (Num. 9:11), celebrated in Temple times by those unable to celebrate *Passover in Nisan, and still marked in the synagogue by the omission of the *Taḥanun prayer; (7) 18th of Iyyar, corresponding to *Lag ba-Omer, the 33rd day of the *Omer*; (8) 23rd of Iyyar, commemorating the Hasmoneans' expulsion of the Hellenists from Jerusalem's Acra (fortified area) in 141 B.C.E., their entrance with thanksgiving, hymns, and songs, and their ordaining that that day should be an annual occasion for rejoicing (I Macc. 13:51–52; Meg. Ta'an. 2); (9) 27th of Iyyar, formerly observed as the anniversary of another Hasmonean victory of an obscure nature (Meg. Ta'an. 2; but cf. JE, 7 (1904), 15; it cannot be identified with the events in I Macc. 13:41–42); (10) 28th of Iyyar, the anniversary of the death of the prophet *Samuel, once observed as a fast (Meg. Ta'an. 13; according to a manuscript variant, the date is the 27th of Iyyar, but not the 29th of Iyyar).

[Ephraim Jehudah Wiesenberg]

IZATES II, called Zotos in the Midrash (Gen. R. 46:10), king of *Adiabene (c. 35–60 C.E.). In his youth, Izates was sent by his father to the court of Abnerigos, king of Mesene, where he received his education. He married Samakhos (or Simakho), the king's daughter, and was appointed ruler of Ḥaran by his father through the efforts of his mother *Helena. Although Izates was the youngest son, he succeeded his father as king of Adiabene. While still in Mesene he became attracted to Judaism, like his mother, and on the occasion of a famine in Ereẓ Israel, they both gave considerable help to the hungry. He sent five of his sons to Jerusalem, "that they should acquire a thorough knowledge of our ancestral language and ethics" (Jos., Ant., 20:51f., 71). His conversion aroused opposition in Adiabene and his opponents, in a desire to depose him, called on Abias, king of Arabia, for assistance. After a temporary setback Izates succeeded in defeating his opponents and attacked Abias, who committed suicide rather than be taken captive.

In general Izates' foreign policy was prudent and was directed toward preserving the independence of his country. He avoided involvement in the wars between the two great powers of his day, the Roman Empire and Parthia, to whose overall authority he was subject. He pursued this policy when the Parthian king Vardanes demanded his participation in war against Rome. When he refused, Vardanes threatened him with war but was assassinated before he could implement his threat. Later the nobility of Adiabene requested Vologases I, king of the Parthians, to appoint a new king, and Vologases made preparations to invade the country. However, external events compelled him to change his plans.

On Izates' death, he left 48 sons and daughters, but bequeathed the throne to his brother, *Monobaz II. When Helena (who was then living in Jerusalem), learned of his death she hastened back to Adiabene but died there shortly after. Monobaz transferred the remains of his mother and brother to Jerusalem, burying them in the mausoleum built by Helena north of Jerusalem and called "the tombs of the kings" (or, by Jews, "the cave of Kalba Savu'a"). In the Roman war many of Izates' sons fought on the side of the Jews and were put in chains after their surrender.

BIBLIOGRAPHY: Schuerer, Gesch, 3 (1909⁴), 169–73; M.Kon, *Kivrei ha-Melakhim* (1947); Klausner, Bayit Sheni, 5 (1951²), 45–9; Schalit, in: *Annual of the Swedish Theological Institute*, 4 (1965), 163–81.

[Abraham Schalit]

IZBAN, SHMUEL (1905–1995), Yiddish novelist. Born in Gostynin, Poland, he grew up in Wloclawek, where he attended a Hebrew gymnasium. In 1921 he immigrated to Palestine with his parents. At his father's cafe, he met artists, actors, and writers, including Aḥad *Ha-Am, *Bialik, and *Rawnitzky and was stimulated to compose sketches and short stories in Hebrew for local periodicals and in Yiddish for American and Polish newspapers. Later, he contributed to several Yiddish publications printed in Palestine, which he also coedited. His first novel, *Masn* (1929), dealt with the Russian revolution of 1905, and his second, *Kver 1914–1918* (1936), with Poland during World War I. He published numerous short stories about the exotic mixture of populations and life styles in Palestine, collected in *Tsvishn Hundert Toyern* ("Within Hundred Gates," 1942), and *A Valfish in Yafo* ("A Whale in Jaffa," (1980). His stories about New York, where he settled in 1937, also have a special flavor. He aroused much attention with his reports collected in *Umlegale Yidn Shpaltn Yamen* ("Illegal Jews Split the Sea," 1948), and with his two-volume novel about Palestine in the 1920s, *Familye Karp* (1949). Izban's mastery of the historical novel is displayed in *Di Kenigin Izabel* ("Queen Jezebel," 1959) and *Yerikho* ("Jericho," 1966), which vividly recreate Israel's past. Several of Izban's stories and historical novels have been translated into Hebrew, Spanish, and English.

BIBLIOGRAPHY: LNYL, 1 (1956), 52–3; J. Glatstein, *In Tokh Genumen* (1956), 430–6; S. Bickel, *Shrayber fun Mayn Dor*, 2 (1965), 386–96. **ADD. BIBLIOGRAPHY:** A Liss, *Di Goldene Keyt*, 104 (1981), 90–4.

[Sol Liptzin]

IZBICA LUBELSKA, town in Lublin province, Poland. In 1856 the Jewish population together with that of Tarnogora numbered 1,594 (62.8% of the total population). In Izbica proper the number of Jews was 3,019 (95%) in 1897 and 2,862 (92.7%) in 1921. At that time the Polish authorities opposed the establishment of a municipal council so as to prevent its being in Jewish hands. The town was known in the ḥasidic world through the *ẓaddik* Mordecai Joseph Leiner of Izbica, a disciple of Mendel of *Kotsk. Mordecai Joseph, founder of the ḥasidic dynasty of Izbica, was followed by his son Jacob, author of *Beit Ya'akov* and father of the *ẓaddik* Gershon Henikh *Leiner of Radzyn.

At the outbreak of World War II there were some 4,000 Jews in Izbica Lubelska. In December 1939 about 2,500 Jews from Lodz and Kolo were forced to settle there, and during March and April 1942 an additional 1,000, mostly from Czechoslovakia, were deported to the town. On March 24, 1942, about 2,200 Jews were deported from Izbica Lubelska to *Belzec death camp. By the end of that year the entire Jewish population of the town, including the deportees, had been exterminated in the Belzec and *Sobibor death camps or shot.

BIBLIOGRAPHY: B. Wasiutyńsski, *Ludność żdowska w Polsce w wiekach XIX I XX* (1930), s.v.; Poland, Główny Urząd Statystyczny, *Skorowidz miejscowości Rzeczypospolitej Polskiej*, 4 (1924), s.v.; T. Brustin-Bernstein, in: *Bleter far Geshikhte*, 3:1–2 (1950), 51–78.

[Stefan Krakowski]

IZBICA RADZYN, ḥasidic dynasty in Poland. R. MORDECAI JOSEPH LEINER OF IZBICA (1800–1854), the founder of the dynasty, was born in Tomaszow, Poland, to a rabbinic family of means. He was 19 when he sold all his possessions and traveled to Przysucha to become *Simḥah Bunim's disciple for nine years, until the latter passed away in 1827. After Simhah Bunim's death he moved back to Tomaszow and accepted his older friend, Menaḥem Mendel Morgenstern of *Kotsk, as his rebbe. Gradually he realized that he opposed Menaḥem Mendel's religious leadership. He started teaching his own original, independent ideas, until the schism became evident on Simḥat Torah in 1839, which he spent in Kotsk, after which he parted company with Menaḥem Mendel. He returned to Tomaszow, but because of the hostility of Menaḥem Mendel's followers he moved to Izbica, where he lived until his death in 1854. Unlike Menaḥem Mendel, he was in constant company with his followers, challenging them by upsetting religious conventions on the one hand and comforting them with his guidance on the other. Continuing Przysucha's strong emphasis on the study of Talmud, he lectured on the Talmud a few hours each weekday.

Among his eminent disciples were Judah Leib Eiger of Lublin and. *Ẓadok ha-Kohen of Lublin, both of whom became *rebbes* and central ḥasidic leaders in the second half of the 19th century.

Mordehai Joseph did not leave behind any writings. After his death his grandson GERSHON ḤANOKH HENIKH (1839–1891) collected testimonies of his homilies and published them under the name *Mei ha-Shiloaḥ* (1860). After publication, Gershon continued collecting testimonies and they were published by his brother Mordecai Joseph as *Mei ha-Shiloaḥ*, Part 2 (1922).

Mordecai Joseph generated much controversy, initially because of the schism between him and Menaḥem Mendel. Afterwards it was his novel and daring teachings that were under attack. Gershon Ḥanokh Henikh, being aware of this, writes in the introduction to *Mei ha-Shiloaḥ* (1860) that some of the ideas expressed in the book are going to be "difficult to hear." From the early 1960s, Mordecai Joseph attracted attention in academic circles as well as in religious movements seeking religious renewal. R. Shlomo *Carlebach was a key figure in this trend.

JACOB (1818–1878), his son, succeeded him and relocated the dynasty to Radzyn. His writings include *Beit Ya'akov* (1890–1937), homilies on the Torah, and *Sefer ha-Zemanim* (1903–73), homilies on the holidays. Jacob's son, Gershon Ḥanokh Henikh, succeeded his father to become the "Radzyner Rebbe." The latter's grandson, SAMUEL SOLOMON, was the *rebbe* of Radzyn during the Holocaust. He called upon his followers to flee to the forest and fight against the Nazis. Upon hearing this, the Nazis murdered him. He is the hero of Yitzhak *Katzenelson's poem "Dos Lied vegan Radziner" (1943).

Mordecai Joseph's Teachings

The principal innovation of Mordecai Joseph's thought is introduced in his homilies, where he endorses the sins of biblical heroes (the famous and most controversial example being Zimri). He states that they acted in accordance with "God's will" – a phrase that suggests an alternate way of life to the rational, halakhic route. The very idea that "God's will" is at variance with *halakhah* undermines the common traditional view.

This path, in harmony with "God's will," may be called voluntarism – the view that at the dawn of history, when God created the world, he determined its course according to his will. God's will is understood as the only free will in existence. Mordecai Joseph asserts that God's free will, as the very definition of free will, does not lend itself to formulation in general rules – the identifying feature of rationality. In contrast, *halakhah* is a system that follows general rules. In accordance with "God's will" different and even opposed actions can be justified when they are performed by different people or by the same person in different contexts, as long as they are consistent with God's will. "God's will" can manifest itself in infinite possibilities of human action.

"God's will" is described as a deterministic awareness in people who follow this path, understanding themselves as vehicles executing God's will. The belief that God's will determines the entire course of our lives is a way of thinking that calls for the humble overcoming our illusion of free will. Rare individuals who attain such a spiritual level live and act decisively (*tekufot*). At the same time, some homilies characterize the followers of "God's will" as people who bravely bring themselves to face uncertainty (*safek*). In doing so they put aside all halakhic conventions, all norms, trying to do God's will despite the uncertainty and danger of failure. In the hereafter the commonly shared illusion of human free will will give way to the true understanding of "God's will," which will be recognized by all.

In contrast to the path of "God's will," homilies that emphasize the important religious role of *halakhah* can be found as well. This makes it necessary to interpret the relationship between "Gods will" and the halakhic approach in Mordecai Joseph's' teachings. There are several ways to overcome this difficulty. One is to understand "God's will" as relevant only in the messianic era. Another reads "God's will" as relevant for the pre-messianic era as well, seeing the *halakhah* as a first necessary stage on the way to perfection – then only can "God's will" become a practical way of life. Yet another interpretation is to understand *halakhah* as worship of God out of fear, an inferior way to worship God. *Halakhah*, which is the veneer (*gavan*) of God's will, contrasts with worshiping God out of love, which enables one to find the depth (*omek*) of God's Will. It is also possible to understand "God's will" and *halakhah* as two systems that Mordecai Joseph approves of. He is aware that they are in conflict with each other, as he realizes that the nature of human religious experience is complex and incoherent.

As daring as Mordecai Joseph's ideas are, we should understand that he was the leader of an orthodox ḥasidic community which organized its praxis according to *halakhah*, just as he did.

It is generally agreed that his thought was strongly individualistic, a tendency typical of Przysucha Ḥasidism. Yet the social environment in which he was rooted was one of intense community life. Accordingly, his individualism should be seen not as a call for seclusion but rather as a quest for one's personal religious path while part of a meaningful community.

BIBLIOGRAPHY: H.S. Leiner, *Dor Yesharim* (1925); idem, *Zikkaron la-Rishonim* (1950); R. Mahler, *Ha-Ḥasidut ve-ha-Haskalah* (1961), 343–49; J. Weiss, in: F. Baer Jubilee Volume (1961), 447–53; idem, in: *Studies in Eastern European Jewish Mysticism* (1985), 209–48; R. Schatz, in: *Molad*, 21 (1963), 554–61; S.Z. Shragai, *Bi-Netivei Ḥasidut Izbiza-Radzyn* (1972–74); M.M. Faierstein, *All Is in the Hands of Heavens* (1989); R. Elior, in: Tarbiz, 62/63 (1993), 402–32; J.I. Gellman, *The Fear, the Trembling, and the Fire* (1994), 23–58.

[Y. Ben-Dor (2nd ed.)]

IZENBERG, JERRY (1930–), U.S. sportswriter. Izenberg, whose father was born on the Polish-Russian border in a village with no name called "the Jew village," grew up in Newark, N.J., where his father worked dyeing furs seven days a week. Izenberg attended college at Newark-Rutgers, where he was a sports reporter and later editor-in-chief of the *Observer*, the student newspaper. After graduating in 1952, Izenberg worked at the *Newark Star-Ledger* for a summer, and then enlisted and served in Japan and Korea for two years. After being discharged, Izenberg worked first at weekly newspapers in New Jersey, and then at the *Paterson News, the Newark Star-Ledger*, and the *New York Herald Tribune*. In August 1962, the *Newark Star-Ledger* offered Izenberg a job as a columnist, and he remained there ever since, writing 10,000 nationally syndicated columns in the ensuing four decades.

Izenberg was a weekly sports commentator on New York's Channel 5 in the 1970s, spent two years as host of the NBC Radio Network's *Sports at Large with Jerry Izenberg*, and taught journalism at both Rutgers University and the New School for Social Research. Izenberg was also producer, director, writer, and narrator for more than 30 television specials, winning an Emmy Award for writing and directing *A Man Named Lombardi*, and he is one of only five sportswriters who has attended every Super Bowl since its inception in 1967. He is a five-time winner of the N.J. Sportswriter of the Year Award, has been nominated for the Pulitzer Prize numerous times, and is a member of the N.J. Literary Hall of Fame, in which he is the only sportswriter; the National Sportscasters and Sportswriters Hall of Fame; the N.J. State Athletic Hall of Fame; the Rutgers University's Hall of Distinguished Alumni; and winner of the Red Smith Award from the Associated Press Sports Editors, which Izenberg considers his proudest accomplishment. Smith once called him "one of the best-informed conscientious writers in sports," and his politically active stance sometimes drew the wrath of readers, as when he defended Muhammad Ali's refusal to fight in Vietnam in the 1970s.

"We got well over a thousand letters, and only two agreed with me," Izenberg said. "One of the letters was written in crayon. But all the mail had a common thread: 'Dear Communist Jew Bastard,' or 'Dear Facist Jew Bastard.'"

Izenberg is the author of nine books, including *At Large, With Jerry Izenberg* (1968), *The Rivals* (1968), *How Many Miles To Camelot?: The All-American Sport Myth* (1972), *Great Latin Sports Figures: The Proud People* (1976), *The Greatest Game Ever Played* (1987), and *No Medals for Trying: A Week in the Life of a Pro Football Team* (1990).

[Elli Wohlgelernter (2nd ed.)]

IZIS (**Izrael Bidermanas**; 1911–1980), French photographer. Izis was born in Mariampol, Lithuania. In 1930 he went to Paris. During World War II, he was captured by the Nazis but escaped and joined the Resistance. There he taught himself to produce expressive human studies with small, fast cameras instead of his former sophisticated commercial photographs. In 1946 Izis had his first exhibition in Paris; a second one four years later brought him a contract with the French magazine *Paris Match*. His roving mission, which took him all over Europe and the Middle East, resulted in beautifully designed photographs that were lyrical, humane, and exciting. His book of this period, *Paris des Rêves* (1950), with text by 40 French poets, ran into many editions. His other collections include *Charmes de Londres* (1952), *Paradis terrestre* (1953) with text by Colette, and *Israël* (1955) with a preface by André Malraux. In 1963 *Chagall designed a frontispiece for *The Circus of Izis*, for which Jacques Prévert wrote the text, and in 1968 Izis published *The World of Marc Chagall*.

[Peter Pollack]

IZMAIL (Rom. **Ismail**), city in Bessarabia, Romania, today Ukraine. Jews are first mentioned in Izmail in 1769. The community developed after the Russian annexation of Bessarabia in 1812; Jewish immigrants received the same privileges as other new settlers in the city. In 1827 there were 549 Jews in Izmail and in 1847, 1,105. As the community grew, the "great synagogue" (1825) and a *bet midrash* (1826) were built. In the middle of the 19th century a government-run Jewish school was opened. After the region was incorporated into Romania in 1856, the Jews were oppressed by the Romanian authorities. Severe anti-Jewish riots occurred in 1872 when money and church vessels were stolen from the main church by a convert to Christianity, who when arrested accused several Jews, including one of the heads of the community and the rabbi, of sending him to desecrate the church. The riots aroused international opinion which resulted in the vigorous intervention of the representatives of the great powers in Romania. When the district of Izmail was ceded to Russia in 1878, many Jews were considered aliens and the authorities expelled them to Romania. The Romanians, however, returned them to Russia. They were not granted the status of Russian citizens until 1892. At that time, the Jews of Izmail suffered from the restrictions in force in Russia on Jewish residence in border areas. On October 23 1905, 50 Jews were killed in a pogrom and shops and houses were looted and destroyed. There were 2,781 Jews in Izmail (12.5% of the total population) in 1897 and 1,623 (6.5%) in 1930. The communal institutions then included a kindergarten and a *Tarbut elementary school. During Soviet rule (1940–41) many wealthy Jews were exiled to Bolgrad and Siberia. The community was destroyed when the Germans and Romanians entered Bessarabia in July 1941. Those exiled to Bolgrad were murdered there and those remaining in Izmail were taken by Romanian soldiers to Vadui Lui Traian and killed there. In 1970 the Jewish population of Izmail was estimated at 1,000 persons. Though many left in the 1990s, Jewish life began to revive under Rabbi Shneur Alperovich, with a synagogue, day school, and kindergarten in operation.

BIBLIOGRAPHY: Y. Reicher, in: *Sinai, Sefer ha-Shanah shel ha-Ḥevrah le-Ḥokhmat Yisrael be-Romanyah*, 3 (1931), ix–xii; E. Feldman, in: *Sefer Yahadut Bessarabia* (1971), passim; L.P. Gartner, in: AJHSQ, 58 (1968), 68–74.

[Eliyahu Feldman / Shmuel Spector (2nd ed.)]

IZMIR (**Smyrna**), provincial capital and principal harbor of W. Anatolia, *Turkey, on the coast of the Aegean Sea. There were Jews settled in Izmir at the beginning of the Christian era as attested by the New Testament (Rev. 1:11; 2:8). It is thought that many pagans became proselytes as a result of Jewish influence. Christianity was accepted by only a few Jews there. A few Greek inscriptions of the second and third centuries C.E. have been preserved. From one of them it appears that the community was authorized to impose punishments on any person who showed disrespect toward it, and that a woman named Rufina was then "Mother of the synagogue." One of the seals found in the proximity of the town has a fine representation of a *menorah* very similar to the one on the arch of Titus at Rome. During the Middle Ages the number of Jews decreased and they may have disappeared completely from the town. However, when the descendants of the Spanish exiles arrived in the 16th century, they found a small *Romaniot community.

The development of Izmir dates from the beginning of the 17th century, when it was a flourishing center of Mediterranean commerce. The Jewish community increased in numbers and became one of the most important of the Ottoman Empire. Jews from *Salonika, Constantinople, and neighboring towns also settled in Izmir. The new settlers established their own communities (*Eẓ Ḥayyim, Gerush, Portugal*, etc.) and appointed R. Joseph *Escapa of Salonica as their rabbi (before 1630). After some time R. Azariah Joshua Ashkenazi, also from Salonika, arrived in the town. A controversy broke out between Escapa and Ashkenazi, as a result of which the community split into two factions. However, after the death of the latter in 1648, Escapa was appointed rabbi over all the Jewish population, which was thus of diverse origins and had different customs. Escapa endeavored to unite the community. He issued important *takkanot* still in force in Izmir and the neighboring localities. He instituted tax laws and appointed councils for the spiritual and material administration of the community. As a result religious and social standards improved; one of the eminent rabbis of Salonika during that period, R. Samuel Isaac Modigliano, said of Izmir that it was "a holy and pure community, all of whose regulations are decreed with ability and justice, through the counsel of sages and wise men."

This period was the golden era of the Izmir community. Large yeshivot, schools, synagogues (i.e, the Portuguese synagogue in 1710, the Algazi synagogue – Kal de Ariva – in 1728, etc.) and a Hebrew printing press (1658) were founded. The local Jewish population included prosperous merchants, translators, agents of European merchants, banks and consulates, customs officials, usurers and eminent rabbis who ranked among the most distinguished of that generation – R. Aaron *Lapapa, R. Solomon *Algazi, and R. Ḥayyim *Benveniste, all of them during the 17th century. *Shabbetai Ẓevi was born in Izmir and began his activities there. His appearance shook the Jewish world, and the violent conflict which ensued in Izmir in its wake had an adverse influence on the community. The dispute subsequently subsided and the community returned to its former prosperity. Jews then held important economic positions and Jewish merchants maintained commercial relations with the Balkan countries, the Near East and Far East, Africa, and the large European cities. In addition to the six existing synagogues, another three were erected. Literature also flourished. Important and fundamental works in the fields of *halakhah* and ethics were written. These include the works of Ḥayyim Benveniste on the Shulḥan Arukh entitled *Keneset ha-Gedolah* ("Great Assembly"), and that of *Elijah ha-Kohen of Izmir, *Shevet Musar* ("Rod of Admonition").

The most renowned rabbis of the late 17th and early 18th centuries were Jacob b. Na'im, who headed a large yeshivah from which many disciples graduated; his disciple R. Abraham ibn Ezra, author of the important work *Battei Kenesiyyot* (Salonika, 1806); R. Joseph Ḥazzan, author of the well-known commentaries on *Ein Yosef* (Izmir, 1675); and R. Aaron *Alfandari, author of *Yad Aharon* (Izmir, 1735). Special mention should be made of R. Ḥayyim *Abulafia, who was chief rabbi of Izmir from 1720 to 1740 and was a distinguished and active scholar. In 1740 he emigrated, together with his disciples, to Tiberias.

The most prolific of the 19th century's rabbis was R. Ḥayyim Palacci (*Palache), who represented the old generation of strict old-fashioned rabbis. He wrote over 72 works in all the fields of scholarship (54 of his books were lost in the great fire of 1841).

Towards the end of the 18th century, many of Izmir's Jews were engaged in the manufacture of wool from goats' fleece. There was both an organization of workshop owners and a workers' organization. Two manufacturers (not among the biggest) employed 130 workmen (*Ḥikrei Lev* of R. Joseph Ḥazzan, Sh. Ar. YD, 2:37, Salonika, 1806). Over a period of some 180 years five great fires broke out (1743, 1772, 1841, 1881, 1922), in which large sections, mostly of the Jewish quarters of Izmir, were destroyed. There were also frequent epidemics, mostly between 1770 and 1892, and big earthquakes. The Greek population of the town frequently brought *blood libels against the Jews; there were six cases between 1864 and 1901. In the 19th century, there were 15,000–20,000 Jews in Izmir. At the end of the 19th century a general decline of Izmir Jewry set in. In 1905, an Ashkenazi community was founded in Izmir by Russian refugees. Its last rabbi was Meir Melammed. After the Turco-Greek War (1919–21), many Jews left the town for Greece or emigrated to France and the United States.

Social institutions that were established between the 16th and 18th centuries, such as Ḥevrat Bikkur Ḥolim, were still active in the 19th century, together with new modern institutions – pharmacies, hospitals, etc.

Modern Period

Beginning from the 19th century, Izmir – a commercial city situated on a major transportation route – became one of the most prominent financial and cultural centers in the world. This financial growth and the consequent cultural and spiritual recrudescence attracted many Jews to Izmir.

The westernization and modernization of the Ottoman Empire, stepped up from the end of 18th century, had a profound impact on Ottoman Jewry in general and on the Izmir community in particular. This outside influence was further strengthened by the settlement of the Francos (European Jewish merchants) from the 17th century in Izmir, and brought changes to the social and financial infrastructure of the Izmir community. Also strengthening the modernization processes in Izmir was the establishment of new *Alliance schools there starting in 1873 and accompanied by the invasion of Western cultural ideas. It was also Izmir where the first Jewish journal, *La Buena Esperansa* ("The Good Hope"), was published in 1843, testifying to the flourishing of Jewish journalism that went hand in hand with the accelerated cultural development of the city. The local Jewish theater performed original plays in Ladino and foreign plays in their original language. Groups of dancers appeared for the first time outside religious frameworks. These changes were accompanied by the partial adoption of European dress; by new living quarters, i.e., the move from the Jewish Quarter near the market (Çarşı) to new mixed neighborhoods in the western part of the city: Göstepe, Karataş, and Karantina; by the use of European languages (French and later Turkish) at the expense of Ladino; and by new professions made possible by an Alliance education.

These processes of modernization, westernization, and progress at the same time underscored the polaritization that spread within Jewish society. The disintegration of traditional frameworks was also felt within the religious establishment. With the enforcement of the Tanzimat regulations and the legislation of the Chief Rabbinate Law in 1865, the prestige of the rabbis began to decline. The constitution weakened the rabbis and strengthened, in their stead, the rich community leaders. As Izmir was known for the strict religious attitude of its rabbis, spirited struggles, sometimes violent, took place among different groups in the community.

In the beginning of the 20th century there were over 20,000 Jews in Izmir. After World War I, many emigrated to South America. After the establishment of the State of Israel and between 1948 and 1950, about 10,000 immigrated to Israel as well, so that, in 1965, the chief rabbinate of the town reported that there were about 4,000 Jews there. In 1968 their number was estimated at around 3,000, and at the beginning of the 21st century at approximately 2,000, mostly concentrated in the Alsancak quarter. As a result of the large-scale emigration, the Jewish orphanage was closed. The only Jewish talmud torah was closed in 1999, probably as a consequence of changes in the educational system in Turkey (Tevhid-i Tedrisat). Wealthy Jews sent their children to the French St. Joseph School, which is located in the old Jewish school building, or to private schools such as the American College. If the family was not wealthy, its children were sent to public schools. Seven of the synagogues in the town remained in some use, usually on the High Holidays; two of them were in constant use: Shaar Shamayim situated in Alsancak and Beth Israel in Karataş. The most significant events in those two were the festivals. The community retained a hospital which was mainly used for deliveries, and a Moshav Zekenim Retirement Home (Assyl De Viar) in Karataş. The community also operated a Ḥevra Kaddisha, a youth club (called the Liga (League)), and the La Dame de Bonne volunteer organization. There was also a rabbinical court headed by R. Nissim Barmaimon.

There are three cemeteries in Izmir, only one in use: the Bornova Cemetery located in Bornova, was established in 1881 by Alexandre Sidi; the Gurt Çeşme, or Kan Çeşme, Cemetery, which was in use from 1885 to 1934, where the Izmir rabbis' tombstones are located at the entrance; and the New Cemetery, which was opened in the 1930s and is the only one still in use.

Most of the Jews who remained in Izmir are merchants, some of them exporters and industrialists, and the economic situation of the community is relatively good, since thousands of the poor left for Israel. There were no assaults on Jews, apart from attacks on Jewish shops during the demonstrations connected with the problem of Cyprus in September 1955.

[Haim J. Cohen / Efrat E. Aviv (2nd ed.)]

Hebrew Printing

Izmir was one of the three printing centers in the Ottoman Empire, following Constantinople and Salonika. The first Jewish printer in Izmir was Abraham b. Jedidiah Gabbay (1657–75). His first book was J. Escapa's *Rosh Yosef* (1657). Besides several Hebrew works, Gabbay also printed two in Spanish, in Latin characters: a second edition of *Mikveh Yisrael (Esperanza de Israel)* by Manasseh Ben Israel; and *Apologia por la noble nación de los Judíos, por Eduardo Nicholas*, translated from English into Spanish by R. Manasseh. In 1675 he printed 16 books; he left Izmir in 1683 and from that year all printing activity ceased for the next 50 years. Jonah b. Jacob of Zalocze established a new printing house in 1728 in partnership with Rabbi David Hazzan. It was closed in 1739. In 1754 a new printing house was established by Judah Hazzan and Jacob Valensi. The printing house of Osta Maragos, the Greek printer, was also active during this period. Printing activity ceased in Izmir after this period for nearly 60 years for unknown reasons

From the fourth decade of the 19th century on, several printing houses were active in Izmir. In 1838, the English printing house of Griffith was established, mainly to serve the Anglican Mission. Griffith also printed some journals in Ladino which appeared in Izmir.

In the 1850s another printing house was in operation, the one of Judah Samuel Ashkenazi's two sons. It ceased operation at some stage and Benzion Benjamin began printing in 1857 using the equipment of this printing house after its closure. In 1862 Roditi was given the opportunity to use a new printing house. By 1884 he had published no fewer than 71 books, among them many important religious works, such as *Me-Am Lo'ez*. The printing house of the De Seguras was founded in 1862 and existed until 1906. Abraham Pontremoli founded a new printing house which operated from 1876 to 1889. Pontremoli published some of Palacci's books.

In the last quarter of the 19th century, a few other printing houses were founded but operated for only a short while (i.e., Shevet Ahim, 1876, etc.). During the 20th century the most prominent printer was Ephraim Melamed, whose printing house operated between 1901 and 1924. Hebrew books continued to be issued in Izmir until the 1950s. These printers produced more than 400 books, ranging over the entire field of biblical, talmudic and rabbinic literature, besides a large amount of liturgy and *Kabbalah. Many of the authors were local scholars. From 1838, 117 books were printed entirely, or partially, in Ladino. These were at first religious works only, but toward the end of the 19th century stories, novels, poetry, etc., were also published. Additionally, from 1842, Jewish newspapers such as *La Buena Esperanza* (1842), *El Novelista* (1889–1922), and *El Messerret* (1897–1922) were printed in Ladino.

[Avraham Yaari / Efrat E. Aviv (2nd ed.)]

BIBLIOGRAPHY: Rosanes, Togarmah, index; A. Galanté, *Histoire des Juifs d'Anatolie*, 1 (1937); idem, *Appendice à l'Histoire des Juifs d'Anatolie* (1948), 5–15; Werses, in: *Yavneh*, 3 (1942), 93–111; Scholem, Shabbetai Ẓevi, 1 (1957), 298–353; Yaari, in: *Aresheth*, 1 (1958), 97–222; C. Roth, in: KS, 28 (1952/53), 390–3; Frey, *Corpus*, 2 (1952) 9–12. **ADD. BIBLIOGRAPHY:** Y. Ben Na'eh, "Hebrew Printing Houses in the Ottoman Empire," in: G. Nassi (ed.), *Jewish Journalism and Printing Houses in the Ottoman Empire and Modern Turkey* (2000); S. Bora, *Izmir Yahudileri Tarihi* (1995); H. Nahum, *Izmir Yahudileri 19–20 yüzyıl* (2000); E. Bashan, "Contacts between Jews in Smyrna and the Levant Company of London in the Seventeenth and Eighteenth Centuries," in: *Transactions of the Jewish Historical Society of England*, 29 (1988), pp. 53–73; E. Eldem, D. Goffman and B. Masters (eds.), *The Ottoman City between East and West-Aleppo, Izmir and Istanbul* (1999); D. Goffman, *Izmir and the Levantine World, 1550–1650* (1990); S.J. Shaw, *The Jews of the Ottoman Empire and the Turkish Republic* (1991); A. Levy, *The Sephardim in the Ottoman Empire* (1992); A. Levy (ed.), *The Jews of the Ottoman Empire* (1994); H. Gerber and J. Barnai, *The Jews of Izmir in the 19th Century – Ottoman Documents from Shar'i Court* (1984) (Hebrew); E. Benbassa and A. Rodrigue, *The Jews of the Balkans. The Judeo-Spanish Community, 15th to 20th Centuries* (2001) (Hebrew).

IZMIT, port on the Sea of Marmara, in the Kocaeli Province, Turkey; in rabbinic literature its name appears as Isnimit, while its older Turkish name was Izniknid and its Greek name is Nicomedia. Its Jewish community has a long history and is first mentioned in various sources in the sixth century. The Karaite philosopher *Aaron b. Elijah (d. 1369), known as "Nicomedio," lived in Izmit. It is probable that the Karaites appeared in Nicomedia already before the 14th century, although no documentary or literary confirmation is as yet available. In the 16th century several families of Jewish refugees from Spain settled in Izmit, and in the middle of the 17th century there were about 60 Jewish families there. During the Ottoman period the Jews lived in a special quarter, known as *Yahudi Mahallesi*. The community had its rabbinical court, a synagogue and religious school, and two cemeteries. Some of the Jews engaged in petty trade, while others were artisans, working in silk, wool, cotton, glass, and pottery. In the 17th century emissaries from Ereẓ Israel visited the community and the local Jews turned with their halakhic questions to *Istanbul and *Salonica, especially to Rabbi Moses *Benveniste and Rabbi Ḥayyim Sabettai. There is some information about Jewish courts of law in 1622 and 1635. Rabbi Abraham Donozo served the community in 1635–70. According to censuses 199 Jews lived there in 1893, 428 in 1912, and 512 in 1911–12. The last rabbis of the community from 1911 were Abraham Habib, Daniel Tazartes, and Raphael Tazartes. In 1919, when the Greeks invaded western Anatolia, most of the Jews took refuge in Istanbul. The remaining Jews fled in 1921, when a great fire raged in the town, and Jewish settlement in Izmit came to an end.

BIBLIOGRAPHY: A. Galanté, *Histoire des Juifs d'Anatolie*, 2 (1939), 262–4; Z. Ankori, *Karaites in Byzantium* (1959), index. **ADD. BIBLIOGRAPHY:** A. Galanté, in: ISIS, 1:88; 4:225–28, 300, 338; J. McCarthy, in: A. Levy (ed), *The Jews of the Ottoman Empire* (1994), 380, 382, 392.

[Abraham Haim / Leah Bornstein-Makovetsky (2nd ed.)]

IZRAELITA, Polish Jewish weekly of assimilationist tendencies (1866–1908). During the 40 years it appeared, *Izraelita* promoted Polish culture within the Jewish community. The editor, Samuel Henryk *Peltin, continued the tradition of *Jutrzenka*, edited by Daniel *Neufeld. The forerunner of both these journals was the short-lived *Izraelita Polski*, which appeared during the November Revolution (1830–31) under the editorship of Stanislaw Harnisch. The *Izraelita* opposed antisemites who rejected the services of the Jewish youth who had enthusiastically volunteered in the ranks of the revolution. The *Izraelita* had a varied readership. Since its editor was not an extreme assimilationist, he maintained contact with the Jewish intelligentsia of differing ideologies. Among those who contributed to the journal were Wilhelm *Feldman, historian of Polish literature; the lawyer Joseph Kirszrot; the author Leo Belmont; the lawyer A.J. Cohen; Adolf *Gruenbaum; the lawyer Nikodem Lekert; and Nahum *Sokolow. The journal carried news of Jews throughout the world, Jewish historical and literary articles, and reports on the Warsaw Jewish community, and performed an important function in opposing the antisemitic incitement of the journal *Rola* edited by Jan *Jeleński. It supported community philanthropy and attempted to strengthen Jewish commitment among the assimilationists in Poland. In this context, the paper aroused interest in research into the Jewish past in Poland, encouraging scholarship into folklore and history. The Polish press accused the *Izraelita* of encouraging separatism even to the extent of supporting an independent Jewish school system. Despite the strong trend to polonization, the journal never achieved a significant circulation. In 1872 it had 460 subscribers, 300 of them from Warsaw. By 1895, it had still not achieved a readership of one thousand. *Izraelita* opposed the Orthodox camp and Zionism, regarding emigration as an act of treachery toward the Polish homeland. During the short period of Nahum Sokolow's editorship after the death of Peltin (1896), the journal did, however, give some expression to national-Zionist ideas. In 1915, publication of the *Izraelita* was briefly resumed by Joseph Wasserzug, an extreme assimilationist who opposed the efforts of Georg *Brandes to defend the Jews against Polish antisemitism.

BIBLIOGRAPHY: EG, 1 (1953), 246, 509; J. Shatzky, *Geshikhte fun Yidn in Varshe*, 3 (1953), 318–21; I. Schiper (ed.), *Zydzi w Polsce Odrodzonej*, 2 (1933), 151. **ADD. BIBLIOGRAPHY:** M. Fuks, *Prasa zydowska w Warszawie 1823–1939* (1979), index.

[Moshe Landau]

IZRAELITA MAGYAR IRODALMI TÁRSULAT (Imit; "Jewish-Hungarian Literary Society," 1894–1950), literary society founded mainly at the urging of I. *Goldziher, S. Kohn, and I. *Loew, and its first president was Samuel *Kohn. According to the society's bylaws its main function was to publish an annual and a Hungarian translation of the Bible. The latter was published under the editorship of W. *Bacher, J. *Banoczi, and S. *Krauss (4 vols., 1898–1907). The annual, a publication of rich scholarly and literary merit, appeared in the years 1895–1918, 1929–43, and 1948. Its first editors were W. Bacher, F. *Mezey, and J. Banoczi. From 1929 S. *Szemere served as editor. In addition, the society published important monographs, such as, among others, M. Pollak, *A zsidók története Sopronban* ("History of the Jews in Sopron"); S. Buechler, *A zsidók története Budapesten…* ("History of the Jews in Budapest," 1901); *Monumenta Hungariae Judaica* (vols. 1–4, 1903–38).

The society arranged lecture series in Budapest and other cities. In 1909 the Jewish Museum of Budapest was established at the initiative of the society. In 1947 the society was reorganized, but in its new form it was short-lived.

BIBLIOGRAPHY: B. Heller, in: *Emlékkönyv Bánóczi Józsefnek* (1919), 80–96.

[Alexander Scheiber]

IZYASLAV (formerly **Zaslavl**), city in Khmelnitski district (former Kamenets-Podolski), Ukraine. The first information about the Jewish community there dates from the first half of the 16th century. Most of the Jews fled to neighboring cities during the *Chmielnicki massacres of 1648; approximately 200 who had remained behind were killed. After the massacres, the community was rebuilt. With the beginning of the *Haidamack movement in 1708 the community was destroyed and most of its members killed. In 1747 five Jews from a neighboring village were put to death in the city as a result of a *blood libel. The Jewish population was 2,807 in 1765 and 5,998 (47% of the total population) in 1897. Towards the end of Polish rule, Izyaslav was a center of *Ḥasidism. Due to the influence of Leib Bolekhovski (d. 1883), the rabbi, the community was culturally in advance of other settlements in the area. In 1897 Izyaslav had 6,000 Jews (almost 50% of the total population). After the Russian Revolution of 1917, the Zionist movement flourished in Izyaslav. Most of the city's Jewish children were enrolled in Hebrew kindergartens and schools. With the establishment of Soviet rule in 1920, Jewish community life in the city declined. By 1926, 3,820 Jews (one third of the population) remained there, dropping to 3,208 (28% of the total) in 1939. The Germans captured Izyaslav in July 1941 and murdered 1,000 Jews on August 24. A ghetto was set up and Jews from neighboring towns were brought there. In the course of 1942, some 5,000 Jews were murdered. A group of essential workers was put into a local labor camp and executed on January 20 1943. Izyaslav was the home of Nathan Nata *Hannover, author of *Yeven Meẓulah*. A Hebrew printing press was active there from 1807 to 1808 and five books, three of them liturgical, were issued.

BIBLIOGRAPHY: J. Kontorshchik, in: *Ha-Meliẓ*, 32 (1892), 195, 198; N.N. Hannover, *Yeven Meẓulah* (1923), 30–33; E. Ehrenburg, *Merder fun Felker* (1945), 77–79; I. Vogel, in: *Yalkut Vohlin*, 7 (1947), 6–9; A. Yaari, in: KS, 19 (1943), 277–9. **ADD. BIBLIOGRAPHY:** PK.

[Yehuda Slutsky / Shmuel Spector (2nd ed.)]

ABBREVIATIONS

GENERAL ABBREVIATIONS

This list contains abbreviations used in the Encyclopaedia (apart from the standard ones, such as geographical abbreviations, points of compass, etc.). For names of organizations, institutions, etc., in abbreviation, see Index. For bibliographical abbreviations of books and authors in Rabbinical literature, see following lists.

*	Cross reference; i.e., an article is to be found under the word(s) immediately following the asterisk (*).
°	Before the title of an entry, indicates a non-Jew (post-biblical times).
‡	Indicates reconstructed forms.
>	The word following this sign is derived from the preceding one.
<	The word preceding this sign is derived from the following one.

ad loc.	*ad locum*, "at the place"; used in quotations of commentaries.
A.H.	*Anno Hegirae*, "in the year of Hegira," i.e., according to the Muslim calendar.
Akk.	Addadian.
A.M.	*anno mundi*, "in the year (from the creation) of the world."
anon.	anonymous.
Ar.	Arabic.
Aram.	Aramaic.
Ass.	Assyrian.
b.	born; *ben, bar.*
Bab.	Babylonian.
B.C.E.	Before Common Era (= B.C.).
bibl.	bibliography.
Bul.	Bulgarian.
c., ca.	Circa.
C.E.	Common Era (= A.D.).
cf.	*confer*, "compare."
ch., chs.	chapter, chapters.
comp.	compiler, compiled by.
Cz.	Czech.
D	according to the documentary theory, the Deuteronomy document.
d.	died.
Dan.	Danish.
diss., dissert,	dissertation, thesis.
Du.	Dutch.
E.	according to the documentary theory, the Elohist document (i.e., using Elohim as the name of God) of the first five (or six) books of the Bible.
ed.	editor, edited, edition.
eds.	editors.
e.g.	*exempli gratia*, "for example."
Eng.	English.
et al.	*et alibi*, "and elsewhere"; or *et alii*, "and others"; "others."
f., ff.	and following page(s).
fig.	figure.
fl.	flourished.
fol., fols	folio(s).
Fr.	French.
Ger.	German.
Gr.	Greek.
Heb.	Hebrew.
Hg., Hung	Hungarian.
ibid	*Ibidem*, "in the same place."
incl. bibl.	includes bibliography.
introd.	introduction.
It.	Italian.
J	according to the documentary theory, the Jahwist document (i.e., using YHWH as the name of God) of the first five (or six) books of the Bible.
Lat.	Latin.
lit.	literally.
Lith.	Lithuanian.
loc. cit.	*loco citato*, "in the [already] cited place."
Ms., Mss.	Manuscript(s).
n.	note.
n.d.	no date (of publication).
no., nos	number(s).
Nov.	Novellae (Heb. *Ḥiddushim*).
n.p.	place of publication unknown.
op. cit.	*opere citato*, "in the previously mentioned work."
P.	according to the documentary theory, the Priestly document of the first five (or six) books of the Bible.
p., pp.	page(s).
Pers.	Persian.
pl., pls.	plate(s).
Pol.	Polish.
Port.	Potuguese.
pt., pts.	part(s).
publ.	published.
R.	Rabbi or Rav (before names); in Midrash (after an abbreviation) – *Rabbah.*
r.	recto, the first side of a manuscript page.
Resp.	Responsa (Latin "answers," Hebrew *She'elot u-Teshuvot* or *Teshuvot),* collections of rabbinic decisions.
rev.	revised.

Rom.	Romanian.
Rus(s).	Russian.
Slov.	Slovak.
Sp.	Spanish.
s.v.	*sub verbo, sub voce*, "under the (key) word."
Sum	Sumerian.
summ.	Summary.
suppl.	supplement.
Swed.	Swedish.
tr., trans(l).	translator, translated, translation.
Turk.	Turkish.
Ukr.	Ukrainian.
v., vv.	*verso*. The second side of a manuscript page; also verse(s).
Yid.	Yiddish.

ABBREVIATIONS USED IN RABBINICAL LITERATURE

Adderet Eliyahu, Karaite treatise by Elijah b. Moses *Bashyazi.
Admat Kodesh, Resp. by Nissim Ḥayyim Moses b. Joseph |Mizraḥi.
Aguddah, Sefer ha-, Nov. by *Alexander Suslin ha-Kohen.
Ahavat Ḥesed, compilation by *Israel Meir ha-Kohen.
Aliyyot de-Rabbenu Yonah, Nov. by *Jonah b. Avraham Gerondi.
Arukh ha-Shulḥan, codification by Jehiel Michel *Epstein.
Asayin (= positive precepts), subdivision of: (1) *Maimonides, *Sefer ha-Mitzvot;* (2) *Moses b. Jacob of Coucy, *Semag.*
Asefat Dinim, subdivision of *Sedei Ḥemed* by Ḥayyim Hezekiah *Medini, an encyclopaedia of precepts and responsa.
Asheri = *Asher b. Jehiel.
Aeret Ḥakhamim, by Baruch *Frankel-Teomim; pt, 1: Resp. to Sh. Ar.; pt2: Nov. to Talmud.
Ateret Zahav, subdivision of the *Levush*, a codification by Mordecai b. Abraham (Levush) *Jaffe; *Ateret Zahav* parallels Tur. YD.
Ateret Ẓevi, Comm. To Sh. Ar. by Ẓevi Hirsch b. Azriel.
Avir Ya'akov, Resp. by Jacob Avigdor.
Avkat Rokhel, Resp. by Joseph b. Ephraim *Caro.
Avnei Millu'im, Comm. to Sh. Ar., EH, by *Aryeh Loeb b. Joseph ha-Kohen.
Avnei Nezer, Resp. on Sh. Ar. by Abraham b. Ze'ev Nahum Bornstein of *Sochaczew.
Avodat Massa, Compilation of Tax Law by Yoasha Abraham Judah.
Azei ha-Levanon, Resp. by Judah Leib *Zirelson.

Ba'al ha-Tanya – *Shneur Zalman of Lyady.
Ba'ei Ḥayyei, Resp. by Ḥayyim b. Israel *Benveniste.
Ba'er Heitev, Comm. To Sh. Ar. The parts on OḤ and EH are by Judah b. Simeon *Ashkenazi, the parts on YD AND ḤM by *Zechariah Mendel b. Aryeh Leib. Printed in most editions of Sh. Ar.
Baḥ = Joel *Sirkes.
Baḥ, usual abbreviation for *Bayit Ḥadash*, a commentary on Tur by Joel *Sirkes; printed in most editions of Tur.
Bayit Ḥadash, see *Baḥ*.
Berab = Jacob Berab, also called Ri Berav.
Bedek ha-Bayit, by Joseph b. Ephraim *Caro, additions to his *Beit Yosef* (a comm. to Tur). Printed sometimes inside *Beit Yosef*, in smaller type. Appears in most editions of Tur.
Be'er ha-Golah, Commentary to Sh. Ar. By Moses b. Naphtali Hirsch *Rivkes; printed in most editions of Sh. Ar.
Be'er Mayim, Resp. by Raphael b. Abraham Manasseh Jacob.
Be'er Mayim Ḥayyim, Resp. by Samuel b. Ḥayyim *Vital.
Be'er Yizḥak, Resp. by Isaac Elhanan *Spector.
Beit ha-Beḥirah, Comm. to Talmud by Menahem b. Solomon *Meiri.
Beit Me'ir, Nov. on Sh. Ar. by Meir b. Judah Leib Posner.
Beit Shelomo, Resp. by Solomon b. Aaron Ḥason (the younger).
Beit Shemu'el, Comm. to Sh. Ar., EH, by *Samuel b. Uri Shraga Phoebus.
Beit Ya'akov, by Jacob b. Jacob Moses *Lorberbaum; pt.1: Nov. to Ket.; pt.2: Comm. to EH.
Beit Yisrael, collective name for the commentaries *Derishah, Perishah*, and *Be'urim* by Joshua b. Alexander ha-Kohen *Falk. See under the names of the commentaries.
Beit Yizḥak, Resp. by Isaac *Schmelkes.
Beit Yosef: (1) Comm. on Tur by Joseph b. Ephraim *Caro; printed in most editions of Tur; (2) Resp. by the same.
Ben Yehudah, Resp. by Abraham b. Judah Litsch (ליטש) Rosenbaum.
Bertinoro, Standard commentary to Mishnah by Obadiah *Bertinoro. Printed in most editions of the Mishnah.
[Be'urei] Ha-Gra, Comm. to Bible, Talmud, and Sh. Ar. By *Elijah b. Solomon Zalmon (Gaon of Vilna); printed in major editions of the mentioned works.
Be'urim, Glosses to Isserles *Darkhei Moshe* (a comm. on Tur) by Joshua b. Alexander ha-Kohen *Falk; printed in many editions of Tur.
Binyamin Ze'ev, Resp. by *Benjamin Ze'ev b. Mattathias of Arta.
Birkei Yosef, Nov. by Ḥayyim Joseph David *Azulai.
Ha-Buẓ ve-ha-Argaman, subdivision of the *Levush* (a codification by Mordecai b. Abraham (Levush) *Jaffe); *Ha-Buẓ ve-ha-Argaman* parallels Tur, EH.

Comm. = Commentary

Da'at Kohen, Resp. by Abraham Isaac ha-Kohen. *Kook.
Darkhei Moshe, Comm. on Tur Moses b. Israel *Isserles; printed in most editions of Tur.
Darkhei No'am, Resp. by *Mordecai b. Judah ha-Levi.
Darkhei Teshuvah, Nov. by Ẓevi *Shapiro; printed in the major editions of Sh. Ar.
De'ah ve-Haskel, Resp. by Obadiah Hadaya (see *Yaskil Avdi).*

Derashot Ran, Sermons by *Nissim b. Reuben Gerondi.
Derekh Ḥayyim, Comm. to *Avot* by *Judah Loew (Lob., Liwa) b. Bezalel (Maharal) of Prague.
Derishah, by Joshua b. Alexander ha-Kohen *Falk; additions to his *Perishah* (comm. on Tur); printed in many editions of Tur.
Derushei ha-Ẓelaḥ, Sermons, by Ezekiel b. Judah Halevi *Landau.
Devar Avraham, Resp. by Abraham *Shapira.
Devar Shemu'el, Resp. by Samuel *Aboab.
Devar Yehoshu'a, Resp. by Joshua Menahem b. Isaac Aryeh Ehrenberg.
Dikdukei Soferim, variae lections of the talmudic text by Raphael Nathan*Rabbinowicz.
Divrei Emet, Resp. by Isaac Bekhor David.
Divrei Ge'onim, Digest of responsa by Ḥayyim Aryeh b. Jeḥiel Ẓevi *Kahana.
Divrei Ḥamudot, Comm. on *Piskei ha-Rosh* by Yom Tov Lipmann b. Nathan ha-Levi *Heller; printed in major editions of the Talmud.
Divrei Ḥayyim several works by Ḥayyim *Halberstamm; if quoted alone refers to his Responsa.
Divrei Malkhi'el, Resp. by Malchiel Tenebaum.
Divrei Rivot, Resp. by Isaac b. Samuel *Adarbi.
Divrei Shemu'el, Resp. by Samuel Raphael Arditi.

Edut be-Ya'akov, Resp. by Jacob b. Abraham *Boton.
Edut bi-Yhosef, Resp. by Joseph b. Isaac *Almosnino.
Ein Ya'akov, Digest of talmudic *aggadot* by Jacob (Ibn) *Habib.
Ein Yiẓḥak, Resp. by Isaac Elhanan *Spector.
Ephraim of Lentshitz = Solomon *Luntschitz.
Erekh Leḥem, Nov. and glosses to Sh. Ar. by Jacob b. Abraham *Castro.
Eshkol, Sefer ha-, Digest of *halakhot* by *Abraham b. Isaac of Narbonne.
Et Sofer, Treatise on Law Court documents by Abraham b. Mordecai *Ankawa, in the 2nd vol. of his Resp. *Kerem Ḥamar.*
Etan ha-Ezraḥi, Resp. by Abraham b. Israel Jehiel (Shrenzl) *Rapaport.
Even ha-Ezel, Nov. to Maimonides' *Yad Ḥazakah* by Isser Zalman *Meltzer.
Even ha-Ezer, also called *Raban* of *Ẓafenat Pa'ne'aḥ,* rabbinical work with varied contents by *Eliezer b. Nathan of Mainz; not identical with the subdivision of Tur, Shulḥan Arukh, etc.
Ezrat Yehudah, Resp. by *Isaar Judah b. Nechemiah of Brisk.

Gan Eden, Karaite treatise by *Aaron b. Elijah of Nicomedia.
Gersonides = *Levi b. Gershom, also called Leo Hebraecus, or Ralbag.
Ginnat Veradim, Resp. by *Abraham b. Mordecai ha-Levi.

Haggahot, another name for *Rema.*
Haggahot Asheri, glosses to *Piskei ha-Rosh* by *Israel of Krems; printed in most Talmud editions.
Haggahot Maimuniyyot, Comm,. to Maimonides' Yad Ḥazakah by *Meir ha-Kohen; printed in most eds. of Yad.
Haggahot Mordekhai, glosses to *Mordekhai* by Samuel *Schlettstadt; printed in most editions of the Talmud after *Mordekhai.*
Haggahot ha-Rashash on Tosafot, annotations of Samuel *Strashun on the Tosafot (printed in major editions of the Talmud).
Ha-Gra = *Elijah b. Solomon Zalman (Gaon of Vilna).
Ha-Gra, Commentaries on Bible, Talmud, and Sh. Ar. respectively, by *Elijah b. Solomon Zalman (Gaon of Vilna); printed in major editions of the mentioned works.
Hai Gaon, Comm. = his comm. on Mishnah.
Ḥakham Ẓevi, Resp. by Ẓevi Hirsch b. Jacob *Ashkenazi.
Halakhot = Rif, *Halakhot.* Compilation and abstract of the Talmud by Isaac b. Jacob ha-Kohen *Alfasi; printed in most editions of the Talmud.
Halakhot Gedolot, compilation of *halakhot* from the Geonic period, arranged acc. to the Talmud. Here cited acc. to ed. Warsaw (1874). Author probably *Simeon Kayyara of Basra.
Halakhot Pesukot le-Rav Yehudai Ga'on compilation of *halakhot.*
Halakhot Pesukot min ha-Ge'onim, compilation of *halakhot* from the geonic period by different authors.
Ḥananel, Comm. to Talmud by *Hananel b. Ḥushi'el; printed in some editions of the Talmud.
Harei Besamim, Resp. by Aryeh Leib b. Isaac *Horowitz.
Ḥassidim, Sefer, Ethical maxims by *Judah b. Samuel he-Ḥasid.
Hassagot Rabad on Rif, Glosses on Rif, *Halakhot,* by *Abraham b. David of Posquières.
Hassagot Rabad [on Yad], Glosses on Maimonides, *Yad Ḥazakah,* by *Abraham b. David of Posquières.
Hassagot Ramban, Glosses by Naḥmanides on Maimonides' *Sefer ha-Mitzvot;* usually printed together with *Sefer ha-Mitzvot.*
Ḥatam Sofer = Moses *Sofer.
Ḥavvot Ya'ir, Resp. and varia by Jair Ḥayyim *Bacharach
Ḥayyim Or Zaru'a = *Ḥayyim (Eliezer) b. Isaac.
Ḥazon Ish = Abraham Isaiah *Karelitz.
Ḥazon Ish, Nov. by Abraham Isaiah *Karelitz
Ḥedvat Ya'akov, Resp. by Aryeh Judah Jacob b. David Dov Meisels (article under his father's name).
Heikhal Yiẓḥak, Resp. by Isaac ha-Levi *Herzog.
Ḥelkat Meḥokek, Comm. to Sh. Ar., by Moses b. Isaac Judah *Lima.
Ḥelkat Ya'akov, Resp. by Mordecai Jacob Breisch.
Ḥemdah Genuzah, , Resp. from the geonic period by different authors.
Ḥemdat Shelomo, Resp. by Solomon Zalman *Lipschitz.
Ḥida = Ḥayyim Joseph David *Azulai.
Ḥiddushei Halakhot ve-Aggadot, Nov. by Samuel Eliezer b. Judah ha-Levi *Edels.
Ḥikekei Lev, Resp. by Ḥayyim *Palaggi.
Ḥikrei Lev, Nov. to Sh. Ar. by Joseph Raphael b. Ḥayyim Joseph Ḥazzan (see article *Ḥazzan Family).
Hil. = Hilkhot … (e.g. *Hilkhot Shabbat).*
Ḥinnukh, Sefer ha-, List and explanation of precepts attributed (probably erroneously) to Aaron ha-Levi of Barcelona (see article *Ha-Ḥinnukh*).
Ḥok Ya'akov, Comm. to Hil. Pesaḥ in Sh. Ar., OḤ, by Jacob b. Joseph *Reicher.
Ḥokhmat Sehlomo (1), Glosses to Talmud, *Rashi* and Tosafot by Solomon b. Jehiel "Maharshal") *Luria; printed in many editions of the Talmud.
Ḥokhmat Sehlomo (2), Glosses and Nov. to Sh. Ar. by Solomon b. Judah Aaron *Kluger printed in many editions of Sh. Ar.
Ḥur, subdivision of the *Levush,* a codification by Mordecai b. Abraham (Levush) *Jaffe; *Hur* (or *Levush ha-Hur)* parallels Tur, OḤ, 242–697.
Ḥut ha-Meshullash, fourth part of the *Tashbeẓ* (Resp.), by Simeon b. Zemaḥ *Duran.

Ibn Ezra, Comm. to the Bible by Abraham *Ibn Ezra; printed in the major editions of the Bible *("Mikra'ot Gedolot")*.
Imrei Yosher, Resp. by Meir b. Aaron Judah *Arik.
Ir Shushan, Subdivision of the *Levush*, a codification by Mordecai b. Abraham (Levush) *Jaffe; *Ir Shushan* parallels Tur, ḤM.
Israel of Bruna = Israel b. Ḥayyim *Bruna.
Ittur. Treatise on precepts by *Isaac b. Abba Mari of Marseilles.

Jacob Be Rab = *Be Rab.
Jacob b. Jacob Moses of Lissa = Jacob b. Jacob Moses *Lorberbaum.
Judah B. Simeon = Judah b. Simeon *Ashkenazi.
Judah Minz = Judah b. Eliezer ha-Levi *Minz.

Kappei Aharon, Resp. by Aaron Azriel.
Kehillat Ya'akov, Talmudic methodology, definitions etc. by Israel Jacob b. Yom Tov *Algazi.
Kelei Ḥemdah, Nov. and *pilpulim* by Meir Dan *Plotzki of Ostrova, arranged acc. to the Torah.
Keli Yakar, Annotations to the Torah by Solomon *Luntschitz.
Keneh Ḥokhmah, Sermons by Judah Loeb *Pochwitzer.
Keneset ha-Gedolah, Digest of *halakhot* by Ḥayyim b. Israel *Benveniste; subdivided into annotations to *Beit Yosef* and annotations to Tur.
Keneset Yisrael, Resp. by Ezekiel b. Abraham Katzenellenbogen (see article *Katzenellenbogen Family).
Kerem Ḥamar, Resp. and varia by Abraham b. Mordecai *Ankawa.
Kerem Shelmo. Resp. by Solomon b. Joseph *Amarillo.
Keritut, [Sefer], Methodology of the Talmud by *Samson b. Isaac of Chinon.
Kesef ha-Kedoshim, Comm. to Sh. Ar., ḤM, by Abraham *Wahrmann; printed in major editions of Sh. Ar.
Kesef Mishneh, Comm. to Maimonides, *Yad Ḥazakah*, by Joseph b. Ephraim *Caro; printed in most editions of *Yad Ḥazakah*.
Keẓot ha-Ḥoshen, Comm. to Sh. Ar., ḤM, by *Aryeh Loeb b. Joseph ha-Kohen; printed in major editions of Sh. Ar.
Kol Bo [Sefer], Anonymous collection of ritual rules; also called *Sefer ha-Likkutim*.
Kol Mevasser, Resp. by Meshullam *Rath.
Korban Aharon, Comm. to *Sifra* by Aaron b. Abraham *Ibn Ḥayyim; pt. 1 is called: *Middot Aharon*.
Korban Edah, Comm. to Jer. Talmud by David *Fraenkel; with additions: *Shiyyurei Korban;* printed in most editions of Jer. Talmud.
Kunteres ha-Kelalim, subdivision of *Sedei Ḥemed*, an encyclopaedia of precepts and responsa by Ḥayyim Hezekiah *Medini.
Kunteres ha-Semikhah, a treatise by *Levi b. Ḥabib; printed at the end of his responsa.
Kunteres Tikkun Olam, part of *Mispat Shalom* (Nov. by Shalom Mordecai b. Moses *Schwadron).

Lavin (negative precepts), subdivision of: (1) *Maimonides, *Sefer ha-Mitzvot;* (2) *Moses b. Jacob of Coucy, *Semag*.
Leḥem Mishneh, Comm. to Maimonides, *Yad Ḥazakah*, by Abraham [Ḥiyya] b. Moses *Boton; printed in most editions of *Yad Ḥazakah*.
Leḥem Rav, Resp. by Abraham [Ḥiyya] b. Moses *Boton.
Leket Yosher, Resp and varia by Israel b. Pethahiah *Isserlein, collected by *Joseph (Joselein) b. Moses.
Leo Hebraeus = *Levi b. Gershom, also called Ralbag or Gersonides.
Levush = Mordecai b. Abraham *Jaffe.
Levush [Malkhut], Codification by Mordecai b. Abraham (Levush) *Jaffe, with subdivisions: *[Levush ha-] Tekhelet* (parallels Tur OḤ 1–241); *[Levush ha-] Ḥur* (parallels Tur OḤ 242–697); *[Levush] Ateret Zahav* (parallels Tur YD); *[Levush ha-Buẓ ve-ha-Argaman* (parallels Tur EH); *[Levush] Ir Shushan* (parallels Tur ḤM); under the name *Levush* the author wrote also other works.
Li-Leshonot ha-Rambam, fifth part (nos. 1374–1700) of Resp. by *David b. Solomon ibn Abi Zimra (Radbaz).
Likkutim, Sefer ha-, another name for *[Sefer] Kol Bo*.

Ma'adanei Yom Tov, Comm. on *Piskei ha-Rosh* by Yom Tov Lipmann b. Nathan ha-Levi *Heller; printed in many editions of the Talmud.
Mabit = Moses b. Joseph *Trani.
Magen Avot, Comm. to *Avot* by Simeon b. Ẓemaḥ *Duran.
Magen Avraham, Comm. to Sh. Ar., OḤ, by Abraham Abele b. Ḥayyim ha-Levi *Gombiner; printed in many editions of Sh. Ar., OḤ.
Maggid Mishneh, Comm. to Maimonides, *Yad Ḥazakah*, by *Vidal Yom Tov of Tolosa; printed in most editions of the *Yad Ḥazakah*.
Maḥaneh Efrayim, Resp. and Nov., arranged acc. to Maimonides' *Yad Ḥazakah* , by Ephraim b. Aaron *Navon.
Maharai = Israel b. Pethahiah *Isserlein.
Maharal of Prague = *Judah Loew (Lob, Liwa), b. Bezalel.
Maharalbaḥ = *Levi b. Ḥabib.
Maharam Alashkar = Moses b. Isaac *Alashkar.
Maharam Alshekh = Moses b. Ḥayyim *Alashekh.
Maharam Mintz = Moses *Mintz.
Maharam of Lublin = *Meir b. Gedaliah of Lublin.
Maharam of Padua = Meir *Katzenellenbogen.
Maharam of Rothenburg = *Meir b. Baruch of Rothenburg.
Maharam Shik = Moses b. Joseph Schick.
Maharash Engel = Samuel b. Ze'ev Wolf Engel.
Maharashdam = Samuel b. Moses *Medina.
Maharḥash = Ḥayyim (ben) Shabbetai.
Mahari Basan = Jehiel b. Ḥayyim Basan.
Mahari b. Lev = Joseph ibn Lev.
Mahari'az = Jekuthiel Asher Zalman Ensil Zusmir.
Maharibal = *Joseph ibn Lev.
Mahariḥ = Jacob (Israel) *Ḥagiz.
Maharik = Joseph b. Solomon *Colon.
Maharikash = Jacob b. Abraham *Castro.
Maharil = Jacob b. Moses *Moellin.
Maharimat = Joseph b. Moses di Trani (not identical with the Maharit).
Maharit = Joseph b. Moses *Trani.
Maharitaẓ = Yom Tov b. Akiva Ẓahalon. (See article *Ẓahalon Family).
Maharsha = Samuel Eliezer b. Judah ha-Levi *Edels.
Maharshag = Simeon b. Judah Gruenfeld.
Maharshak = Samson b. Isaac of Chinon.
Maharshakh = *Solomon b. Abraham.
Maharshal = Solomon b. Jeḥiel *Luria.
Mahasham = Shalom Mordecai b. Moses *Sschwadron.
Maharyu = Jacob b. Judah *Weil.
Maḥazeh Avraham, Resp. by Abraham Nebagen v. Meir ha-Levi Steinberg.
Maḥazik Berakhah, Nov. by Ḥayyim Joseph David *Azulai.

*Maimonides = Moses b. Maimon, or Rambam.
*Malbim = Meir Loeb b. Jehiel Michael.
Malbim = Malbim's comm. to the Bible; printed in the major editions.
Malbushei Yom Tov, Nov. on *Levush*, OḤ, by Yom Tov Lipmann b. Nathan ha-Levi *Heller.
Mappah, another name for *Rema.*
Mareh ha-Panim, Comm. to Jer. Talmud by Moses b. Simeon *Margolies; printed in most editions of Jer. Talmud.
Margaliyyot ha-Yam, Nov. by Reuben *Margoliot.
Masat Binyamin, Resp. by Benjamin Aaron b. Abraham *Slonik
Mashbir, Ha- = *Joseph Samuel b. Isaac Rodi.
Massa Ḥayyim, Tax *halakhot* by Ḥayyim *Palaggi, with the subdivisions *Missim ve-Arnomiyyot* and *Torat ha-Minhagot.*
Massa Melekh, Compilation of Tax Law by Joseph b. Isaac *Ibn Ezra with concluding part *Ne'ilat She'arim.*
Matteh Asher, Resp. by Asher b. Emanuel Shalem.
Matteh Shimon, Digest of Resp. and Nov. to Tur and *Beit Yosef,* ḤM, by Mordecai Simeon b. Solomon.
Matteh Yosef, Resp. by Joseph b. Moses ha-Levi Nazir (see article under his father's name).
Mayim Amukkim, Resp. by Elijah b. Abraham *Mizraḥi.
Mayim Ḥayyim, Resp. by Ḥayyim b. Dov Beresh Rapaport.
Mayim Rabbim, , Resp. by Raphael *Meldola.
Me-Emek ha-Bakha, , Resp. by Simeon b. Jekuthiel Ephrati.
Me'irat Einayim, usual abbreviation: *Sma* (from: *Sefer Me'irat Einayim*); comm. to Sh. Ar. By Joshua b. Alexander ha-Kohen *Falk; printed in most editions of the Sh. Ar.
Melammed le-Ho'il, Resp. by David Ẓevi *Hoffmann.
Meisharim, [*Sefer*], Rabbinical treatise by *Jeroham b. Meshullam.
Meshiv Davar, Resp. by Naphtali Ẓevi Judah *Berlin.
Mi-Gei ha-Haregah, Resp. by Simeon b. Jekuthiel Ephrati.
Mi-Ma'amakim, Resp. by Ephraim Oshry.
Middot Aharon, first part of *Korban Aharon,* a comm. to *Sifra* by Aaron b. Abraham *Ibn Ḥayyim.
Migdal Oz, Comm. to Maimonides, *Yad Ḥazakah,* by *Ibn Gaon Shem Tov b. Abraham; printed in most editions of the *Yad Ḥazakah.*
Mikhtam le-David, Resp. by David Samuel b. Jacob *Pardo.
Mikkaḥ ve-ha-Mimkar, Sefer ha-, Rabbinical treatise by *Hai Gaon.
Milḥamot ha-Shem, Glosses to Rif, *Halakhot,* by *Naḥmanides.
Minḥat Ḥinnukh, Comm. to *Sefer ha-Ḥinnukh,* by Joseph b. Moses *Babad.
Minḥat Yiẓḥak, Resp. by Isaac Jacob b. Joseph Judah Weiss.
Misgeret ha-Shulḥan, Comm. to Sh. Ar., ḤM, by Benjamin Ze'ev Wolf b. Shabbetai; printed in most editions of Sh. Ar.
Mishkenot ha-Ro'im, Halakhot in alphabetical order by Uzziel Alshekh.
Mishnah Berurah, Comm. to Sh. Ar., OḤ, by *Israel Meir ha-Kohen.
Mishneh le-Melekh, Comm. to Maimonides, *Yad Ḥazakah,* by Judah *Rosanes; printed in most editions of *Yad Ḥazakah.*
Mishpat ha-Kohanim, Nov. to Sh. Ar., ḤM, by Jacob Moses *Lorberbaum, part of his *Netivot ha-Mishpat;* printed in major editions of Sh. Ar.
Mishpat Kohen, Resp. by Abraham Isaac ha-Kohen *Kook.
Mishpat Shalom, Nov. by Shalom Mordecai b. Moses *Schwadron; contains: *Kunteres Tikkun Olam.*
Mishpat u-Ẓedakah be-Ya'akov, Resp. by Jacob b. Reuben *Ibn Ẓur.
Mishpat ha-Urim, Comm. to Sh. Ar., ḤM by Jacob b. Jacob Moses *Lorberbaum, part of his *Netivot ha-Mishpat;* printed in major editons of Sh. Ar.
Mishpat Ẓedek, Resp. by *Melammed Meir b. Shem Tov.
Mishpatim Yesharim, Resp. by Raphael b. Mordecai *Berdugo.
Mishpetei Shemu'el, Resp. by Samuel b. Moses *Kalai (Kal'i).
Mishpetei ha-Tanna'im, Kunteres, Nov on *Levush,* OḤ by Yom Tov Lipmann b. Nathan ha-Levi *Heller.
Mishpetei Uzzi'el (Uziel), Resp. by Ben-Zion Meir Hai *Ouziel.
Missim ve-Arnoniyyot, Tax *halakhot* by Ḥayyim *Palaggi, a subdivision of his work *Massa Ḥayyim* on the same subject.
Mitzvot, Sefer ha-, Elucidation of precepts by *Maimonides; subdivided into *Lavin* (negative precepts) and *Asayin* (positive precepts).
Mitzvot Gadol, Sefer, Elucidation of precepts by *Moses b. Jacob of Coucy, subdivided into *Lavin* (negative precepts) and *Asayin* (positive precepts); the usual abbreviation is *Semag.*
Mitzvot Katan, Sefer, Elucidation of precepts by *Isaac b. Joseph of Corbeil; the usual, abbreviation is *Semak.*
Mo'adim u-Zemannim, Rabbinical treatises by Moses Sternbuch.
Modigliano, Joseph Samuel = *Joseph Samuel b. Isaac, Rodi (Ha-Mashbir).
Mordekhai (Mordecai), halakhic compilation by *Mordecai b. Hillel; printed in most editions of the Talmud after the texts.
Moses b. Maimon = *Maimonides, also called Rambam.
Moses b. Naḥman = Naḥmanides, also called Ramban.
Muram = Isaiah Menahem b. Isaac (from: Morenu R. Mendel).

Naḥal Yiẓḥak, Comm. on Sh. Ar., ḤM, by Isaac Elhanan *Spector.
Naḥalah li-Yhoshu'a, Resp. by Joshua Ẓunẓin.
Naḥalat Shivah, collection of legal forms by *Samuel b. David Moses ha-Levi.
*Naḥmanides = Moses b. Naḥman, also called Ramban.
Naẓiv = Naphtali Ẓevi Judah *Berlin.
Ne'eman Shemu'el, Resp. by Samuel Isaac *Modigilano.
Ne'ilat She'arim, concluding part of *Massa Melekh* (a work on Tax Law) by Joseph b. Isaac *Ibn Ezra, containing an exposition of customary law and subdivided into *Minhagei Issur* and *Minhagei Mamon.*
Ner Ma'aravi, Resp. by Jacob b. Malka.
Netivot ha-Mishpat, by Jacob b. Jacob Moses *Lorberbaum; subdivided into *Mishpat ha-Kohanim,* Nov. to Sh. Ar., ḤM, and *Mishpat ha-Urim,* a comm. on the same; printed in major editions of Sh. Ar.
Netivot Olam, Saying of the Sages by *Judah Loew (Lob, Liwa) b. Bezalel.
Nimmukei Menaḥem of Merseburg, Tax *halakhot* by the same, printed at the end of Resp. Maharyu.
Nimmukei Yosef, Comm. to Rif. *Halakhot,* by Joseph *Ḥabib (Ḥabiba); printed in many editions of the Talmud.
Noda bi-Yhudah, Resp. by Ezekiel b. Judah ha-Levi *Landau; there is a first collection *(Mahadura Kamma)* and a second collection *(Mahadura Tinyana).*
Nov. = Novellae, Ḥiddushim.

Ohel Moshe (1), Notes to Talmud, *Midrash Rabbah,* Yad, *Sifrei* and to several Resp., by Eleazar *Horowitz.

Ohel Moshe (2), Resp. by Moses Jonah Zweig.
Oholei Tam. Resp. by *Tam ibn Yaḥya Jacob b. David; printed in the rabbinical collection *Tummat Yesharim.*
Oholei Ya'akov, Resp. by Jacob de *Castro.
Or ha-Me'ir Resp by Judah Meir b. Jacob Samson Shapiro.
Or Same'aḥ, Comm. to Maimonides, *Yad Ḥazakah,* by *Meir Simḥah ha-Kohen of Dvinsk; printed in many editions of the *Yad Ḥazakah.*
Or Zaru'a [the father] = *Isaac b. Moses of Vienna.
Or Zaru'a [the son] = *Ḥayyim (Eliezer) b. Isaac.
Or Zaru'a, Nov. by *Isaac b. Moses of Vienna.
Orah, Sefer ha-, Compilation of ritual precepts by *Rashi.
Oraḥ la-Ẓaddik, Resp. by Abraham Ḥayyim Rodrigues.
Oẓar ha-Posekim, Digest of Responsa.

Paḥad Yiẓḥak, Rabbinical encyclopaedia by Isaac *Lampronti.
Panim Me'irot, Resp. by Meir b. Isaac *Eisenstadt.
Parashat Mordekhai, Resp. by Mordecai b. Abraham Naphtali *Banet.
Pe'at ha-Sadeh la-Dinim and Pe'at ha-Sadeh la-Kelalim, subdivisions of the *Sedei Ḥemed,* an encyclopaedia of precepts and responsa, by Ḥayyim Hezekaih *Medini.
Penei Moshe (1), Resp. by Moses *Benveniste.
Penei Moshe (2), Comm. to Jer. Talmud by Moses b. Simeon *Margolies; printed in most editions of the Jer. Talmud.
Penei Moshe (3), Comm. on the aggadic passages of 18 treatises of the Bab. and Jer. Talmud, by Moses b. Isaiah Katz.
Penei Yehoshu'a, Nov. by Jacob Joshua b. Ẓevi Hirsch *Falk.
Peri Ḥadash, Comm. on Sh. Ar. By Hezekiah da *Silva.
Perishah, Comm. on Tur by Joshua b. Alexander ha-Kohen *Falk; printed in major edition of Tur; forms together with *Derishah* and *Be'urim* (by the same author) the *Beit Yisrael.*
Pesakim u-Khetavim, 2nd part of the *Terumat ha-Deshen* by Israel b. Pethahiah *Isserlein' also called *Piskei Maharai.*
Pilpula Ḥarifta, Comm. to *Piskei ha-Rosh, Seder Nezikin,* by Yom Tov Lipmann b. Nathan ha-Levi *Heller; printed in major editions of the Talmud.
Piskei Maharai, see *Terumat ha-Deshen,* 2nd part; also called *Pesakim u-Khetavim.*
Piskei ha-Rosh, a compilation of *halakhot,* arranged on the Talmud, by *Asher b. Jehiel (Rosh); printed in major Talmud editions.
Pitḥei Teshuvah, Comm. to Sh. Ar. by Abraham Hirsch b. Jacob *Eisenstadt; printed in major editions of the Sh. Ar.

Rabad = *Abraham b. David of Posquières (Rabad III.).
Raban = *Eliezer b. Nathan of Mainz.
Raban, also called *Ẓafenat Pa'ne'aḥ* or *Even ha-Ezer,* see under the last name.
Rabi Abad = *Abraham b. Isaac of Narbonne.
Radad = David Dov. b. Aryeh Judah Jacob *Meisels.
Radam = Dov Berush b. Isaac Meisels.
Radbaz = *David b Solomon ibn Abi Ziumra.
Radbaz, Comm. to Maimonides, *Yad Ḥazakah,* by *David b. Solomon ibn Abi Zimra.
Ralbag = *Levi b. Gershom, also called Gersonides, or Leo Hebraeus.
Ralbag, Bible comm. by *Levi b. Gershon.
Rama [da Fano] = Menaḥem Azariah *Fano.
Ramah = Meir b. Todros [ha-Levi] *Abulafia.
Ramam = *Menaham of Merseburg.
Rambam = *Maimonides; real name: Moses b. Maimon.
Ramban = *Naḥmanides; real name Moses b. Naḥman.
Ramban, Comm. to Torah by *Naḥmanides; printed in major editions. ("Mikra'ot Gedolot").
Ran = *Nissim b. Reuben Gerondi.
Ran of Rif, Comm. on Rif, *Halakhot,* by Nissim b. Reuben Gerondi.
Ranaḥ = *Elijah b. Ḥayyim.
Rash = *Samson b. Abraham of Sens.
Rash, Comm. to Mishnah, by *Samson b. Abraham of Sens; printed in major Talmud editions.
Rashash = Samuel *Strashun.
Rashba = Solomon b. Abraham *Adret.
Rashba, Resp., see also; *Sefer Teshuvot ha-Rashba ha-Meyuḥasot leha-Ramban,* by Solomon b. Abraham *Adret.
Rashbad = Samuel b. David.
Rashbam = *Samuel b. Meir.
Rashbam = Comm. on Bible and Talmud by *Samuel b. Meir; printed in major editions of Bible and most editions of Talmud.
Rashbash = Solomon b. Simeon *Duran.
*Rashi = Solomon b. Isaac of Troyes.
Rashi, Comm. on Bible and Talmud by *Rashi; printed in almost all Bible and Talmud editions.
Raviah = Eliezer b. Joel ha-Levi.
Redak = David *Kimḥi.
Redak, Comm. to Bible by David *Kimḥi.
Redakh = *David b. Ḥayyim ha-Kohen of Corfu.
Re'em = Elijah b. Abraham *Mizraḥi.
Rema = Moses b. Israel *Isserles.
Rema, Glosses to Sh. Ar. by Moses b. Israel *Isserles; printed in almost all editions of the Sh. Ar. inside the text in Rashi type; also called *Mappah* or *Haggahot.*
Remek = Moses Kimḥi.
Remakh = Moses ha-Kohen mi-Lunel.
Reshakh = *Solomon b. Abraham; also called Maharshakh.
Resp. = Responsa, *She'elot u-Teshuvot.*
Ri Berav = *Berab.
Ri Escapa = Joseph b. Saul *Escapa.
Ri Migash = Joseph b. Meir ha-Levi *Ibn Migash.
Riba = Isaac b. Asher ha-Levi; Riba II (Riba ha-Baḥur) = his grandson with the same name.
Ribam = Isaac b. Mordecai (or: Isaac b. Meir).
Ribash = *Isaac b. Sheshet Perfet (or: Barfat).
Rid= *Isaiah b. Mali di Trani the Elder.
Ridbaz = Jacob David b. Ze'ev *Willowski.
Rif = Isaac b. Jacob ha-Kohen *Alfasi.
Rif, *Halakhot,* Compilation and abstract of the Talmud by Isaac b. Jacob ha-Kohen *Alfasi.
Ritba = Yom Tov b. Abraham *Ishbili.
Riẓbam = Isaac b. Mordecai.
Rosh = *Asher b. Jehiel, also called Asheri.
Rosh Mashbir, Resp. by *Joseph Samuel b. Isaac, Rodi.

Sedei Ḥemed, Encyclopaedia of precepts and responsa by Ḥayyim Ḥezekiah *Medini; subdivisions: *Asefat Dinim, Kunteres ha-Kelalim, Pe'at ha-Sadeh la-Dinim, Pe'at ha-Sadeh la-Kelalim.*
Semag, Usual abbreviation of *Sefer Mitzvot Gadol,* elucidation of precepts by *Moses b. Jacob of Coucy; subdivided into *Lavin* (negative precepts) *Asayin* (positive precepts).
Semak, Usual abbreviation of *Sefer Mitzvot Katan,* elucidation of precepts by *Isaac b. Joseph of Corbeil.

Sh. Ar. = *Shulḥan Arukh,* code by Joseph b. Ephraim *Caro.
Sha'ar Mishpat, Comm. to Sh. Ar., ḤM. By Israel Isser b. Ze'ev Wolf.
Sha'arei Shevu'ot, Treatise on the law of oaths by *David b. Saadiah; usually printed together with Rif, *Halakhot;* also called: *She'arim of R. Alfasi.*
Sha'arei Teshuvah, Collection of resp. from Geonic period, by different authors.
Sha'arei Uzzi'el, Rabbinical treatise by Ben-Zion Meir Ha *Ouziel.
Sha'arei Ẓedek, Collection of resp. from Geonic period, by different authors.
Shadal [or Shedal] = Samuel David *Luzzatto.
Shai la-Moreh, Resp. by Shabbetai Jonah.
Shakh, Usual abbreviation of *Siftei Kohen,* a comm. to Sh. Ar., YD and ḤM by *Shabbetai b. Meir ha-Kohen; printed in most editions of Sh. Ar.
Sha'ot-de-Rabbanan, Resp. by *Solomon b. Judah ha-Kohen.
She'arim of R. Alfasi see *Sha'arei Shevu'ot.*
Shedal, see Shadal.
She'elot u-Teshuvot ha-Ge'onim, Collection of resp. by different authors.
She'erit Yisrael, Resp. by Israel Ze'ev Mintzberg.
She'erit Yosef, Resp. by *Joseph b. Mordecai Gershon ha-Kohen.
She'ilat Yaveẓ, Resp. by Jacob *Emden (Yaveẓ).
She'iltot, Compilation arranged acc. to the Torah by *Aḥa (Aḥai) of Shabḥa.
Shem Aryeh, Resp. by Aryeh Leib *Lipschutz.
Shemesh Ẓedakah, Resp. by Samson *Morpurgo.
Shenei ha-Me'orot ha-Gedolim, Resp. by Elijah *Covo.
Shetarot, Sefer ha-, Collection of legal forms by *Judah b. Barzillai al-Bargeloni.
Shevut Ya'akov, Resp. by Jacob b. Joseph Reicher.
Shibbolei ha-Leket Compilation on ritual by Zedekiah b. Avraham *Anav.
Shiltei Gibborim, Comm. to Rif, *Halakhot,* by *Joshua Boaz b. Simeon; printed in major editions of the Talmud.
Shittah Mekubbeẓet, Compilation of talmudical commentaries by Bezalel *Ashkenazi.
Shivat Ẓiyyon, Resp. by Samuel b. Ezekiel *Landau.
Shiyyurei Korban, by David *Fraenkel; additions to his comm. to Jer. Talmud *Korban Edah;* both printed in most editions of Jer. Talmud.
Sho'el u-Meshiv, Resp. by Joseph Saul ha-Levi *Nathanson.
Sh[ulḥan] Ar[ukh] [of Ba'al ha-Tanya], Code by *Shneur Zalman of Lyady; not identical with the code by Joseph Caro.
Siftei Kohen, Comm. to Sh. Ar., YD and ḤM by *Shabbetai b. Meir ha-Kohen; printed in most editions of Sh. Ar.; usual abbreviation: *Shakh.*
Simḥat Yom Tov, Resp. by Tom Tov b. Jacob *Algazi.
Simlah Ḥadashah, Treatise on *Sheḥitah* by Alexander Sender b. Ephraim Zalman *Schor; see also *Tevu'ot Shor.*
Simeon b. Ẓemaḥ = Simeon b. Ẓemaḥ *Duran.
Sma, Comm. to Sh. Ar. by Joshua b. Alexander ha-Kohen *Falk; the full title is: *Sefer Me'irat Einayim;* printed in most editions of Sh. Ar.
Solomon b. Isaac ha-Levi = Solomon b. Isaac *Levy.
Solomon b. Isaac of Troyes = *Rashi.

Tal Orot, Rabbinical work with various contents, by Joseph ibn Gioia.
Tam, Rabbenu = *Tam Jacob b. Meir.
Tashbaẓ = Samson b. Zadok.
Tashbeẓ = Simeon b. Zemaḥ *Duran, sometimes also abbreviation for Samson b. Zadok, usually known as Tashbaẓ.
Tashbeẓ [Sefer ha-], Resp. by Simeon b. Ẓemaḥ *Duran; the fourth part of this work is called: *Ḥut ha-Meshullash.*
Taz, Usual abbreviation of *Turei Zahav,* comm., to Sh. Ar. by *David b. Samnuel ha-Levi; printed in most editions of Sh. Ar.
(Ha)-Tekhelet, subdivision of the *Levush* (a codification by Mordecai b. Abraham (Levush) *Jaffe); *Ha-Tekhelet* parallels Tur, OḤ 1-241.
Terumat ha-Deshen, by Israel b. Pethahiah *Isserlein; subdivided into a part containing responsa, and a second part called *Pesakim u-Khetavim* or *Piskei Maharai.*
Terumot, Sefer ha-, Compilation of *halakhot* by Samuel b. Isaac *Sardi.
Teshuvot Ba'alei ha-Tosafot, Collection of responsa by the Tosafists.
Teshjvot Ge'onei Mizraḥ u-Ma'aav, Collection of responsa.
Teshuvot ha-Geonim, Collection of responsa from Geonic period.
Teshuvot Ḥakhmei Provinẓyah, Collection of responsa by different Provencal authors.
Teshuvot Ḥakhmei Ẓarefat ve-Loter, Collection of responsa by different French authors.
Teshuvot Maimuniyyot, Resp. pertaining to Maimonides' *Yad Ḥazakah;* printed in major editions of this work after the text; authorship uncertain.
Tevu'ot Shor, by Alexander Sender b. Ephraim Zalman *Schor, a comm. to his *Simlah Ḥadashah,* a work on *Sheḥitah.*
Tiferet Ẓevi, Resp. by Ẓevi Hirsch of the "AHW" Communities (Altona, Hamburg, Wandsbeck).
Tiktin, Judah b. Simeon = Judah b. Simeon *Ashkenazi.
Toledot Adam ve-Ḥavvah, Codification by *Jeroham b. Meshullam.
Torat Emet, Resp. by Aaron b. Joseph *Sasson.
Torat Ḥayyim, , Resp. by Ḥayyim (ben) Shabbetai.
Torat ha-Minhagot, subdivision of the *Massa Ḥayyim* (a work on tax law) by Ḥayyim *Palaggi, containing an exposition of customary law.
Tosafot Rid, Explanations to the Talmud and decisions by *Isaiah b. Mali di Trani the Elder.
Tosefot Yom Tov, comm. to Mishnah by Yom Tov Lipmann b. Nathan ha-Levi *Heller; printed in most editions of the Mishnah.
Tummim, subdivision of the comm. to Sh. Ar., ḤM, *Urim ve-Tummim* by Jonathan *Eybeschuetz; printed in the major editions of Sh. Ar.
Tur, usual abbreviation for the *Arba'ah Turim* of *Jacob b. Asher.
Turei Zahav, Comm. to Sh. Ar. by *David b. Samuel ha-Levi; printed in most editions of Sh. Ar.; usual abbreviation: *Taz.*

Urim, subdivision of the following.
Urim ve-Tummim, Comm. to Sh. Ar., ḤM, by Jonathan *Eybeschuetz; printed in the major editions of Sh. Ar.; subdivided in places into *Urim* and *Tummim.*

Vikku'aḥ Mayim Ḥayyim, Polemics against Isserles and Caro by Ḥayyim b. Bezalel.

Yad Malakhi, Methodological treatise by *Malachi b. Jacob ha-Kohen.

Yad Ramah, Nov. by Meir b. Todros [ha-Levi] *Abulafia.
Yakhin u-Vo'az, Resp. by Ẓemaḥ b. Solomon *Duran.
Yam ha-Gadol, Resp. by Jacob Moses *Toledano.
Yam shel Shelomo, Compilation arranged acc. to Talmud by Solomon b. Jehiel (Maharshal) *Luria.
Yashar, Sefer ha-, by *Tam, Jacob b. Meir (Rabbenu Tam); 1st pt.: Resp.; 2nd pt.: Nov.
Yaskil Avdi, Resp. by Obadiah Hadaya (printed together with his Resp. *De'ah ve-Haskel).*
Yaveẓ = Jacob *Emden.
Yehudah Ya'aleh, Resp. by Judah b. Israel *Aszod.
Yekar Tiferet, Comm. to Maimonides' *Yad Ḥazakah,*by David b. Solomon ibn Zimra, printed in most editions of *Yad Ḥazakah.*
Yere'im [ha-Shalem], [*Sefer*], Treatise on precepts by *Eliezer b. Samuel of Metz.
Yeshu'ot Ya'akov, Resp. by Jacob Meshullam b. Mordecai Ze'ev *Ornstein.
Yiẓhak Rei'aḥ, Resp. by Isaac b. Samuel Abendanan (see article *Abendanam Family).
Ẓafenat Pa'ne'aḥ (1), also called *Raban* or *Even ha-Ezer,* see under the last name.
Ẓafenat Pa'ne'aḥ (2), Resp. by Joseph *Rozin.
Zayit Ra'anan, Resp. by Moses Judah Leib b. Benjamin Auerbach.
Ẓeidah la-Derekh, Codification by *Menahem b. Aaron ibn Zerah.
Ẓedakah u-Mishpat, Resp. by Ẓedakah b. Saadiah Huẓin.
Zekan Aharon, Resp. by Elijah b. Benjamin ha-Levi.
Zekher Ẓaddik, Sermons by Eliezer *Katzenellenbogen.
Ẓemaḥ Ẓedek (1) Resp. by Menaham Mendel Shneersohn (see under *Shneersohn Family).
Zera Avraham, Resp. by Abraham b. David *Yiẓḥaki.
Zera Emet Resp. by *Ishmael b. Abaham Isaac ha-Kohen.
Ẓevi la-Ẓaddik, Resp. by Ẓevi Elimelech b. David Shapira.
Zikhron Yehudah, Resp. by *Judah b. Asher
Zikhron Yosef, Resp. by Joseph b. Menahem *Steinhardt.
Zikhronot, Sefer ha-, Sermons on several precepts by Samuel *Aboab.
Zikkaron la-Rishonim . . ., by Albert (Abraham Elijah) *Harkavy; contains in vol. 1 pt. 4 (1887) a collection of Geonic responsa.
Ẓiẓ Eliezer, Resp. by Eliezer Judah b. Jacob Gedaliah Waldenberg.

BIBLIOGRAPHICAL ABBREVIATIONS

Bibliographies in English and other languages have been extensively updated, with English translations cited where available. In order to help the reader, the language of books or articles is given where not obvious from titles of books or names of periodicals. Titles of books and periodicals in languages with alphabets other than Latin, are given in transliteration, even where there is a title page in English. Titles of articles in periodicals are not given. Names of Hebrew and Yiddish periodicals well known in English-speaking countries or in Israel under their masthead in Latin characters are given in this form, even when contrary to transliteration rules. Names of authors writing in languages with non-Latin alphabets are given in their Latin alphabet form wherever known; otherwise the names are transliterated. Initials are generally not given for authors of articles in periodicals, except to avoid confusion. Non-abbreviated book titles and names of periodicals are printed in *italics.* Abbreviations are given in the list below.

AASOR	*Annual of the American School of Oriental Research* (1919ff.).
AB	*Analecta Biblica* (1952ff.).
Abel, Géog	F.-M. Abel, *Géographie de la Palestine,* 2 vols. (1933–38).
ABR	*Australian Biblical Review* (1951ff.).
Abr.	Philo, *De Abrahamo.*
Abrahams, Companion	I. Abrahams, *Companion to the Authorised Daily Prayer Book* (rev. ed. 1922).
Abramson, Merkazim	S. Abramson, *Ba-Merkazim u-va-Tefuẓot bi-Tekufat ha-Ge'onim* (1965).
Acts	Acts of the Apostles (New Testament).
ACUM	*Who is who in ACUM [Aguddat Kompozitorim u-Meḥabbrim].*
ADAJ	*Annual of the Department of Antiquities, Jordan* (1951ff.).
Adam	Adam and Eve (Pseudepigrapha).
ADB	*Allgemeine Deutsche Biographie,* 56 vols. (1875–1912).
Add. Esth.	The Addition to Esther (Apocrypha).
Adler, Prat Mus	1. Adler, *La pratique musicale savante dans quelques communautés juives en Europe au XVIIe et XVIIIe siècles,* 2 vols. (1966).
Adler-Davis	H.M. Adler and A. Davis (ed. and tr.), *Service of the Synagogue, a New Edition of the Festival Prayers with an English Translation in Prose and Verse,* 6 vols. (1905–06).
Aet.	Philo, *De Aeternitate Mundi.*
AFO	*Archiv fuer Orientforschung* (first two volumes under the name *Archiv fuer Keilschriftforschung)* (1923ff.).
Ag. Ber	*Aggadat Bereshit* (ed. Buber, 1902*).*
Agr.	Philo, *De Agricultura.*
Ag. Sam.	*Aggadat Samuel.*
Ag. Song	*Aggadat Shir ha-Shirim* (Schechter ed., 1896).
Aharoni, Ereẓ	Y. Aharoni, *Ereẓ Yisrael bi-Tekufat ha-Mikra: Geografyah Historit* (1962).
Aharoni, Land	Y. Aharoni, *Land of the Bible* (1966).

Ahikar	Ahikar (Pseudepigrapha).
AI	*Archives Israélites de France* (1840–1936).
AJA	*American Jewish Archives* (1948ff.).
AJHSP	*American Jewish Historical Society – Publications* (after vol. 50 = AJHSQ).
AJHSQ	*American Jewish Historical* (Society) *Quarterly* (before vol. 50 =AJHSP).
AJSLL	*American Journal of Semitic Languages and Literature* (1884–95 under the title *Hebraica*, since 1942 JNES).
AJYB	*American Jewish Year Book* (1899ff.).
AKM	Abhandlungen fuer die Kunde des Morgenlandes (series).
Albright, Arch	W.F. Albright, *Archaeology of Palestine* (rev. ed. 1960).
Albright, Arch Bib	W.F. Albright, *Archaeology of Palestine and the Bible* (1935^{3}).
Albright, Arch Rel	W.F. Albright, *Archaeology and the Religion of Israel* (1953^{3}).
Albright, Stone	W.F. Albright, *From the Stone Age to Christianity* (1957^{2}).
Alon, Meḥkarim	G. Alon, *Meḥkarim be-Toledot Yisrael bi-Ymei Bayit Sheni u-vi-Tekufat ha-Mishnah ve-ha Talmud*, 2 vols. (1957–58).
Alon, Toledot	G. Alon, *Toledot ha-Yehudim be-Ereẓ Yisrael bi-Tekufat ha-Mishnah ve-ha-Talmud*, I (1958^{3}), (1961^{2}).
ALOR	Alter Orient (series).
Alt, Kl Schr	A. Alt, *Kleine Schriften zur Geschichte des Volkes Israel*, 3 vols. (1953–59).
Alt, Landnahme	A. Alt, *Landnahme der Israeliten in Palaestina* (1925); also in Alt, Kl Schr, 1 (1953), 89–125.
Ant.	Josephus, *Jewish Antiquities* (Loeb Classics ed.).
AO	*Acta Orientalia* (1922ff.).
AOR	*Analecta Orientalia* (1931ff.).
AOS	American Oriental Series.
Apion	Josephus, *Against Apion* (Loeb Classics ed.).
Aq.	Aquila's Greek translation of the Bible.
Ar.	*Arakhin* (talmudic tractate).
Artist.	Letter of Aristeas (Pseudepigrapha).
ARN^{1}	*Avot de-Rabbi Nathan*, version (1) ed. Schechter, 1887.
ARN^{2}	*Avot de-Rabbi Nathan*, version (2) ed. Schechter, 1945^{2}.
Aronius, Regesten	I. Aronius, *Regesten zur Geschichte der Juden im fraenkischen und deutschen Reiche bis zum Jahre 1273* (1902).
ARW	*Archiv fuer Religionswissenschaft* (1898–1941/42).
AS	*Assyrological Studies* (1931ff.).
Ashtor, Korot	E. Ashtor (Strauss), *Korot ha-Yehudim bi-Sefarad ha-Muslemit*, 1(1966^{2}), 2(1966).
Ashtor, Toledot	E. Ashtor (Strauss), *Toledot ha-Yehudim be-Miẓrayim ve-Suryah Taḥat Shilton ha-Mamlukim*, 3 vols. (1944–70).
Assaf, Ge'onim	S. Assaf, *Tekufat ha-Ge'onim ve-Sifrutah* (1955).
Assaf, Mekorot	S. Assaf, *Mekorot le-Toledot ha-Ḥinnukh be-Yisrael*, 4 vols. (1925–43).
Ass. Mos.	Assumption of Moses (Pseudepigrapha).
ATA	Alttestamentliche Abhandlungen (series).
ATANT	Abhandlungen zur Theologie des Alten und Neuen Testaments (series).
AUJW	*Allgemeine unabhaengige juedische Wochenzeitung* (till 1966 = AWJD).
AV	Authorized Version of the Bible.
Avad.	*Avadim* (post-talmudic tractate).
Avi-Yonah, Geog	M. Avi-Yonah, *Geografyah Historit shel Ereẓ Yisrael* (1962^{3}).
Avi-Yonah, Land	M. Avi-Yonah, *The Holy Land from the Persian to the Arab conquest (536 B.C. to A.D. 640)* (1960).
Avot	*Avot* (talmudic tractate).
Av. Zar.	*Avodah Zarah* (talmudic tractate).
AWJD	*Allgemeine Wochenzeitung der Juden in Deutschland* (since 1967 = AUJW).
AZDJ	*Allgemeine Zeitung des Judentums.*
Azulai	Ḥ.Y.D. Azulai, *Shem ha-Gedolim*, ed. by I.E. Benjacob, 2 pts. (1852) (and other editions).
BA	*Biblical Archaeologist* (1938ff.).
Bacher, Bab Amor	W. Bacher, *Agada der babylonischen Amoraeer* (1913^{2}).
Bacher, Pal Amor	W. Bacher, *Agada der palaestinensischen Amoraeer* (Heb. ed. *Aggadat Amora'ei Ereẓ Yisrael*), 2 vols. (1892–99).
Bacher, Tann	W. Bacher, *Agada der Tannaiten* (Heb. ed. *Aggadot ha-Tanna'im*, vol. 1, pt. 1 and 2 (1903); vol. 2 (1890).
Bacher, Trad	W. Bacher, *Tradition und Tradenten in den Schulen Palaestinas und Babyloniens* (1914).
Baer, Spain	Yitzhak (Fritz) Baer, *History of the Jews in Christian Spain*, 2 vols. (1961–66).
Baer, Studien	Yitzhak (Fritz) Baer, *Studien zur Geschichte der Juden im Koenigreich Aragonien waehrend des 13. und 14. Jahrhunderts* (1913).
Baer, Toledot	Yitzhak (Fritz) Baer, *Toledot ha-Yehudim bi-Sefarad ha-Noẓerit mi-Teḥillatan shel ha-Kehillot ad ha-Gerush*, 2 vols. (1959^{2}).
Baer, Urkunden	Yitzhak (Fritz) Baer, *Die Juden im christlichen Spanien*, 2 vols. (1929–36).
Baer S., Seder	S.I. Baer, *Seder Avodat Yisrael* (1868 and reprints).
BAIU	*Bulletin de l'Alliance Israélite Universelle* (1861–1913).
Baker, Biog Dict	*Baker's Biographical Dictionary of Musicians*, revised by N. Slonimsky (1958^{5}; with Supplement 1965).
I Bar.	I Baruch (Apocrypha).
II Bar.	II Baruch (Pseudepigrapha).
III Bar.	III Baruch (Pseudepigrapha).
BAR	*Biblical Archaeology Review.*
Baron, Community	S.W. Baron, *The Jewish Community, its History and Structure to the American Revolution*, 3 vols. (1942).

Baron, Social	S.W. Baron, *Social and Religious History of the Jews,* 3 vols. (1937); enlarged, 1-2(1952^{2}), 3-14 (1957–69).
Barthélemy-Milik	D. Barthélemy and J.T. Milik, *Dead Sea Scrolls: Discoveries in the Judean Desert,* vol. 1 *Qumram Cave* I (1955).
BASOR	*Bulletin of the American School of Oriental Research.*
Bauer-Leander	H. Bauer and P. Leander, *Grammatik des Biblisch-Aramaeischen* (1927; repr. 1962).
BB	(1) *Bava Batra* (talmudic tractate). (2) *Biblische Beitraege* (1943ff.).
BBB	Bonner biblische Beitraege (series).
BBLA	*Beitraege zur biblischen Landes- und Altertumskunde* (until 1949–ZDPV).
BBSAJ	*Bulletin,* British School of Archaeology, Jerusalem (1922–25; after 1927 included in PEFQS).
BDASI	*Alon* (since 1948) or *Hadashot Arkheʾologiyyot* (since 1961), bulletin of the Department of Antiquities of the State of Israel.
Begrich, Chronologie	J. Begrich, *Chronologie der Koenige von Israel und Juda* (1929).
Bek.	*Bekhorot* (talmudic tractate).
Bel	Bel and the Dragon (Apocrypha).
Benjacob, Oẓar	I.E. Benjacob, *Oẓar ha-Sefarim* (1880; repr. 1956).
Ben Sira	see Ecclus.
Ben-Yehuda, Millon	E. Ben-Yedhuda, *Millon ha-Lashon ha-Ivrit,* 16 vols (1908–59; repr. in 8 vols., 1959).
Benzinger, Archaeologie	I. Benzinger, *Hebraeische Archaeologie* (1927^{3}).
Ben Zvi, Eretz Israel	I. Ben-Zvi, *Eretz Israel under Ottoman Rule* (1960; offprint from L. Finkelstein (ed.), *The Jews, their History, Culture and Religion* (vol. 1).
Ben Zvi, Erez̧ Israel	I. Ben-Zvi, *Erez̧ Israel bi-Ymei ha-Shilton ha-Ottomani (1955).*
Ber.	*Berakhot* (talmudic tractate).
Bez̧ah	*Bez̧ah* (talmudic tractate).
BIES	Bulletin of the Israel Exploration Society, see below BJPES.
Bik.	*Bikkurim* (talmudic tractate).
BJCE	Bibliography of Jewish Communities in Europe, catalog at General Archives for the History of the Jewish People, Jerusalem.
BJPES	Bulletin of the Jewish Palestine Exploration Society – English name of the Hebrew periodical known as: 1. *Yediʿot ha-Ḥevrah ha-Ivrit la-Ḥakirat Erez̧ Yisrael va-Attikoteha* (1933–1954); 2. *Yediʿot ha-Ḥevrah la-Ḥakirat Erez̧ Yisrael va-Attikoteha* (1954–1962); 3. *Yediʿot ba-Ḥakirat Erez̧ Yisrael va-Attikoteha* (1962ff.).
BJRL	*Bulletin of the John Rylands Library* (1914ff.).
BK	*Bava Kamma* (talmudic tractate).
BLBI	*Bulletin of the Leo Baeck Institute* (1957ff.).
BM	(1) *Bava Meẓia* (talmudic tractate). (2) *Beit Mikra* (1955/56ff.). (3) British Museum.
BO	*Bibbia e Oriente* (1959ff.).
Bondy-Dworský	G. Bondy and F. Dworský, *Regesten zur Geschichte der Juden in Boehmen, Maehren und Schlesien von 906 bis 1620,* 2 vols. (1906).
BOR	*Bibliotheca Orientalis* (1943ff.).
Borée, Ortsnamen	W. Borée *Die alten Ortsnamen Palaestinas* (1930).
Bousset, Religion	W. Bousset, *Die Religion des Judentums im neutestamentlichen Zeitalter* (1906^{2}).
Bousset-Gressmann	W. Bousset, *Die Religion des Judentums im spaethellenistischen Zeitalter* (1966^{3}).
BR	*Biblical Review* (1916–25).
BRCI	*Bulletin of the Research Council of Israel* (1951/52–1954/55; then divided).
BRE	*Biblical Research* (1956ff.).
BRF	*Bulletin of the Rabinowitz Fund for the Exploration of Ancient Synagogues* (1949ff.).
Briggs, Psalms	Ch. A. and E.G. Briggs, *Critical and Exegetical Commentary on the Book of Psalms,* 2 vols. (ICC, 1906–07).
Bright, Hist	J. Bright, *A History of Israel* (1959).
Brockelmann, Arab Lit	K. Brockelmann, *Geschichte der arabischen Literatur,* 2 vols. 1898–1902), supplement, 3 vols. (1937–42).
Bruell, Jahrbuecher	*Jahrbuecher fuer juedische Geschichte und Litteratur,* ed. by N. Bruell, Frankfurt (1874–90).
Brugmans-Frank	H. Brugmans and A. Frank (eds.), *Geschiedenis der Joden in Nederland* (1940).
BTS	*Bible et Terre Sainte* (1958ff.).
Bull, Index	S. Bull, *Index to Biographies of Contemporary Composers* (1964).
BW	*Biblical World* (1882–1920).
BWANT	*Beitraege zur Wissenschaft vom Alten und Neuen Testament* (1926ff.).
BZ	*Biblische Zeitschrift* (1903ff.).
BZAW	*Beihefte zur Zeitschrift fuer die alttestamentliche Wissenschaft,* supplement to ZAW (1896ff.).
BŻIH	*Biuletyn Zydowskiego Instytutu Historycznego* (1950ff.).
CAB	*Cahiers d'archéologie biblique* (1953ff.).
CAD	*The* [*Chicago*] *Assyrian Dictionary* (1956ff.).
CAH	*Cambridge Ancient History,* 12 vols. (1923–39)
CAH^{2}	*Cambridge Ancient History,* second edition, 14 vols. (1962–2005).
Calwer, Lexikon	*Calwer, Bibellexikon.*
Cant.	Canticles, usually given as Song (= Song of Songs).

Cantera-Millás, Inscripciones	F. Cantera and J.M. Millás, *Las Inscripciones Hebraicas de España* (1956).
CBQ	*Catholic Biblical Quarterly* (1939ff.).
CCARY	Central Conference of American Rabbis, *Yearbook* (1890/91ff.).
CD	*Damascus Document* from the Cairo *Genizah* (published by S. Schechter, *Fragments of a Zadokite Work*, 1910).
Charles, Apocrypha	R.H. Charles, *Apocrypha and Pseudepigrapha . . .*, 2 vols. (1913; repr. 1963–66).
Cher.	Philo, *De Cherubim*.
I (or II) Chron.	Chronicles, book I and II (Bible).
CIG	*Corpus Inscriptionum Graecarum*.
CIJ	*Corpus Inscriptionum Judaicarum*, 2 vols. (1936–52).
CIL	*Corpus Inscriptionum Latinarum*.
CIS	*Corpus Inscriptionum Semiticarum* (1881ff.).
C.J.	Codex Justinianus.
Clermont-Ganneau, Arch	Ch. Clermont-Ganneau, *Archaeological Researches in Palestine*, 2 vols. (1896–99).
CNFI	*Christian News from Israel* (1949ff.).
Cod. Just.	Codex Justinianus.
Cod. Theod.	Codex Theodosinanus.
Col.	Epistle to the Colosssians (New Testament).
Conder, Survey	Palestine Exploration Fund, *Survey of Eastern Palestine*, vol. 1, pt. I (1889) = C.R. Conder, *Memoirs of the . . . Survey*.
Conder-Kitchener	Palestine Exploration Fund, *Survey of Western Palestine*, vol. 1, pts. 1-3 (1881–83) = C.R. Conder and H.H. Kitchener, *Memoirs*.
Conf.	Philo, *De Confusione Linguarum*.
Conforte, Kore	D. Conforte, *Kore ha-Dorot* (1842^{2}).
Cong.	Philo, *De Congressu Quaerendae Eruditionis Gratia*.
Cont.	Philo, *De Vita Contemplativa*.
I (or II) Cor.	Epistles to the Corinthians (New Testament).
Cowley, Aramic	A. Cowley, *Aramaic Papyri of the Fifth Century B.C.* (1923).
Colwey, Cat	A.E. Cowley, *A Concise Catalogue of the Hebrew Printed Books in the Bodleian Library* (1929).
CRB	*Cahiers de la Revue Biblique* (1964ff.).
Crowfoot-Kenyon	J.W. Crowfoot, K.M. Kenyon and E.L. Sukenik, *Buildings of Samaria* (1942).
C.T.	Codex Theodosianus.
DAB	*Dictionary of American Biography* (1928–58).
Daiches, Jews	S. Daiches, *Jews in Babylonia* (1910).
Dalman, Arbeit	G. Dalman, *Arbeit und Sitte in Palaestina*, 7 vols.in 8 (1928–42 repr. 1964).
Dan	Daniel (Bible).
Davidson, Oẓar	I. Davidson, *Oẓar ha-Shirah ve-ha-Piyyut*, 4 vols. (1924–33); Supplement in: HUCA, 12–13 (1937/38), 715–823.
DB	J. Hastings, *Dictionary of the Bible*, 4 vols. (1963^{2}).
DBI	F.G. Vigoureaux et al. (eds.), *Dictionnaire de la Bible*, 5 vols. in 10 (1912); Supplement, 8 vols. (1928–66)
Decal.	Philo, *De Decalogo*.
Dem.	*Demai* (talmudic tractate).
DER	*Derekh Ereẓ Rabbah* (post-talmudic tractate).
Derenbourg, Hist	J. Derenbourg *Essai sur l'histoire et la géographie de la Palestine* (1867).
Det.	Philo, *Quod deterius potiori insidiari solet*.
Deus	Philo, *Quod Deus immutabilis sit*.
Deut.	Deuteronomy (Bible).
Deut. R.	*Deuteronomy Rabbah*.
DEZ	*Derekh Ereẓ Zuta* (post-talmudic tractate).
DHGE	*Dictionnaire d'histoire et de géographie ecclésiastiques*, ed. by A. Baudrillart et al., 17 vols (1912–68).
Dik. Sof	*Dikdukei Soferim*, variae lections of the talmudic text by Raphael Nathan Rabbinovitz (16 vols., 1867–97).
Dinur, Golah	B. Dinur (Dinaburg), *Yisrael ba-Golah*, 2 vols. in 7 (1959–68) = vols. 5 and 6 of his *Toledot Yisrael*, second series.
Dinur, Haganah	B. Dinur (ed.), *Sefer Toledot ha-Haganah* (1954ff.).
Diringer, Iscr	D. Diringer, *Iscrizioni antico-ebraiche palestinesi* (1934).
Discoveries	*Discoveries in the Judean Desert* (1955ff.).
DNB	*Dictionary of National Biography*, 66 vols. (1921–222) with Supplements.
Dubnow, Divrei	S. Dubnow, *Divrei Yemei Am Olam*, 11 vols (1923–38 and further editions).
Dubnow, Ḥasidut	S. Dubnow, *Toledot ha-Ḥasidut* (1960^{2}).
Dubnow, Hist	S. Dubnow, *History of the Jews* (1967).
Dubnow, Hist Russ	S. Dubnow, *History of the Jews in Russia and Poland*, 3 vols. (1916 20).
Dubnow, Outline	S. Dubnow, *An Outline of Jewish History*, 3 vols. (1925–29).
Dubnow, Weltgesch	S. Dubnow, *Weltgeschichte des juedischen Volkes* 10 vols. (1925–29).
Dukes, Poesie	L. Dukes, *Zur Kenntnis der neuhebraeischen religioesen Poesie* (1842).
Dunlop, Khazars	D. H. Dunlop, *History of the Jewish Khazars* (1954).
EA	El Amarna Letters (edited by J.A. Knudtzon), *Die El-Amarna Tafel*, 2 vols. (1907 14).
EB	*Encyclopaedia Britannica*.
EBI	*Estudios biblicos* (1941ff.).
EBIB	T.K. Cheyne and J.S. Black, *Encyclopaedia Biblica*, 4 vols. (1899–1903).
Ebr.	Philo, *De Ebrietate*.
Eccles.	Ecclesiastes (Bible).
Eccles. R.	*Ecclesiastes Rabbah*.
Ecclus.	Ecclesiasticus or Wisdom of Ben Sira (or Sirach; Apocrypha).
Eduy.	*Eduyyot* (mishanic tractate).

EG	*Enẓiklopedyah shel Galuyyot* (1953ff.).
EH	*Even ha-Ezer.*
EHA	*Enẓiklopedyah la-Ḥafirot Arkheologiyyot be-Ereẓ Yisrael,* 2 vols. (1970).
EI	*Enzyklopaedie des Islams,* 4 vols. (1905–14). Supplement vol. (1938).
EIS	*Encyclopaedia of Islam,* 4 vols. (1913–36; repr. 1954–68).
EIS²	*Encyclopaedia of Islam, second edition (1960–2000).*
Eisenstein, Dinim	J.D. Eisenstein, *Oẓar Dinim u-Minhagim* (1917; several reprints).
Eisenstein, Yisrael	J.D. Eisenstein, *Oẓar Yisrael* (10 vols, 1907–13; repr. with several additions 1951).
EIV	*Enẓiklopedyah Ivrit* (1949ff.).
EJ	*Encyclopaedia Judaica* (German, A-L only), 10 vols. (1928–34).
EJC	*Enciclopedia Judaica Castellana,* 10 vols. (1948–51).
Elbogen, Century	I Elbogen, *A Century of Jewish Life* (1960²).
Elbogen, Gottesdienst	I Elbogen, *Der juedische Gottesdienst …* (1931³, repr. 1962).
Elon, Mafteʾaḥ	M. Elon (ed.), *Mafteʾaḥ ha-Sheʾelot ve-ha-Teshuvot ha-Rosh* (1965).
EM	*Enẓiklopedyah Mikra'it* (1950ff.).
I (or II) En.	I and II Enoch (Pseudepigrapha).
EncRel	*Encyclopedia of Religion,* 15 vols. (1987, 2005²).
Eph.	Epistle to the Ephesians (New Testament).
Ephros, Cant	G. Ephros, *Cantorial Anthology,* 5 vols. (1929–57).
Ep. Jer.	Epistle of Jeremy (Apocrypha).
Epstein, Amora'im	J N. Epstein, *Mevoʾot le-Sifrut ha-Amora'im* (1962).
Epstein, Marriage	L M. Epstein, *Marriage Laws in the Bible and the Talmud* (1942).
Epstein, Mishnah	J. N. Epstein, *Mavo le-Nusaḥ ha-Mishnah,* 2 vols. (1964²).
Epstein, Tanna'im	J. N. Epstein, *Mavo le-Sifruth ha-Tanna'im.* (1947).
ER	*Ecumenical Review.*
Er.	*Eruvin* (talmudic tractate).
ERE	*Encyclopaedia of Religion and Ethics,* 13 vols. (1908–26); reprinted.
ErIsr	*Eretz-Israel,* Israel Exploration Society.
I Esd.	I Esdras (Apocrypha) (= III Ezra).
II Esd.	II Esdras (Apocrypha) (= IV Ezra).
ESE	*Ephemeris fuer semitische Epigraphik,* ed. by M. Lidzbarski.
ESN	*Encyclopaedia Sefaradica Neerlandica,* 2 pts. (1949).
ESS	*Encyclopaedia of the Social Sciences,* 15 vols. (1930–35); reprinted in 8 vols. (1948–49).
Esth.	Esther (Bible).
Est. R.	*Esther Rabbah.*
ET	*Enẓiklopedyah Talmudit* (1947ff.).
Eusebius, Onom.	E. Klostermann (ed.), *Das Onomastikon* (1904), Greek with Hieronymus' Latin translation.
Ex.	Exodus (Bible).
Ex. R.	*Exodus Rabbah.*
Exs	Philo, *De Exsecrationibus.*
EZD	*Enẓiklopeday shel ha-Ẓiyyonut ha-Datit* (1951ff.).
Ezek.	Ezekiel (Bible).
Ezra	Ezra (Bible).
III Ezra	III Ezra (Pseudepigrapha).
IV Ezra	IV Ezra (Pseudepigrapha).
Feliks, Ha-Ẓomeʾaḥ	J. Feliks, *Ha-Ẓome'aḥ ve-ha-Ḥai ba-Mishnah* (1983).
Finkelstein, Middle Ages	L. Finkelstein, *Jewish Self-Government in the Middle Ages* (1924).
Fischel, Islam	W.J. Fischel, *Jews in the Economic and Political Life of Mediaeval Islam* (1937; reprint with introduction "The Court Jew in the Islamic World," 1969).
FJW	*Fuehrer durch die juedische Gemeindeverwaltung und Wohlfahrtspflege in Deutschland* (1927/28).
Frankel, Mevo	Z. Frankel, *Mevo ha-Yerushalmi* (1870; reprint 1967).
Frankel, Mishnah	Z. Frankel, *Darkhei ha-Mishnah* (1959²; reprint 1959²).
Frazer, Folk-Lore	J.G. Frazer, *Folk-Lore in the Old Testament,* 3 vols. (1918–19).
Frey, Corpus	J.-B. Frey, *Corpus Inscriptionum Iudaicarum,* 2 vols. (1936–52).
Friedmann, Lebensbilder	A. Friedmann, *Lebensbilder beruehmter Kantoren,* 3 vols. (1918–27).
FRLT	*Forschungen zur Religion und Literatur des Alten und Neuen Testaments* (series) (1950ff.).
Frumkin-Rivlin	A.L. Frumkin and E. Rivlin, *Toledot Ḥakhmei Yerushalayim,* 3 vols. (1928–30), Supplement vol. (1930).
Fuenn, Keneset	S.J. Fuenn, *Keneset Yisrael,* 4 vols. (1887–90).
Fuerst, Bibliotheca	J. Fuerst, *Bibliotheca Judaica,* 2 vols. (1863; repr. 1960).
Fuerst, Karaeertum	J. Fuerst, *Geschichte des Karaeertums,* 3 vols. (1862–69).
Fug.	Philo, *De Fuga et Inventione.*
Gal.	Epistle to the Galatians (New Testament).
Galling, Reallexikon	K. Galling, *Biblisches Reallexikon* (1937).
Gardiner, Onomastica	A.H. Gardiner, *Ancient Egyptian Onomastica,* 3 vols. (1947).
Geiger, Mikra	A. Geiger, *Ha-Mikra ve-Targumav,* tr. by J.L. Baruch (1949).
Geiger, Urschrift	A. Geiger, *Urschrift und Uebersetzungen der Bibel* 1928².
Gen.	Genesis (Bible).
Gen. R.	*Genesis Rabbah.*
Ger.	*Gerim* (post-talmudic tractate).
Germ Jud	M. Brann, I. Elbogen, A. Freimann, and H. Tykocinski (eds.), *Germania Judaica,* vol. 1 (1917; repr. 1934 and 1963); vol. 2, in 2 pts. (1917–68), ed. by Z. Avneri.

GHAT	*Goettinger Handkommentar zum Alten Testament* (1917–22).
Ghirondi-Neppi	M.S. Ghirondi and G.H. Neppi, *Toledot Gedolei Yisrael u-Ge'onei Italyah ... u-Ve'urim al Sefer Zekher Ẓaddikim li-Verakhah* . . .(1853), index in ZHB, 17 (1914), 171–83.
Gig.	Philo, *De Gigantibus.*
Ginzberg, Legends	L. Ginzberg, *Legends of the Jews,* 7 vols. (1909–38; and many reprints).
Git.	*Gittin* (talmudic tractate).
Glueck, Explorations	N. Glueck, *Explorations in Eastern Palestine,* 2 vols. (1951).
Goell, Bibliography	Y. Goell, *Bibliography of Modern Hebrew Literature in English Translation* (1968).
Goodenough, Symbols	E.R. Goodenough, *Jewish Symbols in the Greco-Roman Period,* 13 vols. (1953–68).
Gordon, Textbook	C.H. Gordon, *Ugaritic Textbook* (1965; repr. 1967).
Graetz, Gesch	H. Graetz, *Geschichte der Juden* (last edition 1874–1908).
Graetz, Hist	H. Graetz, *History of the Jews,* 6 vols. (1891–1902).
Graetz, Psalmen	H. Graetz, *Kritischer Commentar zu den Psalmen,* 2 vols. in 1 (1882–83).
Graetz, Rabbinowitz	H. Graetz, *Divrei Yemei Yisrael,* tr. by S.P. Rabbinowitz. (1928 1929^2).
Gray, Names	G.B. Gray, *Studies in Hebrew Proper Names* (1896).
Gressmann, Bilder	H. Gressmann, *Altorientalische Bilder zum Alten Testament* (1927^2).
Gressmann, Texte	H. Gressmann, *Altorientalische Texte zum Alten Testament* (1926^2).
Gross, Gal Jud	H. Gross, *Gallia Judaica* (1897; repr. with add. 1969).
Grove, Dict	*Grove's Dictionary of Music and Musicians,* ed. by E. Blum 9 vols. (1954^5) and suppl. (1961^5).
Guedemann, Gesch Erz	M. Guedemann, *Geschichte des Erziehungswesens und der Cultur der abendlaendischen Juden,* 3 vols. (1880–88).
Guedemann, Quellenschr	M. Guedemann, *Quellenschriften zur Geschichte des Unterrichts und der Erziehung bei den deutschen Juden* (1873, 1891).
Guide	Maimonides, *Guide of the Perplexed.*
Gulak, Oẓar	A. Gulak, *Oẓar ha-Shetarot ha-Nehugim be-Yisrael* (1926).
Gulak, Yesodei	A. Gulak, *Yesodei ha-Mishpat ha-Ivri, Seder Dinei Mamonot be-Yisrael, al pi Mekorot ha-Talmud ve-ha-Posekim,* 4 vols. (1922; repr. 1967).
Guttmann, Mafte'aḥ	M. Guttmann, *Mafte'aḥ ha-Talmud,* 3 vols. (1906–30).
Guttmann, Philosophies	J. Guttmann, *Philosophies of Judaism* (1964).
Hab.	*Habakkuk* (Bible).
Ḥag.	*Ḥagigah* (talmudic tractate).
Haggai	*Haggai* (Bible).
Ḥal.	*Ḥallah* (talmudic tractate).
Halevy, Dorot	I. Halevy, *Dorot ha-Rishonim,* 6 vols. (1897–1939).
Halpern, Pinkas	I. Halpern (Halperin), *Pinkas Va'ad Arba Araẓot* (1945).
Hananel-Eškenazi	A. Hananel and Eškenazi (eds.), *Fontes Hebraici ad res oeconomicas socialesque terrarum balcanicarum saeculo XVI pertinentes,* 2 vols, (1958–60; in Bulgarian).
HB	*Hebraeische Bibliographie* (1858–82).
Heb.	Epistle to the Hebrews (New Testament).
Heilprin, Dorot	J. Heilprin (Heilperin), *Seder ha-Dorot,* 3 vols. (1882; repr. 1956).
Her.	Philo, *Quis Rerum Divinarum Heres.*
Hertz, Prayer	J.H. Hertz (ed.), *Authorised Daily Prayer Book* (rev. ed. 1948; repr. 1963).
Herzog, Instit	I. Herzog, *The Main Institutions of Jewish Law,* 2 vols. (1936–39; repr. 1967).
Herzog-Hauck	J.J. Herzog and A. Hauch (eds.), *Real-encyklopaedie fuer protestantische Theologie* (1896–1913^3).
HḤY	*Ha-Ẓofeh le-Ḥokhmat Yisrael* (first four volumes under the title *Ha-Ẓofeh me-Ereẓ Hagar)* (1910/11–13).
Hirschberg, Afrikah	H.Z. Hirschberg, *Toledot ha-Yehudim be-Afrikah ha-Zofonit,* 2 vols. (1965).
HJ	*Historia Judaica* (1938–61).
HL	*Das Heilige Land* (1857ff.)
ḤM	*Ḥoshen Mishpat.*
Hommel, Ueberliefer.	F. Hommel, *Die altisraelitische Ueberlieferung in inschriftlicher Beleuchtung* (1897).
Hor.	*Horayot* (talmudic tractate).
Horodezky, Ḥasidut	S.A. Horodezky, *Ha-Ḥasidut ve-ha-Ḥasidim,* 4 vols. (1923).
Horowitz, Ereẓ Yis	I.W. Horowitz, *Ereẓ Yisrael u-Shekhenoteha* (1923).
Hos.	Hosea (Bible).
HTR	*Harvard Theological Review* (1908ff.).
HUCA	*Hebrew Union College Annual* (1904; 1924ff.)
Ḥul.	*Ḥullin* (talmudic tractate).
Husik, Philosophy	I. Husik, *History of Medieval Jewish Philosophy* (1932^2).
Hyman, Toledot	A. Hyman, *Toledot Tanna'im ve-Amora'im* (1910; repr. 1964).
Ibn Daud, Tradition	Abraham Ibn Daud, *Sefer ha-Qabbalah – The Book of Tradition,* ed. and tr. By G.D. Cohen (1967).
ICC	International Critical Commentary on the Holy Scriptures of the Old and New Testaments (series, 1908ff.).
IDB	*Interpreter's Dictionary of the Bible,* 4 vols. (1962).
Idelsohn, Litugy	A. Z. Idelsohn, *Jewish Liturgy and its Development* (1932; paperback repr. 1967)
Idelsohn, Melodien	A. Z. Idelsohn, *Hebraeisch-orientalischer Melodienschatz,* 10 vols. (1914 32).
Idelsohn, Music	A. Z. Idelsohn, *Jewish Music in its Historical Development* (1929; paperback repr. 1967).

IEJ	*Israel Exploration Journal* (1950ff.).
IESS	*International Encyclopedia of the Social Sciences* (various eds.).
IG	*Inscriptiones Graecae*, ed. by the Prussian Academy.
IGYB	*Israel Government Year Book* (1949/50ff.).
ILR	*Israel Law Review* (1966ff.).
IMIT	*Izraelita Magyar Irodalmi Társulat Évkönyv* (1895 1948).
IMT	International Military Tribunal.
INB	*Israel Numismatic Bulletin* (1962–63).
INJ	*Israel Numismatic Journal* (1963ff.).
Ios	Philo, *De Iosepho.*
Isa.	Isaiah (Bible).
ITHL	Institute for the Translation of Hebrew Literature.
IZBG	*Internationale Zeitschriftenschau fuer Bibelwissenschaft und Grenzgebiete* (1951ff.).
JA	*Journal asiatique* (1822ff.).
James	Epistle of James (New Testament).
JAOS	*Journal of the American Oriental Society* (c. 1850ff.)
Jastrow, Dict	M. Jastrow, *Dictionary of the Targumim, the Talmud Babli and Yerushalmi, and the Midrashic literature*, 2 vols. (1886 1902 and reprints).
JBA	*Jewish Book Annual* (19242ff.).
JBL	*Journal of Biblical Literature* (1881ff.).
JBR	*Journal of Bible and Religion* (1933ff.).
JC	*Jewish Chronicle* (1841ff.).
JCS	*Journal of Cuneiform Studies* (1947ff.).
JE	*Jewish Encyclopedia*, 12 vols. (1901–05 several reprints).
Jer.	Jeremiah (Bible).
Jeremias, Alte Test	A. Jeremias, *Das Alte Testament im Lichte des alten Orients* 1930[4]).
JGGJČ	*Jahrbuch der Gesellschaft fuer Geschichte der Juden in der Čechoslovakischen Republik* (1929–38).
JHSEM	Jewish Historical Society of England, *Miscellanies* (1925ff.).
JHSET	Jewish Historical Society of England, *Transactions* (1893ff.).
JJGL	*Jahrbuch fuer juedische Geschichte und Literatur* (Berlin) (1898–1938).
JJLG	*Jahrbuch der juedische-literarischen Gesellschaft* (Frankfurt) (1903–32).
JJS	*Journal of Jewish Studies* (1948ff.).
JJSO	*Jewish Journal of Sociology* (1959ff.).
JJV	*Jahrbuch fuer juedische Volkskunde* (1898–1924).
JL	*Juedisches Lexikon*, 5 vols. (1927–30).
JMES	*Journal of the Middle East Society* (1947ff.).
JNES	*Journal of Near Eastern Studies* (continuation of AJSLL) (1942ff.).
J.N.U.L.	Jewish National and University Library.
Job	Job (Bible).
Joel	Joel (Bible).
John	Gospel according to John (New Testament).
I, II and III John	Epistles of John (New Testament).
Jos., Ant	Josephus, *Jewish Antiquities* (Loeb Classics ed.).
Jos. Apion	Josephus, *Against Apion* (Loeb Classics ed.).
Jos., index	*Josephus Works*, Loeb Classics ed., index of names.
Jos., Life	Josephus, *Life* (ed. Loeb Classics).
Jos, Wars	Josephus, *The Jewish Wars* (Loeb Classics ed.).
Josh.	Joshua (Bible).
JPESB	Jewish Palestine Exploration Society Bulletin, see BJPES.
JPESJ	Jewish Palestine Exploration Society Journal – Eng. Title of the Hebrew periodical *Kovez ha-Ḥevrah ha-Ivrit la-Ḥakirat Erez Yisrael va-Attikoteha.*
JPOS	*Journal of the Palestine Oriental Society* (1920–48).
JPS	Jewish Publication Society of America, *The Torah* (1962, 1967[2]); *The Holy Scriptures* (1917).
JQR	*Jewish Quarterly Review* (1889ff.).
JR	*Journal of Religion* (1921ff.).
JRAS	*Journal of the Royal Asiatic Society* (1838ff.).
JHR	*Journal of Religious History* (1960/61ff.).
JSOS	*Jewish Social Studies* (1939ff.).
JSS	*Journal of Semitic Studies* (1956ff.).
JTS	*Journal of Theological Studies* (1900ff.).
JTSA	Jewish Theological Seminary of America (also abbreviated as JTS).
Jub.	Jubilees (Pseudepigrapha).
Judg.	Judges (Bible).
Judith	Book of Judith (Apocrypha).
Juster, Juifs	J. Juster, *Les Juifs dans l'Empire Romain*, 2 vols. (1914).
JYB	*Jewish Year Book* (1896ff.).
JZWL	*Juedische Zeitschift fuer Wissenschaft und Leben* (1862–75).
Kal.	*Kallah* (post-talmudic tractate).
Kal. R.	*Kallah Rabbati* (post-talmudic tractate).
Katz, England	*The Jews in the History of England, 1485-1850 (1994).*
Kaufmann, Schriften	D. Kaufmann, *Gesammelte Schriften*, 3 vols. (1908 15).
Kaufmann Y., Religion	Y. Kaufmann, *The Religion of Israel* (1960), abridged tr. of his *Toledot.*
Kaufmann Y., Toledot	Y. Kaufmann, *Toledot ha-Emunah ha-Yisre'elit*, 4 vols. (1937 57).
KAWJ	*Korrespondenzblatt des Vereins zur Gruendung und Erhaltung der Akademie fuer die Wissenschaft des Judentums* (1920 30).
Kayserling, Bibl	M. Kayserling, *Biblioteca Española-Portugueza-Judaica* (1880; repr. 1961).
Kelim	*Kelim* (mishnaic tractate).
Ker.	*Keritot* (talmudic tractate).
Ket.	*Ketubbot* (talmudic tractate).

Kid.	*Kiddushim* (talmudic tractate).
Kil.	*Kilayim* (talmudic tractate).
Kin.	*Kinnim* (mishnaic tractate).
Kisch, Germany	G. Kisch, *Jews in Medieval Germany* (1949).
Kittel, Gesch	R. Kittel, *Geschichte des Volkes Israel,* 3 vols. (1922–28).
Klausner, Bayit Sheni	J. Klausner, *Historyah shel ha-Bayit ha-Sheni,* 5 vols. (1950/512).
Klausner, Sifrut	J. Klausner, *Historyah shel haSifrut ha-Ivrit ha-Ḥadashah,* 6 vols. (1952–582).
Klein, corpus	S. Klein (ed.), *Juedisch-palaestinisches Corpus Inscriptionum* (1920).
Koehler-Baumgartner	L. Koehler and W. Baumgartner, *Lexicon in Veteris Testamenti libros* (1953).
Kohut, Arukh	H.J.A. Kohut (ed.), *Sefer he-Arukh ha-Shalem,* by Nathan b. Jehiel of Rome, 8 vols. (1876–92; Supplement by S. Krauss et al., 1936; repr. 1955).
Krauss, Tal Arch	S. Krauss, *Talmudische Archaeologie,* 3 vols. (1910–12; repr. 1966).
Kressel, Leksikon	G. Kressel, *Leksikon ha-Sifrut ha-Ivrit ba-Dorot ha-Aḥaronim,* 2 vols. (1965–67).
KS	*Kirjath Sepher* (1923/4ff.).
Kut.	*Kuttim* (post-talmudic tractate).
LA	Studium Biblicum Franciscanum, *Liber Annuus* (1951ff.).
L.A.	Philo, *Legum allegoriae.*
Lachower, Sifrut	F. Lachower, *Toledot ha-Sifrut ha-Ivrit ha-Ḥadashah,* 4 vols. (1947–48; several reprints).
Lam.	Lamentations (Bible).
Lam. R.	*Lamentations Rabbah.*
Landshuth, Ammudei	L. Landshuth, *Ammudei ha-Avodah* (1857–62; repr. with index, 1965).
Legat.	Philo, *De Legatione ad Caium.*
Lehmann, Nova Bibl	R.P. Lehmann, *Nova Bibliotheca Anglo-Judaica* (1961).
Lev.	Leviticus (Bible).
Lev. R.	*Leviticus Rabbah.*
Levy, Antologia	I. Levy, *Antologia de liturgia judeo-española* (1965ff.).
Levy J., Chald Targ	J. Levy, *Chaldaeisches Woerterbuch ueber die Targumim,* 2 vols. (1967–68; repr. 1959).
Levy J., Nuehebr Tal	J. Levy, *Neuhebraeisches und chaldaeisches Woerterbuch ueber die Talmudim . . .,* 4 vols. (1875–89; repr. 1963).
Lewin, Oẓar	Lewin, *Oẓar ha-Ge'onim,* 12 vols. (1928–43).
Lewysohn, Zool	L. Lewysohn, *Zoologie des Talmuds* (1858).
Lidzbarski, Handbuch	M. Lidzbarski, *Handbuch der nordsemitischen Epigraphik,* 2 vols (1898).
Life	Josephus, *Life* (Loeb Classis ed.).
LNYL	*Leksikon fun der Nayer Yidisher Literatur* (1956ff.).
Loew, Flora	I. Loew, *Die Flora der Juden,* 4 vols. (1924 34; repr. 1967).
LSI	*Laws of the State of Israel* (1948ff.).
Luckenbill, Records	D.D. Luckenbill, *Ancient Records of Assyria and Babylonia,* 2 vols. (1926).
Luke	Gospel according to Luke (New Testament)
LXX	Septuagint (Greek translation of the Bible).
Ma'as.	*Ma'aserot* (talmudic tractate).
Ma'as. Sh.	*Ma'ase Sheni* (talmudic tractate).
I, II, III, and IVMacc.	Maccabees, I, II, III (Apocrypha), IV (Pseudepigrapha).
Maimonides, Guide	Maimonides, *Guide of the Perplexed.*
Maim., Yad	Maimonides, *Mishneh Torah (Yad Ḥazakah).*
Maisler, Untersuchungen	B. Maisler (Mazar), *Untersuchungen zur alten Geschichte und Ethnographie Syriens und Palaestinas,* 1 (1930).
Mak.	*Makkot* (talmudic tractate).
Makhsh.	*Makhshrin* (mishnaic tractate).
Mal.	Malachi (Bible).
Mann, Egypt	J. Mann, *Jews in Egypt in Palestine under the Fatimid Caliphs,* 2 vols. (1920–22).
Mann, Texts	J. Mann, *Texts and Studies,* 2 vols (1931–35).
Mansi	G.D. Mansi, *Sacrorum Conciliorum nova et amplissima collectio,* 53 vols. in 60 (1901–27; repr. 1960).
Margalioth, Gedolei	M. Margalioth, *Enẓiklopedyah le-Toledot Gedolei Yisrael,* 4 vols. (1946–50).
Margalioth, Ḥakhmei	M. Margalioth, *Enẓiklopedyah le-Ḥakhmei ha-Talmud ve-ha-Ge'onim,* 2 vols. (1945).
Margalioth, Cat	G. Margalioth, *Catalogue of the Hebrew and Samaritan Manuscripts in the British Museum,* 4 vols. (1899–1935).
Mark	Gospel according to Mark (New Testament).
Mart. Isa.	Martyrdom of Isaiah (Pseudepigrapha).
Mas.	Masorah.
Matt.	Gospel according to Matthew (New Testament).
Mayer, Art	L.A. Mayer, *Bibliography of Jewish Art* (1967).
MB	*Wochenzeitung* (formerly *Mitteilungsblatt*) *des Irgun Olej Merkas Europa* (1933ff.).
MEAH	*Miscelánea de estudios drabes y hebraicos* (1952ff.).
Meg.	Megillah (talmudic tractate).
Meg. Ta'an.	*Megillat Ta'anit* (in HUCA, 8 9 (1931–32), 318–51).
Me'il	*Me'ilah* (mishnaic tractate).
MEJ	*Middle East Journal* (1947ff.).
Mehk.	*Mekhilta de-R. Ishmael.*
Mekh. SbY	*Mekhilta de-R. Simeon bar Yoḥai.*
Men.	*Menaḥot* (talmudic tractate).
MER	*Middle East Record* (1960ff.).
Meyer, Gesch	E. Meyer, *Geschichte des Alterums,* 5 vols. in 9 (1925–58).
Meyer, Ursp	E. Meyer, *Urspring und Anfaenge des Christentums* (1921).
Mez.	*Mezuzah* (post-talmudic tractate).
MGADJ	*Mitteilungen des Gesamtarchivs der deutschen Juden* (1909–12).
MGG	*Die Musik in Geschichte und Gegenwart,* 14 vols. (1949–68).

MGG[2]	*Die Musik in Geschichte und Gegenwart, 2nd edition (1994)*
MGH	*Monumenta Germaniae Historica* (1826ff.).
MGJV	*Mitteilungen der Gesellschaft fuer juedische Volkskunde* (1898–1929); title varies, see also JJV.
MGWJ	*Monatsschrift fuer Geschichte und Wissenschaft des Judentums* (1851–1939).
MHJ	*Monumenta Hungariae Judaica,* 11 vols. (1903–67).
Michael, Or	H.Ḥ. Michael, *Or ha-Ḥayyim: Ḥakhmei Yisrael ve-Sifreihem,* ed. by S.Z. Ḥ. Halberstam and N. Ben-Menahem (1965[2]).
Mid.	*Middot* (mishnaic tractate).
Mid. Ag.	*Midrash Aggadah.*
Mid. Hag.	*Midrash ha-Gadol.*
Mid. Job.	*Midrash Job.*
Mid. Jonah	*Midrash Jonah.*
Mid. Lek. Tov	*Midrash Lekaḥ Tov.*
Mid. Prov.	*Midrash Proverbs.*
Mid. Ps.	*Midrash Tehillim* (Eng tr. *The Midrash on Psalms* (JPS, 1959).
Mid. Sam.	*Midrash Samuel.*
Mid. Song	*Midrash Shir ha-Shirim.*
Mid. Tan.	*Midrash Tanna'im* on Deuteronomy.
Miége, Maroc	J.L. Miège, *Le Maroc et l'Europe,* 3 vols. (1961 62).
Mig.	Philo, *De Migratione Abrahami.*
Mik.	*Mikva'ot* (mishnaic tractate).
Milano, Bibliotheca	A. Milano, *Bibliotheca Historica Italo-Judaica* (1954); supplement for 1954–63 (1964); supplement for 1964–66 in RMI, 32 (1966).
Milano, Italia	A. Milano, *Storia degli Ebrei in Italia* (1963).
MIO	*Mitteilungen des Instituts fuer Orientforschung* 1953ff.).
Mish.	Mishnah.
MJ	*Le Monde Juif* (1946ff.).
MJC	see Neubauer, Chronicles.
MK	*Mo'ed Katan* (talmudic tractate).
MNDPV	*Mitteilungen und Nachrichten des deutschen Palaestinavereins* (1895–1912).
Mortara, Indice	M. Mortara, *Indice Alfabetico dei Rabbini e Scrittori Israeliti ... in Italia ...* (1886).
Mos	Philo, *De Vita Mosis.*
Moscati, Epig	S, Moscati, *Epigrafia ebraica antica* 1935–1950 (1951).
MT	Masoretic Text of the Bible.
Mueller, Musiker	[E.H. Mueller], *Deutisches Musiker-Lexikon* (1929)
Munk, Mélanges	S. Munk, *Mélanges de philosophie juive et arabe* (1859; repr. 1955).
Mut.	Philo, *De Mutatione Nominum.*
MWJ	*Magazin fuer die Wissenshaft des Judentums* (18745 93).
Nah.	Nahum (Bible).
Naz.	*Nazir* (talmudic tractate).
NDB	*Neue Deutsche Biographie* (1953ff.).
Ned.	*Nedarim* (talmudic tractate).
Neg.	*Nega'im* (mishnaic tractate).
Neh.	Nehemiah (Bible).
NG[2]	*New Grove Dictionary of Music and Musicians* (2001).
Nuebauer, Cat	A. Neubauer, *Catalogue of the Hebrew Manuscripts in the Bodleian Library ...,* 2 vols. (1886–1906).
Neubauer, Chronicles	A. Neubauer, *Mediaeval Jewish Chronicles,* 2 vols. (Heb., 1887–95; repr. 1965), Eng. title of *Seder ha-Ḥakhamim ve-Korot ha-Yamim.*
Neubauer, Géogr	A. Neubauer, *La géographie du Talmud* (1868).
Neuman, Spain	A.A. Neuman, *The Jews in Spain, their Social, Political, and Cultural Life During the Middle Ages,* 2 vols. (1942).
Neusner, Babylonia	J. Neusner, *History of the Jews in Babylonia,* 5 vols. 1965–70), 2nd revised printing 1969ff.).
Nid.	*Niddah* (talmudic tractate).
Noah	Fragment of Book of Noah (Pseudepigrapha).
Noth, Hist Isr	M. Noth, *History of Israel* (1958).
Noth, Personennamen	M. Noth, *Die israelitischen Personennamen.* ... (1928).
Noth, Ueberlief	M. Noth, *Ueberlieferungsgeschichte des Pentateuchs* (1949).
Noth, Welt	M. Noth, *Die Welt des Alten Testaments* (1957[3]).
Nowack, Lehrbuch	W. Nowack, *Lehrbuch der hebraeischen Archaeologie,* 2 vols (1894).
NT	New Testament.
Num.	Numbers (Bible).
Num R.	*Numbers Rabbah.*
Obad.	Obadiah (Bible).
ODNB online	*Oxford Dictionary of National Biography.*
OḤ	*Oraḥ Ḥayyim.*
Oho.	*Oholot* (mishnaic tractate).
Olmstead	H.T. Olmstead, *History of Palestine and Syria* (1931; repr. 1965).
OLZ	*Orientalistische Literaturzeitung* (1898ff.)
Onom.	Eusebius, *Onomasticon.*
Op.	Philo, *De Opificio Mundi.*
OPD	*Osef Piskei Din shel ha-Rabbanut ha-Rashit le-Ereẓ Yisrael, Bet ha-Din ha-Gadol le-Irurim* (1950).
Or.	*Orlah* (talmudic tractate).
Or. Sibyll.	Sibylline Oracles (Pseudepigrapha).
OS	*L'Orient Syrien* (1956ff.)
OTS	*Oudtestamentische Studien* (1942ff.).
PAAJR	*Proceedings of the American Academy for Jewish Research* (1930ff.)
Pap 4QS[e]	A papyrus exemplar of IQS.
Par.	*Parah* (mishnaic tractate).
Pauly-Wissowa	A.F. Pauly, *Realencyklopaedie der klassichen Alertumswissenschaft,* ed. by G. Wissowa et al. (1864ff.)

PD	*Piskei Din shel Bet ha-Mishpat ha-Elyon le-Yisrael* (1948ff.)
PDR	*Piskei Din shel Battei ha-Din ha-Rabbaniyyim be-Yisrael.*
PdRE	*Pirkei de-R. Eliezer* (Eng. tr. 1916. (1965^2).
PdRK	*Pesikta de-Rav Kahana.*
Pe'ah	*Pe'ah* (talmudic tractate).
Peake, Commentary	A.J. Peake (ed.), *Commentary on the Bible* (1919; rev. 1962).
Pedersen, Israel	J. Pedersen, *Israel, Its Life and Culture,* 4 vols. in 2 (1926–40).
PEFQS	*Palestine Exploration Fund Quarterly Statement* (1869–1937; since 1938–PEQ).
PEQ	*Palestine Exploration Quarterly* (until 1937 PEFQS; after 1927 includes BBSAJ).
Perles, Beitaege	J. Perles, *Beitraege zur rabbinischen Sprach- und Alterthumskunde* (1893).
Pes.	*Pesaḥim* (talmudic tractate).
Pesh.	Peshitta (Syriac translation of the Bible).
Pesher Hab.	Commentary to Habakkuk from Qumran; see 1Qp Hab.
I and II Pet.	Epistles of Peter (New Testament).
Pfeiffer, Introd	R.H. Pfeiffer, *Introduction to the Old Testament* (1948).
PG	J.P. Migne (ed.), *Patrologia Graeca,* 161 vols. (1866–86).
Phil.	Epistle to the Philippians (New Testament).
Philem.	Epistle to the Philemon (New Testament).
PIASH	*Proceedings of the Israel Academy of Sciences and Humanities* (1963/7ff.).
PJB	*Palaestinajahrbuch des deutschen evangelischen Institutes fuer Altertumswissenschaft,* Jerusalem (1905–1933).
PK	*Pinkas ha-Kehillot,* encyclopedia of Jewish communities, published in over 30 volumes by Yad Vashem from 1970 and arranged by countries, regions and localities. For 3-vol. English edition see Spector, *Jewish Life.*
PL	J.P. Migne (ed.), *Patrologia Latina* 221 vols. (1844–64).
Plant	Philo, *De Plantatione.*
PO	R. Graffin and F. Nau (eds.), *Patrologia Orientalis* (1903ff.)
Pool, Prayer	D. de Sola Pool, *Traditional Prayer Book for Sabbath and Festivals* (1960).
Post	Philo, *De Posteritate Caini.*
PR	*Pesikta Rabbati.*
Praem.	Philo, *De Praemiis et Poenis.*
Prawer, Ẓalbanim	J. Prawer, *Toledot Mamlekhet ha-Ẓalbanim be-Ereẓ Yisrael,* 2 vols. (1963).
Press, Ereẓ	I. Press, *Ereẓ-Yisrael, Enẓiklopedyah Topografit-Historit,* 4 vols. (1951–55).
Pritchard, Pictures	J.B. Pritchard (ed.), *Ancient Near East in Pictures* (1954, 1970).
Pritchard, Texts	J.B. Pritchard (ed.), *Ancient Near East Texts* ... (1970^3).
Pr. Man.	Prayer of Manasses (Apocrypha).
Prob.	Philo, *Quod Omnis Probus Liber Sit.*
Prov.	Proverbs (Bible).
PS	*Palestinsky Sbornik* (Russ. (1881 1916, 1954ff).
Ps.	Psalms (Bible).
PSBA	*Proceedings of the Society of Biblical Archaeology* (1878–1918).
Ps. of Sol	Psalms of Solomon (Pseudepigrapha).
IQ Apoc	. The *Genesis Apocryphon* from Qumran, cave one, ed. by N. Avigad and Y. Yadin (1956).
6QD	*Damascus Document* or *Sefer Berit Dammesk* from Qumran, cave six, ed. by M. Baillet, in RB, 63 (1956), 513–23 (see also CD).
QDAP	*Quarterly of the Department of Antiquities in Palestine* (1932ff.).
4QDeut. 32	Manuscript of Deuteronomy 32 from Qumran, cave four (ed. by P.W. Skehan, in BASOR, 136 (1954), 12–15).
4QEx^a	Exodus manuscript in Jewish script from Qumran, cave four.
4QEx$^\alpha$	Exodus manuscript in Paleo-Hebrew script from Qumran, cave four (partially ed. by P.W. Skehan, in JBL, 74 (1955), 182–7).
4QFlor	*Florilegium,* a miscellany from Qumran, cave four (ed. by J.M. Allegro, in JBL, 75 (1956), 176–77 and 77 (1958), 350–54).).
QGJD	*Quellen zur Geschichte der Juden in Deutschland* 1888–98).
IQH	*Thanksgiving Psalms* or *Hodayot* from Qumran, cave one (ed. by E.L. Sukenik and N. Avigad, *Oẓar ha-Megillot ha-Genuzot* (1954).
IQIs^a	Scroll of Isaiah from Qumran, cave one (ed. by N. Burrows et al., *Dead Sea Scrolls* ..., 1 (1950).
IQIs^b	Scroll of Isaiah from Qumran, cave one (ed. E.L. Sukenik and N. Avigad, *Oẓar ha-Megillot ha-Genuzot* (1954).
IQM	The *War Scroll* or *Serekh ha-Milḥamah* (ed. by E.L. Sukenik and N. Avigad, *Oẓar ha-Megillot ha-Genuzot* (1954).
4QpNah	Commentary on Nahum from Qumran, cave four (partially ed. by J.M. Allegro, in JBL, 75 (1956), 89–95).
IQphyl	Phylacteries *(tefillin)* from Qumran, cave one (ed. by Y. Yadin, in *Eretz Israel,* 9 (1969), 60–85).
4Q Prayer of Nabonidus	A document from Qumran, cave four, belonging to a lost Daniel literature (ed. by J.T. Milik, in RB, 63 (1956), 407–15).
IQS	*Manual of Discipline* or *Serekh ha-Yaḥad* from Qumran, cave one (ed. by M. Burrows et al., *Dead Sea Scrolls* ..., 2, pt. 2 (1951).

IQS^{a}	The *Rule of the Congregation or Serekh ha-Edah* from Qumran, cave one (ed. by Burrows et al., *Dead Sea Scrolls* ..., 1 (1950), under the abbreviation IQ28a).
IQS^{b}	*Blessings* or *Divrei Berakhot* from Qumran, cave one (ed. by Burrows et al., *Dead Sea Scrolls* ..., 1 (1950), under the abbreviation IQ28b).
4QSam^{a}	Manuscript of I and II Samuel from Qumran, cave four (partially ed. by F.M. Cross, in BASOR, 132 (1953), 15–26).
4QSam^{b}	Manuscript of I and II Samuel from Qumran, cave four (partially ed. by F.M. Cross, in JBL, 74 (1955), 147–72).
4QTestimonia	Sheet of Testimony from Qumran, cave four (ed. by J.M. Allegro, in JBL, 75 (1956), 174–87).).
4QT.Levi	*Testament of Levi* from Qumran, cave four (partially ed. by J.T. Milik, in RB, 62 (1955), 398–406).
Rabinovitz, Dik Sof	See Dik Sof.
RB	*Revue biblique* (1892ff.)
RBI	*Recherches bibliques* (1954ff.)
RCB	*Revista de cultura biblica* (São Paulo) (1957ff.)
Régné, Cat	J. Régné, *Catalogue des actes . . . des rois d'Aragon, concernant les Juifs* (1213–1327), in: REJ, vols. 60 70, 73, 75–78 (1910–24).
Reinach, Textes	T. Reinach, *Textes d'auteurs Grecs et Romains relatifs au Judaïsme* (1895; repr. 1963).
REJ	*Revue des études juives* (1880ff.).
Rejzen, Leksikon	Z. Rejzen, *Leksikon fun der Yidisher Literature,* 4 vols. (1927–29).
Renan, Ecrivains	A. Neubauer and E. Renan, *Les écrivains juifs français* ... (1893).
Renan, Rabbins	A. Neubauer and E. Renan, *Les rabbins français* (1877).
RES	*Revue des étude sémitiques et Babyloniaca* (1934–45).
Rev.	Revelation (New Testament).
RGG^{3}	*Die Religion in Geschichte und Gegenwart,* 7 vols. (1957–65^{3}).
RH	*Rosh Ha-Shanah* (talmudic tractate).
RHJE	*Revue de l'histoire juive en Egypte* (1947ff.).
RHMH	*Revue d'histoire de la médecine hébraïque* (1948ff.).
RHPR	*Revue d'histoire et de philosophie religieuses* (1921ff.).
RHR	*Revue d'histoire des religions* (1880ff.).
RI	*Rivista Israelitica* (1904–12).
Riemann-Einstein	*Hugo Riemanns Musiklexikon,* ed. by A. Einstein (1929^{11}).
Riemann-Gurlitt	*Hugo Riemanns Musiklexikon,* ed. by W. Gurlitt (1959–67^{12}), Personenteil.
Rigg-Jenkinson, Exchequer	J.M. Rigg, H. Jenkinson and H.G. Richardson (eds.), *Calendar of the Pleas Rolls of the Exchequer of the Jews,* 4 vols. (1905–1970); cf. in each instance also J.M. Rigg (ed.), *Select Pleas* ... (1902).
RMI	*Rassegna Mensile di Israel* (1925ff.).
Rom.	Epistle to the Romans (New Testament).
Rosanes, Togarmah	S.A. Rosanes, *Divrei Yemei Yisrael be-Togarmah,* 6 vols. (1907–45), and in 3 vols. (1930–38^{2}).
Rosenbloom, Biogr Dict	J.R. Rosenbloom, *Biographical Dictionary of Early American Jews* (1960).
Roth, Art	C. Roth, *Jewish Art* (1961).
Roth, Dark Ages	C. Roth (ed.), *World History of the Jewish People,* second series, vol. 2, *Dark Ages* (1966).
Roth, England	C. Roth, *History of the Jews in England* (1964^{3}).
Roth, Italy	C. Roth, *History of the Jews in Italy* (1946).
Roth, Mag Bibl	C. Roth, *Magna Bibliotheca Anglo-Judaica* (1937).
Roth, Marranos	C. Roth, *History of the Marranos* (2nd rev. ed 1959; reprint 1966).
Rowley, Old Test	H.H. Rowley, *Old Testament and Modern Study* (1951; repr. 1961).
RS	*Revue sémitiques d'épigraphie et d'histoire ancienne* (1893/94ff.).
RSO	*Rivista degli studi orientali* (1907ff.).
RSV	Revised Standard Version of the Bible.
Rubinstein, Australia I	*H.L. Rubinstein, The Jews in Australia, A Thematic History, Vol. I (1991).*
Rubinstein, Australia II	*W.D. Rubinstein, The Jews in Australia, A Thematic History, Vol. II (1991).*
Ruth	Ruth (Bible).
Ruth R.	*Ruth Rabbah.*
RV	Revised Version of the Bible.
Sac.	Philo, *De Sacrificiis Abelis et Caini.*
Salfeld, Martyrol	S. Salfeld, *Martyrologium des Nuernberger Memorbuches* (1898).
I and II Sam.	Samuel, book I and II (Bible).
Sanh.	*Sanhedrin* (talmudic tractate).
SBA	Society of Biblical Archaeology.
SBB	*Studies in Bibliography and Booklore* (1953ff.).
SBE	*Semana Biblica Española.*
SBT	*Studies in Biblical Theology* (1951ff.).
SBU	*Svenkst Bibliskt Uppslogsvesk,* 2 vols. (1962–63^{2}).
Schirmann, Italyah	J.Ḥ. Schirmann, *Ha-Shirah ha-Ivrit be-Italyah* (1934).
Schirmann, Sefarad	J.Ḥ. Schirmann, *Ha-Shirah ha-Ivrit bi-Sefarad u-vi-Provence,* 2 vols. (1954–56).
Scholem, Mysticism	G. Scholem, *Major Trends in Jewish Mysticism* (rev. ed. 1946; paperback ed. with additional bibliography 1961).
Scholem, Shabbetai Ẓevi	G. Scholem, *Shabbetai Ẓevi ve-ha-Tenu'ah ha-Shabbeta'it bi-Ymei Ḥayyav,* 2 vols. (1967).
Schrader, Keilinschr	E. Schrader, *Keilinschriften und das Alte Testament* (1903^{3}).
Schuerer, Gesch	E. Schuerer, *Geschichte des juedischen Volkes im Zeitalter Jesu Christi,* 3 vols. and index-vol. (1901–11^{4}).

Schuerer, Hist	E. Schuerer, *History of the Jewish People in the Time of Jesus,* ed. by N.N. Glatzer, abridged paperback edition (1961).
Set. T.	*Sefer Torah* (post-talmudic tractate).
Sem.	*Semaḥot* (post-talmudic tractate).
Sendrey, Music	A. Sendrey, *Bibliography of Jewish Music* (1951).
SER	*Seder Eliyahu Rabbah.*
SEZ	*Seder Eliyahu Zuta.*
Shab	*Shabbat* (talmudic tractate).
Sh. Ar.	J. Caro Shulḥan Arukh. OḤ – *Oraḥ Ḥayyim* YD – *Yoreh De'ah* EH – *Even ha-Ezer* ḤM – *Ḥoshen Mishpat.*
Shek.	*Shekalim* (talmudic tractate).
Shev.	*Shevi'it* (talmudic tractate).
Shevu.	*Shevu'ot* (talmudic tractate).
Shunami, Bibl	S. Shunami, *Bibliography of Jewish Bibliographies* (1965^{2}).
Sif.	*Sifrei Deuteronomy.*
Sif. Num.	*Sifrei Numbers.*
Sifra	*Sifra* on Leviticus.
Sif. Zut.	*Sifrei Zuta.*
SIHM	Sources inédites de l'histoire du Maroc (series).
Silverman, Prayer	M. Silverman (ed.), *Sabbath and Festival Prayer Book* (1946).
Singer, Prayer	S. Singer *Authorised Daily Prayer Book* (1943^{17}).
Sob.	Philo, *De Sobrietate.*
Sof.	*Soferim* (post-talmudic tractate).
Som.	Philo, *De Somniis.*
Song	Song of Songs (Bible).
Song. Ch.	Song of the Three Children (Apocrypha).
Song R.	*Song of Songs Rabbah.*
SOR	*Seder Olam Rabbah.*
Sot.	*Sotah* (talmudic tractate).
SOZ	*Seder Olam Zuta.*
Spec.	Philo, *De Specialibus Legibus.*
Spector, Jewish Life	*S. Spector (ed.), Encyclopedia of Jewish Life Before and After the Holocaust (2001).*
Steinschneider, Arab lit	M. Steinschneider, *Die arabische Literatur der Juden* (1902).
Steinschneider, Cat Bod	M. Steinschneider, *Catalogus Librorum Hebraeorum in Bibliotheca Bodleiana,* 3 vols. (1852–60; reprints 1931 and 1964).
Steinschneider, Hanbuch	M. Steinschneider, *Bibliographisches Handbuch ueber die . . . Literatur fuer hebraeische Sprachkunde* (1859; repr. with additions 1937).
Steinschneider, Uebersetzungen	M. Steinschneider, *Die hebraeischen Uebersetzungen des Mittelalters* (1893).
Stern, Americans	M.H. Stern, *Americans of Jewish Descent* (1960).
van Straalen, Cat	S. van Straalen, *Catalogue of Hebrew Books in the British Museum Acquired During the Years 1868–1892* (1894).
Suárez Fernández, Docmentos	L. Suárez Fernández, *Documentos acerca de la expulsion de los Judios de España* (1964).
Suk.	*Sukkah* (talmudic tractate).
Sus.	Susanna (Apocrypha).
SY	*Sefer Yeẓirah.*
Sym.	Symmachus' Greek translation of the Bible.
SZNG	*Studien zur neueren Geschichte.*
Ta'an.	*Ta'anit* (talmudic tractate).
Tam.	*Tamid* (mishnaic tractate).
Tanḥ.	*Tanḥuma.*
Tanḥ. B.	*Tanḥuma.* Buber ed (1885).
Targ. Jon	Targum Jonathan (Aramaic version of the Prophets).
Targ. Onk.	Targum Onkelos (Aramaic version of the Pentateuch).
Targ. Yer.	Targum Yerushalmi.
TB	Babylonian Talmud or Talmud Bavli.
Tcherikover, Corpus	V. Tcherikover, A. Fuks, and M. Stern, *Corpus Papyrorum Judaicorum,* 3 vols. (1957–60).
Tef.	*Tefillin* (post-talmudic tractate).
Tem.	*Temurah* (mishnaic tractate).
Ter.	*Terumah* (talmudic tractate).
Test. Patr.	Testament of the Twelve Patriarchs (Pseudepigrapha). Ash. – Asher Ben. – Benjamin Dan – Dan Gad – Gad Iss. – Issachar Joseph – Joseph Judah – Judah Levi – Levi Naph. – Naphtali Reu. – Reuben Sim. – Simeon Zeb. – Zebulun.
I and II	Epistle to the Thessalonians (New Testament).
Thieme-Becker	U. Thieme and F. Becker (eds.), *Allgemeines Lexikon der bildenden Kuenstler von der Antike bis zur Gegenwart,* 37 vols. (1907–50).
Tidhar	D. Tidhar (ed.), *Enẓiklopedyah la-Ḥalutẓei ha-Yishuv u-Vonav* (1947ff.).
I and II Timothy	Epistles to Timothy (New Testament).
Tit.	Epistle to Titus (New Testament).
TJ	Jerusalem Talmud or Talmud Yerushalmi.
Tob.	Tobit (Apocrypha).
Toh.	*Tohorot* (mishnaic tractate).
Torczyner, Bundeslade	H. Torczyner, *Die Bundeslade und die Anfaenge der Religion Israels* (1930^{3}).
Tos.	*Tosafot.*
Tosef.	Tosefta.
Tristram, Nat Hist	H.B. Tristram, *Natural History of the Bible* (1877^{5}).
Tristram, Survey	Palestine Exploration Fund, *Survey of Western Palestine,* vol. 4 (1884) = *Fauna and Flora* by H.B. Tristram.
TS	*Terra Santa* (1943ff.).

TSBA	*Transactions of the Society of Biblical Archaeology* (1872–93).
TY	*Tevul Yom* (mishnaic tractate).
UBSB	United Bible Society, *Bulletin.*
UJE	*Universal Jewish Encyclopedia*, 10 vols. (1939–43).
Uk.	*Ukẓin* (mishnaic tractate).
Urbach, Tosafot	E.E. Urbach, *Ba'alei ha-Tosafot* (1957^2).
de Vaux, Anc Isr	R. de Vaux, *Ancient Israel: its Life and Institutions* (1961; paperback 1965).
de Vaux, Instit	R. de Vaux, *Institutions de l'Ancien Testament,* 2 vols. (1958 60).
Virt.	Philo, *De Virtutibus.*
Vogelstein, Chronology	M. Volgelstein, *Biblical Chronology (1944).*
Vogelstein-Rieger	H. Vogelstein and P. Rieger, *Geschichte der Juden in Rom,* 2 vols. (1895–96).
VT	*Vetus Testamentum* (1951ff.).
VTS	*Vetus Testamentum* Supplements (1953ff.).
Vulg.	Vulgate (Latin translation of the Bible).
Wars	Josephus, *The Jewish Wars.*
Watzinger, Denkmaeler	K. Watzinger, *Denkmaeler Palaestinas,* 2 vols. (1933–35).
Waxman, Literature	M. Waxman, *History of Jewish Literature,* 5 vols. (1960^2).
Weiss, Dor	I.H. Weiss, *Dor, Dor ve-Doreshav,* 5 vols. (1904^4).
Wellhausen, Proleg	J. Wellhausen, *Prolegomena zur Geschichte Israels* (1927^6).
WI	*Die Welt des Islams* (1913ff.).
Winniger, Biog	S. Wininger, *Grosse juedische National-Biographie ...,* 7 vols. (1925–36).
Wisd.	Wisdom of Solomon (Apocrypha)
WLB	*Wiener Library Bulletin* (1958ff.).
Wolf, Bibliotheca	J.C. Wolf, *Bibliotheca Hebraea*, 4 vols. (1715–33).
Wright, Bible	G.E. Wright, *Westminster Historical Atlas to the Bible* (1945).
Wright, Atlas	G.E. Wright, *The Bible and the Ancient Near East* (1961).
WWWJ	*Who's Who in the World Jewry* (New York, 1955, 1965^2).
WZJT	*Wissenschaftliche Zeitschrift fuer juedische Theologie* (1835–37).
WZKM	*Wiener Zeitschrift fuer die Kunde des Morgenlandes* (1887ff.).
Yaari, Sheluḥei	A. Yaari, *Sheluḥei Ereẓ Yisrael* (1951).
Yad	Maimonides, *Mishneh Torah (Yad Ḥazakah).*
Yad	*Yadayim* (mishnaic tractate).
Yal.	*Yalkut Shimoni.*
Yal. Mak.	*Yalkut Makhiri.*
Yal. Reub.	*Yalkut Reubeni.*
YD	*Yoreh De'ah.*
YE	*Yevreyskaya Entsiklopediya,* 14 vols. (c. 1910).
Yev.	*Yevamot* (talmudic tractate).
YIVOA	*YIVO Annual of Jewish Social Studies* (1946ff.).
YLBI	*Year Book of the Leo Baeck Institute* (1956ff.).
YMḤEY	See BJPES.
YMḤSI	*Yedi'ot ha-Makhon le-Ḥeker ha-Shirah ha-Ivrit* (1935/36ff.).
YMMY	*Yedi'ot ha-Makhon le-Madda'ei ha-Yahadut* (1924/25ff.).
Yoma	*Yoma* (talmudic tractate).
ZA	*Zeitschrift fuer Assyriologie* (1886/87ff.).
Zav.	*Zavim* (mishnaic tractate).
ZAW	*Zeitschrift fuer die alttestamentliche Wissenschaft und die Kunde des nachbiblishchen Judentums* (1881ff.).
ZAWB	*Beihefte* (supplements) to ZAW.
ZDMG	*Zeitschrift der Deutschen Morgenlaendischen Gesellschaft* (1846ff.).
ZDPV	*Zeitschrift des Deutschen Palaestina-Vereins* (1878–1949; from 1949 = BBLA).
Zech.	Zechariah (Bible).
Zedner, Cat	J. Zedner, *Catalogue of Hebrew Books in the Library of the British Museum* (1867; repr. 1964).
Zeitlin, Bibliotheca	W. Zeitlin, *Bibliotheca Hebraica Post-Mendelssohniana* (1891–95).
Zeph.	Zephaniah (Bible).
Zev.	*Zevaḥim* (talmudic tractate).
ZGGJT	*Zeitschrift der Gesellschaft fuer die Geschichte der Juden in der Tschechoslowakei* (1930–38).
ZGJD	*Zeitschrift fuer die Geschichte der Juden in Deutschland* (1887–92).
ZHB	*Zeitschrift fuer hebraeische Bibliographie* (1896–1920).
Zinberg, Sifrut	I. Zinberg, *Toledot Sifrut Yisrael,* 6 vols. (1955–60).
Ẓiẓ.	*Ẓiẓit* (post-talmudic tractate).
ZNW	*Zeitschrift fuer die neutestamentliche Wissenschaft* (1901ff.).
ZS	*Zeitschrift fuer Semitistik und verwandte Gebiete* (1922ff.).
Zunz, Gesch	L. Zunz, *Zur Geschichte und Literatur* (1845).
Zunz, Gesch	L. Zunz, *Literaturgeschichte der synagogalen Poesie* (1865; Supplement, 1867; repr. 1966).
Zunz, Poesie	L. Zunz, *Synogogale Posie des Mittelalters,* ed. by Freimann (1920^2; repr. 1967).
Zunz, Ritus	L. Zunz, *Ritus des synagogalen Gottesdienstes* (1859; repr. 1967).
Zunz, Schr	L. Zunz, *Gesammelte Schriften,* 3 vols. (1875–76).
Zunz, Vortraege	L. Zunz, *Gottesdienstliche vortraege der Juden ...* 1892^2; repr. 1966).
Zunz-Albeck, Derashot	L. Zunz, *Ha-Derashot be-Yisrael,* Heb. Tr. of Zunz Vortraege by H. Albeck (1954^2).

TRANSLITERATION RULES

HEBREW AND SEMITIC LANGUAGES:

	General	*Scientific*
א	not transliterated[1]	ʾ
בּ	b	b
ב	v	v, ḇ
גּ	g	g
ג		ḡ
דּ	d	d
ד		ḏ
ה	h	h
ו	v – when not a vowel	w
ז	z	z
ח	ḥ	ḥ
ט	t	ṭ, t
י	y – when vowel and at end of words – i	y
כּ	k	k
כ, ך	kh	kh, ḵ
ל	l	l̲
מ, ם	m	m
נ, ן	n	n
ס	s	s
ע	not transliterated[1]	ʿ
פּ	p	p
פ, ף	f	p, f, ph
צ, ץ	ẓ	ṣ, ẓ
ק	k	q, k
ר	r	r
שׁ	sh[2]	š
שׂ	s	ś, s
תּ	t	t
ת		ṯ
ג׳	dzh, J	ğ
ז׳	zh, J	ž
צ׳	ch	č
—ָ		å, o, ǒ (short) â, ā (long)
—ַ	a	a
—ֲ		a, ^{a}
—ֵ		e, ẹ, ē
—ֶ	e	æ, ä, ę
—ֱ		œ, ĕ, ^{e}
—ְ	only *sheva na* is transliterated	ə, ĕ, e; only *sheva na* transliterated
—ִ —ִי	i	i
—ֹ וֹ	o	o, o, o
—ֻ וּ	u	u, ŭ û, ū
—ֵי	ei; biblical e	
‡		reconstructed forms of words

1. The letters א and ע are not transliterated.
   An apostrophe (') between vowels indicates that they do not form a diphthong and are to be pronounced separately.
2. *Dagesh ḥazak* (forte) is indicated by doubling of the letter, except for the letter שׁ.
3. Names. Biblical names and biblical place names are rendered according to the Bible translation of the Jewish Publication Society of America. Post-biblical Hebrew names are transliterated; contemporary names are transliterated or rendered as used by the person. Place names are transliterated or rendered by the accepted spelling. Names and some words with an accepted English form are usually not transliterated.

YIDDISH

א	not transliterated
אַ	a
אָ	o
בּ	b
בֿ	v
ג	g
ד	d
ה	h
ו, וּ	u
וו	v
וי	oy
ז	z
זש	zh
ח	kh
ט	t
טש	tsh, ch
י	(consonant) y (vowel) i
יִ	i
יי	ey
ײַ	ay
כּ	k
כ, ך	kh
ל	l
מ, ם	m
נ, ן	n
ס	s
ע	e
פּ	p
פֿ, ף	f
צ, ץ	ts
ק	k
ר	r
ש	sh
שׂ	s
תּ	t
ת	s

1. Yiddish transliteration rendered according to U. Weinreich's Modern *English-Yiddish Yiddish-English* Dictionary.
2. Hebrew words in Yiddish are usually transliterated according to standard Yiddish pronunciation, e.g., חזנות = *khazones.*

LADINO

Ladino and Judeo-Spanish words written in Hebrew characters are transliterated phonetically, following the General Rules of Hebrew transliteration (see above) whenever the accepted spelling in Latin characters could not be ascertained.

ARABIC

ء ا	a[1]	ض	ḍ
ب	b	ط	ṭ
ت	t	ظ	ẓ
ث	th	ع	ʿ
ج	j	غ	gh
ح	ḥ	ف	f
خ	kh	ق	q
د	d	ك	k
ذ	dh	ل	l
ر	r	م	m
ز	z	ن	n
س	s	ه	h
ش	sh	و	w
ص	ṣ	ي	y
ـَ	a	ـَا ى	ā
ـِ	i	ـِي	ī
ـُ	u	ـُو	ū
ـَو	aw	ـِيّ	iyy[2]
ـَي	ay	ـُوّ	uww[2]

1. not indicated when initial
2. see note (f)

a) The EJ follows the *Columbia Lippincott Gazetteer* and the *Times Atlas* in transliteration of Arabic place names. Sites that appear in neither are transliterated according to the table above, and subject to the following notes.

b) The EJ follows the *Columbia Encyclopedia* in transliteration of Arabic names. Personal names that do not therein appear are transliterated according to the table above and subject to the following notes (e.g., Ali rather than ʿAlī, Suleiman rather than Sulayman).

c) The EJ follows the *Webster's Third International Dictionary, Unabridged* in transliteration of Arabic terms that have been integrated into the English language.

d) The term "Abu" will thus appear, usually in disregard of inflection.

e) Nunnation (end vowels, *tanwīn*) are dropped in transliteration.

f) Gemination (*tashdīd*) is indicated by the doubling of the geminated letter, unless an end letter, in which case the gemination is dropped.

g) The definitive article *al-* will always be thus transliterated, unless subject to one of the modifying notes (e.g., El-Arish rather than al-ʿArīsh; modification according to note (a)).

h) The Arabic transliteration disregards the Sun Letters (the antero-palatals (*al-Ḥurūf al-Shamsiyya*).

i) The *tā-marbūṭa* (o) is omitted in transliteration, unless in construct-stage (e.g., *Khirba* but *Khirbat Mishmish*).

These modifying notes may lead to various inconsistencies in the Arabic transliteration, but this policy has deliberately been adopted to gain smoother reading of Arabic terms and names.

GREEK

Ancient Greek	*Modern Greek*	*Greek Letters*
a	a	*Α; α; ᾳ*
b	v	*Β; β*
g	gh; g	*Γ; γ*
d	dh	*Δ; δ*
e	e	*Ε; ε*
z	z	*Ζ; ζ*
e; e	i	*Η; η; ῃ*
th	th	*Θ; θ*
i	i	*Ι; ι*
k	k; ky	*Κ; κ*
l	l	*Λ; λ*
m	m	*Μ; μ*
n	n	*Ν; ν*
x	x	*Ξ; ξ*
o	o	*Ο; ο*
p	p	*Π; π*
r; rh	r	*Ρ; ρ; ῥ*
s	s	*Σ; σ; ς*
t	t	*Τ; τ*
u; y	i	*Υ; υ*
ph	f	*Φ; φ*
ch	kh	*Χ; χ*
ps	ps	*Ψ; ψ*
o; ō	o	*Ω; ω; ῳ*
ai	e	*αι*
ei	i	*ει*
oi	i	*οι*
ui	i	*υι*
ou	ou	*ου*
eu	ev	*ευ*
eu; ēu	iv	*ηυ*
–	j	*τζ*
nt	d; nd	*ντ*
mp	b; mb	*μπ*
ngk	g	*γκ*
ng	ng	*νγ*
h	–	ʿ
–	–	ʾ
w	–	*Ϝ*

RUSSIAN

А	A
Б	B
В	V
Г	G
Д	D
Е	E, Ye[1]
Ё	Yo, O[2]
Ж	Zh
З	Z
И	I
Й	Y[3]
К	K
Л	L
М	M
Н	N
О	O
П	P
Р	R
С	S
Т	T
У	U
Ф	F
Х	Kh
Ц	Ts
Ч	Ch
Ш	Sh
Щ	Shch
Ъ	omitted; see note [1]
Ы	Y
Ь	omitted; see note [1]
Э	E
Ю	Yu
Я	Ya

1. Ye at the beginning of a word; after all vowels except ***Ы***; and after ***Ъ*** and ***Ь***.
2. O after ***Ч***, ***Ш*** and ***Щ***.
3. Omitted after ***Ы***, and in names of people after ***И***.

A. Many first names have an accepted English or quasi-English form which has been preferred to transliteration.
B. Place names have been given according to the *Columbia Lippincott Gazeteer*.
C. Pre-revolutionary spelling has been ignored.
D. Other languages using the Cyrillic alphabet (e.g., Bulgarian, Ukrainian), inasmuch as they appear, have been phonetically transliterated in conformity with the principles of this table.

GLOSSARY

Asterisked terms have separate entries in the Encyclopaedia.

Actions Committee, early name of the Zionist General Council, the supreme institution of the World Zionist Organization in the interim between Congresses. The Zionist Executive's name was then the "Small Actions Committee."

***Adar**, twelfth month of the Jewish religious year, sixth of the civil, approximating to February–March.

***Aggadah**, name given to those sections of Talmud and Midrash containing homiletic expositions of the Bible, stories, legends, folklore, anecdotes, or maxims. In contradistinction to **halakhah.*

***Agunah**, woman unable to remarry according to Jewish law, because of desertion by her husband or inability to accept presumption of death.

***Aharonim**, later rabbinic authorities. In contradistinction to **rishonim* ("early ones").

Ahavah, liturgical poem inserted in the second benediction of the morning prayer *(*Ahavah Rabbah)* of the festivals and/or special Sabbaths.

Aktion (Ger.), operation involving the mass assembly, deportation, and murder of Jews by the Nazis during the *Holocaust.

***Aliyah**, (1) being called to Reading of the Law in synagogue; (2) immigration to Ereẓ Israel; (3) one of the waves of immigration to Ereẓ Israel from the early 1880s.

***Amidah**, main prayer recited at all services; also known as *Shemoneh Esreh* and *Tefillah.*

***Amora** (pl. **amoraim**), title given to the Jewish scholars in Ereẓ Israel and Babylonia in the third to sixth centuries who were responsible for the **Gemara.*

Aravah, the *willow; one of the *Four Species used on *Sukkot ("festival of Tabernacles") together with the **etrog, hadas,* and **lulav.*

***Arvit**, evening prayer.

Asarah be-Tevet, fast on the 10th of Tevet commemorating the commencement of the siege of Jerusalem by Nebuchadnezzar.

Asefat ha-Nivḥarim, representative assembly elected by Jews in Palestine during the period of the British Mandate (1920–48).

***Ashkenaz**, name applied generally in medieval rabbinical literature to Germany.

***Ashkenazi** (pl. **Ashkenazim**), German or West-, Central-, or East-European Jew(s), as contrasted with *Sephardi(m).

***Av**, fifth month of the Jewish religious year, eleventh of the civil, approximating to July–August.

***Av bet din**, vice president of the supreme court (*bet din ha-gadol*) in Jerusalem during the Second Temple period; later, title given to communal rabbis as heads of the religious courts (see **bet din*).

***Badḥan**, jester, particularly at traditional Jewish weddings in Eastern Europe.

***Bakkashah** (Heb. "supplication"), type of petitionary prayer, mainly recited in the Sephardi rite on Rosh Ha-Shanah and the Day of Atonement.

Bar, "son of . . . "; frequently appearing in personal names.

***Baraita** (pl. **beraitot**), statement of **tanna* not found in *Mishnah.

***Bar mitzvah**, ceremony marking the initiation of a boy at the age of 13 into the Jewish religious community.

Ben, "son of . . . ", frequently appearing in personal names.

Berakhah (pl. **berakhot**), *benediction, blessing; formula of praise and thanksgiving.

***Bet din** (pl. **battei din**), rabbinic court of law.

***Bet ha-midrash**, school for higher rabbinic learning; often attached to or serving as a synagogue.

***Bilu**, first modern movement for pioneering and agricultural settlement in Ereẓ Israel, founded in 1882 at Kharkov, Russia.

***Bund**, Jewish socialist party founded in Vilna in 1897, supporting Jewish national rights; Yiddishist, and anti-Zionist.

Cohen (pl. **Cohanim**), see Kohen.

***Conservative Judaism**, trend in Judaism developed in the United States in the 20th century which, while opposing extreme changes in traditional observances, permits certain modifications of *halakhah* in response to the changing needs of the Jewish people.

***Consistory** (Fr. *consistoire*), governing body of a Jewish communal district in France and certain other countries.

***Converso(s)**, term applied in Spain and Portugal to converted Jew(s), and sometimes more loosely to their descendants.

***Crypto-Jew**, term applied to a person who although observing outwardly Christianity (or some other religion) was at heart a Jew and maintained Jewish observances as far as possible (see Converso; Marrano; Neofiti; New Christian; Jadīd al-Islām).

***Dayyan**, member of rabbinic court.

Decisor, equivalent to the Hebrew *posek* (pl. **posekim*), the rabbi who gives the decision (*halakhah*) in Jewish law or practice.

***Devekut**, "devotion"; attachment or adhesion to God; communion with God.

***Diaspora**, Jews living in the "dispersion" outside Ereẓ Israel; area of Jewish settlement outside Ereẓ Israel.

Din, a law (both secular and religious), legal decision, or lawsuit.

Divan, diwan, collection of poems, especially in Hebrew, Arabic, or Persian.

Dunam, unit of land area (1,000 sq. m., c. ¼ acre), used in Israel.

Einsatzgruppen, mobile units of Nazi S.S. and S.D.; in U.S.S.R. and Serbia, mobile killing units.

***Ein-Sof**, "without end"; "the infinite"; hidden, impersonal aspect of God; also used as a Divine Name.

***Elul**, sixth month of the Jewish religious calendar, 12th of the civil, precedes the High Holiday season in the fall.

Endloesung, see *Final Solution.

***Ereẓ Israel**, Land of Israel; Palestine.

***Eruv**, technical term for rabbinical provision permitting the alleviation of certain restrictions.

***Etrog**, citron; one of the *Four Species used on *Sukkot together with the **lulav, hadas,* and *aravah.*

Even ha-Ezer, see Shulḥan Arukh.

***Exilarch**, lay head of Jewish community in Babylonia (see also *resh galuta*), and elsewhere.

***Final Solution** (Ger. *Endloesung*), in Nazi terminology, the Nazi-planned mass murder and total annihilation of the Jews.

***Gabbai**, official of a Jewish congregation; originally a charity collector.

***Galut**, "exile"; the condition of the Jewish people in dispersion.

***Gaon** (pl. **geonim**), head of academy in post-talmudic period, especially in Babylonia.

Gaonate, office of *gaon.

***Gemara**, traditions, discussions, and rulings of the **amoraim*, commenting on and supplementing the *Mishnah, and forming part of the Babylonian and Palestinian Talmuds (see Talmud).

***Gematria**, interpretation of Hebrew word according to the numerical value of its letters.

General Government, territory in Poland administered by a German civilian governor-general with headquarters in Cracow after the German occupation in World War II.

***Genizah**, depository for sacred books. The best known was discovered in the synagogue of Fostat (old Cairo).

Get, bill of *divorce.

***Ge'ullah**, hymn inserted after the **Shema* into the benediction of the morning prayer of the festivals and special Sabbaths.

***Gilgul**, metempsychosis; transmigration of souls.

***Golem**, automaton, especially in human form, created by magical means and endowed with life.

***Ḥabad**, initials of *ḥokhmah, binah, da'at*: "wisdom, understanding, knowledge"; ḥasidic movement founded in Belorussia by *Shneur Zalman of Lyady.

Hadas, *myrtle; one of the *Four Species used on Sukkot together with the **etrog*, **lulav*, and *aravah*.

***Haftarah** (pl. **haftarot**), designation of the portion from the prophetical books of the Bible recited after the synagogue reading from the Pentateuch on Sabbaths and holidays.

***Haganah**, clandestine Jewish organization for armed self-defense in Ereẓ Israel under the British Mandate, which eventually evolved into a people's militia and became the basis for the Israel army.

***Haggadah**, ritual recited in the home on *Passover eve at seder table.

Haham, title of chief rabbi of the Spanish and Portuguese congregations in London, England.

***Hakham**, title of rabbi of *Sephardi congregation.

***Hakham bashi**, title in the 15th century and modern times of the chief rabbi in the Ottoman Empire, residing in Constantinople (Istanbul), also applied to principal rabbis in provincial towns.

Hakhsharah ("preparation"), organized training in the Diaspora of pioneers for agricultural settlement in Ereẓ Israel.

***Halakhah** (pl. **halakhot**), an accepted decision in rabbinic law. Also refers to those parts of the *Talmud concerned with legal matters. In contradistinction to **aggadah*.

Ḥaliẓah, biblically prescribed ceremony (Deut. 25:9–10) performed when a man refuses to marry his brother's childless widow, enabling her to remarry.

***Hallel**, term referring to Psalms 113-18 in liturgical use.

***Ḥalukkah**, system of financing the maintenance of Jewish communities in the holy cities of Ereẓ Israel by collections made abroad, mainly in the pre-Zionist era (see *kolel*).

Ḥalutz (pl. **ḥalutzim**), pioneer, especially in agriculture, in Ereẓ Israel.

Ḥalutziyyut, pioneering.

***Ḥanukkah**, eight-day celebration commemorating the victory of *Judah Maccabee over the Syrian king *Antiochus Epiphanes and the subsequent rededication of the Temple.

Ḥasid, adherent of *Ḥasidism.

***Ḥasidei Ashkenaz**, medieval pietist movement among the Jews of Germany.

***Ḥasidism**, (1) religious revivalist movement of popular mysticism among Jews of Germany in the Middle Ages; (2) religious movement founded by *Israel ben Eliezer Ba'al Shem Tov in the first half of the 18th century.

***Haskalah**, "enlightenment"; movement for spreading modern European culture among Jews c. 1750–1880. See *maskil*.

***Havdalah**, ceremony marking the end of Sabbath or festival.

***Ḥazzan**, precentor who intones the liturgy and leads the prayers in synagogue; in earlier times a synagogue official.

***Ḥeder** (lit. "room"), school for teaching children Jewish religious observance.

Heikhalot, "palaces"; tradition in Jewish mysticism centering on mystical journeys through the heavenly spheres and palaces to the Divine Chariot (see Merkabah).

***Ḥerem**, excommunication, imposed by rabbinical authorities for purposes of religious and/or communal discipline; originally, in biblical times, that which is separated from common use either because it was an abomination or because it was consecrated to God.

Ḥeshvan, see Marḥeshvan.

***Ḥevra kaddisha**, title applied to charitable confraternity (**ḥevrah*), now generally limited to associations for burial of the dead.

***Ḥibbat Zion**, see Ḥovevei Zion.

***Histadrut** (abbr. For Heb. **Ha-Histadrut ha-Kelalit shel ha-Ovedim ha-Ivriyyim be-Ereẓ Israel**). Ereẓ Israel Jewish Labor Federation, founded in 1920; subsequently renamed Histadrut ha-Ovedim be-Ereẓ Israel.

***Holocaust**, the organized mass persecution and annihilation of European Jewry by the Nazis (1933–1945).

***Hoshana Rabba**, the seventh day of *Sukkot on which special observances are held.

Ḥoshen Mishpat, see Shulḥan Arukh.

Ḥovevei Zion, federation of *Ḥibbat Zion, early (pre-*Herzl) Zionist movement in Russia.

Illui, outstanding scholar or genius, especially a young prodigy in talmudic learning.

***Iyyar**, second month of the Jewish religious year, eighth of the civil, approximating to April-May.

I.Ẓ.L. (initials of Heb. ***Irgun Ẓeva'i Le'ummi**; "National Military Organization"), underground Jewish organization in Ereẓ Israel founded in 1931, which engaged from 1937 in retaliatory acts against Arab attacks and later against the British mandatory authorities.

***Jadīd al-Islām** (Ar.), a person practicing the Jewish religion in secret although outwardly observing Islām.

***Jewish Legion**, Jewish units in British army during World War I.

***Jihād** (Ar.), in Muslim religious law, holy war waged against infidels.

***Judenrat** (Ger. "Jewish council"), council set up in Jewish communities and ghettos under the Nazis to execute their instructions.

***Judenrein** (Ger. "clean of Jews"), in Nazi terminology the condition of a locality from which all Jews had been eliminated.

***Kabbalah**, the Jewish mystical tradition:
Kabbala iyyunit, speculative Kabbalah;
Kabbala ma'asit, practical Kabbalah;
Kabbala nevu'it, prophetic Kabbalah.

Kabbalist, student of Kabbalah.

***Kaddish**, liturgical doxology.

Kahal, Jewish congregation; among Ashkenazim, *kehillah*.

*__Kalām__ (Ar.), science of Muslim theology; adherents of the Kalām are called *mutakallimūn*.

*__Karaite__, member of a Jewish sect originating in the eighth century which rejected rabbinic (*Rabbanite) Judaism and claimed to accept only Scripture as authoritative.

*__Kasher__, ritually permissible food.

Kashrut, Jewish *dietary laws.

*__Kavvanah__, "intention"; term denoting the spiritual concentration accompanying prayer and the performance of ritual or of a commandment.

*__Kedushah__, main addition to the third blessing in the reader's repetition of the *Amidah* in which the public responds to the precentor's introduction.

Kefar, village; first part of name of many settlements in Israel.

Kehillah, congregation; see *kahal*.

Kelippah (pl. **kelippot**), "husk(s)"; mystical term denoting force(s) of evil.

*__Keneset Yisrael__, comprehensive communal organization of the Jews in Palestine during the British Mandate.

Keri, variants in the masoretic (*masorah) text of the Bible between the spelling (*ketiv*) and its pronunciation (*keri*).

*__Kerovah__ (collective plural (corrupted) from **kerovez̩**), poem(s) incorporated into the **Amidah*.

Ketiv, see *keri*.

*__Ketubbah__, marriage contract, stipulating husband's obligations to wife.

Kevuz̩ah, small commune of pioneers constituting an agricultural settlement in Erez̩ Israel (evolved later into *kibbutz).

*__Kibbutz__ (pl. **kibbutzim**), larger-size commune constituting a settlement in Erez̩ Israel based mainly on agriculture but engaging also in industry.

*__Kiddush__, prayer of sanctification, recited over wine or bread on eve of Sabbaths and festivals.

*__Kiddush ha-Shem__, term connoting martyrdom or act of strict integrity in support of Judaic principles.

*__Kinah__ (pl. **kinot**), lamentation dirge(s) for the Ninth of Av and other fast days.

*__Kislev__, ninth month of the Jewish religious year, third of the civil, approximating to November-December.

Klaus, name given in Central and Eastern Europe to an institution, usually with synagogue attached, where *Talmud was studied perpetually by adults; applied by Ḥasidim to their synagogue ("*kloyz*").

*__Knesset__, parliament of the State of Israel.

K(c)ohen (pl. **K(c)ohanim**), Jew(s) of priestly (Aaronide) descent.

*__Kolel__, (1) community in Erez̩ Israel of persons from a particular country or locality, often supported by their fellow countrymen in the Diaspora; (2) institution for higher Torah study.

Kosher, see *kasher*.

*__Kristallnacht__ (Ger. "crystal night," meaning "night of broken glass"), organized destruction of synagogues, Jewish houses, and shops, accompanied by mass arrests of Jews, which took place in Germany and Austria under the Nazis on the night of Nov. 9–10, 1938.

*__Lag ba-Omer__, 33rd (Heb. **lag**) day of the **Omer* period falling on the 18th of *Iyyar; a semi-holiday.

Leḥi (abbr. For Heb. *__Loḥamei Ḥerut Israel__, "Fighters for the Freedom of Israel"), radically anti-British armed underground organization in Palestine, founded in 1940 by dissidents from *I.Z.L.

Levir, husband's brother.

*__Levirate marriage__ (Heb. *yibbum*), marriage of childless widow (*yevamah*) by brother (*yavam*) of the deceased husband (in accordance with Deut. 25:5); release from such an obligation is effected through *ḥaliz̩ah*.

LHY, see Leḥi.

*__Lulav__, palm branch; one of the *Four Species used on *Sukkot together with the **etrog*, *hadas*, and *aravah*.

*__Ma'aravot__, hymns inserted into the evening prayer of the three festivals, Passover, Shavuot, and Sukkot.

Ma'ariv, evening prayer; also called **arvit*.

*__Ma'barah__, transition camp; temporary settlement for newcomers in Israel during the period of mass immigration following 1948.

*__Maftir__, reader of the concluding portion of the Pentateuchal section on Sabbaths and holidays in synagogue; reader of the portion of the prophetical books of the Bible (**haftarah*).

*__Maggid__, popular preacher.

*__Maḥzor__ (pl. **maḥzorim**), festival prayer book.

*__Mamzer__, bastard; according to Jewish law, the offspring of an incestuous relationship.

*__Mandate, Palestine__, responsibility for the administration of Palestine conferred on Britain by the League of Nations in 1922; mandatory government: the British administration of Palestine.

*__Maqāma__ (Ar. pl. **maqamāt**), poetic form (rhymed prose) which, in its classical arrangement, has rigid rules of form and content.

*__Marḥeshvan__, popularly called Ḥeshvan; eighth month of the Jewish religious year, second of the civil, approximating to October–November.

*__Marrano(s)__, descendant(s) of Jew(s) in Spain and Portugal whose ancestors had been converted to Christianity under pressure but who secretly observed Jewish rituals.

Maskil (pl. **maskilim**), adherent of *Haskalah ("Enlightenment") movement.

*__Masorah__, body of traditions regarding the correct spelling, writing, and reading of the Hebrew Bible.

Masorete, scholar of the masoretic tradition.

Masoretic, in accordance with the masorah.

Meliz̩ah, in Middle Ages, elegant style; modern usage, florid style using biblical or talmudic phraseology.

Mellah, *Jewish quarter in North African towns.

*__Menorah__, candelabrum; seven-branched oil lamp used in the Tabernacle and Temple; also eight-branched candelabrum used on *Ḥanukkah.

Me'orah, hymn inserted into the first benediction of the morning prayer (*Yoz̩er ha-Me'orot*).

*__Merkabah__, *merkavah*, "chariot"; mystical discipline associated with Ezekiel's vision of the Divine Throne-Chariot (Ezek. 1).

Meshullaḥ, emissary sent to conduct propaganda or raise funds for rabbinical academies or charitable institutions.

*__Mezuzah__ (pl. **mezuzot**), parchment scroll with selected Torah verses placed in container and affixed to gates and doorposts of houses occupied by Jews.

*__Midrash__, method of interpreting Scripture to elucidate legal points (*Midrash Halakhah*) or to bring out lessons by stories or homiletics (*Midrash Aggadah*). Also the name for a collection of such rabbinic interpretations.

*__Mikveh__, ritual bath.

*__Minhag__ (pl. **minhagim**), ritual custom(s); synagogal rite(s); especially of a specific sector of Jewry.

*__Minḥah__, afternoon prayer; originally meal offering in Temple.

*__Minyan__, group of ten male adult Jews, the minimum required for communal prayer.

*__Mishnah__, earliest codification of Jewish Oral Law.

Mishnah (pl. **mishnayot**), subdivision of tractates of the Mishnah.

Mitnagged (pl. *__Mitnaggedim__), originally, opponents of *Ḥasidism in Eastern Europe.

*__Mitzvah__, biblical or rabbinic injunction; applied also to good or charitable deeds.

Mohel, official performing circumcisions.

*__Moshav__, smallholders' cooperative agricultural settlement in Israel, see moshav ovedim.

Moshavah, earliest type of Jewish village in modern Ereẓ Israel in which farming is conducted on individual farms mostly on privately owned land.

Moshav ovedim ("workers' moshav"), agricultural village in Israel whose inhabitants possess individual homes and holdings but cooperate in the purchase of equipment, sale of produce, mutual aid, etc.

*__Moshav shittufi__ ("collective moshav"), agricultural village in Israel whose members possess individual homesteads but where the agriculture and economy are conducted as a collective unit.

Mostegab (Ar.), poem with biblical verse at beginning of each stanza.

*__Muqaddam__ (Ar., pl. **muqaddamūn**), "leader," "head of the community."

*__Musaf__, additional service on Sabbath and festivals; originally the additional sacrifice offered in the Temple.

Musar, traditional ethical literature.

*__Musar movement__, ethical movement developing in the latter part of the 19th century among Orthodox Jewish groups in Lithuania; founded by R. Israel *Lipkin (Salanter).

*__Nagid__ (pl. **negidim**), title applied in Muslim (and some Christian) countries in the Middle Ages to a leader recognized by the state as head of the Jewish community.

Nakdan (pl. **nakdanim**), "punctuator"; scholar of the 9th to 14th centuries who provided biblical manuscripts with masoretic apparatus, vowels, and accents.

*__Nasi__ (pl. **nesi'im**), talmudic term for president of the Sanhedrin, who was also the spiritual head and later, political representative of the Jewish people; from second century a descendant of Hillel recognized by the Roman authorities as patriarch of the Jews. Now applied to the president of the State of Israel.

*__Negev__, the southern, mostly arid, area of Israel.

*__Ne'ilah__, concluding service on the *Day of Atonement.

Neofiti, term applied in southern Italy to converts to Christianity from Judaism and their descendants who were suspected of maintaining secret allegiance to Judaism.

*__Neology; Neolog; Neologism__, trend of *Reform Judaism in Hungary forming separate congregations after 1868.

*__Nevelah__ (lit. "carcass"), meat forbidden by the *dietary laws on account of the absence of, or defect in, the act of **sheḥitah* (ritual slaughter).

*__New Christians__, term applied especially in Spain and Portugal to converts from Judaism (and from Islam) and their descendants; "Half New Christian" designated a person one of whose parents was of full Jewish blood.

*__Niddah__ ("menstruous woman"), woman during the period of menstruation.

*__Nisan__, first month of the Jewish religious year, seventh of the civil, approximating to March-April.

Niẓoẓot, "sparks"; mystical term for sparks of the holy light imprisoned in all matter.

Nosaḥ (**nusaḥ**) "version"; (1) textual variant; (2) term applied to distinguish the various prayer rites, e.g., *nosaḥ Ashkenaz*; (3) the accepted tradition of synagogue melody.

*__Notarikon__, method of abbreviating Hebrew works or phrases by acronym.

Novella(e) (Heb. **ḥiddush (im)*), commentary on talmudic and later rabbinic subjects that derives new facts or principles from the implications of the text.

*__Nuremberg Laws__, Nazi laws excluding Jews from German citizenship, and imposing other restrictions.

Ofan, hymns inserted into a passage of the morning prayer.

*__Omer__, first sheaf cut during the barley harvest, offered in the Temple on the second day of Passover.

Omer, Counting of (Heb. *Sefirat ha-Omer*), 49 days counted from the day on which the *omer* was first offered in the Temple (according to the rabbis the 16th of Nisan, i.e., the second day of Passover) until the festival of Shavuot; now a period of semi-mourning.

Oraḥ Ḥayyim, see Shulḥan Arukh.

*__Orthodoxy__ (Orthodox Judaism), modern term for the strictly traditional sector of Jewry.

*__Pale of Settlement__, 25 provinces of czarist Russia where Jews were permitted permanent residence.

*__Palmaḥ__ (abbr. for Heb. *peluggot maḥaẓ*; "shock companies"), striking arm of the *Haganah.

*__Pardes__, medieval biblical exegesis giving the literal, allegorical, homiletical, and esoteric interpretations.

*__Parnas__, chief synagogue functionary, originally vested with both religious and administrative functions; subsequently an elected lay leader.

Partition plan(s), proposals for dividing Ereẓ Israel into autonomous areas.

Paytan, composer of **piyyut* (liturgical poetry).

*__Peel Commission__, British Royal Commission appointed by the British government in 1936 to inquire into the Palestine problem and make recommendations for its solution.

Pesaḥ, *Passover.

*__Pilpul__, in talmudic and rabbinic literature, a sharp dialectic used particularly by talmudists in Poland from the 16th century.

*__Pinkas__, community register or minute-book.

*__Piyyut__, (pl. **piyyutim**), Hebrew liturgical poetry.

*__Pizmon__, poem with refrain.

Posek (pl. *__posekim__), decisor; codifier or rabbinic scholar who pronounces decisions in disputes and on questions of Jewish law.

*__Prosbul__, legal method of overcoming the cancelation of debts with the advent of the *sabbatical year.

*__Purim__, festival held on Adar 14 or 15 in commemoration of the delivery of the Jews of Persia in the time of *Esther.

Rabban, honorific title higher than that of rabbi, applied to heads of the *Sanhedrin in mishnaic times.

*__Rabbanite__, adherent of rabbinic Judaism. In contradistinction to *Karaite.

Reb, rebbe, Yiddish form for rabbi, applied generally to a teacher or ḥasidic rabbi.

*__Reconstructionism__, trend in Jewish thought originating in the United States.

*__Reform Judaism__, trend in Judaism advocating modification of *Orthodoxy in conformity with the exigencies of contemporary life and thought.

Resh galuta, lay head of Babylonian Jewry (see exilarch).

Responsum (pl. ***responsa**), written opinion (*teshuvah*) given to question (*she'elah*) on aspects of Jewish law by qualified authorities; pl. collection of such queries and opinions in book form (*she'elot u-teshuvot*).

***Rishonim**, older rabbinical authorities. Distinguished from later authorities (**aḥaronim*).

***Rishon le-Zion**, title given to Sephardi chief rabbi of Ereẓ Israel.

***Rosh Ha-Shanah**, two-day holiday (one day in biblical and early mishnaic times) at the beginning of the month of *Tishri (September–October), traditionally the New Year.

Rosh Hodesh, *New Moon, marking the beginning of the Hebrew month.

Rosh Yeshivah, see *Yeshivah.

***R.S.H.A.** (initials of Ger. *Reichssicherheitshauptamt*: "Reich Security Main Office"), the central security department of the German Reich, formed in 1939, and combining the security police (Gestapo and Kripo) and the S.D.

***Sanhedrin**, the assembly of ordained scholars which functioned both as a supreme court and as a legislature before 70 C.E. In modern times the name was given to the body of representative Jews convoked by Napoleon in 1807.

***Savora** (pl. **savoraim**), name given to the Babylonian scholars of the period between the **amoraim* and the **geonim*, approximately 500–700 C.E.

S.D. (initials of Ger. *Sicherheitsdienst*: "security service"), security service of the *S.S. formed in 1932 as the sole intelligence organization of the Nazi party.

Seder, ceremony observed in the Jewish home on the first night of Passover (outside Ereẓ Israel first two nights), when the *Haggadah is recited.

***Sefer Torah**, manuscript scroll of the Pentateuch for public reading in synagogue.

***Sefirot, the ten**, the ten "Numbers"; mystical term denoting the ten spheres or emanations through which the Divine manifests itself; elements of the world; dimensions, primordial numbers.

Selektion (Ger.), (1) in ghettos and other Jewish settlements, the drawing up by Nazis of lists of deportees; (2) separation of incoming victims to concentration camps into two categories – those destined for immediate killing and those to be sent for forced labor.

Seliḥah (pl. ***seliḥot**), penitential prayer.

***Semikhah**, ordination conferring the title "rabbi" and permission to give decisions in matters of ritual and law.

Sephardi (pl. ***Sephardim**), Jew(s) of Spain and Portugal and their descendants, wherever resident, as contrasted with *Ashkenazi(m).

Shabbatean, adherent of the pseudo-messiah *Shabbetai Ẓevi (17th century).

Shaddai, name of God found frequently in the Bible and commonly translated "Almighty."

***Shaḥarit**, morning service.

Shali'aḥ (pl. **sheliḥim**), in Jewish law, messenger, agent; in modern times, an emissary from Ereẓ Israel to Jewish communities or organizations abroad for the purpose of fund-raising, organizing pioneer immigrants, education, etc.

Shalmonit, poetic meter introduced by the liturgical poet *Solomon ha-Bavli.

***Shammash**, synagogue beadle.

***Shavuot**, Pentecost; Festival of Weeks; second of the three annual pilgrim festivals, commemorating the receiving of the Torah at Mt. Sinai.

***Sheḥitah**, ritual slaughtering of animals.

***Shekhinah**, Divine Presence.

Shelishit, poem with three-line stanzas.

***Sheluḥei Ereẓ Israel** (or **shadarim**), emissaries from Ereẓ Israel.

***Shema** ([Yisrael]; "hear... [O Israel]," Deut. 6:4), Judaism's confession of faith, proclaiming the absolute unity of God.

Shemini Aẓeret, final festal day (in the Diaspora, final two days) at the conclusion of *Sukkot.

Shemittah, *Sabbatical year.

Sheniyyah, poem with two-line stanzas.

***Shephelah**, southern part of the coastal plain of Ereẓ Israel.

***Shevat**, eleventh month of the Jewish religious year, fifth of the civil, approximating to January–February.

***Shi'ur Komah**, Hebrew mystical work (c. eighth century) containing a physical description of God's dimensions; term denoting enormous spacial measurement used in speculations concerning the body of the **Shekhinah*.

Shivah, the "seven days" of *mourning following burial of a relative.

***Shofar**, horn of the ram (or any other ritually clean animal excepting the cow) sounded for the memorial blowing on *Rosh Ha-Shanah, and other occasions.

Shoḥet, person qualified to perform **sheḥitah*.

Shomer, *Ha-Shomer, organization of Jewish workers in Ereẓ Israel founded in 1909 to defend Jewish settlements.

***Shtadlan**, Jewish representative or negotiator with access to dignitaries of state, active at royal courts, etc.

***Shtetl**, Jewish small-town community in Eastern Europe.

***Shulḥan Arukh**, Joseph *Caro's code of Jewish law in four parts:
Oraḥ Ḥayyim, laws relating to prayers, Sabbath, festivals, and fasts;
Yoreh De'ah, dietary laws, etc;
Even ha-Ezer, laws dealing with women, marriage, etc;
Ḥoshen Mishpat, civil, criminal law, court procedure, etc.

Siddur, among Ashkenazim, the volume containing the daily prayers (in distinction to the **maḥzor* containing those for the festivals).

***Simḥat Torah**, holiday marking the completion in the synagogue of the annual cycle of reading the Pentateuch; in Ereẓ Israel observed on Shemini Aẓeret (outside Ereẓ Israel on the following day).

***Sinai Campaign**, brief campaign in October–November 1956 when Israel army reacted to Egyptian terrorist attacks and blockade by occupying the Sinai peninsula.

Sitra aḥra, "the other side" (of God); left side; the demoniac and satanic powers.

***Sivan**, third month of the Jewish religious year, ninth of the civil, approximating to May–June.

***Six-Day War**, rapid war in June 1967 when Israel reacted to Arab threats and blockade by defeating the Egyptian, Jordanian, and Syrian armies.

***S.S.** (initials of Ger. *Schutzstaffel*: "protection detachment"), Nazi formation established in 1925 which later became the "elite" organization of the Nazi Party and carried out central tasks in the "Final Solution."

***Status quo ante** community, community in Hungary retaining the status it had held before the convention of the General Jew-

ish Congress there in 1868 and the resultant split in Hungarian Jewry.
***Sukkah**, booth or tabernacle erected for *Sukkot when, for seven days, religious Jews "dwell" or at least eat in the *sukkah* (Lev. 23:42).
***Sukkot**, festival of Tabernacles; last of the three pilgrim festivals, beginning on the 15th of Tishri.
Sūra (Ar.), chapter of the Koran.
Ta'anit Esther (Fast of *Esther), fast on the 13th of Adar, the day preceding Purim.
Takkanah (pl. ***takkanot**), regulation supplementing the law of the Torah; regulations governing the internal life of communities and congregations.
***Tallit (gadol)**, four-cornered prayer shawl with fringes (*ẓiẓit*) at each corner.
***Tallit katan**, garment with fringes (*ẓiẓit*) appended, worn by observant male Jews under their outer garments.
***Talmud**, "teaching"; compendium of discussion on the Mishnah by generations of scholars and jurists in many academies over a period of several centuries. The Jerusalem (or Palestinian) Talmud mainly contains the discussions of the Palestinian sages. The Babylonian Talmud incorporates the parallel discussion in the Babylonian academies.
Talmud torah, term generally applied to Jewish religious (and ultimately to talmudic) study; also to traditional Jewish religious public schools.
***Tammuz**, fourth month of the Jewish religious year, tenth of the civil, approximating to June-July.
Tanna (pl. ***tannaim**), rabbinic teacher of mishnaic period.
***Targum**, Aramaic translation of the Bible.
***Tefillin**, phylacteries, small leather cases containing passages from Scripture and affixed on the forehead and arm by male Jews during the recital of morning prayers.
Tell (Ar. "mound," "hillock"), ancient mound in the Middle East composed of remains of successive settlements.
***Terefah**, food that is not **kasher*, owing to a defect on the animal.
***Territorialism**, 20th century movement supporting the creation of an autonomous territory for Jewish mass-settlement outside Ereẓ Israel.
***Tevet**, tenth month of the Jewish religious year, fourth of the civil, approximating to December–January.
Tikkun ("restitution," "reintegration"), (1) order of service for certain occasions, mostly recited at night; (2) mystical term denoting restoration of the right order and true unity after the spiritual "catastrophe" which occurred in the cosmos.
Tishah be-Av, Ninth of *Av, fast day commemorating the destruction of the First and Second Temples.
***Tishri**, seventh month of the Jewish religious year, first of the civil, approximating to September–October.
Tokheḥah, reproof sections of the Pentateuch (Lev. 26 and Deut. 28); poem of reproof.
***Torah**, Pentateuch or the Pentateuchal scroll for reading in synagogue; entire body of traditional Jewish teaching and literature.
Tosafist, talmudic glossator, mainly French ($12–14^{th}$ centuries), bringing additions to the commentary by *Rashi.
***Tosafot**, glosses supplied by tosafist.
***Tosefta**, a collection of teachings and traditions of the *tannaim*, closely related to the Mishnah.
Tradent, person who hands down a talmudic statement on the name of his teacher or other earlier authority.
***Tu bi-Shevat**, the 15th day of Shevat, the New Year for Trees; date marking a dividing line for fruit tithing; in modern Israel celebrated as arbor day.
***Uganda Scheme**, plan suggested by the British government in 1903 to establish an autonomous Jewish settlement area in East Africa.
***Va'ad Le'ummi**, national council of the Jewish community in Ereẓ Israel during the period of the British *Mandate.
***Wannsee Conference**, Nazi conference held on Jan. 20, 1942, at which the planned annihilation of European Jewry was endorsed.
Waqf (Ar.), (1) a Muslim charitable pious foundation; (2) state lands and other property passed to the Muslim community for public welfare.
***War of Independence**, war of 1947–49 when the Jews of Israel fought off Arab invading armies and ensured the establishment of the new State.
***White Paper(s)**, report(s) issued by British government, frequently statements of policy, as issued in connection with Palestine during the *Mandate period.
***Wissenschaft des Judentums** (Ger. "Science of Judaism"), movement in Europe beginning in the 19th century for scientific study of Jewish history, religion, and literature.
***Yad Vashem**, Israel official authority for commemorating the *Holocaust in the Nazi era and Jewish resistance and heroism at that time.
Yeshivah (pl. ***yeshivot**), Jewish traditional academy devoted primarily to study of rabbinic literature; *rosh yeshivah*, head of the yeshivah.
YHWH, the letters of the holy name of God, the Tetragrammaton.
Yibbum, see levirate marriage.
Yiḥud, "union"; mystical term for intention which causes the union of God with the **Shekhinah*.
Yishuv, settlement; more specifically, the Jewish community of Ereẓ Israel in the pre-State period. The pre-Zionist community is generally designated the "old yishuv" and the community evolving from 1880, the "new yishuv."
Yom Kippur, Yom ha-Kippurim, *Day of Atonement, solemn fast day observed on the 10th of Tishri.
Yoreh De'ah, see Shulḥan Arukh.
Yoẓer, hymns inserted in the first benediction (*Yoẓer Or*) of the morning **Shema*.
***Ẓaddik**, person outstanding for his faith and piety; especially a ḥasidic rabbi or leader.
Ẓimẓum, "contraction"; mystical term denoting the process whereby God withdraws or contracts within Himself so leaving a primordial vacuum in which creation can take place; primordial exile or self-limitation of God.
***Zionist Commission (1918)**, commission appointed in 1918 by the British government to advise the British military authorities in Palestine on the implementation of the *Balfour Declaration.
Ẓyyonei Zion, the organized opposition to Herzl in connection with the *Uganda Scheme.
***Ẓiẓit**, fringes attached to the **tallit* and **tallit katan*.
***Zohar**, mystical commentary on the Pentateuch; main textbook of *Kabbalah.
Zulat, hymn inserted after the **Shema* in the morning service.

ISBN-13: 978-0-02-865938-1
ISBN-10: 0-02-865938-4